South America
on a shoestring

James Lyon
Wayne Bernhardson   **Robyn Jones**
Andrew Draffen   **Leonardo Pinheiro**
Krzysztof Dydyński   **María Massolo**
Conner Gorry   **Mark Plotkin**

LONELY PLANET PUBLICATIONS
Melbourne · Oakland · London · Paris

SOUTH AMERICA

GALÁPAGOS ISLANDS

- Isla Santiago (James)
- Isla Santa Cruz (Indefatigable)
- **Puerto Ayora**
- Isla San Cristóbal (Chatham)
- Isla Fernandina (Narborough)
- Isla Isabela (Albemarle)

PACIFIC OCEAN

Equator

92°W 91°W 90°W 1°S

0 50 100 km
0 30 60 miles

Equator

0 1500 3000 km
0 1000 2000 miles

Galápagos Islands (Ecuador)

Easter Island (Chile)

EASTER ISLAND (RAPA NUI)

27°5'S

27°10'S

PACIFIC OCEAN

Hanga Roa

0 5 10 km
0 3 6 miles

109°25'W

Tropic of Capricorn

30°S

ATLANTIC OCEAN

RIO DE JANEIRO

SÃO PAULO

Curitiba
Ilha do Mel
Paranaguá
Ilha de Santa Catarina
Florianópolis

Porto Alegre

Foz do Iguaçu
Puerto Iguazú

ASUNCIÓN
Ciudad del Este
Encarnación
Posadas

PARAGUAY

Río Paraguay

Río Pilcomayo

Corrientes

Rosario

Santa Fe

Río Paraná

URUGUAY
Colonia
MONTEVIDEO

Maldonado
Punta del Este

Mar del Plata

BUENOS AIRES

Peninsula Valdés

Tupiza
Villazón
Tarija
La Quiaca
San Salvador de Jujuy

Calama
Antofagasta

Salta
Tucumán

CÓRDOBA

Ojos del Salado 6880m

Aconcagua 6962m

Mendoza

CHILE

A n d e s

La Serena

Viña del Mar
Valparaíso
SANTIAGO

Chillán
Concepción
Temuco
Valdivia
Osorno
Puerto Montt
Isla Grande de Chiloé

Bariloche
El Bolsón

Pucón

ARGENTINA

The Pampas

Río Salado

Puerto Madryn

P a t a g o n i a

Coihaique

El Calafate

Puerto Natales

Río Gallegos

Punta Arenas

Strait of Magellan

Isla Grande de Tierra del Fuego

Ushuaia

Cape Horn

FALKLAND ISLANDS (ISLAS MALVINAS; UK)

STANLEY

Juan Fernández Islands (Chile)

PACIFIC OCEAN

0 300 600 km
0 200 400 miles

Elevation

Over 4000 m
4000 m
2000 m
500 m
0 m

50°W

60°W

70°W

80°W

90°W

South America
7th edition – January 2000
First published – January 1980

Published by
Lonely Planet Publications Pty Ltd A.C.N. 005 607 983
192 Burwood Rd, Hawthorn, Victoria 3122, Australia

Lonely Planet Offices
Australia PO Box 617, Hawthorn, Victoria 3122
USA 150 Linden St, Oakland, CA 94607
UK 10a Spring Place, London NW5 3BH
France 1 rue du Dahomey, 75011 Paris

Photographs
Roberto Araki/International Stock, Sandra Bao, Wayne Bernhardson,
Jan Butchofsky-Houser, Krzysztof Dydynski, Robert Fried, Dave G
Houser, Robyn Jones, Ken Laffal, Michal Lavi & Aviv Fried, James
Lyon, Guy Moberly, Michael J Pettypool, Kevin Schafer, Sylvia
Stevens, David Tipling

Some of the images in this guide are available for licensing from
Lonely Planet Images.
email: lpi@lonelyplanet.com.au

Front cover photograph
Weaving in Otavalo Market, Ecuador (Sylvia Stevens)

ISBN 0 86442 656 9

text & maps © Lonely Planet 2000
photos © photographers as indicated 2000
climate charts compiled from information supplied by Patrick J Tyson,
© Patrick J Tyson, 2000

Printed by The Bookmaker Pty Ltd
Printed in China

Contents – Text

BOLIVIA   223

BRAZIL   307

CHILE 451

COLOMBIA   583

ECUADOR   669

6   Contents – Text

URUGUAY   967

VENEZUELA   995

LANGUAGE   1081

Contents – Maps

Contents – Maps

CHILE

COLOMBIA

ECUADOR

FALKLAND ISLANDS (ISLAS MALVINAS)

THE GUIANAS

PARAGUAY

PERU

The Authors

James Lyon
An Australian by birth and a skeptic by nature, James studied sociology, economics and Spanish before starting a not very promising career as a public bureaucrat. Travel became a major distraction but eventually qualified him to work as an editor in Lonely Planet's Melbourne office. He jumped at the chance to update LP's guide to *Bali & Lombok* and has since been fully occupied researching and writing guides to *Mexico*, *Maldives*, *California & Nevada*, *South America* and the *USA*.

Wayne Bernhardson
Wayne was born in Fargo, North Dakota, grew up in Tacoma, Washington, and earned a PhD in geography at the University of California, Berkeley. His LP credits include *Buenos Aires*; *Chile & Easter Island*; *Argentina, Uruguay & Paraguay*; *Baja California*; and *Mexico*. Wayne resides in Oakland, California.

Andrew Draffen
Born in Australia, Andrew traveled and worked his way around Australia, Asia, North America and the Caribbean, settling just long enough in Melbourne to complete an arts degree, majoring in history. In 1984, during his first trip to South America, Andrew fell in love with both Brazil and his future wife, Stella. They have since toured extensively in Brazil, Europe and Asia and today travel with their young children, Gabriela and Christopher, whose great-great-grandfather introduced football to Brazil.

Krzysztof Dydyński
Krzysztof was born and raised in Warsaw, Poland. Though he became an assistant professor in electronic engineering, he soon realized that there's more to life than microchips. He took off for Afghanistan and India in the mid-1970s and has returned to Asia several times. In the 1980s, a newly discovered passion for Latin America took him to Colombia, where he lived for more than four years, and elsewhere on the continent. In search of a new incarnation, he made Australia his home and began working for Lonely Planet. He is the author of LP guides to *Colombia*, *Venezuela*, *Poland* and *Krakow* and has also contributed to other Lonely Planet books.

Conner Gorry

Hooked on Latin America since her first trip there as an eight-year-old imp, Conner has traveled extensively, almost exclusively, in the western hemisphere. From archaeological digs in Costa Rica to farms in Cuba, she can't get enough. This interest in Latino culture led her to spend mountains of money and time obtaining a BA in Latin American Studies and an MA in International Policy. Before taking the LP challenge, she had written on such topics as José Martí, Heidi Fleiss, the Arawak Indians and menorahs. She currently calls San Francisco home, though Manhattan and Havana are always beckoning.

Robyn Jones & Leonardo Pinheiro

As a teenager, Robyn traded farm life in rural Victoria, Australia, for a year as an exchange student in the Brazilian megalopolis of São Paulo. While studying for a degree in architecture, she tripped around Australia and Europe. She later returned to Brazil with Leonardo to live in Rio de Janeiro and to get to know her future in-laws. Robyn worked on the 3rd and 4th editions of Lonely Planet's *Brazil* and cowrote *Fiji*. In between travels, Robyn works as an architect in Melbourne.

Leonardo was born and raised in Rio de Janeiro, Brazil. At 15, curious to roam farther than Rio city, he jumped on a bus to the northeast coast. From then on, he traveled throughout Brazil as much as his pocket money and time would allow. After tertiary studies in agricultural science, he came to Sydney to get a master's degree in biotechnology and to check out the Australian surf. He met Robyn and moved to Melbourne, where they now live with their baby son, Alex. Leonardo has also worked on the 3rd and 4th editions of LP's *Brazil* and *Fiji*. He is currently studying for his PhD in biochemistry.

María Massolo

María was born in Olavarría (the 'cement capital of Argentina'), Buenos Aires province, studied literature at the Universidad de Buenos Aires and relocated to California's Bay Area after marrying coauthor Wayne Bernhardson. She holds an MA in folklore and a PhD in anthropology from the University of California at Berkeley, where she is the vice-chair of the Center for Latin American Studies. In between their trips to Latin America, María, Wayne and their daughter, Clio, live in Oakland.

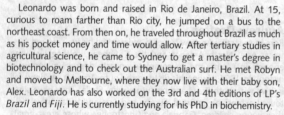

Mark J Plotkin

Mark is an ethnobotanist who has worked and traveled from Mexico to Argentina. His book *Tales of a Shaman's Apprentice*, which chronicles his search for healing plants in the northeast Amazon, is currently in its 16th edition, and he is the coauthor (along with illustrator Lynne Cherry) of a children's version, *The Shaman's Apprentice*. In 1997, Mark played a leading role in the Academy Award-nominated *Amazon*, filmed in IMAX. He currently serves as the president of the Amazon Conservation Team (www.ethnobotany.org), a cyberorganization sponsoring grassroots conservation projects in partnership with local peoples in northern South America. Mark's latest book is *Medicine Quest: In Search of Nature's Healing Secrets*.

FROM THE AUTHORS

From James Bolivia has the most helpful hotel staff anywhere, and I must thank the many desk clerks who answered my many questions – especially Sylvia in La Paz. Thanks also to Yossi, Alistair and Chris, and to all the travelers and local people who freely offered information, support and friendliness. To Pauline – it was great to have you along on this trip; and to Mike and Ben, maybe you can come next time.

From Wayne Special mention to Fito and Mary Massolo of Olavarría, Buenos Aires province, and to all their sons and daughters, nieces and nephews and others. Special mention as well to staff at Argentine, Chilean, Uruguayan, Paraguayan and Falkland Islands tourist authorities, most notably Mónica Kapusta of Buenos Aires and Mariano Besio of Santa Cruz. Thanks also to Alberto Cortez and Buddy Lander of LanChile airlines, Manuel Pérez Bravo of Montevideo, Paula Braun of Asunción, John Fowler of the Falkland Islands Tourist Board and to others whose names, for lack of space here, appear in the 3rd edition of *Argentina, Uruguay & Paraguay*.

From Andrew *Muito obrigado* to the following for their support, advice and insider tips: Vera Miller *(a sogra mais animada da praia)*, Iara Costa da Pinto, Ivana and Portugues, Arnauldo, Craig Bavinton (all São Paulo); John Caralho Malandro Maier, Mike and Ivandy and Astor (all Rio de Janeiro); Tursbahia (Salvador); and my Australian-Brazilian family who make it all worthwhile. I would like to dedicate my section of the book to my beloved father Frank, who passed away just before this research trip. He was a great dad who always encouraged me to travel and keep an open mind. We all miss him very much.

From Krzysztof Warmest thanks to Laura Beccarelli, Urs Diethelm, Doris Dornheim, Germán Escobar, Raquel and Tom Evenou, Nico de Greiff, Oscar Guerrero, Hans Kolland, Roberto Marrero, Jesús Morales and Dirk Enrique Seiffert. My special appreciation goes to Angela Melendro.

From Conner This was an intense trip! Kudos to my faithful partner, logistics guru and all-around best friend John Kochicas, who joined me in this odyssey. Koch, you're the best. A giant thank you goes to my mom for giving me the moxie to be me and introducing the family to the wonders of travel. Thanks also to the NYC literati, especially Stephen Culp, Carolyn Gorry and Andy Long. Queue up Noreen Sanders of Oakland for a big hug as well. I am forever in Mike Maurillo's debt for his tips and encouragement. In Ecuador, thank you to Sheila Corwin of the SAEC and in Amsterdam, to Ivor Netten and Justine Smit. We owe you one!

From Robyn & Leo Special thanks to Leo's family in Rio, especially *titia* Liane and *vovo* Laire for their baby-sitting skills. Thanks to Robyn's mum, Marj, for looking after our bills while we were away. Alex deserves a mention for cooperating most of the time and for making traveling more interesting! Thanks also to the tourist offices in Belém, Manaus, Rio Branco and Porto Velho.

From María I want to thank the following people for their contributions and help: In the US, Wayne Bernhardson and Clio for their relentless support; in Lima, Lily Muñoz and Laura Gómez, Catia Romero and Siduith Ferrer made my stay very pleasant; in Puerto Maldonado, Boris Zlatav and Dora Stepanovich, Manuel Ponce de León, Willy Wither, Fernando Rosemberg and Nadir Gnan; in Nazca, Juan Tohalino and his wife; in Puno, Eliana Pauca and her family; and in Cuzco, Jessica Bertrand de Sasari. Fellow travelers who made my trip a richer experience include Sarah Goodman and Simon Lund; Susan McCusker; Amanda Cavan; Allison Ferguson and Tim Wright; and Brian, Ruth and Karis Eklund. In Peru and the US, Rob Rachowiecki proved a generous colleague and friend.

From Mark Thanks to Bruce Hoffman and the late Kris Woods in French Guiana; Andrew Macushi and Neville Waldron in Guyana; and Neville Gunther, Akoi Jagan, Chris Healy, Henk and Judi Reichart, Frits von Troon, Koita Akapare and Yaloeefuh Jaromata in Suriname.

This Book

The early editions of *South America on a shoestring* were written by Geoff Crowther, but later editions have drawn increasingly on the expertise of authors of Lonely Planet guides to individual South American countries. This 7th edition was revised and updated by a team of writers. James Lyon was the coordinating author, and he updated and revised the introductory chapters and the Bolivia chapter. Wayne Bernhardson researched and updated the chapters on Argentina, Chile, the Falkland Islands, Paraguay and Uruguay; Andrew Draffen did the same for most of Brazil; Leonardo Pinheiro and Robyn Jones, for northwestern Brazil; Krzysztof Dydynski, for Colombia and Venezuela; Conner Gorry, for Ecuador; Mark Plotkin, for the Guianas; and María Massolo, for Peru.

FROM THE PUBLISHER

The 7th edition of *South America on a shoestring* was produced in Lonely Planet's Oakland office. The coordinating editor was Michele Posner, who had the invaluable support of Brigitte Barta, Jacqueline Volin and Ben Greensfelder. Michele's editorial team included Ben, Andrew Nystrom, Paige R Penland, Maia Hansen, Tullan Spitz, Kevin Anglin and Karla Huebner. Kate Hoffman, Tom Downs, Christine Lee and Maureen Klier also lent their editorial eyes to the project. Ken DellaPenta indexed the book. Kimra McAfee was the miracle-working lead cartographer; her mapping crew included John 'S-P-E' Spelman, Annette Olson, Matt DeMartini, Monica Lepe, Andy Rebold, Mary Hagemann, Bart Wright, Tim Lohnes, Dion Good and Guphy. Alex Guilbert supervised the cartography, with help from Amy Dennis and Tracey Croom. Richard Wilson oversaw the layout and design team, which included Larry Hermsen, Tomji Serianni, Josh Schefers and Henia Miedzinski; they were directed by Margaret Livingston. Shelley Firth drew the llama-rific chapter end; Rini Keagy designed the cover; and Beca Lafore designed the color pages.

THANKS

Many thanks to the travelers who used the last edition and wrote to us with helpful hints, advice and interesting anecdotes. Your names appear in the back of this book.

Foreword

ABOUT LONELY PLANET GUIDEBOOKS

The story begins with a classic travel adventure: Tony and Maureen Wheeler's 1972 journey across Europe and Asia to Australia. Useful information about the overland trail did not exist at that time, so Tony and Maureen published the first Lonely Planet guidebook to meet a growing need.

From a kitchen table, then from a tiny office in Melbourne (Australia), Lonely Planet has become the largest independent travel publisher in the world, an international company with offices in Melbourne, Oakland (USA), London (UK) and Paris (France).

Today Lonely Planet guidebooks cover the globe. There is an ever-growing list of books, and there's information in a variety of forms and media. Some things haven't changed. The main aim is still to help make it possible for adventurous travelers to get out there – to explore and better understand the world.

At Lonely Planet we believe travelers can make a positive contribution to the countries they visit – if they respect their host communities and spend their money wisely. Since 1986 a percentage of the income from each book has been donated to aid projects and human-rights campaigns.

Updates Lonely Planet thoroughly updates each guidebook as often as possible. This usually means there are around two years between editions, although for more unusual or more stable destinations the gap can be longer. Check the imprint page (following the color map at the beginning of the book) for publication dates.

Between editions, up-to-date information is available in two free newsletters – the paper *Planet Talk* and email *Comet* (to subscribe, contact any Lonely Planet office) – and on our website at www.lonelyplanet.com. The *Upgrades* section of the website covers a number of important and volatile destinations and is regularly updated by Lonely Planet authors. *Scoop* covers news and current affairs relevant to travelers. And, lastly, the *Thorn Tree* bulletin board and *Postcards* section of the site carry unverified, but fascinating, reports from travelers.

Correspondence The process of creating new editions begins with the letters, postcards and emails received from travelers. This correspondence often includes suggestions, criticisms and comments about the current editions. Interesting excerpts are immediately passed on via newsletters and the website, and everything goes to our authors to be verified when they're researching on the road. We're keen to get more feedback from organizations or individuals who represent communities visited by travelers.

Lonely Planet gathers information for everyone who's curious about the planet – and especially for those who explore it firsthand. Through guidebooks, phrasebooks, activity guides, maps, literature, newsletters, image library, TV series and website, we act as an information exchange for a worldwide community of travelers.

Research Authors aim to gather sufficient practical information to enable travelers to make informed choices and to make the mechanics of a journey run smoothly. They also research historical and cultural background to help enrich the travel experience and allow travelers to understand and respond appropriately to cultural and environmental issues.

Authors don't stay in every hotel because that would mean spending a couple of months in each medium-size city and, no, they don't eat at every restaurant because that would mean stretching belts beyond capacity. They do visit hotels and restaurants to check standards and prices, but feedback based on readers' direct experiences can be very helpful.

Many of our authors work undercover; others aren't so secretive. None of them accept freebies in exchange for positive write-ups. And none of our guidebooks contain any advertising.

Production Authors submit their raw manuscripts and maps to offices in Australia, the USA, the UK or France. Editors and cartographers – all experienced travelers themselves – then begin the process of assembling the pieces. When the book finally hits the shops, some things are already out of date, we start getting feedback from readers and the process begins again....

WARNING & REQUEST

Things change – prices go up, schedules change, good places go bad and bad places go bankrupt – nothing stays the same. So, if you find things better or worse, recently opened or long since closed, please tell us and help make the next edition even more accurate and useful. We genuinely value all the feedback we receive. Julie Young coordinates a well-traveled team that reads and acknowledges every letter, postcard and email and ensures that every morsel of information finds its way to the appropriate authors, editors and cartographers for verification.

Everyone who writes to us will find their name in the next edition of the appropriate guidebook. They will also receive the latest issue of *Planet Talk*, our quarterly printed newsletter, or *Comet*, our monthly email newsletter. Subscriptions to both newsletters are free. The very best contributions will be rewarded with a free guidebook.

Excerpts from your correspondence may appear in new editions of Lonely Planet guidebooks, the Lonely Planet website, *Planet Talk* or *Comet*, so please let us know if you *don't* want your letter published or your name acknowledged.

Send all correspondence to the Lonely Planet office closest to you:

Australia: PO Box 617, Hawthorn, Victoria 3122
USA: 150 Linden St, Oakland, CA 94607
UK: 10A Spring Place, London NW5 3BH
France: 1 rue du Dahomey, 75011 Paris

Or email us at: talk2us@lonelyplanet.com.au

For news, views and updates, see our website: www.lonelyplanet.com

HOW TO USE A LONELY PLANET GUIDEBOOK

The best way to use a Lonely Planet guidebook is any way you choose. At Lonely Planet, we believe the most memorable travel experiences are often those that are unexpected, and the finest discoveries are those you make yourself. Guidebooks are not intended to be used as if they provided a detailed set of infallible instructions!

Contents All Lonely Planet guidebooks follow the same format. The Facts about the Country chapters or sections give background information ranging from history to weather. Facts for the Visitor gives practical information on issues like visas and health. Getting There & Away gives a brief starting point for researching travel to and from the destination. Getting Around gives an overview of the transport options available when you arrive.

The peculiar demands of each destination determine how subsequent chapters are broken up, but some things remain constant. We always start with background, then proceed to sights, places to stay, places to eat, entertainment, getting there and away, and getting around information – in that order.

Heading Hierarchy Lonely Planet headings are used in a strict hierarchical structure that can be visualized as a set of Russian dolls. Each heading (and its following text) is encompassed by any preceding heading that is higher on the hierarchical ladder.

Entry Points We do not assume guidebooks will be read from beginning to end, but that people will dip into them. The traditional entry points are the list of contents and the index. In addition, however, some books have a complete list of maps and an index map illustrating map coverage.

There may also be a color map that shows highlights. These highlights are dealt with in greater detail later in the book, along with planning questions and suggested itineraries. Each chapter covering a geographical region usually begins with a locator map and another list of highlights. Once you find something of interest in a list of highlights, turn to the index.

Maps Maps play a crucial role in Lonely Planet guidebooks and include a huge amount of information. A legend is printed on the back page. We seek to have complete consistency between maps and text, and to have every important place in the text captured on a map. Map key numbers usually start in the top left corner.

Although inclusion in a guidebook usually implies a recommendation, we cannot list every good place. Exclusion does not necessarily imply criticism. In fact, there are a number of reasons why we might exclude a place – sometimes it is simply inappropriate to encourage an influx of travelers.

Introduction

Still a destination for independent travelers, South America offers something for every interest and lots of opportunities to get off the beaten track.

Looking for mountains? The Andes have everything from gentle, scenic treks to high-altitude technical climbs. Beaches? Loll on unspoiled tropical islands, or hit Brazil's *barracas* for cold beer, beautiful bodies and blaring music. Jungles? Despite deforestation, vast tracts of tropical rain forest still contain thousands of plant and animal species. Rivers? The Amazon is the biggest

anywhere. Waterfalls? The world's highest and most voluminous cascades are here. Cities? Try the big-city pulse of megalopolis São Paulo, the European style of Buenos Aires, the sophistication of Santiago or the faded funkiness of Paramaribo.

If your passions are history and culture, you'll want to see the ancient ruins of mysterious Machu Picchu or discover Ciudad Perdida, the 'lost city' of Colombia. Colonial history is visually evident in dozens of cities and towns, where churches, missions, fortresses and palaces are now mellowed

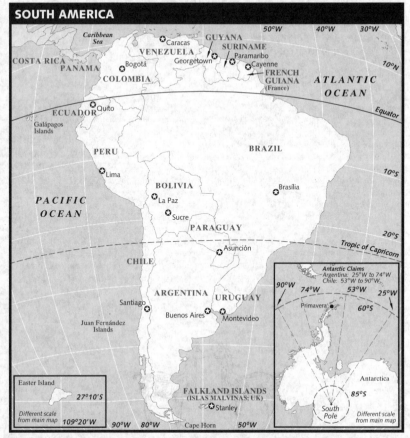

SOUTH AMERICA

19

testaments to European domination. One of the most exciting and accessible forms of contemporary culture is South American music, heard everywhere on the continent, from Caribbean rhythms to Brazilian samba to the haunting flutes of the Andes.

Recent economic instability has made several countries much more affordable for visitors, most notably Brazil, which is once again a worthwhile destination for budget travelers. The Andean countries are still a bargain, and there are economical travel options even in relatively expensive countries such as Argentina and Chile. Economic changes have brought improved infrastructure in many countries – phones work, buses run on time and the electricity supply lasts all night, mostly. But there are downsides: Colombia is riskier than ever due to guerrillas, drug runners, robbers and kidnappers, and there's a lot of thievery in Peru and Brazil, but travelers who avoid dangerous areas and take sensible precautions are unlikely to find trouble.

Transport options range from the roof of a train to a luxury bus, a rickety riverboat, a dugout canoe or your own two feet. You can sleep in a hostel, a high-rise, a love hotel or a hammock; drink sickly-sweet Inca Kola or overproof *cachaça*; and eat anything from pizza to piranha, barbecued beef to spicy sea urchin. Adventurous travelers will find South America is still an adventure.

Facts about South America

HISTORY
Pre-Columbian South America

It's generally accepted that the first people in the Americas came from east Asia, over a land bridge across what is now known as the Bering Strait. The land bridge, called Beringia, occurred when sea levels were lowered during an ice age between 25,000 and 10,000 years ago. Estimates of the timing of this epic migration vary from as recently as 12,500 years ago to as far back as 70,000 years, but the oldest estimates are largely speculative. Subsequent migrations distributed the population southward through both North and Central America and down to the southern tip of South America. Human artifacts from a site in southern Chile, recently carbon dated to be about 12,500 years old, are close to the oldest undisputed evidence of human occupation in the Americas.

The first inhabitants of South America were nomadic hunter-gatherers who lived in small bands. It's likely that agriculture developed gradually in the tropical lowlands, starting around 5000 BC, with the planting of wild tubers such as manioc (cassava) and sweet potato, under systems of shifting cultivation. One of the continent's greatest contributions to the world is the humble potato, a root crop domesticated in the Andean highlands.

About the same time, people began to farm seed crops, such as beans, in the highland areas, and large deposits of animal bones on the continent are the first evidence of the domestication of animals such as the llama. From about 4000 BC, there is evidence of seed agriculture in Peru's coastal lowlands. The cultivation of maize, probably imported from Mexico before 2500 BC (perhaps much earlier), is closely correlated with the development of settled agriculture communities.

Coastal & Highland Civilizations

Complex societies developed first in the valleys of coastal Peru. It's thought that the population of some of these valleys grew until all the cultivable land was occupied, and the need to expand into neighboring valleys led the inhabitants to develop a more organized society for the purpose of conquest. Conquerors became rulers, and the conquered became their subjects, thus developing the social and economic hierarchies of these early states.

These embryonic states ultimately developed into major civilizations, such as the Wari Empire of the Peruvian central highlands, the Tiahuanaco (or Tiwanaku) culture of highland Bolivia, the Chimú of northern coastal Peru and the Inca empire of Cuzco, known more properly as Tahuantinsuyo (or Tawantinsuy). Most of what is known about these cultures is derived from archaeological remains, particularly ceramics (see Nazca, Around Cuzco, Machu Picchu and Around Trujillo in the Peru chapter).

The Inca Empire The Incas developed the most sophisticated of South America's pre-Columbian highland civilizations. At its peak, at the time of the Spanish invasion in the early 16th century, the Inca empire governed at least 12 million people from north Ecuador to central Chile, traversing the Andes with more than 8000km of highways, but it was never able to penetrate deep into the Amazon lowlands. This overextended empire, racked by dissension and civil war, proved vulnerable to invasion by a very small force of Spaniards.

Tropical Rain Forest Peoples The inhabitants of tropical rain forest regions such as the Amazon Basin did not develop complex civilizations such as those found in the Andes. The population of rain forest areas at the time of European contact is not known for certain, but there is evidence of substantial villages of 5000 or more people. Archaeological remains are few because most tools and other artifacts were made of perishable materials such as wood and bone.

Southern South America Inca rule barely touched central Chile or northern Argentina. Native peoples of the Araucanian language groups, including the Picunche and Mapuche peoples of Chile and Argentina, fiercely resisted incursions from the

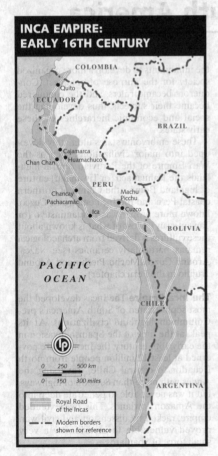

INCA EMPIRE: EARLY 16TH CENTURY

COLOMBIA
Quito
ECUADOR
BRAZIL
Cajamarca
Chan Chan   Huamachuco
PERU
Chancay   Machu
Pachacamac   Picchu
Ica   Cuzco
BOLIVIA
PACIFIC
OCEAN
CHILE

0   250   500 km
0   150   300 miles

ARGENTINA

▭ Royal Road of the Incas
– ∙ – Modern borders shown for reference

South of the mainland, on the islands of Tierra del Fuego, small populations of Indians subsisted on hunting and fishing, including the Chonos, Qawashqar (Alacalufes), Tehuelches, Yamaná (Yahgans) and Onas (Selknam). These isolated, archipelagic peoples long avoided contact with Europeans and have now virtually disappeared as a recognizable cultural group.

European Contact

Christopher Columbus (known in Spanish as Cristóbal Colón) led the first recorded European 'discovery' of the Americas, though in fact he was seeking a new route to Asia's spice islands. Bankrolled by Queen Isabella of Spain and given an exceedingly broad grant of authority over any territory he might discover, the dubiously qualified Genoese mariner sailed westward, making landfalls on several Caribbean islands that he believed to be part of Asia. It was actually the Portuguese navigator Vasco da Gama who found the sea route to Asia, around the Cape of Good Hope and across the Indian Ocean; the Spanish discovery of the New World was a second prize. These momentous discoveries raised the stakes in the rivalry between Spain and Portugal.

Treaty of Tordesillas When Portugal protested that Spanish voyages had encroached on its sphere of influence in the Atlantic, the Spanish monarchs asked Pope Alexander VI to resolve the dispute. In 1494, representatives of the two countries met in the northern Spanish town of Tordesillas, where they established a line of demarcation at about 48° west of Greenwich, giving Africa and Asia to Portugal and all of the New World to Spain. Significantly, however, this agreement placed the coast of Brazil (not discovered until six years later) on the Portuguese side of the line, giving Portugal unanticipated access to the new continent. The treaty was ratified in 1506, though no other European maritime power, and certainly none of the indigenous people of the Americas, ever agreed to the arrangement.

Exploration, Conquest & Colonization

The island of Hispaniola (today shared by the Dominican Republic and Haiti) became the first European settlement and Columbus'

north. The Picunche lived in permanent agricultural settlements, while the Mapuche, who practiced shifting cultivation, were more mobile. Several groups closely related to the Mapuche (Pehuenches, Huilliches and Puelches) lived in the southern lake district, while the Cunco fished and farmed on the island of Chiloé and along the shores of the gulfs of Reloncaví and Ancud.

In the forested delta of the upper Río Paraná, Guaraní shifting cultivators relied on maize and tuber crops. In the Pampas to the south and well into Patagonia, highly mobile peoples hunted the guanaco (a wild relative of the Andean llama) and the rhea (a flightless bird resembling the ostrich) with bows and arrows or *boleadoras* (heavily weighted thongs).

base for further exploration. Between 1496 and 1518, he and other voyagers charted the Caribbean Sea and the Gulf of Mexico, the Venezuelan and Guyanese shores all the way to the mouth of the Amazon, and the Brazilian coastline. This phase of coastal exploration effectively ended when Portuguese navigator Ferdinand Magellan sailed down South America's east coast, through the strait that now bears his name, and across the Pacific Ocean to reach the Philippines in 1521. This demonstrated that America was no shortcut to Asia, and Europeans turned their efforts to occupying, plundering and otherwise profiting from the new territories.

Jamaica, Cuba and Puerto Rico followed Hispaniola as early Spanish settlements. Cortés' conquest of Mexico led to further land expeditions. The members of one of these expeditions returned with rumors of a golden kingdom, Birú (Peru), to the south of Panama. After Francisco Pizarro's preliminary expeditions down South America's Pacific coast (1524 and 1526) confirmed some of these rumors, he went to Spain, where he convinced authorities to finance an expedition of 200 men and grant him authority over the lands he would survey.

Spain's invasion of the Americas was accomplished by small groups of adventurers, lowlifes and soldiers of fortune. Though few in number, the conquerors were determined and ruthless, exploiting factionalism among native groups and frightening indigenous peoples with horses, firearms and vicious dogs.

The Conquest of the Inca

Pizarro's advance into Peru was rapid and dramatic. His well-armed soldiers terrorized the Indians, but his greatest ally was infectious disease, to which indigenous people lacked any immunity. About 1525, the Inca ruler Huayna Capac died, probably of smallpox contracted through messengers who had been in contact with the Spaniards.

Before he died, Huayna Capac divided his empire, giving the northern part to his son, Atahualpa, and the more southerly Cuzco area to another son, Huáscar. Civil war followed, and after several years of fighting, Atahualpa's troops defeated and captured Huáscar outside Cuzco.

Meanwhile, Pizarro had landed in north Ecuador and marched south in the wake of Atahualpa's conquests. On November 16, 1532, a fateful meeting between Atahualpa and Pizarro took place in Cajamarca. Atahualpa was ambushed and captured by the Spanish army, who killed thousands of unarmed Indians. In an attempt to regain his freedom, Atahualpa offered a ransom – one room full of gold and two of silver. Pizarro sent three of his soldiers to Cuzco in early 1533, and they proceeded to strip Coricancha, the 'Gold Courtyard,' of its splendid ornamentation, melting and crushing beautiful artifacts to ensure that the room was really filled with gold. Despite the ransom, the treacherous Spanish put Atahualpa through a sham trial, and he was executed by strangulation.

When Pizarro entered Cuzco on November 8, 1533, he was permitted into the heart of the Inca empire by a people whose sympathy lay more with the defeated Huáscar than with Atahualpa. Pizarro appointed Manco Inca, Huáscar's half-brother, as a puppet Inca ruler. In 1536, Manco Inca fled from the Spanish and raised a huge army, estimated at far more than 100,000 people, and laid siege to Cuzco. Only a desperate breakout from Cuzco and a violent battle saved the Spanish troops from defeat. Atahualpa's nephew, Tupac Amaru, also fought valiantly against the Spanish until his beheading in a Cuzco plaza in 1572.

Spain's Empire in South America

Lima, founded in 1535 as the capital of the new Viceroyalty of Peru, was the base for most of the further exploration and conquest of the continent. Sebastián Benalcázar traveled from Lima via Quito (in modern-day Ecuador) to the highlands of Colombia in 1538, and by 1540, Pedro de Valdivia had penetrated as far as Chile's Río Biobío. Expeditions south, along and over the Andes mountains, founded Tucumán and Mendoza.

Pedro de Mendoza formed a settlement at the mouth of the Río de la Plata in 1535, which later moved upriver to what is now Asunción, Paraguay. The coast of Venezuela was settled from Hispaniola, and it later became part of the Viceroyalty of Nueva Granada.

Administration The Viceroyalty of Peru was the seat of all power in Spanish South America. As the monarch's representative

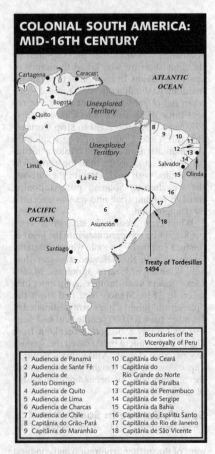

COLONIAL SOUTH AMERICA: MID-16TH CENTURY

ATLANTIC OCEAN

Cartagena
Caracas
Bogotá
Quito
Unexplored Territory
Unexplored Territory
Lima
La Paz
Salvador
Olinda
PACIFIC OCEAN
Asunción
Santiago
Treaty of Tordesillas 1494

– – – Boundaries of the Viceroyalty of Peru

1 Audiencia de Panamá	10 Capitânia do Ceará
2 Audiencia de Sante Fé	11 Capitânia do
3 Audiencia de	Rio Grande do Norte
Santo Domingo	12 Capitânia da Paraíba
4 Audiencia de Quito	13 Capitânia de Pernambuco
5 Audiencia de Lima	14 Capitânia de Sergipe
6 Audiencia de Charcas	15 Capitânia da Bahia
7 Audiencia de Chile	16 Capitânia do Espírito Santo
8 Capitânia do Grão-Pará	17 Capitânia do Rio de Janeiro
9 Capitânia do Maranhão	18 Capitânia de São Vicente

parentage, usually of a Spanish father and an Indian mother, were known as *mestizos* and were generally excluded from higher positions. *Indígenas* (Native Americans) made up the bottom stratum of society.

The administration of the viceroyalty was highly centralized, but there were enormous practical difficulties in imposing imperial control throughout the area. This lack of control led to considerable local autonomy in government and commerce. In addition, abuse, corruption and a flourishing contraband trade served to further undermine peninsular authority.

Spaniards & Indians The primary goal of the first Spaniards was the acquisition of gold and silver, and they ruthlessly appropriated precious metals, through outright robbery when possible, and by other equally brutal means when necessary.

The Spaniards exploited indigenous populations through such mechanisms as the *encomienda* (best translated as 'entrustment'), by which the Spanish Crown granted an individual Spaniard rights to Indian labor and tribute in a particular village or area. In theory, Spanish legislation required the holder of the encomienda, the *encomendero,* to reciprocate with instruction in the Spanish language and the Catholic religion, but in practice, imperial administration could not ensure compliance or avoid serious abuses. Spanish overseers worked Indians mercilessly in the mines and extracted the maximum in agricultural produce.

In the most densely populated parts of the Americas, some encomenderos became extraordinarily wealthy, but the encomienda system itself failed when Native American populations declined rapidly due to introduced diseases, such as smallpox, influenza and typhus. In some parts of the New World, these diseases reduced the indigenous population by more than 95%.

This demographic collapse had a lasting impact on South American societies and economies. As encomiendas became worthless, encomenderos and others assembled *latifundios* (large properties) from the holdings of the depleted Indian communities. As the indigenous populations declined, there was a growth in the number of people of mixed European and Indian descent – the *mestizaje*. In several parts of the continent,

in Lima, the viceroy headed a hierarchy of lesser officials. The main functionaries were the presidents of *audiencias*, who held civil power in areas where no viceroy was resident, and the *corregidores*, who each governed a provincial city and its surrounding area. The corregidor was usually associated with a *cabildo* (town council), which was about the only representative institution.

Only *peninsulares* (those born in Spain) could hold any senior positions. *Criollos* (creoles), born in the New World of Spanish parents, could hold a commission in a colonial army or serve on a cabildo. As the peninsulares generally spent a term in the colonies before returning to Spain, the criollos became the main landholders, merchants and entrepreneurs. People of mixed

African slaves were introduced to make up for the lack of indigenous labor, notably in the plantations of Brazil and the mines of Bolivia.

Colonial Economy After the initial period of plunder, mines were the principal source of revenue; one-fifth of all precious metals, the *quinto real* or 'royal fifth,' went to the Spanish monarchy. To discourage piracy and simplify taxation, all colonial exports had to go to Spain by way of the officials of Lima and the ports of Veracruz (Mexico), Cartagena (Colombia) and Portobelo (Panama). For example, in the early colonial period, goods from Buenos Aires went overland to Lima, by sea to Panama and then overland across the isthmus before being loaded onto ships to cross the Atlantic; officially nothing could be sent directly to Europe.

Under a crown monopoly, a merchant guild based in Spain controlled all trade with the colonies. With their related guilds in Lima and Mexico, Spanish merchants fixed high prices for European goods in the colonies, and taxes were levied on the imports. These taxes and restrictions on trade caused great discontent within the colonies, particularly among criollos, whose prosperity depended more on local development than on generating wealth for Spanish merchants and the crown.

The Church

The conversion of indigenous people to the Catholic faith was the moral rationale for the Spanish conquest. The Catholic Church was an active partner in the Iberian domination of the continent and even held encomiendas in its own right. Nevertheless, some members of the church did protest at the treatment of the Indians. The Dominican priest Bartolomé de las Casas was a one-time conquistador who later spoke out against corrupt officials and encomenderos, even advocating restitution for all the wealth that Spain had plundered from the Americas.

Of the various Catholic orders active in South America, the Jesuits worked most closely with the Indians, especially in Brazil and the south of the continent. They recorded native languages, established missions in which Indians were resettled, and defended the Indians against the worst excesses of the colonial system. Their actions antagonized both Spanish and Portuguese authorities, who eventually expelled the Jesuits from Brazil in 1759 and from the Spanish colonies in 1767. One Brazilian statesman wrote that 'without the Jesuits, our colonial history would be little more than a chain of nameless atrocities.'

Other European Colonies

Portugal's colonization of Brazil was far less systematic than Spain's practices in the rest of South America. Whereas Spain set up a colonial bureaucracy accountable to the crown, Portugal divided the country into parallel strips extending to the Line of Tordesillas, and established *capitânias* (donated or inherited captaincies), which gave the chosen rulers almost unlimited powers within their domains. When this proved unsatisfactory, the crown assumed direct control. For details, see the Brazil chapter.

Other European powers to claim territory in South America were Britain, Holland and France, all of which sought to extend their influences from the Caribbean to the mainland. Though the Spanish and Portuguese always regarded the presence of these countries as an incursion, the territories on the northeast coast of the continent were, relatively, so unattractive that neither peninsular power could spare the resources to eject the rivals. See the Guianas chapter for more details.

Revolution & Independence

Spanish Colonies Pressure for independence came mainly from criollos, who resented both the political and social dominance of the peninsulares and the restrictive trade policies of the colonial administration. Some criollos were educated, and their awareness of the Enlightenment, the American Revolution and the French Revolution contributed to a pro-independence attitude. Events in Europe, though, are what really precipitated the independence movement.

In 1796, Spain formed an alliance with France, making Spanish vessels a target for the British navy (in addition to the unofficial privateers who had been attacking Spanish ships for years). This disrupted Spain's communication and trade with the Americas, forcing the colonies into practical, if not official, independence. The defeat of a British invasion of Buenos Aires in 1806 added to the colonists' growing self-confidence and sense of self-sufficiency.

The following year, Napoléon forced the abdication of Spanish monarch Charles IV, replacing him with Napoléon's own brother, Joseph. Criollo leaders forced royal officials to hand over power to local juntas, supposedly until the restoration of a legitimate monarch. The criollos were reluctant to relinquish power when, after Napoléon's defeat in 1814, Ferdinand VII became King of Spain. The end of the European wars enabled more troops to be deployed in the Americas, but the burden was on the Spanish to reassert control, particularly in Venezuela and Argentina, which had effectively declared independence.

The two main currents of the independence movement converged on Peru from these two areas. Argentina overcame Spain's attempted reconquest, and its forces, under the command of José de San Martín, crossed the Andes to liberate Chile (1817-18) from the Spanish and finally sailed up the coast to take Lima (1821). From 1819 to 1821, Simón Bolívar and his followers advanced overland to Peru from Venezuela via Colombia and Ecuador.

At their famous meeting at Guayaquil in 1822, the apolitical San Martín found himself in conflict with Bolívar, who had strong political ambitions. San Martín saw the installation of a powerful leader, even a monarch, as essential to avoid the disintegration of Peru, while Bolívar insisted on a constitutional republic. In a complicated exchange, which aroused ill-feeling in both camps, Bolívar won the day and San Martín returned to the south.

In the long run, both were disappointed. The proliferation of *caudillos* (local warlords or strongmen) set a deplorable pattern for most of the 19th century. San Martín returned to an Argentina racked by internal dissension and left almost immediately for self-imposed exile in France. Bolívar's dream of a strong republic of Gran Colombia was shattered by difficulties leading to the secession of Ecuador and the separation of Colombia and Venezuela in 1830.

Brazil Brazil became autonomous in 1807, when the Portuguese prince regent, exiled after Napoléon's occupation of Portugal, established himself in Brazil. He later returned to Europe, leaving his son Pedro as prince regent, but when the Portuguese parliament tried to reclaim the colony, Dom Pedro proclaimed himself emperor of an independent Brazil.

After Independence

South America's modern political map reflects, to a great degree, the viceroyalties, audiencias and presidencias of the Spanish Empire. After independence, the former colonies became separate countries whose borders generally followed colonial administrative divisions, modified by the ambitions of the independence leaders. The consolidations, secessions and territorial disputes that followed – in some cases still persist – are outlined in the geography section and in individual country chapters.

The social structures of the new countries changed slowly. Criollos replaced peninsulares at the apex of the hierarchy, while mestizos and indigenous people continued to occupy the lower social and economic strata. Within the criollo elite, divisions emerged between educated, urban liberals and rural landholders who had traditional, conservative, Spanish Catholic values. The former group favored a centralized government that looked to Enlightenment Europe for inspiration, while the latter group sought to retain the privileges it had acquired under colonial rule.

Rural landowners (*hacendados* or *gamonales*) prevailed in the short run. Powerful caudillos with private armies exerted considerable influence on national politics and filled the power vacuum left by the departed colonial regime. Because this strong leadership was based on personality and personal following rather than on ideology or collective interest, it did not offer any continuity beyond that individual leader. The instability and violence that have characterized the South American republics have many roots in this period.

While each country has developed separately since independence, there have been common elements, particularly the alternation between strong dictatorships and periods of instability, and the gross inequality between powerful elites and the powerless masses. Indian populations have fared badly in almost every country, suffering marginalization at best, genocide at worst. Only recently have some groups been able to reassert their identities and exercise political power. Foreign intervention has also factored in the political and economic development of most countries in South America, though direct military involvement has been a rarity, and many of the republics have very independent foreign policies.

GEOGRAPHY

Apart from the main physical and political divisions of the continent, it's common to refer to the 'Andean countries,' Colombia, Ecuador, Peru and Bolivia; and the 'Southern Cone (el Cono Sur),' comprising Argentina, Uruguay, Paraguay, Chile and south Brazil.

Physical Features

The great mountain system of the Andes forms the western margin of the continent, snaking nearly 8000km from Venezuela to southern Patagonia. From its northern extremity in Venezuela, the *cordillera* (range) extends southwest to form the eastern segment of several ranges in Colombia, which join to form a single range in the south of the country. In Ecuador, the Andes divide into two major volcanic chains, separated by a broad plateau. The Central Andes, located in Peru, comprise three southeast trending ranges that meet the *altiplano* (high plateau) on the Bolivian border. South of Bolivia, the mountain range forms the border between Chile and Argentina and extends to the southern tip of the continent.

The other dominant physical feature is the Amazon Basin, which drains an area of about 7 million sq km, extending 3000km from the eastern slopes of the Andes to the Atlantic coast, bounded by the highlands of the Guiana Shield to the north and the Brazilian Shield to the south.

Other physical features are the smaller Orinoco River Basin, which drains the Llanos (plains) of Venezuela; the barren Chaco of southern Bolivia and northwestern Paraguay; the extensive Paraná-Paraguay river system; the fertile Pampas of Argentina and Uruguay; and arid Patagonia, in the far south. A narrow strip of coastal plains around much of the continent, while not prominent on a map, contains some of the most densely populated areas, especially in Brazil, Argentina, Uruguay and Peru.

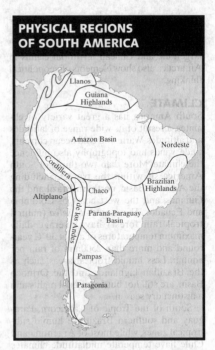

PHYSICAL REGIONS OF SOUTH AMERICA

Political Geography & Borders

South America's colonial political boundaries were indistinct, and the creation of new states resulted in many territorial disputes, some of which persist. A dispute over the Peru-Ecuador border was the subject of armed confrontation in 1995, but in 1998 this was finally settled by diplomatic means. Other countries that dispute borders are Venezuela and Guyana, Guyana and Suriname, and Suriname and French Guiana. Argentina's claim to the Falkland Islands (Islas Malvinas) led to open warfare in 1982. A long-standing dispute between Chile and Argentina over three small islands in the Beagle Channel was settled by arbitration in 1979, but a small area of the Patagonian ice field is still disputed.

Geopolitics One of the mainstays of military ideology, especially in the Southern Cone countries, is the 19th-century European notion of geopolitics. According to this view, the state is like a biological organism that must grow or die. A state must effectively occupy the territories it claims as its own, even if this brings it into conflict with other states. Such thinking was clearly a major factor in Argentine general Galtieri's decision to invade the Falkland Islands in 1982. Argentine and Chilean territorial claims in Antarctica also show elements of geopolitical thinking.

CLIMATE

South America has a great variety of climates, a result of its wide range of latitudes and altitudes. Warm and cold ocean currents, trade winds and topography also influence the climate. More than two-thirds of South America sit within the tropics, including the Amazon Basin, northern Brazil and the Guianas, and the west coast of Colombia and Ecuador. These areas of *selva* (natural tropical rain forest) have average daily maximum temperatures of about 30°C year-round and more than 2500mm of rain per annum. Less humid tropical areas, such as the Brazilian highlands and the Orinoco Basin, are still hot but enjoy cool nights and a distinct dry season.

South of the Tropic of Capricorn, Paraguay and southern Brazil are humid subtropical zones, while most of Argentina and Chile have temperate midlatitude climates with mild winters and warm summers ranging from 12°C in July to 25°C in January, depending on landforms and latitude. Rainfall, occurring mostly in winter, varies from 200mm to 2000mm per annum, depending on winds and the rain shadow effect of the Andes.

The main arid regions are Patagonia, in the rain shadow east of the Andes, and northern Chile and Peru, between the Andes and the Pacific coast, where the cold Humboldt current creates a cloudy but dry climate. About every seven years, large-scale changes in Pacific Ocean circulation patterns and rising sea-surface temperatures create the 'El Niño effect,' which brings heavy rain and floods to these desert areas and disrupts weather patterns all around the world. There are two smaller arid zones, the northeastern Brazilian *sertão*, where severe droughts wreak great hardships on peasant populations, and along the north coast of Colombia and Venezuela.

The high Andes, which have an altitude of more than 3500m, and far southern Chile and Argentina are cool climate zones, where average daily temperatures fall lower than 10°C and temperatures often dip lower than freezing.

ECOLOGY & ENVIRONMENT

The South American continent comprises a number of distinct environments, each with its own ecosystem. The most extensive of these environments is the Amazon Basin, which is the subject of worldwide concern. Other environments are tiny by comparison, but still of great interest. For more detailed information on this subject, see the Flora & Fauna sections in the country chapters.

Amazon Basin Rain Forests

Bolivia, Brazil, Colombia, Ecuador, Guyana, French Guiana, Peru, Suriname and Venezuela all occupy parts of the world's greatest river basin. The Amazon, born inconspicuously in the Peruvian highlands, has a number of enormous tributaries and some imposing statistics. The distance from its source to its mouth is more than 6200km, its flow is 12 times that of the Mississippi, it carries one-fifth of the world's fresh water, and its discharge into the Atlantic every 24 hours equals that of the Thames in a full year. Atlantic tides can be felt at Óbidos, 500km above the river mouth, but early mariners collected fresh water from its discharge more than 250km out to sea; its sediments are identifiable for hundreds of kilometers more.

Tributaries north of the Solimões (the main channel of the Amazon) are mostly 'black water' rivers, whose dissolved organic matter consumes oxygen and renders the streams acidic and relatively lifeless. Those to the south are 'clear water' rivers with higher, more stable banks, and they support a greater amount of aquatic life. The most biologically productive channels are the upper 'white water' tributaries such as the Marañon and Ucayali, which carry suspended sediments from the eastern slopes of the Peruvian Andes. At the Encontro das Aguas ('meeting of the waters'), near Manaus, these white waters flow alongside the black waters of the Rio Negro for some distance without mixing.

The tropics are far richer in species than the midlatitudes, and tropical rain forest is the earth's most complex ecosystem. The Amazonian forest may contain as many as 50,000 species of higher plants, one-fifth of the world's total. In some two-hectare plots in the Amazon, one can find more than 500 tree species; a comparable plot in a midlatitude forest might have no more than three or four. This is correlated with a great diversity of animal species. One study found 3000 species of beetles in five small plots of rain forest and estimated that each species of tree supported more than 400 different unique species of animal.

The physical structure of the tropical rain forest consists of an overstory of large trees buttressed by vines and a lower story of smaller trees. The canopy is so dense that almost no sunlight penetrates to the forest floor. So little grows in this shade that, except near watercourses, the forest floor itself is surprisingly open and not at all like the dense jungle many people imagine.

More than 98% of the area drained by the Amazon is of low fertility, despite the exuberant appearance of the natural vegetation. Heavy rainfall leaches almost all important chemical nutrients from the soil and, because of high temperatures and bacterial activity, there is almost no accumulation of humus; nutrients from the decayed material are almost immediately reabsorbed into the living trees. This is why the forest is rarely able to regenerate itself after large areas are cleared. Less than 2% of the Amazon Basin is alluvial flood plain suitable for intensive agriculture.

Environmental Problems Environmental threats to the Amazon Basin have been well publicized – vast areas have been deforested for timber, mining and agriculture, while hydroelectric projects have inundated pristine forest and have displaced indigenous peoples.

South American people are well aware of these issues, but powerful entrenched interests and short-term economic considerations have often overwhelmed long-term environmental concerns. There are very different conditions in various parts of the region; in recent years the tributaries of the Amazon have suffered the worst depredations. Brazilian projects such as the Tucuruí dam on the Rio Tocantins, the Transamazon Highway, tree plantations on the Rio Jarí and gold mining in Roraima have brought deforestation, mercury contamination and siltation of rivers.

On a global scale, the Amazon rain forest is believed to moderate climatic patterns, so its destruction will contribute to global warming. Rain forests are also vital for the maintainance of biodiversity. Roughly half of the planet's 1.5 million known species live in tropical rain forests, and millions more species are as yet undocumented. Deforestation results in countless extinctions, and many of the species being lost may have medicinal or agricultural potential that has never been assessed. Deforestation also threatens many indigenous people who still depend on the forest to maintain their way of life.

Efforts are now under way to show that the economic value of the standing rain forest is greater than the mineral, timber and grazing wealth to be realized by deforestation. One way to make tropical rain forest economically productive, without cutting it down, is to protect it and make it accessible to visitors; tourism has boomed in several South American countries though many so-called ecotourism developments are not especially environmentally friendly or sustainable.

The total deforestation may be less than some alarmist estimates have suggested. It's estimated that only around 10% of the Amazon rain forests have been cleared to date, but the *rate* of deforestation is so startling that many fear it is an irreversible trend. Satellite data from 1993 suggests that more than 15,000 sq km of Amazon rain forest is being cut down every year.

Traditional Shifting Agriculture The widespread practice of slash-and-burn agriculture is sometimes seen as a culprit in the deforestation of the Amazon and other rain forest regions, but it is actually a sustainable technique well suited to the rain-forest ecosystem. Indigenous peoples such as the Kuikuru, of Brazil's upper Rio Xingú, have farmed nearby forest for as long as 90 years at a stretch without exhausting its resources or permanently reducing forest cover.

Shifting agriculture certainly appears disruptive – the forest understory is hacked away with a machete, large trees are felled and the debris is piled up and burned. In fact, the burning liberates plant nutrients for growing crops in an accelerated version of the natural cycle, which depends on decomposition and reabsorption of plant materials.

Various crops are planted, in a structure resembling that of a natural rain forest, with an upper story of fruit trees, an intermediate level of plants such as maize and sugar cane, and a surface layer of tubers and ground-cover plants that protect the soil surface. A single plot might contain five varieties of bananas, three types of plantains, several kinds of tubers (including yams, sweet potatoes and cassava), tree crops (like peach palm, avocado and papaya), sugar cane, tobacco and cotton, and annuals such as chilies, maize, beans, tomatoes and squash. The variety of plants discourages natural pests that thrive in large stands of a single crop, thus helping to ensure a steady harvest.

Fertility on these small plots drops rapidly after two or three years, but the tree crops are good for several more years. A long fallow period, up to 30 years, then allows recovery of the forest.

If increased population or market pressures reduce fallow periods, the forest may not have sufficient time to recover. Innovations such as chainsaws can upset the delicate balance on which the system depends. When the system is extended into drier environments, it may fail, and when inexperienced immigrants attempt to farm the forest, results can be disastrous. But travelers who see a smoldering plot in the rain forest should not assume the worst; there is a strong correlation between the presence of indigenous peoples and the preservation of the selva.

Central Andean Region

Another unique ecosystem exists between the coast and the cordillera, from northern Chile to northern Peru. The coastal Atacama desert, the world's driest, is almost utterly barren in the rain shadow of the high Andes. The cold Peru current (also called the Humboldt current) moderates the temperature at this tropical latitude and produces convective fogs, known as *garúa* or *camanchaca*, that support the hillside vegetation known as *lomas* in the coastal ranges. The only other vegetation occurs in the valleys of the several transverse rivers that descend from the Andes.

Precipitation and vegetation increase with altitude and distance from the coast as well as from south to north. Traditionally, Andean peoples in different agropastoral 'niches' produced different, complementary products, which they exchanged with their family in other zones. Coastal products included cotton, fish, guano (for fertilizer) and coca, while the higher *sierra* (mountain range) yielded maize and tubers (notably potatoes), grown on an extensive system of agricultural terraces. On the heights of the altiplano cultivation was impossible, and therefore salt, wool and meat were the bases of subsistence.

This integrated economic system was disrupted by colonization, but it survives in many parts of the Andean region. The Andes are still a repository for a plant genetic diversity that parallels that of the Amazon. Some 6000 varieties of potatoes are raised by Andean peasants; these are important sources of genetic material for improved potato varieties.

Tropical Cloud Forests

In remote valleys at higher elevations, tropical cloud forests create and retain clouds that engulf the forest in a fine mist, allowing some particularly delicate forms of plant life to survive. Cloud forest trees are adapted to steep rocky soils and a harsh climate. They have characteristically low, gnarled growth, dense, small-leafed canopy, and moss-covered branches supporting orchids, ferns, bromeliads and a host of other epiphytes (aerial plants that gather moisture and nutrients without ground roots). Such forests are the homes of rare species such as the woolly tapir, the Andean spectacled bear and the puma. This habitat is particularly important as a source of fresh water and protects the thin soil against erosion.

High-Altitude Grassland

Even higher than the cloud forest, the *páramo* is the natural sponge of the Andes. It catches and gradually releases much of the water eventually used by city dwellers. The páramo is characterized by a harsh climate, high levels of ultraviolet light and wet, peaty soils. It is a highly specialized highland habitat unique to tropical America, and it's found only from the highlands of Costa Rica to the highlands of northern Peru. Flora of the páramo is dominated by hard grasses, cushion plants and small herbaceous plants, which have all adapted well to the harsh environment. The páramo also features dense thickets of the *Polylepis* species *(queñua* in Spanish), members of the rose family. Along with the Himalayan pines, the *queñua* share the world altitude record for trees. Once considerably more extensive, they have been pushed back into small pockets by fire and grazing. A spiky, resistant tussock grass, locally called *ichu*, is also often encountered. It grows in large clumps and makes walking uncomfortable.

Tropical Dry Forest

Hot areas with well-defined wet and dry seasons support dry forests. In South America these climatic conditions are mostly found near the coast in the northern part of the continent. Trees here lose their leaves during the dry season and are more widely spaced than in the rain forest. Because many of these coastal regions have a dense and growing population, tropical dry forest is a fast-disappearing habitat – only about 1% of the continent's natural dry forest remains undisturbed.

Mangroves

Mangroves are trees with the remarkable ability to grow in salt water. They have a broadly spreading system of intertwining stilt roots to support the tree in unstable sandy or silty soils. Mangrove forests trap sediments and build up a rich organic soil, which in turn supports other plants. In between the roots, a protected habitat is provided for many types of fish, mollusk and crustacean as well as other animals, while the branches provide nesting areas for sea birds.

Islands

Island groups off South America's coast are some of the most isolated spots in the world. The Galápagos Islands (1000km off Ecuador's coast) have been known for their wildlife since Darwin's day. Chile's Juan Fernández archipelago (700km west of Valparaíso), Brazil's Fernando de Noronha archipelago (350km east of Natal), and the Falklands, also known as the Malvinas (500km east of the Patagonian coast), also have unique island ecosystems, making them havens for many plant and animal species, birds and marine life.

ECONOMY

Throughout the continent, and even within individual South American nations, apparently modern market economies coexist with near-subsistence third-world economic conditions. The most 'developed' regions are around the urban areas of central Chile, Argentina, Uruguay, Venezuela and southeastern Brazil, but even these regions have problems of poverty and gross inequalities of wealth and income. In many rural areas and especially in the poorer countries (Bolivia, Colombia, Guyana, Paraguay, Peru, Suriname), low living standards and limited infrastructure are the norm. Some economic problems stem in part from a long history of foreign domination, political instability, social inequality and the failure to develop a sound domestic infrastructure. Other economic problems are of more recent origin or result from events elsewhere in the world.

Post-Independence Economies

From about 1850 to the start of WWI, several South American countries enjoyed a period of growth and relative prosperity based on commodity exports such as coffee and sugar (Brazil); guano and copper (Peru); nitrates (Chile); and grain, beef and wool (Argentina and Uruguay). Foreign capital and foreign expertise supported much of this development. Countries such as Colombia, Bolivia and Ecuador lagged behind because of internal instability or lack of exploitable resources.

Wild fluctuations in available foreign capital and demand for exports during WWI and the depression of the 1930s brought greater government intervention in South American economies. Initially, this took the form of regulations and controls aimed at protecting foreign investment, though there was direct government involvement in mining and transport. WWII was a time of strong demand for South America's food and raw materials, but imported, manufactured goods from Europe and North America were in short supply. Industrialization, which was often identified with nationalism, became a key economic goal after the war.

Industrialization required more capital than foreign private investment could readily provide, especially given postwar Europe's ruinous economic situation. Moreover, in projects involving natural resources and infrastructure (roads, telecommunications, electricity), locals worried that overseas capital might compromise economic autonomy, and foreign investors feared nationalization of their assets. The solution was for governments to borrow from abroad and become direct participants in economic enterprises. Argentina set up an organization called YPF (Yacimientos Petrolíferos Fiscales) to develop oil reserves. Brazil's government entered the petroleum and steel industries, Bolivia's invested in tin, Chile's in copper, Colombia's in iron and steel, Uruguay's in meat packing and so on.

Brazil, Argentina and Chile have been the most successful in achieving industrialization, while the Andean countries of Bolivia, Colombia, Ecuador and Peru have fallen behind. Industry, however, has been largely geared to protected local markets rather than international trade; the more traditional primary products of the mines, ranches, plantations and grain farms continue to dominate the export sector. Venezuela is among the wealthiest South American republics, but this is based almost solely on oil revenues. In poorer countries, many rural people survive on small subsistence plots, but the lack of opportunity in the countryside has driven many of them to the shantytowns surrounding modern capitals and other large cities.

Debt Crisis In the 1970s and 1980s, as dictatorships provided an appearance of stability and Western banks were awash with petrodollars, South American governments accelerated their borrowing. Much of the money went to grandiose but unproductive developments, such as Brazil's new capital city, and massive hydroelectric projects such as Itaipú and Yacyretá. Much was also squandered on military hardware and siphoned off by corrupt officials.

This infusion of foreign capital, supplemented by deficit spending without a corresponding increase in productivity, triggered serious inflation in most countries. In Brazil, for example, rates in mid-1993 consistently topped 30% per month. Inflation and other economic problems decreased the ability to service foreign debt, and governments borrowed more just to pay the interest. The crisis emerged when the volume of doubtful debts reached a level

that threatened the stability of Western banks. Countries became unable to pay off the interest on their borrowings, but the banks could not admit that the debts were worthless. The situation led to a series of debt reschedulings and restructurings and also forced countries to adopt economic reforms prescribed by the International Monetary Fund, the World Bank and other international creditors.

Economic Restructuring Most South American countries adopted policies of reduced government spending and tight monetary restraint to prevent severe inflation. Many industries owned by the state – telecommunications, railways and even highways – were privatized. The economic reforms often increased unemployment as inefficient enterprises closed or restructured, and income inequality worsened as the incomes of lower-paid workers and government employees were pegged back. The total debt burden remained, but economic growth and stronger currencies improved the capacity to service debt. In the late 1990s, as current account deficits increased, and the value of currencies came under pressure, debt-to-export ratios seemed likely to emerge as a cause for concern.

Tequila Effect In December 1994, a panic withdrawal of private capital from Mexico led to a collapse in its stock market and a 40% currency devaluation. This was followed by a big sell-off of all South American stocks and a dive on the markets – the so-called Tequila Effect. The effect has underscored the problems of depending on foreign capital. The country that came out best in 1995 was Chile, notably for its strategy of boosting domestic savings with a national pension plan.

Trade Blocks In an attempt to gain more benefits from trade within the region, two major trading blocks emerged. Argentina, Uruguay, Paraguay and Brazil make up the Mercosur group; while Colombia, Venezuela, Ecuador, Peru and Bolivia form the Andean Group. Neither of these groups, however, has yet achieved a complete elimination of internal trade barriers or a uniform policy on external trade. Chile is pressing for admission to NAFTA (the

North American Free Trade Association, comprising the USA, Canada and Mexico), but this is not likely to happen in the near future. Guyana and Suriname are members of Caricom, the so-called Caribbean Common Market, while French Guiana is officially a part of France and therefore part of the European Union.

Asian Meltdown Most of South America experienced several years of stability and growth in the late 1990s. In 1998, however, the Asian economic meltdown had a severe negative impact on Brazil, and the continent's largest economy was forced to devalue its currency. This in turn will have adverse consequences for Brazil's regional trading partners in the Mercosur group, especially for Argentina. Meanwhile, low oil prices have caused a contraction in Venezuela's economy and have had an adverse effect on Colombia, and this is likely to flow to other members in the Andean Group. Ecuador has been one of the first countries to experience this new round of economic woes.

POPULATION & PEOPLE

While the population of South America is growing at a fairly modest rate of around 2% per annum, that growth rate varies widely both among and within countries. The Southern Cone nations of Argentina, Chile and Uruguay have relatively stable populations, while numbers in the tropical countries are increasing rapidly. Infant mortality rates are shockingly high in some countries, most notably Bolivia, Brazil and Peru.

Nearly three-quarters of all South Americans live in cities, while large areas such as the Amazon Basin and Atacama desert are almost uninhabited. Population growth and internal migration has seen the emergence of supercities, such as São Paulo (population 20 million), Buenos Aires (13 million), Rio de Janeiro (10 million), Lima (eight million) and Bogotá (seven million). These megalopolises concentrate some of the most severe social and environmental problems on the continent.

South America has a high proportion of people (32%) younger than 15 years old, but some of the countries (in particular Bolivia, Ecuador, Peru, Colombia, Brazil and Venezuela) have even more youthful populations,

with nearly 40% of the people younger than 15. Not only does this mean that populations will continue to grow rapidly as these individuals reach childbearing ages, but it is doubtful whether local economies will be able to provide employment for so many in such a short time.

ARTS

While it is common to refer to Latin America as a single cultural entity, most of the arts have a distinctly national or even regional character. South America, the largest geographical part of Latin America, is best known for its music, especially Brazilian and Andean styles, and for dances such as tango and samba. See individual country chapters for more information.

South American literature is also well established – see the country chapters for more about the continent's most famous writers, who include Jorge Luis Borges (from Argentina); Jorge Amado (Brazil); Pablo Neruda, Gabriela Mistral and Isabel Allende (Chile); Gabriel García Márquez (Colombia); and Mario Vargas Llosa (Peru). All of the greatest works are available in English; see the Books section in Facts for the Visitor for a few suggestions.

SOCIETY & CONDUCT
Traditional Cultures

Peasant populations of the Andean highlands are often considered to have the most 'traditional' way of life; they still raise potatoes on small plots and herd llamas and alpacas on the pastures of the altiplano.But over centuries they have adopted many European customs, sold their surpluses in local markets and shipped wool to European mills. Similarly, indigenous peoples of the Amazon, even in very isolated areas, have long used European goods like metal axes, fishhooks and machetes.

Access is restricted to many of the areas where people retain the most 'traditional' ways of living, and it is essential to respect these restrictions. They help to protect the indigenous people from unwanted interference and from diseases to which they have little immunity.

Avoiding Offense

In general, South Americans are friendly, gregarious and not easily offended, but they will almost always expect to exchange pleasantries before getting to the point of a conversation; not to do so is considered the mark of an unrefined person. Public behavior can be very formal, especially among government officials, who expect respect and deference.

Don't photograph individuals without obtaining their permission, especially indigenous people. If someone is giving a public performance, such as a street musician or a dancer at Carnaval, or is incidental to a photograph, such as someone in a broad cityscape, it is not usually necessary to request permission – but if in doubt, ask or refrain.

Appearance & Conduct

Casual dress has become more acceptable in recent years, but most South Americans still take considerable pride their personal appearance. Foreign visitors should, at the very least, be clean and neatly dressed if they wish to conform to local standards and be treated with respect by officials, business people or professionals.

To the poorest local people, even shoe-string travelers possess considerable wealth. Flaunting items such as expensive cameras, watches and jewelry is likely to attract thieves. Police and military officials are often poorly paid and may resent affluent visitors who do not behave appropriately.

Prostitution

Prostitution exists in most of the continent, but is most prevalent in Brazil, where the distinction between prostitution and promiscuity can sometimes be hazy. Sexual contact between locals and visitors, male and female, straight and gay, is quite common, and some areas could be described as sex-tourism destinations. AIDS is widespread among gay and straight people alike. Child prostitution is not common, but unfortunately it does exist. There are severe penalties for those convicted of involvement in child prostitution and very real risks of entrapment.

RELIGION

About 90% of South Americans are at least nominally Roman Catholic. Virtually every town and city has a central church or cathedral and a calendar loaded with Catholic holidays and celebrations. Spreading the faith was a major objective of colonization.

Among Indian peoples, allegiance to Catholicism was often just a veneer, disguising precolonial beliefs ostensibly forbidden by the Church. Similarly, black slaves in Brazil gave Christian names and forms to their African gods, whose worship was discouraged or forbidden. Cults and sects have proliferated to this day, but they do not exclude Christianity. There is no conflict between attending mass on Sunday and seeking guidance from a *brujo* (witch) the next day.

Activist elements within the Catholic Church have promoted social justice in the name of 'liberation theology,' the belief that Christians have a duty to reform oppressive economic and political systems. This is less important than in Central America, but it has nevertheless attracted the ire of reactionary elements in several South American countries.

In recent decades, various Protestant sects have made inroads among the traditionally Catholic population. This is partly because of evangelical efforts, partly as a response to the uncertainty created by rapid social and economic change and perhaps partly due to complacency in the established Catholic Church.

LANGUAGE
Latin American Spanish

Spanish is the first language of the vast majority of South Americans; Brazilians speak Portuguese, but they often understand Spanish as well. Without a basic knowledge of Spanish, travel in South America can be difficult, and your interaction with local people will be limited.

Before going, try to attend an evening course in Spanish or borrow a recorded course from the library. Buy a book on grammar and a phrasebook (such as Lonely Planet's *Latin American Spanish phrasebook*) and try to find a Latin American person with whom to practice. Quite a few foreigners start their South American trip with a short Spanish course, commonly in Quito, Ecuador, or Cuzco, Peru. Learning Spanish is not especially difficult for an English speaker; there are many related words, and Latin Americans are very tolerant of grammatical errors and poor pronunciation.

There are significant differences between European and American Spanish. Even within the Americas, accents, pronunciation and vocabulary vary considerably from one country to the next. Chilean and Argentine Spanish, in particular, can be awkward for inexperienced speakers. Some words that are totally innocuous in one country can be grievous insults in another – avoid slang unless you are certain of its every meaning.

For a very brief introduction to Spanish and some useful phrases, see the Language section at the back of this book.

Portuguese

For information on Brazil's official language, see the Language entry in the Facts about Brazil section of that chapter and the Language section at the back of this book.

Indigenous Languages

There are hundreds of distinct South American Indian languages; some of them are spoken by only a few people. In Suriname, locals converse in Sranan Tongo, a language spoken along the Maroni and Lawa Rivers. In the Andean countries and parts of Chile and Argentina, millions of people speak Quechua or Aymara as a first language, and many do not use Spanish at all. Quechua was the official language of the Inca Empire, and is most widely spoken in the old Inca heartland of Peru and Ecuador. Aymara was the language of the pre-Inca Tiwanaku culture, and though the Aymara speakers were subjugated by the Inca empire, and later by the Spanish, their language survives around Lake Titicaca and in much of Bolivia.

English-speakers may find grammar and pronunciation of these languages quite difficult. For a few useful words and phrases, see the Language section at the back of this book.

If you're serious about learning more, or will be spending a lot of time in remote areas, look around La Paz or Cuzco for a good language course. Dictionaries and phrasebooks are available through Los Amigos del Libro and larger bookstores in La Paz, but the translations are in Spanish. Lonely Planet's *Quechua phrasebook* is primarily for travelers to Peru and contains grammar and vocabulary in the Cuzco dialect but will also be useful for visitors to the Bolivian highlands.

Facts for the Visitor

HIGHLIGHTS

Highlights of a trip to South America depend on what you like most. There are specific suggestions in each country chapter, but here are some more general considerations.

If you like mountains, any part of the Andes, from Venezuela to Chile, will present opportunities for climbing and trekking in addition to alpine scenery. Argentina and Chile have the best ski areas. Some scenic highlights include the Chilean-Argentine Lake District, the Torres del Paine and the fjords of southern Chile, and Argentina's Moreno Glacier. The continent boasts some spectacular waterfalls: Angel Falls in Venezuela; Kaieteur in Guyana; and Iguazú, on the Brazil-Argentina border.

Brazil is the best known beach destination, but there are also great beaches in Venezuela and on Colombia's Caribbean coast. Brazil has the best surf.

Many travelers go to Brazil to experience tropical rain forest, but there are also accessible areas of pristine Amazon rain forest in Bolivia, Ecuador and Colombia, while the Guianas have possibilities for ecotourism that have scarcely been developed. Other areas to see birds and wildlife include Brazil's Pantanal, Esteros del Iberá in Argentina and on some of the offshore island groups: the Galápagos, the Juan Fernández archipelago and the Falkland Islands (Islas Malvinas).

For archaeology enthusiasts, the most famous ruins are those of Peru's Machu Picchu, but other highlights include Ciudad Perdida (the Lost City) in Colombia and the mysterious statues of Easter Island. More recent ruins are the abandoned missions of Argentina and Paraguay.

Fine colonial architecture is found all over the continent, but some of the best examples are in Cartagena (Colombia); Salvador da Bahia, Ouro Prêto, Olinda, and at least a half-dozen more towns in Brazil; Colonia in Uruguay; Cajamarca in Peru; and Sucre and Potosí in Bolivia.

A real highlight of contemporary South America is the various types of music, and the best places to hear it are the towns and cities of Brazil, the Caribbean coastal areas (especially if you like reggae), and Ecuador, Peru and Bolivia (for Andean music).

PLANNING

When to Go

When you go depends on what you want to do. Hikers and trekkers should avoid the rainy season, which varies from country to country: In most of Peru, the winter months of June, July and August are the driest, while in Chile, the summer months of December, January and February are best. Visitors to the Southern Cone also find that longer summer days (around December) allow more opportunities for outdoor activities. Brazilian beaches are great in the northern winter, and you can stay on until Carnaval, around the end of February. Skiing is best from June to September. For more information, see the Climate section in Facts about South America and the individual country chapters.

How Long?

A month is good, a year is better, a lifetime is not enough. For most travelers, South America is a remote destination, and just getting there can be expensive business, so budget travelers often plan to stay for some time – perhaps six months or more. Good planning, however, can make even a short trip worthwhile.

Maps

ITM (International Travel Maps; ☎ 604-687-3320), 345 W Broadway, Vancouver, BC, V5Y 1P8, Canada, produces a range of excellent maps, especially of Central and South America. For the whole continent, they have a reliable three-sheet map at a scale of 1:4,000,000 and a memorial edition of their classic 1:500,000 map by the late Kevin Healey. In Europe, ITM maps are distributed by Bradt Publications (☎ 01494-873478), 41 Nortoft Rd, Chalfont St Peter, Bucks, SL9 0LA, England. The maps might be a bit big for field use, but they are helpful for planning a trip.

World Map has a good, but expensive, three-sheet set at 1:4,000,000. Collins and Halliwag both have OK maps of the continent at 1:7,000,000, but the continent is so large that it's impossible to map it in detail on a single sheet. See the country chapters for suggestions on country and regional maps. More detailed ITM maps are available for the Amazon Basin, Ecuador, Bolivia and Venezuela.

What to Bring

Travel light – overweight baggage soon becomes a nightmare, especially in hot weather and on public transport. Official prejudice against backpacks has dissipated in recent years, so most budget travelers prefer them; internal-frame packs are more suitable than those with external frames. If you travel very light, a bag with a shoulder strap is still easy to carry and perhaps more secure – a backpack is vulnerable to a thief with a razor.

A robust convertible backpack with zip-away straps is a good compromise. For long, dusty bus trips, carry a large, strong plastic bag or even a lockable duffel for the luggage compartment or roof.

Unless you're staying exclusively in the lowland tropics, bring a sleeping bag. Above 3000m and in the far south, nights get very cold; not all budget hotels provide enough blankets, and buses, trains and especially trucks are often unheated. You can buy additional warm clothing at reasonable prices in the Andean countries. A sleeping-bag liner can discourage mosquitoes, but a mosquito net is better. A hammock is essential for river travel and can be bought locally.

Some people take a small tent and portable stove, which give you greater independence in out-of-the-way places and expand your budget alternatives in the costlier Southern Cone. Hired equipment is available in popular trekking areas such as Peru's Inca Trail, but if you want to camp regularly, you should bring your equipment with you.

Don't forget small essentials. A combination pocketknife such as a Swiss Army knife; a needle, cotton and a small pair of scissors; a padlock; and one or two good long novels (English-language books are usually expensive in South America). Most toiletries (toilet paper, toothpaste, shampoo, etc) are easily found in large cities and even small towns. Bring some condoms, whether you think you will need them or not. Virtually every small shop sells packets of washing powder just large enough for a pile of laundry. A 'universal' sink plug is also useful. See the Health section for suggestions for a personal medical kit.

VISAS & DOCUMENTS

As well as a passport, you'll need visas, air tickets and a health certificate. Make copies of all these documents and details of your credit cards and traveler's checks, and carry them separately from the originals. The copies will be invaluable if originals are lost or stolen. Certified copies will have more credibility. Leave a second copy of your documents with someone at home.

Passport

A passport is essential – make sure it's valid for at least six months beyond the projected end of your trip and has plenty of blank pages for stamp-happy officials.

Visas

A visa is an endorsement in your passport, usually a stamp, permitting you to enter a country and remain for a specified period of time. It is obtained from a foreign embassy or consulate of that country. You can often get them in your home country, but it's usually possible to get them en route, which may be better if your itinerary is flexible: Most visas are only good for a limited period after they're issued. Ask other travelers about the best places to get them, since two consulates of the same country may enforce different requirements – the fee might vary, one might want to see your money or an onward ticket, another might not ask, or one might issue them on the spot while another might take days to do so.

If you really need a visa in a hurry, ask nicely and explain your reasons. Consulates can often be very helpful if the officials sympathize and your papers are in order. Sometimes they will charge a fee for fast processing, but don't mistake this for a bribe.

Nationals of most European countries and Japan require few visas, but travelers from the USA need some, and those from Australia, New Zealand or South Africa might need quite a few. Carry a handful of passport-size photographs for visa applications (though most border towns have a photographer who can do them).

Visa requirements are given in the Facts for the Visitor section of each individual country chapter, but here is a summary (subject to change). Some countries issue tourist cards to visitors on arrival; while traveling within these countries, carry your tourist card with you at all times.

Argentina Residents of New Zealand require visas.

Bolivia Visas are not required for residents of most countries.

Brazil Residents of Canada, the US, Australia, New Zealand and Japan require visas.

Chile Residents of New Zealand require visas.

Colombia Residents of South Africa require visas.

Ecuador Visas are not required for residents of most countries.

Falkland Islands For non-Britons, visa requirements are generally the same as those for foreigners visiting the UK, though Argentines must obtain an advance visa.

Guyana Residents of Japan and Israel require visas.

Suriname Residents of Canada, the US, Australia, New Zealand and citizens of some EC countries, including the Netherlands, require visas.

French Guiana Citizens of Japan require visas when staying longer than one month.

Paraguay Residents of Canada, Australia, New Zealand, South Africa and Japan require visas.

Peru Visas are not required for residents of most countries.

Uruguay Residents of Canada, Australia and New Zealand require visas.

Venezuela Officially, no one needs a visa if arriving by air, but everyone must obtain a tourist card or visa before arriving at a land border.

If you need a visa for a certain country and arrive at a land border without one, you will probably have to return to the nearest town with a consulate and obtain a visa before being admitted. Airlines will not normally let you board a plane for a country to which you don't have the necessary visa. Also, a visa in itself may not guarantee entry: you may still be turned back at the border if you don't have 'sufficient funds' or an onward or return ticket.

Sufficient Funds Getting visas is generally a routine procedure, but officials may ask, either verbally or on the application form,

about your financial resources. If you lack 'sufficient funds' for your proposed visit, officials may limit the length of your stay, but once you are in the country, you can usually renew or extend your visa by showing a wad of traveler's checks. A credit card or two is often convincing evidence of sufficient funds.

Onward or Return Tickets Several countries require you to have a ticket out of the country before they will admit you at the border or grant you a visa. The onward or return ticket requirement can be a major nuisance for overland travelers who want to fly into one country and travel overland through others. Peru, Colombia, Venezuela, Bolivia, Brazil, and French Guiana officially demand onward or return tickets, but only Brazil and French Guiana are strict about it.

Sometimes you can satisfy the return ticket requirement by purchasing an MCO (miscellaneous charge order), a document that looks like an airline ticket but can be refunded in cash or credited toward a specific flight with any International Air Transport Association (IATA) carrier. Check whether consular or immigration officials will accept an MCO as an onward ticket. If not, try to buy a refundable onward or return ticket – ask specifically where you can get a refund, as some airlines will only refund tickets at the office of purchase or at their head office.

Any ticket out of South America plus sufficient funds might be a sufficient substitute for an onward ticket. Having a recognized international credit card or two might help. A prosperous appearance and a sympathetic official also will improve your chances.

Airlines flying to Colombia or Venezuela may be reluctant to sell a one-way ticket – if you're not admitted they'll have to fly you back. In practice, they may sell an open-jaw ticket or any deal that means you've paid for a ticket out of the country, so work out in advance where you'll go after leaving Colombia or Venezuela.

Proof of Vaccination

Also essential for travel to, and especially from, many parts of South America is proof of vaccination against yellow fever. In some countries, health authorities issue the 'International Certificate of Vaccination' (a yellow booklet with a WHO logo on it), in which the dates and types of vaccinations are recorded (in the USA, order one at ☎ 202-512-1800). If this isn't available, ask the doctor or clinic to provide you with a certificate that details vaccination, and carry it with your passport. Yellow fever vaccination takes at least ten days to be fully effective, so don't leave it to the last week.

Travel Insurance

A travel insurance policy to cover theft, loss, accidents and illness is highly recommended. Many policies include a card with toll-free numbers for 24-hour assistance, and it's a good idea to carry that with you. The policy document will have details about coverage and claims, and you should also carry that or a copy.

There is a wide variety of policies available and your travel agent will be able to make recommendations. The policies handled by STA Travel and other student-travel organizations usually offer good values. If a policy offers lower and higher medical-expense options, the low-expenses policy should be OK for South America – medical costs are not nearly as high there as they are in the USA.

Some policies specifically exclude 'dangerous activities,' which can include scuba diving, motorcycling, even trekking. If such activities are on your agenda, you don't want this sort of policy.

You may prefer a policy that pays doctors or hospitals directly instead of one that requires you to pay on the spot and claim later. If you do have to claim later, make sure you keep all documentation. Some policies ask you to call back (reverse charges) to a center in your home country where an immediate assessment of your problem is made.

Check that the policy covers ambulances or an emergency flight home. If you have to stretch out you will need two seats, and somebody has to pay for them!

Driver's License & Permits

If you're planning to drive anywhere, obtain an International Driving Permit or Inter-American Driving Permit (Uruguay theoretically recognizes only the latter). For about US$10, any motoring organization will issue one on presentation of a current state or national driver's license.

Hostel Cards

A Hostelling International-American Youth Hostel (HI-AYH) membership card can be useful in Brazil, Chile, Argentina and Uruguay, where there are quite a few hostels and accommodations tend to be costlier. Hostels may accept nonmembers, but at a higher rate.

Student Cards

An International Student Identity Card (ISIC) is useful in some places for reductions on admission charges to archaeological sites and museums. At times, it will also entitle you to reductions on bus, train and air tickets. In some countries, such as Argentina, almost any form of university identification will suffice.

EMBASSIES

For embassy addresses and phone numbers, see the individual country chapters.

Your Own Embassy

As a visitor in a South American country, it's important to realize what your own embassy – the embassy of the country of which you are a citizen – can and can't do.

Generally speaking, it won't be much help in emergencies if the trouble you're in is remotely your own fault. Remember that you are bound by the laws of the country you are in. Your embassy will not be sympathetic if you end up in jail after committing a crime locally, even if such actions are legal in your own country.

In genuine emergencies you might get some assistance, but only if other channels have been exhausted. For example, if you need to get home urgently, a free ticket home is exceedingly unlikely – the embassy would expect you to have insurance. If you have all your money and documents stolen, it might assist in getting a new passport, but a loan for onward travel is out of the question. Some embassies may repatriate a penniless citizen as a last resort but will probably confiscate your passport until you repay the debt – and it won't be a cheap flight. French embassies don't usually repatriate their citizens and US embassies rarely do so.

Embassies used to keep letters or have a small reading room with home newspapers for travelers, but these days the mail holding service has been stopped, and even newspapers tend to be out of date.

MONEY
Exchanging Money

Change traveler's checks or foreign cash at a *casa de cambio* (exchange house) or a bank. Rates are usually similar, but in general casas de cambio are quicker, less bureaucratic and open longer hours. Street money changers, who may or may not be legal, will only handle cash. Sometimes you can also change money unofficially at hotels or in shops that sell imported goods (electronics dealers are an obvious choice).

The unofficial exchange rate for the US dollar can be higher than the official bank rate because official rates do not always reflect the market value of local currency. Official rates may be artificially high for political reasons, or they may not be adjusted sufficiently for inflation, which has at times been very high in South America. The unofficial rate is often known as the *mercado negro* (black market) or *mercado paralelo* (parallel market). Nowadays, official exchange rates are quite realistic in most South American countries, so the role of the black market is declining.

You might still want to use street money changers, if only because they are so much faster and more convenient than banks, but observe a few precautions. Be discreet, as it's often illegal, though it may be tolerated. Have the exact amount handy, to avoid pulling out large wads of notes. Beware of sleight-of-hand tricks: Insist on personally counting out the notes you are handed one by one, and don't hand over your dollars until satisfied you have the exact amount agreed upon. One common trick is to hand you the agreed amount, less a few pesos, so that, on counting it, you will complain that it's short. They take it back, recount it, discover the 'mistake,' top it up and hand it back, in the process spiriting away all but one of the largest bills. For certainty, recount it yourself and don't be distracted by supposed alarms like 'police' or 'danger.'

Cash Carry some cash in US dollars, because it's exchangeable for local currency just about anywhere, anytime. It's convenient when you're about to leave a country to change some small dollar bills rather than a traveler's check. Greenbacks are also convenient when there's a black market, parallel market or unofficial exchange rate. In some places you can exchange US-dollar traveler's checks for US dollars in cash at banks and casas de cambio, in order to top up on cash from time to time.

Sometimes it's useful to get a relatively large amount of local currency cash in a big city, before venturing into the boondocks where facilities may be limited. But if you have too much local cash, it might not be worth much at the border, even less in a neighboring country.

Of course there is a risk in carrying cash rather than traveler's checks – nobody will give you a refund for lost or stolen cash.

Traveler's Checks Traveler's checks are the safest way to carry money. American Express, Thomas Cook, Citibank and Visa are among the best known brands and, in most cases, offer instant replacement in case of loss or theft. Checks issued by smaller banks with limited international affiliations may be difficult to cash, especially in more remote areas. To facilitate replacement in case of theft, keep a record of check numbers and the original bill of sale in a safe place. Even with proper records, replacement can take time.

Have some traveler's checks in small denominations, say US$50. If you carry only large denominations, you might find yourself stuck with a large amount of local currency when leaving a country.

In some countries, notably Argentina and to a lesser extent Peru, traveler's checks are more difficult to cash, and banks and casas de cambio charge commissions as high as 10%. Often there is a fixed transaction fee for cashing traveler's checks, regardless of the number and value of the checks, so it can be more economical to change large amounts.

ATMs Automatic teller machines (ATMs) are available in most cities and large towns, and they are usually a convenient, reliable, secure and economical way of getting cash when you need it. The rate of exchange is usually as good as, or better than, any bank or legal moneychanger. Many ATMs are connected to the Cirrus or Plus network. If you rely on ATMs, take two or more cards. If you only have one, and it's lost or swallowed by an ATM, you could be in big trouble.

Credit & Debit Cards The big-name credit cards are accepted at most big stores, travel agencies and better hotels and restaurants. Credit-card purchases sometimes attract an extra premium *(recargo)* on the price (2% to 5% or even more), but they are usually billed to your account at quite favorable exchange rates. Some banks will issue cash advances on major credit cards. The most widely accepted is Visa, followed by MasterCard (those with UK Access should insist on its affiliation with MasterCard). American Express, Diners Club and others are also accepted in many places. Beware of credit-card fraud (especially in Brazil) – never let the card out of your sight.

With a debit card, you can only access money you have previously deposited in the account, but otherwise it works like a credit card, and can be used for purchases, cash advances and in ATM machines.

Keep your cards separately and note the numbers of the cards and the emergency phone numbers of the card companies.

International Transfers If you're out of money, ask your bank at home to send a draft, specifying the city, the bank and the branch of destination. Cable transfers should arrive in a few days, but you can run into complications, even with supposedly reliable banks. Mail drafts will take at least two weeks and often longer to process. Some banks delay releasing transferred money because they earn interest on hard-currency deposits.

Some countries will let you have your money in US dollars, while others will only release it in local currency. Be certain before you arrange the transfer; otherwise, you could lose a fair amount of money if there is a major gap between official and unofficial exchange rates. Bolivia, Ecuador, and Chile will let you have all your money in dollars, but regulations change frequently, so ask for the latest information.

What to Carry

It is preferable to bring money in US dollars, though banks and *casas de cambio* (exchange houses) in capital cities will change pounds sterling, Deutschmarks, Japanese yen and other major currencies. Changing these currencies in smaller towns and on the street can be next to impossible.

Everyone has a preferred way to carry money. Some use money belts, others have hidden pockets inside their trousers or leg pouches with elastic bands, and others hang a pouch round their neck. Leather money belts, which appear from the outside to be ordinary belts, seem to be effective but their capacity is limited. If you use a neck pouch, consider incorporating a length of guitar string into the strap so that it can't be cut without alerting you.

Ideally, have some traveler's checks *and* a stash of US$ cash *and* at least two pieces of plastic, and carry them in two or three separate places.

Costs

Generally speaking, it will cost less (per person) if you travel as a couple or in a small group, and you will spend less if you travel slowly with long stops. It will cost more if you want comforts like air-conditioning and a private bathroom, if you want to eat in good restaurants, if you do expensive tours to places such as the Galápagos Islands, or if you indulge in expensive activities like skiing or going to nightclubs.

The cost of traveling varies greatly among the different countries of South America. To give a very rough idea of relative costs, let's assume you're traveling with another person, mostly by bus, staying in cheap but clean hotels, eating in cheap restaurants and food stalls, with the occasional splurge on sightseeing or whatever. You could budget on the following as a minimum, per person per day.

Argentina – US$30 to US$40 (less expensive if you camp out a lot; more in Buenos Aires)

Bolivia – less than US$20 (less than US$15 is feasible)

Brazil – US$30 to US$50, depending on how much comfort you want (this may come down somewhat with currency depreciation)

Chile – around US$30

Colombia – US$20 to US$25

Ecuador – less than US$20 (quite a bit more with a trip to the Galápagos)
Falkland Islands – at least US$50
French Guiana – at least US$50
Guyana – US$20 to US$30
Paraguay – less than US$30
Peru – around US$25, maybe less
Suriname – around US$25
Uruguay – US$25 to US$35
Venezuela – US$20 to US$30

Inflation rates are now much lower than the astronomical levels some countries achieved in the 1980s, but prices can still be unpredictable. A currency devaluation means that local prices drop in relation to hard currencies like the US dollar, but normally local prices soon rise, so dollar costs soon return to previous levels (or higher). These factors make it difficult to quote prices in local currencies, but one thing is certain: If a hotel or restaurant was cheap before price increases, it's still going to be cheap compared to other hotels and restaurants after a price rise. Prices tend to be more stable in terms of US dollars, so prices have been quoted in dollars throughout most of this book.

Bargaining

Probably the only things you'll have to haggle over are long-term accommodation and purchases from markets, especially craft goods, the prices of which are normally very negotiable. Haggling is the norm in the Andean countries, but in the Southern Cone, it's much less common. Patience, humor and an ability to speak the local language will make the process more enjoyable and productive.

POST & COMMUNICATIONS
Post

The quality of postal service varies between countries. International postal rates can be quite expensive. Generally, important mail and parcels should be sent by registered or certified service.

Sending parcels can be awkward, as often a customs officer must inspect the contents before a postal clerk can accept them. In Peru and Bolivia, the parcel must also be stitched up in linen before the clerk can accept it. The place for posting overseas parcels is sometimes different from the main post office.

UPS, FedEx, DHL and other private postal services are available in some countries – an efficient but expensive alternative.

Receiving Mail The simplest way of receiving mail is to have letters sent to you c/Lista de Correos, followed by the name of the city and country where you plan to be. Mail addressed in this way will always be sent to that city's main post office. In most places, the service is free or has a small fee. In Argentina, it's very expensive; try to use a hotel or private address if possible. Most post offices hold mail for a month or two, then return it to sender, destroy it or lose it.

American Express operates a mail service for clients, including those who use American Express traveler's checks. Some embassies will hold mail for their citizens, among them Australia, Canada, Germany, Israel and Switzerland. British and US embassies are very poor in this regard; letters addressed to a British embassy will be sent to the main post office.

To collect mail from a post office, American Express office or elsewhere, you need to produce identification, preferably a passport. If expected correspondence does not arrive, ask the clerk to check under every possible combination of your initials, even 'M' (for Mr, Ms, etc). There may be particular confusion if correspondents use your middle name, since Spanish Americans use both paternal and maternal surnames for identification, with the former listed first. Thus a letter to Augusto Pinochet Ugarte will be filed under 'P' rather than 'U,' which is fine for a Chilean, whereas a letter to George Bernard Shaw may be found under 'B,' even though 'Shaw' is the surname. Note that in Brazil the maternal surname is listed first.

Local Addresses Many South American addresses in this book contain a post-office box number as well as a street address. A post-office box is known as an *apartado* (abbreviated to 'Ap' or 'Apto') or a *casilla de correos* ('Casilla,' 'CC').

Telephone & Fax

Traditionally, governments have operated the national and international telecommunications systems and, traditionally, services have been wretched. Quite a few countries have now privatized their phone systems, choosing high charges over poor service, but sometimes getting both. International calls are particularly expensive, especially from Bolivia, Colombia and Ecuador; they are perhaps cheapest from Chile.

Direct lines abroad, accessed via special numbers and billed to an account at home, have made international calls much simpler. There are different access numbers for each telephone company in each country – get a list from your phone company before you leave home.

It is sometimes cheaper to make a reverse-charge (collect) or credit-card call to Europe or North America than to pay for the call at the source. Often the best way is to make a quick international call and have the other party call you back (some telephone offices allow this).

Nearly every town and city will have a telephone office with a number of phone booths for local and international calls. Commonly these are run by the telephone company, but sometimes they are private businesses. They often provide a public fax service and will accept an incoming fax for you at a dollar or so per page.

There's a wide range of local and international phonecards. Lonely Planet's eKno Communication Card (see the insert in this book) is aimed specifically at travelers and provides cheap international calls, a range of messaging services and free email; for local calls, you're usually better off with a local card. The card does not yet cover all the countries in this book, though new countries are being added all the time. You can join online at www.ekno.lonelyplanet.com. To join by phone from the countries covered in this book, dial the relevant registration number. Once you have joined, to use eKno, dial the access number. As we go to print, you can access the eKno service from the following countries:

country	registration	access number
Brazil	☎ 000816-550-0251	☎ 000816-550-0252
Colombia	☎ 980-918-0097	☎ 980-918-0096

Email & Internet Access

Public Internet access is available in most countries, especially those that are popular with foreign travelers. Many towns and cities have 'cybercafés' or 'Internet cafés' (very few actually serve coffee) that let you use a PC and access the Internet for something between US$0.50 and US$5 per hour. These places have become something of a travelers' scene in themselves, with a bunch of backpackers huddled over keyboards, typing out messages to friends and family back home – even to other travelers on the road.

Some budget-travelers' lodgings now provide economical Internet access for their guests. Other possible spots to get online include universities (if you befriend a student or staff member), computer schools and stores selling computer equipment and software. This book lists Internet access points in many towns and cities, and you can also ask at a tourist office or your hotel.

Email is faster, cheaper and usually more reliable than international post and much cheaper than telephone calls or faxes. The most straightforward way to send and receive email while traveling is to sign up for a Web-based email account that you can access from any online computer with a Web browser. Hotmail (www.hotmail.com) and Yahoo (www.yahoo.com) are the most popular of these, but sometimes they are very slow (too many subscribers logged on at one time?) and not totally reliable (messages do get delayed or lost). Netscape (www.netscape.com) is another option, and there are many smaller Web-based email services, such as Pobox (www.pobox.com) and Bigfoot (www.bigfoot.com), that may work better for you. Try a few out before you leave home, and use the one that works best for you.

With a little technical savvy, you can access your home email on the road from any online computer. Change the POP3 email settings on the computer to connect to your home ISP (before you leave home, ask your ISP what settings to use). Just be sure to switch the settings back to the defaults, or the next person to use the computer will download your email.

INTERNET RESOURCES

The World Wide Web is a rich resource for travelers. You can research your trip, track down bargain air fares, book hotels, check on weather conditions or chat with locals and other travelers about the best places to visit (or avoid!).

There's no better place to start your Web explorations than the Lonely Planet Web site (www.lonelyplanet.com). Here you'll find succinct summaries on traveling to most places on earth, postcards from other travelers and the Thorn Tree bulletin board, where you can ask questions before you go or dispense advice when you get back. You can also find travel news and updates to many of our most popular guidebooks, and the sub-WWWay section links you to the most useful travel resources elsewhere on the Web. The site has destination profiles on all South American countries, feedback from travelers on the road and links to other sites.

Most of the other interesting Internet sites about South America are devoted to specific countries within the continent – see the individual country chapters for other suggestions.

The South American Explorers Club site, www.samexplo.org, is also an excellent starting point for research on the Web. For background information on every country in the region, check the US CIA Factbook, www.odci.gov/cia/publications/factbook. For travel advisories and more, check out the US State Department site, www.state.gov/www/services.html, or the UK Foreign & Commonwealth Office (FCO) http://193.114.50.10/travel. The Latin American Travel Advisor site, at www.amerispan.com/lata/, doesn't give much away, but it does let you order its quarterly newsletter (where you'll find the real information).

BOOKS

Most books are published in different editions by different publishers in different countries. As a result, a book might be a hardcover rarity in one country while it's readily available in paperback in another. Fortunately, bookstores and libraries can search by title or author, so your local bookstore or library is the best place to find out about the availability of the following recommendations and those that appear in individual country chapters.

Of the many books on South America, some are available in general-interest bookstores, but others, particularly older and more specialized titles, will most likely be found in university libraries. Many old titles are still available through booksellers online.

Lonely Planet

It's impossible to cover every detail of travel in South America in this book, so if you need greater detail on specific places, you may want to supplement it with some other guides.

Lonely Planet produces regularly updated travel guide books for individual South American countries, with a wealth of information, numerous maps, illustrations and color photos. Titles to look for are *Argentina, Uruguay & Paraguay; Bolivia; Brazil; Chile & Easter Island; Colombia; Ecuador & the Galápagos Islands; Peru;* and *Venezuela.*

For even more detailed information, see Lonely Planet's city guides, *Buenos Aires, Santiago* and *Rio de Janeiro.*

Also useful are the *Brazilian phrasebook,* the *Latin American Spanish phrasebook* and the *Quechua phrasebook.*

For detailed trekking info, look for Lonely Planet's *Trekking in the Patagonian Andes.* If you're planning to visit Central America as well as South America, get a copy of Lonely Planet's *Central America on a shoestring,* which covers the region from Belize to Panama.

Guidebooks

For general advice, read *The Tropical Traveler* by John Hatt. This is an excellent compilation of information on all aspects of travel in the tropics and is entertainingly written.

William Leitch's beautifully written *South America's National Parks* is essential background for trekkers, superb on environment and natural history, but weaker on practical matters. Bradt Publications also produces guides for trekking in the mountains and off-the-beaten-track excursions. Some of them may be hard to find, but the series includes *Backcountry Brazil, Backpacking in Chile & Argentina, Backpacking & Trekking in Peru & Bolivia, Venezuela* and *Climbing & Hiking in Ecuador.*

Another useful title is *Trails of the Cordilleras Blanca & Huayhuash of Peru,* by Jim Bartle; it contains excellent trail descriptions with maps and color photographs, but may be out of print.

Lynn Meisch's *A Traveler's Guide to El Dorado & the Inca Empire* has excellent coverage of Andean crafts, especially weaving (the subject takes up nearly half the book), but it's thin on practical details and currently out of print.

For information about skiing and surfing in South America, see the publications listed in the Activities section.

Travel

US writer Peter Matthiessen describes a journey from the rivers of Peru to the mountains of Tierra del Fuego in *The Cloud Forest*; this was also the inspiration for his acclaimed novel (see Fiction). Alex Shoumatoff's *In Southern Light* explores firsthand some of the fantastic legends of the Amazon. Chilean writer Luis Sepúlveda's gripping personal odyssey takes him to different parts of the continent and beyond in *Full Circle: A South American Journey*, translated into English for Journeys, Lonely Planet's travel literature series.

Many readers may feel ambivalent about anyone who drives from Tierra del Fuego to the North Slope of Alaska in 23½ days, but Tim Cahill's hilarious encounters with customs officials and other bureaucrats alone make *Road Fever* worth reading. Another funny road book is *Inca Kola*, by Matthew Parris; the book is an Englishman's account of travels in Peru and Bolivia. *Eight Feet in the Andes*, by Dervla Murphy, is a sensitive and insightful description of the author's trip through Peru with her 10-year-old daughter and Juana the mule.

An engaging combination of travelogue and botanical guide, *Tales of a Shaman's Apprentice* is the wonderful story of author Mark Plotkin's travels in Amazonia and the Guianas in search of traditional medicinal plants. *Heart of the Amazon*, by Yossi Ghinsberg, is a true story of survival and rescue on a remote river in Bolivia – the rescuer goes on to become an ecotour operator.

General History

George Pendle's *A History of Latin America* is a readable but very general account of the region since the European invasions.

Eduardo Galeano's *Open Veins of Latin America: Five Centuries of the Pillage of a Continent* is an eloquent polemic from a leftist perspective on the continent's cultural, social and political struggles by a famous Uruguayan writer. The Memories of Fire trilogy, by the same author, is wonderfully readable and highly recommended. John A Crow's *Epic of Latin America* is an imposing, but readable, volume that covers nearly the whole of the region from Mexico to Tierra del Fuego, from prehistory to the present.

Prehistory & the Incas

A key book on early South America is Edward P Lanning's *Peru Before the Incas*, and an innovative approach to Amazonian prehistory is Donald Lathrap's *The Upper Amazon*, which argues for the tropical lowlands as a hearth of South American cultural development.

Several indigenous and Spanish chroniclers left accounts of their times. Garcilaso de la Vega, son of an Inca princess, wrote *Royal Commentaries of the Incas*, available in many editions, but much criticized for exaggerations and misrepresentations of detail. Father Bernabé Cobo's 17th-century *History of the Inca Empire* draws on Garcilaso, but also includes much original material from his own observations. Huamán Poma de Ayala's 17th-century *Letter to a King* is an eloquent letter of protest against Spanish abuses of indigenous peoples.

Conquest of the Incas, by John Hemming, is a fine interpretation of the clash between the Spaniards and the lords of Cuzco. Hemming's *The Search for Eldorado* is a very readable, illustrated account of the European quest for South American gold.

European Invasion & the Colonial Era

Carl O Sauer's *The Early Spanish Main* portrays Columbus as an audacious bumbler whose greed colored his every perception of the New World. On the achievements of other early European explorers, see JH Parry's *The Discovery of South America*. To learn who the conquistadores really were, read James Lockhart's fascinating *The Men of Cajamarca*, a series of biographical studies of the first Europeans in Peru, from Pizarro to his lowliest soldier.

James Lockhart and Stuart Schwartz's *Early Latin America* makes an unusual but persuasive argument that the structures of indigenous societies were more important than Spanish domination in the cultural transitions of the colonial period. Magnus Mörner's *The Andean Past: Land, Societies and Conflicts* deals with the struggles of the Quechua and Aymara peoples in a cultural and ecological context. Charles Gibson's standard *Spain in America* focuses on the institutions of Spanish rule.

Alfred Crosby's *Ecological Imperialism: The Biological Expansion of Europe, 900 to 1900*, chronicles the environmental transformation of southern South America under colonial rule. His earlier book *Columbian Exchange* details the microbial invasion that changed South American demography, evaluating the impact of European plants and animals in the Americas and American plants and animals in Europe and worldwide.

See William Denevan's edited collection, *The Native Population of the Americas in 1492* for a regional approach to the demographic collapse.

Independence & the Republican Era

For the South American wars of independence, a standard work is John Lynch's *The Spanish-American Revolutions 1808 to 1826*. For an overview of social problems in Latin America, see Eric Wolf and Edward Hansen's *The Human Condition in Latin America*. For other titles, see individual country chapters.

Contemporary Issues

Gabriel García Márquez, better known as a novelist, returned to his journalistic roots to write *News of a Kidnapping*, a tragically fascinating account of an abduction by members of Colombia's Medellín drug cartel. For a more general analysis of both the cocaine and anticocaine industries, read *Snowfields: The War on Cocaine in the Andes*, by Clare Hargreaves. The rise and fall of Peru's guerilla insurgency is covered in *Shining Path*, by Simon Strong.

Amazonia

A classic 19th-century account is Henry Walter Bates' *The Naturalist on the River Amazon*. Roughly contemporaneous is AR Wallace's *Travels on the Amazon and Rio Negro*. Anthony Smith's *Explorers of the Amazon* is a series of essays on explorers of various kinds, from conquerors and scientists to plant collectors and rubber barons.

Despite shortcomings, Betty J Meggers' *Amazonia: Man and Culture in a Counterfeit Paradise* is essential reading for its description of traditional rain-forest cultures and the environment. Perhaps the best overall

account of the plight of the global rain forests is journalist Catherine Caufield's *In the Rainforest*, which contains substantial material on Amazonia, but also covers other imperiled areas. More recent is *The Fate of the Forest: Developers, Destroyers, and Defenders of the Amazon*, by Susanna Hecht and Alexander Cockburn.

On the situation of indigenous peoples, see Shelton Davis' *Victims of the Miracle: Development and the Indians of Brazil*. Julie Sloan Denslow and Christine Padoch's *People of the Tropical Rainforest* is an edited and well-illustrated collection of articles on tropical ecology and development that deals with rain-forest immigrants and indigenous peoples. For an assessment of the impact of mining, see David Cleary's *Anatomy of the Amazon Gold Rush*.

Flora & Fauna

Neotropical Rainforest Mammals: A Field Guide, by Louise Emmons and François Feer, provides color illustrations for identification. Birders in the Amazon region might try *South American Birds: A Photographic Aid to Identification*, by John S Dunning; *A Guide to the Birds of Colombia*, by Stephen L Hilty and William L Brown; or *A Guide to the Birds of Venezuela*, by Rodolphe Meyer de Schauensee and William Phelps. More inclusive is Meyer de Schauensee's *A Guide to the Birds of South America*.

Piet van Ipenburg and Rob Boschhuizen's *Ecology of Tropical Rainforests: An Introduction for Eco-tourists* is a booklet packed with intriguing minutiae about sloths, bats, strangler figs and other rainforest biota. It's available in the UK from J Forrest, 64 Belsize Park, London NW3 4EH, or in the USA from M Doolittle, 32 Amy Rd, Falls Village, CT 06031; all proceeds go to the Tambopata Reserve Society, which is funding research in the southeastern Peruvian rain forests.

Fiction

Peter Matthiessen's *At Play in the Fields of the Lord*, set in Peru's Amazon rain forests, is a tale of conflict between the forces of 'development' and indigenous peoples. Another superb novel with similar themes is Raymond Sokolov's *Native Intelligence*.

Nobel Prize-winner Gabriel García Márquez has been the leader of Latin America's fiction boom; his *One Hundred Years of Solitude* is perhaps South America's most famous fictional work. Another major writer is Peru's Mario Vargas Llosa, whose *The Real Life of Alejandro Mayta* offers insights into his country's current political dilemmas; also try his *Aunt Julia and the Scriptwriter*.

Many books by the late Brazilian novelist Jorge Amado, most notably *Dona Flor and Her Two Husbands* and *Gabriela, Clove and Cinnamon*, are easy to find in English. Contemporary satirist Márcio Souza has written *Emperor of the Amazon* and *Mad Maria*, both of which deal with attempts to conquer the rain forest.

NEWSPAPERS & MAGAZINES

The best regular source of South American news in English is the *Miami Herald*, which publishes an overseas edition available in capital cities and a few other centers throughout South America. The *Economist* also has good coverage of the region.

The *Latin American Weekly Report* has about a dozen pages of the latest news from Latin America and the Caribbean. It's available by airmail subscription from Latin American Newsletters (☎ 020-7251-0012, fax 020-7253-8193), 61 Old St, London EC1V 9HX, UK. They also publish a range of more specialized newsletters on specific parts of the region.

For up-to-date information on safety, political and economic conditions, health risks and costs for all Latin American countries, see the *Latin American Travel Advisor*, an impartial 16-page quarterly newsletter published in Ecuador. Current issues cost US$15, back issues are US$7.50; any four issues cost US$39. They're sent by airmail from LATA, PO Box 17-17-908, Quito, Ecuador (fax 593-2-562-566, lata@pi.pro.ec; in the US, fax 888-215-9511).

PHOTOGRAPHY & VIDEO

The latest consumer electronics are available throughout South America, but taxes make cameras and film very expensive in some countries. A good range of film, including B&W and slide film, can now be purchased at reasonable prices in many parts of Bolivia, in Asunción (Paraguay) and in the duty-free zones at Iquique and Punta Arenas (Chile). Paraguay's and Chile's free zones have camera equipment at prices only slightly higher than in North America, even if the selection is not so great. Salvador and Manaus in Brazil are good places to stock up on film and equipment. Be careful to keep film away from excessive heat. Locally manufactured film is reasonably good, but no cheaper than the imported stuff.

In tropical conditions, some photographers prefer to use Fujichrome, which renders greens exceptionally well and is readily available in the cities mentioned above. For the low-light conditions of the Amazonian rain forests, it's a good idea to carry a few rolls of high-speed (ASA 400) film and a flash. Kodachrome (in ASA 64 and 200) is better at capturing true reds and nearby colors of the spectrum and is often more suitable for deserts and urban areas, but it's virtually unobtainable in South America.

Photo processing is relatively expensive, but widely available. E6 slide processing is available in larger centers, but the quality you will receive is unreliable. Have one roll processed and check the results before you hand over your whole collection. It is almost impossible to get Kodachrome processed in South America. Most professionals take their film home for processing. Avoid posting unprocessed film – postal authorities use powerful X rays to screen parcels.

Always protect camera lenses with an ultraviolet (UV) filter. In high-altitude tropical light conditions in the Andes, the UV filter may not be sufficient to prevent washed-out photos; a polarizing filter can correct this problem.

Restrictions

Some tourist sites charge an additional fee for tourists with cameras. It's unwise and possibly illegal to take photos of military installations or security-sensitive places such as police stations.

Photographing People

Ask for permission before photographing individuals, particularly indigenous people. If someone is giving a public performance (such as a street musician or a dancer at Carnaval), or is incidental to a photograph (in a broad cityscape, for example), this is not usually necessary – but if in doubt, ask or refrain.

Video

Cassettes (8mm) for video cameras are available, but they will probably be more expensive than at home. Tourist sites that charge for a still camera may charge more for a video camera. If you want to buy a prerecorded video cassette or record a local TV program for your VCR at home, remember that different countries use different TV and video systems. For example, Colombia and Venezuela use the NTSC system (as in the USA), while Brazil uses PAL, and French Guiana uses the French SECAM system.

TIME

The South American mainland is between three and five hours behind Greenwich mean time (GMT). Chile, Paraguay and parts of Argentina and Brazil adopt 'summer time' from about October to March, when they are one hour closer to GMT.

ELECTRICITY

Most countries use either 110V or 220V, at 50Hz or 60Hz, and plugs with either two flat pins (US style) or two round pins. For details, see the country chapters. You'll need a multi-adapter with your appliance.

Argentina – 220V, 50Hz

Bolivia – 220V + 110, 50Hz; US-type plugs (two flat prongs)

Brazil – 110V, 120V, 127V, + 220V, 60Hz; two round prongs

TIME ZONES

GMT-6

Caribbean Sea

Isla de San Andrés

VENEZUELA

SURINAME

GUYANA

FRENCH GUIANA

COLOMBIA

Galápagos Islands

ECUADOR

GMT-5

PERU

GMT-4

BRAZIL

GMT-3

PACIFIC OCEAN

BOLIVIA

BRAZIL

PARAGUAY

Easter Island

CHILE

GMT-3

URUGUAY

ATLANTIC OCEAN

Juan Fernández Islands

ARGENTINA

Easter Island

GMT-6

Falkland Islands (Islas Malvinas)

GMT-4

Times are shown behind Greenwich mean time (GMT), ignoring local seasonal time variations.

Chile – 220V; two round prongs

Colombia – 110V, 60Hz; US-type plugs

Ecuador – 110V, 60Hz

Falklands – 220-240V, 50Hz; UK-type plugs

Guyana – 110V + 220V

Suriname – 127V; two round prongs

French Guiana – 220V, 50Hz; French-type plugs (two round prongs or two fatter prongs with a protruding earth prong)

Paraguay – 220V, 50Hz

Peru – 220V, 50 or 60Hz; US-type plugs

Uruguay – 220V, 50Hz

Venezuela – 110V, 60Hz; US-type plugs

WEIGHTS & MEASURES

The metric system is used everywhere except Guyana and the Falkland Islands (Islas Malvinas). For metric-imperial conversions, see the end of this book.

HEALTH

Travel health depends on your predeparture preparations, your daily health care while traveling and how you handle any medical problem that does develop. While the potential dangers can seem quite frightening, few travelers experience anything more serious than upset stomachs.

Predeparture Planning

Health Insurance Make sure that you have adequate health insurance. See Travel Insurance under Visas & Documents earlier in this chapter.

Immunizations Plan ahead for getting your vaccinations – some of them require more than one injection, while some vaccinations should not be given together. It is recommended you seek medical advice at least six weeks before traveling. Remember that some vaccinations should not be given during pregnancy or to people with allergies – discuss with your doctor. The risk of disease is often greater for children and pregnant women.

International health regulations require yellow-fever vaccination if you're coming from an infected area, and most of tropical South America is officially infected. Other vaccinations are recommended for travel in various parts of South America for your own protection, even though not required by law.

All vaccinations, but especially yellow fever, should be recorded in an *International Health Certificate*, a yellow booklet available from physicians or government health departments (see Visas & Documents earlier in this chapter). If an official health certificate is unavailable, have the doctor or clinic provide a document certifying the date and type of vaccinations, and carry it with you.

Yellow Fever Yellow-fever vaccination is a legal requirement for entry into many countries when a visitor comes from an infected area. Protection lasts 10 years and is recommended for most lowland tropical areas of South America, where the disease is endemic (see map later in the chapter). Not many doctors stock this vaccine, so you may have to go to a special yellow-fever vaccination center. Vaccination poses some risk during pregnancy, but if you must travel to a high-risk area, it is advisable. People allergic to eggs may not be able to have yellow-fever vaccination.

Hepatitis A The hepatitis A vaccine (eg, Avaxim, Havrix 1440 or VAQTA) provides long-term immunity (possibly for more than 10 years) after an initial injection and a booster at six to 12 months. Alternatively, an injection of gamma globulin can provide short-term protection against hepatitis A – two to six months, depending on the dose given. It is not a vaccine, but is a ready-made antibody collected from blood donations. It is reasonably effective and, unlike the vaccine, it is protective immediately, but because it is a blood product, there are current concerns about its long-term safety.

Hepatitis B Travelers who should consider a hepatitis B vaccination include health workers, those likely to have sexual contacts and those visiting countries with many hep B carriers or countries where blood supplies may not be adequately screened. Vaccination involves three injections, the quickest course being over three weeks with a booster at 12 months. A combined Hepatitis A and Hepatitis B vaccine called Twinrix is also available. Three injections over a six-month period are required, the first two providing substantial protection against hepatitis A.

Malaria This serious disease is spread by mosquito bites and is widespread in tropical South America, where drug-resistant strains of the disease are prevalent (see map). Main areas of risk are along the coasts and in rain-forest regions; areas above 2500m are safe. In malarial areas, it is imperative to protect yourself against mosquito bites and to take antimalaria drugs. These drugs do not prevent you from becoming infected, but kill the malaria parasites during a stage in their development and reduce the risk of serious illness or death. Antimalaria drugs are not vaccinations as such, but it is important to start taking them up to a week before entering a malarial area. Newer drugs such as mefloquine (Lariam) and doxycycline (Vibramycin, Doryx) should be considered for South America, which has chloroquine and multidrug-resistant malaria. Expert advice on medication should be sought, as there are many factors to consider, including the area to be visited, the risk of exposure to malaria-carrying mosquitoes, the side effects of medication, your medical history and whether you are a child or adult or pregnant. Travelers to isolated areas in high-risk countries may wish to carry a treatment dose of medication for use if symptoms occur. (See under Insect-Borne Diseases later in this chapter for more information.)

Diphtheria & Tetanus Vaccinations for these two diseases are usually combined and are recommended for everyone. After an initial course of three injections (usually given in childhood), boosters are necessary every 10 years.

Poliomyelitis A booster of either the oral or injected polio vaccine is required every 10 years to maintain immunity. More frequent boosters may be needed in tropical areas. Polio is a very serious, easily transmitted disease that still occurs in South America.

Typhoid This is an important vaccination to have in areas where hygiene is a problem and recommended if you are traveling for long periods in rural, tropical areas. It is available either as an injection or as oral capsules.

Cholera Cholera outbreaks have occurred recently in South America (see map), as recently as 1998 in Bolivia in addition to other countries. Cholera is usually transmitted by water and is most likely in the presence of unsanitary conditions. Vaccination gives poor protection, lasts only six months, has various side effects and is contraindicated in pregnancy. Though not generally recommended, and not required by international law, cholera vaccination may still be required at some South American border crossings if you're coming from an infected area.

Meningococcal Meningitis This vaccination may be advisable if you plan to travel rough in the Amazon region, but it is not generally recommended. A single injection will give good protection for three years. The vaccine is not recommended for children younger than two years old.

Rabies Pretravel rabies vaccination requires three injections over 21 to 28 days. It should be considered by those who will spend a month or longer in South America, especially if they are handling animals, cycling, caving or traveling to remote areas. Children may not report a bite and are therefore at greater risk than adults. If a vaccinated person is bitten or scratched by an animal, he or she will require two booster injections of vaccine. Those not vaccinated require more.

Tuberculosis TB risk to travelers is usually very low, but the disease is becoming more common in some cities, including São Paulo and Asunción. The main risk is to those living closely with local people in infected areas for extended periods. Vaccination against TB (BCG) is recommended for children and young adults living in these areas for three months or more. Most healthy adults do not develop symptoms, so a skin test is necessary to determine whether exposure has occurred.

Travel Health Guides If you are planning to be away or traveling in remote areas for a long period of time, you may want to consider taking a more detailed health guide.

CDC's Complete Guide to Healthy Travel, Open Road Publishing, 1997. The US Centers for Disease Control & Prevention recommendations for international travel.

Staying Healthy in Asia, Africa & Latin America, Dirk Schroeder, Moon Publications, 1994. Probably the best all-around guide to carry; it's compact, detailed and well organized.

Travelers' Health, Dr Richard Dawood, Oxford University Press and Random House, 1994. Comprehensive, easy to read, authoritative and highly recommended, although it's rather large to lug around.

Travel with Children, Maureen Wheeler, Lonely Planet Publications, 1995. Includes advice on travel health for younger children.

There are also a number of travel health sites on the Internet. From the Lonely Planet website (www.lonelyplanet.com) there are links to the World Health Organization and the Centers for Disease Control & Prevention.

Other Preparations Make sure you're healthy before you start traveling. Make sure your teeth are OK; there are lots of places where a visit to the dentist would be the last thing you'd want.

If you wear glasses, take a spare pair and your prescription. In most of South America you can get new spectacles made up quickly and competently.

If you require a particular medication take an adequate supply, as it may not be available locally. Take part of the packaging showing the generic name rather than the brand; this will make getting replacements easier. It's a good idea to have a legible prescription or letter from your doctor to show that you legally use the medication.

Medical Kit

It's wise to take a basic medical kit; include the following items:

☐ **Aspirin** or **paracetamol** (acetaminophen in the US) – for pain or fever.

☐ **Antihistamine** (such as Benadryl) – a decongestant for colds and allergies, eases the itch from insect bites or stings and helps prevent motion sickness. Antihistamines may cause sedation and interact with alcohol, so care should be taken when using them; take one you know and have used before, if possible.

☐ **Antibiotics** – useful if you're traveling well off the beaten track, but they must be prescribed; carry the prescription with you. If you are allergic to commonly prescribed antibiotics such as penicillin or sulfa drugs, carry this information when traveling.

☐ **Lomotil** or **Imodium** – to treat diarrhea; prochlorperazine (eg, Stemetil) or metaclopramide (eg, Maxalon) is good for nausea and vomiting.

☐ **Rehydration mixture** – to treat severe diarrhea; particularly important when traveling with children.

☐ **Antiseptic,** such as povidone-iodine (eg, Betadine) – for cuts and grazes.

☐ **Multivitamins** – especially useful for long trips when dietary vitamin intake may be inadequate.

☐ **Calamine lotion** or **aluminum sulfate spray** (eg, Stingose) – to ease irritation from bites or stings.

☐ **Bandages** and **Band-aids**.

☐ **Scissors, tweezers** and a **thermometer** – note that mercury thermometers are prohibited by airlines.

☐ **Cold and flu tablets** – Pseudoephedrine hydrochloride (Sudafed) may be useful if flying with a cold to avoid ear damage.

☐ **Throat lozenges.**

☐ **Insect repellent, sunscreen, Chapstick** and **water purification tablets.**

☐ **A couple of syringes** – in case you need injections in a country with medical hygiene problems. Ask your doctor for a note explaining why they have been prescribed.

Basic Rules

Care in what you eat and drink is the most important health rule. It's common to experience stomach upsets, especially in the first couple of weeks, but these are usually minor. Don't become paranoid; trying the local food is part of the experience of travel.

Water Be extremely careful about the water you drink, and this includes ice. If you don't know for certain that the water (or the ice) is safe, assume the worst. Bottled water is widely available, although in some places bottles may be refilled with tap water – make sure the bottle has an intact seal. Some hotels have a container of filtered water available, but this cannot be relied on. Take care with fruit juice, particularly if water may have been added. Milk should be treated with suspicion as it is often unpasteurized, though boiled milk is fine if it is kept hygienically. Tea or coffee should be OK if the water has been boiled.

The simplest method of water purification is to boil it thoroughly. At high altitudes, water boils at a lower temperature, so germs are less likely to be killed. Boil it for longer in these environments.

Consider bringing a water filter, of which there are two main kinds. Total filters take out all parasites, bacteria and viruses and make water safe to drink. They are often expensive, but can they be more cost effective than buying bottled water. Simple filters (which can even be a nylon mesh bag) take out dirt and larger foreign bodies from the water so that chemical solutions work much more effectively; if water is dirty, chemical solutions may not work at all. Simple filtering will not remove all dangerous organisms, so the water should also be boiled or treated chemically. Chlorine tablets (Puritabs, Steritabs or other brand names) will kill many pathogens, but not some parasites like giardia and amoebic cysts. Iodine is more effective in purifying water and is available in tablet form (such as Potable Aqua). Follow the directions carefully and remember that too much iodine can be harmful.

Food Vegetables and fruit should be washed with purified water or peeled when possible. Beware of ice cream that is sold in the street or anywhere it might have been melted and refrozen. Thoroughly cooked food is safest, but not if it has been left to cool or if it has been reheated. Raw shellfish such as mussels, oysters and clams should be avoided, as should undercooked meat, particularly in the form of mince. Steaming does not make shellfish safe for eating.

If a place looks clean and well run, and the vendor also looks clean and healthy, then the food is probably safe. In general, places that are packed with travelers or locals will be fine, while empty restaurants are questionable. The food in busy restaurants is cooked and eaten quickly with little standing around and is probably not reheated.

Nutrition If your food is poor or limited in availability, if you're traveling hard and fast and missing meals, or if you simply lose your appetite, you can soon start to lose weight and place your health at risk.

Make sure your diet is well balanced. Cooked eggs, beans, and nuts are all safe ways to get protein. Fruit you can peel (like bananas, oranges or mandarins, for example) is usually safe and a good source of vitamins (melons can harbor bacteria in their flesh and are best avoided). Try to eat plenty of grains (including rice) and bread. Food is generally safer if it is cooked well, but overcooked food loses much of its nutritional value. If your diet isn't well balanced or if your food intake is insufficient, it's a good idea to take vitamin and iron pills.

In hot climates make sure you drink enough – do not rely on feeling thirsty to indicate when you should drink. Not needing to urinate is a danger sign, as is very dark yellow urine. Always carry a water bottle with you on long trips. Excessive sweating can lead to loss of salt, and muscle cramping can result. Salt tablets are not a good idea as a preventative, but in places where salt is not used much, adding salt to food can help.

Medical Problems & Treatment

Self-diagnosis and treatment can be risky, so you should always seek medical help. Although we do give drug dosages in this section, they are for emergency use only. Correct diagnosis is vital. Generic names are given here for medications – check with a pharmacist for brands available locally.

An embassy, consulate or any well-run hotel can usually recommend a good place to go for advice. In some places standards of medical attention are so low that for some ailments the best advice is to get on a plane and go somewhere else.

Antibiotics should ideally be administered only under medical supervision. Take only the recommended dose at the prescribed intervals and use the whole course even if the illness seems to be cured earlier. Stop immediately if there are any serious reactions, and don't use the antibiotic at all if you are unsure that you have the correct one. If you are allergic to commonly prescribed antibiotics, such as penicillin or sulfa drugs, carry this information (eg, on a bracelet) when traveling.

Environmental Hazards

Sunburn In the tropics, the desert or at high altitude you can get sunburned surprisingly quickly, even through cloud. Use a sunscreen, hat and barrier cream for your nose and lips. Calamine lotion and aloe vera gel are good for mild sunburn. Protect your eyes with good-quality sunglasses, particularly if you will be near water, sand or snow.

Fungal Infections Fungal infections occur more commonly in hot weather and are usually found on the scalp, between the toes or fingers, in the groin and on the body (ringworm). You get ringworm (a fungal infection, not a worm) from infected animals or other people. Moisture encourages these infections.

To prevent fungal infections wear loose, comfortable clothes, avoid artificial fibers, wash frequently and dry carefully. If you do get an infection, wash the infected area at least daily with a disinfectant or medicated soap and water, and rinse and dry well. Apply an antifungal cream or powder like tolnifate (Tinaderm). Try to expose the infected area to air or sunlight as much as possible and wash all towels and underwear often in hot water and let them dry in the sun.

Prickly Heat Prickly heat is an itchy rash caused by excessive perspiration trapped under the skin. It usually strikes people who have just arrived in a hot climate. Keeping cool, bathing often, drying the skin and using a mild talcum or prickly-heat powder will help. Or resort to an air-conditioned hotel.

Heat Exhaustion Dehydration and salt deficiency can cause heat exhaustion. Take time to acclimatize to high temperatures, drink sufficient liquids and do not do anything too physically demanding.

Salt deficiency is characterized by fatigue, lethargy, headaches, giddiness and muscle cramps; salt tablets may help, but adding extra salt to your food is a better idea.

Anhydrotic heat exhaustion, caused by an inability to sweat, is quite rare. It is likely to strike people who have been in a hot climate for some time, rather than newcomers.

Heatstroke This serious, occasionally fatal, condition can occur if the body's heat-regulating mechanism breaks down and body temperature rises to dangerous levels. Long, continuous periods of exposure to high temperatures and insufficient fluids can leave you vulnerable to heatstroke.

The symptoms are feeling unwell, not sweating very much (or at all) and a high body temperature (39°C to 41°C or 102°F to 106°F). Where sweating has ceased the skin becomes flushed and red. Severe, throbbing headaches and lack of coordination will also occur, and the sufferer may be confused or aggressive. Eventually the victim will become delirious or convulse. Hospitalization is essential, but in the interim, get victims out of the sun, remove their clothing, cover them with a wet sheet or towel and fan continually. Give fluids if they are conscious.

Hypothermia Too much cold can be just as dangerous as too much heat. If you are trekking at high altitudes or simply taking a long bus trip over mountains, particularly at night, be prepared. In the Andes, you should always be prepared for cold, wet or windy conditions even if you're just out for a few hours.

Hypothermia occurs when the body loses heat faster than it can produce it and the core temperature of the body falls. It is surprisingly easy to progress from very cold to dangerously cold due to a combination of wind, wet clothing, fatigue and hunger, even if the air temperature is above freezing. It is best to dress in layers; silk, wool and some of the new artificial fibers are all good insulating materials. A hat is important, as a lot of heat is lost through the head. A strong, waterproof and windproof outer layer is essential. Carry basic supplies, including food containing simple sugars to generate heat quickly, fluid to drink, and a 'space' blanket for emergencies.

Symptoms of hypothermia are exhaustion, numbness (particularly in the toes and fingers), shivering, slurred speech, irrational or violent behavior, lethargy, stumbling, dizzy spells, muscle cramps and violent bursts of energy. Irrationality may take the form of sufferers claiming they are warm and trying to take off their clothes.

To treat mild hypothermia, first get people out of the wind or rain, remove their clothing if it's wet and replace it with dry, warm clothing. Give them hot liquids – not alcohol – and some high-kilojoule, easily digestible food. Do not rub victims, instead allow them to slowly warm themselves. This should be enough to treat the early stages of hypothermia. The early recognition and treatment of mild hypothermia is the only way to prevent severe hypothermia, which is a critical condition.

Altitude Sickness At altitudes higher than about 2500m, the lack of oxygen affects most people to some extent until they become acclimatized. The effect may be mild or severe and occurs because less oxygen reaches the muscles and the brain at high altitude, requiring the heart and lungs to compensate by working harder. It's a common hazard in the Andes and the altiplano region, where it's called *apunamiento* or *soroche*.

Symptoms of Acute Mountain Sickness (AMS) usually develop during the first 24 hours at high altitude but may be delayed up to three weeks. Mild symptoms include headache, lethargy, dizziness, difficulty sleeping and loss of appetite. AMS may become more severe without warning and can be fatal. Severe symptoms include breathlessness, a dry, irritative cough (which may progress to the production of pink, frothy sputum), severe headache, lack of coordination and balance, confusion, irrational behavior, vomiting, drowsiness and unconsciousness. There is no hard-and-fast rule as to what is too high: AMS has been fatal at 3000m, although 3500m to 4500m is the usual range at which it becomes dangerous.

Treat mild symptoms by resting at the same altitude until recovery, usually a day or two. Paracetamol or aspirin can be taken for headaches. If symptoms persist or become worse, however, *immediate descent is necessary*; even 500m can help. Drug treatments should never be used to avoid descent or to enable further ascent.

The traditional Andean remedy for mild symptoms is *mate de coca*, a tea made from coca leaves that you can get in most cafés in Peru and Bolivia. You can also buy leaves legally for US$4 to US$5 per kilo in *tiendas* (small general stores) or markets. It's debatable whether mate de coca will actually help a visitor cope with the altitude, but it's a pleasant enough drink.

The drugs acetazolamide (Diamox) and dexamethasone are recommended by some doctors for the prevention or treatment of AMS, but this is controversial. These drugs can reduce the symptoms, but they may also mask warning signs; severe and fatal AMS has occurred in people taking these drugs. For the average traveler, they are probably not a good idea.

To prevent acute mountain sickness, note the following:

- Ascend slowly – have frequent rest days, spending two to three nights at each rise of 1000m. If you reach a high altitude by trekking, acclimatization takes place gradually, and you are less likely to be affected than if you fly directly to high altitude.

- If possible, sleep at a lower altitude than the greatest height reached during the day. Once above 3000m, care should be taken not to increase the sleeping altitude by more than 300m per day.

- Drink extra fluids. The mountain air is dry and cold and moisture is lost as you breathe. Evaporation of sweat may occur unnoticed and result in dehydration.

- Eat light, high-carbohydrate meals for more energy.

- Avoid alcohol as it may increase the risk of dehydration.

- Avoid sedatives.

Jet Lag Jet lag is experienced when a person travels by air across more than three time zones (each time zone usually represents a one-hour time difference). It occurs because many of the functions of the human body (such as temperature, pulse rate and emptying of the bladder and bowels) are regulated by internal 24-hour cycles. When

we travel long distances rapidly, our bodies take time to adjust to the 'new time' of our destination, and we may experience fatigue, disorientation, insomnia, anxiety, impaired concentration and loss of appetite. These effects will usually be gone within three days of arrival, but to minimize the impact of jet lag:

- Rest for a couple of days prior to departure.

- Try to select flight schedules that minimize sleep deprivation; arriving late in the day means you can go to sleep soon after you arrive. For very long flights, try to organize a stopover.

- Avoid excessive eating (which bloats the stomach) and alcohol (which causes dehydration) during the flight. Instead, drink plenty of noncarbonated, nonalcoholic drinks, such as fruit juice or water.

- Avoid smoking.

- Make yourself comfortable by wearing loose-fitting clothes and perhaps bringing an eye mask and ear plugs to help you sleep.

- Try to sleep at the appropriate time for the time zone of your destination.

Motion Sickness Eating lightly before and during a trip will reduce the chances of motion sickness. If you are prone to motion sickness, try to find a place that minimizes movement – near the wing on aircraft, close to midships on boats, near the center on buses. Fresh air usually helps; reading and cigarette smoke don't. Commercial motion-sickness preparations, which can cause drowsiness, have to be taken before the trip commences. Ginger (available in capsule form) and peppermint (including mint-flavored sweets) are believed to be natural preventatives.

Infectious Diseases

Diarrhea Simple things like a change of water, food or climate can all cause a mild bout of diarrhea, but a few rushed toilet trips with no other symptoms is not indicative of a major problem.

Dehydration is the main danger caused by diarrhea, particularly in children or the elderly. Under all circumstances, *fluid replacement* (at least equal to the volume being lost) is the most important thing to remember. Weak black tea with a little sugar, soda water or soft drinks allowed to go flat and diluted 50% with clean water are all good. With severe diarrhea, a rehydrating solution is preferable to replace minerals and salts lost. Commercially available oral rehydration salts (ORS) are very useful; add them to boiled or bottled water. In an emergency you can make up a solution of six teaspoons of sugar and a half-teaspoon of salt to a liter of boiled or bottled water. You need to drink at least the same volume of fluid that you are losing in bowel movements and vomiting. Urine is the best guide to the adequacy of replacement – if you have small amounts of concentrated urine, you need to drink more. Keep drinking small amounts often. Stick to a bland diet as you recover.

Lomotil or Imodium can be used to bring relief from the symptoms, although they do not actually cure the problem. Only use these drugs if you do not have access to toilets – if you *must* travel. For children younger than 12, Lomotil and Imodium are not recommended. Do not use these drugs if the person has a high fever or is severely dehydrated.

In certain situations, antibiotics may be required: diarrhea with blood or mucus (dysentery), any fever, watery diarrhea with fever and lethargy, persistent diarrhea not improving after 48 hours and severe diarrhea. In these situations gut-paralyzing drugs like Imodium or Lomotil should be avoided.

A stool test is necessary to diagnose which kind of dysentery you have, so you should seek medical help urgently. Where this is not possible, the recommended drugs for dysentery are norfloxacin, 400mg twice daily for three days, or ciprofloxacin, 500mg twice daily for five days. These are not recommended for children or pregnant women. The drug of choice for children would be co-trimoxazole (Bactrim, Septrin, Resprim), with dosage dependent on weight. A five-day course is given. Ampicillin or amoxicillin may be given in pregnancy, but medical care is necessary.

Another common cause of persistent diarrhea in travelers is amoebic dysentery, caused by the protozoan *Entamoeba histolytica* and characterized by a gradual onset of low-grade diarrhea, often with blood and mucus. Cramping abdominal pain and vomiting are less likely than in other types of diarrhea, and fever may not be present. It will persist until treated and can recur and cause other health problems.

Diarrhea may also be a symptom of giardiasis, which is caused by a common parasite, *Giardia lamblia*. Symptoms include stomach cramps, nausea, a bloated stomach, watery, foul-smelling diarrhea and frequent gas. Giardiasis can appear several weeks after you have been exposed to the parasite. The symptoms may disappear for a few days and then return; this can go on for several weeks.

You should seek medical advice if you think you have giardiasis or amoebic dysentery, but where this is not possible, tinidazole or metronidazole are the recommended drugs. Treatment is a 2g single dose of tinidazole (known as Fasigyn) or 250mg of metronidazole (Flagyl) three times daily for five to 10 days.

Cholera This is the worst of the watery diarrheas and medical help should be sought. Outbreaks of cholera are generally widely reported, so avoid such problem areas. Fluid replacement is the most important treatment – the risk of dehydration is severe, as you may lose up to 20 liters of fluid per day. If there is a delay in getting to a hospital then begin taking tetracycline. The adult dose is 250mg, four times daily. It is not recommended for children under nine years nor for pregnant women. Tetracycline may help shorten the illness, but adequate fluids are required.

Hepatitis Hepatitis is a general term for inflammation of the liver, and it is a common disease worldwide. There are several different viruses that cause hepatitis, and they differ in the way that they are transmitted. The symptoms are similar in all forms of the illness and include fever, chills, headache, fatigue, feelings of weakness and aches and pains, followed by loss of appetite, nausea, vomiting, abdominal pain, dark urine, light-colored feces, jaundiced (yellow) skin and yellowing of the whites of the eyes. People who have had hepatitis should avoid alcohol for some time after the illness, as the liver needs time to recover.

Hepatitis A is transmitted by contaminated food and drinking water. You should seek medical advice, but there is not much you can do apart from resting, drinking lots of fluids, eating lightly and avoiding fatty foods. Hepatitis E is transmitted in the same way as hepatitis A; it can be particularly serious in pregnant women.

There are almost 300 million chronic carriers of hepatitis B in the world. It is spread through contact with infected blood, blood products or body fluids, for example through sexual contact, unsterilized needles and blood transfusions, or contact with blood via small breaks in the skin. Having tattoos, body piercing, or even shaving with contaminated equipment can be risks. The symptoms of hepatitis B may be more severe than type A and the disease can lead to long-term problems, such as chronic liver damage, liver cancer or a long-term carrier state. Hepatitis C and D are spread in the same way as hepatitis B and can also lead to long-term complications.

There are vaccines against hepatitis A and B, but there are currently no vaccines against other types of hepatitis. Following the basic rules about food and water (hepatitis A and E) and avoiding risk situations (hepatitis B, C and D) are important preventative measures.

Typhoid Typhoid fever is a dangerous gut infection caused by contaminated water and food. Medical help must be sought.

In typhoid's early stages, sufferers may feel they have a bad cold or flu on the way, as early symptoms are a headache, body aches and a fever that rises a little each day until it is around 40°C (104°F) or more. The victim's pulse is often slow relative to the degree of fever present – unlike a normal fever where pulse increases. There may also be vomiting, abdominal pain, diarrhea or constipation.

In the second week, the high fever and slow pulse continue, and a few pink spots may appear on the body; trembling, delirium, weakness, weight loss and dehydration may occur. Complications such as pneumonia, perforated bowel or meningitis may occur.

The fever should be treated by keeping the victim cool and giving them fluids (watch for dehydration). Ciprofloxacin 750mg twice a day for 10 days is good for adults.

Chloramphenicol is recommended in many countries. The adult dosage is two 250mg capsules, four times per day. Children between eight and 12 years old should have half the adult dose; for younger children one-third the adult dose.

Intestinal Worms These parasites are most common in rural and tropical areas.

Different worms have different ways of infecting people. Some may be ingested with food, including undercooked meat, and some enter through your skin. Infestations may not show up for some time, and although they are generally not serious, if left untreated some can cause severe health problems later. Consider having a stool test when you return home to check for these and determine the appropriate treatment.

Schistosomiasis Also known as bilharzia, this disease is present in the coastal regions of northeast Brazil, Suriname and north-central Venezuela. It is carried in water by minute worms that enter through the skin and attach themselves to the intestines or bladder. The first symptom may be a tingling and sometimes a light rash around the area where a worm entered. Weeks later, a high fever may develop. A general feeling of being unwell may be the first symptom, or there may be no symptoms. Once the disease is established, abdominal pain and blood in the urine are other signs. The infection often causes no symptoms until the disease is well established (several months to years after exposure), and damage to internal organs is irreversible.

Avoid swimming or bathing in fresh water where bilharzia is present. Even deep water can be infected. If you do get wet, dry off quickly and dry your clothes as well.

A blood test is the most reliable test, but the test will not show positive until a number of weeks after exposure.

Tuberculosis TB is a bacterial infection usually transmitted from person to person by coughing or spitting, but it can be transmitted through consumption of unpasteurized milk. Milk that has been boiled is safe to drink, and the souring of milk to make yogurt or cheese also kills the bacilli. Travelers are usually not at great risk, as close household contact with the infected person is usually required before the disease is passed on.

HIV & AIDS HIV (Human Immuno-deficiency Virus) develops into AIDS (Acquired Immune Deficiency Syndrome), which is a fatal disease. Called SIDA in Spanish and Portuguese, this is still a growing problem in South America, especially in

Brazil. Any exposure to blood, blood products or body fluids may put the individual at risk. The disease is often transmitted through sexual contact or dirty needles – body piercing, acupuncture, tattooing and vaccinations can be potentially as dangerous as intravenous drug use. HIV and AIDS can also be spread via infected blood transfusions, but blood supplies in most reputable hospitals in South America are now screened, so the risk from transfusions is low.

If you do need an injection, ask to see the syringe unwrapped in front of you, or take a needle and syringe pack with you.

Fear of HIV infection should not preclude treatment for any serious medical conditions.

Sexually Transmitted Diseases Gonorrhea, herpes and syphilis are among these diseases; sores, blisters or rashes around the genitals, discharges or pain when urinating are common symptoms. In some STDs, such as wart virus or chlamydia, symptoms may be less marked or not observed at all, especially in women. Syphilis symptoms eventually disappear completely but the disease continues and can cause severe problems in later years. While abstinence from sexual contact is the only 100% effective prevention, using condoms can also be effective. Gonorrhea and syphilis are treated with antibiotics. Different sexually transmitted diseases each require specific antibiotics. There is no cure for herpes or AIDS.

Insect-Borne Diseases

Malaria If you are traveling in endemic areas (see the Malarial Areas map) it is extremely important to avoid mosquito bites and to take antimalaria tablets (see Immunizations, earlier). Symptoms range from fever, chills and sweating, headache, diarrhea and abdominal pains, to a vague feeling of ill health. Seek medical help immediately if malaria is suspected. Without treatment, malaria can rapidly become more serious and can be fatal.

If medical care is not available, antimalaria tablets can be used for treatment. You need to use a tablet that is different from the one you were taking when you contracted malaria. The treatment dosages are mefloquine (two 250mg tablets and two more six hours later), Fansidar (a single dose

of three tablets). If you were previously taking mefloquine (Lariam) and cannot obtain Fansidar, alternatives are Malarone (atovaquone-proguanil; four tablets once daily for three days), halofantrine (three doses of two 250mg tablets every six hours) or quinine sulfate (600mg every six hours). If used with mefloquine, there is a greater risk of side effects with these dosages than in normal use, so medical advice is preferable. Halofantrine is no longer recommended by the World Health Organization (WHO) as emergency standby treatment because of side effects and should only be used if no other drugs are available.

Because antimalaria tablets are not 100% effective, the primary preventative is protection from mosquito bites. The mosquitoes that transmit malaria bite from dusk to dawn, but precautions should be taken at all times:

• Wear light-colored clothing.
• Wear long pants and long-sleeved shirts.
• Use mosquito repellents containing the compound DEET on exposed areas (prolonged overuse of DEET may be harmful, especially to children, but its use is considered preferable to being bitten by disease-transmitting mosquitoes).
• Avoid highly scented perfumes or deodorants.
• Use a mosquito net impregnated with mosquito repellent (permethrin) – it may be worth taking your own.
• Impregnate clothes with permethrin to effectively deter mosquitoes and other insects.

Malaria can be diagnosed by a simple blood test. Seek examination immediately if there is any suggestion of malaria. Some species of the parasite may lie dormant in the liver, but they can be eradicated using a specific medication. Malaria is curable, as long as the traveler seeks medical help when symptoms occur.

Dengue Fever This serious disease is a rapidly growing problem in tropical South America. The *Aedes aegypti* mosquito, which transmits the dengue virus, is most active during the day and is found mainly in urban areas, in and around human dwellings.

Signs and symptoms of dengue fever include a sudden onset of high fever, headache, joint and muscle pains, nausea and vomiting and sometimes a rash of small

MALARIAL AREAS

Limited Risk Area
Malaria Risk Area

red spots appears three to four days after the onset of fever. In the early phase, dengue may be mistaken for other diseases, including malaria and influenza. Later it can progress to the potentially fatal dengue hemorrhagic fever (DHF), a severe illness characterized by heavy bleeding. Full recovery even from simple dengue fever may be prolonged, with tiredness lasting for several weeks.

If you think you may be infected, seek medical attention quickly. A blood test can exclude malaria and indicate the possibility of dengue fever, for which there is no specific treatment. Aspirin should be avoided, as it increases the risk of hemorrhaging.

There is no vaccine against dengue fever. The best prevention is to avoid mosquito bites at all times, as for malaria.

Yellow Fever This viral disease is endemic in many South American countries and is transmitted by mosquitoes. The initial symptoms are fever, headache, abdominal pain and vomiting. Seek medical care urgently and drink lots of fluids. Vaccination against yellow fever is a requirement for travel to and from many parts of South America.

Chagas' Disease In remote rural areas of South America, this parasitic disease is transmitted by the reduvid bug, locally called the *vinchuca* or *barbeiro*. It infests crevices and palm fronds, often lives in thatched roofs and comes out to feed at night. A hard, violet-colored swelling appears at the site of the bite in about a week. The disease is treatable in the early stages, and the body usually overcomes the disease unaided, but if it continues it can eventually be fatal. Avoid sleeping in thatched-roof huts, or use a mosquito net, insecticides and repellents and check for hidden insects.

Filariasis This is a mosquito-transmitted parasitic infection found in many parts of South America. Possible symptoms include fever, pain and swelling of the lymph glands; inflammation of lymph drainage areas; swelling of a limb or the scrotum; skin rashes and blindness. Treatment is available to eliminate the parasites from the body, but some of the damage already caused may not be reversible. Medical advice should be obtained promptly if the infection is suspected.

Leishmaniasis A group of parasitic diseases transmitted by sandfly bites, leishmaniasis is found in some parts of South America. Cutaneous leishmaniasis affects the skin tissue, causing ulceration and disfigurement. Visceral leishmaniasis affects the internal organs. Seek medical advice as laboratory testing is required for diagnosis and correct treatment. Avoiding sandfly bites is the best precaution. Bites are usually painless, itchy and are yet another reason to cover up and apply repellent.

Typhus Typhus is spread by ticks, mites or lice. It begins with fever, chills, headache and muscle pains followed a few days later by a body rash. There is often a large painful sore at the site of the bite, and nearby lymph nodes are swollen and painful. Typhus can be treated under medical supervision. Seek local advice on areas where ticks pose a danger and always check your skin (including hair) carefully for ticks after walking in a danger area such as a tropical forest. A strong insect repellent can help, and serious

YELLOW FEVER AREAS

walkers in tick areas should consider having their boots and trousers impregnated with benzyl benzoate and dibutylphthalate.

Cuts, Bites & Stings

Bedbugs & Lice Bedbugs live in various places, but particularly in dirty mattresses and bedding, evidenced by spots of blood on bedclothes or on the wall. Bedbugs leave itchy bites in neat rows. Calamine lotion or Stingose spray may help.

All lice cause itching and discomfort. They make themselves at home in hair (head lice), clothing (body lice) or pubic hair (crabs). You can catch lice through direct contact with infected people or by sharing combs, clothing and the like. Powder or shampoo treatment will kill the lice. Infected clothing should then be washed in very hot, soapy water and left in the sun to dry.

Insect Bites & Stings Bee and wasp stings are usually painful rather than dangerous. However, in people who are allergic to them, severe breathing difficulties may occur and require urgent medical care. Calamine lotion

or Stingose spray will give relief, and ice packs will reduce the pain and swelling. Scorpions often shelter in shoes or clothing; their stings are notoriously painful.

Bichos de Pé These small parasites live on beaches and in sandy soil in northeast Brazil. They burrow into the thick skin of the foot at the heel, toes and under the toenails and appear as dark boils. They must be incised and removed completely. Do it yourself with a sterilized needle and blade. To avoid *bichos de pé,* wear footwear on beaches and dirt trails, especially where animals are present.

Cuts & Scratches Wash well and treat any cut with an antiseptic, such as povidone-iodine. When possible, avoid bandages and Band-aids, which can keep wounds wet. Coral cuts are notoriously slow to heal, and if they are not adequately cleaned, small pieces of coral can become embedded in the wound. Avoid coral cuts by wearing shoes if there's a chance that you might step on any coral, and clean any cut thoroughly with an antiseptic. Severe pain, throbbing, redness, fever or generally feeling unwell suggest infection and the prompt need for antibiotics, as coral cuts may result in serious infections.

Tetanus Tetanus occurs when a wound becomes infected by a germ that lives in soil and in the feces of horses and other animals. It enters the body via breaks in the skin, so the best prevention is to clean all wounds promptly and thoroughly and use an antiseptic. Use antibiotics if the wound becomes hot, throbs or pus is seen. The first symptom may be discomfort in swallowing, or stiffening of the jaw and neck; this is followed by painful convulsions of the jaw and whole body. The disease can be fatal, but is preventable with vaccination.

Rabies Rabies is a fatal viral infection found throughout South America. Many animals can be infected (such as dogs, cats, bats and monkeys) and it is their saliva that is infectious. Any bite, scratch or even lick from a warm-blooded, furry animal should be cleaned immediately and thoroughly. Scrub with soap and running water, and then apply alcohol or iodine solution. Medical help should be sought promptly to receive a course of injections to prevent the onset of symptoms and death.

Leeches & Ticks Leeches may be present in damp rain-forest conditions; they attach themselves to your skin to suck your blood. Trekkers often get them on their legs or in their boots. Salt or a lighted cigarette end will make them fall off. Do not pull them off, as the bite is then more likely to become infected. Clean and apply pressure if the point of attachment is bleeding. An insect repellent may keep them away.

Always check all over your body (hikers often get them on their legs or in their boots) after walking through a potentially tick-infested area, as ticks can cause skin infections and more serious diseases. Adult ticks suck blood from hosts by burying their head into skin, but they are often found unattached and can simply be brushed off. Avoid pulling the rear of the body, as this may squeeze the tick's gut contents through the attached mouth parts into the skin, increasing the risk of infection and disease. To remove an attached tick, use a pair of tweezers, grab it by the head and gently pull it straight out – do not twist it. (If no tweezers are available, use your fingers, but protect them from contamination with a piece of tissue or paper.) Do not touch the tick with a hot object like a cigarette or a match – this can cause it to regurgitate noxious gut substances or saliva into the wound. And do not rub oil, alcohol or petroleum jelly on it. If you get sick in the next couple of weeks, consult a doctor.

Snakes To minimize your chances of being bitten, always wear boots, socks and long trousers when walking through undergrowth where snakes may be present. Don't put your hands into holes and crevices, and be careful when collecting firewood.

Snakebites do not cause instantaneous death and antivenins are usually available. Immediately wrap the bitten limb tightly, as you would for a sprained ankle, and then attach a splint to immobilize it. Keep the victim still and seek medical help, if possible bringing the dead snake for identification. Don't attempt to catch the snake if there is a possibility of being bitten again. Using tourniquets and sucking out the poison are now comprehensively discredited.

Women's Health

Antibiotic use, synthetic underwear, sweating and contraceptive pills can lead to fungal vaginal infections when traveling in hot climates. Wearing loose-fitting clothes and cotton underwear will help to prevent these infections.

Fungal infections, characterized by a rash, itch and discharge, can be treated with a vinegar or lemon-juice douche, or with yogurt. Nystatin, miconazole or clotrimazole pessaries or vaginal cream are the usual treatment.

Other vaginal problems include a smelly discharge, painful intercourse and sometimes a burning sensation when urinating. These may be sexually transmitted, so sexual partners must also be treated. Medical attention should be sought, and remember that in addition to these diseases, HIV or hepatitis B may also be acquired during exposure. Besides abstinence, the best preventative is to practice safer sex using condoms.

Pregnancy Safe travel in much of South America requires vaccinations, and some of these are not advisable during pregnancy. In addition, some diseases, such as malaria, are much more serious during pregnancy and may pose a risk to the fetus. Pregnant women should avoid all unnecessary medication, but advice should be sought on vaccination and malaria prophylaxis. Additional care should be taken to prevent illness (eg, avoiding mosquito bites), and particular attention should be paid to diet and nutrition.

Most miscarriages occur during the first three months of pregnancy. Miscarriage is not uncommon and can occasionally lead to severe bleeding. The last three months should also be spent within reasonable distance of good medical care. A baby born as early as 24 weeks stands a chance of survival, but only in a good modern hospital.

WOMEN TRAVELERS

South American women rarely travel alone, and single women travelers may find themselves the object of curiosity – sometimes well-intentioned, sometimes not. In the Andean region, especially in smaller towns and rural areas, modest dress and conduct are the norm, while in Brazil and the more liberal Southern Cone countries, standards are more relaxed, especially in beach areas. A good rule is to follow local practice and take your cues from local women. Local women usually do not go into cheap bars, and those who do are commonly assumed to be prostitutes.

Machista attitudes, stressing masculine pride and virility, are fairly widespread among South American men. They are often expressed in boasting and in exaggerated attention toward women. Snappy put-down lines or other caustic responses to unwanted advances may make the man feel threatened, and he may become aggressive. Most women find it more effective to invent a husband and leave the guy with his pride intact, especially in front of others.

There have been cases of South American men raping women travelers. The greatest risk seems to be in remote or isolated areas to women trekking or on tours. Some cases have involved tour guides assaulting tour group members, so it's worth double checking the identity and reputation of any guide or tour operator. Also be aware that women have been drugged, in bars and elsewhere, using drinks, cigarettes or pills. South American police may not be very helpful in rape cases – if a local woman is raped, her family usually seeks revenge rather than calling the police. Tourist police may be more sympathetic, but it's possibly better to see a doctor and contact your embassy before reporting a rape to police.

GAY & LESBIAN TRAVELERS

Brazil is the most gay-friendly country on the continent, especially the cities of Rio de Janeiro, São Paulo and Salvador. Buenos Aires also has a visible gay scene (though gays may be harassed in parts of Argentina), as does Santiago (although male homosexuality is technically illegal in Chile). Elsewhere on the continent, local gays are discreet, and same-sex couples may provoke negative reactions if they are affectionate in public.

Despite a growing number of publications and websites devoted to gay travel, very few have specific advice about South American destinations. The gay travel newsletter, *Out and About*, has occasionally covered South America – their website, www.outandabout.com, has general information and lets you order back issues on Argentina, Rio and São Paulo.

DISABLED TRAVELERS

South America generally is not well set up for disabled travelers, but the more modernized, Southern Cone countries may be less difficult to deal with – notably Chile, Argentina and perhaps the main cities of Brazil. Unfortunately, expensive international hotels are more likely to cater for guests with disabilities than cheap local lodgings; air travel will be more feasible than inexpensive local buses; and well-developed tourist attractions will be more accessible than more off-the-beaten-track destinations. Careful planning is essential, but there is little detailed information on South America for disabled travelers.

In the US, Mobility International (☎ 541-343-1284, fax 541-343-6812), PO Box 10767, Eugene, OR 97440, advises disabled travelers on mobility issues. It primarily runs educational exchange programs, which could be a good way to visit South America.

Some sources on the Internet include www.access-able.com, which has little specifically on South America, and www.geocities .com/Paris/1502/exotictravel.html, which has two good accounts of disabled travel in South America.

SENIOR TRAVELERS

There are few discounts or special deals for older travelers and few facilities for those of limited mobility, but older people are generally treated with respect and courtesy, and those with a reasonable level of fitness will have no problem enjoying a trip to South America. Some US-based organizations may be able to give advice.

The American Association of Retired Persons (AARP; ☎ 800-424-3410; www .aarp.org), 601 E St NW, Washington, DC 20049, is an advocacy group for Americans 50 years and older and a good resource for travel bargains. Non-US residents can get one-year memberships for $10.

Grand Circle Travel (☎ 617-350-7500, 800-350-7500), 347 Congress St, Boston, MA 02210, offers escorted tours and travel information in a variety of formats, and distributes a useful free booklet, *Going Abroad: 101 Tips for Mature Travelers*.

TRAVEL WITH CHILDREN

A small number of foreigners visit South America with children, and they are usually treated with great kindness throughout the continent. Though there are few attractions or facilities specifically for kids, transport, food and lodging are all quite manageable, and a widespread affection for kids throughout South America makes them something of a social asset. Children with fair hair and light skin are especially likely to receive attention, and this may become tiresome for them.

Civilian airlines let kids younger than 12 fly at half the regular economy fare. Long-distance buses usually charge children full fare if they occupy a seat (but bus fares are usually cheap anyway). Most hotels have some rooms with three or four beds – these rooms cost more, but ask for a special family rate. Restaurants rarely advertise children's meals, but will often offer a child-size serving at a lower price and invariably allow two kids to share an adult meal. For light, cheap meals, bring some cups, plates and utensils and buy cereals, soft drinks and sandwich stuff from a supermarket.

You might find water parks and amusement parks in the more developed countries, but they are uncommon. Kids will enjoy the beaches and perhaps some natural attractions in addition to cable cars, trains, boat rides and the ubiquitous video arcades. They'll also enjoy outdoor activities such as skiing, white-water rafting, snorkeling, horseback riding and even walking. It's a good idea to alternate adult activities (museums, galleries, shopping, scenic tours) with things that kids will enjoy.

A baby backpack is the best way to carry very young children, but a stroller can be very useful too. Strollers may be impossible .o push on many rough pavements, but they're great as a portable place for sitting and sleeping and carrying kids' stuff. Have your child carry a small bag with a few favorite toys or teddies, some books, crayons and paper. For more information, advice and anecdotes, look at Lonely Planet's *Travel with Children*, by Maureen Wheeler.

USEFUL ORGANIZATIONS
South American Explorers Club
This very informative nonprofit organization has offices in Lima (☎ 511-425-0142) and Quito (☎ 593-2-225-228); for addresses, see the Peru and Ecuador chapters. There were plans to open an office in La Paz, Bolivia; check with another branch. The US office

(☎ 607-277-0488), 126 Indian Creek Rd, Ithaca, NY 14850, publishes the quarterly magazine, *South American Explorer,* and maintains the website, www.samexplo.org.

The SAEC was founded in 1977 and functions as an information center for travelers, adventurers and researchers. It supports scientific field work, mountaineering and other expeditions, wilderness conservation and social development in Latin America. The club's Lima office has an extensive library of books, maps and traveler's reports. The club sells maps, books and other items at its offices in Lima and Quito and by mail order.

Membership costs US$40 per person per year (US$60 for a couple) and includes four issues of *South American Explorer* magazine. Members receive access to the club's information service, library, storage facilities, mail service, book exchange, discounts at some hotels and travel services. If you're interested in joining, send US$4 for a sample copy of the magazine and further information.

In 1998, legal eagles representing the Explorers Club of New York advised the South American Explorers Club to stop calling itself the South American Explorers Club, so if you see a T-shirt from the Club Formerly Known as the South American Explorers Club, you'll know what happened.

Environmental Organizations
See the Argentina, Bolivia, Chile, Paraguay, Peru and Falkland Islands chapters for local organizations promoting environmental preservation. The organization Friends of the Earth International office has a website at www.xs4all.nl/~foeint. The following groups may also have suggestions for prospective travelers.

Australia
Friends of the Earth (☎ 03-9419-8700, www.foe .org.au), 312 Smith St, Collingwood, PO Box 222, Fitzroy, Vic 3065

UK
Friends of the Earth (☎ 020-7490-1555), 26/28 Underwood St, London N17JQ
Survival International (☎ 020-7492-1441), 11-15 Emerald St, London WC1N 3QL
WWF (☎ 1483-426-444), Panda House, Weyside Park, Godalming, Surrey GU7 1BP

USA
The Rainforest Action Network (RAN; ☎ 415-398-4404, www.ran.org), 221 Pine St, Suite 500, San Francisco, CA 94104

Conservation International (☎ 202-429-5660, www
.conservation.org), 2501 M St NW, Suite 200,
Washington, DC 20037

The Nature Conservancy (☎ 703-841-5300, www.tnc
.org), 4245 N Fairfax Drive, Suite 100, Arlington,
VA 22203

DANGERS & ANNOYANCES

There are quite a few potential dangers, but
don't be put off. Most areas are quite safe,
and with sensible precautions, you are
unlikely to have any problems.

Theft

Theft can be a big problem in some countries, especially Colombia, Peru and parts of
Brazil. Rob Rachowiecki, author of LP's
Peru and *Ecuador*, makes the following recommendations for situations where there is
a high risk of theft:

As well as pickpockets and bag-snatchers, there are
the razor-blade artists who slit open your luggage
when you're not looking. This includes a pack on
your back or even your trouser pocket. To avoid
this, many travelers carry day packs on their chests
during trips to markets, etc. When walking with my
large pack, I move fast and avoid stopping, which
makes it difficult for anyone intent on cutting the
bag. If I have to stop, at a street crossing for
example, I move gently from side to side so I can
feel if anyone is touching my pack, and I look
around a lot. I don't feel paranoid – walking fast and
looking around on my way from bus station to hotel
has become second nature to me, and I never place
a bag on the ground unless I have my foot on it.

One of the best solutions to the rip-off problem
is to travel with a friend and to watch each other.
An extra pair of eyes makes a lot of difference. I
often see shifty-looking types eyeing luggage at
bus stations, but they notice if you are alert and are
less likely to bother you. They'd much rather steal
something from the tired and unalert traveler who
has put a bag on a chair while buying a coffee. Ten
seconds later, the traveler has the coffee – but the
thief has the bag!

Thieves look for easy targets. Leave your wallet
at home; it's an easy mark for a pickpocket. Carrying a small roll of bills loosely wadded under a
handkerchief in your front pocket is as safe a way as
any of carrying your daily spending money. The rest
should be hidden. Always use at least a closeable
inside pocket or preferably a body pouch, money
belt or leg pouch to protect your money and passport. Carry some of your money in traveler's checks.

Pickpockets are not the only problem. Snatch
theft is also common, so don't wear gold necklaces
and expensive wristwatches or you're liable to
have them snatched from your body. Snatch theft

can also occur if you carry a camera loosely over
your shoulder or place a bag down on the ground
for just a second!

Thieves often work in pairs or groups. While
your attention is being distracted by one, another is
robbing you. Distractions I have seen used include
a bunch of kids fighting in front of you, an old lady
'accidentally' bumping into you, someone dropping something in your path or spilling something
on your clothes – the possibilities go on and on.
The only thing you can do is to try, as much as possible, to avoid being in very tight crowds and to
stay alert, especially when something out of the
ordinary occurs.

On buses and trains, keep an eye on your baggage
at all times, but especially at night. Don't fall asleep
in a railway compartment unless a friend is watching
you and your gear, or you'll wake up with everything
gone. When a bus stops, if you can't see what's happening to your gear, get off and have a look.

Confidence Tricks & Scams

Tricks involving a quantity of cash being
'found' on the street, elaborate hard-luck
stories from supposed travelers, and 'on-the-
spot fines' by bogus police are just some of
the scams used to separate tourists from
their money. Be especially wary if one or
more 'plainclothes' police officers demand
to search your luggage or examine your documents, traveler's checks or cash. Insist that
you will only allow this at an official police
station or in the presence of a uniformed
officer, and don't allow anyone to take you
anywhere in a taxi or unmarked car. A
healthy skepticism is your best defense.

Trouble Spots

Some countries and areas are more dangerous than others; see individual country chapters for details. The more dangerous places
warrant extra care, but don't feel you should
avoid them altogether. Kidnapping for
ransom is a serious and growing problem in
Colombia. Peru has been regarded as the
most hazardous country for travelers, but it's
safer now than in the past. The risk of terrorist action is dramatic, but extremely low;
petty theft is highly likely. Peruvian authorities have improved policing of tourist areas,
but be vigilant. There have been robberies,
some of them armed, on the Inca Trail to
Machu Picchu. It's wise not to go alone.

Robbery, sometimes violent, is also prevalent in Colombia, Brazil, Venezuela and
Guyana, so take extra care, and don't carry
valuables. In Brazil, the main trouble spots

are the beaches of Rio and the northeast, where muggings occur even at midday and gangs roam the beaches watching for unattended articles. Ecuador, Bolivia and Suriname are considerably safer, but travelers shouldn't be complacent. Argentina, Chile, Uruguay, Paraguay and French Guiana are probably the safest places on the continent.

Drugs

Marijuana and cocaine are big business in parts of South America, and are available in many places but illegal everywhere. Penalties are severe. Beware that drugs are sometimes used to set up travelers for blackmail and bribery. Avoid any conversation with someone who offers you drugs. If you are in an area where drug trafficking is prevalent, ignore it, and do not show any interest in it whatsoever.

Don't accept food, drinks, sweets or cigarettes from strangers on buses, trains or in bars. They may be laced with powerful sedative drugs, and you will be robbed while you're unconscious.

Roll-your-own cigarettes or cigarette papers may arouse suspicion.

Coca In Bolivia and Peru, coca leaves are sold legally in *tiendas* (small general stores) or markets for US$4 to US$5 per kilo. Mate de coca is a beverage made by the infusion of coca leaves in boiling water. It's served in many cafes and restaurants in the Andean region, and coca-leaf 'tea bags' are also available. Though mate de coca is widely believed to combat the effects of altitude, there is no evidence that conclusively supports this, and a cup of mate de coca has no immediate stimulant effect.

The practice of chewing coca leaves goes back centuries and is still common among the native people of the Andean altiplano. The leaves are chewed with a little ash or bicarbonate of soda, as the alkalinity releases the mild stimulant contained in the leaf cells. Prolonged chewing will dull the pangs of hunger, thirst, cold and fatigue, but the initial effect is to make the mouth go numb, and it's no better a buzz than a dental anesthetic. Without the alkaline catalyst, chewing coca leaves won't do much at all.

Someone who has chewed coca leaves or taken mate de coca may test positive for cocaine use in the following weeks. If you're about to compete in a major sporting event, or apply for a job with a superstraight corporation, it might be well to abstain.

More refined forms of coca are illegal everywhere. Contrary to some beliefs, smoking coca paste or crystals is probably more harmful and addictive than sniffing cocaine powder.

Baggage Insurance & Theft Reports

Baggage insurance is worth its price in peace of mind. Make sure the policy has a maximum value limit on any one item, and make sure it's sufficient to cover replacement. When you make a claim, especially for a valuable item, the insurance company may demand a receipt to prove that you bought it in the first place. If you have anything stolen, you must usually inform the insurance company by air mail and report the loss or theft to local police within 24 hours. Make a list of stolen items and their value. At the police station, you complete a *denuncia* (statement), a copy of which is given to you for your claim on the insurer. The denuncia usually has to be made on *papel sellado* (stamped paper), which you can buy for a few cents at any stationer.

In city police stations, you might find an English-speaking interpreter, but in most cases, you'll either have to speak the local language or provide an interpreter. Some cities have a tourist police service, which can be more helpful.

It can be expensive and time-consuming to replace a lost or stolen passport. Apart from the cost of backtracking to the nearest embassy or consulate, there will be telex charges to your home country to check the details of your previous passport plus the cost of a new passport.

If you are robbed, photocopies (even better, certified copies) of original passports, visas and air tickets and careful records of credit card numbers and traveler's checks will prove invaluable. Replacement passport applications are usually referred to the home country, so it helps to have a copy of your passport details with someone back home.

Police & Military

Corruption is a very serious problem among Latin American police, who are generally poorly paid, poorly educated and poorly supervised. In many countries, they are not reluctant to plant drugs on unsuspecting travelers or enforce minor regulations to the letter in hopes of extracting *coimas* (bribes).

If you are stopped by 'plain clothes policemen,' *never* get into a vehicle with them. Don't give them any documents or show them any money, and don't take them to your hotel. If the police appear to be the real thing, insist on going to a bona fide police station on foot.

The military often maintains considerable influence, even under civilian governments. Avoid approaching military installations, which may display warnings like 'No stopping or photographs – the sentry will shoot.' In the event of a coup or other emergency, state-of-siege regulations suspend civil rights. Always carry identification and be sure someone knows your whereabouts. Contact your embassy or consulate for advice.

Natural Hazards

The Pacific Rim 'ring of fire' loops through east Asia, Alaska and all the way down through the Americas to Tierra del Fuego in a vast circle of earthquake and volcanic activity that includes the whole Pacific side of South America. In 1991, for example, the eruption of Volcán Hudson in Chile's Aisén Region buried parts of southern Patagonia knee-deep in ash. Volcanoes usually give some notice before blowing and are therefore unlikely to pose any immediate threat to travelers. Earthquakes are common, occur without warning and can be very serious. Andean construction rarely meets seismic safety standards; adobe buildings are particularly vulnerable. A 1998 earthquake in Colombia cost thousands of lives.

ACTIVITIES
Diving

Major destinations for divers are the Caribbean coast of Colombia and Venezuela and islands such as Providencia (a Colombian-owned island that is actually nearer to Nicaragua), the Galápagos and the Brazilian archipelago of Fernando de Noronha, which is out in the Atlantic.

Mountaineering

On a continent with one of the world's great mountain ranges, climbing opportunities are almost unlimited. Ecuador's volcanoes, the high peaks of Peru's Cordillera Blanca, Bolivia's Cordillera Real and Argentina's Aconcagua (the continent's highest verified peak) are all suitable for mountaineering, but perhaps the most challenging technical climbs are in the FitzRoy range of Argentina's Parque Nacional Los Glaciares. Brazil lacks big mountains, but rock climbing is very popular around Rio.

River Rafting

Chile's Río Biobío features some of the world's finest Class V white water, though it may yet be drowned by a proposed hydroelectric project. River running is also possible in Peru on the Urubamba, other rivers near Cuzco and in the very difficult Río Colca canyon near Arequipa; on several rivers around Bariloche in Argentina; and near Tena and Baños in Ecuador.

Sea Kayaking

Southern Chile has some great coastal kayaking, particularly the island of Chiloé and the Canal Moraleda south to Laguna San Rafael.

Skiing

South America's most important downhill ski areas are in Chile and Argentina – see those chapters for more details. The season is from about June to September. There's also plenty of snow in the Andes of Bolivia, Peru, Ecuador, Colombia and Venezuela, where ski touring is a possibility. Chris Lizza's *South America Ski Guide* (Bradt) is the best source of information.

Surfing

South America's best surfing is probably in Brazil, though Brazilian surfers can be possessive about their breaks and aggressive in the water. Brazil has thousands of kilometers of coast, with surf from Santa Catarina to São Luís – the best season is June through August. Other areas with surfing potential include Uruguay, Mar del Plata in Argentina and Chile's central and northern coasts. There are also breaks on the coasts of Peru, Ecuador and Venezuela. Some of the more far-flung possibilities are on the Galápagos Islands, Juan Fernández Archipelago and Easter Island.

For detailed information, get a copy of the *Surf Report* for the specific area that interests you. It has individual reports on many parts of the South American coast – get a full list and order the ones you want from Surfer Publications (☎ 714-496-5922, fax 714-496-7849, surfrpt96@aol.com), PO Box 1028, Dana Point, CA 92629, USA, or check www.surfermag.com.

Trekking

South America is a brilliant destination for trekkers. In the Andean countries, many of the old Inca roads are ready-made for scenic excursions, but lesser-known mountain ranges, such as Colombia's Sierra de Santa Marta, also have great potential. The national parks of southern South America, such as Chile's Torres del Paine and Argentina's Nahuel Huapi, are most like those of Europe and North America in their trail infrastructure and accessibility. Detailed books on trekking are listed in the Books section in this chapter and in individual country chapters.

LANGUAGE COURSES

Spanish language courses are available in most South American cities, with the most popular language learning centers being Quito (Ecuador), Cuzco (Peru) and Buenos Aires (Argentina). For Portuguese, Rio de Janeiro is a great place to spend some time, and there is a variety of courses available. For Quechua and Aymara, try Cochabamba (Bolivia) or Cuzco. For details, see individual country chapters. AmeriSpan (☎ 800-879-6640, www.amerispan.com), PO Box 40007, Philadelphia, PA 19106, USA, can arrange courses with homestays in 10 South American cities.

WORK

Except for teaching or tutoring English, opportunities for employment are few, poorly paid and usually illegal Even tutoring, despite good hourly rates, is rarely remunerative because it takes time to build up a clientele. The best places are probably Buenos Aires and Santiago, where living expenses are also high. Rio and the larger cities of Brazil may also have possibilities.

If you're looking for voluntary work, adequate Spanish (or Portuguese in Brazil) is usually essential, and with some organizations you will have to provide for your own food and lodging. Some prefer to check out the opportunities on the spot, but if you want to see what's available, check the following websites:

Amerispan (www.amerispan.com/volunteer) has recently started a volunteer and internship program with opportunities for various skills in Ecuador and Peru.

Council on International Educational Exchange (www.ciee.org/vol) offers short-term projects in small communities.

Directory on International Volunteer Service (www.astro.viginia.edu/~rd7a) has general information on volunteer opportunities, and links to specific organizations in South America.

Earthwatch (www.earthwatch.org), at 680 Mt Auburn St, or PO Box 9104, Watertown, MA 02471, USA.

WorldTeach (www.igc.org/worldteach) provides volunteers to teach English and basic skills; tertiary qualification required, but not specifically in education.

ACCOMMODATIONS

The cost of accommodations varies greatly from country to country, with Andean countries being the cheapest (as little as US$4 per night) and the Southern Cone being generally the most expensive (more than US$35). Brazil has been expensive, but may be a better value with its currency depreciated. French Guiana and the Falkland Islands are exceptionally expensive.

The cheapest places are *hospedajes, casas de huéspedes*, *residenciales*, *alojamientos*, *pensiones* or *dormitorios*. An *albergue* is a hostel, and may or may not be an official *albergue juvenil* (youth hostel). The terminology varies in each country. Basic accommodations include a bed with clean sheets and a blanket or two, table and chair, sometimes a fan for cooling, but rarely any heating in cold climates. Showers and toilets are shared, and there may or may not be hot water. Cleanliness varies widely, but some places are remarkably good.

Good *hostales* and hotels proper are generally dearer, but distinctions can be unclear. In some countries, especially southern Chile and Argentina, the cheapest places may be *casas familiares*, family houses whose hospitality makes them excellent values.

Many of the cheapest places have partitioned larger rooms to accommodate more guests. These hardboard (or cardboard!) partitions often fail to reach the ceiling – you can't see other occupants, but you can certainly hear them, and vice versa. If the place doubles as a brothel, you may experience several hours of sighs, cries and giggles, banging doors, flushing toilets and testy customers. If you're really tired, the background noise may not disturb you, but light sleepers can find it trying. Since many South Americans are tolerant of noise, complaining rarely helps. One solution is to choose a room well away from the foyer or TV lounge, perhaps at the end of the hall where you'll only have neighbors on one side.

Some cheap hotels specialize in renting rooms by the hour. These 'love hotels' can be an acceptable budget-accommodation alternative, though they may be reluctant to take travelers who want to use a room for the whole night. This applies especially on weekends, when the hotel can make more money from a larger number of shorter stays.

In Brazil and some other places, the room price usually includes breakfast, which can be very good. It's worth paying a little extra for a place with a quality breakfast.

Hot water supplies are often erratic, or may only be available at certain hours of the day. It's something to ask about. Some hotels charge extra for hot showers, and a few have no showers at all – but you can use public baths instead.

Beware the electric shower, a single cold-water shower head hooked up to an electric heating element. Don't touch the heating unit, or anything metal, while in the shower or you may get a shock – never strong enough to throw you across the room, but unpleasant nevertheless. You regulate the temperature by adjusting the water flow – 'Más agua, menos caliente (More water, less hot)' was the succinct advice at one cheap guesthouse.

Toilets can be quite easily blocked: low-grade toilet paper clogs the system and the toilet can overflow. There is usually a basket for used toilet paper, which may seem pretty unhygienic, but is a lot better than a flood on the floor. A well-run place, however cheap, will empty the receptacle and clean the toilet every day.

Camping

Camping is an obvious choice in parks and reserves and a useful budget option in the more expensive countries of southern South America. In the Andean countries, there are few organized camping grounds, and accommodations are so cheap that camping is probably not worth the trouble or risk, but in Argentina, Chile, Uruguay and parts of Brazil, camping holidays have long been popular with local people. It's better to bring your own equipment than to buy locally.

FOOD

There are many national and even regional specialties – see the Food section in each country chapter. Plenty of gringo-style fast food (hamburgers, pizzas, chicken and chips) can be found in most large towns. Good seafood is available in coastal areas. Immigrant groups have introduced other possibilities – you can find Chinese, Korean, Japanese, Middle Eastern or Italian food in some surprising places.

Nearly every town has a market with cheap and plentiful fruit and vegetables, some of which you will have never seen before. At street stalls and small local cafés you might fill yourself for a dollar or two. Lunch is the biggest meal of the day and usually the cheapest – most cafés offer a cheap *comida corrida* or *menú del día* (set meal) for lunch, though eating this way can get monotonous.

Even in carnivorous countries such as Argentina, vegetarianism is no longer the mark of an eccentric. Most restaurants can prepare dishes without meat – plead an allergy *(alergia)*.

DRINKS

South Americans drink prodigious amounts of sugary soft drinks, including the ubiquitous Coca-Cola and 7-Up. In Brazil, *Guaraná* is a popular soft drink made from an Amazonian berry, and Peru has the indigenous Inca Kola, which tastes like boiled lollipops and has a color not found in nature. Mineral water *(agua mineral)*, both carbonated *(con gas)* and plain *(sin gas)*, is widely available.

Most cafés sell bottled lager-type beers, which are usually good, cold, and cost about twice as much as soft drinks. *Chopp* (draught beer, pronounced 'shop') is cheaper and often better. Rum is a popular spirit in Venezuela, Colombia, Ecuador, Guyana and Peru. Sugarcane alcohol, variously called *aguardiente*, *pinga* and *cachaça* is a low-cost, high-proof option for drunks on a budget. The grape brandy *pisco* is popular in Peru and Chile. In Bolivia, *singani* is a spirit made from distilled grape skins, and it's an excellent drink, straight or mixed.

Chile and Argentina produce South America's best wines, along with those from the Tarija region of Bolivia. Wine is also made in Brazil and Peru.

SPECTATOR SPORTS

In South America, sport means soccer. Argentina, Brazil and Uruguay have all won the World Cup, though many of the best athletes have abandoned their own countries to play for higher salaries in Europe. Other sports which enjoy widespread popularity are motor racing, basketball, cycling, tennis and volleyball (especially in Brazil). Bullfighting is popular in Venezuela and Colombia, and can also be seen in Peru and Ecuador.

Getting There & Away

AIR
Airports & Airlines

Every South American country has an international airport in its capital or in its major cities. Main gateways include Buenos Aires (Argentina), Caracas (Venezuela), La Paz (Bolivia), Lima (Peru), Quito (Ecuador), Rio de Janeiro (Brazil) and Santiago (Chile). There are direct, intercontinental flights to all these cities, plus many more flights that will involve at least one stop at an intermediate airport. Less commonly used international gateways include Bogotá, Colombia; Guayaquil, Ecuador; Manaus, Recife, Salvador and São Paulo in Brazil; Montevideo, Uruguay; Asunción, Paraguay; Santa Cruz, Bolivia; and Río Gallegos, Argentina. It's worth considering indirect routes – they may offer the possibility of a stopover, which can be like getting free flights within South America. For example, a Varig flight from London to La Paz may permit a free stopover in Rio de Janeiro.

WARNING

The information in this chapter is particularly vulnerable to change. Prices for international travel are volatile, routes are introduced and canceled, schedules change, special deals come and go, and rules and visa requirements are amended. Airlines and governments seem to take a perverse pleasure in making price structures and regulations as complicated as possible. In addition, the travel industry is highly competitive and there are many hidden costs and benefits.

The upshot of this is that you should get quotes and advice from as many airlines and travel agents as possible, and make sure you understand how a fare (and any ticket you may buy) works before you part with your hard-earned cash. The details given in this chapter should be regarded as pointers and are not a substitute for your own careful, up-to-date research.

The most frequent and direct flights to a South American country are likely to be with its national 'flag carrier' airline. Many of these airlines have websites:

AeroContinente – 200.4.197.130/Acerca-in.htm
Aerolineas Argentinas – www.aerolineas.com.ar
Air France – www.airfrance.fr
Avensa – www.avensa.com
Avianca – www.avianca.com.co
LanChile – www.lanchile.cl
Lloyd Aéreo Boliviano – www.labairlines.com
Saeta – www.saeta.com.ec
Varig – www.varig.com.bra

North American and European airlines that offer regular South American connections include Air France, American, British Airways, Iberia, KLM and Swissair among others.

Buying Tickets

The cost of flying to South America depends on your point of departure, when you're traveling, your destination within South America, your access to discount travel agencies and whether you can take advantage of advance-purchase fares and special offers. Patience and flexibility will get you the best deal. An understanding of some basics will help; see the Air Travel Glossary on the next page.

Airlines are the best source for finding information on routes, timetables and standard fares, but they don't usually sell the cheapest tickets.

Start shopping for airfares as soon as you can, because the cheapest tickets have to be bought months in advance, and popular flights sell out early.

The fares quoted in this book are guides for planning your trip only; they are approximate and based on the rates advertised by most travel agents at press time. Quoted airfares do not imply a recommendation for the carrier.

Bucket Shops, Consolidators & Charter Flights Some travel agencies specialize in selling officially or unofficially

Air Travel Glossary

Baggage Allowance This will be written on your ticket and usually includes one 20kg item to go in the hold, plus one item of hand luggage.

Bucket Shops These are unbonded travel agencies specializing in discounted airline tickets.

Bumped Just because you have a confirmed seat doesn't mean you're going to get on the plane (see Overbooking).

Cancellation Penalties If you have to cancel or change a discounted ticket, there are often heavy penalties involved; insurance can sometimes be taken out against these penalties. Some airlines impose penalties on regular tickets as well, particularly against 'no-show' passengers.

Check-In Airlines ask you to check in a certain time ahead of the flight departure (usually one to two hours on international flights). If you fail to check in on time and the flight is overbooked, the airline can cancel your booking and give your seat to somebody else.

Confirmation Having a ticket written out with the flight and date you want doesn't mean you have a seat until the agent has checked with the airline that your status is 'OK' or confirmed. Meanwhile you could just be 'on request.'

Courier Fares Businesses often need to send urgent documents or freight securely and quickly. Courier companies hire people to accompany the package through customs and, in return, offer a discount ticket that is sometimes a phenomenal bargain. In effect, what the companies do is ship their freight as your luggage on regular commercial flights. This is a legitimate operation, but there are two shortcomings – the short turnaround time of the ticket (usually not longer than a month) and the limitation on your luggage allowance. You may have to surrender all your allowance and take only carry-on luggage.

ITX An ITX, or 'independent inclusive tour excursion,' is often available on tickets to popular holiday destinations. Officially it's a package deal combined with hotel accommodations, but many agents will sell you one of these for the flight only and give you phony hotel vouchers in the unlikely event that you're challenged at the airport.

Lost Tickets If you lose your airline ticket, an airline will usually treat it like a traveler's check and, after inquiries, issue you another one. Legally, however, an airline is entitled to treat it like cash; and if you lose it, then it's gone forever. Take good care of your tickets.

MCO An MCO, or 'miscellaneous charge order,' is a voucher that looks like an airline ticket but carries no destination or date. It can be exchanged through any International Association of Travel Agents (IATA) airline for a ticket on a specific flight. It's a useful alternative to an onward ticket in those countries that demand one, and is more flexible than an ordinary ticket if you're unsure of your route.

---

discounted air tickets. In the UK, they are unbonded agencies called bucket shops. In the USA, the cheapest fares are usually available through what have come to be known as 'consolidators.'

Bucket-shop tickets often cost less than advance-purchase fares, without advance purchase or cancellation penalties, though some agents have their own penalties. Most bucket shops are well established

and honorable, but unscrupulous agents might take your money and disappear before issuing a ticket or issue an invalid or unusable ticket. Check carefully before handing over the money and confirm the reservation directly with the airline.

From continental Europe, the cheapest deal may be on a charter flight, and some agencies specialize in these. The dates of charter flights are fixed.

Air Travel Glossary

No-Shows No-shows are passengers who fail to show up for their flight. Full-fare passengers who fail to turn up are sometimes entitled to travel on a later flight. The rest are penalized (see Cancellation Penalties).

On Request This is an unconfirmed booking for a flight.

Onward Tickets An entry requirement for many countries is that you have a ticket out of the country. If you're unsure your next move, the easiest solution is to buy the cheapest onward ticket to a neighboring country or a ticket from a reliable airline that can later be refunded if you do not use it.

Open-Jaw Tickets These are return tickets on which you fly out to one place but return from another. If available, these can save you backtracking to your arrival point.

Overbooking Airlines hate to fly with empty seats and since every flight has some passengers who fail to show up, airlines often book more passengers than they have seats. Usually excess passengers make up for the no-shows, but occasionally somebody gets bumped. Guess who it is most likely to be? The passengers who check in late.

Point-to-Point Tickets These are discount tickets that can be bought on some routes in return for passengers waiving their rights to a stopover.

Reconfirmation At least 72 hours prior to departure time of an onward or return flight, you must contact the airline and 'reconfirm' that you intend to be on the flight. If you don't do this, the airline can delete your name from the passenger list and you could lose your seat.

Restrictions Discounted tickets often have various restrictions on them – such as advance payment, minimum and maximum periods you must be away (eg, a minimum of two weeks or a maximum of one year), and penalties for changing the tickets.

Round-the-World Tickets RTW tickets give you a limited period (usually a year) in which to circumnavigate the globe. You can go anywhere the carrying airlines go, as long as you don't backtrack. The number of stopovers or total number of separate flights is decided before you set off (usually somewhere between five and seven), and they usually cost a bit more than a basic return flight.

Stand-By This is a discounted ticket on which you only fly if there is a seat free at the last moment. Stand-by fares are usually available only on domestic routes.

Travel Periods Ticket prices vary with the time of year. There is a low (off-peak) season and a high (peak) season, and often a low-shoulder season and a high-shoulder season, too. Usually the fare depends on your outward flight – if you depart in the high season and return in the low season, you pay the high-season fare.

Buying Tickets Online Most airlines have their own websites that offer online ticket sales, often discounted for online customers.

To buy a ticket on the Internet you'll need to use a credit card. Commercial reservation networks offer airline ticketing as well as information and reservations for hotels, car rentals and other services, though South American offerings can be very limited or nonexistent on many booking networks.

CNN Interactive's Travel Guide – www.cnn.com/Travel

Excite Travel by City.Net – www.city.net

Internet Travel Network – www.itn.net

Microsoft Expedia – www.expedia.com

Preview Travel – www.previewtravel.com

There are also some online travel agents that specialize in cheap fares, but only a few have a good selection of flights to South America. In North America, try Cheap Tickets, www.cheaptickets.com; in Europe, www.etn.nl; in Australia, www.travel.com.au.

Air Passes

There are several types of air pass available, some covering several South American countries. Usually, these passes must be bought outside the country in conjunction with an international ticket, so you have to consider this option before you leave. For more information, see the Getting Around chapter.

Stopovers

Flights from North America, Europe, Australia and New Zealand may permit a stopover in South America on the way to your destination city. This can effectively give you a free air connection within the region, so it's worth considering when comparing international flights. International flights may also include an onward connection at a much lower cost than a separate fare.

Travelers with Special Needs

If you have special needs of any sort – you have broken a leg, you're vegetarian, traveling in a wheelchair, taking the baby, terrified of flying – you should let the airline know as soon as possible so that it can make arrangements accordingly. You should remind the airline staff when you reconfirm your reservation (at least 72 hours before departure) and again when you check in at the airport. It may also be worth telephoning around the airlines before you make your booking to find out how each one can handle your particular needs.

Most international airports will provide escorts from check-in desk to plane where needed, and there should be ramps, lifts and accessible toilets and phones. Aircraft toilets, on the other hand, are likely to present a problem; travelers should discuss this with the airline at an early stage and, if necessary, with their doctor.

Guide dogs for the blind will often have to travel in a specially pressurized baggage compartment with other animals, though smaller dogs may be admitted to the cabin. All guide dogs are subject to the same quarantine laws (six months in isolation, etc) as any other animal when entering or returning to countries currently free of rabies, such as the United Kingdom or Australia.

Deaf travelers can ask for airport and in-flight announcements to be written down for them.

Children younger than two years old travel for 10% of the standard fare (or free, on some airlines), as long as they don't occupy a seat. They do not get a baggage allowance, either. 'Skycots' should be provided by the airline if requested in advance; these will take a child weighing up to about 10kg. Children between two and 12 years old can usually occupy a seat for one-half to two-thirds of the full fare and do get a baggage allowance. Strollers can often be taken as hand luggage.

The USA

Major gateways are Miami, New York and Los Angeles; Miami is usually cheapest. Newark, NJ; Washington, DC; Dallas and Houston also have direct connections to South America. As a general rule, Caracas and Lima are probably the cheapest South American cities to fly to, while Buenos Aires and Rio de Janeiro are the most expensive.

Inexpensive tickets from North America usually have restrictions; fares must often be purchased two weeks in advance, and usually you must stay at least one week and no more than three months (prices often double for longer periods). High season for most fares is from early June to mid-August, and mid-December to mid-January.

For an idea of what's available, peruse the Sunday travel sections of papers like the *New York Times*, *Los Angeles Times* and *San Francisco Examiner*. Details change frequently. Free weekly city entertainment newspapers also have ads for travel bargains. It pays to shop around.

Travel agencies known as 'consolidators' generally have the best deals. They buy tickets in bulk, then discount them to their customers, or sell 'fill-up fares,' which can be even cheaper (with additional restrictions). Look for agencies specializing in South America, such as eXito (☎ 510-655-2154, 800-655-4566, www.wonderlink.com), 1212 Broadway, Suite 910, Oakland CA 94612.

Council Travel has 60 offices in the US that specialize in student and youth fares. Its head office (☎ 212-822-2600, 800-226-8624, fax 212-822-2699, www.counciltravel.com) is at 205 E 42nd St, New York, NY 10017; call for the office nearest you.

Another budget and student travel agent is STA (☎ 310-394-5126, 800-777-0112, fax 310-394-4041, www.statravel.com), at 411 Santa Monica Blvd, Santa Monica, CA 90401. It also has offices in Boston, Chicago, Miami, New York, Philadelphia, San Francisco, Seattle, Washington, DC, and other cities. Call the toll-free 800-number for office locations.

Sample Fares The best fares to a country are often with its national airline. The following examples are official excursion fares for the low season (high season is usually June to August and December to January). Tax will add about US$50, and flights on weekends may also be more pricey. A ticket consolidator may be able to sell these fares more cheaply than the official rate.

Aerolineas Argentinas (☎ 800-333-0276)
The best deal is a 60-day excursion fare from Miami to Buenos Aires, which must be a morning flight, for US$470. Apart from this promotional fare, most roundtrip tickets will cost more than US$1100.

Avianca (☎ 800-284-2622)
The Colombian airline has 60-day excursion fares to Bogotá for US$514 from Miami or US$865 from New York. Its 45-day excursion fares to Caracas can be real bargains – US$509 from Los Angeles, US$229 from New York and US$199 from Miami.

LanChile (☎ 800-735-5526)
Several flights depart weekly from New York, Miami, and Los Angeles. The 90-day excursion fare to Santiago is US$1185 from New York, US$1325 from Los Angeles and US$1089 from Miami. A Circle-Pacific fare with LanChile and other airlines can include Hawaii, Papeete, Easter Island, Santiago and back to the US for about US$1645.

Lloyd Aéreo Boliviano (LAB; ☎ 800-327-7407)
LAB has a 90-day excursion fare to La Paz from Miami for US$559, New York for US$852 and Los Angeles for US$938. LAB flights to Santiago, Buenos Aires and Rio de Janeiro can also be good – they all go via La Paz and include a stopover there.

Servivensa (☎ 305-381-8001, 800-428-3672)
Servivensa sometimes offers a cheap Miami-Caracas cut-down fare often for as little as US$100. Servivensa may also have attractive fares from New York (☎ 718-244 6857).

Varig (☎ 800-468-2744)
A 90-day return ticket to Rio de Janeiro costs around US$1200 from Miami or New York and about US$1400 from Los Angeles. You might do better flying to Manaus (US$800 from Miami) and getting an air pass for travel around Brazil.

For details on air passes for travel within South America, see the Getting Around chapter.

Canada

Most flights from Canada involve a connection via one of the US gateways. Canada's national student travel agency is Travel CUTS (☎ 416-977-3703, fax 416-977-4796, www.travelcuts.com), at 171 College St, Toronto, ON M5T 1P7, and at 50 other locations across Canada. It has good deals for students, and it works with the general public as well.

STA (☎ 416-977-5228, fax 416-977-7112, www.statravel.com), at 187 College St, Toronto, ON M5T 1P7, also has travel offices in Montreal, Calgary, Edmonton and Vancouver.

Australia

Excursion fares from Australia to South America have fallen greatly in the last few years. The most direct route is with Aerolíneas Argentinas via Auckland, New Zealand, to Buenos Aires, with connections to Santiago, Lima, La Paz, Santa Cruz or Rio de Janeiro at little or no extra cost. Qantas is now sharing this route with Aerolíneas Argentinas. Fares are usually the same from Melbourne, Sydney or Brisbane, but from other Australian cities you may have to add the cost of getting to Sydney. Low-season 'Discover South America' excursion fares from Sydney or Melbourne are A$1449 for a stay of up to 35 days, A$1640 for up to 45 days.

The other South American route is with Qantas or Air New Zealand and travels from Sydney to Papeete (Tahiti), connecting with a LanChile flight via Easter Island to Santiago, with a free onward flight to either Rio or Buenos Aires. Connections can be awkward on this route, making for a long trip. Discount excursion fares on this route can be as low as A$1599 for 45 days.

In terms of airfares only, it may be marginally cheaper to go to South America via the US, but even a day or so in Los Angeles would cost more than the savings in airfares, so it's not a good value unless you want to visit the US anyway. It may be worth it for travel to Colombia or Venezuela, but not for cities farther south.

The best RTW options are probably those with Aerolíneas Argentinas combined with other airlines (including Air New Zealand, British Airways, Iberia, Singapore Airlines, Thai or KLM). The new Qantas version of an RTW ticket is its 'OneWorld Explorer' fare, which allows you to visit up to six continents with three stopovers in each one. Prices start at A$1999 for three continents in the low season, A$2599 in peak season. Rules are quite complicated, but a routing via South America will probably need to include Europe.

Aerolíneas Argentinas
(☎ 02-9283-3660) Level 2, 580 George St, Sydney 2000
(☎ 03-9650-7111) Level 6, Nauru House, 80 Collins St, Melbourne 3000
LanChile
(☎ 02-9244-2333) 64 York St, Sydney 2000
(☎ 03-9920-3881) 310 King St, Melbourne 3000
Varig
(☎ 02-9244-2111) 403 George St, Sydney 2000
(☎ 03-9920-3856) 310 King St, Melbourne 3000

A number of agents offer cheap air tickets out of Australia. STA (www.statravel.com.au) has offices in all capital cities and on many university campuses. Flight Centres International (www.flightcentre.com.au) also specializes in cheap airfares and has offices in most capital cities and many suburban branches. Inca Tours (☎ 02-4351-2133, 1800-024-955, www .southamerica.com.au) is staffed by very knowledgeable people who arrange tours to South America in addition to giving advice and selling tickets to independent travelers. Destination Holidays (☎ 03-9725-4655, 1800-337-050) also specializes in travel to Latin America. Also, check the advertisements in Saturday editions of newspapers, such as Melbourne's *Age* or the *Sydney Morning Herald*.

New Zealand

The two chief options are to fly Aerolíneas Argentinas (☎ 09-379-3675) from Auckland to Buenos Aires (with connections to neighboring countries) or to fly with Air New Zealand (☎ 09-357-3000) from Auckland to Papeete, Tahiti, connecting with a LanChile (☎ 09-309-8673) flight via Easter Island to Santiago. The excursion fare from Auckland to Santiago or Buenos Aires is about the same for both routes – NZ$1899/2099 in low/high season for 10 to 45 days, NZ$2099/ 2299 for 21 to 90 days and NZ$2986 for up to one year (high season is roughly December through February). You might also be able to get a low-season promotional fare of NZ$1499 for a 10- to 35-day stay.

Onward tickets, eg, to Lima, Rio de Janeiro, Guayaquil, Bogotá or Caracas, are much cheaper if purchased in conjunction with a long-haul flight from the same carrier. A 'Visit South America' fare, good for three months, allows you two stops in South America plus one in the US, then takes you back to Auckland. Various open-jaw options are possible, and you can make the trip in either direction. It costs NZ$2986/3293 in low/high season.

For discount fares, try STA (☎ 09-309-0458), at 10 High St, Auckland, or Flight Center (☎ 800-354-488), National Bank Tower, 205-225 Queens St, Auckland. Both have offices in other cities.

The UK

Fares from London used to be the cheapest in Europe, but some other cities now have similar fares. The cheapest destinations in South America are generally Caracas, Venezuela and Bogotá, Colombia.

Some London agencies specialize in South America. One very good agency is Journey Latin America (JLA; ☎ 020-8747-8315, fax 020-8742-1312), at 12 & 13 Heathfield Terrace, Chiswick, London W4 4JE, sales@journeylatinamerica.co.uk, www .journeylatinamerica.co.uk. The agency can make arrangements via phone or Internet. JLA has another office at Suites 28-30, Barton Arcade (2nd floor), Deansgate, Manchester, M3 2BH (☎ 0161-832-1441, fax 0161-832-1551, man@journeylatinamerica .co.uk). Ask for *Papagaio*, JLA's useful free magazine. JLA is very well informed on South American destinations, has a good range of South American air passes and can issue tickets from South America to London and deliver them to any of the main South American cities (this can be much cheaper than buying the same ticket in South America).

Another place to try is South American Experience (☎ 020-7976-5511, fax 020-7976-6908, sax@mcmail.com), at 47 Causton St, Pimlico, London SW1P 4AT; or Austral

Tours (☎ 020-7233-5384, fax 020-7233-5385, 100532.255@ compuserve.com), 20 Upper Tachbrook St, London SW1.

London has countless bucket shops, with well-advertised services and prices. Travel agents that are 'bonded' (eg, by ATOL, ABTA or AITO) give you some protection if the company goes broke. A good general agency is Trailfinders (☎ 020-7938-3939), at 194 Kensington High St, London W8 7RG. It has cheap flights to a wide variety of destinations; ask about RTW tickets. Its useful travel newspaper, *Trailfinder,* is free. Another well-established budget travel agency is STA (☎ 020-7465-0484, fax 020-7388-0944), 112 Euston Rd, London, NW1 2SX. Trailfinders has offices in Manchester (☎ 0161-839-6969), Birmingham (☎ 0121-236-1234), Bristol (☎ 0117-929-9000), Glasgow (☎ 0141-353-2224) and Dublin (☎ 01-677-7888); STA has offices in nearly every city in the UK – these are good options in regional areas, which are not as well supplied with bucket shops.

Some of the best sources of information about cheap fares are weekend editions of national newspapers. In London, try the *Evening Standard*, the listings magazine *Time Out* and *TNT,* a free weekly magazine, ostensibly for antipodeans but full of relevant travel information for anyone. *TNT* comes out every Monday and is found in dispenser bins outside underground stations.

Current fares advertised from London follow. They are examples of what is possible, but such fares may not necessarily be available when you want to travel. Note that the cheapest fares may have very restrictive conditions and limited availability, and 'come-on' advertisements for cheap fares are common. July, August and December are high-season months.

destination	one-way (low/ high season)	roundtrip
Asunción	£400/465	£601/754
Bogotá	£310/430	£490/673
Buenos Aires	£320/435	£414/660
Caracas	£230/360	£385/593
La Paz	£390/483	£690/790
Lima	£285/398	£399/650
Quito	£285/400	£399/645
Recife	£299/455	£530/740
Rio de Janeiro	£240/405	£415/612
Santiago	£285/405	£450/670

Continental Europe

The best places in Europe for cheap airfares are 'student' travel agencies (you don't have to be a student to use them) in Amsterdam, Brussels, Paris, Berlin, Frankfurt and possibly Athens. If airfares are expensive where you live, try contacting a London agent, who may be able to issue a ticket by mail. The cheapest destinations in South America are generally Caracas (Venezuela), Buenos Aires (Argentina) and possibly Recife or Rio de Janeiro (Brazil). High-season months are usually July, August, September and December. The cheapest flights from Europe are typically charters, usually with fixed dates for both outward and return flights.

The magazine *Aventure du Bout du Monde* at 116 rue de Javel, 75015 Paris, France, covers exotic destinations.

France Council Travel (☎ 01 44 55 55 44) is at 22 rue des Pyramides, 1er. Nouvelles Frontières (☎ 08 03 33 33 33) and Havas Voyages (☎ 01 53 29 40 00) have branches throughout Paris.

Germany STA has offices in Frankfurt (☎ 4969-43-01-91), at Bergerstrasse 118, as does Council Travel (☎ 211-36-30-30), at Graf Adolfstrasse 64.

Netherlands The official student agency, NBBS (☎ 020-624-0989), Rokin 38, Amsterdam, is good, but also check the discount travel agencies along Rokin. Other established agencies include Budget Air (☎ 020-556-3333), Singel 21, and Flyworld/Grand Travel (☎ 020-657-0000), at Schiphol, which does everything by phone and fax.

Asia

There are few direct flights from Asia to South America. The cheapest options are via London to Caracas or Bogotá or via Los Angeles to the rest of South America. The cheapest Asian city in which to buy tickets is Bangkok, but Hong Kong, Kuala Lumpur, and Singapore are pretty good, too. STA has offices in all of these cities.

Central America

Flights from Central American countries are usually subject to high tax, and bucket-shop deals are almost unobtainable. Nevertheless,

TO/FROM CENTRAL AMERICA

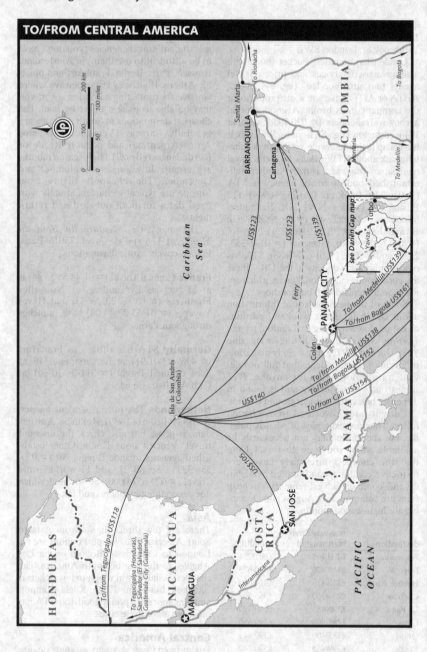

To Riohacha

To Bogotá

Santa Marta

COLOMBIA

BARRANQUILLA

Cartagena

To Medellín

Montería

To Medellín

*Caribbean
Sea*

US$123

US$123

US$139

see Danién Gap map

Turbo

Yaviza

To/from Medellín US$139

PANAMA CITY

Ferry

Colón

To/from Medellín US$161

To/from Bogotá US$138

To/from Medellín US$138

Isla de San Andrés
(Colombia)

To/from Bogotá US$152

US$140

To/from Cali US$154

PANAMA

US$105

HONDURAS

To/from Tegucigalpa US$118

To Tegucigalpa (Honduras),
San Salvador (El Salvador),
Guatemala City (Guatemala)

NICARAGUA

MANAGUA

COSTA
RICA

Interamericana

SAN JOSÉ

*PACIFIC
OCEAN*

200 km

100 miles

0   50   100

0   100   200

it's still cheaper to fly between Central and South America rather than to go overland.

You must have an onward ticket to enter Colombia, and no airline in Panama or Costa Rica will sell you a one-way ticket to Colombia unless you already have an onward ticket or are willing to buy one. If you need a Colombian visa, you will probably have to show an onward ticket anyway. Venezuela also demands an onward ticket. Some airlines will refund the unused portion of a return ticket; check this with the airline before you buy the ticket. The only way to avoid the onward or return ticket requirement is to fly from Central America to Ecuador or Peru.

Via Isla de San Andrés Several airlines land at San Andrés, an island off the coast of Nicaragua that is actually Colombian territory. From San Andrés, you can continue on a domestic Colombian flight to Barranquilla for US$123, Cartagena for US$123 or Bogotá for US$152. From all Central American countries except Panama, it's cheaper to go via San Andrés than to fly directly to the Colombian mainland. For more details, see the San Andrés section of the Colombia chapter.

Costa Rica Flights to South America from Costa Rica (about US$292) are considerably dearer than from Panama. The Costa Rican student organization OTEC offers some cheap tickets.

Panama Panama requires an onward or return ticket before you enter the country (a bus ticket is acceptable, but the return half is not refundable). The cost of living is higher in Panama than nearby countries, so time spent looking for a ticket can be a significant expense. Direct flights from Panama City include ones headed for Bogotá (US$139), Cartagena (US$139) and Medellín (US$123). The Colombian airline, SAM, and the Panamanian carrier, Copa, generally offer the cheapest deals to these places. Copa is not a IATA carrier, so its tickets are not transferable to other airlines. Copa offices in Cartagena, Barranquilla and Medellín should refund unused return halves of tickets, but check in advance. If possible, apply in Barranquilla, since applications in Cartagena are referred to Barranquilla anyway. Refunds, in Colombian currency only, take up to four days.

LAND
Darién Gap

From North America, you can journey overland only as far south as Panama. There is no road connection onward to Colombia: the Carretera Panamericana (Pan-American Highway) ends in the vast wilderness called the Darién, in southeast Panama. Travelers know this roadless area between Central and South America as the Darién Gap – in the past it has been difficult, but possible, to trek across the Darién Gap with the help of local guides, but since around 1998 it has been prohibitively dangerous because of bandit and guerrilla activity, especially on the Colombian side. It is still possible to skirt the north edge of the Darién, trekking and using local boats, but it's not easy or completely safe. It's possible in as little as a week, but allow twice this time. Take dried food, drinking water and purification tablets or equipment.

Remember that both Panama and Colombia demand onward tickets, so get one and any visas you need before setting out from either north or south. Many travelers have been turned back for lack of an onward ticket, especially coming from Colombia to Panama.

Warning Though the Darién Gap is still a wilderness area, it is not unpopulated; there are a fair number of people crossing the region by small boat and on foot. Some are indigenous inhabitants, others are illegal immigrants, smugglers, guerrillas, terrorists or bandits. Don't undertake this trip lightly, and don't even think about the overland route between Yaviza and Parque Nacional Los Katíos.

Information Eco-tours (☎ 263-3077, fax 263-3089) in Panama City can arrange guides and trips in the area and is worth consulting for the latest information. If you want to visit the Darién rain forest, there are reasonably safe parts, but they are not in the border region. Officially you need written permission from Inrenare, Panama's environmental agency, to enter the Parque Nacional del Darién area. Inrenare has offices in Panama City and El Real, and can arrange guides and boats and give good advice.

Environment Densely settled when the Spaniards first arrived, the *selva* (tropical rain forest) ecosystem of the Darién has, since 1980, been declared a World Heritage Site and international biosphere reserve by

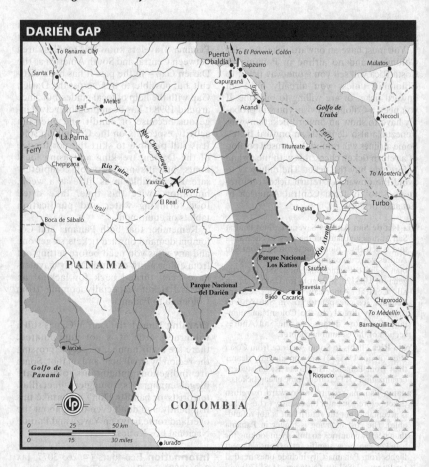

DARIÉN GAP

UNESCO. To protect the natural and human resources of the region, Panama has established the Parque Nacional del Darién, a reserve that covers 90% of the border between Panama and Colombia and at 5790 sq km, is the largest national park in Central America. Across the border, the Colombian government has established an equivalent reserve, Parque Nacional Los Katíos.

Scientists describe this region as one of the most biologically diverse in tropical America, and it has long been the home of the river-dwelling Emberá and Wounaan peoples (often known together as Chocó Indians). The better-known Cuna Indians live along the north coast of the Darién and in the San Blás archipelago.

North-Coast Route

This route starts at Colón (Panama) and goes via the San Blás archipelago to Puerto Obaldía, then on to Capurganá (Colombia), Acandí, Titumate and on to Turbo. It's also possible to travel in the other direction. Either way, make sure you have all necessary documents (passport and tourist card or visa if required) and onward tickets in addition to sufficient funds; US$500 per month of your planned stay is usually enough. You may not be asked for these, but it's worth being sure – it's a long backtrack if you don't have them.

The journey from Colón to Turbo is possible to do in as little as a week, but could easily take double that or longer, especially if you have to wait around for boats or if you stay somewhere on the way. The San Blás archipelago, Sapzurro and Capurganá are the most pleasant places along this route to break the journey.

Panama City to Puerto Obaldía The simplest way to Puerto Obaldía is to fly from Panama City with Aereo Taxi (☎ 264-8644) or Ansa (☎ 226-7891), which have three flights weekly (US$44 one-way). Alternately, make an island-hopping excursion through the Archipiélago de San Blás. From San Blás, you have three options. You can hire a Kuna Indian to take you from the San Blás islands to the border in a long, narrow boat – the only kind the Indians use. You can take one of the slow-moving coconut boats from El Porvenir, in the San Blás islands, to Puerto Obaldía. These boats stop at many islands to pick up coconuts, and for US$30 or so you can often negotiate a ride (you'll want to bring a hammock for sleeping). The third option is to negotiate a ride on a Colombian merchant boat traveling between Colón and Cartagena, Colombia. These boats are notorious for running drugs and contraband; they are not recommended.

Puerto Obaldía is a nine-square-block tropical way station. Its beaches are strewn with litter and there's little to do in the town itself. There's one main road, with a soccer field at one end and the police station at the other. In between are the Panamanian and Colombian immigration offices and the Pensión Conde (no phone), which offers basic rooms with private bathrooms for US$12 per room.

If you're heading into Colombia, you need to check with the Panamanian immigration office for an exit stamp or, if you're heading into Panama, an entry stamp. The office is open 9 am to 5 pm weekdays; it closes at noon on Saturday and is closed all day Sunday. An entry stamp is supposed to cost US$5, but officers have been known to ask for US$10, US$15 or US$20, depending on their moods. Once you have your exit stamp, go to the Colombian immigration office and obtain an entry stamp (US$5) for Colombia.

Puerto Obaldía to Sapzurro (Colombia) This journey is made by boat or on foot. Boats depart for Sapzurro, the first town on the Colombian side of the border, when they collect enough people. The ride costs US$10 and lasts 15 minutes. The boats then continue to Capurganá, an additional 10-minute ride, for another US$10. The boaters often try to make foreign travelers pay more by claiming the journey is an 'international route' or saying that your backpack is heavy. Just laugh about this and pay what the locals are paying.

The alternative is to walk, but the first part of the trail, from Puerto Obaldía to La Miel (the last Panamanian village, about two hours from Puerto Obaldía), is unsafe – there are bandits and smugglers in the area. Also, the trails are so indistinct that you can easily become lost in the jungle. It may be wisest to travel to La Miel by boat and walk from there. From La Miel, you climb a small hill, pass the border marker on the top and descend to Sapzurro in about half an hour.

Small and pleasant Sapzurro is beautifully set on the shore of a deep horseshoe-shaped bay. Here you'll find a couple of guesthouses, several restaurants and a narrow but clean white-sand beach shaded by coconut palms.

Sapzurro to Capurganá From Sapzurro, the footpath (there is no road) climbs again and then drops to the next coastal village, Capurganá. This can be easily walked in 1½ to two hours – go at a leisurely pace and take in the splendid scenery.

Capurganá, with a strip of fine hotels lining a wide sweep of beach, is the most touristy place in the whole area and gets pretty crowded from mid-December to the end of January (the Colombian holiday season), but at other times it's quiet and easygoing. Hotel rates during the low season range from US$15 to US$90. The best of the budget hotels is the Hostal Marlin (no phone). A few businesses in the village change US dollars, though at poor rates. It's a pleasant place to hang around for a day or two, but if you want to get out quickly, you can fly to Medellín for about US$50.

Capurganá to Acandí From Capurganá, you can take a boat to Acandí (US$8, one hour) and continue on another to Turbo, but if you're not in a hurry, continue to Acandí on foot, allowing yourself the best part of a day for a beautiful walk. Start along the beach and follow the path, which at various points cuts across the headlands.

An hour's walk brings you to Aguacate, a cluster of huts with a simple *hospedaje*. Follow the footpath for another hour or so to Rufino, another cluster of houses, where the path continues inland, climbing the coastal ridge, passing it and dropping into the valley of the Río Acandí (it's another hour to this point). Follow the river downstream for a leisurely three-hour walk to Acandí. The path does not always follow the river and includes several fords, so be prepared to wet your shoes. This part of the track is often muddy.

Acandí is a fair-size village with a church, two or three hotels, a few cafés and several small shops selling mostly bottled and canned goods of limited variety and quantity. Some shops will change dollars into Colombian pesos at reasonable rates.

Acandí to Turbo There's a launch from Acandí every morning to Turbo via Titumate, and there may be other boats that go directly to Turbo. The three- to four-hour journey costs around US$10, but is only reliable during the first half of the year, when the sea is not too rough; other times, it leaves in good weather only, but it's never a very smooth journey. Be prepared to get soaked, wrap anything you want to keep dry in plastic, and try to sit in the rear of the boat.

Turbo, a drab and dangerous port on the Golfo de Urabá, has a variety of fresh and canned foods, so travelers heading north should stock up here. Whether northbound or southbound, you need to obtain an exit or entry stamp at the Policía Distrito Especial, two blocks down from the harbor. It's very informal and quick as long as your papers are in order.

Turbo has no bank, but many shops and the more expensive hotels will exchange cash dollars – usually at poor rates. Change just enough to get to Medellín or Cartagena.

Turbo has no Panamanian consulate, so northbound travelers should get a visa beforehand. It may be possible to get one in Sapzurro, but if the consulate there is closed for some reason, you will have to backtrack to Medellín or Barranquilla. To enter Panama, be sure you have an onward ticket as well; many travelers have been forced to go back to Medellín to get one.

SEA

A few cruise ships from Europe and the US call on South American ports, but they are much more expensive than any air ticket. Some cargo ships from ports like Houston, New Orleans, Hamburg and Amsterdam will take a limited number of passengers to South American ports, but they are also expensive. The standard reference for passenger ships is the *OAG Cruise & Ferry Guide*, published by Reed Travel Group (☎ 0158-2600-111), Church St, Dunstable, Bedfordshire LU5 4HB, UK.

The ferry that used to run between Colón, Panama, and Cartagena, Colombia, is no longer in operation. Some small cargo ships sail between Colón and the Colombian port of Barranquilla, but many of them are involved in carrying contraband and may not be very secure or reliable. Nevertheless, some of these ships will take paying passengers, and some will also take motorcycles and even cars. Prices are very negotiable – maybe US$50 for a passenger, US$150 to US$200 for a motorcycle.

Officially, both Panama and Colombia require an onward or return ticket as a condition of entry. This may not be enforced in Colombia, but it's wise to get a ticket anyway, or have plenty of money and a plausible itinerary. Panama requires a visa or tourist card, an onward ticket and sufficient funds and has been known to turn back arrivals who don't meet these requirements. The Panamanian consulate in Cartagena is reportedly helpful.

Getting Around

AIR

Because of vast distances between population centers and geographical barriers to overland travel, South America was one of the first regions to develop air services among and within its countries. There is an extensive pattern of domestic flights, with surprisingly low price tags, especially in the Andean countries. After 18-hour-plus bus journeys across mountains on atrocious roads, you may decide, as many travelers do, to take an occasional flight.

There are drawbacks, however. Airports are often far from city centers, and public buses don't run all the time, so you may have to pay a lot for taxis to and from the airports (it's generally easier to find a cheap taxi *to* an airport than *from* one). Airport taxes can also add to the cost of air travel; they are usually higher for international departures.

In some areas, planes rarely depart on time. A backlog accumulates, with every passenger intent on getting on the next flight, and there is resultant bedlam at the check-in counter. Avoid scheduling a domestic flight with a tight connection for an international flight. Reconfirm all flights 48 hours before departure and turn up at the airport at least an hour before flight time.

Flights from North America and Europe may permit stopovers on the way to the destination city. It's worth considering this when shopping for an international flight, as it can effectively give you a free air connection within South America. Onward connections in conjunction with an international flight can also be a cheap way to get to another South American city.

Air Passes

Air passes offer a number of flights within a country or region, for a specified period, at a fixed total price. There are various conditions and restrictions, but tickets must usually be bought outside the countries for which they are valid.

An air pass can be an economical way to cover long distances if your time is limited, but it can have shortcomings. Some passes are quite inflexible – once you start using the pass, you're locked into a schedule and you can't change it without paying a penalty. The validity period can be restrictive: A Brazil air pass is great for getting to remote parts of the country, but it's only good for 21 days, and you may want to spend much longer in some areas. Some air passes require that you enter the country on an international flight – you can't travel overland to the country and then start flying around on an air pass.

Multicountry Air Passes A few air-pass schemes cover two or more countries and are of particular interest:

Venezuela Airpass
This provides four or more discounted flights within 45 days, using Avensa or Servivensa, between Caracas and Miami (US$80), Mexico City (US$200), Bogotá (US$80), Quito (US$160), Lima (US$180) and major Venezuelan cities (US$40).

Southern Lakes Pass
This is for circle travel in the Chilean and Argentine Lake District using LanChile and Aerolíneas Argentinas. For US$318, the pass allows you to fly from Santiago to Puerto Montt, travel by land through the Lake District to Bariloche, then fly to Buenos Aires and back to Santiago. Other options that include more flights cost US$380 and US$520.

Mercosur Pass
This mileage-based pass allows travelers to fly to cities in Argentina, Brazil, Paraguay, Uruguay and Chile (excluding Easter Island) on the major airlines of those countries. The flights must be completed over a minimum of seven days and a maximum of 30 days, and there's a maximum of two flights in any country. If it's well organized, this can be cheaper than some domestic air passes, but you may need a patient travel agent to arrange the optimum itinerary. The cost is based on the number of standard air miles (not kilometers) you want to cover:

no of miles	cost
1200 to 1900	US$225
1901 to 2500	US$285
2501 to 3200	US$345
3201 to 4200	US$420
4201 to 5200	US$530
5201 to 6200	US$645
6201 to 7200	US$755
more than 7200	US$870

AIRFARES

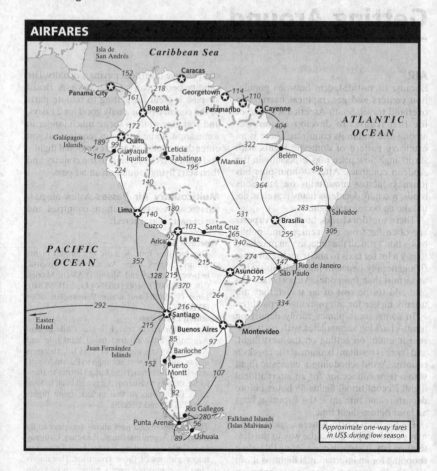

Approximate one-way fares in US$ during low season

Single-Country Air Passes Most air passes are only for use within one country and are usually purchased in combination with a return ticket to that country. The following countries offer domestic air passes; for more details, see the Getting Around section of each country chapter.

Argentina

The Visit Argentina Pass offers a minimum of four flight coupons for Aerolíneas Argentinas and Austral flights, which must be made within 30 days. A pass costs US$420 for those arriving in Argentina on Aerolíneas or Iberia flights, with up to four extra coupons for US$110 each. Those arriving via other airlines pay US$500 for the pass plus US$130 for additional coupons.

Bolivia

The Lloyd Aéreo Boliviano LABpass is a real bargain, permitting as many as five flights to half a dozen Bolivian cities within 30 days for only US$173. The pass can be purchased inside Bolivia.

Brazil

Transbrasil and Varig offer a Brazil Airpass, which is good for five flights within 21 days (on one airline only) for US$490/540 in low/high season; additional flights cost US$100. Cheaper passes are available for travel to south-central Brazil (US$350/400) and northeast Brazil (US$290/340).

Chile

LanChile offers a 30-day Visit Chile Pass, good for three to six flights on LanChile and Ladeco. If you fly in with LanChile, the pass costs

US$250 for three coupons, plus US$60 for any additional coupons. Pass-holders can get a special sector fare to Easter Island for US$525. If you enter Chile with another carrier, the pass is US$350 plus US$80 for additional coupons.

Colombia

Avianca's 21-day Descubra Colombia fare allows as many as five stops for US$180/200 in low/high season or US$260/290 including flights to San Andrés and Leticia. As many as three extra flight coupons can be bought for US$40 each. If you fly into Colombia with any airline other than Avianca, the pass will cost you twice as much.

Peru

AeroContinente's Inka Air Pass offered up to five domestic flights in 30 days for about US$90 each if purchased outside Peru. This may change with the reorganization of air services following the demise of AeroPeru.

BUS

Road transport, especially by bus, is well developed throughout the continent, but road conditions and the quality of the buses vary widely.

Highland Peru has some of the worst roads, and bad stretches can be found in parts of Colombia, Bolivia and the Brazilian Amazon. Much depends on the season – vast deserts of red dust in the dry season become oceans of mud in the rainy season. In Chile, Argentina, Uruguay, coastal and southern Brazil and most of Venezuela, roads are generally better, though poor maintenance can be a problem.

In more remote areas, buses may be stripped to their bare essentials; tires often haven't seen tread for years and they all seem to be held together by a double set of springs at the back, which makes their suspensions rock-hard and ensures that each and every bump is transmitted directly to your backside. When all the seats are taken, the corridor is then packed to capacity and beyond, and the roof is loaded with cargo to at least half the height of the bus, topped by the occasional goat. You may have serious doubts about ever arriving at your destination, but the buses usually make it and may provide some of the most memorable experiences of your trip.

At the other extreme, you'll find very comfortable coaches in Venezuela, Argentina, Brazil, Chile, Colombia, Uruguay and even Bolivia along main routes. You can get

a luxury sleeper bus, called a *bus cama*, on some long routes, but it may cost double the fare on a regular bus.

Most major cities and towns have a *terminal de autobuses* (long-distance bus terminal); in Brazil, it's called a *rodoviária*. Often this is outside the center of town, and you'll need a local bus or taxi to reach it. The biggest and best terminals also have restaurants, shops, showers and other services, and the surrounding area is often a good place to look for cheap accommodations and food. Most bus companies have ticket offices at central terminals and information boards showing routes, departure times, fares and whether the bus is direct. Seats are numbered and booked in advance. At holiday times, all the seats may be filled on major routes, but generally you will get a seat if you turn up an hour or so before the departure time.

Some cities have several terminals, each serving a different route. Sometimes each bus company has its own terminal, which is particularly inconvenient. This is most common in Colombia, Ecuador and Peru, particularly in smaller towns, but notably in Lima. A small, one-company terminal may be nothing more than a parking area and a ticket seller.

TRAIN

South American railways, covering some of the most spectacular routes on earth, are invariably cheaper than buses (even in 1st class) but they're also slower. Many services have closed down, but railway enthusiasts should note the following routes:

Lima-Huancayo (Peru) – Reestablished on a trial basis, this train runs on the last weekend of every month via Galera, which has reputedly the world's highest standard-gauge railway station (4781m).

Arequipa-Juliaca-Cuzco/Puno (Peru) – The section from Arequipa to Juliaca is usually done at night. At Juliaca, change for trains to Cuzco (and Machu Picchu), or continue 40 spectacular kilometers across a 4600m pass to Puno, on the shores of Lake Titicaca.

Oruro-Uyuni-Calama (Bolivia-Chile) – The train line south of Oruro offers great altiplano scenery all the way to Uyuni, where a branch line goes southwest to the Chilean border. After a tediously long border crossing, the line descends dramatically to Calama, through spectacular moonlike landscapes and extinct volcanoes. This is a long and tiresome trip, and there's every chance you'll pass the most scenic sections at night.

Oruro-Uyuni-Tupiza-Villazón (Bolivia) – The main line from Oruro continues south from Uyuni to Tupiza (another scenic rail trip through eroded gorge country) and on to Villazón at the Argentine border. This is a great trip if you can do it in daylight on the comfortable *expreso* train.

Salta-San Antonio de los Cobres (Argentina) – The *Tren a las Nubes* (Train to the Clouds) runs through the arid foothills on the eastern slope of the Andes, offering spectacular bridges and tunnels along the way. It's usually done as an expensive excursion from Salta. It's difficult, but possible, to continue by freight train over the Andes to Chile.

Curitiba-Paranaguá (Brazil) – Descending steeply to the coastal lowlands, this trip offers some unforgettable views.

There are several types of passenger trains in the Andean countries. The *ferrobus* is a relatively fast, diesel-powered single or double car that caters to passengers going from A to B but not to intermediate stations. Meals are often available on board. These are the most expensive trains and can be an excellent value.

The *tren rápido* is more like an ordinary train, pulled by a diesel or steam engine. It is relatively fast, makes only a few stops and is generally cheaper than a ferrobus. Ordinary passenger trains, sometimes called expresos ('express' is a relative term), are slower, cheaper and stop at most stations en route. There are generally two classes, with 2nd class being very crowded. Lastly, there are *mixtos*, mixed passenger and freight trains; these take everything and everyone, stop at every station and a lot of other places, take forever to reach their destination and are dirt cheap.

The few remaining passenger trains in Chile and Argentina are generally more modern, and the salon and pullman classes are very comfortable and quite inexpensive. The *economía* or *turista* classes are slightly cheaper, while the sleeper class *(cama)* is even more comfortable. Brazil still has a few interesting train trips, but they are quite short.

CAR & MOTORCYCLE

In parts of South America, such as Patagonia, where distances are great and buses can be infrequent, a car is worth considering, despite the expense. You must have an International or Inter-American Driving Permit to supplement your driving license from home.

Security can be a problem, most notably in the Andean countries and Brazil. Avoid leaving valuables in the vehicle, and always lock it securely.

Road Rules

Most South American countries drive on the right side; Guyana and Suriname are the two exceptions. Road rules are frequently ignored and seldom enforced, conditions can be hazardous, and many drivers, especially in Argentina and Brazil, are very reckless and even willfully dangerous.

Rental

Major international rental agencies such as Hertz, Avis and A1 have offices in South American capitals and other major cities, but there are also local agencies. To rent a car, you must have a valid driver's license and be at least 25 years old. It may also be necessary to present a credit card, such as MasterCard or Visa, or pay a large cash deposit.

Even at smaller agencies, rental charges are very high, but if several people share expenses, it's feasible. If the vehicle enables you to camp out, the saving in accommodations may offset much of the car-rental cost, especially in Southern Cone countries.

Purchase

If you're spending several months in South America, purchasing a car is worth consideration. It's likely to be cheaper than renting if you can resell it at the end of your stay. On the other hand, any used car can be a financial risk, especially on rugged roads.

The best countries in which to purchase cars are Argentina, Chile and Brazil, but you must often deal with exasperating bureaucracies. By reputation, Santiago de Chile is the best place to buy a car, and Asunción (Paraguay) is the best place to sell one. Be certain of the title; as a foreigner, you may find it very useful to get a notarized document authorizing your use of the car, since the bureaucracy may take some time to change the title. You may find obstacles to taking a vehicle purchased in South America across international borders.

Officially, you'll need a *carnet de passages* or a *libreta de pasos por aduana* to cross most land borders in your own vehicle. In practice, you may never have to show these documents. The best source of advice is the national automobile club in the country where you buy the car. In North America, the Canadian Auto Association may be more helpful in getting a carnet de passages than the American Auto Association.

Shipping a Vehicle

Quite a few people ship their own motorcycle and ride it around South America. Bringing a car or camper van is far less common.

Documents You must submit three notarized copies of the vehicle's title to the shipper, plus a letter of permission from the lienholder if it is not completely paid for. In practice, most countries seem to have dispensed with the requirement for a carnet de passages or a libreta de pasos por aduana, but officially one of these documents is still usually required; check (well before shipping) with the appropriate consulates, especially for any country where your vehicle will arrive by air or sea. Some travelers have had horrendous experiences taking vehicles, especially motorcycles, from Panama to South America without proper documentation.

On arrival, make it clear to customs officials that the vehicle is only in transit; in the case of Chile, for example, the maximum stay is 90 days. Once you have entered South America, border crossings should be routine in a vehicle from your home country.

To/From North America Shipping a car to South America is not cheap, but the bureaucracy is less demanding than in the recent past. Prices are variable, so call several places before committing yourself; look in the yellow pages under 'Automobile Transporters' for toll-free numbers.

It is generally cheaper to ship from US Atlantic ports than from Pacific ports. Miami, New Orleans or Houston to Barranquilla (Colombia), or Maracaibo (Venezuela) are the most direct routes. On the Pacific side, Valparaíso is a good choice, since Chile's bureaucracy is among the most reasonable; Guayaquil (Ecuador) is another possibility. You must usually book transport for your vehicle at least two weeks ahead, and you can't usually travel on the same ship

as your vehicle. Costs from eastern US ports start around US$1500.

To/From Central America An alternative is to drive through Central America and ship your vehicle from Panama to a South American port. There's no regular boat service from Panama to Colombia, and the cargo ships between Colón and the Colombian port of Barranquilla are not very safe or reliable. Prices are very negotiable; they might start out at US$1500 and eventually come down to half of that. More established shippers will be more expensive, but they may help you with the paperwork, which must be handled at both the Colombian and Panamanian ends. You'll need all the papers for car ownership, registration and insurance; an international driving permit and (in theory anyway) a carnet de passage.

You could also ship a car or, more easily, a motorcycle, by air and you may be able to get a special air-cargo rate if you are also flying with the same airline. Ask at airline cargo departments or at the cargo terminal at the international airport in Tocumen near Panama City. Travel agents can sometimes help.

Security

If you can't stay with your vehicle every minute, you can expect that something will be stolen from it. Stealing from vehicles being shipped is big business. If you ship the vehicle with all your possessions in it, take every precaution, and even then, don't be surprised if thieves get your stuff. Remove everything removable (hubcaps, wipers, mirrors), and take everything visible out of the interior. Camper vans are a special target – seal off the living area from the driving compartment, double-lock the living area, cover the windows so no one can see inside, and double-lock your possessions *again* inside the cabinets. Shipping your vehicle in a container is more secure, but more expensive.

BICYCLE

Bicycling is an interesting and inexpensive alternative, especially in Southern Cone countries, where roads are better and transport costs tend to be higher. Road bikes are suitable for paved roads, but on the mostly graveled or dirt roads of the Andes, a *todo terreno* (mountain bike) is a better choice. Bring your own bicycle, since locally manufactured ones are less sturdy and dependable.

There are many good cycling routes, especially in the lake districts of Chile and Argentina. Mountain bikers have even cycled the length of Brazil's Trans-Amazon Highway.

Bicycle mechanics are common even in small South American towns, but will almost invariably lack the parts you'll need. Before coming to South America, make an effort to become a competent bicycle mechanic yourself and purchase spares for the pieces most likely to fail.

Other drawbacks to cycling include the weather (rain in Brazil or wind in Patagonia can slow your progress to a crawl) and high altitude and poor roads in the Andean countries. In addition, Brazilian and Argentine motorists, who have a total disregard for anyone but themselves, can be serious hazards to cyclists.

HITCHHIKING

Hitchhiking is never entirely safe in any country in the world, and for safety reasons it can't be recommended. Travelers who decide to hitchhike should understand that they are taking a small but potentially serious risk. Hitchhiking is less dangerous if you travel in pairs and let someone know where you are planning to go.

Though it is possible to hitchhike all over South America, free lifts are the rule only in Argentina, Chile, Uruguay and parts of Brazil. Elsewhere, drivers expect payment for lifts, and hitching is virtually a form of public transport, especially among poor people and in the highlands, where buses can be infrequent. There are more or less fixed fares over certain routes – just ask the other passengers what they're paying. It's usually less than the bus fare, but can be the same in some places. You get a better view from the top of a truck, and people tend to be friendlier, but if you're hitchhiking on the Andean altiplano, take warm clothing. Once the sun goes down or is obscured by clouds, it gets *very* cold.

There's no need to wait at the roadside for a lift, unless it happens to be convenient. Almost every town has a central truck park, often in or near the market. Ask around for a truck going in your direction and how much it will cost; be there about 30 minutes before the departure time given by the driver. If the driver has a full load of passengers, you'll leave more or less on time, but if not, the driver may spend some time driving around town hunting for more. It is often worth soliciting a ride at *servicentros* on the outskirts of large cities, where drivers refuel their vehicles.

BOAT
Riverboat

Many travelers dream about cruising down big rivers like the Orinoco or Amazon, but you'll have a more idyllic time on one of the smaller rivers such as the Mamoré or Beni, where boats hug the shore and you can see and hear the wildlife. Another alternative is the Río Paraguay, upstream from Asunción (Paraguay) to Brazil.

The Amazon is quite densely settled in its lower reaches, and its upper reaches have fewer passenger boats than in the past. Also, the Amazon is so broad that your boat may be miles from anything interesting on the riverbanks.

Boats vary greatly in size and standards, so it's wise to check the vessel before you buy a ticket. Fares for a given route and class vary a little, and it can be worth shopping around. When you pay the fare, get a ticket with all the details on it. Downriver travel is considerably faster than upriver, but boats going upriver travel closer to the shore and offer more interesting scenery. The time taken between ports is unpredictable: From Manaus to Belém should be about four days, but it commonly takes six or more. River travel is not for those on a tight schedule.

Food is usually included in ticket prices and includes lots of rice and beans and some meat, but bring bottled water, fruit and snacks as a supplement. The evening meal on the first night of a trip is not usually included. Drinks and extra food are generally sold onboard, but at high prices. Bring some spare cash, and insect repellent.

Unless you have cabin space, you'll need a hammock and rope to string it up. It can get windy and cool at night, so a sleeping bag is also recommended. There are usually two classes of hammock space, with space on the upper deck costing slightly more; it's cooler there and worth the extra money. Be on the boat at least eight hours prior departure to get a good hammock space away from engine noise and toilet odors.

Beware of theft on boats – it's a very common complaint. Don't allow your baggage to be stored in an insecure locker – bring your own padlock. Don't entrust your bag to any boat officials unless you are quite certain about their status – bogus officials have been reported.

Lake Crossings

There are outstanding lake excursions in southern Chile and Argentina and on Lake Titicaca in Bolivia (see those chapters).

Sea Trips

The best sea trip in South America is down the Chilean coast from Puerto Montt to Puerto Natales. Short boat rides in some countries take you to islands not far from the mainland, including Ilha Grande and Ilha de Santa Catarina in Brazil, Isla Grande de Chiloé in Chile and Isla Grande de Tierra del Fuego. More distant islands are usually reached by air, but ocean trips to the Galápagos and Juan Fernández islands are a possibility.

ORGANIZED TOURS

The possibilities for organized tours run from comfortable 10-day bus excursions around the main attractions to months of overland travel in an expedition vehicle. More specialized tours cater to the ecotourist with rain forests, wilderness and wildlife, while others arrange skiing, trekking, rafting or kayaking packages for the outdoor enthusiast.

Tours usually cover only part of the continent (eg, the Andean region or southern Chile and Argentina), but some of the tour companies arrange itineraries so that you can join two successive tours and see more than one region.

Two companies of interest are GAP and Encounter (www.encounter-overland.com),

which are both well represented by student, budget and adventure travel agents in Australia, New Zealand, the UK and the US. GAP offers small group tours using local transport and inexpensive accommodations, accompanied by a guide experienced in the region. The trips are similar to independent travel, but a guide takes care of most hassles and decisions. Encounter specializes in overland journeys, typically in their own specially equipped vehicles (trucks, vans or buses), with a driver-mechanic-cook-tour leader. Outside of cities, the tours include tent accommodations and camp meals, and they often include treks, river trips and extended stops at national parks or places of particular interest.

Most travel agents will offer a selection of tours – following are a few of the companies that specialize in South American trips.

Australia
   Inca Tours (☎ 02-4351-2133, 1800-024-955, www.southamerica.com.au), 3 Margaret St, Wyong NSW 2259
   South America Travel Centre (☎ 03-9642-5353, fax 03-9642-5454), 104 Hardware St, Melbourne, Vic 3000
   World Expeditions (☎ 02-9261-1974, 1800-803-688, www.worldexpeditions.com.au), at 377 Sussex St, Sydney, NSW 2000

UK
   Explore Worldwide (☎ 01252-34-4161, fax 01252-34-3170), 1 Frederick St, Aldershot, Hants GU11 1LQ
   Journey Latin America (JLA; ☎ 020-8747-8315, fax 020-8742-1312, www.journeylatinamerica .co.uk), 12 & 13 Heathfield Terrace, Chiswick, London W4 4JE
   South American Experience (☎ 020-7976-5511, fax 020-7976-6908), 47 Causton St, Pimlico, London SW1P 4AT

USA
   Forum International (☎ 925-671-2900, fax 925-946-1500, www.foruminternational.com), at 91 Gregory Lane, Pleasant Hill, CA 94523
   Ladatco (☎ 305-854-8422, 800-327-6162, www.ladatco.com), 2220 Coral Way, Miami, FL 33145

Argentina

The cultural dominance of immigrants in Argentina led historian Alfred Crosby to call the River Plate (Río de la Plata) region a 'neo-Europe,' where transatlantic plants and animals transformed the natural environment and ensured the demise of pre-Columbian cultures. Having fed its European parent with grains and beef, made a mark in literature and exported the tango to continental salons, Argentina is a country in which foreigners feel at ease and inconspicuous. Its persistent regionalisms and unexpected cultural diversity undercut an idealized uniform nationality.

Argentina has a string of alpine parks among the glaciers and blue-green lakes of its southern cordillera. The Central Andes contain some of the continent's highest peaks, the colorful northern deserts are no less impressive, and Iguazú Falls, shared with Brazil, are legendary. Desolate southern Patagonia, with massive concentrations of subantarctic wildlife, forms a striking contrast to Buenos Aires' cosmopolitan frenzy.

Facts about Argentina

HISTORY

In pre-Columbian times, sedentary Diaguita Indians cultivated maize in the Andean Northwest (Noroeste Andino); to the east, in the forested Paraná delta, the Guaraní grew maize and tubers like manioc (cassava). Mostly, though, nomadic peoples hunted the guanaco (a relative of the llama) and the ostrich-like rhea on the Pampas and in Patagonia, though Fuegian Indians gathered shellfish and birds' eggs.

Indian resistance forced early Spaniards from Buenos Aires. Spanish forces established the city anew by 1580, but it languished compared to Tucumán, Córdoba and Salta, which provided mules, cloth and foodstuffs for the mines of Alto Perú (Bolivia). Spaniards from Chile settled the trans-Andean Cuyo region, which produced wine and grain.

At a Glance

Country Name	República Argentina
Area	2,766,890 sq km
Population	36.1 million
Population Density	13 per sq km
Capital	Buenos Aires
Head of State	President Carlos Saúl Menem
Official Language	Spanish
Other Languages	English, Italian, German, Mapuche, Quechua, Toba and other indigenous languages
Currency	Peso (Arg$)
Exchange Rate	US$1 = Arg$1
Per Capita GNP	US$8900
Inflation Rate	0% (1998)

The Northwest's declining Indian population, in conjunction with the Indians' relatively small numbers in the rest of the country, resulted in a peculiarly Argentine maldistribution of land. The hacienda was less important than in Peru or Mexico; instead, the livestock *estancia* dominated development.

91

ARGENTINA

Spaniards returning to the Pampas in the late 16th century found that cattle and horses left behind earlier multiplied profusely. This had a huge impact on the environment. Without horses and cattle, the legendary gaucho could never have existed, but their growing commercial importance brought about his demise.

Growth & Independence

Buenos Aires' designation as capital of the new Viceroyalty of the Río de la Plata, in 1776, demonstrated that it had outgrown Spanish domination. After expelling British invaders in 1806 and 1807, confident criollos revolted against Spain in 1810, declaring independence in 1816.

Despite this unity, provincial *caudillos* (local strongmen) resisted Buenos Aires' authority. President DF Sarmiento castigated demagogic caudillos in his writings, yet they commanded great loyalty. Darwin observed that Juan Manuel de Rosas 'by conforming to the dress and habits of the Gauchos...obtained an unbounded popularity in the country.'

Provincial Federalists, allied to conservative landowners, opposed Buenos Aires' Unitarists, who looked to Europe for capital, immigrants and ideas. The two parties' bloody, vindictive conflicts nearly exhausted the country.

Reign of Rosas

Rosas represented *estancieros*, but also helped centralize power in Buenos Aires, building a large army, creating the ruthless *mazorca* (political police), institutionalizing torture and forcing overseas trade through the port city. In Sarmiento's words, Rosas 'applied the knife of the gaucho to the culture of Buenos Ayres, and destroyed the work of centuries – of civilization, law and liberty.' The Unitarists, and some of Rosas' former allies, forced him from power in 1852.

Roots of Modern Argentina

The 1853 Unitarist constitution allowed the president to dissolve provincial administrations. Its liberal economic ideology opened the Pampas, Mesopotamia and Córdoba to foreign investment, trade and immigration, but barely affected interior provinces.

European immigrants filled key roles in crafts and commerce. Basque and Irish refugees tended the sheep that displaced semi-wild cattle on many estancias. After 1880, Argentina became a major cereal exporter, as immigrant Swiss, Germans and Italians proved successful farmers in Santa Fe and Entre Ríos, but bargain sales of public lands encouraged speculation and reduced such opportunities. Many immigrants, faced with rural sharecropping or seasonal labor, remained in Buenos Aires.

British capital built the extensive rail network that fanned out in all directions from Buenos Aires, but vulnerability to global economic fluctuations stimulated debate over foreign investment and encouraged protectionism. The only sectors to benefit were producers of agricultural commodities like wheat, wine and sugar, whose growth encouraged a speculative boom in land prices and paper money loans, whose depreciation nearly bankrupted the country.

By reducing rural opportunities, speculation also encouraged urban growth; in the 1880s, immigration nearly doubled Buenos Aires' population. Urban services such as transport, power and water improved, but industry could not absorb all the immigrants. At the onset of the 1929 depression, the military took power from ineffectual civilians, but an obscure colonel, Juan Domingo Perón, was the first leader to really confront the crisis.

Perón & His Legacy

As Juan Perón (born 1895) grew to maturity, Argentina was one of the world's most prosperous countries, but many resented the *oligarquía terrateniente* (landed elite) and British interests that had built the railways and flooded local markets with cheap manufactures.

From a minor post in the labor ministry, Perón won the presidency in 1946, and was reelected in 1952. His economic program, which stressed domestic industrialization and economic independence, appealed to conservative nationalists and to working-class elements who mistrusted foreign capital and benefited from improved wages, pensions, job security and working conditions. Remarkably, Perón avoided alienating either sector, despite a virtual civil war between them.

Economic difficulties, due especially to a shortage of capital from war-torn Europe,

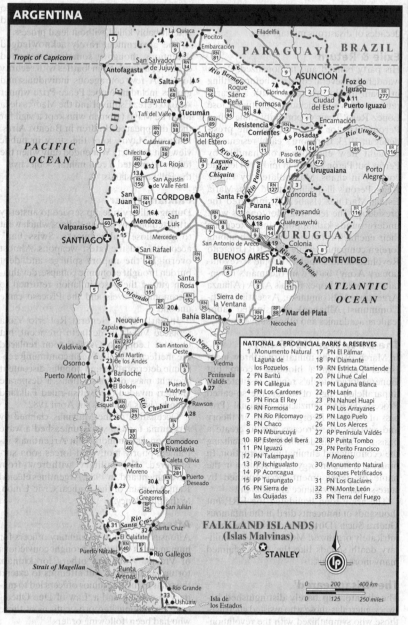

ARGENTINA

Tropic of Capricorn

PARAGUAY

BRAZIL

CHILE

PACIFIC
OCEAN

La Quiaca
Pocitos
Filadelfia
Embarcación
San Salvador
de Jujuy
Antofagasta
Salta
ASUNCIÓN
Foz do
Iguaçu
Roque
Sáenz
Peña
Cafayate
Clorinda
Ciudad
del Este
Puerto Iguazú
Tafí del Valle
Tucumán
Formosa
Encarnación
Catamarca
Santiago
del Estero
Resistencia
Corrientes
Posadas
Río Uruguay
Chilecito
La Rioja
Porto
Alegre
Laguna
Mar
Chiquita
Paso de
los Libres
Uruguaiana
San Agustín
de Valle Fértil
San
Juan
CÓRDOBA
Santa Fe
Concordia
Paraná
Paysandú
SANTIAGO
Valparaíso
Mendoza
San
Luis
Rosario
Gualeguaychú
URUGUAY
San Rafael
Mercedes
San Antonio de Areco
Colonia
MONTEVIDEO
San Rafael
San Antonio de Areco
BUENOS AIRES
La
Plata
*ATLANTIC
OCEAN*
Santa
Rosa
Sierra de
la Ventana
Mar del Plata
Neuquén
Bahía Blanca
Necochea
Zapala
Valdivia
San Antonio
Oeste
Viedma
Osorno
San Martín
de los Andes
Bariloche
Península
Valdés
Puerto Montt
El Bolsón
Puerto
Madryn
Trelew
Rawson
Esquel
Río Chubut
Comodoro
Rivadavia
Caleta Olivia
Perito
Moreno
Puerto
Deseado
Gobernador
Gregores
San Julián
Río Santa Cruz
Santa Cruz
El Calafate
**FALKLAND ISLANDS
(Islas Malvinas)**
STANLEY
Puerto Natales
Río Gallegos
Strait of Magellan
Punta
Arenas
Porvenir
Río Grande
Isla de
los Estados
Ushuaia

NATIONAL & PROVINCIAL PARKS & RESERVES	

1 Monumento Natural
  Laguna de
  los Pozuelos
	17 PN El Palmar
	18 PN Diamante
	19 RN Estricta Otamende

2 PN Baritú	20 PN Lihué Calel
3 PN Calilegua	21 PN Laguna Blanca
4 PN Los Cardones	22 PN Lanín
5 PN Finca El Rey	23 PN Nahuel Huapi
6 RN Formosa	24 PN Los Arrayanes
7 PN Río Pilcomayo	25 PN Lago Puelo
8 PN Chaco	26 PN Los Alerces
9 PN Mburucuyá	27 RP Península Valdés
10 RP Esteros del Iberá	28 RP Punta Tombo
11 PN Iguazú	29 PN Perito Francisco
12 PN Talampaya	P Moreno
13 PP Ischigualasto	30 Monumento Natural
14 PP Aconcagua	Bosques Petrificados
15 PP Tupungato	31 PN Los Glaciares
16 PN Sierra de	32 PN Monte León
las Quijadas	33 PN Tierra del Fuego

0   200   400 km
0   125   250 miles

undermined Perón's second presidency. A 1955 coup against him began nearly three decades of disastrous military rule.

Exile & Return

His party banned and factionalized, Perón wandered to several countries before settling in Spain to plot his return with a bizarre retinue of advisers, including spiritualist José López Rega. Their opportunity came when Peronist Héctor Cámpora won the presidency in 1973. Cámpora's early resignation brought new elections, won handily by Perón, but Perón's death in mid-1974 left the country in chaos. Manipulated by López Rega, Perón's ill-qualified third wife, María Estela Martínez (Isabelita), inherited the presidency. The left-wing Montoneros went underground, kidnapping and executing their enemies, robbing banks and bombing foreign companies, while the ERP (Ejército Revolucionario Popular; People's Revolutionary Army) battled in Tucumán's mountainous forests. López Rega's AAA (Alianza Argentina Anticomunista; Argentine Anti-Communist Alliance) assassinated labor leaders, academics and other 'subversives.'

The Dirty War (1976-83)

In March 1976, the military overthrew inept Isabel Perón in a bloodless coup, but General Jorge Videla's regime instituted an unparalleled reign of terror, the so-called Proceso de Reorganización Nacional (Process of National Reorganization). In theory and rhetoric, the Proceso was to create a basis for enduring democracy by stabilizing the economy and eliminating corruption. In practice, it was an orgy of corruption in the name of development, accompanied by state-sponsored violence and anarchy.

The army soon liquidated the ERP, but thousands of innocents died in the infamous Guerra Sucia (Dirty War) against the more intricately organized Montoneros. Paramilitary death squads like the AAA claimed many more victims.

The 'Disappeared'

The dictatorship barely distinguished between guerrillas, those who assisted guerrillas, those who sympathized with the revolutionaries without assisting them, and those who expressed reservations about the dictatorship's indiscriminate brutality. For at least 9000 people and perhaps three times more, to 'disappear' meant to be detained, tortured and probably killed, without legal process.

The government rarely acknowledged detentions, though it sometimes reported deaths of individuals in 'battles with security forces.' A few courageous individuals and groups, including Nobel Peace Prize winner Adolfo Pérez Esquivel and the Madres de la Plaza de Mayo (women who kept a vigil for their disappeared children in Buenos Aires' Plaza de Mayo), kept the story in public view, but the Dirty War ended only when the forces attempted a real military objective – the Falkland Islands.

Falklands War

During military rule, lip service to austerity attracted billions of loan dollars, which went to grandiose public works, Swiss bank accounts, and the latest weapons. Almost overnight, the import splurge and debt burden brought economic collapse, devaluation gutted the peso, inflation returned to astronomical levels and the Proceso came undone.

In early 1981, General Roberto Viola replaced Videla as de facto president, but General Leopoldo Galtieri soon replaced the ineffectual Viola. When continuing economic deterioration and popular discontent brought mass demonstrations, a desperate Galtieri invaded the British-ruled Falkland Islands (Islas Malvinas) in April 1982.

Occupation of the Malvinas, claimed by Argentina for 150 years, unleashed a wave of nationalist euphoria, but Argentina's ill-trained, poorly motivated forces soon surrendered. The military withdrew from government and, in 1983, Argentines elected Raúl Alfonsín, of the Radical Civic Union, to the presidency.

Aftermath

Alfonsín's pledge to try military officers for human rights violations brought convictions of Videla, Viola and others for kidnap, torture and murder, but attempts to extend the trials to include junior officers led to military discontent and a 'Law of Due Obedience' that eliminated prosecutions of those who had been 'following orders.'

President Carlos Menem, who came to power in 1989, himself a prisoner during the Dirty War, inexplicably pardoned Videla and other top military officers. Revelations from lower-level officials confirmed practices like the execution of drugged prisoners by dropping them from airplanes into the ocean, leading to an unprecedented apology to the Argentine people from army general Martín Balza. Menem's pardon and the Law of Due Obedience seemed to have precluded further legal options, but in 1998 Videla and retired Admiral Emilio Massera, another junta member, were arrested on charges of child kidnapping, an offense specifically excluded from amnesty.

Most of President Menem's second term, which expired in 1999, was uneventful, though many accused him of authoritarian tendencies and his administration acquired a reputation for corruption, particularly in questionable privatizations of state enterprises.

GEOGRAPHY & CLIMATE

Argentina's land area of about 2.8 million sq km, excluding South Atlantic islands and Antarctic claims, makes it the world's eighth-largest country, slightly smaller than India.

Cuyo & the Andean Northwest

The Andes are a formidable barrier in the area colonized from Peru. Perennial streams provide irrigation water, but only a few inhabitants live in scattered mining settlements or herd llamas on the *puna* (Andean highlands). South of Tucumán province, rainfall is inadequate for crops, but irrigation has boosted the wine-producing Cuyo region (Mendoza, San Juan and San Luis provinces). La Rioja and Catamarca provinces are less well-to-do. In western Jujuy and Salta provinces, soaring volcanic peaks punctuate the puna and *salares* (salt lakes), while to the east, foothills give way to dissected river valleys and the lowlands of the Gran Chaco. The hot subtropical lowlands of Santiago del Estero are transitional between the Chaco and the Andes.

Mesopotamia

East of the Andes, northern Argentina is a subtropical lowland with very hot summers. The provinces of Entre Ríos and Corrientes comprise most of the area known as Mesopotamia, between the Paraná and Uruguay Rivers, where heavy rainfall supports swampy lowland forests and upland savan-

nas. Misiones province, even more densely forested and surrounded on three sides by Brazil and Paraguay, contains part of the awesome Iguazú Falls.

The Chaco

The Argentine Chaco includes the provinces of Chaco and Formosa, eastern areas of Salta and Santiago del Estero, and the northern edges of Santa Fe and Córdoba. It is part of the much larger Gran Chaco region, which extends into Bolivia, Paraguay and Brazil. Open savanna alternates with thorn forest, but erratic precipitation makes rain-fed cultivation risky. Summers are brutally hot.

The Pampas

Argentina's agricultural heartland is a nearly level plain of windborne loess and riverborne sediments, once covered by native grasses and now occupied by grain farms and estancias. More properly subdivided into the Humid Pampas, along the littoral, and the Dry Pampas of the west and south, the region comprises the provinces of Buenos Aires, La Pampa and much of Santa Fe and Córdoba. The Atlantic Coast features attractive sandy beaches.

Patagonia & the Lake District

Patagonia is the thinly populated region south of the Río Colorado, consisting of Neuquén, Río Negro, Chubut and Santa Cruz provinces. It is mostly arid, but the far southern Andes have the largest glaciers in the southern hemisphere outside Antarctica. East of the Andes, cool arid steppes pasture huge flocks of sheep, while the Río Negro and Chubut valleys support crop and fruit farming. Patagonia is also an energy storehouse, with oil and coal deposits. The climate is generally temperate, but winter temperatures can drop well below freezing.

Tierra del Fuego

The 'Land of Fire' consists of one large island (Isla Grande de Tierra del Fuego), unequally divided between Chile and Argentina, and many smaller ones. Isla Grande's northern half resembles the Patagonian steppe, while dense forests and glaciers cover its mountainous southern half. The maritime climate is surprisingly mild, even in winter, but changeable.

FLORA & FAUNA

The extensive Pampas are primarily sprawling grasslands, with gallery forests along the major rivers. In the higher altitudes of the Andes, and the high latitudes of Patagonia, pasture grasses are much sparser. The main forested areas are subtropical Misiones province, and the eastward-sloping Andes from Neuquén province south, where species of southern beech predominate.

The guanaco, a wild relative of the llama, once grazed the Pampas, but overhunting and the encroachment of cattle estancias have reduced its range to Patagonia and parts of the Andean Northwest. Bird life is varied along the rivers and coasts, and on low-lying Pampas wetlands. Coastal Patagonia supports dense concentrations of marine fauna, including whales, sea lions, elephant seals and penguins.

National & Provincial Parks

Argentina's national and provincial park systems protect samples of most of these environments. The most notable are Parque Nacional Iguazú, famous for its waterfalls; Reserva Provincial Esteros del Iberá, in Corrientes, for its wetlands wildlife; Parque Provincial Aconcagua, in Mendoza province, with the continent's highest peak; Reserva Faunística Península Valdés, in Chubut province, for its coastal fauna; Parque Nacional Nahuel Huapi, in Río Negro province, for its alpine scenery; Parque Nacional Los Alerces, in Chubut province, for its ancient alerce (false larch) forests; Parque Nacional Los Glaciares, in Santa Cruz province, for its continental glaciers and alpine towers; and Parque Nacional Tierra del Fuego, in Tierra del Fuego province, for its southern beech forests and coastal fauna.

GOVERNMENT & POLITICS

Argentina's 1853 constitution established a federal system, with equal executive, legislative and judicial branches. The president and the National Congress (comprising a 254-member Chamber of Deputies and a 72-member Senate) are popularly elected, as are provincial governors and legislatures. In practice, the president often governs by decree and intervenes in provincial matters.

Administratively, the country consists of the home-rule federal district of Buenos Aires and 23 provinces. Argentina also claims South Atlantic islands (including the British-ruled Falkland Islands, also known as the Islas Malvinas, and South Georgia) and a slice of Antarctica (on hold by international agreement).

Political Parties

Of 22 parties in the Congress, the most important are the Peronists (Justicialists) of former president Carlos Menem, the centrist Radicals, and the left-center Frente de País Solidario (Frepaso); the latter two form the Alianza, a tenuous electoral alliance that wrested control of the Chamber of Deputies from the Peronists in 1997. Until the 1940s, when Peronism absorbed labor unions and other underrepresented sectors, the middle-class Radicals opposed parties tied to conservative landowners.

Within the Peronist party there remain implacable factions that in the mid-1970s conducted open warfare against each other. There is still friction between the Menemist economic 'neoliberals' and leftists who see their policies as capitulation to institutions like the International Monetary Fund.

As of 1999, Buenos Aires city mayor Fernando de la Rúa, a Radical, is the Alianza presidential candidate; his running mate is Frepaso's Carlos 'Chacho' Álvarez. The Peronist candidate is Eduardo Duhalde, governor of Buenos Aires province, a former Menem opponent. His vice presidential running mate is Menemist Ramón Ortega, a former crooner and one-time Tucumán provincial governor. Menem's former economy minister, Domingo Cavallo, is a potential 'spoiler' candidate.

The Military

Since overthrowing Radical president Hipólito Yrigoyen in 1930, the military has often felt 'obliged' to intervene in government because of civilian incompetence and corruption, although, in effect, it usually undermines the civil order. In 1995, army chief of staff Martín Balza made a public apology on nationwide TV for his service's role in the repression of the 1970s, but the navy has remained unrepentant.

ECONOMY

Since colonial times, Argentina's economy has relied on export commodities – hides, wool, beef and grains – from the Pampas, but these have brought only superficial and maldistributed prosperity. Control of the richest agricultural lands by a handful of families relegated many rural people to marginal lands or made them dependent laborers. Perón demonstrated that Argentina needed to develop its industrial base to benefit the general populace, but state intervention outlived its usefulness. The borrowing binge of the 1970s and 1980s funded capital-intensive projects that encouraged graft and fueled inflation that often reached 50% monthly.

The usual response was wage and price indexing, which in turn reinforced the inflationary spiral. The Menem administration managed to break the pattern by reducing the deficit, selling state enterprises and restricting unionism, but side effects have included unemployment approaching 14%. Inflation is near zero, but several privatization projects have gone awry.

Selling off state assets was a one-time bonanza that reduced or eliminated shortterm budget deficits, but greater productivity and a more efficient tax system will have to do so in the future. The legacy of state domination has fostered a large informal sector operating parallel to the official economy in providing goods and services. Repercussions from the Asian meltdown of 1998 have reduced economic growth projections, which could worsen more if Brazil, Argentina's largest trading partner, continues to falter.

POPULATION & PEOPLE

Over a third of Argentina's 36.1 million people reside in Gran Buenos Aires (the Capital Federal and its suburbs in Buenos Aires province). Nearly 90% live in urban areas; other major cities are Rosario, Córdoba, Tucumán, Mendoza and Bahía Blanca. Patagonia's population is small and dispersed.

Following Juan Bautista Alberdi's dictum 'to govern is to populate,' early Unitarists promoted European immigration. From the mid-19th century, Italians, Basques, Welsh, English, Ukrainians and others streamed into Buenos Aires. Some groups have maintained a distinctive cultural identity, like Buenos Aires' Jewish community and Anglo-Argentines across the country.

Middle Easterners, though few, have been influential; President Menem is of Syrian ancestry. Escobar, a Buenos Aires suburb, has an established Japanese community, and Asian faces are becoming more common. Some groups are still marginalized, like Chileans on sheep estancias in Patagonia and Bolivian laborers (peones golondrinas, or 'swallow laborers') who help with the Northwest's sugar harvests, but many Paraguayans and Uruguayans are permanent residents.

The major indigenous nations are the Quechua of the Northwest and the Mapuche of northern Patagonia, but Matacos, Tobas and others inhabit the Chaco and northeastern cities including Resistencia and Santa Fe.

EDUCATION

Argentina's 94% literacy rate is one of Latin America's highest. From age five to 12 education is free and compulsory, though rural attendance may be low. Elite public secondary schools like the Colegio Nacional Buenos Aires, where the teachers are also university instructors, are unequaled by other public or private institutions. Many government ministers have graduate degrees from European and US universities.

SCIENCE & PHILOSOPHY

Argentina has had two Nobel Prize winners in science, Bernardo Houssay (Medicine, 1946) and Luis Federico Leloir (Chemistry, 1972). Traditionally, though, many academics have worked overseas because of Argentina's turbulent politics and for economic reasons.

ARTS

Though in many ways derivative of European precedents, Argentine arts have been influential beyond the country's borders. In the 19th and early 20th centuries Buenos Aires emulated French cultural trends in art, music and architecture. There are many important museums and galleries, especially in Buenos Aires.

Tango & Folk Music

Legendary figures like Carlos Gardel, Julio Sosa and Astor Piazzolla popularized the tango as music and dance, while contemporaries like Susana Rinaldi, Eladia Blásquez and Osvaldo Pugliese carry on the tradition. Folk musicians like Mercedes Sosa, Tarragó Ross, Leon Gieco and the Conjunto Pro Música de Rosario are popular performers.

Dance, Theater & Classical Music

The palatial Teatro Colón, home of the Buenos Aires opera, is one of the world's finest facilities. Classical music and ballet, as well as modern dance, appear here and at similar venues. Buenos Aires has a vigorous theater community, but even in the provinces live theater is an important medium of expression.

Popular Music

Charly García, whose version of the national anthem does what Jimi Hendrix did for *The Star-Spangled Banner*, is the country's best-known musician, but Buenos Aires' thriving blues/rock scene includes groups like Los Divididos, Memphis La Blusera, and the female a cappella group Las Blacanblus. Los Fabulosos Cadillacs won a Grammy for best alternative Latin rock group in 1998.

Les Luthiers, who build many of their unusual instruments from scratch, satirize nationalist sectors in the middle class and the military. Many performers are more derivative – before reporting an Elvis sighting in Buenos Aires, make absolutely sure it isn't Sandro, a living Argentine clone of The King.

Literature

Jorge Luis Borges, known for short stories and poetry, is a world literary figure whose erudite language and references sometimes make him inaccessible to readers weak in the classics. Ernesto Sábato's psychological novel *On Heroes and Tombs*, a favorite among Argentine youth in the 1960s, explores people and places in Buenos Aires.

Parisian resident Julio Cortázar emphasized Argentine characters in novels like *Hopscotch* and *62: A Model Kit*; one of his short stories inspired the 1960s film *Blow-Up*. Manuel Puig's novels *Kiss of the Spider Woman* and *Betrayed by Rita Hayworth* focus on popular culture's ambiguous role in Argentina. Adolfo Bioy Casares' *The Invention of Morel* also deals with the inability or unwillingness to distinguish between fantasy and reality. In Osvaldo Soriano's novel *Shadows*, the protagonist is lost in an Argentina where the names are the same, but all the familiar landmarks and points of reference have lost their meaning.

Visual Arts

Public art tends toward the pompously monumental, and arbiters of official taste rarely acknowledge the thriving alternative and unconventional art scene. Buenos Aires is the focus of the arts community, but there are unexpected outliers like Resistencia, capital of Chaco province.

Cinema

Argentine cinema has achieved international stature through such directors as Luis Puenzo *(The Official Story)*, Eliseo Subiela *(Man Facing Southeast)*, Héctor Babenco *(Kiss of the Spider Woman)*, and the late María Luisa Bemberg *(Camila, Miss Mary)*. Many films are available on video.

SOCIETY & CONDUCT

Foreign travelers are less incongruous in Argentina than in countries with large indigenous populations, and gregarious Argentines often include them in daily activities. One such activity is to *tomar un mate*, a social ritual throughout the region; *mate* ('Paraguayan tea') is drunk bitter in the south, or sweetened with sugar and *yuyos* (herbs) in the north.

RELIGION

Roman Catholicism is the state religion, but popular beliefs diverge from official doctrine. Spiritualism and veneration of the dead, for instance, are widespread – visitors to Recoleta and Chacarita cemeteries will see endless processions of pilgrims communicating with icons like Juan and Evita Perón, Carlos Gardel and psychic Madre María. Cult beliefs like the Difunta Correa of San Juan province attract hundreds of thousands of adherents, while evangelical Protestantism is also growing.

During the Dirty War, the Church generally supported the dictatorship despite persecution, kidnapping, torture and murder of religious workers among the poor and dispossessed. Social activism has resumed in today's more permissive climate.

LANGUAGE

Spanish is universal, but some immigrants retain their language as a badge of identity. Italian is also widely understood. Anglo-Argentines speak a precise, clipped English.

In Chubut, Welsh has nearly disappeared, despite persistent cultural traditions, but is undergoing a revival. Quechua-speakers, numerous in the Northwest, tend to be bilingual in Spanish. At least 40,000 Mapuche-speakers live in the southern Andes, while northeastern Argentina has about 15,000 Guaraní-speakers, as many Tobas and about 10,000 Matacos.

Argentine Spanish

Local characteristics readily identify an Argentine elsewhere in Latin America, or abroad. The most prominent are the *voseo* (usage of the pronoun *vos* in place of *tú*) and pronunciation of 'll' and 'y' as 'zh' (as in 'plea**s**ure') rather than '**y**' (as in English '**y**ou'). The speech of Buenos Aires abounds with *lunfardo*, the city's colorful slang.

See the Language chapter in the back of the book for further information on Spanish and indigenous tongues.

Facts for the Visitor

HIGHLIGHTS

Argentina's attractions are both cultural and natural. The following list, starting north and working south, includes some of the country's best-known tourist features and some lesser but still deserving ones.

Quebrada de Humahuaca
  The Noroeste's scenic desert canyons, with their large Indian populations and colonial churches, are an outlier of the central Andean countries.

Iguazú Falls
  Despite commercialization, the thunderous cascades at Iguazú are still one of the continent's most breathtaking sights.

Esteros del Iberá
  For wildlife, this sprawling wetland in Corrientes province may be superior to Brazil's Pantanal.

Buenos Aires
  A self-consciously European sophistication, combined with the romantic image of the tango, is only the stereotypical trademark of a city that has much more to offer. When you tire of urban life, escape to the lush delta of the Río Paraná.

Cuyo
  Argentina's wine country also features recreational attractions like Parque Provincial Aconcagua and the offbeat Difunta Correa Shrine.

Lake District
  Soaring volcanoes, shimmering lakes, sprawling forests and trout-rich rivers make the eastern Andean slopes a recreational paradise. The traditional focus is San Carlos de Bariloche, on Lago Nahuel Huapi, but many other places are more suitable for extended visits.

Península Valdés
  The unique, abundant wildlife and desert scenery of the Patagonian coast draw visitors to this popular wildlife reserve in Chubut province.

Moreno Glacier
  In Santa Cruz province, one of the world's few advancing glaciers is an awesome sight.

PLANNING

Buenos Aires' urban attractions transcend the seasons, but Patagonian destinations like the Moreno Glacier are best in summer. Iguazú is best in the southern winter or spring, when heat and humidity are less oppressive. Skiers enjoy the Andes from June to September.

Maps

The Automóvil Club Argentino (ACA) publishes excellent provincial road maps, indispensable for motorists and an excellent investment for others (members of ACA's overseas affiliates get discounts). Tourist office maps vary in quality but are usually free.

What to Bring

Argentina is a mostly temperate, midlatitude country, and seasonally appropriate clothing for North America or Europe will be equally suitable here. In the subtropical north, carry lightweight cottons, but at higher elevations in the Andes and Patagonia's high latitudes, warm clothing is important even in summer.

Argentines have no prejudice against backpackers, and many young Argentines take to Patagonia and other remote parts of the country on a shoestring themselves. Bring camping supplies from home, because generally you'll find that they're more expensive in Argentina.

TOURIST OFFICES

Almost every province and municipality has a tourist office, often on the main plaza or at the bus terminal. Each province has a tourist office in Buenos Aires. A few municipalities have separate offices. The Dirección Nacional de Turismo (☎ 011-4312-2232), Av Santa Fe 883 in Buenos Aires, is open weekdays 9 am to 5 pm.

ARGENTINA

Tourist Offices Abroad
Larger Argentine diplomatic missions, such as those in New York and Los Angeles, usually have a tourist representative in their delegation. Below are a few tourist information contacts.

Australia
(☎ 02-6282-4555)
MLC Tower, 1st floor, Woden, ACT 2606

Canada
(☎ 613-236-2351)
90 Sparks St, Suite 620,
Ottawa, Ontario K1P 514

UK
(☎ 020-7318-1340)
27 Three Kings Yard, London W1Y 1FL

USA
(☎ 212-603-0403)
12 W 56th St, New York, NY 10019
(☎ 323-954-9155)
5550 Wilshire Blvd, Suite 210,
Los Angeles, CA 90036

VISAS & DOCUMENTS
Passport
Passports are obligatory for all visitors except for citizens of bordering countries. Argentines are very document oriented, and a passport is essential for cashing traveler's checks, checking into a hotel, and many other routine activities.

Visas
Most foreigners do not need visas, but New Zealanders must pay US$24 for one. At major border crossings, officials issue a free, renewable 90-day tourist card, but at minor crossings, they often ignore this formality.

Tourist Card & Visa Extensions To get 90-day extensions, visit Migraciones (☎ 4312-8661), at Av Antártida Argentina 1365 in Buenos Aires or in provincial capitals, or provincial delegations of the Policía Federal.

EMBASSIES & CONSULATES
Argentine Embassies & Consulates
For lists of Argentina's embassies and consulates in neighboring countries, see those countries' Facts for the Visitor sections.

Australia
(☎ 02-6282-4555)
1st floor, MLC Tower, Woden, ACT 2606
Consulate:

(☎ 02-9251-3402)
Gold Fields House, 1 Alfred St,
Sydney, NSW 2000

Canada
(☎ 613-236-2351)
90 Sparks St, Suite 620,
Ottawa, Ontario K1P 5B4

France
(☎ 01 45 53 27 00)
6 rue Cimarosa, Paris 75016

Germany
(☎ 0228-228010)
Adenauerallee 50-52, 53113 Bonn

UK
Embassy:
(☎ 020-7318-1300)
65 Brook St, London W1Y 1YE
Consulate:
(☎ 020-7318-1340)
27 Three Kings Yard, London W1Y 1FL

USA
Embassy:
(☎ 202-238-6400)
1600 New Hampshire Ave NW,
Washington, DC 20009
Consulate:
(☎ 202-238-6460)
1718 Connecticut Ave NW,
Washington, DC 20009

Embassies & Consulates in Argentina
The Buenos Aires addresses below include the barrio.

Australia
(☎ 011-4777-6580)
Villanueva 1400, Palermo, Buenos Aires

Bolivia
(☎ 011-4381-0539)
Av Belgrano 1670, 1st floor,
Montserrat, Buenos Aires
(☎ 0387-421-1040)
Mariano Boedo 34, Salta
(☎ 0388-423-3156)
2nd floor, Güemes 779, San Salvador de Jujuy

Brazil
(☎ 011-4394-5264)
5th floor, Carlos Pellegrini 1363,
Retiro, Buenos Aires
(☎ 03772-425441)
Mitre 842, Paso de los Libres
(☎ 03752-424830)
Av Corrientes 1416, Posadas
(☎ 03757-420601)
Esquiú and El Mensú, Puerto Iguazú

Canada
(☎ 011-4805-3032)
Tagle 2828, Palermo, Buenos Aires

Chile
  (☎ 011-4394-6582)
  9th floor, San Martín 439, Buenos Aires
  (☎ 02944-422842)
  Juan Manuel de Rosas 180, Bariloche
  (☎ 0261-425-5024)
  Olascoaga 1071, Mendoza
  (☎ 02966-422364)
  Mariano Moreno 148, Río Gallegos
  (☎ 0387-431-1857)
  Santiago del Estero 965, Salta
  (☎ 02901-422177)
  Malvinas Argentinas 236, Ushuaia

France
  (☎ 011-4312-2409)
  3rd floor, Santa Fe 846, Retiro, Buenos Aires

Germany
  (☎ 011-4778-2500)
  Villanueva 1055, Palermo, Buenos Aires

Paraguay
  (☎ 011-4812-0075)
  Viamonte 1851, Balvanera, Buenos Aires
  (☎ 03752-423850)
  San Lorenzo between Santa Fe and Sarmiento,
  Posadas

Switzerland
  (☎ 011-4311-6491)
  10th floor, Santa Fe 846, Retiro

UK
  (☎ 011-4803-7070)
  Dr Luis Agote 2412, Palermo, Buenos Aires

Uruguay
  (☎ 011-4807-3040)
  Las Heras 1907, Recoleta, Buenos Aires
  (☎ 0345-421-0380)
  Pellegrini 709, Concordia
  (☎ 03446-426168)
  Rivadavia 510, Gualeguaychú

USA
  (☎ 011-4777-4533)
  Colombia 4300, Palermo, Buenos Aires

CUSTOMS

Officials usually defer to foreign visitors, but arrivals at Buenos Aires' Ezeiza airport may be asked about electronic equipment, which is much cheaper abroad. Arrivals from the central Andean countries may experience drug searches, and officials will confiscate fruits and vegetables from Chile or Brazil.

MONEY

Banknotes come in denominations of one, two, five, 10, 20, 50 and 100 pesos (Arg$). The peso is subdivided into 100 *centavos*, with coins of one, five, 10, 25 and 50 centavos.

Exchange Rates

Since its adoption in early 1992, the peso has remained on a par with the US dollar. Prices in this chapter are in US dollars, and will be the same in pesos unless the currency devalues. For latest trends, see *Ámbito Financiero* or the *Buenos Aires Herald*.

Approximate official rates at press time were as follows:

country	unit		peso
Australia	A$1	=	Arg$0.64
Canada	C$1	=	Arg$0.67
euro	€1	=	Arg$1.04
France	FF1	=	Arg$0.15
Germany	DM1	=	Arg$0.53
Japan	¥100	=	Arg$0.84
New Zealand	NZ$1	=	Arg$0.52
United Kingdom	UK£1	=	Arg$1.65
USA	US$1	=	Arg$1

Exchanging Money

Cash and ATMs Cash dollars can be exchanged at banks, *cambios* (exchange houses), hotels, travel agencies, in shops or on the street, but are also widely accepted in lieu of pesos. Traveler's checks, increasingly difficult to cash, suffer large commissions. *Cajeros automáticos* (ATMs) are abundant and can also be used for cash advances on major credit cards. Many but not all ATMs dispense either pesos or US dollars.

Credit Cards MasterCard and Visa are the main credit cards, but American Express and others are also valid in many places. MasterCard, affiliated with the local Argencard, is more widely accepted than Visa.

Many businesses add a *recargo* (surcharge) of 10% or more to credit purchases; conversely, some give cash discounts of 10% or more. Be aware of exchange-rate fluctuations, which can bring unpleasant (or pleasant) surprises when a transaction is finally posted to your overseas account.

Costs

The fixed exchange rate has driven some prices to European levels, but budget travel is not impossible. Modest lodging, food and transport are still reasonable; after the initial shock, arrivals from cheaper countries like Bolivia should adapt to local conditions, but allow at least US$30 to US$35 per day for food and lodging. Prices are subject to wild fluctuations.

Tipping & Bargaining

Waiters and waitresses are poorly paid; if you can afford to eat out, you can afford the customary 10% *propina*.

Bargaining is customary in the Noroeste, and in artisans markets countrywide. Even in Buenos Aires, leather shops may listen to offers. Late in the evening, hotels may give you a break on room prices; if you stay several days, they almost certainly will. Many better hotels will give discounts of up to 30% for cash payments. Be sure to ask.

POST & COMMUNICATIONS
Post

Encotesa (also known as Correo Argentino), the privatized postal service, has some of the world's highest overseas rates; surface mail is cheaper but less reliable. Send essential mail *certificado* (registered). Private couriers are expensive but far more dependable.

Encotesa charges for poste restante or *lista de correos* services. Arrange for delivery to a private address, such as a friend's residence or a hotel, to avoid this costly and bureaucratic annoyance.

Telephone

French and Spanish interests control telephone services through their local affiliates Telecom and Telefónica, but there are many private *locutorios* (long-distance offices). Argentina's country code is ☎ 54.

Reverse-charge (collect) calls to North America or Europe are possible from most (but not all) long-distance offices; be certain, or you may have to pay costs out of pocket. Though slowly falling, rates remain so high that even weekend and evening discounts are no bargain.

Most public telephones use tokens (*fichas* or *cospeles*), available from kiosks and telephone offices. Magnetic debit cards (*tarjetas*) are available in values of 25, 50, 100 and 150 fichas. The following toll-free numbers provide direct connections to home-country operators; for other countries dial Telintar at ☎ 000 (a number blocked at many locutorios that do permit access to 800 numbers). The first number for each country is for use from

public telephones; the second from private telephones.

Australia		☎ 0800-5556100
		☎ 0061-800-666111
Canada		☎ 0800-5555500
		☎ 001800-2221111
France		☎ 0800-5553300
		☎ 0033800-999111
Germany		☎ 0800-5554900
		☎ 0044800-999111
Italy		☎ 0800-5553900
		☎ 0039800-555111
UK	(British Telecom)	☎ 0800-5554401
		☎ 0044800-555111
	(Mercury)	☎ 0800-2224400
		☎ 0044800-333111
USA	(AT&T)	☎ 0800-2221001
		☎ 0800-5554288
		☎ 001800-2001111
	(MCI)	☎ 0800-5551002
		☎ 001800-3331111
	(Sprint)	☎ 0800-5551003
		☎ 001800-7771111

Fax & Email

Most locutorios offer fax services. In addition to fax services, Encotesa also provides telegraph and telex services.

Online access is rapidly increasing in Argentina, with a proliferation of Internet cafés and ISPs, but their cost is far higher than in the US or Europe. Recent reductions in phone charges for Internet connections, however, may result in reduced costs for end users.

INTERNET RESOURCES

A private Argentine Internet directory with huge numbers of links organized by category, including arts and humanities, news and media, science and the like (in Spanish and English) is:

Grippo – El Directorio de Argentina
    www.grippo.com/

A wide-ranging, sometimes trivial, but often polemical and irritating Usenet discussion group is soc.culture.argentina

BOOKS

Lonely Planet LP's *Argentina, Uruguay & Paraguay* travel guide and *Buenos Aires* city guide, both by Wayne Bernhardson, are worthwhile if you'd like to explore Argentina in greater depth.

Travel

In *The Voyage of the Beagle*, Darwin's account of the gauchos evokes a way of life to which Argentines still pay symbolic homage. Make a special effort to locate Lucas Bridges' *The Uttermost Part of the Earth*, about his life among the Indians of Tierra del Fuego. Bruce Chatwin's *In Patagonia* is one of the most informed syntheses of life and landscape for any part of the world. Paul Theroux's overrated and patronizing bestseller *The Old Patagonian Express* does not merit attention from serious travelers.

One of the more unusual pieces of recent travel literature is Ernesto Guevara's *The Motorcycle Diaries: A Journey Around South America*, an early 1950s account of two Argentine medical students who rode a dilapidated motorcycle across northern Patagonia and into Chile before abandoning it to continue their trip by stowing away on a coastal freighter. Guevara, who died in 1967 in Bolivia, is better known by the nickname 'Che,' a common Argentine interjection meaning, basically, 'hey!'

History & Politics

For colonial times, see the book section in the Facts about South America chapter. James Scobie's *Argentina: A City and a Nation* is a standard history. David Rock's *Argentina 1516-1987: From Spanish Colonization to the Falklands War & Alfonsín* is more comprehensive. DF Sarmiento's 19th-century classic *Life in the Argentine Republic in the Days of the Tyrants* is an eloquent, but often condescending, critique of Federalist caudillos and their followers.

Several books have compared Argentina with other commodity exporters. These include Carl Solberg's *The Prairies and the Pampas: Agrarian Policy in Canada and Argentina, 1880-1930*. On the gaucho, see Richard W Slatta's *Gauchos & the Vanishing Frontier*. Nicholas Shumway's *The Invention of Argentina* is an intellectual history of the country.

Among many books on the Peróns are Joseph Page's *Perón: A Biography* and Robert Crassweller's *Perón & the Enigma of Argentina*. Tomás Eloy Martínez's *The Perón Novel* is a fascinating fictionalized effort; Martínez also authored *Santa Evita* on Perón's flamboyant second wife. In his grim essay *The Return of Eva Perón*, VS Naipaul argues that state violence has long permeated Argentine politics.

Robert Potash has published two books on military interference in politics: *The Army & Politics in Argentina, 1928-1945: Yrigoyen to Perón* and *The Army & Politics in Argentina, 1945-1962: Perón to Frondizi*. A more general account, also dealing with Chile, Brazil and Paraguay, is César Caviedes' *The Southern Cone: Realities of the Authoritarian State*.

On the democratic transition, see Mónica Peralta-Ramos and Carlos Waisman's *From Military Rule to Liberal Democracy in Argentina*. David Erro's *Resolving the Argentine Paradox: Politics and Development, 1966-1992* provides a good analysis of contemporary politics and policies through the early Menem years, but may be overly optimistic about current trends.

The classic first-person account of 1970s state terrorism is Jacobo Timerman's *Prisoner Without a Name, Cell Without a Number*. See also John Simpson and Jana Bennett's *The Disappeared: Voices from a Secret War*. Horacio Verbitsky's *The Flight* (1996) relates the confessions of naval officer Adolfo Scilingo, who implicated himself and many others in Dirty War atrocities.

NEWSPAPERS

Buenos Aires' most important dailies are *La Prensa*, *La Nación* and the middle-of-the-road tabloid *Clarín*, which has an excellent Sunday cultural section. *Página 12* provides a refreshing leftist perspective and often breaks important stories that mainstream newspapers are slow to cover. *Ámbito Financiero* is the voice of the business sector, but it also provides good cultural coverage.

The English-language daily *Buenos Aires Herald* covers the world from an Anglo-Argentine perspective of business and commerce; the Sunday edition, which features perceptive summaries of Argentine politics and economics, also includes the *Guardian Weekly*. The *Herald* has a well-deserved reputation for editorial boldness, having condemned military and police abuses during the Dirty War.

RADIO & TV
On the AM band, nationwide Radio Rivadavia is a hybrid of top-40 and talk radio. At least a dozen FM stations in Buenos Aires specialize in styles from classical to pop to tango.

Legalization of nonstate TV and the growth of international cable services have brought a wider variety of programming to the small screen.

PHOTOGRAPHY
Film costs at least double what it does in North America or Europe, and processing is even dearer. Print film is widely available, slide film less so.

TIME
Argentina is three hours behind GMT/UTC.

ELECTRICITY
Electric current operates on 220V, 50Hz.

WEIGHTS & MEASURES
The metric system is in official use throughout the country. See the inside back cover for a conversion chart.

HEALTH
Argentina requires no vaccinations, but visitors to nearby tropical countries should consider measures against typhoid, malaria and other diseases (see Health in the Facts for the Visitor chapter); cholera is a concern in parts of Salta, Jujuy and the Chaco. Urban water supplies are usually potable, making salads safe to eat. Many prescription drugs are available over the counter.

USEFUL ORGANIZATIONS
Asatej (☎ 011-4311-6953, fax 011-4311-6840), Argentina's nonprofit student travel agency, is on the 3rd floor, Florida 835, 1005 Buenos Aires. The Administración de Parques Nacionales (☎ 011-4311-0303 interno 165), Santa Fe 690 in Buenos Aires, provides information on national parks. Another useful contact for conservationists is the wildlife organization Fundación Vida Silvestre Argentina (☎ 011-4331-4864), Defensa 245 in Buenos Aires.

BUSINESS HOURS
Traditionally, businesses open by 8 am, break several hours for lunch and a brief *siesta*, then reopen until 8 or 9 pm. This schedule is still common in the provinces, but government offices and many businesses in Buenos Aires have adopted an 8 am to 5 pm schedule for 'greater efficiency' and, especially in government, reduced corruption.

PUBLIC HOLIDAYS & SPECIAL EVENTS
Government offices and businesses close on national holidays. The following list does not include provincial holidays.

Año Nuevo (New Year's Day)
    January 1

Viernes Santo/Pascua (Good Friday/Easter)
    March/April (dates vary)

Día del Trabajador (Labor Day)
    May 1

Revolución de Mayo (May Revolution of 1810)
    May 25

Día de las Malvinas (Malvinas Day)
    June 10

Día de la Bandera (Flag Day)
    June 20

Día de la Independencia (Independence Day)
    July 9

Día de San Martín (Anniversary of
    San Martín's death)
    August 17

Día de la Raza (Columbus Day)
    October 12

Navidad (Christmas Day)
    December 25

ACTIVITIES
Skiing, though expensive, is gaining popularity, as are whitewater rafting, climbing, trekking, windsurfing and hang-gliding. The major ski resorts are Las Leñas in Mendoza province, Chapelco in Neuquén province, and Cerro Catedral near Bariloche, Río Negro province.

The major trekking areas are the Andean Lake District and the southern Patagonian cordillera, while whitewater is best around Mendoza and Bariloche.

ACCOMMODATIONS
Camping & Refugios
Budget travelers *must* consider camping to control expenses. Almost every major city and many smaller towns have woodsy sites where you can pitch a tent for less than US$5,

with hot showers, toilets, laundry, firepits and other facilities. Most Argentines arrive by car, but campgrounds are often central and backpackers are welcome.

Organized sites in national parks resemble those in cities and towns, and more isolated, rustic alternatives exist. Some parks have *refugios*, which are basic shelters for trekkers and climbers.

Hostels

The Red Argentina de Albergues Juveniles (RAAJ, ☎ 011-4381-9760), Moreno 1273 in Buenos Aires, is helping to expand and promote the Argentine hostel system. Travelers can also contact the Asociación Argentina de Albergues de la Juventud (AAAJ, ☎/fax 4476-1001), 2nd floor, Oficina 6, Talcahuano 214, in Buenos Aires, for information on Argentine youth hostels, but the latter is moribund in comparison with RAAJ. The two hostel representatives overlap affiliations with some hostels, but also represent others exclusively.

Hostels, some open in summer only, can be found in Buenos Aires, the Atlantic Coast, Sierra de la Ventana, Córdoba province, Villa Paranacito (Entre Ríos province), Puerto Iguazú, Mendoza, Salta and Jujuy provinces, the Patagonian Lake District and Tierra del Fuego province.

Casas de Familia

Tourist offices in small towns and some larger cities keep lists of inexpensive *casas de familia* (family houses) where you can experience local hospitality. These casas usually offer access to cooking and laundry facilities and hot showers.

Hospedajes, Pensiones & Residenciales

Differences among these types of permanent accommodation are ambiguous, but all may be called hotels. An *hospedaje* is usually a family home with extra bedrooms and shared bath. A *pensión* offers short-term accommodations in a family home, but may have permanent lodgers and serve meals. *Residenciales* are permanent businesses in buildings designed for short stays. Rooms and furnishings are modest; a few have private baths, but toilet and shower facilities are usually shared with other guests.

Hotels

Hotels proper vary from basic one-star accommodation to five-star luxury, but many one-stars are better values than three- or four-star places. Rooms generally have private bath, often telephone, sometimes *música funcional* (elevator Muzak) or TV. Most have a *confitería* or restaurant; breakfast may be included. Those in higher categories have room and laundry service, swimming pools, bars, shops and other luxuries.

FOOD

Traditionally, even ideologically, Argentines consider *carne* (meat) essential to any meal. Carnivores will devour the *parrillada*, a mixed grill of steak, other beef cuts, and offal.

Italian influence is apparent in dishes like spaghetti, lasagna and ravioli, but don't overlook the inexpensive staple *ñoquis* (gnocchi). Since the early 1980s, vegetarian fare has acquired a niche in Buenos Aires and a few other cities. Chinese *tenedor libre* (all you can eat) is often a great value.

From Mendoza northward, Middle Eastern food is common. The Andean Northwest is notable for spicy dishes like those of Bolivia or Peru, while Mesopotamian river fish is truly delectable. In Patagonia, lamb often replaces beef in the parrillada. Trout, boar and venison are also regional specialties.

Budget travelers in the north should frequent central markets for cheap meals; *rotiserías* (delis) have quality chicken, empanadas, pies and *fiambres* (processed meats) for a fraction of restaurant prices.

For fast food, try bus terminals, train stations or the *comedor*, which usually has a limited menu with simple but filling fixed-price meals. Comedores also serve *minutas* (short orders) like steak, eggs, *milanesa* (breaded steak), salad and fries.

Confiterías usually serve sandwiches such as *lomito* (steak), *panchos* (hot dogs) and hamburgers. *Restaurantes* have larger menus, professional waiters and more elaborate decor.

Cafés are important gathering places, the site for everything from marriage proposals to business deals and revolutions. Many Argentines dawdle for hours over a single cup of coffee, but simple meals are available. Cafés also serve alcohol.

Bars are establishments for drinking alcohol. In small towns, they're a male domain and women usually avoid them.

Breakfast

Argentine breakfasts are scanty. Most common is coffee, tea or *mate* with *tostadas* (toast), *manteca* (butter) and *mermelada* (jam). In cafés, *medialunas* (croissants), either sweet or *saladas* (plain), accompany *café con leche* (coffee with milk). A *tostado* is a thin-crust toasted sandwich with ham and cheese.

Snacks

The *empanada* is a pie or turnover with vegetables, hard-boiled egg, olive, beef, chicken, ham and cheese or other filling. Empanadas *al horno* (baked) are lighter than *fritas* (fried).

Pizzerias sell cheap slices at the counter, but there are more options when seated for an entire pizza. Common slices include *fugazza*, a cheap and delicious cheeseless variety with sweet onions, or *fugazzeta* (mozzarella added), which is sometimes eaten with *fainá*, a baked chickpea (garbanzo) dough.

Lunch & Dinner

Argentines compensate for light breakfasts with enormous lunches and dinners (the latter never before 9 pm, often much later). An important custom is the *sobremesa*, dallying at the table to discuss family matters or events of the day.

An *asado* or parrillada is the standard main course, prepared over hot coals and accompanied by the marinade *chimichurri*, with fries or salad on the side. Carnivores will savor the tender, juicy *bife de chorizo*, but try also *bife de lomo* (short loin), *bife de costilla* or *chuleta* (T-bone), *asado de tira* (roast rib) or *vacío* (sirloin). *Matambre relleno* is stuffed and rolled flank steak, baked or eaten cold as an appetizer. Offal dishes include *chinchulines* (small intestines), *tripa gorda* (large intestine) and *morcilla* (blood sausage).

Most restaurants prepare beef *cocido* (well done), but serve it *jugoso* (rare) or *a punto* (medium) on request. *Bife a caballo* comes with two eggs and chips.

Carbonada is a beef stew of rice, potatoes, sweet potatoes, maize, squash, and chopped apples and peaches. *Puchero* is a casserole with beef, chicken, bacon, sausage, blood sausage, maize, peppers, tomatoes, onions, cabbage, sweet potatoes and squash. The cook may add garbanzos or other beans, accompanied by rice cooked in the broth.

Pollo (chicken) sometimes accompanies the parrillada, but usually comes separately, with fries or salad. The most common fish is *merluza* (hake), usually fried in batter and served with mashed potatoes.

Desserts

Fresh fruit is the usual *postre* at home; in restaurants, diners choose *ensalada de fruta* (fruit salad), *flan* (egg custard) or *queso y dulce* (cheese with preserved fruit, also known as *postre vigilante*). Flan comes topped with *crema* (whipped cream) or *dulce de leche* (caramelized milk).

Ice Cream

Argentina's Italian-derived *helados* may be South America's best. Smaller *heladerías* make their own in small batches – look for the words *elaboración propia* or *elaboración artesanal*.

DRINKS
Soft Drinks

Argentines drink prodigious amounts of sugary soft drinks. If carbonated *(con gas)* mineral water is unavailable, *soda,* often in siphon bottles, is usually the cheapest thirst-quencher.

Juices & Licuados

For fresh orange juice, ask for *jugo de naranja exprimido* to avoid canned juice. *Pomelo* (grapefruit), *limón* (lemon) and *ananá* (pineapple) are also common. *Jugo de manzana* (apple juice) is a specialty of northern Patagonia's Río Negro valley.

Licuados are milk-blended fruit drinks. Common flavors include banana, *durazno* (peach) and *pera* (pear).

Coffee, Tea & Chocolate

Foreigners should not decline an invitation for mate ('Paraguayan tea'). Caffeine addicts may overdose; even in the smallest town, coffee will be espresso. *Café chico* is thick, dark coffee in a very small cup. *Cortado* is a small coffee with a touch of milk, usually served in a glass; *cortado doble* is a larger portion. *Café con leche* (a *latté*) is served for breakfast only; after lunch or dinner, request a cortado.

Tea usually comes with lemon slices. If you want milk, avoid *té con leche*, a tea bag immersed in tepid milk; rather, ask for *un poquito de leche*. For breakfast, try a *submarino*, a semisweet chocolate bar dissolved in steamed milk.

Alcoholic Drinks

Beer, wine, whiskey and gin should satisfy most drinkers, but *ginebra bols* (which differs from gin) and *caña* (cane alcohol) are specialties. Both Quilmes and Bieckert are popular beers; in bars or cafés, ask for *chopp* (draft or lager).

Argentine wines are less famous than Chilean, but both reds *(tintos)* and whites *(blancos)* are excellent. When prices on everything else skyrocket, wines miraculously remain reasonable. The major wine-producing areas are near Mendoza, San Juan, La Rioja and Salta. Among the best known brands are Orfila, Suter, San Felipe, Santa Ana and Etchart.

ENTERTAINMENT

Argentines are fond of music and dancing. Dance clubs in Buenos Aires and the provinces get going between about midnight and 2 am and don't close until after sunrise. Live music is best in the tango, rock and jazz clubs of Buenos Aires. Live theater, both the well-supported official variety and low-budget alternatives, is well attended and of good quality. Cinema is experiencing a revival in the capital and larger cities, where major cinemas show the latest films from Europe, the USA and Latin America, and repertory houses, cultural centers and universities screen classics and less-commercial releases.

SPECTATOR SPORTS

Rugby, basketball, field hockey, tennis, polo, golf, motor racing, skiing, cycling and fishing are popular participant sports, but soccer is an obsession – with teams like River Plate and Boca Juniors (based in Buenos Aires' immigrant Italian barrio of La Boca) all over the country. Professional soccer is world-class, but many Argentine stars play for higher salaries in Europe. The national team has twice won the World Cup.

SHOPPING

Argentine leather goods – especially shoes – are famous, and many Buenos Aires shops cater to the tourist trade. Shopkeepers are aggressive but sometimes open to bargaining. Bariloche is well known for woolen clothing. Mate paraphernalia make good souvenirs, and the variety of handicrafts found in *ferias* (artisans markets) throughout the country is extensive. Buenos Aires has a superb selection of bookstores, but foreign-language books are usually expensive.

Getting There & Away

AIR
Airports & Airlines

Buenos Aires' Aeropuerto Internacional Ministro Pistarini (commonly known as Ezeiza) is the main international airport. Some regional flights use close-in Aeroparque Jorge Newbery, commonly known as Aeroparque. Many other cities have international airports, but serve mostly domestic destinations.

Many major European and North American airlines, plus a handful of African and Asian carriers, serve Buenos Aires. There are also, of course, airlines from other South American countries.

Departure Tax

International passengers leaving from Ezeiza pay a US$18 departure tax, also payable in local currency, but a 21% IVA is due to raise this to US$21.78. On flights to Uruguay, the tax is only US$5, but again this is likely to increase by 21%.

Chile

Many airlines fly between Ezeiza and Santiago (Chile), but only LanChile flies to Mendoza. Regional carriers connect Bariloche to Puerto Montt (Chile) and Neuquén and San Martín de los Andes to Temuco (Chile). Provincial airlines fly between Punta Arenas, Chile, and destinations in Santa Cruz province and Argentine Tierra del Fuego.

Bolivia

La Paz is the main destination, but some flights go to Santa Cruz de la Sierra and

Cochabamba, occasionally via Salta, Tucumán and Jujuy.

Paraguay

Asunción is the only Paraguayan city with connections to Argentina.

Brazil

From both Ezeiza and Aeroparque, Rio de Janeiro and São Paulo are the main destinations, with Porto Alegre and Florianópolis secondary. Flights from Córdoba and Rosario also go to Rio and São Paulo, while some from Ezeiza to Montevideo continue to Brazil.

Uruguay

There are numerous flights from Aeroparque to Montevideo; the only other Uruguayan destination is Punta del Este. Some long-distance international flights continue from Ezeiza to Montevideo.

LAND
Chile

The very long border between Argentina and Chile has many crossings. For details, see the Getting There & Away section for Chile, where a map shows many Lake District routes. Except in Patagonia, every land border involves crossing the Andes. The only train, from Baquedano (Chile) to Salta (Argentina), is not a regular passenger service.

Bolivia

Buses from Bolivia to Argentina include the following:

La Quiaca to Villazón Many buses go from Jujuy and Salta to La Quiaca, where you must walk or take a taxi across the Bolivian border.

Aguas Blancas to Bermejo From Orán, reached by bus from Salta or Jujuy, take a bus to Aguas Blancas and then Bermejo, where you can catch a bus to Tarija.

Pocitos to Yacuiba Buses from Jujuy or Salta go to Tartagal and then on to the Bolivian border at Pocitos/Yacuiba, where there are trains to Santa Cruz de la Sierra.

Paraguay

Buses from Paraguay to Argentina include:

Clorinda to Asunción Frequent buses cross the Puente Internacional Ignacio de Loyola to the Paraguayan capital.

Posadas to Encarnación Vehicles use the Puente Internacional Beato Roque González, but launches still connect the Paraná river docks.

Puerto Iguazú to Ciudad del Este Frequent buses connect Puerto Iguazú (Misiones province) to Ciudad del Este (Paraguay) via Foz do Iguaçu (Brazil).

Brazil

The most common crossing is from Puerto Iguazú (Argentina) to Foz do Iguaçu (Brazil), but there are bridges from Paso de los Libres (Corrientes province) to Uruguaiana (Brazil) and Santo Tomé (Corrientes) to São Borja (Brazil).

Uruguay

Buses from Uruguay to Argentina include:

Gualeguaychú to Fray Bentos Several buses daily cross the Puente Internacional Libertador General San Martín.

Colón to Paysandú The Puente Internacional General José Gervasio Artigas links these two cities.

Concordia to Salto The bridge across the Salto Grande hydroelectric complex, north of Concordia, unites these two cities.

RIVER
Departure Tax

Users of Buenos Aires' hydrofoil port at Dársena Norte pay a departure tax of US$6 to Colonia or US$10 to Montevideo.

Boats ply the following routes from Argentina to Uruguay:

Buenos Aires to Montevideo High-speed ferries sail from Buenos Aires to the Uruguayan capital in just 2½ hours.

Buenos Aires to Piriápolis Summer weekend ferries link the Argentine capital and Uruguayan resort.

Buenos Aires to Colonia Morning and evening ferries sail from Buenos Aires to Colonia, Uruguay (2½ hours). Hydrofoils take only 45 minutes.

Tigre to Carmelo Launches cross the Río de la Plata estuary daily from Tigre, a Buenos Aires suburb.

ORGANIZED TOURS

Travel agents specializing in South America (see the Getting There & Away chapter) offer tours to Argentina, usually including Buenos Aires, Iguazú Falls, and parts of Patagonia, usually the Moreno Glacier and Tierra del Fuego. Some companies specialize in outdoor activities or ecotourism.

Getting Around

AIR

Argentine air traffic, routes and fares have undergone a major transformation since the privatization of Aerolíneas Argentinas (domestic and international routes) and Austral (domestic routes only). While these two airlines have the most extensive services, some existing secondary airlines have expanded routes, others have come into existence and both have undercut the fare structure of the established carriers.

Líneas Aéreas Privadas Argentinas (LAPA) competes with Aerolíneas and Austral on many routes, but has lower capacity. Dinar Líneas Aéreas flies to northwestern Argentina and a few other spots. Andesmar and Southern Winds link cities throughout the north and west of the country, offering minimal connections to Buenos Aires.

Líneas Aéreas del Estado (LADE), the air force's passenger service, serves mostly Patagonian destinations, but declining state subsidies have meant reduced services. Transportes Aéreos Neuquén (TAN) has fairly extensive schedules from Córdoba in the north to Bariloche in the south, but other Patagonian carriers have smaller and slower planes. In summer and around holidays, all Patagonian flights may be heavily booked; early reservations are advisable.

Air Passes

Aerolíneas Argentinas' 'Visit Argentina' fare, also valid on Austral, lets you fly anywhere served by either airline so long as you make no more than one stop in any city except for an immediate connection, but it's more expensive and less flexible than in the past. The pass is a good value if you are coming from abroad for a short time, but if your schedule is flexible you can arrange cheaper discount fares on certain routes.

Four flight coupons, valid 30 days, cost US$420; additional coupons, to a maximum total of eight, cost US$110 each. One coupon must be used for each numbered flight, so that a flight from Puerto Iguazú to Bariloche, for example, requires two coupons because there's a change of planes at Aeroparque. Conditions permit one change of itinerary without charge, but each additional change costs US$50. International passengers arriving on other airlines pay US$500 for coupons, plus US$130 for each additional coupon.

An alternative, the mileage-based Mercosur pass, allows travelers to visit areas in Brazil, Paraguay, Argentina and Uruguay on any major carrier in those countries, but must include at least one international flight. Properly organized, this can be cheaper than the Visit Argentina pass, but you need a patient travel agent to design the optimum itinerary.

Timetables

All Argentine airlines publish detailed timetables to which they adhere closely except LADE, which may leave early if its flight is full or nearly full – don't be getting to the airport late. There's a list of principal airline offices, both international and domestic, in the Buenos Aires section, and addresses of regional offices appear in each city entry.

Domestic Departure Tax

Argentine domestic flights carry a departure tax of US$6.05, including 21% IVA. At Chapelco (San Martín de los Andes), Reconquista and Goya, the tax is traditionally lower.

BUS

Most cities have consolidated terminals, but in some, bus companies are clustered downtown. Fares and schedules are usually posted prominently. Long-distance buses are fast and comfortable, have toilets, and serve coffee or snacks. Some provide meals, but others stop at roadside restaurants.

Some buses have *coche cama* recliners at premium prices, but regular buses are fine even on very long trips. Local or provincial *común* services are more crowded, make frequent stops and take longer than *expreso* buses.

Reservations

During holiday periods or on routes with limited seats, buy tickets in advance. The winter holidays around Independence Day (July 9), and international services from Salta to Calama (Chile) and from Comodoro Rivadavia (Chubut province) to Coyhaique (Chile), are often fully booked.

Costs

Bus fares are about US$0.04 per kilometer, but about US$3 per hour is a good rule of thumb. University students and teachers may receive 20% discounts, for cash only.

TRAIN

Most passenger rail services have ceased, but Buenos Aires province operates Ferrocarril Roca services from Buenos Aires to Mar del Plata and the beach resorts, Río Negro province operates the same line from Viedma to Bariloche, and Tucumán province runs the Ferrocarril Mitre to Rosario, Santiago del Estero and San Miguel de Tucumán. Chubut province runs the famous narrow-gauge line from Esquel to El Maitén.

TAXI

In areas like Patagonia, where public transport can be scarce, try hiring a cab with driver to visit remote places. If you bargain, this can be cheaper than a rental car.

CAR & MOTORCYCLE

Especially in Patagonia, where distances are great and buses infrequent, even budget travelers may splurge on an occasional rental. The price of *nafta* (gasoline) has risen to between US$0.80 and US$1 per liter in much of the country, though in Patagonia (from El Bolsón southward on Ruta Nacional 258, and south from Sierra Grande on RN 3), subsidies reduce it to about half that. Argentina requires an International or Inter-American Driving Permit in addition to your national or state driving license. Insurance is obligatory.

Argentine highways consist of national routes (Rutas Nacionales, abbreviated RN in this book) and provincial routes (Rutas Provinciales, abbreviated RP).

Road Rules

Police rarely patrol the highways, where reckless drivers often cause high-speed, head-on crashes, but they do conduct meticulous document and equipment checks at highway junctions and checkpoints. Minor equipment violations carry large fines but are usually opportunities for graft. If uncertain of your rights, calmly state your intention to contact your consulate. Offer a *coima* (bribe) only if certain that it is 'appropriate' and unavoidable.

Automóvil Club Argentino (ACA)

The Automóvil Club Argentino (ACA) has offices, service stations and garages throughout the country, offering free road service and towing in and around major cities. ACA also recognizes members of its overseas affiliates, such as the American Automobile Association (AAA), as equivalent to its own members and grants them the same privileges, including discounts on maps, accommodations, camping, tours and other services.

ACA's headquarters (☎ 011-4802-6061) is at Av del Libertador 1850, Palermo, Buenos Aires.

Rental

Major international agencies have offices in Buenos Aires, major cities and other tourist areas. To rent a car, you must have a valid driving license, be 25 years of age and leave a deposit or present a credit card.

Even at minor agencies, rental charges are now very high, the cheapest and smallest vehicles going for about US$27 per day plus US$0.27 per kilometer (you can sometimes negotiate a lower rate by paying cash rather than by credit card), even higher in Patagonia. Camping rather than staying in hotels offsets some of these costs.

Purchase

For extended visits, buying a car is worth considering, though any used car is a risk, especially on rugged back roads. Argentina's automobile industry has created a reserve of decent used cars, mostly Peugeots and Ford Falcons. A usable car will cost at least US$3500, and prices will be higher for a *gasolero*, which uses cheaper diesel fuel.

Purchasers must deal with an exasperating bureaucracy. Be sure of the title (*tarjeta verde*, or 'green card') and that license tax payments are up to date. Obtain a notarized document authorizing use of the vehicle, since the bureaucracy moves slowly in changing vehicle titles.

Some customs officials may refuse foreigners permission to take a car out of the country, even with a notarized authorization, but certain frontier posts (such as Puerto Iguazú and Bariloche/Osorno) appear to be flexible. Contact your consulate for assistance and advice.

BICYCLE

Recreational cycling is increasingly popular among Argentines, and increasing numbers of travelers are enjoying cycling around the country. Racing bicycles are suitable for paved roads, but on graveled roads a mountain bike *(todo terreno)* is advisable.

The best routes are around Bariloche and in the Andean Northwest: the highway from Tucumán to Tafí del Valle, the direct road from Salta to Jujuy, and the Quebrada de Cafayate are exceptionally beautiful rides on generally good surfaces. Drawbacks include the wind (a nuisance that can slow progress to a crawl in Patagonia) and reckless motorists. Less-traveled secondary roads, carrying little traffic, are excellent alternatives. Rental bikes are increasingly common in tourist areas.

HITCHHIKING

Private cars are often stuffed with families, but at *servicentros* on the outskirts of large cities, where truckers refuel their vehicles, it's worth soliciting a ride. In Patagonia, distances are great and vehicles few, so expect long waits and carry snack foods and warm, windproof clothing. Especially in the desert north, carry extra water as well.

BOAT

Opportunities for internal river travel are few. A passenger ferry runs from Rosario (Santa Fe province) across the Paraná to Victoria (Entre Ríos province). There are also launches around the Paraná delta from Tigre, a Buenos Aires suburb.

LOCAL TRANSPORT
Bus

Even small towns have good bus systems. On boarding, indicate your destination and the driver will tell you the fare and issue a ticket, which may be inspected en route. A few cities use *fichas* (tokens) in lieu of cash, and some have automatic ticket machines or magnetic fare cards. Pay attention to placards indicating a bus's ultimate destination, since identically numbered buses may cover slightly different routes.

Train

Private operators have assumed control of commuter trains from Constitución, Retiro and Once stations to suburbs of Buenos Aires. There are also trains from Rosario to its suburbs.

Underground

Buenos Aires' aged but improving Subte is an excellent way of getting around the city center.

Taxi & Remise

Buenos Aires' reasonably priced taxis have digital-read-out meters. A ride in the downtown area will run between US$2 and US$4. It's customary to leave small change as a tip. *Remises* are radio taxis, marginally cheaper than regular taxis, but without meters, so agree on the fare in advance. Outside Buenos Aires, taxi meters are generally less common.

ORGANIZED TOURS

Companies based in Buenos Aires arrange tours within Argentina. Small operators run tours of local attractions, particularly to out-of-the-way parks and wilderness areas difficult to reach. These are mentioned in individual geographical entries.

Buenos Aires

Argentina's capital and largest city is not part of Buenos Aires province, but a separate federal district, the Capital Federal. Most destinations in Buenos Aires province are covered in later sections on the Atlantic Coast and the Pampas.

History

In 1536, Pedro de Mendoza's 1600 men camped on a bluff above the Río de la Plata, but within five years, Querandí resistance forced them out for nearly half a century.

Spanish mercantile restrictions slowed Buenos Aires' growth, but frustrated criollo merchants exchanged contraband with the Portuguese and British. Independence, in 1816, did not resolve conflicts between conservative provincial landowners and residents of Buenos Aires, who maintained an international orientation, both commercially and intellectually. European immigration swelled the population from 90,000 at the overthrow of caudillo Juan Manuel de Rosas (in 1852) to over a million by the turn of the century, when Buenos Aires was Latin America's largest city.

As families crowded into substandard housing, industry kept wages low, and labor became increasingly militant. In 1919, military suppression of a metalworkers' strike in what became known as La Semana Trágica (The Tragic Week) set an unfortunate precedent for coming decades. In the 1930s, a massive modernization program obliterated narrow colonial streets to create major avenues like Santa Fe, Córdoba and Corrientes.

After WWII, Gran (Greater) Buenos Aires absorbed many once-distant suburbs, and now faces massive pollution, noise, decaying infrastructure and declining public services, unemployment and underemployment, and spreading shantytowns. Since the restoration of democracy in 1984, though, Buenos Aires has enjoyed freewheeling political dialogue, the publishing industry has rebounded, and arts and music flourish within economic limits. Buenos Aires may have seen better days, but survives to offer a rich urban experience.

Orientation

Buenos Aires' size is intimidating, but a brief orientation suffices for its compact downtown and more accessible *barrios* (boroughs or neighborhoods). The major thoroughfare is broad Av 9 de Julio, which runs from Plaza Constitución to Av del Libertador and exclusive northern suburbs. Except for Av 9 de Julio, all north-south street names change at Av de Mayo.

Most *porteños* (residents of Buenos Aires) 'belong' to barrios that tourists rarely see, but five main ones contain most of the capital's attractions. The *microcentro* (north of Av de Mayo and east of Av 9 de Julio) includes popular tourist areas like the Florida and Lavalle pedestrian malls, Plaza San Martín, and the commercial and entertainment areas of Corrientes, Córdoba and Santa Fe. Beyond Santa Fe are chic Recoleta/Barrio Norte and Palermo, while south of Plaza de Mayo are colorful, working-class San Telmo and La Boca.

Information

Tourist Offices All tourist offices have English-speaking staff. The Dirección Nacional de Turismo (☎ 011-4312-2232), Av Santa Fe 883, is open weekdays 9 am to 5 pm.

In the Centro Cultural San Martín at Sarmiento 1551, 5th floor, the municipal Direc-ción General de Turismo, (☎ 011-4476-3612, 4371-1496) organizes free weekend guided walks. There's a municipal tourist kiosk on the Florida *peatonal* (pedestrian mall) near Diagonal Roque Sáenz Peña (open 10 am to 6 pm weekdays, 2 to 6 pm weekends and holidays), and an office in the Galerías Pacífico, at Av Córdoba and Florida (open weekdays 10 am to 4 pm, Saturday 11 am to 6 pm). Both distribute excellent pocket-size maps in English and Spanish, as well as other brochures.

Metrovías, the private Subte operator, publishes an excellent pocket-size map of its service area, available free from most public information offices. For visitors spending some time here, Lumi Transportes' *Capital Federal* (US$10), in compact, ring-binder format, indexes all city streets and bus routes.

Money Dozens of cambios line Calle San Martín, south of Av Corrientes, but the only real reason to use them is to change traveler's checks. American Express, Arenales 707, cashes its own traveler's checks without commission. Visa and MasterCard holders can get cash advances at most downtown banks, and ATMs are ubiquitous.

Post The Correo Central is at Sarmiento 189. For international parcels weighing over 1kg, go to the Correo Postal Internacional, on Antártida Argentina near Retiro station.

Telephone & Fax Public phones are numerous. For local calls, carry a pocketful of cospeles, available from kiosks, or a magnetic phonecard. Telefónica's long-distance office at Corrientes 701 is open 24 hours, but there are many private locutorios.

Email & Internet Access The 2600 Internet Café (☎ 011-4807-4929), Scalabrini Ortiz 3191 in Palermo, charges US$8 per hour. Try also the Leru Bar (☎ 011-4383-4940) at Rivadavia 1475 in San Nicolás (Congreso).

Travel Agencies Asatej (☎ 011-4311-6953), the nonprofit student travel agency, is on the 3rd floor, Oficina 319-B, at Florida 835. Open weekdays 11 am to 7 pm, it seeks out the cheapest airfares, arranges bargain tours, and has a brochure of discount offers for ISIC cardholders.

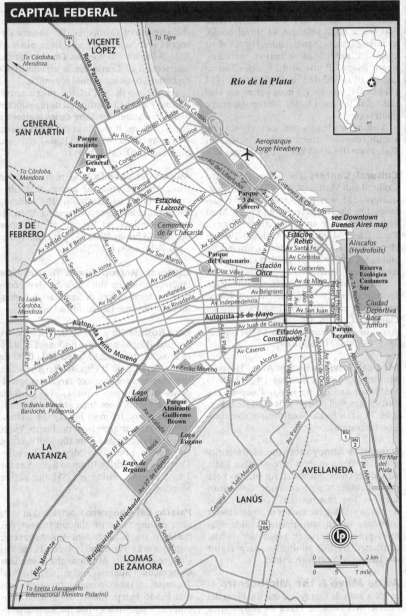

CAPITAL FEDERAL

To Tigre

VICENTE LÓPEZ

To Córdoba, Mendoza

Ruta Panamericana

Río de la Plata

Av B Mitre

Av General Paz

Av Int Cantilo

GENERAL SAN MARTÍN

Parque Sarmiento

Av Ricardo Balbín

Crisólogo Larralde

Monroe

Parque General Paz

Av Congreso

Av Cabildo

Aeroparque Jorge Newbery

To Córdoba, Mendoza

Av de los Constituyentes

Av Moroni

Pampa

Av del Libertador

Av Costanera R Obligado

Av Figueroa Alcorta

8

Av Dorrego

Estación F Lacroze

Parque 3 de Febrero

see Downtown Buenos Aires map

3 DE FEBRERO

Av SM del Carril

Av F Beiró

Av Nazca

Av San Martín

Cementerio de la Chacarita

Av Scalabrini Ortiz

Av Díaz

Av Pueyrredón

Estación Retiro

Av Santa Fe

Aliscafos (Hydrofoils)

Av Segurola

Av A Jonte

Parque del Centenario

Av Córdoba

Reserva Ecológica Costanera Sur

Av Lope de Vega

Av Gaona

Av Díaz Vélez

Estación Once

Av Corrientes

Av Juan B Justo

Avellaneda

Av de Mayo

Ciudad Deportiva Boca Juniors

To Luján, Córdoba, Mendoza

Av Rivadavia

Av Independencia

Av Belgrano

Av 9 de Julio

Av Paseo Colón

Av Ing Huergo

Av TA Rodríguez

Autopista 25 de Mayo

Entre Ríos

Av San Juan

Autopista Perito Moreno

Av Juan de Garay

Parque Lezama

General Paz

Av Emilio Castro

Av Juan B Alberdi

Estación Constitución

Av La Plata

Av Cadañares

Av Caseros

Av Patricios

Av Montes de Oca

Av Almirante Brown

To Bahía Blanca, Bariloche, Patagonia

Av Eva Perón

Av Perito Moreno

Av Amancio Alcorta

Av Vélez Sarsfield

LA MATANZA

Lago Soldati

Parque Almirante Guillermo Brown

Av Escalada

Av Pavón

Av Roca

Lago Lugano

AVELLANEDA

To Mar del Plata

Lago de Regatas

Av 27 de Febrero

Av FF de la Cruz

General J de San Martín

LANÚS

Río Matanza

Rectificación del Riachuelo

10 de Septiembre 1861

LOMAS DE ZAMORA

To Ezeiza (Aeropuerto Internacional Ministro Pistarini)

0   1   2 km

0   .5   1 mile

Bookstores Buenos Aires' landmark bookstore El Ateneo (☎ 011-4325-6801), Florida 340, has a large selection of travel books, including Lonely Planet guides. For the most complete guidebook selection, including nearly every LP title, visit Librerías Turísticas (☎ 011-4963-2855), at Paraguay 2457 (Subte: Pueyrredón), whose prices are also the most reasonable for foreign-language guidebooks.

Visiting academics and curiosity-seekers should explore the basement stacks at Platero (☎ 011-4382-2215), Talcahuano 485.

Cultural Centers The high-rise Centro Cultural San Martín (☎ 011-4374-1251), Sarmiento 1551, has free or inexpensive galleries, live theater, lectures and films. Most visitors enter from Corrientes, between Paraná and Montevideo. At Junín 1930 in Recoleta, the Centro Cultural Ciudad de Buenos Aires (☎ 011-4803-1041) also offers free or inexpensive events.

The US Information Agency's Biblioteca Lincoln, which carries *The New York Times*, the *Washington Post* and English-language magazines, is in the Instituto Cultural Argentino-Norteamericano (☎ 011-4322-3855, 4322-4557), Maipú 672.

Medical Services Buenos Aires' Hospital Municipal Juan Fernández (☎ 011-4801-5555) is at Av Cerviño 3356 in Palermo. The British Hospital (☎ 011-4304-1081) is at Perdriel 74, a few blocks southwest of Constitución train station.

Dangers & Annoyances Personal security is a lesser concern than in most other Latin American cities, but watch for pickpockets, purse-snatchers and common diversions such as the 'inadvertent' collision that results in spilling ice cream or some similar substance on an unsuspecting visitor, who loses precious personal possessions while distracted by the apologetic perpetrator working in concert with a thief.

Av de Mayo & the Microcentro

In 1580, Juan de Garay laid out the Plaza del Fuerte that became **Plaza de Mayo** after 1810. Most public buildings date from the 19th century, when Av de Mayo first connected Plaza de Mayo to **Plaza del Congreso**. Av Santa Fe is the most fashionable shopping area, and Florida and Lavalle are pedestrian malls. Demolition of older buildings created the avenues of Corrientes (the theater district), Córdoba and Santa Fe. Even wider Av 9 de Julio, with its famous **Obelisco** at the intersection of Corrientes, is a pedestrian's nightmare, but has a tunnel beneath it.

At the north end of the microcentro, beyond **Plaza San Martín** and its magnificent *ombú* tree, stands the **Torre de los Ingleses**, a Big Ben clone. It stands in the **Plaza Fuerza Aérea Argentina** (Air Force Plaza), renamed thus after the Falklands War.

Museo del Cabildo Modern construction truncated the colonial arches that once crossed Plaza de Mayo, but the building itself remains more interesting than its scanty exhibits. At Bolívar 65, it's open Tuesday to Friday 12:30 to 7 pm, Sunday 3 to 7 pm. Admission is US$1.

Catedral Metropolitana This religious landmark, also on the Plaza de Mayo, contains the tomb of José de San Martín, Argentina's most venerated historical figure.

Casa Rosada Off-limits during the Proceso, the presidential palace is no longer a place to avoid. Its basement **Museo de la Casa de Gobierno**, entered at Hipólito Yrigoyen 219, provides a chronology of Argentine presidents, but nothing after 1966 – perhaps because events since then are too painfully contemporary. Its most interesting feature, though, is the catacombs of the Fuerte Viejo, a colonial ruin dating from the 18th century.

Museum hours are Monday, Tuesday, Thursday and Friday 10 am to 6 pm, Sunday 2 to 6 pm. Admission is US$1 but is free Monday.

Palacio del Congreso Completed in 1906 after costing twice its allotted budget, this building set a precedent for Argentine public-works projects. It faces Plaza del Congreso and its **Monumento a los Dos Congresos** (Buenos Aires in 1810 and Tucumán in 1816), commemorating events that led to independence. Its granite steps symbolize the Andes, while the fountain represents the Atlantic Ocean.

Teatro Colón Since its opening in 1908, visitors have marveled at the massive Colón

(☎ 011-4382-6632), a world-class facility for opera, ballet and classical music. Occupying an entire block bounded by Libertad, Tucumán, Viamonte and Cerrito (Av 9 de Julio), the imposing seven-story building seats 2500 spectators and has standing room for another 1000.

Guided visits (US$5) take place hourly between 11 am and 3 pm weekdays and 9 am and noon Saturday. They are offered in Spanish, English and sometimes in other languages. There are no January tours.

Montserrat & San Telmo

South of Plaza de Mayo, Montserrat (also known as Catedral al Sur) and parts of San Telmo are still an artists quarter with low rents. The area saw rugged street fighting in 1806 and 1807, when a criollo militia drove British troops back to their ships. It was fashionable until a 19th-century yellow-fever epidemic drove the porteño elite to higher ground and many houses became *conventillos*, sheltering immigrants in cramped quarters with poor sanitary facilities – conditions that have not totally disappeared.

The **Manzana de las Luces** (Block of Enlightenment), bounded by Alsina, Bolívar, Perú and Moreno, includes the Jesuit **Iglesia San Ignacio**, Buenos Aires' oldest church. At Defensa and Humberto Primo, **Plaza Dorrego** hosts the Feria de San Telmo, the famous Sunday flea market. Four blocks south, at Defensa and Brasil, believed to be the site of Pedro de Mendoza's first encampment, **Parque Lezama** contains the **Museo Histórico Nacional** (theoretically open daily except Monday 2 to 6 pm, but frequently closed for repairs).

La Boca

Literally Buenos Aires' most colorful neighborhood, La Boca was built up by Italian immigrants along the **Riachuelo**, a narrow waterway lined by meatpackers and warehouses. Part of its color comes from brightly painted houses along the **Caminito**, a pedestrian walk named for a popular tango; the rest comes from petroleum sludge and toxics that tint the waters of the Riachuelo.

Immigrants could find a foothold here, but British diplomat James Bryce described Boca houses as 'dirty and squalid…their wooden boards gaping like rents in tattered clothes.' Boca's status as an artists colony is the legacy of painter Benito Quinquela Martín, but it's also a solidly working-class neighborhood, whose symbol is the Boca Juniors soccer team. The No 86 bus from Plaza del Congreso is the easiest way to get there.

Once Quinquela Martín's home and studio, the fine-arts **Museo de Bellas Artes de La Boca**, Pedro de Mendoza 1835, is open weekdays 10 am to 6 pm, weekends 11 am to 8 pm. Admission is free.

Recoleta

Upper-class porteños relocated to the now-fashionable Recoleta, north of the microcentro, after the San Telmo yellow fever epidemic of the 1870s. The barrio is famous for the **Cementerio de la Recoleta**, a necropolis where, in death as in life, generations of Argentina's elite rest in ornate splendor. The colonial **Iglesia de Nuestra Señora de Pilar** (1732) is a historical monument; nearby are the **Centro Cultural Ciudad de Buenos Aires** and the **Centro Municipal de Exposiciones**, which host many cultural events. Attractive gardens and open spaces include **Plaza Alvear**, **Plaza Francia** and other parks toward Palermo.

The **Museo Nacional de Bellas Artes** houses works by Renoir, Rodin, Monet, Van Gogh and Argentine artists. At Av del Libertador 1473, it's open daily except Monday 12:30 to 7:30 pm; it opens at 9:30 am Saturday. Admission is free.

Palermo

Rosas' most positive legacy is Palermo's open spaces, which became parkland after his overthrow by Entre Ríos caudillo and former ally Justo José de Urquiza (who sits astride his horse in a massive monument at Sarmiento and Figueroa Alcorta).

Palermo contains the **Jardín Botánico Carlos Thays** (botanical gardens), **Jardín Zoológico** (zoo), **Rosedal** (rose garden), **Campo de Polo** (polo grounds), **Hipódromo** (racetrack) and **Planetario**. Some of these uses were obviously not for the masses, but it's a more democratic place these days.

Language Courses

Among the many options for Spanish instruction are the Instituto de Lengua Española para Extranjeros (ILEE, ☎ 011-4372-0223, fax 011-4782-7173; ilee@overnet.com.ar), Av Callao 339, 3rd Floor; the

DOWNTOWN BUENOS AIRES

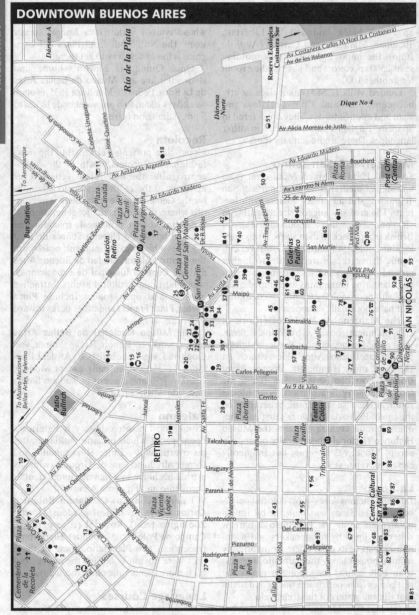

Dársena A

Río de la Plata

Reserva Ecológica
Costanera Sur

Av Costanera Carlos M Noel (La Costanera)
Av de los Italianos

Dársena
Norte

Dique No 4

Av Alicia Moreau de Justo

To Aeroparque

Bus Station

Estación
Retiro

Plaza
Canada

Plaza del
Carril

Plaza Fuerza
Aérea Argentina

Plaza Libertador
General San Martín

Av Antártida Argentina

Av Eduardo Madero

Av Eduardo Madero

Av Leandro N Alem

25 de Mayo

Reconquista

San Martin

Galerías
Pacífico

Florida (Ped Mall)

Maipú

Esmeralda

Suipacha

Carlos Pellegrini

Cerrito

Av 9 de Julio

Plaza
Roma

Bouchard

Post Office
(Central)

Lavalle
(Ped Mall)

SAN NICOLÁS

Av Corrientes

Diagonal
Norte

Plaza
de la
República

Patio
Bullrich

To Museo Nacional
Bellas Aires, Palermo

Plaza
Libertad

Teatro
Colón

Plaza
Lavalle

RETIRO

Acevedo

Av Santa Fe

Talcahuano

Uruguay

Paraná

Montevideo

Del Carmen

Tribunales

Centro Cultural
San Martín

Plaza
Vicente
López

Plaza
R Peña

Rodríguez Peña

Pizzurno

Dellepiane

Tucumán

Lavalle

Sarmiento

Cementerio
de la
Recoleta

Av Gral Las Heras

Callao

Riobamba

DOWNTOWN BUENOS AIRES

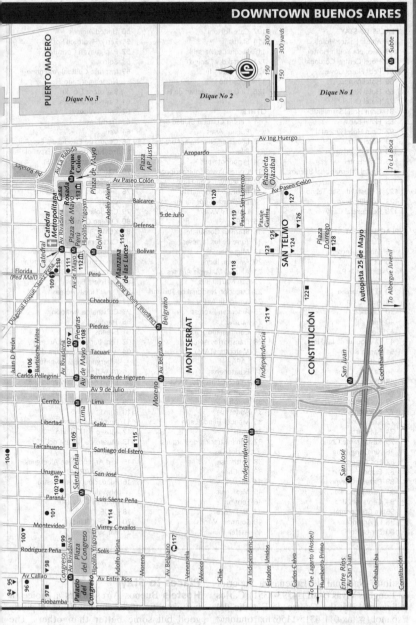

DOWNTOWN BUENOS AIRES

PLACES TO STAY
9 Alvear Palace Hotel
19 Recoleta Youth Hostel
41 Hotel Central Córdoba
57 Petit Hotel Goya
60 Hotel Maipú
65 Hotel Regidor
77 Hotel O'Rei
81 Gran Hotel Sarmiento
89 Hotel Bahía
97 Gran Hotel Oriental
99 Hotel Plaza
103 Hotel Sportsman
105 Chile Hotel
115 Hostel Internacional Buenos Aires
122 El Hostal de San Telmo
123 Hotel Bolívar
128 Residencial Carly

PLACES TO EAT
3 Clark's
5 Munich Recoleta
6 La Biela
7 Café de la Paix
8 Freddo
10 El Sanjuanino
13 Au Bec Fin
30 Payanca
40 Filo
42 Dora
43 La Esquina de las Flores
54 Bar La Robla
55 Coto
56 La Casa China
58 Broccolino
68 Heladería Cadore
69 Los Inmortales
72 La Estancia
73 China Doll
74 La Huerta
75 Restaurante Chino
78 Xin Dong Fang
82 Los Amigos
87 Pippo
88 Pizzería Güerrín
91 Valle Esmeralda
94 Cervantes II
95 La Continental
98 La Americana
100 Bar La Robla

107 Café Tortoni
114 Status
119 Nicole de Marseille
121 Hostal del Canigó
124 Las Marías II
125 Jerónimo
126 La Casa de Esteban de Luca

OTHER
1 Centro Cultural Ciudad de Buenos Aires
2 Iglesia de Nuestra Señora de Pilar
4 Hippopotamus
11 Correo Postal Internacional
12 Uruguayan Consulate
14 Instituto Nacional de Enseñanza Superior en Lenguas Vivas
15 LAPA
16 Brazilian Consulate
17 Torre de los Ingleses
18 Migraciones
20 Avianca, Iberia
21 Alitalia, Malaysia Airlines
22 San Martín Bus
23 Dirección Nacional de Turismo
24 American Airlines
25 American Express
26 Austral
27 Contramano
28 Transportes Aéreos de Mercosur (TAM)
29 LAPA
31 Ecuatoriana
32 French Consulate, Swiss Consulate, Swissair
33 Aeroflot
34 Andesmar
35 Manuel Tienda León
36 Vasp
37 Administración de Parques Nacionales
38 Lufthansa
39 LanChile
44 Buquebus
45 Mexicana
46 Ferrytur
47 Air France
48 Southern Winds
49 Asatej

50 United Airlines
51 Ferry/Hydrofoil Port
52 Paraguayan Consulate
53 Boicot
59 Instituto Cultural Argentino-Norteamericano, Biblioteca Lincoln
61 Canadian Airlines
62 British Airways
63 TransBrasil
64 Varig
66 Centro de Estudio del Español
67 Instituto de Lengua Española para Extranjeros (ILEE)
70 Platero
71 Obelisco
76 Telefónica Long-Distance Office
79 Cacciola
80 Chilean Consulate
81 KLM
83 Cartelera Vea Más
84 Teatro General San Martín
85 Dirección General de Turismo
86 Girondo
88 Cartelera Baires
90 Dinar Líneas Aéreas
92 El Ateneo
93 Cubana de Aviación
96 Tradfax
101 Evenos
102 Leru Bar (Internet Access)
104 Asociación Argentina de Albergues de la Juventud (AAAJ)
106 Lloyd Aéreo Boliviano (LAB)
108 Morocco
109 Municipal Tourist Kiosk
110 Pluna
111 Aerolíneas Argentinas
112 Museo del Cabildo
113 Museo de la Casa del Gobierno
115 Red Argentina de Albergues Juveniles (RAAJ)
116 Fundación Vida Silvestre Argentina
117 Bolivian Consulate
118 LADE
120 La Casa Blanca
127 Bar Sur

Instituto Nacional de Enseñanza Superior en Lenguas Vivas (☎ 011-4393-7351), Carlos Pellegrini 1515; the Centro de Estudio del Español (☎/fax 011-4315-1156; martinduh@act.net.ar), Reconquista 719, 111/4 E; and Tradfax (☎ 011-4373-5581; royal@einstein.com.ar), Av Callao 194, 2nd floor.

Places to Stay

Hostels Buenos Aires offers a choice of hostels, both official and unofficial, all pretty good but some better than others. The cheapest is *Che Lagarto* (☎ 011-4304-7618), Combate de los Pozos 1151 (Subte: Entre Ríos), for US$8 in four- to six-bed rooms.

In a rambling building at Brasil 675 (Subte: Constitución), between Chacabuco and Perú, the HI-affiliated *Albergue Juvenil* (☎ *011-4394-9112*) costs US$10 per person including breakfast but without kitchen privileges. Rates at the new 100-bed *Hostel Internacional Buenos Aires* (☎ *011-4381-9760*), another HI-affiliated facility at Moreno 1273 (Subte: Lima), should be comparable to other BA hostels.

Not affiliated with HI, *El Hostal de San Telmo* (☎ *011-4300-6899; elhostal@satlink .com*), Carlos Calvo 614, is an outstanding facility for US$10 per person in three- and four-bed rooms. The new *Recoleta Youth Hostel* (☎ *011-4812-4419; mpa@interserver .com.ar*), not yet affiliated with HI, occupies a recycled mansion at Libertad 1218 (Subte: Tribunales). Rates are US$10 per person.

Hotels Central, attractive *Hotel Maipú* (☎ *011-4322-5142*), Maipú 735, has simple but pleasant rooms for US$19/24 with shared bath, US$22/29 with private bath. *Hotel O'Rei* (☎ *011-4393-7186*), Lavalle 733, is quiet and clean but sometimes grumpily managed; singles/doubles with shared bath cost US$19/25. Another recommended place is *Hotel Bahía* (☎ *011-4382-1780*), Corrientes 1212, (US$20 single or double), despite reports of thefts.

In San Telmo, amiable, well-kept *Hotel Zavalia* (☎ *011-4362-1990*), Juan de Garay 474 (at Perú), has singles/doubles with shared bath for only US$10/15, but children make it noisy at times. Closer to Plaza Dorrego, run-down but passable *Residencial Carly* (☎ *011-4361-7710*), Humberto Primo 464, charges US$10 single with shared bath, US$12/14 with private bath. At *Hotel Bolívar* (☎ *011-4361-5105*), the barrio's budget favorite at Bolívar 886, several rooms have sunny balconies for US$15/22 with private bath.

Near Congreso, a good budget area, *Hotel Sportsman* (☎ *011-4381-8021*) occupies an older building at Rivadavia 1425; rates are US$12/20 with shared bath, US$20/30 with private bath. At scruffy but passable *Hotel Plaza* (☎ *011-4371-9747*), Rivadavia 1689, small rooms with shared bath cost US$12/15, with private bath US$15/20. Greatly improved *Gran Hotel Oriental* (☎ *011-4951-3371*), Mitre 1840, has rooms with shared bath for US$18/20 and

others with private bath for US$24/28. Still decent value is friendly *Gran Hotel Sarmiento* (☎ *011-4374-8069*), on a quiet block at Sarmiento 1892, where simple but very clean rooms (some a bit cramped) with private bath cost US$25/35.

Travelers able to spend a bit more can find good values. Corner rooms at *Chile Hotel* (☎ *011-4383-7112*), Av de Mayo 1297, have huge balconies with views of the Congreso and the Casa Rosada (US$35/50 with private bath). Once a budget hotel, well-kept *Petit Hotel Goya* (☎ *322-9311*), Suipacha 748, is no longer cheap at US$40/50 (including breakfast if the hotel bill is paid in cash), but it's friendly, spotless, central, quiet and comfortable. Cozy *Hotel Central Córdoba* (☎ *011-4311-1175*), modest but friendly and pleasant, is also central, at San Martín 1021 (US$35/45).

For US$55/65 with breakfast, *Hotel Regidor* (☎ *011-4314-7917*), Tucumán 451, is an excellent value, but can be snooty toward casually dressed visitors. Few places can match the old-world charm of *Hotel Plaza Francia* (☎ *011-4804-9631*), Eduardo Schiaffino 2189 in Recoleta (about US$140/152). At the elegant *Alvear Palace Hotel* (☎ *011-4804-4031*), Av Alvear 1891 in Recoleta, doubles cost US$350 and upward.

Places to Eat

In ordinary restaurants, standard fare is pasta, minutas such as milanesa, and cheaper cuts of beef, plus fries, salads and desserts. For a little more, you can eat similar food of better quality, but meals at top restaurants can be costly.

Parrillas Charles Darwin, crossing the Pampas in the 1830s, expressed astonishment at the gauchos' meat diet, which 'would only have agreed with me with hard exercise.' You can probably indulge yourself on Argentina's succulent grilled meat, so long as you don't make a lifestyle of it.

If you visit only one parrilla, make it *La Estancia*, Lavalle 941, and overlook the rent-a-gauchos to focus on the excellent, moderately priced food. *Dora*, Av Alem 1016, is popular in part for its massive portions; most dishes suffice for two people, and the imposing half-portion of bife de chorizo weighs nearly half a kilo. *Cervantes II*, Perón 1883, serves enormous portions of standard Argentine fare at modest prices, but is often very crowded. One of the most economical parrillas is *Pippo*, Paraná 356.

Italian & Pizzerias Readers and author are unanimous that *Broccolino*, Esmeralda 776, is one of Buenos Aires' best Italian places. *Filo*, San Martín 975, is a lively pizza-and-pasta place whose menu changes frequently; it has friendly service and great decor, but prices are not for the financially challenged.

Unsung *Pizzería Güerrín*, Corrientes 1372, sells inexpensive individual slices of superb fugazza, fugazzeta and other specialties, plus excellent empanadas and cold lager beer. At Callao and Mitre, *La Americana* has very fine pizza and exceptional empanadas, but the best chicken empanadas (usually breast meat) are at *La Continental*, Callao 202.

Visit the original branch of *Los Inmortales*, at Corrientes 1369 beneath the conspicuous billboard of Carlos Gardel, to see historic photographs of Gardel and his contemporaries. Another recommended pizzeria is unpretentious *Las Marías II*, Bolívar 964-66 in San Telmo.

Spanish Spanish restaurants offer the best choices for seafood, generally not a high priority for Argentines. Part of San Telmo's Casal de Catalunya cultural center at Chacabuco 863, *Hostal del Canigó* serves Catalonian specialties like *pollo a la punxa* (chicken with calamari). Prices are not cheap (the fixed-price menú ejecutivo costs US$9), but portions are large. A nice touch is the complimentary glass of sherry.

Bar La Robla, with locations at Viamonte 1613 and Montevideo 194, has both seafood and standard Argentine dishes, in pleasant surroundings at moderate prices. Its US$4 lunch specials, with an appetizer and a small glass of clericó, are an excellent value. San Telmo's *La Casa de Esteban de Luca* has very fine food at moderate prices, served in a restored colonial house at Defensa 1000.

French It's stretching it a bit to call *Nicole de Marseille*, Defensa 714, a French or even Franco-Argentine restaurant, but three-course weekday lunches (US$6) present a wide choice of main courses and desserts. Try also the appealing but pricier *French Bistro*, French 2301 in Barrio Norte.

Widely acknowledged as one of Buenos Aires' best restaurants, *Au Bec Fin*, Vicente López 1825 in Recoleta, has prices to match.

Other European Many new restaurants have opened in Plaza del Pilar, at Av Pueyrredón 2501 alongside the Centro Cultural Recoleta; more easily reached from the Calle Junín entrance to the Centro, they range from modest fast-food offerings to elaborate and sophisticated fare. If price is no object, check out Recoleta institutions like *Munich Recoleta* at RM Ortiz 1871 or *Clark's* at Junín 1777.

An inexpensive choice in San Telmo is *Jerónimo*, Estados Unidos 407, where main courses only cost from US$4 to US$6 and desserts about US$2. *Restaurant Ruso*, Azcuénaga 1562 in Barrio Norte, specializes in Russian food at reasonable (by barrio standards) prices.

Asian Most Asian food is unremarkable Cantonese, but tenedor libre restaurants, as cheap as US$4, are a good budget option. Most have salad bars with excellent ingredients, but tack on a US$1 surcharge if you don't order anything to drink. Try *Restaurante Chino* at Suipacha 477, *China Doll* at Suipacha 544, or *Los Amigos* at Rodríguez Peña 384.

A step up from most all-you-can-eats is *Gran Fu Ia*, Las Heras 2379, a few blocks from Recoleta cemetery; the US$10 price tag reflects its higher quality. Other possibilities for better quality Chinese food include *La Casa China* at Viamonte 1476, or *Xin Dong Fang* at Maipú 512.

Latin American & Regional In Congreso, at Virrey Cevallos 178, the modest but friendly *Status* is a hangout for the capital's Peruvian community; large portions and reasonable prices make it worth a stop if you're nearby. *El Sanjuanino*, Posadas 1515 in Recoleta, serves regional versions of Argentine dishes like empanadas, locro and sweets. Moderately priced *Payanca*, Suipacha 1015, features spicy northern Argentine cuisine from Salta; Jujuy cuisine is the rule at friendly *La Carretería*, Brasil 656 (across from the youth hostel).

Vegetarian Since the mid-1980s, the carnivorous capital has enjoyed a vegetarian boom, and nearly all of these places are tobacco-free. One of the capital's most enduring vegetarian alternatives, also something of a cultural center, *La Esquina de las Flores* has moved its restaurant to the upstairs of its health-food store at Av Córdoba 1587; meals cost around US$10. Reader endorsements include *La Huerta* at Lavalle 893 and *Valle Esmeralda* at Esmeralda 370 (tenedor libre for US$6).

Fast Food Fast-food restaurants are generally inferior to standard inexpensive eateries, but the Patio de Comidas on the lower level of the Galerías Pacífico on the Florida peatonal has a number of moderately priced fast-food versions of very good restaurants for about US$5 to US$7. The express cafetería at supermarket *Coto*, Viamonte 1571, offers a variety of cheap (US$3 or less) meals of good quality.

Cafés & Confiterías Porteños spend hours solving their own problems, the country's and the world's over a chessboard and a cortado at places like century-old *Café Tortoni*, Av de Mayo 829.

Some upper-class porteños dawdle for hours over caffeine from *La Biela*, Quintana 598 in Recoleta. The rest exercise their purebred dogs nearby; watch your step crossing the street to *Café de la Paix*, Quintana 595.

Ice Cream Chocoholics should not miss the exquisite *chocolate amargo* (semisweet chocolate) and *chocolate blanco* (white chocolate), at *Heladería Cadore*, Corrientes and Rodríguez Peña. In Recoleta, try *Freddo*, at Ayacucho and Quintana and several other locations. Many ice-creameries close in winter.

Entertainment

The *carteleras* (ticket offices) along Av Corrientes sell discounted tickets for movies, theater and tango shows; since the number of tickets may be limited, buy them as far in advance as possible. *Cartelera Vea Más* (☎ 011-4372-7285 interno 219) is at Local 19 in the Paseo La Plaza complex at Corrientes 1660, while *Cartelera Baires* (☎ 011-4372-5058) is at Local 25 in the Galería Teatro Lorange at Corrientes 1372.

Tango Finding spontaneous tango is not easy, but plenty of places portray Argentina's most famous cultural export, for up to US$40 per show, in San Telmo and La Boca. The free Sunday performances at Plaza Dorrego are the best value, but chip in when the dancers pass the hat.

At the lower end of the scale, open nightly except Sunday, the cover for shows at *Bar Sur* (☎ 011-4362-6086), Estados Unidos 299 in San Telmo, is US$15, which includes unlimited pizza but not the fairly expensive drinks. From its publicity, *La Casa Blanca* (☎ 011-4331-4621), Balcarce 668 in San Telmo, appears to take pride in hosting disgraced heads of state like Brazil's Fernando Collor de Mello and Mexico's Carlos Salinas de Gortari.

Dance Clubs Discos, such as *Hippopotamus* at Junín 1787, tend to be exclusive and expensive (US$20 and up, with pricey drinks). *Morocco*, Hipólito Yrigoyen 851, is a favorite haunt of Argentine and other Spanish-speaking pop stars, but some porteños argue it's not what it used to be.

Gay & Lesbian Venues Gay visitors will find a cluster of congenial bars and dance clubs in the Recoleta/Barrio Norte area, around Av Santa Fe and Pueyrredón, where it's possible to get free or discount admission tickets.

Contramano (men only), Rodríguez Peña 1082 in Recoleta (Barrio Norte), is one of the city's oldest gay venues. Nearby reader recommendations include *Gasoil*, Anchorena 1179, and *Abaco*, Anchorena 1347. Close to Barrio Norte, *Boicot*, Pasaje Dellepiane 657, is a lesbian club.

Rock & Blues Buenos Aires has a thriving rock and blues scene; for the latest information, consult Friday's 'Suplemento Joven,' which also lists free events, in *Clarín* and the weekend editions of *Página 12*.

El Samovar de Rasputín (☎ 011-4302-3190), Del Valle Iberlucea 1251 in La Boca, presents blues and rock bands on weekends, from 11:30 pm (admission US$5). Another possibility is the *Blues Special Club*, Almirante Brown 102 in La Boca, opposite Parque Lezama.

Jazz For contemporary jazz, try *Girondo* (☎ 011-4371-8838), at Paraná 328, or *Evenos* (☎ 011-4381-7776), at Mitre 1552.

Cinemas The main cinema zones, along Lavalle west of Florida, and on Avs Corrientes and Santa Fe, feature first-run films from around the world, but there's also an audience for unconventional and classic films. Many offer half-price tickets Wednesday. The *Sala Leopoldo Lugones* at the Teatro General San Martín, Av Corrientes 1530, offers thematic foreign-film cycles and occasional reprises of outstanding commercial films.

Translations of English-language titles can be misleading, so check the *Buenos Aires Herald* to be sure what's playing. Foreign films have Spanish subtitles.

Classical Music & Performing Arts The capital's most prestigious performing arts venue is the *Teatro Colón* (☎ *011-4382-6632)*, opposite Plaza Lavalle.

Av Corrientes, between 9 de Julio and Callao, is the capital's Broadway or West End. The *Teatro General San Martín* (☎ *011-4374-8611)*, Corrientes 1530, has several auditoriums and frequent free events. For listings, see the *Buenos Aires Herald* or *Clarín*.

Spectator Sports

Buenos Aires has eight first-division soccer teams. *Entradas populares* (standing room) cost around US$10, while *plateas* (fixed seats) cost $20 and upward. The most popular teams are *Boca Juniors* (☎ *011-4362-2260)*, Brandsen 805 in La Boca, and *River Plate* (☎ *011-4788-1200)*, Av Presidente Figueroa Alcorta 7597 in Belgrano.

Shopping

The main shopping zones are along Florida (see the impressive recycled Galerías Pacífico shopping center at Florida and Córdoba), Av Santa Fe, and Recoleta. The Feria de San Telmo flea market, on Plaza Dorrego, takes place Sunday from 10 am to about 5 pm. Good antique shops and restaurants are nearby, with spontaneous live entertainment from buskers and mimes. Best buys are jewelry, leather, shoes and mate paraphernalia.

Getting There & Away

Air Many of the following international airlines use Ezeiza, but some fly to neighboring countries from Aeroparque.

Aeroflot
(☎ 011-4312-5573) Av Santa Fe 822

Aerolíneas Argentinas
(☎ 011-4320-2000) Perú 2

Air France
(☎ 011-4317-4700) Paraguay 610, 14th floor

Alitalia
(☎ 011-4310-9999) Suipacha 1111, 28th floor

American Airlines
(☎ 011-4318-1111) Av Santa Fe 881

Avianca
(☎ 011-4394-5990) Carlos Pellegrini 1163, 4th floor

British Airways
(☎ 011-4320-6600) Av Córdoba 650

Canadian Airlines
(☎ 011-4322-3632) Av Córdoba 656

Cubana de Aviación
(☎ 011-4326-5291) Sarmiento 552, 11th floor

Ecuatoriana
(☎ 011-4311-3010) Suipacha 1065

Iberia
(☎ 011-4327-2739) Carlos Pellegrini 1163, 1st floor

KLM
(☎ 011-4480-9470) Reconquista 559, 5th floor

LanChile
(☎ 011-4316-2200) Florida 954

Lloyd Aéreo Boliviano (LAB)
(☎ 011-4326-3595) Carlos Pellegrini 141

Lufthansa
(☎ 011-4319-0600) MT de Alvear 636

Malaysia Airlines
(☎ 011-4312-6971) Suipacha 1111, 14th floor

Mexicana
(☎ 011-4312-6152) Av Córdoba 755, 1st floor

Pluna
(☎ 011-4342-4420) Florida 1

South African Airways
(☎ 011-4311-8184) Av Santa Fe 794, 3rd floor

Swissair
(☎ 011-4319-0000) Av Santa Fe 846, 1st floor

Transportes Aéreos de Mercosur (TAM)
(☎ 011-4816-1000) Cerrito 1026

TransBrasil
(☎ 011-4394-8424) Florida 780, 1st floor

United Airlines
(☎ 011-4316-0777) Av Eduardo Madero 900, 9th floor

Varig
(☎ 011-4329-9204) Florida 630

Vasp
(☎ 011-4311-2699) Av Santa Fe 784

The major domestic carriers are Aerolíneas and Austral, serving nearly every major city from Bolivia to the Beagle Channel, but alternatives are increasing. For route details, see the Getting Around section.

Andesmar
(☎ 011-4312-1077) Esmeralda 1063, 1st floor

Austral
(☎ 011-4317-3605) Av Alem 1134

Dinar Líneas Aéreas
(☎ 011-4326-0135) Av Roque Sáenz Peña 933

LADE
(☎ 011-4361-7071) Perú 714

LAPA
(☎ 011-4819-5272) Carlos Pellegrini 1075

Southern Winds
(☎ 011-4312-2811) Florida 868, 13th floor

Bus At the massive Retiro bus station, at Antártida Argentina and Ramos Mejía, near the train station, each company has a desk like an airline ticket counter. The entries below are only a representative sample of very extensive schedules.

International General Urquiza (☎ 011-4313-2771) has a nightly service to Montevideo (US$25, eight hours). La Internacional (☎ 011-4313-3167), Nuestra Señora de la Asunción (☎ 011-4313-2325) and Chevallier Paraguaya (☎ 011-4313-2349) go to Asunción, Paraguay (US$56 to US$73, 20 hours).

Pluma (☎ 011-4313-3901) goes to Brazilian destinations, including Foz do Iguaçu (US$60, 19 hours), São Paulo (US$101, 42 hours) and Rio de Janeiro (US$117, 48 hours). Rápido Yguazú (☎ 011-4315-6981) also serves Brazilian routes.

Several companies cross the Andes to Santiago, Chile (US$60, 21 hours): TAC (☎ 011-4313-2627), Chevallier (☎ 011-4314-5555), and Fénix Pullman Norte (☎ 011-4313-0134).

Atlantic Coast & the Pampas Costera Criolla (☎ 011-4313-2449) and El Cóndor (☎ 011-4313-1700) both go to Mar del Plata (US$25, seven hours) and other beach resorts. La Estrella (☎ 011-4313-1700), El Cóndor and Costera Criolla serve many destinations within Buenos Aires province, as far as Bahía Blanca (US$30, 10 hours). Chevallier (☎ 011-4314-5555) goes to Rosario (US$20, six hours) and points north.

Mesopotamia, Misiones & the Gran Chaco El Rápido Argentino (☎ 011-4315-

2505) and Expreso Río Paraná (☎ 011-4313-3143) serve the littoral cities of Santa Fe (US$21, six hours), Paraná (US$21, seven hours) and Corrientes (US$40, 14 hours). El Norte Bis (☎ 011-4315-1102) goes to Resistencia (US$43, 15 hours).

Empresa Tata (☎ 011-4313-3844) serves Gualeguaychú (US$11, three hours) and other northerly destinations, passing Parque Nacional El Palmar. Expreso Singer (☎ 011-4313-3937) and Empresa Kurtz (☎ 011-4315-1215) have buses to Posadas (US$39, 14 hours) and Puerto Iguazú (US$48, 21 hours).

Córdoba & the Northwest Cacorba (☎ 011-4313-2651) has buses to Córdoba (US$25 to US$30, 10 hours) and Catamarca (US$42 to US$54, 16 hours). Ablo (☎ 011-4313-2995) goes to Rosario, Córdoba and its Sierras, and La Rioja (US$52 to US$62, 17 hours), as does Chevallier (☎ 011-4314-5555).

La Estrella (☎ 011-4315-3058) goes to Termas de Río Hondo (US$42, 15 hours), Santiago del Estero (US$45, 14 hours) and Tucumán (US$30-69, 16 hours). La Veloz del Norte (☎ 011-4315-0800) goes to Salta (US$64 to US$86, 22 hours); La Internacional (☎ 011-4313-3167) also goes to Salta and Jujuy (US$64 to US$80, 22 hours).

Cuyo Chevallier (☎ 011-4314-5555) and Expreso Jocolí (☎ 011-4311-8283) go to San Luis (US$40 to US$45, 12 hours) and Mendoza (US$45 to US$55, 14 hours), as does TAC (☎ 011-4313-3627). Autotransportes San Juan (☎ 011-4313-9625) has buses to San Luis and San Juan (US$40 to US$60, 16 hours).

Patagonia Empresa Pehuenche (☎ 011-4311-8283) goes to Santa Rosa (US$25, nine hours) and to Neuquén (US$45 to US$55, 16 hours). El Cóndor/La Estrella (☎ 011-4313-1700) and Chevallier (☎ 011-4314-5555) have buses to Neuquén and Bariloche (US$75 to US$85, 23 hours). Other Bariloche carriers include El Valle (☎ 011-4313-2441), which also serves San Martín de los Andes (US$65 to US$75, 23 hours); Vía Bariloche (☎ 011-4315-3122); and TAC (☎ 011-4313-3627).

Costera Criolla/Don Otto (☎ 011-4313-5997) is the major carrier to coastal Patagonia, including Puerto Madryn (US$35 to

US$57, 21 hours), Comodoro Rivadavia (US$60 to US$75, 24 hours) and Río Gallegos (US$70 to US$100, 40 hours). La Estrella and La Puntual (☎ 011-4313-2441) run similar routes. Expreso Pingüino (☎ 011-4315-4438) also goes to Río Gallegos.

Train Rail travel in Argentina is generally cheaper but less frequent, swift and comfortable than bus travel.

From Estación Constitución (Subte: Constitución), Ferrobaires (☎ 011-4304-0035) operates the Ferrocarril Roca to the beach resorts of Mar del Plata, Pinamar and other Buenos Aires province destinations. From Estación Retiro (Subte: Retiro), Tucumán Ferrocarriles SA (Tufesa, ☎ 011-4313-8060) operates the Ferrocarril Mitre to Rosario, Santiago del Estero and Tucumán. The Ferrocarril Sarmiento (☎ 011-4861-0041), primarily a commuter line, still links the capital to Santa Rosa, in La Pampa province, from Estación 11 de Septiembre (Subte: Plaza Miserere). Línea C of the Subte links Retiro and Constitución.

River Most ferries and hydrofoils going to Uruguay sail from Dársena Norte, near Madero and Viamonte, but some depart from Dársena Sur, Av Pedro de Mendoza 20 in La Boca. There is now a US$10 departure tax from both terminals.

Ferrytur (☎ 011-4315-6800), Córdoba 699, sails twice each weekday, once a day on weekends, to Colonia (US$23, 2½ hours) and back; its hydrofoil *Sea Cat* goes to Colonia (45 minutes) four times a day weekdays, three times a day weekends (US$32 one way).

Buquebus (☎ 011-4313-4444), Córdoba 867, has two ferry sailings daily to Colonia. Its 'Aviones de Buquebus' are luxurious high-speed passenger ferries that reach Colonia (US$32) in 45 minutes and Montevideo (four times daily weekdays, three times daily weekends) in 2½ hours for US$52 in *turista* class, US$67 in *primera*. Buquebus also has weekend service to Piriápolis (Uruguay) in summer.

Cacciola (☎ 011-4749-0329), at Lavalle 520 in the riverside suburb of Tigre, goes twice daily to Carmelo, Uruguay (US$11). Movilán/Deltanave (☎ 011-4749-4119) also goes to Carmelo twice daily. Also from Tigre, Línea Delta (☎ 011-4749-0537) goes

to Nueva Palmira, Uruguay, daily at 7:30 am (US$15 one way, US$26 return). There's a US$5 departure tax from Tigre.

Getting Around

To/From the Airport Nearly all domestic flights and some to neighboring countries leave from Aeroparque Jorge Newbery (☎ 011-4771-2071), only a few kilometers north of the microcentro. Most international flights leave from Aeropuerto Internacional Ministro Pistarini (commonly known as 'Ezeiza,' ☎ 011-4480-0235), about 35km south of the city center.

To Aeroparque, take city bus No 37C ('Ciudad Universitaria') from Plaza Italia in Palermo; No 45 northbound from Constitución, Plaza San Martín or Retiro; or No 160B from Av Las Heras or Plaza Italia. The fare is about US$0.70.

To Ezeiza, the cheapest way (US$1, 1½ to two hours) is the No 86 bus (US$1.20; be sure it says 'Ezeiza,' since not all No 86s go to the end of the line), which starts in La Boca and comes up Av de Mayo past the Plaza del Congreso. To be assured of a seat, take the more comfortable *servicio diferencial* (about US$5).

Manuel Tienda León (☎ 011-4314-3636, 4314-2577), Santa Fe 790, runs minibuses to Ezeiza (US$14 one way, 45 minutes). Its Aeroparque service costs US$5. San Martín Bus (☎ 011-4314-4747), Av Santa Fe 887, has begun to provide slightly cheaper competition (US$11 one way); it also offers door-to-door service in the downtown area.

Taxis to Ezeiza cost about US$30 plus a US$2 freeway toll, but may prove cheaper than Manuel Tienda León for a group of three or four; negotiate with the driver. Taxis from downtown to Aeroparque cost about US$6.

Bus Sold at nearly all kiosks and bookstores, Ediciones Lumi's *Capital Federal* street atlas details nearly 200 different bus routes. Many porteños have memorized the system and can instantly tell you which bus to take and where to get off, but always check the window placard for the final destination. Fares depend on distance; tell the driver your destination. Most buses now have automatic ticket machines, which also make small change. The minimum fare is US$0.60 to US$0.70, depending on the route.

Train Commuter trains serve most of Gran Buenos Aires from Retiro, Constitución, Lacroze and Once. Fares are cheaper than buses.

Underground Buenos Aires' antique Subte is fast and efficient, but reaches only certain parts of a city much larger than when the system opened in 1913. Four of the five lines (Líneas A, B, D, and E) run from the microcentro to the capital's western and northern outskirts, while Línea C links Retiro and Constitución. Tourist kiosks and ticket booths distribute a map of the system. Buy a pocketful of fichas (US$0.50 each) to avoid standing in line.

Trains operate 5 am to 10 pm except Sunday (8 am to 10 pm); they are frequent weekdays, less so on weekends.

Taxi & Remise Black-and-yellow cabs are numerous and reasonably priced, with new digital-read-out meters. A brief ride should cost around US$3. Drivers customarily receive small change as a tip. Remises (radio taxis) have many offices around town.

AROUND BUENOS AIRES
Isla Martín García
Navigating the densely forested channels of the Delta, en route to historic Martín García, it's easy to imagine colonial smugglers hiding among the rushes. Just off the Uruguayan littoral, directly south of the city of Carmelo, the island is famous – or infamous – as a prison camp; four Argentine presidents have spent time in custody here, and the Servicio Penitenciario of Buenos Aires province still uses it as a halfway house for prisoners near the end of their terms. At present, though, it's more a combination of historical monument, nature reserve, and recreational retreat from the bustling capital.

Without your own boat, the only practical way to the island is the guided tour from Cacciola's Terminal Internacional (☎ 011-4749-0329), at Lavalle 520 in the suburb of Tigre; tickets are also available at the company's microcentro office (☎ 011-4394-5520), at Florida 520, 1st floor, Oficina 113.

The enclosed catamaran leaves Tigre at 8 am Tuesday, Thursday, weekends and holidays, returning from Martín García at 4 pm), and costs US$28 return. For US$39, the tour includes lunch at Cacciola's *La Fragata*, but there are cheaper and better dining alternatives. Bus No 60 from Av Callao goes straight to Tigre.

Luján
Legend says that, in 1630, a wagon would not budge on a rutted cart road until gauchos removed from it an image of the Virgin brought from Brazil. The image's devoted owner built a chapel on the spot, 65km west of Buenos Aires, where Argentina's patron saint now occupies the neo-Gothic **Basílica Nuestra Señora de Luján**, the country's most important devotional site. Her day is May 8. Luján's other main attraction is a colonial museum complex.

Waiters at the many cheap restaurants along Av Nuestra Señora de Luján virtually drag pilgrims off the sidewalk. Luján's best dining is at *L'Eau Vive*, Constitución 2112, a superb, tobacco-free French restaurant with friendly, attentive service by Carmelite nuns from around the world. The US$11 midday menu is a great value, but note the limited hours: noon to 2:15 pm for lunch, 8 to 10 pm for dinner (a very early closing hour for Argentines).

From Plaza Miserere, north of Congreso but reached by Subte, Transporte Luján (Línea 52) runs buses to Luján (US$3), while the Ferrocarril Sarmiento runs commuter trains to and from Once Station. Transportes Atlántida (Línea 57) runs buses from Palermo (Subte Plaza Italia).

San Antonio de Areco
Dating from the early-18th-century construction of a chapel in honor of San Antonio de Padua, this serene village is the symbolic center of Argentina's vestigial gaucho culture and host to the country's biggest gaucho celebration, Día de la Tradición, in November. Nestled in the verdant pampas of northern Buenos Aires province, 113km west of Buenos Aires via RN 8, its main permanent attraction is the **Parque Criollo y Museo Gauchesco Ricardo Güiraldes**, honoring the author of the classic gauchesque novel *Don Segundo Sombra*.

San Antonio is a popular weekend excursion from Buenos Aires, but weekdays are less crowded (accommodation is limited). Local artisans are known for mate paraphernalia, *rastras* (silver-studded belts) and *facones* (long-bladed knives), produced by skilled silversmiths.

Frequent buses from Buenos Aires to San Antonio take 1½ hours (US$3.50).

Atlantic Coast

In summer, millions of porteños take a holiday from friends, families and coworkers, only to meet them on the beaches of Buenos Aires province. Beach access is open, but *balnearios* (resorts) are private – only those renting tents may use showers and toilets. Besides lifeguards and medical services, balnearios usually have confiterías, shops and paddle-ball courts. Prices rise every two weeks from mid-December to mid-February, then decline until late March, when most hotels and residenciales close.

North of Mar del Plata, gentle dunes rise behind generally narrow beaches, while southwest toward Miramar, steep bluffs highlight a changing coastline. Beyond Miramar, broad sandy beaches delight bathers, fishing enthusiasts and windsurfers.

MAR DEL PLATA

Mid-19th-century Portuguese investors established El Puerto de Laguna de los Padres here, about 400km south of Buenos Aires, but developer Patricio Peralta Ramos founded Mar del Plata proper in 1874. First a commercial and industrial center, then a beach resort for upper-class porteño families, Mardel, as it's called, has become the main summer resort for middle-class vacationers. Some travelers may prefer spring or autumn, when prices are lower and the atmosphere more relaxed.

Information

Tourist Offices The Ente Municipal de Turismo (Emtur, ☎ 0223-495-1777), Blvd Marítimo 2267, has an efficient information system, good maps and useful brochures; there's usually an English-speaker on duty.

Money There are cambios and banks along San Martín and Rivadavia, and many ATMs, mostly on Av Independencia.

Post & Communications The post office is at Luro 2460. Locutorio Arenales, Arenales 2344, has phone and fax services.

For Internet access, try the cybercafé Krackers, Mitre 2069.

Medical Services Centro de Salud Municipal No 1 (☎ 0223-495-0568) is at Av Colón 3294.

Walking Tour

A stroll past Mardel's mansions offers vivid evidence of its upper-class origins and erstwhile status as the playground of wealthy Argentines. Now the Italian Consulate, the **Villa Normandy** (1919) at Viamonte 2216 is one of few surviving examples of the French style that underwent a renovation craze in the 1950s. Near the top of the hill, at Almirante Brown and Viamonte, is **Iglesia Stella Maris**, with an impressive marble altar; its virgin is the patron saint of local fishermen. On the summit, at Falucho and Mendoza, the 88m **Torre Tanque** offers outstanding views from its *mirador* (lookout).

After descending Viamonte to Rodríguez Peña, walk toward the ocean to the corner of Urquiza, where **Chalet Los Troncos** gave its name to this distinguished neighborhood; the timber of the gate and fence are *quebracho* and *lapacho* hardwoods from Salta province. Lining Calles Urquiza, Quintana, Lavalle, Rodríguez Peña, Rivas and Almafuerte are examples of more recent but equally elite design. To return downtown, try the longer route along Av Peralta Ramos. It offers fine city views from **Cabo Corrientes**.

Banquina de Pescadores

Barking sea lions monitor the anglers and stevedores at this picturesque wharf in the port; nearby there's fine dining at a complex of restaurants or, more cheaply, at stand-up cafeterias. Take any of several southbound buses from downtown.

Villa Victoria

Victoria Ocampo, founder of the journal *Sur* in the 1920s, hosted literary salons at this prefab Norwegian house at Matheu 1851, open daily 10 am to 1 pm and 5 to 9:30 pm. Admission is US$2.

Places to Stay

It's worth reiterating that prices climb steadily in summer and fall in the off season. Unless indicated otherwise, prices below are from early high season.

ATLANTIC COAST & THE PAMPAS

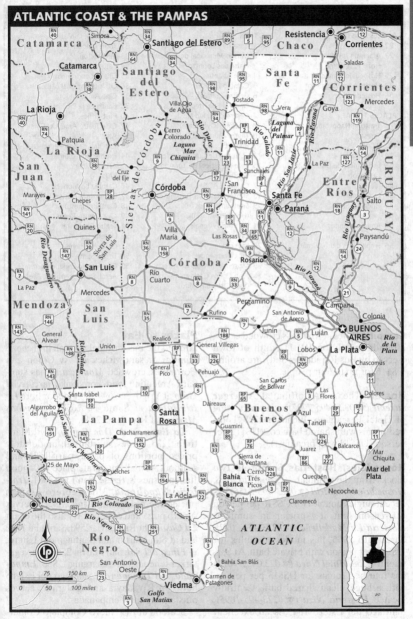

MAR DEL PLATA

ARGENTINA

PLACES TO STAY
22 Hotel Nava
23 Albergue Juvenil,
    Hotel Pergamino
25 Hospedaje Lamadrid
32 Hostería La Madrileña
56 Hostería Niza

PLACES TO EAT
3   Trattoria Napolitana
9   Teresa
12 Il Gato
14 Montecatini
16 La Estancia de Don Pepito
20 La Biblioteca
24 Joe
39 La Casona
41 Finca del Sol
50 La Casona
53 Ambos Mundos
54 La Casona
55 Empanadas del Tucumán

OTHER
1   Casa de Salta
2   Museo Municipal de Ciencias
    Naturales Lorenzo Scaglia
4   Cine Atlantic
5   Cambio Jonestur
6   Centro Cultural
    General Pueyrredón
7   Centro de Salud No 1
8   Krackers (Cybercafé)
10 Teatro Municipal Colón
11 Budget
13 Sociedad de Cultura Inglesa
15 Ente Municipal de Turismo
    (Emtur)
17 Casino, LADE
18 Subsecretaría de Turismo
19 Southern Winds
    (Hotel Provincial)
21 Locutorio Arenales
26 Lave-Quick
27 Laverap
28 Villa Normandy
29 Museo Municipal de Arte
    Juan Carlos Castagnino
    (Villa Ortiz Basualdo)

30 Iglesia Stella Maris
31 Torre Tanque
33 Villa Victoria
34 Patur (Car Rental)
35 Chalet Los Troncos
36 Oti Internacional (Amex)
37 Cine Ambassador
38 Banco de la Provincia
40 Post Office
42 Cine Teatro América, Cine
    Atlas
43 Catedral de San Pedro
44 Exposición Cultural
    Arte y Nácar
45 LAPA
46 Cambio La Moneta
47 Banco de la Nación
48 Cambio Jonestur
49 Cine/Teatro Regina
51 Teatro Corrientes
52 Librería Galerna
57 Cartelera Baires
58 Teatro Santa Fe
59 Cine/Teatro Enrique Carreras
60 Aerolíneas Argentinas, Austral

Camping Rates at Mardel's crowded campgrounds, mostly on RP 11 south of town (served by Bus Rápido del Sud), are around US$16 for up to four people.

Hostels The AAAJ-affiliated *Albergue Juvenil* (☎ 0223-495-7927) occupies a wing of Hotel Pergamino, Tucumán 2728. Four-bed rooms with shared bath cost US$12 per person (US$13 with breakfast).

Hospedajes, Hosterías & Hotels Two blocks from the terminal, at Lamadrid 2518, *Hospedaje Lamadrid* (☎ 0223-495-5456) has decent singles/doubles for US$10 per person off-season, but it's pricier in summer. *Hostería La Madrileña* (☎ 0223-451-2072), Sarmiento 2955, has modest doubles for US$12 per person with private bath. At Sarmiento 2258, *Hotel Nava* (☎ 0223-451-7611) has four-bed rooms for US$15 per person, with a huge, clean shared bath. Centrally located *Hostería Niza* (☎ 0223-495-1695), Santiago del Estero 1843, is an excellent value for US$15 per person with breakfast and private bath, and only US$10 off-season.

Places to Eat

Around the bus terminal you can find cheap *minutas* or sandwiches. At Av Colón and Corrientes, crowded *Montecatini* has standard Argentine food. For similar fare, try *Il Gato* at Yrigoyen 2699, the tenedor libre *La Biblioteca* at Santa Fe 2633, or *Ambos Mundos* at Rivadavia 2644.

La Estancia de Don Pepito, Blvd Marítimo 2235, serves substantial, moderately priced portions of pasta, parrillada and seafood. A small, moderate place with good Italian dishes is *Teresa*, San Luis 2081. *Trattoria Napolitana*, 3 de Febrero 3158, is pricier. *Joe*, at Lamadrid and Alberti, serves superb pizza and calzones. Try also the chain *La Casona* at Rivadavia 2598, Santa Fe 1752 and at San Martín and Santiago del Estero.

Finca del Sol, San Martín 2563, is a vegetarian tenedor libre charging US$6. *Empanadas del Tucumán*, on Santiago del Estero between Rivadavia and Belgrano, serves outstanding spicy empanadas.

Seafood at the Nuevo Complejo Comercial Puerto (the renovated old port) is excellent, though costly – try *La Caracola* at Local 6.

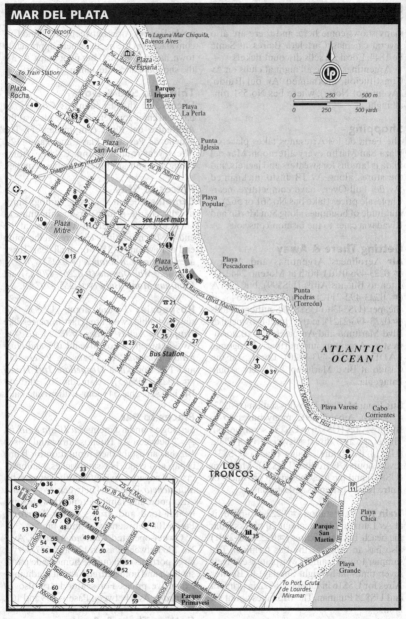

MAR DEL PLATA

To Airport
To Laguna Mar Chiquita,
Buenos Aires
España
Salta
Av Libertad
Balcarce
1
2
Plaza
España
Independencia
11 de Setiembre
To Train Station
3
3 de Febrero
Parque
Irigaray
Playa
La Perla
Plaza
Rocha
4
Av Luro
9 de Julio
25 de Mayo
5
6
Punta
Iglesia
San Martín
Rivadavia
Belgrano
Plaza
San Martín
Moreno
Diagonal Pueyrredón
Bolívar
Av JB Alberdi
(Red Mall)
(Red Mall)
Playa
Popular
7
La Rioja
Yrigoyen
8
9
Buenos Aires
Córdoba
Santa Fe
Santiago del Estero
see inset map
Plaza
Mitre
10
11
16
15
Almirante Brown
Entre Ríos
Corrientes
Av Colón
12
13
Plaza
Colón
17
18
19
Playa
Pescadores
Falucho
Gascón
Alberti
Rawson
Garay
Castelli
20
21
22
Punta
Piedras
(Torreón)
Moreno
Bolívar
29
24
26
25
27
28
ATLANTIC
OCEAN
Buenos Aires
Tucumán
Alsina
23
Bus Station
Las Heras
Garibaldi
32
30
31
Catamarca
Olavarría
Alsina
Güemes
GM de Alvear
Viamonte
Mendoza
Gascón
Playa Varese
Cabo
Corrientes
General Roca
General Paz
Jujuy
Carlos Pellegrini
Alvarado
Av Martínez de Hoz
LOS
TRONCOS
Avellaneda
San Lorenzo
Roca
RdeL Yrigoyen
LN Alem
A del Valle
34
33
43
36
37
25 de Mayo
Av JB Alberdi
San Luis
38
44
45
San Martín (Red Mall)
Av Luro
39
40
46
47
48
Santa Fe
41
42
Córdoba
53
54
55
56
Rivadavia (Red Mall)
Corrientes
Entre Ríos
49
50
51
52
Santiago del Belgrano
57
58
Moreno
60
59
Parque
Primavesi
Rodríguez Peña
Primera Junta
Saavedra
Quintana
Matheu
Formosa
Almafuerte
Parque
San Martín
Av Peralta Ramos (Blvd Marítimo)
Playa
Chica
Playa
Grande
35
To Port, Gruta
de Lourdes,
Miramar

0   250   500 m
0   250   500 yards

Entertainment

When Buenos Aires shuts down in January, many shows come here, and there are also several cinemas. Cartelera Baires, at Santa Fe 1844, Local 33, sells discount tickets.

Argentines dance all night at clubs on Av Constitución, nicknamed 'Av del Ruido' (Avenue of Noise), where bus No 551 runs all night.

Shopping

The Feria de los Artesanos takes place on Plaza San Martín every afternoon. Mar del Plata is famous for sweaters and jackets, and the stores along Av JB Justo, nicknamed 'Av del Pull-Over,' have competitive, near-wholesale prices (take bus No 561 or 562). A multitude of boutiques along San Martín and Rivadavia cater to the fashion-conscious.

Getting There & Away

Air Aerolíneas Argentinas and Austral (☎ 0223-496-0101), both at Moreno 2442, fly often to Buenos Aires (US$99), but LAPA (☎ 0223-492-2112), San Martín 2648, is cheaper (US$43 to US$85). Southern Winds (☎ 0223-493-2121), in the Hotel Provincial at Blvd Marítimo and Arenales, flies to north-western Argentina and northern Patagonia. LADE (☎ 0223-493-8220), Local 5 in the Casino at Blvd Marítimo 2300, serves only Patagonia.

Bus From Mardel's busy bus station (☎ 0223-451-5406), Alberdi 1602, many buses go to Buenos Aires (US$26 to US$33, seven hours). There are also direct services to La Plata (US$18, five hours), Bahía Blanca (US$31, seven hours), Córdoba (US$50), Mendoza (US$75) and the Mesopotamian provinces of Entre Ríos, Corrientes and Misiones.

Train The train station (☎ 0223-475-6076) is at Av Luro and Italia, about 20 blocks from the beach, but Ferrobaires (☎ 0223-451-2501) also has an office at the bus terminal. The summer tourist train El Marplatense travels seven times daily (eight Sunday) to Buenos Aires for US$16 in turista, US$22 in primera and US$28 Pullman. The trip takes about six hours.

VILLA GESELL

Its perceived exclusivity keeps many visitors away from this sedate, woodsy beach resort, 100km northeast of Mar del Plata via RP 11. The Secretaría de Turismo (☎ 02255-458596), on Av Buenos Aires between RP 11 and Circunvalación at the northwestern approach to town, has friendly staff but poor maps. Av 3 is the shopping and entertainment center.

Things to See & Do

Events like the 'Encuentros Corales' (a national choir competition) take place at the **Anfiteatro del Pinar** (amphitheater). The **Muelle de Pesca**, at Playa and Paseo 129, offers year-round fishing. Cycling, horse riding and golf are other possible activities.

Places to Stay

Camping Gesell's dozen campgrounds usually charge a four-person minimum of US$5 to US$8 per person. Most close at the end of March, but three clustered at the south end of town on Av 3 are open all year. These are *Camping Casablanca* (☎ *02255-470771*), *Camping Mar Dorado* (☎ *02255-470963*) and *Camping Monte Bubi* (☎ *02255-470732*).

Hospedajes Figure about US$30 for singles/doubles with breakfast in places like *Hospedaje Aguas Verdes* (☎ *02255-462040*), Av 5 between Paseos 104 and 105, and *Hospedaje Sarimar*, Av 3 between Paseos 117 and 118. Sprawling *Hospedaje Inti Huasi* (☎ *02255-468365*), Alameda 202 and Av Buenos Aires, has 54 rooms with private bath.

Places to Eat

Serving a standard menu, *La Jirafa Azul*, on Av 3 between Av Buenos Aires and Paseo 102, has an established reputation for being cheap and good. For sandwiches, hamburgers and superb service from the owners, try *Sangucheto*, Paseo 104 between Avs 3 and 4. Also good and family-attended, with some health food and drinks, is *La Martona*, Paseo 106 between Avs 3 and 3 bis.

Owner-operated *Cantina Arturito*, Av 3 No 186 between Paseos 126 and 127, serves large portions of exquisite homemade pasta, shellfish and home-cured ham, at medium to expensive prices. For seafood, try also *El Comedor*, Av 3 between Paseos 108 and 109.

Getting There & Away

Air Aerolíneas Argentinas (☎ 02255-468228), at Av Buenos Aires and Av 10, has daily flights to Buenos Aires (US$125) in summer, but LAPA (☎ 02255-458219), Av Buenos Aires and Alameda 211, is cheaper (US$39 to US$85). Líneas Aéreas Entre Ríos (LAER, ☎ 02255-468169), Av Buenos Aires between Paseos 205 and 206, flies to and from Buenos Aires (US$63) 15 times weekly.

Bus The bus station (☎ 02255-476058) is at Av 3 and Paseo 140, on the south side of town. Some long-distance buses stop at the Mini Terminal (☎ 02255-462340) on Av 4, between Paseos 104 and 105. Fares to Buenos Aires (seven hours) are about US$20.

PINAMAR

Planned by elite architect Jorge Bunge for Argentines who needn't work for a living, elegant Pinamar is 120km northeast of Mar del Plata; visitors enjoying the usual outdoor activities must dodge dune buggies on the beach and even along nature trails.

Pinamar acquired notoriety in early 1997 with the still unresolved murder of photo-journalist José Luis Cabezas, which was linked to bodyguards of shady businessman Alberto Yabrán, who committed suicide barely a year later.

Av Libertador, parallel to the beach, and the perpendicular thoroughfare Av Bunge are the main streets; streets on each side of Bunge form large fans, making orientation tricky. The busy Secretaría de Turismo (☎ 02254-491680), Av Bunge 654 at Libertador, has a good pocket map with useful descriptions of Pinamar, Valería, Ostende, and Cariló.

Places to Stay

Several campgrounds, charging about US$18, line the coast between Ostende and Pinamar. The beachfront *Albergue Estudiantil* (☎ 02254-482908), at Nuestras Malvinas and Sarmiento in nearby Ostende, offers 85 dormitory beds at US$12 per person.

Regular accommodations start around US$40 double at *Hospedaje Valle Fértil* (☎ 02254-484799) at Del Cangrejo 1110, rising to US$45 at *Hospedaje Las Acacias* (☎ 85175) at Del Cangrejo 1358 and US$55 *Hospedaje Rose Marie* (☎ 02254-482522), Las Medusas 1381.

Places to Eat

Con Estilo Criollo, Av Bunge and Marco Polo, serves great pork and *chivito a la parri-*

lla (grilled kid goat). *Mamma Liberata*, Av Bunge and Simbad el Marino, and *Club Italiano*, Eneas and Cazón, offer tasty pasta. *Paxapoga*, Avs Bunge and Libertador, is a parrilla and pasta place open all year.

German cooking, mostly breads and cakes, can be found at *Tante*, De las Artes 35. *El Vivero*, Avs Bunge and Libertador, is an enormous but high-quality vegetarian restaurant. For ice cream, there's *Freddo* at Av Bunge and Simbad El Marino.

Getting There & Away

Air Aerolíneas Argentinas (☎ 02254-483663) is at Av Bunge 799, as is Alameda Tur (☎ 02254-481965), the agent for LAPA and LAER. For details, see the Villa Gesell entry.

Bus The bus station is on Shaw between Del Pejerrey and Del Lenguado. Schedules resemble those from Villa Gesell.

Train Trains run in summer from Pinamar's Estación Divisadero to Constitución. Purchase tickets at the bus station.

NECOCHEA

The most attractive feature of this popular, family-oriented resort, 125km southwest of Mar del Plata, is **Parque Miguel Lillo**, a huge green space along the beach whose dense pine woods are popular for cycling, riding or picnicking. The Río Quequén, rich in trout and mackerel, also allows for adventurous canoeing.

The Secretaría de Turismo (☎ 02262-425983, 02262-430158), right on the beach at Av 2 (25 de Mayo) and Calle 83 (Butti), is open 8 am to 8 pm daily.

Places to Stay & Eat

Camping Americano (☎ 02262-435832), in Parque Lillo at Av 2 and Calle 101, costs around US$5 per person. Otherwise, the most reasonable are hospedajes in the US$10 per person range, such as *Hospedaje Regis* (☎ 02262-425870) at Av San Martín 726 and *Hospedaje Bayo* (☎ 02262-423334) at Calle 87 No 338. For off-season prices of US$9 per person with breakfast, large bathrooms and abundant closet space, cheerful *Hostal del Rey* (☎ 02262-425170), on Calle 81 (Moreno) between Calles 6 and 8 is a bargain, but it would be a good deal even at twice the price in summer.

La Romana, on Av 79 between Calles 4 and 6, is a great value with tenedor libre pasta for only US$4.50. Popular even in the off season, *La Rueda*, Calle 4 No 4144, serves excellent, competitively priced parrillada, seafood and Italian cuisine, though the service is awkward.

Getting There & Away

Bus The bus station (☎ 02262-422470) is on Av 58 (Sarmiento) between Calle 47 (Rondeau) and Av 45 (Jesuita Cardiel), near the river. There are many buses daily to Buenos Aires ($25, seven hours) and others to interior destinations including Córdoba, Mar del Plata, Bariloche, Tandil and Santa Rosa, and the Cuyo provinces.

Train The Ferrocarril Roca (☎ 02262-450028) has three trains weekly to Constitución, Buenos Aires.

The Pampas

Unrelentingly flat, Argentina's agricultural heartland contains a surprising number of tourist attractions in the provinces of Buenos Aires, La Pampa, and parts of Santa Fe and Córdoba. An integrated rail and highway network connects the towns of the Pampas to the city of Buenos Aires.

Buenos Aires is Argentina's largest, richest, most populous and most important province. La Plata, the provincial capital, and the port of Bahía Blanca are key cities, while colonial Luján is a major religious center and San Antonio de Areco is the sentimental focus of the country's gaucho culture (both Luján and San Antonio are covered earlier in the Around Buenos Aires section).

Santa Fe city is the capital of its namesake province. Rosario, exporting agricultural produce, challenges Córdoba's status as the republic's 'second city.'

Settled late because of Indian resistance and erratic rainfall, La Pampa did not attain provincial status until 1951. Its varied environments include rolling hills of native *caldén* forests, extensive grasslands, and *salares* (salt lakes) with flamingos. Parque Nacional Lihué Calel justifies a detour from the usual routes to Patagonia.

History

In pre-Columbian times, the aboriginal Querandí hunted guanaco and rhea on the Pampas, but feral European livestock transformed the region. One 18th-century visitor estimated 48 million head of cattle between modern Paraguay and the Río Negro.

Having tamed wild horses, mobile Indians were formidable adversaries, but the Pampas eventually fell to cattle ranchers and farmers. Feral livestock spawned two enduring legacies: the culture of the gaucho, who persisted for decades as a neohunter-gatherer and then a symbol of *argentinidad* (a romantic nationalism); and environmental impoverishment, as grazing and European weeds altered the native pastures.

Only the relatively few estancieros with the luck to inherit or the foresight to grab large tracts of land benefited from hides, tallow and salt beef, which had limited overseas markets. British-built railways made both beef and wool exports feasible, but improved cattle breeds required succulent feeds like alfalfa, which needed preparatory cultivation. Landowners therefore rented to *medieros* (sharecroppers who raised wheat for four or five years before moving on) and thus profited both from their share of the wheat harvest and from new alfalfa fields. Maize, wheat and linseed soon exceeded the value of animal products.

The Pampas are still famous for beef, but some struggling estancias have opened their gates to the tourist trade – not unlike Britain's stately homes or North America's dude ranches. Argentina is still a major grain exporter, while intensive fruit and vegetable cultivation, as well as dairying, takes place near Buenos Aires and other large cities.

LA PLATA

After the city of Buenos Aires became the federal capital, Governor Dardo Rocha founded La Plata, 56km southeast, as the new provincial capital. An important administrative, commercial and cultural center, it has one of the country's best universities.

The superposition of diagonals on a conventional grid forms a distinctive diamond pattern linking several plazas. Most public buildings are on or near Plaza Moreno, but the commercial center is near Plaza San Martín. Almost hostile toward all but the most routine information requests, the Entidad Municipal de Turismo (☎ 0221-482-9656), in the Pasaje Dardo Rocha at Calles 6 and 50, is open 9 am to 6 pm daily except Sunday (9 am to 1 pm).

Things to See

Paseo del Bosque Plantations of eucalyptus, gingko, palm, and subtropical hardwoods cover this 60-hectare park at the northeastern edge of town. Its facilities include the **Anfiteatro Martín Fierro**, an open-air facility that hosts summer drama festivals, the famous natural history **Museo de La Plata** (open daily 10 am to 6 pm; admission US$3), the **Observatorio Astronómico** (open Friday at 9:30 pm for tours), the symbolic United Nations of the **Jardín de la Paz** (Garden of Peace), a small **Jardín Zoológico** (zoo; open daily, except Monday, 9 am to 7 pm) along Av 52, and several university departments.

La República de los Niños A steam train circles this scale reproduction of a city, sponsored for children by Eva Perón and completed shortly before her death in 1952. From Av 7 in La Plata, take bus No 518 or 273 to Camino General Belgrano Km 7, in the suburb of Gonnet. Admission is US$3 per person, which includes aquarium and *granja* (a small zoo of domestic animals), but the train ride and doll museum require separate admission. It's closed Monday.

Places to Stay & Eat

One of few budget hotels, *Hotel Saint James* (☎ 0221-421-8089), Calle 60 No 377, charges US$20/30 single/double without breakfast. *Hotel García*, Calle 2 No 525, is the only other real budget choice. The friendly, remodeled *Hotel Roca* (☎ 0221-421-4916), Calle 47 No 309, costs US$25/30 with shared bath, US$31/38 with private bath.

Among the cheaper restaurants are *Everton*, Calle 14 between Calles 63 and 64, and *Club Matheu*, Calle 63 between Av 1 and Calle 2. A local recommendation is the *Colegio de Escribanos*, Av 13 between Calles 47 and 48.

Chachacha, Calle 10 No 370 between 46 and 47, features an extensive choice of meat, chicken and seafood crêpes, plus draft beer, at moderate prices. A popular Italian place, at Calle 47 and Diagonal 74, is *La Trattoria*.

On warm summer nights, dawdle at the venerable *Cervecería Modelo*, at Calles 54 and 5, with *cerveza tirada* (lager beer), snacks and complimentary peanuts.

Getting There & Away

Bus The bus station (☎ 0221-421-0992) is at Calles 4 and 42. Río de la Plata has half-hourly buses to Once, Constitución and Retiro in Buenos Aires (US$2); there are also long-distance services.

Train Frequent trains to Constitución leave from the Estación Ferrocarril General Roca (☎ 0221-421-9377), Av 1 and Calle 44.

BAHÍA BLANCA

More a crossroads than a tourist destination, 650km south of Buenos Aires, Bahía Blanca is South America's largest naval base, a key port for grain from Buenos Aires province and produce from the Río Negro valley, and the coastal gateway to Patagonia.

Bahía Blanca's Oficina de Información Turística (☎ 0291-455-1110), Alsina 45, is open weekdays 8 am to 1:30 pm, Saturday 10 am to 1 pm. The post office is at Moreno 34, while Locutorio del Sol is at Arribeños 112.

The most worthwhile sight is the **Museo del Puerto**, a 'community museum' that's a whimsical but iconoclastic antidote to Argentina's pompously nationalistic historical museums. At Guillermo Torres 4180 in Puerto Ingeniero White, it's open 8:30 am to noon weekdays and 4 to 7 pm Tuesday and Thursday. From downtown, buses Nos 500 and 501 drop passengers almost at the front door.

Places to Stay & Eat

Open all year, the municipal campground at *Balneario Maldonado* (☎ 0291-452-9511), 4km southwest of downtown, has hot water and electricity in summer only. It charges US$5 per person.

Across from the train station, several cheap but run-down hospedajes charge about US$10 per person. The best is probably simple but clean and friendly *Residencial Roma* (☎ 0291-453-8500), Cerri 759, but there's also *Hotel Molinari* (☎ 0291-452-2871), at Cerri 717, and *Hospedaje Los Vascos* (☎ 0291-452-9290), at Cerri 747. Four blocks west is *Hotel Victoria* (☎ 0291-452-0522), General Paz 84.

For empanadas, there's the take-out *El Mago de la Empanada*, on Undiano near Chiclana. Food is plain, but abundant and inexpensive at *El Jabalí*, Av Cerri 757. There are many parrillas, including *Víctor*, at Chiclana 83, which also serves seafood, and *La Marca*, at Chiclana 417. Plaza Rivadavia features modest eateries like *Pizzería Roma*, at Chiclana 17.

A local institution for more than a century at Arribeños 164, *Gambrinus* is a *choppería* (a beer joint with food) with lively atmosphere, friendly service and some imaginative dishes (try chicken in corn and artichoke sauce).

Getting There & Away
Air Austral (☎ 0291-451-9938), San Martín 298, flies thrice each weekday to Buenos Aires (US$124) and twice a day on weekends; daily except Saturday to Santa Rosa (US$78). LAPA (☎ 0291-456-4522), Soler 68, is less frequent but cheaper (US$39 to US$105) and also flies daily to Río Gallegos (US$97 to US$163) as well as Río Grande (US$125 to US$207). TAN (☎ 0291-451-1305), Euskadi 46, flies to Neuquén (US$50 to US$63) and Bariloche (US$100 to US$114). LADE (☎ 0291-452-1063), Darregueira 21, flies cheaply but slowly to Patagonian destinations.

Bus A key transport node for southern Buenos Aires province and points south, Bahía Blanca's Terminal de Ómnibus San Francisco de Asís (☎ 0291-4818121), Brown 1700, is about 2km east of Plaza Rivadavia. Buses to Buenos Aires (US$30, 10 hours) are frequent, but there are also services to Mar del Plata (US$21, seven hours), Neuquén (US$30, 10 hours) and coastal Patagonia as far as Río Gallegos (US$78, 26 hours).

Train From Estación Ferrocarril Roca (☎ 521168), Av Cerri 750, Ferrobaires goes nightly to Constitución. Fares are US$15 turista, US$17 primera, US$22 Pullman, and US$30 coche cama.

Getting Around
To/From the Airport Aeropuerto Comandante Espora (☎ 0291-4521665) is 15km east of town on the naval base, RN 3 Norte, Km 674. Austral provides its own transport (US$3).

Bus Local buses cost US$0.70; buy magnetic cards from kiosks. Nos 505, 512, 514, 516 and 517 serve the bus terminal, while No 505 goes out Av Colón to Balneario Maldonado.

SIERRA DE LA VENTANA
Granitic bedrock emerges from the deep Pampas sediments only in the ranges of Tandilia and Ventania, trending northwest to southeast. The easterly Sierras de Tandil are rounded hills of around 500m, but the westerly Sierra de la Ventana attracts hikers and climbers to scenic jagged peaks above 1300m. Its charming namesake village, 125km north of Bahía Blanca, also offers conventional facilities including a casino, golf links and swimming pools.

Just south of the train station, the Oficina de Turismo y Delegación Municipal (☎ 0291-491-5303), Roca 15, has a useful packet of maps and brochures.

Places to Stay & Eat
There are several free campsites along the river, with toilets and showers at the nearby municipal swimming pool (US$2.50). If you would prefer an organized campground, try *Camping El Paraíso* (☎ 0291-491-5299), on Diego Meyer, which has good facilities at US$5 per adult, US$2 per child.

In Villa Arcadia, at the east end of Coronel Suárez, the *Ymcapolis* (☎ 0291-491-5004) provides hostel accommodations in a stylish old building for US$10 per person.

Other moderately priced accommodations include *Hospedaje La Perlita* (☎ 0291-491-5020), Islas Malvinas and Pasaje 3, for US$15 per person. For the same price, *Hotel Anay-Ruca* (☎ 0291-491-5191), Rayes and Punta Alta in Villa Arcadia, includes breakfast.

Ser, on Güemes just off San Martín, has good pizza and pasta, with large portions, but drinks are expensive. *El Establo*, on San Martín between Islas Malvinas and Av Roca, is a decent pizzería that also serves fixed-price lunches.

Getting There & Away
From the modest bus station (☎ 0291-491-5091) at Av Roca 80, La Estrella has nightly buses to Buenos Aires (US$25, 7½ hours) at 10:30 pm, plus an 8 am service to La Plata. Expreso Cabildo goes to Bahía Blanca, via Tornquist, at 6:45 am and 7 pm daily.

AROUND SIERRA DE LA VENTANA

Popular for ranger-guided walks and independent hiking, 6700-hectare **Parque Provincial Ernesto Tornquist**, west of the village, is the starting point for the 1136m summit of **Cerro de la Ventana**. It's about two hours routine hiking for anyone except the wheezing porteño tobacco addicts who struggle to the crest of what is probably the country's most climbed peak.

Rangers in the trailer at the trailhead collect a US$1 entry fee and routinely deny permission to climb after 1 pm; insistent hikers can get permission by signing a waiver. The friendly *Campamento Base* has good shade, clean baths and excellent hot showers for US$5 per person.

SANTA FE

Tributaries of the Río Paraná surround Santa Fe, capital of its namesake province and a leading agro-industrial center, but the main channel flows about 10km east; in 1983, the powerful rising river mangled the Puente Colgante (Hanging Bridge), which connected the city with Paraná, 25km east, forcing the province to build a replacement.

Relocated during the mid-17th century because of Indians, floods and isolation, the city duplicates the original plan of Santa Fe La Vieja, but a 19th-century neo-Parisian building boom and more recent construction have left only isolated colonial buildings, mostly near Plaza 25 de Mayo. Av San Martín, north of the plaza, is the main commercial artery.

Information

At the bus terminal, Belgrano 2910, Santa Fe's Dirección Municipal de Turismo (☎ 0342-457-4123) is open daily 7 am to 1 pm and 2 to 8 pm.

Tourfe, San Martín 2500, collects 3% commission on traveler's checks; there are several ATMs along the San Martín peatonal. The post office is at Av 27 de Febrero 2331. Telecom is upstairs at the bus terminal.

Things to See

Some colonial buildings are museums, but the churches still serve their ecclesiastical functions, like the mid-17th-century **Templo de Santo Domingo**, at 3 de Febrero and 9 de Julio. The exterior simplicity of the Jesuit **Iglesia de la Compañía** (1696), on Plaza 25 de Mayo, masks an ornate interior. The restored, two-story **Casa de los Aldao**, Buenos Aires 2861, dates from the early 18th century.

Built in 1680, the **Convento y Museo de San Francisco** at Amenábar 2257, south of Plaza 25 de Mayo, is Santa Fe's most important landmark. Its meter-thick walls support a roof of Paraguayan cedar and hardwood beams fitted with wooden spikes rather than nails. The doors are hand-worked originals, while the baroque pulpit is laminated in gold. Its museum covers secular and religious topics from colonial and republican eras.

In a damp 17th-century building at San Martín 1490, the **Museo Histórico Provincial Brigadier General Estanislao López** has permanent exhibits on the 19th-century civil wars, provincial governors (and caudillos), period furnishings and religious art, plus a room treating more-contemporary themes. The most interesting item at the **Museo Etnográfico y Colonial Juan de Garay**, 25 de Mayo 1470, is a scale model of Santa Fe La Vieja on the Río San Javier. There are also colonial artifacts, Indian basketry, Spanish ceramics, and coins and other money.

Places to Stay

Near the bus terminal, the absolute cheapest is *Residencial Las Vegas*, Irigoyen Freire 2246, where singles/doubles cost US$10/16; *Hotel Alfil* (☎ 0342-453-5044), Belgrano 2859, has air-con rooms with shared bath for US$10/15, with private bath US$13/20.

Residencial Guadalupe (☎ 0342-452-1289), Eva Perón 2575, is slightly dearer at US$12/18. *Hotel Apolo* (☎ 0342-452-7984), Belgrano 2821, is clean but dark; it has rooms for US$15/28 with shared bath, US$22/38 with private bath.

Downtown, friendly but undistinguished *Hotel California* (☎ 0342-452-3988), 25 de Mayo 2190, has only a dozen rooms, all with private bath, for US$17/25. Perhaps the best value in town, *Hotel Emperatriz* (☎ 0342-453-0061), Irigoyen Freire 2440, occupies a remodeled private house once owned by an elite santafesino family. It's quiet, friendly, and dignified for US$25/35 with private bath.

Places to Eat

On Belgrano, across from the bus terminal, several very good, inexpensive places serve

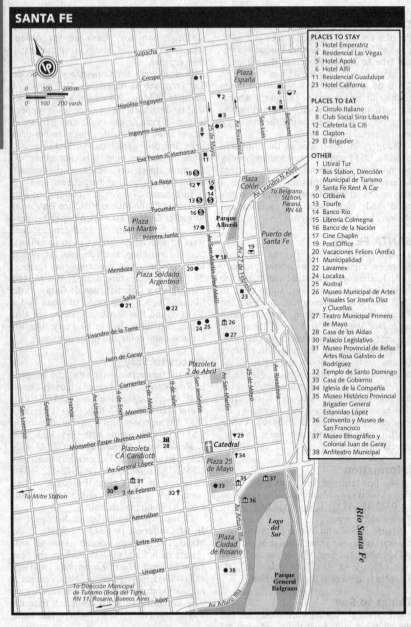

SANTA FE

PLACES TO STAY
3 Hotel Emperatriz
4 Residencial Las Vegas
5 Hotel Apolo
6 Hotel Alfil
11 Residencial Guadalupe
23 Hotel California

PLACES TO EAT
2 Círculo Italiano
8 Club Social Sirio Libanés
12 Cafetería La Citi
18 Clapton
29 El Brigadier

OTHER
1 Litoral Tur
7 Bus Station, Dirección
   Municipal de Turismo
9 Santa Fe Rent A Car
10 Citibank
13 Tourfe
14 Banco Río
15 Librería Colmegna
16 Banco de la Nación
17 Cine Chaplin
19 Post Office
20 Vacaciones Felices (AmEx)
21 Municipalidad
22 Lavamex
24 Localiza
25 Austral
26 Museo Municipal de Artes
   Visuales Sor Josefa Díaz
   y Clucellas
27 Teatro Municipal Primero
   de Mayo
28 Casa de los Aldao
30 Palacio Legislativo
31 Museo Provincial de Bellas
   Artes Rosa Galisteo de
   Rodríguez
32 Templo de Santo Domingo
33 Casa de Gobierno
34 Iglesia de la Compañía
35 Museo Histórico Provincial
   Brigadier General
   Estanislao López
36 Convento y Museo de
   San Francisco
37 Museo Etnográfico y
   Colonial Juan de Garay
38 Anfiteatro Municipal

Argentine staples such as empanadas, pizza, and parrillada. At La Rioja 2609, try *Cafetería La Citi* for coffee and sandwiches. *Clapton*, San Martín 2300, also has good sandwiches and lunches. *El Brigadier*, San Martín 1607, is a cheap parrilla.

The *Círculo Italiano*, Hipólito Yrigoyen 2457, prepares good, moderately priced lunch specials. The *Club Social Sirio Libanés*, on San Martín between Irigoyen Freire and Eva Perón, serves tasty Middle Eastern fare.

Tourists and locals flock to riverside *El Quincho de Chiquito*, some distance north of downtown at Brown and Obispo Vieytes, for grilled river fish – in practice, it's all you can eat for about US$10 to US$15 plus drinks. Take bus No 16 on Av Gálvez, which parallels Suipacha four blocks to the north.

Getting There & Away

Air Austral (☎ 0342-459-8400), Lisandro de la Torre 2633, has 25 weekly nonstops to Buenos Aires (US$81). Litoral Tur (☎ 0342-499-5414), San Martín 2984, represents Líneas Aéreas de Entre Ríos (LAER), which flies daily except Sunday to Buenos Aires' Aeroparque (US$65).

Bus The Oficina de Informes (☎ 0342-454-7124) at the bus station, Belgrano 2940, is open 6 am to 10 pm; it posts all fares for destinations throughout the country, so it's unnecessary to run from window to window for comparison.

Roughly hourly throughout the day and night, Etacer buses leave for Paraná (US$3). Sample long-distance fares include Rosario (US$10, two hours), Buenos Aires (US$26, six hours), Corrientes (US$26, 10 hours), Posadas (US$30, 12 hours), and Puerto Iguazú (US$40, 16 hours). Other carriers go to Córdoba and its Sierras, to Mendoza, and Patagonian destinations such as Neuquén (US$65, 16 hours).

International services go to Porto Alegre (US$51) and Rio de Janeiro (US$92), Brazil; Asunción, Paraguay (US$41 to US$57, 13 hours); and Montevideo, Uruguay (US$45, 12 hours).

ROSARIO

Rosario, the presumptive birthplace of revolutionary leader Ernesto 'Che' Guevara, is 320km upstream from Buenos Aires on the west bank of the Paraná. After independence, the city quickly superseded the provincial capital of Santa Fe as an economic powerhouse, as the railway brought agricultural exports from Córdoba, Mendoza and Tucumán. Curving bluffs and open space above the river channel modify Rosario's regular grid pattern, whose center is Plaza 25 de Mayo. The pedestrian streets of San Martín and Córdoba are the focus of commerce.

Information

Tourist Offices The Ente Turístico Rosario (Etur, ☎ 0341-480-2230; etur@rosario.gov.ar), is on the waterfront at Av Belgrano and Buenos Aires, and is open 8 am to 8 pm weekdays, 9 am to 8 pm weekends. It has a computerized information system and also offers weekend walking tours.

Cambios along San Martín and Córdoba change cash and traveler's checks; there are several ATMs along the Córdoba peatonal. The post office is at Córdoba 721. There are many locutorios. The Berlín Ciber Café, Tucumán 1289, has Internet access and live music as well.

Things to See

Rosario's biggest attraction (literally) is the colossal, boat-shaped **Monumento Nacional a la Bandera** (Monument to the Flag), which shelters the crypt of flag designer General Manuel Belgrano, at the foot of Av Córdoba. Its museum is open 9 am to 7 pm daily; in June, Rosario celebrates **La Semana de la Bandera** (Flag Week).

Focusing on the republican era, Parque Independencia's **Museo Histórico Provincial Dr Julio Marc** is open weekdays 9 am to 6 pm, weekends 3 to 8 pm. The **Museo de la Ciudad**, Oroño 2350, is open weekdays 10 am to 1 pm, weekends 5 to 8 pm. The fine-arts **Museo Municipal de Bellas Artes Juan B Castagnino**, at Pellegrini and Oroño, is open Tuesday to Friday 4 to 10 pm.

Visitors interested in environment and wildlife should visit the **Museo Provincial de Ciencias Naturales Dr Ángel Gallardo**, Moreno 758, Tuesday to Friday 9 am to 12:30 pm and Tuesday, Friday and Sunday 3 to 6 pm. The planetarium, at the **Complejo Municipal Astronómico Educativo Rosario** in Parque Urquiza, has weekend shows

ROSARIO

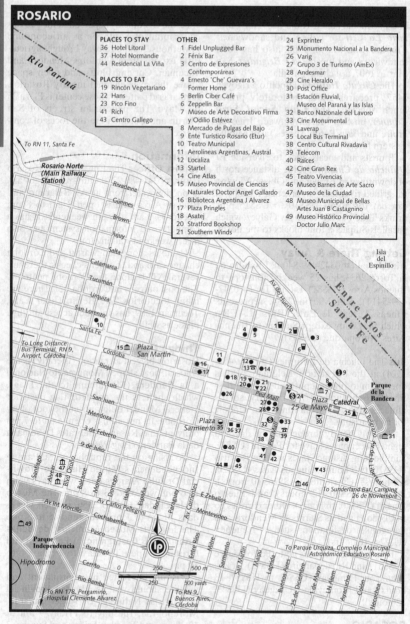

PLACES TO STAY
36 Hotel Litoral
37 Hotel Normandie
44 Residencial La Viña

PLACES TO EAT
19 Rincón Vegetariano
22 Hans
23 Pico Fino
41 Rich
43 Centro Gallego

OTHER
1   Fidel Unplugged Bar
2   Fénix Bar
3   Centro de Expresiones
    Contemporáreas
4   Ernesto 'Che' Guevara's
    Former Home
5   Berlín Ciber Café
6   Zeppelin Bar
7   Museo de Arte Decorativo Firma
    y Odilio Estévez
8   Mercado de Pulgas del Bajo
9   Ente Turístico Rosario (Etur)
10 Teatro Municipal
11 Aerolíneas Argentinas, Austral
12 Localiza
13 Startel
14 Cine Atlas
15 Museo Provincial de Ciencias
    Naturales Doctor Angel Gallardo
16 Biblioteca Argentina J Alvarez
17 Plaza Pringles
18 Asatej
20 Stratford Bookshop
21 Southern Winds

24 Exprinter
25 Monumento Nacional a la Bandera
26 Varig
27 Grupo 3 de Turismo (AmEx)
28 Andesmar
29 Cine Heraldo
30 Post Office
31 Estación Fluvial,
    Museo del Paraná y las Islas
32 Banco Nazionale del Lavoro
33 Cine Monumental
34 Laverap
35 Local Bus Terminal
38 Centro Cultural Rivadavia
39 Telecom
40 Raíces
42 Cine Gran Rex
45 Teatro Vivencias
46 Museo Barnes de Arte Sacro
47 Museo de la Ciudad
48 Museo Municipal de Bellas
    Artes Juan B Castagnino
49 Museo Histórico Provincial
    Doctor Julio Marc

from 5 to 6 pm. On Friday, Saturday and Sunday, from 9 to 10 pm, visitors can view the austral skies through its telescopes.

River life – flora, fauna and people – is the focus of the **Museo del Paraná y Las Islas** in the waterfront Estación Fluvial. Undergoing restoration as of this writing, it's most notable for Raúl Domínguez's romantic but fascinating murals.

Renowned architect Alejandro Bustillo designed the apartment building at **Entre Ríos 480** where, in 1928, Ernesto Guevara Lynch and Celia de la Serna resided after the birth of their son Ernesto Guevara de la Serna, popularly known as 'Che.' According to biographer Jon Anderson, the young Ernesto's birth certificate was falsified (he was born more than a month before the official date of June 14), but this was certainly his first home.

Places to Stay

Friendly, inexpensive *Hotel Normandie (☎ 0341-424-0381)*, Mitre 1030, has singles/doubles for US$18/28 with private bath and breakfast, slightly less with shared bath. Centrally located *Residencial La Viña (☎ 0341-421-4549)*, 3 de Febrero 1244, is a good value for US$20/25. *Hotel Litoral (☎ 0341-421-1426)*, Entre Ríos 1043, has attractive balconies opening out from many of its rooms, which cost US$22/32. Near the long-distance bus terminal, at Pasaje Quintanilla 657, *Hotel Gran Confort (☎ 0341-438-0486)* has rooms with private bath for US$20/30.

Places to Eat

Pico Fino, San Martín 783, has a varied menu of Argentine and international food, outstanding service, and is very reasonable – even reasonable enough to make half-pizzas (four portions) for solo diners.

The *Centro Gallego*, Buenos Aires 1137, serves fixed-price all-you-can-eat meals, while *Hans*, Mitre 777, is also economical. For non-carnivores, *Rincón Vegetariano*, Mitre 720, is a meatless alternative. *Rich*, San Juan 1031, is fine for Italian food, but don't overlook the rotisería alongside.

Rosario's classic eatery is the venerable *Sunderland Bar*, Av Belgrano Sur 2210, with excellent service, superb food at reasonable prices, and great atmosphere, though desserts are expensive.

Getting There & Away

Air Aerolíneas Argentinas and Austral (☎ 0341-448-0372) share offices at Santa Fe 1412. Aerolíneas has 11 weekly flights to Buenos Aires' Aeroparque (US$67), while Austral has 23.

Southern Winds (☎ 0341-425-3808), Mitre 737, flies often to Córdoba (US$59 to US$79) and other northwestern destinations, as well as to northern Patagonia. Andesmar (☎ 0341-424-8070), Rioja 1198, flies to Córdoba (US$39 to US$63), Buenos Aires (US$49 to US$67), Mendoza (US$87 to US$119) and the Northwest.

Rosario's only international service is three times weekly with Varig (☎ 0341-425-6262), Av Corrientes 729, 7th floor, to São Paulo and Belo Horizonte, Brazil.

Bus Reached by bus No 101 from Calle San Juan, Estación Mariano Moreno (☎ 0341-437-2384) is at Cafferata 702, near Santa Fe. Buses go frequently to Buenos Aires (US$15, four hours), Córdoba (US$20, six hours) and Santa Fe (US$10, two hours); Corrientes (US$30, 10 hours) and Puerto Iguazú; less often to Tucumán and Mendoza, and to Bariloche (US$76, 23 hours). International destinations include Asunción, Paraguay (US$40 to US$56, 12 hours), Montevideo, Uruguay (US$51, 10 hours), and Porto Alegre and Rio de Janeiro (Brazil).

Train From the Estación Rosario Norte (☎ 0341-439-2429), Av del Valle 2700, northbound services to Santiago del Estero/La Banda (US$18 primera, US$15 turista) and Tucumán (US$25 primera, US$17 turista) leave Tuesday and Saturday at 2:58 am, while southbound services to Retiro (US$12 primera, US$8 turista) leave at 8:19 am Monday and Friday.

Getting Around

To/From the Airport Aerolíneas runs minibuses to Aeropuerto Fisherton, 8km west of town. A taxi or remise costs about US$12.

Bus The extensive local bus system is centered on Plaza Sarmiento.

SANTA ROSA

Santa Rosa de Toay, 600km from Buenos Aires via RN 5, is a tidy, pleasant city of

82,000. Plaza San Martín is the commercial center of the city's standard grid, north of Av España. The modern centro cívico is on Av Pedro Luro, seven blocks east.

Information

The enthusiastically helpful Dirección Provincial de Turismo (☎ 02954-425060) is at Av Pedro Luro and Av San Martín, directly across from the bus terminal. The staff have maps and brochures, and selected local handicrafts in the Mercado Artesanal on the premises. Hours are weekdays 7 am to 1:30 pm and 5 to 9 pm, weekends 9 am to noon and 5 to 9 pm.

The Municipalidad maintains a tourist information center at the bus terminal, open 24 hours.

Several banks change cash (though not traveler's checks) and there are several ATMs. The post office is at Hilario Lagos 258. Telefónica Centro is on Avellaneda near Quintana.

Museums

At Pellegrini 190, Santa Rosa's **Museo de Ciencias Naturales y Antropológicas** contains natural science, archaeological, historical, artisanal and fine-arts collections. The **Museo de Artes**, at 9 de Julio and Villegas, contains works by Argentine and provincial artists.

Places to Stay & Eat

One of Argentina's last remaining free campgrounds is the *Centro Recreativo Municipal Don Tomás* (☎ 02954-455368), at the west end of Av Uruguay. From the bus terminal, take the local Transporte El Indio bus. *Hospedaje Mitre* (☎ 02954-425432), a short walk from the bus terminal at Emilio Mitre 74, has singles/doubles with shared bath for US$15/27, with private bath for US$21/34. Rates are marginally cheaper at *Hostería Santa Rosa* (☎ 02954-423868), Hipólito Yrigoyen 696.

Restaurant San Martín, Pellegrini 115, is a routine but popular spot for parrilla and pasta, cheap by current standards. At *La Tablita*, Urquiza 336, the US$10 parrillada includes a superb buffet. The *Club Español*, Hilario Lagos 237, has excellent Argentine and Spanish food, outstanding service and reasonable prices.

Getting There & Away

Air Austral (☎ 02954-433076), Rivadavia 258, flies Sunday through Friday to Bahía Blanca (US$78), where there are onward connections.

Bus The bus station (☎ 02954-422952) is at the centro cívico, Av Pedro Luro 365. Chevallier offers the only regular service passing Parque Nacional Lihué Calel (US$22) en route to Neuquén, leaving Wednesday at midnight. Other destinations include Buenos Aires (US$25, six hours), Mendoza (US$41, 12 hours), San Martín de los Andes and Bariloche (US$50, 21 hours), and Comodoro Rivadavia.

Train The Ferrocarril Sarmiento (☎ 02954-433451), at Alsina and Pellegrini, has sluggish services to Estación Once (Buenos Aires) Tuesday, Thursday and Sunday at 8:12 pm (US$13 turista, US$15 primera, US$20 Pullman).

PARQUE NACIONAL LIHUÉ CALEL

Lihué Calel's small, remote mountain ranges, 226km southwest of Santa Rosa via RN 152, were a stronghold of Araucanian resistance during General Roca's so-called Conquista del Desierto (Conquest of the Desert). Its salmon-colored exfoliating granites, reaching 600m, offer a variety of subtle environments, changing with the season or even with the day.

In this 10,000-hectare desert, sudden storms can bring flash floods and create spectacular, temporary waterfalls. Even when there's no rain, subterranean streams nourish the *monte*, a scrub forest of surprising botanical variety.

The author has seen a puma here, but the most common mammals are foxes, guanacos, *maras* (Patagonian hares) and *vizcachas* (relatives of the chinchilla). Bird species include *ñandú* (rhea) and birds of prey like the *carancho* (crested caracara).

Things to See & Do

From the park campground, a signed trail leads through a dense thorn forest of caldén (*Prosopis caldenia*, a local species of a common genus) and similar trees, to a site with petroglyphs, unfortunately vandalized.

From the petroglyphs, another trail reaches the 589m summit of **Cerro de la Sociedad Científica Argentina**, with outstanding views of the entire sierra, surrounding marshes and salares. The boulders are slippery when wet; notice the flowering cacti between them.

Places to Stay
The free *campground* near the visitor center has shade, picnic tables, firepits, cold showers and many birds. Bring food – the nearest supplies are at the town of Puelches, 35km south. The *ACA Hostería*, on the highway, has rooms and a restaurant.

Getting There & Away
The only remaining bus service using RN 152 from Santa Rosa to Chelforó (on RN 22 in Río Negro province) is Chevallier's weekly service to Neuquén at midnight Wednesday, which drops passengers at Lihué Calel in the predawn hours for US$22. Minibuses belonging to Sacra (☎ 02954-428903), Av Luro 1340 in Santa Rosa, pass Lihué Calel en route to the town of Puelches (US$12) Monday, Wednesday and Friday at 6 am.

Mesopotamia

Mesopotamia, the area between the Paraná and Uruguay Rivers, offers varied recreational opportunities on the rivers and in the parks of Entre Ríos and Corrientes provinces. Subtropical Misiones province, nearly surrounded by Paraguay and Brazil, features ruined Jesuit missions and the spectacular Iguazú Falls. Across the Río Paraná, the Gran Chaco is Argentina's 'empty quarter.'

History
After Spaniards reached the upper Paraná, obtaining provisions from the Guaraní, settlement proceeded southward from Asunción (Paraguay). Corrientes was founded in 1588, Santa Fe about the same time. For more information on early Spanish activities, see the Paraguay chapter.

Jesuits established 30 Guaraní *reducciones* in the upper Paraná. These settlements resembled most other Spanish municipalities, but non-Jesuits envied their political and economic autonomy – mostly because Jesuits monopolized Indian labor in an area where the encomienda was weak. Concerned that Jesuits were creating a state within a state, Spain expelled them from the Americas in 1767. Argentina took definitive control of the territory, contested by Brazil and Paraguay, after the War of the Triple Alliance (1865-70).

Briefly an independent republic, Entre Ríos became a Unitarist stronghold after Rosas took power. Local caudillo Justo José Urquiza brought about Rosas' defeat and the eventual adoption of Argentina's modern constitution.

In the dense thorn forests of Chaco and Formosa provinces, oppressive heat and hostile Indians discouraged early exploration. After 1850, woodcutters from Corrientes, exploiting the *quebracho* (axe-breaker) tree for tannin, literally cleared the way for cotton and cattle.

PARANÁ
Capital of the Argentine confederation from 1853 to 1861, now of Entre Ríos province, Paraná takes pride in having cooperated with Santa Fe to build the Hernandarias tunnel beneath the main channel of the Río Paraná, despite active opposition from the federal government.

On the east bank of the river, the city's irregular plan has several diagonals, curving boulevards and complex intersections. From Plaza Primero de Mayo, the town center, Calle San Martín is a peatonal for six blocks. At the west end of San Martín, Parque Urquiza extends more than a kilometer along the riverfront.

Information
Paraná's Dirección Municipal de Turismo (☎ 0343-420-1805 interno 27), on San Martín near La Paz, is open 8 am to 8 pm daily. There are branches at the bus terminal and at the Oficina Parque (☎ 0343-420-1837) on the riverfront at Bajada San Martín and Av Laurencena. Paraná's Dirección Provincial de Turismo (☎ 0343-422-3384) is located at Laprida 5.

There are several ATMs along the peatonal San Martín. The post office is at Av 25 de Mayo and Monte Caseros, while

MESOPOTAMIA

there's a Telecentro on San Martín between Uruguay and Pazos. The Cyber Pub, at La Rioja and Uruguay, has Internet access.

Things to See

The **Iglesia Catedral** has been on Plaza Primero de Mayo since 1730, but the current building dates from 1885. When Paraná was capital of the confederation, the Senate deliberated at the **Colegio del Huerto**, at 9 de Julio and 25 de Mayo.

A block west, at Corrientes and Urquiza, are the **Palacio Municipal** (1889) and the **Escuela Normal Paraná**, a school founded by noted educator (later President) DF Sarmiento. Across San Martín, at Av 25 de Mayo 60, is the **Teatro Municipal Tres de Febrero** (1908). At the west end of the San Martín peatonal, on Plaza Alvear, the **Museo Histórico de Entre Ríos Martín Leguizamón** flaunts provincial pride, as knowledgeable guides go to rhetorical extremes extolling the role of local caudillos in Argentine history. The adjacent subterranean **Museo de Bellas Artes Pedro E Martínez** shows works by provincial artists.

The modern **Museo de la Ciudad** focuses on Paraná's urban past and surroundings. It's on the *costanera* (riverfront road) Av Laurencena in Parque Urquiza, and is open Tuesday through Sunday 4 to 8 pm, Tuesday to Friday 8 am to noon, and Saturday 9 am to noon; winter hours are slightly shorter and earlier. Admission is free.

Activities

From the Puerto Nuevo at Costanera and Vélez Sársfield, the Paraná Rowing Club (☎ 0343-431-2048) conducts hour-long **river excursions** (US$3) at 3:30 and 5 pm Friday, Saturday and Sunday.

Places to Stay

Bus Nos 1 and 6 ('Thompson') link *Camping Balneario Thompson* (☎ 0343-420-1583), the most convenient campground, to downtown. Campsites cost US$4 per tent, plus US$1 per person and per vehicle.

The best budget choice is *Hotel City* (☎ 0343-431-0086) at Blvd Racedo 231, directly opposite the train station. It has a wonderful patio garden and cool rooms with high ceilings. Singles/doubles here are US$20/31 with private bath, slightly less with shared bath.

Prices are similar at downtown *Hotel Roma* (☎ 0343-4312247), Urquiza 1061. *Hotel Bristol* (☎ 0343-4313961), near the bus terminal at Alsina 221, is more expensive at US$25/35, but clean and attractive.

Places to Eat

A good place to stock up on food is the *Mercado Central*, at Pellegrini and Bavio. River fish is the local specialty, though; try *Pollolandia*, Tucumán 418, for a bargain on tasty grilled boga.

One of Paraná's traditional favorites is *Luisito*, 9 de Julio 140. *Don Charras*, Av Raúl Uranga 1127 near the junction to the tunnel, is a highly regarded parrilla, as is *Giovani*, Av Urquiza 1045. Other recommended choices include *Viva El Río* at Av Crespo 71 and *Quinchos de Paja* at Av Laurencena and Bajada San Martín.

Getting There & Away

Air Aerolíneas Argentinas (☎ 0343-423-2425) has offices at Corrientes 563, but flights leave from Santa Fe's Aeropuerto Sauce Viejo (see Getting There & Away for Santa Fe). Líneas Aéreas de Entre Ríos (LAER, ☎ 0343-423-0347), 25 de Junio 77, flies to Buenos Aires (US$65) an average of four times daily from Aeropuerto Ciudad de Paraná, just outside the city limits.

Bus The bus station (☎ 0343-422-1282) is on Av Ramírez between Posadas and Moreno, opposite Plaza Martín Fierro. Roughly hourly throughout the day and night, Etacer buses (☎ 0343-421-6809) leave for Santa Fe (US$3). Other services and fares closely resemble those to and from Santa Fe.

GUALEGUAYCHÚ

In the first sizable city north of Buenos Aires, on a tributary of the Río Uruguay, Gualeguaychú's Carnaval has an international reputation, so stop here if you can't make Rio or Bahia. RN 14 passes west of Gualeguaychú, while RN 136, a side road, bypasses the city center en route to Fray Bentos, Uruguay.

Plaza San Martín marks the city center. Gualeguaychú's Dirección Municipal de Turismo (☎ 03446-422900), on Av Costanera near the bridge over the Río Gualeguaychú, keeps long hours. Several banks have ATMs.

Uruguay has a consulate (☎ 03446-426168), at Rivadavia 510.

The colonial **Casa de Andrade**, at Andrade and Borques, once belonged to 19th-century poet, journalist, diplomat and politician Olegario Andrade. At Fray Mocho 135, **Casa de Fray Mocho** was the birthplace of José S Álvarez, founder of the influential satirical magazine *Caras y Caretas* at the turn of the century; Fray Mocho was his pen name.

At the former Estación Ferrocarril Urquiza, at the south end of Maipú, the **Museo Ferroviario** is an open-air exhibit of locomotives, dining cars and the like. Alongside the station, on Blvd Irazusta, the new **Corsódromo** is the main site for Gualeguaychú's lively Carnaval.

Places to Stay & Eat
Camping La Delfina (☎ 03446-423984), across the Río Gualeguaychú in Parque Unzué, has good facilities (US$10 for two). Clean, friendly *Pensión Gualeguaychú*, Av 25 de Mayo 456, has singles for US$10 with shared bath. At *Hospedaje Mayo* (☎ 03446-427661), Bolívar 550, singles/doubles with private bath cost US$15/20. *Hotel Amalfi* (☎ 03446-425677), 25 de Mayo 579, charges US$15/20 single/double with shared bath, US$20/30 with private bath.

Most better restaurants are along the Costanera, such as *Ducal,* at the corner of Andrade (good fish), but try also the *Círculo Italiano* at San Martín 647 or *Paris* at Pellegrini 180. *Pizzería Don Julián* is at Urquiza 607, while *Pizza San Remo* is at 25 de Mayo 634.

Getting There & Away
The run-down bus station (☎ 03446-427987), very central at Bolívar and Monseñor Chalup, is likely to move in the near future. Several companies go to Buenos Aires (US$20, three hours) and to Paraná (US$20, six hours), and north toward Corrientes. Monday through Friday at noon and 7 pm, Ciudad de Gualeguay goes to Fray Bentos, Uruguay (US$4, one hour), continuing to Mercedes.

PARQUE NACIONAL EL PALMAR
The yatay palm *(Syagrus yatay)* covered much of the littoral until 19th-century agriculture, ranching and forestry destroyed palm savannas and inhibited their reproduc-

tion. On the west bank of the Río Uruguay, 360km north of Buenos Aires, the relict yatays of 8500-hectare El Palmar have again begun to thrive, under protection from fire and grazing. Reaching 18m in height, the larger specimens punctuate a soothing subtropical landscape.

To see wildlife, walk along the watercourses or through the palm savannas early in the morning or just before sunset. The most conspicuous bird is the ñandú, or rhea *(Rhea americana)*, but look for parakeets, cormorants, egrets, herons, storks, caracaras, woodpeckers and kingfishers. The carpincho (capybara), a semiaquatic rodent weighing up to 60kg, and the vizcacha, a relative of the chinchilla, are among the most conspicuous mammals.

At night, squeaking vizcachas infest the campground at Arroyo Los Loros and gigantic toads invade the showers and toilets, but both are harmless. The *yarará*, a highly poisonous pit viper, is not; bites are unusual, but watch your step and wear high boots and long trousers when hiking.

Things to See & Do
Across from the campground, the park's **Centro de Interpretación** (☎ 03447-93031) offers evening slide shows and contains a small reptile house. At the Arroyo Los Loros campground, rental canoes are available for exploring the placid river. A short hike from the campground, **Arroyo Los Loros** is a good place to observe wildlife.

Five km from the campground, **Arroyo El Palmar** is a pleasant stream with a beautiful swimming hole, and a good site for birdwatching. Crossing the ruined bridge, you can walk several kilometers along a palm-lined road being reclaimed by savanna grasses.

Places to Stay & Eat
Arroyo Los Loros campground (☎ 0447-93031) has good sites (US$4 per person plus US$4 per tent the first day only), hot showers, a shop and a *confitería*.

Getting There & Away
Any northbound bus from Buenos Aires to Concordia can drop you at the entrance (admission US$5). No public transport serves the Centro de Interpretación and campground, but hitching is feasible.

CORRIENTES

Just below the confluence of the Paraná and Paraguay Rivers, one of Argentina's oldest cities and capital of its namesake province, Corrientes is 1025km from Buenos Aires. Its once-moribund **Carnaval Correntino** has experienced a revival, attracting crowds up to 80,000 strong. Across the Paraná is Resistencia, capital of Chaco province.

Plaza 25 de Mayo is the center of Corrientes' extremely regular grid plan, but public buildings are more dispersed than in most Argentine cities. The commercial center is the Junín peatonal, between Salta and Catamarca, but the most attractive area is the shady riverside Parque Mitre.

Information

The friendly, helpful Dirección Provincial de Turismo (☎ 03783-427200), 25 de Mayo 1330, is open weekdays 7 am to 1 pm and 3 to 9 pm, weekends 8 am to noon and 4 to 8 pm. The Dirección Municipal de Turismo (☎ 03783-23779) is at Pellegrini 542.

Cambio El Dorado is at 9 de Julio 1341; there are several banks with ATMs around 9 de Julio. The post office is at San Juan and San Martín. There's a Telecentro at Pellegrini 1239.

Things to See

The museum at the colonial **Convento de San Francisco**, Mendoza 450, is open 8 am to noon and 5 to 9 pm weekdays. The east side of Calle San Juan, between Plácido Martínez and Quintana, has become a shady, attractive park whose **Monumento a la Gloria** honors the Italian community; a series of striking historical murals, extending over 100m around the corner, chronicles local history since colonial times.

On Belgrano between Buenos Aires and Salta, visit the **Santuario de la Cruz del Milagro**, whose 16th-century cross, according to local legend, defied Indian efforts to burn it.

The **Museo Histórico de Corrientes**, Av 9 de Julio 1044, features exhibits of weapons, coins and antique furniture, as well as displays on religious and civil history; it's open weekdays 8 am to noon and 4 to 8 pm. The **Museo de Bellas Artes Dr Juan Ramón Vidal**, San Juan 634, emphasizes sculpture. Hours are Tuesday to Saturday 9 am to noon and 6 to 9 pm.

Places to Stay

During Carnaval, the provincial tourist office maintains a list of *casas de familia* ranging from US$10 to US$20 per person. Regular budget choices include *Hospedaje Robert* (no phone) at La Rioja 415, and *Residencial Necochea* (no phone) at Héroes Civiles (the southward extension of La Rioja) 1898, both charging around US$18/30 single/double with shared bath. *Hotel Caribe* (☎ 03783-42197), close to the bus terminal at Maipú 2590, charges US$25/35 with private bath.

Gran Hotel Turismo (☎ 03783-33174), in parklike grounds with a swimming pool, restaurant and bar on the Av Costanera General San Martín (though the street address is Entre Ríos 650), is a good value at US$48/58.

Places to Eat

For cheap eats, look in and around the *Mercado Central* (central market) on Junín between La Rioja and San Juan. *Pizzería Los Pinos*, at Bolívar and San Lorenzo, is a good fast-food choice, but the lively and slightly more expensive *Eco Pizza Pub*, Hipólito Yrigoyen 1108, has better food.

Las Espuelas, Mendoza 847, is an outstanding parrilla, but prices have risen enough that it's not the value it once was. At lunchtime, you may wish to take advantage of its air conditioning, but the outdoor patio can be pleasant for dinner. Prices are high but not outrageous at *La Cueva del Pescador*, Hipólito Yrigoyen 1255, a very fine fish restaurant with good atmosphere.

Getting There & Away

Air Austral (☎ 03783-23918), Junín 1301, flies to Buenos Aires Aeroparque (US$161), but there are also flights from nearby Resistencia, both with Austral and Aerolíneas. LAPA (☎ 03783-31628), 9 de Julio 1261, flies 10 times weekly to Aeroparque (US$59 to US$79).

Bus Frequent buses to Resistencia (US$2) leave from the bus station on Av Costanera General San Martín at La Rioja. Tata/El Rápido goes to Paso de los Libres, on the Brazilian border, via the interior city of Mercedes, for access to Esteros del Iberá.

Sample destinations include Posadas (US$18, 4½ hours), Puerto Iguazú (US$35,

ARGENTINA

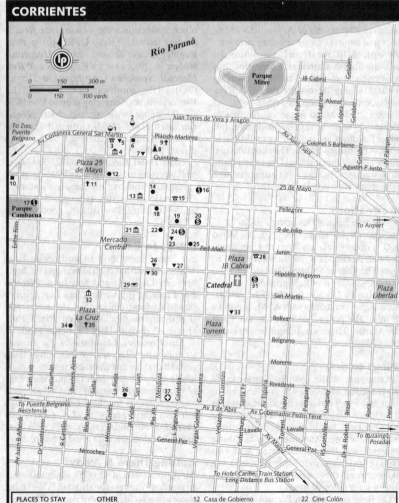

CORRIENTES

Río Paraná

Parque Mitre

0   150   300 m
0   150   300 yards

To Zoo,
Puente
Belgrano

Av Costanera General San Martín

Juan Torres de Vera y Aragón

Plácido Martínez

Quintana

Plaza 25
de Mayo

Parque
Cambacuá

Mercado
Central

Ped Mall

Plaza
JB Cabral

Catedral

Plaza
La Cruz

Plaza
Torrent

JB Cabral

Av Juan Pujol

Colonel S Balbiene

Agustín P Justo

25 de Mayo

Pellegrini

9 de Julio

Junín

Hipólito Yrigoyen

San Martín

Bolívar

Belgrano

Moreno

Rivadavia

To Airport

Plaza
Libertad

JM Pampín   M Larrana   Alvear   López   Gelabert   Gelabert   Gelabert
Av Pampín

Entre Ríos

San Luis   Tucumán   Buenos Aires   Salta   La Rioja   San Juan   Mendoza   Catamarca   San Lorenzo   Santa Fe   Av España   Jujuy   Torrent   Paraguay   Uruguay   Brasil   Roca   Perú

Av Juan B Alberdi   Dr Gustavino   R Castillo   Blas Parera   Héroes Civiles   R Vidal   Pío XII   J Segovia   Vargas Gómez   Velazco   Gutenburg   Lavalle   RS González   Dr JE Robert

To Puente Belgrano,
Resistencia

General Paz

Necochea

Av 3 de Abril   Av Gobernador Pedro Ferré

General Paz

Av Maipú

To Ituzaingó,
Posadas

To Hotel Caribe, Train Station,
Long Distance Bus Station

PLACES TO STAY	OTHER	12 Casa de Gobierno	22 Cine Colón
6 Hospedaje Robert	1 City Bus Station	13 Museo de Bellas Artes	24 Banco de la Nación (ATM)
10 Gran Hotel Turismo	2 Resistencia-Corrientes	Dr Juan Ramón Vidal	25 Austral
	Bus Station	14 Teatro Oficial Juan de Vera	28 Telecentro
PLACES TO EAT	3 Telecentro	15 Telecentro	29 Post Office
5 Heladería Trieste	4 Museo de Artesanía	16 Dirección Provincial	31 Citibank (ATM)
7 Heladería Trieste	Folklórica	de Turismo	32 Museo de Ciencias Naturales
23 Las Espuelas	8 Monumento a la Gloria,	17 Dirección Municipal de Turismo	Amado Bonpland
26 Heladería La Terraza	Historical Murals	18 Quo Vadis	34 Zoca Pub
27 La Cueva del Pescador	9 Convento de San Francisco,	19 LAPA	35 Iglesia de la Cruz/Santuario
30 Eco Pizza Pub	Museo Franciscano	20 Cambio El Dorado	de la Cruz del Milagro
33 Pizzería Los Pinos	11 Iglesia de la Merced	21 Museo Histórico de Corrientes	36 Localiza
			37 Hospital Escuela San Martín

10 hours) and Buenos Aires (US$35 to US$50, 12 hours). There are also services to Asunción, Paraguay, and to Brazil.

Getting Around
To/From the Airport Local bus No 8 goes to Aeropuerto Doctor Fernando Piragine Niveyro (☎ 03783-31628), about 10km east of town on RN 12. Austral runs a minibus to Resistencia in accordance with flight schedules.

Bus The long-distance Estación Terminal de Transporte Gobernador Benjamín S González (☎ 03783-42149) is on Av Maipú, southeast of downtown. From the local bus station on Av Costanera, take bus No 6.

RESERVA PROVINCIAL ESTEROS DEL IBERÁ
Esteros del Iberá, a wetlands wilderness covering 13,000 sq km in the north-central Corrientes is a wildlife cornucopia comparable – if not superior – to Brazil's Pantanal do Mato Grosso. Aquatic plants and grasses, including 'floating islands,' dominate the marsh vegetation, while trees are relatively few. The most notable wildlife species are reptiles like the cayman, mammals like the maned wolf, howler monkey, neotropical otter, capybara, and pampas and swamp deer, and more than 350 bird species.

For independent travelers, the settlement of Colonia Pellegrini, 120km northeast of Mercedes, on Laguna Iberá, is the easiest place to organize trips into the marshes. Launch tours, about US$20 hourly for up to five persons, are outstanding values.

Camping is possible at Colonia Pellegrini and costs about US$2 per person. The rustically styled but comfortable *Hostería Ñandé Retá* (☎ 03773-421741) is a bargain at US$42 per person with full board.

Getting There & Away
There is frequent public transportation between Corrientes and Paso de los Libres to Mercedes, where Itatí buses to Colonia Pellegrini (two hours) leave Monday at 5 am and 2 pm, Tuesday through Friday at 2 pm, and Saturday at 10 am. They return to Mercedes at 6 am Monday through Saturday, and also at 1 pm Saturday.

PASO DE LOS LIBRES
Known for its lively **Carnaval**, Paso de los Libres, 700km north of Buenos Aires, is directly across the Río Uruguay from Uruguaiana (Brazil), by a bridge about 10 blocks southwest of central Plaza Independencia. The main commercial street is Av Colón.

Libres Cambio is at Av Colón 901. The post office is at General Madariaga and Juan Sitja Min. Telecentro Mercosur is at Colón 975. Brazil has a consulate (☎ 03772-425441) at Mitre 842.

The **Cementerio de la Santa Cruz**, just beyond the bus station, holds the tomb of Amado (Aimé) Bonpland, a naturalist and travel companion of Alexander von Humboldt. Ask for directions to 'El sabio Bonpland.'

Places to Stay & Eat
The cheapest lodging is *Residencial Colón Hotel*, Av Colón 1065, at US$15 per person with private bath. Comfortable *Hotel Iberá* (☎ 03772-421848), Coronel López 1091, has rooms with bath and very welcome air-con for US$25/35.

ACA has a mediocre *restaurant* near the border complex, but try also *La Victoria* (☎ 03772-421577), Colón 585.

Getting There & Away
Air LAER (☎ 03772-422395), Colón 1028, flies to Concordia (US$21) and Buenos Aires (US$86) eight times weekly.

Bus The bus station (☎ 03772-421608) is at Av San Martín and Santiago del Estero. Provincial services run three times daily to Corrientes and twice daily to Santo Tomé via Yapeyú. Expreso Singer and Crucero del Norte pass through town three times daily en route between Buenos Aires and Posadas (six hours). There are also daily buses to Paraná and Santa Fe, and except Thursday, Paso de los Libres is a stopover between Córdoba and Puerto Iguazú.

YAPEYÚ
Birthplace of General José de San Martín, Yapeyú is a charming village, 55km north of Paso de los Libres. Founded in 1626, it once had a population of 8000 Guaraní Indians who tended up to 80,000 cattle; after the Jesuits' expulsion, the Indians dispersed and

the mission fell into ruins, but villagers built many houses of salvaged red sandstone blocks.

Things to See

The **Museo de Cultura Jesuítica**, consisting of several modern kiosks on the foundations of mission buildings, has a sundial, a few other mission relics and interesting photographs.

Plaques in the pretentious temple sheltering the **Casa de San Martín**, the modest birthplace of Argentina's greatest hero, include one from pardoned Dirty War lifer General Jorge Rafael Videla, asserting his 'most profound faith' in San Martín's ideals. Next door is the **Museo Sanmartiniano**, temporarily relocated to the Granaderos regiment in early 1998.

Places to Stay & Eat

At the *Camping Municipal* near the river, sites cost US$5, with hot showers. Insects can be abundant, and the most low-lying sites can flood in heavy rain. *Hotel San Martín*, Sargento Cabral 712, is bright and cheerful for US$15/20 single/double.

Restaurant Bicentenario has good food, reasonable prices and friendly, attentive service. *Comedor El Paraíso*, next to Hotel San Martín, serves passable meals as well.

Getting There & Away

Singer stops three times daily at the small bus station, at Av del Libertador and Chacabuco, en route between Paso de los Libres and Posadas.

POSADAS

Posadas (population 250,000), on the south bank of the upper Paraná, became capital of the new territory of Misiones in the 1880s. Travelers stopping here en route to Iguazú should not miss Jesuit ruins at San Ignacio Miní, about 50km east, or at Trinidad (Paraguay), across the river.

Orientation

Plaza 9 de Julio is the center of Posadas' standard grid. Streets were renumbered several years ago, but local preference for the old system has created confusion. Wherever possible, information below refers to locations instead of street numbers (which, if given, list the new number first and the old number in parentheses).

Information

The well-informed provincial Secretaría de Turismo (☎ 03752-447540, 800-555-0297 toll-free; turismo@electromisiones.com.ar) is at Colón 1985 (ex-393) between Córdoba and La Rioja. It's open from 8 am to 8 pm weekdays, 8 am to noon and from 4:30 to 8 pm weekends and holidays.

Open weekdays 8 am to noon, Paraguay's consulate (☎ 03752-423850), on San Lorenzo between Santa Fe and Sarmiento, has brochures and basic maps. Brazil's consulate (☎ 03752-424830), Av Corrientes 1416, offers same-day visa service and does not insist on a photograph. Hours are weekdays 9 am to 1 pm and 4 to 6:30 pm.

Money You can change traveler's checks at Cambios Mazza, on Bolívar between San Lorenzo and Coló. There are several downtown ATMs.

Post & Communications The post office is at Bolívar and Ayacucho. Telecentro Bolívar is at Bolívar and Colón.

Museo de Ciencias Naturales e Históricas

The natural-history section of this museum, on San Luis between Córdoba and La Rioja, focuses on invertebrates, vertebrates, and the province's geology and mineralogy; it also has an excellent serpentarium (every July morning at 10 am there's a demonstration of venom extraction), an aviary and an aquarium. Its historical section stresses prehistory, the Jesuit missions and modern colonization. Weekday hours are 7 am to noon and 2 to 7 pm, weekend hours 9 am to noon.

Places to Stay

Budget travelers should consider staying in Encarnación (Paraguay), for lower prices. *Residencial Misiones* (☎ 03752-430133), on Av Azara between La Rioja and Córdoba, costs US$15/25 single/double with private bath, but some visitors have questioned its standards. A good, comparably priced choice is *Residencial Neumann* (☎ 03752-424675), Roque Sáenz Peña 665 between Mitre and Santiago del Estero. *Residencial Nagel* (☎ 03752-425656), at Pedro Méndez 2148 and Uruguay, charges US$16 per person.

Mid-range accommodations are better values, starting with the outstanding *Hotel*

POSADAS

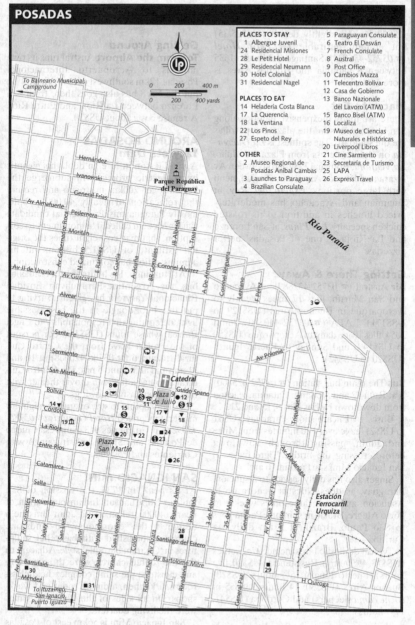

To Balneario Municipal
Campground

0   200   400 m
0   200   400 yards

PLACES TO STAY
1 Albergue Juvenil
24 Residencial Misiones
28 Le Petit Hotel
29 Residencial Neumann
30 Hotel Colonial
31 Residencial Nagel

PLACES TO EAT
14 Heladería Costa Blanca
17 La Querencia
18 La Ventana
22 Los Pinos
27 Espeto del Rey

OTHER
2 Museo Regional de
   Posadas Aníbal Cambas
3 Launches to Paraguay
4 Brazilian Consulate
5 Paraguayan Consulate
6 Teatro El Desván
7 French Consulate
8 Austral
9 Post Office
10 Cambios Mazza
11 Telecentro Bolívar
12 Casa de Gobierno
13 Banco Nazionale
    del Lavoro (ATM)
15 Banco Bisel (ATM)
16 Localiza
19 Museo de Ciencias
    Naturales e Históricas
20 Liverpool Libros
21 Cine Sarmiento
23 Secretaría de Turismo
25 LAPA
26 Express Travel

Río Paraná

Hernández
Ivanowski
General Frías
Av Almafuerte
Pedernera
Moritán
Av JJ de Urquiza
Av Guacurarí
Alvear
Belgrano
Santa Fe
Sarmiento
San Martín
Bolívar
Córdoba
La Rioja
Entre Ríos
Catamarca
Salta
Tucumán
Av Corrientes
Jujuy
San Luis
Junín
Ayacucho
San Lorenzo
Colón
Av Azara
Av Bartolomé Mitre
Barrufaldi
Méndez
To Ituzaingó;
San Ignacio;
Puerto Iguazú

Av Gobernador Roca
N. Castro
F. Ramírez
R. García
A. Aguña
BR. González
JB. Alberdi
L. Torai
Coronel Álvarez
A. De Arechea
Coronel Riguera
Lezcano
F. Pérez

Av Polonia
Tineguela
Av Madariaga
Av Roque Sáenz Peña
Lanusse
Coronel López

Parque República
del Paraguay

Catedral
Guido Spano
Plaza 9
de Julio

Plaza
San Martín

Uruguay
Líbano
Israel
Rademacher
Rivadavia
3 de Febrero
25 de Mayo
General Paz
Santiago del Estero
Rivadavia
General Paz
H. Quiroga

Estación
Ferrocarril
Urquiza

Av De Haro

Colonial (☎ *03752-436149*), Barrufaldi 2419 near the Singer/Tigre bus terminal, for US$22/36. The slightly dearer (US$25/35) but equally desirable *Le Petit Hotel* (☎ *03752-436031*), Santiago del Estero 1635 between Rivadavia and Buenos Aires, is more central.

Places to Eat

There are many inexpensive eateries along San Lorenzo west of the plaza, but parrillas are the standard. The spiffiest is *La Queren-cia* on Bolívar across from Plaza 9 de Julio. *La Ventana*, Bolívar 1725 (580) between Av Azara and Buenos Aires, has a varied menu with large portions. *Espeto del Rey*, at Tucumán and Ayacucho, has moderately priced lunches in addition to its roasted chicken specialty. *Los Pinos*, at San Lorenzo and La Rioja, is one of Posadas' better pizzerias.

Getting There & Away

Air Austral (☎ 03752-432889), at Ayacucho and San Martín, flies 17 times weekly to Aeroparque in Buenos Aires (US$129 to US$171). LAPA (☎ 03752-440300), Junín 2054, flies twice daily to Aeroparque (US$59 to US$149) and Sunday to Puerto Iguazú (US$20 to US$42).

Bus The main bus station (☎ 03752-425800) is at Ruta 12 and Av Santa Catalina, reached from downtown by bus Nos 8, 15 and 21.

Buses to Encarnación, Paraguay (US$1 to US$2) leave every 20 minutes from Mitre and Junín, passing through downtown before crossing the bridge. Tigre buses to San Ignacio Miní start around 6 am.

Singer also has daily service to Asunción, Paraguay, as does Nuestra Señora de la Asunción, and goes three times weekly to Porto Alegre, Brazil, in summer. Penha goes to São Paulo, Brazil, at 5 am daily via Curitiba.

Typical domestic fares include Corrientes (US$18, 4½ hours), Resistencia (US$20, five hours), Puerto Iguazú (5½ hours, US$20) Buenos Aires (US$30, 14 hours; US$55 in *coche cama* sleepers) and Córdoba (US$41, 17½ hours).

Boat Launches across the Paraná to Encarnación (US$1) continue to operate despite the new bridge. They leave from the dock at the east end of Av Guacurarí.

Getting Around

To/From the Airport Austral runs its own minibus to Aeropuerto Internacional Posadas, 12km southwest of town via RN 12, but the No 8 bus also goes there from San Lorenzo between La Rioja and Entre Ríos. A remise costs about US$10.

AROUND POSADAS
Yacyretá Dam

A vivid lesson in foreign debt, this gigantic hydroelectric project will submerge the Paraná over 200km upstream and require the relocation of nearly 40,000 people, mostly Paraguayans. Presidential candidate Carlos Menem called it 'a monument to corruption' that may cost eight times the original estimate of US$1.5 billion, but his administration has continued construction.

At Ituzaingó, 1½ hours from Posadas by bus, the Argentine-Paraguayan Entidad Binacional Yacyretá has given up trying to put this boondoggle in the best possible light, delegating that responsibility to Engel Barrea, whose tours (US$3.50 per person) of the project leave from the Centro Cultural Ituzaingó (☎ 03786-420008) at 10 and 11 am, and at 3, 4 and 5 pm. The Centro Cultural also has a first-run movie theater with free or inexpensive showings.

Visitors opting to stay overnight might try moderately priced *Hotel Géminis* (☎ *03786-420324*) at Corrientes 943. Empresa Ciudad de Posadas and Singer link Ituzaingó with Corrientes and Posadas.

SAN IGNACIO MINÍ

At its peak, in 1733, the mission of San Ignacio Miní had an Indian population of nearly 4000. Italian Jesuit Juan Brasanelli designed the enormous red-sandstone church, embellished with bas-relief sculptures in 'Guaraní baroque' style. Adjacent to the tile-roofed church were the cemetery and cloisters; the same complex held classrooms, a kitchen, a dining room and workshops. On all sides of the Plaza de Armas were the living quarters.

San Ignacio Miní is 56km east of Posadas via RN 12 at the village of San Ignacio. It is an easy day trip from Posadas, but staying overnight allows more time to explore the mission ruins.

Places to Stay & Eat

At *Hospedaje Los Salpeterer*, near the bus terminal, rooms with shared bath cost US$7 per person with kitchen facilities, while those with private bath cost US$10. Two can also pitch a tent on the grounds for US$6.

Farther from the ruins, at Pellegrini 270, *Hospedaje El Descanso* (☎ 03752-70207) is a real find with spartan but spotless rooms and friendly German-speaking management; singles cost US$6 with shared bath, while doubles with a private bath cost US$15.

Near the exit to the ruins on Rivadavia, *Coco* has first-rate, home-style dinners starting at US$4; *La Casa Azul* is an assembly-line comedor. *Don Valentín*, near the Alberdi entrance to the ruins, is also very good.

Getting There & Away

The bus terminal is at the west end of Av Sarmiento, the main road into town. Services are frequent between Posadas (US$4) and Puerto Iguazú (US$17) with several companies, but buses along RN 12 also stop readily en route in either direction.

PUERTO IGUAZÚ

Puerto Iguazú hosts most visitors to the Argentine side of Iguazú Falls (for details of the Brazilian side, see Foz do Iguaçu in the Brazil chapter). The town's very irregular city plan is compact enough for relatively easy orientation. The main drag is the diagonal Av Victoria Aguirre.

Information

The Secretaría de Turismo (☎ 03757-420800), Av Victoria Aguirre 311, is open weekdays 8 am to 1 pm, weekends 8 am to noon, and daily 4 to 8 pm.

Banco de Misiones has an ATM at Av Victoria Aguirre 330. Before buying Brazilian currency, ask other travelers about trends in Foz do Iguaçu.

The post office is at Av San Martín 780. Telecentro Cataratas is on Av Victoria Aguirre between Los Cedros and Aguay. The Las Vegas Coffee Shop (☎ 03757-422962), on Aguirre near Bonpland, offers Internet access.

Brazil's consulate (☎ 03757-420601), at Esquiú and El Mensú, turns around visa applications in as little as half an hour. Hours are weekdays 8 am to 2 pm.

Places to Stay

Foz do Iguaçu, on the Brazilian side, is usually cheaper than Puerto Iguazú, but the overvalued Brazilian *real* has made Puerto Iguazú more competitive.

Camping At Km 3.5 of RN 12 on the edge of town, *Camping El Pindo* charges US$3 per person and US$3 per vehicle.

Hostels HI has two local affiliates. *Residencial Uno* (☎ 03757-420529), at Fray Luis Beltrán 116, charges US$10 with breakfast and has better hostel atmosphere; the slightly more expensive, motel-like *Residencial La Cabaña* (☎ 03757-420564), Av Tres Fronteras 434, offers more privacy but less contact with other travelers.

Residenciales & Hotels *Residencial Arco Iris* (☎ 03757-420636), Curupy 152, is very popular with travelers for US$15/20 single/double with private bath. Shady *Hostería Los Helechos* (☎ 20338), at Paulina Amarante 76 near Beltrán, is a superb value for US$15/25, a bit more in high season. At Victoria Aguirre 915, for about the same price, *Residencial King* (☎ 03757-420360) has attractive grounds and a swimming pool.

Places to Eat

The *Fechoría Bar*, Eppens 294, is a good breakfast choice. *El Criollito*, on Av Tres Fronteras just west of the plaza, has a superb Argentine menu, relaxed atmosphere, outstanding service and sidewalk seating. Recommended parrillas include *Tomás* at the bus terminal and *El Tío Querido* on Bonpland. It's drawn mixed commentary, but *La Esquina*, in the Hotel St George at Av Córdoba 148, remains a personal favorite.

Getting There & Away

Air Aerolíneas Argentinas (☎ 03757-420168), Aguirre 295, flies three or four times daily to Buenos Aires (US$109 to US$203) and Monday, Wednesday and Friday to Rio de Janeiro. LAPA (☎ 03757-420390), Perito

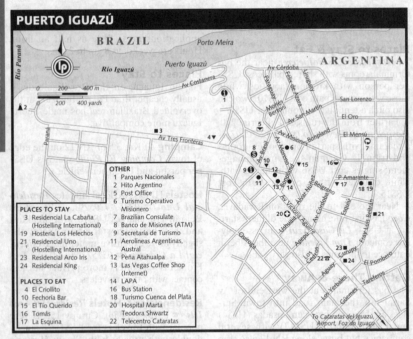

PUERTO IGUAZÚ

BRAZIL

Porto Meira

Río Paraná

Río Iguazú

Puerto Iguazú

ARGENTINA

Av Córdoba

Av Costanera

0   200   400 m

0   200   400 yards

Av Tres Fronteras

OTHER
1   Parques Nacionales
2   Hito Argentino
5   Post Office
6   Turismo Operativo
    Misionero
7   Brazilian Consulate
8   Banco de Misiones (ATM)
9   Secretaría de Turismo
11 Aerolíneas Argentinas,
    Austral
12 Peña Atahualpa
13 Las Vegas Coffee Shop
    (Internet)
14 LAPA
16 Bus Station
18 Turismo Cuenca del Plata
20 Hospital Marta
    Teodora Shwartz
22 Telecentro Cataratas

PLACES TO STAY
3   Residencial La Cabaña
    (Hostelling International)
19 Hostería Los Helechos
21 Residencial Uno
    (Hostelling International)
23 Residencial Arco Iris
24 Residencial King

PLACES TO EAT
4   El Criollito
10 Fechoría Bar
15 El Tío Querido
16 Tomás
17 La Esquina

To Cataratas del Iguazú,
Airport, Foz do Iguaçu

Moreno 184, Local 2, flies to Buenos Aires (US$79 to US$169) daily except Sunday, when it has two flights.

Bus The bus station is at Avs Córdoba and Misiones. Many companies have services to Posadas (US$20, 5½ hours), Buenos Aires (US$45, 22 hours) and intermediate points.

Getting Around
To/From the Airport Expreso Aristóbulo del Valle (☎ 03757-420348), Entre Ríos 239, charges US$3 to the airport and makes hotel pickups; phone for reservations. Remises run about US$15.

Bus Frequent buses to Parque Nacional Iguazú (US$2) leave from the bus station, as do international buses to Foz do Iguaçu (US$2) and Ciudad del Este, Paraguay.

Taxi For groups of three or more hoping to see both sides of the falls as well as Ciudad del Este and the Itaipú hydroelectric project, a shared cab or remise can be a good idea; figure about US$80 for a full

day's sightseeing. Contact the Asociación de Trabajadores de Taxis (☎ 03757-420282), Rolón Hermanos (☎ 03757-420331), or simply approach a driver.

PARQUE NACIONAL IGUAZÚ
Guaraní legend says that Iguazú Falls originated when a jealous forest god, enraged by a warrior escaping downriver by canoe with a young girl, caused the riverbed to collapse in front of the lovers, producing a precipitous falls over which the girl fell and, at their base, turned into a rock. The warrior survived as a tree overlooking his fallen lover.

The falls' geological origins are more prosaic. In southern Brazil, the Río Iguazú passes over a basalt plateau that ends just above its confluence with the Paraná. Where the lava stopped, at least 5000 cubic meters of water per second plunge 70m into the sedimentary terrain below. Before reaching the edge, the river divides into many channels to form several distinctive *cataratas*.

The most awesome is the semicircular Garganta del Diablo (Devil's Throat), a deafening and dampening part of the experience, approached by launch and via a system of *pasarelas* (catwalks). Despite development pressures, the 55,000-hectare park is a natural wonderland of subtropical rain forest, with over 2000 identified plant species, countless insects, 400 bird species and many mammals and reptiles.

Information

Buses from Puerto Iguazú will drop passengers off at the Centro de Informes (☎ 03757-420180), near the Hotel Internacional, where there's a small museum. There's also a gift shop, bar, photo developing and many other services, including restaurants and snack bars.

Dangers & Annoyances

The Río Iguazú's currents are strong and swift; more than one tourist has been swept downriver and drowned near Isla San Martín.

Wildlife is potentially dangerous – in 1997, a jaguar killed a park ranger's infant son. Visitors should respect the big cats and, if should you encounter one, do not panic. Speak calmly but loudly, do not run or turn your back, and try to appear bigger than you are, by waving your arms or clothing for example.

Human predators may abscond with your personal belongings, so watch your things while hiking. This is not exactly epidemic, but it's not unheard of either.

Iguazú Falls

Before seeing the falls themselves, look around the museum, and climb the nearby tower for a good overall view, but plan hikes before midmorning's tour-bus invasion. Descending from the visitor center, you can cross by free launch to **Isla Grande San Martín**, which offers unique views and a refuge from the masses on the mainland.

Flood damage has isolated the pasarelas to **Garganta del Diablo**, but you can still reach the lookout by a road to Ñandú (hourly buses cost US$1) and a launch (US$5). Of all sights on earth, this must come closest to the experience of sailing off the edge of the earth imagined by early European sailors, as the deafening cascade plunges to a murky destination, blurred by the rising vapor soaking the viewer.

Activies

Best in the early morning, the Sendero Macuco nature trail leads through dense forest, where a steep sidetrack goes to the base of a hidden waterfall. Another trail goes to the *bañado*, a marsh abounding in bird life.

To get elsewhere in the forest, hitch or hire a car to go out RN 101 toward the village of Bernardo de Irigoyen. Few visitors explore this part of the park, and it is still nearly pristine forest. Iguazú Jungle Explorer, at the visitor center, can arrange trips to this area.

Floating Iguazú, also at the visitor center, arranges 4WD trips to the Yacaratia forest trail, organizes rafting excursions and rents mountain bikes.

Getting There & Away

For bus information, see the Puerto Iguazú entry. Park admission is US$5 per person and includes the launch to Isla Grande San Martín.

RESISTENCIA

Resistencia, across the Paraná from Corrientes, is capital of Chaco province and a major crossroads for Paraguay, Santa Fe and trans-Chaco routes to the Northwest. Despite a frontier past, it prides itself on a reputation as the 'city of sculptures,' for the statues in almost every public space.

Refurbished Plaza 25 de Mayo occupies four square blocks in the city center. The Dirección Provincial de Turismo (☎ 03722-423547), at Santa Fe 178, is open from 7:30 am to 1 pm and 3 to 7:30 pm weekdays, and there's also a tourist kiosk (☎ 03722-458289) on Plaza 25 de Mayo, open from 8 am to 9 pm weekdays and from 9 am to midnight weekends.

Cambio El Dorado, Jose María Paz 36, changes traveler's checks at reasonable rates. There are several ATMs near Plaza 25 de Mayo. The post office faces the plaza, at Sarmiento and Yrigoyen. There's a Telecentro at JB Justo 136.

Things to See

There's insufficient space to detail the number of sculptures in city parks and on the sidewalks, but the tourist office distributes a map, with their locations, that makes a good introduction to the city. The best starting point is the open-air **Parque de las Esculturas Aldo y Efraín Boglietti**, at Avs Laprida and Sarmiento, a 2500-sq-meter area alongside the old French railroad station.

The **Museo del Hombre Chaqueño** (Museum of Chaco Man), Arturo Illia 655, focuses on the colonization of the Chaco. The **Museo Policial**, Roca 223, is better than one might expect, partially redeeming its trite drug-war rhetoric with absorbing accounts of *cuatrerismo* (cattle-rustling, which is still widespread in the province) and social banditry.

El Fogón de los Arrieros, Brown 350, is famous for its eclectic assemblage of art objects from around the Chaco, Argentina and the world. The driving force behind the city's progressive displays of public art, it's open 9 to 11 pm nightly. Admission is US$2.

Places to Stay

Camping The *Camping Parque 2 de Febrero*, Av Avalos 1100, has excellent facilities for US$4 per site plus US$1 per person.

Residenciales & Hotels Despite a run-down exterior, *Residencial Alberdi*, Av Alberdi 317, has decent rooms with shared bath for US$18 per person, but is often full. Nearby at Frondizi 304, comparably priced *Residencial San José* (☎ 03722-426062) is ramshackle but clean, and one of the rooms is truly enormous. Upgraded *Hotel Marconi* (☎ 03722-421978), Perón 352, is probably the best mid-range value for US$31/41.

Places to Eat

Several attractive confiterías and ice creameries have rejuvenated the area north and northwest of Plaza 25 de Mayo – try, for instance, *Café de la Ciudad*, formerly a sleazy bar, at Pellegrini 109. *Charly*, Güemes 215, has international cuisine and local river fish, but *Kebon*, at Güemes and Don Bosco, is probably Resistencia's best (budget-watchers will find its next-door rotisería a bargain for take-out food.

For variety, try also *Por la Vuelta* at Obligado 33 for international food or *Trattoria Genova* at Yrigoyen 236 for Italian specialties. *La María*, on Lavalle between Av Sarmiento and Güemes, has pizza and sidewalk seating. *Barrilito*, Lavalle 269, is a beer-garden restaurant.

Getting There & Away

Air Aerolíneas Argentinas (☎ 03722-445553) and Austral (☎ 03722-446800) share offices at Frondizi 99, but only Austral has flights from Resistencia, twice daily to Buenos Aires' Aeroparque (US$161) except Sunday (one flight). LAPA (☎ 03722-430201), Pellegrini 100, flies daily to Aeroparque (US$59 to US$129).

Bus Resistencia's sparkling bus station (☎ 03722-461098) is at Av MacLean and Islas Malvinas. Godoy Resistencia buses shuttle frequently between Corrientes and Resistencia.

La Estrella goes to the village of Capitán Solari, near Parque Nacional Chaco, four times daily. Godoy goes to Naick-Neck and Laguna Blanca, near the Parque Nacional Pilcomayo.

Several companies go south to Santa Fe, Rosario and Buenos Aires (US$43, 15 hours), north to Formosa and Asunción, Paraguay, and east to Posadas and Puerto Iguazú (US$38, 10½ hours). There is daily service to Córdoba and the Cuyo provinces, and across the Chaco to Salta and Jujuy.

Getting Around

To/From the Airport Aeropuerto San Martín is 6km south of town on RN 11; take bus No 3 (black letters) from the post office on Plaza 25 de Mayo.

To/From the Bus Terminal Take bus No 3 or No 10 from the Casa de Gobierno (near the post office) on Plaza 25 de Mayo.

PARQUE NACIONAL CHACO

This little-visited park, 115km northwest of Resistencia, preserves 15,000 hectares of marshes, grasslands, palm savannas, scrub and dense gallery forests in the humid eastern Chaco. Mammals are few, but birds include rheas, jabirú storks, roseate spoonbills, cormorants and caracaras. The most abundant species is the mosquito, so visit in the relatively dry, cool winter and bring insect repellent.

Hiking and bird-watching are best in the early morning or around sunset. Some swampy areas are accessible only on horseback – inquire in Capitán Solari for horses and guides.

Information

The Administración (☎ 03725-496190) now collects a US$2 admission charge at the park entrance. Park personnel are extremely hospitable and will accompany visitors if their duties permit.

Places to Stay & Eat

The shaded *camping* area has clean toilets and (cold water) showers, but a tent is essential. Sometimes on weekends, a *snack bar* sells meals, but make sure you bring supplies from Resistencia.

Getting There & Away

La Estrella runs four buses daily from Resistencia to Capitán Solari (2½ hours); from there you must walk or catch a lift to the park entrance.

FORMOSA

From Formosa city, capital of Formosa province, it's possible to cross the northern Chaco to Jujuy, Salta or Bolivia, or continue to Paraguay. In November, the week-long **Fiesta del Río** features an impressive nocturnal religious procession in which 150 boats from Corrientes sail up the Río Paraguay.

Formosa has no real bargain accommodations, but the *Residencial Colonial* (☎ 03717-426346), San Martín 879, is a reasonable value for US$18/20 single/double. Navarro (☎ 03717-423598), at Alberdi and Corrientes, has buses to Clorinda and Laguna Naick-Neck (Parque Nacional Río Pilcomayo) departing daily at 5:30 am and 2 and 8 pm.

PARQUE NACIONAL RÍO PILCOMAYO

West of Clorinda, the wildlife-rich wetlands of 60,000-hectare Parque Nacional Río Pilcomayo hug the Paraguayan border. Its outstanding feature is shimmering **Laguna Blanca** where, at sunset, yacarés lurk on the lake surface. Other wildlife, except for birds, is likelier to be heard than seen among the dense aquatic vegetation.

Parque Nacional Río Pilcomayo's free camping facilities are little used except on weekends; just outside the park entrance, a small shop sells basic food and cold drinks, including beer. There is bus service with Navarro from Formosa and Clorinda along

RN 86 to Laguna Naick-Neck, where a well-marked turnoff leads to the Laguna Blanca ranger station. From the turnoff, visitors have to hike or hitch the last 5km.

Córdoba Province

Córdoba province is bounded by the Andean provinces to the northwest, Cuyo to the southwest, the Chaco to the northeast and the Pampas to the southeast. Popular with Argentine tourists, its key attractions are the capital city of Córdoba and the province's scenic mountain hinterland, the Sierras de Córdoba.

History

Comechingones Indians briefly resisted the Spaniards, but by 1573, Jerónimo Luis de Cabrera founded the city of Córdoba. In colonial times, Córdoba's ecclesiastical importance made it a center for education, arts and architecture, but after independence, the city had to reorient itself to the political and economic whims of Buenos Aires as immigrants flooded the province, thanks to the railway. Between 1882 and 1896, the number of agricultural colonies increased from just five to 176, but Córdoba's national role actually declined because of phenomenal growth on the Pampas.

Eventually the exaggerated conservatism of the local establishment aroused an aggressive reform movement that had a lasting impact locally and nationally. In the late 1960s, a coalition of students and auto workers nearly unseated a de facto military government in an uprising known as the *cordobazo*. After the chaos of the 1970s and early 1980s, the region's economy declined as a result of the automobile industry's obsolete equipment and the country's economic stagnation. There are signs of revival, however, as Fiat has reestablished itself in the provincial capital.

CÓRDOBA

Sited on the south bank of the Río Primero (or Suquía), 400m above sea level at the foot of the Sierra Chica, the city of Córdoba has sprawled north of the river and into the countryside, but its compact downtown is easily explored on foot.

Plaza San Martín is the nucleus for Córdoba's 1 million inhabitants, but the commercial center is northwest of the plaza, where the 25 de Mayo and Indarte pedestrian malls intersect. Calle Obispo Trejos, south of the plaza, has the finest concentration of colonial buildings.

Information

Both the provincial Subsecretaría de Turismo (☎ 0351-421-4027) and the municipal Dirección de Turismo (☎ 0351-433-1542) have desks in the historic Cabildo at Independencia 30, on Plaza San Martín, but both generally take the attitude that 'we're here to hand out brochures, nothing more, nothing less.' Hours are weekdays 8 am to 9 pm, weekends 9 am to noon and 5 to 8 pm. The Subsecretaría's office at the bus terminal (☎ 0351-423-4169) is generally more helpful, and there are two other tourist offices in town with abbreviated hours.

For changing cash or traveler's checks, try Cambio Barujel at Rivadavia and 25 de Mayo. There are ATMs downtown and at the bus station. The post office is at Av General Paz 201. There are Telecentros downtown and at the bus terminal.

Things to See

To see Córdoba's colonial buildings and monuments, start at the **Cabildo**, on Plaza San Martín, and the **Casa del Obispo Mercadillo**, Rosario de Santa Fe 39. At the plaza's southwest corner, crowned by a Romanesque dome, the **Iglesia Catedral** (begun in 1577) mixes a variety of styles.

The Jesuit **Iglesia de La Compañía** (1645), at Obispo Trejos and Caseros, has a modest exterior, but its unique interior features a timber ceiling shaped like an inverted ship's hull. The **Universidad Nacional de Córdoba** (1613) is at Obispo Trejos 242, but see also the nearby **Colegio Nacional de Monserrat** (1782). At Rosario de Santa Fe 218, the **Museo Histórico Provincial Marqués de Sobremonte** is open Tuesday to Saturday 9 am to 1 pm and 3 to 7 pm, Sunday 10 am to 1 pm (mornings only in summer, when it is closed Sunday). Admission is US$1.

Places to Stay

Parque General San Martín, 13km west of downtown, has a spacious but basic *campground* (US$4 per site). Bus No 31 from Plaza San Martín goes to the Complejo Ferial, an exhibition and entertainment complex about 1km from the park.

Among the cheapest regular accommodations is *Residencial Thanoa*, San Jerónimo 479; quiet and friendly but very basic, it costs US$10 per person with shared bath. Comparably priced, family-oriented *Residencial Central* (☎ 0351-421-6667), Blvd Perón 150, is dingy but clean. The spotless *Hospedaje Suzy*, Entre Ríos 528, has singles for just US$13 with shared bath.

Not quite equal to its prestigious Buenos Aires namesake, *Hotel Claridge* (☎ 0351-421-5741), 25 de Mayo 218, has balconied rooms with balky air-con on a quiet pedestrian street for US$14/25; interior rooms cost US$10 per person. At Entre Ríos 687, the modern *Hotel Termini Roma* (☎ 0351-421-8721) has rooms with private bath for US$20/28. The attractive, well-kept *Hotel Garden* (☎ 0351-421-4729), 25 de Mayo 35, is a good value for US$23/40.

Places to Eat

The municipal *Mercado Norte* at Rivadavia and Oncativo, has excellent and inexpensive eats – pizza, empanadas and lager beer. *Mandarina*, Obispo Trejos 171, has reasonable, fixed-price meals in informal surroundings. *La Candela*, on Corrientes near Obispo Trejos, is a student hangout featuring empanadas and locro.

Córdoba has some quality pizzerias, including *Viejos Tiempos* on Corrientes between Ituzaingó and Av Chacabuco, *Tenorio* at San Luis and Av Marcelo T de Alvear, and *Pizza Cero* on Av Hipólito Yrigoyen between Obispo Trejos and Independencia.

Minoliti, Entre Ríos 358, is a good, bargain-priced Italian restaurant. *Guccio*, on Av Hipólito Yrigoyen near Obispo Trejos, is a more expensive Italian choice but has a US$12 fixed-price lunch and dinner.

Estancia La María, 9 de Julio 364, is a parrilla. *La Zete*, Corrientes 455, serves Middle Eastern food.

Getting There & Away

Air Aerolíneas Argentinas and Austral, sharing offices (☎ 0351-426-7600) at Av Colón 520, have more than 100 weekly flights to Buenos Aires and about 25 to Mendoza. There are cheaper, less-frequent services to Buenos Aires' Aeroparque with LAPA

ARGENTINA

CÓRDOBA

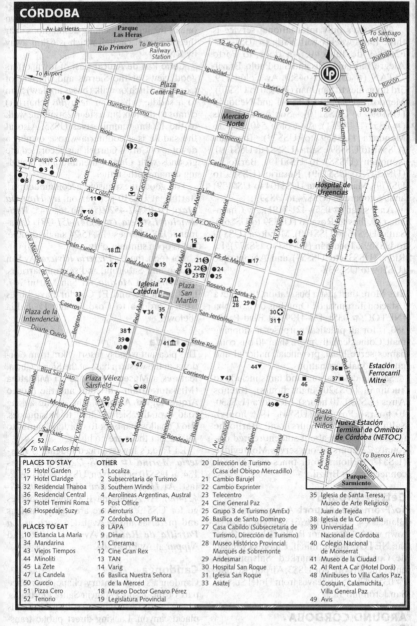

0   150   300 m
0   150   300 yards

PLACES TO STAY
15 Hotel Garden
17 Hotel Claridge
32 Residencial Thanoa
36 Residencial Central
37 Hotel Termini Roma
46 Hospedaje Suzy

PLACES TO EAT
10 Estancia La María
34 Mandarina
43 Viejos Tiempos
44 Minoliti
45 La Zete
47 La Candela
50 Guccio
51 Pizza Cero
52 Tenorio

OTHER
1   Localiza
2   Subsecretaría de Turismo
3   Southern Winds
4   Aerolíneas Argentinas, Austral
5   Post Office
6   Aeroturis
7   Córdoba Open Plaza
8   LAPA
9   Dinar
11 Cinerama
12 Cine Gran Rex
13 TAN
14 Varig
16 Basílica Nuestra Señora
    de la Merced
18 Museo Doctor Genaro Pérez
19 Legislatura Provincial
20 Dirección de Turismo
    (Casa del Obispo Mercadillo)
21 Cambio Barujel
22 Cambio Exprinter
23 Telecentro
24 Cine General Paz
25 Grupo 3 de Turismo (AmEx)
26 Basílica de Santo Domingo
27 Casa Cabildo (Subsecretaría de
    Turismo, Dirección de Turismo)
28 Museo Histórico Provincial
    Marqués de Sobremonte
29 Andesmar
30 Hospital San Roque
31 Iglesia San Roque
33 Asatej

35 Iglesia de Santa Teresa,
    Museo de Arte Religioso
    Juan de Tejeda
38 Iglesia de la Compañía
39 Universidad
    Nacional de Córdoba
40 Colegio Nacional
    de Monserrat
41 Museo de la Ciudad
42 AI Rent A Car (Hotel Dorá)
48 Minibuses to Villa Carlos Paz,
    Cosquín, Calamuchita,
    Villa General Paz
49 Avis

(☎ 0351-426-3336), Av Figueroa Alcorta 181, and Dinar (☎ 0351-426-2020), Av Colón 533.

Córdoba's only international service is three times weekly with Varig (☎ 0351-425-6262), 9 de Julio 40, 7th floor, to Porto Alegre, Florianópolis and São Paulo, Brazil.

TAN (☎ 0351-421-6458), Av Colón 119, 3rd floor, flies to San Juan (US$50 to US$70), Mendoza (US$39 to US$74) and Neuquén (US$69 to US$110). Southern Winds (☎ 0351-424-7251), Av Colón 540, flies to Mendoza (US$59 to US$79), Tucumán (US$67 to US$89), Salta (US$82 to US$109), Neuquén (US$89 to US$119), Bariloche (US$127 to US$169), Rosario (US$59 to US$79), Mar del Plata (US$104 to US$139) and Aeroparque (US$74 to US$99).

Andesmar (☎ 0351-421-7191), Av Chacabuco 80, flies to Rosario (US$39 to US$63), Salta (US$76 to US$100), Mendoza (US$49 to US$69), Tucumán (US$53 to US$77), La Rioja (US$35 to US$59) and Aeroparque (US$69 to US$93).

Bus More than just a bus station, the Nueva Estación Terminal de Ómnibus de Córdoba (NETOC, ☎ 0351-423-4199), at Blvd Perón 380, is for all practical purposes a shopping mall. Coincidentally, more than 40 bus companies serve local, provincial, national and international destinations.

Sample destinations and fares include to Tucumán (US$20, eight hours), Buenos Aires (US$30, 10 hours), Mendoza (US$30, 10 hours), Posadas (US$41, 19½ hours), Salta (US$45, 12 hours) and Bariloche (US$105, but ask about student/retired discounts; 22 hours). Cora serves Montevideo (US$47, 15 hours) four times weekly, with connections to Brazil.

Getting Around
To/From the Airport Aeropuerto Pajas Blancas (☎ 0351-4810696) is 15km north of town via Av Monseñor Pablo Cabrera. From the NETOC bus terminal, Empresa Ciudad de Córdoba buses marked 'Salsipuedes' enter the airport. For US$3, Airport Kombis (☎ 0351-470-1529) leaves from Hotel Sussex, San Jerónimo 125.

AROUND CÓRDOBA
Cosquín
Cosquín's Festival Nacional del Folklore, held every January for more than 30 years,

has declined by most accounts., but the surrounding countryside still makes the town one of the more appealing destinations near the provincial capital, which is 63km away by RN 38.

Cerro Pan de Azúcar, east of town, offers good views of the Sierras and the city of Córdoba. Hitch or walk (buses are few) 5km to a saddle, where an *aerosilla* (chairlift) climbs to the top, but a steep 25-minute walk to the 1260m summit saves US$5. Also at the saddle is a confitería whose owner, a devotee of Carlos Gardel, has decorated the grounds with Gardel memorabilia, including a mammoth statue.

For good, inexpensive accommodations, starting at US$10 per person, try *Hostería Mary* (☎ 03541-452095), Bustos 545. *Residencial Esteleta* (☎ 03541-451473), Catamarca 138, charges US$15/24 single/double, but is open summer only.

For food, there's *Pizzería Riviera*, Av San Martín and Sabattini, and several parrillas, including *San Marino*, Av San Martín 707. La Capillense and El Cóndor have buses from Córdoba to Cosquín and La Falda (below).

La Falda
This pleasant woodsy resort 78km from Córdoba, at the western base of the Sierra Chica, features a **Museo de Trenes en Miniatura** (Miniature Train Museum) and the **Museo Arqueológico Ambato**. The scenic zigzag road over the Sierra Chica to Salsipuedes, Río Ceballos and back to Córdoba climbs to 1500m, but there are no buses.

La Falda's lowest-priced lodging is *Hostería Marina* (☎ 03548-422640), Güemes 134, at US$10 per person, US$12 with breakfast. At *Hospedaje San Remo* (☎ 03548-422409), Av Argentina 108, singles/doubles go for US$13/15. There are many parrillas and pizzerias along Av Edén, such as *La Parrilla de Raúl* at Av Edén 1000 and *Nippur* at Av Edén 164.

Candonga
Candonga's 18th-century chapel was once part of the Jesuit Estancia Santa Gertrudis, whose overgrown ruins are still visible in this placid canyon. Lacking direct public transport, try hitching from El Manzano, 40km north of Córdoba (reached by Empresa Ciudad de Córdoba or Sierras de Córdoba).

A day trip is worthwhile, but there are good accommodations at *Hostería Candonga* (☎ *0351-471-0683 in Córdoba for reservations*), where US$35 per person buys room plus full board, including regional specialties like asado con cuero, locro, empanadas and homemade desserts.

Jesús María
After losing their operating funds to pirates off the coast of Brazil, the Jesuits produced and sold wine from Jesús María to support their university in colonial Córdoba. These days the town, 51km north of Córdoba via RN 9, hosts the annual **Fiesta Nacional de Doma y Folklore**, a celebration of gaucho horsemanship and customs.

Set among very attractive grounds, the church and convent now constitute the **Museo Jesuítico Nacional de Jesús María**, open weekdays 8 am to noon and 2 to 7 pm (3 to 7 pm in summer), weekends 2 to 6 pm (3 to 7 pm in summer) only. Five km away is the colonial posthouse of **Sinsacate**, site of a wake for murdered La Rioja caudillo Facundo Quiroga in 1835. It's open 3 to 7 pm daily from mid-November to mid-March, 2 to 6 pm daily the rest of the year, but the caretaker is rarely punctual. Admission is US$1 to each site.

Ciudad de Córdoba and Cadol run buses between Córdoba and Jesús María.

Alta Gracia
Only 35km southwest of Córdoba, the colonial mountain town of Alta Gracia is steeped in history, its illustrious residents ranging from Jesuit pioneers to Viceroy Santiago Liniers, Spanish composer and civil-war refugee Manuel de Falla and revolutionary Che Guevara. In the first half of the 20th century, the town (whose architecture closely resembles parts of Mar del Plata) was a summer retreat for the Argentine oligarchy, but it's not the social center it once was.

Things to See
From 1643 to 1762, Jesuit fathers built the **Iglesia Parroquial Nuestra Señora de la Merced**, on the west side of the central Plaza Manuel Solares; the nearby Jesuit workshops of **El Obraje** (1643) are now a public school. Liniers, one of the last officials to occupy the post of Viceroy of the River Plate, resided in what is now the **Museo**

Histórico Nacional del Virrey Liniers, alongside the church.

Some blocks west, on Av Vélez Sársfield, squatters inhabit the crumbling **Sierras Hotel**, which, during Alta Gracia's social heyday, was the meeting place for the elite (including Che's black sheep family). From 1939 until his death in 1946, Falla lived in **Villa Los Espinillos**, which is now a museum at Carlos Pellegrini and Calle Manuel de Falla. Though the Guevaras lived in several houses in the 1930s, their primary residence was **Villa Beatriz** (still a private home) at Avellaneda 501 in Villa Carlos Pellegrini.

Places to Stay & Eat
Charming *Hostería Asturias* (☎ *03547-23668*), Vélez Sársfield 127, charges only US$15/20 single/double with private bath, but is often full. *Trattoria Oro*, España 18 opposite Plaza Manuel Solar, has a varied menu and excellent service.

Getting There & Away
From the bus station at Av Sarmiento and Vélez Sársfield, there are many buses to Córdoba and some long-distance services.

Cuyo

Cuyo consists of the Andean provinces of Mendoza and San Juan, and adjacent San Luis. Part of colonial Chile, Cuyo retains a strong regional identity. Despite the rain-shadow effect of Aconcagua (6962m) and other formidable peaks, enough snow accumulates to sustain rivers that irrigate extensive vineyards.

With its varied terrain and climate, Cuyo offers outdoor activities all year round. Summer activities include climbing, trekking, riding, hang-gliding, white-water rafting, fishing, water-skiing, windsurfing and sailing. Skiing is increasingly popular in winter. Many travelers visit Mendoza, but the other provinces, especially San Juan, also provide off-the-beaten-track experiences.

History
Spaniards from Chile crossed 3850m Uspallata Pass to establish encomiendas among the indigenous Huarpe, but Mendoza's winter isolation stimulated economic

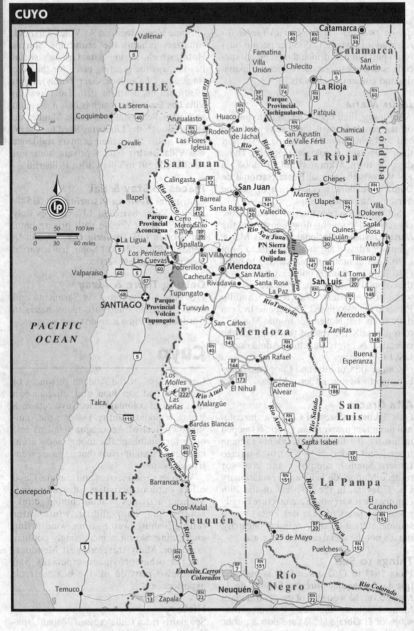

CUYO

PACIFIC OCEAN

CHILE

CHILE

San Juan

Mendoza

San Luis

La Rioja

Córdoba

La Pampa

Neuquén

Río Negro

Catamarca
Catamarca

Vallenar

Famatina
Villa Unión

Chilecito

San Martín

La Rioja

La Serena

Coquimbo

Angualasto

Huaco

Patquía

San Agustín
de Valle Fértil

Chamical

Ovalle

Las Flores
Iglesia

Rodeo

San José
de Jáchal

Chepes

Parque
Provincial
Ischigualasto

Calingasta

San Juan

Marayes

Ulapes

Villa
Dolores

Illapel

Barreal

Santa Rosa

Vallecito

Quines
Luján

Santa
Rosa

Merlo

Parque
Provincial
Aconcagua

Cerro
Mercedario
6770m

PN Sierra
de las
Quijadas

Tilisarao

La Ligua

Uspallata

Villavicencio

San Martín

La Toma

San Luis

Los Penitentes
Las Cuevas

Potrerillos

Cacheuta

Mendoza

Santa Rosa

Valparaíso

Rivadavia

La Paz

Tupungato

SANTIAGO

Parque
Provincial
Volcán
Tupungato

Tunuyán

Mercedes

Zanjitas

San Carlos

Buena
Esperanza

Talca

Los
Molles

Las
Leñas

San Rafael

General
Alvear

San Luis

Malargüe

Bardas Blancas

Santa Isabel

El Nihuil

Concepción

Barrancas

El
Carancho

Chos-Malal

25 de Mayo

Puelches

Temuco

Embalse Cerros
Colorados

Zapala

Neuquén

independence and political initiative. Still, for many decades, links to the viceregal capital in Lima were via Santiago and the Pacific, rather than overland via Tucumán and Bolivia.

Colonial vineyards were important, but independence eliminated traditional outlets for their produce. Arrival of the railway in 1884 and improved irrigation brought expansion of grape and olive cultivation, plus alfalfa for livestock. Modern Cuyo is one of Argentina's most important agricultural regions.

MENDOZA
Founded in 1561, at an altitude of 761m, the provincial capital is a lively city of 880,000, with an important university and, thanks to nearby oilfields, a growing industrial base. Modern quake-proof construction has replaced fallen historic buildings, but Mendoza's *acequias* (irrigation canals) and tree-lined streets create a pleasing environment.

Orientation
Plaza Independencia fills four square blocks downtown. Two blocks from each of its corners are smaller satellite plazas; Plaza España deserves special attention for its Saturday artisans market.

Sidewalk cafés on Av San Martín, which crosses the city from north to south, are good places to meet locals. The poplar-lined Alameda, beginning at the 1700 block of San Martín, was a traditional site for 19th-century promenades.

Information
The municipal Centro de Información y Asistencia al Turismo (☎ 0261-420-1333), on the broad Garibaldi sidewalk near Av San Martín, is the most convenient information source; open 9 am to 9 pm daily, it offers good maps and detailed handouts, and there's usually an English-speaker on hand. Another Centro de Información (☎ 0261-429-6298) is at Las Heras and Mitre. There's also an Oficina de Informes (☎ 0261-431-3001), open 7 am to 11 pm, in the bus terminal. At Av San Martín 1143, the provincial Subsecretaría de Turismo (☎ 0261-420-2800) is open weekdays 7 am to 9 pm.

Cambio Santiago, Av San Martín 1199, takes a 2% commission on traveler's checks. There are many downtown ATMs.

The post office is at Av San Martín and Av Colón. There are many locutorios, such as Fonobar, Sarmiento 33. Fifty, at Colón 199, offers Internet access for US$6 per hour.

Chile's consulate (☎ 0261-425-5024) is at Olascoaga 1071.

Things to See
At Ituzaingó and Fray Luis Beltrán, the misnamed **Ruinas de San Francisco** (1638), in the Ciudad Vieja (Old City) were part of a Jesuit-built church/school later taken over by Franciscans. The Virgen de Cuyo in the **Iglesia, Convento y Basílica de San Francisco**, Necochea 201, was the patron of San Martín's Ejército de los Andes (Army of the Andes). The historical **Museo Sanmartiniano**, at Remedios Escalada de San Martín 1843, is open weekdays 9 am to noon and 5 to 8 pm.

One might call the **Museo Fundacional** empty, but it would be fairer to call the high-ceilinged structure spacious, as it protects the excavations of the colonial Cabildo, destroyed by an earthquake in 1861, and of the slaughterhouse later built on the foundations. Open Monday to Saturday 8 am to 8 pm, Sunday 3 to 10 pm, the air-conditioned facility at Alberdi and Videla Castillo charges US$1.50 admission for adults, US$1 for students.

The unusual **Museo Popular Callejero** along Av Las Heras, between 25 de Mayo and Perú, consists of a series of encased dioramas depicting the changes in one of Mendoza's major avenues since its 1830 creation in a former dry watercourse. Because it's on the sidewalk, the museum is open to viewing 24 hours a day.

Bus No 110 ('Favorita') links Plaza Independencia to the forested 420-hectare **Parque San Martín** and a zoo on the hillside of **Cerro de la Gloria**.

Get a route map of the Municipalidad's Bus Turístico (☎ 0261-420-1333), whose well-versed guides (some English-speaking) offer the best possible orientation to the city for US$10. Good for 24 hours, the ticket allows you to board and reboard at any of several fixed stops throughout the city; the circuit begins at the corner of Garibaldi and Av San Martín and to the summit of Cerro de la Gloria. Hours are 10 am to 8 pm daily; the service runs from January 1 to Semana Santa.

ARGENTINA

MENDOZA

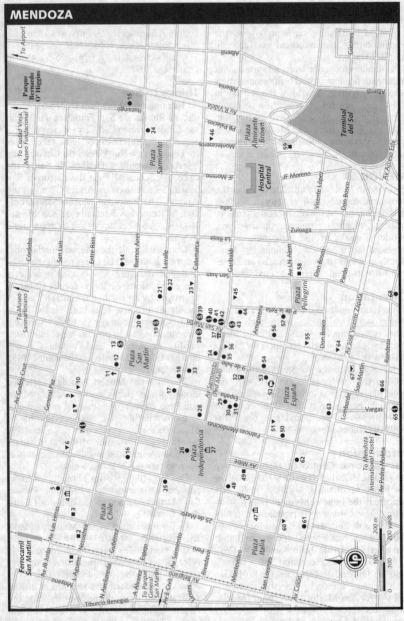

MENDOZA

PLACES TO STAY
1 Hotel Laerte
2 Hotel Vigo
3 Hotel Petit
49 Hostel Campo Base
58 Hotel Galicia
59 Residencial Savigliano

PLACES TO EAT
6 Rincón de La Boca
8 Café La Avenida
9 La Marchigiana
10 Mercado Central
23 Las Vías
36 Il Tucco
45 La Nature
46 Onda Verde
51 El Mesón Español
55 Asia
60 Línea Verde
64 Trattoria La Veneciana

OTHER
4 Museo Popular Callejero
5 Empresa Jocolí
7 Centro de Información y
  Asistencia al Turismo
11 Iglesia, Convento y
  Basílica de San Francisco

12 Migraciones
13 Banco de la Nación
14 Teatro Mendoza
15 Acuario Municipal
16 Localiza Rent A Car
17 Turismo Maipú
18 Andesmar
19 Banco de Mendoza
20 Asatej
21 Cine Opera
22 Cine Emperador (Universidad
  Nacional del Cuyo)
24 Hertz
25 Teatro Independencia
26 Teatro Quintanilla
27 Museo de Arte Moderno
28 Cámara de Diputados
29 Isc Viajes (AmEx)
30 LAPA, TAN
31 Kaikén Líneas Aéreas,
  Southern Winds
32 Café Soul
33 LanChile
34 Dinar
35 Aerolíneas Argentinas, Austral
37 Fonobar
38 Cambio Exprinter
39 Cambio Santiago
40 Subsecretaría de Turismo

41 Mercado Artesanal
42 Centro de Información y
  Asistencia al Turismo
43 Citibank (ATM)
44 Turismo Sepean
47 Museo del Pasado Cuyano
48 Instituto Cultural Argentino
  Norteamericano
50 Club Andino Italiano/
  Centro Italiano
52 German Consulate
53 English House Bookstore
54 Aymará Turismo
56 García Santos Libros
57 Avis
61 Laverap
62 La Lavandería
63 Fifty (Internet Access)
65 Terraza Mirador/Dirección
  Municipal de Turismo,
  Microcine
  Municipal David Eisenchlas
66 English Lending Library
67 Post Office
68 Iaim Instituto Cultural

Special Events

Mendoza's biggest annual event is late February's Fiesta Nacional de la Vendimia, the wine harvest festival.

Places to Stay

Camping The *Churrasqueras del Parque* (☎ 0261-428-0511), in Parque General San Martín, has good facilities but its popular *parrilla* means it can be noisy at night; fees are US$2.50 per person, tent and vehicle. Take bus No 50, 100 or 110 from downtown.

No 110 continues to *El Challao* (☎ 0261-431-6085), 6km north of downtown, and woodsy *Parque Suizo* (☎ 0261-444-1991), 9km from downtown. The former charges US$7 for two persons, while the latter costs US$12 for three. Each has hot showers, laundry facilities, electricity and a grocery.

Hostels Mendoza has two central HI affiliates. *Hostel Campo Base* (☎ 0261-429-0707, cellular 0261-15-569-6036; campobase@lanet .com.ar), Mitre 946, caters to climbers but draws a wider clientele and has good common spaces. Rates are US$8 per person

for hostel bunks. Email access is offered. The *Mendoza International Hostel* (☎/fax 0261-424-0018; mendoza1@hostels.org.ar), España 343, charges US$12 with breakfast; it also offers other meals, email, entertainment and organized tours and activities.

Casas de Familia, Residenciales & Hotels The tourist booth at the bus terminal may help find good rooms at bargain prices, while the downtown office also keeps a list of casas de familia charging US$10 to US$15 single.

Across Av Videla from the bus terminal, at Pedro Palacios 944 (take the pedestrian underpass), the *Residencial Savigliano* (☎ 0261-423-7746) has drawn enthusiastic commentary and charges US$10 per person with breakfast, shared bath, reasonable privacy and cable TV in a common area. For about the same price, try also two in nearby Dorrego, a neighborhood south of the bus terminal: *Hotel Mariani* (☎ 0261-431-9932) at Lamadrid 121, with private bath and breakfast, and the *Casa de Familia* (☎ 0261-432-0645), Sobremonte 1084, with breakfast and kitchen and laundry privileges.

Recommended *Hotel Galicia (☎ 0261-420-2619)*, San Juan 881, is central, clean, and friendly for US$12/20 single/double with shared bath, US$30 double with private bath. Equally central *Hotel Vigo (☎ 0261-425-0208)*, Necochea 749, may be one of the best inexpensive hotels in town, a bit run-down but with a nice garden; rates are US$15/26 for singles/doubles.

For US$25/35, enthusiastically recommended *Hotel Laerte (☎ 0261-423-0875)*, Leonidas Aguirre 19, is modern but homey. Comparable *Hotel Petit (☎ 0261-423-2099)*, Perú 1459, is clean, with friendly staff, for US$25/35.

Places to Eat

The best budget choice is the *Mercado Central*, at Av Las Heras and Patricias Mendocinas, whose various stalls offer pizza, empanadas, sandwiches and groceries. For pizza, try also *Rincón de La Boca*, with good fugazzeta (hard to find in Mendoza) and chopp (draft or lager), at Av Las Heras 485.

Several places specialize in pasta, including traditional favorite *Trattoria La Veneciana*, Av San Martín 739, and *Il Tucco*, Sarmiento 68. Mendoza's finest Italian restaurant is *La Marchigiana*, Patricias Mendocinas 1550; relatively expensive, it's worth the splurge.

El Mesón Español, Montevideo 244, has typical Spanish food, moderately priced. *Praga*, Leonidas Aguirre 413, has drawn praise from local residents. *Asia*, San Martín 821, is one of few tenedor libre Chinese restaurants in town.

For Middle Eastern cuisine, try *Café La Avenida*, Las Heras 341. For regional specialties, locals recommend *El Retortuño (☎ 0261-431-6300)*, on Dorrego near Adolfo Calles, which has live Latin American music on weekends; take the 'Dorrego' trolley from downtown.

Vegetarian options include the reasonably priced *Onda Verde*, Montecaseros 1177; *Línea Verde*, San Lorenzo 550, which also has a take-out *rotisería*; *La Nature*, at Garibaldi 63; and *Las Vías*, Catamarca 76.

Getting There & Away

Air Aerolíneas Argentinas (☎ 0261-420-4185), and Austral share offices at Sarmiento 82. Aerolíneas flies at least three times daily to Buenos Aires (US$57 to US$196). Austral

has 24 flights weekly to Buenos Aires' Aeroparque. LAPA (☎ 0261-429-1061), España 1012, is usually cheaper. Dinar (☎ 0261-420-4520), Sarmiento 69, also flies to Aeroparque (US$85 to US$179).

LanChile (☎ 0261-420-2890), Espejo 128, flies twice daily to Santiago de Chile, Mendoza's only international flight.

TAN (☎ 340240), also at España 1012, has 20 flights weekly to Neuquén (US$85 to US$100) and daily flights to Córdoba (US$39 to US$74). Andesmar (☎ 0261-438-0654), Espejo 189, flies to Córdoba (US$49 to US$69) and northwestern cities.

Kaikén Líneas Aéreas (☎ 0261-438-0243), Rivadavia 209, flies to Patagonian destinations from Neuquén (US$96 to US$100) to Ushuaia (US$265 to US$350). Southern Winds, at the same address, flies to Córdoba (US$59 to US$79) and the northwest, northern Patagonia and Mar del Plata.

Bus Mendoza's Terminal del Sol (☎ 0261-431-1299) lies between Av Gobernador Videla and Av Acceso Este. Hot showers are available for US$2.

International Numerous buses cross the Andes to Santiago or Valparaíso/Viña del Mar for about US$20 (eight hours). Faster taxi colectivos cost about US$25, sometimes less. Empresa General Artigas (EGA) goes to Montevideo, Uruguay (22 hours) at 1:30 pm Sunday, while El Rápido goes there at 8 pm Tuesday.

Provincial & Regional To Uspallata and Los Penitentes (US$9, four hours), for Parque Provincial Aconcagua, there are two buses daily with Expreso Uspallata. Empresa Jocolí and Turismo Maipú, Espejo 207, each has a daily service.

Service is frequent to San Rafael, slightly less frequent to Malargüe (US$20, seven hours). In ski season, several companies directly go to Las Leñas (US$15, 6½ hours), and Malargüe (US$20, seven hours). Buses to San Juan (US$10, two hours) and San Luis are numerous. La Cumbre has daily buses to the Difunta Correa Shrine in San Juan province.

Long Distance Mendoza has frequent long-distance services to almost every province.

Sample fares include Córdoba (US$30, 10 hours), Tucumán (US$39, 14 hours), Neuquén (US$40, 13 hours), Buenos Aires, (US$45 to US$55, 14 hours), Salta (US$62 to US$71, 19 hours), Puerto Iguazú (US$98, 36 hours) and Río Gallegos (US$129, 41 hours).

Getting Around

Mendoza buses now take magnetic fare cards, sold in multiple values of the basic US$0.55 fare.

To/From the Airport Aeropuerto Internacional Plumerillo (☎ 0261-448-7128) is 6km north of central Mendoza on RN 40. Bus No 60 ('Aeropuerto') from Calle Salta goes straight to the terminal.

AROUND MENDOZA
Wineries

Wineries in the province yield nearly 70% of the country's production; several near the capital offer tours and tasting. Southeast of downtown at Ozamis 1040 in Maipú, **Bodega La Colina de Oro** (ex-Giol, ☎ 0261-497-6777) is open weekdays 9 am to 6 pm, weekends 9 am to 11 pm. Take bus No 150 or 151 from downtown.

Bus Nos 170, 172 and 173 go to Coquimbito, Maipú, where **Bodega La Rural** (☎ 0261-497-2013), on Montecaseros, is open weekdays 9 to 11 am and 3 to 6:30 pm, Saturday 9 am to 11 am only. Its Museo Francisco Rutini displays wine-making tools used by 19th-century pioneers, as well as colonial religious sculptures from the Cuyo region.

Los Penitentes

Both scenery and snow cover can be excellent at Los Penitentes, 165km from Mendoza, offering downhill and Nordic skiing at an altitude of 2580m. Lifts and accommodation are very modern; the maximum vertical drop on its 21 runs exceeds 700m. For detailed information, contact the Los Penitentes office (☎ 0261-427-1641) at Paso de los Andes 1615, Departamento C, Godoy Cruz.

USPALLATA

In an exceptionally beautiful valley surrounded by polychrome mountains, 105km west of Mendoza at an altitude of 1751m, this crossroads village along RN 7 is a good base for exploring the surrounding area, which served as a location for the Brad Pitt epic, *Seven Years in Tibet*.

One km north of the highway junction toward Villavicencio, a signed side road leads to ruins and a museum at the **Bóvedas Históricas Uspallata**, a metallurgical site since pre-Columbian times. About 4km north of Uspallata, in a volcanic outcrop near a small monument to San Ceferino Namuncurá, is a faded but still visible set of **petroglyphs**.

Places to Stay & Eat

Uspallata's poplar-shaded *Camping Municipal* (☎ 02624-420009), 500m north of the Villavicencio junction, charges only US$5.60 per site. The quieter north end of the facilities, near the wood-stoked hot showers, is the best place to pitch a tent.

Hotel Viena (☎ 02624-420046), at Av Las Heras 240, east of the highway junction, is a bargain at US$15 per person with private bath and cable TV. Behind the YPF station, *Parrilla San Cayetano* is a convenient stop offering decent food for travelers en route to and from Chile. South of the junction is *El Rancho de Olmedo*, another parrilla.

Getting There & Away

Expreso Uspallata runs three buses every weekday, four on weekends, between Mendoza (US$8) and Uspallata, as far as Puente del Inca. Santiago-bound buses will carry passengers to and across the border, but are often full.

PARQUE PROVINCIAL ACONCAGUA

North of RN 7, nearly hugging the Chilean border, Parque Provincial Aconcagua protects 71,000 hectares of wild high country surrounding the Western Hemisphere's highest summit, 6962m Cerro Aconcagua. Passing motorists can stop to enjoy the view of the peak from **Laguna Horcones**, a 2km walk from the parking lot just north of the highway, where a ranger is available weekdays 8 am to 9 pm, Saturday 8 am to 8 pm.

Cerro Aconcagua

Reaching Aconcagua's summit requires a commitment of at least 13 to 15 days, including time for acclimatization. Potential climbers should acquire RJ Secor's climbing guide *Aconcagua*; there is also an Internet information page (www.aconcagua.com.ar). Non-climbers can trek to base camps and refugios beneath the permanent snow line.

From December to March, permits are obligatory both for trekking and climbing; rangers at Laguna Horcones will not allow visitors to pass without one. These permits, which cost US$30 for trekkers (seven days), US$80 for climbers (20 days) in December and February, and US$120 for climbers in January, are available at the Dirección de Recursos Naturales Renovables (☎ 0261-425-2090), Av Boulogne Sur Mer s/n, in Mendoza's Parque San Martín. It's open weekdays 8 am to 8 pm, weekends 8 am to noon.

Many adventure-travel agencies in and around Mendoza arrange excursions into the high mountains. The most established operators are Fernando Grajales (☎/fax 0261-429-3830), José Francisco Mendoza 898, 5500 Mendoza, and Rudy Parra's Aconcagua Trek (☎/fax 0261-431-7003), Güiraldes 246, 5519 Dorrego, Mendoza.

Puente del Inca

This natural stone bridge over the Río Mendoza, 2720m above sea level and 177km from Mendoza, is one of Argentina's most striking natural wonders. *Camping Los Puquios* is an inexpensive lodging choice, as is the *Albergue El Refugio*. The pleasant *Hostería Puente del Inca* (☎ 02624-420222; ☎ 0261-438-0480) charges US$40/50 single/ double with breakfast, though dorm beds can go for as low as US$25 per person with breakfast.

Cristo Redentor

Pounded by chilly winds, nearly 4000m above sea level on the rugged Argentina-Chile border, this famous monument, erected after settlement of a territorial dispute in 1902, has a fitting backdrop in the high Andes. The view is a must-see either by tour or private car, but the first autumn snowfall closes the hairpin road. At Las Cuevas, 10km before the border, travelers can stay at *Hostería Las Cuevas*.

MALARGÜE

From precolonial times, Pehuenche Indians hunted and gathered in the valley of Malargüe, 189km southwest of San Rafael via paved RN 40, but the advance of European agricultural colonists dispossessed the aboriginal inhabitants. Today petroleum is the principal industry, followed by uranium processing, but Malargüe is also a year-round outdoor activity center: nearby Las Leñas offers Argentina's best skiing.

The Dirección de Turismo y Medio Ambiente (☎ 02627-471659; 0800-666-8569 toll-free) has new facilities at the north end of town, directly on the highway.

Places to Stay & Eat

Open all year, the *Camping Municipal Malargüe* (☎ 02627-470691), on Alfonso Capdevila at the north end of town, charges US$5 per site. *Hotel Bambi* (☎ 02627-471237), Av San Martín 410, is the cheapest in town at US$20/35 single/double with private bath. Plain but comfortable *Hotel Turismo* (☎ 02627-471042), Av San Martín 224, charges US$24/35 with breakfast and private bath.

La Posta, Av Roca 374, serves local specialties such as chivito and trout.

Getting There & Away

Aerolíneas has flights to and from Malargüe during ski season only. Otherwise, the bus station, at Av General Roca and Aldao, has regular service to Mendoza (US$20, 4½ hours), some via San Rafael. There is summer service, once or twice weekly, across the 2500m Paso Pehuenche and down the awesome canyon of the Río Maule to Talca, Chile.

AROUND MALARGÜE
Las Leñas

Designed primarily to attract wealthy foreigners, Las Leñas is Argentina's most self-consciously prestigious ski resort, but despite the glitter it's not totally out of the question for budget travelers. Since opening in 1983, it has attracted an international clientele that spends the days on the slopes and the nights partying until the sun comes up.

Open mid-June to late September, Las Leñas is 445km south of Mendoza and 200km southwest of San Rafael via RN 40 and RP 222; it's only 70km from Malargüe via RN 40 and RP 222. Its 33 runs cover 3300 hectares, with a base altitude of 2200m, but the slopes reach 3430m for a maximum drop of 1230m. Arrange winter holidays through Badino Turismo (☎ 011-4326-1351, fax 011-3493-2568), Perón 725, 6th floor, in Buenos Aires. Las Leñas also has an Internet page (www.laslenas.com/).

Budget travelers will find regular transport from Malargüe, where accommodations are cheaper.

Lift Tickets Lifts function 9 am to 5 pm daily; rental equipment is readily available. Prices vary considerably throughout the season; children's tickets are discounted about 30%. Half-day tickets range in price from US$18 in low season to US$32 in high season; there are corresponding rates for one day (US$27 to US$42), three days (US$80 to US$120), four days (US$105 to US$160), one week (US$160 to US$260), 15 days (US$285 to US$475), one month (US$440 to US$525) and the whole season (US$735).

SAN JUAN

Though a provincial capital, San Juan de la Frontera, 170km north of Mendoza, retains the rhythm and cordiality of a small town. Juan Perón's relief efforts after San Juan's massive 1944 earthquake first made him a public figure; since then, modern construction, wide tree-lined streets and exceptional tidiness characterize the city center.

Orientation & Information

San Juan's grid makes orientation easy, but the addition of cardinal points to street addresses helps even more. East-west Av San Martín and north-south Calle Mendoza divide the city into quadrants; the functional center is south of San Martín.

The Ente Provincial de Turismo (Enprotur, ☎ 0264-422-7219), Sarmiento 24 Sur, has a good map of the city and its surroundings, plus useful information on the rest of the province. Hours are 7 am to 9 pm weekdays, 9 am to 9 pm weekends.

Cambio Santiago is at General Acha 52 Sur, and there are several downtown ATMs. The post office is at Av José Ignacio de la Roza 259 Este. There are many locutorios.

Things to See

At Av San Martín and Entre Ríos, the only surviving part of the earthquake-ravaged 17th-century **Convento de Santo Domingo** is

the cell occupied by San Martín in 1815, with a small museum entered at Laprida 96 Oeste. Inaugurated in 1979, the **Iglesia Catedral**, at Mendoza and Rivadavia, has all the charm of a Soviet apartment block.

At the **Museo de Ciencias Naturales**, at San Martín and Catamarca, the most interesting specimen is the skeleton of the carnivorous dinosaur *Herrerasaurus*, found in Ischigualasto, but the rest of the exhibits are poorly organized and interpreted. In the Parque de Mayo, at Av 25 de Mayo and Urquiza, the **Mercado Artesanal Tradicional** has brightly colored *mantas* (shawls) from Jáchal, pottery, horse gear, basketry, traditional silver knife handles and mate gourds.

The educator and provincial governor Domingo Faustino Sarmiento, also president of Argentina (1868-74), was born in the colonial **Casa de Sarmiento**, Sarmiento 21 Sur. Exiled in Chile during the Rosas regime, he wrote the polemic Life in the Argentine Republic in the Days of the Tyrants, arguing that Unitarism embodied European 'civilization,' while Federalism represented unprincipled 'barbarism.' The nostalgic Recuerdos de Provincia recount his childhood in this house, which is open 9 am to 7 daily except in summer, when hours are slightly shorter.

Places to Stay

Empresa de la Marina buses go to *Camping El Pinar*, the municipal site on Av Benavídez Oeste, 6km west of downtown. Charges are US$3 per person, US$2 per tent.

Near the bus terminal, small rooms at friendly *Hotel Hispano Argentino*, Estados Unidos 381 Sur, cost US$10 per person with shared bath. Similar in standard is *Hotel Susex*, España 348 Sur, for US$15. The *Residencial Embajador* (☎ 0264-422-5520), Av Rawson 25 Sur, has nice, clean rooms at US$15/25 single/double. Tidy *Hotel Central* (☎ 0264-422-3174), Mitre 131 Este, is central but quiet, has firm beds, and costs US$19/36 with private bath. For spotless, spacious rooms with breakfast for US$20/36, try the new *Petit Hotel Dibú* (☎ 0264-420-1034), Av San Martín and Patricias Sanjuaninas.

Places to Eat

One of San Juan's small pleasures are the numerous downtown *carritos* (carts) selling gulps of ice-cold, freshly squeezed orange juice for about US$0.60.

The *Club Sirio Libanés*, Entre Ríos 33 Sur, serves moderately priced Middle Eastern food among beautifully conserved tiles and woodwork. *La Nonna María*, west of downtown at Av San Martín and Perito Moreno, has excellent pasta. *Pirandello*, San Martín 3105 Oeste, is an outstanding sandwich place. The vegetarian *Soychú*, Ignacio de la Roza 223 Oeste, serves a highly recommended tenedor libre lunch.

Bigotes, Las Heras 647 Sur, has reasonably priced tenedor libre beef, chicken and salads. For parrillada, try also *El Castillo de Oro* at Av Ignacio de la Roza 199 Oeste and *Las Cubas*, Av San Martín and Perito Moreno.

Un Rincón de Napoli, Rivadavia 175 Oeste, has varied pizza and good beer; it's a bit dingy, but also prepares take-out food. *Listo El Pollo*, at Av San Martín and Santiago del Estero, specializes in grilled chicken.

Getting There & Away

Air Austral (☎ 0264-422-0205), Av San Martín 215 Oeste, flies twice daily to Buenos Aires' Aeroparque (US$75 to US$149) except Sunday (once only), and to San Luis daily except Saturday. LAPA (☎ 0264-421-6039), Av José Ignacio de la Roza 160, flies three times weekly to Aeroparque (US$59 to US$149), and four times weekly to Mendoza (US$20 to US$35).

TAN (☎ 0264-4275875), Av José Ignacio de la Roza 288 Este, flies several times weekly to Córdoba (US$50 to US$70), Mendoza (US$80 to US$90) and Neuquén (US$98 to US$115).

Bus The bus station (☎ 0264-422-1604) is at Estados Unidos 492 Sur. International services to Santiago (US$30, 10 hours) and Viña del Mar/Valparaíso all involve changing buses in Mendoza (US$10, two hours).

Empresa Vallecito has a daily bus to Caucete, the Difunta Correa Shrine (US$3, one hour) and San Agustín de Valle Fértil, but all eastbound long-distance buses pass the shrine as well; Vallecito also goes to Chilecito nightly at 10:15.

Sample long-distance fares from San Juan include Córdoba (US$25, eight hours), Catamarca (US$26, eight hours), Rosario (US$30, 12 hours), Tucumán (US$33, 13 hours), Buenos Aires (US$40 to US$60, 16 hours), Neuquén (US$49, 15 hours), Salta (US$50, 17 hours), Jujuy (US$55, 18 hours), Mar del Plata (US$70) and Bariloche (US$72).

AROUND SAN JUAN
Museo Arqueológico La Laja

With and emphasis on regional prehistory, this Moorish-style building 25km north of San Juan displays mummies, artifacts, petroglyphs and plant remains in seven separate rooms. Outside are reproductions of natural environments, farming systems, petroglyphs and scale-model house types.

This former hotel's thermal baths are still in use. From Av Córdoba in San Juan, take bus No 20 ('Albardón') at 8 am or 1 or 4 pm. At other times, take any No 20 'Albardón' bus to Las Piedritas and hitch or walk the last 5km.

Vallecito

According to legend, Deolinda Correa trailed her conscript husband on foot through the desert during the civil wars of the 1840s before dying of thirst, hunger and exhaustion, but passing muleteers found her infant son alive at her breast. Vallecito, 60km southeast of San Juan, is widely believed to be the site of her death.

Since the 1940s, the once simple **Difunta Correa Shrine** has become a small town, with its own gas station, school, post office, police station and church, plus 17 chapels or exhibit rooms where devotees leave elaborate ex-votos in exchange for supernatural favors. Her cult may be the strongest popular belief system in a country with a variety of unusual religious practices tenuously related to Roman Catholicism, the official state religion.

Truck drivers are especially devoted believers – from La Quiaca to Ushuaia, roadside shrines display her image, surrounded by candles, small banknotes, and bottles of water left to quench her thirst. Despite official Church antagonism, the shrine has grown rapidly; at Easter, May 1 and Christmas, up to 200,000 pilgrims visit the site.

Vallecito has one inexpensive *hostería* and a decent *restaurant*, but unless you're a believer, it's a better day trip than an overnight. Like the pilgrims, you can camp almost anywhere. Empresa Vallecito buses arrive regularly from San Juan, but any other eastbound bus will drop you at the site.

PARQUE PROVINCIAL ISCHIGUALASTO

At every meander in the canyon of Parque Provincial Ischigualasto, a desert valley between sedimentary mountain ranges, the intermittent waters of the Río Ischigualasto have exposed a wealth of Triassic fossils – up to 180 million years old – and carved distinctive shapes in the monochrome clays, red sandstones and volcanic ash. The desert flora of algarrobo trees, shrubs and cacti complement the eerie landforms.

Camping is permitted at the visitor center, which also has a *confitería* with simple meals (breakfast and lunch) and cold drinks; dried fruits and bottled olives from the province are also available. There are toilets and showers, but water shortages are frequent and there's no shade.

Getting There & Away

Ischigualasto is about 80km north of San Agustín via RP 510 and a paved lateral to the northwest. Given its size and isolation, the only practical way to visit the park is by vehicle. After you pay the US$5 entrance fee, a ranger will accompany your vehicle on a two-hour, 45km circuit over the park's unpaved roads, which may be impassable after rain.

If you have no vehicle, ask the tourist office in San Agustín about hiring a car and driver. Alternatively, contact Noli Sánchez or Jorge Gargiulo (☎ 02646-491100) at the park or Triassic Tour (☎ 0264-423-0358), Hipólito Yrigoyen 294 Sur in San Juan; tour rates are about US$10 per person for a minimum four-person trip in a 10-passenger minibus.

The Empresa Vallecito bus from San Juan to San Agustín and La Rioja stops at the Los Baldecitos checkpoint on RP 510, but improved RN 150 from Jáchal is shorter and may supersede the former route.

SAN LUIS

Capital of its province, San Luis (population 130,000) is 260km east of Mendoza. Its commercial center is along the parallel streets of San Martín and Rivadavia, between Plaza Pringles on the north and Plaza Independencia to the south.

The Dirección Provincial de Turismo (☎ 02652-423957), open weekdays 8 am to 10 pm and weekends 8 am to 8 pm, is at the triangular junction of Junín, San Martín and Av Illia. Alituris, Colón 733, changes US dollars and Chilean pesos. Several banks, mostly around Plaza Pringles, have ATMs. The post office is at Arturo Illia and San Martín. Locutorio San Martín is at San Martín 633.

Things to See

The 1930s Iglesia de Santo Domingo, on Plaza Independencia, replaced a 17th-century predecessor but kept its Moorish style; note the algarrobo doors on remaining parts of the old church next door. Alongside the church, on Av 25 de Mayo, the Mercado Artesanal sells fine handmade wool rugs, as well as ceramics, onyx carvings, and weavings. It's open weekdays, 7 am to 1 pm.

Places to Stay & Eat

In a quiet neighborhood at Buenos Aires 834, *Hotel Buenos Aires* (☎ 02652-424062), has modest but adequate rooms for US$16/29 single/double. Across from the bus terminal are two modest lodgings: *Residencial 17* (☎ 02652-423187), at Estado de Israel 1476, for US$15/26, and *Residencial Rivadavia* (☎ 02652-422437), next door at Estado de Israel 1470, for US$18/22.

A good breakfast choice is the bus station's *Confitería La Terminal*, which serves terrific café con leche with croissants. *Pizza Club*, Av Illia 113, has varied pizza toppings, good service and atmosphere, and excellent takeout empanadas. *Restaurant Argentino*, Av Illia 352, serves large portions of pasta.

Sofía, at Colón and Bolívar, has Spanish cuisine, most notably seafood. *La Buena Mesa*, San Martín 488, also specializes in seafood.

Getting There & Away

Air Austral (☎ 02652-423407), Colón 733, flies twice each weekday to Buenos Aires' Aeroparque, once each weekend day; and daily except Sunday to San Juan. LAPA (☎ 02652-422499), Av Illia 331, flies 10 times weekly to Aeroparque.

Bus San Luis' bus station (☎ 02652-424021) is on España between San Martín and Rivadavia. There are several buses daily to provincial hill resorts like Merlo.

Sample long-distance fares from San Luis include Mendoza (US$16, three hours), San

Juan (US$15, four hours), Rosario (US$33, 11 hours), Buenos Aires (US$40, 12 hours) and Mar del Plata (US$50).

The Andean Northwest

The Northwest (Noroeste) comprises the provinces of Jujuy, Salta, Tucumán, La Rioja, Catamarca and Santiago del Estero. Its pre-Columbian and colonial past makes the trip to the Argentine heartland a journey through time as well as space.

History

In pre-Columbian times, two-thirds of the population of what is now Argentina inhabited the Northwest. The widespread Diaguita, the Lule south and west of modern Salta, the Tonocote of Santiago del Estero, and the Omahuaca of Jujuy were all, in some ways, cultural outliers of the agrarian civilizations of the Central Andean highlands. Even today, the northern provinces resemble the Andean countries, and Quechua communities reach as far south as Santiago del Estero.

Diego de Almagro's expedition from Cuzco to Chile passed through Jujuy and Salta, but the earliest city was Santiago del Estero (1553). Indians destroyed several others before the founding of San Miguel de Tucumán (1565), Córdoba (1573), Salta (1582), La Rioja (1591) and San Salvador de Jujuy (1593). Catamarca was founded more than a century later. Unimpressive in their infancy, these settlements still established the basic elements of colonial rule: the *cabildo* (town council), the church, and the rectangular plaza with its clustered public buildings.

As Indians fell to disease and exploitation, encomiendas lost their economic value, but colonial Tucumán provided mules, cotton and textiles for the mines of Potosí. The opening of the Atlantic to legal shipping in late colonial times relegated Jujuy and Salta to marginality, but the sugar industry increased Tucumán's economic importance.

SAN SALVADOR DE JUJUY

San Salvador de Jujuy was a key stopover for colonial mule-traders en route to Potosí, but sugarcane became a major commodity at Jesuit missions and, later, British plantations. Now commonly known as 'Jujuy,' the town's proper name distinguished it as a Spanish settlement and also avoided confusion with nearby San Pedro de Jujuy. During the wars of independence, General Manuel Belgrano directed the evacuation of the city to avoid royalist capture; every August Jujuy's biggest event, the week-long **Semana de Jujuy**, celebrates the *éxodo jujeño* (Jujuy exodus).

Orientation & Information

At the mouth of the Quebrada de Humahuaca, the colonial center of the city (population 200,000) is Plaza Belgrano. Between Necochea and Lavalle, the 700 block of Belgrano (the main commercial street) is a peatonal. RN 9 leads north up the Quebrada, while RN 66 leads southeast to RN 34, the main route to Salta.

The Dirección Provincial de Turismo (☎ 0388-422-1326) is at Belgrano 690. The staff vary in their attention to visitors but have abundant maps, brochures and other materials. Hours are 7:30 am to 1 pm and 3 to 9 pm daily.

Graffiti Turismo, Belgrano 731, cashes traveler's checks, but commissions are substantial. ATMs are common. The post office is at Lamadrid and Independencia; there's a Telecentro at Belgrano and Lavalle.

Bolivia's consulate (☎ 0388-423-3156), Güemes 779, 2nd floor, is open weekdays 8 am to 1 pm.

Things to See

Opposite Plaza Belgrano, Jujuy's **Iglesia Catedral** (1763) features a gold-laminated Spanish baroque pulpit, built by local artisans under a European master. Across the street, on the plaza, there's an artisans market.

Also opposite Plaza Belgrano, the colonial **Cabildo** deserves more attention than the **Museo Policial** within. The **Museo Histórico Provincial**, Lavalle 256, has rooms dedicated to distinct themes in provincial history. The **Iglesia Santa Barbara**, at Lamadrid and San Martín, contains several paintings from the colonial Cuzco school. The new **Museo Arqueológico Provincial**, at Lavalle 434, has made some good first impressions.

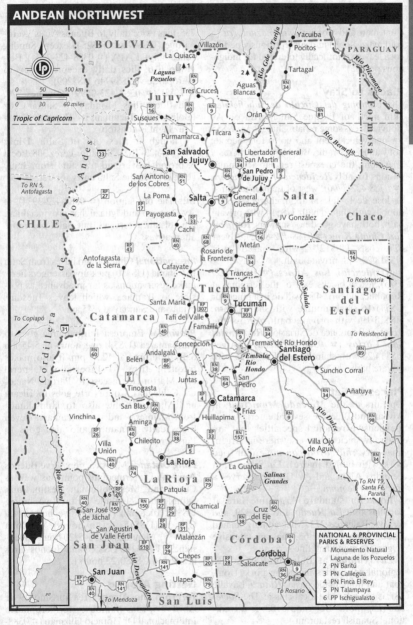

ANDEAN NORTHWEST

BOLIVIA

Yacuiba

Villazón

La Quiaca

Pocitos

PARAGUAY

Laguna
Pozuelos

Tres Cruces

Aguas
Blancas

Tartagal

RN
34

0   50   100 km
0   30   60 miles

Tropic of Capricorn

JUJUY

RN
16

RN
40

RN
9

Orán

RN
81

Formosa

Susques

Purmamarca

Tilcara

San Salvador
de Jujuy

Libertador General
San Martín

Río Bermejo

RP
23

San Antonio
de los Cobres

RP
51

RN
66

San Pedro
de Jujuy

RP
5

To RN 5,
Antofagasta

RP
27

La Poma

Salta

RN
9

General
Güemes

Salta

Chaco

RP
17

Payogasta

RP
33

JV González

CHILE

Cachi

RN
68

RN
16

Cordillera de los Andes

RP
43

Rosario de
la Frontera

Metán

RN
34

RN
16

Antofagasta
de la Sierra

RN
40

Cafayate

Trancas

Río Salado

To Resistencia

Santiago
del
Estero

To Copiapó

RN
31

Santa María

Tucumán

RP
307

Tucumán

RN
9

RP
303

To Resistencia

Catamarca

Tafí del Valle

Famaillá

RN
34

RN
89

RN
40

Concepción

RN
9

Termas de Río Hondo

Santiago
del Estero

RN
60

Andalgalá

RP
46

Embalse
Río
Hondo

Suncho Corral

Belén

RP
38

Añatuya

RP
3

Las
Juntas

RN
64

San
Pedro

RN
34

Tinogasta

RP
4

Catamarca

Río Dulce

RN
98

San Blas

RN
60

Frías

RN
9

Vinchina

Aminga

Huillapima

Villa Ojo
de Agua

RP
26

RN
40

Chilecito

RP
38

RP
33

RN
157

RN
34

Villa
Unión

RP
5

RN
40

La Rioja

La Guardia

Salinas
Grandes

To RN 19,
Santa Fé,
Paraná

RN
74

La Rioja

RN
79

Patquía

RP
26

RN
60

San José
de Jáchal

RN
150

RP
27

Chamical

Cruz
del Eje

RN
9

RN
40

RN
150

RP
29

RN
38

RP
28

San Agustín
de Valle Fértil

RP
510

Malanzán

RP
31

Córdoba

RN
9

San Juan

RP
29

Chepes

RP
20

RP
28

Salsacate

Córdoba

RN
36

Río Desaguadero

RN
141

Ulapes

RN
9

Pilar

San Juan

RP
12

RN
40

RN
141

To Mendoza

San Luis

To Rosario

**NATIONAL & PROVINCIAL
PARKS & RESERVES**
1 Monumento Natural
   Laguna de los Pozuelos
2 PN Baritú
3 PN Calilegua
4 PN Finca El Rey
5 PN Talampaya
6 PP Ischigualasto

Jujuy's **Mercado del Sur**, opposite the bus terminal, is an Indian market where Quechua men and women swig *mazamorra* (a cold maize soup) and surreptitiously peddle coca leaves (unofficially tolerated for indigenous people).

Places to Stay

The *Camping del Círculo de Suboficiales*, 3km north of Parque San Martín on Av Bolivia, needs some rehab. Charges are US$5 for one vehicle, tent and up to four people; hot water is sporadic. Bus No 4 goes there.

Among the cheapest regular accommodations, friendly *Residencial Río de Janeiro* (☎ 0388-422-3700), west of the bus terminal at José de la Iglesia 1356, charges US$13 double with shared bath, US$14 with private bath; both have good hot showers. *Residencial Chung King* (☎ 0388-422-8142), Alvear 627, costs US$12/14 with shared bath, US$18/22 with private bath.

Residencial Los Andes (☎ 0388-422-4315), a few blocks east of the terminal at República de Siria 456, will do in a pinch for US$11/16 single/double with shared bath, US$13/19 with private bath. Across the street, at República de Siria 459, *Residencial San Carlos* (☎ 0388-422-2286) charges US$14/20 with shared bath, US$20/25 with private bath.

Places to Eat

Upstairs at the *Mercado Municipal*, at Alvear and Balcarce, several eateries serve inexpensive regional specialties that are generally spicier than elsewhere in Argentina – try *chicharrón con mote* (stir-fried pork with boiled maize). *La Sucreña*, at Leandro Alem and Av Dorrego, serves a spicy *sopa de maní*.

Look for standard Argentine fare at parrillas like *La Rueda*, Lavalle 329, and *Krysys*, Balcarce 272. Misleadingly named *Chung King*, Alvear 627, has an extensive Argentine menu and fine service.

La Ventana, at Belgrano 749, serves regional specialties including pork, trout, goat and homemade pasta. *Ruta 9*, Lavalle 287, is considered a local classic. The *Sociedad Española*, Belgrano 1102, is a traditional Spanish restaurant.

For vegetarian fare, try *Madre Tierra* at Belgrano and Otero. *El Pan Casero* is a natural-foods bakery at Belgrano 619.

Getting There & Away

Air Austral (☎ 0388-422-7198), San Martín 735, flies twice daily to Buenos Aires' Aeroparque (US$97 to US$254) except Sunday (once only). LAPA (☎ 0388-423-2244), Belgrano 616, flies daily except Sunday to Aeroparque (US$99 to US$209).

LAB (☎ 0388-423-0699), Güemes 779, 2nd floor, flies Monday to Santa Cruz (Bolivia) via Tucumán; its Thursday Santa Cruz flight is nonstop.

Though it flies out of Salta, Dinar (☎ 0388-423-7100), Senador Pérez 308, Local 3, provides overland transfers from Jujuy (US$10). See the Salta entry for details.

Bus The bus station (☎ 0388-422-3934), at Av Dorrego and Iguazú, has provincial and long-distance services, but Salta has more alternatives.

International Chile-bound buses from Salta to Calama (US$50) pick up passengers here; make reservations as far in advance as possible at Tramaca, which leaves Tuesday, Friday and Sunday at 8:45 am.

Provincial Empresa Purmamarca goes to Purmamarca (US$4, one hour) at 5:45 am daily, returning at 12:30 pm. It also makes frequent trips ·to Libertador General San Martín (for access to Parque Nacional Calilegua). Cota Norte goes to Tilcara and Maimará, and also to Humahuaca from Maimará, and to Purmamarca seven times daily. Panamericano also goes to Purmamarca.

Long Distance Many carriers serve Buenos Aires and intermediate points, as well as Cuyo and Mesopotamian destinations. Sample fares include Salta (two hours, US$8), Tucumán (US$15, five hours), La Quiaca (US$15, seven hours), Córdoba (US$25), Mendoza (US$45, 20 hours), Resistencia (US$42 to US$55) and Buenos Aires (US$64 to US$80, 22 hours).

Getting Around

To/From the Airport Tea Turismo, 19 de Abril 485, runs minibuses to Aeropuerto Internacional Dr Horacio Guzmán (☎ 0388-491-1106), 32km southeast of town, for US$5. LAPA provides its own airport transfers, as does Dinar (to Salta).

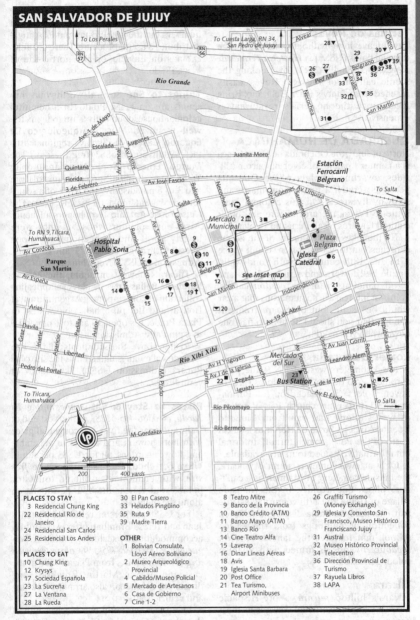

SAN SALVADOR DE JUJUY

ARGENTINA

AROUND SAN SALVADOR DE JUJUY

Termas de Reyes

Don't leave Jujuy without wallowing in the thermal baths (US$6) at *Hostería Termas de Reyes* (☎ 0388-492-2522), overlooking the scenic canyon of the Río Reyes, easily reached from Jujuy's Plaza Belgrano. Bring food, since the hostería's restaurant is expensive.

QUEBRADA DE HUMAHUACA

North of Jujuy, the Quebrada de Humahuaca is a painter's palette of color on barren hillsides, dwarfing hamlets where Quechua peasants scratch a living from maize and scrawny livestock. On this colonial postroute to Potosí, the architecture and other cultural features recall Peru and Bolivia.

Earthquakes leveled many of the adobe churches, but they were often rebuilt in the 17th and 18th centuries with solid walls, simple bell towers, and striking doors and wood paneling from the *cardón* cactus. Points of interest are so numerous that a car would be useful, but buses are frequent enough that you should be able to flag one down when you need it.

Lower Quebrada

A few kilometers west of RN 9, the polychrome Cerro de los Siete Colores (Hill of Seven Colors) is a backdrop for Purmamarca's 17th-century **church**. Part of a chain of way stations that ran from Lima to Buenos Aires, **La Posta de Hornillos** is 11km north of the Purmamarca turnoff. Informal but informative guided tours are available.

Only a few kilometers south of Tilcara, the hillside cemetery of **Maimará** is a can't-miss photo opportunity. In the roadside village of **Uquía**, the 17th-century **Iglesia de San Francisco de Paula** displays a restored collection of paintings from the Cuzco school, that features the famous *Ángeles arcabuceros*, angels armed with Spanish colonial muskets.

Tilcara

Tilcara's hilltop *pucará*, a pre-Hispanic fortress with unobstructed views, is its most conspicuous attraction, but the village's museums and artists-colony reputation help make an appealing stopover. At 2461m above sea level, Tilcara has an irregular street plan beyond the central Plaza Prado; people generally ignore street names and numbers, but the hotel/restaurant El Antigal distributes a useful brochure. There are Telecabinas on Lavalle, on the north side of Plaza Prado.

Things to See Several worthwhile museums are on Plaza Prado. In a beautiful colonial house, open daily 9 am to 6 pm, the well-organized **Museo Arqueológico Dr Eduardo Casanova** displays regional artifacts. Admission is US$2 (free Tuesday). The **Museo Ernesto Soto Avendaño**, open Wednesday through Sunday, 9 am to 1 pm and 3 to 6 pm, displays the work of a sculptor who spent most of his life here. The **Museo José Antonio Terry** honors a Buenos Aires-born painter whose themes were largely rural and indigenous. It's open Tuesday through Sunday 7 am to 7 pm. Admission is US$2 (free Thursday).

Tilcara's newest museum, the **Museo Irureta de Bellas Artes** displays an appealing collection of contemporary Argentine art, at Bolívar and Belgrano, half a block west of Plaza Prado. It's open 10 am to 1 pm and 3 to 6 pm daily. Admission is free.

Rising above the sediments of the Río Grande valley, an isolated hill is the site of **El Pucará** (admission US$2), 1km south of central Tilcara.

Places to Stay & Eat *Autocamping El Jardín* (☎ 0388-495-5128), at the west end of Belgrano near the river, is a congenial place with hot showers and attractive vegetable and flower gardens, all for US$3 per adult, US$2 per child. There's an adequate *free site*, with picnic tables but no toilets or potable water, near the YPF petrol station along the highway.

For US$8 per person, relocated porteños Juan and Teresa Brambati offer excellent HI accommodation at secluded, hilltop *Albergue Malka* (☎ 0388-495-5197; tilcara@hostels .org.ar), four blocks from Plaza Prado at the east end of San Martín. Breakfast and dinner are extra; Juan also arranges trekking and vehicle tours.

One block west and two blocks south of the plaza, *Hospedaje El Pucará Casa de Piedra* (☎ 0388-495-5050) has clean rooms in a garden setting for US$9 per person with shared bath, US$12 with private bath.

Getting There & Away Both north and southbound buses stop on Plaza Prado.

Humahuaca

Straddling the Río Grande, nearly 3000m above sea level, Humahuaca (population 6200) is a mostly Quechua village of cobbled streets lined with adobe houses. The tourist office, in the Cabildo at Tucumán and Jujuy, is rarely open. The post office is across from the plaza. There's a Telecentro at Jujuy 399, behind the Municipalidad.

Things to See From the clock tower in the **Cabildo**, a life-size figure of San Francisco Solano emerges daily at noon. Arrive early, since the clock is erratic and the figure appears only very briefly.

Humahuaca's patron saint resides in the colonial **Iglesia de la Candelaria**, which contains 18th-century oils by Cuzco painter Marcos Sapaca. Overlooking the town, Tilcara sculptor Ernesto Soto Avendaño's **Monumento a la Independencia** is a textbook example of *indigenismo*, a distorted, romantic nationalist tendency in Latin American art and literature.

Local writer Sixto Vázquez Zuleta (who prefers his Quechua name 'Toqo') runs the **Museo Folklórico Regional**, Buenos Aires 435/447, open daily 8 am to 8 pm for formal tours only (US$5 per person for a minimum group of three or four).

Ten km north of Humahuaca by a dirt road on the east side of the bridge over the Río Grande, northwestern Argentina's most extensive pre-Columbian ruins cover 40 hectares at **Coctaca**. Many appear to be broad agricultural terraces on an alluvial fan, but there are also obvious outlines of clusters of buildings.

Places to Stay & Eat The municipal campsite across the bridge remains closed, but it's possible to park or pitch a tent there for free. The *Albergue Juvenil*, Buenos Aires 435, is open year-round and charges US$5 per person, but reports are that standards have fallen.

Posada del Sol (☎ 03887-490508), a short distance across the bridge, is run by the owners of its namesake café, half a block east of the plaza. It's a little ramshackle but, for US$7 per person, the rooms have personality, hot showers, homemade bread, and free tea and coffee. *Residencial Humahuaca* (☎ 03887-421141), at Córdoba 401 near Corrientes, half a block from the bus terminal, charges US$10/18 single/double with shared bath, US$18/30 with private bath.

For regional dishes like tamales, empanadas and chicken, try *Cacharpaya* on Jujuy between Santiago del Estero and Tucumán. *El Humahuaca*, Tucumán 22, is only so-so, but palatable. *El Fortín* on Buenos Aires just north of Salta, is worth a look, as is *Cafetería Belgrano* (good pizza) near the railway line. There's an acceptable *confitería* at the bus terminal.

Getting There & Away From the bus station at Belgrano and Entre Ríos, several carriers run southbound buses to Salta and Jujuy, and northbound buses to La Quiaca (US$15, 2½ hours).

LA QUIACA

North of Humahuaca, graveled RN 9 climbs steeply to the altiplano, where agriculture is precarious and peasants subsist on llamas, sheep, goats and the few cattle that can graze the sparse *ichu* grass. At the end of the road are La Quiaca and its Bolivian twin, Villazón. For more details on the border crossing, see the Villazón entry in the Bolivia chapter.

La Quiaca has no tourist office, but the ACA station on RN 9 has maps. If Banco Nación will not cash traveler's checks, try Universo Tours in Villazón. La Quiaca's Bolivian Consulate, at San Juan and Árabe Siria, charges a hefty US$15 for visas.

Places to Stay & Eat

Accommodation is cheaper on the Bolivian side, but try the unimpressive *Hotel Frontera* on 25 de Mayo, for about US$8 per person. Recommended *Hotel Cristal* (☎ 03885-422255), Sarmiento 543, charges US$17/28 single/double.

El Buen Gusto, a parrilla on Av España between Belgrano and 25 de Mayo, has decent food but slow service. *Rosita*, on 9 de Julio between Balcarce and Árabe Siria, has simple inexpensive meals and fine take-out empanadas.

Getting There & Away

From the bus station at 25 de Mayo and Av España, several carriers provide frequent connections to Jujuy (US$14), Salta and intermediate points, plus long-distance service.

AROUND LA QUIACA

At the village of **Yavi**, 16km east of La Quiaca, the 17th-century **Iglesia de San Francisco** is renowned for its altar, paintings, and carved statues. The nearby **Casa del Marqués Campero** belonged to a nobleman whose marriage to the holder of the original encomienda created a family that dominated the region's economy in the 18th century.

Every half-hour or so, there's a pickup truck that runs from La Quiaca's Mercado Municipal on Av Hipólito Yrigoyen.

SALTA

Salta is in a basin surrounded by verdant peaks, 1200m above sea level. Its agreeable climate attracted early Spaniards, who could pasture animals nearby and raise crops that could not grow in Bolivia's frigid highlands. When the railway made it feasible to haul sugar to the Pampas, the city partly recovered from its 19th-century decline.

Salta's commercial center is southwest of the central Plaza 9 de Julio. Alberdi and Florida are pedestrian malls between Caseros and Av San Martín.

Information

The provincial Secretaría de Turismo (☎ 0387-431-0950), Buenos Aires 93, is open 8 am to 9 pm daily. The Dirección Municipal de Turismo (☎ 0387-437-3341), at Av San Martín and Buenos Aires, is open 8 am to 9 pm daily; in high season, at the bus terminal, it maintains a smaller office that closes from 1 to 4 pm. The Administración de Parques Nacionales (☎ 0387-431-0255), Santa Fe 23, has information on the province's national parks.

Cambio Dinar, Mitre 101, changes cash and traveler's checks; there are many ATMs. The post office is at Dean Funes 140. There's a Telecentros on Buenos Aires half a block south of Plaza 9 de Julio. Shownet, 20 de Febrero 28, has Internet access.

Bolivia's consulate (☎ 0387-421-1040) is at Mariano Boedo 34, while Chile's (☎ 0387-431-1857) is at Santiago del Estero 965.

Things to See

Museums The 18th-century **Cabildo**, at Caseros 549, houses the **Museo Histórico del**

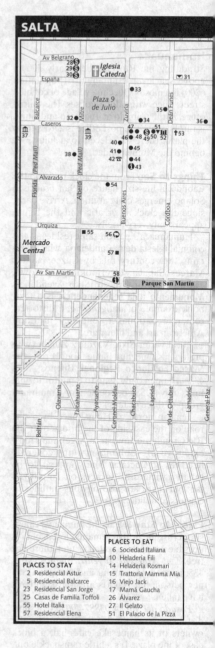

SALTA

PLACES TO STAY
2 Residencial Astur
5 Residencial Balcarce
23 Residencial San Jorge
25 Casas de Familia Toffoli
55 Hotel Italia
57 Residencial Elena

PLACES TO EAT
6 Sociedad Italiana
10 Heladería Fili
14 Heladería Rosmari
15 Trattoria Mamma Mia
16 Viejo Jack
17 Mamá Gaucha
26 Álvarez
27 Il Gelato
51 El Palacio de la Pizza

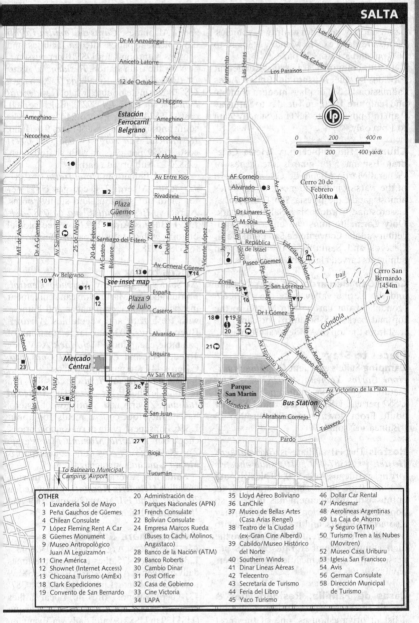

SALTA

Norte (admission US$1), with religious and modern art, period furniture, historic coins, paper money, and horse-drawn vehicles. Hours are daily except Monday 9:30 am to 1:30 pm and 3:30 to 8:30 pm.

In the colonial Casa Arias Rengel, at Florida 18, the **Museo de Bellas Artes** (admission US$1) displays modern painting and sculpture. It's open Tuesday to Saturday 9 am to 1 pm and 4 to 8:30 pm, Sunday 9 am to 1 pm only.

Churches The 19th-century **Iglesia Catedral**, España 596, guards the ashes of General Martín Miguel de Güemes, a hero of the wars of independence. So ornate it's almost gaudy, the **Iglesia San Francisco**, at Caseros and Córdoba, is a Salta landmark. Only Carmelite nuns can enter the 16th-century adobe **Convento de San Bernardo**, at Caseros and Santa Fe, but anyone can admire its carved algarrobo door.

Cerro San Bernardo For views of Salta and the Lerma valley, take the *teleférico* (gondola) from Parque San Martín to the top and back (US$6 return), or climb the trail from the top of Av General Güemes.

Places to Stay

Camping Salta's excellent *Camping Municipal Carlos Xamena* (☎ 0387-423-1341) features a gigantic swimming pool. Fees are US$2 per car, US$3 per tent and US$2 per adult. From downtown, take bus No 13 ('Balneario') south.

Hostels The HI affiliate is *Backpacker's Hostel* (☎ 0387-423-5910; salta@hostels .org.ar) at Buenos Aires 930, 10 blocks south of Plaza 9 de Julio. Though cramped, its enthusiastic management has made it so popular that reservations are advisable; they also arrange tours, and it's a good place to organize a group to rent a car to explore the high country. Member rates are $8 per person with kitchen facilities; nonmembers pay US$9.

Casas de Familia, Residenciales & Hotels The Secretaría de Turismo maintains a list of private houses; one of the most popular and central is at Mendoza 915, run by María de Toffoli (☎ 0387-431-8948), one of three sisters. The other two let rooms in their own houses at Mendoza 917, (☎ 0387-421-2233), and Mendoza 919, (☎ 0387-421-7383). All of these **Casas de Familia Taffoli** have pleasant patios, kitchen facilities, and spotless bathrooms, for US$10 per person.

Near the train station, **Residencial Astur** (☎ 0387-421-2107), Rivadavia 752, charges US$18/25 single/double, while **Residencial Balcarce** (☎ 0387-421-8023), Balcarce 460, costs US$20/25. At Esteco 244, two blocks south and six blocks west of Plaza 9 de Julio, **Residencial San Jorge** (☎ 0387-421-0443) costs US$9 per person with shared bath, US$20/25 with private bath.

Central, Italian-run **Hotel Italia** (☎ 0387-421-4050), Alberdi 231, charges US$19/27 for plain but spacious and sunny rooms. Attractive **Residencial Elena** (☎ 0387-421-1529), Buenos Aires 256, in a neocolonial building with an interior patio, offers rooms for US$20/28.

Places to Eat

At Salta's large, lively **Mercado Central**, Florida and San Martín, you can supplement inexpensive pizza, empanadas and humitas with fresh fruit and vegetables. **Álvarez**, Buenos Aires 302, has large portions of palatable, cheap food. **Viejo Jack**, Av Virrey Toledo 145, and **El Solar del Convento**, Caseros 444, are popular parrillas.

El Palacio de la Pizza Caseros 437, is a reasonable choice for pizza. The **Sociedad Italiana**, Zuviría and Santiago del Estero, has quality four-course meals for about US$6. For superb pasta at reasonable prices, check out **Trattoria Mamma Mia**, Pasaje Zorrilla 1; its very Argentine counterpart is **Mamá Gaucha**, Gurruchaga 225.

Salta has several fine ice creameries, including **Heladería Rosmari** at Pueyrredón 202, **Heladería Fili** at Av Güemes 1009, and **Il Gelato** at Buenos Aires 606.

Getting There & Away

Air Aerolíneas Argentinas (☎ 0387-431-1331), Caseros 475, flies two or three times daily to Buenos Aires' Aeroparque (US$139 to US$248). Dinar Líneas Aéreas (☎ 0387-431-0606), Buenos Aires 46, Local 2, flies nonstop every weekday to Aeroparque (US$139 to US$219) and daily via Tucumán. LAPA (☎ 0387-421-0386), Caseros 492, flies at least once daily to Aeroparque (US$99 to US$209).

Lloyd Aéreo Boliviano (☎ 0387-431-0320), Deán Funes 29, flies Tuesday, Friday and Sunday to Santa Cruz (Bolivia). Lan-Chile (☎ 0387-421-1500), Caseros 322, has seasonal flights over the Andes.

Andesmar (☎ 0387-431-0875), Caseros 489, flies to northwestern destinations from Mendoza to Salta. Southern Winds (☎ 0387-421-0808), Buenos Aires 28, flies mostly to Córdoba and northern Patagonia.

Bus Salta's bus station (☎ 0387-431-5227), on Av Hipólito Yrigoyen southeast of downtown, has frequent services to all parts of the country. A few carriers have offices nearby or elsewhere in town.

International Tramaca (☎ 0387-431-2497) goes Tuesday and Friday to San Pedro de Atacama (12 hours) and Calama, Chile (14 hours; US$55) Tuesday and Friday mornings, connecting to Antofagasta, Iquique and Arica.

Provincial El Indio goes five times daily to Cafayate (US$9 to US$10, three hours) except Sunday (four times); El Cafayateño goes twice daily except Sunday (once). El Quebradeño goes daily to San Antonio de los Cobres.

Empresa Marcos Rueda (☎ 0387-421-4447), Islas Malvinas 393, serves the altiplano village of Cachi (US$14, five hours) twice daily except Monday and Wednesday (once only); it also goes Tuesday through Sunday to Molinos, and Thursday to Angastaco.

Long Distance Long-distance services are frequent in all directions. Some sample fares include Tucumán (US$15 to US$18, four hours), La Quiaca (US$23, nine hours), Resistencia (US$32 to US$42, 13 hours), Rosario (US$57 to US$73, 17 hours), Mendoza (US$61, 19 hours) and Buenos Aires (US$64 to US$86, 22 hours).

Train The Ferrocarril Belgrano (☎ 0387-421-3161), Ameghino 690, lacks regular passenger services, but one of Salta's popular attractions is the scenic but expensive ride to and beyond the mining town of San Antonio de los Cobres (see that section later in this chapter for more details) on the famous Tren a las Nubes (Train to the Clouds) – contact Turismo Tren a las Nubes (☎ 0387-431-4984), Caseros 431.

The local freight, leaving Friday about 9:20 am, is a cheaper alternative to San Antonio (US$10) or to the Chilean border at Socompa (US$15, 29 hours).

Getting Around
Buses to Aeropuerto Internacional El Aybal (☎ 0387-423-1648), 9km southwest of town on RP 51, cost US$3.

PARQUE NACIONAL CALILEGUA
On Jujuy province's eastern border, the arid altiplano surrenders to dense subtropical cloud forest in the Serranía de Calilegua, where 3600m Cerro Hermoso offers boundless views of the Gran Chaco. Bird life is abundant, and the varied flora change with the increasing altitude.

The park headquarters and visitor center (☎ 03886-422046) are in the village of Calilegua, just north of Libertador General San Martín. Donated by the Ledesma sugar mill, the visitor center has exhibits on all the region's national parks.

Beware mosquitoes at the developed *campsite* at Aguas Negras, on a short lateral near the entrance station. Camping is also possible on a level area near the ranger station at Mesada de las Colmenas.

Getting There & Away
Empresa Valle Grande goes to the park from Libertador General San Martín at 7 am Tuesday and Saturday, returning at 11 am Thursday and Sunday. However, inquire at the park visitor center for the most current information.

QUEBRADA DE CAFAYATE
Beyond the village of Alemania, 100km south of Salta, verdant forest becomes barren sandstone in the Quebrada de Cafayate. The eastern Sierra de Carahuasi is the backdrop for distinctive landforms like Garganta del Diablo (Devil's Throat), El Anfiteatro (The Amphitheater), El Sapo (The Toad), El Fraile (The Friar), El Obelisco (The Obelisk) and Los Castillos (The Castles). Nearer Cafayate is an extensive dunefield at Los Médanos.

Getting There & Away
Other than car rental or brief, regimented tours, the only way to see the Quebrada is by bike, bus, thumb or foot. To walk the canyon at your own pace (carry food and water),

disembark from any El Indio bus and catch a later one; a good starting point is the impressive box canyon of Garganta del Diablo. The most interesting portion is too far to walk in a single day, but you can double back from Cafayate. Travelers renting mountain bikes in Cafayate can get off the bus and ride back.

CAFAYATE

Many tourists and major vineyards enjoy Cafayate's warm, dry and sunny climate, at 1600m at the mouth of the Valles Calchaquíes. It's not overrun with visitors, but there are many young artists and artisans. RN 40 (Av Güemes) goes northwest to Molinos and Cachi, while RP 68 goes to Salta.

The tourist information kiosk at the northeast corner of Plaza San Martín is open weekdays 9 am to 8 pm, weekends 9 am to 1 pm and 3 to 9 pm. Change money in Salta before arrival. Telecentros Cafayate is at Güemes and Belgrano.

Things to See & Do

Drop by the late Rodolfo Bravo's house, on Calle Colón, at any reasonable hour to see his personal **Museo Arqueológico** (admission US$1) of Calchaquí (Diaguita) ceramics. Colonial and other artifacts include elaborate horse gear and wine casks.

On Güemes near Colón, the **Museo de Vitivinicultura** details the history of local wines. Three nearby **bodegas** offer tours and tasting; try the fruity white *torrontés*.

Places to Stay

Camping Lorahuasi (US$2 per car, person and tent) has hot showers, a swimming pool and a grocery. The *Cafayate Youth Hostel* (☎ 03868-421440), Av Güemes Norte 441, is not an official HI affiliate, but it's friendly and has good facilities for US$8 per person.

In an old adobe mansion at Salta and Diego de Almagro, *La Casona de Don Luis* is one of Argentina's best hotel values, but it's hard to imagine that prices of US$10 per person, for spotless rooms with private bath, won't go up.

Hospedaje Familiar Basla (☎ 03868-421098), Nuestra Señora del Rosario 153, charges US$10 per person in clean multibed rooms. *Hospedaje Arroyo*, Quintana de Niño 160, is comparably priced.

Places to Eat

Besides *La Casona de Don Luis* (see Places to Stay), *La Carreta de Don Olegario*, Av Güemes 2, has an appealing menu with many regional dishes. Try also *Quijote*, alongside Hotel Briones at the southwest corner of the plaza.

There are several cheaper comedores, such as *El Gordo* on the north side of the plaza, and *Comedor Criollo* on Güemes between Alvarado and La Banda.

Heladería Miranda, at Av Güemes and Carlos Quintana de Niño, has imaginative wine-flavored ice cream – torrontés and cabernet.

Getting There & Away

El Indio, on Belgrano between Güemes and Salta, has five buses daily to Salta (US$9, four hours) except Sunday (four only). There are five daily to San Carlos, up the Valle Calchaquí, and one to Angastaco (US$6). El Cafayateño, at San Martín and Buenos Aires, goes twice daily to Salta except Sunday (once).

Use the daily buses to Santa María to visit the ruins at Quilmes (see next section), in Tucumán province. From Mitre 77, El Aconquija's two buses a day to Tucumán (US$17, 6½ hours) both pass through Tafí del Valle; one goes via Santa María.

AROUND CAFAYATE
Valles Calchaquíes

In this valley north and south of Cafayate, once a principal route across the Andes, Calchaquí Indians resisted Spanish attempts to impose forced labor obligations. Tired of having to protect their pack trains, the Spaniards relocated many Indians to Buenos Aires, and the land fell to Spaniards, who formed large rural estates.

Cachi Northwest of Cafayate is Cachi. Its scenic surroundings, 18th-century church and archaeological museum make it the most worthwhile stopover in the Valles Calchaquíes. For accommodations, try the *municipal campground* and *hostel*, or *Hotel Nevado de Cachi* (US$10 per person).

You can reach Cachi either from Cafayate or, more easily, by Marcos Rueda bus from Salta (US$13), which uses the scenic Cuesta del Obispo route past Parque Nacional Los Cardones.

Quilmes This pre-Hispanic pucará, in Tucumán province only 50km south of Cafayate, is probably Argentina's most extensive preserved ruins. Dating from about 1000 AD, this complex urban settlement covered about 30 hectares, housing perhaps 5000 people. The Quilmes Indians abided contact with the Incas but could not outlast the Spaniards, who, in 1667, deported the last 2000 to Buenos Aires.

Quilmes' thick walls underscore its defensive functions, but evidence of dense occupation sprawls north and south of the nucleus. *Camping* is possible near the small museum, where US$2 admits you to the ruins. There's also a new *hotel* and *restaurant*. Buses from Cafayate to Santa María pass the junction, but from there, it's 5km to the ruins by foot or thumb.

SAN ANTONIO DE LOS COBRES

Colonial pack trains to Peru usually took the Quebrada de Humahuaca, but an alternative crossed the Puna de Atacama to the Pacific and thence to Lima. For travelers on this route, bleak San Antonio (3700m) must have seemed an oasis. Well into this century, it was a stopover for drovers moving stock to Chile's nitrate mines, but railways and roads have now supplanted mules.

San Antonio, a largely Indian town with posters and political graffiti that tell you it's still part of Argentina, has basic lodging for US$8 per person at *Hospedaje Belgrano* or *Hospedaje Los Andes*; the latter has a *restaurant*.

Hostería de las Nubes (☎ 0387-490-9056) has 12 rooms with private baths, double-glazed windows and a *restaurant*; rooms cost US$40/50 a single/double, including breakfast. Make reservations at Turismo Tren a las Nubes (☎ 0387-431-4984), Caseros 443 in Salta.

El Tren a las Nubes

From Salta, the Tren a las Nubes (Train to the Clouds) makes countless switchbacks and spirals to ascend the Quebrada del Toro and reach the high puna. Its La Polvorilla viaduct, crossing a broad desert canyon, is a magnificent engineering achievement.

Tren a las Nubes Turismo (☎ 0387-431-4984), Caseros 443 in Salta, operates full-day excursions as far as La Polvorilla; most trips take place on weekends only from April to October, but can be more frequent during July holidays. The US$95 fare does not include meals, which cost around US$11. Some travelers have purchased slightly less comfortable 'discount carriage' tickets for US$50.

Getting There & Away

Bus There are daily buses that make the trip from Salta to San Antonio (US$14, five hours) with El Quebradeño.

Freight Trains From Salta, Rosario de Lerma or San Antonio, a more economical alternative to the Tren a las Nubes is one of the weekly freights that reach the border at Socompa, where a Chilean freight train goes to Baquedano, about 100km from Antofagasta on the Ruta Panamericana. This segment is not for the squeamish: the Chilean crew is unfriendly and the train truly filthy. Purchase Chilean pesos before leaving Salta to pay for the ticket, which is not guaranteed.

At Socompa, clear Argentine and Chilean immigration before asking permission to ride the train – and expect to wait several days. It descends through vast deserts to the abandoned station of Augusta Victoria, where you may disembark to try hitching to Antofagasta; mining trucks are almost certain to stop.

TUCUMÁN

Independence Day (9 July) celebrations are especially vigorous in San Miguel de Tucumán, which hosted the congress that declared Argentine independence in 1816. Unlike Salta and Jujuy, Tucumán successfully reoriented its post-independence economy, as the railway brought it just close enough to Buenos Aires to take advantage of the federal capital's growing sugar market. The city still preserves notable colonial remnants near Plaza de la Independencia.

Information

Tucumán's provincial Secretaría de Estado de Turismo (☎ 0381-422-2199), at 24 de Setiembre 484 on Plaza Independencia, is open weekdays 7 am to 1 pm and 5 to 9 pm, weekends 10 am to 1 pm and 6 to 9 pm.

Maguitur, San Martín 765, cashes traveler's checks (2% commission), and ATMs are numerous. The post office is at Av 25 de

ARGENTINA

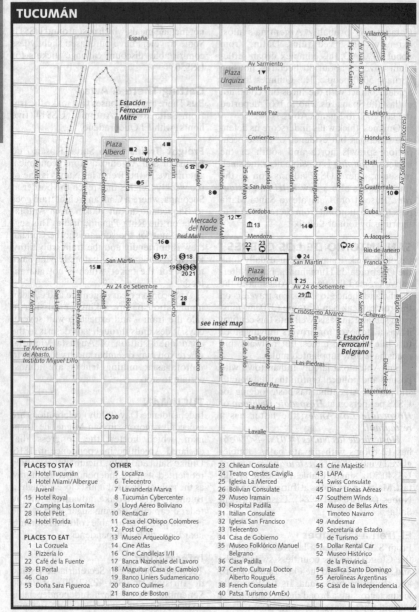

TUCUMÁN

(Map labels, reading by area:)

España · España · Villarroel · Pje. José A. García · Av. Juan B Justo · Gutiérrez · Villafañe

Av Sarmiento · 1 ▼ · Plaza Urquiza · PL García

Santa Fe

Estación Ferrocarril Mitre · Marcos Paz · E Unidos

Corrientes · Honduras

Plaza Alberdi · ■2 3 ■4 · Santiago del Estero · Haiti

Av Mitre · Suipacha · Marcos Avellaneda · Colombres · Catamarca · Salta · Junín · 6 ☎ ●7 · Maipú · Muñecas · 25 de Mayo · Laprida · Rivadavia · Monteagudo · Balcarce · Av Avellaneda · Av Soldati (Los Próceres)

●5 · 8● · San Juan · 9● · Guatemala · 10●

Córdoba · Cuba

Mercado del Norte · 12 ☑ · 🏛13 · 14● · A Jacques

Ped Mall · Mendoza · Rio de Janeiro

Ped Mall · 16● · 22 ▼ · 23 ↻ · ○26

San Martín · Ⓢ17 · Ⓢ18 · ● 24 · Francia · Gutiérrez

15 ■ · 19 ⓈⓈⓈ · San Martín · Brígido Terán

20 21 · Plaza Independencia · † 25

Av 24 de Setiembre · Av 24 de Setiembre

Av Alem · San Luis · Bernabé Aráoz · Alberdi · La Rioja · Jujuy · Ayacucho · 28 ■ · 29 🏛 · Av Sáenz Peña · Moreno · Entre Ríos · Charcas

Crisóstomo Álvarez

see inset map

San Lorenzo · Estación Ferrocarril Belgrano

To Mercado de Abasto, Instituto Miguel Lillo · Chacabuco · Buenos Aires · 9 de Julio · Congreso · Las Heras · Diaz Vélez

Las Piedras

General Paz

○30 · Ingenieros

La Madrid

Lavalle

PLACES TO STAY
2 Hotel Tucumán
4 Hotel Miami/Albergue Juvenil
15 Hotel Royal
27 Camping Las Lomitas
28 Hotel Petit
42 Hotel Florida

PLACES TO EAT
1 La Corzuela
3 Pizzería lo
22 Café de la Fuente
39 El Portal
46 Ciao
53 Doña Sara Figueroa

OTHER
5 Localiza
6 Telecentro
7 Lavandería Marva
8 Tucumán Cybercenter
9 Lloyd Aéreo Boliviano
10 RentaCar
11 Casa del Obispo Colombres
12 Post Office
13 Museo Arqueológico
14 Cine Atlas
16 Cine Candilejas I/II
17 Banca Nazionale del Lavóro
18 Maguitur (Casa de Cambio)
19 Banco Liniers Sudamericano
20 Banco Quilmes
21 Banco de Boston

23 Chilean Consulate
24 Teatro Orestes Caviglia
25 Iglesia La Merced
26 Bolivian Consulate
29 Museo Iramain
30 Hospital Padilla
31 Italian Consulate
32 Iglesia San Francisco
33 Telecentro
34 Casa de Gobierno
35 Museo Folklórico Manuel Belgrano
36 Casa Padilla
37 Centro Cultural Doctor Alberto Rougués
38 French Consulate
40 Patsa Turismo (AmEx)

41 Cine Majestic
43 LAPA
44 Swiss Consulate
45 Dinar Líneas Aéreas
47 Southern Winds
48 Museo de Bellas Artes Timoteo Navarro
49 Andesmar
50 Secretaría de Estado de Turismo
51 Dollar Rental Car
52 Museo Histórico de la Provincia
54 Basílica Santo Domingo
55 Aerolíneas Argentinas
56 Casa de la Independencia

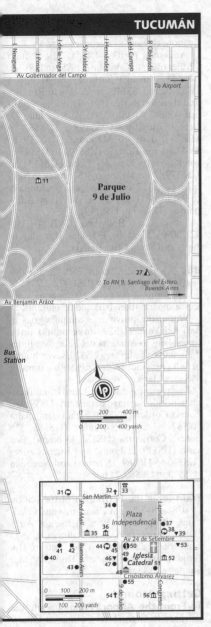

TUCUMÁN

Nougues
I de la Vega
Posse
Sv Valdez
J Hernández
E del Campo
R Obligado

Av Gobernador del Campo

To Airport

🏛 11

Parque
9 de Julio

27 ⚠
To RN 9, Santiago del Estero,
Buenos Aires

Av Benjamín Aráoz

Bus
Station

LP

0   200   400 m
0   200   400 yards

31 ☎   32 ✝ 🏛 33
        San Martín
Red Mall
            34 ●
                    Plaza
        36   Independencia
    🏛 35 🏛   ● 37
                   Av 24 de Setiembre ● 38 ▼ 39
    ■ ■   44 ☎ 45   ❸ 50   ▼ 53
    41 42   49 Iglesia   🏛 52
● 40   46 ✝ 47 Catedral 51
        43 ●   48
                   Crisóstomo Álvarez
                          ● 55
0   100   200 m   54 ✝   56 🏛
0   100   200 yards

Buenos Aires
Laprida
Congreso
de Julio

Mayo and Córdoba. There's a Telecentro at Maipú 480. For Internet access, the Tucumán Cybercenter is at San Juan 612.

Things to See

Downtown's most imposing landmark is the turn-of-the-century **Casa de Gobierno**, which replaced the colonial cabildo on Plaza Independencia.

The **Museo Iramain**, Entre Ríos 27, focuses on Argentine art and sculpture; it's open weekdays 8 am to noon and 2 to 7 pm, Saturday 8 am to noon only. The fine-arts **Museo de Bellas Artes Timoteo Navarro** (1905), 9 de Julio 44, is open weekdays 9:30 am to 12:30 pm and 5 to 8:30 pm, weekends 5:30 to 8:30 pm only.

On July 9, 1816, Unitarist lawyers and clerics declared independence (Federalists boycotted the meeting) at the dazzlingly white colonial house (admission US$2) at Congreso 151 now known as **Casa de la Independencia**. Hours are Tuesday to Friday 9 am to noon and 5 to 7:30 pm, weekends and holidays 9 am to 1 pm and 3:30 to 7:30 pm.

The **Museo Folklórico Manuel Belgrano** displays horse gear, indigenous musical instruments, weavings, and woodcarvings, Quilmes pottery and samples of *randa* lace. The museum shop sells some items. At 24 de Septiembre 565, it's open weekdays 7 am to 1 pm and 3 to 9 pm, weekends 9 am to 1 pm and 4 to 9 pm. Admission is free.

In Parque 9 de Julio (once a plantation), this 18th-century house known as **Casa del Obispo Colombres** (admission US$1) preserves the first ox-powered *trapiche* (sugar mill) of Tucumán's post-independence industry. Guided tours in Spanish explain the mill's operations. Hours are weekdays 8 am to 12:30 pm and 2 to 7 pm, weekends 7 am to 7 pm.

Other noteworthy museums include the **Museo Histórico de la Provincia** at Congreso 56, open 9 am to 12:30 pm weekdays only and 5 to 8 pm daily; and the **Museo Arqueológico**, at 25 de Mayo 265, which focuses on northwestern Argentine prehistory and is open weekdays 8 am to noon and 5 to 9 pm.

Horse-drawn carts from the countryside still haul their goods to the lively **Mercado de Abasto** at San Lorenzo and Miguel Lillo, 10 blocks west and two blocks south of Plaza Independencia. Unlike most markets, it's liveliest from mid- to late afternoon.

Places to Stay

Camping Fees are traditionally very low at *Las Lomitas*, which has reopened in Parque 9 de Julio, about 10 blocks from the new bus terminal via Av Benjamín Aráoz. If tent camping, choose your site carefully; lower-lying parts flood when it rains heavily.

Hostels Tucumán's AAAJ-affiliated *Albergue Juvenil (☎ 0381-431-0265)*, occupying part of the mid-range Hotel Miami at Junín 580, charges US$15 with breakfast.

Hotels At Catamarca 563, try *Hotel Tucumán (☎ 0381-422-1809)*, where singles/doubles cost US$12/15 with shared bath, US$15/25 with private bath. About five blocks south, *Hotel Royal (☎ 0381-421-8697)*, San Martín 1196, charges US$12/25.

Friendly *Hotel Petit (☎ 0381-421-3902)*, Crisóstomo Álvarez 765, has become the best budget choice in town at US$10 per person for small but tidy rooms with shared bath, US$15 for larger rooms with private bath.

Hotel Florida (☎ 0381-422-6674), just off Plaza Independencia at 24 de Setiembre 610, is friendly, quiet, and central, but very small; upstairs rooms have more and better light. Rooms with fans and shared bath cost US$15/25, slightly more with private bath.

Places to Eat

One of the best budget choices is the colorful *Mercado de Abasto* (see separate entry earlier), but the more central *Mercado del Norte*, at Mendoza and Maipú, is another possibility.

For breakfast, try *Café de la Fuente*, 25 de Mayo 183. Half a block east of Plaza Independencia, on 24 de Setiembre, try the chicken empanadas, humitas and other regional specialties at modest-looking *El Portal*. *La Corzuela*, Laprida 866, serves parrillada but also regional specialties.

Middle Eastern food is the rule at *Doña Sara Figueroa*. For pizza, try moderately priced *Ciao*, 9 de Julio 63, or the outstanding but more elaborate and expensive *Pizzería Io*, Salta 602.

Getting There & Away

Air Aerolíneas Argentinas (☎ 0381-431-1030), 9 de Julio 112, flies daily to Salta and Buenos Aires' Aeroparque (US$77 to US$228). LAPA (☎ 0381-430-2630), Buenos

Aires 95, and Dinar Líneas Aéreas (☎ 0381-422-9274), at 9 de Julio and 24 de Setiembre, fly more cheaply to Aeroparque.

Andesmar (☎ 0381-430-4517), 9 de Julio 72, flies often to Córdoba (US$53 to US$77), Monday through Saturday to Mendoza (US$102 to US$149), weekdays to Rosario, and three times weekly to La Rioja. Southern Winds (☎ 0381-422-5554), 9 de Julio 77, flies frequently to Córdoba (US$67 to US$89); daily to Mendoza (US$119 to US$159) and Rosario (US$104 to US$139); weekdays to Mar del Plata (US$134 to US$179); Monday through Saturday to Neuquén (US$127 to US$169); and occasionally to Bariloche (US$142 to US$189) and Aeroparque (US$89 to US$119).

Lloyd Aéreo Boliviano (LAB, ☎ 0381-421-2090), Córdoba 131, flies Thursday to Jujuy and Santa Cruz, Bolivia.

Bus At Brígido Terán 350, Tucumán's sparkling bus station (☎ 0381-422-2221) has 60 platforms, a post office, telephone services, a supermarket, bars and restaurants.

Within the province, Aconquija goes to Tafí del Valle (US$9, three hours) three times daily, to Amaichá del Valle four times daily, and to Cafayate (US$20, seven hours) in Salta province twice daily, with a transfer at Santa María.

Sample long-distance fares from Tucumán include Santiago del Estero (US$9, two hours), Córdoba (US$20, eight hours), Salta (US$21, 4½ hours), Jujuy (US$25, 5½ hours), Corrientes (US$34, 13 hours), Rosario (US$49, 11 hours) and Buenos Aires (US$30 to US$69, 15 hours) and Neuquén (US$72 to US$80, 24 hours).

Train From the Ferrocarril Mitre station (☎ 0381-430-3895) at Catamarca and Corrientes, El Tucumano goes to Buenos Aires (US$25 primera, US$40 Pullman, US$75 camarote) via Santiago del Estero (La Banda) and Rosario on Thursday and Sunday at 2:45 pm.

Getting Around

To/From the Airport From opposite the entrance to Gran Hotel Corona on Calle 9 de Julio, half a block from Plaza Independencia, Empresa Sáenz Alderete runs airport minibuses (US$2.50) to the Aeropuerto Internacional Benjamín Matienzo

(☎ 0381-426-1122), 8km east of downtown. They leave 75 minutes before flight time.

Bus City buses do not accept cash; buy *cospeles* (US$0.60 each) at downtown kiosks.

TAFÍ DEL VALLE

Southwest of Tucumán, RP 307 snakes up a narrow gorge, opening onto a misty valley where, in summer, *tucumanos* seek relief in the cool heights around Tafí del Valle. Beyond Tafí, about 100km from the provincial capital, the road zigzags over the 3050m Abra del Infiernillo, an alternate route to Cafayate and Salta.

At 2000m, a temperate island in a subtropical sea, Tafí grows seed potatoes, sends fruits (apples, pears and peaches) to Tucumán, and pastures cattle, sheep and, at higher altitudes, llamas. At Tafí's centro cívico, the helpful Casa del Turista (☎ 03867-421020) is open weekdays 7:30 am to 7:30 pm, weekends 10 am to 4 pm. Long-distance telephones are also here.

Tafí's 18th-century Jesuit **Capilla La Banda** contains a worthwhile museum. At **Parque Los Menhires**, at the south end of La Angostura reservoir, more than 80 aboriginal granite monuments, collected from nearby archaeological sites, resemble the standing stones of the Scottish Hebrides.

Tafí's recently reopened *Autocamping del Sauce* (☎ 03867-421084) is acceptable for US$2.50 per person; tiny cabañas, with bunks for US$5 per person, would be very cramped at their maximum capacity of four people.

Hospedaje La Cumbre (☎ 03867-421016), Diego de Rojas 311, charges US$10 per person for rooms with shared bath, with meals for US$4. *El Rancho de Félix* serves regional food and is probably the best choice in town, but *La Rueda* is also worth a look.

Getting There & Away

From the bus station on the northern side of the plaza, Empresa Aconquija has six buses daily to Tucumán. Some of the buses from Tucumán continue on to Santa María and Cafayate.

SANTIAGO DEL ESTERO

Founded in 1553, Argentina's oldest city, Santiago del Estero (population 224,000),

was once a stopover between the Pampas and the Bolivian mines, but irrigated cotton now supports the economy. Restoration work is proceeding on the provincial Casa de Gobierno and Palacio Legislativo, both of which were gutted by fire in 1993 after provincial employees went unpaid for four months, bringing federal intervention in the province.

Av Libertad bisects the city, 170km southeast of Tucumán, from southwest to northeast. On either side of Plaza Libertad, Av Independencia and the peatonal Av Tucumán are important commercial areas. Av Belgrano is the main thoroughfare.

Information

The provincial Subsecretaría de Turismo (☎ 0385-421-3253), Av Libertad 417, is normally open 7 am to 1 pm and 3 to 9 pm weekdays, 9 am to noon weekends; from May to October, weekend hours are 9 am to noon and 3 to 6 pm.

Noroeste Cambio, 24 de Setiembre 220, doesn't change traveler's checks, but several banks have ATMs. The post office is at Buenos Aires and Urquiza. There are long-distance phones at the Telecentro Peatonal, Tucumán 64/66.

Things to See

At Avellaneda 355, the **Museo Wagner** offers free guided tours of its well-presented collection of fossils, funerary urns and Chaco ethnography, weekdays 7 am to 1 pm. Exhibits at the **Museo Histórico Provincial**, at Urquiza 354, emphasize postcolonial history; it's open weekdays 8 am to noon.

Places to Stay & Eat

At shady *Campamento Las Casuarinas*, in Parque Aguirre less than 1km from Plaza Libertad, fees are about US$5 per site.

Residencial Santa Rita (☎ 0385-422-0625), Santa Fe 273, has singles/doubles with shared bath for US$15/20, with private bath for US$18/25. Tiny *Residencial Emaus* (☎ 0385-421-5893), Moreno Sur 673, has only five rooms, but is friendly and spotless for US$15/27. *Residencial Iovino* (☎ 0385-421-3311), at Moreno Sur 602, charges US$17/27.

The student-oriented *Comedor Universitario*, Avellaneda 364, has uninspiring cheap food. Better but still reasonably priced meals are available at the **Comedor Centro de Viajantes**, Buenos Aires 37. Moderately priced **Mía Mamma**, 24 de Setiembre 15, has an extensive Italian menu, plus a good, inexpensive salad bar. **Taffik**, at Jujuy and Tucumán, serves Middle Eastern food.

Getting There & Away
Air Austral (☎ 0385-422-4335), Urquiza 235, flies twice each weekday to Buenos Aires (US$119 to US$194), once a day weekends.

Bus Santiago's aging bus station (☎ 0385-421-3746) is at Pedro León Gallo and Saavedra, eight blocks south of Plaza Libertad.

There are hourly buses to Termas de Río Hondo (US$4, one hour), most continuing to Tucumán (US$9, two hours). Sample long-distance fares include Rosario (US$25), Resistencia (US$25, eight hours), San Juan (US$35, 12 hours), Mendoza (US$45, 14 hours) and Buenos Aires (US$45, 14 hours).

Train El Tucumano stops in Ferrocarril Mitre's suburban La Banda station Monday, Wednesday, and Friday on its way northbound to Tucumán, and Tuesday, Thursday and Sunday as it heads south to Buenos Aires.

Getting Around
To/From the Airport Bus No 19 goes to Aeropuerto Mal Paso, 6km southwest of downtown.

To/From the Train Station From Moreno and Libertad in downtown Santiago, bus Nos 10, 14, 18 and 21 all go to the Ferrocarril Mitre station in La Banda.

LA RIOJA
In 1591, Juan Ramírez de Velasco founded Todos los Santos de la Nueva Rioja, at the base of the Sierra del Velasco, 154km south of Catamarca. An earthquake in 1894 destroyed many buildings, but the restored commercial center, near Plaza 25 de Mayo, replicates colonial style.

The province's memorable historical figures include caudillos like Facundo Quiroga – objects of Sarmiento's tirades against provincial strongmen – but the province also nurtured intellectuals like Joaquín V González, founder of La Plata University. Facundo's modern counterparts, including

President Carlos Menem's *riojano* family, are politically influential. Corruption and nepotism are widespread.

Information
La Rioja's Dirección Municipal de Turismo (Dimutur, ☎ 03822-427103), Av Perón 715, distributes a good city map and brochures of other provincial destinations. Hours are 8 am to 1 pm and 4 to 9 pm weekdays, 8 am to noon weekends. Open 8 am to 1 pm and 4 to 9 pm weekdays, the provincial Dirección General de Turismo (☎ 03822-428839), at Av Perón and Urquiza, is also helpful.

La Rioja has no cambios, but several banks have ATMs. The post office is at Av Perón 764. Telecentro Av is at Av Perón 1066.

Things to See
Museums charge US$1 admission. The **Museo Folklórico**, in a re-created 19th-century house at Pelagio Luna 811, displays ceramic reproductions of mythological figures from local folklore. Over 12,000 pieces, from tools and artifacts to Diaguita ceramics and weavings, fill the **Museo Inca Huasi**, Alberdi 650. The **Museo Histórico**, Adolfo Dávila 79, contains memorabilia of Facundo Quiroga.

Built by the Diaguita under Dominican overseers, the **Convento de Santo Domingo** (1623), at Pelagio Luna and Lamadrid, is the country's oldest. The **Convento de San Francisco**, at Av 25 de Mayo and Bazán y Bustos, houses the Niño Alcalde, a Christ Child icon symbolically recognized as the city's mayor. The **Iglesia Catedral**, at San Nicolás and Av 25 de Mayo, contains the image of patron saint Nicolás de Bari, another devotional object.

Special Events
The December 31 ceremony El Tinkunako reenacts San Francisco Solano's mediation between the Diaguitas and the Spaniards in 1593. For accepting peace, the Diaguitas imposed two conditions: resignation of the Spanish mayor and his replacement by the Niño Alcalde.

Places to Stay
Camping At Km 8 on RN 75 west of town, **Country Las Vegas** charges around US$5 per tent and US$4 per person; to get there, catch city bus No 1 southbound on Perón.

Casas de Familia & Residenciales The tourist office maintains a list of casas de familia offering accommodations for about US$12 per person. *Residencial Sumaj Kanki*, at Av Castro Barros and Coronel Lagos, provides modest but clean accommodations for US$10 per person with shared bath, but can get noisy. More central are *Residencial Don José*, Av Perón 407, with small, dark but clean rooms at US$10 per person with private bath, and *Residencial Florida* (☎ 03822-426563), 8 de Diciembre 524, with small but comfy rooms for US$15/26 with private bath.

The family-oriented *Residencial Anita* (☎ 03822-427008), Lagos 476, is new and friendly; it charges US$25 for singles and doubles.

Places to Eat

Places serving both regional specialties and standard Argentine dishes like parrillada include *La Vieja Casona*, Rivadavia 427, and *El Milagro*, Av Perón 1200.

Il Gatto, Pelagio Luna 555, is part of a chain but still has decent pizza and pasta at moderate prices. *Mangattori*, Av Quiroga 1131, is one of the best Italian restaurants in town. *La Marca* is a tenedor libre parrilla on 25 de Mayo between Pelagio Luna and Bazán y Bustos.

Café del Paseo, at Pelagio Luna and 25 de Mayo, is an appealing confitería. *Café de la Bolsa*, at Rivadavia 684, has fixed-price lunches including Middle Eastern dishes. *Rotisería La Rueda*, Rivadavia 461, has good take-out food.

Getting There & Away

Air Aerolíneas Argentinas (☎ 03822-426307), at Belgrano 63, flies twice each weekday, once a day weekends to Aeroparque (US$77 to US$190). LAPA (☎ 03822-435197), San Nicolás de Bari Oeste 516, flies daily to Aeroparque (US$79 to US$149). Andesmar (☎ 03822-437995), San Nicolás de Bari Oeste 729, flies Tuesday, Wednesday and Thursday to Córdoba (US$35 to US$59) and Rosario (US$85 to US$98).

Bus La Rioja's bus station (☎ 03822-425453) is at Artigas and España; a new terminal is being planned.

El Cóndor travels daily to provincial destinations (Sanagasta and Chilecito). La Riojana, Buenos Aires 132, goes to Chilecito (US$8, three hours), as does Rioja Bus, San Nicolás de Bari 743. Maxi Bus (☎ 35979), San Nicolás de Bari 725, runs minibus service to Chilecito.

Sample long-distance fares include Catamarca (US$8, two hours), Tucumán (US$14, five hours), Córdoba (US$15 to US$17, five hours), San Luis (US$25, nine hours), San Juan (US$22, six hours), Mendoza (US$26 to US$29, eight hours), Salta (US$24 to US$35, 11 hours) and Buenos Aires (US$52 to US$62, 17 hours).

CATAMARCA

Settled only in 1683, San Fernando del Valle de Catamarca has remained an economic backwater, but major holidays attract many visitors. Flanked by the Sierra del Colorado in the west and the Sierra Graciana in the east, it is 156km northeast of La Rioja. Shady Plaza 25 de Mayo offers refuge from summer heat in an otherwise treeless city.

Information

The Dirección Municipal de Turismo (☎ 03833-437595), Sarmiento 535, is open weekdays 7 am to 8 pm, weekends 8 am to 8 pm. Open weekdays 7 am to 8 pm, the provincial Subsecretaría de Turismo (☎ 03833-437594) is in the Manzana del Turismo at Av Virgen del Valle and General Roca.

Several downtown banks have ATMs. The post office is at San Martín 753. There's a Telecentro at Rivadavia 758.

Things to See

The neocolonial **Iglesia y Convento de San Francisco**, at Esquiú and Rivadavia, contains the cell of Fray Mamerto Esquiú, famous for his vocal defense of the 1853 constitution. After being stolen and left on the roof years ago, a crystal box containing his heart now sits in a locked room.

Tedious presentation undermines outstanding materials in the **Museo Arqueológico Adán Quiroga**, on Sarmiento between Esquiú and Prado. Opposite the plaza, the **Catedral** contains the Virgen del Valle, one of northern Argentina's most venerated images.

Special Events

On the Sunday after Easter, thousands of pilgrims honor the Virgen del Valle in the Fiesta de Nuestra Señora del Valle.

Places to Stay

Catamarca's **Autocamping Municipal**, about 4km from downtown, gets heavy use on weekends and holidays, and also has ferocious mosquitoes. Rates are US$5 per tent plus US$1 per vehicle; take bus No 10 from Convento de San Francisco, on Esquiú, or from the bus terminal.

The tourist office keeps a list of casas de familia. The cheapest option in town, though, is to share the pilgrims' dormitory accommodations at the **Hospedaje del Peregrino** (☎ 03833-431003), Sarmiento 653, for US$5 per person (with your own sheets) or US$7 (with theirs).

Not as good as it looks from outside, the **Hotel Comodoro** (☎ 03833-423490), República 855, rents small, dark rooms with shared bath for US$10 per person; better rooms with air-con and private bath cost US$20/30 a single/double. Better than it looks from outside, cordial **Residencial Delgado** (☎ 03833-426109) is very central at San Martín 788, and has rooms for US$15/26 with private bath. Attractive **Residencial Esquiú** (☎ 03833-422284), Esquiú 365, charges US$15/25.

Places to Eat

The least expensive eateries cater to pilgrims. In the gallery behind the Catedral, **Comedor El Peregrino** offers two courses (empanadas and pasta) for about US$4, or an option with meat for US$6. **La Tinaja**, Sarmiento 533, also has low prices and occasional live music. **Viejo Bueno**, Esquiú 480, is a central parrilla. **Trattoria Montecarlo**, República 548, specializes in pasta. The **Sociedad Española**, Av Virgen del Valle 725, has traditional Spanish dishes, including seafood.

Shopping

For hand-tied rugs, visit the Mercado Artesanal Permanente y Fábrica de Alfombras, Virgen del Valle 945, which also sells ponchos, blankets, jewelry, red onyx sculptures, musical instruments, hand-spun wool, and baskets.

Getting There & Away

Air Aerolíneas Argentinas (☎ 03833-424460), Sarmiento 589, flies Monday through Saturday to Buenos Aires' Aeroparque (US$77 to US$190). Austral, at the same office, flies daily except Saturday to Santiago del Estero (US$44) and Aeroparque. LAPA (☎ 03833-434772), Sarmiento 506, flies Monday, Friday and Sunday to Aeroparque (US$79 to US$159) via La Rioja.

Bus Catamarca's bus station (☎ 03833-423415) is at Av Güemes 850. Sample fares include La Rioja (US$8, 2½ hours), Tucumán (US$11, 3½ hours), Santiago del Estero (US$12, five hours), Córdoba (US$16, 5½ hours), Salta (US$21, seven hours), Jujuy (US$24, eight hours), San Juan (US$21 to US$25, eight hours) Mendoza (US$27 to US$31, 10 hours), Resistencia/Corrientes (US$47, 14 to 15 hours) and Buenos Aires US$42 to US$54, 15 hours).

Patagonia

Patagonia is the enormous region beyond Buenos Aires province, south of the Río Colorado to the Strait of Magellan. Glaciers dot the mountainous interior of Río Negro and Neuquén provinces, which stretch all the way to the Atlantic. Santa Cruz province features the Moreno Glacier and the pinnacles of the Fitz Roy Range. Near the Andean divide, forests of southern beech, alerce and the distinctive pehuén (monkey puzzle tree) cover the slopes.

Patagonia's most conspicuous economic institution is the sprawling sheep estancia, but large oilfields in Chubut, Neuquén and Tierra del Fuego keep Argentina self-sufficient in petroleum. The Andean national parks have encouraged a major tourism industry.

History

One theory credits Magellan's crew with the toponym Patagonia, after they encountered Tehuelche Indians whose large moccasins made their feet appear huge – in Spanish, *pata* means paw or foot. Bruce Chatwin, however, speculated that Magellan applied the term 'Patagon,' from a fictional monster in a Spanish romance, to the Tehuelches.

Darwin dispelled some of the mystery surrounding the Tehuelches, but he also recognized that the arrival of whites would result in the disappearance or subjugation of the Indian. In his account of a massacre by

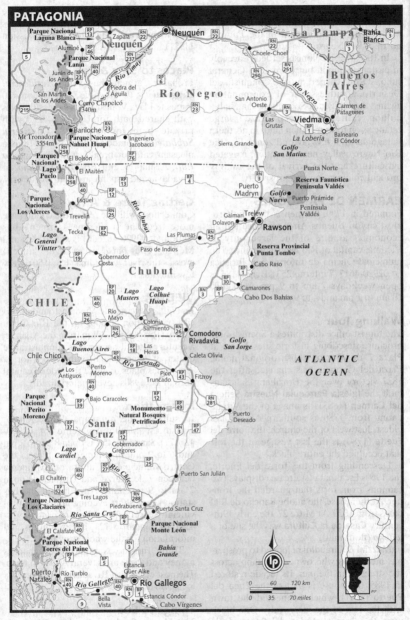

PATAGONIA

Parque Nacional Laguna Blanca
RP 13
Zapala
RN 22
Neuquén
RN 22
La Pampa
Bahía Blanca
RN 3

Aluminé
RP 46
RN 237
Choele-Choel
RN 22

Parque Nacional Lanín
RN 40
RN 250
RN 251
Buenos Aires

Junín de los Andes
RP 23
RP 6

San Martín de los Andes
Piedra del Águila
Río Limay
Río Negro
San Antonio Oeste

215
Cerro Chapelcó 1340m
RN 23
Carmen de Patagones

5
Mt Tronador 3554m
Bariloche
RN 23
Ingeniero Jacobacci
Sierra Grande
RN 3
Viedma
RP 1
Las Grutas
La Lobería
Balneario El Cóndor

Parque Nacional Nahuel Huapi
RN 258
El Bolsón
RP 76
Golfo San Matías

Parque Nacional Lago Puelo
El Maitén
RN 40
RP 13
RP 4
Punta Norte

Parque Nacional Los Alerces
Esquel
RP 12
Puerto Madryn
Reserva Faunística Península Valdés

Trevelin
RN 25
Río Chubut
Gaiman Trelew
Golfo Nuevo
Puerto Pirámide
Península Valdés

Tecka
RP 62
Dolavon
Rawson

Lago General Vintter
Las Plumas
RN 25
Reserva Provincial Punta Tombo

RP 19
Paso de Indios
Cabo Raso

Gobernador Costa
Chubut
RP 30
RN 1

RP 20
Lago Musters
Lago Colhué Huapi
RN 3
RN 1
Camarones
Cabo Dos Bahías

CHILE
RN 40
Río Mayo
RN 26

RN 26
Colonia Sarmiento
RN 26
Comodoro Rivadavia
Golfo San Jorge

Lago Buenos Aires
RP 18
Las Heras
Caleta Olivia
ATLANTIC OCEAN

Chile Chico
RP 43
Río Deseado

Los Antiguos
Perito Moreno
Pico Truncado
RP 43
Fitzroy

RN 40
RP 12

Parque Nacional Perito Moreno
RP 39
Bajo Caracoles
RP 49
RN 281
Puerto Deseado

RP 37
Monumento Natural Bosques Petrificados
RN 3
RP 47

Santa Cruz
RP 12
Gobernador Gregores
RP 25

Lago Cardiel
RP 27
Río Chico
Puerto San Julián

El Chaltén
RN 40
RN 288

RP 524
Tres Lagos
RN 288
Piedrabuena
Puerto Santa Cruz

Parque Nacional Los Glaciares
Río Santa Cruz
RP 9

El Calafate
RN 40
Parque Nacional Monte León

Parque Nacional Torres del Paine
RN 3
Bahía Grande

RP 7
RP 5
Estancia Güer Aike

Puerto Natales
Río Turbio
RN 40
Río Gallegos
Río Gallegos
RN 3
RP 1
Estancia Cóndor

9
Bella Vista
Cabo Vírgenes

0   60   120 km
0   35   70 miles

Argentine soldiers, he observed that 'Great as it is, in another half century I think there will not be a wild Indian in the Pampas north of Río Negro.'

In 1865 Welsh colonists settled peaceably in eastern Chubut, but from 1879 General Julio A Roca carried out the Conquista del Desierto, a ruthless war of extermination against the indigenes. Soon more than half a million cattle and sheep grazed large estancias on former Indian lands in northern Patagonia. In a few favored zones, like the Río Negro valley near Neuquén, irrigated agriculture and the arrival of the railway brought colonization and prosperity.

CARMEN DE PATAGONES

Founded in 1799, Carmen is the southern-most city in Buenos Aires province but an economic satellite of the larger city of Viedma, capital of Río Negro province. The municipal Oficina de Información Turística (☎ 02920-461777 interno 253), Bynon 186, is open weekdays 7 am to 9 pm, weekends 10 am to 1 pm and 4 to 9 pm.

Walking Tour

The tourist office distributes a Spanish-only brochure describing historic sites. Begin at **Plaza 7 de Marzo**, whose original name, Plaza del Carmen, was changed after the 1827 victory over the Brazilians. Salesians built the **Iglesia Parroquial Nuestra Señora del Carmen** (1883); its image of the Virgin, dating from 1780, is southern Argentina's oldest. Just west of the church, the **Torre del Fuerte** (1780) is the last vestige of the fort that occupied the entire block.

Descending from the Torre del Fuerte, the 1960s **Escalinata** (staircase) displays two cannons from forts that guarded the frontier. At their base, the adobe **Rancho de Rial** dates from 1820. At Mitre 27, the early 19th-century **Casa de la Cultura** was the site of a *tahona* (flour mill).

Mazzini & Giraudini belonged to prosper-ous merchants who owned the shop across the street from the pier. Its façade was restored in 1985, the house is part of the **Zona del Puerto** (port), which connected the town with the rest of the viceroyalty. One block west, the **Casa Histórica del Banco de la Provincia de Buenos Aires** originally housed naval stores, but became in succession a girls' school, a branch of the Banco de la

Provincia, then of Banco de la Nación. Since 1988, it has been a museum, open weekdays 9 am to noon and daily 7 to 9 pm (admission US$1).

Places to Stay & Eat

Probably Carmen's best value, **Residencial Reggiani** (☎ 02920-464137), at Bynon 420 opposite Plaza Villarino, has singles/doubles with shared bath for US$14/24 and with private bath for US$18/28. **Confitería Sabbatella**, Comodoro Rivadavia 218, is a pleasant café for breakfast, while **Pizzería Loft**, Alsina 70, and **Pizzería Neptuno,** at Rivadavia and España, are both worth a try.

Getting There & Away

Connections with the rest of the country are more frequent in Viedma. Carmen's bus station (☎ 02920-462666) is at Barbieri and Méjico. The *balsa* (passenger launch) crosses the river to Viedma (US$0.50) every few minutes.

VIEDMA

In 1779, Francisco de Viedma founded this city (population 50,500) on the Río Curru Leuvu (Río Negro), 30km from the Atlantic; a century later, it became the administrative center of Argentina's southern territories. Ambitious plans to move the federal capital here in the 1980s never materialized.

Information

In summer the municipal Dirección de Turismo y Medio Ambiente (☎ 02920-427171), Saavedra 456, is open 8 am to 2 pm and 6 to 9 pm. In summer, its office in the Centro Municipal de Cultura, on Av Viedma between 7 de Marzo and Urquiza, is open 7 am to 9 pm daily. An office at the bus station keeps short evening hours. The pro-vincial Secretaría de Turismo (☎ 02920-422150), Gallardo 121, has brochures and information for the whole province.

Tritón Turismo, Namuncurá 78, changes money and there are several ATMs in town. The post office is at Rivadavia 151. There's a locutorio at Mitre 531.

Things to See

The **Museo Cardenal Cagliero**, Rivadavia 34, chronicles the Salesian catechization of Patagonian Indians. The **Museo Gobernador Eugenio Tello**, San Martín 263, is also a research center in architecture, archaeology, physical and cultural anthropology, and geography.

Places to Stay & Eat

The friendly riverside *Camping Municipal* (☎ 02920-421341) west of RN 3, reached by bus from downtown, charges US$4 per person and US$4 per tent; beware mosquitoes in summer.

Seedy *Hotel Nuevo Roma* (☎ 02920-424510), 25 de Mayo 174, has singles/doubles with shared bath for US$12/15, with private bath for US$17/24. *Hotel Buenos Aires* (☎ 02920-424858), Buenos Aires 153, is basic for US$20/25. A step up is *Residencial Luis Eduardo* (☎ 02920-420669), Sarmiento 366, which charges US$20/30. It also has a good *restaurant*.

Pizzería Acrílico, Saavedra 326, has flashy decor, good pizza, and mid-range prices except for the pasta, which is equally good but expensive by Argentine standards. Almost as popular *Los Tíos*, Belgrano 265, is nothing special. *El Nuevo Munich*, Buenos Aires 161, has good pizza, large tasty sandwiches and good draft beer.

Local parrillas worth trying include *El Tío* at Av Zatti and Colón and *Rancho Grande* at Av Villarino 30.

Getting There & Away

Air Austral (☎ 02920-422018), Mitre 402, flies weekdays to Buenos Aires (US$109 to US$167). LADE (☎ 02920-424420), Saavedra 403, flies cheaply but infrequently to Patagonian destinations and Buenos Aires.

Bus Viedma's bus station (☎ 02920-426850) is 13 blocks south of downtown, at Guido 1580 and Av General Perón. Most services are north-south along RN 3 and west along RN 22.

Sample fares are: Bahía Blanca (US$13, four hours), Puerto Madryn (US$20, five hours), Trelew (US$22, 5½ hours), Neuquén (US$30, eight hours), Esquel (US$32, 10 hours), La Plata (US$34, 12 hours), Comodoro Rivadavia (US$37, 10 hours), Buenos Aires (US$35 to US$45, 13 hours), Bariloche (US$40 to US$52, 14 hours), Río Gallegos (US$48, 20 hours).

Train From Estación Viedma, on the southeast outskirts of town, Sefepa (☎ 02920-422130) still runs westbound trains to Bariloche (15 hours) at 6 pm Wednesday and Sunday. Fares are US$28 primera, US$46 Pullman; children 5 to 12 pay half-fare.

BARILOCHE

In San Carlos de Bariloche, 460km southwest of Neuquén on Lago Nahuel Huapi, architect Ezequiel Bustillo adapted Middle European styles into an attractive urban plan, but the past decade's orgy of construction has overwhelmed Bustillo's efforts and, consequently, destroyed Bariloche's perceived exclusivity. The silver lining is that prices have remained reasonable and have even fallen in recent years. The influx of visitors from South America's largest country has led to the ironic nickname 'Brasiloche.'

At an altitude of 770m, the city has a regular grid between the Río Ñireco and Bustillo's centro cívico; north-south streets rise steeply from the lake. The major commercial zone is Av Bartolomé Mitre.

Information

Bariloche's Secretaría Municipal de Turismo (☎ 02944-423122; secturismo@bariloche .com.ar) at the centro cívico is open 8 am to 9 pm daily; its kiosk at the Paseo de los Artesanos, Perito Moreno and Villegas, is open daily 9:30 am to 1 pm and 5 to 8:30 pm. The provincial Secretaría de Turismo de Río Negro (☎ 02944-426644; secturrn@rnonline .com.ar), at Av 12 de Octubre and Emilio Frey, has information on the province.

The Intendencia de Parques Nacionales (☎ 02944-423111), San Martín 24, and the Club Andino Bariloche (☎ 02944-424531), 20 de Febrero 30, can provide information on Parque Nacional Nahuel Huapi.

Open weekdays 9 am to 2 pm, the Chilean Consulate (☎ 02944-422842) is at Juan Manuel de Rosas 180.

Money You can change foreign cash and traveler's checks at Cambio Sudamérica, Mitre 63. Banks with ATMs are ubiquitous downtown.

Post & Communications The post office is at the centro cívico. Just outside the tourist office are direct lines to the USA, France and several other countries for reverse-charge and credit-card calls. The largest of several locutorios is at Bariloche Center, San Martín and Panozzi.

ARGENTINA

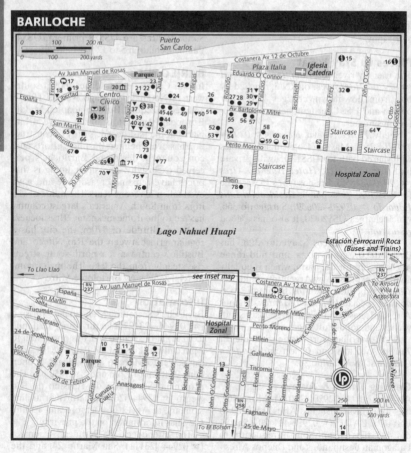

BARILOCHE

CyberClub Bariloche (☎ 02944-421418; cyber@bariloche.com.ar), in the Galería del Sol on Mitre between Rolando and Palacios, offers Internet access.

Centro Cívico

Recent construction has erased much of Bariloche's previous charm, but Bustillo's log-and-stone public buildings still merit a visit.

Features such as lifelike stuffed animals, well-prepared archaeological and ethnographic materials, and critically enlightening historical evaluations on topics like Mapuche resistance to the Conquista del Desierto and Bariloche's urban development make the diverse **Museo de la Patago-** nia one of the country's best. It has a specialized library and a bookstore.

Admission is US$2.50. Hours are Tuesday to Friday 10 am to 12:30 pm and 2 to 7 pm, Monday and Saturday 10 am to 1 pm only.

Skiing

Gran Catedral, the largest and most popular area, amalgamates two formerly separate areas, Cerro Catedral and Lado Bueno, so skiers can buy one ticket valid for both sets of lifts. Adult passes start at US$22 to US$40 per day, depending on the time of the season, but one-week passes entail substantial savings. Rental equipment is available both at Gran Catedral and in Bariloche, but good equipment is costly.

BARILOCHE

PLACES TO STAY
4 Aguilar Cárdenas
5 Lemos de Ferreyra
7 Pirker
8 Arko
9 Residencial Güemes
10 Lamouniere
11 Albergue Patagonia Andina
13 Residencial Torres
14 Hospedaje Monte Grande
62 Hostería Los Andes
63 Hospedaje El Mirador
66 Albergue Mochilero's

PLACES TO EAT
18 Helados Bari
21 La Andinita
29 Zona Sur
30 Bucaneros
31 Ahumadero Familia Weiss
37 Cocodrilos
40 Helados Jauja
41 Lennon
42 La Alpina
50 De la Granja
53 La Vizcacha
64 El Mundo de la Pizza
70 El Vegetariano
75 La Andina
77 Jauja

OTHER
1 Club de Caza y Pesca
2 Bikeway
3 German Consulate
6 Pub Moritz
11 Aguas Blancas
12 Bariloche Mountain Bike
15 Secretaría de Turismo de
Río Negro
16 ACA
17 Chilean Consulate
19 Migraciones
20 Museo de la Patagonia
22 Bariloche Rafting
23 Localiza
24 Budget
25 LAPA
26 Southern Winds
27 Del Turista
28 CyberClub Bariloche
32 Dirty Bikes
33 Al
34 Bariloche Center
35 Secretaría Municipal de Turismo
36 Post Office
38 Cambio Sudamérica
39 Baruzzi Deportes
43 TAN
44 Aerolíneas Argentinas
45 Expediciones Náuticas

46 Rafting Adventure
47 Salón Cultural de Usos
Múltiples (SCUM)
48 Paseo de los Artesanos
49 LADE
51 Karnak Expediciones
52 Laverap
54 Spanish Consulate
55 Fenoglio
56 Hiver Turismo (Amex)
57 Catedral Turismo
58 Kaikén Líneas Aéreas
59 Local Bus Station
60 Codao del Sur
61 Micro Ómnibus 3 de Mayo
65 Avis
67 Lavadero Huemul
68 Intendencia del Parque
Nacional Nahuel Huapi
69 Club Andino Bariloche
71 Museo Arquitectónico
72 Cine Arrayanes
73 Banco de Galicia
74 Laverap
76 Lavandería La Casita
78 La Bolsa del Deporte

Places to Stay

The municipal tourist office's computer tracks current prices of everything from campgrounds and private houses to five-star hotels. Reasonable lodging is available even in high season.

Camping The nearest organized camping area is *La Selva Negra* (☎ 02944-441013), 3km west of town on the Llao Llao road. It charges US$7 per site.

Hostels Bariloche's official HI facility is *Albergue Alaska* (☎/fax 02944-461564; alaska@bariloche.com.ar) at Lilinquen 328, 7.5km west of town just off Av Bustillo; bus Nos 10, 20 and 21 drop passengers nearby. Rates are US$10 per person (US$8 in off season), slightly more for nonmembers.

There are two more central but unofficial hostels. Friendly *Albergue Mochilero's* (☎ 02944-431627; cecilia@bariloche.com.ar), San Martín 82, charges US$5 for floor space, or US$8 with your own sleeping bag (US$10 with sheets) in smaller dorm rooms. There is

also good luggage storage. *Albergue Patagonia Andina* (☎ 02944-422783), Morales 564, charges US$8 to US$10 per person in an older house in an excellent location. Though some rooms are small, there are good common spaces.

Casas de Familia Bariloche's best values are casas de familia, starting around US$10 to US$12 per person. At the east end of town, the *Lemos de Ferreyra* family (☎ 02944-422556), Martín Fierro 1535, and Señora Heydée *Aguilar Cárdenas* (☎ 02944-425072) at Martín Fierro 1541 (firm beds, but the rooms are a little cramped) are both near the bus/train station.

In woodsy Barrio Belgrano, overlooking the centro cívico, are several slightly dearer but agreeable choices; the houses in this area help each other out, so if one is full the owner will contact the neighbors. Try Marianne *Pirker* (☎ 02944-424873) at 24 de Septiembre 230; Rosa *Arko* (☎ 02944-423109) Güemes 691; Carlotta *Baumann* (☎ 02944-429689) at Av Los Pioneros 860;

and Eloisa *Lamouniere* (☎ 02944-422514) at 24 de Septiembre 71.

Hospedajes, Hosterías & Residenciales

Hospedaje El Mirador (☎ 02944-422221), Perito Moreno 652, charges US$8 per person with shared bath or US$12 with private bath. At *Hospedaje Monte Grande* (☎ 02944-422159), 25 de Mayo 1544, rates are US$15/24 single/double. *Residencial Torres* (☎ 02944-423355), Tiscornia 747, charges US$15/25.

Hostería Los Andes (☎ 02944-422222), Perito Moreno 594, costs US$15/28 with shared bath, US$20 per person with private bath. In Barrio Belgrano, at Güemes 715, *Residencial Güemes* (☎ 02944-424785) charges US$30 a double.

Places to Eat

Regional specialties, including *jabalí* (wild boar), *ciervo* (venison), and *trucha* (trout), deserve mention. Some places, like *Ahumadero Familia Weiss*, Palacios 167, specialize in smoked game and fish.

Decorated in a Beatles motif, *Lennon*, Perito Moreno 48, is nominally a parrilla, but the menu is more imaginative than that would suggest. *La Vizcacha*, Rolando 279, is one of the country's best parrillas, offering a pleasant atmosphere and outstanding service. *La Andina*, Elflein 95, has drawn praise for good food, large portions and moderate prices.

Recommended *De la Granja*, Villegas 220, features farm-fresh ingredients at moderate prices. The more expensive *Jauja*, Quaglia 366, has a European-style menu but erratic service and small portions.

Cocodrilos, Mitre 5, serves a very fine fugazzeta at a very reasonable price, as does *La Andinita*, Mitre 56. *Bucaneros*, Palacios 187, is also a good pizza choice, as is *El Mundo de la Pizza*, Mitre 759.

La Alpina, Perito Moreno 98, is a popular confitería. *Zona Sur*, Mitre 396, serves tasty coffee, hot chocolate, and fresh croissants.

The best ice creamery in town is *Helados Jauja*, Perito Moreno 14; the adventurous should try the exquisite *mate cocido* (boiled mate) flavor, which sounds strange even to Argentines.

Shopping

Del Turista and Fenoglio, facing each other on Mitre, are chocolate supermarkets and are also good places for a stand-up cup of coffee, hot chocolate or dessert. Local artisans display their wares in wool, wood, leather and other media at the Paseo de los Artesanos, at Villegas and Perito Moreno.

Getting There & Away

Air Aerolíneas Argentinas (☎ 02944-422425), Quaglia 238, flies to Buenos Aires' Aeroparque (US$97 to US$269) at least twice a day. LAPA (☎ 02944-423714), Villegas 121, flies to Aeroparque (US$99 to US$235) at least daily. TAN (☎ 02944-427889), Quaglia 242, Local 11, flies Saturday to Comodoro Rivadavia (US$75 to US$88), and Tuesday and Friday to Puerto Montt, Chile (US$50 to US$62).

LADE (☎ 02944-423562), Mitre 186, flies cheaply to other Patagonian destinations and Aeroparque. Kaikén Líneas Aéreas (☎ 02944-433494), Palacios 266, flies daily except Sunday to southern Patagonia as far as Ushuaia, and north to Mendoza. Southern Winds (☎ 02944-423704), Mitre 260, flies to Córdoba (US$127 to US$169) and northwestern cities.

Bus The train station, Estación Ferrocarril Roca, does double duty as the bus station (☎ 02944-426999), but some companies retain downtown offices.

Several carriers cover the route between Bariloche and Osorno (US$18, six hours) and Puerto Montt (US$19), usually with early morning departures.

Buses are numerous to most major domestic and regional destinations. Sample fares include Villa la Angostura (US$6.50, two hours), El Bolsón (US$8 to US$11, two hours), Junín de los Andes (US$16, four hours), San Martín de los Andes (US$17, 4½ hours), Esquel (US$18, 4½ hours), Neuquén (US$18 to US$22, 7 hours), Viedma (US$40 to US$50, 16 hours), Trelew (US$40 to US$51, 13 hours), Bahía Blanca (US$45 to US$55, 14 hours), Puerto Madryn (US$48 to US$54, 14 hours), Santa Rosa (US$50, 11 hours), Mendoza (US$55 to US$62, 19 hours), Comodoro Rivadavia (US$47 to US$69, 14 hours), San Juan (US$63 to US$72, 21 hours), Mar del Plata (US$65, 21 hours), Buenos Aires (US$75 to US$85, 22 to 23 hours), Córdoba (US$75 to US$79, 22 hours), Rosario (US$76, 23 hours) and Río Gallegos (US$78 to US$104, 28 hours).

Codao del Sur, Perito Moreno 480, goes to El Maitén (US$14, 3½ hours) Tuesday at 8 am for the narrow-gauge train to Esquel. Transportes Ko-Ko, Perito Moreno 107, has buses to Junín de los Andes and San Martín de los Andes, mostly via the longer paved La Rinconada (RN 40) route rather than the more scenic but chokingly dusty Siete Lagos route, which usually has summer service only.

Bus & Boat Catedral Turismo (☎ 02944-425443), Bartolomé Mitre 399, arranges the bus-boat combination over the Andes to Puerto Montt for US$110; it leaves weekdays at 9 am.

Train Sefepa (Servicio Ferrocarril Patagónico; ☎ 02944-423172) leaves from Estación Ferrocarril Roca across the Río Ñireco along RN 237. Departures for Viedma (16 hours) are Tuesday and Friday at 5 pm; fares are US$28 primera, US$42 Pullman.

Getting Around
To/From the Airport Aeropuerto Teniente Candelaria (☎ 02944-422767) is 15km east of town via RN 237 and RP 80. TAN runs its own airport minibus, while LADE, LAPA, and Aerolíneas use Transporte Alí (US$3), which leaves Aerolíneas' downtown offices, at Quaglia 238, 1½ hours before flight time.

Bus From Perito Moreno between Palacios and Beschtedt, Codao del Sur (☎ 02944-423654) and Ómnibus 3 de Mayo (☎ 02944-433805) run hourly buses to Cerro Catedral (US$2.40).

From 6 am to midnight, bus No 20 leaves every 20 minutes to Llao Llao (US$1.90) and Puerto Pañuelo. The Nos 10 and 11 buses also go to Colonia Suiza (US$2.20) 14 times daily; three of these, at 8:05 am, noon and 5:40 pm continue to Puerto Pañuelo; departures from Puerto Pañuelo back to Bariloche via Colonia Suiza are 9:40 am and 1:40 and 6:40 pm.

Ómnibus 3 de Mayo's Nos 50 and 51 buses go to Lago Gutiérrez (US$1.10) every half-hour, while in summer the company's Línea Mascardi goes to Villa Mascardi (US$3.50) and Los Rápidos (US$5) three times daily. Their Línea El Manso goes twice Friday and once Sunday to Río Villegas and El Manso (US$7.50), on the southwestern border of Parque Nacional Nahuel Huapi.

Car Rental agencies include Avis (☎ 02944-431648), San Martín 130; Budget (☎ 02944-422482), Mitre 106, 1st floor; and Localiza (☎ 02944-423457), Quaglia 161.

Bicycle For rentals, try Bariloche Mountain Bike (☎ 02944-462397) at Gallardo 375, Bikeway (☎ 02944-424202) at Eduardo O'Connor 867, Dirty Bikes (☎ 02944-425616) at Eduardo O'Connor 681 or Martín Ferrer (cellular ☎ 0268-230-2515).

PARQUE NACIONAL NAHUEL HUAPI
Lago Nahuel Huapi, a glacial relic over 100km long, attracts so many visitors that its natural attributes are at risk, though native and introduced fish species still offer excellent sport. To the west, 3554m Monte Tronador marks the Andean crest and the Chilean border. Humid Valdivian forest covers its lower slopes, while summer wildflowers blanket alpine meadows.

Things to See & Do
Travel agencies offer tours of the **Circuito Chico** loop between Bariloche and Llao Llao, but public transport is cheaper and more flexible. En route, **Cerro Campanario's** chairlift (US$10) offers panoramic views, while Llao Llao's **Puerto Pañuelo** is the departure point for the boat-bus excursion to Chile.

From Llao Llao, continue to **Colonia Suiza**, whose modest *confitería* has excellent pastries. The road passes the trailhead to 2075m **Cerro López** (a four-hour climb) while returning to Bariloche. **Cerro Otto** (1405m) is an 8km walk on a gravel road west from Bariloche, but a gondola (US$15) also goes to the summit.

At **Cerro Catedral** (2400m), a ski center 20km west of Bariloche, chairlifts and a large cable car climb to a restaurant/confitería with excellent panoramas (US$16). Several trails begin here, including one to the Club Andino's Refugio Frey.

For US$12 one way, US$20 return, the Club Andino Bariloche organizes transport to Pampa Linda and **Monte Tronador** daily at 9 am, returning at 5 pm; some have found the trip dusty and unpleasant.

ARGENTINE-CHILEAN LAKE DISTRICT

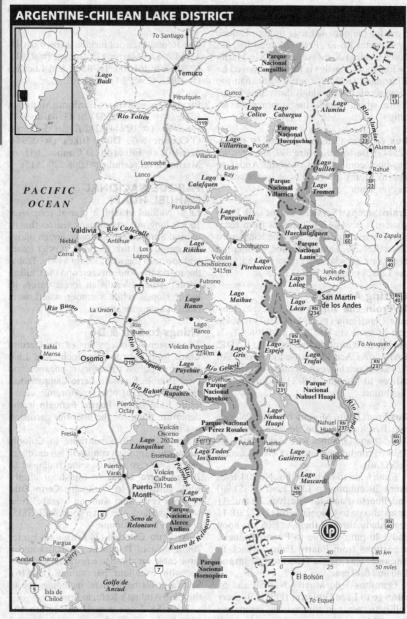

Activities

Fishing For details on licenses and regulations, contact the Club de Caza y Pesca (☎ 02944-422785), at Costanera 12 de Octubre and Onelli, Bariloche. For rental equipment, try Bariloche's Baruzzi Deportes (☎ 02944-424922), Urquiza 250, or Martín Pescador (☎ 02944-422275), Rolando 257.

White-water Rafting Several operators with offices in Bariloche arrange rafting on the Río Manso, a Class III descent with enough rapids to be interesting, for about US$65. Among them are Expediciones Náuticas (☎ 02944-426677), Mitre 125, Oficina 126; Aguas Blancas (☎ 02944-432799), Morales 564 and Rafting Adventure (☎ 02944-432928), Mitre 161.

Places to Stay

Besides campgrounds near Bariloche, there are *sites* at Lago Mascardi, Lago Los Moscos, Lago Roca, Lago Guillelmo and Pampa Linda. With permission from rangers, free camping is possible in certain areas. Alpine *refugios* charge US$6 per night, US$1.50 for day use, and US$3 for kitchen privileges.

EL BOLSÓN

In southwestern Río Negro, 130km from Bariloche, rows of poplars shelter chacras devoted to hops, soft fruits such as raspberries, and orchard crops like cherries and apples. El Bolsón's self-proclaimed status as a 'non-nuclear zone' and 'ecological municipality' is a pleasant relief from Bariloche's commercialism. Most services are on Av San Martín, which runs along the landmark, ovoid Plaza Pagano.

Information

The Dirección Municipal de Turismo (☎ 02944-492604), at the north end of Plaza Pagano, is open in summer 8 am to 10 pm weekdays, 9 am to 10 pm Saturday, and 10 am to 10 pm Sunday; the rest of the year hours are 9 am to 6 pm. Visitors interested in the surrounding mountains can contact the Club Andino Piltriquitrón, on Sarmiento between Roca and Feliciano.

It's better to change money elsewhere, since El Bolsón has no ATMs or cambios. The post office is at Av San Martín 2608. The Cooperativa Telefónica is at the south end of Plaza Pagano.

Places to Stay

For US$3 per person, the dusty but shady riverside *Camping del Sol*, at the west end of Av Castelli, has hot showers and a small *confitería*. For US$5, *Camping La Chacra* (☎ 02944-492111), off Av Belgrano on the eastern edge of town, has more grass, less dust, and increasing shade.

Local buses go hourly to the HI affiliate *Albergue El Pueblito* (☎ 02944-493560; elbolson@hostels.org.ar), in Barrio Luján, about 4km north of town. Rates are US$8 with hostel card, US$9 without; campsites are also available.

Residencial Salinas (☎ 02944-492396), Roca 641, has US$10 rooms that include a private log fire, but the insulation is inadequate in winter. Rates are the same at *Residencial Edelweiss* (☎ 02944-492594), Ángel del Agua 360 with shared bath, while *Residencial La Paz* (☎ 02944-492252), Sarmiento 3212, charges US$12 per person with private bath.

Places to Eat

The periodic *feria artesanal* (see Shopping) is the best value. *Calabaza*, San Martín 2524, has superb breakfasts for just US$2.50. *Cerro Lindo*, Av San Martín 2526, has large, tasty pizzas, good music and excellent, friendly service.

For a splurge, the varied menu at *Jauja*, Av San Martín 2867, is among the best values in Argentina; save room for the astounding homemade, fruit-flavored ice cream next door at *Heladería Jauja*. *Las Brasas*, at Sarmiento and Hube, is a superb choice for beef.

Shopping

Tuesday, Thursday and Saturday, local craftsworkers sell their wares at the *feria artesanal* on Plaza Pagano from 10:30 am to 3 pm. It's also one of the best places in town to eat delicacies like homemade empanadas and sausages, Belgian waffles with fresh raspberries, and locally brewed beer.

Getting There & Away

Air LADE (☎ 02944-492206), on San Martín between José Hernández and Azcona, flies cheaply Wednesday to Bariloche, San Martín de los Andes, Zapala and Neuquén, and Thursday to El Maitén, Esquel, and Comodoro Rivadavia. Flights leave from the

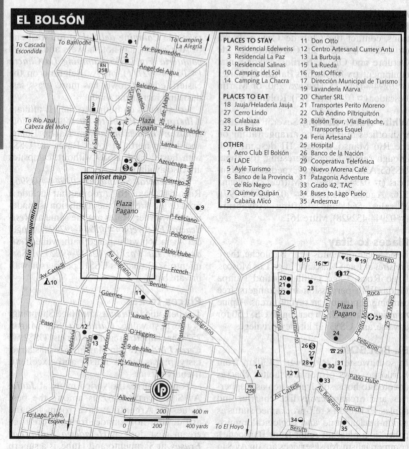

EL BOLSÓN

PLACES TO STAY
2 Residencial Edelweiss
3 Residencial La Paz
8 Residencial Salinas
10 Camping del Sol
14 Camping La Chacra

PLACES TO EAT
18 Jauja/Heladería Jauja
27 Cerro Lindo
28 Calabaza
32 Las Brasas

OTHER
1 Aero Club El Bolsón
4 LADE
5 Aylé Turismo
6 Banco de la Provincia
   de Río Negro
7 Quimey Quipán
9 Cabaña Micó

11 Don Otto
12 Centro Artesanal Cumey Antu
13 La Burbuja
15 La Rueda
16 Post Office
17 Dirección Municipal de Turismo
19 Lavandería Marva
20 Charter SRL
21 Transportes Perito Moreno
22 Club Andino Piltriquitrón
23 Bolsón Tour, Vía Bariloche,
   Transportes Esquel
24 Feria Artesanal
25 Hospital
26 Banco de la Nación
29 Cooperativa Telefónica
30 Nuevo Morena Café
31 Patagonia Adventure
33 Grado 42, TAC
34 Buses to Lago Puelo
35 Andesmar

Aero Club El Bolsón, at the north end of town.

Bus El Bolsón has no central bus terminal, but most companies are within a short walk of Av San Martín.

The most common destinations are Bariloche (US$10, two hours) and Esquel (US$16, three hours). Heading to other destinations, southbound fares are slightly lower than those from Bariloche and northbound fares are slightly higher.

Andesmar (☎ 02944-492178), at Belgrano and Perito Moreno, goes to Bariloche and points north, and to Esquel. Charter SRL (☎ 02944-492333) at Sarmiento and Roca, also goes to Bariloche.

Bolsón Tour (☎ 02944-492161), Roca 359, is the agent for Vía Bariloche, which goes to Esquel, Bariloche and Buenos Aires. Transportes Esquel, at the same address, goes Tuesday and Friday at 8:30 am to Esquel. Grado 42 (☎ 02944-493124), Belgrano 406, is the agent for TAC, which goes to Bariloche and connects in Neuquén for Mendoza and other northern destinations.

Don Otto (☎ 02944-493910), on Bolívar between Perito Moreno and 25 de Mayo, goes to Bariloche and Comodoro Rivadavia, with connections in Esquel for Trelew and Puerto Madryn. Transportes Perito Moreno (☎ 02944-492307), Sarmiento 2786, Local 1, goes to El Maitén, Bariloche, Parque Nacional Los Alerces and local destinations.

AROUND EL BOLSÓN

On a ridge 8km west of town, the metamorphic **Cabeza del Indio** formation resembles a profile of the 'noble savage.' The trail, traversing a narrow ledge, gives superb views of the Río Azul and Lago Puelo. Walk, hitch or take a taxi from El Bolsón to the trailhead.

The granitic ridge of 2260m **Cerro Piltriquitrón** dominates the landscape east of Bolsón. From the 1000m level, reached by road (about US$15 by taxi, or an 11km uphill hike), an hour's walk leads to **Refugio Piltriquitrón** (☎ 02944-492024); US$6 per person, meals extra; sleeping bag essential. Another tiring two hours' walk earns the summit.

Only 15km south of El Bolsón, the windy azure waters of **Parque Nacional Lago Puelo** are suitable for water sports and camping (some sites are free). There are regular buses, but reduced Sunday services.

NEUQUÉN

At the confluence of the Limay and Neuquén Rivers, 265m above sea level, this provincial capital (population 235,000) is an agricultural service center for the Río Negro valley. East-west RN 22 is the main highway through town, while the main north-south thoroughfare is Av Argentina (Av Olascoaga beyond the train station).

Information

Neuquén's Dirección Provincial de Turismo (☎ 0299-442-4089), at Félix San Martín 182, is open weekdays 7 am to 9 pm, weekends 8 am to 8 pm. Neuquén has two cambios: Olano at JB Justo 197 and Pullman at Ministro Alcorta 144, but ATMs are numerous. The post office is at Rivadavia and Santa Fe. There are many locutorios, including one on Mitre across from the bus terminal.

Things to See

The **Sala de Arte Emilio Saraco**, in the old cargo terminal at the railway station, has current art exhibits. **Juntarte en el Andén**, an outdoor art space across the tracks at the former passenger terminal, is also the site of the performing arts **Sala Teatral Alicia F Reyes**.

Across Av Argentina, fronting on Av San Martín, the **Museo Municipal Dr Gregorio Álvarez** (1902) was once the locomotive repair shed for the British-built Ferrocarril del Sud. It now holds exhibits on northern Patagonian dinosaurs, regional prehistory and ethnography and Neuquén's urban development.

Places to Stay & Eat

Basic **Residencial Continental** (☎ 0299-442-3757), near the bus terminal at Perito Moreno 90, has rooms with private bath for US$15/20 for singles/doubles. **Residencial Inglés** (☎ 0299-442-2252), Félix San Martín 534, costs US$15/25, about the same as inviting **Residencial Belgrano** (☎ 0299-442-4311), Rivadavia 283. **Residencial Alcorta** (☎ 0299-442-2652), Ministro Alcorta 84, is probably the pick of the category for US$18/25; breakfast costs US$2.50 extra.

Confiterías along Av Argentina are pleasant for breakfast and morning coffee. **El Plato**, Alberdi 158, has good US$5 lunch specials. **Franz y Peppone**, at 9 de Julio and Belgrano, is an unusual combo of Italian and German cuisine. **Las Tres Marías**, Alberdi 126, deserves special mention for its exceptionally diverse menu at moderate prices, in addition to cheap daily specials. **La Nonna Franchesca**, 9 de Julio 56, has attractive decor in addition to outstanding pasta and French cuisine.

El Plato, Alberdi 158, has a good reputation for its US$5 lunch specials. Nearby **La Fusta**, Alberdi 176, has home-style Argentine cooking. **Fatto dalla Mamma**, 9 de Julio 56, has outstanding pasta, but prices, especially for desserts, are on the high side. **Pop Hot's Pizza**, Yrigoyen 90, has good music and ambience. **La Rural**, a parrilla at Alberdi 126, rates special mention for its diverse menu at mid-range prices.

Getting There & Away

Austral (☎ 0299-442-2409), Santa Fe 52, flies to Buenos Aires's Aeroparque (US$57 to US$196) at least twice daily. LAPA (☎ 0299-438555), Av Argentina 30, flies weekdays to Bariloche (US$41 to US$76) and three times each weekday, twice Saturday and once Sunday to Aeroparque (US$59 to US$149).

Neuquén-based TAN (☎ 0299-442-3076), 25 de Mayo 180, has extensive regional schedules and the only international flights, to Puerto Montt and Concepción, Chile.

LADE (☎ 0299-443-1153), Brown 163, flies to Patagonian destinations, as does Kaikén Líneas Aéreas (☎ 0299-447-1333), Av Argentina 327. Southern Winds (☎ 0299-448-7248), at the same address as Kaikén, flies to Córdoba (US$89 to US$119) and northwestern cities.

Bus Neuquén's bus station (☎ 0299-442-4903) is at Bartolomé Mitre 147. Several carriers offer international services to Temuco, Chile (US$45, 13 to 14 hours) via Zapala and the Pino Hachado pass or over Paso Tromen via Junín de los Andes. There are also services three times weekly to Osorno and Puerto Montt via Paso Cardenal Samoré (US$45, 14 hours).

Sample domestic fares include Zapala (US$9, three hours), Bariloche (US$15 to US$25, five hours), Junín de los Andes (US$22, seven hours), San Martín de los Andes (US$24, eight hours), Santa Rosa (US$25), Villa La Angostura (US$28, seven hours), Bahía Blanca (US$30, eight hours), Puerto Madryn (US$39, 10 hours), Trelew (US$42, 11 hours), El Bolsón (US$42, 10 hours), Mendoza (US$45, 12 hours), Esquel (US$51, 12 hours), Buenos Aires (US$45 to US$55, 16 hours), Comodoro Rivadavia (US$65, 15 hours), Córdoba (US$43 to US$72, 16½ hours), Rosario (US$75, 14 hours) and Río Gallegos (US$111, 28 hours).

JUNÍN DE LOS ANDES

Neuquén's 'trout capital,' a modest livestock center (population 8800) on the Río Chimehuín, is 41km north of San Martín de los Andes, and has better access to many parts of Parque Nacional Lanín. The enthusiastic Secretaría Municipal de Turismo (☎ 02972-491160) is at Padre Milanesio 596, opposite Plaza San Martín. Hours are 8 am to 10 pm daily; it also issues fishing permits. In an adjacent office, Parques Nacionales is open weekdays 9 am to 8:30 pm, weekends 2:30 to 8:30 pm.

Places to Stay & Eat

The riverside *Camping La Isla* (☎ 02972-491461), three blocks east of the plaza, has all facilities for US$6 per person, plus US$1 for showers. *Residencial Marisa* (☎ 02972-491175), Blvd Rosas 360, charges US$20/30 single/double with private bath, as do *Posada Pehuén* (☎ 02972-491569), Coronel Suárez 560, and *Hostería del Montañés* (☎ 02972-491155), San Martín 555.

The varied main courses at *Ruca Hueney*, Padre Milanesio 641, range from US$6 to US$12. *Roble Bar*, Ginés Ponte 331, is

Junín's main pizzeria, with baked empanadas and sandwiches as well. *Rotisería Tandil*, Coronel Suárez 431, has superb take-out empanadas.

Getting There & Away

Air The Aeropuerto Chapelco is midway between Junín and San Martín de los Andes; for flights, see the San Martín entry.

Bus Bus services from the station, at Olavarría and Félix San Martín, closely resemble those from San Martín de los Andes (see below).

SAN MARTÍN DE LOS ANDES

San Martín (altitude 642m), on Lago Lácar, retains some of the charm that once attracted people to Bariloche, but burgeoning hotels, spreading restaurants and insidious timeshares are transforming it into a costly tourist trap. At the centro cívico, San Martín and Rosas, the well-organized Secretaría Municipal de Turismo (☎ 02972-427347) is open 8 am to 10 pm daily.

The only official cambio is Andina Internacional at Capitán Drury 876; there are several ATMs. The post office is at the centro cívico. The Cooperativa Telefónica is at Capitán Drury 761.

Skiing

Cerro Chapelco's Centro de Deportes Invernales (☎ 02972-427460), 20km southeast of San Martín, has a downtown Centro de Informes/Escuela de Ski at Av San Martín and Elordi. Rental gear is available both on site and in town.

Places to Stay

Camping On the eastern outskirts of town, the spacious *Camping ACA* (☎ 02972-427332) charges US$10 per site. San Martín's *Albergue Juvenil*, 3 de Caballería 1164, charges US$10 per person but lacks kitchen facilities.

Hostels San Martín's *La Posta del Caminante* (☎ 02972-428672), 3 de Caballería 1164, charges $10 per person but lacks kitchen facilities. YPF's *Club Cordillerano* (☎ 02972-427431), on Juez del Valle just north of the arroyo, charges US$10 for shared rooms, US$15 per person for double rooms, with better facilities.

Residenciales Conventional accommodations start around US$20 per person at *Residencial Italia* (☎ 02972-427590) at Coronel Pérez 977, remodeled *Residencial Villalago* (☎ 02972-427454) at Villegas 717, and well-located *Residencial Los Pinos* (☎ 02972-427207) at Almirante Brown 420.

Places to Eat

Rotisería Viviana, San Martín 489, has outstanding take-out food, particularly baked empanadas. For coffee, chocolate and croissants, try *Abolengo*, Av San Martín 806.

Traditional favorite *Piscis*, Villegas 598, is a parrilla. Long lines also form outside *Mendieta*, San Martín 713, a more upscale parrilla. *Pura Vida*, Villegas 745, has a small but good and mostly vegetarian menu, plus some chicken and fish items, and first-rate service. At Villegas 744, *Paprika* serves pricey Middle European food.

Getting There & Away

Air Austral (☎ 02972-427003), Capitán Drury 876, flies Thursday through Tuesday to Buenos Aires (US$159 to US$260); Monday, Tuesday and Thursday flights go via Esquel (US$79). LADE (☎ 02972-427672), Av San Martín 915, and TAN (☎ 02972-427872), Belgrano 760, mostly serve Patagonian destinations.

Bus The bus station (☎ 02972-427044) is at Villegas and Juez del Valle.

Igi-Llaima and Empresa San Martín alternate service to Temuco, Chile (US$25, eight hours, Monday through Saturday. Regional carrier El Petróleo serves northern destinations (Aluminé, Junín de los Andes, Zapala), the Río Negro valley to the east, and the Chilean border at Pirehueico (US$5.50). Aluminé buses leave Tuesday only, at 8 am.

Domestic destinations and sample fares include Junín de los Andes (US$3.50, one hour), Pirehueico (US$5.50, two hours), Villa La Angostura (US$13, three hours), Aluminé (US$13, four hours), Bariloche (US$19, 4½ hours), Neuquén (US$22, six hours), Buenos Aires (US$65 to US$75, 22 hours), Mendoza (US$67, 19½ hours) and Córdoba (US$70, 21 hours).

Boat Plumas Verdes (☎ 02972-428427) sails from the Muelle de Pasajeros (passenger pier) on the Av Costanera to Paso Hua Hum on the Chilean border, daily at 10 am. The fare is US$30, plus a US$5 national park fee.

PARQUE NACIONAL LANÍN

Tranquil Lanín, extending about 150km north from Nahuel Huapi to Lago Ñorquinco, has escaped the frantic commercialism blemishing the Bariloche area. Extensive stands of the broadleaved deciduous southern beech *raulí* and the curious pehuén (monkey puzzle tree) flourish on the lower slopes of snowcapped, 3776m Volcán Lanín, in addition to the *lenga*, *ñire*, and *coihue* that characterize more southerly Patagonian forests. Pleistocene glaciers left behind numerous finger-shaped lakes that now have excellent campsites.

For detailed information, contact the Parques Nacionales office in San Martín or Junín.

Things to See & Do

From San Martín, you can sail west on **Lago Lácar** to Paso Hua Hum and cross by road to Pirehueico, Chile, but there is also bus service. Hua Hum has both free and organized camping, plus hiking trails. Fifteen km north of San Martín, almost undeveloped **Lago Lolog** has good camping and fishing.

Source of the Río Chimehuín, **Lago Huechulafquen** is easily accessible from Junín, despite limited public transport. There are outstanding views of Volcán Lanín, and several excellent hikes. Campers at the free sites in the narrow area between the lakes and the road should dig a latrine and remove their rubbish. Mapuche-operated campgrounds at *Raquithue* (US$3 per person) and *Piedra Mala* (US$4.50) are more hygienic, while *Bahía Cañicul* costs US$5.50 to US$6.50 but grants ACA discounts. Bring supplies from Junín de los Andes.

The forested **Lago Tromen** area, the northern approach to Volcán Lanín, opens earlier in the season for hikers and climbers than the route from Huechulafquen.

Getting There & Away

Public transport is limited, but hitching is feasible in high season. Buses to Chile over the Hua Hum and Tromen passes may drop passengers at intermediate points, but are often crowded. Pickup trucks from Junín carry six or seven backpackers to Puerto Canoas, on Huechulafquen, for US$5 each.

VILLA LA ANGOSTURA

On the north shore of Lago Nacional Nahuel Huapi, this placid resort takes its name from the 91m isthmus that connects it to Península Quetrihué, whose most striking natural asset is Parque Nacional Los Arrayanes. The commercial center El Cruce straddles the highway, while residential La Villa (which still has hotels, shops and services) is closer to the lake.

The well-organized Dirección Municipal de Turismo (☎ 02944-494124), at Av Siete Lagos 93 in El Cruce, is open 8:30 am to 9 pm daily. The post office is in El Cruce. There's a locutorio in the Galería Inacayal at El Cruce.

Things to See & Do

Parque Nacional Los Arrayanes On the Quetrihué peninsula, this overlooked park protects the cinnamon-barked arrayán, a myrtle relative. Park headquarters is at the southern end of the peninsula, a three-hour hike from La Villa, but start early in the morning: hikers must leave the park by 4 pm (ask the El Cruce tourist office for brochures). Mountain bikes are available at El Cruce (US$5 per hour, cheaper for a full day).

At La Villa, a very steep, 20-minute hike goes to two panoramic viewpoints over Nahuel Huapi.

Siete Lagos RP 234 follows this scenic but smotheringly dusty route to San Martín de los Andes, usually in summer only. For transport details, see the Getting There & Away entry (below).

Places to Stay & Eat

Camping El Cruce (☎ 02944-494145), on Av Los Lagos 500m beyond the tourist office, charges US$5 per person, but toilets may be dirty. *Residencial Don Pedro (☎ 02944-494269),* at the corner of Belvedere and Los Maquis in El Cruce, charges US$24/34, but don't expect to pay single prices in summer.

Rincón Suizo (☎ 02944-494248), on Av Los Arrayanes near Av Siete Lagos in El Cruce, serves fondue and has outdoor seating. *La Recova,* Av Arrayanes 51, has decent food and excellent service; next-door *Helados Melgari* is worth a stop for ice cream.

Getting There & Away

Villa La Angostura's new bus station is at the junction of Av Siete Lagos and Av Arrayanes in El Cruce. Several carriers link El Cruce with Bariloche (US$6, two hours); there are also services to Neuquén (US$28, nine hours). Albus goes thrice daily to San Martín de los Andes (US$13, three hours) by the Siete Lagos route in summer.

Buses en route from Bariloche to Osorno and Puerto Montt (Chile) pass through El Cruce, but they are often full.

PUERTO MADRYN

Founded by Welsh settlers in 1886, this sheltered desert port on the Golfo Nuevo, 1371km south of Buenos Aires, has taken off as a tourist destination because its proximity to the provincial wildlife sanctuary of Península Valdés attracts foreigners, and the good beaches bring domestic tourists. Street names alone remain of its Welsh past.

Information

The Secretaría de Turismo y Medio Ambiente (☎ 02965-453504; municipio_madryn@cpsarg.com) has a spacious visitor center at Av Roca 223. It's open daily 7 am to 1 am from mid-December to mid-March; the rest of the year 8 am to 2 pm and 3 to 10 pm. There's usually an English-speaker among the efficient, helpful staff.

The several cambios on Av Roca and 28 de Julio belong to travel agencies. Banco Almafuerte, at Roque Sáenz Peña and 25 de Mayo, cashes traveler's checks and there are several ATMs. The post office is at Belgrano and Gobernador Maíz. Telefónica Patagónica is at MA Zar 289.

Nearly all the guides speak English at Sur Turismo (☎ 02965-473585), Av Roca 349, which organizes tours of the Madryn area, Punta Tombo and Península Valdés; there are many similar agencies.

Places to Stay

Camping Toward Punta Cuevas, *Camping Municipal Sud (☎ 02965-455640)* has comfy 'A' and 'B' areas (US$12 per day for four), but perfectly acceptable 'C' and 'D' areas are cheaper.

Hostels At 25 de Mayo 1136, *Hostelling International Puerto Madryn (☎/fax 02965-474426; madryn@hostels.org.ar, hi-pm@satlink.com.ar)* has large rooms, some with private bath, for US$10 per person (HI members) or US$12 (nonmembers). Office

PUERTO MADRYN

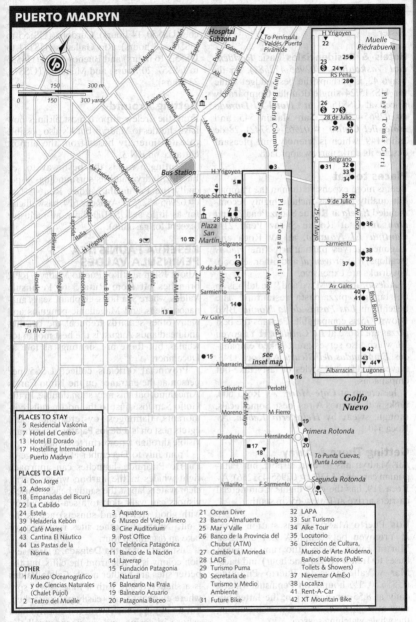

PLACES TO STAY
5 Residencial Vaskonia
7 Hotel del Centro
13 Hotel El Dorado
17 Hostelling International
   Puerto Madryn

PLACES TO EAT
4 Don Jorge
12 Adesso
18 Empanadas del Bicurú
22 La Cabildo
24 Estela
39 Heladería Kebón
40 Café Mares
43 Cantina El Náutico
44 Las Pastas de la
   Nonna

OTHER
1 Museo Oceanográfico
   y de Ciencias Naturales
   (Chalet Pujol)
2 Teatro del Muelle

3 Aquatours
6 Museo del Viejo Minero
8 Cine Auditorium
9 Post Office
10 Telefónica Patagónica
11 Banco de la Nación
14 Laverap
15 Fundación Patagonia
   Natural
16 Balneario Na Praia
19 Balneario Acuario
20 Patagonia Buceo

21 Ocean Diver
23 Banco Almafuerte
25 Mar y Valle
26 Banco de la Provincia del
   Chubut (ATM)
27 Cambio La Moneda
28 LADE
29 Turismo Puma
30 Secretaría de
   Turismo y Medio
   Ambiente
31 Future Bike

32 LAPA
33 Sur Turismo
34 Aike Tour
35 Locutorio
36 Dirección de Cultura,
   Museo de Arte Moderno,
   Baños Públicos (Public
   Toilets & Showers)
37 Nievemar (AmEx)
38 Localiza
41 Rent-A-Car
42 XT Mountain Bike

hours are 8 am to 1 pm and 4 to 9 pm only; it also rents mountain bikes. It closes after Easter.

Hotels & Residenciales Basic *Residencial Vaskonia* (☎ 02965-472581), 25 de Mayo 43, is perhaps the best budget value for US$15/24 single/double. Comparably priced, at US$15/25, are *Hotel El Dorado* (☎ 02965-471026), San Martín 545, and *Hotel del Centro* (☎ 02965-473742), 28 de Julio 149, which is friendly and pleasant despite its dark, narrow approach.

Places to Eat

Beef is more expensive than in the Pampas, but quality parrillas include highly recommended *Estela* at Roque Sáenz Peña 27 and *Don Jorge* at Roque Sáenz Peña 214. *Cantina El Náutico*, at Av Roca and Lugones, serves particularly fine *vieiras* (scallops) *a la provenzal* and other seafood, but drinks are expensive.

Adesso, at 25 de Mayo and 9 de Julio, is an outstanding pizza/pasta restaurant. The beachfront *Las Pastas de la Nonna*, Blvd Brown 775, is comparable. Perhaps the best pizzas are those at *La Cabildo*, H Yrigoyen 36, which also serves great baked empanadas. *Empanadas del Bicurú*, Av Roca 1143, serves 14 different styles of tasty take-out empanadas.

Ice cream at *Café Mares*, Av Roca 600, ranks with Buenos Aires' best. Some locals, though, swear by *Heladería Kebón*, Av Roca 540.

Getting There & Away

Air Madryn has its own airport, but Patagonian carrier LADE (☎ 02965-451256), Av Roca 119, has the only flights. Commercial carriers arrive at Trelew, 65km south.

Bus Puerto Madryn's bus station is on H Yrigoyen between MA Zar and San Martín. Línea 28 de Julio runs frequent buses to Trelew (US$4, one hour) and back. Mar y Valle goes to Puerto Pirámide (US$6.50, 1½ hours), on Península Valdés, daily at 8:55 am and 5 pm; the latter bus runs at peak times, in summer and during the whale-watching season.

Sample long-distance fares include Comodoro Rivadavia (US$18, six hours), Caleta Olivia (US$20, eight hours), Bahía Blanca

(US$24, eight hours), Esquel (US$28, eight hours), Neuquén (US$32, 12 hours), Bariloche (US$50, 14 hours), Córdoba (US$55 to US$61, 18 hours), Río Gallegos (US$44 to US$52, 16 hours) and Buenos Aires (US$35 to US$57, 20 hours) and Mendoza (US$72, 23 hours).

Getting Around

From the Trelew airport, most airlines now have shuttles to Madryn, but it's also possible to catch intercity buses from the airport entrance on RN 3.

Renting a car is the best way to see Puerto Madryn and its surroundings, especially the Península Valdés. Rent-A-Car (☎ 02965-452355), Av Roca 624, has vehicles for as little as US$100 daily, all-inclusive (except for gasoline).

RESERVA FAUNÍSTICA PENÍNSULA VALDÉS

About 18km north of Puerto Madryn, RP 2 branches off from Ruta 3 to Península Valdés, where sea lions, elephant seals, guanacos, rheas, and Magellanic penguins and many other seabirds frequent the beaches and headlands. August is the best month for whales, but there are sightings as late as December.

Provincial officials collect US$5 per person at the entrance on the Istmo Carlos Ameghino, but this may soon double. In the Golfo San José, just to the north, gulls, cormorants, flamingos, oystercatchers and egrets nest on **Isla de los Pájaros**, a sanctuary visible through a powerful telescope.

From July to December at the village of Puerto Pirámide, launches can approach right whales in the harbor, whose warm, clear waters lap at the sandy beach. Carless visitors can walk 4km to a sea-lion colony, with good views (and sunsets) across the Golfo Nuevo; for other sites, rent a car or take an organized tour.

Just north of **Punta Delgada**, a large sea-lion colony is visible from the cliffs, but the better sites are farther north. **Caleta Valdés** is a sheltered bay with a long gravel spit, where elephant seals (easily photographed, but do not approach them too closely) haul ashore in spring and guanacos stroll the beach. Between Caleta Valdés and Punta Norte is a substantial colony of burrowing Magellanic penguins. At **Punta Norte** proper is a huge mixed colony of sea lions and elephant seals; clearly marked trails and fences discourage visitors (and sea lions) from too close an encounter.

Places to Stay & Eat

Puerto Pirámide's *Camping Municipal*, sheltered from the wind by dunes and trees, charges US$4 per person. It has clean toilets, hot showers (US$1; carefully timed because of water shortages) and a shop with basic provisions.

At *Hospedaje El Español* (☎ 02965-495031), simple but clean rooms and toilets, plus hot showers, run US$8 per person. *Hostería El Libanés* (☎ 02965-495007) has modest rooms for US$23 per person with bath in summer, slightly cheaper out of season, and a small *confitería*. The *Hostería Pub Paradise* (☎ 02965-495030) is an expensive B&B, but serves reasonable meals.

Getting There & Away

Tuesday, Thursday, Saturday and Sunday at 8:55 am, the Mar y Valle bus travels from Puerto Madryn to Puerto Pirámide (US$6.50), returning at 7 pm. Tours from Puerto Madryn may drop off visitors at Puerto Pirámide and permit them to return another day for no additional charge, but verify this beforehand.

Getting Around

For sites any distance from Pirámide, the options are renting a car or taking an organized tour. Most Puerto Madryn travel agencies organize day trips for about US$25 to US$30, not including admission; there are also operators in Puerto Pirámide. Some frustrated travelers have complained of too much time at confiterías and too little at wildlife sites, so ask other travelers about their experiences, make sure the operator's expectations are the same as yours, and do not hesitate to relay complaints to Puerto Madryn's Secretaría de Turismo y Medio Ambiente.

Puerto Pirámide also has rental bikes – very convenient for seeing the immediate area but not the major wildlife sites, which are too distant for most day trips, especially with the strong winds.

TRELEW

Actively courting the tourist trade, the Chubut valley town of Trelew is a conven-

ient staging point for the nearby Welsh villages of Gaiman and Dolavon, as well as the massive Punta Tombo penguin reserve. Trelew's center is Plaza Independencia, while most of the sights are on Calles 25 de Mayo and San Martín, and along Av Fontana. Named for early settler Lewis Jones, Trelew is 65km south of Puerto Madryn. The major cultural event is early September's **Eisteddfod de Chubut**, celebrating Welsh traditions.

Information

The cheerful, competent Oficina Municipal de Turismo (☎ 02965-420139), at San Martín 171, is open 8 am to 8 pm weekdays; from September to March it is open weekends 10 am to 1 pm and 5 to 8 pm. Their bus-terminal branch (☎ 02965-420121) is open 9:30 am to 12:30 pm and 6 to 9 pm weekdays, 6 to 8 pm Saturday. There's also an airport branch (☎ 02965-428021), open for incoming flights.

Sur Turismo (☎ 02965-434081), Belgrano 330, changes cash and traveler's checks, and several banks have ATMs. The post office is at Av 25 de Mayo and Mitre. There are many downtown locutorios.

Travel agencies organizing tours to Península Valdés (US$40) and Punta Tombo (US$30) include Sur Turismo; Skua Operadores Turísticos (☎ 02965-420358), at San Martín 150; and Nievemar (☎ 02965-434114), Italia 20.

Things to See

The Dirección Municipal de Turismo distributes an informative brochure, in Spanish and English, describing historic buildings like the **Banco de la Nación** (the first bank); **Salon San David** (a community center where the Eisteddfod takes place); the **Capilla Tabernacl** (1889); the **Teatro Verdi** (1914); **Plaza Independencia** (with its Victorian kiosk); the **Distrito Militar** (which housed Trelew's first school); and the **Teatro Español**.

In the former railway station, at Av Fontana and 9 de Julio, the **Museo Regional** has good artifacts, but lacks any explanatory or interpretive material on the Welsh settlements. It's open 7 am to 1 pm and 2 to 8 pm weekdays; admission is US$2 for adults, US$1 for children.

Fossils, especially dinosaurs, are superb at the spacious new quarters of the **Museo**

Paleontológico Egidio Feruglio, Av 9 de Julio 631, open weekdays 8:30 am to 12:30 pm and 1:30 to 8 pm, Saturday 9 am to noon and 2 to 9 pm, and Sunday and holidays 2 to 9 pm. Admission is US$4 for adults, and US$2 for university students, retirees and children under 12 years old.

Places to Stay & Eat

Hotel Avenida (☎ 02965-434172), Lewis Jones 49, is friendly, quiet and clean for US$12/20 single/double with shared bath and an inexpensive breakfast, but some of the beds sag. *Residencial San Carlos* (☎ 02965-421038), Sarmiento 758, has small but tidy rooms at US$15/23 with bath, while *Hotel Argentino* (☎ 02965-436134), Mathews 186, is clean and comfy for US$15/25. Popular with travelers, the modest rooms at *Residencial Rivadavia* (☎ 02965-434472), Rivadavia 55, are a good value for US$18/30 with private bath, but there are three singles with shared bath for US$13.

The *Comedor Universitario*, at Fontana and 9 de Julio, offers wholesome meals at low prices. For breakfast, the *Confitería Touring Club*, part of its namesake hotel, has classic atmosphere.

For US$8 tenedor libre, *Rancho Aparte*, Av Fontana 236, specializes in Patagonian lamb. *Los Tres Chinos*, San Martín 188, serves Chinese, while *Quimey Quipán*, Pellegrini 53 Norte, has seafood. *La Casa de Juan*, Moreno 360, is nominally a pizzería but has a far more varied menu.

Getting There & Away

Air At 25 de Mayo 33, Aerolíneas Argentinas (☎ 02965-420210) flies twice each weekday to Buenos Aires' Aeroparque (US$77 to US$192), once each weekend day. LAPA (☎ 02965-423440), Belgrano 206, flies twice daily to Aeroparque (US$79 to US$149).

Three carriers serve Patagonian destinations: TAN (☎ 02965-434550), Belgrano 326; LADE (☎ 02965-435740), Av Fontana 227; and Kaikén Líneas Aéreas (☎ 02965-421448), San Martín 146.

Bus Trelew's bus station (☎ 02965-420121) is at Urquiza and Lewis Jones, six blocks northeast of downtown. Empresa 28 de Julio (☎ 02965-432429) has frequent buses to Puerto Madryn (US$4), and 20 daily to Gaiman (US$2.60) and Dolavon (US$1.40) between 7:20 am and 10:45 pm (weekend services are reduced). Empresa Rawson and Empresa 28 de Julio have buses to Rawson (US$1) every 15 minutes, starting at 5:30 am.

Mar y Valle (☎ 02965-432429) has daily service to Puerto Pirámide (US$11, three hours), leaving Trelew at 7:45 am, with additional service in summer; for more detail, see the Puerto Madryn entry. Ñandú goes to Camarones (US$10, three hours) weekdays at 8 am, returning at 5 pm.

Sample long-distance fares include Comodoro Rivadavia (US$17 to US$22, five hours), Caleta Olivia (US$25, six hours), Viedma/Carmen de Patagones (US$28, seven hours), Esquel (US$35, 10 hours), Neuquén (US$38 to US$44, 10 hours), Bahía Blanca (US$45, 12 hours), Río Gallegos (US$51 to US$71, 17 hours), Bariloche (US$56, 13 hours), Buenos Aires (US$60 to US$80, 21 hours), Córdoba (US$78, 19 hours) and Mendoza (US$78, 24 hours).

Getting Around

Local rental agencies include Rent a Car (☎ 02965-420898), San Martín 125; Avis (☎ 02965-434834), Paraguay 105; and Localiza (☎ 02965-435344), Urquiza 310.

AROUND TRELEW
Gaiman

Chubut's oldest municipality and one of the few demonstrably Welsh towns remaining in Patagonia, Gaiman is 17km west of Trelew. Its **Museo Histórico Regional de Gaiman** is staffed by Welsh- and English-speaking volunteers, in the old railway station, at Sarmiento and 28 de Julio. One of Patagonia's oddest sights is eclectic **Parque El Desafío**, built by local political protester and conservationist Joaquín Alonso (admission US$5).

From about 3 pm, several *teahouses* offer a filling *té galés* of homemade cakes and sweets for about US$10; all of them are good, so for better service choose one without a tour bus outside. There is a small, inexpensive riverside *campground*, and several places now offer B&B accommodations.

Empresa 28 de Julio has several buses daily from Trelew (US$2.50 return).

Reserva Provincial Punta Tombo

From September to April, half a million Magellanic penguins breed at Punta Tombo,

110km south of Trelew. Other sea and shore birds include cormorants, giant petrels, kelp gulls, flightless steamer ducks and oyster-catchers.

Early-morning visits beat tourist buses from Trelew, but camping is forbidden. Most of the nesting area is fenced off; this does not prevent approaching the birds for photos, but remember that penguin bites can require stitches. To get there, arrange a tour in Trelew (about US$30), hire a taxi, or rent a car. There is a US$5 entry fee.

COMODORO RIVADAVIA

Founded in 1901, Comodoro Rivadavia boomed a few years later, when well-diggers made a fortuitous petroleum strike. The state soon dominated the sector through now privatized Yacimientos Petrolíferos Fiscales (YPF). Argentina is self-sufficient in petroleum, about one-third of it coming from this area.

Comodoro is a frequent stopover for southbound travelers. The main commercial street is Av San Martín, which trends east-west below 212m Cerro Chenque. With Av Alsina and the Atlantic shoreline, San Martín forms a triangle that defines the city center.

Comodoro's very helpful Dirección de Turismo (☎ 0297-446-2376), Rivadavia 430, is open in summer 8 am to 9 pm weekdays, 2 to 7 pm weekends; winter hours are 8 am to 7 pm weekdays, 8 am to 3 pm weekends. It also has a space at the bus terminal open Monday to Saturday 9 am to 7 pm, Sunday 5 to 9 pm only.

Most banks and ATMs are along Av San Martín, where travel agencies will also change cash. The post office is at San Martín and Moreno. Telefonia Patagonia is at Av San Martín and Belgrano.

Museo del Petróleo

Vivid exhibits on the region's natural and cultural history, early and modern oil technology, and social and historical aspects of petroleum development distinguish this museum, a YPF legacy now managed by the Universidad Nacional de Patagonia. There are also fascinating, detailed models of tankers, refineries and the entire zone of exploitation.

In the suburb of General Mosconi, a few kilometers north of downtown, the museum is on Lavalle between Viedma and Carlos Calvo. From downtown Comodoro, take either the No 7 Laprida or No 8 Palazzo bus. Admission is US$2.50, US$3.50 with a guided tour. Hours are Tuesday to Friday 8 am to 1 pm and Tuesday through Sunday 4 to 9 pm.

Places to Stay

Deservedly, the most popular budget hotel is *Hotel Comercio* (☎ 0297-447-2341), Rivadavia 341, whose vintage bar and restaurant alone justify a visit. Rooms with shared bath cost US$15 per person. Well-located *Hospedaje Cari-Hue* (☎ 0297-447-2946), Belgrano 563, charges US$15/25 with private bath. Others in this category, for US$20/30 with private bath, include *Hostería Rua Marina* (☎ 0297-446-8777), Belgrano 738, and the quiet *Hospedaje Belgrano* (☎ 0297-447-8349), Belgrano 546.

Places to Eat

Dino, upstairs at San Martín 592, is a cheap confitería that's good for breakfast; *La Fonte D'Oro*, San Martín at 25 de Mayo, is more upscale. At Rivadavia and Alvear, *Rotisería Andafuera* prepares a variety of exquisite empanadas for takeout.

Parrillas include *La Rastra*, Rivadavia 348, and the very popular *El Nazareno*, at San Martín and España. *Gran Pizzería Romanella*, 25 de Mayo 866, serves standard fare. *Peperoni*, Rivadavia 619, is a fine restaurant with friendly service, featuring minutas, pasta and fish. *La Barca*, Belgrano 935, also serves seafood.

Getting There & Away

Air Aerolíneas Argentinas (☎ 0297-444-0050), 9 de Julio 870, flies frequently to Buenos Aires' Aeroparque (US$77 to US$199), sometimes via Trelew. LAPA (☎ 0297-447-2400), Rivadavia 396, flies to Aeroparque (US$79 to US$169) twice each weekday and once a day on weekends. Dinar Líneas Aéreas (☎ 0297-444-1111), Rivadavia 242, flies Sunday through Friday to Aeroparque (US$109 to US$170).

Comodoro is the hub for Patagonian carrier LADE (☎ 0297-447-6181), Rivadavia 360. Patagonian carrier TAN (☎ 0297-447-7268), España 928, flies three times weekly to Puerto Montt, Chile (US$103 to US$107). Kaikén Líneas Aéreas (☎ 0297-447-2000),

Rivadavia 240, flies to cities between Mendoza and Ushuaia.

Bus Comodoro's Terminal de Ómnibus Teniente General Ángel Solari (☎ 0297-446-7305) is at Ameghino and 25 de Mayo. There's international service to Coihaique, Chile (US$40), with Transportes Giobbi at 1 am Monday and Thursday, but reservations are advisable for these buses, which are often very full. Turibús goes to Coihaique Tuesday and Saturday at 8 am.

Sample fares include Caleta Olivia (US$4, one hour), San Julián (US$14), Trelew (US$15, six hours), Puerto Deseado (US$17, four hours), Puerto Madryn (US$20, seven hours), Los Antiguos (US$20, six hours), Esquel (US$29, eight hours), Río Gallegos (US$30, 11 hours), Viedma (US$35, 10 hours), Bahía Blanca (US$45), Bariloche (US$47, 14 hours) and Buenos Aires (US$60, 24 hours).

Getting Around
The No 8 Patagonia Argentina (Directo Palazzo) bus goes to Aeropuerto General Mosconi (☎ 0297-443-3355 interno 163) from the bus station.

MONUMENTO NATURAL BOSQUES PETRIFICADOS
In Jurassic times, 150 million years ago, vulcanism leveled this southern Patagonian area's extensive *Proaraucaria* forests and buried them in ash; later erosion exposed mineralized trees 3m in diameter and 35m long. Until legal protection, souvenir hunters regularly plundered the area; do not perpetuate this tradition for even the smallest specimen.

From RN 3, 157km south of Caleta Olivia, a gravel road leads 50km west to the park's modest headquarters. *Camping* is free at the dry creek nearby, but bring water if you have a vehicle; otherwise, the ranger *may* be able to spare some. Buses from Comodoro Rivadavia or Caleta Olivia will drop you at the junction, but you may wait several hours or more for a lift.

LOS ANTIGUOS
Aged Tehuelche Indians frequented this 'banana belt' on the south shore of Lago Buenos Aires, where rows of poplars now shelter irrigated chacras whose abundant fruit, for lack of markets, is absurdly cheap. Los Antiguos' Fiesta de la Cereza (cherry festival) lasts three days in mid-January. The nearby countryside has good fishing and hiking.

Both the tourist office and bank are on Av 11 de Julio, the main street, which runs the length of town. Local fruits (cherries, raspberries, strawberries, apples, apricots, pears, peaches, plums and prunes) are delectable. Purchase these, and homemade preserves, directly from producers – Chacra El Porvenir is within easy walking distance of Av 11 de Julio.

Places to Stay & Eat
The cypress-sheltered *Camping Municipal* (☎ 02963-491265), at the east end of Av 11 de Julio, charges US$3 per person, plus US$2.50 per tent and US$5 per vehicle. Hot showers are available from 5:30 to 10 pm. A handful of tiny cabins sleep up to six people, for US$10 per cabin.

Hotel Argentino (☎ 02963-491132), which charges US$19/35 single/double with private bath, also has excellent lunches and dinners for US$8, with desserts of local produce, and outstanding breakfasts for US$4. *El Disco*, Pallavicini 140, is a parrilla.

Getting There & Away
LADE and Pingüino serve the nearest airport, 64km east at Perito Moreno. La Unión, Alameda 451, has buses to Caleta Olivia (US$18, five hours) and Comodoro Rivadavia (US$20, six hours) at 7 am and 3:30 pm daily. Sportman, Av 11 de Julio 666, goes to Caleta and Comodoro at 4:30 pm daily.

Transportes Padilla (☎ 02963-491140), San Martín 44, and Acotrans cross the border to Chile Chico (US$3 return) several times daily. From November through March, there is Wednesday and Sunday service to El Chaltén (US$73) via RN 40 with Itinerarios y Travesías, at the same address.

ESQUEL
In the foothills of western Chubut, sunny Esquel is the gateway to Parque Nacional Los Alerces and other Andean recreation areas, and the terminus for the picturesque narrow-gauge railway from Ingeniero Jacobacci in Río Negro province. Founded at the turn of the century, the town of 23,000

is also the area's main commercial and livestock center.

Information

Esquel's well-organized Dirección Municipal de Turismo (☎ 02945-452369), at Sarmiento and Alvear, maintains a thorough list of lodging and recreation options.

Banco Nación, at Alvear and Roca, changes AmEx traveler's checks; there are several ATMs. The post office is at Alvear 1192. Unitel is at 25 de Mayo 526.

Things to See

The **Museo Indigenista**, part of the Dirección Municipal de Cultura, is at Belgrano 330. The **Estación Ferrocarril Roca**, at Brown and Roggero, is now also a museum, but travelers arriving by air or bus should still not miss the arrival of **La Trochita**, the narrow-gauge steam train (serious railway fanatics will find the town of El Maitén on the border of Río Negro province, even more interesting because of the extraordinary concentration of antique rail equipment in its workshops).

Places to Stay

Camping A site at *Autocamping La Colina* (☎ 02945-454962), Humphreys 554, costs US$3.50 per person. There are also hostel accommodations for US$8/15 single/double.

Hostels The *Hotel Argentino* (☎ 02945-452237), 25 de Mayo 862, offers backpackers floor space on an informal basis for US$3 per person. The HI affiliate, *Parador Lago Verde* (☎ 02945-452251; esquel@hostels.org.ar), Volta 1081, offers a small discount on its regular accommodations.

Casas de Familia Check the tourist office for latest listings, but try Elvey Rowlands (☎ 02945-452578) at Rivadavia 330, with rooms for US$10 per person with shared bath, or identically priced Ema Cleri (☎ 02945-452083), Alvear 1021, who has rooms with private bath. Isabel Barutta (who speaks some English) runs *Parador Lago Verde* (☎ 02945-452251), Volta 1081, and has rooms for US$15/24 with private bath.

Residenciales & Hosterías *Residencial El Cisne* (☎ 02945-452256), Chacabuco 778, costs US$12/20, while *Hostería Huentru-*

Niyeu (☎ 02945-452576), Chacabuco 606, costs US$17/22. Highly regarded *Residencial Ski* (☎ 02945-452254), San Martín 961, charges US$20/25.

Places to Eat

Confitería Atelier, 25 de Mayo and San Martín, has excellent coffee and chocolate, and is open 24 hours. *Rotisería Donna*, 25 de Mayo 559, serves a variety of inexpensive take-out dishes, along with El Bolsón's extraordinary Jauja ice cream. For a variety of empanadas, there's *La Empanadería*, Molinari 633.

Esquel has several worthwhile pizzerias, starting with *Don Pipo*, Fontana 649, *Pizzería Fitzroya*, Rivadavia 1050, and *Pizzería Dos-22*, Ameghino and Sarmiento. The best Italian choice, though, is *Trattoria Don Chiquino*, 9 de Julio 964, serving varied pasta and pizza, amid informal decor with attentive service (the owner provides puzzles to solve while you wait).

Getting There & Away

Air Austral (☎ 02945-453413), Fontana 406, flies Monday, Tuesday, Thursday, Friday and Saturday to Buenos Aires (US$165 to US$282). LADE (☎ 02945-452124), Alvear 1085, flies to Patagonian destinations.

Bus Esquel's congested bus station is at the junction of Avs Fontana and Alvear, though local authorities have projected a new terminal six blocks north.

Codao (☎ 02945-452924) runs to the nearby destinations of Trevelin (frequently, US$1.40, 30 minutes); La Balsa (Monday at 8 am, Friday at 8 am and 5 pm); and Corcovado (US$10, 4½ hours) and Carrenleufú (Sunday, Monday, Wednesday at 5 pm; Friday at 9 am).

Transportes Jacobsen (☎ 02945-453528) goes to El Maitén at 6:30 am Monday and at 6:30 pm Monday, Wednesday, Thursday and Friday; and to Cholila Tuesday and Thursday at 12:30 pm.

Transportes Esquel (☎ 02945-455059) goes to Parque Nacional Los Alerces (US$3.50 to US$8 depending on the destination), Lago Puelo/El Bolsón (US$18) and intermediate points, daily at 8 am and 2 pm, plus a 7:30 pm that goes only as far as Lago Verde; the first service combines with lake excursions. Winter schedules may differ.

Long-distance fares include El Bolsón (US$8, 2½ hours direct), Bariloche (US$15, five hours), Neuquén (US$28, eight hours), Trelew (US$28, 8½ hours), Puerto Madryn (US$30, nine hours), Comodoro Rivadavia (US$33, nine hours), Río Gallegos (US$64, 19 hours), Mendoza (US$70, 24 hours) and Buenos Aires (US$91, 30 hours).

Train Ferrocarril General Roca (☎ 02945-451403) is at Brown and Roggero. Its narrow-gauge steam train *El Trencito* or *La Trochita* has regular passenger service to El Maitén Thursday at 11 pm (US$15, 6½ hours), but it's now primarily a recreational tourist train.

Getting Around

To/From the Airport Esquel Tours, at Fontana 754, runs airport minibuses according to flight schedules at Aeropuerto Esquel, 20km east of town on RN 40.

AROUND ESQUEL
Trevelin

Only 24km south of Esquel, Trevelin is interior Chubut's only notable Welsh community. The Dirección de Turismo, Deportes y Actividades Recreativas (☎ 02945-480120), on octagonal Plaza Fontana, occasionally has discount coupons for local teahouses, the town's major attraction. The **Museo Molino Viejo**, a restored flour mill, and the **Capilla Bethel** (1910), a Welsh chapel, are landmarks.

Trevelin has a good campground, but lodging is otherwise limited. *Nain Maggie*, Perito Moreno 179, is the oldest teahouse, but *Las Mutisias*, Av San Martín 170, and *Owen See*, Molino Viejo 361, are also worth a visit. There are 11 weekday buses from Esquel (US$1.40), seven on weekends.

PARQUE NACIONAL
LOS ALERCES

West of Esquel, this spacious Andean park protects extensive stands of alerce *(Fitzroya cupressoides)*, a large (up to 60m tall and 4m in diameter) and long-lived (400 years or more) conifer of the humid Valdivian forests. Other common trees include cypress, incense cedar, southern beeches and arrayán. The *chusquea* (solid bamboo) undergrowth is almost impenetrable.

The receding glaciers of Los Alerces' peaks, which barely reach 2300m, have left nearly pristine lakes and streams, with charming vistas and excellent fishing. Westerly storms drop nearly 3m of rain annually, but summers are mild and the park's eastern zone is much drier.

Information

At the Museo y Centro de Interpretación at Villa Futalaufquen, rangers provide information from 8 am to 8 pm weekdays; on weekends, they break for lunch from 1 to 2:30 pm. Park admission is US$5.

Things to See & Do

Traditionally, the most popular excursion sails from Puerto Limonao on Lago Futalaufquen up the Río Arrayanes to Lago Verde, but dry years and low water have eliminated part of this segment. Launches from Puerto Chucao, on Lago Menéndez, cover the second segment of the trip to **El Alerzal**, an accessible stand of alerces. Outside of parks these trees are under logging pressure. Buy advance tickets for the voyage (US$55 from Limonao, US$35 from Chucao) in Esquel.

A one-hour stopover permits a hike around a loop trail that passes Lago Cisne and an attractive waterfall to end up at **El Abuelo** (The Grandfather), the finest single alerce specimen. Guides are knowledgeable, but the group can be uncomfortably large.

Places to Stay

At organized *campgrounds* at Los Maitenes, Lago Futalaufquen, Bahía Rosales, Lago Verde and Lago Rivadavia, charges are US$3 to US$5 per person per day, plus a one-time charge of US$3 per car or tent. There are free sites near some of these locations. Lago Krüger, reached by foot from Villa Futalaufquen, has a *campground* (US$5 per person) and a *refugio* (US$15 per person, US$8 with your own sleeping bag).

Cabañas Los Tepues, on Lago Futalaufquen, rents five-person cabins for US$80 per day (up to eight people). *Motel Pucón Pai* has doubles with private bath and breakfast for US$90; US$118 with half-board.

Getting There & Away

For details, see the earlier Esquel section.

RÍO GALLEGOS

In addition to servicing the wool industry, this port (population 70,000) ships coal and refines oil. Many travelers only pass through en route to El Calafate and the Moreno Glacier, Punta Arenas or Tierra del Fuego, but a day here need not be a wasted one.

Río Gallegos' two main streets, Av Julio Roca and Av San Martín, run at right angles to each other. Most sights and services are in the southwestern quadrant formed by these avenues.

Information

The energetic Subsecretaría de Turismo de la Provincia (☎ 02966-422702), Av Roca 1551, is open weekdays 9 am to 8 pm. The Dirección Municipal de Turismo maintains a Centro de Informes (☎ 02966-442159) at the bus terminal and another at Av San Martín and Av Roca.

El Pingüino, Zapiola 469, changes cash and traveler's checks (with commission). Most banks are on or near Av Roca; there are several ATMs. The post office is at Roca and San Martín. Telefax is at Av Roca 1328. The Chilean Consulate (☎ 02966-422364), Mariano Moreno 136, is open weekdays 9 am to 2 pm.

Things to See

In new quarters on Perito Ramón y Cajal, the **Museo Provincial Padre Jesús Molina** has good exhibits on geology, Tehuelche ethnology (superb photographs) and local history; it's open weekdays 10 am to 6 pm. In a metal-clad house typical of southern Patagonia, the **Museo de los Pioneros** at Elcano and Alberdi documents early immigrant life; it's open daily 3 to 8 pm.

Places to Stay

About 400m southwest of the bus terminal, at Asturias and Yugoslavia, the *Polideportivo Atsa* (☎ 02966-442310) offers camping for US$3 per person, US$3 per vehicle; showers cost US$2. There are also rooms for US$20/30 single/double.

Probably the best inexpensive lodgings are at the family-oriented *Hotel Colonial* (☎ 02966-422329), Rivadavia and Urquiza, for US$15 per person. Boxy *Hotel Ampuero* (☎ 02966-422189), Federico Sphur 38, charges US$20/30, as does *Hotel Cabo Vírgenes* (☎ 02966-422141), Rivadavia 252. *Hotel Nevada* (☎ 02966-422155), Zapiola 486, is also a good value for US$22/38. Simple but spotless, quiet, comfortable,

Hotel Covadonga (☎ 02966-420190), Av Roca 1244, charges US$29/44 with private bath; rooms with washbasin and mirror (shared bath) cost only US$18/30.

Places to Eat

Le Croissant, at Zapiola and Estrada, has attractive baked goods. *Pepino's*, Chacabuco 88, features good fast food, sandwiches and cheap draft beer. Rehabbed *Restaurant Díaz*, Av Roca 1143, has reasonable minutas.

At Av Roca 862 is the attractive and highly regarded *El Horreo*. Next door, equally appealing *Pizzería Bertolo* has indifferent service. *Peperone*, Vélez Sársfield 96, features fine pizza but careless service.

The classic atmosphere at the *Club Británico*, Roca 935, outshines the generally passable food. Comparable, at least in a historical sense, is the *Río Gallego Tennis Club*, Avellaneda 25.

Reservations are advisable at *Casa de Campo* (☎ 02966-424622), Avellaneda 275, for its elaborate afternoon tea. *Heladería Tito*, Zapiola and Corrientes, has imaginative but expensive ice cream.

Getting There & Away

Air On its transpolar flight from Ezeiza to Auckland and Sydney, Aerolíneas Argentinas (☎ 02966-422020), Av San Martín 545, makes a stopover at Río Gallegos Monday, Friday and Sunday. Aerolíneas also flies daily to Buenos Aires' Aeroparque (US$107 to US$217) via Ushuaia (US$56), and twice daily except Sunday (once only) nonstop to Aeroparque. LAPA (☎ 02966-428382), Estrada 71, flies daily to Tierra del Fuego, Bahía Blanca, Trelew and Aeroparque.

LADE (☎ 02966-422316), Fagnano 53, flies to Patagonian destinations and Tierra del Fuego, as does Kaikén Líneas Aéreas, whose agent is Tur Aike (☎ 02966-424503), Zapiola 63.

Bus Río Gallegos' bus station (☎ 02966-442159) is at RN 3 and Av Eva Perón, but some companies have convenient downtown offices.

International Several carriers go to Punta Arenas (US$20, 5½ hours). Travelers bound for northern Chile cannot board through buses from Punta Arenas here, but Terrke Potar (☎ 02966-422701), Av San Martín 565,

RÍO GALLEGOS

PLACES TO STAY
4   Hotel Ampuero
12 Hotel Nevada
17 Hotel Covadonga
21 Hotel Cabo Vírgenes
22 Hotel Colonial

PLACES TO EAT
5   Casa de Campo
8   Río Gallego Tennis Club
11 Heladería Tito
16 Le Croissant
18 Restaurant Díaz
19 Peperone
29 Club Británico
36 Pepino's
44 Pizzería Bertolo

OTHER
1   Artesanías Santacruceñas
2   Museo de los Pioneros
3   Subsecretaría de Turismo
    de la Provincia
6   Localiza
7   Servi-Car
9   Artesanías Keokén
10 Aike Lavar
13 Cambio El Pingüino
14 Telefax
16 LAPA, Quebek Tours
20 TAC
23 Migraciones

24 Chilean Consulate
25 Complejo Cultural Provincial
    (Museo Provincial Padre
    Jesús Molina)
26 Hospital Regional
27 Riestra Rent A Car
28 Museo de la Ciudad
    al Aire Libre
30 Sur Cambio, Terrke Potar
31 Aerolíneas Argentinas, Austral
32 Post Office
33 Bansud (ATM)
34 Transportes Burmeister
35 Deco Bar

37 Banco de la Nación
38 Cine Carrera
39 LADE
40 Tur Aike,
    Kaikén Líneas Aéreas,
    Chaltén Patagonia
41 Escalatur
42 La Caja de Ahorro y
    Seguro (ATM)
43 Centro de Informes
45 Banco de la Provincia
46 Museo de Arte Eduardo
    Minnicelli

Río Gallegos

Estación Ferrocarril
Yacimientos
Carboníferos
Fiscales (YCF)

Plaza
San Martín

0   100   25   200 m
0   100   200 yards

Laguna
María
La Gorda

see inset map

Plaza
San Martín

0   200   400 m
0   200   400 yards

RN
3

To Bus Station,
El Calafate

RN
3

To Tierra del Fuego

sells tickets for these routes; it's necessary to go south to the Monte Aymond border post and board the through bus there.

El Pingüino goes to Puerto Natales (US$18, six hours), Tuesday and Thursday at 11 am, while Bus Sur goes Tuesday and Thursday at 5 pm. Natales-bound travelers can also take buses to Río Turbio, where there are frequent buses across the border.

Provincial & Long-Distance Interlagos goes to El Calafate and the Moreno Glacier; Calafate-bound buses leave from the airport 30 minutes after flight arrivals, but seats may be few. Transporte Greco goes to Gobernador Gregores Tuesday and Friday at 1 pm (eight hours). Transportes Burmeister (☎ 02966-420293), San Martín 470, goes directly to El Chaltén, bypassing El Calafate, Monday, Wednesday and Friday. Chaltén Patagonia (☎ 02966-424503), Zapiola 63, does the same route.

Sample fares include San Julián (US$15, 4½ hours), Río Turbio (US$15, five hours), El Calafate (US$20, 4½ hours), Caleta Olivia (US$27, eight hours), Comodoro Rivadavia (US$31, nine hours), Trelew (US$45, 14 hours), Puerto Madryn (US$52, 15 hours) and Buenos Aires (US$70 to US$100, 40 hours).

Getting Around
To/From the Airport Cabs to or from Aeropuerto Internacional Río Gallegos cost about US$5 to US$8; to save money, share.

To/From the Bus Terminal Bus No 1 or 12 (the placard must say 'terminal') from Av Roca goes to the terminal (US$1.20).

Car Localiza (☎ 02966-424417), Sarmiento 237, rents cars for excursions to outlying places like Cabo Vírgenes.

RÍO TURBIO
Coal deposits, worked by Chilean commuters from Puerto Natales, sustain this town, which, though desolate, has a ski area. Travelers use Río Turbio for connections between Río Gallegos and Puerto Natales. The Centro de Información Turística (☎ 02902-421950), on the Plazoleta Agustín del Castillo in the center of town, is open 8 am to 8 pm weekdays.

Places to Stay & Eat
Albergue Municipal (☎ 02902-422160), at Paraje Mina 1, has four-to-a-room dormitory beds (US$10 per person); *Hotel Nazo* (☎ 02902-421800), Gobernador Moyano 100, has comfortable rooms with private bath, breakfast, telephone and cable TV for US$30/50 single/double. *El Guri*, almost directly opposite the tourist office, prepares excellent pastas (particularly ñoquis) at reasonable prices, but has many other items.

Getting There & Away
LADE (☎ 02902-421224), Av Mineros 375, flies Thursday to Río Gallegos (US$20), and Friday to El Calafate (US$20), Gobernador Gregores (US$29), Perito Moreno (US$55) and Comodoro Rivadavia (US$63).

Buses to the border are frequent, while several companies cross the steppe to Río Gallegos (US$15, six hours).

EL CALAFATE
Gradually overcoming its tourist-trap reputation, El Calafate still swarms with porteños who come to spend a few hours at the Moreno Glacier; try to avoid the January-February peak season. From May to September prices are more reasonable, but the main attractions are less accessible.

Calafate's improved Ente Municipal Calafate Turismo (Emcatur, ☎ 02902-491090), at the bus station, keeps long hours, has good information, and there's usually an English-speaker on hand.

Banco de la Provincia de Santa Cruz, Av Libertador 1285, has an erratic ATM. El Pingüino, Av Libertador 1025, also changes money, but imposes a substantial commission on traveler's checks. The post office is at Av Libertador 1133. Calafate's Cooperativa Telefónica, at Espora 194, does not allow reverse-charge calls.

Places to Stay
Camping Now fenced, the woodsy *Camping Municipal* (☎ 02902-498129), straddling Arroyo Calafate, charges US$8 per site. *Camping Los Dos Pinos* (☎ 02902-491271), at the northern end of 9 de Julio, charges US$4 per person. There are also orchard sites at *Hospedaje Jorgito* (☎ 02902-491323), Moyano 943, for the same price.

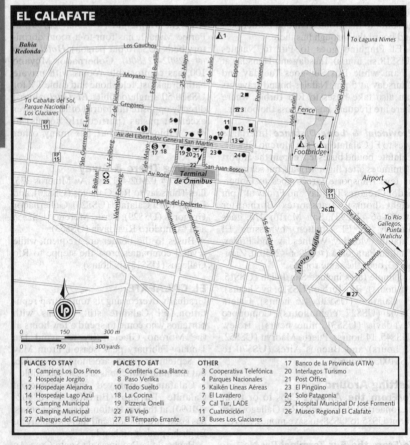

EL CALAFATE

PLACES TO STAY	PLACES TO EAT	OTHER	17 Banco de la Provincia (ATM)
1 Camping Los Dos Pinos	6 Confitería Casa Blanca	3 Cooperativa Telefónica	20 Interlagos Turismo
2 Hospedaje Jorgito	8 Paso Verlika	4 Parques Nacionales	21 Post Office
12 Hospedaje Alejandra	10 Todo Suelto	5 Kaikén Líneas Aéreas	23 El Pingüino
14 Hospedaje Lago Azul	18 La Cocina	7 El Lavadero	24 Solo Patagonia
15 Camping Municipal	19 Pizzería Onelli	9 Cal Tur, LADE	25 Hospital Municipal Dr José Formenti
16 Camping Municipal	22 Mi Viejo	11 Cuatrociclón	26 Museo Regional El Calafate
27 Albergue del Glaciar	27 El Témpano Errante	13 Buses Los Glaciares	

Hostels The HI *Albergue del Glaciar* (☎ 02902-491243), on Calle Los Pioneros, east of the arroyo, charges US$10 for members, US$12 for nonmembers, including kitchen privileges, laundry facilities and access to a spacious, comfortable common room.

Hospedajes Prices vary with the season, but the cheapest places are family inns like highly regarded *Hospedaje Alejandra* (☎ 02902-491328), Espora 60, where rooms with shared bath cost US$10 per person. Identically priced are *Hospedaje Jorgito* (☎ 02902-491323), Moyano 943, and *Hospedaje Lago Azul* (☎ 02902-491419), Perito Moreno 83.

Several readers have praised *Cabañas del Sol* (☎ 02902-491439), Av Libertador

1956, which charges US$30/34 off-season, US$35/44 in summer.

Places to Eat

Confitería Casa Blanca, Av Libertador 1202, has good pizza and reasonable beer; *Pizzería Onelli*, across the street, also has adherents. *Paso Verlika*, Av Libertador 1108, is popular and reasonably priced, especially the pizza. *Mi Viejo*, Av Libertador 1111, is a popular but pricey parrilla.

La Cocina, Av Libertador 1245, has an innovative Italian menu but stubbornly disagreeable service. *El Témpano Errante*, at the youth hostel on Los Pioneros, is worth a try even for visitors from upscale hotels.

Todo Suelto, Av Libertador 1044, prepares a dozen types of empanadas, including trout.

Getting There & Away
Air As airport facilities improve, it's likely major airlines will fly directly here. At present, though, only LADE (☎ 02902-491262), Av Libertador 1080, and Kaikén Líneas Aéreas (☎ 02902-491266), 25 de Mayo 23, serve Patagonian destinations and Tierra del Fuego.

Bus El Calafate's new bus station is on Av Roca, easily reached by a staircase from Av Libertador. Several carriers go to Río Gallegos (US$20, six hours).

Turismo Zaahj (☎ 02902-491631), along with Bus Sur, connects Calafate with Puerto Natales, Chile (US$23) daily except Monday and Thursday. Cootra (☎ 02902-491444) goes Sunday through Friday to Río Turbio (US$18) and Puerto Natales.

Daily at 7:30 am in summer, Buses Los Glaciares (☎ 02902-491158) leaves Calafate for El Chaltén (US$25, four hours) and the Fitz Roy Range. The return service leaves El Chaltén at 5 pm. Cal Tur (☎ 02902-491842) goes to Chaltén half an hour earlier, while Chaltén Travel (☎ 02902-491833) leaves at 8 am. Winter schedules may differ.

PARQUE NACIONAL LOS GLACIARES
Over millennia, Andean snowfields have recrystallized into ice and flowed eastward toward Lago Argentino and Lago Viedma, which in turn feed the Río Santa Cruz, southern Patagonia's largest river. The centerpiece of this conjunction of ice, rock and water is the **Moreno Glacier**, one of the earth's few advancing icefields.

This 60m-high river of ice periodically but erratically dams the Brazo Rico (Rico Arm) of Lago Argentino, so that the ice can no longer support the weight of the rising water and the dam virtually explodes. The dam hasn't formed since 1988, but even in ordinary years, huge icebergs calve and topple into the Canal de los Témpanos (Iceberg Channel). From a series of catwalks and platforms you can see, hear and photograph the glacier safely, but descending to the shores of the canal is now prohibited.

Launches from Puerto Bandera, 45km west of El Calafate, visit the massive **Upsala**

Glacier; many recommend this trip for the hike to iceberg-choked Lago Onelli. It's possible to camp and return to Puerto Bandera another day.

Places to Stay
On Península Magallanes, en route to the glacier, *Camping Río Mitre* and *Camping Bahía Escondida* charge US$5 per person. About 3km east of Bahía Escondida, *Camping Correntoso* is free but dirty; backpackers can camp two nights near the ranger station at the glacier.

Getting There & Away
Calafate operators visit the Moreno (US$25 to US$30) and Upsala (US$55) glaciers, but brief tours can be unsatisfactory if inclement weather limits visibility. Interlagos has English-speaking guides. Park admission is US$5.

CERRO FITZROY
Once a desolate collection of pseudo-chalets pummeled by the almost incessant wind, El Chaltén is becoming a village rather than just a bureaucratic outpost seemingly airlifted onto the exposed floodplain of the Río de las Vueltas. It's a mecca for hikers, climbers and campers, and a more agreeable place to stay than El Calafate.

One popular hike goes to Laguna Torre and the base camp for skilled technical climbers attempting the spire of Cerro Torre (3128m). Another climbs steeply from the park campground to a signed junction, where a lateral leads to backcountry campsites at Laguna Capri. The main trail continues gently to Río Blanco, base camp for climbing Cerro Fitz Roy, and then very steeply to Laguna de los Tres, a tarn named for three members of the French expedition that first climbed it.

Places to Stay & Eat
Parques Nacionales' free *Camping Madsen* has running water and abundant firewood, but no toilets – you must dig a latrine. If you don't mind walking about 10 minutes, shower at friendly *Confitería La Senyera* for about US$1; after drying off, try their enormous portions of chocolate cake and other snacks. Other campgrounds charge from US$6 to US$8 per person.

Albergue Los Ñires (☎ 02962-93009) is a small (eight-bed) hostel that charges US$10 per person or US$5 per person for camping. The larger but homier Dutch-Argentine **Albergue Patagonia** (☎ 0292-493019; chal ten1@hostels.org.ar) charges US$12, plus US$2 for kitchen privileges; reasonable meals are also available. Beds at the spacious new **Rancho Grande Hostel** (☎/fax 02962-493005; , rancho@cvtci.com.ar) cost US$10 for HI members, slightly more for nonmembers.

Josh Aike has drawn praise for its pizzas, desserts and breakfasts, but the best place to eat is **Ruca Mahuida**, part of the eponymous campground, which has creative cuisine in a tobacco-free environment. **La Casita** comes recommended by locals, but the food can't match Ruca Mahuida and the smoke-laden atmosphere is lethal.

Getting There & Away

Most buses stop at The Wall restaurant. There are several daily to El Calafate between 5 and 6 pm, and direct service to Río Gallegos with Transportes Burmeister.

In summer Itinerarios y Travesías (☎ 011-4302-9533 in Buenos Aires), based at Albergue Patagonia, operates twice-weekly minibus service on RN 40 to the small agricultural town of Perito Moreno and to Los Antiguos, including a 2½-hour stopover at Cueva de las Manos (US$92, 18 hours elapsed time).

Tierra del Fuego

Over half of Isla Grande de Tierra del Fuego, and much of the surrounding archipelago, belongs to Chile. For details of Chilean towns, see the Chile chapter.

History

Early European navigators feared and detested the stiff westerlies, hazardous currents and violent seas that impeded their progress toward Asia. None had any serious interest in this remote area, whose indigenous peoples were mobile hunter-gatherers.

The Ona (Selknam) and Haush subsisted on terrestrial animals like the guanaco, while Yahgans and Alacalufes ('Canoe Indians') lived on fish, shellfish and marine mammals. Despite inclement weather, they used little

TIERRA DEL FUEGO

TIERRA DEL FUEGO

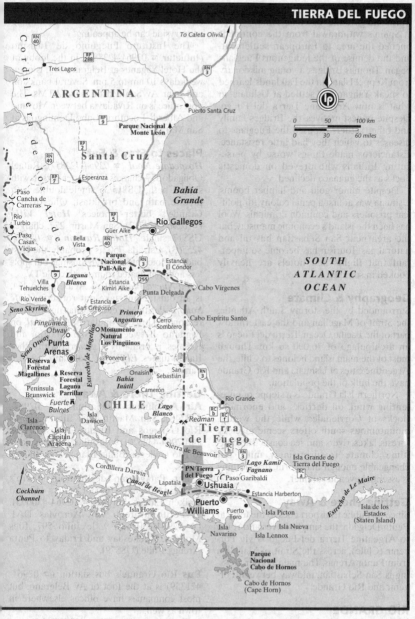

or no clothing, but constant fires kept them warm and gave the region its name.

Spain's withdrawal from the continent opened the area to European settlement, and the demise of the indigenous Fuegians began. Thomas Bridges, a young missionary from Keppel Island in the Falklands, learned to speak Yahgan and settled at Ushuaia, in what is now Argentine Tierra del Fuego. Despite honest motives, the Bridges family and other settlers exposed the Fuegians to diseases to which they had little resistance. Estancieros made things worse by persecuting Indians who preyed on domestic flocks as the guanaco declined.

Despite minor gold and lumber booms, Ushuaia was at first a penal colony for political prisoners and common criminals. Wool has been the island's economic mainstay, but the area near San Sebastián has oil and natural gas. Tourism has become so important that flights and hotels are heavily booked in summer.

Geography & Climate

Surrounded by the stormy South Atlantic, the Strait of Magellan and the easternmost part of the Pacific Ocean, Tierra del Fuego is an archipelago of 76,000 sq km. Though most of the main island belongs to Chile, the Argentine cities of Ushuaia and Río Grande have the bulk of the population.

Northern Isla Grande is a steppe of unrelenting wind, oil derricks and enormous flocks of Corriedales, while the wetter, mountainous south offers scenic glaciers, forests, lakes, rivers and sea coasts. The maritime climate is surprisingly mild, but changeable enough that warm, dry clothing is essential even in summer.

Getting There & Away

Since no public transport goes to the ferry at Punta Delgada, the simplest overland route to Argentine Tierra del Fuego is via Porvenir (Chile), across the Strait of Magellan from Punta Arenas. The main border crossing is San Sebastián, midway between Porvenir and Río Grande.

RÍO GRANDE

Río Grande, a windswept wool and petroleum service center facing the open South Atlantic, is making a genuine effort to beautify and improve itself, but still has a long way to go. Most visitors pass through quickly en route to Ushuaia, but the surrounding countryside can be appealing.

The Instituto Fueguino de Turismo (Infuetur, ☎ 02964-422887), in the lobby of the Hotel Yaganes at Belgrano 319, is open weekdays 10 am to 5 pm. Several banks on and near Av San Martín have ATMs. The post office is on Rivadavia between Moyano and Alberdi. Locutorio Cabo Domingo is at San Martín 458.

Places to Stay & Eat

Hospedaje Noal (☎ 02964-422857), Rafael Obligado 557, charges US$13 per person with shared bath, US$15/35 single/double with private bath and breakfast. One of Río Grande's better choices, **Hotel Villa** *(☎ 02964-422312)*, San Martín 277, charges US$17 single. **Hotel Rawson** *(☎ 02964-425503)*, Estrada 750, is probably the best budget choice, at US$18/28 for small but spotless and well-heated rooms with cable TV.

La Nueva Piamontesa, Av Belgrano 464, is an outstanding take-out rotisería. *Café Sonora*, Perito Moreno 705, has fine pizza at reasonable prices. Popular *La Colonial*, on Fagnano between Av San Martín and Rosales, is primarily a pizzería with other Italian dishes. *El Portal*, Belgrano 383, is a parrilla.

Getting There & Away

Air Aerolíneas Argentinas (☎ 02964-422748), San Martín 607, flies daily to Río Gallegos and Buenos Aires. LAPA (☎ 02964-432620), 9 de Julio 747, flies daily to Río Gallegos, Bahía Blanca and Buenos Aires.

For Patagonian destinations, there's LADE (☎ 02964-421651), Lasserre 447, and Kaikén Líneas Aéreas (☎ 02964-430665), at Perito Moreno 937. Aerovías DAP (☎ 02964-430249), 9 de Julio 597, flies Monday, Wednesday and Friday to Punta Arenas, Chile (US$79).

Bus Río Grande's bus station (☎ 02964-421339) is at the foot of Av Belgrano, but most companies have offices elsewhere in town as well.

Tecni-Austral (☎ 02964-422620), Moyano 516, goes to Ushuaia daily (US$21) at 7:30 am and 6 pm, and also to Punta Arenas Monday, Wednesday and Friday at 11:30 am.

It also sells tickets for Transporte Gesell (☎ 02964-421339), which goes Wednesday and Saturday at 8 am to Porvenir (US$25, seven hours) in Chilean Tierra del Fuego, meeting the ferry to Punta Arenas. Buses Pacheco (☎ 02964-423382) goes to Punta Arenas (US$30) Tuesday, Thursday and Saturday at 7:30 am.

AROUND RÍO GRANDE

The missionary order that proselytized local Indians established the **Museo Salesiano**, 11km north of town on Ruta 3, which has exhibits on geology, natural history and ethnography. **Lago Fagnano** (also known by its Oma/Yahgan name, Kami), the huge glacial trough on RN 3 between Río Grande and Ushuaia, merits a visit. Singles at *Hostería Kaikén* (☎ 02964-492208) cost US$10 to US$15.

USHUAIA

Over the past two decades, fast-growing Ushuaia has evolved from a village into a homely city of 42,000, but the setting is still one of the most dramatic in the world, with jagged glacial peaks rising from sea level to nearly 1500m. The surrounding area offers hiking, fishing and skiing, and the chance to go as far south as highways go: RN 3 ends at Bahía Lapataia, 3242km from Buenos Aires.

In 1870 the British-based South American Missionary Society based itself here, but only artifacts, middens and memories remain of its Yahgan neophytes. Argentina incarcerated notorious criminals and political prisoners at Ushuaia until 1947, when it became a key naval base and, gradually, a tourist destination. Forestry, fishing and electronics assembly have become significant.

Shoreline Av Maipú leads west to Parque Nacional Tierra del Fuego. One block north is parallel Av San Martín, the main commercial street.

Information

The municipal Dirección de Turismo (☎ 02901-424550), Av San Martín 660, keeps a complete list of accommodations and current prices, assists in finding a room with private families, and posts a list of available accommodations after closing time. The friendly, patient and helpful staff usually includes an English-speaker. Hours are weekdays 8 am to 9 pm, weekends and holidays 9 am to 8 pm.

Several banks have ATMs; the best bet for traveler's checks (2% commission) is Banco de la Provincia, San Martín 396. CrediSol, on San Martín between Rosas and 9 de Julio, takes 5%. The post office is at Av San Martín and Godoy. Locutorio Cabo de Hornos is at 25 de Mayo 112. The Oficina Antarctica Infuetur (antartida@tierradel fuego.ml.org), on the Muelle Comercial, has inexpensive email services.

Chile's consulate (☎ 02901-422177), Malvinas Argentinas 236, is open weekdays 9:30 am to 1 pm.

Things to See & Do

At Maipú and Rivadavia, the **Museo Territorial Fin del Mundo** (admission US$5) has exhibits on natural history, Indian life and early penal colonies, and re-creations of an early general store and bank. It's open 10 am to 1 pm and 3 to 8 pm Monday through Saturday in summer, 4 to 8 pm the rest of the year.

Closed as a penal institution since 1947, the former Presidio de Ushuaia, now the **Museo Marítimo,** held as many as 600 inmates in 380 cells designed for one prisoner each. Open 10 am to 1 pm and 4 to 8 pm daily, it charges US$5 admission; use the entrance at Yaganes and Gobernador Paz rather than the military entrance at Yaganes and San Martín.

A magnificent walk to **Martial Glacier** starts at the west end of San Martín, climbing the zigzag road (with hiker short cuts) to a ski run 7km northwest of town. About two hours from the base of the lift, the glacier yields awesome views of Ushuaia and the Beagle Channel. There are several buses daily from Av Maipú.

Places to Stay

Camping Ushuaia's inexpensive *Camping Municipal*, 8km west of town on RN 3, has minimal facilities. The *Camping del Rugby Club Ushuaia*, 5km west of town, charges US$5 per person for reasonable facilities. Far more central but still a steep uphill walk, *La Pista del Andino* (cellular ☎ 0266-296-8626), Alem 2873, charges US$5 per person. It has a bar/restaurant with good atmosphere (you can also crash in the refugio upstairs), but could do with a few more

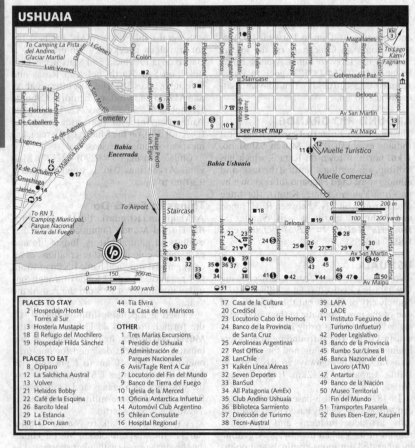

USHUAIA

PLACES TO STAY	44 Tía Elvira	17 Casa de la Cultura	39 LAPA
2 Hospedaje/Hostel Torres al Sur	48 La Casa de los Mariscos	20 CrediSol	40 LADE
3 Hostería Mustapic		23 Locutorio Cabo de Hornos	41 Instituto Fueguino de Turismo (Infuetur)
18 El Refugio del Mochilero	OTHER	24 Banco de la Provincia de Santa Cruz	42 Poder Legislativo
19 Hospedaje Hilda Sánchez	1 Tres Marías Excursions	25 Aerolíneas Argentinas	43 Banco de la Provincia
	4 Presidio de Ushuaia	27 Post Office	45 Rumbo Sur/Línea B
PLACES TO EAT	5 Administración de Parques Nacionales	9 LanChile	46 Banca Nazionale del Lavoro (ATM)
8 Opíparo	6 Avis/Tagle Rent A Car	31 Kaikén Línea Aéreas	47 Antartur
12 La Salchicha Austral	9 Locutorio del Fin del Mundo	33 BanSud	49 Banco de la Nación
13 Volver	10 Banco de Tierra del Fuego	35 All Patagonia (AmEx)	50 Museo Territorial Fin del Mundo
21 Helados Bobby	10 Iglesia de la Merced	35 Club Andino Ushuaia	51 Transportes Pasarela
22 Café de la Esquina	11 Oficina Antarctica Infuetur	36 Biblioteca Sarmiento	52 Buses Eben-Ezer, Kaupén
26 Barcito Ideal	14 Automóvil Club Argentino	37 Dirección de Turismo	
29 La Estancia	15 Chilean Consulate	38 Tecni-Austral	
30 La Don Juan	16 Hospital Regional		

showers and toilets. They offer free transport to the campground on your arrival in Ushuaia.

Hostels The HI affiliate, highly regarded *Torres al Sur Hostel* (☎ 02901-430745; *ushuaia@hostels.org.ar*), Gobernador Paz 1437, charges US$10 in low season, US$12 in summer. Deservedly popular *El Refugio del Mochilero* (☎ 02901-436129), 25 de Mayo 241, is not an HI affiliate, but has excellent facilities and great ambience for US$13 per person.

Casas de Familia The Dirección de Turismo arranges accommodations in private homes, but usually only in peak season. Prices are around US$20 per person, sometimes slightly cheaper.

Hospedajes & Hosterías The *Hospedaje Torres al Sur* (☎ 02901-430745; see Hostels, above), Gobernador Paz 1437, charges $15 single for non-hostellers. The Dirección de Turismo discourages visitors from *Hospedaje Hilda Sánchez* (☎ 02901-423622), Deloquí 391, but many travelers have found her place congenial, if crowded and a bit noisy at times. Rates are US$15 per person, and it's open all year.

Hostería Mustapic (☎ 02901-421718), Piedrabuena 230, charges US$25/40 for singles/doubles with shared bath, US$35/50 with private bath.

Places to Eat

On the waterfront, informal *La Salchicha Austral* is among the most reasonable places in town. *Opíparo*, Maipú 1255, specializes in varied, moderately priced pizza and pasta. The US$10 tenedor libre at lively *Barcito Ideal*, Av San Martín 393, is no bargain, but some travelers making it their only meal of the day find it a good choice.

La Don Juan, San Martín 193, is Ushuaia's main parrilla, but *La Estancia*, on San Martín between Godoy and Rivadavia, offers some competition. *La Casa de los Mariscos*, San Martín 232, specializes in fish and shellfish, most notably crab. *Tía Elvira*, Maipú 349, also has a good reputation for seafood, along with *Volver*, Maipú 37.

Café de la Esquina, San Martín 601, is Ushuaia's most popular confitería. *Helados Bobby*, San Martín 621, features deliciously unusual ice cream flavors like rhubarb and calafate.

Getting There & Away

Air Aerolíneas Argentinas (☎ 02901-421091), Roca 116, flies at least twice daily to Buenos Aires' Aeroparque (US$147 to US$252). LAPA (☎ 02901-422150), 25 de Mayo 64, flies daily to Aeroparque (US$149 to US$245) via Trelew, sometimes with a stop in Río Gallegos.

For Patagonian destinations, try LADE (☎ 02901-421123), in the Galería Albatros at Av San Martín 564, and Kaikén Líneas Aéreas (☎ 02901-432963), San Martín 880, which goes as far north as Mendoza.

LanChile (☎ 02901-431110), Godoy 169, flies to Punta Arenas (US$100), with connections to northern Chile, in summer only, as do Kaikén and (sometimes) Aerovías DAP, which primarily flies out of Río Grande.

Bus Tecni-Austral (☎/fax 02901-423396), in the Galería del Jardín at 25 de Mayo 50, goes to Río Grande (US$21, four hours) at 7:30 am and 6 pm daily. The Monday, Wednesday and Friday morning services continue to Punta Arenas (US$51, 14 hours).

Boat The 12-passenger *Piratur* makes the crossing between Puerto Almanza, east of Ushuaia near historic Estancia Harberton, to Puerto Williams, across the Beagle Channel in Chile. Large enough to carry a few bicycles, the *Piratur* (☎ 02901-423875) has an office at the Muelle Turístico, where it connects to Puerto Almanza by bus. Ferry service may soon commence from Almanza to Puerto Williams.

PARQUE NACIONAL TIERRA DEL FUEGO

Argentina's first coastal national park, 18km west of Ushuaia, extends north from the Beagle Channel to encompass rivers, lakes, forests and glaciers beyond Lago Fagnano. Southern beeches like the evergreen coihue and deciduous lenga thrive on heavy coastal rainfall, and the deciduous ñire tints the hillsides in autumn. Sphagnum peat bogs on the self-guided nature trail at Laguna Negra support ferns, wildflowers, and insectivorous plants. Marine mammals are most common on offshore islands.

Inland, there are guanacos and foxes, but visitors are most likely to see two unfortunate introductions: the European rabbit and the North American beaver. The Andean condor and the maritime black-browed albatross overlap ranges on the coast, but neither is common. Shore birds such as cormorants, gulls, terns, oystercatchers, grebes, steamer ducks and kelp geese are common. The large, striking upland goose *(cauquén)* is common inland.

Park admission is US$5.

Trekking

It's possible to hike from Lapataia along the north shore of Lago Roca to the Chilean border, but authorities have inexplicably closed the upper Río Pipo toward Lago Kami/Fagnano, the park's best trekking area.

Places to Stay

The only campground with hot showers is *Camping Lago Roca*, which charges US$5 per person and also has a *confitería* and a small grocery. *Camping Las Bandurrias*, *Camping Laguna Verde* and *Camping Los Cauquenes* are improved and improving sites charging US$1 to US$2 per person, while *Camping Ensenada* and *Camping Río Pipo* are free sites that, unfortunately, can be disgracefully filthy.

Getting There & Away

Several bus companies charge US$10 return from Ushuaia. In summer, Transporte Pasarela leaves from the YPF station at Av Maipú and Fadul six times daily. Buses Eben-Ezer leaves from Maipú and 25 de Mayo five times daily, while Kaupén leaves the same location seven times daily.

Bolivia

Bolivia is the Tibet of the Americas – the highest and most isolated of the Latin American republics. A landlocked country lying astride the widest stretch of the Andean Cordillera, Bolivia spills through a maze of torturous hills and valleys into the vast forests and savannas of the Amazon and Paraná basins, its geographical and climatic zones ranging from snowcapped peaks to vast, low-lying grasslands and jungles. With two major indigenous groups and several smaller ones, Bolivia is also the most Indian country on the South American continent. More than 50% of the population are of pure Amerindian blood, and many people maintain traditional cultural values and belief systems.

Bolivia has certainly had a turbulent and explosive history, but nowadays its image as a haunt of revolutionaries and drug barons is greatly overstated. The country combines unimaginable landscapes, colonial treasures, colorful indigenous cultures and remnants of mysterious ancient civilizations; and despite its former political strife and problematic drug trade, it remains one of South America's most peaceful, secure and inviting countries. These, together with its natural beauty and cultural wealth, makes Bolivia ideal for independent adventuring.

Facts about Bolivia

HISTORY
Pre-Columbian Times

There's much speculation about humanity's earliest history in Bolivia. It's certain that early advances toward agricultural civilization took place on the altiplano.

From about 1500 BC, Aymara-speaking Indians, possibly from the mountains of what is now central Peru, swept across into the Bolivian Andes to occupy the altiplano. The years between about 500 AD and 900 AD were marked by the imperial expansion and increasing power and influence of the new Tiahuanaco (or Tiwanaku) culture. The society's ceremonial center (also known as Tiahuanaco), near Lake Titicaca, grew and

At a Glance

Country Name	República de Bolivia
Area	1,098,580 sq km
Population	7,826,352 (1998 estimate)
Population Density	7.12 per sq km
Capitals	La Paz & Sucre
Head of State	Hugo Banzer Suárez
Official Language	Spanish
Other Languages	Quechua, Aymara
Currency	Boliviano (B$)
Exchange Rate	US$1 = B$5.75
Per Capita GNP	US$3000
Inflation Rate	6.8% (1997-98)

prospered, developing into the religious and political center of the altiplano.

Around the 9th century AD however, Tiahuanaco's power waned and its civilization declined. One theory attributes this decline to a drop in the level of Lake Titicaca that left the lakeside settlement far from shore. Another theory postulates that Tiahuanaco was attacked and its population massacred by the warlike Kollas (or Collas), also known as Aymara, from the west. Finely made Tiahuanaco artifacts are displayed in museums around the country.

Before the Spanish conquest, the Bolivian altiplano had been incorporated into the Inca empire as the southern province of Kollasuyo. The Quechua-speaking Indians around Lake Titicaca today are descended from those who immigrated under an Inca policy of populating newly conquered colonies with Quechua-speaking tribes.

Spanish Conquest

By the late 1520s, internal rivalries had begun to take their toll on the Inca empire. It was the arrival of the Spaniards, first thought to be emissaries of the Inca sun god, however, that dealt the final blow. The Inca emperor Atahualpa was captured in 1532, and by 1537, the Spanish had consolidated their forces in Peru and securely held Cuzco (the seat of Inca power).

After the fall of the Inca empire, Alto Perú, as the Spaniards called Bolivia, fell briefly into the possession of the conquistador Diego de Almagro. Francisco Pizarro dispatched his brother, Gonzalo, to head an expedition to subdue the southern province of Kollasuyo. The Pizarros were, no doubt, attracted by the prospect of silver mines that had been worked in Inca times. Gonzalo Pizarro organized the Charcas administrative unit in what is now central Bolivia and there, in 1538, Pedro de Anzures founded the township of La Plata. La Plata later changed its name to Chuquisaca, and then to its present name, Sucre. It soon grew into the administrative, religious and educational center of the eastern Spanish territories.

In 1545, vast deposits of silver were discovered in Potosí which quickly gained prominence due to the abundant, high-quality ores. Before long, the settlement had grown into the largest city on the continent – but not without cost. The atrocious conditions in the Potosí mines led to the deaths of perhaps 8 million Indian and African slaves.

In 1548, Alonso de Mendoza founded the city of La Paz on the main silver route from Potosí to the Pacific coast, where it served as a staging post and administrative center. In 1574, the Spaniards founded Cochabamba, which soon became the granary of Bolivia, and Tarija, which served to contain the uncooperative Chiriguano Indians. Thus, at the close of the 16th century, Bolivia's settlement patterns had been established within the realm of Spain's South American empire.

Independence

In 1781, a futile attempt was made to expel the Spaniards and reestablish the Inca empire. Three decades later, in May 1809, Chuquisaca (Sucre) became the scene of an overt call for independence, and a local government was established. From Chuquisaca, one of the most fertile centers of liberal thinking on the continent, advanced political doctrines radiated throughout Spanish America.

In 1824, after 15 years of war, the liberation of Peru from Spanish domination was finally won in the battles of Junín and Ayacucho. However, in Alto Perú (Bolivia), the royalist general Pedro Antonio de Olañeta still opposed the liberating forces. In 1825, when offers of negotiation failed, Simón Bolívar dispatched an expeditionary force to Alto Perú under General Antonio José de Sucre. With the defeat of Olañeta at the battle of Tumusla, resistance came to an end. On August 6, 1825, independence was proclaimed, and Alto Perú became the Republic of Bolivia. Bolívar and Sucre, incidentally, became the first and second presidents of the new republic.

In 1828, Andrés de Santa Cruz (who had a Spanish father and an Indian mother) took power and in 1836, influenced by romantic attachments to Inca ideals, formed a confederacy with Peru. This triggered a protest by Chile, whose army defeated Santa Cruz in 1839, breaking the confederation and submerging Bolivia in political chaos. The confusion peaked in 1841, when three different governments claimed power simultaneously.

The pattern of spontaneous and unsanctioned changes of government took root at this time and continued through the 1980s in a series of coups and military interventions. One military junta after another usurped power from its predecessor; as of 1992, Bolivia had endured 188 changes of government in its 167 years as a republic. With such internal strife, it is not surprising that external affairs haven't always run smoothly either.

Loss of Territory

By the mid-19th century, the discovery of rich deposits of guano and nitrates in the

Llama at Machu Picchu, Peru

MICHAEL J PETTYPOOL

Man on the street, Santiago, Chile

ROBERT FRIED

Paseo de la República, Lima, Peru

ROBERT FRIED

Homestyle barbecueing at a Buenos Aires *parrilla*, Argentina

DAVE G HOUSER

Isla Isabela blossom, Galápagos Islands

These iguanas' eyes are smiling, Galápagos Islands

Andean condor, Chile

Red and blue macaws, Manu, Peru

Atacama region changed a desolate and sparsely populated desert into an economically strategic area. As Bolivia lacked the population and resources to settle, develop and exploit its coastal area, it contracted Chilean companies to carry out development projects. In 1879, when the Bolivian government proposed a tax on the minerals, Chile occupied Bolivia's Litoral department, prompting Bolivia and Peru to declare war on Chile.

Between 1879 and 1883, in the War of the Pacific, Chile took 350km of coastline, leaving Bolivia with no outlet to the sea. Though Chile tried to compensate Bolivia with a railway from Antofagasta to Oruro and duty-free facilities for the export of Bolivian commodities, Bolivians refused to accept their *enclaustramiento* (landlocked status) and have taken every opportunity to voice their demand for access to the sea. Even now, the government uses the issue as a rallying cry whenever it wants to unite the people in a common cause.

Bolivia's next loss was in 1903, when Brazil annexed some 100,000 sq km of the Acre region, which stretched from Bolivia's present Amazonian border to halfway up Peru's eastern border. The reason this time was rubber. Centered in Manaus (Brazil), the rubber boom took off in the second half of the 19th century and by 1890 accounted for 10% of Brazil's export earnings. Bolivia participated in the boom by plundering the

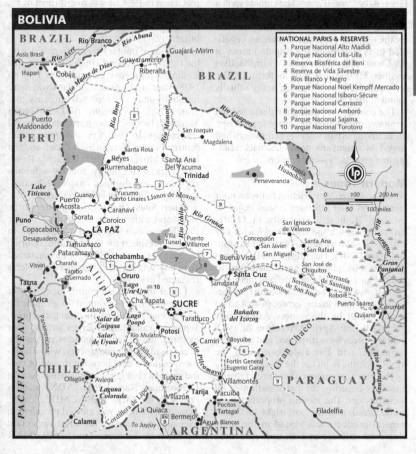

BOLIVIA

NATIONAL PARKS & RESERVES
1. Parque Nacional Alto Madidi
2. Parque Nacional Ulla-Ulla
3. Reserva Biosférica del Beni
4. Reserva de Vida Silvestre
   Ríos Blanco y Negro
5. Parque Nacional Noel Kempff Mercado
6. Parque Nacional Isiboro-Sécure
7. Parque Nacional Carrasco
8. Parque Nacional Amboró
9. Parque Nacional Sajama
10. Parque Nacional Torotoro

forests of the Acre, until Brazil eventually engineered a dispute over sovereignty, and the Brazilian army was sent in.

Between 1932 and 1935, Bolivia fought a third devastating war, this time against Paraguay for control of the Chaco region. This area had previously been of little interest to either country, as it had very limited agricultural potential and was inhabited only by a few indigenous tribes.

The trouble started when North American and European oil companies began to speculate about potential oil deposits in the area. In a bid to secure favorable franchises, a quarrel was engineered, with Standard Oil supporting Bolivia and Shell siding with Paraguay. Although Bolivia had more soldiers, fighting conditions in the Chaco favored the Paraguayans. The climate took a heavy toll on the highland Indian troops of Bolivia, and Bolivia was gradually beaten. By the terms of the peace settlement negotiated in 1938, most of the disputed areas of the Chaco went to Paraguay, costing Bolivia another 225,000 sq km of its territory. The anticipated oil reserves were never actually found in the Chaco.

The conflict with Paraguay disrupted the economy, discredited the army, spread new ideas among urban workers and miners, and sowed discontent among intellectuals, resulting in a process of social ferment.

Modern Times

After the Chaco War, friction between poor miners and their absentee bosses began to escalate. Radicals, especially in Oruro, gathered beneath the banner of Victor Paz Estenssoro's Movimiento Nacional Revolucionario (MNR). The presidential elections of 1951 took place in an atmosphere of general unrest and finally brought victory to Paz Estenssoro, but a military coup that prevented him from taking power provoked an armed revolt by the miners. After heavy fighting in the April Revolution of 1952, military forces were dispersed and forced to capitulate, and Paz Estenssoro and the MNR took the helm for the first time.

The new government announced reforms aimed at ensuring the participation of all social sectors. The mining properties were nationalized, and the sole right to export mineral products was vested in the state. Universal suffrage and an unprecedented policy of agrarian and educational reform were introduced, including a redistribution of estates among peasants and the restructuring of the educational system to provide elementary schooling for everyone.

For the first time since the Spanish conquest, indigenous people felt that they had a voice in the Bolivian government. The MNR government lasted 12 years under various presidents; Paz Estenssoro himself returned to power in 1960 and was reelected again in 1964.

The party, however, was unable to substantially raise the standard of living or increase food production, and Paz Estenssoro was forced to become more and more autocratic as dissension in his own ranks increased. Shortly after Paz Estenssoro's reelection in 1964, he was overthrown by his vice president, General René Barrientos, plunging Bolivia into renewed political instability.

A series of military regimes ensued, with the right-wing general Hugo Banzer Suárez leading a repressive regime from 1971 to 1978. After elections in 1978, there was more instability and more repressive military governments – the regime of Luis García Mendez (1980-82) was particularly brutal and corrupt. In 1982 a civilian government returned under Hernán Siles Zuazo and the left-wing Movimiento de la Izquierda Revolucionaria (MIR), but the country suffered a period of labor disputes, monetary devaluation and a staggering inflation rate.

When Siles Zuazo gave up after three years and called general elections, Victor Paz Estenssoro returned to politics to become president for the third time. During his four-year term (1985-89), the shattered economy was revived, but social problems remained unsolved.

Under the Bolivian constitution, 50% of the popular vote is required for a candidate to become president in direct elections. When no candidate emerges with a clear majority, the Bolivian congress makes the decision, usually in conjunction with a backroom coalition deal between the major candidates. In 1989, the right-wing Acción Democrática Nacionalista (ADN) made a deal with the MIR, and the MIR's leader, Jaime Paz Zamora, was elected president in exchange for leaving the most important ministries to the opposition. In 1993, MNR leader Gonzalo Sánchez de Lozada ('Goni'), won the greatest number of votes, but had to form an alliance with an Indian party to secure the presidency. He embarked on an ambitious program of privatization of state industries, notable because much of the proceeds of the sales have been vested in a public pension program. The new economic policies were accompanied by protests and strikes, while antidrug programs sparked more unrest.

In the 1997 presidential elections, Hugo Banzer and his rightist ADN party won just 23% of the vote, but a coalition with other parties saw Banzer become president. Partly because of pressure from the International Monetary Fund, economic reforms have continued, the currency has stabilized and more major industries, including telecommunications, airlines, and the petroleum industry, are set to be privatized (or 'capitalized' as they say in Bolivia).

The GDP grew steadily in the 1990s, and the foreign debt has been brought under control, but Bolivia is still the poorest country in South America. It remains to be seen how Bolivia will cope with effects of the Asian economic meltdown, and whether enough economic progress can be made to contain social unrest.

Coca, Cocaine & the Drug War

From time immemorial, coca has been part of Bolivian culture. The Inca love goddess was represented with coca leaves in her hands, and legend has it that Manco Capac, the son of the sun god, brought the divine coca leaf, which alleviates hunger and strengthens the feeble. At first, the use of coca was restricted to privileged families and religious ceremonies, but by the time of the Spanish conquest it was widespread among Indians, sustaining them through prolonged periods of exhausting labor under severe conditions.

When coca leaves are chewed with a catalyst (usually the ashes of other plants, mainly quinoa), the juices extracted give a high degree of insensitivity to hunger, cold, fatigue and pain and indifference toward hardship and anxiety. The Spaniards soon learned that coca was a perfect stimulant to increase the output of Indian labor and promoted its use. The first commercial plantations were in the Yungas, which is still the

country's leading coca producer. The success of La Paz as a city was partly due to the traffic of coca from the Yungas to the Potosí mines.

The alkaloid drug extracted from coca leaves has been refined and used widely as a stimulant and topical anesthetic. Numerous 19th-century patent medicines, as well as Coca-Cola, were based on coca, while synthetic versions are still used in products such as medical anesthetics and hemorrhoid creams. When coca derivatives like cocaine became popular recreational drugs, especially in the USA, demand grew hugely for Bolivian coca leaves. Today, at least 50,000 hectares are cultivated, with most of the leaf refined into coca paste and taken to other Latin American countries for processing. Much of the workforce, perhaps 30%, is involved in illicit coca production and trafficking, and they bring a large amount of foreign revenue into the country – estimates vary from US$350 to US$700 million per year. The trade has resulted in widespread corruption, social problems and foreign interference in the country's affairs.

As early as 1987, the USA sent Drug Enforcement Agency (DEA) squadrons into the Beni and Chapare regions of northern Bolivia to 'assist' in coca eradication. Instead of eliminating the trade, however, the US eradication program brought about the organization of powerful and vociferous peasant unions and interest groups. With lax enforcement, corruption and skyrocketing profit potential, the program actually resulted in an increase in cocaine production.

By 1995, the USA had grown impatient, and set a deadline of June 30th for the eradication of nearly 2000 hectares of coca in the Chapare and an additional 3500 hectares by the end of the year. It also demanded Bolivia's signature on an extradition treaty that would send drug traffickers to trial in the USA. If Bolivia refused or failed, US loans, aid and funding would be cut off.

In April, a geographically challenged US Congressman, Dan Burton, suggested the USA spray the Bolivian coca crop with herbicides dropped by planes based on ships 'off the Bolivian coast.' After the laughter subsided, protests were launched against the US and Bolivian governments for ever suggesting such a thing and the Coca Leaf Growers Association again pointed out that

BOLIVIA

the problem lay not with Bolivian coca growers, but with a burgeoning US market for cocaine.

Bolivia met the June 30 deadline by paying farmers US$2500 for each hectare destroyed, which placed a heavy strain on government resources. Of course, this also created an incentive to plant more coca, and as the eradication campaign intensifies in one area, coca cultivation is started up in new ones.

In August 1995, the Bolivian government rejected a US proposal for militarization of the antidrug war because it would compromise Bolivian self-determination and obfuscate the real problem, the profitability of cocaine, which was thanks mainly to the US market. The absurdities of the drug war arouse great cynicism in Bolivia, where it is widely seen as a pretext for US interference in Latin America and a cover for US interests in the international drug trade. At the same time, there's a burgeoning antidrug industry bankrolled by Washington with hundreds of millions of US dollars and conflicts between campesinos, guerrillas, paramilitary groups and armed forces continue in the main coca-growing region of Chapare. There is a fear that substantial areas of the countryside could pass out of the government's control, as has happened in much of Colombia.

GEOGRAPHY

Despite the loss of huge chunks of territory in wars and concessions, landlocked Bolivia is South America's fifth-largest country. It encompasses 1,098,000 sq km (the area of France and Spain combined) and is bounded by Peru, Brazil, Paraguay, Argentina and Chile.

Two Andean mountain chains run through western Bolivia, with many peaks rising higher than 6000m. The western Cordillera Occidental stands as a barrier between Bolivia and the Pacific coast. The eastern Cordillera Real runs southeast past Lake Titicaca, then turns south across central Bolivia, joining with the other chain to form the Cordillera Central in the south of the country.

The altiplano, or high plain, with an altitude ranging from 3500m to 4000m, is bounded by these two great cordilleras. The Andean altiplano itself is a haunting place –

an immense, nearly treeless plain punctuated by mountain barriers and solitary volcanic peaks. At the northern end of the Bolivian altiplano, straddling the Peruvian border, Lake Titicaca is considered the world's highest navigable lake. At its southern end, the land is much drier and less populated. Here are the remnants of two other great lakes, the Salar de Uyuni and the Salar de Coipasa, which form an eerie expanse of salty desert plains.

East of the Cordillera Central are the highland valleys, a region of scrambled hills, valleys and fertile basins. Olives, nuts, wheat, maize and grapes are cultivated in this Mediterranean climate.

North of the Cordillera Real, where the Andes fall away into the Amazon Basin, the Yungas form a transition zone between arid highlands and humid lowlands.

Though most people live on the altiplano, more than half of Bolivia's total area is part of the Amazon Basin. The northern and eastern lowlands are sparsely populated and flat, with swamps, savannas, scrub and rain forest.

In the southeastern corner of Bolivia lies the flat, nearly impenetrable scrubland of the Gran Chaco, which extends into northern Paraguay. The level terrain is covered by a tangled thicket of small thorny trees and cacti. As the region is almost completely uninhabited, native flora and fauna thrive undisturbed.

CLIMATE

Because of its topography, Bolivia has a wide range of altitude-affected climatic patterns. Within its frontiers, every climatic zone can be found, from steaming rainforest heat to arctic cold. The 1998 El Niño season brought both droughts and flooding and some US$500 million in damage, especially to crops, farms and roads.

The rainy period lasts from November to March (summer) through most of the country. Of the major cities, only Potosí receives regular snowfalls (between February and April), though snow is possible in Oruro and La Paz at the end of the rainy season. On the altiplano and in the highlands, subzero temperatures are frequent, especially at night. Winter in Cochabamba, Sucre and Tarija is a time of clear skies and optimum temperatures.

The Amazon Basin is always hot and wet, with the drier period falling between May and October. The Yungas region is cooler but fairly wet year-round.

FLORA & FAUNA

Bolivia's several national parks and reserves are home to a myriad of animal and bird species. Parks that are accessible to visitors – albeit often with difficulty – include:

Parque Nacional Alto Madidi This park protects a wide range of wildlife habitats and is thought to be home to more than 1000 species of birds. Populated portions of the park along the Río Tuichi have been given a special distinction under UNESCO's Biosphere statutes, which will allow the indigenous Chimane and Tacanas people to retain with their traditional lifestyles. It's accessed by boat tours from Rurrenabaque, and the new Laguna Chalalan ecotourist complex sets a new standard for rain-forest resorts.

Parque Nacional Amboró Amboró, near Santa Cruz, was expanded and classified as a national park in 1990. It is home to the rare spectacled bear, jaguars, capybaras, peccaries and an astonishing variety of bird life. Information is available from Fundación Amigos de la Naturaleza (FAN, see Useful Organizations, later in this section).

Parque Nacional Carrasco This remote extension to Amboró attempts to protect some remaining stands of rain forest in the volatile Chapare region. The most accessible site is the Cuevas de los Pájaros Nocturnos, which is most easily reached from Cochabamba with Fremen Tours.

Parque Nacional Isiboro-Sécure Due to a 1905 policy to colonize this area of the Chapare (northern Cochabamba Department), the Indian population has been either displaced or exterminated, and most of the wildlife has vanished, except in the more remote areas. Access is difficult, and because this park lies along a major coca and cocaine-trafficking route, extreme caution is advised. Fremen Tours runs river trips from Cochabamba into the park's best-known site, Laguna Bolivia.

Parque Nacional Noel Kempff Mercado This remote park near the Brazilian border is named in honor of the distinguished Bolivian biologist who was murdered by renegades in 1986. It contains a variety of Amazon wildlife and some of the most inspiring natural scenery in Bolivia. Overland access is possible from either Bolivia or Brazil, but requires fortitude; most visitors fly from Santa Cruz. Contact FAN (see Useful Organizations) or Santa Cruz tour operators for more information.

Parque Nacional Sajama This national park, which adjoins Chile's magnificent Parque Nacional Lauca, contains Volcán Sajama (6542m), one of Bolivia's highest peaks. The park lies on the main route between La Paz and Arica, Chile, but apart from a couple of private *alojamientos,* no tourist facilities are available on the Bolivian side.

Parque Nacional Torotoro Paleontologists will be interested in the biped and quadruped dinosaur tracks from the Cretaceous period, which can be found in the enormous rock formations near the village of Torotoro. The park also boasts caves, ancient ruins and lovely landscapes. The Asociación Experimental Torotoro (☎ 042-225843) in Cochabamba provides visitor information.

Parque Nacional Tunari This park, right in Cochabamba's backyard, features the Lagunas de Huarahuara, small lakes containing trout and pleasant mountain scenery. Picnic areas and campsites are available. The entrance lies within hiking distance of the city center.

Parque Nacional Ulla-Ulla Excellent hiking is possible in this remote park abutting the Peruvian border beneath the Cordillera Apolobamba. It was established in 1972 as a vicuña reserve and presently contains 2500 vicuñas and a large population of condors. For information see Instituto de Fomento Lanero (INFOL; ☎ 02-379048), Casilla 732, Calle Bueno 444, La Paz.

Reserva Biosférica del Beni The 334,200-hectare Beni Biosphere Reserve, near San Borja in the Amazon Basin, exists in conjunction with the adjacent Reserva Forestal Chimane. It is home to at least 500 species of tropical birds and more than 100 species of mammals. The entry station, at Porvenir, is on the main La Paz-Trinidad road.

Reserva de Vida Silvestre Ríos Blanco y Negro This remote 1.4 million-hectare wildlife reserve takes in vast tracts of rain forest, but there has been logging encroachment along the eastern boundaries. Wildlife includes anteaters, peccaries and tapirs, and more than 300 bird species. Accommodations and transportation are expensive, but a visit is highly worthwhile. For information, contact Amazonas Adventure Tours (☎ 03-422760, fax 03-422748), Av San Martín 756, 3° Anillo Interno, Barrio Equipetrol, Casilla 2527, Santa Cruz.

GOVERNMENT

Bolivia is a republic with legislative, executive and judicial branches of government. The first two convene in La Paz and the supreme court sits in Sucre, the legal capital. The president is elected to a four-year term and cannot hold more than one consecutive

BOLIVIA

term. The legislature consists of a senate and a chamber of deputies. After many years of rapidly changing regimes and military coups, Bolivia has been, since the early 1980s, one of the most politically stable nations in South America.

ECONOMY

Bolivia is rich in natural resources – tin, tungsten, antimony, sulfur, copper, iron, oil, natural gas, silver and gold – but despite this wealth it remains among the poorest Latin American nations. It has been described as 'a donkey burdened with silver' and 'a beggar sitting on a golden chair.'

Thanks to the remoteness of many mines and the distances over which raw metals must be freighted, Bolivia is a high-cost mineral producer. This, together with lack of skill and capital, corruption, disorganization, and internal strife makes the mining industry uncertain. Low mineral prices, especially those from the collapse of the tin market in the 1980s, have also hurt the mining sector. On the bright side, deposits of oil and natural gas have been discovered in the eastern lowlands, pipelines have enabled gas to exported to Argentina and new pipelines to Brazil and Paraguay are under construction.

Bolivia satisfies most of its own food and fiber requirements, and big agribusinesses are now growing cotton, soya, sunflowers and sugar for export in the fertile eastern lowlands. Illicit coca exports still exceed all legal agricultural exports combined.

Sustained economic growth rates of more than 4% were achieved during most of the 1990s. Infrastructure has improved greatly, unemployment has fallen and there has even been some progress in reducing poverty, though a wide gap remains between rich and poor.

POPULATION & PEOPLE

With just 7.8 million people, Bolivia is thinly populated. Despite its cold, arid climate, the altiplano has long been the country's most inhabited region, home to 70% of the population.

Between 50% and 60% of the total population is of pure Indian descent, and most people speak either Quechua or Aymara as a first language. They are traditionally oriented and strongly resist cultural change. About 35% of the population is made up of *mestizos* (of Spanish and Indian blood), and nearly 1% is of African heritage, mostly descendants of slaves conscripted to work the Potosí mines. The remainder of the population is primarily of European descent, with a small Asian minority. The sparsely populated northern and eastern lowlands – where Mennonite farmers have established dairy industries – are currently in the relatively early stages of settlement. By comparison, Santa Cruz is a cosmopolitan city, with immigrants from many countries.

The standard of living of most Bolivians is low, and in places, housing, nutrition, education, sanitation and hygiene are appalling. About 8% of infants die before their first birthday, and the average life expectancy is only 60 years for men and 65 years for women.

ARTS
Dance

The pre-Hispanic dances of the altiplano celebrated war, fertility, hunting prowess, marriage and work. After the Spanish arrived, traditional European dances and those of the African slaves were introduced and developed into the hybrid dances that characterize Bolivian festivities today.

If Bolivia has a national dance, it is the *cueca*, danced by handkerchief-waving couples to three-quarter time. It is derived from the Chilean cueca, which in turn is a Creole adaptation of the Spanish fandango. Its liberally interpreted choreography is danced primarily during fiestas by whirling couples, called *pandillas*. The dance is intended to convey a story of courtship, love, love lost and reconciliation. Another popular dance is the *huayno*, which originated on the altiplano.

The *auqui-auqui* (old-man dance) parodies high-born colonial gentlemen by portraying them ludicrously with a top hat, gnarled cane and exaggerated elderly posture. Another tradition is the *tinku*, a ritual fight that loosely resembles a dance. It's most practiced during festivals in northern Potosí Department. Tinkus may begin innocently enough but, near the end of the celebrations, they can often erupt into drunken mayhem.

The unique traditions of Tarija, in the south, have developed the *chapaqueada*. It's associated with religious celebrations, particularly San Roque, and is performed to the strains of Tarija's unusual musical instruments. Also popular in Tarija is *la rueda* (the wheel), which is danced throughout the year.

In San Ignacio de Moxos and around the Beni lowlands, festivities are highlighted by the *machetero*, a commemorative folkloric dance accompanied by drums, violins and *bajones* (pan flutes). Dancers carry wooden machetes and wear crowns of brilliant macaw feathers, wooden masks and costumes of cotton, bark and feathers.

Other popular dances in the northern lowlands include the *carnaval* and the *taquirari beniano*, both adapted from the altiplano, and the *chovena*, from northeastern Bolivia.

The most unusual and colorful dances are performed at festivals on the high altiplano, particularly during Carnaval. Oruro's *La Diablada* (Dance of the Devils) fiesta draws crowds from all over. The most famous and recognizable Diablada dance is *la morenada*, which reenacts the dance of African slaves brought to the courts of Viceroy Felipe III. Costumes consist of hooped skirts, shoulder mantles and dark-faced masks adorned with plumes. Another dance with African origins is *los negritos*. Performers beat on drums, the rhythm reminiscent of the music of the Caribbean.

Los llameros represent Andean llama herders, *waca takoris* satirize Spanish bullfighters and *waca tintis* represent the bullfighting *picadores*. *Los Incas* commemorates the original contact between the Incan and southern European cultures, while *las tobas* is performed in honor of the lowland Indians who were forcefully absorbed into the Inca empire.

Music

Although the musical traditions of the Andes have evolved from a series of pre-Inca, Inca, Spanish, Amazonian and even African influences, each region of Bolivia has developed distinctive musical styles and instruments. Andean music, from the cold, bleak altiplano, is suitably haunting and mournful, while music from the warmer lowland areas like Tarija has more vibrant and colorful tones.

Although the original Andean music was exclusively instrumental, popularization of the melodies has inspired the addition of appropriately bittersweet lyrics. Bolivian folk-music shows are called *peñas* and operate in most larger cities for both locals and tourists. Under the military regimes, the peña became a venue for protest, but this role has now diminished and most peñas purely entertain.

In the far northern and eastern lowland regions of Bolivia, Jesuit influences upon Chiquitano, Moxos and Guaraní musical talent left a unique legacy still in evidence here and in neighboring Paraguay. The Jesuits encouraged education and the study of European culture, and the Indians learned to handcraft musical instruments (the renowned violins and harps featured in Chaco music today) and to perform Italian baroque music, including opera.

Musical Instruments Although the martial honking of tinny and poorly practiced brass bands seems an integral part of most South American celebrations, Andean musical traditions employ a variety of instruments that date back to precolonial days.

The popular, ukulele-like *charango* was originally based on the Spanish *vihuela* and *bandurria*, early forms of the guitar and mandolin. By the early 17th century, Andean Indians had blended and adapted the Spanish designs into the charango, an instrument with five pairs of llama-gut strings and a *quirquincho* (armadillo carapace) soundbox that produced the Indians' pentatonic scale. Modern charangos are scarcely different from the earliest models, though the soundbox is now usually of wood. Another stringed instrument, the *violín chapaco*, originated in Tarija and is a variation on the European violin. Between Easter and the Fiesta de San Roque (held in early September), it is the favored instrument.

Prior to the advent of the charango, melody lines were carried exclusively by woodwind instruments. Best recognized are the *quena* and the *zampoña* (pan flute), which star in the majority of traditional musical performances. Quenas are simple reed flutes played by blowing into a notch at one end. The more complex zampoñas are played by forcing air across the open ends of reeds lashed together in order of size, often in double rows. Both quenas and zampoñas come in a variety of sizes and tonal ranges. Although the quena was originally intended

BOLIVIA

for solo interpretation of musical pieces known as *yaravies*, the two flutes are now played as part of a musical ensemble. The *bajón*, an enormous pan flute with separate mouthpieces in each reed, accompanies festivities in the Moxos communities of the Beni lowlands. While played, it must be rested on the ground or carried by two people.

Other Bolivian wind instruments include the *tarka* and the *sikuri*, lead instruments in the breathy *tarkeadas* and *sikureadas* of the rural altiplano, and the *pinquillo*, a Carnaval flute that comes in various pitches.

Woodwinds unique to the Tarija area are the *erke*, the *caña* and the *camacheña*. The erke, also known as the *phututu*, is made from a cow's horn and is played exclusively between the New Year and Carnaval. From San Roque (in early September) to the end of the year, the camacheña, a type of flute, is used. The caña, a 3m-long cane pole with a cow's horn on the end, is similar in appearance and tone to an alpenhorn. It's played year-round in Tarija.

Percussion also figures in most festivals and folkloric performances as a background for the typically lilting strains of the woodwind melodies. In highland areas, the most popular drum is the humongous *huankara*. The *caja*, a tambourine-like drum played with one hand, is used exclusively in Tarija.

Artists & Recordings Although there is a wealth of yet-to-be-discovered musical talent in Bolivia, key players are influencing musical trends and tastes worldwide with their recordings and occasional performances abroad.

Visitors who have attended peñas or fiestas and enjoy the music can buy compact discs or cassettes. Many cassettes are low-quality bootleg copies (US$3 to US$5); CDs cost around US$10, but have higher quality and longer durability. Selection is best in La Paz, but tapes are also available in the USA through the South American Explorers Club. Discolandia (☎ 02-354253) Casillo 422, La Paz, also distributes Bolivian music.

Major artists to look for include charango masters Celestino Campos, Ernesto Cavour and Mauro Núñez. Look out for the recording *Charangos Famosos*, a selection of well-known charango pieces. The Bolivian group that's been the most successful abroad is Kjarkas. The group has recorded at least a dozen albums, including the superb *Canto a la Mujer de Mi Pueblo*. The track entitled 'Llorando se fue' was recorded by the French group Kaoma in 1989 and became a worldwide hit as the 'Lambada.' Other groups worth looking for are Altiplano, Savia Andina, Chullpa Ñan, K'Ala Marka, Rumillajta, Los Quipus, Wara, Los Masis and Yanapakuna.

Weaving
Methods of spinning and weaving have changed little in Bolivia for centuries. In rural areas, girls learn to weave before they reach puberty and women spend nearly all their spare time spinning with a drop spindle or weaving on heddle looms. Prior to Spanish colonization, llama and alpaca wool were the materials of choice, but sheep's wool has now emerged as the most readily available and least expensive material, along with synthetic fibers.

Bolivian textiles come in diverse patterns, and the majority display a degree of skill that results from millennia of tradition. The beautiful and practical creations are true works of art. Touristy places such as Calle Sagárnaga (La Paz) and Tarabuco (near Sucre) have the widest range of goods for sale, but buying them here may be more expensive than buying direct from a craftsperson. The most common piece is a *manta*, a square shawl made of two handwoven strips joined edge to edge. Also common are the *chuspa* (coca pouch), the *falda* (skirt) with patterned weaving on one edge, woven belts and touristy items such as camera bags made from old remnants. Prices vary greatly with the age, quality, color and extent of the weaving – a new and simple manta might cost US$20, while the finest examples, especially those with a red background, will cost several hundred–not much for a few months work.

Regional differences are manifest in weaving style, motif and use, but tourist markets sell textiles from all over the country, so it's hard to pick up regional characteristics. Weavings from Tarabuco often feature intricate zoomorphic patterns, while distinctive and sought-after red-and-black designs come from Potolo, northwest of Sucre. Some woven designs are fanciful combinations of animal forms; horses figure prominently, as do avian aberrations. Zoomorphic paterns are also prominent in the wild Charazani country north of Lake Titicaca and in several areas in the vicinity of La Paz, including Lique and Calamarka.

Some extremely fine weavings originate in Sica Sica, one of the many dusty and non-descript villages between La Paz and Oruro, while in Calcha, southeast of Potosí near the boundary of Chuquisaca, expert spinning and an extremely tight weave – more than 150 threads per inch – combine in some of Bolivia's best clothing textiles.

Those interested in Bolivian textiles may want to browse *A Traveler's Guide to Eldo-rado and the Inca Empire*, by weaving expert Lynn Meisch; the hard-to-find *Weaving Tra-ditions of Highland Bolivia*, by Laurie Adelson and Bruce Takami, published by the Los Angeles Craft & Folk Art Museum; and *Bolivian Indian Textiles,* an excellent booklet on Bolivian textile arts, by Tamara Wasserman and Jonathon S Hill.

Architecture

The pre-Columbian architecture of Bolivia is seen in the largely ruined walls and struc-tures of Tiahuanaco and in Inca remains throughout the country. Restoration of these sites has been based on architectural inter-pretation by archaeologists, without reveal-ing much about their artistic values. The classic Inca polygonal-cut stones that domi-nate many Peruvian sites are unusual in Bolivia, found only on Isla del Sol and Isla de la Luna, both in Lake Titicaca.

Some colonial-era houses and street facades survive, notably in Potosí, Sucre and La Paz. Look for courtyards, colonnades of semicircular arches and overhanging bal-conies, all derived from Spanish styles. The vast majority of colonial buildings are reli-gious, and their styles are divided into several major overlapping periods.

Renaissance (1550-1650)
Renaissance churches are simple in design. They were constructed primarily of adobe, with court-yards, massive buttresses and naves without aisles. One of the best surviving examples is in the village of Tiahuanaco. Some Andean Renaissance churches indicate Moorish Mudejar influences. Two examples of Mude-jar Renaissance churches are San Miguel, in Sucre, and Copacabana, on the shores of Lake Titicaca.

Baroque (1630-1770)
Baroque churches were constructed in the form of a cross, with an elaborate dome and walls made of either stone or reinforced adobe. The best exam-ples of the pure baroque churches are the Compañía in Oruro, San Agustín in Potosí and Santa Bárbara in Sucre.

Mestizo (1690-1790)
Mestizo elements in the form of whimsical decorative carvings were introduced late in the baroque period and were applied with what appears to be wild abandon. Prominent themes include densely packed tropical flora and fauna, Inca deities and designs and bizarre masks, sirens and gargoyles. The interesting results are best seen at the churches of San Fran-cisco (in La Paz), San Lorenzo, Santa Teresa and the Compañía (in Potosí) and the rural churches of Sica Sica and Guaqui (in La Paz department).

Neoclassical (post 1790)
Neoclassical design, which dominated between 1790 and the early 20th century, is observed in the church of San Felipe Neri in Sucre and the cathedrals in Potosí and La Paz.

Eclectic
During mainstream church con-struction in the mid-18th century, the Jesuits in the Beni and Santa Cruz lowlands designed churches showing Bavarian rococo and Gothic influences. Their most unusual effort was the bizarre mission church at San José de Chiquitos. Its direct European origins aren't clear, but it bears superficial resemblance to churches in Poland and Belgium.

Contemporary
Since the 1950s, many new and high-rise buildings have appeared in La Paz and other cities. Though most reflect bland, modern, international style, there are some traditional echoes – look for triangular pediments on the rooflines and new versions of the Spanish balcony.

RELIGION

As a legacy of their Spanish colonial past, 95% of Bolivians are at least nominally Roman Catholic. There is, however, a blend-ing of ancient traditions and beliefs with the Christian faith, particularly among Indian communities. Evangelical protestant sects, including Mormons, Pentecostals and

BOLIVIA

Jehovah's Witnesses, are making some converts.

LANGUAGE
Spanish is the official language of Bolivia, and most people speak and understand it to some extent. However, more than half of Bolivia's people speak Quechua or Aymara as a first language.

Facts for the Visitor

HIGHLIGHTS
Adventure opportunities afforded by Bolivia's dramatic geography are the real highlights of any visit to this relatively untouristed and inexpensive country. The *salars* (salt pans) and deserts of Bolivia's far southwest make for a mindbending landscape. Elsewhere the towering Andes are reflected in brilliant blue Lake Titicaca lowlands. There's exciting trekking in the canyon country around Tupiza and in the misty valleys of the Yungas and the Cordillera Real. In the lowlands, riverboats take ecotourists deep into the pampas and Amazon rain forest. The bustling atmosphere of historic cities such as Sucre and Potosí contrasts with small, old-fashioned towns such as Coroico, Rurrenabaque, Sorata and Tarija, which retain a delightful easygoing charm. Home to a large indigenous population, the altiplano is a great place to hear Andean music and see traditional textiles.

PLANNING
Most travelers visit Bolivia on the way to or from Peru. The main gringo trail traverses the altiplano from Lake Titicaca in the north, via the capital city La Paz, to the superb salars in the southwest. The most popular detours are to the Yungas (especially around Coroico and Sorata), the lowlands for a rain-forest excursion, and to Potosí and Sucre. There are good overland connections to northern Chile and Argentina, but the road, rail and river routes into Paraguay and Brazil are more demanding and less traveled.

When to Go
Bolivia lies in the Southern Hemisphere; winter runs from May to October and summer from November to April. The high-

lands and altiplano can be cold in the winter and wet in the summer, but the only serious barrier to travel will be the odd road washout. In the tropical lowlands, however, summer can be miserable with mud, steamy heat, bugs and relentless downpours. Travel is difficult, and services may be stifled by mud and flooding. On the other hand, these conditions necessitate an increase in river transport, so it can be the best season to look for cargo boats in northern Bolivia.

Also consider that the high tourist season falls in the winter (late June to early September), due not only to climatic factors, but also to the timing of European and North American summer holidays and the fact that it's also Bolivia's major fiesta season. This means that both overseas visitors and lots of South Americans are traveling during this period. This can be an advantage if you're looking for people with whom to form a tour group for the southwestern circuit or the Cordillera Apolobamba, but prices for most everything tend to be a bit higher during this period than in other seasons.

Maps
Government topographical sheets and speciality maps are available from the Instituto Geográfico Militar (IGM), whose head office is on Av Bautista Saavedra in Miraflores, La Paz. It's in a military compound, and visitors must present their passports at the entrance. There's also a smaller outlet at Oficina 5, Calle Juan XXIII 100, off Calle Rodríguez between Calles Linares and Murillo, also in La Paz. Here, you select and pay for maps, and they'll be ready for collection the following day.

Both offices sell topo sheets and thematic national maps at a scale of 1:50,000 and 1:250,000, covering some 70% of Bolivia, and if the sheet you want is sold out, they'll provide photocopies at discounted prices. Maps of some areas are unavailable for security reasons.

Bolivian geologic maps are sold at Geobol, on the corner of Ortiz and Federico Zuazo in La Paz; take your passport. For trekking maps of the Cordillera Real and Sajama, the colorful contour maps produced by Walter Guzmán (US$5 to US$8.25) are good. Try the Librería Don Bosco and the Librería del Turista, both in La Paz. Climbing maps of Illimani and Illampu at a scale of 1:50,000 are published in Munich by the Deutscher Alpenverein and distributed internationally. The excellent *Cordillera Real Recreation Map*, published by O'Brien Cartographics (www.mountainmaps.com), is available at various gringo hangouts for US$10. O'Brien also publishes the *Travel Map of Bolivia*, which is about the best country map available.

What to Bring
The range of climates and activities can require an assortment of clothing. Warm, waterproof and windproof clothing is essential for trekking in the altiplano, while the lowland areas require tropical dress and strong insect repellent. Effective sun protection is essential throughout the country.

TOURIST OFFICES
The national tourist authority, the Vice-Ministerio de Turismo, formerly known as Senatur, has an office in La Paz (☎ 02-367464), but doesn't really provide information to tourists, though it may have copies of the *Bolivia EthnoEcoTourism* booklet. Municipal and departmental tourist offices are usually more helpful and hand out what little printed information is available as well as the odd map.

VISAS & DOCUMENTS
Passports must be valid for one year beyond the date of entering the country. Entry or exit stamps are free of charge and attempts at charging should be met with polite refusal; in hopes of stamping out corruption, immigration offices now display notices to this effect.

Personal documents – passports, visas, *cédulas* (identification cards) or photocopies of these items – must be carried at all times. If you don't have them during a police check, you will probably waste some time at the police station while paperwork is shuffled and may have to pay a fine. This is most strictly enforced in lowland regions.

Tourist Cards & Visas
Bolivian visa requirements can be subject to arbitrary change and interpretation. Each Bolivian consulate and border crossing may have its own entry requirements and prices.

Citizens of most South American and Western European countries can get a tourist card on entry for stays up to 90 days.

Citizens of the USA, Canada, Australia, New Zealand, Japan, South Africa, Israel and many other countries are usually granted stays of 30 days without a visa – if you want to stay longer, ask at the point of entry and officials may give you 90 days anyway. Otherwise, you have to extend your tourist card (apply at the immigration office in any major city – it charges about US$2 for every extra day), or apply for a visa. Visas are issued by Bolivian consular representatives, including those in neighboring South American countries. Costs vary according to the consulate and the nationality of the applicant – up to US$50 for a one-year multiple-entry visa.

Overstayers can be fined US$2 per day and may face a measure of red tape at the border or airport when leaving the country.

Onward Tickets
Officially, everyone entering Bolivia is required to have proof of onward transport and sufficient funds for their intended stay; in practice officials rarely enforce these rules.

Vaccination Certificates
Anyone who is coming from a yellow-fever infected area needs a vaccination certificate to enter Bolivia. Many neighboring countries, including Brazil, require anyone arriving from Bolivia to have proof of a yellow-fever vaccination.

EMBASSIES & CONSULATES
Bolivian Embassies
Bolivia is represented in the following countries:

Australia
   (☎ 07-3221-1606)
   Suite 512, 5th floor, Pennys Building, 210 Queen St, GPO Box 53, Brisbane, Qld 4001

Canada
   (☎ 613-236-5730)
   130 Albert St, Suite 416, Ottawa, Ontario K1P SG4

France
   (☎ 01 45 27 84 35)
   12 Av du Presidente Kennedy, 75016 Paris 16

Germany
   (☎ 0228-362-038)
   Konstantinstrasse 16, D-5300 Bonn 2

UK
   (☎ 020-7235-4248, 020-7235-4255)
   106 Eaton Square, SW1 9AD London

BOLIVIA

USA
  Consulate General: (☎ 212-687-0530)
  211 E 43rd St, Room 802, New York, NY 10017
  Embassy: (☎ 202-483-4410)
  3014 Massachusetts Ave NW, Washington, DC,
  20008

Embassies in Bolivia

The following countries are among those with representation in La Paz unless otherwise noted.

Argentina
  (☎ 02-369266, fax 02-391083)
  Calle Aspiazu 497;
  open weekdays 9 am to 1 pm
  Santa Cruz: (☎ 03-347133)
  Banco de la Nación Argentina, Plaza 24 de
  Septiembre; open weekdays 9 to 11:30 am
Brazil
  (☎ 02-430303)
  Capitan Ravelo, Edificio Metrobol;
  open weekdays 9 am to 1 pm
  Santa Cruz: (☎ 03-344400)
  Av Busch 330; open weekdays 9:30 am to
  12:30 pm and 3:30 to 6:30 pm
Canada
  (☎ 02-431215)
  Plaza Avaroa, Av 20 de Octubre 2475;
  open weekdays 9 am to noon
Chile
  (☎ 02-783018)
  Av Hernando Siles 5843, Calle 13, Obrajes;
  open weekdays 8:30 am to 1 pm and 3 to 6 pm
  Santa Cruz: (☎ 03-434272)
  Barrio Equipetrol, Calle Elvira de Mendoza
  275; open weekdays 8 am to 1 pm
Colombia
  (☎ 02-786841)
  Plaza Avaroa, Av 20 de Octubre 2427, 2nd floor;
  open weekdays 9 am to 1 pm and 3 to 5 pm
France
  (☎ 02-786125)
  Av Hernando Siles 5390 at Calle 8, Obrajes;
  open weekdays 9 am to 12:30 pm
  (☎ 03-433434)
  Calle Avaroa 70; open weekdays 3 to 6 pm
Germany
  (☎ 02-431502)
  Av Aniceto Arce 2395;
  open weekdays 9 am to noon
  Santa Cruz: (☎ 03-324825)
  Av de las Américas 241;
  open weekdays 8:30 am to noon
Israel
  (☎ 02-358 676)
  Av Mariscal Santa Cruz, Edificio Esperanza
  10th floor; open by appointment only
Netherlands
  (☎ 02-432020)
  Av 6 de Agosto 2455, 8th floor, Sopocachi;
  open weekdays 9 am to 1 pm

Paraguay
  (☎ 02-432201)
  Av 6 de Agosto, Edificio Illimani;
  open weekdays 8:30 am to 1 pm
Peru
  (☎ 02-352031)
  Av 6 de Agosto y Guachalla, Edificio Alianza;
  open weekdays 9 am to 1 pm and 2:30 to
  5:30 pm
UK
  (☎ 02-433424)
  Av Aniceto Arce 2732; open weekdays 9 am to
  noon and 1:30 to 4:30 pm
USA
  (☎ 02-430251)
  Av Aniceto Arce 2780, esquina Cordero;
  open weekdays 8:30 am to noon
  Santa Cruz: (☎ 03-363842)
  Barrio Equipetrol, Calle Guemes 6;
  open weekdays 9 to 11:30 am

CUSTOMS

Visitors are permitted to import duty-free two bottles of alcohol, up to 500g of tobacco, 50 cigars and 200 cigarettes. Drugs and firearms are prohibited. Departing air passengers are searched thoroughly.

MONEY

Currency

Bolivia's unit of currency is the *boliviano* (B$), which is divided into 100 *centavos*. Bolivianos come in five, 10, 20, 50, 100 and 200 denomination notes, with coins worth five, 10, 20 and 50 centavos and one and two bolivianos. Bolivian currency is extremely difficult to change outside Bolivia, so don't wind up with more than you'll need.

Exchange Rates

The official rate represents the currency's actual value, and there's no black market offering a better rate of exchange. At press time, these were exchange rates:

country	unit		boliviano
Australia	A$1	=	B$3.72
Canada	C$1	=	B$3.86
euro	€1	=	B$5.99
France	FF1	=	B$0.91
Germany	DM1	=	B$3.06
Japan	¥100	=	B$4.83
New Zealand	NZ$1	=	B$3.01
United Kingdom	UK£1	=	B$9.05
USA	US$1	=	B$5.76

Exchanging Money

Cash & Traveler's Checks As a rule, visitors fare best with US dollars, the only foreign currency accepted throughout Bolivia. Currencies of neighboring countries may be exchanged in border areas and at certain casas de cambio in La Paz. American Express traveler's checks seem to be the most widely accepted brand, though you shouldn't have problems with other major brands.

Currency may be exchanged at casas de cambio and at some banks in larger cities. All casas de cambio change cash dollars and some also change traveler's checks. You can often change money in travel agencies, jewelry or appliance stores and pharmacies. These establishments deal mainly with cash, though a few also accept traveler's checks. *Cambistas* (street moneychangers) operate nights and weekends in most cities and towns but only change cash dollars, paying roughly the same as casas de cambio and other establishments. They're convenient after hours, but you must guard against rip-offs.

The rate for cash doesn't vary much from place to place, although rates may be slightly lower in border areas. The rate for traveler's checks is best in La Paz, where it nearly equals the cash rate; in other large cities it's 3% to 5% lower, and in smaller towns it may be impossible to change traveler's checks at all. Some banks and casas de cambio charge a commission of 1% to 3% to exchange traveler's checks. Carry cash dollars (or bolivianos) if you are heading off the beaten track.

When exchanging money, ask for the cash in small denominations, as it can be difficult to get change for large notes. Beware of mangled notes; unless both halves of a repaired banknote bear identical serial numbers, the note is worthless.

Credit & Debit Cards Major cards, such as Visa, MasterCard and American Express, may be used in larger cities at better hotels, restaurants and tour agencies.

Because traveler's checks may be difficult to change in some places, a credit card is a useful backup. Cash advances of up to US$300 per day are available on Visa (and often MasterCard) with no commission and a minimum of hassle from city branches of Banco de Santa Cruz, Banco Mercantil and Banco Nacional de Bolivia. Banco de La Paz

charges 1.75% commission on all cash advances.

ATMs Just about every sizable town has an ATM – look for the 'Enlace' sign. They dispense bolivianos (sometimes greenbacks as well) on Visa, Plus and Cirrus cards.

POST & COMMUNICATIONS
Post

All major and minor cities have post offices – some are signposted 'Ecobol,' which is short for 'Empresa Correos de Bolivia.' From major towns, the post is generally reliable, but when posting anything important, it's still wise to pay an additional US$0.20 to send it by certified mail. Poste restante (occasionally called *lista de correos*) is available in larger cities and towns. The only posting boxes are inside post offices. A postcard costs about US$1 to the USA, US$1.20 to Europe and US$1.40 to the rest of the world. A 10kg parcel will cost about US$58 to the USA or US$91 by air; to airmail it to Australia will cost US$167.

Telephone

The Empresa Nacional de Telecomunicaciones (Entel) has a telephone office in nearly every town, usually open 7 am to 11:30 pm daily. Local calls from Entel offices cost just a few centavos. Alternatively, small street kiosks are often equipped with telephones that may be used for brief local calls (US$0.20). In La Paz and in some tiny villages, you'll find pay telephone boxes, but card phones are much more common.

Bolivia's country code is ☎ 591. The international direct-dialing access code is 00. For reverse-charge (collect) calls from a private line, dial the international operator (☎ 356700 in La Paz) and explain that the call is *por cobrar*. Entel offices will not accept reverse-charge calls, but some will give you the office's number and let you be called back. International calls from Entel offices are expensive to the USA ($1.56 per minute), more expensive to Europe (US$2.90 per minute) and exorbitant to Asia, Australia and Oceania (US$3.40). Some calls are cheaper nights, weekends and on Sunday.

Fax

You can send faxes at most Entel offices, which charge a per-page rate depending on

BOLIVIA

the distance. Within Bolivia it's from US$0.50 to US$1 per page. Internationally, it's about US$3.60 per page to the USA, US$4.80 to Europe, and US$5.60 to Australia. Some Entel offices have a number for incoming faxes, which cost about US$1 per page, and faxes can be delivered to a street address for an extra charge. Many hotels will accept incoming faxes for their guests, which may be more convenient.

Email & Internet Access

Cybercafés have blossomed in towns all over Bolivia. Rates run from US$0.60 to US$2 per hour for the use of an online PC with a Web browser.

INTERNET RESOURCES

Two good starting points are Bolivia Web (www.boliviaweb.com) and the Café Boliviana (jaguar.pg.cc.md.us). Bolivia's National Institute of Statistics is at www.ine.gov.bo (in Spanish only).

BOOKS

For more travel information, pick up Lonely Planet's *Bolivia*, which gives a complete rundown on the country. If you intend to go hiking or trekking, look for *Backpacking and Trekking in Peru & Bolivia*, by Hilary Bradt, which covers major hikes in the Cordillera Real and the Yungas.

For a good general introduction to the country, *Bolivia in Focus,* by Paul van Lindert and Otto Verkoren, provides an excellent synopsis of Bolivia's history, economics, politics and culture.

English-, German- and French-language publications are available from Los Amigos del Libro, with outlets in La Paz and Cochabamba. The goods are quite pricey (due mainly to a weighty import duty), but the store does offer a good selection of popular paperbacks, Latin American literature, magazines, dictionaries, histories and glossy coffee-table books on Bolivia. The Librería del Turista on Plaza San Francisco in La Paz sells a limited range of books and maps on Bolivia and its history.

Spanish-language books, including novels and classic literature, are found at Los Amigos del Libro and similar shops. Most *librerías* (bookstores) and street sellers, however, sell only stationery, pulpy local publications, comics and school texts.

MEDIA

Cochabamba, La Paz, Potosí, Oruro and Santa Cruz all have daily newspapers. There's also an English-language weekly, *The Bolivian Times*, that is sold at newsstands and bookstores in major cities. *Newsweek*, the *International Herald Tribune, Time, The Economist* and the *Miami Herald* are sold at some street kiosks in larger cities and at Los Amigos del Libro in La Paz, Cochabamba and Santa Cruz.

Bolivia has two government-run and five private TV stations and 125 radio stations broadcasting in Spanish, Quechua and Aymara. Recommended listening includes FM 96.7 in La Paz, which plays classic rock and pop music, and Radio Latina in Cochabamba, at the upper end of the FM band, which plays a mix of Andean folk music, salsa and local rock. Cable TV (with CNN, ESPN and BBC) is available in some hotels.

TIME

Bolivian time is four hours behind GMT/UTC. Bolivia doesn't go on summer time, but Chile does, so there's an hour difference between them from about November to March.

ELECTRICITY

Bolivia uses a standard current of 220V at 50Hz except in La Paz and a few selected locations in Potosí that use 110V at 50Hz. Ask before you plug in. In a few areas, the water and power are routinely turned off at certain times of day or at night. If you're a night owl, keep a flashlight on hand.

WEIGHTS & MEASURES

Like most countries in South America, Bolivia uses the metric system. Local units of measurement occasionally used in Bolivia include the *arroba*, which is equal to 11.25kg, and the *quintal*, which is equal to four arrobas, or 45kg.

HEALTH

Bolivia is not a particularly unhealthy country, but sanitation and hygiene are poor in some areas, and you should pay attention to what you eat. Some tap water is safe to drink, but if you'd rather not chance it and can't boil it, opt for bottled mineral water. Avoid the Viscachani brand, in which the main mineral appears to be salt.

The altiplano lies between 3000m and 4000m, and many visitors to places like La Paz, Cocabana and Potosí will have problems with altitude sickness. Complications like cerebral edema have killed otherwise fit and healthy travelers. Read the information on altitude-related health problems in the Health section of the Facts for the Visitor chapter.

Bolivia is officially in a yellow-fever zone, so a vaccination is recommended – it may be obligatory for return or onward travel. If you'll be in the lowlands, take precautions against malaria.

USEFUL ORGANIZATIONS
The following groups in Bolivia promote environmental conservation:

Armonía
(☎ 02-792337) Casilla 3045, La Paz
(☎ 03-522919, fax 03-324971) Casilla 3081, Santa Cruz

Conservación Internacional
(☎ 02-434058, ci-bolivia@conservation.org) Calle Macario Pinilla 291, 2nd Piso, Casilla 5633, La Paz

Fundación Amigos de la Naturaleza (FAN)
(☎ 03-337475, ecotourism@fan.scbbs-bo.com) Casilla 4200, Santa Cruz

Instituto de Ecología
(☎ 02-792582, fax 02-391176) Casilla 10077, Calle 27, Cotacota, La Paz

BUSINESS HOURS
Very few businesses open before 9 or 9:30 am, although markets may see dribbles of activity as early as 6 am. In the cities, an increasing number of restaurants are opening at 8 am to serve breakfast. Shops, travel agencies and banks open around 9 am.

At noon, cities virtually shut down, with the exception of markets and restaurants serving lunch-hour crowds. The afternoon resurrection begins between 2 and 4 pm, and most businesses remain open until 8 or 9 pm. Bars and restaurants generally close around 10 pm. On Saturday, shops, services and some eateries close down at 1 pm, but street markets run until at least mid-afternoon and often into the evening. Sundays are generally dead, but ice-cream parlors, street vendors and some markets operate during the day.

The leisurely business hours can be frustrating for foreigners and can result in four traffic jams per day in La Paz. In April 1999, the national government introduced a 'continuous workday' policy for government offices in main cities in the departments of Beni, Cochabamba, La Paz and Santa Cruz. Initially, the new working hours were set at 8 am to 4 pm with a half-hour for lunch, but this schedule may be modified as the new system evolves. The change is intended to reduce traffic problems in the middle of the day, and to enable employees to undertake evening studies or a second job. It was expected that many private companies would follow this lead and adopt the shorter lunch break, but they are not required to do so.

PUBLIC HOLIDAYS
Bolivian public holidays include:

New Year's Day
January 1
Carnaval
February/March (dates vary)
Easter Week
March/April (dates vary)
Labor Day
May 1
Corpus Christi
May (dates vary)
Independence Days
August 5-7
Columbus Day
October 12
All Souls' Day
November 2
Christmas Day
December 25

In addition, each department has its own holiday: February 22 in Oruro, April 1st in Potosí, April 15 in Tarija, May 25 in Chuquisaca, July 16 in La Paz, September 14 in Cochabamba, September 24 in Santa Cruz and Pando and November 18 in Beni.

SPECIAL EVENTS
Bolivian fiestas are invariably of religious or political origin, normally commemorating a Christian or Indian saint or god, or they commemorate a political event such as a battle or revolution. They typically include lots of folk music, dancing, processions, food, alcohol, ritual and general unrestrained behavior. Water balloons (tourists are especially vulnerable!), fireworks and brass bands figure prominently.

The following is a list of major events:

Alasitas (La Paz & Copacabana)
    January 24
Virgen de Candelaria (Copacabana)
    First week in February
La Diablada (Oruro)
    February/March (week before Lent; dates vary)
Phujllay (Tarabuco)
    Second Sunday in March
El Gran Poder (La Paz)
    Late May or early June
Santo Patrono de Moxo (San Ignacio de Moxos)
    July 31
San Lorenzo (San Lorenzo, Tarija & Santa Cruz)
    August 10 to 13
Virgen de Urcupiña (Quillacollo)
    August 15 to 18
Chu'tillos (Potosí)
    Late August
San Roque (Tarija)
    First week in September

ACTIVITIES

Hiking, trekking and mountaineering are among the most rewarding ways to gain an appreciation of the Andes. The mountain backbone of South America is not a wilderness area – it has been inhabited for thousands of years by herders and farmers. Many areas of the country are suitable for hiking, but most of the popular hikes and treks begin near La Paz, traverse the Cordillera Real along ancient Inca routes and end in the Yungas.

An increasing number of La Paz agencies organize technical climbs and expeditions into the Cordillera Real and to Volcán Sajama (6542m, Bolivia's highest peak), near the Chilean border. For a list of recommended agencies, see Organized Tours in this chapter's Getting Around section.

For something different in downhill skiing, you may want to check out Chacaltaya, near La Paz, which is the world's highest developed ski resort. The words 'developed' and 'resort' are used rather loosely: facilities are limited to a drafty hut and a challenging makeshift ski-tow. The ski area is on a glacier and snow cover is limited – the best chance is in January or February, but don't count on it (see the Around La Paz section for details).

Mountain biking outisde of La Paz is another adventure option.

WORK

There are a great number of voluntary and nongovernmental organizations at work in Bolivia, and quite a few international companies have offices, too, but travelers looking for paid work on the spot probably won't have much luck.

Qualified English teachers wishing to work in La Paz or other cities may want to try the professionally run Centro Boliviano Americano (☎ 02-351627), at Parque Zenón Iturralde off Av Aniceto Arce, in La Paz. New, unqualified teachers must forfeit two months salary in order to pay for their training. Alternatively, try the Pan American English Language Institute (☎ 02-340796).

ACCOMMODATIONS

Most accommodations are inexpensive throughout Bolivia, though price and value are not uniform. Bigger cities, like La Paz, Sucre and Santa Cruz, tend to be more expensive than small places such as Copacabana and Uyuni. Prices in this chapter reflect the standard, mid-season rates – prices can be 10% to 20% more expensive in the high season (late June to early September) and can double during major fiestas. At slow times most places will give a substantial discount if you negotiate.

Room availability in Bolivia is rarely a problem. The main exception is during fiestas and at places such as Coroico that are popular with Bolivians on weekends.

The Bolivian hotel rating system divides accommodations into categories that, from bottom to top, include *posadas, alojamientos, residenciales, casas de huéspedes, hostales* and *hoteles*. This rating system reflects the price scale and, to some extent, the quality.

Posadas are the bottom end – the cheapest basic roof and bed available; they're frequented mainly by *campesinos* (peasants) visiting the city. They cost between US$1 and US$2.50 per person and provide minimal cleanliness and comfort. Shared bathrooms are the norm, some have no showers at all and hot water is unknown.

A step up are alojamientos, which are considerably better and cost a bit more, but are still quite basic. Bath facilities are almost always communal, but some do offer hot showers. Some are clean and tidy, while others are disgustingly seedy. Prices range from US$1.20 to US$4 per person.

Residenciales, casas de huéspedes and hostales all serve as budget hotels, but quality varies – officially they are graded from one to four stars. The cheapest ones are basic alojamientos trying to improve their image, while the best ones are comparable to a nice hotel. Most are acceptable, and you'll often have a choice between shared or private bath. Plan on US$8 to US$20 for a double with private bath, about 30% less without.

Moving upmarket, there's a whole constellation of hotels that vary in standards from literal dumps to five-star luxury. The lower-range hotels can be amazingly cheap, while the most expensive hotels top US$100 per person.

Most Bolivian hotel owners are friendly, honest people who demand the same standards of their staff. Still, use common sense and don't leave valuables in hotel rooms unless you're certain they are secure. If you'll be away for a few days, most hotels will watch luggage free of charge.

Bolivia offers excellent camping, especially along trekking routes and in remote mountain areas. There are very few organized campsites, but you can pitch a tent almost anywhere outside population centers. Remember, however, that highland nights can be freezing. Theft from campers is reported in some areas – inquire locally about security.

FOOD

Bolivia offers a diversity of traditional cuisines, thanks to its various climatic zones. Generally, the food is palatable and filling, but unremarkable. Altiplano fare tends to be starchy and loaded with carbohydrates. Potatoes come in dozens of varieties, most of them small and colorful. Freeze-dried potatoes, called *chuño* or *tunta*, often accompany meals. In the lowlands, the potato and its relatives are replaced by *yuca* (cassava), and other vegetables figure more prominently.

Beef, chicken and fish are the most common meats. Poorer campesinos eat *cordero* (mutton), *cabrito* (goat), llama and, on special occasions, *carne de chancho* (pork). The most popular fish on the altiplano is *trucha* (trout), which has been introduced to Lake Titicaca. The lowlands have a great variety of freshwater fish, including *sábalo*, *dorado* and the delicious *surubí*.

Some popular Bolivian dishes include *chairo* (a kind of lamb or mutton broth with potatoes, chuños and other vegetables), *sajta* (chicken served in hot pepper sauce), *saice* (a spicy meat broth), *pacumutu* (filleted beef chunks), *silpancho* (pounded beef schnitzel) and *pique a lo macho* (chopped beef served with onions and other vegetables). Pizza, fried chicken, hamburgers and Chinese restaurants *(chifas)* provide some variety.

The tastiest Bolivian snack is the *salteña*, usually enjoyed for breakfast or as midmorning sustenance. These delicious meat and vegetable pasties originated in Salta, Argentina, but achieved perfection in Bolivia. They come in several varieties, stuffed with beef or chicken, olives, egg, potato, onion, peas, carrots and other surprises – they will squirt juice over the unwary eater. A similar concoction is the *tucumana*, which is square-shaped and generally contains more juice.

Standard meals are *desayuno* (breakfast), *almuerzo* (lunch, although the word normally refers to a set lunch served at midday) and *cena* (dinner). For almuerzo, many restaurants, from backstreet cubbyholes to classy establishments, offer bargain set meals consisting of soup, a main course and coffee or tea. In some places, a salad and simple dessert are included. Almuerzos cost roughly half the price of à la carte dishes – from US$1.50 to US$3, depending on the class of restaurant. Reliable market *comedores* (basic eateries) are almost always the cheapest option.

DRINKS

Beyond the usual coffee, tea and hot chocolate, typical hot drinks include *mate de coca* (coca leaf tea) and *api*. Api, a sweet breakfast drink made of maize, lemon and cinnamon, is served mainly in markets. Major cola brands are available, as well as locally produced soft drinks of varying palatability. Many restaurants and markets serve up *licuados*, delicious fruit shakes blended with either milk or water.

Most of Bolivia's wine is produced around Tarija with varying degrees of success. The best – and most expensive – is Concepción San Bernardo de la Frontera, which sells for around US$5 per bottle. The same wineries also produce *singani*, a spirit obtained by distilling grape skins and other by-products.

The most popular cocktail is *chuflay*, a refreshing blend of singani, 7-Up (or ginger ale), ice and lemon. Bolivian beers aren't bad either; popular brands include Huari, Paceña, Tropical Extra, Sureña and Potosina. Beer is ridiculously fizzy at the higher altitudes, where it can be difficult to get the brew from under the foam.

The favorite alcoholic drink of the Bolivian masses is *chicha cochabambina*, obtained by fermenting maize. It is made all over Bolivia, especially in the Cochabamba region. Other versions of chicha, often nonalcoholic, are made from maize, sweet potato, peanuts, cassava and other fruits and vegetables.

Getting There & Away

Only a few airlines offer direct services to Bolivia, and fares are typically high; those from Peru and Chile are the most economical. It can be cheaper to fly into Peru or northern Chile, then travel overland to Bolivia. The same goes with departure; it's very difficult to find a discounted fare out of the country.

AIR

The national airline is Lloyd Aéreo Boliviano (LAB; ☎ 02-367-710, 800-4321, www .labairlines.com), which offers both domestic and international flights. International airfares purchased in Bolivia are subject to 19.05% tax. The main international gateway is La Paz, but quite a few international flights go to Santa Cruz – this can be cheaper, and Santa Cruz has a warmer and more oxygenated atmosphere for new arrivals.

Departure Tax

Airports charge US$20 departure tax on international flights for those who have spent fewer than 90 days in Bolivia. Those who've stayed longer than 90 days pay US$50.

Argentina

LAB flies from Buenos Aires to La Paz via Santa Cruz on Tuesday, Wednesday, and Thursday and to Cochabamba on Sunday. Fares are US$370 to La Paz, US$256 to Santa Cruz. From Salta, Argentina, there are several flights each week to Cochabamba.

Aerolíneas Argentinas (☎ 02-351711, fax 02-391059) flies regularly between Buenos Aires and La Paz via Santa Cruz, with some flights stopping at Salta and Córdoba.

Brazil

LAB flies between Rio de Janeiro, São Paulo and La Paz via Santa Cruz on Monday, Thursday and Saturday. One-way fares from Rio are US$340 to La Paz and US$273 to Santa Cruz. From São Paulo, the fare is US$340 to La Paz and US$262 to Santa Cruz. Varig (☎ 02-314040) flies the same route every day except Sunday. In addition, LAB runs two flights per week between Manaus and Santa Cruz for US$210 one way.

Chile

LanChile (☎ 02-358377) and LAB both fly daily between La Paz, Arica, Iquique and Santiago. The fare is US$92 to Arica and US$215 to Santiago. Inquire about LanChile's airpass deal for solid discounts on Santiago-La Paz return flights.

Paraguay

LAB flies between Asunción, Santa Cruz and La Paz on Tuesday and Friday. One-way fares from La Paz to Asunción are US$215; from Santa Cruz, US$168. TAM Mercosur (☎ 02-376001 in La Paz, 03-371999 in Santa Cruz) also flies Santa Cruz-Asunción on Monday, Wednesday and Saturday.

Peru

LAB, KLM (☎ 02-323965) and Lufthansa (☎ 02-372170) fly between Lima and La Paz. LAB has service on Tuesday, Thursday, Saturday and Sunday for US$180 one way. From Cuzco to La Paz, KLM flies twice weekly. Peru levies a tax of 18% on air tickets purchased in the country.

BUS, TRAIN & BOAT
Argentina

From Salta or Jujuy in northwestern Argentina, buses leave every couple of hours during the day for La Quiaca, which lies opposite the Bolivian town of Villazón. It takes about 20 minutes to walk between the Argentine and Bolivian bus terminals, excluding immigration procedures, but taxis are available.

From Villazón, buses run to Tupiza and Potosí, and slow local trains leave for Tupiza,

Uyuni and Oruro on Wednesday and Sunday; the comfortable expreso train does the run on Saturday.

The border crossing at tiny Pocitos is a short distance south of Yacuiba, Bolivia, and north of Tartagal, Argentina. Walking across the border between Pocitos, Argentina, and Pocitos, Bolivia, takes about 10 minutes. There are taxis between Pocitos and Yacuiba and buses to and from Tartagal. From Tucumán in north-central Argentina, take a bus to Embarcación and Tartagal and another from there to Pocitos on the frontier. From Yacuiba, buses run to Tarija, Santa Cruz and the rest of Bolivia.

The third Bolivia-Argentina border crossing sometimes used by travelers is at Bermejo and Aguas Blancas. It's accessed via Tarija in Bolivia and Oran in Argentina.

Daily long-distance buses go between La Paz and Buenos Aires ($130, 72 hours) via Tarija, Yacuiba, Salta and Cordoba.

Brazil
Corumbá, opposite the Bolivian border town of Quijarro, is the busiest port of entry between Bolivia and Brazil, with bus connections from São Paulo, Rio de Janeiro, Cuiabá and southern Brazil.

Once in Corumbá, take a bus to the border, and from there go by taxi (US$1 per person) to the Quijarro railhead. From Quijarro, passenger trains leave for Santa Cruz daily except Sunday, and more frequent freight trains will also accept passengers in the *bodegas* (boxcars). During the wet, you may wait several days.

From Cáceres, southwest of Cuiabá, you can cross to San Matías in Bolivia, and from there either take a bus to San Ignacio de Velasco or fly to Santa Cruz (via Roboré).

From Brasiléia, in the state of Acre, you can cross into Cobija, Bolivia, where you'll find buses to Riberalta. From there, dry-weather roads run to La Paz and Guayaramerín.

A more popular crossing is by ferry from Guajará-Mirim in Brazil across the Río Mamoré to Guayaramerín, Bolivia. From there, you can travel by bus to Riberalta and on to Cobija or Rurrenabaque and La Paz.

Chile
Flota Litoral, Andes Mar and other bus companies run between La Paz and Arica, in northern Chile, via the Chungará-Tambo Quemado border crossing. This once-rough route is now paved, and the trip takes eight or nine hours; fares start at US$17 and run up to US$22 for a luxury bus. Some go through to Iquique, Chile (US$24, 11 hours). Trans-Sabaya also has a twice-weekly service between Oruro and Chungará (Lauca National Park), with direct connections to Arica.

Coming from Antofagasta, you must first take a bus to Calama (US$5, three hours). From there, a Wednesday evening train goes to Ollagüe on the Bolivian border, eight hours uphill from Calama. In Ollagüe, passengers cross the border to Avaroa on foot to connect with the Bolivian train to Uyuni (US$5.50). Trains are slow and this connection is subject to very long delays. The Tramaca bus company in Antofagasta sells a combination bus- and train-ticket all the way to Uyuni, Oruro or La Paz. On all routes between Chile and Bolivia, warm clothes are vital.

An interesting alternative is from San Pedro de Atacama in Chile by bus or 4WD tour through Bolivia's southwestern desert, arriving in Uyuni.

Paraguay
Pan Americana has buses from La Paz to Asunción, via Santa Cruz (US$100, 24 hours, longer if the Chaco road has been heavily rained on). From Santa Cruz to Asunción it's around US$75.

Peru
There are two routes from Puno, which is Peru's main access point for Bolivia. The quicker but less interesting way is by *micro* (small bus) from Puno to the frontier at Desaguadero, where you can connect with Bolivian transport to La Paz. A direct bus from La Paz to Puno leaves at 8 am (US$5.40, six hours).

The more scenic and interesting route is via Copacabana and the Estrecho de Tiquina (Straits of Tiquina). Minibuses leave from Puno and enter Bolivia at Yunguyo, 11km south of Copacabana. There you connect with another minibus to Copacabana, where there are regular buses to La Paz (US$5, five hours), including a boat across the straits. The entire run from Puno to La Paz can be done in a day, but the

BOLIVIA

Copacabana area merits a couple of days for exploration.

There are other obscure border crossings, such as the one via Puerto Acosta north of Lake Titicaca, and a couple of ports of entry along the northern rivers, but these require some effort and there's no public transport available.

Getting Around

AIR

Most domestic air services are operated by national airline LAB and AeroSur. Both have a wide network with frequent flights and services to virtually everywhere you might wish to go. Service on LAB is usually OK, but delays and cancellations are still frequent in the Amazon lowlands. AeroSur generally offers better service, but fares are slightly higher, especially in the Amazon region.

The military airline, Transportes Aéreos Militares (TAM), is an inconvenient alternative for some hard-to-reach places. Fares are cheaper than LAB's, but you often can't book a seat in advance, and flights are often late or canceled; don't confuse it with the new Paraguayan airline Transportes Aéreos del Mercosur, which is also called TAM.

The following are sample one-way LAB fares from La Paz:

Cochabamba	US$46
Puerto Suárez	US$158
Riberalta	US$126
Santa Cruz	US$103
Sucre	US$67
Tarija	US$104
Trinidad	US$64

LAB offers a special LABpass, an air pass that allows five flights between any of the main cities served by LAB if you return to your starting point; eg, you can go from La Paz to Cochabamba to Sucre to Santa Cruz to Tarija and back to La Paz (Trinidad is another possible destination). If you don't want to return to your start point, you can just use four flights. The LABpass costs US$173 from LAB offices and travel agencies.

The domestic *derecho del aeropuerto* (airport departure tax) ranges from US$1.50

to US$2 and is collected after check-in at the airport.

BUS & CAMIÓN

The Bolivian road network is improving as more and more kilometers are paved. Unpaved roads range from good-grade dirt to mud, sand or potholed gravel. Modern coaches use the best roads, while older vehicles cover minor secondary routes.

Long-distance bus lines are called *flotas*. Large buses are called *buses* and small ones are called *micros*. A bus terminal is a *terminal terrestre*.

To be safe, reserve bus tickets at least several hours in advance. Many buses depart in the afternoon or evening, to arrive at their destination in the wee hours of the morning. On most major routes, such as La Paz–Cochabamba, there are also daytime departures.

An alternative on many routes is a *camión* (truck), which will normally charge around one-half to two-thirds the bus fare. This is a very popular mode of transport among campesinos, but it can be excruciatingly slow and rough, depending on the cargo and the number of passengers being carried. Camiones offer a very non-tourist experience and the best views of the often spectacular countryside. Each town has one or two places where camiones gather to wait for passengers; some even have scheduled departures. Otherwise, the best place to hitch lifts will be the appropriate *tranca*, a police checkpoint at every town exit.

On any bus or camión trip in the highlands, day or night, take plenty of warm clothing. At night on the altiplano, temperatures can drop well below freezing. Even in the lowlands, nights can be surprisingly chilly.

TRAIN

Bolivian railroads have been privatized and the passenger services have been cut back. The western network, now run by FCA, runs from Oruro to Uyuni and Villazón (on the Argentine border); a branch line runs southwest from Uyuni to Avaroa, on the Chilean border. Between Oruro, Tupiza and Uyuni, the very comfortable Expreso del Sur trains run twice per week – they have 'premier' and 'salon' classes, dining cars and video entertainment. Once a week the train continues to Villazón. The cheaper, less comfortable and even slower Tren Especial also runs twice a week from Oruro to Villazón.

In the east, there's a line from Santa Cruz to Quijarro on the border, where you cross to Corumbá on the Brazilian side. Another service goes south from Santa Cruz to Yacuiba on the Argentine border three times a week.

Rail travel in Bolivia can require determination and patience. Few stations have printed timetables and information is hard to get. Departure times may be scrawled on a blackboard, but cannot be relied on. When buying tickets, take your passport. For most trains, tickets are available only on the day of departure, but you can reserve seats on the better trains, sometimes through a travel agent.

BOAT

Half of Bolivia's territory lies in the Amazon Basin, where rivers are the main transport arteries and transport is by cargo boats, which carry everything from livestock to vehicles to human passengers. The main 'highways' of the region are the Ichilo, Mamoré, Beni, Madre de Dios and Guaporé rivers – all Amazon tributaries. For more information about boats, see the Amazon Basin section.

ORGANIZED TOURS

Organized tours, from La Paz and other centers, are normally arranged through hotels, agencies or tourist offices. They're a convenient way to visit an attraction when you're short of time and sometimes the easiest way to visit a remote area. They're also relatively inexpensive, from US$18 for a day trip, but the cost often depends on the number of people in your group.

Tours are excellent for visiting Tiahuanaco, for example. An English-speaking guide is normally included, and the ruins can become more than an impressive heap of rocks. A short tour is also useful for visiting the Chacaltaya ski slopes, which are difficult to reach on your own. Similarly, longer excursions to such remote attractions as Laguna Colorada or the Cordillera Apolobamba are most conveniently done through tour agencies in the nearest town.

For the more adventurous, who nevertheless don't want to strike out into the wilderness alone, there are a number of outfits that offer trekking, mountain climbing, and rainforest exploration packages. For mountain trekking or climbing in the Cordilleras, tour operators offer customized expeditions. They can arrange anything from just a guide and transport right up to equipment, porters and even a cook. Some also rent trekking equipment. Adventure-tour companies include:

Amazonas Adventure Tours (☎ 03-422760, fax 03-422748), 756 Av San Martín, 3rd Anillo Interno, Barrio Equipetrol, Casilla 2527, Santa Cruz. Specializes in visits to the remote Reserva de Vida Silvestre Ríos Blanco y Negro and the Perseverancia jungle resort

America Tours (☎ 02-374204, fax 02-328584), Av 16 de Julio 1490, ground floor, Casilla 2568, La Paz. Specializes in cultural and ecotourism trips to the Sajama and the far southwest, Rurrenabaque and Beni, and Jesuit missions

Andean Summits (☎ 02-317497, andean@latinwide.com), Calle Sagárnaga 189, 1st floor, Casilla 6976, La Paz. Offers mountaineering and trekking all over Bolivia, plus other adventure tours and archaeology trips

Colibri (☎ 02-371936, fax 02-355043, acolibri@ceibo.entelnet.bo), Calle Sagárnaga 309, Casilla 7456, La Paz. Offers comprehensive adventure-travel services: trekking, mountaineering, mountain biking, jungle trips and 4WD tours; rents climbing and trekking gear

Diana Tours (☎ 02-375374, fax 02-360831, hotsadt@ceibo.entelnet.bo), Calle Sagárnaga 328, Hotel Sagárnaga, La Paz. Good-value city tours as well as day trips to Tiahuanaco, Valle de la Luna, Chacaltaya and the Yungas and cheap tours to Copacabana and Puno

Fremen Tours (☎ 02-417062), Calle Pedro Salazar 537, La Paz; (☎ 042-259392, fax 042-117790) Casilla 9682, Calle Tumusla 0245, Cochabamba. Upmarket company specializing in the Amazon area, including the Chapare region, Parque Nacional Isiboro-Sécure, La Puente – a wilderness resort near Villa Tunari – and the *Reina de Enin* riverboat based in Trinidad

Huayna Potosí Tours (☎ 02-323584, fax 02-378226), Hotel Continental, Calle Illampu 626, Casilla 731, La Paz. Agency owner and A-1 character Dr Hugo Berrios built the luxurious Refugio Huayna Potosí (US$7 per night), which serves as expedition base camp. Dr Berrios speaks both English and French and organizes good-value treks and climbs in the Cordillera Real and Cordillera Apolobamba as well as in other areas of Bolivia

Inca Land Tours (☎ 02-365515, incaland@ceibo.com.entelnet.bo), Hotel Pando, Av Pando 248, La Paz. Established Peruvian operation now running tours out of Rurrenabaque; it arranges its own SAVE charter flights to Rurre and will book tickets in advance with TAM – at a premium

Ozono (☎/fax 02-323101, ozono@bolivia.com), Calle Salazar 2485, Casilla 7243, La Paz. An innovative adventure travel company specializing in mountaineering, trekking, rock climbing, extreme skiing, 4WD trips and lowland expeditions. Run by two British mountain and trekking guides and a local enthusiast, the emphasis is on well-off-the-beaten path destinations

TAWA Tours (☎ 02-325796, fax 02-391175), Calle Sagárnaga 161, 1st floor, Casilla 8662, La Paz. Offers a wide selection of adventure options, including mountaineering, cross-country skiing, jungle trips, trekking, horseback riding and mountain biking in all parts of Bolivia

Warning Lonely Planet has received several credible reports of very serious incidents involving the drugging and rape of women tourists who've taken guided jungle and pampas tours with independent guides around Rurrenabaque. Avoid unlicensed guides – ask to see *la autorización* – and see the warning in the Organized Tours heading in the Rurrenabaque section.

La Paz

The home of more than a million Bolivians, more than half of Indian heritage, La Paz is the country's largest city and its center of commerce, finance and industry. Although Sucre remains the judiciary capital, La Paz has usurped most government power and is now the de facto capital.

La Paz was founded by Alonso de Mendoza in 1548, following the discovery of gold in the Río Choqueyapu. Although gold fever didn't last long, the town's location on the main silver route from Potosí to the Pacific assured stable progress. It wasn't until the mid-20th century that peasant migration from the countryside caused the city to expand rapidly.

A visitor's first view of La Paz will be unforgettable. The city's bleak approaches are flanked by the gray, littered and poverty-plagued sprawl of El Alto, which was once merely a La Paz suburb but has now burgeoned into a separate entity with more than 500,000 inhabitants. At its edge, however, the earth drops away as if all the poverty and

LA PAZ

PLACES TO STAY
6 Residencial Illimani
26 Hostal Sucre
29 Residencial
    La Paz City Annex
37 Residencial La Paz City

PLACES TO EAT
12 Andromeda
14 Pronto Ristorante
18 Clap
19 La Québecoise
22 Mongo's Rock
    Bottom Café
28 Restaurant San Pedro
31 Eli's Pizza Express
33 McDonalds
35 La Bodeguita Cubana
41 Café Ciudad
42 Club Social Japón
43 Restaurant Vienna
44 Café Oro

OTHER
1 Main Bus Terminal
2 Transportes Larecaja
   Buses to Sorata
3 Autolineas Ingavi Buses to
   Tiahuanaco & Desaguadero
4 Transportes 2 de
   Febrero Buses
   to Copacabana
5 Transportes Manco Capac
   Buses to Copacabana
7 Museo de Aire Libre
   Templete Tiahuanaco
8 Tourist Police
9 Museo Marina
   Nuñez del Prado
10 Argentine Consulate
11 Peruvian Embassy
13 Café Montmartre,
    Alliance Française
15 German Embassy
16 Brazilian Consulate
17 Sopocachi Market
20 Plaza Avaroa
21 Canadian Embassy
23 Instituto Geográfico Militar
24 British Embassy
25 US Embassy
27 Plaza San Pedro
    (Plaza Sucre)
30 Magri Turismo
    (American Express)
32 AeroSur
34 Museo Arqueológico
    de Tiwanaku

BOLIVIA

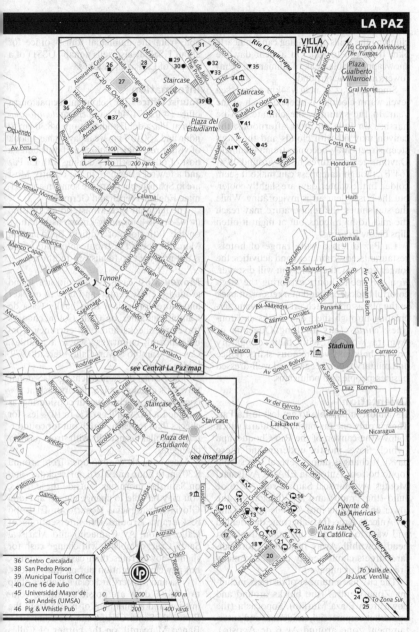

36 Centro Carcajada
38 San Pedro Prison
39 Municipal Tourist Office
40 Cine 16 de Julio
45 Universidad Mayor de
   San Andrés (UMSA)
46 Pig & Whistle Pub

ugliness has been obliterated, and there, 400m below, is La Paz, filling the bowl and climbing the walls of a gaping canyon nearly 5km from rim to rim. On a clear day, the snowcapped triple peak of Illimani (6402m) towers in the background.

Since La Paz is nearly 4km above sea level, warm clothing is needed much of the year. In the summer, the climate can be harsh; rain falls on most afternoons, the canyon may fill with clouds and the city's steep streets may become stream channels. Daytime temperatures hover around 18°C (64°F), though dampness can make it seem colder. In the winter, days are slightly cooler, but the crisp, clear air is invigorating. While the sun shines, the temperature may reach the mid- to high teens, but at night it often dips below freezing.

La Paz offers a wide range of hotels, restaurants, entertainment and activities; the longer you stay, the more you will discover. You can spend hours exploring the city's colorful backstreets and markets, or sit back in the plazas and watch urban Bolivians circulating through their daily tasks and routines: *cholas* (city-dwelling Quechua or Aymara women) with their obligatory bowler hats and voluminous skirts, police and military types, beggars and well-dressed businesspeople and politicians.

Orientation

It's almost impossible to get lost in La Paz. There's only one major thoroughfare, which follows the canyon of the Río Choqueyapu (which flows mostly underground these days). It changes names several times from top to bottom: Autopista El Alto, Av Ismael Montes, Av Mariscal Santa Cruz, Av 16 de Julio (the Prado) and Av Villazón. At the lower end, it splits into Av 6 de Agosto and Av Aniceto Arce. If you become disoriented and want to return to this main street, just head downhill. Away from this thoroughfare, streets climb steeply uphill, and many are cobbled or unpaved.

The city has a number of districts, including Zona Central (the blocks around and down from Plaza Murillo), Sopocachi (the upmarket commercial, residential and entertainment zone around Av 6 de Agosto), Miraflores (climbing the slope east of Zona Central) and Zona Sur (the most expensive residential area, farther down the valley).

Maps The best tourist map of the city is *Guía de Atractivos Turísticos y Rutas*, available from the municipal tourist office for about US$2. It also sells a map (US$1) of a couple of La Paz-area hikes.

Information

Tourist Offices The helpful municipal tourist office (☎ 02-371044) has a *caseta de información* at Plaza del Estudiante, open 8:30 am to noon and 2:30 to 7 pm weekdays. It has a book of visitor recommendations and distributes a host of other brochures dealing with La Paz and a few for elsewhere in the country. Most are in Spanish, but there are some in approximate English, French and German.

The national Vice-Ministerio de Turismo (☎ 02-367464; formerly known as Senatur), on the 18th floor of Edificio Ballivián, on Mercado, doesn't distribute information and is not really set up to answer questions.

Money Most casas de cambio are found around the city center, and they're quicker and more convenient than banks. Casa de Cambio Sudamer, on Calle Colón, changes traveler's checks and sells currency from neighboring countries (when available). Casa de Cambio Silver, Calle Mercado 979, is also good.

Some casas de cambio change US dollar traveler's checks for US dollars cash at 1% commission, which is worth considering, as outside La Paz you'll get 3% to 10% less for checks than for cash. Watch out for counterfeit US dollars, especially with street money-changers.

Most casas de cambio open from around 8:30 am to noon and 2 to 6 pm weekdays and on Saturday mornings. Outside these times, you may be able to change checks at Hotel Gloria, Residencial Rosario or El Lobo restaurant. Around the intersections of Calle Colón, Av Camacho and Mariscal Santa Cruz, cambistas will change cash for slightly lower rates than casas de cambio, but pay close attention during transactions.

Visa and MasterCard cash advances of up to US$300 daily are possible, with no commission and a minimum of hassle, from the Banco de Santa Cruz, Calle Mercado 1077; Banco Mercantil, on the corner of Calles Mercado and Ayacucho; and Banco Nacional de Bolivia, on the corner of Calle Colón and Av Camacho. Banco de La Paz charges

1.75% commission on cash withdrawals. Cash withdrawals, in bolivianos or dollars, are also possible at Enlace ATMs around the city.

The local American Express representative is Magri Turismo, 5th floor, Av 16 de Julio 1490.

Post The main post office, on the corner of Av Mariscal Santa Cruz and Calle Oruro, is open 8:30 am to 8 pm weekdays, 9 am to 7 pm Saturday and 9 am to noon on Sunday. Mail should be addressed to: Simon BOLÍVAR (with surname underlined and capitalized), Poste Restante, Correo Central, La Paz, Bolivia.

Mail is held for three months. The service is free, but you must present your passport when collecting post. Poste restante is sorted into foreign and Bolivian stacks, so those with Latin surnames should check the Bolivian stacks as well.

Telephone The Entel office, Calle Ayacucho 267, is open 7 am to 11:30 pm daily for national and international telephone calls. Entel also has telegram and telex services. There is also an increasing number of convenient *entelitos,* or 'little Entels,' scattered around the city.

Fax You can send and receive faxes at the main Entel office, but it's not very efficient. The public fax numbers are ☎ 02-391784 and 02-367625.

Email One of the best places for Internet access is on the ground floor of the Casa de Cultura Franz Tamayo, near Plaza Velasco, which charges US$1.80 per hour and has a good snack bar. WaraNet Cyber Cafe, in the basement of Galería Cristal, corner of Yanacocha and Potosí, charges US$3.60 an hour, has shorter hours and no coffee. Popular with backpackers, Angelo Colonial Cafe, upstairs at Linares 922, charges US$2.70 an hour, US$1.60 in the evenings. The café at Hotel Torino, near Plaza Murillo, is another good place to meet wired gringos.

Embassies & Consulates See the Facts for the Visitor section for a list of countries with representation in La Paz.

Visa Extensions Extensions for visas and lengths of stay are given with little ado at the immigration office (☎ 02-370475), at Av Camacho 1433. It's open 9 am to noon and 2:30 to 6 pm weekdays.

Photography Fujichrome color slide film is widely available for around US$7 per roll; be cautious when purchasing film at street markets, where it may be exposed to strong sun. Fujicolor is the most widely available print film.

For processing slides or print film, reliable laboratories include Casa Kavlin, at Calle Potosí 1130, and Foto Linares, in the Edificio Alborada, on the corner of Calle Loayza and Juan de la Riva. The latter sells a selection of Agfa film.

If you have camera problems, see Rolando Calla at Foto Linares (☎ 02-327703). He's there 10:15 am to 12:30 pm; from 3 to 7 pm, you can contact him at home (☎ 02-373621), Av Sánchez Lima 2178.

Medical Services The Unidad Sanitario Centro Piloto, near the brewery just off upper Av Ismael Montes, is open weekdays 8:30 am to noon and 2:30 to 6:30 pm and on Saturday morning. Anyone heading for the lowlands can pick up yellow-fever vaccinations and free chloroquine to be used as a malaria prophylaxis. (See the antimalarials segment of the Health section in the Facts for the Visitor chapter.)

Rabies vaccinations are available for US$1. Anyone bitten or scratched by a suspect animal must take daily vaccinations for seven subsequent days and three more over the next two months.

If you're in need of an English-speaking doctor, try Clínica Americana (☎ 02-783509), at 5809 Av 14 de Septiembre, Calle 9, in Obrajes. The sign outside says 'Hospital Metodista.' The German clinic, Clínica Alemana (☎ 02-329155, 02-373676), is at Av 6 de Agosto 2821.

Tourist Police If you have to report a crime, or if you're ripped off and need a police report for an insurance claim, go to the Policía Turistica (☎ 02-225016), Plaza del Estadio.

Things to See
La Paz has conventional tourist attractions such as churches and museums. It's also a city that invites leisurely exploration to

BOLIVIA

CENTRAL LA PAZ

appreciate the architectural mishmash, colorful street scenes, busy market life and the pervasive influence of the country's Indian cultures, which is more in evidence here than in other Latin American capitals.

Walking Tour A good place to start is the **Iglesia de San Francisco**, on the plaza of the same name. This imposing church was started in 1549 but was not finished until the mid-18th century, and its architecture reflects the mestizo style, emphasizing natural forms. Look for colorful Indian wedding processions on Saturday mornings.

From **Plaza San Francisco**, stroll up Calle Sagárnaga, which is lined with handicraft shops and street stalls selling beautiful Indian weavings (ponchos, mantas, chuspas), musical instruments, silver antiques, 'original' Tiahuanaco artifacts and a wealth of other tourist-oriented stuff. Turn right at Linares and walk through the most unusual **Mercado de Hechicería,** or **Mercado de los Brujos,** the 'Witches Market,' where merchants peddle magical ingredients, herbs,

seeds, figurines and strange things such as dried llama fetuses, intended as remedies for any combination of ills or as protection from the malevolent spirits that populate the Aymara world.

Higher up, along and around Buenos Aires, Graneros and Max Paredes, you'll find the **Mercado Negro**, a congested maze of makeshift stalls that sprawls over several blocks. The name means 'black market,' but it's mainly above board and is a good place to bargain for clothing and ordinary household goods. It is, however, notorious for pickpockets and skillful rip-offs; don't let yourself become distracted and avoid carrying anything of value.

From here, wander downhill, north and east of the markets, through bustling streets to the Plaza Alonso de Mendoza. Nearby is the **Museo Tambo Quirquincho**, a former *tambo* (wayside market and inn) that displays old-fashioned dresses, silverware, photos, artwork and a collection of Carnaval masks. It's open 9:30 am to 12:30 pm and 3:30 to 7 pm Tuesday to Friday, and 10 am to

CENTRAL LA PAZ

PLACES TO STAY
1 Alojamiento Universo
9 Hostal Ingavi
13 Hotel Continental
16 Hostal Austria
17 Hostal Yanacocha
18 Hotel La Joya
19 Residencial Rosario
23 Hotel Torino
25 Residencial El Lobo
26 Hotel Alem
27 Hotel Sagárnaga
29 Hostal Naira
41 Hotel Viena
43 Hostal República

PLACES TO EAT
5 Casa de los Paceños
6 El Gran Palacio
19 La Fuente
21 Hotel Gloria: Restaurant
  Vegetariano, Café Pierrot

23 Café Torino
24 El Lobo
31 Pollo Copacabana
33 Snack El Montañés
35 Clap
36 Imperial (Indian Restaurant)
40 Boutique del Pan Bakery
42 El Vegetariano
44 Acuario II
47 Confitería Club de La Paz
49 Restaurant Verona
51 Wall Street Cafe
54 Chifa Galaxia

OTHER
2 TAM Airline Office
3 Calle Jaén Museums
4 Marka Tambo (Peña)
7 Plaza Alonso de Mendoza
8 Museo Tambo Quirquincho
10 Cinemateca Boliviana
11 Teatro Municipal

12 Plaza Vicenta Juariste Eguino
14 Plaza Pérez Velasco
15 Museo de Etnografía y
  Folklore
20 Casa de Cultura, Internet Cafe
22 Museo Nacional del Arte
28 Iglesia de San Francisco
29 Peña Naira
30 Galería Cristal, Internet Cafe
32 Peña Huari
34 Museo de Coca
35 Angelo Colonial Cafe, Internet
  Cafe
37 Casa del Corregidor (Peña)
38 Entel (Main Office)
39 Amigos del Libro
45 Plaza Belzu
46 Main Post Office
48 Street Money Changers
50 Casa de Cambio Sudamer
52 LAB Office
53 Immigration

BOLIVIA

12:30 pm on weekends. Admission is US$0.50 on weekdays and free on Saturday.

Plaza Murillo Area This plaza is the formal center of the city, with various monuments, the imposing Congreso Nacional, the Palacio Presidencial and the 1835 catedral. The **Museo de la Catedral**, just down Socabaya, houses a collection of religious art and artifacts.

Just off the west side of the plaza, the **Museo Nacional del Arte** is in the superbly restored Palacio de los Condes de Arana, an impressive 18th-century mansion. This fine building houses a small but rewarding collection of indigenous, colonial and contemporary arts, with regular special exhibitions. It's open 9:30 am to 12:30 pm and 3 to 7 pm Tuesday to Friday and 10 am to 1 pm on weekends; admission is US$0.60.

Walk a block west on Ingavi to see the impressive facade of the **Iglesia de Santo Domingo**, on the corner of Yanacocha.

Calle Jaén Museums Four or five blocks northwest of the plaza, this beautifully restored colonial street has four small museums that can easily be appreciated in one visit. **Museo de Metales Preciosos Precolombinos** has amazing gold and silver artifacts; **Museo Casa Murillo** displays items

from the colonial period; **Museo del Litoral Boliviano** is about the 1884 war in which Bolivia lost its Pacific coast (may be closed for improvements); and **Museo Costumbrista Juan de Vargas** has good displays on the colonial period. All these museums open 9:30 am to 12:30 pm and 3 to 7 pm Tuesday to Friday and 10 am to 12:30 pm on weekends. Foreigners pay US$0.70 for admission to all four museums.

Other Museums Between the plaza and Calle Jaén, the free **Museo de Etnografía y Folklore**, in a restored colonial mansion, has a diverse collection of weavings and crafts from throughout the country. It's open 8:30 am to noon and 2:30 to 6:30 pm weekdays.

Down near Plaza Estudiante, the **Museo Nacional Arqueológico** holds a fascinating collection of Tiahuanaco (Tiwanaku) pottery, sculptures, textiles and other artifacts. It's open 9 am to noon and 3 to 7 pm Tuesday to Friday, and 10 am to 12:30 pm and 2:30 to 6:30 pm on Saturday; admission is US$1.80. Over in Miraflores, the **Museo de Aire Libre Templete Tiahuanaco** is a reproduction of part of the Tiwanaku archeological site.

In Sopocachi, the **Museo Marina Núñez del Prado**, Calle Ecuador 2034, is dedicated to Bolivia's most renowned sculptor. It's open 9:30 to 1 pm and 3 to 7 pm weekdays.

A new attraction is the **Museo de Coca**, which describes the place of coca in traditional societies, its use and exploitation by the soft-drink and pharmaceutical industries and the growth of cocaine as a major illicit drug. The displays are very educational, provocative and nonpropagandist. The museum is upstairs from a Calle Linares courtyard, and is open 10 am to 1 pm and 2 to 6 pm weekdays; admission is US$1.25. It may move to new premises at some stage, but it's well worth seeking out.

San Pedro Prison The 1500 prisoners here engage in various activities to get the money they need to survive – the most successful (or ruthless) are ensconced in comfortable cells with all the conveniences of a good hotel. One such enterprise for an English-speaking inmate is to conduct escorted tours of the prison, making it one of the world's most bizarre tourist attractions. To do it, approach the main gate (facing Plaza Sucre) between 9:30 am and 4 pm and tell one of the prisoners what you want. You'll need about US$5.50 for the 'tour,' US$1 for the guard, a few more bolivianos to pay the messenger and perhaps another US$20 worth in small bills if you want to buy any of the toys or other handicrafts made by the prisoners. Bring some identification, but no valuables or cameras.

Activities

Mountain Biking
For a fantastic outing, try a trip with Gravity Assisted Mountain Biking (☎ 02-374204): Staff members drive you to the top, you ride down. Two trip options (around US$45 per person) are to descend from Chacaltaya to La Paz and from La Cumbre down to Coroico.

Skiing
The world's highest downhill ski area (5320m down to 4900m) lies on the slopes of Chacaltaya, a rough 35km drive north from La Paz. The ski season (February to late April) has become uncertain because the ski area is on a glacier that is retreating due to global warming. There is just one primitive rope-tow, and the high altitude means most people can manage only a couple of runs before they're gasping for oxygen. Skiing here is strictly for enthusiasts.

Club Andino Boliviano (☎ 02-324682), Calle México 1638, operates the lift and the dilapidated ski lodge, where you can buy snacks and hot drinks, rent ski gear and even stay the night (US$3). It arranges weekend ski trips when conditions are suitable – make sure you're well acclimatized and bring good UV protection. A number of La Paz tour agencies offer daily tours to Chacaltaya (US$12), but they don't include skiing.

Organized Tours
A growing number of companies operate tours in and around La Paz. As well as those listed in the introductory Getting Around section, try Vicuña Tours (☎ 02-331999) or Pachamama Tours (☎ 02-318176). Prices depend on the size of the group – with four to six people, a three-hour city tour is around US$14 per person, a day trip to Tiwanaku around US$15 and to Chacaltaya about US$23.

Special Events
La Paz enjoys several local festivals and holidays during the year, but El Gran Poder (late May-early June) and Alasitas, the festival of abundance (January 24), will be of particular interest to visitors. The Fiestas Universitarias take place during the first week in December, accompanied by riotous merrymaking.

Places to Stay
Most budget hotels lock up at midnight; all places listed here have hot water at least part of the day.

A cheap, clean, secure and friendly place with hot showers is *Alojamiento Universo* (☎ 02-340341), Calle Inca Mayta Capac 175, which charges just US$2.50 per person for a dorm bed, slightly more for a double room with shared bath. Ground-floor rooms are nicer than those upstairs.

A friendly favorite of Peace Corps volunteers is *Residencial La Paz City* (☎ 02-322177), near Plaza San Pedro, at US$4.75 per person in a single or double room with shared bath. Larger rooms are US$4 per person. It also has an annex on Calle México.

Once travelers' most popular crash pad, the very central *Hotel Torino* (☎ 02-341487), Calle Socabaya 457, has slumped in its standards but is now being remodeled. Singles/

doubles without bath cost US$4.50/8, but prices will rise for renovated rooms.

The current backpackers' favorite is **Hostal Austria** (☎ 02-351140), at 531 Yanacocha. It has safe, gas-heated showers and cooking facilities. One- to four-bed rooms with shared bath cost US$5.40 per person – check the room first, because some are windowless cells. It's a bit of a scene and always full. When booking, give a clear arrival time, and don't be late. As an alternative, **Hostal Yanacocha** (☎ 02-369835), just across the road, is a faded, old-fashioned, family place and not at all a traveler's scene. Rooms are US$5.50 per person with shared bath, and a few have private baths. A new budget place is the **Residencial El Lobo**, on Illampu just east of the not unrelated Cafe El Lobo.

Conveniently close to the center, **Hostal Ingavi** (☎ 02-323645), Calle Ingavi 727, is a more modern place, with motellike rooms for US$8/16 with private bath – some have views across the valley. It's a bit noisy and less than sparkling-clean, but definitely OK.

In a quiet area not far from the stadium, **Residencial Illimani** (☎ 02-325948), Av Illimani 1817, is a friendly, family place that offers singles/doubles without bath for US$5.40/8.20.

Slightly more expensive, the almost modern, two-star **Hotel Continental** (☎/fax 02-378226), Calle Illampu 626, is used by climbers, low-budget tour groups and Bolivian business travelers. It's quite clean and OK at US$7.30/12.70 without bath or US$11/16.40 with bath.

The **Hostal Sucre** (☎ 02-328414), Calle Colombia 340, has helpful management and a good location facing Plaza San Pedro. Rooms of various sizes and standards are set around a courtyard. Singles/doubles cost US$12/20 with private bath, or US$9/12 without.

Another modern place is the relatively elegant **Hotel La Joya** (☎ 02-324346, fax 02-350959), near Plaza Garita de Lima in the Mercado Negro. The best rooms, with TV, phone, private bath and breakfast, cost US$20/25, but smaller rooms with shared bath are US$13/17, and discounts are possible when space is available.

A more interesting mid-range option is **Hotel Vienna** (☎ 02-323572), Calle Loayza 420, a baroque building with a grand courtyard and immense, high-ceilinged rooms;

room No 113 is especially nice. Singles/doubles with shared bath cost US$8/12 or US$11/16 with private bath.

Also recommended for its historic character and helpful staff, the sparkling **Hostal República** (☎ 02-357966), Calle Comercio 1455, was once the home of a Bolivian president. Singles/doubles/triples around the cobbled courtyards cost US$10/16/21 with shared bath, US$15/24/33 with private bath. Get breakfast treats just across the street and down a little in the unnamed place with the purple tiles.

The once widely recommended **Residencial Rosario** (☎ 02-325348), Calle Illampu 704, has converted all available space into a rabbit warren of rooms, passages and stairways to accommodate its enormous popularity. Still, it's kind of quaint, ultraclean and pleasantly quiet: A sort of gringo capsule with Bolivia just outside the door. Singles/doubles without bath cost US$18, around US$27/35 with private bath. Tour groups often reserve most of the better rooms.

Overlooking 'artesanía alley' on steep and bustling Calle Sagárnaga, the modern **Hotel Alem** (☎ 02-367400) has roomy singles/doubles for US$7/13 without bath, US$13.50/18 with bath and breakfast. Just downhill is the recommended **Hotel Sagárnaga** (☎ 02-350252), where a double with shared bath costs US$15; with private bath, cable TV and phone, a comfortable double is around US$25. Farther down, at Sagárnaga 161, the brand new **Hostal Naira** (☎ 02-355645), upstairs from the well-established Peña Naira, was charging US$18/24 for bright, spiffy rooms around an airy courtyard, but will probably up the price to over US$30 as it becomes better known.

Places to Eat

La Paz has a wealth of inexpensive eateries and quite a few quality restaurants that are excellent values. Most budget options offer set meals (typically almuerzo but sometimes cena too) and a short list of the most common dishes such as lomo, churrasco, milanesa and silpancho (all meat dishes). Some also include regional specialties such as sajta and chairo (see the Food section earlier in this chapter) and *ranga* (tripe with yellow pepper, potato and tomato and onion sauce). Most of La Paz's upmarket restaurants are southeast of the center, around Avs 20 de Octubre, 6 de

BOLIVIA

Agosto and 16 de Julio and farther down in the posh Zona Sur district.

Breakfast Because most breakfast venues don't open until 8:30 or 9 am, early risers desperate for a caffeine jolt head to the markets' cheap bread rolls and riveting coffee concentrate. Vendors in *Plaza San Francisco* also sell salteñas, empanadas and api.

You'll find a good early breakfast near some popular hotels. At Residencial Rosario, *La Fuente* serves fresh fruit, juices, delicious bread and all the other components of continental and American breakfasts. Another is *Café Torino*, beside the Hotel Torino, which opens at 7:30 am and serves good almuerzos, US$2.

Next to Hotel Vienna on Calle Loayza, *El Vegetariano* has healthy breakfasts of porridge, yogurt, juice, granola and crêpes. It opens at 8:30 am. If you prefer a quick coffee and a roll or salteña, go to *Confitería Club de La Paz*, a literary café and haunt of politicians and other interesting habitués, at the sharp corner of Avs Camacho and Mariscal Santa Cruz.

Snacks & Fast Food If you don't mind the hectic setting, markets are your best budget eating option. The best one is *Mercado Camacho*, on the corner of Camacho and Bueno, where you'll find takeaway snack stands selling empanadas and chicken sandwiches and comedores with covered sitting areas. A filling meal of soup, a meat dish, rice, lettuce and *oca* or potato is less than US$1. Other places for cheap informal market meals include the Buenos Aires and cemetery areas.

For excellent empanadas, go to the first landing on the steps between the Prado and Calle México. For US$0.40, you'll get an enormous beef or chicken empanada especial served with your choice of sauces.

The *Boutique del Pan* bakery, on Calle Potosí near Loayza, has every imaginable bread concoction: brilliant fruit bread, rolls, brown bread and so on. Some of the best coffee in town is served up at *Café Oro* on Av Villazón below Plaza del Estudiante. Another friendly coffee shop is *Pierrot*, on the ground floor of the Hotel Gloria. Sweettooths can stuff themselves with European coffee, decadent pastries, biscuits and other taste treats at *Kuchen Stube*, Calle Rosendo Gutiérrez 461.

Apart from *McDonald's,* on El Prado, and *Denny's,* on Mariscal Santa Cruz, there are several imitation American fast-food places, including the unfortunately named *Clap*, with two locations – Av Aniceto Arce and Belisario Salinas. A local favorite is *Eli's Pizza Express,* at 1491 and 1800 Av 16 de Julio as well as at other locations. You can choose between pizza, pasta, pastries and rather unusual tacos. The food is only mediocre, but there's no waiting.

For quick chicken, try *Pollo Copacabana*, where you'll get roast chicken, chips and fried plantains smothered in ketchup, mustard and *ají* (chili sauce) for US$2. There are locations on Calle Potosí and Calle Comercio. Beside the former is a wonderful sweet shop selling Bolivia's own Breick chocolate – some of the best!

Lunch Afternoon meals can be the best budget deal of the day. Apart from the markets, where US$1 buys a filling plateful, the almuerzo offered at a thousand family-run hole-in-the-wall restaurants can be excellent, varied and almost as cheap – look for the chalkboard menus out front. As a general rule, the higher you climb from the Prado, the cheaper the meals will be.

Snack El Montañés, directly opposite Hotel Sagárnaga, has good light meals and desserts. In an arcade farther down Calle Sagárnaga, inexpensive *Imperial* features a selection of Indian (ie, from India) and vegetarian dishes.

Along Calle Rodríguez, several places serve almuerzos for less than US$1. The same street also boasts several excellent ceviche restaurants, where Peruvian-style ceviche costs under US$2. The best is *Acuario II* (no sign), opposite Acuario I. *Playa Brava Cevichería,* on Fernando Guachalla opposite Sopocachi market, is another option for great marinated fish.

Bolivian specialties such as *charque kan* (mashed hominy with strips of dried llama meat), *chorizo* (spicy sausage), *anticuchos* (beef-heart kebabs) and *chicharrón* (grilled chicken or beef) are available at *Típicos*, on the 6th level of the Shopping Norte arcade, at Potosí and Socabaya. On weekdays, *Restaurant San Pedro*, near Plaza San Pedro, serves four-course almuerzos for US$1. On Sunday, it does an elaborate 'executive lunch' (US$1.75), served with wine.

Perhaps the best pizzas in town are tossed at *Sergio's*, a tiny place on Av Villazón near the Aspiazu steps. *Café Montmartre*, at Alliance Française on Calle Fernando Guachalla, has lunch specials (US$3) with some vegetarian choices. Also recommended is *Andromeda*, at the bottom of the Aspiazu steps on Av Arce. It serves US$3 almuerzos, with meat dishes and vegetarian options on other days. On Friday, there's always a fish dish.

At *Café Ciudad*, on Plaza del Estudiante, service is slow and the food is ordinary, but the full menu is available 24 hours a day, seven days a week, and they don't mind travelers lingering over coffee and snacks – try the apple pie. *Restaurant Verona*, on Calle Colón near Av Mariscal Santa Cruz, is recommended for its sandwiches (US$1.50), pizzas (US$3) and almuerzos (US$3.50). Also very popular is *La Fiesta*, on Mariscal Santa Cruz opposite the bottom of Calle Socabaya. Lunches (US$1.75) are good but breakfasts are overpriced.

The restaurant in *Hotel Gloria*, Calle Potosí 909, is recommended for vegetarian set lunches (US$2.50). It's popular, so arrive before 12:30 pm. Tiny *El Vegetariano* (see Breakfast earlier) has excellent vegetarian salteñas (US$0.40) and great-value veggie almuerzos.

Dinner Many of the suggested lunch places also serve dinner. An excellent choice for homemade pasta and other good-value Italian meals is *Pronto Ristorante*, Calle Jáuregui 2248, a half-block from Av 6 de Agosto.

Fish fans will relish *El Gran Palacio*, on Av América, where surubí, pacu, trucha, pejerrey and sábalo dishes average US$2.

Inexpensive lunches and dinners are also available at *El Lobo*, upstairs on the corner of Calles Santa Cruz and Illampu, where the curry and chicken dishes are particularly good. It's popular with young Israelis and the menu is in English and Hebrew.

Another great choice is the friendly, family-run *La Casa de los Paceños*, Calle Sucre 856, handy to the Calle Jaén museums. In addition to set almuerzos (US$1.50), try the typical La Paz dishes, including saice, sajta, *fricasé* (stew with ground maize), *chairo paceño* (mutton or beef soup with chuño and hominy) and *fritanga* (fried

pork). It's open for lunch every day except Monday and for dinner from Tuesday to Friday.

Few places are open on Sunday for dinner. *Restaurant Verona* is one of the few lights on Sunday evenings around the usually bright Prado. Other Sunday alternatives include *Mongo's Rock Bottom Café*, an American-style bar and restaurant at Hermanos Manchego 2444 above Plaza Isabel la Católica. Specialties include onion rings, nachos, enormous burgers (from US$3), Miller beer and American football on a big-screen TV. It's an expat hangout.

Inexpensive Chinese *Chifa Galaxia*, on Calle Buena, is frequented by locals. Not far away, *Wall Street Cafe*, Camacho 1363, has American-style meals and good coffee until late at night. It's a little on the expensive side but very relaxed. Some other international offerings in the same part of town include the very agreeable *La Bodeguita Cubana*, Zuazo 1653, with filling Cuban specialties; *Club Social Japón*, around the corner, which has a good, unpretentious Japanese eatery upstairs; the classy *Restaurant Vienna* (☎ 02-391660), Zuazo 1905, possibly the best continental cuisine in town (main courses run US$5 to US$7); and its classy rival *La Québecoise* (☎ 02-361782), Calle 20 de Octubre 2355, recommended for its excellent French-Canadian food and atmosphere (main meals are US$7 to US$10).

Entertainment

Typical of La Paz (and all of Bolivia) are folk music venues known as peñas. Most present traditional Andean music, featuring zampoñas, quenas and charangos, but also often include guitar shows and song recitals. The best known is probably *Peña Naira* (☎ 02-350530), Sagárnaga 161, just above Plaza San Francisco, with shows geared toward foreign tourists on Friday and Saturday evenings; cover is around US$3. *Peña Huari* (☎ 02-316225), Sagárnaga 339, is also popular with tour groups. The *Casa del Corregidor* (☎ 02-363633), Murillo 1040, and *Marka Tambo* (☎ 02-340416), Calle Jaén 710, attract local music fans as well.

There are scores of inexpensive local drinking dens scattered around the city, especially on and around El Prado. Unaccompanied women should steer clear and

BOLIVIA

nobody should sit down to drink with Bolivians in one of these unless they intend to pass out later in the evening.

An alternative venue is **Centro Carcajada** (☎ 02-317967), Almirante Grau 525, a feminist center hosting cultural activities, theater, music and sociopolitical discussion. It serves coffee and snacks and opens 8 am to 10 pm Monday to Thursday, later on Friday and Saturday.

There are also a few more elegant bars, which are frequented by foreigners and middle-class Bolivians. **La Luna**, Calle Oruro 197, is a central and friendly pub, with music and a mixed clientele. **Mongo's,** at Calle Hermanos Manchego 2444, offers American beer and is open until 2 am, seven nights a week. Near Alliance Française, **Café Montmartre** is more a bar than a café, but it has interesting decor and a varied crowd of twenty- and thirtysomethings. For novelty value, the **Pig & Whistle,** on Calle Goitia near Av Arce, is a plausible impersonation of a British pub, though it doesn't have British beer on tap. It's lively on Friday, but pretty quiet at other times.

The local gilded youth mingle with upmarket expats in Zona Sur, where US-style bars and discos have sprouted along Av Ballivián and Calle 21. You'll need more than a backpacker's budget and wardrobe to make the scene here.

For classic and current movies from South America and elsewhere, check the program at the **Cinemateca Boliviana**, on the corner of Pichincha and Indaburo (US$1.50). Modern cinemas on the Prado, including **Cine 16 de Julio**, show recent international releases (about US$2.50), usually in the original language with Spanish subtitles. The Teatro Municipal, on the corner of Sanjinés and Indaburo, has an ambitious program of folk-music concerts and foreign theatrical presentations.

Getting There & Away

Air El Alto airport, on the altiplano at 4018m, is 10km from the center of La Paz. Micro 212 (US$0.75) runs between Plaza Isabel la Católica and the airport; the radio taxi fare is US$5. Heading into town from the airport, catch micro 212 outside the terminal. It will drop you anywhere along the Prado. Airline offices in La Paz include the following:

Aerolíneas Argentinas
(☎ 02-351711, fax 02-391059)
Av 16 de Julio 1486, edificio Banco de la Nación Argentina, ground floor

AeroSur
(☎ 800-3030, 02-369292, fax 02-390457)
El Prado 1616, Edificio Petrolero

American Airlines
(☎ 02-351360, fax 02-391080)
Plaza Venezuela 1440, Edificio Herrmann P Busch

British Airways
(☎ 02-373857, fax 02-391072)
Edificio Mariscal de Ayacucho, Calle Loayza

Faucett Peruvian Airlines
(☎ 02-325764, fax 02-350118)
Edificio Cámara de Comercio Office 4, ground floor

Iberia
(☎ 02-320270, fax 02-391192)
Av 16 de Julio 1616, Edificio Petrolero, 2nd floor

KLM
(☎ 02-376001, fax 02-362697)
Plaza del Estudiante 1931

LanChile
(☎ 02-358377, fax 02-392051)
Av 16 de Julio 1566, Edificio Mariscal de Ayacucho, Suite 104 ground floor

LAB
(☎ 800-4321, 02-367707)
Av Camacho 1460

Lufthansa
(☎ 02-372170, fax 02-431267)
Av 6 de Agosto 2512

TAM
(☎ 02-366654, fax 02-362697)
Av Ismael Montes 728

United Airlines
(☎ 02-372462, fax 02-391505)
Calle Mercado 1328, Edificio Ballivián 1606

Varig
(☎ 02-314040, fax 02-391131)
Av Mariscal Santa Cruz 1392, Edificio Cámara de Comercio,

Bus The main bus terminal (☎ 02-367275) is at Plaza Antofagasta, 1km or so uphill from the city center. Bus fares are relatively uniform between companies, but competition on most routes is such that they're amazingly cheap.

Buses to Oruro run about every half-hour (US$2.70, 3½ hours). To Uyuni, Panasur departs on Tuesday and Friday at 5:30 pm (US$7.30, 14 hours). Plenty of flotas go to Cochabamba (US$5.40, six hours), leaving

Patagonian sky – Argentina's finest

Stanley resident, Falkland Islands

Colorful La Boca, Buenos Aires, Argentina

Buenos Aires' sultry tango

Woman with vicuña, Isla del Sol, Bolivia

Train cemetery near Uyuni, Bolivia

Tiahuanaco ruins, Bolivia

Building a dock on Isla del Sol

either in the morning or between 8 and 9 pm. Many of these continue on to Santa Cruz or connect with a Santa Cruz bus in Cochabamba. Direct Santa Cruz buses depart every evening (US$22, 17 hours).

There are a few direct buses to Sucre (US$13, 14 hours), but most pass through Cochabamba, and some stop there for several hours, so the trip can take 19 hours altogether. Numerous flotas run daily to Potosí (US$8.20, 11 hours), departing between 6 and 7 pm. Have warm clothes handy for this typically chilly trip. Some Potosí buses continue on to Tarija, Tupiza, Yacuiba and Villazón. There are also direct buses to Villazón (US$14.50, 20 hours).

Manco Capac and Transtur 2 de Febrero run to Copacabana (US$3.60, 3½ hours) several times daily from Calle José María Aliaga, near the cemetery. Alternatively, for US$6, there are more comfortable tourist minibuses (see Tours) that do hotel pick-ups. From Copacabana, numerous minibuses and micros run to Puno (Peru).

Autolíneas Ingavi has four buses daily to Desaguadero via Tiahuanaco, leaving from Calle José María Asín near the cemetery (US$1, 1½ hours). Nearby are Transportes Larecaja and Flota Unificado Sorata, both on Calle Angel Babia, which operate daily morning and early afternoon buses to Sorata. Seats are in short supply, so book your ticket at least the day before.

A number of flotas in Barrio Villa Fátima, which you can reach by micro or minibus trufi (see the following Getting Around section) from the Prado or Calle Camacho, offer daily services to the Yungas and beyond: Coroico, Chulumani, Rurrenabaque, San Borja, Riberalta and Guayaramerín. Turbus Totai and Flota Yungueña minibuses to Coroico leave from near the gas station in Villa Fátima.

Flota Litoral and Tours Andes Mar have several buses daily to Arica, Chile (US$16, eight hours), traveling via Tambo Quemado and Lauca National Park, and regular buses to Iquique (US$24, 11 hours). Warm clothing is essential for either option.

Getting Around

La Paz is well served by its public transport system. There are full-size buses and medium-size 'Bluebird'-type buses (called micros), which charge US$0.22 (B$1.20) for

trips around the center of town. Kombi minibuses charge US$0.24 (B$1.30) around town and US$0.36 (B$2) to the Zona Sur. Buses, micros and minibuses usually announce their destination or route with a sign inside the windshield. Trufis are shared taxis that follow a fixed route, and they cost around US$0.45 (B$2.50) per person around the center, although the fare may be a bit more for long uphill routes. Any of these vehicles can be waved down anywhere, except near intersections or in areas cordoned off by the police.

Radio taxis, which you can phone or flag down, charge US$1.10 (B$6) around the center and US$2.70 (B$15) to the cemetery district, but a bit more at night. Charges are for up to four passengers and include pick-up, if necessary.

To the airport, minibus No 212 costs US$0.55 (B$3); a taxi is US$7. From the airport, be sure to get a proper taxi from the rank.

AROUND LA PAZ
Valle de la Luna

The Valle de la Luna (Valley of the Moon) is a pleasant and quiet half-day break from urban La Paz. It isn't a valley at all, but a bizarre eroded hillside maze of canyons and pinnacles technically known as badlands. It lies about 10km down the canyon of the Río Choqueyapu from the city center.

To get there, catch a Mallasa-bound micro (No 231 or 273) from the Prado. Get off at the junction near Malasilla Golf Course, and walk for a few minutes toward Mallasa village. When you see a soccer field, you're at the top of Valle de la Luna. Be careful walking through the valley – the route is badly eroded, slippery and dangerous.

Afterwards, you can also visit the blossoming resort village of Mallasa and La Paz's spacious new zoo. From the top of Valle de la Luna, catch a micro marked 'Mallasa' or 'Zoológico,' or continue on foot; it's just a couple of kilometers. The zoo (US$0.70) is open from 9 am to 7 pm daily.

Chacaltaya

Skiing at 'the world's highest ski area' is problematic (see Skiing earlier in the Activities section), but several La Paz tour companies run sightseeing trips (from US$18 to US$35). At present, there's no public transport.

Tiahuanaco

Tiahuanaco, also spelled Tiwanaku, is Bolivia's most significant archaeological site, 72km west of La Paz on the road toward Desaguadero, on the Peruvian border.

Little is known of the Tiahuanaco people who constructed this great ceremonial center on the southern shore of Lake Titicaca. Archaeologists generally agree that the civilization that spawned Tiahuanaco rose about 600 BC. The ceremonial site was under construction around 700 AD, but after 1200 AD the group faded into obscurity. However, evidence of its influence, particularly religious influence, has been found throughout the area of the later Inca empire.

There are a number of large stone slabs (up to 175 tons in weight) strewn around the site, a ruined pyramid, the remains of a ritual platform and many other ruins. Much has been restored, not always with total authenticity. Across the railway line from Tiahuanaco is the excavation of **Puma Punku** (Gateway of the Puma) and a site museum.

Foreigners pay about US$2.70 admission to the site and museum. If you're not in a tour group, you can hire a guide who will provide a greater appreciation of Tiahuanaco's history. They're available outside the fence for around US$2.50 after bargaining.

Getting There & Away You can stop at Tiahuanaco en route between La Paz and Puno, Peru, but most travelers prefer to do La Paz-Puno via Lake Titicaca and visit Tiahuanaco as a day trip from La Paz. Autolíneas Ingavi has four buses daily to Tiahuanaco, leaving from Calle José María Asín near the cemetery (US$1, 1½ hours) – some of which continue to Desaguadero. To return to La Paz after a day trip to Tiahuanaco, flag down a bus, almost always a crowded option, or walk into Tiahuanaco village, about 1km west of the site, and catch one along the main street.

A dozen or more La Paz tour agencies offer guided tours to Tiahuanaco for around US$15.

The Yungas

The dramatic Yungas, northeast of La Paz beyond the Cordillera Real, are characterized by steep forested mountainsides that drop into humid, cloud-filled gorges. They form a natural division between the cold, barren altiplano and the lush Amazonian rain forests of northeastern Bolivia. Going north from La Paz, the road winds up to the 4600m La Cumbre pass, then descends a dramatic 4343m to the lowlands of the Beni region. Tropical fruits, coffee, sugarcane, cacao and coca all grow in the Yungas with minimal tending. The climate is moderate, with rain or mist possible at any time of year.

COROICO

Deservedly popular with travelers, the small village of Coroico is perched on the shoulder of Cerro Uchumachi at an altitude of 1500m. It's a holiday spot and weekend getaway for middle-class *paceños* (citizens of La Paz), a retreat for a few European immigrants, a perfect place for relaxation and a base for short hiking trips into the countryside.

Hire horses from Coroico a Caballo (☎ 0811-6015) at about US$6.50 per hour. Banco Unión does Visa cash advances, but won't change traveler's checks. It's best to bring bolivianos.

Places to Stay

The cheapest places are the *Alojamiento de la Torre*, a little northeast of the plaza, at US$2 per person for a tiny room, and the very basic *Alojamiento 20 de Octobre*, at US$2.50 per person with shared cold shower. Southwest of the plaza, popular *Hostal Kory* has a pool, great views, and small, clean rooms from US$5.50; nicer rooms with private bath cost US$11/18, but 20% more on weekends – its restaurant is ordinary. Slightly more expensive, *Hostal La Casa* (☎ 0811-6024) is downstairs from the Kory and has a pool, views and an excellent restaurant. The German-run *Hostal Sol y Luna*, a 20-minute walk east of town, has double *cabañas* (cabins) at US$6 per person, rooms at US$4 per person and campsites at US$3 per person.

The exceptionally friendly and good-value *Hotel Don Quixote* (☎ 0811-6007), 800m northeast of the plaza, is popular with Bolivians and an excellent mid-range option – rooms with all the amenities cost US$15/23.

One of Bolivia's nicest backpackers' haunts is the friendly and comfortable *Hotel Esmeralda* (☎ 0811-6017), 600m up the hillside east of the plaza. The restaurant and the views defy description and for relaxation, there's a pool and a sunny patio. Single/double rooms cost US$7/14, or US$15/30 with private bath. Book ahead if you can, or phone from the plaza for free pick-up.

Places to Eat

For its size, Coroico offers a great choice of excellent eateries. Try *Bamboo's* for tasty Mexican dishes and the *Back-Stube Konditorei*, near Hostal Kory, for pizza, pasta, Yungas coffee and German-style cakes and pastries. *Hostal La Casa* also has fine European cuisine – book ahead for fondue or raclette (closed Monday). The culinary highlight of Coroico, and some say all Bolivia, is the French-run *Ranch Beni* – it's a 15-minute walk east of town and worth every step.

Getting There & Away

The frightening road between La Paz and Coroico drops over 3000m in 80km, flanked by stunning vertical scenery. It's called the most dangerous road in the Americas, but it's probably a bit less dangerous on weekdays than weekends – a new road is under construction. Buses and minibuses leave from near the gas station in La Paz's Villa Fátima neighborhood. Minibuses with Trans Totai or Flota Yungueña are probably the best way to go (US$2, four hours). Most departures are in the mornings and on weekends.

Minibuses stop first at the junction of Yolosa, from where many buses and trucks continue down to Guanay, Rurrenabaque and farther into Bolivian Amazonia. Coroico is 7km uphill from Yolosa.

TREKS IN THE CORDILLERA REAL

There are several interesting treks between the altiplano and the Yungas, all of which cross the Cordillera Real on relatively low passes. The most popular are the Choro (La Cumbre to Coroico), Taquesi and Yunga Cruz. These two- to four-day walks all begin with a brief ascent into the Cordillera Real, then head down from spectacular high-mountain landscapes into the exuberant vegetation of the Yungas. Hikers should carry food and camping equipment, including a tent, sleeping bag, rainproof gear, stove and flashlight. Security is a concern, espe-

cially on the Choro trek, where there have been several nasty incidents.

Serious hikers should consult Lonely Planet's *Bolivia* or Bradt Publications' *Backpacking and Trekking in Peru & Bolivia*. They include maps and detailed descriptions of these treks, as well as other routes.

GUANAY

Isolated Guanay makes a good base for visits to the gold-mining operations along the Río Mapiri and Río Tipuani. The miners and panners are down-to-earth, and if you can overlook the devastation of the landscape caused by their hunt for gold, a visit will prove interesting. Guanay is a detour from the Coroico-Rurrenabaque road, and it's at the end of the El Camino del Oro trek, which descends from Sorata. Access to the mining areas is by jeep along the Llipi road, or by motorized dugout canoes up the Río Mapiri.

Places to Stay & Eat

The *Hotel Pahuichi*, one block downhill from the plaza, is far and away the best value in town for about US$2 per person. Other possibilities are the slightly more expensive *Panamericana* and several other basic but friendly places within a block of the plaza, which will all be under US$2.50 per person.

The Pahuichi has Guanay's best and most popular restaurant, but there are plenty of others on the main drag and around the plaza.

Getting There & Away

The bus offices are all around the plaza, but buses leave from a block away. Four companies offer daily runs both to and from La Paz, via Caranavi and Yolosa (US$8, 11 hours). A Trans Totaí bus leaves Guanay at 8 am, but the others are all in the afternoon, between 4:30 and 5 pm. For Coroico, get off at Yolosa and catch a pickup truck up the hill. For Rurrenabaque, get off in Caranavi to connect with a northbound bus.

Alternatively, you can go to and from Rurrenabaque by motorized canoe along the Río Beni. Make arrangements at the Agencia Fluvial in Guanay or Rurrenabaque. Canoes take about 10 people, at around US$15 to US$20 each. Allow eight to 10 hours to Rurre.

SORATA

Sorata is often described as having the most beautiful setting in Bolivia, and this is no exaggeration – it sits at an altitude of 2695m beneath the towering snowcapped peaks of Illampu (6362m) and Ancohuma (6427m). It's popular with mountaineers and trekkers as well as with people who just want a cool place to relax.

Most visitors make a day trip of the 12km hike to the Gruta de San Pedro (San Pedro Cave), a 2½-hour walk from Sorata (a car one way costs about US$2.50).

Trekking

Ambitious hikers may want to try the six- or seven-day trek along El Camino del Oro, an ancient route used as a commerce and trade link between the altiplano and the Río Tipuani gold fields. Alternatively, there's the challenging Mapiri Trail (five days) or the steep climbs up to Laguna Challata (a long day hike), Comunidad Lakathiya (another long day hike) or Laguna Glacial (three days). Inquire locally about security before attempting any treks in this area.

The Asociación de Guías Turísticas Sorata (☎ 0811-5044) is a local group that can rent equipment (around US$6 per day for tent, stove and sleeping bag) and arrange treks. Budget around US$13 per day for a guide and a pack-mule.

Places to Stay

The cheapest place is *Hotel San Cristóbal*, just off the plaza, at less than US$2 per person with cold water in the shared bathroom. *Hostal Panchita* (☎ 0811-5038), on the plaza, is cheap, friendly and popular with travelers at about US$2.70 per person.

Another popular spot is the German-run *Hotel Copacabana* (☎ 0811-5042), 15 minutes from the plaza toward San Pedro. Singles/doubles cost US$3/3.70 with shared bath, US$6.40/7.30 with private bath. It has trekking information, a good restaurant and a large video collection.

For its friendly antique atmosphere and brilliant flower garden, the Canadian-run *Residencial Sorata* (☎ 0811-5044), on the main plaza, is an accommodation highlight. Grand rooms in this colonial mansion cost US$5/9 with shared bath; smaller rooms are US$3.50/7, and rooms with private bath are US$6.50/13. There's a spacious restaurant and lounge area, a book exchange and trekking information.

Places to Eat & Drink

Small, inexpensive restaurants around the plaza and the market sell filling almuerzos for less than US$2. One good choice is *Restaurant-Café Altai*, with a healthy yogurt-muesli breakfast (US$2) and an outstanding selection of vegetarian and international dishes (around US$5). The classiest place is *Casa de Papaco*, signposted as 'Ristorante Pizzeria Italiano,' which offers genuine Italian cuisine, homemade pasta and even good espresso in a garden setting overlooking town. Plan on US$6 per person. Backpackers drink at the little *Spider Bar*, 250m west of the plaza.

Getting There & Away

Sorata is a long way from the other Yungas towns and there's no road connecting it directly with Coroico. From La Paz, Transportes Larecaja and Flota Unificado Sorata leave two to six times daily (from 6 am to 2 pm) from Calle Angel Babia, near the cemetery (US$2, 4½ hours). Buses get crowded, so book tickets a day ahead to be sure of a seat. Foreigners must register at the military post near Achacachi, so have your passport handy. There are no direct buses from Copacabana to Sorata. You must get off at the junction town of Huarina and wait for another bus, which may be full anyway – it can be a long wait.

Lake Titicaca

Lake Titicaca, more than 230km long and 97km wide, is one of the world's highest navigable lakes. Straddling the Peru-Bolivia border, it lies in a depression of the altiplano at an elevation of 3820m and covers an area of more than 8000 sq km. It's a remnant of the ancient inland sea known as Lago Ballivián, which covered much of the altiplano before geological faults and evaporation caused the water level to drop.

The lake offers an incongruous splash of clear, blue waters amid the parched dreariness of the altiplano. According to ancient myths, this was the birthplace of the sun, and the Incas believed that their first emperor rose from the rock called Titicaca, or 'rock of

LAKE TITICACA

1 Isla Taquiri
2 Isla Suriqui
3 Isla Pariti
4 Isla Kalahuta

BOLIVIA

the puma,' on the northern tip of Isla del Sol. The lake is still revered by the Aymara people who live on its shores.

COPACABANA

Copacabana is an untidy town on the southern shore of Lake Titicaca, near the Peruvian border – it's not too attractive, but some people get to like it. In the 16th century, after Copacabana was presented with an image of the Virgin of Candelaria, there was a rash of miracles in the town. Since then, Copacabana has been a pilgrimage site, and today, the Virgin is the patron saint of Bolivia.

Copacabana is well known for its fiestas, which bring the town to life. At other times, it's a sleepy, dusty little place, but it's a convenient base for visiting Isla del Sol, and a popular stop between La Paz and Puno (Peru). It rains some in December and January, but for the rest of the year it's pleasant and sunny, with cool or cold nights.

Information

A casa de cambio on 6 de Agosto, beside the Hotel Playa Azul, exchanges cash and trav-

eler's checks for a 4% commission, and there's a Banco Unión up the street, which does Visa cash advances every day except Monday.

During festivals in Copacabana, be especially wary of light-fingered revelers. Also, stand well back during fireworks displays; crowd safety is a rather low priority.

Things to See

The sparkling Moorish-style **catedral**, built between 1605 and 1820, dominates the town. The famous statue of the Virgen de Copacabana, carved in wood by the Indian artist Francisco Tito Yupanqui, is housed upstairs in the Camarín de la Virgen. It's open 11 am to noon and 2 to 6 pm daily (US$0.60). The blessing of cars, trucks and buses is a colorful scene that often takes place in front of the catedral.

Another local tradition is the blessing of miniature objects, like cars or houses, at the Alasitas festival (January 24) as a prayer that the real thing will be obtained in the coming year. Sometimes these cute miniatures are exhibited in town or sold in stalls.

The hill to the north of town is **Cerro Calvario**, which can be reached in half an hour and is well worth the climb, particularly in the late afternoon, to see the sunset over the lake. Many pilgrims make this climb, and lots of stalls sell miniatures on Sundays. Less impressive are the minor Inca sites around town: the **Tribunal del Inca**, near the cemetery; **Horca del Inca**, on the hill Niño Calvario; and **Baño del Inca**, north of the village.

Special Events

Following Alasitas, Fiesta de la Virgen de Copacabana is celebrated on the first two days of February. Indians and dancers from both Peru and Bolivia perform traditional Aymara dances; there's much music, drinking and feasting. On Good Friday, the town fills with pilgrims, who join a solemn candlelit procession at dusk. The biggest fiesta lasts for a week around Independence Day, the first week in August, and features parades, brass bands, flute and panpipe ensembles, fireworks and plenty of chicha.

Places to Stay

Copacabana has many lodgings, including the least expensive residenciales and alojamientos in Bolivia as well as some quite good mid-range hotels. During fiestas, however, everything fills up and prices increase up to threefold.

The cheapest places in town are less than US$2/3 for basic singles/doubles with shared bath. In this range are alojamientos such as the *Emperador*, with bright colors and a sunny mezzanine; *Aroma*, where some rooms upstairs have a fine view; *Kota Kahuaña*, closer to the lake, with kitchen facilities; and *Bolívar*, which is well recommended by readers.

Moving up a notch, try residenciales such as *La Porteñita* (☎ 0862-2006), *Aransaya* (☎ 0862-2229) and *Copacabana* (☎ 0862-2220), which charge around US$4/5.50 for rooms without bath and a bit more for the few rooms with private baths. Also in this range is *Residencial Brisas del Titicaca*, nicely located by the lake.

By far the best mid-range option is the well-run *La Cúpula* (☎ 0862-2029), on a hillside overlooking town and the lake. Very pleasant rooms cost US$8/15 with shared bathroom or US$9/16 with private bath. The

restaurant is excellent, and there's a video room, games and regular arts and language workshops. *Hotel Ambassador* (☎ 0862-2216) is an uninspiring alternative at US$9/18, but the rooftop restaurant is a bonus. *Rosario de Lago* (☎ 0862-2141) is the best hotel in town, where well-finished rooms with lake views cost US$34/45.

Places to Eat

The local specialty is *trucha criolla* from Lake Titicaca, which may be the world's largest trout. As usual, the cheapest meals are in the market food hall. If you need a sugar rush in the morning, head there and treat yourself to a breakfast of hot *api morado* (a purple maize drink) and syrupy *buñuelos* (doughnuts).

The most interesting restaurant is *Sudna Wasi* (☎ 0862-2091), with delightful courtyard tables and a varied menu including many Bolivian specialties – allow US$5 or US$6 per person and enough time to really enjoy your meal. *Pacha Cafe* is cozy place with a bar, excellent pizza and occasional live entertainment. Climbing up to *La Cúpula* is well worthwhile for the atmosphere and the view from the restaurant as much as the tasty vegetarian dishes.

Otherwise, Copacabana cuisine is inexpensive but unexciting. On the main drag, *Snack 6 de Agosto* is a good value, *Restaurant Flores* has been recommended by some readers and *Puerta del Sol* is pretty ordinary. Down by the lake, *El Rey* is very pleasant in the evening, and a row of stalls serves snacks and beer, especially on weekends, when you can have a drink and observe Bolivian beach life. *Bar Milagro*, up near the Entel office, is a congenial stop for snacks and drinks.

Getting There & Away

Transportes Manco Capac and Transtur 2 de Febrero have daily connections from La Paz (near the cemetery) to Copacabana (on Plaza 2 de Febrero), with extra departures on Sunday (US$2.50, four hours). You pay a few bolivianos extra for the boat across the straits at Tiquina.

The cheapest way to reach Puno (Peru) is to catch a bus or minibus from Plaza Sucre to the border at Yunguyo (US$0.90), where you'll find onward transport to Puno (two hours).

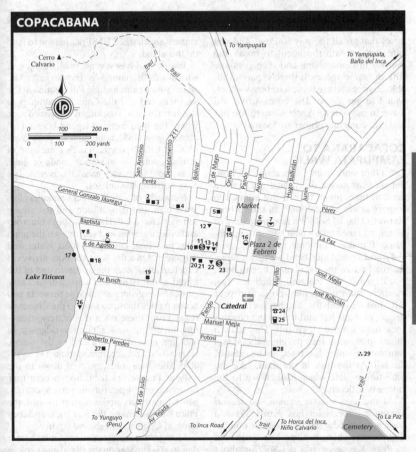

COPACABANA

PLACES TO STAY

1 Residencial La Cúpula
2 Alojamiento Bolívar
3 Alojamiento Aroma
4 Hotel Ambassador
5 Residencial Copacabana
10 Hotel Playa Azul
15 Residencial La Porteñita
18 Residencial Brisas del Titicaca
19 Alojamiento Kota Kahuaña
21 Residencial Aransaya
27 Hotel Rosario del Lago
28 Alojamiento Emperador

PLACES TO EAT

8 El Rey
12 Sudna Wasi
13 Puerta del Sol
14 Restaurant Flores
20 Pacha Cafe
22 Snack 6 de Agosto
26 Snack & Beer Stalls

OTHER

6 Transtur 2 de Febrero Bus
  Terminal
7 Post Office

9 Tour Company Offices & Bus
  Stop
11 Casa de Cambio
16 Transportes Manco Capac Bus
  Terminal
17 Canoe Rentals
23 Banco Unión
24 Entel Office
25 Bar Milagro
29 Tribunal del Inca

BOLIVIA

Comfortable tour buses from La Paz to Copacabana cost about US$5. Many are buses that go all the way to Puno, and you can arrange with the agent to break the journey in Copacabana and then continue with the same agency. If there's space available, anyone can use these tour buses – book ahead to get a seat. The buses arrive and leave from Av 6 de Agosto, where the bus and tour company offices are located.

COPACABANA TO YAMPUPATA WALK

The 17km walk from Copacabana to Yampupata (just across the strait from the Isla del Sol) takes about four or five hours. The scenery is superb, and you can take a boat across to Isla del Sol for a few more days of hiking, and then take a boat back to Copacabana – it makes a fabulous trip.

From Copacabana, head northeast along the road across the flat plain. After an hour, you'll reach the isolated Hinchaca fish hatchery and reforestation project on your left. Just beyond the hatchery, cross the stream on your left and follow the obvious Inca road up the steep hill. This stretch shows some good Inca paving and makes a shortcut, rejoining the track at the crest of the hill. At the fork in the road, take the road turning left, which leads down to the village of Titicachi.

At the next village, Sicuani, the *Hostal Yampu* has meals for less than US$1 and basic accommodations. It's another hour to Yampupata, where you can hire a rowboat to Pilko Kaina, on Isla del Sol, for about US$3. Going back to Copacabana, a minibus leaves Yampupata at 9:30 am daily.

ISLA DEL SOL & ISLA DE LA LUNA

Isla del Sol (Island of the Sun) is the legendary site of the Incas' creation and has been credited as the birthplace of all sorts of important entities, including the sun itself. It was there that the bearded white god Viracocha and the first Incas, Manco Capac and his sister-wife Mama Huaca (or Mama Ocllo) all made their mystical appearances. The Aymara and Quechua people accept these legends as history and Isla del Sol remains sacred.

Isla de la Luna (the Island of the Moon, also called Koati) is smaller and less visited by tourists. Isla de la Luna was the site of the convent housing the virgins of the sun. Foreigners are charged US$1 per person to land on the island.

Isla del Sol has several small villages, of which Cha'llapampa is the largest. The island's Inca ruins include Pilko Kaina at the southern end and the Chincana complex in the north, which is the site of the sacred rock where the Inca creation legend began. Foreigners pay US$1 admission to each complex. At Cha'llapampa, there's a museum of artifacts, some of which are made of gold, from the underwater excavations near Isla Koa, north of Isla del Sol.

Networks of walking tracks make exploration easy, but the altitude and the strong sun may take a toll. The island has numerous archeological sites, and you can see the main ones in a long day. Bring food, water and sunscreen. On a day tour, the boat arrives at Cha'llapampa, near the northern end of the island, about 10 am, and a Spanish-speaking guide shows groups around the museum and accompanies them, on foot, to the Chincana ruins. From there it's a moderately strenuous three-hour walk along the ridgeline to Yumani, near the south end of the island, where food and accommodations are available. The 'Inca stairway' goes down to the jetty at Fuente del Inca, from where tour boats leave at 4 pm for the return journey. Most tour boats make a stop to visit the Pilko Kaina ruins on the way back, and they finish at Copacabana around 6 pm.

Most tour tickets let you return on a later day, so you can stay on the island and explore more. Half-day tours let you see only a little of either the north end or the south end of the island and are not worthwhile.

Places to Stay & Eat

Facilities on Isla del Sol are basic, but improving. There are now a half-dozen simple alojamientos on the hilltop in Yumani, including *Hostal Inti Wayra*, a large white house, *La Casa Blanca*, also a white house, and *Templo del Sol*. They all charge around US$1.50 per person with shared cold showers, they all prepare meals for less than US$2 and they all have spectacular views. The very elegant place near the church, *La Posada del Inca,* is a restored hacienda now used by upmarket tour groups – book through Crillon Tours (☎ 02-350363) in La Paz.

ISLA DEL SOL & ISLA DE LA LUNA

Legend:
1 Marka Pampa
2 Chincana Ruins (Palacio del Inca or El Laberinto)
3 Titicaca Rock (Rock of the Puma)
4 Templo del Inca
5 Piedra Sagrada, Snack Bar
6 Posada del Inca (Alojamiento Juan Mamani)
7 Escalera del Inca (Inca Stairway), Fuente del Inca (Inca Springs)
8 Pilko Kaina Ruins, Albergue Inca Sama
9 Acllahuasi Ruins

BOLIVIA

At the north end of the island, you'll be able to find lodging and meals in houses around the plaza in Cha'llapampa. Farther down the east coast, on the beautiful sandy beach at Cha'lla, *Posada del Inca* (also called Alojamiento Juan Mamani) is a friendly place with a few rooms at around US$1.40 per person, and it serves drinks and snacks to passing hikers. (Don't confuse this place with the expensive La Posada del Inca in Yumani.)

Near the southern tip of the island, beside the Pilko Kaina ruins, *Albergue Inca Sama* offers very basic accommodations and quite expensive meals. For more information, ask at the Hotel Playa Azul in Copacabana.

It's also possible to camp, with the best locations being on beaches and on the west side of the island. Don't camp near villages or on cultivated land.

Getting There & Away

Day tours by boat from Copacabana to Isla del Sol and back – with stops at Cha'llapampa, Fuente del Inca and the Pilko Kaina ruins – cost US$3.60 per person. Tickets may be purchased at the ticket offices on the beach or at agencies in town. Admission to the ruins is extra. A tour costs the same if you walk from Cha'llapampa to Yumani.

It's also possible to walk from Copacabana to Yampupata, and cross to Isla del Sol by a rowboat (see previous section).

The Southwest

Geographically, southwestern Bolivia consists of the southern altiplano and highlands, one of the country's most hauntingly marvelous regions. The southern altiplano is a harsh, sparsely populated wilderness of scrubby windswept basins, lonely volcanic peaks and glaring salt deserts – a land of lonely mirages and indeterminable distances. Farther to the east, the altiplano drops into spectacular red-rock country and then, lower still, into dry, eroded badlands, vineyards and orchards.

ORURO

Oruro, the only city of the southern altiplano, lies at an altitude of 3702m. It's immediately north of the lakes Uru Uru and Poopó, crowded against a colorful range of low, mineral-rich hills. The approximately 160,000 inhabitants of Oruro, of whom 90% are of pure Indian heritage, are for some reason known as *quirquinchos* (armadillos). The city is three hours south of La Paz by quite a good road and is the northern limit of Bolivia's diminished rail network.

If you can manage, try to attend La Diablada, a wild annual fiesta that takes place on the Saturday before Ash Wednesday, during Carnaval. The main attraction is a spectacular parade of devils, performed by dancers in very elaborate masks and costumes. However, during the fiesta, accommodations are extremely tight, so advance booking is essential and inflated prices are the norm.

Oruro gets extremely cold and windy, so come prepared with warm clothing.

Information

The helpful tourist information service is in a fishbowl of an office one block east of the plaza, open 8 am to noon and 2 to 6 pm weekdays.

The Banco Boliviano Americano and the Banco de Santa Cruz both change cash and traveler's checks at 5% commission. You can change cash dollars at shops with a 'Compro Dólares' sign or with street moneychangers, but it's best to bring a good supply of bolivianos to Oruro. But be careful with your cash – local pickpockets and bag-slashers are quite competent.

Things to See

The **Casa de la Cultura Museo Patiño**, on Calle Galvarro in the center, is a former residence of tin baron Simon Patiño. Exhibits include period furnishings, paintings, photographs and some nice toys. It's open 8:30 am to noon and 3:30 to 6 pm weekdays; admission is US$1.50.

Adjacent to the Santuario de la Virgen del Socavón, the **Museo Etnográfico Minero** is in a disused mine, with displays on mines, miners and the miners' god, El Tío. Descend daily from 9 am to noon and 3 to 6 pm (US$0.55).

The **Museo Antropológico Eduardo López Rivas**, at the south end of town, focuses on the Oruro area, with information and artifacts from the early Chipayas and Uru tribes. It's open 9 am to noon and 3 to 6 pm weekdays, 10 to noon and 3 to 6 pm weekends (US$0.55). Take micro 'C' marked 'Sud' from the northwestern corner of the plaza or opposite the railway station, and get off just beyond the tin-foundry compound.

The **Museo Mineralógico**, on the university campus south of the city center, has worthwhile exhibits of minerals, precious stones, fossils and crystals (open 9 am to noon and 2 to 5 pm weekdays; US$1.25). From the center of town, take micro 'A,' marked 'Sud.'

On weekends, local rock climbers enjoy the area called Rumi Campana, about 2km northwest of town.

Places to Stay

Close to the train station, three cheap alojamientos on Calle Velasco Galvarro are convenient, if not classy: *Alojamiento Ferrocarril* is like a prison but without showers; *Alojamiento San Juan de Dios* is a little better; and *Alojamiento Hispano Americano* is almost acceptable. They all charge about US$2.50/5 for a single/double. The *Residencial Ideal* (☎ 052-52863), Calle Bolívar 386, is basic, but more traveler-friendly and only a little more expensive at US$3.50/7.

Not so central, but clean and well-run, *Hotel Bernal* (☎ 052-79468), Av Brasil 701, is a solid mid-range hotel opposite the bus terminal. It's a good value, with clean singles/doubles at US$4.50/7.50 or US$11/13 with private bath. For the Carnaval festival

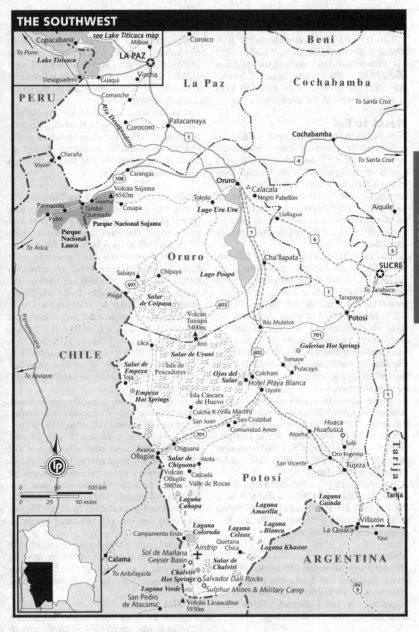

THE SOUTHWEST

BOLIVIA

period, it's US$120 for a minimum stay of three days.

The relaxed *Hotel Repostero* (☎ 052-50505), Calle Sucre 370, charges US$14.50/22 with private bath, but is nothing special. *Sucre Hotel* (☎ 052-53838), Calle Sucre 510, is more upmarket and has OK rooms for US$6.50/11 or US$14.50/18 with private bath.

Places to Eat

Most places in Oruro don't open until 11 am or later, so the Campero market is the only option for an early breakfast. Stalls serve mostly api and pastries in the morning, but later on, look for *falso conejo* ('false rabbit,' a rubbery meat-based concoction), mutton soup, beef and *thimpu de cordero,* boiled potatoes, oca, rice and carrots over mutton, smothered with hot llajhua (a spicy tomato-based sauce).

The best salteñas are found at *La Casona*, on Av Presidente Montes, just off the Plaza 10 de Febrero, and *Super Salteñas*, on Soria Galvarro. Both of these places serve sandwiches for lunch and pizza in the evening.

For bargain lunch specials, check out the small eateries around the train station or *Rabitos* on Ayacucho, *SUM* on Calle Bolívar, *Confitería Mateos*, also on Bolívar, and *Gaviota* on Calle Junín. *Unicornio* is good for snacks and lunches, and it's even open Sunday afternoons.

Nayjama, on the corner of Pagador and Aldina, has good lunches and typical dishes for around US$5. Vegetarian dishes are available at *El Huerto* on Calle Bolívar; almuerzos cost around US$1.50. For typical Bolivian dishes in a pleasant setting, try *La Cabaña* on Calle Junín.

An interesting place for an evening drink is *Pub the Alpaca* at Calle La Paz 690, near Plaza Ranchería. It's styled after an English pub, and owners Eva and Willy speak a range of European languages.

Shopping

The design, creation and production of Diablada costumes and masks has become an art and a small industry. On Av La Paz, between León and Villarroel, you can find shops selling these devilish things.

Getting There & Away

Bus All buses leave from and arrive at the Terminal de Omnibuses Hernando Siles, northeast of the center. Buses to La Paz run every half-hour or so (US$2.70, 3¼ hours). There are also several daily buses to Cochabamba (US$3, four hours) and Potosí (US$4, eight hours) and one daily to Uyuni (US$6, nine hours), but the train is better on this route. To Sucre, you must go via either Cochabamba or Potosí.

Two buses a week leave for Tambo Quemado and Chungará (Chile), with connections to Arica, but most travelers prefer the more southerly route via Pisiga to Iquique, or even farther south through Uyuni and the salares.

Train Oruro became a railway center because of its mines, but the only surviving passenger connection is with Uyuni and points south. The privatized service is run by FCA and offers two types of trains. The excellent *Expreso del Sur* has comfortable salon seats and even more comfortable premier-class seats. Videos are shown, and the dining car is a delight. It departs Oruro Monday and Friday at 10:10 am for Uyuni (US$8/10 in salon/premier; 6½ hours) and Tupiza (US$12/15; 11 hours); the Friday train continues to Villazón (US$20/25.50; 14½ hours). It's a thoroughly enjoyable trip with beautiful scenery as far as Uyuni, but unfortunately the stretch to Tupiza is mostly after dark.

A 2nd-class train, called the *tren especial,* departs Oruro 7 pm Wednesday and Sunday, stopping at numerous stations on the way to Uyuni (US$3.60), Tupiza (US$6.50) and Villazón (US$8). Scheduled trip times are the same as for the *Expreso,* but actual trip times are much longer. These trains can be crammed with campesinos who have vast amounts of luggage and who spread themselves across several seats to sleep. There's no dining car, but vendors offer snacks at every stop.

From Uyuni a slow train goes southwest to Avaroa, on the Chilean border, leaving Monday at 5 am. None of the trains from Oruro connect with the Uyuni-Avaroa train.

UYUNI

This isolated desert community thrives from growing tourist interest in visiting the superb surrounding salar country. The largest and most important town in the region, Uyuni can be cold, windy and otherworldly. The

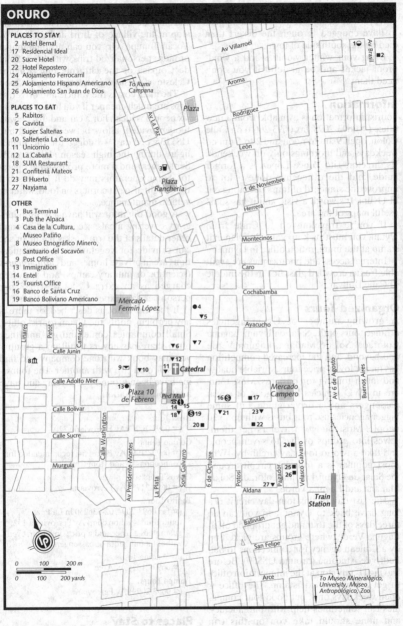

ORURO

PLACES TO STAY
2 Hotel Bernal
17 Residencial Ideal
20 Sucre Hotel
22 Hotel Repostero
24 Alojamiento Ferrocarril
25 Alojamiento Hispano Americano
26 Alojamiento San Juan de Dios

PLACES TO EAT
5 Rabitos
6 Gaviota
7 Super Salteñas
10 Salteñería La Casona
11 Unicornio
12 La Cabaña
18 SUM Restaurant
21 Confitería Mateos
23 El Huerto
27 Nayjama

OTHER
1 Bus Terminal
3 Pub the Alpaca
4 Casa de la Cultura,
   Museo Patiño
8 Museo Etnográfico Minero,
   Santuario del Socavón
9 Post Office
13 Immigration
14 Entel
15 Tourist Office
16 Banco de Santa Cruz
19 Banco Boliviano Americano

BOLIVIA

Av Villarroel
Av Brasil
Aroma
To Rumi Campana
Av La Paz
Plaza
Rodríguez
León
1 de Noviembre
PlazaRanchería
Herrera
Montecinos
Caro
Cochabamba
Mercado Fermín López
Ayacucho
Linares
Petot
Camacho
Calle Junín
Calle Adolfo Mier
Catedral
Plaza 10 de Febrero
Calle Bolivar
Mercado Campero
Ped Mall
Calle Washington
Calle Sucre
Murguía
Av Presidente Montes
La Plata
Soria Galvarro
6 de Octubre
Potosí
Pagador
Velasco Galvarro
Aldana
Train Station
Ballivián
San Felipe
Arce
Av 6 de Agosto
Buenos Aires

To Museo Mineralógico, University, Museo Antropológico, Zoo

0   100   200 m
0   100   200 yards

town itself is of little interest except for the graveyard of steam locomotives that appear to have chugged through the desert then died on the south side of town.

Bring your winter woollies and a windproof jacket and be grateful if you don't need them.

Information

Tourist information is available from a new office (☎ 0693-2098, fax 0693-2060) on Calle Colón, open 9 am to noon and 2 to 5 pm on weekdays and mornings only on weekends. Its director, Tito Ponce López, is a former guide, and the office has done a lot to improve the standard of tours operating out of Uyuni. It's worth a visit, and it has some useful maps of the area.

If you're traveling on to Chile from Uyuni, you must pick up your Bolivian exit stamp at the immigration office in Uyuni.

Internet access and photocopies are available from a crowded glass box in the middle of Calle Bolívar.

Organized Tours

A growing number of Uyuni agencies arrange tours of the Salar de Uyuni, Laguna Colorada, Sol de Mañana, Laguna Verde and beyond, and the increased competition has meant lower-price tours, variable quality and much touting for business. Most tours are in 4WD vehicles holding six or seven passengers and a driver-guide, but some bigger agencies use tour buses with up to 30 people. Most budget travelers get themselves into groups of five to seven people and take a two-to-four day circuit by 4WD. Most popular is a four-day circuit around the Salar de Uyuni, Laguna Colorada, Sol de Mañana and Laguna Verde.

The last day of this four-day circuit is a long drive back to Uyuni, and you can do three days of the tour and get dropped off at Laguna Verde, where groups are picked up by a Chilean agency for connections to San Pedro de Atacama (around US$50). Before leaving Uyuni, stop at the immigration office to get a Bolivian exit stamp. The office is open weekdays only, but good tour companies can sometimes help with bureaucracy, and none should take you on this trip without first ensuring that you have an exit stamp. A trip finishing at Laguna Verde is no cheaper than the full circuit back to Uyuni.

Shorter trips take in the northern part of the Salar de Uyuni, often with an overnight stop at the village of Jiriri and a climb on Vocán Tunupa. Or, you can arrange longer or more personalized trips, with Llica, Salar de Coipasa or the chlorine blue Laguna Celeste as possible destinations.

The main cost is the vehicle and driver, so trips are much cheaper if you have a group – six people is ideal. For a car and driver, with food provided, allow between US$90 and US$135 per day – budget for the higher figure during the high season (July to early September) and a more professional operator. Some operators may do it for less, but they might also cut corners on food, water or vehicle maintenance.

A good operator will have a written itinerary covering meals, accommodations and other details of the trip – ask what he or she can provide for vegetarians. Accommodations are in private homes and *campamentos* (scientific or military camps) and are often charged as an extra US$2 or US$3 per person per day. Expect basic conditions.

If the trip is not as described, or there is any problem, notify the Uyuni tourist office. Small companies come and go, and they often share passengers to fill up a group – you may book with one company and find yourself on a trip with another. The following have been around a few years and have a reliable reputation:

Brisa Tours
  (☎ 0693-2096) Av Ferroviaria 320
Colque Tours
  (☎ 0693-2199) Av Potosí 54; recommended for connections to and from Chile
Olivos Tours
  (☎ 0693-2173) Av Ferroviaria
Toñito Tours
  (☎/fax 0693-2094, 02-336250 in La Paz, tonitotours@yahoo.com) Av Ferroviaria 152; guarantees a place and a price on a tour, even without a full quota of passengers
Trans-Andino Tours
  (☎ 0693-2132) Av Arce
Tunupa Tours
  (☎ 0693-2099) Av Ferroviaria

Places to Stay

Uyuni's tourism boom means that hotels fill up quickly; an advance booking may offer some peace of mind. A couple of cheap

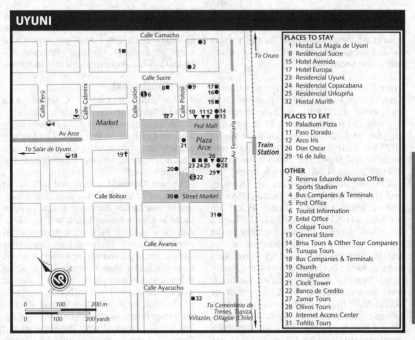

UYUNI

PLACES TO STAY
1 Hostal La Magia de Uyuni
8 Residencial Sucre
15 Hotel Avenida
17 Hotel Europa
23 Residencial Uyuni
24 Residencial Copacabana
25 Residencial Urkupiña
32 Hostal Marith

PLACES TO EAT
10 Paladium Pizza
11 Paso Dorado
12 Arco Iris
26 Don Oscar
29 16 de Julio

OTHER
2 Reserva Eduardo Alvaroa Office
3 Sports Stadium
4 Bus Companies & Terminals
5 Post Office
6 Tourist Information
7 Entel Office
9 Colque Tours
13 General Store
14 Brisa Tours & Other Tour Companies
16 Tunupa Tours
18 Bus Companies & Terminals
19 Church
20 Immigration
21 Clock Tower
22 Banco de Credito
27 Zamar Tours
28 Olivos Tours
30 Internet Access Center
31 Toñito Tours

BOLIVIA

places are on Av Ferroviaria, near the train station. Popular **Hotel Avenida** (☎ 0693-2078) has clean singles/doubles at around US$3.50/7.50 or US$7.50/15 with private bath; hot water is usually available until noon. If it's full, continue to **Hotel Europa** (☎ 0693-2126), which has various size rooms for about US$3 per person with shared bathroom.

Around the corner, **Residencial Sucre** (☎ 0693-2047) is also OK, with basic rooms around US$2.70 per person with shared bath. Another good cheapie is the new **Hostal Marith** (☎ 06993-2174), a few blocks south at Potosí 61, where rooms are the usual US$2.70 per person with shared bath, US$6.50 with private bath.

If you're desperate, there is a trio of cheap places on Plaza Arce: The unappealing **Residencial Uyuni** (no sink or shower), the almost adequate **Residencial Copacabana** and the slightly better **Residencial Urkupiña**. All of them ask around US$2.50 per person.

For something pleasant, go to **Hostal La Magia de Uyuni** (☎ 0693-2541), where a spotless room costs US$15/20, including breakfast.

Places to Eat

The most popular gringo eatery is **Arco Iris**, on Plaza Arce, a cozy place with good pizzas, cold beer and occasional live music. Ask around here for people with whom to make up a tour group. A little farther west, **Paso Dorado** has quite good food too, with main meals around US$3.50 and assorted pizzas up to US$11 – it's not so crowded. Nearby **Paladium Pizza** serves up more of the Uyuni staple. Places on the south side of Plaza Arce, such as **Don Oscar**, have breakfast from 7 am, and some do pizzas in the evening. Old favorite **16 de Julio** has moved around the corner, but still serves up solid food in a pleasant atmosphere for slightly upmarket prices.

Getting There & Away

Bus A bus goes at 10 am daily to Potosí (US$3.40, five to six hours) and Sucre (US$6.40, eight hours). Flota 11 de Julio goes to Tupiza on Wednesday and Sunday at

10 am (US$5.40, 10 to 11 hours), and there are buses at 7 pm daily to Oruro (US$6, nine hours). All buses leave from the dusty street behind the church, where the bus company offices are located.

Train Uyuni has an impressive new station. Comfortable *Expreso del Sur* trains go north to Oruro (US$8/10 in salon/premier; 6½ hours) on Saturday at 11:30 pm and Tuesday at 11:20 am and south to Tupiza (US$10/13, five hours) on Friday and Monday at 4:30 pm. The Friday train continues to Villazón (US$14/18, eight hours).

Cheaper local trains leave on Thursday and Monday at 1:30 am for Oruro (US$3.60) and on Wednesday and Sunday at 2:35 am for Tupiza (US$3) and Villazón (US$4.50). Scheduled journey times are similar to the expreso trains, but local trains are always late. In either direction, local trains are likely to be crowded before they arrive in Uyuni.

On Monday at 5 am, a slow train heads west for Avaroa, on the Chilean border (US$5.40, 12 to 20 hours), where you cross to Ollagüe and have to wait maybe six hours to clear Chilean customs. Then another train continues the trip to Calama (US$5, six hours). The whole trip takes 20 to 40 hours and is strictly for masochistic rail enthusiasts.

SOUTHWESTERN CIRCUIT
Salar de Uyuni

The Salar de Uyuni, an immense saltpan at an altitude of 3653m, stretches over an area of about 12,000 sq km. It was part of a prehistoric salt lake, Lago Minchín, which covered most of southwestern Bolivia. When it dried up, it left a couple of puddles, Lago Poopó and Lago Uru Uru, and several salt pans, including the Salar de Uyuni and Salar de Coipasa.

Apart from Uyuni, the most important villages are Colchani on the eastern shore and Llica on the west, where there is a basic alojamiento and accommodations in the *alcaldía* (town hall) for US$1.50. A maze of tracks crisscrosses the salar and connects settlements around it. Several islands are scattered over this salt desert. Isla de Pescadores, in the heart of the salar, bears amazing stands of cactus and a stranded colony of *vizcachas* (long-tailed rabbitlike rodents related to chinchillas). Isla Cáscara de Huevo is known for its roselike salt formations.

Hotel Playa Blanca, constructed entirely of salt, is in the Salar de Uyuni 16km west of Colchani. Beds cost US$10 per person and may be booked through Turismo AS (☎ 0693-2772), Av Ferroviaria 304, in Uyuni.

Far Southwest

The spectacular Laguna Colorada and Laguna Verde, among other attractions, lie in the far southwest, the most remote highland area of Bolivia, in a surreal and nearly treeless landscape interrupted by gentle hills and high volcanoes rising abruptly near the Chilean border.

Laguna Colorada, a fiery red lake about 25km east of the Chilean border, is inhabited by rare James' flamingos. On its western shore is Campamento Ende, and beside it, there's a squalid meteorological station, where those with marginal tour companies endure the night and where visitors without tents will find a place to crash. The Reserva Eduardo Alvaroa runs a much better lodge – contact its Uyuni office.

The clear air is bitterly cold, and at night the temperature drops below -20°C (-4°F). The air is perfumed with the scent of the *llareta* – a dense-growing, mosslike shrub that is almost as hard as rock and must be broken apart to be burned for fuel.

Most transport to and around Laguna Colorada will be supplying or servicing mining and military camps or the developing geothermal project 50km south at Sol de Mañana. The real interest here is the 4800m-high geyser basin, with its bubbling mud pots, fumaroles and sulphur fumes. Be extremely careful when approaching the site; any damp or cracked earth is potentially dangerous, and cave-ins do occur, sometimes causing serious injury.

Laguna Verde, a stunning blue-green lake at 5000m, is tucked into the southwestern corner of Bolivia. Behind the lake rises the dramatic cone of 5930m Volcán Licancábur.

Getting There & Around

The easiest way to visit far southwestern Bolivia is with an organized tour from Uyuni. See Organized Tours under the earlier Uyuni section. Some good tour companies can make the arrangements in La Paz, but agents in Potosí don't offer good values. The best time to explore the region is between April and September, when the

BOLIVIA

days are cold but dry. During the rest of the year, the roads can turn into quagmires and transport is scarce.

This sparsely populated region is even more remote than the salares (salt lakes), but there are several mining and military camps and weather stations that will often provide a place to crash. You must nevertheless be self-sufficient; bring camping gear, warm clothing, food, water, compass, maps and so on.

TUPIZA

Tranquil and friendly Tupiza, with a population of around 21,000, is set in the valley of the Río Tupiza, surrounded by the rugged Cordillera de Chichas – an amazing landscape of rainbow-colored rocks, hills, mountains and canyons. Hiking opportunities are numerous and, whichever route you take, you'll be amazed by the variety of strange rock formations, deep gorges and canyons, chasms of rugged spires and pinnacles, dry washes and cactus forests.

The landscape is a vision from the US Old West and appropriately so. Tupiza lies in the heart of Butch Cassidy and the Sundance Kid country. After robbing an Aramayo payroll at Huaca Huañusca, about 40km north of Tupiza, the pair reputedly met their untimely demise in the mining village of San Vicente.

Information

There's no tourist office, but Tupiza Tours (☎/fax 0694-3001), at Hotel Mitru, has information about the area. You'll see lots of 'Compro Dólares' signs around town – casas de cambio on Calle Avaroa seem to give a good deal, but they don't change traveler's checks. In an emergency, Señor Umberto Bernal, at Empresa Bernal Hermanos, may be able to help. For the best maps, go to Instituto Geográfico Militar, upstairs at the Municipalidad building on Plaza Independencia.

Things to See & Do

A short walk up **Cerro Corazón de Jesús** will provide lovely views over the town, particularly at sunrise or sunset. The town also has an unexciting museum.

The main attraction is the surrounding countryside, best seen on foot or horseback. Recommended destinations include the Quebrada de Palala (5km each way), El Sillar (16km each way), Quebrada Seca (5km to 10km each way), the Quebrada de Palmira (5km each way) and El Cañon (5km each way).

Organized Tours

Tupiza Tours, at Hotel Mitru, offers good-value day trips (US$80) exploring Tupiza's wild quebradas (mountain streams). It also runs tours (US$260 for a group of six to eight people) along the trail of Butch and Sundance to Huaca Huañusca (worthwhile for the scenery alone) and the bleak and lonely mining village of San Vicente where, in 1908, the outlaws' careers abruptly ended. They can also arrange horseback trips from about US$4 per hour.

To learn more about the story, see the very readable *Digging Up Butch & Sundance* by Anne Meadows (Bison Books, University of Nebraska Press, 1996). If you want to reach San Vicente on your own, ask Hotel Mitru about arranging a taxi; expect to pay US$80 to US$100 for the 10-hour return trip.

Places to Stay

The friendly, bright and airy *Hotel Mitru* (☎ 0694-3001) and the affiliated *Hotel Mitru Anexo* (☎ 0694-3002) are both good choices, with rooms at US$3.60 per person or US$6.40 per person with private bath.

The *Residencial Centro*, on Av Santa Cruz, is decent, with singles/doubles for US$3.60/6.50 or US$6/10 with private bath. Popular *Residencial My Home*, at Avaroa 288, is a recommended low-budget option with rooms at US$3.40 per person, or US$5 per person with private bath. *Residencial Valle Hermoso* (☎ 0694-2592) is another OK in the same price range.

Places to Eat

Confitería Los Helechos, beside the Hotel Mitru Anexo, is the only restaurant that reliably serves three meals a day. Breakfasts are especially nice, served with quince jam and real coffee. Later in the day, it does good burgers, milanesa, chicken, licuados and a variety of cocktails. *Residencial My Home* serves a good almuerzo. You'll find Tupiza's best salteñas at the friendly *Il Bambino*, which also has almuerzos for US$1.20. A half-block north of the plaza on Cochabamba, look for another small *family*

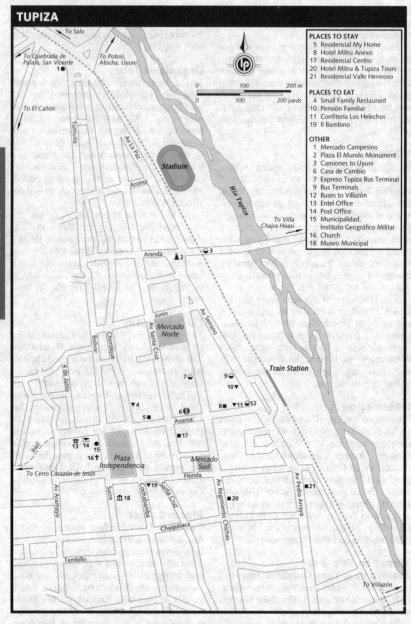

TUPIZA

0   100   200 m
0   100   200 yards

To Salo
To Quebrada de
Palala, San Vicente ● 1
To Potosí,
Atocha, Uyuni
To El Cañón

Tumusla
Av La Paz
Aroma
Stadium
Río Tupiza
To Villa
Chajra Huasi

Aranda   ▲ 2   ○ 3

Junín
Av Santa Cruz
Mercado
Norte
Av Serrano
Chorolque
Bolívar
4 de Junio

Train Station

7 ○   9 ○
10 ▼

▼ 4   8 ■   ▼ 11 ○ 12
5 ■   6 ⑤
Avaroa
■ 17

13 ☎ 14 ✉ ● 15
16 ✝
Plaza
Independencia
To Cerro Corazón de Jesús

Mercado
Sud
Florida

Av Regimiento Chichas
Av Pedro Araya

▼ 19
Sucre   Cochabamba   Santa Cruz
🏛 18

■ 21

■ 20

Av Aramayo
Chuquisaca

Tambillo

To Villazón

PLACES TO STAY
5 Residencial My Home
8 Hotel Mitru Anexo
17 Residencial Centro
20 Hotel Mitru & Tupiza Tours
21 Residencial Valle Hermoso

PLACES TO EAT
4 Small Family Restaurant
10 Pensión Familiar
11 Confitería Los Helechos
19 Il Bambino

OTHER
1 Mercado Campesino
2 Plaza El Mundo Monument
3 Camiones to Uyuni
6 Casa de Cambio
7 Expreso Tupiza Bus Terminal
9 Bus Terminals
12 Buses to Villazón
13 Entel Office
14 Post Office
15 Municipalidad,
   Instituto Geográfico Militar
16 Church
18 Museo Municipal

BOLIVIA

restaurant that does delicious almuerzos for appreciative locals. Inexpensive lunches and dinners are also served in the small restaurants around the bus terminals; the *Pensión Familiar* is recommended.

Getting There & Away

Bus Most buses depart from Av Serrano, opposite the train station. Several companies have morning and evening departures to Potosí (US$5.40, six to eight hours or more, depending on road conditions). Transporte Juaréz goes to Tarija daily at 7:30 pm (US$5.40, eight to nine hours), with connections to Yacuiba. Both Expreso Tupiza and El Chicheño run buses to Villazón (US$2.70, three hours) several times daily.

Flota 11 de Julio has two buses per week to Uyuni (US$5.40, 10 to 11 hours), but the train is better. Trucks to Uyuni leave in the morning from Calle Aranda just east of Plaza El Mundo, a traffic circle around an enormous globe.

Train The ticket window has no set opening hours, so ask for local advice regarding when to queue up. The scenery from the train is brilliant, so travel in daylight if possible. The comfortable *Expreso del Sur* train goes north to Uyuni (US$10/13 in salon/premier, five hours) and Oruro (US$12/15; 11 hours) on Saturday at 6:20 pm and Tuesday at 6 am. At 9:25 pm Friday, an expreso goes south to Villazón (US$4/4.50, three hours).

Cheaper local trains leave at 7 pm on Thursday and Monday for Uyuni (US$3) and Oruro (US$6.40), and on Wednesday and Sunday at 8:40 am for Villazón (US$4.50). Scheduled times are similar to those of the expreso trains, but the local trains are always late and will be crowded before they reach Tupiza.

TARIJA

Tarija (population 111,000, elevation 1854m) has a distinctly Mediterranean flavor in its architecture and vegetation. The main plaza is planted with stately date palms, while the surrounding landscape combines wildly eroded badlands and lush grape-growing valleys – this is Bolivia's main wine-producing region. The valley climate is idyllic, though winter nights may be cool. As in most of Bolivia, the dry season lasts from April to November.

Chapacos (Tarija residents) are said to consider themselves more Spanish or Argentine than Bolivian. The city is known for its colorful fiestas and the unique musical instruments used to celebrate them. The student population adds to the liveliness.

Information

The municipal tourist office (☎ 066-38081), on the corner of Bolívar and Sucre, has information about the city itself. The departmental tourist office (☎ 066-31000), on the main plaza, is helpful with queries about the city and surroundings as well. It sells an OK map of the town (US$0.25). Both offices are open 8 am to noon and 2:30 to 6:30 pm weekdays.

The casas de cambio on Bolívar between Sucre and Daniel Campos change only US dollars and Argentine pesos. For traveler's checks, try Café Irubana in the central market, or Banco Bidesa, at Sucre N-651.

Post and Entel offices are a block southeast of the plaza. Torcasnet Cafe, in an arcade at Ingavi 449, offers Internet access until 10 pm (8 pm on weekends) at US$6.50 per hour. Hostal Gran Buenos Aires also offers public access on its single machine for US$3.60 per hour.

Things to See

Tarija retains some of its colonial atmosphere and it's worth a quick stroll around the center. The **Museo Universitario** provides an overview of history, geology and the prehistoric creatures and early peoples that once inhabited the Tarija area. It's open 8 am to noon and 3 to 6 pm weekdays, 9 am weekends (which are free).

Tarija was the home of the wealthy merchant Moisés Navajas, who left behind two curious buildings. One is the **Castillo de Moisés Navajas**, an obtrusive home at Calle Bolívar E-644. The other is the **Casa Dorada**, now the Casa de la Cultura, on the corner of Ingavi and General Trigo. The size is imposing, but it's really just an extravaganza of large, lurid and overdecorated rooms – nouveau-riche kitsch. For brief guided tours, foreigners pay a token boliviano. Art exhibitions on the ground floor can be worth a look.

There is a **zoo** on the western outskirts of the town but it is small and rundown. Nearby, the **Mirador Loma de San Juan**,

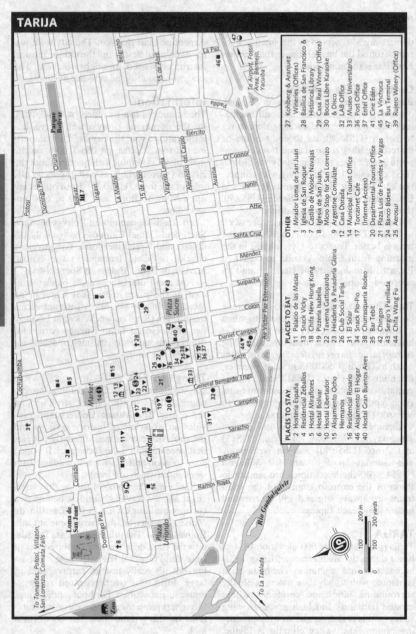

TARIJA

PLACES TO STAY

- 2 Hostería España
- 4 Residencial Zeballos
- 5 Hostal Miraflores
- 6 Hostal Bolívar
- 10 Hostal Libertador
- 15 Alojamiento Ocho Hermanos
- 16 Residencial Rosario
- 46 Alojamiento El Hogar
- 40 Hostal Gran Buenos Aires

PLACES TO EAT

- 11 Palacio de las Masas
- 13 Snack Vicky
- 18 Chifa New Hong Kong
- 19 Pizzería Isabella
- 22 Taverna Gattopardo
- 23 Heladería & Panadería Gloria
- 26 Club Social Tarija
- 31 El Solar
- 34 Snack Pio-Pio
- 38 Churrasquería Rodeo
- 35 Bar Tebit
- 42 Chingos
- 43 Sergio's Parrillada
- 44 Chifa Wang Fu

OTHER

- 1 Mirador Loma de San Juan
- 3 Iglesia de San Roque
- 7 Castillo de Moisés Navajas
- 8 Iglesia de San Juan, Micro Stop for San Lorenzo
- 9 Argentine Consulate
- 12 Casa Dorada
- 14 Municipal Tourist Office
- 17 Torcasnet Cafe (Internet Access)
- 20 Departmental Tourist Office
- 21 Plaza Luis de Fuentes y Vargas
- 24 Banco Bidesa
- 25 Aerosur
- 27 Kohlberg & Aranjuez Wineries (Offices)
- 28 Basílica de San Francisco & Historical Library
- 29 Casa Real Winery (Office)
- 30 Bocca Libre Karaoke & Disco
- 32 LAB Office
- 33 Museo Universitario
- 36 Post Office
- 37 Entel Office
- 41 Cine Edén
- 45 La Vinchuca
- 47 Bus Terminal
- 39 Rujero Winery (Office)

0   100   200 m
0   100   200 yards

To Airport, Fossil Area, Bermejo, Yacuiba

To Tomatitas, Potosí, Villazón, San Lorenzo, Coimata Falls

To La Tablada

above the tree-covered slopes of Loma de San Juan, affords a view over the city and is popular with students.

To visit the **wineries**, inquire at their town offices: Kohlberg (Calle 15 de Abril O-275), Aranjuez (Calle 15 de Abril O-241), Casa Real (Calle 15 de Abril O-246) and Rujero (☎ 066-25040, on the corner of La Madrid and Suipacha). The managements are friendly and you may be able to get a lift with the staff. Only the Aranjuez vineyard is close to town; Kohlberg and Casa Real are in Santana, 15km from Tarija, and Rujero is near Concepción, 35km from town. The offices of Kohlberg, Aranjuez and Casa Real have small shops where they sell wine at factory prices. Rujero has shops at Calle Ingavi E-311 and at O'Connor N-642. Besides the wine, they produce singani, a distilled grape spirit.

Outside the city are several natural attractions. One popular weekend venue for *tarijeños* is **San Lorenzo**, 15km northwest, where there's a museum in the home of the Chapaco hero, Moto Méndez. Another is **Tomatitas**, 5km away, which has a natural swimming hole, and a hike to 50m-high **Coimata Falls**. Micros to Tomatitas leave every few minutes from the west end of Av Domingo Paz. For Coimata Falls, walk or hitch 5km to Coimata, where there's a small cascade. The falls are a 40-minute walk upstream.

Places to Stay

Alojamiento Ocho Hermanos (☎ 066-42111), at Sucre N-782, has tidy, pleasant singles/doubles with shared bath for US$4.50/7.30. The *Alojamiento El Hogar* (☎ 066-43964), opposite the bus terminal, offers a friendly atmosphere and comfortable accommodations at US$4/7 with shared bathroom, but it's a 20-minute walk east of the center.

Residencial Zeballos (☎ 066-42068), at Calle Sucre N-966, has bright, comfortable rooms for US$4.50 per person or US$7.30 with bath.

Residencial Rosario (☎ 066-42942), a favorite haunt of volunteer workers, is known as a value-for-money option. Rooms cost US$4.50/7.30 per person with shared bath.

Hostería España (☎ 066-41790), Calle Corrado 546, is a good all-around choice,

with a nice flowery patio. It costs US$4.50 per person or US$7.30 per person with bath. *Hostal Bolívar* (☎ 066-42741), Calle Bolívar 256, offers hot showers, TV room and a sunny courtyard. Singles/doubles with bath cost US$10/18, plus US$2 for a TV. *Hostal Miraflores* (☎ 066-43355), Calle Sucre N-920, charges US$11.50/18 for singles/doubles with private bath. Some slightly more comfortable places include *Hostal Gran Buenos Aires* (☎ 066-36802), Daniel Campos 448, where the best rooms cost US$17/28, and *Hostal Libertador* (☎ 066-44580), Bolívar 649, at US$14/22.

Places to Eat

In the northeast corner of the market, at Sucre and Domingo Paz, street vendors sell local pastries and snacks unavailable in other parts of Bolivia, including delicious crêpe-like *panqueques*.

At the *Palacio de las Masas*, on Campero near Bolívar, you'll find a variety of cakes, pastries and breads, including French-style baguettes and meringue confections. *Heladería y Panadería Gloria* is also recommended for cakes, French bread and biscuits. Nearby *Snack Vicky* is a good option for a quick bite.

For lunch, the popular *El Solar* vegetarian restaurant attracts Tarija's New Age crowd. Four-course vegetarian lunches (US$1.60) are served from noon to 2 pm; arrive early to beat the herd.

For more conservative lunches, try *Club Social Tarija*, on the Plaza Luis de Fuentes y Vargas. The extremely popular Swiss and Czech-run *Taverna Gattopardo*, also on the plaza, is recommended for its pizza, pasta, burgers and very pleasant atmosphere – a good lunch will be less than US$5. Sidewalk seating is available.

With Argentina so close, it's not surprising that steaks are popular. Two options for hungry carnivores are the *Churrasquería Rodeo*, opposite Entel, and *Sergio's Parrillada*, on Plaza Sucre, which is lively in the evenings. Also on Plaza Sucre, *Chingos* is a local youth hangout serving chicken and other things fried.

A couple of good Chinese restaurants provide a change of style – try the classy *Chifa New Hong Kong*, at La Madrid 478, or the cheaper *Chifa Wang Fu*, at Daniel Campos 179.

BOLIVIA

Entertainment

Near the south end of Daniel Campos, *La Vinchuca* is a bar and 'cultural center' popular with expats and foreign-aid workers. It presents live music, discussions and art films most nights of the week. The classic old *Cine Edén* has reasonably recent release movies, and on Friday and Saturday you can catch live music and local karaoke at *Boca Libre*.

Getting There & Away

Air The Oriel Lea Plaza airport lies 3km east of town along Av Victor Paz Estenssoro. LAB (☎ 066-42282), a couple of blocks south of the main plaza, has regular flights between Tarija, La Paz and Cochabamba, and several flights per week to and from Santa Cruz and Sucre. Taxis to the airport cost US$1.25 per person; taxis into town cost twice as much from the terminal as from the road just outside.

Bus The bus terminal is at the east end of town, on Av Victor Paz Estenssoro. It's a 20-minute walk from the city center.

Several buses a day travel to Potosí (US$13.70, 14 hours), with connections to Oruro, Cochabamba and Sucre. For Tupiza, there are daily departures in the evening (US$5.40, eight to nine hours). Buses to Villazón, which follow a spectacular route, depart daily in the evening (US$5.40, eight to 10 hours). Other connections to Argentina, via Bermejo or Yacuiba, also involve long night bus rides through beautiful scenery.

VILLAZÓN & LA QUIACA (ARGENTINA)

Villazón (population 13,000, altitude 3447m) is the main border crossing between Bolivia and Argentina. It's a dusty, busy haphazard settlement that contrasts sharply with sleepy La Quiaca (see the Argentina chapter), just over the border. In addition to being a point of entry, Villazón serves as a warehouse and marketing center for contraband (food products, electronic goods and alcohol) smuggled into Bolivia on the backs of peasants, who form a human cargo train across the frontier.

Information

The Argentine Consulate is on a street facing the railway line, one block west of Av República Argentina. It's open 9 am to 1 pm weekdays. There's a Bolivian consulate in La Quiaca, near the train station.

Money To change dollars or Argentine pesos into bolivianos, you'll get reasonable rates from the casas de cambio along Av República Argentina. However, not all places offer the same rates, so shop around. Casa de Cambio Trebol is reputed to change traveler's checks, but not at good rates.

On the Argentine side, dollars and Argentine pesos are exchanged at a par, but be warned that dollar notes with even the slightest flaws aren't accepted anywhere.

Time From October to April, there's a one-hour time difference between Bolivia and Argentina (noon in Villazón is 1 pm in La Quiaca). From May to September, the Argentine province of Jujuy, where La Quiaca is located, operates on Bolivian time (only a bit more efficiently).

Dangers & Annoyances You need to be more on your guard in Villazón than in other parts of Bolivia. There have been reports of fake police scams, baggage theft, pickpocketing and counterfeit US banknotes.

Places to Stay & Eat

Residencial Martínez (☎ 0596-3353), opposite the bus terminal, is an OK place to crash. Singles/doubles with shared bath cost US$3.60/7. Across the street, the *Grand Palace Hotel* (☎ 0596-5544) isn't quite as traveler-friendly, but has clean rooms at US$4.50/9 with shared bath, US$9/18 with private bath. Check the room first – some have no windows.

A travelers' favorite is *Residencial El Cortijo* (☎ 0596-2093), two blocks north of the bus terminal. Singles/doubles with shared bath cost US$7.30/12.70. Farther north, the basic *Residencial Panamericano* costs about US$3/6.50 without bath or hot water. Accommodations on the Argentine side are better, but more expensive.

For meals, there isn't much choice. Try the *Charke Kan Restaurant*, opposite the bus terminal, which is good but rather grimy. There are also some basic Bolivian eateries around the plaza. Alternatively, pop over to La Quiaca for an expensive steak at *Rosita* or *Parrillada El Buen Gusto*.

VILLAZÓN & LA QUIACA

PLACES TO STAY
1 Residencial Panamericano
4 Residencial El Cortijo
7 Grand Palace Hotel
8 Residencial Martínez
13 Alojamiento Pequeño
16 Hotel Frontera
17 Hotel Crystal
21 Hotel de Turismo
24 Hotel La Victoria

PLACES TO EAT
6 Charke Kan Restaurant
14 Parrillada El Buen Gusto
15 Rosita

OTHER
2 Entel Office
3 Post Office
5 Church
9 Argentine Consulate
10 Casa de Cambio Trebol
11 Bolivian Customs & Immigration
12 Argentine Customs & Immigration
18 Gas Station, ACA Representative
19 La Quiaca Bus Terminal
20 Telephone Office
22 Church
23 Banco de la Nación Argentina
25 Post Office
26 Bolivian Consulate

BOLIVIA

Getting There & Away

Bus All northbound buses depart from around the large central terminal building in Villazón. Buses leave for Tupiza at 8:30 am and 6 pm (US$2, two to three hours). Some continue or make connections to Potosí (US$5.40, nine to 13 hours) with connections to Sucre, Cochabamba and La Paz. Buses to Tarija leave between 7 and 8 pm daily (US$5.40, eight hours).

Agencies close to the terminal sell bus tickets to major destinations in northern Argentina and all the way to Buenos Aires.

Train The train station is at least 1km north of the border crossing – a taxi there will cost about US$2.50. Comfortable *Exspreso del Sur* departs Saturday at 3:30 pm for Tupiza (US$4/4.50 in salon/premier, two to three hours), Uyuni (US$14/17.25, eight hours) and Oruro (US$20/25.50, 16 hours). This is an enjoyable trip, with great scenery for the first few hours. The more basic and crowded local train departs Monday and Thursday at 3:30 pm for Tupiza (US$1.60, three hours), Uyuni (US$4.50, 10 hours) and Oruro (US$8.10, 17 hours). It's a good option as far as Tupiza, but after that you'll be traveling in the dark, and the trip is potentially tedious.

There's no longer onward passenger rail service into Argentina.

To/From Argentina Bolivian immigration, on the north side of the international bridge, opens from 6 am to 8 pm to issue tourist cards and exit stamps – there is no official charge for these services. Formalities are normally minimal and friendly, but those entering Argentina can count on an exhaustive customs search about 20km south of the border.

COCHABAMBA

After its founding in 1574, Cochabamba quickly developed into the country's foremost granary, thanks mainly to its fertile soil and mild climate. It long held the title of Bolivia's second city, but has now been knocked into third place by booming Santa Cruz. Nonetheless, Cochabamba remains a progressive and economically active city, with a growing population of more than 580,000. Cochabamba is commonly abbreviated to CBBA.

The city has a warm, dry and sunny climate, offering pleasant relief after the chilly altiplano. It also has a congenial nightlife, but apart from that, there's little for tourists. Once you've seen the museums and done some shopping, it's time to head for the hinterlands. At some point, try to sample *chicha cochabambina*, an alcoholic maize brew typical of the region.

Information

Tourist Offices Información Turistica is in a glass office on Av Achá, near the handicrafts market a half-block block west of the plaza – it's open 9 am to noon and 2 to 6 pm weekdays. It sells a good color map of town for US$1.80. Good maps are also available at kiosks and shops on the west side of the plaza or at Los Amigos del Libro, on Av de las Heroínas.

Money Banks and casas de cambio charge a commission to change traveler's checks – Exprint-Bol, on the plaza, gives OK rates and charges 2% commission. To change cash, you may find street moneychangers along Av Heroínas and around the Entel office on Achá.

Email &Internet Access The best place is on España, just south of Ecuador. There are dozens of computers in a big upstairs room; it's open 7 am to 11 pm weekdays and charges US$1.30 per hour. There's a smaller place on Achá, in an arcade opposite the tourist office.

Things to See

The **Museo Arqueológico**, on the corner of Jordán and Aguirre, has a fine little collection of Bolivian artifacts. Exhibits date from as early as 12,000 BC and as late as the colonial period. Admission is US$1. It's open 8:30 am to noon and 2:30 to 6:30 pm weekdays.

The **Palacio de Portales** (☎ 042-243137), in the barrio of Queru Queru, north of the center, is more evidence of the wealth of tin baron Simón Patiño, though he never actually lived in this imposing French-style mansion. It was built between 1915 and 1925 and everything except perhaps the bricks was brought from Europe – the floors, fireplaces, furniture, windows, tiles, tapestries, etc. It's now a cultural center, used for music recitals, art exhibitions and teaching. Called the Centro Pedagógico y Cultural Simón I Patiño, the sumptuous house and its lovely garden can be visited by guided tour only (US$1.80), 5 to 6 pm weekdays and 11 am to 12:30 pm weekends – call ahead to verify tour times. Take micro 'G' north on Av San Martín.

The **Cristo de la Concordia** statue, which towers over the east side of the city, is best reached by taxi (about US$5 return from the center).

Two to three hours' walk from the village of Sipe-Sipe, 27km southwest of Cochabamba, are the worthwhile ruins of **Inca-Rakay**. Sipe-Sipe is accessible by micro via Quillacollo.

Language Courses

Cochabamba is probably the best place in Bolivia to hole up for a few weeks of intensive Spanish instruction. Private teachers charge around US$5 per hour, but not all are experienced. One of the best is Señor Reginaldo Rojo (☎ 042-242322). Also recommended is Marycruz Almanza Bedoya (☎ 042-550604). Alternatively, ask for recommendations at the Centro Boliviano-Americano (☎ 042-221288), Calle 25 de Mayo N-0365.

Organized Tours

To visit any of the nearby national parks, contact Fremen Tours (☎ 042-259392, fax 042-259686), Casilla 1040, Calle Tumusla 0245.

Special Events

The Fiesta de la Virgen de Urcupiña, around August 14-18, is the biggest annual event in Cochabamba department. It happens in Quillacollo, 13km west of Cochabamba.

Places to Stay

The cheapest decent accommodations are at *Alojamiento Cochabamba* (☎ 042-225067), at Nataniel Aguirre S-591. Although basically a flophouse, it's popular with budget travelers. Rooms with common bath cost US$2.70 per person, without breakfast.

Near nerve-racking Av Aroma are the adequate *Residencial Escobar* (☎ 042-229275), at Uruguay E-0213, which charges US$3.60 per person with common bath, and the much more basic *Alojamiento Escobar* (☎ 042-225812), at Aguirre S-0749, which only charges US$2.70 per person.

They're nothing to write home about, but they are cheap.

One of Bolivia's nicest inexpensive digs is *Hostal Elisa* (☎ 042-235102), at Agustín López 834 near Av Aroma. It's conveniently close to the bus station, though the location is unattractive. Inside the door it's a different world, with friendly management and a sunny courtyard. It's popular with travelers and has good local information. Singles/doubles are US$4.50/9 with shared bath, US$9/16.30 with private bath.

Another excellent choice is *Residencial Florida* (☎ 042-257911), at 25 de Mayo S-0583. There's hot water until 1 pm, and the friendly owner cooks a mean breakfast for her guests. It's US$5.50 per person without bath, or US$13.60 with both.

Residencial Familiar (☎ 042-227988), Sucre E-554, and *Residencial Familiar Anexo* (☎ 042-227986), 25 de Mayo N-0234, are popular with both Bolivian and foreign travelers. Slightly overpriced rooms without bath are US$4.50 per person; note that the door locks aren't always secure.

The very clean and secure *Hostal Colonial* (☎ 042-221791) has pleasant rooms, especially the ones upstairs overlooking the courtyard garden. It costs US$7.20 per person with bath. Quiet *Hostal Central* (☎ 042-223622), on General Achá, is an excellent value at US$8.20/14.50 with private bath, TV and continental breakfast.

For more mid-range comfort, *Hostal Jordan* (☎ 042-225010), 25 de Mayo S-0651, has small but very clean rooms with phone and cable TV for US$12.70 per person, including breakfast.

Places to Eat

For breakfast or lunch, the market is cheap for simple but varied and tasty meals, and you'll find a variety of fruits grown in the Cochabamba Valley. The most central market is on Calle 25 de Mayo between Sucre and Jordán. Other markets include the *Mercado de Ferias*, just east of the old train station, and *Mercado Cancha Calatayud*, along Av Aroma between San Martín and Lanza. For a glimpse of Cochabamba's trendy side, don't miss the amazing North American-style *IC Norte* supermarket.

For a big breakfast, *Kivón Helados*, Av Heroínas E-352, serves great juice, eggs, toast, coffee, pancakes and salteñas. On the

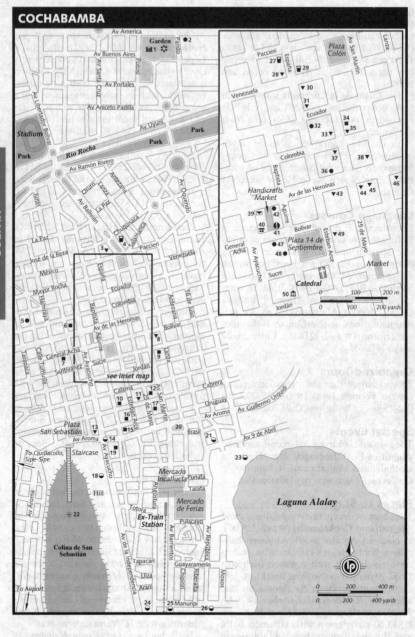

COCHABAMBA

Av America

Garden
1 🌿   2

Av Buenos Aires
Av Santa Cruz
Av Portales
Av Aniceto Padilla

Paniado
Potosí

Plaza
Colón

Av San Martin
Lanza

Paccieri
España
27
28
29

Venezuela

30
31

Ecuador

34
35

32
33

Av Uyuni

Av Oquendo

Stadium
Park
Río Rocha
Park
Park

Av Liberador Bolívar

Av Ramón Rivero

Oruro
Jama
Americana
Junín
Av Ballivián
La Paz

Chuquisaca
Salamanca

Colombia

Baptista

37
38

36

Paccieri

Venezuela

Handicrafts
Market
39
42
40
41

Av de las Heroínas
43

Aguirre

44 45
46

La Paz
José de la Reza
México
Mayor Rocha
Hamiraya

3

España

Ecuador

Colombia

Av de las Heroínas

Baptista

Aguirre

16 de Julio
Antezana

Bolívar
General
Achá

Sucre

Plaza 14 de
Septiembre

Esteban Arce

49

25 de Mayo

Av Ayacucho

47
48

Market

5

6

General Achá
Santivañez

Ayacucho

Sucre

see inset map

Jordán
8
9

Lanza

Sucre

Catedral
50

Jordán

0   100   200 m
0   100   200 yards

Calama
11
10
Esteban Arce
16
15

12
San Martin
17

Av 16 de Mayo

Cabrera
Uruguay
Av Guillermo Urquidi

Plaza
San Sebastián
13
14
Av Aroma
19

Brasil

Av Aroma

20

21

Av 9 de Abril

To Quillacollo,
Sipe-Sipe
Staircase

18

Hill

23

Mercado
Incallucta
Punata
Tarata

Laguna Alalay

22

Colina de San
Sebastián

Totora

Ex-Train
Station

Mercado
de Ferias

Pulacayo

Av República

Av Barrientos

Av de la Independencia

Tapacari
Lliza
Arani

Guayaramerin

Chipiri
Ribercalta
Moxos

0   200   400 m
0   200   400 yards

To Airport

24

25 Manuripi   26

COCHABAMBA

PLACES TO STAY
6 Hostal Colonial
7 Hostal Central
9 Residencial Familiar
10 Alojamiento Cochabamba
12 Residencial Florida
15 Alojamiento Escobar
16 Residencial Escobar
17 Hostal Jordan
19 Hostal Elisa
34 Residencial Familiar Anexo

PLACES TO EAT
3 El Prado Ice Cream
8 Café Express Bolívar
11 Restaurant Marvi
13 Churrasquerías
28 La Cantonata
30 Café Bistro El Carajillo
31 Metrópolis

33 La Salsa Café
35 Rondevu
37 Confitería Bambi
38 Tea Room Zürich
43 Heladería Dumbo
44 California Burgers & Donuts
45 Confitería Cecy & Kivón Helados
46 Snack Uno
49 Restaurant Lose

OTHER
1 Palacio de Portales
2 IC Norte
4 Top Chop
5 Fremen Tours
14 Micros to Quillacollo, Payrumani, Sipe-Sipe
18 Bus Terminal
20 Mercado Cancha Calatayud

21 Flota 7 de Junio
22 Heroínas de la Coronilla Monument
23 Micros & Buses to Chapare
24 Micros to Tarata
25 Micros to Cliza
26 Micros to Punata, Arani
27 Viking Pub
29 Aladin's Pub
32 Internet Access
36 Los Amigos del Libro
39 Post Office
40 Entel Office
41 Tourist Information
42 LAB Office
47 Internet Access
48 Exprint-Bol Casa de Cambio
50 Museo Arqueológico

BOLIVIA

corner of General Achá and Av Villazón, street vendors sell delicious *papas rellenas* (potatoes filled with meat or cheese).

Economical almuerzos are everywhere. One nice, family-run place is **Restaurant Marvi**, on Av Cabrera, where you'll get a meal of salad, soup, a main course and a dessert for less than US$1.50. At dinner you'll pay a bit more for hearty helpings of 'comida tipica.' **Café Express Bolívar**, Av Libertador Bolívar 485, offers what may be Cochabamba's best espresso drinks. A convenient spot for lunch or dinner on the plaza is **Restaurant Lose** – it's Korean-run, but does equally inexpensive Chinese meals.

Av Heroínas is fast-food row, and the **Confitería Cecy** is good for chicken, burgers, pizza and other snacks – super salteñas are available midmorning. **California Burgers & Donuts** serves up what it says and good coffee too. **Heladería Dumbo**, with its landmark flying elephant, and **Confitería Bambi**, at Colombia and 25 de Mayo, may infringe Disney copyright, but both serve good light meals and ice cream.

For something healthier, Cochabamba's best vegetarian food is found at **Snack Uno**, farther east on Heroínas. Almuerzos cost US$1.30; pizza and pasta dishes are also available. The salteñería next door is also recommended.

For something classier, take tea and eclairs at **Tea Room Zürich**, around the corner at Av San Martín 143. It's open 9:30

to 11:30 am and 2 to 7:30 pm daily except Tuesday. Much less refined are the smoky **churrasquerías** at the south end of Hamiraya near Av Aroma, where carnivores gorge on barbecued flesh.

The liveliest area at night is up Av 25 de Mayo and Av España, which features restaurants, bars, pubs and people. You could start with dinner at **La Salsa Café**, Calle 25 de Mayo N-217, for Bolivia's finest Mexican food, including tacos, enchiladas, burritos, quesadillas and other treats. It also offers a variety of international fast food and Bolivian specialties. Big main courses cost less than US$4.50. Alternatively, cross the road for a pizza at **Rondevu**.

A block west on España, on the corner of Ecuador, **Metrópolis** is a popular eating, drinking and socializing spot, especially with expats. It serves mostly light meals such as soup, salad and pasta. Pizza by the slice is US$0.60 and draft beer is US$1.60. Farther north, **Café Bistro El Carajillo** is another lively place for a drink and bar snacks. Diagonally opposite, concealed behind rose-colored stucco, is one of the city's best restaurants, **La Cantonata**, an exceptionally good splurge.

Entertainment

Moving north on España, there's more drinking and less eating at **Aladin's Pub** and the **Viking Pub**, which both feature loud music.

Av Ballivián, at the north end of the city, is another popular area. Look for *El Prado*, an upmarket ice-creamery with sidewalk seating, and *Top Chop*, a Bolivian beer barn. There's a karaoke bar and a disco nearby.

Getting There & Away

Air Cochabamba is served by both LAB (☎ 042-250750) and AeroSur (☎ 042-223206). LAB charges US$41 to La Paz, US$53 to Santa Cruz and US$39 to Sucre. The airport is accessible on micro 'B' from the main plaza. Taxis from the center cost about US$1 per person.

Bus Cochabamba's central bus terminal is on Av Ayacucho, just south of Av Aroma. Super comfortable *bus cama* service is available on the main routes for about double the price. There are frequent buses to La Paz, most in the morning or the evening but some in the middle of the day (US$5, seven hours). Most buses to Santa Cruz leave before 9 am or after 5 pm (US$6, seven hours).

Five to 10 buses leave for Sucre daily between 4:30 and 7 pm (US$7, 10 hours). Some then continue to Potosí (at least US$2 more). To Villa Tunari (US$2, five to six hours) and Puerto Villarroel in the Chapare region, micros leave in the morning from the corner of 9 de Abril and Oquendo. Flota 7 de Julio has several morning buses.

Trufis and micros to eastern Cochabamba villages leave from along Calle Manuripi; to the western part of the valley, they leave from the corner of Avs Ayacucho and Aroma.

POTOSÍ

The renown of Potosí – its fame and splendor but also its tragedy and horror – is inextricably tied to silver. The city was founded in 1545, following the discovery of ore in silver-rich Cerro Rico, the hill that overlooks the town. The veins proved to be so rich that the mines quickly became the world's most prolific. Despite its setting at an altitude of 4070m, Potosí blossomed and toward the end of the 18th century grew into the largest and wealthiest city in Latin America. Silver from Potosí underwrote the Spanish economy and its monarch's extravagance for more than two centuries. Millions of conscripted laborers were put to work in the mines – both Indians and imported African

slaves. Conditions were appalling, with many workers dying from accidents and diseases or from contact with toxic chemicals. It's estimated that as many as eight million workers died at Potosí during the three centuries of colonial rule.

In the early 19th century, silver production began to wane. During the present century, it was only a demand for tin that rescued Potosí from ruin and brought a slow recovery. Silver extraction continues on only a small scale, but reminders of the grand colonial city are still evident in the narrow streets, formal balconied mansions and ornate churches.

Superlatives buffs will be happy to learn that Potosí is the world's highest city, and the fact will be driven home when you're climbing the streets or shivering with cold at night. Warm clothing is essential!

Information

Tourist Offices The regional department of tourism (☎ 062-25288), upstairs on the corner of Matos and Quijarro, is theoretically open 9 am to noon and 3 to 6 pm weekdays, but it's not very helpful. There's also an information office on Plaza 6 de Agosto, supposedly keeping similar hours. The various tour agencies have better information, even if they're not objective.

Money Lots of businesses along Bolívar, Sucre and in the market change cash US dollars at a reasonable rate – look for the 'Compro Dólares' signs. Casa Fernández, on Sucre, will also change traveler's checks, as will Banco Nacional on Junín, but rates for checks are not so good. Visa cash advances (bolivianos or dollars) are available at Banco de La Paz, on the plaza.

Post & Communications In addition to the post office and Entel, there's an Internet place (US$2.20 per hour) on Bolívar. It's upstairs in the shopping center opposite the market.

Things to See

The entire central area of Potosí contains a wealth of colonial architecture, so allow a couple of hours to stroll the quaintly irregular streets. Unfortunately, many worthwhile churches are closed to the public or open only

POTOSÍ

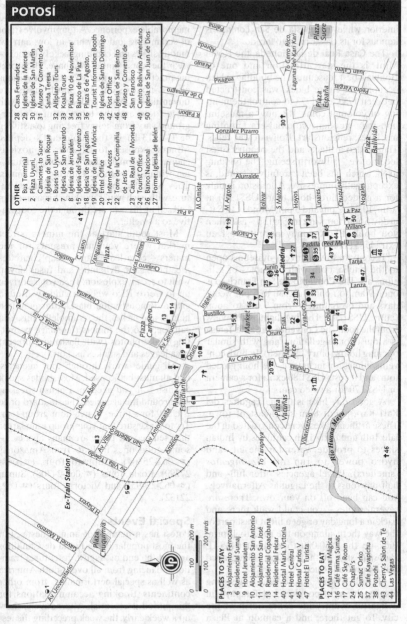

OTHER
1 Bus Terminal
2 Plaza Uyuni,
   Camiones to Sucre
4 Iglesia de San Roque
5 Buses to Uyuni
7 Iglesia de San Bernardo
8 Iglesia de Jerusalén
15 Iglesia del San Lorenzo
18 Iglesia de San Agustín
19 Iglesia de Santa Mónica
20 Entel Office
21 Internet Access
22 Torre de la Compañía
   de Jesús
23 Casa Real de la Moneda
24 Tourist Office
26 Banco Nacional
27 Former Iglesia de Belén

28 Casa Fernández
29 Iglesia de la Merced
30 Iglesia de San Martin
31 Museo y Convento de
   Santa Teresa
32 Altiplano Tours
33 Koala Tours
34 Plaza 10 de Noviembre
35 Banco de La Paz
36 Plaza 6 de Agosto,
   Tourist Information Booth
39 Iglesia de Santo Domingo
42 Post Office
46 Iglesia de San Benito
48 Museo y Convento de
   San Francisco
49 Centro Bolivano Americano
50 Iglesia de San Juan de Dios

BOLIVIA

PLACES TO STAY
3 Alojamiento Ferrocarril
6 Residencial Sumaj
9 Hotel Jerusalem
10 Alojamiento San Antonio
11 Alojamiento San José
13 Residencial Copacabana
40 Residencial Felcar
41 Hostal María Victoria
45 Hotel Central
45 Hostal Carlos V
47 Hotel El Turista

PLACES TO EAT
12 Manzana Mágica
16 Café Imma Sumac
16 Café Sky Room
24 Chaplin's
25 Sumac Orko
37 Cafe Kayapichu
38 Potochi
43 Cherry's Salon de Té
44 Las Vegas

rarely. The **catedral,** open for tours (US$1) Monday to Saturday, has a particularly fine interior, while the **Iglesia de San Lorenzo** is famous for its classic mestizo façade.

The **Casa Real de la Moneda,** the Royal Mint, is the star attraction and one of Bolivia's best museums. The building, which occupies an entire block, was constructed between 1753 and 1773 to control the minting of colonial coins. It's now a museum housing wooden colonial-era minting machines, religious art, Bolivian war relics, Tiahuanaco artifacts and the country's first locomotive – all worth seeing. The building itself, which has been carefully restored, is exceptionally impressive. Admission is only for a guided three-hour tour (US$1.80) at 9 am, 10 am, 2 pm and 3 pm, Monday to Saturday. Some tours are in English – ask when you book. Photography permits cost an extra US$1.80.

The city has two convent-museums open to the public, both with examples of religious art. The **Convento de San Francisco** is open 9 am to noon and 2:30 to 5 pm weekdays and on Saturday from 9 am to noon (entry US$1.50). The highlight is the view from the roof. The **Convento de Santa Teresa** is a must for flagellation fans, with similar opening hours (entry US$1.80). In both convents, admission includes a one-hour guided tour, and it costs US$1.80 extra for a camera or US$2.70 for a video cam.

A good day hike is to the **Lagunas del Kari Kari,** about 8km southeast of town. These artificial lakes were constructed in the late 16th and early 17th centuries by Indian slaves to provide water for the city and hydro power to run its 132 *ingenios* (smelters). Travel agencies offer full- and half-day tours to the Lagunas. Alternatively, you can head off on your own. There are several routes – you could walk there and back in a long day or get a lift at least part of the way there, along on the road to Tupiza. Pick up the 1:50,000 topo sheet 6435-II, *Potosí (Este),* at the Instituto Geográfico Militar on Calle Sucre.

Outside Potosí are several hot spring resorts; the most popular is at **Tarapaya,** in delightful countryside 25km north of the city. To get there, find a camión at Plaza Chuquimia, uphill from the bus terminal. Micros also run until mid-afternoon and cost US$0.50.

Cooperative Mines A visit to the cooperative mines is a demanding, shocking and memorable experience. A tour involves a lot of scrambling and crawling in low, narrow, muddy shafts and climbing rickety ladders – wear the worst clothes you have. The working practices are primitive, safety provisions almost nonexistent and most shafts are unventilated. Work is done by hand with basic tools, and the temperatures underground vary from below freezing to a stifling 45°C (113°F) in the mountain's depths. Miners, exposed to all sorts of noxious chemicals, normally die of silicosis pneumonia within 10 years of entering the mines. They work the mine as a cooperative venture, with each miner working his own claim and selling his own ore through the cooperative to a smelter.

Most tours start at the miners' street market where you buy presents for the miners – coca leaves and cheap cigarettes are the basics; dynamite and fuses if you want to see an explosion. Then you're driven up to Cerro Rico where a guide will often give a demonstration blast. After getting a helmet and jacket, the scramble begins. You can speak to the miners (language permitting), take photos (with flash) and present coca leaves and smokes as a tip.

All guides work through tour agencies, and all must be licensed. Most guides speak Spanish – if you need an English speaker, ask around the agencies. The standard price is US$9 for a three- to five-hour group tour. Try to make sure that your group is no larger than ten people. There are many agencies – some good ones include TransAmazonas (☎ 062-25304), Altiplano Tours (☎ 062-27299), Koala Tours (☎ 062-24708), Sumaj (☎ 062-22495), and Victoria Tours (☎ 062-22132).

Special Events

Potosí has a number of annual fiestas, but the most popular is the Fiesta de Chu'tillos around the end of August. It features traditional dancing from all over South America as well as special performances from other continents. Booking accommodations for this period is essential. Alternatively, show up a week early; the week preceding the festival is given over to practicing for the big event and can be nearly as exciting as the real thing.

Places to Stay

Only top-end hotels have heating, and there may be blanket shortages in cheaper accommodations, so you may want to bring a sleeping bag. Budget places charge extra for hot showers – maybe US$0.50.

The somewhat ramshackle *Residencial Sumaj* (☎ 062-062-23336), near the Plaza del Estudiante, is still a popular budget place, although its appeal escapes many people – maybe it's because it's close to the bus terminal. Small, dark rooms with a basic shared bathroom cost about US$4.50 per person; a matrimonial is US$7.50. Hot-water availability is hit or miss.

More deservedly popular is the friendly *Hostal Carlos V* (☎ 062-25121), close to the middle of town. It's in a cozy old colonial building with a covered patio. Rooms with shared bath cost US$5.50 per person, while double rooms with bath are around US$20. Even nicer is the *Hostal María Victoria* (☎ 062-22132), in a colonial home just downhill from the main plaza. It has a pleasant outlook, a sunny courtyard and a friendly atmosphere. Dorm beds cost US$3.60, while singles/doubles are US$4.50/9. Breakfast and snacks are available for reasonable prices.

Residencial Central (☎ 062-062-22207), in a quiet old part of town, has a traditional *potosino* overhanging balcony, a load of character and rooms at around US$4.50/9. It's friendly if not fancy. *Hotel El Turista* (☎ 062-22492), Lanza 19, is a long-standing favorite and charges US$8.20/12.70 for rooms with private baths – ask for a top-floor room with a view.

Residencial Felcar (☎ 062-24966), Serrudo 345, offers free hot showers, a sunny patio and clean rooms for US$4.50/7.30. It doesn't look like much, but some travelers really like it. On the same street and with the same prices, *Residencial Copacabana* (☎ 062-22712), Av Serrudo 319, is an uninspiring alternative – singles are very small.

As its name would imply, *Alojamiento Ferrocarril* (☎ 062-24294) is near the old train station, but since rail service is defunct this is no great convenience. It's still a friendly and inexpensive option though, at US$4.50/9, and the showers are good.

There are a few places along Calle Oruro, starting with the scummy *Alojamiento San José* (☎ 062-22632), Calle Oruro 173, the cheapest in town at US$2.40 per person – the dodgy showers are extra. *Alojamiento San Antonio* (☎ 062-23566), Oruro 136, costs US$4.50 per person for small, plain rooms and minimal shared bathrooms. Much nicer is *Hotel Jerusalem* (☎ 062-24633), Oruro 143, where a comfortable room with bath, TV and phone costs US$14.50/21.80 including breakfast. It has an Internet connection and its own tour agency, and it's one of the best values in town.

Places to Eat

The market *comedor* offers inexpensive breakfasts, and the *ice-cream shop* beside the catedral and a couple of small *bakeries* along the pedestrian stretch of Padilla do American and continental breakfasts. Most hotels and residenciales offer some sort of breakfast option, but nearly everything else is locked up until midmorning. For great salteñas, go to *Café Imma Sumac*, at Calle Bustillos 987. In the morning, meatless *salteñas potosinas* are sold on the street near Iglesia de San Lorenzo for US$0.20. Meat empanadas are sold around the market until early afternoon, and in the evening, street vendors sell cornmeal humitas.

If you're up near Calle Oruro, *Manzana Mágica* (Apple Magic) is a good vegetarian restaurant serving muesli and yogurt for breakfast, a US$1.50 almuerzo lunch and dinners and snacks until 9 pm. Another good veggie place is *Cafe Kayapichu*, on Millares, with a selection of main courses less than US$2.20. On the other side of Millares, *Potochi* is pleasant and inexpensive, and it hosts a peña (US$1.50 cover) several nights a week.

Good for its relaxed atmosphere and US$3 almuerzo, *Las Vegas* is upstairs from the pedestrian Calle Padilla, near the Linares corner. The house specialty is pique a lo macho. On the other side of Padilla, *Cherry's Salon de Té* is the place for apple strudel, chocolate cake and lemon meringue pie – take tea, but the coffee is mediocre. It's open all afternoon.

Sumac Orko, Calle Quijarro 46, offers filling almuerzos with salad, soup, a meat dish and dessert for just US$1.50. In the evening it's more expensive, with à la carte options such as *trucha al limón* (lemon trout) for US$3.50. The slightly cheaper

Café Sky Room, near the market on Calle Bolívar, does excellent beef and chicken specialties – it's not fast food, and you can enjoy the view while you wait.

An especially friendly choice is *Chaplin's*, on Matos near Quijarro – delicious vegetarian lunches (US$1.60) include noodle soup, spicy lentils, potatoes, rice, fruit juice and papaya. It's also popular for dinner, and it makes excellent tacos on weekends. Nearby, the *Dansk Cafe* is popular with travelers and once had a Danish owner.

Getting There & Around

Walking is the best way to enjoy Potosí, but there's a comprehensive system of micros cruising the streets, and taxis cost only US$1 or so.

Air Potosí boasts the world's highest commercial airport, but it doesn't have any scheduled flights with LAB or AeroSur. The closest air connections are in Sucre.

Bus The bus terminal is 1km or so northwest of town, reached by frequent micros or by taxi. Several buses go to La Paz every evening (US$5.50, 11 hours). There are morning and evening buses to Oruro (US$4, seven hours), and you can get a daytime bus from there to La Paz.

Buses to Sucre (US$2.70, three hours) leave daily at 7 or 7:30 am and after 5 pm. There are also charter taxis to Sucre (from US$4 per person, two hours) if you're in a hurry and camiones and micros if you're not. They leave from Plaza Uyuni when full and can take a long time to reach Sucre.

Heading south, buses leave for Tupiza around 8 am and 7 pm daily (US$5.50, eight hours) with some continuing to Villazón (10 hours). Buses to Tarija run at 7 am, 11 am and 4:30 pm (US$13.70, 14 hours).

Buses to Uyuni (US$5.50, eight hours) depart between 11 am and noon – a scenic and popular route. Some go from the bus terminal, others from Av Universitario.

SUCRE

Set in a valley surrounded by low mountains, Sucre is a small, pleasant city of 132,000 people with a rich heritage evident in its colonial churches and streetscapes. Although La Paz has usurped most of the governmental power, the supreme court still convenes in Sucre and with a sort of wistful pride, *sureños* (as the city's inhabitants are known) maintain that their city remains the real heart of Bolivian governance.

Sucre was founded in 1538 (under the name La Plata) as the Spanish capital of the Charcas, a vast region stretching from southern Peru to Río de la Plata in present-day Argentina. In 1776, when the new territorial division was created by the Spaniards, the city's name was changed to Chuquisaca.

During the long colonial period, La Plata/Chuquisaca was the most important center in the eastern Spanish territories and influenced much of Bolivia's history. It was here that independence was declared on August 6, 1825, and here that the new republic was created and named after its liberator, Simón Bolívar. Several years later, the name of the city was changed again to Sucre in honor of the general who promoted the independence movement.

Information

Tourist Offices Sucre has several tourist offices. The Direccíon Departamental de Turismo office (☎ 064-55983), in the Caserón de la Capellanía, is not terribly helpful. On the plaza, in the Museo Gutiérrez Valenzuela, the university has a tourist information desk, which sometimes has enthusiastic English speakers on the job – ask about guides for a city tour. The municipality also has a tourist information office in the Casa de Cultura, on Argentina – the staff are knowledgeable and some speak English.

Money There are a couple of casas de cambio around the main market. Casa de Cambio Ambar changes traveler's checks at good rates quickly and without hassles. Banco Nacional changes traveler's checks at 4% commission. Street moneychangers operate along Av Hernando Siles, behind the main market. Businesses displaying 'Compro Dólares' signs only change cash. Visa cash advances are available at Banco de Santa Cruz.

Post & Communications In addition to the usual correos and Entel offices, Sucre has several Internet access places – the best is Fotocopias Osiris, on Grau.

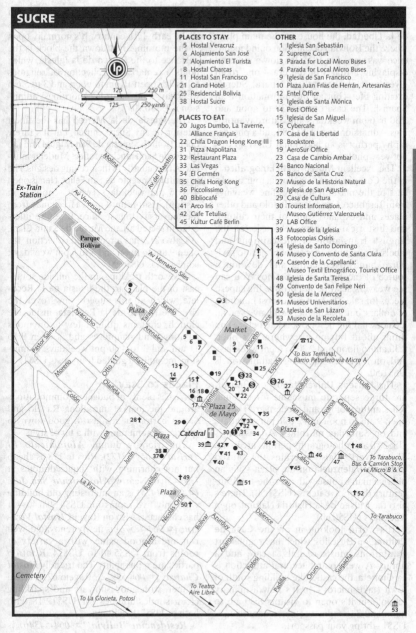

SUCRE

0   125   250 m
0   125   250 yards

PLACES TO STAY
5   Hostal Veracruz
6   Alojamiento San José
7   Alojamiento El Turista
8   Hostal Charcas
11 Hostal San Francisco
21 Grand Hotel
25 Residencial Bolivia
38 Hostal Sucre

PLACES TO EAT
20 Jugos Dumbo, La Taverne,
    Alliance Français
22 Chifa Dragon Hong Kong III
31 Pizza Napolitana
32 Restaurant Plaza
33 Las Vegas
34 El Germén
35 Chifa Hong Kong
36 Piccolissimo
40 Bibliocafé
41 Arco Iris
42 Cafe Tetulias
45 Kultur Café Berlin

OTHER
1   Iglesia San Sebastián
2   Supreme Court
3   Parada for Local Micro Buses
4   Parada for Local Micro Buses
9   Iglesia de San Francisco
10 Plaza Juan Frías de Herrán, Artesanías
12 Entel Office
13 Iglesia de Santa Mónica
14 Post Office
15 Iglesia de San Miguel
16 Cybercafe
17 Casa de la Libertad
18 Bookstore
19 AeroSur Office
23 Casa de Cambio Ambar
24 Banco Nacional
26 Banco de Santa Cruz
27 Museo de la Historia Natural
28 Iglesia de San Agustín
29 Casa de Cultura
30 Tourist Information,
    Museo Gutiérrez Valenzuela
37 LAB Office
39 Museo de la Iglesia
43 Fotocopias Osiris
44 Iglesia de Santo Domingo
46 Museo y Convento de Santa Clara
47 Caserón de la Capellanía:
    Museo Textil Etnográfico, Tourist Office
48 Iglesia de Santa Teresa
49 Convento de San Felipe Neri
50 Iglesia de la Merced
51 Museos Universitarios
52 Iglesia de San Lázaro
53 Museo de la Recoleta

BOLIVIA

Ex-Train Station

Parque Bolívar

Cemetery

Market

Plaza 25 de Mayo

Catedral

Plaza

Plaza

Plaza

To Bus Terminal,
Barrio Petrolero via Micro A

To Tarabuco,
Bus & Camión Stop
via Micro B & C

To Tarabuco

To La Glorieta, Potosí

To Teatro
Aire Libre

Things to See

For a dose of Bolivian history, visit the **Casa de la Libertad**, the house on the main plaza where the Bolivian declaration of independence was signed in 1825. It's now a museum displaying artifacts of the era – one room gives a good account of General Sucre's exciting life – but all the information is in Spanish. The casa opens 8:30 to noon and 2:30 to 6 pm weekdays and Saturday mornings. Admission costs US$1.80 and a photography permit is an additional US$1.80 (it's not very photogenic).

The excellent **Museo Textil Etnográfico** is in the Caserón de la Capellanía, four blocks east of the plaza. It displays fine weavings from Tarabuco, Candelaria, Potolo and other places and explains some of their cultural and historical importance – ask for the English translation of the captions and labels. It's part of a successful project to revitalize handwoven crafts and develop a source of income for campesinos. You can see weavers at work and browse the superb pieces for sale. The best pieces cost hundreds of dollars, but looking here will give you an idea of what the best work is like before you think about buying elsewhere. It's open 8:30 am to noon and 2:30 to 6 pm weekdays and on Saturday mornings; admission is US$1.50.

The **Museos Universitarios**, on Bolívar, are three separate museums for colonial relics, anthropology and modern art. They're open 9 am to noon and 2 to 6 pm weekdays and on Saturday mornings. Admission is US$2.70 and photography permits are extra. The university also operates the **Museo Gutiérrez Valenzuela** on the plaza – it's an old rich man's house with over-the-top 19th-century decorative items (US$1.50). There's also the **Museo de la Historia Natural**, open weekdays (US$0.60).

It's worth looking in on the **Casa de Cultura**, on Bustillos, which has regular art exhibitions, music recitals, a café and a library. A weirdo architectural attraction is **La Glorieta**, the castle-like building south of town (take micro 'G'). It's now a military school, but it's open to visitors 8:30 am to noon and 2 to 6 pm weekdays; admission is US$1 – bring your passport.

Churches & Religious Art Sucre boasts a number of lovely colonial churches. The **catedral**, on the plaza, dates from the 16th century, though there were major additions in the early 17th century. It's normally open in the morning. Just down the block is the entrance to the **Museo de la Iglesia**, which holds a remarkable collection of religious relics. It's open 10 am to noon and 3 to 5 pm weekdays and Saturday mornings; admission is US$0.90.

The **Iglesia de la Merced** has the finest interior of any Sucre church, but it's rarely open. Both the **Iglesia de San Miguel** and the **Iglesia de San Francisco** reflect Mudéjar influences, particularly in their ceiling designs. The beautiful **Convento de San Felipe Neri** is open 4 to 6 pm weekdays (when school is in session). Visitors must have a free guide from the university tourist office. If you're interested in sacred art, the **Museo de Santa Clara**, at Calvo 212, has a renowned collection. It's open 9 am to noon and 3 to 6 pm weekdays; admission is US$0.90.

It's worth trekking up the hillside southeast of the plaza to the **Iglesia de la Recoleta**, which affords superb views over the city. The **Museo de la Recoleta**, inside the church, contains quite a few anonymous paintings and sculptures and is open 9 to 11 am and 3 to 4:30 pm weekdays. Admission, including a guided tour, costs US$1.

Places to Stay

Sucre has plenty of budget accommodations around the market and along Ravelo and San Alberto, but it's also a good town to splurge on something with a bit of style.

The friendly, dumpy *Alojamiento El Turista* (☎ 064-53172), Ravelo 118, is cheap but not charming, with singles/doubles at US$4.50/6. Nearby *Alojamiento San José* (☎ 064-51475) is an interesting old building with only five rooms for US$4.50/6.40 – it has character. Also on Ravelo, *Hostal Veracruz* (☎ 064-42576) is newly renovated, well run and a good value, with a variety of rooms from US$5.40 to US$24. Rooftop parties are a possibility. The friendly *Hostal Charcas* (☎ 064-53972), Ravelo 62, is a real winner, with good showers and sparkling clean singles/doubles for US$12/18 with bath or US$7/12 without.

Residencial Bolivia (☎ 064-54346) is farther along at San Alberto 42, with clean and spacious rooms for US$9/15.50 with bath or US$5.40/10 without. Going up Calle

Aniceto Arce you'll find ***Hostal San Fran-cisco*** *(☎ 064-52117)*, a rambling place with OK rooms for US$10/16.50 with bath.

One of the cheapest options is the mis-named ***Alojamiento Central*** *(☎ 064-62634)*, opposite the bus terminal, where rooms without bath cost US$3.40 per person.

The delightful ***Grand Hotel*** *(☎ 064-52104)*, Aniceto Arce 61, is a refurbished old building with very comfortable rooms and slightly erratic service. Singles/doubles with bath, cable TV and phone cost US$18/20, including breakfast, but prices will probably go up. ***Hostal Sucre*** *(☎ 064-51411)* is one of the nicest places to stay in town, with a lovely antique dining room and a sunny, flowery courtyard. At US$19/25, it's a rewarding splurge.

Places to Eat

Sucre has a variety of quality restaurants and is a good place to lounge around coffee shops and observe Bolivian student life.

Upstairs in the market, you can have a delicious and typical breakfast of api and *pasteles* (pastries) or salteñas for a dollar or two. ***Jugos Dumbo***, just up from the plaza on Arce, is open early for salteñas, coffee, tea, juice and licuados.

Lots of lunch possibilities surround the plaza. The attractive ***Chifa Dragon Hong Kong III*** does a good-value Chinese al-muerzo. ***Chifa Hong Kong***, one block south-east on Calle Calvo, is less elegant but has good standard Chinese meals (less than US$2) and a blaring big-screen TV. Upstairs on the opposite side of Calvo, popular ***El Germén*** is a vegetarian restaurant with great set lunches and German pastries.

On the east side of the plaza, the long-running ***Las Vegas*** is a good place to hang out, though the food is nothing special. Next door, ***Restaurant Plaza*** has an ordinary menu, but the balconies upstairs are a great place for an afternoon beer. Farther down, ***Pizza Napolitana*** has reasonably priced pizza and pasta, excellent ice cream and a good mix of locals and visitors.

Continuing downhill from the plaza, a selection of eateries and bars offers plenty of choice in the evening. ***Cafe Tetulias*** is slightly pricey with US$5 main courses, but the food is good and the bar is cozy. Another above-average option is the Swiss-run ***Arco Iris***, where the menu includes such delights as *roeschti* (Swiss hash browns), fondue bourguignonne and chocolate mousse – you can eat well for US$5 or US$6. Vegetarian meals are available, and there are occasional show videos and peñas featuring local bands. Farther down again, ***Bibliocafé*** opens in the evening, with a selection of German magazines, light meals and light music. The pasta is recommended, as are the crêpes.

A German coffee shop and restaurant, ***Kultur Café Berlin***, Calle Avaroa 326, serves tasty pastries and light meals – try the papas rellenas. It's also the German-Bolivian cul-tural institute, so there's usually something happening. Alliance Française runs a rival restaurant, ***La Taverne***, just north of the plaza, which serves a mean ratatouille for US$1.80, as well as coq au vin, quiche lor-raine and llama steak. Films (mostly French) are shown nightly.

For Italian food, there's ***Piccolissimo***, which is about as elegant as Sucre gets. Plan on US$6 to US$8 per person, more with a bottle of Chilean wine. Afterward, enjoy a real espresso or cappuccino.

For back-to-basics Bolivian, check the chicken-and-chips shops along Av Her-nando Siles between Tarapaca and Junín, or revisit the market where the fruit salads and juices are among the best in the country. Try *jugo de tumbo* (juice of unripe yellow passion fruit) or any combination of melon, guava, pomelo, strawberry, papaya, banana, orange, lemon and lime; find the vendors with the blenders.

Entertainment

Some of the bars and restaurants on and around the plaza have live music and peña nights. For discos and karaoke, check ***Calle España*** just up from the plaza. The ***Teatro Aire Libro***, southeast of the center, is a won-derful outdoor venue for music and other performances.

Getting There & Away

Air LAB *(☎ 064-54445)* and AeroSur *(☎ 064-62141)* both have flights to and from La Paz (US$67), Cochabamba (US$39), Santa Cruz (US$41), Tarija (US$43) and other towns. You can reach the airport on micro 'F' for US$0.10 or by taxi for US$1.50.

Bus The bus terminal is accessed by micro 'A' from the center (it goes along Calle

BOLIVIA

España), though the micros are too tiny for lots of luggage. There are numerous daily buses to Cochabamba (US$4.50, 10 hours), all of which leave around 6 or 7 pm. Direct buses to Santa Cruz (ie, not via Cochabamba) run most days (US$9, 16 hours). Several companies leave daily for Potosí (US$2, three hours) at 7 or 7:30 am and at 5 pm. A number of flotas connect Sucre and La Paz, with the best buses taking only 12 hours (US$14.50 for a bus cama).

Camión Camiones for Punilla, Chataquila, Potolo, Ravelo and points north and west leave in the morning from the Río Quirpinchaca bridge en route to the airport. Camiones to Tarabuco, Candelaria and points south depart from the stop on Av de las Américas – get there on a 'B' or 'C' micro.

Getting Around
Very cheap local micro buses take circuitous routes around Sucre's many one-way streets. Most eventually converge on the parada on Hernando Siles, north of the market, but they can be waved down on the street.

AROUND SUCRE
Tarabuco
This small, predominantly Indian village, 65km southeast of Sucre, is widely known for its beautiful handmade weavings and for the colorful Sunday market that spreads over the length and breadth of the town. It's an extremely touristy scene, but you can buy amazingly woven ponchos, mantas, bags and belts as well as charangos (buy only wooden ones – have mercy on endangered armadillos). In fact, much of the work for sale in the small shops is not local but acquired by traders. So don't expect to get a bargain, but enjoy the huge variety of quality textiles on sale.

You can do it with a tour group or take a bus from Av de las Américas in Sucre between 6:30 and 9:30 am on Sunday (US$1, 2½ hours). Buses and camiones returning to Sucre wait at the top of the main plaza in Tarabuco.

Cordillera de los Frailes
This imposing range runs through much of western Chuquisaca and northern Potosí departments and offers some wonderful trekking opportunities. Sites in the Sucre area worth visiting include the Capilla de Chataquila, the 6km Camino del Inca, the rock paintings of Pumamachay, the weaving village of Potolo, pastoral Chaunaca, dramatic Maragua Crater and Talula's hot springs.

There are plenty of trekking routes, but they traverse little-visited areas; to minimize cultural impact and avoid getting hopelessly lost, a guide is essential. Two good local guides are Lucho and Dely Loredo, at Barrio Petrolero, at the end of Calle Panamá at Calle Comarapa 127 (get a taxi). They offer a variety of itineraries, charging from around US$25 per person per day. Several Sucre travel agencies also arrange brief jaunts around Pumamachay – try Sur Andes (☎ 064-52632).

Santa Cruz

Santa Cruz de la Sierra was founded in 1561 by the Spaniard Ñuflo de Chaves; the town was originally 220km east of its current location. Around the end of the 16th century, however, it proved vulnerable to Indian attack and was moved to its present position, 50km east of the Cordillera Oriental foothills.

Over the past four decades, Santa Cruz mushroomed from a backwater cow town of 30,000 to its present position as Bolivia's second-largest city, with 950,000.

Santa Cruz today is a big city near the edge of a retreating wilderness. Though growth continues at a phenomenal rate, this cosmopolitan city retains traces of its dusty past. A hub of trade and transport, it has direct flights to Miami and Europe, but forest-dwelling sloths still hangs out in trees in the main plaza. Visitors enjoy the tropical ambience and frontier feel, and it's a good base for exploring some still-pristine rain forests and 18th-century Jesuit missions.

Reputed to be a center for drug trafficking, the city has recently become the focus of a boom in tropical agriculture. Large corporate plantations of sugar, rice, cotton, soybeans and other warm-weather crops now thrive in the lowlands east of the city, where rain forest grew just a few years ago.

Orientation
Santa Cruz is laid out in *anillos* (rings), the Primer (1st) Anillo to Quinto (5°, or 5th)

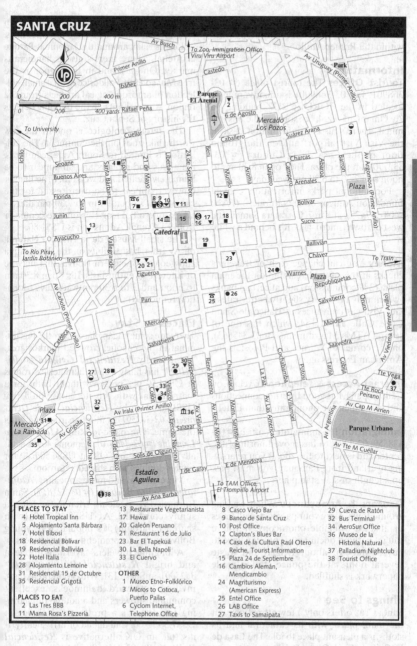

SANTA CRUZ

BOLIVIA

PLACES TO STAY
4 Hotel Tropical Inn
5 Alojamiento Santa Bárbara
7 Hotel Bibosi
18 Residencial Bolívar
19 Residencial Ballivián
22 Hotel Italia
28 Alojamiento Lemoine
31 Residencial 15 de Octubre
35 Residencial Grigotá

PLACES TO EAT
2 Las Tres BBB
11 Mama Rosa's Pizzería
13 Restaurante Vegetarianista
17 Hawaï
20 Galeón Peruano
21 Restaurant 16 de Julio
23 Bar El Tapekuä
30 La Bella Napoli
33 El Cuervo

OTHER
1 Museo Etno-Folklórico
3 Micros to Cotoca,
   Puerto Pailas
6 Cyclom Internet,
   Telephone Office
8 Casco Viejo Bar
9 Banco de Santa Cruz
10 Post Office
12 Clapton's Blues Bar
14 Casa de la Cultura Raúl Otero
   Reiche, Tourist Information
15 Plaza 24 de Septiembre
16 Cambios Alemán,
   Mendicambio
24 Magriturismo
   (American Express)
25 Entel Office
26 LAB Office
27 Taxis to Samaipata
29 Cueva de Ratón
32 Bus Terminal
34 AeroSur Office
36 Museo de la
   Historia Natural
37 Palladium Nightclub
38 Tourist Office

Anillo, which form concentric circles around the city center. The entire central area lies within the Primer Anillo.

Information

Tourist Offices The tourist office (☎ 03-368901, fax 03-368900) is inconveniently located in the CORDECRUZ building on Av Omar Chávez, 400m south of the bus terminal. There's also an information desk at the Viru Viru airport and on the ground floor of the Casa de la Cultura (☎ 03-332770), on the plaza. They open 8:30 am to noon and 2:30 to 6:30 pm weekdays.

For national parks information, contact Fundación Amigos de la Naturaleza (FAN; ☎ 03-337475), at Km 7, Carratera Samaipata, west of town (micro 44) – it's behind a white wall.

Money You can change cash or traveler's checks at the casas de cambio on the main plaza (2% commission) and at certain banks (which may have very slightly better rates). Get Visa cash advances at Banco de Santa Cruz, Calle Junín 154, which has one of several ATMs. Magriturismo (☎ 03-345663), on the corner of Warnes and Potosí, is the American Express agent.

Internet Access & Telephone Cyclom, on Calle España, has good Internet connections and less-expensive phone rates than Entel.

Immigration The immigration office (☎ 03-438559, 03-332136) has moved north of the center and is next to the zoo. If you're arriving overland from Paraguay, you must pick up a length-of-stay stamp here.

Dangers & Annoyances When walking around town, carry your passport at all times or at least a legible photocopy. If you're caught without documents, you may have to pay a 'fine' of about US$50 and waste several hours at the police station while paperwork is shuffled.

Things to See

Santa Cruz offers only a few attractions, but the main plaza, with its cathedral and its sloths, is a pleasant place to idle. The **Casa de la Cultura Raúl Otero Reiche**, on the west side of the plaza, hosts free exhibitions of contemporary Bolivian art and music in addition to theater performances. It's open 8:30 am to noon and 2:30 to 6 pm weekdays.

Locals relax around the lagoon at **Parque El Arenal**, where there's also a handicrafts market. On an island in the lagoon is the free **Museo Etno-Folklórico**, with a small collection of anthropological artifacts from the region. A mural outside the building depicts the history of Santa Cruz.

The **Jardín Zoológico** is one of the few worthwhile zoos on the continent. The collection is limited to South American birds, mammals and reptiles, and all appear to be humanely treated and well fed. (The llamas, however, appear to be overdressed for the climate.) It's open 9 am to 7:30 pm daily – take a micro 8, 11 or 17 from the center or from El Arenal. Admission is US$1.80.

The small **Museo de la Historia Natural**, on Av Irala, has exhibits on the flora, fauna and geology of eastern Bolivia that may be of interest to enthusiasts. It's open 8:30 am to noon and 3 to 6:30 pm weekdays (donation requested).

Places to Stay

There are some cheap places near the bus terminal in the chaotic, crowded market area. The friendly *Residencial Grigotá* (☎ 03-541699) has fairly clean, characterless rooms at US$4.50 per person without bath; for a matrimonial with private bath, you'll pay US$14.60. Nearby, *Residencial 15 de Octubre* (☎ 03-342591) is more spartan, but costs the same. The basic-looking *Alojamiento Lemoine* (☎ 03-346670), Lemoine 469, is actually very clean and OK at US$4.50/6.40 for singles/doubles with shared bathroom.

More central and more appealing, *Alojamiento Santa Bárbara* (☎ 03-321817), Santa Bárbara 151, is clean, friendly and has a sunny courtyard. At US$5.40/7.30 (with shared bathroom) it's popular with young Bolivians and recommended by travelers.

A longtime travelers' favorite is the clean and bright *Residencial Bolívar* (☎ 03-342500), at Sucre 131. With good breakfasts, inviting courtyard hammocks, excellent communal showers and a couple of charming toucans, it's a pretty good choice at US$7.30/13.60. Call ahead or arrive early. If it's full, an OK alternative is *Residencial Ballivián* (☎ 03-321960), which has a courtyard and reasonable rooms for US$4.50 without bath.

Slightly more upmarket *Hotel Bibosi* (☎ *03-348548*), Junín 218, has very helpful staff and a great rooftop view. A clean, spacious room with fan, phone, bath and breakfast costs US$20/33. The central *Hotel Italia* (☎ *03-323119*), René Moreno 167, charges US$10/15 with shared bath and breakfast, US$15/25 with private bath, US$20/30 with air con, TV and phone. Modern, well-run *Hotel Tropical Inn* (☎ *03-346666*), España 351, is equipped for business travelers and is not a bad value at US$30/36.

Places to Eat

For simple and inexpensive eats, try *Mercado La Ramada* and *Mercado Los Pozos*. They can be unpleasantly hot during the day, but they're cool places to eat breakfast. Mercado Los Pozos is especially good for a variety of unusual tropical fruits. For inexpensive roast chicken, churrasco, french fries and fried plantains, stroll up *Pollo Alley* (also known as Av Cañoto), north of the bus station, where there are dozens of nearly identical grill restaurants.

Inexpensive vegetarian lunches and dinners are served at *Restaurant Vegetarianista*, near the corner of Ayacucho and Sara, where the almuerzo costs US$2.40. For a slight splurge, popular *Mama Rosa's Pizzeria*, on the north side of the plaza, serves feisty pizzas, chicken and fast food from noon to midnight. A local favorite lunch spot is *Galeón Peruano*, on Ingavi, with main meals around US$3 and almuerzo less than US$2. Nearby, *Restaurant 16 de Julio* is similarly priced and has tables in a shady courtyard.

Hawai, one block east of the plaza, is a big and popular place for ice cream, sundaes, cakes, light meals and good coffee.

The cozy Swiss-Bolivian-owned *Bar El Tapekuá*, on the corner of Ballivián and La Paz, serves pub grub from Wednesday to Saturday evenings, with live music most nights (US$1 cover). Opposite Parque El Arenal is the oddly named *Las Tres BBB*, which serves ceviche and other fish dishes.

La Bella Napoli, in a rustic barn six blocks south of the plaza, serves fine pasta dishes on chunky outside tables. It's good but expensive, at US$5.50 for a small pizza and US$7 for main courses; it's a dark walk back to the center at night. A couple of blocks away, *El Cuervo* is a friendly little family restaurant where the filling almuerzo costs US$2.50.

Japanese immigrants run several sushi joints in town. If you're craving sashimi or tempura, try *Yorimichi* (☎ 03-347717), out at Av Busch 548. It's a bit pricey (around US$10 for a meal with a beer), but it's pretty good and certainly a change from the usual Bolivian eating options.

Entertainment

The *Casco Viejo* bar, upstairs and a block from the plaza, is one of the few places in the central area where you can socialize and slake your thirst most nights of the week – look for the punters at the balcony bar. *Clapton's Blues Bar* is also central at Murillo and Arenales – it can be fun, but it only opens on weekends. You might expect *Cueva de Ratón* (the Rat's Cave) to be an intimate venue, but it's a barnlike bar with big-screen music videos – it's open most nights but is only lively on weekends.

There's a full quota of discos and karaoke bars, but most are outside the central area, so you'll need a taxi (US$1 to US$2). Cover charges start at around US$2 and drinks can be expensive. Most places only get lively on weekends after 11 pm. Try *Tombstone*, Perú 275, a tourist-friendly karaoke-disco near the studious Av Busch area, or *Palladium*, a nightclub at Boquerón 83.

Getting There & Away

Air LAB (☎ 03-344411) and AeroSur (☎ 03-364446) both have flights most days to Cochabamba, La Paz, Sucre and most other Bolivian cities. Quite a few flights from neighboring countries come direct to Santa Cruz and are worth considering if you're coming from sea level and don't want to spend days acclimatizing in La Paz. The modern Viru Viru international airport, 15km north of the center, handles both domestic and international flights. The frequent minibus service from the terminal costs US$0.75 and takes a half-hour; a taxi costs US$5. El Trompillo Airport, south of town, is very small and for light planes only. Some tour operators use it for small groups visiting the remote national parks.

Bus The long-distance bus terminal (☎ 03-340772) is on the corner of Avs Cañoto and Irala. There are plenty of daily services to

BOLIVIA

Cochabamba (US$7.30, 10 hours), from where you'll find connections to La Paz, Oruro, Sucre, Potosí and Tarija. Most flotas offer both morning and evening services.

Several companies offer direct service to Sucre (ie, not via Cochabamba), usually departing around 5 pm (US$9, 12 hours). Most services south to Camiri and Yacuiba (on the Argentine border) depart around 6 pm (US$12.70, 11 hours). Buses to Comarapa and Vallegrande leave both in the morning and afternoon. Flota Chiquitano leaves nightly at 6 pm for Concepción (US$7.30, six hours) and San Ignacio.

To Trinidad and beyond, a number of buses leave between 5:30 and 7 pm nightly (US$12.70, 12 hours or more). Although the road is theoretically open year-round, the trip gets rough in the rainy season.

Train The new railway station (☎ 03-463388, 03-467795), on Av Brasil, is east of the center, beyond easy walking distance, but you can get there in 10 minutes or so on micro 12.

The *Expreso del Oriente* runs to Quijarro, on the Brazilian border, and fares cost US$14.60 for Pullman class (1st-class) and US$7.30 for especial class (2nd-class), but it's a long trip. It takes at least 19 hours, sometimes well more than 24 hours, and in the wet season it may not run at all. The train passes through soy plantations, forest, scrub and oddly shaped mountains to the steamy, sticky Pantanal region on the Brazilian frontier. Carry plenty of food and water and enough mosquito repellent to help you cope with long and unexplained stops in low-lying, swampy areas.

Trains arrive in Quijarro late the following morning, and taxis meet them to take passengers to the Brazilian border town of Corumbá, 2km away. You shouldn't have to pay more than US$1 per person for the taxi, but rip-offs are common. You can change dollars or bolivianos into *reais* (pronounced *HAY-ice*) on the Bolivian side, but the boliviano rate is poor. Note that there's no Brazilian consulate in Quijarro, so if you need a visa, get it in Santa Cruz. Bolivian officials may demand a US$10 bribe for an exit stamp at Quijarro, so it may be easier to pick up the stamp from immigration at the Santa Cruz train station. From Corumbá there are good bus connections into southern Brazil, but no more passenger trains.

During times of high demand, tickets are hard to come by and carriages become so crowded with people and luggage that there's no room to sit. Ticket windows (supposedly) open at 8 am, and you can only buy your ticket on the day of departure. A funkier alternative is to stake out a place in the *bodegas* (boxcars) of a mixed train and purchase a 2nd-class ticket from the acrobatic conductor (for 20% more than the ticket window price). The upmarket option is to buy a 1st-class ticket through one of the travel agents in Santa Cruz – try Bracha (☎ 03-322209), Florida 11.

The rail service to Yacuiba (on the Argentine border) is a reasonably quick and comfortable Automotor. It supposedly departs 5 pm on Monday, Thursday and Friday and costs US$15 for Pullman, US$7 for 1st class and US$6 for 2nd class.

AROUND SANTA CRUZ
Samaipata
The village of Samaipata, at 1660m in the foothills of the Cordillera Oriental, is a popular weekend destination for *cruceños* and a great place to kick back and relax for a couple of days. For a small village, it's almost cosmopolitan.

The main attraction is El Fuerte, a pre-Inca ceremonial site on a hilltop 10km from the village. The view from the ruins takes in the characteristic hills and valleys of the transitional zone between the Andes and low-lying areas farther east. Hitchhiking from the village is easiest on weekends, but it also makes a fine day walk. It's open 9 am to 5 pm daily and foreigners pay US$2 admission. Taxis for the return trip, including a 1½-hour stop at the ruins, cost US$8 for up to four people. In the village is a small archaeological museum open 9 am to noon and 2:30 to 6:30 pm daily. Admission for foreigners is US$1.

Places to Stay The cheapest accommodations are at basic but friendly *Residencial Panorama* (☎ 0944-6175) for about US$3 per person with shared bath. *Residencial Don Jorge* (☎ 0944-6086) charges US$4 per person, or US$7 with private bath, plus US$1 for a continental breakfast. Another inexpensive place is *Hotel Mily* (☎ 0944-6151).

Hospedaje La Víspera (☎ 0944-6082) is on an experimental biological farm 800m southwest of the plaza. There's a great view, and the owners hire horses and organize trekking trips. A self-catering guesthouse costs US$38 for up to six people, plus US$4 for each extra person (a little more on weekends). Book through Tropical Tour (☎ 03-361428) in Santa Cruz. When there's space, they may accept backpackers for US$5.40 per person. Bring a flashlight; there's no street lighting between the village and the guesthouse.

Achira Kamping at Km 113, 8km east of Samaipata, has cabañas, campsites, baths, showers and sinks as well as a social hall with a restaurant and game room. For information, call (☎ 03-522288 or 03-525777) in Santa Cruz. More basic is the secluded *Mama Pasquala's*, 500m upstream from the river ford en route to El Fuerte. Campsites cost US$1 per person; cabañas are US$2.

Places to Eat For snacks, try the hamburgers, chicken and delicious jugo de mandarina at *Hamburguesa Tobby*. You'll find great pizza and home-baked goodies at the *Churrasquería-Pizzería El Chancho Rengo*. For excellent European gourmet meals, try *Landhaus*, a good value, below the airplane near the northern end of the village. It's open Thursday to Sunday evenings.

Getting There & Away Taxis to Samaipata leave when full from the corner of Lemoine and Cañoto, near the bus terminal in Santa Cruz (US$4.50 per person). Alternatively, micros depart approximately twice daily (US$3, 2½ hours).

Parque Nacional Amboró

The village of Buena Vista, two hours northwest of Santa Cruz, is the staging point for trips into the forested lowland section of Parque Nacional Amboró. For information, visit the park's information office just south of the plaza in Buena Vista, or speak to the people at Hotel Amboró (☎ 0932-2054), 1km southwest of Buena Vista.

Rooms at *Hotel Amboró* cost US$20 per person, including breakfast. Camping is also permitted. More basic accommodations are available for US$2.70 per person at *Residencial Nadia* (☎ 0932-2049) in the village. The owner is a good source of information on Amboró. In the park itself, four basic cabañas cost US$2 per person; reserve through the office in Buena Vista (☎ 0932-2054).

Chiquitos Missions Circuit

From the late 17th century, Jesuits established mission settlements called *reducciones* in Bolivia's eastern lowlands, building churches, establishing farms and instructing the Indians in religion, agriculture, music and crafts. A circuit east and north of Santa Cruz takes in a number of old mission sites, with mission buildings in various stages of decay or reconstruction. Tours are organized by agents in Santa Cruz, or you can do it independently. Food and lodging (sometimes quite basic) are available in most of the towns.

Going clockwise from Puerto Pailas and Pailon, east of Santa Cruz:

San Ramón is just a transport junction

San Javier has the oldest mission (1692), recently and sympathetically restored

Concepción is an attractive town with a gaudy restored 1756 church

San Ignacio de Velasco is much less attractive, with an elaborate mission and church (1748) demolished in 1948

San Miguel is a sleepy town with a beautiful church (1721) that has been accurately and painstakingly restored

Santa Ana is another tiny village, with a rustic 1755 church

San Rafael's church (1740s) is noted for its fine interior

San José de Chiquitos has an impressive stone church (1748) in a complex of mission buildings – it's on the train line between Santa Cruz and Quijarro on the Brazilian border, but taking the four-times-a-week buses may be less hassle

If you want to take the train, it's probably better to catch it to San José first and then proceed counterclockwise. You can also take buses to San Ignacio, visit the villages south of there as an excursion, miss San José and return by bus from San Ignacio. Renting a car in Santa Cruz is another option, affordable between a few people.

The Amazon Basin

The Bolivian part of the Amazon Basin, which takes in half of Bolivia's total territory, is an excellent place to experience rainforest ambience. Though the Brazilian Amazon is much better known and more easily accessible, much of it is degraded and

BOLIVIA

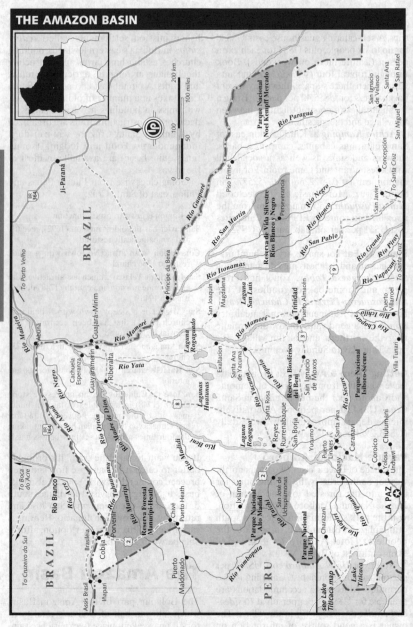

THE AMAZON BASIN

heavily populated. By contrast, Northern Bolivia remains relatively undeveloped Also, the rivers are narrower, so boat travelers can see more wildlife.

There are no scheduled passenger services; boats that ply the northern rivers are cargo vessels with no passenger comforts. Most passages include meals, but the menu is typically monotonous and the water comes straight from the river. Cabins are for the crew and rarely available to passengers, so travelers should bring a hammock and a sleeping bag (nights can be chilly). Other necessities are a water container, water purification tablets, antimalarials, mosquito protection and some snacks. The most popular river routes are Puerto Villarroel to Trinidad on the Río Ichilo and Trinidad to Guayaramerín on the Río Mamoré.

Increasingly ecotourism companies are offering river tours better for wildlife spotting and certainly more comfortable. Some excellent rain-forest lodges are also appearing to meet ecotourism demands. Towns with air services include Cobija, Guayaramerín, Riberalta, Trinidad, Rurrenabaque, Reyes, San Borja, Santa Ana, San Joaquín and Magdalena, but timetables are flexible, and flights are often delayed, postponed or canceled, especially during the rainy season.

RURRENABAQUE
Rurrenabaque (often called 'Rurre'), a bustling frontier settlement on the Río Beni, is the most appealing town in the Bolivian lowlands. The sun sets superbly over the river, and clouds of mist can create beautiful effects, especially during the full moon. The main draw for tourists is the surrounding forest and grasslands, which still support pockets of Amazonian wildlife. While waiting for your excursion you can relax and enjoy a swim in Rurrenabaque's pleasant swimming pool for less than US$2.

Information
There's no bank, but traveler's checks and cash US dollars may be changed with Tico Tudela at Hotel Tuichi.

Organized Tours
Jungle and pampas tours are the basic ecotourism alternatives out of Rurrenabaque, with combination tours a possibility. Rain, mud and especially voracious insects make the wet season (January to March) unsuitable for the usual tours, but some agencies have well-set-up jungle camps for good wildlife watching at this time. The usual price for jungle tours (with a group of four or more) is around US$25 per person per day, including transport, guides and food. Pampas tours are usually around US$30 per day. These trips are excellent values, and most people are very happy with them (biting insects are the main complaint – strong insect repellent is essential). Most of the guides have grown up in the area and can provide insights on the fauna, flora, indigenous people and forest lore.

The original tour operator is Agencia Fluvial (☎ 0892-2372) at the Hotel Tuichi, and it still has an excellent reputation. Other reputable operators include Amazonia Adventures (☎ 0892-2100), Bala Tours (☎ 0892-2527), Águila Tours and Inca Land Tours (☎ 02-365515 in La Paz). All guides should be licensed – ask to see what's known as *la autorización*.

Jungle tours typically include a motorized canoe trip up the Beni and Tuichi rivers, camping and taking rain-forest walks along the way. You'll sleep on the river sand beneath a tarpaulin tent surrounded by a mosquito net.

If you're more interested in seeing birds and animals than visiting the rain forest, opt for a pampas trip, which takes in the wetland savannas north of Rurrenabaque. It includes guided walks and both daytime and evening wildlife-viewing trips by boat.

Warning Lonely Planet has received several credible reports of very serious incidents involving the drugging and rape of female tourists who have taken guided jungle and pampas tours with independent guides around Rurrenabaque. Women tourists should not in any circumstances take tours on their own or in pairs with independent guides, but should stick to larger group tours run by reputable agencies. Avoid rogue guides or those who have broken away from established agencies, including any that may be recommended in this book.

Places to Stay
The old favorite travelers' haunt is friendly *Hotel Tuichi (☎ 0892-2372),* with plain but

BOLIVIA

RURRENABAQUE

PLACES TO STAY
1 Safari Hotel
5 Hostal Beni
20 Hotel Berlin
22 Hotel El Porteño
25 Hotel Tuichi,
   Agencia Fluvial
27 Hotel Rurre
28 Alojamiento Aurora
29 Hotel Taquara
30 Hotel Santa Ana

PLACES TO EAT
8 Tacuara Restaurant
11 Playa Azul
12 Social Club
18 Heladería Bambi
21 Bar/Restaurant
   Patuju
24 Camila's Snack
26 Los Osos

OTHER
2 Gas Station
3 Bus Station
4 Entel
6 Market Area
7 Inca Land Tours
9 Agencia Fluvial
   Floating Dock
10 Boats to San
   Buenaventura
13 Amazonia
   Adventures
14 Local Bus Stop
15 TAM Office
16 Bala Tours
17 Águila Tours
19 Swimming Pool
23 Tuoro's Disco
31 Church

decent rooms for US$2.70 per person, US$3.60 with private bath. Also recommended is *Hotel Rurre*, which is similarly priced and may have even cheaper dormitory beds.

The basic *Hotel Santa Ana* has a nice courtyard with tables, and costs US$2.70 per person with shared bath. Avoid the unkempt *Hotel Berlin*, which is less than US$2 per person. *Alojamiento Aurora* costs the same and is a much better deal. One of the best values is *Hotel El Porteño*, at US$2.70 per person; US$5.40 per person with private bath.

More comfortable places include the newish *Hostal Beni*, near the river, for US$12.70 a double with hot water, fan and TV; newly renovated *Hotel Taquara*, on the plaza, at US$15 per person, with a good swimming pool; and the Korean-run *Safari Hotel*, north of town with spacious grounds, river views and good singles/doubles for US$15/30.

Places to Eat
The *Social Club* (Sede Social), on Calle Comercio, has outdoor tables overlooking the river and is a very pleasant place to enjoy lunch or dinner – main courses cost around US$3.50, but the set almuerzo is much cheaper.

Several fish restaurants occupy shelters along the riverfront – *La Playa Azul* has a good atmosphere and serves good-size meals. *Heladería Bambi* is recommended for snacks, ice cream, soda and beer. It's across the road from *Camila's Snack*, which is also popular with travelers. Farther north on Calle Avaroa, friendly *Tacuara Restaurant* is recommended especially for its breakfasts and its lasagna.

Entertainment
There's not a whole lot of action, but Rurre does have some bars and a couple of discos, of which *Unicornio* is the most popular with gringos and gringas.

Getting There & Away
Air In theory, TAM has US$50 flights from La Paz on Monday, Thursday and Saturday. In reality, they're often canceled, and it can be hard to get seats. Occasional charter flights are provided by SAVE aircraft (US$68), which can be booked through Inca Land Tours in La Paz (☎ 02-365515). The airport, a tin shed beside a grassy strip in the jungle, is a few kilometers north of town on a dirt road. Airport transport costs about US$1, whether by battered bus, packed taxi

or (if you don't have much luggage) on the back of a motorcycle.

Bus When the roads are dry, buses run daily between Rurrenabaque and La Paz (US$10.80, 18 hours), but it's best to break the journey at Coroico, which is 'only' 14 hours from Rurre (actually, you get off at Yolosa, 7km west of Coroico).

There are also daily runs to Trinidad (US$22, 12 hours) via Yucumo, San Borja and San Ignacio de Moxos. There are also several buses a week to Riberalta and on to Guayaramerín (US$16, 15 hours).

Boat Thanks to the Guayaramerín road, there's now very little cargo transport down the Río Beni to Riberalta. You can find motorized canoe transport upriver to Guanay for around US$15 to US$20 per person (12 hours). Ask at the Hotel Tuichi for information. Taxi ferries to San Buenaventura, on the opposite shore of the Río Beni, cost US$0.20.

AROUND RURRENABAQUE
Parque Nacional Alto Madidi
The Río Madidi watershed, which has been slated for oil exploration, still contains one of the most intact ecosystems in all of South America. The most ecologically sound section of it is protected by Parque Nacional Alto Madidi, which takes in a range of wildlife habitats, from steaming lowland rain forests to 5500m Andean peaks. It's thought that the park is home to more than one thousand species of birds – more than 10% of all known species in the world.

The populated portions of the park along the Río Tuichi have been given a special distinction under UNESCO's biosphere statutes, which will allow indigenous people to continue with their traditional lifestyles – hunting, fishing and utilizing other forest resources. Hence, for the Chimane and Tacanas tribes, the national park has very little effect on their lifestyles.

Logging activity around the Tuichi and at the northern end of the park, near Ixiamas, is a major threat to the park, with independent loggers still cutting mahogany, cedar and other valuable trees. There is also a proposal to build a dam in the Bala Gorge area, just upstream from Rurre, which would inundate vast areas of rain forest, including an Indian

reserve. This huge project would generate more than three times Bolivia's current total electricity supply, mostly for export to Brazil.

Places to Stay One positive development has been the opening of the *Chalalán Eco-lodge*, near San José de Uchupiamonas, built with the support of Conservation International with the aim of providing local employment and ecologically sustainable tourism. Accessed by road and river from Rurre, a three-day, two-night stay at the lodge costs US$198 per person with a group of four, with transport and full board. It's a wonderful place. For more information, visit the office in Rurre, next to Agencia Fluvial, or contact America Tours (☎ 02-374204, fax 02-328584) in La Paz.

TRINIDAD
The city of La Santísima Trinidad (the Most Holy Trinity), at an altitude of 237m, was founded on June 13, 1686, by Padre Cipriano Barace as the second Jesuit mission in the flatlands of the southern Beni. 'Trini' is now the capital of Beni, with a population around 60,000 and growing, but it still looks and feels like a country town and a charmless one at that – the open sewers are enough to put anyone off.

Trinidad is a stop for overland travelers between Santa Cruz and Rurrenabaque or a place to organize a river trip on the Mamoré. There are some ecotour operations based here too, but apart from that, there's little for the visitor.

Information
The tourist office (☎ 046-21722) is in the back of the administrative building on Joaquin de Sierra, next to Farmacia Beniani. Tour agencies are along Av 6 de Agosto.

Things to See
The most interesting sight in town is the locals cruising around the plaza on motorcycles – for US$2 per hour you can rent a bike and join the action. If that's too much excitement, the plaza is also good for some quiet sloth-watching.

Organized Tours
Moxos Turismo (☎ 046-21141) and Fremen Tours (☎ 046-22276) both offer live-on-board boat trips in the surrounding area.

BOLIVIA

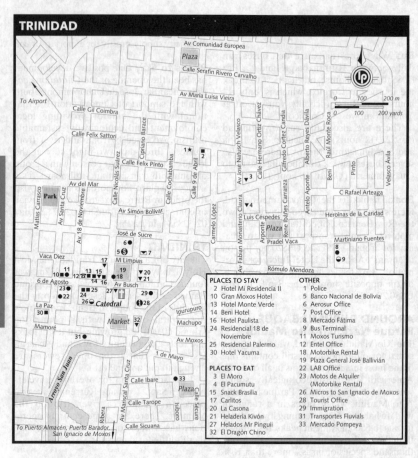

TRINIDAD

PLACES TO STAY	OTHER
2 Hotel Mi Residencia II	1 Police
10 Gran Moxos Hotel	5 Banco Nacional de Bolivia
13 Hotel Monte Verde	6 Aerosur Office
14 Beni Hotel	7 Post Office
16 Hotel Paulista	8 Mercado Fátima
24 Residencial 18 de	9 Bus Terminal
Noviembre	11 Moxos Turismo
25 Residencial Palermo	12 Entel Office
30 Hotel Yacuma	18 Motorbike Rental
	19 Plaza General José Ballivián
PLACES TO EAT	22 LAB Office
3 El Moro	23 Motos de Alquiler
4 El Pacumutu	(Motorbike Rental)
15 Snack Brasilia	26 Micros to San Ignacio de Moxos
17 Carlitos	28 Tourist Office
20 La Casona	29 Immigration
21 Heladería Kivón	31 Transportes Fluviales
27 Helados Mr Pinguii	33 Mercado Pompeya
32 El Dragón Chino	

Places to Stay

Venerable **Hotel Yacuma** (☎ 046-22249) is an old-style building with a faded tropical ambience, but unfortunately it's unkempt, poorly run and security is not good. Big but basic rooms cost about US$3 per person, or US$7 with private bath.

Other basic, budget places are along Av 6 de Agosto, including **Residencial 18 de Noviembre** (☎ 046-21272, and **Residencial Palermo** (☎ 046-20470). They both charge around US$3.60 per person with shared bath, US$5 with private bath. **Hotel Paulista** (☎ 046-20018) is slightly better but nothing special, and it's more expensive at US$4.50 per person, or US$9/US$15 for the best rooms with private bath.

The mid-range places along 6 de Agosto have air conditioning in their better rooms, which cost US$30/35 for singles/doubles at the **Beni Hotel** (☎ 046-20522), US$35/50 at **Hotel Monte Verde** (☎ 046-22750) and US$50/65 at **Gran Moxos Hotel** (☎ 046-22240). If you're willing to pay this sort of money, **Hotel Mi Residencia II** (☎ 046-21529) may be a better deal – it's a few blocks north of the center of town, but it does have a swimming pool.

Places to Eat

If your budget is a major concern, there's always the **Mercado Municipal**. For a pittance, you can try the local specialty, *arroz con queso* (rice with cheese), plus kebab, yuca, plantain and salad. Trinidad is cattle country, so beef is plentiful.

On the east side of the plaza, *La Casona* is a welcoming, open-fronted place with sidewalk tables, good pizzas and inexpensive almuerzos. *Carlitos*, on the other side of the plaza, looks pretty posh and also has inexpensive almuerzos, but doesn't seem too friendly. Also on the plaza, *Heladería Kivón* serves snacks, light meals and full breakfasts, and the balcony tables upstairs offer good views of the motorcycle cruising scene. *Mr Pinguii* is an ice cream and snack place on the south side of the plaza.

On 6 de Agosto, *Snack Brasilia* does a standard menu of good, inexpensive lunch options. Also recommended is the Chinese *El Dragón Chino*, opposite the market. For fish, try *El Moro*, on the corner of Avs Simón Bolívar and José Natusch Velasco. Farther down Velasco, *El Pacumutu* specializes in the chopped chunks of beef called *pacumutus* – it's a very filling meal.

Getting There & Away
Air LAB (☎ 046-20595) and AeroSur (☎ 046-20765) operate flights to Trinidad, La Paz, Cochabamba and Santa Cruz. Both carriers also fly to Riberalta, Guayaramerín and Cobija. TAM (☎ 046-22363) connects Trini with Santa Cruz, Riberalta, San Borja and Guayarmerín.

The airport is northwest of town, a half-hour walk from the center. A taxi into town is around US$1.50, but if you don't have much luggage, a motorcycle taxi is only US$0.40.

Bus The rambling bus 'terminal' is on Rómulo Mendoza. In the dry season, flotas depart nightly for Santa Cruz (12 hours). Fares seem somewhat arbitrary on this route but should be between US$7.30 and US$12. Several companies leave daily for Rurrenabaque (US$22, 12 hours) via San Borja. Frequent micros and camionetas run to San Ignacio de Moxos (US$2.70, three hours) from the small terminals on Av La Paz.

Boat The closest river ports are Puerto Almacén, on the Ibare, 8km southwest of town, and Puerto Barador, on the Río Mamoré, 13km in the same direction. Trucks charge US$1 to Puerto Almacén and US$2 to Puerto Barador.

If you're looking for river transport north to Guayaramerín or south to Puerto Villarroel, ask first at the Transportes Fluviales office (☎ 046-20991) on Mamoré in Trinidad, then check with the boat captains or Policia Naval at the ports. The Guayaramerín run takes up to a week (larger boats do it in three to four days) and costs around US$33, including food. To Puerto Villarroel in the Chapare, smaller boats take eight to 10 days.

Getting Around
Motorcycles can be rented on the plaza for around US$2 per hour, US$20 per 24-hour day. Rental agencies may wish to hold your driver's license (car or motorcycle) and passport or other document as deposit. Motorcycle taxis cost US$0.40 around town; car taxis charge US$1 and up.

AROUND TRINIDAD
Outside of town, the **Llanos de Moxos** have more than 100km of canals and causeways, and hundreds of pre-Columbian *lomas* (artificial mounds) built to permit cultivation during the seasonal floods. At **Chuchini**, 17km northwest, there's a small archaeological museum, a restaurant, a campground and pricey bungalows (US$35 per person). They charge day visitors US$10, but it's not worth it. However, wildlife viewing in the area can be good. Trinidad agencies can arrange tours (see Organized Tours in previous section).

Five km southeast of Trinidad, **Laguna Suárez** is an artificial lake popular with local families for a Sunday outing. Food and drink are available at lakeside restaurants. There is no public transport; you'll have to walk, take a taxi, rent a motorcycle or hitch – there's a small charge to use the access road.

The lovely Ignaciano Indian village of **San Ignacio de Moxos** is 89km west of Trinidad. The annual Fiesta del Santo Patrono de Moxos, held every July 31, is the town's highlight event.

GUAYARAMERÍN
Guayaramerín (population 35,000), Bolivia's back door to Brazil, lies on the banks of the Río Mamoré in the country's northeastern corner. It's a dusty frontier settlement that lives on the thriving trade with the Brazilian town of Guajará-Mirim, just across the river.

Formerly isolated from the rest of Bolivia and accessible only by plane or riverboat, there's now a road from Guayaramerín to Riberalta, connecting south to Rurrenabaque and La Paz, and west to Cobija.

Information

The Brazilian consulate is open 11 am to 1 pm weekdays. Exchange US dollars at the Hotel San Carlos, or with moneychangers around the port area. For traveler's checks, Bank Bidesa charges 2% commission.

Places to Stay & Eat

The mellowest budget place is the *Hotel Litoral*, near the airport, which charges US$7.30/12.70. Opposite is the quiet and shady *Hotel Santa Ana* (☎ 0855-2206) with similar amenities for US$5 per person without bath. The *Hotel Plaza Anexo* (☎ 0855-2086), on the plaza, has clean rooms with bath and a pleasant ambience for US$5 per person. If you can't cope with the heat, the *Hotel San Carlos* (☎ 0855-2419) has a swimming pool and singles/doubles with bath and air con for US$25/40.

Guayaramerín has the Beni's best restaurant, called the *Only Restaurant*, with an extensive international menu and a cool outdoor garden. There's also the *Only Restaurant Chifa*, which is not as good. *Made in Brasil*, near the plaza, provides home cooking for the town's many Brazilian expats. Prices, which are quoted in reais, are generally higher than in Bolivian establishments. *Los Bibosis*, also on the plaza, serves meals and snacks but is primarily a drinking joint.

Getting There & Away

Air LAB (☎ 0855-2140) and AeroSur (☎ 0855-2384) both fly between Trinidad and Guayaramerín, with connections to and from La Paz. With LAB, you can fly to or from Cobija on Monday and Friday. TAM has Tuesday flights from La Paz to Cobija, Riberralta and Guayaramerín.

Bus Most bus terminals are at the western end of town, beyond the market. Several companies have services to Riberalta (US$2, three hours); each has two to four departures daily. Cars and camiones to Riberalta leave from opposite the 8 de Diciembre bus terminal. In the dry season, several flotas leave daily for Rurrenabaque (US$16, 15 hours)

and La Paz (US$27, 35 hours), and there are three buses weekly to Cobija (US$15, 14 hours). Trans-Amazonas goes to Trinidad (US$21, 17 hours) on Thursday at 8:30 am.

Boat Boats up the Río Mamoré to Trinidad leave almost daily (US$33 with food, seven days). A notice board outside the port captain's office lists departures.

To/From Brazil Frequent motorboat ferries cross the river between the two ports (US$1.50; at night, fast motorboats cost US$4). There are no restrictions on crossing between Guayaramerín and Guajará-Mirim, but if you intend to travel farther into Brazil or are entering Bolivia here, you must pick up entry-exit stamps. The Bolivian immigration office is on the Brazilian side of the port area. Have your passport stamped at the Polícia Federal. A yellow-fever vaccination certificate is required to enter Brazil from Bolivia

RIBERALTA

On the banks of the Río Beni, Riberalta (population 60,000) is the major town in Bolivia's northern frontier region. It was once a center of rubber production, but now relies on the cultivation, production and export of brazil nuts and their oil. Since the opening of the road link with La Paz, Riberalta's importance as a river port has declined.

There isn't a lot for visitors to see, but Riberalta is a pleasant enough town. In the paralyzing heat of the day, strenuous activity is suspended and the locals search out the nearest hammock; visitors should follow their examples. On fine evenings, the place comes to life with Technicolor sunsets, cruising motorcycles and a general buzz of activity.

Places to Stay

The spotless *Residencial Los Reyes* (☎ 0852-8018), near the airport, is very nice. It costs US$3.60 per person or US$5.40 with private bath. The cheapest place is *Alojamiento Navarro*, where dormitory accommodations cost US$1.80 per person (don't leave your things in the rooms) and double rooms are US$3.60.

Alojamiento Comercial Lazo (☎ 0852-8326) has basic singles/doubles for US$5.50/6.20 with bath and US$2/3 without. *Residencial Katita*, a friendly place with a public restaurant, charges just US$3.60 per person.

A good lower mid-range choice is *Hotel Amazonas* (☎ *0852-2339*), which charges US$6.40/12 with bath. *Hostal Tahuamanu* (☎ *0852-8006*) is the most comfortable option in town, with air-conditioned double rooms from around US$27 including breakfast.

Places to Eat

The most interesting places are around the plaza, such as *La Cabaña de Tío Tom*, which has good coffee, ice cream, juices, shakes, flan and sandwiches as well as Beni beef. Nearby, *Club Social* serves inexpensive set lunches, superb filtered coffee, drinks and fine desserts. A half block away, *Hotel Colonial* serves a solid breakfast for US$1.50 from 7 am.

The *Club Social Japonés*, near the market, doesn't serve anything Japanese, but it does offer Bolivian and Amazonian dishes. Also near the market, *Churrasquería El Pahuichi* is big on Beni beef. The outdoor seating is particularly pleasant.

Getting There & Away

Air LAB (☎ 0852-2239) and AeroSur (☎ 0852-2798) serve Riberalta with several flights per week to Trinidad and connections to La Paz, Santa Cruz and Cochabamba. The airport is a 15-minute walk from the main plaza.

Bus Several flotas make daily runs between Riberalta and Guayaramerín (US$2, three hours). Alternatively, wait for a car or camión along Av Héroes del Chaco. All flotas from Guayaramerín to Cobija, Rurrenabaque and La Paz stop at Riberalta en route.

Boat Boats up the Río Beni to Rurrenabaque are now rare, and run only at times when the road becomes impassable in the wet season (October to May). If you do find something, plan on US$20 to US$35 for the five- to eight-day trip. For information, check the board in the port captain's office.

Brazil

From the mad passion of Carnaval to the enormity of the dark Amazon, Brazil is a country of mythical proportions – a vast and vibrant landscape of unexplored rain forests, pristine tropical beaches and endless rivers. Best of all are the people themselves, who delight the visitor with their energy, fantasy and joy.

Facts about Brazil

HISTORY
Pre-Columbian Times
The Brazilian Indians did not develop a bureaucratic, centralized civilization like those of the Andes. They left little for archaeologists to discover because their artifacts were largely made of perishable materials. Some scholars believe that when the Portuguese arrived, at least seven million Indians were living in the territory that is now Brazil. Today, there are fewer than 200,000, most in the jungles of the interior.

Some Indians lived in small groups and were primarily hunter-gatherers, but most were shifting agriculturists who lived in villages, some of which may have had as many as 5000 inhabitants. They lived in long communal huts, and music, dance and games played very important roles in their culture. They produced very little surplus and had very few possessions. Every couple of years, the village would pack up and move on. This relatively peaceful life was punctuated by frequent tribal warfare and ritual cannibalism.

The Colonial Period
In 1500, Pedro Cabral sailed from Lisbon, bound for India. Nobody knows exactly why, but he veered west across the Atlantic and 'discovered' Brazil, landing at present-day Porto Seguro. Cabral and his crew stayed only nine days in the land they dubbed Terra da Vera Cruz (Land of the True Cross), then sailed on.

Subsequent Portuguese expeditions were disappointed by what they found. The Indians produced nothing considered valuable for the European markets, though a few Portuguese merchants sent ships to harvest

At a Glance

Country Name	República Federativa do Brasil
Area	8,547,403 sq km
Population	165 million
Population Density	19 per sq km
Capital	Brasília
Head of State	President Fernando Henrique Cardoso
Official Language	Portuguese
Other Languages	Indian languages
Currency	real
Exchange Rate	US$1 = 1.78 reais (July 1999)
Per Capita GNP	US$5030
Inflation Rate	8.1% (1999)

the *pau do brasil* (brazil wood tree), which produced a red dye. Brazil wood remained the country's only exportable commodity for the first half of the 16th century – long enough for the colony to change its name from Terra da Vera Cruz to Brazil.

In 1531, King João III of Portugal sent the first settlers to Brazil, under the direction of Martim Afonso de Sousa. They founded São Vicente, near the modern-day port of

Santos. In 1534, fearing the ambitions of other European countries, the king divided the coast into 12 hereditary captaincies, to be given to friends of the crown. Four of these captaincies were never settled and four were destroyed by Indians. Only Pernambuco and São Vicente proved profitable. In 1549, the king appointed Tomé de Sousa as the first governor of Brazil, with orders to centralize authority and save the remaining captaincies. The new capital of Portuguese Brazil was established at Bahia.

The colonists soon discovered that the land and climate were ideal for growing sugar cane. They needed labor, however, so they enslaved the Indians. The capture and sale of Indian slaves became Brazil's second-largest commercial enterprise, dominated by the *bandeirantes*, São Paulo men who were usually the sons of Portuguese fathers and Indian mothers. They hunted the Indians into the interior and by the mid-1600s had reached the peaks of the Peruvian Andes. Their exploits, more than any treaty, secured the huge interior of South America for Portuguese Brazil.

Jesuit priests, seeking to protect Indians fleeing from bandeirante attacks, built missions in the remote interior, near the present-day borders with Paraguay and Argentina. These settlements were not, as they had hoped, beyond the grasp of the bandeirantes. The Jesuits armed the Indians and desperate battles took place. Eventually, through the collusion of the Portuguese and Spanish crowns, the missions fell. The Jesuits were expelled from Brazil in 1759.

During the 17th century, African slaves largely replaced Indian prisoners on the plantations. They were considered better workers and were less vulnerable to European diseases, but they resisted slavery strongly. *Quilombos*, communities of runaway slaves, were common throughout the colonial period. They ranged from *mocambos*, small groups hidden in the forests, to the great republic of Palmares in northern Alagoas and the southern Pernambuco states, which survived for much of the 17th century.

In the 1690s gold was discovered in south-central Minas Gerais, and soon the rush was on. Brazilians and Portuguese immigrants flooded the territory, and countless slaves were brought from Africa to dig and die in

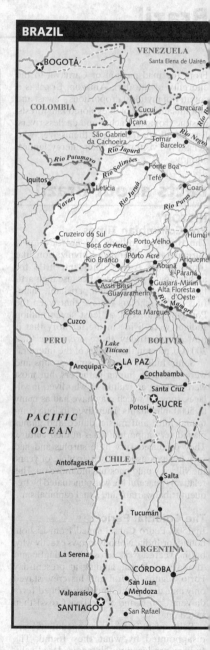

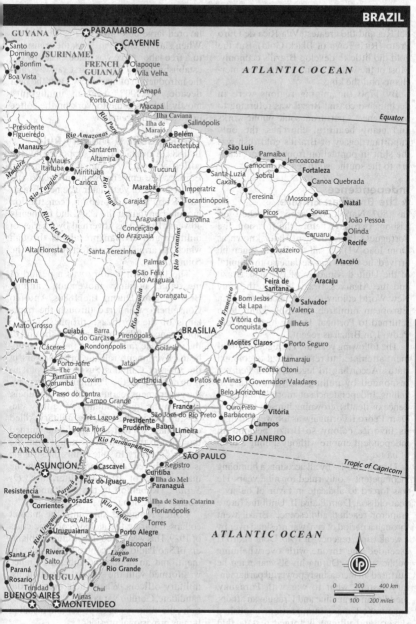

BRAZIL

Minas. Wild boom towns sprang up in the mountain valleys: Sabara, Mariana, São João del Rei and the greatest, Vila Rica de Ouro Prêto (Rich Town of Black Gold). But the gold did little to develop Brazil's economy: Most of the wealth went to Portuguese merchants and the king.

By 1750 the mining regions were in decline and coastal Brazil was returning to prominence. Apart from some public works and many beautiful churches, the only important legacy of Brazil's gold rush was the shift in population from the northeastern to the southeastern regions.

Independence & the Brazilian Empire

In 1807 Napoleon's army marched on Lisbon. Two days before the invasion, the Portuguese Prince Regent (later known as Dom João VI) set sail for Brazil. When he arrived, he made Rio de Janeiro the capital of the United Kingdom of Portugal, Brazil and the Algarves. Brazil became the only New World colony to serve as the seat of a European monarch. In 1821, Dom João returned to Portugal, leaving his son, Dom Pedro I, in Brazil as regent.

The following year, the Portuguese parliament attempted to return Brazil to colonial status. According to legend, Dom Pedro I responded by pulling out his sword and yelling 'Independência ou morte!' (Independence or death), crowning himself Emperor Dom Pedro I. Portugal was too weak to fight its favorite colony, so Brazil became an independent empire without spilling a drop of blood.

Dom Pedro I – by all accounts a bumbling incompetent – only ruled for nine years. He was forced to abdicate in favor of his five-year-old son, Dom Pedro II. Until the future emperor reached adolescence, Brazil went through a period of civil war presided over by a weak triple regency. In 1840, Dom Pedro II ascended the throne with overwhelming public support. During his 50-year reign he nurtured an increasingly powerful parliamentary system, went to war with Paraguay, meddled in Argentine and Uruguayan affairs, encouraged mass immigration, abolished slavery and ultimately forged a state that would do away with the monarchy for ever.

During the 19th century, coffee replaced sugar as Brazil's primary export, at one time supplying three-quarters of world demand. At first, production was labor-intensive and favored large enterprises using slave labor. When slavery ended in 1888, the transition to a free labor force was made easier by the establishment of Brazil's first railways and the introduction of machinery. Over the next decade, 800,000 European immigrants, mostly Italians, came to work on the coffee estates, called *fazendas*.

The Republic & Military Rule

In 1889, a military coup supported by the coffee aristocracy toppled the Brazilian Empire. The emperor went into exile and died a couple of years later. The new Brazilian Republic adopted a constitution modeled on that of the USA, and for nearly 40 years Brazil was governed by a series of military and civilian presidents through which the armed forces effectively ruled the country.

The late 19th century was a period of messianic popular movements among Brazil's poor. During the 1880s, Antônio Conselheiro wandered through the backlands of the northeast, prophesying the appearance of the Antichrist and the end of the world. He railed against the new republican government, rallying his followers in the town of Canudos. Suspecting a plot to return Brazil to the Portuguese monarchy, the government set out to subdue the rebels. Only on the fourth attempt were they successful, but in the end, the military killed every man, woman and child, and burned the town to the ground to erase it from the nation's memory. In spite of this, the struggle is remembered, even immortalized, in the masterpiece of Brazilian literature, *Os Sertões* (Rebellion in the Backlands), by Euclides da Cunha.

Coffee remained king until the market collapsed during the global economic crisis of 1929. This weakened the position of planters of São Paulo, who controlled the government, and an opposition Liberal Alliance was formed with the support of nationalist military officers. When their presidential candidate, Getúlio Vargas, lost the 1930 elections, the military seized power and installed him as provisional president.

Vargas proved a skilled strategist, and dominated the political scene for the next 20 years. In 1937, on the eve of a new election,

Vargas sent in the military to shut down Congress and took complete control of the country. His regime was inspired by the Italian and Portuguese fascist states of Benito Mussolini and Antonio de Oliveira Salazar, but during WWII he sided with the Allies. At the end of the war Vargas was forced to step down, but he remained popular. After winning a legitimate election in 1951, he served as president for three more years, until the military called for him to step down. Vargas shot himself in the heart.

Juscelino Kubitschek, the first of Brazil's big spenders, was elected president in 1956. He built Brasília, the new capital, hoping to stimulate the interior's development. By the early 1960s, the Brazilian economy was battered by inflation, and fears of communism were fueled by Castro's victory in Cuba. Again, Brazil's fragile democracy was crushed in 1964 when the military overthrew the government.

Borrowing heavily from various international banks, the generals benefited from the Brazilian 'economic miracle' of steady growth throughout the late 1960s and early 1970s. But in the 1980s, with the miracle petering out and popular opposition growing, the military announced the *abertura* (opening) and began a cautious return to civilian government. A presidential election was held in 1985, under an electoral college system designed to ensure the victory of the military's candidate. Surprisingly, the opposition candidate, Tancredo Neves, was elected. He died of heart failure the day before he was take office, however, and vice-president elect José Sarney, a relative unknown, took office as president.

In 1987, with Sarney at the helm, politicians hammered out a new, more liberal constitution. But the military remained powerful in the background, and little changed in the day-to-day lives of most Brazilians.

Modern Times

November 1989 saw the first presidential election by popular vote in nearly 30 years. Voters elected Fernando Collor de Mello over the socialist Luiz da Silva (known as Lula) by a narrow but secure majority.

Collor gained office promising to fight corruption and reduce inflation, but in 1992 he was removed from office. Indicted by Federal Police on charges of corruption, he was accused of being the leader of a gang that used extortion and bribery to suck more than US\$1 billion from the economy. Collor joined the long of Brazilian presidents who left office before the end of their mandate list (11 out of 24).

Vice President Itamar Franco became president in December 1992 after Collor's forced resignation. Considered provincial and unprepared to take office, Itamar surprised his critics with a competent and honest administration. His greatest achievement was the 1994 Plano Real, which began the long-awaited stabilization of the economy.

The architect of the plan, Itamar's finance minister Fernando Henrique Cardoso (FHC), became known as 'Father of the Real' and rode its success all the way to a landslide victory in the 1994 presidential elections.

An ex-sociology professor from São Paulo, Cardoso is a social democrat committed to economic progress and growth, as well as tackling Brazil's social problems.

During his first four years in office, FHC succeeded in keeping inflation in check. He also oversaw the flood of foreign capital that entered Brazil as he continued to 'globalize' Brazil's economy and sell off inefficient, state-owned enterprises. The resulting chronic unemployment created other problems, especially in São Paulo, Brazil's industrial heartland, where unemployment levels reached 20%.

The 'Asian Economic Crisis' of 1997 rocked Brazil, showing just how much the country's stability depended on the whims of Wall Street traders.

Nevertheless, FHC was reelected in 1998, beginning his second term with the words: 'It doesn't mean much to be the world's eighth largest economy if we continue to be first in inequality.' It's clear that social justice and economic growth don't always coincide, especially in a country as volatile as Brazil. Many problems remain: corruption, violence, urban overcrowding, lack of essential health and education facilities, environmental abuse and dramatic extremes of wealth and poverty.

Brazil has long been known as a land of the future, but the future never seems to arrive.

BRAZIL

GEOGRAPHY

The world's fifth-largest country, after Russia, Canada, China and the USA, Brazil borders every country in South America except Chile and Ecuador. Its 8.5 million sq km cover almost half the continent.

Brazil can be divided into several major geographic regions: the southeastern coastal area of São Paulo and its hinterland; the Paraná Basin of the far south; the 'drought polygon' of the northeast; the central west of the Brazilian Shield; the tropical north of the Amazon Basin; and the southward-draining Guiana Shield.

The southeastern coastal area is bordered by the mountain ranges that lie between it and Brazil's central plateau. From Rio Grande do Sul to Bahia, the mountains come right to the coast, but beyond Bahia, in the drought-prone northeast, the coastal lands are flatter.

South of the Amazon, the Brazilian Shield is an extensive area of weathered bedrock featuring the Planalto, a plateau with an average altitude of only 500m. Several minor mountain ranges rise from it, the highest of them in Minas Gerais. The western Planalto is a huge expanse of savanna grassland known as the Mato Grosso.

Many rivers drain into the Amazon Basin from the Brazilian Shield to the south, the Andes to the west and the Guiana Shield to the north. The 6275km Amazon is the

world's largest river, and its tributaries carry about 20% of the world's fresh water. The basin contains some 30% of the world's remaining forest.

The Paraná Basin is characterized by open forest, low woods and scrub land. Its two principal rivers, the Paraná and the Paraguay, run south through Paraguay and Argentina. The swampy area of the basin toward the Paraguayan border is known as the Pantanal.

CLIMATE

The Brazilian winter takes place from June to August, but it is only cold south of Rio de Janeiro, where the average temperature during the winter months stays between 13°C and 18°C (55°F and 65°F).

In most of Brazil, short tropical rains are frequent all year round but rarely interfere with travel plans. The *sertão* (the dry interior of the northeast) is an exception: Here, there are heavy rains for a few months of the year, and periodic droughts devastate the region.

The Amazon Basin receives the most rain in Brazil. It is not nearly as hot as most people presume – the average temperature is 13°C (80°F) – but it *is* humid.

FLORA & FAUNA

The richness and diversity of Brazilian flora and fauna are astounding, and the country ranks first in the world for its variety of primate, amphibian and plant species; third for bird species; and fourth for butterfly and reptile species. See the Pantanal and Amazonas sections for further information.

GOVERNMENT & POLITICS

Brazil slowly returned to democracy in the 1980s, enacting a new constitution in 1988. It allows the president to choose ministers of state, initiate legislation and maintain foreign relations, and gives him or her the right of total veto. The president is also commander-in-chief of the armed forces.

These presidential powers are balanced by a bicameral legislature, which consists of a 72-seat senate and a 487-seat chamber of deputies. Presidential, state and congressional elections are held every four years. Municipal elections are held every three years. In 1998 Fernando Henrique Cardoso won an unprecedented second term as president, elected by popular vote.

Elections are colorful affairs, regarded by the democracy-starved Brazilians as yet another excuse for a party, but politics itself remains largely the estate of the wealthy. Corruption is rife, especially at the state and local government levels.

ECONOMY

Before 1994 the only certainty in the Brazilian economy was its uncertainty. Wild boom-and-bust cycles had decimated the economy in the previous decade. Then came the Plano Real, stabilizing the currency, ending the inflation that had corroded the salaries of the lowest wage earners, and provoking a rise in consumption. Of the seven economic plans introduced in the eight years up to 1994, the Real was the first to achieve any real success. Backed by a record volume of foreign investment, the real began on a one-for-one parity with the US dollar.

Because the currency was overvalued by about 20%, the real was devalued in 1999. Naysayers predicted rampant inflation, the specter of which has not been seen. Indeed, the economy, exchange rates and most other economic indicators have remained relatively stable.

At least the Plano Real has shown the Brazilian economy's great potential. All the ingredients for progress are here: a large labor force, the means of production, transportation systems and an expanding market. The question is whether or not they can be coordinated efficiently.

The harsh reality is that the richest 10% of Brazilians control 54% of the nation's wealth – the poorest 10% have just 0.6% – and the gap is widening. Unemployment is rampant and seven out of 10 Brazilians still live in poverty.

POPULATION & PEOPLE

Brazil's population is around 165 million, making it the world's sixth most populous country. Still, Brazil is one of the least densely populated countries in the world, averaging only 15 people per sq km. The population is concentrated along the coastal strip and in the cities, where two out of every three Brazilians live. Greater São Paulo has more than 20 million residents, and greater Rio has more than 10 million.

In this developing country, 40 million people are malnourished, 25 million live in

BRAZIL

favelas (shantytowns), 12 million children are abandoned and more than seven million children between the ages of seven and 14 don't attend school. Sixty million people live without proper sanitation, clean water or decent housing. Brazil, with its dreams of greatness, has misery that compares with the poorest countries in Africa and Asia.

The Portuguese colonized Brazil largely through miscegenation with both the Indian and African populations. Blacks and Indians also intermarried, and the three races became thoroughly mixed. This legacy continued, almost as a semiofficial colonial policy, for hundreds of years, and has led to a greater blending of these races than in any other country on the continent.

At present, the number of Indians in Brazil is estimated at less than 200,000. Of the several hundred tribes, most are concentrated in the Amazon region, and virtually all Brazilian Indians face a host of problems that threaten to destroy their environment and way of life.

ARTS

Brazilian culture has been shaped not only by the Portuguese, who gave the country its language and religion, but also by Indians, Africans and settlers from Europe, the Middle East and Asia.

Although often ignored, denigrated or feared by urban Brazilians, Indian culture has helped shape modern Brazil and its legends, dance and music. Many indigenous foods and beverages, such as tapioca, manioc, potatoes, *mate* and *guaraná*, have become Brazilian staples. The Indians also gave the colonizers numerous objects and skills that are now used daily in modern Brazil, such as hammocks, dugout canoes, thatched roofing, and weaving techniques.

The influence of African culture is also very powerful, especially in the northeast. The people enslaved by the Portuguese brought with them their religion, music and cuisine, all of which have profoundly influenced Brazilian identity. *Capoeira*, an African martial art developed by slaves to fight their oppressors, has become very popular in recent years. Throughout Brazil, you will see *rodas de capoeiras*, semicircles of spectator-musicians who sing the initial *chula* before the fight and provide the percussion during it.

RELIGION

Religion in Brazil is notable for its diversity. There are dozens of religions and sects, though the differences are often ill-defined. Although Catholicism retains its status as the official religion, it is declining in popularity. The largest number of converts are being attracted to Protestantism, including popular evangelical churches such as Bishop Edir Macedo's Universal Church of the Kingdom of God. Up to 30 million Brazilians now call themselves evangelicals, and the Catholic church estimates 600,000 Catholics convert annually.

Afro-Brazilian cults such as Macumba and Candomblé, which incorporate aspects of Indian religions and European spiritualism, are also thriving in Brazil. Other, less well-known religions also thrive, some involving animal sacrifice, black magic and hallucinogenic substances.

In Candomblé, each person has a particular orixá to protect them and their spirit, with Exú serving as mediator between the material and spiritual worlds. To keep them strong, the orixás and Exú must be given food and other gifts. Exú likes alcoholic drinks, tobacco, strong perfumes, fruit and meat. The orixás, like the Greek gods, are often involved in struggles for power.

Candomblé is also a medium for incorporating African traditions such as music, dance and language into Brazilian culture.

The Afro-Brazilian rituals are practiced in a *casa de santo* or *terreiro*, directed by a *pai* or *mãe de santo* (literally, father or mother of the saint – the Candomblé priest or priestess). In Bahia and Rio, millions of Brazilians go to the beach during the festivals at the year's end to pay homage to Iemanjá, the queen of the sea. Flowers, perfumes, fruit and jewelry are tossed into the sea to please the mother of the waters and to gain her protection in the new year.

LANGUAGE

When they settled Brazil in the 16th century, the Portuguese encountered many diverse Indian languages. These, together with the various dialects spoken by Africans brought into the country as slaves, extensively changed the Portuguese spoken by the early settlers. Along with Portuguese, the Indian language Tupi-Guaraní, written down and simplified by the Jesuits, became a common language. It was spoken by the majority of Brazilians until the middle of the 18th century, but its usage diminished as Portuguese gold-rush immigrants flooded westward, and a royal proclamation in 1757 prohibited its use. With the expulsion of the Jesuits in 1759, Portuguese was truly established as the national language.

Still, many words remain from the Indian and African languages. From Tupi-Guaraní come lots of place names (Guanabara, Tijuca and Niterói), animal names *(capivara, piranha and urubu)* and plant names *(mandioca, abacaxí, caju and jacarandá)*. Words from the African dialects, mainly those from Nigeria and Angola, are used in Afro-Brazilian religious ceremonies (Orixá, Exú and Iansã), cooking *(vatapá, acarajé and abará)* and general conversation *(samba, moleque* and *mocambo)*.

Within Brazil, accents, dialects and slang *(gíria)* vary regionally. The *carioca*, or inhabitant of Rio de Janeiro, inserts the 'sh' sound in place of 's.' The *gaúcho* speaks a Spanish-sounding Portuguese, the *baiano* (from Bahia) speaks slowly, and the accents of the *cearense* (from Ceará) are often incomprehensible to outsiders.

Portuguese is similar to Spanish on paper, but sounds completely different. You will do quite well if you speak Spanish in Brazil, although in general, Brazilians will understand you better than you understand them. Try to develop an ear for Portuguese – it's a beautiful language. Brazilians are easy to befriend, but the vast majority speak little or no English. This is changing, as practically all Brazilians in school are learning English.

Most phrasebooks are not very helpful; their vocabulary is often dated and covers the Portuguese spoken in Portugal, not Brazil. Notable exceptions are Lonely Planet's *Brazilian phrasebook*, and the Berlitz phrasebook for travel in Brazil. Make sure any English-Portuguese dictionary uses Brazilian Portuguese. It's easy to arrange tutorial instruction through any of the Brazilian-American institutes where Brazilians go to learn English, or at the IBEU (Instituto Brasil Estados Unidos) in Rio.

Body Language

Brazilians accompany their oral communication with a rich body language, a sort of parallel dialogue. The thumbs up of *tudo bem* is used as a greeting or to signify OK or thank you. The authoritative *não, não* finger-wagging is most intimidating when done right under a victim's nose, but it's not a threat. To indicate *rápido!* (speed and haste), thumb and middle finger touch loosely while rapidly shaking the wrist. If you don't want something *(não quero)*, slap the back of your hands as if ridding yourself of the entire affair.

For useful words and phrases in Brazilian Portuguese, see the Language chapter at the end of the book.

Facts for the Visitor

HIGHLIGHTS

The city of Rio de Janeiro, despite a full set of urban problems, is a marvelous place. Rio's Carnaval is the most famous festival, but the Brazilian passion for music and dance can be seen everywhere and every day, from impromptu gatherings to the thousands of annual celebrations all over the country. There are miles of quiet coastline, but the real Brazilian beach scene features *barracas* (stalls or huts) with loud music, wild dancing, cold beer and beautiful bodies; check it out anywhere from Ilha de Santa Catarina to the northeast.

Many of the historic colonial cities have been restored and are truly gorgeous; some of the best are Ouro Prêto, Congonhas, Diamantina, Parati, Salvador da Bahia, Olinda and São Luís. Ecotourists and wildlife buffs will want to take a trip into the Amazon rain forest, but the Pantanal and the Atlantic rain forest also feature fantastic biodiversity and are well worth a visit. For a scenic highlight, it's hard to top the Iguaçu Falls.

PLANNING
When to Go

See the information under Climate in the Facts about Brazil section for details of seasonal factors that may influence your decision about when to visit. There are few regions that can't be comfortably visited all year round. During summer (December to February), when many Brazilians are on vacation, travel is difficult and expensive. School holidays begin in mid-December and continue until Carnaval, which usually takes place in late February.

BRAZIL

What to Bring

The happiest travelers are those who can slip all their luggage under a plane seat. Pack light.

What you bring will depend on what you want to do. If you're planning a river or jungle trip, read the Amazon section in advance. If you're traveling cheap, a sleeping-sack, made by sewing a cotton sheet together like a light sleeping bag, will come in handy.

With its warm climate and informal dress standards, you don't need to bring many clothes to Brazil. Except for the south and Minas Gerais, where it gets cold in the winter, the only weather you need to contend with is heat and rain, and whatever you're lacking you can purchase while traveling. Buying clothes in Brazil is easy and has the added advantage of helping you appear less like a tourist.

You don't need to pack more than a pair of shorts, long pants, a couple of T-shirts, a long-sleeved shirt, bathing suit, towel, underwear, walking shoes, thongs and a light rain jacket. Quick-drying, light cotton clothes are the most convenient. Suntan lotion and sun-protection cream are readily available in Brazil. Most other toiletries are also easy to get.

Usually, one set of clothes to wear and one to wash is adequate. It's probably a good idea if one set of clothes is somewhat presentable for a visit to a good restaurant or club (or to renew your visa at the federal police station). While dress is informal, many Brazilians are very fashion conscious and pay close attention to both their own appearance and yours.

TOURIST OFFICES

The headquarters of Embratur, the Brazilian Tourist Board (☎ 061-224-2872), is at Setor Comercial Norte, Quadra 2, Bloco G, Brasília, DF, CEP 70710. There is also an Embratur office (☎ 021-509-6017) in Rio de Janeiro, at Rua Uruguaiana 174, 8th floor.

Tourist offices elsewhere in Brazil are generally sponsored by individual states and municipalities. In many places, these offices rely on shoestring budgets, which are chopped or maintained according to the whims (or feuds) of regional and local politicians. Keep your sense of humor, prepare for potluck and don't expect too much!

VISAS & DOCUMENTS
Passports

By law you must carry a passport with you at all times, but many travelers opt to carry a photocopy (preferably certified) when tripping around town and leave their passport secure at their hotel. It's convenient to have extra passport photos for any documents or visas you might acquire in Brazil.

Visas

American, Canadian, Australian and New Zealander citizens require visas, but UK citizens do not. Tourist visas are issued by Brazilian diplomatic offices. They are valid for arrival in Brazil within 90 days of issue and then for a 90-day stay. Visas can be renewed in Brazil for 90 additional days.

It should only take about three hours to issue a visa, though this can vary; you will need a passport (valid for at least six months), a single passport photograph (either B&W or color) and either a return ticket or a statement from a travel agent, addressed to the Brazilian diplomatic office, stating that you have the required ticketing.

People less than 18 years of age who hope to visit must submit a notarized letter of authorization from their parents or legal guardian.

Visa Extensions The Polícia Federal handles visa extensions, but you must go to them before your visa lapses, preferably 15 days in advance. They have offices in major cities. An extension costs about US$12, and in most cases it is granted automatically. However, the police may require you to have a ticket out of the country and proof of sufficient funds. If you leave Brazil, you cannot return until your current visa expires, but you are not obliged to extend your visa for the full 90 days.

Tourist Card

When you enter Brazil, you will be asked to fill out a tourist card, which has two parts. Immigration officials will keep one part. The other part will be attached to your passport, to be detached by immigration officials when you leave. Make sure you don't lose it; otherwise, your departure could be delayed while officials check your story.

Onward Tickets

If you only have a one-way ticket to Brazil, visa officials may accept a document from a bank or similar organization proving that you have sufficient funds to stay and buy a return ticket.

Driver's License & Permits

Your home driver's license is valid in Brazil, but because local authorities probably won't be familiar with it, you should do them (and yourself) a favor and also carry an International Driver's Permit. IDPs are issued by your national automobile association.

To rent a car, you must be at least 25 years old, have a credit card in your name and a valid driving license.

Hostel Card

A Hostelling International membership card is essential if you plan to stay in the *albergues de juventude* (youth hostels). Most hostels in Brazil will let you in without one, but will charge more. HI cards are available in any hostel for varying fees, usually less than US$20. For information on the growing network of Brazilian youth hostels, contact the head office of the Federação Brasileira dos Albergues de Juventude (FBAJ; ☎ 021-286-0303) in Botafogo, in the hostel at Rua General Dionísio 63.

EMBASSIES & CONSULATES
Brazilian Embassies & Consulates

The Federative Republic of Brazil maintains embassies and consulates in the following countries:

Australia
(☎ 02-6273-2372)
19 Forster Crescent, Yarralumla, ACT 2600

Canada
(☎ 613-237-1090)
450 Wilbrod St, Ottawa, Ontario KIN 6MB

Chile
(☎ 2-639-8867)
Calle Enrique Mac-Iver 225, Ed Banco Exterior, Piso 15, Centro, Santiago

Colombia
(☎ 571-218-0800)
Calle 93 NR 14-20, Piso 8, Apartado Aerea 90540, Bogotá 8

France
(☎ 01 45 61 63 00)
34 Cours Albert, 1er, 75008 Paris

Germany
(☎ 030-883-1208)
Esplanade 11, Poste 13187, Berlin 15

New Zealand
(☎ 04-473-3516)
Level 9, 10 Brandon St, Wellington

Paraguay
(☎ 21-448-069)
Calle General Díaz C/14 De Mayo NR 521, Edificio Faro Internacional, 3rd floor, Caixa Postal 1314, Asunción

UK
Embassy: (☎ 020-7499-0877)
32 Green St, London, W1Y 4AT
Consulate: (☎ 020-7930-9055)
6 St Alban's St, London, SW1Y 4SQ

USA
Embassy: (☎ 202-238-2828, fax 202-238-2818)
3006 Massachusetts Av, NW,
Washington, DC 20008
Consulate: (☎ 212-827-0976)
531 5th Av, Room 210, New York, NY 10176

Venezuela
(☎ 2-261-7553)
Centro Gerencial Mohedando, Piso 6, Calle Los Chaguaramos Con Av Mohedano, La Castellana 1060, Caracas

Embassies & Consulates in Brazil

Most countries maintain embassies in Brasília, but many also have offices in Rio and São Paulo, any of which can take care of most travelers' needs. Following is a list of embassies in Brasília; SES stands for Setor de Embaixadas Sul:

Australia
(☎ 061-248-5569)
Setor de Habitações Individuais Sul, Q I-9, cj 16, casa 1

Canada
(☎ 061-321-2171)
SES, Av das Nações Q 803, lote 16 sl 130

France
(☎ 061-312-9100)
SES, Av das Nações, lote 4

Germany
(☎ 061-224-7273)
SES, Av das Nações 25

Israel
(☎ 061-244-7675)
SES, Av das Nações, Q 809, lote 38

UK
(☎ 061-225-2710)
SES, Av das Nações, Q 801, cj K lote 8

USA
(☎ 061-321-7272)
SES, Av das Nações, Q 801, lote 3

BRAZIL

Consulates with representation in Manaus include:

Bolivia
  (☎ 092-234-6661)
  Av Eduardo Ribeiro 520, sala 1410, Centro

Colombia
  (☎ 092-234-6777)
  Rua Dona Libânia 262

France
  (☎ 092-233-6583)
  Av Joaquim Nabuco 1846, Bl A, sala 02, Centro

Peru
  (☎ 092-642-1646)
  Conj Morada do Sol, Rua KL c/6, Aleixo

Venezuela
  (☎ 092-233-6004)
  Rua Ferreira Pena 179, Centro

CUSTOMS

Travelers entering Brazil are allowed to bring in one radio, tape player, typewriter, video and still camera. Personal computers are permitted, but you may be required to fill out paperwork promising to take it with you when you leave.

Airport customs sometimes use a random check system: After collecting your luggage you pass a post with two buttons; if you have nothing to declare, you push the appropriate button. A green light means walk straight out; a red light means that you've been selected for a baggage search. Customs searches at land borders are more thorough, especially if you're coming from Bolivia.

MONEY
Currency

The monetary unit of Brazil is the *real* (pronounced '**hay**-ow'); its plural is *reais* (pronounced '**hay**-ice'). It's made up of 100 *centavos*. There are now two sets of coins in circulation: the older, frustratingly similar coins in denominations of one, five, 10, 25 and 50 centavos are slowly being replaced by a new set with different sizes. There's also a one-real coin as well as a one-real note. The notes are different colors, so there's no mistaking them; along with the green one-real note, there's a blue/purple five, a red 10, a brown 50 and a blue 100.

Exchange Rates

There are currently three exchange rates in Brazil: official (also known as *comercial* or *câmbio livre*), *turismo* and *paralelo*. You'll get the turismo rate from most banks and exchange places. Rates are written up every day on the front page and in the business sections of the major daily papers, and announced on the evening TV news.

Approximate exchange rates in June 1999 were as follows:

country	unit		reais
Australia	A$1	=	R$1.49
Canada	C$1	=	R$1.20
France	FF1	=	R$0.28
euro	€1	=	R$1.83
Germany	DM1	=	R$0.94
Japan	¥100	=	R$1.46
New Zealand	NZ$1	=	R$0.94
UK	UK£1	=	R$2.81
USA	US$1	=	R$1.76

Exchanging Money

Changing money in Brazil's larger cities is easy. Almost anyone can direct you to a *casa de câmbio* (money exchange house), where Brazilians and foreigners can buy and sell dollars with no restrictions. In small towns without a bank, you'll have to ask around. Someone will usually be able to direct you to a person who buys cash.

Change, variously referred to as *troco* or *miúdo*, is often unobtainable. When you change money, ask for lots of small bills.

Changing money on weekends, even in the big cities, can be extremely difficult, so make sure you have enough to last until Monday. If you do get stuck, the best places to try are the large hotels, expensive restaurants, travel agents, jewelry shops and souvenir shops.

Don't change money on the street, follow moneychangers into unfamiliar areas, or give money or unsigned checks up front.

Cash US dollars are easier to exchange and are worth a bit more than other currencies. Have some US dollars in cash to use when the banks are closed.

Traveler's Checks Get traveler's checks in US dollars and carry some small denominations for convenience.

American Express is the most recognized brand, but Thomas Cook, Barclays and First National City Bank traveler's checks are also good.

Most Brazilian banks, including the Banco do Brasil, charge absurdly high fees for cashing travelers checks (up to US$20 regardless of the amount cashed).

ATMs A good national network of automatic teller machines (ATMs) operates throughout Brazil. Bradesco machines are in most cities and can usually give you cash from a Visa card (if you've activated your four-digit Personal Identification Number, or PIN), as well as from bank cards on the Plus network. Banco do Brasil (which has distinctive red booths in almost every sizable town) ATMs are increasingly offering this service as well. Citibank ATMs are in major cities and also accept Visa/Plus cards.

Credit & Debit Cards Visa is the most versatile credit and debit card in Brazil, and getting cash advances is becoming easier.

International credit cards such as Visa, American Express and MasterCard are accepted by many expensive hotels, restaurants and shops. It's surprising, however, how many don't accept credit cards. Make sure you ask first if you plan to use one. At present, you get billed at the turismo rate in reais.

American Express cardholders can purchase traveler's checks in US dollars from American Express offices in most large cities. MasterCard holders can pay for many goods and services with their card, but cash advances are difficult.

Credit-card fraud is rife in Brazil. Never let your card out of your sight, especially in restaurants.

International Transfers Transferring money from a bank in your home country to you while in Brazil is either cheap and extremely problematic or easy and usuriously expensive.

If you have an account at a Brazilian bank, the procedure is straightforward: forward your account number, your Brazilian bank's SWIFT address, physical address and ABA routing number to whoever is sending the money, and anywhere from 24 to 72 hours later (depending on your Brazilian banker's overnight Fed Fund habits) it should be in your Brazilian account.

If you don't have an account in Brazil, ask your bank at home for the name of the bank they have a correspondent relationship with in Brazil and ask them about the best possible way to transfer funds.

Costs

After the long-expected devaluation of the real in 1999, many people predicted a higher inflation rate. So far, however, exchange rates and prices have held steady. Unfortunately, money has been harder to exchange since the devaluation. Many of the smaller câmbios have closed or are reluctant to change some currencies and particularly traveler's checks. Make sure you have enough cash on hand when visiting out-of-the-way places, particularly on weekends.

Before the devaluation, Brazil could not be considered even remotely cheap. Prices are still similar to those in Australia or the southeastern USA. However, despite the real's relative stability, bargains might still be had by the budget-savvy traveler.

If you plan to lie on a beach for a month, eating rice, beans and fish every day, US$20 to US$30 a day would be enough.

During the holiday season (December to February) accommodations costs generally increase by around 25% to 30%, sometimes more in popular resorts.

Bargaining

Bargaining for hotel rooms should become second nature. Before you agree to take a room, ask for a better price. '*Tem desconto?*' ('Is there a discount?') and '*Pode fazer um melhor preço?*' ('Can you give a better price?') are the phrases to use. There's often a discount for paying *ávista* (cash) or for staying during the *baixa estaço* or *época baixa* (low season) when hotels need guests to cover running costs. It's also possible to reduce the price if you state that you don't want a TV, private bath or air-con. If you're staying longer than a couple of days, ask for a discount. Once a discount has been quoted, make sure it is noted on your bill at the same time to avoid misunderstandings at a later date. Also bargain in markets and in unmetered taxis.

POST & COMMUNICATIONS
Post

Postal services are usually pretty good in Brazil, although LP has heard plenty of complaints from readers. Most mail seems to get through, and airmail letters to the US and Europe usually arrive in a week or so. For Australia, allow two weeks. Rates for mail leaving Brazil are almost US$1 for an international letter or postcard. Most *correios* (post offices) are open weekdays from 9 am to 6 pm and Saturday mornings.

The *posta restante* system seems to function reasonably well and will hold mail for 30 days. A reliable alternative for American Express customers is to have mail sent to an American Express office.

Telephone

International Calls Brazil's international telephone code is ☎ 55. To the USA and Canada, it costs approximately US$1.35 a minute. To the UK and France, the charge is US$1.80 a minute. Prices are 25% lower from 8 pm to 6 am daily and all day Sunday. To Australia and New Zealand, calls cost US$2.50 a minute (there are no cheaper times to call these two countries).

Every town has a *posto telefônico* (phone company office) for making long-distance calls that require a large deposit. If you're calling direct from a private phone, dial ☎ 00, followed by the country code number, the area code and finally, the phone number. For information on international calls, dial ☎ 000333.

International reverse-charge (collect) calls *(a cobrar)* can be made from any phone. To get the international operator, dial ☎ 00-0111 or ☎ 107 and ask for the *telefônista internacional*. Embratel, the Brazilian telephone monopoly, now offers direct services for the following countries:

Australia	☎ 000-8061
Canada	☎ 000-8014
France	☎ 000-8033
Germany	☎ 000-8049
Israel	☎ 000-8097
Italy	☎ 000-8039
Japan	☎ 000-8081
Netherlands	☎ 000-8031
UK	☎ 000-8044
USA (AT&T)	☎ 000-8010
(MCI)	☎ 000-8012
(Sprint)	☎ 000-8016

National Calls National long-distance calls can also be made at the local phone com-

pany office, unless you're calling collect. For reverse-charge calls within Brazil, dial ☎ 9, the area code, then the phone number. A recorded message in Portuguese will ask you to say your name and where you're calling from after the beep. The person at the other end then decides if they will accept the call.

Local Calls Brazilian public phones are nicknamed *orelhôes* (big ears). They use *fichas* (coinlike tokens) or *cartão telefônicos* (phonecards). Both can be bought at newsstands, pharmacies and other places. Phonecards range in value from 30 centavos (good for 10 local calls) to three reais. When your time is up, you will be disconnected without warning. To call the operator, dial ☎ 100; for information, call ☎ 102.

Fax

Post offices send and receive faxes. Faxes generally cost US$5 for the first page and US$3 for each additional page to the USA and Canada, US$8/4.50 to Australia and New Zealand, and US$6/4 to the UK.

Email & Internet Access

Internet access is taking off in larger cities, where Internet cafés are becoming more popular. Access is still limited in rural areas. Try *escolas de informatica* (computer schools), which often have Internet connections. Staff are usually happy to rent you some time.

INTERNET RESOURCES

For the latest, up-to-date links in and about Brazil, visit Lonely Planet's website (www.lonelyplanet.com) for destination profiles, relevant links, recent (unconfirmed) reports from other travelers and much more. You can also visit Lonely Planet on America Online (keyword: lp), or on the French Minitel system at 3615 lonelyplanet. Another useful website is lanic.utexas.edu /ilas/brazctr/school.html, which originates at the University of Texas and has heaps of links and *Real Brazil*, an English language journal of Brazilian affairs. Other websites dedicated to Brazil include:

Embratur National Tourism –
    www.embratur.gov.br

Brazilian Embassy, Washington, DC –
    www.brasil.emb.nw.dc.us/embing6.htm;

this is probably the most reliable set of Brazil links around plus constantly updated visa information

Brazilian Consulate in San Francisco – www.crl.com/~brazil/address.htm; listings of addresses and telephone numbers of US and some international Brazilian consular offices

Green Globe – www.wttc.org

Nature Conservancy – www.tnc.org; this and Green Globe run websites with information about natural history and links to Amazon and ecotourism sites.

BOOKS
Lonely Planet

Lonely Planet publishes an excellent *Brazilian phrasebook* that covers practically anything you'd ever need to say in Brazilian Portuguese. Lonely Planet's *Brazil* covers the country in detail.

The French-language Lonely Planet Guides de Voyage publishes *Brésil.*

Guidebooks

Quatro Rodas publishes the best series of Brazil guides. They're in Portuguese, but keyed in English and extremely easy to follow.

The bigger sellers are readily available at most newsstands and all are available in Brazilian bookstores. The prices aren't marked, so you'll have to ask the vendor – they generally cost about US$20.

The flagship title is *Quatro Rodas: Guia Brasil,* which contains a wealth of information about accommodations, restaurants, transportation, sights, etc. If you buy it in Brazil it comes with an excellent fold-out map of the country, but doesn't cover budget options.

Other titles include *Guia São Paulo Ruas* and *Guia Rio de Janeiro Ruas,* both superb atlases to São Paulo and Rio. *Guia Rodoviário* is a comprehensive road atlas with excellent countrywide maps that also cover main roads into other Mercosur countries. *Guia de Estradas* is *Guia Rodoviário* on steroids. Then there's the beautiful and pricey *Guia de Praias,* which is geared toward beach freaks on driving tours with maps and stunning satellite photographs of the country's beaches plus information on accommodations and parks. *Mapa das Capitais* gives detailed street plans of all Brazilian state capitals.

Travel

Travelers' Tales Brazil, edited by Lonely Planet author Scott Doggett and Annette Haddad, is a fine anthology of tales about travel and life in Brazil, with submissions from Bill McKibben, Joe Kane, Petru Popescu and Alma Guillermoprieto. It will keep you riveted and laughing – great bus reading.

Peter Fleming's *Brazilian Adventure* is about the young journalist's expedition into Mato Grosso in search of missing explorer Colonel Fawcett, who was the inspiration for Indiana Jones. At the time this area was the world's last, vast unexplored region. What Fleming actually discovered is less important than his story. Written with the humor of the disenchanted Briton, travel adventures don't get any funnier than this.

Running the Amazon, by Joe Kane, is the story of the 11 people who in 1986 began the only expedition to cover the entire length of the Rio Amazonas, from the Andes to the Atlantic, by foot raft and kayak.

It's not hard to guess what *Eat Smart in Brazil: How to Decipher the Menu, Know the Market Foods & Embark on a Tasting Adventure* (Ginkgo Press) is about.

We really enjoyed Paul Rambali's *It's all True – in the Cities and Jungles of Brazil.* Rambali, founding editor of *The Face* magazine, writes of his travel experiences in Brazil with shrewd and humorous insight. Among other things, he looks at favela gangsters, street kids, soap operas and neo-evangelism.

History & Politics

A History of Brazil, by E Bradford Burns, is an in-depth look at the history of the country up to 1993.

John Hemming's *Red Gold: The Conquest of the Brazilian Indians* follows the colonists and Indians from 1500 to 1760, when millions of indigenous people were either eliminated or pacified. Hemming, a founder of Survival International and an eloquent campaigner for Indian rights, extends his analysis of Indian history in *Amazon Frontier: The Defeat of the Brazilian Indians*

The most famous book on Brazil's colonial period is Gilberto Freyre's *Masters and the Slaves: A Study in the Development of Brazilian Civilization.* Freyre's other works include *The Mansions and the Shanties: The*

BRAZIL

Making of Modern Brazil and *Order and Progress: Brazil from Monarchy to Republic*.

Freyre argues that Brazilian slavery was less harsh than slavery in the USA, and through interracial pairing, Brazil has avoided the USA's racial problems. His views have contributed to the myth of racial democracy in Brazil and have been severely rebuked by academics over the past 20 years. Still, Freyre's books can be read on many levels, and he makes fascinating comments on folklore, myth, superstition, religion and sexuality.

Finally, the unbelievable rebellion in Canudos by the followers of the mystic Antônio Conselheiro has been immortalized in *Rebellion in the Backlands* by Euclides da Cunha. Mixing history, geography and philosophy, *Os Sertões* (in Portuguese) is considered the masterpiece of Brazilian literature. It's an incredible story about outcasts of the northeast and a sort of meditation on Brazilian civilization. The story of da Cunha and the rebellion is told by Mário Vargas Llosa in his novel, *The War of the End of the World*. It's light, entertaining reading for the traveler.

For readers who like their history with a dose of fiction, *Brazil*, by Errol Lincoln Uys, is an interesting novel that traces the history of two Brazilian families from pre-Cabral times to the foundation of Brasília.

The Amazon

Amazonia, by renowned explorer and photographer Loren McIntyre, records in magnificent photographs the gradual demise of the region and its original inhabitants.

Alex Shoumatoff has written some excellent books about the Amazon, all of them entertaining combinations of history, myth and travelogue. *The World is Burning* recounts the Chico Mendes story.

The Fate of the Forest: Developers, Destroyers and Defenders of the Amazon by Susanna Hecht and Alexander Cockburn is one of the best analyses of the complex web of destruction and provides ideas on ways to mend the damage.

NEWSPAPERS & MAGAZINES

English By far the best English-language newspaper is the Latin American edition of the *Miami Herald*, which costs about US$5. *Time* and *Newsweek* magazines are available throughout Brazil. In the big cities, you can find imported newspapers and magazines at some newsstands, but they are very expensive.

Portuguese The *Folha de São Paulo* is Brazil's finest newspaper. It has excellent coverage of national and international events and is a good guide to entertainment in São Paulo. The *Jornal do Brasil* and *O Globo* are Rio's main daily newspapers. Among weekly magazines, *Veja*, the Brazilian *Time* clone, is the country's best-selling magazine.

TV

English Cable TV is a recent addition and includes ESPN (the sports network), CNN (Cable News Network), RAI (Radio Televisione Italiana) and, of course, MTV (music television) available to those few who can afford them.

Portuguese The most popular programs on Brazilian TV are *novelas* (soap operas) that go on the air between 7 and 9 pm. The news is on several times a night, but broadcast times vary from place to place.

PHOTOGRAPHY & VIDEO

Brazilian video and television operate on the PAL system. American (NTSC) and French (SECAM) machines and pre-recorded tapes won't play on Brazilian machines and vice versa.

Video cameras are no longer a big deal in Brazil, so you won't get any weird stares as you shoot. Some churches charge special admission for video camera operators.

Film & Equipment

Kodak and Fuji print film are sold and processed almost everywhere, but you can only get slide film developed (expensively) in big cities. If you're shooting slides, it's best to bring film with you and have it processed back home.

Photography equipment is expensive, so buy accessories before arriving. Disposable cameras are readily available at reasonable prices.

Photographing People

Some Candomblé temples do not permit photography. Respect the wishes of the locals and ask permission before taking a photo of them.

TIME

Brazil has four official time zones, generally depicted on maps as a neat series of lines, though in reality these zones are subject to the whims of bureaucracy. The standard time zone covers the eastern, northeastern, southern and southeastern parts of Brazil. This zone is three hours behind GMT/UTC. Brazil uses daylight saving time, which requires clocks to be set one hour ahead in October and one hour back in March or April.

ELECTRICITY

Electrical current is not standardized in Brazil, so it's a good idea to carry an adapter if you can't travel without your hair dryer. In Rio de Janeiro and São Paulo, the current is almost exclusively 110V or 120V, 60Hz AC. Salvador and Manaus have 127V service. Recife, Brasília and various other cities have 220V service. Check before you plug in. The most common power points have two round sockets.

WEIGHTS & MEASURES

Brazil uses the metric system. There is a metric conversion table at the back of this book.

TOILETS

Brazilians are quite nice about letting you use toilets in restaurant and bars. Public toilets can be found in most cities and towns; there's usually an entrance fee between US$0.25 and US$0.75. There are public toilets at every bus and train station and airport.

HEALTH

Your chances of contracting a serious illness in Brazil are slight. You will be exposed to environmental factors, foods and sanitation standards that are probably quite different from what you're used to, but if you take the recommended jabs, faithfully pop your anti-malarials and use common sense, there shouldn't be any problems.

While there's no worry of any strange tropical diseases in Rio and points farther south, remember that Amazonas, Pará, Mato Grosso, Amapá, Rondônia, Goiás, Espírito Santo and the northeast have some combi-

nation of: malaria, yellow fever, dengue fever, leprosy and leishmaniasis. Health officials periodically announce high rates of tuberculosis, polio, sexually transmitted diseases, hepatitis and other endemic diseases.

Bichos de pé are small parasites that live on Bahian beaches and in sandy soil. They burrow into the thick skin of the heel, toes and under toenails, appearing as dark boils. Bichos de pé must be incised and removed completely; if you do it yourself, use a sterilized needle and blade. Better still, avoid them by wearing footwear on beaches and dirt trails.

For more information on Health see the Facts for the Visitor chapter.

WOMEN TRAVELERS

In São Paulo, where there are many people of European ancestry, white women without traveling companions will scarcely be given a sideways glance. In the more traditional rural areas of the northeast, however, where a large percentage of the population is a mix of European, African and Indian, blond-haired and light-skinned women – especially those without male escorts – may arouse curiosity. It may be best to dress conservatively. What works in Rio will not necessarily be appropriate in a northeastern city or a Piauí backwater.

Flirtation (often exaggerated) is a prominent element in Brazilian male-female relations. It goes both ways and is nearly always regarded as amusingly innocent banter. If unwelcome attention is forthcoming, you should be able to stop it by merely expressing distaste or displeasure.

It's a good idea, however, to keep a low profile in cities at night and avoid going alone to bars and nightclubs. Similarly, women should not hitchhike, either alone or in groups, and men and couples should exercise discretion when hitchhiking. Most importantly, the remote, rough-and-ready areas of the north and west, where there are lots of men but few local women, should be considered off limits to lone female travelers.

GAY & LESBIAN TRAVELERS

Brazilians are pretty laid back when it comes to most sexual issues, and homosexuality is widely accepted in most larger urban areas. Bisexuality, or at the very least, bisexual sex, is condoned if not winked at.

BRAZIL

Especially in Rio, Salvador and São Paulo, the gay bars are all-welcome establishments attended by fun-loving crowds of heterosexuals, homosexuals and who-gives-a-sexuals – people are far more concerned with dancing and having a good time than determining your sexual preference.

That said, the degree to which you can be out in Brazil varies greatly by region, and in some smaller towns flamboyance is not appreciated.

USEFUL ORGANIZATIONS

The Brazilian American Cultural Center (BACC) (☎ 212-730-0515, 800-222-2746), 16 W 46th St, New York, NY 10036, USA, is a tourism organization and travel agency that offers its members discounted flights and tours. It also sells discounted air passes and other air tickets for travel within Brazil. Members receive a monthly newspaper about Brazil and the USA's Brazilian community and can send money to South America using BACC's remittance service. BACC also has offices in Rio de Janeiro (☎ 021-267-3499) and São Paulo (☎ 011- 231-3100).

DANGERS & ANNOYANCES

Robberies on buses, city beaches and in areas frequented by tourists are extremely common. Thieves tend to work in gangs, are armed with knives and guns and are capable of killing those who resist them. Much of the petty street crime in Rio, São Paulo, Salvador and Manaus is directed at tourists – Rio's thieves refer to them as *filet mignon*.

Be especially careful on the city beaches. Take enough money for lunch and drinks and nothing else. Don't hang out on the beaches at night.

When reporting a theft, be wary of the police. They have been known to plant drugs and sting gringos for bribes. For advice on security precautions, see the Dangers & Annoyances information in the Facts for the Visitor chapter.

BUSINESS HOURS

Most shops and government services are open weekdays from 9 am to 6 pm and Saturday from 9 am to 1 pm. Some shops stay open later than 6 pm in the cities, and the huge shopping malls often stay open until 10 pm and are open on Sunday as well. Banks are generally open from 10 am to 4:30 pm. Business hours vary by region and are taken less seriously in remote locations.

PUBLIC HOLIDAYS & SPECIAL EVENTS
Public Holidays
National holidays fall on the following dates:

New Year's Day
  January 1
Epiphany
  January 6
Carnaval
  February/March (four days before Ash Wednesday)
Easter
  March/April (dates vary)
Tiradentes Day
  April 21
May Day
  May 1
Corpus Christi
  June
Independence Day
  September 7
Our Lady of Aparecida Day
  October 1
All Souls' Day
  November 2
Proclamation Day
  November 15
Christmas Day
  December 25

Special Events
Major cultural events and festivals include:

New Year & Festa de Iemanjá (Rio de Janeiro), Procissão do Senhor Bom Jesus dos Navegantes (Salvador, Bahia)
  January 1
Folia de Reis (Parati, Rio de Janeiro)
  January 1-20
Bom Jesus dos Navegantes (Penedo, Alagoas)
  Second Sunday in January
Lavagem do Bonfim (Salvador, Bahia)
  Second Thursday in January
NS de Nazaré (Nazaré, Bahia)
  January 24-February 2
Grande Vaquejada do Nordeste (Natal, Rio Grande do Norte)
  February
Festa de Iemanjá (Salvador, Bahia)
  February
Lavagem da Igreja de Itapuã (Itapuã, Bahia)
  Shrove Tuesday (and the preceding three days to

two weeks, depending on the place)
February

Drama da Paixão de Cristo
(Brejo da Madre de Deus, Pernambuco)
Mid-April

Cavalhadas (Pirenópolis, Goiás)
April/May (15 days after Easter)

Festa do Divino Espírito Santo
(Parati, Rio de Janeiro)
Late May/early June

Festas Juninas and Bumba Meu Boi
celebrated throughout June in much of the
country, particularly São Luis, Belém and
throughout Pernambuco and Rio states

Festival Folclórico do Amazonas
(Manaus, Amazonas)
June

São João (Cachoeira, Bahia and Campina
Grande, Paraíba)
June 22-24

Festa do Divino (Diamantina, Minas Gerais)

Regata de Jangadas Dragão do Mar
(Fortaleza, Ceará)
July

Festa de Iemanjá (Fortaleza, Ceará)
August 15

Festa da NS de Boa Morte (Cachoeira, Bahia)
Mid-August

Cavalhada (Caeté, Minas Gerais)
September

Festa de NS Aparecida (Aparecida, São Paulo)
October 12

Círio de Nazaré (Belém, Pará)
October (starting second Sunday)

NS do Rosário (Cachoeira, Bahia)
October (second half)

NS da Ajuda (Cachoeira, Bahia)
November

Festa do Padre Cícero (Juazeiro do Norte, Ceará)
November 1 & 2

Festa de Iemanjá
(Belém, Pará & João Pessoa, Paraíba)
December 8

Celebração de Fim de Ano and Festa do Iemanjá
(Rio de Janeiro)
December 31

ACTIVITIES
Surfing

Surfing is popular all along the coast and
there are some excellent waves to be had,
especially in the south. Santa Catarina has
the best surfing beaches in the country and
Joaquina Beach, near Florianópolis, hosts the
Brazilian championships. In Rio state,
Saquarema has the best surf, but Búzios and

Itacoatiara beach in Niterói are also popular
breaks. There's also plenty of surf close to the
city of Rio; see the Rio de Janeiro section for
details. The waves are best in winter.

Hiking & Climbing

Hiking and climbing in Brazil are best during
the cooler months of the year – April to
October. During the summer, the tropical sun
heats the rock up to oven temperatures and
turns the jungles into steamy saunas. People
still climb during the summer, although
usually in the early morning or late afternoon
when the sun's rays are not so harsh.

Brazil offers lots of fantastic rock climbs,
ranging from the beginner level to routes
still unconquered. Rio de Janeiro is the
center of rock climbing in Brazil: There are
350 documented climbs within 40 minutes of
the city center.

There are lots of great places to hike in
Brazil, both in the national and state parks
and along the coastline. Several good hikes
are mentioned in the appropriate sections.
It's also a good idea to contact some of the
climbing clubs (see the Rio city section for
addresses), for details of trekking options.

ACCOMMODATIONS

Camping is becoming increasingly popular
in Brazil, and is a viable alternative for travelers on limited budgets or those who want
to explore some of the country's national
and state parks. For detailed information on
campgrounds, buy the *Guia Quatro Rodas
Camping Guide* from any newsstand. You
may also want to contact the Camping Club
of Brazil, Rua Senador Dantas 75, 25th floor,
Rio de Janeiro. The club has 52 sites in 14
states.

Most state capitals and popular tourist
areas have at least one YHA hostel and
some non-affiliated hostels. A night in a
hostel will cost around US$10 per person,
more if you're not a YHA member. International Youth Hostel cards are accepted, but
if you arrive in Brazil without one, you can
buy guest membership cards. For the
address of the Brazilian Youth Hostel Fed-
eration (FBAJ), see the Hostel Card section
earlier in this chapter. The FBAJ publishes a
useful directory of Brazilian hostels.

The cheapest places to stay are *dormi-
tórios*. These have several beds to a room,
and may cost as little as US$5 per night.

BRAZIL

Most budget travelers stay at a cheaper *pousada* (small guesthouse) or *hotel*, where a *quarto* (room without a bathroom) costs between US$8 and US$15. Rooms with a private bathroom are called *apartamentos*.

Most hotels in Brazil are regulated by Embratur, the Brazilian tourism authority, which rates the quality of hotels from one to five stars. Regulated hotels must have a price list with an Embratur label, and a copy is usually posted on the wall in each room. Even so, it pays to bargain.

If you're traveling in the Amazon or the northeast, where there are no hotels, a hammock and a mosquito net are essential. With these basics and help from friendly locals, you can get a good night's rest almost anywhere. Most fishing villages along the coast have seen an outsider or two and will put you up for the night. If they've seen a few more outsiders, they'll probably charge you a couple of dollars.

FOOD

The staples of the Brazilian diet are *arroz* (white rice), *feijão* (black beans) and *farofel* (manioc flour), also called *farinha*. These are usually combined with *carne* (beef), *frango* (chicken) or *peixe* (fish) to make up the *prato feito* (set meal) or *prato do dia* (plate of the day). These set meals are typically enormous and cheap, but can become monotonous. Lunch is the big meal of the day, and *lanchonetes* (snack bars) throughout the country will have a prato do dia on offer. In the cities, there is more variety. Many restaurants and lanchonetes also offer pay-by-weight *(comida por kilo)* buffets.

A *churrascaria* is a restaurant serving barbecued meat, and many offer *rodízio* (a meat smorgasbord). They are especially good in the south.

Brazilian Dishes

The following are some common dishes:

Acarajé – This is what the baianas, Bahian women in flowing white dresses, traditionally sell on street corners throughout Bahia. Acarajé is made from peeled brown beans mashed with salt and onions, then fried in *dendê* (palm) oil. These delicious fried balls often contain *vatapá*, dried shrimp, pepper and tomato sauce. Dendê oil is strong stuff; many stomachs can't handle it.

Carne de sol – This tasty salted beef is grilled and served with beans, rice and vegetables.

Caruru – One of the most popular Brazilian dishes brought from Africa, Caruru is made with okra or other vegetables cooked in water. The water is then drained, and onions, salt, shrimp and malagueta peppers are added, mixed and grated together with okra paste and dendê oil. Traditionally, a sea fish such as garoupa is then added.

Cozido – The term refers to any kind of stew, usually with more vegetables (eg, potatoes, sweet potatoes, carrots and manioc) than other stew-like Brazilian dishes.

Feijoada – The national dish of Brazil, feijoada is a meat stew served with rice and a bowl of beans. It's served throughout the country, and there are many variations.

Moqueca – This is both a kind of sauce or stew and a style of cooking from Bahia. There are many kinds of moqueca: fish, shrimp, oyster, crab or any combination thereof. The moqueca sauce is defined by its heavy use of dendê oil and coconut milk, often with peppers and onions. A moqueca must be cooked in a covered clay pot.

Pato no tucupi – Roast duck, flavored with garlic and cooked in the *tucupi* sauce made from the juice of the manioc plant and *jambu*, a local vegetable, is a very popular dish in Pará.

Peixe a delícia – This dish of broiled or grilled fish is usually made with bananas and coconut milk. It's delicious in Fortaleza.

Pirarucu ao forno – Pirarucu is the most famous fish from the rivers of Amazônia. It's oven-cooked with lemon and other seasonings.

Tutu á mineira – This bean paste with toasted bacon and manioc flour, often served with cooked cabbage, is typical of Minas Gerais.

Vatapá – A seafood dish with a thick sauce made from manioc paste, coconut and dendê oil, vatapá is perhaps the most famous Brazilian dish of African origin.

FRUIT

From the savory nirvana of *graviola* to the confusingly clinical taste of *cupuaçú*, fruits and juices are a major Brazilian highlight. Many of the fruits of the northeast and Amazon have no English-name equivalent; you'll just have to try their exotic tastes.

DRINKS

Fruit juices, called *sucos*, are divine in Brazil. If you don't want sugar and ice, ask for them *sem açúcar e gelo* or *natural*. To avoid getting water mixed with them, ask for a *suco com leite*, also called a *vitamina*, which is juice mixed with milk. Orange juice is rarely diluted. The Brazilian soft drink *guaraná* is made from the berry of an Amazonian plant and has a delicious, distinctive taste.

A *cerveja* is a 600ml bottled beer. A *cervejinha* is a 300ml bottled or canned beer. *Chopp* (pronounced 'shoppee') is a pale blond pilsner draft, lighter than and far superior to canned or bottled beer.

Cachaça, pinga or *aguardente* is a high-proof, dirt-cheap sugarcane alcohol, produced and consumed throughout the country. Cachaça literally means 'booze.' Pinga (literally, 'drop') is considered more polite, but by any name, it's cheap and toxic. An inexpensive cachaça can cut a hole in the strongest stomach lining. Velho Barreiro, Ypioca, Pitú, Carangueijo and São Francisco are some of the better labels.

Caipirinha is the Brazilian national drink. The ingredients are simple (cachaça, lime, sugar and crushed ice), but a well-made caipirinha is a work of art. *Caipirosca* is a caipirinha made with vodka instead of cachaça. *Caipirissima* is still another variation, using Bacardi rum instead of cachaça. *Batidas* are wonderful mixes of cachaça, sugar and fruit juice.

ENTERTAINMENT
Music
Brazilians must be among the most musical people on the planet. Everywhere you travel, you'll see and hear marvelous music. From the *samba* of Rio to the *sertanejo* love songs; from the pounding *baterias* of Salvador to the *repentistas* of the northeast, Brazil is a music lover's paradise.

SPECTATOR SPORTS
Brazilians are passionate about soccer. The men's team has won the World Cup a record four times, and the remarkable women's team is also a consistent top contender in international competition. Soccer is played everywhere, and the average four-year-old Brazilian can probably run rings around you. Professional games are played on the weekend and midweek all year round. Don't miss this vibrant spectacle of fancy footwork.

SHOPPING
Shopping malls are a hit with Brazil's upper- and middle-classes, who love to spend time and money in complete security away from the masses. Everything is more expensive, but who cares? Saying you bought it at the *shopping* confers instant status on both you and your purchase. For homesick gringos,

malls usually have cinemas and fast-food outlets. But watch out – it's easy to get lost in these monsters.

Getting There & Away

For information on getting to South America, see the introductory Getting There & Away chapter.

AIR
For international flights, the departure tax is a whopping US$40.

The most popular international gateway is Aeroporto Galeão in Rio de Janeiro. From there, connecting flights to airports throughout the country leave regularly. Be warned that construction after a 1998 fire in Rio's domestic terminal, Aeroporto Santos Dumont, may continue to cause inconvenience. See the Rio de Janeiro City section for more information. São Paulo's Aeroporto São Paulo-Guarulhos is probably the second most popular gateway.

Varig, Brazil's international airline, flies to many of the world's major cities. Basic carriers serving Brazil from the USA include Varig, Continental Airlines, Delta Airlines, American Airlines, United Airlines and Japan Airlines (JAL); from the UK, British Airways and Varig; and from Australia, Qantas and Aerolíneas Argentinas.

Several flights per day go between Buenos Aires (Argentina) and Rio de Janeiro, and there are several good air connections between Argentina and other large Brazilian cities.

There are five Varig flights per week between La Paz (Bolivia) and Rio, all of which stop over in São Paulo. TAM operates flights each way between Cáceres and San Matías and Santa Cruz (via Roboré) in Bolivia on Saturday. Varig also has two flights a week between Bogotá (Colombia) and Rio, daily flights from Asunción (Paraguay) to Rio, two flights per week between Caracas (Venezuela) and Rio and several weekly flights between Lima (Peru) and Rio. Cruzeiro do Sul flies twice a week from Iquitos (Peru) to Manaus. Other airlines fly fairly frequently from Rio to Montevideo (Uruguay).

BRAZIL

Suriname Airways (SLM) and TABA fly to and from Belém (Brazil), Cayenne (French Guiana) and Paramaribo (Suriname). There are also flights from Macapá. There are no direct flights to Guyana from any Brazilian city.

LAND
Argentina
Most travelers pass through Foz do Iguaçu (see the Foz do Iguaçu entry in the Paraná section for more information).

Bolivia
Points of entry to Brazil from Bolivia include the following:

Corumbá Opposite the Bolivian border town of Quijarro, Corumbá is the busiest port of entry along the Bolivia-Brazil border. It has bus connections from São Paulo, Rio de Janeiro, Cuiabá and southern Brazil. During the dry season there's a daily train between Quijarro and Santa Cruz, but during the wet season there may be waits of several days. For further information, see Corumbá in the Central West section.

Cáceres From Cáceres, west of Cuiabá, you can cross to San Matías in Bolivia. Daily buses do the 4½-hour trip for US$10. During the dry season, there's also a daily bus between the border town of San Matías and San Ignacio de Velasco (see the Jesuit Missions section in both this and the Bolivia chapters), where you'll find flights and bus connections to Santa Cruz.

San Ignacio Coming from Bolivia, there are daily *micros* (again, only during the dry season) from San Ignacio de Velasco to the border at San Matías, where you'll find onward transportation to Cáceres and Cuiabá.

Guajará-Mirim Another possible crossing is between Guajará-Mirim in Brazil and Guayaramerín, Bolivia, via motorboat ferry across the Rio Mamoré. Guayaramerín is connected with Riberalta by a road that should be extended to Cobija and Brasiléia in the near future. Another route runs south to Rurrenabaque and La Paz, with a spur to Trinidad. For further information see Guajará-Mirim and Guayaramerín in the Rondônia section of this chapter.

Brasiléia In Acre state, there's a border crossing between Brasiléia and Cobija, Bolivia. For more details, see Brasiléia in the Acre section of this chapter.

Colombia
The Colombian border crossing is at Leticia-Tabatinga. For further information on the Triple Frontier region, refer to Benjamin Constant and Tabatinga in the Amazonas section of this chapter.

French Guiana
You can cross the Oiapoque River between Oiapoque (Brazil) and St Georges de l'Oiapoque (French Guiana), where there are heavily booked flights to Cayenne, but no road connections as yet. For further information, see Oiapoque in the Amapá section of this chapter.

Guyana
Cross the border from Bonfim (reached via Boa Vista), in Roraima state, to Lethem, which is connected to Georgetown by a very rough road or an often full flight. See the Roraima section for more details.

Paraguay
Foz do Iguaçu to Ciudad del Este and Ponta Porã to Pedro Juan Caballero are the two major border crossings. See Foz do Iguaçu in the Paraná section and Ponta Porã in the Mato Grosso section for details.

Peru
There is a border crossing to Iñapari (Peru) at Assis Brasil. For more details, see Brasiléia and Assis Brasil in the Acre section.

Uruguay
Coming from Uruguay, travelers usually pass through the border towns of Chuy, Uruguay, and Chuí, Brazil; the international border is the main street. There are four other border crossings: at Aceguá; from Rivera to Santana do Livramento; from Artigas to Quaraí; and at Barra do Quaraí, near the Argentine border.

If you're driving from Brazil, you'll need to stop at the Brazilian checkpoint to get an exit stamp, then at the Uruguayan checkpoint so the Uruguayans can make sure that you have a Brazilian exit stamp and a Uruguayan visa (if you need one). Buses will stop at all checkpoints.

Venezuela
From Boa Vista (Roraima state), you can cross into Venezuela through the border town of Santa Elena.

RIVER
Peru
The main route between Brazil and Peru is along the Amazon between Iquitos and Islandia, the Peruvian island village at the

confluence of the Rio Yauari and the Amazon, opposite Benjamin Constant. Some boats leave from Ramón Castilla, a few kilometers farther upstream in Peru. For further information, see the Amazonas section later this chapter.

ORGANIZED TOURS

Most tour operators include Brazil as part of a South American tour; see the introductory Getting There & Away chapter for details.

Getting Around

AIR

Flying within Brazil is becoming cheaper, thanks to a recent deregulation. This is great for travelers, but you now need to shop around for promotional specials. Many flights are cheaper at night, for example.

Brazil has four major national carriers and several smaller regional airlines. The biggies and their toll-free numbers are:

VASP	☎ 0800-998-277
Varig	☎ 0800-997-000
TAM	☎ 0800-123-100
Transbrasil	☎ 9021-297-4422

Every major city is served by at least one of these airlines. It's usually not difficult to get on a flight, except between December and Carnaval (late February) and in July. There are also many air-taxi companies that mostly fly in the Amazon region.

Aeronautica, the military air-transport service, has been known to give away free flights when there is extra space, but you might have to wait for a while. First the officers get a seat, then the soldiers, then the civilians. Go to the desk marked 'CAN' in the airport and ask about the next military flight, then show up again two days before scheduled departure time and sign up. It helps to have a letter of introduction from a consulate.

Air Passes

The Brazil Airpass can be a good deal. It now costs between US$490 and US$540, depending on the carrier. This buys you five flight coupons for flights anywhere in the country. It's possible to pay US$100 each for four additional flight coupons, totaling from

US$890 to US$940 for nine flights. All travel must be completed within 21 days.

Airpasses are also available for areas of limited travel; the Airpass II, covering the central and south of the country, costs from US$350 to US$400 depending on the carrier; the Airpass III, covering the northeast, costs from US$290 to US$340.

Before buying an airpass, sit down and work out whether it is really a good investment for your purposes. There are often delays flying in Brazil and it's rare that you don't waste a day in transit. Unless you're intent on a whistle-stop tour of the country, there are only so many flights that you will want to take in two or three weeks.

The pass *must* be purchased outside Brazil, where you'll get an MCO (miscellaneous charges order) in your name with 'Brazil Airpass' stamped on it, which you exchange for an airpass from one of the Brazilian airlines. All three airlines offer the same deal, and all three fly to most major cities, although Varig/Cruzeiro flies to more cities than the other two. If you are buying an airpass and have specific plans to go to a smaller city, you may want to check with a travel agent to see which airline goes there.

Airpass holders who get bumped from a flight for any reason should reconfirm *all* their other flight reservations.

Domestic Departure Tax

Passengers on domestic flights pay an airport tax. This tax varies, depending on the classification of the airport, but it is usually about US$8.

BUS

Except in the Amazon Basin, buses are the primary form of long-distance transportation for the vast majority of Brazilians. Bus services are generally excellent: Departure times are usually strictly adhered to, and the buses are clean, comfortable and well-serviced. Bus travel is very cheap, with fares that work out to approximately US$3 per hour.

All major cities are linked by frequent buses, and there is a surprising number of scheduled long-distance buses. It's rare that you will have to change buses between two major cities, no matter what the distance. For tips on security and bus travel, see the Dangers & Annoyances information in the introductory Facts for the Visitor chapter.

BRAZIL

There are two types, or classes, of long-distance buses. The *comum* (common) is comfortable and usually has air-con and a toilet. The *leito* or *executivo* is Brazil's version of the couchette or sleeper. Leitos, which often depart late at night, usually take as long to reach their destination as a comum and cost twice as much, but they are exceptionally comfortable. If you don't mind missing the scenery, a leito bus can get you there in comfort and save you the cost of a hotel room. Long-distance buses generally make pit stops every three or four hours.

In every big city, and most small ones, there is a central bus terminal (*rodoviária*), usually on the outskirts of the city. Some are modern and comfortable, and all have restaurants, newsstands and toilets. Some even have post offices and long-distance telephone facilities. Most importantly, all the long-distance bus companies operate out of the same place, making it easy to find your bus. A combined train and bus station is a *ferrorodoviária*.

In general, it's advisable to buy a ticket at least a few hours in advance or the day before departure. On weekends, holidays and from December to February, this is always a good idea.

You don't always have to go to the rodoviária to buy your bus ticket. Selected travel agents in major cities sell long-distance bus tickets. Agents do this at no extra charge and can save you a long trip out to an often chaotic rodoviária.

TRAIN

There are very few railway passenger services in Brazil, and the trend to cut more and more services continues.

Enthusiasts should not despair, however, as there are still some interesting train rides. The Curitiba-Paranaguá train offers some unforgettable views, and the 13km run from São João del Rei to Tiradentes, in Minas Gerais, is great fun.

TAXI

Taxis are reasonably priced, if not cheap, but you should be aware of various tricks used by some drivers to increase the charges.

As a general rule, Tarifa I (standard tariff) applies from approximately 6 am to 10 pm Monday to Saturday; Tarifa II (higher tariff) applies outside these hours, on holidays and

beyond city limits. Sometimes there is a standard charge, typically for the trip between the airport and the city center. Many airports and rodoviárias now have a system that allows you to purchase a taxi ticket from a *bilheteria* (taxi ticket office). In many cases, this ticketed fare is much more than you'd pay if you just hailed a taxi at the regular metered rate. If you need an early-morning taxi to the airport, consider asking drivers the day before about the going rate and arranging to be picked up.

The same general advice applies to taxis without meters. You *must* agree on the price beforehand and make sure there is no doubt about it. Learn the numbers in Portuguese.

If the driver claims to have no change, hold firm and see if this is just a ploy to extract more from you. Avoid this scenario by carrying change.

If possible, orient yourself before taking a taxi, and keep a map handy in case you find yourself being taken for a blatant detour. Never use a taxi tout, which is almost certainly a rip-off. The worst place to get a cab is wherever the tourists are, so don't hire one near one of the expensive hotels. In Rio, walk a block away from the beach at Copacabana to flag down a cab. Many airports have special airport taxis, which are about 50% more expensive than a regular taxi. If you are carrying valuables, however, the special airport taxi or a radio-taxi can be a worthwhile investment. These are probably the safest taxis on the road.

For more tips on security see the Dangers & Annoyances information in the introductory Facts for the Visitor chapter.

CAR & MOTORCYCLE

Roads in Brazil are not policed. This and the national cult of speed, as well as the poor quality of the roads in many areas, makes for hazardous driving.

Car Rental

Renting a car is expensive, with prices similar to those in Europe. Familiar multinationals dominate the car rental business. Hiring a car is safe and easy if you have a driver's license, a credit card and a passport.

Shop around, as companies often have promotional deals. In times of high inflation, some companies are slower to put up their prices than others.

Volkswagen Golfs and Fiat Unos are the cheapest cars to rent. If the rental companies claim to be out of these, shop around. Also, when you get a price quoted on the phone, make sure it includes insurance, which is legally required.

The big companies have offices at the airport in most cities and often in the city center as well.

Motorcycle Rental & Purchase

Hiring a motorcycle is almost as expensive as hiring a car. If you want to buy a motorcycle, Brazil manufactures its own, but they are also expensive.

Motorcycles are popular in Brazil, especially in and around the cities. Theft is a big problem, and as a result you can't even insure them. Most people keep their motorcycles in guarded places, at least overnight. For the traveler, this can be difficult to organize, but if you can maneuver around the practical problems, Brazil is a great place to have a motorcycle.

HITCHHIKING

Hitchhiking in Brazil, with the possible exception of the Amazon and Pantanal areas, is difficult. The word for hitchhiking in Portuguese is *carona*, so '*Pode dar carona?*' is 'Can you give me a lift?' The best way to hitchhike is to wait at a gas station or truck stop and talk to the drivers, but even this can be difficult. A few years back, there were several assaults on drivers by hitchhikers, and the government started making public announcements to discourage people from giving rides.

BOAT

Many travelers take a boat trip on the Amazon or one of Brazil's other rivers. The government-operated Empresa de Navegação da Amazônia (ENASA) has reduced its passenger-boat services, but private companies have improved their standards and surpassed ENASA in passenger transportation. For more suggestions about river travel, see the Getting Around chapter.

LOCAL TRANSPORT

Local bus services tend to be pretty good, with a comprehensive network of routes. Municipal buses are usually frequent, always cheap and very crowded. You enter most city buses at the back and exit from the front. Crime can be a problem on buses; for tips about security and travel on local buses, see the Dangers & Annoyances section in the Facts for the Visitor chapter.

ORGANIZED TOURS

Brasil Ecotravel Center (☎ 021-512-8882), Rua Garcia D'Avila 72, 3rd floor, Rio de Janeiro, is one of the largest ecological tour operators in Brazil. It specializes in the Amazon and Pantanal but runs many other programs for the special-interest traveler. It is highly recommended.

Focus Tours (☎ 031-332-4627; speak to Regina Caldeira in English or Portuguese), in Belo Horizonte, Minas Gerais, runs a variety of tours with strong emphases on the environment and ecology.

Rio de Janeiro State

The west coast, or Costa Verde, of Rio de Janeiro State is lined with hundreds of islands that shelter the coast and make for easy swimming and boating.

Due north of Rio city in the Serra dos Órgãos are the mountain resort cities of Petrópolis and Teresópolis. There is superb hiking and climbing in the Parque Nacional da Serra dos Órgãos.

The clean and quiet stretches of sand east of Rio city are a welcome change from the famous beaches of Rio and Guanabara Bay, with their high-rise hotels and bars spilling out onto the sands.

RIO DE JANEIRO

The city of Rio de Janeiro is known as *a cidade maravilhosa* (the marvelous city). Jammed between ocean and escarpment are nine million *cariocas*, as the inhabitants are called, making Rio one of the most densely populated places on earth. Despite the city's enormous problems, the cariocas pursue pleasure like no other people. Carnaval is the best known expression of their Dionysian spirit, but there are many others.

History

A Portuguese navigator, Gaspar de Lemos, discovered Guanabara Bay in 1502. He

BRAZIL

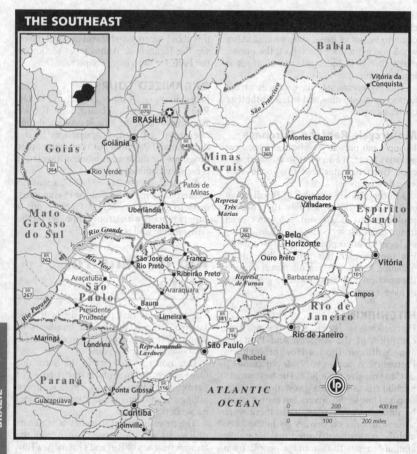

THE SOUTHEAST

mistook the bay for a river and named it Rio de Janeiro. The French established the first settlement in the bay under Nicolas de Villegagnon in 1555. Antarctic France, as it was called, was not a success, and despite the French alliance with the formidable Tamoio Indians, it fell to the Portuguese five years later, in 1560.

During the 17th century, Rio became an important sugar town and port. The city flourished with the Minas Gerais gold rush at the beginning of the 18th century, and in 1763 it replaced Salvador as the colonial capital. Rio was the capital of independent Brazil until Brasília took over in 1960, and it remains the tourist capital of Brazil.

Orientation

Rio is divided into a *zona norte* (north zone) and a *zona sul* (south zone) by the Serra da Carioca, a steep mountain range in the Parque Nacional da Tijuca. Favelas cover steep hillsides on both sides of town.

Centro (the city center) is all business during the day and deserted at night. The main airline offices are here, as are foreign consulates, Brazilian government agencies, money-exchange houses, banks and travel agencies. Centro is also the site of Rio's original settlement, and most of the city's important museums and colonial buildings are here.

Two wide avenues cross the center: Av Rio Branco, where buses leave for the zona

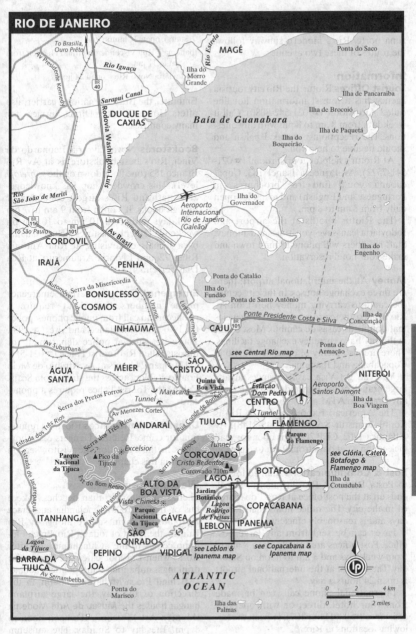

sul, and Av Presidente Vargas, which heads out to Maracaná football stadium and the zona norte. Rio's modern subway follows the routes of these two avenues.

Information

Tourist Offices Riotur, the Rio city tourism agency, has a tourist information hot line called Âlo Riotur (☎ 021-542-8080). Call it weekdays from 8 am to 8 pm with any questions. The receptionists speak English and should be able to help you.

At Riotur's helpful 'tourist room' (☎ 021-541-7522), Av Princesa Isabel 183, Copacabana, you'll find free brochures (in Portuguese and English) and maps. It's open daily from 8 am to 8 pm.

The Riotur booths at the airport and rodoviária can save you time and money: Staff members will phone around town and make your hotel reservation.

Money At the international airport, there are three exchange houses. In the city center (be cautious carrying money here), on Av Rio Branco, there are several travel agencies that double as casas de câmbio. Most banks in the city have currency exchange facilities. There are also plenty of casas de câmbio in Copacabana and Ipanema.

You can get Visa cash advances at any large branch of the Banco do Brasil or from any Bradesco ATM.

The American Express agent in Rio is Kontik-Franstur SA (☎ 021-548-2148), Av Atlântica 1702, CEP 20040, is open for mail pick-up on weekdays from 9 am to 6 pm.

Post & Communications Mail addressed to Posta Restante, Rio de Janeiro, Brazil, ends up at the post office at Rua 1 de Março 64 in the city. The office holds mail for 30 days and is reasonably efficient.

Faxes can be sent from any large post office. Post offices are usually open 8 am to 6 pm weekdays and 8 am to noon on Saturday. The branch at the international airport is open 24 hours a day.

International phone calls can be made from your hotel, direct or with operator assistance (☎ 000111 or 107), or from the following locations in Rio:

Aeroporto Internacional (Galeão) – open 24 hours
Aeroporto Santos Dumont – open 6 am to 11 pm
Centro – Praça Tiradentes 41, open 24 hours
Copacabana – Av NS de Copacabana 540 (upstairs), open 24 hours
Ipanema – Rua Visconde de Pirajá111, open from 6 am to 11 pm
Rodoviária Novo Rio – open 24 hours

Embratel, the Brazilian national carrier, also offers Home Country Direct Services for many countries.

Bookstores Nova Livraria Leonardo da Vinci, Rio's best bookstore, is at Av Rio Branco 185 (one floor down on the *sobreloja* level). This crowded shop has knowledgeable staff and Rio's largest collection of foreign books. It's open from 9 am to 7 pm weekdays and from 10 am to 10 pm on weekends. Other bookstores include Guanabara Jornais e Revistas, at Rua Antonia Ribas 72, and Livraria Argumento, at Rua Dias Ferreira 417.

Emergency There are certain emergency phone numbers that don't require a phonecard to call from public phones: police (☎ 190) and ambulance and fire (☎ 193). There is a special police department for tourists called Rio Tourist Police (☎ 021-511-5112), open 24 hours at Av Afrânio de Melo Franco, Leblon, across the street from Scala. Calling the Tourist Police requires a phonecard.

Dangers & Annoyances Rio has a reputation for crime. Refer to Dangers & Annoyances in the Facts for the Visitor section earlier in this chapter.

Walking Tour

There's more to Rio than beaches. Take a bus or the metro to Cinelândia and **Praça Floriano**, the main square along Av Rio Branco, the heart of today's Rio. Praça Floriano comes to life at lunchtime and after work, when outdoor cafés are filled with drinking, samba music and political debate.

Behind Praça Mahatma Gandhi, in the direction of the bay, the large airplane hangar houses the **Museu de Arte Moderna** (Modern Art Museum). It's open noon to 8 pm, Tuesday to Sunday. The museum grounds were designed by Brazil's most famous landscape architect, Burle Marx (who landscaped Brasília).

BRAZIL

The most impressive building on Praça Floriano is the **Teatro Municipal**, home of Rio's opera, orchestra and gargoyles. The theater was built in 1905, then renovated in 1934 under the influence of the Paris opera. Visit the ostentatious Assyrian Room Restaurant & Bar downstairs (entrance on Av Rio Branco). Built in the 1930s, it's completely covered in beautiful mosaic tiles.

On Av Rio Branco, the **Museu Nacional de Belas Artes** houses some of Brazil's best paintings. The most important gallery is the Galeria de Arte Brasileira, with 20th-century classics such as Cândido Portinari's *Café*. The museum is open 10 am to 6 pm, Tuesday to Sunday.

Head back to the other side of the Teatro Municipal and walk down the pedestrian-only Av 13 de Maio (on your left are some of Rio's best juice bars). Cross Av Almirante Barroso and you're in the Largo da Carioca. Up on the hill is the **Convento de Santo Antônio**. The church's sacristy, which dates from 1745, has some beautiful jacaranda-wood carving and *azulejos* (Portuguese ceramic tiles with a distinctive blue glaze). The original church here was begun in 1608, making it Rio's oldest.

If you have time for a side trip, head over to the nearby *bondinho* (little tram) that goes up to **Santa Teresa**, a beautiful neighborhood of cobblestone streets and old homes. The tram goes from the corner of Av República do Chile and Senador Dantas over the old aqueduct to Santa Teresa. The **Museu Chácara do Céu**, Rua Murtinho Nobre 93, has a good collection of art and antiques. This is a high-crime area; don't take valuables.

Returning to the city center, check out the shops along 19th-century **Rua da Carioca**. The old wine and cheese shop has some of Brazil's best cheese and bargains on Portuguese and Spanish wines. Other shops here sell fine instruments made in Brazil, including all the Carnaval rhythm-makers. Try Casa Oliveira, at Rua da Carioca 70. There are several good jewelry shops off Rua da Carioca, on Rua Ramalho Ortigão.

When you get to Rua da Carioca 39, stop at the **Bar Luis** for a draft beer and lunch or snack. Rio's oldest restaurant (opened in 1887), Bar Luis was called Bar Adolf until WWII. For decades, this is where Rio's intellectuals chewed the fat while drinking the best chopp in Centro.

At the end of the block, you'll pass the **Cinema Iris**, once Rio's most elegant theater, and then you'll emerge into the hustle of Praça Tiradentes. It's easy to see that this used to be a fabulous part of the city. On opposite sides of the square are the **Teatro João Caetano** and the **Teatro Carlos Gomez**, both of which present plays and dance performances. The narrow streets in this part of town are lined with old, mostly dilapidated small buildings. It's worth exploring along Rua Buenos Aires as far as **Campo de Santana**, then returning along Rua da Alfândega to Av Rio Branco. Campo de Santana is a pleasant park, where – a scene re-enacted in every Brazilian classroom – Emperor Dom Pedro I proclaimed Brazil's independence from Portugal.

Back near Av Rio Branco, at Rua Gonalves Dias 30, hit the ornate **Confeitaria Colombo** for coffee and 19th-century opulence. Offering relief to shopping-weary patrons since 1894, the Colombo is best for its desserts and very strong coffee.

From here, cross Av Rio Branco, go down Rua da Assembléia to **Praça Quinze de Novembro**. In the square is the **Pyramid Fountain**, built in 1789, and a crafts market. As you face the bay, on your right is the **Paço Imperial**, which was once the imperial palace and is now a popular cultural center.

On the opposite side of the square is the historic **Arco de Teles**, running between two buildings. The shops that line the stone streets have a waterfront character. There are several restaurants, bars (crowded during 'happy hour'), fishing supply shops and a couple of simple colonial churches. It's a colorful area.

Back at Praça Quinze de Novembro, stroll over to the **waterfront**, where ferries and hydrofoils depart to **Niterói** and **Ilha da Paquetá**. The ferry to Niterói takes only 15 minutes, so you never have to wait long. Consider crossing the bay and walking around central Niterói if you have some time (the feel is different from Rio – it's much more like the rest of Brazil). Even if you return immediately, the trip is worth it just for the view.

When you're facing the bay, **Restaurant Alba Mar** is a few hundred meters to your right in the green gazebo. The food is good and the atmosphere just right. On Saturday, the building is surrounded by the tents of

CENTRAL RIO

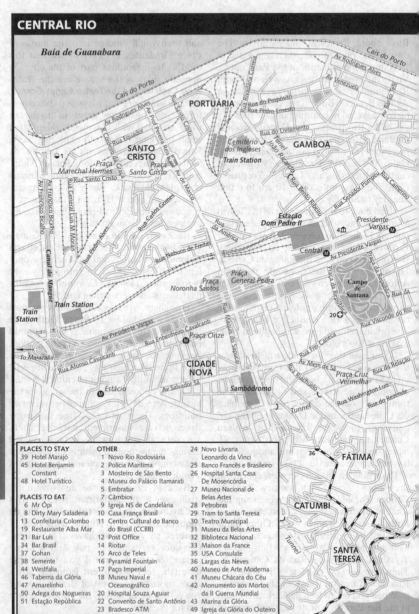

Baía de Guanabara

Cais do Porto

PORTUÁRIA

Cemitério dos Ingleses

SANTO CRISTO

GAMBOA

Estação Dom Pedro II

Presidente Vargas

Central

Av Presidente Vargas

Praça General Pedra

Campo de Santana

Praça Noronha Santos

Train Station

Train Station

CIDADE NOVA

Estácio

Sambódromo

FÁTIMA

CATUMBI

Largas das Neves

SANTA TÉRESA

PLACES TO STAY
39 Hotel Marajó
45 Hotel Benjamin Constant
48 Hotel Turístico

PLACES TO EAT
6 Mr Ópi
8 Dirty Mary Saladeria
13 Confeitaria Colombo
19 Restaurante Alba Mar
21 Bar Luís
34 Bar Brasil
37 Gohan
38 Semente
44 Westfalia
47 Amarelinho
50 Adega dos Nogueiras
51 Estação República

OTHER
1 Novo Rio Rodoviária
2 Policia Marítima
3 Mosteiro de São Bento
4 Museu do Palácio Itamaratí
5 Embratur
7 Câmbios
9 Igreja NS de Candelária
10 Casa França Brasil
11 Centro Cultural do Banco do Brasil (CCBB)
12 Post Office
14 Riotur
15 Arco de Teles
16 Pyramid Fountain
17 Paço Imperial
18 Museu Naval e Oceanográfico
20 Hospital Souza Aguiar
22 Convento de Santo Antônio
23 Bradesco ATM

24 Novo Livraria Leonardo da Vinci
25 Banco Francês e Brasileiro
26 Hospital Santa Casa De Misericórdia
27 Museu Nacional de Belas Artes
28 Petrobras
29 Tram to Santa Teresa
30 Teatro Municipal
31 Museu da Belas Artes
32 Biblioteca Nacional
33 Maison de France
36 USA Consulate
40 Museu de Arte Moderna
41 Museu Chácara do Céu
42 Monumento aos Mortos da II Guerra Mundial
43 Marina da Glória
49 Igreja da Glória do Outeiro

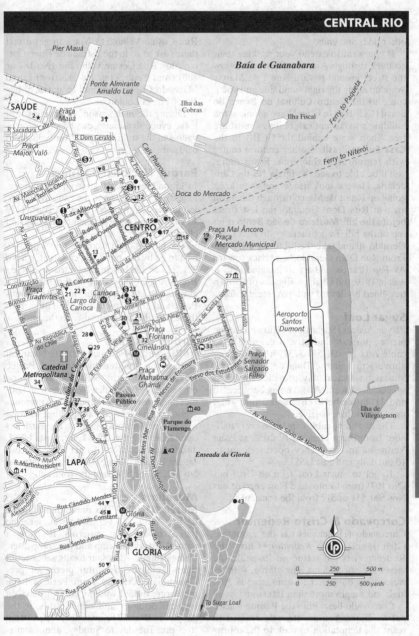

CENTRAL RIO

Baía de Guanabara

Pier Mauá

Ponte Almirante Arnaldo Luz

Ilha das Cobras

Ilha Fiscal

Ferry to Paquetá

Ferry to Niterói

SAÚDE

Praça Mauá

R Sacadura Cabral

R Dom Geraldo

Praça Major Valô

Cais Pharoux

Doca do Mercado

Av Presidente Kubitschek

Av Rio Branco

Av Marechal Floriano

Rua Teófilo Otoni

Uruguaiana

R da Alfândega

R do Rosário

R do Ouvidor

CENTRO

Rua 7 de Setembro

Rua da Assembléia

Praça Mal Âncoro

Praça Mercado Municipal

R Buenos Aires

Av Presidente Antônio Carlos

Av Central Justo

Av Santa Lúcia

Av Marechal Câmara

Aeroporto Santos Dumont

Constituição

Praça Tiradentes

R da Carioca

Carioca

Largo da Carioca

Av Almirante Barroso

Av Rio Branco

Av Almirante Barroso

Araujo Porto Alegre

Praça Floriano

Cinelândia

Av Pres Vargas

Av República do Chile

Catedral Metropolitana

R Evaristo da Veiga

Praça Mahatma Ghandi

Passeio Público

Trevo dos Estudantes

Praça Senador Salgado Filho

Rua Riachuelo

Aqueducto da Carioca

Rua da Lapa

R do Passeio

Parque do Flamengo

Ilha de Villegaignon

LAPA

R Joaquim Murtinho

R Murtinho Nobre

Rua Cândido Mendes

Av Beira Mar

Av Dom Henrique

Enseada da Gloria

R Almirante Alexandrino

Rua Benjamin Constant

Glória

GLÓRIA

Rua Santo Amaro

Rua Pedro Américo

Av Almirante Silvio de Noronha

Rua do Russel

To Sugar Loaf

0   250   500 m
0   250   500 yards

BRAZIL

the **Feira de Antiguidades**, a strange and fun hodgepodge of antiques, clothes, food and other odds and ends.

If you want to extend your walking tour, go back through Arco de Teles and follow the street around toward Rua 1 de Março. Walk up along the right-hand side and you'll come to the **Centro Cultural do Banco do Brasil** (CCBB). Go in and have a look at the building and current exhibitions – most are free. Then, walk behind the CCBB to the **Casa França-Brasil**, another cultural center with temporary exhibitions. From there, you'll be able to see the **Igreja NS de Candelária**. Have a look inside and then keep going up Rua 1 de Março through the naval area to Rua Dom Geraldo, the last street before the hill. **Mosteiro de São Bento** is on top of the hill. To get there, go to Rua Dom Geraldo 40 and take the lift to the 5th floor. From Rua Dom Geraldo, head back toward Av Rio Branco, and try to imagine it as it was in 1910, the Champs-Élysées of Rio – a tree-lined boulevard with pavement cafés.

Sugar Loaf

Pão de Açúcar (Sugar Loaf), Rio's gift to the picture-postcard industry, is dazzling. Two cable cars (☎ 021-541-3737) lift you 396m above Rio and the Baía de Guanabara. Sunset on a clear day provides the most spectacular ascent. Avoid going between 10 and 11 am or between 2 and 3 pm, when most tourist buses arrive.

The two-stage cable cars leave every half-hour from Praça General Tibúrcio, at Praia Vermelha in Urca. They operate 8 am to 10 pm daily and cost US$15.

To get to Sugar Loaf, take an Urca bus (No 107) from Centro and Flamengo or bus Nos 500, 511 or 512 from the zona sul.

Corcovado & Cristo Redentor

Corcovado (Hunchback) is the mountain (709m), and *Cristo Redentor* (Christ the Redeemer) is the statue on its peak; the views are spectacular. The statue, with its welcoming outstretched arms, stands 30m high and weighs more than 1000 tons.

Corcovado lies within the Parque Nacional da Tijuca. You are strongly advised to resist the temptation to walk to the top, as there's a good chance you will be robbed. You can get there by car or by taxi, but the best way is to go up in the cog train; for the best view going up, sit on the right-hand side. The roundtrip costs US$15 and leaves from Rua Cosme Velho 513. You can get a taxi there (ask to go to the Estrada de Ferro Corcovado); Rua Cosme Velho bus (No 184 or 180) from Centro; bus No 583 from Largo Machado, Copacabana and Ipanema; or bus No 584 from Leblon.

During the high season, the trains, which leave every 30 minutes, can be slow. Corcovado and the train are open from 8:30 am to 6:30 pm.

Parque Nacional da Tijuca

In 15 minutes you can go from the concrete jungle of Copacabana to the exuberant tropical jungle of Parque Nacional da Tijuca (120 sq km), a good place for picnics, walking and climbing.

The park is open from 7 am to 7 pm. It's best to go by car, but if you can't, catch a No 221, 233 or 234 bus from Centro to Alto da Boa Vista, in the heart of the forest. An alternative is to take the metro to Saens Peña and then any Barra da Tijuca bus; these pass the main entrance to the park.

Jardim Botânico

At Rua Jardim Botânico 920, the botanical garden was planted by order of Prince Regent Dom João in 1808. Quiet and serene on weekdays, the garden blossoms with families and music on weekends. The Amazonas section, with a lake containing huge *Victoria regia* water lilies, is a highlight. The garden is open 8 am to 5 pm daily. Entry costs US$2. Take insect repellent. To get there, catch a Jardim Botânico bus, No 170 from Centro, or No 571, 572 or 594 from the zona sul.

Museums

Museu Nacional This museum, at Quinta da Boa Vista, São Cristóvão, was once the palace of Brazil's emperors. It's now a natural history museum and has some interesting exhibits – dinosaur fossils, saber-tooth tiger skeletons, beautiful pieces of pre-Columbian ceramics from Peru, a huge meteorite, stuffed wildlife, gory displays on tropical diseases and exhibits about the peoples of Brazil. The museum is open 10 am to 5 pm, Tuesday to Sunday; admission is about US$3 (free on Thursday). Rio's **zoo** is just behind the museum and worth a visit. To get there, take the metro from Centro to São

Cristóvão, or catch bus No 472 or 474 from either Centro or the zona sul.

Museu do Folclore Edson Carneiro At Rua do Catete 181 is this small gem of a museum with excellent displays of folk art, a folklore library and a bookstore that sells recorded folk music. It's open 11 am to 6 pm Tuesday to Friday and 3 to 6 pm on weekends and holidays.

Museu da República & Palácio do Catete The Museu da República and the Palácio do Catete have been wonderfully restored. Built between 1858 and 1866 and easily recognized by the bronze eagles on the eaves, the palace was occupied by the president of Brazil from 1896 until 1954, when President Getúlio Vargas killed himself here. Now a museum, it has a good collection of art and artifacts from the Republican period. It's open noon to 5 pm Tuesday to Friday. Admission is US$2 (free on Wednesday).

Beaches

Rio is, of course, famous for its beaches. The beach is a ritual and a way of life for the carioca, and every 20m of coastline is populated by a different group of regulars. Some beaches, such as Copacabana, are more notorious for theft than others, but wherever you go, don't take valuables. It's also not a good idea to walk down by the water at night.

Sweeping around southeast from the center, the beaches are Flamengo, Botafogo, Leme, Copacabana, Arpoador, Ipanema, Leblon, Vidigal, Pepino and Barra da Tijuca. The last two are cleaner and less crowded.

Copacabana Perhaps the world's most famous beach, it runs for 4.5km in front of one of the world's most densely populated areas. There's always something happening on the beach during the day and on the footpaths at night – drinking, singing, eating and all kinds of people checking out the scene.

Ipanema This is Rio's richest and most chic beach, lacking the frenzy of Copacabana. Ipanema is an Indian word for dangerous, bad waters: Waves can get big and the undertow is often strong, so be careful. Swim only where the locals are swimming.

Different parts of the beach attract different crowds. Posto 9 is the 'Girl from Ipanema' beach, right off Rua Vinícius de Morais. Today it's also known as the Cemetério dos Elefantes, because of the old leftists, hippies and artists who hang out there. The Farme de Armoedo, also called Land of Marlboro, at Rua Farme de Armoedo, is the gay section. In front of the Caesar Park Hotel there's a very young crowd.

Carnaval

Rio's glitzy Carnaval is a big tourist attraction. Here, more than anywhere else in Brazil, it is a spectator event, and it's a fantastic spectacle. Every year, wealthy and spaced-out foreigners descend on Rio en masse, get drunk, get high, bag some sun rays and exchange exotic diseases. Everyone gets a bit unstuck and there are lots of car accidents. Room rates and taxi fares triple and quadruple, and some thieves, in keeping with the spirit of the season, rob in costume.

A couple of months before Carnaval starts, rehearsals at the *escolas de samba* (samba clubs) are open to visitors on Saturday. These are usually in the favelas. They're fun to watch, but for your safety, go with a carioca.

The escolas de samba are, in fact, predated by *bandas* (nonprofessional equivalents of the escolas de samba). These are returning to the Carnaval scene as part of the movement to bring Rio's Carnaval back to the streets. The bandas are great fun, good places to loosen up your hip joints for samba and excellent photo opportunities; transvestites always keep the festivities entertaining.

Riotur has information on the scheduled bandas, or you could just show up in Ipanema (many of them are in here), at Praça General Osório or at Praça Paz around 5 pm or so, a couple of weekends before the official Carnaval begins. Other street festivities are held in Centro, on Av Rio Branco.

Carnaval balls are surreal and erotic events. Tickets go on sale about two weeks before Carnaval starts, and the balls are held nightly for the week preceding the festivities and throughout Carnaval. If you go, don't take more money than you're willing to lose. Buy a copy of the *Veja* magazine with the Veja Rio insert. It has details about all the balls and bandas.

BRAZIL

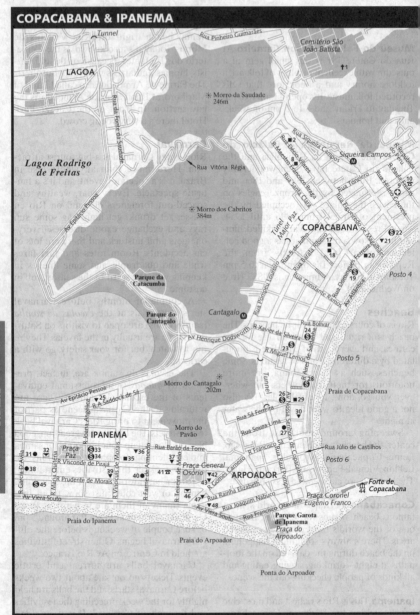

COPACABANA & IPANEMA

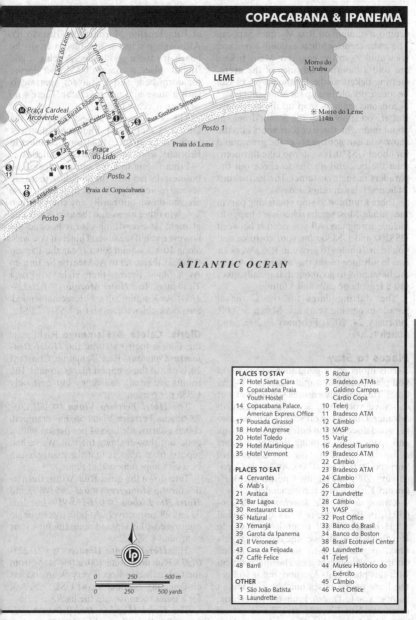

COPACABANA & IPANEMA

LEME

Morro do
Urubu

✳ Morro do Leme
114m

Praça Cardeal
Arcoverde

Praça
do Lido

Posto 1

Praia do Leme

Posto 2

Praia de Copacabana

Posto 3

ATLANTIC OCEAN

BRAZIL

PLACES TO STAY
2 Hotel Santa Clara
8 Copacabana Praia
  Youth Hostel
14 Copacabana Palace,
   American Express Office
17 Pousada Girassol
18 Hotel Angrense
20 Hotel Toledo
29 Hotel Martinique
35 Hotel Vermont

PLACES TO EAT
4 Cervantes
6 Mab's
21 Arataca
25 Bar Lagoa
30 Restaurant Lucas
36 Natural
37 Yemanjá
39 Garota da Ipanema
42 Il Veronese
43 Casa da Feijoada
47 Caffè Felice
48 Barril

OTHER
1 São João Batista
3 Laundrette

5 Riotur
7 Bradesco ATMs
9 Galdino Campos
  Cárdio Copa
10 Telerj
11 Bradesco ATM
12 Câmbio
13 VASP
15 Varig
16 Andesol Turismo
19 Bradesco ATM
22 Câmbio
23 Bradesco ATM
24 Câmbio
26 Câmbio
27 Laundrette
28 Câmbio
31 VASP
32 Post Office
33 Banco do Brasil
34 Banco do Boston
38 Brasil Ecotravel Center
40 Laundrette
41 Telerj
44 Museu Histórico do
   Exército
45 Câmbio
46 Post Office

0   250   500 m
0   250   500 yards

The 16 top-level samba schools prepare all year for an hour of glory in the Sambódromo, a stadium on Rua Marques Sapucai. The extravaganza starts around 7 pm and goes until 9 am the next day. Many tickets are sold a month in advance of the event. Getting tickets at the legitimate prices can be tough; people line up for hours, and travel agents and scalpers snap up the best seats. But, if you show up at the Sambódromo at about midnight, three or four hours into the show, you can get tickets at the grandstand for about US$10. It's safer to take the metro than the bus, and it's fun to check out the paraders in their costumes. The metro runs 24 hours a day during Carnaval.

There's nothing to stop you taking part in the parade. Most samba schools are happy to include foreigners. All you need is between US$200 and US$300 for your costume and you're in. It helps to arrive in Rio a week or two in advance to get this organized. Ask at the hotel how to go about it. It usually takes just a few phone calls and a fitting.

The starting dates for the Carnaval parade in coming years are: March 5, 2000; February 24, 2001; February 9, 2002; and March 1, 2003.

Places to Stay

Reservations are a good idea, especially if you plan to stay in a mid-range or top-end hotel. This not only ensures you a room, but can save you up to 30% for booking in advance. During the off season, you can also get good discounts on hotels in Copacabana and Ipanema by booking through a travel agent in Rio after you arrive. Andesol Turismo (☎ 021-541-0748), Av NS de Copacabana 209, is run by English-speaking Gustav Kirby, and is recommended.

Chave do Rio de Janeiro (☎ *021-286-0303*), in Botafogo, is Rio's only official AYH hostel. You'll meet lots of young Brazilians from all over the country. It gets busy, so you need to make reservations during peak holiday times. The only problem with this place is its location, but if you get the hang of the buses quickly, it shouldn't hamper you too much. From the rodoviária, catch bus Nos 170, 171 or 172 and get off after the Largo dos Leões. Go up Rua Voluntários da Pátria until you hit Rua General Dionísio, then turn left. The hostel is at No 63.

Unofficial hostels include the *Copacabana Praia Youth Hostel* (☎ *021-547-5422*), at Rua Tenente Marones de Gusmão 85. Although it's just a few blocks from the beach, it's still a good value. A relaxed and friendly place, it charges US$15 per person for dorm beds and US$40 for apartments with a stove and a refrigerator. There's no sign, but it's easy to find.

The best areas for budget hotels are the Glória, Catete and Flamengo districts. Hotels here are often full from December to February, so reservations are a good idea.

From Glória to Lapa, on the edge of the business district near the aqueduct, there are several more budget hotels. In general, these are run-down, but hardly any cheaper than hotels in other areas, and the area is less safe at night. If everything else is booked up, however, you'll see several hotels if you walk along Rua Joaquim Silva (near the Passeio Público), then over to Av Mem de Sá, turn up Av Gomes Freire, then right to Praça Tiradentes. The *Hotel Marajó* (☎ *021-224-4134*), Av Joaquim Silva 99, is recommended. Singles/doubles/triples go for US$25/28/54.

Glória, Catete & Flamengo Right near the Glória metro station, the *Hotel Benjamin Constant*, Rua Benjamin Constant 10, is one of the cheapest places around. The rooms are small and dingy but cost only US$8 per person.

The *Hotel Ferreira Viana* (☎ *021-205-7396*, Rua Ferreira Viana 58, has cramped, cheap quartos for US$14 per person with a good hot shower down the hall. We've had reports from readers that the manager can be a bit temperamental at times.

Turn down the quiet Rua Arturo Bernardes for the *Monterrey* (☎ *021-265-9899*) and *Hotel Rio Lisboa* (☎ *021-265-9599*), at Nos 39 and 29, respectively. At both places, single quartos cost US$15 and apartamentos start at around US$18/25.

The *Hotel Monte Blanco* (☎ *021-225-0121*), Rua do Catete 160, a few steps from the Catete metro stop, is very clean and has air-con. Singles/doubles cost US$20/25. Ask for a quiet room toward the back.

The *Hotel Hispáno Brasileiro* (☎ *021-265-5990*), Rua Silveira Martins 135, has big, clean apartamentos for US$20/30.

The *Hotel Paysandú* (☎ *021-558-7270*), Rua Paissandú 23, is a two-star Embratur hotel with quartos for US$20/35 and apartamentos for US$30/40. It's a good value for the money.

The *Hotel Turístico* (☎ 021-557-7698), Ladeira da Glória 30, is one of Rio's most popular budget hotels, and there are always plenty of gringos staying here. It's across from the Glória metro station, 30m up the street that emerges between two pavement restaurants. The rooms are clean and safe, with small balconies. The hotel is often full but does take reservations. Single quartos cost US$25 and apartamentos start at US$30.

Decent mid-range hotels in the area include the clean and cozy *Regina Hotel* (☎ 021-556-1647), at Rua Ferreira Viana 29. All rooms have double beds, air-con, TV and hot water. Apartamentos are US$35/43, singles/doubles.

Copacabana The *Pousada Girassol* (☎ 021-256-6951), Travessa Angrense 25-A, is a cheerful pousada featuring comfortable apartamentos with ceiling fans for US$25/40/50. It's in a good location and English is spoken. Next door at No 25 is *Hotel Angrense* (☎ 021-548-0509), one of Copacabana's cheapest budget hotels. Clean, dreary singles/doubles cost US$30/50 with bath, US$25/40 without. Travessa Angrense isn't on most maps, but it intersects Av NS de Copacabana just past Rua Santa Clara.

Often considered the best two-star hotel in Copacabana, the *Hotel Toledo* (☎ 021-257-1990) is at Rua Domingos Ferreira 71. The rooms, as fine as those in many higher priced hotels, start at US$36/40, and there are also some tiny singles (US$30).

Near the youth hostel, at Rua Décio Vilares 316, the delightful mid-range *Hotel Santa Clara* (☎ 021- 256-2650) has apartamentos starting at US$43/50.

The *Hotel Martinique* (☎ 021-521-1652) combines a perfect location with good rooms at a moderate cost. It's at quiet Rua Sá Ferreira 30, one block from the far end of Copacabana beach. Clean, comfortable rooms with air-con start as low as US$45/60, and they have a few very small singles (US$30).

The *Grande Hotel Canada* (☎ 021-257-1864), Av NS de Copacabana 687, has modern rooms with air-con and TV for US$50/60, but they do good deals in low season.

Leblon & Ipanema The *Hotel Carlton* (☎ 021-259-1932), Rua João Lira 68, is on a very quiet street, one block from the beach in Leblon. It's a small, friendly hotel, away from the tourist scene. Singles/doubles are US$48/52. The family room, for two adults and two children, costs US$62.

The *Hotel São Marco* (☎ 021-239-5032), Visconde do Piraja 524 and the *Hotel Vermont* (☎ 021-521-0057), Visconde do Piraja 254, are two relatively inexpensive hotels in Ipanema, a couple of blocks from the beach. Both have simple, modern rooms with air-con, TV and refrigerator, and charge US$55/65. The Hotel Vermont is located on the Copacabana & Ipanema map.

Places to Eat

As in most of Brazil, restaurants in Rio are abundant and cheap. Try the *galetos*, which serve barbecued chicken with rice, beans, potatoes and salad for around US$5. There are several in Copacabana and Cinelândia. Rio is also full of juice places offering a huge range of fruits. Most of these also serve healthy sandwiches.

There are several lanchonetes that sell food por kilo for the lunchtime crowd. If your budget is tight, these are the places to look for. If you don't feel like a big lunch, lanchonetes also serve tasty snacks called *salgados*. Popular ones include the *coxinha*, savory chicken pieces wrapped in dough and deep-fried, as well as Arab *quibe* and *pasteis,* deep-fried pastry puffs with cheese, mincemeat or *palmitos* (palm hearts) inside.

If you want a little more atmosphere without paying too much, try one of Rio's more traditional restaurants, mentioned below.

Make a habit of asking for an *embalagem* (doggie bag) when you don't finish your food. Wrap it and hand it to a street person.

Centro The *Bar Luis*, Rua da Carioca 39, is a Rio institution that opened in 1887. The city's oldest *cervejaria* (public house) on Rio's oldest street is a dining room serving good German food and dark draft beer at moderate prices. It's open for lunch and dinner until midnight, Monday to Saturday.

Confeiteria Colombo is at Rua Gonçalves Dias 34, one block from and parallel to Rio Branco. It's an ornate coffee house and restaurant where you can either sit

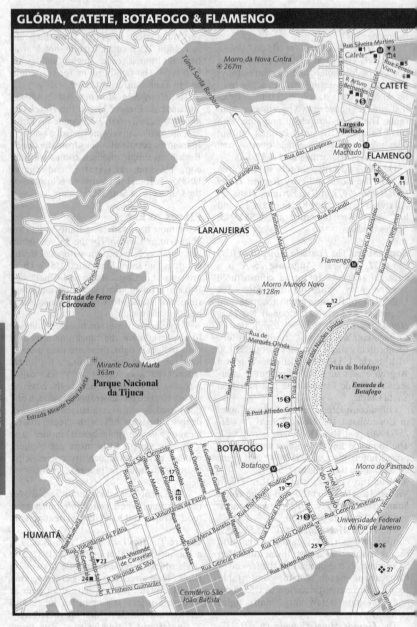

GLÓRIA, CATETE, BOTAFOGO & FLAMENGO

GLÓRIA, CATETE, BOTAFOGO & FLAMENGO

PLACES TO STAY
1 Hotel Hispáno Brasileiro
2 Hotel Monte Blanco
5 Hotel Ferreira Viana
6 Regina Hotel
7 Monterrey
8 Hotel Rio Lisboa
11 Hotel Paysandú
24 Chave do
Rio de Janeiro YHA

PLACES TO EAT
3 Palácio do Catete,
Museu da República
10 Café Lamas
23 Café Brasil
25 Adega do Valentim

OTHER
4 Museu Folclorico Edson Carneiro
9 Banco do Brasil
12 Telerj - Phones
13 Museu Carmen Miranda
14 Post Office
15 Banco do Brasil
16 Bradesco ATM
17 Museu do Índio
18 Museu Villa Lobos
19 Post Office
20 Late Clube do Rio de Janeiro
21 Bradesco ATM
22 Buses to Centro & Zona Sul
26 Canecão
27 Rio Sul Shopping Mall

Parque do Catete

Parque do Flamengo

Baía de Guanabara

Morro Cara de Cão
72m

Fortaleza de São João

Praia de Fora

Av João Luís Alves

Rua Cândido Gaffré

Rua São Sebastião

Av São Sebastião

URCA

Alameda Ferrano

Praia da Urca

Av Portugal

Rua Marechal Cantuária

Pão de Açúcar (Sugar Loaf)
395m

Morro da Urca
218m

Trilha Claudio Coutinho

Av Portugal

Praça
Euzebio Oliveira

Av Pasteur

Praça General
Tiburcio

Praia Vermelha

Cable-Car Station

PRAIA VERMELHA

0   250   500 m
0   250   500 yards

BRAZIL

down for a meal or stand if you're just having a dessert. The Colombo is best for coffee, cake or a snack. During the week it has a reasonably priced lunch buffet.

The green gazebo near the Niterói ferry houses *Restaurante Alba Mar* at Praça Marechal Áncora 184. Go for the seafood and the view of Baía de Guanabara and Niteroi. It stays open from 11:30 am to 10 pm Monday to Saturday. Dishes start at US$20 (enough for two). The *peixe brasileira* is recommended. Two better (and more expensive) self-serve places downtown are *Mr Ôpi*, Rua da Alfândega 91, and *Dirty Mary Saladeria*, Rua Teófilo Otoni 50.

Lapa & Santa Teresa *Bar Brasil*, at Av Mem de Sá 90 in Lapa, is a traditional bar and restaurant with decent German food. It's open 11:30 am to 11 pm weekdays and 11:30 am to 3 pm on Saturday. Lapa also has a couple of decent vegetarian places: *Semente* and *Gohan*, both on Rua Joaquim Silva. Semente, at No 138, gets a big lunch crowd attracted by the mix of natural and Asian cuisine. It's inexpensive and open from 11 am to 11 pm on weekdays. In Santa Teresa, at Rua Almirante Alexandrino 316-B, *Bar do Arnaudo* serves Rio's best northeastern food. The *carne do sol* is excellent and cheap. It's closed on Monday.

Glória, Catete & Largo do Machado In Glória & Catete, two good, cheap, self-serve places are *Estaçao Republica*, on the corner of Rua do Catete and Rua Andrade Pertence, and the restaurant upstairs at Rua do Catete 152. *Westfalia*, Rua da Gloria 318, serves good German food. *Taberna da Glória*, Rua do Russel 32A, has friendly service and is good for Brazilian staple dishes such as the Sunday *cozido*, roast piglet on Thursday and *feijoada* on Saturday. On the other corner of Ladeira da Gloriais *Amarelinho*, an air-con, self-serve lunch place that's packed at lunchtime. *Adega dos Nogueiras*, Rua Pedro Americo, has a wonderful *picanha* that 'serves three' for around US$10.

Restaurant Amazónia, upstairs at Rua do Catete 234, has good steak and a tasty broiled chicken with creamed-corn sauce, both for about US$12. Avoid the lanchonete downstairs. For a splurge, eat at the *Museum* restaurant in the Museu da Republica. It has excellent food and a relaxed atmosphere.

Botafogo & Flamengo The popular *Churrascaria Majórica*, Rua Senador Vergueiro 11/15, Flamengo, has good meat, reasonable prices and an interior done in gaúcho kitsch. It's open for lunch and dinner.

Café Lamas, at Rua Marques de Abrantes 18-A in Flamengo, has been operating since 1874 and is one of Rio's most renowned eateries. It has a lively and loyal clientele. It's open for lunch and dinner with a typical meaty menu and standard prices; try the grilled *linguiça* or filet mignon.

In Botafogo, *Café Brasil*, Rua Capitão Salomão 35, is a Brazilian restaurant open from 11:30 am to 1 pm (2 pm on Friday and Saturday). Its speciality is *comida mineira* (food from Minas Gerais), eaten for lunch, not dinner.

Adega do Valentim is a highly recommended Portuguese restaurant at Rua da Passagem 176. It's open from noon until 2 am daily. The baked rabbit with spicy rice is excellent, as are the codfish dishes. They have a Portuguese dance show on Friday and Saturday nights.

There are also decent restaurants in the Rio Sul shopping center, such as the *Fun Club*, which serves pastas and steaks. It's popular with teenagers and happy-hour revelers. The *T-Bone* barbecue house is also good.

Copacabana *Restaurante Lucas*, Av Atlântica 3744, is across from Rua Sousa Lima. It offers reasonably priced German dishes starting at US$10.

Arataca, Rua Domingos Ferreira 41, is one of several restaurants in Rio featuring the exotic cuisine of the Amazon. This place is actually a lunch counter and deli around the corner from one of its sit-down restaurants. You'll get the same food for only half the price at the deli. In addition to the regional dishes such as *vatapáand pato* (duck), they serve real guaraná juice (try it) and delicious sorbets made from Amazonas fruits.

Mab's, Av Atlântica (the Copacabana side of Princesa Isabel, across from the Meridien), has excellent seafood soup in a crock, chock-full of piping hot creepy-crawlies for US$10.

Cervantes is Rio's best sandwich joint and a late-night hangout for a strange and colorful crew. It's on the infamous Av Prado

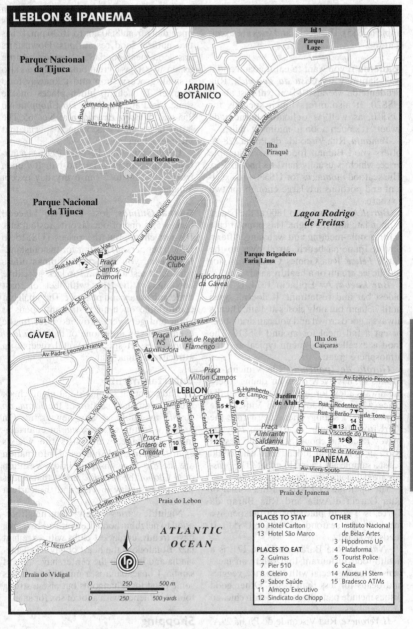

LEBLON & IPANEMA

Parque Nacional
da Tijuca

JARDIM
BOTÂNICO

Rua Fernando Magalhães

Rua Pachaco Leão

Jardim Botânico

Ilha
Piraquê

Parque Nacional
da Tijuca

Rua Jardim Botânico

Lagoa Rodrigo
de Freitas

Rua Major Rubens Vaz

Praça
Santos
Dumont

Jóquei
Clube

Parque Brigadeiro
Faria Lima

Rua Marquês de São Vicente

Rua Artur Araripe

GÁVEA

Rua Mário Ribeiro

Hipódromo
da Gávea

Av Padre Leonel Franca

Av Bartolomeu Mitre

Praça
NS
Auxiliadora

Clube de Regatas
Flamengo

Ilha dos
Caiçaras

Praça
Milton Campos

Av Viscondé de Albuquerque

Rua General Urquiza

LEBLON

Rua Humberto de Campos

R Humberto
de Campos

Jardim
de Alah

Av Epitácio Pessoa

Rua José Linhares

Rua Carlos Góis

Rua Aristides Espínola

Rua Almirante Guilhem

Av Ataulfo de Paiva

Av Afrânio de Mélo Franco

Redentor

Rua
Barão

da Torre

Rua General San Martins

Rua Dias Ferreira

Artigas

Praça
Antero de
Quental

Praça
Almirante
Saldanha
Gama

Rua Henrique Dumont

Rua Prudente de Morais

Rua Visconde de Pirajá

IPANEMA

Rua Maria Quitéria

Av Delfim Moreira

Av Viera Souto

Praia do Lebon

Praia de Ipanema

ATLANTIC
OCEAN

Av Niemeyer

Praia do Vidigal

| 0 | 250 | 500 m |
| 0 | 250 | 500 yards |

PLACES TO STAY
10 Hotel Carlton
13 Hotel São Marco

PLACES TO EAT
2 Guímas
7 Pier 510
8 Celeiro
9 Sabor Saúde
11 Almoço Executivo
12 Sindicato do Chopp

OTHER
1 Instituto Nacional
 de Belas Artes
3 Hipodromo Up
4 Plataforma
5 Tourist Police
6 Scala
14 Museu H Stern
15 Bradesco ATMs

BRAZIL

Junior, where everyone and everything goes at night. Meat sandwiches come with pineapple (US$5). The steaks and fries are excellent too.

Ipanema If you want to eat feijoada and it isn't Saturday, try *Casa da Feijoada*, Rua Prudente de Morais 10-B; it will cost about US$20. It also offers lunch specials for US$10, as well as delicious homemade sweets. It's open noon to midnight daily.

Yemanjá, Rua Visconde de Pirajá 128-A, offers good Bahian food at a reasonable price, which is usually hard to find in Rio. The seafood *moquecas* for US$30 are excellent and portions are large enough for two to share.

Barril, Av Vieira Souto 1800 at the beach, is open late into the night. This popular café is for people-meeting and watching. After a day at Ipanema beach, stroll over to the *Caffè Felice*, Rua Gomes Carneiro 30, for terrific ice cream or a healthy sandwich.

Bar Lagoa, Av Epitácio 1674, is Rio's oldest bar and restaurant. It doesn't open until 7:30 pm but only closes at 3 am. There's always a good crowd and you can drink beer or eat a full meal for around US$10. The food is excellent, the menu typical and the atmosphere great.

Garota de Ipanema, Rua Vinícius de Morais 49, has lively open-air dining. There are always a few foreigners checking out the place where Tom Jobim and Vinícius de Moraes were sitting when they wrote the 'Girl from Ipanema.' A Brazilian *Playboy* survey rated the chopp here as the best in Rio – a bold claim indeed, but who could resist a sample after a rap like that? The *petiscos* are delicious – try their famous *kibes*.

The open-air *Pier 510*, on the corner of Rua Garcia d'Avila and Rua Barão da Torre, is a good place for an inexpensive meal. Try the seafood risotto for US$10. It feeds two easily.

Natural, Rua Barão da Torre 171, is a health-food restaurant that offers an inexpensive lunch special with soup, rice, veggies and beans for less than US$5. Other good dishes include pancakes served with chicken or vegetables.

Il Veronese, Rua Visconde de Pirajá 29A, off Gomes Carneiro serves inexpensive takeaway Italian pastas (the best in Rio, according to local sources), pizzas and pastries.

Leblon *Sabor Saúde*, Av Ataulfo de Pavia 630, is Rio's best health-food emporium. It's open daily from 8:30 am to 10:30 pm. It has two natural food restaurants: Downstairs has good meals for US$6; upstairs is more expensive (it has a great buffet). There's also a small grocery shop and takeaway-food counter. Two cheap lunch places on the same street are *Sindicato Do Chopp* at No 355 and *Almoço Executivo* at No 365. The latter has a daily US$5 lunch special that includes a beverage.

Celeiro, Rua Dias Ferreira 199, has a fantastic (and expensive) salad bar. It's open from 11:30 am to 5 pm every day except Sunday.

Gávea *Guimas*, Jose Roberto Macedo Soares 5, is one of our favorite restaurants. It's not cheap, but the prices (US$15 to US$30 per person) are fair for the outstanding cuisine you're served. Guimas offers what most restaurants in Rio lack – creative cooking. Try the trout with leek or roast duck with honey and pear rice. The small but comfortable open-air restaurant opens at noon and gets very crowded later in the evening. If you order one of their *boa lembrança* dessert specials, you'll receive an attractive ceramic plate.

Entertainment

To find out what's going on at night, check the entertainment section of the *Jornal do Brasil*, available at any newsstand. On Friday it features *Programa*, an entertainment magazine, which lists the week's events. Other good sources of information are the *Rio Show* insert in Friday's edition of *O Globo*, the *Veja Rio* insert that comes out every Sunday in *Veja* and the current *Riotur*.

Nightlife varies widely from neighborhood to neighborhood. Leblon and Ipanema have trendy, upmarket clubs with excellent jazz. Botafogo is the heart of gay Rio. Cinelândia and Lapa, in the center, have a lot of samba. Copacabana is a mixed bag: It has some good local hangouts but also a strong tourist influence, with a lot of sex for sale.

Shopping

Most shops are open 9 am to 7 pm (some stay open even later) on weekdays, and 9 am to 1 pm Saturday. The malls usually open from 10 am to 10 pm weekdays, and from 10 am to 8 pm on weekends.

In Laranjeiras, on Rua Ipiranga 53, Pé de Boi is open until 7 pm weekdays and from 10 am to 1 pm Saturday. This shop sells the traditional artisan handicrafts of Brazil's northeast and Minas Gerais. Although the items are not cheap, it's all fine work.

Artíndia, a tiny craft shop at the Museu do Índio, Rua das Palmeiras 55, Botafogo, has woven papoose slings, jewelry and musical instruments. It's open 9 am to noon and 1 to 6 pm weekdays.

Casa Olveira, a beautiful music shop, is in Centro on Rio's oldest street, at Rua da Carioca 70. It sells a wide variety of musical instruments, including all the noisemakers that fuel the Carnaval *baterias* (rhythm sections).

The Hippie Fair is an arts and crafts fair, featuring booths that sell jewelry, leather goods, paintings, samba instruments and clothes. Stuff here runs the gamut from awful to all right. The fair takes place every Sunday at the Praça General Osório in Ipanema.

The nordeste (northeast) fair is held at the Pavilhão de São Cristóvão, on the north side of town, every Sunday. It starts early and goes until about 3 pm. The fair is very northeastern in character. Besides food, stallholders sell cheap clothes, hammocks at bargain prices and a few good nordeste gifts such as leather *vaqueiro* (cowboy) hats.

Getting There & Away

Air From Rio, flights go to all parts of Brazil and Latin America. Shuttle flights to São Paulo leave from the conveniently located Aeroporto Santos Dumont in the city center, right along the bay.

Almost all other flights – domestic and international – leave from Aeroporto Galeão. See the Getting There and Away section at the beginning of this chapter for more information.

The major Brazilian airlines have their main offices in the center (metro stop Cinelândia). You can also walk over to Aeroporto Santos Dumont, where there are ticket counters and staff members will make reservations for you.

Varig (☎ 021-292-6600) has its main office in Centro, at Av Rio Branco 277G. VASP (☎ 021-292-2112) has a city office at Rua

Santa Luzia 735. TAM (☎ 021-240-8217) is downtown at Av Franklin Roosevelt 194. Transbrasil (☎ 021-297-4422) is also in the center, at Rua Santa Luzia 651. International airlines include:

Aerolíneas Argentinas
(☎ 021-275-0440)
Rua São José 70, 8th floor, Centro

Air France
(☎ 021-532-3642)
Av Presidente Antônio Carlos 58, 9th floor, Centro

Alitalia
(☎ 021-292-4424)
Av Presidente Wilson 231, 21st floor, Centro

American Airlines
(☎ 021-210-3126)
Av Presidente Wilson 165, 5th floor, Centro

Avianca
(☎ 021-220-7697)
Av Presidente Wilson 165, No 801

British Airways
(☎ 021-221-0922)
Av Rio Branco 108, 21st floor, Centro

Continental
(☎ 021-531-1142)
Rua da Assembléia 10, room 3710, Centro

Delta Airlines
(☎ 021-507-7227)
Rua da Ouvidor 161, 14th floor, Centro

Iberia
(☎ 021-282-1336)
Av Presidente Antônio Carlos 51, 9th floor, Centro

Japan Air Lines
(☎ 021-220-6414)
Av Rio Branco 156, No 2014, Centro

KLM
(☎ 021-292-7747)
Av Rio Branco 311A, Centro

LanChile
(☎ 021-220-0299)
Rua Sete de Setembro 111, room 701, Centro

Lloyd Aero Boliviano (LAB)
(☎ 021-220-9548)
Av Calógeras 30 A, Centro

Lufthansa
(☎ 021-217-6111)
Av Rio Branco 156 D, Centro

South African
(☎ 021-262-6252)
Av Rio Branco 245, 4th floor, Centro

United Airlines
(☎ 021-532-1212)
Av Presidente Antônio Carlos 51, 5th floor, Centro

BRAZIL

Bus All long-distance buses leave from the Novo Rio Rodoviária (☎ 021-291-5151 for information in Portuguese), Av Francisco Bicalho in Santo Cristo, just north of the center. Many travel agents in the city and zona sul sell bus tickets; it's best to purchase these a couple of days in advance.

Getting Around

To/From the Airport

There are three options: air-conditioned buses, local buses and taxis. If you have any valuables, an air-con bus or a taxi is safer than a local bus.

Empresa Real air-con buses run on two routes to and from Aeroporto Galeão. The buses operate from 5:20 am to 12:10 pm, and leave every 40 minutes to one hour. One route goes to the city center and the Santos Dumont airport (US$2.50); the other route goes to the city center and along the beaches of Copacabana, Ipanema, Leblon, Vidigal, São Conrado and Barra da Tijuca (US$4.50).

You can catch the bus on the 1st floor of the main terminal at the Galeão sign. If you ask the driver, the bus will stop anywhere along the route. Buses on both routes stop at the rodoviária, if you want to catch a bus out of Rio immediately.

If you're heading to the airport, you can catch the Empresa Real bus in front of the major hotels along the beach, but you have to flag it down. 'Aeroporto Internacional' should be written on the direction sign.

There is a small terminal for city buses on Rua Ecuador (on the far corner to your right as you leave the main terminal at Galeão).

A taxi is a good option if you have valuables, though many drivers will try to rip you off. The safest and most expensive option is to take a white radio-taxi, where you pay a set fare at the airport. A yellow-and-blue comum taxi is about 25% cheaper if the meter is working and if you pay what is on the fare schedule. A trip from the airport to Copacabana costs about US$25 in a comum taxi, US$35 in a radio-taxi. If you're entering Brazil for the first time, on a budget, a good compromise is to take a bus to somewhere near your destination, then take a short taxi ride to your hotel. Sharing a taxi from the airport is a good idea. Taxis will take up to four people.

Bus The buses are a mixture of the good, the bad and the ugly. The good: Rio's buses are fast, frequent, cheap (US$0.70) and, because Rio is long and narrow, it's easy to get the right bus and usually no big deal if you're on the wrong one. The bad: Rio's buses are often crowded, slowed down by traffic and driven by raving maniacs who drive the buses as if they were motorcycles. The ugly: Rio's buses are the scene of many of the city's robberies, so don't carry any valuables. In addition to their numbers, buses have their destinations, including the areas they go through, written on the side. Nine out of 10 buses going south from the center will go to Copacabana and vice versa. All buses have the prices displayed above the head of the money collector. The buses you need to catch for specific destinations are listed under individual sights.

Since bus numbers and routes are posted, it's pretty easy to work out which bus to catch from the rodoviária. For Copacabana, the best are bus Nos 126, 127 and 128. The fastest bus to Ipanema and Leblon is No 128, but you can also take No 126 or 127 to Copacabana and then transfer. For budget hotels in Catete and Glória, take the Gávea via Jóquei bus (No 170), which goes down Rua do Catete and then turns up Rua Pedro Américo and cruises along Rua Bento Lisboa. If you want the Catete budget hotels, get off at the stop near the corner of Bento Lisboa and Rua Silveira Martins, then walk a block down to Rua Catete.

An alternative is to take any bus that goes to the center along Av Rio Branco. Get off near the end of Av Rio Branco and hop on the metro. Get off the metro at Catete station, in the heart of the budget hotel area.

If you're staying in the Catete-Flamengo area and want to get to the beaches by bus, you can either walk to the main roadway along Parque Flamengo and take any Copacabana bus, or you can walk to Largo do Machado and take bus No 570.

Metro Rio's excellent subway system extends to Copacabana. It's open from 5 am to 11 pm daily except Sunday. The two air-con lines are cleaner and faster than the buses. It's US$1 per ride. The main stops for Centro are Cinelândia and Carioca.

Car You can find car rental agencies at the airport or clustered together on Av Princesa

Isabel in Copacabana. Rental is not cheap (up to US$100 a day), but promotional rates vary, so it's worth shopping around. When agencies quote prices on the phone, they usually leave out the cost of insurance, which is mandatory. Most agencies will let you drop off their cars in another city without extra charge.

Taxi Rio taxis are quite reasonably priced if you're dividing the fare with a friend or two. They are particularly useful late at night and when carrying valuables, but are not a completely safe and hassle-free ride. There have been a few cases of people being assaulted and robbed by taxi drivers. More commonly, the drivers have a marked tendency to exaggerate fares. See the information on taxis in the Getting Around section for more hints. The white radio-taxis (☎ 021-260-2022) are 30% more expensive than the comums, but they will come to you and they are safer.

ANGRA DOS REIS

Angra dos Reis is a transit point for nearby islands and beaches, not a tourist attraction in itself. The Centro de Informações Turísticas is in Largo da Lapa, right across from the bus station. Helpful, English-speaking staff have information about attractions and places to stay in Angra and Ilha Grande. It's open 8 am to 7 pm Monday to Saturday. The closest beaches are at Praia Grande and Vila Velha. Take the Vila Velha municipal bus.

Angra dos Reis is almost three hours (US$15) by bus from Rio de Janeiro's Novo Rio Rodoviária. To Parati, it's a two-hour trip (US$5).

ILHA GRANDE

Ilha Grande is all beach and tropical jungle, with only three towns on the island: Freguesia de Santana (a small hamlet without accommodations), Parnaioca (a collection of homes beside a lovely strip of beach near the old prison) and Abraão (which has plenty of pousadas, campgrounds and ferry connections to Mangaratiba and Angra dos Reis). If you really want to get away from it all, Ilha Grande may well be the place.

There are trails through the jungle to Praia Lopes Mendes (said by some to be the most beautiful beach in Brazil) and the island's other 102 beaches.

Places to Stay & Eat

The cheapest option is to camp. *Camping Renato*, up a small path beside Dona Penha's, has well-drained, secure sites and basic facilities, as well as an on-site café and bar. They charge US$5 per person.

The youth hostel, *Ilha Grande* (☎ 021-264-6147), Getúlio Vargas 13, is a good option here. It's well located, with friendly staff, and costs US$12/15 for members/nonmembers. Reservations are a good idea, especially on weekends and holidays.

Most of the pousadas in Abraão cost between US$15 and US$25 for a double in low season (April to November). In summer, prices double. All prices quoted here are for low season. A good option is the *Pousada Beira Mar* (☎ 021-987-4696), right on the beach, 300m from the dock. Lutz, the owner, speaks German and English; he charges US$15/25 singles/doubles. Close by is the *Tropicana* (☎ 021-225-1286 in Rio), Rua da Praia 28. It's a very pleasant place with apartamentos for US$30/40.

The three best places to eat in town are *Bar Casarão da Ilha*, which is expensive but serves very high quality seafood; *Restaurant Minha Deusa*, with cheap, good home cooking; and *Bar Restaurant Lua & Mar*, which serves good seafood dishes if you don't mind waiting a while.

Getting There & Away

Catch a Conerj ferry from either Mangaratiba or Angra dos Reis. From Mangaratiba to Abraão, the ferry leaves weekdays at 8 am and weekends at 9 am. It returns from Abraão daily at 5 pm.

The ferry from Angra dos Reis to Abraão leaves at 3 pm on weekdays and 2:30 pm on weekends, returning from Abraão at 9:30 am on weekdays and 11 am on weekends. It's a 1½-hour, US$5 ride.

PARATI

Parati, one of Brazil's most enchanting colonial towns, is a good place to explore a dazzling section of the coast. It is now one of the most popular holiday spots between Rio and São Paulo, and prices are high.

Information The Centro de Informações Turísticas (☎ 024-371-1266, ext 218), on Av Roberto Silveira, is open daily from 9 am to 9 pm.

BRAZIL

Parati Tours (☎ 024-371-1327) is on Av Roberto Silveira 11, just before you hit the colonial part of town. It's also useful for information. Its five-hour schooner cruises are US$15 (US$20 with lunch), and it also rents bicycles (US$2 an hour, or US$10 per day).

Things to See & Do

Parati's 18th-century prosperity is reflected in its beautiful old homes and churches. In the 18th century, the population was divided among the three main churches: **NS do Rosário** (1725) for slaves, **Santa Rita dos Pardos Libertos** (1722) for free mulattos and **NS das Dores** (1800) for the white elite.

The **Forte Defensor Perpétuo** was built in 1703 to protect the gold being exported from Minas Gerais, which was subject to attack by pirates. It's a 20-minute walk north from town. The fort houses the **Casa de Artista e Centro de Artes e Tradições Populares de Parati**.

To see the **beaches** and **islands**, many tourists take one of the schooners that leave from the docks around noon. The boats normally make three beach stops of about 45 minutes each.

An alternative is to rent a small motorboat at the port. For US$10 per hour (somewhat more in summer) the skipper will take you where you want to go. Bargaining may be difficult.

The mainland beaches tend to be better than the ones on the islands. The closest fine beaches on the coast – Vermelha, Lula and Saco – are about an hour away by boat; camping is allowed. The most accessible beaches, just north of town, are Praia do Pontal, Praia do Forte and Praia do Jabaquara.

Places to Stay

Parati has two very different tourist seasons. From December to February hotels book up and room prices double, so reservations are a good idea. The rest of the year, finding accommodations is easy and inexpensive. The town is quiet and some of the boutiques and restaurants close for the winter. The prices quoted here are low-season rates.

There are several campgrounds on the edge of town, just over the bridge. The **Pouso Familiar** (☎ 024-371-1475), Rua José Vieira Ramos 262, is close to the bus station and charges US$14/22 for singles/doubles,

including a good breakfast. It's a friendly place, run by a Belgian/Brazilian couple, Joseph and Lúcia. Joseph speaks English, French, German, Spanish and, of course, Flemish, and is very helpful. The pousada also has clothes-washing facilities.

Another recommended place is the **Pousada Marendaz** (☎ 024-371-1369), Rua Dr Derly Ellena 9. Run by Rachel and her four sisters, it's more of a family home than a hotel. They charge US$10 per person.

The **Hotel Solar dos Gerânios** (☎ 024-371-1550), Praça da Matriz, is a beautiful old hotel with wood and ceramic sculptures, flat brick and stone, rustic heavy furniture and azulejos. Apartamentos start as low as US$15/25.

Places to Eat

Parati has many pretty restaurants, but prices go up the minute your feet touch the cobblestones. To beat inflated costs in the old part of town, try **Sabor da Terra**, Rua Roberto Silveira 80. Also popular is **Bar da Terra**, across the bridge and up the hill on the left-hand side. They also have live music from Thursday to Sunday nights. The best restaurants in the old town include the **Galeria do Engenho**, Rua da Lapa, which serves large and juicy steaks for US$15, and **Vagalume**, Rua da Ferraria. **Hiltinho**, Rua da Cadeia, is more expensive, but the menu is good and the portions ample.

Getting There & Away

The new rodoviária is at Parque Imperial, 500m up from old town. There are 12 daily buses from Parati to Rio. The first bus leaves at 2 am and the last at 9:15 pm. Buses leave Rio for Parati at 6 and 9 am, and 12:30, 3, 6:20 and 8 pm. It's a four-hour, US$15 trip.

Eighteen buses a day go from Parati to Angra dos Reis, the first leaving at 5 am and the last at 7:20 pm (US$5, two hours).

PETRÓPOLIS

Petrópolis is a lovely mountain retreat with a decidedly European flavor. Only 60km from Rio de Janeiro, it's an ideal day trip. The main attraction is the **Museu Imperial**, the perfectly preserved and impeccably appointed palace of Dom Pedro II.

Information

Petrotur has a handy information booth on Praça Dom Pedro. It has brochures, maps and information on places to stay. It's open 9 am to noon and 2 to 5 pm Tuesday to Saturday, 9 am to 3 pm Sunday.

Places to Eat

Two good places for self-serve, por kilo lunch are *Farfalle*, upstairs on the corner of Rua do Imperador and Rua Marechal Deodoro, and *Artesão*, on Rua Imperador near the post office.

Rua 16 de Março has lots of eateries, such as *Kafta*, the Arab restaurant at No 52, *Maurício's* seafood place at No 154, and the *Midas Steak House* at No 170.

Getting There & Away

From Rio, buses to Petrópolis leave every half hour from 5:15 am onward. The trip takes 1½ hours and costs US$5.

TERESÓPOLIS

Teresópolis is the climbing and trekking center of Brazil. The city itself is modern, prosperous and dull; the principal attraction is the surrounding landscape of the **Serra dos Orgãos.**

There are extensive hiking trails, and it's possible to trek to Petrópolis. The trails aren't marked, but guides are inexpensive.

The main entrance to the Parque Nacional Serra dos Orgãos is open 8 am to 5 pm daily. There's a 3.5km walking trail, waterfalls, swimming pools, tended lawns and campsites. It's a very pretty park for a picnic. There are also some campsites and chalets for rent at the park substation, 12km toward Rio.

Places to Stay & Eat

The cheapest place is the *Hotel Comary* (☎ 021-742-3463), Av Almirante Lúcio Meira 467, with quartos for US$8 without breakfast. For faded grandeur, try the *Várzea Palace Hotel* (☎ 021-742-0878), Rua Prefeito Sebastião Teixeira 41/55, behind the Igreja Matriz. It's been a Teresópolis institution since 1916. Classy quartos are US$21/30 singles/doubles; apartamentos are US$30/45. *Cheiro de Mato*, Rua Delfim Moreira 140, is a decent vegetarian restaurant. *Sand's*, Av Almirante Lúcio Meira near the bus station, has a cheap self-serve lunch spread.

Getting There & Away

The rodoviária is on Rua 1 do Maio, off Av Tenente Luiz. Buses to Rio depart every half hour from 5 am to 10 pm (US$6, 1½ hours). There are seven buses to Petrópolis (from 6 am to 9 pm), and several to Novo Friburgo.

NOVA FRIBURGO

This mountain town was established by Swiss immigrants in 1818. The Cónego neighborhood is interesting for its German-style architecture and its flowers, which seem to bloom perpetually.

You can survey the surrounding area from **Morro da Cruz** (1800m). The cable-car station is in the center, at Praça do Suspiro, and gondolas run up to the top from 10 am to 6 pm on holidays and weekends. **Pico da Caledônia** (2310m) offers fantastic views.

The more energetic can hike to **Pedra do Cão Sentado** or explore the **Furnas do Catete** rock formations. Interesting nearby villages include the mountain towns of **Bom Jardim** (23km north on BR-492) and **Lumiar** (25km from Mury, just before the entrance to Friburgo). Hippies, cheap pensions, waterfalls, walking trails and white-water canoe trips abound in Lumiar.

Places to Stay

Primus (☎ 024-523-2898), up a steep hill on Rua Adolfo Lautz 128, is the best deal in town. Very comfortable apartamentos with everything (including padded toilet seats!) go for US$25/35, complete with a huge breakfast spread. The views are great and it's nice to watch the birds come to the feeders outside. Another good deal is the *Hotel São Paulo* (☎ 024-522-9135), Rua Monsenhor Miranda 41. In a restored old building, it has a pool and apartamentos for US$31/40. Also recommended is the *Hotel Maringá* (☎ 024-522-2309), Rua Monsenhor Miranda 110. They have quartos for US$15/25, apartamentos for US$25/35, and a restaurant downstairs.

Places to Eat

Crescente, Rua General Osório 4, is a classy little place serving, among other things, some very tasty trout dishes. The *Churrascaría Majórica*, Praça Getúlio Vargas 74, serves a decent cut of filet mignon (US$15) that's enough for two. *Friburgo Shopping*, a shopping mall on the other side of Praça Getúlio Vargas, has a few bars and cafés. *Dona Mariquinha* in the Hotel Maringá serves excellent comida mineira (from Minas Gerais) for lunch.

BRAZIL

Getting There & Away

Nova Friburgo is a little over two hours (US$6) by bus from Rio via Niterói on 1001 Lines. From Novo Friburgo, buses to Rio leave at least every hour from 6 am to 9:30 pm. There are four daily buses to Teresópolis, at 7 and 11 am, and 3 and 6 pm (US$5, two hours).

There are two long-distance bus terminals in Novo Friburgo: the Rodoviária Norte, where you catch buses for Petropolis and Teresópolis, and the Rodoviária Sul, with buses to Rio. From either one, you'll need to catch a local bus to the central, local bus terminal on Praça Getúlio Vargas.

ITATIAIA

The Itatiaia region, in the Serra da Mantiqueira, is a curious mix of old-world charm and new-world jungle. Food and lodging are expensive. You can reach this region via Resende.

Parque Nacional do Itatiaia

This 120-sq-km national park contains alpine meadows and Atlantic rain forests, lakes, rivers and waterfalls. It is home to jaguars, monkeys and sloths.

The park headquarters, museum and Lago Azul (Blue Lake) are 10km in from the Via Dutra highway. The museum, which is open 8 am to 4 pm Tuesday to Sunday, has glass cases full of stuffed animals, pinned moths and snakes in jars.

Every two weeks, a group scales the 2787m Agulhas Negras peak, the highest in the area. For more information, contact the Grupo Excursionista de Agulhas Negras (☎ 024-354-2587).

It's a 26km, eight-hour trek from the park entrance to the Abroucas refuge, at the base of Agulhas Negras. The refuge sleeps 24 people. Reservations are required. Call IBAMA (the national parks service; ☎ 024-352-1461) in Resende, to get maps and advice before setting off.

Simpler hikes include the walk between Hotel Simon and Hotel Repouso, and the 20-minute walk from the Sítio Jangada to the Poronga waterfalls.

Places to Stay

Camping is the cheapest option inside the park. There's the campground *Aporaoca*, 4km from the main entrance to the park.

(When you get to the Gula & Artes store and the ice-cream shop, there's a signpost; the campground is 200m up from and behind these places.) Sites with running water and firepits are US$3 per person.

A YHA youth hostel, *Ipê Amarelo* (☎ 352-1232), at Rua João Mauricio de Macedo Costa 352, is in Campo Alegre, a suburb of Itatiaia. The hostal rents bicycles.

The *Pousada do Elefante*, close to the Hotel Simon, is the cheapest hotel in the park. It's basic but well located. Doubles cost US$40, including three filling but repetitive meals a day.

Getting There & Away

Buses from Resende to Itatiaia run every 20 minutes on weekdays and every 40 minutes on weekends, from 7 am to 11:20 pm. From Praça São José in Itatiaia, take the Hotel Simon's Kombi up to the park. It leaves at 8 and 10 am, noon, and 2, 5 and 7 pm. The ride costs US$3, and you'll also have to pay the park entry fee (US$2) as you go through the main gate. A taxi costs US$15.

SAQUAREMA

Saquarema, 100km from Rio de Janeiro, is a horse-breeding and fruit-growing center. You can visit the orchards and pick fruit, or hire horses and take to the hills. The beaches are a major attraction: Bambui, Ponta Negra and Jaconé, south of town, are long and empty except for a couple of fishing villages. The waves are big, particularly in Ponta Negra, about 3km north of Saquarema in Praia Itaúna, where an annual surfing contest is held during the first two weeks of October.

Places to Stay

The *Pousada Ilhas Gregas* (☎ 024-651-1008), is excellent. Only 100m from the beach, at Rua do Prado 671 in Itaúna, it has bicycles, a swimming pool, a sauna and a bar-restaurant. It's easy to catch a taxi here from the bus station in Saquarema, but if you feel like a hike, get off the bus at the gas station 'Sudoeste.' Walk for half an hour along Av Oceânica until you get to the center of Itaúna (where there are lots of beachfront bars and kiosks). Go along Av NS de Nazareth and take the second street on the left (Rua das Caravelas), then the first street on your right (Rua do Prado). It's US$18 per person.

There are stacks of places charging around US$60 for a double. A couple of the popular ones are the **Pousada Pedra d'Agua Maasai** (*☎ 024-651-1092*), near Itaúna beach, and the **Pousada Pratagi** (*☎ 024-651-2161*), Av Salgado Filho 4484.

Getting There & Away
Buses leave every hour from Rio to Saquarema, from 6:30 am to 8:30 pm. The two-hour trip costs US$6. To get to Cabo Frio, take a local bus to Bacaxá. From there, buses to Cabo leave every half-hour.

ARRAIAL DO CABO
Ten kilometers south of Cabo Frio (take the municipal bus from Cabo Frio; US$0.60), Arraial do Cabo has beaches that compare with the finest in Búzios. Praia dos Anjos has beautiful turquoise water, but there's a little too much boat traffic for swimmers to feel comfortable.

Things to See & Do
The favorite beaches in town are **Praia do Forno**, **Praia Brava** and **Praia Grande**. The **Museu Oceanográfico** on Praia dos Anjos is open 9 am to noon and 1 to 4:30 pm Tuesday to Sunday.

The **Gruta Azul** (Blue Cavern), on the far side of Ilha de Cabo Frio, is another beautiful spot. Be alert to the tides: The entrance to the underwater cavern isn't always open. Arrail Sub (*☎ 024-622-1149*) and Send-Mar (*☎ 024-622-1356*) both run diving trips.

Places to Stay & Eat
Prices quoted here are for the low season. Expect prices to rise by around 30% in high season.

The Camping Club do Brasil has a campground, **CCB-RJ05**(*☎ 024-622-1023*), at Praia dos Anjos. They charge US$10 per person. The **Hotel Praia Grande** (*☎ 024-622-1369*), Rua Dom Pedro 41, is a good cheapie in the center of town, with US$15/30 singles/doubles. At Praia dos Anjos, the **Porto dos Anjos** (*☎ 024-622-1629*), Av Luis Correa 8, is a house that's been converted into a pousada. The double rooms (US$30) have sea views.

Garrafa de Nansen Restaurante is a classy seafood place where you can eat very well for about US$15. Cheaper eats are available in the center at **Meu Cantinho**, Rua Dom Pedro I, No 18, where the US$10 fish dinners will easily feed two.

BÚZIOS
Búzios is on a peninsula scalloped by 17 beaches. It was a simple fishing village until Brigitte Bardot and her Brazilian boyfriend discovered it. Now it's a highly developed, expensive resort.

Búzios actually comprises three settlements on the peninsula (Ossos, Manguinhos and Armação) and one farther north, on the mainland (Rasa). Ossos (which means bones), at the northernmost tip of the peninsula, is the oldest and most attractive.

Information
The Secretaria de Turismo (*☎ 024-623-2099*), Praça Santos Dumont 111 in Armação, is open 8 am to 6 pm on weekdays and 8 am to 4 pm on weekends. Pick up a copy of *Guia Verão Buzios* (US$4) at any newsstand. It provides information in English as well as Portuguese, including a list of places to stay.

Things to See & Do
In general, the southern beaches are trickier to get to, but they're prettier and have better surf. The northern beaches are more sheltered and closer to the settlements.

The schooner *Queen Lory* makes daily trips to Ilha Feia, Tartaruga and João Fernandinho. They offer a 2½-hour trip (US$15) and a five-hour trip (US$20). These trips are excellent values, especially since caipirinhas, soft drinks, fruit salad and snorkeling gear are included in the price. To make a reservation, ask at your pousada or visit Queen Lory Tours (*☎ 024-623-1179*), Rua Angela Diniz 35.

Places to Stay
Accommodations are expensive, especially in summer, so consider looking in Saquarema or Cabo Frio, or renting a house and staying a while. In the low season, however, you should be able to find a room as cheap as those in Cabo Frio or Arraial. In Armação, **Estalagem**(*☎ 024-623-1243*), Av José Bento Ribeiro 156, is right in the middle of the action. This is where Bardot stayed all those years ago. Doubles go for US$40 in low season and US$70 in high season.

The **Pousada Mediterrânea** (*☎ 024-623-2353*), Rua João Fernandes 58, is a whitewashed and tiled little hotel. Low-season doubles with a lovely inland view will cost you US$48.

Places to Eat

For good, cheap food, have grilled fish and a beer right on the beach. Brava, Ferradura and João Fernandes beaches have fish restaurants. Most of the better restaurants are in or near Armação. *Restaurante David*, Rua Manoel Turibe de Farias, is a good value – an ample US$8 prato feito usually includes shark fillet (*cassão*) with rice, beans and salad. *Chez Michou Crêperie*, on Rua das Pedras, makes almost any kind of crepe you want. The most happening bar in town is *Takatakata*, Av José Bento Ribeiro Dantas 144. Kijzer Van Derhoff is a showman as well as a barman, and his fiery concoctions are legendary.

Getting There & Away

Buses to Rio depart daily from the bus stop on Rua Turibe de Faria in Armação (US$11, three hours). From Cabo Frio to Búzios (Ossos), it's a 50-minute trip on the municipal bus.

Minas Gerais

The main attractions for visitors to this state are the national parks and historic gold-rush cities with their Baroque churches and sacred art, nestled into the Serra do Espinhaço.

BELO HORIZONTE

Belo Horizonte has nothing of special interest to the traveler. Mostly, those who stop here are on their way to Ouro Prêto or Diamantina. Belotur (☎ 031-277-7667), puts out a comprehensive monthly guide in Portuguese, English and French. It lists the main tourist attractions and how to get there using local buses. It also includes flight times and detailed long-distance bus schedules.

Belotur has booths at Confins airport (open daily from 8 am to 10 pm), and at the rodoviária and in front of the Parque Municipal (both open weekdays from 8 am to 8 pm and weekends from 8 am to 4 pm). Staff speak a bit of English and can also supply you with state tourist information.

Places to Stay

The youth hostel is your cheapest option, though it's a bit of a hike from the bus station. The *Pousadinha Mineira* (☎ 031-446-2911), Rua Araxá 514, has dormitory rooms for US$7.50 with an HI card, US$11 without one. It's open from 7 am to midnight. From the rodoviária, follow Av Santos Dumont to Rua Rio de Janeiro, then turn left and go up a couple of blocks to Av do Contorno. Cross it and follow Rua Varginha up a few blocks to Rua Araxá.

The *Pousada Beagá*, Rua Santa Catarina 597, is in the Lourdes district. From the rodoviária, follow Av Paraná to Rua dos Tupis and turn right, then turn left on Rua Santa Catarina. It's open from 7 am to 11 pm.

Two central places offer good deals on rooms: *Hotel Contijo* (☎ 031-272-1177), Rua Dos Tupinambás 731, with quartos (ask for a clean one until you get it) from US$18/31 singles/doubles, apartamentos for US$26/37; and the slightly nicer *Hotel Bragança* (☎ 031-212-6688), Av Paraná 109, with decent rooms for US$30/45.

The simple, well-kept *Hotel Magnata* (☎ 031-201-5368), Rua Guarani 124, is an island in the sleaze of the rodoviária's red-light district. It has apartamentos for US$24/35, but you can get them for a little less on slow days. It's strictly *familiar* – no rooms by the hour.

Places to Eat

At the southern end of Praça da Savassi is the popular *Cafeteria 3 Corações*, good for coffee and cakes. There are lots of lanchonetes and fast-food places clustered around Praça Sete. *Padaria Zona*, Av Parana 163, has super roast chickens for US$3 each. The *Demave Lanches* chain has a good outlet at Rua Dos Tupinambas 736. *Torino*, at Rua dos Tupinambas 253, has a wood-fired oven, varied menu and por kilo lunch.

There are wonderful vegetarian offerings at *Naturalis*, Rua Tome de Souza 689 in Savassi, with terrific set-lunch specials for about US$6, plus delicious fresh-squeezed juices.

Getting There & Away

Air There are flights from Belo's two airports to just about anywhere in Brazil, and frequent VASP, Varig, Transbrasil and TAM flights linking Belo with Rio, Brasilia, Vitória and São Paulo.

Bus Buses will take you to Rio (US$22, seven hours), São Paulo (US$25, 9½ hours), Brasília (US$24, 12 hours) and Salvador (US$57, about 22 hours). There are hourly departures for Ouro Prêto (US$6, 1¾ hours), and daily buses to Mariana (US$5, two hours), Diamantina (US$17, 5½ hours) and São João del Rei (US$11, 3½ hours).

CONGONHAS

Little is left of Congonhas' colonial past except for Aleijadinho's extraordinary *12 Prophets*. Aleijadinho, the son of a Portuguese architect and a black slave, lived from 1730 to 1814. He lost the use of his hands and legs at the age of 30, but with hammer and chisel strapped to his arms, he advanced Brazilian sculpture from the excesses of the baroque style to a finer, more graceful rococo. The *12 Prophets*, in front of the Basílica do Bom Jesus do Matosinhos, is his masterwork.

The town warrants a visit for these statues alone, but it's not worth staying here. With an early start, you can go by bus from São João del Rei to Congonhas, spend a few hours at the *12 Prophets*, then go on to Conselheiro Lafaiete and Ouro Prêto (or vice versa), all in one day.

Getting There & Away

There are six buses daily from Belo Horizonte to Congonhas (US$6, 1¾ hours). The last bus returning to Belo Horizonte leaves Congonhas at 8:20 pm. Buses leave every 45 minutes for Conselheiro Lafaiete. To get from Congonhas to Ouro Prêto, you can go to Belo Horizonte or make a connection in Conselheiro Lafaiete.

To get from Congonhas to São João del Rei, catch one of the Belo Horizonte to São João del Rei buses that stop off at Congonhas. There are seven a day, between 7:30 am and 8:20 pm.

OURO PRÊTO

Vila Rica, the predecessor of Ouro Prêto, was founded in 1711, in the early days of the gold rush. It became the capital of Minas Gerais in 1721. At the height of the boom, in the mid-18th century, the city had a population of 110,000 and was the richest in the Americas.

As the boom declined, however, miners found it more and more difficult to pay the ever-increasing gold taxes exacted by the Portuguese crown. In 1789, the Inconfidência Mineira, an attempt to overthrow the Portuguese, was crushed in its early stages.

By decree of Emperor Dom Pedro I, Vila Rica became the Imperial City of Ouro Prêto. In 1897, the state capital moved from Ouro Prêto to Belo Horizonte, thus preserving Ouro Prêto's colonial flavor. It's now a university town.

Orientation

Praça Tiradentes, a few blocks down from the rodoviária on the main road, is the town center. The town is very hilly and the rain-slicked, cobblestone streets are steep. Bring good walking shoes.

Information

The tourist office, Praça Tiradentes 41, is open from 8 am to 6 pm on weekdays, and from 8 am to 5 pm on weekends. The friendly staff speaks English, provides leaflets, sells maps and arranges guides. It also has a complete list of places to stay, including the cheapest, and they'll ring around to find a vacancy for you.

To pack in a lot of sightseeing with little effort, hire an official guide (US$30 for a four-hour tour) at the tourist office. Cássio speaks excellent English and really knows his Baroque. The tourist office also organizes treks into the surrounding hills and horseback rides to Itacolomy. Either costs around US$50 for the day. Speak to João, Alexandre or Renaldo a day before you wish to go, to give them enough time to get the horses ready.

If you plan to spend only one day in Ouro Prêto, make sure it's not a Monday, when virtually everything is closed.

Things to See & Do

To see the town properly, you'll need a couple of days. Keep quirky opening times in mind when planning your itinerary.

The **Museu da Inconfidência**, on Praça Tiradentes, was formerly the municipal building and jail. It contains Tiradentes' tomb, documents of the Inconfidência Mineira, torture instruments and important works by Ataíde and Aleijadinho. Also on Praça Tiradentes, in the old governor's palace, the **Escola de Minas** has a very fine museum of mineralogy.

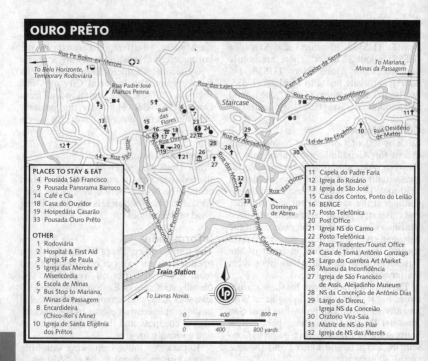

OURO PRÊTO

PLACES TO STAY & EAT
4 Pousada Saõ Francisco
9 Pousada Panorama Barroco
14 Café e Cia
18 Casa do Ouvidor
19 Hospedária Casarão
33 Pousada Ouro Prêto

OTHER
1 Rodoviária
2 Hospital & First Aid
3 Igreja SF de Paula
5 Igreja das Mercês e Misericórdia
6 Escola de Minas
7 Bus Stop to Mariana, Minas da Passagem
8 Encardideira (Chico-Rei's Mine)
10 Igreja de Santa Efigênia dos Prêtos
11 Capela do Padre Faria
12 Igreja do Rosário
13 Igreja de São José
15 Casa dos Contos, Ponto do Leilão
16 BEMGE
17 Posto Telefônica
20 Post Office
21 Igreja NS do Carmo
22 Posto Telefônica
23 Praça Tiradentes/Tourist Office
24 Casa de Tomá Antônio Gonzaga
25 Largo do Coimbra Art Market
26 Museu da Inconfidência
27 Igreja de São Francisco de Assis, Aleijadinho Museum
28 NS da Conceição de Antônio Días
29 Largo do Dirceu, Igreja NS da Conceião
30 Oratorio Vira-Saia
31 Matriz de NS do Pilar
32 Igreja de NS das Mercês

There are many magnificent churches in Ouro Prêto. **Matriz NS da Conceição de António Dias** and **Matriz de NS do Pilar** are the cathedrals of two parishes. The **Igreja de Santa Efigênia dos Prêtos** was built by and for the black slave community. The **Igreja de São Francisco de Assis** has exterior carvings by Aleijadinho and is particularly interesting.

Places to Stay & Eat

Student lodgings, known as *repúblicas*, are the cheapest accommodations, but they are usually closed from Christmas to Carnaval. Another problem with repúblicas is their lack of security. Regular lodging tends to be expensive and scarce on weekends, holidays and during exam periods.

The two cheapest pousadas have great views. The best deal in town is the ***Pousada São Francisco,*** Rua Padre José Marcos Penna 202 next to the Igreja de São Francisco de Paula (*not* São Francisco de Assis). It has absolutely spectacular views and seriously friendly staff. Spotless dormitory beds are US$10 per person (US$15 with view); apartamentos are US$20/30 for singles/

doubles. There's a communal kitchen and breakfast is included. From the rodoviária, walk 100m down the hill to the church; facing downhill, look for the break in the fence on the left and follow the path down to the pousada. If you pass the church you've missed the turn.

The ***Pousada Panorama Barroco*** (☎ 031-551-2582), Rua Conselheiro Quintiliano 722, northeast of the center, charges US$10 per person in quartos, plus US$4 for breakfast.

Hospedaria Casarão (☎ 031-551-2056), at Rua Direita 94-B, is a family home above a store. There are eight rooms costing US$10 per person.

A fine bet is the ***Pousada Ouro Prêto*** (☎ 031-551-3081), Largo Musicista José das Anjos Costa (also called das Mercês) 72, right below the Igreja NS das Mercês. It's a friendly place and Gerson, who runs it, speaks English. It has a fantastic view and all the comforts that delight the traveler. Apartamentos cost US$30/50/60 for singles/doubles/triples.

The typical dish of Minas is tutu a mineira, a black-bean feijoada. ***Restaurante***

Casa Do Ouvidor, on Rua Direita, is the place to try it. If the mineiro food is a bit heavy for you, *Café e Cia*, Rua São José 187, has good sandwiches and a great view of the town. It also has a por-kilo buffet lunch.

Getting There & Away

There are frequent bus connections between Belo Horizonte and Ouro Prêto (US$6, 1¾ hours). During the peak tourist period, buy bus tickets at least a day in advance. One bus a day goes to Rio, at 11 pm (US$19, seven hours).

MARIANA

Mariana is a beautiful old mining town founded in 1696. Only 12km from Ouro Prêto, it's much less touristy than its neighbor, and a great place to unwind. The **18th-century churches** of São Pedro dos Clérigos, NS da Assunção and São Francisco, and the Catedral Basílica da Sé, with its fantastic German organ dating from 1701, are all worthwhile. The **museum** at Casa Capitular is also worth a look. Walking through the old part of town, you'll come across painters and wood sculptors at work in their studios.

Places to Stay & Eat

Hotel Providência (☎ 031-557-1444), Rua Dom Silveiro 233, is an interesting cheapie. It was originally the living quarters for nuns, who still run a school next door. It also has an excellent swimming pool. Quartos are US$15 per person, apartamentos US$20/32 singles/doubles. *Hotel Central* (☎ 031-557-1630), Rua Frei Durão 8, is a real budget hotel, with quartos for US$15/27. The best hotel in town is the *Pouso da Typographia* (☎ 031-557-1577), at Praça Gomes Freire 220. Apartamentos cost US$50/80, but discounts are available during the week.

Frango na Brasa Lua Cheia, Rua Dom Viçoso 23, is a good value. Near the town square, there are wonderful breads and sweets at *Pão Pão Restaurante*. *Tambaú* also has good regional food at reasonable prices.

Getting There & Away

A bus leaves Ouro Prêto for Mariana every half hour from the far side of the Escola de Minas (US$0.85, 35 minutes).

SÃO JOÃO DEL REI

Unlike many of the other historic cities in Minas Gerais, São João del Rei has not been frozen in time. The old central section, with its fine churches and colonial mansions, is surrounded by a small but thriving modern city.

The city is sandwiched between two hills, both of which provide excellent views, particularly at sunset. The tourist office (☎ 032-379-2952) is at Praça Frei Orlando 90, in front of the Igreja São Francisco. It's open from 8 am to 5 pm.

Things to See & Do

The exquisite Baroque **Igreja de São Francisco de Assis** looks out on a lyre-shaped plaza lined with palm trees. This church was Aleijadinho's first complete project, though much of his plan was not realized. It is open 8 am to noon.

The **Igreja de NS do Carmo** was also designed by Aleijadinho. In the second sacristy is a famous unfinished sculpture of Christ. The church is open 8 to 11 am and 4 to 7 pm. The **Catedral de NS do Pilar** has exuberant gold altars and fine azulejos. It's open from 8 to 11 am. Make sure to take a walk at night, when floodlights illuminate the churches.

One of the best museums in Minas Gerais is the **Museu Regional do SPHAN**, a well-restored colonial mansion (1859). It has sacred art on the first two floors and an industrial section on the 3rd floor. It's open from noon to 5:30 pm daily, except Monday.

A must for railroad fanatics is the **Museu Ferroviário**, in the train station. This expertly renovated railway museum houses a wealth of artifacts and information about the trains of the late 19th century. Don't forget to walk down the track to the large roundhouse; it's the best part. The museum is open 9:30 to 11:30 am and 1:30 to 5 pm Tuesday to Sunday. Entry costs US$1. See also the discussion of the 'Maria Fumaça' (Smoking Mary) train in the Getting There & Away section later in this chapter.

Special Events

The Semana da Inconfidência, from 15 to 21 April, celebrates Brazil's first independence movement and the locals who led it. São João also has a very lively Carnaval.

BRAZIL

Places to Stay & Eat

There is a good stock of inexpensive hotels in the old section of the city, right where you want to be. The once-grand *Hotel Brasil* (☎ *032-371-2804*), Av Presidente Tancredo Neves 395, faces the river and is a real bargain at US$10 per person, US$15 in apartamentos.

Another good cheapie option is the *Aparecida Hotel* (☎ *032-371-2540*), Praça Dr Antônio Viegas 13, with quartos for US$10 per person and apartamentos for US$20/30 singles/doubles.

The *Hotel Hespanhol* (☎ *032-371-7677*), Rua Marechal Deodoro 131, offers clean and relatively spacious quartos for US$15/29 and apartamentos for US$30/48.

Canecão Lanches, Praça Dr Antônio Viegas, is a great lanchonete and super-cheap juice bar – a huge mixed fruit milkshake is US$0.80. It has sandwiches and snacks, too.

Getting There & Away

Bus Buses leave Rio direct for São João three times daily (US$20, 5½ hours). There are seven buses a day from São João to Belo Horizonte (US$11, 3½ hours) This is also the bus to Congonhas (US$6, two hours).

Train Chugging along at 25km/h on the steam-powered Maria Fumaça, down a picturesque stretch of track from São João to Tiradentes, makes a great half-hour train ride. The line has operated nonstop since 1881 with the same Baldwin locomotives and has been restored to perfect condition. The train runs only on Friday, Saturday, Sunday and holidays, leaving São João at 10 am and 2:15 pm and returning from Tiradentes at 1:20 and 5 pm. Arrive early to buy your one-way/roundtrip ticket for US$6.60/13.20. Going to Tiradentes, sit on the left-hand side for a better view.

Getting Around

Local buses get you from the small bus stop in front of the train station to the rodoviária in 10 minutes. To get to the center from the rodoviária, catch any yellow bus (US$0.50) from the stop to your left as you walk out (in front of the butcher), not from the more obvious stop directly in front.

TIRADENTES

This very pretty town, 10km down the valley from São João del Rei, has changed little over the last two centuries. The best source of English-language information is John Parsons, an Englishman, who owns the Solar da Ponte hotel. If you call in advance (☎ 032-355-1255) he can help with information about the town's excellent hiking and horseback riding opportunities, even if you don't stay at his hotel.

Things to See & Do

Named after the town's patron saint, the **Igreja Matriz de Santo Antônio** stands on top of the hill. There are two bell towers, and a frontispiece by Aleijadinho, who also made the sundial in front of the church. The church is open from 8 am to 5 pm, but usually closes from noon to 1 pm for lunch.

The **Museu do Padre Toledo** is dedicated to another hero of the Inconfidência, Padre Toledo. He lived in this 18-room house where the *inconfidêntes* used to meet. The museum features regional antiques and documents from the 18th century.

From the beautiful **Chafariz de São José** fountain, it's a 3km walk (25 minutes) to Mãe d'Agua, at the base of the **Serra de São José**, a range renowned for its untouched segments of Atlantic rain forest. Other walks include A Calçada (a stretch of the old road that linked Ouro Prêto with Rio de Janeiro), Cachoeiras do Mangue (the falls where you can see an old gold mine) and Cachoeira do Bom Despacho (a waterfall on the road from Tiradentes to Santa Cruz). Each of these walks takes four or five hours. A seven-hour walk will allow you to cross the range. For guides and information about walks into the mountains, ask at the tourist office.

Places to Stay

Tiradentes has lots of good but expensive pousadas and only a few cheap places. If you can't find anything within your budget, ask around for homes to stay in, or commute from São João del Rei. Try to avoid staying in Tiradentes on the weekend as it gets crowded and prices double.

Pousada do Laurito is the best cheapie in town, with a good central location and singles/doubles for US$18/27. Next to the bus station, *Pousada Tiradentes* (☎ *032-355-1232*) has charm and costs US$15/30. *Quatro Encantos,* near the Santo Antônio church, has a great little garden and charges around US$35/45. The *Porão Colonial* (☎ 032-355-1251) is near the train station. It has a pool and charges US$28/40.

Getting There & Away

The way to get to Tiradentes is by train from São João del Rei (see the section on that city for details). Buses come and go between São João and Tiradentes every 40 minutes. They run slightly less frequently on weekend afternoons.

SÃO TOMÉ DAS LETRAS

São Tomé das Letras is a small village in a beautiful mountainous region of southern Minas, 310km from Belo Horizonte. The name refers to inscriptions in some of the local caverns. These have inspired strange stories of flying saucers, extraterrestrials and a subterranean passageway to Machu Picchu. There are also great walks and several waterfalls.

Places to Stay & Eat

The run-down *Pousada Mahã-Mantra* (☎ 035-989-5563), 10m behind the stone church, is the cheapest cot in town at US$5 per person without breakfast. Camping at *Gruta do Leão*, which is supposedly stocked with enchanted water, costs US$3 per person.

The spotlessly clean *Pousada Reino dos Magos* (☎ 035-237-1300), Rua Gabriel Luiz Alvarez 27, has dorm and private rooms for US$15 per person.

The *Hospedaria Dos Sonhos I* (☎ 035-237-1235), Rua Gabriel Luiz Alvarez 28, has private rooms for US$17 per person with breakfast. It's even nicer than the *Hospedaria Dos Sonhos II* (same ☎), under the same management and with similar prices, right near the stone church.

Ximan, Rua Camilo Rios 12, has awesome hot foods and salads. *Bar do Gê*, Rua Gabriel Luiz Alves 28, is another surprisingly good restaurant. The bar *All Days of Peace and Music Woodstock*, in Rua Camilo Rios, is a good place to meet people who've seen UFOs.

Getting There & Away

The town is best reached from Três Corações, 38km to the west. Buses (US$2.75) leave at 6 and 11 am and 3:30 pm Monday to Saturday, and on Sunday at 7 am and 2 pm.

There are several buses a day from São João del Rei to Três Corações (US$4.50, 2¼ hours).

DIAMANTINA

Diamantina boomed when diamonds were discovered in the 1720s, shortly after the gold finds in Minas. The diamonds are gone, but fine colonial mansions and excellent hiking in the surrounding mountains still draw visitors.

The house of Padre Rolim, one of the inconfidêntes, is now the **Museu do Diamante** (Diamond Museum) and houses furniture, coins, instruments of torture and other relics of the diamond days. It's open from noon to 5:30 pm daily except Monday. The **Igreja NS do Carmo**, built in 1758, is the most opulent church in town.

Places to Stay & Eat

The *Hotel Nosson* (☎ 038-531-1565), opposite the bus station, is a classic cheapie (US$9 per person), but it's a long uphill walk from the center. For a bit extra, the *Hotel Dália* (☎ 038-531-1477), Praça Juscelino Kubitschek 25, is much better. It's in a nice old building in a good location, almost next door to the diamond museum. Quartos cost US$20/35 singles/doubles and apartamentos go for US$25/40. Romantic cheapies can be had at the charming *Pousada Dos Cristais* (☎ 038-531-2897), Rua Jogo de Bola 53, with clean quartos (with separate but private bath) for US$15 per person and apartamentos from US$20/35.

A popular pick of Diamantina's eateries is the *Cantinha do Marinho*, Beco do Motta 27, with good mineiro dishes and a cheap buffet lunch. *Restaurante Grupiara*, Rua Campos Carvalho 12, is also recommended.

Getting There & Away

There are six buses running daily between Diamantina and Belo Horizonte (US$17, five hours).

São Paulo State

São Paulo is the industrial engine that powers Brazil's economy: Thirty of Brazil's 50 largest companies are in São Paulo, as is 50% of the nation's industry. Unfortunately, government mismanagement in recent years has left the state almost bankrupt and unable to finance vital infrastructure projects.

SÃO PAULO

With more than 20 million inhabitants, the city of São Paulo is South America's biggest. Its extraordinary growth over the past century has been boosted by migration from both inside and outside Brazil, encouraged by the area's industrial development. Rapid growth has created massive problems, including traffic congestion, pollution and housing shortages. Compared to the rest of Brazil, São Paulo is expensive, and shoestring travelers should prepare for a shock.

Orientation

São Paulo is a difficult city in which to orient yourself. The solution is to go underground: São Paulo's subway system (metro) is one of the best in the world. Pick up *Veja* at a newsstand or go to a tourism booth for a good list of attractions.

As a city of immigrants, certain districts of São Paulo are associated with the nationalities that settled there. Liberdade, just south of Praça da Sé, is the Asian area. Bela Vista and nearby Bixiga are Italian. Bom Retiro, near Estação da Luz train station (the metro also runs through here is the old Jewish quarter. A large Arab community is based around Rua 25 de Março, to the north of Praça da Sé. In all these areas, you'll find restaurants that match the tastes of their inhabitants.

Av Paulista, to the southwest of the center, is an avenue of skyscrapers. The adjoining district of Cerqueira César contains the city's highest concentration of good restaurants, cafés and nightclubs. When people refer to São Paulo as the 'New York of the Tropics,' this is the area they have in mind. Adjoining Cerqueira César is the stylish Jardins Paulista district, home to many of the city's middle- and upper-class residents.

Information

Tourist Offices The city's tourist information booths have excellent city and state maps. They are also good for bus and metro information. The tourist information booth on Praça da República (along Av Ipiranga) is helpful; members of the staff speak English, French, Italian and Spanish. It's open 9 am to 6 pm daily. The phone number for the main tourist office is ☎ 011-267-2122, ext 627 (ext 640 on weekends).

Other tourist offices are at Av Paulista, near MASP (open 9 am to 6 pm); Av São Luís, on the corner of Praça Dom José Gaspar (open 9 am to 6 pm daily) and Aeroporto de Congonhas (open 24 hours a day). There is also a tourist information booth in front of the shopping center Iguatemi.

Money There are several travel agencies and casas de câmbio across from the airline offices on Av São Luis, close to Praça da República. Most banks in this area have foreign-exchange counters.

Post & Communications The main post office is on Praça do Correio. The posta restante service downstairs holds mail for 30 days. Fax services are available in the same building. The Telesp long-distance telephone office is close to Praça da República, on the Ipiranga side.

Bookstores For an OK selection of English books, visit the Book Center, at Rua Gabus Mendes 29 (near Praça da República), or Livraria Cultura at Av Paulista 2073. Livraria Francesa at Rua Barão de Itapetininga 275 deals exclusively with books in French. Other bookstores include Agencia Siciliano, at Av Pereira de Megalhaes 3305 and Laselva Comercial, Rua Gomez de Carvalho 243.

Emergency Deatur, the English-speaking tourist police service, has two offices in the city: Av São Luis 115 (☎ 011-214-0209) and Rua 15 de Novembro (☎ 011-607-8332). They're closed on weekends. For serious health problems, Einstein Hospital (☎ 011-845-1233) is one of the best in Latin America.

Dangers & Annoyances Pickpockets and bag-snatchers are common around Praça da Sé: Don't carry valuables. Be careful in the center at night, and around the cheap hotels in Rua Santa Efigênia.

Things to See & Do

The **Museu de Arte de São Paulo** (MASP) is at Av Paulista 1578. It has a good collection of European art and some great Brazilian paintings. The museum is open 9 am to 9 pm

CENTRAL SÃO PAULO

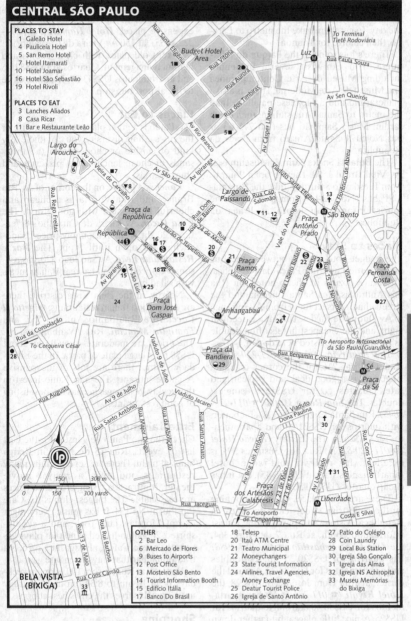

PLACES TO STAY
1 Galeão Hotel
4 Pauliceia Hotel
5 San Remo Hotel
7 Hotel Itamarati
10 Hotel Joamar
16 Hotel São Sebastião
19 Hotel Rivoli

PLACES TO EAT
3 Lanches Aliados
8 Casa Ricar
11 Bar e Restaurante Leão

OTHER
2 Bar Leo
6 Mercado de Flores
9 Buses to Airports
12 Post Office
13 Mosteiro São Bento
14 Tourist Information Booth
15 Edifício Itália
17 Banco Do Brasil
18 Telesp
20 Itaú ATM Centre
21 Teatro Municipal
22 Moneychangers
23 State Tourist Information
24 Airlines, Travel Agencies, Money Exchange
25 Deatur Tourist Police
26 Igreja de Santo Antônio
27 Patío do Colégio
28 Coin Laundry
29 Local Bus Station
30 Igreja São Gonçalo
31 Igreja das Almas
32 Igreja NS Achiropita
33 Museu Memórias do Bixiga

BRAZIL

Tuesday to Sunday; on Thursday, entry is free. Go early, as the light can be bad late in the day. To get there, take the metro to Paraiso, then change for Trianon.

There's lots to do in the **Parque do Ibirapuera**. You can visit several museums, including Museu de Arte Contemporânea and Museu de Arte Moderna. There is also a planetarium and a Japanese pavilion. Take the metro to Santa Cruz station, then catch Jardim Maria Sampião bus (No 775-C) or bus No 5121 Santo Amaro from Praça da República.

The **Butantã Snake Farm & Museum** is at Av Vital Brasil 1500. They're open 9 am to 5 pm Tuesday to Saturday. Take the Butantã-USP bus (No 702-U) from in front of the tourist information booth at Praça da República.

Places to Stay

The budget hotel area is between the Luz metro station and the Praça da República. There are dozens of cheap hotels on Rua dos Andradas, Rua Santa Efigênia and the streets that intersect them from Av Ipiranga to Av Duque de Caxias. This area is seedy at night, and the cheapest hotels often double as brothels. Those listed here do not.

The *Pauliceía Hotel* (☎ 011-220-9733), Rua Timbiras 216 (at the corner of Santa Efigênia), is a good deal, and is clean and safe. Quartos go for US$15/25 singles/ doubles. The *San Remo Hotel* (☎ 011-229-6845), Rua Santa Efigênia 163, is a bit better, with quartos for US$21/28 and apartamentos for US$25/35. The friendly *Galeão Hotel* (☎ 011-220-8211), Rua dos Gusmões 394, is excellent. It's really a mid-range hotel (apartamentos start at US$28/45), but it has cheap quartos (US$20/30).

There are a few places worth mentioning on the pedestrian streets close to Praça da República. A stone's throw from the tourist information booth, at Rua 7 de Abril 364, the *Hotel São Sebastião* (☎ 011-257-4988) has quartos for US$20/25 singles/doubles and apartamentos for US$28/33. Around the corner, at Rua Dom José de Barros 28, the *Hotel Rivoli* (☎ 011-231-5633) has apartamentos for US$30/40 and single quartos for US$25. A nice little place a bit farther down at No 187 is *Hotel Joamar* (☎ 011-221-3611), with apartamentos for US$28/35.

On the other side of Praça da República, on Av Vieira de Carvalho, are some more expensive places. *Hotel Itamarati* (☎ 011-222-4133), at 150 Av Vieira de Carvalho, is a well-kept old place, with clean rooms and helpful management. Quartos are US$32/46 and apartamentos US$43/57. It's quite close to the airport bus stop.

Places to Eat

São Paulo is a great place to eat. Because of the city's ethnic diversity, you can find every kind of cuisine or choose from the thousands of cheap lanchonetes, pizzerias and churrascarias.

Lanches Aliados, on the corner of Av Rio Branco and Rua Vitória, is a cheap and cheerful lanchonete with good food. The *Casa Ricar*, Av Vieira de Carvalho 48, features 20 different reasonably-priced sandwiches. It's open until 7 pm. The *Bar e Restaurante Leão*, Av São João 320, has reasonably priced all-you-can-eat Italian meals with salad bar.

Nearby, in the Bela Vista district, there are some good Italian restaurants: *Gigetto Il Cacciatore*, Rua Santo Antônio 855, and *Famiglia Mancini*, Rua Avanhandava 81. The prices are moderate – you'll pay about US$8 for a large plate of pasta. In the Liberdade district there are lots of inexpensive Asian restaurants. The São Paulo insert in the weekly *Veja* magazine has the best listing of good restaurants.

Entertainment

Check the São Paulo *Veja* insert for the best list of events. Rua 13 de Maio in Bixiga hums at night. There are several clubs, many restaurants and even a revival movie theater. It attracts a young crowd, so prices are reasonable. The biggest club is the Café Piu-Piu, at No 134. It has music every night except Monday: jazz, rock, and a sequin-shirted, 20-gallon-hatted band that plays US country music. Café do Bixiga, at No 76, is a traditional bar that stays open late.

Bar Leo, at Rua Aurora 100, is open weekdays from 10 am to 8:30 pm and Saturday until 3 pm. It serves the city's best chopp.

Shopping

Shopping is almost as important to paulistanos as eating out. Much more interesting than the endless shopping malls are the many markets and fairs that take place around town, especially on weekends. One of the most popular is held in the Praça da República, 8 am to 2 pm on Sunday. Liberdade, the Oriental district (only 5 minutes from the center by metro), also has a big street fair all day on Sunday. An excellent handicraft market takes place every weekend in Embu, 28km from São Paulo.

Getting There & Away

Air There are flights from São Paulo to anywhere in Brazil and many of the world's major cities. Before buying your ticket, check which airport the flight departs from; see the Getting Around section for details. The São Paulo to Rio shuttle flies at least every half-hour from Congonhas airport to Santos Dumont airport in central Rio. The flight takes less than an hour, and you can usually go to the airport, buy a US$150 ticket and be on a plane within the hour.

Most major airlines have offices on Av São Luis, near the Praça da República.

Bus Terminal Tietê is easy to reach – it's connected to the Tietê metro station. It's an enormous but easily navigated building. There's an information desk in the middle of the main concourse. Bus tickets are sold on the 1st floor.

Buses leave for destinations throughout Brazil, as well as to major cities in Argentina, Paraguay, Chile and Uruguay.

All of the following buses leave from the Terminal Tietê. Frequent buses traverse the Via Dutra highway to Rio (429km, six hours). It costs US$15 for the regular bus, US$22 for the leito. There are also buses to Brasília (US$48, 14 hours), Foz do Iguaçu (US$45, 15 hours), Cuiabá (US$62, 23 hours), Campo Grande (US$62, 15 hours), Salvador (US$85, 32 hours), Curitiba (US$19, six hours) and Florianópolis (US$32, 12 hours).

Buses to Santos, Guarujá and São Vicente leave every five minutes from a separate bus station at the end of the southern metro line (Jabaquara station). Buses to Minas Gerais (Belo Horizonte, US$25, 9½ hours) leave from Rodoviária Bresser; take the metro to Bresser.

Getting Around

To/From the Airport Three airports serve São Paulo: Aeroporto de Congonhas (14km south of the center), Aeroporto Internacional de São Paulo/Guarulhos (30km east of the center) and Aeroporto Viracopos (97km from the center, near Campinas).

At Congonhas, avoid the radio-taxis at the front of the terminal and ask for the comums; there's a small sign marking the stop. The ride into town is about US$12. To catch a bus into the city, walk out of the terminal and to your right, where you'll see a busy street with a pedestrian overpass. Head to the overpass, but don't cross; you should see a crowd of people waiting for the buses along the street – ask for the Banderas bus. The trip takes about an hour, and the last bus leaves around 1 am.

From Aeroporto Internacional de São Paulo/Guarulhos, there's a bus that goes to Praça da República, Terminal Tietê rodoviária and Congonhas airport. It costs US$12. For the same price, another bus does a circuit of upmarket hotels in the Jardims area and the center. The cheapest alternative is to catch the local EMTU bus (US$1.50) to the Bresser bus terminal and then catch the metro to your destination. From Guarulhos to the center, a comum taxi will cost US$36, a radio-taxi US$50.

Avoid Aeroporto Viracopos if possible. A taxi from here into town will cost about US$90.

Bus Buses are slow, crowded during rush hours and not too safe. When you can, use the metro.

Metro If you're on a limited budget, a combination of walking and hopping the metro is the best way to see the city. The metro, open from 5 am to midnight, is modern, cheap, safe and fast. There are currently three lines. Two intersect at Praça da Sé; the other line runs under Av Paulista. Tickets cost US$1.25 for a single ride, or buy a *multiplo 10*, which gives you 10 rides for US$10.

Taxi Both the comum and radio-taxi services are metered. Radio-taxis (☎ 011-251-1733) cost 40% more than the comums but will pick you up anywhere in the city.

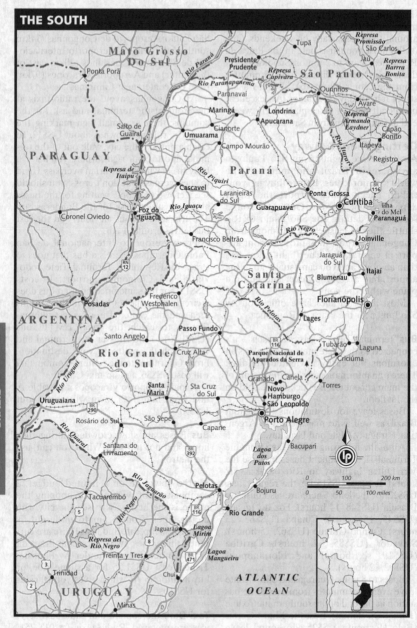

THE SOUTH

Paraná

CURITIBA

Curitiba, the capital of Paraná, is one of Brazil's urban success stories. There's not much for the traveler, but it's possible to spend a pleasant day waiting for your bus or train to leave.

Information

The Departamento de Turismo (☎ 041-352-4021), on the 3rd floor at Rua da Glória 362, has English- and French-speaking staff. They offer a useful map and some brochures about the city's attractions. There are also branches in the airport, Rua 24 Horas, and Galeria Schaffer.

Largo da Ordem

Close to Praça Tiradentes and the Catedral Metropolitana, take the pedestrian tunnel and you'll be in the cobblestoned historical quarter, Largo da Ordem. It's a good place for a drink and some music at night.

Train Ride to Paranaguá

The railway journey from Curitiba to the port of Paranaguá, descending a steep mountainside to the coastal lowlands, is the most exciting and spectacular in Brazil.

There are two types of train: a regular train *(trem)* and a tourist train *(litorina)*. The trem (US$15 one-way) runs to Paranaguá at 8 am and returns at 4 pm from Tuesday to Sunday, stopping at every station along the way. The air-con litorina (US$25/40) leaves Curitiba at 9 am and starts back at 3:30 pm. Both trains take about three hours each way. For the best view on the way to the coast, sit on the left-hand side.

Tickets for the trem and the litorina are sold at the train station behind the rodoviária. Buy them as far in advance as possible. Getting tickets during the week should be no problem, except during January and on holidays. For information, call ☎ 041-323-4007 in Curitiba.

Places to Stay

Across from the rodoferroviária, there are lots of inexpensive hotels. *Hotel Imperio* (☎ 041-264-3373), Av Presidente Afonso Camargo 367, is very clean and friendly.

Quartos cost US$15/25 singles/doubles. Another good one to head for is the *Hotel Itamarati* (☎ 041-222-9063), Rua Tibagi 950, with quartos for US$17/30 and apartamentos for US$30/42.

A good mid-range alternative in the center is the *Cervantes Hotel* (☎ 041-222-9593), Travessa Alfredo Bufren 35. It has old-world charm and comfortable apartamentos with TV and fridge for US$26/48.

Places to Eat

The *Vherdejante* vegetarian restaurant, Rua Presidente Faria 481, has good fixed-price buffet lunches and is open daily except Sunday. In Rua 24 Horas, there are several places: *Le Lasagne* serves five types of lasagne in individual portions for US$6, while *Le Mignon* serves a varied menu, with cheap 'chef's suggestions.' The *Schaffer*, Rua das Flores 424, is a classic Curitiban confeitaria famous for its coffee and cakes.

Getting There & Away

Air There are flights from Alfonso Pena Airport to all major cities in Brazil.

Bus The entrance to the rodoferroviária is on Av Presidente Afonso Camargo. There are several daily buses to São Paulo (US$19, six hours), Rio (US$40, 12 hours) and all major cities to the south. There are 13 buses a day to Foz do Iguaçu (US$30 regular and US$64 leito). From Curitiba, you can also get direct buses to Asunción (US$37), Buenos Aires (US$82) and Santiago (US$122).

Train See earlier in the Curitiba section for information on scenic train rides to the port of Paranaguá.

Getting Around

Alfonso Pena airport is 17km from the city. An Aeroporto bus leaves every half hour from outside the Hotel Promenade, on the corner of Av 7 de Setembro and Rua Mariano Torres. A taxi to the airport costs about US$25.

PARANAGUÁ

The train ride isn't the only reason to go to Paranaguá. It's a colorful city, with an old section near the waterfront that has a feeling of tropical decadence. Paranaguá also

CURITIBA

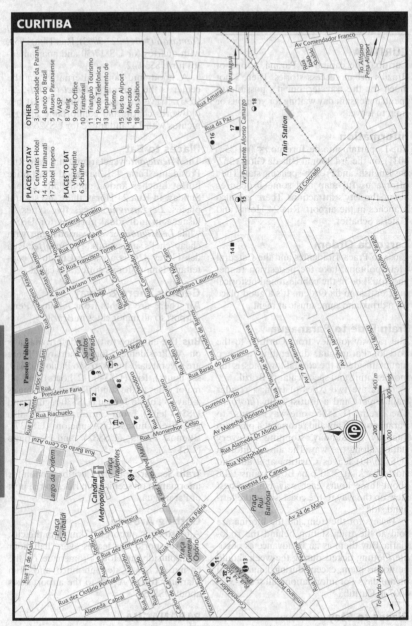

PLACES TO STAY
2   Cervantes Hotel
14 Hotel Itamarati
17 Hotel Imperio

PLACES TO EAT
1   Vherdejante
6   Schaffer

OTHER
3   Universidade da Paraná
4   Banco do Brasil
5   Museu Paranaense
7   VASP
8   Varig
9   Post Office
10 Transbrasil
11 Triangulo Tourismo
12 Posto Telefonica
13 Departamento de
    Turismo
15 Bus to Airport
16 Mercado
18 Bus Station

provides access to Ilha do Mel. There's a tourist office in front of the train station.

Museu de Arqueologia e Etnologia

Don't miss this museum at Rua 15 de Novembro 567, in the old section near the waterfront. Housed in a beautifully restored Jesuit school, the museum has many Indian artifacts, primitive and folk art, and some fascinating old tools and machines. It's open noon to 5 pm from Tuesday to Sunday.

Places to Stay & Eat

The cheapest places are along the waterfront, on Rua General Carneiro, but this area is dark and nearly deserted at night, so you need to be careful. *Hotel Karibe*(☎ 041-423-4377), Rua Fernando Simas 86, has bright quartos for US$10 per person with a good breakfast. The *Hotel Litoral* (☎ 041-423-1734), Rua Correia de Freitas 66, offers the best deal in town. Its rooms are large and open onto a sunny courtyard. Singles/doubles are US$10/15.

Restaurante Bobby, Rua Faria Sobrinho 750, has excellent seafood for only US$7 a meal. The *Mercado Municipal do Café* is a good place to have lunch. It's been restored and contains five small restaurants, all serving cheap seafood.

Getting There & Away

All long-distance buses leave from the rodoviária on the waterfront. There are frequent buses to Curitiba (US$5.50, 1½ hours). If you're going south, 12 buses a day go to Guaratuba, where you can catch another bus to Joinville.

For details of the train ride between Paranaguá and Curitiba, see the Curitiba section.

ILHA DO MEL

Ilha do Mel is an oddly shaped island at the mouth of the Baía de Paranaguá. It is popular in summer because of its excellent surf beaches, scenic walks and relative isolation.

Ilha do Mel consists of two parts connected by the beach at Nova Brasília. The larger side is an ecological station, little visited except for Praia da Fortaleza. The main attractions of the island are close to Nova Brasília. On the ocean side (east) are the best beaches – Praia Grande, Praia do Miguel and Praia de Fora. The best walks are also along the ocean side, from the southern tip of the island up to Praia da Fortaleza. There are bichos de pé, so keep your shoes on when you're off the sand.

Places to Stay & Eat

If you arrive on the island on a holiday weekend or during peak season, rooms may be in short supply, but it's easy to rent some space to sling a hammock. There's also plenty of room to camp. If you decide to crash out on the beach, watch out for the tides.

There are plenty of camping areas on the island: Just about every second backyard in Praia dos Encantadas, Nova Brasília, and Praia Farol das Conchas is designated for camping. All have electricity and water and cost US$3 per person. You're not supposed to camp outside designated areas.

There are pousadas at Nova Brasília, Praia da Fortaleza, Praia Farol and Praia dos Encantadas. Prices range from US$10 per person for simple quartos to US$40 for doubles. During high season, prices go up 20% to 50%. *Pousadinho* (☎ 041-978-3662) is highly recommended. The staff speaks French, English and Italian. Low-season prices are US$30 for a double quarto and US$40 for a double apartamento.

At Praia da Fortaleza, 200m past the fort, there are a few accommodations. Try the *Pousada dos Prazeres*(☎ 041-978-3221) with rooms for US$30 per person with all meals. Pousada do Barata (☎ 041-978-3795) has small quartos for US$25 per person with all meals.

At Praia dos Encantadas, there are several beachfront places. *Pousada Estrela do Mar* (☎ 041-991-9296) has good-value, clean quartos for US$15/30 with a breakfast. The *Pousada Ilha Verde* (☎ 041-978-2829) has quartos for US$20 per person and double apartamentos for US$50 in a pleasant garden setting.

You will find barracas with food and drink at Encantadas, Brasília and Fortaleza. There is music and dancing on Friday and Saturday night.

Getting There & Away

Boats for Nova Brasília and Praia dos Encantadas leave from Paranaguá at 3 pm

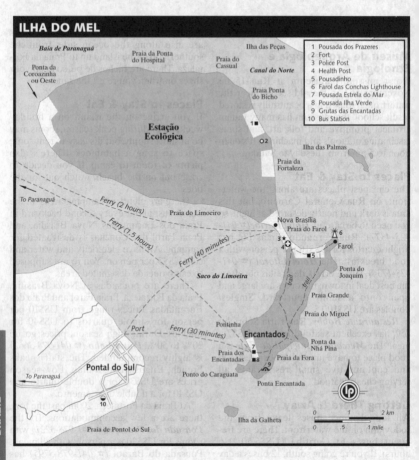

ILHA DO MEL

Baía de Paranaguá

Praia da Ponta do Hospital

Ponta da Coroazinha ou Oeste

Ilha das Peças

Praia do Cassual

Canal do Norte

Praia Ponta do Bicho

Estação Ecológica

Ilha das Palmas

Praia da Fortaleza

To Paranaguá

Ferry (2 hours)

Ferry (1.5 hours)

Praia do Limoeiro

Ferry (40 minutes)

Nova Brasília
Praia do Farol

Farol

Saco do Limoeira

Ponta do Joaquim

Praia Grande

Praia do Miguel

Port

Ferry (30 minutes)

Pontinha

Encantados

Ponta da Nhá Pina

Praia dos Encantados

Praia da Fora

Pontal do Sul

Ponto do Caraguata

Ponta Encantada

To Paranaguá

Ilha da Galheta

Praia de Pontol do Sul

1	Pousada dos Prazeres
2	Fort
3	Police Post
4	Health Post
5	Pousadinho
6	Farol das Conchas Lighthouse
7	Pousada Estrela do Mar
8	Pousada Ilha Verde
9	Grutas das Encantadas
10	Bus Station

0   1   2 km
0   .5   1 mile

every weekday and at 10 am on Saturday. The boats return from Ilha do Mel to Paranaguá at 8 am on weekdays and 4 pm on Sunday.

From Pontal do Sul (US$1, one hour by bus), there are at least two boats daily to both Nova Brasília and Encantadas at 2:50 pm and 4:30 pm. They return to Pontal do Sul at 4 pm and 5:30 pm. The trip takes about 40 minutes and costs US$3. Check at the tourist information office in Paranaguá for the latest schedule.

FOZ DO IGUAÇU

People visit Foz do Iguaçu to see Iguaçu Falls. The town has settled down since the frenzied period when Itaipu dam was under construction, but can still be dangerous, particularly at night, when you should avoid the riverfront area. On the Paraguayan side of the river, Ciudad del Este is pretty shabby, while Puerto Iguazú, in Argentina, is much more mellow. Most budget travelers stay in Foz because there are more and cheaper accommodations. For information about Puerto Iguazú and the falls see the Argentina chapter.

Information

Tourist Offices Foztur maintains five tourist information booths, all with the same information: maps, lists of hotels, and tourist newspapers with English-language descriptions of the attractions. Staff members are helpful and most speak English. Some also speak Italian, Spanish and German. There are booths at Rua Barão do Rio Branco, in the city (open from 6:30 am to 10 pm); at the rodoviária (6 am to 6 pm); at the airport (9 am until the last plane); just before the Ponte da Amizade, on the Paraguayan border (8 am to 8 pm); and at the entrance to the city, on highway BR-27 (7 am to 6 pm).

Teletur (☎ 045-1516) maintains a 24-hour information service with English-speaking operators.

Money The Banco do Brasil on Av Brasil changes money and has ATMs that accept Visa. It charges around US$10 to change traveler's checks. There are dozens of casas

de câmbio all over town, but not many change traveler's checks. Readers have recommended Caribe Tourismo at the airport; it will change traveler's checks without charging a commission.

Visas Visitors who spend the day outside Brazil do not require visas, but those who intend to stay longer must go through all the formalities. In Foz do Iguaçu, the Argentine Consulate (☎ 045-574-2969) is at Travessa Eduardo Branchi 26. The Paraguayan Consulate (☎ 045-523-2898) is at Rua Bartolomeu de Gusmão 738.

The Falls
Argentina has more of the falls than Brazil, but to see them properly, which takes at

FOZ DO IGUAÇU

PLACES TO STAY
3 Hotel Del Ray

PLACES TO EAT
4 Del Churrascaria Búfalo Branco
6 Maria & Maria's Confeitaria No 1
8 Andreolli's
12 Ver o Verde
14 Maria & Maria's Confeitaria No 2

OTHER
1 Urban Bus Terminal
   (Buses to Iguaçu Falls,
   Argentina, Paraguay)
2 Bus to Itaipu
5 Posto Telefônica
7 Paraguayan Consulate
9 Varig
10 VASP
11 Coart Artists Cooperative
13 Transbrasil
15 Posto Telefônica
16 Foztur Tourist Information
17 Post Office
18 Banco do Brasil
19 Argentine Consulate

To Paraguay,
Itaipu Dam

To Curitiba,
São Paulo

To Bus Station

Rua Duarte da Costa
Rua Mem de Sá
Av República Argentina
Rua Rebouças
Rua Xavier da Silva
Rua Rui Barbosa
Rua Bartolomeu de Gusmão
Rua Jorge Sanways
Rua Quintino Bocaiuva
Rua Edmundo de Barros
Av Jorge Schimmelpfeng
Rua Berlamindo de Mendonça
Rua Antônio Raposo

Rio Paraná

Av Beira Rio
Rua Naipi
Rua Tarobá
Rua Juscelino Kubitscheck
Av Brasil
Rua Almirante Barroso
Rua Marechal Floriano Peixoto
Rua Marechal Deodoro da Fonseca
Rua Santos Dumont
Rua Pres Castelo Branco
Rua Patrulheiro Vernanto
Av Paraná

Rua Barão do Rio Branco

Rio M Boicy

To Iguaçu Falls,
Pousada Evelina,
Airport

To Argentina,
Porto Meira

0   200   400 m
0   200   400 yards

BRAZIL

least two full days, you must visit both sides – the Brazilian park for the grand overview and the Argentine park for a closer look. The best season to see them is from August to November. From May to July, you may not be able to approach the falls on the catwalks, due to the increased volume of water, but this can make them even more impressive.

Places to Stay

Camping Club do Brasil (☎ 045-574-1310) is the closest to the falls. Just before the entrance to the park, there's a dirt road to the left. The campground is about 600m along it. The popular YHA hostel *Paudimar* (☎ 045-572-2430), at Km 12.5, also provides camping facilities. They have a booth at the rodoviária (open 5 am to 3 pm) and will do free transfers to the hostel.

The best place for budget travelers is the *Pousada Evelina* (☎ 045-574-3817), Rua Irlan Kalichewski 171, 3.5km out of Foz on the way to the falls. Scrupulously clean apartamentos cost US$12 per person, including a good breakfast. Staff members speak English, French and Spanish, and there are easy connections to the center and both sides of the falls. To get there from the rodoviária, take either a Jd Copacabana or J das Flores bus and ask to get off at Supermercado Chemin. Walk down the hill toward the city and turn left at the third street.

Hotel Del Rey (☎ 045-523-2027), Rua Tarobá 1020, is a cheap, friendly hotel with a pool. Singles/doubles go for US$20/30.

Places to Eat

Cheap buffets abound. *Andreolli's*, Rua Jorge Samways 681, has a good one – all you can eat for US$3. *Maria & Maria's Confeitaria* has good cakes, sandwiches and hot chocolate. There are two locations, at No 495 and No 1285 Av Brasil. *Búfalo Branco* is a good churrascaria at Rua Rebouças 530. Vegetarians can lunch at *Ver o Verde*, Rua Edmundo do Barros 111.

Getting There & Away

Air There are frequent flights from Foz do Iguaçu to Asunción, Buenos Aires, Rio and São Paulo.

Bus Foz's international bus terminal is on Av Costa e Silva, 6km outside town, and buses from Argentina go directly there after stopping at the local bus terminal in the town center.

From Foz do Iguaçu, there are 14 buses a day to Curitiba (US$30, 9½ hours), four to São Paulo (US$45, 14 hours) and four to Rio (US$70, 21 hours). There are two direct buses from Foz to Asunción (US$20, five hours) at 6:30 pm and 12:05 am. There are also several buses a day from Ciudad del Este to Asunción (US$13), if you want to save a few bucks.

Getting Around

To/From the Airport Catch a Parque Nacional bus for the half-hour journey (US$0.90). Buses depart every 22 minutes from 5:30 am to 7 pm, then every hour until 12:40 pm. A taxi costs US$18.

Bus To get to the center from the rodoviária, walk down the hill to the local bus stop, just around the corner to the right, and hop on any bus. All local buses leave from the urban bus terminal on Av Juscelino Kubitschek.

To get to the Brazilian Falls, catch a Cataratas (US$1.60) bus to get to the Brazilian side of the falls. At the park entrance, the bus waits while you get out and pay the US$6 entry fee. The park's open 7 am to 6 pm daily. On weekdays, buses depart every hour from 8 am until 6 pm. On weekends and public holidays, the first bus departs at 8 am and the second at 10 am; thereafter, buses leave every hour until 6 pm. Buses leave the falls every hour on the hour until 6 pm.

Buses for Ciudad del Este depart from the urban terminal in Foz every 10 minutes from 7am.

In Foz, catch a Puerto Iguazú bus to the Argentine side of the falls. Buses leave every 13 minutes (every 50 minutes on Sunday) from 7 am until 8:50 pm. The fare is US$1.60. In Puerto Iguazú, transfer to an El Pratico bus.

At the bus station in Puerto Iguazú, you can pay for everything at once: the bus fares to and from the park, the bus to and from Puerto Canoas, and entry to the park. The entrance fee can be paid in Argentine pesos or in US dollars. If you only have reais, the ticket seller at the bus station will change into pesos the amount required for the park entrance fee; this can then be paid on arrival at the park. The bus costs US$4, plus US$5 for park entry and US$4 for the boat at Puerto Canoas to the Garganta do Diablo.

The bus leaves every hour from 6:40 am to 8:15 pm, but not at 1 pm (siesta time).

Santa Catarina

Santa Catarina is one of Brazil's most prosperous states. Most travelers come for the beaches, many of which have become 'in' vacation spots for well-to-do Brazilians and Argentines. Rapid growth is changing the coastline at an unbelievable pace, often with ugly results.

FLORIANÓPOLIS

Florianópolis, the state capital, is a modern city (map on next page). It spreads across the mainland and the Ilha de Santa Catarina, linked by a causeway. The central section is on the island, facing the Baía Sul. The island side of the city is easy to get around on foot, and there are regular public buses to the island's beautiful beaches.

Information

The information desks at the rodoviária, the airport, and next to the old *Alfandega* (customs house) on Av Paulo Fontes are good for transportation and hotel information. Staff members can speak Spanish and make hotel reservations.

Places to Stay & Eat

There's a good youth hostel (☎ 048-222-3781) at Rua Duarte Schutell, a 10-minute walk from the rodoviária. All the cheap hotels are in the center of town. On Rua Conselheiro Mafra at No 324, the *Hotel Cruzeiro*(☎ 048-222-0675) is seedy but friendly, with basic quartos for US$10 per person. The *Felippe Hotel* (☎ 048-222-4122) is a couple of blocks past Praça 15 de Novembro, at Rua João Pinto 26. It charges US$15 per person with breakfast.

There are plenty of cheap lanchonetes in the market; *Box 32* and *O Mercador* have great seafood snacks. Vegetarians can get a healthy lunch at *Vida*, on Rua Visconde de Ouro Prêto, next door to the Alliance Française building.

Getting There & Away

Air There are daily direct flights to São Paulo and Porto Alegre, as well as connections to most other cities.

Bus Long-distance buses travel to Porto Alegre (US$21, seven hours), Curitiba (US$15, 4½ hours), São Paulo (US$32, 11 hours), Rio (US$52, 18 hours), Foz do Iguaçu (US$41, 16 hours), Buenos Aires, Argentina (US$70, 26 hours) and Montevideo, Uruguay (US$56, 20 hours).

Getting Around

To/From the Airport The airport is 12km south of the city. A taxi costs US$22. Red *Correador Sudoeste* buses shuttle to the airport every 15 minutes until midnight (departing from the second platform away from Rua Antonio Luz) from the eastern rodoviária.

ILHA DE SANTA CATARINA

The east coast's beaches are the prettiest and emptiest, and have the biggest waves. Most do not have hotels. The north coast beaches are calm, baylike and feature resorts, while the west coast has great views of the mainland and a quiet Mediterranean feel.

In the interior, the beautiful Lagoa da Conceição is surrounded by mountains and sand dunes. It's a great place for walks or boat rides.

Getting Around

Local buses serve all of the island's beach towns, but they are infrequent and the times change with the season. Get the schedule at the tourist office or the central rodoviária in Florianópolis. During the tourist season, additional microbuses leave from the center and go directly to the beaches. Unfortunately, surfboards aren't allowed on local buses, only on microbuses.

A one-day car rental is a good (though fairly expensive) way to see most of the island and pick a beach to settle on. Alternately, take one of the bus tours offered by the Florianópolis travel agencies. Itaguatur (☎ 048-241-0333) has a good eight-hour bus tour that costs US$15.

Scuna-Sul (☎ 048-224-1806) operates three-hour sailboat cruises in Baía Norte for US$15.

BRAZIL

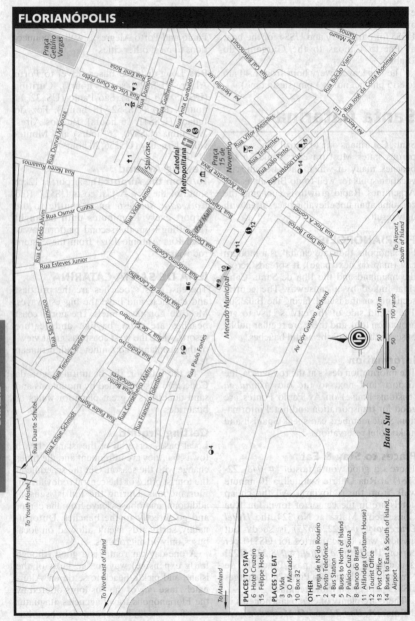

FLORIANÓPOLIS

Praça Getúlio Vargas

Rua Emir Rosa

Rua Visc de Ouro Preto

Rua Dumont

Rua Guilherme

Rua Anita Garibaldi

Rua Duval M Souza

Rua Nereu Ramos

Av Hercilio Luz

Rua Cel Bittencourt

Av Mauro Ramos

Rua Balção Viana

Rua José da Costa Moelmann

Rua Vitor Meirelles

Av Hercilio Luz

Rua Tiradentes

Rua João Pinto

Rua Antônio Luz

Catedral
Metropolitana

Praça
15 de
Novembro

Rua Arcipreste Paiva

Rua Vidal Ramos

Rua Osmar Cunha

Rua Cel Melo Alvim

Rua Esteves Junior

Rua Deodoro

Rua Trajano (Ped Mall)

Rua Jerônimo Coelho

Rua Álvaro de Carvalho

Rua São Francisco

Rua Tenente Silveira

Rua 7 de Setembro

Rua Pedro Ivo

Rua Paulo Fontes

Mercado Municipal

Rua Dep J Bertoli

Rua Proc A Gomes

Av Gov Gustavo Richard

To Airport,
South of Island

Rua Duarte Schutel

Rua Felipe Schmidt

Rua Conselheiro Mafra

Rua Bento Gonçalves

Rua Frei Caneca Roma

Rua Francisco Tolentino

To Youth Hostel

To Northeast of Island

To Mainland

Baía Sul

To Airport,
South of Island

0   50   100 m
0   50   100 yards

PLACES TO STAY
6 Hotel Cruzeiro
15 Felippe Hotel

PLACES TO EAT
3 Vida
9 O Mercador
10 Box 32

OTHER
1 Igreja de NS do Rosário
2 Posto Telefônica
4 Bus Station
5 Buses to North of Island
7 Palácio Cruz e Souza
8 Banco do Brasil
11 Alfândega (Customs House)
12 Tourist Office
13 Post Office
14 Buses to East & South of Island,
    Airport

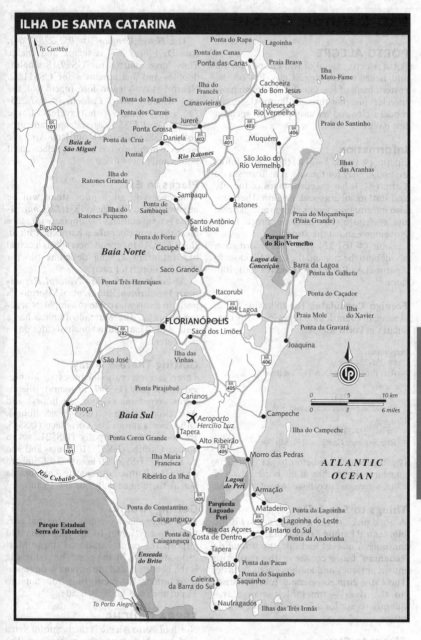

ILHA DE SANTA CATARINA

To Curitiba
Ponta do Rapa
Lagoinha
Ponta das Canas
Ponta das Canas
Praia Brava
Ilha
Mato-Fame
Cachoeira
do Bom Jesus
Ilha do
Francês
Ponta do Magalhães
Canasvieiras
Ingleses do
Rio Vermelho
Ponta dos Currais
Jurerê
Praia do Santinho
BR 101
BR 403
Ponta Grossa
Daniela
BR 402
BR 401
Muquém
BR 406
Baía de
São Miguel
Ponta da Cruz
Pontal
Rio Ratones
São João do
Rio Vermelho
Ilhas
das Aranhas
Ilha do
Ratones Grande
Sambaqui
Ratones
Ilha do
Ratones Pequeno
Ponta de
Sambaqui
Praia do Moçambique
(Praia Grande)
Biguaçu
Santo Antônio
de Lisboa
Parque Flor
do Rio Vermelho
Ponta do Forte
Cacupé
Baía Norte
Lagoa da
Conceição
Barra da Lagoa
Ponta da Galheta
Saco Grande
Ponta Três Henriques
Itacorubi
Ponta do Caçador
BR 404
Lagoa
Ilha
do Xavier
FLORIANÓPOLIS
Praia Mole
BR 282
Saco dos Limões
Ponta da Gravatá
Ilha das
Vinhas
Joaquina
São José
BR 406
Ponta Pirajubaé
Carianos
BR 405
Palhoça
Baía Sul
Aeroporto
Hercílio Luz
Campeche
BR 101
Tapera
Ilha do Campeche
Ponta Coroa Grande
Alto Ribeirão
BR 405
Rio Cubatão
Ilha Maria
Francisca
Morro das Pedras
ATLANTIC
OCEAN
Ribeirão da Ilha
Lagoa
do Peri
Parque Estadual
Serra do Tabuleiro
Armação
Ponta do Constantino
Parque da
Lagado
Peri
Matadeiro
Ponta da Lagoinha
Caiaganguçu
BR 406
Lagoinha do Leste
Praia das Açores
Pântano do Sul
Ponta da
Caiaganguçu
Costa de Dentro
Ponta da Andorinha
Tapera
Enseada
do Brito
Solidão
Ponta das Pacas
Ponta do Saquinho
Caieiras
da Barra do Sul
Saquinho
To Porto Alegre
Naufragados
Ilhas das Três Irmãs

0   5   10 km
0   3   6 miles

BRAZIL

Rio Grande do Sul

PORTO ALEGRE
Porto Alegre, capital of Rio Grande do Sul and Brazil's sixth-biggest city, lies on the eastern bank of Rio Guaíba. Although most travelers just pass through, Porto Alegre is a modern city and an easy place to spend a few days.

Information
Epatur (☎ 051-225-4744), the tourist information agency for the city, is at Travessa do Carmo 84. It has excellent maps of the city and staff members speak English. There are also information booths at the rodoviária, in the *prefeitura* (city hall) on Praça 15 de Novembro, and at the airport.

Setur (☎ 051-224-4784) has information about both the city and the state. It's close to Epatur at Av Borges de Medeiros 1501, 10th floor.

Foreign Consulates The following South American countries are represented by consulates in Porto Alegre:

Argentina
  (☎ 051-224-6799)
  Rua Prof Annes Dias 112, 1st floor
Paraguay
  (☎ 051-346-1314)
  Quintino Bocaiuva 554, sala 302
Uruguay
  (☎ 051-224-3499)
  Rua Siqueira Campos 1171, 6th floor

If you need one, it's better to get your Uruguayan visa here than at the border town of Chuí, where you may have to wait overnight.

Things to See & Do
A good place to see gaúchos at play is the big, central **Parque Farroupilha**. On Sunday morning, a market and fair, the **Brique da Redencão**, fills a corner of the park with music, antiques and leather goods for sale. The *Cisne Branco* operates tourist cruises on the river – timetables change frequently, so ask for a schedule at the tourist office.

Places to Stay
The *Hotel Ritz* (☎ 051-225-3423), Av André da Rocha 225, is Porto Alegre's youth hostel.

It's well located close to the center of town. The staff speaks English and Spanish.

The *Hotel Uruguai* (☎ 051-228-7864), Rua Dr Flores 371, is secure and cheap. They have quartos for US$9/18 singles/doubles and apartamentos for US$11/22. Nearby, at Av Vigarió José Inácio 644, the very friendly *Hotel Palácio* (☎ 051-225-3467) is popular with travelers. Large quartos cost US$20/30 and apartamentos go for US$28/36. Check out Rua Andrade Neves, which also has a good selection of hotels and places to eat.

Places to Eat
Wherever you go, a juicy steak will be nearby. At Rua Riachuelo 1331, *La Churrasquita* is a vegetarian's nightmare, with more meat than you can poke a barbecue fork at. *Bar Lider*, Av Independência 408, is a casual bar/restaurant serving delicious filé for US$13 (enough for two).

At lunchtime, the *Ilha Natural Restaurante Vegetariano*, Rua General Vitorino 35, packs in locals who come to sample its vegetarian buffet. The Mercado Público has a central food hall with a bunch of cafés on its perimeter.

Getting There & Away
There are international buses to Montevideo, Uraguay (US$47, 12 hours), Buenos Aires, Argentina (US$76, 22 hours) and Asunción, Paraguay (US$48, 15 hours). Other buses run to Foz do Iguaçu (US$45, 16 hours), Florianópolis (US$21, seven hours), Curitiba (US$25, 10 hours) and Rio de Janeiro (US$68, 26 hours). To Cambará do Sul (for Parque Nacional de Aparados da Serra), there's one daily bus at 6:15 am.

Getting Around
Porto Alegre has a one-line metro that goes from the city center to the rodoviária and airport. The central station, Estação Mercado Modelo, is by the port. The rodoviária is the next stop, and the airport is three stations farther. The metro runs from 5 am to 11 pm and costs US$0.50 a ride.

SERRA GAÚCHA
North of Porto Alegre is the beautiful Serra Gaúcha, which is popular with hikers. The mountain towns of Gramado and Canela are popular resorts.

PORTO ALEGRE

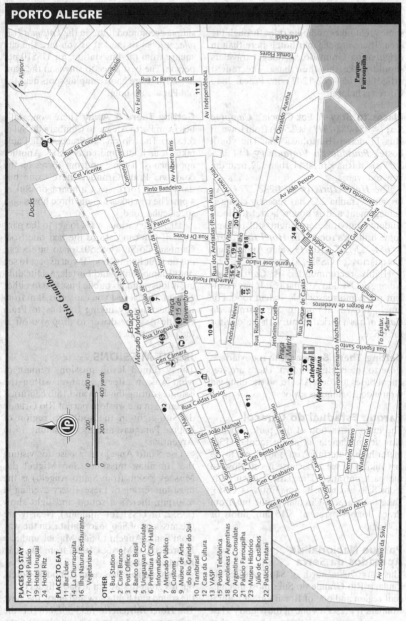

To Airport

Rio Guaíba

Docks

Garibaldi

Tomás Flores

Parque Farroupilha

Av Farrapos

Rua Dr Barros Cassal

Av Independência

Rua da Conceição

Cel Vicente

Comend Pereira

Av Alberto Bins

Pinto Bandeiro

Passos

Voluntários da Pátria

Rua Dr Flores

Rua Prof Annes Dias

Rua dos Andradas (Rua da Praia)

Rua General Vitorino

Av Salgado Filho

Av Osvaldo Aranha

Sarmento Leite

Av João Pessoa

Av André da Rocha

Av Des Cal Lima e Silva

Vigário José Inácio

Staircase

Av Júlio de Castilhos

Praça 15 de Novembro

Rua Uruguai

Gen Câmara

Estação Modelo

Mercado Modelo

Av Maua

Marechal Floriano Peixoto

Andrade Neves

Jerônimo Coelho

Rua Riachuelo

Praça da Matriz

Av Borges de Medeiros

Rua Duque de Caxias

Genuíno

To Epatur, Setur

Rua Espírito Santo

Coronel Fernando Machado

Rua Caldas Júnior

Rua Riachuelo

Rua Riachuelo

Catedral Metropolitana

Gen João Manoel

Rua Siqueira Campos

Rua 7 de Setembro

Gen 7 de Setembro

Gen Bento Martins

Gen Canabarro

Gen Portinho

Demetrio Ribeiro

Washington Luis

Rua Duque de Caxias

Vasco Alves

Av Loureiro da Silva

0   200   400 m
0   200   400 yards

BRAZIL

PLACES TO STAY
17 Hotel Palácio
19 Hotel Uruguai
24 Hotel Ritz

PLACES TO EAT
11 Bar Líder
14 La Churrasquita
16 Ilha Natural Restaurante Vegetariano

OTHER
1   Bus Station
2   Cisne Branco
3   Post Office
4   Banco do Brasil
5   Uruguayan Consulate
6   Prefeitura (City Hall)/ Information
7   Mercado Público
8   Customs
9   Museu de Arte do Rio Grande do Sul
10 Transbrasil
12 Casa da Cultura
13 VASP
15 Posto Telefônica
18 Aerolíneas Argentinas
20 Argentine Consulate
21 Palácio Farroupilha
23 Museu Histórico Júlio de Castilhos
22 Palácio Piratini

Canela

Canela is the best jumping-off point for some great hikes and bike rides through the area. There are cheaper hotels here than in neighboring Gramado, so budget travelers should make this their base. The tourist office (☎ 054-282-1287) in Praça João Correa is helpful.

Places to Stay & Eat

Canela's *Camping Sesi (☎ 054-282-1311)* is 2.5km from town at Rua Francisco Bertolucci 504. The youth hostel, *Pousada do Viajante (☎ 054-282-2017)*, is at Rua Ernesto Urban 132, near the new rodoviária.

The *Hotel Turis (☎ 054-282-2774)*, Av Osvaldo Aranha 223, has recently changed management and is now a hostel for local students, but travelers might still be welcome if there's room. The *Hotel Bela Vista (☎ 054-282-1327)*, Rua Osvaldo Aranha 160, has quartos for US$20/30.

Highly recommended is *Cantina de Nono*, Av Osvaldo Aranha 161. It has excellent pizza and reasonable Italian food. For lunch, the restaurant in the *Parque do Caracol* has a varied menu, with prato feitos for US$6.

Getting There & Away

The rodoviária is close to the center of town. There are frequent buses to Porto Alegre, all traveling via Gramado, 15 minutes away.

Parque Estadual do Caracol

The major attraction of this park, which is 8km from Canela, is a spectacular, 130-meter-high waterfall. You don't have to do any hiking to see it because it's so close to the park entrance. The park is open daily from 8:30 am to 6:30 pm. Entry is US$3. Take the Caracol Circular public bus from Praça João Correa at 8:15 am, noon or 5:30 pm.

Parque Nacional de Aparados da Serra

This park, 70km north of São Francisco de Paula, is Rio Grande do Sul's most magnificent region and one of Brazil's great natural wonders. It preserves one of the country's last forests of *araucária* (a pine-like tree that stands up to 50m tall), and contains the Itaimbézinho, a fantastic narrow canyon 120m deep, as well as the Canyon da Fortaleza.

Places to Stay

The closest town to the park is Cambarádo Sul, where you can find simple accommodations in the *Pousada Fortaleza*, 300m to the left as you face the city square from the bus station, for US$10 per person. The best place to stay is in the park itself. There are good camping spots near the old Paradouro hotel.

Getting There & Away

There's one daily bus from Porto Alegre to Cambará do Sul at 6:15 am. The trip via São Francisco de Paula takes four hours and costs US$8. Another approach is to come up from Torres on the coast via Praia Grande. There's one bus daily from Torres to Cambará do Sul at 4 pm. The trip takes around three hours on a spectacular road.

There are various ways to get to the park itself. If you can't afford the taxi ride from Cambará do Sul (US$50), or to hire a car, put on your hiking shoes if you expect to see both Itaimbézinho and Fortaleza. Hitchhiking is lousy, and no public buses go to either canyon. The closest you can get is 3km from Itaimbézinho by taking the bus to Praia Grande. Ask the driver to drop you off at the park entrance.

JESUIT MISSIONS

Thirty ruined Jesuit missions remain of what was, in effect, a nation within the colonies during the 17th and 18th centuries. Seven lie in the western part of Rio Grande do Sul, eight in the southern region of Itapúa, Paraguay, and the remaining 15 in Argentina.

Use Santo Angelo as a base for visiting the Brazilian missions. São Miguel das Missões (58km from Santo Angelo) is the most interesting of these. Every evening at 8:30 pm, there's a sound and light show (US$2, or US$1 for students). Nearby are the missions of São João Batista, on the way from Santo Angelo to São Miguel, and São Lourenço das Missões, 10km from São João Batista by dirt road.

Santo Angelo has several modest hotels, but it's great to stay out at São Miguel to see the sound and light show and enjoy the view. The *Hotel Barichello (055-381-1104)* is the only place to stay and a good place to eat, too. It's run by a friendly family. Very clean singles cost US$18, and doubles with a shower are US$28.

Brasília

Brasília is in a federal district, Distrito Federal, and does not belong to any of the states. It must have looked good on paper and still looks good in photos, but the city was built for cars and air-conditioners, not people. It's a lousy place to visit and no one wants to live there. It's probably better to read about it instead: Try Alex Shoumatoff's *The Capital of Hope.*

Orientation
The city is divided into two halves: Asa Sul and Asa Norte. Av W3, the main commercial thoroughfare, and Av L2 both run the length of the city. They are also divided into north and south.

Information
Tourist Offices The Setur tourist information desk at the airport is open 8 am to 1 pm and 2 to 6 pm on weekdays, and 10 am to 1 pm and 4:30 to 7:30 pm on weekends. If you just need a map or a list of attractions, pick up a brochure from the front desk of any large hotel or travel agency.

Money Banks with money-changing facilities are in SBS (the Setor Bancário Sul, Banking Sector South) and SBN (Setor Bancário Norte, Banking Sector North).

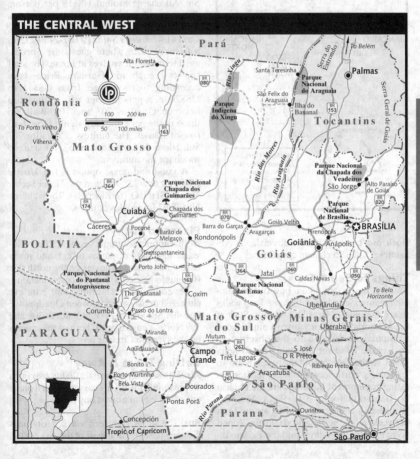

THE CENTRAL WEST

BRAZIL

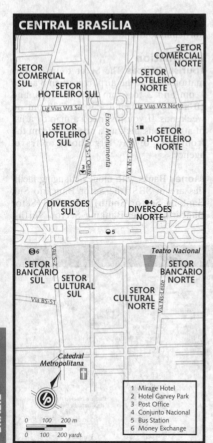

CENTRAL BRASÍLIA

SETOR COMERCIAL NORTE

SETOR COMERCIAL SUL

SETOR HOTELEIRO SUL

SETOR HOTELEIRO NORTE

Lig Vias W3 Sul   Lig Vias W3 Norte

Eixo Monumental

SETOR HOTELEIRO SUL

SETOR HOTELEIRO NORTE

DIVERSÕES SUL

DIVERSÕES NORTE

Teatro Nacional

SETOR BANCÁRIO SUL

SETOR CULTURAL SUL

SETOR BANCÁRIO NORTE

SETOR CULTURAL NORTE

Via BS-S1

Catedral Metropolitana

0   100   200 m
0   100   200 yards

1 Mirage Hotel
2 Hotel Garvey Park
3 Post Office
4 Conjunto Nacional
5 Bus Station
6 Money Exchange

Both are close to the rodoviária. Travel agencies will also change cash dollars.

Things to See & Do

You can rent a car, take a bus tour or combine riding a city bus with some long walks to see the bulk of Brasília's edifices. Start at the **Memorial JK**, open 9 am to 6 pm Tuesday to Sunday, then head to the observation deck of the **TV tower**. It's open 9 am to 9 pm. The **Catedral Metropolitana**, open 8 am to 7:30 pm, is worth seeing too. The most interesting **government buildings** are the Palácio do Itamaraty (open 3 to 5 pm, Monday, Wednesday and Friday, and 10 am to 2 pm on weekends), the Palácio da Justiça (open noon to 7 pm weekdays) and the Palácio do

Congresso (open 10 am to noon and 2 to 5 pm weekdays).

The **Parque Nacional de Brasília**, an ecological reserve, is a good place to relax if you're stuck in the city. The Grande do Torto bus that leaves from the city rodoviária goes past the front gate.

To get a bus tour, visit the Hotel Garvey-Park (full of travel agencies offering sightseeing tours) or book one at the airport.

Places to Stay

Camping is possible not far from the city in the Setor de Garagens Oficiais. To get there, take the Buriti bus (No 109 or No 143) from the rodoviária. Campsites cost US$5.

There are no cheap hotels in Brasília, but there are a few cheap pensions, mostly in W3 Sul. All charge around US$15 per person. *Pousada 47* (☎ 061-224-4894) is a clean, well-kept place at Quadra 703, Bloco A, Casa 41/47. *Cury's Solar* (☎ 061-243-6252) is a friendly place where guests are encouraged to make themselves at home. The staff speaks French and German. Prices vary according to room size, from US$15 to US$20 per person. Get off at the stop between Quadras 707 and 708. Walk up through the park and turn right at the third row of houses. The address is Quadra 707 Sul, Bloco I, Casa 15. There's no sign, so watch for the numbers.

A good mid-range option is the *Mirage Hotel* (☎ 061-225-7150) in the Hotel Sector North (SHN Q 02 Bloco N). They charge US$38/62 for singles/doubles.

Places to Eat

Both shopping complexes near the rodoviária have lots of places to eat, and many have lunch specials. The one on the north side (Conjunto Nacional) has the best selection.

Several good restaurants and bars are clustered in two strips between Quadras 405 and 404 Sul and between Quadras 308 and 309 Norte. You can get to both of these areas on the Grande Circular bus.

Getting There & Away

Air With so many domestic flights making a stopover in Brasília, it's easy to catch a plane out of the city at almost any time.

Bus The giant rodoferroviária (for long-distance buses) is due west of the city center.

BRAZIL

Destinations include Goiânia (US$9, three hours), Anápolis (US$7, 2½ hours), Belém (US$94, 34 hours), Belo Horizonte (US$33, 11 hours), Rio (US$67, 17 hours), São Paulo (US$46, 14 hours) and Salvador (US$68, 24 hours). There are five buses a day to Pirenópolis (US$6, 2½ hours). There are also buses to Cuiabá (US$49, 19 hours) and Porto Velho (US$126, 44 hours) for a connection to Manaus.

Getting Around

The international airport is 12km south of the center. There are two buses marked Aeroporto that go from the city rodoviária to the airport every 15 minutes. The fare is US$1.75 and the trip takes 35 minutes. A taxi between the airport and the city center costs US$20.

To get from the city rodoviária to the rodoferroviária, take the local bus No 131 (you can also flag it down along the main drag).

There are car rental agencies at the airport, the Hotel Nacional and the Hotel Garvey-Park.

Goiás

GOIÂNIA

The capital of the state of Goiás, Goiânia is 200km southwest of Brasília. It's a fairly pleasant place, with lots of open spaces laid out around circular streets in the center. The *Mini Guia de Goiânia*, available in hotels, includes a city map and useful listings.

Places to Stay & Eat

The *Hotel Del Rey* (☎ 062-224-0035) is centrally located in the Rua 8 pedestrian mall at No 321. Dingy apartamentos cost US$15 per person. *Lord Hotel* (☎ 224-0385), Av Anhanguera 4999, is a better value. Comfortable apartamentos with fan and fridge go for US$23/34, singles/doubles. Ask for a room with a balcony. Another cheapie nearby on Av Anhanguera is the *Goiânia Palace* (☎ 224-4874), which charges US$18/30 for basic quartos.

For typical Goiânian dishes, head for *Fogão Caipira*, No 570 Rua 83, Setor Sul, or *Tacho de Cobre* in the Serra Dourada stadium, Jardim Goiás. Our favorite dish is the *empadão de Goiás*, a tasty meat, vegetable and olive pie.

Vegetarian food is available at *Reserva Natural*, upstairs at No 485, Rua 7. It's open for lunch weekdays. *Micky's,* on Rua 4 near the Parthenon Center, is a popular place for a drink and snack.

Getting There & Away

Air If you're interested in an air taxi call Sete Taxi Aereo (☎ 062-207-1519) or União (☎ 062-207-1600).

Bus The rodoviária is at No 399 Rua 44. There are buses to Brasília (US$9, three hours), Goiás Velho (US$10, 2½ hours, every hour from 5 am to 8 pm), Cuiabá (US$41, 13 hours), and Pirenópolis (US$6, two hours, 4 pm).

Getting Around

Aeroporto Santo Genoveva is 6km from the city. A taxi there will cost US$8. To get from the rodoviária to the hotels and restaurants at the corner of Av Anhanguera and Av Goiás is a hot, 15-minute walk. From outside the rodoviária, take a No 163 Vila União – Centro or No 404 Rodoviária – bus to town.

GOIÁS VELHO

The historic city of Goiás Velho, formerly known as Vila Boa, enjoyed a brief gold rush in the 18th century and was once the state capital.

Things to See & Do

Walking through Goiás Velho you quickly notice the main legacies of the gold rush: 18th-century architecture and a large mulatto and mestizo population. Of the seven churches, the most impressive is the oldest, the **Igreja de Paula** (1761), on Praça Zaqueu Alves de Castro. The **Museu das Bandeiras**, in the old town council building (1766) on Praça Brasil Caiado, is also worth a visit.

Special Events

The big occasion here is Semana Santa (Holy Week). The main streets of town are lit by hundreds of torches, carried by the townsfolk and dozens of hooded figures in a procession which reenacts Christ's removal from the cross and burial.

Places to Stay & Eat

You can camp in town at the *Chafariz da Carioca*, just behind the Pousada do Ipê.

Camping is free, and there are lots of horses and locals wandering among the sites.

The best budget place is the **Pousada do Ipê** (☎ 062-371-2065), a colonial house on Praça da Boa Vista with rooms set around a shady courtyard. Apartamentos start at US$20/30 for singles/doubles, including a healthy breakfast. Another good option is the **Pousada do Sol** (☎ 062-371-1717), Rua Dr Americano do Brasil 17, with apartamentos at the same prices. **Flor do Ipê** on Praça da Boa Vista offers very good regional food served in a garden setting overlooking the river for around US$6 per person.

Getting There & Away
There are frequent buses to Goiânia, 144km away.

PIRENÓPOLIS
Another historic gold city, Pirenópolis is 70km from Anápolis and 128km from Goiânia on the Rio das Almas. Cerrado Ecoturismo (☎ 062-331-1240), Rua do Bonfim 46, organizes treks, mountain-bike rides and tours at reasonable prices.

The city is famous for the **Festa do Divino Espírito Santo**, 45 days after Easter. If you're in the area, don't miss this curious spectacle, which is more folkloric than religious. Among the attractions are medieval tournaments, dances and festivities, including a mock Iberian battle between Moors and Christians.

There are bus services from Pirenópolis to Anápolis, Goiânia and Brasília.

Places to Stay & Eat
There are lots of pousadas in town. **Pousada Dona Geny** (062-331-1128), Rua dos Pirineus 29, costs US$8 a head. The **Rex Hotel** (☎ 062-331-1121), Emmanoel Lopes 15, is basic but clean, with quartos for US$10 per person. The pink-and-white **Pousada Matutina Meiapontense** (☎ 062-331-1101) is a friendly, comfortable place with a swimming pool. Apartamentos with fans go for US$20 per person.

All these places fill up during the festival, so most visitors either camp out near the Rio das Almas or rent a room.

The **Restaurante As Flor**, on Av São Jayme, serves huge plates of good regional cuisine. There are 18 different desserts, each sweeter than the last. **Nena**, Rua Aurora 4, has an excellent buffet lunch of regional dishes for US$6. **Restaurante Aravinda** on Rua do Rosário has an extensive menu with some vegetarian dishes.

PARQUE NACIONAL DA CHAPADA DOS VEADEIROS
Just over 220km north of Brasília, this scenic park in the most mountainous area of the Central West is a popular destination for Brazilian ecotourists. The best time to visit is between May and October. The entry fee is US$3. Visitors must enter the park with an IBAMA guide, who charge US$30 per group (up to 15 people) and give a rundown of the local flora and fauna. Take lunch and water with you, as there are no facilities inside the park.

You can camp at **Parada Obrigatória**, 400m from the entrance to the park, for US$6 a night. There are also a couple of cabins for around US$15 per person. In the small town of São Jorge, a few kilometers from the park, **Pousada Trilha Violeta** (☎ 061-646-1109 in Brasília) is a friendly, family-run place with apartamentos for US$25 per person, including a big breakfast.

Getting There & Away
From Goiânia, there's a daily bus to Alto Paraíso at 10 pm. You can get a local bus from there to São Jorge. There are two buses a day from Brasília to Alto Paraíso, at 10 am and 10:30 pm.

Mato Grosso & Mato Grosso do Sul

Mato Grosso and Mato Grosso do Sul are separate states, although until the late 1970s, the entire region was considered Mato Grosso state. The vast wetlands of the Pantanal extend across parts of both states.

The Mato Grosso is home to many of Brazil's remaining Indians, whose lands have been threatened by rapid agricultural development following the construction of the roads from Belém to Brasília and Cuiabá to Santarém.

CUIABÁ
Cuiabá is a lively place and a good base for excursions into the Pantanal and Chapada dos Guimarães.

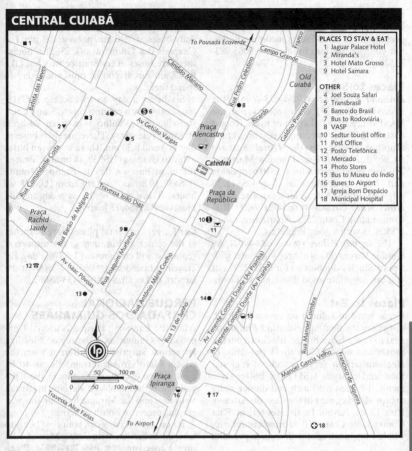

CENTRAL CUIABÁ

PLACES TO STAY & EAT
1 Jaguar Palace Hotel
2 Miranda's
3 Hotel Mato Grosso
9 Hotel Samara

OTHER
4 Joel Souza Safari
5 Transbrasil
6 Banco do Brasil
7 Bus to Rodoviária
8 VASP
10 Sedtur tourist office
11 Post Office
12 Posto Telefônica
13 Mercado
14 Photo Stores
15 Bus to Museu do Indio
16 Buses to Airport
17 Igreja Bom Despácio
18 Municipal Hospital

To Pousada Ecoverde
Campo Grande
Old Cuiabá
Cândido Mariano
Av Getúlio Vargas
Praça Alencastro
Catedral
Praça da República
Rua Pedro Celestino
Rua Comandante Costa
Batista das Neves
Travessa João Diaz
Rua Barão de Malgaço
Praça Rachid Jaudy
Av Isaac Póvoas
Rua Joaquim Murtinho
Rua Antônio Maria Coelho
Rua 13 de Junho
Av Tenente Coronel Duarte (Av Prainha)
Av Tenente Coronel Duarte (Av Prainha)
Rua Manoel Coimbra
Manoel Garcia Velho
Francisco de Siqueira
Praça Ipiranga
Travessa Alice Farias
To Airport
Franco
Galdino Pimentel
Ricardo

0 50 100 m
0 50 100 yards

BRAZIL

Orientation & Information

Cuiabá is actually two cities separated by the Rio Cuiabá: old Cuiabá, where the modern town's center is located; and Várzea Grande, to the southwest where the airport is. The tourist office (☎ 065-624-9060) is on Praça da República, near the post office. It provides maps and lists of attractions, and is open 8 am to 6 pm weekdays. Staff members speak English and Spanish.

Things to See & Do

The **Museu do Indio** (Rondon) has exhibits on the Xavantes, Bororos and Karajas tribes. It's worth a visit. It is at the university, on Av Fernando Correia da Costa, and is open 8 to 11:30 am and 1:30 to 5:30 pm on weekdays.

The university contains a small zoo, which is also worth a look. Entry is free. The **market** by the Rio Cuiabá bridge is interesting.

Organized Tours

Travel agencies in town arrange reservations, guides and transportation for photo-safaris into the Pantanal and day trips to Chapada dos Guimarães. They can also help with the logistics of more ambitious trips to Emas. Anaconda (☎ 065-624-4142), Rua Joaquim Murtinho 242, has been recommended. Their tours are expensive (around US$80 a day), but well organized. A relatively cheap alternative excursion is with Joel Souza, a very enthusiastic guide who is fluent in English, Italian and German. His two-day Pantanal trips cost around US$120 including food, accommodations and transportation. He often meets incoming flights, but you can call him toll-free (☎ 9065-983-3552).

Places to Stay

Pousada Ecoverde (☎ 065-623-4696), Rua Pedro Celestino 391, is two blocks from the VASP office in the old part of town. Rooms cost US$10 per person with breakfast. Another cheapie is the *Hotel Samara* (☎ 065-322-6001), Rua Joaquim Murtinho 270, with basic quartos for US$10 per person and boxy apartamentos for US$15/20 singles/doubles. A traveler's favorite is the *Hotel Mato Grosso* (☎ 065-321-9121), Rua Comandante Costa 2522. Apartamentos are US$28/33 with a good breakfast.

The *Jaguar Palace* (☎ 065-624-4404), Av Getúlio Vargas 600, is a three-star hotel with a pool. Singles/doubles go for US$72/86, but you can negotiate good discounts with cash.

Places to Eat

If you want to splurge on exotic local fish dishes, try the floating restaurant *Flutuante*, next to Ponte Nova bridge. It's 6km from the center and open 11 am to 11 pm daily. *O Regionalissimo* serves excellent regional food and charges US$12 for buffet-style meals. It's open for lunch and dinner, daily except Monday, next to the Casa do Artesão, Rua 13 de Junho. In the center, at Rua Comandante Costa 710, *Miranda* is a cheap, wholesome lunch spot with comida por kilo.

Getting There & Away

Air The airport is in Várzea Grande, 7km from Cuiabá. To catch the local bus to town, cross the road and walk to the left toward Las Velas hotel. The bus stop is opposite the hotel entrance. Catch a Jardim Marajoara, Cohab Canelas or Imperial bus to the center.

There are flights between Cuiabá and the rest of Brazil. Make reservations well in advance if you're traveling in July, when many Brazilians are on vacation.

Bus Cuiabá's rodoviária is on the highway toward Chapada dos Guimarães. To get there, catch a municipal bus from Praça Alencastro in the center. Five buses a day make the trip to Poconé (US$8.50, 1½

hours); the first leaves at 6 am. To Barão de Melgaço (US$11, 3½ hours) there are three daily buses at 7:30 am, noon and 3 pm. For Chapada dos Guimarães (US$6, 1½ hours) there are buses every hour or two, but take the 7 am bus if you've only got a day to spend there.

Six buses a day go to Cáceres (US$16, four hours) with connections to Santa Cruz, Bolivia. Porto Velho is a hard 24-hour (US$65) ride away. There are two buses a day, at 4 and 8:30 pm. There are seven buses a day to Goiânia (US$39, 14 hours). Most of the eight buses a day to Campo Grande (US$30, 10 hours) stop at Coxim (US$21, six hours). There are four buses a day to Alta Floresta (US$54, 13 hours).

Car Larger car rental places have branches in the center and in or near the airport. A rental car will cost around US$70 a day. Try Trescinto Locadora (☎ 065-627-3500) at the airport, or Localiza (☎ 065-433-5866).

PARQUE NACIONAL CHAPADA DOS GUIMARÃES

After the Pantanal, Parque Nacional Chapada dos Guimarães is the region's leading attraction. Surprisingly different from the typical Mato Grosso terrain, it's not to be missed. Two exceptional sights in the Chapadas are the 60m Véu de Noiva (Bridal Veil) falls and the Mirante lookout, the geographic center of South America.

If you don't have a car, your best bet is to take an excursion with Jorge Mattos, who runs Ecoturismo (☎ 065-791-1393), Praça Dom Wunibaldo 57, in the town of Chapada. He speaks English and meets the 7 and 8 am buses from Cuiabá every day.

An alternative is to hire a car and explore the area on your own, stopping at different rock formations, waterfalls and bathing pools at your leisure. If you travel by car, visit the Secretaria de Turismo, on the left-hand side as you enter town, just before the square. It's open 8 to 11 am and 1 to 4 pm weekdays, and they have a useful map. You'll need it.

Places to Stay & Eat

There is good camping at Salgadeira, just before the climb into Chapada. If you want to rough it, however, you can camp basically anywhere.

Cheap accommodations in the area include the very basic but friendly *Hotel São José* (☎ 065-791-1454), Rua Vereador José de Souza 50, which charges US$8 per person. The *Turismo Hotel* (☎ 065-791-1176), Rua Fernando Correo Costa 1065, is run by a German family. Apartamentos cost US$23/33 for singles/doubles. The *Hotel Quincó* (☎ 065-791-1404), Praça Dom Wunibaldo 464, has good-value apartamentos for US$13 per person.

On the main square, *Nivios* has excellent regional food, including an all-you-can-eat lunch for US$8.

Getting There & Away

Buses leave for Chapada dos Guimarães from Cuiabá's rodoviária every 1½ hours from 7 am to 7 pm (US$6).

THE PANTANAL

The Amazon may have all the fame and glory, but the Pantanal is a far better place to see wildlife. This vast area of wetlands, about half the size of France, lies mostly within the states of Mato Grosso and Mato Grosso do Sul, but also extends into the border regions of Bolivia and Paraguay.

The Pantanal is a vast alluvial plain, much of which is flooded by the Rio Paraguai and its tributaries during the wet season (October to March). It is what remains of an ancient inland sea called the Xaraés, which began to dry out at the same time as the Amazon Sea, about 65 million years ago.

Birds are the most frequently seen wildlife, but the Pantanal is also a sanctuary for giant river otters, anacondas, iguanas, jaguars, cougars, crocodiles, deer, anteaters, black howler monkeys and capybaras.

The area has few people and no towns. The only road that plunges deep into the Pantanal is the Transpantaneira, which ends 145km south of Poconé, at Porto Jofre. Only a third of the intended route from Poconé to Corumbá has been completed, delayed because of ecological concerns and lack of funds. The best way for the budget traveler to see Pantanal wildlife is to drive or hitch-hike down the Transpantaneira, preferably all the way to Porto Jofre.

The best time to visit is during the dry season (April until September or October). The best time to see birds is July to September. Flooding, incessant rains and extreme heat make travel difficult from November to March.

If language or time is a problem and money isn't, you can write to Douglas Trent of Focus Tours (☎ 505-466-4688, focustours@aol.com), 103 Moya Rd, Santa Fe, NM 87505 USA; in Brazil, contact Focus (☎ 031-332-4627) in Belo Horizonte, Minas Gerais. Focus specializes in nature tours and Doug is active in trying to preserve the Pantanal.

Places to Stay

Pantanal accommodations are divided into four general categories: *fazendas*, *pousadas*, *pesqueiros* and *botels*. Fazendas are ranch-style hotels that usually have horses, and often boats, for hire. Pousadas range from simple to top-end accommodations. Pesqueiros are hangouts for anglers; they usually rent boats and fishing gear. A botel (a contraction of boat and hotel) is a floating, and usually very expensive, lodge. Reservations are needed for all accommodations, especially in July, when lots of Brazilian tourists holiday in the Pantanal.

Unfortunately, nearly all accommodations are expensive. They usually include good food, modest lodging and transportation by plane, boat or 4WD from Corumbá or Cuiabá. More often than not, reservations are handled through a travel agent, and you must pay in advance. It's also a good idea to call ahead for weather conditions.

Along the Transpantaneira At Km 30, *Pousada do Araras* charges US$60 a day. It has a pool and shows films about the Pantanal.

At the Rio Pixaim, Km 65, you'll find two places. *Pousada do Pixaim* (☎ 065-721-1899) is the more rustic of the two, a classic Pantanal building (wooden, on stilts). It has air-con, tasty meals (included in the price), clean rooms with electric showers, and the last álcool and gas pump until you return to Poconé – so fill up! Prices are US$40 per person. Across the bridge, the much more modern *Fazenda-Hotel Beira Rio* (☎ 065-721-1642) is more expensive at US$50/60 for singles/doubles. It's popular with package tourists from São Paulo. Boats can be rented for US$20 an hour and horses for US$12 an hour.

Forty km farther down the road is the cheapest pousada on the Transpantaneira,

BRAZIL

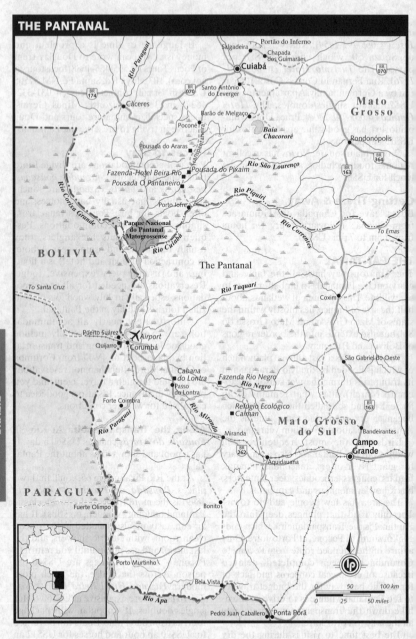

THE PANTANAL

the **Pousada O Pantaneiro** (☎ 065-721-1545), run by Lerinho and his son Eduardo. It's a simple place, charging US$30 per person for room and board.

Porto Jofre is a one-hotel hamlet. Campers can stay at Senhor Nicolino's **fishing camp**, near the river, for US$5 per person. He provides clean bathrooms and cooking facilities, and also rents boats.

Mato Grosso do Sul Eight km from Miranda is the **Hotel Beira Rio** (☎ 067-242-1262 in Miranda). It costs US$42 per person (meals included) for rooms with air-con and hot showers.

There are a few accommodations at Passo do Lontra, 120km and two hours (in the dry season) deeper into the Pantanal from Corumbá. The excellent **Cabana do Lontra** (☎ 067-241-2121) is another classic Pantanal structure, with lots of wildlife around. It costs US$40 per person, including full board, but they are quite willing to bargain, especially out of season. To get there, take the dirt road leading off the main road to Campo Grande.

The top-end place in the southern Pantanal is the **Refúgio Ecológico Caiman** (☎ 067-725-5267 in Campo Grande, 067-242-1102 in Corumbá, 011-246-9934 in São Paulo), 36km from Miranda. Caiman offers 25 different programs that can be done on foot, on horseback or by truck. All are led by one of the multilingual guides who live on the fazenda. This is real ecotourism. It isn't cheap (around US$200 a day per person), but it's highly recommended.

Getting There & Away

There are two main approach routes to the Pantanal: via Cuiabá in the north and via Corumbá in the south. From Cuiabá there are three gateways to the Pantanal – Cáceres, Barão de Melgaço and Poconé – all of which lead to Porto Jofre on the Transpantaneira. Corumbá is best accessed by bus from Campo Grande; the route runs via Aquidauana and Miranda.

If you're driving in the dry season, try the 120km stretch of newly upgraded road from Passo do Lontra to Corumbá that runs deep into the Pantanal. Coxim, a small town on the east of the Pantanal, is a third point of entry to the Pantanal, but has a very limited tourist infrastructure.

Getting Around

Car Since the lodges are the only places to sleep, drink and eat, and public transportation doesn't exist, independent travel is difficult in the Pantanal. Driving is an option, but it's not easy. Only a few roads reach the periphery of the Pantanal; they are frequently closed by rain and reconstructed yearly. Only the Transpantaneira goes deep into the region.

Wildlife is abundant along the length of the Transpantaneira, so if your budget is limited and you can get a group together, a cheap way to visit the Pantanal is driving a rental car all the way to Porto Jofre. Unfortunately, if you go without a guide, you miss a lot. Also, the many wooden bridges along the road are getting worse each year, and you'll probably have to do a little plank-reconstruction along the way.

If you are driving from Cuiabá, get going early. Leave at 4 am and you'll reach the Transpantaneira by sunrise, when the animals begin their day. You'll have a full day's light in which to drive to Porto Jofre.

The approach road to the Transpantaneira begins in Poconé (two hours from Cuiabá), by the Texaco station. Follow the road toward Hotel Aurora. The official Transpantaneira Highway Park starts 17km south of Poconé. There's a sign and guard station (where you pay a small entry fee) at the entrance.

Hitchhiking Hitchhiking from Poconé may be the cheapest way to go, but it doesn't allow you to stop whenever you want to observe wildlife. There aren't a lot of cars or trucks, but many stop to give rides. The best time to hitchhike is on weekends, when the locals drive down the Transpantaneira for a day's fishing. Make sure you get on the road early.

CORUMBÁ

Corumbá, a port city on the Rio Paraguai (the Bolivian border), is the southern gateway to the Pantanal. The town has a reputation for drug trafficking, gun-running and poaching, so be cautious.

Information

Tourist Offices The tourist office at the rodoviária (☎ 067-231-6091) provides information on hotels, travel agencies and boat trips. It also sells airline tickets to Bolivia. The Polícia Federal staff are also helpful, if they're not busy shaking down small-time drug runners.

Foreign Consulates The Bolivian consulate (☎ 067-231-5605) is at Rua Antônio Maria Coelho 881, near the intersection of Rua América. It's open from 8:30 am to 1:30 pm weekdays. At the time of writing, Bolivia had waived its visa requirements for nearly all western travelers.

The Paraguayan consulate (☎ 067-231-1691) is at Rua Firmo de Matos 508.

Organized Tours

Corumbá's star attraction is the Pantanal, and you can get a preview from Morro Urucum (1100m). Daily boat tours of the Corumbá area are available from all travel agencies. An all-day trip on the boat *Pérola do Pantanal* costs US$35, including lunch.

Many budget travelers to Corumbá choose to go on cheap three- to four-day tours into the southern Pantanal. Gil Tours (☎ 067-231-8486), run out of the Hotel Londres, and Colibri Pantanal Safari (☎ 067-231-3934), run by Swiss Claudine Roth at Rua Frei Mariano 1221, both organize Pantanal excursions and offer similar deals. Tours don't come much cheaper: US$30 per day for the first three days and US$10 per day for additional days. You can usually pay half before you leave and the rest when you return.

Panatanal trips can be rough-and-ready affairs. Accommodations are at bush camps, in tents or hammocks. Food is generally pretty good, though you should take extra water. Some of the guides are former jacaré hunters and their attitude toward animals can be less than sensitive. You'll see lots of birds, capybaras and jacarés, but jaguars and otters are harder to spot.

If you want something more comfortable and riding around in the back of a pickup truck doesn't grab you, you can pay a bit more and stay at a hotel or fazenda for a few days.

While the main operators are well organized, during the high season (June-August) some dodgy outfits pop up to get a slice of the tourist dollar. These characters generally offer cut-rate prices compared to the more reputable operators. Before joining one of these trips, there are a few things you should check out. Ask for a detailed itinerary, in writing if possible. Check out the truck. Does it look OK? Does it have a radio and carry a first-aid kit in case of emergency? A bite from the boca da sapo snake will kill you in half an hour if left untreated.

Expect to spend at least half a day traveling into the Pantanal. Finding wildlife depends less on how far you travel than on how well your guide knows the Pantanal. Allow at least two days to see wildlife at close quarters. Definitely insist on doing this on foot – vehicles should be used only for access, *not* for pursuit. Your chances of enjoying the Pantanal and its wildlife are greatly increased if you go with a reputable guide who: forsakes the 'mechanical chase' approach; accompanies small groups (preferably no more than eight people); camps out at night (away from drinking dens!); and takes you on walks at the optimum times to observe wildlife (before sunrise, at dusk and during the night). A trip like this will require at least four days (preferably five).

Places to Stay & Eat

There are some cheap hotels close to the rodoviária that are OK if you're just spending a night before heading out. Otherwise, consider some of the better places closer to the waterfront and the restaurants and bars in the center of town. Near the rodoviária, the *Hotel Londres* (☎ 067-231-6717) has run-down apartamentos for US$10 per person. The *Hotel Beatriz* (☎ 067-231-8465), Rua Porto Carrero, has basic quartos for US$6/12/18 singles/doubles/triples.

In the center, the *Condor*, on Rua Delamere, has quartos with fans for US$7 per person. *Hotel Santa Rita* (☎ 067-231-5453), Rua Dom Aquino 860, has good, big apartamentos for US$17/28.

Bar El Pacu, on Rua Cabral, is a good fish restaurant. Enjoy as much meat and salad as you can eat for US$7 at *Laco do Ouro*, on Rua Frei Mariano.

The hippest eatery in town is *Vivabella*, a small bar and restaurant tucked away near the corner of the park at the bottom of Rua 7 de Setembro.

Getting There & Away

Like Campo Grande, Corumbá is a transit point for travel to and from Bolivia and Paraguay.

Air The airport is 3km from the town center. VASP (☎ 067-231-4441, 067-231-4468 at the airport), Rua 15 de Novembro 392, is the only large company flying into Corumbá.

Bus From the rodoviária, buses run to Campo Grande eleven times a day (US$25, six hours). There's one daily bus to Bonito (US$25, seven hours) at 5:30 am.

Boat Passenger boat services between Corumbá and Asunción (Paraguay) have been discontinued. Boat transportation through the Pantanal is infrequent – inquire at the Porto Geral.

To/From Bolivia Brazilian immigration is at the federal police post in the Corumbá rodoviária. Anyone entering or exiting Brazil must check in here for complete immigration formalities. For about US$0.70, a city bus will take you into Corumbá, 5km from the border. Everyone entering Brazil from Bolivia is required to have a yellow fever vaccination certificate.

Getting Around
A taxi to the center of Corumbá from either the bus or the train station costs US$7. For a taxi from the center to the Bolivian border, expect to pay US$10. A city bus between the center and the Brazilian border departs every 40 minutes (US$0.70).

Bahia

Bahia is Brazil's most African state. Its capital, Salvador da Bahia, is a fascinating city and a major tourist attraction. The Bahian coast has many fine beaches, while the inland regions, though less well known, are well worth a visit. Lençois provides a handy base for hiking trips inside the spectacular Parque Nacional da Chapada Diamantina.

Bahia also has some of Brazil's best artisans, who usually have small shops or sell their folk art in the local market. You can buy many crafts in Salvador, but the best place to see or purchase the real stuff is from the artists themselves.

SALVADOR DA BAHIA
Salvador da Bahia is often abbreviated to Bahia by Brazilians, but also commonly called Salvador. It's the capital of Bahia state and one of Brazil's highlights.

On November 1, 1501, All Saints' Day, Amerigo Vespucci sailed into the bay, which was accordingly named Baía de Todos os Santos. In 1549, on the shores of the bay, Tomé de Souza founded what would be Brazil's most important city for 300 years.

Thriving on the sugar trade until the mid-18th century, Salvador was the Portuguese empire's second most important city, after Lisbon. It was famous for its gold-filled churches, beautiful mansions and many festivals, as well as its sensuality and decadence. The historic city center has been attractively renovated, though the redevelopment displaced many of the former residents, and purists say that it's not a totally authentic restoration. While visitors throng the central areas and new industries have transformed the suburbs, many of the city's 2.1 million people are still jobless, homeless and hungry.

Orientation
Salvador sits on a peninsula at the mouth of Baía de Todos os Santos. A steep bluff divides central Salvador into two parts (see map on p392): historic Cidade Alta (Upper City) and Cidade Baixa (Lower City), the commercial and financial center. These are linked by the Plano Inclinado Gonçalves (funicular railway), the Lacerda Elevator and some very steep roads (*ladeiras*).

The heart of the historic center, which attracts most of the tourists and nightlife, is called Pelourinho. This refers, very roughly, to the area between and around Largo do Pelourinho and Terreiro de Jesus. Farther south, at the tip of the peninsula, the area known as Barra has a pretty beach and is also popular. There are many other beaches along the coast to the east.

Information
Tourist Offices Bahiatursa (☎ 071-322-2403), the state tourism authority, has offices on the Belvedere da Sé, Rua Francisco Muniz Barreto 12, Pelourinho, Mercado Modelo, the rodoviária, the airport, the Centro de Convenções da Bahia, Shopping Iguatemi and Shopping Barra.

Bahiatursa also operates an alternative accommodations service to locate rooms in private houses and other accommodations during Carnaval and summer holidays.

BRAZIL

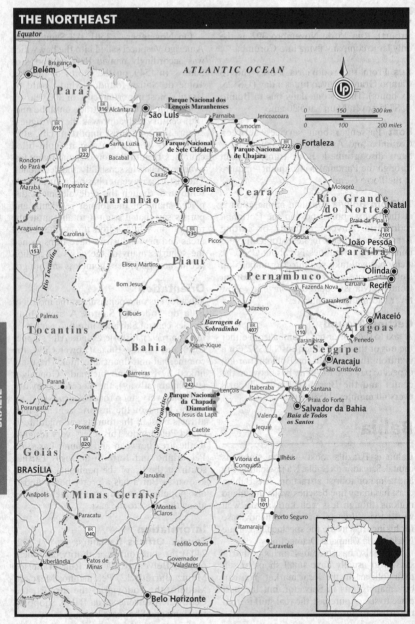

THE NORTHEAST

Equator

ATLANTIC OCEAN

BRAZIL

Money In Cidade Alta, two good places to change money are Toursbahia and Vertur, both near Terreiro de Jesus. Banco do Brasil's main branch is at Av Estados Unidos 561, in Cidade Baixa. Visa withdrawals can be made from Bradesco ATMs at the airport, rodoviária, Shopping Iguatemi, Shopping Barra and Largo Teresa Batista in the Pelourinho.

Post The central post office is in Cidade Baixa on Praça da Inglaterra, but there's a more convenient one at Rua Alfredo de Brito 43, Pelourinho.

Telephone For international long-distance calls, direct dial international (DDI) public telephones may be more convenient than running off to a telephone station. They work with phonecards, preferably the 90-unit ones that allow longer conversations, and are located in major hotels and tourist areas. If you can't find one, some of the convenient Telebahia posto telefônica stations are at the airport, rodoviária, Shoppings Barra and Iguatemi, and the Centro de Convenções da Bahia.

Emergency DELTUR tourist police (☎ 071-242-3504) operate 24 hours a day in the Pelourinho at Cruzeiro de São Francisco 14. Other useful numbers include: Disque Turismo (dial tourism, ☎ 131); Pronto Socorro (first aid, ☎ 192); and Polícia Civil (police, ☎ 197).

Dangers & Annoyances Salvador has a reputation for theft and muggings, though the Pelourinho area is now thick with patrolling police and pretty safe. Elsewhere, be careful.

Walking Tour

Historic Salvador is easy to see on foot, and you should plan on spending a couple of mornings wandering through the old city. The most important sections of Salvador's colonial quarter extend from Praça Castro Alves along Rua Chile, past Praça Tomé de Souza, along Rua da Misericórdia to Praça da Sé and Terreiro de Jesus, then down through Largo do Pelourinho and up the hill to Largo do Carmo.

Starting at the Praça da Sé, look north to the big **Catedral Basílica**, built between 1657 and 1672, which is being restored; the deteriorating ceiling is being replaced with fiberglass. Next to the cathedral, the **Antiga Faculdade de Medicina** (old medical faculty) is a handsome building that houses two museums. The **Museu Afro-Brasileira** has displays on black cultural traditions, with orixás from Africa and Bahia. The museum is open 9 am to 5 pm Tuesday to Saturday. In the basement is the **Museu de Arqueologia e Etnologia**.

To the southeast is a large square, the **Terreiro de Jesus**, with a fountain and some bars with outdoor tables that are popular in the evenings. Walk to the far end of the plaza and continue on the narrower Praça Anchieta, which has a large carved stone cross. Beyond that is the Baroque **Igreja São Francisco**, which is crammed with displays of wealth and splendor.

To see the city's oldest architecture, go northeast off the Terreiro down Rua Alfredo de Brito. You'll descend to **Largo do Pelourinho**, the old slave auction site and the place where the slaves were tortured and sold. *Pelourinho* means 'whipping post'; the whipping of slaves was legal in Brazil until 1835.

The building facing the Largo has been restored and converted into two museums: The **Casa da Cultura Jorge Amado** is dedicated to novelist Jorge Amado, who lived near here; and the **Museu da Cidade** has interesting exhibits including costumes of the orixás of Candomblé and the personal effects of the Romantic poet Castro Alves, one of the first public figures to protest against slavery. The museums are open 10 am to 6 pm Tuesday to Friday, and 1 to 5 pm weekends.

From Pelourinho, go down the hill past **Igreja NS do Rosário dos Pretos**, an 18th-century church built by (and for) slaves. It has some lovely azulejos. Follow Ladeira do Carmo uphill, where you'll see a set of steps to the left, reminiscent of the Spanish steps of Rome. They lead up to **Igreja do Santíssimo Sacramento da Rua do Paço**.

At the top of the hill is **Igreja da Ordem Terceira do Carmo**. Founded in 1636, it contains a Baroque altar and an organ dating from 1889. For a glimpse of old Salvador, walk a few blocks farther, past very old, dilapidated buildings teeming with life.

Return to Praça da Sé (try a detour through some other old streets south of

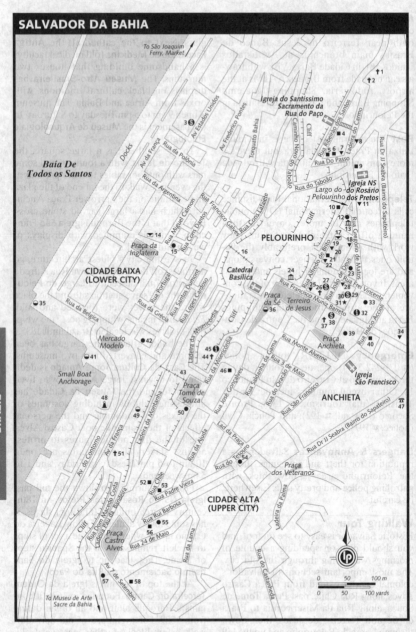

SALVADOR DA BAHIA

To São Joaquim Ferry, Market

Baía De Todos os Santos

Docks

CIDADE BAIXA (LOWER CITY)

Praça da Inglaterra

Mercado Modelo

Small Boat Anchorage

Av do Contorno

Av da França

Rua Dom Macedo Costa

Cliff

Praça Castro Alves

To Museu de Arte Sacre da Bahia

Rua da França

Rua da Polónia

Av da França

Rua da Argentina

Rua Miguel Calmon

Rua Lons Dantos

Rua Francisco Galves

Rua Cons Lafaiete

Av Estados Unidos

Av Frederico Pontes

Torquato Bahia

Caminho Novo do Taboão

Rua Ribeiro dos Santos

Ladeira do Carmo

Rua Dr JJ Seabra

Igreja do Santíssimo Sacramento da Rua do Paço

Rua Do Passo

Rua do Taboão

Rua do Taboão

Largo do Pelourinho

Igreja NS do Rosário dos Pretos (Bairro do Sapateiro)

PELOURINHO

Rua Gregório de Matos

Rua Alfredo de Brito

Rua João de Deus

Rua Frei Vincente

Catedral Basílica

Rua Francisco Muniz Barreto

Praça da Sé

Terreiro de Jesus

Praça Anchieta

Rua Inácio Accioli

Rua Monte Alverne

Igreja São Francisco

ANCHIETA

Rua Dr JJ Seabra (Bairro do Sapateiro)

Rua Santos Dumont

Rua Portugal

Rua da Grécia

Rua Lopes Cardoso

Ladeira da Misericórdia

Rua da Misericórdia

Praça Tomé de Souza

Rua José Gonçalves

Rua Saldanha da Gama

Rua 3 de Maio

Rua do Oração

Rua São Francisco

Ladeira da Montanha

Rua da Ajuda

Lad da Praça

Rua do Tesouro

Praça dos Veteranos

CIDADE ALTA (UPPER CITY)

Rua Chile

Rua Padre Vieira

Rua Rui Barbosa

Rua 24 de Maio

Rua da Lama

Rua da Palma

Rua do Castanheda

Av 7 de Setembro

Ladeira Paula da Bandeira

BRAZIL

0   50   100 m
0   50   100 yards

SALVADOR DA BAHIA

PLACES TO STAY
4 Albergue de Juventude Solar
5 Albergue de Juventude do Pelô
6 Albergue Pousada do Passo
9 Hotel Solara
10 Hotel Pelourinho
21 Albergue de Juventude Vagaus
40 Albergue de Juventude das Laranjeiras
46 Hotel Themis
52 Hotel Chile
53 Palace Hotel
56 Hotel Pousada da Praça
58 Hotel Maridina

PLACES TO EAT
7 Kilinho
8 Casa do Benin
11 Senac
18 Uauá
19 Micheluccio
22 Mamabahia
25 Cantinha da Lua
28 Tempero da Dada
34 Glojú

OTHER
1 Igreja e Convento de NS do Carmo, Museu do Carmo
2 Igreja da Ordem Terceira do Carmo
3 Banco do Brasil
12 Casa da Cultura Jorge Amado
13 Museu da Cidade
14 Post Office
15 VASP
16 Plano Inclinado Gonçalves (Funicular Railway)
17 Post Office
20 Praça Quincas Berro d'Agua (Praça Dois M)
23 Didá Music & Dance School
24 Antigua Faculdade de Medicina, Museu Afro-Brasileiro, Museu de Arqueologia e Ethnologia
26 Igreja Sáo Pedro dos Clérigos
27 Toursbahia
29 Bradesco ATM
30 Largo de Tereza Batista

31 DELTUR Tourist Police
32 Bahiatursa Tourist Office
33 Largo do Pedro Arcanjo
35 Terminal Turístico Marítimo (Boat to Ilha de Itaparica)
36 Bus Station
37 Igreja da Ordem Terceira de São Domingus
38 Vertur
39 Mercado Artesenato
41 Small Boats to Ilha de Itaparica
42 Casa dos Azulejos
43 Lacerda Elevator
44 Igreja da Misericórdia
45 Bahiatursa (Main Office)
47 Posto Telefônica
48 Bunda Statue
49 Av de França Bus Station, Buses to Mercado São Joaquim, Ferry & Igreja NS do Bonfim
50 Palácio Rio Branco
51 Igreja NS da Conceição
54 Casa de Ruy Barbosa
55 Livraria Brandão Bookshop
57 Varig

Alfredo de Brito), and continue to Praça Tomé de Souza, with the beautiful **Palácio Rio Branco** on one side and the ugly, modern office of the mayor on the other. There's a great view over the harbor from the top station of the **Lacerda Elevator**, which carries up to 50,000 passengers a day (including quite a few pickpockets). The elevator will take you down to the Cidade Baixa (lower city), close to the **Mercado Modelo**, a touristy market that often has live music and entertainment. The blocks to the northeast are the main commercial district.

Back at the top of the elevator, walk southwest along Rua Chile to **Praça Castro Alves**, where there's an imposing statue and good sea views. From there it's a short walk to the **Museu de Arte Sacra da Bahia**, at Rua do Sodré 276. The sacred art is displayed in a beautifully restored 17th-century convent. It's open 12:30 to 5:30 pm weekdays.

Solar do Unhão

On the bay, southwest from the center toward Campo Grande, this old sugar estate now houses the small Museu de Arte Moderna, a good restaurant, a ceramic workshop and the ghosts of tortured slaves. This area has a reputation for crime (espe-

cially tourist muggings), so take a taxi there and back. Opening hours are 1 to 5 pm Tuesday to Sunday.

Barra

Five km southwest of the center, the **Forte de Santo Antonio da Barra** (1598) is at the very tip of the peninsula. There are nearby beaches on the bay and the Atlantic Ocean. The first stretch of sand along the Atlantic has a lively beach scene, but heavy pollution makes swimming inadvisable. The bay beach, Praia do Porto, is also popular and looks much cleaner. There are plenty of bars and restaurants.

Monte Serrat & Itapagipe

North of the center, Baía de Todos os Santos curves around to the Itapagipe peninsula, with the old Monte Serrat Lighthouse and the Igreja de Monte Serrat at its tip. Nearby Igreja NS do Bonfim was built in 1745, and is famous for its miraculous power to effect cures. It's an important church for Candomblistas. Nearby is **Praia da Boa Viagem**, a popular beach lined with barracas that's lively on weekends. Buses from the Lacerda Elevator base station go to Boa Viagem.

BRAZIL

Beaches

Beautiful beaches dot the Atlantic coast east of Barra, but those close to the city are polluted. If you want to swim, it's advisable to head out to Placaford, Itapuã or beyond.

Candomblé

Much of Bahian life revolves around the Afro-Brazilian cults known as Candomblé (see under Religion in the Facts about the Country section). Don't miss a night in a terreiro. Bahiatursa can provide a complete list and advise you on the schedule for the month. The center for Candomblé in Salvador is Casa Branca, Av Vasco da Gama 463, in the Engenho Velho neighborhood.

Capoeira

To visit a capoeira school, it's best to get the up-to-date schedule from Bahiatursa. The Associação de Capoeira Mestre Bimba is an excellent school.

Carnaval

Carnaval, usually held in late February or early March, starts on a Thursday night and continues until the following Monday. Anything, but anything, goes during these four days, especially the trios elétricos (fast frevostyle electric music, frequently played from a truck). Carnaval here is becoming more commercialized, but this trend is still light-years behind Rio.

Many clubs have balls just before and during Carnaval. If you're in the city before the festivities start, you can also see the *blocos* (musical street groups) practicing; don't miss the *afoxés* (African blocos). The best place to see them is Liberdade, Salvador's largest black district.

Violence can be a problem during Carnaval, and some women travelers have reported threatening approaches from locals, but wild dancing behind a trio elétrico is a more common danger!

Places to Stay

Salvador has many hotels, but they are often full during summer holidays, big festivals and Carnaval. Bahiatursa can help you find lodging if you don't look too burnt-out or broke.

Camping On the outskirts of Itapuã, there are several campgrounds. One, *Camping*

Ecológico (☎ 071-374-0201), is on Alameda da Praia at Praia do Flamengo. *Camping Pituaçu*, (☎ 071-231-7413) on Av Pinto d'Aguiar at Pituaçu, is about 14km from the center.

Hostels There are some excellent youth hostels close to the city center. They all charge around US$10 for members, a little more for nonmembers, and sometimes a couple of dollars extra for breakfast.

There are a few excellent hostels close to the city center, mostly clustered around Pelourinho. *Albergue Pousada do Passo* (☎ 071-326-1954), Rua do Passo 3, is popular with backpackers. The friendly owner, Fernando, speaks English, French and Spanish. He offers very clean dormitories for US$10/25 singles/doubles. Another favorite is the *Albergue de Juventude das Laranjeiras* (☎ 071-321-1366), a very flashy Pelourinho hostel at Rua Inácio Acciolli 13. The YHA *Albergue de Juventude do Pelô* (☎ 071-242-8061) is also popular and conveniently located at Rua Ribeiro Santos 5. Close by is the YHA *Albergue de Juventude Solar* (☎ 071-241-0055), Rua Ribeiro Santos 45. *Albergue de Juventude Vagaus* (☎ 071-321-1179), on Rua Alfredo Brito, has basic dorm rooms for US$10 per person and friendly owners.

There are two hostels close to the beaches. The *Albergue do Porto* (☎ 071-247-8228), Rua Barão de Sergy 197, is close to the beach in Barra. Next to Praia Pituba is the *Albergue de Juventude Casa Grande* (☎/fax 071-248-0527), Rua Minas Gerais 122.

Hotels Cheap, good-value hotels are hard to find near the historic center. One of the cheapest is the *Hotel Solara* (☎ 071-326-4583) on the downhill side of Largo do Pelourinho, offering apartamentos that start at US$18/25 for singles/doubles including breakfast.

Another cheapie is *Hotel Themis* (☎ 071-243-1668), on the 7th floor of the ugly Edifício Themis, Praça da Sé 57. It has a bar and restaurant with great views, but rooms are pretty run-down. Apartamentos without a view cost US$17/24/30 for singles/doubles/triples, apartamentos with a view cost US$20/28/36.

The *Hotel Chile* (☎ 071-321-0245), Rua Chile 7 (1st floor), has quartos starting at

US$17/25 for singles/doubles. Apartamentos cost US$28/40 with air-con. A little farther away, *Hotel Pousada da Praça* (☎ *071-321-0642*), Rua Rui Barbosa 5, offers basic but clean quartos for US$18/23 and apartamentos for US$30. It's very pleasant and a good value. Just down from Praça Castro Alves, *Hotel Maridina* (☎ *071-242-7176*), Av 7 de Setembro, Ladeira de São Bento 6 (1st floor), is a friendly, family-run hotel that's a good value for the money. Quartos with fan cost US$17/28 and apartamentos with air-con cost US$25/35.

The *Hotel Pelourinho* (☎ *071-243-2324*), in an old converted mansion at Rua Alfredo de Brito 20, is in the heart of Pelourinho. It has long been a favorite with travelers, but is getting pricey. Small apartamentos with fan cost US$30/45/60 for singles/doubles/triples. The modern *Palace Hotel* (☎ *071-322-1155*), Rua Chile 20, is a reasonable mid-range option offering comfortable quartos with fan for US$33/38 and air-con apartamentos for US$45/53.

The pleasant *Hotel Caramuru* (☎ *071-336-9951*), Av 7 de Setembro 2125, is in a quiet location halfway between the center and Barra. It's in a large colonial mansion and has spotless quartos for US$25/30 and big double apartamentos for US$35. The hotel also organizes Candomblé excursions and other trips.

In Barra, *Pousada Azul* (☎ *071-245-9798*), Rua Praguer Fróis 97, is a friendly, comfortable, highly recommended pousada. There are dorms and some rooms for singles and couples. At US$15 per person with a good breakfast, it's only a couple of blocks from the beach.

Also in Barra, *Pousada Âmbar* (☎ *071-235-6956*), Rua Afonso Celso 485, is a lovely family-run pousada with a relaxed, friendly atmosphere. They charge US$12 per person without breakfast and US$15 with – it's definitely worth the extra three bucks. Right on Praia do Porto da Barra at Av 7 de Setembro 3801, the *Pousada Malu* (☎ *071-237-4461*) is a relaxed place offering clean apartamentos with fan for US$20/25.

Along the beach, in Itapuã, the *Pousada Bruta Flor*, Rua Passagarda 20, is a beautiful, small pousada. It's a five-minute walk from clean beaches and has a nice pool for a swim before breakfast. It has spotless six-bed, four-bed and two-bed quartos for US$15 or US$25, depending on the season and whether you'll be having breakfast.

Places to Eat

Bahian cuisine is an intriguing blend of African and Brazilian recipes based on ingredients such as coconut cream, ginger, hot peppers, coriander, shrimp and dendê oil. For names and short descriptions of typical Bahian dishes, see Food in the Facts for the Visitor section of this chapter.

The Pelourinho area is packed with restaurants, but many of them cater to tourists and are expensive, especially at lunch time. The popular self-serve restaurants are the best value for lunch. *Glojú*, at the bottom of Rua Francisco M Barreto, and *Kilinho,* close to the Pousada do Passo, are a couple of the best places.

A long-time favorite on Terreiro de Jesus is *Cantinho da Lua*, which serves good-value refeições and is a popular hangout. Nearby, at Rua Alfredo Brito 21, *Mamabahia* has a popular churrasco lunch for US$7.

Other popular places for dinner are on the block around Praça Quincas Berro D'Agua. *Micheluccio*, at Rua Alfredo Brito 33, has excellent pizza. *Tempero da Dada*, Rua Frei Vicente 5, is a lively, casual restaurant with tasty seafood – the moqueca de peixe is good. Two people can eat for around US$20.

The restaurant at *Hotel Pelourinho* has a great view of the bay and OK food, but it's a bit overpriced. On Largo do Pelourinho is *Senac*, a cooking school that offers a huge buffet of 40 regional dishes. It's not the best Bahian cooking, but for US$14 you can discover which Bahian dishes you like – and eat till you explode. Senac is open 6 to 9 pm daily except Sunday.

Downhill from Largo do Pelourinho is *Casa do Benin*, a superb restaurant serving excellent African food in a small, attractive courtyard. The main dishes start around US$15; try the delicious *frango ao gengibre* (ginger chicken). Another terrific restaurant for African-influenced cuisine is the colorful *Uauá*, Rua Gregório de Matos 36.

Entertainment

Salvador is justly renowned for its music. The blend of African and Brazilian traditions produces popular styles, such as trio

BRAZIL

elétrico (which dominates Carnaval), tropicalismo, afoxé, caribé, reggae and lambada. Bars and clubs go in and out of fashion, so ask around.

Pelourinho is the nightlife capital of Salvador; its cobbled streets are lined with bars, and blocos practice almost every night, especially Tuesday, when bands set up on Terreiro de Jesus, Largo do Pelourinho and anywhere else they can find space. Crowds pour in to eat, drink, dance and party until the early hours. There are lots of locals and tourists, including quite a few professional and semiprofessional prostitutes.

The city sponsors free live music at several outdoor venues in the Pelourinho, including *Largo de Tereza Batista*, *Largo do Pedro Arcanjo* and *Praça Quincas Berro d'Agua* (known locally as Praça Dois M).

Praça Dois M is also home to several hip bars – *Habeus Copos* and *Kibe & CIA* are two of the popular spots. *Bar do Reggae*, right on the Pelourinho, tends to have dancers spilling out into the street just about every night.

Folklore shows, usually consisting of mini-displays of Candomblé, capoeira, samba and lambada are presented in the evening at *Senac* in Pelourinho, *Solar do Unhão*, south of the city center, and *Moenda*, at Jardim Armação next to the Centro de Convenções. The monthly *Agenda Cultural* includes a comprehensive rundown of music events, theater, dance and art exhibitions.

Getting There & Away

Air There are regular international flights between Salvador and Miami, New York, Frankfurt, Paris, Rome and Buenos Aires. There are good connections to other large Brazilian cities with the major domestic airlines. Nordeste (☎ 071-341-2866) flies to smaller cities in the region, like Ilhéus and Porto Seguro.

Bus There are numerous departures daily to Rio (US$75, 28 hours), Brasília (US$70, 22 hours) and four to Belo Horizonte (US$60, 22 hours).

There are eight departures daily to Aracaju (US$15) via the Linha Verde, three to Recife (US$40, 13 hours), two to Fortaleza (US$60, 20 hours), and one to Belém (US$93, 34 hours). Two buses daily go to Lençois (US$18, six hours), Ilhéus (US$23,

seven hours), and Porto Seguro (US$42, 12 hours), as well as frequent departures to Valença (US$13, five hours) and Cachoeira (US$6, two hours) – take the São Felix bus.

Getting Around

The Lacerda Elevator runs 24 hours daily, linking the lower and upper cities. The Plano Inclinado funicular stops at 10 pm.

The rodoviária is 5km from the city center. The best way there is the executivo bus from Praça da Sé to Iguatemi shopping center, then walk over the pedestrian footbridge to the rodoviária. A taxi from Praça da Sé will cost about US$6, but the fixed-price taxi tickets from the bilheteria at the rodoviária cost US$11. If you want to go from the center to the rodoviária by local bus, descend the Lacerda Elevator and take either a Rodoviária or Iguatemi bus (US$0.70) heading southwest.

To/From the Airport Aeroporto Dois de Julho is more than 30km from the city center, inland from Itapuã. At the airport, there's a bilheteria for overpriced taxis: It costs US$35 to Praça da Sé during the day, and US$50 at night. It's best to take the executivo Praça da Sé-Aeroporto bus (US$1.80) from the stop at Praça da Sé. You can flag it down along the coastal road. Allow at least an hour for the ride, 1¾ hours if there's traffic. If you have an early flight, stay the night at Itapuã.

Bus There are two types of local buses. Municipal buses are very cheap (US$0.70) but crowded, slow, and not recommended if you have any baggage. Executivo buses cost two or three times as much, but everyone gets a seat and enjoys air-con comfort. They are available on an increasing number of routes, including from Praça da Sé. Praça da Sé-Aeroporto executivo buses go along the beaches from Barra to Itapuã.

The Av da França bus terminal is in Cidade Baixa, beside the Lacerda Elevator base station. From here, you can take Ribeira or Bonfim buses to the Itaparica ferry, Mercado São Joaquim market, and the Itapagipe peninsula.

ITAPARICA

This is the largest island in Baía de Todos os Santos. It is quite pretty and popular with

Salvadoreans on weekends, but is not really a must-see destination. The best part of the island is owned by Club Med, but there are still a few clean beaches, including Barra Grande, with good views of the city. At the northern tip of the island is the city of Itaparica and the São Lourenço Fort. South of the city is Ponte da Areia, a thin strip of sand with barracas serving excellent food.

You can stay at the *Albergue de Juventude Enseada de Aratuba* at Quadra H, lotes 12/1, or at campgrounds at Praia de Berlinque, Praia de Barra Grande and Praia de Cacha Pregos. In Mar Grande, a good cheap option is the *Pousada Koisa Nossa (☎ 071-833-1028)*, Rua da Rodagam 173, with apartamentos for US$18/25 singles/doubles.

Getting There & Away

There are three types of boat from Salvador to Itaparica. The first is a small boat that leaves from the Terminal Turístico Marítimo behind the Mercado Modelo and goes directly to Mar Grande. The trip costs US$1.45 and takes around 50 minutes.

The second option is a giant car-and-passenger ferry that operates between São Joaquim and Bom Despacho. The fare is US$1.45 and the ride takes 45 minutes. Ferries operate every hour from 5:30 am to 10:30 pm (until midnight in summer). Expect a long wait to get on the ferry during weekends, especially in summer.

The fastest way to do the trip is on one of the air-con catamarans. The journey takes 20 minutes and costs US$4.50, beginning at 6:30 am and running frequently from Mar Grande until 7 pm (later in summer).

CACHOEIRA

Cachoeira – the jewel of the recôncavo (a fertile region around the Baía de Todos os Santos) – is a small city in the center of Brazil's best tobacco-growing region. It is full of beautiful colonial architecture, uncompromised by modern buildings. It sits on the Rio Paraguaçu, with the town of São Felix on the other side. Cachoeira is 120km from Salvador de Bahia, so plan to stay overnight.

Information

The tourist office on Praça da Aclimação should be able to help with accommodations and general information.

Things to See & Do

Cachoeira is an important center for **Candomblé**. The ceremonies are held in small homes and shacks up in the hills, usually at 8 pm on Friday and Saturday nights. Visitors are not as common here as in Salvador, so the tourist office is sometimes reluctant to give out information about the ceremonies. They may help, however, if you show an interest in Candomblé and respect for its traditions.

Cachoeira and São Felix are best seen on foot. The restored **Igreja da Ordem Terceira do Carmo** features a gallery of suffering polychrome Christs imported from the Portuguese colonies in Macau. You can visit 2 to 5 pm Tuesday to Saturday and on Sunday morning.

The **Museu Hansen Bahia** displays the powerful work of German Brazilian artist Hansen Bahia. It's open 9 am to 5 pm weekdays and 9 am to 2 pm weekends.

The tiny **NS d'Ajuda**, on Largo da Ajuda, is Cachoeira's oldest church. Attached to the church is the **Museu da Boa Morte**, an interesting museum with displays featuring photos and ceremonial apparel of the exclusively female Boa Morte (Good Death) cult, a secret religious society.

Special Events

One of Cachoeira's many festivals is the fascinating Festa da NS de Boa Morte, organized by the Sisterhood of the Good Death. The festival falls on the Friday closest to 15 August and lasts three days. The Festa de São João (22-24 June) is the biggest popular festival of Bahia's interior.

Places to Stay

The *Pousada do Pai Thomáz (☎ 075-725-1288)*, Rua 25 de Junho 12, has comfortable apartamentos for US$15/30 singles/doubles. The *Pensão Tia Rosa (☎ 075-725-1792)*, opposite Museu Hansen Bahia, has basic quartos for US$12 per person, including a good breakfast. The *Pousada do Guerreiro*, Rua 13 de Maio 14, has ragged but clean quartos for US$12/20 and apartamentos for US$15/25.

Pousada do Convento de Cachoeira (☎ 075-725-1716) is a lovely old hotel with a courtyard and swimming pool. The darkwood rooms of what was once a convent now have air-con and hot showers. They cost US$46/52.

BRAZIL

Places to Eat

The *Gruta Azul*, Praça Manoel Vitorino 2, is Cachoeira's best restaurant; ask for the *boa morte* drink. It opens only for lunch.

Nair restaurant (often called 'Rian') provides excellent moqueca dishes and local specialties: Try *maniçoba*, a typical Cachoeira dish. There's more good food at *Cabana do Pai Thomáz*, across the road from the pousada.

Getting There & Away

Buses depart hourly from 4:30 am to 6:30 pm for Salvador (US$6, two hours).

PRAIA DO FORTE

Praia do Forte is 80km north of Salvador on the Rodovia do Coco (the Coconut Highway). It has fine beaches, a beautiful ruined castle fortress, and a sea-turtle reserve. Until recently a fishing village, Praia do Forte is being developed as an ecologically minded, upmarket beach resort.

TAMAR Turtle Reserve

The reserve is on the beach, right next to the lighthouse. Tartaruga Marinha (TAMAR) is a project started in 1982 to protect several species of marine turtle.

Places to Stay & Eat

There's a campground about 10 minutes from the beach. The friendly new YHA hostel *Praia do Forte* (☎ 071-876-1094), Rua Aurora 3, is 200m from the beach. They charge US$12 for members and US$15 for nonmembers. Also recommended is the *Pousada Brasil,* opposite the church near TAMAR. Double rooms with veranda and sea view cost US$40. *Casa da Lagosta* on Rua da Aurora serves seafood dishes large enough for two.

Getting There & Away

The Catuense company runs buses from Salvador to Praia do Forte between 7:30 am and 6 pm daily. The trip takes 1½ hours and costs US$3.50.

MORRO DE SÃO PAULO

Morro de São Paulo, at the northern tip of Ilha do Tinharé, was an isolated fishing village 'discovered' by Brazilian and international tourists 15 years ago. It now receives some 120,000 visitors each year. The beaches

are wonderful and the village is loaded with pousadas, restaurants and bars. It's still quite a relaxing place, except during the summer.

Places to Stay & Eat

Accommodations in Morro can be tight during summer. Still, there are more than 100 pousadas, so it's definitely worth hunting around. Close to the action, *Pousada Gaucho* (☎ 075-783-1115) and *Pousada Giras Sol*, both on Caminho da Praia, are two good, cheap options, with quartos for around US$10 per person in the low season. *Pousada Ilha do Sol* (☎ 075-783-1118), next to the steep concrete ramp at the beach end of Caminho da Praia, has spacious apartamentos with hammocks and beach views. It charges US$13/25 singles/doubles in the low season and US$20/40 in the high.

There are a few campgrounds, but for longer stays the best deal is to rent a house.

The main street, Caminho da Praia, is a regular restaurant strip. *Ponte de Econtro* offers a wide range of excellent, tasty vegetarian food por kilo. *Canto do Mar* and *Sabor da Terra* both have good-value seafood prato feito for around US$6. *La Strega* is a tiny restaurant with excellent pasta. *Forno a Lenha Pizzaria* is the place to head for good-value, wood-fired pizza.

Getting There & Away

To get to the island take a relaxed 1½-hour ride (US$2) on the *Brisa Biônica* or *Brisa Triônica* from Valença to Morro de São Paulo. It's a beautiful trip.

During the summer, seven boats per day depart Valença for Morro between 7:30 am and 5 pm. During summer, there are direct boats to and from Salvador. During the rest of the year boats are less frequent, except on weekends; Bahiatursa should know the schedule. At any time of year, try to arrive early.

ILHÉUS

Ilhéus, the town where Jorge Amado lived and wrote about in *Gabriela, Clove & Cinnamon,* retains some of the charm and lunacy that Amado fans know well. The colonial center is interesting and the beaches are superb.

Things to See & Do

The best thing to do in Ilhéus is just wander. If you walk up the hill to the **Convento NS**

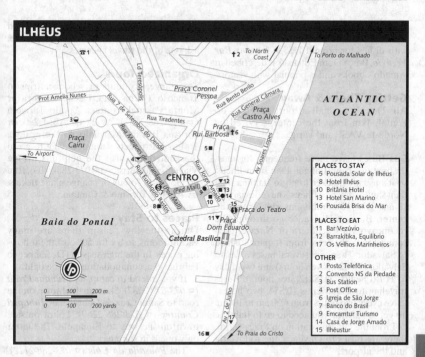

ILHÉUS

ATLANTIC OCEAN

Baia do Pontal

Praça Coronel Pessoa

Praça Castro Alves

Praça Rui Barbosa

CENTRO (Ped Mall)

Praça do Teatro

Praça Dom Eduardo

Catedral Basílica

Praça Cairu

To Airport

To North Coast

To Porto do Malhado

To Praia do Cristo

PLACES TO STAY
5 Pousada Solar de Ilhéus
8 Hotel Ilhéus
10 Britânia Hotel
13 Hotel San Marino
16 Pousada Brisa do Mar

PLACES TO EAT
11 Bar Vezúvio
12 Barrakítika, Equilibrio
17 Os Velhos Marinheiros

OTHER
1 Posto Telefônica
2 Convento NS da Piedade
3 Bus Station
4 Post Office
6 Igreja de São Jorge
7 Banco do Brasil
9 Emcamtur Turismo
14 Casa de Jorge Amado
15 Ilhéustur

0   100   200 m
0   100   200 yards

BRAZIL

da Piedade, there's a good view of the city and littoral. The **Igreja de São Jorge** (1534), the city's oldest church, houses a small sacred-art museum. It's on Praça Rui Barbosa and is open 8 to 11 am and 2 to 5:30 pm Tuesday to Sunday.

The **Museu Regional do Cacao**, at Rua AL Lemos 126, displays cacao artifacts and contemporary paintings by local artists. It's open most afternoons, and also mornings from December to March.

Places to Stay

Ilhéus boasts a good range of accommodations. In summer, expect prices to rise at least 25% from those quoted here. For camping, try **Camping Estância das Fontes** (☎ 073-212-2505), 15km from Ilhéus. It's close to the beach and charges US$8 per person for a campsite.

Pousada Solar de Ilhéus (☎ 073-231-5125), Rua General Câmara 50, is a friendly, secure, family-run place with spotless quartos from around US$15/22, including a superb breakfast; get a room with windows. The central **Hotel San Marino** (☎ 073-231-

6511), Rua Jorge Amado 29, has four-bed quartos for US$10 per person, and double apartamentos from US$35.

The **Britânia Hotel** (☎ 073-634-1722), Rua Jorge Amado 16, is a pleasant, old-style hotel with quartos from US$15 and apartamentos from US$20.

Even better places include **Pousada Brisa do Mar** (☎ 073-231-2644), on the beachfront at Av 2 de Julho 136. It's in a deco-style building and has large, comfortable apartamentos starting at US$30/40. **Hotel Ilhéus** (☎ 073-634-4242), Rua Eustáquio Bastos 44, in the center, offers fading grandeur from US$30 a double.

Places to Eat

Behind the Catedral Basílica, along the beach, there are several reasonably priced seafood stands with outdoor tables. The center is filled with cheap restaurants offering self-serve lunches for a few dollars. **Barrakítika** is a popular hangout with outdoor tables, seafood and pizza. There's good live music here on Thursday, Friday and Saturday. Next door, **Equilibrio** has a self-serve lunch spread.

For seafood with great views of the beach, try *Os Velhos Marinheiros*, Av 2 de Julho, with dishes for around US$20 for two. *Bar Vezúvio*, Praça Dom Eduardo, is described in Amado's books and is popular with visitors.

Getting There & Away

Air There's a small airport at Praia do Pontal, 4km from the center, serviced by Nordeste, VASP and Varig.

Bus Buses leave more frequently for most destinations from Itabuna than from Ilhéus, so it's usually quicker to go to Itabuna first, then shuttle down to Ilhéus. The rodoviária in Ilhéus is a 15-minute bus ride from the center. Buses to Salvador go through the recôncavo via Cachoeira or Nazaré, then connect with the ferry from Itaparica Island to Salvador. There are several buses a day to Salvador (US$28, seven hours) and two a day to Porto Seguro (US$12, five hours). Buses traveling to Canavieiras (US$4, two hours) leave every two hours from 6:30 am to 10 pm. To get to Valença, you need to go to Itabuna.

From the city bus station on Praça Cairu, there are buses to Olivença, the rodoviária and the airport.

PORTO SEGURO

The one-time pioneering settlement of Porto Seguro is just south of where Cabral and his men stepped ashore in 1500. It's now a refuge for swarms of domestic and international tourists who come to party and take in some mesmerizing beaches. Tourism is the primary industry, so this small city has hundreds of hotels and pousadas. The town itself has no beaches, but the nearby coast has plenty, protected by reefs with clear, shallow, safe water. Carnaval here is not at all traditional, but it's one hell of a party.

Things to See & Do

About 1km north along the beach road is **Cidade Alta**, one of the oldest settlements in Brazil. The city has some very old buildings, such as the **churches** of NS da Misericórdia (perhaps the oldest in Brazil), NS da Pena (1535, rebuilt 1773) and NS do Rosário dos Jesuitas (1549). It also has the small Museu Antigo Paço Municipal (1772) and the old fort (1503).

The **Reserva Biológica do Pau Brasil**, a 10-sq-km reserve 15km from town, was set aside principally to preserve the brazil wood tree. For details about visiting this reserve, ask one of the travel agencies.

Organized Tours

To arrange city tours or schooner trips to Trancoso, Coroa Alta, Recife da Fora or Monte Pascoal, contact Apollo Turismo (☎ 073-288-2157), Av 22 de Abril 260, or Nirvana Turismo Maritimo, Av Portugal 90. To buy bus tickets without having to go to the rodoviária, visit the helpful Curuípe Viagems and Turismo (☎ 073-288-2403), Rua do Golfo 10. To buy or change plane tickets, try Adeltur Turismo & Câmbio.

Places to Stay

During the low season there are many vacant rooms, so try for 50% off the following prices. In the high season (December to February) accommodations can be tight.

If you intend to camp, try *Mundaí Praia* (☎ 073-879-2287), 5km north of town on the road to Santa Cruz da Cabrália, or *Tabapiri Country* (☎ 073-288-2269), 1.5km outside town on the way to Eunápolis. The latter only opens in summer.

The *Pousada do Cais* (☎ 073-288-2112), Av Portugal 382, is a rustic place with individually decorated singles/doubles for US$12 per person in the low season and US$24/48 in the high. The friendly German owner, Jochen Heckhausen, speaks English and is always delighted to meet fellow travelers. Other cheapies close to the action and the ferry include: *Raízes Pousada* (☎ 073-288-4717), Praça dos Pataxós 196, with clean, basic apartamentos for US$8 per person (US$15 in summer); and *Pousada Brisa do Mar* (☎ 073-288-2943), Praça Dr Manoel Ribeiro Coelho 188, which charges US$15 per person (US$25 in summer) with breakfast.

Places to Eat

Restaurants in Porto Seguro are becoming expensive, at least in summer, when many places have a minimum charge per table. The cheapest option is to eat at the stalls set up along Av Portugal (better known as the Passarela de Álcoól), where you can get good chicken or meat, salad and farofa plates for US$4.

The *Bar-Restaurant Tres Vintens*, Av Portugal 246, serves a delicious bobó de

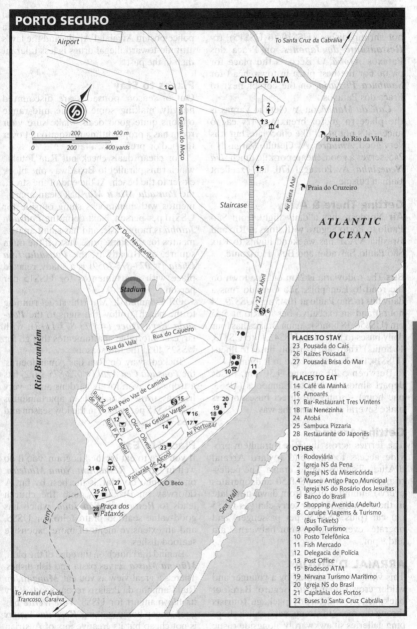

PORTO SEGURO

CICADE ALTA

Airport

To Santa Cruz da Cabrália

Rua Guava do Moço

Praia do Rio da Vila

Praia do Cruzeiro

Staircase

ATLANTIC
OCEAN

Av Dos Navagantes

Av Biera Mar

Av 22 de Abril

Stadium

Rio Buranhém

Rua do Cajueiro

Rua da Vala

Rua 2 de Julho

Rua Pero Vaz de Caminha

Rua Oscar Oliveira

Rua 'A' Cabral

Av Getúlio Vargas

Av Portugal

Passaráa de Álcool

O Beco

Praça dos
Pataxós

Sea Wall

Ferry

To Arraial d'Ajuda,
Trancoso, Caraíva

0   200   400 m
0   200   400 yards

BRAZIL

PLACES TO STAY
23 Pousada do Cais
26 Raízes Pousada
27 Pousada Brisa do Mar

PLACES TO EAT
14 Café da Manhã
16 Amoarês
17 Bar-Restaurant Tres Vintens
18 Tia Nenezinha
24 Atobá
25 Sambuca Pizzaria
28 Restaurante do Japonês

OTHER
1   Rodoviária
2   Igreja NS da Pena
3   Igreja NS da Misericórida
4   Museu Antigo Paço Municipal
5   Igreja NS do Rosário dos Jesuitas
6   Banco do Brasil
7   Shopping Avenida (Adeltur)
8   Curuipe Viagems & Turismo
    (Bus Tickets)
9   Apollo Turismo
10 Posto Telefônica
11 Fish Mercado
12 Delegacia de Polícia
13 Post Office
15 Bradesco ATM
19 Nirvana Turismo Marítimo
20 Igreja NS do Brasil
21 Capitânia dos Portos
22 Buses to Santa Cruz Cabrália

camarão for US$20. With a side dish, this is a meal for two. For good sushi, sashimi and hot shrimp dishes (US$10 to US$15), try *Restaurante do Japonês*, on Praça dos Pataxós. *Atobá*, O Beco, is the place for pasta. For the best pizza in town, head for *Sambuca Pizzaria*, on the corner next to Praça dos Pataxós.

Café da Manhá, on Av Getúlio Vargas, is the place to go for breakfast. Try cacao juice – it's not at all like chocolate, but it is very good. *Amoarés*, Av Getúlio Vargas No 245, serves a good, cheap, por-kilo lunch. *Tia Nenezinha*, Av Portugal 170, has excellent Bahian cuisine.

Getting There & Away
Air Nordeste has a daily flight from São Paulo to Porto Seguro with stops in Rio and Brasília. VASP has weekend flights to Rio, São Paulo, Salvador and Belo Horizonte.

Bus The rodoviária is 2km outside town on the road to Eunápolis. São Geraldo runs a daily bus to São Paulo at 10:45 am (US$79, 24 hours) and an executivo bus to Rio at 5:45 pm (US$58, 18 hours). Aguia Branca has four daily buses to Salvador (US$42; leito US$73, 11 hours). There are two daily buses to Ilhéus (US$14, five hours) and five to Itabuna.

Between 5:20 am and 9:30 pm, buses depart almost hourly to Eunápolis (US$3, one hour) – some are direct buses, others make several stops along the way.

Getting Around
The ferries across the Rio Buranhém provide access to the road toward Arraial d'Ajuda, Trancoso and Caraiva. The pedestrian ferry charges US$0.50 and operates every 15 minutes or so from dawn until late in the evening. The car ferry charges US$5 per car (plus US$0.50 per passenger) and operates every half an hour between 7 am and 9 pm.

ARRAIAL D'AJUDA
This village is frequented by a younger and wilder crowd than Porto Seguro: Barefoot backpackers and trendy package tourists throng the maze of streets, where slick shopping galleries sit awkwardly alongside rustic reggae cafés. Newcomers soon fall into the routine: going crazy every evening, then recovering the following morning to crawl

back onto the beach for more surf, sun and samba. Be warned, however: There's now a police post in Arraial d'Ajuda, and the law's attitude toward illegal drugs is less tolerant than in the past.

Places to Stay
Out of season, pousadas are discounted heavily, making some of the mid-range options quite good deals. Make sure your room has a proper-fitting mosquito net over the bed or, preferably, a fan.

For cheap deals check out Rua Jotobá, which runs parallel to Broadway one block closer to the beach. At the end of the street, the *Pousada Mir a Mar* has clean apartamentos with hammocks slung outside for US$10 per person. Next door, the *Pousada Jatobá* is more basic, and has small apartamentos for the same price. Just off the main square, on Broadway, the *Pousada Lua Cheia* (☎ 073-875-1059) is a shady, relaxed place with apartamentos for US$15 per person.

Off Caminho do Mar (the street running to the beach), follow the signs to the *Pousada Erva Doce* (☎ 073-875-1113), with large, comfortable apartamentos that go for US$25/40 in the low season.

Tucked away on Rua das Amandoeiras, the *Pousada Céu Azul* (☎ 073-875-1312) has a tropical flavor, lovely gardens and a very friendly owner. Small, clean apartamentos cost US$15 per person in the low season and US$30/40 in summer.

Places to Eat
If you like to eat by the kilogram, you'll do well in Arraial. *Restaurant Nóna Madeira*, on Caminho do Mar, is the best by far. A doorway on Broadway near the church leads to *Restaurant São João*, which has good-value seafood prato feito for US$5, and an extensive menu of more expensive seafood dishes.

Behind the church on the edge of the bluff, *Mão na Massa* serves pasta and fish dishes. There's a great view as you eat. *Manguti*, on Rua Caminho da Praia, is recommended. Try its filé manguti for US$8. *Vale Verde* has good, cheap home cooking. *Rosa das Ventas* is not cheap but its creative mix of Austrian Bahian cuisine is definitely worth a try. The barracas down at the beach have excellent fried shrimp and other seafood.

Getting There & Away

Take a ferry from Porto Seguro, then one of four approaches to Arraial d'Ajuda: a lovely four-km hike along the beach, a taxi to town, a bus to town, or a VW Kombi to Praia de Mucugê.

TRANCOSO

This village, 12km southwest of Porto Seguro, is on a grassy bluff overlooking fantastic beaches. The central square is lined with small, colorful colonial buildings and casual bars and restaurants nestled under shady trees.

Places to Stay & Eat

If you're planning a long stay, rent a house on the beach. Next to the school on Rua Itabela, the **Pousada Quarto Cresente** (☎ 073-868-1014), is highly recommended. This is a quiet location, and the pousada has comfortable double quartos with fan starting at US$22 (US$33 in the high season), and double apartamentos for around US$25 (US$45 in the high season). They also have a couple of houses for rent.

The colorful **Pousada Soloamanha** (☎ 073-868-1003), on the Quadrado, is a rustic place with clean, collective rooms for US$20 per person during summer. Also in the Quadrado is **Pousada Seis e Meia** (☎ 073-868-1027), a tranquil little pousada offering singles/doubles with mosquito nets for US$15 per person, including breakfast. Out of season, it charges US$5 per person without breakfast.

The **Pousada Hibisco** (☎ 073-868-1117) is more upmarket, with large grounds and views of the forest and ocean. Double apartamentos start at US$40 (US$60 in the high season). **Pousada Capim Santo** (☎ 073-868-1122), in the Quadrado, very close to the bus stop, is a highly recommended pousada/restaurant. It has comfortable double apartamentos for US$40 (US$60 in the high season).

Maré Cheia, on the Quadrado, has a good self-serve por kilo for US$6 and prato feito for US$4. **Primavera**, close by, serves excellent homemade ice cream.

Getting There & Away

Trancoso is 22km from Arraial d'Ajuda on a good dirt road, or 13km on foot along the beach. The bus from Arraial d'Ajuda to Trancoso leaves every two hours from 8 am until 7:40 pm. It originates at the ferry landing opposite Porto Seguro and stops at the bus depot in Arraial d'Ajuda, behind the main praça. Buses are less frequent during the low season. When the bus reaches Trancoso, it stops at the beach first – if you are looking for accommodations, stay on the bus until it reaches the village. Buses from Trancoso to Porto Seguro leave almost every hour from 7 am to 6 pm.

It's a beautiful 13-km walk along the beach between Trancoso and Arraial d'Ajuda.

CARAIVA

Without running water, electricity or throngs of tourists, the hamlet of Caraiva is primitive and beautiful. Rustic pousadas will put you up for US$15 to US$20 per person.

Two buses a day (8 am and 3 pm) make the 42km trip along the dirt road from Trancoso to Caraiva. There are also two buses daily to Itabela, on BR-101, for connections north and south. Buses stop on the far side of the river, and small dugout canoes ferry passengers across to the village for US$0.50.

LENÇOIS

Lençois lies in a wooded, mountainous region – the Chapada Diamantina, an oasis in the dusty sertão. Here, you'll find old mining towns and great hiking nearby in the Parque Nacional da Chapada Diamantina (see the next section). If you have time for only one excursion into Brazil's northeastern interior, this is the one.

There are plenty of travel agents and English-speaking guides who offer useful information. Try Olivia Taylor (☎ 075-334-1229). The Banco do Brasil changes cash and traveler's checks (for a fee) and has an ATM for Visa withdrawals.

Things to See & Do

The city is pretty and easy to see on foot, although most of the buildings are closed to the public. Check out the 19th-century **French vice-consulate**, a beige building where diamond commerce was negotiated, and **Casa de Afrânio Peixoto**, which houses the personal effects and works of writer Afrânio Peixoto. The **Prefeitura Municipal**, Praça Otaviano Alves 8, is a pretty building with interesting B&W photos of old Lençois. Also worth a visit is **Lanchonete Zacão**, run by local historian Mestre Oswaldo, who displays various mining relics and artifacts.

Places to Stay

Camping Lumiar, on Praça do Rosário, has shady campsites, passable bathrooms, a bar and a restaurant – but watch out for Pablito and his marauding chickens. It costs US$4 per person. Another good camping option is **Alquimia**, opposite Pousada Alcino. It also has some cheap rooms for rent.

The **Pousalegre** (☎ 075- 334-1124) is a favorite with travelers. The rooms are certainly basic (there's a lack of windows and furniture), but the friendly staff and good meals more than compensate. Quartos cost US$5 per person without breakfast or US$8 per person with. Close by, the **Re Pousada** is another good option that charges the same rates.

The **Pousada dos Duendes** (☎ 075-334-1229), at Rua do Pires, is a small pousada with a relaxed atmosphere. Run by Olivia and Rao, it's in a quiet location just a short walk from the center. Collective rooms cost US$5 per person, or US$8 with breakfast. The **Pousada Diangela** (☎ 075-334-1192) is a large, bright building with a pleasant eating area and quartos for US$8 per person (US$10 with breakfast). Apartamentos cost US$15 per person with breakfast.

Pousada Nossa Casa (☎ 075-334-1258), in the center of town, is a friendly place run by Ana and Ze Henrique. An excellent budget option, quartos are US$15 per person with breakfast, a bit less in the low season. The **Pousada Alcino** (☎ 075-334-1171), Rua Tomba Surrão 139, is in a beautifully converted colonial building. Quartos cost US$15 per person, including a highly recommended breakfast. Alcino speaks a bit of English and French. The **Pousada Casa da Hélia** (☎ 075-334-1143), on Rua da Muritiba, is in a quiet area just a short walk from the rodoviária. Quartos cost US$10 per person, with the pousada's famous breakfast included.

Pousada Canto das Águas (☎ 075-334-1154), in a landscaped garden beside the river, has a restaurant, bar, pool, and apartamentos overlooking the cascades for around US$56/63/78.

Places to Eat

Dona Joaninha, on Rua das Pedras, serves an excellent breakfast, as does **Doceria Vai Quem Quer**, also in Rua das Pedras. They also serve cakes, mousses and other sweet, delicious things.

The vegetarian restaurant **Beco da Coruja**, Rua do Rosário, offers tasty soups, pizza and other vegetarian specialties. Carnivores should head for **Picanha na Praça** for a good churrasco. Also in the main square, **Pizzarela Pizza House** and **Grisante** serve good, cheap meals and snacks – try Grisante's *carne do sol with aipim frito* (salted meat and fried manioc). **Lanchonete Zacão** serves great fruit juices and amazing *bolinho de queijo* (hot fried balls of dough filled with melted cheese), a must during cold weather.

Brilhante is a colorful natural-food store and café with healthy sandwiches, snacks and juices. The **Pousalegre** (see Places to Stay earlier in this section) serves inexpensive meals – Rosa's moqueca is justly famous. For the best self-serve in town, try **O Kilo**. Other popular restaurants worth visiting include **Arte Lanches**, for great sandwiches, and **Restaurant Amigo da Onça**, for home cooking and old-time dancing on weekends.

Getting There & Away

The rodoviária is on the edge of town beside the river. There are two buses daily to and from Salvador (US$18, six hours). Lençois also has an airport: Check with a travel agent for flight details.

AROUND LENÇOIS

For day trips around Lençois, walk or hire a horse. Ask around town for Senhor Dazim, who hires horses for about US$3 an hour. Agents in Lençois run trips to Chapada Diamantina. Lentur (☎ 075-334-1271), Av 7 de Setembro, runs day trips by car to several destinations within the park for US$20 per person (a guide, admission fees and flashlights are included in the price). Cirtur (☎ 075-334-1133), Rua da Baderna 41, offers similar deals. Olivia Taylor's Saturno Informações (☎ 075- 334-1229), Rua da Baderna 95, arranges tours by foot or by car.

Parque Nacional da Chapada Diamantina

This park, which occupies 1520 sq km within the Sincora range of the Diamantina plateau, has several species of monkeys, beautiful views, clean waterfalls, rivers and streams, and a seemingly endless network of trails. Rock hounds appreciate the curious geology of the region. Many foreigners and Brazilians living in Lençois have joined a strong ecological movement that is in direct opposition to the extractive mentality of the *garimpeiros* (prospectors), who have caused much damage. Lately, frequent fires have been a major problem in the park.

Information The park has minimal infrastructure for visitors. Knowledgeable guides can greatly enhance enjoyment of trips into the park. In Lençois, contact Olivia Taylor at Saturno Informacões, or Roy Funch, at the Fundação Chapada Diamantina (☎ 075-334-1305), Rua Pé de Ladeira 212. Claude Samuel runs trips into the park from the Pousada Candombá (☎ 075-332-2176) in Palmeiras.

Short Hikes A pleasant 1½-hour hike can be taken upstream along the Rio Lençois to Salão de Areias Coloridas (Room of Colored Sands), where artisans gather material for bottled sand paintings, then on to Cachoeira da Primavera waterfall.

Another relaxing 45-minute hike leads to Ribeirão do Meio, a series of swimming holes with a natural waterslide (bring old clothes or borrow a burlap sack). Bathers have had nasty accidents walking up the slide: Swim across to the far side of the pool and climb the dry rocks.

Lapa Doce About 70km northwest of Lençois, followed by a 25-minute hike, is a huge cave formed by a now-dry subterranean river. You will need a guide and a flashlight.

Rio Mucugêzinho This river, 30km from Lençois, is a super day trip. Take the 7 am bus and ask the driver to let you off at Mucugêzinho bar; the bus passes through again at around 4 pm on its return trip to Lençois. From Barraca do Pelé, pick your way about 2km downstream to Poço do Diabo (Devil's Well), a swimming hole with a 30m waterfall.

Morro do Pai Inácio At 1120m, this is the most prominent peak in the immediate area.

It's 27km from Lençois and easily accessible from the highway. An easy but steep trail goes 200m to the summit for a beautiful view. The trail along **Barro Branco** between Lençois and Morro do Pai Inácio is a good four- or five-hour hike.

Palmeiras, Capão & Cachoeira da Fumaça

Palmeiras is a drowsy little town 56km west of Lençois, with a scenic riverside location and streets lined with colorful houses. There are several cheap pensões.

The hamlet of **Capão** is 20km from Palmeiras by road (or use the hiking trail connecting Capão with Lençois). From here, there's a 6km trail (two hours on foot) to the top of **Cachoeira da Fumaça**, also known as the Glass Waterfall (after missionary George Glass). It plummets 420m, making it the longest waterfall in Brazil. The route to the bottom is very difficult and not recommended.

Visiting the bottom of Cachoeira da Fumaça is a tiring three-day walk, but much easier than the Inca Trail. The walk itself is extremely beautiful, passing other waterfalls on the way. You leave Lençóis in the morning of the first day, sleep in caves at night, and arrive in Capão on the third day. You can add an extra day by walking back to Lençóis, or you can continue with the Grand Circuit.

The **Grand Circuit Route**, a 100km walk, is a much longer trip best done in a counterclockwise direction. It takes about five days, but allow eight days if you include highly recommended side trips such as Igatú and Cachoeira da Fumaça.

Sergipe

Sergipe, north of Bahia, is Brazil's smallest state. There are a couple of interesting historic towns, but the beaches are not expecially good and the capital, Aracaju, is not overwhelmingly attractive.

ARACAJU

Aracaju has little to offer the visitor, but it's a pleasant enough base for trips to the colonial villages of Laranjeiras and São Cristóvão. The Centro do Turismo houses the Emsetur tourist office (☎ 079-224-5168), open 8 am to 8 pm daily, and an *artesanato* market. Praia Atalaia Velha, on Av Atlântica, is an overdeveloped and mediocre beach.

Places to Stay

For camping, try *Camping Clube do Brasil* (☎ 079-243-1413) on Atalaia Velha. There are many hotels out at Praia Atalaia Velha, but the ones in the center are more convenient and a better value. Ask for low-season discounts between March and June and during August and September.

For rock-bottom accommodations, *Hotel Sergipe* (☎ 079-222-7898) charges US$6 per person for quartos and US$10/15 for apartamentos, and is the choice of locals wanting a quickie. The best budget option is the central *Hotel Amado* (☎ 079-211-9937), Rua Laranjeiras 532, with clean single/double quartos for US$12/18 and apartamentos for US$16/22, or US$20/30 with air-con.

Also try the good-value *Hotel Oasis* (☎ 079-224-1181), which has bright apartamentos from US$22/30, or *Hotel Brasília* (☎ 079-224-8020), with apartamentos for US$25/38. A popular mid-range hotel is the *Jangadeiro* (☎ 079-211-1350), in the city center, for US$30/35.

Places to Eat

Tempero Nordestino, Rua Santa Luzia 59, has a good self-serve lunch. It's open 11 am to 3 pm daily. *Cacique Chá* (closed on Sunday) is a garden restaurant on Praça Olímpio Campos and a popular meeting place. *Artnatus,* at Rua Santo Amaro 282, is a well-stocked health-food store that serves vegetarian lunches. The cafés in Rua 24 Horas are good for snacks and drinks.

Recommended seafood restaurants at Atalaia Velha include *Taberna do Tropeiro* (with live music in the evening), Av Oceânica 6; and *O Miguel* (closed on Monday), Rua Antônio Alves 340.

Getting There & Away

Air Major airlines fly to Rio, São Paulo, Salvador, Recife, Maceió, Brasília, Goiânia and Curitiba.

Bus Long-distance buses leave from the rodoviária nova (new bus terminal), about 4km east of the center. There are eight buses a day to Salvador (US$11). Some take the new Linha Verde route along the coast (4½

hours), and the rest go inland via Entre Rios (6 hours). There are four departures daily to Maceió (US$12, five hours), and two to Recife (US$21, nine hours).

Buses to São Cristóvão and Laranjeiras operate from the rodoviária velha (old bus terminal). The shuttle service between the bus terminals costs US$0.70 and takes 15 minutes.

SÃO CRISTÓVÃO

Founded in 1590, São Cristóvão was the capital of Sergipe until 1855. The old part of town, up a steep hill, has a surprising number of 17th- and 18th-century buildings along its narrow stone roads. Of particular distinction are the **Igreja e Convento de São Francisco**, on Praça São Francisco, and the **Igreja de Senhor dos Passos**, on Praça Senhor dos Passos.

São Cristóvão is 25km south of Aracaju and 7km off BR-101. The rodoviária is down the hill, below the historical district on Praça Dr Lauro de Freitas. There are frequent buses to Aracaju, but no direct buses south to Estância.

LARANJEIRAS

Nestled between three lush, church-topped hills, Laranjeiras is the colonial gem of Sergipe. It has several churches and museums worth visiting, and the surrounding hills offer picturesque walks with good views.

The city tourist office is in the Trapiche building in the Centro de Tradições, on Praça Samuel de Oliveira. It's open from 8 am to 5 pm Tuesday to Sunday.

The only pousada in town is the *Pousada Vale dos Outeiros* (☎ 079-281-1027), Rua José do Prado Franco 124. There are good views of the surrounding hills from the back rooms. Double quartos and apartamentos with air-conditioning cost US$20 and US$30 respectively.

Buses (US$1, 35 minutes) run between Laranjeiras and Aracaju's rodoviária velha every half hour from 5 am to 9 pm, but any bus traveling the BR-101 can let you off at the turnoff for Laranjeiras.

Alagoas

The small state of Alagoas is one of the pleasant surprises of the northeast. Its beaches are enchanting, and inland there is a fabulous stretch of lush sugar-cane country.

MACEIÓ
Maceió, the capital of Alagoas, has a small historical area but is mostly modern. A recent boom in tourism has encouraged the rapid development of the city beaches, particularly between Ponta Verde and Praia de Jatiúca.

Information
Ematur (☎ 082-221-9393), the state tourism organization, is at Av da Paz 2004. Emturma (☎ 082-223-4016), the municipal tourism body, has convenient tourist information booths at Praia Pajuçara, Ponte Verde, Praia Jatiúca, the rodoviária and the airport.

Things to See & Do
The **Museu do Instituto Histórico**, Rua João Pessoa, has exhibits about regional history.

Beaches close to Centro are polluted, and Praia Pajuçara and Praia dos Sete Coqueiros (3km and 4km away) are becoming dirtier. The best **beaches** are farther north, including Ponta Verde (5km), Jatiúca (6km), Jacarecica (9km), Guaxuma (12km), Garça Torta (14km), Riacho Doce (16km) and Pratagi (17km).

These tropical paradises get busy on weekends and throughout the summer. On Pajuçara, *jangadas* (traditional sailboats) will take you out to the reef for US$4; the marine life there is most visible at low tide.

Schooners depart daily from Pontal da Barra for a five-hour cruise to islands and beaches (US$30 with lunch, US$20 without); contact Ematur. Small motorboats make similar cruises from Pontal da Barra (US$15).

Locals reckon Barra de São Miguel has the best Carnaval in the area. Festa do Mar takes place in December.

Places to Stay
For camping try *Camping Jatiúca* (☎ 082-235-1251), Praia Cruz das Almas, around 6km from the center. Most hostels in Maceió have closed, except for French-run *Albergue de Juventude Nossa Casa* (☎ 082-231-2246), Rua Prefeito Abdon Arroxelas 327, on Praia de Ponta Verde. Call before arriving to make sure it's still open.

In the city, try *Hotel dos Palmares* (☎ 082-223-7024), Praça dos Palmares 253, with quartos for US$8 per person without breakfast or apartamentos for US$15/28 singles/doubles, including breakfast. Nearby, the *Hotel Maceió* (☎ 082-221-1883), Rua Dr Pontas de Miranda 146, offers cell-like but clean apartamentos for US$15/30.

Praia de Pajuçara, between the city center and the better beaches, has plenty of budget accommodations. The cheapies are all one block from the beach on Rua Dr Antônio Pedro de Mendonça. Prices quoted here are for the low season – expect hikes of 20% to 30% in summer. *Pousada Rex* (☎ 082-231-4358), No 311, is a family-run place with apartamentos starting at US$10/20. Staff can also arrange boat trips. Next door at No 315, *Hotel Pousada Zeide* (☎ 082-231-1008) is another family-run place with clean apartamentos for US$15/25. The nearby *Mar Amar* (☎ 082-231-1551), No 343, has air-conditioned apartamentos with TV for US$15/20.

For better beachside places, try the older hotels along Praia de Pajuçara. *Hotel Praia Bonita* (☎ 082-231-2565), at Av Antônio Gouveia 943, Praia de Pajuçara, has clean apartamentos with air-con for US$25/30. *Pousada Cavalo Marinho* (☎ 082-335-1247), 17km from the center at Rua da Praia 55, Praia Riacho Doce, has been recommended, and has doubles from around US$30.

Places to Eat
A very cheap, decent lunch place in the center is *Estação Centro*, opposite the ferroviária. It has an all-you-can-eat buffet for US$2.50.

Most of the beaches offer a wide choice of food, with barracas and snack bars serving seafood and local dishes. At Praia de Pajuçara, *Paraíso* is a casual little café with a great range of juices and snack foods. *Gulosão Nobre*, on Rua Domingos S Leens, is a friendly place with reasonably priced seafood, meat and chicken refeições. *King's* is a breezy restaurant along the beachfront with self-serve lunches and dinners.

Getting There & Away
Maceió is connected by air with Rio, São Paulo, Brasília and all the major centers of the northeast.

BRAZIL

MACEIÓ

R Melo Morais
Rua Ladislau Neto
Av Moreira Lima
Rua do Livramento
Praça dos
Palmares
Mercado do
Artesanato
Av Santos Pacheco
Rua Pedro Monteiro
Rua Rosa de C Rua Zacarias de Azevedo
Rua Rosa de Fonseca
To Praia do Francês,
Marechal Deodoro,
Pontal da Barra
Praia do Sobral

R João Pessoa
R Const. Comerciatório
R do Sol
R do Comércio
Rua Saldanha da Gama
CENTRO
Av Arsêu de Andrade
Av Barão de Atalaia
Rua Ferroviário
Av Buarue de Macedo RFFSA
R Comendador
R Comendador Leão

To Shopping Center

JARAGUÁ
Rua Silvério Jorge
Rua Barão de Jaraguá
Rua Sá Albuquerque
Rua Ind Cícero Toledo

Av Duque de Caxais
Praia da Avenida

Porto
de Jaraguá

0   300   600 m
0   300   600 yards

Aeroporto dos Palmares is 20km from the center; get a bus (US$4) at Praça Sinibu, or a taxi for around US$15.

There are frequent bus departures daily to Recife (US$10, four hours), Aracaju (US$12, five hours), and Salvador (US$28, 10 hours).

PENEDO

Penedo, known as the capital of the lower São Francisco, is a fascinating colonial city almost untouched by tourism. Attractions include many baroque churches and colonial buildings, and the opportunity to travel on the Rio São Francisco. Penedo bustles with people from the surrounding villages who come to buy and sell goods.

Saturday is the major market day and the easiest day to find a boat up or down the São Francisco. For a short excursion take one of the motorboats that departs every half hour to Neópolis, a few kilometers downriver, or one of the frequent boats to Carrapicho, a small town noted for its ceramics.

The tourist office is open 8 am to 6 pm daily. It is housed with a small city museum in the Casa da Aposentadoria, just up from the fort on Praça Barão de Penedo. Portuguese-speaking guides are available for a one-hour walking tour of the town.

Places to Stay & Eat

For a budget option, try the **Pousada Familiar** (☎ 082-551-3194), Rua Siqueira 77, with quartos for US$8 with a basic breakfast (coffee, bread and an egg) or US$10 with a better breakfast. If you prefer a place where the walls reach the ceiling, walk a bit farther up the same street to the **Hotel Turista** (☎ 082-551-2237), at No 143, which offers clean, basic apartamentos with ceiling fans for US$15/20 with breakfast.

The **Pousada Colonial** (☎ 082-551-2677), Praça 12 de Abril, is a beautiful converted colonial home on the waterfront with spacious apartamentos from US$25. Make sure you get one with a view of the river.

The **Hotel São Francisco** (☎ 082-551-2273), Av Floriano Peixoto, is a 1960s-style hotel that's been in a time warp for the last 30 years. It's clean, quiet and has comfortable apartamentos with balconies and great

BRAZIL

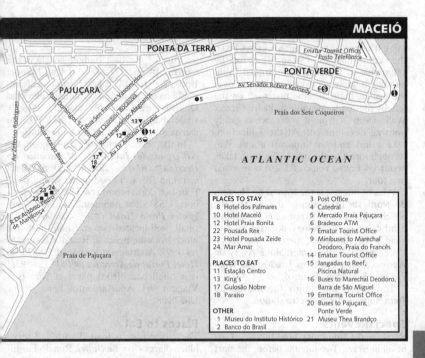

MACEIÓ

PONTA DA TERRA

Ematur Tourist Office
Posto Telefônica

PONTA VERDE

PAJUÇARA

Av Senador Robert Kennedy   6

Rua Domingos S Lemos
Rua Sen Firmino Vasconcelos
Rua Quintino Bocaiúva
Rua Jangadeiros Alagoanos
Av Dr Antônio Gouveia

Praia dos Sete Coqueiros

Av Zeferino Rodrigues
Rua Arnaldo Bivar

5

13

12   14
15

ATLANTIC OCEAN

17
18

23 24
22

R Dr Antônio Pedro
de Mandonça

Praia de Pajuçara

PLACES TO STAY	3	Post Office
8	Hotel dos Palmares	4	Catedral
10	Hotel Maceió	5	Mercado Praia Pajuçara
12	Hotel Praia Bonita	6	Bradesco ATM
22	Pousada Rex	7	Ematur Tourist Office
23	Hotel Pousada Zeide	9	Minibuses to Marechal
24	Mar Amar		Deodoro, Praia do Francês
		14	Ematur Tourist Office
PLACES TO EAT	15	Jangadas to Reef,
11	Estação Centro		Piscina Natural
13	King's	16	Buses to Marechal Deodoro,
17	Gulosão Nobre		Barra de São Miguel
18	Paraíso	19	Emturma Tourist Office
		20	Buses to Pajuçara,
OTHER		Ponte Verde
1	Museu do Instituto Histórico	21	Museu Thea Brandço
2	Banco do Brasil		

hot showers. Prices start at US$42/61, but you can usually get a 30% discount.

Forte da Rocheira, in an old fort overlooking the river, is recommended for lunch and dinner. There are plenty of cheap bars and lanchonetes around town.

Getting There & Away
The rodoviária is on Av Duque de Caxias. There are seven buses daily to Maceió (US$5). The 11 am bus to Propriá continues on to Aracaju (US$6.50, three hours). Alternately, take a ferry to Neópolis, then one of the frequent buses to Aracaju.

Pernambuco

RECIFE
Recife, the capital of Pernambuco, is a sprawling city with an eclectic mix of baroque churches, 19th-century public buildings and '60s and '70s high-rise buildings, all in various states of decay. The upmarket beach suburb of Boa Viagem is OK, but the main attraction is nearby Olinda.

Information
Tourist Offices Empetur (☎ 081-241-2111), the state tourism bureau, has tourist information desks at the airport and at the Casa de Cultura, in the Terminal Integrado de Passageiros (TIP), a combined metro terminal and rodoviária.

Post & Communications The main post office is at Av Guararapes 250. There are also post offices at the airport and TIP. TELPE (the state telephone company) has 24-hour telephone stations at TIP and the airport; there are also telephones in the center at Rua do Hospício 148.

Things to See & Do
The **Casa da Cultura**, a former prison, now houses many craft and souvenir shops. Good traditional music and dance shows are often performed outside the building. It's open 9 am to 7 pm Monday to Saturday and 2 to 7 pm Sunday.

The **Olaria de Brennand**, a ceramics factory and exhibition hall, is set in a forested suburb of Recife. The gallery and museum houses a permanent exhibition of around 2000 original ceramic pieces (*not* for sale). It's open 8 am to 4 pm weekdays. From the center, take the Caxangá bus for the 11km ride to Caxangá bus terminal. Walk another 100m away from the city and over the bridge, then take the first road on the left, by the roadside statue of Padre Cicero. Walk about 2km until you reach a gaudy housing development. At the T-junction, take a left and continue for about 3km through forest to the office. The walk takes about 1¼ hours. You could also take a taxi or a tour.

Also of interest is the **Museu do Homem do Nordeste** (Museum of the Northeast), which is Recife's best museum. It features exhibits on anthropology, popular art and local herbal medicine (open till 5 pm daily). It's east of the city center, along Av 17 de Agosto. Catch the Dois Irmãos bus from Parque 13 de Maio, Centro.

Train buffs may enjoy the **Museu do Trem**, adjacent to the metro station.

Special Events

Recife and Olinda may hold the best Carnaval in Brazil. Two months before the start of Carnaval, there are *bailes* (dances) in the clubs and Carnaval blocos practicing on the streets. Galo da Madrugada, Recife's largest bloco, has been known to bring 20,000 people onto the beaches at Boa Viagem. The main Carnaval dance in Pernambuco is the frenetic *frevo*. Most of the action takes place around the clock from Saturday to Tuesday. Along Av Guararapes, there's a popular frevo dance that begins on Friday night.

Places to Stay

Although most budget travelers prefer to stay in Olinda, Recife has a couple of options.

The **Brasil Hotel** (☎ 081-222-3534), at Rua do Hospício 687, has grungy quartos for US$8/11 singles/doubles and apartamentos with fan for US$10/15. Much better value is the friendly family-run **Hotel Inter Laine**, Rua do Hospício 186. It has clean apartamentos for US$20/25/35 for singles/doubles/triples. The owner, José Carlos, speaks English and French. He also gives discounts for longer stays. Closer to the nightlife in the old city, **Hotel Nassau** (☎ 081-224-3977), Rua Largo do Rosário, has large, clean rooms with good-sized bath-

rooms. Located in a pedestrian mall, it's a good value, with apartamentos that go for US$20/30.

One of the best budget hotels is the **Central** (☎ 081-221-1472) at Rua Manoel Borba 209. It's a '30s hotel with a pleasant, rambling design and classic antique elevator. Quartos are a reasonable value at US$18/20, while apartamentos start at US$25/29. You can negotiate a discount for longer stays.

In the beach suburb of Boa Viagem, the **Albergue de Juventude Maracatus do Recife** (☎ 081-326-1221), Rua Dona Maria Carolina 185, is a good hostel with a pool. Four-bed dorm rooms cost US$12 for members, US$15 for nonmembers. The **Navegantes Praia Hotel** (☎ 081-326-9609) is a small, well-located two-star hotel just one block from the beach at Rua dos Navegantes 1997. Apartamentos start at US$33/36. **Hotel Portal de Arrecifes** (☎ 081- 326-5921) is a small beachfront place at Rua Boa Viagem 864. Apartamentos here go for US$28/38.

Places to Eat

The city center is loaded with self-serve lunch places – try **Le Buffet**, Rua do Hospício 147, or **Geranio's**, nearby on Rua 7 de Setembro. At night in the center, it should be easy to find something to your liking around the lively Pátio de São Pedro or at the Polo Bom Jesus in the old city. Both areas offer a surprising variety of prices and styles.

Boa Viagem has many restaurants, but apart from those in the Polo Pina (see the following Entertainment section), which has a concentrated assortment of bars and restaurants, they're widely scattered. **Comida Gostosa**, Av Conselheiro Aguiar, is a classy self-serve lunch place that's very popular with locals. **Chapagrill**, Rua Mamanguape 157, is a self-serve place with stacks of different salads and cold cuts. The **Lobster**, Av Rui Barbosa 1649, is good if you want to splurge on lobster. It provides live music at dinner and opens noon to midnight daily.

Entertainment

Recife has two major leisure areas. One is in the old city and is called **Polo Bom Jesus**; the other is at the northern end of Boa Viagem and is known as **Polo Pina**. Polo Bom Jesus is more interesting than Polo Pina. Every night of the week, both places are crowded with

RECIFE

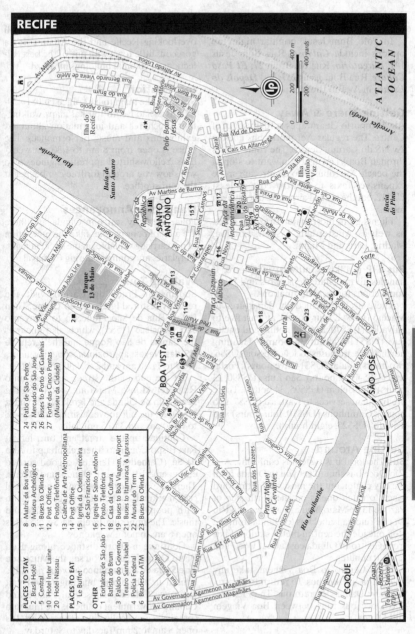

PLACES TO STAY
1 Fortaleza de São João
2 Brasil Hotel
5 Central
10 Hotel Inter Laine
20 Hotel Nassau

PLACES TO EAT
7 Le Buffet

OTHER
1 Fortaleza de São João
Batista do Brum
3 Palácio do Governo,
Teatro Santa Isabel
4 Polícia Federal
6 Bradesco ATM
8 Matriz da Boa Vista
9 Museu Archeológico
11 Buses to Olinda
12 Post Office,
Posto Telefônica
13 Galeria de Arte Metropolitana
14 Post Office
15 Igreja da Ordem Terceira
de São Francisco
16 Igreja de Santo Antônio
17 Posto Telefônica
18 Casa da Cultura
19 Buses to Boa Viagem, Airport
21 Buses to Itamaracá & Igarassu
22 Museu do Trem
23 Buses to Olinda
24 Pátio de São Pedro
25 Mercado de São José
26 Buses to Porto de Galinhas
27 Forte das Cinco Pontas
(Museu da Cidade)

BRAZIL

locals, and it's a trip just hanging around watching them party.

In Polo Bom Jesus, popular nightclub options include *Calypso*, Rua Bom Jesus 147; *Purgatório*, Rua do Brum 27; *El Paso Cabaré*, Rua Bom Jesus 237; and *Depois do Escuro* in Av Rio Branco.

Getting There & Away
Air Aeroporto Guararapes is 10km south of Centro. The regular Aeroporto bus goes to Av NS do Carmo, Centro. The route passes through Boa Viagem, if you want to stop at the beach. Microbuses to Centro are more expensive. Taxis to Centro cost at least US$12, but the special airport taxis cost even more.

Flights go to most major Brazilian cities, as well as Amsterdam, Lisbon, London, Madrid, Paris and Miami.

Bus TIP is 14km southwest of Centro. It handles all interstate departures and many connections for local destinations.

There are frequent daily departures to Maceió (US$11, four hours), at least five to Salvador (US$40, 12 to 14 hours) and one to Rio (US$110, about 36 hours). Heading north, there are buses to João Pessoa (US$6, two hours), Natal (US$14, five hours), Fortaleza (US$43, 12 hours), São Luis (US$90, 23 hours) and Belém (US$95, 34 hours). There are frequent services to Caruaru (US$7, two hours), Garanhuns (US$10, four hours) and Triunfo (US$23, eight hours).

Getting Around
Bus The local bus system is confusing. Any Rio Doce bus should get you to Olinda from the city center, but the most straightforward place to catch one is on the north side of Parque 13 de Maio. You can also catch a Rio Doce/Princesa Isabel bus to Olinda from the stop outside the central metrô station. Taxis from Centro to Olinda cost about US$7 and take 20 minutes.

From Centro to Boa Viagem, take any CDU/Boa Viagem bus. To return to Centro, take any Dantas Barreto bus. The Piedade/ Rio Doce bus runs between Boa Viagem and Olinda.

Metro The metro system is very useful for the 25-minute trip (US$0.50) between TIP and the metro station in Centro.

OLINDA
Olinda, Brazil's first capital, sits on a hill overlooking Recife and the Atlantic. It's a gorgeous little town with one of the best collections of colonial buildings in Brazil.

Information
Sepactur, the main tourist office (☎ 081-429-927), Rua São Bento 160, has maps, walking-tour brochures and information about art exhibitions and music performances. The office is open from 8 am to 1:30 pm weekdays. Yellow-shirted apprentice guides who will show you around for free can be met at the tourist office.

Dangers & Annoyances
Police are fairly scarce in Olinda, and there are a lot of poor people. Take the precaution of not carrying valuables in the street at night. Burglaries are common during Carnaval.

Walking Tour
Starting at Praça do Carmo, visit the recently restored **Igreja NS do Carmo**. Then follow Rua de São Francisco to **Convento São Francisco** (1585), which also encloses the **Capela de São Roque** and the **Igreja de NS das Neves**: approximate opening hours are 8 to 11:30 am and 2 to 4:30 pm daily.

At the end of the street, turn left onto Rua Frei Afonso Maria and you'll see the **Seminário de Olinda** and **Igreja NS da Graça** (1549) on the hill above. Visiting hours are 8 to 11:30 am and 3 to 5 pm daily.

Continue up the street and turn left at Rua Bispo Coutinho. Then, climb up to **Alto da Sé**, (Cathedral Heights), a good spot to enjoy superb views of Olinda and Recife. There are outdoor restaurants and a small craft market. It's a popular hangout at night, with people coming for food, drink and music. The imposing **Igreja da Sé** (1537) is open 8 am to noon weekends.

Continue a short distance along Rua Bispo Coutinho until you see the **Museu de Arte Sacra de Pernambuco** on your right. It's housed in a beautiful building (1696) that was once Olinda's Episcopal Palace and Camara (government council). The museum contains a good collection of sacred art. It's open 8 am to 2 pm Tuesday to Saturday.

Keep going about 75m farther down the street and turn right into a patio to visit **Igreja NS da Conceição** (1585).

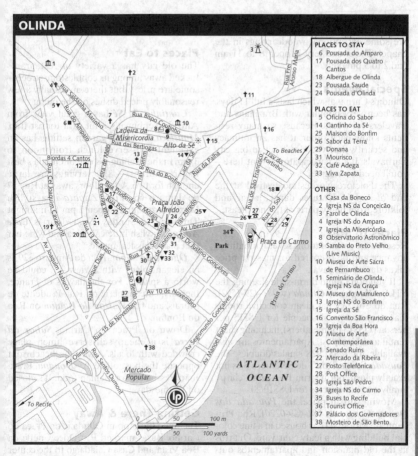

OLINDA

PLACES TO STAY
6 Pousada do Amparo
17 Pousada dos Quatro Cantos
18 Albergue de Olinda
23 Pousada Saude
24 Pousada d'Olinda

PLACES TO EAT
5 Oficina do Sabor
14 Cantinho da Sé
25 Maison do Bonfim
26 Sabor da Terra
29 Donana
31 Mourisco
32 Café Adega
33 Viva Zapata

OTHER
1 Casa da Boneco
2 Igreja NS da Conceição
3 Farol de Olinda
4 Igreja NS do Amparo
7 Igreja da Misericórdia
8 Observatorio Astronômico
9 Samba do Preto Velho (Live Music)
10 Museu de Arte Sacra de Pernambuco
11 Seminário de Olinda, Igreja NS da Graça
12 Museu do Mamulenco
13 Igreja NS do Bonfim
15 Igreja da Sé
16 Convento São Francisco
19 Igreja da Boa Hora
20 Museu de Arte Comtemporânea
21 Senado Ruins
22 Mercado da Ribeira
27 Posto Telefônica
28 Post Office
30 Igreja São Pedro
34 Igreja NS do Carmo
35 Buses to Recife
36 Tourist Office
37 Palácio dos Governadores
38 Mosteiro de São Bento

BRAZIL

Retrace your steps and continue down the street, now named Ladeira da Misericórdia, to **Igreja da Misericórdia** (1540), which has fine azulejos and gilded carvings inside. It's open 8 to 11:30 am and 2 to 5 pm daily.

Turn right onto Rua Saldanha Marinho to see **Igreja NS do Amparo** (1581), which is under renovation.

Descend Rua do Amparo until you see the **Museu do Mamulenco**, on your right, with its colorful collection of antique wooden puppets. A few doors down, at Rua do Amparo 45, is the house of Silvio Botelho, the creator of the *Bonecos Gigantes de Olinda*, giant papier-mâché puppets that are used in Carnaval festivities.

Continue along Rua do Amparo to Rua 13 de Maio and see the **Museu de Arte Contemporânea** (MAC). This contemporary art museum is recommended for its permanent and temporary exhibits. It's housed in an 18th-century *ajube*, a jail used by the Catholic church during the Inquisition. With its new paint job it's hard to imagine its grim past. It's open 9 am to noon and 2 to 5 pm Tuesday to Friday, and 2 to 5 pm on weekends.

Rua 13 de Maio continues in a tight curve to a junction with Rua Bernardo de Melo and Rua São Bento. If you walk up Rua Bernardo de Melo, you'll come to **Mercado da Ribeira**, an 18th-century structure that is now home to art and artisan galleries.

Go down Rua São Bento to the huge Mosteiro de São Bento (1582), where there are some exceptional woodcarvings in the chapel. The monastery is open 8 to 11 am and 2 to 5 pm daily.

Special Events

Olinda's Carnaval, which lasts a full 11 days, has been very popular with Brazilians and travelers for years. Because so many residents know each other, it has an intimacy and security that you don't get in big city Carnavals. It's a participatory event here – you'll need a costume!

The Folclore Nordestino festival at the end of August features dance, music and folklore from many parts of the northeast.

Places to Stay

Reserve accommodations several months in advance and be prepared for massive price hikes during Carnaval.

If you don't mind dorm-style sleeping, the YHA *Albergue de Olinda* (☎ 081-429-1592), Rua do Sol 233, has clean collective rooms that sleep two to six people for US$15 per person (US$13 for members), including sheet rental and breakfast. Apartamentos are also available for US$15/28 singles/doubles. The *Pousada Saude*, Rua 7 de Setembro 8, is not exactly plush, but it's run by a large, chirpy family and has quartos for US$10/20.

Moving up in price, the *Pousada dos Quatro Cantos* (☎ 081-429-0220), Rua Prudente de Morais 441, is housed in a fine colonial building with a leafy courtyard. Quartos in the old mansion and apartamentos outside cost around US$36/42, though they sometimes offer discounts for longer stays or those outside the high season. Splurge on a suite (with two rooms plus a veranda) for US$75/85. Staff members speak English.

The *Pousada d'Olinda* (☎ 081-439-1163), Praça João Alfredo 178, is a friendly place with a swimming pool and garden. It has a variety of options: dorm rooms for US$15 per person, quartos with fan for US$25/30, apartamentos with fan for US$30/40, and apartamentos with air-conditioning for US$45/50. The staff speaks English, French and German.

The *Pousada do Amparo* (☎ 081 439-1749), Rua do Amparo 191, is a charming place with a lovely garden, pool and view. Very tasteful air-con suites range from US$30 to US$40 (20% more in the high season). Staff members speak English, German and Spanish.

Places to Eat

The old city has a variety of restaurants tucked away among its cobblestone streets – some are pricey, but there are usually a few reasonably priced dishes on the menu.

Cantinho da Sé has a great view from Alto da Sé, but it's a bit of a tourist trap. *Mourisco*, in a lush garden setting, has an excellent self-serve lunch from noon to 3 pm. In the evening it's one of Olinda's best fish restaurants – the servings are large enough for two. A few doors away at Rua 27 de Janeiro 65, *Viva Zapata* is a stylish Mexican restaurant open 7 pm to midnight Thursday to Sunday. Next door is *Café Adega*, a stylish little cafeteria and wine bar that plays classical music.

Oficina do Sabor, Rua do Amparo 329, is an elegant place with a view – it could be worth a splurge. For the flavors of France, there's a cute crêperie on Rua Prudente de Morais, and the *Maison do Bonfim* on Rua do Bonfim.

Down on Praça do Carmo, *Sabor da Terra* is a cheap self-serve lunch place crowded with locals. Along the beachfront opposite the post office, try *Donana*, Praça João Pessoa 55, for Bahian food. It's closed on Wednesday.

Getting There & Away

The main bus stop in Olinda is on Praça do Carmo. Buses marked Rio Doce/Conde da Boa Vista and Casa Caiada go to the center of Recife. The Rio Doce/Princesa Isabel bus stops outside the metrô station. Taxis cost about US$6. Long-distance buses depart from TIP in Recife, but you can book tickets at the Itapema office in Olinda.

Getting Around

Chartering a minibus between a few people is a good way to see surrounding attractions like Porto de Galinhas, Itamaracá, Caruaru, Fazenda Nova (Nova Jerusalém), and Olaria Brennand. There are a few small operators around; ask for a recommendation at the place where you are staying.

CARUARU

On Wednesday and Saturday, Caruaru has a folk-art fair featuring the town's famous ceramic artwork. Singers and poets perform the *literatura de cordel* (literally, string literature) – folk poetry, sold in little booklets which hang by string from the vendors' stands. Caruaru is a day-trip from Recife on shuttle buses (US$6, two hours) that depart every half hour.

FAZENDA NOVA & NOVA JERUSALÉM

The small town of Fazenda Nova, 50km from Caruaru, is famous for its reconstruction of Jerusalem, known as Nova Jerusalém. The time to visit is during Semana Santa, when several hundred inhabitants of Fazenda Nova perform the Paixão de Cristo (Passion Play).

Places to Stay

There's a campground, *Camping Fazenda Nova*, or you can stay in the center of town at the *Grande Hotel* (☎ 081-732-1137), Av Poeta Carlos Pena Filho, which has apartamentos for US$20/25 singles/doubles.

Getting There & Away

During Semana Santa, there are frequent buses from Recife. Special package tours are also offered by travel agencies. At other times, there are daily buses between Fazenda Nova and Caruaru.

Paraíba

JOÃO PESSOA

João Pessoa, the capital of Paraíba, is a noisy, bustling place that's worth a quick look before you head to the beaches.

Information

PBTUR (☎ 083-226-7078), Av Almirante Tamandaré 100, in Praia Tambaú, east of town, provides maps and leaflets. There are also helpful tourist information stands at the rodoviária and the airport. All are (supposedly) open 8 am to 8 pm daily.

Igreja São Francisco

This is João Pessoa's principal tourist attraction and one of Brazil's finest churches. Its construction was interrupted by battles with the Dutch and the French, so the result is a beautiful but architecturally confused complex built over three centuries. The church is open 8 to 11 am and 2 to 5 pm Tuesday to Saturday.

Beaches

Praia Tambaú, 7km directly east of the city center, is rather built up, but clean and nice. South of Tambaú is Praia Cabo Branco. From there, it's a glorious 15km walk along Praia da Penha to Ponta de Seixas, the easternmost tip of South America. There are good beaches north of Tambaú, too.

Places to Stay

At the easternmost tip of Brazil, *Camping-PB-01* is run by Camping Clube do Brasil at Praia de Seixas, 16km from João Pessoa.

In the city center, *Hotel Aurora* (☎ 083-241-3238), Praça João Pessoa 51, has adequate quartos for US$7/12 singles/doubles and apartamentos with fan for US$15/20. Rooms overlooking the street can be noisy. The *Rio Verde* (☎ 222-4369), Rua Duque de Caxias 111, has clean, basic, windowless apartamentos for US$10/13 with fan or US$13/17 with air-con. The price includes a surprisingly decent breakfast.

The best deal in Tambaú is the *Hotel Pousada Mar Azul* (☎ 083-226-2660), Av João Maurício 315. Huge apartamentos with a kitchen and refrigerator cost US$15 (US$20 in the high season). Breakfast is not included. The *Hotel Gameleira* (☎ 083-226-1576), Av João Maurício 157, has standard apartamentos with fan for US$15/18 and apartamentos with air-con for US$18/20; it charges 30% more in summer. Both these hotels are opposite the beach.

Places to Eat

In the center, *Cassino da Lagoa* has an open patio and a fine position beside the Lagoa. Seafood and chicken dishes are recommended. For Italian food try *La Veritta*, at Rua Desembargador Souto Maior 33. Vegetarians can head for *Komida Kilo*, Rua Rodrigues de Aquino 177, for lunch.

Tambaú has a strip of restaurants on Rua Coração, a block back from the beachfront, near the Tropical Hotel Tambaú. *Peixada do Duda* makes superb *ensopado de caranguejo* (crab stew). *O Cariri*, opposite the Tropical Hotel Tambaú on the corner of Av Olinda, is a good lunch spot with cold meats, salads and hot food priced by the kilogram.

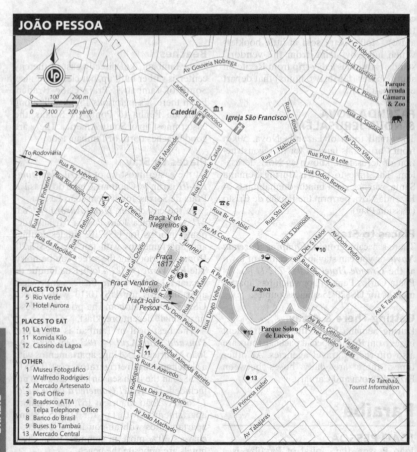

JOÃO PESSOA

PLACES TO STAY
5 Rio Verde
7 Hotel Aurora

PLACES TO EAT
10 La Veritta
11 Komida Kilo
12 Cassino da Lagoa

OTHER
1   Museu Fotográfico
    Walfredo Rodrigues
2   Mercado Artesenato
3   Post Office
4   Bradesco ATM
6   Telpa Telephone Office
8   Banco do Brasil
9   Buses to Tambaú
13 Mercado Central

Entertainment

Nightlife in Tambaú centers around the beachfront along Rua João Maurício and Av Olinda. The latter runs off the beachfront near the Tropical Hotel Tambaú.

Getting There & Around

Air Aeroporto Presidente Castro Pinto (☎ 083-232-1200) is 11km from the city center. Flights operate to Rio, São Paulo and the major cities of the northeast and the north.

Bus The rodoviária is on Av Francisco Londres. There are frequent buses to Recife (US$6, two hours), Natal (US$8, 2½ hours) and Fortaleza (US$22, 10 hours).

Local buses can be boarded at the rodoviária, at the bus stop next to the main post office, and at the bus stops next to the Lagoa. Bus Nos 510 and 511 run frequently to Tambaú (US$0.55, 25 minutes). Bus No 507 runs to Cabo Branco.

Taxi Taxis here like to overcharge. A taxi to the airport should cost around US$18; from the rodoviária to the center, around US$3. To call for a taxi, dial Teletaxi (☎ 083-222-3765).

AROUND JOÃO PESSOA

Thirty-five km south of João Pessoa, **Praia Jacumã** is a long, thin strip of sand featuring colored sand bars, natural pools, mineral springs, shady palms, and barracas on weekends. There are several campsites, and the Swedish-run **Pousada Valhall** (*☎ 083-290-1015*) offers ocean views and comfortable apartamentos from around US$25.

About 10km south of Jacumã is **Praia de Tambaba**, one of the best beaches in Brazil and the only official nude beach in the northeast. There are two barracas along the beach, and you may be able to camp nearby.

Rio Grande do Norte

NATAL

On a peninsula flanked by the Rio Potengi to the northwest and Atlantic reefs and beaches to the southeast, Natal, the capital of Rio Grande do Norte, is a clean, bright city. It's also being developed at top speed into the beach capital of the northeast.

Information

There's a private tourist information booth at the rodoviária nova, open 8 am to 6 pm daily.

Staff has maps and brochures, and can book hotels. Setur's headquarters in the Centro Convenções de Natal is a bit out of the way. More convenient and useful are the information booths at Praia das Artistas and the airport. They have maps, tour pamphlets, touch-screen multimedia, and multilingual information terminals that might be working.

Things to See & Do

The pentagonal **Forte dos Reis Magos** and the **Museu da Câmara Cascudo**, at Av Hermes da Fonseca 1398, are Natal's principal sights. The museum features a collection of Amazon Indian artifacts. It's open 8 to 11 am and 2 to 5 pm Tuesday to Friday, and 10 am to 4 pm Saturday.

Natal's **city beaches** stretch well over 9km, from the fort to the lighthouse. Most have bars, nightlife, big surf and petty crime.

Beach-buggy excursions are offered by a host of *bugeiros* (buggy drivers), for about US$60 per buggy per day. Encourage the driver to stay in established buggy areas and not to damage the more remote and pristine beaches.

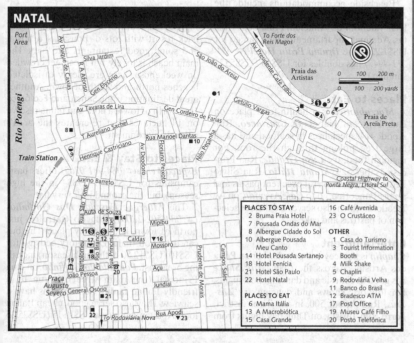

NATAL

PLACES TO STAY
2 Bruma Praia Hotel
7 Pousada Ondas do Mar
8 Albergue Cidade do Sol
10 Albergue Pousada Meu Canto
14 Hotel Pousada Sertanejo
18 Hotel Fenícia
21 Hotel São Paulo
22 Hotel Natal

PLACES TO EAT
6 Mama Itália
13 A Macrobiótica
15 Casa Grande
16 Café Avenida
23 O Crustáceo

OTHER
1 Casa do Turismo
3 Tourist Information Booth
4 Milk Shake
5 Chaplin
9 Rodoviária Velha
11 Banco do Brasil
12 Bradesco ATM
17 Post Office
19 Museu Café Filho
20 Posto Telefônica

BRAZIL

Places to Stay

In the city center, *Albergue Pousada Meu Canto* (☎ *084-212-2811)*, Rua Manoel Dantas 424, is in a beautiful garden setting. It offers quartos for US$10 per person (US$8 for YHA members) with a good breakfast. There's another nice central hostel, the *Albergue Cidade do Sol* (☎ *084-211-3233)*, near the rodoviária velha at Av Duque de Caxias 190.

The *Hotel Pousada Sertanejo* (☎ *084-221-5396)*, Rua Princesa Isabel, is stylish and moderately priced; spotless apartamentos with fan go for US$15/25 singles/doubles.

Along Av Rio Branco you'll find *Hotel Natal* (☎ *084-222-2792)*, with standard single/double apartamentos for US$18/25 (slightly more with air-con); *Hotel São Paulo* (☎ *084-211-4130)*, with apartamentos for US$10 per person without breakfast; and the well-worn *Hotel Fenícia* (☎ *084-211-4378)*, offering apartamentos for US$15/20 without breakfast. The two-star *Hotel Sol Natal* (☎ *084-221-1154; fax 084-221-1157)*, Rua Heitor Carrilo 107, has nice double apartamentos for US$50, but often offers huge discounts.

Beachside accommodations include the *Pousada Ondas do Mar* (☎ *084-211-3481)*, Rua Valentim de Almeida, Praia dos Artistas. Adequate apartamentos with fan go for US$12/20. The *Bruma Praia Hotel* (☎ *084-211-4947)* has doubles for US$35 (US$55 in summer).

Places to Eat

A Macrobiótica is a health-food place on Rua Princesa Isabel. *O Crustáceo*, Rua Apodi 414, specializes in seafood and has a large tree poking through the roof. For regional food, try *Casa Grande*, Rua Princesa Isabel 529. *Mama Itália*, Rua Silvio Pedrosa 43, has several excellent pastas and pizzas. For coffee, go to *Café Avenida*, on Av Deodoro, which also serves a delicious selection of pastries and cakes.

Entertainment

Chaplin is a pricey and popular bar on Praia dos Artistas. Across the road, *Milk Shake* has good live music and dancing most nights. For folkloric shows and dancing, try *Zás-Trás*, Rua Apodi 500, in the Tirol district. Forró com Turista, on Thursday nights from 10 pm in the *Casa do Turismo*, sounds corny but is a lot of fun.

Getting There & Away

Air There are flights from Natal to all major cities in the northeast and the north, as well as Rio and São Paulo.

Bus Long-distance buses use the rodoviária nova, 6km south of the city center. There is one departure daily at noon to Salvador (US$60, 18 hours); six daily to Recife (US$12, 4½ hours); and frequent departures to João Pessoa (US$8.50, 2½ hours. Five regular buses (US$29, eight hours) and one *leito* (US$48) depart daily for Fortaleza. Two executivo buses a day depart for Rio (US$90, 44 hours), at 3:30 and 3:45 pm. There are eight departures a day for Mossoró (US$11, 4½ hours) and one a day for Juazeiro do Norte (US$14, nine hours), leaving at 7 pm.

Getting Around

The rodoviária velha is the hub for bus services to the airport, and the rodoviária nova is the terminal for buses to the beaches.

PRAIA DA PIPA

Pipa, 95km south of Natal, is a small, laid-back resort with lots of pousadas, a hostel and some good restaurants and bars. The main beach is lovely, but it can get crowded on weekends. There are plenty of isolated beaches north and south of town. Another great destination is the Sanctuário Ecológico 1km north of town, a flora and fauna reserve on 14 hectares that re-creates the area's natural environment.

Places to Stay & Eat

Espaço Verde(☎ *084-981-0765)* offers basic campsites for US$2.50 (US$4 in the high season), but the ground isn't very flat.

The *Albergue Enseada Dos Golfinhos* (☎ *084-502-2303)*, Rua do Barreiro, just north of town, is a friendly place. The bus can drop you there. Dormitory beds go for US$10 (US$12.50 in the high season) including breakfast. *Pousada do Golfinho*, on Rua Principal (the main street), is run by a friendly Italian family. Some rooms have a sea view. They also serve good, cheap Italian food. Apartamentos cost US$10/15 (US$25/35 in the high season). *Pousada Aconchego*, just up from the main street opposite Pousada do Golfinho, has comfortable, spacious chalets with individual verandas and hammocks for US$10/15 (US$15/25 in the high season). The best chalet is No 5, with a view of the sunset and Mata Atlântica.

Other good options include *Oásis* (☎ 084-502-2340), on Rua Principal, with apartamentos for US$35 (US$50 in the high season) and *Pousada da Pipa* (☎ 084-982-2753), Rua do Cruzeiro, in a small cul-de-sac off the main road opposite the Oásis. Apartamentos are US$15 (US$20 in the high season).

There are some very good restaurants in Pipa. *A Vivenda*, on Rua Principal, serves pasta, grilled meat and seafood in an ambient setting. *Creperia da Pipa*, also on Rua Principal, is a good option if you're sick of prato feito and pizza. *Cruzeiro do Pescador*, near Pousada da Pipa, has great seafood. Two excellent French restaurants in town are *La Provence* and *Chez Liz*. *Espaço Verde* has the cheapest self-serve lunch in Pipa.

Getting There & Away

From the rodoviária nova in Natal, there are two buses a day to Pipa (US$4, two hours) from Monday to Saturday at 8 am and 3:15 pm. On Sunday, there's one bus, at 8 am. From Pipa, buses leave for Natal daily at 5 am and 4 pm. Another option is to go to Canguaretama and cross on the ferry at Sibaúma. It's also possible to take a boat from Tibaú across to Senador Georgino Alevino. Ask around at the port in Tibaú.

Ceará

Ceará's glorious coastline has nearly 600km of magnificent beaches. The state also has a rich cultural and craft tradition, but economically it is largely poor and undeveloped. Poverty and disease are rampant. Dengue and yellow fevers are prevalent.

FORTALEZA

Fortaleza, the capital of Ceará, is a major fishing port and commercial center. It also boasts the fastest-growing tourist trade in Brazil.

Orientation & Information

The city center forms a grid above the old historical section and includes the Mercado Central (Central Market), the cathedral, major shopping streets and government buildings.

East of the center are the beaches of Praia de Iracema and Praia do Ideal. Continuing eastward, Av Beira Mar (also called Av Presidente John Kennedy in places) links Praia do Diário and Praia do Meireles, both of which are lined with big hotels.

Setur runs the helpful Centro de Turismo (☎ 085-231-3566), Rua Senador Pompeu 350, inside a renovated prison. It's open 7 am to 6 pm Monday to Saturday. They also have booths at the airport and rodoviária.

Beaches

Nightlife is hot around Praia de Iracema and the Ponte dos Ingleses jetty. Farther east, the seashore at Praia do Meireles has lots of craft stalls and outdoor entertainment. These beaches may be polluted, but locals do swim at them. Praia do Futuro, several kilometers east of the city, is much cleaner. The barracas here are popular party places, but don't hang around when the beach is deserted.

Special Events

The Regata de Jangadas, a regatta of traditional balsa-log sailing-craft between Praia do Meireles and Praia Mucuripe, is held during the second half of July. The Iemanjá festival is held on August 15 at Praia do Futuro. The Semana do Folclore, the town's folklore week, takes place in the Centro do Turismo from August 22 to 29.

Places to Stay

There are some cheap dives around the city center, but no real reason to stay there. *Hotel Passeio* (☎ 085-252-2104), Rua Dr João Moreira 221, is a nice old place, with reasonable single/double apartamentos for US$20/28. Between the center and the beaches, the friendly and clean *Pousada do Tourista* (☎ 085-226-5662), Rua Dom Joaquim 351, has quartos for US$12/23. Nearby, *Hotel Savoy* (☎ 085-226-8426) has apartamentos with fan for US$15/25.

Praia de Iracema is a more interesting area to stay. The YHA *Albergue de Juventude Praia de Iracema* (☎ 085-219-3267),

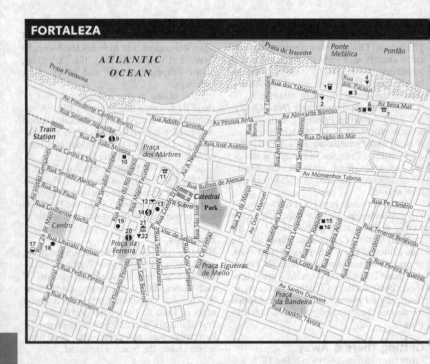

FORTALEZA

Av Almeida Barroso 998, on Praia de Iracema, is a convenient distance from the center. The YHA *Albergue de Juventude Coqueiro Verde* (☎ 085-267-1998), Rua Frei Mansueto 531, is a friendly, comfortable hostel close to the glitz of Praia do Meireles. It charges US$15 (US$10 for members). The *Pousada Vitória de Iracema*, Rua dos Tabajaras 673, is a friendly place with clean, basic quartos for US$10/18. It also has a kitchen you can use. The *Abril em Portugal* (☎ 085-219-9509), Av Almirante Barroso 1006, has apartamentos for US$12/20.

The *Solar da Praia Hotel* (☎ 085-224-7323), Rua Silva Paulet 205, is a good deal at US$15 per person, with a huge buffet breakfast. Not far from the beach at Praia Meireles, the French-owned *Pousada Arara* (☎ 085-263-2277), Rua Frei Mansueto 343, has colorful, comfortable air-con apartamentos for US$35/45.

Places to Eat

Fortaleza features fantastic fruit and fish. The center is OK for snacks and por kilo lunches. *Self L'escale*, just off Praça da Ferreira, does big buffet lunches on weekdays.

In the evening, look around the city beaches. Along Rua dos Tabajaras in Iracema, near the Ponte dos Ingleses, there are some excellent restaurants, including *La Boheme*, a sophisticated, arty place where the chairs are individually painted. For Italian food, stop at *La Trattoria*, Rua dos Pacajus 125.

Lots of eateries line the beachfront at Praia do Meireles, from snack bars to barracas. *Terrace Grill* is a churrascaria on the beach, with tables set out in the open to catch the breeze. The Japanese restaurant *Mikado*, Av Barão de Studart 600, specializes in teppanyaki.

Entertainment

Pirata Bar, near Praia de Iracema, hosts live music for avid forró and lambada fans, who can dance until they drop for a US$10 cover charge. There's plenty more action in the area. During the holiday season, the hotel strip on Praia do Meireles is lined with outdoor bars featuring live music.

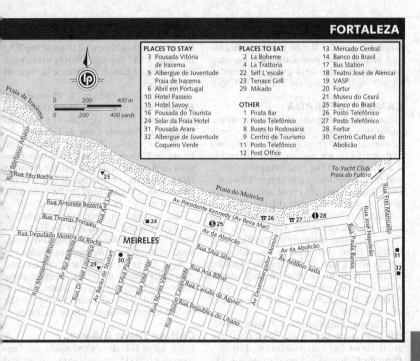

FORTALEZA

PLACES TO STAY
3 Pousada Vitória
  de Iracema
5 Albergue de Juventude
  Praia de Iracema
6 Abril em Portugal
10 Hotel Passeio
15 Hotel Savoy
16 Pousada do Tourista
24 Solar da Praia Hotel
31 Pousada Arara
32 Albergue de Juventude
  Coqueiro Verde

PLACES TO EAT
2 La Boheme
4 La Trattoria
22 Self L'escale
23 Terrace Grill
29 Mikado

OTHER
1 Pirata Bar
7 Posto Telefônico
8 Buses to Rodoviária
9 Centro de Tourismo
11 Posto Telefônico
12 Post Office

13 Mercado Central
14 Banco do Brasil
17 Bus Station
18 Teatro José de Alencar
19 VASP
20 Fortur
21 Museu do Ceará
25 Banco do Brasil
26 Posto Telefônico
27 Posto Telefônico
28 Fortur
30 Centro Cultural do
  Abolicão

BRAZIL

Shopping

Fortaleza is one of the most important centers in the northeast for crafts. Lacework, embroidery, raw leather goods, ceramics, and articles made of straw are available from many organizations. Try one of the following: the Central de Artesanato Luiza Távora, Av Santos Dumont 1589, in Aldeota district; the Centro do Turismo, Rua Senador Pompeu 350; the Mercado Central (which has cheaper prices) on Rua General Bezerril; and tourist boutiques (clothing, jewelry, fashion) along Av Monsenhor Tabosa. Cashew nuts are also an excellent value in Fortaleza.

There is a craft fair every night on Praia Meireles, where you can purchase sand paintings, watch the artists work and have them customize your designs.

Getting There & Away

Air Aeroporto Pinto Martins is 7km south of the center. Flights operate to Rio, São Paulo and major cities in the northeast and the north.

Bus The rodoviária, (☎ 085-272-1566, ☎ 186 in Ceará, for scheduling information) is 5km south of the center. Take any local bus marked 13 de Maio or Aguanambi (passes the Centro de Turismo). Bus services run daily to Salvador (US$60, 22 hours), Natal (US$22, eight hours), Teresina (US$26, 10 hours), São Luis (US$46, 16 hours), Recife (US$42, 12 hours), and Belém (US$66, 22 hours).

The Redencão bus company runs buses at 9 am and 9 pm daily to Jericoacoara (US$15, 6½ hours). Empresa São Benedito runs three buses daily to Canoa Quebrada (US$7, 3½ hours). Ipu Brasileira has buses to Ubajara six times a day (US$14, six hours).

Getting Around

From the airport there are buses (No 404 Aeroporto/Benfica) to Praça José Alencar in the center. A taxi to the center costs US$16 from the airport (with a ticket), or about US$10 from the road outside.

The air-conditioned Guanabara Top Bus is highly recommended if you're coming or going to the rodoviária or airport. The route loops from the airport and rodoviária through the center and on to Praias Iracema and Meireles, and passes the local bus stop outside the rodoviária every 30 minutes from 7 am to 10 pm daily. The fare is US$2.

CANOA QUEBRADA
Once a tiny fishing village cut off from the world by its huge, pink sand dunes, Canoa Quebrada, 13km from Aracati, is still small and pretty, but it is no longer the Shangri-la it was in the past. The road to town is sealed, and there's electricity and chopp. There are lots of gringos running about, and it's a party town on weekends, when the tourist buses roll in. Other than the beach, its main attractions are watching the sunset from the dunes, tearing around in buggies and dancing forró or reggae. If you still have energy after a night of dancing, the beautiful 70km walk south to Tibaú is well worthwhile – take a hammock.

Don't go barefoot: Bichos de pé are prevalent here.

Albergue Lua Estrela is a youth hostel that looks more like a resort hotel. There are great views from its restaurant. Friendly *Pousada Holandes* is a good value at US$5 without breakfast. Other budget options include *Pousada Quebra Mar*, *Pousada Lua Morena* and *Pousada Oasis do Rei*. Highly recommended is *Pousada do Toby*, Rua Nascer do Sol, which has a pool on the roof with a great view; it also provides a good breakfast. Doubles go for around US$30.

There are three buses daily to Canoa Quebrada from Fortaleza's rodoviária, at 8:30 am and 1:40 and 3:30 pm (US$7, 3½ hours).

JERICOACOARA
This remote beach and small fishing village, 290km northwest of Fortaleza, is now popular with backpackers and Brazilians. Avoid bichos de pé by not walking barefoot. Forró is featured every Wednesday and Saturday – just follow the music. You can also play in the sand dunes, hire horses, sail on a jangada, or walk to Pedra Furada, 3km east along the beach.

Places to Stay & Eat
There are plenty of cheap accommodations in Jericoacoara, but also several upmarket options – the latter have generators. For longer stays, ask about renting a local house – you should be able to get something for about US$5 per night. Words to the wise: Bring a large cotton hammock or bedroll with sleeping sack.

An excellent cheapie is *Pousada da Renata*, 500m from town along the beach. Other good budget options are *Pousada Islana*, and *Pousada Casa do Turismo*.

More upmarket lodgings include: the *Pousada Matusa*, Rua São Francisco; *Pousada do Avalon*, Rua Principal; the *Pousada Hippopotamus* (☎ 088-603-1616); and the *Jericoacoara Praia Hotel* (☎ 088-603-1602). The last two are both on Rua Forró.

The best place in town to eat is *Isabel*, on the beach at the end of Rua do Forró. On Rua Principal, *Mama na Égua* also serves good-value seafood. *Restaurant Avalon* has a wide range of salads and crêpes, and *Alexandre Bar* is the prime location along the beach for afternoon drinks, sunset-gazing and seafood dishes. Most of the budget accommodations also serve food.

Getting There & Away
Buses leave Fortaleza's rodoviária for Jericoacoara (US$15, seven hours) at 9 am and 9 pm. In Jijoca, you are transferred to a truck (included in the price) for the 24km rodeo ride to Jericoacoara. The night bus is quicker and cooler, but you arrive in Jericoacoara at around 3:30 am; people from the pousadas meet the bus. Operators in Fortaleza offer package tours of the park for around US$30 a day.

PARQUE NACIONAL DE UBAJARA
The main attractions of this park, near the small town of Ubajara, 290km west of Fortaleza, are the caves and the cable-car ride down to them. There are also beautiful vistas, forests, waterfalls and cooler temperatures – it's 750m above sea level.

The *teleférico* (cable car) operates 10 am to 4 pm daily. It costs US$4, including a guided tour through the caves.

Sítio do Alemão, 1.5km from the park entrance, has spotless chalets for US$10 per person, and provides useful information about local attractions. Near the park entrance, *Pousada da Neblina* (☎ 088-634-1297) has a swimming pool and apartamentos from US$28, while *Pousada Gruta de Uba-jaras* (☎ 088-634-1375) has apartamentos for US$10/20. Both have restaurants. In Ubajara, *Churrascaria Hotel Ubajara* (☎ 088-634-1261) has single/double quartos for US$9/18.

Ipu-Brasília has four buses to Ubajara (US$14, six hours), leaving Fortaleza between 6:30 am and 9 pm. There are also buses from Teresina (US$11, six hours). From Ubajara, walk 3km to the park entrance, or take a taxi.

Piauí

Although travelers usually bypass Piauí state, it has superb beaches along its short coast, plus the friendly city of Teresina and interesting hikes in the Parque Nacional de Sete Cidades.

TERESINA
Teresina, the capital of Piauí and the hottest city in Brazil, is a quirky place that likes to show its Middle Eastern influence in the names of its streets, hotels and sights.

Information
Piemtur (☎ 086-223-4417), the state tourism organization, has a convenient booth inside the Centro Artesanal, on Praça Dom Pedro II. It's open from 8 am to 6 pm weekdays. Servitur Turismo (☎ 086-223-2065), Rua Eliseu Martins 1136, arranges tours of Piauí's attractions.

Things to See & Do
The Museu Histórico do Piauí displays an eclectic assortment of fauna, flora, antique radios and other ancient wonders. It's open Tuesday to Sunday. The entrance fee is nominal and a guide is provided. The Centro Artesanal is a center for artisans from Piauí and a pleasant spot to browse among shops that sell leatherwork, fiber furniture, intricate lacework, colorful hammocks, opals and soapstone.

Places to Stay & Eat
Camping Club do Nordeste (☎ 086-222-6202) is 12km out of the city on Estrada da Socopo, the road running east toward União.

The best cheapie is *Hotel São Benedito*, Rua Senador Teodoro Pachêco 1199, a friendly place with quartos for US$9/14 singles/doubles, and apartamentos for US$15. The two-star *Teresina Palace Hotel* (☎ 086-221-2770), Rua Paissandu 1219, is a good value and worth considering. It has a pool, and its air-con apartamentos start at US$23/30.

Gustavo's, on the corner of Rua David Caldas and Rua Alvaro Mendes, is an excellent por-kilo lunch place, with a great variety of salads and an air-conditioned dining room upstairs. For seafood, try *Camarão do Elias*, Av Pedro Almeida 457. For a splurge, visit the *Forno e Fogão*, inside the Hotel Luxor Palace, for a gigantic buffet lunch. There's also a good restaurant inside the Teresina Palace Hotel that serves regional food.

Getting There & Away
The airport, 6km north of the center, has flights to Rio, São Paulo and the major cities of the northeast and north.

Teresina has regular bus connections with Sobral (US$17, six hours), Fortaleza (US$28, 10 hours), São Luís (US$20, seven hours) and Belém (US$34, 15 hours).

There are two executivo buses to Parnaíba (US$22, five hours) and several standard buses (US$10, six hours) daily. There are bus connections twice daily to São Raimundo Nonato (US$25, 10 hours) and hourly to Piripiri (US$5, three hours).

Getting Around
From the rodoviária to the center, the cheapest, slowest and hottest option is to take the bus (US$2) from the stop outside the rodoviária. A taxi costs US$9 at the bilheteria, but much less if you flag it down outside. A taxi to the airport from the center is US$5.

PARNAÍBA
Parnaíba, once a major port at the mouth of the Rio Parnaíba, is being developed as a beach resort, as is the town of Luís Correia, 18km away. Porto das Barcas, the old warehouse section along the riverfront, has been restored. It boasts a Piemtur tourist office, an artesanato center, art galleries, bars and restaurants.

Praia Pedra do Sal is a good beach about 15km northeast of town on Ilha Grande Santa Isabel. Lagoa do Portinho, a lagoon surrounded by dunes, is about 14km east on the road to Luís Correia.

Parnaíba is also the starting point for trips into the Delta do Parnaíba, a 2700-sq-km expanse of islands, beaches, lagoons, sand dunes and mangroves that are home to abundant wildlife. The region straddles the border of Piauí and Maranhão.

Places to Stay

The friendly hostel *Pousada Porto das Barcas* (☎ 086-321-1856) is in a converted warehouse right in Porto das Barcas. Dormitory rooms cost US$10 per person with breakfast. The *Hotel Cívico* (☎ 086-322-2470), Av Governor Chagas Rodrigues 474, in the center of town, has a swimming pool and apartamentos starting at US$20/30 for singles/doubles with a huge buffet breakfast. On the beach at Pedra do Sal, the *Pousada do Sol* has been recommended by readers.

Getting There & Away

There are daily buses to and from Teresina. A small wooden boat plies a route daily through the Delta do Parnaíba to Tutóia (US$5, about six hours).

PARQUE NACIONAL DE SETE CIDADES

Sete Cidades is a small national park with interesting rock formations, estimated to be at least 190 million years old, that resemble *sete cidades* (seven cities). The appeal for visitors lies in the walking opportunities; the loop through the seven cities is a two-hour (or so) leisurely stroll. The park is open from 6 am to 6 pm. Entry is US$3 for 24 hours.

Abrigo do IBAMA, 6km from the park entrance, is the most popular place to stay. Apartamentos with fan cost US$20 and can sleep up to four people. There's a restaurant attached to the hostel. Designated campsites are also available for US$6.

Just outside the park entrance is the *Hotel Fazenda Sete Cidades* (☎ 086-276-2222), a two-star resort hotel with attractive apartamentos for US$34/48. It's a cool and shady spot with a restaurant and pool.

The park is 180km from Teresina and 141km from Ubajara (Ceará state) on a fine paved road. Take any bus between Fortaleza and Teresina, and get off at Piripiri. From there, an IBAMA courtesy bus makes the 26km trip to the park from Piripiri at 7 am and returns from Abrigo do IBAMA at 5 pm. A taxi from Piripiri costs around US$20. A *mototaxi* (motorcycle taxi) costs US$8. Hitchhiking is easier here than elsewhere. In the park itself, you can drive on the roads or follow the trails on foot – they're well marked.

Maranhão

Maranhão is the northeast's second-largest state (after Bahia) and has a population of more than five million.

SÃO LUÍS

São Luís, the capital of Maranhão, is a city with unpretentious colonial charm and a rich folkloric tradition – definitely a highlight for travelers to the northeast. It was recently declared a World Heritage Site by UNESCO. In the historic center of São Luís, Projeto Reviver (Project Renovation) has created a charming and beautifully restored colonial precinct.

Information

Tourist Offices The most useful tourist office in São Luís is run by Funtur (☎ 098-222-5281), on Praça Dom Pedro II. It has brochures and maps in English and French, as well as helpful English-speaking attendants. It's open 8 am to 7 pm weekdays, 9 am to 6 pm Saturday. Maratur, the state tourism organization, has its head office on Rua da Estrêla, in the historical district, and information booths at the rodoviária and elsewhere around town.

Travel Agencies Giltur (☎ 098-232-6041), Rua do Giz 46, offers organized tours of the Alcântara, the city's historic center, and Parque Nacional dos Lençóis Maranheses, for very reasonable prices. In the shopping gallery at Rua do Sol 141, there are several travel agencies offering package tours. Many sell bus tickets at the same price as at the rodoviária. An efficient travel agency in the shopping gallery is Taguatur (☎ 098-232-0906) at loja 14.

Things to See & Do

The whole historical district is a must-see, with its cobbled streets and azulejo facades. Some worthwhile museums are housed in various historic buildings, and there are frequent outdoor cultural performances-cum-parties. **Museu de Artes Visuais** has good examples of traditional arts. It's open 9 am to 6 pm Tuesday to Saturday). Nearby is the interesting old circular marketplace. The **Museu do Negro**, open afternoons Tuesday to Saturday, records the history of slavery in Maranhão. On the hill north of the historical district is **Catedral da Sé**, constructed by Jesuits in 1726, and the **Palácio dos Leões**, a French fortress built in 1612 that is now the state governor's pad.

The **Museu Histórico e Artístico**, on Rua do Sol, is a restored 1836 mansion with attractive displays of artifacts from wealthy Maranhão families.

Across the river north of town is the modern suburb of São Francisco. There are also a number of good **beaches** that turn into total party scenes on weekends and holidays.

Special Events

Distinctive local dances and music are performed all year round, with active samba clubs turning it up especially for Carnaval. The Tambor de Mina festivals, in July, are important Afro-Brazilian religious occasions. The famous Bumba Meu Boi festival runs from late June to mid-August.

Places to Stay

Unicamping (☎ 098-222-2552) is near Calhau beach, 8km from town.

A decent budget option in the city is *Hotel Casa Grande* (☎ 098-232-2432), an old building on Rua Isaac Martins. Large, clean, basic apartamentos cost US$15/17/20 for singles/doubles/triples, with a bread-and-coffee breakfast. *Hotel Estrêla* (☎ 098-222-7172), Rua da Estrêla 370 in the heart of the historical district, is basic but clean, with quartos for US$15/20/30. *Hotel Lord* (☎ 098-222-5544), Rua de Nazaré 258, is a large, timeworn hotel with comfortable quartos for US$18/24, as well as air-con apartamentos. The *Hotel São Marcos* (☎ 098-232-3763), Rua do Saúde 178, has recently been renovated. Smallish apartamentos cost US$19/25. There's a swimming pool and restaurant.

Pousada Colonial (☎ 098-232-2834), Rua Afonso Pena 112, in a restored colonial mansion, has comfortable little apartamentos for US$42/50, maybe less if you pay cash. *Pousada do Francês* (☎ 098-231-4844), at Rua 7 de Setembro 121, is even nicer, with well-equipped air-con single/double apartamentos for US$40/50.

Places to Eat

Across from the Fonte do Ribeirão, you'll find a couple of decent self-serve lunch spots. *Fonte de Sabor* is a good one.

The *Base da Lenoca*, Praça Dom Pedro II, is a popular restaurant with a great position overlooking the Rio Anil – order a beer and a snack and enjoy the breeze. In the heart of the historic district, on Rua da Estrêla, there's the *Restaurante Antigamente*. It has tables on the street and serves seafood and meat dishes. There's live music here on weekend evenings. *Senac*, Rua de Nazaré 244, offers fine dining in a lovely colonial building. *Naturista Alimentos*, Rua do Sol 517, has the best vegetarian food in the city.

Entertainment

São Luís is the reggae center of the northeast, and several places have ear-splitting sound systems and hordes of *reggeiros*. The action is at a different place each night; ask the tourist office for suggestions, and don't bring valuables. For pagode music and dancing, barracas and *boates* (nightclubs) blast it day and night.

Getting There & Away

Air There are flights to and from Rio, São Paulo and major northern cities. By the time you read this, a new international airport will be servicing direct flights from Europe. Check travel agents for details.

Bus The rodoviária is 8km southeast of the city center. There are daily buses: frequently to Teresina (US$20, seven hours); two to Belém (US$38, 12 hours); three to Fortaleza (US$46, 18 hours); and two to Recife (US$55, 24 hours).

Boat From the *hidroviária* (boat terminal) west of the center, there are regular ferries to Alcântara. Sailing times depend on the tides. The tourist boat leaves at about 9 am, returns at about 4 pm, and takes about 50 minutes (US$6 one way). More crowded public boats leave at 7 am (US$3). Two anti-quated sailboats also ply the route, leaving the hidroviária at around 7 am and 4 pm. This pirates-of-the-Caribbean experience takes about 1½ hours and costs about US$3.

BRAZIL

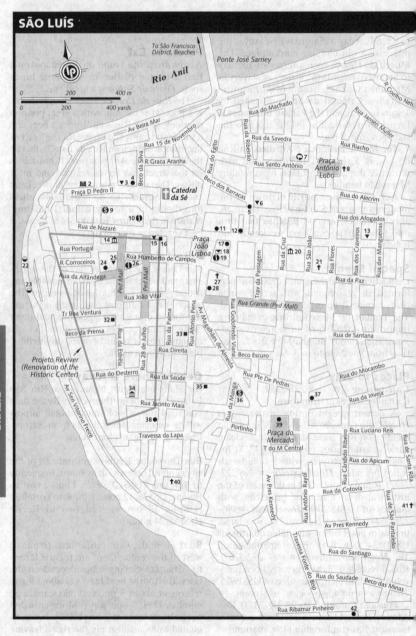

SÃO LUÍS

To São Francisco District, Beaches

Ponte José Sarney

Rio Anil

R Coelho Netc

Av Beira Mar

Rua 15 de Novembro

Rua do Machado

Rua da Ribeirão

Rua da Savedra

Rua Jansen Muller

Rua Santo Antônio

Rua Riacho

R Graça Aranha

Beco da Silva

Rua do Egito

Praça Antônio Lobo †8

Catedral da Sé

Beco dos Barracas

Rua do Alecrim

Praça D Pedro II

Rua dos Afogados

Rua de Nazaré

Rua da Cruz

Rua dos Craveiros

Rua das Mangueiras

Praça João Lisboa

Trav da Passagem

Rua São João

Rua Flores

Rua Portugal

Rua Humberto de Campos

Ped Mall

Ped Mall

Rua da Palma

Rua da Paz

R Corroceiros

Rua da Alfândega

Rua João Vital

Rua Grande (Ped Mall)

Rua Afonso Pena

Av Magalhães de Almeida

Rua Godofredo Viana

Tr Boa Ventura

Beco da Prensa

Rua da Estrela

Rua 28 de Julho

Rua Direita

Beco Escuro

Rua de Santana

Projeto Reviver (Renovation of the Historic Center)

Rua do Desterro

Rua da Saúde

Rua Pte De Pedras

Rua do Mocambo

Av Sen Vitorino Freire

Rua Jacinto Maia

Rua da Manga

Rua da Inveja

Portinho

Praça do Mercado

T do M Central

Travessa da Lapa

Rua Luciano Reis

Rua Cândido Ribeiro

Rua do Apicum

†40

Rua da Cotovia

Rua Antônio Rayol

Rua Pres Kennedy

Av Pres Kennedy

Rua de São Pantaleão

Rua de Santa Rita

Travessa Fonte do Bisp

Rua do Santiago

Rua do Saudade

Beco das Minas

Rua Ribamar Pinheiro

0   200   400 m
0   200   400 yards

BRAZIL

SÃO LUÍS

Getting Around

São Cristóvâo buses run to the airport from the bus stop on Praça Deodoro (45 minutes). To get to the rodoviária, catch a Rodoviária bus from the same place. Bilheteria taxi tickets from the airport are a rip-off at US$15. Buses to the beaches leave from the Praia Grande terminal west of the center.

ALCÂNTARA

Across the Baía de São Marcos from São Luís is the old colonial town of Alcântara. Built in the early 1600s with extensive slave labor, the town was the hub of the region's sugar and cotton economy, and home to Maranhão's rich landowners. The new rocket-launching facility, Centro do Lançamento de Alcântara, provides a modern contrast.

As you walk around the picturesquely decrepit town, look in particular for the beautiful row of two-story houses on Rua Grande, the **Igreja de NS do Carmo** (1665) on Rua Amargura, and the **pelourinho** on Praça da Matriz. The **Museu Histórico** displays a collection of sacred art, festival regalia and furniture (closed Monday).

On the first Sunday after Ascension Day, Alcântara celebrates the **Festa do Divino**, one of the most colorful annual festivals in Maranhão.

Places to Stay & Eat

Alcântara has simple *campsites* close to Praça da Matriz and near the lighthouse. Inexpensive hotels include *Pousada do Imperador*, on Rua Grande, *Pousada Pelourinho*(☎ 098-337-1150), beside Praça da Matriz, and the recommended *Pousada do Mordomo Régio* (☎ 098-337-1221). *Chale da Baronesa* (☎ 098-337-1339), on the beachfront at Praia da Baronesa, is particularly quiet and relaxing.

The hotels all have restaurants, and there are others along Rua Neto Guteirrez.

Getting There & Away

The only way to Alcântara is by ferry from São Luís.

PARQUE NACIONAL DOS LENÇÓIS MARANHENSES

Natural attractions here include 1550 sq km of beaches, mangroves, lagoons, sand dunes and local fauna, including turtles and migratory birds. The dunes are thought to resemble

BRAZIL

lençóis (bedsheets) strewn across the landscape. Tourist infrastructure is minimal.

Information is available in São Luís, from the tourist office or from one of the travel agencies. Giltur in São Luis runs tours to the park. A three-day trip costs around US$195, including accommodations in Barreirinhas and bus and boat transport.

It's also possible to arrange a visit from the pretty little town of **Barreirinhas**, two hours away by boat. *Pousada Lins (☎ 098-349-1203)*, Av Joaquim Soeiro de Cavalho 550, is a nice, inexpensive place to stay. They have quartos from US$10 per person.

Buses make the rough trip to Barreirinhas at 9:30 am and 9:45 pm daily from the rodoviária in São Luís (US$21, around eight hours). Book tickets at Taguatur, well in advance if possible.

Pará

The state of Pará covers more than one million sq km. It includes a major stretch of the Amazon and huge tributaries such as the Rio Trombetas, Rio Tapajós and Rio Xingu. Much of the southern part of the state has been deforested, and there are serious ecological problems as a result of uncontrolled mining, land disputes and ranching.

BELÉM
Belém is the economic center of the north and the capital of the state of Pará. Parts of the city are almost decrepit, but the central area is pleasant. Belém is one of the rainiest cities in the world, but each cloudburst brings with it brief, welcome relief from the oppressive heat. (See map on pp 432-433.)

Information
Tourist Offices Belémtur (☎ 091-241-3194), the municipal tourism agency, is at Av Governador José Malcher 592. It also has an information booth at the airport. Paratur (☎ 091-223-6198), the state tourism agency, Feira de Artesanato do Estado, Praça Kennedy, is open 8 am to 6 pm weekdays.

Money The main branch of Banco do Brasil is at Av Presidente Vargas 248. There are several câmbios that change traveler's checks, such as Casa Cruzeiro Câmbio, Rua 28 de Setembro.

Travel Agencies Many agencies offer city tours, river tours, excursions to Ilha de Marajó, and very worthwhile trips to Icoaraci pottery village. Prices are around US$50 per person for a standard full-day river tour, but it's worth shopping around. Agencies include:

Amazon Star Turismo
  (☎ 091-224-6244) Rua Henrique Gurjão 236
Amazon Incoming Services
  (☎ 091-249-4904) Av Gentil Bittencourt 3552
Mururé Turismo
  (☎ 091-241-0891) Av Presidente Vargas 134

Dangers & Annoyances Pickpockets are a problem at Mercado Ver-o-Peso. Geptur (the tourist police) has an office in the Solar da Beira building at the market, almost opposite the Hotel Ver-o-Peso. Theft is also common on riverboats and from rooms in cheap hotels. Avoid walking alone around deserted commercial areas and docks at night.

Things to See & Do
Av Presidente Vargas is the main street. It's an interesting walk from the waterfront to the **Praça da República**, where people relax and socialize in the early evening. Facing the praça, the richly decorated, neo-classical **Teatro da Paz** (1874) is open on weekdays. Admission is US$1.10.

Southwest of Vargas, there are narrow shopping streets and the **Cidade Velha** (Old Town). There are some colonial buildings, but most are run down or unsympathetically modernized. On the waterfront, **Mercado Ver-o-Peso** covers several blocks and is open all day, every day. There's an amazing variety of produce and people.

Next to the fishing port is **Praça do Mercado**, with its replica of Big Ben. The next block is **Praça Dom Pedro II**, with two grand and beautifully restored museums on its east side. **Palácio Antônio Lemos** houses the Art Museum and the mayor's offices. Also called the Palácio Azul (blue palace), it's a late-19th-century building in Brazilian imperial style, with vast rooms and opulent imported furniture. It's open from 9 am to noon and 2 to 6 pm Tuesday to Friday and on weekend mornings; admission is free.

Palácio Lauro Sodré, built in 1771, houses the State Museum. It has a good collection of paintings, a small chapel, stables and a

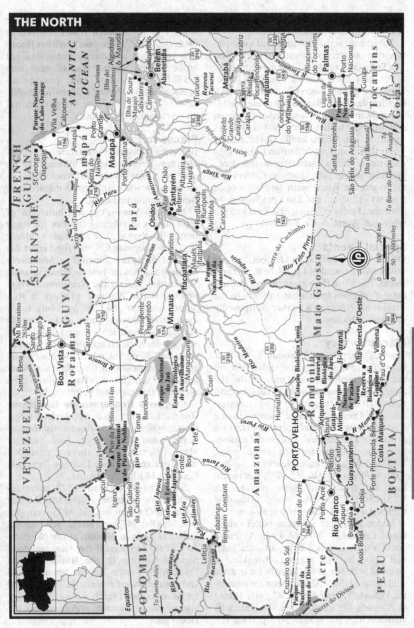

THE NORTH

slaves' dungeon It's open 12:15 to 5:30 pm Tuesday to Friday; admission is free.

To the west is the cathedral and some picturesque old streets around the waterfront. The **Forte do Castelo** is pleasant at dusk.

About 1.25km east of Praça da República, facing Praça Justo Chermont, the 1909 **Basílica de NS de Nazaré** has a fine marble and gold interior and a sacred-art museum downstairs. Another block east is Belém's top attraction, **Museu Emílio Goeldi**, featuring a park, zoo, aquarium and ethnology museum. Exhibits include manatees, huge pirarucu, jungle cats, giant river otters and many strange Amazonian birds. It's open from 9 to 11:45 am and 2 to 5 pm Tuesday to Thursday, Friday morning, and 9 am to 5 pm weekends. Admission is US$2.70.

Special Events

On the second Sunday in October, the city wakes to the sound of hymns, bells and fireworks. The Círio de Nazaré, one of Brazil's biggest religious festivals, is a tribute to the Virgin of Nazaré, a statue supposedly sculpted in Nazareth.

Places to Stay

The very cheapest accommodations are near the waterfront; security and cleanliness are not guaranteed and most will rent by the hour. The *Transamazonas* is rock-bottom basic, with quartos for US$7/11 singles/doubles. There are better options in the Comércio, such as *Hotel Fortaleza*, Travessa Frutuoso Guimarães 276, with almost-tolerable quartos for the same price, US$10/16 with breakfast. Nearby, at No 260, *Vitória Régia* (☎ 091-212-2077) has rooms that are clean and more private for US$14.50/18/22.50 for singles/doubles/triples. An extra US$4 gets you air-con.

Mid-range places are much better values. *Hotel Central* (☎ 091-242-3011), Av Presidente Vargas 290, is a large, art-deco hotel that's popular with travelers. Breakfast is included with rates of US$16/21 for quartos with fan and US$27/32 for air-con apartamentos. *Vidonho's Hotel* (☎ 091-242-1444), Rua Ó de Almeida 476, is an OK, modern place with apartamentos for US$27/34. Opposite the market, *Hotel Ver-o-Peso* (☎ 091-241-1093), has single air-con apartamentos for US$20, and better ones for US$27/32. The rooftop restaurant has good views.

There are also upmarket options for slightly more. *Manacá Hotel Residência* (☎ 091-222-6227), Travessa Quintino Bocaiúva 1645, is a charmingly renovated old house with immaculate apartamentos from US$27/34. Breakfast and air-con are optional extras. *Hotel Le Massilia* (☎ 091-224-7147), Rua Henrique Gurjão 236, has air-con rooms for US$36/50.

Places to Eat

Belém has a distinct regional cuisine featuring a bewildering variety of fish and fruit. Try *pato no tucupi*, a lean duck cooked in fermented manioc extract, and maniçoba, a stew of manioc and meat.

Mercado Ver-o-Peso has hundreds of food stands serving big lunches for small prices – it's a good place to sample local fish. Iguatemi Shopping Center's *food court* has a range of options, including *Sorveteria Cairu*, which has the best ice cream in town. Vegetarians can try the *Restaurante Vegetariano Nutre Natural*, upstairs at Rua Santo Antônio 264. For heavenly sucos made from Amazon fruits, go to *Casa do Suco*, at Av Presidente Vargas 794; there's also self-serve lunch upstairs. *Inter Restaurant*, Rua 28 de Setembro 304, has typical, good-value Brazilian fare; *Spazzio Verde* and *Bon Apetit*, Travessa Rua Barbosa 1059, are more expensive but better quality.

Chopperia Restaurante do Boêmio, on Rua Carlos Gomes, is one of the few budget dinner options close to downtown. *Restaurante Casa Portuguesa*, Rua Senador Manoel Barata 897, is also recommended and *Cantina Italiana*, Travessa Benjamin Constant 140, has good pasta.

Expect to pay US$9 to US$22 for entrées at the more upmarket restaurants. *Lá Em Casa* and *O Outro*, both at Av Governador José Malcher 247, have all the best regional dishes. *O Círculo Militar*, at the old Forte do Castelo, has a great bay view and good regional cooking. Try the *Miako*, Travessa Primeiro de Março 766, for Japanese food and *Restaurante Le Massilia*, in the Hotel Le Massilia, for French cuisine. There are also several restaurants and bars near the Docas area.

Entertainment

Belém has some hot nightlife – it's the main attraction for some visitors. The Docas area along Av Visconde de Souza Franco is home to Belém's busiest scene. There are some good bars, including **Chopperia Colarinho Branco** and **Chopp Mill Doca**, many of which have live music. **Bar do Parque**, a 24-hour outdoor bar at Praça da Republica, is a popular, if seedy, meeting place. **Cosanostra Caffè** east of downtown at Travessa Benjamim Constant 1499, is a hangout for intellectual types. It has a bar, a restaurant and live music.

There's great traditional music and dance, such as *carimbó*, but performances are hard to find. Ask at the tourist office. **Sabor da Terra** (☎ 091-241-5377) is a restaurant and club with regular folkloric shows. Boates with music, shows and dancing include **Bora-Bora** (☎ 091-241-5848), Rua Bernal do Couto, just off Av Visconde de Souza Franco down at the Docas area, and the **African Bar** (☎ 091-241-1085), at Praça Kennedy near Paratur.

If you want to escape the Amazon, there are cinemas on Av Nazaré at Travessa São Pedro near Iguatemi Shopping Center.

Getting There & Away

Air Flights go to Macapá, Santarém, Manaus and major Brazilian cities, as well as Cayenne, French Guiana, Paramaribo, Suriname, and Miami, Florida.

Bus There are regular bus services to São Luís (US$34, 12 hours), Fortaleza (US$63, 25 hours), Recife (US$86, 34 hours) and Rio de Janeiro (US$131, 52 hours). There are also direct buses to Belo Horizonte (US$77, 30 hours), São Paulo (US$123, 46 hours) and Brasília (US$85, 36 hours). There are no direct buses to Santarém; you might get there in the dry season via Marabá, but boats are a much better option.

Boat Private companies provide most of the river transport. You can book a ticket with an agency or go to the docks and find a boat yourself. The agencies have booths along Rua Castilho França near Escadinha Port. The best place to look yourself is Portão 17 (Armazém 9), where Av Visconde de Souza Franco meets Av Marechal Hermes.

Boats depart almost daily for the upriver trip to Manaus via Santarém and numerous other ports. A ticket to Manaus is around US$75 for hammock space and US$110 per person in a four-berth cabin; tickets to Santarém cost about US$40/65. Shop around for discounts. There isn't usually much advantage in taking a cabin; they can be hot, stuffy and unclean. It takes at least two days to reach Santarém and five to reach Manaus, but may take much longer.

The government line, ENASA (☎ 091-242-5870), Av Presidente Vargas 41, leaves Belém every Wednesday at 8 pm, arrives in Santarém at noon on Saturday, and reaches Manaus on Tuesday morning. Prices are US$55 to Santarém and US$73 to Manaus for hammock space. Boats are apparently very crowded and magnets for thieves. The food is poor. Arrive early on the day of departure and take your own snacks and water.

There are boats leaving most days for Macapá. Souzamar agency has boats departing from Belém to Macapá 10 am Tuesday and Thursday. The 24-hour trip costs US$27/32 for hammock space/shared cabin.

For Ilha de Marajó, the Arapari boat service to Câmara leaves Escadinha port Monday to Saturday at 7 am (US$8, three hours), returning at 10 am. Paraense boats also depart three times daily, Monday to Saturday. The ENASA ferry to Soure departs at 8 pm Friday and at 2 pm Saturday (US$8, five hours), returning 3 pm Sunday.

Getting Around

The rodoviária is a 15-minute bus ride east of the city. To get to the city, take an Aeroclube (Presidente Vargas) bus. Cidade Nova (Ver-o-Peso) buses run via Mercado Ver-o-Peso.

To/From the Airports The main airport, Aeroporto Internacional Val de Cans is a few kilometers north of town. Take the Marex-F Patroni to and from the city center (a half-hour). A taxi costs around US$13. Air taxis fly from Aeroporto Júlio César (☎ 091-223-3986).

AROUND BELÉM

There are regular buses from the rodoviária to the pottery village of Icoaraci, and to Ilha do Mosqueiro, which has a few places to stay. Ilha de Cotijuba is also worth a visit. It has nice beaches and the rustic **Pousada Trilha Dourada** (☎ 091-266-2277). Take a boat from Rodomar port or bus to Icoaraci, then a local boat.

BRAZIL

BELÉM

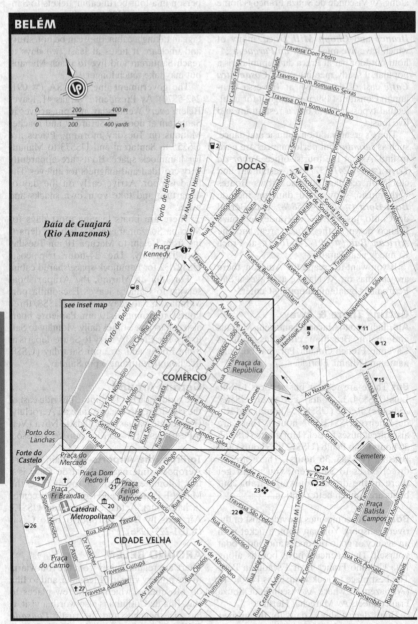

Baía de Guajará (Rio Amazonas)

Porto de Belém

DOCAS

Praça Kennedy

see inset map

Porto de Belém

COMÉRCIO

Praça da República

Porto dos Lanchas

Forte do Castelo

Praça do Mercado

Praça Dom Pedro II

Praça Felipe Patrone

Praça Fr Brandão

Catedral Metropolitana

CIDADE VELHA

Praça do Carmo

Praça Batista Campos

Cemetery

Travessa Dom Pedro
Travessa Dom Romualdo Seixas
Travessa Dom Romualdo Coelho
Travessa Almirante Wandenkolk

Av Castilho França
Rua da Municipalidade
Av Senador Lemos
Av Jerônimo Pimentel
Rua Bernal do Couto

Av Marechal Hermes
Rua da Municipalidade
Rua Gaspar Viana
Av 28 de Setembro
Av Visconde de Souza Franco
Av Visconde de Souza Franco
Rua Sen Manoel Barata
Rua Ó de Almeida
Rua Aristides Lobo
Rua Tiradentes
Rua Boaventura da Silva

Travessa Piedade
Travessa Benjamin Constant
Travessa Rui Barbosa

Av Assis de Vasconcelos
Av Clauíba França
Rua S Antônio
Av Pres Vargas
Rua Aristides Lobo
Rua Osvaldo Cruz
Rua Henrique Gurjão

Rua 15 de Novembro
Rua João Alfredo
13 de Maio
Rua Sen Manoel Barata
Rua Ó de Almeida
Padre Prudencio
Travessa Campos Sales
Travessa Carlos Gomes
Av Nazaré
Travessa Dr Morais
Av Serzedelo Correia

7 de Setembro
Av Portugal

Rua João Diogo
Travessa Padre Eutiquio
Tv Pres Pernambuco

Des Inacio Guilhon
Rua Aver Roche
Travessa São Pedro
Rua São Francisco
Av Arcipreste M Teodoro
Rua dos Tamoios
Rua dos Mundurucus

Siqueira Mendes
Dr Assis
Dr Malcher
Rua Joaquim Tavora
Av 16 de Novembro
Rua Veiga Cabral
Av Conselheiro Furtado
Rua dos Apinajés

Travessa Gurupá
Travessa Alenquer
Av Tamandaré
Rua Óbidos
Rua Triunvirato
Rua Cezário Alvim
Rua dos Tupinambás
Rua dos Pariquís

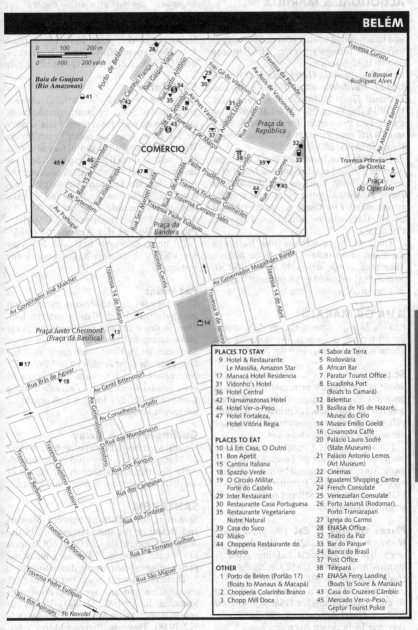

BELÉM

PLACES TO STAY
9   Hotel & Restaurante
    Le Massilia, Amazon Star
17 Manacá Hotel Residencia
31 Vidonho's Hotel
36 Hotel Central
42 Transamazonas Hotel
46 Hotel Ver-o-Peso
47 Hotel Fortaleza,
    Hotel Vitória Regia

PLACES TO EAT
10 Lá Em Casa, O Outro
11 Bon Apetit
15 Cantina Italiana
18 Spazzio Verde
19 O Círculo Militar,
    Forte do Castelo
29 Inter Restaurant
30 Restaurante Casa Portuguesa
35 Restaurante Vegetariano
    Nutre Natural
39 Casa do Suco
40 Miako
44 Chopperia Restaurante do
    Boêmio

OTHER
1   Porto de Belém (Portão 17)
    (Boats to Manaus & Macapá)
2   Chopperia Colarinho Branco
3   Chopp Mill Doca

4   Sabor da Terra
5   Rodoviária
6   African Bar
7   Paratur Tourist Office
8   Escadinha Port
    (Boats to Camará)
12 Belemtur
13 Basílica de NS de Nazaré,
    Museu do Círio
14 Museu Emílio Goeldi
16 Cosanostra Caffè
20 Palácio Lauro Sodré
    (State Museum)
21 Palácio Antonio Lemos
    (Art Museum)
22 Cinemas
23 Iguatemi Shopping Centre
24 French Consulate
25 Venezuelan Consulate
26 Porto Jarumã (Rodomar),
    Porto Transarapari
27 Igreja do Carmo
28 ENASA Office
32 Teatro da Paz
33 Bar do Parque
34 Banco do Brasil
37 Post Office
38 Telepará
41 ENASA Ferry Landing
    (Boats to Soure & Manaus)
43 Casa do Cruzeiro Câmbio
45 Mercado Ver-o-Peso,
    Geptur Tourist Police

BRAZIL

ALGODOAL & MARUDÁ

Algodoal, a remote fishing village on the Atlantic coast northeast of Belém, has dunes and beaches that attract younger *belenenses* and a few foreign travelers. Hotel prices double in high season.

Double rooms at *Hotel Bela Mar* start at US$27. *Caldeirão* (☎ 091-227-0984) and *Cabanas Hotel* both have basic rooms for US$9/14 singles/doubles. The latter also has a cute two-story room for US$18/33. *Pousada ABC* near Praia da Vila offers simple rooms for US$18/23.

The *Bela Mar* restaurant has a set menu offering fish and meat. *Cabanas Hotel* also serves meals. At Praia da Vila, *Restaurant Prato Cheio* has good views and a more varied menu. *Lua Cheia* is a haunt of local youth. Bars can be found on Praia da Princesa.

There are regular buses from Belém to the town of Marudá (US$7, three hours). Then take a boat across the bay (US$2.50, 30 minutes) followed by an optional donkey cart taxi to Algodoal village.

ILHA DE MARAJÓ

Ilha de Marajó, one of the world's largest fluvial islands, lies where the Amazon and Tocantins Rivers pour into the Atlantic.

Soure

Soure is the island's principal town and is probably the best place to visit, with good beaches and fazendas. It's primarily a fishing village, but is also the commercial center for the island's big buffalo business.

Praia Araruna is a beautiful beach, 5km from town, and Praia do Pesqueiro is 13km away. Both can be reached by taxi. Bike Tur, on the corner of Rua Terceira and Travessa 14, hires bikes for US$9 per hour. You can negotiate a daily rate.

Places to Stay & Eat The plain *Soure Hotel* (☎ 091-741-1202), in the center of town, has the cheapest lodging. Apartamentos are US$15, US$23 with air-con. *Hotel Marajó* (☎ 091-741-1396), at Praça Inhangaíba 351, has a swimming pool and air-con apartamentos for US$23/36 singles/doubles. *Hotel Araruna* (☎ 091-741-1347), Travessa 14, between Avenidas 7 and 8, has air-con rooms for similar prices. *Hotel Ilha do Marajó* (☎ 091-741-1315), at Travessa 2 is more upmarket, with rooms for US$45/54.

Restaurante O Canecão, Terceira Rua facing the market plaza, has a cheap prato feito. *Restaurante Minha Deusa*, Travessa 14, near Praia do Araruna, serves excellent fish.

Salvaterra

Just across the Rio Paracauari, Salvaterra is connected to Soure by hourly shuttle boats. A 10-minute walk from town, **Praia Grande de Salvaterra** is a long, pretty beach on the Baía de Marajó with beautiful fenced corrals that use the falling tide to trap fish. There are restaurants and accommodations along the beach. *Pousada Anastácia* has simple rooms for US$7/14 singles/doubles, and a rustic restaurant. *Pousada Tropical* (☎ 091-765-1155) has apartamentos for US$11/18. *Pousada Bosque dos Aruãs* (☎ 091-765-1115) has comfortable huts with bay view for US$25/27. It also has a good-value restaurant.

Fazendas

The fazendas are enormous estates that occupy most of the island's eastern half. They're rustic refuges with birds, monkeys and roaming buffalo. Some have dorms for tourists; contact Paratur for more information. *Fazenda Bom Jardim* (☎ 091-241-6675) is recommended. It's about three hours by boat or taxi from Soure. *Fazenda Carmo Camará* (☎ 091-223-5696) is well organized for tourist visits.

Getting There & Away

Several agencies in Belém offer tours to Ilha de Marajó, but it's easy to do it independently. See the Belém section for details of the daily boat services to Soure and Câmara.

SANTARÉM

Santarém, about halfway between Manaus and Belém, is the third-largest city in the Amazon (population 265,000), but it feels like a quiet backwater. The area has some pretty beaches and unspoiled rain forests.

There is no tourist office, but you can get information and arrange excursions with Santarém Tur (☎ 091-522-4847), Rua Adriano Pimentel 44, or Amazon Tours (☎ 091-522-1928), Travessa Turiano Meira 1084. Santarém Tur will exchange cash dollars and traveler's checks.

Things to See & Do
Walk along the waterfront on Av Tapajós from the Docas do Pará to Rua Adriano Pimentel. Then, continue to the Praça Barão, where the **Centro Cultural João Fona** has a collection of pre-Columbian pottery.

Places to Stay
Hotel Beira Rio (☎ 091-522-2519) Rua Adriano Pimentel 90, has simple rooms for US$9/14 singles/doubles. Nearby, the *Brisa Hotel* (☎ 091-522-1296), on Rua Senador Lameira Bittencourt 5 near the waterfront, has clean but small and windowless rooms for the same price. Air-con apartamentos are US$25/34. *Hotel Alvorada* (☎ 091-522-5340), opposite the Restaurante O Mascote on Praça do Pescador, is a friendly, old-fashioned place that has quartos for US$9/14 with fan and US$14/23 with air-con. The *Brasil Grande Hotel* (☎ 091-522-5660), Travessa 15 de Agosto 213, has clean, fan-cooled rooms from US$14/23, and air-con apartamentos for US$32/42.

For something a bit better, try the *New City Hotel* (☎ 091-522-3764), Travessa Francisco Correia 200. Rooms start at US$32/47, including transportation from the airport.

Places to Eat
Casa da Vinoca, on the third block up from Av Rui Barbosa on Travessa Turiano Meira, serves cheap and excellent regional dishes. It's open 4:30 to 9 pm. Another place for good cheap meals is *Restaurante Refeição,* Av Tapajós, next door to lobrás shop. *Mistura Brasileira,* also on the waterfront, has good-value buffet lunches.

Restaurante O Mascote, on Praça do Pescador, is Santarém's best restaurant and music venue. Its sibling restaurant, *Mascotinho,* is good for pizza and beer overlooking the river.

Getting There & Away
Air The airport is 15km from the center; a shuttle operates from 6 am to 7 pm. Taxis ask for US$20 from the airport, but may settle for US$9.

Varig provides connections to major Brazilian cities via Manaus and Belém. Santarém is a free stop on its Brazil Airpass. Penta (☎ 091-522-4021) has inexpensive flights to Manaus and Belém by light plane.

Bus The rodoviária is 6km from the center. During the dry season, there are buses on the Transamazônica highway to Marabá. From there you can continue to Belém via Imperatriz, all for US$118. Bus services to Cuiabá have been discontinued due to poor conditions on highway BR-163. Bus travel can be miserable or impossible during the wet season. Most travelers still rely on river transportation.

Boat Larger boats go from Docas do Pará, west of the old part of town. There are ticket agents here. Cabins will usually be fully booked when boats stop at Santarém. Hammock space costs about US$40 downstream to Belém or US$40 upstream to Manaus. Shop around. Both trips should take two or three days, but don't count on it. There are also boats to Porto Santana, near Macapá, and up the Rio Tapajós to Itaituba (12 to 24 hours).

ALTER DO CHÃO
Popular for its lovely lagoon, beaches and fishing, Alter do Chão is 35km west of Santarém, and is easily reached by bus. The excellent **Centro de Preservação da Arte Indígena Cultura e Ciências** has Indian art and artifacts on display and for sale. Entry costs US$3.

Pousada Alter-do-Chão (☎ 091-522-3410), Rua Lauro Sodré 74, has a great view of the beach from the veranda and simple apartamentos with fan for US$23. It also has a good restaurant. A block away, *Pousada Vila da Praia* (☎ 091-522-1161), has simple chalets with four beds for US$36.

Pousada Tupaiulândia (☎ 091-522-2980), Rua Pedro Teixeira 300, offers comfortable accommodations with air-con, TV, and fridge for US$27/32 singles/doubles. *Tia Marilda* (☎ 091-522-3629), Travessa Antônio Agostinho 599, has doubles with shower and fan for US$18, US$23 with air-con. There are good restaurants on the square.

Amapá

Amapá is Brazil's second-most sparsely populated state, after Roraima, home to only about 290,000 people, two thirds of whom live in Macapá. Most of the state is inaccessible during the wet season.

MACAPÁ

Macapá, the state capital, was officially founded in 1815 in a strategic position on the Amazon estuary. The town has few attractions apart from an old Portuguese fort and a pleasant riverfront. From Macapá it is possible to take an excursion to see the *pororoca* (the thunderous collision between the Atlantic tide and the Rio Amazonas).

Information

The Detur/AP tourist office (☎ 096-241-1136), Rodovia JK, Km 2, is underneath the monument that marks where the equator crosses Macapá, about 5km from the fort at the southern end of town (open 8 am to noon and 2 to 6 pm weekdays). Catch a Universidade or Fortaleza bus from the municipal bus terminal near the fort.

The French consulate (☎ 096-222-4378) is at Rua Jovino Dinoá, 1693. Many countries don't require a visa for French Guiana. It takes around 30 days to get one from Macapá because applications go to Belém, Cayenne and Paris. Get one at home.

Things to See & Do

The **Forte São José de Macapá** was built in 1782 by the Portuguese for defense against French invasions. The village of **Curiaú**, 8km from Macapá, was founded by escaped African slaves. To see more traditional Amazon culture, you can also catch a bus at Praça São José that goes via **Marco Zero do Ecuador** and **Fazendinha**, which has a few seafood restaurants, then to Porto Santana, finally returning to Macapá. **Bonito** and the **Igarapé do Lago**, 72km and 85km from Macapá respectively, are good places for swimming, fishing and jungle walks.

Places to Stay & Eat

Hotel Santo Antonio (☎ 096-222-0226), Av Coriolando Jucá 485, about 800m northwest of the fort, is probably Macapá's best budget option. Dorm beds are US$8, quartos US$9 and apartamentos US$14/21 single/doubles, US$19/25 with air-con. The *Emerick Hotel* (☎ 096-223-2819), Av Coaracy Nunes 333, west of the fort, has small fan-cooled rooms for US$11/18 and apartamentos for US$18/23, US$27/33 with air-con. Farther west, *Hotel Glória* (☎ 096-222-0984), Rua Leopoldo Machado 2085, charges US$20/23 for neat, air-con rooms with hot shower. For

a splurge, try *Pousada Ekinox* (☎ 096-222-4378), Rua Jovino Dinoá 1693, at the rear of the French consulate. Rooms are US$63/81 with breakfast; book in advance.

Por-kilo restaurants near the fort include *Só Assados*, Av Henrique Galúcio 290, and *Restaurante Kilão* on the corner of Av Coaracy Nunes and Rua São José. West of the theater at Av Presidente Vargas 456, *Bom Paladar Kilos* is a bit more expensive but better quality. *Chalé Restaurant,* Av Presidente Vargas 499, is good for regional dishes. A block away, toward the river, *Sorvetaria Macapá*, Rua São José 1676, has the best ice cream in town.

Kiosks line the waterfront to the north of the fort and are popular for evening snacks. There are two good fish restaurants on the waterfront south of the fort: *Peixaria Amazonas* and *Martinhos Peixaria*.

Getting There & Away

The airport is about 3.5km northwest of the center. Varig and VASP both have daily flights from Macapá to most other Brazilian capitals. Penta Air Taxis fly small planes to Belém, Santarém, and Manaus. Suriname Airways (☎ 096-222-1477) flies to and from Macapá and Cayenne, French Guiana, and Georgetown, Guyana.

Bus The road to Oiapoque, BR-156, is on the border of French Guiana. It's paved for the first 380km to Calçoene. The remaining 210km are unpaved, but passable, though it may be slow going in the wet season. There are almost no services on the way.

Buses (US$45, 15 hours) leave daily from a stop at Policia Técnica, 5km outside Macapá. Take the local Nova Esperança bus or a taxi (US$7) into town. Tickets are sold at the Viação Catani booth on Rua Candido Mendes next to the municipal bus terminal. Pickup trucks also take paying passengers on this route and are slightly faster.

Boat The Souza Mar boat agency has an office two doors from the church opposite the main plaza. Several boats per week go to Santarém (US$50 for hammock space, at least two days) and Belém (US$27 for hammock space, one day), from Porto Santana, 20km southwest of Macapá. There are also frequent buses. If you stay in Porto Santana, try *Hotel Muller* (☎ 096-281-2018).

OIAPOQUE

This remote town is the only legal border crossing between Brazil and French Guiana, and is also a gateway to backcountry mining camps. Smuggling and illegal immigration are rife. There are some cheap and nasty hotels; *Hotel do Governo* (☎ *096-521-1355*) and *Kayama* (☎ *096-521-1355*) are probably the best. Oiapoque can be reached by rough road or by plane from Macapá.

To/From French Guiana

Get your Brazilian exit stamp from the Polícia Federal in Oiapoque. Cross the Oiapoque River by motorboat (20 minutes, US$5), and get a French Guianese entry stamp at the *gendarmerie* in St Georges. The casa de câmbio at Oiapoque's harbor has poor rates, and there's nowhere to change money in St Georges, so bring francs with you.

From St Georges you'll have to fly to Cayenne, or perhaps catch one of the coastal freight boats. A trail has been cut, but there's no road yet.

It's much easier to fly directly to Cayenne from Macapá or Belém. Traveling overland to/from French Guiana is also problematic because of the official requirement for an onward or return ticket from the territory.

Tocantins

The state of Tocantins was created by a constitutional amendment in 1989, encompassing what was the northern half of Goiás state. The small town of Palmas became the state capital and the site of grandiose developments. Since the city's inception, its population has grown from 2000 to 86,000, but there's really no reason to visit. Miracema and Gurupi are OK places to break up a long bus trip.

ILHA DO BANANAL

The Rio Araguaia begins in the Serra dos Caiapós and flows 2600km northward to join the Rio Tocantins near Marabá in Pará. At the southwestern corner of Tocantins state, the Rio Araguaia bifurcates into the greater and lesser Araguaia rivers. These rivers later rejoin, forming one of the largest river islands in the world, the Ilha do Bananal, which covers some 20,000 sq km. The majority of the island is covered with forest, and a big chunk is sectioned off into the **Parque Nacional do Araguaia**, which is inhabited by Carajás and Javaés Indians. Ilha do Bananal is rich in wildlife, but it's difficult to access.

You can obtain permission to visit the park at the IBAMA office in Brasília or Palmas (☎ 063-215-1873). Of course, if you just show up, you may get in anyway. There are simple accommodations available on the island, but no food other than what you bring.

Getting There & Away

It's probably easiest to reach Araguaia from Goiânia, Goiás. The town of Aruanã, accessible by bus from Goiânia (310km via the town of Goiás), is the gateway to the Araguaia.

There is a campground at Aruanã that's only open in July. Hire a *voadeira* (a small aluminium motorboat) and guide for a river trip to Ilha do Bananal.

From Barra do Garças, Mato Grosso, there's a bus to São Felix do Araguaia, which also has access to Bananal.

Another way to reach Parque Nacional da Araguaia is from the small fishing village of Barreira da Cruz, on the shore of Rio Javaés. It's 52km from Lagoa da Confusão in Tocantins state. Contact the Secretaria Municipal de Turismo (☎ 063-864-1148) in Lagoa da Confusão.

Amazonas

Amazonas, covering more than 1.5 million sq km, is Brazil's largest state. With only two million people, it's quite sparsely populated.

MANAUS

Manaus is on the Rio Negro, 10km upstream from the confluence of the Solimões and Negro rivers, which join to form the Amazon. A fort was built here in 1669, but the town really grew during the late-19th-century boom in the rubber industry.

At its peak, Manaus had a rich elite of plantation owners, rubber traders and bankers. Ocean-going steamships brought every luxury up the Amazon and returned to Europe or America laden with latex. When the rubber boom ended, around 1914, Manaus fell into decline.

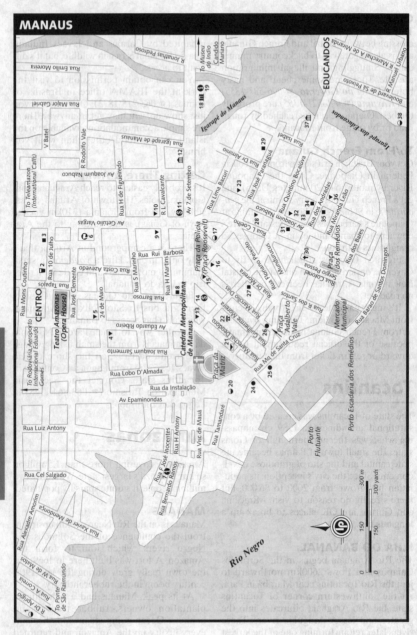

MANAUS

BRAZIL

MANAUS

PLACES TO STAY
3 Hospedaria de
  Turismo 10 de Julho
8 Hotel Krystal
27 Hotel Rei Salomão
29 Hotel Sol
31 Pensão Sulista
33 Hotel Ideal
34 Hotel Jangada
35 Hotel Rio Branco

PLACES TO EAT
4 Skina dos Sucos
5 Mandarim
9 Sorveteria Glacial I
10 Sorveteria Glacial II

13 O Naturalista
15 Restaurant Fiorantina
16 Mister Pizza
23 Churrascaria Búfalo
28 Big Frango
32 Você Decide
36 Galo Carijó

OTHER
1 Porto de São Raimundo
  (Low Water Port)
2 Bar do Armando
6 Colombian Consulate
7 Fumtur (Municipal Tourist
  Office)
11 Casa de Câmbio Cortéz

12 Museu do Homem do Norte
14 Banco do Brasil
17 Bus to Praia da Ponta Negra
18 Palácio Rio Negro
19 Emamtur (State Tourist Office)
20 Local Bus Station
21 Post Office
22 Teleamazon (National Calls)
24 Rodomar
25 Alfândega (British Customs
  House)
26 Praça Adalberto Vale, Artíndia
30 Igreja Nossa Senhora dos
  Remédios
37 Arts Centre Chiminé
38 Educandos Port Area

It has revived since it was declared a free trade zone in the 1960s. Roads to the north and south, the establishment of new factories, and the growth in tourism have led to rapid population increase – from 250,000 to more than a million in the last 30 years.

The city had become somewhat run-down but is now improving, though you still need to be careful of theft. Much of the central shopping area (the Zona Franca) has been renovated, with many pedestrian precincts. The older streets to the southeast retain a certain sleazy charm. There's also some raunchy nightlife. Some opulent buildings remain from the boom days.

Manaus is interesting, but it's not pretty. Most visitors come to arrange a rain-forest excursion with one of the many tour operators, but there is no primary rain forest close to Manaus; you need a few days to reach an area that is reasonably pristine.

Orientation
The most interesting parts of Manaus are close to the waterfront. Av Eduardo Ribeiro is lined with airline offices, banks and Manaus' fancier shops.

Information
Tourist Offices Manaus' municipal tourist office, Fumtur (☎ 092-622-4948), is at Rua Bernardo Ramos 173. For information about jungle lodges and operators contact Emamtur (☎ 092-633-2983), the state tourism organization, Av 7 de Setembro 1456. It's open 7:30 am to 1:30 pm weekdays. Both organizations have information booths at

the airport. For details about national parks, contact IBAMA (☎ 092-237-3710), Rua Ministro João Gonçalves de Souza, Hwy BR-319, Km 01, Distrito Industrial.

Money There are plenty of banks, but Casa de Câmbio Cortéz, on Av 7 de Setembro, is quicker and is open longer hours weekdays and on Saturday mornings.

Post & Communications Manaus' main post office is on Rua Marechal Deodoro. Teleamazon, for international calls, is on Av Getúlio Vargas 950. It's open from 8 am to 11 pm daily. National calls can also be made at the Teleamazon office on Rua Guilherme Moreira.

Emergency Useful emergency telephone numbers include ☎ 192 for *pronto socorro* (first aid) and ☎ 190 for *polícia*.

Foreign Consulates Most Western European countries and the USA have consulates in the city. Fumtur and Emamtur have all the addresses. Visas for French Guiana will take weeks, as applications are referred to Brasília.

Things to See & Do
The **Porto Escadaria dos Remédios** and the **Porto Flutuante** are good places to watch the locals at work. There are a few interesting pre-fabricated buildings, including the **Alfândega** (British customs house, 1906) and the cast-iron **Mercado Municipal**, designed in 1882 by Adolfo Lisboa after Les Halles in

BRAZIL

Paris. You can buy provisions for jungle trips in the market area.

The famous opera house, **Teatro Amazonas** (1896), was built in Italian Renaissance style at the height of the rubber boom. It's open 9 am to 4 pm daily. Admission is US$4.50.

The **Museu do Homem do Norte**, Av 7 de Setembro 1385, is dedicated to the river-dwelling *caboclos* (people of white and Indian mix). It's open 9 am to noon and 1 to 5 pm Monday to Thursday, and Friday afternoon. It costs US$1. The **Museu do Indio**, off Av 7 de Setembro on Av Duque de Caxias 356, has good exhibits on the tribes of the upper Rio Negro. It's open 8:30 to 11:30 am and 2 to 4:30 pm weekdays, and on Saturday morning. Admission is US$2.25.

The INPA research institute has a botanical garden and zoo, the **Bosque da Ciência**. It's open 9 am to noon and 2 to 4 pm Tuesday to Friday, 9 am to 4 pm weekends. Admission is US$3.50. Take the São José bus from the city center. The **Museu de Ciencias Naturais da Amazônia** (☎ 092-644-2799), at Estrada Belém, Colônia Cachoeira Grande, is out of the way but worth a look. It exhibits regional fish, insects and butterflies. It's open 9 am to 5 pm Tuesday to Sunday, and costs US$5.50. Take the São José bus to INPA, then catch a taxi.

The **Encontro das Águas** (meeting of the waters), where the inky-black flow of Rio Negro meets the yellow waters of the Rio Solimões, is well worth seeing, but it's not absolutely necessary to take a tour. It can also be seen from the ferry that shuttles between Careiro and the Porto Velho highway (BR-319).

Organized Tours

Most visitors' top priority is a jungle tour to experience the rain forest at close quarters. It's possible to arrange anything from standard day trips to month-long expeditions in the hinterland.

Tour-agency representatives (or touts) meet new arrivals at the airport, and can offer useful information, and maybe transport to the center, but hold off booking a tour until you've had time to shop around. There are dozens of agencies with trendy names ('eco' and 'green' are standard prefixes) and glossy brochures. Many of the small agencies are working together, and competing agencies actually book people on the same trips.

A standard one-day boat tour goes downstream to the Encontro das Águas, returns to the Lago Janauário reserve for a short guided jungle walk, stops at a shop selling Indian souvenirs, spends some time fishing for piranha and looking for jacaré by flashlight, and includes lunch, dinner, and cachaça on the boat. During the wet season, trips should include a canoe trip on the *igarapés* (small jungle streams), but this isn't possible in the dry season. As a rain-forest experience, it's better than nothing, but it's not as satisfying as a longer trip into a more pristine area. Agencies charge from US$45 to US$75 and up for these trips, and they're not great value if you pay the higher price.

On a three- or four-day boat trip, you can expect to see jungle flora, including abundant bird life and a few jacaré. This kind of trip also offers a chance to see what life is like for the caboclos in the vicinity of Manaus. You *cannot* expect to meet remote Indian tribes or see lots of free-ranging wildlife. Most of the longer trips go up the Rio Negro.

Ignore the flowery propaganda and ask the tour operator or agent for exact details. Who will be the guide, and do they speak English? Does the tour include extended travel in small boats (without motors) along igarapés? How much time is spent getting to and from your destination? What is the breakdown of the costs for food, lodging, gasoline and guides? You may want to pay some of these expenses en route, thereby avoiding fanciful markups. Insist on paying a portion of the costs at the beginning of the trip and the rest at the end. This encourages operators and guides to define and stick to a schedule, and gives you some leverage if promises are not kept.

If you want to do an extended trip in the Amazon region, try a short trip from Manaus first. This will help you plan longer trips, either from Manaus or from other parts of the Amazon. The latter option is becoming increasingly popular among travelers disenchanted with Manaus. Jungle trips are probably cheaper in Peru, Ecuador and Bolivia.

The bigger tour operators are pricey (US$75 to US$135 per person per day), but should be relatively hassle-free and have English-speaking guides. Most of them operate 'jungle lodges' that provide a comfortable base well outside Manaus and with access to relatively unspoiled rain forest. They are often booked by overseas travel agents as part of an international package. Reputable firms include:

Amazonia Expeditions
(☎/fax 092-671-2731) Hotel Tropical; organizes trips to the Tropical Lago de Salvador, a small hotel about 30km west of Manaus

Ecotéis
(☎/fax 092-233-7642) Rua Doutor Alminio 36; has trips to Acajatuba Jungle Lodge

Guanavenas Turismo
(☎ 092-656-3656; fax 092-656-5027) Rua Constantino Nery 2486; organizes trips to Pousada dos Guanavenas, 300km east of Manaus

Nature Safaris
(☎ 092-622-4144; fax 092-622-1420 in Manaus, or ☎/fax 021-502-2208 in Rio de Janeiro) organizes trips to Amazon Lodge, a cute small-scale floating lodge on Lago Juma

Rio Amazonas Turismo
(☎ 092-234-7308; fax 233-5615) Rua Silva Ramos 20; organizes trips to Manaus' largest jungle lodge, Ariaú Jungle Tower

If you speak a little Portuguese and don't mind traveling a bit roughly, there are plenty of smaller operators and independent guides offering tours. Allow at least a day to hammer out a deal, change money, arrange supplies and buy provisions. Prices with the smaller operators are often not much cheaper than the larger operators. As a rough rule of thumb, expect prices to start around US$70 per person per day, including boat transportation, guide, food, and hammock space (minimum two people on a three-day, two-night trip).

The guide should be registered with Emamtur and have an identity card. Smaller agencies and operators include:

Amazonas Indian Turismo
(☎ 092-233-3104) Rua dos Andrades 335; takes trips up the Rio Urubu, staying overnight in rustic cabanas

Swallows & Amazons
(☎/fax 092-622-1246) Rua Quintino Bocaiuva 189, Andar 1, Sala 13, Centro; a reliable small operator offering various trips including camping or accommodations at its Over Look Lodge

Moaçir Fortes
(☎ 092-671-2866); runs a small, first-class operation; book in advance

Another option is a trip with a member of the canoe guides association, Associação dos Canoeiros (☎ 092-238-8880). While these trips are less predictable than the organized tours, they may be more authentic. Usually you stay with caboclo families from the surrounding river settlements. Ask at the Porto Flutuante for Bacuri or Samuel. A trip to the Encontro das Águas (minimum four people) will cost US$18 per person. Overnight jungle trips involving boat transportation will cost US$36 to US$72 per day; and by bus, you may negotiate as low as US$27 to US$36 per day.

Special Events
During the month of June, Manaus has a variety of regional folklore events, including the competition of the *boi-bumbás* (two rival bulls, Caprichoso and Garantado), with dancing, parades and outlandish costumes. A folklore festival held during the second half of June coincides with a number of saints' days and culminates in the Procissão Fluvial de São Pedro, when hundreds of boats parade on the river for the patron saint of fishermen.

Places to Stay
There's plenty of cheap lodging that ranges from grungy to decent. *Pensão Sulista* (☎ 092-234-5814), Av Joaquim Nabuco 347, has clean quartos with fan for US$9/14, while air-con doubles are US$23.

Hotel Rio Branco (☎ 092-233-4019), Rua dos Andradas 484, is also a popular budget place. Dorm beds cost US$7/9 for fan/air-con; rooms cost US$8/14 for singles/doubles, US$14/18 with air-con. *Hotel Ideal* (☎ 092-233-9423), across the street, is OK. Single/double apartamentos (some without windows) cost US$11/16 with fan, US$16/26 with air-con. On the same street, *Hotel Jangada* (☎ 092-232-2248) offers basic dorm beds with fan for US$8 and double rooms for US$14. There are other cheapies on Rua José Paranaguá, two streets to the north. Some rent by the hour, but the *Hotel Sol* should be OK.

Hospedaria de Turismo 10 de Julho (☎ 092-232-6280), Rua 10 de Julho 679, is in a nice area near the opera house. It has clean, secure, good-value air-con apartamentos for US$18/23.

Modern-style, mid-range hotels are mostly in the Zona Franca, where it is hectic

BRAZIL

during the day and dead at night. Discounts are common, but check the room and ensure that the facilities work. *Hotel Rei Salomão* (☎ 092-234-7344), Rua Dr Moreira 119, has single/double apartamentos for US$39/48. *Hotel Krystal* (☎ 092-233-7305), Rua Barroso 54, is in a quieter location and has clean apartamentos for US$60/74.

Places to Eat

Street stalls serve hamburgers, sandwiches, and local specials like tacacá, a gummy soup made from manioc root, lip-numbing jambu leaves and dried shrimp.

Av Joaquim Nabuco, near the cheap hotel area, has several eateries (and quite a few prostitutes in the evening). Try *Big Frango* for cheap chicken. The bar *Você Decide*, opposite Pensão Sulista, has OK prato feito. A more expensive option is *Churrascaria Búfalo*, Av Joaquim Nabuco 628, which serves massive steaks and a meaty per-kilo buffet. *Galo Carijó*, nearby on Rua dos Andradas, is favored by locals for fresh fish.

There are some good places around the center, such as *O Naturalista* upstairs at Av Sete de Setembro 752, with a good vegetarian self-serve lunch. *Mandarim*, at Av Eduardo Ribeiro 650, serves inexpensive Chinese food and a buffet lunch. Diagonally opposite, *Skina dos Sucos* has tasty snacks and great juices of strange fruits such as guaraná, acerola, cupuaçu or graviola.

For pizza and pasta, there's *Mister Pizza* or the more upmarket *Restaurante Fiorentina*, both on Praça da Policia. *Sorveteria Glacial*, with two locations across Av Getúlio Vargas from one another, is the most popular ice cream parlor in town.

Entertainment

Você Decidé, an open-air bar on Av Joaquim Nabuco, is something of a hangout for travelers, with beer, snacks, music and a not entirely respectable clientele. *Bar do Armando*, near the Teatro Amazonas, is a traditional rendezvous open from noon to midnight. Most dancing establishments are clustered in the Cachoeirinha district, northeast of the center. *Nostalgia*, at Av Ajuricaba 800, is a hot spot for forró. There are lots of bars and restaurants along Praia da Ponta Negra that are popular at weekends.

Shopping

The best place in Manaus to buy Indian crafts is Artíndia (☎ 092-232-4890), on the Praça Adalberto Vale. It's open 7:30 am to noon and 1:30 to 5 pm weekdays, and on Saturday morning. For hammocks, try Casa das Redes on Rua Floriano Peixoto or the street vendors around Praça Adalberto Vale. For some local music, check out the group *Carrapicho*.

Getting There & Away

Air There are international flights to Caracas, Bogotá, La Paz, Georgetown and Miami (five hours). Manaus is not a good place to buy cheap tickets.

Bus The rodoviária is 7km north of the center. Phone for information on road conditions. The BR-319 road south of Manaus is in disrepair, and no buses serve the route. The 770-km BR-174 road north to Boa Vista is now mostly paved (US$57, 13 hours, three buses daily).

Boat Boats from Porto Flutuante serve most large Amazon destinations – Belém, Santarém, Tefé and Benjamin Constant – and is used by ENASA. Three major ports in Manaus function according to high and low water levels, Bairro Educandos is the port for sailing to Porto Velho. For sailing on the Rio Negro as far as Caracaraí, the requisite high-water port is Ponte de São Raimundo; the low-water port is Bairro de São Raimundo, about 2.5km away.

For information, visit the Rodomar at the Porto Flutuante. The Rodomar has a complex of counters arranged like those at a bus terminal, with fares and destinations prominently posted. The ENASA ticket office (☎ 092-633-3280) is at Rua Marechal Deodoro 61.

Various companies operate passenger boats between Manaus, Santarém and Belém. Prices for hammock space average US$40 to Santarém (24 to 36 hours) and US$75 to Belém (3½ days). The weekly ENASA boat to Belém (US$60) leaves on Thursday and can get very crowded.

Ports of call are marked on the boats, and fares are pretty much standardized according to distance. The boats usually pull out at 6 pm regardless of the destination. Bring bottled water and extra food.

It's a seven-day trip (if all goes well) to Tabatinga, or longer if the boat makes many stops. It's about US$77/225 for hammock space/cabin. There is onward service from Tabatinga to Iquitos, Peru.

Another long river journey is from Manaus up the Rio Madeira to Porto Velho (one week, US$68/95 for hammock space/cabin).

In the wet season, you may be able to find a cargo boat to Caracaraí on the Rio Branco (four days). From Caracaraí there's a bus to Boa Vista (four hours). Another remote river destination is São Gabriel da Cachoeira, about five or six days up the Rio Negro.

Getting Around

The rodoviária is 6km north of the city center. The Ileia, Santos Dumont and Aeroporto Internacional buses run between the center and rodoviária. A taxi to the center costs around US$11.

To/From the Airport Aeroporto Internacional Eduardo Gomes is 14km north of the city center on Av Santos Dumont. Taxis between the airport and the center can cost up to US$25. However, the Aeroporto bus runs every half hour between the airport and the local downtown bus station from 6 am to midnight (US$0.60, 40 minutes).

Bus The local bus station is on Praça da Matriz, near the cathedral. From here you can catch the bus to Praia da Ponta Negra (about 30 minutes). Alternately, take the Tropical Hotel shuttle bus (US$5.50) from Rua Dr Moreira.

TABATINGA & BENJAMIN CONSTANT

These two Brazilian ports are on opposite sides of the Rio Solimões (Amazonas) on the border of Brazil, Colombia and Peru, known as the **Triple Frontier**. Neither is particularly attractive, and most travelers view them as transit points. Tabatinga has a couple of hotels and an excellent restaurant, *Restaurante Tres Fronteiras*, on Rua Rui Barbosa. You can change traveler's checks at CNM Câmbio e Turismo, Av da Amizade, 2217. If you have to wait a few days for a boat, however, the Colombian border town of Leticia is a more interesting place to hang out.

Tabatinga and Leticia are practically the same town, and locals and foreigners can cross the border freely. If you plan to travel farther into either country, however, you must complete immigration formalities. There are frequent colectivo buses between the Leticia and Tabatinga ports (US$0.35). It's a 20-minute walk.

Get your Brazilian entry and exit stamps at the Polícia Federal (dress neatly), toward the southern end of Av da Amizade near the hospital. It's open 8 am to noon and 2 to 6 pm daily. On the Colombian side, have your passport stamped at DAS, the security police office on Calle 9. It's open 24 hours. You can also get your Brazilian entry and exit stamps from the Polícia Federal in Benjamin Constant.

Getting There & Away

Air From Tabatinga airport, Varig flies four times weekly to Manaus. Apart from these commercial passenger flights, cargo planes operate irregularly between these cities. You can fly from Leticia to Bogotá, Columbia, with Air Avianca.

Boat Boats down the Amazon to Manaus leave from Benjamin Constant, but usually call at Tabatinga, too. Regular boats depart from Tabatinga (theoretically) Wednesday and Saturday mornings, and from Benjamin Constant Wednesday and Saturday nights for US$72/234 for hammock space/double cabin (three to six days). In the opposite direction, upstream from Manaus to Benjamin Constant, the trip takes between five and 10 days. Food is included but it is usually of poor quality.

Two daily ferries shuttle between Tabatinga and Benjamin Constant (US$3, two hours,). There are also *deslizadores* (small boats) that do the same run in 40 minutes for US$4.50. Both services depart from Porto da Feira in Tabatinga.

There are four companies operating rápido passenger services, each with two to three boats per week (US$45, eight hours) from Leticia, Colombia upstream to Iquitos, Peru. The boats call at the Peruvian immigration post in Santa Rosa, across the river from Tabatinga, that has replaced the old port of Ramón Castilla.

There are irregular cargo boats to and from Puerto Asís (Colombia), on the upper reaches of the Rio Putumayo. However, river travel may be restricted in the dry season.

Roraima

The area north of Roraima is perhaps the ultimate Amazon frontier, a rugged land that is home to the Yanomami, who represent about one-third of the remaining tribal Indians of the Amazon. Although the Brazilian government has declared their lands a special Indian reserve, miners, timber cutters and new roads encroach on the area.

BOA VISTA

This new, planned city is fairly unattractive, and most travelers just pass through going to and from Venezuela or Guyana. However, there are some attractions in the surrounding area, which is becoming more accessible.

Information

There are information booths at the rodoviária (☎ 095-623-1238) that are open 8 am to noon and 2 to 7 pm on weekdays.

There are also booths at the airport, open 7 pm to 11 pm.

Casa de Câmbio Pedro José keeps longer hours than Banco do Brasil or Timbó Viagens e Turismo. It's on Av Benjamin Constant 170, and is open on Saturday mornings.

The Venezuelan Consulate (☎ 095-224-2182), Av Benjamin Constant 525E, is open 8 am to noon weekdays. Free tourist cards are issued for most nationalities who intend to stay in Venezuela for less than 90 days and only enter once. Longer term multiple-entry visas are US$30; if you arrive early with a photo and a photocopy of your passport, you may be able to pick up your visa by noon.

Things to See & Do

About 1.5km northwest of the center, **Parque Anauá** has gardens, a lake, a museum and an amphitheater. You might even catch a concert in the *forródromo*. The main beach is **Praia Grande**, opposite Boa Vista on Rio Branco; take a boat from Porto do Babá (US$2).

Places to Stay

Pousada Beija-Flor (☎ 095-224-8241), Av NS da Consolata 939, is the best budget

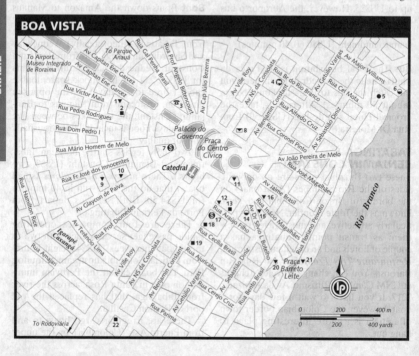

BOA VISTA

option, with dorm beds for US$9. There are also a few cheap dives such as *Hotel Brasil*, Av Benjamin Constant 331, with singles/doubles for US$7/9. *Hotel Imperial* (☎ 095-224-5592), Av Benjamin Constant 433, offers basic apartamentos with fan for US$15/16. Double air-con apartamentos are not bad value for US$18. *Hotel Tres Nações* (☎ 095-224-3439), Av Ville Roy 188W, São Vicente (near the bus terminal), charges US$14/18 for air-con rooms.

For more comfort, try *Hotel Euzebio's* (☎ 095-623-0300), Rua Cecília Brasil 1107, with apartamentos for US$24/30, or *Hotel Barrudada* (☎ 095-623-9335), Rua Araújo Filho 228. It has spotlessly clean air-con apartamentos and an excellent breakfast for US$36/40.

Places to Eat
La Gondola, Av Benjamin Constant 35W, and *Mister Kilo*, Rua Inácio Magalhães 346, have good-value, self-service meals. *Banana Paçoca Restaurante*, on the grounds of Palácio da Micro Empresa, Av Glaycon de Paiva, has excellent regional fare. The *Bistro Restaurante* at the front of Pousada Beija-Flor also serves local favorites. *Black & White* and *Restaurante Peixada Panorama* are both good for fish. For pizza and pasta try *Pigalle* or *Margô Pizzaria*. *Só Caldos*, open 24 hours, has good-value soups. *Pik Nik*, Rua Inácio Magalhães 325, is the best place for ice cream.

Getting There & Away
Air The airport is 4km from the city center; take the Aeroporto bus from the municipal bus terminal. A taxi will cost US$15. Varig offers daily flights to and from Manaus, while META air taxi (☎ 095-224-7677) has weekday flights.

Bus The rodoviária is 3km west of the center; get a Joquey Clube or 13 de Setembro bus along Av Villa Roy from the center. A taxi there runs about US$6. Buses to Manaus depart three times daily between 8:30 am and 4 pm (US$63, 13 hours).

To/From Venezuela There's interesting scenery on the ride to Santa Elena, about 15km north of the border. There are four departures daily between 6:30 am and 5:30 pm, from the rodoviária in Boa Vista (US$12, 3½ hours). The bus stops at the Venezuelan and Brazilian immigration posts. Several buses a week go directly to Ciudad Bolívar (US$25, 14 hours). Reserve a seat the day before.

AROUND BOA VISTA
Pedra Pintada About 140km north of Boa Vista is a mushroom-shaped boulder about 60 meters across and 35 meters high, with painted inscriptions on its external face and caves at its base. Also worth visiting is **Estação Ecológica da Ilha de Maracá**, an ecological reserve 120km away, accessed with permission from IBAMA (☎ 095-623-9513). The easiest way to visit these places is with a local tour operator such as Iguana Tours (☎ 095-971-7006) or Beija Flor Tours (☎ 095-224-8241). **Mt Roraima** (2875m) straddles the Brazil-Venezuela-Guyana border, but the easiest access is from Venezuela (see that chapter for details).

To/From Guyana
Buses leave Boa Vista for Bonfim twice daily at 7:30 am and 3 pm (US$6, 125km, two hours). Take the earliest bus to avoid being stuck in Bonfim for the night. Tell the driver you're heading for Guyana, and ask where to get off. Sometimes buses stop at a

BRAZIL

BOA VISTA

PLACES TO STAY
2 Hotel Euzebio's
13 Hotel Barrudada
18 Hotel Brasil
19 Hotel Imperial
22 Pousada Beija-Flor

PLACES TO EAT
1 Pigalle
9 Banana Paçoca Restaurante

10 Só Caldos
11 La Gondola
12 Margô Pizzaria
15 Pik Nik
16 Mister Kilo
20 Black & White
21 Restaurante Peixada Panorama

OTHER
3 Posto Telefônico
4 Venezuelan Consulate
5 Iguana Tours
6 Porto do Babá
7 Banco do Brasil
8 Post Office
14 Municipal Bus Terminal
17 Casa de Cambio Pedro José
22 Beija Flor Tours

checkpoint before Bonfim, where you may be able to get an exit stamp from the Polícia Federal and a jeep or taxi to the border post (US$2.50, 5km). Otherwise, stay on the bus until the stop after the bus station, then walk 2km or catch a taxi or jeep to the border crossing.

The border is open until 6 pm, and you should be able to get an exit stamp from the Brazilian immigration post. Then, hire a boat (US$0.40) across the Rio Tacutu to Lethem, in Guyana. Guyanese officials tend to scrutinize travelers carefully, so be sure your papers are in order. If you do have to stay in Bonfim, try *Possada Fonteira*, with US$9 doubles. *Restaurant Tia Chica* has good value meals.

Overland travel from Lethem to Georgetown is feasible but difficult. There are trucks every few days and four flights per week to Georgetown, but they are usually heavily booked. See under Lethem in the Guianas chapter for more information.

Rondônia

Previously an undeveloped frontier region, Rondônia has undergone rapid change with the construction of BR-364. Massive deforestation has left vast tracts of land looking like the aftermath of a holocaust. Most travelers only pass through on the way to or from Peru or Bolivia. Rondônia is also a route for the distribution of cocaine, which should not affect travelers, provided they mind their own business.

PORTO VELHO

Porto Velho, the capital of Rondônia, is on the east bank of the Rio Madeira, near the Amazonas border. There's not much of interest for visitors, but there's access to Rio Branco, Guajará-Mirim and the Bolivian border.

Information

The state tourist office, Funcetur (☎ 069-221-1881), is on Av 7 Setembro 237, first floor, above the Museu Estadual. It's open 8 am to noon and 2 to 6 pm weekdays.

IBAMA (☎ 069-223-33607), Av Jorge Teixeira 3477, Bairro C E Silva, has information and permits for visiting national parks in Rondônia.

Estação Madeira-Mamoré & Museu Ferroviário

The Madeira-Mamoré railway was completed in 1912, taking many years and many lives, although it quickly fell into disuse. The Maria Fumaça steam locomotive now does 7km tourist excursions to Santo Antônio on Sunday and holidays (US$2 roundtrip). The free museum displays train memorabilia, photographs, and the 1872 *Colonel Church* steam locomotive It's open 8 am to 6 pm weekdays.

Organized Tours

Nossa Viagens e Turismo (☎ 069-221-1567), Rua Terneiro Aranha 2125, offers package tours to Rio Madeira tributaries.

Places to Stay

Hotel Cuiabano (☎ 069-221-4084), Av 7 de Setembro 1180, has double quartos for US$9, and apartamentos for US$14. *Hotel Sonora* has coffin-size quartos for a similar price. *Hotel Tia Carmem* (☎ 069-221-7910), Rua Campos Sales 2895, is in a better location and offers good-value, basic quartos with fan for US$9/14 singles/doubles, and better air-con versions for US$15/23. *Hotel Angra dos Reis,* on Av Dom Pedro II, is the best budget option near the rodoviária, offering clean rooms with fan and bath for US$12/14.

Better places include the *Hotel Regina* (☎ 069-224-3411), Rua Almirante Baroso 1127, where clean air-con apartamentos with fridge and TV cost US$23/36. *Hotel Central* (☎ 069-224-2099), Rua Terneiro Aranha 2472, offers similar facilities for US$39/52 singles/doubles.

Places to Eat

Porto Velho has a few decent restaurants. *Restaurante Mirante II*, at the end of Dom Pedro II, right on the river, and out-of-the-way *Remanso do Tucunaré*, Av Brasília 1506, are good places for fish. *Pizzaria Agua na Boca* has Porto Velho's best pizza, served on outdoor tables facing a large TV screen so you won't escape the Brazilian soapies.

Restaurante e Pizzaria TuttiFrutti has good juices and a per-kilo lunch. *Kamila Restaurante* is also recommended for self-serve meals. *Confeitaria Delicerse* has excellent-quality snacks and delicious juices. *Sanduba's*, two doors from Hotel Tia Carmen, has good-value hamburgers.

PORTO VELHO

PLACES TO STAY		OTHER	
3	Hotel Tia Carmem	4	Bangalô Bar
12	Hotel Central	6	Caixas d'Agua
15	Hotel Angra dos Reis		(Water Towers)
21	Hotel Sonora	7	Teleron
22	Hotel Cuiabano	8	Palácio do Governador
24	Hotel Regina	10	Banco do Brasil
		13	VIP's Tour
PLACES TO EAT		14	Bus Station
1	Pizzaria Agua na Boca	16	Estação Madeira-Mamoré
2	Restaurante e Pizzaria		& Museu Ferroviário
	TuttiFrutti	17	Maretur Flutuante
5	Restaurante Mirante II	18	Funcetur, Museu Estadual
9	Kamila Restaurante	19	Post Office
11	Confeitaria Delicerse	20	Nossa Viagens e Turismo.
		23	Buses to Airport, Rodoviária

Entertainment

The *Bangalô Bar* has a good atmosphere and live music Thursday to Saturday night. *Maretur Flutuante* is a popular floating bar at the docks – it can get a bit seedy late at night, so check to see if police security is around. Restaurante Mirante II also has live music on weekends.

Getting There & Away

Air The airport is 7km north of town. There are regular local buses to and from the center. Taxis to the town have a set price of US$14, while metered taxis cost US$9 from the center to the airport. There are flights from Porto Velho to all major Brazilian cities.

Bus The rodoviária is about 2km east of the center, on Av Jorge Teixeira. The Hospital de Base bus runs to the rodoviária from Av 7 de Setembro in the city center. It's best to travel overnight for Rio Branco (leaving 11:30 pm) to avoid the heat (US$23, eight hours, four buses daily). For information on buses to Guajará-Mirim, see that section.

Boat Boats run between Porto Velho and Manaus three times per week. The three-day trip costs US$54/90 for hammock space/cabin. Meals are included but take bottled water. Most boats go directly to Manaus; others require a transfer halfway down the Rio Madeira, at Manicoré. The trip can take up to a week, depending on the level of the water, the number of breakdowns and the availability of onward connections. Taking a bus to Humaitá (203km from Porto Velho) and then catching a boat to Manaus saves about 24 hours.

GUAJARÁ-MIRIM

Guajará-Mirim is on the Bolivian border, with the town of Guayaramerín on the other side. The Bolivian Consulate (☎ 069-541-2862), Av Costa Marques 495, is open on weekday mornings. Citizens of most countries do not require visas to travel to Bolivia.

Places to Stay & Eat

Most of the places to stay and eat are on or to the north of Av 15 de Novembro. It runs east-west from the rodoviária to the river.

BRAZIL

It's worth ringing ahead to book a hotel if you'll arrive on a weekend.

The cheapest place in town is *Hotel Chile* (☎ 069-541-3846), with quartos for US$9/14 singles/doubles and musty air-con apartamentos for US$18/23. *Hotel Pousada Tropical* (☎ 069-541-3308), at Av Leopoldo de Matos, offers clean, good-value apartamentos for US$9/18, US$14/27 with air-con. The popular *Hotel Mini-Estrela Palace* (☎ 069-541-4798), Av 15 de Novembro, charges US$14/23 for fan-cooled apartamentos, US$25/35 with air-con. The *Alfa Hotel* (☎ 069-541-3121), Av Leopoldo de Matos 239, is more upmarket. It charges US$27/40 for air-con apartamentos with TV, fridge and hot shower.

Guajará-Mirim's best restaurant, the *Oasis*, is next door to the Hotel Mini-Estrela Palace. It offers a good, all-you-can-eat lunch for US$7. Across the road, *Pizzaria Stop Drinks* is popular at night. Another option for good-value meals is the *Restaurante da Mariza*, open for lunch and dinner, except Sunday night.

Getting There & Away

Bus There are five bus connections daily from Porto Velho to Guajará-Mirim (US$14, five hours). Alternately, catch a shared cab at any time of day for US$23.

Boat It's possible to travel by boat up the Mamoré and Guaporé rivers to Costa Marques via Forte Príncipe da Beira. Ask about schedules at the not-terribly-helpful Capitânia dos Portos (☎ 069-541-2208).

To/From Bolivia It's easy to pop across the Rio Mamoré to visit Guayaramerín, which has cheaper accommodations than Guajará-Mirim. Between early morning and 6:30 pm, small motorized canoes and larger motor ferries cross every few minutes (US$1.50). After hours, there are only express motorboats (about US$4 per boat). Those traveling beyond the frontier area will have to complete border formalities.

To leave Brazil, you may need to have your passport stamped at the Bolivian Consulate in Guajará-Mirim before getting a Brazilian exit stamp at the Polícia Federal (☎ 069-541-2437) on Av Presidente Dutra. Once across the river, get an entrance stamp from Bolivian immigration at the ferry terminal.

If you are leaving Bolivia, have your passport stamped by Bolivian immigration, then get a Brazilian entry stamp at the Polícia Federal in Guajará-Mirim. Officials don't always check, but technically everyone needs a yellow-fever vaccination certificate to enter Brazil here. If you don't have one, the convenient clinic at the Brazilian port can do it hygienically.

Acre

The state of Acre has become a favored destination for developers and settlers, who have followed BR-364 through Rondônia and started claiming lands, clearing forest and setting up ranches. The resulting conflict over land ownership and sustainable use of the forest received massive national and international attention when Chico Mendes, a rubber-tapper and opponent of rain forest destruction, was assassinated in 1988.

RIO BRANCO

Rio Branco, the capital of Acre state, was founded in 1882 on the banks of the Rio Acre.

Information

The Departamento de Turismo (☎ 068-229-2134), Estrada Dias Martins, Km 5, Distrito Industrial, is a bit far out of town. It's open 8 am to 1 pm weekdays. In the city center, you can try SEBRAE (☎ 068-223-2100) at Rua Rio Grande do Sul.

Things to See & Do

The **Parque Ambiental Chico Mendes** has walking paths and theme huts representing different ways people in the region live. It's about 10km from Rio Branco at Rodovia AC-40, Km 3, near Vila Acre. To get there, catch one of the regular Rio Branco-Vila Acre buses.

The free **Museu da Borracha** has interesting exhibits. It's open 9 am to noon and 2 to 5 pm weekdays. **Casa do Seringueiro**, also free, has exhibits on the life of a typical *seringueiro* (rubber-tapper). It's open from 7 am to 1 pm and 2 to 5 pm Tuesday to Friday.

It's possible to visit the **Colônia Cinco Mil**, a religious community that follows the doctrine of Santo Daime. They are known for their use of a hallucinogenic drink called *ayahuasca*. Take a local bus from the city center or a taxi (US$13.50).

The **Parque Ecológico Plácido de Castro**, 94km east of Rio Branco on the Brazil-Bolivia border, offers good swimming at river beaches, and forest walks along paths originally used by rubber-tappers. There are five buses daily from Rio Branco to Plácido de Castro. There is a hotel and several inexpensive pensões.

Organized Tours

Biotur Eco-Turismo (☎ 068-985-2272) takes excursions to Parque Ecológico Plácido de Castro US$27. Enquire at Hotel Rio Branco's reception.

Places to Stay & Eat

Most of the places to stay and eat are on or near Rua Rui Barbosa, which is perpendicular to the main street, Av Getúlio Vargas. *Hotel Rio Branco* (☎ 068-224-1785), Rua Rui Barbosa 193, is a classic lodging with good service, breakfast and dated decor. Apartamentos cost US$27/36/54 for singles/doubles/triples. The *Inácio Palace Hotel* (☎ 068-224-6397), Rua Rui Barbosa 72, is a bit old and tacky but offers reasonably clean and comfortable apartamentos for US$27/36.

Albemar Hotel (☎ 068-224-1938), nearby at Rua Franco Ribeiro 99, has clean, small air-con apartamentos for US$18/23. *Hotel Triangulo* (☎ 068-224-4117), Rua Floriano Peixoto 227, has good-value, air-con apartamentos with TV for the same price.

The Mira Shopping *food court* on Rua Rui Barbosa, opposite the praça, is an air-con oasis. It has pizzas, self-serve lunch and simple dinners. It also has the *Café do Ponto,* for good coffee, pastries and ice cream. A block south, *Casarão*, on Av Brasil 310, has good-value self-serve lunch and is popular with locals. Meat-eaters should try *Churrascaria Triangulo* at the Hotel Triangulo, where all-you-can-eat meat rodizio costs U$7. *Restaurante Flutuante,* at the end of Rua Floriano Peixoto, is a pleasant floating restaurant.

Getting There & Away

Access to Rio Branco has improved. You can get there year-round along sealed roads from Brazil's eastern states. However,

between October and June, when the rivers are at their highest, the roads to the more isolated towns (off Hwy BR-364) are precarious and often impassable, leaving plane or boat the only viable transport options. From July to September, when the rivers are at their lowest levels, the roads are passable, but river traffic is restricted.

Air The Aeroporto Internacional Presidente Medici is about 2km from town on Hwy AC-40, at Km 1. Varig is the main airline operating interstate flights. At the time of writing, regular flights to Puerto Maldonado (in Peru) had been discontinued, but it was possible to hire an air-taxi there for US$1250 total, six passengers maximum.

Bus The rodoviária is a couple of kilometers out of town on the Norte/Sul bus route. There are regular buses to other state capitals: four daily to Porto Velho (US$22, 10 hours); twice weekly to Belém (US$200, 4 days); weekly to Fortaleza (US$225, 4 days); and daily to Goiania (US$115, 48 hours). Services to Manaus have been suspended indefinitely. Other destinations include Brasiléia, Xapuri, Plácido de Castro and Boca do Acre in Amazonas state.

Boat Enquire about boats at the port, at the eastern end of Av Epaminondas Jácome. If there's a group, a 1½ day trip to Boca do Acre (Amazonas) costs around US$60. From Boca do Acre, there is river traffic along the Rio Purus as far as the Amazon, even to Manaus.

BRASILÉIA

The small town of Brasiléia lies on Brazil's border with Bolivia, separated from Cobija (its Bolivian counterpart) by the Rio Abunã and the Rio Acre. Brasiléia has nothing to interest travelers except an immigration stamp into or out of Brazil.

The Bolivian Consulate, Rua Major Salinas 205, is open 8 to 11 am weekdays. For a Brazilian entry or exit stamp, dress nicely and visit the Polícia Federal, 2km northeast of the center. It's open 8 am to noon and 2 to 5 pm daily.

If you're stuck in Brasiléia, try *Hotel Fronteiras* (☎ 068-546-3045), near the church in the center, with apartamentos for US$8/15. The similarly priced *Hotel Kador*

(☎ 068-546-3283), Av Santos Dumont 25, is on the road between the international bridge and the Polícia Federal.

From the rodoviária, five daily buses go to Rio Branco (US$15, six hours). Buses also go to Assis Brasil, on the Peruvian border, during the dry season. During the rainy season you may be able to organize a ride in a truck. Contact Transport Acreana in Brasiléia.

To/From Bolivia

You'll have to get stamps from both Bolivian Migración in Cobija and the Brazilian Polícia Federal just outside Brasiléia. A yellow-fever vaccination certificate is technically required to enter Brazil from Cobija.

They don't usually check, but if you need a vaccination you'll have to find a local doctor. There's no vaccination clinic in Brasiléia.

It's a long slog across the bridge from Cobija to Brasiléia, but taxis will take you from Cobija to the Polícia Federal in Brasiléia, wait while you complete immigration formalities, then take you to the city center or to the rodoviária. It's about US$3 if you negotiate the route and fare in advance. Going the other way, taxis try to charge double this price.

Alternately, take a rowboat ferry (US$0.40 per person) across the Rio Acre to the landing in the center of Brasiléia. From here it's about 1km to the rodoviária and another 1.5km to the Polícia Federal.

Chile

Chile stretches 4300km from Peru to the Strait of Magellan. Its contrasts include the scenic but nearly sterile Atacama Desert in the north, the metropolis of Santiago and its Valle Central (Central Valley), a verdant lake district and the glacial landscapes of southern Patagonia. Within just hours of each other are world-class Andean skiing and scores of Pacific beach resorts.

Many Chileans are of European descent, but indigenous traditions persist. In the north, Aymara Indians farm the Andean foothills and tend llamas and alpacas on the *altiplano*. Mapuche Indians still inhabit the south, where they earned respect for their resistance to Chilean expansion in the 19th century.

Adventurous visitors will appreciate Polynesian Easter Island (Rapa Nui) with its giant stylized statues, and the Juan Fernández Islands, a botanical wonderland best known for marooned Scotsman Alexander Selkirk, who inspired the novel *Robinson Crusoe*.

Facts about Chile

HISTORY
Pre-Columbian Chile
Inca rule touched Chile, but northern Aymara and Atacameño farmers and herders predated the lords of Cuzco, while Changos fished coastal areas and Diaguitas farmed the interior of Coquimbo. Beyond the central valley, Araucanian (Mapuche) Indians resisted Inca aggression. Cunco Indians fished and farmed on the island of Chiloé. Smaller groups long avoided European contact in the far south, but are now nearly extinct.

Colonial Times
A year after leaving Peru in 1540, Pedro de Valdivia reached the Mapocho valley to found the city of Santiago. Mapuche assaults threatened the fledgling capital, but the determined Spaniards held out and Valdivia gradually worked southward, founding Concepción, Valdivia and Villarrica. Before his death in 1553 at the hands of the Mapuche,

he had laid the foundation for a new country.

Finding little gold or silver, the Spanish invaders set up *encomiendas* (forced labor systems) to exploit the north's relatively large, sedentary population. The Spaniards also dominated central Chile, but Mapuche defenders made the area south of the Río Biobío unsafe for over three centuries.

Spanish men interbred with Indian women, and their descendants, or *mestizos*,

Rise of the Latifundio

As population-based encomiendas lost their value, Valdivia rewarded his loyalists with land grants like those of his native Extremadura. Landless and 'vagrant' Spaniards became *inquilinos* (tenants) on units that evolved from livestock *estancias* into agricultural *haciendas* or *fundos*. These estates *(latifundios)*, many intact into the 1960s, became the dominant force in Chilean society.

Paying little or no rent, inquilino families could occupy a shack, raise a garden and graze animals on hacienda land. In return, they provided labor during annual rodeos (cattle roundups) and defended the interests of the *hacendado* (owner). This 'man and master' relationship permeated society.

Other groups, like immigrant Basques, purchased large properties as their families flourished in commerce. Adopting landowners' values, they have remained important in politics, society and business. Mining and commerce brought more wealth than land per se.

Revolutionary Wars & the Early Republic

Part of the Viceroyalty of Peru but distant from Lima, the Audiencia of Chile stretched roughly from modern Chañaral to Puerto Aisén. By 1818, José de San Martín's Ejército de los Andes (Army of the Andes), part of the South American independence movement, marched from Argentina into Chile, took Santiago and sailed north to Lima. San Martín appointed the Chilean Bernardo O'Higgins, the son of an Irishman, to be his second-in-command, and O'Higgins became 'supreme director' of the Chilean republic.

Independent Chile shared ambiguous boundaries with Bolivia, Argentina and the Mapuche. It lost the Cuyo region to Argentina, but managed rapid progress in agriculture, mining, industry and commerce.

O'Higgins dominated politics for five years after independence, decreeing political, social, religious and educational reforms, but landowners' objections to his egalitarian measures forced his resignation.

The landowners' spokesman was businessman Diego Portales who, as interior minister, was de facto dictator until his execution in 1837. His custom-drawn constitution centralized power in Santiago and established Catholicism as the state religion. It also limited suffrage to literate, propertied adult males, and established indirect elections for president and senate. This constitution lasted, with some changes, until 1925.

Territorial Expansion & Economic Development

At independence, Chile was small and compact, but triumphs over Peru and Bolivia in the War of the Pacific (1879-83) and treaties with the Mapuche placed the nitrate-rich Atacama Desert and the southern lake district under Chilean rule. Chile also annexed remote Easter Island (Rapa Nui) in 1888.

British, North American and German capital turned the Atacama into a bonanza, as nitrates brought prosperity, at least to certain sectors of society, and funded the government. The nitrate ports of Antofagasta and Iquique grew rapidly until the Panama Canal (1914) reduced traffic around Cape Horn and development of petroleum-based fertilizers made mineral nitrates obsolete.

Mining also created a new working class and a class of nouveau riche, who both challenged the landowners. Elected in 1886, President José Manuel Balmaceda promoted government services and public works to tackle the dilemma of unequally distributed wealth and power, but a congressional attempt to depose him in 1890 triggered a civil war that resulted in 10,000 deaths, including his own suicide. His successors continued many of his projects, but on a lesser scale, and also opened the Congress to popular elections.

20th-Century Developments

As late as the 1920s, up to 75% of Chile's rural population still lived on latifundios holding 80% of prime agricultural land. Inquilinos' subsistence depended on the haciendas, and their votes belonged to landowners. As industry expanded and public works advanced, urban workers' welfare improved, but that of rural workers declined, forcing day laborers to the cities. Inquilinos suffered reduced privileges, while their labor obligations became more onerous. An abundant labor force gave haciendas little incentive to modernize, and production stagnated until the crisis of the 1960s.

Despite hard times due to declining nitrate income, President Arturo Alessandri Palma instituted land and income taxes to fund health, education and welfare reforms, but conservative obstruction and army opposition forced his resignation in 1924. For several years the dictatorial General Carlos Ibáñez del Campo held the presidency and other powerful positions, but opposition to his policies (exacerbated by global depression) forced him into exile.

Stalinists, Trotskyites and other radicals and reformists created a bewildering mix of new political entities in the 1930s and 1940s, but the democratic left dominated politics. Corfo, the state development corporation, played a major economic role, and North American companies gained control of copper mines, now the cornerstone of the economy.

Christian Democratic Ascendancy

In 1952, Ibáñez del Campo again won the presidency, but his surprising attempts to curtail landowners' power faltered. In the 1958 presidential elections, Arturo Alessandri's popular son, Jorge Alessandri Rodríguez, representing a coalition of conservative and liberal parties, won a close race, defeating leftist Salvador Allende Gossens and Christian Democrat Eduardo Frei Montalva. In 1961 congressional elections, opposition gains forced Alessandri to accept modest land reforms that began a decade's battle with the fundos.

In the 1964 presidential election Frei decisively defeated Allende, who was undermined by party factionalism. Frei's genuinely reformist policies threatened both the elite's privileges and the left's working-class base, but improvements stalled as economic decline drove displaced rural workers to urban squatter settlements (*callampas*, or mushrooms, since they seemed to spring up overnight). Opportunistically attacking the US-dominated export sector, Frei advocated Chileanization of the copper industry, while Allende and his backers demanded nationalization.

The Christian Democrats also faced challenges from violent groups like MIR (the Leftist Revolutionary Movement), who found support among coal miners, textile workers and other urban laborers, and also agitated for land reform. Too slow for leftists, Frei's reforms were too rapid for obstructionist conservatives – and, in this increasingly polarized society, there was even dissension among Christian Democrats.

Allende Comes to Power

In 1970, Allende's Unidad Popular (Popular Unity or UP) coalition offered a radical program advocating nationalization of industry and expropriation of latifundios. After winning a small plurality and agreeing to constitutional guarantees, Allende took office with congressional approval, but the coalition quarreled over the administration's objectives.

Allende's program, evading rather than confronting Congress, included state control of many private enterprises and massive income redistribution. Increased public spending briefly stimulated growth, but falling production brought shortages, soaring inflation and black marketeering.

Politics grew more confrontational as peasants, frustrated with agrarian reforms that favored inquilinos over sharecroppers and *afuerinos* (day laborers), seized land, and harvests declined. Expropriation of copper mines and other enterprises, plus conspicuously friendly relations with Cuba, provoked US hostility. Compromise was impossible between extreme leftists, who believed that only force could achieve socialism, and their rightist counterparts, who believed that only force could prevent it.

Golpe de Estado

On September 11, 1973, General Augusto Pinochet Ugarte led a brutal *golpe de estado* (coup d'état) that resulted in the death of Allende (an apparent suicide) and thousands of his supporters. The military argued that force was necessary because Allende was planning to overthrow the constitutional order.

Inept policies had led to economic chaos, but reactionary forces also undercut Allende's government by manipulating scarcities of commodities and food. Allende's pledges to the opposition were credible, but his inability or unwillingness to control forces to his left terrified the middle classes and outraged the oligarchy, underlining his failure.

CHILE

CHILE (NORTH)

PERU
Tacna
BOLIVIA
Arica
11
Panamericana
1
2
3
4
I
Iquique
5
Chuquicamata
Calama
San Pedro
de Atacama
7
Antofagasta
II
6
0   100   200 km
0   75   150 miles
PACIFIC
OCEAN
8
1
Caldera
9
Copiapó
III
10
Vallenar
RN
40
11
La Serena
Vicuña
12
RN
150
13
Ovalle
IV
ARGENTINA
Los Vilos
5
V
14
Viña del Mar
15
Valparaíso
68
16
17
SANTIAGO
18
VI
Rancagua
19
RN
7
Curicó
VII
Talca
22
20
21
Chillán
RN
143
Concepción
RN
151

CHILE (SOUTH)

Concepción
Chillán
VIII
RN
151
Los Ángeles
24
23
5
IX
Temuco
25
26
Villarrica
27
Pucón
Valdivia
Lican
Ray
28
RN
40
X
29
Osorno
30
Puerto Varas
Puerto Montt
Bariloche
Ancud
31
32
33
Castro
34
35
Quellón
Chaitén
RN
25
37
38
39
36
40
7
41
42
43
Coihaique
44
Camino
Austral
XI
45
Cochrane
RN
40
RN
26
RN
3
46
47
El Calafate
ATLANTIC
OCEAN
48
49
RP
7
RP
5
Puerto Natales
XII
50
Punta
Arenas
Porvenir
Río Grande
51
52
53
Ushuaia
PACIFIC
OCEAN
54

ARGENTINA

CHILE

ADMINISTRATIVE REGIONS
- I Región de Tarapacá
- II Región de Antofagasta
- III Región de Atacama
- IV Región de Coquimbo
- V Región de Valparaíso (includes Easter Island & Archipiélago Juan Fernández) Región Metropolitana
- VI Región del Libertador General Bernardo O'Higgins
- VII Región del Maule
- VIII Región del Biobío
- IX Región de La Araucanía
- X Región de Los Lagos
- XI Región de Aisén del General Carlos Ibáñez del Campo
- XII Región de Magallanes y Antártica Chilena

PARQUES NACIONALES
- 1 Lauca
- 4 Volcán Isluga
- 8 Pan de Azúcar
- 9 Nevado Tres Cruces
- 10 Llanos de Challe
- 13 Fray Jorge
- 14 La Campana
- 23 Nahuelbuta
- 24 Laguna del Laja
- 25 Tolhuaca
- 26 Conguillío
- 27 Huerquehue
- 28 Villarrica
- 30 Puyehue
- 31 Vicente Pérez Rosales
- 32 Alerce Andino
- 33 Hornopirén
- 34 Chiloé
- 36 Isla Guamblín
- 38 Isla Magdalena
- 40 Queulat
- 41 Río Simpson
- 45 Laguna San Rafael
- 47 Bernardo O'Higgins
- 49 Torres del Paine
- 50 Pali-Aike
- 54 Cabo de Hornos

RESERVAS NACIONALES
- 2 Las Vicuñas
- 5 Pampa del Tamarugal
- 6 La Chimba
- 7 Los Flamencos
- 11 Pingüino de Humboldt
- 15 Lago Peñuelas
- 18 Río Clarillo
- 19 Río de los Cipreses
- 20 Los Ruiles
- 21 Altos del Lircay
- 37 Las Guaitecas
- 39 Lago Rosselot
- 42 Coihaique
- 44 Cerro Castillo
- 46 Katalalixar
- 48 Alacalufes

OTHER PROTECTED AREAS
- 3 Monumento Natural Salar de Surire
- 12 Monumento Natural Pichasca
- 16 Santuario de la Naturaleza Yerba Loca
- 17 Monumento Natural El Morado
- 22 Area de Protección Radal Siete Tazas
- 29 Monumento Natural Alerce Costero
- 35 Parque Natural Pumalín
- 43 Monumento Natural Dos Lagunas
- 51 Reserva Forestal Magallanes
- 52 Reserva Forestal Laguna Parrillar
- 53 Monumento Natural Los Pingüinos

Military Dictatorship

Most politicians expected a quick return to civilian rule, but Pinochet took 16 years to remake Chile's political and economic culture, largely by terror – more than 4000 Chileans and foreigners 'disappeared' during his dictatorship, mostly in the first few years. International assassinations were not unusual; most notorious was that of Allende's ex-Foreign Minister Orlando Letelier by a car bomb in Washington, DC, in 1976. In 1980, Pinochet submitted a new constitution to the voters; about two-thirds approved it and ratified his presidency until 1989, despite many abstentions.

Early Transition

In October 1988, voters rejected Pinochet's bid to extend his presidency until 1997. In 1989, 17 parties formed the coalition Concertación para la Democracia (Consensus for Democracy). Patricio Aylwin, the Concertación's compromise presidential candidate, easily defeated both Pinochet's reluctant protégé, Hernán Büchi, of the Renovación Nacional party, and right-wing independent Francisco Errázuriz. Pinochet's custom-made constitution limited Aylwin's well-intentioned presidency which, however, did see the publication of the Rettig report documenting deaths and disappearances during the dictatorship.

For more on the transition, see Government & Politics below.

GEOGRAPHY & CLIMATE

Chile's 800,000 sq km contains stony Andean peaks, snowcapped volcanoes, broad river valleys and deep canyons, sterile deserts, icy fjords, deep blue glaciers, turquoise lakes, sandy beaches and rocky headlands. Continental Chile extends from tropical Arica to subantarctic Punta Arenas; less than 200km wide on average, it rises from sea level to above 6000m. Its Antarctic claims overlap Argentina's and Britain's.

Chile's 13 administrative regions are numbered ordinally from north to south, except for the Metropolitan Region of Santiago. The regions of Tarapacá and

CHILE

Antofagasta comprise the Norte Grande (Great North), dominated by the barren Atacama Desert.

The regions of Atacama and Coquimbo form the mineral-rich Norte Chico (Little North), an area of scrub and scattered forests. Beyond the Río Aconcagua begins the fertile heartland of Middle Chile, containing the capital Santiago, the port of Valparaíso and most of the country's industry and employment. It enjoys a Mediterranean climate of warm dry summers and mild wet winters.

South of Concepción, the Río Biobío marks Chile's 19th-century frontier and the Mapuche homeland. South of Temuco, the scenic Lake District has snowcapped volcanoes, many still active, framing its numerous foothill lakes. South of Puerto Montt, Chiloé is the largest island wholly within Chile, with a lengthy coastline, dense forests and many small farms. It has a marine west coast climate, with rainfall spread evenly throughout the year.

Chilean Patagonia, comprising the regions of Aisén and Magallanes, experiences cool summers but relatively mild winters, as does the island of Tierra del Fuego, divided between Chile and Argentina.

The Andes run the length of the country. The Norte Grande's volcanoes reach above 6000m, as does the imposing wall of sedimentary and volcanic peaks east of Santiago. South of the Biobío, the Andes are a less formidable barrier.

FLORA & FAUNA

Chile's northern deserts and high-altitude steppes, soaring mountains, alpine and subantarctic forests and extensive coastline all support distinctive flora and fauna. To protect these environments Chile's Corporación Nacional Forestal (Conaf) administers an extensive national park system.

The northern highlands support the endangered vicuña, most notably in Parque Nacional Lauca, and huge nesting colonies of flamingos, mostly near San Pedro de Atacam. The Pacific coastal deserts offer pelicans, penguins, otters and sea lions. The Andean portion of La Araucanía houses large forests of araucaria (monkey-puzzle tree), cypress and southern beech in several national parks. In the extreme south, Parque Nacional Torres del Paine is a UNESCO Biosphere Reserve with a wealth of wildlife, including the Patagonian guanaco.

ECOLOGY & ENVIRONMENT

Major environmental issues, not well-addressed by a government whose priority is short-term economic gain, are urban growth and air pollution (sprawling Santiago has some of the world's worst smog), water pollution (usually associated with mining), questionable hydropower projects (the damming of the Río Biobío has displaced indigenous peoples) and the destruction of old-growth forests (particularly in the Aisén region and Tierra del Fuego).

GOVERNMENT & POLITICS

The constitution allows a popularly elected president and establishes a Congress with a 46-member Senate and a 120-member Chamber of Deputies, but eight institutional senators are the legacy of Pinochet's dictatorship. The president resides in Santiago but the Congress meets in Valparaíso. Despite regionalization, administration is highly centralized.

In late 1993 Chileans chose Eduardo Frei Ruiz-Tagle, son of former president Frei, to succeed Patricio Aylwin. Frei has continued Pinochet's (and Aylwin's) economic policies with more enlightened social programs; despite proposed divorce legislation (Chile is the last western democracy without a divorce law), Frei's initiatives have met limited success because the conservative opposition controls the Senate. Frei has also drawn criticism for inattention to or disregard for environmental matters.

The front-runner in the 1999 presidential race is Socialist Ricardo Lagos, formerly Frei's public works minister. The wild card in Chilean politics is Pinochet himself, a senator-for-life on his own terms, whose recent arrest in London at the request of a Spanish judge investigating human rights violations unleashed an international furor. The general's detention, whatever its final outcome, has brought unresolved issues into the open for the first time in decades.

The Military in Politics

Thanks to constitutional provisions assuring them 10% of state copper sales profits, Chile's armed forces enjoy a larger budget than their counterparts in any neighboring country. All the services enjoy autonomy, despite a proposed constitutional amendment to strengthen presidential authority.

Of Chile's 123,000 uniformed personnel, more than half are in the army; nearly half of those are officers and noncommissioned officers. Historically, the services are highly disciplined, cohesive and more loyal to their commanders than to civilian authority, but there are indications of change. The military continues to have direct political influence through the constitutionally mandated Consejo de Seguridad Nacional (consisting of heads of the armed forces) and the so-called designated senators, some chosen from the ranks of retired military commanders.

ECONOMY

In an early experiment in neoliberal economics, Pinochet's government enlisted University of Chicago economists to reduce public expenditures and encourage foreign investment. For some years after, inflation remained high, industrial production declined and some inefficient industries disappeared, but 'nontraditional' exports like off-season temperate fruits helped compensate for falling copper prices. The new policies had great social costs; only soup kitchens prevented starvation in some callampas.

Chile is often cited as a success story because of a decade-plus of 6% growth, though the recent Asian meltdown has slowed the economy. Still, exports are more diverse and less vulnerable to international market fluctuations, Chile has repaid some of its foreign debt and inflation has fallen to a modest 6%. However, the growth of national income has benefited the poor only incidentally, and already inequitable income distribution has worsened.

Much of the growth has been in natural resources exports, which may not be sustainable. Chile is the world's largest copper producer and exporter, but also sells other metals and minerals, wood and other forest products, fish, fish meal and fruits to the EU, Japan, the USA, Argentina and Brazil. When a 1996 forestry study concluded that in 25 to 30 years the country might have no more trees worth cutting down, the industry's strong reaction forced dismissal of the study's director.

While Chile is keen to join NAFTA – the North American free-trade bloc that includes the US, Canada and Mexico – changing political considerations in the US have blocked NAFTA expansion for the time being. Meanwhile, Chile has managed to reduce trade barriers with Mercosur countries as an associate member.

POPULATION & PEOPLE

Over a third of Chile's 14.8 million people reside in Gran Santiago (the capital and its suburbs). About 75% live in Middle Chile, only 20% of the country's total area. More than 85% live in cities, but south of the Biobío, the peasant population is still dense.

As most Chileans are mestizos, class is a greater issue than race. La Araucanía has a large Mapuche population. In the north, Aymara and Atacameño peoples farm terraces in the *precordillera*, and pasture llamas and alpacas in the altiplano.

After 1848, many Germans settled in the Lake District. Other immigrants came from France, Italy, Yugoslavia (especially to Magallanes and Tierra del Fuego) and Palestine.

ARTS

Famous Chilean writers include Nobel Prize poets Gabriela Mistral and Pablo Neruda (also an important political activist). Much of their work is available in English translation – see the Facts for the Visitor section. Chile's best-known contemporary writers are novelist Isabel Allende (a niece of the late President) and playwright-novelist-essayist Ariel Dorfman, both of whom live in the US but maintain close links to their homeland.

Until 1973, Chilean cinema was among Latin America's most experimental. Director Alejandro Jodorowsky's surrealistic *El Topo* (The Mole) was an underground success overseas, while exiled Miguel Littín's *Alsino and the Condor*, nominated for an Academy Award in 1983, is readily available on video.

La Nueva Canción Chilena (the New Chilean Song Movement) wedded Chile's folkloric heritage to the political passions of the late 1960s and early 1970s. Its most legendary figure is the late Violeta Parra, whose performing children, Isabel and Angel, established the first of many *peñas* (musical and cultural centers) in the mid-1960s. Individuals such as Victor Jara (executed in

CHILE

1973) and contemporary groups such as Quilapayún and Inti-Illimani have acquired international reputations. In recent years, Chilean rock music has come into its own through the efforts of groups like La Ley and Los Tres.

SOCIETY & CONDUCT

Because of the European influence, English-speaking visitors will find Chile more accessible than some other Latin American countries. Many Chileans are exceptionally hospitable and frequently invite foreigners to their homes.

Chile's indigenous peoples, however, may be distrustful of strangers in their midst, though they are usually polite and gracious. Travelers should be circumspect, for example, of aggressively photographing Mapuche and Aymara peoples except in the context of a public performance, such as a parade or dance demonstration.

RELIGION

About 90% of Chileans are Catholic, but the Church has many factions – its Vicaria de la Solidaridad staunchly defended human rights during the dictatorship, but members of the ultraconservative Opus Dei collaborated with the dictatorship. Evangelical Protestantism is growing, but Mormon proselytizing has made their churches targets of leftist bombings.

LANGUAGE

Spanish is the official language, dominant even for many if not most speakers of the handful of Indian languages. In the north, over 20,000 speak Aymara; in the south there are at least 400,000 Mapudungun (Mapuche) speakers and another 150,000 of the related Huilliche. About 2200 speak Rapa Nui, the Polynesian language of Easter Island.

Chilean Spanish

Chileans relax terminal and even some internal consonants, making it difficult to distinguish plural from singular: *las islas* (the islands) may sound more like *la ila*. They also speak more rapidly than other South Americans, and rather less clearly: The conventional *¿Quieres...?* (Do you want...?) sounds like *¿Querí...?* on the tongue of a Chilean.

Facts for the Visitor

HIGHLIGHTS

Chile's myriad natural attractions range from northern deserts to the southern Lake District and the mountains of Patagonia. For outdoor enthusiasts, highlights include trekking, climbing and skiing. The adobe houses and colonial churches of the high Andean villages, and the vernacular architecture of Chiloé, complement the natural landscape, while Mapuche textiles and silver jewelry appeal to shoppers. Fabulous seafood, superb wines and Chilean cordiality also make for a memorable visit.

PLANNING

Chile is mostly a midlatitude country: The seasons are reversed from North America and Europe, except in the subtropical northern deserts, which have mild weather year-round.

Santiago and Middle Chile are best in spring or during the autumn harvest, but skiers will prefer the northern-hemisphere summer. Natural attractions like Torres del Paine and the Lake District are best in summer, but rain is always possible. Rapa Nui is cooler, slightly cheaper and less crowded outside after summer. Likewise, March is an excellent time to visit the Juan Fernández archipelago.

At high altitudes, carry warm clothing even in summer. The altiplano's summer rainy season usually means only a brief afternoon thunderstorm.

Maps

LP's *Chile & Easter Island Travel Atlas* (1997) has detailed highway maps of the entire country. Now hard to find, the Instituto Geográfico Militar's *Plano Guía del Gran Santiago* (1989) is the equivalent of *London A–Z*, but needs updating. The IGM's 1:50,000 topographic series is valuable for trekkers but costly (about US$15 per sheet).

TOURIST OFFICES
Local Tourist Offices

Sernatur, the national tourist service, has offices in Santiago, regional capitals and several other cities. Many localities have their own tourist offices, usually on the main plaza or at the bus terminal, sometimes only open in summer.

Tourist Offices Abroad

Chilean consulates abroad often provide tourist information. Try also LanChile, the major international airline, for information.

VISAS & DOCUMENTS

Passports are obligatory except for nationals of neighboring countries, and essential for cashing traveler's checks, checking into hotels and other routine activities.

On arrival, most nationalities receive a 90-day tourist card, renewable for 90 more at the Departamento de Extranjería (☎ 02-6725320), Moneda 1342 in Santiago, but renewals now cost about US$100. A few nationalities, most notably New Zealanders, need advance visas, but requirements change, and Chilean embassies recommend that people check before their visit for the latest information. If staying longer than six months, make a brief visit to a neighboring country, then return.

Chilean authorities take the tourist card very seriously; for a replacement, go to the Policía Internacional (☎ 02-7371292), General Borgoño 1052 (Metro: Puente Cal y Canto) in Santiago.

Motorists need an International Driving Permit as well as a state or national license. International Health Certificates are optional. There is a growing network of youth hostels; the Asociación Chilena de Albergues Turísticos Juveniles (☎/fax 02-2333220, achatj@entelchile.net), at Hernando de Aguirre 201, Oficina 602, Providencia, Santiago (Metro: Tobalaba), sells the HI Card, which can also be purchased at the Santiago hostel, Cienfuegos 151.

EMBASSIES & CONSULATES
Chilean Embassies & Consulates

Chilean embassies and consulates include:

Australia
(☎ 06-6286-2430)
10 Culgoa Circuit, O'Malley, ACT 2606
(☎ 02-9299-2533)
8th floor, National Mutual Centre,
44 Market St, Sydney 2000
(☎ 03-9654-4479)
Level 43, Nauru House, 80 Collins St,
Melbourne 3000

Canada
(☎ 613-235-4402)
151 Slater St, Suite 605, Ottawa, Ontario
(☎ 416-366-9570)
Bay Street, Suite 1003, Toronto, Ontario

(☎ 514-861-8006)
1010 St Catherine West, Suite 731,
Montréal, Québec

France
(☎ 01-47054661)
4 Blvd de la Tour, Maubourg, Paris

Germany
(☎ 0228-955840)
Kronprinzenstrasse 20, Bonn
(☎ 069-550194)
Humboldstrasse 94, Frankfurt
(☎ 030-2044990)
Leipzigerstrasse 63, Berlin

UK
(☎ 0171-580-1023)
12 Devonshire Rd, London

USA
(☎ 202-785-1746)
732 Massachusetts Ave NW, Washington, DC
(☎ 212-980-3366)
866 United Nations Plaza, Room 302,
New York, NY
(☎ 310-785-0047)
1900 Avenue of the Stars, Suite 1250,
Los Angeles, CA
(☎ 415-982-7662)
870 Market St, Suite 1062, San Francisco, CA
(☎ 305-373-8623)
1110 Brickell Ave, Suite 616, Miami FL
(☎ 708-654-8780)
875 N Michigan Ave, Suite 3352,
Chicago IL 60611

Embassies & Consulates in Chile

The following countries maintain embassies in Santiago:

Argentina
(☎ 02-2228977)
Vicuña Mackenna 41

Australia
(☎ 02-2285065)
Gertrudis Echeñique 420, Las Condes

Bolivia
(☎ 02-2328180)
Av Santa María 2796, Las Condes

Canada
(☎ 02-3629660)
Nuevo Tajamar 481, 12th floor, Las Condes

France
(☎ 02-2251030)
Av Condell 65, Providencia

Germany
(☎ 02-6335031)
Agustinas 785, 7th floor

Israel
(☎ 02-2461570)
San Sebastián 2812, 5th floor, Providencia

CHILE

New Zealand
(☎ 02-2314204)
Isidora Goyenechea 3516, Las Condes

Peru
(☎ 02-2352356)
Andrés Bello 1751, Providencia

UK
(☎ 02-2313737)
3rd floor, Av El Bosque Norte 0125,
Las Condes

USA
(☎ 02-2322600)
Andrés Bello 2800, Las Condes

Argentina maintains additional consulates in the following locations:

Antofagasta
(☎ 055-222854)
Díaz Gana at Hermógenes Alfaro;
open 9 am to 2 pm weekdays

Puerto Montt
(☎ 065-253996)
Cauquenes 94, 2nd floor;
open 8 am to 1 pm weekdays

Punta Arenas
(☎ 061-261912)
21 de Mayo 1878;
open 10 am to 3 pm weekdays

Valparaíso
(☎ 032-256117) Blanco 725, Oficina 26

Bolivia maintains additional consulates in the following locations:

Antofagasta
(☎ 055-225010)
Washington 2562; open 9 am to 2 pm weekdays

Arica
(☎ 058-231030)
21 de Mayo 575; open 8 am to 2 pm weekdays

Calama
(☎ 055-344413)
Madame Curie 2388;
open 10 am to 1:30 pm weekdays

Iquique
(☎ 057-421777)
Arturo Fernández 1081

Peru maintains additional consulates in the following locations:

Arica
(☎ 058-231020)
San Marcos 786;
open 8:30 am to 1:30 pm weekdays

Iquique
(☎ 057-411466)
Zegers 570

The UK maintains an additional consulate in Valparaíso (☎ 032-256117), at Blanco 725, Oficina 26

CUSTOMS

There are no currency restrictions. Duty-free allowances include 400 cigarettes or 50 cigars or 500 grams of tobacco, 2.5 liters of alcoholic beverages and perfume for personal use.

Inspections are usually routine, but some travelers have undergone more thorough examinations because of drug smuggling from Peru and Bolivia. Arrivals from duty-free zones in the First Region (Tarapacá) and the 12th Region (Magallanes) are subject to internal customs checks. The Servicio Agrícola-Ganadero (SAG) inspects luggage for fresh produce at international borders and domestic checkpoints.

MONEY

The unit of currency is the *peso* (Ch$). There are banknotes for 500, 1000, 2000, 5000, 10,000 and 20,000 pesos; and coins for one, five, 10, 50 and 100 pesos. One peso coins are disappearing and even fives and tens are uncommon.

US dollars are the preferred currency, but Argentine pesos can be readily exchanged in Santiago, at border crossings and in tourist areas like Viña del Mar and the Lake District.

Exchange Rates

Approximate official rates as of July 1999 are as follows:

country	unit		pesos
Australia	A$1	=	Ch$342
Canada	C$1	=	Ch$348
euro	€1	=	Ch$526
France	FF1	=	Ch$80
Germany	DM1	=	Ch$269
Japan	¥100	=	Ch$427
New Zealand	NZ$1	=	Ch$271
UK	UK£1	=	Ch$807
USA	US$1	=	Ch$516

Exchanging Money

It's quicker and simpler to change money at *cambios* than at banks. Cash earns a better rate than traveler's checks and avoids commissions (though these are usually modest). Hotels, travel agencies, street changers and some shops also change cash.

ATMs are abundant and work with both credit and debit cards. ATM users also get Santiago rates, which are better than in other regions.

Costs

Chile is no longer a bargain, but modest lodgings, food and transport are still cheaper than in Europe, North America or Argentina. Allow at least US$25 per day for food and accommodations; by purchasing market food or eating at modest restaurants, you may get by for less.

Tipping & Bargaining

In restaurants, a 10% *propina* is customary. Bargaining is customary only in markets. Hotel prices are generally fixed and prominently displayed, but try haggling in a slow summer or during the off-season.

POST & COMMUNICATIONS

Postal services are sometimes slow, but Chile's much-improved telephone services are also cheap. Telegraph, telex and fax services are also good.

Post

Post offices are open 9 am to 6 pm weekdays and 9 am to noon Saturdays. Send essential overseas mail *certificado* to ensure its arrival. Parcel post is efficient, though customs may inspect your package before a clerk will accept it. Vendors near the post office wrap parcels for a small charge.

Poste restante and *lista de correos* are equivalent to general delivery. Lista de correos charges a nominal fee (about US$0.20 per letter). Santiago's American Express office holds client mail, as do some embassies for their citizens. Instruct correspondents to address letters clearly and to indicate a pick-up date (*'Guardar hasta...'* means 'Keep until...'). International Federal Express services are available in Santiago.

Telephone

Entel, the former state monopoly, Compañía de Teléfonos de Chile (CTC) and several other companies offer domestic and international long-distance services throughout the country.

Domestic long-distance calls are generally less than US$1 for three minutes. Approximate charges to North America are

US$1 per minute, to England or Australia US$2.50 per minute, and to other Latin American countries US$2 per minute. Late-evening and weekend discounts make calls to the USA less than US$1 per minute.

Local calls from public phones cost Ch$100 (about US$0.20) for three minutes, half that evenings and weekends. When the liquid-crystal readout reaches zero, insert another coin. Phone boxes do not provide change, but if there is at least Ch$50 credit remaining, you may make another call by pressing a button. Magnetic telephone cards are more convenient than coins.

Long-distance domestic and overseas calls are possible from phone boxes, which accept coins and cards. Reverse-charge overseas calls are simple to make but credit-card calls are possible only from private phones or from the gray-blue *teléfonos inteligentes*. Phone offices are ubiquitous, and private ones are often cheaper than Entel or CTC.

Chile's country code is ☎ 56.

INTERNET RESOURCES

Sernatur, the official Chilean government tourist agency has a website in English and Spanish at: www.segegob.cl/sernatur/inicio.html.

The Usenet discussion group soc.culture.chile is wide-ranging but often polemical and irritating.

BOOKS
Travel Guides & Literature

For detailed travel information, there's the 5th edition of LP's *Chile & Easter Island*.

The annually updated, reasonably priced Turistel series, published by the Compañía de Teléfonos, has separate volumes on northern, central and southern Chile, plus an additional one on camping, and good maps. Oriented toward motorists, Turistel provides excellent maps and thorough background, but ignores budget alternatives. The single-volume English-language version is badly out of date.

Sara Wheeler's *Travels in a Thin Country* has also drawn favorable commentary.

History & Politics

For general history, read Arnold Bauer's *Chilean Rural Society from the Spanish Conquest to 1930*.

CHILE

James Petras and Morris Morley's *The United States & Chile: Imperialism & the Overthrow of the Allende Government* and Robert J Alexander's *The Tragedy of Chile* are opposing visions of the fall of Allende. Thomas Hauser's *The Execution of Charles Horman: An American Sacrifice*, which implicated US officials in the death of a US activist in the 1973 coup, was the basis of the 1982 film *Missing*.

Chile: The Pinochet Decade, by Phil O'Brien and Jackie Roddick, covers the dictatorship's early years and radical economic measures. Genaro Arriagada's *Pinochet: The Politics of Power* details the regime's evolution from a collegial junta to a personalistic, but institutionalized, dictatorship. Pamela Constable and Arturo Valenzuela's *A Nation of Enemies* eschews partisan rhetoric to focus on the intricacies and implications of events since 1973.

Literature

Poets Pablo Neruda and Gabriela Mistral are Nobel Prize winners. Available in translation are Neruda's *The Heights of Machu Picchu, Canto General, Passions and Impressions* and his rambling prose *Memoirs*. US poet Langston Hughes translated *Selected Poems of Gabriela Mistral* (1957); the Library of Congress and Johns Hopkins Press published a different book with the same title in 1971.

Though often repetitive, Isabel Allende's magical realist novels have made her popular overseas and in Chile; *House of Spirits, Of Love and Shadows, Eva Luna* and the nonfiction *Paula* are available in paperback. José Donoso's novel *Curfew* (1988) offers a view of life under dictatorship through the eyes of a returned exile. Antonio Skármeta's novel *Burning Patience* (1987) became the award-winning Italian film *Il Postino* (The Postman).

Easter Island (Rapa Nui)

See the Easter Island section for details on literature available about this island.

NEWSPAPERS

Santiago's oldest daily, *El Mercurio*, follows a conservative editorial policy, while *La Nación* is the official government daily. *Estrategia*, voice of the financial sector, is the best source of information on exchange rates. The weekly *News Review* serves the English-speaking population.

The following Chilean news sources have Internet homepages:

Estrategia
www.estrategia.cl

El Mercurio (Santiago)
www.elmercurio.cl

Santiago Times (Internet only, in English)
www.chip.cl

RADIO & TV

Radio broadcasting is less regulated than before, with many stations on both AM and FM bands. TV stations include state-owned TVN (Televisión Nacional), the Universidad Católica's Channel 13 and several private stations. International cable services are widely available.

TIME

Most of the year Chile is four hours behind GMT/UTC, but from mid-December to mid-March (summer), the country observes daylight saving time and is three hours behind. Easter Island is two hours behind the mainland.

ELECTRICITY

The electricity supply is 220V. Sockets take two round prongs, and adapters are readily available.

WEIGHTS & MEASURES

The metric system is official.

LAUNDRY

Self-service laundries have become more common, but it's only slightly dearer to leave your load and pick it up later. Most budget hotels have a place to wash clothes; maid service is usually reasonable, but agree on charges beforehand.

HEALTH

In some areas, raw vegetables may be suspect. *Ceviche* (marinated seafood) may also be questionable, and red tide conditions can make all shellfish toxic. Santiago's drinking water is adequately treated, and the author has drunk tap water in most areas without problems, but bottled mineral water is a good alternative. In the south there have been isolated cases of rodent-borne hantavirus which, while rare, is frequently lethal.

Basic Rules & Precautions
Most Chilean food is relatively bland and shouldn't cause problems, but take care with shellfish, such as mussels and scallops, served raw. Take precautions with rural drinking water, as latrines may be close to wells or local people may take untreated water from streams or ditches. Water in the Atacama has a strong taste, often salty, due to its high mineral content; Easter Island's water has a similar reputation, but the author found it both safe and tasty.

WOMEN TRAVELERS
Chile is generally safe for women in groups or alone, though it's important to take certain precautions. Avoid hitching a ride in a vehicle in which you are outnumbered by males, and remember that in certain areas population centers are few and widely separated so the rides are long. A Swedish reader complained that the prejudice Chilean men have toward Scandinavian women accompanied her wherever she went. Although the fantasy of sexual liberalism is extended to European and North American women, it does not seem to translate into aggressive behavior toward them beyond the occasional *piropo* (a comment made out loud to a woman passing in the street), which is best ignored.

Chilean women are very gregarious so it's rare to see them alone in public places. Since waiters find it unusual to see a woman dining alone, they may allow time for your expected companion to arrive!

GAY & LESBIAN TRAVELERS
While Chile is a strongly Catholic country and homosexuality or even talk of it is taboo to many, there are enclaves of tolerance, most notably in Santiago. Since Chilean males in general are more physically demonstrative than their counterparts in Europe or North America, behaviors like a vigorous embrace will seem innocuous even to some who dislike homosexuals. Likewise, lesbians walking hand-in-hand will attract little attention, since Chilean women frequently do so, but this would be indiscreet for males.

Chile's only gay-rights organization is the Movimiento Unificado de Minorías Sexu-

ales (MUMS; ☎ 02-6347557, www.minorias.in.cl), Viollier 87, Santiago.

USEFUL ORGANIZATIONS
The Corporación Nacional Forestal (Conaf, ☎ 02-6711850), administers national parks from Av Bulnes 259, Departamento 206, Santiago; its regional offices are also helpful.

Travelers interested in environmental conservation might contact Comité Pro Defensa de la Fauna y Flora (Codeff; ☎ 02-2510287), Av Francisco Bilbao 691, Providencia, Santiago. Climbers should call the Federación de Andinismo (☎ 02-2220888), Almirante Simpson 77, Santiago. The Sociedad Lonko Kilapán (☎ 02-213134), Aldunate 12, Temuco, promotes sustainable development among indigenous peoples.

DANGERS & ANNOYANCES
Personal Security & Theft
Truly violent crime is rare in Santiago, but purse snatchings are not unusual. Valparaíso has a reputation for robberies in some neighborhoods. Summer is the crime season at beach resorts – be alert for pickpockets and be careful with valuables.

Unauthorized political protests can be contentious, especially on the September 11th anniversary of the 1973 coup. After the arrest of General Pinochet in London in late 1998, both the British and Spanish embassies were targets of ugly rightist demonstrations. US institutions, such as banks and Mormon churches, have also been past targets of protest.

For emergencies call ☎ 133, the nationwide number for *carabineros* (police); updated information on border crossings is also available.

Police & the Military
In routine types of circumstances, carabineros behave professionally and politely; *never* attempt to bribe them. Avoid photographing military installations. In the unlikely event of a coup or similar emergency, carry identification and contact your embassy or consulate for advice.

Carabineros may use tear gas or water cannons – known as *guanacos*, after the spitting wild camelids – to break up demonstrations.

CHILE

Natural Hazards

Volcanic eruptions are not rare: in 1991 Volcán Hudson, in the Aisén Region, buried Chile Chico and Los Antiguos, Argentina, knee-deep in ash. Earthquakes are common and can be serious.

Volcanoes usually give notice before blowing big, but a few resorts are especially vulnerable, notably Pucón, beneath Volcán Villarrica. Earthquakes strike without warning and local buildings, especially adobe constructions, are often unsafe; travelers in budget hotels should make contingency plans for safety or evacuation before going to sleep.

Recreational Hazards

Many of the finest beach areas have dangerous offshore currents. While some beaches are polluted, there are usually warning signs. Because of accidents, authorities discourage solo trekking in wilderness areas like Torres del Paine.

BUSINESS HOURS

Most businesses open by 8 am, but shops close at midday for several hours, then reopen until closing at 8 or 9 pm. In Santiago, government offices and many businesses have adopted a 9 am to 6 pm schedule. Banks and some government offices are open to the public mornings only.

PUBLIC HOLIDAYS & SPECIAL EVENTS

Throughout the year, Chileans celebrate a variety of local and national cultural festivals. Other than religious holidays, the most significant are the mid-September *fiestas patrias*. Government offices and businesses close on the following national holidays:

Año Nuevo (New Year's Day)
  January 1
Semana Santa (Holy Week)
  March/April (dates vary)
Día del Trabajo (Labor Day)
  May 1
Glorias Navales (Naval Battle of Iquique)
  May 21
Corpus Christi
  May 30
San Pedro y San Pablo (St Peter's and
  St Paul's Day)
  June 29

Asunción de la Virgen (Assumption)
  August 15
Día de Unidad Nacional (Day of National Unity)
  replaces the contentious September 11 Pronunciamiento Militar de 1973 (Military Coup of 1973), but the latter is not likely to disappear from the consciousness of both pro- and anti-Pinochet forces
  First Monday of September
Día de la Independencia Nacional (Independence Day)
  September 18
Día del Ejército (Armed Forces Day)
  September 19
Día de la Raza (Columbus Day)
  October 12
Todos los Santos (All Saints' Day)
  November 1
Inmaculada Concepción (Immaculate Conception)
  December 8
Navidad (Christmas Day)
  December 25

ACTIVITIES

Soccer is the most widespread spectator and participant sport. Others include tennis, basketball, volleyball and cycling, while summer outdoor activities like canoeing, climbing, kayaking, mountain biking, trekking, windsurfing and hang gliding are gaining popularity. Rivers such as the Maipo, Claro, Futaleufú and Biobío are popular for whitewater rafting, but hydroelectric development threatens the Biobío.

In summer, most Chileans head to the beach. In winter, skiing, although expensive, can be world-class. The country's best downhill skiing is found in Middle Chile's high cordillera, from June to September.

WORK

Many travelers work as English-language instructors in Santiago, but wages are fairly low and full-time employment is rare. Reputable employers insist on work or residence permits (increasingly difficult to obtain) from the Departamento de Extranjería (☎ 02-6725320), Moneda 1342 in Santiago, open 9 am to 1:30 pm weekdays.

Other possibilities include bar work, street performing or volunteering with Chilean environmental organizations.

ACCOMMODATIONS

Accommodations, ranging from basic hostels and campgrounds to five-star hotels, are reasonable by North American or European standards. Summer prices may be 10 to 20% higher than the rest of the year.

Camping & Refugios

Sernatur has a free brochure listing campgrounds nationwide. The usually woodsy sites generally have hot showers, toilets and laundry, firepits, a restaurant or snack bar and a grocery; some have swimming pools or lake access. The Turistel camping guide has more detail and superb maps.

Many campgrounds discriminate against backpackers by imposing a five-person minimum, so for singles or couples they are often dearer than basic hotels. Free camping is possible in some remote areas, but usually with no facilities.

Refugios are rustic shelters, either free or very cheap, in national parks.

Hostels

Chile has a growing network of youth hostels; for details, contact the Asociación Chilena de Albergues Turísticos Juveniles (☎ 02-2333220), Hernando de Aguirre 201, Oficina 602, Providencia, Santiago. In summer (January and February), inexpensive local hostels often occupy temporary sites at stadiums, campgrounds, schools and churches.

Casas de Familia & Hospedajes

In summer, especially in the Lake District, families offer inexpensive rooms with kitchen and laundry privileges, hot showers, breakfast and local hospitality. Longer established, more permanent places tend to adopt the name *hospedaje*. Ask at tourist offices.

Pensiones & Residenciales

Differences between these inexpensive permanent forms of accommodations are vague – both may be called hotels.

FOOD

The cool waters of the Humboldt Current provide superb fish and shellfish, while the fields, orchards and pastures of Middle Chile fill the table with fine produce and meat. The best Chilean cuisine, though, may be priced beyond the reach of budget travelers.

Places to Eat

Distinctions among 'restaurants,' which range from simple snack bars to sumptuous international venues, are ambiguous. Central markets in most cities have small, cheap eateries of surprisingly high quality.

Bars serve snacks and drinks (alcoholic and nonalcoholic), while *fuentes de soda* offer tea, coffee and sandwiches. *Cafeterías* serve modest meals. A *salón de té* is not literally a teahouse, but a bit more upmarket than a cafetería. A *picada* or *picá* is a modest informal restaurant in a family home, frequented by locals, with a limited menu (often seafood) and substantial portions.

Quality and service distinguish fully fledged *restaurantes*. Many places offer a cheap set meal *(comida corrida* or *colación)* for lunch or, less often, for dinner. Some common dishes are listed below.

Breakfast

Toast, marmalade, *paila* (eggs, named after the pan in which they are fried and served), coffee and tea are usual breakfast fare. Sandwiches are common throughout the day; among the fillings are *churrasco* (steak), *jamón* (ham) and *queso* (cheese). Cold ham and cheese make an *aliado* which, when heated to melt the cheese, is a Barros Jarpa, after the Chilean painter. Steak with melted cheese is a Barros Luco, after former president Ramón Barros Luco (1910-15). Beefsteak with tomato and other vegetables is a *chacarero*.

Snacks

The cheapest fast food is a *completo*, a hot dog oozing absolutely everything. Arrivals from Argentina will find the individual Chilean *empanada* larger and more filling than its trans-Andean counterpart, so don't order a dozen for lunch or your bus trip. Chilean empanadas are *de pino* (ground beef) or *de queso* (cheese), fried or baked. *Humitas* are corn tamales. *Onces* (literally 'elevens') are Chilean teatime snacks, usually served in the afternoon.

Main Meals

Lunch is the day's biggest meal. Set menus, almost identical at cheaper restaurants, usually consist of *cazuela* (a broth with potato or maize and beef or chicken), a main course of rice with beef or chicken and a simple dessert. *Porotos* (beans) are a common budget dish. *Pastel de choclo*, a maize casserole filled with vegetables, chicken and beef, is delicious and hearty.

CHILE

The biggest standard meal is *lomo a lo pobre*, an enormous slab of beef topped with two fried eggs and buried in fries – monitor your cholesterol count. Beef, in a variety of cuts and styles of preparation, is the most popular main course at *parrillas* like those in Argentina. *Pollo con arroz* (chicken with rice) is another common offering.

Seafood

Chilean seafood is varied. *Curanto*, a hearty stew of fish, shellfish, chicken, pork, lamb, beef and potato, is a specialty of Chiloé and Patagonia.

Sopa de mariscos is a brothy seafood soup, while *cazuela de mariscos* is more a stew. Fish soup is *sopa de pescado*, while *paila marina* is a fish chowder. Try *chupe de congrio* (conger eel stew) or, if available, *chupe de locos* (abalone stew), both cooked in a thick sauce of butter, bread crumbs, cheese and spices. Locos may be in *veda* (quarantine) because of over-exploitation. Some dishes, like *erizos* (sea urchins), are acquired tastes.

Do not miss market restaurants in cities like Iquique, Concepción, Temuco and Puerto Montt, but insist on thorough cooking of all shellfish. A few seafood terms are worth knowing:

cangrejo, jaiva	crab
centolla	king crab
cholgas, choritos	mussels
ostras	oysters
camarones grandes	prawns
machas	razor clams
ostiones	scallops
mariscos	shellfish
camarones	shrimp
calamares	squid

Ethnic Food

Santiago's ethnic restaurants fill many pages in the phone book. French, Italian, Spanish, German and Chinese are the most common, but Brazilian, Middle Eastern, Mexican and others are also available. Northern Chilean cities have many *chifas* (Chinese restaurants), offering a pleasant change of pace.

Vegetarian Food

Most Chileans are very fond of meat, but vegetarianism is no longer the mark of an eccentric. Santiago has excellent vegetarian fare and every town has a produce market.

Desserts

Dessert is commonly fresh fruit or ice cream. Also try *arroz con leche* (rice pudding), *flan* (egg custard) and *tortas* (cakes). Lake District bakers of German descent prepare exquisite *kuchen* (pastries) filled with local fruit – especially raspberries.

DRINKS
Nonalcoholic Drinks

Chileans guzzle all the usual soft drinks and some local varieties, plus mineral water.

Mote con huesillo, sold by street vendors, is a peach nectar with barley kernels. *Licuados* are milk-blended fruit drinks, sometimes made with water and often with too much sugar. Common flavors are banana, *durazno* (peach) and *pera* (pear).

In the past semisoluble instant coffee was the norm, but espresso is becoming more common. Normally, tea is served black, usually with lemon. Try *aguas* (herbal teas) such as *manzanilla* (chamomile) or the digestive *boldo*.

Alcoholic Drinks

Chilean wines should satisfy most alcoholic thirsts, but don't miss the powerful *pisco* (grape brandy), often served in the form of a *pisco sour* (with lemon juice, egg white and powdered sugar). Pisco may also be served with *chilcano* (ginger ale) or *capitán* (vermouth).

Escudo is the best bottled beer, but *chopp* (draft beer, pronounced 'shop') is cheaper and often better. A cherrylike fruit, *guinda*, is the basis of *guindado*, a fermented alcoholic drink with brandy, cinnamon and clove.

Wines & Wine Regions Wine-growing districts stretch from the Norte Chico's Copiapó valley to the Biobío. The number of regions and the abrupt topography produce a diverse harvest. Atacama wineries specialize in pisco, but also produce small quantities of white and sparkling wines. Middle Chile's *zona de regadío* produces mostly cabernets and other reds, but acreages planted for whites are increasing. Reds give way to whites in the transitional Maule region, while the Biobío drainage has only recently converted to grape growing. Farther south, commercial production is precarious.

Wine-lovers should read Harm de Blij's *Wine Regions of the Southern Hemisphere* (1985).

ENTERTAINMENT
Nightclubs
In cities like Santiago and Viña, nightclubs can be tacky affairs where traditional music and dances are sanitized and presented in glitzy settings for foreigners. In port cities, they can be disreputable joints.

Cinemas
In the capital and in larger cities like Valparaíso and Viña del Mar, theaters screen the latest films from Europe, Hollywood and Latin America. Repertory houses, cultural centers and universities offer the classics or less commercial films. Prices have risen in recent years, but are still reasonable; midweek discounts are common.

Theater
Throughout the country, live theater is well attended and of high quality; it ranges from the classics and serious drama to burlesque. In the Lake District, many towns offer seasonal productions at cultural festivals.

Peñas
Peñas are nightclubs whose performers offer unapologetically political, folk-based material. The New Chilean Song Movement had its origins in the peñas of the 1960s.

SPECTATOR SPORTS
The most popular spectator sport is soccer, whose British origins are obvious in team names like Santiago Morning and Everton; the main teams are Colo Colo, Universidad de Chile and Universidad Católica. Other popular spectator sports include tennis, boxing and, increasingly, basketball.

SHOPPING
Artisans *ferias* (markets) display varied crafts, especially in the Santiago borough of Bellavista, Viña del Mar, Valdivia, the Puerto Montt suburb of Angelmó and the village of Dalcahue (Chiloé). Copper and leather goods are excellent, and northern woolens resemble those of Peru or Bolivia.

Mapuche artisans produce ceramics, basketry, silverware, woven goods and carvings.

Getting There & Away

AIR
Airports & Airlines
Santiago's Aeropuerto Internacional Arturo Merino Benítez, the main port of entry, also has a domestic terminal. Most major cities the length of the country have good airports, some with international service to neighboring countries.

LanChile is the traditional flag carrier, but major North American and European airlines, and South American carriers also serve Santiago. Only LanChile flies to Rapa Nui (Easter Island).

Entrance & Departure Taxes
US citizens arriving by air pay an entrance fee of US$45, valid for the life of the passport; this is a Chilean response to US visa-processing charges for Chileans. Australians pay US$30 and Canadians US$55. The international departure tax of US$18 is payable in US dollars or pesos.

Peru
LanChile, Lacsa and Copa fly to Lima, but since the demise of AeroPerú there are no direct flights to Cuzco.

Bolivia
LAB flies daily from Santiago to various Bolivian cities, including La Paz (US$215 one way), Santa Cruz (US$261 one way) and Cochabamba (US$240 one way), sometimes via Iquique or Arica. LanChile also flies to La Paz and Santa Cruz.

Argentina
Many airlines fly from Santiago to Buenos Aires (from US$150 return), and there are also flights to Mendoza (US$91) and Córdoba. The Argentine carrier TAN links Puerto Montt to Bariloche (US$62) and Temuco to Neuquén (US$88).

Falkland Islands
In April 1999 flights between Chile and Stanley were suspended in retaliation for

CHILE

Pinochet's arrest. See the Falklands chapter's Getting There & Away section for further information on air services.

Other South American Countries

Santiago also offers connections to every other South American country except the Guianas, often via intermediate stops like Lima and Buenos Aires. LanChile usually has the most direct services.

LAND & WATER
Peru

Tacna to Arica is the only land crossing from Peru; for details, see the Arica section.

Bolivia

Road connections between Bolivia and Chile are improving. There are also buses from Oruro (Bolivia) to Iquique. A popular connection for travelers is between San Pedro de Atacama (Chile) and Uyuni (Bolivia) on a 4WD tour of the remote and beautiful salar region of southwest Bolivia.

A weekly train and occasional buses link Calama to Ollagüe, connecting to Oruro and La Paz. For details, see the Calama section.

Argentina

Except in far southern Patagonia and Tierra del Fuego, travel to Argentina involves crossing the Andes; some passes close in winter. The Salta-Baquedano rail crossing is not a regular passenger service. For information on passes call the Carabineros (☎ 133).

Lake District crossings, involving bus-boat shuttles, are popular in summer, so make advance bookings. Since the opening of the Camino Austral south of Puerto Montt, it has become more common to cross the border there. The most common routes to Argentina follow.

Calama to Salta Buses on this route now use the Paso de Jama via Jujuy, but bookings are heavy. A weekly Argentine freight train also carries passengers from Salta to Socompa, but it's difficult to catch the uncomfortable Chilean freight to Baquedano.

La Serena to San Juan The 4779m Agua Negra pass is open to automobile traffic, but there's no bus service.

Santiago to Mendoza Many buses and *taxi colectivos* serve the Libertadores crossing.

Talca to Malargüe Open summer only, this spectacular crossing has weekly bus service.

Temuco to Zapala & Neuquén Occasional buses use the 1884m Pino Hachado pass along the upper Biobío in summer. An alternative is the 1298m Icaima pass.

Temuco to San Martín de los Andes On this popular route, regular summer buses use the Mamuil Malal pass (Paso Tromen to Argentines).

Valdivia to San Martín de los Andes This is a bus-ferry combination over Paso Hua Hum.

Osorno to Bariloche via Paso Cardenal Samoré (Puyehue) Frequent buses use this rapid Lake District crossing.

Puerto Montt to Bariloche via Parque Nacional Vicente Pérez Rosales This bus-ferry combination crosses scenic Lago Todos los Santos.

Puerto Ramírez to Esquel There are two options here, via Futaleufú or Carrenleufú.

Coihaique to Comodoro Rivadavia The several weekly bus services are usually heavily booked.

Chile Chico to Los Antiguos Frequent buses shuttle between these small towns on the south shore of Lago General Carrera (Lago Buenos Aires to Argentines).

Puerto Natales & Parque Nacional Torres del Paine to Río Turbio & El Calafate Frequent buses connect Puerto Natales to Río Turbio, with connections to Río Gallegos and El Calafate. At least twice weekly in summer, buses go from Torres del Paine and Puerto Natales to El Calafate, the gateway to Argentina's Parque Nacional Los Glaciares.

Punta Arenas to Río Gallegos There are many buses daily on this route (5½ hours).

Punta Arenas to Tierra del Fuego From Punta Arenas, it's a three-hour ferry ride or a 10-minute flight to Porvenir, on Chilean Tierra del Fuego, with two buses weekly to Río Grande (Argentina), connecting to Ushuaia. Some buses go straight to Ushuaia from Punta Arenas.

Getting Around

AIR
Domestic Air Services
LanChile, Ladeco and Avant offer domestic services, including some discount seats. All have computerized booking services, accept phone reservations and publish detailed timetables. Avant fares are generally lower, but the difference is not as great as it once was.

Regional airlines include DAP (from Punta Arenas to Tierra del Fuego and Antarctica), and Lassa and Líneas Aéreas Robinson Crusoe (to the Juan Fernández archipelago). Air taxis connect settlements in the Aisén region.

Air Passes
For US$250, LanChile's 30-day Visit Chile Pass allows flights to and from selected airports either north or south of Santiago (or, for an additional fee, both), but international passengers arriving on other airlines pay US$350. Available only to nonresidents, passes must be purchased outside Chile. Ladeco has a similar pass.

Domestic Departure Tax
The domestic airport departure tax, about US$7, is usually included in the fare.

BUS
Long-distance buses are comfortable (sometimes luxurious), fast and punctual. They usually have toilets and either serve meals or make regular food stops. By European or North American standards, fares are a bargain, but they differ among companies. *Ofertas* (promotions) can reduce normal fares by half; ask for student discounts.

Most cities have a central terminal, but in a few towns, companies have separate offices. Except near holidays, advance booking is unnecessary.

Types of Buses
Long-distance buses are either *Pullman* (with ordinary reclining seats) or *salón cama* (sleepers, with extra leg room).The latter may cost double ordinary buses, but merit consideration on long hauls. Ordinary fares are reasonable; a good rule of thumb is US$2 per hour or less.

On back roads, transport is slower and less frequent, the buses older and more basic. They often lack reclining seats and may be packed with peasants and their produce. *Micros* or *liebres* are city buses.

TRAIN
Southbound trains connect Santiago with Temuco. Classes of service are *economía*, *salón* and *cama* (sleeper). Hardbacked economy seats, though very cheap, are uncomfortable; most travelers will prefer salón.The costlier cama class has upper and lower bunks.

Schedules change, so check an official timetable. Major destinations (with salón fares) include Concepción (US$17, nine hours) and Temuco (US$21, 13 hours).

Commuter trains run from Rancagua to Santiago, and from Quillota to Viña del Mar and Valparaíso.

CAR & MOTORCYCLE
Operating a car is cheaper than in Europe but dearer than in the USA; the price of gasoline *(bencina)* is about US$0.50 per liter in Santiago. There is little price difference between 97-octane *(ultra verde)* and 81-octane *(común)*; unleaded gas is widely available. Foreign drivers need an International or Inter-American Driving Permit.

The Automóvil Club Chileno (Acchi, ☎ 02-2125702), Av Vitacura 8620, Vitacura, Santiago, offers members of affiliated overseas clubs low-cost road service and towing, plus discounts on accommodations, camping, rental cars, tours and other services.

Rental
To rent a car you must have a valid driver's license, be at least 25 years of age and present either a credit card or a large cash deposit.

The cheapest vehicles can be hired for US$50 to US$65 per day with 150km to 200km included (sometimes with unlimited mileage), plus insurance, gas and tax.

Weekend rates (about US$125) or unlimited mileage weekly rates (US$340 to US$450) are a better value.

BICYCLE
Racing bicycles are suitable for paved routes, but on gravel roads, a mountain bike (*todo terreno*) is a better choice. Southwards from Temuco, be prepared for rain; north of Santiago, water is scarce. In some areas, the wind can slow your progress; north to south is generally easier than south to north. Motorists are usually courteous, but on narrow roads they can be a hazard.

HITCHHIKING
Chile is one of the best countries on the continent for hitching. Vehicles are often packed with families but truckers can be helpful – try asking for rides at *servicentros* on the Panamericana. In Aisén and Magallanes, where distances are great and vehicles few, expect long waits and carry warm, windproof, waterproof clothing. Also carry snacks and water, especially in the desert.

Along the Panamericana, hitching is fairly easy as far as Puerto Montt, but competition is heavy in summer. In the Atacama, you may wait for some time, but almost every lift will be a long one. Along the Camino Austral, vehicles are few, except from Coihaique to Puerto Aisén.

Bear in mind, however, that although many travelers hitchhike, it's potentially hazardous. Just because hitching tips appear in this book doesn't mean hitching is recommended.

BOAT
Although buses cover parts of the Camino Austral between Puerto Montt and Coihaique, it's easier to take a ferry from Puerto Montt or Chiloé to Chaitén or Puerto Chacabuco. For detailed information, see the respective geographical entries.

Puerto Montt to Puerto Chacabuco & Laguna San Rafael Navimag and Transmarchilay boats sail from Puerto Montt to Puerto Chacabuco (the port of Coihaique). Transmarchilay runs the tourist ship *Skorpios* and Navimag runs the ferry *Evangelistas* to Laguna San Rafael. Patagonia Connection also runs a catamaran from Puerto Chacabuco to Laguna San Rafael.

Puerto Montt to Puerto Natales Navimag's *Puerto Edén* covers this route weekly in four days and three nights.

Chiloé to the Mainland The most frequent connection is with Transmarchilay or Cruz del Sur ferries from Chacao, at the northern tip of the island, to Pargua, across the Canal de Chacao. There are other Navimag and Transmarchilay services from Quellón (on Chiloé) to Chaitén or Puerto Chacabuco (on the mainland).

La Arena to Puelche Transmarchilay's shuttle ferry, about 45km southeast of Puerto Montt, connects two northerly segments of the Camino Austral year-round.

Hornopirén to Caleta Gonzalo The last mainland stop southbound on the Camino Austral, Hornopirén is a scenic village where, in summer, Transmarchilay ferries sail to Caleta Gonzalo, about 60km north of Chaitén.

Puerto Ibáñez to Chile Chico There's an automobile/passenger ferry between Puerto Ibáñez, on Lago General Carrera south of Coihaique, to the border town of Chile Chico.

Punta Arenas to Tierra del Fuego There are daily ferry crossings from Punta Arenas to Porvenir.

LOCAL TRANSPORT
To/From the Airport
Airport shuttles and buses are cheap and frequent in Santiago. Elsewhere, airlines often provide airport shuttles. In a few places, public transport and taxis are the only options.

Bus
Even small towns have extensive bus systems; buses are clearly numbered and usually carry a sign indicating their destination. Pay your fare and the driver will give you a ticket, which may be checked by an inspector.

Taxi
Most cabs are metered but fares vary. Where there's no meter, agree upon the fare in advance. Tipping is unnecessary, but round off the fare for convenience.

Santiago

Chile's sprawling capital is really many cities in one – Santiago proper, the former colonial core, is surrounded by another 31 *comunas* of greater or lesser antiquity that have coalesced to form the present megacity. Highrises have sprouted in the downtown area and in the comuna of Providencia, which is rapidly becoming the city's commercial and financial center. With more than 4 million inhabitants, Santiago is one of South America's largest cities.

History

Indians nearly obliterated Santiago six months after Pedro de Valdivia founded it in 1541. Even in the late 16th century, only 700 Spaniards and mestizos, plus Indian laborers and servants, inhabited its 200 adobe houses. Occasionally flooded by the Río Mapocho, it still lacked a safe water supply and communications between town and country were hazardous.

By the late 18th century, new *tajamares* (dikes) restrained the Mapocho, and improved roads carried increased commerce. By the 19th century, a railway linked the capital's more than 100,000 inhabitants to the port of Valparaíso.

Poverty and paternalistic *fundos* drove farm laborers and tenants north to the nitrate mines and then into the cities; from 1865 to 1875, Santiago's population rose from 115,000 to more than 150,000.

Industrialization created jobs, but never enough to satisfy demand. In the 1960s, continued rural turmoil resulted in squatter settlements around Santiago. Planned decentralization has eased the pressure, and regularization, including granting of titles, has transformed many callampas, but they still contrast with affluent eastern comunas like Vitacura and Las Condes.

Orientation

Santiago's core is a compact, triangular area bounded by the Río Mapocho in the north, the Vía Norte Sur in the west, and Av General O'Higgins (the Alameda) in the south. Key public buildings line the Plaza de Armas, from which the pedestrian Paseo Ahumada leads south. Paseo Huérfanos is a block south of the plaza.

Attractive Cerro Santa Lucía overlooks the Alameda near Plaza Baquedano. The other main park is Cerro San Cristóbal (Parque Metropolitano), north of Av Providencia. Between the park and the Río Mapocho, on either side of Av Pío Nono, is the lively Bellavista area. South of the Río Mapocho, Parque Forestal forms a verdant buffer between downtown and residential zones.

Information

Tourist Offices Sernatur (☎ 02-2361416), Av Providencia 1550 (Metro: Manuel Montt), is open 9 am to 5 pm weekdays, 9 am to 1 pm Saturday. English is spoken, and the office has maps and abundant leaflets on the entire country. There's another office at the airport, and at the San Borja bus terminal.

The Municipalidad de Santiago maintains a tourist kiosk in the middle of the Ahumada pedestrian mall just south of Paseo Huérfanos that is open 9 am to 9 pm daily. The personnel are helpful but this office does not have as ample a supply of written information.

Sernatur offices and the Municipalidad all provide a free pocket-size *Plano del Centro de Santiago*, a map of downtown, Providencia and other inner comunas, with a useful Metro diagram.

Money Cambios on Agustinas between Bandera and Ahumada change cash and traveler's checks. Some open Saturday mornings. American Express Bank, Agustinas 1360, exchanges traveler's checks for cash dollars. ATMs are everywhere downtown and in Providencia.

Post & Communications The main post office (Correo Central), on the Plaza de Armas, handles poste restante and also has a philatelic desk. For long-distance calls, you can go to Entel, Paseo Huérfanos 1133, or CTC at Moneda 1151. The Café Virtual (☎ 02-6355548), Alameda 145, has Internet access.

Travel Agencies For bargains on air tickets, try the Student Flight Center (☎ 02-3350395, stflictr@ctc-mundo.net), Hernando de Agurre 201, Oficina 401 (Metro: Tobalaba). The AmEx representative is Turismo

SANTIAGO

PLACES TO STAY		PLACES TO EAT	
9	Hotel Caribe	2	El Caramaño
10	Hotel Indiana	5	Tasca Mediterránea
11	Nuevo Hotel Valparaíso	7	El Antojo de Gauguin
12	Hotel Cervantes	23	Da Carla
17	Residencial del Norte	28	Bar Nacional
18	Hotel España	29	Chez Henry
31	Hotel Santa Lucía	33	Izakaya Yoko
40	Hotel Los Arcos	34	Les Assassins
47	Hotel Montecarlo	36	Pérgola de la Plaza
49	Hotel Principado	39	Ocean Pacific's
52	Albergue Hostelling	41	Tú y Yo
	International	42	Café Haití
53	Hotel Turismo Japón	43	Café Caribe
56	Hotel Carrera	45	Le Due Torri
74	Residencial Alemana	46	San Marco
75	Residencial Mery	51	Plaza Garibaldi
80	Hotel Vegas	58	El Novillero
82	Hotel París	63	Puente de los
83	Residencial Londres		Suspiros

INDEPENDENCIA

Río Mapocho

Av Balmaceda

Parque
Los Reyes

Parque
Quinta
Normal

Parque
Portales

Estación
Santa Ana

Catedral

Plaza Brasil

Estación
Los Héroes

Estación
República

Av O'Higgins (Alameda)

Estación Unión
Latino Americana

Universidad
de Santiago

Estación
Central

Estación Universidad
de Santiago

Terminal
San Borja

Estación
Central

To Terminal
de Buses Alameda

Parque
O'Higgins

Club Hípico

Blanco Encalada

0   200   400 m
0   200   400 yards

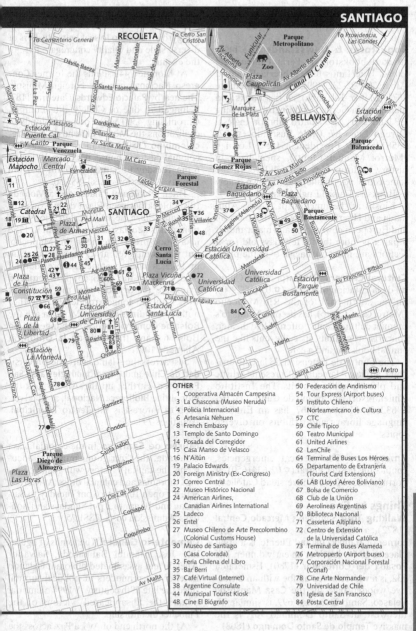

SANTIAGO

OTHER

1 Cooperativa Almacén Campesina
3 La Chascona (Museo Neruda)
4 Policía Internacional
6 Artesanía Nehuen
8 French Embassy
13 Templo de Santo Domingo
14 Posada del Corregidor
15 Casa Manso de Velasco
16 N'Aitún
19 Palacio Edwards
20 Foreign Ministry (Ex-Congreso)
21 Correo Central
22 Museo Histórico Nacional
24 American Airlines,
   Canadian Airlines International
25 Ladeco
26 Entel
27 Museo Chileno de Arte Precolombino
   (Colonial Customs House)
30 Museo de Santiago
   (Casa Colorada)
32 Feria Chilena del Libro
35 Bar Berri
37 Café Virtual (Internet)
38 Argentine Consulate
44 Municipal Tourist Kiosk
48 Cine El Biógrafo

50 Federación de Andinismo
54 Tour Express (Airport buses)
55 Instituto Chileno
   Norteamericano de Cultura
57 CTC
59 Chile Típico
60 Teatro Municipal
61 United Airlines
62 LanChile
64 Terminal de Buses Los Héroes
65 Departamento de Extranjería
   (Tourist Card Extensions)
66 LAB (Lloyd Aéreo Boliviano)
67 Bolsa de Comercio
68 Club de la Unión
69 Aerolíneas Argentinas
70 Biblioteca Nacional
71 Cassetería Altiplano
72 Centro de Extensión
   de la Universidad Católica
73 Terminal de Buses Alameda
76 Metropuerto (Airport buses)
77 Corporación Nacional Forestal
   (Conaf)
78 Cine Arte Normandie
79 Universidad de Chile
81 Iglesia de San Francisco
84 Posta Central

CHILE

Cocha (☎ 02-2301000), Av El Bosque Norte 0430, Las Condes (Metro: Tobalaba).

Bookstores & Newsstands The best-stocked bookstore is Feria Chilena del Libro, Huérfanos 623. Librería Eduardo Albers (☎ 02-2327499), 11 de Septiembre 2671 (Metro: Tobalaba), carries books and magazines in German and English, including LP guides. Try also Kuatro Librería Inglesa, Orrego Luco 87. Chile Ilustrado (☎ 02-2358145), Av Providencia 1652, Local 6 (Metro: Manuel Montt), specializes in history, anthropology and folklore. In the same complex, a smaller shop, known simply as Books, sells used English paperbacks.

Kiosks at the junction of Paseos Ahumada and Huérfanos carry North American and European newspapers and magazines. If a paper is more than a few days old (or if sections are missing), haggle over the price.

Cultural Centers The Corporación Cultural de la Estación Mapocho (☎ 02-6972990), on the south bank of the Río Mapocho (Metro: Cal y Canto), has become Santiago's premier cultural center, offering live theater, concerts, art exhibits, special events like the annual book fair and a café.

The Centro de Extensión de la Universidad Católica, Alameda 390, presents artistic and photographic exhibits. The Instituto Chileno-Norteamericano de Cultura (☎ 02-6963215), Moneda 1467, has an English-language library and exhibits on diverse topics.

Emergency For medical emergencies, contact the Posta Central (☎ 02-6341650), at Portugal 125 (Metro: Universidad Católica).

Things to See

Walking Tour Santiago's **Mercado Central** (1872), a wrought-iron structure at the corner of Balmaceda and Puente, is a great place to go for lunch or an early dinner. The **Posada del Corregidor** (1780), Esmeralda 732, is a whitewashed adobe with an attractive wooden balcony; the **Casa Manso de Velasco**, Santo Domingo 699, is similar. To the west, at Santo Domingo 961, is the massive **Templo de Santo Domingo** (1808).

Santiago's historical center is the Plaza de Armas, flanked by the main post office, the **Museo Histórico Nacional** and the colonial

Catedral. At its southwest corner is Paseo Ahumada, where hawkers peddle everything from shampoo to seat belts. Buskers of diverse style and quality congregate here in the evening.

At Morandé 441 stands the former **Congreso Nacional**, now the Foreign Ministry. The nearby **Palacio Edwards**, Catedral 1187, belonged to one of Chile's elite families. Chronicling 4500 years of pre-Columbian civilizations, the **Museo Chileno de Arte Precolombino** (1805), Bandera 361, was the colonial customs house; it's open 10 am to 6 pm Tuesday to Saturday, 10 am to 1 pm Sunday. Admission costs US$3.50.

The late-colonial **Palacio de La Moneda** fills a block between Plaza de la Constitución and Plaza de la Libertad. Construction of this neoclassical mint began in 1788 in a flood-prone site near the Mapocho, but was completed at its present location in 1805; it later became the presidential palace. After the 1973 coup, it required extensive restoration, and the president works but no longer resides here. Other notable buildings near La Moneda are the **Bolsa de Comercio** (stock exchange), at La Bolsa 64, and the **Club de la Unión**, at Alameda 1091.

Just across the Alameda are the **Universidad de Chile** and the colonial **Iglesia de San Francisco**. Farther up the Alameda is the monolithic **Biblioteca Nacional**, at MacIver. Also of interest is the **Teatro Municipal**, Agustinas 794.

Museo de Santiago In the colonial Casa Colorada, this intriguing museum documents the capital's history with maps, paintings, dioramas and colonial dress. At Merced 860, it's open 10 am to 6 pm Tuesday to Saturday and 10 am to 2 pm Sundays and holidays. Admission costs US$1.25.

Cementerio General The tombs of figures like José Manuel Balmaceda, Salvador Allende and assassinated diplomat Orlando Letelier are reminders of political turmoil since the late 19th century. A 1994 memorial honors the 'disappeared' victims of the Pinochet dictatorship.

At the north end of Av La Paz, across the Mapocho via the Cal y Canto bridge, the Cementerio General is open daily during daylight hours.

Cerro Santa Lucía Covered with gardens, footpaths and fountains, Santa Lucía (Huelén to the Mapuche) is a hilltop sanctuary from the congested city center. It's an easy walk from downtown and free guided tours (in Spanish and English) are offered daily by the municipal tourist office.

La Chascona (Museo Neruda) The Fundación Neruda (☎ 02-7778741), Márquez de La Plata 0192, conducts tours of the poet's eclectic Bellavista house on a first-come, first-served basis daily except Monday, 10 am to 1 pm and 3 to 6 pm. Admission costs US$4.50 for adults, half that for children; tours last an hour and are very thorough. The Fundación also arranges tours of Neruda's houses at Isla Negra and Valparaíso.

Cerro San Cristóbal North of the Mapocho, 860m San Cristóbal towers above Santiago. Reached by funicular railway, *teleférico* (cable car), bus or foot, it's part of **Parque Metropolitano**, the capital's largest open space.

In summer, the funicular from Plaza Caupolicán, at the north end of Pío Nono, operates 10 am to 8:30 pm daily; hours are slightly shorter the rest of the year. A short walk from the Terraza Bellavista, the 2000m teleférico departs from the Estación Cumbre and connects San Cristóbal to Av Pedro de Valdivia Norte (a short hike from Metro Pedro de Valdivia); its schedule is slightly different. For about US$4, the funicular-teleférico combination offers a good introduction to Santiago's complex geography.

Places to Stay – Budget

Hostels The custom-built *Albergue Hostelling International* (☎ 02-6718532) is at Cienfuegos 151 (Metro: Los Héroes); plain but clean and comfortable rooms have four to six single beds and private lockers. It has attractive common spaces, a no-frills café, cheap laundry service and luggage storage. Rates are US$12.50 for nonmembers (after six days you automatically become a member), US$10 for members.

Hotels & Residenciales Budget accommodations are abundant and differ more in quality than in price. In the main budget zone, a seedy area near the former Terminal de Buses Norte, lodgings range from squalid to passable.

Dilapidated *Hotel Indiana* (☎ 02-6714251), Rosas 1343, is Santiago's Israeli hangout; beds cost around US$5. Labyrinthine *Hotel Caribe* (☎ 02-6966681), San Martín 851, is better value at US$7.50 per person with shared bath. Though popular, it's large and there's usually a room, though not always a single. Rivaling the Caribe is the more central, slightly cheaper *Nuevo Hotel Valparaíso* (☎ 02-6715698), at San Pablo and Morandé.

In Barrio París Londres, south of the Alameda, *Residencial Londres* (☎ 02-6382215), Londres 54, is great value at US$12 per person; it has clean, secure rooms and pleasant staff, but fills up quickly and singles are few. At *Hotel Paris* (☎ 02-6394037), around the corner at París 813, singles/doubles cost US$15/25.

West of Via Norte Sur, Barrio Brasil's warmly recommended *Residencial del Norte* (☎ 02-6951876), Catedral 2207 (Metro: Santa Ana), charges US$11 per person in a family atmosphere. Also recommended is comparably priced *Residencial Alemana* (☎ 02-6712388), República 220 (Metro: República). Closer to the Metro, but slightly dearer, is *Residencial Mery* (☎ 02-6968883), Pasaje República 36.

Places to Stay – Mid-Range

Rates start around US$17/22 at well-located *Hotel España* (☎ 02-6966066), Morandé 510, for clean but stark rooms, some with balky plumbing. Opinions differ on nearby *Hotel Cervantes* (☎ 02-6965318), Morandé 631, where rooms vary greatly. Rates are US$28/39 with private bath, but there are slightly cheaper doubles with shared bath.

In Barrio Brasil, at Agustinas 2173, family-oriented *Hotel Los Arcos* (☎ 02-6990998) is a good value at US$26/35 without breakfast. Nearby, with spacious gardens, *Hotel Turismo Japón* (☎ 02-6984500), Almirante Barroso 160, is an excellent value at US$35/45 with breakfast. No longer a bargain but still a good value, clean and spacious *Hotel Vegas* (☎ 02-6322498), Londres 49, costs US$43/51.

A perennial favorite, with gracious management, is *Hotel Santa Lucía* (☎ 02-6398201), Huérfanos 779, 4th floor. Attractive rooms are US$47/56 with TV, telephone, safe deposit box, fridge and private bath. Quieter interior rooms are better values.

At friendly *Hotel Montecarlo* (☎ 02-6381176), Victoria Subercaseaux 209 near Cerro Santa Lucía, rooms are small but cheery; beware of street noise. Rates are US$45/52. The quieter *Hotel Principado* (☎ 02-2228142), at Arturo Buhrle 015, just off Vicuña Mackenna (Metro: Baquedano), costs US$60/70.

Places to Stay – Top End

In a well-preserved building at Pedro de Valdivia 027 (Metro: Pedro de Valdivia), dignified *Hotel Orly* (☎ 02-2318947) reflects the Providencia of less commercial times; for US$84/95, rooms are a little small, but the hospitable staff is a big plus.

Charging US$140/160, *Hotel Aloha* (☎ 02-2332230), Francisco Noguera 146 in Providencia (Metro: Pedro de Valdivia), has drawn praise for friendly, attentive staff. At venerable *Hotel Carrera* (☎ 02-6982011), Teatinos 180, rates start at US$210/220.

Places to Eat

Restaurants range from basic (around the bus terminals) and better (around Huérfanos and Ahumada, the Plaza de Armas and the Alameda) to elegant (in Providencia, Las Condes and Bellavista).

There's a string of cheap stand-up places in the south arcade of the Plaza de Armas, where highly regarded *Chez Henry* is no longer cheap, but not outrageous either – try the filling pastel de choclo (about US$7) or take-away dishes. Also serving Chilean specialties, *Bar Nacional*, Bandera 317, is a lunchtime favorite with downtown office workers.

The cheapest fixed-price lunches are at *Peters*, Marchant Pereira 132 (Metro: Pedro de Valdivia); weekdays before 1 pm or after 3 pm, four-course meals, including salad bar, cost only US$2.50. For good, cheap espresso and cocoa, try stand-up bars like *Café Haití* and *Café Caribe*, on Paseo Ahumada.

Carnivores should try *El Novillero*, Moneda 1145. The best vegetarian restaurant is Providencia's expensive *El Huerto*, Orrego Luco 054 (Metro: Pedro de Valdivia), but its café *La Huerta* has bargain lunches. For seafood, visit the historic *Mercado Central*, 4 blocks north of the Plaza de Armas. The tables among the fruit

and vegetable stands, like the classic *Donde Augusto*, have great atmosphere, but the smaller, cheaper places on the periphery are just as good. At Ricardo Cumming 221 (Metro: República), *Ocean Pacific's* is a reasonably priced, family-style seafood restaurant with friendly service and superb homemade bread.

Eateries near Pablo Neruda's old Bellavista haunts, north of the Mapocho, include *El Antojo de Gauguin*, Pío Nono 69; the Spanish *Tasca Mediterránea*, Purísima 165; and *El Caramaño*, Purísima 257 (no sign – ring bell), serving Chilean delicacies in a non-conformist setting. South of the Mapocho, try *Pérgola de la Plaza*, Lastarria 305-321, for wine and pastries.

For pasta, try *Da Carla*, at MacIver 577, or *San Marco*, at Huérfanos 618. More than one reader has found *Le Due Torri*, San Antonio 258, among Santiago's best values. French cuisine is the rule at *Les Assassins*, Merced 297. At Merced 457, *Izakaya Yoko* is authentically Japanese and remarkably inexpensive.

For good Peruvian food at modest prices, try *Puente de los Suspiros*, Brasil 75. *Tú y Yo*, at Brasil 249 in an improving neighborhood, is a good pub/restaurant with Chilean food. The best Mexican (as opposed to Tex-Mex) restaurant is moderately priced *Plaza Garibaldi*, Moneda 2319 (Metro: República). Also good is the *Casa de la Cultura de México*, Bucarest 162 (Metro: Los Leones).

For ice cream, the traditional favorites are *Sebastián*, Andrés de Fuenzalida 26 in Providencia (Metro: Pedro de Valdivia), or *Bravissimo*, Av Providencia 1406 (Metro: Manuel Montt), also good for tea and pastries. They have tough competition, though, from the classy Buenos Aires transplant *Freddo*, at Providencia and Av Suecia (Metro: Los Leones).

Entertainment

For music and drinks Santiago has several pubs in Bellavista, Providencia and Las Condes. *Bar Berri*, at Rosal and Lastarria, is a reasonably priced place to meet locals, as is *Flannery's Irish Geopub* at Encomenderos 83 (Metro: Tobalaba). *N'Aitún*, at Ricardo Cumming 453 in Barrio Brasil, is a bookstore pub with live folk music in an intimate setting.

The cinema district is along Paseo Huérfanos and nearby streets; many cinemas offer Wednesday discounts. The Universidad Católica's **Centro de Extensión**, Alameda 390, has low-priced screenings of international films on a regular basis, as do **Cine Arte Normandie**, Tarapacá 1181, and **Cine El Biógrafo**, Lastarria 181.

Shopping

Crafts and gemstones on sale include lapis lazuli, pottery and copperware, plus carved wooden *moai* (statues) from Easter Island. The Feria Artesanal Indígena, on Cerro Santa Lucía near the Alameda entrance, is a good place for an overview, and there's also well-stocked Chile Típico at Moneda 1025, Local 149.

Bellavista is a popular crafts area, both at Pío Nono's weekend street fair and at shops like Artesanía Nehuen, Dardignac 59, which has a wide selection of materials from throughout the country. Nearby is the Cooperativa Almacén Campesina, Purísima 303.

Several readers enjoyed the market at Los Graneros del Alba, Av Apoquindo 9085; take the Metro to Escuela Militar and catch a bus out Av Apoquindo; from downtown, bus No 344 from the Alameda or No 327 from Av Providencia. For Latin American and Andean music try Cassetería Altiplano in the Arteferia Santa Lucía, Alameda 510.

Getting There & Away

Air Nearly every visitor to Chile arrives in Santiago or passes through the capital at some time. International airlines with Santiago offices include:

Aerolíneas Argentinas
(☎ 02-6393922) Moneda 756

Aeroméxico
(☎ 02-2340001) Ebro 2738, Las Condes

Air New Zealand
(☎ 02-2318626) Andrés de Fuenzalida 17, Oficina 62, Providencia

American Airlines
(☎ 02-6790000) Huérfanos 1199

British Airways
(☎ 02-2329560) Isidora Goyenechea 2934, Oficina 302

Canadian Airlines International
(☎ 02-6883580) Huérfanos 1199, Oficina 311

Continental Airlines
(☎ 02-2044000) Nuevo Tajamar 445, Local 10, Las Condes

KLM
(☎ 02-2017460) San Sebastián 2939, Oficina 202, Las Condes

LAB (Lloyd Aéreo Boliviano)
(☎ 02-6951290) Moneda 1170

Lacsa
(☎ 02-2355500) Barros Borgoño 105, 2nd floor, Providencia

LanChile
(☎ 02-6323442) Agustinas 640
(☎ 02-2323448) Pedro de Valdivia 0139, Providencia

United Airlines
(☎ 02-6320279) Tenderini 171

LanChile, its subsidiary Ladeco and Avant are the main domestic carriers.

Avant
(☎ 02-3353080) Santa Magdalena 75, Oficina 2, Providencia

Ladeco
(☎ 02-6395053) Huérfanos 1157 Pedro de Valdivia 0210, Providencia

Bus Santiago has four domestic-bus terminals. Most northbound buses leave from Terminal San Borja (Metro: Estación Central), Alameda 3250, whose inconspicuous access is via the market alongside the train station. Tur-Bus and Pullman Bus use the Terminal de Buses Alameda at Alameda and Jotabeche (Metro: Universidad de Santiago); Valparaíso/Viña del Mar buses and many southbound carriers depart from the nearby Terminal de Buses Sur (☎ 02-7791385), Alameda 3800. Some northbound buses use Terminal de Buses Los Héroes, on Tucapel Jiménez near the Alameda.

Sample fares (in US dollars) and journey times from Santiago include:

to/from	price	duration
Antofagasta	US$45	18 hours
Arica	US$55	26 hours
Chillán	US$11	6 hours
Concepción	US$14	8 hours
Copiapó	US$28	11 hours
La Serena	US$18	7 hours
Puerto Montt	US$25	16 hours
Punta Arenas	US$100	60 hours
Temuco	US$16	11 hours
Valparaíso	US$4	2 hours

Most international buses use Terminal Sur. Mendoza, Argentina (US$20, seven hours)

CHILE

is the most frequent destination. Other typical fares include Bariloche (US$45), Córdoba (US$60) and Buenos Aires (US$70).

Taxi colectivos to Mendoza are quicker and slightly more expensive (around US$25) than buses; try haggling for discounts outside the peak season.

Train Southbound trains use the Estación Central (☎ 02-6895199), Alameda 3222 (Metro: Estación Central); it's open 7 am to 11 pm daily for ticket sales. Otherwise book at the Venta de Pasajes (☎ 02-6398247), in the Galería Libertador, Alameda 853, Local 21; it's open 8:30 am to 7 pm weekdays, 9 am to 1 pm Saturdays. For sample fares, see this chapter's Getting Around section.

Getting Around
To/From the Airport Aeropuerto Internacional Arturo Merino Benítez (☎ 02-6019001) is in Pudahuel, 26km northwest of downtown Santiago. Tour Express (☎ 02-6717380), Moneda 1529, has about 30 airport buses daily (US$2, ½ hour), between 6:30 am and 9 pm. Metropuerto provides a similar, slightly cheaper service from Los Héroes Metro station. Transfer (☎ 02-7777707) offers door-to-door minibus service for US$5.50 to US$7.50; call a day ahead. Delfos (☎ 02-2266020) has comparable services. Negotiated cab fares are about US$10 (if your Spanish is good).

Bus Buses go to all parts of Santiago, but the system is complex – check destination signs or ask waiting passengers. Fares are usually a flat rate of around US$0.45.

Metro The three-line Metro operates Monday to Saturday 6 am to 10:30 pm, Sundays and holidays 8 am to 10:30 pm. On Línea 1, Dirección Las Condes heads toward Escuela Militar in the eastern suburbs, while Dirección Pudahuel goes to San Pablo (It does *not* reach the international airport.) On the north-south Línea 2, Dirección Centro goes to Puente Cal y Canto near the Mapocho, while Dirección La Cisterna heads toward Lo Ovalle. The newer north-southeast Línea 5 runs between Baquedano, on Línea 1, and La Florida. Baquedano and Los Héroes are the only transfer stations.

Fares vary slightly depending on time of day, but range between US$0.30 and US$0.45. A multiride *boleto inteligente*, available at a small discount, saves time.

Car For details of car-rental rates, see this chapter's Getting Around section. Less well-known companies tend to be cheapest. Several well-known companies have offices in the international airport terminal. City offices include:

Automóvil Club de Chile (Acchi)
  (☎ 02-2746261) Vitacura 8620, Vitacura
Avis
  (☎ 02-3310121) Guardia Vieja 255, Oficina 108, Providencia
Budget
  (☎ 02-2208292) Manquehue Sur 600, Las Condes
Hertz
  (☎ 02-2359666) Costanera Andrés Bello 1469, Providencia

Taxi Colectivo Taxi colectivos, quicker than buses, carry up to five passengers on fixed routes. The fare is about US$0.75 within the city limits, more to outlying suburbs.

Taxi Santiago's abundant metered taxis are moderately priced. Most drivers are honest, courteous and helpful, but a few take roundabout routes and a handful have 'funny' meters. Flag fall costs about US$0.55.

AROUND SANTIAGO
Wineries
The nearest winery is **Viña Santa Carolina** (☎ 02-2382855), Rodrigo de Araya 1341, Nuñoa. The sprawling capital has displaced the vineyards, but the historic *casco* (big house) and *bodegas* (cellars) are open weekends. Also within city limits is **Viña Cousiño Macul**, Av Quilín 7100; tours of the bodegas take place daily at 11 am. Take bus No 39 or 391 from Santo Domingo out Américo Vespucio Sur.

In Pirque, southeast of Santiago, **Viña Concha y Toro** (☎ 02-8503123) is Chile's largest winery. Tours take place daily, except Sunday, 10 am to 1 pm and 3 to 6 pm. To Pirque, take Línea 5 of the Metro to the end of the line at Bellavista, then catch connecting Metrobús No 5.

Viña Undurraga (☎ 02-8172308), 34km southwest of Santiago on the old Melipilla

AROUND SANTIAGO (REGIÓN METROPOLITANA)

road, is open weekdays 9:30 am to noon and 2 to 4 pm. Take Buses Peñaflor's 'Talagante' micro (☎ 02-7761025) from Terminal San Borja, Alameda 3250.

Cajón del Maipo

Southeast of the capital, the Cajón del Maipo (canyon of the Río Maipo) is a major weekend destination for *santiaguinos*.

One of Santiago's closest nature reserves, 10,000-hectare **Reserva Nacional Río Clarillo** has short hiking trails in a scenic tributary canyon of the Cajón, 23km from Pirque. From Pirque (see above), Buses Lac has hourly departures to within 2km of the reserve.

Near the village of San Alfonso, the private nature reserve **Cascada de las Animas**

arranges outings ranging from picnics, day trips and camping to more strenuous activities like hiking, horseback riding and rafting/kayaking, The Santiago office, Expediciones Las Cascadas (☎ 02-2519223) is at Orrego Luco 040, 2nd floor, Providencia.

Only 93km from Santiago, 3000-hectare **Parque Nacional El Morado** rewards hikers with views of 5060m Cerro El Morado at **Laguna El Morado**, a two-hour walk from the humble hot springs of Baños Morales. Conaf maintains a small Centro de Información at the park entrance, where rangers collect US$1.25 admission. T-Arrpue (☎ 02-2117165) runs weekend buses from Santiago's Plaza Italia (Metro: Baquedano) directly to Baños Morales.

CHILE

Overlooking the canyon from a southside perch above the Río Volcán, across from Baños Morales and surrounded by poplars, the **Refugio Alemán** (☎ 02-8501773 in Santiago) is a popular weekend destination throughout the year. Shoestring travelers with their own sleeping bags can crash in the attic for US$12. Its restaurant also serves fine breakfasts, onces and dinners.

Ski Resorts

Chilean ski resorts, mostly above 3300m, are open June to October. Rates are lower in early and late season. Three major resorts are barely an hour from the capital, while the fourth is about two hours away on the Argentine border.

El Colorado, 45km east of the capital up the Mapocho valley, has 16 lifts (mostly drag, four chairs) and 25 runs; tickets cost US$29 weekdays, US$37 weekends. For day trips, contact the Centro de Ski El Colorado (☎ 02-2463344), Av Apoquindo 4900, Local 48, Las Condes.

Only 4km from Farellones, **La Parva** has 13 separate runs ranging from 2662 to 3630m (968m vertical drop); lift tickets cost US$29 in low season, US$39 in peak season. For information, contact Centro de Ski La Parva (☎ 02-2641466), La Concepción 266, Providencia.

Another 14km beyond Farellones, well-planned **Valle Nevado** ranges from 2805 to 3670m, with nine runs up to 1.7km in length. Lift tickets cost US$29 to US$37. For bookings or more details, contact Valle Nevado (☎ 02-2060027) at Gertrudis Echeñique 441, Las Condes.

Portillo, 145km southeast of the capital on the international border, has a dozen lifts and 23 runs with a maximum vertical drop of 340m; it has been the site of several downhill speed records. Day lift tickets cost US$37. Costly packages at **Hotel Portillo** include all meals and eight days of lift tickets; non-residents of Chile can avoid the 21% IVA by paying in US dollars. Cheaper packages, with bunks and shared bath, start at US$620. Moderately priced accommodations are available in the town of Los Andes, below the snow line, 69km to the west. Otherwise contact Centro de Ski Portillo (☎ 02-2630606; portillo@skiarea.mic.cl), Renato Sánchez 4270, Las Condes.

Middle Chile

Middle Chile comprises the Metropolitan Region, plus the regions of Valparaíso, O'Higgins, Maule and Biobío. Its fertile central valley, endowed with rich soils, a pleasant climate and snowmelt for irrigation, is ideal for cereals, fruit and vineyards.

Northwest of Santiago, the port of Valparaíso is one of South America's most distinctive cities, while Viña del Mar and other coastal towns are favorite summer playgrounds. South of Santiago is a string of agricultural and industrial centers.

VALPARAÍSO

Mercantilism retarded colonial Valparaíso's growth, but foreign merchants quickly established themselves after independence – in 1822 one visitor remarked that 'a stranger might almost fancy himself arrived at a British settlement.' After the completion of the Santiago railroad in 1880, Valparaíso (or Valpo) became Chile's financial powerhouse, with over 100,000 residents, but the opening of the Panama Canal in 1914 clobbered the local economy as shipping avoided the Cape Horn route. The Great Depression was a further calamity as it reduced the demand for minerals until after WWII.

The capital of the Fifth Region and site of the National Congress, Valparaíso (population 265,000) is 120km northwest of Santiago. It is an administrative center whose key industries are food processing and fruit and mineral exporting. It depends less on tourism than neighboring Viña del Mar, but many vacationers arrive from nearby beach towns. The navy also plays an important economic role.

Orientation

Probably only a native *porteño* or lifetime resident can fathom Valparaíso's complex geography. In its congested center of sinuous cobbled streets and irregular intersections, most major streets parallel the shoreline, which curves north toward Viña del Mar. Av Errázuriz runs the length of the waterfront, alongside the railway. Behind and above the downtown, the hills are an almost medieval warren of steep footpaths, zigzag roads and blind alleys where even the best map often fails.

MIDDLE CHILE

To Mendoza

To La Serena

La Ligua

V Región

San Felipe

Los Libertadores Tunnel

Parque Provincial Aconcagua

Los Andes

Parque Provincial Volcán Tupungato

Viña del Mar
Valparaíso

Parque Nacional La Campana

Reserva Nacional Lago Peñuelas

Colina

Santuario de la Naturaleza Yerba Loca

SANTIAGO

Cartagena

Puente Alto

San Antonio

Talagante

San Bernardo

Monumento Natural El Morado

Melipilla

Región Metropolitana

Reserva Nacional Río Clarillo

Chapa Verde

Lago Rapel

Rancagua

Sewell

Termas de Cauquenes

Pichilemu

Reserva Nacional de los Cipreses

VI Región

Bucalemu

▲ Volcán El Palomo 4850m

San Fernando

Curicó

Paso del Planchón 2938m

PACIFIC OCEAN

Constitución

Talca

Malargüe

Area de Protección Radal Siete Tazas

Mendoza

Reserva Nacional Los Ruiles

▲ **Reserva Nacional Altos del Lircay**

Cauquenes

Linares

VII Región

Paso Pehuenche 2553m

Ninhue

San Carlos

Tomé

Chillán

Penco

Concepción

San Pedro

Termas de Chillán

Coronel

Lota

VIII Región

ARGENTINA

Laguna de la Laja

Chos Malal

Curanilahue

Los Ángeles

Parque Nacional Laguna del Laja

Lebú

Renaico

Mulchén

Cañete

Parque Nacional Nahuelbuta

Angol

Laguna Agria

Los Sauces

Collipulli

Neuquén

Laguna Lleulleu

Purén

IX Región

To Temuco

Cordillera de los Andes

Río Biobío

Panamericana

0   30   60 km
0   20   40 miles

CHILE

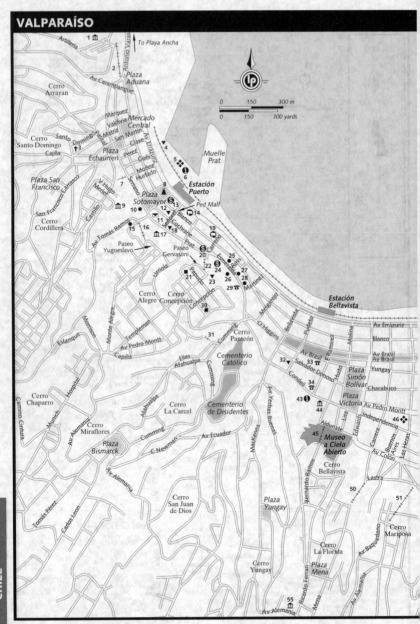

VALPARAÍSO

VALPARAÍSO

PLACES TO STAY
21 Residencial Latina
30 Hospedaje Carrasco
38 Residencial Veracruz
39 Casa Familiar
   Mónica Villegas
47 Hostal Kolping

PLACES TO EAT
4 Bote Salvavidas
12 Valparaíso Eterno
18 La Rotonda
23 Café Turri
32 Bambú
48 Club Peruano

OTHER
1 Museo Naval y Marítimo
3 Iglesia Matriz
5 Feria de Artesanías
6 Departamento de Turismo Kiosk
8 Monumento a los Héroes de Iquique
9 Museo del Mar Lord Cochrane

10 Primera Zona Naval
11 Post Office
13 Inter Cambio
14 British Consulate
15 Tribunales
17 Palacio Baburizza (Museo de Bellas Artes)
19 Argentine Consulate
20 Cambio Exprinter, Reloj Turri
24 Cambios Gema
25 Ladeco
26 LanChile
27 Instituto Chileno-Norteamericano
   de Cultura
28 Centro Cultural Valparaíso
29 CTC
33 Chilesat
34 Entel
35 CTC
36 Cine Metroval
37 Terminal Rodoviario
43 Municipalidad, Departamento
   de Turismo

44 Palacio Lyon (Museo de Historia
   Natural, Galería Municipal de Arte)
46 Mercado Artesanal Permanente
54 Hospital Carlos van Buren
55 La Sebastiana
   (Fundación Neruda)

ASCENSORES
2 Ascensor Artillería
7 Ascensor Cordillera
16 Ascensor El Peral
22 Ascensor Concepción (Turri)
31 Ascensor Reina Victoria
40 Ascensor Barón
41 Ascensor Lecheros
42 Ascensor Larraín
45 Ascensor Espíritu Santo
49 Ascensor Polanco
50 Ascensor Florida
51 Ascensor Mariposa
52 Ascensor Monjas
53 Ascensor Cerro La Cruz

Muelle
Barón

To Viña
del Mar

Cerro
Barón

Bahía de
Valparaíso

Av España

Av Diego Portales

Estación
Barón

40

Magallanes

Cerro
Lecheros

41

Av Errázuriz

Av Brasil
Av Brasil

Yungay

Rawson

12 de Febrero

Av Argentina

Eusebio Lillo

Cerro
Larraín

Chacabuco

☎ 35   ● 36

Av Pedro Montt

38
37

39

42

Parque
Italia

Victoria

48

Plaza
O'Higgins

Congreso
Nacional

Cerro
Rodríguez

Rodríguez

Freire

Vergara

Cruz

47

Av Francia

Independencia

San Ignacio

Simón Bolívar

Morris

Av Uruguay

Retamo

Barroso

Juana Ross

Rancagua

Av Colón

54

Van Buren

Blas Cuevas

Pocuro

Hontáneda

Simpson

49

Cerro
Monjas

52

53

Cerro
Molino

To Santiago
Av Santos Ossa

68

Casablanca

Plaza
Esmeralda

Parque
El Litre

Cerro
La Cruz

Cerro El Litre

Cerro de
las Cañas

Cerro
de la
Merced

Cerro
O'Higgins

CHILE

Information

Tourist Offices The municipal Departamento de Turismo (☎ 032-251071), Condell 1490, is open 8:30 am to 2 pm and 3 to 5 pm weekdays. From mid-December to mid-March, its kiosk on Muelle Prat (the pier), near Plaza Sotomayor, is open 10 am to 2 pm and 3 to 7 pm daily, but the rest of the year it's open Thursday through Sunday only. There are also seasonal offices in the Terminal Rodoviario (the bus station, ☎ 032-213246) and on Plaza Victoria.

Money Besides ATMs, try Inter Cambio on Plaza Sotomayor, or Cambio Exprinter at Prat 895.

Post & Communications Correos de Chile is on Plaza Sotomayor. CTC has offices at Esmeralda 1054, Pedro Montt 2023 and the bus terminal.

Medical Services Hospital Carlos van Buren (☎ 032-254074) is at Av Colón 2454.

Dangers & Annoyances Hillside neighborhoods have a reputation for thieves and robbers, but with the usual precautions they're safe enough. Do watch for suspicious characters and diversions in the area west of Plaza Sotomayor and even downtown. Avoid poorly lit areas at night, and if possible, walk with a companion.

Because of this major port's sex industry, Valparaíso has Chile's highest AIDS rate.

Things to See & Do

The Muelle Prat This area, at the foot of Plaza Sotomayor, is lively on weekends, with a good Feria de Artesanías (crafts market). Do not photograph naval vessels on harbor tours (US$1.50).

Chile's imposing new **Congreso Nacional** (National Congress) is at the junction of Avs Pedro Montt and Argentina, opposite the bus terminal.

On a sunny Sunday, you can spend hours riding Valparaíso's *ascensores* (funiculars) and strolling the back alleys of its picturesque hillside neighborhoods. Some ascensores, built from 1883 to 1916, are remarkable engineering feats – **Ascensor Polanco**, on Av Argentina, is more like an elevator.

One of the best areas for urban explorers is Cerro Concepción, reached by **Ascensor Concepción** at Esmeralda and Gómez Carreño, across from the **Reloj Turri**, a landmark clock tower. Cerro Alegre, behind Plaza Sotomayor, is reached by **Ascensor El Peral**, near the **Tribunales** (law courts), just off the plaza.

The **Museo Municipal de Bellas Artes** (fine arts museum, also known as the Palacio Baburizza), on Paseo Yugoeslavo (take Ascensor El Peral), is closed for a major rehab. The **Museo del Mar Lord Cochrane** (1842), overlooking the harbor on Calle Merlet near Plaza Sotomayor (take Ascensor Cordillera), housed Chile's first observatory and now displays a good collection of model ships. The hilltop **Museo Naval y Marítimo**, on Paseo 21 de Mayo (take Ascensor Artillería from Plaza Aduana), focuses on the War of the Pacific.

At Ferrari 602 on Cerro La Florida, **La Sebastiana** (☎ 032-256606), Pablo Neruda's least-known house, reflects the poet's eclectic taste, his humor and his passion for ships. It's open 10:30 am to 2:30 pm and 3:30 to 6 pm daily (except Monday). Admission costs US$3. Take the Verde Mar bus 'O' or 'D' on Serrano near Plaza Sotomayor and disembark in the 6900 block of Av Alemania, a short walk from the house.

Places to Stay

More travelers stay in Viña, where there's a wider choice of accommodations. The family-oriented *Residencial Latina* (☎ 032-237733), at Papudo 462 on Cerro Concepción, reached by Ascensor Concepción (Turri), comes highly recommended at US$10 per person. Also recommended is *Hospedaje Carrasco* (☎ 032-210737), Abtao 668, a mansion on Cerro Concepción, offering US$10 per person rooms and spectacular rooftop views.

Near the bus terminal is quiet, comfortable and agreeable *Casa Familiar Mónica Villegas* (☎ 032-215673), Av Argentina 322-B, charging US$10 per person. Try also appealing *Residencial Veracruz*, opposite the Congreso Nacional at Pedro Montt 2881. One of Valpo's best values is *Hostal Kolping* (☎ 032-216306), Francisco Valdés Vergara 622, where singles/doubles cost US$19/28 with shared bath, US$24/34 with private bath, breakfast included.

Places to Eat

Downtown, informal *Valparaíso Eterno*, upstairs at Señoret 150, oozes bohemian ambience and is also an inexpensive lunch favorite for the downtown business crowd. Recommended *Bambú*, Pudeto 450, has vegetarian lunches for as little as US$2.50, while the *Club Peruano*, Victoria 2324, serves moderately priced Peruvian specialties.

At *La Rotonda*, Prat 701, consider splitting a la carte dishes – portions are huge – from the extensive menu. Both the seafood and service are excellent. *Bote Salvavidas*, on Muelle Prat, is a traditional, expensive seafood restaurant. *Café Turri*, on Paseo Gervasoni at the upper exit of Ascensor Concepción (Turri), has superb seafood and panoramic views of Valparaíso's harbor.

Getting There & Away
Nearly all bus companies have offices at the Terminal Rodoviario, Av Pedro Montt 913. Several have direct buses to northern cities like Arica and Iquique, with fares comparable to those from Santiago. Tur-Bus has the most frequent departures to Santiago (US$4, two hours).

Services to Mendoza, Argentina (US$25 to US$28) leave between 8 and 9 am, stopping in Viña but bypassing Santiago.

Getting Around
Valpo and Viña are connected by local buses (US$0.40) and commuter trains that leave from the Estación Puerto, Plaza Sotomayor 711.

AROUND VALPARAÍSO
Neruda's outlandish oceanside house on Isla Negra, a rocky headland roughly 80km south of Valparaíso, is now the Museo Neruda, housing the poet's collections of bowsprits, ships in bottles, nautical instruments and other memorabilia. Isla Negra is *not*, incidentally, an island.

In summer, reservations (☎ 035-461284) are imperative for the half-hour weekday tours (US$4.50), which run between 10 am and 8 pm, but you can hang around the grounds as long as you like.

From Santiago's Alameda terminal, buses beyond Algarrobo leave pilgrims almost at the door. Buses also leave frequently from Valparaíso's Terminal Rodoviario.

VIÑA DEL MAR
Popularly known as the Ciudad Jardín (Garden City), Viña del Mar has been Chile's premier beach resort ever since construction of the railway between Valparaíso and Santiago, even though the ocean here is cold for swimming. The porteños of Valparaíso flocked to Viña because of its easy beach access and broad green spaces, and soon built grand houses and mansions away from the congested port. Today, though, it's a more democratic destination than in the past.

Orientation
Ten km north of Valparaíso, Viña (population 310,000) consists of an older area south of Estero Marga Marga and a newer residential grid to its north, where most streets are identified by number and direction, either Norte (north), Oriente (east) or Poniente (west). These streets are usually written as a number, but are sometimes spelled out, for example, 1 Norte is also written Uno Norte. Av Libertad separates Ponientes and Orientes. The main activity centers are south of the Marga Marga, on Plaza Vergara and Avs Arlegui and Valparaíso.

Information
Tourist Offices The Central de Turismo e Informaciones (☎ 032-883154), north of Plaza Vergara, is open 9 am to 2 pm and 3 to 7 pm weekdays, 10 am to 2 pm Saturday, but in summer it's open 9 am to 7 pm daily, except Sunday. It provides an adequate map and a useful calendar of events.

Money For US cash or traveler's checks, try Cambios Symatour, Arlegui 684/686.

Post & Communications Correos de Chile is at Valparaíso 846. The CTC long-distance office is at Valparaíso 628.

Medical Services Hospital Gustavo Fricke (☎ 032-680041) is east of downtown, at Viana Álvarez 1532.

Things to See
Specializing in Mapuche silver and Easter Island archaeology, the Museo de Arqueológico e Historia Francisco Fonck, at 4 Norte 784, is open 10 am to 6 pm Tuesday to Friday, 10 am to 2 pm weekends; admission is US$1. Two blocks east at Quillota 214, the Museo Palacio Rioja is a one-time mansion that's now a municipal museum, open 10 am to 2 pm and 3 to 6 pm daily, except Monday.

CHILE

VIÑA DEL MAR

PLACES TO STAY
- 4 Hotel Royal House (Hostelling International)
- 13 Residencial Caribe
- 14 Residencial Victoria
- 24 Residencial Agua Santa
- 25 Residencial La Nona
- 28 Residencial La Gaviota
- 40 Residencial Ona Berri
- 45 Hotel Quinta Vergara

PLACES TO EAT
- 1 Ital Burger
- 3 Santa Fe
- 34 Anayak
- 35 Samoiedo
- 42 El Sin Nombre
- 43 Panzoni
- 44 México Lindo

OTHER
- 2 Laverap
- 5 Casino Municipal
- 6 Conaf
- 7 Inter-Cambio
- 8 Centro Cultural Viña del Mar
- 9 Museo de Arqueológico e Historia Francisco Fonck

- 10 Museo Palacio Rioja
- 11 Museo de la Cultura del Mar Salvador Reyes
- 12 Reloj de Flores
- 15 Ladeco
- 16 Cyber Blues Café
- 17 Manhattan
- 18 CTC
- 19 Sernatur
- 20 Cine Rex
- 21 Scratch
- 22 Terminal Rodoviario
- 23 Mercado Municipal
- 26 Palacio Vergara (Museo Municipal de Bellas Artes)
- 27 Anfiteatro
- 29 Cambios Afex
- 30 Sala Viña del Mar
- 31 Post Office
- 32 Central de Turismo e Informaciones, Aguitur
- 33 Acuario Municipal
- 36 Cambios Symatour
- 37 Cine Arte
- 38 Teatro Municipal
- 39 Cine Olimpo
- 41 CTC

PACIFIC OCEAN

Muelle Vergara

Playa Acapulco

Av San Martín

0   150   300 m
0   150   300 yards

Av Perú

6 Poniente

5 Poniente

4 Poniente

3 Poniente

Puente Casino

Av Marina

Plaza Mexico

Av San Martín

Iberia

Callao

Berger

Von Schroeders

Nieto

Libertad

Balmaceda

13

15

17

Av Valparaíso

16

18

19

Ecuador

Traslaviña

Villanelo

Echevers

Quinta

Caleta Abarca

Av Marina

12

Av España

To Valparaíso

Av Portales

Agua Santa

Estación Miramar

14

24

25

Bellavista

Viana

Álvarez

CHILE

VIÑA DEL MAR

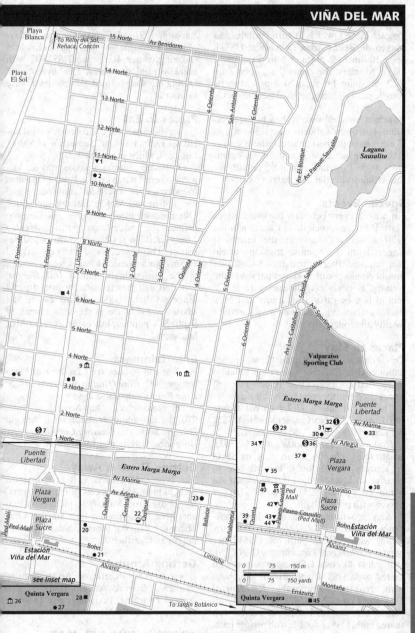

Playa Blanca

To Reloj del Sol, Reñaca, Concón

Playa El Sol

15 Norte
Av Benidorm
14 Norte
13 Norte
12 Norte
11 Norte
● 2
10 Norte
9 Norte

4 Oriente
San Antonio
6 Oriente

Laguna Sausalito

Av El Bosque
Av Parque Sausalito

2 Poniente
4 Poniente
Av Libertad
1 Oriente
2 Oriente
3 Oriente
Quillota
4 Oriente
5 Oriente

8 Norte
7 Norte
■ 4
6 Norte
5 Norte
4 Norte
9 🏛
3 Norte
● 8
10 🏛
● 6
2 Norte
💲 7
1 Norte

Subida Sausalito
Av Los Castaños
Av Sporting

Valparaíso Sporting Club

6 Oriente

Puente Libertad

Plaza Vergara

Estero Marga Marga
Av Marina
Plaza Sucre
Ped Mall
Ped Mall
Av Arlegui
Quillota
Central
22 ●
Quilpué
23 ●
Batuco
Peñablanca

Estación Viña del Mar
● 20
Bohn
● 21
Alvarez
Limache

see inset map

🏛 26
Quinta Vergara
28 ■
● 27

To Jardín Botánico →

Inset map

Estero Marga Marga

Puente Libertad

💲 29
34 ▼
32 🛈
31 ✉
30 ●
💲 36
37 ●
▼ 35
■ 40
☎ 41 ▼
Ped Mall
42 ▼
39 ●
43 ▼
44 ▼

Av Marina
● 33
Av Arlegui
Plaza Vergara
Av Valparaíso
● 38
Plaza Sucre
Paseo Cousiño
Paseo Cousiño (Ped Mall)
Quinta
Bohn
Estación Viña del Mar
Alvarez

0   75   150 m
0   75   150 yards

Quinta Vergara
■ 45
Errázuriz
Montaña

CHILE

The magnificently landscaped **Quinta Vergara** contains the Venetian-style **Palacio Vergara** (1908), which in turn contains the **Museo de Bellas Artes** (admission US$1), open 10 am to 2 pm and 3 to 6 pm daily, except Monday. The grounds are open 7 am to 7 pm daily. Frequent summer concerts complement the song festival (see below).

Beaches Most downtown beaches are polluted. Northern suburbs like Reñaca and Concón have the best beaches, where surfing is becoming increasingly popular – take Bus No 1 from Libertad. For more details, see the Around Viña del Mar entry, below.

Special Events

For a week every February the ostentatious Festival Internacional de la Canción, in the Quinta Vergara, features the kitschiest singers from the Spanish-speaking world (for balance, there's usually at least one insipid Anglo performer) and paralyzes the country, as ticketless Chileans gaze at TV sets in homes, cafés, restaurants and bars. Patient, selective listeners may discover worthwhile folk performers.

Places to Stay

This is only a sample of available accommodations. After Chileans finish their holidays in February, supply exceeds demand and prices drop but the weather is still ideal.

The HI affiliate is *Hotel Royal House* (☎ 032-681922), 5 Norte 683; rates are US$12 per person off-season, US$20 in summer.

Residencial Agua Santa (☎ 32-901531), an attractive blue Victorian at Agua Santa 36, charges US$20 double in peak season. Nearby, at Agua Santa 48, *Residencial La Nona* (☎ 032-663825) costs US$10 per person with private bath.

At Von Schroeders 46, remodeled *Residencial Caribe* (☎ 032-976191) has tiny rooms with private bath for US$12 per person. *Residencial Victoria* (☎ 032-977370), Valparaíso 40, costs US$12 per person with shared bath, US$14 with private bath, both with breakfast. Comparable *Residencial Ona Berri* (☎ 032-688187), upstairs at Valparaíso 618, charges US$12 per person with shared bath, US$17 double with private bath.

Near the Quinta Vergara, at Alcalde Prieto Nieto 0332, *Residencial La Gaviota* (☎ 032-974439) is a good value at US$16 per person with shared bath, US$19 per person with private bath, both with breakfast. Worth a splurge is *Hotel Quinta Vergara* (☎ 032-685073), Errázuriz 690, which has an English-speaking owner. Rates are US$38/47 with breakfast, but rise about 15% in summer. During the song festival, this can be a noisy location.

Places to Eat

For sandwiches, coffee and desserts, try *Anayak* at Quinta 134 or, *Samoiedo* at Valparaíso 637, which is even better.

On Pasaje Cousiño, a passageway off Valparaíso near Plaza Vergara, *Panzoni* features friendly service, excellent atmosphere and fine Italian and Middle Eastern specialties. Other possibilities clustered on Cousiño include the modest, inexpensive *México Lindo* (credible Tex-Mex enchiladas and burritos, but bland sauces and pricey drinks) and *El Sin Nombre* (cheap lunches, tobacco-free).

The misleadingly named *Ital Burger*, Libertad 920, has reasonably priced pasta dinners (about US$6). *Santa Fe*, at San Martín and 8 Norte, is the Viña branch of Santiago's popular but expensive Tex-Mex landmark.

Entertainment

For first-run movies, try *Cine Arte* at Plaza Vergara 142, *Cine Olimpo* at Quinta 294, or *Cine Rex* at Valparaíso 758.

For dancing, Viña has *Scratch* at Bohn 970, the enormous *Manhattan* at Arlegui 302, 2nd floor, and *Cantina Cocodrilo* at Av Borgoño 13101, in nearby Reñaca.

Getting There & Away

The Terminal Rodoviario is at Valparaíso and Quilpué, 2 blocks east of Plaza Vergara. Most buses from Valparaíso pick up passengers here, though a few lines start in Viña. There are frequent buses to San Felipe, Los Andes and Santiago.

Getting Around

Buses marked 'Puerto' or 'Aduana' go to Valparaíso from Av Arlegui. There are also commuter trains. Taxis here are twice as expensive as in Santiago.

AROUND VIÑA DEL MAR

North of Viña are less celebrated but attractive beach towns. **Reñaca** has its own tourist

CHILE

office (☎ 032-900499) at Av Borgoño 14100, plus the area's most extensive beach, but few budget accommodations.

Concón, 15km from Viña, is another exclusive *balneario* (bathing resort), known for its seafood restaurants – make a special effort to try the congrio margarita (conger eel) at hard-to-find *La Picá Horizonte*, San Pedro 120. From the Muelle de Pescadores (Fisherman's Pier), climb the steps (behind Restaurant El Tiburón) and, at the top, walk one short block along the dirt road to San Pedro.

Another 23km beyond Concón is **Quintero**, a peninsula community once part of Lord Cochrane's hacienda. For reasonable accommodations, try *Residencial María Alejandra* (☎ 032-930266), Cochrane 157, where singles with shared bath cost about US$8.

Farther north, the fishing port of **Horcón** is an artists' colony with a bohemian flavor and outstanding seafood restaurants like *Santa Clara*. Sol del Pacífico buses from Viña's Av Libertad go directly to Horcón.

Parque Nacional La Campana

In the coast range, this park's 8000 hectares of jagged scrubland shelter the rare Chilean palm (with edible fruit) and the northernmost remaining stands of southern beech. Darwin's ascent of 1840m **Cerro La Campana**, now easily reached from the Administración at Granizo on the southern approach to the park, was one of his most memorable experiences. Figure at least four hours to the summit, and three hours down.

Access is more difficult to **Palmar de Ocoa**, the park's northern entrance. The saddle of the **Portezuelo de Granizo**, a two-hour climb through a palm-studded canyon, offers some of the views which impressed Darwin. Camping is possible (US$6) but water is limited and there is wildfire risk, especially in summer and autumn.

Getting There & Away Sectors Granizo and Cajón Grande can be reached by Línea Ciferal from Valparaíso and Viña del Mar, every half hour in the summertime. Agdabus leaves every 20 minutes from Limache and Olmué. Both involve a 1km walk to the Administración.

For Sector Ocoa, any northbound bus from Santiago will drop you at Hijuelas (watch for the poorly marked turnoff before the bridge over the Río Aconcagua); from Hijuelas you must hitch or walk 12km.

RANCAGUA

Capital of the Sixth Region, 86km south of Santiago, the agricultural service center of Rancagua (population 160,000) also depends on copper from El Teniente, the world's largest subsurface mine. In 1814, Chilean self-determination suffered a temporary setback at the Desastre de Rancagua (Disaster of Rancagua), at the hands of Spanish Royalist troops.

Sernatur (☎ 072-230413) is at Germán Riesco 277, 1st floor; there's also a municipal Kiosco de Turismo on Paseo Independencia, opposite Plaza Los Héroes. Forex, Campos 363, is the only place to cash traveler's checks. Conaf (☎ 072-221293), Cuevas 480, has information on Reserva Nacional Río de los Cipreses.

Things to See & Do

Late colonial buildings include the **Iglesia de la Merced** (O'Higgins' headquarters during the battle of Rancagua), the **Casa del Pilar de Esquina** and the **Museo Histórico Regional**.

In early autumn (late March), the **Campeonato Nacional de Rodeo** (national rodeo championship) takes place at the Medialuna de Rancagua, on Av España.

Places to Stay & Eat

Easily the cheapest accommodations are at barebones *Hotel Rosedal de Chile*, near the train station at Calvo 435, about US$9 per person. Several travelers have recommended *Hotel España* (☎ 072-230141), San Martín 367, which has singles/doubles with private bath, cable TV and breakfast starting at US$24/35.

Yuly's Bar, Cuevas 745, has simple and cheap well-prepared lunches, as does *Casas Viejas*, Rubio 216. *Reina Victoria*, Independencia 667, has lunches for about US$4 and excellent ice cream.

Getting There & Away

Rancagua's new Terminal Rodoviario is on Av Viña del Mar, just north of the Mercado Central. Many buses covering the Panamericana between Santiago (US$2, one hour) and Puerto Montt stop here.

Long-distance trains stop at the station on Viña del Mar between Ocarrol and

Carrera Pinto; there are also commuter services to Santiago.

AROUND RANCAGUA
Termas de Cauquenes

Only 28km east of Rancagua, these hot springs were visited by both O'Higgins and Darwin (who called the facilities 'a square of miserable little hovels, each with a single table and bench,' but also said it was 'a quiet solitary spot with a good deal of quiet beauty'). Subsequent improvements have placed accommodations beyond shoestring travelers, but you can still spend the afternoon here by taking an Empresa Micro Termas de Cauquenes bus (US$2), at 11 am and 6:15 pm weekdays, from Rancagua's Terminal Rodoviario. Buses Coya goes to Termas de Cauquenes at 9:30 am and 1:30 pm, returning at 11 am and 5:15 pm.

Reserva Nacional Río de los Cipreses

Fifty km southeast of Rancagua, condors soar above the volcanic landforms, hanging glacial valleys and riverscapes of 37,000-hectare Los Cipreses, whose forests shelter guanacos, foxes and vizcachas. There are many petroglyphs and places to camp and hike.

No direct public transport exists, though buses to Cauquenes go within 15km; try to arrange transport with Conaf in Rancagua.

CURICÓ

Surrounded by orchards and vineyards, Curicó (population 75,000), 195km south of Santiago, is a good base for trips into the countryside, coastal areas and parts of the Andes. Its palm-lined Plaza de Armas, one of Chile's prettiest, has a wrought-iron bandstand and cool fountains with black-necked swans.

Sernatur operates out of a kiosk on the east side of the Plaza, open 9 am to 6:30 pm daily. Forex, Carmen 477, is the only casa de cambio. There's an ATM at Banco de Crédito, Merced 315. Correos de Chile is at Carmen 556, while CTC has long-distance offices at Peña 650 and Camilo Henríquez 414. Entel, Prat 373, is open until midnight.

Wineries

Bodega Miguel Torres (☎ 075-310455) is just south of Curicó on the Panamericana. Phone ahead and take a taxi colectivo toward the village of Molina. On the same route, near the village of Lontué, is **Viña San Pedro** (☎ 075-491517).

Places to Stay & Eat

Friendly *Hotel Prat* (☎ 075-311069), Peña 427, is a bargain at US$9 per person with shared bath and hot showers, US$15 with private bath, but some rooms are dark and drab. *Residencial Rahue* (☎ 075-312194), across the street at Peña 410, is satisfactory for US$9 with shared bath.

Donde Iván, at Prat and Membrillar, has typical Chilean fare. Also try *Centro Italiano*, Estado 531.

Getting There & Away

Bus Buses to Santiago (US$4, 2½ hours) leave every half hour from the long-distance Terminal Rodoviario on Camilo Henríquez, 3 blocks north of the plaza. Buses Lit (☎ 075-315648), at Las Heras 0195 and Tur-Bus (☎ 075-312115) at Manso de Velasco 0106, have their own offices. For local and regional services, the Terminal de Buses Rurales is at the west end of Calle Prat.

Train Passenger trains between Santiago and Temuco stop at the Estación de Ferrocarril (☎ 075-310028), Maipú 567, at the west end of Calle Prat, 5 blocks from the Plaza de Armas.

AROUND CURICÓ
Radal Siete Tazas (Reserva Nacional)

This national reserve east of Molina features a series of falls and pools in the upper Río Claro. There are scenic trails up Cerro El Fraile and at Valle del Indio, with camping in the Radal and Parque Inglés sectors, and across the Claro drainage to Reserva Nacional Altos del Lircay (difficult without a guide). Conaf's visitor center, 50km from Molina, can be reached from Curicó and Molina by buses which run daily in summer, less often in other seasons.

TALCA

Founded in 1690 but refounded in 1742 after shaky beginnings (a major earthquake), Talca is capital of the Seventh Region of Maule, 257km south of Santiago. Long the residence of landowners, it's also an important commercial center. For information, Sernatur (☎ 071-233669), 1 Poniente 1281, is open 10 am to 2 pm daily except Sunday and 4 to 8 pm only on weekdays. Conaf (☎ 071-225622) is at 3 Sur and 2 Poniente.

The **Museo O'Higginiano y de Bellas Artes** occupies the house where Bernardo O'Higgins signed Chile's declaration of independence in 1818.

Places to Stay & Eat
The remodeled *Hotel Cordillera* (☎ *071-221817)*, at 2 Sur 1360, has singles/doubles with shared bath for US$17/29, while those with private bath cost US$26/43. Probably the best value is well-kept *Hotel Amalfi* (☎ *071-233389)*, set among attractive gardens at 2 Sur 1265, for US$32/47.

One of Chile's best bargains is *Picada José Barrera*, 1 Sur 530, jammed with downtown diners enjoying tasty, filling three-course lunches costing barely US$2. The Mercado Central, bounded by 1 Norte, 5 Oriente, 1 Sur and 4 Oriente, has several economical cocinerías. Relatively expensive *El Alero de Gastón*, 2 Norte 858, has shady patio dining, but the food is good rather than exceptional. *Gobelino*, at 1 Sur and 1 Oriente, is one of Talca's best.

Getting There & Away
Many north-south buses stop at the Rodoviario Municipal (☎ 071-243270) at 2 Sur 1920, behind the train station. There is a separate terminal, mostly for international buses, 1 block south at 3 Sur 1960; weekly summer buses to Malargüe, Argentina, pass through some of the Andes' most scenic terrain.

Trains from Santiago stop at the station (☎ 071-226254), 11 Oriente 1000, at the east end of 2 Sur.

AROUND TALCA
In the Andean foothills 65km east of Talca, **Reserva Nacional Altos del Vilches** offers camping in the upper Río Lircay basin and hiking to Laguna El Alto, Laguna Tomate, up the canyon of the Valle del Venado and to the spectacular basaltic plateau of El Enladrillado. Buses to Vilches depart daily, except Sunday, at 1 and 5 pm from Talca.

CHILLÁN
The birthplace of the famous Bernardo O'Higgins, Chillán marks the approximate northern border of La Frontera, a Mapuche-controlled area until the late 19th century. Of all the towns on the Panamericana between Santiago and Temuco, Chillán most deserves a stopover.

Orientation & Information
Chillán (population 135,000), 400km south of Santiago, sits on an alluvial plain between the Río Ñuble and the Río Chillán. Sernatur (☎ 042-223272) is at 18 de Septiembre 455, half a block north of the Plaza de Armas. There's also an information kiosk at the bus terminal.

Correos de Chile is at Libertad 505, while CTC is at Arauco 625. For changing cash or traveler's checks, try Schüler Cambios, Av Collín 585-A.

Things to See
Murales de la Escuela México After a 1939 earthquake, Mexican president Lázaro Cárdenas donated a new school to Chillán. At Pablo Neruda's urging, Mexican artist David Alfaro Siqueiros decorated the library with murals honoring indigenous and post-Columbian figures in each country's history – the northern wall devoted to Mexico and the southern wall to Chile. *Hermanos Mexicanos*, a simple but powerful work by Siqueiros' countryman Xavier Guerrero, flanks the library stairs.

At O'Higgins 250, the building still functions as a school but the staff welcome visitors.

Feria de Chillán One of Chile's most colorful markets, the Feria has a great crafts selection (leather, basketry and weaving) and mountains of fresh produce. It happens daily, but is especially lively Saturdays, and occupies the entire Plaza de la Merced and spills into adjacent streets.

Places to Stay
Budget accommodations start around US$8 at *Hospedaje Sonia Seguí*, Itata 288, including a generous breakfast, and US$10 at *Residencial Su Casa* (☎ *042-223931)*, at Cocharcas 555, with shared bath but without breakfast. Also try *Hospedaje Tino Rodríguez Sepúlveda* (☎ *042-216181)*, Purén 443, for US$10 with shared bath and breakfast.

Places to Eat
In the remodeled *Mercado Municipal*, bounded by 5 de Abril, El Roble, Isabel

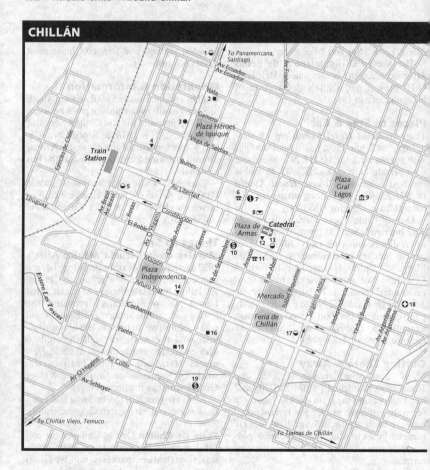

CHILLÁN

Riquelme and Maipón, several simple but excellent and reasonably priced cocinerías prepare local specialties such as pastel de choclo for as little as US$3 in season.

For pizza, try **Pizzería Ficus** at Bulnes and Rosas, or **Venecia** at Prat and Carrera. The **Centro Español**, Arauco 555, has excellent food and service.

Getting There & Away

Bus Chillán's Terminal María Teresa (☎ 042-231119) is at Av O'Higgins 010, just north of Av Ecuador. A few companies still sell tickets and leave from the old Terminal de Buses Inter-regionales (☎ 042-221014) at Constitución 01. There are frequent north-south services, plus connections to Argen-

tina via Temuco and Osorno. Fares to Santiago (six hours) are about US$11.

For local and regional services, the Terminal de Buses Rurales (☎ 042-223606) is on Sargento Aldea, south of Maipón.

Train Trains between Santiago and Temuco use the train station (☎ 042-222424) on Av Brasil, at the west end of Libertad.

AROUND CHILLÁN

Renowned for hot springs and skiing, **Termas de Chillán** is 80km east, at 1800m, on the slopes of Volcán Chillán. Accommodations are costly, but check travel agencies for day trips. Buses Loyola (☎ 042-217838), 5 de Abril 594 in Chillán, runs buses to Termas.

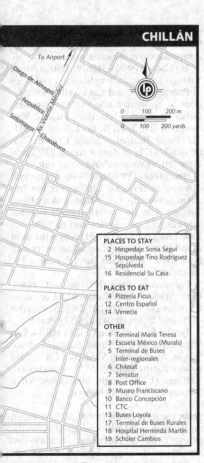

CHILLÁN

To Airport

Diego de Almagro
Republica
Sotomayor
Av Vicente Méndez
Chacabuco

0   100   200 m
0   100   200 yards

PLACES TO STAY
2 Hospedaje Sonia Seguí
15 Hospedaje Tino Rodríguez Sepúlveda
16 Residencial Su Casa

PLACES TO EAT
4 Pizzería Ficus
12 Centro Español
14 Venecia

OTHER
1 Terminal María Teresa
3 Escuela México (Murals)
5 Terminal de Buses Inter-regionales
6 Chilesat
7 Sernatur
8 Post Office
9 Museo Franciscano
10 Banco Concepción
11 CTC
13 Buses Loyola
17 Terminal de Buses Rurales
18 Hospital Herminda Martín
19 Schüler Cambios

CONCEPCIÓN

Menaced by Indians and devastated by earthquakes, Concepción moved several times in the colonial era, but maintained seaborne communications with Santiago. After independence, coal on the Península de Lebú supported an autonomous industrial tradition, and glass-blowing, timber and textile industries emerged. The railway arrived in 1872 and, when the Mapuche threat receded, a bridge over the Biobío gave the city a strategic role in further colonization.

Since WWII, the major industrial project has been the steel plant at Huachipato, but wages and living standards remain low. Coupled with activism at the Universidad de Concepción, these conditions fostered a highly politicized labor movement that strongly supported Salvador Allende.

Orientation & Information

On the north bank of the Biobío, Concepción is capital of the Eighth Region. Few older constructions have survived around pleasantly landscaped Plaza Independencia, whose utilitarian buildings reflect the earthquake risk. Near the plaza the main commercial streets, Barros Arana and Aníbal Pinto, are pedestrian malls. With the nearby port of Talcahuano, the urban area has roughly half a million people.

Well-stocked Sernatur (☎ 041-227976), Aníbal Pinto 460, is open 8:30 am to 8 pm daily in summer; otherwise, hours are 8:30 am to 1 pm and 3 to 5:30 pm weekdays only. To exchange money, try Inter-Santiago at Caupolicán 521, Local 58.

Correos de Chile is at O'Higgins 799. CTC has offices at Colo Colo 487, while Entel is at Barros Arana 541, Local 2.

Things to See

On the grounds of the **Barrio Universitario**, at Chacabuco and Larenas, the highlight of the **Casa del Arte** (art museum) is Mexican muralist Jorge González Camarena's *La Presencia de América Latina*.

On the edge of Parque Ecuador, the **Galería de Historia de Concepción** features vivid dioramas of local and regional history. Subjects include Mapuche subsistence, battles with the Spaniards (note Mapuche tactics), literary figure Alonso de Ercilla, the 1939 earthquake and a finely detailed model of a local factory.

Places to Stay

In summer, when university students vacate the town, there's plenty of inexpensive accommodation, but the rest of the year it's hard to find anything reasonable. ***Residencial Metro*** *(☎ 041-225305)*, Barros Arana 464, has spacious rooms with high ceilings for US$13/22 with breakfast; equally spacious ***Residencial O'Higgins*** *(☎ 041-228303)*, O'Higgins 457, is marginally cheaper, around US$10 per person.

Friendly, recommended ***Residencial Colo Colo*** *(☎ 041-234790)*, Colo Colo 743, costs US$15/23 with shared bath, but is rundown and has just two showers for 20

CHILE

rooms. *Residencial Antuco* (☎ 041-235485), Barros Arana 741, Departamento 28, charges US$17/27 with breakfast.

Places to Eat

Filling the entire block bounded by Caupolicán, Maipú, Rengo and Freire, the *Mercado Central* has many excellent eateries, though aggressive waiters try to literally drag customers into some venues. Try pastel de choclo, a meal in itself.

El Naturista, Barros Arana 342, serves vegetarian food, while *El Novillo Loco*, Pasaje Portales 539, is for carnivores. The *Centro Español*, Barros Arana 675, and the *Centro Italiano*, Barros Arana 935, add a European touch. For cheap cappuccinos, try *Café Haití* at Caupolicán 511, or *Café Caribe* at Caupolicán 521.

Shopping

Look for woolens, basketry, ceramics, carvings and leather at the Mercado Central; La Gruta, Caupolicán 521, Local 64.

Getting There & Away

Air Aeropuerto Carriel Sur is 5km northwest of town. LanChile (☎ 041-229138), Barros Arana 451, averages four flights daily to Santiago (US$64 to US$91), and flies daily except Monday and Saturday to Puerto Montt. Ladeco (☎ 041-248824), O'Higgins 533, averages three flights daily to Santiago, and flies daily to Valdivia and Wednesday and Saturday to Punta Arenas.

Avant (☎ 041-246710), Barros Arana 455, flies often to Santiago (US$61 to US$83), daily to Temuco and Valdivia, and weekends to Puerto Montt and Punta Arenas (US$80 to US$134).

Bus Concepción's Terminal de Buses Puchacay (☎ 041-316666) is at Tegualda 860, on the northern outskirts of town. Many bus companies have downtown offices, indicated below where appropriate.

Tur-Bus (☎ 041-315555), Tucapel 530, has 13 buses daily to Santiago, some continuing to Valparaíso and Viña del Mar, and goes southbound to Puerto Montt and intermediates. It leaves from the separate Terminal Chillancito at Camilo Henríquez 2565, the northward extension of Bulnes.

Sol del Pacífico has ten buses daily to Santiago, six of them continuing to Valparaíso and Viña del Mar. Buses Lit (☎ 041-230722) has another four to Santiago; several other companies cover the same route.

Tas Choapa (☎ 041-312639), Barros Arana 1081, goes twice daily to Santiago and twice to Puerto Montt, and has excellent connections to northern Chile and to Argentina. Other southbound carriers include Varmontt (☎ 041-314010), Igi Llaima (☎ 041-312498) at Tucapel 432, and Cruz del Sur (☎ 041-314372) at Barros Arana 935, Local 9; the latter two go to Valdivia as well.

Buses Biobío (☎ 041-310764), Arturo Prat 416 and at Terminal Chillancito, has frequent service to Los Ángeles, Angol and Temuco; Jota Be (☎ 041-312652) also has services to Los Ángeles and to Salto del Laja. Línea Azul (☎ 041-311126) is the most frequent to Los Ángeles, about every half hour from Chillancito, but Igi Llaima has another ten.

For services down the coast to Coronel, Lota, Arauco, Lebu, Cañete and Contulmo, try Buses Los Alces (☎ 041-240855), Prat 699 or Buses J Ewert (☎ 041-229212), Prat 535.

Typical fares include Chillán (US$4, two hours), Talca (US$8, four hours), Temuco (US$8, four hours), Valdivia (US$10, six hours), Puerto Montt (US$12, seven hours), Santiago (US$14, eight hours) and Viña/Valparaíso (US$18, 10 hours).

Train The train station (☎ 041-227777) shown on the map is closed for remodeling; in the interim you'll find a temporary station northwest toward the airport. EFE also has a Venta de Pasajes (ticket office, ☎ 041-225286) at Aníbal Pinto 478, Local 3. Santiago-bound trains leave daily at 1 and 10 pm.

AROUND CONCEPCIÓN
La Costa del Carbón

As an advertising slogan, the 'Coast of Coal' may sound unappealing, but beach towns south of the Biobío draw crowds to and around Coronel (which reeks of fish meal), Lota, Arauco and Península Lebú. The best day trip is Lota, site of the 14-hectare **Parque Isidora Cousiño**; the town's mid-century company-town architecture is also worth a look. Open 10 am to 8 pm daily, the park is a remarkable demonstration of the ability of cultivated beauty to survive alongside massive slag heaps. Admission costs US$1.25 for adults, half that for children.

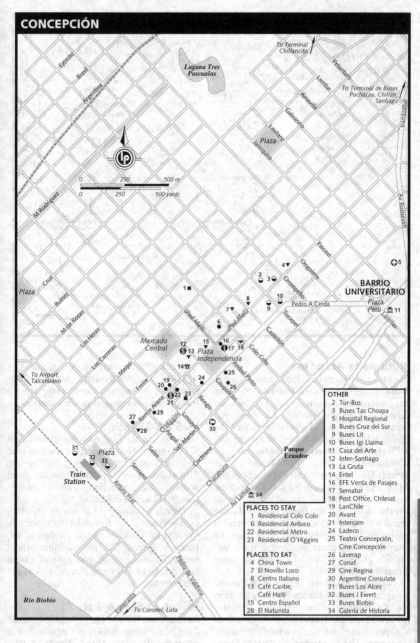

CONCEPCIÓN

Laguna Tres Pascualas

To Terminal Chillancito

To Terminal de Buses Puchacay, Chillán, Santiago

0   250   500 m
0   250   500 yards

BARRIO UNIVERSITARIO

Plaza Perú

Mercado Central

Plaza Independencia

To Airport Talcahuano

Parque Ecuador

Train Station

Plaza

Río Biobío

To Coronel, Lota

To Terminal de Buses Puchacay, Chillán, Santiago

OTHER
2   Tur-Bus
3   Buses Tas Choapa
5   Hospital Regional
8   Buses Cruz del Sur
9   Buses Lit
10 Buses Igi Llaima
11 Casa del Arte
12 Inter-Santiago
13 La Gruta
14 Entel
16 EFE Venta de Pasajes
17 Sernatur
18 Post Office, Chilesat
19 LanChile
20 Avant
21 Intercam
24 Ladeco
25 Teatro Concepción,
     Cine Concepción
26 Laverap
27 Conaf
29 Cine Regina
30 Argentine Consulate
31 Buses Los Alces
32 Buses J Ewert
33 Buses Biobío
34 Galería de Historia

PLACES TO STAY
1   Residencial Colo Colo
6   Residencial Antuco
22 Residencial Metro
23 Residencial O'Higgins

PLACES TO EAT
4   China Town
7   El Novillo Loco
8   Centro Italiano
13 Café Caribe,
     Café Haití
15 Centro Español
28 El Naturista

CHILE

AROUND CONCEPCIÓN

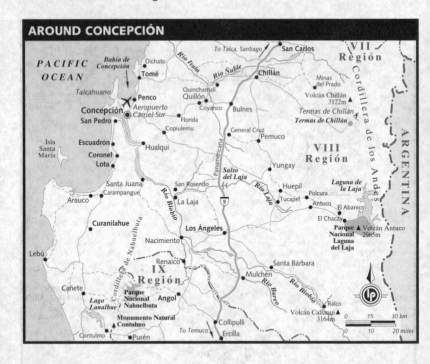

Ruta de la Araucana

South of Concepción, local and regional authorities have erected historical markers memorializing soldier-poet Alonso de Ercilla y Zúñiga's epic tale *La Araucana*, which honored the Mapuche resistance. At Escuadrón, 22km south of Concepción, the **Hito Histórico Galvarino** marks the battle of Lagunillas (1557), where the Mapuche *toqui* (chief) Galvarino submitted stoically as the Spaniards severed both his hands with their swords, after which he placed his own head on the block. The Spaniards refrained from executing Galvarino, who continued to resist; on being recaptured years later, he may have been executed, though some historians believe he killed himself to avoid Spanish retribution.

Near Arauco, about 2km west of Carampangue, the **Hito Histórico Prueba y Elección de Caupolicán** commemorates the site where Mapuche leader Colo Colo chose Caupolicán to lead the resistance against the Spaniards. The Mapuche defeated the Spaniards at Tucapel (1553) and executed Pedro de Valdivia.

If continuing south to Angol and Los Ángeles, visit **Monumento Natural Contulmo**, an 84-hectare forest reserve with trails, but no camping or picnic facilities.

LOS ÁNGELES

Santa María de Los Ángeles (population 97,000) is not Hollywood, and the two-lane Panamericana is not a freeway, but the city, 110km south of Chillán, provides good access to the upper Biobío and to Parque Nacional Laguna del Laja.

There's a municipal Oficina de Información Turística on Caupolicán, alongside Correos de Chile on the south side of the Plaza de Armas. CTC long-distance offices are at Paseo Quilpué, just east of Colón between Colo Colo and Rengo, and at the bus terminal.

Places to Stay & Eat

Residencial Winser (☎ 043-323782), Colo Colo 335, charges US$10 per person, but is often full. Its sister *Hotel Winser* (☎ 043-313845), at Colo Colo 327, is an excellent alternative for US$17/32 singles/doubles with shared bath, with some cheaper singles; the annex (☎ 043-315140) next door has identical prices.

An excellent breakfast choice, **Café Prymos**, Colón 400, also has sandwiches and outstanding ice cream. **Julio's Pizza**, Colón 452, is part of a small chain with excellent food; for more varied fare try the **Centro Español**, Colón 482.

Getting There & Away
Los Ángeles' main Terminal de Autobuses has moved to Av Sor Vicenta 2051 on the northeastern outskirts of town, most easily reached via Av Villagrán. Sample fares include Chillán (US$2.50, 1½ hours), Concepción (US$4, two hours), Temuco (US$7, four hours), Puerto Montt (US$13, eight hours) and Santiago (US$14, eight hours).

From Terminal Santa Rosa, at Villagrán and Rengo, ERS goes to the village of Antuco, gateway to Parque Nacional Laguna del Laja, seven times daily on weekends, three times daily on weekdays.

AROUND LOS ÁNGELES
The **Río Biobío** has South America's finest white water, though hydroelectric development threatens the river and the livelihood of the Pehuenche Indians. Between December and March, three-day trips cost in the US$500 range with Santiago operators like Cascada Expediciones (☎ 02-2342274), Orrego Luco 054, 2nd floor, Providencia, or Altué Expediciones (☎ 02-2321103), Encomenderos 83, Las Condes.

PARQUE NACIONAL LAGUNA DEL LAJA
Lava from 2985m Volcán Antuco dammed the Río Laja to form this reserve's centerpiece lake, 95km east of Los Ángeles, with forests of mountain cypress and pehuén (monkey puzzle tree). Nearly 50 bird species, including the condor, frequent the area.

The best of several hikes circles Antuco, but the higher Sierra Velluda to the southwest offers a series of impressive glaciers. Summer is dry but rain and snow are common the rest of the year. The ski season lasts June to October.

Places to Stay & Eat
Near the park entrance, at Km 90, **Camping Lagunillas** charges US$15 per site. In winter, Concepción's Dirección General de Deportes y Recreación operates the **Refugio Digeder**, which has beds for 50 skiers and a restaurant. They also rent ski equipment and *may* open in summer. Rates are US$10 per person; for reservations, contact Digeder (☎ 041-229054), O'Higgins 740, Oficina 23, in Concepción. Try also Los Ángeles' **Refugio Municipal** (☎ 043-322333).

Getting There & Away
From Los Ángeles' Terminal Santa Rosa, at Villagrán and Rengo, ERS goes to the villages of Antuco and Abanico (1½ hours), gateways to the park, seven times daily on weekends, three times daily on weekdays. It takes several hours to walk the 11km to Conaf's administrative offices and visitor center at Chacay.

Norte Grande

The Norte Grande's main features are the Pacific Ocean and its beaches, the desolate Atacama Desert and the Andean altiplano and high peaks. Many Indians remain, and earlier populations left huge, stylized geoglyphs of humans and animals on barren hillsides.

The Atacama is arid, but El Niño events (sea surface circulation changes in the western Pacific, occurring every seven years or so) can bring phenomenal downpours. Coastal *camanchaca* (fog) moistens scattered semidesert *lomas* vegetation, and rainfall and vegetation increase with elevation and distance from the sea. In the precordillera (foothills), Aymara farmers cultivate potatoes up to altitudes of 4000m, while herders pasture llamas and alpacas in the higher *puna* (highlands).

After the War of the Pacific, Chile annexed these copper and nitrate-rich lands from Peru and Bolivia; most Atacama cities owe their existence to minerals. Nitrate *oficinas* like Humberstone flourished in the early 20th century, then withered or died when artificial fertilizers superseded mineral nitrates, and they are now ghost towns. Copper has supplanted nitrates in economic importance and is still extracted at open-pit mines like Chuquicamata, the world's largest.

CHILE

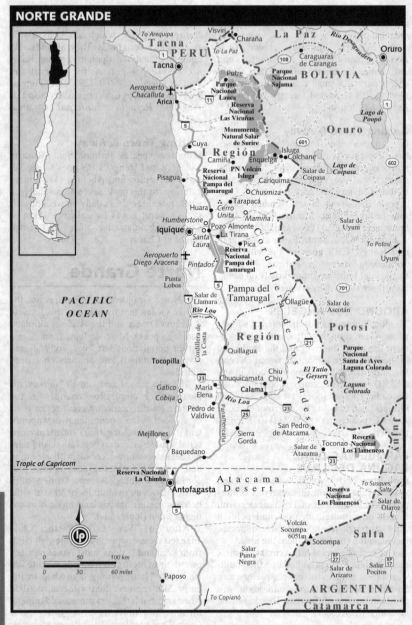

Militant trade unions first developed in this area, introducing a new force into Chilean politics. Chuquicamata dominates the mining sector, but fishing and tourism have growing significance.

ARICA

A 19th-century visitor called Arica 'one bleak, comfortless, miserable, sandy waste,' but even before Inca times it had been the terminus of an important trade route. In colonial times it was an export point for silver from Potosí (in present-day Bolivia). Where Chile and Peru battled in the War of the Pacific, tourists now lounge on the beach and Aymara Indians sell handicrafts, vegetables and trinkets. Industrialization failed in the 1960s, but international trade and a duty-free zone *(zona franca)* brought a dramatic population increase.

Orientation

At the foot of El Morro, a dramatic headland, the downtown is a slightly irregular grid. The Chile-Peru border is 20km north.

Tourist Offices & Information

Sernatur (☎ 058-232101), at Prat 305 (2nd floor), is open 8:30 am to 1 pm and 3 to 7 pm weekdays. It distributes a useful city map, plus brochures on Tarapacá and other regions. Conaf (☎ 058-250207) is at Vicuña Mackenna 820.

Money Besides ATMs, cambios on 21 de Mayo change US cash and traveler's checks plus Peruvian, Bolivian and Argentine currency. They're closed Sundays, so try the street changers at 21 de Mayo and Colón.

Post & Communications Correos de Chile is at Prat 305. For long-distance calls, go to Entel at 21 de Mayo 345, CTC at Colón 476 or Chilesat at 21 de Mayo 372. The alcove outside Sernatur has overseas direct lines, but it's accessible only during regular business hours.

Immigration To replace a lost tourist card or extend a visa, go to the Departamento de Extranjería (☎ 058-232411), 7 de Junio 188, 3rd floor.

Medical Services Hospital Dr Juan Noé (☎ 058-229200) is at 18 de Septiembre 1000.

Things to See & Do

Take the footpath from the top of Calle Colón for exceptional views from **El Morro de Arica**, site of a crucial War of the Pacific battle. Alexandre Gustave Eiffel designed the **Iglesia San Marcos** (1875) on Plaza Colón. **Pasaje Bolognesi**, a narrow passage between Sotomayor and 21 de Mayo, has a lively artisans market.

Beaches The most-frequented beaches are south of town, along Av Comandante San Martín. The closest is **Playa El Laucho**, just south of the Club de Yates, followed by **Playa La Lisera** 2.5 km south of downtown; both have little surf and are suitable for swimming. Bus No 8 from General Velásquez and Chacabuco serves this area.

Beaches along the Panamericana Norte are cleaner than those to the south. **Playa Chinchorro**, 2km north of downtown, is suitable for swimming and diving, while **Playa Las Machas**, a few kilometers north, is ideal for surfing and fishing. Take bus No 12 from General Velásquez and Chacabuco.

Places to Stay

Arica usually has an inexpensive student hostel in January and February, but the location changes. Ask Sernatur for current information.

Residencial Sur (☎ 058-252457), Maipú 516, has hot water and clean sheets for US$6 per person. Frequented by many travelers, *Residencial Madrid (☎ 058-231479)* at Baquedano 685 has singles/doubles at US$7/12, but is sometimes noisy and the management can be brusque. *Residencial Rachell (☎ 058-231560)*, in a quiet neighborhood at Sotomayor 841, is a good value for US$7 per person.

Residencial Chungará (☎ 058-231677), Patricio Lynch 675, is probably the pick of the litter – bright, friendly and quiet (except near the TV), for US$9 per person with breakfast. French-run *Residencial Leiva (☎ 058-232008)*, Colón 347, is quiet and well-located; rates are US$7 to US$9 per person with shared bath, depending on the number of beds, US$10 per person with private bath.

One of Arica's traditional favorites is *Hotel Lynch (☎/fax 058-231581)*, Patricio Lynch 589, where simple but clean rooms with shared bath start at US$16/25; with private bath, expect about US$28/39.

CHILE

Places to Eat

Foreign travelers congregate at *Café 21*, 21 de Mayo 201, for snacks, coffee and excellent lager beer. For breakfast, try sandwiches and licuados at *Buen Gusto No 2*, Baquedano 559. *Restaurant Casino La Bomba*, within the fire station at Colón 357, is an Arica institution for inexpensive lunches.

Govinda, Bolognesi 430, has cheap vegetarian specials. In the Mercado Colón, at Colón and Maipú, *Caballito del Mar* has well-prepared corvina, cojinova and other tasty fish for US$5 to US$6, though service can be erratic. Upstairs in the same building, *El Rey del Marisco* is better but more expensive.

El Arriero, 21 de Mayo 385, is an outstanding parrilla with pleasant atmosphere and friendly service (closed Monday). *D'Aurelio*, Baquedano 369, is a fine Italian restaurant with attentive service and exceptional appetizers.

Getting There & Away

Air Santiago-bound passengers should sit on the left side of the plane for awesome views of the Atacama and the Andes.

Ladeco (☎ 058-252021), 21 de Mayo 439, and LanChile (☎ 058-251641), 21 de Mayo 345, have several daily flights to Santiago (US$128 to US$215) and intermediates. Avant (☎ 232328), 21 de Mayo 277, has similar schedules and is slightly cheaper (US$124 to US$156).

LAB (☎ 058-251919), Patricio Lynch 298, flies Thursday and Saturday to La Paz, where LanChile flies daily.

Bus & Colectivo All major companies have offices at the Terminal de Buses (☎ 058-241390), Diego Portales 948. Frequent buses go to Iquique (US$6, four hours); faster taxi colectivos charge about US$12. Other typical southbound fares are Calama (US$20, 11 hours), Antofagasta (US$23, 12 hours) and Santiago (US$50 to US$55, 26 hours).

For altiplano destinations, including Parinacota (US$6.50), Visviri (US$8) and Charaña, contact Buses Martínez (☎ 058-232265), Pedro Montt 620, or Transporte Humire (☎ 058-253497). La Paloma (☎ 058-222710), Germán Riesco 2071, goes to the precordillera villages of Socoroma (US$2), Putre (US$4, daily), Codpa and Belén.

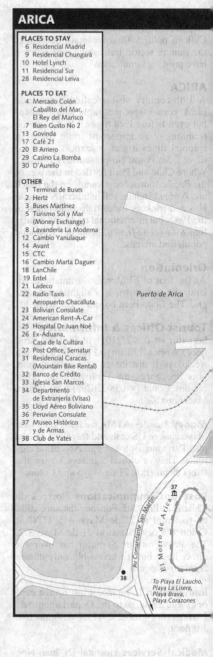

ARICA

PLACES TO STAY
6 Residencial Madrid
9 Residencial Chungará
10 Hotel Lynch
11 Residencial Sur
28 Residencial Leiva

PLACES TO EAT
4 Mercado Colón
    Caballito del Mar,
    El Rey del Marisco
7 Buen Gusto No 2
13 Govinda
17 Café 21
20 El Arriero
29 Casino La Bomba
30 D'Aurelio

OTHER
1 Terminal de Buses
2 Hertz
3 Buses Martínez
5 Turismo Sol y Mar
    (Money Exchange)
8 Lavandería La Moderna
12 Cambio Yanulaque
14 Avant
15 CTC
16 Cambio Marta Daguer
18 LanChile
19 Entel
21 Ladeco
22 Radio Taxis
    Aeropuerto Chacalluta
23 Bolivian Consulate
24 American Rent-A-Car
25 Hospital Dr Juan Noé
26 Ex-Aduana,
    Casa de la Cultura
27 Post Office, Sernatur
31 Residencial Caracas
    (Mountain Bike Rental)
32 Banco de Crédito
33 Iglesia San Marcos
34 Departamento
    de Extranjería (Visas)
35 Lloyd Aéreo Boliviano
36 Peruvian Consulate
37 Museo Histórico
    y de Armas
38 Club de Yates

Puerto de Arica

Av Comandante San Martín

El Morro de Arica

To Playa El Laucho,
Playa La Lisera,
Playa Brava,
Playa Corazones

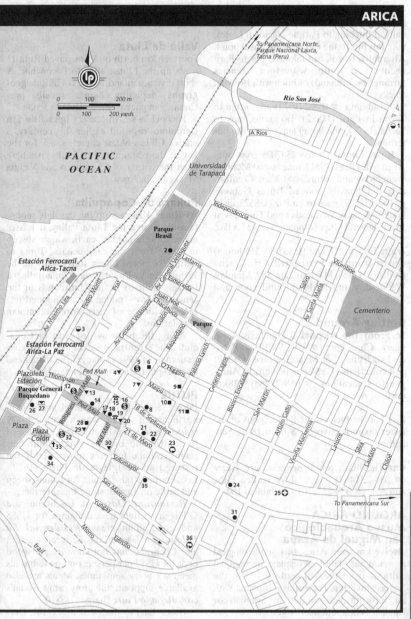

ARICA

PACIFIC
OCEAN

Río San José

JA Ríos

Universidad
de Tarapacá

Independencia

Parque
Brasil

2

Cementerio

Estación Ferrocarril
Arica-Tacna

Estación Ferrocarril
Arica-La Paz

3

Plazoleta
Estación

Parque General
Baquedano

Ped Mall   4

5   6

7

Maipú   9

O'Higgins

10

11

18 de Septiembre

8

12
13
14
15 16
17 18
19
20

26   27

28

29

21

22

23

30

27 de Mayo

Sotomayor

35

24

25

31

San Marcos

Yungay

Ejercito

36

trail

To Panamericana Norte,
Parque Nacional Lauca,
Tacna (Peru)

To Panamericana Sur

CHILE

Bus Lluta serves Poconchile from Chacabuco and Vicuña Mackenna four times daily; if hitching to Parque Nacional Lauca, take this bus to the Carabineros checkpoint. Alternatively, you can take the bus to Parinacota and return with tour agencies (arrange beforehand) or hitch with Bolivian trucks.

Adsubliata (☎ 058-241972) goes often to Tacna in Peru (US$2). Taxi colectivos to Tacna (US$4, one hour) leave from the bus terminal.

Buses Litoral (☎ 058-254702) goes from Arica to La Paz (US$17, nine hours) Monday, Wednesday and Saturday at 7 am. Comfortable but heavily booked Buses Géminis (☎ 058-241647) goes to La Paz (US$22, eight hours) Monday, Wednesday and Thursday at 10 am. Several other companies serve La Paz.

Train Trains to Tacna (US$1.30, 1½ hours) depart from the Ferrocarril Arica-Tacna (☎ 058-231115), Máximo Lira 889, Monday, Wednesday and Friday around noon and 4 pm.

Getting Around
To/From the Airport Radio Taxis Aeropuerto Chacalluta (☎ 058-254812), at Patricio Lynch and 21 de Mayo, has taxis (US$10) and colectivos (US$4 per person) to Aeropuerto Chacalluta (☎ 058-222831), 18km north of Arica.

Bus For the bus terminal, take a bus or the faster taxi colectivo No 8 from 18 de Septiembre.

Car The main rental agencies are Hertz (☎ 058-231487), General Velásquez 1109, and Avis (☎ 058-232210), Chacabuco 180.

AROUND ARICA
Museo Arqueológico San Miguel de Azapa
Twelve km from Arica, this archaeological museum has elaborate displays on regional cultures from the 7th century BC to the Spanish invasion. The visit is self-paced, with an informative booklet in Spanish or English. Ask about nearby geoglyphs.

It's open 9 am to 8 pm daily in January and February, 10 am to 6 pm the rest of the year; admission is US$1.25 for adults, US$0.50 for children. From Maipú and Patricio Lynch in Arica, taxi colectivos charge about US$1 to the front gate.

Valle de Lluta
Fourteen km north of Arica, paved Ruta 11 leads up the Lluta valley to Poconchile. A short distance inland, a series of hillside **geoglyphs** depicting llamas recalls pre-Columbian pack trains to Tiahuanaco.

Poconchile's 17th-century **Iglesia de San Gerónimo**, restored earlier this century, is one of Chile's oldest churches; ask for the key at the restaurant. Bus Lluta goes here from the corner of Chacabuco and Vicuña Mackenna in Arica.

Pukará de Copaquilla
As Ruta 11 zigzags up the desolate mountainside above the Lluta valley, it passes many 'candle-holder' cacti, which absorb moisture from the camanchaca. Tours to Parque Nacional Lauca stop briefly at the 12th-century Pukará de Copaquilla, a fortress built to protect farmlands in the canyon below – notice the abandoned terraces, evidence of larger pre-Columbian populations.

Along the highway just west of Copaquilla, the eccentric Posada Pueblo Maiko is a survivor of 1994's solar eclipse mania and a good spot for a drink and a sandwich.

PUTRE
Putre, 3500m above sea level and 150km northeast of Arica, was a 16th-century *reducción* (a Spanish settlement established to control the Indians). Many buildings retain colonial features, most notably the restored adobe **Iglesia de Putre** (1670). Local farmers raise alfalfa for llamas, sheep and cattle on ancient stone-faced terraces.

Restaurant Oasis, at Cochrane and O'Higgins, offers basic lodgings for US$5 and good plain meals. *Residencial La Paloma*, on Baquedano between Carrera and Cochrane, has hot showers and good beds for US$7 per person, but the thin walls mean it's noisy sometimes. Meals are also available. Opposite the army camp, Conaf's cozy *Refugio Putre* charges US$10.

Buses La Paloma (☎ 058-222710), Germán Riesco 2071 in Arica, serves Putre daily, departing Arica at 6:45 am, returning in early afternoon. Buses to Parinacota, in Parque Nacional Lauca (see below), pass the turnoff to Putre, which is 5km off the main highway.

PARQUE NACIONAL LAUCA

Parque Nacional Lauca is a 138,000-hectare altiplano biosphere reserve with vicuña, vizcacha and 150 bird species, plus cultural and archaeological landmarks. The Pallachata volcanoes behind sprawling Lago Chungará are dormant, but nearby Guallatire smokes ominously.

Lauca is 160km northeast of Arica, between 3000 and 6300m above sea level. Visitors should adapt to the altitude gradually; do not exert yourself at first and eat and drink moderately. If you suffer altitude sickness try the herbal tea remedy *chachacoma*. You'll need sunblock against the brutal tropical rays, but it can also snow during *invierno boliviano* (Bolivian winter, the summer rainy season).

Flocks of vicuña graze the verdant *bofedales* (boglands) and lower mountain slopes, alongside domestic llamas and alpacas. Note the ground-hugging llareta, a bright green shrub with a deceptive cushion-like appearance; the Aymara use a pick or mattock to crack open dead plants for fuel.

The park is under siege from regional authorities and mining interests who want to reduce its size by a third for a highly speculative gold extraction project that would pollute precordillera waters and lower air quality. It has also come under pressure, more appropriately, from Aymara herders with legitimate but only recently acknowledged land titles for much of the altiplano.

Things to See & Do

The Las Cuevas entrance is an excellent place to photograph vicuñas, whose numbers have increased from barely 1000 in the early 1970s to over 17,000 today. Try a soak in the rustic thermal baths.

Domestic stock graze the Ciénegas de Parinacota between the villages of Chucuyo and Parinacota, and wildlife and cultural relics are abundant; have a look at Chucuyo's colonial chapel. *Guallatas* (Andean geese) and ducks drift on the Río Lauca and nest on the banks, and chinchilla-like vizcachas peek out from rockeries. Parinacota, an Aymara village 5km off the highway, has a 17th-century church, with Bosch-like interior murals.

Lava from 6350m Volcán Parinacota dammed a snowmelt stream to form shallow Lago Chungará, over 4500m above sea level and 28km from Las Cuevas. Birds at Chungará include flamingos, giant coots and Andean gulls, but Arica's demand for hydroelectricity and the Azapa valley's thirst have created an intricate system of pumps and canals that may compromise the area's ecological integrity.

Places to Stay & Eat

In a pinch *Refugio Las Cuevas*, at the park entrance, may offer a bed. In Chucuyo, Matilde and Máximo Morales usually have an inexpensive spare bed, and Matilde prepares alpaca steaks and other simple meals for about US$3. There are two other cheap restaurants, but buy most supplies in Arica.

At spacious but sparsely furnished *Refugio Parinacota*, Conaf charges US$11 for beds and solar-heated hot water; bring a sleeping bag. Tent sites cost US$7 here and at Chungará, which has picnic tables, some shelter and *very* cold nights. *Refugio Chungará* also has eight beds at US$11 per person.

Getting There & Away

The park straddles the Arica-La Paz highway, which is now paved to La Paz. For buses, see the Arica entry.

Many Arica travel agencies, mostly on or near Paseo Bolognesi, offer tours (about US$20), leaving around 7:30 am and returning about 8:30 pm. Birding Alto Andino (☎ 058-241322), Baquedano 299 in Putre, runs guided birding trips in the precordillera and altiplano.

Tours are a good introduction, but try to arrange a longer stay – a rental car lets you visit more remote areas like Guallatire, Caquena and Salar de Surire. Carry extra fuel.

IQUIQUE

Iquique (population 140,000) was a collection of shanties until the 19th-century mining boom, when nitrate barons built mansions and authorities piped in water from the Andes. Its Plaza de Armas, with a Victorian clock tower and a theater with Corinthian columns, reflects this boom.

Iquique's port now ships more fish meal than any other in the world, while the

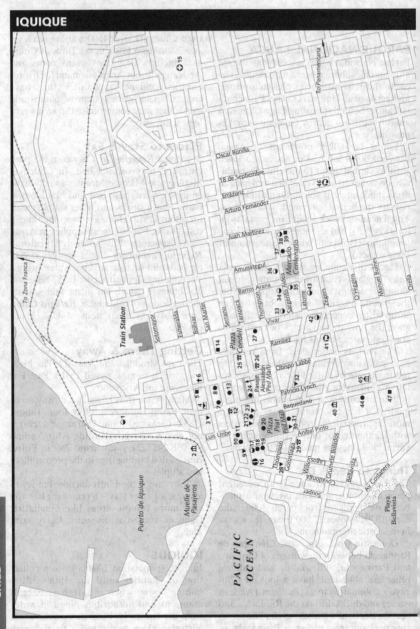

IQUIQUE

To Panamericana

To Zona Franca

Train Station

Oscar Bonilla

18 de Septiembre

Errázuriz

Arturo Fernández

Juan Martínez

Amunátegui

Barros Arana

Thompson

Tarapacá

Vivar

Ramírez

Obispo Labbé

Patricio Lynch

Baquedano

Aníbal Pinto

Thompson

Gorostiaga

Covadonga

Souper

Sotomayor

Esmeralda

Bolívar

San Martín

Serrano

Plaza Condell

Pasaje Alessandri (Ped Mall)

Luis Uribe

Plaza Prat

Lagos

Wilson

Bellavista

Av Costanera

Mercado Centenario

Sargento Aldea

Latorre

Zegers

O'Higgins

Manuel Bulnes

Orella

Plaza Prat (Ped Mall)

Gumete Bolados

PACIFIC OCEAN

Puerto de Iquique

Muelle de Pasajeros

Playa Bellavista

CHILE

Av Héroes de la Concepción

To Playa Brava,
Airport, Tocopilla

Playa
Cavancha

Playa
Saint Tropez

Av Presidente Balmaceda

Libertad

Céspedes y Gónzalez

Manuel Rodríguez

Av Portales

Hernán Fuenzalida

Bonilla

José Miguel Carrera

Tl Pérez

Riquelme

0   100   200 m
0   100   200 yards

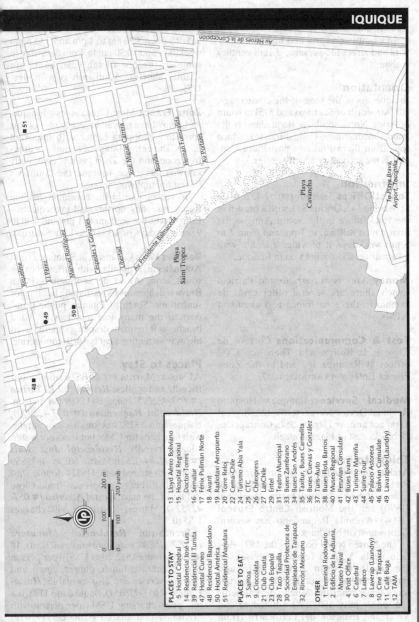

PLACES TO STAY
5 Hostal Catedral
14 Residencial José Luis
39 Residencial El Turista
47 Hostal Cuneo
48 Residencial Baquedano
50 Hostal America
51 Residencial Manutara

PLACES TO EAT
3 Samoa
9 Cioccolata
21 Club Croata
23 Club Español
28 Taco Taquilla
30 Sociedad Protectora de
     Empleados de Tarapacá
32 Rincón Mexicano

13 Lloyd Aéreo Boliviano
15 Hospital Regional
     Doctor Torres
16 Sernatur
17 Fénix Pullman Norte
18 Avant
19 Radiotaxi Aeropuerto
20 Torre Reloj
22 Cema-Chile
24 Turismo Abía Yala
25 CTC
26 Chilexpress
27 LanChile
29 Entel
31 Teatro Municipal
33 Buses Zambrano
34 Buses San Andrés
35 Taxitur, Buses Carmelita
36 Buses Cuevas y González
37 Turis-Auto
38 Buses Flota Barrios
40 Museo Regional
41 Peruvian Consulate
42 Buses Evans
43 Turismo Mamiña
44 Surire Tour
45 Palacio Astoreca
46 Bolivian Consulate
49 Lavarápido (Laundry)

OTHER
1 Terminal Rodoviario
2 Edificio de la Aduana,
    Museo Naval
4 Post Office
6 Catedral
7 Ladeco
8 Laverap (Laundry)
10 Cine Tarapacá
11 Café Buga
12 TAM

CHILE

modern duty-free shopping center (zona franca), has added to prosperity. Downtown's ramshackle wooden houses, sailors' bars and street life preserve a 19th-century feeling.

Orientation

Iquique sits at the base of the coast range, 1853km north of Santiago and 315km south of Arica. North-south Av Baquedano is the main thoroughfare. Calle Tarapacá, which runs from Plaza Prat east past Plaza Condell, is the secondary activity center.

Information

Tourist Offices Sernatur (☎ 057-427686) is at Serrano 145, Oficina 303, with a branch at the zona franca in the Sector Antiguo, 1st floor. Open 8:30 am to 1 pm and from 3 to 6 pm weekdays, it provides a leaflet with information about what's on in Iquique.

Money Afex is at Serrano and Patricio Lynch; there are several other casas de cambio in the zona franca and abundant ATMs.

Post & Communications Correos de Chile is at Bolívar 458. There are CTC offices at Ramírez 587 and in the Zona Franca. Entel is at Gorostiaga 287.

Medical Services Iquique's Hospital Regional Doctor Torres (☎ 057-422370) is at Tarapacá and Av Héroes de la Concepción, 10 blocks east of Plaza Condell.

Things to See

Architectural landmarks on or near Plaza Prat include the 1877 **Torre Reloj** (clock tower), the neoclassical **Teatro Municipal** (1890) and the Moorish **Centro Español** (1904). Avenida Baquedano has several Georgian-style buildings.

The Museo Naval occupies the 1871 Edificio de la Aduana (customs house), on Esmeralda between Aníbal Pinto and Baquedano. Just west of the Aduana, harbor tours leave from the Muelle de Pasajeros (passenger jetty, 1901). At Sotomayor and Vivar, the Estación del Ferrocarril (train station) once served nitrate oficinas.

Once a courthouse, the Museo Regional features pre-Columbian artifacts, a mock altiplano village, Aymara crafts, historical

photos and a detailed model of Oficina Peña Chica, near Humberstone. At Baquedano 951, it's open 8:30 am to 1 pm and 3 to 8 pm weekdays and 10:30 am to 1 pm Saturday in summer; the rest of the year, hours are slightly shorter. Admission is a modest US$0.70.

Zona Franca Most Chileans visit Iquique, and many have moved here, because of this sprawling shopping center with imported goods. The entire Tarapacá region is a duty-free zone, and the *Zofri* (as it is commonly known) has given Iquique the country's lowest unemployment rate.

To see or join in the consumer feeding frenzy, take any northbound taxi colectivo from downtown 9:30 am to 1 pm and 4:30 to 9 pm weekdays, or 9:30 am to 1 pm Saturday.

Beaches Playa Cavancha, at Balmaceda and Amunátegui, is popular with surfers; farther south, along Av 11 de Septiembre, Playa Brava is dangerous for swimming but fine for sunbathing. South of Iquique, public transport to the many fine and less crowded beaches is infrequent despite a superb paved highway, so renting a car is worth considering.

Places to Stay

At Juan Martínez 849-857, simple but friendly and spotless *Residencial El Turista* (☎ 057-422245), charges US$8 per person. *Residencial Baquedano* (☎ 057-422990), Baquedano 1315, has small clean singles with firm beds for US$9, but lacks hot water. Clean, friendly *Residencial José Luis* (☎ 057-422844), San Martín 601, costs US$9 single with shared bath, US$14 double with private bath, but gets short-stay trade. Close to Playa Cavancha, *Hostal América* (☎ 057-427524), Manuel Rodríguez 550, charges US$10.

French-run *Residencial Manutara* (☎ 057-418280; manutara@hotmail.com), 18 de Septiembre 1512, costs US$10 per person with breakfast; lunch, dinner, email and laundry service are also available. *Hostal Cuneo* (☎ 057-428654), Baquedano 1175, is a fine place charging US$11 per person with breakfast and shared bath, US$19 with private bath, but some interior rooms lack windows. Not the value it once was but still often full, tidy *Hostal Catedral* (☎ 057-412184), Obispo Labbé 233, charges US$12 with shared bath, while rooms with private bath are US$26/32.

Places to Eat

At the **Mercado Centenario**, on Barros Arana between Sargento Aldea and Latorre, several upstairs cocinerías offer varied seafood at moderate prices. **Ciocco-lata**, Aníbal Pinto 487, is good for breakfast or onces. Reader-recommended **Samoa** Bolívar 396, has economical fixed-price lunches, as does the **Sociedad Protectora de Empleados de Tarapacá**, Thompson 207.

The **Club Croata**, Plaza Prat 310, has excellent lunches for US$6. Not to be missed are the ornate Moorish interior and artwork at the **Club Español**, at the northeast corner of Plaza Prat, but it's become expensive.

Iquique has two Mexican restaurants: the Tex-Mex **Taco Taquilla** at Thompson 123, and the more genuinely Mexican **Rincón Mexicano** at Patricio Lynch 754, which has fine food, excellent service, real corn tortillas and tasty but pricey margaritas.

Getting There & Away

Air LanChile (☎ 057-427600), Vivar 675, averages six flights daily to Arica and to Santiago (US$127 to US$213); most of the latter stop in Antofagasta. There are daily flights to La Paz, Bolivia and Tuesday, Thursday and Sunday flights to Santa Cruz, Bolivia.

Ladeco (☎ 057-413038), San Martín 428, Local 2, flies five times daily to Santiago, usually stopping in Antofagasta but also once in La Serena, and three times daily to Arica. Avant (☎ 057-428800), Aníbal Pinto 555, has similar routes but is slightly cheaper (US$122 to US$154 to Santiago).

LAB (☎ 057-426750), Serrano 430, flies Monday to Santa Cruz and Cochabamba, Bolivia. TAM (☎ 057-410155), Patricio Lynch 455, flies Tuesday, Thursday and Saturday to Asunción, Paraguay.

Bus Iquique's shabby Terminal Rodoviario (☎ 057-416315) is at the north end of Patricio Lynch, but passengers can also board at company ticket offices, mostly near the Mercado Centenario. Services north (to Arica) and south are frequent; nearly all southbound services now use Ruta 1, the coastal highway to Tocopilla (for connections to Calama), Antofagasta, Santiago and intermediates.

Buses to Arica (four hours) cost US$7, while faster taxi colectivos charge US$12. Sample long-distance bus fares include Calama (US$15), Antofagasta (US$20, eight hours), Caldera/Copiapó (US$30, 14 hours), La Serena (US$35, 18 hours) and Santiago (US$45, 24 hours). Try Turis-Auto, Sargento Aldea 931, for colectivos to these destinations.

Buses San Andrés (☎ 057-413953), Sargento Aldea 798, goes daily to Pica, Arica and Santiago. Turismo Mamiña (☎ 057-420330) at Latorre 779, goes to interior destinations like Pica, Mamiña and Matilla. Taxitur (☎ 057-422044), Sargento Aldea 791, has taxi colectivos to Mamiña and Pica.

Monday and Thursday at 11:15 pm, Tramaca (☎ 057-413884) offers service to Jujuy and Salta, Argentina (US$65) via Calama. Mass y Kiss (☎ 057-417106) goes to Oruro, Bolivia (US$9, 12 hours) via Colchane, Tuesday, Thursday, Friday and Saturday at 11 pm. Chilebus (☎ 057-423065), at the terminal, also has Bolivian services.

Getting Around

Ladeco and LanChile taxi colectivos and minibuses (US$4) go to Aeropuerto Diego Aracena, 41km south of downtown via Ruta 1.

For car rental try Hertz (☎ 057-426316) at Souper 650, or Budget (☎ 057-429566) at O'Higgins 1361.

AROUND IQUIQUE

Because public transport to some areas is difficult, tours are worth considering. Sernatur has a full list of agencies: Try Turismo Abia Yala (☎ 057-422676), Patricio Lynch 554, Surire Tour (☎ 057-445440), Baquedano 1035, or Transtours (☎ 057-428984).

Humberstone

In this eerie nitrate ghost town, 45km northeast of Iquique, nearly all the original buildings, including the market and the theater, remain standing; some are being restored. For recreation there were tennis and basketball courts and an enormous swimming pool. At the west end are the power plant and the railway to the older Oficina Santa Laura.

Any bus from Iquique to Arica passes the ruins, where it's easy to catch a lift or bus back. Take food, water and your camera;

CHILE

there's a kiosk with snacks at the entrance. Admission costs US$2.50.

El Gigante de Atacama

The 86m pre-Columbian Giant of the Atacama, 14km east of Huara on the slopes of Cerro Unita, is best seen from a distance on the desert *pampa*; avoid climbing the hill and damaging the figure. The best way to visit the site is to hire a car or taxi.

La Tirana

In mid-July, up to 30,000 dancing pilgrims invade La Tirana (population 250), 72km southeast of Iquique, to honor the Virgin of Carmen. The **Santuario de La Tirana** is a broad plaza with one of Chile's oddest churches. There are no hotels or residenciales – pilgrims camp in open spaces to the east – but there are several restaurants around the plaza. The **Museo del Salitre** exhibits a haphazard assortment of artifacts from nitrate oficinas.

RESERVA NACIONAL PAMPA DEL TAMARUGAL

The dense groves lining the Panamericana south of Pozo Almonte are not a natural forest, but they are a native species; the tamarugo *(Prosopis tamarugo)* covered thousands of square kilometers until woodcutting for the mines nearly destroyed it. Conaf's 108,000-hectare reserve has restored much of this forest, which flourishes in highly saline soils by reaching deep for ground water.

Within the reserve, over 400 geoglyphs of humans, llamas and geometric shapes blanket the hillside at **Pintados**, 2km west of the Panamericana, nearly opposite the turnoff to Pica. It's actually a derelict railroad yard, a dry and dusty but easy walk from the highway – figure about 1½ hours each way, perhaps with a detour to avoid the junkyard dogs. Take food and water.

Conaf's visitor center, 24km south of Pozo Almonte, has fine displays on local ecology. Its guesthouse charges US$11 single; across the highway is a campground (US$7 for shaded sites with tables and benches).

MAMIÑA

Mamiña, 73km east of Pozo Almonte, has been a popular hot-springs resort since the nitrate era, but is much older – the **Pukará**

del Cerro Inca is a pre-Columbian fortress, while the **Iglesia de Nuestra Señora del Rosario** dates from 1632.

Residencial Sol de Ipla, Ipla s/n, offers the most economical accommodation, charging US$12 per person with shared bath. The friendly *Residencial Cholele,* has comfortable rooms for US$10 per person, including breakfast. The Spanish-run *Hotel La Coruña,* with a nice pool and restaurant (US$25 per person) is a better-value splurge than expensive *Hotel Refugio del Salitre.* For transport, see the Iquique entry.

PICA

Diego de Almagro skirmished with Indians at Pica, now a popular hot-springs resort, 119km southeast of Iquique on the road from La Tirana. In late colonial times, it was famous for wines and fruits, while in the 19th century, it supplied wheat, wine, figs, raisins and alfalfa to the oficinas.

Pica was so dependent on outside water that the Spaniards developed an elaborate delivery system of more than 15km of tunnels. When Iquique boomed, the Tarapacá Water Company piped water to the coast, and Pica became a 'hill station' for the nitrate barons.

Places to Stay & Eat

Nearly shadeless *Camping Miraflores* (☎ 057-741333), the municipal site at Miraflores 4, charges US$2.50 per person; it's adequate but crowded, especially weekends. Simple but clean *Hotel Palermo* (☎ 057-741129), Arturo Prat 233, charges US$7.50 per person with private bath, and also has a restaurant. Friendly, ramshackle *Hotel San Andrés* (☎ 057-741319), Balmaceda 197, is a non-smoking facility charging US$20 per person for spacious rooms with shared bath and full board.

For best menu, the hands-down winner is *El Edén*, Riquelme 12, which has patio dining, but items like seafood, quinoa and juices are not always available

For transport, see the Iquique section.

ANTOFAGASTA

Antofagasta (population 225,000), 1350km north of Santiago and 700km south of Arica, exports most of the Atacama's minerals, especially copper. Founded in 1870, it offered the easiest route to the interior and soon handled the highest tonnage of any South American Pacific port.

Freak floods in 1991 briefly obliterated the southern access road to the Panamericana, but the climate is usually clear and dry, neither too hot nor too cold. New port facilities at nearby Mejillones may reduce Antofagasta's economic importance.

Orientation

Downtown's western boundary is north-south Av Balmaceda, which eventually becomes Aníbal Pinto; to the south, it becomes Av Grecia. Within this central grid, bounded also by Bolívar and Ossa, streets run southwest to northeast. Plaza Colón is at the center.

Information

Tourist Offices Sernatur (☎ 055-264016), Maipú 240, is open 9:30 am to 1 pm and 3:30 to 7:30 pm weekdays. In front of Hotel Antofagasta, at Balmaceda and Prat, there's an information kiosk (☎ 055-224834) that keeps similar hours.

Money Besides downtown ATMs, try Cambio San Marcos at Baquedano 524, or Cambio Ancla Inn at Baquedano 508.

Post & Communications The post office is at Washington 2613. CTC long-distance services are at Condell 2527.

Medical Services The Hospital Regional (☎ 055-269009) is at Av Argentina 1962.

Things to See

The British community left a visible imprint in the **Torre Reloj**, a Big Ben replica on Plaza Colón; the **Barrio Histórico**, between Plaza Colón and the old port; and the **Muelle Salitrero** (nitrate pier), at the foot of Bolívar.

At Balmaceda and Bolívar, the former **Gobernación Marítima** (port authority) houses the **Museo Regional**. Across the street is the former **Aduana** (customs house), moved from the town of Mejillones in 1888. Across Bolívar is the **Estación Ferrocarril** (1887), former terminus of the La Paz railway.

Places to Stay

Plain, friendly *Residencial Riojanita* (☎ *055-268652)*, Baquedano 464, costs US$8 per person. *Hotel Capri* (☎ *055-263703)*

Copiapó 1208, is US$10 per person with shared bath. *Hotel Rawaye* (☎ *055-225399)*, Sucre 762, is US$8.50/13 for singles/doubles with shared bath, but its standards have declined. Recommended *Hotel Brasil* (☎ *055-267268)*, Ossa 1978, has spacious rooms with shared bath for US$9 per person; the hot showers are excellent.

Places to Eat

The best value is the unpretentious *Terminal Pesquero*, at the old port, where simple stands peddle tasty fresh shellfish and masses of pelicans lurk for scraps. Similar fare is available at the *Mercado Central*, on Ossa between Maipú and Uribe.

The *Casino de Bomberos*, Sucre 763, has set lunches for about US$4. *Bavaria*, Ossa 2424, is part of a reliable but uninspired chain. The always crowded, inexpensive *Spiedo*, at Prat and Ossa, specializes in grilled chicken.

D'Alfredo, Condell 2539, is a chain with pizza at reasonable prices, but Antofagasta's best pizzería is *Pizzanté*, Carrera 1857. Carnivores will enjoy *El Arriero*, Condell 2644, for large portions, attentive service and classic decor. Perhaps worth a look is *Mexall*, an expensive Mexican restaurant at Orchard and Poupin.

Getting There & Away

Air LanChile (☎ 055-265151) is at Washington 2552; Ladeco (☎ 055-269170) is nearby at Washington 2589. Flight schedules resemble those at Iquique and Arica, though Ladeco also has a daily flight to Calama and one southbound flight stops in La Serena. Several LanChile flights also continue to Calama. Santiago fares are US$111 to US$189.

Avant (☎ 055-284412), Prat 268, has similar itineraries but slightly cheaper fares (US$107 to US$150 to Santiago).

Bus Most bus companies have their own downtown terminals, but a few long-distance and most locally-based carriers use the Terminal de Buses Rurales, Riquelme 513. Nearly all northbound services now use coastal Ruta 1, via Tocopilla, en route to Iquique and Arica. International buses fill rapidly, so purchase tickets as far in advance as possible.

Tramaca (☎ 055-251770), Uribe 936, has frequent buses to Calama, some continuing

ANTOFAGASTA

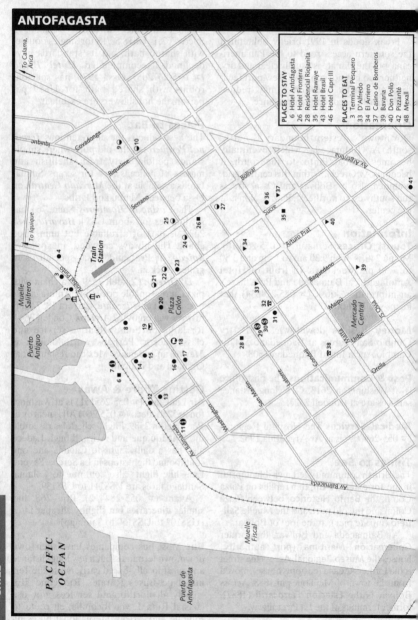

PLACES TO STAY
6   Hotel Antofagasta
26 Hotel Frontera
28 Residencial Riojanita
35 Hotel Rawaye
43 Hotel Brasil
46 Hotel Capri III

PLACES TO EAT
3   Terminal Pesquero
33 D'Alfredo
34 El Arriero
37 Casino de Bomberos
39 Bavaria
40 Don Pollo
42 Pizzanté
48 Mexall

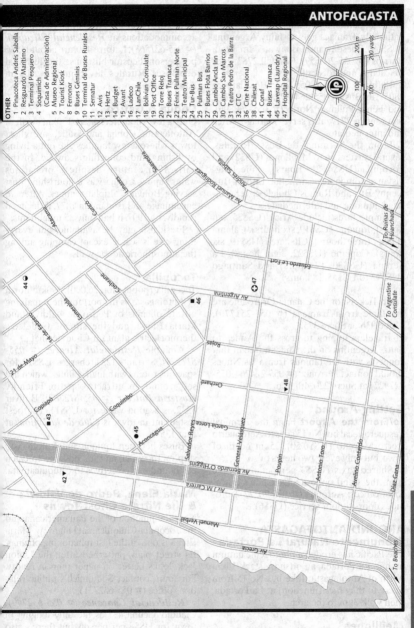

ANTOFAGASTA

OTHER
1 Pinacoteca Andrés Sabella
2 Resguardo Marítimo
3 Terminal Pesquero
4 Soquimich
   (Casa de Administración)
5 Museo Regional
7 Tourist Kiosk
8 Ferronor
9 Buses Geminis
10 Terminal de Buses Rurales
11 Sernatur
12 Avis
13 Hertz
14 Budget
15 Avant
16 Ladeco
17 LanChile
18 Bolivian Consulate
19 Post Office
20 Torre Reloj
21 Buses Tramaca
22 Fénix Pullman Norte
23 Teatro Municipal
24 Tur-Bus
25 Pullman Bus
27 Buses Flota Barrios
29 Cambio Anda Inn
30 Cambio San Marcos
31 Teatro Pedro de la Barra
32 CTC
36 Cine Nacional
38 Chilesat
41 Conaf
44 Buses Tramaca
45 Laverap (Laundry)
47 Hospital Regional

To Ruinas de Huanchaca

To Argentine Consulate

To Beaches

CHILE

to San Pedro de Atacama, plus daily service to Arica, Santiago and intermediates. Internationally, Tramaca goes to Jujuy, Argentina (US$60), Tuesday and Friday at 7 am. Flota Barrios (☎ 055-268559), Condell 2782, goes to Calama and Tocopilla.

Pullman Bus (☎ 055-262591), Latorre 2805, Tur-Bus (☎ 055-264487), Latorre 2751, and Fénix Pullman Norte (☎ 055-268896), San Martín 2717, also serve Santiago, Arica and intermediates.

From the Terminal de Buses Rurales, several carriers go to Mejillones (US$2) and Tocopilla (US$4, 2½ hours), while long-distance companies Carmelita, Litoral Bus, Kenny Bus and Ramos Cholele cover Santiago, Iquique and intermediates.

Sample fares include Arica (US$25, ten hours), Iquique (US$19, six hours), Calama (US$5, three hours), Chañaral (US$19, six hours), Copiapó (US$22, eight hours), La Serena (US$30, 12 hours) and Santiago (US$42 to US$45, 18 hours).

Train Tickets for the Calama-Oruro line are available from Tramaca (☎ 055-251770), Uribe 936 or Sucre 375.

Travelers hoping to cross the Andes to Salta, Argentina on the Chilean freight that connects with the famous Tren a las Nubes should contact Ferronor (☎ 055-224764, 055-227927) at Sucre 220, 4th floor.

Getting Around
To/From the Airport From the Terminal Pesquero, local bus No 15 goes to Aeropuerto Cerro Moreno (US$0.50), 25km north of town, but only every two hours or so.

Shared taxis (US$3 per person) leave from the stand opposite LanChile's downtown offices; Aerobus (☎ 055-262727) provides door-to-door service (US$6).

AROUND ANTOFAGASTA
Monumento Natural La Portada
The Pacific has eroded a photogenic natural arch in La Portada, an offshore stack 16km north of Antofagasta. Take bus No 15 from Sucre to the *cruce* (junction) at La Portada, then walk 3km to the arch.

Mejillones
Mejillones, a small beach resort 60km north of Antofagasta, is poised to become a major

port after completion of the paved highway across the Andes to Argentina. Reasonable accommodations at **Residencial Elizabeth** *(☎ 055-621568)*, Latorre 440, are about US$6 per person. Fepstur buses use the Terminal de Buses Rurales at Riquelme 513 in Antofagasta.

Cobija & Gatico
Only a few kilometers apart, 130km north of Antofagasta, Cobija and Gatico are ghost towns where a few families eke out a living by fishing and collecting seaweed. In the early 19th century, despite a precarious water supply, Cobija was a flourishing port serving Bolivia's altiplano mines. After an earthquake and tsunami in 1877, it declined rapidly; by 1907, it had only 35 inhabitants.

Fresh fish may be available, but everything else is scarce except camping among the atmospheric adobe walls.

Tocopilla
Tocopilla (population 26,000), 190km north of Antofagasta, is the port for the remaining nitrate oficinas of Pedro de Valdivia and María Elena, and the site of Codelco's thermoelectric plant for Chuquicamata.

Amiable **Residencial Álvarez** *(☎ 055-811578)*, Serrano 1234, charges US$10 for spacious rooms with high ceilings, which are set around an attractive patio. Friendly **Hostería Bolívar** *(☎ 055-812783)*, Bolívar 1332, is a good value for US$11. The best restaurant in town is **Club de la Unión**, at Prat 1354.

Buses between Iquique and Antofagasta stop in Tocopilla, and it's possible to catch eastbound taxi colectivos to Chuquicamata.

María Elena, Pedro de Valdivia & the Nitrate Ghost Towns
Near the junction of the Panamericana and the Tocopilla-Chuquicamata highway, María Elena is one of the last functioning oficinas. Its street plan, patterned after the Union Jack, looks better on paper than in reality. For tours, contact Soquimich's public relations office (☎ 055-632731).

Residencial Chacance *(☎ 055-632749)*, Claudio Vicuña 437, is the only lodging in town, for US$8 per person, but there's also camping on the Río Loa on the east side of the Panamericana. Decent food is available at *Yerco* and the *Club Social*. Some Tramaca and Flota Barrios buses from Antofagasta to Calama stop here.

Pedro de Valdivia, 40km south, is also open to the public. Meals are available at the *Club Pedro de Valdivia*. Tramaca and Flota Barrios buses go directly to Antofagasta.

Dozens of ghost towns line both sides of the Baquedano-Calama road and the Panamericana north of the Tocopilla-Chuquicamata highway.

Baquedano

Between Antofagasta and Calama, Baquedano was a major rail junction where the Longino (longitudinal railway) met the Antofagasta-La Paz line. Its **Museo Ferroviario** is a notable open-air rail museum. An infrequent, agonizingly slow and indescribably filthy freight train still runs from here to the Argentine border at Socompa – for truly intrepid travelers only. See the Antofagasta Getting There & Away entry for details.

CALAMA

Calama (population 110,000), 220km from Antofagasta and 2700m above sea level, is the gateway to Chuquicamata, the oases of San Pedro de Atacama and Toconao and the eerie El Tatio geysers. It's also the western terminus of the Calama-Uyuni (Bolivia) railway.

Orientation

Plaza 23 de Marzo is the center of Calama. Though the town has sprawled on the north bank of the Río Loa because laborers prefer it to higher, colder Chuquicamata, its core is pedestrian-friendly.

Information

Tourist Offices The municipal Oficina de Turismo (☎ 055-345345), Latorre 1689, is open 9 am to 1 pm and 3 to 7 pm weekdays. There's usually an English speaker on duty in summer, when it's also open Saturday mornings.

Money Besides ATMs, Money Exchange, Sotomayor 1837, pays good rates, with no commission for traveler's checks.

Post & Communications Correos de Chile is at Vicuña Mackenna 2167. Entel is at Sotomayor 2027.

Medical Services Hospital Carlos Cisterna (☎ 055-342347) is at Av Granaderos and Cisterna, 5 blocks north of the plaza.

Organized Tours

Limited public transport makes tours a reasonable alternative. Itineraries vary, but the most complete one (for about US$25) goes from Calama to the El Tatio geysers and returns via villages with traditional Andean churches.

Other tours involve overnighting in San Pedro de Atacama, stopping at Valle de La Luna (Valley of the Moon) before visiting El Tatio. Another visits the Salar de Atacama, including the village of Toconao (US$15 from San Pedro). In general, it's more convenient to make arrangements for El Tatio in San Pedro, because it's cheaper and the trip is shorter and less tiring. Tours to El Tatio leave as early as 3 am.

Calama operators include Turismo El Sol (☎ 055-340152), on Cobija between Abaroa and Latorre, and Desert Adventure (☎ 055-3344894) at Latorre 1602.

Places to Stay

Tolerable by budget standards but avoided by some travelers, *Residencial Capri* (☎ 055-342870), Vivar 1639, is Calama's cheapest at US$5.50 per person. Tidy *Nuevo Hotel Los Andes* (☎ 055-341073), Vivar 1920, costs US$7.50. Long popular with foreign visitors, tranquil *Residencial Toño* (☎ 055-341185), Vivar 1970, provides clean sheets and lots of blankets for the same price.

Friendly *Hotel El Loa* (☎ 055-341963), Abaroa 1617, offers spotless rooms with shared bath for US$11/20. Reader-endorsed *Hostal Internacional* (☎ 055-342927), General Velásquez 1976, is OK but a bit rundown for US$12/23.

At the very good *Residencial John Kenny* (☎ 055-341430), Ecuador 1991, rates start at US$13 per person; rooms with private bath cost US$25 per person. A big step up, the architecturally distinctive *Hotel El Mirador* (☎ 055-340329), Sotomayor 2064, costs US$50/65.

Places to Eat

At the Mercado Central, on Latorre between Ramírez and Vargas, there are several inexpensive cocinerías. The inexpensive *Osorno*,

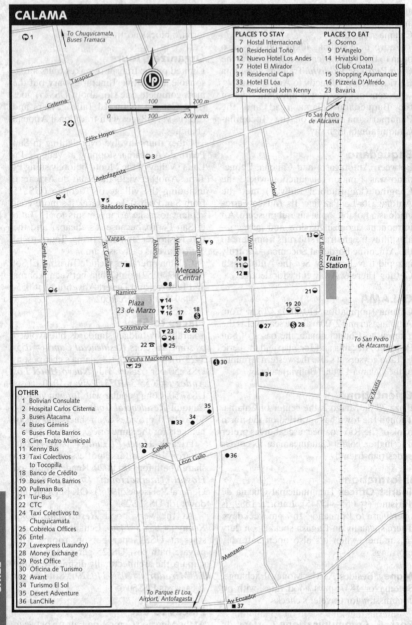

CALAMA

To Chuquicamata,
Buses Tramaca

Tarapacá

Cisterna

Félix Hoyos

0   100   200 m
0   100   200 yards

To San Pedro
de Atacama

Antofagasta

Bañados Espinoza

Vargas

Santa María

Av Granaderos

Abaroa

Velásquez

Latorre

Vivar

Av Balmaceda

Ramírez

Plaza
23 de Marzo

Mercado
Central

Train
Station

Sotomayor

Vicuña Mackenna

To San Pedro
de Atacama

Av Matta

Cobija

León Gallo

Manzano

To Parque El Loa,
Airport, Antofagasta

Av Ecuador

PLACES TO STAY	PLACES TO EAT
7 Hostal Internacional	5 Osorno
10 Residencial Toño	9 D'Angelo
12 Nuevo Hotel Los Andes	14 Hrvatski Dom
17 Hotel El Mirador	(Club Croata)
31 Residencial Capri	15 Shopping Apumanque
33 Hotel El Loa	16 Pizzería D'Alfredo
37 Residencial John Kenny	23 Bavaria

OTHER
1   Bolivian Consulate
2   Hospital Carlos Cisterna
3   Buses Atacama
4   Buses Géminis
6   Buses Flota Barrios
8   Cine Teatro Municipal
11 Kenny Bus
13 Taxi Colectivos
    to Tocopilla
18 Banco de Crédito
19 Buses Flota Barrios
20 Pullman Bus
21 Tur-Bus
22 CTC
24 Taxi Colectivos to
    Chuquicamata
25 Cobreloa Offices
26 Entel
27 Lavexpress (Laundry)
28 Money Exchange
29 Post Office
30 Oficina de Turismo
32 Avant
34 Turismo El Sol
35 Desert Adventure
36 LanChile

upstairs at Granaderos 2013-B, is also a functioning peña.

The *Hrvatski Dom* (Club Croata or Croatian Club), facing Plaza 23 de Marzo, is more upmarket but has good fixed-price lunches. Next-door *Shopping Apumanque*, Abaroa 1859, also has good fixed-price meals, but the a la carte menu is more expensive. Around the corner at Sotomayor 2093, *Bavaria* has reliable breakfasts and other meat-and-potatoes fare.

Pizzería D'Alfredo, Abaroa 1835, is the local branch of a regional chain; also try *D'Angelo*, Latorre 1983.

Getting There & Away

Air Ladeco (☎ 055-312626), Ramírez 1858, flies 12 times weekly to Antofagasta and Santiago (US$126 to US$185), while Lan-Chile (☎ 055-341477), Latorre 1499, flies 20 times weekly. Avant (☎ 055-341614), Cobija 2188, flies similar routes but is slightly cheaper (US$116 to US$156).

Bus Calama has no central terminal, but most companies are within a few blocks of each other.

Tramaca (☎ 055-340404) has its terminal at Av Granaderos 3048. It has frequent buses to Antofagasta, plus several daily to Santiago, Arica and Iquique. Tur-Bus (☎ 055-316699), Ramírez 1802, has similar services, as do Flota Barrios (☎ 055-341497), Ramírez 2298 and on Sotomayor between Vivar and Balmaceda; Pullman Bus (☎ 055-311410), Sotomayor 1808; and Géminis (☎ 055-341993), Antofagasta 2239. Kenny Bus (☎ 055-342514), Vivar 1954, serves Iquique via María Elena and Pozo Almonte.

Several carriers serve San Pedro de Atacama (US$2.50), including Buses Atacama (☎ 055-314757), Abaroa 2105-B.

Taxi colectivos to Tocopilla leave from Balmaceda and Vargas, 1 block north of the Tur-Bus terminal.

Sample fares include Antofagasta (US$5.50, three hours), Arica (US$22, nine hours), Copiapó (US$25, 11 hours), La Serena (US$35, 16 hours) and Santiago (US$44, 20 hours).

International buses are invariably full, so make reservations as far in advance as possible. Tramaca crosses the Andes to Jujuy and Salta, Argentina leaving Tuesday and Friday at 10 am (US$52).

Train Thursday at 3 am there's train service to Ollagüe, on the Bolivian border, with connections to Uyuni (US$15) and Oruro (US$22). Tickets are available either at the Tramaca bus terminal or from Calama's train station (☎ 055-342004), Balmaceda 1777; tickets may also be available at Tramaca offices in Antofagasta and Santiago.

Getting Around

Aeropuerto El Loa (☎ 055-311331) is a short taxi ride south of town.

Calama has many car-rental agencies, but to visit El Tatio geyser field, rent a jeep or pickup truck – passenger cars are unsuitable for the rugged roads.

CHUQUICAMATA

Chuquicamata (population 13,000), a company town 16km north of Calama, provides half of Chile's copper output and about 25% of its total export income. The 400m-deep open-pit mine is the world's largest.

Chuqui changed hands several times before the US Anaconda Copper Mining Company began excavations in 1915. Out of nothing, Anaconda created a city with housing, schools, cinemas, shops, a hospital and clinics – though many accused it of taking out more than it put in.

By the 1960s, Anaconda was a target for those who advocated the nationalization of the copper industry. During the Frei Montalva administration, the state gained a majority shareholding and, in 1971, Congress enthusiastically approved nationalization. After 1973, the junta compensated foreign companies for loss of assets, but retained ownership through the Corporación del Cobre de Chile (Codelco). Over the next few years Chuqui's entire population will be relocated to Calama, and the town will exclusively serve as a workplace.

Chuqui is an orderly town whose landscape recalls its history. The stadium is the **Estadio Anaconda**, while the **Auditorio Sindical** is a huge theater with an interior mural commemorating a contentious strike. A prominent statue honors workers who operated equipment like the behemoth power shovel nearby.

Organized Tours

For weekday two-hour tours, report to the Oficina Ayuda a la Infancia, at the top of

Av JM Carrera, by 9 am. Bring your passport and make a modest donation (about US$2.50). Demand is high in January and February, so get there early; with enough demand, there are afternoon tours.

Places to Eat
Good lunches are available at the *Club de Empleados* and the *Arco Iris Center*, both across from the plaza on Av JM Carrera, and the *Club de Obreros*, on Mariscal Alcázar 2 blocks south of the stadium. Try also *Carloncho*, on Av Comercial O'Higgins.

Getting There & Away
Taxi colectivos (US$1.50) leave Calama from Abaroa near Vicuña Mackenna. There are also buses from Granaderos and Ramírez.

SAN PEDRO DE ATACAMA
San Pedro de Atacama is an oasis village at the north end of the Salar de Atacama, a vast saline lake, 120km southeast of Calama. To its east rise immense volcanoes, both active and extinct. Nearby is the Valle de la Luna (Valley of the Moon).

At 2440m above sea level, San Pedro's adobe houses preserve a colonial feeling. In the early 20th century, the village was a major stop on cattle drives from Argentina to the nitrate mines, but the Salta-Antofagasta railway ended this era.

No longer on the cattle trail, San Pedro is now on the 'gringo trail.' Many young Chileans also spend their holidays here, and the newly paved highway from Jujuy, Argentina, is bringing other South American tourists along with Mercosur truck traffic headed for Iquique and Mejillones. Despite the increasing tourist trade, San Pedro remains attractive and affordable.

Information
Tourist Offices San Pedro's Oficina de Información Turística (☎ 055-851084), on the northeast corner of the Plaza de Armas at Toconao and Padre Le Paige, is open 10:30 am to 2:30 pm and 4 to 7:30 pm weekdays, 9 am to 1 pm weekends.

Money Cambios Atacama is on Caracoles between Tocopilla and Toconao. Money Exchange is on Toconao near Solcor, but don't expect good rates for traveler's checks.

Post & Communications Correos de Chile is on Padre Le Paige, opposite the museum. Entel is at the southwest corner of the Plaza, while CTC, on Caracoles half a block south of the Plaza, is open 8:30 am to 8 pm daily.

Warnings Some local residents, especially the indigenous Atacameño peoples, are sensitive to what they perceive as an overwhelming presence of outsiders. Visitors should make a special effort to behave appropriately and blend in as well as possible.

San Pedro's water has a high mineral content, and some visitors react poorly to it. If in doubt, drink bottled water.

Things to See
Museo Gustavo Le Paige In 1955, Belgian priest and archaeologist Gustavo Le Paige, assisted by villagers and the Universidad del Norte, began to assemble artifacts of the area's cultural evolution for this well-organized museum. It also includes exhibits on the Inca conquest, the Spanish invasion and contemporary cultural anthropology.

Half a block east of the plaza, on Padre Le Paige, the museum (☎ 055-851002) charges US$2.50 admission, half that with student ID.

Around the Plaza Over 450 years ago, Pedro de Valdivia's entourage passed through here with seeds, pigs and chickens and farming tools. On the east side of the plaza stands the **Casa de Pedro de Valdivia**, a restored adobe reportedly built around 1540. On the west side, the modified 17th-century **Iglesia San Pedro** was built with local materials – adobe, wood from the *cardón* cactus and leather straps in lieu of nails.

Organized Tours
San Pedro's many travel agencies compete fiercely, and not always ethically, to provide tours to nearby attractions. Among the best-established are Dutch-run Cosmo Andino (☎ 055-851069), at the corner of Tocopilla and Caracoles; Desert Adventure across the street; Inca Tour (☎ 055-851034) on the east side of the plaza; Expediciones Corvatsch Florida (☎ 055-851021) on Caracoles between Calama and Tocopilla.

To Bolivia Turismo Colque (☎ 055-851109), at Caracoles and Calama, is the best choice if you want to cross the Bolivian border at

Portezuelo del Cajón and continuing to Lago Verde and Uyuni, on the Bolivian side – Chilean operators have had problems with Bolivian authorities at this legally ambiguous border crossing. Colque's three-day trip goes to Laguna Colorada, the Salar de Uyuni and intermediate points before ending in the town of Uyuni. The price is US$80 per person with food; modest lodging is extra at Laguna Colorada and Hotel San Juan, near Chiguana. Travelers clear Chilean immigration at San Pedro and Bolivian immigration on arrival at Uyuni.

Places to Stay

Accommodations can be scarce around holiday periods like Chile's mid-September independence days.

Several campgrounds charge from US$2.50 to US$6 per person. *Residencial El Pukará*, on Tocopilla between Antofagasta and Caracoles, offers the cheapest but by no means bad lodgings for about US$8. At Domingo Atienza and Antofagasta, look for *Residencial Chiloé* (☎ *851017*), a good value at US$9 per person.

Other establishments in the same range include recommended *Residencial Rayco* (☎ *851008*), on Antofagasta, and *Residencial Puri* (☎ *851049*), on Caracoles west of Domingo Atienza, while next-door *Hostal Takha Takha* (☎ *851038*) charges US$11. *Casa Corvatsch* (☎ *851101*), on Antofagasta between Domingo Atienza and Calama, has firm beds and hot water for US$11 per person.

Places to Eat

Quitor, at the corner of Licancábur and Domingo Atienza, and *Juanita*, on the Plaza de Armas, both prepare simple but nourishing meals for US$4 or less.

On Calama between Licancábur and Antofagasta, *Café al Paso Sonchek* has drawn praise from visitors. *Tambo Cañaveral*, at Caracoles and Toconao, doubles as a night spot, with live Andean music Friday and Saturday nights. *La Estaka*, on Caracoles near Tocopilla, has excellent food, including vegetarian specials, and a lively bar. Highly recommended *Paachá*, Caracoles and Domingo Atienza, is a good splurge.

Shopping

For handicrafts, including cardón carvings and llama and alpaca ponchos, try the crafts market at the east end of Licancábur, by the museum.

Getting There & Away

San Pedro's 'bus terminal' is an open area on Licancábur, across from the Paseo Artesanal. There are about 10 buses daily to Calama (US$2.50, 1½ hours) with Buses Atacama, which also has two daily to Toconao (US$2).

AROUND SAN PEDRO DE ATACAMA

Swimming Holes

For year-round swimming check the enormous pools at Pozo 3, 3km east of town on the Toconao road, reached by foot or with a minivan that stops in front of Residencial La Florida. There are campsites and a restaurant here.

Pukará de Quitor & Catarpe

Ruins of a 12th-century fortress sit on a promontory above the Río San Pedro at Quitor, 3km northwest of San Pedro; across the river, Catarpe was an Inca administrative center. The best way to get here is to walk or bicycle.

Reserva Nacional Los Flamencos

Consisting of several scattered sectors near San Pedro, this Conaf-administered reserve has many attractions; the most accessible is **Valle de la Luna**, an area of strikingly eroded landforms 15km west of San Pedro. If driving, don't get stuck in the sand; if hiking or cycling, carry water and food, and smear yourself with sunblock.

South of San Pedro, the Salar de Atacama affords great views of the Andean chain of volcanoes, including imposing Licancábur, as well as the lower Cordillera Domeyko. At **Laguna Chaxa**, on the eastern edge of the Salar, nest three species of flamingos (James, Chilean and Andean) as well as smaller plovers, coots and ducks.

Conaf maintains an information center at Solcor, about 2km past San Pedro's customs and immigration post on the Toconao road. It's open 10 am to 1 pm and 2:30 to 4:30 pm daily. There's also a ranger station at Laguna Chaxa, where admission is US$1.50.

El Tatio Geysers

At an altitude of 4300m, 95km north of San Pedro, El Tatio is the world's highest geyser

CHILE

field. In the azure clarity of the altiplano, the steaming fumaroles at sunrise are unforgettable, and there are strikingly beautiful individual structures formed by mineral deposits where the boiling water evaporates. Watch your step everywhere – visitors have suffered severe burns after plunging through the thin crust into scalding water. Camping is possible but nights are freezing. It's also possible to stay at Corfo's no-frills refugio, about 3km before the geysers, for next to nothing; a sleeping bag is essential here.

About 6 am is the best time to see the geysers; most tours return by about 8:30 am. Tours from San Pedro (about US$20 with lunch) stop at Puritama. Fording streams is impossible in low-clearance vehicles and difficult even for high-clearance 4WD vehicles. The route is signposted, but in the dark it's easier to follow tour agencies' minibuses (who do not, however, appreciate the practice). Alternatively, head out a day in advance and camp halfway, or at the Corfo refugio. If you rent a car in Calama, you can return via the villages of Caspana, Toconce, Ayquina and Chiu Chiu, rather than via San Pedro.

TOCONAO
Known for finely hewn volcanic stone, Toconao is a fruit-growing oasis about 40km south of San Pedro, which has the pace that San Pedro had 15 years ago. The **Iglesia de San Lucas**, with a separate bell tower, dates from the mid-18th century. Its interior reveals an interesting altar and meter-thick walls.

The **Quebrada de Jeria**, with an intricate irrigation system, is a delightful place for a walk or even a swim. Affluent San Pedro families once dispatched peons with mules here to fetch casks of drinking water.

Near the plaza are several inexpensive residenciales and restaurants. See the San Pedro entry for bus services; hitching is possible, but leave San Pedro early and be prepared to return early or stay the night.

Norte Chico

A semiarid transition zone from the Atacama to the Valle Central, the Norte Chico (Little North) is also the 'region of 10,000 mines.' Politically, it comprises the Third

Region of Atacama (capital Copiapó) and the Fourth Region of Coquimbo (capital La Serena), but its customary boundaries encompass a slightly greater area. The main attractions are a pleasant climate, fine beaches and the city of La Serena, but intriguing mountain villages lie off the beaten track. Near the Panamericana are the Pan de Azúcar and Fray Jorge national parks.

History
Decades before the Spaniards, the Incas subdued Diaguita farmers, but the area was always peripheral to the Central Andean civilizations. Europeans first arrived in 1535, when Diego de Almagro crossed the Andes from Salta.

A few years later, Pedro de Valdivia founded La Serena, but Copiapó lagged until an 18th-century gold boom. When gold failed, silver took its place and Copiapó really took off, tripling its population to 12,000 after a bonanza find at Chañarcillo in 1832.

When silver declined in the late 19th century, copper took its place in Potrerillos and, later, in El Salvador. Recently, La Serena and Bahía Inglesa have enjoyed tourist booms, but mining remains significant. The area is also important culturally – Nobel Prize-winning poet Gabriela Mistral was a native of Vicuña, in the Elqui valley. The Copiapó, Huasco and Elqui valleys have contributed to Chile's flourishing fruit exports.

COPIAPÓ
The discovery of silver at nearby Chañarcillo provided Copiapó with several firsts: South America's first railroad (completed in 1852 to the port of Caldera), Chile's first telegraph and telephone lines and the first gas works. While not a major travelers' destination, its pleasant climate and historical landmarks make it a worthwhile stopover between La Serena and Antofagasta.

Orientation & Information
Copiapó (population 98,000) is 800km north of Santiago and 565km south of Antofagasta. Sernatur (☎ 052-217248), in a concrete bunker facing Plaza Prat, is open 8:30 am to 5:30 pm weekdays; it distributes a list of accommodations, an excellent map and

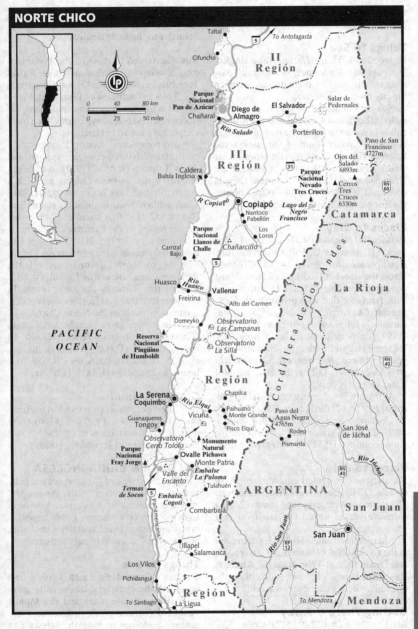

NORTE CHICO

Taltal
To Antofagasta
Cifuncho
II Región
Parque Nacional Pan de Azúcar
Diego de Almagro
El Salvador
Salar de Pedernales
Chañaral
Río Salado
Porterillos
Paso de San Francisco 4727m
III Región
Ojos del Salado 6893m
Caldera
Bahía Inglesa
R Copiapó
Copiapó
Parque Nacional Nevado Tres Cruces
Cerros Tres Cruces 6330m
Catamarca
Nantoco
Pabellón
Lago del Negro Francisco
Los Loros
Parque Nacional Llanos de Challe
Carrizal Bajo
Chañarcillo
Huasco
Río Huasco
Vallenar
Freirina
Alto del Carmen
La Rioja
Domeyko
Observatorio Las Campanas
PACIFIC OCEAN
Observatorio La Silla
Reserva Nacional Pingüino de Humboldt
IV Región
Chapilca
La Serena
Coquimbo
Río Elqui
Paihuano
Monte Grande
Paso del Agua Negra 4765m
Guanaqueros
Tongoy
Vicuña
Pisco Elqui
Rodeo
San José de Jáchal
Observatorio Cerro Tololo
Monumento Natural Pichasca
Pismanta
Parque Nacional Fray Jorge
Ovalle
Monte Patria
Río Jáchal
Valle del Encanto
Embalse La Paloma
ARGENTINA
Termas de Socos
Tulahuén
San Juan
Embalse Cogotí
Panamericana
Combarbalá
San Juan
Illapel
Salamanca
Río San Juan
San Juan
Los Vilos
Pichidangui
V Región
To Santiago
La Ligua
To Mendoza
Mendoza

Cordillera de los Andes

CHILE

many brochures. Conaf (☎ 052-239067), Juan Martínez 55, had national parks information.

Things to See

Founded in 1857, the **Museo Mineralógico**, at Colipí and Rodríguez, is a literally dazzling tribute to the raw materials to which the city owes its existence.

Notable buildings from the mining boom include the **Iglesia Catedral** and the Municipalidad, on Plaza Prat. At the foot of Batallón Atacama, directly south of the station, the **Palacete Viña de Cristo** was the town's most elegant mansion. A few blocks west, at the Universidad de Atacama (the former Escuela de Minas), is the Norris Brothers locomotive, the first on the Caldera-Copiapó line.

Places to Stay

Residencial Benbow (☎ 052-217634), Rodríguez 541, charges US$6/10 single/double. *Residencial Rodríguez* (☎ 052-212861), across the street at Rodríguez 528, is almost equally reasonable at US$7/11 with shared bath, but twice that with private bath. *Residencial Chañarcillo* (☎ 052-213281), Chañarcillo 741, has small but clean rooms for US$9 per person, but also a noisy TV lounge. Funky but friendly, the identically priced *Anexo Residencial Chañarcillo* (☎ 052-212284), O'Higgins 804, has hot water mornings only.

At Infante 766, the very fine *Hotel Montecatini I* (☎ 052-211363) costs US$28/38. One of Copiapó's best values is *Hotel Palace* (☎ 052-212852), Atacama 741, with attractive patio rooms for US$28/41 with private bath.

Places to Eat

For inexpensive grilled chicken, try *Pollo Spiedo*, O'Higgins 461. *Di Tito*, Chacabuco 710, is a modest pizzería. At Atacama 245, *El Corsario* serves varied Chilean food in a patio setting.

Alternatives include Middle Eastern food at the *Club Social Libanés*, Los Carrera 350, and Italian food at *Villa Rapallo*, Atacama 1080. *Hao Hwa*, Colipí 340, is one of northern Chile's better Chinese restaurants.

Getting There & Away

Air LanChile (☎ 052-213512), Colipí 526, flies twice daily to La Serena and Santiago. Ladeco (☎ 052-217285), Colipí 354, flies twice each weekday and once Saturday and Sunday to La Serena and Santiago. Avant (☎ 052-219775), Colipí 350, flies daily except Saturday to the same destinations.

Bus Conveniently close to the Panamericana, Copiapó's Terminal de Buses Rafael Torreblanca (☎ 052-212577) is at Chacabuco 112, 3 blocks southwest of Plaza Prat. Virtually all north-south carriers, and many for interior destinations, have offices here, but a couple have separate terminals.

Many companies cover the Panamericana and intermediates between Santiago and Arica. Tramaca (☎ 052-213979), in addition, has two buses daily to Calama and half a dozen to Taltal. Tas Choapa (☎ 052-213793), Chañarcillo 631, works the same routes. Tur-Bus (☎ 052-213050), Chacabuco 249, covers similar routes on the Panamericana.

Pullman Bus (☎ 052-211039), Colipí 109, covers the Panamericana and serves Viña as well as southerly destinations off the Panamericana. Inca Bus/Lasval (☎ 052-213488) runs virtually the same routes. In the same terminal, Los Corsarios serves destinations throughout the Norte Chico.

Some sample fares include Antofagasta (US$22, eight hours), Arica (US$40, 16 hours), Calama (US$25, 11 hours), Iquique (US$35, 14 hours), La Serena (US$8, four hours) and Santiago (US$25, 11 hours).

Getting Around

LanChile operates its own minibus to Aeropuerto Chamonate (☎ 052-214360), 7km west of town, and Transfer (☎ 09-5540364) also runs an airport service for US$3.

CALDERA & BAHÍA INGLESA

Caldera, 75km west of Copiapó, grew rapidly with silver discoveries in the Andes and arrival of the railway, which gave people in Copiapó easy beach access. Bahía Inglesa, a privateers' refuge in colonial times, has better beaches, but Caldera is livelier and cheaper.

Things to See

Caldera's **Cementerio Laico**, Chile's first non-Catholic cemetery, has artistic ironwork. Between the plaza and the **Muelle Pesquero** (fishing pier), distinctive 19th-century buildings include the **Iglesia San Vicente**, with its Gothic tower, the **Municipalidad**, the **Aduana** (customs house) and the **Estación de Ferrocarriles** (train station).

Activities
Besides swimming and sunbathing, windsurfing is a popular pastime at Bahía Inglesa; rental equipment is available.

Places to Stay
Camping Bahía Inglesa (☎ 052-315424), at Playa Las Machas, has good facilities but costs nearly US$30 per site in high season. The cheapest option is rundown *Residencial Molina* (☎ 052-315941) at Montt 346, charging around US$10 per person. *Hotel Fenicia* (☎ 315171), Gallo 370, has singles/doubles with shared bath for US$18/30, with private bath for US$24/43.

Places to Eat
Popular *New Charles*, Ossa Cerda 350, specializes in Chilean food. Bahía Inglesa's upscale *El Coral*, El Morro 564, serves superb seafood, including local scallops.

Getting There & Away
The bus terminal is at Galleo and Vallejos. Pullman Bus (☎ 052-315227) at Cousiño and Gallo, Inca Bus (☎ 052-315261) at Gana 225, and Tramaca (☎ 052-316235) at Edwards 415 all have long-distance services. Recabarren (☎ 052-315034), Cousiño 260, serves Copiapó (US$2.50, one hour).

Getting Around
Buses and taxi colectivos shuttle visitors from Caldera to Bahía Inglesa.

PARQUE NACIONAL PAN DE AZÚCAR
Just 30km north of the dilapidated mining port of Chañaral, Pan de Azúcar comprises 44,000 hectares of coastal desert and precordillera, sheltered coves among stony headlands, white sandy beaches, abundant wildlife and unique flora. The rich Humboldt current feeds otters, sea lions and many birds; pelicans, cormorants and penguins nest on Isla Pan de Azúcar, but access is restricted – bring binoculars. At higher altitudes, the camanchaca nurtures cacti and succulents; farther inland, guanacos and foxes are common.

Places to Stay
A private concessionaire (☎ 052-480551) operates campgrounds at Playa Piqueros (25 sites) and Caleta Pan de Azúcar (29 sites).

Charges are US$10 per site; facilities include toilets, water, showers, picnic tables and shade. Reservations are advisable in summer and on weekends. There's a small store, otherwise Chañaral has the nearest supplies; try buying fish from local families.

Getting There & Away
Turismo Chango (☎ 052-490484), Comercio 265 in Chañaral, buses depart opposite the Municipalidad (summer only) at 8:30 am and 3 pm, returning at 8 pm. Alternatively, you can arrange a taxi from Chañaral for about US$20 – double that if you want to be picked up. On weekends, try hitching. Conaf collects a US$4 admission fee at the south entrance.

LA SERENA
Founded in 1544, La Serena (population 107,000) maintains a colonial façade, thanks to President Gabriel González Videla's 'Plan Serena' of the late 1940s, when silver and copper were its economic backbone, along with irrigated agriculture. Capital of the Fourth Region of Coquimbo and 470km north of Santiago, it's an agreeable place that's rapidly supplanting Viña del Mar as Chile's premier beach resort.

Orientation
Centered on the Plaza de Armas, the city plan is a regular grid. Most areas of interest fall within the area bounded by Av Bohón and Parque Pedro de Valdivia to the west, the Av Almagro to the north, Calle Benavente to the east and Av Aguirre to the south.

Information
Tourist Offices Sernatur (☎ 051-225199), Matta 461, is open 8:30 am to 6:30 pm weekdays. The Municipalidad's office at the bus terminal keeps long hours but closes for lunch.

Hotelga, the private hotel and restaurant association, operates an information kiosk (☎ 051-227771) in front of Iglesia La Merced, at Prat and Balmaceda (open 10 am to 2 pm and 5 to 9 pm daily, except Sunday), and at Mercado La Recova at Cienfuegos and Cantournet (open 10 am to 2 pm daily except Sunday, weekdays only 4:30 to 8 pm).

Money Exchange money at Gira Tour, Prat 689, or bank on ATMs.

Post & Communications Correos de Chile is at Matta and Prat, opposite the plaza. CTC has offices at Cordovez 446 and O'Higgins 536, Entel at Prat 571.

Medical Services Hospital Juan de Diós (☎ 051-225569) is at Balmaceda 916, but the emergency entrance is at Larraín Alcalde and Anfión Muñoz.

Things to See

Many key features are on or near the pleasingly landscaped Plaza de Armas. On the east side is the **Iglesia Catedral** (1844), while at the southwest corner, facing a smaller plaza, is the colonial **Iglesia Santo Domingo**.

In an annex of the colonial **Iglesia San Francisco**, at Balmaceda 640, the **Museo Colonial de Arte Religioso** features polychrome sculptures from Cuzco and paintings from 17th-century Quito.

La Serena's native son and Chile's president from 1946 to 1952, González Videla was a controversial figure who drove Pablo Neruda out of the senate and into exile. Exhibits on González Videla's life in the **Museo Histórico Gabriel González Videla**, Matta 495, omit such episodes, but the museum does include material about regional history.

The **Museo Arqueológico** is at Cordovez and Cienfuegos; add this collection of Diaguita artifacts to the González Videla and you'd have one fine museum instead of two mediocre ones. The US$1.25 admission is valid for both.

Check **Mercado La Recova** for musical instruments, woolens and dried fruits and artisanal jewelry.

Beaches On a two-week vacation, you can visit a different beach every day, but watch for strong currents. Safest for swimming are Canto del Agua, Las Gaviotas, El Pescador, La Marina, La Barca, Playa Mansa, Los Fuertes, Playa Blanca, El Faro (Sur) and Peñuelas (Coquimbo).

Suitable only for sunbathing are Cuatro Esquinas, El Faro (Norte), Playa Changa (Coquimbo), Punta de Teatinos, Los Choros, Caleta Hornos, San Pedro and Chungungo.

There's no bus service along beachfront Av del Mar. From downtown take bus Liserco (which runs between La Serena and

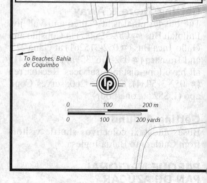

LA SERENA

PLACES TO STAY		15	Entel
1	Residencial Suiza	16	Gira Tour
5	Residencial El Loa	17	Iglesia San Agustín
6	Residencial Lorena	20	Iglesia Santo Domingo
18	Hotel Casablanca	22	Conaf
19	Residencial La Casona	23	Diaguitas Tour
	de Cantournet	24	Cine Centenario
21	Hotel Pacífico	25	Galería Cema-Chile
38	Residencial Limmat (HI)	26	Fray Jorge Tour Service
44	Residencial Jofré	27	Buses Tal,
			Diamontes de Elqui
PLACES TO EAT		28	Buses Tas Choapa
4	El Cedro	31	Museo Arqueológico
10	Café Plaza Real	32	Covalle Bus
14	Café do Brasil	33	Buses Libac
29	Rincón Oriental	34	Iglesia San Francisco,
30	Quick Biss Dos		Museo Colonial de
			Arte Religioso
OTHER		35	Linea Ruta 41,
2	Café del Patio		Tasco Taxi Collectivos
3	Iglesia La Merced,	36	Pullman Bus, Los Corsarios
	Hotelga Tourist Kiosk	37	Lasval/Inca Bus
7	Post Office, Sernatur	39	Buses Tramaca
8	Museo Histórico	40	Laverap (Laundry)
	Gabriel González Videla	41	Hospital Juan de Diós
9	Municipalidad	42	Museo Mineralógico
11	Catedral		Ignacio Domeyko
12	CTC	43	Bus Station
13	Ladeco		

To Beaches, Bahía de Coquimbo

| 0 | 100 | 200 m |
| 0 | 100 | 200 yards |

Coquimbo) and get off at Peñuelas and Cuatro Esquinas, 1 block from the beach.

Places to Stay

Hostels The local HI affiliate is **Residencial Limmat** (☎ 051-211373), Lautaro 914, charging US$10 with shared bath.

Residenciales & Hotels The pick of the cheapies is **Residencial Lorena**, (☎ 051-223380), Cantournet 950, where spacious rooms with shared bath cost only US$9; during the school year, though, university students monopolize most of the quieter rooms at the back. **Residencial La Casona de Cantournet** (☎ 051-226439), Cantournet 815, has spacious singles with comfy beds

LA SERENA

and hot showers for US$7 per person with shared bath, US$11 with private bath. The entrance is through top-end Hotel Casablanca, Vicuña 414. Near the bus terminal, recommended *Residencial Jofré* (☎ 051-222335), Regimiento Coquimbo 964, charges US$9 with breakfast and shared bath, US$15 with private bath. Some rooms are dark at *Residencial El Loa* (☎ 051-224663), O'Higgins 362, which charges US$10 per person.

Comfortable, friendly *Hotel Pacífico* (☎ 051-225674), Eduardo de la Barra 252, costs US$13/19 single/double with shared bath, US$17/26 with private bath, but maintenance is lagging. Not really Swiss, tidy *Residencial Suiza* (☎ 051-216092), Cienfuegos 250, charges US$22/39.

Places to Eat

For quality cafeteria fare at low prices, try *Quick Biss Dos*, Cienfuegos 545, 2nd floor. For seafood, any locale in the *Mercado La Recova*, at Cienfuegos and Cantournet, is a winner. *Café Plaza Real*, Prat 465, has decent fixed price lunches. For coffee, snacks and sandwiches, there's *Café do Brasil*, Balmaceda 465.

El Cedro, Prat 568, is a recommended but pricey Chilean/Middle Eastern restaurant in pleasant surroundings. *Rincón Oriental*, O'Higgins 570, is Chilean for Chinese.

Entertainment

Café del Patio, Prat 470, keeps long hours every day of the week, and becomes a lively

CHILE

jazz and blues venue Friday and Saturday nights. *Cine Centenario*, Cordovez 399, shows recent films.

Getting There & Away

Air There are three to five flights daily to Santiago (US$68 to US$100) and to Copiapó with LanChile (☎ 051-221531), Eduardo de la Barra 435-A, and Ladeco (☎ 051-225753), Cordovez 484. Avant (☎ 051-219275), Cordovez 309, flies daily except Saturday to Santiago (US$64 to $89), and to Copiapó (US$28 to US$34).

Bus Southwest of downtown, at Amunátegui and Av El Santo, La Serena's bus station (☎ 051-224573) also serves nearby Coquimbo. Many companies have downtown offices as well; when no address appears below, the office is at the station.

Several regional carriers serve Vicuña, including Via Elqui (☎ 051-225240) and Frontera Elqui (☎ 051-221664) at Juan de Dios Pení and Coquimbo, which also goes to the upper Elqui valley destinations of Monte Grande and Pisco Elqui.

Los Diamantes de Elqui (☎ 051-225555) goes to Vicuña and Ovalle, as does Expreso Norte (☎ 051-224857, 051-225503). Other carriers serving Ovalle include Tas Choapa (☎ 051-225959) at O'Higgins 599 and Lasval/ Inca Bus (☎ 051-225627) at Cienfuegos 698. Fares to regional destinations range from US$3 to US$5.

Many long-distance bus companies ply the Panamericana, from Santiago to points north, including Buses Tal (☎ 051-225555, with the cheapest fares), Géminis (☎ 051-224018), Tramaca (☎ 051-226071) at Av Aguirre 375, Buses Lit (☎ 051-224880) at Cordovez 533, Flota Barrios (☎ 051-213394, 051-226361) at Domeyko 550, Los Diamantes del Elqui, Tas Choapa, Buses Libac (☎ 051-226101) at Francisco de Aguirre 432, and Pullman Bus (☎ 051-225284), O'Higgins 663. Los Corsarios (☎ 051-225157), Lasval/ Inca Bus and Pullman Bus all serve Valparaíso and Viña del Mar.

Typical fares include Antofagasta (US$30, 11 hours), Arica (US$45, 19 hours), Calama (US$31, 14 hours), Copiapó (US$8, four hours), Iquique (US$40, 17 hours), Santiago (US$17, seven hours) and Viña del Mar or Valparaíso (US$17, seven hours).

In summer, Wednesdays and Sundays at 12:45 pm, Covalle Bus (☎ 051-213127), Infante 538, connects La Serena with the Argentine cities of Mendoza (US$39, 12 hours) and San Juan (US$45, 14 hours) via the Libertadores pass.

Taxi Colectivo Línea Ruta 41 (☎ 051-224517), Domeyko 524, goes to upper Elqui valley destinations like Vicuña faster and more frequently than ordinary buses.

Getting Around

To/From the Airport Cabs to La Serena's Aeropuerto La Florida, a short distance east of downtown on Ch 41, cost only a couple dollars.

AROUND LA SERENA

At 2200m above sea level, 88km southeast of La Serena, the **Observatorio Cerro Tololo** is one of the southern hemisphere's most important observatories. Make tour reservations by calling the La Serena office (☎ 051-225415) well in advance. There is no public transport; hitching is feasible from the junction on the highway to Vicuña, but allow plenty of time.

VICUÑA

Around the upper Elqui valley town of Vicuña (population 7700), 62km east of La Serena, logos bearing the names of Capel, Control and Tres Erres piscos are as conspicuous as international soft drink billboards in the rest of the country. Farmers surrounding this quiet village of adobe houses grow avocados, papayas and other fruits, but most notably the grapes that local distilleries transform into Chile's powerful brandy. The area has also acquired an oddball reputation thanks to several groups convinced that UFOs frequent the area.

The Municipalidad's Oficina de Información (☎ 051-209125), in the landmark Torre Bauer clocktower at the northwest corner of the Plaza de Armas, is open 9 am to 1 pm and 1:45 to 5:30 pm weekdays.

Things to See & Do

Vicuña's **Museo Gabriela Mistral** is a tangible eulogy to the famous literary figure, born Lucila Godoy Alcayaga in 1889, in the village of Montegrande. Her house, since moved to Vicuña, is on show at the museum entrance.

Tours of the **Planta Capel** distillery, across the bridge from town, take place every half-hour, 9:30 am to noon and 2:30 to 6 pm weekdays, 10 am to 12:30 pm only Saturdays and holidays.

Places to Stay & Eat

Camping is available at shady *Las Tinajas* (☎ *051-411731*) for US$6 per site, which includes access to the municipal swimming pool. *Hostal Michel,* Gabriela Mistral 573, charges US$7 per person. Warmly recommended *Residencial La Elquina* (☎ *411317*), O'Higgins 65, costs US$9 per person with shared bath, US$11 with private bath, in an attractive house with lush gardens and fruit trees. Breakfast is included.

Halley, Mistral 404, is specifically recommended for pastel de choclo. The *Club Social de Vicuña*, Mistral 445, is expensive but offers a good menu in an attractive setting.

Getting There & Away

Vicuña's Terminal de Buses is at Prat and O'Higgins, 1 block south of the plaza. Several companies go to La Serena, Coquimbo and Pisco Elqui (US$2), and there are also long-distance services.

Across the street is the separate Terminal de Taxis Colectivos, the departure point for shared taxis to Vicuña and up the Elqui valley.

OVALLE

Ovalle (population 52,000), half an hour east of the Panamericana, is the tidy capital of Limarí, a prosperous agricultural province. The tourist information kiosk, at the southeast corner of the Plaza de Armas, is rarely staffed.

The **Museo del Limarí**, Independencia 329, is a modest endeavor stressing the trans-Andean links between the Diaguita peoples of coastal Chile and northwestern Argentina. The **Feria Modelo**, a lively fruit and vegetable market with several restaurants, occupies the former railway workshops.

Places to Stay & Eat

Hotel Roxy (☎ *053-620080*), Libertad 155, is one of Chile's best values for US$10/17

single/double with shared bath, US$14/24 with private bath.

For good fixed-price lunches, try *Casino La Bomba* at Aguirre 364, the *Club Comercial* at Aguirre 244, or the *Club Social Arabe*, Arauco 255. A personal favorite, though, is the unrepentantly political *El Quijote*, Arauco 295, which covers its walls with images of leftist icons and delivers excellent meals with friendly but unobsequious service.

Getting There & Away

The bus terminal is on the corner of Maestranza and Balmaceda. North-bound bus services resemble those from La Serena. Most companies have offices on the west side of Ariztía, with others across the street or nearby.

AROUND OVALLE

The **Monumento Arqueológico Valle del Encanto**, 19km west of Ovalle, is a rocky tributary canyon of the Río Limarí, with pre-Columbian petroglyphs, pictographs and mortars. Any westbound bus will drop you at the highway marker, where it's an easy 5km walk on a clearly marked road.

PARQUE NACIONAL FRAY JORGE

Moistened by the camanchaca, Fray Jorge is an ecological island of Valdivian cloud forest in a semiarid region, 110km south of La Serena. Of its 10,000 hectares, only 400 contain this truly unique vegetation – still enough to make it a UNESCO International Biosphere Reserve. Some believe this area is evidence of dramatic climate change, but others argue that such forests were more extensive before their destruction by humans.

Fray Jorge is open to the public 8:30 am to 6 pm Thursday to Sunday (plus holidays) in summer (January 1 to March 15); the rest of the year, it's open weekends only.

Places to Stay

El Arrayancito, 3km from the visitor center and 7km west of El Bosque, has 13 campsites (US$10) with fireplaces, picnic tables, water and toilets.

Getting There & Away

Fray Jorge is reached by a westward lateral off the Panamericana, about 20km north of

CHILE

the Ovalle junction. Several agencies offer tours from La Serena and Ovalle; it's possible to leave the tour, stay overnight in the park and then return to La Serena or Ovalle the next day. North-south buses will drop you at the clearly marked turnoff, 22km from the gate; walking is not easy, so try hitching.

La Araucanía & Los Lagos

Beyond the Biobío, glaciated volcanoes tower above deep blue lakes, ancient forests and verdant farmland, while waterfalls spill into limpid pools. Temuco, capital of the Ninth Region (La Araucanía), is the staging point for visits to Parque Nacional Conguillío, the upper Biobío and lakeside resorts like Villarrica and Pucón. Farther south, near Osorno, there's an easy land crossing to Argentina along the southern shore of Lago Puyehue, and a more scenic bus-boat combination.

Puerto Montt, on the Seno de Reloncaví, is the capital of the 10th Region (Los Lagos) and gateway to the Chiloé archipelago and Chilean Patagonia. Hikers should acquire the 2nd edition of LP's *Trekking in the Patagonian Andes*, by Clem Lindenmayer, which also covers southern Argentina.

History
South of Concepción, the Spaniards found small gold mines, good farmland and a large potential workforce, but constantly suffered Mapuche attacks or natural disasters. By the mid-17th century, they had abandoned most settlements, except for heavily fortified Valdivia. Early-19th-century travelers still referred to 'Arauco' as a separate country, and it was not safe for European settlers until the 1880s.

Today, several hundred thousand Mapuche still live in La Frontera, the area between the Biobío and the Río Toltén, earning a precarious livelihood from farming and crafts. Nineteenth-century German immigrants started industries and left a palpable architectural heritage, while Chilean-Germans made their mark on the region's food and agricultural landscape.

TEMUCO
Fast-growing Temuco (population 215,000), 675km south of Santiago, is the service center for a large hinterland and supports a range of industries, including steel, textiles, food processing and wood products. The gateway to the Lake District, it's also a market town for Mapuche produce and crafts.

Information
Tourist Offices Sernatur (☎ 045-211969), at Claro Solar and Bulnes, has city maps. In January and February, it's open 8:30 am to 8 pm weekdays, 9 am to 2 pm and 3 to 7 pm Saturday and 10 am to 2 pm Sunday. Otherwise, it's open 9 am to 12:30 pm and 3 to 6 pm weekdays.

Money Intercam is at Bulnes 743 and ATMs are abundant around the Plaza de Armas.

Post & Telecommunications Correos de Chile is at Diego Portales and Prat. Entel is at the corner of Manuel Montt and Carrera, Chilesat on Vicuña Mackenna between Manuel Montt and Claro Solar.

Medical Services Temuco's Hospital Regional (☎ 045-212525) is at Manuel Montt 115, 6 blocks west and 1 block north of Plaza Aníbal Pinto.

National Parks Conaf (☎ 045-211912) is at Av Bilbao 931, 2nd floor.

Things to See
In 1881, Mapuche leaders ceded land for Temuco at **Monumento Natural Cerro Ñielol**, a popular site for Sunday outings that also has trails and an environmental information center.

The **Mercado Municipal**, 3 blocks north of the plaza at Portales and Aldunate, has food, clothing, restaurants and crafts, but closes by 7 pm (2 pm Sunday). Open daily from 9:30 am until the last Mapuche vendors pack up, the **Feria Libre** (produce market) fills several blocks along Barros Arana near the train station.

At Alemania 084, reached by bus No 9 from downtown, the **Museo Regional de la Araucanía** chronicles Mapuche history since pre-Columbian times, alongside materials on European colonization, historical maps and a gallery of regional art. In summer, it's open daily 9 am to 7 pm Monday to Saturday, and 10 am to 1 pm Sunday; otherwise, hours are slightly abbreviated and it's closed Monday.

Places to Stay

HI affiliate *Residencial Temuco* (☎ 233721), Rodríguez 1341, 2nd floor, offers warm, clean and comfortable family ambience for US$9 with breakfast.

Despite short-term clientele, *Hospedaje Furniel* (☎ 045-237095), Vicuña Mackenna 570, is an OK place charging US$7.50 per person (US$9 with breakfast). Clean, friendly *Hospedaje Espejo* (☎ 045-238408), Aldunate 124, has singles with shared bath for US$7.50. Across the street at Aldunate 187, attractive, friendly *Hospedaje Aldunate* (☎ 045-212976) charges US$11.

At Varas 708 for over a century, rambling *Hotel Continental* (☎ 045-238973) has hosted the likes of poet Pablo Neruda, and presidents Pedro Aguirre Cerda and Salvador Allende. Rates begin at US$18/31 for singles/doubles with shared bath. *Hotel Espelette* (☎ 045-234805), Claro Solar 492, compares favorably for US$12/22 single/double with shared bath; breakfast costs US$2.

Places to Eat

Temuco's best value is the seafood at various *puestos* (stands) in the Mercado Municipal. *Restaurant Caribe*, Puesto 45, is outstanding, and the slightly more formal and upscale *La Caleta* is a recommended splurge. Market restaurants close around 7 pm.

For Mediterranean food, check the *Centro Español* at Bulnes 483. For heartier middle-European fare, the *Club Alemán* is at Senador Estebáñez 772. *Il Gelato*, Bulnes 420, has good ice cream.

Shopping

The Mercado Municipal has the best crafts, especially Mapuche woolens. Look for jewelry, pottery and musical instruments like *zampoñas* (pan pipes) and drums.

Getting There & Away

Air LanChile (☎ 045-211339), Bulnes 655, flies three times daily to Santiago (US$80 to US$115) and once each to Valdivia, Osorno and Puerto Montt. Ladeco (☎ 045-213180), Prat 565, Local 102, has similar schedules. Avant (☎ 045-270670), Prat 565, Local 101, flies frequently to Santiago (US$76 to US$108), twice daily to Valdivia (US$15) and has 20 flights weekly to Puerto Montt (US$26 to US$34), seven of which continue to Balmaceda (US$70 to US$91) and eight of which continue to Punta Arenas (US$116 to US$138).

For US$88, Transportes Aéreos Neuquén (TAN, ☎ 045-210500), Portales 840, connects Temuco with Neuquén (Argentina) five times weekly.

Bus Temuco has a new bus terminal at the north end of town, just off the Panamericana. All companies are supposed to move there, as buses are now banned from downtown. How effective this will be is uncertain, so the map indicates companies who still maintain downtown offices.

For regional destinations, the Terminal de Buses Rurales (☎ 045-210494) is at Av Balmaceda and Av Pinto. Schedules change often, with fewer buses in winter.

Buses Biobío (☎ 045-210599), Lautaro 853, goes to Angol, Los Ángeles and Concepción. Cruz del Sur (☎ 210701), Vicuña Mackenna 671, serves Concepción, Santiago, Puerto Montt and intermediates, some continuing to Chiloé.

Tas Choapa (☎ 045-212422), Varas 609, has frequent service to Valdivia, Puerto Montt, Santiago and intermediates, and a nightly direct service to Valparaíso and Viña del Mar without transfer in Santiago. Carriers with similar routes include Fénix (☎ 045-212582), at Claro Solar 609; Tur-Bus (☎ 045-234349), Lagos 538; Buses Lit (☎ 045-211483), San Martín 894; Igi Llaima (☎ 045-210364), at Miraflores 1535; Varmontt (☎ 045-211314), Bulnes 45; Inter Sur (☎ 045-234278); Balmaceda 1378; Buses Power (☎ 045-236513), Bulnes 178.

Buses Jac (☎ 045-210313), Vicuña MacKenna 798, goes frequently to Villarrica and Pucón, Lican Ray and Coñaripe. Panguisur (☎ 045-211560), Miraflores 871, has 11 buses daily to Panguipulli.

Sample fares include Ancud (US$13, seven hours), Castro (US$15, eight hours), Chillán (US$6, four hours), Concepción

LA ARAUCANÍA & LOS LAGOS

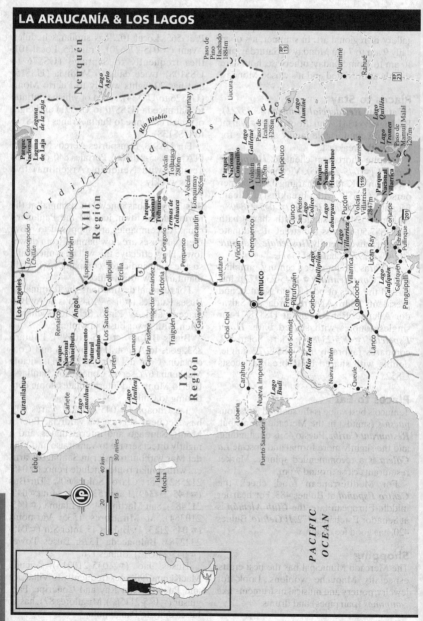

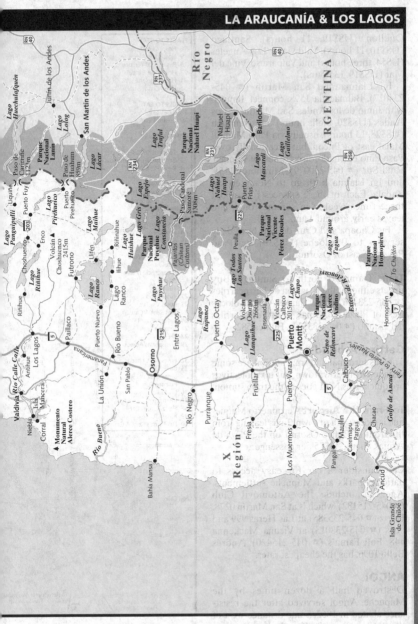

(US$8, five hours), Osorno (US$7, three hours), Puerto Montt (US$10, five hours), Quellón (US$19, 11 hours), Santiago (US$16, 11 hours), Valdivia or Los Ángeles (US$4, three hours) and Valparaíso/Viña del Mar (US$19, 13 hours).

Igi Llaima and San Martín (☎ 045-234017), Balmaceda 1598, connect Temuco with Junín de los Andes, San Martín de Los Andes (US$20, eight hours) and Neuquén (US$28, 13 hours), usually via Paso Mamuil Malal east of Pucón, but occasionally over Paso Pino Hachado, directly east of Temuco. Ruta Sur (☎ 045-210079), Miraflores 1151, and Igi Llaima both go to Neuquén via Zapala. Each of these services runs about three times weekly in summer only, and leaves early, around 4 am.

Tas Choapa and Cruz del Sur have daily services to Bariloche (US$30), via Paso Puyehue east of Osorno.

Train Trains go north to Santiago. Buy tickets either at the Estación de Ferrocarriles (☎ 045-233416), on Av Barros Arana 8 blocks west of Plaza de Armas, or at Ferrocarriles del Estado (☎ 045-233522), Bulnes 582.

Getting Around
The bus terminal and train station are some distance from downtown, but taxi colectivos are quick. Bus No 1 goes to the train station.

To/From the Airport Aeropuerto Maquehue is 6km south of town. Taxis leaving from the front of Banco Osorno, on the Plaza de Armas, charge US$5 per passenger.

Car Consider a car for easy access to national parks and Mapuche settlements. Agencies include the Automóvil Club (☎ 045-215132), which is at San Martín 0278, Hertz (☎ 045-235385) at Las Heras 999 and Avis (☎ 045-238013) at Vicuña Mackenna 448. Full Fama's (☎ 045-215420), Andrés Bello 1096, has the cheapest rates.

ANGOL
Destroyed half a dozen times by the Mapuche, Angol survived after the resistance abated in 1862. Some distance west of the Panamericana, it offers the best access to Parque Nacional Nahuelbuta, which preserves the largest remaining stands of coastal araucarias (monkey puzzle trees).

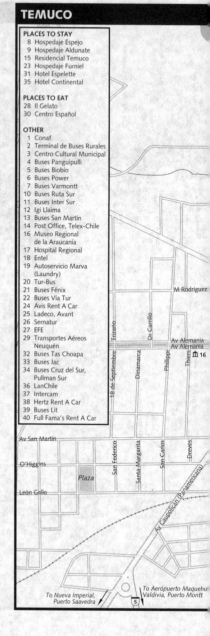

TEMUCO

PLACES TO STAY
8 Hospedaje Espejo
9 Hospedaje Aldunate
15 Residencial Temuco
23 Hospedaje Furniel
31 Hotel Espelette
35 Hotel Continental

PLACES TO EAT
28 Il Gelato
30 Centro Español

OTHER
1 Conaf
2 Terminal de Buses Rurales
3 Centro Cultural Municipal
4 Buses Panguipulli
5 Buses Biobío
6 Buses Power
7 Buses Varmontt
10 Buses Ruta Sur
11 Buses Inter Sur
12 Igi Llaima
13 Buses San Martín
14 Post Office, Telex-Chile
16 Museo Regional
    de la Araucanía
17 Hospital Regional
18 Entel
19 Autoservicio Marva
    (Laundry)
20 Tur-Bus
21 Buses Fénix
22 Buses Vía Tur
24 Avis Rent A Car
25 Ladeco, Avant
26 Sernatur
27 EFE
29 Transportes Aéreos
    Neuquén
32 Buses Tas Choapa
33 Buses Jac
34 Buses Cruz del Sur,
    Pullman Sur
36 LanChile
37 Intercam
38 Hertz Rent A Car
39 Buses Lit
40 Full Fama's Rent A Car

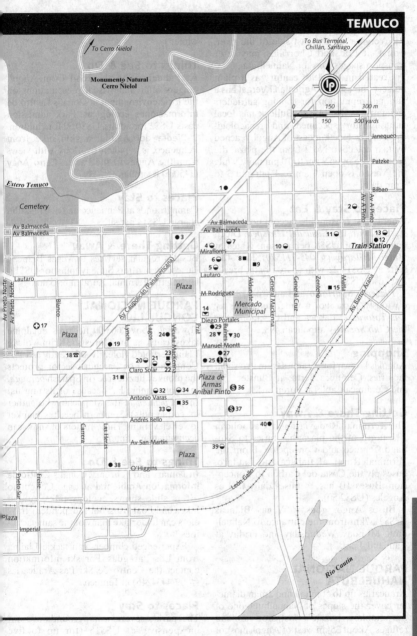

TEMUCO

Angol's Oficina Municipal de Turismo (☎ 045-711255) is near the bridge across the Río Vergara, on the east side of the river. Conaf, at Prat and Chorrillos, may offer transport suggestions for Nahuelbuta.

Created in the 19th century as a plant nursery, the **Escuela Agrícola El Vergel** has a national reputation for training gardeners and farmers. Its **Museo Bullock** has local natural history specimens and archaeological artifacts. Five km east of Angol, reached by taxi colectivo No 2 from the plaza, the grounds are open 9 am to 10 pm daily, while the Museo is open 9 am to 1 pm and 3 to 7 pm daily.

Places to Stay & Eat

Angol has reasonable accommodations, starting with the *Casa del Huésped*, Dieciocho 465, for US$8 per person. Rates at *Hotel Millaray* (☎ 045-711570), Prat 420, start at US$14/22 with shared bath; breakfast costs US$3.

Pizzería Sparlatto at Lautaro 418 has, obviously, pizza. For a wider selection, try *Las Totoras* at Ilabaca and Covadonga, or the *Club Social*, Caupolicán 498.

Shopping

Angol is known for ceramics from two small factories: Cerámica Serra, at Bunster 153, and Cerámica Lablé, at Purén 864.

Getting There & Away

The Terminal Rodoviario, at Caupolicán 200, north of the plaza, has buses to Santiago, Temuco and Concepción. From the Terminal Rural, at Ilabaca and Lautaro, buses ply the Costa del Carbón to Concepción. Buses JB has 14 buses daily to Los Ángeles (US$2.50).

Buses Angol goes to Vegas Blancas (US$2), 7km from the entrance to Nahuelbuta, Monday, Wednesday and Friday at 7 am and 4 pm.

PARQUE NACIONAL NAHUELBUTA

Araucarias up to 50m tall and 2m in diameter cover the slopes of Nahuelbuta, one of the monkey puzzle's last non-Andean refuges. About 35km west of Angol, most of the park is a slightly undulating plain, 950m above sea level, but permanent streams have cut deep canyons beneath jagged granitic peaks that reach 1565m. Summers are warm and dry but snow touches the summits in winter.

Things to See & Do

At Pehuenco, on the road from Angol, rangers offer audiovisual presentations on the local environment at Conaf's **Centro de Informaciones Ecológicas**. Park admission costs US$2 for adults, US$0.50 for children.

Piedra del Águila, a 4km hike from Pehuenco, is a 1400m overlook with views from the Andes to the Pacific. **Cerro Anay** (1450m) is similar.

Places to Stay

Campgrounds at Pehuenco and at Coimallín charge US$14 per site.

Getting There & Away

Besides regular services to Vegas Blancas, Buses Angol offers Sunday tours for US$13, leaving the Terminal Rural at 6:45 am.

PARQUE NACIONAL CONGUILLÍO

Towering above 60,000 hectares of alpine lakes, canyons and forests, 3125m Volcán Llaima erupted violently as recently as 1957. Conguillío's Los Paraguas sector protects the monkey puzzle tree (in Spanish *paragua*, meaning 'umbrella,' because of its unusual shape; *pehuén* to the Mapuche, who gather its edible nuts). Southern beeches blanket lower elevations. Three meters of snow can accumulate in winter.

Things to See & Do

In January and February, Conaf's **Centro de Información Ambiental** at Lago Conguillío offers slide shows, ecology talks, guided hikes and boat trips, but independent travelers can undertake many of the same activities.

Experienced climbers can tackle Llaima from Los Paraguas. For ski information contact the Centro de Ski Las Araucarias (☎ 09-4434246) in Temuco.

Places to Stay

The park's several campgrounds are not inexpensive, at US$15 (for up to five people), but Conaf reserves a limited number of sites for backpackers (US$4 per person) at *El Estero*.

Getting There & Away

For Los Paraguas, take Erbuc or Nar Bus from Temuco's Terminal de Buses Rurales to Cherquenco (US$2), then walk or hitch the 17km to the ski lodge.

For the northern entrance to the Conguillío sector, take a bus to Curacautín, 42km from park headquarters, via Victoria (US$2) or Lautaro (US$2.50). From Curacautín, it's necessary to hitch. A southern approach passes through Cunco and Melipeuco (US$2), where buses leave Hostería Hue-Telén for park headquarters. With a rental car, you can make a loop from Temuco.

VILLARRICA

Founded in 1552, colonial Villarrica withered under repeated Mapuche attacks until treaties were signed in 1883. The present resort, 86km southeast of Temuco, on Lago Villarrica, shares its name with a smoldering, snowcapped volcano.

Information

Tourist Offices The municipal Oficina de Turismo (☎ 045-411162) is at Pedro de Valdivia 1070. From January to mid-March, it's open 8:30 am to 11 pm daily; otherwise, hours are 8:30 am to 1 pm and 2:30 to 6:30 pm daily.

Money Banks and their ATMs are the only places here to get your money fix.

Post & Communications Correos de Chile is on General Urrutia, near Anfión Muñoz. CTC long-distance offices are at Henríquez 544.

Medical Services Hospital Villarrica (☎ 045-411169) is at San Martín 460.

Things to See

Next to the tourist office, the **Museo Histórico-Arquelógico Municipal** displays Mapuche jewelry, musical instruments and rough-hewn wooden masks. Nearby is an oblong Mapuche **ruca**, with thatched walls and roof. Behind the tourist office, the **Feria Artesanal** has a selection of crafts and traditional Mapuche food.

Places to Stay

Camping Dulac (☎ 045-412097), 2km east of town, can be crowded, but the shady sites

(US$19) provide reasonable privacy. Try asking for discounts with smaller parties.

Many places offer seasonal accommodation only for around US$8 per person (US$10 with breakfast); the tourist office provides current information. One of the cheapest year-round accommodations is *Hotel Fuentes* (☎ 045-411595), Vicente Reyes 665, for about US$9/16 single/double with simple breakfast and shared bath; the downstairs bar and restaurant provide a cozy winter hearth. *Residencial Villa Linda* (☎ 045-411392), Pedro de Valdivia 678, is comparable at US$9 per person with shared bath, US$22 double with private bath.

Hostería Rayhuén (☎ 045-411571), Pedro Montt 668, is a charming place with hot showers, well-heated rooms and a fine restaurant. Rates with breakfast are US$22/31.

Places to Eat

Café Bar 2001, Henríquez 379, is typical of Villarrica's tourist cafés, with its selection of sandwiches and kuchen. *Hostería Rayhuén*, Pedro Montt 668, has hearty fixed-price lunches.

El Rey del Marisco, Valentín Letelier 1030, is nothing fancy, but serves fine fish and other seafood at midrange prices. The popular *Club Social Treffpunkt*, Valdivia 640, serves German cuisine and Chilean seafood. *The Traveller*, Valentín Letelier 753, is a Sino-Chilean bar with a nice ambience and good food.

Getting There & Away

Villarrica's main Terminal de Buses is at Pedro de Valdivia 621, though a few companies have separate offices nearby. There are frequent buses to Santiago (US$19 to US$28, 12 hours) and many regional destinations, but most southbound services require a change in Temuco. International services to Argentina are extensions of those from Temuco.

Carriers to Santiago not at the main terminal are Buses Lit (☎ 045-411555) at Anfión Muñoz 640, and Fénix (☎ 045-419098) at Pedro de Valdivia 599. Regionally, Buses Jac (☎ 045-411447), Bilbao 610, goes to Pucón (US$0.65) and Temuco (US$2) every half hour, four times daily to Valdivia (US$3), frequently to Lican Ray (US$0.65) and six times daily to Coñaripe

(US$2). It also goes twice daily to Caburgua via Pucón (US$2), and daily to Curarrehue (US$2). Buses Regional Villarrica (☎ 045-411871), at the main terminal, leaves daily for Pucón, Curarrehue and the Puesco border post.

PUCÓN

Home to a growing numbers of hikers, climbers, mountain bikers, windsurfers, white-water rafters and kayakers, Pucón resembles Wyoming's Jackson Hole in its youthful vitality. At least until the next major eruption of Volcán Villarrica obliterates it, this lakeside resort will remain the focus of Chile's adventure tourism industry and a locus of environmental activism.

Information

Tourist Offices The private Cámara de Turismo (☎ 045-441671), at Brasil 115, is commercially oriented but helpful. It's open 8 am to midnight in January and February, 10 am to 1 pm and 4 to 9 pm the rest of the year.

Money Banco de Crédito has an ATM at the corner of Alderete and Fresia. Turismo Christopher at O'Higgins 335 changes cash and traveler's checks.

Banco de Chile maintains an ATM in the Galería Alto Pucón, at O'Higgins and Lincoyán. Turismo Money Exchange is at Fresia 547.

Travel Agencies On Av Bernardo O'Higgins, Chile's adventure travel mecca, numerous companies arrange climbing, white-water rafting, mountain biking (including rentals) and similar activities. Among them are reader-recommended, Colombian-American Sol y Nieve Expediciones (☎ 045-441070) at O'Higgins and Lincoyán, Expediciones Trancura (☎ 045-441189) at O'Higgins 211, Turismo Apumanque (☎ 045-441085, fax 045-441361) at O'Higgins 412, and Andén Sport (☎ 045-441048, fax 441236) at O'Higgins 535.

National Parks Conaf (☎ 045-441261) has moved east of town to Camino Internacional 1355.

Places to Stay

Camping Mapu-Rayen (☎ 045-441378), about 1km south of O'Higgins on Colo Colo, is quieter than areas closer to the beach. Peak season rates are US$20 per site, but small parties might try negotiating.

The local HI affiliate is *Hostería ¡Ecole!* (☎ 045-441081), General Urrutia 592, which charges US$9 to US$12, depending on the number of people per room. It also has a superb vegetarian restaurant and a book exchange, holds parties and dances and organizes informal tours to nearby attractions.

Budget accommodations start around US$8 to US$10, usually with breakfast and/or kitchen privileges, at places like *Hospedaje Eliana*, Pasaje Chile 225; *Hospedaje Juan Torres* (☎ 045-441248), Lincoyán 445; *Hospedaje Lucía*, Lincoyán 565; *Hospedaje González* (☎ 045-441491), General Urrutia 484; *Hospedaje La Casita* (☎ 045-441712), Palguín 555; and *Residencial Lincoyán* (☎ 045-441144), Lincoyán 323.

For US$12 per person with breakfast and kitchen privileges, congenial *Hospedaje Sonia* (☎ 045-441269), Lincoyán 485, is a good place to meet people.

Places to Eat

Los Hornitos de Pucón, Caupolicán 710, has fine empanadas. For cheap eats, try *El Amigo*, at Urrutia 407, and the *Strogen Bar* at Urrutia 417. The vegetarian specialties at tobacco-free *Hostería ¡Ecole!*, General Urrutia 592, are one of Pucón's special attractions. *Marmonch*, Ecuador 175, has a different, inexpensive fixed-price lunch daily, while *Café Brasil*, Fresia 472, is recommended for trout and sandwiches.

Las Terrazas de Pucón, O'Higgins 323, is highly regarded for pizza, pancakes, meat and seafood, with patio dining. *El Fogón*, O'Higgins 480, is a parrilla. *Puerto Pucón y Tequila*, Fresia 245, is a decent if overpriced Spanish and Mexican restaurant, but worth consideration.

For breakfast or onces, you can't do better than Swiss-run *La Tetera*, General Urrutia 580. For exquisite sweets, try the *Holzapfel Bäckerei*, Clemente Holzapfel 524.

Getting There & Away

Long-distance services and prices resemble those from Villarrica. Long-distance carriers include Buses Lit (☎ 045-441055), Power (the cheapest but also least comfortable)

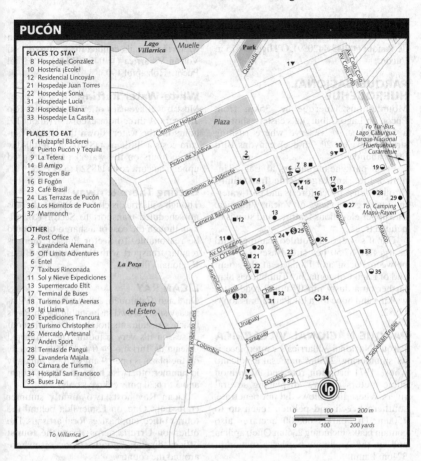

PUCÓN

PLACES TO STAY
- 8 Hospedaje González
- 10 Hostería ¡Ecole!
- 12 Residencial Lincoyán
- 21 Hospedaje Juan Torres
- 22 Hospedaje Sonia
- 31 Hospedaje Lucia
- 32 Hospedaje Eliana
- 33 Hospedaje La Casita

PLACES TO EAT
- 1 Holzapfel Bäckerei
- 4 Puerto Pucón y Tequila
- 9 La Tetera
- 14 El Amigo
- 15 Strogen Bar
- 16 El Fogón
- 23 Café Brasil
- 24 Las Terrazas de Pucón
- 36 Los Hornitos de Pucón
- 37 Marmonch

OTHER
- 2 Post Office
- 3 Lavandería Alemana
- 5 Off Limits Adventures
- 6 Entel
- 7 Taxibus Rinconada
- 11 Sol y Nieve Expediciones
- 13 Supermercado Eltit
- 17 Terminal de Buses
- 18 Turismo Punta Arenas
- 19 Igi Llaima
- 20 Expediciones Trancura
- 25 Turismo Christopher
- 26 Mercado Artesanal
- 27 Andén Sport
- 28 Termas de Pangui
- 29 Lavandería Majala
- 30 Cámara de Turismo
- 34 Hospital San Francisco
- 35 Buses Jac

Lago Villarrica

Muelle   Park

To Villarrica

0   100   200 m
0   100   200 yards

---

and Empresa San Martín, all at the main Terminal de Buses at Palguín 383; Tur-Bus (☎ 045-441965) 200m east of corner of O'Higgins and Colo Colo; Longitudinal Sur (☎ 045-442004) at Ansorena 343; Igi Llaima at O'Higgins and Colo Colo, and on Ansorena between Urrutia and O'Higgins.

Buses Jac (☎ 045-441923), in a new terminal at Uruguay and Palguín, has countless departures to Villarrica (US$0.65, ½ hour), also serves Valdivia daily, and adds local service to Caburgua (US$2) and Paillaco three times daily except Sunday (twice only). Other companies serving nearby rural destinations include Buses Regionales Villarrica (to Currarehue and Puesco for the border crossing to Argentina); and Taxibus

Rinconada (to Palguín), on Urrutia between Ansorena and Palguín.

AROUND PUCÓN

The hot-springs resorts **Termas de Huife** and **Termas de Palguín,** both within 30km of Pucón, are upmarket but not prohibitively expensive for day use. At the rustic **Termas Los Pozones**, a few kilometers beyond Huife, admission costs only US$4. Buses Cordillera (☎ 045-441903), Ansorena 302, goes to Huife at 12:30 and 5 pm weekdays, and Taxibus Rinconada serves Palguín.

Unorthodox **Termas de Panqui**, 58km east of Pucón via a 4WD road, is a deep ecology enclave. Admission costs US$10, tipi accommodations another US$10 (more for hotel

CHILE

rooms) and full board around US$20, plus IVA. Make arrangements through Termas de Panqui (☎ 045-442039), O'Higgins 615 in Pucón.

PARQUE NACIONAL HUERQUEHUE

Mountainous Huerquehue, 35km from Pucón on Lago Caburgua's eastern shore, is a 12,500-hectare reserve where rushing streams have cut 2000m-deep canyons. Bird life is abundant.

From park headquarters at Lago Tinquilco, the 7km **Lago Verde Trail** climbs through dense beech forests and past waterfalls, with great views of Volcán Villarrica. The upper elevations feature solid stands of pehuén trees.

Conaf's Lago Tinquilco campground charges US$7.50 per site. Buses Jac goes between Pucón and Paillaco, at the south end of Lago Caburgua, but Tinquilco is 8km farther on a dusty, mostly uphill road; start walking and hope for a lift. Park admission is US$2.

PARQUE NACIONAL VILLARRICA

Parque Nacional Villarrica's centerpiece is its smoldering, 2850m namesake volcano whose 1971 eruption released 30 million cubic meters of lava, displacing several rivers. Where these flows did not penetrate, southern beech and pehuén reach up to 1500m. The park's 60,000 hectares also contain peaks including 2360m Quetrupillán and, on the Argentine border, a section of 3746m Lanín.

Trekking & Climbing
Volcán Villarrica

Only 12km from Pucón, Volcán Villarrica is a hikers' and climbers' mecca. Though not technically demanding, the summit climb is tiring and requires equipment and a local guide or express permission from Conaf. Many Pucón travel agencies rent equipment and lead one-day excursions (about US$35 per person).

The most convenient of several treks circles the volcano's southern flank and exits the park at Palguín; from Palguín, another route goes to Puesco, near the Argentine border. Those not wishing to ascend the volcano can still hike the base of the mountain and get great views of caves, volcanic debris and lava flows.

Skiing

Refugio Villarrica accommodates skiers in winter; for details, contact the Centro de Ski Volcán Villarrica (☎ 045-441176), at Hotel Pucón, Holzapfel 190.

White-Water Rafting

Most travel agencies offer trips on the Río Trancura. A three-hour excursion (about 1½ hours on the water) down the lower Trancura costs as little as US$10, and a full-day (three hours on the water) on the rugged upper Trancura costs US$20 to US$25.

Getting There & Away

Though Villarrica is close to Pucón, there is no scheduled transport to Sector Rucapillán, though the cost of a shared taxi should be reasonable. To Sector Puesco, there is regular transport with the company Buses Regional Villarrica.

LICAN RAY

On Lago Calafquén, 30km south of Villarrica, visitors crowd fashionable Lican Ray's beaches, restaurants, hotels and cafés, but out of season it's very tranquil. The municipal Oficina de Turismo (☎ 045-431201), directly on the plaza, is open 9 am to 10:30 pm daily in summer; otherwise, hours are 9 am to 1 pm and 3 to 6:30 pm weekdays only.

Lican Ray hosts two nightly summer crafts fairs. One, on Esmeralda behind the tourist office, emphasizes local artisans. The other, on Urrutia across from the tourist office, displays goods from elsewhere around the country.

Places to Stay

Residencial Temuco (☎ 045-431130), Gabriela Mistral 515, is passable for US$9 per person, with sagging beds and breakfast included at the downstairs restaurant. Woodsy, friendly *Residencial Catriñi*, Catriñi 140, costs about US$10 with breakfast. Unfortunately, the eight beds in two-plus rooms take up nearly all the floor space, and also sag a bit; there's one single.

Places to Eat

The Ñaños, Urrutia 105, is one of the town's most popular establishments for Chilean specialties. *Cafetería Alemana*, facing the beach at Punulef 440, is nothing special, but not bad either. *Guido's*, Urrutia 405, specializes in meat, seafood and trout. *Madonna*, Urrutia 201, has a wider variety of toppings than most other Chilean pizzerías.

Getting There & Away
Buses Jac goes often to Villarrica (45 minutes) from its own terminal at Urrutia and Marichanquín, but most buses leave from the corner of Urrutia and Huenumán. Every morning at 7:30 am, a local bus goes to Panguipulli (US$2, two hours) via back roads. There is direct service to Santiago.

COÑARIPE
At the east end of Lago Calafquén, 22km from Lican Ray, Coñaripe's black-sand beaches sprout multicolored tents in summer. *Hotel Entre Montañas* (☎ 045-317298), opposite the plaza, has singles/doubles with private bath for US$13/25, including breakfast. The drab cafeteria opposite the hotel has fabulous humitas (tamales), but *El Mirador* is better for a more leisurely meal.

Buses Jac has several buses daily to and from Villarrica (US$2) via Lican Ray; others go to Panguipulli.

PANGUIPULLI
Quieter and slower paced than other resorts, 115km east of Valdivia by paved highway, Panguipulli has sensational views across Lago Panguipulli to Volcán Choshuenco. On the east side of Plaza Prat, the Oficina Municipal de Turismo (☎ 063-311311, Anexo 731), is open 10 am to 9 pm daily from mid-December to mid-March, but keeps shorter hours the rest of the year.

Places to Stay & Eat
Several hospedajes are in the US$10 range, including reader-endorsed *Hospedaje Berrocal* at JM Carrera 834, and *Hospedaje Pozas* on Pedro de Valdivia between Gabriela Mistral and JM Carrera. Friendly *Hotel Central* (☎ 063-311331), Pedro de Valdivia 115, has rooms with shared bath and breakfast for US$11 per person; airy rooms with private bath (even bathtubs) for US$18/26 single/double. Upstairs rooms are quieter and larger.

Try either *El Chapulín*, Martínez de Rozas 639, for meat and seafood, or reader-recommended *Girasol* on Martínez de Rozas near Matta.

Getting There & Away
Panguipulli's Terminal de Buses is at Gabriela Mistral and Diego Portales, but Tur-Bus has its own terminal at Pedro de Valdivia and JM Carrera. There are a number of buses to Temuco, Valdivia, Puerto Montt and Santiago.

Buses Hua Hum has several crowded daily buses to Choshuenco, Neltume and Puerto Fuy. For information on the ferry from Puerto Fuy to Puerto Pirehueico and the Argentine border at Paso Hua Hum, ask at Hostería Quetropillán. There are also numerous buses to Coñaripe.

CHOSHUENCO
Tiny Choshuenco, at the southeast end of Lago Panguipulli, survives from farming, a sawmill and visitors enjoying its attractive black-sand beach. Tidy *Hotel Rucapillán* (☎ 063-224402), San Martín 85, has heated rooms, a good restaurant, hot showers and friendly staff; rates are about US$12 per person.

Getting There & Away
Buses from Panguipulli to Puerto Fuy pass through Choshuenco. From Puerto Fuy, there are daily ferries to Puerto Pirehueico, but times vary.

VALDIVIA
Pedro de Valdivia himself founded Santa María La Blanca de Valdivia. After Mapuche raids, it became a military camp, but 19th-century German immigrants transformed its architecture and regional cuisine. Valdivia (population 123,000), also known as the City of the Rivers, is 160km southwest of Temuco, 45km west of the Panamericana. The leafy suburb of Isla Teja is across the bridge just west of town.

Information
Tourist Offices The Sernatur office (☎ 063-215396), Prat 555, is open 9 am to 8:30 pm weekdays, 10 am to 4 pm Saturdays, 10 am to 2 pm Sundays. There is an Oficina de Informaciones (☎ 063-212212) at the bus terminal, Anfión Muñoz 360, that is open 8:30 am to 10 pm daily.

Money Besides ATMs, try Cambio Global, Arauco 331, Local 24, or Cambio Arauco, Carampangue 325.

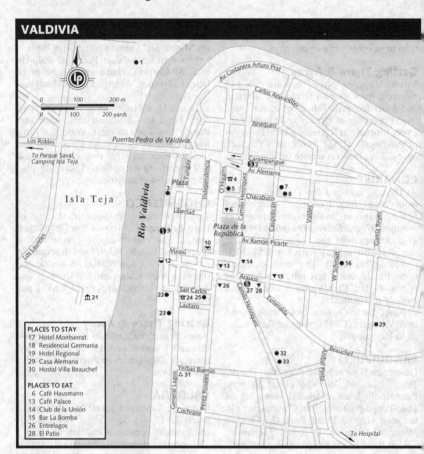

VALDIVIA

0   100   200 m
0   100   200 yards

Los Robles

To Parque Saval,
Camping Isla Teja

Puente Pedro de Valdivia

Isla Teja

Río Valdivia

Los Laureles

Av Costanera Arturo Prat

Carlos Anwandter

Janequeo

Carampangue

Av Alemania

Plaza

Yungay

Independencia

O'Higgins

Camilo Henríquez

Chacabuco

Caupolicán

Valdés

García Reyes

Libertad

Plaza de la
República

Maipú

Av Ramón Picarte

W Schmidt

San Carlos

Lautaro

Arauco

Camilo Henríquez

Esmeralda

Beauchef

Aníbal Pinto

Yerbas Buenas

General Lagos

Pérez Rosales

Cochrane

To Hospital

PLACES TO STAY
17 Hotel Montserrat
18 Residencial Germania
19 Hotel Regional
29 Casa Alemana
30 Hostal Villa Beauchef

PLACES TO EAT
6 Café Hausmann
13 Café Palace
14 Club de la Unión
15 Bar La Bomba
26 Entrelagos
28 El Patio

Post & Communications Correos de
Chile is at O'Higgins 575. Telefónica del Sur
is at San Carlos 107.

Medical Services The Hospital Regional
(☎ 063-214066) is at Bueras 1003, near
Aníbal Pinto.

Things to See
On Sunday, *valdivianos* jam the **Feria Fluvial**,
a riverside market north of the tourist office,
to buy fish and fruit. On Isla Teja, shady
Parque Saval has a riverside beach and a
pleasant trail to lily-covered **Laguna de los
Lotos**. Nearby, the **Universidad Austral** operates a first-rate dairy outlet, with ice cream,
yogurt and cheese at bargain prices.

In an erstwhile riverfront mansion on Isla
Teja, the **Museo Histórico y Arqueológico**
has a well-arranged collection of Mapuche
artifacts and household items from early
German colonists. You can get there by
walking across the bridge to Isla Teja or by
rowboat from the Sernatur office. Informative tours (Spanish only) are a bit rushed but
guides respond well to questions. Admission
is about US$1.25.

Places to Stay
For US$20 per site, try **Camping Isla Teja**
(☎ 063-213584), which is located at the west
end of Calle Los Robles. It has a pleasant
orchard setting, good facilities and a riverside beach.

VALDIVIA

OTHER		20	Torreón del Barro
1	Universidad Austral	21	Museo Histórico
2	Cambio Arauco		y Arqueológico
3	Feria Fluvial	22	Feria Artesanal
4	LanChile		Camino de Luna
5	Cine Cervantes	23	Centro Cultural El Austral
7	Ladeco	24	Telefónica del Sur
8	Avant	25	Café Fértil Provincia
9	Sernatur, Corporación	26	Chocolatería Entrelagos
	Cultural de Valdivia	27	Cambio Global
10	Post Office	31	Torreón de los Canelos
11	Terminal de Buses	32	Artesanía Cema-Chile
12	Puerto Fluvial	33	Artesanía Ruca Indiana
16	Lavamatic (Laundry)		

Río Calle Calle

Q11

17   18
19

20∴

Av Picarte
Av Picarte

To Train Station,
Puerto Montt, Osorno

30

Parque Municipal

To Temuco,
Santiago

Stadium

Valdivia's HI affiliate is **Residencial Germania** (☎ 063-212405), Picarte 873, charging US$9 per person.

Sernatur provides a thorough list of seasonal accommodation, much of it on Avs Ramón Picarte and Carlos Anwandter.

Friendly **Hotel Regional** (☎ 063-216027), Picarte 1005, is plain but clean, with hot water for US$6.50 per person with shared bath, US$11 with private bath, both with breakfast. In the same range is readers' choice **Hostal Villa Beauchef** (☎ 063-216044), Beauchef 844. The hospitable German-speaking owner at **Casa Alemana** (☎ 063-212015), García Reyes 658 (interior), charges US$11/20 single/double with shared bath and breakfast. **Hotel Montserrat**

(☎ 063-215401), Picarte 849, has small but clean and bright rooms for US$16/27 with shared bath and breakfast.

Places to Eat

El Patio, Arauco 347, is a worthwhile choice for beef and seafood. **El Conquistador**, O'Higgins 477, has a simple downstairs café and a fancier upstairs restaurant with balcony seating. **Club de La Unión**, Camilo Henríquez 540, offers filling, well prepared three-course meals, with tea or coffee, for about US$6. Try also **Bar La Bomba**, Caupolicán 594.

For coffee and snacks, check out **Café Palace**, Pérez Rosales 580. For pastries and desserts, try **Establecimientos Delicias** at Henríquez 372, or **Café Hausmann** at O'Higgins 394. **Entrelagos** at Pérez Rosales 630 has good ice cream.

Shopping

For crafts, browse the Feria Artesanal Camino de Luna, at the corner of Costanera and San Carlos. You can buy specialty chocolates at Chocolatería Entrelagos, Pérez Rosales 622.

Getting There & Away

Air LanChile (☎ 063-213042), O'Higgins 386, flies daily to Temuco and Santiago (US$95 to US$124). Ladeco (☎ 063-213392), Caupolicán 364, Local 7/8, flies daily to Temuco and Santiago, and weekdays to Concepción and Santiago. Avant (☎ 063-251431), Chacabuco 408, flies six times weekly to Santiago (US$85 to US$111), via either Concepción (US$39 to US$45) or Temuco (US$15).

Bus Valdivia's Terminal de Buses (☎ 063-212212) is at Anfión Muñoz 360. Companies serving the Panamericana to Santiago, Puerto Montt and intermediates include:

Tur-Bus (☎ 063-212430), Tas Choapa (☎ 063-213124), Bus Norte (☎ 063-212800), Igi Llaima (☎ 063-213542), Buses Lit (☎ 063-212835) and Cruz del Sur (☎ 063-213840). Typical fares are Temuco (US$3.50, two hours), Puerto Montt (US$6, three hours), Concepción (US$10, six hours) and Santiago (US$20, 13 hours).

Regionally, Línea Verde, Pirehueico (☎ 063-218609), Valdivia and Chile Nuevo all go to Panguipulli. Buses Jac has regular

CHILE

service to Temuco, Villarrica and Pucón. Fares to Panguipulli and Villarrica are around US$4.

Getting Around

To/From the Airport Transfer (☎ 063-225533) offers door-to-door minibus service to Aeródromo Las Marías, north of the city via the Puente Calle Calle.

AROUND VALDIVIA

At Corral, Niebla and Isla Mancera, at the mouth of the Río Valdivia, is a series of 17th-century Spanish forts. Largest and most intact is the **Fuerte de Corral** (1645), site of a naval encounter between Chilean patriots and Spanish loyalists in 1820.

Corral and nearby Armagos are most easily reached by boat (US$3 to US$10), but buses from Valdivia's Mercado Municipal go directly to Niebla (US$1.50), where launches across the river cost US$0.75. The best option is a morning cruise from Valdivia's Puerto Fluvial, returning by afternoon bus.

OSORNO

In the late 16th century, huge encomiendas supported over 1000 Spaniards and mestizos in San Mateo de Osorno, but rebellion in 1599 forced them to flee to Chiloé. Only in 1796 was resettlement successful, and well after independence the Mapuche still made overland travel dangerous.

German immigrants have left their mark in dairy farming and manufacturing. Tourism is increasing because Osorno (population 110,000), 910km south of Santiago, is a key road junction for Lagos Puyehue and Rupanco, Parque Nacional Puyehue and the Argentine border.

Information

Tourist Offices Sernatur (☎ 064-237575), on the ground floor of the Edificio Gober-ñación Provincial on the Plaza de Armas, is open 8:30 am to 1 pm and 2:30 to 6:30 pm weekdays. In summer, there's usually an English speaker on duty.

From mid-December through March, the municipal Departamento de Turismo operates an information kiosk at the northwest corner of the Plaza, 10 am to 8 pm Monday through Saturday, 10 am to 2 pm Sunday. There's also a private information office (☎ 064-234149), coordinated with Sernatur.

You'll find it at the main Terminal de Buses, Errázuriz 1400.

Money Besides ATMs, try Cambiotur, Juan Mackenna 1010.

Post & Communications Correos de Chile is at O'Higgins 645. You'll find Entel at Ramírez 1107.

Medical Services The Hospital Base (☎ 064-235572) is on Av Bühler, the southward extension of Arturo Prat.

Things to See

Between the Plaza de Armas and the Estación de Ferrocarril (train station, 1912), new construction is threatening many intriguing buildings in Osorno's **Distrito Histórico** (historic district). Some, however, have been well restored, like the silos of the **Sociedad Molinera de Osorno**, an early grain mill.

West of the railway station, the bulwarks of **Fuerte Reina Luisa** (1793) once guarded riverine access to Osorno. Although the well-restored ruins are unspectacular, they're a pleasant site for a lunchtime breather.

At Mackenna 949, the **Casa Mohr Pérez** (1876) is Osorno's oldest surviving Germanic construction. The **Cementerio Católico** (Catholic cemetery), at Manuel Rodríguez and Eduvijes, has ornate family crypts with numerous German surnames. There's also a larger **Cementerio Alemán** on Los Carrera, between Arturo Prat and Angulo.

The **Museo Histórico Municipal**, Matta 809, traces the region and the city from prehistory to the present.

Places to Stay

Near the bus terminal, *Hospedaje de la Fuente* (☎ 064-239516), Los Carrera 1587, charges about US$9 for spotlessly clean rooms with sagging beds and breakfast. Identically priced *Hospedaje Sánchez* (☎ 064-232560), Los Carrera 1595, also includes breakfast and kitchen privileges. *Hospedaje Central* (☎ 064-231031), Bulnes 876, is comparable. At Colón 602, simple but clean *Residencial Ortega* (☎ 064-232592) is an excellent value for US$9 with breakfast, shared bath and pleasant common spaces.

Places to Eat

La Naranja, in the Mercado Municipal at Prat and Errázuriz, has good, inexpensive meals. The *Kaffeestube*, at Supermercado Las Brisas, Mackenna 1150, serves decent cafeteria food.

Los Platos, Mackenna 1027, has cheap lunchtime dishes for about US$4. *Los Troncos*, Cochrane 527, serves pizza. The *Deutscher Verein* (German Club), O'Higgins 563, is more typically Chilean, but offers good food with fine service at reasonable prices. *Bavaria*, O'Higgins 743, is part of a chain specializing in beef and seafood.

For a splurge, try *Casa del Altillo*, Mackenna 1011, or the German *Peter's Kneipe*, Manuel Rodríguez 1039.

Getting There & Away

Air LanChile (☎ 064-236688), Matta 862, flies daily to Santiago (US$95 to US$124) via Temuco, as does Ladeco (☎ 064-234355), Mackenna 1098.

Bus The long-distance Terminal de Buses (☎ 064-234149) is at Av Errázuriz 1400, near Angulo, but buses to local and regional destinations leave from the Terminal de Buses Rurales in the Mercado Municipal, 2 blocks west at Errázuriz and Prat.

Buses Puyehue (☎ 064-236541), at the Mercado Municipal, has several buses daily to Termas de Puyehue en route to Aguas Calientes (US$2), and to Chilean customs and immigration at Pajaritos (US$3), within Parque Nacional Puyehue. Expreso Lago Puyehue (☎ 064-243919) goes to Entre Lagos (US$1.50) many times daily, Sundays to Aguas Calientes (US$3).

Transur (☎ 064-234371), at the main terminal, goes to Las Cascadas (US$3), on the eastern shore of Lago Llanquihue. Buses Via Octay (☎ 064-237043), also in the main terminal, serves Puerto Octay (US$1.50) and Frutillar on Lago Llanquihue. Mini Buses Puerto Octay, at the same office, also goes to Puerto Octay.

Many companies cover Panamericana destinations between Santiago and Puerto Montt. Typical fares include Concepción (US$13, nine hours), Puerto Montt (US$3, 1½ hours), Santiago (US$19, 14 hours), Temuco (US$5, three hours) and Valparaíso (US$22, 16 hours). Many services originate in Puerto Montt; for more details,

see the Puerto Montt Getting There & Away entry.

International services to Bariloche and other Argentine destinations begin at Puerto Montt; for details, see the Puerto Montt Getting There & Away entry.

Getting Around

To/From the Airport Osorno's Aeropuerto Carlos Hott Siebert (also known as Cañal Bajo) is 7km east of downtown, across the Panamericana via Av Buschmann. A cab costs about US$12.

AROUND OSORNO

One of Chile's most famous hot-springs resorts, **Termas de Puyehue** is an expensive place to stay, but worth a visit for its old-world elegance. It's 76km east of Osorno, where paved Ruta 215 forks; the north fork goes to Anticura and the Argentine border, while its southern lateral goes to Aguas Calientes and Antillanca, in Parque Nacional Puyehue.

PARQUE NACIONAL PUYEHUE

Puyehue's 107,000 hectares of verdant montane forest and starkly awesome volcanic scenery are about 75km east of Osorno. In its lower Valdivian forest, the dominant tree is the multitrunked *ulmo*. The dense understory includes the delicate, rust-barked *arrayán* (a myrtle), *quilla* (a solid bamboo that makes some areas impenetrable) and wild fuchsia. At higher altitudes, southern beeches predominate.

Birds are the most visible fauna. On the peaks, you may spot the Andean condor; look for the Chilean torrent duck in river rapids.

Altitudes range from 250m on the Río Golgol to 2236m on Volcán Puyehue. January and February are best for the high country, but winter skiing is also popular. Despite the moist climate, many areas north of Ruta 215 have been barren since Volcán Puyehue erupted in the 1960s. On the western slopes are many extinct fumaroles and still active hot springs.

Aguas Calientes

Conaf's **Centro de Información Ambiental**, open 9 am to 1 pm and 2:30 to 8:30 pm daily, has an informative display on natural history and geomorphology, with slide presentations daily at 5 pm.

CHILE

OSORNO

To Temuco

Estero Pilauco

Villa Olímpica

Estadio Llanquihue

Parque Cuarto Centenario

Río Damas

Baquedano

Los Carrera

Río Rahue

Train Station

Estero Ovejería

Eleuterio Ramírez

Plaza de Armas

Juan Mackenna

Rosas

Francisco Bilbao

Manuel Rodriguez

Amthahuer
Amthahuer

Mendoza

Arana

Julio Montt

Guillermo Francke

Pérez

M. de Rosas

Av. Portales

Manuel Bulnes

O'Higgins

Av. Matta

Cochrane

Freire

Ejército

Inés de Suárez

1 ●   2 ●   ● 3

5 ▼   ● 7   8 ▼

☎ 6

● 4

17 ❶   ☎ 20

15 ✉
16 ❶   19 ●
   $ 18

23 ▼   ⛪ 24   ▼ 25

27 ⛪

■ 26   ● 28   ▼ 29

∴ 14

PLACES TO STAY	OTHER	17 Departamento de
10 Residencial Ortega	1 Conaf	Turismo Kiosk
12 Hospedaje Sánchez	2 Automóvil Club de Chile	18 Cambiotur
13 Hospedaje de la Fuente	3 Instituto Chileno-	19 Ladeco
26 Hospedaje Central	Norteamericano	20 Entel
	4 Cine Showtime 1 & 2	22 Lavandería Limpec
PLACES TO EAT	6 Centro de Llamados	(Laundry)
5 Deutscher Verein	7 Centro Cultural	24 Casa Mohr Pérez
8 Los Troncos	9 Terminal de Buses Rurales	27 Museo Histórico
21 Kaffeestube	11 Terminal de Buses	Municipal
23 Bavaria	14 Fuerte María Luisa	28 LanChile
25 Los Platos	15 Post Office, Chilesat	
29 Peter's Kneipe	16 Sernatur	

CHILE

OSORNO

Nearby **Sendero El Pionero** is a steep 1800m nature trail with splendid views of Lago Puyehue, the Río Golgol valley and Volcán Puyehue. Watch for the rhubarb-like *nalca*, whose edible stalks support leaves the size of umbrellas, and the ulmo, which grows to 45m. For a longer excursion, take the 11km trail to **Lago Bertín**.

Conaf rangers lead free overnight trips to Lago Paraíso, Volcán Puyehue, Lago Constancia and Pampa Frutilla. For schedules and to reserve a spot, contact Conaf here or in Osorno (☎ 064-234393) at Martínez de Rozas 430. Bring your own tent, food and rain gear.

Skiing
For some of the finest views of Puyehue and its surroundings, visit the Antillanca ski lodge, at the foot of Volcán Casablanca. The season runs early June to late October.

Anticura
Anticura is the base for exploring Puyehue's wildest areas. The highway follows the Río Golgol, but the finest scenery is the desolate plateau at the base of Volcán Puyehue, reached by an overnight hike from El Caulle, 2km west of Anticura.

On Puyehue's western slope, a steep morning's walk from El Caulle, Conaf's well-kept refugio is a good place to lodge or camp. From the refugio, it's another four hours over a moonscape of lava flows and fumaroles to a spring with rustic thermal baths, and a fine, private campsite.

Places to Stay & Eat
Conaf charges US$5 for campsites at Catrue, near Anticura, which has fresh water, picnic tables, firepits and toilets. At Aguas Calientes, concessionaires operate **Camping Chanleufú** (US$25 per site for up to eight people) and **Camping Los Derrumbes** (US$20). Fees include access to thermal baths, but these sites are crowded and noisy in summer.

Getting There & Away
From Osorno's Mercado Municipal, Buses Puyehue (☎ 064-236541) and Expreso Lago Puyehue have several buses daily to Aguas Calientes (US$2), and Chilean customs and immigration at Pajaritos (US$3). In winter, the Club Andino Osorno (☎ 064-232297),

CHILE

O'Higgins 1073, offers direct services to the ski lodge at Antillanca.

PUERTO OCTAY

In the early days of German settlement, Puerto Octay linked Puerto Montt and Osorno via Lago Llanquihue. The Oficina Municipal de Turismo (☎ 064-391491, anexo 727) is on Esperanza, on the east side of the Plaza de Armas.

Puerto Octay's **Museo El Colono**, Independencia 591, displays antique farm machinery and other artifacts.

Places to Stay & Eat

Several travelers have complimented *Hospedaje La Cabaña*, upstairs at German Wulf 712, for US$10 per person with breakfast. The same folks run *Restaurant Cabañas*, nearby at Pedro Montt 713. A few kilometers south of town, on Península Centinela, well-located *Hostería La Baja (☎ 064-391269)* is a basic but agreeable place for US$10 per person with breakfast and shared bath, US$14 with private bath. Shady *Camping La Baja (☎ 064-391251)* is the municipal site, charging US$20 for up to eight people, but backpackers and cyclists get a break at US$4 per person.

Getting There & Away

Puerto Octay's bus stop is on Esperanza just south of Amunátegui. Via Octay goes to Osorno's main bus terminal several times daily, while Thaebus goes to Puerto Montt. At 5 pm weekdays, Minibus Turismo Express Vergara runs from Puerto Octay south to Las Cascadas.

LAS CASCADAS

On the eastern shore of Lago Llanquihue, Las Cascadas has an attractive black-sand beach. Recommended *Hostería Irma*, 1km south of town on the Ensenada road, charges about US$15 per person. Diagonally opposite, along the lake, is a placid free *campsite* with almost no facilities. *Camping Las Cañitas (☎ 064-238336)*, 3km down the road, charges US$13 per site for basic services, including cold showers.

The bus from Puerto Octay arrives in the early evening, but there is no service on the poor 20km road to Ensenada, the entry point to Parque Nacional Vicente Pérez Rosales – either walk or hitch, or return to

the Panamericana and take the bus from Puerto Varas.

FRUTILLAR

From Frutillar, 70km south of Osorno, snow-capped Volcán Osorno seems to float on the horizon above Lago Llanquihue. Noted for its Germanic architecture, Frutillar consists of lakeside Frutillar Bajo and, 2km west near the Panamericana, Frutillar Alto.

For information, Frutillar's Oficina de Información Turística (☎ 064-421198), on Av Philippi between San Martín and O'Higgins, is open 10 am to 9 pm in summer; otherwise, hours are 10 am to 6 pm.

Museo de la Colonización Alemana

Set among manicured gardens, the Museum of German Colonization's perfectly reconstructed buildings include a water mill, a functioning smithery and a typical mansion (as typical as mansions can be), all displaying immaculate 19th-century farm implements and household artifacts.

A short walk from the lakeshore, it's open 9 am to 2 pm and 3 to 7 pm in summer; mid-March to mid-December hours are 10 am to 6 pm. Admission costs US$2 for adults, US$1 for children.

Places to Stay

Camping Los Ciruelillos (☎ 064-339123) at the far south end of Frutillar Bajo, has shady sites with beach access for US$18 (up to six persons). There are hot showers and fresh homemade bread in the morning.

For US$10, there are official HI accommodations at *Hostería Winkler* (☎ 064-421388), Philippi 1155, though regular rooms are in the midrange category.

On the escarpment above the lake, at Las Piedras 60, *Residencial Bruni* (☎ 064-421309) charges a very reasonable US$11 per person.

Places to Eat

Frutillar's best value is the *Casino de Bomberos*, Philippi 1065, serving four-course lunches for about US$5. *Salón de Té Trayen*, Philippi 963, specializes in onces but also offers full lunches. *Café del Sur*, Philippi 775, and the *Andes Café*, Philippi 1057, are good for light meals. The *Bauernhaus*, across O'Higgins from Café del Sur, has superb kuchen. The **Club Alemán**, San Martín 22, has fixed price lunches for about US$10.

Shopping

Local specialties include fresh raspberries, jams and kuchen and miniature wood-carvings of museum buildings.

Getting There & Away

Varmontt and Cruz del Sur, on Alessandri in Frutillar Alto, run buses to Puerto Montt and Osorno every half hour most of the day.

Getting Around

Taxi colectivos shuttle between Frutillar Alto and Frutillar Bajo.

PUERTO VARAS

Attractive Puerto Varas, a 19th-century lakeport 20km north of Puerto Montt, is the gateway to Parque Nacional Vicente Pérez Rosales and the popular boat-bus crossing to Bariloche, Argentina.

Information

Tourist Offices The municipal Oficina de Información Turística (☎ 065-232437), San Francisco 441, is open 9 am to 9 pm daily in summer; otherwise, hours are 10 am to 2 pm and 4 to 6 pm daily.

Money Besides ATMs, change cash and traveler's checks at Turismo Los Lagos, Local 11 in the Galería Real at Del Salvador 257.

Post & Telecommunications Correos de Chile is at San Pedro and San José. Entel is at the corner of San José and San Francisco.

Medical Services Clínica Alemana (☎ 065-232336) is at Dr Bader 810.

Activities

Puerto Varas is a major center for trekking, climbing, white-water rafting and kayaking, mountain biking and birding. Local operators include Aqua Motion (☎ 065-232747), San Pedro 422, and Alsur (☎ 065-232300), Del Salvador 100.

Places to Stay

For updated information on budget accommodations, check the Oficina de Información Turística, Del Salvador 328. Even when the office is closed, there are usually postings in the entryway.

For about US$10, at Verbo Divino 427, **Hospedaje Elsa** (☎ 065-232803) is an excellent choice. Friendly **Hospedaje Florida** (☎ 065-233387), Florida 1361, is comparably priced but less central. Several others are slightly dearer, including recommended **Hospedaje Ceronni** (☎ 065-232016) at Estación 262, and spacious but gloomy **Residencial Hellwig** (☎ 065-232472) at San Pedro 210.

Congenial, German-run **Casa Azul** (☎ 065-232904), Mirador 18, charges US$14 per person in comfortable surroundings. The **Outsider Inn** (☎ 065-232910), San Bernardo 318, is a stylish, immaculate midrange choice at US$25/40 single/double.

Places to Eat

Café Real, upstairs at Del Salvador 257, has cheap set lunches, while **Asturias** at San Francisco 302 features sandwiches and desserts. **Café Mamusia**, San José 316, serves excellent Chilean specialties.

El Gordito and **El Mercado**, both in the Mercado Municipal at Del Salvador 582, are fine upscale seafood venues. Highly regarded **Merlin** (☎ 065-233105), Walker Martínez 584, is expensive, but worth it by all accounts. Several readers have testified that **Ibis**, Pérez Rosales 1117, is also worth a splurge.

Getting There & Away

Puerto Varas has no central terminal, but most bus companies have offices downtown. Northbound buses from Puerto Montt usually pick up passengers in Puerto Varas. Fares and times closely resemble those from Puerto Montt.

Varmontt (☎ 065-232592) San Francisco 666, has daily buses to Santiago and many to Puerto Montt. Cruz del Sur (☎ 065-233008), San Pedro 210, has eight daily to Osorno, Valdivia and Temuco, plus frequent service to Chiloé.

Other nearby companies include Tas Choapa (☎ 065-233831), at Walker Martínez 230, and Buses Norte at San Pedro 210. Both operate buses to Santiago, with regular services to Bariloche over the Puyehue pass.

In summer, at 11 am daily except Sunday, Buses Erwin, San Pedro 210, goes to Ensenada (US$1.25) and Petrohué (US$2.50), returning to Puerto Varas at 1 pm. The rest

CHILE

of the year, these buses run Tuesday, Thursday and Saturday only.

Andina del Sud (☎ 065-232511), Del Salvador 72, runs daily buses to Ensenada and Petrohué, with connections for bus-boat crossing to Bariloche, daily in summer, less frequently the rest of the year.

PARQUE NACIONAL VICENTE PERÉZ ROSALES

Beneath Volcán Osorno's flawless cone, the scoured glacial basin of Lago Todos los Santos offers dramatic views and a scenic boat-bus route to Argentina. Volcán Puntiagudo's needle point lurks to the north, while Volcán Tronador marks the Argentine border.

Chile's first national park (established in 1926), 251,000-hectare Vicente Pérez Rosales is 50km east of Puerto Varas via paved Ruta 225. Its forests and climate (more than 200 rainy days yearly) resemble those of Puyehue, but January and February are fairly dry.

Volcán Osorno

Many agencies in Puerto Varas and Puerto Montt organize guided ascents of Osorno, which requires snow and ice gear, but skilled climbers can handle it solo. In winter, try skiing at the **Centro de Esquí La Burbuja**, 1250m above sea level, reached from Ensenada.

The *Refugio Teski Ski Club* (☎ 065-338490, 212012), just below snow line, has outstanding views of Lago Llanquihue. Beds are available for US$10 per night; breakfast costs US$5, lunch or dinner US$9.

Petrohué

In the shadow of Volcán Osorno, Petrohué is the departure point for the ferry to Peulla, which leaves early in the morning and returns after lunch.

Conaf's **Centro de Visitantes**, opposite Hotel Petrohué, presents displays on the park's geography, geology, fauna and flora and history. From Hotel Petrohué, a dirt track leads to **Playa Larga**, a long black-sand beach. The **Sendero Rincón del Osorno** is a 5km trail on Lago Todos los Santos's western shore.

Aqua Motion, the Puerto Varas adventure travel operator, maintains an office at Petrohué, where it's possible to arrange climbs of Volcán Osorno (US$100), rafting on the Río Petrohué (US$35) and full-day 'canyoning' excursions in Río León gorge (US$79).

Across the river, reached by rowboat, *Hospedaje Küscher* has rooms for US$10 per person, with camping possible for US$5.

Peulla

Approaching the village of Peulla, which bustles in summer with tourists en route to Argentina, Lago Todos los Santos' deep blue becomes emerald green. **Cascada de los Novios** is a waterfall just a few minutes walk from upscale Hotel Peulla along an easy footpath. For a longer excursion, take the 8km **Sendero Laguna Margarita**, a rewarding climb.

There's a *campsite* opposite Conaf, or you can stay at *Hospedaje Hernández*, on the right side as you leave the jetty, for US$9.

Getting There & Away

Bus For bus services to Petrohué, see Getting There & Away for Puerto Varas and Puerto Montt.

Boat Andina del Sud's ferry (☎ 065-232511) departs Petrohué early for the three-hour voyage to Peulla, the first leg of the journey to Bariloche. Get tickets (US$30) at the kiosk near the jetty, or from Andina del Sud in Puerto Varas or Puerto Montt.

PUERTO MONTT

Puerto Montt (population 90,000), capital of the 10th Region (Los Lagos), on the Seno de Reloncaví, resembles Seattle or Vancouver in site, but its older architecture is Middle European. It has excellent transport connections to Chiloé, Aisén and Patagonia. The mountains of wood chips at the port of Angelmó are fast becoming a symbol of uncontrolled exploitation in southern Chile's temperate forests.

Information

Tourist Offices Puerto Montt's Oficina Municipal de Turismo (☎ 065-253551, Anexo 2307) is at Varas and O'Higgins. Open 8:30 am to 1:30 pm and 2 to 7:30 pm Monday through Saturday, 10 am to 2 pm on Sunday, it's more convenient than hilltop Sernatur (☎ 065-252720), O'Higgins 480.

Money Besides ATMs, cambios include Turismo Los Lagos at Varas 595, Local 3, and La Moneda de Oro (at the bus terminal).

Post & Communications Correos de Chile is at Rancagua 126. Chilesat is at Talca 70, Entel at Varas 567, Local 2.

Travel Agency English-run Travellers (☎/fax 065-258555, travlers@chilepac.net), Av Angelmó 2456, arranges guides and equipment for Volcán Osorno and other adventure trips, sells IGM topographic maps and travel books (including LP guides) and reserves flights, rental cars, and ferry trips. They also operate a used paperback exchange and a café with cable TV and a message board.

Medical Services Puerto Montt's Hospital Base (☎ 065-253991) is on Seminario, behind the hilltop Intendencia Regional.

Things to See
About 3km west of downtown, the port of **Angelmó** has an outstanding crafts market, with handmade boots, curios, copperware, ponchos and woolen sweaters, hats and gloves. For a quieter perspective on the gulf, launches from the docks go to **Isla Tenglo**.

Places to Stay
Puerto Montt has two HI affiliates, both charging US$10 per person: *Residencial Independencia* (☎ 065-277949), Independencia 167, and another *Residencial Independencia* (☎ 065-257938), Av Angelmó 2196, across from the ferry terminal.

Residencial El Talquino (☎ 065-253331), near the bus terminal at Pérez Rosales 114, is a bargain at US$6 per person, plus US$1 for breakfast. *Hospedaje Emita* (☎ 065-250725), Miraflores 1281, is reasonable at US$8 per person with firm beds, shared bath and hot showers. Convenient to the Angelmó ferry port, *Hospedaje Marazul* (☎ 065-256567), Ecuador 1558, charges US$9 with shared bath, US$11 with private bath.

Several others are in the US$9 range, including friendly *Hospedaje González*, at Gallardo 552, with spacious, sunny rooms, breakfast, hot water and kitchen privileges; equally friendly but sometimes noisy *Hostal Yelcho* (☎ 065-262253), Ecuador 1316, with three beds per room; and *Residencial Los*

Helechos (☎ 065-259525), Chorrillos 1500, where some rooms lack windows.

Lively *Hospedaje Suizo* (☎ 065-252640), Independencia 231, is an excellent value for US$11 with shared bath, plus US$1.50 for a generous breakfast. It's straight uphill from the mountain of wood chips at the entrance to the port at Angelmó.

Places to Eat
For drinks, snacks and kuchen, try *Pastelería Alemana* at Rancagua 117, *Café Real* at Rancagua 137 or *Kaffeeschatz* at Varas 629. *Mykonos*, Antonio Varas 326, has moderately priced lunches. At Gallardo 119, Puerto Montt's best pizzería, Italian-run *Di Napoli* is a tiny venue that gets crowded and stuffy – ventilation is better downstairs.

Don't leave Puerto Montt without tasting curanto or other regional seafood specialties at Angelmó's waterfront cafés – among the recommended choices are the aggressively touristy *Marfino*, Av Angelmó 1856, and the much less pretentious *Asturias*, Av Angelmó 2448-C. Downtown seafood choices include the *Centro Español* at O'Higgins 233, renowned for paella, and *Balzac* at Urmeneta 305.

Getting There & Away
Air LanChile and Ladeco (☎ 065-253315), both at O'Higgins 167, Local 1-B, fly several times daily to Balmaceda/Coihaique (US$42 to US$82), Punta Arenas (US$82 to US$160) and Santiago (US$95 to US$164), usually nonstop but sometimes via Temuco or Concepción. Avant (☎ 065-258277), at Benavente 305, flies twice daily to Santiago (US$85 to US$121), daily to Balmaceda (US$45 to US$76) and eight times weekly to Punta Arenas (US$85 to US$134).

Transportes Aéreos Neuquén (TAN, ☎ 065-250071), Varas 445, flies Tuesday and Friday to Bariloche (US$62), Comodoro Rivadavia (US$107) and Neuquén (US$105), and Saturday to Comodoro and Neuquén only.

Aeromet (☎ 065-253219), Quillota 127, and Aerosur (☎ 065-252523), Urmeneta 149, fly air taxis to the Aisén region.

Bus Puerto Montt's waterfront Terminal de Buses (☎ 065-253143) is at Av Portales and Lillo. There are services to all regional destinations, Chiloé, Santiago, Coihaique, Punta

CHILE

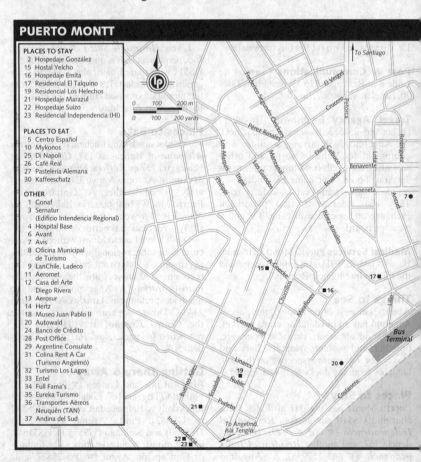

PUERTO MONTT

PLACES TO STAY
2 Hospedaje González
15 Hostal Yelcho
16 Hospedaje Emita
17 Residencial El Talquino
19 Residencial Los Helechos
21 Hospedaje Marazul
22 Hospedaje Suizo
23 Residencial Independencia (HI)

PLACES TO EAT
5 Centro Español
10 Mykonos
25 Di Napoli
26 Café Real
27 Pastelería Alemana
30 Kaffeeschatz

OTHER
1 Conaf
3 Sernatur
   (Edificio Intendencia Regional)
4 Hospital Base
6 Avant
7 Avis
8 Oficina Municipal
   de Turismo
9 LanChile, Ladeco
11 Aeromet
12 Casa del Arte
   Diego Rivera
13 Aerosur
14 Hertz
18 Museo Juan Pablo II
20 Autowald
24 Banco de Crédito
28 Post Office
29 Argentine Consulate
31 Colina Rent A Car
   (Turismo Angelmó)
32 Turismo Los Lagos
33 Entel
34 Full Fama's
35 Eureka Turismo
36 Transportes Aéreos
   Neuquén (TAN)
37 Andina del Sud

Arenas and Argentina. Services down the Camino Austral are limited but increasing.

There are frequent buses to nearby Puerto Varas (US$0.70), Frutillar (US$1.40) and Puerto Octay. Buses Fierro (☎ 065-253022) goes to Lenca, the turnoff for the southern approach to Parque Nacional Alerce Andino, and Chaica (US$1.50) five times daily, and to Lago Chapo (US$1.75), the northern approach to Alerce Andino, four times daily. Other destinations include the villages of Ralún (US$4), Cochamó (US$4.50) and Río Puelo (US$5.50). Buses Pirehueico (☎ 065-252926) goes to Panguipulli four times daily.

Buses Fierro has two buses daily to Hornopirén (US$7, three hours) on the Camino Austral, where there are summer ferry connections to Caleta Gonzalo. There is, however, no consistent public transport for the 56km between Caleta Gonzalo and the mainland port of Chaitén, which is more easily reached by ferry from either Puerto Montt or Quellón (Chiloé). Since conditions and traffic on the Camino Austral change rapidly, check details on arrival in Puerto Montt.

Several carriers go south to Chiloé, including Cruz del Sur (☎ 065-254731) and Transchiloé (☎ 065-254934). To Santiago and intermediates, there's Varmontt (☎ 065-254410), Igi Llaima (☎ 065-254519), Buses Lit (☎ 065-254011) Etta Bus (☎ 065-257324), Turibús (☎ 065-253245), Bus Norte (☎ 065-

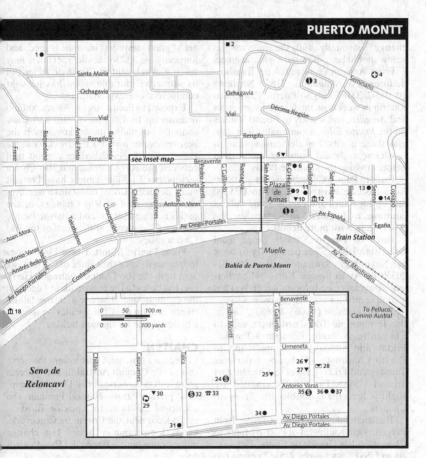

PUERTO MONTT

252783), Tas Choapa (☎ 065-254828), Tur-Bus (☎ 065-253329) and Vía Tur (☎ 065-253133). Buses Lit and Tur-Bus have daily service to Valparaíso and Viña del Mar.

For the marathon to Punta Arenas (US$70), via Argentina's Atlantic coast, contact Turibús, Buses Ghisoni (☎ 065-256622) or Bus Sur (☎ 065-252926). Turibús also goes to Coihaique (US$33) daily via Argentina.

Sample fares include Ancud (US$5, two hours), Castro (US$7, three hours), Concepción (US$14, nine hours), Osorno (US$2.50, 1½ hours), Quellón (US$10, five hours), Santiago (US$25, 16 hours), Temuco (US$9, five hours), Valdivia (US$6, 3½ hours) and Valparaíso (US$28, 18 hours).

Bus Norte, Cruz del Sur and Río de La Plata (☎ 065-253841) have daily buses to Bariloche, Argentina (US$20) via Puyehue, while Tas Choapa goes twice daily.

Buses Andina del Sud and Varastur (☎ 065-252203), both at Varas 437, offer daily bus-boat combinations to Bariloche (US$106), via Ensenada, Petrohué and Peulla. These depart Puerto Montt around 8:30 am, arriving in Bariloche early in the evening.

Boat Ferries or bus-ferry combinations go to Chiloé and Chaitén, in the 10th Region; those to Chiloé leave from Pargua, on the Canal de Chacao. Some sail to Puerto Chacabuco (port of Coihaique), in the 11th

Region (Aisén), or to Puerto Natales, in the 12th Region (Magallanes). Schedules change seasonally and the information below should be considered a general guide.

From Angelmó's Terminal de Transbordadores, Av Angelmó 2187, Navimag (☎ 065-253318) sails to Puerto Chacabuco four times weekly on the ferries *Evangelistas* and *Amadeo*, and weekly to Puerto Natales on the *Puerto Edén*, a memorable four days and three nights. Travelers susceptible to seasickness should consider medication before crossing the Golfo de Penas.

Fares to Puerto Chacabuco start at US$26 for a basic seat without meals, to US$100 and up for bunks and cabins. Some sailings continue to Laguna San Rafael; see the Aisén section for more details.

Fares to Puerto Natales range from US$210 to US$515 per person. Try to book at Navimag's Santiago office (☎ 02-2035030), Av El Bosque Norte 0440; otherwise, Travelers (see Information above) has a good record for arranging passages.

Transmarchilay (☎ 065-253683), also at the Terminal de Transbordadores, sails to Chaitén (eight hours, departures Tuesday, Friday and Sunday) in summer and to Puerto Chacabuco (23 hours, departures Tuesday and Friday). Fares to Chaitén start around US$18. Fares to Chacabuco are slightly less than double the fares to Chaitén.

Transmarchilay also runs car ferries from Pargua, 60km southwest of Puerto Montt, to Chacao, on Isla Grande de Chiloé. Fares are about US$1 for walk-ons, US$12 per car (no matter how many passengers).

Getting Around

To/From the Airport ETM buses (US$1.50, ½ hour) go to Aeropuerto El Tepual (☎ 065-252019), 16km west of town.

Car Rental Rental agencies include the Automóvil Club (☎ 065-254776) at Esmeralda 70, First (☎ 065-252036) at Antonio Varas 447, Hertz (☎ 065-259585) at Varas 126, and Full Fama's (☎ 065-258060) at Portales 506.

PARQUE NACIONAL ALERCE ANDINO

Only 40km southeast of Puerto Montt, this 40,000-hectare reserve of Andean peaks and glacial lakes shelters the alerce (*Fitzroya cupressoides*), a conifer resembling California's giant sequoia in appearance and longevity. A 3000-year-old specimen may reach 40m in height and 4m in diameter, but its attractive, durable wood has brought commercial overexploitation.

Exposed to Pacific storms, Alerce Andino receives up to 4500mm of rain and snow annually, but hiking the backcountry is the best reason for a visit. LP's *Trekking in the Patagonian Andes* describes a good trail between the Río Chamiza and Río Chaica sectors, but El Niño winters have brought many deadfalls. Conaf maintains a free five-site campground at Río Chamiza, in the park's northern sector, and a six-site facility at Lago Chaiquenes, at the head of the Río Chaica valley.

From Puerto Montt, Buses Fierro goes four times daily to the village of Correntoso, 3km from the Río Chamiza entrance. Fierro also has buses to the crossroads at Lenca, on the Camino Austral, where a narrow lateral climbs 7km up the Chaica valley – probably a better choice for the non-trekker.

CHAITÉN

Chaitén is a tiny, quiet port toward the north end of the Camino Austral. It is the access point for US conservationist Douglas Tompkins' private Parque Natural Pumalín. The municipal Caseta de Información Turística, on Todesco near the Costanera Corcovado, keeps long summer hours, but change money elsewhere – Banco del Estado gives poor rates.

Places to Stay & Eat

For budget accommodations, look for private houses, some of them open only in summer. Several places offer beds for about US$9 with breakfast, including *Hospedaje Sebastián* (☎ 065-731225) at Todesco 188. Slightly more expensive is *Hostería Llanos* (☎ 065-731332), Corcovado 378.

For seafood, try the simple restaurants on the Costanera Corcovado, including *Cocinería Marita III* at Carrera Pinto, and *Hostería Corcovado*, at Pedro Aguirre Cerda.

Getting There & Away

Air Aerosur (☎ 065-731228), at Carrera Pinto and Almirante Riveros, flies daily except Sunday to Puerto Montt (US$43), as does Aeromet (☎ 065-731275), Todesco 42.

Bus The Terminal de Buses is at O'Higgins 67. Buses Futaleufú (☎ 065-731278) makes the journey weekdays to Futaleufú (US$10), on the Argentine border, while Buses Alcón goes to Palena Monday, Wednesday and Friday at 1 pm.

Buses Becker, on Corcovado between Todesco and O'Higgins, and B y V Tour, Libertad 432, alternate services to Coihaique (US$25 to US$30, 12 hours). B y V also serves Caleta Gonzalo on Monday, Wednesday and Saturday (more frequently on demand), departing at 7 am.

Boat Transmarchilay (☎ 065-731611), Corcovado 266, has eight ferries monthly to Quellón, on Isla Grande de Chiloé, and four weekly to Puerto Montt. Navimag (☎ 065-731570), at Carrera Pinto and Almirante Riveros, runs the spacious ferry *Alejandrina* to Quellón thrice weekly. Confirm schedules at Transmarchilay; for fares, see entries for Quellón, Chonchi and Puerto Montt.

In January and February, Transmarchilay sails daily except Tuesday and Wednesday from Caleta Gonzalo, 56km north of Chaitén, to Hornopirén, which has bus connections to Puerto Montt.

FUTALEUFÚ

Futaleufú, at the confluence of the Río Espolón and the Río Futaleufú, is 155km from Chaitén via an indirect route around Lago Yelcho. Only a few kilometers from Argentina's Chubut province, it's renowned for fishing and Class V whitewater.

Reasonable accommodations are available for US$8 to US$10 at *Residencial Carahue* (☎ 065-258633, Anexo 260), O'Higgins 332; *Hospedaje El Campesino* (☎ 065-258633, Anexo 275) at Prat 107; and *Hospedaje Cañete* (☎ 065-258633, Anexo 214) at Gabriela Mistral 374.

Buses Futaleufú, at Balmaceda and Prat, has buses to Chaitén (US$10), Monday, Wednesday, Thursday and Saturday at 4 pm, Tuesday at 1 and 4 pm. Buses Codao goes to the border, where it meets an Argentine bus.

PARQUE NACIONAL QUEULAT

Fronting the Camino Austral between Chaitén and Coihaique, 154,000-hectare Queulat is a zone of steep-sided fjords, rushing rivers, evergreen forests, creeping glaciers and high volcanic peaks. The Río Cisnes and the glacial fingers of Lago Rosselot, Lago Verde and Lago Risopatrón offer excellent fishing.

Queulat is popular with adventure travel agencies, but also attracts independent travelers – though dense brush inhibits off-trail exploration. There's a good 2km trail to the **Ventisquero Colgante** (Hanging Glacier), 36km south of Puyuhuapi, and another up the **Río Guillermo**. Consult rangers at Pudú, Ventisquero, Puyuhuapi, El Pangue or La Junta.

Places to Stay

Camping Ventisquero, convenient to the Ventisquero Colgante, has attractive but rocky sites with covered barbecues and picnic tables (US$10), but the showers sprinkle glacial meltwater. On Lago Risopatrón, 15km north of Puyuhuapi, Conaf's *Camping Angostura* charges US$4 per site in a sopping rain forest, but the facilities are good (cold showers only, though).

Getting There & Away

Buses from Chaitén or Coihaique drop passengers at points along the park's western boundary. Renting a car in Coihaique is more flexible, but expensive without several people to share the cost.

Chiloé

Isla Grande de Chiloé, a well-watered, forested island of undulating hills, is 180km long but just 50km wide. Surrounded by smaller islands, it has a temperate maritime climate. Distinctive shingled houses line the streets and dot the verdant countryside. When the sun finally breaks through the rain and mist, it illuminates majestic panoramas of snowcapped mainland volcanoes.

Huilliche Indians first raised potatoes and other crops in the fertile volcanic soil. Jesuits were among the earliest European settlers, but mainland refugees arrived after the Mapuche uprising of 1599. A Spanish royalist stronghold, Chiloé resisted *criollo* attacks on Ancud until 1826.

Chiloé is part of the 10th Region (Los Lagos); Ancud and Castro are the only

CHILE

CHILOÉ (& THE CAMINO AUSTRAL)

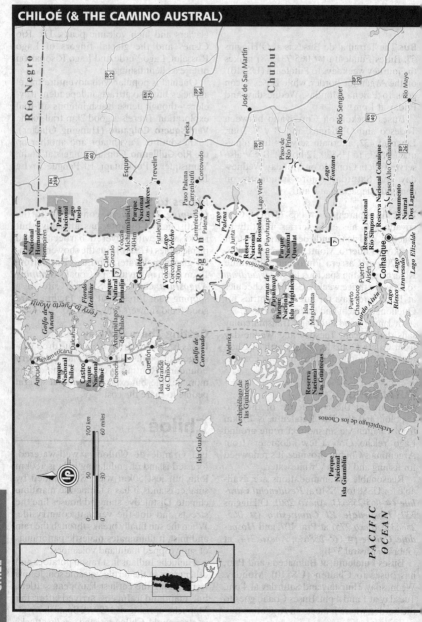

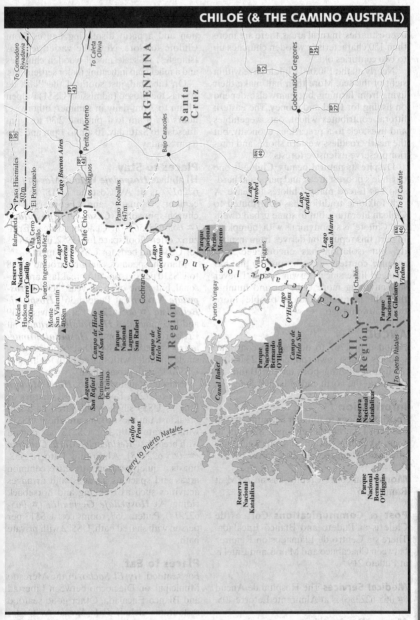

CHILOÉ (& THE CAMINO AUSTRAL)

large towns. Castro and some villages have picturesque rows of *palafitos*, stilted houses over estuaries. In rural areas, there are more than 150 characteristic wooden churches up to two centuries old.

Nearly all the 130,000 Chilotes live within sight of the sea. More than half make their living from farming, but many also depend on fishing for food and money. The eastern littoral contributes wheat, oats, vegetables and livestock to a precarious economy, but the nearly roadless western shores and interior preserve extensive forests.

Despite its natural beauty, Chiloé is one of Chile's poorest areas, and perpetual hardship has forced many Chilotes to leave. A rich folkloric tradition has contributed to Chilean literature, but to some urban dwellers, 'Chilote' is synonymous with 'bumpkin.' In part, this reputation derives from insularity, but isolation has encouraged self-reliance, courtesy and a hospitality that has changed little since Darwin wrote: 'I never saw anything more obliging and humble than the manners of these people' more than 150 years ago.

ANCUD
Founded in 1767 to defend the coastline, Chiloé's largest town (population 23,000) is a bustling fishing port on the Bahía de Ancud, at the north end of Isla Grande.

Information
Tourist Offices In summer Sernatur (☎ 065-622665), Libertad 665, is open 8:30 am to 8 pm weekdays, 10 am to 4 pm weekends; otherwise, it's open weekdays only.

Money Banco de Crédito has an ATM at Ramírez 257.

Post & Communications Correos de Chile is at Pudeto and Blanco Encalada. There's a Centro de Llamados on Ramírez between Chacabuco and Maipú, and Entel is at Pudeto 219.

Medical Services The Hospital de Ancud (☎ 065-622356) is at Almirante Latorre 405.

Museo Regional Aurelio Bórquez Canobra
Also known as the Museo Chilote, this attractive facility maintains ethnographic and his-

torical materials (including outstanding photographs), a fine natural-history collection and a patio displaying figures from Chilote folklore. Note the varied *tejuelas* (shingles) on scale model wooden churches and a relief map indicating major settlements.

On Libertad, just south of the Plaza de Armas, the Museo (admission US$1) is open 11 am to 7 pm daily in summer; otherwise, hours are 9 am to 1 pm and 2:30 to 7 pm Tuesday to Saturday, 10 am to 1 pm and 3 to 6 pm Sunday.

Places to Stay
HI affiliate *Hospedaje Vista al Mar* (☎ 065-622617) is at Av Costanera 918. In December, January and February, the church-sponsored *Casa del Apostulado* (☎ 065-623256), on Chacabuco near Errázuriz, offers floor space for US$2, mattresses for US$4 and beds for US$5 per night.

Many hospedajes, charging around US$8 to US$10 per person with breakfast, are seasonal, but some open all year include *Hospedaje Navarro* at Pudeto 361, *Hospedaje Bellavista* (☎ 065-622384) at Bellavista 449 and recommended *Hospedaje Miranda,* at Errázuriz and Mocopulli. *Hospedaje Montenegro* (☎ 065-622239), Dieciocho 191, has singles/doubles with shared bath for around US$10/15 with private bath.

Praised by many readers, *Hotel Madryn* (☎ 065-622128), Bellavista 491, charges as little as US$9 single with shared bath and breakfast, but most rooms are about US$11 with private bath. For US$13 per person with breakfast, *Residencial María Carolina* (☎ 065-622458), Almirante Latorre 558, boasts a quiet location, attractive common areas and spacious gardens, and arranges activities such as trekking and horseback riding. At *Hospedaje Germania* (☎ 065-622214), Pudeto 357, rooms cost US$13 per person with shared bath, US$22 with private bath.

Places to Eat
For seafood, try *El Sacho*, in the Mercado Municipal, on Dieciocho between Libertad and Blanco Encalada. Other good seafood restaurants include *Polo Sur*, at Av Costanera 630; *La Pincoya*, Prat 61; and *Capri*, at Mocopulli 710.

For good dinners, desserts and coffee, try *Café Lydia*, Pudeto 256. Highly recommended *Kurantón*, Prat 94, specializes in Chilean cuisine, notably curanto (mostly in summer).

Shopping
Ancud has a plethora of outlets for woolens, carvings and pottery. Besides the museum, try Artesanía Francisquita, Libertad 530.

Getting There & Away
All long-distance bus companies have moved their offices to Ancud's shiny new Terminal de Buses, at Aníbal Pinto and Marcos Vera, east of downtown. For buses to other destinations on Isla Grande, try the two rural bus terminals: on Pedro Montt opposite Prat and at Prat and Libertad.

Cruz del Sur (☎ 065-622265) has a dozen buses daily to Puerto Montt, some continuing to Santiago and intermediates, and many southbound to Castro and Quellón. Varmontt (☎ 065-623049) has similar routes. Transchiloé (☎ 065-622876) covers all the stops from Puerto Montt to Quellón. Turibús (☎ 065-622289) goes to Santiago and intermediates and to Punta Arenas and Puerto Natales.

Sample fares include Castro (US$2, one hour), Concepción (US$19, 11 hours), Puerto Montt (US$5, two hours), Quellón (US$5, three hours), Temuco (US$14, seven hours) and Santiago (US$28, 18 hours).

CASTRO
Founded in 1567, 90km south of Ancud, Castro is the capital of Chiloé province. When Darwin visited in 1834, he found it 'a most forlorn and deserted place.' Today, the town is a popular summer destination, attracting many Chilean and Argentine tourists. The distinctive waterfront palafitos, with their handcrafted tejuelas, are emblematically Chilote. The most conspicuous landmark – the bright, incongruously painted cathedral – dates from 1906.

Information
Tourist Offices The private Asociación Gremial Hotelera Gastronómica funds the kiosk on the north side of the Plaza de Armas, which is open 9 am to 9 pm daily in summer; otherwise, it's open weekdays 9 am to 1 pm and 3 to 7 pm, Saturday 9 am to 1 pm.

Money For best rates, try Julio Barrientos (☎ 065-625079) at Chacabuco 286, or Banco de Crédito's ATM at O'Higgins and Gamboa.

Post & Communications Correos de Chile is at O'Higgins 388. Telefónica del Sur is at Latorre 289.

Medical Services The Hospital de Castro (☎ 065-632445) is at Freire 852.

National Parks Conaf (☎ 065-632289), Gamboa 424, has the latest on Parque Nacional Chiloé.

Things to See
At the north end of the Plaza de Armas, Castro's **Iglesia San Francisco** assaults the eyes with its dazzling exterior – salmon with violet trimmings. On Esmeralda, half a block south of the plaza, the **Museo Regional de Castro** houses an idiosyncratic collection of Huilliche Indian relics, farm implements and exhibits on Chilote urbanism.

The waterfront **Feria Artesanal** has a selection of woolens and basketry. Note the bundles of dried seaweed and nalca, both eaten by Chilotes, and the chunks of peat fuel.

Palafitos All around Castro, shingled houses on stilts stretch into the estuaries and lagoons. Look especially along Costanera Pedro Montt, at the north end of town, at the Feria Artesanal (where some of the palafitos house restaurants), and at both ends of the bridge over the Río Gamboa.

Places to Stay
Hostels In summer, the *Albergue Juvenil* (☎ 065-632766), in the Gimnasio Fiscal at Freire 610, charges about US$4.

Hospedajes Hospedajes start around US$6, but some are seasonal – look for handwritten signs along San Martín and O'Higgins, near Sargento Aldea. At *Hospedaje Central*, on Los Carrera between Blanco Encalada and Gamboa, spotless but small and spartan rooms with firm beds and shared bath cost US$8.

At Barros Arana 140, cordial *Hospedaje El Molo* (☎ 065-635026) charges only US$9 with breakfast, an outstanding value. For

US$10 per person with breakfast, rooms at recommended *Hospedaje Agüero* (☎ 065-635735), in a quiet location at Chacabuco 449, have views of the sea and Castro's southern palafitos.

Places to Eat

The waterfront palafito restaurants have the best food for the fewest pesos – try *Brisas del Mar* or *Mariela* for set lunches as well as seafood specialties. *Don Octavio*, at Costanera Pedro Montt 261, is no longer a budget choice but is still a good value for seafood. Try *Chilos*, at Sotomayor and San Martín, for meat and seafood, and *Sacho*, Thompson 213, for curanto.

Café La Brújula del Cuerpo, O'Higgins 308, has sandwiches, coffee and desserts. *La Tavolata*, Balmaceda 245, is a moderately priced pizzería.

Getting There & Away

The Terminal de Buses Rurales is on San Martín near Sargento Aldea; most but not all long-distance companies have offices nearby.

Buses Arroyo (☎ 065-635604) has two to three buses a day to Cucao (US$2.50), the west coast entrance to Parque Nacional Chiloé; Ocean Bus (☎ 065-635492) has two daily services on the same route. There are frequent buses to Dalcahue, Chonchi and offshore islands, the latter via short ferry links.

Long-distance services and fares resemble those from Castro. The main carriers are Cruz del Sur (☎ 065-632389), San Martín 486; Regional Sur (☎ 065-632071); and Transchiloé (☎ 065-635152). There's direct service, via Argentina, to Puerto Natales and Punta Arenas with Buses Ghisoni (☎ 065-632358), Turibús (☎ 065-635088), Bus Sur and Buses Queilén.

DALCAHUE

A 1960 tsunami washed away Dalcahue's palafitos, but its 19th-century church and gorgeous vernacular architecture survived. Taking its name from Chiloé's seagoing *dalcas* (canoes), the town, 20km northeast of Castro, is the gateway to Quinchao, one of archipelagic Chiloé's most interesting and accessible islands. The tourist information kiosk at Freire and O'Higgins keeps erratic hours.

Every Sunday, artisans from offshore islands bring a fine selection of woolens, wooden crafts and basketry to Dalcahue's waterfront **Feria Artesanal,** which also has good cheap food.

Places to Stay & Eat

For about US$7 to US$8 per person, try very friendly *Residencial Playa*, Rodríguez 009, or *Residencial San Martín*, San Martín 001, which also serves moderately priced meals. For excellent food and waterfront atmosphere, try *Brisas Marinas*, in palafitos above the Feria Artesanal.

Getting There & Away

Buses load and unload at the market. Expreso Dalcahue has half-hourly buses to Castro weekdays, but fewer on weekends. Taxi colectivos charge US$1 for the half-hour trip. There are ferries to Isla Quinchao, with bus connections to Achao and its landmark 18th-century church.

CHONCHI

Chonchi dates from 1767, though its **Iglesia San Carlos**, with its three-story tower and multiple arches, is a 19th-century landmark. Connected by launch and ferry to Isla Lemuy, the town is 23km south of Castro. Its Oficina de Información Turística (☎ 065-671223) is at Sargento Candelaria and Centenario.

Hospedaje El Mirador (☎ 065-671351), Ciriaco Álvarez 198, offers the most economical lodging at US$7.50 per person with breakfast and hot showers. English and German are spoken at comparably priced, beachfront *Hospedaje La Esmeralda* (☎ 065-671328), Irarrázabal s/n, which also rents mountain bikes, boats and fishing gear. For seafood dinners, try *El Trébol* at the Mercado Municipal.

Getting There & Away

Cruz del Sur and Transchiloé have several buses daily from Castro. Taxi colectivos from the corner of Chacabuco and Esmeralda in Castro cost US$1; in Chonchi, they leave from Pedro Montt, opposite Iglesia San Carlos.

There are launches to Ichuac, on Isla Lemuy, and the ferry leaves every two hours from 8 am to 8 pm from Puerto Huichas, 5km south, with connections to Puqueldón.

PARQUE NACIONAL CHILOÉ

Nowhere in South America can a traveler follow Darwin's footsteps more closely than in Parque Nacional Chiloé. The great naturalist's account of his passage to Cucao merits lengthy citation:

At Chonchi we struck across the island, following intricate winding paths, sometimes passing through magnificent forests, and sometimes through pretty cleared spots, abounding with corn and potato crops. This undulating woody country, partially cultivated, reminded me of the wilder parts of England, and therefore had to my eye a most fascinating aspect. At Vilinco (Huillinco), which is situated on the borders of the lake of Cucao, only a few fields were cleared...

The country on each side of the lake was one unbroken forest. In the same periagua (canoe) with us, a cow embarked. To get so large an animal into a small boat appears at first a difficulty, but the Indians managed it in a minute. They brought the cow alongside the boat, which was heeled towards her; then placing two oars under her belly, with their ends resting on the gunwale, by the aid of these levers they fairly tumbled the poor beast, heels overhead into the bottom of the boat, and then lashed her down with ropes.

Chiloé's Pacific coast still harbors native coniferous and evergreen forests, plus an almost pristine coastline. The Chilote fox and pudú (miniature deer) scurry beneath the shadowy trunks of the contorted tepú, while the 110 bird species include the Magellanic penguin. About 30km west of Chonchi and 54km southwest of Castro, the park is open all year, but fair weather is more likely in summer.

Huilliche communities are ambivalent about Conaf's park management plan, which has restricted access to traditional subsistence while allowing some commercial exploitation. Darwin, more than 150 years ago, also wrote of the 'harsh and authoritative manner' of government officials toward Chilotes.

Bruce Chatwin, the late gifted travel writer, left a superlative essay on Cucao in his *What Am I Doing Here?*

Sector Chanquín

Park admission costs US$1.50. Conaf's **Centro de Interpretación**, across the suspension bridge from Cucao, is open 9 am to 7:30 pm daily, with good displays on flora and fauna, the Huilliche people, the early mining industry and local folklore. The **Sendero Interpretivo El Tepual** is a winding nature trail through gloomy forest where you might meet up with the Trauco, a troll-like creature from Chilote folklore. The **Sendero Dunas de Cucao** is another trail, that leads to a series of dunes behind a long, white-sand beach, but the sea is too cold for swimming.

Three km north on the coastal trail, at **Lago Huelde**, is a Huilliche community. At Río Cole Cole, 12km north of Chanquín, and at Río Anay, 8km beyond, are rustic refugios, but a tent is advisable in this changeable climate. Wear water-resistant footwear and wool socks since, in Darwin's words, 'everywhere in the shade the ground soon becomes a perfect quagmire.'

Places to Stay & Eat

Camping Chanquín, 200m beyond the visitor center, has secluded sites with running water, firewood and cold showers for US$6. Within easy walking distance of the park entrance, *Hospedaje El Paraíso* and *Hospedaje Pacífico* have B&B for US$7.50 per person, while *Posada Cucao* costs about US$10.

Getting There & Away

Between them, Buses Arroyo and Ocean Bus run four to five buses daily to Castro (US$2.50).

QUELLÓN

From Quellón, 92km south of Castro, ferries sail to Chaitén and Puerto Chacabuco. From December to March, Quellón maintains a Caseta de Información Turística at Gómez García and Santos Vargas, open 9:30 am to 1 pm and 2:30 to 10:30 pm daily.

Places to Stay & Eat

On the waterfront at Pedro Montt 427, *Hotel Playa* (☎ 065-681278) is a decent place charging US$8 per person with breakfast. *Hotel La Pincoya* (☎ 065-681285), La Paz 64, is a comfortable place with friendly staff and hot water, charging US$13/22 single/double with shared bath and breakfast, US$22/32 with private bath.

For a small town, Quellón has fine seafood in the waterfront restaurants near the jetty and at *La Quila*, La Paz 385 and *El Coral*, 21 de Mayo 251.

CHILE

Getting There & Away

Bus Services to Castro (US$2.50, 1½ hours) are frequent with Cruz del Sur (☎ 065-681284) and Transchiloé, both at Aguirre Cerda 52.

Boat Transmarchilay (☎ 065-681331) is at Pedro Montt 457, near the pier. You can reach the Aisén region by ferry from Quellón, either via Chaitén or directly to Puerto Chacabuco (the port of Coihaique). Ferries run to a timetable but sometimes leave late and schedules change seasonally, so verify the information below at Transmarchilay offices.

The car ferry *La Pincoya* sails to Chaitén (five hours) Mondays and Wednesdays at 4 pm and to Puerto Chacabuco (18 hours) Saturdays at 4 pm. Passenger fares to Chaitén range from US$13 to US$20, depending on the seat, while those to Chacabuco range from US$20 to US$32.

Aisén

Aisén's islands, fjords and glaciers resemble those of Alaska's Inside Passage and New Zealand's South Island. Air and sea access, and overland routes from Argentina, are better than the Camino Austral, which supposedly links the area to Puerto Montt, but the highway is improving.

For millennia, Chonos and Alacalufes Indians fished and hunted the intricate canals and islands. Several expeditions visited the area in the late 18th and early 19th centuries; Chilean naval officer Enrique Simpson's 1870s survey mapped areas as far south as the Península de Taitao.

Chile later promoted colonization with grazing and timber leases, allowing a single company to control nearly a million hectares near Coihaique. The bleached trunks of downed trees still litter hillsides where, encouraged by a land law that rewarded clearance, the company and colonists burned nearly three million hectares of lenga forest in the 1940s.

See the Southern Patagonia map later in this chapter for destinations south of Coihaique.

COIHAIQUE

Founded in 1929, Coihaique (sometimes spelled Coyhaique) has outgrown its pioneer origins to become a modest but tidy regional capital with a population of 34,000. Most visitors arrive by air from Puerto Montt or by ferry at Puerto Chacabuco, 80km west.

Information

Tourist Offices Sernatur (☎ 067-231752), Bulnes 35, is open 9 am to 1 pm and 3 to 7 pm weekdays. The Oficina Municipal de Turismo (☎ 067-232100) is at Baquedano 310.

Money Change cash or traveler's checks at Turismo Prado, 21 de Mayo 417. Banco Santander has an ATM at Condell and 21 de Mayo.

Post & Communications Correos de Chile is at Cochrane 202. Entel is at Prat 340, Chilesat at Ibáñez 347.

Medical Services Coihaique's Hospital Base (☎ 067-231286) is on Calle Hospital, at the west end of JM Carrera.

National Parks Conaf (☎ 067-212128) is at Bilbao 234.

Things to See & Do

The **Museo Regional de la Patagonia**, Baquedano 310, has a fine collection of labeled photographs on regional history, plus miscellaneous pioneer artifacts.

From May to September, the **Centro de Ski El Fraile** (☎ 067-231690), 29km from Coihaique, operates two lifts on five different runs. On most lakes and rivers, the fishing season runs November to May.

Places to Stay

The woodsy, attractive HI affiliate *Albergue las Salamandras* (☎/fax 065-211865), about 2km southwest of town, has cooking facilities and great common spaces for US$10 per person (US$5 if camping).

Family-run *Hospedaje Los 4 Hermanos* (☎ 067-232647), Colón 495, has singles for US$8 per person; breakfast (US$3) is additional. Amiable, slightly dearer *Hospedaje Nathy* (☎ 067-231047), Almirante Simpson 417, permits garden camping as well. *Hospedaje Guarda* (☎ 067-232158), Simpson 471, has spacious rooms in a garden setting for US$17 per person, with an excellent breakfast and private bath.

AISÉN & MAGALLANES

CHILE

Archipiélago de los Chonos

Parque Nacional Las Guaitecas

RP 19 · José de San Martín

Camino Austral

7 · Paso de Río Frías · To Chaitén

Lago La Plata

Puerto Chacabuco

Lago Fontana · Alto Río Senguer

Chubut

Reserva Provincial Punta Tombo

RN 3 · Cabo Raso

RP 30 · Camarones

RP 1 · Cabo Dos Bahías

Puerto Aisén · Paso Alto Coihaique

RP 40 · Coihaique

RP 20 · Lago Musters

Lago Colhué Huapi

Coihaique

RP 26 · Paso Huemules

Río Mayo

Colonia Sarmiento

RN 26

Golfo San Jorge

Balmaceda

RP 55 · El Portezuelo

Comodoro Rivadavia

Puerto Ingeniero Ibáñez

Lago Buenos Aires

Las Heras

Caleta Olivia

Chile Chico

Los Antiguos

Perito Moreno

RP 43

Parque Nacional Laguna San Rafael

Península de Taitao

Ferry

Paso Roballos

Pico Truncado

ARGENTINA

Fitzroy

Cochrane

Lago Pueyrredón

XI Región

Campo de Hielo Norte

Bajo Caracoles

Monumento Natural Bosques Petrificados

RN 3

RN 281 · Puerto Deseado

Reserva Nacional Katalalixar

Laguna Posadas

RP 12 · Tres Cerros

RP 47

Campo de Hielo Sur

Parque Nacional Perito Moreno

RP 37

Gobernador Gregores

Santa Cruz

Lago O'Higgins

RP 25

Parque Nacional Bernardo O'Higgins

Lago San Martín

RN 40

San Julián

El Chaltén

Lago Viedma

RP 27

Tres Lagos

RN 288

Parque Nacional Los Glaciares

Piedrabuena

Lago Argentino

El Calafate

RP 9

Santa Cruz

XII Región

RP 2

RN 40

Parque Nacional Torres del Paine

Esperanza

RP 5

Bahía Grande

SOUTH ATLANTIC OCEAN

Paso Cancha de Carreras

Puerto Natales

Río Turbio

Estancia Güer Aike

SOUTH PACIFIC OCEAN

Paso Casas Viejas

Bella Vista

RN 40 · Río Gallegos

9

Estancia Cóndor

Punta Delgada · Cabo Vírgenes

Punta Arenas

Porvenir

Strait of Magellan

San Sebastián

RN 3 · Río Grande

Reserva Nacional Alacalufes

Tierra del Fuego

CHILE

Parque Nacional Tierra del Fuego

Isla Grande de Tierra del Fuego

Ushuaia

Puerto Williams

Isla Navarino

Islas de los Estados

Parque Nacional Cabo de Hornos

Cabo de Hornos (Cape Horn)

Cordillera de los Andes

0   50   100 km
0   30   60 miles

Places to Eat
Café Samoa, Prat 653, is a cozy bar/restaurant with cheap meals and snacks. *Café Ricer*, Horn 48, has good lunches and dinners with large portions and fine service. Lively *Café Oriente*, at Condell and 21 de Mayo, has snacks and light meals, as does the more sedate *Cafetería Alemana*, at Condell and Moraleda.

The *Casino de Bomberos*, General Parra 365, also has fine meals at reasonable prices. For seafood, try *Loberías de Chacabuco*, Prat 386, and *Corhal*, Bilbao 125. *La Olla* is an upscale restaurant at Prat 176.

Getting There & Away
Air Both at General Parra 402 (☎ 067-231188), LanChile and Ladeco fly several times daily to Puerto Montt (US$42 to US$82) and Santiago (US$124 to US$200). Avant (☎ 067-237571), General Parra 302, flies daily to Puerto Montt (US$45 to US$76) and Santiago (US$113 to US$172), sometimes via Temuco.

Aerotaxi Don Carlos (☎ 067-232981), Subteniente Cruz 63, flies to Cochrane (US$65), Villa O'Higgins (US$98), Lago Verde and Chile Chico (US$40) once or twice weekly.

Bus Coihaique's Terminal de Buses is at Lautaro and Magallanes, but a number of companies have offices elsewhere in town.

To Puerto Aisén (US$2.50) and Puerto Chacabuco, try Transaustral (☎ 067-231333) at Baquedano 1171, or Taxi Bus Don Carlos (☎ 067-231981) at Cruz 63.

Artetur (Becker; ☎ 067-233768), General Parra 337, goes Tuesday and Saturday to Puyuhuapi (US$13), La Junta and Lago Verde (US$15). Transaustral goes to Puyuhuapi and La Junta (US$15) Tuesday and Saturday at 8:30 am.

Artetur's Wednesday bus to Chaitén (US$25) leaves at 10:30 am, overnighting in La Junta (US$6) before continuing Thursday morning. B y V Tour (☎ 067-231793), Simpson 1037, goes Tuesday, Thursday and Saturday at 9 am to Chaitén (US$30, 11 hours).

Southbound, Colectivo Puerto Ibáñez (☎ 067-233064), at Presidente Ibáñez 30, goes to Puerto Ibáñez (US$7), connecting with the Chile Chico ferry. Buses Australes Pudú (☎ 067-231008) goes Wednesday and Saturday mornings to Villa Cerro Castillo (US$10), Cochrane (US$22) and intermediates. Taxi Bus Don Carlos and Río Baker Taxi Bus (☎ 067-231052) have slightly cheaper service, on Monday, Wednesday and Friday mornings, to Cochrane and intermediate stops.

Long-distance buses to Osorno and Puerto Montt (US$33) go via Argentina. Turibús (☎ 067-231333), Baquedano 1171, leaves Tuesday and Saturday at 4 pm, while La Cascada goes Wednesday at 10 am in summer only.

Buses Giobbi (☎ 067-232067), at the terminal, has Tuesday and Saturday buses to Comodoro Rivadavia, Argentina (US$40), at 8:30 am. Turibús goes to Comodoro Monday and Friday at 11 am.

Boat Ferries to Chiloé and Puerto Montt leave from Puerto Chacabuco, two hours from Coihaique by bus. Schedules are subject to change; for fares, see the Quellón and Puerto Montt entries.

Transmarchilay (☎ 067-231971), upstairs at 21 de Mayo 417, sails to Puerto Montt Monday at 4 pm and Wednesday at 10 pm, and to Quellón Monday at 6 pm. Navimag (☎ 067-223306), at Presidente Ibáñez 347, Oficina 1, also sails to Puerto Montt, Wednesday at 8 pm and Friday at 7 pm.

Getting Around
To/From the Airport Aeropuerto Teniente Vidal, 5km south of town, has a short runway and a steep approach, so most commercial flights now use Balmaceda, 50km southeast of Coihaique. Many taxi colectivos and minibuses ply the paved road to Balmaceda, an hour's ride.

Car Shoestring travelers might consider pooling resources to rent a car to explore the region. Shop around, since prices vary, but try Automotora Traeger (☎ 067-231648) at Baquedano 457, Automundo (☎ 067-231621) at Bilbao 510, or Turismo Prado (☎ 067-231271) at 21 de Mayo 417.

AROUND COIHAIQUE
Reserva Nacional Coihaique
Despite its proximity to Coihaique, this 2150-hectare reserve is wild country, with exhilarating panoramas of the town and the

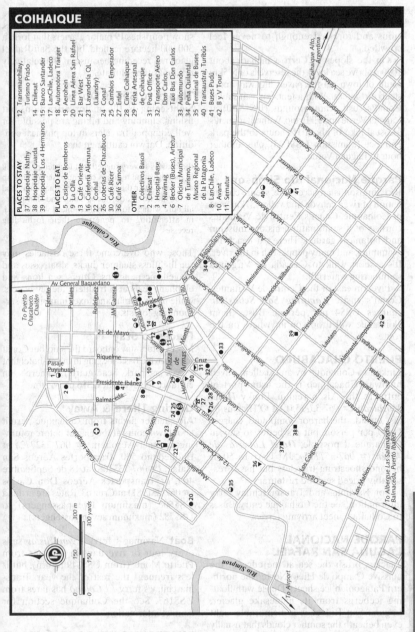

COIHAIQUE

PLACES TO STAY
37 Hospedaje Nathy
38 Hospedaje Guarda
39 Hospedaje Los 4 Hermanos

PLACES TO EAT
5 Casino de Bomberos
9 La Olla
13 Café Oriente
16 Cafetería Alemana
22 Corhal
26 Loberías de Chacabuco
30 Café Ricer
36 Café Samoa

OTHER
1 Colectivos Basoli
2 Chilesat
3 Hospital Base
4 Navimag
6 Becker (Buses), Artetur
7 Oficina Municipal
  de Turismo,
  Museo Regional
  de la Patagonia
8 LanChile, Ladeco
10 Avant
11 Sernatur
12 Transmarchilay,
  Turismo Prado
14 Chilesat
15 Banco Santander
17 LanChile, Ladeco
18 Automotora Traeger
19 Aerohein
20 Línea Aérea San Rafael
21 Bar West
23 Lavandería QL
  (Laundry)
24 Conaf
25 Cambios Emperador
27 Entel
28 Cine Coihaique
29 Feria Artesanal
  de Coihaique
31 Post Office
32 Transporte Aéreo
  Don Carlos,
  Taxi Bus Don Carlos
33 Automundo
34 Peña Quilantal
35 Terminal de Buses
40 Transaustral, Turibus
41 Buses Pudú
42 B y V Tour

CHILE

enormous basalt columns of Cerro Macay in the distance. A popular local retreat, it's spacious and forested enough to never feel crowded.

On the slopes of Cerro Cinchao, about 1000m above sea level, the reserve is only 5km south of town via the paved highway and a steep dirt lateral. With a tent, you can stay at Conaf's rustic campgrounds (US$3.50) at Laguna Verde and El Brujo. Without a car, it's a casual hike of about 1½ hours to the park entrance (admission US$1.25), plus another hour to Laguna Verde.

Parque Nacional Río Simpson

Río Simpson is an accessible, scenic combination of river, canyon and valley, 37km west of Coihaique. Conaf's Centro de Visitantes consists of a small natural history museum and botanical garden. There's a beach for swimming, and many people fish in the river. It's a short walk to Cascada La Virgen, a shimmering waterfall.

Five km east of the Centro de Visitantes, Conaf's rustic *Camping San Sebastián* charges US$4 per person. Buses from Coihaique will drop you anywhere on the route.

PUERTO CHACABUCO

Linked to Coihaique by an excellent paved highway, Chacabuco is the usual port of entry to the Aisén region. Funky *Hotel Moraleda* (☎ 067-351155), at O'Higgins 82 just outside the harbor compound, charges US$9 per person, but it's better to stay in Coihaique if possible. *Hotel Loberías de Aisén* (☎ 067-351115), JM Carrera 50, is beyond shoestring travelers but has a reasonably priced seafood restaurant.

For Navimag and Transmarchilay ferry information, see the Coihaique entry. Buses to Coihaique meet arriving ferries.

PARQUE NACIONAL LAGUNA SAN RAFAEL

Glaciers brush the sea at the edge of the massive Campo de Hielo Norte (the northern Patagonian ice sheet). Dense with floating icebergs from its namesake glacier, Laguna San Rafael is a memorable sight even beneath the somber clouds that usually hover over the surrounding peaks.

Laguna San Rafael is 225km southwest of Puerto Chacabuco via a series of channels between the Chonos archipelago and the Patagonian mainland. At higher elevations, snow nourishes 19 major glaciers that form a 300,000-hectare icefield, but the San Rafael glacier is receding because of the relatively mild maritime climate.

Things to See & Do

Sightseeing is the major attraction, but fishing, climbing and hiking are possible for well-equipped travelers in top physical condition. Darwin cautioned that

the coast is so very rugged that to attempt to walk in that direction requires continued scrambling up and down over the sharp rocks of mica-slate; and as for the woods, our faces, hands and shin-bones all bore witness to the maltreatment we received, in attempting to penetrate their forbidding recesses.

Those who overcome these obstacles may see flightless steamer ducks, albatrosses and Magellanic penguins. Otters, sea lions and elephant seals also frequent the icy waters, while pudú, pumas and foxes inhabit the surrounding forests.

Places to Stay

Most visitors stay onboard the ship, but Conaf may provide basic lodging in the ex-hotel that serves as park headquarters. There's an entrance fee of about US$6 per visitor.

Getting There & Away

Air Charter flights from Coihaique permit about two hours at the glacier before returning; contact Aerohein (☎ 067-232772) at Baquedano 500, Transportes Aéreos San Rafael (☎ 067-233408) at 18 de Septiembre 469, or Transportes Aéreos Don Carlos (☎ 067-231981) at Cruz 63. Rates are around US$608 (maximum five passengers) to US$782 (maximum seven passengers).

Boat Navimag's ferry *Evangelistas* sails every four or five days in summer from Puerto Montt (from US$149 return), but is less frequent the rest of the year. Transmarchilay's ferry *El Colono* has fares from US$167. See the Coihaique section for contact information.

PUERTO INGENIERO IBÁÑEZ

Puerto Ingeniero Ibáñez, on the north shore of Lago General Carrera, has recovered quickly from the 1991 eruption of Volcán Hudson, which nearly buried it in ash. Local *huasos*, counterparts to the Argentine *gauchos*, drive cattle and sheep along the roads, and orchard crops do well in the lakeside microclimate; rows of poplars separate the fields. Ferries cross the lake to Chile Chico.

Residencial Ibáñez (☎ 067-423227), Dickson 31, has unheated singles with plenty of extra blankets for about US$9 with breakfast; other meals are available. Next door, at Dickson 29, *Hotel Mónica* (☎ 067-423226) is slightly dearer.

Getting There & Away
For transport from Coihaique, see the Coihaique entry.

Naviera Sotramin (☎ 067-234240), Portales 99 in Coihaique, sails the ferry *El Pilchero* to Chile Chico daily except Sunday. The passenger fare is US$3.50 per person, but students pay half and bicycles cost US$3.

RESERVA NACIONAL CERRO CASTILLO
Blanketed by southern beech forests, overshadowed by the 2700m basalt spires of Cerro Castillo and flanked by three major glaciers on its southern slopes, this 180,000 hectare reserve is one of Aisén's most impressive sights. On the Camino Austral, 67km south of Coihaique, Conaf operates a modest but sheltered and shady campground at *Laguna Chaguay* (US$3.50 per site).

There's an excellent four-day trek from Km 75, at the north end of the reserve, to Villa Cerro Castillo, at the south end, detailed in LP's *Trekking in the Patagonian Andes*. At Villa Cerro Castillo, *Pensión El Viajero* has rooms (US$6 single), a bar and a cheap restaurant.

CHILE CHICO
On the south shore of Lago General Carrera, tiny Chile Chico derived its early prosperity from copper, but fruit cultivation in its sunny microclimate has kept it alive – though not prosperous, since it's remote from markets. Gold mining has brought a recent revival, and it's one of few southern Patagonian border crossings with good public transport.

At O'Higgins and Lautaro, the Oficina de Información Turística is part of the newly opened museum. *Hospedaje Alicia* (☎ 067-411265), Freire 24, is worth a look for US$9 per person, but the best accommodations are at spotless *Hospedaje Don Luis* (☎ 067-411384), Balmaceda 175, a friendly place charging US$11 per person without breakfast. For snacks and drinks, try congenial *Café Elizabeth y Loly*, Pedro González 25.

Getting There & Away
Aerotaxi Don Carlos, O'Higgins 264, has three flights weekly from Coihaique, but there are regular ferries to Puerto Ibáñez. Acotrans, O'Higgins 424, crosses the border to Los Antiguos, Argentina, for connections to southern Argentine Patagonia.

Magallanes

Unless arriving by air or sea, visitors to rugged, mountainous, stormy Magallanes must pass through Argentina (See Aisén and Magallenes map earlier). The region's original inhabitants were Ona, Yahgan, Haush, Alacaluf and Tehuelche Indians, who lived by fishing, hunting and gathering. Early Spanish colonization failed, and Chile did not assume definite control until 1843.

The California gold rush nurtured the port of Punta Arenas, which further developed with the wool and mutton trade in the late 19th century, but maritime traffic declined when the Panama Canal opened. Wool, commerce, petroleum and fisheries have made this one of Chile's most prosperous regions, and its natural assets, particularly Parque Nacional Torres del Paine, attract many travelers.

PUNTA ARENAS
On the western shore of the Strait of Magellan, wool-boom mansions and other landmarks preserve a late-19th-century atmosphere in Patagonia's most interesting city. The best port for thousands of kilometers, Punta Arenas (population 113,000) attracts fishing fleets as well as Antarctic research and tourist vessels, while a duty-free zone (zona franca) has promoted commerce and encouraged immigration. It's utterly dead on Sunday, so this is a good time to explore the surrounding area or start a trip to Torres del Paine.

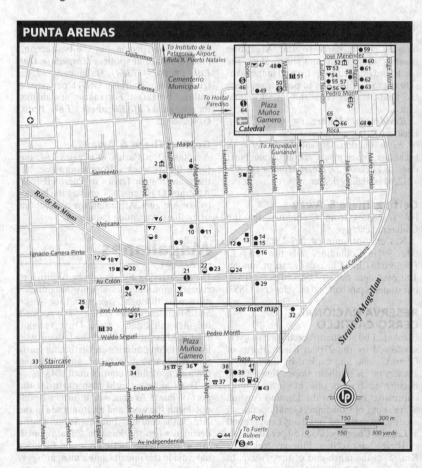

PUNTA ARENAS

History

Punta Arenas' early economy relied on wild-animal products like sealskins, guanaco hides and feathers; mineral products like coal, gold and guano; and firewood and timber. Though well situated for the California gold rush, it really flourished after 300 purebred sheep arrived from the Falkland Islands in the late 19th century; soon two million animals were grazing the territory's pastures.

As the wool market boomed, Asturian entrepreneur José Menéndez became one of South America's wealthiest and most influential individuals. First engaged solely in commerce, his Sociedad Explotadora de Tierra del Fuego eventually controlled nearly a million hectares in Magallanes, and other properties in Argentina.

Menéndez and his colleagues built their empires with European immigrant labor; in the municipal cemetery, modest markers on all sides of his opulent mausoleum recall those who made the great wool fortunes possible.

Information

Tourist Offices Open 8:30 am to 5:45 pm weekdays, plus extended summer hours, Sernatur (☎ 061-225385), Waldo Seguel 689, publishes a list of accommodations and transport, and maintains a message board. The municipal Kiosko de Informaciones (☎ 061-223798), in the 700 block of Av

PUNTA ARENAS

PLACES TO STAY
5 ¡Ecole! Patagonia
13 Hospedaje Manuel
15 Albergue Backpacker's Paradise
19 Residencial Coirón
43 Hostal O'Higgins
60 Hostal Calafate II

PLACES TO EAT
6 222
7 El Mercado
18 Rotisería La Mamá
27 Golden Dragon
28 Café Calipso
36 Centro Español
41 Sotito's Bar
54 Asturias
65 Quijote

OTHER
1 Hospital Regional
2 Museo Regional Salesiano
  Mayorino Borgatello
3 Southern Patagonia
  Souvenirs & Books
4 Internacional Rent A Car
8 Transportes Polo Sur
9 Austro Internet

10 Sala Estrella
11 Turismo Aonikenk
12 Arka Patagonia
14 Canadian Institute
16 Chile Típico
17 Buses Punta Arenas
20 Buses Fernández, Buses
   Pingüino, Turibús, Queilén
21 Kiosko de Informaciones
22 Bus Sur
23 Operatur Patagónica
24 Buses Pacheco, Australmag
   Rent A Car
25 Turismo Cordillera Darwin
26 Turismo Comapa, Magallanes
   Tour
29 Gabriela Mistral Mural
30 Milward's Stone Castle
31 Austral Bus
32 Conaf
33 Mirador La Cruz
34 Turismo Viento Sur
35 CTC
36 Teatro Cervantes
37 Chilexpress
38 Tercera Zona Naval
39 Turismo Pali Aike
40 Ladeco

42 Olijoe Pub
44 Navimag
45 Pingüi Tour
   (Casa de Cambio)
46 Redbanc (ATM)
47 Post Office
48 Lubag Rent A Car
49 Club de la Unión
50 Citibank
51 Casa Braun-Menéndez
52 Museo Militar de la Quinta
   División del Ejército
53 Entel
55 LanChile
56 Buses Ghisoni, Tecni-Austral
57 Buses Transfer
58 Budget Rent A Car
59 Aerovías DAP
61 Automóvil Club de Chile
62 Lavasol
63 Hertz
64 Sernatur
66 British Consulate, Avant
67 Museo Naval y Marítimo
68 Emsa/Avis

Colón, is open 9 am to 7 pm weekdays all year, plus 9 am to 7 pm Saturday in summer.

Money Besides ATMs, travel agencies along Lautaro Navarro change cash and traveler's checks on weekdays and Saturday mornings. Bus Sur, at Magallanes and Colón, cashes traveler's checks for Saturday afternoon arrivals.

Post & Communications Correos de Chile is at Bories 911. CTC is at Nogueira 1116, on Plaza Muñoz Gamero. For Internet access, try Austro Internet, Croacia 690, Oficina 3, or the Canadian Institute (☎ 061-227943), O'Higgins 694.

Walking Tour

Landscaped with exotic conifers, **Plaza Muñoz Gamero** is the setting for landmarks like **Club de la Unión** (the former Sara Braun mansion), the **Catedral** and the headquarters of the powerful **Sociedad Menéndez Behety** (now a branch of Citibank).

Half a block north, at Magallanes 949, the spectacular **Casa Braun-Menéndez** (the family's mansion) is now a cultural center

and regional history museum. Three blocks west of the plaza, the outlandish **stone castle** at Av España 959 belonged to Charly Milward, whose eccentric exploits inspired his distant relation Bruce Chatwin to write *In Patagonia.*

Four blocks south of the plaza, at the foot of Av Independencia, is the entrance to the port, a harbor for seafarers from Spain, Poland, Japan, France, the USA and many other countries, as well as local fishing boats, the Chilean navy and countless seabirds. At Colón and O'Higgins, 4 blocks northwest of the Plaza, is a very fine **mural** of Gabriela Mistral.

Six blocks north of the Plaza, at Bories and Sarmiento, is the **Museo Salesiano**. Another 4 blocks north, the **Cementerio Municipal** (municipal cemetery) is an open-air historical museum in its own right.

Places to Stay

Open November through March, *Albergue Backpacker's Paradise* (☎ *061-222554*), Ignacio Carrera Pinto 1022, charges US$6 for dark, crowded dormitory accommodations, but has pleasant common spaces. At

CHILE

Bellavista 697 (6 blocks south of Plaza Muñoz Gamero), *Colegio Pierre Fauré* (☎ 061-226256) operates a hostel in January and February. Singles cost US$7 with breakfast, US$6 without; campers can pitch tents in the garden for US$4 per person.

Homey *Hospedaje Guisande* (☎ 061-243295), JM Carrera 1270, US$9 with breakfast, has earned exuberant recommendations. *Hospedaje Manuel* (☎ 061-220567), O'Higgins 648, has similar accommodations for US$9/15 and also organizes tours. In the southern port zone are *Hospedaje Carlina* (☎ 061-247687), Paraguaya 150 and *Hospedaje Nena* (☎ 061-242411), Boliviana 366, both charging about US$9 per person with breakfast.

At recommended *Hostal O'Higgins* (☎ 061-227999), O'Higgins 1205, rates are US$12 per person. *Residencial Coirón* (☎ 061-226449), Sanhueza 730, has spacious, sunny singles for US$13 with breakfast. Recommended *Hostal Calafate II* (☎ 061-241281), José Menéndez 1035, charges US$16/30 with shared bath. *Hostal Parediso* (☎ 061-224212), Angamos 1073, is an excellent value for US$18/20 with shared bath.

Places to Eat
222, Mejicana 654, offers good pizza and sandwiches. *Quijote*, Lautaro Navarro 1087, also has reasonable lunches. Family-run *Rotisería La Mamá*, Sanhueza 720, offers fine, moderately priced lunches. A good choice for breakfast, onces and people-watching is *Café Calipso*, Bories 817. *Lomit's*, José Menéndez 722, also serves sandwiches.

A local institution at Mejicana 617 (the ground-level entrance to this upstairs restaurant is inconspicuous), *El Mercado* prepares fish and shellfish at moderate prices. The *Centro Español*, above the Teatro Cervantes on the south side of Plaza Muñoz Gamero, is another fine seafood choice. *Golden Dragón*, Colón 529, is a very good Chinese restaurant.

Highly regarded *Sotito's Bar*, O'Higgins 1138, serves outstanding if pricey dishes such as centolla. *Asturias*, Lautaro Navarro 967, is worth a splurge.

Shopping
The Zona Franca (Zofri or duty-free zone), open daily except Sunday, is excellent for cameras, film and other luxuries. Taxi colectivos to the shopping center are numerous.

Getting There & Away
Air LanChile (☎ 061-241232), Lautaro Navarro 999, flies twice daily to Santiago (US$152 to US$292) via Puerto Montt (US$82 to US$160). Ladeco (☎ 061-244544), Lautaro Navarro 1155, flies twice daily to Santiago via Puerto Montt except Wednesday and Saturday, when the afternoon flight stops in Concepción.

Avant (☎ 061-228312), Roca 924, flies twice daily to Santiago (US$139 US$215) via Puerto Montt (US$80 to US$133); most flights also stop in either Temuco or Concepción.

Aerovías DAP (☎ 061-223340), O'Higgins 891, flies to Porvenir (US$22) and back at least twice daily except Sunday. Tuesday, Thursday and Saturday, it flies to and from Puerto Williams, on Isla Navarino (US$66). In summer it flies daily except Sunday to Río Grande, Argentina (US$79), where connections to Ushuaia are available.

Kaikén Líneas Aéreas (☎ 061-227061), Colón 521, flies daily except Sunday to Río Grande (US$69) and nine times weekly to Ushuaia (US$78) in summer.

Bus Services to Puerto Natales (US$7, three hours) are frequent with Buses Fernández (☎ 061-242313), Armando Sanhueza 745; Bus Sur (☎ 061-244464), at Magallanes and Colón; Transfer Austral (☎ 061-229613), Pedro Montt 966; and Austral Bus (☎ 061-241708), José Menéndez 565.

Overland buses to destinations like Puerto Montt (US$70 to US$95), Isla Grande de Chiloé and Santiago take up to 48 hours via Argentina. Among the carriers are Buses Ghisoni (☎ 061-222078), Lautaro Navarro 971; Buses Punta Arenas (☎ 061-249868) at José Menéndez 556 and Magallanes 775; and Turibús (☎ 061-227970), Armando Sanhueza 745.

There are numerous services to Río Gallegos, Argentina (US$13 to US$18, five hours). The most frequent is Buses Pingüino (☎ 061-221812, 061-242313), Armando Sanhueza 745, daily at 12:45 pm. Buses Ghisoni goes Monday, Wednesday, Thursday and Saturday at 11 am, while Magallanes Tour (☎ 061-221936), Colón 521, plies the route Tuesday at 9 am.

Buses Pacheco (☎ 061-242174), Av Colón 900, goes Monday, Wednesday and Friday at 7:15 am to Río Grande (US$27), in Argentine Tierra del Fuego, with connections to Ushuaia. Tecni-Austral (☎ 061-223205), Lautaro Navarro 971, goes to Río Grande (US$30) and Ushuaia (US$51) Tuesday, Thursday and Saturday at 7 am, without changing buses.

Boat From the Tres Puentes ferry terminal (taxi colectivos going here leave from Casa Braun-Menéndez), Transbordador Austral Broom (☎ 061-218100) sails to Porvenir, Tierra del Fuego (US$7, 2½ hours). Boats depart daily, except Monday and Thursday, at 9 am and return at 2 pm, except Sundays and holidays (5 pm). Arrange vehicle reservations at Av Bulnes 05075.

Broom is also the agent for the ferry *Patagonia*, which sails twice monthly to Puerto Williams, on Isla Navarino; seats on the 38-hour trip cost US$50 including meals, while bunks cost US$80.

Getting Around
To/From the Airport Transportes Polo Sur (☎ 061-243173), Chiloé 873, offers airport transfers for US$5, as does Buses Transfer (☎ 061-220766), Pedro Montt 966.

Bus & Colectivo Taxi colectivos are quicker, more comfortable and only slightly dearer than buses at about US$0.40 or a bit more late at night and Sunday.

Car Rental Rental agencies include Hertz (☎ 061-248742) at O'Higgins 987, Budget (☎ 061-241696) at O'Higgins 964, the Automóvil Club de Chile (☎ 061-243675) at O'Higgins 931, Australmag (☎ 061-242174) at Av Colón 900, and Lubag (☎ 061-242023) at Magallanes 970.

AROUND PUNTA ARENAS
Northwest of Punta Arenas is a substantial colony of Magellanic penguins (also gulls, cormorants and sea lions) at **Seno Otway** (Otway Sound). *Spheniscus magellanicus*, also known as the jackass penguin for its characteristic braying, comes ashore in the spring to nest in burrows or beneath shrubs. Naturally curious, jackasses will back into their burrows or toboggan into the water if approached too quickly. Their bills can inflict

serious cuts – *never* stick your hand or face into a burrow, rather sit nearby and wait for them to emerge.

About 55km south of Punta Arenas, the military outpost of **Fuerte Bulnes** was abandoned soon after its founding in 1843 because of poor soil and pastures, lack of potable water and exposed site. Across the Strait are **Isla Dawson** (a 19th-century Salesian mission to the Yahgans and a notorious prison camp after the 1973 coup) and the Cordillera Darwin.

Several agencies organize tours of the Otway penguin colony (about US$11), Fuerte Bulnes and other nearby sites. These include Turismo Pali Aike (☎ 061-223301); Lautaro Navarro 1129; Arka Patagonia (☎ 061-248167); Carrera Pinto 946; Turismo Aonikenk (☎ 061-228332); Magallanes 619; and Turismo Viento Sur (☎ 061-225167), Fagnano 565.

Porvenir
Populated by Yugoslav immigrants in the 1880s, Chilean Tierra del Fuego's largest settlement (population 5083) is a cluster of corroding, metal-clad Victorian buildings belying its optimistic name (the future). For most travelers, it's a brief stopover en route to Ushuaia, Argentina, but it makes a good Sunday ferry excursion from Punta Arenas.

The improved Oficina Municipal de Turismo (☎ 061-580636), upstairs at Padre Mario Zavattaro 402, is open 9 am to 5 pm weekdays.

The cheapest rooms are at *Residencial Colón* (☎ *061-580108*), Damián Riobó 198, where singles with shared bath and breakfast cost US$7. *Hotel España* (☎ *061-580160*), Croacia 698, charges US$12. The midrange *Hotel Rosas* has a fine seafood restaurant. *Club Croata* – formerly the Club Yugoslavo – also serves meals.

Buses Gesell (☎ 061-580488), Dublé Almeyda 257, departs Tuesday and Saturday at 2 pm for Río Grande, in Argentine Tierra del Fuego (US$17, seven hours). See the Punta Arenas entry for air and ferry services.

PUERTO NATALES
On the shores of Seno Última Esperanza (Last Hope Sound), 250km northwest of Punta Arenas, Puerto Natales (population 18,000) is the southern terminus of the spectacular ferry trip through the Chilean fjords.

CHILE

Once dependent on wool, mutton and fishing, it's now a burgeoning destination for visitors to Parque Nacional Torres del Paine, the Balmaceda Glacier and the Cueva del Milodón.

Information

Sernatur (☎ 061-412125), on the Costanera Pedro Montt at the junction with the Philippi diagonal, is open 8:30 am to 1 pm and 2:30 to 6:30 pm weekdays all year, and 9 am to 1 pm weekends December to March only.

Stop Cambios, Baquedano 380, changes cash and traveler's checks. Banco Santiago, Bulnes 598, has an ATM.

Correos de Chile is at Eberhard 423. CTC, Blanco Encalada 169, offers long-distance services 8 am to 10 pm daily.

Places to Stay

Competition keeps accommodations reasonable – as cheap as US$5 at *Residencial Lago Pingo* (☎ 061-411026), Bulnes 808. Convenient to the ferry, *Hospedaje Tierra del Fuego* (☎ 061-412138), Av Bulnes 23, charges US$7 with breakfast and shared bath, as do *Residencial Asturias* (☎ 061-412105), Prat 426, enthusiastically recommended *Hospedaje Teresa Ruiz*, Esmeralda 483, and *Residencial Patagonia Aventura* (☎ 061-411028), Tomás Rogers 179.

Charging US$9 per person, Swiss-Chilean *Casa Cecilia* (☎ 061-411797), Tomás Rogers 64, is famous for its delicious breakfasts with fresh bread and sweets, though some rooms are small. Slightly more expensive, around

PUERTO NATALES

PLACES TO STAY
2   Casa Cecilia
9   Residencial Lago Pingo
10 Residencial Temuco
22 Residencial Patagonia
    Aventura
36 Residencial Sutherland
42 Hospedaje Teresa Ruiz
43 Residencial Asturias
46 Hostal Amerindia
51 Hospedaje Tierra del Fuego

PLACES TO EAT
11 La Frontera
23 Última Esperanza
32 Gelatería Bruna
33 La Tranquera
37 Gelatería Bruna
48 El Marítimo
52 Café Andrés

OTHER
1   Sernatur
3   Ladeco
4   Pub Tío Cacho
5   Buses Lagoper
6   Turis Sur
7   Cootra
8   Entel
12 Turismo Cutter 21
    de Mayo
13 Turismo Luis Díaz
14 Buses Fernández
15 Andescape, Onas Patagonia
16 Andes Patagónicos
17 Cambio Mily
18 CTC
19 Southern Patagonia
    Souvenirs & Books
20 Emsa/Avis
21 Chile Express
24 Post Office
25 Gobernación Provincial
26 Municipalidad
27 Iglesia Parroquial
28 Turismo Zaahj
29 Buses JB
30 Banco Santiago
31 Servilaundry
34 Stop Cambios
35 Transfer Austral
38 Cambios Sur
39 Museo Histórico
    Municipal
40 Onas Aventuras
41 Buses Servitur
44 Conaf
45 Bus Sur, Austral Bus
46 Amerindia Concept
47 Turismo Cutter 21
    de Mayo
49 Ñandú Artesanía
50 Navimag
53 Hospital Puerto Natales

To Puerto Bories, Cueva del Milodón, Punta Arenas, Torres del Paine

Estero Natales

Stadium

Plaza de Armas

Cemetery

Plaza

Seno Última Esperanza

Pier

Pier

To Museo Salesiano

0   100   200 m
0   100   200 yards

CHILE

US$10, are *Residencial Temuco* (☎ *061-411120)*, at Ramírez 310, and the friendly, Scottish-Chilean *Residencial Sutherland* (☎ *061-410359)*, Barros Arana 155.

Hostal Amerindia (☎ *061-410678)*, Ladrilleros 105, is becoming a traveler's hangout, partly due to the downstairs pub/café (which closes early enough, however, for a good night's sleep) and the climbing wall outside. Rates are US$12 in multi-bed rooms or US$30 double, but if it's not crowded they'll give you a single at the lower price.

Places to Eat

Open for lunch only, *La Frontera*, Bulnes 819, has superb home-cooked meals for only US$4, but haphazard service. *El Marítimo*, a moderately priced seafood choice at Costanera Pedro Montt 214, does excellent business, but has become self-consciously touristy.

With walls covered with bric-a-brac worthy of some regional museums, popular *La Tranquera*, Bulnes 579, has good food, friendly service and reasonable prices. Relatively few foreigners patronize cheaper-than-it-looks *Última Esperanza*, Eberhard 354, despite its fine seafood in huge portions (salmon is a specialty) and good service.

Another good seafood choice is *Café Andrés*, Ladrilleros 381. Unpretentious *La Bahía* (☎ *061-411297)*, Serrano 434, can accommodate large groups for a superb curanto, with sufficient notice.

Rhubarb-flavored ice cream is a local specialty at *Gelatería Bruna*, Bulnes 585 and Eberhard 217.

Getting There & Away

Bus Puerto Natales has no central bus terminal, though several companies stop at the junction of Valdivia and Baquedano. To Punta Arenas (US$7, three hours), carriers include Buses Fernández (☎ 061-411111) at Eberhard 555, Bus Sur (☎ 061-411325) and Austral Bus (☎ 061-411859), both at Baquedano 534, and Transfer Austral (☎ 061-412616) at Baquedano 414.

In summer, Bus Sur also goes daily to Parque Nacional Torres del Paine (US$9 one way, US$16 return), weekdays to Río Turbio, Argentina (US$4) and Tuesday and Thursday at 6:30 am to Río Gallegos, Argentina (US$19). El Pingüino, at the Fernández terminal, goes Wednesday and Sunday at 11 am to Río Gallegos (US$18). Other carriers

include Servitur (☎ 061-411858) at Prat 353 and Buses JB (☎ 061-412824) at Prat 258.

Turismo Zaahj (☎ 061-412260), Prat 236, goes to El Calafate, Argentina (5½ hours, US$23), in summer only, Tuesday, Thursday and Saturday at 10 am. Bus Sur goes daily, except Wednesday and Sunday, at 9 am to El Calafate.

Lagoper (☎ 061-411831), Angamos 640 and Cootra (☎ 061-412785), Baquedano 244, have frequent buses to Río Turbio, for connections to both Río Gallegos and Calafate. Turis Sur, on Angamos near Valdivia, also goes to Río Turbio.

Boat Navimag (☎ 061-411421), Costanera Pedro Montt 380, operates the car ferry MV *Puerto Edén* to Puerto Montt weekly all year, though dates and times can vary according to weather conditions and tides. Reserve ahead in summer, when the four-day, three-night voyage is heavily booked. Thursday is the usual departure day from Puerto Natales.

Fares start around US$170 in mid season (September-October, March-April) and around US$200 in summer (November through February). Accommodations in all categories are comfortable (though claustrophobes may find the cheapest class cramped) and include breakfast, lunch and dinner, but incidentals like drinks and snacks are extra.

Getting Around

Car Emsa/Avis (☎/fax 061-412770), in Hotel Martín Gusinde at Bories 278, charges around US$80 per day.

Organized Tours Puerto Natales' many travel agencies offer visits to attractions like Bories, Cueva del Milodón and Torres del Paine. Among them are Andes Patagónicos (☎ 061-411594, a good place to confirm airline reservations) at Blanco Encalada 226; Turismo Luis Díaz (☎ 061-411654) at Blanco Encalada 189; Onas Aventuras (☎ 061-412707), Bulnes 453, which also does sea kayaking and trekking; and Amerindia Concept (☎ 061-410678, amerindia@chilnet .cl), Ladrilleros 105, which does a traverse of Glaciar Grey (US$85), a one-day kayaking and climbing course (US$100) and several overnights within the Torres del Paine (US$180 to US$280).

CHILE

AROUND PUERTO NATALES

At **Cueva del Milodón**, 24km northwest of Puerto Natales, Hermann Eberhard discovered the well-preserved remains of an enormous ground sloth in the 1890s. Nearly 4m high, the herbivorous milodon ate the succulent leaves of small trees and branches, but became extinct in the late Pleistocene. The 30m-high cave contains a life-size replica of the animal.

Conaf charges US$4 admission; camping and picnicking are possible. Torres del Paine buses pass the entrance, which is several kilometers from the cave proper. Alternatively, take a taxi or hitch.

PARQUE NACIONAL TORRES DEL PAINE

The Torres del Paine, granite pillars soaring almost vertically above the Patagonian steppe, are only one feature of this miniature Alaska of shimmering turquoise lakes, roaring creeks and rivers, cascading waterfalls, sprawling glaciers, dense forests and abundant wildlife. A UNESCO Biosphere Reserve, the 180,000-hectare park has a well-developed trail network and hut system for trekkers, who can also camp at designated sites (bring a warm sleeping bag, waterproof gear and a tent). Weather is changeable, but long summer days permit outdoor activities late into the evening.

Paine's major conservation success has been the guanaco (*Lama guanicoe*), which grazes the open steppes. The elusive huemul, or Andean deer, is more difficult to spot.

Information

Conaf charges an entry fee of US$15 per person at Guardería Lago Sarmiento, where maps and information brochures are available, and at Guardería Laguna Amarga (where most inbound buses stop), Guardería Laguna Verde and Guardería Laguna Azul. There are additional climbers' fees, but these recently dropped.

At the Administración, Conaf's Centro de Visitantes features a good exhibit on local ecology. Visitors should be aware that, because of pressure on park resources, Conaf is likely to institute restrictions during heavy usage periods, especially in January and February, when reservations may be necessary in some parts of the park.

Trekking

Most trekkers start the inordinately popular Paine circuit, now approaching gridlock, at Guardería Laguna Amarga. Trekkers must register with rangers or at the Conaf administration office at Río Serrano, and give their passport number.

In some ways, the circuit is less challenging than in past years, as sturdy bridges have replaced log crossings and stream fords, and park concessionaires have built comfortable refugios (US$18) with hot showers and meals (extra) along the trail. In theory, this makes it possible to walk between refugios without carrying a tent, but the changeable weather and distance between them still makes a tent desirable. Camping is possible only at designated sites; there is a modest charge for camping near the new refugios.

While the trek is tamer than it once was, it is still hazardous – hikers have died or disappeared on the trail. Conaf therefore no longer permits solo treks, but it is not difficult to link up with others. Allot at least five days, preferably more for bad weather; consider at least one layover day.

Both the Sociedad Turística Kaonikén in Puerto Natales and Kiosko Puma in Punta Arenas publish good topographic maps of the park at a scale of 1:100,000, with 100m contour intervals. Another source for trekkers and campers is LP's *Trekking in the Patagonian Andes*.

Places to Stay & Eat

The most central, organized campsites are **Camping Pehoé** (☎ 061-410684), US$19 for up to six people, and **Camping Río Serrano** (US$15). Fees include firewood and hot showers, available all morning but evenings by request only.

At Guardería Laguna Amarga, Conaf has a free camping area with a very rustic refugio and pit toilets. Only river water is available at this site, usually frequented by recent arrivals or people waiting for Puerto Natales buses. **Camping Las Torres**, on the grounds of Estancia Cerro Paine, charges US$5 per person and is popular with hikers taking the short hike up the Río Ascencio before hitting the circuit. At the more remote **Camping Laguna Azul**, charges are US$21 per group.

A short distance from the Conaf administration office, **Refugio Lago Toro** has bunks for US$6 (US$2 for hot showers), but your

PARQUE NACIONAL TORRES DEL PAINE

9 Campamento Torres
10 Refugio & Camping Chileno
11 Hostería & Camping Las Torres
12 Guardería & Camping
   Laguna Amarga
13 Refugio & Camping Grey
14 Campamento Italiano
15 Refugio & Camping Cuernos
16 Portería Sarmiento,
   Camping Lago Sarmiento
   & Guardería
17 Refugio & Camping Pehoé
18 Refugio Pudeto,
   Guardería Lago Pehoé
19 Refugio Zapata
20 Refugio Pingo
21 Hostería & Guardería Lago Grey
22 Hostería Pehoé
23 Camping Lago Pehoé
24 Hotel Salto Chico
25 Hostería Estancia Lazo
26 Guardería Lago Verde
27 Hostería Río Serrano,
   Refugio Lago Toro
28 Park Administration (Conaf)
29 Camping Río Serrano

1 Guardería & Refugio Lago Paine
2 Campamento Zapata
3 Campamento Coirón
4 Campamento Serón
5 Camping Laguna Azul
6 Guardería Laguna Azul
7 Refugio & Camping
   Río de los Perros
8 Campamento Británico

own sleeping bag is essential. Other refugios, such as *Pudeto* on Lago Pehoé, are free but *very* rustic.

The lakeside *Hostería Pehoé* and most other park lodgings are beyond the budgets of shoestring travelers, but their restaurants and bars are open to the public.

Getting There & Away

For details, see the Puerto Natales entry; in summer, buses go to El Calafate, Argentina. Hitching competition is heavy.

Getting Around

Hikers can save time and effort by taking the launch *Tzonka* from Refugio Pudeto, at the east end of Lago Pehoé, to Refugio Pehoé at the west end of the lake. The launch runs two to four times daily (US$14), but sometimes erratically – visitors should not rely on it to make connections.

PARQUE NACIONAL BERNARDO O'HIGGINS

A scenic four-hour cruise up Seno Última Esperanza ends at Puerto Toro and the Balmaceda and Serrano glaciers; on a clear day, the Torres del Paine are visible in the distance. En route are the *frigorífico* (meat freezer) at Bories, several estancias, waterfalls, a large cormorant rookery and a smaller sea-lion colony and the occasional condor.

Daily in summer and on demand in other seasons (weather permitting), Turismo

CHILE

Cutter 21 de Mayo, (☎ 061-411978) at Eberhard 554, or (☎ 061-411176) in Puerto Natales at Ladrilleros 171, runs its namesake cutter or the motor yacht *Alberto de Agostini* to Puerto Toro (US$45 per person). Decent, moderately priced meals are available on board, along with hot and cold drinks.

Archipiélago Juan Fernández

In 1966, a tourist-motivated government renamed Isla Masatierra to Isla Robinson Crusoe, after literature's most renowned castaway. Scotsman Alexander Selkirk, who spent more than four years in complete isolation on Masatierra, was the real-life model for Daniel Defoe's fictional character.

The tranquil Juan Fernández archipelago is also a national park and UNESCO World Biosphere Reserve. It's a storehouse of rare plants and animals that evolved in isolation and adapted to specific ecological niches. Its native flora have suffered from the introduction of non-native species, but much remains in areas where even the agile goat could not penetrate.

Local flora have evolved into something very distinct from their continental origins. Of the 87 plant genera, 16 are endemic, found nowhere else on earth; of 140 plant species, 101 are endemic.

The most notable animal species is the only native mammal, the Juan Fernández fur seal. It was nearly extinct a century ago, but about 2500 individuals now breed here. Of 11 endemic bird species, the most eye-catching is the bright-red male Juan Fernández hummingbird; the female is a more subdued green, with a white tail. About 250 of these birds survive, feeding off the endemic cabbage that grows in many parts of San Juan Bautista, but the species does best in native forest. Introduced rodents and feral cats have endangered nesting marine birds like Cook's petrel, by preying on their eggs and young.

History

In 1574, Juan Fernández discovered the islands that still bear his name. For over two centuries, the islands sheltered pirates and sealers, but were most renowned for Selkirk's exile on Masatierra after going ashore, at his own request, in 1704. Most castaways soon starved or shot themselves, but the adaptable Selkirk survived on feral goats (a Spanish introduction).

In 1708, Commander Woodes Rogers, of the privateers *Duke* and *Duchess*, rescued Selkirk who, on returning to Scotland, became a celebrity. Defoe's fictionalized account, set in the Caribbean, became a classic.

After Selkirk's departure, the presence of privateers and sealers compelled Spain to found the village of San Juan Bautista in 1750, but there was no really permanent presence until 1877. During WWI the British navy sank a German cruiser in Cumberland Bay.

Since then, the islands have played a less conspicuous but more significant role. In 1935, Chile declared them a national park for their unique flora and fauna, then began to remove the feral goats. Mainland demand for the tasty local lobster provides substantial income for some Islanders. Recently, Isla Robinson Crusoe made headlines when North American treasure hunters reportedly discovered US$10 billion in buried gold ingots – presumably a legacy of the pirate era – but the stories proved erroneous, or at least premature.

Geography & Climate

Separated from Valparaíso by 670km of open Pacific, Juan Fernández consists of Isla Robinson Crusoe, Isla Alejandro Selkirk (ex-Masafuera) and Isla Santa Clara. The islands are really emergent peaks from a submarine mountain range. Robinson Crusoe's area is only 93 sq km, its length a maximum 22km and its width a maximum 7.3km. Cerro El Yunque (the Anvil) reaches an altitude of 915m. The climate is Mediterranean, but rainfall varies greatly because of irregular topography.

Books

Defoe's classic is an obvious choice, but Rogers' *A Cruising Voyage Round the World* is available as a Dover Publications facsimile. The most thorough history is Ralph Lee Woodward's *Robinson Crusoe's Island*.

Getting There & Away

Air Two companies fly air taxis almost daily in summer, less often in other seasons, from Santiago's Aeropuerto Los Cerrillos. Travelers should allow for an extra two or three days' stay when poor weather makes landings risky at Robinson Crusoe's dirt airstrip.

Lassa (☎ 02-2731458), in the Aeródromo Tobalaba, Av Larraín 7941 in the eastern Santiago suburb of La Reina, flies six-passenger taxis, as does Transportes Aéreos Robinson Crusoe (☎ 02-5314343), at Monumento 2570 in the suburb of Maipú. Fares are about US$405 return, depending on currency fluctuations.

From the airstrip, it's about 1½ hours by a combination of 4WD (to the jetty at Bahía del Padre) and subsequent motor launch (sailing along the island's awesome volcanic escarpments) to San Juan Bautista. Both the flight and voyage can be rough. The roundtrip from the airstrip to San Juan Bautista costs US$18.

Boat Sailing to Juan Fernández is not easy, but quarterly naval supply ships carry passengers cheaply. Since even the most innocuous naval movements are top secret, it's hard to learn departure dates, but try calling the Comando de Transporte (☎ 032-032-258457) at the Primera Zona Naval, opposite Plaza Sotomayor in Valparaíso. There may also be monthly private transport to Juan Fernández and Rapa Nui from Valparaíso by the time you read this.

Getting Around

Getting around sometimes requires hiring a fishing boat (rates are fixed by the Municipalidad) or accompanying lobster-catchers on their rounds. To arrange a launch, contact Polo González at Lassa's office on the plaza. Conaf rangers visiting outlying sites may take along passengers.

ISLA ROBINSON CRUSOE

Yielding great views, the **Mirador de Selkirk**, in the center of Isla Robinson Crusoe, is at the end of a steep 3km walk west of San Juan Bautista. Hikers can continue on the same trail to the airstrip for the flight back to the mainland, but should confirm reservations in San Juan.

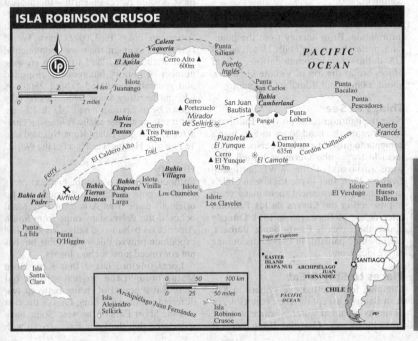

ISLA ROBINSON CRUSOE

Plazoleta El Yunque, half an hour south of San Juan, is a tranquil forest clearing with picnic and camping areas. Only 15 minutes from San Juan by launch, **Puerto Inglés** has a reconstruction of Selkirk's shelter, ruins of a cowherd's shed and adequate water for camping, but no firewood. The boat is expensive without a group; alternatively, there's a steep trail from San Juan which takes about two hours.

Robinson Crusoe's only colony of fur seals breeds in **Bahía Tierras Blancas**, just east of the airstrip. The trail to the airstrip from San Juan passes near the colony, which lacks drinking water. If you can't visit Tierras Blancas, you can still see fur seals at Bahía del Padre on arrival, or just north of San Juan's cemetery.

SAN JUAN BAUTISTA

San Juan Bautista (population 600) is one of Chile's most tranquil villages. Most visitors stay here or at nearby Pangal, and camping is possible.

The economy depends on fishing, mostly for lobsters, which are flown to Santiago by air taxi, but most islanders rarely visit the continent.

The Municipalidad, near the plaza, has Sernatur leaflets with decent maps and information. Bring money from the mainland, preferably in small bills. Hotels accept US dollars for accommodations. Conaf offices are at the top of Vicente González, about 500m inland from the Costanera.

Things to See

Near the lighthouse, the polyglot European surnames on the headstones in San Juan's **cementerio** provide a unique perspective on local history – the Germans buried here were survivors of the WWI battleship *Dresden*. More that 40 participants in Chile's independence movement spent many years imprisoned in the **Cuevas de los Patriotas** after defeat at Rancagua in 1814. Directly above the caves is **Fuerte Santa Bárbara**, built by the Spaniards in 1749 to discourage pirate incursions.

Places to Stay & Eat

Camping is permitted everywhere in San Juan Bautista except the *zona intangible*, an off-limits area, but water is scarce in some areas. Inexpensive *Camping Municipal* is at

the foot of Vincente González. There is another site at *Plazoleta El Yunque*. The nearest shower (cold water only) is at the jetty.

Hostería Villa Green (☎ 032-751049), on Larraín Alcalde opposite the plaza, charges US$40/70 single/double with breakfast, US$65/107 with half-board and US$77/145 with full board. On beautiful grounds on the Costanera, *Hostería Selkirk* (☎ 032-751107) has singles for US$50 and doubles for US$90, with half-board. If not staying at a hotel, give restaurants several hours' notice for lunch or dinner.

Hostería Daniel Defoe serves lobster and *Restaurant Remo* on the plaza has sandwiches and drinks. *El Nocturno,* at the north end of Larraín Alcalde, keeps long hours for dinner. At last report, *Restaurant La Bahía* was closed due to illness.

Easter Island (Rapa Nui)

Tiny Easter Island (117 sq km) is one of the most isolated places on earth – the nearest populated landmass is the even tinier Pitcairn Island, 1900km west, while the South American coast is 3700km east. World famous for its enigmatic *moai* (monumental stone statues), the island attracts a growing number of visitors, but remains unspoiled and sparsely populated (about 2800). A Chilean territory since 1888, it's officially known by its Spanish name, Isla de Pascua, but it retains an essentially Polynesian character. Locally, it is called Rapa Nui, and also Te Pito o Te Henua, 'The Navel of the World.'

History

Orthodox opinion is that the first occupants of this remote island were Polynesians, who originally came from Asia. Thor Heyerdahl believed the Polynesians came from South America on balsa wood rafts – his *Kon Tiki* expedition proved this was possible but has not convinced most archaeologists.

Local folklore has it that King Hotu Matua brought the original settlers, but there was a period of rivalry between two different peoples, the Long Ears of the east and the Short Ears of the west. Some have speculated that the Long Ears arrived with

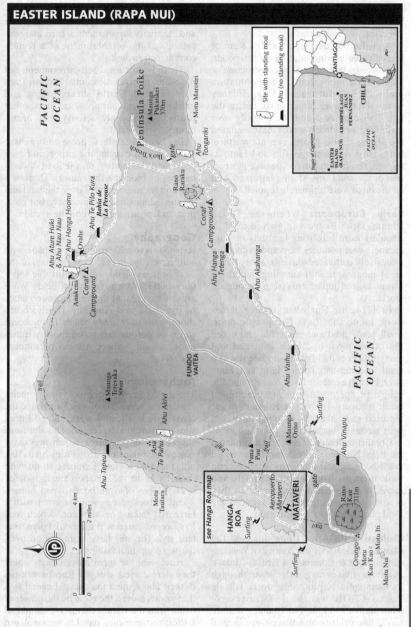

EASTER ISLAND (RAPA NUI)

PACIFIC OCEAN

Site with standing moai

Ahu (no standing moai)

SANTIAGO

CHILE

ARCHIPIÉLAGO JUAN FERNÁNDEZ

EASTER ISLAND (RAPA NUI)

PACIFIC OCEAN

Tropic of Capricorn

Península Poike

▲ Maunga Pukatikei 370m

□ Motu Marotiri

Iko's Trench

gate

Ahu Tongariki

Rano Raraku

Ahu Te Pito Kura

Bahía de La Perouse

Ahu Ature Huki & Ahu Nau Nau

Ahu Hanga Hoonu

Ovahe

Anakena

Conaf Campground

Conaf Campground

Ahu Hanga Tetenga

Ahu Akahanga

PACIFIC OCEAN

▲ Maunga Terevaka 500m

Ahu Akivi

trail

FUNDO VAITEA

Ahu Vaihu

Ahu Tepeu

Ana Te Pahu

Motu Tautara

trail

trail

Puna Pau ▲

▲ Maunga Orito

Surfing

Ahu Vinapu

Aeropuerto Mataveri

see Hanga Roa map

HANGA ROA

MATAVERI

gate

Rano Kau 311m

Surfing

Surfing

Surfing

Orongo

Motu Kao Kao

Motu Nui

Motu Iti

0   2   4 km

0   1   2 miles

CHILE

Hotu Matua from Polynesia, followed by Short Ears under Tuu-ko-ihu from South America.

A civilization developed, with a form of hieroglyphic writing engraved on wooden *rongo-rongo* tablets, and the construction of many stone monuments. The population probably peaked at around 15,000, and they were erecting ever larger moai, but in the late 17th century a conflict, possibly over dwindling resources, nearly exterminated the Long Ears. More recent warfare, between peoples of the Tuu and Hotu-iti regions, resulted in the progressive destruction of the *ahu* (large stone platforms), and all the moai were ultimately toppled.

Early Europeans When the Dutch admiral Jacob Roggeveen arrived in 1722, islanders were subsisting healthily on sugarcane, sweet potatoes, taro and yams from intensively cultivated gardens. Many of the great moai were still standing, but there was no sign of implements from the outside world.

In 1774, the English navigator James Cook found the Rapa Nui people poor, small, lean, timid and miserable and noted that many moai had been damaged and many topknots had fallen – apparently as a result of inter-tribal wars. Fourteen years later, French explorer La Perouse found the people prosperous and calm, suggesting a quick recovery. In 1804, a Russian visitor reported more than 20 standing moai, but later accounts suggest further disruption.

Contact with outsiders nearly annihilated the Rapa Nui people. A Peruvian slave raid in 1862 conscripted a thousand islanders and took them to work guano deposits and mines. A few eventually returned, but they brought back smallpox which reduced the local population to a few hundred.

Chilean Rule After Chile annexed the island, it came under the control of Williamson, Balfour & Company, a British-Chilean enterprise that managed the island through its Compañía Explotadora de la Isla de Pascua. CEDIP was the de facto government until the 1950s, but islander welfare was a low priority and there were several uprisings against the company. In 1953, the Chilean government revoked CEDIP's lease and the navy took charge. After 1967 a

civilian administration proved more benevolent and there were improvements to water and electricity supply, medical care, and education and the establishment of a regular commercial air link.

There is now local self-government, but the island receives substantial support from the mainland. Cattle, sheep, fishing and market gardens supply local needs, but tourism is the only activity that brings money to the island.

In 1990, islanders protested airfare increases by occupying the airport and even prevented the landing of a jetload of carabineros by blocking the runway. There is a demand for more control over the land and greater administrative autonomy, but complete independence is not on the agenda.

Geography

Rapa Nui is roughly triangular in shape, with a volcanic cone in each corner. Much of the interior is grassland, where cultivable soil is interspersed with rugged lava fields. Wave erosion has created steep cliffs around much of the coast, and Anakena, on the north shore, is the only sandy beach. The volcanic soil is so porous that water quickly drains underground – there are no permanent streams.

Archaeology

The most common archaeological remains are the ahu, some 245 of which surround the coast. Originally, ahu were village burial sites and ceremonial centers. The *ahu moai* supported massive moai, which may have represented clan ancestors. From 2m to 10m tall, these stony-faced statues stood with their backs to the Pacific Ocean, looking over villages of oval, boat-shaped houses. Some statues were even crowned with a large red *pukao*, or 'topknot,' which may have represented a traditional Polynesian hair style (or may have been just an over-the-top sculptural fashion).

How were the moai moved from where they were carved at Rano Raraku volcano to their ahu around the coast? Legend says that priests moved the moai by the power of *mana*, with the statues themselves 'walking' a short distance each day. US archaeologist William Mulloy proposed that a sledge was fitted to the moai, which was then lifted with a bipod and dragged forward (or 'walked'?)

Carnaval, Rio de Janeiro, Brazil

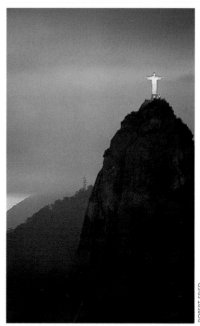

Corcovado Mountain, Rio – oh, how lovely

Teatro Amazonas, Manaus, Brazil

JAMES LYON

Hanga Roa fishing harbor, Easter Island, Chile

AVIV FRIED & MICHAL LAVI

Parque Nacional Torres del Paine, Chile

ROBERT FRIED

Plaza de la Constitución, Santiago, Chile

SYLVIA STEVENS

Chiloé child, Chile

a short distance at a time. Heyerdahl and 180 islanders managed to pull a 4m moai across a field at Anakena and figured that they could have moved a larger one with wooden runners and more labor. The use of timber to help move the statues may partly explain the island's deforestation.

Many stone structures have been demolished, damaged, recycled or rebuilt during tribal conflicts and under CEDIP. For example, the pier at Caleta Hanga Roa is built on stones from dismantled ahu. Several moai and numerous smaller artifacts have been taken by collectors and museums. Some moai have been completely restored, while others have been re-erected but are eroded. Many more lie on the ground, toppled over near an ahu or abandoned on the long drag from Rano Raraku. Most of them lie facedown, but the newest ones, freshly carved only 300 years ago, are buried up to the shoulders in the grassy slopes of the old volcano.

Language
Spanish is the official language, but the indigenous language is Rapa Nui, an Eastern Polynesian dialect related to Cook Islands Maori. Many people in the tourist business speak English.

When to Go
The island is hottest in January and February and coolest (but still warm) in July and August. May is the wettest month, but downpours can occur at any time. Most visitors come in late December-January (the South American summer holidays), in February for the Semana de Rapa Nui festival and in August-September (the Northern Hemisphere summer holidays). Allow at least three days to see the major sites.

Information
Sernatur, Chile's national tourist service, provides some information on the island and has an office in Hanga Roa (☎ 032-100255). The unofficial Easter Island homepage (www.netaxs.com/~trance/rapanui .html) is excellent. For a graphic but very fictionalized version of the island's history, see the corny 1994 movie *Rapa Nui*.

Maps The outstanding 1:30,000-scale *Isla de Pascua-Rapa Nui: Mapa Arqueológico-*

Turístico is available at local shops for about US$10. JLM Mapas publishes the excellent *Isla de Pascua Trekking Map*, at 1:32,000, also available locally for US$10. The annotated *Easter Island* map by ITM, at 1:30,000, is also excellent.

Books On geography and environment, the most thorough source is Juan Carlos Castilla's edited collection (in Spanish) *Islas Oceánicas Chilenas*, which also covers the Juan Fernández Islands.

Thor Heyerdahl's *Kon-Tiki* and *Aku-Aku: The Secret of Easter Island* are well known. The Bavarian priest Sebastian Englert, a longtime resident, retells Easter Island's history through oral tradition in *Island at the Center of the World*.

Time Easter Island is two hours behind mainland Chile, six hours behind GMT, or five hours behind GMT in summer.

Dangers & Annoyances The weather can be hot, and there is little shade or fresh water available outside town. On excursions, bring water bottles, a long-sleeved shirt, sunglasses, hat and a powerful sunblock.

Activities
Steep drop-offs, abundant marine life and clear water make for good diving. Centro de Buceo Orca (☎ 032-100375) is the only dive operator. Dives cost from US$50 to US$80. Three main surf breaks in the south corner of the island can get good swells at any time of year.

Getting There & Away
LanChile, the only airline serving Easter Island, has four flights per week to and from Santiago, and three per week to and from Papeete (Tahiti), but it's an expensive detour. A standard economy roundtrip fare from Santiago costs US$865, with promotional excursion fares from US$584.

It's much cheaper to do a stopover at Easter Island on your way to or from South America. From Asia or Australia, you can fly via Auckland (New Zealand) and join a Qantas flight to Papeete, connecting with LanChile's Papeete-Easter Island-Santiago service (see Getting There & Away at the start of the book). There's a free stopover in Easter Island on this route. Easter Island

CHILE

can be included in any round-the-world deal that involves LanChile and is a possible stopover on some fares from North to South America via the Pacific.

Flights can be heavily booked, especially in summer, so reconfirm at both ends. The airport departure tax is US$8.

Getting Around
Car & Motorcycle Agencies and bigger hotels rent Suzuki jeeps for US$90 per day in peak season, but locals and some guesthouses do it for as little as US$50 per 8-hour day. A 24-hour day is up to US$80 or US$90, but you can get a few consecutive days for US$50 per day. On Policarpo Toro, try Easter Island Rent-a-Car (☎ 032-100328), Commercial Insular (☎ 032-100480), Puna Pau Rent-a-Car (☎ 032-100978) or Te Aiki (☎ 032-100366, at Residencial Tekena), or look for signs in windows. Outside the high season, prices are negotiable. Insurance is not usually included, and some cars are very imperfect.

Motorcycles are rented for about US$20 per eight hours, US$30 to US$35 a day. Given rough roads and occasional tropical downpours, a jeep is more convenient and more economical for two or more people.

Taxi Taxis cost a flat US$2 for most trips around town. Longer trips can be negotiated, with the cost depending mainly on the time – an all-day trip will be expensive.

Bicycle Bikes can be rented at a few places for around US$20 per day – try Comercial Insular. If you bring your own bike, you may be able to sell it here.

Horse For sites near Hanga Roa, horses can be hired for about US$20 to US$25 per day. Horse gear is very basic and potentially hazardous for inexperienced riders. Hotel Hotu Matua (☎ 032-100242) or Hotel Hanga Roa (☎ 032-100299) can organize riding excursions with proper saddles, bridles and guides. Residencial Ana Rapu (☎ 032-100540) runs five-day horseback camping tours around the island from around US$250 per person.

Organized Tours Plenty of small operators do tours of the sites, for US$35 to US$40 per person for a full day, US$20 to US$25 for a half day.

HANGA ROA
Nearly all the islanders live in Hanga Roa, a sprawling town with irregular, uncrowded streets. Tourism, fishing, government services and retailing are the main activities, but the tourist sector is so informal that the town doesn't seem touristy at all.

Orientation
Av Policarpo Toro, the main north-south road, has the island's few shops and several eateries. The bank, tourist office, school and some other public buildings are in the blocks between Policarpo Toro and the small bay called Caleta Hanga Roa. Only small fishing boats can enter the bay, which has a nice little surf break and a protected swimming area. The restored moai Ahu Tautira stands with its back to the bay, overlooking the football field.

Information
Tourist Offices Sernatur (☎ 032-100255), near Caleta Hanga Roa, is open 9 am to 1 pm and 2 to 7 pm weekdays and on Saturday morning. Some staff speak English, French or Rapa Nui, but most information is in Spanish. Conaf (☎ 032-100236), on Atamu Tekena, gives advice on hiking and camping.

Money Banco del Estado, next to Sernatur, changes US dollars at reasonable rates but charges a US$7 commission on traveler's checks. The gas station may change traveler's checks at OK rates without commission. Many businesses accept cash dollars, though some use very approximate exchange rates. It's handy to bring Chilean currency from the mainland. As yet there is no ATM on the island.

Post & Communications The post office is on Te Pito o Te Henua, open 9 am to 5 pm weekdays and on Saturday mornings. The Entel telephone office, with its conspicuous satellite dish, is in a cul-de-sac opposite Sernatur, open 8 am to 6 pm daily. Easter Island is under Chile's country code (56). International calls are expensive (US$2 per minute minimum). Someone will probably open an Internet café soon.

Medical Services The hospital (☎ 032-100131) is on Simón Paoa east of the church.

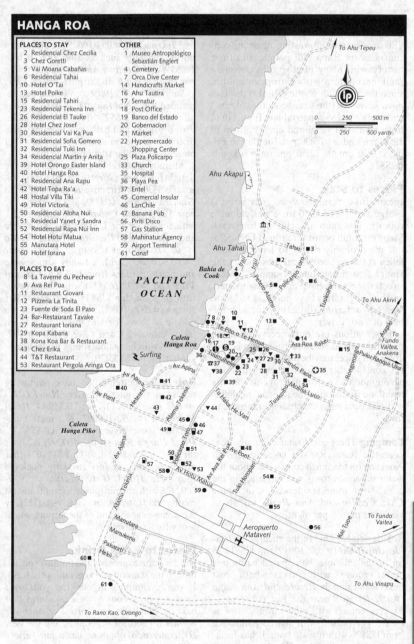

HANGA ROA

PLACES TO STAY
2   Residencial Chez Cecilia
3   Chez Goretti
5   Vai Moana Cabañas
6   Residencial Tahai
10 Hotel O'Tai
13 Hotel Poike
15 Residencial Tahiri
23 Residencial Tekena Inn
26 Residencial El Tauke
28 Hotel Chez Josef
30 Residencial Vai Ka Pua
31 Residencial Sofia Gomero
32 Residencial Tuki Inn
34 Residencial Martín y Anita
39 Hotel Orongo Easter Island
40 Hotel Hanga Roa
41 Residencial Ana Rapu
42 Hotel Topa Ra'a
48 Hostal Villa Tiki
49 Hotel Victoria
50 Residencial Aloha Nui
51 Residecial Yanet y Sandra
52 Residencial Rapa Nui Inn
54 Hotel Hotu Matua
55 Manutara Hotel
60 Hotel Iorana

PLACES TO EAT
8   La Taverne du Pecheur
9   Ava Rei Pua
11 Restaurant Giovani
12 Pizzeria La Tinita
23 Fuente de Soda El Paso
24 Bar-Restaurant Tavake
27 Restaurant Ioriana
29 Kopa Kabana
38 Kona Koa Bar & Restaurant
43 Chez Erika
44 T&T Restaurant
53 Restaurant Pergola Aringa Ora

OTHER
1   Museo Antropológico
    Sebastián Englert
4   Cemetery
7   Orca Dive Center
14 Handicrafts Market
16 Ahu Tautira
17 Sernatur
18 Post Office
19 Banco del Estado
20 Gobernacion
21 Market
22 Hypermercado
    Shopping Center
25 Plaza Policarpo
33 Church
35 Hospital
36 Playa Pea
37 Entel
45 Comercial Insular
46 LanChile
47 Banana Pub
56 Piriti Disco
57 Gas Station
58 Mahinatur Agency
59 Airport Terminal
61 Conaf

To Ahu Tepeu

0   250   500 m
0   250   500 yards

PACIFIC OCEAN

Ahu Akapu

Ahu Tahai

Tahai

To Ahu Akivi

Bahía de Cook

Caleta Hanga Roa

Surfing

To Ahu Anakena

To Fundo Vaitea, Anakena

Caleta Hanga Piko

Aeropuerto Mataveri

To Fundo Vaitea

To Ahu Vinapu

To Rano Kao, Orongo

CHILE

Museo Antropológico Sebastián Englert

This moderately interesting museum concentrates on Rapa Nui people and their history, with many photographs depicting their encounters with European culture since the mid-19th century. It also displays *moai kavakava* (the strange 'statues of ribs') and replica rongo-rongo tablets. It's north of town near Ahu Tahai and open 9:30 am to 12:30 pm and 2 to 5:30 pm Tuesday to Fridays; 9:30 am to 12:30 pm on weekends (US$2).

Places to Stay

Inexpensive residenciales (guesthouses) charge about US$25/40 for a single/double room in low season, including breakfast. Many offer full board for around US$45/75, but it's probably better to have a picnic lunch at the archaeological sites and try the Hanga Roa restaurants for dinner. Neither streets nor residenciales are well signposted, and buildings rarely have numbers, so locate places by referring to the map, or with the help of a taxi driver.

Reservations are only necessary in the peak times of August and January to February, when prices may be 30% to 50% higher. It's considerably more expensive to book accommodations through agents on the mainland. Touts often meet incoming flights with discount offers, including transport to town.

Camping There are Conaf camping areas near the Rano Raraku volcano, and at Anekena on the north coast – ask about the water supply. In town, you can camp in the grounds of some residenciales, including *Chez Cecilia* and *Ana Rapu*, for about US$8 per person per night.

Residenciales One of the cheapest is *Residencial Tahai* (☎ 032-100395), at US$14/25 for a single/double with shared bathroom; better rooms with private bath cost US$25/40. Friendly *Residencial Ana Rapu* (☎ 032-100540), near the bay, is the backpackers' choice, with rooms from as low as US$15 per person with shared bathroom, from US$20 with private bath. It has facilities for campers, and staff will arrange car and horse rentals, conduct tours and do the occasional Rapa Nui barbecue.

Other popular residenciales include the centrally located *El Tauke* (☎ 032-100253) and *Tekena Inn* (☎ 032-100289); quiet places on the outskirts such as *Tuki Inn* (☎ 032-100859) and *Martín y Anita* (☎ 032-100593); and those closer to the airport such as *Yanet y Sandra* (☎ 032-100365) and the recommended *Rapa Nui Inn* (☎ 032-100228). They all cost around US$25/50 for singles/doubles with breakfast and bath, and they may give discounts in the off-season. Plenty of other places have similar standards and prices.

More comfortable places include the delightful *Chez Goretti* (☎ 032-100459), from US$30/50; attractive *Residencial Sofía Gomero* (☎ 032-100313), at US$35/60; the new *Vai Moana Cabañas* (☎ 032-100626), with sea views for US$40/60; comfortable and well-managed *Residencial Chez Cecilia* (☎ 032-100499), at US$40/70; *Hotel Poike* (☎ 032-100283), with a family atmosphere and pretty gardens from US$40/60; *Hostal Villa Tiki* (☎ 032-100327), which has a beautiful outlook, for US$45/70; *Hotel Chez Joseph* (☎ 032-100373), on a hilltop near the middle of town, for US$45/85 (get a room facing outwards); and *Chez Erika* (☎ 032-100474), with bungalow rooms in a spacious garden, from US$35/70.

Hotels The better hotels have swimming pools but are quite expensive. *Hotel O'Tai* (☎ 032-100250) is OK for US$59/94. *Hotel Manutara* (☎ 032-100297) is a more comfortable, motel-style place for US$78/121. *Hotel Hanga Roa* (☎ 032-100299) is about the best on the island, at US$90/110. Other pricey options, mainly used by package tours, are *Hotel Hotu Matua* (☎ 039-100242), with an uninspiring location and no charm, and *Hotel Iorana* (☎ 039-100312), by the ocean near the end of the airport, which is due for a renovation.

Places to Eat & Drink

Food is quite expensive and nothing special, though the seafood and vegetables are fresh. If you're camping or cooking your own food, get provisions at general stores and bakeries on Policarpo Toro. The *open-air market* is good for vegetables, and the new *Hypermercado*, opposite, has a fair variety of cheese and Spam.

Inconspicuous *Restaurant Giovani* is one of the cheapest eateries and popular with locals – you eat what they serve. Reach it up the lane beside *Pizzeria La Tinita*. A few places along Policarpo are OK but uninspiring – try *Fuente de Soda el Paso*, *Ioriana*, or the *T&T Restaurant*. *Bar-Restaurant-Café Tavake* is OK for hot dogs and snacks, but pricey for main meals. *Kopa Kabana* serves some typical Rapa Nui dishes and other excellent offerings in a pleasant indoor-outdoor setting. *Pérgola Aringa Ora*, opposite the airport, is also recommended.

The French-run *La Taverne du Pecheur* has a lovely, rustic seaside setting, some excellent dishes and high prices – main courses are well over US$10. *Kona Koa* (☎ 038-100415), near the Entel office, is a somewhat pricey restaurant with a popular bar and regular Rapa Nui folkloric shows.

The *Banana Pub*, on Policarpo Toro, attracts young locals with off-beat decor inside and a surfboard outside. Other nightspots are *Playa Pea*, near the seafront, and *Piriti Disco*, opposite the airport, which both open Thursday to Saturday nights.

Shopping

For crafts, the best selection and prices (open to some negotiation) are at the recently reconstructed handicrafts market across from the church. The classic souvenir is a miniature carved stone moai, usually sold with a red stone topknot. Smaller ones begin at about US$15 and are not too heavy. Stuffed soft moai toys are a cuddly variant. Wooden 'statues of ribs' and rongo-rongo tablets are also good, as are necklaces of obsidian or seashells.

PARQUE NACIONAL RAPA NUI

Since 1935, much of Easter Island's land and all the archaeological sites have been a national park administered by Conaf. Non-Chileans are supposed to buy admission tickets (US$10) at Ahu Tahai or Orongo, valid for the whole park for the length of one's stay, but the fee is not always collected.

Though Chilean government agencies have promoted tourism and enabled the restoration of some moai, many islanders view the park as a land grab. A native rights organization, the Consejo de Ancianos (Council of Elders), wants the park (about a third of the island's area) returned to its aboriginal owners, who control almost no land outside Hanga Roa.

Near Hanga Roa

Several sites of interest are close to town, and all can be seen in a few hours by car or motorcycle.

Ahu Tahai A short hike north of town, this site contains three restored ahu, especially photogenic at sunset. Ahu Tahai proper is in the middle, with a solitary moai. Ahu Ko Te Riku is to the north, with a topknotted and eyeballed moai. Ahu Vai Uri has five eroded moai of varying sizes.

Ahu Akapu A solitary moai stands on the coast just north of Ahu Tahai. It's another great sunset spot.

Ahu Tepeu Four kilometers north of Tahai on a rough but scenic road, this large ahu has several fallen moai and an extensive village site. Walk around to find foundations of *hare paenga* (elliptical houses) and the walls of several round houses.

Ana Te Pahu Off the dirt road between Ahu Akivi and the west coast, Ana Te Pahu is a former cave dwelling where the entry-way is a garden of sweet potatoes, taro and bananas. The caves here are lava tubes, created when rock solidified around a flowing stream of molten lava.

Ahu Akivi Unusual for its inland location, this ahu has seven restored moai. They are the only ones that face toward the sea, but like all moai they overlook the site of a village, traces of which can still be seen.

Puna Pau The soft, red stone of this volcanic hill was used to make the reddish cylindrical *pukao* (topknots) that were placed on many moai. Half-finished topknots have been rolled down the hill and remain in a scattered line. Look for the partly hollow underside designed to slot onto a moai's head. Puna Pau is only a couple kilometers east of town, reachable by a rough and very roundabout road.

The Northeast Circuit

This loop takes in the three finest sites on the island and can be done in a long day with motorized transport. It's good to go counter-clockwise, because Rano Raraku is a magnificent highlight in the late afternoon.

CHILE

Heading northeast from the airport, a good paved road runs 13km to the north coast.

Anakena The legendary landing place of Hotu Matua, Anakena has several caves and is popular for swimming and sunbathing. The curving, white-sand beach is a perfect backdrop for Ahu Nau Nau, with its fine row of moai. A 1979 excavation and restoration revealed that the moai were not 'blind' but had inlaid coral and rock eyes – 'eyes that look to the sky,' in a Rapa Nui phrase.

On a rise south of the beach stands Ahu Ature Huki and its lone moai. Heyerdahl and a dozen islanders took nine days to lever up this statue with wooden poles and ropes.

You can stay overnight at the small Conaf camping ground, just inland from the beach, but bring supplies from Hanga Roa. Ask in town whether water is available.

Ovahe Just east of Anakena, this cove has a sandy beach, small caves, a ruined ahu, rough water and the occasional shark.

Ahu Te Pito Kura Overlooking La Perouse Bay, a massive 10m-high moai lies facedown with its neck broken. It is the largest moai ever moved from Rano Raraku and erected on an ahu. Its resemblance to the uncompleted figures at Rano Raraku suggest that this moai is also one of the most recent.

Poike Peninsula Rapa Nui's eastern corner is a peninsula formed by the extinct volcano Maunga Pukatikei. Legend says that the Long Ears retreated to Poike and built a 2km defensive trench that was filled with wood and set ablaze. Carbon dating of ash and charcoal in the area is consistent with genealogical research in dating an island conflict to around 1680.

Ahu Tongariki In 1960, a tsunami demolished several moai and scattered topknots far inland from this, the largest ahu ever built. A Japanese project has restored the 15 imposing moai at this stunning oceanside location. The statues gaze over a large, level village site, with ruined remnants scattered about and some petroglyphs nearby.

Rano Raraku This volcano where moai were cut out from the porous gray rock is a wonderfully evocative place. Groups of moai are partly buried, their heads grouped on the grassy slopes. Others are in the early stages of carving and seem to be sleeping in niches in the cliffs – the largest is a 21m giant, but most range from 5.5m to 7m. More than 600 of these wonderful figures stand and lie around Rano Raraku, and a number are scattered face-down in an irregular line to the southwest, never to reach their ahu on the coast.

Most were carved face up, horizontal or slightly reclined. Be sure to walk up and around to the inside of the crater, which has a reedy lake and an amphitheater full of handsome heads. Climb right to the top for a fabulous 360° view.

There are no facilities at the site, but Conaf maintains a shady campground on a side track a little to the southwest. Rano Raraku is a detour off the rugged south coast road, about 18km northeast of Hanga Roa. There are several ruined ahu along the way.

The Southwest

The southwest corner of the island is dominated by the Rano Kau crater. On its seaward slopes, the low stone houses of **Orongo Ceremonial Village** were used during the bizarre rituals of the 'bird cult' in the 18th and 19th centuries.

The climax of the rituals was a competition to retrieve an egg of the sooty tern (*Sterna fuscata*), which breeds on the small *motu* (islets) just offshore. Young men climbed down the steep cliffs and swam out to the islands to search for an egg. The egg was then tied to the forehead for the return swim and climb. Whoever returned first with an intact egg won the favor of the god Makemake and great community status. Also (as if that were not enough), local lore has it that seven virgins became birdman groupies for the whole year. Birdman petroglyphs are visible on a cluster of boulders between the cliff top and the crater's edge. Orongo is a steepish 2km climb from town or a short scenic drive.

Ahu Vinapu Beyond the eastern end of the airport runway, a road heads south past some large oil tanks to Ahu Vinapu. Several toppled moai lie around, but Vinapu is most famous for its tight-fitting, Inca-like stonework.

Colombia

For most travelers, Colombia is unknown territory – a land of myths, of cocaine barons, guerrillas, emeralds and the mysterious El Dorado. It is the land of Gabriel García Márquez and his famous novel, *One Hundred Years of Solitude* – a tale as magical as the country itself. And it is the land that bears the name of Columbus, discoverer of the Americas, but where people have rearranged the name to spell 'Locombia,' or 'the mad country.'

Colombia's geography is among the most varied in South America, as are its flora and fauna. The inhabitants form a palette of ethnic blends uncommon elsewhere on the continent and include a few dozen Indian groups, some of which still maintain traditional lifestyles. It's a country of amazing natural and cultural diversity and contrast, where climate, topography, wildlife, crafts, music and architecture change within hours of overland travel – it's as if Colombia were several countries rolled into one.

Through its turbulent history, Colombia has been soaked in blood in innumerable civil wars and has endured the continent's most massive and persistent guerrilla insurgency. The country is also the world's major producer of cocaine. With such a background, it's no wonder that violence occurs here more frequently than in neighboring countries, and that Colombia is not as safe.

However, if you take the necessary precautions, Colombia may be worth the challenge. It is exotic, sensual, wild, complex and fascinating. And it's difficult to find people more hospitable, spirited and stimulating than Colombians.

At a Glance

Country Name	República de Colombia
Area	1,141,748 sq km
Population	approx 39 million (1999)
Population Density	34 people per sq km
Capital	Santa Fe de Bogotá
Head of State	President Andrés Pastrana (1998-2002)
Official Language	Spanish
Other Languages	More than 50 Indian languages
Currency	peso (Col$)
Exchange Rate	US$1 = Col$1840
Per Capita GNP	$6,200 (1997)
Inflation Rate	16.7% (1998)

Facts about Colombia

HISTORY

Pre-Columbian Times

Colombia is the northwestern gateway to South America and undoubtedly part of the route pioneered by the continent's first inhabitants who migrated from North and Central America. Some tribes headed farther south, while others established permanent settlements in what is now Colombia and, in time, reached a remarkably high level of development. However, these groups are little known internationally, partly because few left spectacular, enduring monuments. There are only three important archaeological sites in Colombia: San

Agustín, Tierradentro and Ciudad Perdida. Other communities left behind not much more than artifacts – mainly gold and pottery – some of which are now held in museums across the country. Yet their art reveals a high degree of skill, and their goldwork is the continent's best, both for the techniques used and for its artistic design.

In contrast to the Aztecs or Incas, who dominated vast regions, several independent Colombian groups occupied relatively small areas scattered throughout the Andean region and along the Pacific and Atlantic (Caribbean) coasts. Despite trading and cultural contacts, these cultures developed largely independently. Among the most outstanding were the Calima, Muisca, Nariño, Quimbaya, San Agustín, Sinú, Tayrona, Tierradentro, Tolima and Tumaco. The Tierradentro and San Agustín flourished before the Spanish conquest, while the other groups are believed to have reached the height of their cultural and social development when the Spaniards arrived.

San Agustín, one of the most extraordinary ceremonial centers in South America, is noted for hundreds of monolithic statues and tombs scattered over a wide area. Another culture with developed funeral rites flourished in Tierradentro, an area separated by a mountain range from San Agustín. There, the Indians built a number of underground burial chambers, where they kept the remains of tribal elders. These funeral chambers, laboriously carved out of the soft rock and decorated with paintings, are unique in South America.

The Muisca culture is widely known for the myth of El Dorado, created by the Spaniards. The Muiscas (also confusingly called the Chibchas because they formed the largest group of the Chibcha linguistic family) were known far and wide for their wealth, and had a flourishing civilization that occupied what are now the Boyacá and Cundinamarca departments. Beginning in the 3rd century BC, they took good advantage of fertile soils and rich salt and emerald mines, creating extensive trading links with other cultures.

In the mountainous jungles along the Caribbean coast, *huaqueros* (grave-robbers who search for pre-Columbian treasures) discovered Ciudad Perdida (Lost City) in 1975. The find has shed new light on the

Tayrona (or Tairona) culture, which developed from about the 5th century AD in the Sierra Nevada de Santa Marta. The Tayrona had long been considered one of the most advanced early Indian civilizations, yet it was only after the discovery of the Lost City that their greatness as architects was confirmed. Ciudad Perdida, thought to be their major center, is one of the largest ancient cities ever found in the Americas; resplendent with several hundred stone terraces linked by a network of stairs, it is spectacularly situated in the heart of a tropical rain forest.

The Spanish Conquest

In 1499, Alonso de Ojeda was the first conquistador to set foot on Colombian soil and to see indigenous people using gold objects. Attracted by the presumed riches of the Indians, the shores of present-day Colombia became the target of numerous coastal expeditions by the Spaniards. Several short-lived settlements were founded, but it was not until 1525 that Rodrigo de Bastidas laid the first stones of Santa Marta, the earliest surviving town. In 1533, Pedro de Heredia founded Cartagena, which soon became the principal center of trade.

In 1536, a general advance toward the interior began independently from three different directions, under Jiménez de Quesada, Sebastián de Benalcázar (known in Colombia as Belalcázar) and Nikolaus Federmann.

Quesada set off from Santa Marta, pushed up the Magdalena valley, then climbed the Cordillera Oriental, arriving in Muisca territory early in 1537. After conquering the Muiscas, he founded Santa Fe de Bogotá in 1538. Quesada didn't actually find gold, despite the elaborate rituals of the Indians, who threw gold offerings into the waters of their sacred lake, the Laguna de Guatavita, and thus gave birth to the mysterious legend of El Dorado.

Belalcázar deserted from Francisco Pizarro's army, which was conquering the Inca empire, and mounted an expedition from Ecuador. He subdued the southern part of Colombia, founding Popayán and Cali along the way, and reached Bogotá in 1539. Federmann started from the Venezuelan coast and, after successfully crossing Los Llanos, arrived in Bogotá shortly after Belalcázar.

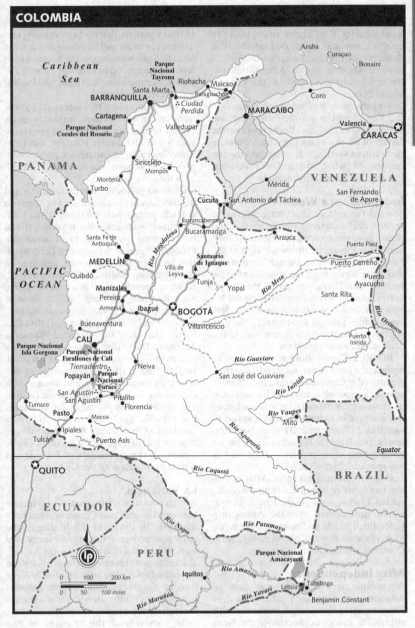

COLOMBIA

Caribbean Sea

PANAMA

PACIFIC OCEAN

Parque Nacional Tayrona

Riohacha · Maicao
Santa Marta · Paraguachón
BARRANQUILLA
· *Ciudad Perdida*
Cartagena
Parque Nacional Corales del Rosario
Valledupar

Sincelejo
Mompós
Montería
Turbo

Santa Fe de Antioquia

MEDELLÍN
Quibdó
Manizales
Pereira
Armenia · Ibagué
Buenaventura
CALI
Parque Nacional Isla Gorgona
Parque Nacional Farallones de Cali
Tierradentro
Popayán
San Agustín
San Agustín
Tumaco
Pasto
Ipiales
Tulcán · Puerto Asís

QUITO

ECUADOR

PERU

Aruba
Curaçao · Bonaire

Coro

MARACAIBO

Valencia
CARACAS

VENEZUELA

Mérida
San Fernando de Apure

Cúcuta · San Antonio del Táchira
Barrancabermeja
Bucaramanga
Arauca
Puerto Páez

Santuario de Iguaque
Villa de Leyva
Tunja
Yopal
Río Meta
Santa Rita
Puerto Carreño
Puerto Ayacucho

BOGOTÁ
Villavicencio

Río Guaviare
San José del Guaviare

Puerto Inírida

Río Orinoco

Neiva
Parque Nacional Puracé
Pitalito
Florencia
Mocoa

Río Inírida

Río Vaupés
Mitú

Río Apaporis

Equator

Río Caquetá

BRAZIL

Río Napo

Río Putumayo

Parque Nacional Amacayacu

Río Amazon
Iquitos
Leticia · Tabatinga
Benjamin Constant
Río Yavarí

Río Marañón

0   100   200 km
0   50   100 miles

The three groups fought tooth and nail for supremacy, and it was not until 1550 that King Charles V of Spain, in an effort to establish law and order, created the Real Audiencia del Nuevo Reino de Granada, a tribunal based in Bogotá. Administratively, the new colony was subject to the Viceroyalty of Peru.

With the growth of the Spanish empire in the New World, a new territorial division was created in 1717, and Bogotá became the capital of its own viceroyalty, the Virreinato de la Nueva Granada. It comprised the territories of what are today Colombia, Panama, Ecuador and Venezuela.

Independence Wars

Toward the end of the 18th century, the general disillusionment with Spanish domination gave rise to open protests and rebellions. This, together with events such as the North American and French revolutions and, most importantly, the invasion of Spain by Napoléon Bonaparte, paved the way to independence. When Napoleon placed his own brother on the Spanish throne in 1808, the colonies refused to recognize the new monarch. One by one, Colombian towns declared their independence.

In 1812, Simón Bolívar, who was to become the hero of the independence struggle, arrived in Cartagena to take the offensive against the Spanish armies. In a brilliant campaign to seize Venezuela, he won six battles but was unable to hold Caracas, and had to withdraw to Cartagena. By then, Napoléon had been defeated at Waterloo, and Spain set about reconquering its colonies. Colonial rule was re-established in 1817.

Bolívar took up arms again. After assembling an army of horsemen from the Venezuelan Llanos, strengthened by a British legion, he marched over the Andes into Colombia. The last and most decisive battle took place at Boyacá on August 7, 1819. Colombia's independence was won.

After Independence

A revolutionary congress was held in Angostura (modern-day Ciudad Bolívar, in Venezuela) in 1819. Still euphoric with victory, the delegates proclaimed the Gran Colombia, a new state uniting Venezuela, Colombia and Ecuador (although Venezuela and Ecuador were still under Spanish

rule). The congress was followed by another, held in Villa del Rosario, near Cúcuta, in 1821. It was there that the two opposing tendencies, centralist and federalist, came to the fore. Bolívar, who supported a centralized republic, succeeded in imposing his will. The Gran Colombia came into being and Bolívar was elected president.

From its inception, the state started to disintegrate. It soon became apparent that a central regime was incapable of governing such a vast and diverse territory. The Gran Colombia had split into three separate countries by 1830, soon before Bolívar's death later the same year.

The two political currents, centralist and federalist, were formalized in 1849 when two political parties were established: the Conservatives (with centralist tendencies) and the Liberals (with federalist leanings). Colombia became the scene of fierce rivalries between the two forces, resulting in complete chaos. During the 19th century, the country experienced no less than eight civil wars. Between 1863 and 1885, there were more than 50 antigovernment insurrections.

In 1899, a Liberal revolt turned into a full-blown civil war, the so-called War of a Thousand Days. That carnage resulted in a Conservative victory and left 100,000 dead. In 1903, the USA took advantage of the country's internal strife and fomented a secessionist movement in Panama (at that time a Colombian province). By creating a new republic, the USA was able to build a canal across the Central American isthmus. It wasn't until 1921 that Colombia finally recognized the sovereignty of Panama and settled its dispute with the USA.

La Violencia

After a period of relative peace, the struggle between Liberals and Conservatives broke out again in 1948 with La Violencia, the most destructive of Colombia's many civil wars, which left a death toll of some 300,000. The urban riots broke out on April 9, 1948 in Bogotá following the assassination of Jorge Eliécer Gaitán, a charismatic populist Liberal leader. Liberals soon took up arms throughout the country.

To comprehend the brutality of this period, one must understand that for a century Colombians were raised either Liberal or Conservative from birth and reared with a mistrust of the other party. In the 1940s and 1950s, these 'hereditary hatreds' were the cause of countless atrocities, rapes and murders, particularly in rural areas. Hundreds of thousands of people took to the hills and shot each other for nothing more than just the name of their party.

By 1953, some groups of the Liberal guerrillas had begun to demonstrate a dangerous degree of independence, in some cases making alliances with the small bands of communist guerrillas that also operated during this period. As it became evident that the partisan conflict was taking on revolutionary overtones, the leaders of both the Liberal and Conservative parties decided to support a military coup as the best means to retain power and pacify the countryside. The 1953 coup of General Gustavo Rojas Pinilla was the only military intervention the country has experienced in this century.

The dictatorship of General Rojas was not to last. In 1957, the leaders of the two parties signed a pact to share power for the next 16 years. The agreement, later approved by a plebiscite (in which women were, for the first time, allowed to vote), became known as the Frente Nacional (National Front). During the life of the accord, the two parties alternated in the presidency every four years.

In effect, despite the enormous loss of lives in what turned out to be the bloodiest civil war in the Americas, the same people returned to power. Moreover, they no longer needed to contest it. The party leaders repressed all political activity that remained outside the scope of their parties, thus sowing the seeds for the appearance of guerrilla groups.

Guerrillas & Paramilitaries

Guerrillas have been quite an important part of Colombian political life, and a headache for the government. With roots that extend back to La Violencia, they are the oldest insurgent forces in Latin America. They continue to engage in armed struggle and are more active than ever.

Colombia saw the birth of perhaps a dozen different guerrilla groups, each with its own ideology and its own political and military strategies. The movements which have had the biggest impact on local politics (and left the largest number of dead)

include the FARC (Fuerzas Armadas Revolucionarias de Colombia), the ELN (Ejército de Liberación Nacional) and the M-19 (Movimiento 19 de Abril).

Until 1982, the guerrillas were treated as a problem of public order and persecuted by the military forces. President Belisario Betancur (1982-86) was the first to open direct negotiations with the guerrillas in a bid to reincorporate them into the nation's political life. Yet the talks ended in failure. The rupture was poignantly symbolized by the takeover of Bogotá's Palacio de Justicia by the M-19 guerrillas in November 1985.

The Liberal government of Virgilio Barco (1986-90), after long and complicated negotiations with the M-19, signed an agreement under which this group handed over its arms, ceased insurgent activity and transformed itself into a political party. However, the FARC and the ELN remain under arms and currently control about 40% of the country's area. Having lost support from Moscow and Havana, they now rely on extortion, robbery and kidnapping to finance their struggle. They are also increasingly involved in the drug production and trade.

Since the state has been unable to control areas lost to the guerrillas, private armies – the so-called *paramilitares* or *autodefensas* – have mushroomed, with the army turning a blind eye or even supporting them. These right-wing armies operate against rebels in many regions, including Urabá, Cesar, Córdoba, Antioquia, Magdalena Medio, Santander, Cundinamarca and Caquetá, and have committed some horrendous massacres on civilians allegedly supporting the guerrillas. They form a loosely woven alliance known as the United Self-Defense Forces of Colombia (AUC), with an estimated 5000 fighters nationwide.

Drug Cartels

Colombia is the biggest producer of cocaine, controlling some 80% of the world market. The mafia started in a small way in the early 1970s but, within a short time, developed the trade into a powerful industry, with their own plantations, laboratories, transport services and protection.

The boom years began in the early 1980s. The Medellín Cartel, led by Pablo Escobar, became the principal mafia, and its bosses lived in freedom and luxury. They even founded their own political party and two newspapers, and in 1982 Escobar was elected to the Congress.

In 1983 the government launched a campaign against the drug trade, which gradually turned into an all-out war. The cartel responded violently and managed to liquidate many of its adversaries. The war became even bloodier in August 1989, when Luis Carlos Galán, the leading Liberal contender for the 1990 presidential election, was assassinated. The government responded with the confiscation of nearly 1000 mafia-owned properties, and announced new laws on extradition – a nightmare for the drug barons. The cartel resorted to the use of terrorist tactics, principally car bombs.

The election of the Liberal César Gaviria (1990-94) brought a brief period of hope. Following lengthy negotiations, which included a constitutional amendment to ban extradition of Colombians, Escobar and the remaining cartel bosses surrendered and the narco-terrorism subsided. However, Escobar escaped from his palace-like prison following the government's bumbling attempts to move him to a more secure site. An elite 1500-man special unit sought Escobar for 499 days, until it tracked him down in Medellín and killed him in December 1993.

Despite this, the drug trade continued unaffected. While the military concentrated on hunting one man and persecuting one cartel, the other cartels were quick to take advantage of the opportune circumstances. The Cali Cartel, led by the Rodríguez Orejuela brothers, swiftly moved into the shattered Medellín Cartel's markets and became Colombia's largest trafficker. It also diversified into opium poppies and heroin. Although the cartel's top bosses were captured in 1995 and are now behind bars, the drug trade continues to flourish, with other regional cartels and guerrillas filling the gap left behind by the two original mafias.

The Controversial Samper Government

The 1994 elections put the Liberal Ernesto Samper into the presidency. Just before he took office, his major opponent, Andrés Pastrana, released tapes (called 'narco-cassettes') of wire-tapped telephone conversations, in which Cali Cartel bosses discussed making 'donations' to Samper's presidential campaign. The issue was discreetly maneuvered out, but resurfaced in August 1995, when Santiago Medina, Samper's campaign treasurer, testified that the party had received some US$6 million from the cartel. A further blow came from Fernando Botero, the campaign manager, who in a televised interview confirmed that Samper knowingly took the cartel's money.

Both Medina and Botero, plus several members of parliament, former ministers and a former attorney general, were linked to an amazing web of corruption (referred to as the Proceso 8000) and went to jail. Meanwhile, the president maintained he was unaware that drug money had gone to his campaign fund. Even though he was cleared of charges by congress in June 1996, the investigation was widely considered a farce, and several influential groups, including the business lobbies, the Church and even some factions of Samper's own Liberal party demanded the president's resignation.

While the 'Colombian Watergate' occupied the top of the political agenda, the government largely lost control of domestic affairs and guerrilla and paramilitary activities intensified dramatically. By the end of Samper's term, the country was in the worst economical and public order situation in recent decades.

Recent Developments

The 1998 elections brought 12 years of Liberal domination to an end by placing Conservative Andrés Pastrana into the top office. Just after the elections and before taking the office, Pastrana met secretly with the FARC's top commander Manuel Marulanda, known as Tirofijo (Sure Shot), in order to end 34 years of bloody guerrilla war. Talks began in January 1999, but the prospects for peace remain tenuous.

Before entering into talks, the FARC insisted on the withdrawal of government troops from some guerrilla-controlled areas and on exchange of some 250 jailed rebels for the police and soldiers captured in recent years. They also wanted the government to dismantle the right-wing paramilitary groups, a condition virtually impossible to satisfy as long as the guerrillas operate. And they refused a cease-fire as a precondition to the peace dialogue. Pastrana made some concessions, but is cautious not to go too far.

Adding to the endless list of Colombia's problems, a serious earthquake hit the prosperous coffee-growing region around Armenia in January 1999. Measuring 6.0 on Richter scale, the 12-second quake was the strongest in the region for a century. It ruined an estimated 60% of Armenia, a provincial capital city of 250,000 people, and two dozen towns and villages across the region, leaving behind more than 1900 dead and 250,000 homeless.

GEOGRAPHY

Colombia covers 1,141,748 sq km, roughly equivalent to the area of France, Spain and Portugal combined. It is the fourth-largest country in South America, after Brazil, Argentina and Peru. Colombia occupies the northwestern part of the continent and is the only country in South America with coasts on both the Pacific (1448km long) and the Caribbean (1760km). Colombia is bordered by Panama, Venezuela, Brazil, Peru and Ecuador.

The country's physical geography is amazingly diverse. The western part, almost half of the total territory, is mountainous, with three Andean chains – the Cordillera Occidental, Cordillera Central and Cordillera Oriental – running roughly parallel north-south across most of the country.

The Sierra Nevada de Santa Marta, an independent and relatively small formation, rises from the Caribbean coastline to permanent snows. It is the highest coastal mountain range in the world, and its twin peaks of Simón Bolívar and Cristóbal Colón (both 5775m) are the country's highest.

More than half of the territory east of the Andes is a vast lowland, which is generally divided into two regions: the savanna-like Los Llanos in the north and the mostly jungle-covered Amazon in the south.

Colombia has several small islands. The major ones are the archipelago of San Andrés and Providencia (in the Caribbean Sea, and closer to Nicaragua's Atlantic Coast than to mainland Colombia), the Islas del Rosario and San Bernardo (near the Caribbean coast) and Gorgona and Malpelo (in the Pacific Ocean).

CLIMATE

Its proximity to the equator means Colombia's temperature varies little throughout the year. However, the temperature does change with altitude, creating various climatic zones, from hot lowlands to the alpine Andean cordilleras, so you can experience completely different climates within just a couple of hours of travel.

Colombia has two seasons: dry or *verano* (summer) and wet or *invierno* (winter). The pattern of seasons varies in different parts of the country, and have been largely affected over recent years by El Niño and La Niña.

As a rough guideline only, in the Andean region there are two dry and two rainy seasons per year. The main dry season falls between December and March, with a shorter and less dry period between July and August. This general pattern has wide variations throughout the Andean zone.

The weather in Los Llanos has a more definite pattern: there is one dry season, between December and March, and the rest of the year is wet. The Amazon doesn't have a uniform climate but, in general, is quite wet year-round.

FLORA & FAUNA

Colombia claims to have more plant and animal species per unit area than any other country in the world. Its variety of flora and fauna is second only to Brazil's, even though Colombia is seven times smaller than its neighbor. This abundance reflects Colombia's numerous climatic zones and microclimates, which have created many different habitats and biological islands in which wildlife has evolved independently.

Colombia is home to the jaguar, ocelot, peccary, tapir, deer, armadillo, spectacled bear and numerous species of monkey, to mention just a few of the 300-odd species of mammals. There are more than 1900 recorded species of birds (about 20% of the world's total), ranging from the huge Andean condor to the tiny hummingbird. There is also abundant marine life in Colombia's extensive river systems and along its two coastlines.

Colombia's flora is equally impressive and includes some 3000 species of orchid alone. The national herbariums have classified more than 130,000 plants, including many endemic species. This richness is still not the whole picture, because large areas of the country, such as inaccessible parts of the Amazon, have never been investigated by botanists.

NATIONAL PARKS & NATURE RESERVES
National Parks

Colombia has 34 national parks and a dozen other state-run nature reserves. Their combined area constitutes 7.9% of the country's territory. This figure may sound impressive but, unfortunately, there have never been sufficient funds or personnel to properly guard the parks. In many areas, simply decreeing a national park has not eliminated colonization, logging, ranching and poaching.

Only a dozen parks provide accommodation and food; several more offer only camping. The remaining parks have no tourist amenities at all and some, especially those in remote regions, are virtually inaccessible.

All national parks are operated by the Unidad Administrativa Especial del Sistema de Parques Nacionales, a department of the Ministry of the Environment. Their central office is in Bogotá, and there are regional offices in Bucaramanga, Cali, Medellín, Popayán and Santa Marta. If you plan on visiting the parks, you must (in theory, at least) first visit a Unidad office to pay the entrance fee (around $US5 per person). Accommodations, when available, cost US$10 to US$15 per bed. The Bogotá office handles all parks, whereas subsidiary offices only service the parks in their regions. The more popular parks include Tayrona, Corales del Rosario, Isla Gorgona, Farallones de Cali, Puracé and Amacayacu.

Private Nature Reserves

Growing ecological awareness has led to the creation of privately owned and run nature reserves. They are administered by individual proprietors, rural communities, foundations and other nongovernmental organizations. They are usually small, but often contain an interesting sample of habitat. As of 1998, they numbered about 80. They are scattered countrywide, although most are in the Andean region. Some reserves offer tourist facilities, including accommodation, food and guides and may be an interesting (and cheaper) alternative to national parks. The reserves are affiliated with the Red de Reservas Naturales de la Sociedad Civil, an association based in Cali (see that section for details).

GOVERNMENT & POLITICS

A new constitution came into effect in July 1991. The president is directly elected for a four-year term and cannot be re-elected. The Congress consists of two houses, the 102-seat Senate and the 165-seat Chamber of Representatives. The members are also elected in a direct vote for a four-year term. The cabinet is appointed by the president.

Administratively, the country is divided into 32 departments, plus Bogotá's Special District.

ECONOMY

Colombia managed to avoid the debt crises and bouts of hyper-inflation which plagued most of its neighbors in the 1980s, and has long had one of the continent's steadiest economies. Despite social and political problems, the country's GDP growth rate oscillated around 5% annually for the past three decades. This remarkable economic performance was badly affected during the Samper presidency. The GDP growth rate fell below 3% in 1998 and the prospects for 1999 are just zero. Some economists say that this is the worst state of economy since the 1930s.

Colombia is the world's second-largest coffee producer, after Brazil. Other main agricultural products are sugar (with production concentrated in the Cali region), cotton, flowers and bananas. Thanks to the diverse climate, there is a variety of other crops, such as rice, maize, potatoes, tobacco, barley, beans and cocoa.

Mineral resources are plentiful but underexploited, and the extent of deposits has still not been thoroughly explored. Colombia possesses the largest deposits of coal in Latin America, and coal mining has become one of the most dynamic sectors of the economy.

With the discovery of new oilfields in Casanare in the early 1990s (thought to be the biggest new fields found in the world in the last 10 years), Colombia has joined the ranks of the world's oil-exporting nations, with oil currently accounting for about 10% of fiscal revenues.

The country also has deposits of gold, silver, platinum, nickel, copper and iron, to list just a few. It produces half of the world's emeralds, and Colombian stones are considered to be the best.

Industry has grown notably in recent decades, mainly in the fields of petrochemicals, metallurgy, car assembly (Renault, Chevrolet, Mazda), textiles, domestic electrical appliances and food and agriculture.

And then, behind the official economic statistics, there are the illegal exports of drugs, principally cocaine, which account for a significant portion of the GNP. Cocaine alone earns an estimated US$5 billion annually, US$3 billion of which is thought to be re-invested in Colombia. The country is also the world's third-largest producer of marijuana. The new illegal export is heroin, which is quickly making inroads into northern markets, pushing out the traditional Asian suppliers.

POPULATION & PEOPLE

By 1998, the population had reached 39 million, making Colombia the second-most populous country in South America, after Brazil. Population growth is about 1.9%, which is among the highest rates in Latin America.

Population density varies a great deal across the country. The western half of Colombia consists of the Andean region and the two coasts, is home to more than 90% of the total population.

About 75% of people are of mixed blood, comprising 50 to 55% *mestizos* (of European-Indian blood) and 15 to 20% *mulatos* (of European-African blood). There are also some *zambos* (of African-Indian blood).

Whites, who are mainly descendants of the Spaniards, constitute about 20% of the population and live almost entirely in the urban centers. Blacks represent about 4% of the population and are most numerous on the Caribbean and Pacific coasts.

Indians number between 300,000 and 400,000, representing roughly 1% of the population. This number comprises more than 50 Indian groups, speaking 66 indigenous languages belonging to a dozen linguistic families.

ARTS
Architecture

The most outstanding example of pre-Columbian urban planning is the Ciudad Perdida (Lost City) of the Tayrona Indians in the Sierra Nevada de Santa Marta.

Although the dwellings haven't survived, the stone structures, including a complex network of terraces, paths and stairways, remain in remarkably good shape.

After the arrival of the Spaniards, bricks and tiles became the main construction materials. The colonial towns followed rigid standards laid down by the Spanish Crown. They were constructed on a grid plan, centered around the Plaza Mayor (main square). This pattern was applied both during and after the colonial period, and is the dominant feature of most Colombian settlements.

Spain's strong Catholic tradition left behind loads of churches and convents in the colony – the central areas of Cartagena, Tunja, Bogotá, Popayán and Pasto are good examples. Unlike in Mexico or Peru, colonial churches in Colombia have rather sober exteriors, but their interiors are often richly decorated.

In the 19th century, despite independence, the architecture continued to be predominantly Spanish in style. Modern architectural trends only began to appear in Colombia after WWII. This process accelerated during the 1960s when city skyscrapers appeared.

Visual Arts

The colonial period was dominated by Spanish religious art, and although the paintings and sculptures of this era were generally executed by local artists, they reflected the Spanish trends of the day. With the arrival of independence, visual arts departed from strictly religious themes, but it was not until the turn-of-the-19th-century revolution in European painting that Colombian artists began to experiment and create original work.

Among the most distinguished modern painters and sculptors are Pedro Nel Gómez, known mainly for his murals but also for his watercolors, oils and sculptures; Luis Alberto Acuña, a painter and sculptor who used motifs from pre-Columbian art; Alejandro Obregón, a painter tending to abstract forms; Edgar Negret, an abstract sculptor; Rodrigo Arenas Betancur, Colombia's most famous monument-maker; and Fernando Botero, the most internationally renowned Colombian artist, whose somewhat ironic style of painting and sculpture is easily recognizable by the characteristic fatness of the figures.

Literature

During the independence period and up to WWII, Colombia produced few internationally acclaimed writers other than José Asunción Silva (1865-96), perhaps the country's best poet, considered the precursor of modernism in Latin America.

A postwar literary boom thrust at least a dozen great Latin American authors into the international sphere, including the Colombian Gabriel García Márquez (born 1928). His novel *One Hundred Years of Solitude*, published in 1967, immediately became a worldwide best seller. It mixed myths, dreams and reality, and amazed readers with a new form of expression which critics dubbed *realismo mágico* (magic realism). In 1982, García Márquez won the Nobel Prize for literature.

In one of his most recent works, *Noticia de un Secuestro*, which appeared in May 1996 and was translated into English as *News of a Kidnapping*, García Márquez returned to journalism, where his career began. The book relates a series of kidnappings ordered by Medellín Cartel boss, Pablo Escobar. The combination of the author's literary talents and Colombia's action-movie-like modern history makes the book a fascinating if terrifying read.

Music

In very broad terms, Colombia can be divided into four musical zones: the two coasts, the Andean region and Los Llanos. All the rhythms described below have corresponding dance forms.

The Caribbean coast vibrates with hot African-related rhythms, such as the *cumbia*, *mapalé* and *porro*, which share many similarities with other Caribbean musical forms. The music of the Pacific coast, such as the *currulao*, is more purely African, with strong use of drums, but tinged with Spanish influences.

Colombian Andean music has been strongly influenced by Spanish rhythms and instruments, and differs notably from the Indian music of the Peruvian and Bolivian highlands. Among the typical forms are the *bambuco*, *pasillo* and *torbellino*, all of which are instrumental and feature predominantly string instruments.

The music of Los Llanos, *música llanera*, is sung and usually accompanied by a harp, *cuatro* (a sort of four-string guitar) and maracas. It has much in common with the music of the Venezuelan Llanos.

Apart from these traditional forms, several newer musical styles have conquered large parts of the country. These include the *salsa*, which spread throughout the Caribbean in the 1960s, and the *vallenato*, which emanated from the northern regions of La Guajira and Cesar. The latter is based on the European accordion.

RELIGION

The great majority of Colombians are Roman Catholic. Other creeds are officially permitted but their numbers are small. However, over the past decade there has been a proliferation of various Protestant congregations, which have succeeded in converting some three million Catholics.

Many Indian groups have adopted the Catholic faith, sometimes incorporating some of their traditional beliefs. Only a few indigenous communities, particularly those living in isolation, still practice their ancient native religions.

The Protestant faith predominates on the islands of San Andrés and Providencia – a legacy of British colonization.

LANGUAGE

The official language is Spanish, and apart from some remote Indian groups, all inhabitants speak it. On San Andrés and Providencia, English is still widely used.

The Spanish spoken in Colombia is generally clear and easy to understand, though there are regional variations which Colombians easily recognize. For the visitor, these differences won't be so noticeable, except for the *costeños*, the inhabitants of the Caribbean coast, who speak quickly and are more difficult to understand.

Facts for the Visitor

HIGHLIGHTS

Colombia's highlights include San Agustín, Tierradentro and Ciudad Perdida (archaeological sites); Cartagena and Popayán (colonial cities); Mompós, Barichara and Villa de Leyva (small colonial towns); and the

Museo del Oro in Bogotá (arguably the world's best gold museum).

SUGGESTED ITINERARIES

This will largely depend on your particular interests, your budget and your points of entry and exit the country. Some travelers arrive from Central America via San Andrés or San Blás and head south to Ecuador (or vice versa), in which case the usual route includes Cartagena, Bogotá, San Agustín and Popayán. There are also a number of visitors coming from Venezuela via Cúcuta; some of these take a detour to Colombia's Caribbean coast (Cartagena, Tayrona), while others head straight south via Bogotá, San Agustín and Popayán. Given widespread guerrilla activity in many rural areas, few travelers these days explore off-the-beaten-track sights.

PLANNING
When to Go

The most pleasant time to visit Colombia is in the dry season (December to March and July to August), but there are no major obstacles to general sightseeing in the wet months. Most Colombians take their holidays between late December and mid-January, so transport is more crowded and hotels tend to fill up faster at this time.

Maps

The widest selection of maps of Colombia is produced and sold by The Instituto Geográfico Agustín Codazzi (IGAC), the government mapping body, with its head office in Bogotá (see that section). Folded national road maps are produced by several publishers and distributed through bookstores.

TOURIST OFFICES

The national tourist information board, the Corporación Nacional de Turismo (CNT), has closed down. Municipal tourist information bureaus fill the void, with varying degrees of success. By and large, the staff are friendly but few of them speak English.

VISAS

Nationals of most countries, including almost all of Europe (except for the Czech Republic and Slovakia), the Americas (save for Cuba, Nicaragua and Haiti), Japan, Australia and New Zealand, don't need a visa to enter Colombia. They will simply get an entry stamp in their passport from DAS (the security police who are also responsible for immigration) upon arrival at any international airport or land border crossing. DAS will note on the stamp the period you can stay in the country. The maximum allowed is 90 days, but you may receive only 60 or 30 days. Technically, an onward ticket is required, but this requirement is rarely enforced.

If you receive a 90-day stay at the border, you are entitled to one 30-day extension. If you receive less, you're allowed extensions up to a total of 90 days (including your original stay). Extensions (US$30) can be obtained from DAS in any departmental capital. Apply shortly before the expiration of your allowed stay, as the extension runs from the day it is stamped in your passport. If you have used all the extensions, you can still apply for a *salvoconducto*, which costs US$18 and can last for up to 30 days. Before issuing it, however, DAS officials will probably want to see an onward plane ticket.

Upon departure, immigration officials put an exit stamp in your passport. Travelers have reported that some immigration stations no longer stamp passports. However, the central DAS office in Bogotá firmly states that you do need this stamp; without it you may have problems entering Colombia next time around.

EMBASSIES & CONSULATES
Colombian Embassies & Consulates Abroad

Colombia has embassies and consulates in all neighboring countries, and also in:

Australia
  (☎ 02-6257-2027)
  101 Northbourne Ave, Turner, ACT 2601
  (☎ 02-9955-0311)
  100 Walker St, North Sydney, NSW 2060
Canada
  (☎ 514-849-4852, 514-849-2929)
  1010 Sherbrooke St West, Suite 420, Montreal, Quebec H3A 2R7
  (☎ 416-977 0098, 416-977-0475)
  1 Dundas St West, Suite 2108, Toronto, Ontario M5G 1Z3
France
  (☎ 01-53 93 91 91)
  12 rue de Berri, Paris 75008

Germany
(☎ 030-229 26 69)
Dorotheenstrasse 89, 10117 Berlin
(☎ 0228-92 37 00)
Friedrich Wilhelm Strasse 35, 5300 Bonn 1

UK
(☎ 020-7495-4233)
Suite 14, 140 Park Lane, London W1Y 3AA

USA
(☎ 202-387-8338)
2118 Leroy Place NW, Washington, DC 20008
(☎ 305-444-5084, 305-441-1235)
280 Aragon Ave, Coral Gables, Miami, FL
33134
(☎ 212-949-9898)
10 East 46th St, New York, NY 10017

Embassies & Consulates in Colombia

Foreign diplomatic representatives in Bogotá include:

Brazil
(☎ 1-218-0800)
Calle 93 No 14-20, 8th floor

Canada
(☎ 1-313-1355)
Calle 76 No 11-52

Costa Rica
(☎ 1-256-6007)
Carrera 15 No 102-25

Ecuador
(☎ 1-218-3526)
Carrera 11 No 86-32, oficina 404

France
(☎ 1-618-0511)
Carrera 11 No 93-12

Germany
(☎ 1-348-4040)
Carrera 4 No 72-35, piso 6

Guatemala
(☎ 1-259-1496)
Transversal 29A No 139A-41

Honduras
(☎ 1-610 2403)
Carrera 10 No 96-25, oficina 211

Israel
(☎ 1-232-0764)
Calle 35 No 7-25, piso 14

Panama
(☎ 1-257-5067)
Calle 92 No 7-70

Peru
(☎ 1-257-6846)
Calle 90 No 14-26, oficina 417

UK
(☎ 1-317-6690)
Carrera 9 No 76-49, piso 9

USA
(☎ 1-315-0811)
Calle 22D Bis No 47-51

Venezuela
(☎ 1-636-4011)
Av 13 No 103-16

Foreign diplomatic representatives in Cartagena include:

Panama
(☎ 5-666-2079)
Calle 67 No 4-97, near the airport in Crespo

Venezuela
(☎ 5-665-0382, 5-665-0353)
Edificio Centro, at Carrera 3 No 8-129,
Bocagrande

Foreign diplomatic representatives in Leticia include:

Brazil
Calle 13 No 10-51; open 8 am to 2 pm weekdays

Peru
Calle 10 No 9-82; open 8 am to noon and 2 to 4 pm weekdays

Foreign diplomatic representatives in Medellín include:

Panama
(☎ 4-268-1157)
Calle 10 No 42-45, oficina 233, in El Poblado

Venezuela
(☎ 4-351-1614)
Calle 32B No 69-59

CUSTOMS

You are also allowed to bring in still, cine or video cameras plus accessories, a personal computer, a portable radio or cassette recorder, camping equipment, sporting accessories, etc – in effect, one item of each class.

Customs procedures are usually a formality, both on entering and on leaving the country. However, thorough luggage checks occasionally occur, more often at the airports than at the overland borders, and they can be very exhaustive, with a body search included. They aren't looking for your extra Walkman, but for drugs. Trying to smuggle dope through the border is the best way to see what the inside of a Colombian jail looks like, for quite a few years.

On departure, you may be asked for receipts for any emeralds, antiques and articles of gold and platinum purchased in Colombia.

MONEY

Given the country's hazards, it's better to carry traveler's checks (American Express ones are by far the most easy to change) than cash, though some US dollar bills may be useful. With the recent proliferation of ATMs, however, the best way to carry money in Colombia is a credit card (see Credit Cards).

Note that large amounts of counterfeit US dollars 'made in Cali' circulate on the market. According to rough estimates, about a quarter of all fake US dollars circulating worldwide are printed in Colombia. They are virtually indistinguishable from the genuine article.

Currency

Colombia's official currency is the peso (Col$). There are 50-, 100-, 200-, 500- and 1000-peso coins, and paper notes of 2000, 5000, 10,000 and 20,000 pesos. Forged peso notes do exist, so watch exactly what you get. In contrast to perfect dollar fakes, peso forgeries are generally of poor quality and easy to recognize.

Exchange Rates

Approximate official exchange rates at press time were as follows:

country	unit		peso
Australia	A$1	=	Col$1216
Canada	C$1	=	Col$1242
euro	€1	=	Col$1878
France	FF1	=	Col$286
Germany	DM1	=	Col$960
Japan	¥1	=	Col$15
New Zealand	NZ$1	=	Col$965
UK	UK£1	=	Col$2881
USA	US$1	=	Col$1840

Banks change traveler's checks at rates 2% to 5% lower than the official rate, and usually pay about a further 1% to 3% less for cash. Exchange rates vary from bank to bank, so shop around. Some banks charge a commission for changing checks.

The depreciation of the peso against the US dollar averages roughly 15% to 20% per year.

Exchanging Money

Some banks change cash and traveler's checks, but others don't. Some branches of a bank will change your money while other branches of the same bank will refuse.

Banks (except for those in Bogotá – see that section for details) are open 8 to 11:30 am and 2 to 4 pm Monday to Thursday, and 8 to 11:30 am and 2 to 4:30 pm on Friday. However, they usually offer currency exchange services within limited hours, which may mean only one or two hours daily; your best chances are in the morning. Banks close at noon on the last working day of the month, and it may be difficult to change money on that day; plan ahead.

Your passport is required for any banking transaction. Some banks will also request a photocopy of your passport (two pages are required, the one with your photo and personal details and the one with the entry stamp), while other banks won't change your traveler's checks before seeing the purchase receipt for the checks. Banks are often crowded and there's much paperwork involved in changing money, so the process may be time-consuming – set aside up to an hour.

Banks that are most likely to exchange your cash or traveler's checks include: Banco Anglo Colombiano, Banco Unión Colombiano, Bancolombia, Banco Sudameris Colombia, Bancafé and Banco Santander.

You can also change cash (but rarely traveler's checks) at *casas de cambio* (authorized money exchange offices), found in most major cities and border towns. These are open weekdays till 5 or 6 pm, and usually till noon on Saturday. They deal mainly with US dollars, offer rates comparable to, or slightly lower than, banks. The whole operation takes seconds.

You can change cash dollars on the street, but it's not recommended. The only street money markets worth considering are those at the borders, where there may be simply no alternative. There are moneychangers at every land border crossing.

Never change money that is not yours, particularly on behalf of Colombians you meet in the street. Travelers were arrested and jailed for this favor after the bank discovered that the dollars were faked.

The Tierra Mar Aire (TMA) travel agency, which has offices in major cities,

COLOMBIA

represents American Express. It doesn't change traveler's checks, but is the place to go if your checks are lost or stolen.

Credit Cards

Plastic is becoming an increasingly popular method of payment for services, including car rental, air tickets, and in most top-class hotels and restaurants. Also, you can get a peso advance on credit cards at the bank – this is much faster than changing traveler's checks. Furthermore, you get more money on cards because these transactions are calculated on the basis of the official exchange rate.

Visa is by far the best card for Colombia, and most banks will give advance payments on it. MasterCard is the next best, but it's only useful for advances at Bancolombia and Banco de Occidente. Other cards are of limited use.

There are an increasing number of *cajeros automáticos* (ATMs), which accept Visa, MasterCard and some other major cards and dispense pesos.

Costs

Colombia is now up to 50% more expensive to travel in than it was five years ago. This is mostly due to the rapid rise of prices of transport and accommodation. Backpackers should be prepared to shell out US$20 to US$30 per day, unless hanging a hammock somewhere on the beach.

POST & COMMUNICATIONS
Post

The Colombian postal service is operated by two companies, Avianca and Adpostal. Both cover international post, but Avianca only deals with airmail, so if you want to ship a parcel overseas, you'll need Adpostal.

Both companies seem to be efficient and reliable and have similar rates for letters, postcards and packages. Domestic rates are cheap but international airmail is fairly expensive. Adpostal's surface-mail rates are cheaper.

The poste restante system is operated by Avianca. You can receive poste restante letters in any city where Avianca has a post office, but not all provincial offices do a good job. The most reliable office is in Bogotá (Your Name, c/o Poste Restante, Lista de Correo Aéreo Avianca, Edificio Avianca, Carrera 7 No 16-36, Santa Fe de Bogotá).

They hold letters for up to one month and charge US$0.40 per letter.

Telephone

The telephone system is largely automated for both domestic and international calls. Until recently, Telecom was the only national telecommunication company, with its offices even in the most remote villages. In November 1998 two new companies, Capitel and Orbitel, entered the market and began a price war.

Public telephones dot the streets of the larger cities, but many are out of order. Most accept coins, although newly installed telephones accept phonecards *(tarjeta telefónicas)*. Phonecards can be used for international, intercity and local calls, so it's worth buying one (from a Telecom office) if you are going to use public telephones more than sporadically.

You can call direct to just about anywhere in Colombia. Area codes are included before all the local numbers listed in this chapter, but before them you need to dial the index of the provider you want to use – '05' for Orbitel, '07' for Capitel and '09' for Telecom. As yet, Orbitel and Capitel provides connections only between some major cities, so in the vast majority of cases you'll be using Telecom.

The international service is expensive, but again, competition means that the tariffs may drop and various special deals will be available. Calling abroad from Colombia, you dial ☎ 005, ☎ 007 or ☎ 009, respectively, then the country code etc. Details about services and tariffs of the three companies can be obtained from ☎ 150, ☎ 170 or ☎ 190, respectively.

Reverse-charge *llamadas de pago revertido* (collect calls) are possible to most major countries and can be cheaper. Following are the international direct-dialing numbers of some selected countries.

Australia	☎ 9809 61 00 57
Canada	☎ 9809 19 00 57
France	☎ 9809 33 00 57
Germany	☎ 9809 49 00 57
UK	☎ 9809 44 00 57
USA (AT&T)	☎ 9809 11 00 10
(MCI)	☎ 9809 16 00 01
(Sprint)	☎ 9809 13 00 10

Colombia's country code is ☎ 57. If you are dialing Colombian number from abroad, drop the prefix (05, 07 or 09) and dial only the area code and the local number.

Fax & Email
Most larger Telecom offices offer fax services. Internet and email are becoming increasingly popular and a number of places provide access to the public (US$4 to US$5 per hour). There are some Internet cafés, but the major providers are computer companies and hostels and hotels catering to travelers.

INTERNET RESOURCES
Some of the most up-to-date information about Colombia is available from local newspapers and magazines (in Spanish), most of which are available on the Web. The major ones include:

El Espectador: www.elespectador.com

El Tiempo: www.eltiempo.com

Publicaciones Semana: www.semana.com.co

Cambio: www.cambio16.com

The Colombian Yellow Pages (www.quehubo.com; English version available) lists hotels, tourist attractions, sporting events, etc.

BOOKS
For more detailed travel information, there's Lonely Planet's *Colombia*.

In Focus: Colombia – A Guide to the People, Politics and Culture by Colin Harding is a good brief introduction to the country's history, economy and society. The *Colombia: Portrait of Unity and Diversity* by Harvey F Kline is a well-balanced overview of Colombian history.

Titles covering Colombia's modern history include: *The Politics of Colombia* by Robert H Dix; *Colombia: Inside the Labyrinth* by Jenny Pearce; *The Politics of Coalition Rule in Colombia* by Jonathan Hartlyn; and *The Making of Modern Colombia: A Nation in Spite of Itself* by David Bushnell.

The Fruit Palace by Charles Nicholl is a good introduction to Colombia's crazy reality. A journalist's account of what was intended to be an investigation into cocaine trafficking, the book does not delve into the

heart of the Colombian cartels, but the author nevertheless provides a vivid picture of the country.

NEWSPAPERS & MAGAZINES
All major cities have a daily newspaper. Bogotá's leading newspapers, *El Tiempo* and *El Espectador*, are distributed nationwide. Both have reasonable coverage of national and international news, culture, sports and economics. *Semana* is the biggest national weekly magazine. It features local and international affairs and has an extensive cultural section. Another major weekly, *Cambio 16*, was bought by Gabriel García Márquez and several fellow journalists in early 1999, which may help transform it into an opinion-forming paper.

RADIO & TV
More than 500 FM and AM radio stations operate in Colombia and mainly broadcast music programs. There are three nationwide and four regional TV channels. Satellite TV has boomed in Bogotá and to a lesser extent in other major cities.

TIME
All of Colombia lies within the same time zone, five hours behind GMT/UTC. There's no daylight saving time.

ELECTRICITY
Electricity is 110V, 60Hz AC throughout the country. Plugs are the flat two-pin US type

WEIGHTS & MEASURES
The metric system is commonly used, except for gasoline, which is measured in US gallons.

HEALTH
A yellow fever vaccination certificate is required if you arrive from an infected area; no other vaccinations are necessary, though some are recommended. In particular, guard against malaria and hepatitis.

The pharmacy network is extensive, and there are *droguerías* or *farmacias* even in small towns. In the cities, they are usually well stocked. Many drugs are available without prescription, but always check the expiration date.

In most of the larger cities, the water can be safely drunk from the tap, though it is best to avoid it if possible. Outside these areas, drink boiled or bottled water.

DANGERS & ANNOYANCES

Colombia definitely isn't the safest of countries, and you should be careful at all times. The biggest potential dangers are being ripped off or robbed. The problem is more serious in the major cities, Bogotá, Medellín and Cali being the worst.

Keep your passport and money next to your skin and your camera inside your bag, and don't wear jewelry or expensive watches. If you can, leave your money and valuables somewhere safe before walking the streets. In practice, it's good to carry a decoy bundle of small notes, the equivalent of US$5 to US$10, ready to hand over in case of an assault; if you really don't have a peso, robbers can become frustrated and, as a consequence, unpredictable. Always carry your passport with you, as document checks on the streets are not uncommon. Some police officers may accept a photocopy of the passport, but legally, only the genuine document is valid.

Robbery can be very dangerous. Armed hold-ups become more common every year, mainly in slum *barrios* of the large cities. Avoid dubious-looking areas, especially if you are alone and particularly at night. If you are accosted by robbers, it is best to give them what they are after, but try to play it cool and don't rush to hand them all your valuables at once – they may well be satisfied with just your decoy wad.

Be exceptionally careful about drugs – never carry them. The police and army can be extremely thorough in searching travelers, often looking for a nice fat bribe. Don't buy dope on the street; the vendors may well be setting you up for the police. There have been reports of drugs being planted on travelers, so keep your eyes open. Never try to smuggle dope across borders.

Burundanga is more bad news. It is a drug obtained from a species of tree widespread in Colombia and is used by thieves to render a victim unconscious. It can be put into sweets, cigarettes, chewing gum, spirits, beer – virtually any kind of food or drink – and it doesn't have any particular taste or odor. The main effects are loss of will and memory, and sleepiness lasting from a few hours to several days. An overdose can be fatal. Think twice before accepting a cigarette from a stranger or a drink from a new 'friend.'

Keep an eye on guerrilla movements, so as not to get caught in the crossfire. Unfortunately, certain regions of Colombia (parts of the Amazon Basin, Los Llanos, Urabá and the Sierra Nevada de Santa Marta) are becoming off limits for secure travel.

Kidnapping for ransom has been part of guerrilla activity for quite a while and is on the increase. The main targets are well-off locals and foreign executives and the ransoms go up to US$1 million or more. In 1998 about 2000 people were kidnapped in Colombia (a world's record), including 40 foreigners (half of whom hadn't been released by the end of that year). These are official figures, but it's estimated that there may be up to 50% more unreported cases negotiated privately with the abductors.

Guerrillas don't normally target tourists, but cases are reported more and more frequently. Statistically, backpackers traveling by bus face slim risk, at least far smaller than VIPs moving around in 4WD Toyotas, yet you should know about the potential danger.

More frequent than kidnapping is ambushing cars and buses for possessions, not for people. These normally occur at night at roadblocks and the perpetrators essentially target passengers' valuables. To minimize the risk, avoid nighttime travel. In any case, it's best to stick to the main routes and avoid off-the-beaten-track travel.

PUBLIC HOLIDAYS

The following days are observed as public holidays in Colombia:

La Circuncisión (Circumcision)
January 1

Los Reyes Magos (Epiphany)
January 6*

San José (St Joseph)
March 19*

Jueves Santo (Maundy Thursday)
Viernes Santo (Good Friday)
March/April (Easter, dates vary)

Día del Trabajo (Labor Day)
May 1

La Ascensión del Señor (Ascension)
May (date varies)*

Corpus Cristi (Corpus Christi)
May/June (date varies)*

Sagrado Corazón de Jesús (Sacred Heart)
    June (date varies)*

San Pedro y San Pablo (St Peter and St Paul)
    June 29*

Día de la Independencia (Independence Day)
    July 20

Batalla de Boyacá (Battle of Boyacá)
    August 7

La Asunción de Nuestra Señora (Assumption)
    August 15*

Día de la Raza (Discovery of America)
    October 12*

Todos los Santos (All Saints' Day)
    November 1*

Independencia de Cartagena (Independence of
    Cartagena)
    November 11*

Inmaculada Concepción (Immaculate
    Conception)
    December 8

La Navidad (Christmas Day)
    December 25

When the dates marked with an asterisk do not fall on a Monday, the holiday is moved to the following Monday to make a three-daylong weekend, referred to as the *puente*.

SPECIAL EVENTS

Colombians love fiestas. There are more than 200 festivals and events ranging from small, local affairs to international festivals lasting several days. Most of the celebrations are regional, and the most interesting ones are listed in the sections on individual places.

ACTIVITIES

With its amazing geographical diversity, Colombia offers wide opportunities for hiking, though some regions are infiltrated by guerrillas and should be avoided. Trails in some national parks and private reserves are good places for viewing wildlife.

Colombia's coral reefs provide good conditions for snorkeling and have prompted development of scuba-diving facilities. The main centers are San Andrés, Providencia, Santa Marta and Cartagena, each of which has several diving schools offering courses (NAUI and PADI) and the full complement of diving services.

Other possible activities include mountaineering, rock climbing, windsurfing, canoeing, rafting, fishing, caving and even bathing in a mud volcano (see the Around Cartagena section).

ACCOMMODATIONS

There is a constellation of places to stay in Colombia, from large cities to the smallest villages. Except for a handful of places which have gained popularity among travelers, the rest are straight Colombian hotels where you are unlikely to meet foreigners.

Accommodation appears under a variety of names including *hotel*, *residencias*, *hospedaje*, *pensión*, *hostería*, *hospedería*, *estadero*, *apartamentos*, *amoblados* and *posada*. Residencias and hospedaje are the most common names for budget places. A hotel generally suggests a place of a higher standard, or at least a higher price, though the distinction is often academic.

On the whole, residencias and hospedajes are unremarkable places without any style or atmosphere. This is particularly true in the cities, where the budget places are often poor or overpriced, or both. Hardboard partitions instead of walls are not unusual, making noise and security a problem.

Some budget hotel rooms have a toilet and shower attached. Note that cheap hotel plumbing can't cope with toilet paper, so throw it in the box or basket that is usually provided.

In hot places (ie, the lowland areas), a ceiling fan or table fan is often provided. Always check the fan before you take a room. On the other hand, above 2500m, where the nights can be chilly, look to see how many blankets you have, and check the hot water if they claim to have it.

By and large, residencias (even the cheapest) provide a sheet and some sort of cover (another sheet or blankets, depending on the temperature). Most will also give you a towel, a small piece of soap and a roll of toilet paper. The cheapies cost around US$4 to US$10 for a single room, US$8 to US$15 for a double.

Many hospedajes have *matrimonios*, rooms with a double bed intended for couples. A matrimonio is usually cheaper than a double and can be only slightly more expensive than a single (or even the same price).

Some residencias offer a safety deposit facility, which means that they will store your valuables, as there are no other safe places. Better hotels usually have the reception desk open round the clock, with proper facilities to safeguard your things. Remember that a hotel (no matter what hotel it is) is almost always safer than the streets of a big city at night.

Brothels are not uncommon in Colombia, so check before booking – these places are usually easy to recognize by the hordes of *putas* (prostitutes) at the entrance or on the closest corner.

More common than brothels are love hotels, which rent rooms by the hour. Many cheap residencias double as love hotels. Intentionally or not, you are likely to find yourself in such a place from time to time. This is actually not a major problem, as love hotels are usually as clean and safe as other hotels, and usually do not allow prostitutes.

Colombia has just two youth hostels, in Bogotá, and an overpriced and inconvenient one in Cali.

Camping is not popular in Colombia and there are only a handful of campsites in the country. Camping wild is theoretically possible outside the urban centers but you should be extremely careful. Try to pitch your tent under someone's protection (next to a *campesino* house or in the grounds of a holiday center), after getting permission from the owners, guards or management. Don't leave your tent or gear unattended.

FOOD

Colombian cuisine is varied and regional. Among the most typical regional dishes are:

Ajiaco – a soup with chicken and three varieties of potato, served with corn and capers; a Bogotan specialty

Bandeja paisa – a typical Antioquian dish made up of ground beef, a sausage *(chorizo)*, red beans *(fríjoles)*, rice, fried green banana *(plátano)*, a fried egg, a piece of fried salt pork *(chicharrón)* and avocado

Chocolate santafereño – a cup of hot chocolate accompanied by a piece of cheese and bread (traditionally, you put the cheese into the chocolate); another Bogotan specialty

Cuy – grilled guinea pig, typical of Nariño

Hormiga culona – large fried ants; probably the most exotic Colombian specialty, unique to Santander

Lechona – a pig carcass, stuffed with its own meat, rice and dried peas and then baked in an oven; a specialty of Tolima

Tamales – chopped pork with rice and vegetables folded in a maize dough, wrapped in banana leaves and steamed; there are many regional varieties

Variety does not, unfortunately, apply to the basic set meal *(comida corriente)*, which is the principal diet of the majority of Colombians eating out. It is a two-course meal consisting of *sopa* (soup) and *bandeja* or *seco* (main course), and usually includes a *sobremesa* (a bottled fizzy drink or juice). At lunchtime (from noon to 2 pm), it is called *almuerzo*; at dinnertime (after 6 pm), it becomes *comida*, but it is in fact identical to lunch. Despite some local additions, it's almost exactly the same throughout the country.

The almuerzos and comidas are the staple, and sometimes the only, offering in countless budget restaurants. Some serve them continuously from noon until they close at night, but most only serve them during lunchtime and, less often, at dinnertime. The comida corriente is the cheapest way to fill yourself up, costing between US$1.50 and US$3 – roughly half the price of an à la carte dish.

Barbecued chicken restaurants (there are plenty of them) are a good alternative to the comida. Half a chicken with potatoes will cost around US$3 to US$5. Another budget option, particularly in smaller towns and villages, is the market, where food is usually fresh, tasty and cooked in front of you.

Western food is readily available, either in fast-food outlets (including chains such as McDonald's and Pizza Hut) or in up-market restaurants. Over the last decade there has been a trend toward vegetarian food, and most major cities have budget vegetarian restaurants.

Colombia has an amazing variety of fruits, some of which are endemic to the country. You should try *guanábana, lulo, curuba, zapote, mamoncillo, uchuva, feijoa, granadilla, maracuyá, tomate de árbol, borojó, mamey* and *tamarindo*, to name just a few.

DRINKS

Coffee is the number one drink – *tinto* (a small cup of black coffee) is served everywhere. Other coffee drinks are *perico* or *pintado*, a small milk coffee, and *café con leche*, which is larger and uses more milk.

Tea is of poor quality and not very popular. On the other hand, the *aromáticas* – herb teas made with various plants like *cidrón* (citrus leaves), *yerbabuena* (mint)

and *manzanilla* (chamomile) – are cheap and good. *Agua de panela* (unrefined sugar melted in hot water) is tasty with lemon.

Beer is popular, cheap and generally not bad. This can't be said about Colombian wine, which is best avoided.

Aguardiente is the local alcoholic spirit, flavored with anise and produced by several companies throughout the country; Cristal from Caldas and Nectar from Cuidinamarca are the most popular. *Ron* (rum) is another popular distilled spirit, particularly on the Caribbean coast.

In some regions, mostly in rural areas, you will find *chicha* and *guarapo* (fermented maize or fruit drinks), which are homemade and low (or not so low) in alcohol.

Getting There & Away

Sitting on the northwestern edge of the continent, Colombia is a convenient gateway to South America from the USA and Central America, and even from Europe.

Colombia still, technically, has an onward ticket requirement, which means that you are officially not allowed into the country if you don't have a ticket out. This is practically never enforced by immigration officials, either at international airports or at land border crossings.

AIR

Colombia is not a good place to buy international air tickets. Airfares to the USA, Europe and Australia are expensive and there are hardly any attractive discounted tickets available, except for some reasonable student fares offered by a handful of student travel agencies (see the Bogotá section). Furthermore, if you buy an international ticket in Colombia, you pay 10% tax (5% for return tickets) on top of the fare. Airfares given in this chapter don't include this tax.

Departure Tax

The airport tax on international flights out of Colombia is US$24 if you have stayed in the country up to 60 days, and US$46 if you've stayed longer. It can be paid in pesos or dollars (but not by credit card).

Europe

The cheapest flights are from London – low-season airfares to Bogotá start at around £300 one-way, £480 return.

North America

Avianca may have discount return flight offers from New York and Miami to Colombia. Other options to check include the New York/Miami-San José-Barranquilla flight with Lacsa, and the New York/Miami-Caracas-Bogotá flight with Avensa.

Central America

Colombia has regular flight connections with most Central American capitals. Sample fares include: Guatemala City-Bogotá US$321 (US$417 for a 60-day return) and San José-Bogotá US$292 (US$362 return). It may work out cheaper to go via the Colombian island of San Andrés and then get a domestic flight to the Colombian mainland. See the San Andrés section for details.

Several carriers, including Copa, Avianca/Sam and Aces, operate direct flights between Panama and Colombia. One-way fares out of Panama City include: Cartagena US$139, Medellín US$161, Bogotá US$161 and Cali US$174. Discount fares are available on return flights.

Ecuador

There are more than a dozen regular flights a week between Quito and Bogotá, operated by Avianca, Saeta, Aces and Servivensa (US$172 one-way, US$199 30-day return). Tame (an Ecuadorian carrier) has twice weekly connections between Esmeraldas and Cali (US$70).

Venezuela

There are several flights daily between Caracas and Bogotá, with Avianca, Saeta, Servivensa and a few other carriers. The regular one-way fare is US$218; a discount 30- or 60-day return ticket, originating from either end, costs US$251/281.

Other connections between Venezuela and Colombia include Caracas-Cartagena with Aeropostal (US$180 one-way, US$220 30-day return), Maracaibo-Barranquilla with Santa Bárbara (US$135, US$190) and San Antonio del Táchira-Medellín with Servivensa (US$63). Servivensa suspended their San Antonio del Táchira-Bogotá flights in 1999.

LAND
Central America
The Darién Gap very effectively separates Colombia from Panama. There are no through roads, and it is unlikely that one will be built to complete the missing link in the Carretera Panamericana (Pan-American Highway) anytime soon. The trek through the jungle from Yaviza to Los Katíos is extremely dangerous these days, so the only viable overland route is along the northern coast, from Puerto Obaldía to Capurganá. See the Getting There & Away chapter for more details and other options.

Ecuador
Almost all travelers use the Carretera Panamericana border crossing through Ipales and Tulcán. See the Ipiales section in this chapter and the Tulcán section in the Ecuador chapter for more information.

Venezuela
There are several border crossings between Colombia and Venezuela. By far the most popular with travelers is the route via Cúcuta and San Antonio del Táchira, on the main Bogotá-Caracas road. See the Cúcuta section in this chapter and the San Antonio del Táchira section in the Venezuela chapter for details.

Another Venezuelan entry point is Paraguachón, on the Maicao-Maracaibo road. You may use this route if you are heading for the Caribbean coast. There are buses and shared taxis between Maicao and Maracaibo. Your passport should be stamped by both Colombian and Venezuelan officials in Paraguachón, on the border. See the Maracaibo section of the Venezuela chapter for transportation information.

Yet another possible route leads to the Orinoquia, via Colombia's Puerto Carreño to either Puerto Páez or Puerto Ayacucho (both in Venezuela). See the Puerto Ayacucho section of the Venezuela chapter for details.

RIVER
There is an official tripartite Colombia-Peru-Brazil border crossing at Leticia, in the far southeastern corner of the Colombian Amazon. Leticia is downriver from Iquitos (Peru) and upriver from Manaus (Brazil), and is a hub of Amazon exploration. For details, see the Leticia section in this chapter.

SEA
There are now sailboats between Porvenir in the San Blás Archipelago (Panama) and Cartagena. See the Cartagena section for details.

Getting Around

AIR
Colombia has a well-developed airline system and a dense network of domestic flights. Main passenger airlines include Avianca, Sam, Aces, Aires, Intercontinental de Aviación, AeroRepública and Satena, most of which also have international flights. There are also a number of small airlines, which operate over limited areas, as well as several cargo carriers.

Airfares can differ between the carriers. Avianca and Sam (which operate jointly) keep their regular fares high, while Aero-República and Intercontinental may be cheaper. All airlines offer various and frequently changing discounted fares, so shop around. There's a 10% tax on domestic airfares (5% on return tickets), except for flights to the localities inaccessible by road – eg, San Andrés, Leticia and Puerto Carreño – and a US$5 airport tax on domestic flights.

Fares quoted in this chapter are regular fares including taxes. Given the volatile state of affairs, however, consider them as guidelines only, and always re-confirm your reservations 72 hours before departure.

Avianca Air Pass
Visitors who fly into Colombia with Avianca can take advantage of the 30-day Descubra Colombia pass. This pass can only be purchased outside the country and allows for five domestic stopovers of your choice serviced by Avianca/Sam (but you cannot visit the same place twice). In the high season (June to August and December) the pass costs US$290 (including San Andrés and Leticia as two of the five stopovers) or US$200 (excluding these two destinations). The rest of the year, it's US$260 or US$180, respectively. You are allowed to buy up to

three additional stopovers for US$40 each. There's also a cheaper 21-day version of the pass, which allows only three stopovers (plus purchase of two extra) and doesn't include San Andrés and Leticia.

BUS

Buses are the main means of getting around Colombia. The bus system is well developed and extensive, reaching even the smallest villages, if there is a road. There are three principal classes of bus: ordinary (called *corriente*), 1st class (*pullman*) and air-conditioned (*climatizado*).

The corriente buses are older and mostly service side roads. The Pullmans are more modern, reliable and comfortable. They ply both side and main routes. Climatizados are the best. They have plenty of leg room, reclining seats, large luggage compartments, and some have toilets. They are predominantly long-distance buses covering main routes; many travel at night. The climatizado is becoming the dominant means of intercity transport. Carry warm clothes – drivers usually set the air-con on full blast.

On the main roads, buses run every hour, or more frequently, so there is little point in booking a seat in advance. In some places off the main routes, where there are only a few buses daily, it's better to buy a ticket some time before departure. The only time you need to book is during the Christmas and Easter periods, when hordes of Colombians are on holiday.

There is one more kind of bus – the *chiva*. This trolley-type vehicle was the principal means of transport several decades ago. Its body is made almost entirely of wood, covered with colorful decorative patterns, with a main painting on the back. Today, the chivas have disappeared from the main roads, but they still play an important role on back roads between small villages.

The *colectivo* is a cross between a bus and a taxi. They are usually large cars (sometimes jeeps or minibuses) that cover fixed routes, mainly over short and medium distances. They leave when full, not according to a schedule, and are a good option if there is a long wait for the next bus or if you are in a hurry.

All major cities have a central bus terminal, often well outside of the center but linked by urban transport. In smaller locali-ties, where there is no terminal, bus company offices tend to cluster along one or two adjacent streets.

Bus travel is not that cheap in Colombia. As a rule of thumb, the corriente bus costs about US$3 to US$4 for every 100 km, pullmans cost about 20% more than corrientes and climatizados 20% more than pullmans.

BOAT

With more than 3000 km of Pacific and Atlantic coastline, there is a considerable amount of shipping traffic, consisting mostly of irregular cargo boats, which may also take passengers.

Rivers are also important transport routes, particularly in the Chocó and the Amazon, where there is no other way of getting around. Very few riverboats run on regular schedules, and as most are primarily cargo boats, they are far from fast. Conditions are primitive and food (when provided) is poor.

Bogotá

The capital of the country, Bogotá is the quintessence of all things Colombian. It's a city of splendid colonial churches, brilliant museums, universities, futuristic architecture, intellectuals and artists, offering a vibrant and diverse cultural life. Yet it is also a city of vast shantytowns, street urchins, beggars, thieves, drug dealers, itinerant vendors, wild traffic and graffiti.

The city was founded in 1538 and named Santa Fe de Bogotá, but after independence the name was shortened to Bogotá. Though it always played an important political role as the capital, its rapid progress only came in the 1940s, with industrialization and consequent migrations from the countryside. Over the past 50 years, Bogotá has grown 20-fold to its present population of between six and seven million. The city's official name was changed back to Santa Fe de Bogotá in 1991.

The city lies at an altitude of about 2600m, and the temperature averages 14°C year-round, with cold nights and warm days. The dry season is from December to March, and there is also a semidry period from July to August.

Bogotá is a bustling, noisy and aggressive metropolis – amazing but awful, fascinating

CENTRAL BOGOTÁ

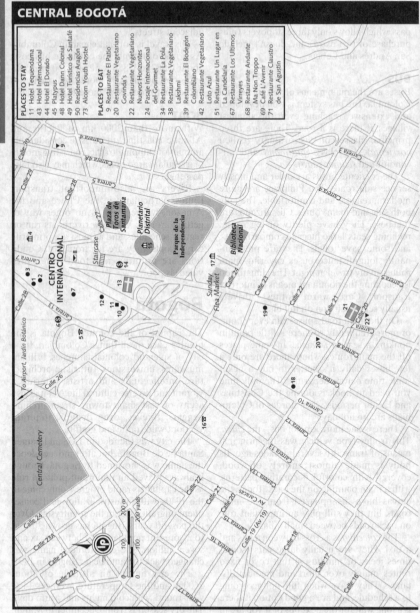

PLACES TO STAY
- 11 Hotel Tequendama
- 43 Hotel Internacional
- 44 Hotel El Dorado
- 45 Platypus
- 48 Hotel Dann Colonial
- 49 Hotel Turístico de Santafé
- 50 Residencias Aragón
- 73 Alcom Youth Hostel

PLACES TO EAT
- 9 Restaurante El Patio
- 20 Restaurante Vegetariano Govinda's
- 22 Restaurante Vegetariano Nuevos Horizontes
- 24 Pasaje Internacional del Gourmet
- 34 Restaurante La Pola
- 38 Restaurante Vegetariano Lakshmi
- 39 Restaurante El Bodegón Colombiano
- 42 Restaurante Vegetariano Loto Azul
- 51 Restaurante Un Lugar en La Candelaria
- 67 Restaurante Los Últimos Virreyes
- 68 Restaurante Andante
- 69 Ma Non Troppo
- 70 Café L'Avenir
- 71 Restaurante Claustro de San Agustín

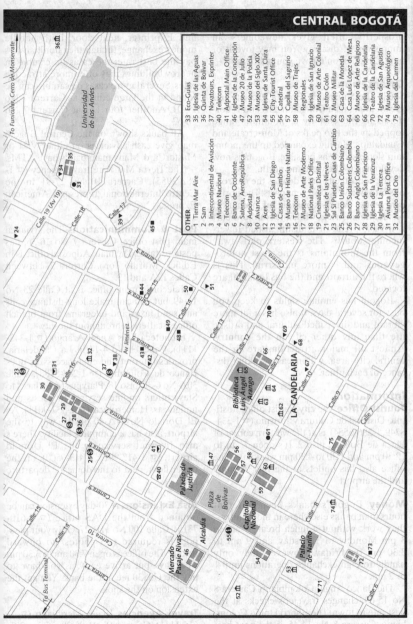

OTHER

1 Tierra Mar Aire
2 Sam
3 Intercontinental de Aviación
4 Museo Nacional
5 Telecom
6 Banco de Occidente
7 Satena, AeroRepública
8 Adpostal
10 Avianca
12 Aces
13 Iglesia de San Diego
14 Casas de Cambio
15 Museo de Historia Natural
16 Telecom
17 Museo de Arte Moderno
18 National Parks Office
19 Cinemateca Distrital
21 Iglesia de las Nieves
23 Sal Si Puedes; Casas de Cambio
25 Banco Unión Colombiano
26 Banco Sudameris Colombia
27 Banco Anglo Colombiano
28 Iglesia de San Francisco
29 Iglesia de la Veracruz
30 Iglesia La Tercera
31 Avianca Post Office
32 Museo del Oro

33 Eco-Guías
35 Iglesia de las Aguas
36 Quinta de Bolívar
37 Novatours, Expinter
40 Telecom
41 Adpostal Main Office
46 Iglesia de la Concepción
47 Museo 20 de Julio
52 Museo de la Policía
53 Museo del Siglo XIX
54 Iglesia de Santa Clara
55 City Tourist Office
56 Catedral
57 Capilla del Sagrario
58 Museo de Trajes Regionales
59 Iglesia de San Ignacio
60 Museo de Arte Colonial
61 Teatro Colón
62 Museo Militar
63 Casa de la Moneda
64 Casa Luis López de Mesa
65 Museo de Arte Religioso
66 Iglesia de la Candelaria
70 Teatro de la Candelaria
72 Iglesia de San Agustín
74 Museo Arqueológico
75 Iglesia del Carmen

but dangerous. The bizarre mixture of everything from oppressive poverty to sparkling prosperity often gives newcomers an impression of disarray. You may love it or hate it, but it won't leave you indifferent.

Orientation

Set in the Sabana de Bogotá, the city has grown along its north-south axis and is bordered to the east by a mountain range topped by the two peaks of Monserrate and Guadalupe. Having expanded up the mountain slopes as far as possible, Bogotá is now developing to the west and north.

The central city area divides the metropolis into two very different parts. The northern sector consists mainly of upmarket residential districts, while the southern part is a vast spread of undistinguished lower-income suburbs. The western part, away from the mountains, is the most heterogeneous and is more industrial. This is where the airport and the bus terminal are located.

Bogotá has enough sights to keep you busy for several days. It also has a far more vibrant and diversified cultural and artistic life than any other city in the country. Almost all major attractions are in the central city area, within easy walking distance of each other.

Information

Tourist Office The city tourist office, Instituto Distrital de Cultura y Turismo (☎ 1-334-8749, 1-286-6554), is at the western corner of Plaza de Bolívar, piso 2. It's open 7 am to 12:30 pm and 1:30 to 4:30 pm weekdays. The office also has outlets at the bus terminal and the airport.

Money Bogotá's banks keep different hours than banks elsewhere in the country – they work without a lunch break, 9 am to 3 pm Monday to Thursday, and 9 am to 3:30 pm on Friday. However, they only handle foreign exchange operations until 1 or 2 pm.

The Banco Anglo Colombiano, Carrera 8 No 15-60, changes traveler's checks at the best rate in town. The Banco Unión Colombiano, Carrera 8 No 14-45, is the next best place for cashing checks, but service is slow.

These banks also change cash, but check the casas de cambio beforehand, which may pay the same amount and do it much quicker. Novatours, Carrera 6 No 14-64, and Exprinter, next door, both handle money exchange, though they don't always pay the best rate; the casas de cambio in nearby buildings may offer more attractive rates. Several more casas de cambio can be found in the large edifice at Carrera 7 No 17-01. Another four are at Carrera 7 No 26-62.

All banks shown on the Central Bogotá map give cash advances on either Visa or MasterCard. Many main banks have ATMs.

The Tierra Mar Aire travel agency (☎ 1-283-2955), Carrera 10 No 27-91 in the Centro Internacional, represents American Express.

Post & Communications The Avianca main post office, Carrera 7 No 16-36, has poste restante. The main Adpostal office is in Edificio Murillo Toro, Carrera 7, between Calles 12A and 13.

Telecom's main office is at Calle 23 No 13-49, but you can make long-distance calls and send faxes and telegrams from branch offices scattered throughout the city.

Biblioteca Luis Angel Arango (☎ 1-342-1111), Calle 11 No 4-14 in La Candelaria, provides Internet and email access, as does Banco de Colombia (☎ 1-288-5788), Calle 30A No 6-38, piso 18. Platypus (see Places to Stay) offers on-line services to guests and nonguests. Hemeroteca (☎ 1-337-9011), Av El Dorado No 44A-40 on the way to the airport, also has a computer facility. There's also Internet service in the El Dorado airport, (☎ 1-413-9913, 1-413-9500), on the upper floor, next to the domestic departure gate.

Visa Extensions A 30-day extension can be obtained from the DAS office (☎ 1-610-7315), Calle 100 No 11B-27. Only your passport is required (no photos, no onward ticket). The office is open 7:30 am to 3:30 pm weekdays, but arrive early, as you have to pay the US$30 fee at the bank. You get the extension on the spot.

Travel Agencies Viajes Meridiano (☎ 1-616-1111), Carrera 15 No 85-29, oficina 201, and Educamos Viajando (☎ 1-214-1817), Calle 108A No 18-64, specialize in student travel, especially cheap airfares.

National Parks The Unidad Administrativa Especial del Sistema de Parques Nacionales (☎ 1-283-0964), Carrera 10 No 20-30, piso 4, issues permits and provides information for parks nationwide.

Maps IGAC, Carrera 30 No 48-51, next to the Universidad Nacional, sells general, regional and city maps. The institute is open 8 am to 3:30 pm weekdays.

Laundry There are no self-service laundries, but a lot of places offer cheap laundry services, including Lava Rápido, Calle 15 No 4-14; Lavandería, Calle 13 No 3-55; and Lavandería Burbuja, Carrera 3 No 18-57, local S-104.

Dangers & Annoyances Bogotá is not a safe place. Parts of the city center become quite dangerous after dark and are notorious for robbery. Keep nighttime strolls to a minimum and don't carry money or other valuables.

Things to See & Do

Historic Quarter The **Plaza de Bolívar** is the heart of the original town, but what you see around it is a mishmash of architectural styles. The massive stone building in classical Greek style on the southern side is the **Capitolio Nacional**, the seat of the Congress. Opposite is the equally monumental **Palacio de Justicia**. It replaces an earlier building which was taken by the M-19 guerrillas in November 1985 and gutted by fire in a fierce 28-hour offensive by the army, which left more than 100 dead, including 11 Supreme Court justices.

The western side of the plaza is taken up by the French-style **Alcaldía** (mayor's office), dating from the early 20th century. The neoclassical **Catedral**, on the eastern side of the square, was completed in 1823 and is Bogotá's largest church. Next door, the **Capilla del Sagrario** is the only colonial building on the square.

To the east of the plaza is the colonial quarter of **La Candelaria**. Some of the houses have been meticulously restored, while others are dilapidated. On the whole the sector preserves an agreeable old-world appearance, even though a number of modern edifices have replaced historic buildings. The best preserved part of the district is between Calles 9 and 13 and Carreras 2 and 5.

Museums Bogotá has a number of good museums (all closed on Monday). The star attraction is the **Museo del Oro** (Gold Museum), Calle 16 No 5-41, the most important of its kind in the world. It contains more than 33,000 gold pieces from all the major pre-Hispanic cultures in Colombia. Most of the gold is displayed in a huge strong room on the top floor. The museum is open from 9 am to 4:30 pm Tuesday to Saturday and 10 am to 4:30 pm on Sunday. Admission is US$2 (US$1.50 on Sunday).

The **Museo Arqueológico**, in a beautifully restored colonial house at Carrera 6 No 7-43, has an extensive collection of pottery from Colombia's main pre-Hispanic cultures. Other important museums in the historic quarter include the **Museo de Arte Colonial**, Carrera 6 No 9-77, and **Museo de Arte Religioso**, Calle 12 No 4-33.

In the northern part of the city center, be sure to visit the **Museo Nacional**, accommodated in an old prison at Carrera 7 No 28-66. It is divided into anthropology, ethnography, history and fine arts sections, and also hosts temporary exhibitions. For contemporary art, visit the **Museo de Arte Moderno**, Calle 24 No 6-00, which runs frequently changing displays of national, and sometimes foreign, artists.

The **Quinta de Bolívar**, Calle 20 No 2-23 Este, is an old country house which was donated to Simón Bolívar in gratitude for his services. Today, it's a museum displaying documents, maps, weapons, uniforms and Bolívar's personal effects.

Churches A center of evangelism since the early days of Spanish rule, Bogotá boasts many colonial churches, most dating from the 17th and 18th centuries. Unlike the outwardly ornate churches typical of other colonial capitals, Bogota's churches have austere exteriors, though internal decoration is often quite elaborate.

One of the most remarkable is **Santa Clara**, open as a museum. Other churches worth a look include: **San Francisco**, for the extraordinary decoration of its chancel; **La Concepción**, home of Bogotá's most beautiful Mudejar vault; **San Ignacio**, distinguished by both its size and its valuable art collection; **La Tercera**, with its walnut and cedar carvings; and **San Diego**, a charming country church (it was well outside the town when built) now surrounded by a forest of high-rise buildings.

Cerro de Monserrate For a spectacular view of the city, go to the top of the Cerro de Monserrate, the mountain overlooking the city center from the east. There is a church on the summit, with a statue of the Señor Caído (Fallen Christ), to which many miracles have been attributed.

There are three ways to get to the top: by cable car *(teleférico)*, funicular railway or foot-path. The cable car operates daily (US$5 return), while the funicular only runs on Sunday (US$4 return). If you want to do the trip on foot (one hour uphill), do it only on Sunday, when crowds of pilgrims go; on weekdays, take it for granted that you will be robbed along the way. The lower stations of the cable car and the funicular are close to the city center, but the access road leads through a poor suburb, so take the bus marked 'Funicular' from Av Jiménez, or a taxi.

Other Sights The **Jardín Botánico José Celestino Mutis**, at Calle 57 No 61-13, has a variety of national flora from different climatic zones. On Sunday, don't miss the colorful **Mercado de las Pulgas**, a flea market held at the car park on Carrera 7 between Calles 24 and 26.

Language Courses
Bogotá's best known facility is the Universidad Javeriana's Centro Latinoamericano (☎ 1-212-3009), Carrera 10 No 65-48, which offers regular one-year courses (260 hours, US$880) and three-week intensive courses (72 hours, US$370). The Universidad Nacional has seven-week courses (56 hours, US$280).

Organized Tours
There are loads of travel agencies organizing tours. Eco-Guías (☎ 1-284-8991, 1-334-8042), Carrera 3 No 18-56A, oficina 202, focuses on ecotourism and organizes customized trips at reasonable prices to various regions, including many national parks.

Viajes Chapinero (☎ 1-612-7716), Av 7 No 124-15, is one of the biggest operators and has a wide number of tours, including out-of-the-way trips.

Sal Si Puedes (☎ 1-283-3765), Carrera 7 No 17-01, oficina 640, is an association of hiking enthusiasts who organize weekend walks in the countryside. These are mostly one-day excursions to Cundinamarca, but longer hikes in other regions are also arranged. Other associations of this type include Clorofila Urbana (☎ 1-310-2009), Calle 67 No 4A-80, oficina 101, and Vagabundos del Cosmos (☎ 1-222-1079).

Places to Stay
The most popular budget place among backpackers is *Platypus* (☎ 1-341-2874, 1-341-3104), Calle 16 No 2-43 (no sign on the door, just a picture of the platypus). It has three dorms (US$7 per person) and several singles (US$10) and doubles (US$15). Although conditions are quite simple and only a few rooms have private baths, the place is safe, clean and pleasant and has hot water in the communal baths. The hostel offers book exchange, Internet access, laundry and kitchen facilities, and there's a cozy dining room where you can relax and have a tinto, which is provided free of charge. The friendly owner, Hermann, a longtime traveler himself, speaks several languages and is an excellent source of practical information. He also offers a poste restante service (c/o your name, AA 3902, Bogotá, Colombia).

There are several cheap places nearby. You can try *Residencias Aragón* (☎ 1-284-8325), Carrera 3 No 14-13, which has fairly large rooms with shared bath and hot water for US$7 per person. Alternatively, check *Hotel El Dorado* (☎ 1-334-3988), Carrera 4 No 15-00, which has smaller rooms, some with private bath (US$8 per person). Similarly priced is *Hotel Internacional* (☎ 1-341-8731), Carrera 5 No 14-45.

Cheaper than any of the above is the *Alcom* youth hostel (☎ 1-280-3202, 1-280-3318), Carrera 7 No 6-10, 4 blocks south of Plaza de Bolívar. It's not ideally located but often hosts foreign travelers. Clean six- and eight-bed dorms with shared bath (hot water in the morning only) cost US$6 per person (US$5 with an HI membership card). The hostel has a cheap restaurant.

For somewhere a bit better, go to *Hotel Turístico de Santafé* (☎ 1-342-0560), Calle 14 No 4-48, which has large rooms with bath and TV for US$16/24/32 a single/double/

Historic center of Cartagena, Colombia

Fruit vendor in traditional attire, Cartagena

Caribbean coast near Santa Marta, Colombia

Mt Cotopaxi, near Latacunga, Ecuador

Grilled guinea pigs, a delicacy in Quito, Ecuador

Friends in the Plaza de la Independencia, Quito

Jugos de frutas on offer in Zumbahua, Ecuador

triple. Better still is *Hotel Dann Colonial* (☎ 1-341-1680), opposite at Calle 14 No 4-21, but it's far more costly (around US$40/50/60 with breakfast). Don't be confused by the name: The hotel is modern, not colonial.

All the hotels listed above are in or near La Candelaria, the most popular area to stay among budget travelers. While it's not a particularly safe area at night, neither is the rest of the city center.

There are also hotels in Bogotá's northern part, which is considered to be safer, but it's more expensive and inconvenient for sightseeing. One of the cheaper options is the *Casona del Patio Amarillo* (☎ 1-212-8805), Carrera 8 No 69-24. At US$11/13 per person in rooms or dorms without/with bath, it's not a great value, but the place is OK and offers some facilities, including laundry and a restaurant.

Places to Eat

Innumerable places have set meals for US$1.50 to US$3 – the best way to choose is to drop into one, see what people are eating and stay or move on to the next one. *Pasaje Internacional del Gourmet* (several establishments), Carrera 4 No 19-44/56; *El Bodegón Colombiano*, Calle 17 No 2-55; and *Un Lugar en La Candelaria* at Carrera 3 No 13-86 are just a few examples.

For cheap vegetarian food try *Lakshmi*, Av Jiménez No 5-32; *Loto Azul*, Carrera 5 No 14-00; *Nuevos Horizontes*, Calle 20 No 6-37; or *Govinda's*, Carrera 8 No 20-55. Some open for lunch only.

Bogotá has a number of barbecued-chicken restaurants, where a half-chicken with potatoes or chips makes a filling meal for US$3 to US$5. For pizza, there's a row of *pizzerias* on Calle 19, between Carreras 3 and 7.

Claustro de San Agustín, in the Museo de Artes y Tradiciones Populares, has delicious local food (served until 3 pm weekdays). *Los Ultimos Virreyes*, Calle 10 No 3-16, is one of the better restaurants in La Candelaria, serving local and international cuisine. Marginally cheaper are *Andante Ma Non Troppo*, Carrera 3 No 10-92, and *Café L'Avenir*, Calle 11 No 2-98.

La Pola, Calle 19 No 1-85, has fine regional food at reasonable prices. *El Patio*, a cozy place with only a few tables, at Carrera 4A No 27-86, serves excellent, if pricey, Italian food, and is one of the trendiest places for lunch or dinner. Encouraged by its success, several similar restaurants have mushroomed nearby.

Entertainment

Check the entertainment columns of the leading local papers, *El Tiempo* and *El Espectador*. The Thursday edition of *El Tiempo* has the goings-on section called 'Eskpe,' while *El Espectador* includes its entertainment section, 'Pync' on Friday. Also, get a copy of the *Suburbia*, a what's-on weekly, distributed free in hotels and restaurants. Online, check bogota.eureka.com.co, which covers cinemas, theaters, nightclubs and cultural events.

Bogotá has lots of cinemas offering the usual Hollywood fare. For something more thought provoking, check the programs of the *cinematecas* (art cinemas). The two most popular places of this kind are *Cinemateca Distrital* at Carrera 7 No 22-79 and *Museo de Arte Moderno*, which has its own screening room (enter from Calle 26).

Leading theaters include *Teatro de la Candelaria*, Calle 12 No 2-59; *Teatro Libre de Bogotá*, Calle 62 No 10-65; and *Teatro Nacional*, in its two locations at Calle 71 No 10-25 and Calle 95 No 30-13.

For classical music, check the program of the *Biblioteca Luis Angel Arango*, which hosts performances in its own concert hall.

The main area of nighttime entertainment is the Zona Rosa, in the northern sector of the city, between Carreras 11 and 15, and Calles 81 and 84. There's a maze of music spots, bars, restaurants, cafés and snack bars in the area, which become particularly vibrant on weekend nights. The better known *salsotecas* (discos that play mostly son and salsa) include *Salomé* at Carrera 14A No 82-16, *Galería Café Libro* at Calle 81 No 11-92 and *Quiebra Canto* at Carrera 15 No 79-28, but there are plenty of other places playing reggae, rock and heavy metal. One of the most popular these days is *Mister Babilla*, on Calle 82, next door to the Hotel La Bohème.

Spectator Sports

Soccer is Colombia's national sport. The principal venue is the Estadio El Campín, on the corner of Carrera 30 and Calle 55. Matches are played on Wednesday nights and Sunday afternoons. Bullfighting is also very popular, with fights held at the Plaza de Toros de Santamaría, Carrera 6, on most Sundays in January and February.

Getting There & Away

Air El Dorado airport, which handles all domestic and international flights, is 13km northwest of the city center. It has two terminals. The main one, El Dorado, houses the tourist office and money-changing facilities. Aerocambios, on the ground floor (open 7 am to 9 pm daily), changes cash. The Banco Popular, at the next window (the same opening hours), changes both cash and traveler's checks, but rates for checks are lower than those at banks in the city center. There are several ATMs on the upper level.

The other terminal, Puente Aéreo, is about 1km before El Dorado. It handles Avianca's international flights to the USA, and domestic flights to Cali, Medellín and a few other destinations. Make sure to check which terminal your flight departs from.

There are plenty of domestic flights to destinations all over the country, including Cali (US$76), Cartagena (US$118), Leticia (US$142), Medellín (US$71) and San Andrés (US$152). Discounted fares are sometimes offered. Aerosucre has cargo flights to Leticia (see the Leticia section near the end of this chapter).

There are also a lot of international departures, including ones to Caracas (US$218), to Guatemala City (US$290), to Panama City (US$161), to Quito (US$172) and to San José (US$266).

Bus The bus terminal is a long way west of the city center. Take a bus or colectivo marked 'Terminal' from Av Jiménez. Taxis between the terminal and the city center shouldn't cost more than US$4.

The bus terminal is large, functional and well organized. It has a tourist office, restaurants, cafeterias, showers and left-luggage rooms plus a number of well-dressed thieves who will wait for a moment's inattention to grab your stuff and disappear: Watch your bags closely.

The terminal handles buses to just about every corner of the country. On the main roads, buses run frequently round the clock to Bucaramanga (US$22, 10 hours), Cali (US$26, 12 hours) and Medellín (US$25,

nine hours). There are also direct buses to Cartagena (US$52), Cúcuta (US$32), Ipiales (US$46), Popayán (US$33), San Agustín (US$24) and Santa Marta (US$45). All prices are for air-conditioned buses, the dominant class on these routes.

Getting Around

To/From the Airport Both El Dorado and Puente Aéreo terminals are accessible from the center by *busetas* (small buses) and colectivos marked 'Aeropuerto'; catch them on Calle 19 or Carrera 10. Alternatively, take a taxi (US$6).

Bus & Buseta Buses and busetas run the length and breadth of the city. On most streets you just wave the vehicle down, but on Carrera 7, Av Caracas and some other routes there are now bus stops. The flat fare (US$0.25 to US$0.60) is always posted by the door or windshield. Colectivos operate on the major routes and cost about US$0.40.

Taxi Bogotá's taxis all have meters and most drivers use them; insist, or take another taxi. Fares are calculated by units that are translated to pesos using the chart which should be displayed in every taxi. A 10km ride (eg, from Plaza de Bolívar to Av 100 in northern Bogotá) shouldn't cost more than US$4. There's a US$1.25 surcharge on rides to the airport.

A warning: When taxiing from the bus terminal or the airport to a budget hotel, your driver may insist that your chosen hotel no longer exists, is now a brothel, has security problems or some other story, and will offer a 'much better option.' Don't trust a word – many taxi drivers have agreements with hotel owners and get kickbacks for delivering tourists.

AROUND BOGOTÁ
Zipaquirá

Zipaquirá, 50km north of Bogotá, is noted for its salt mines. Although the mines date back to the Muisca period and have been intensively exploited, they still contain vast reserves; they tap into virtually a huge mountain of rock salt. In the heart of the mountain, an underground **salt cathedral** has been carved out of the solid salt and was opened to the public in 1954. It was closed in 1992 for safety reasons, but a new cathedral was scooped out 60m below the old one and opened for visitors in December 1995. It is 75m long and 18m high and can accommodate 8400 people.

The cathedral is open 10 am to 4 pm Tuesday to Sunday. The entrance fee is US$6 (half-price Wednesday). Tours are guided and take one hour. Guides with basic English are sometimes available at no extra charge.

Buses to Zipaquirá run from Bogotá every 10 minutes, departing from the corner of Calle 19 and Carrera 20 (US$1, 1½ hours). The mines are a 15-minute walk uphill from the town center.

Guatavita

Also called Guatavita Nueva, this town was built from scratch in the late 1960s when the old colonial Guatavita was flooded by the waters of a hydroelectric reservoir. The town is an architectural blend of old and new, and is a popular weekend destination for *bogotanos*.

About 15km from the town is the famous **Laguna de Guatavita**, the ritual center and sacred lake of the Muisca Indians, and a cradle of the myth of El Dorado. The lake was an object of worship, where gold pieces, emeralds and food were offered by the Muisca. The myth of incalculable treasures at the bottom gave rise to numerous attempts to salvage the riches. Despite enormous efforts by the Spanish and later the Colombians, very little has actually been recovered. Legend claims that the lake retains its treasures.

Buses to Guatavita Nueva depart from Carrera 15 No 14-59 in Bogotá's center (US$2, two hours). They run every hour on weekdays and every half-hour on Sunday. For the lake, get off 11km before town (drivers will let you off at the right place) and walk 7km uphill along a dirt track. On weekends, it's possible to hitch a lift with bogotano tourists.

Boyacá, Santander & Norte de Santander

The three departments of Boyacá, Santander and Norte de Santander cover the part of the Cordillera Oriental to the north of Bogotá. The region offers a variety of landscapes, from fertile green valleys, such as the Valle de Tenza (southern Boyacá), to the arid Cañón del Chicamocha (Santander) and the snowy peaks of the Sierra Nevada del Cocuy (northern Boyacá).

Once the territory of the Muiscas (Boyacá) and the Guane Indians (central Santander), the region was one of the first to be explored and settled by the Spaniards. There are many well-preserved colonial towns in the region; Villa de Leyva, Barichara and Girón are among the best.

Of the three departments, Boyacá is perhaps the safest, easiest and most pleasant in which to travel. It is also the most traditional province, widely known for its handicrafts, particularly pottery, basketwork and weaving.

TUNJA

Tunja, the capital of Boyacá, was founded in 1539 on the site of Hunza, the pre-Hispanic Muisca seat. Though almost nothing is left of the Indian period, much colonial architecture remains. The central sector was restored for the town's 450-year anniversary and many historic public buildings have recovered their original splendor. Tunja is a city of churches: Several imposing examples from the 16th century stand almost untouched by time.

Information

Tourist Office The municipal tourist office (☎ 87-423272) is in the Casa del Fundador, on Plaza de Bolívar. It's open 8 am to noon and 2 to 6 pm weekdays.

Money Banks in Tunja won't change cash. Try the Joyería Francesa or Agencia de Viajes Roka, which may buy US dollars. Only the Banco de Bogotá exchanges traveler's checks (morning only). All banks marked on the map give cash advances on Visa and MasterCard.

Things to See

The **Casa del Fundador Suárez Rendón** (house of the founder of Tunja) and **Casa de Don Juan de Vargas** have both been converted into colonial art museums. The ceilings in both houses are covered with intriguing paintings featuring human figures, animals and plants, coats of arms and mythological scenes. A similar ceiling can be

COLOMBIA

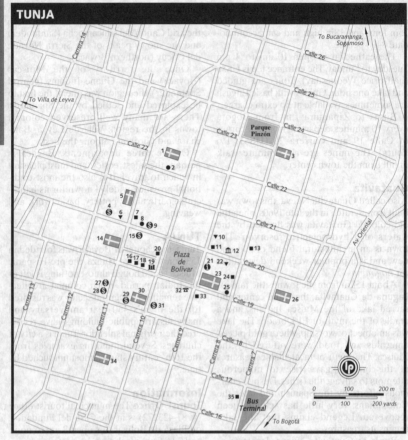

TUNJA

seen in the **Casa de Don Juan de Castellanos**, now the public library.

Among the churches, **Santo Domingo** and **Santa Clara La Real** are the most beautiful and richly decorated. The latter is also a museum. Also worth a visit are the churches of **Santa Bárbara** and **San Francisco** and the **Catedral**. Tunja's churches are noted for their Mudejar art, an Islamic-influenced style which developed in Christian Spain between the 12th and 16th centuries. It is particularly visible in the ornamented, coffered vaults.

Places to Stay

Tunja sits at an altitude of about 2800m and has a cool climate; you'll need warm clothing, especially at night. Not all cheap hotels provide enough blankets. Ask for more if

you think you might get frozen solid. Another problem of local cheapies (and even some of the mid-range hotels) is that they have erratic hot water supply, usually only for a few hours in the morning.

There are several basic hotels close to the bus terminal, of which **Hotel Príncipe** (☎ 87-403580), Carrera 7 No 16-47, is possibly the best, for US$4 a bed.

It's more pleasant, although more expensive, to stay in the heart of the city, around Plaza de Bolívar. The cheapest there is the very simple **Hotel Don Camilo** (☎ 87-426574), on the west side of the plaza, which costs US$6/10/15 per single/double/triple without bath.

The cheapest central option with private bath is **Hotel Lord** (☎ 87-423556), Calle 19

TUNJA

PLACES TO STAY
7 Hostería San Carlos
11 Hotel Conquistador
13 Hotel Casa Colonial
16 Hotel Dux
17 Hotel Lord
18 Hotel Saboy
20 Hotel Don Camilo
24 Hostería Pila del Mono
33 Hotel San Francisco
35 Hotel Príncipe

PLACES TO EAT
6 Restaurante Estar de
   Hunzohua

10 Restaurante El Maizal
22 Restaurante Pila del Mono

OTHER
1 Iglesia de San Francisco
2 Agencia de Viajes Roka
3 Iglesia de San Agustín
4 Banco Popular
5 Iglesia de Santa Clara La
   Antigua
8 Joyería Francesa
9 Banco de Bogotá
12 Casa de Don Juan de Vargas
14 Iglesia de Santo Domingo
15 Banco Industrial Colombiano

19 Casa de la Cultura
21 Tourist Office & Casa del
    Fundador Suárez Rendón
23 Catedral
25 Casa de Don Juan de
    Castellanos
26 Iglesia de Santa Clara La Real
27 Bancafé
28 Banco del Estado
29 Banco de Occidente
30 Iglesia de San Ignacio
31 Banco Santander
32 Telecom
34 Iglesia de Santa Bárbara

No 10-64, which has clean but dark singles/doubles/triples for US$7/15/17. *Hotel Saboy* (☎ 87-423492) and *Hotel Dux* (☎ 87-425736), on either side of the Lord, offer much the same but are more expensive. In the same class is *Hotel San Francisco* (☎ 87-426645), Carrera 9 No 18-90, which costs US$12/20/26 with bath.

For something a bit nicer, try *Hotel Casa Colonial* (☎ 87-422169), Carrera 8 No 20-40 (US$18/28 a single/double); *Hostería San Carlos* (☎ 87-423716), Carrera 11 No 20-12 (US$20/28); *Hotel Conquistador* (☎ 87-431465), Calle 20 No 8-92 (US$22/32); or *Hostería Pila del Mono* (☎ 87-403380), Carrera 8 No 19-67 (US$28/40).

Places to Eat

Plenty of restaurants serve inexpensive set meals, including: *Estar de Hunzohua*, Calle 20 No 11-30; *El Maizal*, Carrera 9 No 20-30; and the restaurant in *Hostería San Carlos*. There are also a number of outlets serving snacks, fast food and chicken. *Pila del Mono*, Calle 20 No 8-19, is one of the better restaurants in the central area.

Getting There & Away

The bus terminal is on Av Oriental, a short walk southeast of the Plaza de Bolívar. There are frequent buses to Bogotá (US$6, 2½ to three hours) and Bucaramanga (US$17, seven hours). Buses to Villa de Leyva (US$2, one hour) leave every couple of hours. For marginally more, you can get there faster by colectivo; they also depart from the terminal and are more frequent than buses.

VILLA DE LEYVA

This small colonial town, founded in 1572, remains largely unspoiled, and is one of the finest architectural gems in the country. As it lies relatively close to the capital, it has become a trendy weekend spot for bogotanos. This has made the town somewhat artificial, with a noticeably split personality – on weekdays, it is a sleepy, lethargic village, but on weekends and holidays it comes alive, crammed with tourists and their cars. It's up to you to choose which of the town's faces you prefer, but don't miss it.

Information

Tourist Office The tourist office (☎ 87-320232), at the east corner of the main square, is open 8 am to 1 pm and 2 to 5 pm Tuesday to Saturday, and 9 am to 1 pm and 2 to 4 pm on Sunday.

Money Traveler's checks are useless in Villa de Leyva. Probably the only place you can change cash (at a poor rate) is the Miscelánea, the shop a few doors from the parish church. The Banco Popular, on the main square, may give advances on Visa cards.

Things to See

The **Plaza Mayor**, an impressive central square, is paved with massive cobblestones and lined with whitewashed colonial houses. The **parish church**, on the square, and the **Iglesia del Carmen**, a block northeast, both have interesting interiors. Next to the latter is a museum of religious art, the **Museo del Carmen**, open weekends only.

COLOMBIA

The **Museo de Luis Alberto Acuña**, on the main square, features various works of the painter, sculptor, writer and historian. Other museums worth visiting include the **Casa de Antonio Nariño**, in the house where the forefather of independence lived; the **Casa de Antonio Ricaurte**, the home of another national hero; and the **Museo Paleontológico**, 1km northeast of town on the road to Arcabuco, displaying fossils dating from the period when the area was a seabed (100 to 150 million years ago). Most local museums are open roughly 10 am to 1 pm and 3 to 5 pm Wednesday to Sunday.

Give yourself a couple of hours to wander about the charming cobbled streets and to climb the hill behind the Hospedería Duruelo for a marvelous bird's-eye view of the town. Inspect handicrafts shops noted for fine basketry and good-quality woven items, such as sweaters and *ruanas* (ponchos). The colorful Saturday **market**, on Carrera 6, is best early in the morning.

Places to Stay

The town has more than two dozen places to stay, and most hotels, particularly the upmarket ones, are stylish and pleasant. Accommodation becomes limited on weekends, and can fill up completely on puentes and during Easter week, despite the fact that the prices tend to rise, sometimes significantly, at these times.

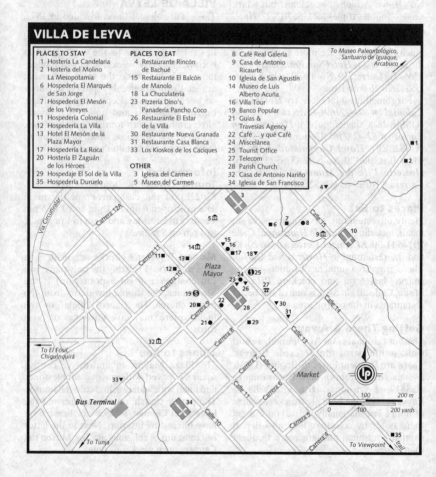

VILLA DE LEYVA

PLACES TO STAY
1 Hostería La Candelaria
2 Hostería del Molino La Mesopotamia
6 Hospedería El Marqués de San Jorge
7 Hospedería El Mesón de los Virreyes
11 Hospedería Colonial
12 Hospedería La Villa
13 Hotel El Mesón de la Plaza Mayor
17 Hospedería La Roca
20 Hostería El Zaguán de los Héroes
29 Hospedaje El Sol de la Villa
35 Hospedería Duruelo

PLACES TO EAT
4 Restaurante Rincón de Bachué
15 Restaurante El Balcón de Manolo
18 La Chuculatería
23 Pizzería Dino's, Panadería Pancho Coco
26 Restaurante El Estar de la Villa
30 Restaurante Nueva Granada
31 Restaurante Casa Blanca
33 Los Kioskos de los Caciques

OTHER
3 Iglesia del Carmen
5 Museo del Carmen
8 Café Real Galería
9 Casa de Antonio Ricaurte
10 Iglesia de San Agustín
14 Museo de Luis Alberto Acuña
16 Villa Tour
19 Banco Popular
21 Guías & Travesías Agency
22 Café ... y qué Café
24 Miscelánea
25 Tourist Office
27 Telecom
28 Parish Office
32 Casa de Antonio Nariño
34 Iglesia de San Francisco

To Museo Paleontológico, Santuario de Iguaque, Arcabuco

Plaza Mayor

Market

Bus Terminal

To El Fósil, Chiquinquirá

To Tunja

To Viewpoint

0   100   200 m
0   100   200 yards

The cheapest place in town is the basic *Hospedería La Villa* (☎ 87-320416), on the west corner of the main square. It has rooms of varying quality, so have a look before paying. The price is US$6 per person, but it's negotiable, especially if you come in a larger party on weekdays.

The revamped *Hospedería Colonial*, a few steps from La Villa on Calle 12, offers slightly better standards, but charges US$10 per person in rooms with bath; bargaining also is possible here.

Hospedería La Roca (☎ 87-320331), on the main square, has a nice patio but otherwise isn't significantly better than the Colonial, and it charges US$20/25/40 a single/double/triple with bath.

Better is *Hospedaje El Sol de la Villa* (☎ 87-320224), Carrera 8 No 12-28. Neat rooms with bath and TV cost US$15 per person (US$18 on weekends), breakfast included.

More upmarket, there is a range of charming hotels, most of which are set in colonial mansions with flower-filled patios. One of the cheapest is *Hospedería El Marqués de San Jorge* (☎ 87-320240), costing US$20 per person. If you are willing to pay up to US$60 for a double, check *Hostería La Candelaria* (☎ 87-320534), *Hotel El Mesón de la Plaza Mayor* (☎ 87-320425), *Hospedería El Mesón de los Virreyes* (☎ 87-320252) or *Hostería El Zaguán de los Héroes* (☎ 87-320476).

At the top are *Hostería del Molino La Mesopotamia* (☎ 87-320235), in a lovely 400-year-old flour mill, and the beautifully maintained hacienda-style *Hospedería Duruelo* (☎ 87-320222).

Places to Eat

Villa de Leyva has a fair choice of restaurants, but some don't open on weekdays. *El Estar de la Villa* and *Nueva Granada* serve some of the cheapest set meals (US$2.50). Other budget restaurants include *Casa Blanca* and *Los Kioskos de los Caciques*. *El Balcón de Manolo* also has inexpensive food and the balcony overlooking the plaza is a nice place for a cold beer. *Rincón de Bachué* is a pleasant place for the comida típica. *La Chuculatería* serves hearty food, including good salads.

Among the hotel restaurants, you might want to try those in *La Candelaria* (Spanish

cuisine), *La Mesopotamia* and *El Duruelo*. All are good but expensive.

Panadería Pancho Coco, next to the parish church, has good pasteles and other pastries. *Pizzería Dino's*, next door, serves pizza and spaghetti. For a decent cup of coffee try *Café…y qué Café* or *Café Real Galería*.

Getting There & Away

There are several direct buses daily to Bogotá (US$8, four hours). There are some buses to Tunja, but colectivos ply this route more frequently (US$2.50, 45 minutes). The bus terminal is southwest of the plaza on the Tunja road.

AROUND VILLA DE LEYVA

Villa de Leyva is a good jumping-off place for short excursions around the surrounding region, which is noted for a variety of attractions and is a great place for fossil hunting.

You can move around the area on foot, using some local buses. The Villa Tour agency, on the main square in Villa de Leyva, runs tours in chivas, an easy way of visit local sights. Tours depart on weekends, and by request on weekdays if there are at least six people.

The Guías & Travesías agency (☎ 87-321384), Carrera 8A No 11-59 in Villa de Leyva, also organizes tours (which cover all the sights listed below) and rents bicycles (US$2/12 per hour/day).

El Fósil

This is a reasonably complete fossil of a kronosaurus, a 120-million-year-old prehistoric marine reptile vaguely resembling a crocodile. It is off the road to Chiquinquirá, 6km east of Villa de Leyva. You can walk there by a path in one hour, or the Chiquinquirá bus will drop you 1km from El Fósil.

El Infiernito

About 2km north of El Fósil, this Muisca astronomic observatory was also a ritual site, notable for a number of large, phallic stone monoliths.

Convento del Santo Ecce Homo

This convent, 13km from Villa de Leyva, was founded in 1620. It's a large stone and adobe construction with a lovely courtyard. The colectivo to Santa Sofía will drop you within a 15-minute walk of the convent.

Ráquira

A small village 25km southwest of Villa de Leyva, Ráquira is known countrywide for its quality pottery, everything from kitchen utensils to copies of indigenous pots. There are a number of small workshops in the village, where you can watch the production process. Most of the houses have been painted in bright colors, which gives the village much life and charm. There are two hotels on the main square (neither is very cheap) and a couple of restaurants.

Two or three buses run daily from Villa de Leyva to Ráquira (US$2, 30 minutes). The morning bus returns to Villa de Leyva around noon, giving you several hours to look around. A return taxi trip from Villa de Leyva can be arranged for around US$15 (up to five people), allowing a couple of hours in Ráquira.

La Candelaria

This tiny hamlet, 7km beyond Ráquira, is noted for the Monasterio de la Candelaria, founded in 1597 by the Augustinians. Part of it is open to the public; the monks will show you around. The *Parador La Candelaria*, close to the monastery, is a nice (but not cheap) place to stay and eat. Only two buses a day call at La Candelaria. Otherwise, walk by a shortcut from Ráquira (one hour).

Santuario de Iguaque

About 15km northeast of Villa de Leyva, at an altitude of some 3600m, is a group of eight small lakes, including the Laguna de Iguaque, which the Muiscas considered sacred. The area is now a nature reserve. The visitor center, a couple of km off the Villa de Leyva-Arcabuco road, offers accommodation for about US$13 per person and collects the US$5 reserve entrance fee. From the center, it's a leisurely three-hour walk uphill to Laguna de Iguaque.

SAN GIL

This 300-year-old town on the Bogotá-Bucaramanga road may deserve a stop to see El Gallineral, a riverside park where the trees are covered with *barbas de viejo*, long silvery fronds of tillandsia that form spectacular transparent curtains of foliage. San Gil also has a pleasant main square with huge old ceibas and an 18th-century cathedral.

If you stop in San Gil, be sure to make the short trip to Barichara, a beautiful small colonial town (see the next section). You may also take a trip to the village of Curití, 12km northeast of San Gil, known for its 17th-century church and the Quebrada Curití, a mountain-like river with waterfalls and ponds to swim in.

Places to Stay & Eat

There are several cheap residencias in the center, including *San Gil*, at Carrera 11 No 11-25, and *Villas del Oriente*, at Calle 10 No 10-47, where you shouldn't pay more than US$5 per person. If you need something better, *Hostal Isla Señoral*, at Calle 10 No 8-14, has comfortable singles/doubles/triples with bath and TV for US$16/24/30.

Plenty of budget restaurants around the residencias serve basic meals. There's an agreeable restaurant in the park of El Gallineral, with typical food at reasonable prices.

Getting There & Away

The bus terminal is 2km west of the town center, and is linked to it by half-hourly urban buses. Frequent air-conditioned buses run south to Bogotá (US$18, 7½ hours) and north to Bucaramanga (US$5, 2½ hours). There are also half-hourly minibuses to Bucaramanga (US$6, two hours). Buses to Barichara leave every hour or two from the bus terminal and call at the company office at Carrera 10 No 14-82, in the town center.

BARICHARA

This well preserved small colonial town was founded on Guane Indian territory 250 years ago. The streets are paved with massive stone slabs and lined with fine whitewashed single-story houses. There are some sights, including a few churches and a small museum, but the town's charm lies rather in its beauty as a whole, and its easygoing, old-world atmosphere.

From Barichara, you might want to visit the tiny old village of Guane, 10km to the northwest, where time seems to have frozen a century or two ago. It has a fine rural church and a museum with a collection of fossils and Guane Indian artifacts. There's no reliable transport except for the morning milk truck, so you may have to walk by road (a good two hours) or by the path (half an hour shorter).

Places to Stay & Eat

There are several hotels in Barichara, including *Coratá*, Carrera 7 No 4-02, *Bahía Chalá*, Calle 7 No 7-61, and *Posada Real*, Carrera 6 No 4-69. All charge about US$8 to US$10 per person, and have their own restaurants. There are a couple of other budget restaurants around the square and some locals rent out rooms in their houses, which may be cheaper than staying in hotels. Check the homes of *Rosario García*, Calle 10 No 7-46; *Jairo Pinto*, Carrera 3A No 6-31; and *Vitelma*, Calle 7 No 5-38.

The *Hostal Misión Santa Bárbara*, Calle 5 No 9-12, offers more comfortable accommodations in a tastefully refurbished colonial house; meals are available for guests.

Getting There & Away

There are several buses daily between Barichara and San Gil (US$1.25, 45 minutes).

BUCARAMANGA

Bucaramanga, the capital of Santander, is a fairly modern, busy commercial and industrial center with an agreeable climate. It is noted for its cigars and the *hormiga culona*, a large ant that is fried and eaten.

There is not much to do here, but it may be a stopover on the long route from Bogotá to the coast or Cúcuta. If so, take a side trip to Girón, 10km away (see the next section).

Information

Tourist Office The tourist office, the Secretaría de Cultura y Turismo (☎ 7-643-0947, 7-643-3139) is at Calle 48 No 27A-48, piso 2.

Money Banks which might deal with your cash, traveler's checks and credit cards (Visa or MasterCard) are marked on the map; they are within a small central area.

Things to See

You can visit the **Casa de Bolívar**, which contains ethnographic and historic collections (closed on Sunday and Monday), and have a walk in the **Jardín Botánico Eloy Valenzuela**, in the suburb of Bucarica (open daily). To get there, take the Bucarica bus from Carrera 15 in the city center.

Places to Stay

Budget accommodation is centered near the Parque Centenario, particularly on Calle 31 between Carreras 19 and 22, where you'll be able to find a single/double for below US$6/8. They are mostly basic, but some have private baths. One of the better cheapies is *Hotel Elena* (☎ 7-642-8845), Carrera 21 No 30-55 (US$5 for a single without bath, US$9 for a double with bath).

If the Elena is full (as often happens), try *Residencias ABC* (☎ 7-633-7352), Calle 31 No 21-44, or *Residencias Amparo* (☎ 7-630-4098), Calle 31 No 20-29, both just around the corner and costing the same.

For somewhere a bit flashier, try *Hotel Balmoral* (☎ 7-642-6232), Carrera 21 No 34-85, which is pleasant and friendly. Singles/doubles/triples with private bath and hot water are US$14/18/24. Alternatively, consider *Hotel Morgan No 2* (☎ 7-642-4732), Calle 35 No 18-83, just off the Parque Santander, which has ample rooms for US$16/22/28; choose one with a window facing the street.

If you want somewhere upmarket, choose between *Hotel Bucarica* (☎ 7-630-1592), overlooking Parque Santander, and *Hotel Chicamocha* (☎ 7-634-3000), Calle 34 No 31-24, in the more easygoing residential district, 1km to the east.

Places to Eat

There are plenty of cheap restaurants around, or attached to, the budget hotels, where you can grab a set meal for US$2. There are few remarkable restaurants in the city center, save perhaps the expensive one in Hotel Bucarica. At more affordable prices are *El Paisa*, Carrera 21 No 36-28, and *El Consulado Antioqueño*, Carrera 19 No 33-81, both serving local and Antioquian food.

A better area for dining is the eastern sector of the city, particularly on and around Carreras 27 and 33, where you'll find some of the best of the city eateries. Try, for example, *La Pampa*, Carrera 27 No 42-27, serving Argentine food, or the *Casona de Chiflas*, Carrera 33 at Calle 36, for its parrillada and other meat dishes.

On weekend evenings, stroll around the Hotel Chicamocha, where a string of live music bars and discos attract young locals.

COLOMBIA

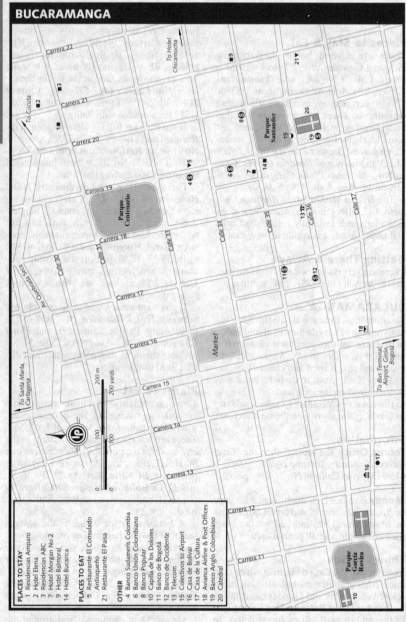

BUCARAMANGA

PLACES TO STAY
1 Residencias Amparo
2 Hotel Elena
3 Residencias ABC
9 Hotel Morgan No 2
9 Hotel Balmoral
14 Hotel Bucarica

PLACES TO EAT
5 Restaurante El Consulado Antioqueño
21 Restaurante El Paisa

OTHER
4 Banco Sudameris Colombia
6 Banco Unión Colombiano
8 Banco Popular
10 Capilla de los Dolores
11 Banco de Bogotá
12 Banco de Occidente
13 Telecom
15 Colectivos to Airport
16 Casa de Bolívar
17 Casa de la Cultura
18 Avianca Airline & Post Offices
19 Banco Anglo Colombiano
20 Catedral

Parque García Rovira

Parque Centenario

Parque Santander

Market

Carrera 22
Carrera 21
Carrera 20
Carrera 19
Carrera 18
Carrera 17
Carrera 16
Carrera 15
Carrera 14
Carrera 13
Carrera 12
Carrera 11

Calle 30
Calle 31
Calle 33
Calle 34
Calle 35
Calle 36
Calle 37

AV Quebrada Seca

To Cúcuta
To Santa Marta, Cartagena
To Hotel Chicamocha
To Bus Terminal, Airport, Girón, Bogotá

0   100   200 m
0   100   200 yards

Getting There & Away

Air The Palonegro airport is on a meseta high above the city, off the Barrancabermeja road. The landing here is breathtaking. Local buses marked 'Aeropuerto' link the airport and the city center every hour or two; you catch them on Carrera 15. It's much faster to go by colectivo (US$2.50), which park in the Parque Santander, opposite the cathedral. There are flights to some major Colombian cities, including Bogotá (US$75) and Medellín (US$85).

Bus Bucaramanga's bus terminal is quite a distance southwest of the center, off the road to Girón, but you can get there easily by frequent city buses marked 'Terminal,' which you wave down on Carrera 15. There are plenty of air-conditioned buses to Bogotá (US$22, 10 hours), Cartagena (US$32, 13 hours), Cúcuta (US$12, six hours) and Santa Marta (US$24, nine hours).

GIRÓN

Girón is a pretty old town 10km southwest of Bucaramanga. It was founded in 1631 and has preserved much of its colonial character. It's a nice place to stroll around looking at the fine houses, charming patios and a few small bridges. The Plazuela Peralta and Plazuela de las Nieves are among its most enchanting spots.

Girón has become a trendy place, and is home to some intellectuals and artists. Due to its proximity to the city, the town fills up with *bumangueses* on weekends.

Places to Stay & Eat

Girón is a short trip from Bucaramanga, but if you wish to stay longer there is the good if expensive *Hotel Las Nieves* (☎ 7-646-8968), on the main square. A cheaper alternative is the *Hotel Río de Oro*, also on the plaza.

Antón García, Calle 29 No 24-47, and *El Carajo*, Carrera 25 No 28-08, serve cheap meals. More upmarket are *La Casona*, Calle 28 No 27-47, and *Mansión del Fraile*, on the main square, both pleasant and serving hearty, typical food. On weekends, riverside stalls offer a choice of regional dishes.

Getting There & Away

There are frequent city buses from Carrera 15 in Bucaramanga, which will deposit you at Girón's main square in half an hour.

CÚCUTA

Cúcuta is a hot, uninspiring city of around half a million people. It's the capital of Norte de Santander and a busy commercial center, fueled by its proximity to Venezuela, just 12km away. The city doesn't have significant tourist attractions, so unless you're en route to or from Venezuela, there's little reason to visit.

Information

Tourist Office The tourist office (☎ 75-713395) is at Calle 10 No 0-30.

Money No banks in Cúcuta will change cash dollars, but there are plenty of casas de cambio, including a dozen at the bus terminal and a number in the center. They all change dollars, pesos and bolívares. There's also a rash of casas de cambio in San Antonio (on the Venezuela side of the border), paying much the same as those in Cúcuta.

Only a few of Cúcuta's banks, including the Banco del Estado and Bancolombia, change traveler's checks. Other banks marked on the map give advances on Visa or MasterCard (available from the bank's ATM or the cashier).

Venezuelan Consulate The consulate (☎ 75-780797, 75-781034) is on Av Camilo Daza (the road that goes to the airport), about 3km north of the center. You can get there with local buses marked 'Consulado' from the bus terminal or from Calle 13 in the center. The consulate issues free tourist cards for nationals who don't need visas, but not visas for those who need one.

Immigration The DAS post (where you get an exit/entry stamp in your passport) is just before the frontier on the Río Táchira, on the left side of the road going toward Venezuela. The office is open 7:30 am to noon and 2 to 6:30 pm daily. You can also have your passport stamped in the main DAS office in Cúcuta, Av 1 No 28-57, San Rafael suburb, but it's less convenient.

Things to See

If you have a couple of hours to spare, visit the **Museo de Arte e Historia de Cúcuta** (closed Sunday and Monday), Calle 14 No 1-03, which has a private collection of objects relating to the town's history.

COLOMBIA

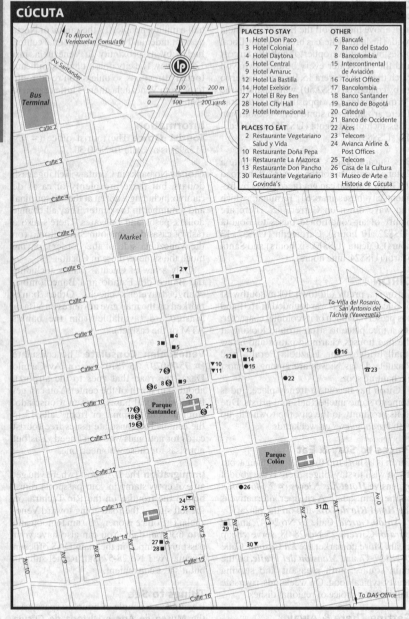

CÚCUTA

To Airport,
Venezuelan Consulate

Av Santander

Bus
Terminal

Calle 2

Calle 3

Calle 4

Calle 5

Market

Calle 6

Calle 7

Calle 8

Calle 9

Calle 10

Parque
Santander

Calle 11

Calle 12

Parque
Colón

Calle 13

Calle 14

Calle 15

Calle 16

To Villa del Rosario,
San Antonio del
Táchira (Venezuela)

To DAS Office

0   100   200 m
0   100   200 yards

PLACES TO STAY
1 Hotel Don Paco
3 Hotel Colonial
4 Hotel Daytona
5 Hotel Central
9 Hotel Amaruc
12 Hotel La Bastilla
14 Hotel Exelsior
27 Hotel El Rey Ben
28 Hotel City Hall
29 Hotel Internacional

PLACES TO EAT
2 Restaurante Vegetariano
   Salud y Vida
10 Restaurante Doña Pepa
11 Restaurante La Mazorca
13 Restaurante Don Pancho
30 Restaurante Vegetariano
   Govinda's

OTHER
6 Bancafé
7 Banco del Estado
8 Bancolombia
15 Intercontinental
   de Aviación
16 Tourist Office
17 Bancolombia
18 Banco Santander
19 Banco de Bogotá
20 Catedral
21 Banco de Occidente
22 Aces
23 Telecom
24 Avianca Airline &
   Post Offices
25 Telecom
26 Casa de la Cultura
31 Museo de Arte e
   Historia de Cúcuta

Outside the city, about 10km east of Cúcuta on the road to the border, is **Villa del Rosario**, where the constitution of Gran Colombia was drawn up and passed in 1821. The central park, on the main road, contains several historic buildings, including the Casa de Santander and the Templo del Congreso. The Casa de la Bagatela, across the road, houses a modest archaeological collection.

Places to Stay

There are plenty of residencias around the bus terminal, particularly along Av 7, but they range from basic to ultra-basic and most double as love hotels or brothels. The area is far from attractive and gets dangerous at night. It's safer and more pleasant to stay in the city center, though hotels there are not as cheap. All those listed below have rooms with fans (or air-conditioning where indicated) and private bath.

Among the cheapest central options are *Hotel La Bastilla* (☎ 75-712576), Av 3 No 9-42, *Hotel Daytona* (☎ 75-717927), Av 5 No 8-57, and *Hotel Central* (☎ 75-713673), Av 5 No 8-89. Any of these will cost about US$8/12 a single/double. For a dollar more, you can stay in the more pleasant *Hotel Colonial* (☎ 75-712661), Av 5 No 8-82. Similarly priced is *Hotel Don Paco* (☎ 75-710575), Calle 7 No 4-44, but the surrounding area isn't particularly attractive.

Hotel Internacional (☎ 75-712718), Calle 14 No 4-13, is good value. It has a fine patio, a swimming pool and spacious rooms for US$10 per person. If you want to have air-conditioning, some of the cheapest to offer it are *Hotel City Hall* (☎ 75-726962), Av 6 No 14-38, and *Hotel El Rey Ben* (☎ 75-729678), Av 6 No 14-24. Both have air-conditioned rooms for US$15/18/20 a single/double/triple, and also some cheaper rooms with fan (US$12/14/16).

Hotel Amaruc (☎ 75-717625), overlooking the main square from the corner of Av 5 and Calle 10, is an option for those who don't need to count every peso. It has singles/doubles/triples with air-conditioning for US$30/35/40. *Hotel Exelsior* (☎ 75-730862), Av 3 No 9-65, provides similar standards for the same price.

Places to Eat

Acceptable set meals and other dishes are served at *La Mazorca*, Av 9 No 9-67, *Don Pancho*, Av 3 No 9-21, and *El Chócolo*, Av 2E No 13-12. *Doña Pepa*, Av 4 No 9-57, specializes in typical Colombian food. For vegetarians, *Salud y Vida*, on Av 4, and *Govinda's*, at Calle 15 No 3-48, are good budget lunch places. There are a number of more upmarket restaurants in town.

Getting There & Away

Air The airport is 4km north of the center; city buses, which you catch on Av 3 in the center, will drop you nearby. There are flights to most major Colombian cities, including Bogotá (US$92), Cartagena (US$118) and Medellín (US$85). Cheaper fares may be found sometimes.

There are no direct flights to Venezuela – you must go to San Antonio, the Venezuelan border town, 12km from Cúcuta. See San Antonio del Táchira in the Venezuela chapter.

Bus The bus terminal is on the corner of Av 7 and Calle 1. It's very dirty and very busy – one of the poorest in Colombia. Watch your belongings closely. If you are arriving from Venezuela, you may be approached by well-dressed English-speaking characters who will kindly offer their help in buying bus tickets. They may also advise that you need to insure your cash and invite you to 'their office.' Ignore them – they are con men. Buy tickets directly from company offices.

There are frequent buses to Bucaramanga (US$12, six hours). At least a dozen air-con buses daily run to Bogotá (US$32, 16 hours). There are also direct air-con buses to Cartagena (US$44) and Medellín (US$38).

Heading to Venezuela, take one of the frequent buses or shared taxis that run from Cúcuta's bus terminal to San Antonio (US$0.30 and US$0.50 respectively, paid in either pesos or bolívares). You can also catch colectivos and buses to San Antonio from the corner of Av 0 and Calle 8, closer to the center. Don't forget to get off just before the bridge to have your passport stamped at DAS.

Caribbean Coast

The Colombian Caribbean coast stretches more than 1760km from the dense jungles of the Darién Gap, on the border with Panama, to the desert of La Guajira in the east, near

Venezuela. To the south, the region extends to the foot of the Andes. Administratively, the area falls into the departments of La Guajira, Cesar, Magdalena, Atlántico, Bolívar, Sucre and Córdoba, plus the northern tips of Antioquia and Chocó.

The coast is steeped in sun, rum and tropical music. Its inhabitants, the costeños, are an easygoing, fun-loving people who give the coast a touch of carnival atmosphere.

Special attractions include Cartagena, one of the most beautiful colonial cities in Latin America, and the town of Mompós, a small architectural gem. You can take it easy on the beach – some of the best are in the Parque Nacional Tayrona – or go snorkeling or scuba diving amid the magnificent coral reefs of the Islas del Rosario. There's also Ciudad Perdida, the pre-Hispanic lost city of the Tayrona Indians, hidden deep in the lush tropical forest on the slopes of the Sierra Nevada de Santa Marta.

SANTA MARTA

Founded in 1525, Santa Marta is the oldest surviving town in Colombia, though its colonial character has virtually disappeared. The climate is hot, but the sea breeze, especially in the evening, cools the city and makes it pleasant to wander about, or to sit over a beer in any of the numerous open-air waterfront cafés.

Santa Marta has become a popular tourist center, not for the city itself but because of its surroundings. Nearby El Rodadero is one of Colombia's most fashionable beach resorts, though it's being dangerously polluted by the Santa Marta port. Most visitors to the city take trips to Taganga and the Parque Nacional Tayrona. Santa Marta is also the place to arrange a tour to Ciudad Perdida.

Information

Tourist Offices The Etursa city tourist office (☎ 54-211295) is on the corner of Calle 19 and Carrera 2A. The departmental tourist office (☎ 54-211167) is in the former Convent of Santo Domingo at Carrera 2 No 16-44. Both offices are open 8 am to noon and 2 to 6 pm weekdays.

Money The Banco Santander and Bancolombia change traveler's checks and cash. Before you change your dollars here,

however, check the casas de cambio, which may give comparable rates and save long waits in banks. There are plenty of casas de cambio in the bank area, especially on Calle 14 between Carreras 3 and 4. All banks marked on the map give advances on Visa or MasterCard, and some of them have ATMs.

Internet Access Compucesco (☎ 54-232640), Calle 15 No 7-93, is the most central option.

Things to See

The **Museo Arqueológico Tayrona** (closed weekends), in the Casa de la Aduana on the corner of Calle 14 and Carrera 2, features a good collection of Tayrona objects, mainly pottery and gold. Don't miss the model of Ciudad Perdida, especially if you plan on visiting the real thing.

The **Quinta de San Pedro Alejandrino**, the hacienda where Simón Bolívar spent his last days and died, is today a national monument. You can visit the house, arranged in the style of Bolívar's days, and the old *trapiche* (sugarcane mill). There are also a few monuments built on the grounds in remembrance of Bolívar, and the **Museo Bolivariano**, which features contemporary works of art donated by artists from Colombia, Venezuela, Panama, Ecuador, Peru and Bolivia, the countries liberated by Bolívar. The Quinta is in the far suburb of Mamatoco (take the Mamatoco bus from the waterfront to get there), and is open daily (may be closed on Tuesday in the off season); entry is US$3.50.

The **Catedral**, a large whitewashed building on the corner of Carrera 4 and Calle 17, is supposedly the oldest church in Colombia, but work was not actually completed until the end of the 18th century. It holds the ashes of the town's founder, Rodrigo de Bastidas (just to the left of the entrance).

Organized Tours

Santa Marta's tour market revolves principally around Ciudad Perdida and the Parque Nacional Tayrona (see those sections). Tours to Ciudad Perdida are monopolized by Turcol (☎ 54-212256), Carrera 1C No 22-79. You can book and pay for the tour through some hotels (eg, the Hotel Miramar or Casa Familiar), which will then transfer your application and payment to

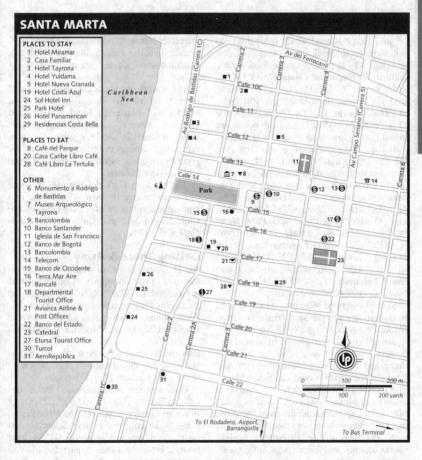

SANTA MARTA

PLACES TO STAY
1 Hotel Miramar
2 Casa Familiar
3 Hotel Tayrona
4 Hotel Yuldama
5 Hotel Nueva Granada
19 Hotel Costa Azul
24 Sol Hotel Inn
25 Park Hotel
26 Hotel Panamerican
29 Residencias Costa Bella

PLACES TO EAT
8 Café del Parque
20 Casa Caribe Libro Café
28 Café Libro La Tertulia

OTHER
6 Monumento a Rodrigo de Bastidas
7 Museo Arqueológico Tayrona
9 Bancolombia
10 Banco Santander
11 Iglesia de San Francisco
12 Banco de Bogotá
13 Bancolombia
14 Telecom
15 Banco de Occidente
16 Tierra Mar Aire
17 Bancafé
18 Departmental Tourist Office
21 Avianca Airline & Post Offices
22 Banco del Estado
23 Catedral
27 Etursa Tourist Office
30 Turcol
31 AeroRepública

Turcol. Tours to the Parque Nacional Tayrona are run by several operators, of which the Hotel Miramar is the cheapest.

Places to Stay

There are plenty of hotels throughout the city center, and their prices are reasonable. All places listed below have rooms with fan, unless specified otherwise.

Hotel Miramar (☎ 54-214756), Calle 10C No 1C-59, provides the cheapest accommodations in town (US$3.50/6 a single/double without bath, US$5/8 with bath), or you can string up your hammock for US$2. The hotel has a café serving meals, snacks, soft drinks and beer. The place has long been the archetypal gringo hotel, with a hippie-type atmosphere, but if you find it too noisy or freak-filled, go to *Casa Familiar* (☎ 54-211697), a few steps away at Calle 10C No 2-14. It's quieter, costs US$7/12 a single/double with bath, US$4 a bed in a dorm without bath, and serves meals. The place is also frequented by backpackers and the staff are friendly.

For somewhere with a more individual style, try *Hotel Tayrona* (☎ 54-212408), Carrera 1C No 11-41, in an old house with a fine wooden interior and beautiful tiling. It costs US$8 per person in rooms with bath. You might also consider the quiet and well-kept *Hotel Nueva Granada* (☎ (54-211337), Calle 12 No 3-17, which costs US$7/12/16 a single/double/triple in rooms with bath overlooking a spacious flowered patio.

There's also a choice of budget accommodation farther south, around Calles 17 and 18, in a pleasant area which has preserved some of its colonial appearance, yet few travelers stay here. The budget hotels here include *Residencias Costa Bella* (☎ *54-213169)*, at Calle 18 No 3-93, asking US$7/10/12 a single/double/triple with bath, and *Hotel Costa Azul* (☎ *54-212236)*, Calle 17 No 2-09, for US$10/12/16. Both hotels are in old houses arranged around leafy patios.

If you need somewhere with a view over the sea (particularly attractive at sunset), there are several modern hotels on the waterfront (Carrera 1C). In ascending order of price and value they are *Sol Hotel Inn* (☎ *54-211131)*, Carrera 1C No 20-23 (US$16/20/24 a single/double/triple with bath); *Park Hotel* (☎ *54-211215)*, at Carrera 1C No 18-67 (US$22/28/32); *Hotel Panamerican* (☎ *54-214751)*, Carrera 1C No 18-23 (US$24/35/45 with fan, US$35/46/60 with air-con); and *Hotel Yuldama* (☎ *54-210063)*, Carrera 1C No 12-19 (US$40/54/66 with air-con).

Should you need somewhere budget in El Rodadero, try the pleasant *Hostería Tima-Uraka* (☎ *54-228433)*, Calle 18 No 2-59.

Should you want to escape from heat and people altogether and relax for a while, there are two lovely places high on the slopes of the Sierra Nevada de Santa Marta. The German-run *Hospedaje Las Piedras* is at 700m in Minca, 35km southeast of Santa Marta. Pickup trucks depart from the city's market every hour or two (US$1, 45 minutes). The hospedaje offers budget rooms, dorms and hammocks, plus meals and the use of the kitchen. It's a good place to relax, walk, rent a mountain bike or ride horses or mules. Information is available from the Casa Natalie (☎ 5-656-4857) in Cartagena.

The other place, Belgian-run *Finca Carpe Diem* is an ecological farm at 600m above sea level, 15km from Santa Marta by a partly rough road. It also provides accommodation and meals (made mostly from products raised on the farm) and is a good place to take it easy while walking, horseback riding and bird watching. There's no public transport all the way to the farm; you need to walk a fair bit. You can get more information from the Hotel Casa Francesa (☎ *54-234002)* in Taganga.

Places to Eat

There are a lot of cheap restaurants around the Hotel Miramar, particularly on Calles 11 and 12 near the waterfront, where you can get an unsophisticated set meal for about US$2.

The waterfront is packed with cafés and restaurants offering almost anything from snacks and pizzas to local cuisine and seafood. Several thatched restaurants between Calles 26 and 28, south of the town center and close to the beach, are noted for good fish. Choose between *Terraza Marina* and *El Gran Manuel*.

The open-air *Café del Parque* has some of the best coffee in town. Also try the two enjoyable arty cafés *Café Libro La Tertulia*, Calle 18 No 2-82, and *Casa Caribe Libro Café*, Calle 17 No 2-29.

Getting There & Away

Air The airport is 16km south of the city on the road to Barranquilla. City buses marked 'El Rodadero Aeropuerto' will take you there in 45 minutes from Carrera 1C. Avianca and AeroRepública have flights to Bogotá (US$118) and Medellín (US$102).

Bus The terminal is on the southeastern outskirts of the city. Frequent minibuses go there from Carrera 1C in the center.

Half a dozen air-conditioned buses run daily to Bogotá (US$45, 16 hours). Plenty of buses go to Barranquilla (US$3.50 ordinary, US$4.50 air-con; two hours). Some air-con buses go direct to Cartagena (US$9, four hours). Frequent buses depart for Maicao (US$11, four hours), where you change for a colectivo or bus to Maracaibo (Venezuela); go early.

AROUND SANTA MARTA
Taganga

Taganga is a small fishing village set in a beautiful bay, 5km north of Santa Marta and easily accessible by frequent minibuses from Carrera 1C. The village's beach is packed with boats and open-air cafés blasting out music at full volume. Boat excursions along the coast are offered by locals, or you can walk around the surrounding hills, which provide splendid views.

Go to **Playa Grande**, a magnificent bay northwest of the village. Either walk there

(20 minutes) or take a boat from Taganga (US$1). The beach is lined with palm-thatched restaurants serving good fish. You can walk farther along the coast on a path which winds along the slopes of the hilly coast up to Playa Granate.

Taganga is a popular scuba-diving center; there are half a dozen dive shops and schools offering dives and courses. They are slightly cheaper than those in Cartagena and San Andrés.

Places to Stay & Eat There's a choice of accommodation in Taganga, though it's not as cheap as in Santa Marta. The cheapest and best value is the French-run *Hotel Casa Francesa (☎ 54-234002)*, Calle 12 No 4-09, which has simple but pleasant rooms with bath and fan for US$6 per person. There's a bar/restaurant and Internet access is available to hotel guests.

Otherwise, there are a string of hotels along the waterfront, including *Hotel El Delfín (☎ 54-216189)*, for US$8 per person, and *Hotel Playa Brava (☎ 54-216419)*, for US$16 a double with fan, US$20 with air-con. *Hotel La Ballena Azul (☎ 54-216668)* focuses on more affluent clientele (US$50 a double with fan, US$60 with air-con) and has a good (though not cheap) restaurant.

Parque Nacional Tayrona

One of the most popular national parks in the country, Tayrona is set on the jungle-covered coast just east of Santa Marta. The park's beaches, set in deep bays and shaded with coconut palms, are among the loveliest in Colombia. Some are bordered by coral reefs, and snorkeling is good, but be careful of the treacherous offshore currents. The region was once the territory of the Tayrona Indians, and some remains have been found in the park, the most important being the ruins of the pre-Hispanic town of **Pueblito**.

The park's main entrance is in **El Zaíno** (where you pay the US$4 entrance fee), 35km from Santa Marta on the coastal road to Riohacha. From El Zaíno, walk 4km north on a paved road to **Cañaveral**, on the seaside. Here you'll find the administrative center of the park, which runs cabañas (US$50/70 a double/quad) and an over-priced campground. There is also a restaurant. Most travelers walk for 50 minutes

west along a trail to **Arrecifes**, where the beaches are more spectacular and locals run cabañas, a campground (US$4) and restaurants and hire hammocks (US$3).

From Arrecifes, you can walk to Pueblito in two hours along a path with splendid tropical forest scenery. There have been some cases of robbery on this route, so don't walk alone.

The Hotel Miramar in Santa Marta runs a chiva to Cañaveral and is the cheapest operator (US$11 return, including park entrance fee). The chiva shuttles daily, and you can return any day you want.

Other popular sites in the park include **Bahía Concha** and **Naguange**, but they are difficult to get to as there is no public transport. Several travel agents in Santa Marta organize tours to both these places.

CIUDAD PERDIDA

Ciudad Perdida (literally, the Lost City) is one of the largest pre-Columbian towns discovered in the Americas. Known by its indigenous name, Teyuna, it was built between the 11th and 14th centuries, on the northwestern slopes of the Sierra Nevada de Santa Marta, and was most probably the Tayrona's biggest urban center. During their conquest of South America, the Spaniards wiped out the Tayronas, and their settlements disappeared without trace under the lush tropical vegetation. So did Ciudad Perdida, until its discovery in 1975 by huaqueros.

Ciudad Perdida lies on the relatively steep slopes of the Buritaca valley, at an altitude of between 1000 and 1300m. The central part of the city is set on a ridge, from which various stone paths descend to other sectors on the slopes. There are about 150 stone terraces – some in remarkably good shape – which once served as foundations for the houses. Originally, the urban center was completely cleared of trees, before being reclaimed by the jungle. Today, the city is quite overgrown, which gives it a somewhat mysterious air.

Getting There & Away

There are two ways of getting to Ciudad Perdida: a helicopter tour or a trek. Both begin and end in Santa Marta. The former takes less than three hours; the latter takes six days.

Helicopter The Aviatur travel agency has irregular helicopter tours during the peak holiday seasons (Christmas and Easter). It is a 20-minute flight from Santa Marta airport to Ciudad Perdida, followed by a two-hour guided visit and the return journey. In all, it takes about two hours and 40 minutes and costs US$450 per person. If you are captivated by this whirlwind speed, and are not deterred by the price, contact an Aviatur office in any major city.

Trekking There are two trails leading to the Lost City: through La Tagua and Alto de Mira; and through El Mamey and up along the Río Buritaca. The former trail was abandoned several years ago, and now all visitors take the Buritaca trail, which is shorter and easier but perhaps less spectacular. The section between Santa Marta and El Mamey is done by vehicle.

Access to Ciudad Perdida is by tour only, organized by Turcol in Santa Marta (☎ 54-212256). You cannot do the trip on your own, or hire an independent guide. The price is about US$220 (non-negotiable) per person for the all-inclusive tour. This includes transport, food, accommodation (in hammocks), porters, guides and all necessary permits. You carry your own personal belongings. Take a flashlight, water container and insect repellent.

Tours are in groups of four to 10 people, and depart year-round as soon as a group is assembled. In the high season, expect a tour to set off every few days. In the off season, there may be just one tour a week.

The trip takes three days uphill to Ciudad Perdida, one day at the site and two days back down. The hike is not very difficult in technical terms, though it may be tiring due to the heat, and if it's wet (as it is most of the year) the paths are pretty muddy. The only relatively dry period is from late December to February or early March, but global climatic changes have altered this pattern in recent years.

CARTAGENA

Cartagena de Indias is legendary, for both its history and its beauty. It is Colombia's most fascinating city, and shouldn't be missed. Don't be in a hurry either, as the city's charm will keep you here for at least several days.

Dating from 1533, Cartagena was one of the first cities founded by the Spaniards in South America. Within a short time, the town blossomed into the main Spanish port on the Caribbean coast and the gateway to the north of the continent. It was the place where treasure plundered from the Indians was stored until the galleons could ship it back to Spain. As such, it became a tempting target for pirates and, in the 16th century alone, suffered five dreadful sieges, the best known of which was that led by Francis Drake in 1586.

In response to pirate attacks the Spaniards decided to make Cartagena an impregnable port, and constructed elaborate walls encircling the town and a chain of outer forts. These fortifications helped save Cartagena from subsequent sieges, particularly the fiercest attack of all, led by Edward Vernon in 1741.

In spite of these attacks, Cartagena continued to flourish. During the colonial period, the city was the key outpost of the Spanish empire, and influenced much of Colombia's history.

Today, Cartagena has expanded dramatically and is surrounded by vast suburbs. It is now Colombia's second largest port and an important industrial center of 750,000 inhabitants. Nevertheless, the old walled town has changed very little. It is a living museum of 16th- and 17th-century Spanish architecture, with narrow winding streets, palaces, churches, monasteries, plazas and large mansions with overhanging balconies, shady patios and formal gardens.

Over the past decades, Cartagena has become a fashionable seaside resort, though its beaches are actually not very good. An expensive modern tourist district has sprung up on Bocagrande and El Laguito, an L-shaped peninsula south of the old town. This sector, packed with top-class hotels and expensive restaurants, has become the main destination point for moneyed Colombians and international charter tours. Most backpackers, however, stay in the historic part of town.

Cartagena's climate is hot, but a fresh breeze blows in the evening, making this a pleasant time to stroll around the city. Theoretically, the driest period is from December to April, while October and November are the wettest months.

CARTAGENA – OLD TOWN

PLACES TO STAY
3 Hotel Santa Clara
12 Hostal Colonial
13 Hotel Bucarica
14 Hostal Arthur
16 Hotel Montecarlo
17 Hotel del Lago
23 Hostal Santo Domingo
37 Hotel San Felipe
38 Hotel Santa Teresa
46 Casa Viena
49 Hotel Holiday
56 Hotel Familiar
57 Hotel Chalet Suizo
58 Hotel Doral

PLACES TO EAT
4 Restaurante Fellini
7 Restaurante Vegetariano
Girasoles
8 Restaurante Nautilus
20 Restaurante La Vitrola
24 Restaurante Donde Olano

27 La Crêperie
32 Restaurante Vegetariano
Govinda's
40 El Bodegón de la Candelaria
45 El Café del Portal de los Dulces
47 Restaurante La Campiña
48 Restaurante Los 4 Vientos

OTHER
1 Casa de Rafael Núñez
2 Las Bóvedas
5 Teatro Heredia
6 Iglesia de Santo Toribio de
Mangrovejo
9 Monumento a la India Catalina
10 Casa del Marqués de
Valdehoyos
11 Universidad de Cartagena
15 Banco Santander
18 Telecom
19 Iglesia de Santo Domingo
21 Banco Anglo Colombiano
22 Paco's

25 Palacio de la Inquisición
26 Plaza de Bolívar
28 Museo del Oro y
Arqueología
29 Catedral
30 Compu Internet
31 Plaza de los Coches,
Puerta del Reloj
33 Banco Unión Colombiano
34 Bancolombia
35 Bancolombia
36 Adpostal
39 La Escollera de la Marina
41 Planet Cyber Café
42 Plaza de la Aduana
43 Avianca Office
44 Tu Candela
50 Museo Naval del Caribe
51 Iglesia de San Pedro
Claver
52 Convento de San Pedro
Claver
53 Museo de Arte Moderno

54 Iglesia de la Santa Orden
55 Quiebra Canto
59 Iglesia de San Roque
60 Convention & Visitors Bureau
61 Banco Sudameris Colombia
62 Mister Babilla
63 Iglesia de la Santísima Trinidad

*To Airport, Marbella Beach,
Hotel Bellavista*

*Caribbean
Sea*

Las Murallas

SAN DIEGO

Las Murallas

Av Venezuela

LA MATUNA

Av Daniel Lemaitre

EL CENTRO

Av Santander

*Parque del
Centenario*

Calle de la Media Luna

GETSEMANI

Muelle de los Pegasos

*Centro de
Convenciones*

To Bocagrande, El Laguito

Bahía de las Ánimas

Av del Arsenal

Las Murallas

To Manga Island

0   100   200 m
0   100   200 yards

Information

Tourist Office The privately run Convention & Visitors Bureau (☎ 5-660-2415), in the Centro de Convenciones, has taken over the task of providing information for visitors from city-run Proturismo, until (if ever) the local government finds a reliable long-time solution for a state-run tourist office. Alternatively, try the Hotel Chalet Suizo or the Casa Viena, two backpacker hostels (see Places to Stay), which can provide free tourist information.

Money Banks which change traveler's checks or cash include the Banco Anglo Colombiano, Banco Unión Colombiano, Banco Santander, Banco Sudameris Colombia and Bancolombia. Most major banks will accept Visa cards, while MasterCard is recognized only by Bancolombia and Banco de Occidente. Some banks have ATMs.

There are plenty of casas de cambio, particularly around Plaza de los Coches. They all change cash but usually not traveler's checks. The few that do cash checks include the Casa América (☎ 5-660-0543), Calle del Colegio No 34-34 in El Centro, and Titan Intercontinental (☎ 5-665-8197), Calle 8 No 2-24 in Bocagrande.

Tierra Mar Aire (☎ 5-665-5751) is in Bocagrande at Carrera 4 No 7-196.

Cartagena is the only Colombian city where you be propositioned (sometimes quite persistently) by street moneychangers, who offer attractive rates. Give the street changers a big miss – they are all con men.

Internet Access Central places providing Internet access include Planet Cyber Café (☎ 5-664-4320), Calle de las Damas No 3-102; Compu Internet (☎ 5-660-2034), Calle del Arzobispado No 34-18 next to the cathedral; and Hotel Chalet Suizo and Casa Viena (see Places to Stay).

Consulates The Venezuelan and Panamanian consulates issue visas and tourist cards. See the Facts for the Visitor section for contact information.

Things to See & Do

Old Town This is the principal attraction, particularly the inner walled town, consisting of the historical districts of El Centro and San Diego. Almost every street is worth strolling down. Getsemaní, the outer walled town, is less impressive and not so well preserved, but it is also worth exploring. Be careful – this part of the city may not be safe, especially after dark.

The old town is surrounded by **Las Murallas**, the thick walls built to protect it. Construction was begun toward the end of the 16th century, after the attack by Francis Drake; until that time, Cartagena was almost completely unprotected. The project took two centuries to complete, due to repeated storm damage and pirate attacks.

The main gateway to the inner town was what is now the **Puerta del Reloj** (the clock tower was added in the 19th century). Just behind it is the **Plaza de los Coches**, a square once used as a slave market. Note the fine old houses with colonial arches and balconies, and the monument to Pedro de Heredia, the founder of the city, in the middle of the square.

A few steps southwest is the **Plaza de la Aduana**, the oldest and largest square in the old town. It was used as a parade ground, and all governmental buildings were gathered around it. In the center stands a statue of Christopher Columbus.

Close by is the **Iglesia y Convento de San Pedro Claver**, built by the Jesuits, originally under the name of San Ignacio de Loyola. The name was changed in honor of the Spanish-born monk Pedro Claver, who lived and died in the convent. He spent his life ministering to the slaves brought from Africa. The convent, built in the first half of the 17th century, is a monumental three-story building surrounding a tree-filled courtyard, and part of it, including Claver's cell, is open to visitors (8 am to 6 pm daily). You can also climb a narrow staircase to the church's choir and, at times, get on to the roof. The church alongside was built long after, and has an imposing stone façade. The remains of San Pedro Claver are kept in a glass coffin in the high altar.

Nearby, on Calle de las Damas, is a beautiful mansion, the **Casa de la Candelaria**, housing an expensive restaurant. You can visit the house without eating; go up to the bar in the tower for good views of town.

The **Plaza de Bolívar** is in a particularly beautiful area of the old town. On one side of the square is the **Palacio de la Inquisición**, completed in 1776 and a fine example of late colonial architecture, with its overhanging balconies and magnificent Baroque stone gateway. It is now a museum (open daily) displaying Inquisitors' instruments of torture, pre-Columbian pottery and works of art from the colonial and independence periods.

Across the plaza, the **Museo del Oro y Arqueología** (open weekdays) has a good collection of gold and pottery from the Sinú culture. The **Catedral** was begun in 1575 but was partially destroyed by Drake's cannons in 1586, and not completed until 1612. The dome on the tower was built early this century. Apart from this, the church basically retains its original form; it is a massive structure with a fortlike exterior and a simply decorated interior.

One block west of the plaza is **Calle Santo Domingo**, a street which has hardly changed since the 16th century. On it stands the **Iglesia de Santo Domingo**, the city's oldest church. It is a large, heavy construction, and buttresses had to be added to the walls to support the naves. The convent is right alongside, and you can see its fine courtyard. Farther north is the **Casa del Marqués de Valdehoyos**, a mighty colonial mansion from the 18th century, now a museum.

At the northern tip of the old town are **Las Bóvedas**, 23 dungeons built in the defensive walls at the end of the 18th century. This was the last construction done in colonial times, and was destined for military purposes. Today, the dungeons are tourist shops.

While you're wandering around, call at the **Muelle de los Pegasos**, a lovely old port full of fishing, cargo and tourist boats, just outside the old town's southern walls.

Other Attractions Several forts were built at key points outside the walls to protect the city from pirates. By far the greatest is the **Castillo de San Felipe de Barajas**, a huge stone fortress, begun in 1639 but not completed until some 150 years later. It is open 8 am to 5 pm daily, and the entrance is US$4 (US$2 for students). Don't miss the impressive walk through the complex system of tunnels, built to facilitate the supply and evacuation of the fort.

The **Convento de la Popa**, perched on top of a 150m hill beyond the San Felipe fortress, was founded by the Augustinians in 1607. It has a nice chapel and a lovely flower-filled patio, and offers panoramic views of the city. There have been some cases of armed robbery on the zigzagging access road to the top – take a taxi (no public transport).

Special Events
The most important annual event is the national beauty contest held every November 11th, to celebrate the Cartagena's independence; the fiesta strikes up several days before and the city goes wild. An international film festival takes place every March.

Places to Stay
Cartagena has a reasonable choice of budget accommodations and despite its touristy status, the prices of its residencias are not higher than in other cities. The tourist peak is from late December to late January but, even then, it's relatively easy to find a room.

If you're on a tight budget, walk to the Getsemaní area, where you'll find plenty of cheapies on Calle de la Media Luna and nearby streets. Many are dives that double as love hotels or brothels, but there are several 'clean' and safe options frequented by travelers.

One of the more popular backpacker haunts is *Casa Viena* (☎ 5-664-6242), Calle San Andrés No 30-53. It has a variety of simple rooms, some with bath, and there's even an air-conditioned dorm ($4 beds). It's one of the cheapest places around; the best room, a double with bath and cable TV costs US$11. Run by a helpful Austrian, Hans, the hotel offers a typical range of western facilities, including laundry service, Internet access, book exchange, poste restante, individual strongboxes and cooking facilities.

Another well known traveler shelter is the German-owned *Hotel Chalet Suizo* (☎ 5-664-7861), Calle de la Media Luna No 10-36. It's not a posh place either, but also very cheap, at US$4 per dorm bed, US$7/10/14 for singles/doubles/triples without bath. It also provides many amenities, including laundry, bike rental, Internet access and free luggage storage.

The friendly *Hotel Holiday* (☎ 5-664-0948), Calle de la Media Luna No 10-47, is another popular traveler's hangout. Its neat airy double rooms with bath (US$11) are one of the best deals in town.

Other budget places in the area include *Hotel Doral* (☎ 5-664-1706), Calle de la

Media Luna No 10-46 (US$6/7 a bed in rooms without/with bath), with its spacious courtyard with umbrella-shaded tables, and the smaller and slightly cheaper *Hotel Familiar* (☎ 5-664-8374), Calle del Guerrero No 29-66.

The hotels in El Centro, the heart of the old town, are more expensive and rather poor value. One of the few acceptable budget places is *Hotel Bucarica* (☎ 5-664-1263), Calle San Agustín No 6-08, which costs about US$15/20 a double/triple with fan and private bath.

If you don't mind staying outside the old town, try the waterfront *Hotel Bellavista* (☎ 5-664-6411), on Av Santander at Marbella Beach, a 10-minute walk northeast of the walled city. Rooms with bath and fan cost US$9 per person. Another good budget option outside the city walls is the German-run *Hotel Natalie* (☎ 5-656-4857), Calle José María Pasos No 17-198, in the suburb of Torices (take bus from India Catalina), where rooms with bath cost about US$6 per person.

There are several mid-price hotels scattered throughout the old town area. They are nothing special but do have air-con. Try *Hostal Arthur* (☎ 5-664-2633) in El Centro (US$30/35 a double/triple); *Hostal Colonial* (☎ 5-660-1432) opposite, with singles/doubles at US$22/30; *Hotel Montecarlo* (☎ 5-664-4329) in La Matuna (US$25/35/48); nearby *Hotel del Lago* (☎ 5-664-0526; US$26/38/50); and *Hotel San Felipe* (☎ 5-664-5439) in Getsemaní (US$24/30/38). All of them also offer slightly cheaper rooms with fans.

The small *Hostal Santo Domingo* (☎ 5-664-2268) is quite simple and overpriced (US$35 a double with bath and fan), but it's quiet and ideally located in an attractive area of El Centro.

Most of the city's mid-range and top-end hotels are in Bocagrande. In the old town, there are two extraordinary places to stay, *Hotel Santa Clara* (☎ 5-664-6070) and *Hotel Santa Teresa* (☎ 5-664-9494). Even if you're not staying (US$230/300 a double room/suite in each), go and see them.

Places to Eat

Cartagena is a good place to eat, particularly at the upmarket level, but cheap places are also plentiful. Dozens of simple old town restaurants serve set almuerzos for less than US$2, and many also offer set comidas. Some better restaurants also do set lunches. *Govinda's* in El Centro, *Girasoles* in San Diego and *La Campiña* in Getsemaní provide cheap vegetarian meals.

Plenty of cafés all over the old town serve arepas de huevo (toasted or fried maize pancakes), dedos de queso (deep-fried cheese sticks), empanadas, buñuelos (deep-fried maize and cheese ball) and a variety of other snacks. A dozen stalls on the Muelle de los Pegasos operate round the clock and have an unbelievable selection of fruit juices.

La Crêperie on Plaza de Bolívar does appetizing crêpes and tortillas, while *El Café del Portal de los Dulces* has good sandwiches and pasta. The cozy *Restaurante Donde Olano* offers fine French and Creole cooking at reasonable prices. In Getsemaní, one of the most popular places among travelers is *Los 4 Vientos*, which has tasty Italian, Spanish and Mexican food at good prices, plus plenty of drinks.

There are a number of upmarket restaurants in the old town, most of which are set in historic interiors. Some include *El Bodegón de la Candelaria* (try the lobster), *Fellini* (Italian), *Nautilus* (seafood) and *La Vitrola* (international cuisine). The posh *Hotel Santa Clara* and *Hotel Santa Teresa* both have good restaurants. Bocagrande also has many upmarket establishments.

Entertainment

A number of bars, taverns, discos and other venues stay open late. Several of them are on Av del Arsenal in Getsemaní, close to the Centro de Convenciones; *Mister Babilla* is one of the most popular discos in this area. *Quiebra Canto*, near the Parque del Centenario, is a good salsa spot. *Tu Candela*, an informal bar on Plaza de los Coches, serves beer and plays taped music till late.

There are several upmarket restaurants in El Centro that have bands playing Caribbean and Cuban music, usually Wednesday or Thursday to Saturday. Check *La Vitrola*, *La Escollera de la Marina* and *Paco's*.

In Bocagrande, the place to go is *La Escollera* (corner of Carrera 1 and Calle 5), a disco in a large thatched open hut, which goes nightly till 4 am. On the beach beside La Escollera, vallenato groups play till dawn.

Getting There & Away
Air The airport is in the Crespo suburb, 3km northeast of the old city, and is serviced by frequent local buses. All major Colombian carriers operate flights to and from Cartagena. There are flights to Bogotá (US$118), Cali (US$125), Cúcuta (US$118), Medellín (US$102), San Andrés (US$123) and other major cities. You may find cheaper fares, so shop around. A small local carrier, Aerocorales, flies twice weekly to Mompós (US$75).

Avianca flies to Miami and New York, Aeropostal flies to Caracas, and Copa, the Panamanian airline, has daily flights to Panama City (US$139 plus 10% tax).

Bus The bus terminal is on the eastern outskirts of the city, a long way from the center. Air-conditioned urban buses shuttle between the two every 10 minutes (US$0.50, 30 minutes). In the center, you can catch them on Av Daniel Lamître.

There are a dozen air-conditioned buses daily to Bogotá (US$52, 19 hours) and another dozen to Medellín (US$37, 13 hours). Buses to Barranquilla run every 15 minutes or so (US$4.50 ordinary, US$6 aircon; two hours). Unitransco has one bus to Mompós, at 7 am (US$14, eight hours); see the Mompós section for more details. There are daily buses direct to Caracas (US$80) via Maracaibo (US$45).

Boat Large cargo boats depart for San Andrés from the Muelle de los Pegasos but they don't take passengers. Smaller unscheduled cargo boats go to Turbo (about US$35 including food, up to two days), and it's relatively easy to get a ride; take a hammock. From Turbo, you can take a boat to Capurganá, then walk to Puerto Obaldía in Panama (or, safer, take another boat), and then get a flight to Panama City (US$45).

There's no longer a ferry service between Cartagena and Colón in Panama, and there are very few cargo boats. More boats operate between Colón and Barranquilla, some of which will take passengers, motorcycles and even cars, but these services are irregular and infrequent and sometimes disreputable.

A more reliable way of getting to Panama is the new sailboat service. Two sailboats shuttle between Cartagena and Porvenir at San Blás Archipelago (Panama). They depart as soon as they collect four to six passengers, usually once or twice a week. The trip each way normally takes four to five days and costs US$185 (US$250 return). Porvenir has a Panamanian immigration office, accommodation and an airport with daily flights to Panama City (US$27). Check www.salelawrence.com/sailing.htm for more details. Booking is available through Casa Viena and Hotel Chalet Suizo in Cartagena.

Note that Panama requires a visa or tourist card from some nationals (check if you need one), onward ticket and sufficient funds (a minimum of US$500 in cash or traveler's checks) and has been known to turn back those who don't meet the requirements. Don't forget to get an exit stamp in your passport from the DAS immigration officials in Cartagena.

While strolling about Cartagena, you may be approached by men offering fabulous trips around the Caribbean in 'their boats' for a little help on board; if you seem interested, they will ask you to pay some money for a boarding permit or whatever. Don't pay a cent – you'll see neither the man, nor your money, again.

AROUND CARTAGENA
Islas del Rosario
This archipelago of small coral islands is about 35km southwest of Cartagena. There are about 25 islands, including tiny islets only big enough for a single house. The archipelago is surrounded by coral reefs, where the color of the sea ranges from turquoise to purple. The whole area has been declared the Corales del Rosario National Park.

Cruises through the islands are a well-established business. Tours depart year-round from the Muelle de los Pegasos in Cartagena. Boats leave between 7 and 9 am daily and return about 4 or 5 pm. The cruise office at the Muelle sells tours in big boats for about US$20, but independent operators hanging around offer cheaper tours in smaller vessels, for US$15 or even less. It's probably best (and often cheapest) to arrange the tour through one of the budget gringo hotels. Tours normally include lunch, but neither the entrance fee (US$4) to the aquarium on one of the islands nor the port tax (US$2).

COLOMBIA

La Boquilla

This is a small fishing village populated mostly by blacks, 7km north of Cartagena on a peninsula between the sea and the seaside lagoon. The locals fish with their famous *atarrayas* (a kind of net), and you can arrange boat trips with them along the narrow water channels cutting through the mangrove woods. Negotiate the price and only pay after they bring you back.

Plenty of beachfront palm-thatched restaurants attract people from Cartagena on weekends; most are closed at other times. The fish is good but not that cheap. Frequent city buses run to La Boquilla from India Catalina in Cartagena, taking half an hour.

Jardín Botánico Guillermo Piñeres

A pleasant half-day escape from the city rush, these botanical gardens are on the outskirts of the town of Turbaco, 15km southeast of Cartagena. Take the Turbaco bus departing regularly from next to the Castillo de San Felipe and ask the driver to drop you at the turnoff to the gardens (US$0.75, 45 minutes). From there it's a 20-minute stroll down the largely unpaved side road.

The 20-acre gardens (closed Monday) feature plants typical of the coast, including two varieties of coca plant. While buying your entry ticket (US$2) you get a leaflet which lists 250 plants identified in the gardens.

Volcán de Lodo El Totumo

About 50km northeast of Cartagena, on the bank of the shallow Ciénaga del Totumo, is an intriguing 15m mound, looking like a miniature volcano. It's indeed a volcano but instead of lava and ashes, it spews mud, a phenomenon due to the pressure of gases emitted by decaying organic matter underground.

El Totumo is the highest mud volcano in Colombia. Lukewarm mud with the consistency of cream fills its crater. You can climb to the top by specially built stairs, then go down into the crater and have a refreshing mud bath (US$2). It's a unique experience – surely volcano-dipping is something you haven't yet tried! The mud contains minerals acclaimed for their therapeutic properties. You can wash the mud off in the ciénaga. There are several restaurants around the volcano.

To get to the volcano from Cartagena, take a city bus from the old town to Mercado Bazurto, from where hourly buses depart in the morning to Galerazamba. Be on your guard, as aggressive thieves frequent the bus stop. Get off at Loma de Arena (US$1.75, 1¾ hours) and walk along the main road for 20 minutes, then to the right to the volcano for another 10 minutes. The last direct bus from Loma de Arena back to Cartagena departs at 3 pm.

Several operators in Cartagena, including Casa Viena and Hotel Chalet Suizo, organize tours to the volcano.

MOMPÓS

Mompós, about 200km southeast of Cartagena, was founded in 1537 on the eastern branch of the Río Magdalena, which in this region has two arms: Brazo Mompós and Brazo de Loba. The town soon became an important port, through which all merchandise from Cartagena passed to the interior of the country. Several imposing churches and many luxurious mansions were built.

Toward the end of the 19th century, shipping was diverted to the other branch of the Magdalena, ending the town's prosperity. Mompós has existed in isolation ever since. Today its colonial character is very much in evidence, as are the airs of a bygone era.

Mompós has a long tradition in hand-worked filigree gold jewelry, which is of outstanding quality. Nowadays the gold is slowly being replaced by silver. Another specialty of the town is its furniture, particularly rocking chairs.

It's fun to wander aimlessly about this tranquil town, discovering its rich architectural legacy and absorbing the old-time atmosphere. In the evening, when the heat of the day finally eases, people relax in front of their homes, sitting in – of course – Mompós-made rocking chairs.

Information

The tourist office, in the Alcaldía, may have some information about the town, but if not, try La Casona or Doña Manuela (see Places to Stay). They can also put you in contact with Chipi, who organizes reasonably priced city tours and boat trips. Boys hang around to guide tourists through the town and into some private colonial homes.

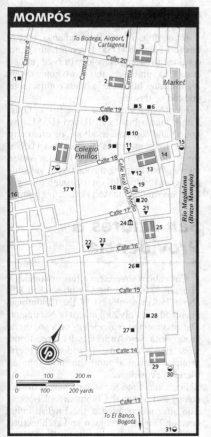

MOMPÓS

PLACES TO STAY
1 Residencias La Cuarta
5 Residencias La Valerosa
6 Hotel Colonial
9 Residencias San Andrés
10 Residencias La Casona
18 Hostal Doña Manuela
20 La Posada del Virrey
26 Residencias Aurora
27 Residencias La Isleña
28 Residencias Villa de Mompox

PLACES TO EAT
11 Restaurante Tebe's
12 Restaurante Milena Paola
17 Asadero A y M
21 La Pizzería
22 Piqueteadero Lo Sabroso
23 Asadero Pollo Rico

OTHER
2 Iglesia de San Juan de Dios
3 Iglesia de San Francisco
4 Tourist Office
7 Jeeps to Bodega & El Banco
8 Iglesia de Santo Domingo
13 Iglesia de la Concepción
14 Plaza Real de la Concepción
15 Boats to El Banco & Magangué
16 Cemetery
19 Museo Cultural
24 Casa de la Cultura
25 Iglesia de San Agustín
29 Iglesia de Santa Bárbara
30 Unitransco Office (Buses to Cartagena)
31 La Veloz Office (Buses to Bosconia)

Bring enough pesos with you, as money may be difficult to change, and rates are poor.

Things to See

Most of the central streets are lined with fine whitewashed colonial houses with characteristic metal-grill windows, imposing doorways and lovely hidden patios. Six colonial churches complete the scenery; all are interesting, though rarely open. In particular, don't miss the **Iglesia de Santa Bárbara**, with its Moorish-style tower, unique in Colombian religious architecture.

The **Casa de la Cultura**, in a historic mansion, houses memorabilia relating to the town's history, and the **Museo Cultural**, in a house where Simón Bolívar once stayed, displays some religious art. There's a small **Jardín Botánico**, with lots of hummingbirds and butterflies, 3 blocks west of Iglesia de Santa Bárbara on Calle 14. Knock to be let in. Also worth a visit is the local **cemetery**, with its decorative old tombstones.

There are some workshops near the museum where you can see and buy local jewelry. Hostal Doña Manuela can provide addresses of artisans who work at home.

Special Events

Holy Week celebrations are very elaborate in Mompós. The solemn processions circle the streets for several hours on Maundy Thursday and Good Friday nights.

Places to Stay

Except for Holy Week, you won't have problems finding somewhere to stay. There are a dozen hotels in town, most of them pleasant and friendly.

Among the cheapest options are *Residencias La Valerosa* and *Residencias La Cuarta*, both basic, charging about US$4/8 a single/double without bath. Better, though also without bath, is *Residencias La Isleña*, which costs US$5 per person. The cheapest places with private baths are *Residencias San Andrés* and *Hotel Colonial*, both offering singles/doubles for US$7/13.

Other reasonably priced, pleasant places to stay include *Residencias Villa de Mompox* (☎ 52-855208), *Residencias Aurora* and *La Posada del Virrey* (☎ 52-855630). All cost about US$8 per person in rooms with bath. The newer *Residencias La Casona* (☎ 52-855307) is the best of the lot, costing US$10/16/25 a single/double/triple with bath.

At the top end is *Hostal Doña Manuela* (☎ 52-855620), which is set in a restored colonial mansion with two ample courtyards, a swimming pool and restaurant. Singles/doubles with bath and fan cost US$35/45 (US$45/60 with air-con). The pool can be used by nonguests (US$3).

Places to Eat

Food stalls at the riverfront market provide cheap meals. There are several budget restaurants around the small square behind Iglesia de la Concepción, near the corner of Carrera 2 and Calle 18.

Piqueteadero Lo Sabroso has inexpensive typical food (such as *mondongo*, or tripe). For chicken, try *Asadero Pollo Rico*; for pizza, check *La Pizzería*, though neither is anything special. *Hostal Doña Manuela* has a reasonable restaurant.

Getting There & Away

Mompós is well off the main routes, but can be reached relatively easily by road and river. Most travelers come here from Cartagena (from where you can also fly to Mompós, twice weekly with Aerocorales for US$75). Unitransco has one direct bus daily, leaving Cartagena at 7 am (US$14, eight hours). Otherwise, take a bus to Magangué (US$10, 3½ hours; at least a dozen departures per day with Unitransco and Brasilia), take a boat to Bodega (US$2, 20 minutes; frequent departures till about 3 pm) and continue by jeep to Mompós (US$2, one

hour). There may also be direct boats from Magangué to Mompós.

If you depart from Bucaramanga, take a bus to El Banco (US$14, seven hours) and continue to Mompós by jeep or boat (either costs US$5 and takes about two hours); jeep is a bit faster but the trip is less comfortable and can be dusty.

From Santa Marta, there are two options. Either take a bus to El Banco (US$12, six hours) and continue as above, or catch any of the frequent buses to Bosconia (US$6, three hours), from where the La Veloz morning bus (coming through from Valledupar) goes to Mompós on the rough road via La Gloria and Santa Ana (US$8, five hours).

San Andrés & Providencia

A Colombian sovereignty, this archipelago of small islands in the Caribbean Sea lies about 750km northwest of the Colombian mainland and only 230km east of Nicaragua. The archipelago is made up of a southern group, with San Andrés as its largest and most important island, and a northern group, centered around the mountainous island of Providencia.

For a long time, the islands were a British colony and, although Colombia took possession after independence, the English influence on language, religion and architecture remained virtually intact until modern times. In the 1950s, when a regular domestic air service was established with the Colombian mainland and San Andrés was declared a duty-free zone, the situation began to change. A significant migration of Colombians to the islands, a boom in tourism and commerce and changing government policies have meant that much of San Andrés' original character has disappeared. Providencia, however, has managed to preserve much more of its colonial character.

The islands, especially Providencia, provide a good opportunity to experience the unique Caribbean ambiance. The turquoise sea, extensive coral reefs and rich underwater life are a paradise for snorkelers and scuba divers. The easygoing pace, friendly locals (descendants of Jamaican slaves), adequate (though not cheap) tourist facilities and general safety also attract visitors to the islands.

San Andrés is often used by travelers as a bridge between Central America and Colombia. All visitors staying more than one day are charged a local government levy of US$10 on arrival and handed the so-called Tarjeta de Turista.

The dry season on the archipelago is from January to May, with another not-so-dry period from August to September. Tourist season peaks from mid-December to mid-January, during the Easter week, and from mid-June to mid-July.

SAN ANDRÉS

San Andrés is about 13km long and 3km wide. It is relatively flat and largely covered by coconut palms. A 30km scenic paved road circles the island, and several roads cross inland.

The urban center and capital of the archipelago is the town of San Andrés (known locally as El Centro), in the extreme north of the island. It has two-thirds of the island's 60,000 inhabitants and is the principal tourist and commercial area, packed with hotels, restaurants and stores.

Information

Tourist Offices The municipal tourist office, the Secretaría de Turismo (☎ 8-512-2543), is in the park next to the huge, new Sunrise Beach Hotel. There's also the tourist office (☎ 8-512-1149) on the ground floor of the airport terminal. The departmental tourist office (☎ 8-512-4230) is in a small free-standing building on Av Colombia, near the airport.

Money Some banks, including Bancolombia and the Banco del Estado, exchange traveler's checks and cash. All banks marked on the map advance cash on either MasterCard (Bancolombia and Banco de Occidente) or Visa (the remaining ones). Some banks have ATMs.

There are a number of casas de cambio in the central area (eg, Boulevard Los Reyes or Titan Intercontinental) that change cash at bank rates. Some also change traveler's checks.

Some shops and hotels accept payments in cash dollars and will change them for pesos, but usually at a lower rate than the banks or casas de cambio.

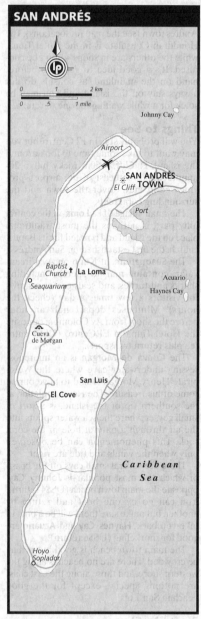

Consulates Costa Rica, Guatemala, Honduras and Panama all have consulates in San Andrés town (see the map for locations). The Honduran Consulate is in the Hotel Tiuna, while the others are in shops – don't be confused. It's a good idea to get visas beforehand on the mainland, as consuls do not always stay on the island and you may be stuck for a while waiting for one to return.

Things to See

You will probably stay in El Centro, but you may want to take some time to look around the island. **El Cliff**, a 50m rocky hill, a 20-minute walk southeast of the airport, provides good views over the town and the surrounding coral reefs.

The small village of **La Loma**, in the central hilly part, is perhaps the most traditional place on the island and is noted for its Baptist church, the first established on San Andrés.

The **Seaquarium**, at Km 6 on Av Circunvalar, contains marine species including sharks and turtles, and seals perform shows for visitors a few times a day (check the hours). Minibuses depart half an hour before the show from Av Colombia opposite the Hotel Tiuna in El Centro (US$7 entry fee plus return transport).

The **Cueva de Morgan** is an unprepossessing underwater cave where the Welsh pirate Henry Morgan is said to have buried some of his treasure. The **Hoyo Soplador**, at the southern tip of the island, is a sort of small geyser where the sea water spouts into the air through a natural hole in the coral rock. This phenomenon can be observed only when the winds and tide are right.

There are several small cays off the coast, of which the most popular is **Johnny Cay**, opposite the main town beach (US$4 return). You can go by one boat and return by another, but make sure there will be a boat to take you back. **Haynes Cay** and **Acuario** are good for snorkeling (US$6 return).

The main town beach is good but it may be crowded. There are no beaches along the western shore, and those along the east coast are nothing special, except for the good beach in San Luis.

Places to Stay

Accommodations in San Andrés are expensive. The cheapest place to stay is *Hotel Restrepo* (☎ 8-512-6744), just north of the airport terminal. It is a mecca for foreign backpackers; Colombian guests are rare. It is basic and unkempt but friendly, and costs US$5 per person, regardless of what room you get – some have their own bath, others don't, but all rooms have fans. There is a dining room, where you can get breakfast, lunch and dinner (US$2.50 per meal). If the rooms are full and if you don't mind mosquitoes (they are only a problem during certain periods), rent a hammock (US$2) or string up your own.

The only other low-budget hotel in San Andrés is *Apartamentos El Español* (☎ 8-512-3337), 1 block south of the airport terminal. This is essentially the Colombian budget hotel, and it is not an attractive place to stay, nor is its vicinity. Yet all rooms have private bath, and are cheap by San Andrés standards – US$10 for a very poor dark double, US$12 for the marginally better one with a window.

If you can't get a room at either the Restrepo or El Español, or you need more comfort, be prepared to pay at least US$12/20 for a single/double. One of the cheapest is *Posada Doña Rosa* (☎ 8-512-3649), which costs US$12/22/30 a single/double/triple with bath and fan, but it has four rooms only and is often full. Better is the small and friendly *Hotel Mary May Inn* (☎ 8-512-5669), which costs US$20/28/34.

Affordable hotels with private baths and air-conditioning include *Hotel Natania* (☎ 8-512-6286), which costs US$25/32 a single/double; *Hotel Hernando Henry* (☎ 8-512-3416), for US$32/36; and *Hotel Capri* (☎ 8-512-6531), for US$24/36. *Apartahotel Tres Casitas* (☎ 8-512-7115) is one of the reasonable options facing the sea, for US$45/60 per room with fan/air-con (up to three people per room).

If money is not a problem, San Andrés has a good choice of upmarket hotels, some of which are marked on the map.

Places to Eat

Given that food is rather expensive on the island, meals at the *Hotel Restrepo* are a good idea. There are a number of simple backstreet restaurants in El Centro which serve the usual undistinguished comida corriente for around US$3.

If you prefer something typical of the island, be prepared to pay more. One of the

SAN ANDRÉS TOWN

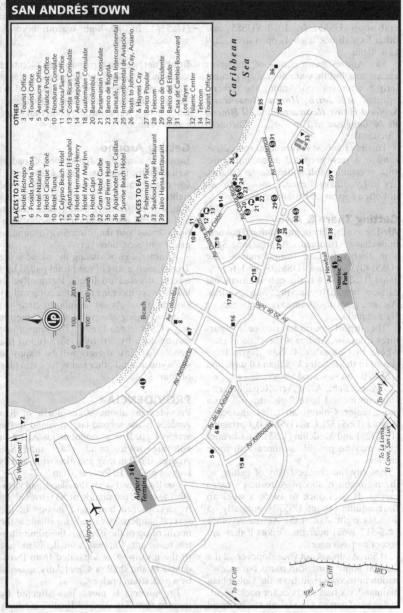

PLACES TO STAY
1 Hotel Restrepo
6 Posada Doña Rosa
7 Hotel Natania
8 Hotel Cacique Toné
10 Hotel Tiuna
12 Calypso Beach Hotel
15 Apartamentos El Español
16 Hotel Hernando Henry
17 Hotel Mary May Inn
19 Hotel Capri
22 Gran Hotel Caribe
35 Lord Pierre Hotel
38 Sunrise Beach Hotel

PLACES TO EAT
2 Fisherman Place
33 Seafood House Restaurant
39 Jairo Hansa Restaurant

OTHER
3 Tourist Office
4 Tourist Office
5 Aerosuce Office
9 Avianca Post Office
10 Honduran Consulate
11 Avianca/Sam Office
13 Costa Rican Consulate
14 AeroRepublica
18 Guatemalan Consulate
20 Bancolombia
21 Panamanian Consulate
23 Banco de Bogotá
24 Bancafé, Titan Intercontinental
25 Intercontinental de Aviación
26 Boats to Johnny Cay, Acuario
   & Haynes Cay
27 Banco Popular
28 Telecom
29 Banco de Occidente
30 Banco del Estado
31 Casa de Cambio Boulevard
   Los Reyes
32 Islamic Center
34 Telecom
37 Tourist Office

Caribbean Sea

cheapest restaurants is **Fisherman Place** on the seafront near the Restrepo, which has crab soup (US$5), fried fish (US$5) and other local dishes. It's only open from 12:30 to 4:30 pm.

San Andrés has a choice of upmarket restaurants, but they are not cheap, particularly not for seafood. Among the top-end options are **Jairo Hansa Restaurant**, **Seafood House Restaurant** and **El Rincón de la Langosta** at Km 7 of the Carretera Circunvalar.

Possibly the best known local specialty is *rondón*, a stew prepared in coconut milk, with vegetables, fish and *caracoles* (snails). Try it if you have a chance, though it does not often appear on restaurant menus.

Getting There & Away

Air The availability of international connections changes frequently. At press time, Sam, with flights to and from Panama City (US$140), San José (US$105) and Tegucigalpa (US$118), was the only international carrier regularly serving San Andrés. Avianca goes to Miami via Cartagena or Barranquilla.

The airport tax on international departures from San Andrés is the same as elsewhere in Colombia: US$24 if you have stayed in the country less than 60 days, and US$46 if you've stayed longer.

Avianca/Sam, Aces, AeroRepública and Intercontinental have flights to and from most major Colombian cities, including Bogotá (US$152), Cali (US$154), Cartagena (US$123) and Medellín (US$138). Cheaper fares may be possible at times with some carriers.

Possibly the cheapest way of getting to the mainland is aboard Aerosucre's cargo carrier. It flies once or twice a week to Barranquilla (about US$70), normally on Tuesday night. Ask at the Aerosucre office (☎ 8-512-4967) near the airport if they are accepting passengers.

If San Andrés is not your stopover on the Central-South American route, but a destination in its own right from the Colombian mainland, it's best to check for package ads in weekend papers. Good deals can be found in the low season, with offers including return airfare and a decent hotel for far less what you'd pay buying your ticket and accommodation separately.

Sam and Satena have several flights daily between San Andrés and Providencia (US$36). In the high season, book in advance.

Boat There are no ferries to the Colombian mainland or elsewhere. Cargo ships run to Cartagena every few days, but they don't take passengers. Cargo boats to Providencia leave once a week, but they don't take passengers either.

Getting Around

Buses run along the circular coastal road, as well as on the inner road to La Loma and El Cove, and can drop you near any of the sights. Otherwise, hire a bicycle (US$2 per hour or US$10 a day). Motorbikes, scooters and cars can also be hired at various locations throughout the town. Shop around, as prices and conditions vary.

Another way of visiting the island is the Tren Blanco, a sort of road train pulled by a tractor dressed up like a locomotive. It leaves every morning from the corner of Av Colombia and Av 20 de Julio to circle the island, stopping at several sights along the way (US$4, three hours). The same route can be done by taxi for US$18 (up to five people fit). Taxi drivers will be happy to show you around other sights, for extra fare, of course.

PROVIDENCIA

Providencia, about 90km north of San Andrés, is the second-largest island in the archipelago. It is a mountainous island of volcanic origin, much older than San Andrés. It's 7km long and 4km wide, and its highest peak is El Pico, at 320m.

An 18km road skirts the island, and virtually the entire population of 5000 lives along it, in scattered houses or in one of the several hamlets. Santa Isabel, a village at the northern tip of the island, is the administrative seat. Santa Catalina, a smaller island just to the northwest, is separated from Providencia by the shallow Canal Aury, spanned by a pedestrian bridge.

Providencia is much less affected by tourism than San Andrés. English is widely spoken, and there's still much Caribbean English-style architecture to be seen. The locals are even friendlier than those on San Andrés, and the duty-free business fever is unknown. However, the island is quite rapidly becoming a fashionable spot for Colombian tourists. Aguadulce, on the west coast, has already been converted into a tourist center, with hotels and restaurants, and boat, motorbike and snorkeling gear for hire. So far, the rest of the island is largely unspoiled, though the situation is changing.

The coral reefs around Providencia are more extensive than those around San Andrés, and snorkeling and scuba diving are even better. The interior of the island provides for pleasant walks, with El Pico being the major goal. The trail to the peak begins from Casabaja, on the south side of the island. It's a steady hour's walk to the top.

Getting around the island is pretty straightforward. Two chivas and several pickups run the circular road, charging US$0.50 for any distance. Providencia is an expensive island for food and accommodation, even more so than San Andrés.

Information

There's a tourist office at the airport, theoretically open 8 am to noon and 2 to 6 pm. The Banco Central Hipotecario in Santa Isabel may change cash (but not traveler's checks), but at a poor rate. Bring enough pesos with you from San Andrés.

Places to Stay

The only really cheap place to stay is the basic *Residencias Sofía* (☎ 8-514-8109), in Pueblo Viejo, 2km south of Santa Isabel. Get off by the SENA center and take the rough track that branches off the main road next to a shop and leads toward the seaside; the residencias is just 200m away, on the shore. It costs US$6 per person in very rustic doubles or triples, and simple meals (around US$3 each) are available on request.

The overwhelming majority of places to stay are in Aguadulce, which is apparently exclusively a tourist village. A dozen cabañas line the main road, charging from about US$20 per person upward. The cheapest option is *Residencias Miss Elma* (☎ 8-514-8166), at about US$12 a bed. Don't confuse this place with the comfortable but expensive *Cabañas Miss Elma* (☎ 8-514-8229).

There are some accommodation options elsewhere on the island, if you're looking to escape tourists. In Santa Isabel, you can stay in the simple *Residencia Santa Isabel*

(☎ 8-514-8097), which costs US$10/12 per person in rooms without/with bath, or in the slightly better but more expensive *Hotel Flaming Tree* (☎ 8-514-8049). There are a couple of places on the island of Santa Catalina, just opposite Santa Isabel by the pedestrian bridge, including *Cabañas Santa Catalina* (☎ 8-514-8392), for US$25 a double with private bath.

Places to Eat

Food is expensive, though usually good, particularly the seafood. Most restaurants are in Aguadulce. One of the reasonable options for comida isleña (the local food) is *Miss Elma*. There are also a few restaurants in Santa Isabel. You can buy good, fresh coconut bread in some shops.

Getting There & Away

Sam and Satena fly between San Andrés and Providencia several times per day (US$36). Buy your ticket in advance, and be sure to reconfirm your return flight at the Satena office at the airport, or at the Sam office in Santa Isabel.

The Northwest

In broad terms, the northwest is made up of two regions, quite different in their geography, climate, people and culture. The first, the Chocó department, along the Pacific coast, is essentially a vast wet tropical forest, with a sparse, mainly black population. Roads are few and poor, so most transport is by boat or plane.

The other part, the departments of Antioquia, Caldas, Risaralda and Quindío, is comprised of picturesque mountainous country, covering parts of the Cordillera Occidental and the Cordillera Central. In contrast to 'black' Chocó, this is Colombia's 'whitest' region, with a large Creole population. It's well crisscrossed by roads linking little towns noted for their distinctive architecture.

MEDELLÍN

Medellín was founded in 1675, but only at the beginning of the 20th century did it begin to expand rapidly, first during the region's coffee boom and then as the center of the textile industry. Today, it's a dynamic industrial and commercial city with a

COLOMBIA

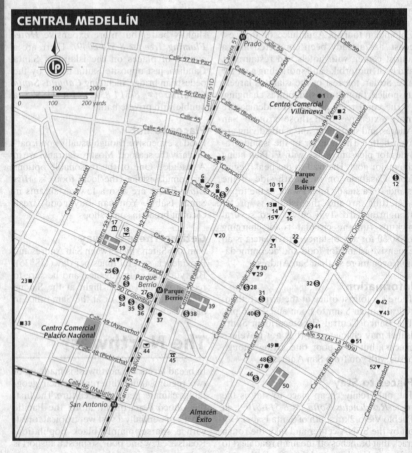

CENTRAL MEDELLÍN

population of nearly two million, the country's largest urban center after Bogotá.

Spectacularly set in the Aburrá valley, with the modern center in the middle and vast slum barrios blanketing surrounding slopes, Medellín is the capital of Antioquia. Not a top traveler's destination, it's a vibrant and friendly city with a pleasant climate, and it does have some museums and tourist facilities. Although no longer the world's cocaine trafficking capital, Medellín may not be safe, so keep your nighttime strolls to a minimum.

Information

Tourist Office The Oficina de Turismo de Medellín (☎ 4-254-0800), at Calle 57

No 45-129, is open 7:30 am to 12:30 pm and 1:30 to 5:30 pm weekdays.

Money Banks that change traveler's checks at reasonable rates include the Banco Sudameris Colombia, Banco Santander and Banco Anglo Colombiano. All these and some other banks will also change cash, but you'll probably get similar or even better rates (and will save a lot of time) at casas de cambio. There are several in the Edificio La Ceiba at Calle 52 No 47-28; before changing at the Intercambio 1A on the ground floor, check the casas on the 3rd floor, which may pay better. Also worth checking is the Titan Intercontinental, Carrera 46 No 49A-27, which exchanges both cash and traveler's

CENTRAL MEDELLÍN

PLACES TO STAY
2 Hotel El Capitolio
3 Aparta Hotel El Cristal
5 Hotel La Mirada
6 Aparta Hotel Santelmo
8 Hotel La Bella Villa
10 Hotel Odeón
13 Hotel Plaza
14 Hotel Americano
23 Hotel Conquistadores
33 Hotel Comercial
49 Hotel Residencias Gómez
   Córdoba

PLACES TO EAT
11 Restaurante La Estancia
15 Salón Versalles
16 Restaurante Aleros del Parque,
   El Café del Parque
20 Restaurante Vegetariano
   Palased
21 Restaurante Hato Viejo

24 Restaurante Vegetariano
   Govinda's
29 Hacienda Real
30 Boulevard de Junín
43 Restaurante Vegetariano Trigo y
   Miel
52 Restaurante Vegetariano
   Paracelso

OTHER
1 Copa Office
4 Basílica Metropolitana
7 Minibuses to José María
   Córdoba Airport
9 Bancafé
12 Tourist Office
17 Museo de Antioquia
18 Avianca Airline & Post Offices
19 Ermita de la Veracruz
22 AeroRepública Office
25 Banco Sudameris Colombia
26 Banco Industrial Colombiano

27 Banco Anglo Colombiano
28 Banco Industrial Colombiano
31 Edificio La Ceiba
32 Banco Industrial Colombiano
34 Banco Santander
35 Banco de Bogotá
36 Bancolombia
37 La Gorda (Botero's Sculpture)
38 Banco Popular
39 Basílica de la Candelaria
40 Banco de Occidente
41 Banco Santander
42 Centro Colombo Americano
44 Adpostal
45 Telecom
46 Banco Unión Colombiano
47 Aces Office
48 Titan Intercontinental
50 Iglesia de San José
51 Tierra Mar Aire

checks at competitive rates. Cash advances on credit cards are available at most banks, some of which have ATMs.

Tierra Mar Aire (☎ 4-242-0820) is at Calle 52 No 43-124.

Internet Access PuntoWeb (☎ 4-230-9403), Carrera 69A No 42-68, close to the Universidad Bolivariana, offers Internet access and food until 10 pm daily, except Sunday.

Consulates See the Facts for the Visitor section for Panamanian and Venezuelan consulate contact information.

Things to See
Apart from a couple of churches, the city's colonial architecture has virtually disappeared. Perhaps the most interesting of the churches is the **Basílica de la Candelaria**, in Parque Berrío. You also might like to visit the **Basílica Metropolitana**, in the Parque de Bolívar, completed early this century to become one of the largest brick churches on the continent (1.2 million bricks were used).

The **Museo de Antioquia**, Carrera 52A No 51A-29, features a collection of paintings and sculptures by Fernando Botero, the most internationally known Colombian contemporary artist. It's open 9:30 am to 5:30 pm weekdays, 9 am to 2 pm Saturday. The city has a fine botanical garden, the **Jardín**

Botánico Joaquín Antonio Uribe, Carrera 52 No 73-182. You may also want to visit the local zoo, the **Zoológico de Santa Fe**, Carrera 52 No 20-63, which specializes in species typical of Colombia. Both the garden and the zoo are open 9 am to 5 pm daily.

For panoramic views of the city, go to the **Cerro Nutibara**, a hill southwest of the center. The **Pueblito Paisa**, a replica of a typical Antioquian village, has been built on the summit and is home to several handicrafts shops.

Special Events
The Mercado de San Alejo, a colorful craft market, is held in the Parque de Bolívar on the first Saturday of every month.

On the last Friday of February, May, August and December, the Tangovía springs to life on Carrera 45 in the Manrique district. This is tango night, when you can listen and dance to the nostalgic rhythms. Medellín is Colombia's capital of tango; it was here that Carlos Gardel, the legendary tango singer, died in an airplane crash in 1935.

Medellín's biggest event, the Feria de las Flores, takes place in early August. Its highlight is the August 7 Desfile de Silleteros, when hundreds of campesinos come down from the mountains and parade along the streets carrying *silletas* full of flowers on their backs.

Places to Stay

Some of the cheapest central hotels are in the busy commercial area between Carreras 52 and 54 and Calles 48 and 50. The most popular with travelers here is probably **Hotel Conquistadores** (☎ 4-512-3229), at Carrera 54 No 49-31, which costs about US$11 for a double with TV and private bath. Alternatively, stay in the large, well-run **Hotel Comercial** (☎ 4-513-0006), Calle 48 No 53-102, which costs US$7/9/12/15 a single/double/triple/quad without bath, US$9/13/17/22 with bath.

If you consider the area too dirty and noisy, try some of the hotels farther west, eg **Hotel Residencias Gómez Córdoba** (☎ 4-513-1676), Carrera 46 No 50-29, which is one of the cheapest acceptable places near Parque de Bolívar. It costs US$9/11/14 per single/couple/double with bath.

At Parque de Bolívar itself is the slightly better **Hotel Plaza** (☎ 4-231-8984), Calle 54 No 49-23, which costs US$12/16 for a couple/double with bath. **Hotel Americano**, next door, is a cheap love dive and won't accept you for the whole night until after 7 pm (never on weekends). Better to check **Hotel La Mirada** (☎ 4-511-2334), Calle 54 No 50-74, a small, family-run place which is simple but cheap.

If you can afford to pay more, **Aparta Hotel El Cristal** (☎ 4-512-0911), Carrera 49 No 57-12, is good value and therefore often full. It costs US$26/34/40 a single/double/triple with bath, telephone, fan, TV and fridge. Next door is the marginally more expensive **Hotel El Capitolio** (☎ 4-512-0003), Carrera 49 No 57-24. **Hotel Odeón** (☎ 4-511-1360), Calle 54 No 49-38, is a bit more modest and cheaper option in the immediate environs of Parque de Bolívar.

In the same price range are **Hotel La Bella Villa** (☎ 4-511-0144), Calle 53 No 50-28, and **Aparta Hotel Santelmo** (☎ 4-231-2728), Calle 53 No 50A-08. They are perhaps not in the most pleasant surroundings but convenient if you are coming by plane, as airport minibuses will deposit you just a few steps away.

Places to Eat

La Estancia, Carrera 49 No 54-15, in Parque de Bolívar, is the cheapest place to eat. It's not very clean or pleasant but does have filling set meals for just US$1.

Vegetarians have several budget options, including **Govinda's**, Calle 51 No 52-17; **Palased**, Carrera 50 No 52-38 (in the Union Plaza commercial center); **Trigo y Miel**, Calle 53 No 43-54; and **Paracelso**, Calle 52 No 43-17.

There are many moderately priced restaurants and cafés on and around the pedestrian walkway Pasaje Junín (Carrera 49), between Parque de Bolívar and Calle 52. **Salón Versalles**, Pasaje Junín No 53-39, has a tasty menú económico, good cakes, fruit juices and tinto. The first floor is more pleasant.

Several restaurants on Pasaje Junín are set on the first floor overlooking the street. **Aleros del Parque**, **El Café del Parque** and **Hacienda Real** are pleasant places for lunch or dinner or for watching the world go by while sipping a beer. If you just want to grab something quickly, try **Boulevard de Junín**, where several self-service joints offer pizza, chicken, pasteles, salpicón (cold mixed fruit cocktail) and ice cream.

Hato Viejo, on the first floor of the Centro Comercial Los Cámbulos, on the corner of Pasaje Junín and Calle 53, is one of the best places in the area. It serves regional dishes and grilled meats.

Getting There & Away

Air The José María Córdoba airport, 30km southeast of the city, takes all international and most domestic flights, except for some regional flights on light planes which use the old Olaya Herrera airport right inside the city. The terminal houses the tourist office (on the lower level by the exit of the domestic arrival hall) and the Banco Santander (on the upper level at the departure hall), which exchanges cash, traveler's checks and gives advances on Visa 8 am to 4 pm weekdays.

Frequent minibuses shuttle between the city center and the airport from the corner of Carrera 50A and Calle 53 (US$2, one hour). A taxi will cost US$16.

There are flights throughout the country – to Bogotá (US$71), Cali (US$81), Cartagena (US$102), Cúcuta (US$85) and San Andrés (US$138). Cheaper fares may be available on some routes with some carriers.

Sam and Copa fly daily to Panama City (US$161), while Servivensa flies to San Antonio del Táchira in Venezuela (US$63); add a 10% tax on top of these fares, if you buy the tickets in Colombia.

Bus Medellín has two bus terminals. The Terminal del Norte, 3km north of the city center, handles buses to the north, east and southeast (Turbo, Cartagena, Barranquilla, Bucaramanga, Bogotá). It's easily reached from the center by metro in six minutes. The new Terminal del Sur, 4km southwest of the center, handles all traffic to the west and south (Quibdó, Manizales, Cali, Popayán). It's accessible by the Guayabal bus (Ruta No 160), which you catch on Av Oriental near the Almacén Exito in the center.

Frequent air-conditioned buses depart to Bogotá (US$25, nine hours), Cali (US$24, nine hours) and Cartagena (US$37, 13 hours).

Getting Around
Medellín is Colombia's first (and for the foreseeable future the only) city to have the Metro, or fast metropolitan train. It consists of the 23km north-south line and a 6km western leg, and is clean, cheap, safe and efficient. The train operates on the ground level except in the central area where it goes on viaducts above the streets.

AROUND MEDELLÍN
The picturesque, rugged region surrounding Medellín is sprinkled with haciendas and *pueblos paisas*, lovely little towns noted for their distinctive architectural style. The temperate climate encourages the luxuriance of a variety of plants and flowers, including many orchids.

With a couple of days to spare, it's a good idea to do a trip around Medellín to see what Antioquia is really like. Among the most interesting places are the towns of **La Ceja**, **El Retiro** and **Marinilla** (all good examples of the regional architecture), **Carmen de Viboral** (well known for its hand-painted ceramics) and the spectacular, 200m granite rock of **El Peñón**. All these places provide food and accommodation, and the buses are frequent.

The most recent addition to the region's attractions is the **Parque de las Aguas**, an enjoyable amusement park full of waterslides, pools and other distractions, open 9 am to 5 pm daily. It's about 20km northeast of Medellín and has good transportation links with the city. Take the metro to the northern end of the line at Niquía and change for a bus. Metro stations sell a US$4 package which includes the return metro fare and the park's entrance ticket (but not the US$1 bus ride each way, which you pay separately).

SANTA FE DE ANTIOQUIA
Founded in 1541, this is the oldest town in the region. It was an important and prosperous center during the Spanish days and the capital of Antioquia until 1826. It retains its colonial character and atmosphere. The town is about 80km northwest of Medellín, on the road to Turbo.

Things to See
Give yourself a couple of hours to wander about the streets to see the decorated doorways of the houses, the windows with their carved wooden guards and the patios with flowers in bloom. Of the town's four churches, the nicest is the **Iglesia de Santa Bárbara**. The **Museo Juan del Corral** (closed Monday) displays historic objects collected in the region. The **Museo de Arte Religioso** (open weekends only) features religious art.

There is an unusual 291m bridge, the **Puente de Occidente**, over the Río Cauca, 6km east of town. When built in 1886, it was one of the first suspension bridges in the Americas. Walk there, or negotiate with taxi drivers in Santa Fe.

Places to Stay & Eat
Residencias Colonial, Calle 11 No 11-72, set in an old mansion, is quiet and friendly. Rooms on the upper floor (US$10 a double) are more pleasant and have a balcony. The hotel serves cheap set meals. ***El Mesón de la Abuela***, Carrera 11 No 9-31, is in the same price range. It's quite simple, but clean and with a friendly atmosphere. It also provides meals.

There are several cheaper residencias in town, including ***Franco***, Carrera 10 No 8-67, and ***Dally***, Calle 10 No 8-50. Top of the range is ***Hotel Mariscal Robledo***, Carrera 12 No 9-70, which costs US$25/40 a single/double. It has a swimming pool and a restaurant.

Apart from the hotel restaurants, there are at least half a dozen other places to eat. The cheapest places are in the market on the main square, where you can get a tasty bandeja for a little more than US$1. Don't miss the pulpa de tamarindo, a local tamarind sweet sold in the market.

COLOMBIA

Getting There & Away

There are several buses daily to and from Medellín's northern terminal (US$4, three hours), and also hourly minibuses until 7 pm (US$5, 2½ hours).

The Southwest

The southwest covers the departments of Cauca, Valle del Cauca, Huila and Nariño. The region is widely diverse, both culturally and geographically. The biggest tourist attractions are the two outstanding archaeological sites of San Agustín and Tierradentro, and the colonial city of Popayán. Cali is the region's largest urban center.

CALI

Cali is a prosperous and lively city with a fairly hot climate. Although founded in 1536, its growth came only in this century, primarily with the development of the sugar industry, followed by dynamic progress in other sectors. Today, Cali is Colombia's third-largest city, with a population of about 1.75 million.

Apart from a few fine churches and museums, the city doesn't have many tourist attractions. Its appeal lies rather in its atmosphere and its inhabitants, who are, in general, friendly and easygoing.

The women of Cali, *las caleñas*, are considered to be the most beautiful in the nation. Cali is also noted for its salsa music. These hot rhythms originated in Cuba in the 1940s, matured in New York and spread throughout the Caribbean, reaching Colombia in the 1960s. The Cali region and the Caribbean coast remain Colombia's major centers of salsa music.

Finally, Cali is notorious as the home of the Cali drug cartel and as the world capital of cocaine trafficking. Since many syndicate leaders were jailed in 1995, this is no longer true, though lower-rank bosses still run the business quite efficiently. Be wary of thieves and muggers, who are as tough and persistent as in other large cities, and avoid unnecessary nighttime strolling.

Orientation

The city center is split in two by the Río Cali. To the south is the historic heart, laid out on a grid plan and centered around the Plaza de Caycedo. This is the area of tourist sights, including historic churches and museums.

To the north of the river is the new center, whose main axis is Av Sexta (Av 6N). This sector is modern, with trendy shops and restaurants, and it comes alive in the evening when a refreshing breeze tempers the daytime heat. This is the area to come and dine, drink and dance after a day of sightseeing on the opposite side of the river.

Information

Tourist Office The Cortuvalle departmental tourist office (☎ 2-660-5000), Av 4N No 4N-10, is open 7:30 am to 12:30 pm and 2:30 to 6 pm weekdays. There's also a Cortuvalle branch at the airport.

Money Most of the major banks are around Plaza de Caycedo, but few will exchange foreign cash or traveler's checks. Try the Banco Anglo Colombiano, Bancolombia or Banco Unión Colombiano (there's a new branch of the latter bank at Calle 22N No 6N-22). Also check the Casa de Cambio Titan Intercontinental on the 2nd floor of the Edificio Ulpiano Lloreda on Plaza de Caycedo, which is more efficient and may give comparable rates for both cash and checks. All banks marked on the map will give peso advances on credit cards.

Tierra Mar Aire (☎ 2-667-6767) is at Calle 22N No 5BN-53.

Internet Access Central facilities include Cafeweb (☎ 2-660-5299), at Calle 15N No 6N-28; Cyancopias (☎ 2-668-8395), at Av 6N No 13N-23; and Mail Boxes (☎ 2-660-5190), at Av 8N No 18N-36. Also see Calidad House and Guest House Iguana in the Places to Stay section.

National Parks & Private Reserves The Ministerio del Medio Ambiente (☎ 2-654-3719, 2-654-3720), Av 3GN No 37N-70, deals with the region's national parks. It has information on Isla Gorgona, issues permits and takes bookings.

The Red de Reservas Naturales de la Sociedad Civil (☎ 2-661-2581), Calle 23N No 6AN-43, 3rd floor, has a list of nature reserves operated by nongovernment organizations, complete with their locations, features, tourist facilities and names and phone numbers of people who can provide further details.

Things to See

The beautiful **Iglesia de la Merced**, on the corner of Carrera 4 and Calle 7, is Cali's oldest church. The adjacent monastery houses two good museums (both closed on Sunday): the **Museo de Arte Colonial**, with mostly colonial religious art, and the **Museo Arqueológico**, with pre-Columbian pottery from several southern Colombia cultures.

One block away, the **Museo del Oro** (open weekdays) has a collection of gold from the pre-Hispanic Calima culture. The **Museo de Arte Moderno La Tertulia**, Av Colombia No 5 Oeste-105, presents temporary exhibitions of contemporary painting, sculpture and photography.

For a view of the city center, go to the hilltop **Iglesia de San Antonio**, a short walk southwest of the center.

Special Events

The main city event is the Feria de Cali, which begins annually on December 25 and goes till the end of the year, with parades, salsa concerts, bullfights and a beauty pageant.

Places to Stay

Most choice budget accommodations are in the Av Sexta area in the new city center. One of the most popular with foreign backpackers is *Calidad House* (☎ 2-661-2338), Calle 17N No 9AN-39, which costs US$5 a person in rooms without bath. It's pretty basic but provides a range of facilities, including laundry and kitchen, Internet access and free luggage storage.

Better is *Guest House Iguana* (☎ 2-661-3522), in a nice house with a patio at Calle 21N No 9N-22. Run by a friendly Swiss couple, the hotel has ample clean rooms (US$7 a person) and many services, such as tours, breakfasts and laundry service (Internet access is in the works).

Other budget options include *Residencial Chalet* (☎ 2-661-2709), Av 4N No 15N-43, charging US$8/11 per couple/double with bath; *Casa Hotel Calima* (☎ 2-661-6214), Av 8N No 10N-104, for US$9/14 a single/double; and *Hotel JJ* (☎ 2-661 8979), Av 8N No 14N-47, for US$9/16. None of them are anything special.

There aren't many budget accommodations south of the Río Cali, except for the maze of seedy hospedajes east of Calle 15,

but don't walk there – this is one of the most dangerous areas of central Cali. Farther west, in a more pleasant area near Iglesia de San Antonio, is the basic *Hostal El Castillo* (☎ 2-888-1339), Carrera 3 No 1-74 (US$6 a person without bath); and the better *Casa Turística Sharon* (☎ 2-884-4885), Carrera 12 No 2-54 (no sign). The latter is a friendly family house that offers 12 neat rooms (US$12/16 a single/couple), plus cooking and laundry facilities.

There's a choice of mid-price hotels around the Plaza de Caycedo, including *Hotel Astoria* (☎ 2-883-0140), Calle 11 No 5-16, which has airy singles/doubles/triples with TV and bath for US$28/34/42. Ask for a room on one of the top floors, for less noise and better views. A little better is *Hotel Royal Plaza* (☎ 2-883-9243), Carrera 4 No 11-69, at US$40/50/62.

If you want something with more character and are prepared to pay more, *Pensión Stein* (☎ 2-661-4927), in a fine house just north of the Río Cali at Av 4N No 3N-33, is a good choice. Run by a Swiss couple, the hotel offers spotlessly clean rooms with bath and also has a restaurant. Singles/doubles cost US$50/80, breakfast included.

Places to Eat

There are loads of cafés and restaurants on and around Av Sexta, offering everything from simple snacks, burgers and pizzas to regional Colombian cuisine and Chinese, Arab and German specialties. It won't take you long to find a cheap restaurant that serves set meals for less than US$2.50, such as *Restaurante Balocco*, Av 6N No 14N-06, and *El Punto Paisa*, at Av 6N No 14N-55. *Sancochos con Sabor a Leña*, at Av 9N No 16N-32, is also inexpensive and does typical food. *Pizza Cuadritos*, Av 6N No 13N-17, tosses cheap pizzas.

Some other upmarket options include *Granada*, Av 9 No 15AN-02 (international), *Mi Tierra*, Av 8N No 10N-18 (local specialties and seafood), and *El Caballo Loco*, Calle 16N No 6N-31 (international).

For vegetarian food, try *La Edad de Oro*, Av 5BN No 20 N-30. There are three more budget places close to each other on Carrera 6, on the south side of the Río Cali: *Casona Vegetariana*, *Sol de la India* and *Punto Verde*. All places listed in this paragraph only open weekdays for lunch.

CENTRAL CALI

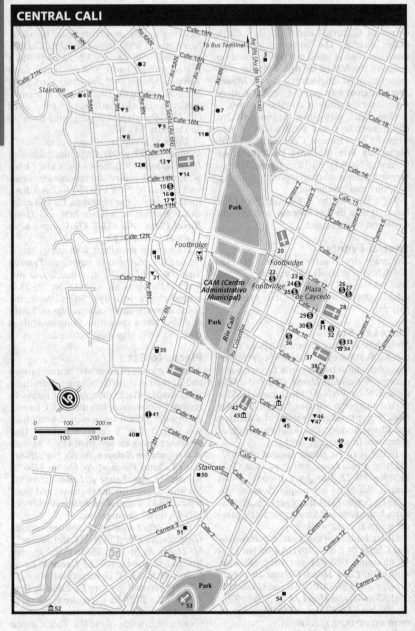

COLOMBIA

CENTRAL CALI

PLACES TO STAY
1 Guest House Iguana
3 Hotel La Torre de Cali
4 Calidad House
11 Residencial Chalet
12 Hotel JJ
18 Casa Hotel Calima
23 Hotel Royal Plaza
31 Hotel Astoria
40 Pensión Stein
50 Hotel Intercontinental
51 Hostal El Castillo
54 Casa Turística Sharon

PLACES TO EAT
5 Sancochos con Sabor a Leña
8 Restaurante Granada
9 Restaurante El Caballo Loco
13 El Punto Paisa
14 Restaurante Balocco
17 Pizza Cuadritos
21 Restaurante Mi Tierra

46 Comedor Vegetariano Punto
    Verde
47 Restaurante Vegetariano Sol de
    la India
48 Casona Vegetariana

OTHER
2 Mail Boxes
6 Bancafé
7 Zaperoco
10 Cafeweb
15 Banco Santander
16 Cyancopias
19 Avianca Post & Airline Offices
22 Banco Unión Colombiano
24 Banco de Bogotá
25 Casa de Cambio Titan
    Intercontinental
26 Banco de Occidente
27 Banco Santander
28 Catedral

29 Banco Anglo Colombiano
30 Banco de Bogotá
32 Banco de Colombia
33 Banco Industrial Colombiano
34 Telecom
35 Sifonería Martyn's
36 Banco Popular
37 Iglesia de San Francisco
38 Capilla de la Inmaculada
39 Torre Mudéjar
41 Cortuvalle Tourist Office
42 Iglesia de la Merced
43 Museo de Arte Colonial &
    Museo Arqueológico
44 Museo del Oro
45 Teatro Municipal
49 Teatro Experimental de Cali
    (TEC)
52 Museo de Arte Moderno La
    Tertulia (Cinemateca La
    Tertulia)
53 Iglesia de San Antonio

Entertainment

Check the entertainment columns in the local newspaper *El País* for theater, cinema and music listings. Colombia's national theater started in Cali with the foundation of *Teatro Experimental de Cali (TEC)*, at Calle 7 No 8-63. If you understand Spanish by all means see one of their plays. The *Cinemateca La Tertulia* art cinema is beside the Museo de Arte Moderno La Tertulia.

There are lots of bars, taverns, discos and nightclubs around the Av Sexta area. *Zaperoco*, Av 5N No 16N-46, is a trendy salsateca (disco playing Latin Caribbean music, mostly salsa). *London Bar*, Calle 22N No 5AN-54, is the place to sit on the terrace and drink to the nostalgic western beats of the '60s and '70s. The English-run *Sifonería Martyn's*, Av 4N No 7N-10, is another place for a nighttime drink.

There's another collection of salsotecas on and around Calle 5 in southern Cali, including *Taberna Latina*, Calle 5 No 38-75, and *Tin Tin Deo*, Carrera 22 No 4A-27.

Also well known is Juanchito, a popular outer suburb largely populated by blacks. Far away from the center on the Río Cauca, Juanchito was traditionally an archetypal salsa haunt dotted with dubious cafés and bars. Today, sterile and expensive salsotecas have replaced the old shady but charming venues.

Night tours in a chiva depart from the Hotel Intercontinental, Av Colombia No 2-72, on Friday and Saturday at 8 pm. The five-hour tour covers a few nightspots (usually one in Juanchito) and costs about US$20, including half a bottle of aguardiente and a snack. Chivas also leave from the CAM (Centro Administrativo Municipal).

Getting There & Away

Air The Palmaseca airport is 16km northeast of the city. Minibuses between the airport and the bus terminal run every 10 minutes till about 8 pm (US$1, 30 minutes).

There are plenty of flights to most major Colombian cities, including Bogotá (US$76), Cartagena (US$125), Medellín (US$81), Pasto (US$73) and San Andrés (US$154).

Copa and Avianca fly to Panama City (US$174), while TAME has flights to Esmeraldas in Ecuador (US$70). Add 10% tax.

Bus The bus terminal is a 20-minute walk northeast the city center, or less than 10 minutes by one of the frequent city buses. Air-conditioned buses run regularly to Bogotá (US$26, 12 hours), Medellín (US$24, nine hours) and Pasto (US$17, nine hours). Pasto buses will drop you off in Popayán (US$5, three hours) and there are also minibuses to Popayán every other hour.

AROUND CALI
Parque Nacional
Farallones de Cali

This fine mountain national park, southwest of Cali, covers 1500 sq km of rugged Cordillera Occidental terrain. It's noted for its lush vegetation and diverse wildlife.

If you just want to do a day trip, take a bus from Cali's terminal to Pance, a weekend resort popular with *caleños*, on the border of the park; from there, footpaths lead into the park. There are hotels and restaurants in the Pance area.

If you intend to hike deeper into the park, contact the Fundación Farallones (☎ 2-556-8335) in Cali, Carrera 24B No 2A-99, which operates the Reserva Natural Hato Viejo in the park, 8km uphill from Pance (a three-hour walk). The reserve offers accommodations, food and guides.

Historic Haciendas

There are a number of old haciendas around Cali, most of which date from the 18th and 19th centuries. Some of them were engaged in the cultivation and processing of sugarcane, the region's most common crop.

The two best known are the **Hacienda El Paraíso** and **Hacienda Piedechinche**, both about 40km northeast of Cali and open as museums. There are tours from Cali, or you can visit them on your own using public transport, though the latter option is a bit time-consuming as both places are off the main roads. The tourist office in Cali can provide more information.

San Cipriano

This is a village lost deep in the tropical forest near the Pacific coast, off the Cali-Buenaventura road. There's no road leading to the village, just a railway with occasional trains, but the locals have set up their own rail network with small human-propelled trolleys. This ingenious means of transport is a great attraction and justifies a San Cipriano trip if only for the ride.

San Cipriano has a crystal-clear river, ideal for swimming (the best part of the river is beyond the village), informal budget accommodations and some simple places to eat. The village is a popular weekend destination with caleños, but it's quiet on weekdays.

To get there from Cali, take a bus or colectivo to Buenaventura, get off at the village of Córdoba (US$5, 2½ hours) and walk down the hill into the village to the railway track. From here, locals will take you to San Cipriano in their rail cars – a great journey through the rain forest.

ISLA GORGONA

Lying 55km northeast of the mainland, the 9km-long and 2.5km-wide Gorgona is Colombia's largest Pacific island. It's a mountainous island of volcanic origin, with its highest peak reaching 330m. It's covered with lush tropical rain forest and shelters diverse wildlife, including various monkey, lizard, turtle, snake and bird species, a number of which are endemic. There are some beaches and coral reefs along the shores, and the surrounding waters seasonally host dolphins, humpback whales and sperm whales. The climate is hot and wet, with high humidity and no distinctive dry season.

The island was a cruel high-security prison during La Violencia until 1984, but is now a national park. It offers accommodations (US$75 a night per quad with bath), food (US$16 full board of three set meals) and trips around the island (all excursions are accompanied by guides). You can also swim, sunbathe and snorkel (bring your own gear).

To visit Gorgona, you need a permit (US$7) from the national park office in Cali or Bogotá. Booking long in advance is advisable, especially for Colombian vacation periods. All visits are fixed four-day/three-night stays, which must be paid for in advance.

Getting There & Away

This is a bit of an adventure. The usual departure point for Gorgona is Buenaventura (a three-hour bus from Cali), where you catch a (usually overcrowded) cargo boat for a 10 to 12-hour night trip to the island (about US$30). It can be a hellish experience if the sea is rough.

If you desire more comfort, several tour companies organize trips to Gorgona for US$250 to US$400. The all-inclusive four-day and three-night package covers permit, accommodation, food and transport, and may include other services, such as scuba diving. In Cali, contact Ecotur (2-552-8634), at Carrera 56 No 5-31, or Ecolombia Tours (☎ 2-557-1957), Carrera 37A No 6-18.

POPAYÁN

Popayán is one of the most beautiful colonial cities in Colombia. Founded in 1537 by Sebastián de Belalcázar, the town quickly became an important political, cultural and religious center, and was an obligatory stopover on the route between Cartagena and Quito. Its mild climate attracted wealthy Spanish settlers from the sugar haciendas of the hot Cali region. Several imposing churches and monasteries were built in the 17th and 18th centuries, when the city was flourishing.

During the 20th century, while many Colombian cities were caught up in the race to modernize and industrialize, Popayán somehow managed to retain its colonial character. Ironically, much of this historic fabric, including most of the churches, was seriously damaged by a violent earthquake in March 1983, just moments before the much-celebrated Maundy Thursday religious procession. The difficult restoration work continued for a decade, and the results are admirable: Little damage can be seen today and the city looks even better than it did before the disaster. Apart from its beauty, Popayán is a friendly, tranquil and clean city. It has a good tourist office and a range of places to stay and eat and is not expensive by Colombian standards.

Information

Tourist Office The helpful Caucatur tourist office (☎ 28-242251), Calle 3 No 4-70, has good information about the city and the region. It's open 8 am to noon and 2 to 6:30 pm weekdays and 10 am to noon and 2 to 5 pm weekends.

Money Few of Popayán's banks change money, but fortunately the efficient Casa de Cambio Titan Intercontinental, in the Caucatur building, does exchange both cash and traveler's checks. Banks, however, are useful for cash advances on credit cards. Note that San Agustín and Tierradentro, two popular destinations from Popayán, don't have banks.

National Parks The national park office (☎ 28-239932) is at Carrera 4 No 0-50. You don't need a permit for a day trip to the Parque Nacional Puracé, but check with the office in case you plan on staying longer. The office takes bookings for cabañas in Pilimbalá (see Around Popayán, later).

Things to See

Churches All the colonial churches have been meticulously restored but most are only open for mass, usually early in the morning and late in the afternoon, so plan your sightseeing accordingly.

Don't miss the **Iglesia de San Francisco**, the city's best church, which has exquisite side altars. Other churches noted for their rich original furnishings include the **Iglesia de Santo Domingo** and the **Iglesia de San Agustín**.

Iglesia La Ermita is Popayán's oldest church (1546), worth seeing for its fine high altar and for the fragments of old frescoes, which were only discovered after the 1983 earthquake. The **Catedral** dates from the second half of the 19th century. It was almost completely destroyed by the same earthquake and subsequently rebuilt from the ground up.

The **Capilla de Belén** offers good views over the town, but it's better not to walk there: There have been some armed attacks on travelers in the access alley.

Museums The **Casa Museo Mosquera** contains a collection of colonial art, including some religious objects. More sacred art is displayed in the **Museo de Arte Religioso**. The **Casa Museo Negret** features abstract sculpture by Edgar Negret and works of art by some Latin American contemporary artists, while the **Museo Guillermo Valencia** is dedicated to the poet who once lived here. The **Museo de Historia Natural** is noted for its collections of insects, butterflies and stuffed birds. Part of the top floor is taken up by an archaeological display of pre-Columbian pottery from southern Colombia. Most local museums are open 9 am to noon and 2 to 5 pm Tuesday to Sunday (some don't open on weekend afternoons).

Other Attractions Churches and museums are only a part of what Popayán has to offer. The best approach is to take a leisurely walk along the streets lined with whitewashed colonial mansions, savor the architectural details and drop inside to see the marvelous patios (many are open to the public). Have a

COLOMBIA

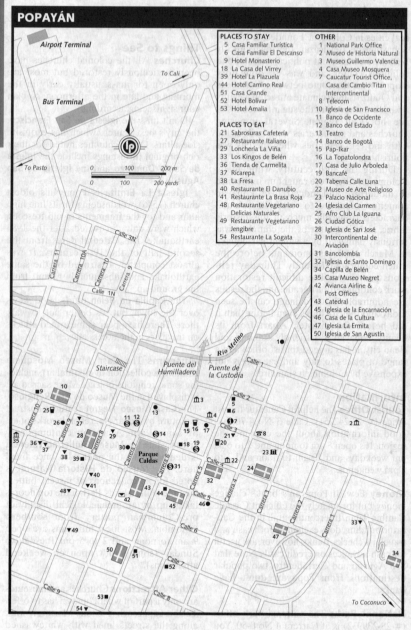

POPAYÁN

PLACES TO STAY
5   Casa Familiar Turística
6   Casa Familiar El Descanso
9   Hotel Monasterio
18 La Casa del Virrey
39 Hotel La Plazuela
44 Hotel Camino Real
51 Casa Grande
52 Hotel Bolívar
53 Hotel Amalia

PLACES TO EAT
21 Sabrosuras Cafetería
27 Restaurante Italiano
29 Lonchería La Viña
35 Los Kingos de Belén
36 Tienda de Carmelita
37 Ricarepa
38 La Fresa
40 Restaurante El Danubio
41 Restaurante La Brasa Roja
48 Restaurante Vegetariano
    Delicias Naturales
49 Restaurante Vegetariano
    Jengibre
54 Restaurante La Sogata

OTHER
1   National Park Office
2   Museo de Historia Natural
3   Museo Guillermo Valencia
4   Casa Museo Mosquera
7   Caucatur Tourist Office,
    Casa de Cambio Titan
    Intercontinental
8   Telecom
10 Iglesia de San Francisco
11 Banco de Occidente
12 Banco del Estado
13 Teatro
14 Banco de Bogotá
15 Pap-Ikar
16 La Topatolondra
17 Casa de Julio Arboleda
19 Bancafé
20 Taberna Calle Luna
22 Museo de Arte Religioso
23 Palacio Nacional
24 Iglesia del Carmen
25 Afro Club La Iguana
26 Ciudad Gótica
28 Iglesia de San José
30 Intercontinental de
    Aviación
31 Bancolombia
32 Iglesia de Santo Domingo
34 Capilla de Belén
35 Casa Museo Negret
42 Avianca Airline &
    Post Offices
43 Catedral
45 Iglesia de la Encarnación
46 Casa de la Cultura
47 Iglesia La Ermita
50 Iglesia de San Agustín

look at the **Palacio Nacional**, the **Casa de la Cultura**, the **Puente del Humilladero** and the **Puente de la Custodia**.

Special Events
If you are in the area during Holy Week, you'll have the chance to see the famous nighttime processions on Maundy Thursday and Good Friday. Popayán's Easter celebrations are the most elaborate in the country. The festival of religious music is held concurrently. Note that hotels are full around that time, so get there early or book in advance.

Places to Stay
Popayán has a good array of accommodations to suit every budget. Many hotels are in stylish old colonial houses.

The recommended *Casa Familiar Turística* (☎ 28-244853), in a colonial building at Carrera 5 No 2-11, has huge rooms, a lot of old-time charm and a family atmosphere. It costs US$5 per person for rooms with shared facilities, and serves an excellent breakfast for US$2. Laundry service and free luggage storage are also available.

Just half a block away is *Casa Familiar El Descanso* (☎ 28-240019), at Carrera 5 No 2-41. Its rooms are clean and comfortable, but much smaller than in the other casa. They don't have private baths either and cost US$7/13 a single/double. There's a 11 pm curfew. Neither casa displays its name on the door – just ring the bell.

If both the casas are full and you need somewhere really cheap, try the simple *Hotel Amalia* (☎ 28-241203), at Carrera 6 No 8-58, which costs US$6/8/11 a single/couple/double without bath. The more basic *Hotel Bolívar* (☎ 28-244844), Carrera 5 No 7-11, charges about the same.

More expensive, but much better, *Casa Grande* (☎ 28-240908), Carrera 6 No 7-11, costs US$12/20/26 a single/double/triple with bath. Better yet and more central, colonial *La Casa del Virrey* (☎ 28-240836), Calle 4 No 5-78, has comfortable rooms with bath attached (choose one facing the street) for US$20/32/40 a single/double/triple, or US$8 per person without bath.

Several splendid historic mansions have been refashioned as stylish hotels. *Hotel La Plazuela* (☎ 28-241084), Calle 5 No 8-13, and *Hotel Camino Real* (☎ 28-241254), Calle 5 No 5-59, both cost about US$50/70 a

single/double including breakfast; ask for a room facing the street. Top-notch *Hotel Monasterio* (☎ 28-242191), on Calle 4, is a restored monastery charging US$70/85.

Places to Eat
Numerous restaurants serve cheap set lunches and dinners. To name just a few: *Restaurante El Danubio*, at Carrera 8 No 5-53; *Restaurante La Brasa Roja*, corner of Calle 6 and Carrera 8; and *Lonchería La Viña* (open till midnight), Calle 4 No 7-85. For vegetarian food, try *Delicias Naturales*, Calle 6 No 8-21, *Jengibre*, Carrera 8 No 7-19, or *La Sogata*, Calle 9 No 6-31 (the latter also has meat dishes).

Popayán has a number of places serving local food. *Los Kingos de Belén*, at Calle 4 No 0-55, has good regional specialties; try their bandeja típica and wash it down with champús. For delicious, cheap empanadas de pipián, the place to go is *La Fresa*, a small cubbyhole (no sign) at Calle 5 No 8-89. Half a block away, *Ricarepa*, Calle 5 No 9-35, has great arepas con maíz y queso. Next door, the unsigned place known locally as *Tienda de Carmelita*, Calle 5 No 9-45, serves good tamales de pipián. You can also find tamales and other typical snacks in *Sabrosuras Cafetería*, Calle 3 No 4-31.

The Swiss-run *Restaurante Italiano*, Calle 4 No 8-83, has a variety of hearty spaghettis and lasagnas at reasonable prices. The restaurant in the *Hotel Camino Real* is one of the best in town: You won't find such mouthwatering steaks and French specialties for miles around. An excellent six-course meal costs about US$18.

Entertainment
If you want a drink to the rhythms of tropical music, try *La Topatolondra*, Calle 3 No 5-69, *Afro Club La Iguana*, Calle 4 No 9-67, *Taberna Calle Luna*, Carrera 5 No 3-49, or *Pap-Ikar*, at Carrera 6 No 3-25. *Ciudad Gótica*, Carrera 9 No 4-42, is a popular disco.

Getting There & Away
Air The airport is just behind the bus terminal, a 15-minute walk north of the city center. Avianca and Intercontinental have daily flights to Bogotá (US$79).

Bus The bus terminal is a short walk north of the city center. Plenty of buses run to Cali

(US$5, three hours), and there are also colectivos every two hours. You shouldn't wait more than an hour for a bus to Pasto (US$10 pullman, US$12 air-con; six hours). Day-time travel is recommended on this route for two reasons: spectacular scenery and the risk of nighttime ambushes. Air-conditioned buses to Bogotá run every hour or two (US$31, 14 hours).

For Tierradentro, take the Sotracauca bus at 8 am, which will take you directly to San Andrés de Pisimbalá (US$8, five to six hours), passing the museum en route. Other buses (three daily) will drop you off in El Cruce de San Andrés, from where you have to walk 20 minutes to the museum plus another 25 minutes to the village.

Half a dozen buses daily (with Cootrans-huila, Cootransmayo, Sotracauca and Trans-ipiales) run to San Agustín on a short road via Coconuco and Isnos (US$11, seven to eight hours). The Cootranslaboyana minibus is a faster alternative (US$13, six hours). The road is very rough, but the trip through the lush cordillera cloud forest is spectacular. Keep an eye on your bags – some cases of theft in the bus have been reported on this route. If you prefer to get to San Agustín in a more adventurous way, there's an attractive trek from Valencia via the Laguna de la Magdalena (see the Laguna de la Magdalena section). The Caucatur tourist office can give you the necessary information.

AROUND POPAYÁN
Silvia

A small town 60km northeast of Popayán, Silvia is the center of the Guambianos, one of the most traditional Indian communities in Colombia. Though the Indians don't live in the town, they bring fruit, vegetables and handicrafts to the Tuesday market. That's the best day to visit Silvia – a pleasant day trip from Popayán. You'll see plenty of Indians in town in their traditional dress, the women in hand-woven garments and beaded necklaces, busily spinning wool. This is possibly the most colorful Indian gathering in the country, but cameras are not welcome.

Bring a sweater – it can get cold when the weather is cloudy. If you decide to stay longer in Silvia, there are at least half a dozen cheap residencias, and also some upmarket options.

To get to Silvia from Popayán, take the Coomotoristas bus (US$2, 1½ hours). You can also take any of the frequent buses to Cali, get off in Piendamó (US$1, 40 minutes), then take a colectivo to Silvia (US$1, another 40 minutes). On Tuesday, there are also direct colectivos between Popayán and Silvia.

Parque Nacional Puracé

This picturesque mountainous park, about 60km east of Popayán, offers a variety of landscapes and sights, from volcanoes and mountain lakes to waterfalls and hot springs. Among the highlights are the **Termales de San Juan**, spectacular sulfur springs set in beautiful surroundings. Multicolored moss, algae and lichens bloom where the hot waters meet the ice-cold mountain creeks. The springs are in the northern part of the park and can be easily reached by the Popayán-La Plata buses which pass nearby. There are two fine waterfalls and a lake within walking distance of the springs.

About 10km west of the springs is **Pilimbalá**, which has accommodation in cabins, a restaurant and thermal pools. A cabin with attached bath and hot water costs US$60 and can sleep up to six people (in the low season individual beds go for US$10). You may be able to find cheaper accommodations and meals with families nearby.

If you feel fit enough, hike to the top of the **Volcán Puracé** (4780m) – it's about a four-hour steady ascent from Pilimbalá. You can do it easily in a day, but start early. The weather is precarious year-round, so take good rain gear. Generally, only the early mornings are sunny; later on, the volcano is covered with clouds.

In the southern part of the park, you can hike from Valencia to Quinchana (or vice versa) – see the following section.

LAGUNA DE LA MAGDALENA TREK

This is a popular if hard two-day hike between the villages of Quinchana and Valencia, passing by a small lake, Laguna de la Magdalena (at 3300m), headwaters of the Río Magdalena. The walk is likely to be wet, cold and muddy, but it's certainly a memorable experience. The trip is an adventurous way of getting between Popayán and San Agustín, and you can get information about the route in both these towns. It can also be done on horseback.

Valencia is linked to Popayán by road and one bus daily (US$8, seven hours). Quinchana, at the other end of the trail, is accessible by road from San Agustín, and serviced by one or two chivas per day (US$2, two hours). Both Valencia and Quinchana have simple informal accommodations, food and horse rental. On the trail, you stay the night and eat in the place known as San Antonio (a nine-hour walk from Valencia, five hours from Quinchana), which is a solitary country house overlooking the valley. You therefore don't need any camping gear, but take some food and snacks along.

SAN AGUSTÍN

This is one of the continent's most important archaeological sites. The area was inhabited by a mysterious pre-Columbian civilization which left behind several hundred freestanding monumental statues carved in stone and a number of tombs. The site was a ceremonial center where locals buried their dead and placed the statues next to the tombs. Pottery and gold objects were left in the tombs of the tribal elders.

San Agustín culture flourished between the 6th and 14th centuries AD, though its initial stages are thought to have been perhaps a millennium earlier. The best statuary was made only in the last phase of the development, and the culture had presumably vanished before the Spaniards came. Perhaps, like some other civilizations of the Andean region, it fell victim to the Incas – this area of Colombia was the northernmost point of the Inca empire. The statues were not discovered until the middle of the 18th century.

So far, some 500 statues have been found and excavated. A great number are anthropomorphic figures – some of them realistic, others very stylized, resembling masked monsters. Others are zoomorphic, depicting sacred animals such as the eagle, the jaguar and the frog. The statues vary both in size, from about 20cm to 7m, and in their degree of detail.

The statues and tombs are scattered in groups over a wide area on both sides of the gorge formed by the upper Río Magdalena. The main town of the region is San Agustín, where you'll find most of the accommodation and restaurants. From there, you can explore the region; give yourself three days for leisurely visits to the most interesting places.

The weather is variable, with the driest period from December to February and the wettest from April to June.

The area around San Agustín has witnessed some intensive guerrilla activity in recent years. There have been a number of ambushes on buses (mainly along the San Agustín-Popayán road), as well as armed robberies of hikers (mainly between La Chaquira and Alto de los Idolos and in the La Pelota area). Also, there have been continuing problems with the theft in buses on routes to and from San Agustín.

Information

Tourist Office The tourist office has closed down, so try some of the travel agencies. Fortunately, there's a number of them, including the helpful Viajes Patrimonio Mundial (☎ 88-373940), Calle 3 No 10-84.

Money As yet, no banks or casas de cambio in San Agustín change cash or traveler's checks. Travel agents may know where to change them, but be prepared for poor exchange rates. It's better to come with a cache of pesos.

The Caja Agraria, corner of Carrera 13 and Calle 4, is likely to give peso advances on Visa, but MasterCard is useless; the closest place which may accept it is the Concasa in Pitalito.

Things to See

The most important place is the **Parque Arqueológico**, 2.5km west of the town, where you can see some of the best examples of San Agustín statuary. The park covers several archaeological sites featuring statues, tombs and burial mounds. It also has a museum displaying smaller statues and pottery, and the **Bosque de las Estatuas** (Forest of Statues), where 35 statues of different origins are placed along a footpath that snakes through the woods.

The park is open 8 am to 6 pm daily, but most sites and the museum close at 5 pm. The ticket office closes at 4 pm. The ticket (US$2.50) bought here also covers entry to the Alto de los Idolos and is valid for two consecutive days.

SAN AGUSTÍN AREA

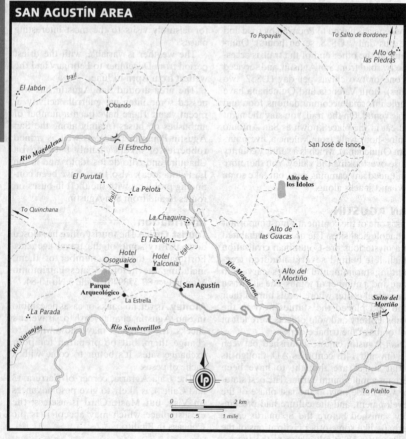

The **Alto de los Idolos** is another archaeological park, noted for burial mounds and large stone tombs. The largest statue, 7m tall, is here. The park is a few km southwest of San José de Isnos, on the other side of the Río Magdalena from San Agustín town. However, the walk from San Agustín through the gorge is not recommended for security reasons – tourists have been robbed on this route.

There are some 15 other archaeological sites scattered over the area. The region is also noted for its natural beauty, with two lovely **waterfalls**, Salto de Bordones and Salto del Mortiño. **El Estrecho**, where the Río Magdalena passes through a 2m narrows, is also an attractive sight.

Places to Stay

On the whole, accommodations in San Agustín are good and cheap. There are a dozen budget residencias in and around town, most of which are clean and friendly and have hot water. Unless stated otherwise, all hotels listed below charge about US$3 to US$4 per person in rooms without bath, or US$5 with private bath.

There are several hotels near the bus offices, which may be convenient if you are coming late or tired. Possibly the best budget option is *Hospedaje El Jardín* (☎ 88-373455), Carrera 11 No 4-10, which has neat rooms with bath and a little garden.

Two blocks west, *Hotel Ullumbe* (☎ 88-373799), at Carrera 13 No 3-36, is another good budget place with rooms with private baths and laundry service. Just a few steps up the street, *Hotel Imperio* (☎ 88-373055), Carrera 13 No 3-42, is a reasonable option with private bath, hot water and laundry.

Another two blocks west, you'll find more cheap places. Your first option might be *Hotel Ixchel* (☎ 88-373492), Calle 5 No 15-39, which offers good rooms, satellite TV, Internet access and a restaurant. Just around the corner, the friendly proprietors of *Residencias Menezú* (☎ 88-373693), Carrera 15 No 4-74, offer clean rooms with shared baths and hot water. *Mi Terruño*, Calle 4 No 15-85, has some rooms with private bath and a pleasant balcony overlooking the garden.

There are some interesting budget options outside the town. *Posada Campesina Silvina Patiño* (☎ 88-373956), a pleasant family house 1km toward El Tablón, offers just three rooms and is probably the cheapest in the whole area. You can also camp and superb meals are available by request. Another good choice is *La Casa del Sol Naciente* (☎ 88-379002), 1km northeast of town (US$5 with breakfast). A little further down the same road is *Casa de Christian*, a friendly hotel with views over the Magdalena gorge. *Casa de Nelly* (☎ 88-373221), run by a French woman, is a lovely tranquil place 1km west of the town off the dirt road to La Estrella. It has four rooms and two cabañas.

There are two upmarket hotels, *Osoguaico* (☎ 88-373069), costing US$35/40/45 a single/double/triple, and *Yalconia* (☎ 88-373013), costing US$50/65/80. Both are outside the town, on the road to the Parque Arqueológico. There are two simple campgrounds, *Camping San Agustín* and *Camping Ullumbe*, near the Hotel Yalconia.

Should you need somewhere to stay in San José de Isnos, there are two budget residencias on the main square: *El Balcón* and *Casa Grande.*

Places to Eat

Brahama, Calle 5 No 15-11, serves cheap set meals, vegetarian food and fruit salads. *Surabhi*, Calle 5 No 14-09, also has inexpensive meals. *Arturo Pizza*, Calle 5 No 15-58, has tasty pizza and spaghetti. *Bambú Café*, Calle 5 No 13-34, does tacos, burritos, sandwiches, spaghetti, salads etc, some of which will suit vegetarians. You'll find several other eateries in the area.

There are half a dozen eating outlets near the Hotel Yalconia, including *La Brasa* (grilled meat) and *Para y Coma* (local dishes). *La Antigua*, 800m from the town on the road to the Casa de Christian, has a diverse menu which includes pasta, salads, pizza, sandwiches and vegetarian food. It also offers rooms and camping.

Getting There & Away

Half a dozen buses a day go to Popayán via a rough but spectacular road through Isnos (US$11, seven to eight hours); watch your luggage closely. Cootranslaboyana runs minibuses to Popayán (US$13, six hours).

Coomotor has two buses daily to Bogotá (US$24, 12 hours). On this route, too, you should keep your luggage next to you, never on the floor or up on the racks (so far, there has been no problem with the luggage traveling in the compartment beneath the floor). There's also a faster and more comfortable Taxis Verdes service in air-conditioned vans (US$27, 10 hours).

Frequent jeeps shuttle between San Agustín and Pitalito (US$1.50, 45 minutes). Here, again, keep a constant eye on your backpack (which is put on the roof). There have been reports that packs which were loaded in Pitalito disappeared somewhere along the way.

There are no direct buses to Tierradentro; go to La Plata (US$9, five hours, one or two buses daily) and change. Buses from La Plata will let you off at El Cruce de San Andrés (US$3, 2½ hours), from where it's a 20-minute walk to the Tierradentro museum. You can stay overnight in La Plata – there are several cheap residencias.

Getting Around

You can visit some of San Agustín's attractions on foot, in conjunction with infrequent public transport. This is the cheapest way, but also the most time-consuming, as some of the sites are distant and involve long hikes. If you are not up to that, plenty of operators in San Agustín arrange jeep and horseback excursions.

Jeep tours can be arranged at Asotranstur (☎ 88-373340) at Calle 5 No 14-50, Viajes Patrimonio Mundial (☎ 88-373940) and other travel agencies. The standard tour includes El Estrecho, Alto de los Idolos, Alto de las Piedras, Salto de Bordones and Salto de Mortiño. The trip takes seven to eight hours and costs US$16 per person.

Horse rental is operated by the Asociación de Alquiladores y Baquianos, corner of Calle 5 and Carrera 17, but you can arrange a horse through most travel agencies, hotel managers or directly with horse owners who frequently approach tourists. Horses are hired out for a specific route, or by the hour (US$2.50) or the day (US$10).

TIERRADENTRO

Tierradentro is an archaeological site known for its underground burial chambers. They are circular tombs scooped out of the soft rock and ranging from two to seven meters in diameter. The domelike vaults of the larger tombs are supported by massive columns. The chambers were painted in geometric patterns, and the decoration in some of them has been remarkably well preserved. These funeral temples contained the cremated remains of tribal elders. The ashes were kept in ceramic urns, which are now displayed in the museum.

About a hundred tombs have been discovered to date, as well as several dozen stone statues similar to those of San Agustín. Not much is known about the people who built the tombs and the statues. Most likely, they were of different cultures, and the people who scooped out the tombs preceded those who carved the statues. Today, the region is inhabited by the Páez Indians, who have lived here since before the Spanish conquest, but it is doubtful whether they are the descendants of the sculptors.

Information

There are no tourist office or money changing facilities. The owner of Los Lagos de Tierradentro (see Places to Stay) is a good source of information about the area.

Things to See

There are four sites with tombs and one with statues, as well as a museum and the village of San Andrés de Pisimbalá. Except for El Aguacate, all the sights are quite close to each other.

TIERRADENTRO

To Santa Rosa

El Duende

To Calderas

El Tablón

Segovia

San Andrés
de Pisimbalá

Museum

Museum

Alto de San Andrés

To El Cruce de
San Andrés

El Aguacate

0   250   500 m
0   250   500 yards

You begin your visit from the museum, where you buy one combined ticket (US$2.50), valid for two consecutive days to all archaeological sights and the museum itself (actually two museums in separate buildings across the road from one another). The **Museo Arqueológico** contains pottery urns which have been found in the tombs, while the **Museo Etnográfico** has utensils and artifacts of the Páez Indians. Both museums are open 8 am to 5 pm daily.

A 15-minute walk up the hill north of the museum will bring you to **Segovia**, the most important burial site. There are 28 tombs here, some with well-preserved decoration. Seven of the tombs are lit; for the others, you need a flashlight – don't forget to bring one.

Other burial sites include **El Duende** (four tombs without preserved decoration) and the more interesting **Alto de San Andrés** (five tombs, two of which have their original paintings). Statues have been gathered together at **El Tablón**.

The village of **Pisimbalá**, a 25-minute walk west of the museum, is noted for its beautiful thatched church.

Places to Stay

As in San Agustín, the accommodation in Tierradentro is good and cheap – expect to pay US$3 to US$4 per person for a simple but clean room. You can stay either close to the museum or in San Andrés de Pisimbalá.

Lucerna, in a house just up the road from the museum, is clean, pleasant and friendly. Some 150m farther on is *Pisimbalá*, one of the cheapest places in the area. Another 150m farther up the road is the *Ricabet*. Next to it is the more expensive *El Refugio* (US$20/25 a single/double), but prices falls considerably in the slow season. The hotel has a swimming pool and a restaurant, and you may be allowed to camp on the grounds.

In San Andrés de Pisimbalá, there are three budget residencias, of which *Los Lagos de Tierradentro* is the cheapest and friendliest. The family who run it serve meals and rent horses.

Places to Eat

In the museum area, *Pisimbalá* (see Places to Stay) is the cheapest place to eat, serving set meals for about US$2. Slightly more expensive is the *Restaurante 86*, just across the road. You can also eat in the restaurant

at *El Refugio*, but it's a bit pricier. In San Andrés de Pisimbalá, the obvious choice is *Los Lagos*.

Getting There & Away

Only one or two buses a day call at San Andrés de Pisimbalá. Most buses ply the Popayán-Belalcázar road, passing El Cruce de San Andrés, so you need to walk to El Cruce (20 minutes from the museum). Three or four buses daily pass via El Cruce on their way to Popayán (US$8, five to six hours). It's a bumpy but spectacular trip on a winding mountain road.

Three or four buses pass through El Cruce to La Plata (US$3, 2½ hours), plus there's one morning bus from San Andrés to La Plata. There are two direct buses from La Plata to Bogotá and two to San Agustín, or take a colectivo to Pitalito and change.

PASTO

Founded in 1537 at the foot of the Volcán Galeras, Pasto was for centuries an important cultural and religious center, and today it's the capital of the Nariño department. Though much colonial character has faded, its churches still reflect some of the town's past splendor. The city lies at an altitude of more than 2500m, so it gets cold at night – have warm clothes handy.

Pasto is noted for its *barniz de Pasto*, a kind of processed vegetable resin (known to the local Indians as *mopa mopa*) used to decorate wooden bowls, plates and boxes with colorful patterns.

Information

Tourist Office The Oficina de Turismo de Nariño (☎ 27-234962), Calle 18 No 25-25, is open 8 am to noon and 2 to 6 pm weekdays.

Money Most major banks are around the main square, Plaza de Nariño. They pay advances on Visa or MasterCard, and some, including the Banco Santander and Banco Anglo Colombiano, also change cash and traveler's checks.

Things to See

There are half a dozen colonial churches in town, most of which are large constructions with richly decorated interiors. The **Iglesia de Cristo Rey**, with its fine stained-glass windows, is arguably the most beautiful. The

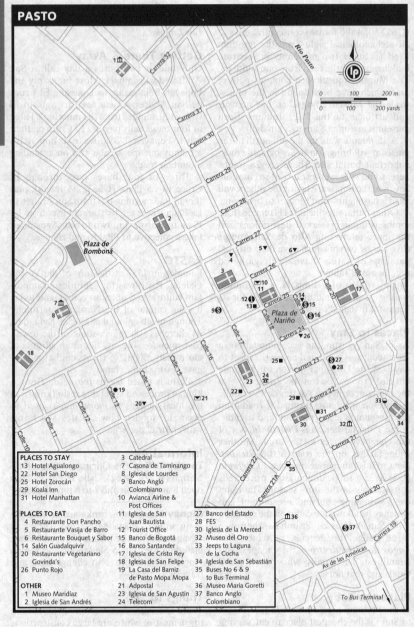

PASTO

Plaza de Bomboná

Río Pasto

Plaza de Nariño

Carrera 32
Carrera 31
Carrera 30
Carrera 29
Carrera 28
Carrera 27
Carrera 26
Carrera 25
Carrera 24
Carrera 23
Carrera 22
Carrera 21B
Carrera 21A
Carrera 21
Carrera 20
Carrera 19

Calle 21
Calle 20
Calle 18
Calle 17
Calle 16
Calle 15
Calle 14
Calle 13
Calle 12
Calle 11
Calle 10

Av de las Américas

To Bus Terminal

PLACES TO STAY		3 Catedral	27 Banco del Estado
13 Hotel Agualongo		7 Casona de Taminango	28 FES
22 Hotel San Diego		8 Iglesia de Lourdes	30 Iglesia de la Merced
25 Hotel Zorocán		9 Banco Anglo	32 Museo del Oro
29 Koala Inn		Colombiano	33 Jeeps to Laguna
31 Hotel Manhattan		10 Avianca Airline &	de la Cocha
		Post Offices	34 Iglesia de San Sebastián
PLACES TO EAT		11 Iglesia de San	35 Buses No 6 & 9
4 Restaurante Don Pancho		Juan Bautista	to Bus Terminal
5 Restaurante Vasija de Barro		12 Tourist Office	36 Museo María Goretti
6 Restaurante Bouquet y Sabor		15 Banco de Bogotá	37 Banco Anglo
14 Salón Guadalquivir		16 Banco Santander	Colombiano
20 Restaurante Vegetariano		17 Iglesia de Cristo Rey	
Govinda's		18 Iglesia de San Felipe	
26 Punto Rojo		19 La Casa del Barniz	
		de Pasto Mopa Mopa	
OTHER		21 Adpostal	
1 Museo Maridíaz		23 Iglesia de San Agustín	
2 Iglesia de San Andrés		24 Telecom	

COLOMBIA

elaborately decorated Iglesia de San Juan Bautista is the city's oldest church.

The small but good **Museo del Oro** (open weekdays), in the Banco de la República building at Calle 19 No 21-27, contains pre-Columbian Nariño gold and pottery. Accommodated in a meticulously reconstructed 17th-century house at Calle 13 No 27-67, the **Casona de Taminango** houses a museum (closed Sunday), which features artifacts and historic objects from the region.

The **Museo Maridíaz** and **Museo María Goretti** both have missionary collections and, as such, resemble antique shops crammed with anything from images of the saints to cannonballs.

Special Events

The city's major event, the Carnaval de Blancos y Negros, is held at the beginning of January. Its origins go back to the time of Spanish rule, when slaves were allowed to celebrate on January 5th and their masters showed approval by painting their faces black. The following day, the slaves painted their faces white. On these two days the city goes wild, with everybody painting one another with anything available. It's a serious affair – wear your least favorite outfit.

Places to Stay

By far the most popular place with backpackers is **Koala Inn** (☎ 27-221101), Calle 18 No 22-37. Set in a fine old building, the hotel offers spotlessly clean, spacious rooms without/with bath for US$6/7 per person, laundry facilities, book exchange, Internet access, a budget restaurant and cable TV in the patio. The friendly manager, Oscar, speaks several languages and is a good source of information.

Alternatively, try **Hotel Manhattan** (☎ 27-215675), Calle 18 No 21B-14. It's also a stylish historic building with large rooms, and charges the same as the Koala.

There are plenty of hotels throughout the central area which can provide more comfort, but they generally lack style and atmosphere. Check **Hotel Zorocán** (☎ 27-233243), Calle 18 No 23-39 (US$16/24/30 a single/double/triple), or **Hotel San Diego** (☎ 27-235050), at Calle 16A No 23-27 (US$18/24/30). The refurbished **Hotel**

Agualongo (☎ 27-235216), at Carrera 25 No 17-83, is the best upmarket option.

Places to Eat

There are loads of cheap restaurants and cafés in the city center, where you can get a set meal for just US$2. For vegetarian food, go to **Govinda's**, Carrera 24 No 13-91 (lunch only). Self-service **Punto Rojo**, on the main square, is a good place to put together a reasonably priced meal. It's clean and is open 24 hours. The tiny restaurant in **Koala Inn** is a good value.

Salón Guadalquivir, on the main square, makes hearty tamales. **Don Pancho**, Calle 18 No 26-93, serves filling plates of comida criolla, such as sobrebarriga, chuleta or arroz con pollo, for US$3. **Vasija de Barro**, Calle 19 No 26-65, and **Bouquet y Sabor**, Carrera 26 No 19-73, both have good, reasonably priced food.

Getting There & Away

Air The airport is 31km north of the city on the road to Cali. Colectivos go there from the corner of Calle 18 and Carrera 25 (US$2.50). Pay the day before your flight at the airline office or at a travel agency, and the colectivo will pick you up from your hotel. Avianca has daily flights to Bogotá (US$105) and Cali (US$73); Intercontinental may be cheaper.

Bus The bus terminal is 2km south of the city center. Urban buses go there from several points in the central area, including the corner of Carrera 21A and Calle 17, or take a taxi (US$1.25).

Frequent buses, minibuses and colectivos go to Ipiales (US$3 to US$4, 1½ to two hours); sit on the left for better views. Plenty of buses ply the spectacular road to Cali (US$15 pullman, US$17 climatizado; nine hours). These buses will drop you off in Popayán in six hours. Avoid traveling this route at night – buses have been ambushed and passengers robbed. A dozen direct air-conditioned buses to Bogotá (US$42, 22 hours) depart daily.

AROUND PASTO
Laguna de la Cocha

This is one of the biggest and most beautiful lakes in Colombia, about 25km east of Pasto. The small island of **La Corota** is a nature reserve, covered by dense forest and home to highly diverse flora. It is accessible by boat from the lakeshore.

Scattered around the lake are two dozen small private nature reserves, collectively known as the **Reservas Naturales de la Cocha**, established by locals on their farms. They will show you around, and some provide accommodation and food. They can also arrange boat excursions. One of the best known reserves is **Tunguragua** (☎ 27-235369). For more information about the reserves, inquire at the Asociación de la Red de las Reservas (☎ 27-231022) in Pasto, Calle 10 No 36-28.

Some reserves (including Tunguragua) are reached by boat – the main departure point is Puerto El Encano on the northern side of the lake. Here you'll find *Cabaña Naturalia* (☎ 27-219329), a good budget place to stay and eat; try the delicious smoked trout.

Jeeps for the lake (US$1, 45 minutes) depart on weekdays from the Iglesia de San Sebastián (known as La Panadería) in central Pasto (weekends from the back of the Hospital Departamental, corner of Calle 22 and Carrera 7).

Volcán Galeras

A hike or ride to the top of this volcano (4267m) was a popular trip from Pasto until the volcano's activity rose dangerously in mid-1989, putting the city and the surrounding region in a state of emergency. Since that time, the volcano has erupted several times and is still smoking. The access is currently closed; check the tourist office for updates.

Volcán Azufral

This volcano (4070m) lies about 14km west of the town of Túquerres, about 80km southwest of Pasto. It's extinct, and its crater shelters a lovely emerald-colored lake, the **Laguna Verde**.

Buses and colectivos run regularly from Pasto to Túquerres, from where it's a four-hour walk uphill to the volcano (three hours back down) along a dirt jeep road. Túquerres has a choice of accommodation and restaurants. *Residencias Quito* on the Pasto road is possibly the best budget place to stay, while *Restaurante Real Danesa*, corner of Carrera 13 and Calle 20, is the best place to eat.

Reserva Natural La Planada

Roughly midway between Pasto and Tumaco, this private reserve is administered by the FES foundation. It's largely covered by lush cloud forest, and is home to rich and diverse wildlife, including the rare spectacled bear and a variety of birds. Food and accommodation are available (about US$25 for three meals and a bed) and guides can show you around (US$16 per day). To get there from Pasto, take a bus to Tumaco, get off in the village of Chucunés (which has two cheap residencias), from where it's a 1½-hour walk to the reserve. For further information, contact FES (☎ 27-238594), Calle 19 No 22-64 in Pasto. You need to call the reserve (☎ 27-753396) in advance to make reservations.

IPIALES

Ipiales, a couple of kilometers from the Ecuadorian border at Rumichaca, is an uninspiring commercial town driven by contraband trade across the frontier. There is little to see or do in town, except for the colorful Saturday market, where the campesinos from surrounding villages come to buy and sell goods. A short side trip to the Santuario de Las Lajas is a must (see the next section).

Information

Money No bank in Ipiales changes cash or traveler's checks. The banks marked on the map are likely to give advances on Visa (Banco de Occidente on MasterCard). Bancolombia and Banco de Bogotá have ATMs. Plenty of moneychangers on the Plaza La Pola (the main square) and a number of casas de cambio in the town's center will change US dollars, Colombian pesos and Ecuadorian sucres. There are also moneychangers at the Ecuadorian border in Rumichaca.

Ecuadorian Consulate The consulate is on the road to the border, opposite the upmarket Hostería Mayasquer, about half a kilometer before the border proper. It's your last chance to get a visa, if you need one.

Immigration All passport formalities are processed in Rumichaca, not in Ipiales or Tulcán. The DAS office, on the Colombian side of the border, is open 8 am to 8 pm daily, but the Ecuadorian post, just across the river, may close for lunch from noon to 2 pm.

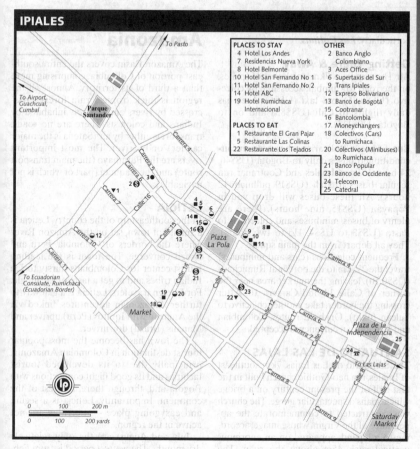

IPIALES

PLACES TO STAY
- 4 Hotel Los Andes
- 7 Residencias Nueva York
- 8 Hotel Belmonte
- 10 Hotel San Fernando No 1
- 11 Hotel San Fernando No 2
- 14 Hotel ABC
- 19 Hotel Rumichaca Internacional

PLACES TO EAT
- 1 Restaurante El Gran Pajar
- 5 Restaurante Las Colinas
- 22 Restaurante Los Tejados

OTHER
- 2 Banco Anglo Colombiano
- 3 Aces Office
- 6 Supertaxis del Sur
- 9 Trans Ipiales
- 12 Expreso Bolivariano
- 13 Banco de Bogotá
- 15 Cootranar
- 16 Bancolombia
- 17 Moneychangers
- 18 Colectivos (Cars) to Rumichaca
- 20 Colectivos (Minibuses) to Rumichaca
- 21 Banco Popular
- 23 Banco de Occidente
- 24 Telecom
- 25 Catedral

Places to Stay

There are plenty of hotels in the center, but some may fill up early (particularly on Saturday), so book as soon as you arrive. The nights are quite chilly, so check the number of blankets before you book a room in a cheapie.

One of the cheapest is *Residencias Nueva York*, on the corner of Carrera 4 and Calle 13, which has acceptable rooms (US$3 per person), but no private baths or hot water. Round the corner, *Hotel Belmonte* (☎ 27-732771), Carrera 4 No 12-111, is a small, friendly, family-run place, possibly the most popular with backpackers. It has no private baths, but does have hot water and costs US$4 per person.

Hotel San Fernando No 1, at Carrera 5 No 12-132, has rooms with private baths and hot water (US$6/10 for a couple/double). *Hotel San Fernando No 2*, next door, has shared baths only, for the same price. A bit better is *Hotel ABC* (☎ 27-732311), Carrera 5 No 14-43, which has singles/doubles/triples with bath and hot water for US$6/10/13.

For something appreciably better, check *Hotel Rumichaca Internacional* (☎ 27-732692), Calle 14 No 7-114 (US$15/25/34), or *Hotel Los Andes* (☎ 27-734338), Carrera 5 No 14-44 (US$22/36/48).

Places to Eat

Several cheap restaurants on the main square serve set meals, and many more are scattered around town. Better eating places include *El Gran Pajar*, *Los Tejados* and, particularly, *Las Colinas*.

Getting There & Away

Air The airport is 7km northwest of Ipiales, on the road to Cumbal, accessible by colectivo (US$0.75) and taxi (US$6). Aces has daily flights to Cali (US$83) and on to Bogotá (US$115).

Bus Expreso Bolivariano has a dozen air-conditioned buses daily to Bogotá (US$46, 24 hours). Trans Ipiales and Cootranar run regular buses to Cali (US$19 pullman, 12 hours). All these buses will drop you in Popayán (US$15, nine hours). There are plenty of buses, minibuses and colectivos to Pasto (US$3 to US$4, 1½ to two hours). They all depart from the main square.

Frequent colectivos (cars and minibuses) travel the 2½ km to the border at Rumichaca (US$0.50), leaving the market area near the corner of Calle 14 and Carrera 10. After crossing the border, take another colectivo to Tulcán (6km). On both routes, Colombian and Ecuadorian currency is accepted.

SANTUARIO DE LAS LAJAS

The Santuario de Las Lajas, 7km southeast of Ipiales, is a neo-Gothic church built in the first half of the present century on a bridge which spans a spectacular gorge. The church was constructed to commemorate the appearance of the Virgin, whose image, according to a legend, appeared on an enormous vertical rock 45m above the river. The church is set up against the gorge cliff in such a way that the rock with the image is its main altar.

Pilgrims from all over Colombia and from abroad come here year-round. Many leave thanksgiving plaques along the alley leading to the church. Note the number of miracles which are said to have occurred.

You can stay in Las Lajas in *Casa Pastoral*, overlooking the gorge. Double rooms with bath cost US$4 per person.

Colectivos run regularly from Ipiales to Las Lajas, leaving from the corner of Carrera 6 and Calle 4 (US$0.50, 15 minutes). A taxi from Ipiales' main square to Las Lajas costs about US$4. A return taxi trip for four people, including one hour of waiting in Las Lajas, shouldn't cost more than US$10.

Colombian Amazonia

The Amazon Basin covers the entire southeast portion of Colombia, comprising more than a third of its territory. Almost all the region is thick tropical rain forest, crisscrossed by rivers and sparsely inhabited by Indians and colonists. There are no roads; transport is either by air (Satena is the major carrier) or by river. The most important rivers are the Putumayo (the main transport route) and the Caquetá (part of which is not navigable).

LETICIA

In the southeast tip of the country, Leticia is a small hot town, set on the Amazon River where the borders of Colombia, Peru and Brazil converge. The town is the leading tourist center for Colombians thirsty to see Indian tribes and to get a taste of the jungle. For foreign travelers, Leticia is a gateway to further Amazonian adventures, linked via the Amazon with Iquitos (Peru) upriver and Manaus (Brazil) downriver.

The town has become the most popular tourist destination in Colombian Amazonia, principally due to its developed tourist facilities and its good flight connections with Bogotá and, through there, the rest of the continent. Importantly, Leticia is a secure and easygoing place – guerrillas are not active in the region.

July and August are the only relatively dry months. The wettest period is from February to April. The Amazon River's highest level is in June, while the lowest is from August to October. The difference between low and high water can be as great as 15m.

Orientation

Leticia lies right on the Colombia-Brazil border. Just south across the frontier sits Tabatinga, smaller and poorer than Leticia, but with its own airport. Leticia and Tabatinga are virtually merging together, and there are no border checkpoints between the two. Frequent colectivos link the two towns, or you can just walk. Both locals and foreigners are allowed to come and go between the two towns without visas, but if you plan on heading further into either country, you must get your passport stamped

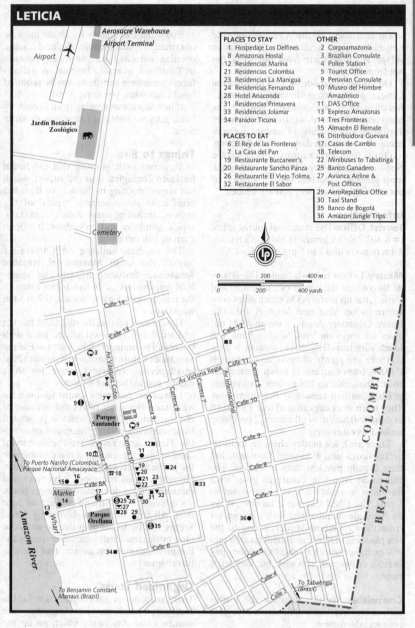

LETICIA

PLACES TO STAY
1 Hospedaje Los Delfines
8 Amazonas Hostal
12 Residencias Marina
21 Residencias Colombia
23 Residencias La Manigua
24 Residencias Fernando
28 Hotel Anaconda
31 Residencias Primavera
33 Residencias Jolamar
34 Parador Ticuna

PLACES TO EAT
6 El Rey de las Fronteras
7 La Casa del Pan
19 Restaurante Buccaneer's
20 Restaurante Sancho Panza
26 Restaurante El Viejo Tolima
32 Restaurante El Sabor

OTHER
2 Corpoamazonía
3 Brazilian Consulate
4 Police Station
5 Tourist Office
9 Peruvian Consulate
10 Museo del Hombre Amazónico
11 DAS Office
13 Expreso Amazonas
14 Tres Fronteras
15 Almacén El Remate
16 Distribuidora Guevara
17 Casas de Cambio
18 Telecom
22 Minibuses to Tabatinga
25 Banco Ganadero
27 Avianca Airline & Post Offices
29 AeroRepública Office
30 Taxi Stand
35 Banco de Bogotá
36 Amazon Jungle Trips

Aerosucre Warehouse
Airport Terminal
Airport
Jardín Botánico Zoológico

Cemetery

0   200   400 m
0   200   400 yards

Calle 14
Calle 13
Calle 12
Calle 11
Calle 10
Calle 9
Calle 8
Calle 8A
Calle 7
Calle 6
Calle 5
Calle 4
Calle 3

Av Vásquez Cobo
Av Victoria Regia
Av Internacional
Carrera 11
Carrera 9
Carrera 7
Carrera 5
Carrera 2
Carrera 8
Carrera 10

Parque Santander
Parque Orellana

Market
Wharf

Amazon River

To Puerto Nariño (Colombia),
Parque Nacional Amacayaco

To Benjamin Constant,
Manaus (Brazil)

To Tabatinga (Brazil)

COLOMBIA
BRAZIL

at DAS in Leticia and at Polícia Federal in Tabatinga (not on the actual border).

On the island in the Amazon opposite Leticia/Tabatinga is Santa Rosa, a Peruvian village. Boats go there from Tabatinga, but not from Leticia.

On the opposite side of the Amazon from Leticia, about 20km downstream, is the Brazilian town of Benjamin Constant, the main port for boats downstream to Manaus. Tabatinga and Benjamin Constant are connected by two boats daily in each direction.

Of the four border towns, Leticia has the best-developed tourist facilities and is the most pleasant – the best place to hang your hat no matter which way you are headed.

Information

Tourist Office The municipal tourist office (☎ 8-592-7505), Carrera 11 No 11-35, is open 7 am to noon and 2 to 5 pm weekdays.

Money Leticia has two banks. The Banco de Bogotá, on the corner of Carrera 10 and Calle 7, has an useful ATM which gives peso advances on Visa and MasterCard. The Banco Ganadero doesn't have an ATM but gives advances on Visa. Neither bank will touch your traveler's checks or cash dollars.

There are plenty of casas de cambio on Calle 8, from Carrera 11 down toward the river. They change US dollars, Colombian pesos, Brazilian reais and Peruvian soles. They open weekdays around 8 or 9 am till 5 or 6 pm and Saturday till around 2 pm. Shop around, as rates vary.

There are a few money-changing facilities in Tabatinga and Benjamin Constant, but they usually pay less than in Leticia. The Banco do Brasil in Tabatinga gives cash advances in reais on Visa (from 8 am to 1 pm). The CNM Câmbio e Turismo on Av da Amizade in Tabatinga, half a kilometer from the Colombian border, is one of the few places in the Leticia-Tabatinga area that will exchange traveler's checks, and they pay in reais or pesos, as you wish, but the rate is poor.

Consulates See the Facts for the Visitor section for Brazilian and Peruvian consulate contact information.

Immigration The DAS office, on Calle 9, is open 8 am to noon and 2 to 6 pm daily. This is where you get your passport stamped when leaving or entering Colombia.

Entry and exit stamps for Brazil must be obtained at the Polícia Federal (same opening hours as DAS), on Av da Amizade in Tabatinga, near the hospital. A yellow-fever vaccination certificate may be required by officials when you enter Brazil.

If heading for or coming from Iquitos by boat, get your entry or exit stamp in Santa Rosa.

Things to See

In the town itself, you can visit the **Jardín Botánico Zoológico**, near the airport, which has almost nothing in the way of flora but does have some animals typical of the region, including anacondas, manatees, tapirs, monkeys and crocodiles. It's open 7 am to 5:30 pm daily.

The modern building on Carrera 11 houses the small **Museo del Hombre Amazónico**, featuring artifacts and household implements of Indian tribes living in the region, open 8 am to noon and 2 to 5 pm weekdays.

Have a look around the riverfront market and stroll along the waterfront, lined with boats and fishmonger stalls. Visit the Parque Santander before sunset, when thousands of small *pericos* (parrots) arrive for their nightly rest in the park's trees.

Leticia has become a tourist spot not for what the town itself offers but because of the surrounding region, which is populated by several indigenous groups, among which the Ticuna and Yagua are the dominant communities. This is also a place to explore the jungle and its exuberant flora and fauna. However, as all transport is by river and there are almost no regular passenger boats, it's difficult to get around cheaply on your own. All trips are monopolized by travel agents and by locals with their own boats. One of the few easily accessible sites is the Parque Nacional Amacayacu (see later in this chapter).

Organized Tours

There are a dozen travel agencies in Leticia focusing on jungle trips. Some agencies offer standard one-day tours, which go up the Amazon to Puerto Nariño and include lunch and a visit to an Indian village. These excursions are usually well organized, comfortable and trouble-free, but can hardly give you a real picture of the jungle or its inhabitants.

The real wilderness begins well off the Amazon proper, along its small tributaries. The further you go, the more chance you have to observe wildlife in relatively undamaged habitat and visit indigenous settlements. This involves more time and money, but the experience is much more rewarding.

Amazon Jungle Trips (☎ 8-592-7377), Av Internacional No 6-25, specializes in adventure trips, centered on its jungle lodge on a tributary of the Río Yavarí (in Peru, but no visas necessary). Unfortunately, the agency has almost doubled its prices in the past few years: Expect to pay around US$70 per person per day in a group of six, all-inclusive. Four people are usually the minimum for a trip (about US$80 per person per day), unless you are prepared to pay substantially more. Given swiftly rising tour prices, an increasing number of travelers visit the Amacayacu National Park instead of taking a tour.

Check other agencies to compare their tours and prices. Try Tramonto Viajes y Turismo (☎ 8-592-8147) at Calle 8 No 9-87, Selva Tour (☎ 8-592-7069) at Carrera 6 No 11-84, Anaconda Tours (☎ 8-592-7891) and Amaturs (☎ 8-592-7018), both at Carrera 11 No 7-34.

There are many independent guides who don't have offices; they will find you and offer their services, usually starting their show by presenting thick albums of photos from their previous trips. The prices they quote may be similar to those offered by the agencies, but are open to negotiation. Always clearly fix the conditions, places to be visited, time and price. Insist on paying only a part of the cost of the trip before departure and the rest at the end.

Luis Daniel González and Jugalvis Valencia Pérez have been recommended by some travelers as good guides. On the other hand, there have been repeated complaints about the services of Joel Mendoza, known locally as Tattoo.

Bring enough mosquito repellent from Bogotá because you can't get good stuff in Leticia. Take high-speed film – the jungle is always dark.

Places to Stay

There are a dozen places to stay in Leticia, which is generally sufficient to cope with the tourist traffic. Most hotels have private bath and all have either fans or air-conditioning.

Probably the cheapest is the basic *Residencias Colombia* (☎ 8-592-7034), Carrera 10 No 8-56, which costs US$8/10 a single/double with hard beds and shared bath. Also basic but with private bath is *Residencias Primavera* (☎ 8-592-7862), Calle 8 No 9-43 (no sign), which costs US$7 per person. Avoid it if you're a light sleeper – salsa and vallenato may blare till late.

Better is *Residencias La Manigua* (☎ 8-592-7121), Calle 8 No 9-22, which has clean singles/doubles with bath for US$13/18. For marginally more you can enjoy similar standards at *Residencias Jolamar* (☎ 8-592-7016), Calle 8 No 7-99, or *Hospedaje Los Delfines* (☎ 8-592-7388), Carrera 11 No 12-81.

Other reasonable options include *Residencias Marina* (☎ 8-592-7309), Carrera 9 No 9-29, and *Residencias Fernando* (☎ 8-592-7362), Carrera 9 No 8-80, both charging about US$16/24 a single/double with bath and TV. You can also try the pleasant *Amazonas Hostal* (☎ 8-592-7069), Av Internacional No 11-84, which, however, seems to be overpriced at US$15/18 per bed in a dorm/double with shared facilities.

There are several upmarket hotels, all with air-conditioning and swimming pools. The most pleasant of these is *Parador Ticuna* (☎ 8-592-7243), with a spacious courtyard filled with tropical plants. Large rooms cost US$60/80/100 a single/double/triple, and there's a restaurant.

Hotel Anaconda (☎ 8-592-7119), Carrera 11 No 7-34, is modern and costs US$75/105/130. It offers good views over the Amazon (particularly at sunset), if you are lucky enough to get the room on the top floor facing the river. Otherwise it's probably not worth the money.

Tabatinga, across the border, also has a collection of hotels, but it's less attractive than Leticia. One of the cheapest (US$16 for a double with bath) is the *Hotel Cristina*, Rua Marechal Mallet No 248, near the wharf. It's convenient if you plan on taking the early-morning boat to Iquitos (see Getting There & Away in this section). One of the best options is the *Hotel Te Contei*, at Av da Amizade No 1813 (US$30/40/50 for an air-con single/double/triple with bath and TV).

Places to Eat

The local specialty is fish: Don't miss the delicious *gamitana*. Also try *cupuasú* juice, from a local fruit (in season from February to March). Beer and soda are expensive.

There's a line of cheap restaurants on Carrera 10 between Calles 8 and 9, of which *Sancho Panza* is perhaps the most popular. It serves set almuerzos and comidas (US$2.50) and reasonably priced à la carte dishes. *El Viejo Tolima* and *El Sabor*, both on Calle 8, have similar offerings and prices. *Buccaneer's* is marginally more expensive but has air-conditioning. Upmarket options include the restaurants at *Hotel Anaconda* and *Parador Ticuna*. *La Casa del Pan*, near Parque Santander, is a good budget breakfast place. For chicken, try *El Rey de las Fronteras*.

Getting There & Away

Air Avianca and AeroRepública fly to and from Bogotá several days a week (US$142); both carriers may offer discounted fares.

Before you book a commercial flight, check for cargo flights with Aerosucre, which shuttles between Leticia and Bogotá almost daily and usually takes passengers for about US$80. You have to hunt for the plane at the airport, sometimes very early in the morning – inquire at the Aerosucre *bodega* (warehouse), behind the passenger terminal. In Bogotá, the Aerosucre planes depart from the cargo building (Edificio de Carga No 1) just before the El Dorado passenger terminal, but they rarely take passengers.

There are no flights into Brazil from Leticia, but from Tabatinga, Varig and Tavaj have flights to Manaus on Monday, Wednesday and Friday, and Rico flies on Tuesday, Thursday and Saturday. Varig's fare is US$200, while the other carriers charge US$180. The airlines' offices are on Av da Amizade near the border. The airport is 2km from Tabatinga; colectivos from Leticia will drop you off nearby. Remember to get your exit/entry stamps before departure.

There are no longer flights to Iquitos, but check when you come as the situation changes frequently.

Boat Leticia is *the* transit point for travelers looking for backwater Amazonian adventures. Although boat fares have risen considerably over the past few years, they are worth the adventure they provide.

Boats down the Amazon to Manaus (Brazil) leave from Benjamin Constant but normally come up to Tabatinga to unload/load. They anchor in Porto de Tabatinga, 1km south of the town's wharf, near the market.

Theoretically, there are two boats per week, leaving Tabatinga on Wednesday and Saturday around noon and Benjamin Constant the same evenings (the Wednesday boat is more reliable). The trip to Manaus takes three days and four nights and costs US$60 in your own hammock, or US$250 for a double cabin. Food is included but is poor and monotonous. Bring snacks and bottled water. The cheapest places to buy an ordinary cloth hammock (US$10 to US$12) are Lojas Esplanada Tecidos, on Rua Marechal Mallet, near Hotel Cristina in Tabatinga; and Almacén El Remate and Distribuidora Guevara, both on Calle 8A in Leticia.

Boats come to Tabatinga one or two days before their scheduled departure back down the river. You can string up your hammock or occupy the cabin as soon as you've paid the fare, saving on hotels. Food, however, is only served after departure. Beware of theft on board. If the boat doesn't come up to Tabatinga but only to Benjamin Constant, you must go there via passenger boat, which departs twice daily from Tabatinga's wharf (US$3.50, 1½ hours).

Upstream from Manaus to Tabatinga, the trip usually takes six days, and costs US$80 in your hammock or US$300 for a double cabin.

Three small companies, Transportes Amazónicos de Turismo, Expreso Loreto and Transporte Pluma Hermanos, all on Rua Marechal Mallet near the wharf in Tabatinga, run high-powered passenger boats *(rápidos)* between Tabatinga and Iquitos. Each company has several departures a week, so there is at least one boat practically every day. The boats depart Tabatinga's wharf at 5 am and arrive in Iquitos about 10 hours later. The boats call at Santa Rosa's immigration posts. The journey costs US$50 in either direction, including lunch.

There are irregular cargo boats to Iquitos once or twice a week, departing from Santa Rosa. The journey takes three days and costs US$25 to US$30, after some negotiations. Downstream from Iquitos to Santa Rosa, it takes around 36 hours.

Note that there are no roads out of Iquitos into Peru. You have to go by air or continue by river to Pucallpa (another four to seven days), from where you can go overland to Lima and elsewhere.

PARQUE NACIONAL AMACAYACU

This national park takes in 2935 sq km of jungle on the northern side of the Amazon, 75km upstream from Leticia. A spacious visitor center with food and accommodation facilities has been built on the bank of the Amazon. Accommodation in a bed or hammock costs US$15/12 per person, and three meals will run to about US$10. The entry fee is US$5. You can book and pay at the national park office in Bogotá, or in Leticia at Corpoamazonía (☎ 8-592-7124), at Carrera 11 No 12-45.

Two small boat companies, Tres Fronteras and Expreso Amazonas (both with offices near the waterfront in Leticia), operate fast passenger boats to Puerto Nariño, daily around noon. They will drop you off at the visitor center (US$10, 1½ hours). Buy your ticket early in the morning.

From the center, you can explore the park, either by paths or by water. Local guides accompany visitors on all excursions and charge roughly US$15 to US$30 per group, depending on the route. In the high-water period (May to June), much of the land turns into swamps and lagoons, greatly reducing walking options, but then trips in canoes are organized. Bring plenty of mosquito repellent, a flashlight, long-sleeve shirt and waterproof gear.

Ecuador

Lying along the equator with Peru to the south and Colombia to the north, Ecuador is a country both blessed and cursed by mother nature. Its blessing is a geography so varied, with so many species, that Ecuador boasts some of the greatest biodiversity on earth. But this astounding landscape is due to the shifting tectonic plates that Ecuador sits on, and when they're feeling capricious, the country gets rocked by earthquakes and volcanic eruptions.

Luckily, this doesn't happen often, and travelers will appreciate the positive results of nature's volatility, as one can venture from white-sand beaches to Andean summits in one day and visit the rain forest the next (all by bus!). Add to this the Galápagos Islands, 1000km off the coast, and it's surprising every adventurous soul among us isn't roaming around Ecuador.

Facts about Ecuador

HISTORY

Ecuadorian Stone Age tools have been dated to 9000 BC, and the oldest signs of a more developed culture date back to 3400 BC. These are mainly ceramics of the Valdivia period, found in the central coastal area of Ecuador.

Early Peoples

Pre-Inca Ecuador is less well known than areas in Peru, but the existence of numerous raised-field earthworks (*camellones*) for cultivation suggests a large population in very early times. In the 11th century AD, there were two dominant cultures: the expansionist Caras along the coast and the peaceful Quitus in the highlands. These peoples merged to form the Shyri nation. In about 1300, the Puruhás of the southern highlands became powerful, and the marriage of a Shyri princess to Duchicela, a Puruhá prince, forged a successful alliance. Duchicela's descendants ruled more or less peacefully for about 150 years.

At a Glance

Country Name	República del Ecuador
Area	272,045 sq km
Population	11,700,000 (1998 estimate)
Population Density	43 per sq km
Capital	Quito
Head of State	President Jamil Mahuad
Official Language	Spanish
Other Languages	Quechua, Quichua, other indigenous languages
Currency	Sucre (S/)
Exchange Rate	US$1 = S/11,580
Per Capita GNP	US$1390
Inflation Rate	30% (1997); 35.9% (1998 estimate)

Inca Conquest

By the mid-1400s, Duchicela's descendants dominated the north. The south was ruled by the Cañari people, who defended themselves fiercely against the Inca invaders. It was some years before the Inca Tupac-Yupanqui was able to subdue them and turn his attention north. During this time, a Cañari princess bore him a son, Huayna Capac.

The subjugation of the north took many years and Huayna Capac grew up in Ecuador. He succeeded his father on the Inca throne and spent years traveling all over his empire, from Bolivia to Ecuador, constantly suppressing uprisings. Wherever possible, he strengthened his position by marriage. His union with a secondary wife, Paccha, the daughter of the defeated Cacha Duchicela, produced an illegitimate son, Atahualpa, while from his principal marriage came Huáscar, his son born of Inca tradition.

Huayna Capac died in 1526 and left his empire not to one son, as was traditional, but to the two half-brothers, thus dividing the Inca Empire for the first time. In the same year the first Spaniards, led by Bartolomé Ruiz de Andrade, landed near Esmeraldas in northern Ecuador, a portent of the invasion that would subjugate the empire some years later.

Meanwhile, the rivalry between the Incas, led by Huáscar of Cuzco and Atahualpa of Quito, flared into civil war. After years of fighting, Atahualpa defeated Huáscar in a battle near Ambato in central Ecuador. Atahualpa thus ruled a weakened and still divided Inca Empire when Pizarro landed in Peru in 1532.

Colonial Era

Francisco Pizarro appointed his brother Gonzalo governor of Quito in 1540. Gonzalo, hoping to find more gold, sent his lieutenant Francisco de Orellana to explore the Amazon. Orellana and his force ended up floating clear to the Atlantic – the first men to descend the Amazon and cross the continent.

Lima was the seat of Ecuador's political administration during the first centuries of colonial rule. Ecuador was at first a *gobernación* (province), but in 1563 it became the Audiencia de Quito, a more important political division. In 1739, the audiencia was transferred from the Viceroyalty of Peru to the Viceroyalty of Colombia (then known as Nueva Grenada).

Ecuador remained peaceful during these centuries, and agriculture and the arts flourished. Cattle, as well as bananas and other agricultural products, were introduced by Europeans. There was prolific construction of churches and monasteries; these were

decorated with unique carvings and paintings resulting from the blend of Spanish and Indian artistic influences.

Life was comfortable for the ruling Spaniards, but Indians and mestizos were treated abysmally. Systems of forced labor and tribute were not only tolerated but encouraged, and it is no surprise that, by the 18th century, there were several uprisings of Indians against their Spanish rulers.

One of the best remembered heroes of the early revolutionary period was Eugenio Espejo, born in Quito in 1747 of an Indian father and a mulatto mother. A brilliant man who obtained his doctorate by the age of 20, Espejo became a major literary voice for independence. He wrote political satire, founded a liberal newspaper and spoke out strongly against colonialism. He was imprisoned several times and died in jail in 1795.

Independence

The first serious attempt at independence was made on August 10, 1809, by a partisan group led by Juan Pío Montúfar. The group took Quito and installed a government, but this lasted for only 24 days before royalist troops regained control.

Independence was finally achieved when Simón Bolívar, the Venezuelan liberator, freed Colombia in his march southward from Caracas in 1819. Bolívar then supported the people of Guayaquil when they claimed independence on October 9, 1820. It was almost two years before Ecuador was entirely liberated from Spanish rule. The decisive battle was fought on May 24, 1822, when Field Marshal Sucre, one of Bolívar's best generals, defeated the royalists at Pichincha and took Quito.

Bolívar's idealistic dream was to form a United South America. He began by amalgamating Venezuela, Colombia and Ecuador into the independent state of Gran Colombia, which lasted eight years. Ecuador became fully independent in 1830. That same year, a treaty was signed with Peru, establishing a boundary between the two nations. After a war between the two nations, the boundary was redrawn by a conference of foreign government ministers in the 1942 Protocol of Rio de Janeiro. Ecuador never recognized this border, and minor skirmishes with Peru have occurred because of it; the most serious was the short war in early 1995, when several dozen soldiers on both sides were killed. Hostilities were confined to remote border areas in the jungle, and travelers were not directly affected. Following more fighting in 1998, Peru and Ecuador negotiated a settlement to the dispute. Peru retained a majority of the land in question, save for a portion known as Tiwintza, a 247-acre area Ecuadorian troops successfully defended in 1995.

Independent Ecuador's internal history has been a typically Latin American turmoil of political and open warfare between liberals and conservatives. Quito emerged as the main center for the church-backed conservatives and Guayaquil has traditionally been considered liberal and socialist. This rivalry continues on a social level today: *quiteños* have given *guayaquileños* the nickname *monos* (monkeys), and the lively coastal people consider the highland inhabitants very staid and dull.

The rivalry between these groups frequently escalated to extreme violence: conservative President García Moreno was shot and killed in 1875 and liberal President Eloy Alfaro was killed and burned by a mob in Quito in 1912. The military began assuming control, and the 20th century has seen more periods of military rule than civilian.

Ecuador's most recent period of democracy began in 1979, when President Jaime Roldos Aguilera was elected. He died in an airplane crash in 1981 and his term of office was completed by his vice president, Osvaldo Hurtado Larrea.

In 1984 the conservative León Febres Cordero was elected. On August 10, 1988, following democratic elections, Social Democrat Rodrigo Borja became president and the government leaned to the left. The elections in 1992 resulted in the victory of the conservative quiteño Sixto Durán Ballén, of the Republican Unity Party.

In 1996, left-wing populist Abdalá Bucaram was elected president. After just six months, Bucaram (known as 'El Loco'), was deemed mentally unfit to rule by the Ecuadorian Congress and was removed from office. Congress named Fabián Alarcón interim president until the 1998 elections. The former mayor of Quito, Jamil Mahuad, emerged victorious over Alvaro Noboa in a hotly contested race.

Jamil, as he's affectionately known, has had his political savvy put to the test. A severe financial crisis in March 1999 led to riots, protests and, ultimately, a government imposed state of emergency. While policies such as austerity measures brought things under a modicum of control, critics accused him of dealing with the symptoms of economic collapse, rather than the problems. Ecuador's economy is still not the most hale.

GEOGRAPHY

Ecuador straddles the equator on the Pacific coast of South America and is bordered by Colombia to the north and Peru to the south. Despite its small size, Ecuador has some of the world's most varied geography.

The country is divided into three regions. The backbone of Ecuador is the Andean range, within which lies the capital, Quito. At 2850m above sea level, it is the second-highest capital in the world (after La Paz, Bolivia). The mountains split the country into the western coastal lowlands and the eastern jungles of the upper Amazon Basin, called the Oriente. In only 200km, as the condor flies, you can climb from the coast to snowcaps over 6km above sea level, then descend to the jungle on the eastern side. The Galápagos Islands (Islas Galápagos) lie on the equator, 1000km west of Ecuador's coast, and constitute one of the country's 21 provinces.

CLIMATE

Ecuador has two seasons: wet and dry. The local weather patterns vary greatly, depending on which geographical region you are in.

The Galápagos and coastal areas have a hot and rainy season from January to April. It doesn't rain constantly but you can expect torrential downpours that often disrupt communications. Daytime temperatures average about 31°C (89°F) but are often much higher, and it is generally unpleasant to travel in the coastal regions during this time. From May to December, temperatures are slightly lower and it rains infrequently.

In the Oriente it's usually almost as hot as on the coast, and it rains during most months. September to December are the driest, and June to August the wettest, with regional variations.

The dry season in the highlands is from June to September, and a short dry season also occurs during the month around Christmas. It doesn't rain daily in the wet season: April, the wettest month, averages one rainy

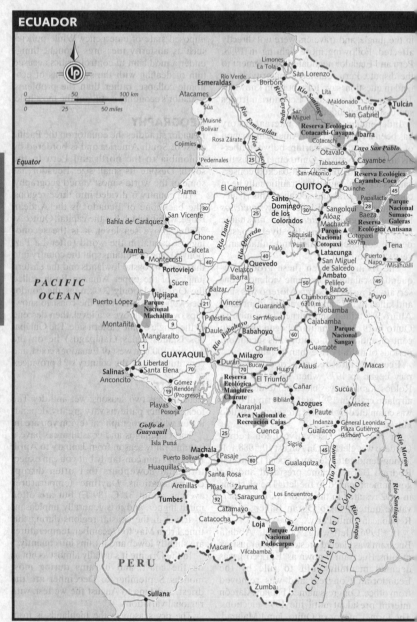

ECUADOR

Limones
La Tola
San Lorenzo
Río Verde Borbón
Esmeraldas
Atacames
Súa
Muisné
Rosa Zárate
Cojimíes
Pedernales

Lita
Maldonado Tufiño **Tulcán**
San Miguel San Gabriel
**Reserva Ecológica
Cotacachi-Cayapas** **Ibarra**
Cotacachi
Otavalo *Lago San Pablo*
Tabacundo Cayambe
San Antonio

Équator

Jama El Carmen
San Vicente
Bahía de Caráquez
Chone
Manta Calceta
Montecristi
Portoviejo
Sucre

**PACIFIC
OCEAN**

Puerto López
Jipijapa
**Parque
Nacional
Machalilla**
Montañita
Manglaralto

Salinas
Santa Elena
Anconcito

*Golfo de
Guayaquil*
Isla Puná

San Antonio
**Reserva Ecológica
Cayambe-Coca**
Quinche Papallacta
QUITO **Parque
Nacional
Sumaco-
Galeras**
Sangolquí Baeza
Aloág **Reserva
Ecológica
Antisana**
Machachi
**Parque
Nacional
Cotopaxi** Cotopaxi
5897m
Saquisilí Pujilí Puerto
Napo Misahuallí
Latacunga
San Miguel
de Salcedo
Ambato Tena
Pelileo
Baños Puyo
Chimborazo Mera
6310 m
Riobamba
Cajabamba
**Parque
Nacional
Sangay**
Guamote
Macas

Santo
Domingo
de los
Colorados
Quevedo
Velasco
Ibarra
Balzar
Vinces Guaranda
Palestina San Miguel
Daule **Babahoyo**
Chillanes

GUAYAQUIL
Milagro
Durán Bucay
Gómez Huigra
Rendón
(Progreso)
Playas
Posorja

**Reserva
Ecológica
Manglares
Churute**
Naranjal
**Area Nacional de
Recreación Cajas**
Cuenca

Alausí
El Triunfo Cañar
Biblián **Azogues**
Sucúa
Paute Méndez
Indanza General Leonidas
Gualaceo Plaza Gutiérrez
(Limón)
Sigsig

Machala
Puerto Bolívar
Huaquillas
Santa Rosa
Arenillas Piñas
Tumbes Zaruma
Catamayo Saraguro
Catacocha

Pasaje
Gualaquiza
Los Encuentros
Loja Zamora
**Parque
Nacional
Podocarpus**
Macará Vilcabamba

PERU

Cordillera del Cóndor
Río Zamora
Río Morona
Río Santiago
Río Cenepa

Sullana

Zumba

0   50   100 km
0   25   50 miles

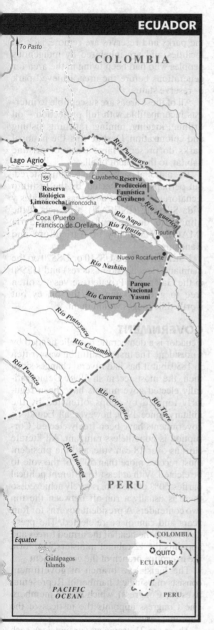

day in two. Daytime temperatures in Quito average a high of 20°C to 22°C (68°F to 72°F) and a low of 7°C to 8°C (44°F to 47°F) year round. Remember, however, that the most predictable aspect of Ecuador's weather is its unpredictability.

FLORA & FAUNA

Though small, Ecuador has many more plant and animal species than do much larger countries. Acre for acre, Ecuador is one of the most species-rich countries on the globe. For example, there are more than 20,000 plant species in Ecuador, with new ones discovered every year. In comparison, there are only 17,000 plant species on the entire North American continent. Scientists have long realized that the tropics harbor many more species than do more temperate countries, but the reasons for this are still a matter of debate and research. The most commonly held belief is that the tropics acted as a refuge for plants and animals during the many ice ages affecting more temperate regions; the much longer and relatively stable climatic history of the tropics has enabled more speciation to occur.

Another reason for Ecuador's biodiversity is simply that there are a great number of different habitats within this small country. Obviously, the Andes will support very different species from the tropical rain forests, and when intermediate biomes and the coastal areas are included, the result is a wealth of habitats, ecosystems and wildlife. Ecologists consider Ecuador to be one of the world's 'megadiversity hot spots.' This has attracted increasing numbers of nature lovers from the world over.

Bird-watchers enjoy Ecuador because of the great number of bird species recorded here – some 1500, or about twice the number found in any one of the continents of North America, Europe or Australia. New species are often added to the list. But Ecuador isn't just for the birds: some 300 species of mammal have been recorded, from monkeys in the Amazonian lowlands to the rare Andean spectacled bear in the highlands. Bats represent the most diverse mammal species, with well over 100 species in Ecuador alone.

Conservation

Ecotourism has become important to the economy of Ecuador and other nations with similar natural resources. Somewhat like Costa Rica in this respect (though more affordable, less overrun and with a palpable indigenous culture), Ecuador has the flora and fauna craved by nature lovers, but it's in perilously scarce supply these days. Eco-tourists spend money on hotels, transport, food etc. Many people who spend time in the tropics gain a better understanding of the problems facing the forests and of the importance of preserving them. As a result, visitors return home and become goodwill ambassadors for tropical forests. Be aware, however, that some 'ecotourism' companies are more interested in short-term profit than long-term protection.

Innovative projects for the sustainable development of tropical forests are being researched and implemented. For example, programs such as 'debt-for-nature' swaps allow local groups to receive funds for pre-serving crucial habitats, and part of Ecuador's national debt are paid off in return.

Local conservation groups have blos-somed in the last decade. Some have been quite successful in providing legal protec-tion for forests. Others have concentrated on improving environmental data collection and on training members to create a strong information base for national conservation research. Perhaps most important are the small local groups that protect specific natural areas. These groups involve nearby communities through environmental educa-tion, agroforestry and community develop-ment projects. Such grassroots community involvement is essential for viable conserva-tion in Ecuador.

NATIONAL PARKS

Ecuador's first national park was the Islas Galápagos, formed in 1959. The first mainland park was Cotopaxi, established in 1975, fol-lowed by Machalilla, Yasuní and Sangay in 1979, Podocarpus in 1982, and Sumaco-Galeras in 1994. As well as these six national parks, there are various reserves and pro-tected areas. These include Manglares-Churute, Cotacachi-Cayapas, Cuyabeno and Cajas. Additionally, local conservation organ-izations have set aside private nature reserves. All of Ecuador's major ecosystems are partly protected in one (or more) of these areas.

These parks lack the tourist infrastructure found in many other parts of the world.

There are few campgrounds, ranger stations, museums, or information centers. Some of the parks and reserves are remote, lack all facilities and are inhabited by indigenous peoples who had been living in the area for generations before the area achieved park or reserve status.

All of these areas are susceptible to inter-ests incompatible with full protection – oil drilling, logging, mining, ranching, fishing and colonization. Despite this, the national parks do preserve large tracts of pristine habitat, to the benefit of all.

The national park system is administered, but perhaps not protected, by the Instituto Ecuatoriano Forestal de Areas Naturales y Vida Silvestre (INEFAN), a branch of the Ministerio de Agricultura y Ganadería (MAG), or Ministry of Agriculture and Ranching.

Entrance fees are US$10 or US$20 on the mainland (less if paid in sucres) and US$80 in the Galápagos. Private reserves are often free to guests staying at the pricey but worthwhile lodges within them.

GOVERNMENT

Ecuador is a democratic republic headed by a president. The first constitution was written in 1830, but it has had several changes since then, the most recent in 1998. Democrati-cally elected governments have been regu-larly toppled by coups, often led by the military. Since 1979, however, all Ecuador's governments have been freely elected. Cor-ruption is nonetheless rampant. All literate citizens over 18 can vote, and the president must receive more than 50% of the vote to be elected. With at least 13 different political parties, 50% of the vote is rarely achieved, so there is usually a run-off between the top two contenders. A president governs for four years and cannot be re-elected. The presi-dent is also the head of the armed forces and appoints the 12 cabinet ministers who form the executive branch of the government.

The legislative branch of government consists of a single Chamber of Representa-tives (or Congress), which has 77 members. The Congress appoints the justices of the Supreme Court.

There are 21 provinces (*provincias*), each with a governor appointed by the president and democratically elected prefects. The provinces are subdivided into smaller political units called *cantones*; each cantón has a democratically elected *alcalde*, or mayor.

ECONOMY

Bananas were the most important export until the early 1970s. This changed with the discovery of oil. Petroleum exports rose to first place in 1973, and by the 1980s accounted for about half of total export earnings. Ecuador's current output of about 3.5 billion barrels per year does not provide as much income as it did in the early to mid-1980s. New reserves discovered in 1993 mean that current rates of production can continue until at least 2030. However, most oil reserves are in the Amazon region and extraction is posing serious threats to the rain forest.

Ecuador's main trading partner is the USA. Bananas remain important, comprising about 22% of the nation's exports, followed by shrimp (17.5%). These are cultivated on farms, which are having devastating effects on coastal habitats.

Tourism is a significant part of the economy. According to the World Bank, tourism is the economic sector with the most growth potential, though more comprehensive protection and conservation of the natural areas that attract tourists must be implemented if Ecuador is to realize this potential.

Despite the new-found wealth produced by oil exportation, Ecuador remains a poor country. Distribution of wealth has been patchy, and much of the rural population continues to live at the same standards it did in the 1970s. Yet education and medical services have improved.

Nonetheless, a financial crisis in March 1999 brought another currency devaluation, protests and riots, and transportation systems were disrupted for several days.

POPULATION & PEOPLE

Ecuador has the highest population density of any South American country. The birth rate is 25 per 1000 inhabitants, which means the population will double by about 2028.

About 40% of the population are Indians and an equal number are mestizos. Whites account for 15%, blacks for 5% and other races for less than 1%.

Most of the Indians speak Quechua or Quichua and live in the highlands. A few other small groups live in the lowlands.

About 48% of the population lives on the coast (and the Galápagos) and about 46% in the highlands. The remainder live in the Oriente, where colonization is slowly increasing. The urban population is 55%. In recent years, the indigenous peoples have become more involved in national politics and have mobilized to protect their special interests.

EDUCATION

Six years of elementary education are compulsory, but many children drop out. In the highlands, the school year is from October to July. On the coast, the school year is from May to January. There are about 20 universities and technical colleges. Adult literacy in 1995 was 90%.

ARTS
Visual Arts

The Spanish conquistadors trained indigenous artists to produce the colonial religious art that is now seen in many churches and museums. Thus arose the *escuela quiteña* (Quito school) of art – Spanish religious concepts portrayed by Indian artists, who incorporated their own beliefs. The Quito school died out with independence.

The 19th century is referred to as the Republican period, and its art is characterized by formalism. Favorite subjects included heroes of the revolution, important members of the new republic's high society, and florid landscapes.

The 20th century saw the rise of the indigenist school, whose unifying theme is the oppression and burdens of Ecuador's indigenous inhabitants. Important artists include Eduardo Kingman, Endara Crow, Camilo Egas and Oswaldo Guayasamín. These and other artists have works in modern galleries and museums in Quito; Egas (1889-1962) and Guayasamín (born 1919) have museums in their homes.

Architecture

Many of Quito's churches were built during the colonial period, and the architects were influenced by the Quito school. In addition, churches often have Moorish influences. The overall appearance of the architecture of colonial churches is overpoweringly ornamental, and almost cloyingly rich – in short, baroque.

ECUADOR

Many colonial houses have two stories, with the upper floors bearing ornate balconies. The walls are whitewashed and the roofs are red tile. Quito's colonial architecture has been well preserved and UNESCO declared the city's Old Town a World Cultural Heritage Site in 1978. Several other towns, notably Cuenca, also have attractive colonial architecture.

Music

Traditional Andean music has a distinctive and haunting sound that has been popularized in Western culture by songs such as Paul Simon's version of *El Cóndor Pasa*.

There are two main reasons for this otherworldly quality of traditional music. First, the scale is pentatonic, or composed of five notes, rather than the eight-note octaves Westerners are used to. Second, pre-Columbian instruments consisted of wind and percussion, which effectively portrayed the windswept quality of *páramo* (highland) life; string and brass instruments arrived only with the Spanish.

Most traditional music is a blend of pre-Columbian and Spanish influences. It is best heard in a *peña*, or folk music club.

Literature

Ecuadorian literature is little known outside Latin America, but indigenous novelist Jorge Icaza's *Huasipungo*, a naturalistic tale of the miserable conditions on Andean haciendas in the early 20th century, is available in English translation as *The Villagers*. Also worth checking out is *Fire from the Andes: Short Fiction by Women from Bolivia, Ecuador & Peru*, edited by Susan E Benner and Kathy S Leonard. Rarely is the Latina literary perspective so readily accesible to English readers; kudos to the publishers and editors for making this one available.

RELIGION

The predominant religion is Roman Catholicism, though a small minority of other churches are found. The indigenous peoples tend to blend Catholicism with their own traditional beliefs.

LANGUAGE

Spanish is the main language. Most Indians are bilingual, either Quechua or Quichua being their mother tongue and Spanish their second language. (See the Spanish, Quechua and Quichua sections of the Language chapter in the back of the book.) Also, some small lowland groups speak their own languages. English is understood in the best hotels, airline offices and tourist agencies.

Facts for the Visitor

HIGHLIGHTS

Ecuador is an adventure for both intrepid travelers and those decidedly less so. There are tours to cool, less-traveled spots, and with a bit of patience and energy, bushwhacking the rugged course is also possible. Highlights include visiting the humming outdoor markets (Otavalo is the first choice for shopping, and Saquisilí for watching the locals shop), riding atop a train through the hair-raising Devil's Nose railway pass, visiting the Amazon – a chance to check out nature's splendor and/or stay with indigenous communities in the forest deep – and, if you can afford it, the Galápagos. These islands are a superlative place if there ever was one to get a scuba-diving certification. Surfers will find decent waves along the coast from November to February.

PLANNING
When to Go

There's no perfect time for a general tour of Ecuador. The coast is hot and wet from January to May (rainstorms may make poorer roads impassable), overcast and humid from June to September, and drier and cooler the rest of the year. The dry season in the highlands is late May to September, which coincides with the wettest months in the Oriente, where roads may be closed.

The high seasons are June to August, December and January.

Maps

Ecuadorian bookstores have a limited selection of Ecuadorian maps. The best selection is available from the Instituto Geográfico Militar (IGM) or the SAEC; both are in Quito. *The Pocket Guide to Ecuador*, published in Quito, has maps of the country plus major city maps. The International Travel Maps website (www.nas.com/~travelmaps) has good, affordable maps that can be purchased before you set off. It offers regional

South American maps as well as individual country maps of Ecuador. Most maps cost US$8.95.

What to Bring

Clothes are relatively cheap in Ecuador, though shoes bigger than size 43 Ecuadorian (size 10 American, size nine British) are hard to find.

The highlands are often cold, so bring a windproof jacket and a warm layer to wear underneath, or plan on buying a thick sweater. Cheap highland hotels often lack heating; they may provide extra blankets on request, but a sleeping bag is useful.

Tampons are expensive and available in regular sizes only in major cities; sanitary pads are cheaper and more common. Stock up before traveling away from the cities. Condoms are widely sold, but spermicidal jelly for diaphragms is hard to find. The choice of oral contraceptives is limited, so bring your preferred brand from home. Good insect repellent and sunscreen are expensive and hard to find. Luggage storage is offered by many hotels in the bigger towns; bring an extra bag so you can ditch unnecessary weight before venturing out on short trips around the country.

TOURIST OFFICES

The government tourist information agency, CETUR, has offices in the major cities. CETUR seems geared mostly toward helping affluent tourists and it is rarely of much help with information about budget hotels etc. English is rarely spoken.

VISAS & DOCUMENTS

Most tourists entering Ecuador need a passport (valid for six months or more) and a T-3 tourist card, which is obtainable on arrival. The T-3 is free, but don't lose it, because you'll need it for stay extensions, passport checks and leaving the country. Lost cards can be replaced at the immigration office in Quito or Guayaquil, or at the exit point from Ecuador.

On arrival, you get identical stamps on both your passport and T-3, indicating how long you can stay. The maximum is 90 days but less is often given. You can get an extension in Quito at the immigration office.

Tourists can stay for 90 days in any 12-month period. (If you leave with only some of your 90 days used, you receive the balance upon re-entry.) UK citizens may stay longer. People with business, work, student or residence visas (difficult to get in Ecuador) may also stay longer. To extend your stay, leaving the country and returning doesn't usually work because the border officials check for entry and exit dates (though they aren't always thorough). If you leave the country and return with a new passport, it's a different story. With no Ecuadorian stamps in that passport, you have no problem.

Officially, a ticket out of Ecuador and sufficient funds for your stay (US$20 per day) are required, but they are rarely asked for. If you're flying in, it's safest to buy an onward ticket. It can be refunded if you don't use it. In Ecuador, this can take a couple of weeks, but they'll give you the money in US dollars.

Always carry your passport and T-3 card for document checks on public transport. You can be arrested if you have no ID and deported if you don't have a visa or T-3.

International vaccination certificates are not required by law, but some vaccinations, particularly against yellow fever, are advisable. Student cards are sometimes useful, especially in the Galápagos. Cards should bear your photograph and be issued by your own college or university. International student cards are treated with suspicion because fakes are available.

If you plan on driving, get an International Driver's License.

Travel insurance, obtainable from some credit card and insurance companies or Council Travel, isn't a bad idea. Typical coverage includes loss, theft or damage to baggage, trip cancellation, and various medical expenses including evacuation and repatriation of remains.

EMBASSIES & CONSULATES
Ecuadorian Embassies

Ecuador has embassies in Colombia and Peru, and also in the following countries:

Australia
  (☎ 02-9223-3266, 02-9223-0041)
  388 George St, Suite 1702A,
    American Express Tower, Sydney, NSW 2000
Canada
  (☎ 613-563-8206, fax 613-235-5776)
  50 O'Connor St, Suite 1311, Ottawa K1P 6L2

France
(☎ 01 45 61 10 21)
34 Avenue de Messine, 75008 Paris

Germany
(☎ 0228-35-25-44)
Koblenzer Strasse 37, 5300 Bonn 2

New Zealand
(☎ 09-309-0229, fax 09-303-2931)
Ferry Building, Quay St, Auckland

UK
(☎ 020-7584-1367)
3 Hans Crescent, Knightsbridge, London
SW1X 0L5

USA
(☎ 202-234-7200)
2535 15th St NW, Washington, DC 20009

Embassies & Consulates in Ecuador

Most don't operate all day so call ahead for hours. Also check the address, which may change every year or two, though the same phone number is often retained.

Australia
(☎ 04-298-823, fax 04-288-822)
Calle San Roque and Av Francisco de
Orellana, Ciudadela Kennedy, Guayaquil

Canada
(☎ 02-506-162)
6 de Diciembre 2816 and J Orton, Quito
(☎ 04-563-580, fax 04-314-562)
Córdova 800 and VM Rendón, 21st floor,
Guayaquil

Colombia
(☎ 02-458-012, fax 02-460-054)
Atahualpa 955 and República, 3rd floor, Quito
(☎ 04-563-308, fax 04-563-854)
Córdova 812 and VM Rendón, 2nd floor,
Guayaquil (☎ 07-836-311)
Luis Cordero 955 and Pasaje Hortensia Mata,
2nd floor, Cuenca

France
(☎ 02-560-789, fax 02-566-424)
Leonidas Plaza 107 and Patria, Quito

Germany
(☎ 02-225-660, fax 02-563-697)
Edificio Banco Consolidado, Patria and 9 de
Octubre, 6th floor, Quito

Ireland
(☎ 02-451-577, fax 02-567-220)
Montes 577 and Las Casas, Quito

Peru
(☎ 02-527-678)
Edificio España, Amazonas 1429 and Colón,
2nd floor, Quito
(☎ 04-322-738, fax 04-325-679)
9 de Octubre 411 and Chile, 6th floor,
Guayaquil

(☎ 07-930-680)
Bolívar near Colón, Machala
(☎ 07-571-668)
Sucre 1056, Loja
(☎ 07-694-030)
Bolívar 127, Macará

UK
(☎ 02-560-670, fax 02-560-730)
González Suárez 111 and 12 de Octubre, Quito
(☎ 04-560-400, fax 04-562-641)
Córdova 623 and Padre Solano, Guayaquil

USA
(☎ 02-562-890, fax 02-502-052)
Patria and 12 de Octubre, Quito
(☎ 04-323-570, fax 04-325-286)
9 de Octubre and García Moreno, Guayaquil

CUSTOMS

One liter of alcohol and 300 cigarettes are allowed duty free. It is illegal to export pre-Columbian artifacts and illegal to bring them into most countries. Taking endangered animal products home is also illegal.

MONEY

The currency in Ecuador is the *sucre* (S/). There are bills of 50,000, 20,000, 10,000, 5000, 1000, 500 and 100, though bills smaller than S/1000 are rare. There are coins of 1000, 500, 100 and 50. The last are usually only in antique shops.

Exchanging Money

The sucre is regularly devalued, so it is impossible to give accurate exchange rates, but at press time rates were as follows:

country	unit		sucre
Australia	A$1	=	S/7438
Canada	C$1	=	S/7684
euro	€1	=	S/12,166
France	FF1	=	S/1855
Germany	DM1	=	S/6221
Japan	¥100	=	S/9882
New Zealand	NZ$1	=	S/6061
UK	UK£1	=	S/18,408
USA	US$1	=	S/11,422

The US dollar is the easiest currency to exchange, and all prices in this chapter are given in US dollars. Other hard currencies can be exchanged in Quito, Guayaquil and Cuenca, but carry sucres or US dollars. Exchange rates are lower in smaller towns.

In some places, notably the Oriente, it is difficult to exchange money. Exchange houses, or *casas de cambio*, are normally the best places to change money; banks also will, but are slower. Usually, exchange rates are within 2% of one another in any given city. There is little difference between exchange rates for cash and traveler's checks.

Banks are open from 9 am to 1:30 pm weekdays. In some cities, banks may stay open later or open on Saturday, especially if Saturday is market day. ATMs are found in the bigger cities. Casas de cambio are usually open from 9 am to 6 pm weekdays, and until noon on Saturday. A lunch hour is common.

You can buy back dollars at international airports when leaving the country. You can also change money at the major land borders.

There is a black market in major towns, usually near the big casas de cambio. Rates are about the same, but street changing is illegal, and forged currency and cheating have been reported.

Credit cards are useful, particularly when buying cash from a bank. Visa and Master-Card are the most widely accepted.

International Transfers
You can receive money from home by finding an Ecuadorian bank that will cooperate with your bank and telexing someone to deposit the money in your name at the Ecuadorian bank of your choice. Allow at least three days. You can also have money sent to Western Union in the cities; this is fast but expensive (US$75 to receive US$1000). Ecuador allows you to receive the money in the currency of your choice. Ecuador is one of the best Latin American countries to have money sent to.

Costs
Costs in Ecuador are low. If you're on a strict budget and being really economical, you can survive on US$5 to US$7 per day by staying in the cheapest pensiones and eating the meal of the day in restaurants. (Quito and touristy places are more expensive.) For about US$6 a double, a simple room with private hot shower, table and chair can be had. Typical à la carte meals start at about US$2.50.

A taxi isn't expensive, particularly when you're in a group; a short ride usually costs about US$1. It helps if you are fluent in

Spanish. Buses cost roughly US$1 per hour of travel. Trains have a dual pricing system with foreigners paying several times more than locals. The same is true of some air fares. National park fees are US$10 to US$20 per person for foreigners. There is a recent trend to charge 'rich' foreigners more. Most budget hotels and restaurants will charge locals and foreigners the same, especially if you speak Spanish and act like you know what you're doing.

The biggest problem for budget travelers is reaching the Galápagos archipelago. Getting there is very expensive and staying there isn't particularly cheap; see the Galápagos Islands section in this chapter for more information.

Tipping
Better hotels and restaurants add 10% tax and 10% service charge to the bill. Cheaper restaurants don't include tax or service charge and tipping is not necessarily expected. If you want to tip your waiter, do so directly – don't just leave the money on the table.

Tip porters at the airport US$0.25 per bag (US$0.50 minimum). Taxi drivers do not receive a tip, though you can leave small change from a metered ride. On a guided tour, a tip is expected. About US$2 to US$3 per passenger per day is average, or rather more in the Galápagos.

POST & COMMUNICATIONS
Most letters sent from Ecuador arrive at their destinations, sometimes in as little as a week to the USA or Europe. Incoming mail is another matter. Some letters take as long as two months to arrive, and a few never do.

Sending Mail
Postcards are available at post offices, and because they contain no enclosure, are more likely to arrive safely. Rates are about US$0.35 to the Americas and US$0.45 elsewhere. For a few cents extra, you can send them *certificado* (certified). Sending parcels of 2kg to 20kg is best done from the post office on Calle Ulloa near Calle Dávalos, in Quito. A 20kg airmail parcel will cost almost US$100 within the Americas and well over US$200 elsewhere. Combination surface/air rates are about US$50 to the Americas and US$75 elsewhere.

ECUADOR

Receiving Mail

Mail sent to the post office is filed alphabetically, so make sure that your last name is clear, eg John PAYSON, Lista de Correos, Correo Central, Quito (or town and province of your choice), Ecuador. American Express will hold mail for its clients (c/o American Express, Apartado 2605, Quito, Ecuador; the street address is Av Amazonas 339). The SAEC holds mail for members. You have to recover your mail from customs (and pay high duty) if it weighs over 2kg.

Telephone

EMETEL provides long-distance national and international telephone, fax and telegram services. EMETEL offices are open from 6 am to 10 pm daily (except in small towns or in hotels and airports, where they keep shorter hours). Service is expensive and inadequate. The privatization of EMETEL is in the works, so maybe this will improve.

Even the most remote villages can often communicate with Quito and connect you into an international call. These cost about US$9 for three minutes to the USA, and about US$12 to Europe. Rates are cheaper on Sunday. Waiting time to make a connection can vary from 10 minutes to more than an hour. Reverse-charge (collect) phone calls are possible to the USA, Brazil, Colombia, Argentina, Spain and the UK only. Direct dialing to a North American or European operator is technically possible, but EMETEL and hotels don't like to deal with these calls because they don't make any money on them. In Quito, you can make Internet phone calls for about US$0.35 a minute to the USA and US$0.55 to Europe. The connection isn't great and the delay is annoying, but it's cheap (see Quito's Internet Access section later in this chapter).

Local numbers are made up of six digits. Area codes are divided by province. Dial ☎ 09 for mobile phones. If calling from abroad, drop the 0 from all codes. Ecuador's country code is ☎ 593.

To call locally, (US$0.15 a minute) you can use coins, phonecards or tokens, depending on the telephone. If you anticipate making a lot of calls, consider purchasing a Porto Alo (cellular payphone) card. They come in denominations of S/20,000 and S/50,000 and are available wherever the phones are found. You can also call internationally with these cards. Porto Alo technology has not yet hit the smaller towns.

Fax services are available from EMETEL, and from private companies and hotels in the larger cities. Rates for sending are about US$9 per page; it costs a small amount, which varies between agencies, to receive. Internet cafés offer fax services at a fraction of this cost.

Email

Internet services are fast on the rise in Ecuador and email is available in the bigger cities, plus tourist spots such as Otavalo and Baños. Set up an email address before you leave. See the Email section of the Facts for the Visitor chapter for more information on setting up email accounts.

INTERNET RESOURCES

A good description of Ecuador and its attractions is available at the Ecuador Explorer website (www.ecuadorexplorer.com). For current events, visa requirements, historical data and the like, visit either the Ministry of Tourism homepage (www.ecua.net.ec/mintur/ingles) or www.ecuador.org, the site of the Ecuadorian Embassy in the US. The SAEC maintains an up-to-date site (www.samexplo.org) with a great search feature and good links.

BOOKS

For more detailed travel information, there is Lonely Planet's *Ecuador & the Galápagos Islands. Ecuador: Fragile Democracy* by David Corkill and David Cubitt (out of print) takes an academic look at the history and trends of Ecuadorian politics. Tom Miller's *The Panama Hat Trail* is a good travel book on Ecuador focusing on the hat industry.

The best general book on the Galápagos is Michael Jackson's *Galápagos: A Natural History Guide. Climbing & Hiking in Ecuador* by Rob Rachowiecki & Betsy Wagenhauser is a detailed guide to climbing Ecuador's mountains. It also describes many beautiful hikes, some of which are day hikes suitable for the beginner. *The Ecotourist's Guide to the Ecuadorian Amazon*, by Rolf Wesche et al, is available in Quito and covers the Baeza, Tena, Misahuallí and Coca regions in detail. Other books are listed in the Facts for the Visitor chapter.

NEWSPAPERS & MAGAZINES

The best newspapers – *El Comercio* and *Hoy*, published in Quito, and *El Telégrafo* and *El Universo*, published in Guayaquil – cost about US$0.40. Two English-language newspapers, *Q.* and *Inside Ecuador*, are published periodically and have interesting articles. The *Explorer* is a free monthly booklet in English and Spanish listing what's on in Quito. *City* is a free magazine with helpful tourist information about Quito.

Foreign newspapers and magazines are sold at good bookstores and at the international airports. Latin American editions of *Time* and *Newsweek* (in English) are available for about US$2.

PHOTOGRAPHY

Camera gear is very expensive in Ecuador and film choice is limited. Always check expiration dates. Slide film is hard to find, and slide developing tends to be shoddy. Print film is cheaper and better developing is available. A roll of 24 photos costs about US$5.50 to develop. Try the El Globo stores in major cities for film, and Ecuacolor, at Amazonas 848 in Quito, for same-day printing. Fotomania, at 6 de Diciembre and Patria in Quito, is quite good for printing.

TIME

The mainland is five hours behind GMT/UTC and the Galápagos are six hours behind. There is no daylight saving time.

ELECTRICITY

Ecuador uses 110V, 60Hz AC.

HEALTH

Decent, affordable care is available at hospitals and clinics in most towns. Dentistry is another story, however, and you should get that filling or extraction dealt with before you venture off. Treat tap water with caution. Unsanitary preparation of street food is blamed for many illnesses countrywide.

Some coastal and eastern regions are malarial areas, so take precautions. A mosquito net, insect repellent, and staying indoors at dawn and dusk are the usual recommendations. As far as malarial medications (and side effects) go, everyone has different reactions, from extreme to negligible. If you'll be visiting malarial areas for an extended period, consider taking anti-malarial pills (see the Health section in the Facts for the Visitor chapter). Some people experience breathlessness and headaches while adjusting to the altitude in Quito.

WOMEN TRAVELERS

Ecuador is among the least (outwardly) macho of the Latin American countries, but it can manifest itself subtly. For instance, if you speak Spanish and have a male traveling companion who doesn't, Ecuadorian men may still ignore you and try to converse with your language-challenged friend. Brazen come-ons and whistles are rare, but less so with some alcohol-induced courage. *Pensiones* that let dirt-cheap rooms are often rented by the hour, and female travelers may be mistaken for prostitutes or be subjected to annoying, run-of-the-mill harassment by johns on a bender.

DANGERS & ANNOYANCES

Although Ecuador is safer than Peru and Colombia, you should still be careful. Pickpocketing is definitely on the increase and is common in crowded places. Armed robbery is still unusual in most of Ecuador, although parts of Guayaquil, some coastal areas, and the stairs up the Panecillo in Quito have a reputation for being very dangerous. Holdups in Quito's new town are not unheard of; steer clear of Parque La Carolina at night.

Every year or so, a couple of long-distance night buses are robbed in the Guayaquil area. Avoid taking night buses through Guayas province unless you have to.

Take the normal precautions as outlined in Dangers & Annoyances in the Facts for the Visitor chapter. If you are robbed, get a *denuncia* (police report) within 48 hours – they won't process a report after that. In Quito, go to the police station at the intersection of Cuenca and Mideros, in the Old Town, between 9 am and noon. In other towns, go to the main police headquarters.

Talk to other travelers and the folks who work at the SAEC in Quito for advice and current information.

BUSINESS HOURS

Most stores, businesses, casas de cambio and government offices are open from about 9 am to 5:30 pm weekdays; usually an hour of this time is taken for lunch. In smaller towns, lunch breaks of two or more hours

ECUADOR

are common. On Saturday, many stores and businesses are open from 9 am to noon.

Restaurants tend to remain open late in the big cities, where 10 pm is not an unusual time to eat the evening meal. In smaller towns, restaurants often close by 9 pm (much earlier in villages). Many restaurants are closed on Sunday.

PUBLIC HOLIDAYS & SPECIAL EVENTS

Many of the major festivals are oriented around the Roman Catholic liturgical calendar. They are often celebrated with great pageantry, especially in highland Indian villages, where a Catholic feast day is often the excuse for a traditional Indian fiesta with drinking, dancing, rituals and processions. Other holidays are of historical or political interest. On major holidays, banks, offices and other services are closed and public transport is often very crowded; book ahead if possible.

The following list describes the major holidays and festivals; they may well be celebrated for several days around the actual date.

New Year's Day
   January 1

Epiphany
   January 6

Carnaval
   March/April – the last few days before Lent, celebrated with water fights; Ambato has its fruit and flower festival

Easter
   March/April (dates vary) – Palm Sunday, Holy Thursday, Good Friday, Holy Saturday and Easter Sunday, celebrated with religious processions

Labor Day
   May 1 – workers' parades

Battle of Pichincha
   May 24 – national holiday commemorating the decisive battle for independence from Spain in 1822

Corpus Christi
   June – religious feast day combined with the traditional harvest fiesta in many highland towns; includes processions and street dancing

St John the Baptist
   June 24 – fiestas in Otavalo area

St Peter & St Paul
   June 29 – fiestas in Otavalo area and other northern highland towns

Simón Bolívar's Birthday
   July 24 – national holiday

Founding of Guayaquil
   July 25 – major festival for Guayaquil

Quito's Independence Day
   August 10

Fiesta del Yamor
   September 1-15 – held in Otavalo

Guayaquil's Independence Day
   October 9

Columbus Day (locally called Día de la Raza)
   October 12 – national holiday

All Saints' Day/All Souls' Day
   November 1-2 – celebrated by flower-laying ceremonies in the cemeteries; especially colorful in rural areas, where entire Indian families show up at the cemeteries to eat, drink, and leave offerings in memory of their departed relatives

Cuenca's Independence Day
   November 3

Founding of Quito
   December 6 – celebrated throughout the first week of December with bullfights, parades and dancing

December 24-25
   Christmas Eve/Christmas Day

End-of-year Celebrations
   December 28-31 – parades and dances culminate in the burning of life-size effigies in the streets on New Year's Eve

ACTIVITIES

Climbing and hiking adventures around Cotopaxi, the Baños area, Las Cajas (near Cuenca) and on Chimborazo (Ecuador's highest mountain) are all worthwhile. Gear can be rented in Quito and some other towns.

The Islas Galápagos have all the big attractions for nature lovers, including bird watching, romping with wildlife and snorkeling. Scuba diving is also available for both experienced and novice divers. The Galápagos may be too expensive for budget travelers (though a great number do get there anyway), but the Amazon can be visited easily and relatively cheaply. All manner of cultural and natural wonders dwell in Ecuador's Amazonian rain forest. Indigenous guides can unlock that world for interested travelers.

LANGUAGE COURSES

Spanish language courses are taught in Quito, Cuenca and a few smaller towns.

WORK

Officially you need a work visa to be allowed to get a job in Ecuador. You might, however, teach English in language schools, usually in Quito. Pay is low but enough to live on. Schools, such as the American School in Quito, will often hire teachers with bona fide teaching credentials in mathematics, biology and other subjects, and may help you get a work visa if you want to stay on. They also pay much better than the language schools.

Another way of making money is by selling good-quality equipment such as camping or camera items. You can post notices about equipment you wish to sell at the SAEC in Quito.

Volunteer opportunities abound; check at the SAEC in Quito or surf the Internet.

ACCOMMODATIONS

There is no shortage of places to stay in Ecuador, but during major fiestas or the night before market day, accommodations can be tight, so plan ahead. If you are going to a town specifically for a market or fiesta, try to arrive a day early, or at least by early afternoon the day before the event.

Single rooms may be hard to find, and you might get a room with two or three beds. Often, you are only charged for one bed and won't have to share, unless the hotel is full. Check that you won't be asked to share with a stranger or to pay for all the beds – there is usually no problem. There are nearly 20 youth hostels in Ecuador, though they're rarely the best value. Pensions are the cheapest accommodations, though rooms are often rented by the hour and cleanliness may be suspect. Staying with families is another option. The SAEC can provide information about homestays. Ask about discounts at hotels for SAEC members.

Most beds in Ecuador will challenge tall people: expect to hang off the end if you're at all lanky.

FOOD

For breakfast, eggs and bread rolls or toast are available. A good alternative is a sweet corn tamale called *humitas* that is often served with coffee.

Lunch is the main meal of the day for many Ecuadorians. A cheap restaurant will serve a decent *almuerzo* (lunch of the day) for as little as US$1. An almuerzo consists of a *sopa* (soup) and a *segundo* (second dish), which is usually a stew with plenty of rice.

Sometimes, the segundo is *pescado* (fish) or a kind of lentil or pea stew *(lenteja, menestra)*. Some places serve salad (often cooked), juice and *postre* (dessert) as well as the two main courses.

The evening meal is usually similar to lunch. Ask for the *merienda*. If you don't want the almuerzo or merienda, you can choose from the menu, but this is always more expensive.

A *churrasco* is a hearty dish of fried beef, fried eggs, vegetables (usually boiled beet slices, carrots and beans), fried potatoes, slices of avocado and tomato, and the inevitable rice. *Arroz con pollo* is a mountain of rice with little bits of chicken mixed in. *Pollo a la brasa* is roast chicken, often served with french fries. *Gallina* is usually boiled chicken, as in soups, and *pollo* is more often spit-roasted or fried. Pollo tends to be underdone, but you can return it and ask for it to be cooked a bit more.

Parrilladas are mixed grills. Steaks, pork chops, chicken breasts, blood sausages, liver and tripe are all served on a table-top grill – it's a lot of food! If you don't want the whole thing, choose just a chop or a steak. Although parrilladas aren't cheap, they are reasonably priced and good values.

Seafood is good, even in the highlands, as it is brought fresh from the coast. The most common types of fish are *corvina* (white sea bass) and *trucha* (trout). *Ceviche* is popular throughout Ecuador; this is uncooked seafood marinated in lemon and served with popcorn and sliced onions, and it's delicious. Ceviche can be *de pescado* (fish), *de camarones* (shrimp), *de concha* (shellfish, such as clams, mussels or oysters) or *mixto*. Unfortunately, improperly prepared ceviche is a source of cholera, so avoid it if in any doubt.

Chifas (Chinese restaurants) are generally inexpensive and a good value. Apart from rice dishes, they serve *tallarines*, or noodles mixed with your choice of pork, chicken, beef, or vegetables *(legumbres, verduras)*. Portions tend to be filling, with a good dose of MSG. Vegetarians will find that chifas offer the best choice for meatless dishes. Vegetarian restaurants are rare in Ecuador.

Restaurants usually have a wide range of dishes, including the following:

Caldo – Soups and stews are very popular and are often served in markets for breakfasts. Soups are

ECUADOR

known as *caldos, sopas,* or *locros*. Chicken soup, or *caldo de gallina*, is the most popular. *Caldo de patas* is soup made by boiling cattle hooves and is, to one author's taste, as bad as it sounds.

Cuy – Whole roasted guinea pig is a traditional food dating back to Inca times. It tastes rather like a cross between rabbit and chicken. The sight of the little paws and teeth sticking out and tightly closed eyes is a little unnerving, but it's considered a local delicacy and some people love it.

Lechón – Suckling pig is often roasted whole and is a common sight at Ecuadorian food markets. Pork is also called *chancho*.

Llapingachos – Fried mashed-potato-and-cheese pancakes are often served with *fritada*, scraps of fried or roast pork.

Seco – Literally 'dry' (as opposed to a 'wet') soup, this is stew, usually meat served with rice. It may be *seco de gallina* (chicken stew), *de res* (beef), *de chivo* (goat) or *de cordero* (lamb).

Tortillas de maíz – These are tasty fried corn pancakes.

Yaguarlocro – This potato soup has chunks of barely congealed blood sausage floating in it. Many people prefer straight *locro*, which usually has potatoes, corn and an avocado or cheese topping.

DRINKS
Nonalcoholic Drinks
Purify all tap water or buy bottled water. Bottled mineral water, *agua mineral*, is carbonated. *Güitig* (pronounced *weetig*) is the most popular brand. *Agua sin gas* is not carbonated.

Bottled drinks are cheap, but the deposit on the bottle is usually worth more than the drink. All the usual soft drinks are available, and some local ones have endearing names such as Bimbo or Lulu. Ask for your drink *helada* if you want it out of the refrigerator, *al clima* if you don't. Remember to say *sin hielo* (without ice) unless you really trust the water supply.

Jugos (juices) are available everywhere. Make sure you get *jugo puro* (pure) and not *con agua* (with water). The most common kinds are *mora* (blackberry), *tomate de árbol* (a strangely appetizing fruit with a greenish taste), *naranja* (orange), *toronja* (grapefruit), *maracuyá* (passion fruit), *piña* (pineapple), *sandía* (watermelon), *naranjilla* (a local fruit that tastes like bitter orange) and *papaya*.

Coffee is widely available but is often disappointing. Instant served either with milk *(en leche)* or water *(en agua)* is the most

common. Otherwise, coffee is served as a liquid concentrate in cruets and you dilute it with milk or water. It doesn't taste that great and looks like soy sauce, so always check before pouring it into your milk (or over your rice)! Espresso is available in the better restaurants.

Tea, or *té*, is served black with lemon and sugar. *Té de hierbas* (herb tea) and hot chocolate are also popular.

Alcoholic Drinks
Local *cervezas* (beers) are good and inexpensive. Pilsener is available in 650ml bottles and Club comes in 330ml bottles.

Local wines are terrible but imported wines are expensive.

Ron (rum) is cheap and good. The local firewater, *aguardiente* (sugar-cane alcohol), is an acquired taste but is also good. It's very cheap. Imported spirits are expensive.

SHOPPING
Souvenirs are good, varied and cheap. If you have time for only one big shopping expedition, the Saturday market at Otavalo is both convenient and varied. In markets and smaller stores, bargaining is expected, though don't expect to reduce the price by more than about 20%. In Quito's 'tourist stores,' prices are usually fixed. Some of the best shops are quite expensive but the quality of their products is often superior.

Woolen goods are popular and are often made of a pleasantly coarse homespun wool. The price of a thick sweater will begin at less than US$10, depending on size and quality. Wool is also spun into a much tighter textile used for making ponchos. *Otavaleño* Indian ponchos are among the best in Latin America. Hand-embroidered clothes are also attractive, but it's worth getting them from a reputable shop. Otherwise they may shrink or the colors may run.

Panama hats are worth buying. A really good panama is so finely made that it can be rolled up and passed through a man's ring. They are made from a palmlike bush that grows abundantly in the coastal province of Manabí; Montecristi is a major center.

Weavings are found all over the country; there's a good selection in Otavalo. Two small weavings are often stitched together to make a shoulder bag. Agave fiber is used to make macramé bags or tough woven bags called *shigras*. Cotacachi and Ambato are centers for leatherwork.

San Antonio de Ibarra, between Otavalo and Ibarra, is Ecuador's major woodworking center. Balsa-wood models, especially of brightly colored birds, are popular; these are made in the Oriente and sold in many of Quito's gift shops. Painted and varnished ornaments made of bread dough are unique to Ecuador and are best obtained in Calderón, north of Quito.

Getting There & Away

AIR
The main international airports are in Guayaquil and Quito.

Latin America
Direct flights go to Bogotá (Colombia), Buenos Aires (Argentina), Caracas (Venezuela), Curaçao, Guatemala City, Havana (Cuba), Lima (Peru), Panama City, Rio de Janeiro (Brazil), San José (Costa Rica), Santiago (Chile) and São Paulo (Brazil). There are connecting flights to Asunción (Paraguay) and La Paz (Bolivia) via Lima. In addition, Esmeraldas and Tulcán airports each have a few flights a week to Cali (Colombia).

North America
There are direct flights to Miami, Houston, Los Angeles, New York and Mexico City, and connecting flights to other cities.

Europe
Direct flights go to Amsterdam, Barcelona, Madrid and Paris, with connections to other European cities.

Other Continents
Flights to Sydney, Auckland and Johannesburg all have connecting flights through Buenos Aires or Santiago. Flights to Tokyo go via Miami or Lima. Flights to Tel Aviv go via Madrid.

LAND
International bus tickets sold in Quito require a bus change at the border. It is cheaper and as convenient to buy a ticket to the border and then another ticket in the next country.

Colombia
Buses go from Colombia to Ecuador via Tulcán. See Tulcán in this chapter for further details.

Peru
Buses go from Peru to Ecuador via either Huaquillas or Macará (both in Ecuador). Huaquillas is the main route. See Huaquillas and Macará in this chapter for further details.

LEAVING ECUADOR
A US$25 departure tax (payable in cash dollars or sucres) is levied for international flights, unless you are in transit.

Getting Around

You can usually get anywhere quickly and easily. The bus is the most common form of transport; buses can take you from the Colombian to the Peruvian border in 18 hours. Airplanes and boats (especially in the Oriente) are also used frequently, but trains less so. Rental cars are very expensive.

Whatever form of transport you use, remember to have your passport with you, as you may need to show it to board planes and boats. People without documents may be arrested. Buses go through a transit police checkpoint upon entering some towns, and passports may be requested. If your passport is in order, these procedures are cursory. If you're traveling anywhere near the borders or in the Oriente, expect more frequent passport checks.

AIR
Domestic flights have no seat reservations and there's always a race to get the choice seats. Flights are subject to frequent delays, changes and cancellations. Some flights give good views of the snowcapped Andes. When flying from Quito to Guayaquil, the mountain views are on the left-hand side. Going north from Quito, sit on the right.

With the exception of flying to the Galápagos, most internal flights are fairly cheap. Almost all flights originate or terminate in Quito or Guayaquil. Flights between Quito

ECUADOR

and Coca, Lago Agrio and Macas all have a surcharge for foreigners, and cost US$52 each way (about twice what locals pay). The Quito to Guayaquil route also carries a surcharge (US$99). All other mainland flights are cheaper.

Flights from Guayaquil to the Galápagos cost US$334 roundtrip for foreigners (US$378 from Quito). Students with a valid college ID should ask about discounts to the Galápagos.

Ecuador's major domestic airline is TAME, which flies between Quito and Guayaquil, Cuenca, Loja, Macas, Coca, Lago Agrio, Tulcán, Esmeraldas, Manta, Machala, Portoviejo, Bahía de Caráquez and Baltra in the Galápagos. TAME may also fly to Tarapoa, east of Lago Agrio. From Guayaquil TAME flies to and from Quito, Cuenca, Loja, Machala, Manta, Bahía and Baltra. SAN-Saeta has flights between Quito, Guayaquil and Cuenca, and flights to San Cristóbal in the Galápagos. The prices of TAME and SAN-Saeta flights are the same. Other small, local airlines have light aircraft that fly mainly along the coast.

Ten to 12 flights a day connect Quito and Guayaquil. There are one to three flights a day between Quito and Cuenca, daily flights to Baltra, and several flights a week to other towns. There are no Sunday flights to the Oriente.

If you can't get a ticket for a particular flight (especially out of small towns), go to the airport early and get on the waiting list in the hope of a cancellation. If you have a reservation, confirm it and reconfirm it or you may be bumped.

BUS
Long-Distance Bus
Most towns have a central bus terminal (terminal terrestre). In some towns, buses leave from other places (where possible, these are indicated on the maps). Timetables change frequently and are not always adhered to.

Busetas are fast, small buses that carry 22 passengers in rather cramped seats. Service is direct and sometimes frighteningly speedy. Larger coaches allow standing passengers and can get crowded. They are generally slower than the busetas, but they can be more interesting.

To get your choice of seat, buy tickets in advance from the terminal. You'll get two:

one for the passage and another for the terminal exit tax (about US$0.10). Avoid the cramped seats over the wheels, and the back seats, which are the bumpiest. Some companies have frequent departures and don't sell advance tickets. During holiday weekends, buses can be booked up for several days in advance. For immediate travel, go to the terminal and listen for your destination to be yelled out. Make sure your bus goes direct to your destination if you don't want to change.

If you're traveling light, keep your luggage with you inside the bus. If your luggage won't fit under the seat, it will go on top or in a luggage compartment. Watch your stuff: it can get soaked on top, stained with grease in a luggage compartment, and stolen anywhere.

Vendors selling fruit, rolls, ice cream or drinks suddenly appear on buses whenever they slow down. Long-distance buses usually stop for 20-minute meal breaks at the appropriate times. The food in the terminal restaurants is basic. Most buses lack toilets, but there are rest stops every few hours.

Local Bus
These are usually slow and crowded but cheap. You can get around most towns for about US$0.10. Local buses often go out to nearby villages, and this is a good way to see an area.

TRUCK
In remote areas, camiones (trucks) and camionetas (pickup trucks) often double as buses. If the weather is OK, you get fabulous views; if not, you have to crouch underneath a dark tarpaulin. Truck drivers charge standard fares, depending on distance, that are almost as much as bus fares.

TRAIN
Trains run from Quito to Huigra (near Guayaquil) via Riobamba and Alausí. In the north, trains (sometimes) run from Ibarra to San Lorenzo, on the coast. Autoferros, which are buses mounted on railway chassis, are often used instead. Foreigners are charged much more than locals on the scenic and exciting Alausí-Huigra and Ibarra-San Lorenzo sections. Serendipity is on your side if you get to these towns and catch a train, as service is sporadic and beholden to weather and track conditions. If you're determined to

ride the rails, try the more reliable Quito-Cotopaxi or Quito-Riobamba routes.

HITCHHIKING
Private cars are not very common and trucks are used as public transport in remote areas, so trying to hitch a free ride isn't easy. If the driver is stopping to drop off and pick up other passengers, assume that payment will be expected. If you are the only passenger, the driver may have picked you up just to talk to a foreigner, and may waive payment.

BOAT
Motorized dugout canoes are the only ways to get around many roadless areas. Regularly scheduled boats are quite affordable, though not as cheap as a bus for a similar distance. Hiring your own boat and boatman is possible but expensive. You are most likely to travel in dugouts in the Misahuallí and Coca regions of the Oriente, and on the northwest coast.

Seating is on hard, low wooden benches; bring something padded to sit on. Luggage is stashed under a tarpaulin, so bring a daypack containing essentials for the journey. Pelting rain and glaring sun are major hazards and an umbrella is excellent defense against both. Use good sunscreen lotion, or wear long sleeves, long pants and a hat. A light jacket is worth having against chilling rain, and insect repellent is useful during stops along the river. A water bottle and food will complete your hand baggage. Keep your spare clothes in plastic bags or they'll get soaked by rain or spray.

TAXI
Taxis are cheap. Bargain the fare beforehand, or you're likely to be overcharged. A long ride in a large city (Quito or Guayaquil) shouldn't go over US$4, and short hops can cost less than US$1. Meters are obligatory in Quito but rarely seen elsewhere. On weekends and at night, fares are always about 25% to 50% higher.

A full-day taxi hire might cost about US$50. If you hire a taxi to take you to another town, expect to pay about US$1 for every 10km. Remember to include money for the return trip. Pickups can be hired to remote places such as climbers' refuges.

ORGANIZED TOURS
Visitors to the Galápagos are required to go on tours (see Galápagos Islands section). Some of the cheapest are offered by Galasam Galápagos Tours in Quito and Guayaquil. Many travelers also opt to visit the Amazon on organized tours, as these are efficient and educational. If staying with indigenous communities is your bag, contact an indigenous guide who can explain the customs and culture and act as translator. IKIAAM Shuar Travel in Macas is a good outfit for this type of trip; there are others in the Oriente. For longer rain forest tours, head to Lago Agrio, but if time is a problem, you can set off from Baños or Tena.

Quito

At 2850m above sea level and only 22km south of the equator, Quito has a wonderful springlike climate. It's in a valley flanked by mountains and, on a clear day, several snow-capped volcanoes are visible from the capital.

Quito was a major Inca city that was destroyed by Atahualpa's general, Rumiñahui, shortly before the arrival of the Spanish conquistadors; there are no Inca remains. The present capital was founded on top of the Inca ruins by Sebastián de Benalcázar on December 6, 1534, and many colonial buildings survive in the Old Town. In 1978, UNESCO declared Quito a World Cultural Heritage site, and building and development in Quito's Old Town is now strictly controlled. There are few modern buildings next to centuries-old architecture, and no flashing neon signs to disrupt the ambience of the past.

Orientation
With a population of about 1.2 million, Quito is Ecuador's second-largest city. It can be divided into three segments. In the center is the Old Town, which has white-washed and red-tiled houses and colonial churches. The north is modern Quito, with major businesses, airline offices, embassies, shopping centers and banks. This area also contains the airport and middle- and upper-class residences. Av Amazonas is the best known street, though Avs 10 de Agosto and 6 de Diciembre are the most important

QUITO – OLD TOWN

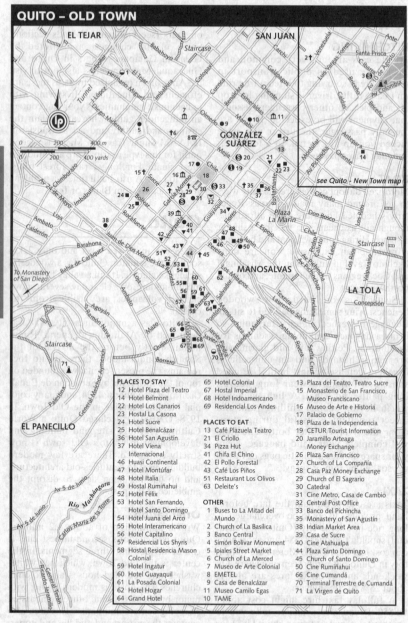

PLACES TO STAY
12 Hotel Plaza del Teatro
14 Hotel Belmont
22 Hotel Los Canarios
23 Hostal La Casona
24 Hotel Sucre
25 Hotel Benalcázar
36 Hotel San Agustín
37 Hotel Viena
     Internacional
46 Huasi Continental
47 Hotel Montúfar
48 Hotel Italia
49 Hostal Rumiñahui
52 Hotel Félix
53 Hotel San Fernando,
     Hotel Santo Domingo
54 Hotel Juana del Arco
55 Hotel Interamericano
56 Hotel Capitalino
57 Residencial Los Shyris
58 Hostal Residencia Mason
     Colonial
59 Hotel Ingatur
60 Hotel Guayaquil
61 La Posada Colonial
62 Hotel Hogar
64 Grand Hotel
65 Hotel Colonial
67 Hostal Imperial
68 Hotel Indoamericano
69 Residencial Los Andes

PLACES TO EAT
13 Café Plazuela Teatro
21 El Criollo
34 Pizza Hut
41 Chifa El Chino
42 El Pollo Forestal
43 Café Los Piños
51 Restaurant Los Olivos
63 Deleite's

OTHER
1 Buses to La Mitad del
   Mundo
2 Church of La Basílica
3 Banco Central
4 Simón Bolívar Monument
5 Ipiales Street Market
6 Church of La Merced
7 Museo de Arte Colonial
8 EMETEL
9 Casa de Benalcázar
11 Museo Camilo Egas
10 TAME
13 Plaza del Teatro, Teatro Sucre
15 Monasterio de San Francisco,
    Museo Franciscano
16 Museo de Arte e Historia
17 Palacio de Gobierno
18 Plaza de la Independencia
19 CETUR Tourist Information
20 Jaramillo Arteaga
    Money Exchange
26 Plaza San Francisco
27 Church of La Compañía
28 Casa Paz Money Exchange
29 Church of El Sagrario
30 Catedral
31 Cine Metro, Casa de Cambio
32 Central Post Office
33 Banco del Pichincha
35 Monastery of San Agustín
38 Indian Market Area
39 Casa de Sucre
40 Cine Atahualpa
44 Plaza Santo Domingo
45 Church of Santo Domingo
50 Cine Rumiñahui
66 Cine Cumandá
70 Terminal Terrestre de Cumandá
71 La Virgen de Quito

thoroughfares. The south comprises mostly working-class housing areas.

Information

Tourist Offices The main CETUR tourist information office (☎ 02-225-101) is at Eloy Alfaro 1214. There are also branches at the airport's domestic terminal and at Venezuela 914 (☎ 02-514-044) in the Old Town. Hours are 9 am to 5 pm weekdays.

Tourist Card Extensions For tourist card extensions, go to Migraciones (☎ 02-454-122), Av Amazonas 2639 (also numbered 3149) at Av de la República, open 8 am to noon and 3 to 6 pm weekdays. It takes anywhere from 10 minutes to two hours to get an extension. Onward tickets out of Ecuador and 'sufficient funds' are rarely asked for. Bring airline tickets or traveler's checks if you have them, just in case.

Money Many banks are on Amazonas; hours are from 9 am to 1:30 pm. ATMs are becoming commonplace. Casas de cambio are the usual places to exchange money; hours are from 9 am to 6 pm weekdays and on Saturday mornings. Casa Paz is the best known, and has an Old Town office at Sucre and Venezuela, and a New Town office at Av Amazonas 370. The casa de cambio at the airport is open on Sunday, and the one at the Hotel Colón is open on Sunday and often until 7 pm on weekdays. There are several other good casas de cambio. Western Union (☎ 02-502-194) is at Av República 396.

You can receive cash with your credit card at the following places, all in the New Town; commissions vary. MasterCard and Visa are most often accepted.

American Express
   (☎ 02-560-488) Amazonas 339 and Jorge Washington, 5th floor
Diners Club
   (☎ 02-221-372) Av República 710 and Eloy Alfaro
MasterCard
   (☎ 02-262-770) Naciones Unidas 825 and Los Shyris
Visa
   (☎ 02-566-800) Banco de Guayaquil, Av Colón and Reina Victoria; Filanbanco, Amazonas 530 and Roca

Post & Communications The central post office is in Old Town, at Espejo 935 and Guayaquil. This is where you pick up lista de correos mail. Alternatively, you can have mail sent to the New Town office at Eloy Alfaro 354 and 9 de Octubre. To do so, drop the 'Correo Central' line in the address and insert 'Eloy Alfaro.' The main branch office in the New Town is at Av Cristobal Colón and Reina Victoria. Hours are 7:30 am to 7:30 pm weekdays, and 8 am to 2 pm Saturday. To mail a package over 2kg, use the office in the New Town at Calle Ulloa 273, near Ramírez Dávalos.

The main EMETEL office for international calls is at 10 de Agosto and Colón; it's open 6 am to 9:30 pm daily. There are smaller EMETEL offices at the Terminal Terrestre, at the airport and at Benalcázar and Mejía, in the Old Town.

Internet Access Internet cafés are appearing throughout Quito; the following places are recommended. Mundo Net, on Pinto next to the youth hostel, is staffed by friendly, computer-savvy, English-speaking folks. Sixty minutes of surfing costs US$2.25. The hipsters hang out at Papaya Net, Calamá 413, which costs US$2.65 an hour. Nearby, Cyber Coffee, Calamá 362, has (surprise!) coffee and computers. Fees are US$3.50 an hour for Internet usage and US$0.35 per minute for Net Phone calls to the USA and US$0.55 to Europe. Monkey On-line, JL Mera at Jorge Washington, also has Net Phone capabilities at similar prices and Internet access for US$2.50 an hour. CyberNet, Colón at Reina Victoria, is conveniently located below the post office and charges US$3.25 an hour.

South American Explorers Club The SAEC clubroom (☎/fax 02-225-228, explorer @saec.org.ec) is in the New Town at Jorge Washington 311 and Leonidas Plaza Gutiérrez. Hours are 9:30 am to 5 pm weekdays. Mail should be sent to Apartado 17-21-431, Eloy Alfaro, Quito, Ecuador. See Useful Organizations in the introductory Facts for the Visitor chapter for a full description of the club and its services.

Cultural Centers Fundación Pueblo Indio (☎ 02-529-361), Ruíz de Castilla 216 and Sosaya, and CONAIE (☎ 02-248-930), at

ECUADOR

Los Granados 2553 and 6 de Diciembre, provide information on indigenous issues.

Bookstores Libri Mundi, JL Mera 851, has a good selection of books in English, German and French. Another recommended bookstore is Libro Express, at Amazonas 816. Confederate Books, Calamá 410, has thousands of used books in French, English and German.

Maps The Instituto Geográfico Militar (IGM), on top of steep Calle Paz y Miño, is open 8 am to 4 pm weekdays. Mornings are recommended. Bring your passport; you'll need to leave it at the gate.

Laundry At Lava Hotel Self Service, Almagro 818 and Colón, they wash, dry and fold your clothes in 24 to 48 hours. Opera de Jabón, Pinto 325 and Reina Victoria, will wash your clothes the same day, or you can do it yourself if there is a machine available.

Emergency The Hospital Voz Andes (☎ 02-262-142), at Juan Villalengua 267 (near América and 10 de Agosto) is an American-run hospital with outpatient and emergency rooms. Fees are low. Good, but pricier, is the Metropolitano (☎ 02-261-520), Av Mariana de Jesús and Occidental. A private clinic specializing in women's health is Clínica de la Mujer (☎ 02-458-000), Amazonas 4826 and Gaspar de Villarroel.

Recommended dental clinics include the Clínica de Especialidades Odontológicas (☎ 02-521-383, 02-237-562), Orellana 1782 and 10 de Agosto, Clínica Dental Arias Salazar (☎ 02-524-582), Amazonas 239 and 18 de Septiembre, and Clínica Dental Dr Pedro Herrera (☎ 02-554-316), Amazonas 353 and Jorge Washington.

Emergency services include police (☎ 101), fire department (☎ 102), general emergency (☎ 111) and Red Cross-ambulance (☎ 131 or 02-580-598).

Dangers & Annoyances The 2850m elevation will make you somewhat breathless if you arrive from sea level. This symptom of altitude sickness *(soroche)* usually disappears after a day or two. Take things easy on arrival: don't overexert yourself, eat lightly and cut back on cigarettes and alcohol.

Robberies and petty theft are on the rise due to the chronic devaluation of the sucre. A veritable financial crisis rocked Ecuador in late 1998 and early 1999 and crime is increasing as a result. Pickpockets ply crowded public buses, markets and church plazas, often working in groups to distract your attention; see the Facts for the Visitor chapter for more details. If you are robbed, obtain a police report within 48 hours from the Old Town station at Mideros and Cuenca from 9 am to noon.

There have been many reports of thefts at Plaza San Francisco. Definitely avoid the climb up El Panecillo hill; armed muggers work this route. Take a tour or hire a taxi for the return trip to the top and stay in the paved area around the statue of the Virgin. Generally, the New Town is safer than the Old Town, but you should still stay alert, especially at night.

Watch your luggage closely when traveling: snatch thefts of poorly attended luggage occur at the bus terminal and airport.

Despite the above warnings, Quito does not seem particularly dangerous. If you avoid attracting undue attention to yourself, it's unlikely you'll have many problems.

Things to See & Do

Opening hours and fees of museums, churches and so forth change often. Many museums are closed on Monday. The Casa de Cultura has the best museums. Seeing the old colonial center is worthwhile, although narrow colonial streets, bustling crowds and constant traffic jams make walking around Old Town a noisy, grimy experience. There's much less traffic and fewer people on Sunday.

Walking Tour The area bounded by Flores, Rocafuerte, Cuenca and Manabí has most of the colonial charm, including the **Plaza de la Independencia**, with the **Palacio de Gobierno** and **Catedral**. If you're short on time, at least see this plaza and continue southwest on García Moreno for two blocks to the church of **La Compañía**. From here, it's one block to the northwest (right) along Sucre to the **Plaza y Monasterio de San Francisco** – a wonderful area, but watch for thieves. Two blocks to the southeast (left) of La Compañía brings you to Guayaquil; turn southwest (right) for a block to see the **Plaza y Iglesia de Santo Domingo**.

From the Old Town, head northeast along Guayaquil toward the New Town. Turn left on 10 de Agosto and pass the Banco Central on your left. Opposite the bank is an impressive **monument** to Simón Bolívar; it's the southernmost point of the triangular **Parque La Alameda**. Head north through the park, past the astronomical observatory and continue north around the lake onto the important thoroughfare of 6 de Diciembre.

After three blocks you pass the modern **Palacio Legislativo** building on your right, on Montalvo. If you continue on 6 de Diciembre you pass the popular **Parque El Ejido** on your left and the huge, circular, mirror-walled **Casa de la Cultura Ecuatoriana** building (with museums) on your right. Past the Casa de la Cultura, go left for three blocks along Patria, with Parque El Ejido to your left, and you reach a small **stone arch**. Opposite this is the beginning of Quito's most famous modern street, **Av Amazonas**.

It is about 3km from the Old Town center to the beginning of Amazonas, which has banks, boutiques, souvenir stands and sidewalk cafés, and is a great meeting place. The parallel street of JL Mera has fine bookstores and craft shops.

Casa de la Cultura Ecuatoriana There are several collections here (☎ 02-565-808), Av 12 de Octubre 555 at Patria, representing 19th-century and contemporary periods. It also has a fascinating display of traditional musical instruments and examples of traditional Ecuadorian regional dress. Hours are 9 am to 6 pm Tuesday to Friday, and 9 am to 5 pm weekends. Entry is US$2, US$1 for students.

Museo del Banco Central This museum (☎ 02-223-259) is in the Casa de la Cultura Ecuatoriana, and is Quito's best archaeological museum, housing ceramics, gold ornaments, skulls showing deformities and early surgical methods (trepanning), a mummy and many other interesting items. There is also a display of colonial furniture and religious art. Hours are 9 am to 5 pm Tuesday to Friday, and 10 am to 3 pm weekends. Entry is US$2, US$1 for students.

Museo de Jacinto Jijón y Caamaño This interesting private archaeology museum (☎ 02-521-834) is on the 3rd floor of the library in the Catholic University, on 12 de Octubre. Hours are 9 am to 4 pm weekdays; entry is US$0.40.

Museo Guayasamín The renowned Ecuadorian Indian painter Oswaldo Guayasamín maintains this museum in his home (☎ 02-242-779), at José Bosmediano 543. It's an uphill walk, or you can take a bus along 6 de Diciembre to Eloy Alfaro, then a Bellavista bus up the hill. Hours are 9 am to 12:30 pm and 3 to 5:30 pm weekdays, and Saturday morning; entry is US$1.

Museo Amazónico Here you'll find a small collection of jungle Indian artifacts collected by the Salesians (☎ 02-562-633), 12 de Octubre 1436. Indian cultural publications (in Spanish) are for sale. Hours are from 11:30 am to 12:30 pm and 1 to 5 pm weekdays, and from 11:30 am to 12:30 pm Saturday. Entry is US$0.50.

Instituto Geográfico Militar (IGM) High on the hill at the end of steep Calle Paz y Miño, southeast of the Parque El Ejido, the IGM (☎ 02-522-066) has a geographical museum and planetarium and sells topographical maps. Museum hours are from 8 to 11 am and 2:30 to 4:30 pm Tuesday to Friday. There are several half-hour shows daily in the planetarium; admission is US$0.35. You must leave your passport at the gate.

Museo de Ciencias Naturales This museum (☎ 02-449-824) houses a natural history collection. It is at Parque La Carolina, on the Los Shyris (eastern) side, opposite República de El Salvador. Hours are 9 am to 6 pm weekdays, and 9 am to 1 pm Saturday. Entry is US$1, less for students.

Vivarium The Vivarium (☎ 02-452-280), Reina Victoria 1576 and Santa María, is the place to check out live reptiles like the highly venomous fer-de-lance, boa constrictors, turtles and tortoises, lizards and iguanas. Hours are from 9 am to 1 pm and 2:30 to 6 pm Tuesday to Sunday. Entry is US$2.

Museo de Arte e Historia This museum (☎ 02-210-863), Espejo 1147, contains a wealth of 16th- and 17th-century colonial art. Hours are 8 am to 4 pm Tuesday to Friday, and 9 am to 2 pm weekends; entry is free.

ECUADOR

QUITO – NEW TOWN

PLACES TO STAY	
10 Hostal Coqui	54 Hotel Pickett
11 Residencial Carrión	57 Hostal Tortuga Verde
12 Residencial Santa Clara	59 Magic Bean
13 Hotel Majestic	69 El Cafecito
15 Residencial Nueve	72 Hotel Alston
de Octubre	75 HI Youth Hostel
24 La Casa de Eliza	78 El Centro del Mundo
29 La Casona	80 Loro Verde
33 El Ciprés	82 Posada del Maple
34 Hostal Farget	83 ECOhostal
39 Hostal Margarita	86 Hostal Bavaria
41 Residencial Marsella	87 Residencial Italia
42 Hostal Margarita 2	91 Hostal Kapuli
47 Albergue El Taxo	93 Hostal Florencia
48 Hostal Adventure	97 Hotel Lafayette
53 Amazonas Inn	98 Hotel Viena

QUITO – NEW TOWN

PLACES TO EAT
3 Windmill Vegetarian Restaurant
18 La Casa de Mi Abuela
19 La Bodega de Cuba
21 Chifa Pekin
45 Cevichería Viejo José
53 Café Al Paso
59 Magic Bean
61 El Marqués
65 El Maple
68 Vitalcentro
67 El Cafecito
73 Super Papa
77 Mama Clorindas
79 Café Hindu
84 Sidewalk Cafés

85 Ch'Farina
92 Café Cultura
95 El Holandés
96 Chifa Mayflower
99 Chifa Hong Kong

ENTERTAINMENT
6 Café Libro
8 Cine Universitario
14 Cine Colón
17 British Council
23 Ñucanchi Peña
30 Teatro Prometeo
31 Casa de la Cultura Ecuatoriana
58 Spaghettería Romulo y Remo
63 No Bar
67 Arribar

OTHER
1 Immigration (Migraciones)
2 CETUR Tourist Information
4 EMETEL
5 Post Office
7 Canadian Consulate
9 Parcel Post Office
16 MM Arteaga Money
   Exchange, SAN-Saeta Airline
20 Centro Comercial Multicentro
22 UK Embassy
24 Fundación Golondrinas
25 French Embassy
26 South American Explorers Club
27 Museo de Jacinto Jijón y
   Caamaño, Universidad Católica

28 Museo Amazonico
31 Casa de la Cultura Ecuatoriana
32 US Embassy
35 Church of El Belén
36 Palacio Legislativo
37 Banco Central
38 Simón Bolívar Monument
40 Cine Capitol
43 Instituto Geográfico Militar
44 Children's Playground
46 Sierra Nevada Expediciones
49 Galasam Economic Galápagos
   Tours
50 TAME Airline
51 Vivarium
52 Emerald Forest Tours
55 Native Life Travels
60 Flying Dutchman
62 Papaya Net
64 Confederacy Books
66 Safari Tours,
   Cyber Coffee
70 Branch Post Office,
   CyberNet
71 Pamir Adventure
74 Libri Mundi Bookshop,
   Galería Latina
76 Mundo Net
81 Children's Playground
88 Metropolitan Touring
89 American Express,
   Ecuadorian Tours
90 Casa Paz
94 La Reina Victoria

ECUADOR

LA PAZ

GUÁPULO

Río Machángara

MARISCAL SUCRE

Park

0   100   200 m
0   100   200 yards

Casa de Sucre The hero of the revolution, Antonio José de Sucre lived in this house at Venezuela 573. It contains period (1820s) furniture and a small museum. Hours are 8:30 am to 4 pm weekdays, and 8:30 am to 1:30 pm Saturday. Entry is US$1.25.

Museo de Arte Colonial This museum (☎ 02-212-297), on Cuenca near Mejía, houses what many consider Quito's best collection of colonial art. Hours are from 8:30 am to 4:30 pm Tuesday to Friday, and 10 am to 2:30 pm weekends. Entry is US$2, US$1 for students.

Museo Camilo Egas Works by Ecuadorian painter Camilo Egas and others are contained in this museum (☎ 02-514-511), Venezuela 1302. Hours are 10 am to 1 pm and 3 to 5:30 pm Tuesday to Friday, and 10 am to 2 pm weekends. Entry is US$0.35.

Churches The most interesting colonial churches are in the Old Town. Photography is not usually permitted because camera flashes damage the pigment in the many valuable religious paintings.

The **Monasterio de San Francisco** is on the plaza of the same name. Construction began a few days after the founding of Quito in 1534, but it was not finished until 70 years later. It is the largest and one of the oldest colonial structures in Quito. Much of the church has been rebuilt because of earthquake damage, but some is original. The chapel of Señor Jesús de Gran Poder, to the right of the main altar, has original tile work. The main altar itself is a spectacular example of Baroque carving, and the roof and walls are also intricately detailed and richly covered in gold leaf. It is open 9 to 11 am and 3 to 6 pm Monday to Saturday. To the right of the main entrance is the **Museo Franciscano** (☎ 02-581-281) with some of the monastery's finest paintings, sculptures and furniture dating from the 16th century. Hours are 9 to 11 am and 3 to 6 pm Tuesday to Saturday, and 9 am to noon Sunday; entry is US$0.50.

It is claimed that 7 tons of gold were used to decorate **La Compañía**, Ecuador's most ornate church. Moorish influence can be seen in the detailed designs carved on the red and gold columns and ceilings. There is a beautiful cupola over the main altar. The remains of the quiteña saint Mariana de Jesús, who died in 1645, lie here. The church is on García Moreno near Sucre, and is open 9:30 to 11 am and 1 to 6 pm daily.

The **Catedral**, the oldest colonial church in South America (1562), though much remodeled, is a stark structure overlooking the Plaza de la Independencia. Plaques on the outside walls commemorate Quito's founders. General Sucre, the leading figure of Quito's independence struggle, is buried inside. To the left of the main altar is a statue of Juan José Flores, Ecuador's first president. Behind the main altar, a plaque marks the spot where President Gabriel García Moreno died on August 6, 1875; he was shot outside the presidential palace and was carried, dying, to the cathedral. Hours are 8 to 10 am and 2 to 4 pm Monday to Saturday; entry is free. Next door, the church of **El Sagrario** is still being renovated; it's interesting to watch how the restoration work is carried out.

Two blocks from the Plaza de la Independencia is the monastery of **San Agustín**, where Ecuador's declaration of independence was signed on August 10, 1809. A museum (☎ 02-515-525), with independence mementos and colonial art, is in the convent to the right of the church. Hours are 9 am to 1 pm and 3 to 6 pm. Entry is free.

In the evening, the domes of the **Santo Domingo** church are floodlit, making it especially attractive. It, too, dates back to early Quito. In the busy Plaza Santo Domingo, in front of the church, is a statue of General Sucre. He is pointing in the direction of Pichincha, where he won the decisive battle for independence in 1822.

Begun in 1700 and completed in 1742, **La Merced**, on Cuenca near Chile, is one of colonial Quito's most recent churches. Its tower is the highest (47m) in the Old Town and contains the largest bell of Quito's churches. The church has a wealth of fascinating art. Paintings depict scenes of volcanoes glowing and erupting over the church roofs of Quito, the capital covered with ashes, General Sucre going into battle and many others. The stained-glass windows also show scenes of colonial life, such as priests and conquistadors among the Indians of the Oriente. Hours are 3 to 8 pm Monday to Saturday; entry is free.

The 17th-century monastery, museum and cemetery of **San Diego** are east of the Panecillo, between Calicuchima and Farfán.

The monastery's colonial art includes a pulpit by the noted Indian woodcarver Juan Bautista Menacho; it is one of the country's finest. The cemetery, with its numerous tombs and mausoleums, is also worth a visit. Hours are 9 am to noon and 3 to 6 pm Tuesday to Sunday.

High on a hill, on Venezuela, is the unfinished church of **La Basílica**. Construction commenced in 1926, so the tradition of taking decades to construct a church is obviously still alive. At the north end of Parque La Alameda is the small church of **El Belén**, built where the first Catholic mass in Quito was held.

The **Santuario of Guápulo**, in a precipitous valley on the east side of town, was built between 1644 and 1688. Good views of this delightful colonial church can be seen from behind the Hotel Quito, at the end of 12 de Octubre. A steep footpath leads down to Guápulo. It's a pleasant walk, though strenuous coming back. The No 21 Santo Domingo-Guápulo bus goes there. Hours are 8 to 11 am and 3 to 6 pm Monday to Saturday.

Other Sights The historic alley of **La Ronda** (also called Juan de Dios Morales) is just off 24 de Mayo, between García Moreno and Venezuela, and on to Maldonado. This street is perhaps the best preserved in colonial Quito and is full of old, balconied houses. Just walk along the street (in daylight) and you'll see some open to visitors; they usually sell handicrafts.

The **Palacio Presidencial** is the low, white building on the northwestern side of the Plaza de la Independencia. The entrance is flanked by a pair of handsomely uniformed presidential guards. Sightseeing is limited to the entrance area.

Language Courses

Quito is one of the better places in South America for learning Spanish. All levels are available, private or group, live-in with family or not – talk to several schools to see what is best for you. Most schools charge about US$4 to US$5 per hour, though both cheaper and rather more expensive places exist. Quito schools that come recommended include: Instituto Superior de Español (☎ 02-223-242), Ulloa 152, which also has an office in Otavalo, (see Things to See & Do in Otavalo), Swiss-owned Bipo & Toni's (☎ 02-

540-618), Carrión 300, and Luz de América (☎ 02-210-192), Rocafuerte 1001, which also offers dance and cooking classes.

Organized Tours

Tours are usually cheaper if they are booked in the town closest to where you want to go rather than in Quito. However, if you prefer to start in Quito, the following operators are reliable. Safari (☎ 02-552-505, fax 02-220-426), Calamá 380 and JL Mera, Apartado 17-11-6060, arranges all kinds of adventure tours from bird-watching to volcano climbing. Emerald Forest Tours (☎ 02-526-403), Amazonas 1023 and Pinto, specializes in jungle tours around Coca, and Native Life Travels (☎ 02-505-158), Pinto 446 and Amazonas, specializes in Cuyabeno Reserve jungle trips. Sierra Nevada Expediciones (☎ 02-553-658) at Pinto 637 and Cordero, and Pamir Adventure (☎ 02-220-892, fax 02-547-576), JL Mera 721, have experienced climbing guides. Sierra Nevada offers river rafting and mountain biking as well. Flying Dutchman (☎ 02-542-806, fax 02-449-568), Foch 714 and Mera, has recommended bike tours. Andes Adrenalline Adventures (☎ 02-821-111), Reina Victoria 24150 and Foch is the place for bungee jumping (at your own risk!).

Fundación Golondrinas (☎ 02-226-602, golondrinas@ecuadorexplorer.com), in La Casa de Eliza hotel at Isabel La Católica 1559, is a conservation project with volunteer opportunities. It arranges four-day walking tours in the páramo and forests west of Tulcán. It costs US$50 per day.

Places to Stay

The cheapest hotels are in the Old Town. However, a big increase in theft there and the opening of cheap hotels in the New Town have resulted in more budget travelers staying in the New Town than before.

Old Town Many cheap hotels are at the south end, on the streets heading toward the bus terminal. You'll find scores of cheap hotels within a few blocks of one another. Many budget travelers stay in this area, but some (particularly single women) do not feel comfortable lodging here. Watch your belongings on the streets and ensure your room is always locked.

The **Grand Hotel** (☎ 02-210-192), Rocafuerte 1001, is popular with international budget travelers and is good value. Basic but clean rooms are US$3/5.50 for singles/doubles or US$3.75/7.50 with private bath. The hotel is family-run and friendly, with hot water, laundry service, and a restaurant. A block away, *La Posada Colonial* (☎ 02-282-859), at Paredes 188, is also a popular choice, with similar facilities at US$4/6 for singles/doubles or US$8/10 with private bath. Another recommended place for travelers is the *Hotel Belmont* (☎ 02-516-235), on Antepara, between the Old and New Towns. This clean, safe, family-run hotel charges US$4 per person.

On the Plaza Santo Domingo is the *Hotel Santo Domingo* (☎ 02-512-810), Rocafuerte 1345, charging US$3 per person or US$3.50 with private hot bath. It's noisy but OK. Next door, the similarly priced *Hotel San Fernando* is grimy. The pleasant, friendly but noisy *Hotel Juana del Arco* (☎ 02-214-175), Rocafuerte 1311, has hot water and charges US$3 each or US$5/7 with bath. Some rooms are quite dark, whereas others have plaza views. Just off the plaza, *Hotel Félix* (☎ 02-514-645), Guayaquil 431, has pretty flowers on the balconies. There is only one hot shower for about 30 basic rooms but the place is clean and secure; ring the bell to get in. It's a good deal for US$2 per person.

There are several cheap and basic hotels on La Ronda. The best is *Residencial Los Shyris* (☎ 02-515-536), La Ronda 691, at US$3 each or US$9 for a double with bath. There are cheaper but worse places on this street, which can be unsafe after dark.

There are many hotels on Maldonado near the terminal terrestre. These are convenient to the terminal, but the street attracts pickpockets. The following are OK and have hot water. The basic but secure and reasonably clean *Hotel Ingatur* (☎ 02-216-461) is only US$2.25/3.50 for singles/doubles or US$3/6 with bath. Next door, the more upscale *Hostal Residencia Mason Colonial* has rooms with bath for US$7.50/11.50. The *Hotel Guayaquil* (☎ 02-959-937) is depressing. Rooms are US$6.50 for a double or US$9.50 with bath.

Basic but decent is the *Hotel Capitalino* (☎ 02-513-433) at US$2/4. The *Hotel Indoamericano* (☎ 02-515-094) is the best of a cluster of dives by the terminal. It charges US$3/5 or US$6/9.50 with bath. Nearby is the sparse but friendly *Residencial Los*

Andes, with doubles for US$3; a classic cold-water cheapie. The new and spotless *Hostal Imperial* across the street is a good choice if you want an Old Town location with New Town amenities. Carpeted rooms with TV, bath and phone are US$7.50/13. The *Hotel Colonial* (☎ 02-510-338), down an alley from Maldonado 3035, is quiet and has hot water in the morning. Basic but clean rooms are US$3/6.50 with toilet only. The *Hotel Interamericano* (☎ 02-214-320) charges US$3 to US$7 for a single and US$6 to US$13 for a double, depending on whether or not you have a bathroom, telephone, or TV in your room.

Going from Plaza Santo Domingo along Calle Flores, there's the friendly *Huasi Continental* (☎ 02-517-327), Flores 332, with spartan but clean rooms for US$3.25/5.50 or US$4/7.25 with private hot bath. The nearby *Hotel Montúfar* (☎ 02-211-419), Sucre 160, is recommended. It's basic but quiet and clean, has warm water and is US$3 per person. Farther along Flores is the better *Hotel San Agustín* (☎ 02-216-051), at No 626, costs US$4.50/9 for dark interior rooms or US$6.50/9 for better ones with private bath, and the *Hotel Los Canarios* (☎ 02-959-103), at No 856, which is US$4.50/9 with bath.

The *Hotel Hogar* (☎ 02-218-183), Montúfar 208, is US$7.50 for a clean double with bath and hot water in the mornings. The clean *Hostal Rumiñahui* (☎ 02-211-407), Montúfar 449, is US$10 for a double with bath. Nearby the friendly *Hotel Italia* (☎ 02-518-643), Junín 765, has clean but basic rooms for US$3 per person.

The *Hotel Sucre* (☎ 02-514-025), on Calle Cuenca at the corner of Plaza San Francisco, has a bustling business renting rooms by the hour. They charge US$1 per person (but maybe the manager misjudged me!). Better on the plaza is the *Hotel Benalcázar* (☎ 02-518-302), Benalcázar 388, which is US$2.50/4.50 for singles/doubles without bath. Though there are great views of the Plaza, it's a rough and shady scene.

The *Hotel Plaza del Teatro* (☎ 02-954-293), Guayaquil 1317, in a nice old house by the theater plaza, charges about US$10/16 for good rooms with private bath. Nearby, the pleasant old *Hostal La Casona* (☎ 02-514-764), Manabí 255, has clean rooms for US$8/16, including breakfast.

Casa Patty (☎ 02-510-407), Iquique 233 and Manosalvas (in La Tola, six blocks east from Plaza Marin on Chile to Iquique, then three blocks south – a steep walk), is run by the same family that has Pensión Patty in Baños. The large house has double rooms for US$4.50. Kitchen facilities are available and the management is friendly. Call ahead to see if there's room.

The *Hotel Viena Internacional* (☎ 02-519-611), Flores 600, is popular with travelers wanting comfort in the Old Town. Large, carpeted rooms, some with balconies and all with telephones, bathrooms and hot water, are US$9 per person. There's a book exchange and restaurant.

New Town A popular (and often full) budget hotel at the edge of the New Town is the *Residencial Marsella* (☎ 02-955-884), Los Ríos 2035. The hotel is family-run and clean, with hot water, laundry service, luggage storage, a cafeteria, garden and a roof terrace. Rates are about US$3.50 to US$5 per person; rooms vary widely in quality, from comfortable doubles with bath to a few airless singles with shared bath. If this is full, try the newer *Hostal Margarita 2* across the street. Clean rooms are US$3.75/6.50 for singles/doubles. They also have the *Hostal Margarita* (☎ 02-512-599), around the corner at Elizalde 410 and Los Ríos, with clean rooms at US$5.50 each with bath.

The small, family-run *Residencial Italia* (☎ 02-224-332), 9 de Octubre 237, is in an old building with plenty of kids running around. Basic rooms are US$4.50 per person or US$5.50 with bath; this place is often full. Another OK value at this price is the *Hostal Florencia*, Reina Victoria 542.

Several small, family-run hostales cater to backpackers, budget travelers and students, and have been well received. Hot showers, kitchen and laundry facilities, luggage storage, a living room, a notice board and information are available in a friendly and relaxed environment. They normally have a few double and triple rooms and a larger dormitory-style room. Single rooms are less common. Showers are usually shared. It is best to phone ahead for availability and prices. The following are all in the small hostal category.

Casapaxi (☎ 02-542-663), Pasaje Navarro 364, near Av La Gasca, is about 1km north and uphill from Av América; the No 19 bus

passes by. It is friendly, clean and helpful, and costs about US$5 for one night, with long-stay discounts given (as is true for most hostales). If this is full, try the similarly priced and named *Casa Paxee* a few doors down. *La Casona* (☎ 02-230-129), Andalucía 213, is US$6 per person, and is in a lovely house. *La Casa de Eliza* (☎ 02-226-602), Isabel La Católica 1559, is also US$6 per person. Owners Eliza and Piet arrange excellent treks through northern Ecuador in association with the Cerro Golondrinas Cloudforest Conservation Project. If La Casa is full, Eliza can send you to her sister's house a few blocks away.

El Centro del Mundo (☎ 02-229-050), Lizardo García 569, is a backpackers hostal with dorm rooms at US$3 and US$4 per person and doubles/triples at US$11/14. There are electric showers, laundry and kitchen facilities, and TV room. It's a nonstop party that even the hard-core tire of eventually. Bring a padlock. Other places at US$6 or US$7 per person are *El Cafecito* (☎ 02-234-862), Cordero 1124, over the restaurant of the same name, and *El Ciprés* (☎ 02-549-561), Lérida 381 and Toledo, a block southwest of Madrid and Toledo. *Hostal Kapuli* at Robles 625 is a good deal in carpeted rooms with private hot bath for US$5 per person including breakfast.

The *Magic Bean* (☎ 02-566-181), Foch 681, above the popular restaurant of that name, is a great meeting place. It's US$8 in dorm rooms, US$22 for a double, US$26 with bath. *Hostal Eva Luna* (☎ 02-234-799), Roca Pasaje 630 and Amazonas, is down a little alley off Roca and Amazonas. It is a hostal for women run by Safari Tours. Rates are US$5 each. *Albergue El Taxo* (☎ 02-225-593), Foch 909, charges US$10 per person. It is run by artists who are a good source of local information.

There are many places to stay along Pinto, including the friendly *Amazonas Inn* (☎ 02-222-666), Pinto 471, which has modern, clean singles/doubles/triples at US$8/11/15. All rooms have hot-water bath, TV and fan; some have balconies. The new *Hostal Tortuga Verde* (☎ 02-556-829), Pinto at JL Mera, is OK for US$5 per person in dorm rooms. The *HI Youth Hostel* (☎ 02-543-995, fax 02-226-271), Pinto 325, has pricey rooms with three or four beds at US$9 per bed (private bath) or US$8 (shared bath). Youth hostel members pay about US$8/7. *Hostal Adventure* (☎ 02-226-340), Pinto 570, has small, scruffy rooms without bath at US$4.50 per person. Rooms with bath are a dollar more. The *Hotel Pickett* (☎ 02-551-205), Wilson at JL Mera, has cleanish, cramped singles/doubles for US$8/11 with bath or US$6/8.50 without. A block away, the *Hotel Lafayette* (☎ 02-224-529), Baquedano 358, looks good for $5.50 per person.

The clean *Hotel Viena* (☎ 02-235-418), Tamayo 879, has private hot showers. It's decent value for US$7.25 per person. At US$8 per person, the *Residencial Nueve de Octubre*, 9 de Octubre and Colón, is a bit haggard, but passable. The clean and friendly *Hostal Coqui* (☎ 02-223-148, fax 02-565-972), Versalles 1075, is good at US$10/13 for rooms with bath or US$7/10 without. There is a cafeteria. The *Residencial Santa Clara* (☎ 02-541-472), Darquea Teran 1578, is clean and OK for US$6.50/9 without bath.

For cozy accommodations in a converted house, try *ECOhostal* (☎ 02-224-483), 9 de Octubre 599, which has quiet, clean rooms for US$10 including breakfast. There is a café, book exchange, and free email for guests. The *Hostal Bavaria*, (☎ 02-509-401), Paez 232 and 18 de Septiembre, also has rooms for US$10 per person; parking is available. The *Loro Verde* (☎ 02-226-173), Rodríguez 241, has a great central location and spacious rooms with bath for US$11/16. Nearby, the *Posada del Maple* (☎ 02-544-507), Rodríguez 148, is a pleasant and friendly little hotel charging US$18/25 with bath and breakfast, US$12/20 without and US$7 per bed in a dorm. Also in the thick of things is the *Hotel Alston* (☎ 02-508-956), JL Mera 741 and Baquedano, with carpeted, spacious doubles sporting two full-size beds and bath at US$24. The clean *Hostal Farget* (☎ 02-570-074), Farget 109 and Santa Prisca, has nice rooms for US$13/20. Two other decent choices in this price range are the *Hotel Majestic* (☎ 02-546-388), Mercadillo 366 and Versalles, and the *Residencial Carrión* (☎ 02-234-620), Carrión 1250 and Versalles.

Homestays The SAEC (see Information, earlier in this section) lists a dozen families that offer homestays for US$5 to US$12 per person. Some include meals.

Places to Eat

If economizing, stick to the standard almuerzos or meriendas.

Old Town Many simple, inexpensive restaurants serve Ecuadorian food in the Old Town, but most are unremarkable. Some recommended ones include the cheap restaurants on the 1400 block of Rocafuerte, near the Plaza Santa Domingo. The *Restaurant Los Olivos*, at Rocafuerte 1421, has decent, cheap almuerzos. Around the corner, *Pollo El Forestal*, Rocafuerte at Venezuela, serves huge portions of roast chicken for US$2. On the plaza, *Café Los Piños* has good coffee and breakfast. Others include *Pizza Hut*, Espejo near Flores, with pizzas less than US$4, and the more expensive *El Criollo*, at Flores 825. The *Chifa El Chino*, on Bolívar near Guayaquil, is a decent Chinese place.

For desserts, snacks and coffee, a good choice is *Café Plazuela Teatro* on the Plaza del Teatro Sucre – a lovely place for rest and refreshment during a sightseeing visit to the Old Town. For ice cream and *batidos* (fresh fruit milkshakes), visit *Deleite's* on Rocafuerte near the Grand Hotel.

New Town There is an international range of eateries here, as behooves a capital city. Even the most expensive restaurants are reasonable by gringo standards. Budget travelers frequent either the simple Ecuadorian places, or the European and US-style restaurants catering to travelers. These are a little pricier, but it's worth it to meet other folks.

Cevichería Viejo José, Veintimilla 1254, has friendly service and good, cheap seafood. *El Marqués*, Calamá 443, has good vegetarian food, including US$2 set lunches that are popular with Ecuadorians. *Vitalcentro*, Lizardo García 630, is another decent vegetarian place. *Mamá Clorindas*, Reina Victoria 1144, is a good place to try local food, particularly at lunch time; meals are less than US$2. For fast food, the block of Carrión east of Amazonas is nicknamed 'Hamburger Alley' for the many places serving burgers and their usual accompaniments. It's popular with students. If you're hankering for Chinese, try *Chifa Mayflower*, Carrión 442 and 6 de Diciembre, or the more expensive *Chifa Hong Kong*, L García 235 and 12 de Octubre. Other inexpensive places can be found by wandering around and seeing where the locals eat.

Av Amazonas is a good place to watch the world go by. The sidewalk cafés on Amazonas near Roca are popular meeting places and are not exorbitant. They serve a decent cup of coffee and don't hassle you if you sit there for hours. Superlative coffee and breakfasts are available at *Café Al Paso*, Pinto 471, on the ground floor of the Amazonas Inn.

El Holandés (☎ 02-522-167), Reina Victoria 600 and Carrión, serves excellent international vegetarian meals for less than US$3. (It's also the contact for mountain-bike tours.) Other good vegetarian places are *El Maple*, Calamá at JL Mera, where you can eat salad, though portions are disappointingly small, and the *Windmill Vegetarian Restaurant*, Colón 2245. In the US$3 to US$5 range, the *Taco Factory*, at Foch 713 and JL Mera, has good Mexican food; *Ch'Farina*, Carrión 619, serves Italian and pizza. For reasonably priced homemade pasta, try *Spaghetteria Romulo y Remo*, JL Mera 1012. *La Bodega de Cuba*, Reina Victoria 1721, is great for Cuban food and ambience. Carnivores may want to splash out at *La Casa de Mi Abuela*, JL Mera 1649, where a steak dinner runs about US$8.

Travelers congregate in the following places. The *Magic Bean*, Foch 681, is popular for slightly pricey breakfasts and good coffee (that's the magic bean!); it's open all day with appetizing snacks and meals, and occasional live music at night. There is indoor and outdoor dining and, among other sporadic surprises, bottled Guinness at not much above the price in a London pub. *Café Colibri*, Pinto 619 and Cordero, is good for hearty breakfasts in pleasant surroundings. Not for the super thrifty, it opens at 7 am. English and German are spoken.

The *Café Cultura*, Robles 513, has great breakfasts and English afternoon teas – again, good but not cheap by Ecuadorian standards. *El Cafecito*, Luis Cordero 1124, has a warming fireplace and a variety of light meals. *Super Papa*, JL Mera 741, serves baked potatoes with about a dozen different fillings. Its notice board is full of useful information. *Café Hindu*, Lizardo García 580 at Reina Victoria, serves a good chicken shawerma and a variety of other Middle-Eastern dishes. There are dozens of other places, especially along Calamá, but this will get you started.

Entertainment

Entertainment reaches its height during the fiestas, such as those celebrating the founding of Quito (first week of December), when there are bullfights at the Plaza de Toros. On New Year's Eve, life-size puppets (often of politicians) are burned in the streets at midnight. Carnaval is celebrated with intense water fights – no one is spared. Colorful religious processions are held during Easter week.

Pubs & Bars There are several 'pubs' and bars, which are not cheap by Ecuadorian standards, but they're popular with travelers and expats. Popular bars, usually with loud music and dancing, include the *Arribar*, JL Mera 1238 and García; *No Bar*, Calamá 442; *Blues Bar*, La Granja 112 and Amazonas; *Reggae Bar*, Amazonas 1691 and Orellana (popular late at night); and *Seseribó* in the Edificio El Girón at Veintimilla and 12 de Octubre – a great place to salsa. *Hopp y Ex*, Reina Victoria 854 and Baquedano, is gay-friendly. *Café Libro*, Diego de Almagro 1500 and Pradera, has jazz, poetry readings, drama and peñas. *Ñucanchi Peña*, Universitaria 496 and Armero, has good peñas with a US$4 cover. A quiet place run by a friendly US-British couple is *La Reina Victoria*, Reina Victoria 530, with a fireplace, dart board, bumper pool and excellent pub ambience.

Music, Theater & Dance Dances, concerts and plays in Spanish are presented at various venues. *El Comercio* newspaper has the best entertainment listings. The *Teatro Sucre*, on Guayaquil in the Old Town, is the most elegant but is being renovated. *Jacchigua*, an Ecuadorian folk ballet, is presented at *Teatro San Gabriel* (☎ 02-506-650), on América at Mariana de Jesús. At the time of writing, performances were offered at 7 pm on Wednesday and Friday; call ☎ 02-952-025 for information and reservations. Entry is US$8 to US$16. The National Symphony plays at *Teatro Politécnico* in the Escuela Politécnica on Andalucía (two blocks east of the Universidad Católica). Concerts are mainly on Friday night (except from mid-August to mid-September) and costs range from free to

US$4. The *Casa de la Cultura* and, behind it, the *Teatro Prometeo*, on 6 de Diciembre, both have a variety of performances. There are several other venues.

Cinemas There are some 20 cinemas; a few show good English-language films with Spanish subtitles. These include the *Cine Colón*, at the intersection of Av Colón and 10 de Agosto, and the *Cine Universitario*, at the Indoamerican Plaza, on Av América across from Pérez Guerrero. Entry is less than US$2. English and French movies are shown at the *British Council* (☎ 02-540-225), Amazonas 1646, and *Alliance Française*, Eloy Alfaro 1900.

Getting There & Away

Air The airport (☎ 02-430-555), 10km north of the center, has a domestic and international terminal. Services include tourist information, money exchange, post office, cafeteria and bar, EMETEL international telephone office and gift shops.

Flight schedules and prices change frequently. TAME and SAN-Saeta have from eight to 14 daily flights to Guayaquil (US$99), most frequently on weekdays. Flights to Cuenca (US$52) leave one to three times daily. Other cities served (several times a week and sometimes daily) are: Tulcán, Esmeraldas, Portoviejo, Manta, Bahía de Caráquez, Macas, Coca, Lago Agrio, Loja, Machala and the Galápagos. See the Getting Around section earlier this chapter for more detail.

In the Old Town, TAME is at Manabí 653 (☎ 02-512-988); in the New Town, TAME has an office at Av Colón 1001 (☎ 02-554-900). SAN-Saeta shares an office at Guayaquil 1228 (☎ 02-211-431) in the Old Town and Colón and Amazonas (☎ 02-502-706) in the New Town. There are other airline offices and most travel agents sell plane tickets for the same price as the airlines.

Bus The Terminal Terrestre de Cumandá (☎ 02-570-529 for information) is in the Old Town on Maldonado, a few hundred meters south of the Plaza Santo Domingo. The terminal is reached along Maldonado on foot, by bus, or by light-rail trolley (El Trole); get off at the Cumandá stop. If arriving by taxi, ask to be let off at the pedestrian stairway at the top of the hill.

Dozens of bus companies serve most destinations and there is an information booth. Book in advance to travel during holiday periods and on Friday evening. Watch your luggage carefully in the terminal.

Several buses a day go to most destinations, and there are several departures an hour to some places, including Ambato and Otavalo. Approximate one-way costs and journey times are shown in the following table. More expensive luxury services are available for long trips.

destination	duration in hours	cost
Ambato	2½	US$2.00
Bahía de Caráquez	8	US$5.50
Baños	3½	US$2.50
Coca	13	US$10.00
Cuenca	8	US$6.00
Guaranda	5	US$3.00
Guayaquil	8	US$6.00
Ibarra	3	US$2.00
Lago Agrio	8	US$8.50
Latacunga	1½	US$1.20
Loja	14	US$10.00
Machala	11	US$7.25
Manta	8	US$5.50
Otavalo	2¼	US$1.60
Portoviejo	8	US$5.50
Puyo	8	US$4.00
Riobamba	4	US$3.00
Santo Domingo	2½	US$2.20
Tena	6	US$4.00
Tulcán	5½	US$4.00

Panamericana has opened a terminal in the New Town at Colón and Reina Victoria with comfortable (and more expensive) long-haul buses to Guayaquil, Huaquillas, Manta, Loja, Esmeraldas and Cuenca.

Companies will sell international tickets to Peru or Colombia. These involve bus changes at the border and are expensive.

Train The train station (☎ 02-656-142) is on Sincholagua near Maldonado, 2km south of the Old Town. There is an 8 am Saturday train to Riobamba (US$16; six hours) and a train tour to Cotopaxi at 8 am on Sunday (US$20 return). Tickets are sold at Bolívar 443 and Benalcázar (☎ 02-513-422) in the Old Town and, on Friday. These train routes are the most reliable (though not the most dramatic) in the country.

Getting Around

To/From the Airport Many of the northbound buses on Amazonas and 10 de Agosto go to the airport. Some have 'Aeropuerto' placards and others say 'Quito Norte.' From the airport, cross Amazonas and flag a southbound bus. It costs about US$0.20 to the New Town. From there, catch a bus or El Trole to the Old Town. A taxi to the airport from the New Town should be less than US$4, or US$5 from the Old Town. From the airport, taxi drivers try to overcharge: bargain hard.

Bus The crowded local buses have a flat fare of US$0.10, which you pay as you board. There are also *ejecutivo* and *selectivo* buses; these don't allow standing, and charge about US$0.20. Generally, buses run north-south and have a fixed route. The ejecutivo and selectivo buses are found primarily on 10 de Agosto and 6 de Diciembre. Buses have destination placards in their windows and drivers usually will tell you which bus to take if they are not going your way. Traffic in the Old Town is very heavy, and it's sometimes faster to walk than to take a bus, particularly during rush hour.

Trolley Quito's trolley service, El Trole, runs between the Estación Trolebús Sur, on Av Maldonado south of Villaflora, and the Estación Trolebús Norte, on 10 de Agosto just north of Av de La Prensa. Trolleys run along Maldonado and 10 de Agosto about every 10 minutes from 6 am to 12:30 am and stop every few blocks. The fare is US$0.20 and the service efficient, if crowded. The government has restricted the number of buses on city routes, which should result in better air quality, especially in the Old Town.

Taxi Cabs are yellow and have red 'TAXI' stickers in the window. Quito cabs have meters and drivers should use them. Sometimes a fare is arranged beforehand so the driver can take a roundabout route to avoid traffic, thus saving time. Cabs cost US$1 to US$2 for short journeys; up to US$5 for a long trip. Cabs can be rented by the hour or longer, about US$50 for a day.

AROUND QUITO

The most famous excursion is to the equator at **La Mitad del Mundo**, 22km north of Quito. Here, a large monument houses a viewing platform and an excellent ethnographical museum. Hours are 10 am to 5 pm weekdays and 9 am to 6 pm weekends; admission is US$0.80. A planetarium, a wonderful scale model of Quito's Old Town and other attractions cost extra. **Rumicucho** is a small pre-Inca site under excavation about 3.5km north of Mitad del Mundo. About 5km north of Mitad del Mundo, on the way to the village of Calacalí, is the ancient volcanic crater of **Pululahua**, into which one can descend on foot – an interesting walk.

From Quito, the Mitad del Mundo bus (US$0.25; one hour) leaves frequently from the short street of J López, between Hermano Miguel and El Tejar, near the Ipiales street market in the Old Town. It's not an obvious bus stop, so ask. The bus also passes the roundabout where Avs Universitaria and América meet.

Several companies offer tours for US$20, or you can take a return-trip taxi for the same price (including waiting time).

The **Reserva Forestal de Pasochoa** is operated by the Fundación Natura (☎ 02-242-758), Rumibamba 1019 and Yugoslavia. The reserve is 30km southeast of Quito and has one of the last stands of undisturbed humid Andean forest left in central Ecuador. More than 100 species of bird and many rare plants have been recorded; it is recommended to naturalists and bird-watchers. Trails range from easy to strenuous. This makes a good day trip. Get the bus to the village of Amaguaña at La Marin in the Old Town; the reserve is 7km beyond the village.

The daily fee for foreign visitors is US$7. Overnight camping in designated areas is US$12 per person (including the daily fee); it may be full on weekends. There are latrines, picnic areas and water. There is also a refuge charging US$6 for basic accommodations. Check with the Fundación Natura to obtain directions, maps, information and permits.

Quito's closest volcano is **Pichincha**, looming over the western side of the city. There are two summits, the closer Rucu Pichincha (about 4700m) and the higher Guagua Pichincha (4794m). Both can be climbed from Quito in a very long day, but the hiking routes are plagued with thieves, rapists and rabid dogs. Go in a large group and get up-to-date information from the SAEC.

North of Quito

The Andean highlands north of Quito are among the most popular destinations in Ecuador. Few travelers spend any time in the country without visiting the famous Indian market in the small town of Otavalo, where you can buy a wide variety of weavings, clothing and handicrafts.

The dramatic mountain scenery of the region is dotted with shining white churches set in tiny villages, and includes views of Cayambe, the third-highest peak in the country, as well as a beautiful lake district. Several small towns are noted for specialty handicrafts such as woodcarving and leatherwork.

Ibarra is a small, charmingly somnolent colonial city that is linked to San Lorenzo on the coast by railway. If you are traveling overland to or from Colombia, it's almost impossible to avoid this region.

OTAVALO

This town of 25,000 inhabitants, 95km from Quito, is justly famous for its friendly people and their Saturday market. The market dates from pre-Inca times, when jungle products were brought up from the eastern lowlands and traded for highland goods.

The most evident feature of the otavaleños' culture is their traditional dress. The men wear long single pigtails, calf-length white pants, rope sandals, reversible gray or blue ponchos and dark felt hats. The women are very striking, with beautifully embroidered blouses, long black skirts and shawls, and interesting folded head cloths. They also wear many strings of gold-colored blown-glass beads around their necks, and bracelets made of long strands of red beads.

The inhabitants of Otavalo are mainly whites or mestizos. There are about 40,000 Indians, most of whom live in the many nearby villages and come into Otavalo for market day. However, quite a few Indians own craft shops in Otavalo.

Information

Casas de cambio (see map) give good rates and are open early mornings and Saturdays. The Banco de la Previsora gives cash advances on credit cards. The post office is at the corner of Sucre and Salinas on the 2nd floor and Internet services are available at Microcontrol, Bolívar 1422 and Centro de Computers on Plaza de los Ponchos, next to the Shenandoah pie shop.

Warning Lonely Planet received a reader's letter from two women who were robbed and raped by three armed men in December 1998, near Lake Mojanda, 16km from Otavalo. Apparently, two other tourists suffered a similar attack there in January 1999. The men were described as well-dressed, affluent Ecuadorians. Be extremely cautious in this area and report to your consulate or embassy for help.

Things to See & Do

The main market day is Saturday. There are three main plazas, with the overflow filling the streets around them. **Plaza de los Ponchos** is for crafts (a 'market' happens most days, especially Wednesday). Bargaining is expected. You can get better deals on weekdays when business is slow. The Saturday market gets under way soon after dawn and continues until about noon. It gets crowded mid-morning, when the big tour groups arrive. Thieves and bag-slashers have been reported. There is an **animal market** from 6 to 8 am on the outskirts of town.

The **Instituto Otavaleño de Antropología** has a museum; admission is free.

The Quito-based **Instituto Superior** (☎ 06-922-414), Sucre 1110 and Morales, has Spanish language classes.

Organized Tours

Zulaytour (☎ 06-921-176), on the eastern corner of Sucre and Colón, 2nd floor, is the longest standing and best known information and guide service. It's run by the knowledgeable Rodrigo Mora, who speaks English. A variety of guided tours enable you to visit local Indian homes, learn about the entire weaving process, buy products off the loom and take photographs. An emphasis on anthropological and sociological background information makes these tours very worthwhile. The most popular visits several local villages and takes all day. Transport is included and the tour costs about US$10 per person. Other companies nearby

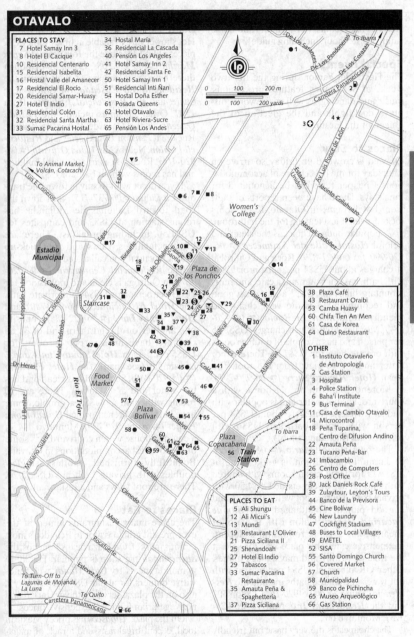

OTAVALO

PLACES TO STAY
- 7 Hotel Samay Inn 3
- 8 Hotel El Cacique
- 10 Residencial Centenario
- 15 Residencial Isabelita
- 16 Hostal Valle del Amanecer
- 17 Residencial El Rocio
- 20 Residencial Samar-Huasy
- 27 Hotel El Indio
- 31 Residencial Colón
- 32 Residencial Santa Martha
- 33 Sumac Pacarina Hostal
- 34 Hostal María
- 36 Residencial La Cascada
- 40 Pensión Los Angeles
- 41 Hotel Samay Inn 2
- 42 Residencial Santa Fe
- 50 Hotel Samay Inn 1
- 51 Residencial Inti Nan
- 54 Hostal Doña Esther
- 61 Posada Queens
- 62 Hotel Otavalo
- 63 Hotel Riviera-Sucre
- 65 Pensión Los Andes

PLACES TO EAT
- 5 Ali Shungu
- 12 Ali Micui's
- 13 Mundi
- 19 Restaurant L'Olivier
- 21 Pizza Siciliana II
- 25 Shenandoah
- 27 Hotel El Indio
- 32 Tabascos
- 33 Sumac Pacarina Restaurante
- 35 Amauta Peña & Spaghetteria
- 37 Pizza Siciliana
- 38 Plaza Café
- 43 Restaurant Oraibi
- 53 Camba Huasy
- 60 Chifa Tien An Men
- 61 Casa de Korea
- 64 Quino Restaurant

OTHER
- 1 Instituto Otavaleño de Antropología
- 2 Gas Station
- 3 Hospital
- 4 Police Station
- 6 Baha'i Institute
- 9 Bus Terminal
- 11 Casa de Cambio Otavalo
- 14 Microcontrol
- 18 Peña Tuparina, Centro de Difusion Andino
- 22 Amauta Peña
- 23 Tucano Peña-Bar
- 24 Imbacambio
- 26 Centro de Computers
- 28 Post Office
- 30 Jack Daniels Rock Café
- 39 Zulaytour, Leyton's Tours
- 44 Banco de la Previsora
- 45 Cine Bolivar
- 46 New Laundry
- 47 Cockfight Stadium
- 48 Buses to Local Villages
- 49 EMETEL
- 52 SISA
- 55 Santo Domingo Church
- 56 Covered Market
- 57 Church
- 58 Municipalidad
- 59 Banco de Pichincha
- 65 Museo Arqueológico
- 66 Gas Station

ECUADOR

run similar tours. Leyton's Tours (☎ 06-922-388) has bike rentals (US$1/hour) and horse riding (US$5/hour, including guide).

Special Events

The **Fiesta del Yamor**, during the first two weeks of September, features processions, music and dancing, as well as fireworks displays, cockfights and the election of the Queen of the Fiesta.

Places to Stay

Otavalo is crowded on Friday, so arrive on Thursday for the best choice of accommodations. Cheaper rates can be negotiated for long stays. There have been reports of theft from hotel rooms in Otavalo. Keep doors locked, even if just leaving for the bathroom.

A popular budget choice is the clean and helpful **Hostal Valle del Amanecer** (☎ 06-920-990, fax 06-921-819), Roca and Quiroga. It charges about US$4 per person or US$6 with bath, has hot water and a café, and rents mountain bikes for US$7 a day. Also good and recommended is the very clean and friendly **Residencial El Rocío** (☎ 06-920-584), Morales 1170, which charges US$2.75 per person and has a couple of double rooms with private bath for US$7.50. There is hot water and a nice view from the roof. The clean **Hotel Riviera-Sucre** (☎ 06-920-241), G Moreno 380, is in an old house with a courtyard, has hot water and is popular with budget travelers. Rates are about US$4 per person with shared bath and US$6 with private bath (including a tub!).

The new **Hostal María** (☎ 06-920-672), M Jaramillo and Colón, is good value at US$3.75 for large, clean rooms with shared bath and plenty of closets or US$4.50 with private bath. There is hot water, parking and a good panadería attached. The **Sumac Pacarina Hostal**, Colón 610, is a dollar cheaper, has a game room and a decent, inexpensive café. This place was for sale at the time of writing and may change names. Other OK places at US$3 per person with hot water and shared baths include the **Residencial Santa Fe** (☎ 06-920-161), Colón 507 and the **Residencial Inti Ñan** (☎ 06-921-373), Montalvo 602.

The cheapest is the very basic but friendly **Pensión Los Andes**, Montalvo 375, at about US$2 per person. It has cold water and a private archaeology museum! For about US$3 per person, the **Residencial Samar-Huasy**, Jaramillo 611, has clean, small rooms. Hot showers are available at times. Other OK places at US$3 include the **Residencial Santa Martha** (☎ 06-920-568), Colón 704 (though there have been reports of theft here), the **Residencial La Cascada**, on Colón near Sucre, and the **Residencial Isabelita**, Roca 1107. Other cheapies include the **Posada Queens**, in the Casa de Korea restaurant, Roca 711, **Pensión Los Ángeles** and **Residencial Colón**. Nearby, the **Hotel Otavalo** (☎ 06-920-416), Roca 504, is in a nice old building and has rooms without bath for US$4/7.

If you don't want to stay in town, the tranquil **La Luna** (☎ 06-737-415), 4km down the road toward Lagunas de Mojanda, has rooms starting at US$3 and campsites for US$1.50, including breakfast. There are kitchen facilities, views and free pick-up from Otavalo if you call ahead.

The **Residencial Centenario** (☎ 06-920-467) on Quiroga is clean and looks good for US$3 per person or US$4 with private bath. The **Hotel El Cacique** (☎ 06-921-740), and **Hotel Samay Inn 3** (☎ 06-922-438), opposite one another on the northern end of 31 de Octubre, have nice, carpeted rooms for US$5 per person. **Hotel Samay Inn 1 and 2** are similar (see map). The **Hotel El Indio** (☎ 06-920-060), Sucre 1214, is clean and has hot water and a restaurant. There are 10 rooms with bath at US$6 a double; some have balconies. French-owned **Hostal Doña Esther** (☎/fax 06-920-739), Montalvo 444, in a colonial house with a courtyard, has some of the loveliest accommodations in Otavalo. Beautifully furnished, spotless singles/doubles with private bath are US$15/20. There are roof views and a restaurant.

Places to Eat

There are many restaurants aimed at the ever-present gringo visitor to Ecuador's most famous market. On Plaza de los Ponchos, the **Shenandoah** pie shop is popular. For more upmarket meals, try **Café Mundi**, with innovative dinners for about US$5. **Ali Micuy's**, also on the plaza, serves both vegetarian and nonvegetarian food at inexpensive prices.

Off the plaza, **Tabascos** has pricey Mexican food, decent breakfasts, and a rack of magazines in English. For good breakfasts, the German-run **Sumac Pacarina Restaurante** has been recommended. **Pizza Siciliana**,

Morales 510, and *Pizza Siciliana II* have good pizzas. *Plaza Café* on Sucre is popular for coffee and snacks late into the evening. The *Quino Restaurant* is popular and has good – though not cheap – seafood. *Agua Fresca Ñanpi* has been recommended for breakfasts and vegetarian meals. The *Restaurant Oraibi* has cheap vegetarian food. *Restaurant L'Olivier* has medium-priced French food. *SISA*, next to the Hotel Coraza, is mid-priced and serves a good variety.

The best chifas are the *Chifa Tien An Men* and the *Casa de Korea*, on the same block. If you're after fried chicken, try the *Camba Huasy*. All these are reasonably priced. The *Hotel El Indio* does good local food, particularly fritada (not always available). For a splurge, try the excellent *Ali Shungu*, in the hotel of the same name, on Quito near Egas.

Entertainment

Otavalo is quiet during the week but lively on the weekend. The popular *Amauta Peña*, Jaramillo 614, has spawned another bar around the corner that serves spaghetti dinners. Music gets under way after 10 pm, and there is a US$1 cover charge. The music and ambience can vary but are usually pretty good. The newer *Peña Tuparina*, on Morales near 31 de Octubre, is similar and popular; the cover charge here is about US$0.50. The *Tucano Peña-Bar*, at Morales 5-10, has both folk and salsa music and may open midweek. The place can get rather wild. *Jack Daniels Rock Café*, off Plaza de los Ponchos is a popular hangout. These places have all been around for a while, and you'll probably find newer ones. *SISA* (see Places to Eat, above) shows films on Thursday, Friday and Saturday at 8:30 pm.

Getting There & Away

All buses leave from the new terminal terrestre at Atahualpa and Jacinto Collahuazo, two blocks north of Quito. Transportes Otavalo has frequent buses to Ibarra, where you change for buses farther north. Transportes Otavalo and Transportes Los Lagos have many Quito-bound buses (under US$2; 2½ hours), which take you into Otavalo. Many other companies go from Quito past Otavalo heading north (and vice versa), and will drop you off on the Panamericana, about a 10-minute walk from the center.

AROUND OTAVALO

Many of the Indians live and work in the nearby villages of **Peguche**, **Ilumán** and **Agato**. These are loosely strung together on the northeastern side of the Panamericana, a few kilometers from Otavalo. There are many other otavaleño villages in the area, and a visit to Otavalo tour agencies will yield more information. You can walk or take local buses to these villages. The *Aya Huma* (☎ 06-922-663) in Peguche, 3km northeast of Otavalo, has clean beds for US$5 per person (US$8 with private bath), serves good, cheap homemade meals, and often has live music in the evenings. There's a pretty **waterfall** 2km south of Peguche. Sunday is not a good day to visit the villages: many people would rather get blind drunk than deal with gringos.

Lago San Pablo can be reached on foot from Otavalo by heading roughly southeast on any of the paths heading over the hill behind the railway station. When you get there, you'll find a paved road that goes all the way around the lake, with beautiful views of both the water and Volcán Imbabura behind it. There have been isolated reports of robberies: plan your walks to return before nightfall and go with a friend.

COTACACHI

This small village, some 15km north of Otavalo, is famous for its leatherwork, which is sold in stores all along the main street. There are hourly buses from Otavalo. Affordable accommodations are available.

LAGUNA CUICOCHA

About 18km east of Cotacachi is an extinct, eroded volcano, famous for its deep crater lake. The lake is part of the Reserva Ecológica Cotacachi-Cayapas, established to protect the large area of western Andean forest that extends from Volcán Cotacachi (4939m) to the Río Cayapas in the coastal lowlands. The official entrance fee is US$10, but collection is lax.

There are half-hour boat rides around the islands on the lake (US$0.50). These are popular with locals on weekends, but may not operate midweek. A walk around the lake takes about six hours. Don't eat the blue berries; they are poisonous. Trucks, taxis and occasional buses go from Cotacachi.

ECUADOR

IBARRA

About 22km north of Otavalo and 135km north of Quito is the attractive colonial town of Ibarra, the provincial capital of Imbabura. One of the main reasons for coming here is to take the train to the coastal city of San Lorenzo, though service is sporadic.

Horse-drawn carts still clatter along cobbled streets flanked by 19th-century buildings, while dark-suited old gentlemen sit in the shady parks discussing the day's events. Most people are in bed by 10 pm. It's a fairly quiet town, and some travelers prefer to stay here when visiting Otavalo.

Information

CETUR is at Olmedo 956. Change US traveler's checks at the Banco Continental, Olmedo near Colón. Quito has better rates. Casas de cambio and many travel agencies are located at Oviedo and Bolívar. Plane tickets bought in Ibarra take at least a day to issue, as they have to come from Quito. Ecuahorizons, Bolívar 4-67, offers expensive email services.

Places to Stay

Ibarra has some of the cheapest hotels in Ecuador and it's a good base for budget travelers wanting to visit Otavalo and northern Ecuador. Nightlife is poor, however.

Hotels charging US$2.75 per person include the *Residencial San Lorenzo*, Olmedo 1056, and *Residencial Paraíso*, Flores 953. Both have warm showers sometimes and are the best of the super-cheapies.

Other similarly priced, very basic places are the *Pensión Varsovia*, *Residencial Guayas*, *Residencial Girasol* and *Residencial El Príncipe*. At about US$2.25 per person are *Pensión Olmedo 1*, which looks OK from the outside but is pretty basic inside, the *Pensión Olmedo 2*, the *Residencial Tahuando*, the *Hotel Berlín*, and the *Residencial Atahualpa*. All are very basic. The *Residencial Majestic*, Olmedo 763, has pretty reliable hot water and charges US$2 per person or US$2.50 with private bath in basic rooms.

The clean and popular *Hotel Imbabura* (☎ 06-950-155), Oviedo 933, has a mellow courtyard with flowers. The best rooms are on the quiet street; inside rooms can be dark. There are hot, shared showers and comfortable beds. Rates are US$2.75 per

person. Similarly priced and also fair value is the *Residencial Imperial*, Bolívar 622, which has rooms with private bathrooms. Others at this price are the *Residencial Primavera*, where rooms vary from poor to OK, and the *Residencial Yahuarcocha*; both have hot water. The *Residencial Vaca*, Bolívar 753, has basic rooms with shared bath for US$2.75 per person, as does the *Residencial Imperio*, which is not too clean.

The friendly *Residencial Colón* (☎ 06-950-093), at Narváez 862, is clean and has hot showers at times. Rooms with bath are US$3.75 per person; those with shared bath, a little less. It has a laundry service. For the safety of your valuables, lock your doors. The newer *Hostal El Retorno* (☎ 06-957-722), Moncayo 432, has fair-size rooms, with private bath and 24-hour warm showers, for about US$4.50 per person – a good deal. Some rooms have TV. It also has a restaurant, as does the *Hostal Ecuador* (☎ 06-956-425), Mosquera 554. This is one of the best budget values at US$4 per person in clean, spacious rooms with private hot shower. There is parking available.

For something a bit more upmarket, try the *Residencial Madrid* (☎ 06-951-760), Olmedo 857, with carpeted rooms and TV; the *Hotel Madrid* (☎ 06-956-177), Moncayo 741, with restaurant and parking; and the *Hostal El Ejecutivo* (☎ 06-956-575), Bolívar 969. All these places have doubles with private hot shower for about US$10, and a few singles.

Places to Eat & Drink

Restaurant La Chagra, Olmedo 7-48, has large helpings, reasonable prices and is popular with locals, perhaps due to the large-screen TV. There are several good and cheap chifas on this street. *Luchino Pizza & Bar*, on the Parque Pedro Moncayo, has Italian food and snacks; there's another *Luchino Pizzería* at Moncayo 630. A block west, *Manolo's* serves snacks and beer, and is popular with young people. *El Encuentro*, Olmedo 9-35, is a nice bar to hang out in. *Pan Danes*, next to the Residencial Imperial, has tasty breads and sweets. If you're hankering for a sit-down dinner, try the *Bar Restaurant El Dorado*, Oviedo 545. If budget is a concern, the *Restaurant Venecia*, Moncayo 728, is an option.

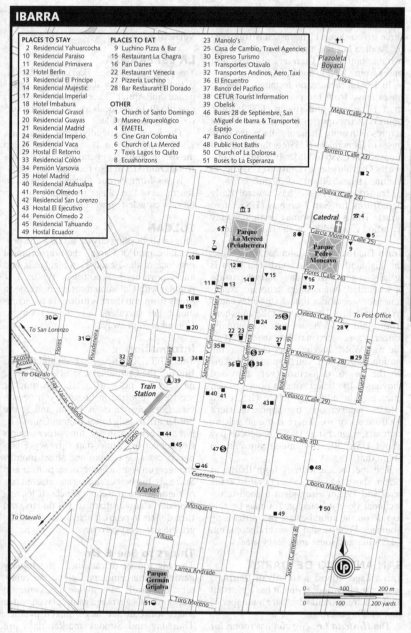

IBARRA

PLACES TO STAY
2 Residencial Yahuarcocha
10 Residencial Paraiso
11 Residencial Primavera
12 Hotel Berlin
13 Residencial El Principe
14 Residencial Majestic
17 Residencial Imperial
18 Hotel Imbabura
19 Residencial Girasol
20 Residencial Guayas
21 Residencial Madrid
24 Residencial Imperio
26 Residencial Vaca
29 Hostal El Retorno
33 Residencial Colón
34 Pensión Varsovia
35 Hotel Madrid
40 Residencial Atahualpa
41 Pensión Olmedo 1
42 Residencial San Lorenzo
43 Hostal El Ejecutivo
44 Pensión Olmedo 2
45 Residencial Tahuando
49 Hostal Ecuador

PLACES TO EAT
9 Luchino Pizza & Bar
15 Restaurant La Chagra
16 Pan Danes
22 Restaurant Venecia
27 Pizzería Luchino
28 Bar Restaurant El Dorado

OTHER
1 Church of Santo Domingo
3 Museo Arqueológico
4 EMETEL
5 Cine Gran Colombia
6 Church of La Merced
7 Taxis Lagos to Quito
8 Ecuahorizons

23 Manolo's
25 Casa de Cambio, Travel Agencies
30 Expreso Turismo
31 Transportes Otavalo
32 Transportes Andinos, Aero Taxi
36 El Encuentro
37 Banco del Pacifico
38 CETUR Tourist Information
39 Obelisk
46 Buses 28 de Septiembre, San
   Miguel de Ibarra & Transportes
   Espejo
47 Banco Continental
48 Public Hot Baths
50 Church of La Dolorosa
51 Buses to La Esperanza

ECUADOR

Getting There & Away

Bus Buses from Quito leave hourly (US$2, three to four hours). The fastest is Transportes Andina but the buses are small, uncomfortable and scary. There are also frequent buses from Otavalo and Tulcán.

In Ibarra, there is no terminal terrestre; buses leave from the places shown on the map. For Quito and Tulcán (US$2; three hours) use Transportes Andina, Aero Taxi or Expreso Turismo. These also have five daily buses to Esmeraldas (US$6; eight hours) and Guayaquil (US$6 to US$8; 10 hours). Transportes Otavalo goes to Otavalo (US$0.30; 40 minutes) from 5:30 am to 9:30 pm.

Transportes Espejo has several daily departures for San Lorenzo (US$5; five hours). This is an awesome ride, though only a portion is paved; sit on the right for views.

Train The Ibarra-San Lorenzo railway links the highlands with the coast. The train is usually an autoferro. A daily 7 am departure is scheduled, but is often canceled, sometimes for weeks at a time. Landslides cause frequent delays. The trip can take anywhere from eight to 15 hours, and occasionally longer. Passengers may be bussed part of the way. Watch luggage very closely in the station. Supposedly, you have to buy tickets on the day of departure (very crowded shoving at the ticket window) but you can often buy them the day before. (If you are told 'No reservations,' try slipping the clerk 5000 sucres or so.) There is a dual pricing system; foreigners pay US$22 and locals pay about US$2.50 – not much you can do about that.

The spectacular journey from Ibarra, at 2225m above sea level, to San Lorenzo, at sea level and 193km away, gives a good cross-sectional view of Ecuador. You may be able to ride on the roof; beware of overhanging branches. Food is sold at several stops, but take water and some emergency snacks.

SAN ANTONIO DE IBARRA

This village, almost a suburb of Ibarra, is famous for its woodcarving. It has a pleasant main square, around which are a number of shops selling carvings.

The *Hostería Los Nogales* has rooms for US$3.

Buses leave frequently for San Antonio from Guerrero and Sánchez y Cifuentes in Ibarra, or you can walk 5km south on the Panamericana (the western extension of Velasco).

LA ESPERANZA

This pretty little village, 7km south of Ibarra, is the place to stay if you're looking for peace and quiet. There's nothing to do except talk to the locals and stroll in the surrounding countryside.

The basic but friendly *Casa Aida* costs US$2.50 per person. It serves good, cheap meals, including vegetarian dishes. The *Restaurant María* also rents basic rooms.

Buses from Parque Germán Grijalva in Ibarra serve the village frequently, but can be very crowded on weekends.

TULCÁN

This small, bustling city of 40,000 is the provincial capital of Carchi, the northernmost province of the Ecuadorian highlands, and an important market town. While it is popular with Colombian shoppers, it's not a pretty town and there is little here to recommend. For travelers, it is the gateway to Colombia, 7km away.

Information

The CETUR office is at Pichincha and Bolívar. The Colombian consul is on Bolívar next to the post office, though quicker service is reported in Quito if you need a visa. Exchange rates in Tulcán and at the border are usually lower than in Quito. The bus between Tulcán and the border accepts Colombian or Ecuadorian currency. Filanbanco, casas de cambio and street moneychangers on Ayacucho between Bolívar and Sucre are the best exchange choices, but few of them accept traveler's checks. If leaving Ecuador, change sucres to US dollars, and then dollars to pesos. If arriving, cash dollars are the strongest currency.

Things to See & Do

The big tourist attraction is the **topiary garden** in the cemetery. Behind the cemetery, the locals play *pelota de guante* on weekends. It's a strange game, played with a small, soft ball and large, spiked paddles. Thursday and Sunday **market** days are crowded with Colombian bargain hunters.

West of Tulcán is the **Páramo de El Ángel**, dropping down into the **Cerro Golondrinas** cloud forests. A recommended trek through remote villages of this area is organized by the Casa de Eliza (see Quito, Places to Stay).

Places to Stay

Hotels are busy, mainly with Colombian visitors. The closest alternative town is San Gabriel, 40 minutes away, which has a few basic hotels.

All hotels claim to have hot water. The basic but reasonably clean *Residencial Quito* (☎ 06-980-541), at Ayacucho 450, is US$3 per person. The *Pensión Avenida*, opposite the bus terminal, has adequate but dark rooms and not-too-clean showers at US$2 per person. The *Hotel Sucre* is US$2.50 per person, but bathrooms are poor and some lack hot water. The *Residencial Florida* (☎ 06-983-849) has rooms from US$2.50 to US$4.50 per person – only the latter have hot water. The *Hotel Atahualpa* has basic rooms at US$3 per person.

There are two other decent places near the bus station. The *Hotel Acacias* (☎ 06-982-501) has singles/doubles at US$7/9 with private bath and TV (some rooms have a balcony). The *Hotel Los Alpes* (☎ 06-982-235) has singles/doubles for US$5.50/9. There is a restaurant.

The *Hotel Granada* (☎ 06-984-595) is OK for US$3 per person with shared bath, as is the *Residencial Oasis* (☎ 06-980-342) at US$3.25 per person with private bath. The *Hotel Imperial* (☎ 06-981-094) has nice, light rooms with shared showers at US$3.75 per person and the *Hotel San Francisco* (☎ 06-980-760) seems OK at the same price and has private showers.

Nice places for about US$10 a double with bath include the *Hotel Unicornio* (☎ 06-980-638), with TV or balconies in some rooms, the *Hotel Alejandra* (☎ 06-981-784), and the *Hotel San Andrés*, which also has a few singles with shared bath for US$4.

Places to Eat

El Patio, Bolívar 13-91, has large servings and good breakfasts, and is one of Tulcán's best restaurants. *Café Tulcán* has ice cream, pastries and decent breakfasts. *Max Pan* has also been recommended for breakfasts. The *Chifa Pack Choy* is the best chifa in town, according to most travelers. For Ecuadorian-style food, the cheap

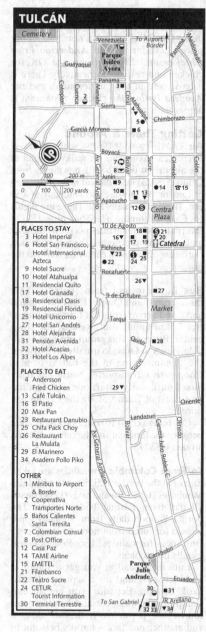

TULCÁN

0   100   200 m
0   100   200 yards

PLACES TO STAY
3 Hotel Imperial
6 Hotel San Francisco, Hotel Internacional Azteca
9 Hotel Sucre
10 Hotel Atahualpa
11 Residencial Quito
17 Hotel Granada
18 Residencial Oasis
19 Residencial Florida
25 Hotel Unicornio
27 Hotel San Andrés
28 Hotel Alejandra
31 Pensión Avenida
32 Hotel Acacias
33 Hotel Los Alpes

PLACES TO EAT
4 Andersson Fried Chicken
12 Café Tulcán
16 El Patio
20 Max Pan
23 Restaurant Danubio
25 Chifa Pack Choy
26 Restaurant La Mulata
29 El Marinero
34 Asadero Pollo Piko

OTHER
1 Minibus to Airport & Border
2 Cooperativa Transportes Norte
5 Baños Calientes Santa Teresita
7 Colombian Consul
8 Post Office
12 Casa Paz
14 TAME Airline
15 EMETEL
21 Filanbanco
22 Teatro Sucre
24 CETUR Tourist Information
30 Terminal Terrestre

ECUADOR

Restaurant Danubio is OK but has a limited menu. The *Restaurant La Mulata*, in the Hotel Frailejón, has much better but pricey Ecuadorian food. *Andersson Fried Chicken* and *El Marinero* are OK for chicken and ceviche, respectively. There is a basic café in the bus terminal, and the *Asadero Pollo Piko* chicken restaurant is across the street.

Getting There & Around

Air TAME (☎ 06-980-675), with offices on Sucre near Ayacucho (in walkway) and at the airport (☎ 06-982-850), has flights from Quito (US$23) weekdays at noon, returning at 1 pm or, on Tuesday and Thursday, at 4:50 pm. These are usually full. There are flights to Cali, Colombia (US$68, plus US$25 international departure tax), on Tuesday and Thursday afternoons. The airport is 2km northeast of the town center en route to the border.

Bus Buses to and from Ibarra (US$2; three hours) and Quito (US$4; 5½ hours) leave and arrive from the terminal terrestre, 2.5km uphill southwest of the town center. Buses to Guayaquil are also available. Buses to Otavalo usually drop you on the Panamericana in the outskirts; ask. Cooperativa Transportes Norte has daily buses until early afternoon for destinations west of Tulcán, along the Colombian border.

City buses (US$0.10) run along Av Bolívar between the terminal and the center. A taxi is around US$0.75.

To/From Colombia Formalities are taken care of at the border, 6.5km north of Tulcán. Minibuses (US$0.50) and taxis (US$3) leave all day from Parque Isidro Ayora. The border is open daily from 6 am to 9 pm (closed for lunch from noon to 1 or 2 pm). Entrance formalities for Ecuador are usually no problem.

Entering Ecuador, you get a stamp in your passport and on a separate tourist card. Leaving Ecuador, you get an exit stamp in your passport and hand in your tourist card. If you lose it, they should give you another one free – but it's best not to lose it. (See Visas & Embassies and Documents in the Facts for the Visitor section of this chapter.)

South of Quito

The Panamericana heads almost directly south from Quito along a long valley flanked by parallel ranges of mountains, many of which are volcanoes. This central valley contains almost half of Ecuador's population. The relatively rich volcanic soils are suitable for agriculture and the valley makes a good communication route between north and south. A string of towns stretches south from the capital to Ecuador's third-largest city, Cuenca, some 300km away. In between is some of Ecuador's wildest scenery, with nine of the country's 10 highest peaks, and scores of tiny Andean Indian villages where lifestyles have changed little in centuries.

LATACUNGA

Latacunga (population 40,000) is the capital of Cotopaxi province and is a good base for several excellent excursions. The drive from Quito is magnificent. Cotopaxi, the second-highest Ecuadorian peak at 5897m, is the cone-shaped mountain looming to the east of the Panamericana. The two Ilinizas (Sur and Norte), also snowcapped and over 5000m, are on your right, and several other peaks are visible during the 90km drive.

Special Events

The major annual fiesta honors La Virgen de las Mercedes and is held from September 23 to 24. This is more popularly known as the Fiesta de la Mama Negra, and there are processions, costumes, fireworks, street dancing and Andean music. This is one of those festivals that, although superficially Christian, has much Indian influence and is worth seeing.

Places to Stay

Latacunga is a primary flower-growing region and most hotels sport vases of roses, carnations and other visual delights.

The best (but not cheapest) budget hotel is the *Hotel Estambul* (☎ 03-800-354), at US$4.75 per person or US$13 for a double with bath in very clean, well-maintained rooms. They can provide transport to Cotopaxi and Laguna Quilotoa. Also recommended is the *Residencial Santiago* (☎ 03-800-899), 2 de Mayo and Guayaquil, at US$3.75 per person for large rooms (shared bath) or US$4.75 per person for

LATACUNGA

PLACES TO STAY
2 Hostal Residencial Jackeline
3 Residencial El Salto
4 Hotel Amazonas
7 Hostal Quilotoa
10 Residencial La Estación
14 Hotel Los Nevados,
    Hotel Turismo
18 Residencial Santiago
19 Hotel Estambul
22 Hotel Rodelu
25 Hotel Central
26 Hotel Cotopaxi

PLACES TO EAT
5 Restaurante El Mashca,
   La Borgoña
13 Restaurant Costa Azul
20 Kahlua Bar
21 Café Pasaje
22 Pizzería Rodelu
23 Gran Pan
24 Pingüino
29 Parrilladas Los Copihues

OTHER
1 Buses to Saquisilí
6 La Merced Market
8 Buses (Passing) to
   Ambato, Baños, Riobamba
9 Gas Station
11 Transportes Cotopaxi Buses
    to Zumbahua & Quevedo
12 Buses to Pujilí
15 Buses to Ambato
16 Buses (Passing) to Quito
17 Church
27 Molinos de Monserrat Museum
28 EMETEL, Post Office
30 Town Hall
31 General Hospital
32 Old Hospital

ECUADOR

smaller, darker rooms with private bath. Both places have hot water, and are helpful and secure.

For US$3.75 per person, the basic, friendly and cleanish **Hostal Residencial Jackeline** (☎ 03-801-033), is OK. The **Residencial El Salto** is also basic and charges US$5.50. Both have warm showers. The **Hotel Turismo** (☎ 03-800-362), has a cheap restaurant and very basic rooms with shared bathrooms at US$3 per person. A friendly, more basic cold-water cheapie is the **Residencial La Estación**. The **Hotel Los Nevados** has simple rooms and shared electric hot showers for US$2.75 per person.

The **Hotel Amazonas** (☎ 03-812-673) has clean doubles/triples with private bath-

rooms, hot water and TV for US$7.50/13. Some rooms are dark; look before leaping. The **Hostal Quilotoa** (☎ 03-800-099) has good, clean, carpeted single/double rooms with bath and hot water for US$8/13. Similar is the **Hotel Rodelu** (☎ 03-800-956), with small, clean doubles for US$15, including parking. The **Hotel Cotopaxi** (☎ 03-801-310) is a good deal at US$6.50 per person in carpeted rooms with private bath and hot water. Some rooms have plaza views. Also good is the friendly **Hotel Central** with similar amenities at US$3.75 or US$4.75, depending on the room.

Hotels fill fast on Wednesday afternoon for the Thursday morning Indian market at Saquisilí.

Places to Eat

Parrilladas Los Copihues, steaks and meat dishes, and *Pizzería Rodelu* are supposedly the best places and they aren't terribly expensive. *Restaurantes La Borgoña* and *Costa Azul* (simple Ecuadorian food) and *El Mashca* (for chicken) are cheaper and quite good. *Pingüino* is a good place for ice cream and *Gran Pan* bakery is good for bread. For super cheap burgers and sandwiches, try *Café Pasaje*. The *Kahlua Bar* next door has live music on Saturday nights.

Most restaurants close by 8 pm. *Pollos Gus*, near the Hostal Quilotoa on the Panamericana, serves fast-food-style hamburgers and roast chicken, and is open late. It's hard to find a place for early breakfasts.

Getting There & Away

Buses drop off and pick up passengers on the Panamericana, at the corner of Av 5 de Junio. Some go direct to and from Latacunga's Plaza Chile (also known as El Salto); these may be slower but a seat is usually guaranteed. Buses go to Quito (US$1.20; two hours), Ambato (US$0.75; 45 minutes), Riobamba (2¼ hours) and Baños (1½ hours).

The bus stop west for Pujilí (US$0.25) and beyond is near the Panamericana. Beyond Pujilí the road goes past Zumbahua (US$1.50; two hours), and down the western Andes to Quevedo (US$3; four hours). This rough but spectacular ride from the highlands to the western lowlands leaves about seven times a day.

Buses for Saquisilí (US$0.25; 30 minutes) leave from M Benavídez, near the river. Those to nearby villages (Sigchos, Chugchilán and Mulaló) leave from Plaza Chile, near the market. Departures are every few minutes on market-day mornings, but less frequently otherwise.

SAQUISILÍ

Saquisilí's Thursday morning market is for the inhabitants of remote Indian villages, most of whom are recognized by their little felt 'pork pie' hats and red ponchos. Ecuadorian economists consider this to be the most important Indian village market in the country and many travelers rate it as the most interesting in Ecuador. Be alert for pickpockets.

There are a couple of cold-water cheapies in town. Buses leaving from Quito's terminal terrestre on Thursday morning go directly to Saquisilí. Many buses also leave from Latacunga.

WEST OF LATACUNGA

Ten kilometers west of Latacunga, **Pujilí** has a Sunday market and interesting Corpus Christi and All Soul's Day celebrations.

The tiny village of **Zumbahua** (3500m, 67km west of Latacunga) has a small but fascinating Saturday market, but the two residenciales fill up fast on Friday, so get there early. The better of the two is the *Hostal Quiroga* below the square. Accommodations and food are basic. From Zumbahua, a 14km unpaved road leads north to the beautiful volcanic **Laguna Quilotoa**. Carry water – the lake is alkaline; camping is possible. The basic but friendly *Cabaña Quilotoa* near the lake provides US$2 beds, typical meals, horses and local guides.

About 14km north of the lake is the little village of **Chugchilán**, where you can stay at the *Black Sheep Inn* for US$18 a double, including two vegetarian meals. The staff speak English and this is a good base for hiking and mountain biking. A farther 23km north is the village of **Sigchos**, which has a couple of basic pensiones. From here, it's about 52km east to Saquisilí.

Getting There & Away

There are several daily buses for either Zumbahua or Sigchos, but there are few between these towns. A daily 11 am bus from Latacunga goes to Chugchilán via Sigchos. Buses from Sigchos going past Chugchilán and on to Zumbahua leave well before dawn on Wednesday, Friday and Saturday. Buses from Zumbahua to Sigchos leave on Thursday and Saturday mornings. There are occasional trucks, or you can walk.

PARQUE NACIONAL COTOPAXI

This is mainland Ecuador's most frequently visited national park, but it is almost deserted mid-week. There is a small **museum**, a llama herd, a climbers' refuge (*refugio*), and camping and picnicking areas. The entrance fee is US$20 and the gate is open from 8 am to 6 pm (longer on weekends). Camping is about US$1 per person. A bunk in the climbers' refuge costs US$10. Cooking facilities are available, but you should definitely bring a warm sleeping bag.

Getting There & Around

There are two entrances on the Panamericana, about 20km and 26km north of Latacunga. Buses will drop you at these entrances – you can then follow the signposted dirt roads to the administration building and museum, about 15km from either entrance. You can walk or hitchhike into the park, but there is very little traffic, except on weekends. Pickups from Latacunga cost about US$20 to US$30, but bargain. Hotel Estambul provides a truck service to the park; clarify how far in you want to go.

The Limpiopungo lake area for camping (very cold) and picnicking is about 4km beyond the museum, and the climbers' refuge is about 12km farther on. You can drive up a very rough road to a parking area about 1km before the refuge. The lake is at 3800m and the refuge is 1000m higher; it is very hard walking at this altitude if you are not used to it. Altitude sickness is a very real danger, so acclimatize for several days in Quito before attempting to walk in.

Continuing beyond the climbers' refuge requires snow- and ice-climbing gear and expertise. Guides and gear are available in Quito and Ambato. Ask at the SAEC in Quito for advice.

AMBATO

Ambato (population 125,000), the Tungurahua provincial capital, is 40km south of Latacunga. Badly damaged in a 1949 earthquake, it is now a modern and growing city, famous for its flower festival in the second half of February, when hotels tend to be full. The Monday market is huge. Most travelers just pass through Ambato on their way to Baños, but the museum in the Colegio Bolívar on the Parque Cevallos, open weekdays (US$2), is worth a visit.

Information

CETUR (☎ 03-821-800) is on Guayaquil by the Hotel Ambato. Several banks, and Cambiato, at Bolívar 1715, change dollars at fair rates. Surtrek (☎ 03-844-448, fax 03-844-512), L Cordero 2-10 and Los Shyris, rents climbing equipment and has guides.

Places to Stay

The area around the Parque 12 de Noviembre and the nearby Mercado Central has many cheap and basic hotels, including the *Residencial América*, JB Vela 737, which has tepid electric showers. It is one of the better cheapies at about US$2.75 per person. Next door is the similarly priced *Residencial Europa*, which claims to have hot water but often doesn't. For US$2 the *Residencial Laurita* (☎ 03-821-377), JL Mera 333, is basic but friendly, and has hot water in one bathroom; so does the similar *Hotel Guayaquil* (☎ 03-821-194), at JL Mera 311. The *Residencial 9 de Octubre* (☎ 03-820-018), at JL Mera 325, is also US$3, but has only cold water. There are several other very basic, grungy-looking hotels in this area (which we enjoyed researching – ha!). The *Hotel Nacional* (☎ 03-823-820), on Vela near Lalama, charges US$2.75 and has hot water – sometimes.

The noisy *Hotel Carrillo* (☎ 03-827-200), above the bus terminal, has hot showers and charges US$3 per person. The *Hotel San Francisco* (☎ 03-821-739), M Egüez 837, is quite clean and friendly (though one critic calls it 'seedy') at US$5 per person or US$7 with private hot bath. More upmarket are the *Hostal Señorial* (☎ 03-826-249), on Cevallos at Quito, where carpeted rooms with bath are US$15 per person, and the *Hotel Pirámide Inn* (☎ 03-842-092), on Cevallos at Egüez, which is US$8/15 (one bed) for carpeted rooms with bath and TV.

Places to Eat

Chifa Jao Fua, on Cevallos near JL Mera, has good meals for less than US$2. Cheaper and almost as good is the *Chifa Nueva Hong Kong*, at Bolívar 768. For breakfast pastries and coffee, try *Panadería Enripan* on JL Mera. *Oasis Heladería*, Sucre near M Egüez, is a popular café. *Mama Miche Restaurant*, on 13 de Abril, behind the Centro Comercial Ambato, is quite good value and open 24 hours.

For good, medium-priced steak, try *Parrilladas El Gaucho*, on Bolívar near Quito, or *Parrilladas Favid* on Bolívar near JL Mera. The *Pizzería La Cigarra*, at Bolívar 373, has reasonable pizza.

ECUADOR

Getting There & Away

The terminal terrestre, 2km from the center, has many buses to Baños (US$0.60; 45 minutes), Riobamba (1½ hours), Quito (US$2; three hours) and Guayaquil (six hours). Less frequent are buses to Guaranda (US$1.60; 2½ hours), Cuenca (seven hours) and Tena (six hours).

Local buses marked 'Terminal' leave from Parque Cevallos in the center. Outside the terminal, buses marked 'Centro' go to Parque Cevallos for US$0.10. There are also other local buses.

BAÑOS

This small town, famous for its hot springs, is popular with Ecuadorian and foreign tourists alike. Baños' elevation of 1800m gives it an agreeable climate. The surroundings are green and attractive, offering good walking and climbing opportunities. Baños is also one gateway to the jungle via Puyo and Misahuallí. East of Baños, the road descends and fabulous views of the upper Amazon Basin stretch away before you. The annual fiesta is held on December 16 and preceding days.

Information

Tourist information is available at the terminal terrestre. The Banco del Pacífico changes dollars and traveler's checks at Quito rates. Internet services are available at Café.com, 12 de Noviembre 500, for US$0.25 a minute to read mail and US$1 to compose. Modems are slow. For inexpensive, efficient laundry service, try Victor's House, Martínez and 16 de Diciembre.

Things to See & Do

The **Santuario de Nuestra Señora de Agua Santa** and museum within the basilica are worth seeing. An annual October celebration in the Virgin's honor has Indian musicians flocking to the streets. Museum hours are 7:30 am to 4 pm; entry is US$0.30. The **zoo**, 3km west of town, has local animals in small but clean cages. Entry is US$0.50.

Activities

Clarify with all tour operators whether you will be entering a park and, if so, who will pay the entrance fees. Though contracting a tour with unlicensed guides may be financially tempting, so think twice; a group of

European tourists perished while rafting near Baños with unlicensed guides in 1998. See Organized Tours.

There have been isolated robberies on some trails and at the climbers' refuge. Don't leave anything unattended or it will disappear. Seek local updates and go with a group.

Hot Baths There are two baths in Baños and a third outside town. All have changing rooms and bathing suit rental. The best known bath is **Piscina de La Virgen**, by the waterfall. Hours are 4:30 am to 4:30 pm; entrance is US$0.80. It's busy by 7 am and crowded on weekends. The **Piscina El Salado**, 2km west of town, is similar but has more pools of different temperatures. The water is natural but the pools are concrete – better for soaking than swimming. Catch the bus outside Residencial La Delicia 1.

Hiking & Climbing From the bus terminal there is a short trail to the San Francisco bridge across the Río Pastaza. Continue up the other side as far as you want. South on Maldonado is a footpath to Bellavista (the white cross high over Baños) and then to the settlement of **Runtún**, two hours away. South on JL Mera, a footpath leads to the Mirador de La Virgen del Agua Santa and on to Runtún. There are good views from both these steep paths.

Climbers with crampons can climb **Tungurahua** (5016m) in two days (an easy ascent for experts). The volcano is part of **Parque Nacional Sangay**, with a US$20 entrance fee and US$5 to overnight in the climbers' refuge. A road goes halfway up from Baños; a ride in a truck will cost US$2.50. Ask at Pensión Patty about their 8 am truck departures and guides, Carlos and José. Expediciones Amazónicas (☎ 03-740 506), on Rocafuerte at Maldonado, has rental equipment and guides. Willie Navarrete (contact at Café Higuerón) is a recommended guide. A two-day climb with a group costs about US$50 per person. Beware of cheap but inexperienced guides.

The jagged, extinct volcano **El Altar** (5319m) is hard to climb but the wild páramo surrounding it is a target for adventurous backpackers with gear. Get there by bus to Penipe, halfway between Baños and Riobamba. Continue on via occasional

BAÑOS

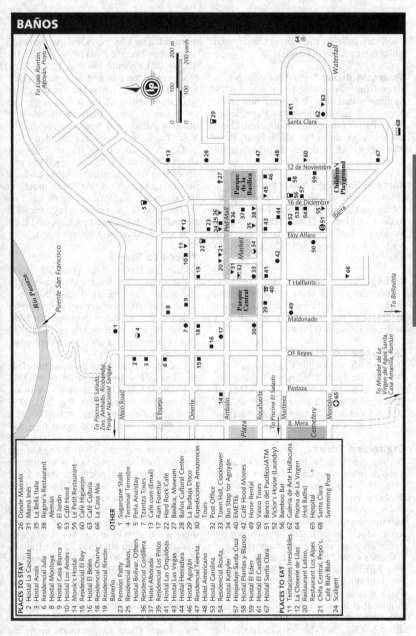

ECUADOR

PLACES TO STAY
2 Hostal La Cascada
3 Hostal Anais
6 Residencial Julia
8 Hostal Montoya
9 Hostal Casa Blanca
10 Hostal Los Andes
14 Monik's Hostal
15 Residencial El Rey
16 Hostal El Belén
18 Residencial Charvic
19 Residencial Rincón
   Baneño
23 Pensión Patty
25 Residencial Baños,
   Hostal Bolívar, Others
36 Residencial Cordillera
37 Hotel Alborada
39 Residencial Los Piños
41 Hostal Las Orquídeas
43 Hostal Las Vegas
44 Hostal Herradura
46 Residencial Teresita
47 Residencial Charvic
48 Hotel Americano
53 Hostal Carolina
54 Residencial Rosita,
   Hostal Kattyfer
57 Hospedaje Santa Cruz
58 Hostal Plantas y Blanco
59 Hostal El Eden
61 Hostal El Castillo
67 Hostal Santa Clara

PLACES TO EAT
11 Tentaciones Irresistibles
12 La Closerie de Lilas
20 Restaurant Latino,
   Restaurant Los Alpes
21 Chifa Central, Pepo's,
   Café Blah Blah
24 Scaligeri

26 Donde Marcelo
31 Mamá Inés
35 La Bella Italia
38 Regine's Restaurant
   Alemán
45 El Jardin
53 Café Hood
55 Le Petit Restaurant
60 Café Higueron
63 Café Cultura
66 La Casa Mia

OTHER
1 Sugarcane Stalls
4 Terminal Terrestre
5 Peña Ananitay
7 Tzantza Tours
13 Café.com (Email)
17 Rain Forestur
22 Hard Rock Café
27 Basílica, Museum
28 Baños Cultural Center
29 La Burbuja Disco
30 Expediciones Amazonicas
   Tours
32 Post Office
33 Town Hall, Clocktower
34 Bus Stop for Agoyán
40 EMETEL
42 Café Hood Movies
49 Horse Rental
50 Vasco Tours
51 Banco del Pacífico/ATM
52 Victor's House (Laundry)
56 Bamboo Bar
62 Galeria de Arte Huillacuna
64 Piscina de La Virgen
   (Hot Baths)
65 Hospital
68 Santa Clara
   Swimming Pool

trucks to Candelaria, 15km away. From here, it is 2km to the Parque Nacional Sangay. It is a full-day hike to the crater. Guides and mules can be hired in Candelaria.

Mountain Biking Several companies rent bikes from about US$4 per day. Check equipment carefully. A popular ride is the dramatic descent (mainly) to Puyo, about 70km. Parts of the road are unpaved. There is a passport control at Shell. From Puyo take a bus back to Baños with the bike on the roof.

Horse Riding Ángel Aldaz (☎ 03-740-175), Montalvo and JL Mera, rents horses for about US$10 per half-day, more with a guide. Christian, at Hostal Isla del Baños, has guided half- and multi-day horse trips. Both are recommended. There are also other places.

Rafting Geotours (☎ 03-740-152), on Maldonado half a block south of the bus terminal, has half-day raft trips on the Río Patate, northwest of Baños (US$20), and full days on the Río Pastaza (US$40).

Language Courses

The Spanish School for Foreigners (☎ 03-740-612), on 16 de Diciembre and Espejo; Elizabeth Barrionuevo (☎ 03-740-314), at T Halflants 656; and Pepe Eras (☎ 03-740-232), at Montalvo 526, are recommended for private lessons at US$3 per hour.

Organized Tours

Visiting the Amazon is generally cheaper (though more time consuming) from the Oriente. If you're looking for a *Heart of Darkness* type of jungle experience, Coca or Lago Agrio is your best bet. For those with time constraints, however, jungle tours are available from Baños, though not all guides are experienced or recommended.

Guides should have a Patente de Operación Turística license issued by INEFAN. The bottom left box shows the areas in which they are authorized to work. They should also have a CETUR card, which ranks them as Naturalista 1 (lowest), Naturalista 2 or Nacional (highest), and states the languages in which they guide. Buyer beware if a guide is reticent to produce a license on request.

Rain Forestur (☎ 03-740-743), on Ambato near Maldonado, has been repeatedly recommended for Cuyabeno Reserve tours and other areas. Tzantza Tours (☎ 03-740-957, fax 03-740-717), Oriente 556 near Eloy Alfaro, has been recommended also, particularly Sebastian Moya. Guides are Shuar Indians who are sensitive of the local people and environment. Vasco Tours (☎ 03-740-017), on Eloy Alfaro and Martínez, run by the Vasco family, has been recommended.

Three- to seven-day jungle tours are about US$35 to US$45 per person per day, depending on destination (three- or four-person minimum). Some focus more on Indian culture and plants; others more on wildlife. Don't expect to see many animals in the rain forest; you need patience and luck. June to September is the busy season.

Places to Stay

Because of Baños' huge popularity, most popular places are full for the weekend by mid-Friday (or earlier), though there is a construction frenzy underway. Hotels prefer guests to stay for a few days. Ask for long-stay discounts. Most hotels are less than US$5 per person – a good town for budget travelers.

One of the cheapest is the basic but clean *Residencial Rincón Baneño* (☎ 03-740-316), Oriente 662 (enter from Halflants), with hot water and doubles for less than US$6. The family-run *Pensión Patty* (☎ 03-740-202), Eloy Alfaro 556, has basic rooms for US$2 per person and is very popular with gringos. Rooms vary in quality. There is one hot and several cold showers, and a communal kitchen. Other basic places for about US$2 per person include the *Residencial Julia* with cold water and kitchen facilities, by the bus station, and the nearby *Residencial El Rey* (☎ 03-740-332) where three rooms share a hot shower and newer rooms with private bathroom are US$4.50. The friendly *Hostal El Belén* (☎ 03-740-024), Reyes near Ambato, has clean, hot-water doubles with refrigerator and TV for US$6.

The *Hostal Santa Clara* (☎ 03-740-349), 12 de Noviembre near Ibarra, is popular and has kitchen, laundry facilities and steaming-hot showers. Clean, simple rooms in the old house are US$2.75 per person and new cabins are US$5.50/9 for singles/doubles with hot shower. The new *Hostal Las Vegas* (☎ 03-

740-426), is US$4 per person in clean rooms with private hot bath or US$3 with shared bath. There is parking and a roof terrace.

Other very basic hotels for about US$3 or less per person include the following. The friendly *Hotel Americano* (☎ 03-740-352), 12 de Noviembre near Martínez, has a simple restaurant and large rooms. The *Residencial Teresita* (☎ 03-740-471), 12 de Noviembre near Rocafuerte, has some rooms overlooking the Parque de la Basílica. Both have hot water and kitchen facilities on request. Nearby, the similar *Hostal Agoyán* is US$3.50 per person. The *Residencial Los Piños* (☎ 03-740-252) has some rooms with Parque Central views.

The very popular *Hostal Plantas y Blanco* (☎/fax 03-740-044), Martínez and 12 de Noviembre, is attractively decorated with plants, has a rooftop terrace that's pleasant for breakfast and a steam bath. Clean rooms are US$5 per person with private bath or US$4 with shared bath. There is a laundry and bike rental, and service is helpful. The well-recommended *Hostal El Eden* (☎ 03-740-616), around the corner at 12 de Noviembre at Montalvo, has sunny, clean rooms overlooking a courtyard for US$5.50 per person. All have private bath and hot water; some are wheelchair accessible.

There are several places to stay on 16 de Diciembre between Montalvo and Martínez, including the *Hospedaje Santa Cruz* (☎ 03-740-648), which is clean but pricey at US$7 per person with bath and hot water. The more economical *Residencial Rosita* has rooms for US$3 per person. The *Hostal Carolina,* above Café Hood, has small, clean doubles with private hot-water bathrooms for US$9. Similarly priced, with laundry and kitchen facilities, is the *Hostal Residencial Kattyfer* (☎ 03-740-856).

The good *Hostal Las Orquídeas* (☎ 03-740-911), on the corner of the Parque Central, has light, clean rooms, some with balconies, for US$3.75 per person with private hot shower. The *Hostal El Castillo* (☎ 03-740-285), Martínez 255, is OK at US$4 per person in rooms with tepid showers. It offers guests three meals for US$2.50.

Others for about US$4.50 per person include the hotels on the busy pedestrian block of Ambato, such as the *Residencial Baños* (☎ 03-740-284), *Residencial Cordillera*

(☎ 03-740-536) and the *Hostal Bolívar* (☎ 03-740-373). Also in this price range are the modern *Hotel Alborada* (☎ 03-740-614), with a terrace, laundry facilities and hot water; *Monik's Hostal* (☎ 03-740-428), with hot water and parking; the *Hostal Casa Blanca* (☎ 03-740-092) which has good, hard beds; and the *Hostal Herradura* (☎ 03-740-913). Other good choices at this price are the new *Hostal Montoya* (☎ 03-740-124), with clean, modern rooms and the *Hostal Los Andes*.

Near the terminal terrestre are the *Hostal La Cascada* (☎ 03-740-946) with carpeted rooms and hot water for US$4 per person and the new *Hostal Anais* with rooms for US$5 per person. About a block from the terminal is the decent *Residencial Charvic* (☎ 03-740-113), with doubles without bath for US$5.

Places to Eat

Donde Marcelo, on Ambato near 16 de Diciembre, has adequate Ecuadorian food with a very popular bar upstairs. On the same block, the cheaper *Restaurant Latino* and *Restaurant Los Alpes* are good. The *Chifa Central* is good for Chinese and local food. Almost next door, *Pepo's* has a delicious selection of seafood and Italian dishes. *Café Blah Blah* serves decent coffee. *Mamá Inés* has Mexican and other meals and is very popular. There are several other cheap restaurants and bakeries on Ambato and around the market. *El Jardín* is good for a variety of food and snacks, which can be enjoyed in the outdoor area. *Tentaciones Irresistibles* has rich coffee and sweets and good salads prepared with sterilized water.

Several international restaurants are slightly pricey but popular with travelers. *Café Hood* features international vegetarian food, has a book exchange and hosts nightly movies. It's open from 8 to 11 am and 1:30 to 9 pm daily except Tuesday. *Café Higuerón* has a good variety of meat and meatless dishes, teas and desserts, and is open from 8 am to 10 pm daily except Wednesday. *La Closerie de Lilas* has good, French-influenced meals at very reasonable prices. *Le Petit Restaurant* is similar, but pricier.

Several places serve good-value Italian food; our favorite is the friendly *La Bella Italia*. Others prefer *Paolo's Pizzería* next to

Café Hood or *Scaligeri* at Eloy Alfaro and Ambato. For a little splurge, try the Italian dishes at *La Casa Mía* on T Halflants. *Regine's Restaurant Alemán*, on Rocafuerte near 16 de Diciembre, is good for breakfast (from 8 am), light meals and drinks – it's German in style. The British-run *Café Cultura*, on Montalvo near Santa Clara, features homemade breads, quiches, fruit pies, fresh fish etc.

Entertainment
The *Hard Rock Café* plays rock classics and is popular, as is the somewhat pricier bar above, *Donde Marcelo*, which also plays rock music and has a dance floor. The friendly and hip *Bamboo Bar* has Latin music and dancing. The *Peña Ananitay* has live folklórico music late on weekend nights. *El Marqués* has weekend peñas with varied music. *La Burbuja* disco has dancing on weekends (US$2 cover). *Baños Cultural Center* screens classic movies nightly at 8 pm (US$1.25) and has a book exchange.

Getting There & Away
From many towns, it may be quicker to change buses in Ambato, where there are frequent buses to Baños (US$0.60; 45 minutes).

From the Baños terminal terrestre, many buses leave for Quito (US$2.40; 3½ hours) and Riobamba (US$0.75; one hour), and less often to Puyo (US$1.50; two hours), Tena (US$3.50; five hours) and points north.

GUARANDA
This small, quiet provincial capital is worth a visit for the spectacular views of Chimborazo on the wild, unpaved road from Riobamba or the paved road from Ambato. Saturday is market day. EMETEL is on Rocafuerte near Sucre.

Places to Stay
Basic cold-water cheapies include the *Pensión San José* on Sucre near Rocafuerte, with large, clean rooms at US$1.75 per person. Others, though not as good, are the *Pensión Rosita Elvira* (opposite the San José), and the *Residencial La Posada*, on Arregon near 10 de Agosto. The clean *Residencial Acapulco* (☎ 03-981-953), on 10 de Agosto near 9 de Abril, has hot showers and is US$3 per person or US$5.50

with private bath. Try to get a room upstairs and bargain. The similarly priced *Residencial Santa Fé* has an overly amorous manager and the *Pensión Tequendama*, on Rocafuerte near José García, is used by short-stay couples (and prostitutes). The *Hotel Matiaví* (☎ 03-980-295), at the bus terminal, has hot water and charges US$4 per person without bath. The pleasant *Hotel Bolívar* (☎ 03-980-547), Sucre 7-04 near Olmedo, has clean rooms and hot showers. Rooms are US$5 per person with shared bath, US$6 with private bath, US$10 with TV and phone. The overrated *Hotel Cochabamba* (☎ 03-981-958, fax 03-982-125), on García Moreno near 7 de Mayo, charges US$6 per person or US$8 with private bath, TV and phone. Rooms vary widely in quality.

Places to Eat
Most restaurants close by 7:30 pm. The *Restaurante Rumipamba*, on the Parque Bolívar, is nothing great, but is one of the better ones. Nearby, the *Chifa Hong Kong* has cheap almuerzos and meriendas, as well as inexpensive à la carte choices. The cafetería attached to the *Hotel Santa Fé* serves a decent, cheap breakfast. *Bar Héroes* at García Moreno and General Enriques is a comfortable, open-air place for drinks.

Getting There & Away
The bus terminal is half a kilometer east of town. Buses leave for Ambato (US$1.60; two hours), Quito (US$3; five hours), Babahoyo (US$2.25; four hours), Riobamba (US$2; three hours), and Guayaquil (US$3; 4½ hours). This last is a beautiful ride; sit on the left. There are also buses to remote towns and villages.

RIOBAMBA
Riobamba is the heart of an extensive and scenic road network. Plan your journey for daylight hours to enjoy the great views. The town is a traditional and old-fashioned city, which both bores and delights travelers.

Information
The helpful CETUR office is on the corner of 10 de Agosto and 5 de Junio and is open from 8 am to noon and 2:30 to 5 pm Tuesday to Saturday. The Casa de Cambio Chimborazo is a good place to change money.

ECUADOR

RIOBAMBA

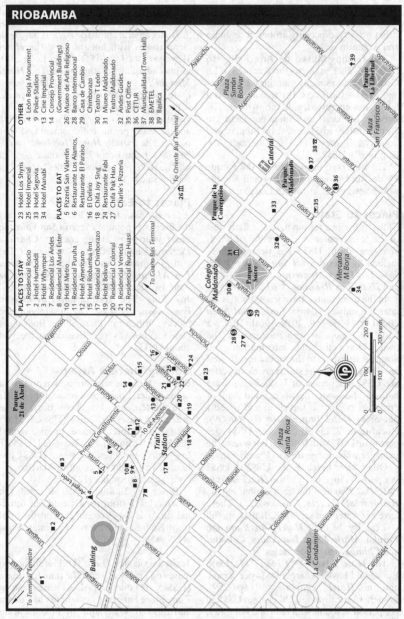

PLACES TO STAY
1 Residencial Rocío
2 Hotel Humboldt
3 Hotel Whymper
7 Residencial Los Andes
8 Residencial María Ester
10 Hotel Metro
11 Residencial Puruha
12 Hotel Americano
15 Hotel Riobamba Inn
17 Residencial Chimborazo
19 Hotel Bolívar
20 Residencial Colonial
21 Residencial Venecia
22 Residencial Ñuca Huasi

23 Hotel Los Shyris
25 Hotel Imperial
33 Hotel Segovia
34 Hotel Manabí

PLACES TO EAT
5 Pizzería San Valentín
6 Restaurante Los Álamos,
   Restaurante El Paraíso
16 El Delirio
18 Chifa Joy Sing
24 Restaurante Fabi
27 Chifa Pak Hao,
   Charlie's Pizzería

OTHER
4 León Borja Monument
9 Police Station
13 Cine Imperial
14 Consejo Provincial
   (Government Buildings)
26 Museo de Arte Religioso
28 Banco Internacional
29 Casa de Cambio
   Chimborazo
30 Teatro T León
31 Museo Maldonado,
   Teatro Maldonado
32 Andes Guides
35 Post Office
36 CETUR
37 Municipalidad (Town Hall)
38 EMETEL
39 Basílica

Things to See & Do

Saturday is market day and there's much street activity, especially around 5 de Junio and Argentinos.

The famous **Museo de Arte Religioso** (☎ 03-965-212), in the restored church of La Concepción, has many paintings, sculptures and religious artifacts. The major piece is a huge, gem-encrusted, gold monstrance. The museum is open from 9 am to noon and 3 to 7 pm Tuesday to Saturday; on Sunday and holidays, it may open in the morning. Entrance is US$2.

The observation platform in the **Parque 21 de Abril** gives good views and has tile work showing the history of Ecuador.

Places to Stay

Close to the bus terminal, nearly 2km west of the town center, are a handful of hotels charging about US$3 per person. These include the **Residencial San Carlos** (☎ 03-968-417), **Hotel Monterrey** (☎ 03-962-421) and **Hotel Las Retamas** (☎ 03-965-005).

In the town center, the cheapest hotels are near the railway station. **Residencial Ñuca Huasi** (☎ 03-966-669), 10 de Agosto 1024, is a basic place popular with backpackers. The owner has climbing information and arranges transport to the mountains. Rooms are a bit grimy but the sheets are clean. Rates are US$2 per person or US$3 with private bath and hot water between 7 and 9 am or pm. Also popular is the clean and friendly but noisy **Hotel Imperial** (☎ 03-960-429), Rocafuerte 2215. Rooms are US$4 per person or US$7 with bath and hot water. The manager will arrange trips to Chimborazo.

Other basic hotels in the US$2 to US$3 per person range include the **Hotel Bolívar** (☎ 03-968-294) near the train station, and the **Residencial Venecia**, Dávalos 2221. These have hot water and seem OK. If they are full you can try the basic **Hotel Americano** and **Puruha, María Ester, Los Andes, Colonial** and **Chimborazo** residenciales.

The **Hotel Metro** (☎ 03-961-714), León Borja and J Lavalle charges US$4 per person, and the **Hotel Segovia** (☎ 03-961-259), Primera Constituyente 2228, charges US$5.50 per person in rooms with bath and hot water; these are just OK. Better at this price is the quiet and clean **Residencial Rocío** (☎ 03-961-848), Brazil 2168. All of these places have cheaper rooms with shared bathroom.

For US$6.50 per person, the friendly and recommended **Hotel Los Shyris** (☎ 03-960-323), Rocafuerte and 10 de Agosto, has good, clean rooms with hot showers. The **Hotel Whymper** (☎ 03-964-575), Ángel León 2310, is just adequate at this price. The **Hotel Manabi** (☎ 03-967-967), Colón 1958, seems quite good at US$5 per person. More upscale is the **Hotel Riobamba Inn** (☎ 03-961-696), Carabobo 2320, with carpeted rooms, parking and hot-water private bathrooms at US$8 per person. The friendly **Hotel Humboldt** (☎ 03-961-788), León Borja 3548, is quite good at US$12/16/22 for singles/doubles/triples, but was for sale in 1998.

Places to Eat

A favorite place for both locals and tourists is the lively and popular **Pizzería San Valentín**; order your pizza at the counter. **Charlie's Pizzería** is more sedate but very good. The budget conscious can try the **Restaurantes Los Álamos**, **El Paraíso** and **Restaurante Fabi**. Two decent chifas are the **Pak Hao** and **Joy Sing**. The **Restaurante Bellavista**, Buenos Aires 1234 and Darquea (about nine blocks northeast of Plaza Simón Bolívar), is good for above-average Ecuadorian meals at about US$3.

Getting There & Away

Bus The terminal terrestre is 2km northwest of the center. Local buses connect the center with the terminal along León Borja. There are many buses to Quito (US$2.80; four hours) and intermediate points, Alausí (US$1.20; 1½ hours) and Guayaquil (US$3.5; five hours), and a few to Cuenca (US$4; five hours). Two night buses go to Machala (10 hours) and Huaquillas (12 hours).

Buses to Baños (US$0.80) and the Oriente leave from the Oriente bus terminal, on Av E Espejo some 2km northeast of town. No buses link the two terminals. A taxi is US$0.80.

Train Service for Quito (US$16; six hours) leaves on Friday at 9 am. The train to Huigra (US$15; six hours) via Alausí leaves daily at 7 am. From Huigra it's two hours to Cuenca and three to Guayaquil by bus; the train goes all the way to Durán via Bucay when track conditions permit (☎ 03-961-909 for information); don't get your hopes up. Roof riding is permitted.

CHIMBORAZO

At 6310m, this is Ecuador's highest peak. The climbers' refuge at 5000m, named after Edward Whymper (the first climber to ascend the Matterhorn, in 1865), can almost be reached by taxi or truck from Riobamba (you have to walk the last couple of hundred meters); this costs US$20 with hard bargaining at the railway station or a few dollars more if arranged in one of the hotels. For example, the Hotel Imperial arranges one-day trips to the refuge, allowing three hours to look around, for US$12 per person (US$36 minimum) and can return another day if you want to climb. A night at the refuge costs US$8. There are mattresses, water and cooking facilities; bring warm sleeping bags.

Beyond the refuge, technical gear and experience are needed to get much higher on Chimborazo. The following guides in Riobamba have been recommended: Marco Cruz at Expediciones Andinas (☎ 03-964-915), Argentinos 3860, is very expensive but perhaps Ecuador's best climber; Silvio Pesantz (☎ 03-962-681), Argentinos 1140, Casilla 327, is well recommended; Marcelo Puruncajas at Andes Climbing & Trekking (☎ 03-940-964, fax 03-940-963), Colón 2221, rents gear and is the cheapest of the recommended guides; and Enrique Veloz (☎ 03-960-916), Chile 3321, is president of the Asociación de Andinismo de Chimborazo. A guided climb costs nearly US$300 for two people, everything included. Other, cheaper guides may be inexperienced. A climb at this altitude is not to be taken lightly.

ALAUSÍ

Just below Alausí is the famous Nariz del Diablo, where a hair-raising series of railway switchbacks negotiate the steep descent toward the lowlands. This spectacular ride is the main reason to visit this small town.

Places to Stay & Eat

Hotels are along the one main street (Av 5 de Junio) and are often full on Saturday night. The clean, family-run *Hotel Tequendama* (☎ 03-930-123) has hot water and charges US$3.50 per person. Breakfast is available. Other possibilities are the friendly *Hotel Panamericano* (☎ 03-930-278), which has electric showers and a basic restaurant below, and charges US$6 for a double, or the *Hotel Europa*, which also has a restaurant. The *Hotel Gampala* (☎ 03-930-138) has erratic hot water and is a rip-off at US$15 for a basic double with private bath. Bargain; it's not worth more than US$10. It has a restaurant but overcharges here too. The best is the *Hotel Americano* (☎ 03-930-159), García Moreno 159, near the railway station. Good, clean rooms with shared bath are about US$3 per person.

Apart from the hotel restaurants, there's little choice, just a couple of basic eateries along the main street. *Danielito's* opposite the Tequendama, is simple but friendly.

Getting There & Away

Bus There are hourly buses to and from Riobamba and several a day to Cuenca. Riobamba-Cuenca buses leave passengers on the Panamericana – a kilometer walk into town. *Camionetas* (pickup trucks) act as buses to various local destinations.

Train The train for Huigra, three hours shy of Guayaquil and two of Cuenca, supposedly leaves at 10 am daily and costs US$12 for foreigners, wherever you get off; expect delays. Tickets go on sale at 7:30 am. It's about three hours to Huigra and six to Bucay (if it's running that far). The train no longer goes all the way to Durán. Passengers can ride on the roof; wear old clothes because of steam, soot and cinders (though a non-steam train runs more often). Derailments and accidents sometimes occur on this treacherous ride.

The train from Huigra passes through in the afternoon and goes to Riobamba.

BUCAY

The most spectacular part of the train ride to Durán is between Alausí and Bucay (General Elizalde on most maps). Unfortunately, the train stopped running even as far as Bucay in 1998 and the farthest you could get was to Huigra. You can get off the train here and continue to Bucay by bus. It is three hours to Guayaquil and two to Cuenca. Buses also go to El Triunfo, where there are frequent buses to Cuenca (four hours). You can take the train from Riobamba or Alausí to Huigra and get to Cuenca by nightfall.

Cuenca & the Southern Highlands

CUENCA

Founded by the Spanish in 1557, Cuenca is Ecuador's third-largest city and its prettiest. The old center has cobblestone streets and churches dating from the 16th and 17th centuries. Nearby is the Inca fortress of Ingapirca, Ecuador's best preserved precolonial ruin.

Information

CETUR (☎ 07-839-337) is at Hermano Miguel 686. INEFAN is at Simón Bolívar 533. Cambistral, on Mariscal Sucre near Borrero, changes various currencies at good

rates. Of several hospitals and clinics, Clínica Santa Inés (☎ 07-817-888), on D Córdova two blocks west of Fray Vicente Solano, has been recommended. The immigration office is in the Municipio on Parque Calderón. The Asociación Hotelera de Azuay (☎ 07-836-925), at Presidente Córdova and Padre Aguirre, has local hotel information.

Internet access is available at the Abraham Lincoln Cultural Center, Borrero 518 for US$3 an hour. Heladería Holandesa (see Places to Eat) and @, Aguirre 1096, 2nd floor, also have (pricier) access. The Fast Kiln Lavandería, Hermano Miguel 668, has efficient laundry service for US$1/kg. Nearby, La Química, Borrero 734, is also good, but more expensive.

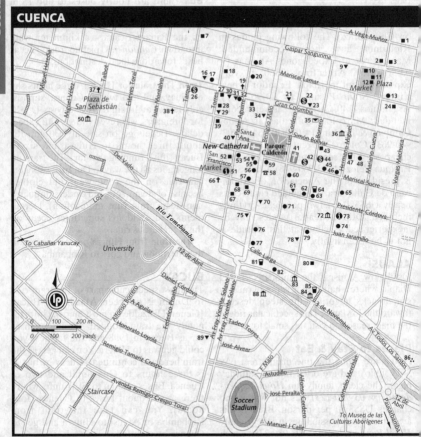

CUENCA

Warning A local man used to ask female travelers to write letters for him in English for 'friends' abroad. He claimed to be a businessman, but was a known rapist, friendly with the police. He was active for years but has not been reported recently. Nonetheless, be aware.

Things to See & Do

The **Río Tomebamba** is attractively lined with colonial buildings, and people dry their laundry on the river's grassy banks. There is a pleasant walk along Av 3 de Noviembre, following the northern bank of the river.

The **Museo del Banco Central** (☎ 07-831-255), on Larga at Huayna Capac, has old black-and-white photographs of Cuenca,

ancient musical instruments and temporary exhibitions. Hours are 9 am to 6 pm weekdays, and 9 am to noon Saturday; entry is free. The **Museo de las Culturas Aborígenes** (☎ 07-811-706), 10 de Agosto 470 (about 1.5km from the town center), has 5000 archaeological pieces representative of about 20 Ecuadorian pre-Columbian cultures. Hours are 8 am to noon and 2:30 to 6:30 pm weekdays and 8:30 am to 12:30pm Saturday; entry is US$1. Call ahead for tours in English.

There are **Inca ruins** near the river. Most of the stonework was destroyed to build colonial buildings but there are some fine niches and walls (though don't expect to compare them with those you'll see in Peru). There is a small site museum.

ECUADOR

CUENCA

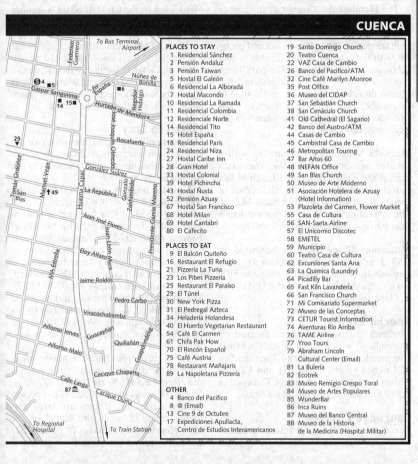

PLACES TO STAY
1 Residencial Sánchez
2 Pensión Andaluz
3 Pensión Taiwan
5 Hostal El Galeón
6 Residencial La Alborada
7 Hostal Macondo
10 Residencial La Ramada
11 Residencial Colombia
12 Residenciale Norte
14 Residencial Tito
15 Hotel España
18 Residencial Paris
24 Residencial Niza
27 Hostal Caribe Inn
28 Gran Hotel
33 Hostal Colonial
39 Hotel Pichincha
43 Hostal Ñusta
52 Pensión Azuay
67 Hostal San Francisco
68 Hotel Milan
69 Hotel Cantabri
80 El Cafecito

PLACES TO EAT
9 El Balcón Quiteño
16 Restaurant El Refugio
21 Pizzería La Tuna
23 Los Pibes Pizzería
25 Restaurant El Paraíso
29 El Túnel
30 New York Pizza
31 El Pedregal Azteca
34 Heladería Holandesa
40 El Huerto Vegetarian Restaurant
54 Café El Carmen
61 Chifa Pak How
70 El Rincón Español
75 Café Austria
78 Restaurant Mañajaris
89 La Napoletana Pizzería

OTHER
4 Banco del Pacifico
8 @ (Email)
13 Cine 9 de Octubre
17 Expediciones Apullacta,
  Centro de Estudios Interamericanos

19 Santo Domingo Church
20 Teatro Cuenca
22 VAZ Casa de Cambio
26 Banco del Pacifico/ATM
32 Cine Café Marilyn Monroe
35 Post Office
36 Museo del CIDAP
37 San Sebastián Church
38 San Cenáculo Church
41 Old Cathedral (El Sagario)
42 Banco del Austro/ATM
44 Casas de Cambio
45 Cambistral Casa de Cambio
46 Metropolitan Touring
47 Bar Años 60
48 INEFAN Office
49 San Blas Church
50 Museo de Arte Moderno
51 Asociación Hotelera de Azuay
  (Hotel Information)
53 Plazoleta del Carmen, Flower Market
55 Casa de Cultura
56 SAN-Saeta Airline
57 El Unicornio Discotec
58 EMETEL
59 Municipio
60 Teatro Casa de Cultura
62 Excursiones Santa Ana
63 La Química (Laundry)
64 Picadilly Bar
65 Fast Kiln Lavandería
66 San Francisco Church
71 Mi Comisariato Supermarket
72 Museo de las Conceptas
73 CETUR Tourist Information
74 Aventuras Río Arriba
77 TAME Airline
79 Abraham Lincoln
  Cultural Center (Email)
81 La Bulería
82 Ecotrek
83 Museo Remigio Crespo Toral
84 Museo de Artes Populares
85 WunderBar
86 Inca Ruins
87 Museo del Banco Central
88 Museo de la Historia
  de la Medicina (Hospital Militar)

The **Museo del CIDAP** (☎ 07-829-451), Hermano Miguel 323, has a small but good exhibit of traditional instruments, clothing and crafts. Hours are 9:30 am to 1 pm and 2:30 to 5 pm weekdays, and 10 am to 1 pm Saturday; entry is free. The **Museo de las Conceptas** (☎ 07-830-625), Hermano Miguel 633, has a fine display of religious art and artifacts housed in a 17th-century convent. Hours are 2 pm to 5:30 pm Monday, 9 am to 5:30 pm Tuesday to Friday and 10 am to 1 pm Saturday. Entry is US$0.80.

The **Parque Calderón** (main plaza) is dominated by the rather stark **new cathedral**, with its huge blue domes. Opposite is the squat **old cathedral** (El Sagrario). At the southwestern corner is the **Casa de la Cultura**, with a local art gallery.

The **Plazoleta del Carmen**, at the corner of Sucre and Padre Aguirre, has a colonial church and a colorful flower market.

Plaza de San Sebastián is quiet and pleasant with the interesting old Church of San Sebastián at the north end. The park has a mural, a couple of art galleries, and the **Museo de Arte Moderno** (☎ 07-831-027) at the southern end. Hours are 9 am to 1 pm and 3 to 7 pm weekdays, and 9 am to 3 pm weekends; entry is free.

Markets Market day is Thursday, with a smaller market on Saturday. The main market areas are around the Church of San Francisco and at the plaza by the corner of Avs Mariscal Lamar and Hermano Miguel. The vibrant market is aimed more at locals than tourists. Watch out for pickpockets.

Mountain Biking Bikes can be rented for US$15 a day (helmet included) from Explorbike (☎ 07-833-362), J Jaramillo 5100 at Hermano Miguel. For an extra US$10 you can hire a guide.

Special Events

Cuenca's independence is celebrated on November 3 with a major fiesta. Christmas Eve parades are very colorful. The founding of Cuenca (April 10 to 13) and Corpus Christi are also busy holidays. Carnaval is celebrated with boisterous water fights.

Language Courses

The Centro de Estudios Interamericanos (☎ 07-839-003, fax 07-833-593), at Gran Colombia 1102, offers courses in Spanish, Quichua, Portuguese, Latin American literature, indigenous culture etc. English classes are taught by native English speakers with a college degree – an opportunity to work.

Organized Tours

English-speaking Eduardo Quito (☎ 07-823-018) is a good local guide. Ecotrek (☎ 07-842-531, fax 07-835-387), on Larga at Luis Cordero, is run by local adventurers who speak English and are recommended for adventure travel. Expediciones Apullacta (☎ 07-837-681), Gran Colombia 1102, has day tours to Ingapirca, Cajas and other places for US$35 per person. English-speaking naturalist guide Edgar Aguirre at Aventuras Río Arriba (☎ 07-840-031), Hermano Miguel 714, by the CETUR office, is another choice. Excursiones Santa Ana (☎ 07-832-340), Córdova and Borrero, and Yroo Tours, on Benigno Malo and Larga, run somewhat pricier tours. English-speaking Humberto Chico at Cabañas Yanuncay (see Places to Stay) organizes overnight tours to Cajas (three days, US$100), the Southern Oriente (five days US$250) and other areas.

Places to Stay

Hotels are often full (and prices rise) for the celebrations mentioned above, so arrive early. At other times, try bargaining and ask if breakfast is included.

Near the bus terminal is ***Residencial La Alborada*** (☎ 07-831-062), Olmedo 392, charging US$3.50/4.50 for singles/doubles with shared hot baths. Nearby, the ***Hotel España*** (☎ 07-824-723), Sangurima 119, is US$9/14 with private bath. Rooms vary in quality – some have TVs – and there is a reasonably priced restaurant. The modern, clean ***Hostal El Galeón*** (☎ 07-831-827), Sangurima 236, has spacious rooms and is similarly priced. The ***Residencial Tito*** (☎ 07-829-734), Sangurima 149, is US$6/11 for singles/doubles, though many rooms lack windows.

There are cheaper hotels with more character in the center. A decent basic place is the ***Residencial Norte*** (☎ 07-827-881), Mariano Cueva 1163, for US$3.75 per person without bathroom. Rooms are large and there's plenty of hot water. Next door, the basic ***Residencial Colombia*** (☎ 07-827-851) is similarly priced but worse. Both get hectic on market days. The basic but adequate *Residencial La Ramada* (☎ 07-833-862), Sangurima 5-51, charges from US$3.50/5.50. The *Residencial Sánchez* (☎ 07-831-519), A Vega Muñoz 428, is similar. The *Residencial Niza* (☎ 07-823-284), Mariscal Lamar 451, is clean and friendly. Rooms are $3.50 per person, or US$4.50 with private bath.

The *Hotel Pichincha* (☎ 07-823-868), on Torres near Bolívar, has large, clean rooms for US$3.75 per person with towels and plenty of hot water in the shared bath; a good value in a homey atmosphere. The friendly *Hotel Milan* (☎ 07-835-351), Presidente Córdova 989, is popular and charges US$5.50/11 with bath, US$3.75/6.50 with shared bath. Some rooms have balconies, and there's plenty of hot water and a simple restaurant. The aging *Gran Hotel* (☎ 07-831-934), Torres 970, is US$7/10 without bath and US$9/12 with; some rooms are dark, with funky carpet. There is a restaurant and an attractive courtyard (which can get noisy). The clean *Residencial Paris* (☎ 07-842-656), Torres 1048, has a helpful English-speaking manager. Rooms are US$5.50 per person with bath, including breakfast.

Other basic places that are not as good but are cheap and OK include the *Pensión Azuay*, Padre Aguirre 761, *Pensión Taiwan*, and *Pensión Andaluz*, all with doubles for about US$4 or US$5. Cheaper but worse are the *Hostal San Francisco* and the run-down *Hotel Cantabri*.

The *Hostal Macondo* (☎ 07-840-697, fax 833-593), Tarqui 1164, is affiliated with Hostelling International. It is quiet and friendly and has kitchen privileges and a nice courtyard. Good-size rooms are US$8/12 (shared bath) and a few have private bath for US$12/16. Reservations are recommended in the high season. Similarly priced are the *Hostal Colonial* and the *Hostal Caribe Inn*.

Two current hot spots for backpackers are the *Hostal Ñusta* (☎ 07-830-862), Borrero 844, with huge carpeted rooms, all with modern, private hot-water bathrooms for US$6 per person including breakfast, and *El Cafecito* (☎ 07-832-337), H Vásquez 736, which has rooms fronting a loud courtyard/bar with shared bath for US$4 per person. Those with private bath are US$2 more. The restaurant is good and there's an economical happy hour.

About 3km southwest of the center is the well-recommended *Cabañas Yanuncay* (☎ 07-810-265, fax 07-819-681), Calle Canton Gualaceo 2149. Take a taxi or bus out on Av Loja and take the first right after 'Arco de la Luz,' 200m along the river. Rooms are in a private house or in two cabins in the garden. Rates are US$8/12 per person with shared/private bath and breakfast, and US$4 more for a delicious dinner made with organic products from the owners' farm. One of the owners is a recommended local guide, and the place is family-run and friendly; English is spoken.

Places to Eat

Those on a tight budget will find set lunches at the hotels with restaurants (see Places to Stay) to be a good deal. *El Túnel*, Torres 860, has a good, filling lunch for less than US$2. *Restaurant El Refugio*, Gran Colombia 1124, looks quite elegant and is good value for lunch. Also inexpensive are the vegetarian restaurants, such as *El Huerto*, Aguirre 815, the homely little *Restaurant El Paraíso*, Tomás Ordóñez 1019, and *Restaurant Mañajaris*, Borrero 533, which has vegetarian specials. For good, affordable Spanish food, try *El Rincón Español*, Benigno Malo 634. A bit pricier are the locally popular *El Balcón Quiteño*, Gaspar Sangurima 649, and *Chifa Pak How*, Córdova 546.

The *Heladería Holandesa*, Benigno Malo 945, a popular hangout for travelers, has excellent ice cream, cakes, coffee, yogurt and fruit salad. Also good is *Café Austria*, Benigno Malo 545, with delicious Austrian-style cakes and coffee. *Café El Carmen*, on the southwest corner of the Parque Calderón, has good snacks and inexpensive local dishes, many of which are not on the menu; ask.

Two good pizzerias on Gran Colombia, on either side of Luis Cordero, are *Los Pibes Pizzería* and *Pizzería La Tuna*. Down the block, *New York Pizza*, Gran Colombia 1043, serves a good, cheap slice, though hardly up to New York standards. The best Italian place is said to be *La Napoletana Pizzería*, Fray Vicente Solano 304. *El Pedregal Azteca*, Gran Colombia 1033, is in an attractive old building, serves Mexican food and is popular with travelers, but it's expensive. For dinner, *Raymipampa* (☎ 07-834-159), Benigno Malo

859, under the new cathedral, is a reasonable and recommended choice.

On Gran Colombia, about 1km west off the map, is an area of restaurants and bars that are popular with young locals. Recommended places include *Doña Charito*, Gran Colombia 2033, with good Ecuadorian and international food and *El Tequila*, Gran Colombia 2059, with good *cuencano* dishes. Prices are mid-range to high.

Entertainment

Apart from the area on Gran Colombia (see Places to Eat), popular bars for young people include the *WunderBar*, on Hermano Miguel, and the *Cine Café Marilyn Monroe*, Gran Colombia 1029, which shows music videos. There are good peñas at *La Morada del Cantor*, on Ordóñez Lazo (the western extension of Gran Colombia). *La Bulería*, Larga 849, has a pool table, and *Bar Años 60*, Bolívar 569, has a disco. You can get pints of Guinness and similar quaffs at the (expensive) *Picadilly Bar* on Borrero. There are several cinemas showing Hollywood action flicks for US$2.

Getting There & Around

Air The airport is 2km from the center on España. There are two or three daily flights to Quito (US$52), but the last one gets canceled quite often. Guayaquil (US$30) is served every weekday. The TAME and SAN-Saeta offices are shown on the map.

Local buses (US$0.10) to the airport pass the flower market on Aguirre. A taxi to the airport is about US$2.

Bus The terminal terrestre is also on España, 1.5km from the center. It has an information desk and a 24-hour cafeteria.

Many buses go to Guayaquil (US$4; five hours) and Quito (US$6 to US$10; eight to 11 hours). Several go to Machala (US$3.50; four hours); a few continue to Huaquillas. Hourly buses go to Azogues (US$0.50; 45 minutes), many continuing to Cañar (US$1; 1½ hours) and Alausí. Several buses a day leave for Saraguro and Loja (US$4; six hours). There are a few daily buses to Macas (US$6; 11 hours) and other Oriente towns. Buses for Gualaceo (1½ hours) leave from the corner of the terminal. Buses for El Tambo leave every 30 minutes; at 9 am and 1 pm on weekdays they continue to Ingapirca (US$1.25).

AROUND CUENCA
Ingapirca

The Incan site of Ingapirca, 50km north of Cuenca, was built with the same mortarless, polished-stone technique as those in Peru, but the site is less impressive than Peruvian ones. Excavation and reconstruction work is still going on. Admission to the ruins and museum is US$4. The museum is open 9 am to 5 pm Monday to Saturday. Guides (both the human and the written varieties) are available.

Ingapirca village has a craft shop, simple restaurants and a basic pensión. A shelter by the ruins may be available for overnighting. Friday is market day.

Direct buses go from Cuenca on weekdays, and there's a bus to El Tambo (7km beyond Cañar) from where it's an 8km walk. Trucks (US$0.50) and taxis are available in El Tambo; beware of overcharging. El Tambo has a basic hotel and Cañar has two.

Area Nacional de Recreación Cajas

This high páramo 30km west of Cuenca is famous for its many lakes (good fishing) and rugged camping and hiking. Buses (two hours) leave San Sebastián church in Cuenca at 6:30 am daily except Thursday from and return in the afternoon. Entry is US$10. You may be able to sleep in a refuge and camping is allowed. The INEFAN office in Cuenca has information and basic maps, but hiking solo in Cajas can be dangerous – the abundance of lakes and fog is disorienting. A group of tourists was lost there in 1998.

GUALACEO, CHORDELEG & SÍGSIG

These villages are famous for their Sunday markets. If you start early from Cuenca, you can visit all three and be back in the afternoon. Gualaceo has the biggest market, with fruit and vegetables, animals and various household goods. Chordeleg's market, 5km away, is smaller and more touristy. Sígsig's market is 25km from Gualaceo and less visited by tourists. This is a good place to see the art of panama-hat making. The **María Auxiliadora**, an all-women's association of hat manufacturers, has demonstrations and hats for sale.

There are a few cheap hotels in Gualaceo and a basic one in Sígsig. Chordeleg has a small but interesting museum on the plaza.

Getting There & Away
Buses from Cuenca to Gualaceo leave about every hour (more often on Sunday). Walk or take a local bus to Chordeleg. A 40-minute local bus ride will take you to Sígsig, from where there are buses to Cuenca.

LOJA
Loja is an attractive provincial city surrounded by beautiful countryside. It makes a convenient stopover on the route to Peru via Macará. The village of Vilcabamba and the Parque Nacional Podocarpus are delightful attractions close to Loja.

Information
CETUR (☎ 07-572-964) is at B Valdivieso 0822. INEFAN (☎ 07-571-534) is on Azuay between Olmedo and B Valdivieso. Banks on the Parque Central give poor exchange rates and are excruciatingly slow. It's better to change in Cuenca or Macará.

The main market day is Sunday. The annual fiesta of the Virgen del Cisne is on September 8; it's celebrated with huge parades and a produce fair.

Hidaltur (☎ 07-571-031), Bolívar 1033, sells discounted tickets for domestic Peruvian flights.

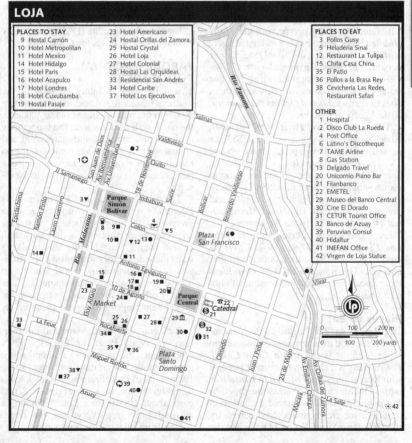

LOJA

PLACES TO STAY
9 Hostal Carrión
10 Hotel Metropolitan
11 Hotel Mexico
14 Hotel Hidalgo
15 Hotel Paris
16 Hotel Acapulco
17 Hotel Londres
18 Hotel Cuxabamba
19 Hostal Pasaje
23 Hotel Americano
24 Hostal Orillas del Zamora
25 Hostal Crystal
26 Hotel Loja
27 Hotel Colonial
28 Hostal Las Orquídeas
33 Residencial San Andrés
34 Hotel Caribe
37 Hotel Los Ejecutivos

PLACES TO EAT
3 Pollos Gusy
5 Heladería Sinaí
12 Restaurant La Tullpa
15 Chifa Casa China
35 El Patio
36 Pollos a la Brasa Rey
38 Cevichería Las Redes, Restaurant Safari

OTHER
1 Hospital
2 Disco Club La Rueda
4 Post Office
6 Latino's Discotheque
7 TAME Airline
8 Gas Station
13 Delgado Travel
20 Unicornio Piano Bar
21 Filanbanco
22 EMETEL
29 Museo del Banco Central
30 Cine El Dorado
31 CETUR Tourist Office
32 Banco de Azuay
39 Peruvian Consul
40 Hidaltur
41 INEFAN Office
42 Virgen de Loja Statue

ECUADOR

A short walk east crosses the Río Zamora and climbs a hill to the statue of the Virgen de Loja; there are good views.

Places to Stay

The basic but clean and friendly *Hostal Carrión* (☎ 07-561-127), Colón 1630, has shared hot showers and charges US$2.75 per person. Also good at this price is the *Hostal Crystal*. The clean and decent *Hotel Caribe* (☎ 07-572-902), Rocafuerte 1552, is US$3 per person, and has hot water. Other OK places with hot water at this price include the friendly *Hostal Pasaje*, Antonio Eguiguren and Bolívar, the *Hotel México* (☎ 07-570-581), 18 de Noviembre and Antonio Eguiguren, the *Hotel Londres* (☎ 07-561-936), Sucre 741, *Hotel Loja* (☎ 07-570-241), Rocafuerte 1527, and the *Hotel Americano*, 10 de Agosto 1662, which was for sale at the time of writing. The *Residencial San Andrés* lacks hot water. At US$3 per person, the *Hotel Hidalgo* is OK and it has hot water; the lively *Hotel Colonial* doesn't. At US$3.50 per person, the *Hotel Cuxubamba* (☎ 07-578-570), next to the Hotel Londres, has hot water and some rooms with private bath, as does the caustic *Hostal Orillas del Zamora*, 10 de Agosto and Sucre.

The popular *Hotel Paris* (☎ 07-561-639), 10 de Agosto 1637, charges about US$3 per person or US$5.50 with private hot bath and TV. The *Hotel Acapulco* (☎ 07-570-651), Sucre 761, is clean, safe and has hot water in rooms with private bath for US$8/11. Downstairs rooms are wheelchair accessible and there is a restaurant. The *Hotel Metropolitan* (☎ 07-570-007), 18 de Noviembre 641, charges US$5.50 per person and the *Hotel Los Ejecutivos* (☎ 07-960-004), Universitaria 1096, is US$2 cheaper; both are similar and OK. The new *Hostal Las Orquídeas* looks good for US$4.50 per person with hot water bath.

Places to Eat

The *Restaurant La Tullpa*, 18 de Noviembre 512, is good for inexpensive Chinese and other food, as is the *Chifa Casa China*. *Pollos Gusy* is a chicken restaurant popular with local youngsters. *Pollos a la Brasa Rey* is also OK for chicken. Across the street, *El Patio* has reasonably priced Ecuadorian food. For ice cream, snacks and coffee, try the *Heladería Sinai*, Colón 143. We like the *Cevichería Las Redes*, 18 de Noviembre 1041, with seafood and other dishes in pleasant surroundings for less than US$3. Nearby, the *Restaurant Safari* is popular with locals.

Getting There & Away

Air The airport is in Catamayo, 30km west. TAME (☎ 07-570-248) has morning flights (except Sunday) to Quito (US$50) and on Tuesday, Thursday and Saturday to Guayaquil (US$25). Catamayo has basic hotels.

Bus The terminal terrestre is 1km north of town. Be sure to book seats early. There are several buses a day to Quito (US$9 to US$11; 12 to 14 hours), Macará (US$4.50; six hours), Guayaquil (US$6; nine hours), Machala (US$4.50; seven hours), Huaquillas (US$4; six hours), Zamora (US$2; three hours), Cuenca (US$4; six hours) and other destinations.

Buses for Vilcabamba (US$1) leave every 30 minutes, as do buses for Catamayo.

PARQUE NACIONAL PODOCARPUS

This park protects many habitats in the southern Ecuadorian Andes at altitudes from 3600m in the páramo near Loja to 1000m in the rain forests near Zamora. The topography is rugged and complex, and many plant and animal species exist here, some unique to the area. This is one of the most biologically rich areas in a country known for its biodiversity.

The park's namesake, *Podocarpus*, is Ecuador's only native conifer. *Cinchona succirubra*, the tree from which the malarial preventative quinine was first extracted, is also found here. Nature and walking trails provide visitors with good opportunities for bird-watching, plant study and maybe glimpses of various mammals. The park is officially protected, but poaching, illegal ranching and logging threaten its integrity.

Park entry is US$10. Maps and information are available at the Loja INEFAN office. Reach the park on a Vilcabamba bus; get off at the Cajanuma entrance, some 10km south of Loja. From here, a track leads 8.5km up to Cajanuma ranger station. A taxi costs about US$10 from Loja. Camping is allowed, but carry everything you need. Access from Vilcabamba is possible.

ECUADOR

VILCABAMBA

This village, 45km south of Loja, is in the 'valley of longevity,' where people supposedly live to be over 100. Scientists find no basis for this claim, but the area is attractive and travelers enjoy relaxing here for a few days. Tourism is booming and both locals and gringos sometimes complain that it's a bit of a scene. Travel sensitively and responsibly here.

Information

A local tourist office is on the plaza. Money exchange is poor so think ahead. The telephone service is unreliable.

Activities

Orlando Falco, a trained, English-speaking naturalist guide, can be contacted in his craft shop, Primavera, on the plaza. He leads recommended tours to the Parque Nacional Podocarpus and other areas for about US$20 per person, plus US$10 park fee. The folks at the Cabañas Río Yambala have a private reserve, camping gear, horse rental and plenty of hiking and riding opportunities with or without guides. Gavilan (ask at tourist information) rents horses for three-day treks at US$75 per person. Several other people rent horses, and hotels will arrange this as well. Massages are advertised – nice after riding or hiking. Spanish lessons are available.

Places to Stay & Eat

The basic, cold-water *Hotel Valle Sagrado* (☎ 07-673-179), on the plaza, is US$2 per person and often filled with budget travelers. It has a popular vegetarian restaurant. The similarly priced *Hostal Mandango* behind the bus station also has some rooms with private bath for US$3 per person. There's a cheap restaurant. For a family stay, call *Señora Libia Toledo* (☎ 07-673-130), a block from the plaza. She charges US$2 per person with shared hot bath and kitchen privileges. Near the plaza, the peaceful *Hidden Garden* has clean and airy singles/doubles/triples for US$6/10.50/14.25. There is a garden, pool, kitchen facilities and a restaurant. For good, cheap lunches (some vegetarian) try *Huilcopamba* on the northwestern corner of the plaza. Orlando Falco, at the Primavera shop. rents the *Pole House*, a serene hideaway with hammocks, kitchen and a private drinking well on the Chamba

River. Rates are US$14/15/16 for two, three or four people.

The *Hostal Madre Tierra* (☎ 07-673-123), 2km north of town (reservations to PO Box 354, Loja), is a rustic, laid-back hostal run by an Ecuadorian-Canadian couple. Rooms are in damp cabins spread over a steep hillside, sometimes reached by long, slippery paths (flashlight needed). Lodging is US$5 to US$11 (depending on the room) per person. Meals are available. Showers are shared. Local hiking and riding information, a book exchange, a steam bath, a video room and table games are available. It's popular and often full, but it's not to everyone's taste.

About 4km southeast of town, the rustic *Cabañas Río Yambala* (☎ 07-580-299) is run by friendly Charlie and Sarah. This place may be full in the high season but you can leave a message. You can walk there or hire a taxi or pickup for US$4. Miguel Carpio, half a block from the plaza, is their recommended driver. They have rooms and cabins, some with private baths, from US$5 to US$16 per person. A vegetarian restaurant and kitchen privileges are available and the owners arrange camping, hiking, and horse riding. Also on this road are the *Hostería Las Ruinas de Quinara* (☎/fax 07-580-314), which charges US$6 per person and has a pool, game room and restaurant, and the well-recommended *Cabañas Tasca* (☎ 07-673-186), with spacious cabins for US$3 per person. Nearby is *El Bistro*, an affordable, French-owned restaurant that serves 'the best steak I've ever eaten,' according to one fan.

Getting There & Away

Transportes Loja has hourly buses to Loja, several daily departures for Cuenca, Machala, and Guayaquil and two buses to Macará, Huaquillas, and Lago Agrio.

MACARÁ

The small border town of Macará offers a more scenic and less traveled route to Peru than the conventional border crossing at Huaquillas.

Places to Stay & Eat

In the town center are a few cheap, basic, cold-water hotels charging about US$3 to US$6 per person. The *Hotel Paraíso*, Veintimilla 553, the *Hotel Amazonas*, M Rengel 418, and *Hotel Espiga de Oro* (with restaurant) are among the better ones and may have private baths. There are a few basic restaurants near the corner of Bolívar and M Rengel, open only at meal times.

Getting There & Away

Transportes Loja has six buses a day (last one at 3 pm) to Loja (US$4.50; six hours), and a morning bus to Guayaquil and Quito (20 hours). Transportes Cariamanga has two morning buses to Loja.

To/From Peru Pickup trucks leave the market often for the border, less than 3km away. Bargain hard or walk. Border hours are 8 am to 6 pm daily. Formalities are OK if your papers are in order. Peru doesn't have many accommodations until Sullana, 150km away. Cross in the morning for bus connections.

Moneychangers are found in the market and at the border. Banks don't change money. Arrive with minimal Ecuadorian or Peruvian money and change into US dollars before crossing.

The Oriente

The Oriente is that part of Ecuador east of the Andes in the lowlands of the Amazon Basin. It features deep jungle, isolated indigenous communities and, sadly, a gigantic oil pipeline. Still, there are many superb opportunities for wildlife viewing, river trips and cross-cultural exchanges in these far reaches of the country.

A 1942 treaty ceded a large portion of the Oriente to Peru. Though Ecuador continued to claim the land as far as Iquitos and the Amazon and went to war with Peru several times over it, a settlement was reached in 1998. The agreement stipulates the creation of adjacent national parks. Travelers may be able to pass between the two countries via the Oriente in the future.

More travelers visit the northern Oriente: Puyo, Tena, Coca, Misahuallí and Lago Agrio. The region south of the Río Pastaza has a real sense of remoteness; it's a good place to get off the beaten track. Buses from Cuenca go through Limón (officially General Plaza Gutiérrez) to Macas. Buses from Loja go via Zamora to Limón and onto Macas. From Macas, there is a road to Puyo and the northern Oriente. Buses from Quito frequently go to the northern Oriente towns of Puyo, Tena, Coca and Lago Agrio. There are many passport checks en route.

The following section describes the Oriente from south to north.

ZAMORA

Three hours from Loja by bus, this town on the edge of the jungle has boomed since the discovery of gold in Nambija, a few kilometers to the north. Food prices are relatively high. Zamora has a few cheap hotels, and there's an entrance to the Parque Nacional Podocarpus, described earlier.

Continuing by bus into the southern Oriente, you will find basic hotels in the small towns of Gualaquiza, Limón, Méndez and Sucúa.

MACAS

This small, old and friendly town is the capital of the province of Morona-Santiago, and it's the biggest in the southern Oriente. Andres Vizuma of IKIAAM Shuar Travel (☎/fax 07-700-380), runs several recommended jungle trips emphasizing Shuar culture. He speaks the language and has a good relationship with interior communities. Tours start at US$35 for a group of two or more.

The best hotel is the *Peñón del Oriente* (☎ 07-700-124), near the bus terminal. It's US$5 per person with private hot bath or US$3 with cold bath. The second-best is the *Hotel Orquídea* (☎ 07-700-970) for US$4 per person with hot water or US$3 with cold. Similarly priced are the *Residencial Mayflower* and the *Hotel Splendit* (☎ 07-700-120). The *Residencial Upano* (☎ 07-700-057) is the best of the cheapies at US$2.25 per person. Slightly cheaper are the *Residencial Upano* and the *Hotel Sangay* (☎ 07-700-457). Also in this price range are the Residencial Macas and the Residencial Emperatriz. The best restaurants are considered to be the *Pagoda*, near the Hotel Peñón del Oriente, and *El Jardín*.

TAME (☎ 07-700-162) has Monday, Wednesday and Friday flights to Quito (US$52). TAO (☎ 07-700-174) flies light aircraft to jungle destinations. The bus terminal has several daily departures for Cuenca, Gualaquiza, Riobamba and Ambato. Several buses a day leave for Puyo; you have to cross the Ríos Pastaza and Pano by foot-

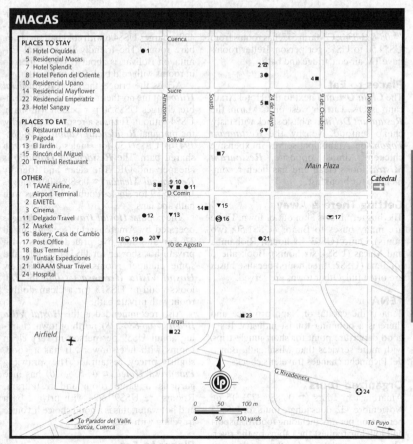

MACAS

PLACES TO STAY
4 Hotel Orquídea
5 Residencial Macas
7 Hotel Splendit
8 Hotel Peñon del Oriente
10 Residencial Upano
14 Residencial Mayflower
22 Residencial Emperatriz
23 Hotel Sangay

PLACES TO EAT
6 Restaurant La Randimpa
9 Pagoda
13 El Jardín
15 Rincón del Miguel
20 Terminal Restaurant

OTHER
1 TAME Airline,
  Airport Terminal
2 EMETEL
3 Cinema
11 Delgado Travel
12 Market
16 Bakery, Casa de Cambio
17 Post Office
18 Bus Terminal
19 Tuntiak Expediciones
21 IKIAAM Shuar Travel
24 Hospital

bridges. Once across, buses wait to continue to Puyo. It's well synchronized.

PUYO

North of the Río Pastaza are the provinces of Pastaza, Napo and Sucumbios, which make up the northern Oriente. Two good roads, with impressive views, go from Quito to this region.

Puyo, on the edge of the jungle, is an important town used as a stopover by travelers. There may be good views of the volcanoes to the west. CETUR is on the corner of Ruales and Amazonas and shares an office with Canelos Tour (☎ 03-795-162). This outfit uses crackerjack guides and offers all

manner of jungle tours, starting at US$30 per person for a group of three. EMETEL is on Villamil near Atahualpa. The post office is on 27 de Febrero near the market. INEFAN is on the road to Tena, just outside of town.

Places to Stay

Hotel Granada (☎ 03-885-578), by the market, charges US$2.75 per person or US$3.75 with bath, and is just OK. *Hotel Chasi* (☎ 03-883-054), on 9 de Octubre, north of the market, is quite good for US$2.50 per person or US$4.50 with bath. There are several other cheapies near the market. The clean *Hotel Barandua* (☎ 03-885-604),

Villamil at Atahualpa, charges US$3 per person with bath. The good *Hotel Araucano* (☎ 03-883-834), C Marin 575, has rooms from US$4.50 to US$8 per person. Better rooms have TV, air-con, fridge and bath.

Places to Eat
The *Chifa Oriental* next to the Hotel Araucano is OK. Farther west on C Marin, the *Restaurant Delfín* is a basic shack with tasty, cheap seafood. Nearby, the *Restaurant Fogón*, on Atahualpa, serves inexpensive chicken. Almost opposite, *Restaurant Mistral* looks clean and has been recommended for breakfast.

Getting There & Away
The bus terminal is 3km out of town. There are many buses to Baños (US$1.50; two hours), Quito (US$3; six hours) Riobamba and Macas (US$4; six hours). Book ahead for Tena (US$2; three hours) because buses are often full. Other towns are served.

TENA
Tena is the capital of Napo province and there is a booming tourist industry. It's a good departure point for short jungle trips, with more services than Misahuallí. Banco del Pichincha changes traveler's checks.

Organized Tours
Amarongachi Tours (☎ 06-886-372), 15 de Noviembre 432, does jungle tours for US$35 per person per day, including food, transport and lodging; request the cabins by the river. These are good tours for the jungle wary. Also with tours at this price is the well recommended Sacharicsina (☎ 06-886-250), run by the Quichua-speaking Cerda brothers. Apart from jungle, you can visit nearby caves and petroglyphs, or go white-water rafting with Ríos Ecuador (☎ 06-887-438). They have an office in the Hostal Camba Huasi. Day trips (no experience required) cost US$50 per person.

Places to Stay
The cheapest hotels suffer from water shortages. The basic Hotel Amazonas, on the corner of the plaza, is about US$2 per person and is OK if you can get an outside room. The Residencial Jumandy, a block north of the main plaza, and the Hotel Baños, near the bus terminal, are similarly

priced and just acceptable. By the bus terminal, the Hostal Camba Huasi (☎ 06-887-429) charges US$4/6 with cold bath in clean, bare rooms. The friendly Residencial Enmita, on Bolívar, is about US$4 per person in rooms with cold bath (less without).

Across the bridge, the clean *Residencial Hilton*, at the northern end of 15 de Noviembre, charges US$5.50 per person with bath, US$4 without. There is a restaurant. Nearby, the marginal *Residencial Napoli* (☎ 06-886-194) is US$5/7.50 for singles/doubles with shared bath. The *Residencial Danubio* is cheaper and OK. The clean and friendly *Residencial Alemán* (☎ 06-886-409) charges US$5.50/9 for singles/doubles in rooms with bath and fans.

The popular *Hostal Travellers Lodging* is operated by Amarongachi (see Organized Tours) and has overpriced rooms with private hot shower for US$14 double, and some cheaper rooms. Nearby, the new *Hostal Visita Hermosa* (☎ 06-886-521), looks good at US$13 for a clean double room with private bath.

Also recommended is the *Hostal Villa Belén* (☎ 06-886-228), north of town, charging about US$9 per person in very clean rooms with hot showers. It has a good, slightly pricey, restaurant. The sprawling *Pumarosa Hotel* (☎ 06-886-320) has nice gardens, a game room and restaurant. Rooms are US$9/16/24 with private bath and hot water; this is a good choice if you're traveling with kids.

Places to Eat
Cheap, decent meals are served at *Chuquitos* and *Restaurant Viena*, in the center. The *Enmita Restaurant*, in Residencial Enmita, is simple but good. Attached to the Travellers Lodging, the clean and recommended *Cositas Ricas* restaurant has tasty vegetarian and Ecuadorian dishes in the US$2 to US$4 range, and juices prepared with boiled water. *Le Massilia* has large pizzas and mouthwatering pies. *Petro's Restaurant*, across from the bus terminal, has breakfasts with good coffee for less than US$2. Nearby on 15 de Noviembre, *La Estación Restaurant* is another convenient choice near the bus terminal. The *Riverside Bar*, with open-air tables, is a good place to have a cocktail or two.

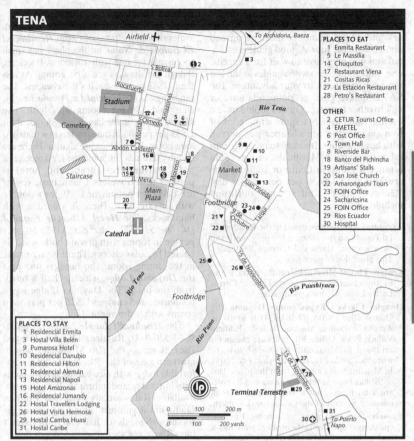

TENA

Airfield
To Archidona, Baeza
S Bolívar
Rocafuerte
Stadium
Cemetery
Río Tena
Olmedo
Abdón Calderón
Market
Staircase
Main Plaza
Footbridge
Catedral
Río Tena
Footbridge
Río Pano
Río Paushiyacu
9 de Octubre
15 de Noviembre
Río Pano
Av Pano
15 de Noviembre
Terminal Terrestre
To Puerto Napo

PLACES TO EAT
1 Enmita Restaurant
5 Le Massilia
14 Chuquitos
17 Restaurant Viena
21 Cositas Ricas
27 La Estación Restaurant
28 Petro's Restaurant

OTHER
2 CETUR Tourist Office
4 EMETEL
6 Post Office
7 Town Hall
8 Riverside Bar
18 Banco del Pichincha
19 Artisans' Stalls
20 San José Church
22 Amarongachi Tours
23 FOIN Office
24 Sacharicsina
25 FOIN Office
29 Ríos Ecuador
30 Hospital

PLACES TO STAY
1 Residencial Enmita
3 Hostal Villa Belén
9 Pumarosa Hotel
10 Residencial Danubio
11 Residencial Hilton
12 Residencial Alemán
13 Residencial Napoli
15 Hotel Amazonas
16 Residencial Jumandy
22 Hostal Travellers Lodging
26 Hostal Visita Hermosa
29 Hostal Camba Huasi
31 Hostal Caribe

ECUADOR

0   100   200 m
0   100   200 yards

Getting There & Away

The terminal terrestre is less than 1km (south) from the center of town. There are several buses a day for Quito via Baeza (US$4; six hours), Lago Agrio (US$7; 10 hours), Coca (US$6; seven hours), Baeza (US$2), Baños (US$3.50; five hours) and other places. Misahuallí buses depart hourly from in front of the terminal.

Military planes fly to Shell and Coca; ask at the airstrip. Seats are hard to get.

MISAHUALLÍ

This village is popular for jungle tours. However, little is virgin jungle: the area has been colonized and most animals are gone. What you can see is many birds, tropical

flowers, army ants and dazzling butterflies. Excursions deeper into the jungle are also possible. This requires patience and money but is still less expensive than most jungle expeditions.

Money-changing facilities are limited, so bring sucres. Telephone service is rare indeed.

Organized Tours

Guided tours of up to 18 days are available, but few guides speak English. Longer tours are recommended if you hope to see wildlife. Some tours visit Huaorani villages. Most are degrading for the Indians and not recommended. A small number of guides have good relationships with the Huaorani; they are mostly in Coca.

Plan details carefully to avoid disappointment. Costs, food, equipment, itinerary and group numbers must be agreed upon before the tour. A good guide is essential and you may have to wait for a specific one. Some outfitters switch guides at the last moment; this is not to your advantage. The SAEC makes good recommendations, or talk to other travelers. Guides should have a license. Tours usually require a minimum of four people and are cheaper per person with larger groups. It's easy to meet up with other travelers in Misahuallí, or you could arrange a group in Quito or Baños. Costs are US$20 to US$50 per person per day. Recommended guides and outfitters include:

Aventuras Amazónicas, based in the Residencial La Posada on the plaza, is the only outfit run by a woman, María del Carmen Santander. This place does a good job.

Crucero Fluvial Misahuallí, off the plaza, is run by the cheerful and knowledgeable Carlos Lastra Lasso. He uses good guides.

Douglas Clarke's Expediciones Dayuma The Quito office (☎/fax 02-564-924) is at 10 de Agosto 38-15, near Mariana de Jesús, Edificio Villacís Pasos, Office 301. Tours are cheaper if arranged in Misahuallí (☎ 06-584-964), or write to: Casilla 291, Tena, Provincia de Napo. In Misahuallí, it's a block from the plaza. This outfit has been around for years and its costs are a bit higher, but it will arrange tours in advance. Several of the guides speak English.

Ecoselva, on the plaza, is run by English-speaking Pepe Tapia González, who has a biology background and is recommended.

Expediciones El Albergue Español is based at the hotel of the same name. Several of its guides have been recommended.

Fluvial River Tours (☎ 06-886-189, or in Quito: ☎ 02-239-044) Héctor Fiallos runs this company (also called *Sacha Tours*); it has also been here for years. The office is on the plaza. Fiallos is good but has used inferior guides in the past; check guides' licenses.

Quindy Tours (☎ 06-887-444) is a block from the plaza. This agency is run by María's brother Pepe Santander, who speaks English and is very knowledgeable.

Other Guides They should produce a license on request. Recommended are Sócrates Nevárez, Alfredo Andrade, Luis Duarte, Billy Clarke (a woman), Marcos Estrada (affiliated with *France Amazonia* on the plaza) and Elias Arteaga. There are others; they have signs on the plaza.

Places to Stay

Water and electricity failures are frequent. Water may stop after about 7 pm. *Residencial El Balcón de Napo*, on the plaza, has small rooms; ask for one with a window. It's clean, though the showers are a bit grungy. At less than US$2 per person, it's the cheapest. The rambling old *Residencial La Posada*, nearby, charges US$6 for rooms with bath. The *Hostal Sacha*, on the beach, is a good deal for US$3 per person in quiet rooms in a thatched long house. Bathrooms are shared. There are laundry facilities, but mind the feral monkeys.

El Paisano restaurant and hotel is popular with travelers. Clean, basic rooms are US$4 per person, or US$9 for a double with private bath. There is a garden with hammocks. The *Hotel Albergue Español* (☎ 06-553-857), charges US$5.50 per person in rooms with private bath; water is heated by solar energy. There is jazz music in the dining room. The hotel is just past the *Dayuma Lodge*, which is half a block from the plaza. The Dayuma Lodge has a restaurant and charges US$5 per person in rooms with a shower and fan.

The *Misahuallí Jungle Lodge* (in Quito ☎ 02-520-043), Ramírez Dávalos 251 and Páez, is across the Río Misahuallí on the northern side of the Río Napo. It's a comfortable lodge with nice cabins, private baths with hot water, and nature trails. Guides are available. Rates are about US$60 a day in Quito, but if you just show up you can get rooms with meals for half that if they aren't busy. There are various other lodges downriver; most are more expensive.

Places to Eat

Most of the hotels have some kind of restaurant. The *Albergue Español* is the best, the *El Paisano* is good for vegetarian food, and the *Dayuma* is also good. The restaurant attached to *La Posada* has great coffee, juices and vegetarian fare. *Doña Gloria* near Ecoselva serves good, cheap *almuerzos*. For something a bit more upscale, try *Le Perroquet Bleu* on the corner of the plaza.

Getting There & Away

Bus Buses to Tena (one hour) leave frequently from the plaza.

Boat Motorized dugout canoes take all day to reach Coca; they leave every few days.

Tickets are US$17. If there is a group of eight or so, you can go any day. You must register your passport with the Capitanía (port captain). Be prepared for strong sun: bring sunscreen and a hat.

Daily canoes go to various villages along the river, and as far up as halfway to Coca.

AROUND MISAHUALLÍ

Jatun Sacha, a rain-forest conservation and research foundation, operates the highly recommended *Cabañas Aliñahui (in Quito ☎ 02-253-267, fax 02-253-266)*, Río Coca 1734 and Isla Fernandina. The lodge is on the southern bank of the Río Napo, about 7km east of Misahuallí, and can be reached by canoe or by road (backtrack 17km west to Puerto Napo, then 26km east to the lodge). The Jatun Sacha research facility is 3km away. Information is also available from co-owners Health and Habitat (☎ 415-383-6130, fax 415-381-9214), 76 Lee St, Mill Valley, CA 94941, USA.

There are eight cabins, each boasting a bathhouse with solar-heated showers. The lodge is near primary rain forest, and guided hikes to both the forest and the research facility are offered. Professional scientists and volunteers can work and stay at Jatun Sacha. Profits from Aliñahui go toward research, conservation, education and training programs. Rates are US$61 per day, including good meals; guided tours are extra. Children younger than 12 get a 40% discount. This place is well recommended.

COCA

This dusty, sprawling oil town, at the junction of the Coca and Napo rivers, is officially named Puerto Francisco de Orellana. River travelers must report to the Capitanía by the landing dock. Money-changing and telephone facilities are poor. INEFAN on the corner of Bolívar and Amazonas has park information. Hitching local boats is possible and some guides rent camping gear; ask around.

Organized Tours

There is a burgeoning tourist industry and Coca is closer to large tracts of virgin jungle than Misahuallí, but it's a pretty depressing place. Trips down the Río Tiputini and into the **Parque Nacional Yasuní**

are possible. This is the largest Ecuadorian national park, and it contains a variety of rain forest habitats, wildlife and a few Huaorani communities. Unfortunately, there is no money for staffing and protection so poaching and, increasingly, oil exploration are damaging the park.

Some guides offer tours to visit Huaorani villages. The Huaorani remain ambivalent about tourism; some villages have arrangements with particular guides whereas others prefer no tourism. A good source of information about this is Randy Smith (☎ 06-880-606) who works with Amazon Jungle Adventures in Coca. This company employs Huaorani staff with the support of the tribe. Safari Tours in Quito can put you in contact with this outfit or you can ask at Pappa Dan's restaurant in Coca.

Other guides who have positive relationships with the Huaorani are Ernesto Juanka at Pankitour Alternativo (☎ 06-880-405), 6 de Diciembre and García Moreno in Coca; Julio Jarrín (☎ 06-880-251) opposite the Hotel Oasis; and Juan Enomenga – ask for him on the waterfront. They don't speak English.

Places to Stay

Water shortages are frequent and food is expensive. The *Hotel El Auca (☎ 06-880-127)* is popular (often full before nightfall) and isn't bad for US$10 a double, or in cabins for US$7/13 for singles/doubles with bath. It has the nicest garden in Coca and an acceptable restaurant. Three very basic residenciales near the Auca charge US$2.50 to US$3.50 per person, are popular with oil workers, and are not recommended for women alone. The similarly poor *Residencial Rosita* is by the port. Other cheapies are the *Residencial Macará*, *Hotel Cofan* and *Residencial Las Brisas*. A better place is the *Residencial Cotopaxi* at US$4 per person with bath. The *Hotel Oasis (☎ 06-880-164)*, is OK for US$7 a single with bath and fan. The *Hotel Florida (☎ 06-880-177)* and the *Hotel Delfín Azul* are similarly priced and OK. The *Amazonas Hostería (☎ 06-880-444)*, on Espejo and 12 de Febrero, in a quiet neighborhood by the river, has clean, comfortable rooms with private bath for US$7.50 per person. The *Hostería La Misión (☎ 06-880-260)* is the best hotel at US$15/22 with fan, or US$18/26 with air-con.

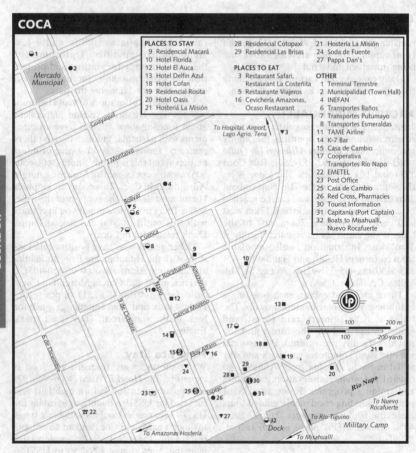

COCA

PLACES TO STAY		28 Residencial Cotopaxi	21 Hostería La Misión
9 Residencial Macará		29 Residencial Las Brisas	24 Soda de Fuente
10 Hotel Florida			27 Pappa Dan's
12 Hotel El Auca		PLACES TO EAT	
13 Hotel Delfin Azul		3 Restaurant Safari,	OTHER
18 Hotel Cofan		Restaurant La Costeñita	1 Terminal Terrestre
19 Residencial Rosita		5 Restaurante Viajeros	2 Municipalidad (Town Hall)
20 Hotel Oasis		16 Cevichería Amazonas,	4 INEFAN
21 Hosteria La Misión		Ocaso Restaurant	6 Transportes Baños
			7 Transportes Putumayo
			8 Transportes Esmeraldas
			11 TAME Airline
			14 K-7 Bar
			15 Casa de Cambio
			17 Cooperativa
			Transportes Río Napo
			22 EMETEL
			23 Post Office
			25 Casa de Cambio
			26 Red Cross, Pharmacies
			30 Tourist Information
			31 Capitanía (Port Captain)
			32 Boats to Misahuallí,
			Nuevo Rocafuerte

Places to Eat

Hostería La Misión has a good, pricey restaurant. Locals recommend the *Cevichería Amazonas* and *Ocaso Restaurant* as the best outside the hotels. The *Safari* and *La Costeñita* are cheaper and quite good too. The *Soda de Fuente* is a basic chicken place with ice cold drinks. *Restaurante Viajeros* serves early, cheap breakfasts. *Pappa Dan's* opens at 4 pm and is a recommended bar with burgers and similar food.

Getting There & Around

Air TAME flies to Quito (US$52) daily except Sunday. Book well ahead. The airport is 2km north of town.

Bus There are bus offices in town and at the terminal terrestre, north of town. Make sure you know where your bus leaves from. Several buses a day go to Quito (US$10; nine hours via Loreto; 14 hours via Lago Agrio), Tena (US$6; seven hours), Lago Agrio (US$2; three hours), and other jungle towns. There are night buses to Ambato.

Boat Boats to Misahuallí (US$17; up to 14 hours against the current) leave every few days. Boats to Nuevo Rocafuerte (US$25; nine to 12 hours), on the Peruvian border, require a military permit. Boats leave on Monday and return Friday. Passenger boats to intermediate destinations leave most days. Ask at the dock. Hiring your own boat is pricey but you can often get rides for a few dollars on boats heading downriver.

DOWN THE RÍO NAPO
Several villages and lodges east of Coca can be reached down the Río Napo. Ask at the Coca docks for boats. *Hacienda Primavera* (in Quito ☎ 02-565-999), José Trevinio 114 and 12 de Octubre, is an hour from Coca. It costs about US$20 a day including meals, more if you make arrangements in Quito. Guided excursions are available at extra cost.

Two hours east of Coca is the mission of **Pompeya**. From here an 8km road goes north to **Limoncocha** village, where there is a basic place to stay (US$2.50 per person) and eat. Nearby is the locally run Limoncocha Biological Reserve, with a beautiful lake recommended for bird-watching at dawn and dusk. Entry is US$16 per person. Limoncocha can also be reached by several buses a day from the oil base of **Shushufindi** (which is a two- or three-hour bus trip from either Coca or Lago Agrio).

Pañacocha village, five hours east of Coca, has several simple places to stay for about US$2.50 a person. Food and local guides are available. About five more hours brings you to the border at **Nuevo Rocafuerte**, where a basic *pensión* (US$3.50) and local guides are available. Tours up the Río Yasuní into the **Parque Nacional Yasuní** can be arranged.

LAGO AGRIO
Built in virgin jungle after oil was discovered in the 1970s, Lago (Nueva Loja on some maps) is Ecuador's largest new oil town. A tourism industry is developing around visits to the nearby **Reserva Faunística Cuyabeno**. This protects the rain forest home of Siona and Secoya Indians, and conserves the Cuyabeno river and lake system, but there have been numerous oil spills. Nevertheless, parts of the reserve are still pristine and well worth a visit (US$20 entry). Most visitors make arrangements in Quito, Tena, Misahuallí or Coca. Outfitters in Lago Agrio include Harpía Eagles Tours (☎ 06-830-779), on Colombia and 18 de Noviembre and *Cuyabeno Tours*, next to the Willigran Hotel. Tours cost about US$40

ECUADOR

LAGO AGRIO

PLACES TO STAY
2 Hotel San Carlos
5 Hotel Paris
10 Hotel La Cabaña
11 Residencial Secoya
12 Hotel Oro Negro
13 Residencial Ecuador
15 Hotel Sayonar
17 Hostal Machala 2
18 Hotel Imperial Lago
21 Residencial Putumayo, Hotel Willigran
23 Hotel D'Marios, Hotel Villa Colombia
25 Hotel Los Guacamayos

PLACES TO EAT
20 Panadería Jackeline
23 Hotel D'Marios

OTHER
1 TAME Airline
3 EMETEL
4 Harpia Eagles Tours
6 Banco Internacional
7 Banco del Pichincha
8 Cinema
9 Police
11 Transportes Baños, Other Bus Companies
14 Colombian Consulate
16 Casa de Cambio
19 Post Office
22 Transportes Occidentales (Buses)
24 Transportes Esmeraldas

9 de Octubre
Plaza
☎3
18 de Noviembre
Eloy Alfaro
Francisco de Orellana
12 de Febrero
Manabí
Añasco
Pasaje
Gran Colombia
Quinzanana
6
Av Quito
7
8
9
10
11
12
13
14
15
16
25
17
18
To Airport
23
Market
Sucre
19
Río Amazonas
20
21
22

0   50   100 m
0   50   100 yards

including food, transport, accommodations and equipment.

A Sunday morning market is visited by the local Cofan Indians. They may take you to their village of Dureno, from which further explorations are possible with Cofan guides. Two highly recommended guides are Alejandro Quezada and Delfin Criollo.

Places to Stay

Mosquito nets or fans are worth having in your room. Water shortages are common. The cheapest places are about US$3 per person but they are very basic and run-down. These include the *Chimborazo, Residencial Ecuador* and *Putumayo*. Better places at US$4 per person are the *Residencial Secoya*, *Hotel Willigran* (you'll need a padlock for the doors) and the *Hotel Oro Negro*.

The *Hotel La Cabaña* (☎ 06-830-127) is a good value for US$4.50 per person in sunny, clean rooms with bath, less without. Ask for a room on the roof or with a balcony. You can wash clothes here. The *Hotel Imperial Lago* (☎ 06-830-460) is another good deal at US$5.50 per person for clean rooms with fan and private bath. Upstairs rooms are better, downstairs rooms are wheelchair accessible. The clean *Hotel San Carlos* (☎ 06-830-122) has some simple rooms at US$4 per person and some with bath for US$5.50. The *Hotel D'Marios*, US$7 per person with bath, is clean and good. The *Hostal Machala 2* (☎ 06-830-073) is not as good at US$6 per person with cramped bath and TV. The *Hotel Sayonara* (☎ 06-830-562) is US$5 per person with bath and fan. Others at this price are the *Hotel Paris, Hotel Los Guacamayos* and *Hotel Villa Colombia*.

Places to Eat

Of several restaurants, the one under the *Hotel D'Marios* is the best, with a choice of (small) dishes for about US$3. *Panadería Jackeline* serves a tasty, cheap breakfast with fresh juices from 6 am.

Getting There & Away

Air The airport is 5km east of town (taxi, US$2). TAME has Monday to Saturday flights to Quito (US$52); it's best to book in advance.

Bus Transportes Baños has eight buses daily to Quito (US$8.50; eight hours), but Occidental is faster. There are several other companies serving Loja, Machala, Cuenca and Esmeraldas. For Tena, take a bus to Baeza and wait. Open-sided *rancheros* go from the market area to Coca and other jungle towns.

To/From Colombia Get your exit stamp at Migración, Quito 111, near the Colombian Consulate. Rancheros from the market go 21km north to La Punta, on the Río San Miguel. Canoes cross here to Puerto Colón or go downriver one hour to San Miguel, both in Colombia. San Miguel has a basic hotel and Colombian immigration. From Puerto Colón or San Miguel, buses continue into Colombia via the towns of Puerto Asís (about five hours) and Mocoa (about nine hours), both with hotels. Mocoa has an immigration office.

Western Lowlands

West of the Andes is a large coastal plain with banana and palm plantations. The descent from the mountains is dramatic, particularly if you take the route from Quito to Santo Domingo.

SANTO DOMINGO DE LOS COLORADOS

This city is an important road hub and a convenient place to break the journey to the coast, though there's little of interest here. The road from the highlands is spectacular, and best done in the morning to avoid afternoon fog.

The area was famous for the Colorado (Tsachila) Indians, who painted their faces with black stripes and dyed their hair a brilliant red. Their traditions are now almost lost and they prefer to be left alone. Taxis go to **Chihuilpe**, 7km south of Santo Domingo, where there is a small cultural museum.

Sunday is the main market day, so the town closes down on Monday.

Places to Stay

The basic but clean and helpful *Residencial San Martín* (☎ 02-750-913), on 29 de Mayo, is US$2 per person. The very basic *Hotels*

SANTO DOMINGO DE LOS COLORADOS

To Esmeraldas
To Post Office
To Lions Traffic Circle (Rotary), Río Toachi, Quito

Market
Macará

Quininde
Las Tsachilas
Montecristi
Ibarra
Tulcán
Lena

29 de Mayo
Market

3 de Julio

To Terminal Terrestre
Cuenca
Riobamba
Ambato
Latacunga
Quito

Galápagos

Iturralde
Main Plaza

PLACES TO STAY	20 Residencial Ontaneda	27 Elite Restaurant
1 Hotel Turistas 2	21 Pensión San José,	
2 Hotel Genova	Hotel Turistas 1	**OTHER**
5 Hotel El Colorado	22 Hostal Galápagos	4 EMETEL
8 Hotel Ejecutivo	25 Pensión El Oro	6 Banco del Pacífico, ATM
9 Residencial Madrid	28 Hostal Las Brisas	7 Local Buses
10 Residencial Viajero		11 Police
13 Hostal Jennefer	**PLACES TO EAT**	19 Banco del Pichincha
14 Hotel Caleta	3 King Pollo	23 Muncipalidad
15 Hotel Turistas 3	12 Pollos Gus	(Town Hall)
16 Pensión Guayaquil	14 Hotel Caleta Cebichería	24 Teatro Amazonas
18 Residencial San Martín	17 Chifa Happy	26 Filanbanco

0   100   200 m
0   100   200 yards

Turistas 1, 2 and **3** (at three locations) claim to have hot water and charge US$1.25 per person. The **Pensión Guayaquil** is acceptable at US$2 per person. Other basic cheapies for less than US$2 per person are the **Pensión San José**, **Residencial Ontaneda**, **Residencial Viajero**, **Pensión El Oro** and **Residencial Madrid**. The best budget choice is the **Hostal Jennefer** (☎ 02-750-577), 29 de Mayo and Latacunga, at US$5 per person with bath and TV.

Also OK are the **Hotel Ejecutivo** (☎ 02-763-305), 29 de Mayo and Ambato, the **Hostal Las Brisas** (☎ 02-753-283), on Quito near Iturralde, and the **Hostal Galápagos**, all at US$5 per person with bath. For something more upmarket, the **Hotel Genova** (☎ 02-759-694), 29 de Mayo and Ibarra, is clean and friendly and costs US$7/10 for singles/doubles with hot bath. For US$1 less, the **Hotel Caleta** (☎ 02-750-277), Ibarra and 29 de Mayo, and **Hotel El Colorado** (☎ 02-750-226), 29 de Mayo and Esmeraldas, are OK.

Places to Eat

Pollos Gus, a clean fried-chicken restaurant, and the expensive **Elite Restaurant** are both on the main plaza and recommended. **Chifa Happy**, on the western side of the plaza, has decent Chinese food. **King Pollo** serves huge, cheap and good almuerzos. There's a well-stocked supermarket next door. The **Hotel Caleta Cebichería** has tables on the street and serves good snacks and meals, but it's pricey.

Getting There & Away

The terminal terrestre is 2km west of the center. Buses into town (US$0.10) pass the rotary. There are frequent buses to most destinations, including the Oriente and the Peruvian border.

QUEVEDO

This is another convenient stopover between the highlands and the coast, particularly on the wild descent from Latacunga. The town is important commercially and is known for its Chinese community and chifas, but it has no special attractions.

Places to Stay & Eat

Hotels are poor. Basic hotels around US$3 per person include the *Hotel Turistas* (which also has rooms for US$6 per person with bath and TV). This is a good budget choice. Others at this price are the *Guayaquil* and *Charito*. The *Hotel Imperial*, by the river at Séptima, has safe, clean rooms with cold showers for US$4 per person. The similarly priced *Hotel Condado*, on Quinta near the river, is OK and friendly, as is the *Hotel Hilton* (☎ 05-751-359), Novena 429. Its 2nd floor is better. The cheapest place with air-con is the basic *Hotel Continental* (☎ 05-750-080), 7 de Octubre and Octava, at US$5 per person. The *Hotel Ejecutivo Internacional* (☎ 05-751-780), Quarta 214, has frayed air-con singles/doubles with bath and TV for US$8/13.

Most cheap restaurants are along 7 de Octubre.

Getting There & Away

Many bus companies are at the west end of 7 de Octubre. There are several buses to Guayaquil (US$2; three hours) but only two to Quito. Buses go to Santo Domingo (US$1; 1½ hours), Babahoyo, Portoviejo and other towns. Transportes Cotopaxi, by the market, has Latacunga buses.

The Coast

The mainland has a 2800km coastline with warm currents, so swimming is pleasant year round. The north coast is wet from December to June and the south coast (the provinces of Guayas and El Oro) is drier and more barren, with a rainy season January to April. These months are humid and uncomfortable, and people flock to the beaches for relief during the weekends. There are mosquitoes in the wet months, so bring repellent and consider using antimalarial medication, especially in the north.

The north coast is less developed and has some tropical rain forest. Farther south, remnants of tropical dry forest are found in the Parque Nacional Machalilla.

Guayas and El Oro provinces use irrigation to produce bananas, rice, coffee, cacao and African palm. Shrimping is a fast-growing industry fraught with environmental problems.

Fishing villages and popular beach resorts are scattered along the coast, but none are outstanding. As a general rule, theft is a major problem on beaches: never leave anything unattended.

The coast is described from north to south.

SAN LORENZO

Travelers arrive by train or bus from Ibarra and continue south by bus or boat. San Lorenzo is hardly attractive, but it's friendly. A new road links Esmeraldas and San Lorenzo, making it possible to reach Esmeraldas from Ibarra in one (long) day. You can break the journey at Rio Verde – more pleasant than Esmeraldas – where there is a recommended hostel (see Borbón).

Orientation & Information

The center is a 15-minute walk from the station and a few minutes from the port. Money changing is poor. Excursiones El Refugio (☎/fax 06-780-134), 30m from the EMETEL office, has local beach, mangrove and cultural excursions from US$10 per day.

Places to Stay & Eat

Hotels are basic. Mosquito nets and fans are recommended and water shortages are frequent. Friendly but persistent kids badger travelers for tips to show them to a hotel.

The new *Hotel Pampa de Oro* (☎ 06-780-214), off Calle Imbabura, has spacious, clean rooms with fan, mosquito net and private bath for US$5 per person. Rooms without bath are US$4. The standoffish *Gran Hotel San Carlos* (☎ 06-780-267), Imbabura and Garces (near the train station), has clean rooms for US$3 per person or US$4 with tepid shower. Most rooms have TV, fan and mosquito net. The *Hotel Imperial* (☎ 06-780-242), on the right side of Calle Imbabura as you walk in from the station, and the *Hotel Continental* (☎ 06-780-125), on the left, are decent. They charge US$5 per person in rooms with private bath. Attached to the Imperial is the OK *Hotel San Lorenzo* at US$2.25 per person. The friendly *Hotel Carondolet* (☎ 06-780-202) has clean rooms with nets and baths for US$3.75 per person and some cheaper ones.

Meals are pricey. *La Estancia*, next to Hotel Pampa de Oro is good. The nearby *El Fogón* is considered the 'best' but is expensive.

Getting There & Away

Bus Buses leave from the Hotel Carondolet. There are several daily to Ibarra (US$5; five hours) and eight to Esmeraldas (US$4.50; five hours), Borbón (US$2; two hours) and intermediate points. The last Esmeraldas bus leaves at 2:30 pm; this may change.

Train The autoferro for Ibarra (US$22) leaves daily at 7 am (supposedly). See Ibarra for details.

Boat The Capitanía on the waterfront has boat information. Motorized dugouts are used; prepare for sun, wind and spray. Locals pay less than foreigners. There are hourly departures for **La Tola** (US$4.50; 2½ hours), from 5:30 am to 2:30 pm. The ride through coastal mangroves, with pelicans and frigatebirds, is interesting. Some boats connect with a bus to Esmeraldas (US$7 from San Lorenzo), and you can reach Atacames or Quito in one day from San Lorenzo. La Tola has a very basic pensión. Boats for Borbón (US$6; 3½ hours) leave twice a day. Boats for other destinations can be arranged, though services may dwindle due to the new road.

BORBÓN

This small port with a predominantly black population of 5000 is on the Río Cayapas. There are buses to Esmeraldas and boats up the Cayapas and San Miguel rivers to the **Reserva Ecológica Cotacachi-Cayapas** – an interesting trip to a remote area.

Places to Stay & Eat

Ángel Cerón, the school principal, runs the *Pampa de Oro Hotel* (US$3 per person) and is a good source of information. The basic *Hotel Panama City* charges US$2 per person and has been recommended. There are several simple restaurants, most closing by 7:30 pm.

An hour beyond Borbón is the friendly seaside village of Rio Verde. The *Hostería Pura Vida* (☎ 06-455-337) is 2km past the Rio Verde bridge on the Esmeraldas road and offers clean rooms near the beach for US$6 per person. There are also cabañas (US$8 per person) and a restaurant. Swiss co-owner Thomas Meier speaks five languages. There may be volunteer opportunities.

Getting There & Away

Bus Buses to Esmeraldas (US$2.50; three hours) and San Lorenzo leave frequently.

Boat Boats to San Lorenzo leave at 7 and 11 am. A daily boat leaves at 11 am for San Miguel (US$8; five hours), passing the Catholic mission of **Santa María** and the Protestant mission of **Zapallo Grande** (both have basic accommodations).

SAN MIGUEL

This primarily black community is the access for the **Reserva Ecológica Cotacachi-Cayapas** (US$20 fee). A shop sells a few supplies, and basic meals are available for US$5. Cayapas Indians live across the river and can be visited.

The ranger station has four beds (US$3, no running water or mosquito nets), or you may camp outside. Beware ferocious chiggers; put repellent on ankles and legs upon arrival. Rangers will guide you into the reserve by dugout and on foot for about US$10 per guide per day (two guides are needed on some trips), plus food. Camping is possible. There are waterfalls, rain forest trails, great bird-watching, and there's a chance you'll see monkeys and other wildlife. September to December is recommended.

The boat back to Borbón leaves before dawn. Arrange in advance which day you want to return.

ESMERALDAS

This has been a major port for centuries and the oil refinery is a major source of income and employment. The beaches are dirty and the city has theft, drug and dust problems (locals walk around with kerchiefs over their mouths). Avoid ill-lit areas and the southern end of the malecón. Most travelers pass through quickly. Filanbanco and Banco del Pichincha change traveler's checks.

Places to Stay

The cheapest hotels are in poor condition. Many places turn on water on request only.

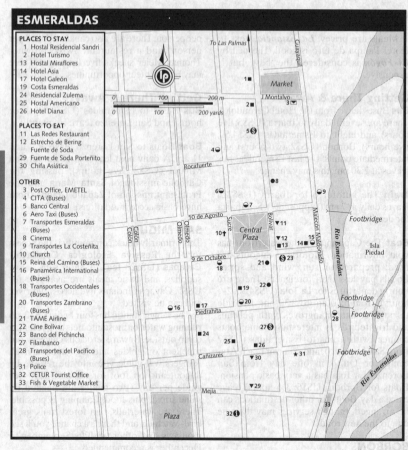

ESMERALDAS

PLACES TO STAY
1 Hostal Residencial Sandri
2 Hotel Turismo
13 Hostal Miraflores
14 Hotel Asia
17 Hotel Galeón
19 Costa Esmeraldas
24 Residencial Zulema
25 Hostal Americano
26 Hotel Diana

PLACES TO EAT
11 Las Redes Restaurant
12 Estrecho de Bering
   Fuente de Soda
29 Fuente de Soda Porteñito
30 Chifa Asiática

OTHER
3 Post Office, EMETEL
4 CITA (Buses)
5 Banco Central
6 Aero Taxi (Buses)
7 Transportes Esmeraldas
   (Buses)
8 Cinema
9 Transportes La Costeñita
10 Church
15 Reina del Camino (Buses)
16 Panamérica International
   (Buses)
18 Transportes Occidentales
   (Buses)
20 Transportes Zambrano
   (Buses)
21 TAME Airline
22 Cine Bolívar
23 Banco del Pichincha
27 Filanbanco
28 Transportes del Pacífico
   (Buses)
31 Police
32 CETUR Tourist Office
33 Fish & Vegetable Market

For less than US$3 per person, try *Hostal Miraflores* or *Hotel Turismo* (☎ 06-712-700), which are just OK. The *Residencial Zulema* (☎ 06-712-424), Olmedo near Cañizares, isn't bad for US$8 for a double with bath. The clean *Hotel Asia* (☎ 06-723-148), 9 de Octubre 116, is OK for US$3 to US$5 per person (some rooms with bath).

For US$4 per person with bath and fan, the friendly *Hotel Diana* (☎ 06-726-962), Cañizares 224, and the clean *Hostal Residencial Sandri* (☎ 06-726-861), Libertad and J Montalvo, are both recommended. The *Hostal Americano* (☎ 06-713-978), Sucre 709, is also OK for US$4 per person or US$5 with TV. The family-run *Costa Esmeraldas* (☎ 06-723-912), Sucre 813, has clean rooms with

bath for US$5.50. The *Hostal El Galeón* (☎ 06-713-116), Olmedo near Piedrahita, is similarly priced and well kept.

Places to Eat
Las Redes Restaurant on the plaza is good for seafood, and the nearby *Fuente de Soda Estrecho de Bering* is good for ice cream and people-watching. The *Chifa Asiática*, Cañizares near Sucre, has good Chinese food. The *Fuente de Soda Porteñito*, Sucre and Mejía, is locally popular and good.

Getting There & Away
Air The airport is 25km away (taxi US$5). TAME (☎ 06-726-862), on Bolívar by the

plaza, has late morning flights to Quito (US$27) on weekdays and an evening flight on Sunday. There are also weekday flights to Cali (US$68).

Bus Aero Taxi is frighteningly fast to Quito (US$6, five hours); Transportes Occidentales, Esmeraldas and Panamérica International (with luxury buses) are slower. Occidentales and Esmeraldas have many buses to Guayaquil (US$5.50 to US$7; eight hours), Ambato, Machala and other cities. CITA has buses to Ambato. Reina del Camino has buses to Manta and Bahía de Caráquez.

For provincial buses, use Transportes La Costeñita or del Pacífico. There are frequent buses for Atacames and Súa (US$0.60) and Muisne (US$1.40; 2½ hours). Several buses go to La Tola, Borbón (US$2.75; three hours) and San Lorenzo. These buses pass the airport.

ATACAMES

This small town, 30km west of Esmeraldas, is crowded with folks looking for a party. The nightlife is loud and boisterous, and the beaches littered.

Warning A powerful undertow causes drownings every year, so keep within your limits. Bring insect repellent, especially in the wet season. The cheapest hotels may have rats, and water shortages are frequent. The water in bathrooms is often brackish – no paradise here.

We have received many reports of assaults on late-night beach walkers and on single people or couples in quiet areas during the day. Stay in brightly lit and well-traveled areas, and go with friends. Don't leave anything unattended on the beach.

Places to Stay

Hotels are full on weekends and holidays, so arrive early. April to October is the high season and prices rise to what the market will bear. Bargain, especially if you're staying a few days.

Many hotels are near the beach, which is reached by a footbridge. Rooms are geared to families and have several beds, so go in a group to economize. Cheap singles are hard to find. Always check your room or cabin for security before renting it.

The cheapest is *Hotel Doña Pichu* (☎ 06-731-441), on the main street in town, not on the beach. Basic rooms are US$2.50 per person and bathrooms are primitive. There are other basic places in the town. On the beach, US$10 for a double is cheap. *Cabañas Rincón del Mar* (☎ 06-731-064), to the left after crossing the footbridge, is clean and secure but small. It charges US$10 for a double with bath, more on weekends. *La Casa del Manglar*, by the footbridge, is clean and friendly and charges US$8 a person with bath. The *Cabañas Los Bohios* (☎ 06-731-089) has decent double cabins with bath at US$10, and has singles midweek. The *Rincón Sage* (☎ 06-731-246) has OK rooms with bath for US$6/10. The *Hostal Jennifer* (☎ 06-710-482) has some singles and charges about US$7 per person with bath, less without. The *Hotel El Tiburón* has also been recommended at this price. The popular *Hotel Galerias Atacames* (☎ 06-731-149) has English-speaking owners, and rooms for US$18 a double with bath on weekends. There are many others, usually more expensive.

Places to Eat

Comedores near the beach all serve the same thing – that morning's catch. Ask the price before ordering or you may be overcharged. Many places double as bars or discos in the evening, and their popularity changes with the seasons. *Marco's* and *Paco Foco* are currently popular.

Getting There & Away

Buses stop on the road near the footbridge to the beach. There are many from Esmeraldas to Súa and back. Buses to Muisne may be full; ride on the roof or return to Esmeraldas for a seat.

SÚA

This friendly fishing village is 6km west of Atacames. Follow the beach at low tide – but join a large group to avoid robbery.

Places to Stay & Eat

There are fewer places than in Atacames but they are quieter and often a better value if you aren't looking for nightlife. The very basic *Residencial Quito* charges less than US$2 for a room without bath. The *Hotel Chagra Ramos* (☎ 06-731-006) has a little beach and nice views, and charges US$4 or

ECUADOR

US$5 per person in decent rooms with bath. It has a good, inexpensive restaurant. *Hotel El Peñón de Súa* (☎ 06-731-013) is not on the beach but has nice rooms with bath at US$5 per person. Other OK places in the US$4 to US$6 per person range are the *Hostal Mar y Sol* (☎ 06-731-293), *Hotel Las Buganvillas* (☎ 06-731-008) and the *Hotel Hostal Shaman* (☎ 06-731-486). The friendly *Hostal Los Jardines* (☎ 06-731-181) has clean rooms around a courtyard, all with bath and four beds for US$4 per person. For breakfast, try *Restaurante Bahia* on the beach.

MUISNE

Muisne is on an island, 1½ hours from Atacames by bus. Boats across the river (leaving from the terminus of the road from Esmeraldas) are US$0.20. From the dock, the main road heads into the 'center' and becomes a track to the beach, 1.5km away. The beach is nicer than at Atacames, but the usual precautions apply.

In the center, Fundación de Defensa Ecológica (☎ 06-480-167) arranges ecologically sensitive boat trips (US$30 per person) to local mangroves. All profits go to environmental protection of the area.

Places to Stay & Eat

There's a residencial on the mainland side of the river, and a few in the center of Muisne. All are cheap and basic. The *Residencial Sarita* and *La Isla* are OK. Halfway to the beach, the good *Hotel Galápagos* (☎ 06-780-758) charges US$5 per person with bath. On the beach are several cabins; check that the rooms have locks, as thefts have occurred. The *Cabañas San Cristobal* has clean cabins for US$7 per person. *Hotel Calade* (☎ 06-480-279) is quite good for US$5 each, as is the *Playa Paraíso*. The *Cabañas Ipanema* are US$5 for basic doubles.

There are basic *comedores* on the beach and in the center.

Getting There & Away

Bus La Costeñita has hourly buses to Esmeraldas (US$1.30; 2½ hours) via Atacames. Transportes Occidentales has night buses to Quito (US$5.75; seven hours) and Guayaquil (US$6.25).

Boat Two boats a day make the journey between Muisne and Cojimíes (US$6; two hours), each direction.

SOUTH OF MUISNE

It's possible to walk along the beach from Muisne at low tide to **Bolívar**, crossing rivers by canoes. It takes all day. Bolívar (no hotels) can also be reached by bus. Boats go to **Cojimíes** for US$2 per person, but it is more easily reached by direct boat from Muisne. Cojimíes has cheap and very basic hotels.

From Cojimíes, buses go via **Pedernales** (with cheap and basic hotels) and **Jama** (there's a basic pensión) to San Vicente (US$5.50; five hours). Buses depend on low tides and services are disrupted in the wet season. Pedernales has buses to Santo Domingo (US$3).

SAN VICENTE

This resort village is a short ferry ride across the Río Chone from Bahía de Caráquez. It has nice beaches and an airport.

Places to Stay & Eat

The basic *Hostal San Vicente* is US$4 each. There are several fancier hotels with decent restaurants.

Getting There & Away

Air The airstrip is behind the market, 10 minutes' walk from the pier (turn right). TAME has flights to Quito (US$29) on Friday and Sunday. AECA and NICA (☎ 05-690-377) offer occasional flights from Guayaquil to San Vicente and Esmeraldas via Pedernales in small aircraft. Flights may go to Cojimíes and other places on demand. Travel light, as there are baggage restrictions.

Boat Launches to Bahía de Caráquez (US$0.20) leave often but charge more after 9 pm. A car ferry takes passengers for free.

Bus Costa del Norte, near the pier, has hourly departures to Pedernales, one or two a day to Cojimíes, and two inland to Chone.

BAHÍA DE CARÁQUEZ

This small port and resort across the river from San Vicente has decent beaches. The

BAHÍA DE CARÁQUEZ

PLACES TO STAY
2 Hotel Palma
6 Hostal Los Andes
7 Bahía B&B
8 Pensión Miriam
9 Pensión Victoria
11 Residencial San José
13 Hotel Vera
23 Bahía Hotel
27 Hostal La Querencia

PLACES TO EAT
12 Restaurant El Galpón
14 Chifa China
16 La Chozita

OTHER
1 Guacamayo Adventures,
  NICA Airline
3 TAME Airline
4 EMETEL
5 CETUR Tourist Office
10 Teatro Municipal
15 Banco Comercial
17 Mirador (Lookout)
18 Church
19 Post Office
20 AECA Airline
21 Filanbanco
22 Casa de la Cultura
24 Coactur (Bus Terminal)
25 Reina del Camino
  (Bus Terminal)
26 Capitanía (Port Captain)

ECUADOR

best are half a kilometer north on Av Montúfar. The mouth of the Río Chone is quite busy, and you can watch the boats go by from a riverside café. It's a quiet and pleasant town, known to locals as 'Bahía.' A massive earthquake devastated this town in 1998.

Information
The CETUR office is near the river. Guacamayo Adventures (☎ 05-691-412) is a good source of local information and arranges tours to islands with seabird colonies, tours to coastal forests, cultural tours and mountain bike rentals. Banco Comercial changes traveler's checks.

Places to Stay
The cheapest places have water supply problems. The very basic *Pensión Victoria* is US$2 per person. The *Pensión Miriam* is a bit cleaner at US$2.50. Other cheapies are the *Residencial San José*, at US$3.50 each, and the better *Hotel Vera*, which has some rooms with bath. The OK *Hotel Palma* (☎ 05-690-467) is US$4 each or US$6 with

bath, but many rooms lack windows. The *Hostal Los Andes* (☎ 05-690-587) is basic but clean at US$6 each. The *Hostal La Querencia* (☎ 05-690-009) is good value for Bahía at US$8 and the *Bahía Hotel* is US$10 and pleasant. The clean but basic *Bahía B&B* is also US$10, and includes breakfast.

Places to Eat
The *Chifa China* is simple but serves decent Chinese food. The *Restaurant El Galpón* is cheap and good. *La Chozita* is a good place to watch the river happenings.

Getting There & Away
Air & Boat See San Vicente, earlier this chapter.

Bus Sit on the left leaving Bahía for good views of the Chone estuary. Coactur serves Portoviejo (US$1.50; two hours) and Manta (US$2; 2½ hours) every hour. Reina del Camino has buses to Portoviejo, Quito (US$6; eight hours), Esmeraldas (US$6;

eight hours), Santo Domingo (US$3.75) and Guayaquil (US$5; six hours).

PORTOVIEJO
The provincial capital of Manabí, with 133,000 inhabitants, is little visited by tourists, who prefer to head to the coast.

There are plenty of hotels. The airport, 2km northwest of town, has flights to Quito with TAME and to Guayaquil with AECA. The bus terminal, 1km west of town, has services to many cities.

MANTA
With 126,000 inhabitants, Manta is a major port, commercial center and Ecuadorian resort.

It is named after the Manta culture (500 to 1550 AD), known for its pottery and navigational skills. The Mantas sailed to Central America and Peru and, possibly, the Galápagos. Balsa sailing rafts, similar to one captured by the Spanish in 1526, are still seen along the coast.

Information
An inlet divides the town into Manta (west side) and Tarqui (east side). They are joined by a road bridge. Manta has the main offices, shopping areas and bus terminal. Tarqui has more hotels and beaches. Streets numbered 100 and up are in Tarqui.

CETUR (☎ 05-622-944) is on the pedestrian-only block of Av 3. The Banco del Pacífico, Banco del Pichincha and casas de cambio change traveler's checks.

Things to See & Do
The **Museo del Banco Central** (☎ 05-622-878) has a small but good exhibit on the Manta culture. Hours are 8:30 am to 4:30 pm weekdays.

Playa Murciélago, 2km west of Manta's center, is a popular beach with decent waves. Beware of theft on the beaches and assaults in Tarqui.

The annual agricultural, fishing and tourism show is from October 14 to 18.

Places to Stay
Prices rise during holiday weekends and the December-to-March and June-to-August high seasons. Single rooms are hard to find.

The *Hotel Chimborazo* is a dive charging US$6 a double, but is the only cheap place in Manta. Most people stay in Tarqui.

In Tarqui, the clean and secure *Residencial Villa Eugenia*, on the Malecón near Calle 105, is a good budget choice for US$3 per person. It's poorly marked, but it's there. The *Residencial Los Ángeles*, on Av 108 near Calle 102, is reasonably clean and charges US$4/6 for singles/doubles. The *Residencial Viña del Mar*, on Calle 104, is OK for US$6 a double. Other cheap, basic hotels at US$3 or US$4 per person are the *Acapulco*, *Residencial Montecarlo*, *Residencial Astoria* and *Residencial Ideal*.

The youth-group oriented *Boulevard Hotel* (☎ 05-625-333), on Calle 103 near Av 105, is cleanish and charges US$6 per person in the high season; bargain hard at other times. The *Hotel Miami,* Calle 108 and Malecón, has simple rooms for US$4 per person. The safe *Hotel Clarke* (☎ 05-625-835), on Calle 102 near Av 109, is US$6 per person in clean, basic rooms with private bath. The clean *Hotel Americana* (☎ 05-623-069), on Calle 105 near Av 106, is US$18 for a basic double with private bath and air-con; rooms with fans are cheaper. The *Hotel Inca* (☎ 05-620-440) is another good choice at this price.

Places to Eat
The eastern end of Tarqui beach has cheap outdoor comedores serving fresh seafood. The market also has cheap food. The *Bar Comedor Boulevard* has large servings and outdoor dining. There are other places nearby; some are cheaper. *Panificadora Buen Pan* on Av 107, has sublime baked goods. Near the bridge joining Tarqui with Manta is *Chifa Popular* at 4 de Noviembre and Av 109. It's cheap and good, as is the *Chifa Oriental* on Calle 8 near Av 4 in Manta. There are inexpensive restaurants near the Hotel Chimborazo. Near Playa Murciélago is *Pizzería Topi*, on the Malecón near Av 15. It's open late.

Getting There & Away
Air The airport is 3km east of Tarqui. TAME (☎ 05-613-210), on the Manta waterfront, has daily flights to Quito (US$39). AECA may fly to Guayaquil with light aircraft.

ECUADOR

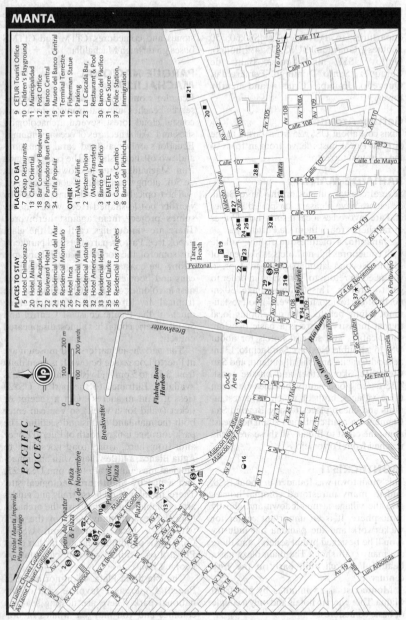

MANTA

PLACES TO STAY

5 Hotel Chimborazo
20 Hotel Miami
21 Hotel Acapulco
22 Boulevard Hotel
24 Residencial Viña del Mar
25 Residencial Montecarlo
26 Hotel Inca
27 Residencial Villa Eugenia
28 Residencial Astoria
32 Hotel Americana
33 Residencial Ideal
35 Hotel Clarke
36 Residencial Los Angeles

PLACES TO EAT

7 Cheap Restaurants
13 Chifa Oriental
18 Bar Comedor Boulevard
29 Panificadora Buen Pan
34 Chifa Popular

OTHER

1 TAME Airline
2 Western Union
   (Money Transfers)
3 Banco del Pacifico
4 EMETEL
6 Casas de Cambio
8 Banco del Pichincha
9 CETUR Tourist Office
10 Children's Playground
11 Municipalidad
12 Post Office
14 Banco Central
15 Museo del Banco Central
16 Terminal Terrestre
17 Fisherman Statue
19 Parking
23 La Cascada Bar,
    Restaurant & Pool
30 Banco del Pacifico
31 Cine Sucre
37 Police Station,
    Immigration

Bus The terminal terrestre is in front of the fishing-boat harbor. There are frequent departures to Portoviejo (US$0.60; 50 minutes), Guayaquil (US$3.75; 4½ hours), Quito (US$7; nine hours), Bahía de Caráquez, Santo Domingo, Esmeraldas, Quevedo, Jipijapa, Crucita and nearby towns.

Getting Around
Taxis cost about US$1.25 from Tarqui to the airport. Local buses leave from in front of the terminal terrestre.

BAHÍA DE MANTA
Several coastal villages on the large Bahía de Manta have pleasant, unspoiled beaches and are favored as local resorts. Local buses or rancheros reach them via Portoviejo.

Jaramijó, a picturesque fishing village with comedores but no hotels, is 8km east of Manta. Beyond Jaramijó, the road stops, so you need to return to Portoviejo in order to get to **Crucita**. This fishing village, 30km north of Portoviejo, has several good restaurants, a long beach, and a developing local tourist industry. There is a basic pensión, some cabins and several hotels for about US$16 a double. Next are **San Jacinto**, 13km beyond Crucita and slightly inland, and **San Clemente**, 3km farther and on the coast. There are good sandy beaches between these villages, both of which have restaurants and cheap places to stay. Beyond San Clemente, a road continues 20km northeast along the coast to Bahía. All these are easily reached from Portoviejo.

MONTECRISTI
This small town was founded in about 1628, and its many unrestored colonial houses give the village a tumbledown and ghostly atmosphere. It is an important center for wickerwork and the panama hat industry (you'll be besieged by hat sellers), and there are many craft shops. The main plaza has a beautiful church built early in the 19th century.

Montecristi is 15 minutes by bus from Manta. There are no hotels and only a couple of basic comedores.

JIPIJAPA
Pronounced 'hipihapa,' this is the main town on the Manta-Guayaquil road. Parque Nacional Machalilla is a short distance to the southwest. There are a couple of basic pensiones and comedores. CITM and CITMS buses go through Machalilla.

PARQUE NACIONAL MACHALILLA
Ecuador's only coastal national park preserves beaches, unusual tropical dry forest, coastal cloud forest, several archaeological sites, and 20,000 hectares of ocean containing Ecuador's only mainland coral formations and two offshore islands. The coastal region from Machalilla south is known as 'La Ruta de Sol,' along which there is good camping.

The tropical dry forest is characterized by weirdly bottle-shaped trees whose heavy spines protect them against herbivores. There are various figs, cacti and the giant kapok tree. Parrots, parrotlets and parakeets are some of the forest's many inhabitants. Along the coastal edges, frigate birds, pelicans and boobies are seen, some of which nest in colonies on the offshore islands. The tropical dry forest used to stretch along much of the Pacific coast of Central and South America but it has almost disappeared entirely.

The park headquarters and museum are in Puerto López (see below). It is open daily from 8 am to 5 pm and visitor information is available. Entrance to the park is US$20 (less if paid in sucres). Get a receipt or ticket (valid for a week) so you can enter both the mainland and island sections. The park entrance is 6km north of Puerto López and, from here, a dirt road goes 5km to **Agua Blanca**, a little village with an archaeological museum (8 am to 6 pm; US$1.25) and a nearby Manta archaeological site. There are hiking and horse trails, and guides are available. You cannot visit the archaeological site and many parts of the park without a local guide (from US$8). Camping is permitted here and farther on at Playa Los Frailes, or you can stay in people's houses.

The **Isla de la Plata**, 40km northwest of Puerto López, is a favorite part of the national park. There are nesting sea-bird colonies and you may see whales or dolphins, particularly from mid-June to mid-October. Boat tours, some with snorkeling, can be arranged in Puerto López or at Alandaluz, 11km south of Puerto López. The park office may know of other boats. Some boats lack life jackets. It takes two to three hours to reach the island, where there are hiking trails. Camping is not permitted.

PUERTO LÓPEZ

This coastal fishing village houses the national park headquarters. Money-changing facilities are poor. Pacarina Travel (☎ 05-604-03) uses boats that take up to eight passengers to Isla de la Plata for US$160, including snorkeling. Pacarina is also a general travel agency. Salangome (☎ 05-604-20) has guided tours in larger boats for US$34 per person. The park entry fee is extra. Salangome will also arrange tours to the mainland part of the park and other areas.

Places to Stay & Eat

There are a few very basic but friendly pensiones charging US$3 to US$4 per person. The *Villa Colombia*, a block from the park headquarters has good, clean rooms with bath for about US$5. The pricier *Albergue La Cueva del Oso* (☎ 05-604-200), A Lascano 116, is part of Hostelling International.

Carmita's, on the shorefront, is a good, cheap restaurant that also has a few simple rooms with bath for US$6 per person. Next door, the *Mayflower* is a locally popular restaurant.

Getting There & Away

Buses between La Libertad (2½ hours) and Jipijapa (US$1.60; 1½ hours) stop in Puerto López every 45 minutes. They can drop you at the national park entrance and at other coastal points. Buses stop running in the late afternoon and, depending on road conditions, may not go to points south. In this case, get a camioneta to La Entrada (US$2 with pack; 45 minutes), from where there are buses continuing south.

SOUTH OF PUERTO LÓPEZ

Salango, 5km south of Puerto López, has a decent archaeological museum (US$0.80) and *El Delfín*, a good seafood restaurant.

The *Alandaluz Ecocultural Hostal* (☎/fax 02-543-042) is 6km south of Salango. This unusual hotel, run by Ecuadorians, built from fast-growing (and easily replaced) local bamboos and palm leaves and designed as a minimum impact project, is a popular getaway for travelers. An undisturbed beach

is nearby, horses can be rented, there is volleyball, and the atmosphere is very relaxed. Some people love it; others find it hard to take. Rustic rooms are US$12 to US$14 per person, most with shared solar showers outside. Toilets are latrines, designed to conserve water and fertilize the orchard. You can sleep in a hammock or camp (US$4). Meals are US$3 for breakfast and US$6 for lunch or dinner. Food is quite good but you have to eat what is available (rice, vegetables and seafood usually). Reservations can be made in Quito (☎/fax 02-543-042), Baquedano 330 and Reina Victoria, 2nd floor. Otherwise, show up early, especially in summer when it's often full. The hostel works in conjunction with Pacarina Travel (see Puerto López) to arrange tours.

About 12km south of Alandaluz is the coastal village of **Olón**, where there is a nice beach. There is a cheap pensión and a pricey hotel. Three kilometers farther south is the village of **Montañita**, with good surfing (some say the best in Ecuador). Fast becoming the hip spot, Montañita has a bohemian (albeit gringo) feel. Prices rise when the surf's up. In town, *Hostal D Lucho* is a popular, locally owned place, charging US$2 for rooms with shared bath and mosquito nets. There is a restaurant with impromptu guitar jams at night. Nearby, the low-key *Hostal La Piraya* has immaculate bamboo cabins amid lush gardens for US$2 to $5 per person. Attached is *Café Art Tam Tam*, so named because Belgian owner Fina Hermans is an accomplished drum maker; she offers the best coffee in town. There are several tasty *comedores* on this block. Around the corner is the popular hangout *La Luna Bar and Café*. *La Casa Blanca* has rustic, clean rooms with balconies, hammocks and bath for US$4 per person. On the beach, *Centro del Mundo* and *Vitos Cabañas* are similarly priced, but not as good. Farther down the beach is the *Casa del Sol*, with clean, modern rooms ranging from US$5 to $12, depending if you share a room and/or bath. Bike and surfboard rentals are available in town.

Manglaralto is 4km farther south, with a few basic pensiones and comedores, as well as a regional hospital. Good waves are found around here too. Ten kilometers south is **Valdivia**, where Ecuador's oldest archaeological site is. The best artifacts are in museums in Quito and Guayaquil, but there

ECUADOR

is a small museum at the site. (Artifacts offered for sale are fakes.)

LA LIBERTAD

This fishing port of 50,000 inhabitants is the largest town and bustling hub of Península de Santa Elena. Although lively, it is not an attractive place.

Places to Stay

If you must stay, the basic and ugly *Residencial Libertad* charges US$2 per person or US$6 for a double with bath. The *Residencial Collins* on 9 de Octubre is similar at US$2 per person or US$8 for a double with bath. Nearby, the *Turis Palm* is slightly better at the same price. The basic *Residencial Seven Seas* on the Malecón is US$3 per person or US$5 with bath. *Hotel Viña del Mar* (☎ 04-785-979), Av 3 and Guayaquil, is US$7.50/13 with bath; it's the only decent cheap hotel. Manager Ignacio Rivera is very knowledgeable about Parque Machalilla.

Getting There & Away

Buses for Guayaquil (US$2; 2½ hours) leave from several places along 9 de Octubre. Buses going north along the coast leave from the market on Guayaquil. Various local destinations are also served.

PLAYAS

The nearest beach resort to Guayaquil, Playas is busy from January to April (when prices rise) but almost deserted at other times.

Places to Stay & Eat

The cheapest places have brackish running water. Get a room with mosquito nets or a fan. The cheapest are the basic *Hotel Turismo* at US$3 per person and the similar *Hotel Caracol*, which also has rooms with bath at US$6 per person. The best of the cheapies is the *Hostal Brisas Marina* (☎ 04-760-324) at US$10 for a double with bath, fan and mosquito nets. Also decent is the *Hotel Marianela* (☎ 04-760-058), at US$4 per person or US$6 with mosquito nets and private bath. The basic but clean and safe *Hostería Costa Verde* (☎ 04-760-645) is US$4 per person or US$6 with bath and nets. The *Residencial El Galeón* (☎ 04-760-270),

with a good cheap restaurant, is clean and friendly at US$5 per person or US$6 with bath and nets.

The *Hotel Playas* (☎ 04-760-121) is near the beach and quite good at US$8/12 for singles/doubles. It has a restaurant. The *Hostería La Gaviota* (☎ 04-760-133) is friendly and has a decent restaurant, though the rooms are very basic at US$8 per person with bath. The *Hostería El Delfín* (☎ 04-760-125), 1km east of the center, has decent rooms, some with sea views, for US$18 a double with bath. It has a restaurant and bar. Nearby is the good *Hostería Estrella del Mar* (☎ 04-760-430) charging US$16 for a double with hot water. It also has a restaurant.

Apart from the hotel restaurants, you'll find several inexpensive comedores on the beach.

Getting There & Away

Buses to Guayaquil (US$1.75; 1-3/4 hours) leave every half hour with Transportes Villamil.

GUAYAQUIL

With more than 1.5 million inhabitants, Guayaquil is Ecuador's largest city and has all the attendant hustle and problems of a major metropolis. Crime and traffic in the city center are two attributes often bemoaned by travelers, but Guayaquil can be manageable, safe and comfortable if you keep your wits about you. It's actually fairly charming, with striking colonial architecture, abundant parks and agreeable walks along the waterfront, but you'll have to tolerate fierce heat and pollution to enjoy it. If you're not enamored of big cities, however, you won't like this one.

Information

Tourist Offices CETUR (☎ 04-328-312), Aguirre 104 near the Malecón, is open 8 am to 5 pm weekdays.

Consulates Many countries have consulates in Guayaquil; see Visas & Embassies in the Facts for the Visitor section of this chapter, or consult the phone book.

Tourist Card Extensions T-3 tourist card extensions are available from Migraciones (☎ 04-322-539), in the Palacio de Gobierno.

Money Casas de cambio are on the first few blocks of 9 de Octubre and the first blocks of Pichincha. Few are open Saturday. The one at the airport is open on weekends for incoming international flights. The Banco del Pacífico has ATMs and is also good.

Post & Communications The main post office is on P Carbo near Aguirre. Ecuanet, Edificio San Francisco 300, 6th floor, on the Plaza de San Francisco has email for US$5 per hour (one-hour minimum).

Bookstores The best shop for books in English is the Librería Científica, Luque 223.

Laundry Laundry services are generally poor. Many places don't have dryers, so your clothes return in a damp, smelly heap. The youth hostel, near the airport, is an exception.

Medical Services The best hospital is the Clínica Kennedy (☎ 04-286-963, 04-289-666), in the northwest suburb of Nueva Kennedy.

Dangers & Annoyances Guayaquil has a reputation for thefts and muggings. Be alert at all times, everywhere.

Things to See & Do

The **Museo Municipal** (☎ 04-516-391), P Carbo at Sucre, is small but varied: there are rooms devoted to archaeology, colonial art, modern art and ethnography. The last houses the famous *tsantsas*, or shrunken heads. Hours are 10 am to 1 pm and 3 to 6 pm Tuesday to Sunday. Nearby, the **Museo Nahim Isaías B**, Pichincha and Ballén, has religious art and some archaeological pieces, and is open from 10 am to 5 pm daily except Sunday. The **Museo de Arqueología del Banco Central** (☎ 04-327-402), 9 de Octubre and José de Antepara, is open 10 am to 6 pm weekdays and from 10 am to 2 pm weekends. It is well laid out, and has a varied and changing display of ceramics, textiles, metallurgy (some gold) and ceremonial masks. The **Museo Arqueológico del Banco del Pacífico** (☎ 04-566-010), Icaza 113, has ceramics and other artifacts documenting the development of Ecuadorian cultures from 3000 BC to 1500 AD. Hours are 10 am to 6 pm weekdays and 11 am to 1 pm weekends. The archaeology and gold museum in the **Casa de Cultura** (☎ 04-300-500), 9 de Octubre 1200, is open Tuesday to Saturday from 8 am to noon and 3 to 6 pm. Good foreign movies (US$1) are screened at 7:30 pm on Monday, Wednesday and Friday. All these museums are free.

There are several impressive monuments and government buildings along the waterfront, at the northern end of which is the picturesque colonial district of **Las Peñas**. This area is unsafe after dark, but is recommended by Ecuadorian guides as 'typical and historical,' so ask at CETUR about visiting the area. The most interesting street is **Calle Numa Pompillo Llona**, at the end of the Malecón. Here, a short flight of stairs leads to the small **Plaza Colón**, where there are two cannons pointing toward the river. The short, narrow and winding Calle Numa Pompillo Llona begins from the corner of the plaza. Several past presidents had their residences here, and the colonial architecture is interesting. Several artists now live in the area and there are a few art galleries.

The **Parque Bolívar**, between Ballén and 10 de Agosto, has small, well-planned gardens, which are home to prehistoric-looking iguanas, some a meter long. The modern cathedral is on the west side.

The **Parque del Centenario** is the city's biggest plaza, covering four blocks. There are many monuments, the most important of which is the monument to patriotism – a huge work.

The most impressive church is **San Francisco**, which has been reconstructed and beautifully restored since a devastating fire in 1896. Also worth seeing is the dazzling white **city cemetery**, at Coronel and Machala, but beware of robbers.

The '**black market**,' by the waterfront north of Olmedo, is a huge open-air affair selling almost anything. It's colorful, interesting and reasonably safe, but watch for pickpockets.

Special Events

The whole city parties in the last week of July, celebrating Simón Bolívar's birthday (July 24), followed by Guayaquil Foundation Day (July 25); hotels may be full. Banks and other services are also disrupted. Guayaquil's Independence Day (October 9), combined with Día de la Raza (Columbus Day, October 12), is an important local

ECUADOR

CENTRAL GUAYAQUIL

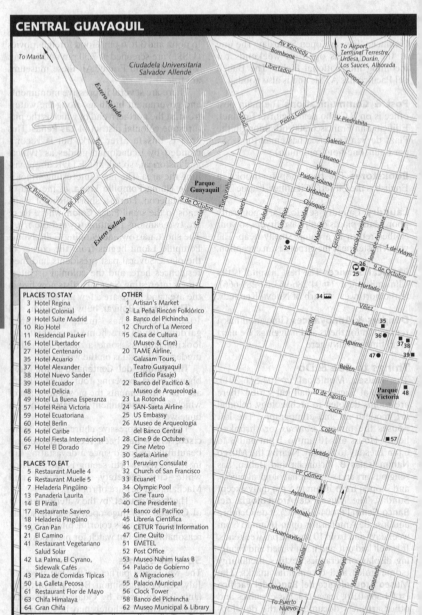

To Manta

Ciudadela Universitaria
Salvador Allende

Estero Salado

Av Kennedy
Bombona
Libertador

To Airport,
Terminal Terrestre,
Urdesa, Durán,
Los Sauces, Alborada

Coronel

Pedro Gual

V Piedrahita

Galecio

Lascano

Vernaza

Padre Solano

Urdaneta

Quisquis

Parque
Guayaquil

9 de Octubre

Av Primera

5 de Junio

Tola

Estero Salado

24

26
25

9 de Octubre

Hurtado

34

Vélez

Luque   35

36   37 38

Aguirre

47   39

Ballén

Parque
Victoria   48

10 de Agosto

Sucre

Colón

57

Alcedo

PP Gómez

Ayacucho

Manabí

Huancavilca

Nájera

Cordero

To Puerto
Nuevo

Quito

Montcayo

Montúfar

Guaranda

PLACES TO STAY
3   Hotel Regina
4   Hotel Colonial
9   Hotel Suite Madrid
10 Río Hotel
11 Residencial Pauker
16 Hotel Libertador
27 Hotel Centenario
35 Hotel Acuario
37 Hotel Alexander
38 Hotel Nuevo Sander
39 Hotel Ecuador
48 Hotel Delicia
49 Hotel La Buena Esperanza
57 Hotel Reina Victoria
59 Hotel Ecuatoriana
60 Hotel Berlin
65 Hotel Caribe
66 Hotel Fiesta Internacional
67 Hotel El Dorado

PLACES TO EAT
5   Restaurant Muelle 4
6   Restaurant Muelle 5
7   Heladería Pingüino
13 Panadería Laurita
14 El Pirata
17 Restaurante Saviero
18 Heladería Pingüino
19 Gran Pan
21 El Camino
41 Restaurant Vegetariano
    Salud Solar
42 La Palma, El Cyrano,
    Sidewalk Cafés
43 Plaza de Comidas Típicas
50 La Galleta Pecosa
61 Restaurant Flor de Mayo
63 Chifa Himalaya
64 Gran Chifa

OTHER
1   Artisan's Market
2   La Peña Rincón Folklórico
8   Banco del Pichincha
12 Church of La Merced
15 Casa de Cultura
    (Museo & Cine)
20 TAME Airline,
    Galasam Tours,
    Teatro Guayaquil
    (Edificio Pasaje)
22 Banco del Pacífico &
    Museo de Arqueología
23 La Rotonda
24 SAN-Saeta Airline
25 US Embassy
26 Museo de Arqueología
    del Banco Central
28 Cine 9 de Octubre
29 Cine Metro
30 Saeta Airline
31 Peruvian Consulate
32 Church of San Francisco
33 Ecuanet
34 Olympic Pool
36 Cine Tauro
40 Cine Presidente
44 Banco del Pacífico
45 Librería Científica
46 CETUR Tourist Information
47 Cine Quito
51 EMETEL
52 Post Office
53 Museo Nahim Isaías B
54 Palacio de Gobierno
    & Migraciones
55 Palacio Municipal
56 Clock Tower
58 Banco del Pichincha
62 Museo Municipal & Library

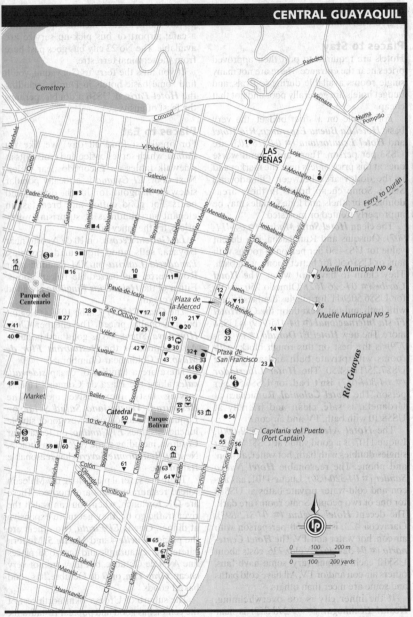

ECUADOR

holiday period. New Year's Eve is celebrated with bonfires.

Places to Stay

Hotels are required to post their approved prices near the entrance. There are not many single rooms available during festivals, and budget hotels are generally poor and not that cheap.

For people on a strict budget, the very basic *Hotel La Buena Esperanza*, *Río Hotel* and *Hotel Ecuatoriana* (☎ 04-518-105) are US$3 per person. There are several worse ones at this price or less near the market and in the dodgy area between Olmedo and Sucre. Some cheap hotels in these areas double as brothels, and lone females may be improperly treated or molested.

The clean *Hotel Suite Madrid* (☎ 04-414-907), Quisquis and Rumicacha, is a decent value for US$4.50 per person in rooms with fans or US$6.50 for better rooms with bath. They claim to have hot water. The *Hotel Caribe* (☎ 04-526-162), Olmedo 250, is OK for US$6.50/9/11 for singles/doubles/triples with bath and fan. Next door, the OK *Hotel Fiesta Internacional* (☎ 04-415-979) is US$1 more. The new *Hotel El Dorado* (☎ 04-323-779) is the best on this rough block, with rooms with private bath and air-con for US$7.25/11/14.50. The *Hotel Libertador* (☎ 04-304-637) isn't bad for US$6.50 per person. The *Hotel Colonial*, Rumichaca at Urdaneta, is safe, clean and friendly at US$8/10 with bath, TV and air-con.

The *Hotel Alexander* (☎ 04-532-000), Luque 1107, is a good value at US$14/18 for singles/doubles with bath, hot water, air-con, and phone. The reasonable *Hotel Nuevo Sander* (☎ 04-320-030), Luque 1101, has air-con and cold-water private baths at US$10 for one or two people. Some rooms are dark. The decent *Hotel Regina* (☎ 04-312-893), Garaycoa 423, is US$7.50 per person with air-con, hot water and TV. The *Hotel Centenario* (☎ 04-524-467), Vélez 726, costs about US$12 each. Rooms vary: some have fans, others air-con and/or TV. All have cold baths and some are nicer than others.

If the inner city is too overwhelming, *Hostal Ecuahogar* (☎ 04-248-357) is near the airport on Isidro Ayora in the suburb of Los Sauces. It is part of the Hostelling International chain and charges US$11 per person or US$9 in dorms (cheaper for hostel members), including breakfast. There are private baths, kitchen facilities, laundry and a café; airport or bus pick-up service are available. The No 22 city bus goes past here from the terminal terrestre.

If you miss the ferry to Guayaquil, you'll find some basic hotels in Durán, including the *Hotel Paris* at US$6 a double, perhaps the least offensive.

Places to Eat

For breakfast (and all day) we like *La Palma*, which serves coffee and croissants at sidewalk tables on Escobedo near Vélez. Next door, *El Cyrano* is a locally popular sidewalk hangout for lunch, dinner and beers. For good coffee and breakfast in elegant surroundings at surprisingly low prices, try the fancy hotels.

La Galleta Pecosa, on 10 de Agosto near Boyacá, sells good homemade cookies. *Panadería Laurita* on VM Rendón near Rocafuerte, has incredible baked goods. Either of the *Heladerías Pingüino* are good for ice cream.

The *Gran Chifa*, P Carbo 1016, is elegant but reasonably priced. The cheaper *Chifa Himalaya*, Sucre 308, is good and popular. Also popular is the *Restaurant Flor de Mayo*, on Colón near Chimborazo.

There are a handful of cheap sidewalk cafés along the Plaza de Comidas Típicas, serving tasty, inexpensive meals. The *Restaurant Vegetariano Salud Solar*, on Luque near Moncayo, serves good, simple lunches, as does *El Camino*, on Icaza near Córdova, including some vegetarian choices. Nearby, *Restaurante Saverio* has reasonable Italian fare.

There are several piers along the Malecón where restaurant boats are moored. These are OK for lunch, when you can watch the river traffic go by; they get more expensive at dinner. One is *El Pirata*, two others are the pricier *Muelle 4* and *Muelle 5*. Modern cafeterias, restaurants and fast-food places line Av 9 de Octubre, but they are not very cheap. *Gran Pan*, on 9 de Octubre, has good baked goods.

The suburb of Urdesa, 6km northwest of the center, has good and popular restaurants, some reasonably priced but none dirt cheap. There is some nightlife – a good area to hang out. The main drag is VE Estrada, and most of the restaurants, bars and clubs are found along this street. *La Parrillada del Ñato*, on VE Estrada near Laurales, serves good Ecuadorian-style steaks, grills and barbecues, as well as pizza. *La Tablita*, Ebanos 126 near VE Estrada, also has good grills and steaks. For Mexican dinners, try *Paco's*, at Acacias 725 near Guayacanes. Mariachi bands play here sometimes. *El Caribe* on VE Estrada has Caribbean specialties.

Entertainment

El Telégrafo and *El Universo* publish entertainment listings. There are some 18 cinemas; English-language movies with Spanish subtitles are often shown. Friday newspapers advertise weekend peñas, which are rarely cheap and always start late. A good one is *La Peña Rincón Folklórico*, at Malecón 208. It opens at 10 pm for food and drinks, the show starts about midnight and goes until the wee hours; the cover charge is US$3 and drinks aren't cheap. *Los Checitos*, PP Gómez and Garaycoa, has live salsa bands and dancing from Wednesday to Sunday. A US$6 cover charge includes five beers! It's a lively spot.

Along VE Estrada in Urdesa, there are plenty of clubs, bars and discos. Calle Principal, in the suburb of La Alborada just north of Hostal Ecuahogar, is also peppered with bars. Our favorite is the cozy *Rob Roy*, on Aguilera Malta 739, near the Burger King. Here, a hospitable blend of expats, travelers and locals kick back over drinks to a classic mix of reggae, rock and blues.

Getting There & Away

Air The main airport is on Av de las Américas, 5km north of the center. The international and domestic terminals are side by side. International flights (to Latin America, USA and Europe) out of Guayaquil are subject to a US$25 departure tax.

There are many daily flights to Quito (US$99) with TAME (☎ 04-565-806) or SAN-Saeta (☎ 04-200-600). One or two flights a day go to Cuenca (US$30), three a week to Loja (US$25), and one every weekday to Machala (US$22).

Flights to the Galápagos (US$334 round-trip) go to Baltra with TAME, or to San Cristóbal with SAN-Saeta (most days).

One kilometer south of the main airport is the *avioneta* (light aircraft) terminal. Avio-Pacífico (☎ 04-283-304/5), AECA (☎ 04-290-849), and CEDTA (☎ 04-561-954) have flights to many coastal destinations. Baggage limit is 10kg and passenger weight limit is 100kg.

Bus The terminal terrestre is 2km beyond the airport. There are dozens of bus offices, stores, restaurants, tourist information, a bank, and so on. You can get buses to most towns; ask at the passenger information desk. For fares and hours, see under the town you wish to go to. There are many daily buses to Quito (US$6; eight hours), Manta (US$4; 3½ hours), Esmeraldas (US$5 to US$7; eight hours) and Cuenca (US$4; five hours). There are also several buses a day to Huigra (three hours) from where you catch the train for Alausí, which includes the Devil's Nose ride.

Train Technically, the train runs all the way to Durán (a suburb on the opposite side of the Río Guayas from Guayaquil) – via Bucay, Huigra and Alausí – but this is the exception, rather than the rule. Daily trains for Alausí (US$12) and on to Riobamba (US$15) do leave from Huigra at 7 am; try calling ☎ 04-800-031 for more information. Huigra is a three hour bus ride from Guayaquil. Passengers who do manage to take the train all the way to Durán will find the ferry to Guayaquil just west of the station but may arrive too late to catch it. (Getting off at Huigra avoids this problem.) A taxi from Guayacil to Durán will cost about US$5. The train ride from Huigra to Alausí includes the infamous and phenomenal pass through the Devil's Nose.

Boat The daily ferry to Durán across the Río Guayas (US$0.10; 15 minutes) leaves a few times an hour from 7 am to 6:30 pm. This is a good sightseeing trip for the impecunious! The dock is on the Malecón near Montalvo.

The cargo boat *Piquero* leaves Guayaquil for the Galápagos around the 25th of every month. See the Galápagos section for more information.

Getting Around

A taxi from the center to the airport or terminal terrestre is about US$2.50, but from the airport, higher fares are charged. For cheaper taxis, cross Av de las Américas in front of the airport and bargain. From this street, there are buses to the center or bus terminal.

From the center, buses run along the Malecón and pass the airport (US$0.25; 30 minutes); allow plenty of time if catching a flight. Buses to the terminal terrestre leave from Parque Victoria, near 10 de Agosto and Moncayo.

MACHALA

This is the capital of El Oro province and the self-proclaimed 'banana capital of the world.' With 150,000 inhabitants, it's Ecuador's fourth-largest city. Most travelers to and from Peru pass through here, but few stay more than a night – with reason. Puerto Bolívar, the international port, is 7km away. Several boats a day go to **Jambelí** (US$1; 30 minutes), with a beach and basic hotels.

Information

CETUR (☎ 07-932-106) is upstairs at 9 de Mayo and Pichincha.

Banco del Pacífico, on Rocafuerte at Junín, and Delgado Travel, on 9 de Mayo near the plaza, change traveler's checks.

The No 1 bus to Puerto Bolívar (US$0.20) plies 9 de Octubre from the central plaza. Boats can be hired to visit the mangroves.

Places to Stay

Most hotels have only cold water and those near bus terminals fill up fast. The cheapest are the very basic *Residencial Machala* and *Almache* at US$1.75 per person. You get what you pay for. The *Residencial Pichincha* is somewhat better at US$1 more. Better still

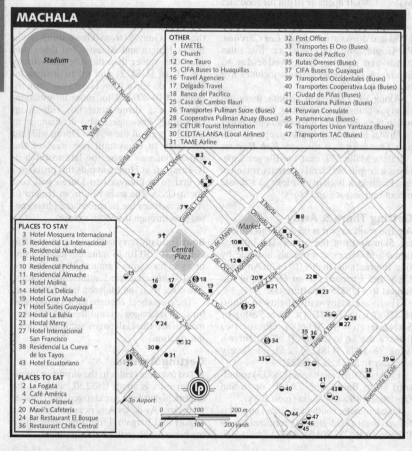

MACHALA

OTHER
1 EMETEL
9 Church
12 Cine Tauro
15 CIFA Buses to Huaquillas
16 Travel Agencies
17 Delgado Travel
18 Banco del Pacífico
25 Casa de Cambio Illauri
26 Transportes Pullman Sucre (Buses)
28 Cooperativa Pullman Azuay (Buses)
29 CETUR Tourist Information
30 CEDTA-LANSA (Local Airlines)
31 TAME Airline
32 Post Office
33 Transportes El Oro (Buses)
34 Banco del Pacífico
35 Rutas Orenses (Buses)
37 CIFA Buses to Guayaquil
39 Transportes Occidentales (Buses)
40 Transportes Cooperativa Loja (Buses)
41 Ciudad de Piñas (Buses)
42 Ecuatoriana Pullman (Buses)
44 Peruvian Consulate
45 Panamericana (Buses)
46 Transportes Union Yantzaza (Buses)
47 Transportes TAC (Buses)

PLACES TO STAY
3 Hotel Mosquera Internacional
5 Residencial La Internacional
6 Residencial Machala
8 Hotel Inés
10 Residencial Pichincha
11 Residencial Almache
13 Hotel Molina
14 Hotel La Delicia
19 Hotel Gran Machala
21 Hotel Suites Guayaquil
22 Hostal La Bahía
23 Hostal Mercy
27 Hotel Internacional San Francisco
38 Residencial La Cueva de los Tayos
43 Hotel Ecuatoriano

PLACES TO EAT
2 La Fogata
4 Café América
7 Chusco Pizzería
20 Maxi's Cafetería
24 Bar Restaurant El Bosque
36 Restaurant Chifa Central

Stadium

Central Plaza

Market

To Airport

0   100   200 m
0   100   200 yards

are the *Hotel Molina* (☎ 07-932-712) at US$3/5 for singles/doubles, the *Hotel La Delicia* and *Hotel Gran Machala*, both at US$3 per person, and the friendly *Residencial La Internacional,* at US$3.50 per person. The *Hostal La Bahía* (☎ 07-920-518) is a good cheap place at US$4.50 for a double or US$5.50 per person with bath.

One of the best cheap hotels, often full by lunch time, is the clean *Hostal Mercy* (☎ 07-920-116) at US$4 per person with bath or US$6 with air-con; rooms are wheelchair accessible. The friendly *Residencial La Cueva de los Tayos* (☎ 07-935-600) is clean at US$4.50 per person or US$5 with bath and fan. The *Hotel Ecuatoriano* (☎ 07-930-197) is rather noisy but convenient if you arrive late at the adjoining bus terminal. Dark, shabby rooms, some with air-con, are US$4 per person.

The *Hotel Suites Guayaquil* (☎ 07-922-570) is OK for US$4 per person with bath and fan. Watch for cockroaches. The *Hotel Mosquera Internacional* (☎ 07-931-140) is US$6 per person in small clean rooms with fan and US$8 with air-con. All have private hot showers and most of them have a TV and telephone. Also with hot showers are rooms at the decent *Hotel Inés* (☎ 07-932-301), US$10/14, with air-con and TV and the *Hotel Internacional San Francisco* (☎ 07-922-395) at US$7.25 apiece with fan or US$10 with air-con. Both have good restaurants.

Places to Eat

Chusco Pizzería, off the central plaza, has good, inexpensive pizzas. *Restaurant Chifa Central*, on Tarqui near 9 de Octubre, is good and reasonably priced, especially the filling chaulafan (fried rice with pork, chicken, egg, etc). Many locals eat lunch here. Other cheap places are along 9 de Octubre, including *La Fogata* for grilled chicken. *Bar Restaurant El Bosque*, on 9 de Mayo near Bolívar, has an outdoor dining area and simple but decent meals for US$2. *Café América* is quite good and open till midnight. For breakfast and coffee, try *Maxi's Cafetería*, across from the *Hotel Suites Guayaquil*.

Puerto Bolívar has seafood restaurants.

Getting There & Away

Air The airport is 1km southwest of town along Montalvo (taxi US$1). At the airport,

CEDTA and LANSA have light aircraft for Guayaquil. TAME (☎ 07-930-139), on Montalvo near Pichincha, has weekday flights to Guayaquil (US$22) and less often to Quito (US$59).

Bus To the Peruvian border at Huaquillas (US$1.20; two hours), use CIFA, which operates frequent buses from the corner of Bolívar and Guayas. Be prepared for passport checks en route. You must leave the bus to register, but the driver will wait.

CIFA buses also go to Guayaquil (US$3; 3½ hours) from 9 de Octubre near Tarqui. Rutas Orenses and Ecuatoriana Pullman also serve Guayaquil, the latter providing air-conditioned coaches.

Panamericana has several coaches a day to Quito (US$7.50; 10 to 12 hours). Ciudad de Piñas has several daily buses to Piñas, and the 6 am bus continues to Loja. It also has one or two buses to Cuenca (US$3.50; 4½ hours). Transportes Cooperativa Loja goes to Loja (US$2.20; eight hours). Pullman Azuay has eight buses daily to Cuenca.

HUAQUILLAS

Huaquillas, 80km from Machala, is the main border town with Peru. It is called Aguas Verdes on the Peruvian side. There is a busy street market on the Ecuadorian side of the border, which is full of Peruvians shopping on day passes. Almost everything happens on the long main street.

Information

Banks don't change money, but there are street moneychangers. They offer poor rates, are pushy, and may use 'fixed' calculators or offer outdated bills. Check with travelers going the opposite way for up-to-date exchange rates and information. It is best to use US dollars for exchange, so arrive with as few sucres (or Peruvian nuevos soles) as possible. Beware of thieves in the street market on the border.

Places to Stay & Eat

Several cheap but poor hotels (less than US$3 per person) are near the border. *Residencial Huaquillas* is the best of these. There are cheap and basic restaurants nearby.

For about US$8 for a double with bath, the **Hotel Rodey**, Teniente Cordovez and 10 de Agosto, is clean and reasonable. Nearby, the similarly priced **Hotel Hidalgo** is also good. The **Parador Turístico Huaquillas** (☎ 07-907-374), is 1.5km from the border on the main road out of town, with the best restaurant around and simple clean doubles with bath for US$14.

Getting There & Away
CIFA buses run frequently to Machala (US$1.20; two hours) from the main street, two blocks beyond the border when heading away from Peru. Panamericana has four daily buses to Quito (US$8; 13 hours). Ecuatoriana Pullman has buses to Guayaquil (US$4; 5½ hours). For Loja, (US$4; six hours) use Transportes Loja, with departures at 1:30 and 8 pm.

To/From Peru The Ecuadorian immigration office is 5km outside of Huaquillas. Entrance and exit formalities are carried out here. It is open daily from 8 am to noon and 2 to 5 pm. The bus doesn't wait, but taxis are US$1.25, or you can jump on another passing bus for US$0.20. If you do, you must brave the crowded market for about 75m before reaching the international bridge.

Those entering Ecuador need an exit stamp in their passport from the Peruvian authorities. Entrance formalities are usually straightforward. Travelers need a T-3 tourist card, which is available free at the immigration office. Usually only 30 days are given, but it is easy to obtain a renewal in Quito or Guayaquil. Show of funds or onward tickets are very rarely asked for.

Those leaving Ecuador need an exit stamp from the Ecuadorian immigration office before entering Peru. If you have lost your T-3 card, you should be able to get a free replacement, as long as the stamp in your passport has not expired.

After showing your passport to the international bridge guard, take a shared moto-taxi (US$0.50) to the Peruvian immigration building, about 2km beyond the border. Officially, an onward ticket is required to enter Peru, but this is not often asked for and, if it is, you can (politely) talk your way

out of it. Border officials may be looking for a bribe; don't give in. From here, shared colectivos go to Tumbes (US$1). Beware of overcharging by drivers – everyone is out to make a fast buck.

Galápagos Islands

The Galápagos archipelago is famous for its fearless and unique wildlife. Here, you can swim with sea lions, float eye-to-eye with penguins, stand next to a blue-footed booby feeding its young, watch a giant 200kg tortoise lumbering through a cactus forest, and try to avert iguanas scurrying over the lava. The scenery is barren and volcanic, with its own haunting beauty, though some people find it bare and ugly. Visiting the islands is very expensive, however, so this trip is for the nature and wildlife enthusiast, not the average sun-seeker.

The islands were uninhabited when they were discovered by the Spanish in 1535. They lie on the equator, about 1000km west of Ecuador, and consist of 13 major islands and many small ones. Five islands are now inhabited. The archipelago's most famous visitor was Charles Darwin, who came here in 1835. The Galápagos comprise one of Ecuador's 21 provinces.

Planning
Plan on spending more money than you want to. You can count on a minimum of $800 for a one-week trip in the low season, or $1000 in high season. Getting to and touring the Galápagos is expensive, but everything that comes from the mainland (eg, beer, rice, taxis) is also expensive. The cheapest (though not the best) time to go is between September and November when seas are rough and business is dead. You can save money if you arrange a tour independently; the place to do this is Puerto Ayora.

What to Bring Many things are unavailable in the Galápagos. Stock up on seasickness pills, sunscreen, insect repellent, film, batteries, toiletries and medication on the mainland.

Books Lonely Planet's *Ecuador & the Galápagos Islands* by Rob Rachowiecki has plenty of Galápagos information, plus a wildlife guide for the nonspecialist. The best general wildlife guide, with background information on history and geology, is Michael H Jackson's *Galápagos: A Natural History Guide*. Bird-watchers consult *A Field Guide to the Birds of the Galápagos* by Michael Harris. Amateur botanists use the pocket-size *Plants of the Galápagos Islands* by Eileen K Schofield. There is also *A Field Guide to the Fishes of Galápagos* by Godfrey Merlen. Most are available at major bookstores in Quito and Guayaquil or from the SAEC.

Orientation

The most important island is Isla Santa Cruz in the middle of the archipelago. On the southern side of the island is Puerto Ayora, the largest town in the Galápagos and where most budget tours are based. There are many hotels and restaurants. North of Santa Cruz, separated by a narrow strait, is Isla Baltra, with the islands' major airport. A public bus and a ferry connect the Baltra airport with Puerto Ayora.

Isla San Cristóbal, the most easterly island, has the provincial capital, Puerto Baquerizo Moreno. There are hotels and an airport.

The other inhabited islands are Isla Isabela, with the small port of Puerto Villamil, and Isla Santa María (Floreana), with Puerto Velasco Ibarra; both have places to stay. Inter-island transport is by infrequent public ferries or private boat.

Information

The islands are a national park. All foreign visitors must pay US$80 upon arrival (US$40 for children under 12; students under 26 with ID from their home university may also pay US$40, but this is subject to change). There's an additional city tax of US$30 per person at Puerto Baquerizo Moreno and US$20 at Puerto Ayora. The high seasons are from December to January, around Easter, and from June to August; during these periods, budget tours may be difficult to arrange. Note that most of the islands have two or even three names. Galápagos time is one hour behind mainland Ecuador.

Tourist Offices CETUR has a Puerto Ayora office. Next door, CAPTURGAL

also has tourist information. Adatur Boat Co-operative is an agency dealing with budget boats. The SAEC in Quito has recent travel information.

Money Banco del Pacífico in Puerto Ayora changes money at reasonable rates and has an ATM. Tours can be paid for in US dollars or traveler's checks.

Post & Communications Mail is slow. Have stamps hand-canceled to avoid them being removed. EMETEL occasionally doesn't work.

Electricity This is cut off at 11 pm or earlier in some places.

Getting There & Away

Flying to the Galápagos is recommended. If you go by boat, you'll probably waste a lot of time in the Guayaquil port getting one of the infrequent passages. With the extra food and accommodations costs, you are unlikely to save much money.

Air Most visitors fly to Isla Baltra, from where public buses and a ferry go to Puerto Ayora, on Isla Santa Cruz. (Tour groups are sometimes picked up directly from Baltra by their boats.) There are flights to Puerto Baquerizo Moreno, on Isla San Cristóbal, but there are more facilities in Puerto Ayora, and travelers wanting to arrange tours on-site should go there.

TAME flies daily from Quito (US$378 roundtrip) via Guayaquil (US$334 roundtrip; 1½ hours) to Baltra. Flights are 20% less in the low season. Ecuadorians or foreigners on residence visas pay about half price. Students with ID from their home university can get discounts.

SAN-Saeta flights to Puerto Baquerizo Moreno are similarly priced with departures daily except Thursday and Sunday. TAME and SAN-Saeta do not honor one another's tickets. You can buy one-way tickets to one island and leave from the other. It's possible to buy tickets with open return dates. Always reconfirm flights.

If you are signed up with a tour, make sure you are flying to the right island! People occasionally end up in the wrong place and miss their tour.

If you fly Miami-Ecuador-Galápagos with SAETA, the Galápagos portion is about US$100 cheaper.

Military *logístico* (supply) flights leave on Wednesday and Saturday from Quito to Baltra (US$140 one way) but getting on is difficult. Go to the military airport (☎ 02-445-043) just north of the civil airport to make reservations. If successful, you have to pay for the ticket in exact US dollars.

If flights are full, try going to the airport. Agencies book blocks of seats for their tours and release unsold seats on the day of the flight (these are full-price tickets). Tuesday is the quietest day to fly.

Boat Cargo ships leave irregularly from Guayaquil and charge about US$150 to US$200. It takes 3½ days to get to the islands. Conditions are tolerable but basic. These ships normally do roundtrips and are for cargo purposes, not for wildlife viewing. If you stay aboard while the boat spends about a week making deliveries around the islands you are charged about US$50 a day, or you can get off and return later. The most reliable boat is the *Piquero*, which leaves Guayaquil around the 25th of every month. The agent for the *Piquero* is Acotramar (☎ 04-401-004), at General Gómez 522 and Coronel. Naval vessels may take passengers. Try at Transnave (☎ 04-561-453), 9 de Octubre 416 and Chile. Also ask the Capitanía in Guayaquil, or at the boats, which anchor near dock No 4. Be prepared to wait weeks for a boat – though you might get lucky.

Getting Around

Arriving air passengers in Baltra are met by a crew member (if on a prearranged tour) or take a bus-ferry-bus combination to Puerto Ayora (US$3; two hours). Buy tickets in the airport.

From Puerto Ayora, buses leave at 8 am from the park for the return trip to Baltra.

Air passengers arriving in Puerto Baquerizo Moreno can walk into town in a few minutes.

Interisland transport is with INGALA (☎ 05-526-151 in Puerto Ayora) open 7:30 am to 12:30 pm and 1:30 to 4 pm weekdays. Recently, boat schedules were as follows:

from	to	departure
Puerto Ayora	Puerto Baquerizo Moreno	Tue 9 am
Puerto Baquerizo Moreno	Puerto Ayora	Wed 10 am
Puerto Ayora	Puerto Velasco Ibarra (Isla Floreana) and on to Puerto Villamil (Isla Isabela)	Thu 9 am
Puerto Villamil	Puerto Ayora	Fri 10 am
Puerto Ayora	Puerto Baquerizo Moreno	Sat 9 am
Puerto Baquerizo Moreno	Puerto Ayora	Mon 10 am

Buy tickets the night before. Fares are US$36 on any passage (US$24 for locals) and subject to change. If you can't get on an INGALA boat, ask around for private trips, which are more expensive.

PUERTO AYORA

This is the main population center of the archipelago and the heart of the tourist industry. It's a friendly town to chill out in.

Things to See & Do

See the following Around Puerto Ayora section for places to visit.

You can rent bicycles (see map) for about US$12 a day. Daily **glass-bottom boat tours** leave from the municipal pier at 8:30 am and 2:30 pm. Galápagos Sub-Aqua (☎ 02-565-294, in Quito) provides everything you'll need for **scuba diving**. It is well recommended and its rates are very competitive. A one-week certification course for beginners, including all gear, boat, instructor and certificate, costs from US$410. Diving only, including gear, boat and guide, is from US$75 a day (two dives). Divemaster Fernando Zambrano speaks English and is very experienced. Clients have free email use. Also recommended and similarly priced is Galápagos Diving (☎ 05-526-193). Both these outfits also offer **snorkeling** trips for about US$15 per person.

Places to Stay

Try bargaining in the off season. The *Residencial Los Amigos* is a popular budget

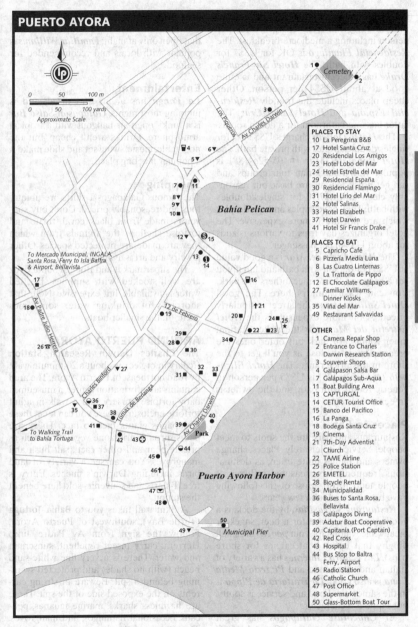

PUERTO AYORA

0   50   100 m
0   50   100 yards
Approximate Scale

Bahía Pelican

To Mercado Municipal, INGALA,
Santa Rosa, Ferry to Isla Baltra
& Airport, Bellavista

12 de Febrero

To Walking Trail
to Bahía Tortuga

Puerto Ayora Harbor

Municipal Pier

ECUADOR

PLACES TO STAY
10 La Peregrina B&B
17 Hotel Santa Cruz
20 Residencial Los Amigos
23 Hotel Lobo del Mar
24 Hotel Estrella del Mar
29 Residencial España
30 Residencial Flamingo
31 Hotel Lirio del Mar
32 Hotel Salinas
33 Hotel Elizabeth
37 Hotel Darwin
41 Hotel Sir Francis Drake

PLACES TO EAT
5 Capricho Café
6 Pizzería Media Luna
8 Las Cuatro Linternas
9 La Trattoría de Pippo
12 El Chocolate Galápagos
27 Familiar Williams,
    Dinner Kiosks
35 Viña del Mar
49 Restaurant Salvavidas

OTHER
1 Camera Repair Shop
2 Entrance to Charles
    Darwin Research Station
3 Souvenir Shops
4 Galápason Salsa Bar
7 Galápagos Sub-Aqua
11 Boat Building Area
13 CAPTURGAL
14 CETUR Tourist Office
15 Banco del Pacífico
16 La Panga
18 Bodega Santa Cruz
19 Cinema
21 7th-Day Adventist
    Church
22 TAME Airline
25 Police Station
26 EMETEL
28 Bicycle Rental
34 Municipalidad
36 Buses to Santa Rosa,
    Bellavista
38 Galápagos Diving
39 Adatur Boat Cooperative
40 Capitanía (Port Captain)
42 Red Cross
43 Hospital
44 Bus Stop to Baltra
    Ferry, Airport
45 Radio Station
46 Catholic Church
47 Post Office
48 Supermarket
50 Glass-Bottom Boat Tour

hotel with clean rooms for US$3 per person. The *La Peregrina B&B* charges US$9 per person including a mediocre breakfast. The *Residencial Flamingo* is OK for US$7 for doubles with bath. The *Hotel Sir Francis Drake* has a decent restaurant and is quite good at about US$4 per person. Other cheap places include the friendly *Residencial España* and *Hotel Santa Cruz*. The latter has one bathroom for a dozen rooms.

The *Hotel Darwin* charges US$3/5/7 for singles/doubles/triples with private bath. The *Hotel Lobo del Mar* (☎ 05-526-188) is popular with Ecuadorian tour groups and can get noisy. Rooms are basic but reasonably clean at US$7/10 for singles/doubles with bath. They have triples and quadruples which are not much more expensive. The hotel organizes day trips to various islands for about US$40 per passenger.

The *Hotel Lirio del Mar* is a good value at US$6 per person with bath and fan if you get a room on the terrace; others are dark. You can wash laundry here. The good *Hotel Salinas* across the street is similarly priced. A bit more expensive is the *Hotel Estrella del Mar* near the police station; inner rooms are dark but outer ones are breezy. This is as close as you'll get to the shore in this price range. The *Hotel Elizabeth* (☎ 05-526-178) is US$5 per person in generic rooms with bath, and the owner is an eerie character.

Places to Eat

Restaurants and bars are the spots to meet people. Service is leisurely. Places change owners and names quite often, as destinations frequented by seasonal influxes of people tend to do. Most of the following have been around for a few years.

Restaurant Salvavidas, by the dock, is a good, expensive place for a beer, snack or meal while waiting for your *panga* (the small dinghy that every boat carries for shore trips). *Las Cuatro Linternas* has a variety of Italian and other food and *Pizzería Media Luna* is also good. *La Trattoría de Pippo* is in the same vein. Food and service is spotty, but Pippo is a character.

El Chocolate Galápagos has great breakfasts and burgers, and *Capricho Café* is good for coffee and juices. Along Av Padre Julio Herrera are some good, inexpensive places to eat, particularly *Viña del Mar*, which has *meriendas* for US$1.50. Charles Binford is lined with food kiosks that open only at night; *Familiar Williams* is popular with locals and recommended for seafood.

Entertainment

La Panga has a bar and disco, and is jumping most nights. *Galápason Salsa Bar* is a funky open-air hangout with a tropical atmosphere. Drinks aren't cheap, but the pool table, music, swing set and slide make it a popular meeting place.

Shopping

The famous Galápagos T-shirts are ubiquitous and reasonably priced. Don't buy souvenirs made from black coral, turtle and tortoise shell, as the animals from which they are made are protected species. Other jewelry and art is available.

The supermarket and Bodega Santa Cruz are well-stocked with supplies. Bottled water is available, but expensive. Note that shortages of drinking water sometimes occur on the smaller boats.

AROUND PUERTO AYORA

The **Charles Darwin Research Station** (fcdarwin.org.ec), is about a 20-minute walk by road northeast of Puerto Ayora. The area contains an information center, a museum, a baby tortoise nursery, and a walk-in adult tortoise enclosure where you can meet these Galápagos giants face to face. There are paths through arid-zone vegetation such as prickly pear and other cacti, salt bush and mangroves. You can see a variety of land birds, including Darwin's finches. Entry is free. T-shirts and souvenirs sold here benefit the station.

A 3km trail takes you to **Bahía Tortuga** (Turtle Bay), southwest of Puerto Ayora. Follow the sign from Av Padre Julio Herrera; carry insect repellent, sunscreen and water. There is a very fine white-sand beach (with no shade) and protected swimming behind a spit. Beware of strong currents on the exposed side of the spit. There are harmless sharks, marine iguanas, pelicans, occasional flamingos, and mangroves. This is one of the few sites you can visit without a guide.

Buses from Puerto Ayora go to the villages of Bellavista or Santa Rosa, from where you can explore some of the interior. Neither of these villages has hotels, and sometimes the return bus is full of passengers from the airport. Buses to Santa Rosa leave from the corner of Padre Julio Herrera and Charles Binford at 6:30 am and 12:30 and 4:30 pm Monday to Saturday. If there's room, you can hop the airport bus at 8 am from the park. To ensure you don't get stuck, hire a camioneta for the day with a group of other travelers. Tours are available or you can rent a bike. It's uphill to get there.

From the village of Bellavista, 7km north of Puerto Ayora, you can turn either west on the main road toward Santa Rosa, or east and go about 2km to the **lava tubes**. These are underground tunnels more than 1km in length. They are in private property and the owners charge a US$2 entrance fee; bring a flashlight.

A footpath north from Bellavista leads toward **the highlands**, including Cerro Crocker and other hills and extinct volcanoes. This is a good chance to see local vegetation and birds. It is about 6km from Bellavista to the crescent-shaped hill of Media Luna, and a farther 3km to the base of Cerro Crocker.

The twin craters called **Los Gemelos** are 5km beyond Santa Rosa, which is about 12km west of Bellavista. They are sinkholes rather than volcanic craters and are surrounded by *Scalesia* forest. Vermilion flycatchers are often seen, and short-eared owls are spotted on occasion. Although less than 100m from the road, the craters are hidden by vegetation, so go with a guide.

Near Santa Rosa, there is a **tortoise reserve**, with giant tortoises in the wild. There is a trail from the village (ask for directions) that leads through private property to parkland about 3km away. The trail is downhill and often muddy. It forks at the park boundary, with the right fork going up to the small hill of Cerro Chato (3km more) and the left fork going to La Caseta (2km). Bring water.

These sites cannot be visited without an official guide because tourists have become lost. In 1991 an Israeli tourist entered the tortoise reserve without a guide, became lost, and died of thirst. All manner of locals will offer to guide you, as competition is tough. If you want an informed, bilingual guide, stop in at any of the boat tour offices and ask for a recommendation. Otherwise, find your own. Horses can be hired in Santa Rosa.

Near the reserve is a ranch owned by the Devine family. This place always has dozens of giant tortoises and you can wander around at will and take photos for a US$3 fee, which includes a cup of coffee or herbal tea that's welcome if the highland *garúa* (mist) has soaked you. Remember to close the gates as you go through.

PUERTO BAQUERIZO MORENO

This town is mostly the haunt of rich tourists getting off luxury cruises – it's a grandmother's Galápagos. You'll have much better luck finding a tour and other travelers to hang out with in Puerto Ayora.

Places to Stay & Eat

The cheapest hotels include the *Pensión San Francisco* (☎ 05-520-104), which is clean and good (US$8 a double with bath), the *Residencial Northia*, the *Cabañas Don Jorge* (☎ 05-520-208) and several others.

Rositas Restaurant serves tasty bacalao (a local fish) and is one of the best cheap restaurants in town. The *Casa Blanca* is pricier but good, and there are several other restaurants, cafés and bars.

AROUND PUERTO BAQUERIZO MORENO

Frigatebird Hill (locally called Cerro de las Tijeretas) is about 1.5km southwest of Puerto Baquerizo Moreno and can be reached on a trail without a guide. There is a national park information office en route. From the hill, there are beautiful views. Frigate birds nest here and you might see lizards.

A few buses a day go from Baquerizo Moreno to the farming center of El Progreso, about 8km to the east and at the base of the Cerro San Joaquín (896m), the highest point on San Cristóbal. From here, there are occasional buses, or you can hire a jeep or walk 10km to the visitor site of **El Junco Lagoon**, a freshwater lake at about 700m above sea level. The road continues beyond the lagoon, but it's in poor shape. At the northern end of the island, is the **Los Galápagos** visitor site, where giant tortoises can be seen in the wild.

ECUADOR

GALÁPAGOS ISLANDS VISITOR SITES

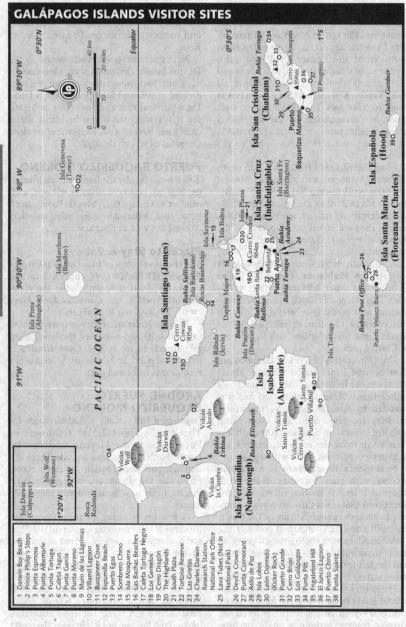

1 Darwin Bay Beach
2 Prince Philip's Steps
3 Punta Espinosa
4 Punta Albemarle
5 Punta Tortuga
6 Caleta Tagus
7 Punta García
8 Punta Moreno
9 Muro de las Lágrimas
10 Villamil Lagoon
11 Buccaneer Cove
12 Espumilla Beach
13 Puerto Egas
14 Sombrero Chino
15 Isla Mosquera
16 Las Bachas Beaches
17 Caleta Tortuga Negra
18 Los Gemelos
19 Cerro Dragón
20 The Highlands
21 South Plaza
22 Las Grietas
23 Tortoise Reserve
24 Charles Darwin
   Research Station,
   National Park Office
25 Lava Tubes (Not in
   National Park)
26 Devil's Crown
27 Punta Cormorant
28 Asilo de Paz
29 Isla Lobos
30 León Dormido
   (Kicker Rock)
31 Puerto Grande
32 Cerro Brujo
33 Los Galápagos
34 Punta Pitt
35 Frigatebird Hill
36 El Junco Lagoon
37 Puerto Chino
38 Punta Suárez

About an hour north of Puerto Baquerizo Moreno by boat is the tiny, rocky **Isla Lobos**, which is the main sea-lion and blue-footed booby colony open to visitors to San Cristóbal. There is a 300m trail, and you can see lava lizards here.

ISLA ISABELA

Most hotels are in Puerto Villamil, from which an 18km road leads up to the tiny village of Santo Tomás.

There are a handful of places to stay, all fairly affordable (about US$10 a double or less). One of the cheapest is *Posada San Vicente* in Puerto Villamil, which has rooms with private bath. The owner, Antonio Gil, is a local guide and offers tours up the volcano on horseback. The *Hotel Ballena Azul* is one of the most popular places; you can contact the staff in Puerto Ayora by asking around. It arranges tours and is one of the more expensive hotels (though still quite cheap). Others include the *Hotel Alexandra* and *El Refugio del Capitán*, both by the beach, and the *Tero Real* and the *Hotel Loja*, on the road to the highlands.

The Hotel Loja has a good restaurant. Most hotels can arrange meals. There are some cheap *comedores* in the port, but you need to ask them in advance to cook a meal for you – giving you an idea of how few visitors there are.

ISLA SANTA MARÍA

This island has fewer than 100 inhabitants, most centered around Puerto Velasco Ibarra. There is a small *hotel* and *restaurant*, run by the famous Margaret Wittmer and her family, and a small gift shop and post office. Call or write for reservations (☎ 05-520-148, Señora Wittmer, Puerto Velasco Ibarra, Santa María, Galápagos; allow a couple of months) or just show up. The place is rarely full.

GALÁPAGOS ISLANDS VISITOR SITES

To protect the islands, the national park authorities allow access to about 50 visitor sites, in addition to the towns and public areas. Other areas are off limits. The visitor sites are where the most interesting wildlife and geology are seen. Apart from the ones mentioned above (near Puerto Ayora and Baquerizo Moreno), most sites are reached by boat.

Normally, landings are made in a panga. Landings are 'wet' (where you hop overboard and wade ashore in knee-deep water) or 'dry' (where you get off onto a pier or rocky outcrop). Take care with these landings; cameras should be wrapped in plastic. People occasionally fall in the surf of a wet landing or slip on the algae-covered rocks of a dry one. Boat captains will not land groups in places other than designated visitor sites. In addition, there are many designated marine sites for snorkeling or diving.

On a cruise of less than a week, try to visit the following islands. **South Plaza** has land iguana, sea-lion and swallow-tailed gull colonies, an *Opuntia* cactus forest and good snorkeling. **Seymour** has nesting colonies of both blue-footed boobies and magnificent frigate birds. **Caleta Tortuga Negra** (Black Turtle Cove), on the north shore of Santa Cruz, has marine turtles and white-tipped sharks.

Isla Bartolomé has a volcanic cone that is easy to climb and gives one of the best views of the islands. There are also penguins, sea lions and good snorkeling. On **San Salvador**, you can walk on a lava flow by Bahía Sullivan, and see marine iguanas, sea lions, fur seals, Galápagos hawks and many kinds of sea birds near Puerto Egas. **Rábida** has a flamingo colony, as well as a colony of irascible bachelor sea lions. You'll see other species almost everywhere. Masked and blue-footed boobies, pelicans, mockingbirds, finches, Galápagos doves, frigate birds, lava lizards and red Sally lightfoot crabs are common.

If you have a full week or more, visit some outlying islands. The red-footed booby is found on **Genovesa** and the small islets surrounding Santa María. The waved albatross breeds only on **Española**, and the flightless Galápagos cormorant is found on the western islands of **Isabela** and **Fernandina**.

Organized Tours

The two kinds of trips within reach of budget travelers are day trips and boat-based trips, with nights spent aboard. Arranging trips in Puerto Ayora is the cheapest way to go, though deals can be found in Guayaquil or Quito. Note that tips are not included. On a cheap one-week tour, the crew and guide are tipped at least US$20 per passenger (about half to the guide).

ECUADOR

Day Trips Most are based in Puerto Ayora, and a few in Puerto Baquerizo Moreno. Several hours are spent sailing to the visitor site(s), the island is visited during the middle of the day, and you'll probably be part of a large group. Only a few islands are close enough to either Santa Cruz or San Cristóbal to be visited on day trips.

Because time is spent going back and forth and because you don't visit the islands early or late in the day, we don't recommend day tours. The cheapest boats may be slow and overcrowded. The island visits may be too brief, the guides poorly informed and the crew lacking an adequate conservationist attitude.

Day-trip operators in Puerto Ayora charge about US$50 per person per day. Talk to other travelers about how good the guide and boat are, or ask at CETUR.

Boat Tours Most visitors go on boat tours and sleep aboard overnight. Tours from four to eight days are the most common. You can't really do the Galápagos justice on a tour shorter than a week, although five days gives a reasonable look. To visit the outlying islands of Isabela and Fernandina, two weeks are recommended. On the first day of a prearranged tour, you arrive from the mainland by air at about noon, so this leaves only half a day in the Galápagos; on the last day, you have to be in the airport in the morning. Thus a 'five-day' tour gives only three full days in the islands. Arranging a tour in Puerto Ayora avoids this.

Tour boats range from small yachts to large cruise ships. The most common type of boat is a motor sailer, which carries six to 16 passengers.

Arranging Tours on Site It is cheaper to arrange a tour independently in Puerto Ayora than to pay for a prearranged tour from the mainland, though the better boats may be full. Arranging a tour can take days or more in the high season, though you can get lucky and find a boat leaving the next day. This is not an option, therefore, for people with a limited amount of time. July and August are especially busy months when cheap tours are difficult to organize. In the low season, tour operators will chase you down as you alight from the bus.

If you are alone or with a friend, find some more people, as even the smallest boats take four passengers and most take eight or more. Check the hotels and restaurants for other travelers and ask around for boats. Your hotel manager can often introduce you to someone. After all, this is a tight little town.

The cheapest and most basic boats are available for about US$50 per day per person, and this should include everything (except park fees, tips and bottled drinks). The cheaper the boat, the more simple the food and more crowded the accommodations. Bargaining over the price is acceptable and sometimes necessary.

The most important thing is to find a boat whose crew you like and which has a good, enthusiastic guide who can point out and explain the wildlife and other items of interest. It is worth paying a little more for a good guide. The cheapest boats often have Spanish-speaking Naturalista II guides, whose function is to fulfill the legal obligation that every boat has a certified guide aboard. Some Naturalista II guides know little about the wildlife and simply act as rangers, making sure groups stay together on the trails and don't molest the wildlife. (You cannot land without a guide and you must always walk around more or less in a group.) Naturalista III guides, on the other hand, are trained, multilingual guides with degrees in biology. Note that all guides are required to carry a guiding card.

Owners, captains, guides and crews change frequently and, in addition, many boats make changes and improvements from year to year. Generally speaking, a boat is only as good as its crew. You should be able to meet the guide and captain and inspect the boat before you leave, and you should have an itinerary agreed upon with the boat owner or captain. You can deal with a crew member or boat representative during your search, but don't hand over any money until you have a signed itinerary. Dealing with tour operators in Puerto Ayora can be tricky because most are booking the same boats and fighting for the same tourist dollar. Stick with the established agencies and ask travelers coming off tours for their impressions.

Get the itinerary in writing to avoid disagreements between you and other passengers and the crew during the cruise. It is particularly important to discuss seasickness and what happens if you have to turn back with a sick passenger. This is more common than anyone will admit and hospitalization is not unheard of. Get it in writing. Even with a written agreement, the itinerary may sometimes be changed, but at least it gives you some bargaining power. The SAEC in Quito has a current Galápagos information packet, which includes a detailed contract in Spanish and English.

Conditions can be cramped and primitive. Washing facilities vary from a bucket of sea water on the cheapest boats to freshwater deck hoses or showers on the better boats. However, it is possible to find a cheap boat with adequate freshwater showers. If you don't want to stay salty, ask about washing facilities. Also inquire about drinking water. We recommend treating the water on most of the cheaper boats or bringing your own fresh water. Agree on the price of bottled drinks before you leave, and make sure that enough of your favorite refreshments are aboard if you don't want to run out. There have been reports of thefts on boats, so watch your stuff.

Because a boat is only as good as the crew running it, it is difficult to make foolproof recommendations. However, although there have been a number of complaints about boats, none of them consistently complain about the same vessel. Adatur, on the waterfront in Puerto Ayora, is a cooperative of economic boat owners and it can assist with tour arrangements.

Although this is the cheapest option, even in the low season total costs (with flight) will be US$750 minimum for a week-long tour. Budget travelers will find that mainland operators (and other guidebooks) discourage them from attempting to make arrangements on the islands, citing the difficulty of finding appropriate boats. As long as you avoid the high season and are flexible with your schedule, you shouldn't have major problems.

Arranging Tours in Advance If you don't have the time or patience to arrange tours on site, you can arrange tours from Quito or Guayaquil. Still, you may have to wait several days or weeks during the high season.

You might get a substantial discount by checking various agencies and seeing if they have any spaces to fill on boats leaving in the next day or two. This applies to the cheaper tours and some of the more expensive ones. Particularly when business is slow, agencies may let you travel cheaply at the last minute rather than leave berths empty. This depends on luck and your bargaining skills.

Some of the cheapest prearranged tours that we know of are the economy tours run by Galasam (Economic Galápagos Tours) in Quito (☎ 02-225-255), at Cordero 1354 and Amazonas, and in Guayaquil (☎ 04-306-289), at 9 de Octubre 424. Galasam has three levels of tour: economy, tourist and luxury.

Seven-day economy tours are aboard small boats with six to 12 bunks in double, triple and quadruple cabins. Bedding is provided and the accommodations are clean but damp and cramped, with little privacy. Plenty of simple but fresh food and juice is served at all meals and a Naturalista II guide accompanies the boat (few guides on economy tours speak English).

There are toilets, and fresh water is available for drinking. Bathing facilities may be saltwater deck hoses or freshwater showers on some boats. There are pre-set itineraries, which allow you to visit most of the central islands and give enough time to see the wildlife.

We have received some letters criticizing the economy-class Galasam tours. Things go wrong occasionally, and when they do, a refund is extremely difficult to obtain. Problems have included last-minute changes of boat (which the contractual small print allows), poor crew, lack of bottled drinks, not sticking to the agreed itinerary, mechanical breakdowns and overbooking. Passengers have to share cabins and are not guaranteed that their cabin mates will be of the same gender; if you are uncomfortable sharing a cabin with a stranger of the opposite sex, make sure you are guaranteed in writing that you won't have to do this. Generally speaking, the cheaper the tour the less comfortable the boat and the less knowledgeable the guide. On the other hand, for every letter saying a tour was poor, another letter says they had a great trip that was a good value.

Eight-day economy tours start at about US$500 to US$600 per person. The US$80 park fee, city tax, airfare and bottled drinks are not included. There are weekly departures. Typically, you'll leave Quito on a specific morning, say Monday, and begin the boat tour on Monday evening. The tour may finish on Sunday night or, possibly, Monday morning at the airport for your flight back. Shorter and cheaper tours are available. Often, a one-week tour is a combination of two shorter tours, for example a Monday to Thursday tour combined with a Thursday to Monday tour. People on the full week spend most of Thursday dropping off and picking up passengers. Try and avoid one-week trips such as this.

Safari Tours in Quito runs a booking service for a number of Galápagos boats and agencies and charges a straight US$25 fee on top of the tour cost. The advantage of this service is that it has a wide variety of

contacts and can help you make the best choice, saving yourself a lot of legwork and uncertainty. It can tell you which boats are more comfortable or have better satisfaction records.

If you add up the cost of the cheapest one-week tour plus airfare and park fees, you get almost no change out of US$1000. If you're going to spend that much, the Galápagos are an important destination for you and you want to get as much out of it as possible. The economy-class boats are usually OK, but if something is going to go wrong, it's more likely to happen on the cheaper boats. If this is all you can afford and you really want to see the Galápagos, go! It'll probably be the adventure of a lifetime. But you might consider spending an extra few hundred dollars and go on a more comfortable, reliable boat and get a decent guide (though more expensive boats have their problems too).

Falkland Islands (Islas Malvinas)

In the South Atlantic Ocean, 300 miles (500km) east of Argentine Patagonia, the controversial Falklands consist of two large islands and many smaller ones.

FACTS ABOUT THE ISLANDS
History

Despite a possible early Indian presence, the Islands were unpeopled when 17th-century European sailors began to frequent the area. Their Spanish name, Malvinas, derives from French navigators of St Malo.

In 1764, French colonists settled at Port Louis, East Falkland, but soon withdrew under Spanish pressure. Spain expelled a British outpost from Port Egmont, West Falkland, in 1767, but Britain restored it under threat of war; Port Egmont was later abandoned by the British under ambiguous circumstances.

Spain placed a penal colony at Port Louis, then abandoned it to whalers and sealers. In the early 1820s, after the United Provinces of the River Plate claimed successor rights to Spain, a Buenos Aires entrepreneur named Louis Vernet attempted a livestock and sealing project. Vernet's seizure of American sealers, however, triggered reprisals that damaged Port Louis beyond recovery. Buenos Aires then maintained a token force, which was expelled by the British Royal Navy in 1833.

The Falklands languished until wool became an important commodity in the mid-19th century. The Falkland Islands Company (FIC) became the Islands' largest landholder, and the population, mostly stranded mariners and holdover gauchos, grew with the arrival of English and Scottish immigrants. A few of these consolidated the remaining pasturelands not claimed by the FIC into large holdings. Half the population resided in the port capital of Stanley, founded in 1844, while the rest worked on sheep stations. Most original landowners lived and worked locally, but their descendants often returned to Britain, running their businesses as absentees.

At a Glance

Country Name	Falkland Islands
Area	4700 sq mi (12,176 sq km)
Population	2564
Population Density	0.21 per sq km
Capital	Stanley
Head of State	Queen Elizabeth II (Governor Donald Lamont)
Official Language	English
Currency	Falkland Islands Pound/Pound Sterling (£)
Exchange Rate	US$1 = FI£0.63 FI£1 = UK£1
Per Capita GNP	£18,010 (1997)
Inflation Rate	3% (1997)

From the late 1970s, local government encouraged subdivision of large landholdings to benefit family farmers. The 1982 Falklands War, subsequent expansion of deep-sea fishing and preliminary offshore petroleum exploration have brought rapid change and prosperity.

FALKLAND ISLANDS (ISLAS MALVINAS)

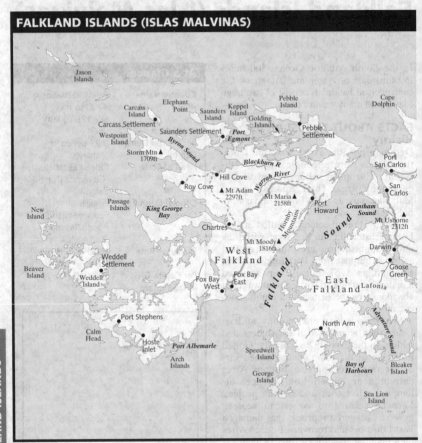

Falklands War Although Argentina had persistently claimed the Falklands since 1833, successive British governments were slow to publicly acknowledge the claim's seriousness. By 1971, however, the Foreign & Commonwealth Office (FCO) reached a communications agreement giving Argentina roles in air transport, fuel supplies, shipping and even immigration. Concerned about Argentina's chronic instability, Islanders and their UK supporters thought the agreement ominous, and suspected the FCO of secretly arranging transfer of the Islands. This process dragged on for a decade, during which Argentina's brutal 'Dirty War' gave Islanders more reason for concern.

Facing pressure from Argentines fed up with corruption, economic chaos and totalitarian ruthlessness, General Leopoldo Galtieri's disintegrating military government invaded the Islands on April 2, 1982. Seizure of the Malvinas briefly united Argentina, but Prime Minister Margaret Thatcher of Britain, herself in shaky political circumstances, sent a naval task force to retake the Islands. Experienced British ground troops routed ill-trained, poorly supplied Argentine conscripts; Argentina's surrender averted Stanley's destruction.

Geography & Climate
The land area of 4700 sq miles (12,176 sq km) is equivalent to Northern Ireland or

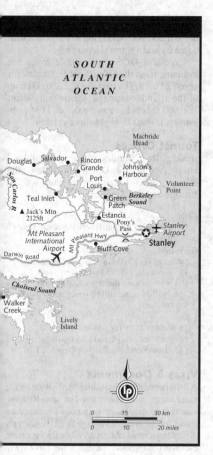

SOUTH
ATLANTIC
OCEAN

Every part of the Falklands outside Stanley is known colloquially as 'camp,' including those parts of East Falkland accessible by road from Stanley, all of West Falkland, and the numerous smaller islands.

Flora & Fauna

Grasses and prostrate shrubs dominate the flora. Native tussock grass once lined the coast but proved vulnerable to overgrazing and fire. Most pasture is rank white grass *(Cortaderia pilosa),* supporting only one sheep per four or five acres.

Beaches, headlands and estuaries support large concentrations of sub-Antarctic wildlife. Five penguin species breed regularly: the Magellanic (jackass), rockhopper, macaroni, gentoo and king.

One of the most beautiful breeding birds is the black-browed albatross, but there are also striated and crested caracaras, cormorants, gulls, hawks, peregrine falcons, oystercatchers, snowy sheathbills, sheldgeese, steamer ducks and swans – among others. Most are present in large, impressive colonies, easily photographed.

Elephant seals, sea lions and fur seals breed on shore, while six species of dolphin have been observed offshore. Killer whales are common, but not the larger South Atlantic whales.

Over the past decade, local government has encouraged nature-oriented tourism by constructing small lodges at outstanding sites, but there are also less-structured opportunities.

Government & Politics

A London-appointed governor administers the Falklands, but the locally elected Legislative Council (Legco) exercises significant power. Five of its eight members come from Stanley; the remainder represent the camp. Selected Legco members advise the governor as part of executive council (Exco).

Economy

Traditionally, the economy depended almost entirely on wool, but fishing has eclipsed agriculture as a revenue-producer. Licensed Asian and European fleets have funded improvements in public services like schools, roads, telephones and medical care. Local government issued the first offshore oil exploration licenses in 1996, a matter

the state of Connecticut. Falkland Sound separates East and West Falkland; only a few smaller islands have settlements. Despite a dismal reputation, the oceanic climate is temperate (if windy). Summer temperatures rarely reach 75°F (24°C), but sustained subfreezing temperatures are unusual. Annual rainfall here is only about 24 inches (600mm).

Except for East Falkland's low-lying Lafonia peninsula, terrain is hilly to mountainous, reaching about 2300 feet (705m). The most interesting geological features are 'stone runs' of quartzite boulders descending from many ridges and peaks. Bays, inlets, estuaries and beaches form an attractive coastline that is home to abundant wildlife.

FALKLAND ISLANDS

about which some Islanders feel ambivalent because of the potential environmental impact. Results from the earliest test wells are inconclusive.

Most Stanley residents work for Falkland Island Government (FIG) or FIC. While FIC has sold all its pastoral property, it continues to provide shipping and other commercial services. In camp, nearly everyone is involved in wool production on relatively small, widely dispersed, family-owned units. Farmers are struggling economically because of low wool prices. Tourism is economically limited, but facilities are always adequate and often excellent.

Population & People

By the 1996 census, the population is 2564; two-thirds live in Stanley, the rest in camp. Over 60% of permanent residents are native-born, some tracing their ancestry back seven generations. Most others are immigrants or temporary residents from the UK. Islanders' surnames indicate varied European backgrounds, but all speak English.

Because of their isolation and small numbers, Falklanders are versatile and adaptable. They are also hospitable, often welcoming strangers for 'smoko,' the traditional midmorning tea or coffee break, or for a drink. This is especially true in camp, where visitors can be infrequent. It is customary to bring a small gift – rum is a special favorite.

About 2000 British military personnel (squaddies) reside at Mt Pleasant Airport, about 35 miles (56km) southwest of Stanley, and at a few other scattered sites.

FACTS FOR THE VISITOR

In many ways the Falklands are a small country, with their own immigration and customs regulations, currency and other unique features. Wildlife, particularly penguins, attracts most visitors, but there are also historical sites.

Planning

From October to March, migratory birds and mammals return to beaches and headlands. Very long daylight hours permit outdoor activities even if poor weather spoils part of the day.

Visitors should bring good waterproof clothing; a pair of rubber boots is useful. Summer never gets truly hot and high winds can lower the ambient temperature, but the climate does not justify Antarctic preparations. Trekkers should bring a sturdy tent with a rain fly and a warm sleeping bag.

Excellent DOS topographic maps are available from the Secretariat in Stanley for about £2 each. The two-sheet, 1:250,000 map of the Islands is suitable for most uses, but 1:50,000 sheets have more detail. ITM publishes a 1:300,000 single-sheet version.

Tourist Offices

Besides their Stanley office and Falkland House (see Visas & Documents below), the Islands have tourist representation in Europe and the Americas.

Chile
  (☎ 61-228312) Broom Travel, Roca 924, Punta Arenas
Germany
  (☎/fax 61-05-1304) HS Travel & Consulting PO Box 1447, 64529 Moerfelden;
  this is no longer officially affiliated with the Tourist Board, but still provides up-to-date information
USA
  (☎ 860-868-1710, fax 860-868-1718; patread@aol.com) Tread Lightly Travel, One Titus Road, Washington Depot, CT 06794

Visas & Documents

All nationalities, including British citizens, must carry valid passports. For non-Britons, visa requirements are generally the same as those for foreigners visiting the UK, though Argentines must obtain an advance visa (not easily accomplished, though some have traveled on second passports). According to a joint statement released by the FCO and Argentine Foreign Relations Ministry at the time of this writing, Argentines should soon find it easier to travel to the Islands. For details, consult Falkland House (☎ 020-7222-2542, fax 020-7222-2375; rep@figo.u-net.com), 14 Broadway, Westminster, London SW1H 0BH, or the Falkland Islands Tourist Board (☎ 22215, fax 22619, manager@tourism.org.fk).

Customs

Customs regulations are few except for limits on alcohol and tobacco, which are heavily taxed.

Money

The Falkland Islands pound (£), divided into 100 pence (p), is on par with the British pound. There are banknotes for £5, £10, £20 and £50, and coins for 1p, 2p, 5p, 10p, 20p, 50p and £1. Sterling circulates alongside local currency, which is not valid in the UK.

Approximate official rates at press time were as follows:

country	unit		pounds
Australia	A$1	=	£0.41
Canada	C$1	=	£0.41
euro	€1	=	£0.67
France	FF1	=	£0.10
Germany	DM1	=	£0.34
Japan	¥100	=	£0.53
New Zealand	NZ$1	=	£0.33
USA	US$1	=	£0.62

Credit cards are becoming more widely used, but traveler's checks are also readily accepted. Britons with guarantee cards can cash personal checks up to £50 at Standard Chartered Bank.

Costs Recent development has encouraged short-stay accommodations at prices around £50 per day (meals included), but B&Bs in Stanley start around £15. Cheaper, self-catering cabins are available in camp, as are opportunities for trekking and camping; some isolated families still welcome visitors without charge.

Air travel within the Falklands costs approximately £1 per minute. See Getting Around for sample fares.

Food prices are roughly equivalent to the UK, but fresh meat (chiefly mutton) is cheap. Stanley restaurants are expensive, except for short orders and snacks.

Post & Communications
Postal services are good. There are one or two airmails weekly to the UK, but parcels heavier than 1 pound (0.45 kg) go by sea four or five times yearly. The Falkland Islands Government Air Service (FIGAS) delivers to outer settlements and islands. Correspondents should address letters to Post Office, Stanley, Falkland Islands, via London, England.

Cable and Wireless PLC operates both local and long-distance telephones; local numbers have five digits. The international country code is ☎ 500, valid for numbers in Stanley and in camp.

Local calls cost 5p per minute, calls to the UK 15p for six seconds, and calls to the rest of the world cost 18p per six seconds. Operator-assisted calls cost the same, but have a three-minute minimum. Reverse-charge (collect) calls are possible only locally and to the UK.

Internet Resources
Internet connections are recent but rapidly improving. The Tourist Board has an informative website (www.tourism.org.fk).

Books
The most readily available general account is Ian Strange's *The Falkland Islands*, 3rd edition. For a summary of the Falklands controversy, see Robert Fox's *Antarctica and the South Atlantic: Discovery, Development and Dispute*. On the war, try Max Hastings and Simon Jenkins' *Battle for the Falklands*.

Robin Woods' *Guide to Birds of the Falkland Islands* is a detailed account of the Islands' bird life. Strange's *Field Guide to the Wildlife of the Falkland Islands and South Georgia* is also worth a look. Trekkers should acquire Julian Fisher's *Walks and Climbs in the Falkland Islands*.

Media
The Falkland Islands Broadcasting Service (FIBS) produces local programs and carries BBC news programs from the British Forces Broadcasting Service (BFBS). The nightly public announcements, to which people listen religiously, are worth hearing.

Television is available through BFBS and via cable. The only print media are the *Teaberry Express* and the weekly *Penguin News*.

Photography
Color and B&W print film are readily available at reasonable prices. Color slide film is less dependably available.

Time
The Falkland Islands are four hours behind GMT/UTC. In summer, Stanley observes daylight saving time, but camp remains on standard time.

Electricity
Electric current operates on 220/240V, 50Hz. Plugs are identical to those in the UK.

FALKLAND ISLANDS

Weights & Measures

The metric system is official, but most people use imperial measures. There's a conversion table at the back of this book.

Health

No special precautions are necessary, but carry adequate insurance. Flights from Britain may be diverted to yellow fever zones in Africa, so authorities recommend vaccination.

Wind and sun can combine to burn unsuspecting visitors severely. Wind also contributes to the danger of hypothermia in inclement weather. Stanley's King Edward VII Memorial Hospital has excellent medical and dental facilities.

Useful Organizations

Based in both the UK and Stanley, Falklands Conservation is a nonprofit organization promoting wildlife conservation research as well as the preservation of shipwrecks and historic sites. Membership is available from Falklands Conservation (☎ 020-8346-5011), 1 Princes Rd, Finchley, London N3 2DA, England. The representative in Stanley (☎ 22247, fax 22288) is on Ross Rd, opposite Malvina House Hotel.

The Falkland Islands Association (☎ 020-7222-0028), 2 Greycoat Place, Westminster, London SW1P 1SD, is a political lobbying group that publishes a quarterly newsletter.

Dangers & Annoyances

Near Stanley and in a few camp locations on both East and West Falkland, there remain unexploded plastic land mines, but minefields are clearly marked and no civilian has ever been injured. *Never* enter a minefield: mines bear the weight of a penguin or even a sheep, but not of a human. Report suspicious objects to the Explosive Ordnance Disposal office (☎ 22229), near Town Hall, which has free minefield maps.

Despite its firm appearance, 'soft camp,' covered by white grass, is very boggy, though not dangerous.

Business Hours

Government offices are open on weekdays 8 am to noon and 1:15 to 4:30 pm. Most larger businesses in Stanley stay open until 7 or 8 pm, but smaller shops may open only a few hours daily. Weekend business hours are reduced. Camp stores keep limited schedules but often open on request.

Public Holidays & Special Events

In a land where most people lived in physical and social isolation, the annual sports meetings provided a regular opportunity to share news, meet new people and participate in friendly competitions like horse racing, bull riding and sheepdog trials.

In late February, the rotating camp sports meeting on West Falkland maintains this tradition the best, hosting 'two-nighters.' Islanders party till they drop, sleep a few hours, and get up and start all over again. Independent visitors are welcome, but arrange accommodations (usually floor space for your sleeping bag) in advance.

The following holidays are observed:

New Year's Day	January 1
Camp Sports	Late February (dates vary)
Good Friday	March/April (date varies)
Queen's Birthday	April 21
Liberation Day	June 14
Falklands Day	August 14
Battle of the Falklands (1914)	December 8
Christmas Day	December 25
Boxing Day/Stanley Sports	December 26/27

Activities

Wildlife is the major attraction. Penguins, other birds and marine mammals are easily approached, even at developed sites like Sea Lion Island, but there are other equally interesting, undeveloped areas. Keep a respectful distance.

Fishing can be excellent; early March to late April is the best season for hooking sea trout, which requires a license (£10) from the Stanley post office. Trekking and camping are feasible, though some landowners and the tourist board discourage camping because of fire danger and disturbance to stock and wildlife. It is also possible to visit the 1982 battlefields.

Accommodations

Stanley has several B&Bs and hotels, while some farms have converted surplus buildings into comfortable lodges. Others have self-catering cottages, trailers or Portakabin shelters. (These are modular units resembling cargo containers with added doors and windows. Many were left on the Islands by the British military.)

In areas not frequented by tourists, Islanders often welcome houseguests; many farms have 'outside houses' or shanties that visitors may use with permission. Camping is possible only with permission.

Food & Drinks

Mutton, the dietary staple, is very cheap. Islanders usually consume their own produce, but a hydroponic market garden now produces aubergines (eggplant), tomatoes, lettuce and other salad greens.

Stanley snack bars offer fish and chips, muttonburgers, pizza, sausage rolls and pasties, while the hotels have decent restaurants. At pubs, beer and hard liquor, particularly whisky and rum, are the favorites.

GETTING THERE & AWAY

From RAF Brize Norton, in Oxfordshire, England, there are regular flights to Mt Pleasant International Airport (16 hours, plus an hour's layover on Ascension Island). Southbound flights leave Brize Norton Monday and Thursday; northbound flights leave Mt Pleasant Wednesday and Saturday.

The return fare is £2302, but reduced Apex fares cost £1414 with 30-day advance purchase. Groups of six or more pay £1192 each. Travelers who are continuing on to Chile can purchase one-way tickets for half the return fare.

For reservations in London, contact Gail Spooner at Falkland House (☎ 020-7222-2542), 14 Broadway, Westminster SW1H 0BH. In Stanley, you can contact the Falkland Islands Company (☎ 27633), on Crozier Place.

From Santiago, LanChile flies to Mt Pleasant every Saturday via Punta Arenas. Santiago fares are US$410 one way, US$680 return (US$370 one way, US$630 return with seven-day advance purchase). Punta Arenas fares are US$320 one way, US$490 return (US$280 one way, US$420 return with seven-day advance purchase). Though, at the time of writing, LanChile flights were suspended due to the detention of General Pinochet in London, flights were expected to resume after the Anglo-Argentine agreement, by whose terms two monthly flights to

the Falklands from Punta Arenas would make stops in Río Gallegos, Argentina.

GETTING AROUND

Outside the Stanley-Mt Pleasant area the only regular flights are provided, on demand, by FIGAS. Sample return fares from Stanley include Salvador (£50), Darwin (£76), San Carlos (£78), Port Howard (£94), Sea Lion Island (£95), Pebble Island (£106), Fox Bay East or West (£121) and Carcass Island (£145). Some grass airstrips only accept a limited payload, and baggage is limited to 30 pounds (14kg) per person.

Rental vehicles are available in Stanley, and visitors may use their own state or national driving licenses in the Falklands for up to 12 months. Some lodges provide 4WDs with drivers or guides for their guests.

Byron Marine Ltd (☎ 22245, fax 22246), carries a small number of passengers on its freighter *MV Tamar* while delivering wool and other goods to outlying settlements. Berths are limited; day trips cost £20, while overnights cost £25.

STANLEY

Stanley's metal-clad houses, brightly painted corrugated metal roofs and large kitchen gardens make a striking contrast to the surrounding moorland. Founded in 1845, the new capital was a supply and repair port, but Cape Horn shipping began to avoid it when boats were scuttled under questionable circumstances. In the late 19th century, Stanley grew more rapidly as the transshipment point for wool between camp and the UK.

As the wool trade grew, so did the influence of the Falkland Islands Company, Stanley's largest employer. Although its political and economic dominance was uncontested, its relatively high wages and good housing offered a paternalistic security. 'Tied houses,' however, were available only while the employee remained with FIC.

Stanley remains the service center for the wool industry, but has also become a significant port for Asian and European fishing fleets.

Orientation

On a steep north-facing hillside, Stanley has sprawled east and west along Stanley

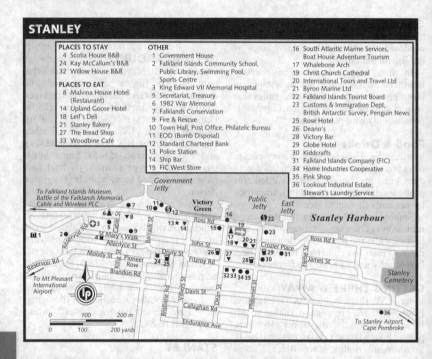

STANLEY

PLACES TO STAY
4   Scotia House B&B
24 Kay McCallum's B&B
32 Willow House B&B

PLACES TO EAT
8   Malvina House Hotel
    (Restaurant)
14 Upland Goose Hotel
18 Leif's Deli
21 Stanley Bakery
27 The Bread Shop
33 Woodbine Café

OTHER
1   Government House
2   Falkland Islands Community School,
    Public Library, Swimming Pool,
    Sports Centre
3   King Edward VII Memorial Hospital
5   Secretariat, Treasury
6   1982 War Memorial
7   Falklands Conservation
9   Fire & Rescue
10 Town Hall, Post Office, Philatelic Bureau
11 EOD (Bomb Disposal)
12 Standard Chartered Bank
13 Police Station
14 Ship Bar
15 FIC West Store

16 South Atlantic Marine Services,
    Boat House Adventure Tourism
17 Whalebone Arch
19 Christ Church Cathedral
20 International Tours and Travel Ltd
21 Byron Marine Ltd
22 Falkland Islands Tourist Board
23 Customs & Immigration Dept,
    British Antarctic Survey, Penguin News
25 Rose Hotel
26 Deano's
28 Victory Bar
29 Globe Hotel
30 Kiddcrafts
31 Falkland Islands Company (FIC)
34 Home Industries Cooperative
35 Pink Shop
36 Lookout Industrial Estate,
    Stewart's Laundry Service

Harbour. Ross Rd, the main street, runs the length of the harbor, but most government offices, businesses and houses are within a few blocks of each other.

Information

Tourist Offices The Falkland Islands Tourist Board (☎ 22215, fax 22619; manager@tourism .org.fk), at the public jetty, distributes an excellent guide to Stanley, as well as other useful brochures. Hours are 8 am to noon and 1:15 to 4:30 pm weekdays.

At Mt Pleasant International Airport, the Mount Pleasant Travel Office (☎ 76691) is at 12 Facility Main Reception,

Money Standard Chartered Bank, on Ross Rd between Barrack and Villiers Sts, changes foreign currency and traveler's checks, and cashes personal checks drawn on UK banks. Hours are 8:30 am to noon and 1:15 to 3 pm weekdays.

Post & Communications The Post Office is in Town Hall, on Ross Rd at Barrack St. Cable Wireless PLC, on Ross Rd West near Gov-

ernment House, operates phone, telegram, telex and fax services. Magnetic cards are cheaper than operator-assisted overseas calls. Counter hours are 8:30 am to 5 pm, but public booths are open 24 hours.

Emergency King Edward VII Memorial Hospital (☎ 27328 for appointments, or ☎ 27410 for emergencies), at the west end of St Mary's Walk, has superb facilities.

Things to See

Distinguished **Christ Church Cathedral** (1892), is a massive brick-and-stone construction with attractive stained-glass windows. On the small nearby plaza, the restored **Whalebone Arch** commemorates the 1933 centennial of British rule.

Since the mid-19th century, London-appointed governors have inhabited rambling **Government House** on Ross Rd. Just beyond it, the **Battle of the Falklands Memorial** commemorates a WWI naval engagement, while the **Falkland Islands Museum** is a recent project, featuring professional exhibits on history and natural history.

Just opposite the Secretariat, on Ross Rd, is the **1982 War Memorial,** designed by a Falklander living overseas, paid for by public subscription and built with volunteer labor. At the east end of Ross Road, the Islands' dead rest at **Stanley Cemetery**, where surnames like Felton and Biggs are as common as Smith and Jones are in the UK.

Activities
Stanley's swimming pool, on Reservoir Rd, has become very popular. There are also sites for squash, badminton, basketball and the like.

Fishing for sea trout, mullet and smelt is popular on the Murrell River, which is walking distance from Stanley, but there are many other suitable places. Some are easily accessible from the Mt Pleasant highway.

Special Events
The Stanley Sports, held after Christmas, feature horse racing (with betting), bull riding and other events. In March, the competitive Horticultural Show displays the produce of kitchen gardens in Stanley and camp, plus a variety of baked goods, and includes a spirited auction. The July Crafts Fair presents the work of local weavers, leatherworkers, photographers and artists. There are many talented illustrators and painters; watercolorist James Peck has exhibited his paintings in Buenos Aires.

Places to Stay
Accommodations are good, but limited and not cheap; reservations are advisable. Breakfast is always included; inquire about full board. The most economical is homey *Kay McCallum's B&B* (☎ 21071), at 14 Drury St, charging £16 per person. Nick and Sheila Hadden's *Willow House B&B* (☎/fax 21014), 27 Fitzroy Rd, also charges £16, while Bob and Celia Stewart's *Scotia House B&B* (☎ 21191), 12 St Mary's Walk, costs £18.50.

Places to Eat
Two bakeries serve bread, snacks and light meals: *The Bread Shop* on Dean St (open daily 7:30 am to 1:30 pm), and *Stanley Bakery*, Waverley House, Philomel St (open weekdays 8:30 am to 3:30 pm, Saturday 9 am to 12:30 pm). *Woodbine Café*, 29 Fitzroy Rd, serves fish and chips, pizza, sausage rolls

and similar items. *Leif's Deli*, 23 John St, has specialty foods and snacks.

The upscale *Malvina House Hotel*, 3 Ross Rd, has beautiful grounds and an excellent conservatory restaurant. The venerable *Upland Goose Hotel*, a mid-19th-century building at 20/22 Ross Rd, also serves meals.

Entertainment
Of Stanley's several pubs, the most popular is the *Globe Hotel* on Crozier Place, but try also the *Rose Hotel* on Brisbane Rd and the *Victory Bar* on Philomel St. The Upland Goose Hotel houses the *Ship Bar*, and Monty's Restaurant, on John St, also has a bar, *Deano's*.

In winter, the pubs sponsor a darts league, with tournaments in Town Hall, where there are also dances with live music throughout the year. There are no cinemas, but hotels and guesthouses have video lounges.

Shopping
For locally spun and knitted woolens, visit the Home Industries Cooperative on Fitzroy Rd. Kiddcrafts, 2-A Philomel St, makes stuffed penguins and other soft toys with great appeal for children.

The Pink Shop, 33 Fitzroy Rd, sells gifts and souvenirs, Falklands and general-interest books (including selected LP guides), and excellent wildlife prints by owner Tony Chater.

Postage stamps, available from the Post Office and from the Philatelic Bureau, are popular with collectors. The Bureau also sells stamps from South Georgia and British Antarctic Territory. The Treasury, in the Secretariat behind the Liberation Monument, sells commemorative coins.

Getting There & Around
For international flight information, see the Getting There & Away section earlier in this chapter.

From Stanley, FIGAS (☎ 27219) serves outlying destinations in nine-passenger aircraft, arranging itineraries by demand; contact FIGAS when you know where and when you wish to go, and listen to FIBS at 6:30 pm the night before to learn your departure time. Occasionally, usually around holidays, flights are heavily booked and seats may not be available.

Passage may also be arranged through the Tourist Board on the public jetty.

To/From the Airport Mt Pleasant International Airport is 35 miles southwest of Stanley by road, while Stanley Airport is about 3 miles east of town.

Falkland Islands Tours and Travel (☎/fax 21775) takes passengers to Mt Pleasant for £13 each; you can call for reservations the day before. They will also take groups to Stanley Airport or meet them there. For cabs, contact Ben's Taxi Service (☎ 21191) or Lowe's Taxis (☎ 21381).

AROUND STANLEY
Stanley Harbour
Maritime History Trail

See the Tourist Board for a brochure on wrecks and condemned ships. There are informational panels near vessels like the *Jhelum* (an East Indiaman deserted by her crew in 1871 when she began to sink), whose hulk is still visible above the water; the *Charles Cooper* (an American packet still used for storage); and the *Lady Elizabeth* (a three-masted freighter that struck a rock in 1913).

Penguin Walk & Gypsy Cove

The Falklands' most convenient penguin colonies are about 1½ hours' walk from Stanley. From the east end of Ross Rd, continue beyond the cemetery and cross the bridge over the inlet known as the Canache, past the *Lady Elizabeth* and Stanley Airport to Yorke Bay.

Penguins crowd the sandy beach where, unfortunately, the Argentines buried plastic mines; get your views of the birds by walking along the minefield fence. Further on, at Gypsy Cove, are nesting Magellanic penguins (avoid stepping on burrows) and other shorebirds.

Kidney Island

Covered with tussock grass, this small reserve supports a wide variety of wildlife, including rockhopper penguins and sea lions. You can arrange visits through the agricultural officer (☎ 27355).

CAMP

Nearly everyone in 'camp' (a term for all of the Falklands outside Stanley) is engaged in

sheep ranching. Camp settlements began as company towns, hamlets near sheltered harbors where coastal shipping could collect the wool. Single shepherds lived at 'outside houses' that still dot the countryside.

Many wildlife sites are on smaller offshore islands like Sea Lion Island and Pebble Island, where there are comfortable but fairly costly tourist lodges. These are described in detail below, but there are also alternatives for budget travelers.

East Falkland

East Falkland's road network consists primarily of a good highway to Mt Pleasant International Airport and Goose Green, with a spur to San Carlos. From Pony's Pass on the Mt Pleasant Hwy, there is a good road north to the Estancia (a farm west of Stanley) and Port Louis, and an excellent road west from Estancia toward Douglas and Port San Carlos. Most other tracks are for 4WDs only.

Several Stanley operators run day trips to East Falkland settlements, including Tony Smith's Discovery Tours (☎ 21027, fax 22304), Sharon Halford's Ten Acre Tours (☎ 21155, fax 21950), Dave Eynon's South Atlantic Marine Services (☎ 21145, fax 22674; sams@horizon.co.fk) and Montana Short's Photographic Tours (☎/fax 21076).

Port Louis Dating from the French foundation of the colony in 1764, Port Louis is the Falklands' oldest settlement. One of the colony's original buildings is an ivy-covered, 19th-century farmhouse, still occupied by farm employees, but there are also ruins of the French governor's house and fortress and Louis Vernet's settlement scattered nearby. Visit the grave of Matthew Brisbane, Vernet's lieutenant, murdered by gauchos after the British left him in charge of the settlement in 1833.

It is possible to trek from Port Louis along the northern coast of East Falkland to Volunteer Beach, a scenic itinerary with an extraordinary abundance of wildlife. To visit the settlement or seek permission for the trek, contact manager Michael Morrison (☎ 31004).

Volunteer Beach Volunteer Beach, part of Johnson's Harbour Farm, is east of Port Louis. It has the Falklands' largest concentration of king penguins, a growing colony of about 150 breeding pairs. At Volunteer Point, several hours walk east, is an offshore breeding colony of southern fur seals (bring binoculars). Return along Volunteer Lagoon to see more birds and elephant seals. If attempting the trip on your own, contact owner George Smith of Johnson's Harbour (☎ 31399) for permission.

San Carlos In 1982, British forces came ashore at San Carlos, on Falkland Sound; in 1983, the sheep station there was subdivided and sold to half-a-dozen local families. There is fishing on the San Carlos River, north of the settlement. Comfortable Blue Beach Lodge (☎ 32205) charges £55 with full board and offers boat excursions.

Across San Carlos Water, but four hours away by foot, is the **Ajax Bay Refrigeration Plant**, a 1950s CDC (Colonial Development Corporation) boondoggle. Gentoo penguins wander through its ruins, which served as a field hospital in 1982. Take a flashlight if you plan to explore.

Darwin & Goose Green At the narrow isthmus that separates Lafonia from northern East Falkland, Darwin was the site of an early *saladero*, where gauchos slaughtered feral cattle and tanned their hides. It later became the center of FIC's camp operations and, with nearby Goose Green, the largest settlement outside Stanley. The heaviest ground fighting of the Falklands War took place at Goose Green, site of the **Argentine Cemetery**.

Sea Lion Island Off East Falkland's south coast, tiny Sea Lion is less than a mile across, but teems with wildlife, including five penguin species, enormous cormorant colonies, giant petrels, and the charmingly tame predator known as the Johnny rook (striated westerly). Hundreds of elephant seals crowd the island's sandy coastline, while sea lions dot the narrow gravel beaches below its southern bluffs or lurk in the towering tussock.

Much of the credit for Sea Lion's wildlife has to go to Terry and Doreen Clifton, who farmed it from the mid-1970s until they sold it recently. The Cliftons developed their 2300-acre (920-hectare) ranch with the idea that wildlife and livestock were compatible,

and Sea Lion was one of few working farms with any substantial cover of native tussock grass. Through improved fencing and other conscientious practices, the Cliftons made it a successful sheep station and a popular tourist site, mostly for day trips from Stanley and Mt Pleasant.

Sea Lion Lodge (☎ 32004) offers twin-bed rooms with full board for £55 per person. At least two full days would be desirable for seeing the island in its entirety.

West Falkland

Pioneers settled West Falkland only in the late 1860s, but within a decade new sheep stations covered the entire island and others offshore. One of the most interesting experiments was the Keppel Island Mission for Indians from Tierra del Fuego.

West Falkland (nearly as large as East Falkland) and adjacent islands have fine wildlife sites. The only proper roads run from Port Howard on Falkland Sound to Chartres on King George Bay and south to Fox Bay, with a northwestward extension toward Hill Cove. But a system of rough tracks is also suitable for Land Rovers and motorcycles, and there is good trekking in the mountainous interior. Only a few places have formal tourist facilities.

Port Howard Scenic Port Howard, at the foot of 2158-foot (658m) Mt Maria, remains intact after sale to its local managers in 1987. About 50 people live on the station, which has its own dairy, grocery, slaughterhouse, social club and other amenities. It will be the West Falkland port for the anticipated ferry across Falkland Sound.

Port Howard's immediate surroundings offer hiking, riding and fishing; wildlife sites are more remote. Visitors can view shearing and other camp activities, and there is a small war museum. Accommodation at *Port Howard Lodge* (☎/fax 42187), the former manager's house, costs £55 per person with full board.

It's possible to hike up the valley of the Warrah River, a good trout stream, and past Turkey Rocks to the Blackburn River and Hill Cove, another pioneer farm. Ask permission to cross property boundaries, and remember to close gates; where the track is faint, look for old telephone lines. There are longer hikes south toward Chartres, Fox Bay and Port Stephens. Mt Maria makes a good day hike.

Pebble Island Off the north coast of West Falkland, elongated Pebble has varied topography, extensive wetlands and a good sample of wildlife. *Pebble Island Hotel (☎/fax 41093)* charges £47.50 per person with full board, but you can ask for self-catering cottages at the settlement. *Marble Mountain Shanty*, at the west end of the island, charges £15 per night.

Keppel Island In 1853, the South American Missionary Society established itself on Keppel to catechize Yahgan Indians from Tierra del Fuego and teach them to grow potatoes. The settlement was controversial because the government suspected that the Yahgans had been brought against their will, but it still remained until 1898.

Interesting ruins include the chapel, the bailiff's house, and the stone walls of Indian dwellings. Keppel is also a good wildlife site, but visits are difficult to arrange because it has no permanent residents. If interested in visiting, contact Mr LR Fell (☎ 41001).

Saunders Island In 1767, Spanish forces dislodged the British from Port Egmont, site of the first British garrison (1765), and nearly precipitated a general war. After the British left in 1774, Spain razed the settlement, but extensive ruins still remain.

Saunders has plenty of wildlife and good trekking to 'The Neck,' whose sandspit beach links it to Elephant Point peninsula, about four hours from the settlement. Near The Neck is a colony of black-browed albatrosses and rockhopper penguins, along with a few king penguins and a solitary chinstrap; farther on are thousands of Magellanic penguins, kelp gulls, skuas and a colony of elephant seals.

David and Suzan Pole-Evans on Saunders (☎ 41298) rent a comfortable self-catering *cottage* in the settlement for £10 per person per night, as well as a six-bunk Portakabin (bedding supplied), with a gas stove and outside chemical toilet, at The Neck. Fresh milk and eggs are usually available, but otherwise visitors should bring their own food. Depending on the farm

workload, transportation to The Neck is available for £10 per person. Inexpensive mountain bikes are for rent.

Port Stephens Port Stephens' rugged headlands, near the settlement's sheltered harbor, host thousands of rockhoppers and other sea birds, while Calm Head, about two hours' walk, has excellent views of the jagged shoreline and the powerful South Atlantic. One longer trek goes to the abandoned sealing station at Albemarle and past huge colonies of gentoo penguins. The Arch Islands, inaccessible except by boat, take their name from the huge gap that the ocean has eroded in the largest of the group.

If interested in visiting Port Stephens and trekking in the vicinity, contact Peter or Anne Robertson (☎ 42307) at the settlement or Leon and Pam Berntsen (☎ 42309) at Albemarle Station.

Weddell Island Scottish pioneer John Hamilton acquired this western offshore island, the third largest in the archipelago, to experiment with tussock grass restoration and forest plantations, and import Highland cattle, Shetland ponies, and exotic wildlife like guanacos, Patagonian foxes and otters. The abundant local wildlife includes gentoo and Magellanic penguins, great skuas, night herons, giant petrels and striated caracaras.

Farm owners John and Steph Ferguson (☎ 42398) welcome guests at *Seaview Cottage, Hamilton Cottage* or the newly remodeled *Mountain View House* for £15 per person per night (self-catering) or £30 per person per night with full board.

New Island The Falklands' most westerly inhabited island was a refuge for whalers from Britain and North America from the late 18th century well into the 19th. There remain ruins of a shore-based, turn-of-the-century Norwegian whaling factory that failed because there simply were not enough whales.

On the precipitous western coast are large colonies of rockhopper penguins and black-browed albatrosses, and a rookery of southern fur seals. Potential visitors should contact Tony or Annie Chater (☎ 21399), or Ian or María Strange (☎ 21185) in Stanley.

The Guianas

On the north coast of South America, the independent republics of Guyana and Suriname and the territory of French Guiana (Guyane Française) exhibit a curious political geography left by British, Dutch and French colonization. The entire region takes its name from an English corruption of the Spanish spelling of a Surinamese Indian tribe. 'Wayana' is the correct name, but the Spanish wrote it as 'Juayana' or 'Guayana,' and the English misread it as 'Guyana.' The name does not mean 'Land of Many Waters' as is often alleged. Collectively referred to as the Guianas, these three territories are culturally more Caribbean than South American and are a fascinating contrast with the rest of the continent. The interior regions, which were never dominated by Europeans, retain some of the world's best remaining tropical forests, although these ecosystems (particularly those in Guyana and Suriname) are constantly threatened by both uncontrolled gold-mining and the advent of multinational timber companies operating with just a few environmental safeguards.

History

The muddy Guiana coastline, covered by mangroves and sparsely populated with warlike Carib Indians, did not attract early European settlement. Spaniards first saw the coast in 1499, but there was no prospect of gold or cheap labor, though they made occasional slave raids. Interior forest peoples such as the Macushi and Tirió survived in relative isolation. Several 16th-century explorers, including Sir Walter Raleigh, placed the mythical city of El Dorado in the region, but Spain's European rivals displayed no sustained interest until the mid-17th century.

The Netherlands made the first move, placing a settlement on the lower Essequibo River in 1615. After forming the Dutch West India Company in 1621, the colonists traded with Indian peoples of the interior and established riverside plantations of sugar, cocoa and other tropical commodities. Indigenous peoples were almost wiped out by introduced diseases, so the Dutch imported West African slaves to construct dikes and polders and work the plantation economies. From the mid-18th century, escaped slaves formed Maroon (also called Bushnegro) settlements in the interior, and these West African-oriented cultures persist in central Suriname and parts of western French Guiana.

England established sugar and tobacco plantations on the west bank of the Suriname River around 1650, followed by the founding of what is now Paramaribo. After the second Anglo-Dutch War, under the Treaty of Breda (1667), the Dutch retained Suriname and their colonies on the Guyanese coast (in exchange for New York), but ceded the area east of the Maroni (Marowijne in Dutch) River to the French. For the next 150 years, sovereignty of the region shifted between the three powers in response to the fortunes of their navies in the Caribbean and various wars and alliances in Europe. By 1800, Britain had become the dominant power, though Suriname remained under Dutch control and France retained a precarious hold on Cayenne in what is now French Guiana.

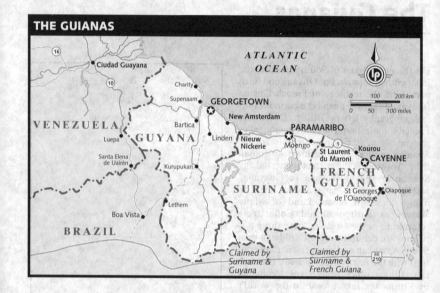

THE GUIANAS

VENEZUELA

GUYANA

SURINAME

FRENCH GUIANA

BRAZIL

ATLANTIC OCEAN

Ciudad Guayana

Charity
Supenaam
GEORGETOWN
New Amsterdam
Bartica
Luepa
Linden   Nieuw Nickerie
Santa Elena de Uairén
Kurupukari
Boa Vista
Lethem

PARAMARIBO
Moengo
St Laurent du Maroni   Kourou
CAYENNE
St Georges de l'Oiapoque   Oiapoque

Claimed by Suriname & Guyana
Claimed by Suriname & French Guiana

0   100   200 km
0   50   100 miles

At the end of the Napoleonic Wars, the Treaty of Paris reaffirmed the sovereignty of the Dutch in Suriname and of the French east of the Maroni, while Britain formally purchased the Dutch colonies in what became British Guiana. By 1834, slavery was abolished in all British colonies, and the Royal Navy suppressed the slave trade in the Caribbean. This created a need for more plantation labor, and the subsequent immigration of indentured labor from other colonies created a unique ethnic mix in each of the Guianas.

Colonial rule left an unfortunate legacy of border disputes. Venezuela claims 130,000 sq km of Guyanese territory west of the Essequibo, while Suriname claims another 13,000km along its border with Guyana and Brazil. Suriname also claims the area between the upper Maroni River and the Litani River, which is currently under French control.

Flora & Fauna

An extensive and largely pristine tropical rain forest covers the interior of the Guianas and is the habitat of many plant and animal species. The jaguar is the most spectacular wild mammal, but the region teems with huge, relatively undisturbed populations of splendid creatures, such as the scarlet macaw, the giant anteater and also the sun parakeet. The Guianas are also home to flourishing populations of creatures endangered in other parts of lowland South America, like the tapir, the black caiman and the giant river otter. The many rivers abound with side-neck turtles, electric eels, spectacled caimans, black piranhas and *tucunares* (peacock bass). Along the coasts are seasonal nesting sites for the awe-inspiring giant leatherback turtle, as well as green and olive ridley turtles. The Guianas are probably the best place in South America to see two of the most unforgettable species of Amazonian birds, the harpy eagle and the cock-of-the-rock.

Getting Around the Guianas

It is possible to travel overland across all three Guianas, but only in the coastal area. From the west, you can get into Guyana from Boa Vista in northern Brazil, but the road connection to Georgetown is not always open, and you may have to take a flight. From Georgetown, roads follow the coast eastward, with a river crossing into Suriname and another into French Guiana, with several others along the way. There's no road yet from Cayenne to the Brazilian border, but you could fly to St Georges de l'Oiapoque in French Guiana, cross the Oiapoque River to

Brazil and continue by road to Macapá, at the mouth of the Amazon.

There is a lot of illegal immigration (called 'backtracking') across all of these borders, and papers are scrutinized carefully. French Guiana requires an onward ticket, so currently it's best to do the trip from west to east and fly out of Cayenne to Macapá or Belém in Brazil.

Guyana

FACTS ABOUT GUYANA
History
In 1831, the three colonial settlements of Essequibo, Demerara and Berbice merged to become British Guiana. After the abolition of slavery, Africans refused to work on the plantations for wages, and many established their own villages in the bush. Plantations closed or consolidated because of the shortage of labor. A British company, Bookers, resurrected the sugar industry by importing indentured labor from India. From 1846 to 1917, nearly 250,000 laborers entered Guyana, drastically transforming its demography and laying the basis of fractious racial politics.

British Guiana was run very much as a colony until 1953, when a new constitution provided for home rule and an elected government. In 1966, the country became an independent member of the British Commonwealth with the name Guyana, and in 1970, it became a republic with an elected president. Guyana hit world news in 1979 with the mass suicide-murder of nearly a thousand cultists in the expatriate religious community of Jonestown.

A new constitution was proclaimed in 1980 by socialist president Forbes Burnham. The current state controls the two main export industries, sugar and bauxite, but the recent trend is to reduce government involvement in the economy, so both of these industries may be privatized.

Geography
Though Caribbean in culture, Guyana actually fronts the Atlantic Ocean and is roughly the size of the UK or the US state of Idaho. The three major rivers – all north-flowing – in Guyana are (east to west) the Demerara, Essequibo and Berbice. The narrow strip of coastal lowland, from 16km to 60km wide,

At a Glance	
Country Name	Co-operative Republic of Guyana
Area	214,970 sq km
Population	770,000 (1998 estimate)
Population Density	3.58 per sq km
Capital	Georgetown
Head of State	President Bharrat Jagdeo
Official Language	English
Other Languages	Amerindian languages; Creole dialects
Currency	Guyanese dollar (G$)
Exchange Rate	US$1 = G$176
Per Capita GNP	US$633 (1996)
Inflation Rate	3.3% (1998)

comprises 4% of the total land area, but is home to 90% of the population. The Dutch, using a system of drainage canals, sea walls and groins, reclaimed much of the marshy coastal land from the Atlantic. These polders support most of Guyana's agriculture. There are very few sandy beaches.

Tropical rain forest covers most of the interior, though southwestern Guyana features an extensive savanna between the Rupununi River and the Brazilian border. The most prominent geological feature here is the Guiana Shield, an extensive, weathered crystalline upland. Once part of the larger Brazilian Shield to the south, it became separated in Tertiary times when the rising Andes reversed the course of west-flowing rivers and created the Amazon Basin. The Shield falls away in steps from 2772m Mt Roraima, on the Brazilian border, down to sea level.

Climate
The equatorial climate has high temperatures with little seasonal variation, though coastal breezes moderate the heat. Guyana has two distinct rainy seasons: May to mid-August and mid-November to late January.

Government
Guyana's 1980 constitution established an executive branch with an elected president and a prime minister appointed by the

president; the 65-member national assembly is also elected, mostly by proportional representation. The High Court is the supreme judicial authority.

The main political parties are the People's National Congress (PNC) and the Marxist-oriented People's Progressive Party (PPP). The PPP is supported principally by the East Indian community, while the PNC is supported by Afro-Guyanese. In October 1992, in an election marred by violence, PPP candidate Cheddi Jagan easily defeated the incumbent PNC president, Desmond Hoyte. Since independence, most of the important posts in the Guyanese Defense Force, the police and the civil service have been occupied by Afro-Guyanese, but with the change of government, more East Indians have been appointed to influential positions. Jagan died in office and was replaced by his US-born wife, who was elected in her own right in late 1997. The PNC refused to accept the results of the election, which led to strikes and rioting. Negotiations ended the violence, but the political situation remains somewhat tense. In summer 1999, Janet Jagan retired from the presidency and named Bharrat Jagdeo her successor.

Economy

Guyana's economy relies on exports of primary commodities, especially bauxite, but also gold, sugar, rice, timber and shrimp. East Indians control most of the small business, while the Afro-Guyanese dominate the government sector. Guyana is a member of the Caribbean economic group, Caricom.

Guyana Sugar Company (Guysuco), the state-controlled sugar enterprise, employs more Guyanese than any other industry and produces 28% of Guyana's export earnings. The company has a 300-year history, and the Demerara River has given its name to a type of raw cane sugar.

Multinational corporations, including US-based Reynolds Metals and Canada's Alcan, are major investors in the mineral sector. There are substantial gold-mining ventures – one gold extraction plant spilled a huge quantity of cyanide in the Essequibo River in 1995.

The Barama Company, owned by Koreans and Malaysians, has an enormous logging concession in the northwest (8% of the country), and most of the local and many international environmentalists are skeptical of this company's capacity (or intention) to carry out a truly sustainable operation.

Though the PPP also used to express skepticism about multinationals, the government has permitted – even encouraged – foreign investment. Economic reforms have led to a resumption of foreign aid, but despite some debt cancellations and rescheduling, the country still has a large foreign debt. The infrastructure, once very run-down, is improving, with more reliable phones and fewer electricity blackouts.

Population & People

There are about 770,000 people in Guyana, but it has been estimated that more than 500,000 Guyanese live abroad, mostly in Canada, the UK, the USA, Trinidad and other English-speaking Caribbean countries. About 51% of the population in Guyana is East Indian (ie, from the Indian subcontinent), 43% is Afro-Guyanese and 2% is of Chinese or European extraction. Amerindians, in scattered interior settlements, make up about 4% of the population; the main groups are Arawak, Carib, Macushi and Wapishana.

Public education is free of charge through the university level, but physical facilities have deteriorated, books and supplies are limited and qualified teachers are few. The literacy rate is about 89%, but many educated Guyanese live abroad.

Arts

To see contemporary Guyanese painting and sculpture, look for special exhibitions at the Georgetown Museum.

Religion

Most Afro-Guyanese are Christian, usually Anglican, but a handful are black Muslim. The East Indian population is mostly Hindu, with a sizable Muslim minority, but Hindu-Muslim friction is uncommon.

Language

English is the official national language, but most Guyanese speak a Creole incomprehensible to outsiders. Some East Indians speak Hindi or Urdu. Each Amerindian tribe speaks its own language. Along the Brazilian border, many Guyanese speak both English and Portuguese.

GUYANA

VENEZUELA

San José de Amacuro

Mabaruma

Shell Beach

Amakura

Kaituma

Barima

Port Kaituma

Waini

Matthews Ridge

Barama

Rio Cuyuni

Charity

Anna Regina

Adventure

Supenaam

Supenaam

Leonora

Parika

GEORGETOWN

Mahaica

Mahaicony

Venamu (Rio Venamo)

Mazaruni

Puruni

Cuyuni

Bartica

Essequibo

Demerara

Cheddi Jagan International Airport

Linden

New Amsterdam

Rosignol

Rose Hall

Pakaraima Mountains

Issano

Semang

Mazaruni

Kaburi

Hinterland Road

Mara

Nieuw Nickerie

Corriverton

(Springlands & Skeldon)

To Paramaribo

Berbice

Ituni

Canje

Mt Roraima ▲2810m

▲ Ayanganna

Potaro

Mahdia

Kwakwani

Wasjabo

Nickerie River

Kaieteur Falls

Kurupukari

Corentyne (Corantijn) River

Kabalebo River

Orinduik Falls

Siparuni

Burro-Burro

BRAZIL

Annai

Apoteri

SURINAME

Lucie River

Rio Ireng

Good Hope

Rewa

Essequibo

Kwitaro

Coeroeni

Rio Tacutu

Bonfim

Lethem

Rupununi

Boa Vista

New

Aishalton

Claimed by Suriname & French Guiana

Kuyuwini

Essequibo

Oronoque

Caracarai

Rio Branco

BR 210

BRAZIL

To Manaus

ATLANTIC OCEAN

0   50   100 km

0   30   60 miles

10

FACTS FOR THE VISITOR
Highlights
The single most spectacular attraction is Kaieteur Falls, which are much more majestic than the more ephemeral (yet higher) Angel Falls in neighboring Venezuela. No visit to Guyana should be considered complete without a wildlife-viewing excursion to Karanambo (or one of the other local ranches) in the Rupununi savannas. For the more adventurous types, the overland trek from Georgetown to Lethem on the back of a truck during the dry season is an unforgettable journey.

Planning
When to Go The best time to visit Guyana may be at the end of either rainy season, in late January or late August, when the discharge of water over Kaieteur Falls is greatest. Some locals recommend mid-October to mid-May, which may be wet, but not as hot. If you want to travel overland to the interior, visit during the dry seasons (see Climate under Facts about Guyana).

Maps Maps are available at Kojac Marketing Agency (☎ 02-52387), 140B Quamina St, Cummingsburg, Georgetown.

What to Bring Dress is informal; coats and ties are exceptional, even among businesspeople and state officials, though Guyanese men seldom wear shorts. Downpours can occur even in the 'dry' seasons, so bringing an umbrella is worthwhile. For trips into the interior, bring light, easy-to-dry clothing, a poncho, a hat and sunscreen.

Tourist Offices
The government has no official tourism representative abroad. The private Tourism Association of Guyana (☎ 02-50807, fax 02-50817), 157 Waterloo St, Georgetown, is more active in promoting the country and publishes the 'Guyana Tourist Guide,' a useful brochure. Guyanese embassies and consulates abroad provide relatively up-to-date information.

UK
   (☎ 020-7229-7684, fax 020-7727-9809)
.   Guyanese High Commission, 3 Palace Court, Bayswater Rd, London

USA
   (☎ 203-431-1571)
   Mary Lou Callahan, Unique Destinations, 307 Peaceable St, Ridgefield, CT 06877

Visas & Documents
All visitors require a passport, but those travelers from the US, Canada, EU countries, Australia, New Zealand and the British Commonwealth do not need a visa. A 30-day stay is granted on arrival in Guyana. If you do need a visa, file your application at least six weeks before you leave your home country.

As well as a passport, carry an international yellow-fever vaccination certificate with you, and keep other immunizations up to date.

Embassies & Consulates
Foreign embassies in Guyana include the following, all of which are in Georgetown:

Brazil
   (☎ 02-57970)
   308-309 Church St
Canada
   (☎ 02-72081)
   High commission on the corner of High and Young Sts
Colombia
   (☎ 02-71410)
   306 Church St
France
   Consular agent:
   (☎ 02-75435)
   7 Sherriff St, Subryanville; if you need a visa for French Guiana, get it at the French embassy in Suriname.
Suriname
   (☎ 02-67844)
   304 Church St; tourist visas are usually issued in two working days (sometimes straightaway) and cost US$42 for Canadians, US$30 for other nationalities.
UK
   High commission:
   (☎ 02-65881)
   44 Main St
USA
   (☎ 02-54900)
   100 Young St
Venezuela
   (☎ 02-60841)
   Thomas St, between Quamina and Church Sts

Guyana's diplomatic representation abroad is limited:

Belgium
  (☎ 02-675 62 16)
  12 Avenue de Brasil, Brussels

Canada
  (☎ 613-235-7249)
  151 Slater St, Suite 309, Ottawa
  (☎ 416-494-6040)
  505 Consumers Rd, Suite 900, Willowdale, Toronto

UK
  (☎ 020-7229-7684, fax 020-7727-98093) Palace Court, Bayswater Rd, London

USA
  (☎ 202-265-6900)
  2490 Tracy Place, Washington, DC
  (☎ 212-527-3215)
  866 United Nations Plaza, New York, NY

Money

The currency is the Guyanese dollar (G$), available as both coins and notes. The notes are in denominations of G$20, G$100, G$500, G$1000; coins are in denominations of G$1, G$5 and G$10. The currency is more or less stable, but it's declining in line with domestic inflation. The official exchange rate is about the same as the parallel rate offered by *cambios* (exchange houses). Rates at press time included the following:

country	unit		Guyanese dollars
Australia	A$1	=	G$116
Canada	C$1	=	G$119
euro	€1	=	G$180
France	FF1	=	G$27
Germany	DM1	=	G$92
Japan	¥100	=	G$145
New Zealand	NZ$1	=	G$92
UK	UK£1	=	G$276
USA	US$1	=	G$176

Cash and traveler's checks can be exchanged in banks and cambios. Sometimes you can change cash unofficially at hotels for 10% or 15% less – there is no real black market. Rates are almost the same for traveler's checks and cash. Credit cards are accepted at many of Georgetown's better hotels and restaurants.

Post & Communications

Postal services are generally unreliable; use registered mail for essential correspondence. UPS (☎ 02-71853), 265 Thomas St, and DHL (☎ 02-57772), 50 E 5th St, Albert-town, are better alternatives for important shipments.

Atlantic Tele-Network Company operates the new Guyana Telecommunications Corporation, a joint venture with the government, and has made major improvements in the telephone service. The country code for Guyana is ☎ 592.

At blue public telephones scattered around Georgetown, Berbice, Mabaruma, Lethem and Linden, you can make home-country direct and reverse-charge (collect) calls abroad. Credit-card calls have been suspended because of frequent fraud, but it's possible to purchase prepaid phone cards in Georgetown. For a USA Direct (AT&T) line, dial ☎ 165; to Canada, dial ☎ 161; and for the UK, dial ☎ 169. For the international operator, dial ☎ 002. Yellow public telephones are for local calls, which are free. Hotels and restaurants generally allow free use of their phones for local calls.

Internet Resources

The 'Welcome to Guyana' site at www.lasalle .edu/~daniels/guyexp/bgintro.htm, is the best website on the country. It's a smorgasbord of information that offers everything from news to weather to history. The Guyana News and Information site, www.guyana.org, also offers a wealth of data, with a heavy emphasis on current affairs. The Guiana Shield Media Project site, www.gsmp.org, focuses primarily on environmental issues.

Books

The classic account of travel in Guyana is Charles Waterton's 1825 *Wanderings in South America*. Though out of print, it is widely available in used bookstores and libraries in the US and UK. The late Gerald Durrell's *Three Tickets to Adventure* is also popular. Evelyn Waugh described a rugged trip from Georgetown across the Rupununi savannas in *Ninety-Two Days*, recently re-issued as a Penguin paperback. Shiva Naipaul wrote a moving account of the Jonestown tragedy in *Journey to Nowhere*, published in the UK as *Black and White*.

GUIANAS

Media

Georgetown has two daily newspapers, *Stabroek News* and the *Guyana Chronicle*, plus the weekly *Kaieteur News* and influential *Catholic Standard*. Local television programming is limited, but international cable services are widely available.

Time

Guyanese time is four hours behind GMT/UTC and one hour behind Suriname.

Electricity

The electricity supply (when it's working) is 110V in Georgetown and 220V in most other places.

Weights & Measures

The metric system is official but imperial measures are still more commonly used. See the conversion table at the back of this book.

Health

Adequate medical care is available in Georgetown, at least at private hospitals, but elsewhere, facilities are few. Chloroquine-resistant malaria is endemic, and dengue fever is also a danger, particularly in the interior – protect yourself against mosquitoes and take a malaria prophylaxis. Typhoid inoculation is recommended. Guyana is regarded as a yellow-fever infected area, and your next destination may require a vaccination certificate, as does Guyana if you arrive from another infected area. Tap water is suspect, especially in Georgetown.

Cholera outbreaks have occurred in areas with unsanitary conditions, but precautions are recommended everywhere. See the Health section in the introductory Facts for the Visitor chapter.

Dangers & Annoyances

Guyana in general, and Georgetown in particular, are notorious for street crime and physical violence. Avoid potentially hazardous situations, and be aware of others on the street. For further information, see the Dangers & Annoyances section under Georgetown.

At the Cheddi Jagan International Airport, try to arrive during daylight and use only registered airport taxis. Drivers are easily recognizable as they all have official IDs attached to their shirt pockets. All baggage should be locked. Backpacks are particularly prone to pilfering hands.

Business Hours

Many businesses close at 4:30 or 5 pm. There are numerous national holidays, on which government offices and businesses are closed. Muslim holidays occur on a different date each year.

Public Holidays & Special Events

Republic Day celebrations in February are the most important national cultural event of the year, though Hindu and Muslim religious festivals are also important. The recently established Amerindian Heritage Month (September) features a series of cultural events such as handicraft exhibits and traditional dances. Regatta, an aquatic event featuring innumerable speedboats of different design, takes place every Easter at both Bartica and Canaan. An annual Easter rodeo is held in the Rupununi savannas at Lethem.

New Year's Day
  January 1
Youman Nabi
  Early January
Republic Day (Slave Rebellion of 1763)
  February 23
Phagwah (Hindu New Year)
  March (date varies)
Good Friday and Easter
  March or April
Labor Day
  May 1
Caricom Day
  July 3
Emancipation Day
  First Monday in August
Divali
  November
Christmas Day
  December 25
Boxing Day
  December 26

Activities

Guyana has few facilities for recreational activities. The coast is generally unsuitable for water sports, but the interior offers possibilities for river rafting and trekking, best arranged through a local tour operator.

Accommodations

In Georgetown there are modest hotels that are clean, secure and comfortable for US$15 to US$25. Better accommodations, with air-con, cost from US$40, while the growing number of rain-forest lodges tend to be even more expensive.

Food & Drinks

Guyanese food ranges from the tasty (pepperpot, an Amerindian game stew) to the inedible (souse, jellied cow's head). Chinese food is widespread but not noteworthy. Two ubiquitous dishes in local restaurants are 'cook-up' (rice and beans – boring) and 'roti' (chicken curry in a crêpe – delicious). Local rum is available everywhere; D'Aguiar's 5-Year-Old and El Dorado 5 Star are two of the best local brands. Banks beer, brewed at Thirst Park in South Georgetown, comes in both regular and premium versions. Also try fruit punch (or, better yet, rum punch) at any of Georgetown's better restaurants.

Entertainment

There's hot nightlife in Georgetown, where quite a few places have live reggae and rock until the early hours. Most discos in central Georgetown are safe and welcome foreigners, but discos on the outskirts may harbor thieves.

Spectator Sports

In racially polarized Guyana, sport is one of the few unifying factors, and sport mainly means cricket. Internationally, Guyanese play with the West Indies; Clive Lloyd is the best known local cricketer.

Shopping

Nibbee fiber, extracted from forest vines, is the most distinctive and appealing local product and is used to make everything from hats to furniture. The Macushi Indians of the southwest have developed a unique art form based on carving forest scenes and creatures from the hardened latex of the *balata* tree. Pieces created by master craftsman George Tancredo are particularly prized.

GETTING THERE & AWAY
Air

Travelers departing from Cheddi Jagan International Airport pay a departure tax of US$15.

Europe There are no direct flights to Guyana from Europe. The most direct route is from the UK through Barbados.

North America BWIA offers the most extensive schedule, with direct flights daily from New York and Miami. ALM and Guyana Airways also have flights, from New York, Miami and Toronto. Most stop over in Trinidad. Both ALM and BWIA include overnight hotel accommodations at Trinidad or Curaçao on flights from Miami.

Suriname SLM (Surinam Airways; ☎ 02-53473, 02-54894) flies between Georgetown and Paramaribo twice a week (US$114).

Land

Brazil From Bonfim (Brazil) you can cross the river to Lethem, in Guyana's southwestern Rupununi savanna. Bonfim has a good road connection to the Brazilian city of Boa Vista, but the road from Lethem to Georgetown is rough and may be impassable in wet weather – see the Lethem section.

Suriname A ferry from Corriverton (Springlands) crosses the Corentyne River to the Surinamese border town of Nieuw Nickerie. Another, new ferry makes the 25-minute crossing twice daily.

Venezuela There are no road connections west to Venezuela and no legal border crossing points. The only overland route is through Brazil via Boa Vista and Bonfim.

GETTING AROUND
Air

Charter services are available. The best pilot is M Chan-A-Sue of Torong Tours (☎ 02-65298). Roraima Airways (☎ 02-59648, fax 02-59646), 101 Cummings St, Bourda, Georgetown, sends small planes into the interior for US$180 roundtrip. The same goes for Trans Guyana Airways (☎ 022-3535, fax 022-5462), at the Ogle Aerodrome, Ogle East Coast Demerara.

Bus

Minibuses link Georgetown with secondary towns, including Parika, Linden, New Amsterdam and Corriverton. These have no fixed schedules and leave when full from bus stops around Stabroek Market.

GUIANAS

Taxi

Because of frequent robberies and generally unsafe conditions on the streets, it's best for visitors to Georgetown to take taxis around town, especially after dark.

Car & Motorcycle

Rental cars are available in Georgetown. They are quite expensive, and you'll need an International Driving Permit. You are better off in a taxi or a bus.

Bicycle

Guyana's modest road network also limits cycling, but truly dedicated mountain bikers might be able to follow the road to Lethem and Bonfim (Brazil). Beware of bandits.

Hitchhiking

Hitchhiking is not recommended – the threat of robbery is real.

Boat

Ferries cross most major rivers. There is regular service on the Essequibo between Charity and Bartica, stopping at Parika (reached by paved highway from Georgetown). More frequent, but relatively expensive, speedboats (river taxis) carry passengers from Parika to Bartica.

Ferry docks are known as *stellings*, a term adopted from Dutch.

Organized Tours

Many Guyanese companies promote 'adventure tourism' in rain-forest and riverside lodges. Costs are US$110 to US$150 per person per night. For details, contact the Tourism Association of Guyana (☎ 02-50807, tag@solutions2000.net), 157 Waterloo St, or one of the following operators, all based in Georgetown.

Highly regarded are Malcolm and Margaret Chan-A-Sue, at Torong Guyana (☎ 02-50749, fax 02-50749), 56 Coralita Ave, Bel Air Park East, who arrange tours into the interior. Although trips with them are not cheap, they will advise budget travelers on alternatives, and their day trips to Kaieteur Falls and Orinduik Falls (US$150) are excellent.

Horizon Tours (☎ 02-64615, fax 02-75024, horizonpix@usa.net) puts together superb customized trips to the interior. Shell Beach Adventures (☎ 02-54483, fax 02-65220,

sbadventures@solutions2000.net), which is headquartered in Le Meridien Hotel, Seawall Rd in Georgetown's Kingstown area specialize in three-day trips to the coast (US$380) to observe the egg-laying of the giant leatherback sea turtle as well as three other species of sea turtle. Timberhead Resorts (☎ 02-53760), also headquartered at Le Meridien, offers trips to the Timberhead Lodge and other parts of the interior. Wilderness Explorers, (☎ 02-62085, fax 02-65220, wilderness-explorers@solution2000 .net), 61 Hadfield, Werk-en-Rust runs trips to the Santa Mission of Carib Indians (US$50) and around Georgetown (US$35).

GEORGETOWN

Originally designed by the Dutch on a regular grid pattern, Georgetown (population 350,000) is Guyana's capital and only large city. It retains some 19th-century colonial architecture, though many buildings are in poor condition.

Orientation

Low-lying Georgetown sits on the east bank of the Demerara River where it empties into the Atlantic. A long sea wall prevents flooding, while the Dutch canal system drains the town. Tree-lined pedestrian paths pass between the traffic lanes of the town's broad avenues, and there are many open spaces, but the canals can be smelly.

Street numbering is discontinuous in Georgetown's various boroughs – the same number may appear twice on the same street, say in Cummingsburg and Lacytown. Some streets change names west of Main St and Avenue of the Republic.

Georgetown is divided into several districts. Kingston is in the northwest of the city, bounded by the Atlantic and the Demerara River. Kitty is just east of Thomas Lands and the National Park. Lamaha St runs east to west, forming the north boundary for Cummingsburg, Alberttown, Queenstown and Newtown, located west to east, respectively; Church St is roughly the southern border. South of Church St, from west to east, sit Robbstown, Lacytown, Starbroek and Bourda (Bourda lines the western border of the botanical gardens). South of those areas are Werk-en-Rust, Wortmanville, Charlestown and Le Repentir.

Information

Tourist Offices The Ministry of Trade, Tourism and Industry (☎ 02-62505), at 229 South Rd, Lacytown, is supposedly open weekdays from 8 am to 4:30 pm. Much more helpful is the private Tourism and Hospitality Association of Guyana (☎ 02-50807, fax 02-50817, tag@solutions2000.net), 157 Waterloo St, South Cummingsburg, open from 8 am to 5 pm weekdays. It publishes the useful 'Guyana Tourist Guide.'

Money Cambios offer better rates and less red tape than banks; a reliable one is Kayman Sankar Cambio (☎ 02-71560), 216 Lamaha St, North Cummingsburg. Globe Trust and Investment, at 92 Middle St next to Rima Guest House, is also dependable.

Post & Communications The main post office, the GPO, is on North Rd, just west of Avenue of the Republic. Guyana Telephone & Telegraph (GT&T), on Church St west of the National Bookseller (see Bookstores), is open daily 7 am to 10 pm.

Visa Extensions The immigration office (☎ 02-51744, 02-63011) is on Camp Rd, just north of Cowan St. It's open weekdays 8 am to 11:30 am and 1 to 3 pm.

Bookstores For a good selection of paperback novels, mostly by Caribbean writers, visit the National Bookseller at 78 Church St.

Cultural Centers The National Cultural Centre (☎ 02-63845), on Mandela Ave in D'Urban Park, frequently puts on plays and concerts.

Medical Services Georgetown Public Hospital (☎ 02-56900), on New Market St, has inadequate and run-down facilities. Travelers may prefer private clinics and hospitals, such as St Joseph's Mercy Hospital (☎ 02-72070), 130-132 Parade St (behind the US embassy).

Dangers & Annoyances Georgetown vies with Bogotá for the most dangerous capital city in South America. Street crime, often violent, is common in Georgetown. Electricity blackouts are quite frequent, and street lighting is poor at the best of times. Avoid walking anywhere after dark; be alert even in daylight. *Never* enter the Tiger Bay area (north of Church St and west of Main St), avoid Middle St between Main and Waterloo St and stay out of the Promenade Garden. Call Horizon Tours (☎ 02-64615), or speak with the concierge at any of the major hotels to arrange a driver-escort to get around the city. It may seem extreme to hail a taxi to go a block or two, but defer to the judgment of local people.

Things to See

Georgetown can be seen in a day. The best 19th-century buildings are along Main St and especially along Avenue of the Republic, just east of the Demerara River.

On an oval on the corner of Church and Carmichael Sts is the Gothic-style **St George's Cathedral**. Built mostly with local materials, most notably a hardwood called greenheart, it's said to be the world's tallest wooden building.

Farther south on Avenue of the Republic is the distinctive neo-Gothic **Town Hall** (1889); just beyond that are the **Victoria Law Courts** (1887). At the south end of the avenue is the well-kept **Parliament Building** (1833), while to its west is the landmark **Stabroek Market**, on Water St, a striking cast-iron building with a corrugated-iron clock tower. Don't go in unless accompanied by Guyanese friends – there are plenty of petty thieves lurking within.

At Avenue of the Republic and Church St is the **National Library**. Three blocks farther north, at Main and New Market Sts, is the **State House** (1852), now the president's residence. The fenced **Promenade Garden**, at Middle and Carmichael Sts, is a welcome relief from midday heat, but enter at your own risk; it's dark and dangerous at night.

Opposite the post office on North Rd is the **Museum of Guyana**, a curious institution with some very old-fashioned exhibits. Occasional special exhibitions of Guyanese painting and sculpture are imaginative and first-rate. It's open weekdays 9 am to 5 pm, Saturdays from 9 am to noon. Admission to the museum is free.

At the east end of Regent Rd, Georgetown's **botanical gardens** are worth visiting (stick to the main paths and avoid the southeastern corner). The **zoo** (☎ 02-59142), which

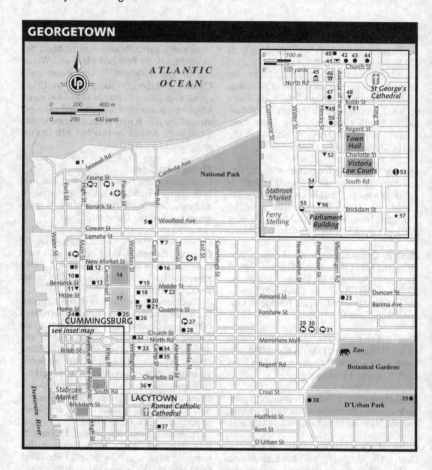

GEORGETOWN

focuses on the local fauna is located in the garden. The most remarkable exhibit is a stunning young jaguar. Admission is a token US$0.70, but it's US$7 with a video camera. The open court on the next block south of the botanical gardens is the **Square of the Revolution**, which houses the monument to the famous Cuffy, the leader and hero of the 1763 rebellion on the Berbice sugar estate. When the statue is viewed from the north, one realizes that the sculptor had a peculiar sense of humor.

Places to Stay

One of Georgetown's cheapest lodgings is **Hotel Tropicana** (☎ 02-62108), 177 Waterloo St, which has singles for US$7/12 with shared/private bathrooms. It's very basic, but it has character, and it's in a good location.

Highly recommended is **Florentene's Hotel** (☎ 02-62283), 3 North Rd, where a very clean single with bath and fan costs US$14. For a friendly family place, try the central and secure **Rima Guest House** (☎ 2-57401), 92 Middle St, which has singles with shared bath for US$18.

German's Hotel (☎ 02-53972), 53 Robb St, is similarly priced. OK and slightly more expensive is **Alpha Hotel** (☎ 02-54324), 203 Camp St, at US$20. The **Water Chris Hotel** (☎ 02-71980), 184 Waterloo St, has a variety of rooms that start at US$25 for a basic single, up to US$35 for a twin room with air-con and private bath, though some consider it unsafe.

GEORGETOWN

PLACES TO STAY
1 Le Meridien Pegasus Hotel
9 Woodbine International Hotel
10 Park Hotel
13 Rima Guest House
18 Hotel Ariantze
19 Hotel Tropicana
20 Alpha Hotel
26 Water Chris Hotel
32 Florentene's Hotel
34 German's Hotel
35 Friends Hotel
37 Campala International
40 Hotel Tower

PLACES TO EAT
1 Brown's Café
7 Orient
11 Palm Court
15 Caribbean Rose
22 Del Casa
33 Salt & Pepper
34 German's

36 Camp Site
40 Main Street Cafe, Cazabon
48 Rice Bowl
49 Coal Pot
51 Country Pride
52 Hack's Halaal
56 Idiho Food Service

OTHER
2 Canadian High Commission
3 US Embassy
4 St Joseph's Mercy Hospital
5 Immigration Office
6 British High Commission
8 Georgetown Public Hospital
12 State House
14 Promenade Garden
16 Library Club & Disco
17 Independence Square
21 Blue Note
23 Xanadu
24 Basket Shop
25 Kojac Marketing Agency

27 Venezuelan Embassy
28 N&R Car Rental
29 Surinamese Embassy
30 Colombian Embassy
31 Brazilian Embassy
38 Square of the Revolution
39 National Cultural Centre
41 GPO
42 National Bookseller
43 National Library
44 Wieting & Richter Travel
   Agency
45 Museum of Guyana
46 Guyana Telephone
   & Telegraph, LIAT
47 BWIA
50 Houseproud
53 Ministry of Trade, Tourism
   & Industry
54 Minibuses to Rosignol, Parika
55 Minibuses to
   Jagan International Airport
57 Brickdam Police Station

At *Friends Hotel* (☎ 02-72383), 82 Robb St in Lacytown, rates start around US$30 for a nice, clean single with private bath and fan.

The *Campala International* (☎ 02-52951), 10 Camp St in Werk-en-Rust, south of Lacytown, charges US$32 for doubles. Rambling *Park Hotel* (☎ 02-54911), 37 Main St, is a pleasantly old-style place, with fan-cooled rooms from just US$32/38 singles/doubles and air-con rooms at US$60/70. *Hotel Ariantze* (☎ 02-65363), 176 Middle St, is a mid-range option with pleasant rooms from US$45 for singles to US$50 for doubles. The modern *Woodbine International* (☎ 02-59430), 41 New Market St, asks US$50 for a single and US$65 for a double.

For upmarket comfort, *Hotel Tower* (☎ 02-72011, hotel.tower@solutions2000.net), 74-75 Main St, has a large pool and rooms from US$85/104 per single/double, but you may be able to negotiate a slightly better rate. The most expensive is the *Le Meridien Pegasus Hotel* (☎ 02-52856), on Seawall Rd, whose rates start at US$129 for singles and peak at US$200 for luxury suites.

Places to Eat

Some of the staff at Georgetown's better restaurants don't like faded jeans or sneakers – so check first. Many of the cheaper places open only for lunch.

The *Coal Pot*, 17 Hincks St, has a diverse lunch menu; it's often crowded, but its seafood is much cheaper than elsewhere in town; meals start at US$2 to US$3. For East Indian food, try *Hack's Halaal*, on Commerce St near Avenue of the Republic. The *Rice Bowl*, 34 Robb St, is also worth a try, as is *Country Pride*, across the road at 64 Robb St. Two places for cheap, authentic local food are *German's*, in German's Hotel, and *Salt & Pepper*, they're both on Robb St. *Idiho Food Service* is a snack place near Stabroek Market on Brickdam St. *Camp Site*, at the corner of Camp St and South Rd, offers Chinese food, pastries and snacks. *Back to Eden*, 85 David St, 1½ blocks west of Sherriff St in Subryanville, serves good vegetarian cuisine (ask for the special of the day).

Palm Court, 35 Main St, is lively and popular, with good seafood. *Caribbean Rose*, 175 Middle St, is a rooftop restaurant, though the tasty fare is not cheap. *Del Casa*, at 232 Middle St, is fairly expensive and formal, with a dress code and surprisingly indifferent service, but it has good meat and seafood (avoid the Indian restaurant they've opened on the second floor, though). The *Orient*, on Lamaha St, is a fine Chinese place with good service. In the Hotel Tower, *Main Street Cafe* is good for breakfast, while the *Cazabon* is also highly regarded. The

GUIANAS

Le Meridien Pegasus features two good but relatively expensive restaurants, including **Brown's Café**, which stays open 24 hours.

Entertainment

Georgetown's popular discos stay open very late. The best nightlife is along Sherriff St, east of the town center, where **The Sheriff**, **C&S** and **Tennessee** are all popular spots that feature local dance music and Chinese restaurants that are open until the wee hours. The **Night Flight** (☎ 02-50811), on Pere St in Kitty, is the hottest disco in town and is jammed with both locals and visitors on the weekend. The **Library Club & Disco**, 226 Camp St, attracts Brazilian and Guyanese gold miners and offers local and Brazilian music. Other possibilities include **Xanadu**, on Vliessengen Rd at Duncan St, and the **Blue Note**, on Camp St. Most places have a cover charge of a few dollars, which is worth it for the live music. The **Tower** and **Le Meridien** hotels also have discos.

Shopping

For pottery, paintings and woodcarvings, try Houseproud at 6 Avenue of the Republic, Creation Craft at 7A Water St, or the Basket Shop at 72 6th St. A newcomer worth visiting is the Hibiscus Plaza, on the ground floor of the post office building, next to the national museum, which specializes in local handicrafts.

Getting There & Away

Air Cheddi Jagan International Airport is 41km south of Georgetown. Regional airlines link the capital to Caribbean islands and to Suriname but not directly to Venezuela or Brazil. Airline offices in Georgetown include:

BWIA
  (☎ 02-58900, 02-71250) 4 Robb St
LIAT
  (☎ 02-61260) Bank of Guyana Building, at
  Church St and Avenue of the Republic
SLM
  (☎ 02-54894, 02-53473) 230 Camp St

SLM has two flights per week to Paramaribo (US$98) and Cayenne (US$114). Barbados-based LIAT (☎ 02-64011) has daily flights with connections to Caribbean islands, including Antigua, Dominica, Grenada, Martinique, Port of Spain, St Lucia and St Vincent.

Bus Minibuses to Parika (No 32; Parika has ferries to Bartica and Charity), to Rosignol (No 44; for the ferry to New Amsterdam, connecting to Corriverton) and to Linden leave from Stabroek Market. If you're interested in overland travel to Lethem, ask around at Stabroek Market about trucks going that way or, better yet, arrange it through Horizon Tours (US$30 to US$75, depending on the truck; see Dangers & Annoyances earlier). This is an unforgettable trip, but it is rustic and not for the fainthearted. Bring your own food and tent or hammock with mosquito net.

Getting Around

To/From the Airport Minibuses connect Jagan Airport with Georgetown for about US$1; they are safe enough in the daytime, but at night, a taxi is a better choice, despite the US$20 price tag (taxis may be shared). For early-morning flights from Jagan, make taxi arrangements the day before.

Bus Minibuses within the city limits cost about US$0.15.

Taxi Taxis within central Georgetown cost about US$1 per ride or US$5 per hour. Try Tower Taxi Service (☎ 02-72011), in front of Hotel Tower, or City (☎ 02-52853).

THE COASTAL PLAIN
Corriverton

Together known as Corriverton, the towns of Springlands and Skeldon, on the west bank of the Corentyne River, are at the eastern end of the coastal road from Georgetown. From Springlands, an old passenger ferry crosses the river to Suriname while the new ferry departs slightly upriver. The town's Main St is a long strip with mosques, churches, a Hindu temple, cheap hotels, eateries and bars. Brahman (zebu) cattle roam round the market like the sacred cows of India. At the north end of town, the Skeldon Estate of Guysuco is quite a large complex and the biggest local employer.

Places to Stay & Eat On Main St south of the stelling, **Hotel Par Park** is clean, cheap and secure. It charges US$8.50 to US$10 for a single with private bath – check the room first. **Mahogany Hotel** (☎ 03-2289), farther south on Main St, is a nice old place with rooms from US$10.50 to US$21, some with good views over the river. The *Arawak Hotel* is dirt cheap, but it should be avoided.

The *restaurant* at the Mahogany Hotel serves some tasty food, which you can enjoy at a table on the veranda overlooking Main St. *Station View*, on Main St, is a good place for lunch. There are a couple of 'snackettes' and *Chinese restaurants*, but avoid the one next to the Hotel Par Park.

Getting There & Away For travelers heading to Suriname from Corriverton, a ferry sails to Nieuw Nickerie daily except Sundays and holidays (check Suriname and Guyana holidays). Catching the ferry is a hassle. The booking office near the stelling opens around 8 am, but people start queuing as early as 7 am. There's a US$2 booking fee (payable in Guyanese dollars), and staff there check your passport. Around 10 am you go out onto the stelling and queue up for Guyanese emigration formalities – after giving you an exit stamp, staff members hold your passport until you board the boat. Some time after 11:30 am the boat arrives, docks and unloads; it may be loaded again and ready to make the return trip sometime between noon and 1:30 pm. The fare is US$2.50 (payable on board in Surinamese guilders only, but sometimes US dollars are accepted), and there may be an extra charge for luggage. It takes around 25 minutes to cross the Corentyne River to Nieuw Nickerie. Flying from Georgetown to Paramaribo in Suriname is the recommended way to travel if you can afford it (and if you can get a seat). Air travel allows you to avoid the headaches involved in crossing the river otherwise.

Smuggling and backtracking are rife here – frequently small, fast boats cross the river in about 15 minutes. Travelers may be tempted to take one of these boats to save the hassle of the ferry, but this is inadvisable. You may be robbed on these boats, and at best you'll wind up in Suriname without the proper stamps in your passport.

Moneychangers on the stelling sell Surinamese guilders and buy excess Guyanese currency at fair rates. Although it is reasonably safe to change money with them, you should still be careful. You'll need enough guilders to pay for the ferry and for your first night in Suriname.

THE NORTHWEST COAST

The west bank of the Essequibo River can be reached by boat from **Parika** to **Supenaam**. A coastal road will take you, via **Adventure**, as far as the charming town of **Charity**, about 50km away. From there, you will need a boat to get any farther. There are several expensive jungle lodges in the western part of the country, mainly reachable by air. **Shell Beach** extends for about 140km along the coast near the Venezuelan border and is a nesting site for turtles, including olive ridleys, hawksbills and the magnificent giant leatherbacks.

THE INTERIOR
Kaieteur Falls

Guyana's best known attraction, majestic Kaieteur Falls, is the most impressive of a series of three falls on the upper Potaro River, a tributary of the Essequibo. In its own way, Kaieteur is only slightly less impressive than the better-known Iguazú Falls of Argentina and Brazil. Its waters drop precipitously 822 feet (250m) from a sandstone tableland, much higher than Iguazú. Depending on the season, the falls range in width from 250 feet (76m) to 400 feet (122m). Swifts nest under the overhang of the falls and dart in and out of the waters.

There is an ancient guesthouse near the airstrip but it is out of commission. Camping is possible, but there are no formal facilities. The hike to the foot of the falls is spectacular, but be sure to carry a tent, as malaria is common due to itinerant gold miners ('pork knockers') who frequent the area.

Getting There & Away Several operators offer day trips in small planes for about US$175 per person; make early inquiries, since the flights go only when a full load of eight passengers can be arranged. For details, see Organized Tours in the Getting Around section earlier in this chapter.

It's possible to reach the falls overland, but it's a difficult trip that takes about a week. Call Horizon Tours (see Organized Tours, earlier).

Lethem

In the Rupununi savanna along the Brazilian border, Lethem itself has little of interest, but it serves as the stepping-off point to the incredible Kanuku Mountains nearby. The term 'Kanuku' means 'rich forest' in the

Macushi Indian language, a reflection of the fact that these mountains harbor an extraordinary diversity of wildlife – fully 70% of all bird species found in Guyana can be found in the Kanukus.

The ranches near Lethem are home to Guyana's cowboys (vaqueros), and there's a rodeo at Easter.

The Guyanese are suspicious about drug smuggling in this area, so make sure you go through proper bureaucratic channels when crossing the border. Keep in mind that you need permission to visit Amerindian communities – inquiries can be made at the Ministry of Amerindian Affairs in the Office of the President (☎ 02-66453), at New Garden and Vliessengen Rd in Georgetown. If traveling with an organized tour, this should be taken care of for you.

Don & Shirley's shop at the airstrip is the best place to get information about the local attractions, guides and other points of interest in the area. The *Takaku Guest House* (☎ 072-2040) charges about US$7 for an OK room and serves three meals a day (US$3 to US$5). The *Cacique Guest House* (☎ 072-2083) is a bit more expensive but the Takatu is nicer. The (newly constructed) *Savanna Inn Guest House* (☎ 072-2035), about 100m north of the Takatu, offers more comfortable accommodations for US$20 per single room with fan and private bath.

The *Karanambo Ranch* feels more like East Africa than tropical America. Owned and run by the extraordinary Diane McTurk, Karanambo is a nature-lovers' paradise. It is one of the best places to see two spectacular endangered species – the giant river otter and the black caiman. The ranch also offers great fishing and bird-watching. The houses are modeled after Amerindian dwellings; prices run US$100 per person for tourists, US$75 for researchers and US$50 for students (meals are included). Torong Guyana in Georgetown (☎ 02-65298) handles bookings. If Karanambo is full, try less-expensive *Dadanawa Ranch* (US$95/115 singles/doubles) south of town, the *Pirara Ranch* (US$50) north of town, or the *Rock View Ecotourism Resort* (☎ 02-65412) near the Macushi village of Annai at the foothills of the scenic Pakaraima mountains (US$95 per single; negotiate a better rate if you are staying longer). The Rock View has an office in Subryanville in Georgetown at 52 4th St.

Getting There & Away Two local airlines, Roraima and Trans Guyana, make trips from Georgetown for US$180 (see Getting Around under Guyana, earlier). If you're coming overland, try booking a ticket by phone from Brazil, through Weiting & Richter Travel Agency in Georgetown (from Brazil ☎ 02-65121) and paying with a credit card.

In the dry season, overland truck transport is feasible between Lethem and Linden (via Kurupukari), but this is only for travelers with both time and stamina – it takes from two days to two weeks.

To/From Brazil To reach and enter Guyana from Brazil, take an early bus from Boa Vista (see Around Boa Vista in the Brazil chapter) to Bonfim, get off at the last stop (after the bus station) and walk about 2.5km to the Brazilian customs police post. After obtaining an exit stamp in your passport, hire one of the small boats (about US$3) for crossing the Takatu River to Guyana. Officially, the border crossing closes at 6 pm. Go immediately to the police station in Lethem (about 1.5km from the crossing point) to have your passport stamped. There's also an immigration office at the airport, usually open only in the morning.

Going to Brazil is the same in reverse – do it early to ensure you are in time for a bus to Boa Vista. Make sure your papers are in order, as illegal immigration and smuggling are rife here, and checks can be thorough. Note also that Americans need a visa to enter Brazil. While local officials may be amenable to Americans who are entering the country for a meal, making an international phone call or doing some quick shopping, do not overstay your welcome or travel farther into Brazil without a visa or you risk serious problems later.

Suriname

Suriname is an unusual cultural enclave whose extraordinary ethnic variety derives from indigenous cultures, British and Dutch colonization, the early importation of African slaves and, later, workers from China and then indentured laborers from India and Indonesia. Paramaribo, the capital, retains some fine Dutch colonial architecture, but for many the greatest attraction is the country's extraordinary system of nature parks and reserves.

FACTS ABOUT SURINAME
History

Suriname was the last outpost of a once substantial Dutch presence in South America – the Netherlands controlled large parts of Brazil and most of the Guianas until territorial conflicts with Britain and France left them only Dutch Guiana and a few Caribbean islands.

Suriname's 19th-century influx of Hindustanis and Indonesians (locally referred to as 'Javanese') resulted in less overt racial tension than in Guyana, though manipulative Creole politicians were said to have limited the representation of immigrants in the colonial Staten (parliament). Despite limited autonomy, Suriname remained a colony until 1954, when the area became a self-governing state; another 21 years passed before it became independent in 1975.

Since independence, political developments have been uneven. A coup in 1980, led by Sergeant Major (later Lieutenant Colonel) Desi Bouterse, brought a military regime to power. The regime brutally executed 15 prominent opponents in 1982. The government then carried out a vicious campaign to suppress a 1986 rebellion of Maroons (Bushnegros), many of whose villages were destroyed or severely disrupted. Many fled to neighboring French Guiana.

In 1987, a civilian government was elected, but it was deposed by a bloodless coup in 1990. Another civilian government was elected in 1991, and a treaty was signed with the Jungle Commando (the Maroon military) and other armed bands in 1992. A series of strikes and street demonstrations in 1999 have now paralyzed the government.

Suriname's economy resembles that of Guyana. Multinationals like Suralco (a subsidiary of Alcoa) and Billiton (a subsidiary of Royal Dutch Shell) control the bauxite industry.

Geography

With an area of 164,000 sq km, Suriname is about four times the size of the Netherlands and roughly equal in size to the US state of Georgia. To the west, the Corantijn River (Corentyne in Guyana) forms the border, disputed in its most southerly

At a Glance	
Country Name	Republiek Suriname
Area	163,270 sq km
Population	427,980
	(1998 estimate)
Population Density	2.62 per sq km
Capital	Paramaribo
Head of State	President
	Jules Wijdenbosch
Official Language	Dutch
Other Languages	Sranan Tongo,
	Creole, Amerindian
	languages
Currency	Suriname Guilder (Sf)
Exchange Rate	US$1 = Sf695
Per Capita GNP	US$3400 (1997)
Inflation Rate	225%

reaches, with Guyana; the Marowijne (Maroni in French Guiana) and Litani Rivers form the border with French Guiana (also disputed in the south).

The majority of Surinamese inhabit the Atlantic coastal plain, where most of the country's few roads are located. The major links to the interior are by air or north-south rivers, though there is a road to the WJ van Blommensteinmeer (known locally as 'Brokopondo'). The nearby Afobakka Dam created one of the world's largest reservoirs (1550 sq km), Brokopondo, on the upper Suriname River. Rapids limit the navigability of most rivers. Interior mountain ranges are not as high as Guyana's; 1230m Julianatop is the highest point in the country.

Climate

Temperatures and humidity are high. The major rainy season is from April to July, with a shorter one in December and January.

Government

The current constitution, approved in 1987, establishes a 51-seat national assembly that chooses the president. Most parties run along ethnic lines, but a broad coalition of Hindu, Creole and Indonesian parties, known as the Front for Democracy and Development (later the New Front) came to power in 1991 and won a provisional total of 24 seats (out of 51) in the 1996 election. The New Front's Ronald Venetiaan became president, but he was unable to assemble a working majority, and a candidate from Bouterse's party (the NDP), Jules Wijdenbosch, took over as president.

Economy
Suriname relies on bauxite for 70% of its foreign exchange, though its ore deposits are less accessible than those of Guyana. Agriculture, particularly irrigated rice cultivation, is a major industry, as are bananas, and the fishing industry (including aquaculture) is growing. The country is also making a conscious effort to develop tourism in the interior.

After independence, Suriname benefited from a massive aid program from the Netherlands, but the former colonial power suspended assistance in 1983. The economic situation has become increasingly difficult, despite restoration of aid in 1987, and in recent years there have been serious budget deficits. Dutch assistance was again suspended in 1991. This, and a fall in the world price of alumina, led to an economic crisis in Suriname.

A structural-adjustment package included the reduction of the official rate of exchange to realistic (ie, parallel-market) levels, but inflation increased, and key imported commodities were rationed to contain the trade deficit. Shortages have eased, and the exchange rate is holding, but the country still has serious long-term economic problems. Limited Dutch aid has resumed.

Population & People
Of Suriname's population of more than 400,000 people, about 35% are East Indian (both Hindu and Muslim), 32% are Afro-Surinamese, 15% are Indonesian and about 10% are Maroons (the descendants of escaped slaves; they inhabit the forests of the interior), with much smaller numbers of Amerindians, Chinese and Europeans. Many Surinamese people live, or have lived at one time, in the Netherlands, partly because of the greater economic opportunities that exist there and partly to escape military repression.

Education
Innovative literacy programs in past years have raised the level higher than 90%. Paramaribo's Anton de Kom University offers degrees in law, social sciences, physical sciences and engineering.

Arts
Because the language of literacy is Dutch, Surinamese literature is not easily accessible to English-speaking visitors. Some cultural forms derive from the immigrant populations, such as Indonesian *gamelan* music, which can be heard at some special events. The Amerindians weave wonderful baskets, there are a number of excellent painters and the Maroons are widely regarded as the best woodcarvers in tropical America.

Religion
About 40% of the country's population is nominally Christian, mostly Roman Catholic (22% of the total) and Moravian Brethren, but some adherents of these and other Christian groups also practice traditional African beliefs. Hindus compose 26% of the population (most of the East Indian community), while 19% are Muslim (ethnic Indonesians plus a minority of the East Indians). There are also small numbers of Buddhists, Jews and followers of Amerindian religions.

Language
Dutch is the official national language, and standard English is understood by most people. The common, vernacular language in Suriname is Sranan Tongo, an English-based Creole, which is also called Surinaams. Other languages spoken in Suriname include Hindi, Javanese and Chinese. Each of the five Maroon tribes has its own language; they are Aucans, Kwinti, Matawai, Paramaccans and Saramaccans. Amerindian languages that are spoken in Suriname include Akuriyo, Arawak, Carib, Tirió and Wayana.

FACTS FOR THE VISITOR
Highlights
The nature reserves are superb (although the infrastructure is not). Standing atop the Voltzberg dome at sunrise is mind-bendingly spectacular, watching giant leatherback sea turtles lay their eggs is breathtaking, and Surinamese cooking is magnificent (see Food & Drink later in this section).

Planning
When to Go Suriname's dry seasons, from early February to late April and from mid-

SURINAME

August to early December, are the best times for a visit. From March to July, several species of sea turtles come ashore to nest at Wia Wia and Galibi reserves.

Maps Good maps of Suriname are available at Vaco, which is located at Domineestraat 26 in Paramaribo.

What to Bring Bring light clothes that dry quickly and a poncho. If you are planning a trip to the interior, bring fishhooks and knives as trade items, available in Paramaribo, to trade with Indians and Maroons. Maroons also like welcoming gifts of rum (Palm is the preferred brand), but don't bring rum into Indian villages.

Tourist Offices

The Tourist Department office (☎ 471163, fax 420425) is in Paramaribo; its postal address is PO Box 656. People planning a visit should contact a Surinamese embassy if possible – the one in Washington provides a good collection of tourist information, including a nice publication on biological conservation, to correspondents who send a self-addressed envelope (22cm by 28cm) with US$2.50 postage.

Visas & Documents

Passports are obligatory, and those who don't need a visa will be given a tourist card.

In theory, visitors spending more than a week in Suriname require an exit visa (blue card) from the Vreemdelingendienst (Immigration) office (☎ 473101), in the Nieuwe Haven area of Paramaribo. Getting an exit visa involves completing a rather long form and submitting two passport photographs, then crossing town to the District Commissaris Paramaribo (☎ 471131), on Wilhelminastraat, to pay a Sf10 (US$0.20) fee and then returning to the Nieuwe Haven office, in the Havenkomplex off Van't Hogerhuystraat, for the stamp. It may also be wise to keep a record of any official bank currency exchanges.

That said, Suriname is becoming more liberal with its entry requirements, and visas are not required by citizens of Denmark, Finland, Guyana, Israel, Norway, Sweden, Switzerland and the UK. Visas are still needed by Australian, Canadian, Dutch, German, New Zealand and US nationals.

Suriname's overseas representation is very limited, so you can contact the nearest embassy for an application form, but allow four weeks for a postal application. Consulates in Georgetown (Guyana) or Cayenne (French Guiana) charge US$30 for a visitor visa and US$175 for a one-year multiple-entry visa and issue them within a couple of days.

The visitor visa is usually good for two months, but on arrival you will be given only a one-week entry stamp. You will probably finish up having to get an extension from the immigration office in Paramaribo. There is talk of doing away with this foolish requirement, but inquire at immigration when you arrive.

Embassies & Consulates
Foreign Embassies in Suriname Most are in central Paramaribo.

Brazil
(☎ 491011)
Maratakastraat 2, Zorg-en-Hoop
Canada
(☎ 471222)
Honorary consulate: Waterkant 92-94
France
(☎ 476455)
Gravenstraat 5-7
Germany
(☎ 410382)
Consulate: Maagdenstraat 46 bv
Guyana
(☎ 477895)
Gravenstraat 82

Netherlands
(☎ 477211)
Dr JC Mirandastraat 10
UK
(☎ 472870)
VSH United Bldg, Van't Hogerhuysstraat
USA
(☎ 477881)
Dr Sophie Redmondstraat 129
Venezuela
(☎ 475401)
Gravenstraat 23-25

Surinamese Embassies Abroad There are representatives in Guyana, French Guiana, Brazil and Venezuela (for addresses, see the chapters on those countries). Outside of South America, you can refer to the following:

Germany
(☎ 089-55-33-63)
Adolf-Kolping-Strasse 16, Munich

Netherlands
(☎ 070-365-08-44)
Alexander Gogelweg 2, The Hague
(☎ 020-642-61-37)
De Cuserstraat 11, Amsterdam

USA
(☎ 202-244-7488)
4301 Connecticut Ave NW, Suite 108, Washington, DC
(☎ 305-593-2163)
7235 NW 19th St, Miami, FL

Customs
Surinamese regulations permit the duty-free importation of two cartons of cigarettes, 100 cigars or 200 cigarillos or one-half kilo of tobacco; two liters of spirits or four liters of wine may also be imported.

Money
US dollars are the most common foreign currency in Suriname, but Dutch guilders and other major foreign currencies are accepted at most banks. However, you may run into difficulty trying to change Guyanese dollars and sometimes even Brazilian currency. Banks are open weekdays from 7 am to 2 pm.

Currency & Exchange Rates The Surinamese guilder (Sf) is divided into 100 cents. There are banknotes for five, 10, 25, 50, 100 and 500 guilders.

At press time, exchange rates included the following:

country	unit		guilder
Australia	A$1	=	Sf459
Canada	C$1	=	Sf469
euro	€1	=	Sf709
France	FF1	=	Sf108
Germany	DM1	=	Sf362
Japan	¥100	=	Sf574
New Zealand	NZ$1	=	Sf364
UK	UK£1	=	Sf1089
USA	US$1	=	Sf695

Exchanging Money Changing money can involve time-consuming paperwork. Black-market rates are much higher than bank rates – more than 50%. This type of currency exchange is technically illegal and not without risk – short-changing is the most frequent problem. In practice, many businesses will accept US dollars at the usual rate, and many quote prices in dollars.

Credit Cards Credit cards are accepted at major hotels and at travel agencies. American Express is much more commonly accepted than either MasterCard or Visa.

Costs Suriname is neither expensive nor cheap in relation to other South American countries. The cheapest accommodations are very basic and cost US$6 per night, while good rooms are at least US$25. A reasonable restaurant meal is at least US$5. Budget travelers can get by on around US$25 per day. It's possible but difficult to use and exchange traveler's checks in Suriname, and rates are poorer than in other South American countries.

Post & Communications
Postal services in Paramaribo are reliable, but may be less so in other places.

TeleSur (Telecommunicatiebedrijf Suriname) is the national telephone company. Calls abroad can be made from blue public phones. You can pay with *fiches* (coinlike tokens) purchased from a TeleSur office, call reverse charges (collect) or use a home-country direct service (☎ 156 to the US; ☎ 157 to the Netherlands).

Internet Resources
A good introduction to Suriname is 'Welcome to Parbo,' www.parbo.com. The Suriname Tourism Foundation offers a wealth of information for the traveler at mhw.org/tourism. The Amazon Conservation Team site at www.ethnobotany.org often features articles on conservation projects in Suriname.

Books
The *Guide to Suriname,* by Els Schellekens and famous local photographer Roy Tjin, has just been published in English and is available in Parbo at the Vaco Bookstore on Domineestraat. It can also be ordered from Brasa Publishers at sranansani@aol.com or by sending a check for US$20 to HA Reichart, PO Box 6545, San Rafael, CA 94903 in the USA. The most popular book on Suriname is Mark Plotkin's *Tales of a Shaman's Apprentice,* which also includes information on Brazil, Venezuela and the other Guianas. Other good introductions to the region are Henk E Chin and Hans Buddingh's *Surinam: Politics, Economics & Society* and Betty Sedoc-Dahlberg's edited collection, *The Dutch Caribbean: Prospects for Democracy.*

Media
There are two daily newspapers, *De Ware Tijd* and *De West.* The *Suriname Weekly,* in both English and Dutch, is a bit skeletal.

The Surinaams Nieuws Agentschaap (Suriname News Agency, or SNA) prints a daily bulletin in readable if imperfect English. Copies are at the front desk of the Royal Torarica Hotel in Paramaribo.

There are five TV stations and ten commercial radio stations. TV broadcasts are in Dutch, but radio transmissions are also in Hindustani, Javanese and Sranan Tongo (Surinaams).

Time
Suriname is three hours behind GMT/UTC.

Electricity
Electricity supply is 127V and quite reliable. Sockets take a European-style plug with two round pins.

Weights & Measures
Suriname uses the metric system.

GUIANAS

Health

A yellow-fever vaccination certificate is required for travelers arriving from infected areas. Typhoid and chloroquine-resistant malaria are present in the interior. Tap water is safe to drink in Paramaribo but not elsewhere – drink bottled water outside of Parbo. See the Health section in the introductory Facts for the Visitor chapter.

Dangers & Annoyances

Paramaribo is probably the safest capital city in tropical America, but one should be a bit careful after dark. Female travelers will find local males less aggressive than in many Latin American countries.

Business Hours

Most businesses and government offices open weekdays by 7 am and close by mid-afternoon, slightly earlier on Fridays. Banks are open weekdays from 7:30 am to 2 pm. Shops mostly open from 8 am to 4 pm weekdays but close by 1 pm on Saturdays.

Public Holidays & Special Events

The Hindu New Year festival, Holi Phagwah, is held in March or April, while the Muslim holiday, Idul Fitr (Lebaran or Bodo in Indonesian), celebrates the end of fasting at Ramadan. Government offices and businesses are closed on national holidays.

New Year's Day
   January 1
Day of the Revolution
   February 25
Phagwah (Hindu New Year)
   Early March
Good Friday/Easter Monday
   March/April
Labor Day
   May 1
National Union Day
   July 1
Independence Day
   November 25
Christmas Day
   December 25
Boxing Day
   December 26

Activities

There are few facilities for outdoor recreational activities. The coast is not suitable for water sports, though the interior is perfect for ecotourism. Outdoor activities need to be arranged with a local tour operator.

Accommodations

The cheapest hotels and guesthouses cost around US$5, though these places also tend to rent rooms by the hour. Some unappetizing places ask more than US$15 for a room, while modern hotels often cost more than US$35.

Food & Drink

Suriname's food reflects its ethnic diversity and is often superb. The cheapest eateries are *warungs* (Javanese food stalls) serving *bami goreng* (fried noodles) and *nasi goreng* (fried rice), but some of the best upmarket restaurants are also Javanese. Creole cooking mixes African and Amerindian elements into unique combinations. Chinese and Hindustani food is cheap and tasty.

Parbo, the local beer, is of good quality and cheaper than imported Heineken. Boergoe and Black Cat are the best local rums.

Spectator Sports

Sports are important to the Surinamese, and it was a source of great pride when swimmer Anthony Nesty won a gold medal in the 100m butterfly at the 1988 Olympic Games. There are national organizations promoting soccer, basketball, boxing, tennis, volleyball, cycling, weightlifting and many other sporting activities.

Shopping

Maroon handicrafts, especially folding chairs and stools carved from single pieces of white cedar, are very appealing, and cheaper than in Guyana or French Guiana. Amerindian and Javanese crafts are also attractive.

GETTING THERE & AWAY
Air

Those leaving Suriname pay an international departure tax of US$15.

Europe The most direct connection is with KLM, which flies from Amsterdam to Paramaribo twice per week. SLM (Surinam Airways) does the route twice weekly also – a two-month, low-season roundtrip fare costs US$1050. It may be cheaper to fly Air France from Paris to Cayenne (French Guiana) and then go overland to Paramaribo.

North America SLM flies to Paramaribo from Miami several times per week, mostly via the Netherlands Antilles. A 30-day Apex fare is US$560.

Caribbean From Paramaribo, there are connections to the islands of Curaçao, Barbados, Martinique and Trinidad.

Brazil SLM flies between Paramaribo and Belém, in the Brazilian state of Pará, for US$251 one way; US$255 for a 30-day roundtrip fare.

French Guiana Air France and SLM both connect Paramaribo with the city of Cayenne for US$110 one way, US$155 roundtrip.

Guyana SLM flies to Georgetown five times weekly, for a one-way fare of US$103.

Land
French Guiana From Albina, a passenger ferry and, more frequently, canoes cross the Marowijne (Maroni) River to St Laurent de Maroni, from which there's a good road to Cayenne.

Guyana A new ferry that carries both passengers and vehicles crosses the Corantijn (Corentyne) River daily except Sundays and holidays between Corriverton (Springlands) in Guyana and Nieuw Nickerie in Suriname.

GETTING AROUND
Air
Gum Air and SLM operate services to the interior. Although Gum is mostly a charter airline, it is regarded as the most reliable local operator and one of the best in tropical America.

Bus
Medium-size buses on the coastal highway are frequent and cheap. Government buses cost less than private buses, but may be more crowded. There are very few buses off the main routes.

Car
Rental cars are available but expensive. Avis has opened an office in the Hotel Torarica (☎ 421567, fax 456392, paragrp@sr.net).

Taxi
Shared taxis cover routes along the coast, from Paramaribo to Nieuw Nickerie in the west and to Albina in the east. Cab fares are negotiable and generally reasonable. Though several times more expensive than buses, they are notably faster.

Bicycle
Bicycles are a popular means of transport, particularly in Paramaribo.

Boat
To visit many parts of the interior, river transport is the least expensive option. Some coastal areas, such as the Galibi marine turtle reserve near Albina, are accessible only by boat. There are few scheduled services, and prices are negotiable. Ferries and launches cross some major rivers, such as the Suriname and the Coppename, and are very cheap.

Local Transport
Bus There are many local bus and minibus services in Paramaribo. They are crowded, cheap and a real cultural experience.

Taxi Taxis are reasonably priced but unmetered, so set a price before getting in; within town, a fare is US$2 to US$3. Most Paramaribo taxi drivers speak English.

Organized Tours
Visitors interested in Suriname's exemplary system of national parks and reserves should contact Stinasu (Stichting Natuur Behoud Suriname, the Foundation for Nature Preservation in Suriname), which coordinates research and tourism in these areas. Stinasu (☎ 475845, fax 478710) has an office in Paramaribo at Cornelis Jongbawstraat 10, just a few doors east of the Hotel Torarica, and runs some inexpensive guided trips. Travelers with limited time and budget should visit the rain forest in Brownsberg Nature Park just three hours from Paramaribo. Those with more time and resources should not miss the Raleighvallen/Voltzberg Nature Reserve.

METS (☎ 477088, fax 497062), Nassylaan Wagenwegstraat 2, Paramaribo, arranges ecotours in conjunction with Surinam Airways. It has three resorts in the interior and conducts a wide range of trips, from a three-hour tour of Paramaribo (US$15) to an eight-day expedition to Mt Kasikasima (US$575). The best offering is a multiday river tour of Kumalu and the Awarra Dam in the heart of Maroon country (US$375). Tours include all meals, accommodations, transport and guides. There is usually a minimum and maximum number of people for each trip, so it is a good idea to make arrangements in advance.

Ara Cari Tours (☎ 498888, fax 497308, henkgum@sr.net) at Kwattaweg 242, is one of the best local operators and runs a great tour to the Tafelberg, the easternmost of the 'Lost World Mountains.' It also organizes excellent trips to Tonka Island in Broko-pondo and to Frederik Willem rapids in southwest Suriname.

Suriname Safari Tours (☎ 424025, fax 478710, plibre@sr.net), Waterkant 54 bv, runs multiday trips into the interior. Amar's Tour Service (☎ 400372), Estalbrielstraat 16, offers shorter and cheaper trips and are a lot of fun (Jodensavanne is their specialty). Independent Tours (☎ 474770), at Roo-seveltkade 20, features tours of Brownsberg Nature Park. Wild Coast Expeditions (☎ 454900) at Poseidenstraat 62, and Cardy Adventures (☎ 476676, fax 410555), Heeren-straat 19, are well-respected companies that offer tours throughout northern Suriname.

PARAMARIBO

Suriname's capital city, Paramaribo (a cor-ruption of the Amerindian term meaning 'place where the maramara tree grows'), is a curious hybrid of northern Europe, tropical Asia, tropical Africa and tropical America. Imposing buildings overlook grassy squares, wooden houses crowd narrow streets, mosques and synagogues sit side by side and enticing aromas waft from streetside food stalls. The vigorous street life of Paramaribo (often abbreviated to 'Parbo' by locals) includes Javanese vendors peddling fragrant satays, Maroons selling fabulous woodcarv-ings and Dutch-speaking Creoles guzzling beer at pavement cafés.

Orientation

Sprawling Parbo sits on the west bank of the meandering Suriname River. Its core is a compact triangular area whose boundaries are Gravenstraat on the north, Zwarten-hovenbrugstraat on the west, and the river to the southeast. Regular ferries cross the river to Meerzorg, on the east bank. The letters 'bv' in an address mean 'boven' – 'above,' or upstairs.

Information

Tourist Offices The Suriname Tourist Department office (☎ 471163) is at Nassylaan Wagenwegstraat 2, opposite the Star Theater. It's open from 7 am to 3 pm Monday to Thursday, but sometimes closes earlier. The staff members speak English, Dutch and German and have an excellent city map (sometimes out of stock), brochures and a map of the country.

Money The Centrale Bank van Suriname is at Waterkant 20, while the ABN Amro Bank is at Kerkplein 1. Both change traveler's checks and stamp foreign-exchange transac-tion forms. Changing money near Waterkant Market is quicker, but exercise caution – don't pull out your wallet, carry only a modest amount of cash, and count your money carefully, twice. Shopkeepers and hotels may also change money at about the same rate as the banks.

Post & Communications The main post office is at the southwest corner opposite the Dutch Reformed Church. To send urgent or important packages call DHL (☎ 474007). TeleSur's long-distance telephone office is a block south of the post office.

Internet Access Cyber Café (☎ 400162, cafe@cyberlinksr.net), Coppenamestraat 19, offers Internet access as well as some desktop publishing facilities and computer rentals. At press time, several major hotels began to offer Internet access to guests.

Stinasu The Foundation for Nature Preser-vation in Suriname (Stinasu; ☎ 475845) is at Cornelis Jongbawstraat 14, several doors east of the Hotel Torarica. The staff members are very helpful, and many of them speak English.

Bookstores The major bookstore, Vaco, at Domineestraat 26, offers a poor selection of books in Dutch and an even poorer one in English.

Emergency Paramaribo's only hospital for emergency services is the Academisch Ziekenhuis (also called AZ), on Flustraat, west of the city center off of Dr Sophie Redmondstraat.

Things to See

Central Paramaribo's focus is the **Onafhankelijksplein** (Independence Square), which fronts the **Presidential Palace**, on Gravenstraat. Immediately behind the palace is the **Palmentuin**, an attractive park with tall royal palms, picnic tables and benches, some birds and a troop of capuchin monkeys. The finance building, on the west side of the square, looks like it's straight from Amsterdam.

To the east is **Fort Zeelandia**, a pentagonal 17th-century fort that overlooks the river. It has been well restored and is being developed as a venue for small exhibitions – it's well worth a look. Going southwest along Waterkant, you pass some of the city's most impressive colonial buildings, mostly merchants' houses built after the fires of 1832. The streets inland from here, particularly **Lim-a-Po Straat**, have many old wooden buildings, some restored, others in picturesque decay.

Another block inland, on Gravenstraat, is the Roman Catholic **Kathedraal** (1885), which is closed until its sagging wooden superstructure can be repaired. A few blocks to the southwest are some other religious buildings – the main **mosque** and the **Dutch Israeli synagogue** – side by side on Keizerstraat.

Paramaribo's commercial center is along **Domineestraat** and nearby streets. **Central Market** is at the foot of Jodenbreestraat; ferries to Meerzorg leave from nearby.

Out in the suburbs, the **Surinaams Museum**, at Commewijnstraat 18, Zorg-en-Hoop, has a small collection of Amerindian artifacts and worthwhile special exhibits. It's open 7:30 am to 2 pm Monday to Thursday, 5 to 8 pm on Friday, Saturday and Sunday. Admission is cheap, but a cab from the city center will cost about US$6. The museum has a modest selection of souvenirs and books, including some in English.

Special Events

On Sundays, people engage in birdsong competitions on the Onafhankelijksplein. Everyone brings his or her favorite 'twatwa' – usually a seed finch purchased from Indians in the interior. This competition is something of a national obsession and is well worth observing.

Places to Stay

Fanna Guest House (☎ 476789), Prinsessestraat 31, is cheap but unattractive, with ramshackle rooms for about US$6.

Highly regarded is the **YWCA Guest House** (☎ 476981), Heerenstraat 14-16, which has clean, simple singles/doubles for US$12/14. Commonly referred to as 'wyka,' it often fills up, so make a reservation if you can. Paramaribo's best budget accommodation is the *Albergo Alberga* (☎ 74286), Lim-A-Po Straat 13, which has lodging with kitchen and laundry facilities for US$12.50.

Flair Guesthouse (☎ 422455), Kleine Waterstraat 7, just across from the Torarica Hotel (see the end of this section), is clean and recommended and costs about US$14 for a room. Prostitutes operate out of a place just a few doors down, however, and they can be aggressive and persistent as you approach. *Lisa's Guest House* (☎ 476927), Burenstraat 6, is quite a bit better, but overpriced at US$16/20 for singles/doubles with shared bath.

Hotel ABC (☎ 472429, fax 477588), at Mahonielaan 55, is near the Torarica and costs US$40/45 for per single/double. *Hotel Ambassador* (☎ 477555), Dr Sophie Redmondstraat 66, has been renovated and rooms go for US$45/60 singles/doubles. The *Hotel Krasnapolsky* (☎ 475050, fax 420139, krasnam@sr.net), in the heart of downtown at Domineestraat 39, is one of Paramaribo's more upscale places, at US$55/66 for singles/doubles. A bit nicer is the *Eco-Resort* (☎ 425522, fax 411682), next to Stinasu at Cornelis Jongbawstraat 16, which is surprisingly popular with backpackers. Though at $65/75 it is not cheap, the price includes the use of the facilities at the exclusive *Hotel Torarica* (☎ 471500, fax 411682, tor.bc@ sr.net). The Torarica, which is at Mr LJ Rietbergplein 1, is the best and most expensive hotel in the country and is something of a national crossroads; rooms here start at US$99/$107. Even if you don't stay here, be sure to visit on a Friday or Saturday night to people-watch at the bar or behind the hotel at the pavilion built above the Suriname River.

Places to Eat

The absolute cheapest way to eat is to buy fruit or snacks at the *Central Market* (which is much cleaner than those in many other

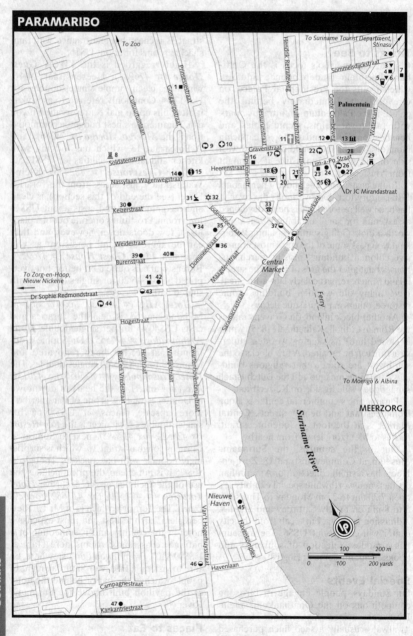

PARAMARIBO

To Zoo

To Suriname Tourist Department, Stinasu

Sommelsdijckstraat

Palmentuin

Central Market

Suriname River

Ferry

To Moengo & Albina

MEERZORG

Nieuwe Haven

To Zorg-en-Hoop, Nieuw Nickerie

0   100   200 m
0   100   200 yards

PARAMARIBO

PLACES TO STAY
1 Fanna Guest House
4 Flair Guesthouse
7 Hotel Torarica
16 YWCA Guest House
23 Albergo Alberga
36 Hotel Krasnapolsky
40 Lisa's Guest House
41 Hotel Ambassador

PLACES TO EAT
3 De Punt
6 La Bastille
21 Roopram's
34 Roopram's

OTHER
2 District Commissaris Paramaribo
5 'K Vat

8 Hindu Temple
9 Guyanese Embassy
10 Hospital
11 Roman Catholic Kathedraal
12 National Assembly
13 Presidential Palace
14 SLM (Surinam Airways), METS
15 Suriname Tourist Department
17 Venezuelan Embassy
18 ABN Amro Bank
19 Post Office
20 Dutch Reformed Church
22 French Embassy
24 KLM Airlines
25 Centrale Bank van Suriname
26 Netherlands Embassy
27 Air France
28 Onafhankelijksplein
29 Fort Zeelandia

30 National Car Rental
31 Mosque
32 Dutch Israeli Synagogue
33 TeleSur
35 Vaco Bookstore
37 Heiligenweg, Local Bus Terminal
38 Ferry Terminal, Buses to
   Moengo & Albina
39 ALM Airlines
42 Touché Disco
43 Minibuses to Nieuw Nickerie,
   Western Suriname
44 US Embassy
45 Vreemdelingendienst
   (Immigration) Office
46 POZ minibus to Johan Pengel
   Airport
47 De Paarl Airport Service

South American countries) or to eat at the *Javanese stalls* along Waterkant (try the salt fish or *petjil*, a type of green bean). Many varieties of Asian cuisine make Suriname a relative paradise for vegetarians (especially since they aren't cooked in lard, as is often the case in Spanish-speaking tropical America). *De Punt*, opposite the Hotel Torarica, serves local fare. When the locals want roti, a tasty Hindustani concoction made by filling a tortilla with meat or vegetables and a fiery curry sauce, they go to *Roopram's* at either Zwarthovenbrugstraat 23 or its other location at the corner of Grote Hofstraat and Watermolenstraat.

Despite the name of the place, *La Bastille* (☎ 473991), Kleine Waterstraat 3, is best known for the 'Chinese hot pot,' a fantastic combination of soup and fondue. Some of the best places are a taxi ride from the center; worth a visit are *Chi Min*, on Cornelis Jongbawstraat, for Chinese food, and *Chez Domi,* on Anton Drachtenweg, which runs along the river northeast of the Torarica, for French and local cuisine. The Javanese section, known as Blauwgrond, north of the center, features people cooking in their kitchens and serving dinner to customers on their patios. The best is *Pawiro's*, at Samson Greenstraat 114.

The best upscale Indonesian restaurants are a bit farther out of town but worth the trip: Don't leave Suriname before trying a *rijstaffel* (multicourse feast) at either

Sarinah's (☎ 430661) or *Jawa* (☎ 492691), both of which are southwest of the center.

Entertainment
After dinner at Pawiro's (see Places to Eat), have a cold beer across the street at *Zanzibar*, whose English-speaking proprietor used to run the forest service and can speak knowledgeably about foreign timber companies coveting Suriname's resources.

On weekends, people gather around *'K Vat,* at the south end of Klein Waterstraat, where there are outdoor tables and sometimes live music. You could also try *Touché* disco, near the Hotel Ambassador on Dr Sophie Redmondstraat. The Torarica Hotel always has live music at the *Saramacca Bar* on both Friday and Saturday nights. Clubs gain and lose popularity very rapidly in Parbo – ask the locals about what is in vogue.

Shopping
Several shops along Domineestraat near the Hotel Krasnapolsky sell attractive souvenirs, most notably woodcarvings, batik and basketwork.

Getting There & Away
Air Paramaribo has two airports, nearby Zorg-en-Hoop (for domestic flights and some flights to Georgetown, Guyana) and the larger Zanderij (for all other international flights), also known as Johan Pengel airport.

GUIANAS

Airlines with offices in Paramaribo include:

Air France
(☎ 473838) Waterkant 12
ALM
(☎ 476066) Burenstraat 34
Gum Air
(☎ 498888) Kwattaweg 254
KLM
(☎ 472421) Dr JC Mirandastraat, near Lim-a-Po Straat
SLM
(☎ 465700) Nassylaan Wagenwegstraat 2

Bus Minibuses to Nieuw Nickerie (US$3.60 for a private bus) and other western destinations leave from the corner of Dr Sophie Redmondstraat and Hofstraat. Buses make two-hour trips to Moengo and four-hour ones to Albina (US$2) at hour intervals. These buses and others bound for eastern destinations leave from the ferry terminal at the foot of Heiligenweg.

Car The most reliable agency in town is Avis, which has an office in the Hotel Torarica (see Places to Stay). Rental agencies include Torarica (☎ 479977), Kankantriestraat 44-48, and Para (☎ 450447). Rental cars are expensive and may not be in perfect condition.

Taxi Taxis leave from the same areas as the minibuses (see Bus, earlier). Going east, it might be better to catch a taxi on the Meerzorg side of the river rather than from the ferry terminal.

Getting Around
To/From the Airport Johan Pengel airport is 45km south of Parbo. A taxi will cost about US$30, but De Paarl Airport Service (☎ 479600), Kankantriestraat 42, is cheaper and will pick you up at your hotel. The much cheaper POZ minibus goes to Pengel from the corner of Campagnestraat and Van't Hogerhuysstraat, near Nieuwe Haven, in daytime hours only.

A taxi to Zorg-en-Hoop airfield from central Parbo is about US$8.

Bus The tourist office has photocopied route maps of Paramaribo's extensive bus system; most buses leave from Heiligenweg, just above the Meerzorg ferry terminal.

Taxi Taxis are usually reasonably priced but unmetered, so agree on the fare in advance; most drivers speak passable English. A short trip will cost around US$2.

AROUND PARAMARIBO
Brownsberg Nature Park & Tonka Island
Brownsberg Nature Park is an area of montane tropical rain forest overlooking WJ van Blommensteinmeer (also called Brokopondo), about 2 hours south of the capital with paved highway most of the way. Stinasu (see that section in Paramaribo) operates occasional day trips with short walks (about US$30, including lunch and transport) on the Mazaroni plateau with fine views of the reservoir and a longer hike down into a canyon with pretty waterfalls. Birds and primates are particularly plentiful. Worth a special trip from Brownsberg is a visit to Tonka Island in the lake, a rustic ecotourism project run by the Saramaccaner Maroons. This can be arranged through Ara Cari Tours in Parbo.

NIEUW NICKERIE
Near the mouth of the Nickerie River, Nieuw Nickerie is Suriname's second port city, exporting rice and bananas. It has a daily ferry to Springlands (Corriverton) in Guyana.

Places to Stay & Eat
Hotel De President, at Gouverneurstraat 104 at St Jozefstraat, is much less pleasant but cheaper than *Hotel de Vesting*, Balatastraat 6, a motel-style place with air-con doubles for around US$18. The most comfortable place in town is the *Residence Inn*, at the corner of W Kanaalstraat and Bharostraat across from the police headquarters; coming in second is the *Hotel Ameerali* (☎ 231265), Maynardstraat 32, with clean but smallish air-con singles/doubles for US$20/30.

Places to eat include the Chinese restaurants *Pak Hap*, at Gouverneurstraat 97, and *New Kowloon*.

Getting There & Away
Air SLM (Surinam Airways; ☎ 031359), Gouverneurstraat 96, has information on irregular flights to Paramaribo. Chartering a plane is possible; private ones usually carry

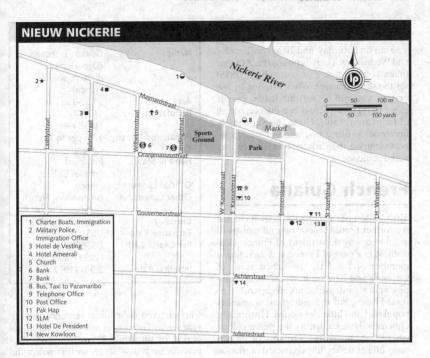

NIEUW NICKERIE

Nickerie River

0   50   100 m
0   50   100 yards

Maynardstraat

Sports Ground

Market

Park

Oranjenassaustraat

Gouverneurstraat

Achterstraat

Julianastraat

Lasthystraat
Batatastraat
Wilhelminstraat
Landingstraat
W. Kanaalstraat
E. Kanaalstraat
Emmenstraat
St Jozefstraat
J.H. Wixstraat

1   Charter Boats, Immigration
2   Military Police,
    Immigration Office
3   Hotel de Vesting
4   Hotel Ameerali
5   Church
6   Bank
7   Bank
8   Bus, Taxi to Paramaribo
9   Telephone Office
10 Post Office
11 Pak Hap
12 SLM
13 Hotel De President
14 New Kowloon

up to five passengers or 400kg total weight
for US$372.

Bus Government buses to Paramaribo
(US$1.85, four hours) leave from the market
on Maynardstraat at 6 am and 1 pm. A
private bus leaves when full, but only after
the departure of the government bus and
costs around US$3.60. A bridge spanning
the Coppename River is scheduled to be
completed sometime in 2000 that could cut
the trip from Nieuw Nickerie to Paramaribo
by at least one hour.

Taxi Taxis to Paramaribo also leave from the
market. With five passengers to share the
cost, the charge is around US$12.50 per
person. They're slightly faster than the buses.

Boat Although the public ferry service was
recently suspended, it is possible to charter a
boat to Springlands (Corriverton) in
Guyana. Expect a thorough customs check
and tedious formalities on each side; see
Corriverton in the Guyana section, earlier in
this chapter.

ALBINA

Albina is a small village that was destroyed in
the civil war of the 1980s and early '90s and is
still recovering. It is located on the west bank
of the Marowijne (Maroni) River, which
forms the border with French Guiana. With
permission from Carib Indians – ask your
boat driver – and a hired canoe, it is possible
to visit the nearby **Galibi Nature Reserve**,
where ridley, green and leatherback turtles
nest in June and July. Trips are best arranged
by Stinasu – contact them in Paramaribo.

The only place to stay in Albina is the
Creek Guesthouse (☎ 458075), a clean and
friendly place with rooms starting at US$15.
The proprietors speak some English and
may be able to help find a guide to the turtle
beaches.

Getting There & Away

Minibuses and taxis to Paramaribo (a four-
hour trip) leave from just outside the
customs and immigration office.

Boat The French ferry crosses to St Laurent
du Maroni in French Guiana two or four

GUIANAS

times daily. The last boat departs at 5 pm on Monday, Thursday, Friday and Sunday; 9:30 am on Saturday; and 10 am on Tuesday and Wednesday. There is no charge. At other times, you can hire a dugout (about US$5) for the short crossing. When arriving by bus or taxi, you will be surrounded by people eager to take you across in a dugout; not all of them are reliable. Go to the Surinamese immigration office first and get your passport stamped, then ask the official to recommend someone.

French Guiana

The smallest of the Guianas, French Guiana is a former French colony now administered as an overseas department of France. Officially, it is a part of France and therefore a member of the EU. The urban areas of Cayenne and Kourou have excellent facilities and an infrastructure comparable to rural France, but the hinterland is sparsely populated and little developed. Historically, Guiana is best known as the penal colony where Captain Alfred Dreyfus (a French army officer wrongfully convicted of treason in 1894) and Papillon (see Books under Facts for the Visitor later) were imprisoned, but today it's famous as the home of the Centre Spatial Guyanais, the launch site for the Ariane rockets of the European Space Agency.

FACTS ABOUT FRENCH GUIANA
History
The earliest French settlement was in Cayenne in 1643, but development of plantations was very limited because of tropical diseases and the hostility of the local Indians. After various conflicts with the Dutch and British and an eight-year occupation by Brazil and Portugal, the French resumed control in 1817. Slavery was abolished in 1848, and the few plantations almost collapsed. A small gold rush in the 1850s saw more laborers desert the plantations, and it precipitated border disputes with Suriname and Brazil.

About the same time, it was decided that penal settlements in Guiana would reduce the cost of prisons in France and contribute to the development of the colony. Convicts

At a Glance	
Name	Guyane Française (Département d'Outre-Mer de France)
Area	91,250 sq km
Population	162,547 (1998 estimate)
Population Density	1.78 per sq km
Capital	Cayenne
Head of State	President Jacques Chirac
Official Language	French
Other Languages	Amerindian, French Guianese Creole
Currency	French Franc (FF)
Exchange Rate	US$1 = FF6.43
Per Capita GNP	US$6000 (1993 estimate)
Inflation Rate	2.5% (1992)

who survived their initial sentences had to remain in Guiana as exiles for an equal period of time, but 90% of them died of malaria or yellow fever, so this policy did little for population growth. French Guiana became notorious for the brutality and corruption of its penal system and was associated with some infamous cases. The last penal settlement closed in 1953.

Guiana became an overseas department of France in 1946, and it receives substantial economic support from the *metropole*. In 1964, work was started on the European space center, which has brought an influx of engineers, technicians and service people from Europe, turning the city of Kourou into a sizable town with every modern amenity.

Geography
French Guiana is roughly the size of Portugal or the US state of Indiana. It borders Brazil in the east and south, while to the west, the Maroni (Marowijne in Suriname) and Litani Rivers form the border with Suriname (the southern part is disputed).

The majority of Guyanais live in the Atlantic coastal zone, which contains most of the country's limited road network. Most of the coast is mangrove swamp, but there are a few sandy beaches.

FRENCH GUIANA

ATLANTIC OCEAN

To Paramaribo

Moengo

Awala
Mana
Albina
St Laurent
du Maroni

Organabo
Iracoubo
Sinnamary

Îles du Salut

Fleuve Mana

Crique Portal

Apatou

Centre Spatial Guyanais

Kourou

Camp Voltaire

Rivière Maroni (Marowijne)

Fleuve Iracoubo

Fleuve Mana

Fleuve Kokioko

St Elie

Tonate

CAYENNE
Rémire

Montsinéry

Matoury

Rivière Koursibo

Roura

Rivière de Kaw

Baie de Oiapoque

Rivière Comté

Tapanahoni River

Grand Santi

Grand Abounami

Lawa River

Crique Sinnamary

Rivière Orapu

Régina

Ouanary

Rivière Arataï

Rivière Matarani

St Georges de l'Oiapoque

Oiapoque

To Macapá

Maripasoula

▲ Montagne Machoulou 782m

Saül

Crique Grand Inini

Rivière Waki

Rivière Tampoki

Fleuve Approuague

SURINAME

▲ Pic Coudreau 711m

Camopi

Fleuve Oiapoque

Rivière Maroni (Marowijne)

Luani River

BRAZIL

Rivière Camopi

Rivière Yaloupi

Claimed by Suriname & French Guiana

Mont St Marcel ▲ 635m

S e r r a   T u m u c u m a q u e

0   50   100 km
0   25   50 miles

The densely forested interior, whose terrain rises gradually toward the Tumac-Humac Mountains on the Brazilian frontier, is very thinly populated. The highest peaks barely exceed 900m.

Climate

French Guiana's rainy season runs from January to June, with the heaviest rains occurring in May.

Government & Politics

French Guiana elects one representative to the French senate and one to the national assembly. It also elects a member to the European parliament. Locally, there are two elected legislative houses, a 19-member general council and a 34-member regional council. Executive authority resides with the commissioner of the republic, usually a career civil servant, appointed for a term of two to three years.

Conservatives have traditionally ruled French Guiana, but the Parti Socialiste Guyanaise has done well since the early 1980s. Some Guyanais favor greater autonomy from France, but very few support complete independence – not surprising given the high level of French economic assistance.

Economy

French Guiana's economy is traditionally dependent on metropolitan France and, to some degree, benefits from its membership in the EU. Successive French governments have provided state employment and billions of francs in subsidies, resulting in a near-European standard of living in the urban areas. Rural villages are much poorer, and in the hinterland many Amerindians and Maroons still lead a subsistence lifestyle. Ironically, the relatively generous welfare benefits provided by the French government have been criticized by locals who feel it provides a disincentive to work.

Historically, the main export product has been rain-forest timber. There is virtually no manufacturing, and agriculture is very poorly developed, except for a few plantations and Hmong market gardens – the vast majority of food and consumer goods are imported. The space center employs nearly 1000 people and comprises about 15% of economic activity.

The main industries now are fishing (fresh and processed shrimp constitute nearly three-quarters of total exports by value), forest products and mining (particularly gold). There are large reserves of bauxite yet to be developed. The tourist industry is embryonic, but growing.

Population & People

French Guiana has only about 150,000 permanent inhabitants, with temporary and migrant workers from Haiti and Brazil making up the balance. Estimates of the ethnic mix vary, but probably around 70% are Creole (of African or Afro-European descent, including Maroons and Haitians), 10% European, 8% Asian, 8% Brazilian and 4% Amerindian. The Boni represent the only endemic tribe of Maroons, although members of the Aucaner (Djuka) and Para-maccaner tribes live in both Suriname and French Guiana. There are two separate Hmong groups, the 'green' and 'white.' Intermarriage between the groups was forbidden in Laos, but permitted in French Guiana to prevent inbreeding.

Education in French Guiana is compulsory until the age of 16, and school attendance is fairly high, but literacy is only about 80%.

Arts

Music and dance are the liveliest art forms – Caribbean rhythms with a French accent. Maroon woodcarvings and Hmong textiles are sold along the roadside. Maroon art is also available in Suriname, whereas the Hmong products are not found elsewhere in the Guianas.

Religion

French Guiana is predominantly Catholic, but Maroons and Amerindians follow their own religious traditions. The Hmong also tend to be Roman Catholics, due to the influence of Sister Anne-Marie Javouhey, the nun instrumental in bringing them to French Guiana.

Language

French is the official language, but French Guianese is a Creole spoken primarily by the blacks of the coastal plain. Amerindians speak tribal languages: Arawak, Carib, Emerillon, Oyapi, Palicur and Wayana.

Sranan Tongo (the lingua franca of Suriname) is spoken all along the Maroni and Lawa Rivers bordering Suriname.

FACTS FOR THE VISITOR
Highlights
The most unforgettable experience is a trip to the pristine rain forests of the interior, although the lack of infrastructure makes this a difficult undertaking without the assistance of a local guide or tour company. Visiting the beach at Les Hattes to watch the spectacular giant leatherback turtles lay their eggs is also highly recommended.

The space center and the Îles du Salut are well worth a visit. Carnaval in Cayenne is a highlight for anyone.

Planning
When to Go The dry season, from July to December, may be more comfortable, but Carnaval, usually in February, is a great attraction.

Maps France's Institut Géographique National publishes a superb 1:500,000 map of French Guiana, with fine city maps of Cayenne and Kourou (FF59 in Cayenne) as well as more detailed maps of the populated coastal areas. There are also 1:25,000 topographic maps available. Both can also be purchased at Le Pou d'Agouti in St Laurent (11 rue Victor Hugo).

What to Bring Travel with light clothing and a poncho. Bring fishhooks and knives as trade goods if visiting the interior.

Tourist Offices
French tourist offices can supply basic information about French Guiana.

Visas & Documents
Passports are obligatory for all visitors, except those from France. Visitors should also have a yellow-fever vaccination certificate.

EU nationals and citizens of Switzerland and the US are not required to have a visa. If you are traveling from Suriname and planning to return to Suriname, be sure to obtain a multiple-entry Surinamese visa. Other visitors (particularly those from Latin America) need a visa: Apply with two passport photos at a French embassy and be prepared

to show an onward or return ticket, to pay a fee of about US$25, and to wait for two or three days. It might take a lot longer at a consulate if they have to refer the application to an embassy. Officially all visitors, even French citizens, should have onward or return tickets, though they may not be checked at land borders.

Embassies & Consulates
French Embassies France has embassies and consulates in neighboring countries in addition to the following:

Australia
(☎ 02-6216-0100) 6 Perth Ave,
Yarralumla, ACT 2600

Canada
(☎ 613-789-1795) 42 Sussex Drive,
Ottawa, Ontario K1M 2C9,

Ireland
(☎ 01-260 1666) 36 Ailesbury Rd, Dublin 4

New Zealand
(☎ 04-472-0200) 1-3 Willeston St, Wellington

South Africa
(☎ 021-23 1575) 2 Dean St, Gardens,
Cape Town

UK
(☎ 020-7823-9555) 6A Cromwell Place,
London SW7

USA
(☎ 202-328-2600) Belmont Rd NW,
Washington, DC

Embassies in French Guiana Several countries have representatives in Cayenne. The nearest US representatives are in Martinique, at 14 rue Blenac, Fort-de-France (☎ 71-9493), or Suriname (see the Suriname section earlier in this chapter).

You can obtain visas for neighboring countries. The Surinamese consulate may charge up to FF150 for the privilege.

Brazil
(☎ 30-0467) 23 Chemin St Antoine

Suriname
(☎ 30-0461) 38 rue Christophe Colomb; visas take one or two days, cost FF150 and require a photo and a ticket out of South America

UK
(☎ 31-1034) 16 Avenue du Président Monerville

Money
The French franc (FF) is the official currency and will be replaced eventually by the euro. It is easy to change cash or traveler's checks in

US dollars in Cayenne (but not Dutch traveler's checks) yet the rates are about 5% lower than official published rates – bring some francs with you. Credit cards are widely accepted, and it is easy to get Visa or MasterCard cash advances at an ATM (*guichet automatique*). Eurocard and Carte Bleue are also widely accepted, and the ATMs at post offices are on the Plus and Cirrus networks. Credit-card charges are billed at a better rate of exchange. At press time official rates of exchange included the following:

country	unit		franc
Australia	A$1	=	FF4.24
Canada	C$1	=	FF4.34
euro	€1	=	FF6.56
Germany	DM1	=	FF3.35
Japan	¥100	=	FF5.32
New Zealand	NZ$1	=	FF3.37
UK	UK£1	=	FF10.01
USA	US$1	=	FF6.43

Costs French Guiana is probably the most expensive country in South America, with prices comparable to metropolitan France. It is difficult to find decent accommodations for less than FF170, but meals are better values, from about FF35. Public transport is limited and far more expensive than in neighboring countries. Tourist services to the interior are very costly. Even parsimonious travelers should budget at least FF250 per day.

Post & Communications

The postal service is very reliable, though all mail is routed through France. There are no central telephone offices, but you can make an international call from any pay phone – dial ☎ 00, then the country code, then the area code, then the local number. For an operator, dial ☎ 00, then 594. You need a telephone card to use public telephones – cards should be available at post offices, newsstands and tobacconists, but they are often in short supply. The country code for French Guiana is ☎ 594.

Internet Resources

French Guiana offers slimmer pickings on the Internet than any other South American country. Check Lonely Planet's 'Destination French Guiana' at www.lonelyplanet.com.au/dest/sam/fgu.htm. The Guiana Shield Media Project features some good information on environmental issues at www.gsmp.org.

Books

The best-known book on French Guiana as a penal colony is Henri Charrière's autobiographical novel, *Papillon*, which was made into a Hollywood film. A factual but very readable account is Alexander Miles' *Devil's Island: Colony of the Damned*. A good overview of the country is featured in *France's Overseas Frontier* by R Aldrich and J Connell. Ann Fadiman's brilliant *The Spirit Catches You and You Fall Down*, though set mostly in California, is the best work explaining the Hmong diaspora.

Media

France Guyane is Cayenne's daily newspaper, with good local and international coverage. French newspapers and magazines are readily available. The *International Herald Tribune* arrives regularly at local newsstands. *Petites Annonces*, a free paper with advertisements and entertainment listings, comes out on Thursdays.

Cayenne has two TV channels and several FM radio stations.

Time

French Guiana is three hours behind GMT/UTC.

Health

Chloroquine-resistant malaria is present, particularly in the interior, and French Guiana is regarded as a yellow-fever infected area. Typhoid prophylaxis is recommended. Excellent medical care is available, but few doctors speak English. See the Health section in the introductory Facts for the Visitor chapter.

Dangers & Annoyances

Generally French Guiana is very safe, but parts of Cayenne are definitely not, especially at night. Avoid the Village Chinois (also known as Chicago) after dark unless accompanied by local friends. There has been a sizable increase in crime and drug trafficking around Cayenne in recent years, and there is often a customs roadblock staffed by gendarmes at Iracoubo. Both locals and foreigners may be thoroughly searched for drugs. For the most part, only eastward traffic is stopped.

Business Hours
Many businesses close for lunch, from about noon to 3 pm.

Public Holidays & Special Events
Carnaval is a big and colorful occasion, with festivities every weekend from Epiphany and for four days solid before Ash Wednesday. Public holidays include:

New Year's Day
    January 1
Ash Wednesday (end of Carnaval)
    February
Good Friday/Easter Monday
    March/April
Labor Day
    May 1
Abolition of Slavery
    June 10
Bastille Day
    July 14
Assumption
    August 15
All Saints Day
    November 1
All Souls Day
    November 2
Veterans Day
    November 11
Christmas Day
    December 25

Activities
Surfing, windsurfing and sailing are possible on quite nice beaches near Cayenne (beware of sharks) and Kourou, but there are few public facilities.

Work
High wages draw workers from Brazil, Haiti and Suriname, especially in construction, but illegal workers are deported when demand slackens. Despite official disapproval, travelers sometimes find work, with payment in cash. An EU passport simplifies matters. Kourou is the best place to look for construction employment, legal or otherwise.

Accommodations
Accommodations are quite good, but expensive – cheap hotels start around FF160 for a single. There are also *gîtes* (rooms or apartments in private houses), which cost from FF120 to FF200 per day, but are cheaper by the week or month. In rural areas, it's possible to hang a hammock in some camping areas from about FF30.

Food & Drink
Excellent food is available, though the better restaurants are very expensive, rarely less than FF50 for a meal and frequently more than twice that. Cheaper cafés and delis have meals for around FF35 that are still very tasty. Asian restaurants and food stalls serve truly delicious Chinese, Vietnamese and Indonesian dishes for as little as FF20.

Imported alcoholic and soft drinks are particularly expensive in bars and restaurants, but can be bought from groceries at more reasonable prices.

Entertainment
Bars and restaurants in Cayenne often have excellent live music, but cover charges and drinks can be ruinous – try listening from the sidewalk.

Shopping
Elaborate tapestries, produced by the Hmong peoples who emigrated here from Laos in the 1970s, are not found elsewhere in South America and can be good value though they are not cheap. Excellent Maroon carvings are sold along the roadside, but they tend to be much more expensive than in Suriname.

GETTING THERE & AWAY
Air
To Suriname, Brazil and other international destinations, the departure tax is FF117. Flights from Cayenne to Paris are regarded as domestic, and there's no departure tax.

There are direct flights to the French Caribbean as well as flights to the following destinations.

Europe The most direct route is from Paris to Cayenne with Air France or AOM. The cheapest published fares are about FF3000 roundtrip. There are also connections via the islands of Guadeloupe and Martinique.

North America There are regular flights with Air France from Miami and other US cities to Guadeloupe and Martinique, with connections to Cayenne.

Brazil Penta flies three times per week from Cayenne to Macapá and Belém. SLM flies to and from Belém (FF2220).

Suriname SLM (Surinam Airways) connects Cayenne with Paramaribo six times weekly (FF1200); four flights continue along to Georgetown.

Land
Brazil From St Georges on the Oiapoque River, there are launches to the Brazilian town of Oiapoque, but you'll have to fly to St Georges.

Suriname From St Laurent de Maroni there is a passenger ferry to Albina, Suriname, with road connections to Paramaribo.

GETTING AROUND
Air
Air Guyane has daily flights going to St Georges (FF490), Saül (FF490) and Maripasoula (FF700).

Bus
There is daily service from Cayenne to St Laurent du Maroni via Kourou, Sinnamary and Iracoubo.

Car & Motorcycle
Car rentals are available in Cayenne, Kourou and St Laurent.

Taxi
Taxis collectifs (actually minibuses) are faster, much more comfortable and more expensive (FF200) than taking the bus from Cayenne to St Laurent. They also run frequently from Cayenne to Kourou.

Hitchhiking
Hitchhiking is never entirely safe in any country in the world, and we don't recommend it. Travelers who decide to hitch should understand that they are taking a small but potentially serious risk. People who do choose to hitch will be safer if they travel in pairs and let someone know where they are planning to go.

Because private cars are numerous and roads are fairly good in French Guiana, some budget travelers choose to hitchhike, but competition is considerable in certain areas, such as on the outskirts of Cayenne on the highway to Kourou.

Boat
River transport into the interior is possible, but requires patience and good timing, unless you are taking an expensive tour.

Local Transport
In Cayenne, local SMTC buses service the region around Cayenne, but the line to the beach areas of Rémire-Montjoly has been discontinued. Nonetheless, public transport is fairly limited, so you may need a taxi.

Organized Tours
Because public transport is so limited, especially in the interior, tours are a good way to see the country, but they are not cheap. For example, a five-day trip up the Maroni (Marowijne) river, with transport from Cayenne, costs about FF2790 per person, all-inclusive. Tours of the space center are free.

CAYENNE
Dating from 1664, French Guiana's capital (population 40,000) is one of the loveliest capital cities in South America. Though the city lacks the soaring grandeur of Buenos Aires, its lovely French-colonial architecture gives it a charm reminiscent of New Orleans' French Quarter. The excellent Creole food and the unique ethnic mix – locals, French expatriates, Brazilian fisherman, Surinamese Maroons and Hmong farmers – make this a fun place to spend a few days.

Orientation
Cayenne is at the west end of a small, somewhat hilly peninsula between the Cayenne and Mahury rivers. The center of action is the Place des Palmistes, in the northwest corner of town, where there are many cafés and outdoor food stalls. To its west, the Place Grenoble (also known as Place Léopold Héder) is one of the oldest parts of Cayenne. The area south of the market, called the Village Chinois, has some of the best music and nightlife, but it's not safe unless you're with a local, especially at night.

Information
Tourist Offices The Agence Régionale de Développement du Tourisme et des Loisirs

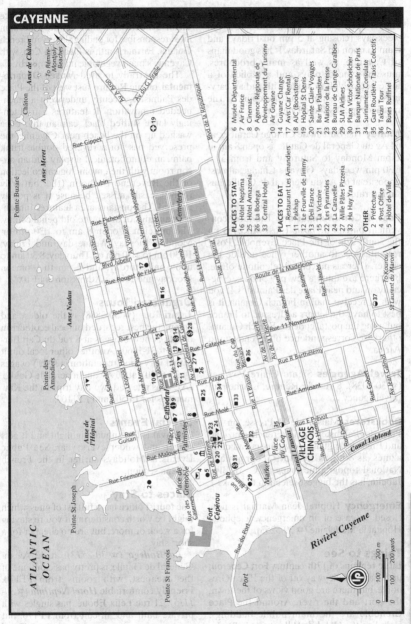

CAYENNE

PLACES TO STAY
16 Hôtel Neptima
25 Hôtel Amazonia
26 La Bodega
33 Central Hotel

PLACES TO EAT
11 Restaurant Les Amandiers
12 Pakhap
13 Le Fourville de Jimmy
15 La Victoire
21 Les Pyramides
24 La Caravelle
27 Mille Pâtes Pizzeria
32 Ha Hay Yan

OTHER
2   Préfecture
4   Post Office
5   Hôtel de Ville
6   Musée Départemental
7   Air France
8   Cinemas
9   Agence Régionale de
    Développement du Tourisme
10 Air Guyane
14 Guyane Change
17 Avis (Car Rental)
18 AJC (Bookstore)
19 Hôpital St Denis
20 Sainte Claire Voyages
21 Bar les Palmistes
23 Maison de la Presse
28 Bureau de Change Caraïbes
29 SLM Airlines
30 Place Victor Schoelcher
31 Banque Nationale de Paris
34 Surinamese Consulate
35 Gare Routière, Taxis Collectifs
36 Takari Tour
37 Buses Ruffinel

de la Guyane (☎ 30-0900), at 12 rue Lalou-ette, is open 8 am to noon and 3 to 6 pm weekdays (closing at 5 pm on Friday) and 8 am to noon on Saturday. It has good maps of Cayenne, as well as many brochures, museum-type displays and a replica of a huge petroglyph (a stone with Indian carvings) from the interior of the country. The manager speaks some English.

Money The Bureau de Change Caraïbes, at 64 Av du Général de Gaulle, is open 8 am to 1 pm Monday to Saturday and from 3 to 6:30 pm weekdays. Guyane Change, almost opposite at 63 Av du Général de Gaulle, has similar rates.

Post & Communications The most convenient *bureau de poste* (post office) is on the south side of the Place Grenoble. Poste restante goes to another office outside the center. There is no central telephone office, but there are quite a few pay phones, especially on and near Place des Palmistes. If you wish to receive mail in French Guiana, it is best to have the letters addressed to France but using the postal code for French Guiana, otherwise correspondence often ends up in Africa.

Travel Agencies Sainte Claire Voyages (☎ 30-0038), 8 rue de Rémire, is a helpful travel agency.

Bookstores Maison de la Presse, on the Place des Palmistes, carries French, Brazilian and English-language newspapers and magazines, as well as Institut Géographique National topographic maps. AJC, 31 Blvd Jubelin, has the biggest selection of books.

Emergency Hôpital Jean Martial is now closed. In case of an emergency, telephone Hôpital la Madelaine (☎ 39-5253).

Things to See
Little remains of 17th-century **Fort Cépérou**, up a narrow alleyway off of the Place Grenoble, but there are good views of the town, the port and the river. Around the **Place Grenoble** are the main public buildings, including the **Hôtel de Ville** (town hall), the **post office** and the **Préfecture**. Across the **Place des Palmistes**, Av du Général de Gaulle is the main commercial street.

South across rue de Rémire, the **Place Victor Schoelcher** commemorates the man most responsible for ending slavery in French Guiana. Farther south is **Place du Coq**, with Cayenne's main vegetable market nearby.

The centrally located **Musée Départemental**, on rue Rémire, just west of the Place des Palmistes, recently underwent a much-needed renovation. It features a frighteningly large stuffed black caiman that once washed up on the beach near Cayenne, the preserved base of a revered double-trunk palm, an ethnobotanical display and an air-con room with the entomological collection of the Reverend Barbotin (the 'butterfly room'), easily missed because it is poorly marked. The upstairs area features intriguing paintings of life in the old penal colony. The museum is open 8 am to 1:30 pm on Monday, Tuesday, Wednesday, and Friday; 10:30 am to 1:30 pm on Thursday; 8:30 am to noon on Saturday; and 3 pm to 6 pm on Monday and Friday. Admission is FF10.

Organized Tours
Takari Tour (☎ 30-3888) is the oldest and among the best regarded of local ecotourism outfits. A new office is at 8 rue du Cap Bernard (☎ 31-1960). Another other local outfit with a very good reputation is JAL Voyages (☎ 31-6820), at 26 Av du Général de Gaulle. JAL runs one and two-day trips to the Kaw marshes for FF500 and FF1100.

Special Events
Carnaval is the annual highlight and it gets bigger and wilder every year. See Public Events & Holidays earlier in the French Guiana section.

Places to Stay
The tourist office has a full list of gîtes, which might be worth considering if you're staying for a week or more, but are no cheaper for a short stay.

La Bodega (☎ 30-2513), at 42 Av du Général de Gaulle, is pretty basic but one of the cheapest, with rooms from FF130. Friendly, comfortable *Hôtel Neptima* (☎ 30-1115), 21 rue Félix Eboué, has singles with private bath and air-con from FF170, but most rooms are more expensive. *Hôtel Ajoupa* (☎ 30-3308) is 2km out of town, on Route de Cabassou, but it's comfortable, with a pool and rooms from FF200 to FF270.

Other places are more expensive, such as *Central Hotel* (☎ 31-3000), on the corner of rue Molé and rue Lt Becker, which has singles/doubles from FF250/280, and *Hôtel Amazonia* (☎ 31-0000), 26 Av du Général de Gaulle, which goes even higher.

A few top-end places, like the *Hôtel Novotel* (☎ 30-3888), start at around FF550. The *Motel Beauregard* (☎ 35-4100) in Rémire-Montjoly (several kilometers out of Cayenne), PK 9, 2 Route de Rémire, has bungalows for two people starting at FF350; the price includes use of health club, tennis court and pool.

Places to Eat
Best quality for the lowest prices are the mobile *food stalls* around the Place des Palmistes in the evening, where delicious crêpes, Indonesian fried noodles or tasty hamburgers will cost from FF10 to FF15.

Deli France, on the corner of rue Justin Catayée and Av du Général de Gaulle, has great coffee, sandwiches and yummy pastries. Nearby, *La Fourville de Jimmy*, 42 rue Justin Catayée, is another good place for a budget breakfast or a snack. *La Victoire*, at 40 rue XIV Juillet, serves very tasty Chinese and Creole dishes at outdoor tables and is an economical and friendly place to eat. *Mille Pâtes Pizzeria* (☎ 31-9019), 52 rue Justin Catayée, is a little more expensive, but it makes a mean pizza for FF30 to FF40. *Pakhap*, 29 rue Arago, is a cheap Chinese place offering very good food.

There are other interesting eateries in the streets south of Place des Palmistes. *Les Pyramides*, on the corner of rue Christophe Colomb and rue Malouet, is a Middle Eastern restaurant with couscous for FF55 and grills for FF45. Going east on rue Christophe Colomb you come to *La Caravelle*, one of the cheaper French restaurants, serving main courses from FF50 to FF90; there's a Wild West-style saloon next door. A couple of blocks away on rue Monerville, *Ha Hay Yan* serves delicious Chinese and Vietnamese dishes to eat in or take away at budget prices.

Perhaps the best restaurant is *Les Amandiers* (☎ 31-3875), facing the pleasant park at Pointe des Amandiers – starters cost FF55 to FF65, fish from FF70 to FF90, and main courses are around FF100. This is pricey, but a good value compared with

Parisian prices, and the set menus, at FF65, FF70 and FF120 for three courses, are almost bargains. The better hotels, like the *Amazon* and *Novotel*, also have good but expensive restaurants.

Entertainment
Bar Les Palmistes, an indoor-outdoor café-bar on Av du Général de Gaulle, at the southwest corner of Place des Palmistes, is an expensive place to drink but sometimes has good live music. *Le Cric Crac*, at Motel Beauregard in Rémire-Montjoly, has a dance band on Saturday nights. Some of the best *reggae music* is in small clubs in Village Chinois, but you'd be ill advised to go there at night without a local friend. *Cinemas* on the east side of Place des Palmistes show European and American films, mostly in French, but sometimes in English with French subtitles.

Shopping
There are several souvenir shops along Avenue du Général de Gaulle. Handicrafts are similar to those in Suriname, but prices are much higher. The most unique offerings are Hmong textiles.

Getting There & Away
Air Rochambeau airport (☎ 35-9350), which is about 15km southwest of Cayenne, has flights to local, regional and international destinations.

Note that SLM offices in Cayenne will not reconfirm Saturday flights from Paramaribo to Georgetown, because those flights leave from Zorg-en-Hoop rather than Johan Pengel airport (also called Zanderij). Airlines with offices in Cayenne include:

Air France
    (☎ 30-2740) 13 Place Léon Gontrand Damas
Air Guyane
    (☎ 35-6555) 2 rue Lalouette
AOM
    (☎ 35-7746)
SLM
    (☎ 31-7298) 915 rue L Blanc
TABA
    (☎ 31-2147) 5 Route de Baduel

Bus Buses Ruffinel (☎ 31-2666), 8 Av Jean Galmot, has a scheduled service to St Laurent du Maroni (FF150, five hours) and intermediate destinations like Kourou (FF50) at 5:30 am Monday to Saturday.

Car Because of limited public transport, car rental is worth considering, even though it's expensive. Eurofranc (☎ 31-9042) is one of the cheapest, with cars from FF85 per day, plus FF95 for insurance and FF1.20 per km. Avis (☎ 30-2522), in town and at the airport, may give you a good deal if you book the car in advance through an Avis agency at home. Other companies include Aria (☎ 30-4050) which is probably the least expensive, Europcar (☎ 35-1827), ACL (☎ 30-4756), Jasmin (☎ 30-8490), Hertz (☎ 351171) and Citer (☎ 30-6512). Most have an office at the airport, but it's easier to shop around by phone.

Taxi Taxis collectifs to Kourou and St Laurent du Maroni leave when full from the Gare Routière on Avenue de la Liberté. They cost FF70 more than the bus to St Laurent, but are much faster and more comfortable. You usually have to wait before they fill with passengers before departing.

Hitchhiking Hitching to Kourou and St Laurent is feasible, but competition is considerable at the junction of the Kourou and Régina highways. On Sunday it may be the only option.

Getting Around
To/From the Airport Taxis to Rochambeau cost about FF100, but they can be shared. It is far cheaper to take a taxi collectif to Matoury, but that still leaves 5km to Rochambeau. Make sure that taxi drivers do not tack on bogus surcharges for each piece of luggage when you arrive at your final destination.

Bus SNTC runs several local bus routes, although the No 6 to the beach area of Rémire-Montjoly has been discontinued. Buses don't run on Sundays.

Taxi Taxis have meters and charge a hiring fee of FF10.60 plus FF5.30 (FF7.42 at night, Sundays and holidays). Settle the rates in advance, or you'll be charged for each piece of luggage.

AROUND CAYENNE
Rémire-Montjoly
Montjoly has Cayenne's best beach, reachable by taxi. It also features historical ruins at **Fort Diamant**, a hiking trail to the top of **Montagne du Mahury** and an early colonial sugar mill at **Vidal de Lingendes**. There is a lovely 5km hiking trail along the lakes at Le Rorota. Another interesting 5km hike goes into the **Grand Matoury Nature Reserve** at La Mirande.

Emerald Jungle Village
The best ecotourism opportunity in the vicinity of Cayenne (and perhaps the best value in all of French Guiana) is Emerald Jungle Village, 97356 Carrefour du Gallion (☎ 28-0089, fax 30-0682), on Route Montsinéry about an hour-long drive from Cayenne. The lodge is in an abandoned French Foreign Legion post and run by expat Dutchman Joep Moenen, a biologist who used to be the director of the Paramaribo Zoo in Suriname. Joep knows both Suriname and French Guiana extremely well and speaks Dutch, English, French and German fluently. The lodge, which holds only eight people (reserve in advance!) is solar powered and features a library and a botanical trail. The staff at the lodge run excursions throughout eastern French Guiana. Emerald Jungle Village also rents canoes to nonguests and lends canoes and mountain bikes to guests.

Roura
In a scenic area on the highway to Kaw, this village on the east bank of the Mahury River has an interesting 19th-century church. Near Roura is the Laotian village of **Dacca**; canoe trips are possible on Gabrielle Creek, and there is a side road to Fourgassier Falls. *Le Relais de Patawa* (☎ 31-9395), on the Kaw highway, has hammock space (FF20); it also rents hammocks (FF40) and offers beds (FF60). Meals cost FF70 to FF90.

Kaw & the Trésor Nature Reserve
Reachable by paved and dirt highway to the Kaw River, then by launch across the river, the Trésor Nature Reserve is one of French Guiana's most accessible wildlife areas. The newly created reserve encompasses a huge swath of the Kaw ecosystem and is an excellent place to observe the giant black caiman as well as spectacular waterfowl like the scarlet ibis. **Mont Favard** features hiking trails and petroglyphs (rock carvings). Basic lodging is available in the village of Kaw. JAL and other agencies run trips from Cayenne. It is also

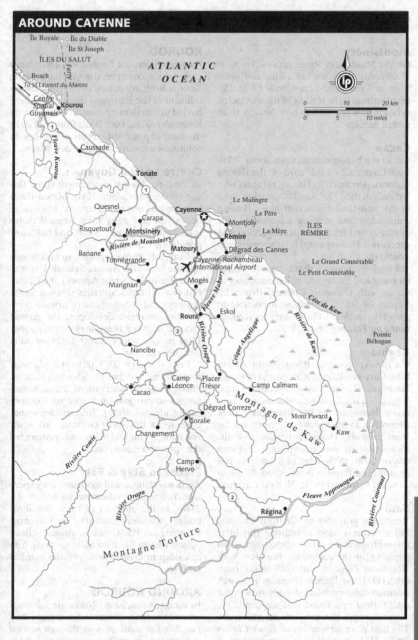

AROUND CAYENNE

Île Royale   Île du Diable
            Île St Joseph
ÎLES DU SALUT

Beach
To St Laurent du Maroni

Centre
Spatial
Guyanais   Kourou

ATLANTIC
OCEAN

0   10   20 km
0   5   10 miles

Caussade

Tonate

Quesnel

Carapa   Cayenne   Le Malingre

Risquetout   Montsinéry   Le Père
                        Montjoly
Banane   Rivière de Montsinéry   Rémire   La Mère
      Tonnégrande   Matoury   Dégrad des Cannes
                Cayenne-Rochambeau
      Marignan   International Airport   Le Grand Connétable
                Mogès   Le Petit Connétable

ÎLES
RÉMIRE

Roura   Eskol

Nancibo   Crique Angélique   Rivière de Kaw   Pointe
                            Béhague

Camp   Placer
Léonce   Trésor   Camp Caïmans
Cacao
        Dégrad Correze   Mont Favard
    Coralie   Kaw
Changement   Montagne de Kaw

Camp
Hervo

Rivière Comte

Rivière Orapu

Rivière Oyac   Fleuve Approuague

Régina   Rivière Courouaï

Montagne Torture

possible to catch a launch downstream from Régina.

Montsinéry

On the Montsinéry River, some 45km west of Cayenne, this town has a little zoo, open 9 am to 7 pm daily; admission is FF70. The big attraction is the feeding of the spectacled caimans at 6 pm on Sundays. Nearby is an orchid garden.

Cacao

Cacao is a beautiful little town about 75km from Cayenne by a side road off the Régina highway, populated by Hmong refugees who left Asia in the 1970s. Sunday – market day – is the best time for a visit here; Hmong embroidery and weaving are available for purchase, and the authentic Asian food (the specialty is Hmong soup) is inexpensive and delicious.

From Cayenne, there are Monday morning and Friday afternoon minibuses to Cacao with Transport Collectif Bruno Le Vessier (☎ 30-5132), making it possible to spend the weekend. For lodging, try *Restaurant Lau Faineng* (☎ 30-2830).

Régina

On the Approuague River, about 100km from Cayenne, Régina is at the end of Route Nationale 2. Once a gold-mining area, Régina is a small village, and somewhat rundown. However, the **Les Nourages Nature Reserve** is located along the river not far from the town. Though generally off-limits to tourists (it was set up as a research station), trips to the edge of the reserve can be arranged through Association Aratie at 2 rue du Lt Goinet (☎ 31-3568) in Cayenne.

Saül

Reachable primarily by air from Cayenne (40 minutes, US$80 roundtrip) this little mining town in the center of the country is a paradise for the ecotourist. The New York Botanical Garden and colleagues from ORSTOM, the French Overseas Research Institute, have established study sites in the undisturbed rain forest that surrounds the town. The area is honeycombed with trails. The best place to stay is *Les Eaux Claires* (☎ 27-0171), north of town; prices start at FF180 per night. Trips through the trails can

be booked through the office of Takari Tours in Cayenne; see the Cayenne section, earlier.

KOUROU

For several decades, Kourou was a moribund ex-penal settlement on the west bank of the Kourou River, 65km west of Cayenne. Establishment of the European space center here has led to a modern new town, overwhelming Kourou's colonial core. Boats from here go to the ruins of penal settlements on the Îles du Salut, now a favorite weekend destination.

Centre Spatial Guyanais

In 1964, the French government chose this site (900 sq km along 50km of coastline) because it's close to the equator, has a large ocean frontage away from tropical storm tracks and earthquake zones, and has a low population density.

Currently, three separate organizations operate here – the Agence Spatiale Européenne (European Space Agency), the Centre National d'Études Spatiales (French Space Agency) and Arianespace (a private commercial enterprise developing the Ariane rocket). Between them, they employ about 1100 people and conduct eight or nine launches per year.

Free tours (☎ 33-4200) take place at 7:45 am and 1:45 pm Monday to Thursday. Phone ahead for reservations, though sometimes you can join on a tour on the spot (bring identification). Tour guides sometimes speak English or German – ask when you book. At the end of the tour, you can see the Spacexpo exhibition.

Places to Stay & Eat

Accommodations and food are very expensive. You might try *Kourou Accueil* (☎ 32-2540), in the old part of town, but most budget travelers will stay in Cayenne. Camping on Île Royale is another cheap option (see the Îles du Salut section). You can sleep in *carbets* (huts) on the beaches for free.

AROUND KOUROU

Beyond Kourou, Route Nationale 1 detours around the space center to Sinnamary, then parallels the coast, passing through several picturesque villages before turning inland at Organabo. A side road goes to the village of

Mana, whereas the main highway continues to St Laurent du Maroni.

Îles du Salut

Best known for the notorious prison at Île du Diable (Devil's Island), the Îles du Salut (Salvation Islands) are 15km north of Kourou over choppy, shark-infested waters. For 18th-century colonists, the islands were an escape from mainland fever and malaria because the sea breezes kept mosquitoes away. The prisons came later, with as many as 2000 convicts.

Île Royale, the largest of the three islands, was the administrative headquarters of the penal settlement, while the smaller Île St Joseph was reserved for solitary confinement. Île du Diable, a tiny islet now covered with coconut palms, was home to political prisoners, including Alfred Dreyfus (see the introduction to the French Guiana section, earlier). Nearly inaccessible because of hazardous currents, the island was linked to Île Royale by a 225m supply cable.

The space center has some installations on Île Royale, but the atmospheric ruins are the main attractions. Surprisingly abundant wildlife includes macaws, agoutis and sea turtles.

Places to Stay & Eat The *L'Auberge des Îles du Salut* (☎ 32-1100) offers hammock space (FF50), dormitory accommodations (FF70) and singles/doubles (from FF210/270). The midday fixed-price meal is good but expensive at FF120. Free camping is possible, but bring food unless you can subsist on coconuts and fallen mangoes; the water is not potable, but mineral water is available at L'Auberge des Îles du Salut.

Getting There & Away From the jetty at Kourou's *marché de poissons* (fish market), a very comfortable launch crosses to Île Royale at 8 am daily (FF190 roundtrip, one hour). Make reservations with Carbet des Îles (☎ 32-0995) or Takari Tours (☎ 31-1969) in Cayenne, though usually it is possible to show up and buy a ticket on the spot. The problem is getting to Kourou from Cayenne in time – a Ruffinel bus is the best bet, but they don't run on Sunday. Taxis collectifs don't leave until they're full, and even the first ones may not make it. On the return

trip, ask drivers in the parking lot for a lift back to Cayenne.

Sinnamary

Sinnamary, a village of 3500 people, is 50km northwest of Kourou. There is an Indonesian community here that produces excellent woodwork and jewelry among other folk arts. The cheapest place to stay is the *Sinnarive Motel* (☎ 34-5646), with rooms at FF220. Local artwork made from bird feathers is based on wholesale slaughter of the scarlet ibis – caveat emptor. Be sure to hike at least part of the 20km old St. Elie mining trail for great birdwatching.

Iracoubo

Iracoubo, 30km west of Sinnamary, is best known for its parish church. The church has an interior elaborately painted by a convict named Huguet, who remained in the area after his release. Ask your bus driver or taxi collectif to stop so you can see it. Accommodations at the *Hôtel au Fil de L'Eau* (☎ 34-6351) cost FF200. Nearby is the Amerindian village of Bellevue, which has attractive Nalina pottery for sale.

ST LAURENT DU MARONI

Once a reception camp for newly arrived convicts, St Laurent retains some picturesque colonial buildings and a certain backwater charm. It is on the east bank of the Maroni (Marowijne) River, which borders Suriname. You can arrange boat trips up the river, which has many Maroon and Amerindian settlements along its banks.

Information

Tourist Offices St Laurent's helpful Office de Tourisme (☎ 34-2398), near the jetty at the north end of town, is open 7:30 am to 6 pm daily (9 am to noon Sunday). Some of the staff speaks English, and the office has maps, brochures and displays. Another good place for getting one's bearings is the Rainforest Information Center (also known as Le Pou d'Agouti, ☎ 34-3325), 11 rue Victor Hugo, which offers maps and books.

Money There is a bureau de change at 19 rue Montravel (open 7:30 to noon daily and 3 to 4 pm except Wednesday and Saturday). There's an ATM at the post office. The

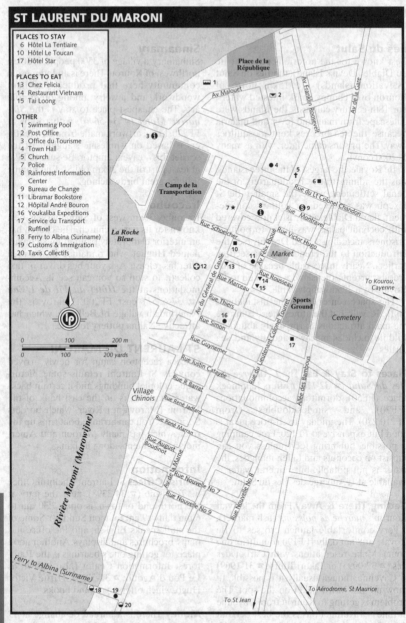

ST LAURENT DU MARONI

PLACES TO STAY
6 Hôtel La Tentiaire
10 Hôtel Le Toucan
17 Hôtel Star

PLACES TO EAT
13 Chez Felicia
14 Restaurant Vietnam
15 Tai Loong

OTHER
1 Swimming Pool
2 Post Office
3 Office du Tourisme
4 Town Hall
5 Church
7 Police
8 Rainforest Information
    Center
9 Bureau de Change
11 Libramar Bookstore
12 Hôpital André Bouron
16 Youkaliba Expeditions
17 Service du Transport
    Ruffinel
18 Ferry to Albina (Suriname)
19 Customs & Immigration
20 Taxis Collectifs

Place de la
République

Av Malouet

Av Franklin Roosevelt

Av de la Gare

Camp de la
Transportation

La Roche
Bleue

Rue du Lt Colonel Chandon

Rue Montravel

Rue Schoelcher

Rue Victor Hugo

Av Félix Eboué

Market

Rue Rousseau

Rue du Général de Gaulle

Rue Marceau

Rue Thiers

Rue Simon

Rue Guynemer

Rue Justin Catayée

Rue R Barrat

Rue René Jadfard

Rue René Maran

Rue August
Boudinot

Av de la Marne

Rue Nouvelle No 7

Rue Nouvelle No 9

Rue Nouvelle No 8

Rue du Lieutenant Colonel Tourtet

Allée des Bambous

Sports
Ground

Cemetery

Village
Chinois

Rivière Maroni (Marowijne)

Ferry to Albina (Suriname)

To Kourou,
Cayenne

To Aérodrome, St Maurice

To St Jean

0   100   200 m
0   100   200 yards

GUIANAS

Banque National has closed, although a new bank will open soon.

Post The post office is at the north end of Av du Général de Gaulle.

Travel Agencies For ecotourism river excursions or fishing trips, contact Youkaliba Expeditions (☎ 34-1645), 3 rue Simon. A half-day trip can be arranged for 150FF, while a 12-day excursion is 3940FF. The Rainforest Information Center also arranges ecotours and has English-speaking guides. Tropic-Cata (☎ 34-2518), which is at 142 rue R Barrat, offers boat tours of the Maroni River.

Medical Services The Hôpital André Bouron (☎ 34-1037) is on Av du Général de Gaulle.

Camp de la Transportation

At the creepy Camp de la Transportation (1857), prisoners arrived for processing and transfer to the various prison camps throughout the territory. You can walk through the same gates as Dreyfus and Papillon – but you can leave more easily than they did.

Many of the buildings have deteriorated, and exuberant tropical vegetation has softened some of the grim history, but you can still see the long common cell blocks, with shackles and open toilets, and the solitary confinement cells with their tiny windows. Several buildings have been restored, and free guided tours (mostly in French) leave from the tourist office seven times daily. The camp is open from 8:30 am to 12:30 pm and 2:30 to 6:30 pm daily. Admission is 15FF for adults and 10FF for students.

Places to Stay & Eat

Hôtel Star (☎ 34-1084), at 109 rue Thiers, has a pool and is a relatively good value, with rooms from FF190 to FF300. *Hôtel La Tentiaire* (☎ 34-2600), at 12 Av Franklin Roosevelt, is the best in town, with very nice rooms from FF240/420. The *Hôtel Toucan* is not recommended if you plan to stay more than an hour.

St Laurent has many good but mostly expensive restaurants; the cheapest alternative is the *Javanese food stalls* along Av Félix Eboué, which offer good and filling bami goreng with a side order of satay for

about FF20. Other Asian eateries include the reasonably priced *Restaurant Vietnam*, 19 Av Félix Eboué, and the nearby *Tai Loong*.

For Creole cuisine, try *Chez Felicia*, on Av du Général de Gaulle. The well-known boat-restaurant *La Goelette* (☎ 34-2897), on the Balate Plage, serves a unique combination of French and Brazilian cuisine.

The Chinese restaurant at the *Hôtel Star* is tasty and inexpensive, and the snack bar at *Le Toucan* is much better than the accommodations there. Worth a trip is the *Les Pieds dans L'Eau* (☎ 34-3884) just south of town (turn right after the Balate bridge), which features excellent French cuisine and a lovely beach setting by the water on rue St Louis.

Getting There & Away

Bus Service de Transport Ruffinel leaves Hôtel Star for Cayenne daily at 5 am (FF150).

Taxi Taxis collectifs leave from the pier when full or nearly so. They are faster, more comfortable and more convenient than buses and are more expensive (FF200 to Cayenne).

Boat The ferry (FF30) crosses to Albina two or four times daily; the last boat is at 4 pm most days, but it would be much wiser to get a morning boat, at 7 or 9 am Monday to Saturday, to make sure you can get through to Paramaribo before dark – you don't want to stay in Albina. At other times, you can hire a motorized dugout pirogue (about FF30) for the short crossing.

Getting Around

Maroni Rent a Car (☎ 34-1430) at 6 rue Jean Jacques Rousseau rents cars for FF230 per day plus mileage. Taxis around town cost FF25.

AROUND ST LAURENT DU MARONI
Mana-Les Hattes

About 50km northeast of St Laurent by a good road is the rustic village of Mana. It has a particularly beautiful waterfront on the Mana River, considered to be one of the loveliest and unspoiled rivers in northern South America.

There are Indian settlements at Awala, 20km west of Mana. At nearby **Plage Les Hattes**, near the Carib Indian village of Yalimapo, giant leatherback turtles come ashore to nest from April to July; their eggs hatch between July and September. This is the highest density of leatherback-turtle nesting sites in the world. The number of turtles that come ashore in the spring is so high that one biologist has likened the scene to a tank battle. The Indians are constructing guesthouses so that they may capture some of the revenue from visiting tourists and researchers, and no one should miss visiting here if it is turtle-egg laying season.

Off the St Laurent-Mana road is **Javouhey**, a Hmong refugee village. It has a popular Sunday market. The **Relais de l'Acarouany** (☎ 341720), which was once a leprosarium, offers accommodations.

Maripasoula

Maripasoula is a popular destination for upstream travelers coming from St Laurent du Maroni because it has an airfield where connections to Cayenne can be made. Going upriver beyond Maripasoula to visit the Wayana Indian villages requires obtaining permission from the Préfecture in St Laurent or Maripasoula.

ST GEORGES DE L'OIAPOQUE

This town on the Brazilian border is not accessible by road, though a track has been cut to Régina, and a road is under construction. Air Guyane sends two flights per day from Cayenne (FF299 one way). Take your chances on food and accommodations at **Chez Modestine** (☎ 37-0013).

From St Georges, you can take a launch (FF25) across the river to the Brazilian town of Oiapoque, where a scheduled daily bus ostensibly departs for Macapá at noon (in fact, it leaves when it's full).

There is much illegal immigration from Oiapoque to Cayenne via precarious, ocean-going dugout canoes. People have died on these voyages, and travelers bound for French Guiana should avoid them. Unscheduled coastal freight boats might take a passenger to Cayenne or Macapá.

Paraguay

Once a notorious police state, Paraguay now welcomes adventurous visitors to the riverside capital of Asunción, the Jesuit missions of the upper Río Paraná and the vast, arid Chaco.

Facts about Paraguay

HISTORY
Pre-Columbian Paraguay
Early Guaraní cultivators occupied most of what is now eastern Paraguay, but several hunter-gatherer groups, known collectively as Guaycurú, inhabited the Chaco, west of the Río Paraguay. Other hunter-gatherers lived in forest enclaves near the modern Brazilian border. Though usually peaceful, the Guaraní sometimes ventured into Guaycurú territory and even raided the Andean foothills.

Arrival of the Spaniards
In 1524, Alejo García walked across southern Brazil, Paraguay and the Chaco with Guaraní guides; his discoveries of silver led to the Río de Solís being renamed the Río de la Plata (River of Silver). Sebastián Cabot sailed up the Paraguay in 1527, but founded no permanent settlements.

Pedro de Mendoza's expedition, fleeing Buenos Aires, settled at Asunción, where Spanish-Indian relations took an unusual course: The Guaraní absorbed the Spaniards into their social system by providing them with women, and therefore food, since women were the farmers in Guaraní society. As heads of household, an informal arrangement ratified by the *encomienda*, the Spaniards adopted Guaraní food, language and other customs, and there emerged a hybrid, Spanish-Guaraní society in which Spaniards dominated politically and *mestizo* children adopted many Spanish cultural values.

Jesuit Missions
Colonial 'Paraguay' encompassed parts of modern Brazil and Argentina, where Jesuit missionaries regimented the Guaraní into

At a Glance

Country Name	República del Paraguay
Area	406,752 sq km
Population	5.2 million
Population Density	12.8 per sq km
Capital	Asunción
Head of State	President Luis González Macchi
Official Languages	Spanish, Guaraní
Other Languages	German, Lengua, Nivaclé, Aché & other indigenous languages
Currency	Guaraní (₲)
Exchange Rate	US$1 = ₲ 3303
Per Capita GNP	US$1600 (1998)
Inflation Rate	14.6% (1998)

settlements where they learned many aspects of European high culture, as well as new crafts, crops and methods of cultivation. Until their expulsion in 1767, the Jesuits deterred Portuguese intervention and protected Spanish interests. For more information on Jesuit missions, see the entry on Argentine Mesopotamia.

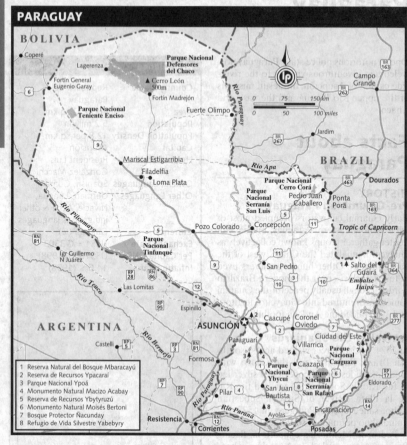

PARAGUAY

BOLIVIA

Coperé

Lagerenza

Parque Nacional
Defensores
del Chaco

Fortín General
Eugenio Garay

▲ Cerro León
500m

Fortín Madrejón

Parque Nacional
Teniente Enciso

Fuerte Olimpo

Campo
Grande

BR 163

BR 262

Jardim

BR 267

Mariscal Estigarribia

Filadelfia

Loma Plata

Río Apa

BRAZIL

Parque Nacional
Cerro Corá

BR 463

Dourados

Parque
Nacional
Serranía
San Luis

Pedro Juan
Caballero

Ponta
Porã

BR 163

Río Pilcomayo

Pozo Colorado

Concepción

Tropic of Capricorn

RN 81

Igr Guillermo
N Juárez

Parque
Nacional
Tinfunqué

San Pedro

Salto del
Guairá

BR 364

RP 28

RN 86

Embalse
Itaipú

Río Teuco

Las Lomitas

RP 95

Espinillo

ARGENTINA

Río Bermejo

Castelli

RP 5

RP 3

RN 81

Caacupé

ASUNCIÓN

Paraguarí

Coronel
Oviedo

Ciudad del Este

BR 277

Formosa

Villarrica

Parque
Nacional
Caaguazú

Parque
Nacional
Ybycuí

Caazapá

Parque
Nacional
Serranía
San Rafael

Eldorado

RP 17

Pilar

San Juan
Bautista

Río Paraná

Encarnación

RN 14

Resistencia

Río Paraguay

RP 7

RP 90

RN 12

Ayolas

Corrientes

Posadas

0   75   150km
0   50   100 miles

Río Paraguay

1   Reserva Natural del Bosque Mbaracayú
2   Reserva de Recursos Ypacaraí
3   Parque Nacional Ypoá
4   Monumento Natural Macizo Acabay
5   Reserva de Recursos Ybytyruzú
6   Monumento Natural Moisés Bertoni
7   Bosque Protector Ñacunday
8   Refugio de Vida Silvestre Yabebyry

The Jesuits were less successful among the
Guaycurú, for whom, wrote one Austrian
father, the Chaco was a refuge 'that the
Spanish soldiers look upon as a theater of
misery, and the savages as their Palestine and
Elysium.' There they had 'mountains for
observatories, trackless woods for fortifications, rivers and marshes for ditches, and
plantations of fruit trees for storehouses.'
After secular Spaniards realized the Chaco
lacked precious metals, they ignored the area.

Independence & the Reign of 'El Supremo'

Within a few years of Paraguay's uncontested
independence in 1811, José Gaspar Rodríguez de Francia emerged as the strongest

member of a governing junta. Until his death
in 1840, the xenophobic 'El Supremo' sealed
the country's borders to promote national
self-sufficiency – large-scale subsistence. He
expropriated the properties of landholders,
merchants and even the Church, controlled
the small agricultural surplus – mostly *yerba
mate* and tobacco – and ruled by fear, impris-
oning opponents in what one visiting Englishman called 'state dungeons.'

Francia himself succumbed to the climate
of terror. After escaping an attack in 1820,
El Supremo so feared assassination that he
had his food and drink checked for poison,
demanded that no one approach him closer
than six paces, ordered streets to be cleared
for his carriage and slept in a different place

every night. Perhaps thanks to these precautions, he died a natural death. In 1870, opponents who knew how to hold a grudge threw his disinterred remains into the river.

López Dynasty & War of the Triple Alliance

By the early 1860s, Francia's successor, Carlos Antonio López, ended Paraguay's isolation, building railroads, telegraph, an iron foundry, a shipyard – and a standing army of 28,000, with another 40,000 reserves (Argentina had only 6000 men in uniform). His megalomaniac son, Francisco Solano López, led the country into a catastrophic war against the triple alliance of Argentina, Uruguay and Brazil. Paraguay lost 150,000 sq km of territory, and perhaps 20% of its population through combat, famine and disease; it is said that only women, children and burros remained.

Reconstruction & the Chaco War

After 1870, a trickle of European and Argentine immigrants resuscitated the agricultural sector, but political life did not stabilize for decades. At the turn of the century, tension arose with Bolivia over the ill-defined borders of the Chaco, but full-scale hostilities did not erupt until 1932. A 1935 cease-fire left no clear victor, but a treaty awarded Paraguay three-quarters of the disputed territory. Petroleum speculation fueled the hostilities, but none was ever discovered.

Modern Developments

After the Chaco War, Paraguay endured a decade of disorder before a brief civil war brought the Colorado party to power in 1949. A 1954 coup installed General Alfredo Stroessner, who ruled harshly for 35 years until his overthrow in 1989. Since then the political environment has improved, but Stroessnerites still dominate a faction of the Colorado party. For more information on the regime and its successors, see the Government & Politics section below.

GEOGRAPHY & CLIMATE

Paraguay appears small on the map, but at 407,000 sq km it is larger than Germany and almost exactly the size of California. About 40% of its territory is east of the Río Paraguay, where a well-watered plateau of rolling grasslands, with patches of subtropical forest, extends all the way to the Río Paraná, which forms much of Paraguay's borders with Brazil and Argentina.

Evenly distributed throughout the year, annual rainfall averages 2000mm near the Brazilian border and declines to about 1500mm near Asunción. Summer highs average 35°C (95°F); winter temperatures average a pleasant 22°C (72°F) in July, the coldest month. Spring and autumn cold fronts can cause temperatures to drop 20°C (68°F) within a few hours.

West of the Río Paraguay, the Gran Chaco is an extensive plain whose principal economic activity is cattle ranching. Hotter than eastern Paraguay, its erratic rainfall and high evaporation make rain-fed agriculture undependable, but Mennonite immigrants have raised cotton and other commercial crops successfully.

FLORA & FAUNA

Like rainfall, vegetation diminishes from east to west. Humid subtropical forests are dense in eastern Paraguay's valleys and occurrences of them are sparse on thinner upland soils. Toward the Río Paraguay, the dominant vegetation is savanna grass, with occasional gallery forests, while to its west, palm savanna gives way to scrub and thorn forest.

Wildlife is diverse, but the dense rural population has put pressure on eastern Paraguay's fauna. A notable international conservation success has been the survival of the Chacoan peccary, once thought extinct. Bird life is abundant, especially in the Chaco, where the most conspicuous species are jabirú and wood storks. Many reptiles, including caiman, anaconda and boa constrictor, inhabit the riverine lowlands.

Paraguay has several national parks and other reserves protecting a variety of habitats. The three largest are in the Chaco, with smaller but more biologically diverse units in eastern Paraguay. Because of corruption, economic pressure and traditionally weak political commitment, some have experienced serious disruption.

For information on Paraguayan parks and reserves, try the Dirección de Parques Nacionales y Vida Silvestre (☎ 021-445214), in the Edificio Ayfra, at Ayolas and Presidente Franco in Asunción. See also the Useful Organizations entry, in the Facts for the Visitor section.

PARAGUAY

GOVERNMENT & POLITICS

Paraguay's 1992 constitution establishes a strong president, popularly elected for a five-year term, who appoints a seven-member cabinet. Congress consists of a lower chamber of deputies and an upper senate elected concurrently with the president. The supreme court is the highest judicial authority.

From 1947 to 1989, under Stroessner and his military-dominated Colorado party, the country experienced one of the continent's most corrupt, odious and durable dictatorships. In 1989 General Andrés Rodríguez (also a Colorado) deposed Stroessner and then won the presidency, unopposed, in a 1991 election in which opposition congressional parties were more successful than ever. In May 1993 Juan Carlos Wasmosy, a civilian engineer from Stroessner's Colorado faction, won a presidential election that, despite an atmosphere of intimidation, was probably the fairest in Paraguayan history.

The prognosis for enduring democracy is uncertain, given Paraguay's authoritarian tradition and the entrenched Colorado elite. Nominated by the Colorados as a figurehead, Wasmosy came into conflict with the still-powerful military, most notably coup-monger General Lino Oviedo, who was forced out of the service and imprisoned in 1996. Oviedo's stalking horse Raúl Cubas won the presidential election of 1998 and immediately pardoned the ambitious general. The Colorados also won 24 of 45 senate seats; 44 of 80 seats in the lower house and 14 of 17 departmental governorships.

When Vice President Luis Argaña was gunned down by assassins in March 1999, popular sentiment linked Cubas and Oviedo to the murder and Cubas was forced to resign from office. Luis González Macchi, who had been president of the senate, was sworn in, while Cubas and Oviedo sought asylum in neighboring countries.

ECONOMY

Historically, the economy depends on exports of beef, maize, sugarcane, soybeans, lumber and cotton, but many rural people cultivate subsistence crops on small holdings. Paraguay's major industry remains contraband, including electronics and agricultural produce, but Mercosur tariff reductions may decrease smuggling by making imported goods cheaper in the neighboring member countries of Argentina, Brazil and Uruguay. Stolen cars and illegal drugs, including cocaine, are other goods that, unfortunately, pass into or through Paraguay.

Paraguay lacks mineral energy resources, but enormous multinational dam projects have developed its hydroelectric potential over the past two decades. A construction slowdown due to completion of Itaipú and continuing problems with Yacyretá have eliminated the economic growth of the 1970s. The growth rate for 1998 was –0.5%, and inflation was at 14.6 also fell to 6%. The official minimum wage is US$240 per month, but lax enforcement means that probably 70% of Paraguayan workers fall below this level.

POPULATION & PEOPLE

Paraguay's population is about 5.2 million, while Asunción (population 500,000) is the largest city; many exiles have returned since the fall of Stroessner, but others remain outside the country for economic reasons. Barely half live in urban areas, compared with 90% in Argentina and Uruguay. More than 95% live in eastern Paraguay. Infant mortality is relatively high at about 3.8.

More than 75% of Paraguayans are mestizos, speaking Guaraní by preference, though almost all speak Spanish. Another 20% or so are descendants of European immigrants, including German Mennonite farmers in the middle Chaco. Japanese immigrants have settled parts of eastern Paraguay, along with Brazilian colonists who have moved across the border in recent years. Asunción has seen an influx of Koreans, mostly involved in commerce.

Most indigenous Paraguayans, about 3% of the population, inhabit the Chaco. The largest groups are the Nivaclé and the Lengua, which each number around 10,000. Isolated peoples like the Ayoreo have lived almost untouched by European civilization, but many others have become dependent labor for immigrant farmers.

ARTS

Paraguay's major literary figures are poet-novelist Augusto Roa Bastos, winner of the 1990 Cervantes Prize, and poet-critic Josefina Pla. Despite many years in exile, Roa

Bastos has focused on Paraguayan themes and history in the context of politics and dictatorship. Little Paraguayan literature is available to English-speaking readers; for suggestions, see Books & Maps in the Facts for the Visitor section.

Theater is popular, with occasional offerings in Guaraní as well as Spanish. Numerous art galleries emphasize modern, sometimes very unconventional works. Venues in Asunción offer classical and folk music.

SOCIETY & CONDUCT

English-speaking visitors may find Paraguay exotic because of its unique racial and cultural mix, but Paraguayans are eager to meet and speak with foreigners. An invitation to drink mate, often in the form of ice-cold *tereré*, can be a good introduction.

An ability to speak German may dissolve barriers in the culturally insular Mennonite communities, but it is more difficult to meet the region's indigenous people, and undiplomatic to probe too quickly into relations between the two. Some Chaco Indians speak German (rather than Spanish) as a second language.

RELIGION

Roman Catholicism is official, but folk variants are important, and the Church is less influential than in other Latin American countries. Native peoples have retained their religious beliefs, or modified them only slightly, despite nominal allegiance to Catholicism or evangelical Protestantism. Protestant sects have made fewer inroads than in other countries, although Mennonites have proselytized among Chaco Indians since the 1930s.

LANGUAGE

Spanish is the language of government and commerce, but Paraguay is officially bilingual. Spanish has influenced the Guaraní language, but Guaraní has also modified Spanish in vocabulary and speech patterns. During the Chaco War against Bolivia, Guaraní enjoyed resurgent popularity when, for security reasons, field commanders prohibited Spanish on the battlefield.

Several other native tongues, including Lengua, Nivaclé and Aché, are spoken in the Chaco and isolated parts of eastern Paraguay.

Facts for the Visitor

HIGHLIGHTS

Southern Paraguay's Jesuit mission ruins are no less appealing than Argentina's, while the riverside capital of Asunción is a livelier city since the overdue return of democracy. The Chaco, with its abundant bird life, is still one of South America's last frontiers.

PLANNING

Visitors from midlatitudes may prefer the winter months from, say, May to August or September, when the country seems positively springlike. During the summer heat, Paraguayans dress very informally in light cottons, but a sweater or light jacket is advisable for changeable spring weather. If you're outdoors in the brutal subtropical sun, don't forget a wide-brimmed hat or baseball cap, a lightweight long-sleeved shirt and sunblock. Mosquito repellent is imperative in many places, including the Chaco.

Maps

For about US$7.50, the *Guía Shell*, despite limited and conventional tourist information, contains the most useful road map of the country, plus a good general country map at a scale of 1:2,000,000 and a very fine map of Asunción, with a street index, at 1:25,000.

TOURIST OFFICES

There are tourist offices in Asunción, Encarnación and Ciudad del Este, but only the Asunción office is really helpful.

Tourist Offices Abroad

The larger Paraguayan consulates (see list) may be able to help with tourist inquiries.

VISAS & DOCUMENTS

All foreigners need a visa, except visitors from bordering countries (who need national ID cards), most Western European countries and the USA. Canadians, Australians and New Zealanders need to obtain visas in advance, but there is no longer a fee. Canadians should apply through the consulate in New York.

Paraguay no longer requires a tourist card, but be sure to get your passport stamped on entering the country or you may be subject to fines on leaving. Paraguay requires that foreign drivers possess the International

Driving Permit, although document checks are usually perfunctory.

EMBASSIES & CONSULATES
Paraguayan Embassies & Consulates
Paraguay has no diplomatic representation in Australia or New Zealand, but has representatives in neighboring countries and in:

UK
(☎ 0171-937-1253)
Braemar Lodge, Cornwall Gardens, London SW7 4AQ
USA
(☎ 202-483-6960)
2400 Massachusetts Ave NW, Washington, DC, 20008
(☎ 305-573-5588)
2800 Biscayne Blvd, Miami, FL 33137
(☎ 212-682-9441)
675 3rd Ave, Suite 1604, New York, NY 10017
(☎ 310-203-8920, fax 310-203-8927)
1801 Ave of the Stars, Suite 421, Los Angeles, CA 90007

Embassies & Consulates in Paraguay
South American countries, the US and most Western European countries have representatives in Asunción, but the nearest Australian and New Zealand embassies are in Buenos Aires. The consulates listed here are all in Asunción, except where noted.

Argentina
(☎ 021-212320)
Av España at Av Perú
Encarnación: (☎ 071-203446)
Mallorquín 788
Bolivia
(☎ 021-210676)
Eligio Ayala 2002
Brazil
(☎ 021-448084)
3rd floor, General Díaz 521
Cuidad del Este: (☎ 061-512308)
Pampliega 337
Encarnación: (☎ 071-203950)
Memmel 452
Canada
(☎ 021-226196)
Profesor Ramírez at Juan de Salazar
France
(☎ 021-212439)
Av España 893

Germany
(☎ 021-214009)
Av Venezuela 241
UK
(☎ 021-496067)
4th floor, Presidente Franco 706
USA
(☎ 021-213715)
Av Mariscal López 1776

CUSTOMS
Paraguayan customs allows you to bring in in 'reasonable quantities' of personal effects, alcohol and tobacco.

MONEY
Currency
The unit of currency is the guaraní (plural guaraníes), indicated by ₲. Banknote values are 500, 1000, 5000, 10,000, 50,000 and 100,000 guaraníes; there are coins for 50, 100 and 500 guaraníes.

Exchange Rates
Prices in this chapter are given in US dollars. No black market exists. At press time, exchange rates were as follows:

country	unit		guaraníes
Australia	A$1	=	₲2182
Canada	Can$1	=	₲2230
euro	€1	=	₲3366
France	FF1	=	₲513
Germany	DM1	=	₲1721
Japan	¥100	=	₲2730
New Zealand	NZ$1	=	₲1732
UK	UK£1	=	₲5168
USA	US$1	=	₲3303

Exchanging Money
Cambios in Asunción and at border towns change both cash and traveler's checks (with small commissions); try banks in the interior. Some travelers have reported that cambios will not cash traveler's checks without the bill of sale. Street changers give slightly lower rates, and for cash only, but can be helpful on weekends or evenings.

Better hotels, restaurants and shops in Asunción accept credit cards, but their use is less common outside the capital. ATMs here often do not recognize foreign credit cards.

Tropical rain forest, Brownsberg NP, Suriname

Kaieteur Falls, Guyana

Penal colony ruins, Île Royale, Îles du Salut, French Guiana

Fishing boats, Punta del Este, Uruguay

Cartmaker, Piribebuy, Paraguay

Architectural detail, Montevideo, Uruguay

Makeshift home in rural Paraguay

Costs

Travel in Paraguay is generally cheaper than in neighboring countries, except for Bolivia.

POST & COMMUNICATIONS

Essential mail should be sent registered. Antelco, the state telephone monopoly, has central long-distance offices; it may soon undergo privatization. Offices in Asunción have fiber-optic lines with direct connections to the USA, Britain, Australia, Germany and Japan. Credit card or collect calls to the USA and other overseas destinations are cheaper than paying locally. For local calls, public phone boxes (which take ficha tokens rather than coins) are few and far between.

Paraguay's international telephone code is ☎ 595. For an international operator, dial 0010; for Discado Directo Internacional (DDI), dial ☎ 002.

BOOKS

Roa Bastos' novel *Son of Man* (1961) links several episodes in Paraguayan history, including the Francia dictatorship and the Chaco War. *I the Supreme* is a historical novel about the paranoid dictator Francia.

Elman and Helen Service's *Tobatí: Paraguayan Town* is a standard account of rural Paraguay in a historical context. Harris Gaylord Warren's *Rebirth of the Paraguayan Republic* analyzes Paraguay's incomplete recovery from the War of the Triple Alliance.

Rule by Fear: Paraguay After Thirty Years Under Stroessner (Americas Watch, 1985) is an account of human rights abuses. Carlos Miranda's *The Stroessner Era* is a thoughtful, nonpolemical analysis with a short political obituary.

MEDIA

Asunción's daily *ABC Color* made its reputation opposing the Stroessner dictatorship; independent Radio Ñandutí also criticized the regime. The editorially bold *Ultima Hora* is very independent, and has broken stories about the deaths of army conscripts – usually termed 'suicides' – under suspicious circumstances; it also has an excellent cultural section. Stroessner cronies control *Hoy* and *Patria* (the official Colorado newspaper). *El Pueblo* is an independent with a small circulation. Asunción's German community publishes the twice-monthly *Neues für Alle* and the weekly *Rundschau*.

TIME

Paraguay is three hours behind GMT except in winter (April 1 to September 30), when daylight-saving time adds an hour.

ELECTRICITY

Electric current operates on 220V, 50Hz.

WEIGHTS & MEASURES

The metric system is official.

HEALTH

Malaria is not a major threat, though Itaipú dam appears to have created a mosquito-vector habitat. Causes for concern, but not hysteria, are tuberculosis, typhoid, hepatitis and hookworm – avoid going barefoot. Cutaneous leishmaniasis, transmitted by biting sandflies and resulting in open sores, is unpleasant and dangerous if untreated.

USEFUL ORGANIZATIONS

For visitors interested in natural history and conservation, the Fundación Moisés Bertoni (☎ 021-608790; mbertoni@pla.net.py), Prócer Carlos Argüello 208 in Asunción, is a private conservation organization that works with landowners and the government and also arranges tours to reserves it helps manage.

Motorists should contact the Touring y Automóvil Club Paraguayo. See Car & Motorcycle under Getting Around for more information.

DANGERS & ANNOYANCES

In Asunción and elsewhere, carjackings of conspicuously valuable vehicles have been a problem, but personal safety concerns are generally less serious than in Brazil. Since the ousting of Stroessner, police and the military operate with less impunity, but try not to aggravate them and always carry your passport.

Poisonous snakes are common in the Chaco, but mosquitoes are a likelier nuisance.

BUSINESS HOURS

Most shops open weekdays and Saturday from 7 am to noon, then close until mid-afternoon and stay open until 7 or 8 pm. Banking hours are usually 7:30 to 11 am

PARAGUAY

weekdays, but casas de cambio keep longer hours. From mid-November to mid-March, government offices open as early as 6:30 am and usually close before noon.

PUBLIC HOLIDAYS & SPECIAL EVENTS

Paraguay's celebration of Carnaval is liveliest in Asunción, Encarnación, Ciudad del Este, and Villarrica. Caacupé is the most important site for the Roman Catholic Día de la Virgen.

Año Nuevo (New Year's Day)
    January 1
Día de San Blas (Patron Saint of Paraguay)
    February 3
Carnaval
    February (date varies)
Cerro Corá
    (Death of Mariscal Francisco Solano López)
    March 1
Viernes Santo/Pascua (Good Friday/Easter)
    March/April (dates vary)
Día de los Trabajadores (Labor Day)
    May 1
Independencia Patria (Independence Day)
    May 15
Paz del Chaco (End of Chaco War)
    June 12
Fundación de Asunción (Founding of Asunción)
    August 15
Victoria de Boquerón (Battle of Boquerón)
    September 29
Día de la Virgen (Immaculate Conception)
    December 8
Navidad (Christmas Day)
    December 25

ACTIVITIES

Conventional beach and river activities such as swimming and fishing are common options, but Paraguay's biological diversity makes it a notable destination for nature-oriented visitors, particularly birders.

ACCOMMODATIONS

Hotels and residenciales resemble those in Argentina, but are generally less expensive. Camping facilities are less common, but in most remote areas you can camp just about anywhere.

FOOD & DRINKS

Parrillada (grilled meat) is popular, but meat consumption is lower than in Argentina or Uruguay. Tropical and subtropical food-stuffs, nourishing the rural poor, play a greater role in the Paraguayan diet.

Grains, particularly maize, and tubers like manioc (cassava) are part of almost every meal. *Locro,* a maize stew, resembles its Argentine namesake, while *mazamorra* is a corn mush. S*opa paraguaya* is corn bread with cheese and onion; *chipa guazú* is a variant. *Mbaipy so-ó* is a hot maize pudding with meat chunks, while *bori-bori* is a chicken soup with corn-meal balls. *Sooyo sopy* is a thick soup of ground meat, accompanied by rice or noodles, while *mbaipy he-é* is a dessert of corn, milk and molasses.

In *chipa de almidón,* manioc flour replaces the corn-meal of c*hipa guazú. Mbeyú,* or *torta de almidón,* is a grilled manioc pancake resembling the Mexican tortilla. During Holy Week, the addition of eggs, cheese and spices transforms ordinary food into a holiday treat.

Paraguayans consume quantities of mate, most commonly as ice-cold *tereré.* Roadside stands offer *mosto* (sugarcane juice), while *caña* (cane alcohol) is a popular alcoholic beverage.

ENTERTAINMENT

Cinema and live theater are popular in Asunción, and the capital's cultural life is livelier since the overthrow of Stroessner.

SPECTATOR SPORTS

Paraguayans in general are very sports minded; the most popular soccer team, Olimpia, has beaten the best Argentine sides. Tennis and basketball are also popular spectator sports.

SHOPPING

The women of Itauguá, a village east of Asunción, produce ñandutí lace, ranging in size from doilies to bedspreads. In the town of Luque, artisans produce handmade musical instruments, particularly guitars and harps.

Paraguayan leather goods are excellent and inexpensive. Chaco Indians produce animal carvings from aromatic palo santo and traditional string bags *(yiscas).*

Asunción and Ciudad del Este are good places to look for electronics, particularly to replace a lost or stolen camera.

Getting There & Away

Asunción is a convenient hub for Southern Cone air transport, but overland travelers may find Paraguay a bit out of the way.

AIR
International departure taxes total US$17, but travelers spending less than 24 hours in the country are exempt. The major airport is Asunción's Aeropuerto Internacional Silvio Pettirossi, though Ciudad del Este is growing in importance.

Paraguay's Transportes Aéreos Mercosur (TAM) flies twice daily to Buenos Aires; daily to Brazilian destinations including Rio de Janeiro, São Paulo and Brasília; and less frequently to the Brazilian cities of Curitiba, Porto Alegre and Belo Horizonte, and to Santa Cruz (Bolivia). TAM also flies several times weekly to Montevideo and Punta del Este (Uruguay), Santiago (Chile) and Lima (Peru).

Aerolíneas Argentinas flies three times weekly to Ezeiza. Lloyd Aéreo Boliviano (LAB) flies Tuesday and Friday to Santa Cruz, with onward connections. Varig flies daily to São Paulo and Rio de Janeiro, Saturday to São Paulo only, and Thursday and Sunday to Florianópolis and Curitiba.

LanChile flies four times weekly to Santiago and three times to Iquique. The Chilean carrier Avant has acquired the routes of Santiago-based National Airlines, which had similar services to LanChile.

See the Asunción Getting There & Away section for a listing of airline offices.

LAND
Argentina
The following are routes between points in Paraguay and Argentina:

Asunción to Clorinda There is frequent bus service from Asunción to Clorinda, in Formosa province.

Encarnación to Posadas Buses use the Puente Internacional Beato Roque González to Argentina, and passenger launches still cross the Río Paraná.

Ciudad del Este to Puerto Iguazú Frequent buses link Ciudad del Este to Puerto Iguazú, Argentina, via the Brazilian city of Foz do Iguaçu.

Bolivia
Regular bus service now links Asunción with Boyuibe and Santa Cruz de la Sierra. Beyond Mariscal Estigarribia, the dirt road is subject to long delays in the event of heavy, if infrequent, rains. In the absence of a bus, there are countless military checkpoints where you can wait days in hope of catching a truck across the border.

Brazil
Routes between Paraguay and Brazil include the following:

Ciudad del Este to Foz do Iguaçu Vehicles and pedestrians move freely across the Puente de la Amistad (Friendship Bridge) over the Río Paraná. If spending more than a day in either country, complete immigration formalities.

Pedro Juan Caballero to Ponta Porã Reached by road from Asunción, Pedro Juan Caballero is a growing contraband center on the Brazilian border. Ponta Porã is its Brazilian counterpart.

RIVER
The only reliable crossing is to Formosa province, Argentina, but there's occasionally upriver traffic to Brazil. See Getting There & Away under Asunción for details.

Getting Around

AIR
The new private carriers Ladesa and Arpa serve Pedro Juan Caballero, Ciudad del Este and Encarnación. Transporte Aéreo Militar (TAM), the Paraguayan air force passenger service, flies to isolated parts of the Chaco. Commercial domestic fares are expensive; the return trip from Asunción to Ciudad del Este costs around US$150, for example.

BUS
Bus quality in Paraguay varies. *Servicio removido* makes flag stops, while *servicio directo* collects passengers only at fixed locations. Larger towns have central terminals, but elsewhere companies are within easy walking distance of each other. Fares are reasonable: For example, Asunción to Filadelfia, a distance of about 450km, costs only about US$11.

TRAIN

Paraguay's antique, wood-burning trains are more entertaining than practical. Asunción visitors should enjoy the short hop to Areguá, on Lago Ypacaraí, but it's basically a day excursion.

CAR & MOTORCYCLE

Paraguay officially requires the International Driving Permit. The Touring y Automóvil Club Paraguayo provides information, road services and excellent maps and guidebooks for its own members and those of overseas affiliates. Its Asunción office (☎ 021-210550) is on Calle Brasil between Cerro Corá and 25 de Mayo.

Car theft is common, so be certain your vehicle is secure. Conspicuously valuable vehicles have been targeted by carjackers. High-wheeled wooden ox-carts and livestock are road hazards, making night driving inadvisable. Super-grade gasoline is relatively inexpensive at about US$0.50 per liter.

LOCAL TRANSPORT

Bus

Asunción and other sizable towns have extensive public transport systems, but late-night buses are infrequent. The usual fare is about US$0.40.

Taxi

Cabs operate on the basis of direct meter readings. Fares are slightly lower than in Argentina, but drivers may levy surcharges after midnight and for luggage.

Asunción

From its central location, Asunción is the pivot of Paraguay's political, economic and cultural life. Only about 15% of Paraguayans live in the capital, but most of the rest live within 150km.

History

Early Spaniards found Asunción more attractive than Buenos Aires because of Guaraní food and hospitality, but the city lost favor when the arid Chaco, with its hostile Indians, proved an unsuitable route to Peru.

When the López dynasty opened the country to foreign influence, newcomers nearly obliterated the city's colonial remains in favor of monumental public buildings, which a British journalist called 'extravagant luxuries' among modest surroundings. Well into the 20th century, much of central Asunción was unpaved, but the city's appearance gradually improved.

The Chaco War retarded progress, but the sprawling capital has encompassed ever more distant suburbs. Despite a recent construction boom, downtown retains a 19th-century feeling, with low buildings lining narrow streets.

Orientation

Its riverside location and some modern developments have created irregularities in Asunción's conventional grid, centered on Plaza de los Héroes. Names of east-west streets change at Independencia Nacional. Nearby Plaza Uruguaya offers shade from the midday heat, but prostitutes frequent the area at night.

North, along the riverfront, Plaza Constitución contains the Palacio Legislativo. Below the bluff, subject to flooding, lie *viviendas temporarias*, Asunción's shanty-towns. The diagonal El Paraguayo Independiente leads northwest to the Palacio de Gobierno (Presidential Palace).

Information

The Dirección General de Turismo (☎ 021-441530 or 021-441620; ditur@infonet.com.py), Palma 468, is friendly but not especially knowledgeable or helpful. It has a good city center map and brochure and several loose-leaf notebooks full of tourist information. It's open 7 am to 7 pm weekdays and 8 to 11:30 am on Saturday; there's a satellite office at the bus terminal.

The weekly 'Fin de Semana,' a calendar of entertainment and cultural events, is widely distributed throughout the city.

Money Cambios along Palma and side streets post exchange rates prominently; street changers hang out at the corner of Palma and Chile. There are also money-changers with name tags near ticket offices on the 2nd floor of the bus terminal.

Post & Communications The Correo Central (main post office) is at Alberdi and El Paraguayo Independiente.

Antelco, at 14 de Mayo and Oliva, has direct fiber-optic lines to operators in North

America, Europe and Australia. There is another office, much less state-of-the-art, at the bus terminal.

At Av España 352, the Centro Cultural Paraguayo-Americano (☎ 021-224772), charges US$1 to send or receive email. Try also the Internet café Patio de Luz (☎ 021-449741, pegaso@uninet.com.py), México 650.

Travel Agencies Inter-Express (☎ 021-490111), the Amex representative, is at Yegros 690. Paula Braun at Paula's Tours (☎ 021-446021), Cerro Corá 795, is an English-speaking Mennonite travel agent who's a good source of information on the Chaco and will help arrange bus tickets to Bolivia.

Cultural Centers Asunción's several international cultural centers offer films at little or no cost, as well as artistic and photographic exhibitions. These include the Casa de la Cultura Paraguaya, 14 de Mayo and El Paraguayo Independiente, the Centro Juan de Salazar (☎ 021-449221) at Herrera 834 and the weirdly neoclassical Centro Paraguayo Japonés (☎ 021-661914), at Julio Correa and Portillo in Barrio San Miguel (take bus No 16), whose modern gym is open to the public.

Bookstores Librería Comuneros, Cerro Corá 289, offers historical and contemporary books on Paraguay. Plaza Uruguay has open-air bookstalls.

Medical Services Asunción's Hospital de Clínicas (☎ 021-80982) is at the corner of Av Dr J Montero and Lagerenza, 1km west of downtown.

Things to See
It is safe to approach and photograph the **Palacio de Gobierno**, on El Paraguayo Independiente near Ayolas. This is a notable improvement over the situation under both Stroessner and Francia – by one 19th-century account, El Supremo ordered that 'every person observed gazing at the front of his palace should be shot in the act.'

The restored colonial **Casa Viola** (1750), at Ayolas and El Paraguayo Independiente, is now a museum. Two blocks east, at 14 de Mayo, is the **Casa de la Cultura Paraguaya** (ex-Colegio Militar). On Plaza Constitución,

which is at the foot of Alberdi, sits the **Palacio Legislativo** (1857).

At the east end of Plaza Constitución are the 19th-century **Catedral** and its museum. At Alberdi and Presidente Franco is the **Teatro Municipal** (1893), while a block west, at Franco and 14 de Mayo, Asunción's oldest building is the **Casa de la Independencia** (1772), where Paraguayans declared independence in 1811.

Panteón de los Héroes On the Plaza de los Héroes, at Chile and Palma, a military guard protects the remains of Carlos Antonio López, Francisco Solano López, Bernardino Caballero, Marshal José Félix Estigarribia and other key figures of Paraguay's catastrophic wars.

Museo Etnográfico Andrés Barbero This anthropological and archaeological museum at España 217 displays indigenous tools, ceramics and weavings, plus superb photographs, and good maps showing where each item comes from. One of Asunción's best, the museum is open 7:30 to 11:30 am and 3 to 5:30 pm weekdays.

Museo de Historia Natural Inside the Jardín Botánico (the former López estate), this museum houses an impressive collection of poorly labeled and displayed specimens, but is worth seeing for the spectacular insects – one butterfly has a wingspan of 274mm. It's open 8 am to 4 pm on weekdays and 8 am to 1 pm on weekends.

Admission to the park, which includes an improving zoo and the municipal campground, is cheap. From downtown, the most direct bus is the No 44-B ('Artigas') from Oliva and 15 de Agosto, which goes directly to the gates. Or take No 23 or 35.

Museo del Barro Asunción's foremost modern art museum displays some very unconventional work, and has other interesting exhibits from colonial times to the present, including political caricatures. To get there, take any No 30 bus out Av Aviadores del Chaco and ask the driver to drop you at Av Molas López in Isla de Francia, where the Museo occupies a contemporary facility at Callejón Cañada and Calle 1. It's open 3:30 to 8 pm Wednesday through Sunday.

ASUNCIÓN

PLACES TO STAY
3 Residencial Ambassador
28 Plaza Hotel
37 Ñandutí Hotel
64 Hotel Hispania
66 Hotel Miami
71 Hotel Nova Itapúa
92 Hotel Azara
95 Residencial Itapúa

PLACES TO EAT
14 Don Vito
16 La Pérgola Jardín
19 Anahí
26 4-D
31 La Flor de Canela
32 Deutsche Bäckerei

33 Heladería Venecia
41 Lido Bar
52 Talleyrand
53 Rincón Chileno
54 La Preferida
55 Café San Francisco
56 Buon Appetito
57 Chiquilín
61 Bolsi Bar
68 Vieja Bavaria
82 Rincón Latino
84 Taberna El Antojo
90 Nick's
98 Alexander Grill
99 Patio de Comidas
(Excelsior Mall)

Río Paraguay

Plaza Constitución

Plaza Juan de Salazar

Catedral Metropolitana

Estación Ferrocarril Central

Av República

El Paraguayo Independiente

Av Mariscal López

Benjamin Constant

Av República

Presidente Franco

Eligio Ayala

Plaza Uruguaya

Palma

Staircase

Mariscal Estigarribia

Estrella

25 de Mayo

Oliva

Plaza de los Héroes

Cerro Corá

General Díaz

Azara

Haedo

Luis A Herrera

Hernandarias

Av Colón

Montevideo

Ayolas

Juan O'Leary

15 de Agosto

14 de Mayo

Alberdi

Chile

Nuestra Señora de la Asunción

Independencia Nacional

Yegros

Iturbe

Caballero

México

Paraguarí

Antequera

Humaitá

Moreno

Staircase

Piribebuy

Manuel Dominguez

Manduvirá

Teniente Fariña

Jejui

República de Colombia

To Hospital

Plaza Italia

Av Ygatymí

Av Doctor R de Francia

Lugano

Bolívar

Ytororó

Abay

Av Ca López

PARAGUAY

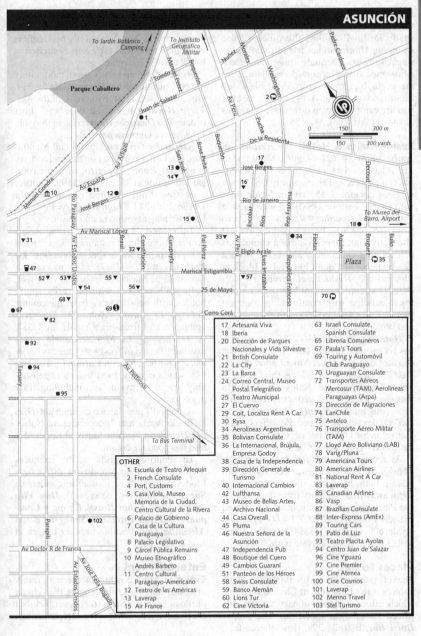

ASUNCIÓN

Parque Caballero

To Jardín Botánico, Camping
To Instituto Geográfico Militar

Manuel Pérez
Boquerón
Nuñez
Morales
Washington
Pucha
Padre Cardozo

Toledo

Juan de Salazar

Av Perú

Av Artigas
Rosa Peña
Boquerón

De la Residenta

Decoud

0   150   300 m
0   150   300 yards

13 ●
14 ▼
José Berges
17
16

Manuel Gondra
Av España
● 11
12 ●
José Berges

Río Paraguay
Av Estados Unidos
Brasil

Río de Janeiro
Escobar
Rio
Tacuarí
Farrá
Iturbe
República Francesa

15 ●
18 ●

To Museo del Barro, Airport

Av Mariscal López

▼ 31
32 ▼
33 ▼
● 34

Constitución
Curupayty
Pai Pérez
Av Perú
Luis Irrazábal
Fleitas
Iturbe
Aquino
Bruguez
Brasil
Plaza
35

Eligio Ayala
Mariscal Estigarribia
25 de Mayo

47
52 ▼   53 ▼   55 ▼
▼ 54   56 ▼
▼ 57

70

68 ▼
69 ●
Cerro Corá

● 67
▼ 82

■ 92

● 94

■ 95

Av Fernández

To Bus Terminal

Tacuarí

OTHER
1   Escuela de Teatro Arlequín
2   French Consulate
4   Port, Customs
5   Casa Viola, Museo
    Memoria de la Ciudad,
    Centro Cultural de la Ribera
6   Palacio de Gobierno
7   Casa de la Cultura
    Paraguaya
8   Palacio Legislativo
9   Cárcel Pública Remains
10 Museo Etnográfico
    Andrés Barbero
11 Centro Cultural
    Paraguayo-Americano
12 Teatro de las Américas
13 Laverap
15 Air France

Parapiti

● 102

Av Doctor R de Francia

Av Estados Unidos
Av José Félix Bogado

17 Artesanía Viva
18 Iberia
20 Dirección de Parques
    Nacionales y Vida Silvestre
21 British Consulate
22 La City
23 La Barca
24 Correo Central, Museo
    Postal Telegráfico
25 Teatro Municipal
27 El Cuervo
29 Coit, Localiza Rent A Car
30 Rysa
34 Aerolíneas Argentinas
35 Bolivian Consulate
36 La Internacional, Brújula,
    Empresa Godoy
38 Casa de la Independencia
39 Dirección General de
    Turismo
40 Internacional Cambios
42 Lufthansa
43 Museo de Bellas Artes,
    Archivo Nacional
44 Casa Overall
45 Pluma
46 Nuestra Señora de la
    Asunción
47 Independencia Pub
48 Boutique del Cuero
49 Cambios Guaraní
51 Panteón de los Héroes
51 Swiss Consulate
59 Banco Alemán
60 Lions Tur
62 Cine Victoria

63 Israeli Consulate,
    Spanish Consulate
65 Librería Comuneros
67 Paula's Tours
69 Touring y Automóvil
    Club Paraguayo
70 Uruguayan Consulate
72 Transportes Aéreos
    Mercosur (TAM), Aerolíneas
    Paraguayas (Arpa)
73 Dirección de Migraciones
74 LanChile
75 Antelco
76 Transporte Aéreo Militar
    (TAM)
77 Lloyd Aéreo Boliviano (LAB)
78 Varig/Pluna
79 Americana Tours
80 American Airlines
83 National Rent A Car
85 Laverap
86 Canadian Airlines
86 Vasp
87 Brazilian Consulate
88 Inter-Express (AmEx)
89 Touring Cars
91 Patio de Luz
93 Teatro Placita Ayolas
94 Centro Juan de Salazar
96 Cine Yguazú
97 Cine Premier
99 Cine Atenea
100 Cine Cosmos
101 Laverap
102 Menno Travel
103 Stel Turismo

PARAGUAY

Places to Stay

Camping Five km from downtown, in the shady Jardín Botánico, the quiet, secure *Camping Municipal* has friendly staff, lukewarm showers, adequate toilets and ferocious ants. Bring mosquito repellent. Fees are negligible; when returning at night, tell the attendant at the Artigas entrance that you are camping. From downtown, take bus No 44-B ('Artigas'), 23 or 35.

Residenciales & Hotels The *Residencial Ambassador* (☎ 021-445901), Montevideo 110, is basic and a bit musty, but it's friendly, has ceiling fans and charges only US$5 for a single. Charging US$7/10 singles/doubles with shared bath or US$10/13 with private bath, *Hotel Hispania* (☎ 021-444108), Cerro Corá 265, has long been a popular budget alternative, but there have been complaints of declining cleanliness and noise from a nearby pub. On a quiet but central block at Moreno 943, *Residencial Itapúa* (☎ 021-445121) occupies an unlikely neocolonial brick building with comfortable common spaces. Rates are US$7/12 with shared bath and breakfast.

Hotel Azara (☎ 021-449754), Azara 850, has rooms with private bath, fridge and aircon for US$10/12. *Hotel Nova Itapúa* (☎ 021-493327), General Díaz 932, is the latest US Peace Corps hangout. Rates are US$10/18 with shared bath, US$12/20 with private bath. The congenial *Ñandutí Hotel* (☎ 021-446780), Presidente Franco 551, offers excellent value for US$12 per person with shared bath, US$16 with private bath.

At recommended *Hotel Miami* (☎ 021-444950), México 449, rates are US$14/18 with private bath, breakfast and air-con; take a room away from the busy front door. Opposite Plaza Uruguaya, clean, quiet, secure and friendly *Plaza Hotel* (☎ 021-444772), Eligio Ayala 609, charges US$14/21 with shared bath, US$21/28 with private bath.

Places to Eat

One of Asunción's best breakfast and lunch choices is the *Lido Bar*, at Chile and Palma, which offers a variety of tasty, reasonably priced Paraguayan specialties. The similar *Bolsi Bar*, Estrella 399, is a tobacco-free, diner-style place with attentive service.

Anahi, at Presidente Franco and Ayolas, is an outstanding confitería with good food

and ice cream at moderate prices. *Nick's*, Azara 348, is a good, inexpensive lunch or dinner choice. For Asunción's best coffee, visit hole-in-the-wall *Café San Francisco* at Brasil and Estigarribia.

Rincón Chileno serves good, moderately priced Chilean food at Estados Unidos 314. One block south, at Estados Unidos 422, *Vieja Bavaria* has good beer and short orders. The *Deutsche Bäckerei*, Eligio Ayala 1189, serves German pastries.

Alexander Grill, at Alberdi and Mandu-virá, is a buffet parrilla. For Italian food, try congenial *Buon Appetito*, in a pleasant garden setting at 25 de Mayo 1199. Another attractive dinner choice is *La Pérgola Jardín*, Perú 240. *Chiquilín*, at Av Perú and Estigarribia, serves pizza and pasta.

Talleyrand, Mariscal Estigarribia 932, a French/international restaurant, is expensive but worthwhile for a special occasion. *La Preferida* (☎ 021-441637), a German restaurant at 25 de Mayo 1005, also merits a visit.

Its walls covered with proverbs, shells, bottles, with bells hanging from the ceiling, *Taberna El Antojo*, Ayolas 631, has great ambiance and fixed-price meals for US$7. At Tacuary 167, *La Flor de Canela* serves excellent Peruvian food – try the *surubí al ajo*, a river fish. *Rincón Latino*, Cerro Corá 948, serves equally good but more reasonably priced Peruvian fare, including tasty pisco sours.

Asunción's popular ice creamery, *4-D,* is at Eligio Ayala and Independencia Nacional. *Heladería Venecia*, Mariscal López 458, also has good ice cream.

The Patio de Comidas at the Excelsior Mall, on Chile near Manduvirá, offers fast-food versions of various ethnic cuisines: *Sugar* (outstanding ice cream), *Don Vito* (empanadas), *Sabor Brasil*, *Chopp y Compañía*, *Taberna Española*, *Shangri-La* and *Ali Baba*. *Don Vito* has another branch at José Berges 595.

Entertainment

Cinemas Most downtown cinemas rarely offer anything more challenging than cheap porno or the latest Schwarzenegger flick, but check out *Fin de Semana* for current listings.

Bars For live rock and roll, try *El Cuervo*, Paraguarí 120. The *Independencia Pub*, Estigarribia 127, also features live music.

Theater Asunción has numerous live theater and music venues; the season generally runs March to October. Possibilities include *Casa de la Cultura Paraguaya* (see Cultural Centers earlier) and *Teatro de las Américas* (☎ 021-224772), José Berges 297.

Shopping

Artesanía Viva, José Berges 993, features Chaco Indian crafts, including ponchos, hammocks and bags, plus books and information on Chaco Indian groups. Casa Overall, Mariscal Estigarribia 397, has a good selection of ñandutí and leather goods. The open-air market on Plaza de los Héroes is a good place for crafts, but remember that items made with feathers are probably subject to endangered species regulations.

Getting There & Away

Air Asunción's centrality on the continent makes it a good place for flights to neighboring countries, Europe and the USA, but domestic services are limited.

Aerolíneas Argentinas
    Av Mariscal López 706

Air France
    (☎ 021-448442) San José 136

Alitalia
    (☎ 021-660435) General Genes 490

American Airlines
    (☎ 021-443331) Independencia Nacional 557

Canadian
    (☎ 021-448917) Juan O'Leary 690

Iberia
    (☎ 021-214246) Av Mariscal López 995

KLM
    (☎ 021-449393) Chile 680

Korean Air
    (☎ 021-495059) Estados Unidos 348

LanChile
    (☎ 021-490782) 15 de Agosto 588

Lloyd Aéreo Boliviano (LAB)
    (☎ 021-441586) 14 de Mayo 563

Lufthansa
    (☎ 021-447962) Nuestra Señora
    de la Asunción 208

National Airlines (Avant)
    (☎ 021-492000) Independencia Nacional 365

Transportes Aéreos Mercosur (TAM)
    (☎ 021-495265) Oliva 761

Varig/Pluna
    (☎ 021-497351) General Díaz and 14 de Mayo

Vasp
    (☎ 021-490555) Juan O'Leary 689

Bus Asunción's bus station (☎ 021-551728) is at Av Fernando de la Mora and República Argentina in the Barrio Terminal. From downtown take buses Nos 8, 10, 25, 31 or 38 from Oliva. Some companies maintain convenient offices on Plaza Uruguaya.

From Presidente Franco and Av Colón, hourly buses leave for Falcón, on the Argentine border, from 5 to 11 am and 12:30 to 5:30 pm. Direct buses leave the terminal for Clorinda (US$2), and there is frequent service to Posadas (US$11, five hours) and Buenos Aires (US$56, 20 hours). Fewer buses run to Córdoba (US$46, 18 hours).

Stel Turismo (☎ 021-450043), Caballero 1340, and Yacyretá (☎ 021-551725) now operate three to four services weekly to Santa Cruz, Bolivia (US$56, 30 hours). There are daily buses to Montevideo, Uruguay (US$70, 18 hours), and less frequent ones to Santiago, Chile (30 hours). Brazilian destinations include Foz do Iguaçu (five hours), Curitiba (14 hours), São Paulo (18 hours) and Rio (US$50, 22 hours).

Countless domestic buses link Asunción with other Paraguayan cities, including Ciudad del Este (US$10 to US$14, 4½ hours) and Encarnación (US$10, five hours). Services to northeastern destinations like Pedro Juan Caballero and Concepción are less frequent, but those to Filadelfia (US$11, eight hours) and other Chaco destinations are dependable. Towns near Asunción, like San Bernardino and Caacupé, have frequent services.

Train From the Estación Ferrocarril Central (☎ 021-447316) on Plaza Uruguaya, an antique steam train tours the backyards of Asunción's shantytowns en route to Areguá, on Lago Ypacaraí (US$0.70 return), but services have become very erratic.

Boat An alternative way of crossing to Argentina is the launch from Puerto Itá Enramada, west of downtown, to Puerto Pilcomayo, Formosa. These leave every half-hour weekdays 7 am to 5 pm, on Saturday irregularly 7 to 10 am.

Up to a dozen naval supply boats per week carry passengers up the Río Paraguay as far as Concepción; inquire at the port at the river end of Calle Montevideo, directly east of the Aduana (customs) at the port of Asunción. These go to Isla Margarita on the Brazilian border, then cross to Porto Murtinho, Brazil, with buses to Corumbá.

Getting Around

City buses go almost everywhere, but few run after about 10 or 11 pm. Bus No 8 runs from Cerro Corá to the bus terminal, as do No 25 from Colón and Oliva, No 38 from Haedo and No 42 from Rodríguez de Francia.

To/From the Airport From downtown, bus No 30A takes 50 to 60 minutes to Aeropuerto Silvio Pettirossi and costs US$0.25. Taxis cost about US$15.

Taxi Cabs are metered and reasonable, but may tack on a surcharge late at night. A cab to the bus terminal costs about US$5.

AROUND ASUNCIÓN
Museo Boggiani

From 1887 to the turn of the century, Italian ethnographer Guido Boggiani conducted fieldwork among the Chamacoco Indians of the upper Río Paraguay, but sent most of his collection of feather art to Berlin; part of it remains in this well-organized, expanding museum (☎ 021-584717), at Coronel Bogado 888 in the suburb of San Lorenzo. Reached by Línea 27 from downtown out Av Mariscal López, it's open 10 am to noon and 3 to 6 pm Tuesday to Saturday.

Villa Hayes

Across the river from Asunción, Villa Hayes honors one of the USA's most undistinguished presidents, Rutherford B Hayes (1877-81). Nearly forgotten even in his home town of Delaware, Ohio, he is here commemorated by a club and local soccer team, a school and a monument.

Why this homage to a man who never set foot in Paraguay? After the War of the Triple Alliance, Argentina claimed the entire Chaco, but the two countries eventually submitted claims over a smaller area to arbitration; in 1878, Argentine and Paraguayan diplomats presented their cases to Hayes in Washington. After he decided in Paraguay's

favor, the Paraguayan Congress immortalized him by renaming Villa Occidental, the territory's largest town.

To reach Villa Hayes, take bus No 46 from downtown Asunción. It leaves every half-hour from 5:30 am to noon, then every 45 minutes from noon to 9 pm.

Eastern Paraguay

East of the Río Paraguay is the nucleus of historical Paraguay. About 90% of Paraguayans live within 100km of Asunción, but the border towns of Encarnación (opposite Posadas, Argentina) and Ciudad del Este (opposite Foz do Iguaçu, Brazil) have grown rapidly because of multinational hydroelectric projects, corruption and contraband.

Attractions convenient to Asunción include the weaving center of Itauguá, the lakeside resorts of San Bernardino and Areguá, the shrine of Caacupé, colonial villages like Piribebuy and Yaguarón and Parque Nacional Ybycuí.

Jesuit ruins near Encarnación match or surpass those of Argentina. In the boom zone of northeastern Paraguay, Brazilian colonists are moving across the border, deforesting the countryside for coffee and cotton, squeezing out Paraguayan peasants and the few remaining Aché Indians.

CIRCUITO CENTRAL

This 200km round trip from Asunción is suitable for day trips, weekend excursions or longer outings.

Areguá

Higher and cooler than Asunción, this resort on Lago Ypacaraí is 28km northeast of the capital. *Hospedaje Ozli* has rooms with fan for US$6 per person, with pleasant gardens and good food.

Train service is erratic (but worthwhile if it's running; inquire at the station in Asunción). There are also frequent buses on Línea 11 from Av Perú in Asunción.

Itauguá

For the women of Itauguá, 30km southeast of Asunción, weaving multicolored ñandutí is a cottage industry from childhood to old age. Pieces range in size from doilies to bedspreads; smaller ones cost only a few dollars

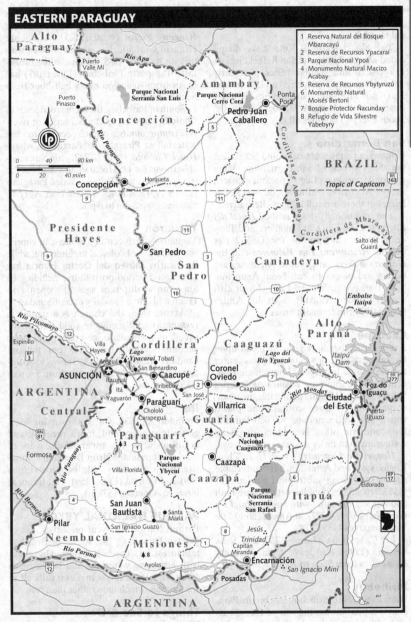

but larger ones range upwards of US$50. In July the town celebrates the annual **Festival del Ñandutí**.

Two blocks south of Ruta 2, the dilapidated **Museo Parroquial San Rafael** displays Franciscan and secular relics, plus early ñandutí samples. It's open 8 to 11:30 am and 3 to 6 pm. From the Asunción bus terminal, buses leave for Itauguá (US$0.50, one hour) about every 15 minutes all day and night.

San Bernardino

Upmarket restaurants, cafés and hotels line the shady streets of San Bernardino, 48km east of Asunción on Lago Ypacaraí's eastern shore. Asunción's elite spend weekends here, but there are still budget alternatives.

The traditionally distinguished *Hotel del Lago* (☎ 0512-2201), at Caballero and Teniente Weiler, has rooms for US$12 per person. *Restaurant Las Palmeras* and the *German bakery* on Colonos Alemanes are both good places to eat. From Asunción, both Transporte Villa del Lago (Línea 210) and Transporte Cordillera de los Andes (Línea 103) run frequent buses.

Caacupé

Every December 8, pilgrims descend upon Paraguay's most important religious center for the Día de la Virgen (Immaculate Conception). The imposing **Basílica de Nuestra Señora de Los Milagros** dominates the townscape from its huge cobblestone plaza, which can accommodate 300,000 faithful. Opposite the plaza is a block of cheap restaurants and tacky souvenir stands.

Hospedaje Uruguayo (☎ 0511-2977), at Eligio Ayala and Asunción, has comfortable rooms set among subtropical gardens for US$12/16 singles/doubles with private bath and fan, slightly more with aircon. *Hotel La Giralda* (☎ 0511-2227), at Alberdi and 14 de Mayo, charges US$12/14.

La Caacupeña (Línea 119) and Villa Serrana (Línea 110) leave Asunción every 10 minutes from 5 am to 10 pm.

Piribebuy

Founded in 1640, Piribebuy was briefly Paraguay's capital during the war of 1865-70; its mid-18th-century church retains some original woodwork and sculpture. Only 74km southeast of Asunción, off of Ruta 2, it's a good place to glimpse rural Paraguay.

The **Museo Histórico**, opposite the church, has deteriorating exhibits. *Hotel Rincón Viejo* (☎ 0515-251), Teniente Horacio Giní 502, has singles/doubles with private bath for US$12/14 including breakfast. Transporte Piribebuy (Línea 197) has buses from Asunción every half-hour from 5 am to 9 pm.

South of Piribebuy, the scenic road leads to **Chololó**, less a village than a series of riverside *campgrounds*; a branch goes to a modest waterfall at **Pirareta**. At **Paraguarí**, where *Hotel Chololó* (☎ 0531-242) offers reasonable rooms for US$16/20 singles/doubles, the road connects with Ruta 1. Ciudad Paraguarí (Línea 193) has buses to Asunción every 15 minutes from 5 am to 8 pm.

Yaguarón

Yaguarón's 18th-century Franciscan church is a landmark of colonial architecture, while the nearby **Museo del Doctor Francia** has some good period portraiture, including El Supremo at different ages. It's open 7 to 11 am and 2 to 5 pm daily except Sunday.

Across from the church is a nameless *restaurant* with mediocre food, except for excellent homemade ice cream, and basic accommodations for US$5 per person. Ciudad Paraguarí (Línea 193) goes to Asunción (48km) every 15 minutes from 5 am to 8:15 pm.

Itá

Founded in 1539, Itá is known for local *gallinita* pottery and, more recently and notoriously, for the apparent discovery of Nazi war criminal Martin Bormann's burial site. Bus companies 3 de Febrero (Línea 159) and Cotrisa (Línea 159) send frequent buses to Asunción (37km).

PARQUE NACIONAL YBYCUÍ

Parque Nacional Ybycuí preserves one of eastern Paraguay's last stands of Brazilian rain forest. Its steep hills, dissected by creeks with attractive waterfalls and pools, reach 400m. The dense forest makes it difficult to see animals, which hide rather than run.

Things to See & Do

Ybycuí is tranquil and undeveloped, though weekenders sometimes disrupt its peacefulness; in this event, take refuge on the extensive hiking trails. Rangers at the visitor center distribute a self-guided nature trail brochure.

The **Salto Guaraní** waterfall is near the campground. Below it, a bridge leads to a pleasant creekside trail with a wealth of butterflies, including the metallic blue morpho, but watch for poisonous snakes. The trail continues to **La Rosada**, an iron foundry destroyed by Brazilian forces in the War of the Triple Alliance; Ybycuí's forest has recovered in the century since the foundry operated on charcoal. Note the water wheel; engineers dammed Arroyo Mina to provide water and power for the bellows, while ox carts brought ore from 25km away.

At La Rosada is a **museum** with irregular hours, at the park entrance 2km west of the campground.

Places to Stay
The only option is *camping* at Arroyo Mina, which has adequate toilets, cold showers and a confitería serving weekend meals. Level sites are few and insects are a nuisance.

Getting There & Away
Parque Nacional Ybycuí is 151km southeast of Asunción. Ruta 1, to Encarnación, leads 84km south to Carapeguá, where a turnoff continues another 67km via the villages of Acahay and Ybycuí. Transporte Emilio Cabrera has eight buses daily to Acahay for local connections to Ybycuí village. A bus leaves daily at noon for the park entrance, returning to the village at 2 pm.

ENCARNACIÓN
Gateway to the nearby Jesuit mission ruins at Trinidad and Jesús, Encarnación is in limbo as the reservoir created by Yacyretá dam slowly inundates the city's riverfront. As established businesses move onto higher ground, the old town has become a tawdry bazaar of imported trinkets – digital watches, Walkmans and the like – and decaying public buildings and housing.

Orientation
Encarnación sits on the north bank of the Río Paraná, directly opposite Posadas, Argentina; the modern Puente Internacional Beato Roque González links the two cities. From the riverside, Av Mariscal JF Estigarribia leads from the old commercial center to the new one around Plaza Artigas.

Information
Tourist Office The Dirección General de Turismo, Monseñor Wiessen 345, is open weekdays only.

Money Cambios Guaraní is at Av Estigarribia 1405, Banco Continental across the street at Av Estigarribia 1418. Moneychangers jam the bus terminal on weekends.

Post & Communications The post office is at Capellán Molas 337, in the old town. Antelco is at PJ Caballero and López.

Consulates The Brazilian vice-consulate here is open 8 am to noon weekdays, while the Argentine consulate is open until 1:30 pm on weekdays. See Facts for the Visitor earlier in this chapter for contact information.

Feria Municipal
At the corner of López and Gamarra, petty merchants are milking every last peso out of visiting Argentines before the flood. The market's liveliness transcends its baubles and gadgets, and it's also an inexpensive place to eat.

Places to Stay
The windowless singles (US$5) at *Hospedaje Karina*, at Cabañas and General Artigas, are the cheapest alternative and the shared toilets are clean. Homey *Hotel Repka* (☎ 071-203546), Tomás Romero Pereira 47, has rooms with shared bath for US$8/12. Much improved *Hotel Germano* (☎ 071-203346), directly across from the bus terminal at Cabañas and Carlos Antonio López, costs US$6/9 with shared bath, US$8/13 with private bath. Near the bus terminal, for US$10/16, *Hotel Itapúa* (☎ 071-205045), on Carlos Antonio López between Cabañas and Kreusser, has air-conditioned rooms with TV, phone and private bath. Rooms at clean, quiet *Hotel Viena* (☎ 071-203486), PJ Caballero 568, are quite reasonable at US$12/20 with private bath.

Places to Eat
Packed with both locals and Argentines, *Cuarajhy*, on Plaza Artigas at Av Estigarribia and Tomás Romero Pereira, is a good, moderately priced 24-hour parrilla. It has branches at Av Estigarribia and 25 de Mayo and at Av Estigarribia 1285.

PARAGUAY

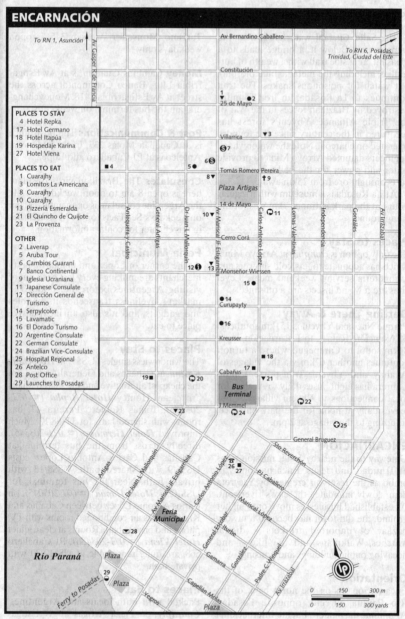

ENCARNACIÓN

To RN 1, Asunción

Av Gaspar R de Francia

Av Bernardino Caballero

To RN 6, Posadas,
Trinidad, Ciudad del Este

Constitución

25 de Mayo

Villarrica

Tomás Romero Pereira

Plaza Artigas

14 de Mayo

Cerro Corá

Monseñor Wiessen

Curupayty

Kreusser

Cabañas

Bus
Terminal

J Memmel

General Bruguez

Sto Reverchón

Pl Caballero

Mariscal López

Feria
Municipal

Río Paraná

Plaza

Ferry to Posadas

Plaza

Plaza

Antequera y Castro
General Artigas
Dr Juan L Mallorquín
Av Mariscal JF Estigarribia
Carlos Antonio López
Lomas Valentinas
Independencia
Gonzáles
Av Irrazábal

Artigas
Dr Juan L Mallorquín
Av Mariscal JF Estigarribia
Carlos Antonio López
General Escobar
General Iturbe
Gamarra
González
Padre C Winiquel
Av Irrazábal

Capellán Molas
Xegros

0   150   300 m
0   150   300 yards

PLACES TO STAY
4 Hotel Repka
17 Hotel Germano
18 Hotel Itapúa
19 Hospedaje Karina
27 Hotel Viena

PLACES TO EAT
1 Cuarajhy
3 Lomitos La Americana
8 Cuarajhy
10 Cuarajhy
13 Pizzería Esmeralda
21 El Quincho de Quijote
23 La Provenza

OTHER
2 Laverap
5 Aruba Tour
6 Cambios Guaraní
7 Banco Continental
9 Iglesia Ucraniana
11 Japanese Consulate
12 Dirección General de
   Turismo
14 Serpylcolor
15 Lavamatic
16 El Dorado Turismo
20 Argentine Consulate
22 German Consulate
24 Brazilian Vice-Consulate
25 Hospital Regional
26 Antelco
28 Post Office
29 Launches to Posadas

PARAGUAY

El Quincho de Quijote, opposite the bus terminal at Carlos A López and General Cabañas, is a good value for its decent food and excellent service at moderate prices. *Lomitos La Americana*, at Villarrica and Carlos Antonio López, serves short orders. *Pizzería Esmeralda* is on Av Estigarribia between Cerro Corá and Monseñor Wiessen. *La Provenza*, Mallorquín 609, has a wider choice of Italian dishes.

Getting There & Away
Air Arpa may begin flights to Asunción; consult travel agencies for details. Posadas, across the river in Argentina, has air connections with Buenos Aires and Puerto Iguazú.

Bus There are frequent buses from Encarnación to Asunción (US$10, five hours) and Ciudad del Este (US$8, four to five hours). From 6 am to 11 pm, local buses cross to Posadas (US$1 regular, US$2 servicio diferencial).

Boat Launches (US$1) cross the Paraná to Posadas frequently.

TRINIDAD & JESÚS
Trinidad, Paraguay's best-preserved Jesuit *reducción*, occupies an imposing hilltop site 28km northeast of Encarnación. Though its church is smaller and its grounds are less extensive than those at San Ignacio Miní, Trinidad is in many ways its equal. From its bell tower, the mission at Jesús de Tavarangue, 10km north, is easily visible. Jesús is strictly speaking not ruins but rather an incomplete construction project, interrupted by the Jesuits' expulsion in 1767.

Trinidad's grounds and museum are open 7:30 to 11:30 am and 1:30 to 5:30 pm Monday through Saturday; Sunday and holiday hours are 8 am to 5 pm. Admission costs US$1 for adults, US$0.50 for children older than 12. Camping is possible outside the ruins.

Jesús, 11km north of Trinidad by a generally good dirt road off Ruta 6, keeps similar hours and collects identical fees. From Encarnación, Empresa Ciudad de Encarnación goes to Trinidad (US$0.80) nine times daily between 6 am and 7 pm, and has two buses daily to Jesús (US$1.25) at 6:30 and 10 am.

SAN IGNACIO GUAZÚ
About 100km northwest of Encarnación, San Ignacio has few ruins, but its **Museo Jesuítico** holds valuable Guaraní carvings. Open 8 to 11:30 am and 2 to 5 pm daily, it charges US$1 admission.

On Ruta 1, near the Ayolas turnoff at the north end of town, *Hotel Piringo* has singles/doubles for US$10/16 with ceiling fans, US$16/24 with aircon, and also has a passable restaurant. There are many buses to Asunción (3½ hours), Encarnación and the village of Santa María.

SANTA MARÍA
Twelve km east of San Ignacio, the former *reducción* of Santa María has a **Museo Jesuítico** with a superb collection of Jesuit statuary, open 8:30 to 11:30 am and 1:30 to 5 pm daily. Admission is US$1.

Basic *Pensión San José* charges US$4 for a single. There are five buses daily from San Ignacio.

CIUDAD DEL ESTE
Ciudad del Este is an important border crossing where Brazilian and Argentine shoppers jam the streets in search of cheap electronic goods. It also has a reputation as one of South America's most corrupt cities, frequented by smugglers, money launderers and, according to intelligence reports from many countries, Islamic terrorists who may have been responsible for attacks on Jewish and Israeli targets in Argentina. On the west bank of the Paraná, across from Foz do Iguaçu, it has an irregular plan, but the downtown area is compact and easily managed on foot. Av San Blas, the westward extension of the bridge from Foz, becomes Ruta 2 to Asunción.

Information
Tourist Office The Dirección de Turismo (☎ 061-512417 or 061-516051) at the immigration border post is friendly, but not particularly well informed or well supplied with printed matter.

Money Ubiquitous street changers give poorer rates than the numerous cambios.

Post & Communications The post office is at Alejo García and Oscar Rivas Ortellado, across from the bus terminal. Antelco is at the corner of Av Alejo García and Paí Pérez.

Consulates The Brazilian consulate is open 7 am to noon weekdays. See Facts for the Visitor earlier in this chapter for contact information.

Places to Stay

Cozy, friendly *Hotel Mi Abuela* (☎ 061-512373), with an attractive garden courtyard at Alejo García and Adrián Jara, has rooms with private bath, ceiling fans and breakfast for US$12/20; for aircon, add US$3 per person. Since it's been up for sale, changes may be in the offing.

Also good value is German-run *Hotel Munich* (☎ 061-500347), at Emiliano Fernández and Capitán Miranda, where rooms with private bath, good breakfast and aircon cost US$13/18. Down the block, at Emiliano Fernández 165, the enthusiastically recommended *Hotel Austria* (☎ 061-504213) is slightly dearer at US$16/18. *City Hotel* (☎ 061-500415), Regimiento Sauce 301 at Capitán Miranda, charges US$20/30.

Places to Eat

Restaurant Oriental, on Adrián Jara near Av Boquerón, has Japanese and Chinese food, with an especially fine *agropicante* (hot-and-sour) soup. Alongside it, *Osaka* has an equally appealing menu but shorter hours. *Taiwan*, on Boquerón between Adrián Jara and Paí Pérez, serves Chinese.

Rotisería Ricky, on Pampliega between Adrián Jara and Paí Pérez, has a variety of short orders and takeout foods. *Mi Ranchito*, a sidewalk parrilla at Curupayty and Av Adrián Jara, offers complete meals for around US$4. *Cavi*, at Monseñor Rodríguez and Nanawa, is a popular Paraguayan choice.

Getting There & Away

Air Ciudad del Este's new Aeropuerto Internacional Guaraní is 30km west of town on Ruta 2. Arpa (☎ 061-512646), Boquerón 310, flies several times daily to Asunción (US$60 to US$90) with onward international connections; in the same office, TAM flies several times weekly to Porto Alegre and Curitiba (Brazil), and three times weekly to Iquique (Chile).

CIUDAD DEL ESTE

PLACES TO STAY	OTHER
1 City Hotel	4 Immigration & Customs,
2 Hotel Munich	Dirección de Turismo
3 Hotel Austria	5 Banco Real
9 Hotel Mi Abuela	7 Transportes Aéreos
	Militares (TAM)
PLACES TO EAT	11 Cosmo's Tours
6 Mi Ranchito	12 Laverap
8 Cavi	15 Banco de Asunción (ATM)
10 Rotisería Ricky	16 Transportes Aéreos
13 Osaka	Mercosur (TAM), Arpa
14 Restaurant Oriental	18 Antelco
17 Taiwan	19 Brazilian Consulate

Bus Buses to Foz do Iguaçu leave from near the bridge every 10 minutes weekdays and Saturday, less frequently Sundays and holidays. On the other side, disembark for Brazilian immigration (unless just crossing for the day); if you hold on to your ticket, any bus will take you to Foz.

The bus terminal, on Av Bernardino Caballero, 2km south of downtown, runs 34 buses daily to Asunción (US$10 to US$14, five hours); nearly as many go to Encarnación (US$8, four to five hours).

ITAIPÚ DAM

Itaipú, the world's largest hydroelectric project, has benefited Paraguay because of the construction activity, and Brazil's purchase of surplus power. However, should the price of competing sources of electricity drop, reduced Brazilian demand could saddle Paraguay with unexpected costs.

Project propaganda omits the US$25 billion price tag and ignores environmental concerns. The 1350 sq km reservoir, 220m deep, drowned Sete Quedas, a more impressive set of waterfalls than Iguazú, and stagnant water has provided a new habitat for anopheles mosquitoes, a malaria vector.

Tours leave from the Centro de Recepción de Visitas, north of Ciudad del Este near the town of Hernandarias. Tours begin at at 8, 9 and 10 am, and 2:30 and 3:30 pm Monday to Saturday; passports are required. A documentary film, also available in English-language video format, airs a half-hour before the tour departs.

From Ciudad del Este, take any Hernandarias Transtur or Tacurú Pucú bus from the roundabout at the intersection of Avs San Blas and Alejo García. These leave every 10 to 15 minutes throughout the day.

PEDRO JUAN CABALLERO

Capital of Amambay department, Pedro Juan Caballero is adjacent to Ponta Porã, Brazil. Locals cross the border at will, but to continue any distance into either country, visit immigration at Naciones Unidas 144, open 8 am to noon Monday to Saturday. There are reports of contraband drugs, so beware of unsavory characters.

Exchange houses are numerous. The Brazilian Consulate (open 8 am to noon and 2 to 6 pm weekdays) is in the now upscale *Hotel La Siesta* (☎ 036-3021), at Alberdi

and Dr Francia, which has singles/doubles for US$36/48. The recommended *Hotel Guavirá* (☎ 036-2743), Mariscal López 1325, charges US$6 single with shared bath, US$10 with private bath.

Ten buses daily serve Asunción (532km, eight to 12 hours). Another 10 go to Concepción and several go to Ciudad del Este. Nasa goes daily to Campo Grande, Brazil.

PARQUE NACIONAL CERRO CORÁ

Visitors to northeastern Paraguay should not overlook Parque Nacional Cerro Corá, 40km west of Pedro Juan Caballero, which protects an area of dry tropical forest and savanna in a landscape of steep, isolated hills. Cultural and historical features include pre-Columbian caves, petroglyphs and the site of Francisco Solano López's death at the end of the War of the Triple Alliance.

The park has nature trails, a camping area and a few basic cabañas. There are rangers, but no formal visitor center.

The Chaco

In Paraguay's Chaco frontier, great distances separate tiny settlements. Its only paved highway, the Ruta Trans-Chaco, leads 450km northwest to Filadelfia, colonized by Mennonites since the late 1920s. At Marical Estigarribia the pavement ends, but the highway continues another 240km to the Bolivian border.

The Chaco is an almost featureless plain of three distinct zones. Across the Río Paraguay, the low Chaco is a soothing palm savanna where ponds and marshes shelter colorful birds. Peasants build picturesque houses of palm logs, but the main industry is cattle ranching. In the middle Chaco, farther west, thorny drought-tolerant scrub replaces the savanna. Only army bases and cattle *estancias* inhabit the denser thorn forests of the high Chaco beyond Mariscal Estigarribia, where rainfall is highly unpredictable.

Historically, the Chaco has been a refuge of Indian peoples who subsisted independently by hunting, gathering and fishing. Later industries included cattle ranching and extraction of the tannin-rich *quebracho*. Place names beginning with the word *fortín* indicate fortifications and trenches from the

Chaco War (1932-35). During this war, Paraguay built a network of roads which are now mostly impassable without 4WD.

Accommodations are sparse outside the few towns, though one can camp almost anywhere. In a pinch, estancias or *campesinos* may offer a bed with a mosquito net.

MENNONITE COLONIES

There are about 10,000 Mennonites and a slightly larger number of Indians in the Chaco. Mennonites believe in adult baptism, separation of church and state and pacifist opposition to military service. They speak Plattdeutsch (Low German) and also Hochdeutsch (High German), which is the language of school instruction. Most adults now speak Spanish and some speak passable English. Indians are as likely to speak German as Spanish.

The first Mennonites to arrive, in 1927, were Sommerfelder (Summerfield) Mennonites, from the Canadian prairies, who left after Canadian authorities reneged on guarantees against conscription. The Sommerfelder formed Menno Colony, centered around the town of Loma Plata. A few years later, refugees from the Soviet Union established Fernheim (Distant Home), with its capital at Filadelfia. Ukrainian Germans, many of whom served unwillingly in WWII, founded Neuland (New Land) in 1947. Its largest settlement is Neu-Halbstadt.

As more Paraguayans settle in the Chaco, Mennonites worry that the government may eliminate their privileges; some have begun to participate in national politics. Others are disgruntled with developments in Filadelfia, where material prosperity has spawned a generation more interested in motorcycles and videos than traditional values. Alcohol and tobacco, once absolutely *verboten*, are now sold openly.

Filadelfia

Filadelfia is the administrative and service center of Fernheim, whose main products are dairy foods and cotton. Still a religious community, Filadelfia shuts down on Sunday, but on weekday mornings farmers cruise the streets in search of Indians for day labor, returning them in the afternoon. At midday, the town is exceptionally quiet, as Mennonites have adopted the custom of the tropical siesta.

Orientation & Information Filadelfia is 480km northwest of Asunción via the Trans-Chaco and a 20km lateral road to its north. Its dusty streets form an orderly grid whose *Hauptstrasse* (main street) is north-south Hindenburg. Perpendicular Calle Trébol leads east to Loma Plata (Menno Colony) and west to the Trans-Chaco and Fortín Toledo.

Filadelfia has no tourist office, but Hotel Florida shows a video cassette on the Mennonite colonies. To change cash, try the Cooperativa Mennonita supermarket, at Unruh and Hindenburg. The post office and Antelco are both at the corner of Hindenburg and Unruh. The modern hospital is at the corner of Hindenburg and Trébol.

Unger Museum On Hindenburg opposite Hotel Florida, the Unger Museum chronicles Fernheim from 1930 to the present and displays materials on Chaco Indians. Hartmut Wohlgemuth, manager of the Florida, provides guided tours in Spanish or German when his schedule permits. Admission is about US$1.

Places to Stay & Eat Camping is free of charge in shady Parque Trébol, 5km east of Filadelfia, but there is no water and only a single pit toilet. Filadelfia's most established accommodation is *Hotel Florida* (☎ 091-258), whose budget annex is an excellent bargain at US$6 per person with comfortable beds, shared bath with cold showers (not a bad idea here) and fans; rooms with private bath cost slightly more.

Besides the restaurant at Hotel Florida, try the parrillada at *La Estrella*, around the corner on Unruh, which has a shady outdoor dining area. *Girasol*, across the street, also serves a good asado. The modern *Cooperativa Mennonita* supermarket has excellent dairy products and other groceries.

Getting There & Away Several bus companies have offices along and near Hindenburg, with daily service to Asunción. Buses are less frequent to Mariscal Estigarribia and Colonia La Patria, farther west on the Trans-Chaco, and Santa Cruz, Bolivia.

Expreso CV connects Filadelfia with Loma Plata (25km) daily at 8 am, returning at 9 am. Buses to Asunción also stop at

Loma Plata and most continue to Neu-Halbstadt.

Around Filadelfia

Fortín Toledo About 40km west of Filadelfia, Fortín Toledo hosts the **Proyecto Taguá**, a small reserve nurturing a population of Wagner's peccary (*Catagonus wagneri*), thought to be extinct for nearly half a century until its rediscovery in 1975. The current project managers, Jakob and María Unger, are English-speaking Mennonites who happily welcome visitors if their schedule permits.

To get to Fortín Toledo, hitchhike or take a bus out along Calle Trébol to the Trans-Chaco. Cross the highway and continue 3km to an enormous tire with the painted words 'pasar prohibido'; continue another 7km on the main road, passing several buildings occupied by squatters, before taking a sharp right leading to a sign marking your destination, 'Proyecto Taguá.' Hitchhiking may be possible along this segment, but do so at your own risk.

Loma Plata The administrative center of Menno Colony is the oldest and most traditional of the Mennonite settlements. Its excellent **museum** has an outdoor exhibit of early farming equipment, a typical pioneer house and an outstanding photographic history of the colony. Ask for keys at the nearby Secretariat.

Accommodations are available at **Hotel Loma Plata** for about US$10 with shared bath. There's also the new **Hotel Algarrobo** (☎ *0918-353*), 1km outside town, for US$12 per person with private bath, aircon and breakfast, and two restaurants, **Churrascaría Amambay** and **La Carreta**.

Neu-Halbstadt Founded in 1947, Neu-Halbstadt is the center of Neuland Colony, south of Filadelfia. **Hotel Boquerón** (☎ *0951-311*) has singles/doubles for US$15/22 and a good restaurant. There's also a **campground** north of town. Nearby Fortín Boquerón preserves a sample of trenches dating from the Chaco War.

South of Neuland are Indian reserves, where many Lengua and Nivaclé have become settled farmers. Neu-Halbstadt is a good place to buy Indian handicrafts such as bags, hammocks and woven goods. For infor-mation and a great selection, contact Verena Regehr, who sells goods on a non-profit basis here as well as at Artesanía Viva in Asunción.

Several buses from Asunción to Filadelfia continue to Neu-Halbstadt, while others come directly from Asunción.

PARQUE NACIONAL DEFENSORES DEL CHACO

Once the province of nomadic Ayoreo foragers, Defensores del Chaco is a wooded alluvial plain about 100m in elevation; isolated 500m Cerro León is its greatest landmark. The dense thorn forest harbors large cats such as jaguar, puma, ocelot and Geoffroy's cat, that survive despite the danger posed by illicit hunting.

Defensores del Chaco is 830km from Asunción over roads impassable to ordinary vehicles. There is no regular public transportation, but the Dirección de Parques Nacionales in Asunción may be able to put you in contact with rangers who must occasionally travel to Asunción and sometimes, if space is available, take passengers on the return trip.

MARISCAL ESTIGARRIBIA

According to LP reader Jerry Azevedo, the last sizable settlement on the Trans-Chaco before the Bolivian border is home to '300 soldiers, half that many civilians and an equal number of roosters.' Mariscal Estigarribia is 540km from Asunción; motorists should be sure to fill up and carry extra gas, food and water.

Lodging is available at **Hotel Alemán** for US$16 per double. The **Restaurant Achucarro** also has simple accommodations. There is also a police checkpoint and a gas station; the latter is a good place to try to catch a lift onward to Bolivia. It's possible to catch a bus to Santa Cruz (Bolivia) here, but be sure to first purchase your ticket in Asunción.

Every Friday at 8 am, a Nasa bus goes to Colonia La Patria (three hours), the last Trans-Chaco outpost accessible by public transport. Buses to Asunción (US$12.50, 10 hours) leave daily, twice on Sunday.

COLONIA LA PATRIA

Only 85km from the Bolivian border, Colonia La Patria is being developed as a rural service center for the estancias of the High Chaco, with running water, a power station, school, hospital, phone system, motel and gas station. Every Friday at 2 pm eastbound buses go to Mariscal Estigarribia (three hours), Filadelfia (five hours) and Asunción (14 hours). Gasoline may be available here.

Peru

Peru is a country of geographic contrasts. Traveling from the dry desert to the lush jungle, the tourist, the anthropologist, the mountain climber and the birdwatcher find a multiplicity of landscapes, peoples, fauna and flora and archaeological monuments.

Culturally, the country is equally diverse: From the Afro-Peruvian music of the coast to the floating islands of the Uros of Lake Titicaca, from the Shipibo pottery of the Amazon, to the fine cuisine of Cuzco, from the white colonial buildings of Arequipa, to the adobe architecture of Cajamarca, a journey across Peru constantly stimulates the traveler's senses.

Facts about Peru

HISTORY

Peru's archaeological wealth is unequaled in South America, thanks to excellent preservation conditions on the arid coast and in highland caves. Its rich pre-Columbian history is the subject of much debate and disagreement among scholars.

The famous Inca civilization is merely the tip of the archaeological iceberg. Numerous cultures preceded the Incas, but they lacked writing so knowledge of them is based almost entirely on archaeological research. The Spanish, however, left written records that give us an insight into the Incas.

A main source of information for archaeologists has been the realistic decoration on the ceramics, textiles and other artifacts of Peru's pre-Columbian inhabitants. These relics often depict everyday life in detail, so it is worth looking for them in Peru's museums.

Early Peoples

The first inhabitants of Peru were nomadic hunter-gatherers who roamed the coast in loose-knit bands. They lived in caves, such as the Pikimachay cave near Ayacucho, the oldest known site in central Peru, dating from approximately 14,000 BC.

Cave paintings depicting hunting scenes (that may date from 8000 BC) have been found near Huánuco at Lauricocha and at Toquepala near Tacna. Domestication of the

At a Glance

Country Name	República del Perú
Area	1,285,216 sq km
Population	26,000,000
	(1999 estimate)
Population Density	19.4 per sq km
Capital	Lima
Head of State	President
	Alberto Fujimori
Official Languages	Spanish, Quechua,
	Aymara
Currency	Nuevo Sol (S/)
Exchange Rate	US$1 = S/3.30
Per Capita GNP	US$2150
Inflation Rate	From 10,000% (early
	1990s) to 6.5%
	(1998 estimate)

llama and guinea pig began between 7000 and 5000 BC.

By about 4000 BC, people began planting seeds and improving crops and a number of small settlements emerged along the coast, which was wetter than it is today. Crops included cotton, chili peppers, beans, squash and, later, corn. Cassava was important in the Amazonian region. Cotton was used for clothing and fishing nets. The people lived in one-room stone-lined pit dwellings, or in branch or reed huts.

Remains in the Virú valley and Guañape area (near Trujillo) and other coastal sites mark the Initial Period (about 2000 to 1000 BC). Ceramics developed from undecorated pots to sculptured, incised and simply colored pots of high quality. Weaving, fishing and horticulture also improved, and large ceremonial temples from this period have recently been found.

Lasting roughly from 1000 to 300 BC, the Early Horizon or Chavín Period – named after the site of Chavín de Huantar, 40km east of Huaraz – indicates some interchange of ideas and increasing cultural complexity. The salient feature of the Chavín is the repeated representation of a stylized jaguar with clear religious overtones. Most importantly, this period represents great cultural developments in weaving, pottery, agriculture, religion and architecture. Around 300 BC the Chavín style inexplicably disappeared, but over the next 500 years several cultures became locally important. Well known are the Salinar culture of the Chicama valley near Trujillo, and the Paracas Necropolis south of Lima. The Salinar ceramics show advanced firing techniques, while the Paracas textiles are considered the finest pre-Columbian textiles in the Americas.

Between about 100 AD and 700 AD, pottery, metalwork and textiles throughout Peru reached a pinnacle of technological development. The Moche (north coast) and the Nazca (south coast) depicted their ways of life on their ceramics, providing archaeologists with invaluable information. The Moche built massive pyramids, such as the Temples of the Sun and Moon near Trujillo and at Sipán near Chiclayo, where amazing graves were discovered in 1987. The Nazca sculpted their enigmatic giant lines and designs in the coastal desert.

From about 600 to 1000 AD Wari (Huari) influence is apparent in the art, technology and architecture of most of Peru. Wari, whose ruins are found in the highlands 25km north of Ayacucho, was the capital of the first Andean expansionist empire.

During the next four centuries several regional states thrived. The best known is the Chimu near Trujillo. Its capital was the immense adobe city of Chan Chan. Roughly contemporary with the Chimu, the Chachapoyas culture left the highland ruin of Kuélap. Other contemporaries include the Chancay, just north of Lima (their artifacts can be seen in Lima's Museo Amano), and the Ica-Chincha culture, further south, whose artifacts are in Ica's Museo Regional. Several small altiplano groups lived near Lake Titicaca and frequently warred with one another. They left impressive, circular funerary towers; the best are at Sillustani. There were also the Chanka (of the Ayacucho-Apurímac area) and the Kingdom of Cuzco, predecessor of the Inca empire.

For all its greatness, the Inca empire existed for barely a century. Prior to 1430, the Incas ruled only the valley of Cuzco, but victory over the Chankas in the 1430s marked the beginning of a rapid expansion. The Incas conquered and incorporated most of the area from southern Colombia to central Chile. Around 1525, a civil war broke out between followers of the Inca Huáscar, in Cuzco, and followers of his half-brother Atahualpa, in Quito. The Spaniards took advantage of the civil war to divide and conquer the Inca empire.

Spanish Conquest

In November 1526, Francisco Pizarro headed south from Panama, and by 1528 had explored as far as Peru's Río Santa. He noted coastal Inca settlements, became aware of the richness of the Inca empire and returned to Spain to raise money and recruit men for the conquest. On his next expedition he left Panama in late 1530, landed on the Ecuadorian coast and began to march overland towards Peru. In September 1532, Pizarro founded the first Spanish town in Peru – San Miguel de Piura. Then he marched into the heart of the Inca empire, reaching Cajamarca in November 1532. Here he captured the Inca Atahualpa and put an end to Inca rule.

Colonial Peru

In 1535, Pizarro founded the coastal city of Lima, which became the capital of the Viceroyalty of Peru. A 30-year period of turmoil ensued, with the Incas resisting their conquerors, who were fighting among themselves for control of the rich colony. Pizarro was assassinated in 1541. Manco Inca nearly regained control of the highlands in 1536, but by 1539 had retreated to his rain forest

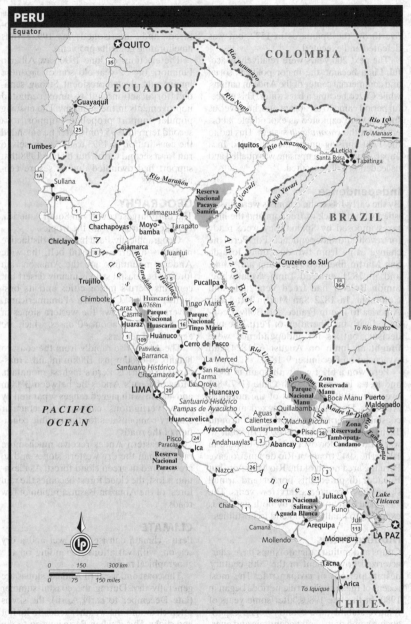

hideout at Vilcabamba, where he was killed in 1544. Inca Tupac Amaru attempted to overthrow the Spaniards in 1572, but was defeated and executed.

The next 200 years were relatively peaceful. Lima became the major political, social and commercial center of the Andean nations, while Cuzco became a backwater. This peaceful period came to an abrupt end, however, as Indians were exploited as expendable laborers under the *encomienda* system. This led to the 1780 uprising under the self-styled Inca Tupac Amaru II. The uprising was quelled and its leaders cruelly executed.

Independence

By the early 1800s, the colonists were dissatisfied with the lack of freedom and the high taxes imposed by Spain. They were ready for revolt and independence. For Peru, the change came from two directions. José de San Martín liberated Argentina and Chile, and in 1821 entered Lima. Meanwhile, Simón Bolívar had freed Venezuela and Colombia. In 1822 San Martín left Latin America to live in France and Bolívar continued with the liberation of Peru. The two decisive battles for independence were fought at Junín on August 6, 1824 and Ayacucho on December 9, 1824.

Peru won a brief war with Spain in 1866, and lost a longer war with Chile (1879-83) over the nitrate-rich areas of the northern Atacama Desert. Chile annexed much of coastal southern Peru but the area around Tacna was returned in 1929. Peru went to war with Ecuador over a border dispute in 1941. The 1942 treaty of Río de Janeiro gave Peru the area north of the Río Marañón, but Ecuador disputed this border and armed skirmishes occurred every few years. The 1998 peace treaty signed by both nations is expected to finally put an end to hostilities.

Modern Times

Coups and military dictatorships have characterized government in the 20th century, despite periods of civilian rule. The most recent of these civilian rule periods began in 1980. In the late 1980s, after some years of relative stability, the country began experiencing some of its worst economic and guerrilla problems in decades.

The Maoist Sendero Luminoso (Shining Path) waged a guerrilla war for more than a decade, resulting in the loss of many thousands of lives. Sendero leaders were captured and imprisoned in 1992, thus ameliorating guerrilla problems.

The elections of June 1990 saw Alberto Fujimori, the 52-year-old son of Japanese immigrants, elected president. Strong, semidictatorial actions led to unprecedented improvements in the economy. The ensuing popular support propelled Fujimori to a second term in 1995 (only after he amended the constitution in 1993 to allow himself to run for a second term), but by late 1998 that support had dwindled due to severe economic crisis.

GEOGRAPHY

The third-largest country in South America, Peru lies entirely within the tropics.

Geographically, Peru has three distinctive regions – a narrow coastal belt, the wide Andean mountains and the Amazon rain forest. The coastal strip is mainly desert but contains Peru's major cities and its best highway, the Carretera Panamericana. Rivers running down the western slopes of the Andes form about 40 oases, which are agricultural centers.

The Andes rise rapidly from the coast to heights of 6000m just 100km inland. Huascarán (6768m) is Peru's highest mountain. Most of Peru's Andes lie between 3000m and 4000m, with jagged ranges separated by deep, vertiginous canyons. Spectacular scenery compensates for the terrible condition of the roads.

The eastern Andes receive much more rainfall than the dry western slopes and so are covered in green cloud forest. As elevation is lost, the cloud forest becomes the rain forest of the Amazon Basin, a region of few roads.

CLIMATE

Peru's climate consists of a wet and a dry season, with variations depending on the geographical region.

The coast and western Andean slopes are generally dry. During the coastal summer (late December to early April), the sky is often clear and the weather tends to be hot and sticky. This is when Peruvians go to the beach. During the rest of the year, the *garúa* (coastal fog) moves in, and the sun is rarely seen on the central and south coasts. Inland, above the coastal garúa, it is hot and sunny for most of the year.

In the Andes proper, the dry season runs from May to September. The mountains can be cold at night, with occasional freezing temperatures in Cuzco (3326m), but the dry weather means beautiful sunshine during the day. The wet season in the mountains extends from October to May, but it doesn't get really wet until late January.

On the eastern Andean slopes, the drier months are similar to the highlands, but the wet season is more pronounced. The wettest months are January to April, when roads are often closed by landslides or flooding. The Amazon lowlands have a similar weather pattern.

FLORA & FAUNA

Peru's varied geography, with long coastal deserts, glaciated mountain ranges, vast tropical rain forests and almost every imaginable habitat in between, allows the country to host one of the world's richest assemblages of plants and animals.

The desert coast has few plants, but marine and bird life are abundant. The Islas Ballestas and Península de Paracas are home to sea lion colonies and vast numbers of sea birds and shore birds such as the Humboldt penguin, guanay cormorant, Peruvian and brown booby, Chilean flamingo, seaside cinclode, Peruvian pelican and the exquisitely beautiful Inca tern.

The Andean condor, among the largest of flying birds, is seen along the coast on occasion, but is normally an Andean inhabitant. Other interesting highland birds include the puna ibis, Andean goose and a variety of hummingbirds, which eke out a precarious existence in the forbidding elevations. The highlands, too, are home to all four South American camelids: llama, alpaca, guanaco and vicuña. In the high country, bleak páramo and puna habitats feature hardy and unique plants adapted to withstand the rigors of high altitude: blazing tropical sun alternating with freezing winds and rains. Small, colorful patches of *Polylepis*, or *queñoa*, woodland are found – this shrubby tree grows at the highest elevation of any tree in the world.

The Amazon Basin begins in Peru – the most distant tributary rises in the southern mountains of the country. The eastern slopes of the Andes, as they tumble to the Amazon Basin, are among the least accessible and least known areas of the planet. These are the haunts of jaguars, Andean spectacled bears and tapirs – spectacular large mammals only rarely seen in the wild. Peru's Amazon is home to most of the country's approximately 1700 bird species, which makes it the world's second-most diverse country for birds, third in mammal diversity and fifth in plant diversity. One protected area, the 5500-hectare Zona Reservada Tambopata, boasts more than 540 bird and 1100 butterfly species recorded. Parque Nacional Manu (1.8 million hectares) has about 1000 bird species (compared to about 700 for the USA) and 13 different species of monkey.

This vast wealth of wildlife is protected through a system of national parks and reserves with 27 areas covering about 7% of the country. This national park system includes remote and inaccessible places rarely visited – but they are there, nonetheless. Protecting these areas is vitally important but difficult because of the lack of finance. Groups like the World Wide Fund For Nature and the Nature Conservancy are active in Peruvian conservation; you can donate money to these organizations and specifically request that your contribution be used in Peru. The Fundación Peruana para la Conservación de la Naturaleza (Nature Conservancy; ☎/fax 01-446-9178), Apartado 18-1393, Lima, is a local conservation organization that provides information and accepts donations.

GOVERNMENT

Peru is a constitutional republic. The president has two vice presidents and 12 cabinet members. A unicameral congress has 120 members. Voting is compulsory for citizens aged 18 to 70.

President Fujimori was reelected for a second five-year term in 1995.

ECONOMY

Peru's disastrous economy in recent years (with inflation at more than 10,000% per year) has been brought under control by the Fujimori administration and inflation dropped to 6% in 1998. In 1996, exports were worth US$6 billion. Major exports include copper (23.1%), fish products (15.4%), agricultural products (11%), zinc

(9.6%), gold (5.6%), and petroleum products (6%). However, unreported revenue from coca (exported for cocaine production, although increasingly refined in-country) is, according to some sources, roughly comparable in value to all legal exports combined.

Peru's major economic partners are the USA and Japan.

POPULATION & PEOPLE

Over half of Peru's 26 million inhabitants are concentrated in the narrow coastal desert. Lima's population is approaching eight million, and the second- and third-largest cities, Arequipa and Trujillo (also in the coastal region) are home to nearly a million people each.

Almost half of the population lives in the highlands, and these people are mainly *campesinos* – peasants who practice subsistence agriculture. There are few large cities in the highlands, but many small towns. The standard of living there is poor, and many campesinos have migrated to the coast, where population growth is a problem.

More than 60% of Peru lies east of the Andes in the Amazon Basin, but only 5% of the population lives there. The region is slowly becoming colonized.

More than half the population is Indian and one-third is mestizo. About 12% are white and 2% are black or of Asian or other descent.

ARTS

The Andes cultural heritage is evident in many folk art forms. For the visitor, the most obvious of these art forms are music, dance and crafts. Pre-Columbian and colonial architecture are also of great interest to the visitor.

Music & Dance

Andean Pre-Columbian Andean music features wind and percussion instruments. Some of those found in archaeological museums date from 5000 BC. Contemporary stringed instruments derive from instruments that were introduced by the Spanish. Traditional Andean music is popularly called *música folklórica* and is frequently heard at fiestas as well as in bars and restaurants. Bars that specifically cater to musical entertainment are called *peñas*.

Wind instruments vary considerably by region. The most representative are the *quena* and the *zampoña*. The quena (or *kena*) is a flute, usually made of bamboo and of varying lengths depending on the pitch desired. The zampoña, or *siku* in Quechua, is a set of panpipes with two rows of bamboo canes – seven in one row and six in the other. Zampoñas come in sizes ranging from the tiny, high-pitched *chuli* to the meter-long, bass *toyo*. Other instruments include the small, oval clay *ocarina*, with up to 12 holes, and horns made of animal horn or sea shells.

Percussion instruments include the inevitable drum, called *bombo*, usually made from a hollowed-out segment of a cedar, walnut or other tree and using stretched goatskin for the head. Rattles, called *shajshas*, are made of polished goat hooves tied together.

Almost all of today's música folklórica groups also use stringed instruments. The guitar is sometimes used, but the most typical is the *charango*, a tiny, five-stringed guitar with a resonance box traditionally made of an armadillo shell, though most are wooden these days.

Of the many regionally based forms of música folklórica, the *huayno*, associated with a dance of the same name, stands out. Hundreds of other dances are known and performed in the highlands. Although dance performances can be seen in theaters and restaurants in the highlands, nowhere are they as colorful as those performed communally during the many fiestas.

Coastal In contrast with its Andean counterpart, the coastal *música criolla* has its roots in Spain and Africa. Its main instruments are guitars and *cajón*, a wooden box on which the player sits and pounds out a rhythm with the hands. The cajón is attributed to African slaves brought by the Spanish. The most popular of the coastal dances is the *marinera*, a graceful, romantic dance employing much waving of handkerchiefs. Marinera competitions are frequent in coastal Peru, the most important taking place in Trujillo, on the north coast.

Afro-Peruvian music has enjoyed a comeback, especially in the Chincha area on the south coast. This music and the dancing that accompanies it are becoming increasingly popular on TV and as a performance art, though Peruvians will go to clubs and dance to it as well. A popular performance dance is the *alcatraz*, during which one partner carrying a candle attempts to light a paper flag tucked into the back of the other's waist.

Modern Other forms of Latin American music that are popular in Peru include omnipresent salsa, as well as *cumbia* and *chicha*, both from Colombia. This is music to dance to in the *salsatecas*, which cram in hundreds of Peruvians for all-night dance-fests.

Crafts

Handicrafts made in the Andes are based on pre-Columbian necessities such as weaving, pottery and metallurgy. Today, woven cloth is still seen in the traditional ponchos, belts and other clothes worn by Andean Indians. Traditionally worked alpaca wool is also in great demand for sweaters and other items. Weaving has extended to cover a variety of rugs and tapestries, which are popular souvenirs. Pottery, well developed among many pre-Columbian cultures, is still important today as a source of souvenirs. Jewelry, especially gold and silver work, is also in demand.

Literature

Peru's most famous novelist is the internationally recognized Mario Vargas Llosa (born 1936), who ran second in the Peruvian presidential election of 1990. Most of his books have been translated into various languages, including English. His novels delve deeply into Peruvian society, politics, and culture. His first novel, *The Time of the Hero*, was publicly burned because of its detailed exposé of life in a Peruvian military academy. Vargas Llosa's work is very complex, with multiple plots and flashbacks.

Peruvian writers noted for their portrayals of the difficulties facing Peru's Indian communities include José María Arguedas (1911-69), who wrote *Deep Rivers* and *Yawar Fiesta*, among others, and Ciro Alegría (1909-67), who authored *The Golden Serpent*, about life in a jungle village on the Río Marañón, and *Broad and Alien is the World*, about repression of Andean Indians. Two contemporary writers deserve attention. Alfredo Bryce Echeñique (born 1939) offers great insight into Peruvian life through the story of a young boy in *A World for Julius*. Julio Ramón Ribeyro (born 1929), one of Latin America's finest narrators,

wrote *Marginal Voices*, a collection of short stories notable for their social commentary and sharp sense of irony.

César Vallejo (1892-1938), considered Peru's greatest poet, wrote *Trilce*, a book of 77 avant-garde poems, which some critics say is one of the best books of poetry ever written in Spanish. Anthologized modern Peruvian poetry is available in English in *Peru: The New Poetry* and *The Newest Peruvian Poetry in Translation*.

Architecture

The Inca architecture of Machu Picchu is perhaps the single greatest attraction in Peru. But there is much more in the way of Inca architecture, especially in (but not limited to) the Cuzco area. Various other pre-Columbian cultures have left us with magnificent examples of their architecture.

Colonial architecture is most importantly represented by the many imposing cathedrals, churches, monasteries and convents built during the 16th, 17th and 18th centuries. These are extremely ornate, both inside and out. Altars are often covered in gold leaf.

Painting & Sculpture

Many of the religious statues and paintings were created by indigenous artists under strong colonial influence. This unique cross-pollination gave rise to the *escuela cuzqueña* (Cuzco school) of art – a syncretic blend of Spanish and Indian sensibilities. Cuzqueña canvases are on display in many of Lima's museums and highland churches.

LANGUAGE

Spanish is the main language. Most Andean people are bilingual in Quechua, their mother tongue (Aymara around Lake Titicaca), and Spanish, their second language. One to two million inhabitants of remote areas speak no Spanish. English, used in airline offices and the best hotels, is becoming more widespread.

Facts for the Visitor

HIGHLIGHTS

Visiting archaeological sites, especially Machu Picchu, is high on everyone's list. Other important sites include Chan Chan (the huge adobe capital of the Chimu) near Trujillo, the 2500-year-old Chavín ruins near Huaraz, the recently discovered site of El Señor de Sipán near Chiclayo, the funerary towers at Sillustani, near Puno, and Kuélap near Chachapoyas.

Trekking, backpacking and mountaineering are popular during the May-to-September dry season. See the Around Cuzco section for details on the Inca Trail, and the Huaraz section for the Cordillera Blanca and Parque Nacional Huascarán.

White-water rafting is possible year-round, with higher water levels in the rainy season. See the Cuzco, Huaraz and Cañete sections.

A few middle- and upper-class young Peruvians enjoy surfing. The water is cold so wet suits must be worn. The surfing is decent but facilities and equipment are basic. Swimming is popular from January to March, but the beaches are very contaminated near cities and there are many dangerous currents.

Wildlife enthusiasts should visit the Islas Ballestas near Pisco for huge sea lion and sea-bird colonies. Seeing the rain forest is also exciting, but expensive.

Finally, try to spend a night with a family on one of Lake Titicaca's islands.

PLANNING
When to go
June to August, the highland dry season, is the most popular time to travel in Peru. At this time, hotels are more likely to be full and to charge full prices. In other months (except for major holidays) expect lower prices and try bargaining. January to March are the 'summer' months on the coast, and many Peruvians vacation then.

Maps
Topographical maps are sold at the Instituto Geográfico Nacional in Lima. The South American Explorers Club (see Information in the Lima section) has hiking maps.

RESPONSIBLE TOURISM
Archaeologists are fighting a losing battle with *huaqueros* (grave robbers), particularly along the coast. Please refrain from buying original pre-Columbian artifacts – there are plenty of nice reproductions for sale. Similarly, do not contribute to wildlife destruction by purchasing souvenirs made from skins, feathers or horns.

Some indigenous communities, like Taquile on the Titicaca, make their living from tourism. Visiting these communities supports their initiatives.

Wool garments and weavings at market stalls in most cities are not sold by the artisans who make them. However, there are a number of venues that benefit craftspeople directly. Patronizing these venues ensures the continuity of traditional techniques and designs.

VISAS & DOCUMENTS
Most travelers do not need a visa to enter Peru. Passports should be valid for at least six months. A free tourist card is given to everybody on arrival. Don't lose this, as it's needed for stay extensions and passport checks and when leaving the country. The Migraciones (immigration) office in Lima, Av España 730, Breña; ☎ 01-330-4020, fax 01-332-1269, deals with replacements. Although you officially need an onward ticket to get in, unless you are traveling on a visa, you will rarely have to show one.

On arrival, you can usually get a 90-day stay if you ask for it, though 30-day admission is the norm. Extensions cost US$20 for 30 days at immigration offices in major cities; it's best to go first thing in the morning for best service. After 180 days you must leave the country, but you are allowed to return the next day and begin again.

Carry your passport and tourist card at all times since you can be arrested if you don't have identification. When walking around town, carry a photocopy of your passport and leave the original in a safe place.

International vaccination certificates are not required by law, though vaccinations are advisable (see Health in the Facts for the Visitor chapter). International student cards save you money at several archaeological sites, museums and hostels.

EMBASSIES & CONSULATES
Peruvian Embassies & Consulates
Peruvian embassies are found in all neighboring countries; addresses are listed in those chapters. There are also Peruvian representatives in the following locations:

Australia
(☎ 02-6290-0922, fax 02-6290-0924)
43 Culgoa Circuit, O'Malley, ACT 2606
Postal address: PO Box 106,
Red Hill, ACT 2603

Canada
(☎ 613-238-1777, fax 613-232-3062)
130 Alver St, Suite 1901, Ottawa K1P 5G4

France
(☎ 01 53 70 42 00, fax 01 47 55 98 30)
50 Ave Kléber, 75007 Paris

Germany
(☎ 0228-37-30-45, fax 0228-37-94-75)
Godesberger Allee 125, 53175 Bonn

Israel
(☎ 03-613-5591, fax 03-751-2286)
37 Revov Ha-Marganit, Shikun Vatikim,
52584 Ramat Gan

New Zealand
(☎ 04-499-8087, fax 04-499-8057)
Level 8, Cigna House, 40 Mercer St, POB 2566,
Wellington

Spain
(☎ 01-431-4242, fax 01-431-2493)
Príncipe de Vergara 36, 5D, 28001 Madrid

UK
(☎ 0171-235-1917, fax 0171-235-4463)
52 Sloane St, London SW1X 9SP

USA
(☎ 202-833-9860, fax 202-659-8124)
1700 Massachusetts Ave, NW,
Washington, DC 20036

Embassies & Consulates in Peru

Almost 50 nations have diplomatic representation in Lima. Some important ones follow. Australian travelers should go to the Canadian Embassy in the event of a lost passport or other emergency; the nearest Australian representation is in Santiago, Chile, and Guayaquil, Ecuador.

Bolivia
(☎ 01-422-8231)
Los Castaños 235, San Isidro, Lima
(☎ 054-351251)
Arequipa 120, Puno; open 8 am to 1 pm and
3 to 6 pm weekdays
Tacna: on Av Piura, at the southeast end of
town; open 9 to 11 am weekdays

Brazil
(☎ 01-421-5650, fax 01-445-2421)
José Pardo 850, Miraflores, Lima
(☎ 094-232081)
Sargento Lores 363, Iquitos

Canada
(☎ 01-444-4015, fax 01-444-4347)
Libertad 130, Miraflores, Lima

Chile
(☎ 01-221-2817, fax 01-221-2816)
Javier Prado Oeste 790, San Isidro, Lima
(☎ 054-724391)
Near the railway station in Tacna;
open 8 am to 12:30 pm weekdays

Colombia
(☎ 01-442-9648, fax 01-441-9806)
Av Jorge Basadre 1580, San Isidro, Lima
(☎ 094-231461)
Putumayo 247, Iquitos

Ecuador
(☎ 01-442-4184, fax 01-422-0711)
Las Palmeras 356, San Isidro, Lima

Germany
(☎ 01-422-4919, fax 01-422-6475)
Arequipa 4210, Miraflores, Lima

Israel
(☎ 01-433-4431)
Natalio Sánchez 125, 6th floor, Lima

New Zealand
(☎ 01-433-8923, fax 01-433-8922)
Natalio Sánchez 125, 4th floor, Lima

South Africa
(☎ 01-422-2280, fax 01-442-7154)
Av Camino Real 1252, 2nd floor,
San Isidro, Lima

Spain
(☎ 01-221-7704, fax 01-440-2020)
Jorge Basadre 498, San Isidro, Lima

UK
(☎ 01-433-4738, fax 01-433-8922)
Natalio Sánchez 125, 4th floor, Lima

USA
(☎ 01-434-3000, fax 01-434-3037)
Av La Encalada, 17th block,
Monterrico-Surco, Lima

CUSTOMS

If bringing a valuable item for personal use (eg, a bicycle or a laptop computer) you may be asked to pay a (supposedly) refundable bond of 25% of its value. It can be hard to get a refund in the few hours that you are at the airport leaving the country. Insist that the item is for personal use and you will not be selling it in Peru. If you have to pay, undervalue the item as much as you dare to minimize potential loss, and check with customs a day or two before you leave.

PERU

It is illegal to export pre-Columbian artifacts and illegal to bring them into most countries. Coca leaves are legal in Peru but shouldn't be brought into most other countries. Objects made from skins, feathers and turtle shells should not be bought; their purchase contributes to wildlife degradation and their importation into most countries is illegal.

MONEY
Currency
The currency, introduced in 1991, is the *nuevo sol* (S/), divided into 100 *céntimos*. The following bills are in circulation: S/10, S/20, S/50, S/100. Counterfeit bills abound, so try to exchange money at banks or *casas de cambio*. Coins of S/0.05, S/0.10, S/0.20, S/0.50, S/1, S/2 and S/5 are also in use.

Exchange Rates
Approximate exchange rates at press time follow:

country	unit		nuevo sol
Australia	A$1	=	S/2.18
Canada	C$1	=	S/2.23
euro	€1	=	S/3.36
France	FF1	=	S/0.53
Germany	DM1	=	S/1.72
Japan	¥100	=	S/2.72
New Zealand	NZ$1	=	S/1.73
UK	UK£1	=	S/5.16
USA	US$1	=	S/3.30

Exchanging Money
Currencies other than US dollars can be exchanged only in major cities and at a high commission, so it pays to obtain US dollars before your trip. All cities or towns of any size can change US dollars. Dollar bills that are slightly torn or damaged are accepted by some street changers but at a very poor rate; torn Peruvian currency is OK.

Banking hours are erratic. In the summer (January to March), banks in Lima may open only from 8:30 to 11:30 am. Expect long queues in banks and go early in the morning. Casas de cambio open from 9 am to 6 pm – or later in touristed towns like Cuzco – and are much faster. Moneychangers, who only take cash, are useful for exchange outside banking hours or at borders where there are no banks. Street rates are equivalent to bank rates, but you may be cheated, so beware. Calculators are often 'fixed' and short-changing is common; count the money carefully before handing over your dollars. With the abundance of counterfeit bills, street vendors now sell devices to detect false currency.

The exchange rates for cash dollars are better than for traveler's checks, which are usually changed at a 1% to 5% commission. Recommended banks are Banco de Crédito, Interbanc and Banco Mercantil. The most widely accepted traveler's checks are American Express and Thomas Cook.

Bills paid by credit card are usually increased by 10%. Visa and MasterCard are widely accepted, and cash withdrawals can be made at ATMs. Acceptance of debit cards is less widespread.

Costs
Prices can triple (in dollar terms) within months and can fall equally rapidly. Costs in Peru increased threefold during the early 1990s but are stable now. On a tight budget, you can get by on US$15 to US$20 per day by staying in the most basic hotels and traveling slowly. Big cities are more expensive than small towns. Most budget travelers spend over US$25 per day because of the large distances that they try to cover.

Tipping & Bargaining
Fancy restaurants add tips and tax to your bill, but cheap restaurants don't. You don't have to tip the server in the cheapest restaurants, but they don't make much money, so leaving some change isn't a bad idea. Don't leave it on the table; give it to the server.

Taxi drivers are not tipped, but bellhops get US$0.50 per bag. Tip a local guide US$3 to US$5 per client for each full day's work if they are good, professional, multilingual guides – less if they aren't. On treks it is customary also to tip the cook and porters. Tip them at least as much as the guide and split it between them.

Bargaining is expected in markets when buying crafts and occasionally in other situations. If you're not sure, try asking for a discount or *descuento*. These are often given in hotels, tour agencies, souvenir shops, and other places where tourists spend money.

POST & COMMUNICATIONS
Post
Postal services have improved since privatization but are expensive: airmail postcards or letters are US$1 to most countries. Letters from major Peruvian cities to other countries take from one to three weeks. Parcel post is not recommended because there is no surface rate and airmail is prohibitively expensive. Regulations change from year to year.

Travelers can receive mail at either the post office (addressed to Lista de Correos, Correo Central, [city], Peru) or American Express (Lima Tours, Casilla 4340, Belén 1040, Lima). The SAEC will hold mail for members, and return or forward it, according to your instructions.

Telephone & Fax
Telefónica del Perú provides national and international telephone and fax services. Main offices are marked on chapter maps, and sub-offices and phone booths are widespread. Calls are expensive. Direct-dial payphones accept coins or telephone cards bought at Telefónica offices. A card for S/30 (US$10) lasts 4½ minutes to the USA, or less to Europe. These are the cheapest calls. In smaller towns you'll need to go through a Telefónica operator. Rates are cheaper on Sunday and after 9 pm. The Telefónica offices are usually open from 8 am to 10 pm – sometimes later in major cities.

Telephone numbers have seven digits in Lima and six digits elsewhere. Area codes begin with 0 (01 in Lima, 0 plus two digits elsewhere; these are given with phone numbers in the text). To call long distance within Peru, include the 0 in the area code.

Peru's country code is 51. To call from abroad, dial your international access code, then 51, the area telephone code *without* the 0 and the six or seven-digit number.

Fax services are available at most Telefónica del Perú offices for US$3 to US$7 per page (rates are higher outside Lima). Telefónica offices will hold faxes clearly marked 'ATENCIÓN (your name),' and charge less than US$1.

Email & Internet Access
Most tourist destinations have Internet offices where you can access email. Hourly rates range from US$1 to US$3.

INTERNET RESOURCES
The University of Texas at Austin's Institute of Latin American Studies hosts a highly recommended website, lanic.utexas.edu/la/peru, featuring frequently updated information, extensive links to news and current events and numerous reference and research resources.

BOOKS
Books in English are expensive in Peru. Many useful books, including Lonely Planet's *Peru*, are listed in the Facts for the Visitor chapter.

Cut Stones and Crossroads by Ronald Wright is a fine travel book by a writer very well informed on archaeology and contemporary Peru. *Exploring Cuzco* by Peter Frost is recommended for anyone planning to spend some time in the Cuzco area.

Readers seriously interested in learning about Peruvian archaeology should read *The Incas and Their Ancestors: The Archaeology of Peru* by Michael E Moseley and Richard L Burger's *Chavín and the Origins of Andean Civilizations*.

MEDIA
The best newspapers are the dry, conservative *El Comercio*, good for what's going on in Lima; the conservative *Expreso* and the moderately left-wing *La República* – all published in Lima. A shorter *El Comercio* (lacking the Lima cultural section) is sold in other cities. There are many trashy tabloids. *Lima Times* is a monthly magazine in English.

Peru has seven TV channels plus cable. Local programming is poor, though evening news broadcasts are OK for local news. Radio stations broadcast in Quechua and Spanish. The BBC World Service and Voice of America can be picked up on shortwave radio.

TIME
Peru is five hours behind GMT/UTC and currently has no daylight saving time.

ELECTRICITY
Peru uses 220V, 60Hz, except Arequipa, which is on 50Hz. Plugs are of the flat, two-pronged type found in the USA.

HEALTH
Definitely avoid salads and fruit you cannot peel, and don't drink tap water or brush your teeth in it. There are good medical services in

the major cities; the best are in Lima, where you should go if seriously ill. See Health in the Facts for the Visitor chapter.

USEFUL ORGANIZATIONS

The South American Explorers Club (SAEC) has a Lima office. See Information in the Lima section for details.

DANGERS & ANNOYANCES

Many travelers report thefts: there are pickpockets, bag-snatchers, razor-blade slashers (slashing your pack or pocket), con artists and crooked police. Take taxis when first arriving in a new city until you get the feel of the place. One scam involves locals spending days befriending you and then, when they have your trust, offering you a joint. You get busted two drags later. Be aware and take precautions but don't be paranoid: violent crime is uncommon. See the Dangers & Annoyances section in the Facts for the Visitor chapter.

Terrorism

The leaders of Peru's major guerrilla groups, the Sendero Luminoso and the Movimiento Revolucionario Túpac Amaru (MRTA), were imprisoned in 1992. Since then, travel has become reasonably safe in most of Peru. Areas to avoid are the Río Huallaga valley between Tingo María and Tarapoto (these towns are safe but the area between is prime drug country) and the Nazca-Puquio-Abancay route, which is a favorite of bandits.

BUSINESS HOURS

Shops open at 9 or 10 am and close around 8 pm. A two or three-hour lunch break is common. There are 24-hour supermarkets in Lima, and shops may stay open through lunch in big cities. Most shops close on Sunday. Banks and offices keep highly variable hours.

PUBLIC HOLIDAYS & SPECIAL EVENTS

Asterisked dates are bank holidays.

Año Nuevo (New Year's Day)
January 1*

La Virgen de la Candelaria (Candlemas) – a colorful highland fiesta, particularly in the Puno area
February 2

Carnaval – many water fights
February-March

Semana Santa (Holy Week) – spectacular religious processions almost daily
March-April*

Labor Day
May 1*

Corpus Christi – Cuzco processions are especially dramatic
June

Inti Raymi – winter solstice, the greatest Inca festival, which brings thousands of visitors to Cuzco
June 24*

San Pedro y San Pablo (St Peter and St Paul)
June 29*

La Virgen del Carmen – especially celebrated in Paucartambo and Pisac near Cuzco and Pucara near Lake Titicaca
July 16

Fiestas Patrias (Peru's Independence) – the biggest national holiday; buses and hotels are booked long in advance and hotel prices can triple
July 28 to 29*

Santa Rosa de Lima –patron saint of Lima and of the Americas; major processions in Lima
August 30*

Battle of Angamos
October 8*

El Señor de los Milagros (Lord of the Miracles) – huge religious processions in Lima; people wear purple
October 18

Todos Santos (All Saint's Day)
November 1*

Día de los Muertos (All Soul's Day) – food, drink and flowers are taken to family graves; especially colorful in the highlands
November 2

Puno Day – spectacular costumes and street dancing in Puno commemorate the legendary emergence of the first Inca, Manco Capac, from Lake Titicaca; celebrated for several days
November 5

Fiesta de la Purísima Concepción (Feast of the Immaculate Conception)
December 8*

Navidad (Christmas Day)
December 25*

WORK

Language centers in Cuzco sometimes hire native speakers to teach English. See Language Courses in Cuzco section for school contact information.

Primary lowland rain forest, Amazon Basin, Manu, Peru

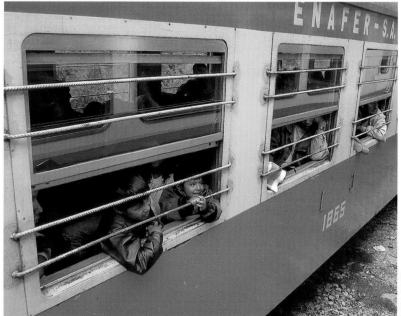

Local train from Cuzco to Quillabamba, Peru

Magnificent Angel Falls, the world's highest waterfall, Venezuela

ACCOMMODATIONS

Accommodations can be scarce during major fiestas and the night before market day. Therefore as many hotels as possible are shown on town maps. If you are going to a town for a fiesta, arrive a day or two early.

Singles may be hard to find, so you may get a room with two or three beds. Check that you won't have to pay for all the beds – usually no problem, unless the hotel is full. Many hotels have triple and quad rooms, which are cheaper for groups. Hotels offering hot water usually have it for a few hours a day; ask when. Young local couples use some cheap hotels for short stays.

Villages off the beaten track may lack a basic *pensión*. If you have a sleeping bag, find somewhere to sleep by asking around; the store owner should know who rents rooms or floor space. People in remote areas are generally hospitable.

FOOD

Those with a tight budget and a strong stomach can eat from street and market stalls provided the food looks hot and freshly cooked. *Chifas* (Chinese restaurants) are often good values. Most will offer *tallarines* (noodles) with chopped chicken, beef, pork or shrimp for less than US$2. Many restaurants offer a *menú del día* (inexpensive set lunch), which consists of a soup and a second course and costs from US$1 to US$3, depending on location. Lunch is the main meal of the day; dinner is usually served late (from 8 pm). Better restaurants add 18% to 31% in tips and tax: ask before you eat. Typical dishes include:

Ceviche de corvina – appetizer of white sea bass marinated in lemon, chili and onions, served cold with a boiled potato or yam; *ceviche de camarones* is the same made with shrimp

Lomo saltado – chopped steak fried with onions, tomatoes and potatoes, served with rice

Palta a la jardinera – avocado stuffed with cold vegetables and mayonnaise; *a la reina* is stuffed with chicken salad

Sopa a la criolla – lightly spiced noodle soup with beef, egg, milk and vegetables; hearty and filling

The term *a la criolla* describes spicy foods. The highlands have their own distinctive cuisine; see the Cuzco section for details.

DRINKS
Nonalcoholic Drinks

Agua mineral (mineral water) is sold *con gas* (carbonated) or *sin gas* (noncarbonated).

The usual soft drinks are available, as well as local ones such as Inca Kola, which is appropriately gold-colored and tastes like fizzy bubble gum. Soft drinks are collectively called *gaseosas*, and the local brands are very sweet. Ask for *helada* if you want a refrigerated drink, *al tiempo* if you don't. Remember *sin hielo* (without ice) unless you really trust the water supply.

Jugos (fruit juices) are available everywhere. Make sure you get *jugo puro* and not *con agua*. The most common kinds of juices are *mora* (blackberry), *naranja* (orange), *toronja* (grapefruit), *piña* (pineapple), *maracuyá* (passion fruit), *sandía* (watermelon), *naranjilla* (a local fruit tasting like bitter orange) and papaya.

Coffee is available almost everywhere but is often disappointing. It doesn't taste that great and it looks very much like soy sauce. Instant coffee is also served. Good espresso and cappuccino are available in the bigger towns. *Café con leche* is milk with coffee, and *café con agua* is black coffee. *Té* (tea) is served black with lemon and sugar. Hot chocolate is also popular. *Mate* and *té de hierbas* are herbal teas. *Mate de coca* is made from coca leaves and served in highland restaurants. It supposedly helps the newly arrived visitor to acclimatize.

Alcoholic Drinks

There are about a dozen kinds of beer, and they are quite palatable and inexpensive. Both light, lager-type beers and sweet, dark beers are available. Dark beer is *malta* or *cerveza negra*. Cuzco and Arequipa are known for their beers, Cuzqueña and Arequipeña.

The traditional highland *chicha* (corn beer) is stored in earthenware pots and served in huge glasses in small Andean villages and markets, but is not commercially available elsewhere. It is homemade and definitely an acquired taste.

Peruvian wines are acceptable but not as good as those from Chile or Argentina. The best labels are Tacama and Ocucaje.

Spirits are expensive if imported and not especially good if made locally, with some

PERU

exceptions. *Ron* (rum) is cheap and quite good. A white grape brandy called *pisco* is the national drink, most frequently served in a pisco sour, a tasty cocktail made from pisco, egg white, lemon juice, syrup, crushed ice and bitters. *Guinda* is a sweet cherry brandy. The local *aguardiente*, sugarcane alcohol, is an acquired taste but is good and very cheap.

SHOPPING

Souvenirs from Peru are good, varied and cheap. You won't necessarily save much money by shopping in villages and markets rather than in shops. In markets and smaller stores, bargaining is expected.

You can buy everything in Lima, be it a blowpipe from the jungle or a woven poncho from the highlands. Although Lima is usually a little more expensive, the choice is varied and the quality is high. Cuzco also has a great selection of craft shops; compare prices and quality before you buy. Old and new weavings, ceramics, paintings, woolen clothing and jewelry are all available.

The Puno-Juliaca area is good for knitted alpaca sweaters and knickknacks made from the *totora* reed, which grows on Lake Titicaca. The Huancayo area is the place for carved gourds, and excellent weavings and clothing are available in the cooperative market. The Ayacucho area is famous for modern weavings and stylized ceramic churches. San Pedro de Cajas is known for its peculiar weavings, which are made of rolls of yarn stuffed with wool. The Shipibo pottery sold in Yarinacocha (near Pucallpa) is the best jungle craft available. Superb reproductions of Moche and Mochica pottery are available in Trujillo; make sure that they are labeled as such.

Getting There & Away

AIR

June to September is the high season; discount fares may be available in other months.

Airports

Lima's Aeropuerto Internacional Jorge Chávez is the main hub for flights to the Andean countries from Europe and North America. There are also some international

flights to Iquitos, in Peru's Amazon region, and from Cuzco to Miami.

Departure Tax

There is a US$25 departure tax (payable in cash dollars or nuevos soles) for travelers leaving Peru on an international flight. An 18% tax is levied on all tickets bought in Peru.

Warning

On March 9, 1999, AeroPerú (☎ 800-777-7717 in the USA, 01-447-0854 or 01-444-2718 in Lima, www.aero-peru.com) announced that they had canceled all flights 'as a result of a company reorganization.' For now, Aero-Continente has effectively monopolized the domestic market. Consequently, fares may be higher than prices quoted in this chapter, and schedules are likely to differ.

Bolivia

Lloyd Aéreo Boliviano (LAB) has daily flights between La Paz and Lima (US$180), which can be heavily booked. There are several flights a week from Santa Cruz to Lima.

Brazil

There are several flights a week between Rio de Janeiro and São Paulo and Lima (US$703) on Varig.

Chile

LanChile has daily flights between Santiago and Lima (US$357).

Colombia

There are daily flights from Bogotá to Lima (US$341) with Avianca and other airlines.

Ecuador

Ecuatoriana and American Airlines fly to Lima from Quito and Guayaquil.

LAND
Bolivia

The overland routes between Peru and Bolivia are around Lake Titicaca. For details, see the Puno section (in this chapter).

Chile

The main border crossing is from Arica in northern Chile to Tacna. For details, see Tacna (in this chapter) and Arica (in the Chile chapter).

Ecuador

This is a straightforward crossing. For details, see Tumbes (in this chapter) and Huaquillas (in the Ecuador chapter).

RIVER
Brazil & Colombia

Boats ply the Amazon from Tabatinga (Brazil), at the Brazil-Colombia-Peru border, to Iquitos (Peru); the passage takes two to three days and the fare is US$20. Express boats from Leticia (Colombia) take 12 hours and charge US$50. Tabatinga and Leticia are adjacent to one another.

Getting Around

When traveling, have your passport with you, not packed in your luggage or left in the hotel safe. Buses may go through police checkpoints. If your passport is in order, these are cursory procedures.

AIR
Domestic Air Services

AeroContinente and Expreso Aéreo are the only carriers still flying regularly. Most connecting flights between smaller cities have disappeared. Expreso Aéreo is flying only to Cajamarca. Other small airlines fly irregularly. The military airline, Grupo Ocho, occasionally provides flights but has infrequent service. Regulations and schedules change often, so check more than once.

Flights are often late. Morning flights are more likely to be on time, but by afternoon things fall an hour or more behind schedule. Show up at least an hour early for all domestic flights, as baggage handling and check-in procedures are chaotic. It is not unknown for flights to leave *before* their official departure time if bad weather has been predicted. Flights are overbooked during holiday periods, so make reservations well in advance and confirm, reconfirm and reconfirm again. Airlines are notorious for bumping you off your flight if you don't reconfirm – and sometimes even if you do! There are no nonsmoking sections on internal flights. Many flights have good views of the Andes, so get a window seat.

One-way flights are half the cost of return flights. An 18% tax is charged on

domestic fares. The same flights are sold in Arica, Chile with a 2% tax.

On internal flights, 20kg of checked luggage is allowed (though you can often get away with more weight). Lost luggage is depressingly frequent. It often turns up on the next day's flight, but you should carry valuables and essentials (a warm coat, medication, etc) in your hand luggage. Lock your checked luggage and label it clearly.

Air Passes

AeroContinente has a special Inka Air Pass for foreigners and non-resident Peruvians, good for 30 days and sold only outside Peru.

Domestic Departure Tax

A US$3.50 departure tax is charged on local flights out of most airports.

BUS

Peru's buses are cheap and go just about everywhere, except for the deep jungle and Machu Picchu. Even the best buses are inferior to those in Chile and Argentina.

Few cities have central bus terminals. Usually, different bus companies have their offices clustered around a few city blocks. It's best to buy your ticket in advance. There may be a separate 'express' window for tickets for another day. Schedules and fares change frequently and vary from company to company. Discounted fares are offered in the low season. Buses occasionally don't leave from the ticket office – ask.

Long-distance buses stop for meals. The driver announces how long the stop will be, but it's your responsibility to be on the bus when it leaves. Many companies have their own restaurants in the middle of nowhere, so you have to eat there. The food is generally inexpensive and unexciting but you can always bring your own. Carry a roll of toilet paper.

During long holiday weekends or special fiestas buses are booked up for several days in advance. Book early. Bus fares often double around Christmas and July 28 and 29 (Fiestas Patrias). Always be prepared for delays and don't plan on making important connections after a bus journey.

A flashlight is useful on an overnight bus. It can get freezing cold on night buses in the highlands, so dress warmly.

PERU

Armed robberies on night buses are occasionally reported. Considering the number of buses, the chance of being held up is remote; nevertheless, travel by day when possible. Some routes (eg, Puno-Cuzco), however, are served only by night buses. Avoid travel between Abancay and Nazca and between Tingo María and Tarapoto.

In remote areas, trucks and pick-ups may carry passengers. Most ride in the back, (though seats in the cab are available at higher cost). Because the trucks double as buses, they usually charge almost as much.

TRAIN

There are two unconnected railway networks; both go from the coast to the highlands. The Central Railroad runs from Lima to Huancayo through Galera station, which, at 4781m, is the world's highest standard-gauge railway station. In 1998 they reopened passenger services on a limited basis; on the last weekend of the month the train goes up on Saturday and returns on Monday. The Southern Railroad runs passenger trains from Arequipa to Puno and Cuzco. Trains from Arequipa to Puno run on Wednesday and Sunday nights. Change at Juliaca, 40km before Puno, for trains to Cuzco. The Arequipa-Juliaca (or Puno) service takes all night; the Puno-Cuzco service takes a day. There are two classes. Second class is cheap but very crowded and uncomfortable. First class is about 25% more expensive, but it is much more comfortable, and cheaper, than a bus journey of comparable length. In addition, there are buffet and Pullman cars, for which you pay a surcharge. There is also a more expensive tourist train from Cuzco to Machu Picchu.

Thieves haunt trains, particularly in second class on the night train from Arequipa to Puno, where a dozing traveler is almost certain to get robbed. Dark stations also have many thieves. Travel with a group or in 1st class. The buffet or Pullman classes are the safest because only ticket holders are allowed aboard.

Buy tickets in advance (the day before is your only option) so you don't have to worry about looking after your luggage while lining up to buy a ticket.

CAR & MOTORCYCLE

Road conditions are poor, distances are great, rental cars are in bad condition – we don't recommend renting cars. Motorcycles can be rented in major Peruvian towns.

HITCHHIKING

Hitching is not considered practical in Peru because there are few private cars. Most vehicles will pick you up space permitting, and most will expect payment. Women are advised against hitching alone.

BOAT

Small motorboats that take about 20 passengers go from Puno to Lake Titicaca's islands. There are departures every day and the costs are low.

In Peru's eastern lowlands, dugout canoes, usually powered by an outboard engine, act as water buses on the smaller rivers. Where the rivers widen, larger cargo boats are normally available. You can travel from Pucallpa or Yurimaguas to Iquitos, where you change boats to the Brazilian border, and on to the mouth of the Amazon. The boats are small but have two or more decks. The lower deck is for cargo, the upper for passengers and crew. Bring a hammock. Food is provided but is basic and not always very hygienic. You may want to bring some of your own. To get a passage, go down to the docks and ask for a boat going to your destination. Arrange a passage with the captain (nobody else). Departure time depends, more often than not, on filling up the hold. Sometimes you can sleep on the boat while waiting for departure, thus saving on hotel bills.

Boats to Iquitos from upriver towns like Yurimaguas or Pucallpa leave every few days and are smaller and slower. Beyond Iquitos, services are more frequent and more comfortable. Things are generally more organized, too: there are blackboards at the docks with ships' names, destinations and departure times.

LOCAL TRANSPORT

Taxis have no meters so ask the fare in advance. Haggle over a taxi fare; drivers often double or triple the standard rate for unsuspecting foreigners. For a short run in Lima, the fare is about US$1.50; it's a little less in other cities. Taxis are recognizable by the small red 'TAXI' sticker on the windshield. More expensive radio taxis (called by telephone) are available.

Lima

Lima, Peru's capital, was founded by Francisco Pizarro on January 6, 1535, the Catholic feast of Epiphany, or the Day of the Kings. Hence the city was first named the City of the Kings. Many colonial buildings have been or are being restored. Unfortunately, much of Lima's colonial charm has been overwhelmed by an uncontrolled population explosion that began in the 1920s. About one-third of the nation's 26 million inhabitants now live in Lima, and most of the city is overcrowded, polluted and noisy.

Much of the growth results from the influx of very poor people from other areas of Peru who come in search of a better life. But jobs are scarce, and most end up living in the *pueblos jóvenes* (literally, young towns). These shantytowns surround the capital and lack electricity, water and adequate sanitation.

Lima has a dismal climate. From April to December, the city gets garúa, a convective coastal fog that blots out the sun and blankets the buildings in a fine gray mist. During the short Lima summer (January to March), the situation is hardly better. Although the sun comes out, the smog makes walking the streets unpleasant, and the city beaches are overcrowded cesspools. The waste products of more than eight million inhabitants have to go somewhere, and they mostly end up in the Pacific; the newspapers routinely publish health warnings about beaches during the summer months.

Despite all this, there are reasons for visiting the city. The inhabitants are generally friendly and hospitable; there are plenty of opportunities for dining, nightlife and other entertainment; and there is a great selection of museums. Besides, it is almost impossible to avoid Lima.

Orientation

The heart of the city is the recently beautified Plaza Mayor (formerly Plaza de Armas), flanked by the Government Palace, the Catedral, the Archbishop's Palace and other important buildings. The Plaza Mayor is linked to the Plaza San Martín by the crowded pedestrian street Jirón (de la) Unión, which is lined with shops. The area around these plazas is historically interesting, and it is here that the majority of budget hotels are found.

South of Plaza San Martín, Jirón Unión continues as Belén and runs to the Paseo de la República. (Many streets in Lima change their names every few blocks, which is confusing for the first-time visitor.) Paseo de la República is graced by the huge Palacio de Justicia, the Sheraton Hotel and many interesting monuments. At the south end of the Paseo is the Plaza Grau, from which the Vía Expresa (locally called 'El Zanjón' – the ditch) is an important expressway to the southern suburbs. Parallel and to the west of the Vía Expresa is Av Garcilaso de la Vega, which runs south into Av Arequipa and is the main street for bus transport to the beachfront suburbs of San Isidro, Miraflores and Barranco. Continuing along Av Arequipa for several kilometers through Miraflores you come to Av Larco, which leads in turn to the Pacific Ocean.

The old heart of Lima is notorious for pickpockets, so keep alert. The southern suburbs, where the better-off *limeños* live, are not as dangerous. Many of the capital's best restaurants and nightspots are in Miraflores, and the cafés are places to hang out, to see and be seen. Barranco is popular with students and artists and has excellent nightlife.

Information

Tourist Offices Infotur (☎ 01-431-0117), Jirón Unión 1066 (interior patio), is open 9:30 am to 6 pm weekdays, and 10 am to 2 pm on Saturday. Lily Muñoz and Laura Gómez provide excellent multilingual information, and will help with your travel arrangements. The municipal office on Pasaje Nicolás de Rivera, behind the Municipalidad (☎ 01-427-6080), open 9 am to 6 pm weekdays, is less helpful. In Miraflores a municipal tourist information booth in Parque Kennedy is open 9 am to 9 pm daily.

Visa Extensions The Migraciones office (☎ 01-330-4020, fax 01-332-1269), Av España 730, in the Breña district near the SAEC, handles visa extensions. Inquire at SAEC about hours and the latest regulations.

Money Interbanc, with branches at Jirón Unión 600, at Larco 690 in Miraflores and elsewhere, changes traveler's checks with low commissions. The American Express

CENTRAL LIMA

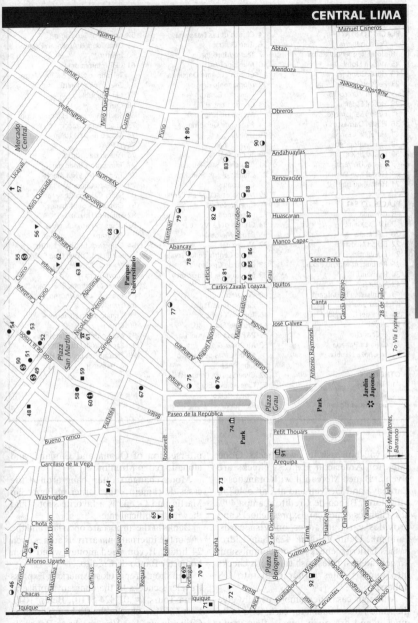

CENTRAL LIMA

CENTRAL LIMA

PLACES TO STAY
5 Pensión Ibarra
8 Hotel Residencial Roma
15 Wilson Hotel
18 Hotel Claridge
23 Pensión Unión
25 Hostal Wiracocha
28 Hostal España
31 Hostal Samaniego
36 Hostal Damascus
41 Hotel La Casona
48 Familia Rodríguez
59 Hostal Belén
63 Hostal Universo
64 Hostal Kori Wasi II
71 Hostal Iquique

PLACES TO EAT
3 Govinda
9 Tic Tac Chifa
20 La Casera
22 El Pan Nuestro
24 El Atlantic
26 Restaurant Machu Picchu
34 Raimondi
42 Natur
43 Manhattan Restaurant
44 L'Eau Vive
56 Casa del Corregidor
62 Heydi
65 El Capricho
70 Chifa La Paisana
72 La Choza Náutica

OTHER
1 Hatuchay
2 Santuario de
   Santa Rosa de Lima

4 Church of Las Nazarenas
6 Cine Central
7 Teatro Municipal
10 Municipalidad
11 Church of Santo Domingo
12 Monumento de
   Francisco Pizarro
13 Correo Central &
   Museo Filatélico
14 Palacio de Gobierno
16 Cine Lido
17 Cine Tacna
19 Teatro Segura
21 Church of San Agustín
27 Church of San Francisco &
   Catacombs
29 Museo de la Cultura Peruana
30 Cine Portofino
32 Interbanc
33 Church of La Merced
35 Banco Mercantil
37 Museo del
   Banco Central de Reserva
38 Banco de Crédito
39 Museo de la Inquisición y
   del Congreso
40 Congreso
45 Palacio Torre Tagle
46 Turismo Chimbote
47 Cruz del Sur
49 P&P Casa de Cambio
50 McDollar &
   Other Casas de Cambio
51 Cine Plaza
52 CyberSandeg (Internet)
53 Cine Adán y Eva
54 Cine Excelsior
55 Banco Wiese

57 Church of San Pedro
58 Lima Tours & American Express
60 Infotur
61 CPT International
   Telephone Office& Cine Metro
66 Telefónica del Perú
67 Cine República
68 Olano
69 South American Explorers Club
73 Cine Conquistador
74 Museo de Arte Italiano
75 TEPSA
76 Palacio de Justicia
77 Transportes Rodríguez
78 Transportes Vista Alegre
79 Buses to Chosica
80 Santa Catalina Convent
81 Ormeño & Subsidiaries
82 Empresa Huaraz
83 Buses to Pachacámac &
   Pucusana
84 Colectivos to Chosica, Cruz del
   Sur Ticket Office, Civa Cial,
   Mariscal Cáceres, Soyuz
85 Movil Tours
86 Buses to Cañete, Chincha, Ica
87 Expreso Sudamericano
88 Transfysa
89 Comité 12 to Huancayo
90 Olano
91 Museo de Arte, Filmoteca
92 Las Brisas del Lago Titicaca
93 Transportes León de Huánuco
   & Transmar

office will not cash its own checks. Good rates for American Express checks are given at Banco Mercantil, with branches at Carabaya and Ucayali and at Larco 467 in Miraflores. Banco de Crédito, Lampa 499, also changes American Express checks and provides cash advances on Visa cards. Citibank, Dean Valdivia 423, San Isidro, cashes Citicorp checks at no commission. To get the best rates cash traveler's checks into nuevos soles rather than into US dollars.

Although casas de cambio usually give the same rate as banks for cash, tend to be quicker and are open longer, they won't always change traveler's checks. There are casas de cambio in the center of Lima at the intersection of Ocoña and Camaná, and along Larco in Miraflores.

Moneychangers often hang around the casas de cambio – the corner of Plaza San Martín and Ocoña is a favorite spot – and they match official rates.

Banks at the airport are open late and the one in the international arrivals area is open 24 hours. If you need money wired from home, try Banco de Crédito.

You should report lost American Express traveler's checks to the company's office at Lima Tours (☎ 01-424-5110), Belén 1040. Lost Citicorp checks should be reported to Citibank, and lost Visa checks to Banco de Crédito (see above). The Thomas Cook representative is Viajes Laser (☎ 01-241-5567),

Comandante Espinar 331, but they won't replace stolen checks.

Visa cards can be used in Unicard ATMs and at Banco de Crédito, Interbanc and Banco Mercantil. MasterCard can be used at Banco Wiese, at Cuzco 245 and at Diagonal 176, Miraflores. The Banco Mercantil also gives cash advances on MasterCard. American Express cards can be used at Interbanc. While debit cards do not always work, obtaining cash with credit cards is easy in the major cities.

Post & Communications The central post office is in the Pasaje del Correo, in the northwest corner of the Plaza Mayor. It is open 8 am to 8 pm Monday to Saturday, and 8 am to 2 pm on Sunday.

Mail held by American Express can be picked up from Lima Tours, Belén 1040, 9 am to noon and 3 to 5 pm weekdays.

There are many Telefónica del Perú offices, most of which can send and receive faxes. The office at Bolivia 347 is open from 7 am to 11 pm (later than most others). International credit card calls are possible from blue street phones.

To send and receive email, go to Cyber-Sandeg in the Galerías Boza, Jirón de la Unión 853, office 210. It's open 9 am to 9 pm Monday through Saturday, and 9:30 am to 1 pm on Sunday. They charge US$2 per hour.

South American Explorers Club The SAEC's (☎/fax 01-425-0142, montague@amauta.rcp.net.pe) Lima office is at República de Portugal 146 in the Breña district. It's open 9:30 am to 5 pm weekdays. The postal address is Casilla 3714, Lima 100, Peru. For more information see Useful Organizations in the Facts for the Visitor chapter.

Bookstores The ABC bookstore (☎ 01-445-8228) and the Librería El Pacífico, at the Ovalo in Miraflores, have good but expensive selections of English, German and French newspapers, magazines and books. Also try an outpost of Ediciones Zeta, at Pachacutec 1414 and Casilla 4050.

The SAEC has English-language guidebooks, hiking maps, road maps and maps of Lima. For topographical maps, try the Instituto Geográfico Nacional (☎ 01-475-3085),

Aramburu 1198, Surquillo; you need your passport to get in.

Cultural Centers The following present a variety of cultural programs (plays, films, art exhibits and lectures) at irregular intervals.

Alliance Française
    (☎ 01-241-7014) Arequipa 4598, Miraflores
British Council
    (☎ 01-221-7552) Alberto Lynch 110, San Isidro
Goethe Institut
    (☎ 01-433-3180) Jirón Nazca 722, Jesús María
Instituto Cultural Peruano-Norteamericano
    (☎ 01-446-0381) Arequipa 4798, Miraflores
    (☎ 01-428-3530) Cuzco 446, Lima
Peruvian British Cultural Association
    (☎ 01-470-5577) Arequipa 3495, San Isidro

Medical Services The best and most expensive general clinic is the Clínica Anglo-American (☎ 01-221-3656), on the third block of Salazar in San Isidro. A consultation costs up to US$45 and a gamma globulin shot costs US$35. In San Borja, try the Clínica San Borja (☎ 01-475-4000), Av Guardia Civil 337. In central Lima, there's the Clínica Internacional (☎ 01-433-4306), Washington 1475. These all have 24-hour service and some English-speaking staff. The Clínica Adventista (☎ 01-445-5395), Malecón Balta 956 in Miraflores, is cheaper – about US$23 for a consultation.

For the cheapest yellow fever, tetanus and typhoid shots, try the Hospital de Niños (☎ 01-330-0022), Brasil 600. For tropical diseases, try Instituto de Medicina Tropical (☎ 01-482-3903, 01-482-3910), at the Universidad Particular Cayetano Heredia, Av Honorio Delgado, San Martín de Porres.

If you are bitten by a dog or other animal and need a rabies shot, call the Centro Antirrábico (☎ 01-425-6313).

There are several opticians along Cailloma, in the center, and around Schell and Larco in Miraflores. Having a new pair of glasses made is not expensive.

Emergency For emergencies ranging from robbery to rabies contact the Policía de Turismo (☎ 01-476-7708, 01-476-9896), Museo de la Nación, Javier Prado Este 2465, 5th floor, San Borja. It's open 8 am to 8 pm daily. Some staff speak English.

PERU

The Spanish- and English-speaking tourist police are available 24 hours a day (☎/fax 01-224-7888 or 01-224-8600, tour@indecopigob .pe) to answer questions, log complaints and give advice in case of emergencies.

Other emergency numbers include police (☎ 105) and fire (☎ 116).

Museums

Museum opening hours change frequently and are often shortened drastically from January to March, when it is best to go in the morning. Photography is usually not allowed.

The **Museo de la Nación** (☎ 01-422-5188), Javier Prado Este 2465, San Borja, is a state-run museum with the best overview of Peru's archaeology and other exhibits. Their lecture and performance schedule is worth checking. It's open 9 am to 7 pm Tuesday to Friday and 10 am to 7 pm weekends. Adults/students pay US$1.80/0.90. This is the best value of Lima's museums and is a must-see.

The **Museo de Oro del Perú** (☎ 01-435-2562), Alonso de Molina 100, Monterrico, has two museums in the same building. The gold museum is in a huge basement vault. There are literally thousands of gold pieces, ranging from ear plugs to ponchos embroidered with hundreds of solid gold plates. There are also many artifacts of silver and precious stones. Unfortunately, there are few signs. The top half of the building houses the **Museo de Armas**, reputedly one of the best arms museums in the world. It's open noon to 7 pm daily. Entry (to both museums) is US$5.

The **Museo Rafael Larco Herrera** (☎ 01-461-1835), Bolívar 1515, Pueblo Libre, contains one of the most impressive collections of ceramics in the world. There are approximately 55,000 pots here, as well as exhibits of mummies, a gold room, a small cactus garden, textiles made from feathers and a Paracas weaving that contains 398 threads to a linear inch – a world record. A separate building houses the famous collection of pre-Columbian erotic pots, depicting the sexual practices of several Peruvian cultures. It's open 9 am to 6 pm daily, except Sunday, when it closes at 1 pm. Adults/students pay US$5/2.50.

Housed in a handsome building, Lima's **Museo de Arte** (☎ 01-423-6332), Paseo de Colón 125, has a collection ranging from colonial furniture to pre-Columbian arti-facts, and includes canvases from four centuries of Peruvian art. It's open 10 am to 1 pm and 2 to 5 pm Tuesday to Sunday. Entry is about US$2. Nearby in a park on the second block of Paseo de la República is the neoclassical building housing the **Museo de Arte Italiano** (☎ 01-423-9932). It displays Italian and other European paintings, sculptures and prints, mainly from the early 20th century. It's open 9 am to 4 pm weekdays. Adults/students pay US$0.50/0.25.

The **Museo Amano** (☎ 01-441-2909), Retiro 160, off the 11th block of Angamos in Miraflores, houses a fine private collection of ceramic pieces, arranged chronologically to show the development of pottery through Peru's various pre-Columbian cultures. The museum specializes in the Chancay culture. Entry is in small groups and by telephone appointment only. Groups are met by a guide; it is best if you understand Spanish. Tours are free, and are available at 3, 4 and 5 pm sharp on weekdays. Guides expect tips.

Another private collection is the **Museo Pedro de Osma** (☎ 01-467-0141), Pedro de Osma 421, Barranco, with a fine selection of colonial art, furniture, sculpture and metal-work from all over Peru. Entry is limited to 10 persons and is by appointment only. Call the day before. Guided tours (US$3.50) last 90 minutes and leave at 11 am or 4 pm on weekdays.

The **Museo Nacional de Antropología, Arqueología e Historia** (☎ 01-463-5070), Plaza Bolívar, Pueblo Libre, used to be Lima's best, but many pieces are now in the Museo de la Nación. It's still worth a visit. It's open 9 am to 6 pm Tuesday to Sunday. Entry is US$1.50.

The **Museo del Banco Central de Reserva** (☎ 01-427-6250 ext 2660), at the corner of Ucayali and Lampa, specializes in ceramics from the Vicus culture, among other exhibits. It offers welcome relief from the hustle and bustle of the city center. It's open 10 am to 4 pm Tuesday to Friday, and 10 am to 1 pm on weekends. Entry is free with a passport.

The **Museo de la Inquisición y del Congreso** (☎ 01-428-7980), Junín 548, is in the building used by the Spanish Inquisition from 1570 to 1820. Visitors can see the base-ment where prisoners were tortured. Student guides give tours (in Spanish and English) of ghoulish life-size waxworks of unfortunates on the rack. There's a remarkable wooden ceiling in the library upstairs. It's open 9 am to 6 pm weekdays. Entry is free.

The **Museo de la Cultura Peruana** (☎ 01-423-5892), Alfonso Ugarte 650, is a small museum concentrating on popular art and handicrafts. Ceramics, carved gourds, contemporary and traditional folk art and regional costumes are exhibited. It's open 10 am to 2 pm Tuesday to Saturday. Adults/students pay US$0.50/0.25.

If you want to familiarize yourself with Peru's fauna, the **Museo de Historia Natural** (☎ 01-471-0117), Arenales 1256, Jesús María, has a modest collection of stuffed animals. It's open 9 am to 2 pm on Monday, 9 am to 5 pm Tuesday to Saturday and 9 am to 1 pm on Sunday. Adults/students pay US$1/0.50.

The **Museo Numismático del Banco Wiese** (☎ 01-427-5060, ext 2009), Cuzco 245, exhibits Peruvian coins, bills and medals from colonial through contemporary times. It's open 9 am to 12:45 pm weekdays and entry is free. The **Museo Filatélico** (☎ 01-428-7931), in Lima's main post office, has an incomplete collection of Peruvian stamps and has stamps for sale. It's open 9 am to 2 pm weekdays, and 10 am to noon weekends. Entry is free.

The **Museo Taurino** (☎ 01-482-3360), Hualgayoc 332, Rimac, is next to Lima's bullring. Exhibits include a holed and bloodstained costume worn by a matador who was gored and killed in the bullring some years ago. It's open 9 am to 4 pm weekdays, 9 am to 2 pm on Saturday. Adults/students pay US$1/0.25.

Religious Buildings

A visit to one of Lima's numerous churches, monasteries and convents provides a quiet break from the incessant sidewalk hustle and bustle. Hours are very erratic; those given below are subject to change.

The original **Catedral** was built on the southeastern side of the Plaza de Armas in 1555 but has been destroyed by earthquakes and rebuilt several times, most recently in 1746. The present reconstruction is based on early plans. The coffin and remains of Francisco Pizarro are in the mosaic-covered chapel to the right of the main door. Also of interest are the carved choir and the small religious museum at the back of the cathedral. It's open 10 am to 5 pm daily. Adults/students pay US$1.50/0.75.

The **San Francisco** monastery is famous for its catacombs, which are estimated to contain the remains of 70,000 people. Less famous is the remarkable library, with thousands of antique texts, some dating back to the Spanish conquest. The church, on the corner of Lampa and Ancash, is one of the best preserved of Lima's early colonial churches, and much of it has been restored to its original baroque style with Moorish (Arab) influence. Guided tours in English and Spanish are worth joining to see the catacombs, library and cloister and a museum of religious art, which nonguided visitors don't see. It's open 9 am to 5:30 pm daily. Entry is US$2 (tour included).

The infrequently visited **Convento de los Descalzos** is at the end of the Alameda de los Descalzos, an attractive if somewhat forgotten avenue in the Rimac district. Tours in Spanish visit the infirmary, typical Franciscan cells, old wine-making equipment in the 17th-century kitchen and 300 colonial paintings. Entry is US$1.50 and it's open 9:30 am to 1 pm and 3 to 6 pm daily (except Tuesday).

The **Santuario de Santa Rosa de Lima** consists of a peaceful garden and chapel on the site where Santa Rosa (the western hemisphere's first saint) was born. The sanctuary itself is a small adobe hut built by Santa Rosa in the early 1600s for prayer and meditation. It's open 9 am to 12:30 pm and 3:30 to 6 pm daily. Entry is free.

The church of **Santo Domingo**, on the first block of Camaná, was built on the land that Francisco Pizarro granted in 1535 to his Dominican friar Vicente Valverde. Construction began in 1540 and finished in 1599, but much of the interior was modernized in the late 1700s. The tombs of Santa Rosa and San Martín de Porres (the Americas' first black saint) are in the church. There is an alabaster statue of Santa Rosa, presented to the church by Pope Clement in 1669, and fine tilework showing the life of St Dominic. It's open from 7 am to 1 pm and 4 to 8 pm daily. The monastery and tombs are open 9 am to 12:30 pm and 3 to 6 pm Monday to Saturday, and 9 am to 1 pm on Sunday and holy days. Entry is US$1.

The church of **La Merced** was built on the site of the first mass said in Lima (in 1534). Inside are an ornately carved chancel and attractively decorated cloister. It is on Jirón Unión, near the corner with Miró Quesada. It's open 8 am to 12 pm and 4 to 8 pm daily.

The cloister is open 9 am to noon and 3 to 5 pm weekdays.

The small baroque church of **San Pedro**, on the corner of Azangaro and Ucayali, is one of the finest examples of early colonial architecture in Lima. Consecrated by the Jesuits in 1638, it has changed little since. The interior is sumptuously decorated with gilded altars and an abundance of beautiful glazed tilework. It's open 11 am and 5 pm Monday to Saturday.

Markets

Lima's **Mercado Central** is on Ayacucho and Ucayali. Although it occupies a whole city block, this is not nearly enough space, and stalls and vendors completely congest the streets for several blocks around. You can buy almost anything, but be prepared for crowds and pickpockets. Don't bring valuables.

The **Handicraft Market** on Petit Thouars, 1½ blocks south of Angamos in Miraflores, offers a wide variety of indigenous crafts in a safe environment.

Plazas

The oldest part of the **Plaza Mayor**, restored in 1997, is the impressive bronze fountain, erected in the center in 1650. The exquisitely balconied Archbishop's palace, to the left of the cathedral, is a modern building dating from 1924. The Palacio de Gobierno, on the northeastern side of the plaza, dates from the same period. The ceremonial changing of the guard takes place at 11:45 am. The other buildings around the plaza are also modern: the Municipalidad (town hall) built in 1945, the Unión Club and various shops and cafés. There is an impressive statue of Francisco Pizarro on horseback, on the corner of the plaza opposite the cathedral.

The major **Plaza San Martín** dates from the early 1900s. The bronze statue of the liberator General José de San Martín was erected in 1921. Five blocks of the pedestrian street **Jirón Unión** connect Plaza San Martín with the Plaza Mayor. Along it are jewelry stores, bookstores and cinemas and the church of La Merced. It is always crowded with shoppers, sightseers, vendors and police trying to control pickpockets.

Activities

Swimming and **surfing** are popular with limeños from January to March, though surfers practice year-round. The water is heavily polluted and newspapers warn of serious health hazards. Thieves on the beach mean you can't leave anything unattended for a second. Despite this and the dirty water, beaches are crowded at weekends in season; hanging out on the beach is free and very popular. Cleaner beaches south of Lima often have dangerous currents and drownings are frequent.

Organized Tours

For various guided tours of Lima, Lima Tours (☎ 01-424-5110, fax 01-330-4488), Belén 1040, is one of the best. Tours start at US$25 per person and comfortable transport and English-speaking guides are included.

For specialized tours for individuals or small groups, the SAEC recommends Tino Guzmán (☎ 01-429-5779). Rates start at US$6 per hour plus expenses.

The Río Cañete, three or four hours south of Lima by car, has white-water rafting opportunities. Organized trips start at US$20. Some agencies organize tours there, ask at SAEC for details. Tours bought in Lima that visit other parts of Peru are much more expensive than tours bought in the nearest major town to the area you wish to visit.

Places to Stay

Hotels are more expensive in Lima than in other cities in Peru. Most of the cheapest are in the center, which is less safe (though not really dangerous) than the more expensive suburb of Miraflores.

Central Lima *Hostal España (no sign; ☎ 01-427-9196)*, Azangaro 105, is a favorite of gringo budget travelers, although we have heard some complaints about it. Accommodations are basic, safe and friendly and cost US$5/8 for a single/double. There are hot showers, laundry facilities, a small café and a roof-top terrace. The friendly *Pensión Unión* (☎ 01-428-4136), Unión 442, 3rd floor, charges US$5 per person (US$4 for students) and sometimes has hot water in the evenings. The old but clean *Hostal Belén* (☎ 01-427-8995), Jirón Belén 1049, has hot water and is popular with young Europeans. Rooms cost US$7/10. The basic but safe *Hostal Universo* (☎ 01-427-2684), Azangaro 754, is near several bus terminals. Rooms with private tepid showers are US$5/7, less without bath.

The friendly *Familia Rodríguez* (☎ 01-423-6465), Nicolás de Piérola 730, 2nd floor, is popular, helpful and recommended. Dormitory-style rooms are US$6 per person, including breakfast. *Hostal Samaniego*, Emancipación 184, Apartment 81, is also friendly and has dorm rooms for US$5 per person. The friendly women who run recommended *Pensión Ibarra* (☎ 01-427-8603), Tacna 359, 16th floor, keep it safe, clean and comfortable. Kitchen facilities are available. Rates are $7 per person, including breakfast.

Hotel Claridge (☎ 01-428-3680), Cailloma 437, has adequate rooms for US$7.50/10 with hot shower. The friendly *Hostal Wiracocha* (☎ 01-427-1178), Junín 284, has rooms with hot water for US$6/10; less without hot water. *Hotel La Casona* (☎ 01-427-6273), Moquegua 289, has a plant-filled lobby that hints at an elegant past. The carpeted rooms are shabby but acceptable and the hot water is reliable. Rooms with bath cost US$5/7. *Wilson Hotel* (☎ 424-8924), Chancay 633, has doubles with hot shower for US$12.

Hostal Iquique (☎ 01-433-4724), Iquique 758, is clean, friendly and has hot water. Rooms are US$7/9.50 or US$9/13 with bath. *Hostal Kori Wasi II* (☎ 01-433-8127), Washington 1137, is clean and has rooms with bath, mini-fridge and TV for $7 a double (one bed), or US$5 without bath. The friendly *Hotel Residencial Roma* (☎ 01-427-7576), Ica 326, is clean, central and attractive; it charges US$13/19 with hot shower and US$10/15 with shared bath. *Hostal Damascus* (☎ 01-427-6029), Ucayali 199, is fairly clean and friendly although the rooms are musty. A double is US$25 with hot shower, US$17 with shared bath.

Miraflores The *Youth Hostel* (☎ 01-442-0162), Casimiro Ulloa 328, charges US$10 per person. There are laundry facilities, travel information and minimal kitchen facilities. The similarly priced *Pensión José Luis* (no sign; ☎ 01-444-1015), east of Parque Reducto at Paula Ugarriza 727, is clean and quiet. Reservations are essential at this popular pensión, which has rooms of various sizes, some with kitchenettes. *Pensión San Antonio* (☎ 01-447-5830), Paseo de la República 5809, is friendly and often full. It costs $10 per person or $12.50 with private hot shower.

The following have rooms in private houses. *M Luisa Chávez* (☎ 01-447-3996), about 8 blocks east of Parque Tradiciones along Av Cáceres at Genaro Castro Iglesias 273, charges US$10 per person with breakfast in a very nice, clean home. *Señora Jordan* (☎ 01-445-9840), Porta 724, is friendly and charges US$15 per person, including breakfast, or US$13 without breakfast. *Rosa Alonso*, Larraboren 231, Jesús María, charges US$10 per person.

Pensión Yolanda (☎ 01-445-7565), at Domingo Elías 230, is run by the friendly English-speaking Yolanda Escobar, who charges US$15/23 for singles/doubles.

Places to Eat
Taxes and service charges on meals can be an exorbitant 31%; check first if you're on a tight budget. Cheaper restaurants don't add taxes.

Central Lima In Central Lima, you can find a decent menú (set lunch) for under US$2. The unnamed *chifa* at Ancash 306 has large, inexpensive portions of tallarines (noodles). Nearby, *Restaurant Machu Picchu*, Ancash 312, is popular with gringos while *El Capricho*, Bolivia 328, is popular with locals. Both are good and cheap. *Tic Tac Chifa*, Callao 184, is cheap and clean. *Chifa La Paisana*, 13th block of Alfonso Ugarte, has large, cheap portions of good food. Most of the chifas are in Chinatown, along Ucayali, near the central market.

The friendly, family-run restaurant *Natur*, Moquegua 132, has vegetarian meals. *Govinda*, Callao 480, is cheaper but worse than the one in Miraflores. *Heydi*, Puno 367, is a popular lunchtime cebichería. *La Casera*, Huancavelica 244, has a good range of typical Peruvian food at reasonable prices. *Manhattan Restaurant*, at Miró Quesada 259, has a pleasant atmosphere and good set lunch for US$3. *El Pan Nuestro*, Ica 129, has a US$2.50 set lunch in very nice surroundings.

On Quilca, between the Plaza San Martín and Av Garcilaso de la Vega, there are several inexpensive restaurants. There are plenty of others all over Lima.

El Atlantic, on Huallaga and Pasaje Olaya, is a pleasant place to sit and watch the activities on the Plaza Mayor. It serves reasonably good coffee and tasty cakes as well as Peruvian cuisine.

PERU

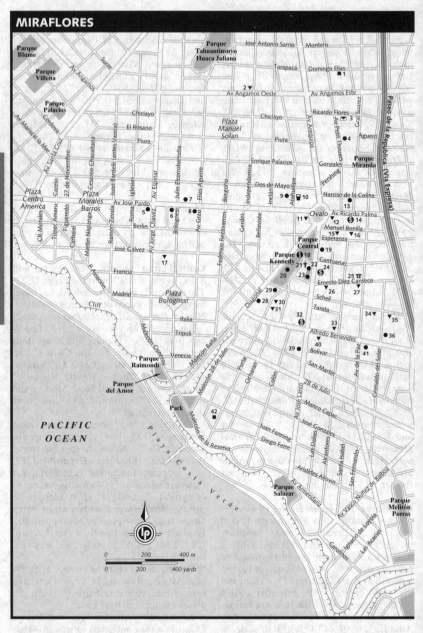

MIRAFLORES

Parque
Blume

Parque
Villena

Parque
Palacios

Parque
Tahuantinsuyo
Huaca Juliana

Jose Antonio Sarrio   Montero

Tarapacá   Domingo Elias
                                              ■ 1

Av Angamos Oeste   Av Angamos Este

2 ▼

Chiclayo   Chiclayo
                                                        Ricardo Flores
El Rosario   Av Petit-Thouars ▼ 3
Piura   Piura
                                                                        ● 4   Aguero

Enrique Palacios   Gonzales   Parque
                                                    Pershing   Miranda

Plaza   Dos de Mayo   Narciso de la Colina
Manuel   9 ● ▼ 10   13
Solan   Ovalo   ● 14
                                                        Av Ricardo Palma $ 14
Av Jose Pardo   7 ●   11 ▼   12 ▼ Manuel Bonilla
5 ●   15 ▼   ▼ 16
        6 ● 8 ●   Esperanza
Berlin   Parque
                                              Central
José Gálvez   Parque ● 18
                                        Kennedy 21 ✝ ● 22   Cantuarias
Francia   17 ▼   20   24 ● 19
                                                  23 ●   25 ☎
Madrid   Ernesto Diez Canseco 27
Cliff   Plaza   ▼ 26
                    Bolognesi   29 ●   Schell
                                        28 ● ▼ 30   Tarata
                                              ▼ 31
Italia   32   33   34 ▼   ▼ 35
Tripoli $ ▼
                                                  Alfredo Benavides   ● 36
Venecia   40 ▼
Parque   39 ● Bolivar
Raimondi   San Martin   ● 41

Parque
del Amor

Park   42 ■

PACIFIC
OCEAN

0   200   400 m
0   200   400 yards

Parque
Salazar

Parque
Melitón
Porras

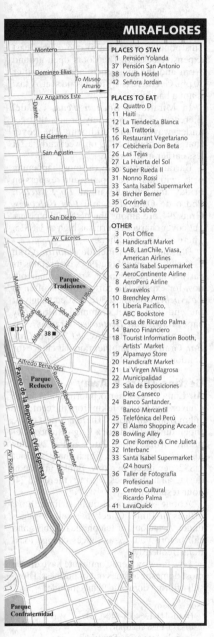

MIRAFLORES

PLACES TO STAY
1 Pensión Yolanda
37 Pensión San Antonio
38 Youth Hostel
42 Señora Jordan

PLACES TO EAT
2 Quattro D
11 Haití
12 La Tiendecita Blanca
15 La Trattoria
16 Restaurant Vegetariano
17 Cebichería Don Beta
26 Las Tejas
27 La Huerta del Sol
30 Super Rueda II
31 Nonno Rossi
33 Santa Isabel Supermarket
34 Bircher Berner
35 Govinda
40 Pasta Subito

OTHER
3 Post Office
4 Handicraft Market
5 LAB, LanChile, Viasa, American Airlines
6 Santa Isabel Supermarket
7 AeroContinente Airline
8 AeroPerú Airline
9 Lavavelos
10 Brenchley Arms
11 Librería Pacífico, ABC Bookstore
13 Casa de Ricardo Palma
14 Banco Financiero
18 Tourist Information Booth, Artists' Market
19 Alpamayo Store
20 Handicraft Market
21 La Virgen Milagrosa
22 Municipalidad
23 Sala de Exposiciones Diez Canseco
24 Banco Santander, Banco Mercantil
25 Telefónica del Perú
27 El Alamo Shopping Arcade
28 Bowling Alley
29 Cine Romeo & Cine Julieta
32 Interbanc
33 Santa Isabel Supermarket (24 hours)
36 Taller de Fotografía Profesional
39 Centro Cultural Ricardo Palma
41 LavaQuick

A favorite seafood restaurant is *La Choza Náutica*, Breña 204. Its fabulous ceviche mixto is US$10, other dishes are cheaper. *Raimondi*, Miró Quesada 110, is popular with Lima's businesspeople. There's no sign and the exterior gives no indication of the spacious comfort within. A set lunch is US$3.50 and there are many more expensive options.

Another favorite is *L'Eau Vive* (☎ 01-427-5712), Ucayali 370, which features dishes from all over the world prepared by a French order of nuns. It's in a quiet colonial-style house and offers welcome relief from the Lima madhouse. Set lunches are US$6 and evening dinners close to US$20, but profits go to charity. The nuns sing an Ave María after dinner (9 pm). For a more upscale meal in a stylish 18th-century house, try *La Casa del Corregidor*, Azángaro 536, first floor.

Miraflores Restaurants in Miraflores are more expensive. The vegetarian places are among the cheapest, including *Govinda*, Schell 634, run by Hare Krishnas, and the *Bircher Berner*, Schell 598, with good food (US$3 lunch menú) but very slow service. *Restaurant Vegetariano*, Manuel Bonilla 178, also bakes bread and has products to take away.

Inexpensive Peruvian-style fast food is available 24 hours a day at the *restaurant* above the *Santa Isabel supermarket*, Benavides 486. The trendy *La Huerta del Sol*, La Paz 522, in the pricey El Álamo shopping plaza, has a reasonable set lunch and other plates for about US$5. Many meals are vegetarian. *Super Rueda II*, Porta 133, is good for tacos and sandwiches. Along Porta there are several restaurants with set lunches for US$2.

Cebichería Don Beta, José Gálvez 667, is a good seafood restaurant and there are several others nearby. They are locally popular for lunch but quiet in the evenings. *Las Tejas,* Diez Canseco 340, has good Peruvian fare.

Lovers of Italian food will find several pricey pizzerias by the Parque Kennedy, which are popular gathering spots. *La Trattoria*, Bonilla 106, has tasty, homemade pasta. Cheaper but still good is *Nonno Rossi*, Porta 185a. Also cheap is *Pasta Subito*, Benavides 446, serving Italian fast food. *Quattro D*, Angamos Oeste 408, has great ice cream, desserts and coffee.

PERU

Miraflores has many outdoor cafés that are pricey but great for people-watching. *Haití*, on the traffic circle next to El Pacífico cinema, and, opposite, *La Tiendecita Blanca*, Larco 111, are among the best known. Others are found on the 200 block of Ricardo Palma and along Larco.

Brenchley Arms, Atahualpa 174, is a British pub run by Englishman Mike Ella and his Peruvian wife, Martha. Prices are steep for budget travelers, but they are worth paying if you're homesick for pub grub. There is a dart board and you can read the British newspapers. It's open 6 pm till late; meals are served till 10 pm daily, except Sunday.

Barranco Budget travelers should try the *anticucho stands* by El Puente de los Suspiros. For dessert try the sweet picarones (fried bread with syrup). Or grab a you-know-what at *Sandwiches Monstruos*, on Piérola near Grau, or a reasonably priced pizza around the corner at *Tío Dan*. *La Canta Rana*, Génova 101, has good ceviches and other seafood for lunch only. *D'Puccio*, San Pedro de Osma at Lavalle, has a cozy atmosphere and seafood and meat dishes.

Entertainment

El Comercio has listings for cinemas, theaters, art galleries and music venues. The monthly English-language magazine *Lima Times* has an abbreviated events listing.

There are dozens of cinemas. Foreign films are normally screened with their original soundtrack and Spanish subtitles. Entry is US$2 to US$4 and may be half-price on Tuesday. Cinema clubs show better films. The *Filmoteca* at Lima's Museo de Arte is good and charges only US$1. The *Cinematógrafo* (☎ 01-477-1961), Pérez Roca 196, Barranco, screens excellent films for about US$3.50.

The *Teatro Municipal* (☎ 01-428-2303), Ica 300, which burned down in 1998, used to host the symphony, opera, plays and ballet. The mayor of Lima has promised to restore it, so check. Another good performance venue is the *Teatro Segura* (☎ 01-426-7206) at Huancavelica 261.

Las Brisas del Lago Titicaca, Wakulski 168, is a good peña folklórica that is popular with limeños. The peña *Hatuchay*, Trujillo 228 in Rimac, just across the bridge behind the Government Palace, presents mainly folklórica, with plenty of audience participation and dancing (during the second half). This popular place is also one of the least expensive (US$3). The doors open around 9 pm and the music gets under way after 10 pm. Get there early for a good seat. A taxi is not a bad idea.

In Miraflores, *Sachún Peña,* Av del Ejército 657, has a variety of acts that get under way around midnight. The cover charge is about US$12 on weekends, a bit less earlier in the week.

Barranco is currently the most happening place, with many bars, peñas and revelers on Friday and Saturday night. *La Estación*, Pedro de Osma 112, and *Los Balcones*, Grau 294, are among the best criolla peñas but cover charges can run as high as US$15. There are several others.

Barranco's bars include *Juanito*, Grau 274, a leftist peña of the 1960s that retains its early simple decor and is a popular hangout now for expats. The party crowd is often in *La Noche,* Bolognesi 307, nestled snugly at the end of a street crammed with trendy bars. *Ludwig Bar Beethoven*, Grau 687, has classical music, often live. *El Ekeko Café Bar,* Grau 266, is another popular choice for libations.

Getting There & Away

Air Lima's Aeropuerto Internacional Jorge Chávez is in Callao, 12km from the center or 16km from Miraflores. There is a post office (open during the day), a long-distance telephone office (open late) and a 24-hour luggage storage room, which charges about US$2 per piece per day. Banks are open during all flight times. Upstairs there is a 24-hour restaurant.

About 30 international airlines have offices in Lima. Check the yellow pages under 'Aviación' for telephone numbers and call before you go, as offices change locations frequently.

Low fares by AeroContinente have driven most domestic airlines out of business. Those still offering domestic flights include:

AeroCóndor
   (☎ 01-441-1354, 01-440-1754;
   01-575-1536 at airport)
   Juan de Arona 781, San Isidro

AeroContinente
   (☎ 01-242-4260, fax 01-446-7638)
   Pardo 651, Miraflores

Transportes Aéreos Andahuaylas (TAA)
(☎ 01-242-1890, fax 01-242-5824)
Pardo 640, Office 2, Miraflores

Flight schedules and ticket prices change frequently; most flights connecting remote towns disappeared in 1998; remaining one-way fares from Lima to interior destinations range from US$50 to US$90.

Getting flight information, buying tickets and reconfirming flights are best done at airline offices (or a reputable travel agent) rather than at the airport counters, where things are often chaotic. You can buy tickets at the airport on a space-available basis, however, if you want to leave for somewhere in a hurry.

Grupo Ocho (the military airline) has sporadic flights to Cuzco, Puerto Maldonado, Pucallpa and some small jungle towns. Flights are half the price of commercial airlines but are subject to overbooking and cancellation, and priority is given to Peruvians so few gringos get on.

Overbooking is the norm on domestic flights, so be there at least an hour early. For all flights, domestic and international, reconfirm several times.

Bus The most important road is the Carretera Panamericana, which runs northwest and southeast from Lima roughly parallel to the coast. Long-distance north and southbound buses leave Lima every few minutes; it takes approximately 24 hours to reach either the Ecuadorian or the Chilean border. Other buses ply the much rougher roads inland into the Andes and across the cordillera into the eastern jungles.

There is no central bus terminal; each bus company runs its own office and terminal. Lima's bus stations are notorious for theft, so find the station and buy your tickets in advance, unencumbered by luggage.

The biggest bus company in Lima is Ormeño (☎ 01-427-5679, 01-428-8453), at Carlos Zavala Loayza 177. There are various subsidiaries at the same address. Among them, they have frequent departures for Arequipa, Caraz, Chiclayo, Cuzco, Huaraz, Ica, Puno, Tacna, Trujillo, Tumbes and various intermediate points. Cruz del Sur (☎ 01-428-2570), corner of Zavala and Montevideo, serves the entire coast plus Arequipa, Cuzco, Huancayo, Huaraz and Puno.

Both companies have normal services and more expensive buses, which are more comfortable and stop less often.

Expreso Sudamericano (☎ 01-427-6548), Montevideo 618, also has buses to most of these destinations, as does TEPSA (☎ 01-427-5642), Lampa 1237. Olano/Oltursa, (☎ 01-428-2370), Grau 617, also has buses to the north and south coast. Coastal routes have 'bus-camas' – buses with seats that recline completely for sleeping.

For the Huaraz region, several companies compete, including Civa Cial (☎ 01-428-5649), Zavala and Montevideo, and Transportes Rodríguez (☎ 01-428-0506), Roosevelt 354. Problems have been reported with this company's luggage storage. Also try Empresa Huaraz, (☎ 01-427-6346), Leticia 655. If going to Chiquian, the best bet is Transfysa (☎ 01-428-0412), Montevideo 724, with departures at 8 am every other day, or TUBSA (☎ 01-428-4510), Leticia 633. Civa Cial also goes to Chachapoyas, Cajamarca and Cuzco.

For Huancayo, there's Cruz del Sur or the recommended Mariscal Cáceres, (☎ 01-427-2844, 01-474-7850), with offices at the corner of Zavala and Montevideo and at 28 de Julio 2195, La Victoria. For Tarma/Chanchamayo, there's Transportes Chanchamayo (☎ 01-470-1189), Manco Capac 1052.

Transportes León de Huánuco (☎ 01-432-9088), 15th block of 28 de Julio, La Victoria, goes to Pucallpa (via Huánuco and Tingo María), and to La Merced. Transmar (☎ 01-424-3214), on the same block, goes to Pucallpa and Ayacucho (via Pisco). Another company that covers Huánuco, Tingo María and Pucallpa is TRANSREY (☎ 01-423-0664), Av 28 de Julio 192, La Victoria. This is a poor neighborhood, use a taxi.

Transportes Vista Alegre (☎ 01-427-6110, 01-427-4155), Abancay 900, has decent buses to Trujillo, Chimbote and Casma. Turismo Chimbote (☎ 01-424-0501), Huarochiri 785, has buses to Chimbote. Soyuz, in the terminal at Zavala and Montevideo, goes to Cañete, Chincha and Ica. Buses for these towns also leave from further down the block on Montevideo.

For approximate fares and journey times, see the respective city sections.

Train The tourist train between Lima and Huancayo has recommenced service. A roundtrip fare (US$20) is available on the last weekend of every month, leaving Lima on Saturday and returning Monday. There are plans to regularize the schedule.

Another train departs from Lima for San Bartolomé, 1600m above sea level and about 70km inland, Sundays at 8:30 am. The train returns at 6 pm and the fare is US$5.

Lima's train station, Desamparados, is on Av Ancash, behind the Presidential Palace.

Getting Around

To/From the Airport The cheapest way to the airport is by city bus No 35 or 11, going from Plaza 2 de Mayo along Alfonso Ugarte to the airport (not recommended if you have a pile of luggage).

A taxi will take you from the center to the airport for about US$5, if you bargain. Taxis are charged US$1.50 to enter the airport but you can get off outside and walk the last 200m. A radio taxi called by telephone will charge US$15. Taxi Seguro (☎ 01-438-5059) has been recommended.

Leaving the airport, you'll find plenty of airport taxis that charge anywhere from US$15 to US$18. You can bargain these down with some insistence. If you don't have much luggage, turn left outside the terminal and walk 100m to a gate, turn right and walk another 100m to the road, where you can get a cab for US$3.50 to US$7 to Lima, depending on bargaining and what time of day (or night) it is.

An airport hotel bus charges US$5 per passenger to your hotel and leaves about every hour.

Maddening traffic and road construction often lead to lengthy delays. Allow at least an hour to the airport, more during rush hours.

Bus Taking the local buses around Lima is a challenge. They are slow and crowded, but very cheap (fares are generally US$0.50). Bus lines are identifiable by their destination cards, numbers and color schemes. At last count, there were nearly 200 bus lines. The last transport map available is now out of date and out of print (though look for an update).

A few colectivo lines operate minibuses that drive up and down the same streets all day long. The most useful goes from Lima to Miraflores along Avs Tacna, Garcilaso de la Vega and Arequipa. You can flag them down

or get off anywhere. The fare is a few cents higher than the bus.

Taxi Taxis usually have a red-and-white taxi sticker on the windshield. Taxi cars can be any make or color. Most are unlicensed. Licensed cabs are usually blue and yellow, often park outside the best hotels and restaurants and charge twice as much as other cabs. Unlicensed cabs charge around US$3 for a Miraflores-Lima run; bargaining is expected.

AROUND LIMA

The closest major archaeological site to Lima is **Pachacamac**, 31km south of the city. Pachacamac's origin predates the Incas by roughly 1000 years. Most of the buildings are now little more than walls of piled rubble, except for the main temples, which are huge pyramids. These have been excavated and are huge mounds with rough steps cut into them. One of the most recent of the complexes, the Mamacuña (House of the Chosen Women), was built by the Incas and has been excavated and reconstructed.

The site is extensive and a thorough visit takes some hours. The visitor center at the entrance has a small museum and a cafeteria. From there, a dirt road leads around the site. Although the pyramids are poorly preserved, their size is impressive and you can climb the stairs to the top of some of them, from where you can get excellent views of the coast on a clear day.

Guided tours to Pachacamac are offered by Lima Tours daily, except Monday, for US$35 per person (six people needed), including return transportation and an English-speaking guide.

From Lima, the No 120 minibus to Pachacamac (US$0.50) leaves from near the corner of Colmena and Andahuaylas, by the Santa Catalina convent. It leaves about every 30 minutes, or as soon as it is full. Tell the driver to let you off near the *ruinas*; otherwise, you will end up at Pachacamac village, 1km beyond the entrance. Alternatively, use the colectivo to Lurín, which leaves from the 900 block of Montevideo.

The ruins are open 9 am to 5 pm daily. Entry costs US$3.50, and a bilingual booklet describing the ruins is available for US$1. It's advisable to leave before noon to avoid getting stuck in the dark with no bus.

South Coast

The Panamericana traverses many places of interest south of Lima and is the preferred route to Lake Titicaca and Cuzco. Thus, the south coast gets more visitors than the north.

CAÑETE & LUNAHUANÁ

The small town of Cañete, 144km south of Lima, is the turnoff from the Panamericana up the Río Cañete toward the village of Lunahuaná, 40km away. White-water rafters begin trips down the Cañete from here during the December-April season. February is the best month, with Class III rapids. (Inquire at SAEC in Lima about recommended agencies as they come and go quite often). Lunahuaná has vineyards, with a harvest festival in March. There are small ruins in the Cañete valley.

Places to Stay

There are a couple of basic but clean hotels on Cañete's Plaza de Armas that charge US$8 to US$12 for a double with bath and cold water.

Lunahuaná has *Hostal Candela* and *Hostal Lunahuaná,* both with doubles for roughly US$10. There are more expensive places here, too.

Getting There & Away

Ormeño subsidiary Expreso Chinchano has several buses daily from Lima to Cañete (US$3, 2½ hours). Minibuses go to Lunahuaná from near the Plaza de Armas in Cañete.

CHINCHA

This small town, 190km south of Lima, has a large black population and is known for its Afro-Peruvian music. The best place to listen and dance the alcatraz is El Carmen, a 30-minute minibus ride from the Plaza de Armas in Chincha. The best times to visit are during Fiestas Patrias in late July, Verano Negro at the end of February, Christmas and a local fiesta in late October. During these times, minibuses run from Chincha to El Carmen all night long and the peña is full of frenzied limeños and local blacks – quite a scene. The cover charge is about US$5.

Places to Stay

During the festivals, hotels double or triple their prices and are completely full. Some people avoid this problem by dancing all night and then taking an early morning bus back to Lima! At other times, cheap places are easy to find.

PISCO

Pisco, a fishing port 235km south of Lima, shares its name with the white grape brandy made in the region. This is a base to see the wildlife of the Islas Ballestas and Península de Paracas, and the area is also of archaeological interest.

In 1925, the Peruvian archaeologist JC Tello discovered burial sites of the Paracas culture, which existed in the area from approximately 1300 BC until 200 AD. The people of ancient Paracas produced the finest textiles in pre-Columbian America. The main Paracas culture is divided into two periods, named Paracas Cavernas and Paracas Necropolis after the two main burial sites discovered.

Paracas Necropolis (300 BC to 100 AD) yielded the treasure-trove of exquisite textiles for which the culture is known today. The necropolis contained over 400 funerary bundles, each of which consisted of a mummy (probably a nobleman or priest) wrapped in layers of weavings.

It is best to visit the Lima museums for a look at the Paracas mummies, textiles and other artifacts. In the Pisco region, visit the JC Tello Museum (on the Península de Paracas) and the Museo Regional de Ica.

Information

There is an Internet office at San Francisco 290, open 7 am to 11 pm Monday to Saturday; on Sunday ring the bell. The charge is US$3 per hour.

Places to Stay

Pisco is occasionally and unpredictably full of people from the fishing boats; hotels are booked up then, and prices rise. It's also full and pricey during national holidays, especially Fiestas Patrias (July 28-29).

Popular with budget travelers, *Hostal Pisco* (☎ 034-532018), on the plaza, charges US$3.50 per person for rooms with shared and not very clean hot baths. Singles/doubles with private bath are US$7/12 and there have been mixed

PERU

PERU

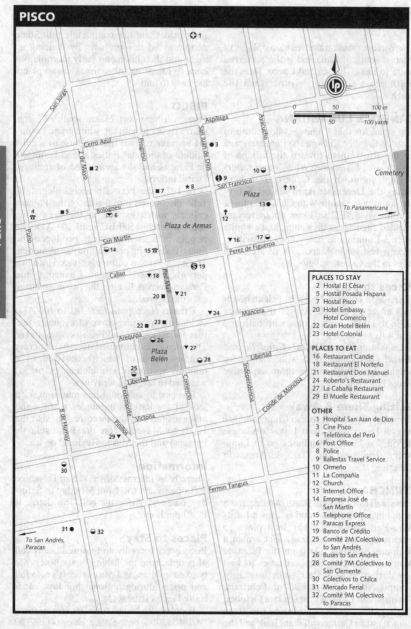

PISCO

Cemetery

To Panamericana

Plaza de Armas

Plaza

Plaza Belén

To San Andrés, Paracas

PLACES TO STAY
2 Hostal El César
5 Hostal Posada Hispana
7 Hostal Pisco
20 Hotel Embassy,
    Hotel Comercio
22 Gran Hotel Belén
23 Hotel Colonial

PLACES TO EAT
16 Restaurant Candie
18 Restaurant El Norteño
21 Restaurant Don Manuel
24 Roberto's Restaurant
27 La Cabaña Restaurant
29 El Muelle Restaurant

OTHER
1 Hospital San Juan de Dios
3 Cine Pisco
4 Telefónica del Perú
6 Post Office
8 Police
9 Ballestas Travel Service
10 Ormeño
11 La Compañía
12 Church
13 Internet Office
14 Empresa José de
    San Martín
15 Telephone Office
17 Paracas Express
19 Banco de Crédito
25 Comité 2M Colectivos
    to San Andrés
26 Buses to San Andrés
28 Comité 7M Colectivos to
    San Clemente
30 Colectivos to Chilca
31 Mercado Ferial
32 Comité 9M Colectivos
    to Paracas

reports about it. *Hotel Colonial*, on Plaza Belén, charges US$9/13 for doubles/triples with clean shared hot showers (no singles).

Hotel Embassy (☎ 034-532809) runs US$11/15 for singles/doubles with private bath and warm water. It may be noisy with tour deportees in the mornings. Next door, the *Hotel Comercio* charges US$5/8 with private tepid showers, but is not very clean. The clean *Gran Hotel Belén* (☎ 034-533046), around the corner, charges US$7/10 or US$10/13 with bath. *Hostal El César* (☎ 034-532512) charges US$8 for a double, US$12 for a double with private hot shower. It's OK and open to bargaining if things are quiet. The very clean *Hostal Posada Hispana* (☎ 034-536363), Bolognesi 236, receives enthusiastic recommendations from travelers. It charges US$14 for a double with bath and hot water.

Places to Eat
A few cafés on the Plaza de Armas are open early enough to buy breakfast before a Ballestas tour, and stay open all day. *Restaurant Candie,* on the plaza, is reasonably priced and there is a *chifa* next door. There are several other cheap places within a block of the plaza: *El Norteño* is popular and *Roberto's* and *La Cabaña* are cheap local places where a set lunch menu will be under US$2. *El Muelle*, 1½ blocks from the plaza, dishes out cheap large portions of local food. *Restaurant Don Manuel* is one of the best, charging US$2 to US$7 for meals.

Discourage poaching of protected and endangered species by refraining for ordering the turtle dishes that appear on many menus.

Getting There & Away
Pisco is 5km west of the Panamericana, and many coastal buses drop you at the turnoff. Ask for a direct bus to Pisco from both Lima and Ica. From the turnoff, local buses go into Pisco sporadically.

Ormeño (☎ 034-532764) has a terminal 1 block from the Plaza de Armas. Buses leave for Lima (US$4, four hours) roughly every two hours. Ormeño also has buses to Nazca (US$3.50, 3½ hours), Ica (US$0.50, 1½ hours) and three to Arequipa (US$12, 12 to 15 hours). To Ayacucho (US$9) there are three daily buses.

Other long-distance bus companies that serve Lima include Paracas Express and Empresa José de San Martín. Empresa also has hourly buses to Ica.

Getting Around
Comité 9M colectivos for Paracas (US$0.50) leave frequently from the market. Comité 2M colectivos for San Andrés (US$0.20) leave every few minutes. A taxi for Paracas is about US$3.

AROUND PISCO
Reserva Nacional de Paracas
The Península de Paracas and Islas Ballestas comprise the Reserva Nacional de Paracas, the most important bird and marine sanctuary on the Peruvian coast. The birds nest on the offshore islands in such numbers that their nitrogen-rich droppings (guano) are commercially exploited for fertilizer. This practice dates from pre-Inca times. The most frequently seen birds are the Guanay cormorant, Peruvian booby and Peruvian pelican. Humboldt penguins and Chilean flamingos may also be seen. Large colonies of sea lions are found on the islands. Jellyfish, some reaching about two-thirds of a meter in diameter and with stinging tentacles trailing a meter or more behind them, get washed up onto the shore. Beachcombers also find sea hares, ghost crabs and seashells.

Organized Tours The bird and sea lion colonies are visited on organized boat tours that are fun, inexpensive and worthwhile. Ballestas Travel Service (☎ 034-533095), San Francisco 249 in Pisco, represents a number of agencies that take turns running trips. They offer the most reputable service.

Tours leave daily from the plaza at 7 am (US$8 and up, depending on bargaining and boat quality). Hotel pick-up is available. Minibuses go to Paracas, where slow motorboats are boarded for the excursion; there's no cabin, so dress for wind and spray and bring sun protection. The outward boat journey takes about 1½ hours, and en route you see the Candelabra, a giant figure etched into the coastal hills, like the Nazca Lines.

About an hour is spent cruising around the islands. You'll see plenty of sea lions on the rocks and swimming around your boat. Wear a hat – there are a lot of birds in the air, and it's not unusual for someone to receive a direct hit!

RESERVA NACIONAL DE PARACAS

Islas Ballestas
Isla Blanca
Islas Farallones
Puerto San Martín
Península de Paracas
Isla San Gallán
PACIFIC OCEAN
Reserva Nacional de Paracas
Lagunillas
Pisco
To Lima
San Andrés
Carretera Panamericana
Bahía de Paracas
Paracas
To Ica

1 Fish Meal Factories
2 Candelabra
3 Fishing Boat Graveyard
4 Hotel Paracas & Boats to Islas Ballestas
5 Playa El Chaco
6 Hotel El Mirador
7 La Vela Monument
8 Flamingo Viewing Area
9 Archaeological Site
10 JC Tello Museum & Information Center
11 Parking, Cliff-Top Trail, Sea Lions & Seabirds

0   5   10 km
0   3   6 miles

Once you return to the mainland, a minibus will take you back to Pisco in time for lunch. Alternatively, you can join the afternoon Reserva de Paracas tour (also US$7). If there are several of you wishing to do both tours in one day, bargain for a reduced rate. The Paracas tour requires an extra US$1 reserve entrance fee and a US$1 museum entrance fee. It visits coastal sea lion and flamingo colonies and geological formations. It is also possible to drive or walk around the reserve by yourself.

ICA

Ica, capital of its department, is a pleasant colonial town of 150,000 inhabitants, 305km south of Lima. The Panamericana heads inland from Pisco, climbing gently to 420m at Ica. The town is high enough to be free of the garúa, and the climate is dry and sunny. The desert surrounding Ica is noted for its huge sand dunes. Río Ica water irrigates vineyards and supports thriving wine and pisco-producing industries. The wineries and distilleries can be visited. Ica has a fine museum and several annual fiestas.

Information

A useless tourist office, Grau 150, is open 8 am to 3:30 pm weekdays. The Banco de Crédito changes cash and traveler's checks,

and has a Visa ATM machine. Banco Latino, Cajamarca 170, has a MasterCard ATM. Street moneychangers hang out nearby. Cetelica, on Huánico between San Martín and Bolívar, provides Internet access.

Things to See

Museo Regional de Ica This museum is in the southwestern suburbs, 1.5km from the center. Take a mototaxi from the plaza (US$0.50), or it's a pleasant walk. It's open from 8 am to 7 pm weekdays, 9 am to 6 pm Saturday and 9 am to 1 pm on Sunday. Adults/students pay US$2/1, with an extra US$1.50 camera fee. It is one of the best small regional museums in Peru, and concentrates on the Paracas, Nazca and Inca cultures.

Museo Cabrera There is no sign to mark this museum, on the Plaza de Armas, at Bolívar 170. It has a collection of 11,000 carved stones and boulders showing pre-Columbian surgical techniques and day-to-day living. The owner, Dr J Cabrera, claims that these stones are centuries old, but most authorities don't believe him. You can see some of the stones in the museum entrance, but a proper look along with a guided tour costs US$3.50. It's open 9 am to 1 pm and 4:30 to 8:30 pm daily.

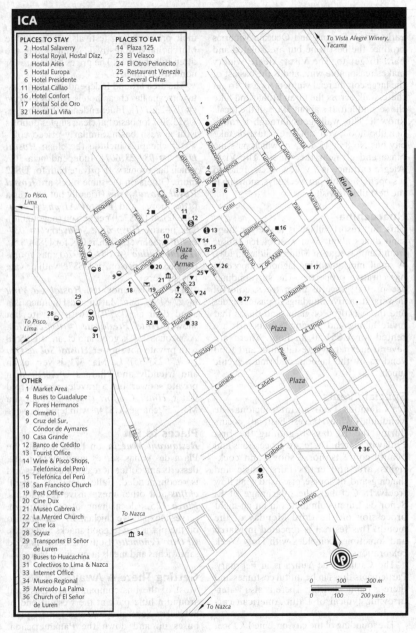

ICA

PLACES TO STAY
2 Hostal Salaverry
3 Hostal Royal, Hostal Díaz,
   Hostal Aries
5 Hostal Europa
6 Hotel Presidente
11 Hostal Callao
16 Hotel Confort
17 Hostal Sol de Oro
32 Hostal La Viña

PLACES TO EAT
14 Plaza 125
23 El Velasco
24 El Otro Peñoncito
25 Restaurant Venezia
26 Several Chifas

OTHER
1 Market Area
4 Buses to Guadalupe
7 Flores Hermanos
8 Ormeño
9 Cruz del Sur,
   Cóndor de Aymares
10 Casa Grande
12 Banco de Crédito
13 Tourist Office
14 Wine & Pisco Shops,
   Telefónica del Perú
15 Telefónica del Perú
18 San Francisco Church
19 Post Office
20 Cine Dux
21 Museo Cabrera
22 La Merced Church
27 Cine Ica
28 Soyuz
29 Transportes El Señor
   de Luren
30 Buses to Huacachina
31 Colectivos to Lima & Nazca
33 Internet Office
34 Museo Regional
35 Mercado La Palma
36 Church of El Señor
   de Luren

To Vista Alegre Winery,
Tacama

To Pisco, Lima

Plaza de Armas

To Pisco, Lima

To Nazca

To Nazca

PERU

0   100   200 m
0   100   200 yards

Vineyards *Bodegas* are best visited during the grape harvest, from late February until early April. Tacama and Ocucaje wineries produce the best wine but are isolated and hard to get to. The Vista Alegre winery makes reasonable wine and is the easiest of the large commercial vintners to visit. To get there, walk across the Grau bridge and take the second left. It's about 3km; all the locals know it. This walk goes through a rough neighborhood; you can hire a taxi or take city bus No 8 or 13, both of which pass the plaza and go near the winery. The Vista Alegre entrance is a yellow-brick arch and it's open 9 am to 4 pm weekdays; morning is the best time to visit.

Huacachina
This tiny resort village is nestled in huge sand dunes about 5km west of Ica (buses from Lambayeque at Municipalidad in Ica). A small, murky-looking lagoon supposedly has curative properties. The surroundings are pretty: graceful palm trees, colorful flowers, attractive buildings in pastel shades and the backdrop of giant sand dunes that invite hiking and playing. Sandboards are rented for US$1.50 an hour. There are several inexpensive restaurants and food vendors by the lagoon, or bring a picnic lunch.

Special Events
Ica's famous Festival Internacional de Vendimia (Wine Harvest Festival) occurs during the 10 days beginning the first Friday in March. There are processions and beauty contests, horse shows and cock-fights, arts and crafts fairs, music and dancing, and, of course, pisco and wine flow freely. In October, the pilgrimage of El Señor de Luren culminates in an all-night procession on the third Monday of the month. This festival is repeated in March and sometimes coincides with Holy Week celebrations.

The Carnaval de Yunza is in February. Participants dress in beautiful costumes and there is public dancing. There is also water-throwing typical of Latin American car-navales.

The founding of the city, on June 17, 1563, is celebrated during Ica Week. The more important Ica tourist festival takes place in the latter half of September.

Places to Stay
The cheapest hotels may double (or more) their prices during festivals, especially the March harvest festival, when hotels are often fully booked. The prices below are for nonfestival times.

The area around Independencia and Castrovirreyna has cheap hotels. *Hostal Europa* (☎ 034-232111), Independencia 258, charges US$3.50/7 for basic but clean singles/doubles with a wash basin. Similarly priced cold-water cheapies include the clean *Hostal Díaz* (☎ 034-231601), Independencia 167, which has rooms with private bath for US$2 more. Others on the same block are *Hostal Royal, Hostal Aries* (friendly but charges a little more) and *Hostal Aleph* (☎ 034-221332), at US$3.50 per person (negotiable). The nearby *Hospedaje Salaverry* (☎ 034-214019), Salaverry 146, is OK for US$4/6.50. *Hostal Callao* (☎ 034-235976), has rooms for US$5 per person, or US$7/9 with private hot showers.

The newly renovated *Hostal La Viña* (☎ 21-8188), San Martín and Huánuco, is a good deal at US$7/12 with private hot shower. *Hotel Presidente* (☎ 034-225977), Amazonas 223, is good and clean at US$5/8 with private hot shower. *Hostal Sol de Oro* (☎ 034-233735), La Mar 371, is very clean and friendly and charges US$8/10 with private shower, but a traveler reports cold water. *Hotel Confort* (☎ 034-233072), La Mar 257, charges US$4/8 with tepid showers.

Places to Eat
Restaurant Venezia, on Lima just off the Plaza de Armas, serves good pizza, pasta, desserts and coffee at reasonable prices and is recommended. Calle Lima has several *chifas* and other inexpensive restaurants. *Plaza 125*, a local hangout on the plaza, serves inexpensive chicken. *El Velasco*, also on the plaza, serves good snacks and cakes. *El Otro Peñoncito*, Bolívar 255, offers good sandwiches and meals at medium prices.

Getting There & Away
Most of the bus companies are clustered around a little park at the western end of Salaverry. Several companies run frequent buses up and down the Panamericana. Ormeño (☎ 034-215600), Lambayeque 180, has the most departures but others may be cheaper. There are many departures for

Lima (US$4.50, five hours), Pisco (US$1, one hour), Nazca (US$2.50, three hours) and Arequipa (US$12 to US$16, 15 hours). Some continue to Tacna or Cuzco. Taxi colectivos for Lima (five passengers) and Nazca (seven passengers) leave from the southwest corner of Municipalidad and Lambayeque as soon as they are full. Fares are US$12 to Lima (3½ hours) and US$3 to Nazca (2 hours).

NAZCA

Nazca, population 30,000, is 450km south of Lima and 598m above sea level, above the coastal garúa.

Like the Paracas culture to the north, the ancient Nazca culture was lost in the drifting desert sands until this century. In 1901, Peruvian archaeologist Max Uhle excavated the Nazca sites and realized that he had rediscovered a distinct coastal culture.

The Nazca culture appeared as a result of the disintegration of the Paracas culture, around 200 AD, and lasted until about 800 AD. The designs on the Nazca ceramics depict their plants and animals, their fetishes and divinities, their musical instruments and household items and the people themselves.

The early Nazca ceramics are very colorful and have a greater variety of naturalistic designs. Pots with double necks joined by a stirrup handle were common, as well as shallow cups and plates. In the late period, the decoration was more stylized.

Information

Hotels provide information biased towards their tours. The Banco de Crédito changes traveler's checks and moneychangers hang out in front. A small archaeological museum on the Plaza de Armas was destroyed in the December 1996 earthquake and has not been rebuilt. Nasca Trails, Alegria Tours and others offer email service for US$3.50 per hour.

Nazca Lines

These spectacular geometric designs drawn in the desert are visible only from the air. Some represent animals, such as a 180m-long lizard, a 90m-high monkey with an extravagantly curled tail and a condor with a 130m wingspan. Others are simple but perfect geometric figures. They were made by removing sun-darkened stones from the desert surface to expose the lighter colored

stones below. The best-known lines are 20km north of Nazca.

María Reiche, a German mathematician who spent her life studying the lines, thought they were made by the Paracas and Nazca cultures from 900 BC to 600 AD, with 7th-century additions by Wari settlers from the highlands. Until her death in 1998, she claimed that the lines were an astronomical calendar used for agriculture. There are other theories.

Flights over the lines are made in light aircraft in the mornings; it is too windy in the afternoon. Tickets are now US$50. (They have been as low as US$30 in low season.) A taxi to the airport is US$3. Flights last 35 minutes.

You can also view the lines from the observation tower beside the Panamericana, 26km north of Nazca. There is an oblique view of three of the figures (lizard, tree and hands), but it's not very good. About 1km south of the tower, a trail leads west to a small hill, from which other lines may be seen. Don't walk on the lines – it damages them, is illegal and you can't see anything anyway. To get to the tower, take a tour or a taxi (US$10), or catch a northbound bus (US$0.50) in the morning and hitchhike back.

Organized Tours

Tour operators are very aggressive here: Some will lie about their qualifications and even impersonate well-known guides in order to get your money. Shop around for the best deal, and do not give money until you get receipts for services.

The popular Hostal Alegría (☎ 034-522085, alegriatours@hotmail.com) organizes inexpensive guided tours. Slightly more expensive but excellent are the tours run by friendly Juan Tohalino at Nasca Trails (☎ 034-522858, nasca@correo.dnet.com.pe), Ignacio Morsesky 122. He speaks very good English, French, German and Italian. Avoid unlicensed agencies: The tours visit uninhabited areas and robberies have occurred, possibly because of collusion between guides and thieves.

One of the most interesting tours is to the **Cementerio de Chauchilla**, 30km away. Here you'll see bones, skulls, mummies, pottery shards and fragments of cloth dating from the late Nazca period. Although everything of value is gone, it's quite amazing to stand

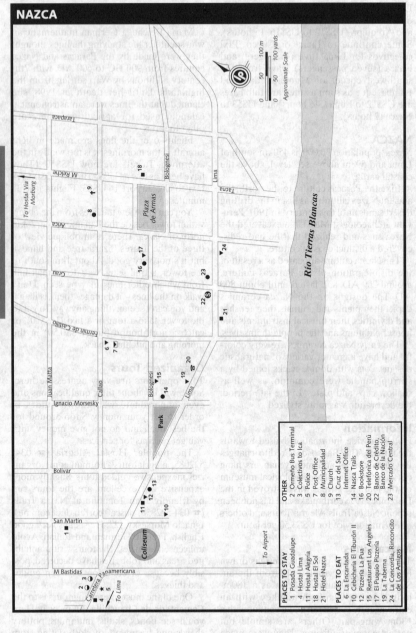

NAZCA

To Hostal Via Morburg

Tarapaca

Bolognesi

M Reiche

Anca

Grau

Fermin de Castillo

Callao

Bolognesi

Lima

Juan Matta

Ignacio Morsesky

Bolivar

San Martin

M Bastidas

Carretera Panamericana

Plaza de Armas

Lima

Tacna

Río Tierras Blancas

Park

Coliseum

To Airport

To Lima

100 m
100 yards
0   50   100
Approximate Scale

PLACES TO STAY
1   Posada Guadalupe
4   Hostal Lima
11 Hostal Alegría
18 Hostal El Sol
21 Hotel Nazca

PLACES TO EAT
6   La Encantada
10 Cebichería El Tiburón II
15 Pizzería La Pua
17 Restaurant Los Angeles
19 El Puquio Pizzería
20 La Taberna
24 La Concordia, Rinconcito de Los Amigos

OTHER
2   Ormeño Bus Terminal
3   Colectivos to Ica
5   Police
7   Post Office
9   Municipalidad
13 Church
13 Cruz del Sur,
     Internet Office
14 Nasca Trails
16 Bookstore
20 Telefónica del Perú
22 Banco de Crédito,
     Banco de la Nación
23 Mercado Central

in the desert and see tombs surrounded by bleached skulls and bones that stretch off into the distance. The tour takes about 2½ hours and costs US$6 per person, with a minimum of three passengers. Most companies include this tour in the price of the Nasca Lines Flight.

There are various other destinations to visit: aqueducts, fossil beds, archaeological sites and vicuña sanctuaries. Ask about them locally. You need three or four people.

Places to Stay

Hotel Nazca (☎ 034-522085), Lima 438, and *Hostal Alegría* (☎ 034-52-2444), Lima 168, are very popular. The Nazca has basic, clean singles/doubles for US$5/8, but there have been negative reports about it. The Alegría is US$3.50 per person for basic, clean rooms with saggy beds. Both have tepid communal showers. The Alegría has double rooms with private bath for US$10. Both hotels have been recommended for cheap tours. It has frequently been reported, however, that the service in both becomes decidedly unfriendly if guests don't want to take a tour with the hotel!

Hostal Lima (☎ 034-522497), Los Incas 117, is friendly and has hot water. Rooms with shared bath are US$5/8, with private showers are US$7/12. The small, family-run *Posada Guadalupe* (☎ 034-522249), San Martín 225, is clean, quiet and friendly with a little garden. Rooms are US$4/7, or US$6/9 with private electric hot showers. At the plaza on Tacna, the *Hostal El Sol* has singles/doubles for US$5/7 without bath, or US$7 singles with bath. The best deal in Nasca is the new *Hostal Via Morburg* (☎ 034-523710), José María Mejía 108, 3 blocks north of the Plaza. Through an agent (Nasca Trails and others) the rates are US$4/8 for clean rooms with bath. Prices are higher if you walk in. It has a restaurant on the third floor with good food but very slow service.

Places to Eat

Cheap restaurants around the market include family run *La Concordia*, offering really good simple food, and, just next to it, *Rinconcito de Los Amigos* for chicken. The friendly *Restaurant Los Angeles*, renovated since the earthquake, has a cheap set lunch, other reasonably priced meals, nice choco-late cake and decent pisco sours. *El Puquío Pizzería* nearby is a small, friendly pizza place. *Pizzería La Pua*, on Lima, has nice atmosphere and good but pricey Peruvian food. *Cebichería El Tiburón II* has good cheap ceviches. At night it becomes *El Huakero Discotec* with music and strange-tasting piña coladas. *La Taberna*, on Lima, is a bit more upmarket, but may have live music on Saturday night. *La Encantada*, Callao 592, is also good for seafood.

Getting There & Away

Ormeño has several buses a day to Lima (US$6, eight hours) and intermediate points. It has two or three buses a day to Arequipa (US$14, 9 hours) and Tacna (US$16, 12 hours). It has a bus to Cuzco every two days, taking 30 to 40 hours and going via Arequipa. A few companies go via Abancay. Other companies along the main street have similar destinations and slightly differing prices, but fewer departures. CIVA has nightly buses to Lima (10:45 pm), and three to Arequipa (11 and 12 pm and 3 am). Cruz del Sur is OK, Sudamericano is cheaper but not as good.

Taxi colectivos to Ica (US$3, 2½ hours) leave when they are full (about every hour) from the Panamericana at Lima.

NAZCA TO TACNA

Apart from Arequipa, places to break the journey on the long haul along the Panamericana from Nazca to Tacna include the small seaside towns of **Chala** and **Camaná** and the inland town of **Moquegua**, all of which have a few simple and inexpensive hotels.

TACNA

Tacna (population 150,000), about 1300km south of Lima by road, is Peru's southernmost town and capital of its department. The elevation is 560m. Only 36km from the Chilean border, Tacna has strong historical ties with that country. It became part of Chile in 1880, during the War of the Pacific, and remained so until 1929, when its people voted to return it to Peru. The main reason to visit Tacna is to cross the border into Chile.

Information

Street moneychangers and banks concentrate at the southeast end of the Plaza de Armas. The Banco de Crédito is the best bet for cashing traveler's checks and has an ATM.

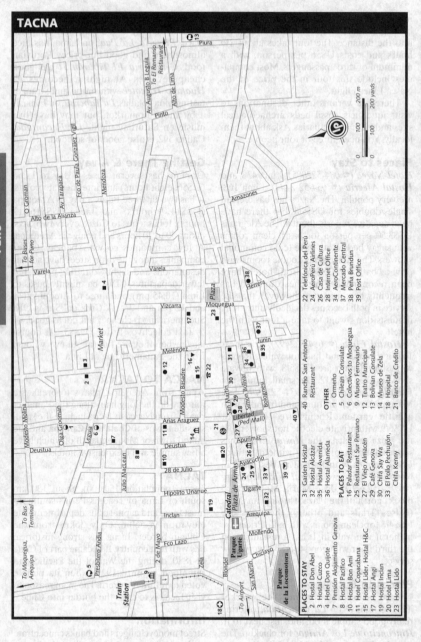

TACNA

Internet service is available at San Martín 611, 9 am to 9 pm Monday to Saturday.

Things to See

The **Museo Ferroviario** is in the railway station and has an interesting display of early 20th-century engines and other rolling stock. It is open 9 am to 3 pm weekdays. Admission is US$0.30.

A British locomotive, built in 1859 and used as a troop train in the War of the Pacific, is the centerpiece of the pleasant **Parque de la Locomotora**, just east of the tracks on Bolognesi.

The small **Museo del Instituto Nacional de Cultura**, in the Casa de Cultura, has paintings and maps explaining the War of the Pacific and a few archaeological pieces. It's usually open weekday mornings. The **Museo de Zela**, on the 500 block of Zela, gives a look at the interior of one of Tacna's oldest buildings. It's open 10 am to 1 pm and 3 to 5 pm daily. Both museums are free.

The main feature of the **Plaza de Armas** is the huge arch flanked by larger-than-life bronze statues of both Admiral Grau and Colonel Bolognesi – a monument to the heroes of the War of the Pacific. The 6m-high bronze fountain was designed by the French engineer Eiffel, who also designed the **Catedral**, noted for its clean lines, fine stained-glass windows and onyx high altar. The plaza is a popular meeting place for locals in the evenings and has a flag-raising ceremony at 10 am on Sunday.

Places to Stay

Cheap Tacna hotels may suffer from water shortages and showers are not always available. Despite this, hotel prices are relatively high, particularly in the center. Arica, Chile, is no cheaper, though hotels may be better.

Hostal Alameda (☎ 054-723071), Bolognesi 780, charges US$5/7 for singles/doubles with private cold showers. The reasonably clean, cold-water *Hostal Pacífico* (☎ 054-713961) charges US$4 per person. The similarly priced *Hostal Bon Ami* (☎ 054-711873), 2 de Mayo 445, is basic but secure, has occasional hot water and is clean.

Other cheap, basic hotels include the *Pensión Alojamiento Genova*, Deustua 559, which also has a restaurant serving cheap lunch menús.

Basic cold-water hotels in the market area (which isn't as safe) include the cheap

Hostal Don Abel and *Hostal Cuzco* and the more upmarket *Hotel Don Quijote* (☎ 054-721514), Augusto B Leguía 940, with rooms for US$5/8 or US$7/10 with private bath.

Several hotels charge about US$10/15 for rooms with private hot showers. *Hostal H&C* (☎ 054-742042), Zela 734, is clean and quite good at US$8.50/12 with private hot showers. *Hostal Lido* (☎ 054-721184), San Martín 876A, is another decent option at US$6/9.50, with bath and hot water. *Hostal Copacabana* (☎ 054-721721), Arias Araguez 370, has clean rooms with hot showers at US$13/15 but is next door to a noisy weekend disco. *Hostal Inclan* (☎ 054-723701), Inclan 171, isn't bad at US$6/10 with bath. *Hostal Alcázar* (☎ 054-724991), Bolívar 295, has clean rooms with bath at US$9.50/13; ask in advance for hot water. The similarly priced *Hotel Lima* (☎ 054-711912), San Martín 442, has a decent restaurant. There is hot water for a couple of hours in the morning and at night. Another reasonable place is *Hostal Angi* (☎ 054-713502), Modesto Basadre 893.

The clean and friendly *Hostal Lider* (☎ 054-715441), Zela 724, has rooms with hot showers, some with TV and phone, for US$12/20. *Hostal Avenida* (☎ 054-724582), Bolognesi 699, and *Garden Hostal* (☎ 054-711825), Junín 78, charge about US$10/14 and look OK.

Places to Eat

Restaurant Sur Peruano, Ayacucho 80, is inexpensive and popular with locals for lunch. Another local favorite is the clean *Paladar*, Meléndez 228, with menús under US$2. The best chicken is at *El Pollo Pechugón*, Bolognesi 378. Next door, *Chifa Kenny* has good lunch menús starting at US$1.50. Good Chinese food is served at *Chifa Say Wa*. Other budget restaurants line Bolognesi between the post office and Junín. *Helados Piamonte* has good ice cream. *El Viejo Almacén*, San Martín 577, has good steaks, pasta, ice cream, coffee, local wine and desserts. Nearby is the cheaper *Café Génova,* which has outdoor tables and good coffee.

The lively *Cevichería El Corsario*, Av Arica and San José near the Ciudad Universitaria (take a taxi), has great ceviche (US$6 and up) and seafood. Nearby, the *Silvia* (☎ 054-724345), Miraflores 702, is another recommended seafood restaurant. *Rancho*

San Antonio, Coronel Bustios 298, serves good Peruvian and international food in a garden setting. *El Remanso*, Lima 2069, also has international food and weekend entertainment including rock music.

Pocollay, 5km northeast of Tacna, has rural restaurants that are popular for weekend lunches.

Getting There & Away

Air There are several daily flights to Arequipa and Lima. Same-day connections are made via Arequipa to Juliaca, Cuzco and Puerto Maldonado and via Lima to major northern Peruvian cities. AeroContinente serves Tacna. Fares are US$90 to Lima and US$22 to Arequipa.

Peruvian airlines have offices in Arica, Chile, where fares are cheaper (2% tax versus Peru's 18%). Ask in Arica about discounts and air passes (see the Getting There & Away chapter at the start of the book).

Fly Lima-Tacna, cross to Arica by land, then fly Arica-Santiago. You'll save US$100 over a Lima-Santiago fare bought in Peru.

Bus The Terminal Terrestre is on Unanue, at the northeast end of town. Passengers pay a US$0.45 departure tax. The terminal can get disorganized with large groups of Peruvians going home after shopping sprees. Flores Hermanos (☎ 054-726691) is the biggest local company, with 14 daily buses to Arequipa, seven to Moquegua, 10 to Ilo and a daily 3:45 pm bus (more on weekends) to Toquepala. Several companies serve Lima (US$17 to US$35, 21 to 28 hours). Some are luxury services and most leave in the evening. Arequipa (US$4 to US$7, seven hours) is frequently served, as are south coast destinations. Cruz del Sur has buses to Cuzco in the evening.

Ormeño (☎ 054-724401), which has buses to Arequipa and Lima, is at Arias Araguez 700. Buses to Puno (US$8, 12 hours) emerge, usually in the evenings, from the jumble of bus companies on Av Circunvalación, north of the city and east of the main terminal. They may move to the main terminal in the future.

Northbound buses are frequently stopped and searched by immigration and/or customs officials not far north of Tacna. Have your passport handy and don't hold packages for strangers.

Train Trains go from Tacna to Arica and back, supposedly daily, but are subject to cancellation. Check locally. They are slower but cheaper than buses.

To/From Chile Formalities at the Peru-Chile border (which closes at 10 pm) are relatively straightforward in both directions. Chile is one hour ahead of Peru (two hours with daylight-saving time). Buses (US$2) and taxi colectivos (US$4) to Arica leave frequently from the terminal. Drivers help with border formalities (if your papers are in order). A new terminal for buses or taxis to Arica is planned on the Panamericana, 2km south of town.

Getting Around

There is no airport bus, so you have to take a taxi (US$4) or walk (about 5km).

Arequipa

Arequipa, 2325m above sea level, is capital of its department and, with almost a million inhabitants, is Peru's second-largest city. It is a beautiful city, surrounded by spectacular mountains, including the volcano El Misti. Many of the buildings are made of a light-colored volcanic rock called *sillar*, hence Arequipa's nickname – 'the white city.'

The founding of Arequipa, on August 15, 1540, is commemorated with a weeklong fair. The fireworks show in the Plaza de Armas on August 14 is particularly spectacular. Unfortunately, the city is built in an earthquake-prone area, and none of the original buildings remain. However, several 17th- and 18th-century buildings survive and are frequently visited. The most interesting of these is the Santa Catalina monastery.

Information

Tourist Office The tourist office (☎ 054-211021, ext 30) is on the Plaza de Armas, opposite the Catedral. It's open 8 am to 5 pm weekdays. The helpful Policía de Turismo (☎ 054-239888), Jerusalén 315, also provide tourist information.

Visa Extensions Migraciones (immigration; ☎ 054-42-1759) is at Urbanización Quinta Tristán, second floor. Av La Pampilla buses will drop you off at the church at La Pampilla;

walk 3 blocks to the left to the urbanización. It's open 8 am to 2 pm weekdays.

Money The Banco de Crédito changes traveler's checks, and moneychangers outside offer competitive rates for cash. Banco Sur has an ATM inside.

Post & Communications The post office (☎ 054-215247) is at Moral 118. The main telephone office is at Alvarez Thomas 201. There is an Internet office on Alvarez Thomas near Palacio Viejo.

Emergency The tourist police are helpful and open 24 hours. The best hospital is Clínica Arequipa (☎ 054-253416, 054-253424), at Av Bolognesi and Puente Grau.

Dangers & Annoyances Pickpockets are plentiful on the busy street of San Juan de Dios, so watch your belongings carefully here – and everywhere else in town. There have been reports of belongings being stolen from restaurants: keep your stuff in sight.

Religious Buildings

The tourist office can give opening hours, but these change often.

The **Monasterio de Santa Catalina** is Peru's most fascinating colonial religious building. It was built in 1580 and enlarged in the 17th century. Surrounded by imposing high walls, it's a city within a city. At one time, 450 nuns and lay servants led a completely secluded life within it. In 1970 it was opened to the public; resident nuns now live in the northern corner of the complex. Visitors are free to wander around other areas. Entry is US$4, multilingual guide services are available (tip expected) and it's open 9 am to 4 pm daily.

The imposing **Catedral** stands on the Plaza de Armas. The original structure, dating from 1656, was destroyed by fire in 1844, and the second building was toppled by the 1868 earthquake, so most of what you see has been rebuilt. The outside is impressive; the interior is luminous, spacious and airy, with high vaults that aren't as cluttered as those of churches in other parts of Peru.

One of the oldest churches in Arequipa is **La Compañía**, on the southeast corner of the Plaza de Armas. This Jesuit church is noted most for its ornate main façade, and it was so solidly built that it withstood several earth-

quakes. Inside, many of the original murals were covered with plaster and white paint by restorers during the 19th century, but the polychrome cupola of the church's San Ignacio chapel survived and is worth seeing. Entry is US$0.45 to the San Ignacio chapel, free otherwise.

The 16th-century church of **San Francisco** has been damaged by earthquakes: check out the large crack in the cupola. There is an impressive silver altar here, too.

La Recoleta, a Franciscan monastery, was built on the western side of the Río Chili in 1648, but has been completely rebuilt. The huge and fascinating library on the grounds contains more than 20,000 books. Many are centuries old and several of them are incunables, or books printed before 1500. Also within the monastery is a museum of Amazonian objects collected by the missionaries, an extensive collection of preconquest artifacts and religious artworks of the Cuzco school, and you can visit the cloisters and monks' cells. It's open 9 am to noon and 3 to 5 pm Monday to Saturday. Entry is US$2. A Spanish-speaking guide is available (tip expected).

Museums

The **Museo Histórico Municipal** has a few paintings, documents, photographs, maps and other historical items. It's open 9 am to 5 pm weekdays and entry is US$0.50. There are craft shops here as well.

Colonial Houses

Many old homes are now being used as art galleries, banks or offices and can be visited. One of the best is the **Casa del Moral**, now owned by the Banco del Sur. In the 1940s and 1950s a visionary British consul bought it and restored it to its colonial splendor, decorating it with a remarkable collection of Cuzco school paintings, colonial furniture, alpaca rugs and adding fireplaces and two bars. In 1996, the house underwent a second restoration. The guided tours (in Spanish and English) are excellent. It is open 9 am to 5 pm Monday to Saturday, and 9 am to 1 pm on Sunday. Admission is US$2. Also spectacular is **Casa Ricketts**. Built in 1738, it was first a seminary, then passed through several hands before being sold to the Banco Central. It now houses a small art gallery, museum and bank offices. Admission is free. It's open 9 am

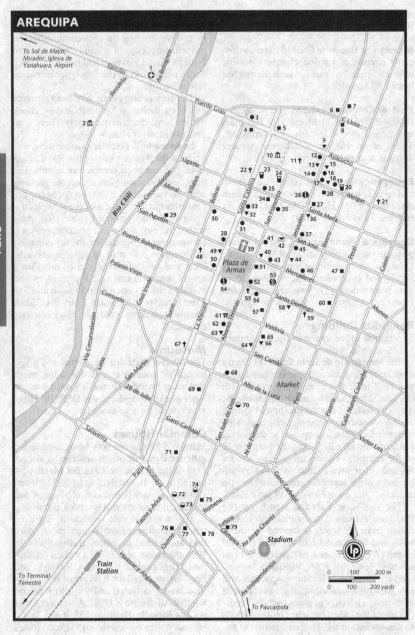

AREQUIPA

PERU

To Sol de Mayo,
Mirador,
Iglesia de
Yanahuara, Airport

To Terminal
Terrestre

Train
Station

Plaza de
Armas

Market

Stadium

To Paucarpata

0   100   200 m
0   100   200 yards

AREQUIPA

PLACES TO STAY
4 Hostal Wilson
5 Hostal Santa Catalina
6 Gran Hotel Jerusalén
7 La Casa de Mi Abuela
8 Hostal Núñez
27 La Casona de Jerusalén
28 La Casa de Melgar
29 Hostal Tumi de Oro
34 Hotel Regis
47 Hostal Mercaderes
51 Hostal Mirador
57 Hostal V Lira
60 Hotel Crillon Serrano,
   Hotel Tito
65 Hostal Royal
69 Hostal Americano
71 Hotel San Gregory
75 Hostal Florida
76 Hostal Grace
77 Hostal Premier
78 Hostal Colonia
79 Hostal Extra

PLACES TO EAT
9 Govinda,
   Other Budget Places
13 Pizzería Los Leños
15 Lakshimivan
18 Snack Faga
32 Café Peña Anuschka
36 Pizzería San Antonio

40 Manolo
44 Bonanza
49 Restaurant Cuzco,
   El Balcón Restaurant
58 Monza
63 Cevichería 45
64 América
66 Dalmacia, Puerto Rico

OTHER
1 Arequipa Clinic
2 Monasterio de La Recoleta,
   Museo
3 Car Rental
10 Museo Histórico Municipal,
   Crafts Shops
11 San Francisco
12 Conresa Tours
14 La Troica
16 Continental Tours
17 Lavandería Rápida
   (Laundromat)
19 Instituto Cultural
   Peruano-NorteAmericano
20 Jenízaro (Pub)
21 Santa Teresa
22 Monasterio de Santa Catalina
23 Las Quenas
24 Blues Bar
25 Instituto Cultural
   Peruano-Alemán
26 Tourist Police, Information

30 Casa del Moral
31 Lima Tours
33 Alianza Francesa
35 Coltur
37 Peña Picantería
38 Casona Iriberry,Complejo
   Cultural Chaves de la Rosa
39 Catedral
41 Casa Ricketts
   (Tristán del Pozo)
42 Post Office
43 Map Store
45 Carnaby Disco
46 Cine Municipal
48 San Agustín
50 AeroContinente
52 Cine Portal
53 Banco de Crédito
54 Tourist Office
55 La Compañía
56 Cine Fénix
59 Santo Domingo
61 Telefónica del Perú
62 Internet Office
67 La Merced
68 Cine Ateneo
69 Cine Variedades
70 Bus Companies
72 Cruz del Sur
73 Sur Peruano
74 Ormeño

to noon and 4 to 6 pm weekdays. Also worth a look are the Casona Iriberry, housing the Complejo Cultural Chaves de la Rosa, and the Palacio Goyeneche.

Suburbs

The suburb of **Yanahuara**, northwest of the center of town, makes a good excursion. Go west on Av Grau, cross the bridge and continue on Av Ejército for six or seven blocks. Turn right on Av Lima and walk 5 blocks to a small plaza with the church of Yanahuara, dating from 1750. There's a viewing platform at the end of the plaza with fine views of Arequipa and El Misti.

If you head back along Av Jerusalén (in Yanahuara), which is the next street parallel to Av Lima, just before Av Ejército you'll see the well-known *Picantería Sol de Mayo* restaurant. The green Yanahuara city bus leaves Arequipa along Independencia and returns from Yanahuara Plaza to the city

every few minutes. There are also vans along Socabaya in Arequipa.

Beyond Yanahuara is **Cayma**, another suburb with an often-visited church. Continue along Av Ejército 3 blocks beyond Av Jerusalén, then turn right on Av Cayma and climb this road for about 1km. The church of San Miguel Arcángel is open from 9 am to 4 pm daily. Buses marked 'Cayma' go there from Arequipa, along Av Grau.

The suburb of **Paucarpata** is 7km southeast of town and has a nice church and great local restaurant. Two km away you'll find the Sabandía mill, which was built in 1621, restored in 1973 and is now working again. Entry is US$2. Gray buses to Paucarpata leave Arequipa along Socabaya.

Places to Stay

Hotel Crillon Serrano (☎ 054-212392), Perú 109, is cheap, basic, clean and friendly and has warm water in the morning. It charges

US$4/7 with private bath. Also clean and friendly are *Hotel Tito* (☎ 054-234424), Perú 105B, which charges US$3/7 with general bath, or US$7/12 with private bath, and *Hotel Regis* (☎ 054-226111), Ugarte 202, which has hot water and a rooftop terrace and charges US$4.50 per person.

Hostal Mercaderes, Peral 117, is basic but OK for US$4/6 or US$6 per person with private warm showers. *Hostal Mirador* charges US$5 per person and receives mixed reports, but a few rooms have great plaza views. The basic *Hostal V Lira* (☎ 054-213161), charges US$3.50/5, or US$8 with bath, has hot water and is secure.

The reasonably clean and friendly *Hostal Royal* (☎ 054-212071), San Juan de Dios 300A, has hot water at US$5 per person, or US$10 for a double with bath. The basic *Hostal Santa Catalina* (☎ 054-243705), Santa Catalina 500, has hot water and is fairly clean and popular. It's US$5 or US$8 with bath. The adequate *Hostal Grace* (☎ 054-235924), Quiroz 121, is US$5/8 with shared warm showers.

The secure *Hostal Núñez* (☎ 054-218648), Jerusalén 528, is US$7/12 or US$12/20 with bath and TV. Some rooms have a strong smoke odor. There is hot water and a terrace, and it's popular with gringos. *Hostal Tumi de Oro* (☎ 054-281319), San Agustín 311A, is clean and friendly and has hot water. It's US$10 per person or US$13 for a double with bath.

The basic but clean *Hostal Americano* (☎ 054-211752), A Thomas 435, has rooms for US$10 (one or two people) with shared hot showers. Also in this price range are the basic *Hostal Colonia* (☎ 054-242766), Cáceres 109, which has large rooms, and the decent *Hotel San Gregory* (☎ 054-245036), A Thomas 535, which has clean rooms with bath and TV. Slightly cheaper is the friendly *Hostal Extra* (☎ 054-221217), which has a garden and charges US$7/9 with bath. The nice *Hostal Wilson* (☎ 054-238781), Grau 306, is US$5 per person or US$6 with bath. *Hostal Florida* (☎ 054-238467), San Juan de Dios 664B, is good at US$15/18 with bath. The clean *Hostal Premier* (☎ 054-241091), Quiroz 100, is US$13/17 with bath.

The very respectable and secure *La Casa de Mi Abuela* (☎ 054-241206), Jerusalén 606, is a good upmarket choice. Rooms are US$26 with bath or US$13 with shared bath. There's an attractive garden full of singing birds where you can enjoy breakfast, a swimming pool, and although the place is usually full, it is efficiently run. Across the street, the very clean *Gran Hotel Jerusalén* (☎ 054-28-8347) is a good deal at US$20, or US$25 (negotiable) with breakfast. Another good choice is the friendly *La Casa de Melgar* (☎ 054-222459), Melgar 108A, in an attractive 18th-century building, with spacious rooms and a good café. Singles/doubles are US$25/35.

Places to Eat

For cheap vegetarian food try *Govinda*, Jerusalén 505, run by Hare Krishnas, or the popular *Lakshimivan*, Jerusalén 402. There are more cheap restaurants on these blocks, including *Lluvia de Oro*, Jerusalén 308. Good Italian food is served at *Pizzería San Antonio* (☎ 054-213950), at Jerusalén 222, and *Pizzería Los Leños*, Jerusalén 407. Both are popular with young locals. *Bonanza*, Jerusalén 114, serves a variety of dishes at US$3 to US$7 and is also locally popular.

El Balcón Restaurant and *Restaurant Cuzco*, on the northwest side of the plaza, 2nd floor, have fine plaza views; the food is OK and cheap but service is very slow. Below El Balcón are other cheap to mid-range restaurants. Three good, reasonably priced restaurants in the 300 block of San Juan de Dios are the *Puerto Rico*, the *Dalmacia* and the *América* – this last has good ice creams and snacks. Several places on this street serve half a grilled chicken for US$3.50. There are restaurants with set lunch menús for US$1.50 along La Merced.

Two upmarket cafés on the first block of San Francisco have good espresso, cappuccino and snacks. There is also good coffee at *Monza*, on Santo Domingo, a block east of the plaza, and at *Manolo*, Mercaderes 109. The best ceviche (and nothing else) is found at the *Cebichería 45*, A Thomas 221, from 9 am to 3 pm. The friendly *Café Peña Anuschka*, Santa Catalina 204 interior, has homemade pastries, German specialties and tropical cocktails. For delicious snacks of empanadas (meat pies), papas rellenas (stuffed potatoes) and tamales stop at the friendly *Snack Faga*, Melgar 101.

An excellent place for arequipeño food is the locally popular *Tradición Arequipeña* (☎ 054-426467), at Av Dolores 111, Paucarpata, with meals in the US$3 to US$6 range. Most taxi drivers know it (under US$2 from the center). Also good for local dishes is the *Sol de Mayo*, Jerusalén 207, Yanahuara. Both places only open for lunch. Other popular *picanterías* include *La Lucila* and *Cau-Cau*, both at the Mirador de Sachaca (a US$1 taxi). Traditional local dishes include chupe de camarones (thick shrimp soup), rocoto relleno (stuffed peppers) and pastel de papa (cottage pie), accompanied with chicha de jora (a high-grade, bright red version of the traditional fermented maize liquor).

Entertainment
Pizzería Los Leños has rock music interspersed with live Peruvian folklórico musicians wandering in during the evening. *Las Quenas*, Santa Catalina 302, has live music nightly from 9 pm. The music varies though folklórico predominates. There is a US$2.50 cover charge and they serve food.

La Troica, Jerusalén 522-A, offers a good folklore show on Saturdays. It's open daily except Sunday. The cover charge is US$2.50, but you can get a free pass at the tourist office. Locals recommend *Yanahuara*, Ejército and Misti, Yanahuara, for *peña criolla* and dancing on Fridays and Saturdays. Occasionally, there is entertainment at the *Peña Picantería*, Jerusalén 204.

The *Blues Bar*, on the last block of San Francisco, has good drinks and music and is the current gathering point of young *arequipeños*. The cover charge is US$3.50. The best disco is the locally popular *Kibosh*, Zela 205, near Plaza San Francisco. Locals also recommend the pub *Jenízaro*, Melgar 119. Ask the tourist office for a free pass. There are several discos, pubs and karaoke bars on Av Dolores.

Getting There & Away
Air The airport is 9km northwest of the city center. AeroContinente (☎ 054-287740, 054-219914) has an office on the plaza. On most days, there are seven flights to Lima (US$89), and one each to Tacna (US$24), Cuzco (US$53) and Juliaca (US$42).

Bus Most buses leave from the modern Terminal Terrestre, 3km south of the center. There is a US$0.50 departure tax. Many bus offices are near the 600 block of San Juan de Dios, where tickets are sold. Adjacent to the

Terminal Terrestre is the Terrapuerto, from where the better class buses depart.

Lima (14 to 16 hours) is served by CIVA, Cruz del Sur, Flores Hermanos, Ormeño, Sudamericano and others, most with buses leaving in the afternoon. Fares range from US$8 for regular service to US$25 for luxury service. Many buses stop in Nazca (US$8 and up, 8 to 10 hours) as well as in Camaná, Chala and Ica. There are also several buses a day via Moquegua to Tacna (US$4 to US$7, six hours).

Ormeño has two night buses to Puno, Cruz del Sur has two day buses to Puno (US$7, 10 to 12 hours) and a bus to La Paz, Bolivia, via Puno (US$20). Other companies also go to Lake Titicaca and beyond. The road to Juliaca is in terrible shape and many travelers prefer the train. There have been cases of night buses to Juliaca being held up. These and other companies also have buses to Cuzco (US$10 to US$12, around 14 hours) on a poor road. The journeys to Juliaca and Cuzco can take much longer in wet weather. This is a cold night trip: dress warmly.

Ormeño has three international buses a week to Santiago, Chile (US$80) and Buenos Aires, Argentina (US$130).

Transportes Transandino, Transportes Prado, Turismo Expreso Cóndor, Transportes El Chasqui, Transportes Colca and Transportes Cristo Rey have departures at 2:30 am, and noon for Chivay (US$4, four hours) continuing through Yanque, Achoma and Maca to Cabanaconde (US$5, seven hours) on the upper Cañón del Colca.

For buses to Corire (US$2.50, three hours) to visit the Toro Muerto petroglyphs, go with Flores Hermanos, El Chasqui or Transportes del Carpio. There are departures almost every hour from about 5:30 am. El Carpio also goes to Valle de Majes (US$2) for whitewater rafting as do Transportes Berrios and Panorama. Transportes Panorama has buses to the Valle de Los Volcanes.

Train The journey to Juliaca is much more comfortable by train than by bus. The train leaves Arequipa at 9 pm on Wednesday and Sunday and arrives at Juliaca at 6 am the following day. You can continue to Puno, an hour away, or connect with the 9 am Juliaca-Cuzco train, arriving at 6 pm. If going to Puno, it is quicker to buy a ticket to Juliaca and then catch one of the many minibuses to Puno waiting for the train.

Many people have been robbed on the night train, especially in crowded 2nd class. You are safest buying a Pullman ticket instead of just a 1st-class ticket. The Pullman car has comfortable reclining seats so you can sleep, and is heated. The doors are locked and only ticket holders are admitted into the carriages.

Fares from Arequipa change frequently and drastically. Current fares to Juliaca are US$7.50 and US$10 for 2nd class or Pullman; to Cuzco they are US$18.50 in executive (a fancy name for 2nd class) and US$25 in Inca class.

Buy your tickets in advance rather than while guarding your luggage. Ticket office hours change constantly, and there are usually long lines with several hours' wait. Travel agencies (eg, Conresa Tours and Continental Tours, on the 400 block of Jerusalén) will sell tickets, for a 25% commission, and provide transport from your hotel to the station. Shop around for the best deal.

Getting Around

Buses go south along Bolívar and Sucre bound for the Terminal Terrestre. A taxi there will cost about US$2.

To/From the Airport Buses marked 'Río Seco,' 'Cono-Norte' or 'Zamacola' go along Puente Grau and Ejército and pass within 1km of the airport; ask the driver where to get off. A taxi from the city center costs about US$3.

AROUND AREQUIPA
Cañón del Colca

The most popular excursion from Arequipa is to the Cañón del Colca (Colca Canyon), which can be visited by public transport or with a guided tour. Controversy rages about whether or not this is the world's deepest canyon. The sections that you can see from the road are very impressive but are not the deepest sections. To see these, you have to hike in on an overnight trip.

Guided tours are US$30 for a day or US$5 more for two days. The one-day trip is rushed, so you get more from a two-day trip, which includes lodging and breakfast in Chivay. Day tours leave before dawn and go through the Reserva Nacional Salinas y **Aguada Blanca**, where vicuñas are often sighted. A breakfast stop is often made at Vizcachani (4150m). The road continues through bleak altiplano to about 4800m, from where the snowcaps of Ampato (6288m) are seen. Then the road drops spectacularly to Chivay, about 160km from Arequipa. The road continues west, following the south side of the Cañón del Colca. The landscape has Inca terracing and several villages whose inhabitants still use the terraces. The end point of the tour is at the Cruz del Cóndor lookout, about 60km beyond Chivay and an hour before you get to the village of Cabanaconde. Andean condors may be seen here and the view is impressive, with the river flowing 1200m below. Overnight tours stop in Chivay, where there are hot springs, continuing to Cruz del Cóndor early the next day.

Several tour companies do the trip; some aren't very good, so check locally before you part with your money. Guides should be able to produce a Tourist Guide card. Operators will often pool their clients. Conresa (☎054-285420, fax 054-247186, conresatours @clubinter.org.pe), Jerusalén 409, or Continental, Jerusalén 402, often provide the vehicle and the lowest prices. Unfortunately, the minibuses used don't have adequate leg room for tall people, so it may be better to go in a smaller group with a car. Guides don't always speak English. A car with driver taking a maximum of three people can be hired for US$177 per day; the hotel is extra. A minivan for four to six people costs US$200 per day.

By public transport, you can get off at Cruz del Cóndor and camp. It is a two-hour walk from the lookout to Cabanaconde, where there are hotels. You could also take the 4 am Arequipa bus from Cabanaconde, get off at the lookout for dawn and condor viewing, then return to Cabanaconde for a second night. The best condor viewing is from 7 to 9 am, but it's not bad in the late afternoon. You can also get directions at Cabanaconde for overnight camping trips into the canyon; bring everything you'll need. The best trips to Colca are unrushed ones.

Places to Stay Chivay, at an altitude of about 3700m, has four basic but friendly cold-water hotels around the plaza for

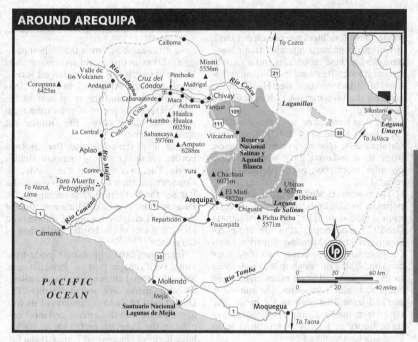

AROUND AREQUIPA

US$3 per person. *Hostal Colca* and *Hostal Posada del Inca* are two or three blocks west of the plaza. Both have restaurants and hot water and charge US$8.50 per person with private bath. The Colca has rooms with shared bath for US$5 per person. There are hot springs 4km northeast of Chivay by road. There is a clean swimming pool (with changing rooms), a basic cafeteria and a US$1.50 fee.

Cabanaconde has three basic *pensiones*, charging US$3.50 per person. Walk 10 minutes west of the plaza to a hill with good views and occasional condors in the early morning. Ask for directions to hike into the canyon. It takes about six hours one way, so you should be prepared to camp. Longer overnight trips are also done; the SAEC clubhouse in Lima has details.

Getting There & Away If you don't want a guided tour, see the Arequipa section for details of bus companies that have daily dawn departures to Chivay. Most continue to Cabanaconde and return from there to Arequipa at 4 am daily. The section of road

between Cabanaconde and Huambo veers away from the canyon. It is also the roughest part, and there is little transport.

White-Water Rafting

Running the Colca is a difficult undertaking, and is for experienced rafters only. The Río Majes is much easier. The best base is the *Majes River Lodge* (☎ 054-255819), 190km by road west of Arequipa. River guide Carlos Zúñiga (☎/fax 054-255819) is the Arequipa contact. The lodge has double rooms with hot water for about US$20, or you can camp for US$2. An 8km white-water run, suitable for beginners, lasts an hour and costs US$16 including transportation from the lodge. Experienced river runners can take a 25km, Class IV run lasting three hours for US$30.

The lodge is a base to visit Toro Muerto (see below). Berrios, Chasqui, Panorama and Carpio bus companies all go there for US$2.

Mountaineering

Many mountains in the Arequipa area are technically easy to climb. Problems are extreme weather conditions (carry warm clothes and a tent), altitude and lack of water (carry four liters per person per day). If you're a beginner, remember that people have died in these mountains and it's not as easy as it looks. Be aware of the main symptoms of altitude sickness (see Health in the Facts for the Visitor chapter). If in doubt, go back down.

The best local guide is Carlos Zárate at the Alianza Francesa (☎ 054-215579), Santa Catalina 208. His wife, Olivia Mazuelos, works there and can tell you where he is. He provides information, gear rental, and guide referral.

The volcano **El Misti** (5822m) is the most popular local climb. There are several routes. One is to take a bus to Chiguata (US$0.75, one hour) at 6 am from Av Sepúlveda in the Miraflores district. From Chiguata to the base camp is an eight-hour hard uphill slog on rough trails. From there to the summit and back takes eight more hours and there's no water. The summit is marked by a 10m-high metal cross. The return from the base camp to Chiguata takes three hours or less. A bus returns from Chiguata to Arequipa at 4 pm.

Chachani (6075m) is one of the easiest 6000m peaks in the world. You need crampons, an ice ax and good equipment. Other nearby peaks of interest include **Sabancaya** (5976m), **Hualca Hualca** (6025m), **Ampato** (6288m), **Ubinas** (5672m), **Mismi** (5556m) and **Coropuna**, which is labeled variously on maps at 6305m or 6425m.

Toro Muerto Petroglyphs & Corire

Hundreds of carved boulders are scattered over 2 sq km of desert; archaeologists aren't sure of their significance. You can see them by taking a bus to Corire (US$2, three hours) and continuing up the valley for several kilometers on foot. The best petroglyphs are on the left and higher up. On the Corire plaza is *Hostal Willy's (054-210232 ext 46 in Corire, or 054-258367 in Arequipa)*, with doubles for US$10 and reasonably priced food. Their rafting trips to the Colca are US$10/14 for beginner/experienced river runners. Crayfish from the local river are sold in several simple restaurants. If you leave Arequipa at dawn, a day trip is possible.

Lake Titicaca Area

Lake Titicaca, at 3820m, is the highest navigable lake in the world. At more than 170km in length, it is also the largest lake in South America. At this altitude, the air is unusually clear, and the deep blue of the lake is especially pretty. If you arrive from the coast, take it easy – the altitude can make you sick.

The lake straddles the Peru-Bolivia border. The most common route into Bolivia is via Yunguyo, crossing the border to Copacabana, then by bus and boat to La Paz; see the To/From Bolivia heading in the Puno section. The Lake Titicaca section of the Bolivia chapter has more information about that side of the border, and a map of the area.

Interesting boat trips can be made from Puno, Peru's major port on Lake Titicaca. Several colonial churches and archaeological monuments are worth visiting. The Department of Puno is famous for its folk dances, which are the wildest and most colorful in the Peruvian highlands. There are huge herds of alpacas and llamas. It is a fascinating area.

JULIACA

With 100,000 inhabitants, Juliaca is the largest town in the department of Puno, has the only commercial airport and is a major railway junction, with connections to Arequipa, Puno and Cuzco. It is of comparatively little interest, however, and most people prefer nearby Puno, which has better hotels and views of Lake Titicaca. According to a recent report, Juliaca has the highest theft rate in the nation. Watch your belongings.

Information

The Banco de Crédito, M Núñez 138, changes traveler's checks. Other moneychangers are on the block north of this bank. Juliaca's Clínica Adventista is the best hospital in the Puno area.

Places to Stay

Cheap hotels have an unreliable water supply. The following are very basic but cheap. *Hotel Don Pedro* and *Hostal Loreto* charge US$3/4.50 for a single/double and are opposite the train station. Nearby, the **Hotel Ferrocarril** is US$2.50 per person, and **Hotel del Sur** is US$3 per person.

Better cheapies include the **Hostal San Antonio** (☎ 054-331803), San Martín 347, at US$3.50/5. Rooms have toilets but showers are shared. Hot water is US$1.20 extra and there's a sauna. **Hostal Sakura** (☎ 054-321194), Unión 133, is OK for US$3 per person or US$5/8 with bath and occasional hot water. Also decent is the friendly **Hostal Aparicio** (☎ 054-321625), Loreto 270, at US$4/6 for rooms with shared bathroom or US$5/7.50 with private bath.

The clean, friendly and often full **Hotel Yasur** (☎ 054-321501), at Núñez 414, is US$4.50/6.50 or US$5/8 with private bath. There is hot water morning and evening. The clean, cosy and recommended **Hostal Perú** (☎ 054-321510), opposite the train station, is US$6/7.50, or US$7.50/10 with bath, and has hot water in the evening.

Getting There & Away
Air The airport serves Juliaca and Puno. There are two daily flights to/from Lima (US$89), via Arequipa (US$54) with Aero-Continente.

Bus San Cristóbal (☎ 054-321181), Cruz del Sur (☎ 054-322011) and others have the same destinations as from Puno. Empresa de Transportes San Martín has night buses to Moquegua, Tacna and Ilo. Transportes 3 de Mayo goes to Huancané (US$1.25, 2½ hours). Minibuses to Puno (US$0.50) pass the railway station looking for passengers.

Train See the Puno section for details about trains, times and fares. Fares from Juliaca are a few soles cheaper than from Puno and trains leave one to two hours after the Puno departure time. Passengers from Arequipa continuing to Cuzco have time between trains to wander around. Alpaca sweaters, ponchos and bags are sold, and you can shop through the carriage window. Bargain hard. Passengers to Puno can take a minibus from Juliaca and beat the train. The poorly lit Juliaca station has a reputation for luggage snatching and pickpocketing. Read the warnings in the Arequipa Train section and watch your belongings.

PUNO
Puno was founded on November 4, 1668, but few colonial buildings remain except the Catedral. The town itself is drab and uninteresting, but there's a good hotel selection and plenty to see nearby.

Information
The tourist office is on the first block of the pedestrian Lima; it's open 8 am to 1 pm and 2 to 6 pm weekdays. The Policía de Turismo is at Deustua 538. Both places offer minimal information. More updated, complete information in several languages is available at All Ways Travel (see below).

Visa Extensions Migraciones (☎ 054-357103) is at Grau 365, second floor. It's open 8 am to 8 pm weekdays.

Money The Banco de Crédito changes traveler's checks and has an ATM. Moneychangers hang out on Calle Lima. Buy or sell Bolivian pesos at the border for the best exchange rates.

Email & Internet Access For email try Punonet (☎ 054-369510), Lambayeque 145. Open daily from 8 am to 10 pm, it charges US$3 per hour.

Travel Agencies All Ways Travel (☎ 054-355552, awtperu@mail.cosapidata.com.pe), Tacna 234, is a reputable agency that offers tours as well as honest tourist information in a variety of languages. Feiser Tours (☎ 054-353112), Valcárcel 153, Kontiki Tours (☎ 054-353473), Melgar 188, and Inca Tours (☎ 35-1062), at Ugarte 112, on the second floor of Hostal Europa have been recommended. There are many others. Avoid the hordes that converge at train and bus stops offering tours; Puno has a reputation for tour rip-offs.

Things to See
The **Museo Carlos Dreyer**, Conde de Lemos 289, is open 8:30 am to noon and 3 to 5 pm weekdays. Entry is US$2.

The **Parque Huajsapata**, a little hill about 10 minutes southwest of town, features a statue of the first Inca, Manco Capac, looking out at Lake Titicaca. The view of the town and the lake is excellent. The **Arco**

PERU

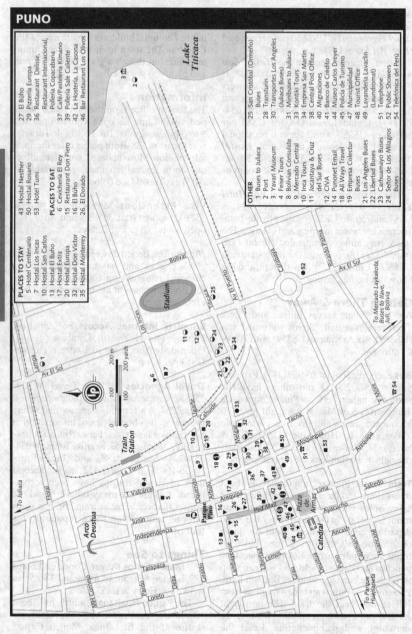

PUNO

PLACES TO STAY
5   Hotel Centenario
7   Hostal Los Incas
10   Hostal San Carlos
13   Hostal El Buho
17   Hostal Extra
20   Hostal Europa
22   Hostal Don Victor
35   Hostal Monterrey
43   Hostal Nesther
50   Hostal Rosario
53   Hotel Tumi

PLACES TO EAT
6   Cevichería El Rey
15   Restaurant Don Piero
16   El Buho
26   El Dorado
27   El Búho
29   Pizzería Europa
36   Restaurant Delisse,
     Restaurant Internacional,
     Pollería Copacabana
37   Café/Pastelería Kimano
39   Pollería Sale Caliente
42   La Hostería, La Casona
46   Bar Restaurant Los Olivos

OTHER
1   Buses to Juliaca
2   Port
3   Yavarí Museum
4   Feiser Tours
8   Bolivian Consulate
9   Mercado Central
11   Inca Tours
12   CIVA
14   Punonet Email
18   All Ways Travel
19   Empresa Colectur
     Buses
21   Los Angeles Buses
23   Carhuamayo Buses
24   Señor de Los Milagros
     Buses
25   San Cristóbal (Ormeño)
     Buses
28   Transturin
30   Transportes Los Angeles
     (Juliaca Buses)
31   Minibuses to Juliaca
33   Kontiki Tours
34   Empresa San Martín
38   Central Post Office
40   Migraciones
41   Banco de Crédito
44   Museo Carlos Dreyer
45   Policía de Turismo
47   Municipalidad
48   Tourist Office
49   Lavandería Lavaclin
     (Laundromat)
51   Telephone
52   Public Showers
54   Telefónica del Perú

Lake Titicaca

Stadium

Train Station

Arco Deustua

Plaza de Armas

Ped Mall

Catedral

To Juliaca

To Mercado Laykakota,
Buses to Ilave;
Juli, Bolivia

To Parque Huajsapata

0   100   200 m
0   100   200 yards

Deustua, an arch on Calle Independencia, also has good views.

The **Yavari Museum** is an iron-hulled boat built in England in 1862 in kit form. Its 1383 pieces were shipped to Arica, transported to Tacna by train, then carried by mule to Puno, where it was reassembled and finally launched onto Lake Titicaca in 1870. After over a century of service, the Yavari was beached, its navigation equipment sent to a naval museum in Arequipa and the hull was abandoned. In 1987, it was acquired by the Yavari Project, and since 1998, the boat is once again afloat and open to the public as an example of one of the oldest seaworthy iron-hulled boats. Visit the ship at the Puno Dock from 9 am to 5 pm, Wednesday to Sunday. Captain Carlos Saavedra, project coordinator, gives fascinating guided tours in English and Spanish.

Special Events

The Department of Puno has a wealth of traditional dances and music. The costumes, often worth more than an entire family's clothes, are ornate and imaginative. Check the tourist office for local fiesta information. Apart from the major Peruvian festivals, the following are important in the Lake Titicaca region:

Día de los Reyes (Epiphany)
    January 6
Virgen de la Candelaria (Candlemas)
    February 2-14
Día de San Juan (St John)
    March 7-8
Alacitas (Puno miniature handicrafts fair),
    Día de Santa Cruz (Holy Cross; Huancané,
    Taquile, Puno)
    May 2-4
Día de Santiago (St James; Taquile)
    July 25
La Virgen de La Merced (Our Lady of Mercy)
    September 24
Semana Cívica de Puno (Puno Week)
    November 1-7

Places to Stay

Hotels fill quickly after the evening train arrives. Prices may double during festivals, and sometimes do so in the evening. Many hotels have triple and quadruple rooms. Water and power shortages are a problem, but there are public hot showers (US$1) on

Av El Sol (the water is reportedly tepid in the first stalls). Lock your luggage; thefts from hotel rooms have been reported.

The following are US$3.50/6 for very basic singles/doubles: *Hostal Extra* (☎ 054-351123), Moquegua 124, which sometimes has hot water and is the best of the super-cheapies; *Hotel Centenario* (☎ 054-352591), Deza 211; *Hostal Rosario* (☎ 054-352272), Moquegua 325; and *Hostal Los Incas*, Los Incas 105, which has no singles, plenty of triples and quads, and hot showers (US$1).

Hostal Europa (☎ 054-353023), Ugarte 112, is popular with gringos. Doubles are US$7. It's OK, with left-luggage facilities and hot water in the evening if the showers work. Probably the best cheap hotel is the quiet *Hostal Los Uros* (☎ 054-352141), Valcarcel 135. It has a cafeteria, open for simple breakfasts, and hot water in the evening. There are a few singles but plenty of triples and even quads. Rates are US$5/7.50 for singles/doubles, or US$6/9.50 with private bath.

The clean *Hostal San Carlos* (☎ 054-351862), Ugarte 161, has telephones in the rooms and claims to have hot water all day. Rates are US$8/12 with private bath. There is a restaurant for breakfast. *Hostal Nesther* (☎ 054-351631), Deustua 268, has hot water from 6 to 8 am and 6 to 8 pm only, is clean and is quite good for US$8/12 with bath. The English translation of the house rules is amusing. *Hotel Tumi* (☎ 054-353270), Cajamarca 253, is another decent choice at US$10/17 with bath. The management is open to bargaining.

Another good choice in this range is the *Hostal Don Víctor* (☎ 054-366087), Melgar 166. Rooms with carpeting, private bath and hot water cost US$8/15. *Hostal Monterrey* (☎ 054-351691), Lima 441, has singles/doubles at US$7.50/11.50 or US$10/15 with bath, but it is not as popular with gringos as it used to be. *Hostal El Buho* (☎ 054-351409), Lambayeque 142, offers very good mid-range accommodations for US$12/15 with hot showers. It has a restaurant downstairs.

Places to Eat

Restaurant Internacional, Libertad 161, serves a wide range of good, abundant dishes at US$3 or US$4. Its international plate is huge. There is often music in the evenings, usually before 8 pm. For vegetarian food, the family run *Restaurant Delisse*,

PERU

Libertad 215, has a good selection of food at reasonable prices. The service by the children is charming but erratic.

Restaurant Don Piero, Lima 354, has local trout meals (US$4) and other cheaper dishes. *El Dorado*, Lima 371, is good and reasonably priced. Nearby, *La Casona*, Lima 517, offers a good variety of highland dishes: cuy chajtado (roasted guinea pig), lomo de alpaca (alpaca steak), quinoa fritters and mote con queso (sweet fruit jam served with cheese). The cozy *La Hostería*, Lima 501, is popular for pizzas (about US$4.50) and other meals. It also has good desserts and alcoholic concoctions and may have music in the evenings.

Popular with locals are the *Café/Pastelería Kimano*, Arequipa 509, for good pastries and pizza in the evening, and the *Bar Restaurant Los Olivos*, Ayacucho 237. *Pollería Sale Caliente*, Tacna 381, is a good chicken place. *El Búho*, Libertad 386 and Lima 347, is a tasty pizza place, and *Pizzería Europa*, on the corner of Tacna and Libertad, is another decent choice. *Cevichería El Rey*, Los Incas 271, looks good and has ceviches from US$3.50.

Quinta La Kantuta (☎ 054-351748), Arequipa 1086 (not in the center), has typical lunch fare (including cuy) daily, except Monday. You must call a day in advance to order a meal.

Shopping

The market near the train station has sheep and alpaca sweaters and other products at good prices. Cuzco has a wider selection.

Getting There & Away

Air Juliaca has the nearest airport; Puno travel agents sell tickets. A taxi from Puno to the airport is about US$13.

Bus The roads are poor, and delays are common in the wet months, especially from January to April. The train is more comfortable. Cruz del Sur (☎ 054-352451), Av El Sol 568, whose service is better along the coast than in the highlands, El Señor de los Milagros, Melgar 308, and CIVA (☎ 054-356882), also on Melgar have buses to Arequipa (US$10, 12 hours). The road is paved only for about 100km, the rest is quite rough. Cruz del Sur also serves Cuzco (US$12, 14 hours) and Lima (US$25, 42 hours), all leaving between

4 and 5 pm, and La Paz, Bolivia, (US$6, five hours) via Desaguadero at 10 am. San Cristóbal (☎ 054-352321), on the 300 block of Titicaca, has slightly cheaper overnight buses to Arequipa and Lima. Cheaper still are Jacantaya (☎ 054-351931), Av El Sol 594, with overnight buses to Arequipa and Lima, and Carhuamayo (☎ 054-353522), Melgar 334, with an overnight bus to Cuzco, but CIVA and Libertad offer better service to Cuzco.

For Tacna (US$10, 15 hours), Transportes Los Angeles has a 6 pm departure. Try also Empresa San Martín. Buses to towns on the south side of the lake and the Bolivian border depart frequently during the day from the Av El Ejército side of the Mercado Laykakota. For travel to Copacabana, Empresa Colectur has a daily bus at 7:30 am (US$3.50), but the schedule changes often. Panamericano, on Tacna, also goes to La Paz via Copacabana.

For Juliaca (US$0.50, about an hour), Transportes Los Angeles buses leave several times an hour from the corner of Tacna and Libertad. Buses also go from the corner of Lampa and El Sol. Slightly faster but more cramped minibuses leave from the corner of Cahuide and Titicaca.

Train The first few kilometers of the journey out of Puno offer good views over Lake Titicaca. Cuzco trains leave at 8 am on Monday, Wednesday, Thursday and Saturday, arriving at 7 pm. Arequipa trains leave at 7:45 pm on Monday and Friday, arriving at 6 am the following day. Departure days can change. Be on the lookout for thieves at the station and on the trains, especially to Arequipa (see the Arequipa section for details).

Cuzco fares are US$23 for Inca (Pullman) class, US$19 in Turismo (1st) and US$8.50 in Económico (2nd) class. Arequipa fares are US$10 for Inca class, US$7.50 for Económico. Fares have varied greatly in past years. There have been complaints of 1st-class tickets being sold for Pullman prices, so check carefully. Pullman class is safest, but 1st class is reasonably safe on the Cuzco day train and 2nd class is OK if you are in a group or have no valuables.

You should buy your Cuzco ticket the day before, but sometimes the numbered 1st-class/Pullman seats get sold out. Lines are always long. Seats sell out fast because travel agencies buy them for resale at a commission of US$2 to US$4. This is OK if you don't want to stand in line for hours but a pain if you are on a budget. The ticket office opens at 8 am; arrive early. Arequipa tickets are sold on the day of travel. It is quicker and cheaper to take the bus to Juliaca and continue by train from there.

To/From Bolivia Bolivia is one hour ahead of Peru. There are two routes to Bolivia: via Yunguyo and via Desaguadero. The former is more attractive and has the added interest of a boat crossing at the Strait of Tiquina. It is longer and a little more complicated than the Desaguadero route. Usually, there's little hassle entering Bolivia at either border crossing, and you can get 90-day permits without difficulty. Beware of immigration officials trying to charge a small 'entry tax': this is not legal. You can either pay or brazen it out.

Via Yunguyo Buses from Puno to Yunguyo ($US1.50, 2½ hours) leave from the Mercado Laykakota – watch for thieves. There are moneychangers in the Yunguyo plaza and by the border, which is about 2km away. Count your money carefully. The border is open from 8 am to 6 pm daily. Bolivian immigration is 1km beyond the border. Taxis are available. Copacabana is the first town in Bolivia, about 10km away. There is more frequent transport on Sunday, market day in Yunguyo. Copacabana is a much more pleasant place than Yunguyo to break the journey, and has several hotels.

Several buses a day leave Copacabana for La Paz (US$5, five hours, including a boat crossing of the Strait of Tiquina). If you leave Puno early, you can reach La Paz in one day. It is more convenient to buy a Puno–La Paz ticket with a company such as Colectur, for a few extra dollars. They will drive you to Yunguyo, stop at the money exchange, show you exactly where to go for exit and entrance formalities and meet a Bolivian bus which will take you to La Paz. This through service costs about US$12.

Via Desaguadero Buses from Puno's Mercado Laykakota leave every hour or two for Desaguadero (US$2, two hours). At Desaguadero, there are basic hotels. Border hours are 8 am to 5 pm daily. There are moneychangers at the border and a casa de cambio around the corner. Several buses a

day go from Desaguadero to La Paz (US$2, 4½ hours), passing the ruins of Tiahuanaco.

Via Lake Titicaca Hydrofoil and catamaran services, combined with bus, link Puno to La Paz but cost about US$150.

Boats from the new Puno dock (a few kilometers north of town) leave for various islands in the lake (see Around Puno). Tickets bought directly from the boats are always cheaper than those from agencies in town.

Getting Around
Tricycle taxis are a popular way of getting around Puno and are a little cheaper than ordinary taxis (US$0.50 per ride).

AROUND PUNO
Sillustani
The southern 'quarter' of the Inca empire was Collasuyo, named after the Collas, who became part of the empire. Colla nobles were buried in *chullpas* (funerary towers) at Sillustani, a small hilltop site on a peninsula in Lake Umayo. The chullpas are up to 12m high and look impressive against the bleak landscape.

Getting There & Away Tours leave at 2 pm from near All Ways Travel on Tacna, or they will pick you up at your hotel. Tours start at US$5, which includes entry to the ruins (US$2.50). Not all guides speak English. The round trip is 3½ hours with 1½ hours at the ruins. For more time at the site, a taxi is US$15.

Floating Islands
The excursion to the floating islands of the Uros people has become somewhat overcommercialized. Despite this, it remains popular because there is nothing quite like it anywhere else.

The Uros have intermarried with Aymaraspeaking Indians, and no pure-blooded Uros remain. Always a small tribe, they began their unusual floating existence to isolate themselves from the Collas and the Incas. About 300 people live on the islands.

The Uros' lives are totally interwoven with the *totora* reed, which grows abundantly in the shallows of Lake Titicaca. They harvest these reeds and use them to make everything, from the islands themselves to little model boats to sell to tourists. The islands are constructed from many layers of reeds, which rot away from the bottom and are replaced at the top. The 'ground' is soft and springy, so step carefully.

The Uros build canoe-shaped boats from tightly bundled reeds. A well-constructed boat carries a whole family and lasts six months. You can pay the Uros to give you a ride on a boat. Begging and selling is common here, and be prepared to tip for taking photographs. One island has a 7m-high rickety platform from which you can view the islands for US$0.50.

Getting There & Away Boats leave the Puno dock every hour from about 7 am until early afternoon. The standard trip (about four hours) takes in the main island and perhaps one other. The boats leave as soon as there are 15 to 20 passengers and charge about US$3.50 each. Tour companies charge US$5 or more, and leave at 9 am for a half-day tour.

Isla Taquile

Taquile is a fascinating island. The people wear colorful traditional clothes, which they make themselves and sell in the island's cooperative store. They speak Quechua and have maintained a strong group identity. The island does not have roads, and electricity was introduced in the 1990s; there are no vehicles and almost no dogs. The island is 6km or 7km long, and has several hills with pre-Inca terracing and small ruins. Visitors can wander around, exploring these ruins and enjoying the peaceful scenery.

Special Events Saint James' Day (July 25) is a big fiesta, and dancing, music and carousing go on from mid-July till the beginning of August, when the Indians traditionally make offerings to Paccha Mama (Mother Earth). New Year's Day is also festive and rowdy.

Many islanders go to Puno for La Virgen de la Candelaria and Puno week, and Taquile is liable to be somewhat deserted then.

Places to Stay & Eat From the dock, a steep stairway leads to the island center. The climb takes at least 20 minutes (not recommended unless you're acclimatized). In the center, individuals or small groups are assigned to families who will put you up in their houses. These are rustic, but there are

no hotels. The charge is US$3 per person and gifts of fresh food are appreciated. You are given blankets, but bring a sleeping bag, as it gets very cold. Facilities are minimal. A flash light is essential.

A few simple restaurants in the island center sell whatever is available: fresh lake trout, boiled potatoes or eggs. Bottled drinks are available, but are pricey and on occasion run out. Beware of overcharging in restaurants. Boiled tea is usually safe to drink, but it's a good idea to bring purified water. Also bring extra food, unless you want to take pot luck on what's available in the restaurants. Bring small bills (change is limited) and extra money for the unique clothes on sale.

Getting There & Away Boats for Taquile leave from the Puno dock daily, at about 8 or 9 am; show up by 7 am. The 24km passage takes four hours (sometimes including a brief stop at the Floating Islands) and costs US$6 one way. You get about two hours on Taquile, and the return trip leaves at 2:30 pm, arriving in Puno around nightfall. Bring sunscreen for this long trip. There is one boat owned by Taquileños, usually with islanders on it, others belong to travel agencies. If you are not planning to stay, an organized tour combining Uros and Taquile costs US$8.

Isla Amantaní

This island a few kilometers north of Taquile is less visited and has fewer facilities. Basic room and board is available for US$4 per day, or pay US$2 to sleep and eat in one of the few 'restaurants.' Boats leave from Puno's dock between 7:30 and 8:30 am on most days. The trip costs US$6.

You can make a roundtrip from Puno to the floating islands, Amantaní and Taquile. Most boats to Amantaní stop at the floating islands, and you stay overnight on Amantaní. There is a boat from Amantaní to Taquile on most days. Puno tour agencies offer two-day trips, staying overnight in Amantaní and also visiting the floating islands and Taquile, for US$12. Two-night tours are also available.

South Shore Towns

An interesting bus excursion can be made to Chimu, Chucuito, Ilave, Juli, Pomata and Zepita, on Lake Titicaca's south shore. If you start early, you can visit all of them in one day and be back in Puno for the night, or continue to Bolivia.

The road east of Puno follows the edge of the lake. After 8km, you reach the village of **Chimu**, famous for its totora-reed industry. Bundles of reeds are seen piled up to dry, and there are often reed boats in various stages of construction.

Juli, 80km southeast of Puno, is famous for its four colonial churches, which are being slowly restored. San Juan Bautista, the oldest, dates from the late 1500s, and has richly framed colonial paintings. This church is now a museum, usually open in the morning. Market day is Thursday. There is a basic alojamiento.

Pomata, 106km from Puno, is dominated by the Dominican church atop a small hill. The church, which is being restored, has many Baroque carvings, and windows made of translucent alabaster; hours are erratic. There is a basic place to stay.

Just beyond Pomata, the road forks. The main road continues southeast through **Zepita** (where there is another colonial church) to the Bolivian border at Desaguadero, while a side road hugs the shore of Lake Titicaca and goes to the other border crossing, at Yunguyo.

Getting There & Away Buses to these places leave frequently from Puno's Mercado Laykakota, on the Av Ejército side. See Puno for details.

Cuzco

Cuzco was the capital of the Inca empire, and most of Cuzco's central streets are lined with Inca-built stone walls, which now form the foundations of colonial or modern buildings. The streets are often stepped and narrow and crowded with Quechua-speaking descendants of the Incas. Cuzco is the archaeological capital of the Americas and the oldest continuously inhabited city on the continent. Today, it is the capital of its department and has 300,000 inhabitants. It is the hub of the South American travel network. The elevation is 3326m.

History
Several poorly known cultures lived here before the Incas arrived in the 12th century.

Around 1438, the ninth Inca, Pachacutec, defeated the Chancas who were attempting to take over Cuzco, and during the next 25 years he conquered most of the central Peruvian Andes. Pachacutec was a great urban developer. He devised the famous puma shape of Cuzco and diverted the Sapphi and Tullumayo rivers into channels that crossed the city, providing water and keeping the city clean. He built agricultural terraces and many buildings, including the famous Coricancha temple and his palace on what is now the western corner of the Plaza de Armas.

By 1532 Atahualpa had defeated his half-brother Huáscar in the Inca civil war. The conquistador Pizarro exploited this situation, marching into Cuzco after taking Atahualpa prisoner, and later having him killed. Pizarro was permitted into the heart of the empire by a people whose sympathy lay more with the defeated Huáscar than with Atahualpa. After Atahualpa was killed, Manco Inca was appointed by Pizarro as a puppet ruler of the Inca. (See History in the Facts about South America chapter.)

Once Cuzco had been captured, looted and settled, its importance declined. In 1535, Pizarro founded his capital at Lima. By 1600, Cuzco was a quiet colonial town, with all the gold and silver gone and many of the Inca buildings pulled down to make room for churches and colonial houses. Despite this, enough remains of the Inca foundations to make a walk around the heart of Cuzco a veritable journey back through time.

Orientation
Cuzco's heart is the Plaza de Armas and Av Sol is the main business street. Streets to the north or east of the plaza have changed little in centuries; many are for pedestrians only. The pedestrian street between the Plaza del Tricentenario and Huaynapata gives great views over the Plaza de Armas. Recently, the city has had a resurgence of Quechua pride and the official names of many streets have changed from Spanish to Quechua spellings. Cuzco has become Qosco, Cuichipunco has become K'uychipunko etc. Many people (and maps) still use the old names.

Information
Tourist Offices The very professional tourist office (☎ 084-263176) is at Portal Mantas 188, across from La Merced church. It's open 8 am

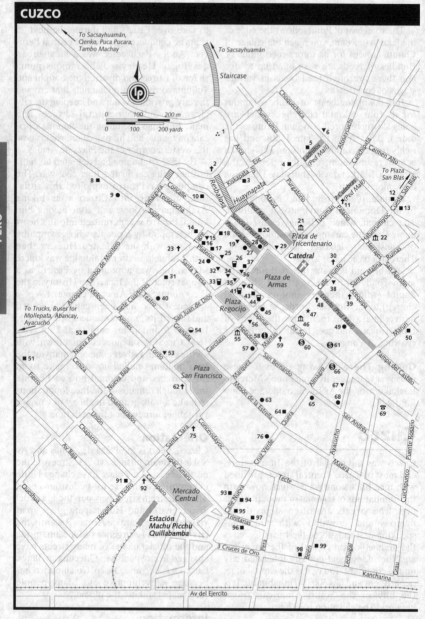

CUZCO

To Sacsayhuamán,
Qenko, Puca Pucara,
Tambo Machay

To Sacsayhuamán

Staircase

0   100   200 m
0   100   200 yards

Plaza de Tricentenario

Plaza de Armas

Plaza Regocijo

Plaza San Francisco

Mercado Central

Estación Machu Picchu Quillabamba

To Trucks, Buses for
Mollepata, Abancay,
Ayacucho

To Plaza
San Blas

Av del Ejercito

CUZCO

PLACES TO STAY
3 Albergue Municipal
4 Hostal Huaynapata
5 Hostal El Arqueólogo
8 Hostal Familiar
10 Hostal Corihuasi
12 Hostal Amaru
13 Hostal San Blas
14 Hostal Residencial Rojas
16 Hospedaje Qoñi Wasi
17 Hostal Cáceres
18 Hostal Royal Qosco
20 Hostal Suecia I
31 Hostal Tumi I
37 Hostal Incawasi
43 Hostal Chaski
50 Hostal Wasichay
51 Pensión Q'oñi Wasi
52 Hostal Qorichaski
64 Gran Hostal Machu Picchu
71 Santo Domingo Convent
91 Hotel Imperio
93 Hostales Comercio &
   San Pedro
94 Hostal La Posada
95 Hostal Milan
96 Hostal San Martín
97 Hostal Trinitarias,
   Hispano
98 Hostal Tambo Real
99 Hotel Belén

PLACES TO EAT
6 Quinta Eulalia
15 Victor Victoria &
   Miski Wasi
19 Chez Maggy & Others
25 Kusikuy
29 El Ayllu & La Yunta
32 Café Haylliy & Others
34 Pucará & Other Restaurants
35 Govinda Vegetarian
   Restaurant, Café Varayoc
36 Inka Restaurant
38 Restaurant El Paititi
42 El Mesón de los Espaderos
53 Restaurant El Tordo
56 La Mamma Pizzería,
   Other Italian Restaurants
67 Chef Victor
102 La Peña de Don Luis

OTHER
1 Colcampata Ruins
2 San Cristóbal Church
7 San Blas Church
9 Teatro Inti Raymi
11 San Antonio Church
21 Museo de Arqueología
22 Museo de Arte Religioso
23 Santa Teresa Church
24 Explorers Inn,
   Tambo Lodge Offices

26 Ukukus Bar
27 Cuzco Amazónico Lodge
28 American Express &
   Lima Tours
30 El Triunfo Church
33 Kamikaze Bar
39 Convento, Museo de
   Santa Catalina
40 Customs
41 Kerara Jazz Bar &
   Mama Africa Pub
44 Cross Keys Pub
45 Café Internet
46 Museo de Historia Natural
47 Policía de Turismo
48 La Compañía Church
52 Craft Market
54 Buses to Abancay,
   Andahuaylas
55 Museo de Historia Regional
57 Farmacia Internacional
58 Tourist Office
59 La Merced
60 Banco Latino
61 Banco de Crédito
62 San Francisco Church
63 Teatro Municipal
65 Inca Craft Market
66 Banco de la Nación
68 Centro Comercial Cuzco
69 Telefónica del Perú

70 Coricancha Ruins,
   Santo Domingo
72 Transportes Chicón &
   Transportes Pitusiray
73 Minibuses to Pisac
74 Ormeño Buses
75 Santa Clara Church
76 Excel Language Center
77 Aventours
78 Manu Nature Tours
79 Milla Turismo
80 Explorandes
81 Peruvian Andean Treks,
   Tambopata Jungle Lodge
82 Qosco Centre of Native
   Dance
83 Migraciones (Immigration)
84 Central Post Office
85 Tumi's Language Center
86 Transportes Oropesa
87 Transportes Collasuyo
88 Expreso Cometa Buses
89 CIVA Buses
90 Cruz del Sur Buses
92 San Pedro Church
100 Waterfall Monument
101 Manu Expeditions

PERU

to 6:45 pm weekdays, and 8 am to 2 pm on Saturday. Cuzco 'Visitor Tickets' are sold here, at Av Sol 106 and at some of the sites. They cost US$10 (US$5 for students with ID), are good for 10 days and are good for admission to 16 sites in the Cuzco area (opening hours for all sites are printed on the back). You need one if you plan to visit any of the sites in and around the city. There is a slightly cheaper option, the *boleto parcial* (US$6) to visit sites near Cuzco, but they are only good for one day.

Visa Extensions The immigration office, on Av Sol next to the post office, renews tourist cards 7:45 am to 2 pm weekdays. An extension costs US$20 for 30 days.

Money Traveler's checks are accepted by a few casas de cambio on the plaza or along Av Sol and at the Banco Latino. Street moneychangers hang out at the plaza end of Av Sol. Rates for cash vary little; street changers and casas de cambio are quicker than banks. Count money carefully before handing over your dollars.

American Express at Lima Tours, on the Plaza de Armas, doesn't refund lost traveler's checks (you must go to Lima).

Post & Communications The central post office, open 8 am to 8 pm Monday to Saturday, holds mail for three months when addressed to you c/o Lista de Correos, Correo Central, Cuzco, Peru. Telefónica del Perú (☎ 084-241111) on Av Sol will hold incoming faxes for a fee. It's open 7 am to 11:30 pm daily. For Internet access, try Café Internet (☎ 084-242424) at Calle del Medio 117, off Plaza de Armas. They charge US$2 per hour, with discounts after 9 pm.

Travel Agencies There are 222 registered travel and tour agencies in Cuzco. The best are expensive. The cheaper ones change addresses often and have been criticized for being unreliable. Compare notes with other travelers and shop around.

Emergency The best clinic is the Hospital Regional (☎ 084-231131), on Av de la Cultura. The Policía de Turismo (☎ 084-252974) are helpful. They are stationed on the Plaza, at Portal de Carrizos 250, but move often.

Dangers & Annoyances Many tourists attract many thieves. Avoid displays of wealth (expensive jewelry, wristwatches, wallets) and leave most of your money in a hotel safe (carry what you need in inside pockets and money belts). Avoid walking alone around town late at night; revelers returning from bars late at night have been mugged. Take special care going to and from the Machu Picchu train station and the nearby market; these are prime areas for pickpockets and bag-slashers. Beware also of con artists who swindle foreigners with elaborate stories. While most visitors leave Cuzco unscathed, there are plenty of travelers who have reported unfortunate experiences. Be vigilant and use common sense.

Things to See

Buy a Cuzco visitor ticket (see Information), which gives entry to the Catedral, Santo Domingo and Coricancha, San Blas, Santa Catalina, the Museo de Historia Regional and the Museo de Arte Religioso. Outside Cuzco it is valid at Sacsayhuamán, Qenko, Puca Pucara, Tambo Machay, Pisac, Chinchero, Ollantaytambo and Piquillacta. Each site can be visited once. Other places in and around Cuzco can be visited for free, or by paying a modest admission fee. Opening hours change frequently.

Plaza de Armas Two flags fly over the plaza: the red-and-white Peruvian flag, and the rainbow flag of Tahuantinsuyo – the four quarters of the Inca empire. The plaza has colonial arcades on all sides. The Catedral is to the northeast and the ornate church of La Compañía to the southeast. Some Inca walls remain, notably from Pachacutec's palace on the western corner. The pedestrian alleyway of Loreto is a quiet and historic way to enter or leave the plaza. Both sides of Loreto have Inca walls.

Churches Begun in 1559, the **Catedral** is one of the city's greatest repositories of colonial art. It is joined with two other churches: to the left is the **Iglesia Jesus María**, dating from 1733, and to the right is the **Iglesia El Triunfo**, which is the tourist entrance to the three-church complex. El Triunfo is the oldest church in Cuzco and dates from 1536.

Near the entrance of El Triunfo is a vault with the remains of the Inca historian Garcilaso de la Vega, born in Cuzco in 1539. In the northeastern corner of the cathedral is a huge painting of the *Last Supper*, by Marcos Zapata, an example of the Cuzco school. The supper includes the Inca delicacy, *cuy* (guinea pig). In the rear of the cathedral is the original wooden altar, behind a new silver altar. Opposite the silver altar is the magnificently carved choir, dating from the 17th century. There are many splendid side chapels. Some contain the elaborate silver trolleys used to cart religious statues around during processions. Others have intricate altars. It's open 10 to 11:30 am and 2 to 5:30 pm. Admission is with the Cuzco visitor ticket. The huge main doors are open for worship from 6 to 10 am (no ticket required, but tourism is forbidden at that time).

La Compañía is also on the plaza and is often lit up at night. It has a painstaking baroque façade and is one of Cuzco's most ornate churches. Its foundations contain stones from the palace of the Inca Huayna Capac. The interior has fine paintings and richly carved altars. Two large canvases near the main door depict early marriages in Cuzco and are noteworthy for their wealth of period detail. The 1986 earthquake damaged the church badly, but it has been repaired.

La Merced dates from 1654; an earlier church was destroyed in the 1650 earthquake. Hours of worship are 7 to 9 am and 5 to 7:30 pm. Left of the church is the monastery and museum, open 8 am to noon and 2 to 5 pm Monday to Saturday. Entry is US$1. The museum contains conquistador/friar Vicente de Valverde's vestments, religious art and a priceless gold monstrance, 1.3m high and covered with 1500 diamonds and 1600 pearls.

The 16th- and 17th-century church and monastery of **San Francisco** has a well-carved cedar choir and a large collection of colonial religious paintings, one of which shows the family tree of St Francis of Assisi and is supposedly the largest in South America. There are two crypts with human bones. San Francisco is currently closed for restoration but will reopen soon.

You can enter the following with the Cuzco visitor ticket. The adobe church of **San Blas** has a pulpit considered the finest

example of colonial woodcarving in the Americas. The gold-leaf main altar has been restored. It's open Monday to Saturday from 10 am to 11:30 and 2 to 5:30 pm. The convent of **Santa Catalina** has a colonial and religious art museum, with statues and ornate wall friezes. It's open Monday to Saturday from 9 am to 5:30 pm. On the site of Coricancha is the church of **Santo Domingo**, which was destroyed by the 1650 earthquake and badly damaged by the 1950 earthquake. Photographs detail the extent of the 1950 damage. Compare the colonial building with the Inca walls, which survived these earthquakes with minimal effects. Inside the cloister are the Inca temple remains. It's open 8 am to 5 pm Monday to Saturday.

Inca Ruins Coricancha is Quechua for 'Golden Courtyard.' In Inca times, the walls of Coricancha were lined with 700 solid-gold sheets weighing 2kg apiece. There were life-size gold and silver replicas of corn, which were ritually 'planted' in agricultural ceremonies. All that remains is the stonework; the conquistadors took the rest. Coricancha was used for religious rites. Mummified bodies of Incas were kept here and brought out into the sunlight every day. Food and drink were offered to them and then ritually burnt. Coricancha was also an observatory, where priests kept track of major celestial events.

A perfectly fitted, curved, 6m wall can be seen from outside the site. It has withstood Cuzco's earthquakes. The courtyard inside has an octagonal font, once covered with 55kg of solid gold. There are Inca temples to either side of the courtyard. The largest, to the right, are said to be temples to the moon and stars, and were perhaps covered with solid silver. The walls taper upwards, and the niches and doorways are fine examples of Inca trapezoidal stonework. Opposite these chambers are the smaller temples, dedicated to thunder and the rainbow.

Leaving the Plaza de Armas along the Loreto alley, you have Inca walls on both sides. On the right is Amarucancha (Courtyard of the Serpents), the site of the palace of Inca Huayna Capac. After the conquest, the church of La Compañía was built here. On the left side is the oldest Inca wall in Cuzco, part of the Acllahuasi (House of the

PERU

Chosen Women). After the conquest, it became part of Santa Catalina.

Leaving the plaza along Calle Triunfo you reach the street of Hatunrumiyoc, named after the great 12-sided stone on the right of the second city block; Indians often sell souvenirs next to it. This excellently fitted stone is part of the palace of the sixth Inca, Roca. There are dozens of other Inca walls to see.

Museums Inside the **Museo de Arqueología**, at the corner of Tucumán and Ataúd, is a massive stairway guarded by sculptures of mythical creatures. A corner window column looks like a statue of a bearded man, until you go outside, from where it appears to be a naked woman. The building has been restored in colonial style and is filled with metal and gold work, jewelry, pottery, textiles, mummies and wooden *queros* (Inca vases). The ceilings are ornate and the views are good, but the collection is poorly labeled in Spanish. Entrance costs US$2 and it's open 8 am to 6 pm daily.

Also known as the Archbishop's Palace, the **Museo de Arte Religioso**, on Hatunrumiyoc, has a fine collection of religious art noted for the accuracy of period detail. There are fine stained-glass windows and colonial-style tilework (not original). It's open 8 to 11:30 am and 3 to 5:30 pm Monday to Saturday. Entry is by Cuzco visitor ticket, as it is for the **Museo de Historia Regional** in the Casa Garcilaso de la Vega, home of the famous Cuzco chronicler. There is a small, chronologically arranged but poorly labeled archaeological collection. Art of the Cuzco school as well as more recent mestizo art is displayed and there are changing local art shows. It's open 8 am to 5:30 pm Monday to Saturday.

Markets The best area to buy local craftwork and see it made is the Plaza San Blas and the streets leading up to it from the Plaza de Armas. The Mercado Central is a colorful affair in front of the church of San Pedro. Don't bring a camera or much money, because the thieves are extremely persistent and professional. There are craft markets on the corner of Quera and San Bernardo, and every night under the arches around the Plazas de Armas and Regocijo. Jewelry, woodcarving, painting and ceramics workshops in the San Blas neighborhood open their doors to visitors.

Language Courses

The Excel language center (☎ 084-235298; esl-ex@qenqo.rep.net.pe), Cruz Verde 336, is recommended. It arranges homestays with local families. Check its website (www.cbc.org.pe/excel/program.htm) for course details. Tumi's, Ahuacpinta 732, offers lessons for US$3 an hour and will arrange homestays. Miguel Gonzalez (☎ 084-222131) offers private lessons.

Organized Tours

Standard tours include a half-day city tour, a half-day tour of the nearby ruins (Sacsayhuamán, Qenko, Puca Pucara and Tambo Machay), a half-day trip to the Sunday markets at Pisac or Chinchero, a full-day tour to the Sacred Valley (Pisac and Ollantaytambo and perhaps Chinchero) and a full-day tour to Machu Picchu. There are many tour companies and most of them do a good job. The cheaper tours are crowded, multilingual affairs. You can visit all the places mentioned using public transport.

Many agencies run adventure trips. Rafting the Urubamba for one or two days is popular (around US$30 a day). The Inca Trail is also popular; you can hire porters, cooks and guides, or just rent equipment (about US$2 per item per day) and carry it yourself. The cheapest tours are US$60 with the highly recommended United Mice, (☎ 084-221139) at Plateros 351. There are several other cheap agencies on Procuradores and around the Plaza de Armas. Mountaineering, horseback-riding, mountain-biking and jungle trekking trips are also available.

Special Events

Inti Raymi, the sun festival, is on June 24 and is Cuzco's most important festival. It attracts tourists from all over the world, and the entire city celebrates in the streets. The festival culminates in a reenactment of the Inca winter solstice festival at Sacsayhuamán. Reserved tourist tickets in the bleachers are US$35 to US$40, or you can sit with the locals on the stone ruins for free.

Held on the Monday before Easter, the procession of El Señor de los Temblores (Lord of the Earthquakes) dates from the 1650 earthquake. The feast of Corpus Christi takes place in early June (usually the ninth Thursday following Easter), with fantastic religious processions and celebrations in the Catedral.

Places to Stay

Accommodations are difficult to find from June to August, especially during the 10 days before Inti Raymi and around the Fiestas Patrias (July 28-29) when prices rise. During other times, try bargaining for better rates; many hotels are half-empty. Budget travelers find the best cheap hotels are in poor areas, and taking cabs or going in groups is advised after dark. The tourist office has a useful new brochure with inexpensive *hospedajes familiares* for Cuzco, Aguas Calientes, Pisac and Ollantaytambo, some of which are listed below. Most hotels will store luggage for a few days while you hike the Inca Trail. Lock and label your luggage, don't leave valuables and ask for a receipt. Haphazard water supplies are the norm and hot water is on for a few hours each day.

Hostal Royal Qosco (☎ 084-226221), Tecsecocha 2, is popular with budget travelers. The *Santo Domingo Convent* (☎/fax 084-225484), on the Colegio Martín de Porres grounds at Ahuacpinta 600, is clean, safe and friendly and has 24-hour hot water. Rates are US$6 per person with shared bath, or US$7 with private bath. The basic, clean and friendly *Hostal Qorichaski* (☎ 084-228974), Nueva Alta 458, is US$6/10 with general bath, hot water and breakfast. *Hostal Tumi I*, Siete Cuartones 245, is friendly with hot water at US$5 per person. *Hostal Suecia I* (☎ 084-233282), Suecia 332, is popular with budget travelers, though thefts have been reported. There is hot water, and rooms are US$7 per person. *Hostal Residencial Rojas* (☎ 084-228184), Tigre 129, is basic but OK for US10/13.50 single/double or US$20 for a double with bath and hot water. *Hostal Cáceres* (☎ 084-228012), Plateros 368, has hot water and is reasonable at US$5 per person. The basic *Hostal Chaski* (☎ 084-236093), Portal Confitería 257 on the plaza, charges US$10 or US$17 with bath.

There are good hotels near the Mercado Central but in an unsafe area. *Hotel Imperio* (☎ 084-228981), Chaparro 121, is clean, very friendly and helpful and has hot water. Rates are US$7 per person without bath. In the same area are the similarly priced *Hostales San Pedro* and *La Posada* and

then, in increasing order of price (up to about US$15 a double with bath), are the *San Martín, Comercio, Belén, Trinitarias, Milan* and *Hispano*. All are OK and have hot water. The friendly and helpful *Hostal Tambo Real* (☎ 084-221621), Belén 588, is US$10/15 with bath and hot showers.

Another area for rock-bottom prices is around the Puno train station, which is unsafe at night. These places aren't marked on the map.

Hostal Chavín II (☎ 084-224175), Cuichipunco 299, charges US$5/7 or a little more with bath. *Hospedaje Qoñi Wasi* (☎ 084-240743), Tigre 124, charges US$4 per person in shared rooms. *Albergue Municipal* (☎ 084-252506), Kiskapata 240, has a balcony with fine city views, helpful owners, hot water, a small café and laundry facilities. Clean rooms have four to eight bunk beds at US$6 each, but the area is not safe at night; take a cab. Also in this area is the friendly *Hostal Huaynapata* (☎ 084-228034), at Huaynapata 369, at US$20/25 for clean rooms with bath and breakfast, or half of that with shared bath. Nearby, the *Hostal El Arqueólogo* (☎ 084-232569), Ladrillos 425, is clean and has hot water, kitchen privileges and a nice garden. It's popular with French tourists. Rates are US$30 for a double with bath, less without. *Hostal Wasichay* (☎ 084-224215), Maruri 312, is a good clean and friendly mid-range choice at US$20/30/40 for singles/doubles/triples with private bath and TV, breakfast included. Another option is the *Hostal Corihuasi* (☎/fax 084-232233), Suecia 561, at US$28/38 a singles/doubles, some with great views, with bath and breakfast. There's a café.

The clean, friendly *Gran Hostal Machu Picchu* (☎ 084-231111), Quera 282, asks US$6 per person, or US$8.50 with private hot water bath, for rooms around two pleasant patios. *Hostal Familiar* (☎ 084-239353), Saphi 661, has doubles for US$5 or US$12 with bath. It is clean, popular and often full. *Hostal Incawasi* (☎ 084-233992), Portal de Panes 143, is well located on the plaza and is US$13/18, with shared bath, or US$18/25 with private bath. The friendly *Hostal San Blas* (☎ 084-225781), Cuesta San Blas 526, is US$12/15 or US$18/22 with bath. Across the street is the *Hostal Amaru* (☎ 084-225933), San Blas 541, with rooms for US$15/20 with bath, or US$7/13 without.

Places to Eat

Breakfast & Snacks The simple and reasonably priced *El Ayllu* café, next to the Catedral, is popular. It plays classical music and has good juices, coffee, tea, yogurt, cakes, sandwiches and other snacks. Next door, the equally popular *La Yunta* also serves juices, good chocolate cake, coffee and light meals. *Café Haylliy*, on the first block of Plateros, is also good for cheap breakfasts and lunches. *Café Varayoc*, on Espaderos, is another good choice.

Peruvian Food A few restaurants serve typical Peruvian food, have outside patios and are open for lunch or afternoon snacks only. Cuy may need to be ordered a day in advance. Also try anticucho de corazón (beef-heart shish kebab), rocoto relleno (spicy bell peppers stuffed with ground beef and vegetables), adobo (spicy pork stew), chicharrones (deep-fried meat chunks), choclo con queso (corn on the cob with cheese), tamales (boiled corn dumplings filled with cheese or meat and wrapped in a banana leaf), cancha (toasted corn) and various locros (hearty soups and stews). Meals are washed down with chicha – either a fruit drink or a fermented, mildly alcoholic corn beer.

Quinta Eulalia (☎ 084-224951), Choquechaca 384 (no sign), has a colorful courtyard. Further afield is *Quinta Zárate* (☎ 084-238219), in a garden on Calle Tortera Paccha – not easy to find, so hire a taxi. *La Peña de Don Luis*, on Av Regional, is popular with locals for lunch. There are hole-in-the-wall places along Pampa del Castillo serving chicharrones right off the grill, which is often placed in the door of the restaurant.

Other local restaurants serve fish, chicken and meat, with a small selection of the more traditional dishes. Just off the plaza, along the first block of Calle Plateros, there are several good restaurants. These include *El Tronquito* and *Los Candiles* (good, cheap set meals), *Kusikuy* (with the best selection of traditional dishes) and *Pucará* that, with dishes in the US$4 to US$10 range, is the most expensive on this block but also serves the best food.

Around the corner on Calle Tigre are recommended budget restaurants *Victor Victoria* and *Miski Wasi*. Other recommended budget places include *Chef Victor*, Ayacucho 217, and the chicken restaurant next to the Hostal del Inca on Quera.

On the Plaza de Armas, the *Inka Restaurant* and *El Paititi* both have Inca walls. El Paititi is pricey but good. Inka is cheaper and hosts a peña at night, for which there is a cover charge. *El Mesón de los Espaderos*, Espaderos 105 (upstairs), serves parrillada (mixed grill), steak, chicken and cuy. Get there early for a seat in the attractively carved balcony overlooking the plaza.

Vegetarian Food *Govinda* vegetarian restaurant on Espaderos is cheap and adequate, with slow service. Their homemade bread lasts for days – good for the Inca Trail. The clean *Restaurant El Tordo*, Tordo 238, has good cheap vegetarian food. Vegetables used for salads are washed in iodized water.

Other Food Procuradores has several popular cheap restaurants including *Chez Maggy Pizzería*, *Mia Pizza* and *Los Cuates* Mexican restaurant. There's another *Chez Maggy* on Plateros, as well as *Pizzería América*. These often have live music (a hat is passed for tips). Other Italian places surround Plaza Regocijo.

Entertainment

Ukukus Bar, Plateros 316, has live and recorded music, with plenty of dancing and is popular with travelers. There's a happy hour from 8 to 9:30 pm, and a US$1.50 cover charge after 9:30 pm. The older *Kamikaze*, at the northwest corner of Plaza Regocijo, has lively taped music and live performers (usually from 10:30 pm). Happy hour is 8:30 to 9:30 pm and the cover charge varies.

The *Cross Keys Pub*, Portal Confituría 233, identified on the plaza by the huge keys hanging outside, is an English pub run by British ornithologist Barry Walker. He knows the area well and is a good contact for the Manu area. There is a dart board and pool and it's a great meeting place where you can talk without having to scream over the music. It's pricier than other places, though there are 6 to 7 pm and 9 to 9:30 pm happy hours (beer not included). *Tumi's Video Bar*, Saphi 456-478, shows films on a 52-inch screen and has a friendly bar. It has pool and darts, is open for lunch and has an 8 to 9 pm happy hour.

A newer upmarket place is the **Kerara Jazz Bar**, on Espaderos featuring seven different bars with various attractions. In the same building is the **Mama Africa Pub**, which has good live music.

Shopping

Cuzco offers a tremendous variety of woolens, gold and silver jewelry and art. Prices and quality vary. For high quality fabrics and other alpaca products, as well as jewelry visit Arte Perú, at the corner of Plateros and Espaderos. Around the plaza look for watercolors by local artists, especially those by Irma Valdivia and her husband. For silver jewelry and ornaments, check the workshop of the Camero family at Palacio 122, where bargaining is acceptable.

Getting There & Away

Air LAB flies almost daily to La Paz (US$96) during the high season.

There are several flights a day to and from Lima (US$120) with AeroContinente. Many get canceled or lumped together with another flight during low periods. The earliest flights are less likely to be canceled. There are one to three flights a day to Arequipa (US$53), Juliaca (US$53) and Puerto Maldonado (US$39). Same-day connections to some northern cities via Lima can be arranged. Flights may be overbooked in the high season, so confirm and reconfirm your flights.

AeroContinente (☎ 084-235666) is at Portal de Harinas 181, on the Plaza de Armas. Other airline offices are along Av Sol or on the Plaza de Armas (see Cuzco map). The military airline, Grupo Ocho, occasionally sells hard-to-get tickets at the airport for its flights to Lima and Puerto Maldonado.

Bus & Truck Buses to Pisac, Calca and Urubamba leave frequently with Transportes Pitusiray from Av Tullumayo from 5:30 am until dusk. Transportes Chicón, nearby, has buses to Chinchero, some continuing to Urubamba and Ollantaytambo, all day. (These stations change locations every year or two.) It takes 2 hours to Urubamba (US$0.80) and one hour to Pisac (US$0.70). Buses are crowded.

Buses to Oropesa, Urcos, Sicuani and Ocongate leave from the Coliseo Cerrado on Manco Capac, 5 blocks east of Tacna. Urcos buses also leave from Av de la Cultura between the university and the Hospital Regional. Take these buses to visit the ruins of Tipón, Pikillacta, Rumicolca and Raqchi.

Trucks for Limatambo, Mollepata, Abancay and other destinations leave from Arcopata, or you can take a bus to Abancay from the same street. A few companies on Granada have buses to Abancay (US$5, eight hours) and Andahuaylas (US$9, 14 hours) leaving at 6 am, 10 am and 1 pm. To continue to Ayacucho, change at Andahuaylas. Empresa Andahuaylas on Arcopata has buses to Ayacucho (US$18) at 6 am, with an overnight stay in Andahuaylas. This road has improved somewhat and is very cold at night. Cramped minibuses are often used.

There are no buses to the southeastern jungles except for those to Quillabamba (US$6, 10 hours) every night with several companies around the Terminal Puqutupampa, near the Almudena Cemetery, in the southwest part of town. A taxi from the Plaza de Armas is US$0.60. In 1998 buses were taking the north route, via Calca on the Valle de Lares, due to the flood damages left by El Niño. Trucks to Puerto Maldonado (2½ days in the dry season, but now even longer because of El Niño) leave from two blocks east of Tacna along Av Garcilaso, or you can get a bus to Urcos or Ocongate and wait for a truck there. Transportes Sol Andino has buses to Paucartambo (US$3.50, six hours) from the Coliseo Cerrado. Get there by 7 am for a seat or book with the Andino office on Av Huáscar. Trucks also do the journey from the Coliseo Cerrado: ask around. From Paucartambo to Manu there are passing trucks or expedition buses. From Cuzco, trucks from the Coliseo Cerrado go to Shintuyo (20 hours) for Manu; for entry restrictions see the Parque Nacional Manu section. Manu Expeditions is a good source of information, or try Explorers Transport, which advertises in popular gringo hangouts in Cuzco and runs expeditions to Manu at irregular intervals.

Cruz del Sur (☎ 084-233383), on Pachacutec, has day buses to Sicuani and night buses to Juliaca and Puno (US$12, 14 hours). The road is bad and the train is more comfortable. The same company has a nightly service to Arequipa via Imata (US$12, 16 hours) – also a rough journey. This service continues to Lima (US$24, 40 hours). Expect delays in the rainy season. Bandits used to work the route to Lima through Abancay and Puquio, but that seems to have stopped now. Other companies on Pachacutec have buses to southern Peruvian towns. Try Expreso Cometa, CIVA, Transportes Collasuyo and others for different prices. Ormeño, on Av Huáscar, also has buses to these destinations.

Train Cuzco has two unlinked train stations. The Huanchac station (☎ 084-233592, 084-221992), near the end of Av Sol, serves Urcos, Sicuani, Juliaca, Puno and Arequipa. The San Pedro station (☎ 084-22-1291, 084-23-8722 for reservations, 084-231207 for information), next to the Mercado Central, serves Machu Picchu and Quillabamba, although since the January 1998 floods, Aguas Calientes (deceptively known as the 'Machu Picchu Station' – it's 8km from the ruins) is now the end of the line. There is uncertainty as to when the track to Puente Ruinas and Quillabamba will be repaired.

Many people try to visit Machu Picchu in a tiring day on the tourist train. It's better to stay overnight near the ruins in Aguas Calientes. See the Machu Picchu entry for more details.

For Machu Picchu there is a cheap local train and an expensive tourist train, and they depart from different stations. The *tren local* (US$5) is the cheapest and stops everywhere. Since it is locals' only means of transportation, it is usually crowded, and it has a reputation for theft. The train leaves Cuzco at 6:45 am daily and takes four hours to Machu Picchu. It barely stops at some stations: descend quickly, particularly at Km 88.

You are better off taking the less crowded *tren expreso* that runs Monday to Saturday, leaving Cuzco at 6:20 am. Buy tickets the day before (US$9 one way). Both trains leave from the San Pedro station. The *autovagón turístico* (tourist train) leaves Cuzco's Estación Huanchac at 6 am daily and only stops at Ollantaytambo and Aguas Calientes (Puente Ruinas before the floods). Passengers may be taken part of the way by bus. The trip takes three hours one way and costs US$55 return. Travel agents sell the trip for about

US$100, including transportation to and from the train station, entry to the ruins and a guide. A cheaper possibility is the *tren Inka* at US$45 return (US$34 for Pullman class). This train leaves at 6:25 am Monday to Saturday.

The Puno train (10½ hours) leaves at 8 am on Monday, Wednesday, Friday and Saturday, reaching Juliaca at 5 pm for night train connections to Arequipa. See the Puno and Arequipa sections for fare details.

Getting Around

To/From the Airport A taxi from the airport to the center of Cuzco costs about US$2.50; the local bus costs about US$0.25.

Around Cuzco

NEARBY RUINS

These are the four ruins closest to Cuzco: Sacsayhuamán, Qenko, Puca Pucara and Tambo Machay. Admission is with the Cuzco visitor ticket. A cheap and easy way to visit them is to take a Cuzco-Pisac bus and get off at Tambo Machay, the ruin farthest from Cuzco (and, at 3700m, the highest). From here, walk 8km back to Cuzco, visiting all four ruins along the way. Colorfully dressed locals with llamas hang around the sites, hoping to be photographed. A tip of about US$0.30 per photograph is expected. This is a popular and rewarding walk, but it's best to go in a group and return before nightfall to avoid potential robbery.

Tambo Machay

This small ruin, about 300m from the main road, is a beautifully wrought ceremonial stone bath, popularly called El Baño del Inca. Opposite it is a small signaling tower, from where Puca Pucara can be seen.

Puca Pucara

The small ruin of Puca Pucara looks red in some lights; the name means 'red fort.'

Qenko

The name of this small, fascinating ruin means 'zigzag.' It is a large limestone rock covered with carvings, including zigzagging channels. These may have been for the ceremonial chicha usage. Tunnels are carved below the boulder, and there's a curious

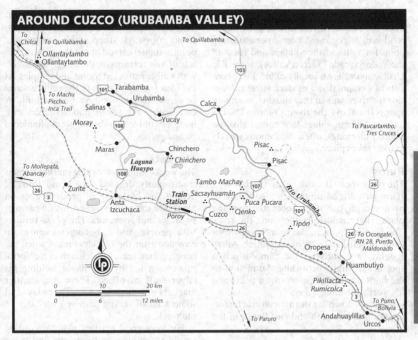

AROUND CUZCO (URUBAMBA VALLEY)

cave with altars carved into the rock. Qenko is on the left side of the road as you descend from Tambo Machay, 4km before Cuzco.

Sacsayhuamán

This huge ruin is the most impressive in the immediate Cuzco area. You can reach it from Cuzco by climbing the steep street of Resbalosa, turning right at the top and continuing until you come to a hairpin bend in the road. Here, take the old Inca road linking Cuzco with Sacsayhuamán. It takes less than an hour from Cuzco.

Sacsayhuamán (which means 'satisfied falcon') is huge, but only about 20% of the original structure remains. The Spaniards used the blocks to build their own houses in Cuzco, but they left the most impressive of the original rocks, one of which weighs more than 300 tonnes. Most of the rocks form the main battlements.

The Incas envisioned Cuzco as having a puma shape. Sacsayhuamán was the head. The site is essentially three different areas, the most obvious being the three-tiered zigzag walls of the main fortifications. These 22 zigzags form the puma's teeth. Opposite is Rodadero hill, with retaining walls, polished rocks and a finely carved series of stone benches, known as the 'throne of the Incas.' In between the zigzag ramparts and Rodadero hill lies a large, flat parade ground, which today is used for the colorful tourist spectacle of Inti Raymi, held every June 24th.

The magnificent zigzag walls are the major attraction even though much has been destroyed. Three towers stood above these walls, but only the foundations remain. It is thought the site had important religious and military significance. This was the site of one of the most bitter battles of the conquest, between the Spanish and the rebellious Manco Inca. Manco lost narrowly and retreated to Vilcabamba, but most of his forces were killed. The dead attracted flocks of Andean condors, which is why there are eight condors on Cuzco's coat of arms.

Robberies have been reported. Avoid visiting early in the morning or in the evening, and don't go alone.

PISAC

Pisac is 32km northeast of Cuzco by paved road and is the most convenient starting point for visits to the villages and ruins of the Valle Sagrado (Sacred Valley), as the Río Urubamba valley is locally called. Pisac consists of a colonial and modern village alongside the river, and an Inca site on a mountain spur 600m above the river. Colonial Pisac is a quiet Andean village that comes alive on Sunday mornings, when the famous weekly market takes place.

Ruins

The ruins above the village are reached by a 10km paved road up the Chongo valley, or by a shorter but steep footpath from the plaza. There is little traffic along the road. The 5km footpath to the ruins leaves town from the left-hand side of the church. Allow roughly two hours for the climb, which is spectacular and worthwhile. Admission to the ruins is with the Cuzco visitor ticket and it's worth spending a day.

Pisac is known for the agricultural terracing around the south and east flanks of the mountain. Above the terraces are some cliff-hanging footpaths, well defended by massive stone doorways, steep stairs and, at one point, a tunnel carved out of the rock. At the top of the terraces is the religious center, with well-constructed rooms and temples. At the back (northern end) of the ruins, a series of ceremonial baths have been rebuilt. A cliff behind the site is honeycombed with hundreds of Inca tombs that were plundered by huaqueros.

Markets

The weekly Sunday morning market attracts traditionally dressed locals and tourists. Selling and bartering of produce goes on alongside the stalls stacked with weavings, sweaters and souvenirs. The plaza throngs with people, and it becomes even more crowded after the Quechua mass, when the congregation leaves the church in a colorful procession led by the mayor holding his silver staff of office. There are smaller markets on Tuesday and Thursday and some kind of selling activity every day of the week.

For very good textiles, made according to old techniques and patterns and using natural dies, visit the weaver-owned store of the Asociación de Tejedoras de Parubamba. It sells superb ponchos, straps and other items at Bolognesi 578 (no sign) on market days. For questions or special arrangements call Dr Gail Silverman (☎ 084-240451), who speaks English and French.

Places to Stay & Eat

Parador Pisaq has two clean rooms with eight beds at US$5 each, and great views of the Plaza. There is food available. **Residencial Beho** is cheaper and has cold showers. Some families rent rooms; ask around. **Hotel & Café Pisaq** is US$10 per person for clean beds and shared hot showers, or US$13 with bath. The food is good. Right next door is the **Hospedaje Kinsa Cocha**, a modest place with basic rooms for US$3. For more accommodation in family **hospedajes** see the brochure offered at Cuzco's tourist office. **Samana Wasi** is one of the better cafés, though a bit overpriced. There are basic eateries near the bridge. Stop by the bakery near the plaza for oven-fresh flat bread rolls typical of the area.

PISAC

Path to
Pisac Ruins

To Bakery,
Road to Ruins

Plaza
de
Armas

Not to Scale

Bolognesi

To Urubamba,
Ollantaytambo

To Road to Ruins

Río Urubamba

To Cuzco

PLACES TO STAY
1 Residencial Beho
3 Parador Pisac
5 Hotel & Café Pisaq
6 Hospedaje Familiar
  Kinsa Cocha

PLACES TO EAT
4 Samana Wasi
7 Restaurant Doña
  Clorinda
9 Small Restaurants

OTHER
2 Church
8 Asociación de
  Tejedoras
  de Parubamba
10 Telefónica del Perú
11 Buses, Police, Post

Getting There & Away

Frequent minibuses leave from Cuzco. To return to Cuzco or continue to Urubamba, wait for a bus by the bridge. Note that buses to Cuzco start in Urubamba and are often full or have standing room only – prime territory for pickpockets. A taxi with four passengers costs about US$10 to Cuzco.

URUBAMBA

Urubamba is 40km beyond Pisac, at the junction of the valley and Chinchero roads. Magnificent views of the valley, more than the village itself, make the trip worthwhile.

The village of Tarabamba is about 6km further down the valley. Here, cross the river by footbridge and continue on a footpath, climbing roughly southwards up a valley for 3km farther to the salt pans of Salinas, which have been exploited since Inca times – a fascinating sight. Admission is US$1.

Places to Stay & Eat

The friendly **Hotel Urubamba** (☎ 084-201062), on Bolognesi 605 near the plaza (10 minutes from the main road), is US$10

for a double with bath, or US$3.50 per person without. Showers are cold. **Hostal Calpulli** is another cheap place in the center and the **Hostal Vera** (☎ 084-201047) on the main road, is also basic. There is nothing in between these and several pricey hotels. There are simple restaurants on the plaza and along the road leading from the main valley road into the town center.

Quinta Los Geranios restaurant, on the main valley road near the petrol station, is good for local lunches.

Getting There & Away

Buses leave Cuzco frequently from the bus stop on Av Tullumayo. Buses back to Cuzco or on to Ollantaytambo stop at the terminal on the main road.

OLLANTAYTAMBO

This is literally the end of the road: Travelers continue by rail or on foot, though there are a few passable dirt tracks into the countryside. Ollantaytambo is a major Inca site and admission is with the Cuzco visitor ticket. The site is one of the few places where the

OLLANTAYTAMBO

To Chilca

To Ocobamba, Huilloc

Car Park

Not to Scale

Main Plaza

To Cuzco

To Machu Picchu

Train Station

Rio Urubamba

To Cuzco

1	Ruins	9	Clinic
2	Juice Stands	10	Hostal Orquídeas
3	Church	11	Café Alcázar
4	Hostal Miranda	12	Telefónica del Perú
5	Hostal La Nusta	13	Ticket Office
6	Hostal Tambo	14	El Albergue
7	Crafts Shops	15	Crafts Market
8	Crafts Shops	16	Albergue Kapuly

PERU

Spaniards lost an important battle during the conquest. Below the ruins is the village of Ollantaytambo, built on traditional Inca foundations; it is the best surviving example of Inca city planning.

The Incas considered Ollantaytambo a temple, but the Spanish, after defeat, called it a fortress, and it has been referred to as such ever since. The temple area is at the top of the terracing. The stone used for these buildings was quarried from the mountainside 6km away and high above the opposite bank of the Río Urubamba. Transporting blocks from the quarry was a stupendous feat, involving the labor of thousands of Indians.

Places to Stay & Eat

Basic places for US$3 per person include the *Hostal Miranda* (☎ 084-204009), *Hostal La Ñusta* on the plaza and the super basic *Hostal Tambo* (☎ 084-204003). All three claim to have warm showers on request. *Hostal Orquídeas* is the best deal at US$10 per person with bath and breakfast. The central courtyard is very tidy, and so are the rooms. At US$15, *El Albergue Ollantaytambo* (☎/fax 084-204014), in the train station, is very tranquil, has a sauna, hot showers and garden and provides meals on request. Next door is the cheaper *Albergue Kapuly* (☎ 084-204017) at US$10 per person without bath. You'll find simple, cheap restaurants around the plaza.

Getting There & Away

Bus Minibuses leave from Urubamba's terminal several times a day, but services peter out in mid-afternoon. Buses from Cuzco are infrequent and many people change in Urubamba. Buses return to Cuzco from the plaza; several go via Chinchero.

Train All trains stop here, 1½ to two hours after leaving Cuzco. The local train is overcrowded by the time it reaches Ollantaytambo and standing room only is the rule, though there may be a few seats in 1st class. The tourist train costs the same from Ollantaytambo to Machu Picchu as it does from Cuzco. The local train is much cheaper.

CHINCHERO

This site (entry with the Cuzco visitor ticket) combines Inca ruins with an Andean Indian village, a colonial country church, mountain views and a colorful Sunday market. There is a smaller Thursday market. The main square of the village has a massive Inca wall with 10 huge trapezoidal niches. Just above the square is the colonial church, which is built on Inca foundations.

Buses leave Cuzco from Av Tullumayo a few times each day, some continuing to Urubamba or even Ollantaytambo. Buses also go from the plazas in Urubamba and Ollantaytambo to Chinchero.

INCA TRAIL

The most famous hike in South America, the Inca Trail is walked by thousands of people every year. The views of snowcapped mountains and high cloud forest are stupendous, weather permitting. Walking from one ruin to the next is a mystical and unforgettable experience.

Conservation

Enjoy the hike, but please don't spoil it for others. Please don't defecate in the ruins, don't leave garbage anywhere, don't damage the stonework by building fires against the walls (it blackens and, worse still, cracks the rocks), use a stove for cooking (the trail has been badly deforested over the past decade) and don't pick the orchids and other plants in this national park. The SAEC organized a trail cleanup in 1980 and collected 400kg of unburnable garbage. More recent clean-up campaigns have recorded similar figures. Please pack out what you pack in.

Preparations

Bring a stove, sleeping pad, warm sleeping bag and a tent. Everything can be rented in Cuzco, but check gear carefully as many rented tents leak. Also bring insect repellent, sunscreen, water purification tablets and basic first-aid supplies. The trek takes at least three full days, overnight temperatures can drop below freezing and it rains even in the dry season. There is nowhere to buy food. The ruins are roofless and don't provide shelter. Caves marked on some maps are usually wet, dirty overhangs. The total distance is only 33km, but there are three high passes and the trail is often steep. One reader dubbed it 'the Inca Trial.'

Detailed maps and information are available in Lima at the SAEC, as well as from

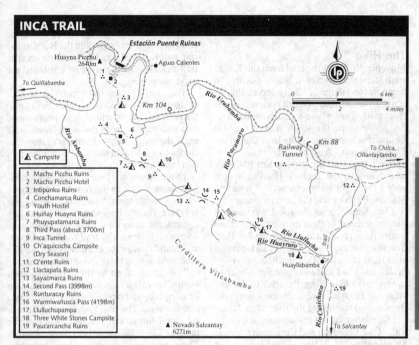

INCA TRAIL

Campsite △

1. Machu Picchu Ruins
2. Machu Picchu Hotel
3. Intipunku Ruins
4. Conchamarca Ruins
5. Youth Hostel
6. Huiñay Huayna Ruins
7. Phuyupatamarca Ruins
8. Third Pass (about 3700m)
9. Inca Tunnel
10. Ch'aquicocha Campsite (Dry Season)
11. Q'ente Ruins
12. Llactapata Ruins
13. Sayacmarca Ruins
14. Second Pass (3998m)
15. Runturacay Ruins
16. Warmiwañusca Pass (4198m)
17. Llulluchupampa
18. Three White Stones Campsite
19. Paucarcancha Ruins

Estación Puente Ruinas
Huayna Picchu 2640m
Aguas Calientes
To Quillabamba
Km 104
Rio Urubamba
Rio Achabamba
Rio Pacamayo
Railway Tunnel
Km 88
To Chilca, Ollantaytambo
Cordillera Vilcabamba
Rio Llullucha
Rio Huayruro
Huayllabamba
Rio Cusichaca
To Salcantay
Nevado Salcantay 6271m
To Salcantay

PERU

trekking agencies and the tourist office in Cuzco. The map in this book is perfectly adequate. Robberies have been reported so you shouldn't hike alone. The most popular period is during the dry season, from June to September. The trail is fairly empty during the rest of the year but is very wet: the mud can be 30cm deep. Nevertheless, the hike is possible all year round.

Organized Tours

Guided tours are offered by outfitters in Cuzco from US$60 per person. This includes the local train to the beginning of the trail at Km 88, a tent, food, a porter, a cook and entrance to the ruins. While this may seem like a good deal, consider the following: The low costs mean that the porters are not provided with camping equipment and food, and so have to fend for themselves. This leads to them cooking and warming themselves with scarce wood from the already badly damaged woodlands. The cheap guided tours generally make no attempt to practice ecologically sensitive camping. Over the past decade, degradation

of the route has become more and more apparent. Do whatever you can to preserve this hike.

There are no easy solutions. You can rent gear in Cuzco (or use your own), avoid outfitters and camp as cleanly as possible. You might even pack out garbage that you encounter. You can go on an expensive guided trip with a local tour operator used by international adventure travel companies. At least these folks make some effort to camp cleanly and provide adequate facilities for porters. They also contribute to clean-up campaigns. Or you can use the cheap outfitters and insist on clean camping by setting an example and ensuring that there is enough fuel and tentage for the porters.

It is normal to tip guides, cooks and porters. Don't forget the porters: they are woefully underpaid and work the hardest of all. Tip them as well as you are able.

Trail Fee

It costs US$17 (or US$8 with international student card) per person to hike the Inca Trail, which includes a one-day entrance fee to Machu Picchu. If joining a guided trek, check to see if this fee is included.

The Hike

Most people begin the trail from the Km 88 train station. However, it is also possible to begin in the village of Chilca (accessible by train, by road from Ollantaytambo or by river raft), from where a relatively flat five-hour hike along the south side of the Río Urubamba brings you to the Inca Trail at the Llactapata ruins. Another abbreviated alternative is to get off the train at Km 104, walk four hours to the Huiñay Huayna hostel, spend the night there and walk 3 hours to Macchu Picchu early the next morning.

From Km 88, cross the Río Urubamba on the suspension bridge, turn left and climb gently through a eucalyptus grove for 1km. You will pass the minor ruin of Llactapata on your right; cross the Río Cusichaca on a foot-bridge and head south along the east bank of the river. It's 6km along the river to the tiny village of Huayllabamba, climbing gently all the way and recrossing the river after 4km.

Huayllabamba is a few minutes above the fork of the Llullucha and Cusichaca rivers, at an elevation of 2750m. The Llullucha is crossed by a log bridge. You can camp in the plaza in front of the school, but beware of thieves slitting your tent at night. Alternatively, if you want to get away from the crowds, you can continue south 3km along the Cusichaca to camp at the ruins of Pau-carcancha.

The Inca Trail climbs steeply along the southern bank of the Río Llullucha. After an hour, the river forks. Continue up the left fork for 500m and then cross the river on a log bridge. There are campsites on both sides of the bridge. The area is called *tres piedras blancas* (three white stones) and is the first camp for many people.

Beyond this camp, the trail turns right after the log bridge and then sweeps back to the Llullucha. It is a long, steep climb to the 4198m high point of the trek, the Warmi-wañusca (Dead Woman's) Pass. The trail passes through cloud forest for 1½ hours before emerging on the high, bare mountain. At some points, the trail and the streambed become one. Llulluchupampa is a flat area above the forest, where water is available and camping is good, though it is cold at night. From here, follow the left-hand side of

the valley and climb for two to three hours to the pass. At Warmiwañusca, you'll see the Río Pacamayo far below and the Runturacay ruin halfway up the hill above the river. The trail descends to the river where there are good campsites.

The trail crosses the river (via a foot bridge) below a small waterfall. Climb up to the right towards Runturacay, an oval-shaped ruin with superb views that is an hour's walk from the river. Above Runturacay, the trail climbs to a false summit, then continues past two small lakes to the top of the second pass at 3998m (about one hour). The trail descends past another lake to the ruin of Sayacmarca, which is visible from the trail 1km before you get there. The site is most impressive: a tightly constructed town on a small mountain spur with superb views. The trail continues down-wards and crosses the headwaters of the Río Aobamba, where there is a small campsite.

The gentle climb to the third pass then begins. There is a causeway across a dried-up swampy lake and later on, a tunnel, both Inca constructions. The trail goes through beauti-ful cloud forest, but the high point of the pass, at almost 3700m, isn't very obvious. There are great views of the Urubamba valley, and soon you reach the beautiful ruin of Phuyupatamarca at 3650m, three hours beyond Sayacmarca. Phuyupatamarca has been well restored and contains a beautiful series of ceremonial baths, which have water running through them. A ridge above the ruin offers campsites with spectacular views.

From Phuyupatamarca a newer section of the trail takes a dizzying drop down hun-dreds of Inca steps into the cloud forest below. It then rejoins the old trail near the electric power pylons, which go down the hill to the dam on the Río Urubamba. Follow the pylons down to the **Albergue Huiñay Huayna** (☎ 084-211147), a red-roofed hostel. Beds are US$7 each or you can sleep on the floor for less. There are hot showers (US$1.25) and meals and bottled drinks are available. Camping is possible nearby. The recently discovered (1993) ter-raced ruin of Conchamarca is about 1km above the hotel.

A 500m trail behind the hostel leads to the small but exquisite Inca ruins of Huiñay Huayna, which cannot be seen from the hostel. Climb down to the lowest part of the town, where it tapers off into a tiny exposed ledge overlooking the Río Urubamba far below. This ruin is a three-hour descent from Phuyupatamarca. The very difficult climb down to the Río Urubamba is prohibited.

From Huiñay Huayna, the trail continues through the cliff-hanging cloud forest and is very thin in places, so watch your step. It takes two hours to reach the penultimate site on the trail, Intipunku (Sun Gate). Machu Picchu comes into view here. There is room for a couple of tents, but no water. This is the last place to camp on the Inca Trail.

From Intipunku, Machu Picchu is an hour's descent. Backpacks aren't allowed into the ruins; on arrival, check your pack at the lower entrance gate and have your trail permit stamped. It is valid only for the day it is stamped, so arrive in the morning.

Getting There & Away

Most hikers take the local train from Cuzco to Km 88. Watch your pack like a hawk. The station at Km 88 is very small and badly marked, so ask where to get off. Cross the river by footbridge and buy a trail permit. An alternative approach begins in Chilca via Ollantaytambo. Finally, for those on a tight schedule, taking the local train to Km 104 is a good option. Doing the hike in reverse is not officially permitted, however it may be possible to pay an extra fee at Intipunku and backtrack to the hostel in Huiñay Huayna.

MACHU PICCHU

This is the best known and most spectacular archaeological site on the continent. From June to September, hundreds of people come daily to visit the 'Lost City of the Incas.' Despite this great tourist influx, the site manages to retain its air of grandeur and mystery, and is a must for all visitors to Peru.

Apart from a few locals, nobody knew of Machu Picchu's existence until American historian Hiram Bingham stumbled upon it in 1911. The ruins were thickly overgrown with vegetation, so his team had to be content with roughly mapping the site. Bingham returned in 1912 and 1915 to clear the thick forest, and further studies and clearings were carried out by Peruvian archaeologist Luis E Valcárcel in 1934 and by a Peruvian-American expedition led by Paul Fejos in 1940-41. Despite these and other, more recent studies, knowledge of Machu Picchu remains sketchy. One thing is

obvious: The quality of the stonework and the abundance of ornamental sites indicate that Machu Picchu must have been an important ceremonial center.

Admission

Visiting Machu Picchu cheaply is possible, once you have budgeted for the US$10 (US$5 with international student card) admission fee. There is a US$15 ticket for two days. A *boleto nocturno* (US$10) allows you in at night. This is popular around full moon. You aren't allowed to bring large packs, food or water bottles into the ruins. Guards check the ruins at closing time, so you can't spend the night. Hours vary from season to season, but officially the ruins are open 7:30 am to 5 pm daily (later with boleto nocturno) and deserve a full day. Going back for a second day (half-price tickets) is worth the money. There is an expensive hotel and restaurant next to the entrance. The nearest cheap place to stay is in Aguas Calientes.

The cheapest way to go is via the local train (*tren local;* 1st class recommended) to Aguas Calientes ($5 one way), but the express train (US$9 one way) is often less crowded. Spend the night there, a full day at Machu Picchu and another night at Aguas Calientes, then return via the local train. This avoids the tourist train completely and maximizes your time at the ruins. The ruins are most heavily visited from June to August, especially on Friday, Saturday and Monday, between 11 am and 2:30 pm.

Ruins

To the left of the central plaza (with the entrance behind you) lie the most significant buildings. A long staircase leads up to the Hut of the Caretaker of the Funerary Rock, where you get some of the best views. Further on, Intihuatana, the major shrine of Machu Picchu, tops a small hill. Although the carved rock at the summit is called a sundial, it was used by the high priests to tell the seasons rather than the time of day. This is the only such Intihuatana that has survived; others were destroyed by the Spaniards.

Short Hikes

Behind the ruins is the steep-sided mountain of Huayna Picchu; it takes an hour to climb and has great views. The entrance to the trail is to the right, at the back of the ruins, and is closed at 1 pm. From the base of Huayna Picchu, a recently cleared trail leads steeply down and up to the Temple of the Moon, from where you can climb to Huayna Picchu – a circuitous route taking two hours. Another option is to walking back to Intipunku along the Inca Trail.

Getting There & Away

Machu Picchu is 700m above the Puente Ruinas train station. Buses take visitors up the 6km zigzag road to the ruins. Tickets cost US$3 each way and are sold at the railway station. Buses are frequent when the tourist train arrives, but there may be an hour or more to wait at other times. Usually, there is a bus for the arrival of the local train. Otherwise, you can walk. Rather than walk up the road, hike up the shorter and steeper footpath, crossing the bridge behind the station, and turn right. Arrows mark the path, which crosses the road at several points on the ascent. Drivers don't stop for passengers at intermediate points unless there are seats, which is unusual. The climb takes 1½ hours from the station, but the descent takes only 40 minutes.

Local and tourist trains depart in the afternoon for the return trip to Cuzco. Departure times vary depending on the season, but the tourist train normally goes first. Buses start descending from the ruins two hours before departure time, and bus lines can get very long during the busy season.

AGUAS CALIENTES

This is the closest village to Machu Picchu and is not a bad spot to hang out in. There are basic hotels, restaurants, hot springs (US$3 per person) and a string of vendors selling crafts along the railroad tracks near the bus stop.

Places to Stay

The basic but clean *Hostal Los Caminantes* (☎ 084-211007) is US$3.50 per person with shared bath or US$11 for a double with bath. Showers are cold. Other cheap and basic cold-water places include *Hostal La Cabaña* and *Hostal Ima Sumac*, both at US$3 per person. Some of the *hospedajes familiares* are *Las Orquídeas*, *Condori* and *Manco Capac*, but there are several others

listed in the brochure given at the tourist office in Cuzco. The popular *Gringo Bill's* (☎ 084-211046) has 24-hour hot water. Rates have gone up after renovations, but the quality is far better than the others. They charge US$15/25 for singles/doubles with shared bath, or US$20/30 for rooms with private bath. There is a good restaurant. *Hostal Machu Picchu* (☎ 084-211034) offers clean doubles with shared hot showers and breakfast at US$25, and singles/doubles with bath for US$38/45. The very clean *Hostal El Inka* (☎ 084-211034) is helpful, friendly and often full. Rooms are US$22/35 with private bath and hot water.

Places to Eat

Some reasonably good and clean places near the tracks include the *Aiko*, *El Refugio*, *Samana Wasi* and *Chez Maggy*, the last of which is quite popular. Away from the tracks is the *Restaurant Huayna Picchu*. All are fairly cheap and there are several others to choose from. The better hotels have restaurants too.

Getting There & Away

Aguas Calientes is 2km before the Puente Ruinas station (for Machu Picchu). Buses for Machu Picchu (US$3.50) depart from the bus stop near the train station. Alternatively, walk 2km to Puente Ruinas and take more frequent buses from there, or walk the entire 8km uphill to the ruins. The tourist train doesn't stop here, but the local train does.

QUILLABAMBA

Quillabamba is on the Río Urubamba, at the end of the train line from Cuzco to Machu Picchu. It is a quiet and pleasant jungle town that can be used as a base for trips further into the jungle.

Places to Stay

Hotel Borranecha, on Espinar 3 blocks north of the Plaza de Armas, is US$3/5 for singles/doubles. Other cheap, basic places are *Hostal Progreso* (no singles) and *Hostal San Antonio* (dormitory accommodations), on Pio Concha just south of the plaza; and *Hostal Thomas* and *Hostal Urusayhua*, near the market. All have cold-water communal bathrooms only.

Clean and recommended, *Hostal Alto Urubamba* (☎ 084-281131), on 2 de Mayo 1

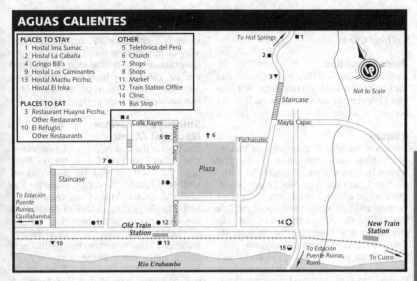

AGUAS CALIENTES

PLACES TO STAY	OTHER
1 Hostal Ima Sumac	5 Telefónica del Perú
2 Hostal La Cabaña	6 Church
4 Gringo Bill's	7 Shops
9 Hostal Los Caminantes	8 Shops
13 Hostal Machu Picchu,	11 Market
Hostal El Inka	12 Train Station Office
	14 Clinic
PLACES TO EAT	15 Bus Stop
3 Restaurant Huayna Picchu,	
Other Restaurants	
10 El Refugio,	
Other Restaurants	

block north of the plaza, is US$6/8 or US$10/14 with private bath. The similarly priced and pleasant *Hostal Cuzco*, near the market, has an erratic water supply. Rooms have private cold showers. Nearby, *Hostal Quillabamba* (☎ 084-281369) has clean rooms with hot showers, a rooftop restaurant, pool and a pleasant garden. Rates are US$14/22. The similarly priced *Hostal Lira* (☎ 084-281324) is also good. The best is *Hostal Don Carlos* (☎ 084-281150), on Libertad just west of the plaza, at US$15/22 with hot bath.

Places to Eat

The *Hostal Quillabamba* restaurant has good views and adequate meals, but slow service. *Hostal Lira* has a reasonable restaurant. *La Trucha* and *Don Felix*, both just south of the plaza, are among the best restaurants in town. A few *heladerías* on the plaza serve ice cream and light snacks.

Getting There & Away

Bus & Truck Trucks and buses for the spectacular drive to Cuzco (US$6, 11 hours) leave from Av Lima south of the market on an irregular basis. Ask around. Pick-up trucks leave every morning from the market area for the village of Kiteni (six to 12 hours) further into the jungle (one cheap hotel). A

reader suggests asking around the plaza for trucks to Huancacalle (a long, bumpy ride), from where you can proceed to Vilcabamba.

Train Due to flooding and avalanches, the train service to Quillabamba has been discontinued. No dates for repairs were available in late 1998. Ask at the train station or tourist office in Cuzco for an update.

SOUTHEAST FROM CUZCO
Tipón

This little-known Inca site is noted for its irrigation system. Take an Urcos bus from Cuzco to the Tipón turnoff, 23km away. A steep dirt road from the turnoff climbs 4km to the ruins.

Pikillacta & Rumicolca

Pikillacta is the only major pre-Inca ruin near Cuzco and was built around 1100 AD by the Wari culture. Entry is with the Cuzco visitor ticket. The site is 32km from Cuzco. It is a large city of crumbling two-story buildings, all with entrances strategically located on the upper floor. A defensive wall surrounds the city. The stonework here is much cruder than that of the Incas. There are local guides available, particularly on weekdays.

About 1km away is the huge Inca gate of Rumicolca, built on Wari foundations. Here, too, the cruder Wari stonework contrasts with the Inca blocks. Get here on the Urcos bus from Cuzco.

Andahuaylillas

Andahuaylillas is 40km from Cuzco and 7km before Urcos. It is famous for its beautiful 17th-century church, comparable to the best in Cuzco, and attractive colonial houses.

Raqchi

These are the ruins of the Temple of Viracocha, which once supported the largest known Inca roof. They are visible from the road and the railway at San Pedro (where there is one hotel), a few kilometers before Sicuani, and look like a huge aqueduct. This was one of the holiest shrines of the Inca empire but was destroyed by the Spanish. Entry is US$2.50. There is a colorful, traditional fiesta in mid-June, good crafts and thermal baths. Both buses and trains from Cuzco go to Sicuani (three hours), which has basic hotels but can be visited in a day trip from Cuzco.

CUZCO TO THE JUNGLE

Two poor roads, in addition to the Quillabamba railway, leave Cuzco for the jungle. One road heads to Paucartambo, Tres Cruces and Shintuya for Parque Nacional Manu, while the other goes through Ocongate and Quince Mil to Puerto Maldonado. Travel on these in the dry months (June to September), as they are muddy and slow in the wet months, especially from January to April.

Paucartambo

This village is 115km east of Cuzco on a very narrow dirt road. There are fine views of the Andes dropping away to the high Amazon Basin beyond. The road is one-way: traffic goes from Cuzco to Paucartambo on Monday, Wednesday and Friday, and in the other direction on Tuesday, Thursday and Saturday. Trucks for Paucartambo leave Cuzco early in the morning from near the Coliseo Cerrado. The journey takes six hours.

Paucartambo is famous for its authentic and colorful annual Fiesta de la Virgen del Carmen, held on and around July 16. Camp, rent a room in one of the two extremely basic small hotels or find a local to give you floor space. Tourist agencies in Cuzco run buses specifically for the fiesta.

Tres Cruces

Tres Cruces, with its locally famous jungle views, is 45km beyond Paucartambo. From May to July, sunrise here tends to be optically distorted, so double images, halos and unusual colors may be seen. During these months, adventure tour agencies run sunrise-watching trips to Tres Cruces.

Shintuya & Parque Nacional Manu

Shintuya is the end of the road, reached by truck from Cuzco (US$15, 20 hours). From here, hire a boat and boatman (about US$100 a day) for the voyage down the Río Madre de Dios to Manu (well-known guide Mario Corisepa charges about US$890 for a nine-day trip including boat, fuel and his service); a minimum of a week is recommended. It is also recommended that you hire a guide with training in ecology and biology; otherwise, your trip will be a meaningless cruise through the rain forest. A good professional guide costs US$50 to US$60 per day, plus food. It is illegal to enter the park without an arranged tour and a guide; only agencies can obtain permits to visit the biosphere. However, you can visit the cultural areas outside the park independently. Guide Jessica Bertram de Sasari (☎ 084-241119 in Cuzco), specializes in native peoples and speaks English and German. You can get to Pillcopata with the Gallito de las Rocas bus from the Coliseo Cerrado in Cuzco. Bring everything you need from there.

Further information can be obtained from the SAEC in Lima or from Manu Expeditions (☎ 084-22-6671, fax 084-23-6706, adventure@manuexpeditions.com), Pardo 895, Cuzco. Because of the expense and hassle of getting a group together, it may be worth taking a tour. Manu Expeditions, which organizes trips all over Peru, has fixed guided departures to Manu leaving every month from May to December. Its nine-day camping tour costs around US$1000 to US$1300 per person, with a minimum of four passengers; smaller groups can band together to make up the numbers. Expert bilingual naturalist guides and all equipment, food and transportation are provided. Staff are very helpful in tailoring itineraries to fit your needs and the tours are a good value. Also recommended is Pantiacolla Tours (☎ 084-238323, fax 084-23-3727), Plateros 360 in Cuzco, which charges about US$650 for a nine-day trip, with larger groups. Cheaper agencies exist, but we haven't heard much in the way of positive reports about them.

The park is closed in January and open only to people staying in the expensive Manu Lodge from February to April. Both Expediciones Manu and Pantiacolla Tours can arrange for you to stay in lodges outside the park, but still in good wildlife areas, for US$40 a day plus transportation.

To Ocongate & Puerto Maldonado

The journey to Puerto Maldonado (see the Amazon Basin section later in this chapter) is a spectacular but difficult journey on poor roads, which takes three days in the dry season (a week in the wet) and costs US$15. The journey can be broken at Ocongate or Quincemil (both with basic hotels). Trucks leave from the little plaza just east of Tacna and Pachacutec (in Cuzco) a few times a week. It may be better to wait in Urcos: all trucks to Puerto Maldonado go via Urcos. This trip involves a degree of hardiness, self-sufficiency and good luck.

From Ocongate, trucks take an hour to reach the village of Tinqui, which is the start of the five- to seven-day trek encircling 6384m Ausangate, southern Peru's highest peak. Tinqui has a very basic hotel and mules can be rented for the trek.

WEST OF CUZCO

Traveling west through Abancay and Andahuaylas to Ayacucho (in the Central Highlands) is a tough ride on a rough road, but is safe. The road is high and night travel is very cold; be prepared. The trip south from Abancay to Nazca through Puquio (the old route to Lima) is not recommended because of banditry near Puquio.

Abancay

This remote town, capital of the Department of Apurímac and 2377m above sea level, is a seven-hour drive west of Cuzco (in the dry season). It's a place to break the Cuzco-Ayacucho trip. The Banco de Crédito changes money. Abancay's carnaval is an especially colorful one.

Places to Stay & Eat *Hostal Sawite* (☎ 084-321692), Núñez 208, charges US$3.50 per person in OK rooms with communal showers (hot water from 6 to 10 am and 1 to 4 pm). *Hostal Leonidas* (☎ 084-321199), Arenas 131, has clean rooms with private electric showers for US$7/10 or with shared showers for a little less. Next door, *Hostal El Dorado* (☎ 084-322005) charges about the same. The new *Hostal Imperial* (☎ 084-321578), Díaz Bárcenas 517, has good rooms with 24-hour hot water for US$13/17 single/double. Opposite, the best hotel in town is the *Hotel de Turistas* (☎/fax 084-321017, 084-321628), Díaz Bárcenas 500, in a pleasant, old-fashioned country mansion. Singles/doubles cost US$21/33 with bath, cable TV and telephone. There is a restaurant and bar. Opposite, there's the *Pizzería Focarela* and the *Restaurant Alicia* for Peruvian food. There are plenty of cheap cafés near the bus stations.

Getting There & Away Buses leave from Arenas near Núñez for Cuzco or Andahuaylas (six hours) at 6 am and 1 pm in both directions. Fares are US$5 to either town and journeys take longer in the wet season. For Ayacucho, change in Andahuaylas. Uncomfortable minibuses are used.

Andahuaylas

Andahuaylas is halfway between Cuzco and Ayacucho and a convenient place to stay overnight. Most inhabitants speak Quechua. This is a very rural and poor part of Peru, and only parts of the town center have electricity. The elevation here is 2980m. Check email at Cenutec, Plaza de Armas, Bolívar 133.

Places to Stay & Eat The basic *Hostal Cusco* (☎ 084-712148) is clean, has hot water in the day and is a good value at US$3/5 for a single/double, or US$5/7 with private bath. There are a couple of cheaper cold-water places. *Hostal Los Libertadores Wari* (☎ 084-721434) is clean, safe and a good value at US$4/6 or US$6/9 with private baths and hot water. *Hostal Las Américas* is US$6/9 with bath. The best hotel in town is the new *El Encanto de Oro Hotel* (☎/fax 084-723066), Pedro Casafranca 424, US$15/20 with bath, hot water and TV.

La Carreta, on the corner of the plaza, is one of several decent inexpensive restaurants; there are others along Ramón Castilla.

Getting There & Away The carrier Transportes Aéreos Andahuaylas (TAA; ☎ 084-721681), Ramón Castilla 429, flies daily to Lima (US$50) except Wednesday. Taxi colectivos charge US$1 into town.

Señor de Huanca (☎ 084-721218) has uncomfortable minibuses to Abancay (US$5, five hours) at 6 am, 1 pm and 8 pm daily. The 6 am departure continues to Cuzco (US$9, 14 hours). Expreso Ayacucho Tours has microbuses to Ayacucho at 6 am and 6 pm, (US$6, 10 hours). Turismo Ayacucho leaves at noon daily for Ayacucho and continues on to Lima (big bus; US$15, 21 hours).

Central Highlands

The central Peruvian Andes are one of the least visited areas of Peru. The mountainous terrain makes overland transport difficult and the region has poor air services. Most of the people of the Central Andes are subsistence farmers.

It was in this environment of isolation and poverty that the Sendero Luminoso, Peru's major terrorist organization, emerged in the 1960s and grew in the 1970s. The violent activities of the Sendero escalated dramatically in the 1980s, and headlines all over the world proclaimed Peru's internal unrest. Tourism declined, and during most of the 1980s the departments of Ayacucho, Huancavelica and Apurímac were almost completely avoided by travelers.

Since the 1992 arrest and imprisonment of many guerrilla leaders, including Abimael Guzmán, founder of the Sendero Luminoso, the power of the guerrilla organizations has been broken and the main routes and towns of the region are safe to visit.

TARMA

This pleasant town, 250km east of Lima, at 3050m, is nicknamed 'the pearl of the Andes.' There are many little-known ruins in the surrounding hills.

Information

Servicios Turísticos Maeedick, 2 de Mayo 547, has tours and information.

Things to See

Trips are made to the village of Acobamba, 10km away, to see the famous religious sanc-

tuary of **El Señor de Muruhuay**. From the village of Palcamayo, 28km northwest of Tarma, it's 4km to the **Gruta de Guagapo**, a huge limestone cave officially protected as a 'national speleological area.' A guide lives opposite the entrance; caving gear is required for a full exploration.

Special Events

The Semana Santa processions, including several candlelit ones after dark, are the big attraction. The Easter Sunday procession to the Catedral follows a route carpeted with flower petals, as does the procession on the annual fiesta of El Señor de Los Milagros, in late October. Other fiestas include Semana de Tarma in late July and San Sebastián (January 20).

Places to Stay

The following places have occasional hot water. The adequate *Hostal Central* is US$4/5.50, or US$5.50/7.50 with private bath. *Hotel Tuchu* is a good value at US$5/7.50 with bath. *Hotel Vargas* has good beds at US$5 per person with private bath, less without. *Hotel El Dorado* is OK at US$6.50/8.50 with bath. The clean, popular *Hotel Galaxia* on the plaza is US$9.50/13 with bath. The good *Hostal Internacional* (☎ 064-321830) is US$13/18 with bath.

Places to Eat

Cheap restaurants line Av Lima. *Restaurant Chavín* on the plaza is good and the *Restaurant Don Lucho* is acceptable and cheap. The best restaurant in town is *El Rosal*.

Getting There & Away

Empresa de Transportes San Juan has frequent buses to Chanchamayo (US$2), some continuing to Villa Rica or Oxapampa. Comité 20 taxi colectivos (US$3.25) leave from the market for Chanchamayo. San Juan also has many buses that go to Huancayo (US$2.25). Los Canarios goes to Huancayo and Lima (US$4). Others for Lima are Transportes DASA, Transportes Chanchamayo and Hidalgo.

HUANCAYO

This modern city, at 3260m, lies in the broad and fertile Río Mantaro valley, in the Central Andes, and is famous for its Sunday market. Huancayo is the capital of the

Department of Junín and the main commercial center for the area. The road from Lima has improved, and the bus (or train) trip is spectacular as you rise from the coast to about 4700m before dropping into the Mantaro valley.

Information

The tourist office is on the corner of Calle Real at Breña. It's open 8 am to 1:30 pm and 4 to 6 pm weekdays and it has good information. Lucho Hurtado, who runs La Cabaña Pizzería and Incas del Perú tour agency (see below), is a recommended source of information.

Casas de cambio and banks are on the 400 and 500 blocks of Calle Real. Banco de Crédito and Banco Wiese have the best rates for traveler's checks. Internet access (US$1.50 an hour) is available 9 am to 8:30 pm daily, at Loreto 337.

Things to See

The Mercado Mayorista (daily produce market) overflows onto the railway tracks from the covered market off Ica east of the tracks. The meat section sells various Andean delicacies, including fresh and dried frogs and guinea pigs.

The Sunday crafts market along Calle Huancavelica has weavings, sweaters and other textile goods, embroidered items, ceramics, woodcarvings and the carved gourds that are a specialty of the area. Watch your wallet.

Walk (or bus) 2km northeast on Giráldez to the Cerro de la Libertad, which has good city views. Continue 2km to see the eroded sandstone towers at Torre Torre.

Activities

Incas del Perú (☎ 064-223303, fax 064-222395, incas&lucho@hys.com.pe), Giráldez 652, offers day hikes, local tours, bicycle rental and Spanish lessons.

Places to Stay

The recommended *La Casa de la Abuela*, Giráldez 691, opposite Incas del Perú, is friendly, very popular with budget travelers, has laundry and breakfast service, a garden, and charges US$4 per person in dorms, or US$7/10 with bath. The popular *Residencial Baldeón*, Amazonas 543, in a friendly family house, costs US$5 per person with hot water,

breakfast and kitchen privileges. Other recommended new budget places include *Casa Alojamiento Bonilla* (☎ 064-232103), Huánuco 332, run by friendly, English-speaking artists Aldo and Soledad Bonilla, who charge US$12 a double with breakfast. A few blocks northeast off the map, *Pension Huanca* (☎ 064-223956), Pasaje San Antonio 113, charges US$4 with breakfast, is friendly and has hot water.

Basic cold-water hotels include *Hostal Roma*, Loreto 447, the *Hostal Tivoli*, Puno 488, and the *Hotel Centro*, Loreto 452, at US$4/6. The Centro also has US$6/8 rooms with cold bath as does the *Hotel Prince*, Calixto 578, and the clean *Hostal Villa Rica*, Calle Real 1291. *Duchas Tina* and *Sauna Blub* have hot showers.

The clean *Hotel Torre Torre*, Calle Real 873, is US$5.50/7.50 or US$2 more with bath. The clean *Hostal Percy's*, Calle Real 1339, is US$8/11 with bath, TV, hot water with 30 minutes notice, or US$6 for a single with shared bath. They also have a restaurant. The clean, safe and friendly *Hostal Pussy Cat* (☎ 064-231565), 300 block of Giráldez, is US$8/12 with bath (30 minutes notice for hot water) or a bit less with shared bath.

The following are clean and have similar rates and private baths, and the *Hostal Roger* (☎ 064-233488), Ancash 460, at US$8/11 with bath and hot water; the *Hostal Palace* (☎ 064-238501), Ancash 1127, which offers the following: singles/doubles US$3.50/7 with shared bath or US$7/10 with bath and TV. Hot water is available 6 to 7 am and 6 to 8 pm only. The simple *Hostal Plaza* (☎ 064-210509, fax 064-236878), Ancash 171, is a good value at US$8/12 for rooms with bath and hot water. *Hotel El Dorado* (☎ 064-223947), Piura 425, has rooms at US$10/12 with hot water and TV. Close by, the *Hostal y Baños Sauna Las Viñas* (☎ 064-231294), Piura 415, has simple rooms with telephone, cable TV and hot water for US$12/15. Saunas (US$2 per person) are available from 6 am to 9 pm.

Places to Eat

The local specialty is *papa a la huancaína*, a boiled potato topped with a tasty white sauce of cheese, milk, hot pepper and butter, served with an olive and eaten as a cold salad.

Restaurants serving good cheap set meals include *Pinky's*, Giráldez 147, and *Chifa Centro* for good Chinese food. The upmarket

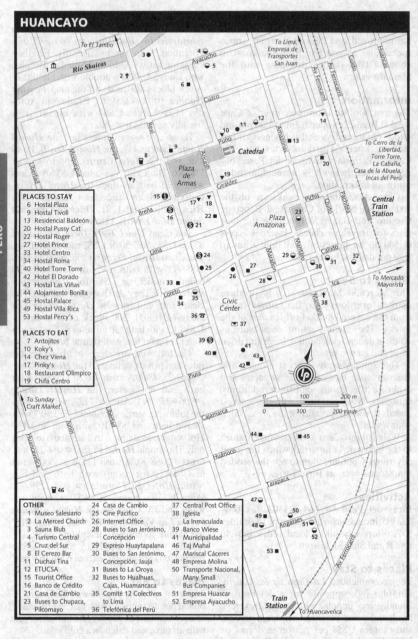

HUANCAYO

To El Tambo

Río Shuicas

To Lima,
Empresa de
Transportes
San Juan

Ayacucho

Cuzco

Puno

Catedral

To Cerro de la
Libertad,
Torre Torre,
La Cabaña,
Casa de la Abuela,
Incas del Perú

Plaza
de
Armas

Giráldez

Central
Train
Station

Breña

Plaza
Amazonas

Lima

To Mercado
Mayorista

Loreto

Civic
Center

Ica

Piura

To Sunday
Craft Market

Cajamarca

Huánuco

Tarapaca

Train
Station

To Huancavelica

PLACES TO STAY
6   Hostal Plaza
9   Hostal Tivoli
13 Residencial Baldeón
20 Hostal Pussy Cat
22 Hostal Roger
27 Hotel Prince
33 Hotel Centro
34 Hostal Roma
40 Hotel Torre Torre
42 Hotel El Dorado
44 Hostal Las Viñas
45 Alojamiento Bonilla
45 Hostal Palace
49 Hostal Villa Rica
53 Hostal Percy's

PLACES TO EAT
7   Antojitos
10 Koky's
14 Chez Viena
17 Pinky's
18 Restaurant Olímpico
19 Chifa Centro

OTHER
1   Museo Salesiano
2   La Merced Church
3   Sauna Blub
4   Turismo Central
5   Cruz del Sur
8   El Cerezo Bar
11 Duchas Tina
12 ETUCSA
15 Tourist Office
16 Banco de Crédito
21 Casa de Cambio
23 Buses to Chupaca,
    Pilcomayo
24 Casa de Cambio
25 Cine Pacifico
26 Internet Office
28 Buses to San Jerónimo,
    Concepción
29 Expreso Huaytapalana
30 Buses to San Jerónimo,
    Concepción, Jauja
31 Buses to La Oroya
32 Buses to Hualhuas,
    Cajas, Huamancaca
35 Comité 12 Colectivos
    to Lima
36 Telefónica del Perú
37 Central Post Office
38 Iglesia
    La Inmaculada
39 Banco Wiese
41 Municipalidad
46 Taj Mahal
47 Mariscal Cáceres
48 Empresa Molina
50 Transporte Nacional,
    Many Small
    Bus Companies
51 Empresa Huascar
52 Empresa Ayacucho

Restaurant Olímpico has good menús for US$2 and Peruvian à-la-carte plates from US$5. The popular *La Cabaña*, Giráldez 652, has good pizzas, sandwiches and anticuchos and live music from Thursday to Saturday nights.

The best place for espresso, cakes, desserts and sandwiches is *Koky's*, at the corner of Ancash and Puno. Another nice coffee/pastry shop is the elegant-looking *Chez Viena*, on Puno just west of the railroad. *Antojitos* is a nice place on the corner of Arequipa and Puno. It opens Monday to Saturday and serves good lunch specials for about US$1, and pizza, barbecue and sandwiches in the evening. They have live music on weekends. There are several budget restaurants on Arequipa in the block south of Antojitos.

Entertainment

La Cabaña has the liveliest action at night and live folklórico and rock from Thursday to Saturday. The *Taj Mahal*, Huancavelica 1052, is a popular club with video karaoke and dancing. You'll also find dancing at *Coconut*, Huancavelica 430, near Puno. *El Cerezo*, on Puno, is a popular bar with loud MTV and many young locals.

Getting There & Away

Bus Mariscal Cáceres (☎ 064-216633, 064-216634), Real 1217, has seven daily buses to Lima for US$7 or US$9 for nonstop 'presidential service.' Others for Lima are ETUCSA (☎ 064-232638), Puno 220, and Cruz del Sur (☎ 064-2356501), Ayacucho 281, both with regular and nonstop buses, and (with cheaper buses) Empresa Molina, Angaraes 334, and Roggero (at Hostal Rogger), with the cheapest bus to Lima, 10 pm departure, US$3.50. Comité 12 (☎ 064-233281), Loreto 421, has cars to Lima (US$12, five hours).

Empresa Molina Trans Nacional and Empresa Hidalgo have buses to Huancavelica (US$3.50, six hours); others in this area go there. Empresa Molina and Empresa Ayacucho have buses to Ayacucho (US$6, 10 to 20 hours). Expect delays in the rainy season.

Empresa de Transportes San Juan, Ferrocarril 131, about 3 blocks north off map, has minibuses to Tarma (US$2.50). Some continue to Chanchamayo. It also has buses to the jungle town Satipo. Turismo Central (☎ 064-223128) Ayacucho 274, has buses to

Tarma, La Merced and many jungle destinations including Pucallpa, Puerto Bermudez, and Satipo. Look also for buses north to Cerro de Pasco, Huánuco and Tingo María.

Local buses to most of the nearby villages leave from the street intersections indicated by arrows on the map.

Train There are two unconnected train stations. The central station serves Lima. This train recently reopened passenger service on a limited schedule. It runs the last weekend of the month, departing 7:40 am Saturday from Lima, arriving at Huancayo 6pm and returning the following Monday from Huancayo (US$18 return, good service, snacks and lunch included). Service may become more frequent.

The Huancavelica train station serves Huancavelica by *expreso* (US$2.50, 4½ hours) at 6:30 am, except Sunday, when it leaves at 2 pm. The *tren extra* (US$2.50/3.50/4 in second/first/buffet – the last guarantees a seat, 6½ hours) leaves at 12:30 pm Monday to Saturday. Advance tickets are recommended.

AROUND HUANCAYO
Mantaro Valley

The twin villages of Cochas Grande and Cochas Chico, 11km from Huancayo, are centers for production of the incised gourds for which the area is famous. San Agustín de Cajas is known for the manufacture of broad-brimmed wool hats, though it seems to be a dying industry now. Hualhuas is famous for wool products. San Jerónimo de Tunán is famous for its filigreed silverware, and its 17th-century church with fine wooden altars.

North of Huancayo is the village of Concepción (with basic accommodations), from which the remarkable 18th-century **Convento de Santa Rosa de Ocopa** can be visited. This beautiful building with an interesting museum and library is open daily, except Tuesday, 9 am to noon and 3 to 6 pm. Admission is US$0.50.

HUANCAVELICA

This city is 147km south of Huancayo, in a high and remote area. It's a pleasant small colonial town with seven 16th- and 17th-century churches with silver-plated altars. Hours are irregular.

Information

The Ministerio de Turismo, Nicolás de Piérola 180, and the Instituto Nacional de Cultura, on Plaza San Juan de Dios, have local information. Traveler's checks may be hard to change. Sunday is market day.

Places to Stay

Hostal Santo Domingo, Barranca 366, has cold water. Very basic rooms are US$2 per person. *Mi Hotel*, Carabaya 481, costs a few cents more but has hot water and is better. *Hotel Tahuantinsuyo*, at Carabaya and M Muñoz, has hot water and charges US$3/4.50 for singles/doubles with private bath. *Mercurio*, Torre Tagle 455, is similar but charges twice as much.

Places to Eat

Cheap restaurants along M Muñoz serve decent set menús for US$1.50. *La Estrellita*, S Barranca 255, has excellent trout. *El Misti*, *La Amistad* and others are on the same block. Also try the *Ganso de Oro*, V Toledo 283, *Restaurant Joy*, V Toledo 230, *Césars*, M Muñoz 390, and *Las Magnolias*, just off the Plaza de Armas. All are reasonable.

Getting There & Away

Bus Most buses leave from Av M Muñoz. Various companies have buses for Huancayo (US$3.50, six hours) and Lima (US$9, 14 hours). There are no direct services to Ayacucho.

Train The tren extra leaves Huancavelica at 6:30 am and the expreso leaves at 12:30 pm, except on Sunday, when it leaves at 7 am. You should buy tickets in advance.

AYACUCHO

Ayacucho is where the Sendero Luminoso arose in the 1960s. Since the capture of the Sendero's founder and leader in 1992, this area is again open to overland travel. This fascinating Andean colonial town is well worth a visit, particularly during the famous Semana Santa celebrations.

Information

La Dirección General de Industria y Turismo, (☎ 064-81-2548, 064-81-3162) Asamblea 481, is good for information. The travel agencies are also helpful. The Banco de Crédito cashes traveler's checks.

Things to See

The center has two museums, a 17th-century Catedral, many churches from the 16th, 17th and 18th centuries and several old mansions around the plaza.

The ruins of **Wari** (Huari), capital of the Wari empire, which predated the Incas by 500 years, are worth seeing. Beyond is the village of Quinua, where a huge monument and small museum mark the site of the Battle of Ayacucho (1824). There is a Sunday market. Wari is 20km and Quinua about 40km northeast of Ayacucho. Agencies on the plaza have tours there, or you can use public transport.

Places to Stay

Reservations are essential during Semana Santa: Hotels are full from Wednesday to Saturday and prices double. Basic cold-water cheapies include the *Hostal Sixtina* (☎ 064-812018), Callao 336, at US$4/7 and the *Hostal Central* (☎ 064-812144), Arequipa 180, at US$4/8, or US$6.50 per person with bath.

The following have hot water at times. The basic *Hotel Santiago* (☎ 064-812132), Nazareno 177, is US$4/6.50 or US$9 for a double with bath. The slightly better *Hotel Crillonesa* (☎ 064-812350), Nazareno 165, is US$4.50/8. The clean *Hostal Magdalena* (☎ 64-812910), Mariscal Cáceres 836 close to the bus stations, which may be unsafe at night, is US$5/9 or US$15 for a double with bath. The simple but clean *Hostal Samary* (☎ 064-812442), Callao 329, has rooftop views and is US$6/8, or US$10/14 with private bath. The often full and recommended *La Colmena Hotel* (☎ 064-812146), Cuzco 140, has a nice courtyard and is US$5/8 or US$7/14 with bath. There are several other cheap and pricier hotels.

Places to Eat

The *Alamo Restaurant* opens at 7 am for varied breakfasts and has good cheap food all day. Marginally more expensive, *La Casona* is popular and recommended. *La Tradición* is also good and the nearby *Restaurant Cámara Comercio* has cheap set menús. For Chinese food try the *Chifa El Dorado*, which also serves Andean dishes. *Restaurant Urpicha*, Londres 272, is a homey place with a small traditional menu, including cuy. Go with a group or take a taxi at night. Occasionally it has folk music on weekends. There are several small peñas.

Getting There & Away

Air AeroContinente flies daily to Lima (US$48). The airport is 4km from the town center; taxis and buses are available.

Bus & Truck For Lima (US$7 via Ica, 10 hours), Transportes Molina, Los Libertadores, Andía and Antezana all have evening buses. Andía, Transportes Antezana and Transportes Molina have nightly buses to Huancayo (US$6, 10 hours. Andía and Ayacucho Tours have 6 am departures to Andahuaylas (US$6, 10 hours). For Cuzco (US$14, 24 hours) Ayacucho Tours and Transportes Chanka have 6 am departures. The cheapest way to Cuzco is to wait at Grifo Chakchi (petrol station) for a truck and ride in the back with the locals. This is slow and uncomfortable but the views are great and you will experience the Andes from a very different perspective.

Pick-up trucks and occasional buses go to many local villages, including Quinua, and to the Wari ruins, departing from Paradero Magdalena, beyond the statue at the east end of Av Centenario.

NORTH OF LA OROYA

A road from Lima to Pucallpa (in the jungle) goes through the central Andes north of La Oroya, via Cerro de Pasco, Huánuco and Tingo María. This route is again safe, but there are several police controls on the Tingo María-Pucallpa section.

Cerro de Pasco

This is a cold, dirty mining town 4333m above sea level – the highest city of its size (population 30,000) in the world. There are a few basic hotels, but it's not worth staying unless you must.

Huánuco

This town, elevation 1894m, is capital of its department and the nicest place between Lima and Pucallpa. There is a decent museum at General Prado 495, and a pleasant Plaza de Armas.

Information A tourism office (☎ 064-512980) is on the plaza at General Prado 714. The Banco de Crédito changes money.

Places to Stay & Eat Hotels fill quickly. The best cheapie is the clean *Hotel Imperial* (☎ 064-513203), Huánuco 581, at US$3.50/5 with shared bath and cold water. Opposite are the similarly priced hotels *Marino* and *Caribe*. *Hostal Santo Domingo* is US$6/8 or US$7/10 with bath, and has cold water, but seems OK. For US$5 per person for rooms with shared bath try *Hotel Paraíso* (☎ 064-511953), on the Plaza de Armas. Also on the plaza are *Hotel Lima* (☎ 064-514773) at US$8/15 with bath, and *Hostal Las Vegas* (☎ 064-512315) at the same price. Both have occasional hot water and a café. *Hotel Kotosh* is US$7/10 with cold bath and the similar *Hotel Tours* is US$8/11.

The pleasant *Hostal Huánuco* (☎ 064-512050), Huánuco 777, has good hot water and is often full. Rates are US$8/13.50 with bath. The clean, well-run *Hostal Garú* (☎ 064-513096), P Puelles 459, is US$17/27 with hot showers.

There's a good choice of restaurants on or near the plaza.

Getting There & Away TAA serves Lima twice a week and continues to Tingo María. AeroCóndor (☎ 064-517728) has flights to Lima on Tuesdays, Thursdays (US$88) and Sundays (US$65). The airport is 8km from town.

For Lima (US$9, nine hours), León de Huánuco has 8 am and 8 pm buses. Others are Transportes Rey and ETNASA, which also has night buses to Pucallpa (US$11.50, 15 hours). León de Huánuco also has buses to Pucallpa. On the other side of the Río Huallaga, 10 minutes walk from the center, shared taxis or minibuses go to Tingo María. You can flag down buses to Pucallpa. Transportes Oriental has day and night buses to Huancayo (US$6, eight hours). Expreso Huallaga has several buses a day to Cerro de Pasco and Huancayo. Turismo Central also goes to Huancayo daily. For remote Andean towns like La Unión and Tantamayo, look around the market.

Tingo María

Just 650m above sea level, Tingo María is surrounded by Andean foothills, but is almost a jungle town. North is the dangerous drug-growing Río Huallaga valley; east is Pucallpa. Tingo María is a busy market town and a safe enough stop.

Places to Stay & Eat Hotels fill quickly and all have cold showers. The basic *Hostal Cuzco* (☎ 064-562095), Raimondi 671, is US$2.50/3.50 for singles/doubles. Across the road, the *Hostal La Cabaña* is reasonably clean at US$5/8. *Hostal Belén* has OK rooms with shared showers for US$5/8. Others include the secure *Hostal Raimondi* (☎ 064-562146), Raimondi 344, the *Hotel Royal* on Benavides, and *Hostal Progreso* on Callao.

The clean *Hostal Viena* (☎ 064-562194), Lamas 254, is US$3.50/5 or US$5/7 with bath. *Hotel Coloso* (☎ 064-562027), Benavides 440, is US$5/8 with bath. *Hotel Palacio* (☎ 064-562319), Raimondi 158, looks OK at US$3.50 per person, or US$7/11 with private bath. The best cheap hotel is the *Hotel Nueva York* (☎ 064-562406), Alameda Perú 553, at US$7.50/12 with tepid showers, a bit more for rooms with cable TV.

There are several inexpensive restaurants along Raimondi.

Getting There & Away Airfare to Lima is US$65. See Huánuco for schedule information.

Bus departures change frequently – ask around. Transtel has dawn buses to Pucallpa (US$9, 12 hours). Empresa La Marginal and others go to Pucallpa. Empresa Transmar and Transportes Rey have night buses to Lima (US$12, 12 hours). León de Huánuco has day buses. Turismo Central has a night bus to Huancayo (US$8, 12 hours). Taxi colectivos and minibuses leave for Huánuco from Raimondi at Callao.

North Coast

The coast road north of Lima passes huge, rolling sand dunes, dizzying cliffs, oases of farmland, busy fishing villages, archaeological sites and some large and historic cities.

BARRANCA & PARAMONGA

The small town of Barranca, 190km north of Lima, is 4km before the Huaraz turnoff. Four km north of the turnoff is the Chimú pyramid of Paramonga, a huge structure that is worth a visit. Admission is US$2.50. There is a small site museum.

There are a few cheap hotels and restaurants in Barranca. No buses go to the ruins,

though local buses going to the port at Paramonga will drop you 3km away.

CASMA

The small town of Casma is 370km north of Lima, and the archaeological site of Sechín is 5km away.

Sechín

This site dates from 1600 BC and is one of the more important and well-preserved coastal ruins. There is a small museum. The outside walls of the main temple are covered with gruesome bas-relief carvings of warriors and of captives being eviscerated. To get there, go 3km south of Casma on the Panamericana, then left on the paved road to Huaraz for 2km more. It's open 9 am to 5 pm daily; entry is US$1.80. Bring your own food.

Places to Stay

The clean *Hostal Gregori* (☎ 044-711073), L Ormeño 579, is US$8/12 for a single/double with cold shower, less with shared bath. *Hostal Indoamericano* (☎ 044-711235) is clean at US$5/8 or US$7/10 with private cold bath. The best is *Hostal El Farol* (☎/fax 084-711064) at US$17/23 with private warm shower, swimming pool and breakfast.

Getting There & Away

Bus offices and stops are clustered together on the main road, near the junction with the Panamericana. There are buses to Lima, Trujillo and Huaraz, but most are just passing through so few seats are available. Alternatively, take a colectivo 50km north to Chimbote (US$1, 1¼ hours), which has better connections.

CHIMBOTE

Even undiscerning noses will know that this is Peru's biggest fishing port. Stop here to take the day bus through the spectacular Cañón del Pato to Huaraz. There are about 15 hotels. Empresa Moreno, Gálvez 1178 (a poor area, take a taxi at night), has an 8 am bus to Huaraz (US$6.50, 10 hours) via the Cañón del Pato.

TRUJILLO

Trujillo, 560km north of Lima, is northern Peru's main city (population 650,000). It is an attractive town, founded in 1535 by

Pizarro, that retains much of its colonial flavor. Nearby are the 1500-year-old Moche Pyramids of the Sun and Moon (Las Huacas del Sol y de la Luna), and the ancient Chimú capital of Chan Chan, which preceded the Incas. There are some pleasant beaches.

Information

The tourist office, Pizarro 402, is open from 8 am to 7:30 pm. Recommended guides are Clara Luz Bravo D (☎ 044-243347), Huayna Capac 542, Santa María district, who speaks English and will provide transport or accompany you on public buses, and José Soto (☎ 044-251489), Atahualpa 514, who also speaks English and some French, and knows the area well. Guía Tours, Independencia 525, has daily tours for US$15. Several banks change traveler's checks at varying rates. For email, Intercall, Zepita 728, charges US$2 per hour. The best hospital is the Clínica Peruana-Americana (☎ 044-231261), Mansiche 702.

Warning Trujillo is a conservative town and local women are not typically seen out alone after dark. Women travelers are thus more likely to receive unsolicited attention here than in other parts of Peru.

Things to See

The spacious and attractive **Plaza de Armas**, with its impressive statue representing commerce, agriculture and science, is fronted by the **Catedral**, which was begun in 1647, destroyed in 1759 and rebuilt soon afterwards. It has a famous basilica and is often open in the evenings around 6 pm. On Sunday at 10 am, there is a flag-raising ceremony and parade on the Plaza de Armas.

There are several elegant **colonial mansions** in the center. Their wrought-iron grillwork and pastel shades are typical of Trujillo. The highly recommended **Casa de la Emancipación** was restored in 1970 by the Banco Continental. Do not miss the 16th-century fountain made of Carabamba marble in the last patio. The **colonial churches** are worth a look, though hours are erratic. La Merced, El Carmen and San Agustín are three of the best.

The **Museo Cassinelli** has an excellent private archaeological collection in the basement of a gas station! It's open Monday to Saturday from 8:30 to 11:30 am and 3:30 to

5:30 pm, and entry is US$1.50. The university-run **Museo de Arqueología**, corner of Ayacucho and Junín, in the restored Casa Risco, has an interesting collection of art and pottery, and a reproduction of the murals in the Moche Pyramid of the Moon. Entry is US$0.60. The university also has a poor **Museo de Zoología**, at San Martín 368. Both are open mornings.

The Catedral and El Carmen church have **art museums** featuring religious and colonial art. **Casona Orbegoso**, on the fifth block of Calle Orbegoso, is a beautiful 18th-century mansion with a period art exhibit. Several colonial buildings contain **art galleries** with changing shows. Admission is normally free or nominal. The **Ganoza Chopitea residence**, recognized by the two lions on the front, on Independencia deserves a look. Hours vary.

Special Events

The marinera dance is the highlight of many of Trujillo's festivals. Caballos de paso are another highlight. The Fiesta de la Marinera, at the end of January, is the biggest in Peru. The Fiesta de la Primavera, held in late September, has Peru's most famous parade, and much dancing and entertainment. Hotels are often booked during festivals.

Places to Stay

Many cheap hotels, especially in the poor area east of Gamarra and Bolívar, are used for short stays by young couples, but aren't very dangerous. The plain, not particularly clean, **Hostal Lima** (☎ 044-244751), Ayacucho 718, is quite popular with gringos. It looks like a jail but is secure and friendly at US$6 for a double. The following places are friendly and have been recommended as good values among the basic hotels. The cold-water **Hotel Oscar** (☎ 044-257033) looks OK for US$5/7.50. The similar **Hotel España** is near the Empresa Antisuyo bus terminal, and the **Hostal JR**, a block away, has rooms with bath for US$6/8.

The popular **Hotel Americano** (☎ 044-241361), Pizarro 767, is in a rambling and dilapidated old mansion with lots of character and cold water. Given the number of complaints received, it may be a better place to visit than to stay. Basic, fairly clean rooms are US$7/10 with bath or a bit less without. **Hostal Roma**, on Nicaragua, is clean and secure (US$9 for a double with cold bath).

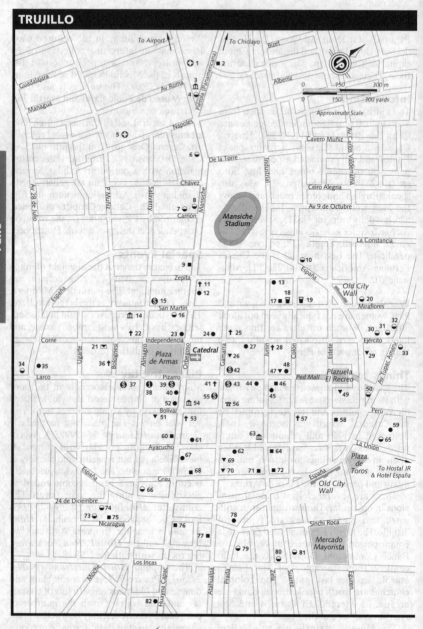

TRUJILLO

TRUJILLO

Av Cesar Vallejo

Puno

The small, family run **Hostal Las Flores** (☎ 044-255681), Atahualpa 282, has been recommended.

The following hotels have rooms with private bath and hot shower. **Hotel Chan Chan** (☎ 044-242964) is basic but OK at US$7/10. **Hotel Primavera** (☎ 23-1915), Piérola 872, is out of the center but clean, modern and a good value (US$8/12). The clean and friendly **Hotel Sudamericano** (☎ 044-243751), Grau 515, is OK for US$8/13, but check the water: some showers are cold. **Hotel San Martín** (☎ 044-234011), 749 San Martín, has over 100 clean rooms. It's a fair value, at US$13/20, but since it is rarely full, prices are negotiable.

Hostal Recreo (☎ 044-246991), Estete 647, has rooms with telephone, TV and (usually) hot water at US$13/17. Other reasonable choices with doubles in the teens are the **Hostal Granada** (☎ 044-256411), Grau 611, with singles/doubles at US$8/12 with bath and hot water, and a bit less without. The friendly **Hostal El Palacio** (☎ 044-258194), Grau 709, has rooms at US$8/12 with bath and TV, or US$6 per person with shared bath. They eagerly offer discounts. The pricier **Residencial Los Escudos** (☎ 044-256131), Orbegoso 676, in an interesting colonial house, charges US$21/25.

To **stay with a local family** (US$5 to US$7 per person), ring Clara Luz Bravo D (☎ 044-243347) or Familia Vanini (☎ 044-233144) at Av Larco 245.

Places to Eat

The market on Ayacucho has the cheapest places to eat in Trujillo. A block away on Gamarra, the **Chifa Oriental** and **Chifa Ah Chau** have decent Chinese chow. Nearby, the **Restaurant 24 Horas** is inexpensive and always open. Next door, the **Restaurant Oasis** is good for local food like fritadas. Simple restaurants on the 700 block of Pizarro include the **Café Romano**, **Café Asturias** for strong espresso coffee and **Café Demarco** for ice cream and homemade desserts. Both have lunch menús under US$2. Also good for menús and chicken dishes are **Las Tradiciones** and **Restaurant La Mochica Ramos**. **Restaurant Big Ben** is good for ceviches and local seafood at reasonable prices. The small **Restaurant Naturaleza** serves vegetarian food.

Entertainment

The *Peña Canana* at San Martín and Colón has live music weekends. There are other peñas away from the center.

Getting There & Away

Air The airport is 10km northwest of town. AeroContinente (☎ 044-244042) has an office in central Trujillo. They fly to Lima (US$45) daily. AeroContinente also has a daily flight to Piura (US$45). Schedules and destinations change often.

Bus Buses are often full, so book as far in advance as you can for the best choice of departure times. Companies are spread out all over town (see Trujillo map).

Many companies have services to Lima and towns to the north along the Panamericana. Fares vary depending on the company (some have luxury buses with videos and toilets), so shop around. Lima is US$8 to US$15 (eight to 10 hours), Piura is US$7 to US$9 (seven to nine hours) and Chiclayo is about US$3 (three hours).

The best services to Lima are said to be Ormeño/Continental (☎ 044-259782) and CIVA (☎ 044-251402). Las Dunas, España 1445, has overnight luxury buses to Lima, and a daily bus to Cajamarca (US$8). EM-TRAFESA (☎ 044-223981), on Miraflores near España, has Chiclayo buses leaving every half-hour during the day, as well as Lima, Cajamarca and Piura buses. Vulkano also has frequent Chiclayo buses as well as service to Cajamarca. El Dorado has good buses north to Piura and Tumbes, and Expreso Sudamericano has cheaper, slower buses. Both also go to Cajamarca. ETHMOPESA also goes north and Cruz del Sur (☎ 044-261801) and ITTSA go north and south. Empresa El Aguila has frequent buses to Chimbote. Olano goes to Chachapoyas and Guadalupe goes to Tarapoto. Chinchaysuyo, Cruz del Sur and Transportes Chimbote go to Huaraz (or change in Chimbote).

Getting Around

To/From the Airport The bus to Huanchaco passes within 1km of the airport. A taxi from the center is about US$3.

Bus 'B' minibuses pass west on the corner of España and Industrial (and other places; see map) for Huaca Esmeralda, Chan Chan and Huanchaco every few minutes. The 'A' minibuses run east on España. Tell the driver where you want to get off. Buses for Esperanza go northeast along Mansiche and can drop you at La Huaca Arco Iris. Colectivos leave every half-hour from Calle Suárez for Las Huacas del Sol y de la Luna, and minibuses leave from José Galvez, near the Mercado Mayorista.

AROUND TRUJILLO

The Moche and the Chimú are the two cultures that have left the greatest mark on the Trujillo area. There are four major archaeological sites.

Archaeology

The Moche (Mochica) culture flourished from 0 to 700 AD and is known especially for its ceramics. The pots are decorated with realistic figures and scenes, and most of what we know about the Moche is from this pottery; there was no written language. They lived around massive ceremonial pyramids such as the nearby Huacas del Sol y de la Luna. The Chimú period lasted from about 1000 to 1470 AD. Chan Chan, the Chimú capital, was the largest pre-Columbian city in Peru, covering 28 sq km and housing about 60,000 people.

Warning

It is dangerous to walk along Buenos Aires beach between Chan Chan and Huanchaco. Single travelers have also been mugged, robbed and raped while visiting archaeological sites. Stay on main footpaths, don't visit the ruins late in the day and go with friends or hire a guide. Beware of pickpockets at all the ruins.

Chan Chan

The city was built around 1300 AD and contained about 10,000 dwellings. There were storage bins for food and other products, huge walk-in wells, canals, workshops and temples. The royal dead were buried in mounds containing a wealth of funerary offerings. The whole city was decorated with designs molded into the mud walls, and the more important areas were layered with precious metals. Although the Incas conquered the Chimú around 1460, the city was not looted until the Spanish arrived.

The Chimú capital consisted of nine subcities, called the Royal Compounds. Each contained a royal burial mound with a rich array of funerary offerings. Visitors today see only a huge area of crumbling mud walls, some decorated with spectacular friezes. The treasures are gone, though a few can be seen in museums. The Tschudi compound has been partially restored and is open to visitors. Since the heavy rains of 1998, some of the walls and graves are protected by necessary if unsightly wooden roofs. Chan Chan is 5km west of Trujillo. Tschudi is to the left of the main road, about 1.5km along a dirt road. You'll see the crumbling ruins of the other compounds all around you. Stick to the road and don't try to visit the ruins on either side, which are muggers' haunts.

The entrance booth is at the Tschudi complex. There is a snack stand, guides are available and tourist police are on duty. It's open 9 am to 4 pm daily; entry is US$3.50. The ticket admits you to the Museo de Sitio de Chan Chan, Huaca Esmeralda and Huaca Arco Iris ruins and is valid for two days. Guides here charge about US$7 for the tour in Spanish or in limited English.

La Huaca Esmeralda

This temple was built by the Chimú at about the time of Chan Chan. Hours and fees are the same as for Chan Chan. Huaca Esmeralda is at Mansiche, halfway between Trujillo and Chan Chan, and it is possible to walk there (check with the tourist police). If returning from Chan Chan to Trujillo, the huaca is to the right of the main road, about four blocks behind the Mansiche church. The site is eroded, but you can make out the characteristic designs of fish, seabirds, waves and fishing nets. The temple consists of two stepped platforms, and an on-site guard will take you around (for a tip).

Huaca Arco Iris

This Chimú site (also called La Huaca del Dragón) is left of the Panamericana, in La Esperanza, 4km northwest of Trujillo. Hours and fees are as for Chan Chan.

This is one of the best preserved Chimú temples, because it was covered by sand until excavation began in 1963. The site has a defensive wall enclosing 3000 sq km. There is one entrance. Inside is a single large structure, the temple itself. This is about 800 sq meters, and has two levels with a combined height of about 7.5m. The walls are covered with repeated rainbow designs, most of which have been restored. Ramps lead to the very top of the temple, from where there are good views.

Huacas del Sol y de la Luna

These Moche temples predate Chan Chan by 700 years and are 10km southeast of Trujillo. The site is open 9 am to 4 pm daily. Entry is US$2.50. The Huaca del Sol is Peru's largest pre-Columbian structure; 140 million adobe bricks were used to build it. Originally, the pyramid had several levels, connected by steep stairs, huge ramps and walls sloping at 77° to the horizon. Now it resembles a giant sand pile, but the brickwork remains impressive from some angles.

In 1990 archaeologists discovered great polychrome friezes in relief at the Huaca de la Luna, about 500m from the Huaca del Sol. The Moche custom of 'burying' old temples under new ones facilitated preservation of the friezes. The excavation revealed six layers or building stages. The walls are decorated with geometrical designs with anthropomorphic figurines or masks, and sea birds, fish and waves. Theft and destruction during colonial times have left archaeologists with many questions unanswered.

Huaca El Brujo

This newly excavated ruin is 60km from Trujillo on the coast and hard to reach without a guide. It has burial sites and some of the best friezes in the area, depicting life-size prisoners, priests, sacrifices and geometric designs.

Huanchaco

This fishing village is a 15km bus ride northwest of Trujillo and has the best beach in the area, though fecal contamination has been reported. The water is too cold for locals most of the year, except from January to March. Totora-reed boats, like those depicted on Moche ceramics, are locally constructed. For a tip fishermen will demonstrate how to use them. They often arrive around 9 or 10 am, and some boats are usually seen stacked up at the north end of the beach.

Warning Robberies and rapes have occurred on Buenos Aires beach between Huanchaco to Trujillo. Take the bus.

Places to Stay & Eat Several families rent rooms; ask around. At Los Piños 451, *La*

PERU

Casa Suiza (no sign; ☎ *044-461285),* charges US$4 per person without bathroom or US$5 with solar powered bathroom. There is a place to barbecue on the terrace, laundry and a book exchange; breakfast is available. Around the corner, *Hostal Solange,* Los Ficus 484, has rooms with kitchen access at US$4 per person. Similarly priced is *Casa Hospedaje Huanchaco (*☎ *044-461719),* Los Ficus 516. The sweet Señora Lola, Manco Capac 136, has cheap rooms.

Hostal/Camping Naylamp (☎ *044-461022),* Prolongación Víctor Larco 3, on the north end of town, has rooms with bath at US$4 per person, kitchen access and a camping area. The clean *Hostal Huanchaco (*☎ *044-461272),* Larco 287, is US$6 per person (communal cold showers). There is a small pool and pleasant courtyard. Best is the *Hostal Bracamonte (*☎ *044-461162),* Los Olivos 503, with a pool and nice gardens. Rooms with private hot showers are US$15/23. Bargain for reduced rates in the off season. Run-down, cold-water *Golden Club Hostal (*☎ *044-461306),* on the waterfront at La Rivera 217, has overpriced rooms but rents surf boards for US$5 a day.

There are simple seafood restaurants at the northern end of the beach, near where the totora-reed boats are stacked. On the plaza, the *Colonial Club* is the best, but pricey.

Getting There & Away Buses leave from Industrial and España in Trujillo at frequent intervals during daylight hours.

CHICLAYO

The next major coastal city is Chiclayo (population 400,000), 200km north of Trujillo. One of Peru's fastest growing cities, it's a major commercial center and the capital of the Department of Lambayeque. Important archaeology sites are nearby.

Information

The tourist office (☎ 074-236701 ext 20), Saenz Peña 830, operated by the friendly tourist police, opens 8 am to 9 pm weekdays. They have limited information, but will keep luggage and take theft reports. Sipán Tours (☎ 074-227022, sipantours@kipu.rednorte .com.pe), Izaga 636, also offers information. It's open 8 am to 8 pm, Monday to Saturday and 8 am to noon on Sunday. The Banco de

Crédito changes traveler's checks. Street moneychangers hang out on the 600 block of Balta. For email, Virtualnet (☎ 074-239538), San José 462 upstairs, opens 8 am to 11 pm Monday to Saturday and charges US$2 per hour.

Things to See

Wander around the Mercado Modelo to see the herbalist stalls and *curanderos* (healers) with their unique healing potions and magic charms. Also look for heavy woven saddlebags, called *alforjas,* which are typical of the area. Watch your belongings. The market is a prime area for *huaco* selling; remember that their commercialization is illegal unless they are marked as reproductions.

Organized Tours Indiana Tours (☎ 074-225751), Colón 556, offers good English language tours to Sipán and Túcume for US$40 (one person), US$15 (three or more people). Other sites can be toured.

Places to Stay

The cheapest hotels on Balta north of the plaza are very basic. Few have hot water. *Hotel Royal (*☎ *074-233421)* on the plaza is old and run-down but OK for US$6/9 a single/double, or US$8/11 with bath.

Better budget hotels include friendly *Hostal Lido (*☎ *074-232810),* E Aguirre 412, at US$7/10 with cold bath or US$4 shared bath, and the quiet and reasonably clean *Hostal Venezuela (*☎ *074-232665),* Lora y Cordero 954, at US$7/12 with bath. Others at this price are the clean *Hostal Tumi de Oro (*☎ *074-227108),* L Prado 1145, with private hot bath for US$7/11 – less on the fourth floor with cold water. *Hotel Santa Rosa (*☎ *074-224411),* L Gonzales 927, one of the cleanest, charges US$13/18 for singles/doubles with bath, hot water, TV and phone, and the nearby *Hotel América (*☎ *074-224476)* is more upscale at US$20/29 with breakfast. *Hostal Señor de los Milagros* looks OK for US$6/10. *Hostal Sol Radiante (*☎ *074-237858),* Izaga 392, is a quiet, family-run place at US$8/12 with hot bath. *Hotel Europa (*☎ *074-222066),* E Aguirre 466, looks nice and charges US$11/14 for rooms with private hot bath or less with communal showers. Also in that range is the recommended *Hostal Miguel Antonio (*☎ *074-226850),* Torres Paz 735, with great showers, firm beds and TV.

CHICLAYO

M Pardo
San Martín
Bolívar
Juan Fanning
1
2
To Terrapuerto Municipal,
Buses to Sipán
Arica
Amazonas
Angamos
8 de Octubre
Mercado
Modelo
3
4
Oriente
5
Balta
2 de Enero
Leticia
Sáenz Peña
P Ruiz
6
7
D Ferre
Parque
Obrero
L Prado
8 de Octubre
9
10
M Cápac
Lora y Cordero
L Prado
11
12
14
Vicente de la Vega
16
17
Mercado
Central
19
To Piura,
Ecuador
13
15
José
18
San José
Plaza
Aguirre
22
23
24
21
E Aguirre
20
Grau
Plaza
de Armas
Catedral
25
26
P Saco
L Ortiz
27
I Gonzales
28
A Ugarte
29
A Carrión
30
J Cuglievan
A La Point
31
Colón
32
33
35
Balta
34
M Izaga
F Sarmiento
37
38
39
40
Torres Paz
36
F Cabrera
41
Tacna
42
43
52
54
55
M Castilla
Sáenz Peña
Tarata
44
45
46
47
48
49
50
51
53
V Dall'Orso
Bolgnesi

0   100   200 m
0   100   200 yards
Approximate Scale

To Trujillo,
Lima

PERU

PLACES TO STAY	OTHER	19 Peña Hermanos Balcázar	43 Expreso
10 Hostal Señor de los Milagros	1 Mini Buses to Sipán	20 Tourist Office,	Sudamericano
11 Hostal Tumi de Oro	2 Sports Stadium	Tourist Police	44 TEPSA Buses
16 Hotels Santa Rosa,	3 Buses to Monsefú	21 Peña El Brujo	45 Vulcano, El Aguila
América	4 Buses to Puerto Etén	24 Cine Colonial	46 Cruz de Chalpon
17 Hostal Venezuela	5 Buses to Monsefú &	25 Telefónica del Perú	47 EMTRAFESA Buses
23 Hotel Royal	Nearby Towns	26 Post Office	48 CIVA, LTTSA,
29 Hostal Lido	6 Buses to Túcume	27 Hospital Las Mercedes	Cruz del Sur, Roggero
30 Hotel Europa	7 Buses to Motupe	28 Santa Cecilia Clinic	49 Peru Express
37 Hostal Sol Radiante	8 Buses to Pimentel	32 AeroContinente	50 Transportes Piura
40 Hostal Miguel Antonio	12 Buses to Chongoyape	33 Cine Tropical	51 Expreso Continental
	13 Empresa Chiclayo	34 Banco de Crédito,	52 Chiclayo Express
PLACES TO EAT	14 Empresa D Olano	600 Block of Balta	53 Empresa D Olano
9 Govinda	15 Transportes San Pablo	36 Cine Oro	54 Transportes
18 La Nueva Barcarola		38 Sipán Tours	El Cumbe
31 Resaurant Mi Tía		42 Atahualpa Buses	55 Empresa Diaz
35 Las Américas			
39 Restaurant Romana			
41 Italian Restaurants			

Places to Eat

There are plenty of cheap restaurants on Av Balta; *Restaurant Romana*, Balta 512, is good and locally popular. Also recommended are *La Nueva Barcarola*, Vicente de la Vega 961, for cheap but tasty meals, *Restaurant Mi Tía* on Aguirre, near the plaza and the nearby *Las Américas*. *Govinda*, Balta 1029, has vegetarian food.

Getting There & Away

Air The airport is 2km southeast of town (a US$1 taxi). AeroContinente (☎ 074-209916) has an office in central Chiclayo by the plaza. There are three or four flights a day to Lima (US$59), two to Tumbes (US$42), one to Trujillo (US$15) and possibly one to Pirua.

Bus Many companies are near the corner of Sáenz Peña and Bolognesi. Look here for long-distance buses to Lima, Tumbes, Trujillo, Cajamarca, Chachapoyas and elsewhere. See the map for stops for buses going to sites around Chiclayo.

AROUND CHICLAYO
Lambayeque

This small town 11km north of Chiclayo has the excellent **Bruning Museum**, with a good collection of artifacts from several cultures. The main exhibit features finds from Sipán. Labels are in Spanish. Entry is US$1 and a guide is US$2.50. It's open 8 am to 6 pm weekdays and 9 am to 6 pm on weekends and holidays. Minivans from Chiclayo drop you at the museum.

Sipán

Hundreds of dazzling and priceless artifacts have been recovered from Sipán, where a royal Moche burial site was discovered in 1987. Excavation continues. One tomb has a replica of one of the several burials and there is a good museum, but the most spectacular finds are on display in Lambayeque's Bruning Museum. Sipán is 30km southeast of Chiclayo. Buses (see map; US$0.50) leave often in the morning, less so in the afternoon. Sipán entry is US$1.

Túcume

This vast and little-known site can be seen from a spectacular cliff-top viewpoint about 30km north of Lambayeque on the Panamericana. It's worth the climb to see over 200 hectares of crumbing walls, plazas and pyramids. There is an on-site museum. Túcume was recently studied by a team led by Thor Heyerdahl (of *Kon Tiki* fame). Entry is US$1, It's open 8:30 am to 4:30 pm weekdays, to 6 pm on weekends. Guides may be available, or hire one in Chiclayo or at the Bruning Museum. Buses go from Chiclayo or from the museum; it's about 1km walk from where the bus drops you in Túcume.

Coastal Villages

Buses from Chiclayo go to the coastal villages of **Pimentel**, **Santa Rosa** and **Puerto Etén**. Pimentel has a decent beach and the many kilometers of coast stretching northwest are good for surfing, though there are no public transport or facilities. There are no hotels but simple rooms can be rented. Both Pimentel and Santa Rosa are active fishing villages and totora-reed boats can be seen in action. Puerto Etén is another fishing town. All three have simple but good seafood restaurants and can be visited easily using frequent minibuses from Chiclayo.

PIURA

Founded by Pizarro in 1532, Piura is Peru's oldest colonial city. The Catedral dates from 1588. The center has some colonial buildings, though many were destroyed in a 1912 earthquake. The city's focal point is the large, shady and pleasant Plaza de Armas. Irrigation of the desert has made Piura a major agricultural center; rice is the main crop. Piura is capital of its department and has over 300,000 inhabitants. December to April is the rainy season and El Niño climatic events occur every few years. The 1992 El Niño washed out roads and bridges; they have all reopened now, but only one car bridge has been rebuilt in town. The old San Miguel bridge reopened as a pedestrian crossing.

Information

There is a tourist office at the Municipalidad that opens 8 am to 5 pm weekdays. The Banco de Crédito changes traveler's checks. Internet services (US$1 per hour) are available at the Universidad de Piura 8 am to 7 pm Monday to Saturday.

Things to See

The small **Museo de la Cultura**, Huánuco and Sullana, houses archaeology and art

PERU

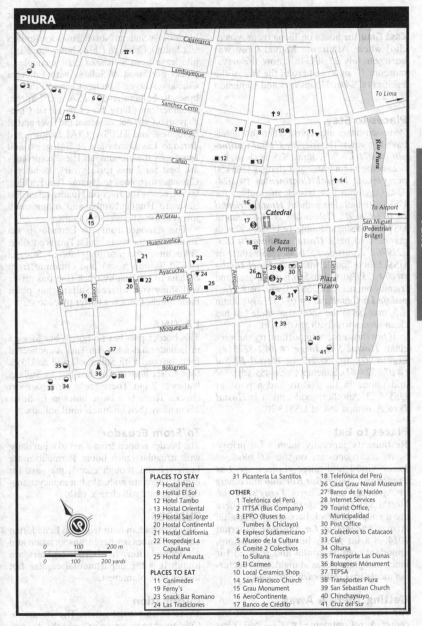

PIURA

PLACES TO STAY
7 Hostal Perú
8 Hostal El Sol
12 Hotel Tambo
13 Hostal Oriental
19 Hostal San Jorge
20 Hostal Continental
21 Hostal California
22 Hospedaje La
     Capullana
25 Hostal Amauta

PLACES TO EAT
11 Canímedes
19 Ferny's
23 Snack Bar Romano
24 Las Tradiciones

31 Picantería La Santitos

OTHER
1 Telefónica del Perú
2 ITTSA (Bus Company)
3 EPPO (Buses to
     Tumbes & Chiclayo)
4 Expreso Sudamericano
5 Museo de la Cultura
6 Comité 2 Colectivos
     to Sullana
9 El Carmen
10 Local Ceramics Shop
14 San Francisco Church
15 Grau Monument
16 AeroContinente
17 Banco de Crédito

18 Telefónica del Perú
26 Casa Grau Naval Museum
27 Banco de la Nación
28 Internet Services
29 Tourist Office,
     Municipalidad
30 Post Office
32 Colectivos to Catacaos
33 Cial
34 Oltursa
35 Transporte Las Dunas
36 Bolognesi Monument
37 TEPSA
38 Transportes Piura
39 San Sebastian Church
40 Chinchaysuyo
41 Cruz del Sur

0   100   200 m
0   100   200 yards

exhibits. It's open 9 am to 1 pm and 4 to 8 pm Tuesday to Saturday; admission is free. **Casa Grau**, the house on Tacna (near Ayacucho) where Almirante Miguel Grau was born, on July 27, 1834, is now the naval museum. Grau was a hero of the War of the Pacific (1879-80). Hours vary and admission is free.

Places to Stay

Water shortages are reported and few hotels have hot water. The friendly *Hostal California* (☎ 074-328789), Junín 835, is clean, has occasional warm water and charges US$4.50 per person. *Hostal Continental* (☎ 074-334531), Junín 924, has clean doubles for US$9 with bath, less without. *Hostal Oriental* (☎ 074-328891), Callao 446, is also clean at US$4.50/8 a single/double, or US$6/9.50 with private cold bath. *Hostal Amauta* (☎ 074-322976), Apurímac 580, is US$6/10.50 or US$12 for a double with bath. *Hotel Tambo* (☎ 074-325379), Callao 546, is good, clean and friendly but noisy at US$7/10 with bath. *Hospedaje La Capullana* (☎ 074-321239), Junín 925, may be in the short stay trade but has clean singles with bath at US$7.50.

If hot showers are important, try the very clean *Hostal San Jorge* (☎ 074-327514), Loreto 960, at US$8/12, or *Hostal El Sol* (☎ 074-324461), Sánchez Cerro 455, with TV and phone in the rooms and a pool, at US$16/23. Another good option is *Hostal Peru*, Arequipa 484, at US$13/20.

Places to Eat

Restaurants generally seem a bit pricey. Some cheap ones are on the 700 block of Junín. Good mid-range choices are *Las Tradiciones, Snack Bar Romano* and others at Ayacucho and Cuzco. *Ferny's*, at the Hostal San Jorge, is clean and good. There are a couple of snack bars on the Plaza de Armas. *Picantería La Santitos*, Libertad 1014, is a bit pricey but serves delicious, abundant comida criolla and seafood for lunch and great pizzas at night. For vegetarian meals, try *Canímedes*, Lima 444.

Getting There & Away

Air The airport is 2km southeast of the center. AeroContinente (☎ 074-325635) has an office in the center. They have three or four daily flights to Lima (US$77) and one daily flight to Trujillo.

Bus & Truck Buses, cars and trucks for various local destinations leave from the fifth block of Av Sullana Norte. Buses for Tumbes (six hours), Chiclayo (three hours) and Trujillo leave from Sánchez Cerro, a couple of blocks northwest of Sullana with Empresa Chiclayo. Also on Sánchez Cerro, EPPO has buses to Sullana and ITTSA and Expreso Sudamericano have buses to Lima; Chinchaysuyo, Cruz del Sur are at the river end of Bolognesi, and TEPSA, CIAL, Oltura and Turismo Las Dunas are at Bolognesi and Loreto, by the monument. These companies are best for Lima (prices vary, 18 hours). Chinchaysuyo goes to Huaraz (via Trujillo). CIVA, across the river on Huancavelica, has buses to Huancabamba and other small towns in the Andes east of Piura.

The standard route to Ecuador is via Tumbes, but the route via La Tina is possible. Take an early morning bus to Sullana (US$0.50, one hour) and continue from Sullana to La Tina by truck (the bus driver will show you where). Sullana has poor, basic hotels; Piura is a better place to stay.

LA TINA

This border post has no hotels, but Macará in Ecuador has a few. La Tina is connected by poor road with Sullana (US$3 to US$6, four to six hours). The last bus to Sullana leaves at 2 pm. There are several passport checks. There is a basic hotel in El Suyo, 15km away, then no hotels until Sullana.

To/From Ecuador

The border is open from 8 am to 6 pm daily, with irregular lunch hours. Formalities are fairly relaxed, though guards may ask for bribes. There are no banks but moneychangers in Macará will change cash.

TUMBES

Although half an hour from the Ecuadorian border, Tumbes is where transportation and accommodations for border-crossers are found. It is the departmental capital, but there's little of interest.

Information

There is no tourist office. The Banco de Crédito changes traveler's checks, though rates are a little better away from the border. Street moneychangers here and at the border give good rates if you know what the

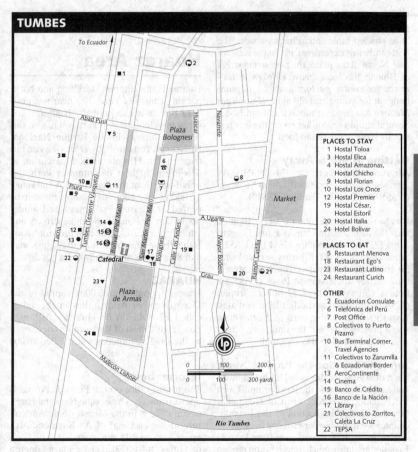

TUMBES

To Ecuador

Abad Pusil

Plaza Bolognesi

Huáscar

Navarrete

Piura

Tumbes (Teniente Vásquez)

Tacna

Bolívar (Ped Mall)

San Martín (Ped Mall)

Calle Los Andes

A Ugarte

Mayor Bodero

Ramón Castilla

Market

Catedral

Bolognesi

Grau

Plaza de Armas

Malecón Lishner

Río Tumbes

| 0 | 100 | 200 m |
| 0 | 100 | 200 yards |

PLACES TO STAY
1 Hostal Toloa
3 Hostal Elica
4 Hostal Amazonas, Hostal Chicho
9 Hostal Florian
10 Hostal Los Once
12 Hostal Premier
19 Hostal César, Hostal Estoril
20 Hostal Italia
24 Hotel Bolívar

PLACES TO EAT
5 Restaurant Menova
18 Restaurant Ego's
23 Restaurant Latino
24 Restaurant Curich

OTHER
2 Ecuadorian Consulate
6 Telefónica del Perú
7 Post Office
8 Colectivos to Puerto Pizarro
10 Bus Terminal Corner, Travel Agencies
11 Colectivos to Zarumilla & Ecuadorian Border
13 AeroContinente
14 Cinema
15 Banco de Crédito
16 Banco de la Nación
17 Library
21 Colectivos to Zorritos, Caleta La Cruz
22 TEPSA

PERU

best rate is and bargain. Otherwise, you'll get poor rates. Beware of 'fixed' calculators.

Places to Stay

During holidays and trade fairs, hotels are often full by noon. At other times, hotels are full by late afternoon. Single rooms are difficult to find. Most hotels have only cold water but are pricey. There are frequent water and electricity outages.

The cheapest basic hotels start at around US$7 for a single and US$10 for a double. The following are the best – friendly and reasonably clean: *Hostal Estoril*, with private hot showers; *Hostal Elica* (☎ 074-523870), Tacna 337, *Hostal Amazonas* (☎ 074-525266), Tumbes 317, and *Hostal Italia*

(☎ 074-526164), at Grau 733, which is slightly cheaper. *Hotel Bolívar* is also cheap and basic but reasonably clean. Others include *Hostal Los Once* (☎ 074-523717), Piura 475, which has private baths, is fairly clean and handy to the buses (but noisy), and the basic but friendly *Hostal Premier* (☎ 074-523077), Tumbes 225, which lacks singles.

Hostal Florian (☎ 074-522464), Piura 414, charges US$12/15 with private hot bath and is recommended. Also decent in this range is *Hostal César* (☎ 074-522883), Huáscar 353, at US$13.50/17. *Hostal Chicho* (☎ 074-522282), Av Tumbes 327, charges US$11/16 for rooms with private bath, TV, fan and phone, and *Hostal Toloa* (☎ 074-523771), Av Tumbes 430, is a bit cheaper at US$8/11.50.

Places to Eat

Bars and *restaurants* on the Plaza de Armas have shaded tables and chairs outside. The best (and most expensive) are on the western side. North of the plaza, the pedestrian street of Bolívar has inexpensive *chicken restaurants, ice-cream parlors* and is a popular hangout for young and old alike. *Restaurant Menova* has good set meals for about US$2. Several simple restaurants near the bus terminals serve good, cheap food.

Getting There & Away

Air AeroContinente (☎ 074-522350), Av Tumbes 217, has one daily flight to Lima (US$59) and one to Trujillo (US$40).

Bus Most bus companies are on Av Tumbes, near the intersection with Av Piura. Fares to Lima (22 to 24 hours) are US$13 to US$25. Some companies offer 'luxury service,' with air con, toilets and video. There are several buses a day; most stop at Piura (US$5, six hours), Chiclayo (US$7, 12 hours), Trujillo (US$10, 15 hours) and other intermediates. If you arrive in Tumbes early in the morning, you'll probably get out the same day; otherwise, be prepared to stay overnight.

To/From Ecuador The Peruvian border town of Aguas Verdes is linked by an international bridge across the Río Zarumilla with the Ecuadorian border town of Huaquillas (see the Huaquillas section in the Ecuador chapter for more border-crossing details.)

Exit formalities as you cross from Peru to Ecuador are fairly quick. Immigration is open 8 am to noon and 2 to 6 pm daily. The Peruvian border post is 2km from the border; *mototaxis* take you to the border for US$0.50. In Aguas Verdes, there are a few simple restaurants, a bank and no hotels. Border guards, taxi drivers and moneychangers all try to rip you off. There are no entry fees into either country so be polite but insistent with border guards, bargain hard with drivers and find out exchange rates ahead of time before changing money. Moneychangers' calculators are sometimes rigged to read low. Buy and sell Peruvian currency in Peru and Ecuadorian in Ecuador for the best rates.

Getting Around

A taxi to the airport is around US$4, to the border about US$7. Colectivos for Aguas Verdes leave from the corner of Bolívar and Piura (US$1, 26km).

Huaraz Area

Huaraz is the climbing, trekking and backpacking center of Peru. The nearby Cordillera Blanca is exceptionally beautiful, and many travelers come to Peru just to visit this region, which is in the **Parque Nacional Huascarán**. You can enjoy great views on bus trips in the Huaraz area: Huascarán, at 6768m the highest mountain in Peru, lies only 14km from the main road. A full range of hiking and climbing equipment can be rented in Huaraz. Trail maps and guidebooks can be bought and mule drivers and guides are available. The best time for hiking is the dry season, from June to August. May and September are usually quite good.

HUARAZ

Huaraz (population 80,000), capital of the Department of Ancash, lies in the valley called El Callejón de Huaylas. Although now rebuilt, most of the town was destroyed by the 1970 earthquake, which killed 70,000 people in central Peru.

Information

The tourist office on the Plaza de Armas is open erratically. The Parque Nacional Huascarán office is in the Ministerio de Agricultura at the east end of Av Raymondi. It's open 7 am to 2:15 pm weekdays. The Casa de Guías (☎ 044-721811), on Plaza Ginebra 1 block northeast of the Plaza de Armas, has a list of registered guides and is a good source of hiking and climbing information. Guide services and equipment rental can be found along Av Luzuriaga. During the dry season, Huaraz swarms with hikers and climbers. They have the best information. Banks are on the north side of the Plaza de Armas and on the 600 block of Luzuriaga. Moneychangers are found on the streets outside. The Banco de Crédito changes traveler's checks.

Things to See

The **Museo Regional**, on the Plaza de Armas, has a small, interesting archaeology exhibit. It's open 9 am to 6 pm Tuesday to Saturday and 9 am to 2 pm Sunday and

Monday. Admission is US$1.50, which includes entry to the small Wari **Ruinas Wilcahuaín**. There is no regular transport, but you can walk or hire a taxi for a few dollars. Head north on Av Centenario to a dirt road to your right a few hundred meters past the Hotel de Turistas. The dirt road climbs 6km (passing through the communities of Jinua and Paria) to the ruins and continues another 20km to Laguna Llaca, where there are excellent mountain views. The site is open daily.

Activities & Organized Tours

Visiting the national park (entry US$1) is the main activity. Several outfitters rent climbing and hiking gear and provide information and guides. Casa de Guías and Montrek (☎ 044-721124), Luzuriaga 646, has a good selection. Maps are sold in Huaraz. Bradt's *Backpacking and Trekking in Peru and Bolivia* is a good guide for independent hikers. Mountain Bike Adventures (☎ 044-724259, olaza@mail.cosapidata.com.pe), Lúcar y Torre 538, rents bikes. You can raft the Río Santa (better in the rainy season). Montrek and Ames River Runners (☎ 044-723375), 27 de Noviembre 773, (at My House B&B) have been recommended.

Bus day tours are another option. One visits the ruins at Chavín de Huantar, another goes through Yungay to the beautiful Lagunas Llanganuco, where there are spectacular views of Huascarán and other mountains and a third goes to see the giant *Puya raimondi* plant and ice caves at Nevado Pastoruri. Prices range from US$5 to US$10 per person, including a guide who doesn't necessarily speak English. There are daily departures in the high season. Some recommended agencies are Pablo Tours (☎ 044-721145), Luzuriaga 501; Chavín Tours (☎ 044-721578), Luzuriaga 508, with the most minibuses; Milla Tours (☎ 044-721742), Luzuriaga 528; and Kike Tours (☎ 044-724818), Luzuriaga 574. These are by no means the only agencies.

Places to Stay

Dry-season prices can be double the off-season rates. The period around Fiestas Patrias (July 28) is especially busy. Most places have warm or hot showers some of the time: ask. Otherwise, you can get a hot shower at Duchas Raimondi, Raimondi 904.

The basic, friendly *Casa de Jaime* (☎ 044-722281), A Gridilla 267, has cooking and laundry facilities and hot water at US$2.50 per person. *Pensión NG*, Pasaje Valenzuela 837 (parallel to and a few blocks south of 28 de Julio), has hot water and charges US$4 each with breakfast. The clean *Edward's Inn* (☎ 044-722692), Bolognesi 121, is friendly and has plenty of local information. It has hot water, laundry facilities and a café, and is popular at US$5 each in dorms or US$13 for a double with bath. *Señora López,* behind Edward's Inn, is another budget option. *Alojamiento El Farolito* (☎ 044-725792), Tarapacá 1466, a two-story green house, has rooms, some with private bath and hot showers, for about US$3.50 per person. They have a TV room, café and laundry service. Nearby is *Hostal Piscis* (☎ 044-722362), Tarapacá 1452, which is clean and helpful, has hot water, breakfast on request, laundry and beds for US$3 to US$5 per person. *Casa de Guías* (☎ 044-721811), Plaza de Ginebra, charges US$5 to US$7 each for dorm beds, depending on the season, and has laundry facilities, hot water and a popular restaurant.

Small, family-run places with occasional hot water include the basic, clean and popular *Hostal Quintana* (☎ 044-726060), M Caceres 411, charging US$4.25 per person, and *Pensión Galaxia* (☎ 044-722230), Romero 638, at US$8 a double. The friendly, helpful *Hotel Los Andes* (☎ 044-721346), Tarapacá 316, charges around US$3.50 each. The basic *Hostal Estoico* (☎ 044-722371), San Martín 635, charges US$5/8 for singles/doubles or US$6/9 with private bath and has hot water some of the time. The family-run *Alojamiento Soledad* (☎ 044-721196), A Figueroa 1267, recommended by a reader as friendly and safe – with free laundry service – charges US$6 per person.

Oscar's Hostal (☎/fax 044-722720), José de la Mar 624, charges about US$8/11 and has hot water. *Hostal Raimondi* (☎ 044-721082), Raimondi 820, has a small café for 6 am breakfasts and charges US$8/14 with bath. Also in this price range is *Hostal Monte Rosa*, Bolívar 419, which is frequently full, and the clean, pleasant and safe *Hostal Yanett* (☎ 044-721466), Centenario 106, which has a small garden and serves breakfast. *Hostal Continental* (☎ 044-721557), 28 de Julio 586, asks US$7 per person and is clean with private baths and

PERU

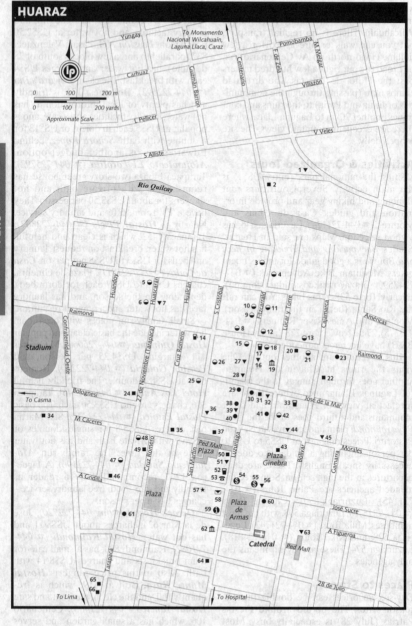

HUARAZ

HUARAZ

PLACES TO STAY	43 Casa de Guías	23 Duchas Raimondi
2 Hostal Yanett	44 Café Andino	25 Civa Cial
20 Hostal Raimondi	45 Bistro de los Andes	26 Transportes Huascarán
22 Hostal Monte Rosa	51 Montrek	& TROME (Buses)
24 Hotel Los Andes	56 Picollo Café & Pizzería	29 Chavín Tours
31 Oscar's Hostal	63 Rinconcito Huaracino	30 Pablo Tours
34 Edward's Inn, Señora López	64 Café Central	33 El Tambo Bar
35 Hostal Quintana		38 Pyramid Adventures,
37 Hostal Estoico	OTHER	Milla Tours
43 Casa de Guías	3 Empresa 14	40 Kike Tours
46 Casa de Jaime	4 Empresa Huandoy (Buses to	41 Mountain Bike Adventures
49 Pensión Galaxia	Monterrey, Carhuaz, Yungay	42 Cruz del Sur
50 Hostal El Pacífico	& Caraz)	47 Transportes Rodríguez
64 Hostal Continental	5 Virgen del Carmen	48 Chavín Express
65 Hostal Piscis	6 El Rápido	51 Montrek
66 Alojamiento El Farolito	8 Empresa Norpacífico	52 La Cueva del Oso Peña
	9 Expreso Sudamericano	53 Telefónica del Perú
PLACES TO EAT	10 Turismo Chimbote	54 Banco de Crédito
1 Recreo La Unión	11 Paradise Tours	55 Interbanc
7 Huaraz Querido	12 Taxis 1 & 2 (Local & to Caraz)	57 Police Station
16 Restaurant Familiar	13 Expreso Ancash	58 Post Office
27 Creperíe Patrick,	14 Gas Station	59 Tourist Office
Chifa Min Hua	15 Transportes Rodríguez	60 Cine Radio
28 Monte Rosa	17 Campo Base	61 Ames River Runners
32 Restaurant Samuels	18 Movil Tours	62 Museo Regional de Ancash
36 Las Puyas	19 Museo de Miniaturas	
39 Chez Pepe	21 Transportes Moreno	

PERU

hot water. Popular with Peruvian tourist groups, *Hostal El Pacífico* (☎ 044-721683), Luzuriaga 630, charges US$8/12 in rooms with private bath and hot water (mornings), but some interior rooms are windowless.

Places to Eat
The following are cheap but good: *Restaurant Familiar* has a wide variety; *Recreo La Unión* serves typical local lunches; *Restaurant Samuels* serves big helpings and is popular with locals and gringos; *Las Puyas* has large meals and is popular with budget travelers; *Recreo de los Jardines*, 1 block from the trout hatchery, is a locally popular for trout dishes under US$3. *Rinconcito Huaracino* serves typical Peruvian food and ceviche. *Huaraz Querido* is also a good spot for ceviche.

For breakfast, *Café Central* is cheap. *Casa de Guías* is very popular and has granola, yogurt and fruit besides the usual fare. The best place for good coffee (including espresso) is the popular *Café Andino*, Morales 753. A block away on Morales and also popular with young foreign visitors is *Picollo Café/Pizzería*, with sidewalk seating and reasonable prices. A new restaurant

worth a look on this street is *Bistro de los Andes*, Morales 823.

There are several good pizzerias and international restaurants, which are pricier than the Peruvian places. Beware – some add a 31% tax. The best pizzerias are *Chez Pepe* (also has other good meals), *Montrek* (with a climbing wall) and the cheaper *Monte Rosa*. *Creperíe Patrick* is recommended for crêpes, ice cream and continental dinners. *Chifa Min Hua* is quite good.

Entertainment
There are several bars, discos and peñas whose popularity waxes and wanes. Entertainment declines outside the tourist season. For a bar atmosphere, *Las Kenas Pub*, Gabino Uribe 620, has a happy hour from 8 to 10 pm and live Andean music from 10:30 pm. *El Tambo Bar*, La Mar 776, is popular with gringos and Peruvians and has good live and recorded music and crowded dancing, though it doesn't get underway until about 10 pm. *La Cueva del Oso Peña*, Luzuriaga 674, also has dancing and a variety of music. *Campo Base*, Luzuriaga 407, is the most recently opened bar with music and dancing.

Getting There & Away

Air Anta (23km north of Huaraz) is the nearest airport. There are no regular commercial flights at the moment.

Bus There are many buses to Lima (US$5 to US$9, eight hours) so shop around. Cruz del Sur (☎ 044-725802) has nightly Imperial non-stop service (the most expensive). Others include Civa Cial (☎ 044-721947), Móvil Tours (☎ 044-722555), Transportes Rodríguez (☎ 044-721353), Expreso Ancash (the Ormeño subsidiary, ☎ 044-72-1102), Empresa 14 (☎ 044-721282) and TROME (☎ 044-721542). Most have day and night buses. Buses to Chimbote (US$5 to US$7, eight hours) go north through the spectacular Cañón del Pato, or west over the 4225m Punta Callán. Both are worth seeing in daylight. Transportes Moreno (☎ 044-721344), Transportes Rodríguez, Comité 14 and Turismo Chimbote (☎ 044-721984) go to Chimbote, some continuing to Trujillo.

Frequent daytime buses north to Yungay and Caraz (US$1.25, 1½ hours) leave from Fitzcarrald north of Raimondi with Empresa Huandoy, which also operates a few buses a week across the Cordillera Blanca to Chacas and Chavín. Faster minibuses to Caraz leave from the same block. Chavín Express goes to Chavín de Huantar (US$3.50, four hours) continuing on to Huari (seven hours) four times daily. For Chiquián (and the Cordillera Huayhuash), Empresa Huallanca, Raimondi at Huascarán, have daily buses (US$2, 3½ hours) and there are others from the same area.

Trucks leave for other villages in the Cordillera Blanca area, ask around.

NORTH OF HUARAZ

The road through the Callejón de Huaylas follows the Río Santa and is paved to Caraz. Five km north is **Monterrey**, where you'll find hot springs. **Carhuaz** is 31km north of Huaraz and has a few basic hotels. It is near the entrance to the Ulta valley, where there is beautiful trekking. Between Carhuaz and Yungay the views of Huascarán are excellent.

Yungay

The town and its 18,000 inhabitants were buried by a catastrophic avalanche during the 1970 earthquake. The site is marked by a white statue of Christ on a knoll overlooking old Yungay. The avalanche path is visible from the road. The mass grave is marked by flower gardens in the **Campo Santo** (US$0.50 admission) culminating in old Yungay's plaza, where parts of the church spire are all that remain. New Yungay has been rebuilt just beyond the avalanche path, about 59km north of Huaraz.

Llanganuco The trip to Lagunas Llanganuco begins from Yungay and is one of the most beautiful and popular excursions in the Cordillera Blanca. To get there, take a tour from Huaraz or buses or taxis from Yungay. From June to August, minibuses (US$5) leave from the plaza in Yungay, stopping for two hours near the lakes. (Trips during the rest of the year depend on passenger demand.) National park entry is US$1. Llanganuco is the start of the popular and spectacular four- or five-day Llanganuco to Santa Cruz hiking loop.

Places to Stay & Eat The very friendly *Hostal Gledel*, near the plaza, is US$5/7.50 with hot water and meals available. The clean *Hostal Yungay* (☎ 044-793053), is US$3.50 per person with hot shared showers. A few other cheap hotels may close in the low season. *Restaurant Turístico Alpamayo* serves typical food; there are others.

Caraz

This pleasant little town (elevation 2270m) is 67km north of Huaraz; it is the end point of the Llanganuco to Santa Cruz trek. Caraz has survived earthquakes and landslides. The Plaza de Armas is attractive, there are several cheap hotels and you can take pleasant walks in the surrounding hills. Run by the amiable English-speaking Alberto Cafferata, Pony's Expeditions (☎/fax 044-79-1642, hcafferata@am1.lima.net.pe), Sucre 1266, open 9 am to 9 pm daily and offers gear rental, maps and trekking services.

Places to Stay The basic, clean and friendly *Caballero Lodging* (☎ 044-791637), Daniel Villar 485, has hot showers and charges US$4 per person. The friendly *Hostal Morovi* (☎ 044-791409), Luzuriaga s/n, is US$4/6 for singles/doubles with bath. *Albergue Los Pinos* (☎ 044-791130), Parque San Martin 103, – ask how to get there – is

US$6 double with hot water and breakfast. *Hostal La Casona* (☎ *044-791334*), Raymondi 319, is clean, has hot water and is US$4/5 or US$5/6 with bath. *Hostal Suizo Peruano* (☎ *044-791166*), San Martín 1133, charges US$4/6 or a bit more for a double with bath. Next door, the *Hostal Chavín* (☎ *044-722171*), one of the best, is friendly, clean and charges US$8/12 in clean rooms with hot showers, and arranges guides and mules. There are other cheapies.

SOUTHEAST OF HUARAZ
Chavín de Huantar

Near this small village are the interesting ruins of Chavín, Peru's oldest major culture (1300 to 400 BC). The site holds highly stylized carvings of the feline, Chavín's principal deity, and of lesser condor, snake and human deities. The most attractive parts of Chavín were built underground (it's lit, but bring a flashlight in case of power failure). It's worth hiring a local guide. In the heart of the underground complex lies an exquisitely carved, 4m dagger-like rock, the Lanzón de Chavín. The site, on the southwest edge of town, is open daily; admission is US$2.

Places to Stay & Eat Hotels are very basic and cheap. The two better ones are *Hostal Chavín* and *La Casona de JB*, which charge about US$5 per person; others are the *Inca* at US$4/6, or try the *Montecarlo* or *Gantu*. Restaurants close soon after sunset, so eat early.

Getting There & Away Tour buses make day trips from Huaraz (US$11). See Huaraz for daily public buses (US$3.50, five hours), but note that they do not return in the afternoon, so you must take a tour or stay overnight.

Chiquián

This village (3400m) is the gateway to the spectacular Cordillera Huayhuash. Few supplies are available but *burros* and *arrieros* (mules and their handlers) can be hired here.

Places to Stay & Eat The basic but clean *Hostal San Miguel*, Comercio 233 (no sign), is US$4 per person. Also friendly *Hotel Inca*, 2 blocks from the plaza, is US$2.50. There are a couple of even more basic places and a few simple restaurants.

Getting There & Away TUBSA and Transfysa go to Lima (US$7.50, 10 hours) every other day. Turismo Cavassa has a night bus to Lima. Transportes Virgen del Carmen and Transportes Huandoy have buses to Huaraz.

Across the Northern Highlands

CAJAMARCA

Cajamarca (2650m) is five hours east of the coast by paved road. It's a tranquil and traditional colonial city (population 70,000) and the capital of its department. The surrounding countryside is green and attractive, particularly during the rainy season.

Cajamarca has impressive colonial architecture, interesting people and customs and excellent Andean food. Pizarro deceived, captured and finally assassinated the Inca Atahualpa (see History in the Facts about South America chapter) here. Relatively few foreigners visit Cajamarca.

Information

The tourist office inside the Complejo de Belén is open 7:30 am to 1 pm and 2:30 to 6:30 pm weekdays. The Banco de Crédito and Interbanc change traveler's checks. Street moneychangers are near the Plaza de Armas. Internet services are available at the university (buses to Baños del Inca go past it) 8 am to 1 pm and 3 to 6 pm weekdays.

There are several travel agencies, but Cumbe Mayo Tours (☎ 044-922938), Puga 635, and Cajamarca Tours (☎ 044-922813), 2 de Mayo 323, are recommended for local tours.

Things to See

The only remaining Inca building in Cajamarca, **El Cuarto del Rescate** (the ransom chamber), is where Pizarro kept Atahualpa prisoner, not where the ransom was stored. It opens daily, except Tuesday, 9 am to noon and 3 to 5 pm. Entry is US$1, and includes admission to the following sites, which have similar hours.

Construction of the **Complejo de Belén** began in the 17th century. Inside what once was the Women's Hospital there is a small archaeology museum, and a few reconstructed minuscule patient cells. In the

PERU

CAJAMARCA

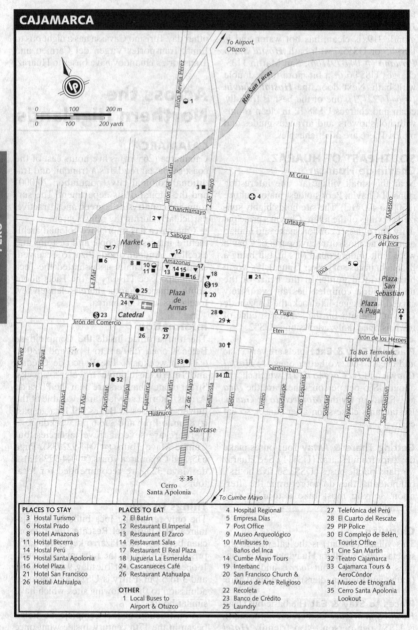

PLACES TO STAY
3 Hostal Turismo
6 Hostal Prado
8 Hotel Amazonas
11 Hostal Becerra
14 Hostal Perú
15 Hostal Santa Apolonia
16 Hotel Plaza
21 Hotel San Francisco
26 Hostal Atahualpa

PLACES TO EAT
2 El Batán
12 Restaurant El Imperial
13 Restaurant El Zarco
14 Restaurant Salas
17 Restaurant El Real Plaza
18 Juguería La Esmeralda
24 Cascanueces Café
26 Restaurant Atahualpa

OTHER
1 Local Buses to
   Airport & Otuzco

4 Hospital Regional
5 Empresa Días
7 Post Office
9 Museo Arqueológico
10 Minibuses to
   Baños del Inca
14 Cumbe Mayo Tours
19 Interbanc
20 San Francisco Church &
   Museo de Arte Religioso
22 Recoleta
23 Banco de Crédito
25 Laundry

27 Telefónica del Perú
28 El Cuarto del Rescate
29 PIP Police
30 El Complejo de Belén,
   Tourist Office
31 Cine San Martín
32 Teatro Cajamarca
33 Cajamarca Tours &
   AeroCóndor
34 Museo de Etnografía
35 Cerro Santa Apolonia
   Lookout

kitchen and dispensary of the hospital there is an art museum. Next door is the **church**, with a fine cupola and a carved and painted pulpit. Woodcarvings include a tired-looking Christ sitting cross-legged on his throne, looking as if he could do with a pisco sour after a hard day's miracle-working. The outside walls display lavish decorations. Close by, the small **Museo de Etnografía** exhibits local costumes and clothing, domestic and agricultural implements, musical instruments and other examples of Cajamarcan culture.

The university-run **Museo Arqueológico** displays artifacts from the under-studied pre-Incan Cajamarca culture. It opens daily, except Tuesday, 8 am to 2:30 pm. Admission is free, knock on the door to get in.

The **Iglesia San Francisco** has catacombs and a religious art museum, open 2 to 6 pm weekdays. Entry is US$1, including a guided tour.

The **Cerro Santa Apolonia** hill overlooks the city from the southwest. Climb the stairs at the end of 2 de Mayo. There are pre-Columbian carvings and pretty gardens. Entry is US$0.50.

Special Events

Water throwing during Carnaval is without respite. Corpus Christi is very colorful and Fiestas Patrias events include a bullfight.

Places to Stay

Prices rise around fiestas and during the dry months. Cheap hotels with hot water have it only a few hours a day – ask when.

Hotel San Francisco (☎ 044-823070), Belén 790, is relatively clean at US$5/8 for singles/doubles with private hot shower. The similar *Hostal Becerra* (☎ 044-823496), JR del Batán 195, charges US$10 per person with bath and shared showers with hot water. A few rooms have full bath. There are several hotels surrounding the plaza. *Hostal Perú* (☎ 044-824030), Puga 605, has private hot showers and is OK at US$8 per person (negotiable). Popular with gringos, the *Hotel Plaza* (☎ 044-822058), Puga 669, is in a colorful old building. It has hot water in the morning and evening, and a few rooms with balconies and plaza views. Rates are US$5/9 or US$9/15 with private bath. The new *Hostal Santa Apolonia* (☎ 044-827207), Puga 649, is clean, with carpeted singles/

doubles at US$14/23 with bath. They also have a couple singles with shared bath for US$8.

The clean *Hostal Prado* (☎ 044-823288), La Mar 582, is a good deal at US$5 per person or US$12/20 with bath, hot water, TV and phone. The bare-looking *Hostal Turismo* (☎ 044-823101), 2 de Mayo 817, has clean, carpeted rooms with comfortable beds and private hot showers at US$10/15. *Hostal Atahualpa* (☎ 044-827840), on Atahualpa near Jr del Comercio, looks quite good for US$10/17 (negotiable) with warm showers in the morning. A few rooms with shared showers are cheaper. The friendly *Hotel Amazonas* (☎ 044-822620), Amazonas 528, has rooms at US$8/12 with bath and communal hot showers.

Places to Eat

Cajamarca is famous for its cheeses and other typical dishes such as *chupe verde*, cuy with spicy potatoes and roasted pork. *Salas*, on the plaza, is a locally popular barn of a place serving various reasonably priced local dishes. Around the corner is the terrific *El Zarco*, which opens 7 am for breakfast, and serves typical dishes at lunch and lighter meals for dinner. *El Real Plaza*, 2 de Mayo 569, has a pleasant courtyard and serves local dishes. *Atahualpa*, next to the hotel, and *El Imperial*, on the 600 block of Amazonas, have good, cheap fixed menús and other meals. Pricier but worth a visit, *El Batán*, Batán 369, on the historical Casona Urteaga, serves varied international cuisine (closed Monday). On Friday and Saturday nights they host live local music shows. and upstairs there is an art gallery. For snacks and fruit shakes, try the new *Jugería La Esmeralda*, 2 de Mayo 568, where they also sell farm-fresh cheese. For those with a sweet tooth, the cakes and coffee at *Cascanueces Café*, Puga 554, are irresistible.

Getting There & Away

Air AeroCóndor (☎ 044-822813, 044-825674), 2 de Mayo 323, has three daily flights to Lima (US$107, direct), via Trujillo and via Chimbote (both US$89). AeroContinente plans future flights. A taxi to the airport is about US$2.

Bus Most bus terminals are on the third block of Atahualpa (not the Atahualpa in

PERU

the town center, but another street of the same name), 1.5km southeast of town on the road to the Baños del Inca. Cumbe Mayo Tours and Cajamarca Tours sell some bus tickets, or you can buy them at the terminals.

Many companies have buses to Trujillo (US$6 to US$8, eight to nine hours), Chiclayo (US$5.50 to US$7.50, six hours) and Lima (US$10 to US$15, 15 to 17 hours). Lima buses go overnight. CIVA (☎ 044-821460), Independencia 386, is the most expensive and comfortable. Atahualpa (☎ 044-823060) also has good buses. Cheaper Lima buses are with Tepsa (☎ 044-823306), Sudamericano (☎ 044-823270), Nor-Perú (☎ 044-824550) and Palacios (☎ 044-825855). For Trujillo, buses leave in the afternoon and arrive late at night. The earliest is with Vulkano (☎ 044-821090) or Empresa Días (☎ 044-827504), Ayacucho 753, near the center. The Lima-bound companies also stop in Trujillo. For Chiclayo, El Cumbe (☎ 044-823088), Independencia 236, has three or four daily buses and goes during the day. Sudamericano and Vulkano also go to Chiclayo. Atahualpa, Nor-Perú and Palacios go to Cajabamba (US$5, seven hours). Días and Nor Perú go to Chota (US$6, nine hours of wild scenery). Atahualpa and Palacios go to Celendín (US$5, five hours).

AROUND CAJAMARCA
Baños del Inca
These natural hot springs are 6km east of Cajamarca. The water is channeled into private cubicles (US$0.50 to US$1.50 per hour), some large enough to hold six people and a cheaper public pool (US$0.50, cleaned on Monday and Friday). Minibuses (US$0.50) leave from the corner of Amazonas and 2 de Mayo in Cajamarca.

Cumbe Mayo
Pre-Inca channels run for several kilometers across the bleak mountain tops, about 23km southwest of Cajamarca by road. Nearby are caves with petroglyphs. The countryside is high, windswept and slightly eerie. The site can be reached on foot from Cerro Santa Apolonia via a signposted road. The walk takes about four hours, if you take the obvious short cuts and ask passersby for directions. Daily tours (US$7) are sold in Cajamarca.

Ventanillas de Otuzco
This pre-Inca graveyard has hundreds of funerary niches built into the hillside. The site is in superb countryside, and you can walk here from Cajamarca or the Baños del Inca. There are local buses and tours from Cajamarca.

Llacanora & Hacienda La Colpa
Llacanora, a picturesque village where the traditional *clarín* (a 3m-long bamboo trumpet) is still played, is 13km southeast of Cajamarca. A few kilometers beyond, the Hacienda La Colpa cattle ranch is often visited on tours to Llacanora.

CELENDÍN
This small, pleasant town is a possible stopover between Cajamarca (five hours) and Chachapoyas (a rough but spectacular 12-hour trip). Buses may be delayed in the wet season (December to April). There are several cheap, basic hotels.

CHACHAPOYAS
This quiet, pleasant little town sits at about 2000m on the eastern slopes of the Andes. Nearby are many little-known archaeological sites. One of the most accessible is the magnificent ruin of Kuélap. Chachapoyas has a small museum, at Merced 800.

Information
The Banco de Crédito changes traveler's checks. Martín Antonio Olivo Chumbe (☎ 074-757212), Piura 909, or at the radio station, is a good local guide.

Places to Stay
The following lodgings charge US$7 per person in rooms with bath and hot water: the *Hostal Johumaji*, Ayacucho 711; *Hotel El Dorado*, Ayacucho 1062; and *Hostal Kuélap*, Amazonas 1057, which also has cheaper rooms with shared bath or cold water. *Hotel Amazonas* (☎ 074-757199) charges US$4/7 or US$7/11 for rooms with bath. There are a couple of more basic pensions: ask around.

Places to Eat
Chacha on the plaza is popular with locals. Opposite, *Mass Burger* has baked goods and fruit salads as well as burgers. Nearby, the Restaurants *Vegas*, *Kuélap*, *Oh Qué*

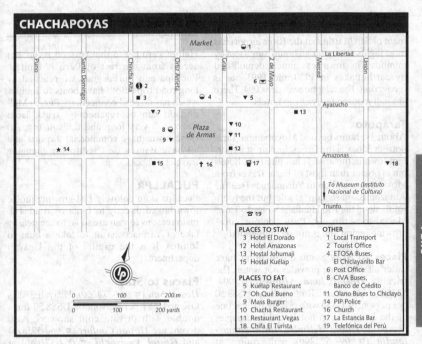

CHACHAPOYAS

PLACES TO STAY
3 Hotel El Dorado
12 Hotel Amazonas
13 Hostal Johumaji
15 Hostal Kuélap

PLACES TO EAT
5 Kuélap Restaurant
7 Oh Qué Bueno
9 Mass Burger
10 Chacha Restaurant
11 Restaurant Vegas
18 Chifa El Turista

OTHER
1 Local Transport
2 Tourist Office
4 ETOSA Buses,
   El Chiclayanito Bar
6 Post Office
8 CIVA Buses,
   Banco de Crédito
11 Olano Buses to Chiclayo
14 PIP Police
16 Church
17 La Estancia Bar
19 Telefónica del Perú

Bueno and *Chifa El Turista* serve OK cheap Peruvian food.

Getting There & Away
Air There are no flights to Chachapoyas at the moment.

Bus Olano, ETOSA and CIVA have buses to Chiclayo (US$9.50, 12 hours) and Lima (US$23, 30 hours).

Minibuses and pick-ups leave from near the market for various destinations. Several a day go to Tingo (US$2, two hours) and on to Leimebamba (from where pick-ups continue to Celendín daily in the dry season). Minibuses go to Pedro Ruiz (US$2, two hours), from where you continue east to the Amazon.

KUELAP
This immense, oval-shaped pre-Inca city is at 3100m on a ridge above the Río Utcubamba, southeast of Chachapoyas. It's a major site with very little tourism. Entry is US$4.

A small, cheap and very basic *hostel* has a few beds and floor space, or you can camp.

You'll need to purify your water. Very simple meals are available. The friendly guardian will show you where to stay, and give a tour – a small tip is appreciated.

To get to Kuelap, take a minibus from Chachapoyas to **Tingo**. This village was badly damaged by floods in 1993 but a couple of basic hotels have reopened. A signposted trail leads from the southern end of Tingo to the ruins, 1200m higher. Allow five hours for the climb and carry water. Mules can be hired.

EAST OF CHACHAPOYAS
First go north to Pedro Ruiz (see Chachapoyas Getting There & Away), where there are a couple of basic hotels. From here a rough road goes east to Yurimaguas (definitely off the gringo trail). Money is changed at the Banco de Crédito and other places in the towns below.

Rioja
About 11 hours east of Pedro Ruiz, Rioja has the regional airport (with flights from Lima) and a few basic hotels.

PERU

Moyobamba

At 860m, this is the capital of the Department of San Martín, but the Rioja airport has most flights. It's under an hour from Rioja by minibus. The town was almost demolished by earthquakes in 1990 and 1991 but is recovering. The telephone code is 094. There are half a dozen fairly cheap hotels.

Tarapoto

About 3½ hours beyond Moyobamba, Tarapoto, at 356m, is the largest and most important town in the area. It has plenty of hotels but is pricier than most of Peru. Travel from Moyobamba and on to Yurimaguas (see the Amazon Basin section) is safe, but the route south along the Río Huallaga valley to Tingo María goes through Peru's major coca-growing region and is not recommended.

Places to Stay Some hotels don't have water all day; none provides hot water. The friendly *Hostal Juan Alfonso* (☎ 094-522179), Ursua and Raimondi, at US$3.50 per person, or US$4 with private bath, is one of the better cheap hotels. Other cheapies nearby are *Hostal Meléndez, Hostal Pasquelandia* (☎ 094-522290) with rooms at US$2.50/3.50, a bit more with bath, *Hostal El Dorado* and *Hostal Viluz*. Within 3 blocks northwest of the plaza are the cheapish *Hostal Las Palmeras* and *Hostal Misti* (☎ 094-522439), at US$3.50 per person with bath. Just off the plaza, the recommended *Hostal San Antonio*, has clean rooms with shower, fan and cable TV (US channels) for US$10/12.50. There are several more expensive places.

Places to Eat *El Mesón* and *La Terraza* on the plaza have decent set lunches. The market has the cheapest places.

Getting There & Away The airport is 2.5km from town (US$1.50 by mototaxi). AeroContinente (☎ 094-524332), San Martín 127, flies daily to Lima (US$55) and Iquitos (US$54).

Buses, taxi colectivos and pick-ups leave from the eighth block of Ramón Castillo for Moyobamba (this departure point may move farther out of town). Pick-ups for Yurimaguas (US$8, five hours) leave from the southeast end of Ursua. Buses to Chiclayo (US$20, 36 hours) and on to Lima leave daily.

Amazon Basin

Half of Peru lies in the Amazon Basin, but access from the rest of Peru is limited. Pucallpa and Yurimaguas are reached by long road trips. Both have boats to Iquitos, which has no road connections. Puerto Maldonado can be reached by truck from Cuzco – a very long and difficult trip. All these towns have commercial airports and all have Bancos de Crédito for changing traveler's checks.

PUCALLPA

Pucallpa is an unlovely, fast-growing jungle town linked directly to Lima by road. The main reasons to visit are to go to the nearby lake of Yarinacocha or to take a boat to Iquitos. It is the capital of the Ucayali department.

Places to Stay

Hostal Sun (☎ 064-574260), Ucayali 380, is OK at US$4 per person, or US$8.50 for a double with private cold showers. Also decent are *Hostal Confort* (☎ 064-575815) and *Hostal Amazonia* (☎ 064-571080) at US$7/9 with bath. The small, friendly and popular *Hostal Residencial Barbtur* (☎ 064-572532), Raimondi 670, is US$4.50/6 or US$8/12 with cold bath and fan. The similarly priced *Hostal Perú* (☎ 064-575128) is also OK. Other cheap and basic places are *Hostal Diamante* at US$6/10, the *Residencial Sisley* (☎ 064-575137) at US$8/12 and *Hotel Marco* (☎ 064-571048) at US$9/12, all with bath and fan. *Hostal Donita* is OK at US$6 each, or US$9 with bath. *Hotel Komby* (☎ 064-571184) is US$12/15 for clean rooms and has a swimming pool. *Hotel Arequipa* (☎ 064-573112) is US$17/20 with bath and TV.

Places to Eat

For cheap local breakfasts, the sidewalk cafés on Portillo near 7 de Junio are OK. *La Baguette* is squeaky clean and sells bread, snacks and pastries. For ceviches and other meals in the range of US$3 to US$6, *Cebichería El Escorpión* is good. Near the intersection of Raimondi and Ucayali are several popular places with outdoor tables, such as *El Chinito* with set lunches for US$1.50, *Restaurant Mi Casa* and the

PERU

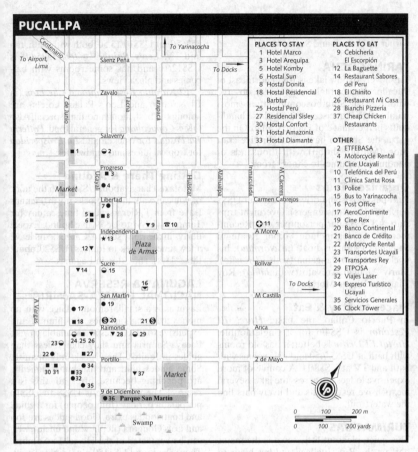

PUCALLPA

PLACES TO STAY	PLACES TO EAT
1 Hotel Marco	9 Cebichería
3 Hotel Arequipa	El Escorpión
5 Hotel Komby	12 La Baguette
6 Hostal Sun	14 Restaurant Sabores
8 Hostal Donita	del Peru
18 Hostal Residencial	18 El Chinito
Barbtur	26 Restaurant Mi Casa
25 Hostal Perú	28 Bianchi Pizzería
27 Residencial Sisley	37 Cheap Chicken
30 Hostal Confort	Restaurants
31 Hostal Amazonia	
33 Hostal Diamante	OTHER
	2 ETFEBASA
	4 Motorcycle Rental
	7 Cine Ucayali
	10 Telefónica del Perú
	11 Clínica Santa Rosa
	13 Police
	15 Bus to Yarinacocha
	16 Post Office
	17 AeroContinente
	19 Cine Rex
	20 Banco Continental
	21 Banco de Crédito
	22 Motorcycle Rental
	23 Transportes Ucayali
	24 Transportes Rey
	29 ETPOSA
	32 Viajes Laser
	34 Expreso Turístico
	Ucayali
	35 Servicios Generales
	36 Clock Tower

PERU

Bianchi Pizzería and Bar, the latter a popular hangout for young people. *Restaurant Sabores del Perú* is a local place with pizza, meat and fish. A couple of cheap, popular chicken restaurants are on Tacna by the Parque San Martín.

Getting There & Away

Air The airport is 5km northwest of town. AeroContinente (☎ 064-575643), 7 de Junio 861, flies daily to and from Lima (US$50) and Iquitos (US$49).

Bus Several companies leave at 6 or 7 am for Lima (US$12 to US$15, 24 hours – longer in the wet season). There are several police checkpoints (because of drugs) between

Pucallpa and Tingo María. Faster minibuses to Tingo María leave from 7 de Junio.

River La Hoyada, Pucallpa's port, is 2.5km northeast of town. During the drier months (June to October) boats leave from El Mangual, 3km farther away. Minibuses go there from the center (US$0.50). Boats along the Río Ucayali from Pucallpa to Iquitos (US$25) take three to five days. There are more boats when the river is high. Hammocks are not provided, but you can buy one in Pucallpa.

Getting Around

Mototaxis are US$1 to the airport and US$2 to Yarinacocha: bargain. Car taxis charge twice that. Buses (US$0.30) and colectivos (US$0.50) to Yarinacocha leave from the corner of Ucayali and Sucre.

YARINACOCHA

This lovely oxbow lake is 10km northeast of Pucallpa. You can take canoe rides, observe wildlife, visit Shipibo communities (most notably San Francisco) and purchase handicrafts in the village of Puerto Callao. On the plaza, the Shipibo have a cooperative craft shop (Maroti Shobo) with thousands of handmade ceramics to choose from.

Organized Tours

Peki-peki boats and drivers are about US$7 per hour (four passengers). Overnight trips start at US$30 per person per day. Recommended guides include Gilber Reategui Sangama (with his boat *La Normita*), his uncle, Nemecio Sangama (with *El Rayito*), Marly Alemán Arévalo (with *Julito*), Roy Riaño and Jorge Morales.

Places to Stay & Eat

In Puerto Callao, the basic *Hotel El Pescador* is US$4/6 for a single/double. *Hostal El Delfín* is better; it has old rooms with bath at US$5/7.50 and new rooms with bath and TV at US$8/11. A couple of more expensive lodges are across the lake. Several inexpensive restaurants and lively bars line the waterfront.

YURIMAGUAS

This quiet, pleasant little town is the major port on the Río Huallaga and has boats to Iquitos. Reaching Yurimaguas involves a hard road trip of several days from Lima. The US Drug Enforcement Agency (DEA) has a high profile but there are no real problems for overland travelers.

Places to Stay & Eat

Hotels don't have hot water. *Quinta Lucy* has private baths at US$3/5 for singles/doubles. *Hostal Baneo* has shared baths and *Hostal El Cisne* and *Hostal La Estrella* have private baths. The best basic cheapie is the clean and quiet *Hostal César Gustavo* at US$7/9 with bath and fan. *Hostal Florinde* has air con and baths in otherwise basic rooms for the same price. *Hostal de Paz* (☎ 094-352123) has clean rooms with bath, fan and TV for US$7/9.50. Also good are

the quiet *Hostal Residencial Cajamarca* at US$11/14 and *Hostal El Naranjo* (☎ 094-352650) at US$10/13.50, both with bath, fan and TV. *Leo's Palace* (☎ 094-352544) is US$12/16 and has some rooms with balconies and plaza views.

El Naranjo Restaurant and *Cheraton* (in El Naranjo and Leo's Palace hotels) are among the best, though nothing special. Also OK is *Copacabana* for general food, *Pollería La Posada* for chicken and *La Prosperidad* for tropical juices and sandwiches.

Getting There & Around

Mototaxis charge about US$0.60 to the port, or you can walk the 13 blocks north. Pickups leave from J Riera several times a day for Tarapoto (US$7 to US$9, five hours). Expect delays in the rainy season. Cargo boats leave a few times a week to Iquitos (US$20, about three days). They stop in Lagunas.

LAGUNAS & RESERVA NACIONAL PACAYA-SAMIRIA

Lagunas is a small, remote village with no moneychanging facilities and limited and expensive food. Guides are available to visit Pacaya-Samiria and they charge less than guides in Iquitos. They speak only Spanish. Some guides hunt and fish but technically are poaching because, after all, this is a reserve! The going rate is US$8 to US$10 per person per day (four people) for a guide and boat; food is extra. Good guides are Job and Luis Gongora (nephew and uncle), who can be contacted at the Hostal La Sombra. They ask around US$150 plus food for a six-day trip for two. Also recommended are Edinson Saldaña Gutiérrez and Juan Huaycama, both well known locally.

Places to Stay & Eat

The friendly *Hostal La Sombra* (also known as Hostal Piñedo) has hot, stuffy rooms at US$2 per person. Shared showers and food are available. The smaller *Hotel Montalbán* is another possibility. You can stay in a *hostal* above the farmacia, but it doesn't have showers (buckets of water are provided). *Doña Dina* in a blue-fronted building just off the plaza serves good cheap meals.

Getting There & Away

Boats from Yurimaguas take about 12 hours and leave most days.

IQUITOS

With 400,000 inhabitants, Iquitos is Peru's largest jungle city, and the capital of the huge department of Loreto. Iquitos is linked with the outside world by air and river; it is the largest city in the Amazon Basin without road links.

Iquitos was founded in the 1750s as a Jesuit mission. In the late 19th century, it was a rubber boomtown, and signs of the opulence of those days remain in some of the mansions and tiled walls. Today, both the oil and tourist industries play an important part in the area's economy.

Being so isolated, Iquitos seems to have been bypassed by the problems of terrorism and thievery – but watch your possessions nevertheless! The people are friendly and easy-going.

Information

The tourist office is unsigned at Napo 176. It's open 7:30 am to 1 pm weekdays. Several banks cash traveler's checks and there are street moneychangers on Lores between Próspero and Arica. Change Brazilian or Colombian currency at the border. Migraciones (☎ 094-231021) is on the 4th block of Yavari.

Things to See

The **Casa de Hierro** (Iron House), designed by Eiffel (of Parisian Tower fame), is on the northeast corner of Putumayo and Raymondi and looks like a bunch of scrap-metal sheets bolted together.

The floating shantytown of **Belén** has a certain charm; it has scores of huts built on rafts, which rise and fall with the river. Thousands of people live here, and canoes float from hut to hut selling and trading. Boatmen will paddle you around. This is a very poor area but seems safe enough in daylight. The **market**, in the blocks in front of Belén, has strange stuff like piles of dried frogs and fish, armadillo shells, piranha teeth and a great variety of tropical fruits. Watch your wallet.

Laguna Quistacocha (entry US$1.50) is 15km south of Iquitos and makes a pleasant day trip. Minibuses leave frequently from Plaza 28 de Julio (US$1.20). There is a small zoo of local fauna, and a fish hatchery with 2m *paiche* swimming around (entry US$1).

Places to Stay

All hotels have private cold baths and fans unless stated otherwise. Erratic water supply is the norm in Iquitos. The following are OK budget places. **Hostal Tacna** (☎ 094-232839), Tacna 516, is basic and noisy but clean at US$4.50/6.50 for singles/doubles. The recommended **Hostal La Pascana** (☎ 094-231418, fax 094-232974), Pevas 133, is good, safe, popular with travelers and often full. Rooms are US$9/11. **Hostal Monterico** (☎/fax 094-235395), Arica 633, is US$7/8. The quiet, clean **Hostal Lima** (☎ 094-235152), Próspero 549, is US$9/12.

The following are cheap and very basic. **Hostal San Antonio** (☎ 094-235221), Próspero 661, is US$3.50/4 and lacks fans. The similarly priced **Hostal Anita,** Hurtado 742, is friendly. **Hostal Lozano** (☎ 094-232486), Hurtado 772, is US$6/9. **Hostal Iquitos** (☎ 094-239015), Hurtado 955, is US$7/10. **Hostal Perú** (☎ 094-234961), Próspero 318, and the **Hostal Fortaleza,** Próspero 311, are reasonably clean for US$7/9. Another recommended cheapie is **Hostal Karina** (☎ 094-235367), Putumayo 467, at US$5/7 with hot water.

Hostal Libertad (☎ 094-235763), Arica 361, has simple rooms with air con for US$8/12. **Hostal Isabel** (☎ 094-234901), Brasil 164, is comparable. The clean **Hostal Dos Mundos** (☎ 094-232635), Tacna 631, is US$17/23, but often offers discounts.

Jungle Lodges & Camps There are about a dozen jungle lodges in the Iquitos area – none for budget travelers. Prices range from US$40 to over US$100 per day depending on services. Lodge offices are found in central Iquitos, or ask at the tourist office. The further away from Iquitos you are, and the further off the Amazon itself, the better your chances of seeing wildlife.

Places to Eat

Inexpensive chifas are near the Plaza 28 de Julio. The best (most expensive) is **Wai Ming**. **El Pollo Suave**, also on this plaza, is a good cheap chicken place, and other cheap restaurants are on Tacna and Huallaga north of Plaza 28 de Julio.

Slightly pricier but good eateries include **La Pascana**, R Hurtado 735, a simple place with good ceviches and fine Amazon river views. **La Olla de Oro**, Araujo 579, has a decent selection of Peruvian food. **Ari's**

IQUITOS

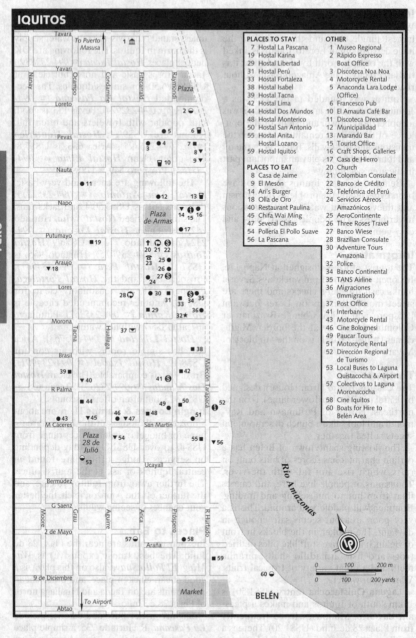

PLACES TO STAY
7 Hostal La Pascana
19 Hostal Karina
29 Hostal Libertad
31 Hostal Perú
33 Hostal Fortaleza
38 Hostal Isabel
39 Hostal Tacna
42 Hostal Lima
48 Hostal Dos Mundos
50 Hostal Monterico
55 Hostal San Antonio
55 Hostal Anita,
     Hostal Lozano
59 Hostal Iquitos

PLACES TO EAT
8 Casa de Jaime
9 El Mesón
14 Ari's Burger
40 Olla de Oro
40 Restaurant Paulina
45 Chifa Wai Ming
47 Several Chifas
54 Pollería El Pollo Suave
56 La Pascana

OTHER
1 Museo Regional
2 Rápido Expresso
   Boat Office
3 Discoteca Noa Noa
4 Motorcycle Rental
5 Anaconda Lara Lodge
   (Office)
6 Francesco Pub
10 El Amauta Café Bar
11 Discoteca Dreams
12 Municipalidad
13 Marandú Bar
15 Tourist Office
16 Craft Shops, Galleries
17 Casa de Hierro
20 Church
21 Colombian Consulate
22 Banco de Crédito
23 Telefónica del Perú
24 Servicios Aéreos
    Amazónicos
25 AeroContinente
26 Three Roses Travel
27 Banco Wiese
28 Brazilian Consulate
30 Adventure Tours
    Amazonia
32 Police
34 Banco Continental
35 TANS Airline
36 Migraciones
    (Immigration)
37 Post Office
41 Interbanc
43 Motorcycle Rental
46 Cine Bolognesi
49 Paucar Tours
51 Motorcycle Rental
52 Dirección Regional
    de Turismo
53 Local Buses to Laguna
    Quistacocha & Airport
57 Colectivos to Laguna
    Moronacocha
58 Cine Iquitos
60 Boats for Hire to
    Belén Area

Burger, on the Plaza de Armas, is a clean, brightly lit joint dubbed 'gringolandia.' It is rarely closed, changes US dollars, is generally helpful and popular with foreign travelers.

El Mesón, Malecón 153, is a little pricey and serves local specialties. *La Casa de Jaime,* Malecón 177 has good local food, steaks and fish. The new and locally popular *Restaurant Paulina,* Tacna 591, serves a good US$2 set lunch with big portions.

Entertainment

For a cold beer and recorded and live music, look in the blocks between the Plaza de Armas and the waterfront. *Marandú Bar* and *Francesco Pub* on the Malecón have both been recommended. *El Amauta Café Bar,* Nauta 250, is a fun place for a drink. It presents live Peruvian music on most nights, and also hosts comedians and theater. *La Pergola,* Napo 735, is a nice bar in a tropical garden and has live music some nights.

For dancing, the *Agricobank* on Condamine is a huge outdoor place where hundreds of locals gather to drink, dance and socialize. A new, very popular dance spot is *Discoteca Noa Noa,* Pevas 298. Another option is *Discoteca Dreams,* on Ocampo.

Getting There & Away

Air Iquitos has a small airport 7km south of town with flights to Miami and Colombia, as well as local flights. Three Roses Travel, Próspero 246, and Paucar Tours, also on Próspero, are recommended travel agents.

AeroContinente (☎ 094-243489) Próspero 232, has two daily flights to Lima (US$59), with some additional flights on weekends. TANS (☎ 094-234632), Lores 127, flies to Caballoc04cha (US$40) near the Colombian border on Saturday. (Caballococha has two simple hotels and daily boats to Leticia, Colombia.) Servicios Aéreos Amazónicos (☎ 094-235776), Arica 273, flies to Caballococha (US$45) and Leticia (US$60). Flights are often full and subject to delay. Schedules, destinations and fares change frequently so check locally.

Boat Boats leave from Puerto Masusa, on Av La Marina, 2 or 3km north of the center. Boats have blackboards saying when they are leaving and for where. Boats to Pucallpa (six to eight days) or Yurimaguas (four to six days) cost about US$20 to US$30 per

person. Boats leave about once a week to Pucallpa, more often to Yurimaguas, less often if the river is low.

Boats to the border with Brazil and Colombia leave every few days, take two to three days and cost under US$20, but gringos have to bargain hard. Expreso Loreto (☎ 094-238652), Loreto 171, has fast launches to the border (US$50, 12 hours) at 6 am on Tuesday, Thursday and Sunday.

Passengers can sleep aboard the boat while waiting for departure. Boats often leave hours or days late!

Getting Around

Buses and trucks for nearby destinations, including the airport, leave from the Plaza 28 de Julio. Taxis to the airport cost US$5 or US$6. *Motocarros* (motorcycle taxis) are cheaper. Motorcycles can be hired (see map).

To/From Colombia & Brazil

Brazil, Colombia and Peru share a three-way border. The biggest town is Leticia (Colombia), which is linked with Tabatinga (Brazil) by road (it's a short walk). You can freely go from one to the other without border hassles unless you are traveling further into Brazil or Colombia. Leticia has the best choice of hotels, restaurants and moneychanging facilities and a hospital. On the south bank of the Amazon, opposite Leticia/Tabatinga, is Santa Rosa (Peru). This is marked on most maps as Ramón Castilla, which is the old port. Because of changes in the flow of the river, Ramón Castilla is no longer on the main Amazon; Santa Rosa is used as the port instead, though there is nowhere to stay here.

Exit formalities when leaving Peru are strict, and Peruvian border officials may send you back to Iquitos if your entry stamp has expired. Riverboats stop at the Peruvian guard post in Santa Rosa for passport formalities, but make sure the captain knows that you need to do this. Check with the immigration office in Iquitos about exit formalities. The Peruvian immigration office moves quite often because of changes in the river.

To enter or leave Colombia, get your passport stamped in Leticia. To enter or leave Brazil, formalities are normally carried out in Tabatinga, although the town of Benjamin Constant, an hour downriver, also has an immigration office. You don't need to get stamps for all three countries – just the one you are leaving and the one you are continuing to. Regulations change, but the boat captains know where to go. Don't try to enter a country without first getting the required exit stamp. You can easily travel between the three countries without having the correct stamps, as long as you stay in the tri-border area. As soon as you leave the border ports, however, your documents must be in order.

Boats to Iquitos leave from Leticia or Tabatinga every few days (about US$20, 2½ days). Alternatively, you can take the thrice-weekly Rápido Expreso from Leticia (US$50, 14 hours).

Boats to Manaus (Brazil) leave from Tabatinga, then spend a night in Benjamin Constant before continuing. The fare is about US$100 in a shared cabin (less for hanging your own hammock) for the three to six-day trip, including very basic meals; as always, bring your own if you have a sensitive stomach. Bottled soft drinks and beer are usually available. Hammocks are airier, and many travelers prefer them to the stuffy cabins.

Leticia and Tabatinga have airports, with flights into the interiors of Colombia and Brazil, respectively.

PUERTO MALDONADO

Founded at the turn of the century, Puerto Maldonado has been a rubber boomtown, a logging center and, recently, a gold and oil center. It is a homely, fast-growing town with a frontier feel and is the capital and most important port of the Department of Madre de Dios. The jungle around Puerto Maldonado is second growth rather than virgin forest. The most inexpensive activity is to take the five-minute ferry ride across the Río Madre de Dios.

Information

The tourist office (☎ 084-571421) is near the market at Fitzcarrald 411 (interior, ask at the entrance). It's open 7:45 am to 4 pm daily. Manuel Ponce de León, the director, is helpful, knowledgeable and friendly. He provides information on budget lodgings with families in small communities. A more central information place is the café La Casa Nostra, León Velarde 515, whose gregarious owners, Dora and Boris, are knowledgeable about the area and about trips to Bolivia and Brazil.

Moreover, the café is the informal 'office' of many well-known local tour guides. The immigration office is down by the river. There are no Brazilian or Bolivian consulates.

Tour Guides

If you do not have a prearranged tour, local arrangements are possible. There are several local guides, some very reputable and experienced, others just interested in making quick money. Shop around, never pay for a tour in full beforehand, and when you agree on a price with a boatman, make sure that it includes the return trip.

An excellent guide is Willy Wither (☎ 084-572014; compured@compured.limaperu.net). His enthusiasm is contagious and he speaks English and German. Nadir Gnan (☎ 084-571900), who speaks English and Italian, also knows the area well and has first hand expertise on mining activities. Victor Yahamona (☎ 084-572613) and his relatives are well known in the area, and Hernán Llave receives high recommendations.

Places to Stay

Hostal Chávez is the cheapest and looks it. Also try *Hotel Tambo de Oro* (☎ 084-572057) at US$3.50 without bath or US$15 for a triple with bath (negotiable). *Hotel El Astro* (☎ 084-572128) and *Kross* are OK, and look clean at US$5/8 for some rooms with private bath. The recommended *Hotel Wilson* (☎ 084-571086), G Prada 355, charges US$5/8, or US$8/12 for a singles/doubles with bath. It has a basic cafeteria. *Hotel Rey Port* (☎ 084-571177) is similarly priced and is just adequate. *Hostal Royal Inn* (☎ 084-571048) has large, clean rooms with bath for US$8/12. Others in this price range are *Hostal Gamboa* and *Hospedaje El Solar* (☎ 084-571571). The pleasant *Hostal Cabaña Quinta* (☎ 084-571045, 084-571864), Cuzco 535, is the best in the center and has a decent restaurant and friendly staff. Rooms are US$11/17, or US$15/23 with private cold shower, fan, TV and breakfast. A good deal in a pleasant setting by the airport is *Lodge Iñapari* (☎ 084-572575), at US$5.50 per person. The friendly owners organize budget horseback and bicycle tours.

Places to Eat

Pizzería El Hornito, on the plaza, is a local hangout that belongs to the owners of *Chez*

PUERTO MALDONADO

Río Madre de Dios

Staircase

Billinghurst

Loreto

Plaza
de Armas

Carrion

Cuzco

2 de Mayo

To Airport,
Laberinto

G Prada

J Troncoso

Tacna

Ica

Mercado
Modelo

Fitzcarrald

Piura

E Rivero

Moquegua

Puno

Velarde

Arequipa

26 de Diciembre

Río Tambopata

0   100   200 m
0   100   200 yards

PLACES TO STAY
8 Hostal Cabaña Quinta
9 Hostal Chávez
10 Hotel Rey Port
12 Hostal Royal Inn
17 Hotel Tambo de Oro
18 Hospedaje El Solar
22 Hotel Wilson
24 Hotel El Astro
26 Hostal Gamboa
27 Hotel Kross

PLACES TO EAT
3 Pizzería El Hornito
6 Chifa Wa-Seng
11 El Tenedor
14 La Casa Nostra
15 Marisquería Libertador
16 La Cusqueñita

OTHER
1 Riverboat Hire
2 Migraciones
   (Immigration)
4 Banco de la Nación
5 Banco de Crédito
7 Explorer's Inn Office
13 AeroContinente
19 Telefónica del Perú
20 De Los Angeles Agency
21 Casa de Cambio
23 Motorcycle Hire
25 Post Office
28 Trucks to Cuzco,
   Buses to Laberinto
29 Tourist Office

PERU

Maggy in Cuzco, and offers really good, thin-crusted pizza and pasta. *La Cusqueñita* is clean and has a good variety of dishes, as does *Marisquería Libertad* next door. *El Tenedor* and *Chifa Wa-Seng* are also satisfactory cheap places, and there are many others that offer a set menú for as little as US$1. One of the best restaurants in Puerto Maldonado is *Brombu's* (☎ 084-573230), on the way to the airport. In a peaceful setting that combines adobe walls and thatched roofs, Fernando Rosemberg and his wife serve local delicacies and international dishes. They plan to offer lodging in the future. The best café in town is *La Casa Nostra*, which serves great juices, snacks and coffee.

Getting There & Away

Air The airport is 7km west of town. Colectivos from the airport are US$1, mototaxis are US$2. AeroContinente (☎ 084-572285), León Velarde 508, has one daily flight to Lima (US$72) via Cuzco (US$41). Light aircraft will fly wherever you hire them to go.

Truck Trucks to Cuzco during the dry season leave from the Mercado Modelo. The rough 500km trip (US$15) takes three days, depending on road and weather conditions.

Boat Boats at the Madre de Dios ferry dock make local excursions and go down to the Bolivian border (US$80 per boat).

Upriver boats to Manu are hard to find and expensive.

To/From Brazil A track to Iñapari, on the Brazilian border, is open but the last stretch is in bad shape. Wet season travel is reportedly not possible but, during the drier months, trucks depart daily from the north side of the Río Madre de Dios (US$14, one day). Iberia, 170km north of Puerto Maldonado, has a couple of basic hotels. Iñapari, 70km beyond Iberia, has a basic hotel and a new airport. Both towns have occasional Grupo Ocho flights from Cuzco, but most people come by road. From Iñapari, wade across the Río Acre to Assis, Brazil, which has a better hotel and a dry-season road to Brasiléia and Río Branco. Peruvian exit and entry formalities are in Puerto Maldonado.

To/From Bolivia Boats can be hired to the Bolivian border at Puerto Pardo (about US$80, half a day). Cheaper passages are available on infrequent cargo boats. From Puerto Heath, on the Bolivian side, it takes several days (even weeks) to arrange a boat (expensive) to Riberalta, where road and air connections are available. Travel in a group to share costs and avoid months when the water is too low. Get exit stamps at the immigration office in Puerto Maldonado before leaving. Reportedly, Bolivian border officials are unfriendly and demand bribes. Few foreigners travel this route. Trips are more frequent in the dry season.

AROUND PUERTO MALDONADO

Lodges and jungle tours are expensive for travelers on a tight budget. The closest lodge to Puerto Maldonado is the deteriorated *Albergue Tambo Lodge*, 10km downriver on the Río Madre de Dios. It has three-day, two-night visits for US$150 per person, including transportation; extra days are US$35. There's not much virgin jungle, but there are tours to Lago Sandoval or to gold-panning areas. Reservations can be made in Cuzco (☎ 084-236159), Plateros 351, or at the AeroContinente office in Puerto Maldonado.

About 15km away, the more comfortable *Cuzco Amazónico Lodge* has local tours and provides a better look at the jungle. Rooms have private cold showers and porch with hammock at US$167 per person for three days and two nights, and US$50 per additional day; ask for low-season discounts. There are 18km of trails in a reserve around the lodge. Reservations can be made in Cuzco (☎ 084-232161, 084-233769) at Procuradores 48. There are other, pricier places – none luxurious.

A pleasant jungle lake, **Lago Sandoval**, is two hours downriver from Puerto Maldonado on the Río Madre de Dios. Half the trip is by boat and half on foot. Bring food and water. You can hire a guide (US$30 to US$35) who knows the local flora and fauna, hire a boat to drop you off and pick you up later or you can do the walk on your own. There are two lodges near the lake, the cheaper, basic, but pleasant *Albergue Mejía* charges US$30 (minimum of four people) for transportation, very good food, lodging and guide service. You can also camp for a small fee. The attractive *Sandoval Lake Lodge* (☎ 084-571428 in Puerto Maldonado, or 084-226392 in Cuzco) is pricier at US$60 for just food and lodging or US$120 including guide and transportation.

Uruguay

Across the Río de la Plata from Buenos Aires, lies Uruguay. Visitors are drawn to the charming town of Colonia, the capital city of Montevideo and Atlantic beach resorts, but towns along the Río Uruguay are also pleasant. The hilly interior is gaucho country.

The República Oriental del Uruguay (Eastern Republic of Uruguay) was long called the Banda Oriental (Eastern Shore) of the Río de la Plata.

Facts about Uruguay

HISTORY

The aboriginal Charrúa Indians, hunter-gatherers who also fished, deterred European settlement – in part because the Spaniards, as William Henry Hudson wrote, 'loved gold and adventure above everything, and finding neither in the Banda, they little esteemed it.' As on Argentina's Pampas, gauchos subsisted on wild cattle until *estancias* pushed them back into the interior.

European Colonization

Jesuit missionaries settled near Soriano, on the Río Uruguay, but in 1680 Portugal established Nova Colônia do Sacramento on the Río de la Plata, forcing Spain to build its own citadel at Montevideo.

National hero José Artigas fought against Spain, but could not prevent Brazil's takeover of the Banda. Exiled to Paraguay, he inspired the '33 Orientales' who, with Argentine support, liberated the area in 1828, establishing Uruguay as a buffer between the emerging continental powers.

Independence & Development

While Uruguay's neighbors threatened its fragile political independence, Britain menaced its economic autonomy. The Argentine dictator Rosas besieged Montevideo from 1838 to 1851; Uruguay's major political parties, the Blancos and Colorados, originated as armed gaucho sympathizers of Federalist and Unitarist causes. As Hudson wrote, 'Endless struggles for mastery ensued,

At a Glance

Country Name	República Oriental del Uruguay
Area	176,215 sq km
Population	3.2 million
Population Density	18.1 sq km
Capital	Montevideo
Head of State	President Julio María Sanguinetti
Official Language	Spanish
Other Languages	Portuguese, Fronterizo
Currency	Peso (Ur$)
Exchange Rate	US$1 = Ur$11.38
Per Capita GNP	US$6000 (1997)
Inflation Rate	10.2% (1998)

in which the Argentines and Brazilians, forgetting their solemn compact, were forever taking sides.'

The Liebig Meat Extract Company of London started operations at Fray Bentos in 1864 and merino wool brought additional opportunities. In 1868 a British railway linked Montevideo with the countryside, where Hereford and shorthorn cattle replaced rangy criollo stock. At the turn of the century, Fray Bentos' massive Anglo plant was the country's first *frigorífico* (meat-freezing factory). Commercialization of livestock meant the demise of the gaucho and rise of the *latifundios* (large landholdings).

Batlle & Uruguayan Modernization

In the early 20th century, visionary president José Batlle y Ordóñez achieved such innovations as pensions, farm credits, unemployment compensation and the eight-hour work day. State intervention led to nationalization of many industries, the creation of others and general prosperity. Taxing the livestock sector financed Batlle's reforms, but when this sector faltered the welfare state crumbled.

Conservatives blamed the state for killing the goose that laid the golden egg, but even earlier, landowners squandered their wealth in conspicuous consumption rather than reinvesting to increase productivity. Redistributive policies worked only as long as there was something to redistribute.

Economic Decline & Political Breakdown

By the 1960s economic stagnation reached a crisis because of patronage and corruption in state enterprises and the government's inability to support a large pensioner class. In 1966 the untimely death of president-elect Oscar Gestido led to his replacement by his running mate Jorge Pacheco Areco.

The authoritarian Pacheco outlawed leftist parties, closed newspapers and invoked a state of siege because of the guerrilla Movimiento de Liberación Nacional (commonly known as Tupamaros), and the country slid into dictatorship. After Tupamaros kidnapped and executed suspected CIA agent Dan Mitrione (as dramatized in Costa-Gavras' film *State of Siege*) and then engineered a major prison escape, Pacheco put the military in charge of counter-insurgency. In 1971 Pacheco's chosen successor, Juan Bordaberry, invited direct military participation in government.

Military Dictatorship & Its Aftermath

As the military occupied almost every position of importance in the 'national security state,' arbitrary detention and torture became routine. The forces determined eligibility for public employment, subjected political offenses to military courts, censored libraries and even required prior approval for large family gatherings.

Voters rejected a new military-drawn constitution in 1980, so four more years passed before Colorado candidate Julio María Sanguinetti became president under the existing constitution. His presidency implied a return to democratic traditions, but he also supported a controversial amnesty, ratified by voters in 1989, for military human rights abuses.

Later in 1989, the Blancos' Luis Lacalle succeeded Sanguinetti in a peaceful transition. Sanguinetti returned to office at the head of a coalition government in the November 1994 elections.

GEOGRAPHY & CLIMATE

Uruguay's 176,000 sq km roughly equal the size of England and Wales combined. Its rolling northern hills are an extension of southern Brazil. West of Montevideo, the terrain is more level, while the Atlantic coast has impressive beaches, dunes and headlands. Rainfall averages about 1000mm, evenly distributed throughout the year. Frosts are unusual.

FLORA & FAUNA

Uruguay's grasslands and gallery forests resemble those of Argentina's Pampas or southern Brazil. Patches of palm savanna persist in the southeast, along the Brazilian border.

Nearly all large land animals have disappeared under human pressure, but the occasional rhea still races across northwestern Uruguay's grasslands. Some offshore islands harbor sea lion colonies.

GOVERNMENT

Uruguay's 1967 constitution establishes three governmental branches. The president heads the executive branch, the legislative branch or Asamblea General, consists of a 99-seat Cámara de Diputados and a 30-member Senado, both chosen by proportional representation. The Corte Suprema is the highest judicial power.

Traditionally, each party would offer several presidential candidates; the winner was the individual with the most votes for the

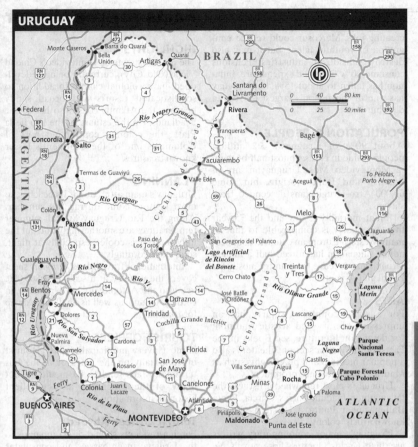

URUGUAY

party with the most votes. Thus the president almost certainly lacked a majority and might not be the candidate with the most overall votes. In eight elections from 1946 to 1984, no candidate won more than 31%. In 1996, Uruguayan voters approved electoral reforms requiring that each party present a single presidential candidate; in the event that no single candidate wins a majority, there is a runoff between the two leading candidates.

The major political parties are the Colorados (heirs of Batlle) and the generally more conservative Blancos; candidates of the two parties have alternated in the presidency since the dictatorship and now form a coalition government at the national level. The leftist coalition Frente Amplio, now the

official opposition, controls the mayoralty of Montevideo. The next presidential elections are scheduled for late 1999.

ECONOMY

Low prices for wool, the primary export, have caused problems in recent years. Only the southwest littoral has intensive agriculture, but this cropland makes a major economic contribution. Many inefficient industries produce inferior products at high cost, surviving because of protective tariffs. Tourism is important, as beaches east of Montevideo attract many Argentines.

In many ways, Uruguay is an economic satellite of both Brazil and Argentina. With those two countries and Paraguay, it now forms the Mercosur common market. Conceivably, by encouraging investment and creating jobs, Mercosur could reduce emigration of youthful talent, but it may also destroy subsidized industries. Pensions consume 60% of public expenditure. Inflation has fallen to about 15%, but Uruguay has one of the region's largest per capita debt burdens.

POPULATION & PEOPLE
About 90% of Uruguay's 3.2 million people reside in cities, almost half of them in Montevideo. Most Uruguayans are of Spanish and Italian origin, but some 60,000 Afro-Uruguayans descended from slaves.

Infant mortality is low and the 75-year life expectancy is comparable to that of many Western European countries, but economic stagnation has forced half a million Uruguayans to leave the country, mostly for Brazil and Argentina.

ARTS
For a small country, Uruguay has an impressive literary and artistic tradition; for details on literature, see Books in the Facts for the Visitor section. Theater is also a popular medium and playwrights such as Mauricio Rosencof are prominent.

Uruguay's most renowned artist was the late painter Joaquín Torres García. Punta Ballena, near Punta del Este, is a well-known artists' colony.

Uruguay's major contemporary writers are Juan Carlos Onetti, whose novels *No Man's Land*, *The Shipyard*, *Body Snatcher* and *A Brief Life* are available in English, and poet, essayist and novelist Mario Benedetti. Journalist Eduardo Galeano, author of *Open Veins of Latin America*, is also Uruguayan.

RELIGION
Mostly Uruguayans are Roman Catholics, but the Church lacks official status. A Jewish minority of about 25,000 lives almost exclusively in Montevideo. Evangelical Protestantism has made some inroads.

LANGUAGE
Spanish is official, but along the Brazilian border many people also speak Portuguese or the hybrid *fronterizo*.

Facts for the Visitor

HIGHLIGHTS
The narrow streets of Montevideo's Ciudad Vieja (Old City), currently being redeveloped, have colonial charm. In addition to sophisticated resorts and broad sandy beaches, the Atlantic coast also has scenic headlands. Up the estuary of the Río de la Plata, the colonial contraband port of Colonia is one of the continent's lesser known treasures.

PLANNING
Uruguay's main attraction is its beaches, so most visitors come during the summer. Along the Río Uruguay littoral, summer temperatures are smotheringly hot, but the hilly interior is cooler, especially at night, so dress accordingly.

International Travel Maps' *Uruguay* sheet covers the country at a scale of 1:800,000. See also the Automóvil Club Uruguayo, in getting Around, as well as Shell and Ancap for road maps.

TOURIST OFFICES
Almost every municipality has a tourist office, usually on the plaza or at the bus terminal. Maps tend to be mediocre, but many of the brochures have excellent historical information.

Tourist Offices Abroad
Foreign residents should direct inquiries to the Uruguayan embassies and consulates listed below.

VISAS & DOCUMENTS
Uruguay requires visas of all foreigners, except nationals of neighboring countries (who need only national identification cards) and those of Western Europe, Israel, Japan and the USA. All visitors need a tourist card, valid for 90 days, renewable for 90 more. Uruguay has also imposed reciprocal visa requirements on Canadians, who must present a return ticket, as well as a photograph and a US$30 payment to a Uruguayan consulate.

To extend your visa or tourist card, visit the Dirección Nacional de Migración (☎ 02-916-0471), Misiones 1513, Montevideo.

EMBASSIES & CONSULATES
Uruguayan Embassies & Consulates Abroad

Uruguay has diplomatic representation in the following countries:

Argentina
(☎ 01-803-6030) Las Heras 1907, Buenos Aires

Australia
(☎ 02-6273-9100) Commerce Bldg, Suite 2, Level 14, 24 Brisbane Lane, Barton, ACT 2604

Brazil
(☎ 61-322-4528) Av das Naçoes, Lote 14, Quadra 803 Sul, Brasilia DF
(☎ 553-6030) Praia de Botafogo 242, 6 Andar, Rio de Janeiro

Canada
(☎ 613-234-2937) Suite 1905, 130 Albert St, Ottawa, Ontario K1P 5G4

Chile
(☎ 02-223-8398) Pedro de Valdivia 711, Santiago

UK
(☎ 020-7589-8735) 140 Brompton Rd, 2nd Floor, London SW31HY

USA
(☎ 202-331-4219) 1918 F St NW, Washington, DC 20006
(☎ 310-394-5777) 429 Santa Monica Blvd, Suite 400, Santa Monica, CA 90401
(☎ 415-986-5222) 546 Market St, Suite 221, San Francisco, CA 94104

Embassies & Consulates in Uruguay

South American countries, the USA and most Western European countries have Montevideo missions, but Australians and New Zealanders must rely on their Buenos Aires embassies.

Argentina
(☎ 02-902-8623) WF Aldunate 1281

Brazil
(☎ 02-901-2024) Convención 1343, 6th floor

Canada
(☎ 02-901-5755) Plaza Cagancha 1335

France
(☎ 02-902-0077) Av Uruguay 853

Germany
(☎ 02-902-5222) La Cumparsita 1435

Israel
(☎ 02-400-4164), Bulevar Artigas 1585

Switzerland
(☎ 02-710-4315) 11th floor, Federico Abadie 2936

UK
(☎ 02-622-3630) Marco Bruto 1073

USA
(☎ 02-203-6061) Lauro Muller 1776

Argentine consulates outside Montevideo include:

Carmelo
(☎ 054-22266) Roosevelt 442

Colonia
(☎ 052-22093) General Flores 350;
open noon to 5 pm weekdays

Paysandú
(☎ 072-22253) Leandro Gómez 1034

Salto
(☎ 073-32931) Artigas 1162

MONEY

The unit of currency is the peso uruguayo (Ur$), which replaced the peso nuevo (N$) in 1993 (the peso nuevo had replaced an older peso in 1975 after several years of hyperinflation). Notes come in denominations of Ur$5, Ur$10, Ur$20, Ur$50, Ur$100, Ur$200, Ur$500 and Ur$1000, while there are coins of 50 centésimos, and one and two pesos. Older bank notes of N$5000 and N$10,000 are still in circulation but gradually disappearing (to get current values, deduct three zeros).

Cambios in Montevideo, Colonia and Atlantic beach resorts change US dollars cash and traveler's checks (the latter at slightly lower rates or modest commissions). Banks are the rule in the interior. Better hotels, restaurants and shops accept credit cards, but Uruguayan ATMs can be fussy about North American or European credit cards. There is no black market.

Annual inflation is about 15%, but steady devaluations keep prices from rising rapidly in dollar terms. Costs are slightly lower than in Argentina, especially with respect to accommodation and transportation.

Exchange Rates

At press time, exchange rates in Uruguay included the following:

country	unit		peso uruguayo
Australia	A$1	=	Ur$7.37
Canada	Can$1	=	Ur$7.60
euro	€1	=	Ur$11.96
France	FF1	=	Ur$1.82
Germany	DM1	=	Ur$6.11
Japan	¥100	=	Ur$9.61
UK	UK£1	=	Ur$15.95
USA	US$1	=	Ur$11.38

URUGUAY

POST & COMMUNICATIONS
Postal rates are reasonable but service is poor. Send important items registered. For poste restante, address mail to the main post office in Montevideo.

Antel, the state telephone monopoly, has central long-distance offices in every town. As in Argentina, public telephones take *fichas* (tokens), each good for about three minutes. More convenient magnetic cards are also available.

International discount rates are in effect between 10 pm and 7 am weekdays, midnight to 7 am and 1 pm to midnight Saturday and all day Sunday.

Credit-card or reverse-charge (collect) calls to overseas destinations are cheaper than paying locally; below are numbers for foreign direct operators:

Canada		☎ 000419
France		☎ 000433
Germany		☎ 000449
Italy		☎ 000439
Netherlands		☎ 000431
Spain		☎ 000434
Switzerland		☎ 000441
UK		☎ 000444
USA	(AT&T)	☎ 000410
	(MCI)	☎ 000412
	(Sprint)	☎ 000417

INTERNET RESOURCES
A guide to Uruguayan Internet resources, the Gran Directorio de Recursos Uruguayos en Internet, can be found at www.civila.com/ uruguay. Mercopress News Agency, at www.mercopress.com, is a Montevideo-based Internet news agency covering politics and business (in English and Spanish) in the Mercosur countries, Argentina, Brazil, Uruguay and Paraguay, in addition to Chile and the Falkland Islands.

BOOKS
History
William Henry Hudson's *The Purple Land* is a 19th-century classic. On Uruguay's welfare system, see George Pendle's *Uruguay; South America's First Welfare State* or Milton Vanger's *The Model Country: Jose Batlle y Ordóñez of Uruguay, 1907-1915*.

Contemporary Government & Politics
A good starting point is Martin Weinstein's *Uruguay, Democracy at the Crossroads*. For an account of Uruguay's own Dirty War, see Lawrence Weschler's *A Miracle, A Universe: Settling Accounts with Torturers*.

FILMS
Costa-Gavras' famous and engrossing *State of Siege* (1973), filmed in Allende's Chile, deals with the Tupamaro guerrillas' kidnapping and execution of suspected American CIA officer Dan Mitrione.

MEDIA
Montevideo dailies include the morning *El Día*, *La República*, *La Mañana* and *El País*. *Gaceta Comercial* is the voice of the business community. Afternoon papers are *El Diario*, *Mundocolor* and *Ultimas Noticias*, the latter operated by disciples of Reverend Sun Myung Moon. Most are identified with political parties, but the weekly *Búsqueda* takes a more independent stance.

There are 20 TV stations (four in Montevideo) and 100 radio stations (about 40 in the capital).

TIME
Like Argentina, Uruguay is three hours behind GMT/UTC.

ELECTRICITY
Electric current operates on 220V, 50Hz.

WEIGHTS & MEASURES
The metric system is official.

USEFUL ORGANIZATIONS
Uruguay's youth-hostel network provides an alternative to standard accommodation. Contact the Asociación de Alberguistas del Uruguay (☎ 02-400-4245), Pablo de María 1583, Montevideo.

BUSINESS HOURS
Most shops open weekdays and Saturday 8:30 am to 12:30 or 1 pm, then close until mid-afternoon and reopen until 7 or 8 pm. Food shops also open Sunday mornings.

From mid-November to mid-March, government offices open weekdays 7:30 am to

1:30 pm; the rest of the year, they are open noon to 7 pm. Banks are open weekday afternoons in Montevideo; elsewhere, mornings are the rule.

PUBLIC HOLIDAYS & SPECIAL EVENTS

Uruguay's Carnaval, the Monday and Tuesday before Ash Wednesday, is livelier than Argentina's but more sedate than Brazil's. The Afro-Uruguayan population of Montevideo's Barrio Sur celebrates traditional *candomblé* ceremonies. Holy Week (Easter) is also La Semana Criolla, with gaucho *asados* (barbecues) and folk music.

Año Nuevo (New Year's Day)
   January 1
Epifanía (Epiphany)
   January 6
Viernes Santo/Pascua (Good Friday/Easter)
   March/April (dates vary)
Desembarco de los 33 (Return of the 33 Exiles)
   April 19
Día del Trabajador (Labor Day)
   May 1
Batalla de Las Piedras (Battle of Las Piedras)
   May 18
Natalicio de Artigas (Artigas' Birthday)
   June 19
Jura de la Constitución (Constitution Day)
   July 18
Día de la Independencia (Independence Day)
   August 25
Día de la Raza (Columbus Day)
   October 12
Día de los Muertos (All Souls' Day)
   November 2
Navidad (Christmas Day)
   December 25

ACTIVITIES

Conventional beach activities like swimming and fishing are the major options for visitors to Uruguay, and surfing is possible on the outer Atlantic beaches.

ACCOMMODATIONS

Accommodations options are virtually identical to those in Argentina. Uruguay has a substantial network of youth hostels and several campgrounds, especially along the coast.

FOOD & DRINKS

Parrillas, confiterías, pizzerías and restaurants resemble their Argentine namesakes. Montevideo, Punta del Este and other beach resorts have good international restaurants. Seafood is usually a good choice.

The standard short order is *chivito*, a steak sandwich with cheese, lettuce, tomato, bacon and condiments. *Chivito al plato* is a larger steak topped with a fried egg, plus potato salad, green salad and chips. Other typical items are *olímpicos* (club sandwiches), *húngaros* (spicy sausages) and blander *panchos* (hot dogs).

Uruguayans consume even more *mate* than Argentines and Paraguayans. *Clericó* is a mixture of white wine and fruit juice, while *medio y medio* is a mixture of sparkling wine and white wine. Local beer is also good.

Getting There & Away

AIR
Departure Tax

International passengers pay a departure tax of US$6 on flights to Argentina, US$12 to other destinations.

Airports & Airlines

Uruguay has two main airports, Montevideo's Aeropuerto Internacional Carrasco and Punta del Este's Aeropuerto El Sauce, which has a few regional flights. While many airlines have offices in Montevideo, only a few fly there directly; it's usually necessary to make connections at Buenos Aires' Aeropuerto Internacional Ezeiza.

Neighboring Countries

There are frequent flights from Carrasco to Buenos Aires' Aeroparque Jorge Newbery, and from Punta del Este to Aeroparque.

Pluna flies to Brazilian destinations, including Porto Alegre, Florianópolis, Rio and São Paulo. Varig has similar routes.

Other South American Countries

Pluna flies to Asunción, Paraguay, Monday and Saturday, and to Santiago, Chile (four

URUGUAY

times weekly). TAM flies Tuesday, Friday and Sunday to Asunción.

Lloyd Aéreo Boliviano flies four times weekly to Santa Cruz de la Sierra and La Paz via Ezeiza. LanChile flies daily except Wednesday to Santiago, with an additional Sunday flight.

Cubana stops Mondays in Montevideo en route to Buenos Aires, whence it returns to Havana.

LAND

Uruguay shares borders with Argentina's Entre Ríos province and the Brazilian state of Rio Grande do Sul.

Argentina

Overland travel to Buenos Aires is slower and less convenient than crossing by boat. For Río Uruguay crossings see the Getting There & Away entry in the Argentina chapter.

Brazil

A number of routes connect Uruguay with points in Brazil.

Chuy to Chuí & Pelotas Only a median strip separates the twin cities of Chuy and Chuí, on the main highway from Montevideo.

Río Branco to Jaguarão This alternative route goes via Treinta y Tres or Melo. There are buses from Jaguarão to Pelotas.

Rivera to Santana do Livramento This route from Paysandú goes via Tacuarembó. Buses continue from Livramento to Porto Alegre.

Artigas to Quaraí This route crosses the Río Quareim, but the main highway goes southeast to Livramento.

Bella Unión to Barra do Quaraí This northwestern crossing leads to Uruguaiana, Brazil, opposite Paso de los Libres in Argentina's Corrientes province.

RIVER

Several crossings link Uruguay to Argentina. Montevideo passengers pay a US$5 port terminal and departure tax, while those from Colonia pay US$3.

Montevideo to Buenos Aires High-speed ferries connect the two capitals in about 2½ hours (US$52 to US$67 one way).

Colonia to Buenos Aires There are morning and evening ferries between Colonia and Buenos

Aires (2½ hours, US$23) and faster hydrofoils (45 minutes, US$32).

Carmelo & Nueva Palmira to Tigre Launches cross the Plata estuary to the Buenos Aires suburb of Tigre (US$11 to US$15).

Getting Around

AIR

Since the military airline Tamu suspended services, there are no flights within Uruguay except for the domestic leg of international flights from Punta del Este via Montevideo to Brazil.

BUS

Buses are frequent to destinations all around the country, so reservations should only be necessary on or around public holidays. Fares are reasonable – for example, Montevideo to Fray Bentos, about 300km, costs only about US$11.

CAR

Uruguayan drivers are less ruthless than Argentines, but there are many Argentines on the road. Uruguay ostensibly requires the Inter-American Driving Permit rather than the International Driving Permit. Arbitrary stops and searches are less common than in Argentina, but police do solicit bribes for traffic violations.

Car rental costs about the same as it does in Argentina, but gasoline is more expensive. The Automóvil Club del Uruguay (☎ 02-901-1251), at Colonia and Yí in Montevideo, is a good source of maps and information.

LOCAL TRANSPORT
Bus

To make sense of Montevideo's extensive public transport, consult routes and schedules in the yellow pages of the telephone directory. Retain your ticket for inspection. The standard fare is about US$0.65.

Taxi

Drivers correlate meter readings with a photocopied fare chart. Fares are higher from midnight to 6 am. There is a small additional luggage charge, and passengers generally round off the fare.

Montevideo

Founded in 1726 as a response to Colonia, Montevideo soon became an important port. It endured a long siege by Argentine dictator Rosas, but normal commerce resumed after his fall in 1851. Montevideo absorbed many immigrants from Spain and Italy in the early 20th century.

Many refugees from rural poverty live in *conventillos*, large, older houses converted into multifamily slum dwellings, in the colonial Ciudad Vieja. Urban redevelopment is displacing people from this picturesque but valuable central area.

Orientation

Montevideo lies on the east bank of the Río de La Plata. Its functional center is Plaza Independencia, east of the Ciudad Vieja. Av 18 de Julio is its key commercial and entertainment area. At the northeast end of 18 de Julio, Parque José Batlle y Ordóñez contains a 75,000-seat stadium, the Estadio Centenario. Perpendicular to its terminus is the major artery of Bulevar Artigas.

Across the harbor, the 132m Cerro de Montevideo was a landmark for early navigators. To the east of downtown, the riverfront Rambla leads past residential suburbs and sandy beaches frequented by *montevideños* in summer and on weekends.

Information

Tourist Offices The Ministerio de Turismo (☎ 02-409-7399) maintains a cubbyhole office on the ground floor at Av Lavalleja 1409, but look for a new office to open in the same building at the corner of Colonia. The better-equipped Oficina de Informes (☎ 02-601-1757) at Terminal Tres Cruces, the bus station at Bulevar Artigas and Av Italia, is open 9 am to 9 pm daily. The *Guía del Ocio*, listing cultural events, cinemas, theaters and restaurants, comes with the Friday edition of *El País*.

Post & Communications The Correo Central (main post office) is at Buenos Aires 451. Antel has Telecentros at San José 1108 (open 24 hours) and Rincón 501.

Travel Agencies Argentina's nonprofit student travel agency Asatej, an affiliate of

STA Travel, has a Montevideo branch (☎ 02-908-0509, fax 02-908-4895) at Río Negro 1354, 2nd floor.

Bookstores Linardi y Risso, at Juan Carlos Gómez 1435, carries a sizable selection of out-of-print books, especially in history and literature.

Medical Services Hospital Maciel (☎ 02-915-6810) is at 25 de Mayo and Maciel, in the Ciudad Vieja.

Dangers & Annoyances Montevideo is sedate by most standards, but there are symptoms of an increasing street crime rate. Take the usual precautions, especially around the Ciudad Vieja's Mercado del Puerto.

Walking Tour

On **Plaza Independencia**, a huge statue of the country's greatest hero tops the **Mausoleo de Artigas**. The 18th-century **Palacio Estévez** served as the Casa de Gobierno until 1985, while the 26-story **Palacio Salvo** was once South America's tallest building. Just off the plaza, the **Teatro Solís** is Montevideo's leading theater.

Beyond the remnant colonial **Puerto de la Ciudadela**, Calle Sarandí leads to **Plaza Constitución**, where the **Iglesia Matriz** (cathedral), at Sarandí and Ituzaingó, is the city's oldest public building (1799). Continue to **Casa Rivera**, corner of Rincón and Misiones, the **Museo Romántico**, 25 de Mayo 428, and **Casa Lavalleja**, corner of Zabala and 25 de Mayo, all part of the Museo Histórico Nacional. A block west is **Casa Garibaldi**, where the Italian hero once lived. From nearby **Plaza Zabala**, continue along Washington to Colón and then to Piedras and the **Mercado del Puerto**.

Museo del Gaucho y de la Moneda

In the Banco de la República, Av 18 de Julio 998, this museum displays artifacts of Uruguay's gaucho past. It's open 4 to 7 pm daily except Monday.

Museo Torres García

On the pedestrian mall at Sarandí 683, this free museum displays the works of Joaquín Torres García (1874-1949), who spent much of his career in France producing abstract

URUGUAY

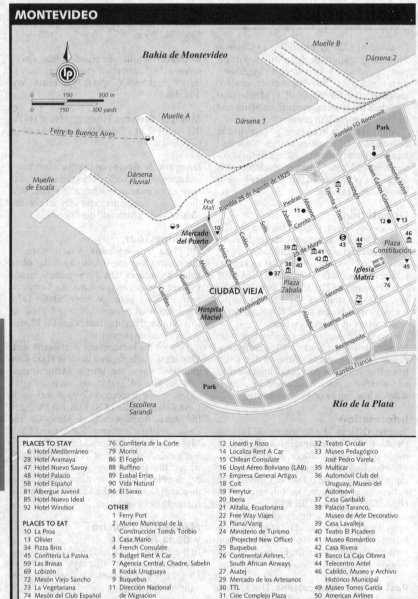

MONTEVIDEO

PLACES TO STAY
6 Hotel Mediterráneo
28 Hotel Aramaya
47 Hotel Nuevo Savoy
48 Hotel Palacio
58 Hotel Español
81 Albergue Juvenil
85 Hotel Nuevo Ideal
92 Hotel Windsor

PLACES TO EAT
10 La Proa
13 Olivier
34 Pizza Bros
45 Confitería La Pasiva
59 Las Brasas
72 Mesón Viejo Sancho
73 La Vegetariana
74 Mesón del Club Español

76 Confitería de la Corte
79 Morini
86 El Fogón
88 Ruffino
89 Eusbal Errias
90 Vida Natural
96 El Sarao

OTHER
1 Ferry Port
2 Museo Municipal de la
   Construcción Tomás Toribio
3 Casa Mario
4 French Consulate
5 Budget Rent A Car
7 Agencia Central, Chadre, Sabelin
8 Kodak Uruguaya
9 Buquebus
11 Dirección Nacional
   de Migracion

12 Linardi y Risso
14 Localiza Rent A Car
15 Chilean Consulate
16 Lloyd Aéreo Boliviano (LAB)
17 Empresa General Artigas
18 Coit
19 Ferrytur
20 Iberia
21 Alitalia, Ecuatoriana
22 Free Way Viajes
23 Pluna/Varig
24 Ministerio de Turismo
   (Projected New Office)
25 Buquebus
26 Continental Airlines,
   South African Airways
27 Asatej
29 Mercado de los Artesanos
30 TTL
31 Cine Complejo Plaza

32 Teatro Circular
33 Museo Pedagógico
   José Pedro Varela
35 Multicar
36 Automóvil Club del
   Uruguay, Museo del
   Automóvil
37 Casa Garibaldi
38 Palacio Taranco,
   Museo de Arte Decorativo
39 Casa Lavalleja
40 Teatro El Picadero
41 Museo Romántico
42 Casa Rivera
43 Banco La Caja Obrera
44 Telecentro Antel
46 Cabildo, Museo y Archivo
   Histórico Municipal
49 Museo Torres García
50 American Airlines

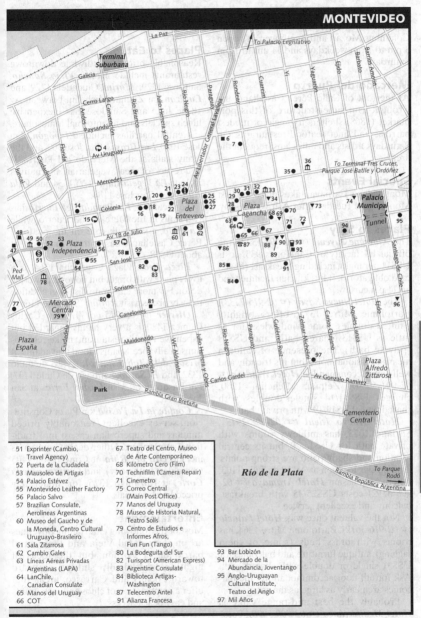

MONTEVIDEO

URUGUAY

51 Exprinter (Cambio,
Travel Agency)
52 Puerta de la Ciudadela
53 Mausoleo de Artigas
54 Palacio Estévez
55 Montevideo Leather Factory
56 Palacio Salvo
57 Brazilian Consulate,
Aerolineas Argentinas
60 Museo del Gaucho y de
la Moneda, Centro Cultural
Uruguayo-Brasileiro
61 Sala Zitarrosa
62 Cambio Gales
63 Líneas Aéreas Privadas
Argentinas (LAPA)
64 LanChile,
Canadian Consulate
65 Manos del Uruguay
66 COT

67 Teatro del Centro, Museo
de Arte Contemporáneo
68 Kilómetro Cero (Film)
70 Technifilm (Camera Repair)
71 Cinemetro
75 Correo Central
(Main Post Office)
77 Manos del Uruguay
78 Museo de Historia Natural,
Teatro Solís
79 Centro de Estudios e
Informes Afros,
Fun Fun (Tango)
80 La Bodeguita del Sur
82 Turisport (American Express)
83 Argentine Consulate
84 Biblioteca Artigas-
Washington
87 Telecentro Antel
91 Alianza Francesa

93 Bar Lobizón
94 Mercado de la
Abundancia, Joventango
95 Anglo-Uruguayan
Cultural Institute,
Teatro del Anglo
97 Mil Años

Río de la Plata

and even cubist work like Picasso's, as well as unusual historical portraits of figures like Columbus, Mozart and Beethoven. It's open 3 pm to 7 pm weekdays and 11 am to 1 pm Saturday.

Mercado del Puerto

At the foot of Calle Pérez Castellano, the wrought-iron superstructure of this port market (1868) shelters a gaggle of modest parrillas and finer seafood restaurants. On Saturdays, artists and musicians frequent the area.

Special Events

Montevideo's Carnaval takes place the first Monday and Tuesday after Ash Wednesday.

Places to Stay

The *Albergue Juvenil* (☎ 02-908-1324), the official HI facility at Canelones 935, costs US$11 per night, including breakfast (hostel card obligatory). It has kitchen facilities and an 11 pm curfew.

The *Hotel Nuevo Savoy* (☎ 02-915-7233), Bartolomé Mitre 1371, offers brightly painted doubles, some windowless, for as little as US$13 (shared bath) and US$18 (private bath). The presence of children means occasional noise, but it's friendly and well run. Recommended *Hotel Windsor* (☎ 02-901-5080), Zelmar Michelini 1260, charges US$11/14 singles/doubles with shared bath, US$14/19 with private bath.

Hotel Nuevo Ideal (☎ 02-908-2913), Soriano 1073, has mildewy rooms with private bath for US$15/20, but its central location and shady patio are strong points. At a noisier location at Av 18 de Julio 1103, otherwise pleasant *Hotel Aramaya* (☎ 02-908-6192) costs US$25/35 with breakfast, balcony and excellent service.

Not the value it once was, *Hotel Palacio* (☎ 02-916-3612), Bartolomé Mitre 1364, has rooms with brass beds (some of them sagging), antique furniture and balconies for US$31 single or double with shared bath. Ask for 6th-floor accommodations; the balconies are nearly as large as the rooms.

Probably the best mid-range value is *Hotel Mediterráneo* (☎ 02-900-5090), Paraguay 1486, charging US$30/40 for well-kept rooms with breakfast and fine service. Enjoying literary cachet as the site of Julio Cortázar's short story 'La Puerta Conde-

nada,' The *Hotel Español* (☎ 02-900-3816), Convención 1317, charges from US$35/45.

Places to Eat

Reasonably priced, worthwhile downtown restaurants include *Mesón Viejo Sancho*, San José 1229, *Morini*, Ciudadela 1229, and *Lobizón*, on Zelmar Michelini between Av 18 de Julio and San José, has inexpensive lunch specials and an informal atmosphere.

Central parrillas include *El Fogón*, San José 1080, *Las Brasas*, San José 909, and the many stalls at the Mercado del Puerto. If you're sick of meat, vegetarian alternatives include *La Vegetariana* at Yí 1334 and *Vida Natural* at San José 1184.

For seafood, *La Posada del Puerto* has two stalls in the Mercado del Puerto, while *La Proa*, a sidewalk café on the peatonal Pérez Castellano, has entrees that start at about US$8.

Pizza Bros, Plaza Cagancha 1364, is a lively place with bright but not overpowering decor. For more elaborate dishes in addition to tasty pizzas, visit *Ruffino*, San José 1166.

Olivier (☎ 02-915-0617), Juan Carlos Gómez 1420, is a very highly regarded but expensive French restaurant; make reservations in advance. Spanish food is available at *Mesón del Club Español*, Av 18 de Julio 1332, and *El Sarao*, Santiago de Chile 1137. For Basque food, visit *Eusbal Errias* at San José 1168.

Confitería La Pasiva, on Plaza Constitución, serves excellent, reasonably priced minutas and superb flan casero in a traditional atmosphere. Other decent confiterías include *Oro del Rhin* at Convención 1403 (the oldest in the city), and *Confitería de la Corte*, at Ituzaingó 1325, for moderately priced lunch specials.

Entertainment

Most of the following entertainment venues are in the Ciudad Vieja and the central barrio of El Cordón, but the focus of nightlife is gradually shifting eastward toward Pocitos and Carrasco, areas that offer a combination of clubs and restaurants and easy beach access.

Cinemas Centrally located cinemas offer films from around the world. The *Cinemateca Uruguaya* (☎ 02-408-2460), a film club at Lorenzo Carnelli 1311, has a modest membership fee allowing unlimited viewing at its five cinemas.

Live Music For live folkloric music, Cuban salsa and the like, the best place is *La Bodeguita del Sur* (☎ 02-902-8649), Soriano 840. For rock and occasional live theater, try the *Sala Zitarrosa* (☎ 02-901-7303), at Av 18 de Julio and Jullo Herrera y Obes.

Theater Like Buenos Aires, Montevideo has an active theater community. Besides the *Teatro Solís*, the most prestigious playhouse in town, there are the *Teatro Circular* (☎ 02-908-1953) at Rondeau 1388; *Casa del Teatro* (☎ 02-402-0773) at Mercedes 1788; *Teatro del Anglo* (☎ 02-902-3773) at San José 1426; *Teatro El Picadero* (☎ 02-915-2337) at 25 de Mayo 390; *Teatro del Centro* (☎ 02-902-8915) at Plaza Cagancha 1164; and *Teatro El Galpón* (☎ 02-408-3366) at Av 18 de Julio 1618. Admission is reasonable, from about US$5.

Tango The informal *Fun Fun* (☎ 02-915-8005), at Ciudadela 1229 in the Mercado Central, offers a good mix of young and old. Visitors interested in lessons can try *Joventango* (☎ 02-901-5561), in the Mercado de la Abundancia at the corner of San José and Yaguarón.

Shopping

El Cordón's Feria De Tristán Narvaja is a Sunday morning outdoor market that sprawls from Av 18 de Julio along Calle Tristán Narvaja. For artisanal items, visit Mercado de los Artesanos on Plaza Cagancha, also a hangout for younger Uruguayans. Another outlet is the recycled Mercado de la Abundancia, at San José and Yaguarón. Manos del Uruguay, at San José 1111 and Reconquista 602, is famous for quality goods.

Getting There & Away

Air Besides the usual international carriers, commuter airlines also provide services to Argentina.

Aerolíneas Argentinas
  (☎ 02-901-9466) Convención 1343, 4th floor
Alitalia
  (☎ 02-908-5828) Colonia 981, 2nd floor
American
  (☎ 02-916-3979) Sarandí 699 bis

Continental
  (☎ 02-908-5828) Río Negro 1380, Oficina 104
Ecuatoriana
  (☎ 02-902-5717) Colonia 981
Iberia
  (☎ 02-908-1032) Colonia 873
LanChile
  (☎ 02-902-3883) Plaza Cagancha 1335, Oficina 801
LAPA
  (☎ 02-900-8765) Plaza Cagancha 1339
Lloyd Aéreo Boliviano (LAB)
  (☎ 02-902-2656) Colonia 920, 2nd floor
Pluna/Varig
  (☎ 02-902-1414) Colonia 1001
South African Airways
  (☎ 02-900-8000) Río Negro 1380, Oficina 104
Transportes Aéreos de Mercosur (TAM)
  (☎ 02-916-6044) Bacacay 1321

Bus Montevideo's Terminal Tres Cruces (☎ 401-8998), at Bulevar Artigas and Av Italia, has superseded the individual bus terminals that once cluttered and congested Plaza Cagancha. It has decent restaurants, clean toilets, a left-luggage facility, telephones, a cambio and other services.

Domestic COT (☎ 02-409-4949) runs 20-plus buses daily to Punta del Este via Piriápolis and Maldonado; Copsa (☎ 02-408-1521) also goes to Maldonado. COT has frequent service to Colonia and also to La Paloma.

Agencia Central, (☎ 1717), Chadre (☎ 1717), Sabelín (☎ 1717), Copay (☎ 02-400-9926) and Intertur (☎ 02-409-7098) all serve littoral destinations like Colonia, Mercedes, Fray Bentos, Paysandú and Salto. Turil (☎ 1990) goes three times daily to Tacuarembó and Rivera and eight times daily to Colonia.

Rutas del Sol (☎ 02-402-5451) goes to Rocha and La Paloma 10 times daily. Cita (☎ 02-402-5425) goes to Chuy, as do COT and Rutas del Sol. Rutas del Plata (☎ 02-402-5129) goes to Minas and Treinta y Tres four times daily. Núñez (☎ 02-408-6670) serves interior destinations like Minas, Treinta y Tres, Salto and Rivera, while El Norteño (☎ 02-908-9212) goes to Salto and Bella Unión. Cynsa (☎ 02-408-6670) runs five buses daily to Chuy and six to La Paloma, and also goes to Paysandú.

CUT/Corporación (☎ 02-402-1920) goes five times daily to Mercedes and Fray

Bentos. Turismar (☎ 02-409-0999) goes to Treinta y Tres three times daily, as does Cota.

Sample fares include Minas (US$5, two hours), Maldonado-Punta del Este (US$6, 2½ hours), Colonia (US$7, 2½ hours), La Paloma (US$9.50, 3½ hours), Fray Bentos (US$11, five hours), Chuy (US$13, five hours), Paysandú (US$15, five hours), Tacuarembó (US$15, 5½ hours) and Salto (US$20, six hours).

International Bus de la Carrera (☎ 02-402-1313) has three buses daily to Buenos Aires. Bus de la Hidrovía (☎ 02-402-5129) departs on Tuesday and Sunday for Corrientes (14 hours).

Several companies go elsewhere in Argentina, including Empresa General Artigas (EGA; ☎ 02-402-5164) to Rosario and Mendoza Saturday, and to Santiago de Chile Monday; Tas Choapa (☎ 02-409-8598) also goes to Santiago. El Rápido Internacional (☎ 02-401-4764) also services Rosario and Mendoza, with connections to Chile. Expreso Encon (☎ 02-408-6670) goes to Rosario, Paraná, Santa Fe, and Córdoba, while Cora (☎ 02-409-8799) goes to Córdoba four times weekly.

Brújula (☎ 02-401-9350) and Coit (☎ 02-401-5628) alternate daily service to Asunción, Paraguay. Cauvi (☎ 02-401-9196) goes to Buenos Aires and the Brazilian cities of Porto Alegre, Curitiba and São Paulo. EGA, TTL (☎ 02-401-1410) and Planalto (☎ 1717) also make Brazilian destinations.

Sample fares include Buenos Aires (US$25, eight hours), Porto Alegre (US$40, 11 hours), Rosario (US$42, 15 hours), Corrientes (US$45, 14 hours), Florianópolis (US$56, 17½ hours), Curitiba (US$67, 23 hours), Asunción (US$70, 18 hours), Mendoza (US$75, 21 hours), São Paulo (US$80, 29 hours) and Santiago de Chile (US$95, 28 hours).

Boat Buquebus (☎ 02-902-0170) is downtown at Río Negro 1400 but also has port offices (☎ 02-916-8801) on Rambla 25 de Agosto, at the foot of Pérez Castellano. Its 'Buqueaviones' (high-speed ferries) cross to Buenos Aires (2½ hours) four times daily. Fares are US$52 in turista, US$67 in primera; children ages two to nine pay US$17.

Ferrytur (☎ 02-900-6617), at Río Branco 1368 and at Tres Cruces (☎ 02-409-8198), does bus-boat combinations to Buenos Aires (US$40, four hours) with their *Sea Cat* hydrofoil, with four departures weekdays and three on weekends.

Cacciola (☎ 02-401-9350), at Terminal Tres Cruces, runs a bus-launch service to Buenos Aires (US$29 one way, US$55 return, eight hours) via the riverside town of Carmelo and the Argentine Delta suburb of Tigre. Services leave Montevideo at 8:30 am daily, 12:40 am Monday through Saturday and 4 pm on Sunday.

Getting Around

Bus Montevideo's bus fleet goes everywhere for about US$0.65. For US$4, Ibat (☎ 02-601-0207) runs an airport bus from Pluna's downtown offices at Colonia 1001. From the Terminal Suburbana at Rambla 25 de Agosto and Río Branco, the No 209 Cutcsa and Copsa buses go to Carrasco (US$1.20) every 15 minutes.

Taxi Drivers correlate meter readings with a photocopied fare chart.

Uruguayan Littoral

West of Montevideo, the littoral's wheat fields and gardens feed the capital. Its main attraction is the 17th-century Portuguese contraband port and fortress of Colonia, but overland travelers from Argentina may find towns along the Río Uruguay pleasant stopovers.

COLONIA

Only an hour from Buenos Aires, Colonia del Sacramento attracts just a handful of the foreigners who visit the Argentine capital. Founded in 1680, it occupied a strategic position across the river from Buenos Aires, as its contraband undercut Spain's mercantile trade monopoly. Spain captured the city in 1762, holding it until 1777, when Spanish reforms finally permitted foreign goods to proceed directly to Buenos Aires.

Orientation

On the east bank of the Río de la Plata, Colonia (population 30,000) is 50km northeast of Buenos Aires by ferry or hydrofoil. Its Barrio Histórico, a jumble of cobblestone streets shaded by sycamores on a small

COLONIA

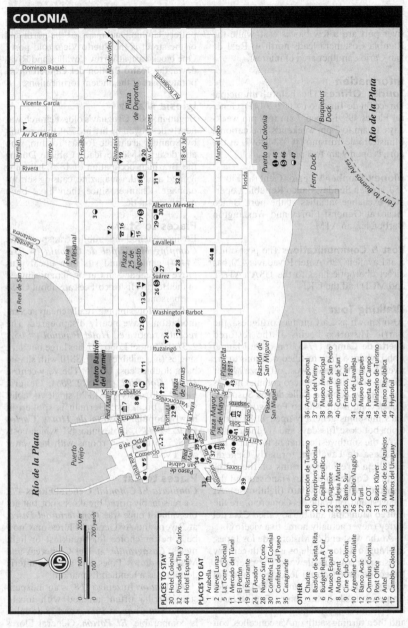

Domingo Baqué

Vicente García

Av JG Artigas

Daymán

Arroyo

Rivera

Plaza de Deportes

To Montevideo

Av Roosevelt

Rivadavia ▼19

Av General Flores

D Fosalba

Manuel Lobo

18 de Julio

●20

Florida

Río de la Plata

Puerto de Colonia

Buquebus Dock

Ferry Dock

Ferry to Buenos Aires

🏧45
$46
○47

Rambla Constanera

Feria Artesanal

Alberto Méndez

3 ◑

▼2

🏛16
▼15

17$

18▼

31▼

32■

29◆
30

Plaza 25 de Agosto

Lavalleja

27▼

▼28

44■

Suárez

14▼

13◑

26◑

To Real de San Carlos

Washington Barbot

12$

▼24

25●

Ituzaingó

Teatro Bastión del Carmen

9●

10◐

▼11

Bastión de San Miguel

Plazoleta
1811

43■

Paseo de San Miguel

Virrey Ceballos

Ped Mall
🏛7

8●

8 de Octubre

Puerto Viejo

Santa Rita

4◑

5●

San José

España

Real

Comercio

Paseo de San Gabriel

▲23

22●

Plaza de Armas

Vasconcellos

Ped Mall

21
36
34
35

Misiones

37

40

Río de la Plata

33

Flores

San Francisco

Solís

San Pedro

San Antonio

Plaza Mayor 25 de Mayo

41
42

39●

PLACES TO STAY
30 Hotel Colonial
32 Posada de Tita y Carlos
44 Hotel Español

PLACES TO EAT
1   Arabella
2   Nueve Lunas
5   La Torre Colonial
11 Mercado del Túnel
19 El Portón
24 El Asador
28 Nuevo San Cono
30 Confitería El Colonial
31 Confitería del Paseo
35 Casagrande

OTHER
3   Chadre
4   Bastión de Santa Rita
6   Budget Rent A Car
7   Museo Español
8   Moto Rent
9   Cine Club Colonia
10 Argentine Consulate
12 Banco Acac
13 Omnibus Colonia
15 Post Office
16 Antel
17 Cambio Colonia

18 Dirección de Turismo
20 Receptivos Colonia
21 Capilla Jesultica
22 Drugstore
23 Iglesia Matriz
25 Barrio Sur
26 Cambio Viaggio
27 Turil
29 COT
31 Buses Klüver
33 Museo de los Azulejos
34 Manos del Uruguay

36 Archivo Regional
37 Casa del Virrey
38 Museo Municipal
39 Bastión de San Pedro
40 Convento de San
    Francisco, Faro
41 Casa de Lavalleja
42 Museo Portugués
43 Puerta de Campo
45 Ministerio de Turismo
46 Banco República
47 Hydrofoil

URUGUAY

0   100   200 m
0   100   200 yards

peninsula, is a must-see. The commercial downtown, near Plaza 25 de Agosto, and the river port are a few blocks east, while the Rambla Costanera leads north to Real de San Carlos, another area of interest.

Information

Tourist Offices The helpful municipal Dirección de Turismo (☎ 052-26141), General Flores 499, is open 7 am to 8 pm weekdays, 10 am to 7 pm weekends. The national Ministerio de Turismo (☎ 052-24897) at the port, is open 9 am to 3 pm daily.

Money Cambio Viaggio, General Flores 350, is open Sunday. Banco República operates exchange facilities at the port. Banco Acac, at General Flores and Washington Barbot, has an ATM.

Post & Communications The post office is at Lavalleja 226. Antel, Rivadavia 420, has direct fiberoptic lines to the USA (AT&T and MCI) and the UK.

Walking Tour

Also known as La Colonia Portuguesa, the Barrio Histórico begins at the restored **Puerta de Campo** (1745), on Calle Manoel Lobo, where a thick fortified wall runs to the river. A short distance west, off Plaza Mayor 25 de Mayo, tile-and-stucco colonial houses line narrow, cobbled **Calle de los Suspiros**; just beyond is the **Museo Portugués**. Colonia's museums generally open 11:30 am to 6 pm, but close Tuesdays and Wednesdays.

At the southwest corner of the Plaza are the **Casa de Lavalleja**, formerly General Lavalleja's residence, ruins of the 17th-century **Convento de San Francisco** and the restored 19th-century **faro** (lighthouse). At the west end, on Calle del Comercio, are the **Museo Municipal** and the so-called **Casa del Virrey** (never actually home to a viceroy).

At the west end of Misiones de los Tapes, the **Museo de los Azulejos** is a 17th-century house with colonial tilework. The riverfront **Paseo de San Gabriel** leads to Calle del Colegio, where a right turn onto Calle del Comercio leads to the ruined **Capilla Jesuítica** (Jesuit chapel). Going east along Flores and then turning south on Vasconcellos, you reach the landmark **Iglesia Matriz** (see the next section), on the **Plaza de Armas** (Plaza Manoel Lobo).

Across Flores, at España and San José, the **Museo Español** exhibits replicas of colonial pottery, clothing and maps. At the north end of the street is the **Puerto Viejo** (old port). One block east, at Virrey Cevallos and Rivadavia, the **Teatro Bastión del Carmen** incorporates part of the ancient fortifications.

Iglesia Matriz

Begun in 1680, Uruguay's oldest church was nearly destroyed by fire in 1799, then rebuilt by Spanish architect Tomás Toribio, who also designed Montevideo's Cabildo. During the Brazilian occupation of 1823, lightning ignited a powder magazine, causing serious damage. Changes since then have been mainly cosmetic.

Places to Stay

Easily reached by public transport, the *Camping Municipal de Colonia* (☎ 052-24444) campground sits in a eucalyptus grove at Real de San Carlos, 5km northwest of the Barrio Histórico. Fees are about US$4 per person.

Except for camping, really cheap accommodations have nearly disappeared. The recently renovated *Hotel Español* (☎ 052-22314), Manoel Lobo 377, has large but dark singles (if available) for US$10 with shared bath; doubles cost US$15. The very central *Hotel Colonial* (☎ 05222906), General Flores 440, costs US$13/20 singles/doubles without breakfast. German is spoken at newly popular *Posada de Tita y Carlos* (☎ 052-24438), 18 de Julio 491, which costs US$25/35 for clean rooms with hot water and TV.

Places to Eat

Confitería El Colonial, General Flores 432, is a reasonably priced breakfast spot, but not the value it once was. *Confitería del Paseo*, at Rivera and Av General Flores, may now be a better choice for breakfast or light meals. *Casagrande*, at Del Comercio and Misiones de los Tapes, is a good confitería doubling as a handicrafts market.

El Asador, Ituzaingó 168, is an inexpensive parrilla often jammed with locals. *Nuevo San Cono*, at Suárez and 18 de Julio, is comparable. *El Portón*, General Flores 333, is a more upscale but appealing parrilla.

At General Flores 229, the extensive menu at *Mercado del Túnel* varies in quality.

Italian *Il Ristorante*, at Rivera and Rivadavia, is a fine choice.

At the tip of the Barrio Histórico, *La Torre Colonial* is a good pizzería in a remodeled tower. Readers recommend the pizza at *Nueve Lunas*, Rivadavia 413, and *Arabella*, Av Artigas 384.

Shopping

Colonia's Feria Artesanal (Crafts Fair) has moved to a permanent spot at Suárez and Fosalba. Manos del Uruguay has an outlet at San Gabriel and Misiones de los Tapes.

Getting There & Away

Bus COT (☎ 052-23121), General Flores 440, runs at least nine buses daily to Montevideo (US$7, 2½ hours), plus 10 daily to Colonia Suiza. Turil (☎ 052-25246), at General Flores and Suárez, goes eight times daily to Montevideo. Klüver (☎ 052-22934), at General Flores and Rivera, goes twice each weekday and daily on weekends to Mercedes.

Chadre, on Méndez between Fosalba and Rivadavia, goes twice daily to Montevideo and to Nueva Palmira, Carmelo, Salto, Paysandú and Bella Unión.

River From the port at the foot of Av Roosevelt, Buquebus (☎ 052-22975) has two daily ferries to Buenos Aires (US$23, 2½ hours); their high-speed 'Buqueaviones' (45 minutes) cost US$32. Ferrytur (☎ 052-22919) makes two ferry crossings every weekday, one every Saturday and Sunday; their hydrofoil Sea Cat goes four times weekdays, three times daily on weekends. Ferrytur and Buquebus prices are almost identical; ask about day tours. All passengers pay a US$3 departure tax.

Getting Around

Local buses go to the Camping Municipal and Real de San Carlos. Otherwise, walking is enjoyable in compact Colonia.

AROUND COLONIA
Real de San Carlos

At the turn of the 20th century, Argentine entrepreneur Nicolás Mihanovich invested US$1.5 million in a huge tourist complex at Real de San Carlos, 5km west of Colonia. Its attractions included a 10,000-seat bullring, a 3000-seat jai alai *frontón*, a racecourse and a hotel-casino with its own power plant. Only the racecourse functions today, but the ruins make for an interesting excursion.

COLONIA SUIZA

Settled by Swiss immigrants in 1862, Colonia Suiza soon provided wheat for Montevideo, 120km away. A quiet destination with a demonstrably European ambiance, its dairy goods are known throughout the country.

On the central Plaza de los Fundadores, the impressive sculpture **El Surco** commemorates Swiss pioneers. Notable buildings include ruins of the first flour mill, the **Molino Quemado**, and the **Hotel del Prado** (1884), which functions as a youth hostel.

Places to Stay & Eat

Dating from 1884, the 80-room *Hotel del Prado* (☎ 055-44169), in the Barrio Hoteles on the outskirts of town, is a magnificent if declining building with huge balconies. Rooms cost US$25 per person, but its hostel wing offers beds with shared bath for US$9 (hostel card obligatory).

For dining, try *La Gondola*, Luis Dreyer and 25 de Agosto, *L'Arbalete* at Hotel Nirvana, on Av Batlle y Ordóñez, and *Don Juan*, 18 de Julio 1214.

Getting There & Away

There are numerous buses to Colonia and Montevideo, fewer westbound to Fray Bentos (three daily) and Paysandú (one daily).

CARMELO

Carmelo, 75km northwest of Colonia, is a center for exploring the Paraná delta. From Plaza Independencia, Av 19 de Abril leads to Arroyo de las Vacas, where a large park offers camping, swimming and a monstrous casino.

The municipal Oficina de Turismo (☎ 054-22001) has moved to Shopping Suhr, a gallery at 19 de Abril and Solís, near the bridge over the arroyo. There are two casas de cambio near the plaza.

Places to Stay & Eat

Camping Náutico Carmelo (☎ 054-22058), on the south side of Arroyo de las Vacas, charges US$3 per person. *Camping Don Mauro* (☎ 054-22390), at Ignacio Barros and Arroyo de las Vacas, charges the same.

URUGUAY

Hotel Paraná (☎ 054-22480), 19 de Abril 585, has singles for US$8 with private bath. At tidy *Hotel La Unión* (☎ 054-22028), Uruguay 368, singles with shared bath cost US$9, singles/doubles with private bath US$12/20.

El Vesubio, 19 de Abril 451, serves an enormous, tasty chivito al plato, plus a variety of other dishes. Other restaurants include *Perrini* at 19 de Abril 440, and the *Yacht Club*, *Morales* and *El Refugio*, all across the bridge in the park.

Getting There & Away
Bus All bus companies are on or near Plaza Independencia. Chadre (☎ 054-22987) goes to Montevideo (US$9, four hours) and north to Fray Bentos, Paysandú and Salto; Sabelín, at the same address, services Nueva Palmira six times daily. Turil goes to Colonia (US$2, one hour), as do Klúver (☎ 054-23411) and Intertur. Klúver also goes to Nueva Palmira and Mercedes.

River Movilán/Deltanave, Constituyentes 263, and Cacciola, Constituyentes 219, each has twice-daily launches to the Buenos Aires suburb of Tigre (US$11 one way).

FRAY BENTOS
In 1864, Uruguay's first meat extract plant opened here, 300km west of Montevideo, across the Río Uruguay from Gualeguaychú, Argentina. In 1902 British interests built the country's first frigorífico, the enormous Anglo plant, now a museum.

Barren Plaza Constitución has only a few palms and a Victorian band shell, but the helpful municipal Oficina de Turismo (☎ 0535-2233) occupies an office in the Museo Solari, on the west side of Plaza Constitución; it's open 8 am to 1 pm and 2 to 8 pm weekdays, with summer hours of 7:30 am to 1:30 pm and 4 to 9 pm weekdays.

Things to See
The landmark 400-seat **Teatro Young**, bearing the name of the Anglo-Uruguayan *estanciero* who sponsored its construction from 1909 to 1912, hosts cultural events throughout the year. It's a block from Plaza Constitución, at the corner of 25 de Mayo and Zorrilla.

In 1865, the Liebig Extract of Meat Company located its pioneer South American plant in the **Barrio Histórico del Anglo**, southwest of downtown. Most of the defunct Frigorífico Anglo del Uruguay, still the dominant landmark in a neighborhood with an active street life, has become the **Museo de la Revolución Industrial** (☎ 0535-2918). Phone for guided tours.

Places to Stay & Eat
The *Club Atlético Anglo* (☎ 0535-2787) maintains a campground, with hot showers and beach access, 10 blocks south of Plaza Constitución. The *Nuevo Hotel Colonial* (☎ 0535-2260), 25 de Mayo 3293, is clean and friendly, with rooms arranged around an interior patio, for US$13 double with shared bath, US$22 with private bath.

The *Hotel 25 de Mayo* (☎ 0535-2586), at 25 de Mayo and Lavalleja, is a modernized 19th-century building offering singles/doubles with shared bath for US$11/20, with private bath for US$15/20.

For dining, *La Enramada*, on España between 25 de Mayo and 25 de Agosto, is cheap and friendly but basic. Try instead *La Olla*, 18 de Julio 1130.

Getting There & Away
Despite a new terminal at 18 de Julio and Varela, most bus companies still use offices around Plaza Constitución, 10 blocks west. ETA runs three buses daily to Gualeguaychú (US$4). CUT (☎ 0535-2286) has five daily to Mercedes (US$1.50) and Montevideo (US$11, five hours). Chadre, 25 de Mayo 3220, conducts two trips daily between Bella Unión and Montevideo via Salto, Paysandú, Fray Bentos, Mercedes, Dolores, Nueva Palmira, Carmelo and Colonia. Agencia Central (☎ 0535-3470) and Sabelín also go to Montevideo.

MERCEDES
The livestock center of Mercedes is also a minor resort on the Río Negro, a tributary of the Uruguay, popular for boating, fishing and swimming. Mercedes has better bus connections than Fray Bentos, 30km northwest.

Plaza Independencia is the center of downtown. The municipal Oficina de Turismo (☎ 053-22733), Artigas 215, has friendly, enthusiastic staff and a good city map. It's open 12:30 to 6:30 pm Monday through Thursday, 9:30 am to 8:30 pm Friday through Sunday. Two nearby cambios change cash but not traveler's checks. The post office is at Rodó 650. Centro Telefónico is at Artigas 290.

Places to Stay & Eat

Eight blocks northwest from Plaza Independencia, linked to the mainland by a bridge, Mercedes' *Camping del Hum* has excellent swimming, fishing and sanitary facilities, but the 1997 and '98 floods disrupted things here. Fees are just US$1 per person plus US$1 per tent. There are hostel accommodations at the *Club Remeros Mercedes* (☎ 053-22534), De la Rivera 949.

Improved *Hotel Mercedes* (☎ 053-23204), Giménez 659, has singles with shared bath for US$9, with private bath for US$12. Quiet, friendly *Hotel Marín* (☎ 053-22987), Rodó 668, has singles for US$10.

La Churrasquera, Castro y Careaga 790, is a parrilla serving large portions. On the Isla del Puerto, near the campground, the *Comedor Municipal* and the *Club Surubí* both have good fish and outdoor seating.

Getting There & Away

Klüver (☎ 053-22046), on Plaza Independencia, runs two buses daily (one on weekends) to Colonia. For nearby Chadre, Mercedes is a stopover en route from Bella Unión to Montevideo (see Fray Bentos section for details). Agencia Central, CUT and Sabelín, all at Artigas 233 (☎ 053-23766), connect Mercedes with Montevideo (US$11, 4½ hours). CUT has five services daily to Fray Bentos. ETA, at the same address, has services to Gualeguaychú, Argentina via Fray Bentos and to interior destinations.

PAYSANDÚ

Uruguay's second-largest city (population 100,000) started as an 18th-century estancia for the Jesuit mission at Yapeyú, Corrientes. Processing beer, sugar, textiles and leather, it's Uruguay's only significant industrial center outside Montevideo.

Across the river from Colón, Argentina, Paysandú is 110km north of Fray Bentos. Av 18 de Julio, the main commercial street, runs along the south side of Plaza Constitución. The flood-prone riverfront mostly consists of parkland.

Opposite Plaza Constitución at 18 de Julio 1226, the Dirección Municipal de Turismo (☎ 072-26221) is open 7 am to 7 pm weekdays, 8 am to 6 pm weekends.

Cambio Fagalde is at 18 de Julio 1002, while Banco Acac has an ATM at 18 de Julio and Montevideo.

Worthwhile museums include the **Museo Salesiano** (Salesian Museum) at 18 de Julio and Montecaseros and the **Museo Histórico** at Zorrilla de San Martín and Sarandí.

Places to Stay & Eat

The cheapest lodging in town is friendly *Hotel Victoria* (☎ 072-24320), 18 de Julio 979, for US$7 per person with shared bath, US$10 with private bath. The comparable *Hotel Concordia* (☎ 072-22417), across the street at 18 de Julio 984, charges US$8 with shared bath, US$9 with private bath.

Good eating spots include highly regarded *Artemisio*, at 18 de Julio 1248, and *Los Tres Pinos*, Av España 1474, which serves outstanding pasta, particularly the *ñoquis,* though prices tend toward the upper end.

Getting There & Away

Paysandú's Terminal de Omnibus (☎ 072-23325) is at 25 de Mayo and Zorrilla de San Martín, directly south of Plaza Constitución. Chadre (☎ 072-25310) passes through Paysandú en route between Bella Unión and Montevideo; for details, see the Fray Bentos section. Agencia Central (☎ 072-25310), Copay (☎ 072-22094), Núñez (☎ 072-29050), and Sabelín (☎ 072-25310) also go to Montevideo (US$17, five hours).

Paccot (☎ 072-22093) goes to Colón, Argentina (US$2.50), three times daily except Sundays and holidays (noon only). There is service to Concepción, Argentina (US$3.50), at 5:30 pm daily except Sunday. Copay goes to Colón and Concepción at 8:15 am daily except Sunday.

SALTO

Directly across the Uruguay from Concordia, Entre Ríos, 520km from Montevideo, the most northerly border crossing into Argentina is the site of the enormous Salto Grande hydroelectric project. The area's main attractions are hot springs resorts at nearby Daymán and Arapey. The Oficina Municipal de Turismo (☎ 073-25194, fax 073-35740) is at Uruguay 1052.

At Brasil and Zorrilla, the erstwhile Mercado Central (Central Market) has become the **Museo del Hombre y la Tecnología** (☎ 073-29898), featuring professional displays on local cultural development and history. Guided visits of Salto Grande (☎ 073-26131) take place 7 am to 2 pm daily except Sunday.

Places to Stay & Eat

Rundown but friendly *Hotel Plaza Artigas* (☎ 073-34824), Artigas 1146, charges US$9 per person with shared bath, US$12 with private bath. The best budget choice, though, is rehabbed *Hotel Plaza* (☎ 073-33744), Uruguay 465, for US$12.

There are many pizzerías, including *Firenze* at Uruguay 945 and *Las Mil y Una* at Uruguay 906. *Azabache*, Uruguay 702, serves fine, inexpensive pasta, sandwiches and reasonably priced fresh juices. The *Club Uruguay*, Uruguay 754, serves parrillada and pasta in fashionable surroundings.

Getting There & Away

Bus The Terminal Municipal de Omnibus (☎ 073-32909) is at Larrañaga and Andrés Latorre. Chadre/Agencia Central (☎ 073-32603) goes to Concordia, Argentina, at 8 am and 2 pm daily except Sunday, while Flecha Bus (☎ 073-32150) goes at 2:30 and 8:30 pm daily except Sunday. Tuesday and Friday mornings, Chadre goes to Uruguaiana, Brazil.

Domestic bus lines to Montevideo (US$20, six hours) include Chadre/Agencia Central, Núñez (☎ 073-35581) and El Norteño (☎ 073-32150), which also goes to Bella Unión (US$5.50). Alonso (☎ 073-34821) goes to Paysandú (US$5, 1½ hours). Agencia Central services interior destinations such as Tacuarembó and Rivera.

Boat From the port at the foot of Brasil, San Cristóbal launches cross the river to Concordia (US$3) five times daily except Sundays and holidays (twice only).

TACUAREMBÓ

In the rolling hills of the Cuchilla de Haedo, 390km north of Montevideo, Tacuarembó's sycamore-lined streets are home to monuments honoring the usual military heroes but also writers, clergy and educators. The late-March **Fiesta de la Patria Gaucho** (Gaucho Festival) merits a visit from travelers in the area.

Tacuarembó is a key highway junction, as roads lead west to Argentina, north to Brazil, east to Brazil and the Uruguayan coast and south to Montevideo. Its center is Plaza 19 de Abril. The municipal Oficina de Turismo (☎ 063-7144), Joaquín Suárez 215, is open 7 am to 7 pm daily. The post office is at Ituzaingó 262. Antel is at Sarandí 240.

The **Museo del Indio y del Gaucho**, at Flores and Artigas, pays romantic tribute to Uruguay's Indians and gauchos.

Places to Stay & Eat

Balneario Municipal Iporá (☎ 063-5344), 7km north of town, has free and paying campsites (US$2). Free sites have clean toilets but lack showers. Buses leave from near Plaza 19 de Abril.

Friendly *Pensión Paysandú* (☎ 063-2453), 18 de Julio 154, offers good, clean but basic accommodations for US$9 per person in a shared room. *Hotel Central* (☎ 063-2341), Flores 300, charges US$19 per person with private bath.

Among the parrillas are *La Rueda*, Beltrán and Flores, and *La Cabaña*, 25 de Mayo 217. *Rotisería del Centro*, on 18 de Julio near Plaza Colón, sells an enormous, tasty chivito that's a meal in itself.

Getting There & Away

The Terminal Municipal is on the northeastern outskirts of town, at the junction of Ruta 5 and Av Victorino Perera. To Montevideo (US$14, 5½ hours), try Buses Chadre/Agencia Central (☎ 063-4122) or Turil (☎ 063-3305). Chadre/Agencia Central also serves interior destinations and the coastal cities of Salto and Paysandú. Copay also goes to Salto and Paysandú (US$10) three times daily.

Uruguayan Riviera

East of Montevideo, countless resorts dot a scenic coastline whose sandy beaches, vast dunes and dramatic headlands extend to the Brazilian border. In summer the area attracts hordes of tourists, but by early March prices drop, the weather is still ideal and the pace more leisurely.

PIRIÁPOLIS

In the 1930s entrepreneur Francisco Piria built the landmark Hotel Argentino and an eccentric residence known as 'Piria's castle,' and ferried tourists directly from Argentina. Almost everything in Piriápolis, about 100km east of Montevideo, is within walking distance of the waterfront Rambla de los Argentinos and defined by proximity to Hotel Argentino. The nearby countryside offers features like Cerro Pan de Azúcar (one of Uruguay's highest points) and the hill resort of Minas.

The Asociación de Fomento y Turismo (☎ 043-22560), Rambla de los Argentinos 1348, has maps, brochures and current hotel prices. In January and February, it's open 9 am to 11 pm daily; in March and April, hours are 9 am to 9 pm. The rest of the year, it's open 10 am to 1 pm and 3 to 8 pm.

There's an ATM at Piria and Buenos Aires. You can change cash, but not traveler's checks, at Hotel Argentino.

Places to Stay & Eat

Many hotels open December to April only; nearly all raise prices from mid-December to March. Bargains come after March 1, when the weather is delightful but crowds are gone.

Open from mid-December to late April, *Camping Piriápolis FC* (☎ 043-23275) is at Misiones and Niza. Sites cost US$5 per person. Its few rooms with shared bath cost US$9 per person.

Albergue Piriápolis 1 (☎ 043-20394), Simón del Pino 1106, and the *Asociación de Alberguistas de Piriápolis* (☎ 043-22157), Simón del Pino 1136, both charge around US$8 per person with HI card. They're open year round, and reservations are essential in January and February.

Hostal La Casona (☎ 043-22441), at Freire and Defensa, costs US$25 double with private bath in mid-season, US$35 in summer. Family-run *Petite Pensión* (☎ 043-22471) is an intimate seven-room hotel at Sanabria 1084, 2 blocks from the beach. Rates are US$18 in the off-season, US$22 per person in summer.

Even if you can't stay at *Hotel Argentino* (☎ 043-22791), visit this elegant, 350-room European-style spa on the Rambla de los Argentinos, with thermal baths, a casino, a classic dining room and other luxuries. Rates are US$137/196 with half-board, US$158/238 with full board.

La Langosta, Rambla de los Argentinos 1212, has fine seafood and parrillada at modest prices. Other appealing restaurants on Rambla include *La Goleta*, at the corner of Trápani, and *Delta*, at the corner of Atanasio Sierra.

Shopping

The Paseo de la Pasiva, an attractive colonnade along the Rambla, is a good place for handicrafts.

Getting There & Away

The Terminal de Omnibus is at Misiones and Niza, 3 blocks from the beach. In high season, COT (☎ 043-24141) and Copsa (☎ 043-22571) run up to 27 buses daily from Montevideo (US$3) to Punta del Este and back via Piriápolis. Guscapar (☎ 043-49253) has 20 buses daily to Pan de Azúcar, where there are connections to Minas.

AROUND PIRIÁPOLIS
Pan de Azúcar

Ten kilometers north of town, there's a trail to the top of 493m **Cerro Pan de Azúcar**, Uruguay's third-highest point, and a small but well-kept zoo at the nearby **Parque Municipal**. Across the highway, the **Castillo de Piria** was Piria's outlandish residence.

Minas & Around

Sixty kilometers north of Piriápolis, this amiable hill town draws its name from nearby quarries. The municipal Oficina de Turismo (☎ 0442-4118) is at Lavalleja 572. The post office is at Rodó 571, Antel at Beltrán and Rodó.

For lodging, try *Residencial 25* (☎ 0442-4272), 25 de Mayo 525, for US$22/30 singles/doubles. Inexpensive camping is possible at *Parque Arequita* (☎ 0440-2503), 9km north on the road to Polanco (public transport available), where two-bed cabañas cost US$11 with shared bath, US$17 with private bath.

Every 19 April, up to 70,000 pilgrims visit the **Cerro y Virgen del Verdún**, 6km west of Minas. **Parque Salus**, source of Uruguay's best-known mineral water and the site of a brewery, is 10km west of town. In **Villa Serrana**, 23km beyond Minas, *Chalet Las Chafas* has hostel accommodations with kitchen facilities, a pool and a lake; make reservations at Montevideo's Asociación de Alberguistas. Buses go no closer than 3km, so you'll need to walk, bike or hitch the rest of the way.

URUGUAY

MALDONADO

In 1755, Spanish authorities founded Maldonado at the mouth of the Río de la Plata as an outpost to provision ships. Downtown retains colonial airs, but the town has sprawled because of tourist development in Punta del Este. It remains a more economical alternative to Punta del Este for food and accommodations.

Orientation

Maldonado is 30km west of Piriápolis. The original grid centers on Plaza San Fernando, but streets are highly irregular between Maldonado and Punta. West, along the river, Rambla Claudio Williman is the main thoroughfare, while to the east,

Rambla Lorenzo Batlle Pacheco follows the Atlantic coast. Locations along these routes are usually identified by numbered *paradas* (bus stops). Both routes have fine beaches, but the ocean beaches have rougher surf.

Information

Tourist Offices Open 12:30 to 6:30 pm weekdays, the Dirección de Turismo (☎ 042-20847) is in the Intendencia Municipal, on Sarandí between Ledesma and Burnett. The Oficina de Informes (☎ 042-25701) at the bus terminal keeps longer hours.

Money Casas de cambio are clustered around Plaza San Fernando.

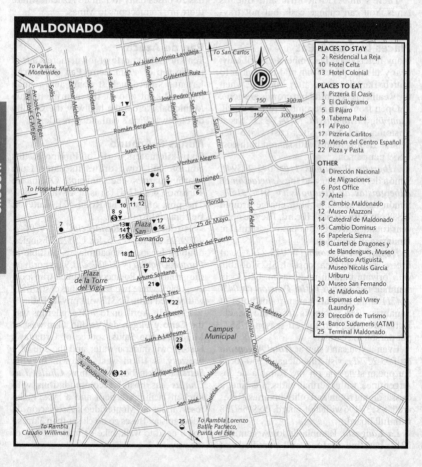

MALDONADO

PLACES TO STAY
2 Residencial La Reja
10 Hotel Celta
13 Hotel Colonial

PLACES TO EAT
1 Pizzería El Oasis
3 El Quilogramo
5 El Pájaro
9 Taberna Patxi
11 Al Paso
17 Pizzería Carlitos
19 Mesón del Centro Español
22 Pizza y Pasta

OTHER
4 Dirección Nacional de Migraciones
6 Post Office
7 Antel
8 Cambio Maldonado
12 Museo Mazzoni
14 Catedral de Maldonado
15 Cambio Dominus
16 Papelería Sienra
18 Cuartel de Dragones y de Blandengues, Museo Didáctico Artiguista, Museo Nicolás García Uriburu
20 Museo San Fernando de Maldonado
21 Espumas del Virrey (Laundry)
23 Dirección de Turismo
24 Banco Sudameris (ATM)
25 Terminal Maldonado

Post & Communications The post office is at Ituzaingó and San Carlos. Antel is at Florida and José G Artigas.

Things to See
On Plaza San Fernando is the Catedral de Maldonado (1895). At Gorriti and Pérez del Puerto, the colonial watchtower at the Plaza de la Torre del Vigía was built with peepholes for viewing the approach of hostile forces.

Built between 1771 and 1797, the Cuartel de Dragones y de Blandengues is a block of military fortifications along 18 de Julio and Pérez del Puerto. Its Museo Didáctico Artiguista, honoring Uruguay's independence hero, is open 8 to 11 pm daily.

The recently renovated Museo San Fernando de Maldonado is a fine arts facility at Sarandí and Pérez del Puerto, open 12:30 to 8 pm Monday to Saturday, 4:30 to 8 pm Sunday. Maldonado's oddest sight is the eclectic Museo Mazzoni (1782) at Ituzaingó 789, open 4 to 10 pm Tuesday to Friday.

Activities
Sportfishing, surfing, windsurfing, diving and other water sports are all possible in the area.

Places to Stay
Peak season accommodations can be costly, but prices fall at summer's end.

Camping San Rafael (☎ 042-86715), on the outskirts of town beyond Aeropuerto El Jagüel, has fine facilities on leafy grounds. Sites cost US$17 for two in January and February, US$12 otherwise. Take bus No 5 from downtown.

Residencial La Reja (☎ 042-23717), 18 de Julio 1092, charges US$25/35 for singles/doubles, but only US$15 per person off-season. Popular with foreign visitors, Irish-owned *Hotel Celta* (☎ 042-30139), Ituzaingó 839, normally charges US$40 to US$55, but has budget rooms even in season. *Hotel Colonial* (☎ 042-23346), on 18 de Julio near the cathedral, charges US$60 for a double with breakfast, but half that in the off-season (without breakfast).

Places to Eat
The modest *El Pájaro*, Ituzaingó and Román Guerra, serves pizza, chivitos and seafood. *El Quilogramo*, on Sarandí between Ventura Alegre and Ituzaingó, is a buffet that charges by weight.

Pizzería Carlitos, Sarandí 834, is inexpensive but ordinary; try instead *Pizzería El Oasis* at Sarandí and Varela or, for more elaborate Italian meals, *Pizza y Pasta* at Sarandí 642.

Al Paso, a favorite parrilla at 18 de Julio 888, is pricey but good value. More upmarket is *Mesón del Centro Español* at 18 de Julio 708, with superb seafood. *Taberna Patxi*, Florida 828, serves Basque specialties, including fish and shellfish.

Getting There & Away
Terminal Maldonado (☎ 042-25701) is at Av Roosevelt and Sarandí, 8 blocks south of Plaza San Fernando. Bus services resemble those from Punta del Este (see later in this chapter). Offices here include COT (☎ 042-25026), Copsa (☎ 042-34733), Expreso del Este (☎ 042-20040), Tur-Este (☎ 042-37323), Núñez (☎ 042-30170), Coom and Olivera Hermanos (☎ 042-28330).

Both COT and Copsa buses go frequently to Montevideo (2½ hours), while COT goes northeast to the Brazilian border. Tur-Este (☎ 042-37323) buses go to Rocha and Treinta y Tres, Núñez buses to Montevideo and Olivera Hermanos and Coom buses to Minas (US$3).

Getting Around
Codesa, Olivera and Maldonado Turismo buses link Maldonado with Punta del Este and other local destinations, including the beach circuit.

AROUND MALDONADO
Casapueblo
At scenic Punta Ballena, 10km west of Maldonado, Carlos Páez Vilaró built this unconventional Mediterranean villa and art gallery (admission US$3) without right angles. Visitors can tour the gallery, view a slide presentation and dine or drink at the bar and cafeteria. It now includes the expensive *Hotel Casa Pueblo* (☎ 042-79836), but nearby *Camping Internacional Punta Ballena* (☎ 042-78902) charges US$12 per site, with tent cabins for US$25.

PUNTA DEL ESTE
Swarming with upper-class Argentines, the tiny peninsula of Punta del Este is strictly speaking part of Maldonado, but economically and socially its elegant seaside homes,

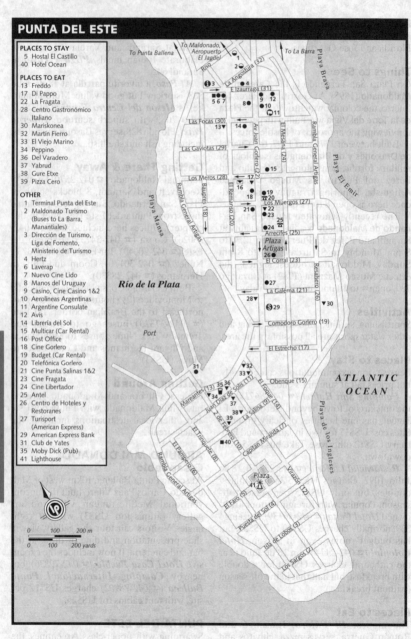

PUNTA DEL ESTE

PLACES TO STAY
5 Hostal El Castillo
40 Hotel Ocean

PLACES TO EAT
13 Freddo
17 Di Pappo
22 La Fragata
28 Centro Gastronómico
    Italiano
30 Mariskonea
32 Martín Fierro
33 El Viejo Marino
34 Peppino
36 Del Varadero
37 Yabrud
38 Gure Etxe
39 Pizza Cero

OTHER
1 Terminal Punta del Este
2 Maldonado Turismo
   (Buses to La Barra,
   Manantiales)
3 Dirección de Turismo,
   Liga de Fomento,
   Ministerio de Turismo
4 Hertz
6 Laverap
7 Nuevo Cine Lido
8 Manos del Uruguay
9 Casino, Cine Casino 1&2
10 Aerolíneas Argentinas
11 Argentine Consulate
12 Avis
14 Librería del Sol
15 Multicar (Car Rental)
16 Post Office
18 Cine Gorlero
19 Budget (Car Rental)
20 Telefónica Gorlero
22 Cine Punta Salinas 1&2
23 Cine Fragata
24 Cine Libertador
25 Antel
26 Centro de Hoteles y
    Restoranes
27 Turisport
    (American Express)
29 American Express Bank
31 Club de Yates
35 Moby Dick (Pub)
41 Lighthouse

To Maldonado,
Aeropuerto
El Jagüel

To Punta Ballena

To La Barra

Río de la Plata

Port

ATLANTIC
OCEAN

Playa Brava

Playa El Emir

Playa Mansa

Playa de los Ingleses

Plaza
Artigas

Plaza

La Angostura (32)
E1 Izaurraga (31)
Las Focas (30)
Las Gaviotas (29)
Los Meros (28)
Los Muergos (27)
Arrecifes (25)
El Corral (23)
La Galerna (21)
Comodoro Gorlero (19)
El Estrecho (17)
Obenque (15)
La Salina (9)
El Foque (13)
Capitán Miranda (7)
Marrantes (13)
Juan Díaz de Solís (11)
El Tiranju+t (8)
El Pampero (6)
Rambla General Artigas
El Faro (5)
Puesta del Sol (4)
Isla de Lobos (3)
Los Sargos (2)
Virazón (2)

Av. Juan Gorlero (22)
El Mesana (24)
Rambla General Artigas
El Remanso (20)
Baupres (18)
Resalero (26)

0   100   200 m
0   100   200 yards

yacht harbor and expensive hotels and restaurants set it a world apart. Budget travelers, too, will find some accommodations.

Orientation

Rambla General Artigas circles the peninsula, passing the protected beach of Playa Mansa and the yacht harbor on the west side and rugged Playa Brava on the east.

Punta has two separate grids. North of a constricted neck east of the harbor is the high-rise hotel zone; the southern area is largely residential. Streets bear both names and numbers: Addresses listed below refer first to the street name, with its number in parentheses. Av Juan Gorlero (22) is the main commercial street, commonly referred to as 'Gorlero.'

Information

Tourist Offices The municipal Dirección de Turismo (☎ 042-46510), in the Liga de Fomento building at Baupres (18) and Inzaurraga (31), is open 9 am to 9 pm weekdays, 9 am to 3 pm weekends. It also maintains an Oficina de Informes (☎ 042-89468) at the bus terminal, open 24 hours in summer, with shorter hours the rest of the year.

Money Nearly all banks and cambios are along Gorlero.

Post & Communications The post office has moved to Los Meros (28) between Gorlero (22) and El Remanso (20). Antel is at Arrecifes (25) and El Mesana (24).

Consulates Argentina operates a high-season consulate (☎ 042-46193) in the Edificio Santos Dumont, on Las Focas (30) between Gorlero (22) and El Mesana (24).

Beaches

Rambla Artigas snakes along the riverside Playa Mansa on the west side of Punta del Este, then circles around the peninsula to the wilder Playa Brava, on the Atlantic. In the other direction from Playa Mansa, along Rambla Williman, the main beach areas are La Pastora, Marconi, Cantegril, Las Delicias, Pinares, La Gruta (Punta Ballena) and Portezuelo. On the ocean side, along Rambla Batlle Pacheco beyond Playa Brava, the prime areas are La Chiverta, San Rafael, La Draga and Punta de La Barra.

All beaches have *paradores* (small restaurants) with beach service. Beach-hopping is common, depending on local conditions and the general level of action.

Places to Stay

Only minutes from the bus terminal *Hostal El Castillo* (cellular 09-409799), on Inzaurraga (31) between El Remanso (20) and Baupres (18), has hostel accommodation for US$10 per person.

In the quiet, residential part of town, affable *Hotel Ocean* (☎ 042-44947), La Salina (9) 636, has rooms with shared bath for US$30 per person with breakfast, but ring ahead for reservations.

Places to Eat

Di Pappo, Gorlero 841, is a reasonable pizzería. Other Italian choices include *Pizza Cero* at La Salina (9) and 2 de Febrero (10), *Peppino* at 2 de Febrero (10) and Rambla Artigas, and several moderately priced restaurants at the *Centro Gastronómico Italiano* at Gorlero (22) and La Galerna (21).

For seafood, try *Mariskonea*, Resalsero (26) 650; *La Fragata*, Gorlero 800; *Del Varadero* on Rambla Artigas between 2 de Febrero (10) and Virazón (12) and *El Viejo Marino* at Solís (11) and El Foque (14). *Martín Fierro* at Rambla Artigas and El Foque (14), is a parrilla. For variety, try the Arab-Armenian *Yabrud* at Solís (11) and Virazón (12), or the Basque *Gure Etxe,* at Virazón (12) and La Salina (9).

The popular Argentine ice creamery *Freddo* has branches here at Las Focas (30) and El Remanso (20), and at Gorlero (22) and Los Muergos (27).

Entertainment

Punta has many cinemas along Gorlero and dance clubs along Rambla Batlle, plus a casino at Gorlero and Inzaurraga (31).

Shopping

For souvenirs, visit the evening Feria Artesanal on Plaza Artigas. Manos del Uruguay has an outlet on Gorlero (22) between Inzaurraga (31) and Las Focas (30).

Getting There & Away

Air Pluna (☎ 042-90101), at Parada 8½ on Rambla Batlle Pacheco, has 29 weekly flights to Buenos Aires' Aeroparque, plus

URUGUAY

summer schedules to São Paulo and other Brazilian destinations. Aerolíneas Argentinas (☎ 042-43801), on Gorlero between Inzaurraga (31) and Las Focas (30), flies to Aeroparque 19 times weekly. Lapa (☎ 042-90840), at Av Roosevelt Parada 14½, flies to Aeroparque Friday and Sunday.

Bus Terminal Punta del Este (☎ 042-89467) is at Riso and Bulevar Artigas. Most services are an extension of those to Maldonado. International carriers include TTL (☎ 042-86755) to Brazil; EGA (☎ 042-92380) to Brazil, Argentina, and Santiago de Chile; and Encon (☎ 042-90012) and Cora to Argentina. Montevideo has more connections.

Nationally, COT (☎ 042-86810) covers the Uruguayan coast from Montevideo to the Brazilian border. Copsa (☎ 042-89205) goes to Montevideo (US$6, 2½ hours) and to José Ignacio.

Getting Around
To/From the Airport Aeropuerto Laguna de Sauce (also known as Aeropuerto Carlos Carbelo), west of Portezuelo, can be reached by Buses Olivera (☎ 042-24039) from Maldonado.

Bus Maldonado Turismo (☎ 042-37181), Gorlero and Las Focas (30), connects Punta del Este with La Barra and Manantiales. Its buses leave from La Angostura behind the bus terminal.

Rocha Department

Conflicts between Spain and Portugal, then between Argentina and Brazil, left Rocha with historical monuments such as the fortresses of Santa Teresa and San Miguel. The fighting also retarded rural settlement, sparing areas like Cabo Polonio, with its extensive dunes and a large sea lion colony, from development. The interior's varied landscape of palm savannas and marshes is rich in bird life.

ROCHA
Late colonial and early independence era houses line the narrow alleyways of Rocha, 220km east of Montevideo, which merits an afternoon's visit for those traveling to La Paloma (see below). The municipal Oficina

de Turismo (☎ 0472-5008) is at General Artigas 176. The post office is at 18 de Julio 131. Antel is at General Artigas and Rodó.

Places to Stay
Try the tidy **Hotel Municipal Rocha** (☎ 0472-2404), 1 block off the plaza on 19 de Abril 87, which was undergoing renovation at press time. **Hotel Trocadero** (☎ 0472-2267), at 25 de Agosto and 18 de Julio, charges US$33/48 plus 14% IVA, including buffet breakfast and cable TV.

Getting There & Away
Rutas del Sol (☎ 0472-3541), at Ramírez and 25 de Agosto, runs 10 buses daily to Montevideo (US$8, 3½ hours) and five daily to Chuy (US$5) via La Paloma, La Pedrera, and Castillos. Cynsa has ten daily to La Paloma and nine from La Paloma back to Rocha, where you can catch the service to Chuy. COT also serves Rocha.

LA PALOMA
Placid La Paloma (population 5000), 28km south of Rocha, is less developed, cheaper and less crowded than Punta del Este, but lacks Punta's nightlife. Beaches to the east are less protected from ocean swells. Streets are named, but hotels and restaurants lack numbers and are more easily located by their relationship to intersections and landmarks.

The Liga de Fomento (☎ 0479-6008), at the east end of Av Nicolás Solari, is open 10 am to 10 pm daily in summer, 10 am to 9 pm daily the rest of the year, except April to October, when it's open weekends only. The post office is on Av Nicolás Solari, just east of the former Onda bus terminal. Antel is on Av Nicolás Solari between Av El Navío and De la Virgen.

Places to Stay & Eat
Camping Parque Andresito (☎ 0479-6107), at the northern approach to town, has excellent beach access and hot showers, a supermarket, restaurant and electricity. Rates are US$12 for two people. Otherwise, the best budget accommodation is the **Albergue Altena 5000** (☎ 0479-6396), also in Parque Andresito, open November through March; rates are US$6 to US$8 for HI members, US$10 for nonmembers.

Charging US$40 for a double, **Residencial Canopus** (☎ 0479-6068) on Av Nicolás

Solari near Sirio, is now one of La Paloma's better values. Room rates are reduced in the off-season.

La Marea, on Av Antares between Av Solari and Canopus, has reasonably priced seafood. Probably the best in town is **La Balconada**, on La Balconada between Perseo and Lira; though fairly expensive, it's worth the difference.

Getting There & Away
Cynsa (☎ 0479-6304), on Antares between Av Solari and Canopus, goes to Rocha (US$1) and to Montevideo (US$10, 4½ to five hours). Rutas del Sol (☎ 0479-6019), at Av Solari and Titania, goes twice daily to Barra de Valizas, Aguas Dulces and Chuy by the coastal Ruta 10.

PARQUE NACIONAL SANTA TERESA
More a historical than a natural attraction, this coastal park 35km south of Chuy contains the hilltop **Fortaleza de Santa Teresa**, begun by the Portuguese but captured and finished by the Spaniards. By international standards, Santa Teresa is a humble place, but Uruguayan and Brazilian visitors enjoy its uncrowded beaches and decentralized forest camping (US$10 per site for basic facilities).

The park gets crowded during Carnaval, but otherwise absorbs visitors without difficulty. Services at headquarters include telephones, post office, supermarket, bakery, butchery and restaurant.

CHUY
Pedestrians and vehicles cross freely between Uruguay and Brazil at Chuy, the grubby but energetic border town at the terminus of Ruta 9, 340km northeast of Montevideo. If proceeding into Brazil, complete Uruguayan emigration formalities on Ruta 9, 2.5km south of town. Travelers needing visas will find the Brazilian Consulate at Fernández 147.

Seven kilometers west of Chuy, do not miss restored **Fuerte San Miguel**, a pink-granite fortress built in 1734 during hostilities between Spain and Portugal and protected by a moat. It's closed Monday.

Places to Stay & Eat
Ten kilometers south of Chuy, a coastal lateral heads to **Camping Chuy** (☎ 0474-2425), which charges US$10 per site, and **Camping de la Barra** (☎ 0474-1611), which costs US$4 per person. Local buses from Chuy go directly to both.

Singles cost only US$15 at **Hotel Internacional** (☎ 0474-2055), Río San Luis 121, but accommodations are usually cheaper on the Brazilian side. For dining, try **Parrillada Jesús**, Av Brasil 603, or the nearby **Bar Restaurante Opal** for pasta.

Getting There & Away
Several bus companies connect Chuy with Montevideo (US$14, five hours) including Rutas del Sol (☎ 0474-2048) on Av Internacional, COT (☎ 0474-2009) at Av Brasil 595 and Cynsa, also on Av Brasil. There is also service to Treinta y Tres.

Venezuela

Contemporary Venezuela has been strongly influenced by oil money, which has turned the country into one of the wealthiest nations in South America. As a result, Venezuela has good road networks, spectacular new architecture and a developed tourism infrastructure. Yet deep in the countryside, people still live traditional lives. A number of Indian groups are still unconquered by encroaching civilization, including the mysterious Yanomami, whose Stone-Age culture seems lost in time along the Venezuela-Brazil border.

The variety of Venezuela's landscapes is unlikely to disappoint visitors. The country boasts the northern tip of the Andes, topped with snowcapped peaks, and the vast Orinoco delta crisscrossed by a maze of natural channels. The southern part of the country is taken up by the legendary wilderness of the Amazon, while the north is bordered by 2800km of Caribbean coastline.

Venezuela's most unusual natural formations are the *tepuis*, flat-topped mountains with vertical flanks that loom more than 1000m above rolling savannas. Their tops are noted for their moonlike landscapes and their peculiar endemic flora. About 100 tepuis are scattered throughout the southeast of the country. From one spills Angel Falls, the world's highest waterfall (979m) and Venezuela's most famous tourist sight.

Venezuela is a reasonably safe and friendly country in which to travel, with fairly inexpensive accommodations, food and domestic transport. Venezuela has South America's cheapest air links to both Europe and the US, and is a convenient gateway to the continent. Don't treat it, however, just as a bridge; give yourself some time to discover this country – it's worth it.

At a Glance

Country Name	República de Venezuela
Area	916,445 sq km
Population	23.5 million (1999)
Population Density	25 people per sq km
Capital	Caracas
Head of State	President Hugo Chávez (1999-2004)
Official Language	Spanish
Other Languages	Indian languages
Currency	bolívar (Bs)
Exchange Rate	US$1 = 612Bs
Per Capita GNP	$8,300 (1997 est)
Inflation Rate	38% (1997)

Facts about Venezuela

HISTORY
Pre-Columbian Period

It's estimated that by the Spanish conquest, up to a half-million Indians inhabited the region that is now Venezuela. They were isolated communities of various backgrounds and belonged to three main linguistic families: Carib, Arawak and Chibcha.

The warlike Carib tribes inhabited the central and eastern coast, living off fishing and shifting agriculture. Various Arawak groups were scattered over a large area of western Llanos and north up to the coast. They lived off hunting and food-gathering and occasionally practiced farming.

The Timote-Cuica, of the Chibcha linguistic family, were the most advanced of Venezuela's pre-Columbian societies. They founded settlements in the Andes linked by a network of trails and had fairly well developed agricultural techniques, including irrigation and terracing.

Spanish Conquest

Columbus was the first European to set foot on Venezuelan soil – indeed, it was the only South American mainland country Columbus landed on. On his third trip to the New World, in 1498, he anchored at the eastern tip of the Península de Paria, opposite Trinidad. He at first thought he had discovered yet another island, but continuing along the coast, he found the voluminous mouth of the Río Orinoco – sufficient proof that the place was much more than an island.

A year later another Spanish explorer, Alonso de Ojeda, accompanied by the Italian Amerigo Vespucci, sailed up to the Península de la Guajira, on the western end of present-day Venezuela. On entering Lago Maracaibo, the Spaniards saw the local Indians living in *palafitos*, thatched huts on stilts above the water. Perhaps as a sarcastic sailor joke, they called the land Venezuela (literally, 'Little Venice'), for these rustic reed-made dwellings didn't exactly match with the opulent palaces of the Italian city they knew.

The first Spanish settlement on Venezuelan soil, Nueva Cádiz, was established around 1500 on the small island of Cubagua, just south of Isla de Margarita. Pearl harvesting provided livelihood for the settlers, and the town developed into a busy port. It was destroyed by an earthquake and tidal wave in 1541. The earliest Venezuelan town still in existence, Cumaná, dates from 1521.

Officially, most of Venezuela was ruled by Spain from Santo Domingo (present-day capital of the Dominican Republic) until 1717, when it fell under the administration of the newly created Viceroyalty of Nueva Granada (with its capital in Bogotá), where it remained until independence. In practice, however, the region was allowed a large degree of autonomy. It was, after all, such an unimportant backwater with an uninviting,

steamy climate that the Spaniards gave it low priority, focusing instead on the gold- and silver-rich Colombia, Peru and Bolivia. In many ways, Venezuela remained a backwater until the oil boom of the 1920s.

Independence Wars

Apart from three brief rebellions between 1749 and 1797, colonial Venezuela had a relatively uneventful history. All this changed at the beginning of the 19th century, when Venezuela gave Latin America its greatest hero, Simón Bolívar. 'El Libertador,' as he is known, together with his lieutenant, Antonio José de Sucre, were largely responsible for ending colonial rule all the way to the borders of Argentina.

The revolutionary flame was lit by Francisco de Miranda in 1806, but his efforts to set up an independent administration in Caracas ended when he was handed over to the Spanish by his fellow conspirators. He was shipped to Spain and died in a Cádiz jail. Leadership of the revolution was taken over by Bolívar. After unsuccessful attempts to defeat the Spaniards at home, he withdrew to Colombia, then to Jamaica, until the opportune moment came in 1817.

The Napoleonic Wars had ended, and Bolívar's agent in London was able to raise money and arms and to recruit more than 5000 British veterans of the Peninsular War. With this force and an army of horsemen from Los Llanos, Bolívar marched over the Andes and defeated the Spanish at the battle of Boyacá, bringing independence to Colombia in August 1819. Four months later in Angostura (present-day Ciudad Bolívar), the Angostura Congress proclaimed 'Gran Colombia,' a new state unifying Colombia, Venezuela and Ecuador (though the last two were still under Spanish rule).

The liberation of Venezuela was completed with Bolívar's victory over Spanish forces at Carabobo in 1821, though the royalists put up a desultory rearguard fight from Puerto Cabello for another two years. Bolívar and Sucre went on to liberate Ecuador, Peru and Bolivia, which they accomplished by the end of 1824.

Although both economically and demographically Venezuela was the least important region of Gran Colombia, it bore the brunt of the fighting. Not only did Venezuelán patriots fight on their own territory, they also fought in the armies that Bolívar led into Colombia and down the Pacific coast. It is estimated that a quarter of the Venezuelan population died in these wars.

Gran Colombia existed for only a decade before splitting into three separate countries. Bolívar's dream of a unified republic fell apart even before he died in 1830.

After Independence

Venezuela's post-independence period was marked by serious governmental problems that continued for more than a century. Mostly these were times of despotism and anarchy, with the country controlled by a series of military dictators known as *caudillos*. It wasn't until 1947 that the first democratic government was elected.

The first of the caudillos, General José Antonio Páez, controlled the country for 18 years (1830-48), though not as president for all that time. Despite his tough rule, he established a certain political stability and put the weak economy on its feet.

The period that followed was an almost uninterrupted chain of civil wars and political strife, stopped only by another long-lived dictator, General Antonio Guzmán Blanco. He came to power in 1870 and kept it, with a few breaks, until 1888. He launched a broad program of reform, including a new constitution and a package of regulations designed to improve the economy. Guzmán Blanco assured some temporary stability, yet his despotic rule triggered wide popular opposition, and when he stepped down the country plunged again into civil war.

Things were not much better on the international front. In the 1840s, Venezuela raised the question of its eastern border with British Guiana (today Guyana). Based on vague pre-independence territorial divisions, the Venezuelan government laid claim to as much as two-thirds of Guiana, up to the Río Essequibo. The issue, which led to severe strains in international relations in the 1890s, was finally settled in 1899 by an arbitration tribunal that gave rights over the questioned territory to Great Britain. Despite this, Venezuela continues to claim it to this day. All Venezuela-produced maps have this chunk of Guyana within Venezuela's boundaries, labeled 'Zona en Reclamación.'

Another conflict during this period was Venezuela's failure to meet payments to Great Britain, Italy and Germany on loans accumulated during the irresponsible government of caudillo General Cipriano Castro. In response, the three European countries sent their navies to blockade Venezuelan seaports in 1902.

20th-Century Dictatorships

The first half of the 20th century was dominated by five successive military rulers from the Andean state of Táchira, the first of whom was Cipriano Castro. The longest-lasting and most despotic was General Juan Vicente Gómez, who seized power in 1908 and didn't relinquish it until his death in 1935. Gómez phased out the parliament, squelched the opposition and monopolized power. He had the support of by a strong army, an extensive police force and a well-developed spy network.

Thanks to the discovery of oil in the 1910s, the Gómez regime was able to stabilize the country. By the late 1920s, Venezuela became the world's largest exporter of oil, which not only contributed notably to economic recovery but also enabled the government to pay off the country's entire foreign debt.

Little of the oil-related wealth filtered down to people on the street. The vast majority continued to live in poverty with little or no educational or health facilities, let alone reasonable housing. Oil money also resulted in the neglect of agriculture. Food had to be imported in increasing amounts, and prices rose rapidly. When Gómez died in 1935, the people of Caracas went on a rampage, burning down the houses of his relatives and supporters and even threatening to set fire to the oil installations on Lago Maracaibo.

Gómez was succeeded by his war minister, Eleázar López Contreras, and six years later by another Táchiran general, Isaías Medina Angarita. Meanwhile, popular tensions rose dangerously, exploding in 1945 when Rómulo Betancourt, leader of the left-wing Acción Democrática (AD) party, took control of the government. A new constitution was adopted in 1947, and noted novelist Rómulo Gallegos became president in Venezuela's first democratic election. On the wave of political freedom, the conservative Partido Social Cristiano (Copei) was founded by Rafael Caldera to counterbalance the leftist AD party.

The pace of reform was too fast, given the strength of old military forces greedy for power. The inevitable coup took place only eight months after Gallegos' election, with Colonel Marcos Pérez Jiménez emerging as leader. Once in control, he began crushing his opposition, at the same time plowing oil money back into public works and into industries that would help diversify the economy and, in particular, modernize Caracas. However, the spectacular buildings mushrooming in the capital were poor substitutes for a better standard of living and access to political power, and opposition grew.

Democracy at Last

In 1958, Pérez Jiménez was overthrown by a coalition of civilians and navy and air force officers. The country returned to democratic rule, and Betancourt was elected president. He ended the former dictator's solicitous policy toward foreign big business, but was careful this time not to act too impetuously.

Betancourt enjoyed popular support and succeeded in completing the constitutional five-year term in office – the first democratically elected Venezuelan president to do so. He voluntarily stepped down in 1963. Since then, all changes of president have been by constitutional means.

Presidents Raúl Leoni (1964-69) and Rafael Caldera (1969-74) had relatively quiet terms, since the steady stream of oil money that flowed into the country's coffers kept the economy buoyant. President Carlos Andrés Pérez (1974-79) witnessed the oil bonanza. Not only did production of oil rise but, more importantly, the price quadrupled following the Arab-Israeli war in 1973. Pérez nationalized the iron-ore and oil industries and went on a spending spree. Imported luxury goods crammed shops, and the nation got the impression that El Dorado had finally materialized. Not for long, though.

Back to Instability

In the late 1970s, the growing international recession and oil glut began to shake Venezuela's economic stability. Oil revenues declined, pushing up unemployment, inflation and foreign debt. Presidents Luis Herrera Campins (1979-84) and Jaime Lusinchi (1984-89) witnessed a slowing down of the economy and an increasing popular sentiment of discontent.

The 1988 drop in world oil prices cut the country's revenue in half, casting doubt on

Venezuela's ability to pay off its foreign debt. Austerity measures introduced in 1989 by President Pérez triggered a wave of protests, culminating in three days of bloody riots, known as Caracazo, and the loss of more than 300 lives. All further measures (basically price increases) spurred protests that often escalated into riots. Strikes and street demonstrations became everyday. Predictably, the crumbling economy affected political stability.

There were two attempted coups d'état in 1992. The first, led by Colonel Hugo Chávez, shocked most Venezuelans. Shooting throughout Caracas claimed more than 20 lives, but the government retained control. Chávez was sentenced to a long term in prison.

The second attempt was led by junior air force officers. The air battle over Caracas, with warplanes flying between skyscrapers, gave the coup a cinematic, if not apocalyptic, dimension. The Palacio de Miraflores (the presidential palace) was bombed and partially destroyed. The army was called to defend the president, and this time, more than 100 people died.

Things became more complicated when Pérez was charged with embezzlement and misuse of public funds. Pérez was automatically suspended, judged and sentenced. He was released in 1996 after 28 months under house arrest.

Caldera's Difficult Second Term

Amid corruption scandals, Rafael Caldera was elected president for a second, nonconsecutive term in 1993. However, 25 years after his first term, the economic situation was quite different, as was the man himself, now 77 years old.

Caldera's problems began before he officially took office. In February 1994, Venezuela's second-largest bank, Banco Latino, collapsed and had to be rescued by a government takeover costing US$2 billion. The domino-like failure of a dozen other banks in 1994 cost the government another US$8 billion, and several more banks failed in 1995. In all, the disaster cost the state coffers 20% of the GDP, making it one of the largest financial collapses experienced by a country in recent history.

In 1995, Caldera devalued the currency by more than 70%, yet Venezuela's economic situation continued to worsen. In 1996, the government introduced drastic rescue measures, including the increase of gas prices by about 500%.

Throughout Caldera's presidency the country was plagued by strikes for higher wages by most major job groups, including teachers, civil servants and doctors. More than three-quarters of Venezuela's 23 million inhabitants were below the poverty line at the end of 1998. Drug-trafficking and crime have increased, and there has been an expansion of Colombian guerrillas into Venezuela's frontier areas in recent years.

Recent Developments

While the country reached one of its deepest crises, challengers for the 1998 presidential election jockeyed for the position. This time there were no candidates from the traditional parties, AD and Copei, among the front-runners. Instead, the campaign was between unusual independents – ex-Miss Universe Irene Sáez and ex-paratrooper Hugo Chávez – a race that reflected the frustration and discontent of the electorate. Yale-educated businessman Henrique Salas Römer joined the race later, but Chávez eventually won with 56% of the vote.

Chávez, the leader of the 1992 failed coup, was pardoned in 1994. He became a radical leftist politician, campaigning with a blend of nationalism, populist rhetoric and anticorruption overtones that made him popular with Venzuela's poor majority. During the campaign he replaced his army uniform with business suits and modeled himself on the UK's Tony Blair, pledging to seek 'a third way between brutal neoliberalism and hard-line socialism.' It was not quite clear what he had in mind, but he showed little enthusiasm for privatization and a free-market economy, vowing to declare a moratorium on repaying the country's US$22 billion foreign debt.

Shortly after taking office, he held a referendum in which a constituent assembly was approved to rewrite the existing constitution. Chávez's presidency may result in some unexpected turns in Venezuelan politics.

GEOGRAPHY

With an area of 916,445 sq km, Venezuela is the sixth-largest country in South America. It occupies the northernmost part of the continent, including the 2800km-long Caribbean coastline. The country has borders with Colombia to the west, Brazil to the south and Guyana to the east.

Venezuela is very varied geographically. Just south of the coast looms a chain of mountain ranges, the Cordillera de la Costa, with a number of peaks exceeding 2000m. The mountains recede southward into vast plains known as Los Llanos, which stretch as far as the Orinoco and Meta rivers and occupy one-third of the country's territory.

The land south of the Orinoco (half of the country's area), known as Guayana, can be broadly divided into three regions. To the southwest is a chunk of the Amazon carpeted with thick rain forest and partly inaccessible. To the northeast lies the Orinoco delta, a vast swamp crisscrossed with a labyrinth of water channels. The central and largest part of Guayana is taken over by the Guiana Highlands, which include a plateau of open savannas known as La Gran Sabana. It's here that the majority of *tepuis* (table mountains) are located. These gigantic mesas, with vertical walls and flat tops, are all that's left of the upper layer of a plateau that has gradually eroded over millions of years.

Northwest Venezuela is another area of geographical contrasts. Here is the Sierra Nevada de Mérida, the north end of the Andean chain and Venezuela's highest mountain range, culminating at 5007m on snowcapped Pico Bolívar. North of the Andes is the marshy lowland basin around Lago Maracaibo. About 200km long and 120km wide, it's South America's largest lake and Venezuela's main oil-producing area.

The 2150km Río Orinoco is Venezuela's main river, its entire course lying within national boundaries. The Orinoco delta covers an area of over 25,000 sq km, almost as large as Belgium.

Venezuela possesses 70-odd islands scattered along the Caribbean coast, the largest of which is Isla de Margarita. Other islands and archipelagos include Las Aves, Los Roques, La Orchila, La Tortuga and La Blanquilla.

CLIMATE

Given Venezuela's latitude close to the equator, average temperatures vary little throughout the year. They do vary with altitude, however, dropping about 6°C (11°F)

VENEZUELA

VENEZUELA

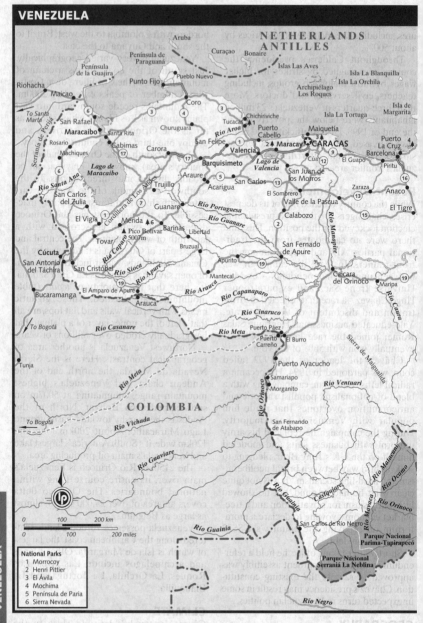

National Parks
1 Morrocoy
2 Henri Pittier
3 El Ávila
4 Mochima
5 Península de Paria
6 Sierra Nevada

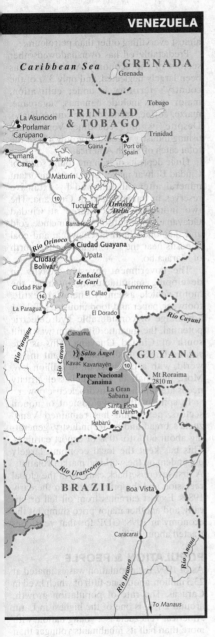

VENEZUELA

Caribbean Sea — GRENADA

Grenada

TRINIDAD & TOBAGO

Tobago

La Asunción
Porlamar
Carúpano

Cumaná
Canipe   Caripito

Maturín

Tucupita   Orinoco Delta

Barrancas

Rio Orinoco   Ciudad Guayana
Ciudad   Upata
Bolívar

Embalse de Guri

Ciudad Piar   El Callao   Tumeremo

La Paragua   El Dorado   Río Cuyuni

Canaima

Salto Ángel
Kavac Kavanayén

Parque Nacional
Canaima   Mt Roraima
2810 m

La Gran Sabana

Santa Elena de Uairén

Icabarú   GUYANA

Rio Paragua
Rio Caroní

Río Uraricoera

BRAZIL   Boa Vista

Caracarai

To Manaus

Rio Branco
Rio Arauá

Trinidad
Güiria   Port of Spain

with every 1000m increase. Since more than 90% of Venezuela lies below 1000m, you'll experience temperatures between 22°C (72°F) and 30°C (86°F) in most places.

Rainfall varies seasonally. Broadly speaking, the dry season goes from December to April, while the wet season lasts the remaining part of the year. There are many regional variations in precipitation and the length of the seasons.

FLORA & FAUNA

As a tropical country with a diverse geography, Venezuela has varied and abundant flora and fauna. Distinctive biohabitats have evolved in different regions, each with its own peculiar wildlife.

There are about 1380 species of bird, including macaw, parrot, toucan, heron, pelican, flamingo, hummingbird, condor and oilbird. Numbering some 250 species, mammals are also well represented and include the jaguar, capybara, armadillo, anteater, tapir, puma, ocelot and peccary. There are also numerous species of reptile, including iguana, five species of cayman (American crocodile) and a variety of snakes.

Possibly the most unusual flora grows on the tops of the tepuis. Isolated from the savanna below and from other tepuis for millions of years, the plant life on each of these plateaus developed independently. In effect, these biological islands have a totally distinctive flora, half of which is considered endemic and typical of only one or a group of tepuis.

Tropical forest – which still covers a quarter of the country's total area – features a maze of plant species uncommon in forests of moderate climates.

NATIONAL PARKS

Venezuela has 43 national parks and 22 other nature reserves. The latter, known as *monumentos naturales*, are usually smaller than the parks and are intended to protect a particular natural feature, such as a lake, a mountain peak or a cave. The whole system of parks and other reserves covers about 15% of the country's area.

The Instituto Nacional de Parques, commonly referred to as Inparques, is the governmental body created to run and take care of national parks and nature reserves. Only

VENEZUELA

a handful of parks have any Inparques-built tourist facilities. Many other parks are either wilderness or have been taken over by private operators, who have built their own tourist facilities and provide transport.

No permits are needed to enter national parks, but some parks charge admission. At the time of writing, the list included Los Roques (US$12), the western part of Canaima (US$5), plus a half dozen others with fees around US$1.

GOVERNMENT & POLITICS

Venezuela is a federal republic. The president, who is head of state and commander-in-chief of the armed forces, is elected by a direct vote for a five-year term and cannot be elected for the two following terms. The national congress is made up of a 50-seat senate and a 204-seat chamber of deputies, both elected for five-year terms simultaneously with presidential elections. Voting is compulsory for citizens from the age of 18.

Of the numerous political parties, the two main traditional movements are Acción Democrática (AD) and Partido Social Cristiano (Copei), both founded in the 1940s. Assailed for corruption and mismanagement of the country's oil wealth, both parties have been gradually losing popularity and influence during the 1990s.

Administratively, the country is divided into 22 states and the federal district of Caracas. The states are further divided into municipalities.

ECONOMY

Oil is Venezuela's main natural resource and the heart of the economy. The main deposits are in the Lago Maracaibo basin, but other important reserves have been discovered and exploited in the Orinoco delta and on the eastern outskirts of Los Llanos.

Since its discovery in 1914, oil turned Venezuela – then poor – into one of South America's richest countries. Until 1970, Venezuela was the world's largest exporter of oil, and though it was later overtaken by Middle Eastern countries, its oil income expanded year after year.

As cofounder of OPEC, Venezuela was influential in the fourfold rise in oil prices introduced in 1973-74. Oil-export earnings peaked in 1981 at US$19.3 billion, representing more than 90% of the country's

exports. On this strength, Venezuela borrowed heavily from foreign banks to import almost everything other than petroleum.

Predictably, oil has overshadowed other sectors of the economy. Agriculture has been largely neglected, and only 3% of the country's territory is under cultivation; major crops include bananas, sugarcane, maize, coffee, cacao, cotton and tobacco. Despite its long coastline, Venezuela's fishing industry accounts for only 4% of the total catch of South America.

Huge deposits of iron ore found south of Ciudad Bolívar make it the most important mineral after oil, followed by extensive reserves of bauxite, also in Guayana. The two industries are centered at Ciudad Guayana. Other subsoil riches include gold and diamonds, both in Guayana, and coal deposits near the Colombian border, north of Maracaibo.

The government invested heavily in developing manufacturing, such as the motor-vehicle assembly, chemical, textile, footwear, paper and food industries. Taking advantage of considerable hydroelectric potential, the gigantic Guri dam was built south of Ciudad Guayana. This is the second-largest hydroelectric plant in the world, with a potential of 10 million kW. More than half of Venezuela's electricity needs are supplied by hydroelectric power.

In spite of the development of nonoil sectors, petroleum has remained Venezuela's bread-and-butter industry, generating about 60% to 70% of export earnings. This has kept the local economy largely dependent on the world oil market volatility. A first severe setback came with the global recession and the price decline in the early 1980s. Export earnings from oil fell drastically, and another major price slump hit the economy in 1998. GDP for that year contracted about 2.5%.

POPULATION & PEOPLE

As of 1999, the population was estimated at 23.5 million, about one-fifth of which lived in Caracas. The rate of population growth, around 2.1%, is one of the highest in Latin America. Venezuela is a young nation, with more than half its inhabitants younger than 18 years old.

The mean population density, about 25 people per square kilometer, is low but varies greatly throughout the country. The central coast, including Valencia, Maracay and Caracas, is the most densely populated, while the Amazon, Los Llanos and Guayana are sparsely populated.

Venezuela is a country of mixed races. About 70% of the population have a blend of European, Indian and African ancestry or any two of the three. The rest are whites (21%), blacks (8%) and Indians (1%). Indians don't belong to a single ethnic or linguistic family, but form about two dozen independent groups throughout the country. Major Indian communities include the Guajiro (north of Maracaibo), the Piaroa, Guajibo, Yekuana and Yanomami (in the Amazon), the Warao (in the Orinoco delta) and the Pemón (in southeastern Guayana). There are more than 40 Indian languages used in the country.

ARTS
Architecture

Since colonial Venezuela was a backwater territory of Spain, local architecture never reached the grandeur that marked its wealthier neighbors like Colombia, Ecuador and Peru. Churches were rather unpretentious, and houses followed the modest Andalusian style. Only in the last 50 years of the colonial era, when a class of wealthier merchants emerged, were residences built that reflected the merchants' social positions. These were few and far between, and only a handful of examples survive, including some in Coro.

Local architectural style followed Spanish fashion for at least a half-century after independence. A thorough modernization program for Caracas was launched in the 1870s by Guzmán Blanco and resulted in a number of monumental public buildings.

The second rush toward modernity came with oil money and culminated in the 1970s. This period was characterized by indiscriminate demolition of the historic urban fabric and its replacement by modern architecture. Many dilapidated colonial buildings fell prey to progressive urban planners. Accordingly, Venezuela's colonial legacy can be disappointing when compared to that of other Andean countries. On the other hand, Venezuela has some remarkable modern architecture. Carlos Raúl Villanueva, who began work in the 1930s, is considered the most outstanding Venezuelan architect.

Visual Arts

Great pre-Columbian creativity is reflected in the petroglyphs, predominantly carved, which have been found at about 200 locations throughout the country. The majority of the petroglyphs are in the central coastal region between Barquisimeto and Caracas and along the Orinoco and Caroní rivers. A number of cave paintings have also been discovered, almost all of them in Bolívar and Amazonas states.

The painting and sculpture of the colonial period had an almost exclusively religious character, and the style followed the Spanish art of the day. Consisting mainly of paintings of saints, carved wooden statues and retables, it can be seen in old churches and museums.

After independence, painting turned to historical themes; outstanding representatives of the genre include Martín Tovar y Tovar (1827-1902), particularly remembered for his monumental works in Caracas' Capitolio Nacional, and Tito Salas (1888-1974), who dedicated himself to commemorating Bolívar's life and achievements.

Modern painting began with Armando Reverón (1889-1954), while Francisco Narváez (1905-82) is commonly acclaimed as Venezuela's first modern sculptor. Remarkable contemporary artists include Héctor Poleo (1918-89), Alejandro Otero (1921-90), Carlos Cruz Díez (born 1923), Marisol Escobar (born 1930) and Jacobo Borges (born 1931). The most internationally renowned Venezuelan artist of the last decades is Jesús Soto (born 1923), noted for his kinetic art.

Literature

Simón Bolívar (1783-1830) left an extensive written heritage, including letters, proclamations, discourses and dissertations, and more literary achievements, such as *Delirio sobre el Chimborazo*. Bolívar was influenced by his close friend Andrés Bello (1781-1865), the first important Venezuelan poet.

Andrés Eloy Blanco (1896-1955) is often considered the best poet Venezuela has produced, while Rómulo Gallegos (1884-1969) is perhaps the Venezuelan writer best known internationally. *Doña Bárbara*, his most famous novel, was first published in Spain in 1929 and has been translated into a dozen languages.

VENEZUELA

Recently, Arturo Uslar Pietri (born 1906) stands out as an authority in the field of literature. A novelist, essayist, historian, literary critic and journalist, he has also been a prominent figure in politics.

Music

Venezuela's most popular folk rhythm is the *joropo*, which developed in Los Llanos. The joropo is usually sung and accompanied by harp, *cuatro* (small, four-stringed guitar) and maracas. There's a dance form of joropo as well.

There are also plenty of regional beats. In the east, depending on the region, you'll hear the *estribillo*, *polo margariteño*, *malagueñas*, *fulías* and *jotas*. In the west, the *gaita* is typical of the Maracaibo region, and the *bambuco* is a popular Andean rhythm. The central coast echoes with African drumbeats. Caracas has absorbed all the influences, both local and international, and blasts as much with joropo and merengue as with salsa and Western rock.

RELIGION

Most Venezuelans are Roman Catholic. Many Indian groups adopted Catholicism, and only a few, primarily living in isolation, still practice ancient beliefs. There are various Protestant churches in Venezuela, and lately they have gained importance, taking adherents away from Catholicism. There are small populations of Jews and Muslims.

LANGUAGE

Spanish is Venezuela's official language and, except for some remote Indian communities, all the population speaks it. Venezuelan Spanish is not the clearest or easiest to understand. Venezuelans (except those from the Andes) speak rapidly and tend to drop some endings, especially plurals. Many people, mostly in large urban centers, speak some English, but it's not commonly understood or spoken.

Facts for the Visitor

HIGHLIGHTS

Few tourists will want to miss a view of Angel Falls (Salto Angel in Spanish), the kilometer-high waterfall that is Venezuela's promotional landmark. For more adventurous travelers, a trek to the top of Roraima is a fascinating and unforgettable experience. Other natural highlights include Andean peaks around Mérida, coral reefs along the coast and offshore islands (Los Roques, for example), the Orinoco delta, Cueva del Guácharo, the tepuis and waterfalls of the Gran Sabana and the wildlife of Los Llanos.

SUGGESTED ITINERARIES

Since Venezuela, more precisely Caracas, is the cheapest entry point to the continent from both the US and Europe, many travelers use it as the beginning (or end) of their South American trips. From Caracas, people usually head west to Colombia or southeast to Brazil and often concentrate just on Venezuela's regions along the route. Those with more time to spend in Venezuela might be inclined to do some detours, at least to visit some of the highlights listed above.

PLANNING
When to Go

Tourist season in Venezuela runs year-round, but the dry season is certainly more pleasant for traveling. Some sights, though – such as waterfalls – are definitely more impressive in the wet season.

Keep in mind that Venezuelans usually take holidays over Christmas, Carnaval (several days prior to Ash Wednesday) and Holy Week (the week before Easter Sunday). In these periods, you'll have to plan ahead and do more legwork before you find a place to stay, but it may be worth it – these times are colorful and alive with a host of festivities.

Maps

The best general map of Venezuela (scale 1:1,750,000) is published by International Travel Maps (Canada). Within Venezuela, folded road maps of the country are produced by several local publishers. Dirección de Cartografía Nacional is the government mapping body; it produces and sells a variety of maps – see the Caracas section for details.

TOURIST OFFICES

Corporación de Turismo, or Corpoturismo, is the government agency based in Caracas that promotes tourism and provides tourist information. Outside the capital, regional tourist bodies have offices in their respective state capitals and in some other cities. Some are better than others, but on the whole they lack city maps and brochures and the staff members rarely speak English.

VISAS & DOCUMENTS

Nationals of the US, Canada, Australia, New Zealand, Japan, the UK and most of Western and Scandinavian Europe don't need visas if they fly into Venezuela; a tourist card (tarjeta de ingreso) is given to these visitors free of charge onboard the airline they fly. The tourist card is normally valid for 90 days (unless immigration officers note on the card a shorter period) and can be extended.

Until recently, all foreigners entering Venezuela by land from neighboring countries needed a visa, but this is currently being changed. Overland visitors bearing passports of the countries listed above are now allowed to enter Venezuela with the tourist card. The card can be obtained free of charge from some consulates, mostly those in border areas. Some may be able to get tourist cards directly at border crossings, but this is a sort of lottery, so don't risk it.

Some consulates may still insist that you have a tourist visa (US$30 to US$40) before issuing a tourist card, others can only issue a 72-hour transit visa (these visas cannot be extended within Venezuela, whatever the consulate tells you!), while still others offer nothing at all. To make matters worse, consulates tend to change their regulations frequently and unexpectedly.

If you plan on traveling overland and want to play it completely safe, you can get a Venezuelan visa in your country of residence. Consulates in most Western countries, including the US, the UK and Australia, issue multiple-entry tourist visas (for about US$30 to US$40) that are valid for one year from the date of issue.

On entering Venezuela, your passport and tourist card will be stamped (make sure this happens) by Dirección de Identificación y Extranjería (DIEX or DEX) border officials. You may be asked for an onward ticket, though it rarely happens these days.

Visa extensions are handled by the Caracas office of DIEX (see the Caracas section for details).

EMBASSIES & CONSULATES
Venezuelan Embassies & Consulates

Venezuela has representatives in neighboring countries and the following locations:

Australia
(☎ 02-6282-4828)
MLC Tower, Phillip, ACT 2606

Canada
(☎ 613-235-5151)
32 Range Rd, Ottawa, Ontario K1N 8J4

France
(☎ 01 45 53 29 98)
11 Rue Copernie, 75116 Paris

UK
(☎ 020-7581-2776, 020-7581-2777)
1 Cromwell Rd, London SW7 2HW

USA
(☎ 202-342-2214)
1099 30th St NW, Washington, DC 20007

Embassies & Consulates in Venezuela

Embassies and consulates in Caracas include:

Australia
(☎ 02-263-4033)
Quinta Yolanda, Av Luis Roche between 6a and 7a Transversal, Altamira

Brazil
(☎ 02-261-7553)
Centro Gerencial Mohedano, Los Chaguaramos at Av Mohedano, La Castellana

Canada
(☎ 02-951-6174)
Torre Europa, Av Francisco de Miranda, Campo Alegre

Colombia
(☎ 02-951-3631)
Edificio Consulado de Colombia, Guaicaipuro, El Rosal

France
(☎ 02-993-6666)
Edificio Embajada de Francia,
Madrid at Av La Trinidad, Las Mercedes

Guyana
(☎ 02-977-1158)
Quinta Roraima, Av El Paseo, Prados del Este

Suriname
(☎ 02-261-2724)
Quinta Los Milagros,
4a Av between 7a and 8a Transversal, Altamira

Trinidad & Tobago
(☎ 02-261-4772)
Quinta Serrana,
4a Av between 7a and 8a Transversal, Altamira

VENEZUELA

UK
(☎ 02-993-4111)
Torre Las Mercedes, Av La Estancia, Chuao
USA
(☎ 02-977-2011)
Calle F at Suapure, Colinas de Valle Arriba

CUSTOMS

Customs regulations don't differ much from those in other countries in South America. You are allowed to bring in personal belongings and presents you intend to give to Venezuelan residents. You can bring cameras (still, video and movie), camping equipment, sports accessories, a personal computer and the like without problems.

According to Venezuelan law, the possession, trafficking and consumption of drugs is a serious offense and subject to heavy penalties. You would have to be crazy to try smuggling them across the border. If you're coming overland from Colombia, your baggage is likely to be searched at the border and at *alcabalas* (police road checkpoints) – considerable drug traffic passes this way.

MONEY
Currency

The unit of currency is the *bolívar* (abbreviated to Bs). There are one, two and five-bolívar coins (which have almost entirely disappeared from the market) and 5, 10, 20, 50, 100, 500, 1000, 2000, 5000 and 10,000-bolívar notes.

Exchange Rates

Approximate exchange rates as of September 1999 included the following:

country	unit		bolivares
Australia	A$1	=	400Bs
Canada	C$1	=	407Bs
euro	€1	=	657Bs
France	FF1	=	100Bs
Germany	DM1	=	336Bs
New Zealand	NZ$1	=	324Bs
UK	UK£1	=	984Bs
USA	US$1	=	612Bs

Exchanging Money

US dollars and American Express traveler's checks are by far the most popular in Venezuela, so stick to them. Among credit cards, Visa and MasterCard are the most useful for getting cash advances and are accepted as a means of payment in a variety of (mostly upmarket) establishments, including hotels, restaurants, airlines and stores. Note that some regional tour operators refuse payment by credit card or charge 10% more if you pay with one.

You can change money at a bank or at a *casa de cambio* (an authorized money-exchange house). Banks change cash and traveler's checks and give cash advances on credit cards. Casas de cambio change cash but seldom travelers' checks.

Banks are plentiful in Venezuela but few of them handle foreign exchange. Furthermore, the availability of this service seems to differ from bank to bank, branch to branch and city to city and changes from day to day. Banks to look for include Corp Banca (which almost always changes American Express traveler's checks and sometimes cash), Banco Unión (which often changes cash and gives advances on Visa and sometimes on MasterCard), Banco de Venezuela (which irregularly changes cash and traveler's checks and accepts credit cards) and Banco Mercantil (which pays advances on MasterCard). Some branches of the banks listed above have ATMs that usually work fine with Visa, MasterCard and some other major cards.

Usual opening hours are 8:30 to 11:30 am and 2 to 4:30 pm on weekdays, but in some cities, banks have adopted a continuous schedule (no lunch break) and are open from 8:30 am to 3:30 pm. Banks are usually crowded, inefficient and often handle exchange operations during limited hours (mostly in the morning). Casas de cambio are much faster.

Costs

Venezuela is still a reasonable country to travel in, even though there has been a recent and massive price increase. Budget travelers should get by on US$20 to US$30 per day for accommodations, food and transport by bus, but that does not apply to tours, which cost US$40 to US$100 per day.

POST & COMMUNICATIONS
Post

The postal service is run by Ipostel, which has post offices throughout the country. The service is slow, inefficient and unreliable. Airmail to the US or Europe can take up to a month, if it arrives at all. Domestic mail is also painfully slow.

Telephone

The telephone system is operated by CANTV and is largely automated for both domestic and international connections. Public telephones exist in larger cities but are often out of order. Since coins disappeared from the market, so did coin phones, and almost all public phones only operate on phonecards (*tarjetas CANTV*). It's worth buying a card as soon as you arrive, unless you don't plan on using public phones at all. Cards come in denominations of 2000 and 5000 bolívares (a three-minute local call costs about 100 bolívares).

International telephone service is expensive. Reverse-charge (collect) phone calls (*llamadas de cobro revertido*) are possible for most countries and may be cheaper. Numbers for making calls include these:

Australia	☎ 800-11610
Canada	☎ 800-11100
France	☎ 800-11330
Germany	☎ 800-11490
UK	☎ 800-11440
USA (AT&T)	☎ 800-11121
(MCI)	☎ 800-11141
(Sprint)	☎ 800-11111

The country code for Venezuela is ☎ 58. To call a number in Venezuela from abroad, dial the international-access code of the country you're calling from, the country code (☎ 58), the area code (drop the initial '0') and the local phone number.

Fax & Email

Faxes can be sent from major branches of CANTV offices. There are also private companies that have fax service. Email providers include computer companies and Internet cafés, so far mostly in Caracas. Expect the service to cost US$5 to US$7 per hour.

INTERNET RESOURCES

For useful information on Venezuela try Lonely Planet's destination profile at www .lonelyplanet.com as well as www.venonweb .com, www.latinworld.com/sur/venezuela/, venezuela.mit.edu and www.veweb.com.

For information on current political, economic and cultural affairs read Venezuela's two leading papers at www.el-universal.com and www.el-nacional.com.

BOOKS

For more detailed travel information, get a copy of Lonely Planet's *Venezuela*. Among other guidebooks, *Venezuela* by Hilary Dunsterville Branch focuses on outdoor activities, predominantly hiking in national parks. *Hiking in the Venezuelan Andes* by Forest Leighty can be useful for those planning walks in the Andes.

A captivating overview of the period of Spanish colonization is provided by John Hemming's *The Search for El Dorado*. *In Focus: Venezuela – A Guide to the People, Politics and Culture* by James Ferguson is a good, concise introduction to the country. *Venezuela: the Search for Order, the Dream of Progress* by John V Lombardi provides general reading on history, politics, geography and people.

For 20th-century history, try *Venezuela: a Century of Change* by Judith Ewell or *Venezuela, Politics in a Petroleum Republic* by David Eugene Blank. *Paper Tigers and Minotaurs* by Moisés Naim provides information on recent economic policies.

Travelers with a serious interest in birdwatching may want to check *A Guide to the Birds of Venezuela* by Rodolphe Meyer de Schauensee and William H Phelps. *Birding in Venezuela* by Mary Lou Goodwin is also a good reference.

NEWSPAPERS & MAGAZINES

All main cities have daily newspapers. The two leading Caracas papers, *El Universal* and *El Nacional*, have countrywide distribution. Both have reasonable coverage of national and international affairs, sports, economics and culture. The *Daily Journal* is the main English-language newspaper published in Venezuela. It's available at major newsstands and at selected bookstores in Caracas. Elsewhere in Venezuela, it can be difficult to find.

RADIO & TV

Most of Venezuela's numerous radio stations are dominated by musical programs, principally Latin music, imported pop, rock, disco and the like. Jazz and classical music

VENEZUELA

are less popular but some stations do grant them airtime.

One government and three private TV stations operate out of Caracas and reach most of the country. They all offer the usual TV fare, including news, music, feature films, sport and culture. Prime time is dominated by *telenovelas*, or soap operas. Almost all programming is in Spanish, including foreign films, which are dubbed.

There are several pay-TV providers, including Omnivisión, Cablevisión, Supercable and DirecTV, which offer mixed Spanish and English packages of feature films, sport, music, soap operas and news. Satellite TV has boomed in Caracas and, to a lesser extent, in other cities.

TIME
All of Venezuela lies within the same time zone, four hours behind GMT/UTC, and there's no daylight saving time.

ELECTRICITY
Electricity is 110V, 60Hz AC all over the country. US-type flat two-pin plugs are used.

WEIGHTS & MEASURES
Venezuela uses the metric system.

HEALTH
Venezuela has quite developed health services, with an array of *farmacias* (pharmacies), private clinics and hospitals. Tap water is safe to drink in Caracas and several larger cities, but if you prefer to avoid it, bottled waters, juices and other drinks are readily available in supermarkets, shops and restaurants.

Sanitary conditions are probably a bit above average South American standards but are declining – yet another effect of economic crisis. No vaccinations are required on entering Venezuela, unless you come from an infected area. However, a vaccination against hepatitis is not a bad idea. Mosquitoes infest many low-lying areas, so use the usual repellents.

DANGERS & ANNOYANCES
Venezuela is a relatively safe country, though robbery is becoming a problem. Common crime is increasing in the large cities; Caracas is by far the most dangerous place in the country, and you should take care while strolling the streets, particularly

at night. Venturing into poor shantytowns is asking for trouble.

Never show disrespect for Bolívar – he is a saint to many Venezuelans. For instance, sitting on a bench in Plaza Bolívar with your feet on the bench, or crossing the plaza carrying bulky parcels (or even a backpack) may be considered disrespectful, and police may hassle you for it.

When traveling around the country, there are plenty of alcabalas, though not all are actually operating. They sometimes check the identity documents of passengers, and occasionally the luggage as well. In the cities, police checks are uncommon, but they do occur, so always have your passport with you. If you don't, you may end up at the police station.

BUSINESS HOURS
The working day is theoretically eight hours, 8 am to noon and 2 to 6 pm, weekdays. Almost all offices, including tourist offices, are closed on Saturday and Sunday.

Usual shopping hours are 9 am to 6 or 7 pm weekdays, and a half-day on Saturday. Many shops close for lunch but some work the *horario corrido*, ie, without a lunchtime break. Many restaurants don't open at all Sunday. Most museums are closed Monday but open Sunday.

PUBLIC HOLIDAYS & SPECIAL EVENTS
Official public holidays include:

New Year's Day
  January 1

Carnaval
  Two days before Ash Wednesday

Maundy Thursday & Good Friday
  March or April

Declaration of Independence
  April 19

Labor Day
  May 1

Battle of Carabobo
  June 24

Independence Day
  July 5

Bolívar's Birthday
  July 24

Discovery of America
  October 12

Christmas Day
  December 25

Given the strong Catholic character of Venezuela, a good number of feasts and celebrations follow the Church calendar. Possibly the biggest event celebrated throughout the country is Carnaval, which takes place on the Monday and Tuesday prior to Ash Wednesday, although feasting breaks out by the end of the preceding week.

One of Venezuela's most colorful events is the Diablos Danzantes, or the Dancing Devils. It's held on Corpus Christi in San Francisco de Yare, about 60km south of Caracas. The ceremony consists of a spectacular parade and the dance of devils, performed by dancers disguised in elaborate masks and costumes.

Cultural events such as theater, film or classical music festivals are mostly confined to Caracas.

ACTIVITIES

Venezuela's national parks provide walks ranging from easy, well-signposted trails to wild jungle paths. Sierra Nevada de Mérida is the best region in Venezuela for high-mountain trekking and, if you're up to it, you can try mountaineering and rock climbing there. Mérida state is also the best area for mountain biking and paragliding.

Some national parks (eg, Henri Pittier) are good for bird-watching. Parts of Venezuela's coast (Mochima) and some islands (Los Roques) have coral reefs, providing good conditions for snorkeling and scuba diving. Other possible activities include sailing, fishing, rafting and caving, to name just a few.

ACCOMMODATIONS

Venezuela has heaps of hotels for every budget, and it's usually easy to find a room, except perhaps on major feast days. With some exceptions, low-budget hotels are uninspiring and styleless, but most do have private baths. As most of the country lies in the lowland tropics, rooms in the cheaper places usually have a fan, and sometimes even air-conditioning, but there's no hot water. Always have a look at the room and check the fan or air-con before you book in and pay.

There's an increasing number of budget places called *posadas*, which are meant to be small, family-run guest houses. They often have more character and offer more personalized attention than the rest, but not always.

In budget hotels and posadas, expect to pay roughly US$5 to US$10 per single and US$8 to US$15 per double. Many budget places have *matrimoniales*, rooms with one wide bed intended for couples, which often cost only marginally more than singles.

Mid-range hotels provide more facilities, though often lack character. They differ wildly in standards and value, but you can usually find a reasonable place for US$25 to US$40 per double. Only Caracas and Isla de Margarita have a choice of hotels with three-digit prices, and a few other cities such as Puerto La Cruz and Maracaibo have one or two such places. Hotels often charge foreigners a 10% tax on top of the room price, though few budget places do it.

Brothels are not uncommon in Venezuela. More numerous, though, are love hotels (places that rent rooms by the hour). Many cheap hotels double as love hotels, and it's often impossible to avoid staying in one from time to time.

Venezuela has no youth hostels. Camping grounds, as the term is understood in the West, are virtually nonexistent, but you can camp rough in the countryside. Camping on the beach is popular, but be cautious and don't leave your tent unattended.

Over the past decades, there has been a rash of places to stay in the countryside called *campamentos* (literally 'camps'). Not to be confused with campsites, campamentos can be anything from rustic shelters with a few hammocks to posh country lodges with swimming pools (most commonly, they're bunches of cabins) that also provide food and usually tours, often selling these services as all-inclusive packages.

FOOD

Venezuelans love to eat out and restaurants are abundant. On the whole, food is good and relatively inexpensive. Apart from a variety of local dishes, there's a choice of international cooking available, including an array of Western fast-food outlets. Spanish and Italian restaurants are well represented, thanks to a sizable immigration population from these two countries. There are also some good Chinese and Middle-Eastern restaurants, mostly in main cities. Gourmets will enjoy their stay in Caracas, which offers the widest range of eating establishments and international cuisines.

Budget travelers should look for restaurants that offer a *menú del día* or *menu ejecutivo*, a set meal consisting of soup and a main course, cheaper than any à-la-carte dish, that will cost roughly US$2 to US$4 (a little more in Caracas). A budget alternative might be spit-roasted chicken, usually called *pollo en brasas*. Or just grab an *arepa*, a wonderful local snack (see Venezuelan Cuisine).

As in most of South America, the market is a good cheap option, offering usually tasty and fresh local food. For breakfast, visit any of the ubiquitous *panaderías* (bakeries), which serve sandwiches, croissants, pastries and a variety of snacks and invariably delicious espresso.

In virtually every dining or drinking establishment, a 10% service charge will automatically be added to the bill. In budget eateries, tipping is uncommon, but in upmarket restaurants, a small tip is customary.

Venezuelan Cuisine

The following list includes some of the most typical Venezuelan snacks and dishes:

Arepa – A small toasted or fried maize pancake, itself plain. It's often included as an accompaniment to some dishes. Popularly, it's served as a snack on its own, stuffed with cheese, beef, ham, sausage, octopus, shrimp, eggs, salad and just about anything you might think of. Snack bars, commonly called *areperas*, serve arepas for about US$1 to US$2.

Cachapa – A round juicy pancake made of fresh corn, usually served with cheese or ham.

Cachito – A sort of croissant filled with chopped ham and served hot.

Hallaca – Chopped pork, beef or chicken with vegetables and olives, all folded in maize dough, wrapped in banana leaves and steamed; particularly popular during Christmas.

Mondongo – A seasoned tripe cooked in bouillon with maize, potatoes, carrots and other vegetables.

Muchacho – Roasted beef served in sauce.

Pabellón – A main course consisting of shredded beef, rice, beans and fried plantain; it's Venezuela's national dish.

Sancocho – A vegetable stew with fish, meat or chicken.

DRINKS

Espresso coffee is strong and excellent in Venezuela. Ask for *café negro* if you want it black; for *café marrón* if you prefer half coffee, half milk; or for *café con leche* if you like more milky coffee.

Fruit juices are readily available in restaurants, *fuentes de soda* (soda fountains), *fruterías*, *refresquerías* and other eating outlets. Given the variety of fruit in the country, you have quite a choice. Juices come as *batidos* (pure or watered down) or as *merengadas,* (milk shakes).

The number-one alcoholic drink is *cerveza* (beer), particularly Polar beer, the dominant brand. It's sold everywhere in cans or small bottles. Among spirits, *ron* (rum) heads the list and comes in numerous varieties and qualities.

SPECTATOR SPORTS

Baseball is the most popular sport, followed by basketball. Venezuelans don't seem to be as crazy about soccer as most other South Americans. Venezuela has several horse racetracks, including the best one, La Rinconada, in Caracas. Most cities have bullrings that attract crowds of *corrida* (bullfighting) fans, with the season peaking during Carnaval.

Getting There & Away

AIR

Set at the northern edge of South America, Venezuela is the cheapest gateway to the continent from both Europe and North America. The official Venezuelan entry requirement is an onward ticket (though nobody now checks it on the border), so it is possible that an airline won't sell you a one-way ticket unless you show them an onward ticket. The airport tax for tourists leaving Venezuela is US$32, payable in either US dollars or bolívares.

Europe

There are cheap airfares available from many European cities. London is often the cheapest jumping-off point (with fares in the low season beginning at £236 one way, £369 return), but there are special deals here and there, so you may also find agents in Paris, Amsterdam, Madrid or Lisbon offering attractive fares.

North America

The major gateway city is Miami, from where several airlines fly to Caracas. Servivensa (a Venezuelan carrier) may be the cheapest operator, with its Miami-Caracas cut-down fares often offered for as little as US$100 to US$130 one way. Contact the Miami office at ☎ 305-381-8001 or toll-free ☎ 800-428-3672. Servivensa may also have attractive fares from New York (☎ 718-244-6857). Check the offers of other airlines as well, which may be some good deals. Before making a final decision, consider Avensa's air pass (see the Getting Around section).

Brazil

Flights between Brazil and Venezuela are expensive. A flight between Caracas and São Paulo or Rio de Janeiro will cost about US$750 (US$850 return). Possibly the cheapest air link between these two countries is the Manaus-Caracas flight serviced by Aeropostal, but it's still pricey at US$450 one way.

Colombia

There are plenty of flights between Bogotá and Caracas with several carriers, including Avianca, Saeta and Servivensa (US$218 one way, US$251 for a 30-day return, US$281 60-day return).

Other possible links between Colombia and Venezuela include Cartagena-Caracas with Aeropostal (US$180, US$220 for a 30-day return), Barranquilla-Maracaibo with Santa Bárbara (US$135, US$190 for a 30-day return) and Medellín-San Antonio del Táchira with Servivensa (US$63). The Bogotá-San Antonio del Táchira flight with Servivensa was the cheapest air link between the two countries (US$50), but this service was suspended indeterminately in April 1999.

Netherlands Antilles

There are flights between Caracas and Aruba (US$115) and Curaçao (US$91), as well as between Las Piedras and Aruba (US$68) and Curaçao (US$96). All these flights are serviced by Servivensa and discount 14-day return fares are available. There are also charter flights on light planes between Coro and Aruba, Curaçao and Bonaire. See the Coro section for information.

Trinidad

Aeropostal flies four times a week from Port of Spain to Caracas (US$114) via Porlamar (Port of Spain to just Porlamar is US$90). Rutaca operates charter flights between Port of Spain and Maturín (US$90).

Guyana & Suriname

There are no direct flights between these countries and Venezuela; you have to use Port of Spain as a bridge. Flights from Georgetown or Paramaribo to Caracas via Port of Spain cost around US$250.

LAND
Brazil

Only one road runs between Brazil and Venezuela; it leads from Manaus through Boa Vista to Santa Elena de Uairén and continues to Ciudad Guayana – see the Santa Elena de Uairén section.

Colombia

You can enter Venezuela from Colombia at four border crossings. In the northwest, there is a coastal smuggling route between Maicao and Maracaibo (see the Maracaibo section). Farther south is the most popular border crossing, between Cúcuta and San Antonio del Táchira (see the San Antonio del Táchira section in this chapter and the Cúcuta section in the Colombia chapter). There is also an unpopular, unsafe and inconvenient crossing from Arauca to El Amparo de Apure. Finally, there's an uncommon but interesting outback route from Puerto Carreño in Colombia to either Puerto Páez or Puerto Ayacucho in Venezuela (see the Puerto Ayacucho section).

Guyana

There are no road links between Guyana and Venezuela; you must go via Brazil.

SEA
Netherlands Antilles

There's no ferry service between Curaçao and La Vela de Coro (the port of Coro), nor between Aruba and Punto Fijo (both were closed in 1992, but they may reopen by the time you arrive).

Lesser Antilles

There's ferry service between the Lesser Antilles (St Lucia, Barbados, St Vincent and

Trinidad) and Güiria and Isla de Margarita (see those sections).

ORGANIZED TOURS

Venezuela is quite a popular destination with tour operators abroad, particularly those in the US, UK and Germany. However, these tours are expensive; you are likely to save a lot of money by arranging one in Venezuela. Information about local tour operators is included in relevant sections.

Getting Around

AIR

Venezuela has a number of airlines and a reasonable network of air routes. Caracas (or, more precisely, Maiquetía, where Caracas' airport is located) is the country's major aviation hub. It handles flights to most cities around the country.

Avensa and its offspring, Servivensa, are the major domestic airlines, landing at two dozen airports throughout the country, and they also operate international flights. Although Avensa and Servivensa planes are labeled with their own distinctive logos, they are the same company. Venezuela's other major passenger airlines include Aeropostal, Santa Bárbara, Aserca and Air Venezuela. There are also a dozen minor passenger carriers that cover mostly regional routes.

Flying in Venezuela is no longer the bargain it used to be several years ago. Fares vary between carriers (sometimes substantially), so if the route you're flying is serviced by several airlines, check all their fares before buying a ticket. Information on routes and fares is included in the relevant sections. Figures listed are approximate mid-price airfares.

Reconfirm your flight at least 72 hours before departure and arm yourself with patience, as not all flights depart on time.

Air Passes

Avensa offers an air pass that allows you to fly within 45 days with Avensa or Servivensa on all domestic and international routes serviced in the Americas. Travel can begin and end in any city on the network, but you can't fly more than once on the same route. The pass can be bought both outside and inside Venezuela.

The pass includes a number of flight coupons (minimum of four, maximum unlimited) of your choice, each with a determined price. Coupons for any of the domestic routes cost US$40 each; those for international routes range from US$55 to US$200. For example, the Mexico City-Caracas coupon costs US$200, the Lima-Caracas coupon is US$180, while Miami-Caracas and Bogotá-Caracas coupons are US$80 each. Contact Avensa's representatives in Europe or the US (there are none in Australia) for details.

BUS

As there is no passenger train service in Venezuela, most traveling is done by bus. Buses are generally fast, and they run regularly day and night between major population centers. They are especially efficient on main roads, which are all surfaced.

There are dozens of bus companies owning buses ranging from archaic pieces to the most recent models. Many major companies offer *servicio ejecutivo* in comfortable air-conditioned buses, which now cover most of the major long-distance routes. Note that the air-conditioning can be *very* efficient, so have warm clothing at hand to avoid being frozen solid. The standard of service may differ from one company to another, as may fares. Figures given in particular sections later in this chapter are approximate mean fares for air-con service (where they exist).

All intercity buses depart from and arrive at the *terminal de pasajeros*, or bus terminal. Every city has such a terminal, usually outside the city center but always linked to it by local transport. Caracas is the most important transport hub, handling buses to just about every corner of the country.

In general, there's no need to buy tickets in advance for major routes, except around Christmas, Carnaval and Easter.

Many short-distance regional routes are serviced by the *por puesto* (literally, 'by the seat'). It's a cross between a bus and a taxi – the same kind of service as a *colectivo* in Colombia or Peru. Por puestos are usually large cars (less often minibuses) that ply fixed routes and depart when all seats are filled. They cost about 40% to 80% more than buses, are faster and usually more comfortable. On some routes, they are the dominant or even the exclusive means of transport.

CAR

Traveling by car is a comfortable and attractive way of getting around Venezuela. The country is sufficiently safe and the network of roads is extensive and usually in acceptable shape. Gas stations are numerous and fuel is cheap: US$0.15 to US$0.30 per liter, depending on the octane level.

There are a number of international and local car rental companies, including Hertz, Avis, Budget and National, that have offices at major airports throughout the country and in the centers of the main cities. Check with tourist offices, travel agencies or top-class hotels for information.

Car rental is expensive. As a rough guide, a small car will cost around US$60 per day, while the discount rate for a full week is about US$350. A 4WD vehicle is considerably more expensive and difficult to obtain.

BOAT

Venezuela has a number of offshore territories, the main one being Isla de Margarita. See the Puerto La Cruz, Cumaná and Isla de Margarita sections for details on ferry service. There's no regular boat service to Venezuela's other islands.

The Río Orinoco is the country's major waterway, navigable from its mouth up to Puerto Ayacucho. However, there's no passenger service on any stretch of the river.

LOCAL TRANSPORT
Bus

All cities and many major towns have their own urban transportation systems, which in most places are small buses or minibuses. They are called, depending on the region, *busetas, carros, carritos, micros* or *camionetas,* and fares are usually not more than US$0.30. In many larger cities, you will also find urban *por puestos*, which are faster and more comfortable.

Metro

Caracas is the only city that has subway transport – see that section.

Taxi

Taxis are fairly inexpensive and are worth considering, particularly for transport between the bus terminal and city center when you are carrying all your bags. Except for some major cities, taxis rarely have

meters, so always fix the fare with the driver *before* boarding the cab. It's a good idea to find out the correct fare beforehand from an independent source, such as terminal officials or a hotel reception desk.

ORGANIZED TOURS

Tours are a popular way to visit some of Venezuela's attractions, largely because vast areas of the country are virtually inaccessible by public transport (the Orinoco delta or Amazon Basin) or because a solitary visit to scattered sights in a large territory (as in the Gran Sabana) may be more time-consuming and eventually more expensive than a tour.

It's cheapest to arrange a tour from the regional center closest to the area you are going to visit. For hikes in the Andes, the place to look for a guide is Mérida; for excursions around the Gran Sabana, the cheapest organized trips are from Santa Elena de Uairén; for the Amazon, book a tour in Puerto Ayacucho; for the Orinoco delta, Tucupita is the right address; and for tours to Angel Falls, Ciudad Bolívar is the place to shop around. Some agencies may tack on a 10 % charge for use of credit cards, or may not accept them at all.

Caracas

Founded by Diego de Losada in 1567, Caracas was for three centuries a small and unhurried place. The first to launch an extensive program of modernization was General Guzmán Blanco, who commissioned monumental edifices in the 1870s, among them the Capitolio Nacional and the Panteón Nacional. However, the town grew at a relatively slow pace well into the 20th century.

Then came the oil boom, and everything began to change at the speed of light. During the last 50 years, the city's population grew from about 350,000 to nearly five million. Oil money has been pumped into modernization, successfully transforming the bucolic colonial town into an urban sprawl of concrete. In the name of progress, colonial architecture, save a handful of buildings, was effectively eradicated and replaced by spanking commercial centers and steel-and-glass towers. In the 1980s, the last important achievement of urban planning was opened: the metro.

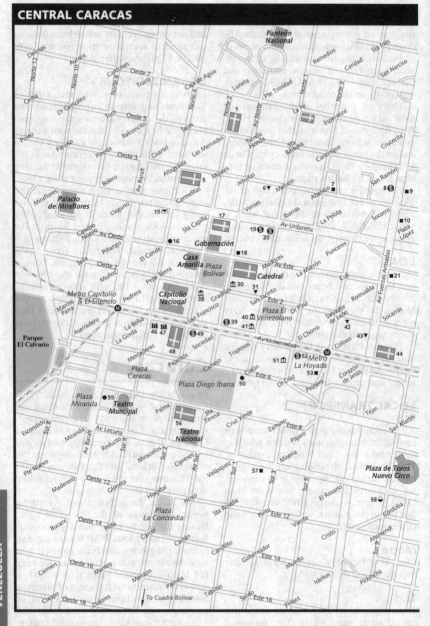

CENTRAL CARACAS

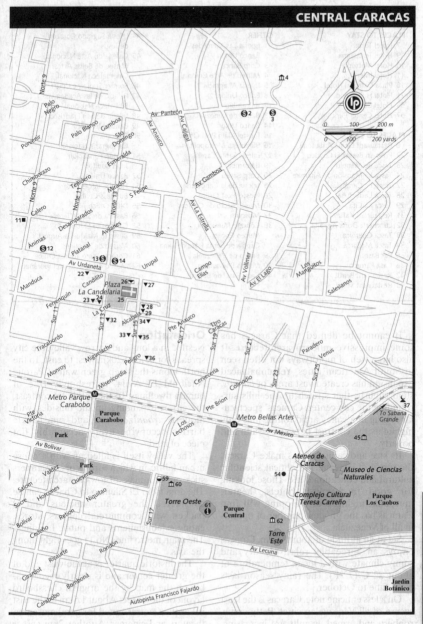

CENTRAL CARACAS

CENTRAL CARACAS

PLACES TO STAY
7   Hotel Turín
9   Hotel Terepaima
10 Hotel Metropol
11 Hotel Inter
18 Plaza Catedral Hotel
21 Hotel Hollywood
53 Hotel Caracol
57 Hotel Center Park

PLACES TO EAT
6   Restaurant Dama Antañona
22 Pollo en Brasas El Coyuco
23 Tasca de Manolo
24 Tasca La Mansión de Altamira
27 Tasca La Carabela
28 Tasca La Tertulia
29 Tasca La Cita
31 Restaurant Kafta
32 Lunchería Doña Agapita
33 Tasca Guernica
34 Tasca Mallorca
35 Bar Basque
36 Casa Farruco
42 Restaurant Beirut
43 Restaurant Sokol

OTHER
1   Iglesia Las Mercedes
2   Banco Unión
3   Corp Banca
4   Museo de Arte Colonial
5   Iglesia Altagracia
8   Banco Unión
12 Italcambio
13 Banco de Venezuela
14 Banco Unión
15 Ipostel Main Post Office
16 Biblioteca Metropolitana
17 Iglesia Santa Capilla
19 Italcambio
20 Corp Banca
25 Iglesia de la Candelaria
26 Ipostel Post Office
30 Museo Sacro de Caracas
37 Mosque
38 Consejo Municipal,
    Museo Criollo,
    Capilla de Santa Rosa de Lima
39 Banco de Venezuela
40 Museo Bolivariano
41 Casa Natal de Bolívar

44 Iglesia Sagrado Corazón
    de Jesús
45 Galería de Arte Nacional,
    Museo de Bellas Artes,
    Cinemateca Nacional
46 Former Supreme Court
47 Palacio de las Academias,
    Biblioteca Nacional
48 Iglesia de San Francisco
49 Banco Mercantil
50 Dirección de
    Cartografía Nacional
51 Museo Fundación
    John Boulton
52 Banco Unión
54 Hotel Caracas Hilton,
    Business Center
55 DIEX Office
56 Basílica de Santa Teresa
58 Carritos to El Junquito
59 Buses to Maiquetía Airport
60 Museo de los Niños
61 Corpoturismo Tourist Office
62 Museo de Arte Contemporáneo

It cannot be denied that Caracas has some impressive modern architecture. It also has a web of motorways not often seen in South American cities. Yet unbalanced expansion has created vast areas of *barrios*, slum suburbs that stretch up the hills surrounding the city center. Caracas' spectacular setting in a valley amid rolling hills only highlights the contrast between wealth and poverty.

Its size and capital status make Caracas the center of Venezuela's political, scientific, cultural and educational life. Those looking for good food, plush hotels, theater, museums, nightlife or shopping will find Caracas has the greatest number of options in all of Venezuela.

Set at an altitude of about 900m, Caracas enjoys an agreeable, relatively dry and sunny climate with a mean temperature of about 22°C (72°F). The rainy season lasts from June to October.

On a less enticing note, Caracas is the least secure of all Venezuelan cities. Petty crime, robbery and armed assaults are increasing, especially at night. Travelers should be cautious and aware of their surroundings.

Orientation

Nestled in a long and narrow valley, the city spreads for at least 20km west to east. To the north looms the steep green wall of Parque Nacional El Avila, refreshingly free of human dwellings. To the south, by contrast, the city is expanding up the hillsides, with modern *urbanizaciones* and ramshackle barrios occupying every acceptably flat piece of land.

The valley itself is filled up with a dense urban fabric, in which forests of skyscrapers stick out of a mass of low-rise architecture. The area from El Silencio to Chacao can be considered the greater nucleus and is packed with commercial centers, stores, eating establishments and public buildings. The main metro line (No 1) goes right along the axis.

The historic quarter is at the west end of the greater center and is clearly recognizable on the map by the original chessboard layout of the streets. About 1.5km to the east is Parque Central, noted for good museums, theaters and cinemas. Another 2km east is Sabana Grande, centered on an attractive pedestrian mall lined with restaurants and shops. Continuing east is the commercial district of Chacao and the trendy Altamira, which boasts a number of good restaurants and nightspots. El Rosal and Las Mercedes, south of Chacao, cater to gourmets and night-trippers.

Most tourist sights are in the central area within walking distance from each other; sights away from the center are easily accessible by metro.

A curiosity of Caracas is the street-address system in the historic quarter. It's actually not the streets that bear names, but the street corners, or *esquinas*. A place is identified by the street corners on either side, and its address is given 'corner to corner.' For example, the address 'Piñango a Conde' means that the place is between these two street corners. If the place is right on the corner, its address would be 'Esquina Conde.' In modern times, authorities have given numbers and cardinal-point designations to the streets (*Este, Oeste, Norte, Sur,* or East, West, North, South), but locals continue to stick to the esquinas.

Other than in the old town, streets and not corners indicate where a place is located. Major streets are commonly called Avenidas. Street numbers are seldom used.

Maps Large-scale maps of the country are sold by the Dirección de Cartografía Nacional (☎ 02-4081-615, 02-408-1637), Calle Este 6, Esquina Colón (metro La Hoyada).

Information

Tourist Office The Corpoturismo tourist office (☎ 02-507-8600, 02-507-8607) is on the 35th floor of the Torre Oeste (West Tower), Parque Central (metro Bellas Artes). The office is open 8:30 am to 12:30 pm and 2 to 5 pm weekdays. There's a Corpoturismo outlet in the international terminal at Maiquetía airport.

Money Few of Caracas' many banks will change traveler's checks or cash, except for the Corp Banca, which normally cashes American Express checks.

A number of casas de cambio change foreign currency and traveler's checks, including Italcambio, which has several outlets throughout the city, plus one at Maiquetía airport. All locations pay marginally less than the banks.

Cash advances on Visa and MasterCard credit cards can be obtained in most branches of Banco de Venezuela, Banco Mercantil, Banco Unión, Banco Provincial and some other banks. Many of these have ATMs.

Post & Communications The main Ipostel post office, Av Urdaneta, Esquina Carmelitas, close to Plaza Bolívar, has poste restante service. Letters sent should be addressed with your name, Lista de Correos, Ipostel, Carmelitas, Caracas 1010.

Caracas' only CANTV office that provides an international call service through the operator is in Centro Plaza, Av Francisco de Miranda, Los Palos Grandes (metro Altamira).

Internet Resources Facilities include Webcenter (☎ 02-261-4151) in Torre Banco Lara (basement level), on Av Principal de la Castellana, and Internet Para Todos (☎ 02-992-4155) in Centro Comercial Paseo Las Mercedes, Local 143 (next door to Cada supermarket). Both are open weekdays and half of Saturday. Also try the small Infoteca (☎ 02-762-0285) in Edificio Rupi, Oficina 42A, Av Casanova in Sabana Grande, and Business Center (☎ 02-503-4367) in the Hotel Caracas Hilton.

Visa Extensions Visa and tourist-card extensions are issued by the DIEX office. It's on Av Baralt. One month's extension will cost you about US$25, and the procedure may take up to a week. Your passport, one photograph, a photocopy of your onward ticket and a letter explaining the purpose of the extension are required in addition to the form you'll fill in at the office.

Travel Agencies IVI Tours (☎ 02-993-6082, 02-993-8738), Residencia La Hacienda, Piso Bajo, Local 1-4-T, Final Av Principal de las Mercedes, issues ISIC and ITIC cards and offers attractive airfares to Europe and elsewhere for foreign students, teachers and those younger than 26.

Fairmont Internacional (02-782-8433, 02-781-7091), Plaza Venezuela, can book a room in some 250 hotels throughout the country (though not the budget ones), charging US$4 for the service.

VENEZUELA

Bookstores Bookstores specializing in English-language publications include the American Book Shop (☎ 02-263-5455), in the Edificio Belveder, Av San Juan Bosco at 1a Transversal (metro Altamira), and the English Book Shop (☎ 02-979-1308), Centro Comercial Concresa, Prados del Este.

The Tecni-Ciencia Libros (☎ 02-959-5547), in the CCCT, Nivel C-2, Chuao, is one of Caracas' best bookstores and has heaps of publications including dictionaries, specialist fare and coffee-table books. Its well-stocked travel section (the best in town) features more than 50 Lonely Planet titles (including *Venezuela* and other regional guidebooks).

Inparques The Inparques office (☎ 02-285-4106, 285-4259), just east of the Parque del Este metro station, can provide general information about national parks and has a small library.

Old Caracas

Caracas' historic quarter has lost much of its identity following a rush toward modernization, during which many colonial houses were replaced with modern architecture. The nucleus is **Plaza Bolívar**, sporting the inevitable monument to the hero in the middle. The equestrian statue was cast in Europe, shipped in pieces, assembled and unveiled in 1874.

The **Catedral**, overlooking the plaza, was built between 1665 and 1713 after an earthquake destroyed the previous church in 1641. A wide, five-nave interior supported on 32 columns was largely remodeled in the late 19th century. The Bolívar family chapel is in the middle of the right-hand aisle, recognizable by the modern sculpture of Bolívar mourning his parents and wife. Next to the cathedral is the **Museo Sacro de Caracas** (closed Monday), which has a collection of religious art.

The Consejo Municipal, on the southern side of the square, houses the **Museo Criollo** (closed Monday), which features exhibits related to the town's history, including dioramas depicting turn-of-the-century Caracas. The west side of the building accommodates the **Capilla de Santa Rosa de Lima**, where, on July 5, 1811, congress declared Venezuela's independence (though it was another 10 years before this became fact).

The entire block southwest of Plaza Bolívar is taken up by the neoclassical **Capitolio Nacional**, a complex of two buildings commissioned in the 1870s by Guzmán Blanco. In the northern building is the **Salón Elíptico**, an oval hall boasting a large mural on its domed ceiling. The painting, depicting the battle of Carabobo, was executed in 1888 by Martín Tovar y Tovar.

Just south of the Capitolio is the **Iglesia de San Francisco**, which shelters a number of richly gilded altarpieces. It was here that, in 1813, Bolívar was proclaimed El Libertador and where his much-celebrated funeral was held in 1842, when his remains were brought from Colombia 12 years after his death.

Two blocks east is the **Casa Natal de Bolívar**, the house where he was born in 1783. Its reconstructed interior is decorated with paintings by Tito Salas depicting Bolívar's battles and other scenes from his life. Just to the north, in another colonial house, the **Museo Bolivariano** displays independence memorabilia, period weapons and banners and portraits of Bolívar. Both museums are open daily.

Seven blocks south is the **Cuadra Bolívar**, one of Bolívar's childhood homes, now a museum restored to its original appearance and stuffed with period furnishings.

The **Panteón Nacional** (open daily), five blocks north of Plaza Bolívar, was rebuilt from a church wrecked by the 1812 earthquake to serve as the last resting place for eminent Venezuelans. The central nave is dedicated to Bolívar – his bronze sarcophagus put in the chancel in place of the high altar – while 163 tombs of other distinguished figures (including three women) have been pushed out to the aisles. Two tombs are empty and open, awaiting the remains of Francisco de Miranda, who died in a Spanish jail in 1816 and was buried in a mass grave, and Antonio José de Sucre, whose ashes are in the Quito cathedral. The vault of the pantheon is covered by paintings depicting scenes from Bolívar's life, all done by Tito Salas in the 1930s.

About 1.5km east of the pantheon is the **Museo de Arte Colonial** (closed Monday), housed in a colonial country mansion known as the Quinta de Anauco. You'll be guided around meticulously restored interiors filled with art, furniture and household implements.

New Caracas

For a taste of modern Caracas, head for **Parque Central**, 1.5km southeast of Plaza Bolívar. Despite its name, it's not a green area, but a concrete complex of high-rise residential slabs of rather apocalyptic appearance, crowned by two 53-story octagonal towers, the tallest in the country. Even if you're not impressed by the architecture, don't retreat, for there are some important sights in the area, especially if you are interested in art, music and theater.

The **Museo de Arte Contemporáneo** (closed Monday), at the east end of the complex, is by far the best in the country and one of the best in South America. Inside you'll find works by prominent national artists, including Jesús Soto, and works by international figures such as Miró, Chagall, Léger and Picasso. The museum's pride is about 100 engravings by Picasso, created in 1931-34. Part of the exhibition space is given to changing displays.

In the opposite (west) end of Parque Central is the good hands-on **Museo de los Niños**, or Children's Museum (closed Monday and Tuesday), where adults have as much fun as kids. Avoid weekends, when the museum is besieged by visitors.

Just east of Parque Central is the **Complejo Cultural Teresa Carreño**, a modern performing-arts center inaugurated in 1983 that hosts concerts, ballet and theater in its 2500-seat auditorium. Hour-long guided tours around the complex are run several times a day. At the back of the building is a small museum dedicated to Teresa Carreño (1853-1917), widely considered the best pianist Venezuela has produced.

North of the complex is the **Ateneo de Caracas**, another cultural center complete with a concert hall, theater, cinema, art gallery, bookstore and café. Behind the Ateneo is the **Museo de Ciencias Naturales** (closed Monday).

Opposite, the **Galería de Arte Nacional** has a permanent collection of some 4000 works of art embracing four centuries of Venezuelan artistic expression, plus some pre-Hispanic art. Adjoining the gallery is the modern **Museo de Bellas Artes**, which features mainly temporary exhibitions. Go to the rooftop terrace for views over the city, including a modern mosque to the north. Both art museums are closed on Monday.

Other Attractions

Stroll along the **Boulevard de Sabana Grande**, a fashionable city mall that stretches between the metro stations of Plaza Venezuela and Chacaíto, or visit the **Jardín Botánico** (Botanical Garden) – the entrance is on Av Interna UCV, south of Plaza Venezuela. South of the garden is the **Universidad Central de Venezuela**, Caracas' largest university that occupies a vast campus dotted with sculptures and murals. There's a good concert hall, Aula Magna, on the grounds – check what's going on.

In the eastern part of the city is the **Parque del Este** (closed Monday), the city's largest park (there's a metro station of the same name). It's good for walks, and you can visit the snake house, aviary and cactus garden and, on weekend afternoons, enjoy a show in the Planetario Humboldt. Next to the park is the **Museo del Transporte** (open Wednesday and Sunday), which features collections of old horse-drawn carts, carriages and vintage cars.

Caracas' main zoo, the **Parque Zoológico de Curicuao**, features a selection of native birds, reptiles and mammals. It's easily accessible by metro.

Organized Tours

There are more than 600 travel agencies in Caracas and most offer tours. Although a tour can send you to virtually every corner of the country, it will always be cheaper to arrive in the region on your own and contract a local operator. If you prefer to have it all organized from Caracas, reputable tour companies include:

Akanan Travel & Tours
    (☎ 02-238-1457) Edificio Claret, Av Sanz at Calle La Laguna, El Marqués

Cóndor Verde
    (☎ 02-975-4306) Torre Humboldt, Av Caura, Prados del Este

Orinoco Tours
    (☎ 02-761-7712) Edificio Galerías Bolívar, Boulevard de Sabana Grande

Turven
    (☎ 02-9511032) Edificio Unión, Boulevard de Sabana Grande

The Centro Excursionista Caracas (CEC) is an association of outdoor-minded people who organize weekend trips around Caracas and the central states (longer journeys to other regions are scheduled for holiday periods). The excursionists use public transport and take their own food and camping gear. Foreign travelers are welcome. Contact persons include Lucy Alió (speaks English and French; ☎ 02-782-4182) and Samuel Bendayán (English; ☎ 02-963-1712).

Younger travelers may be interested in the Centro Excursionista Universitario (CEU), which bands together mostly university students. Contact persons include Virginia Alió (English; ☎ 02-781-3873), and María Grazia Cattinari (English and Italian; ☎ 02-573-4470).

Special Events

The main event is the International Theater Festival, held in April of even-numbered years (it may shift to another month).

Places to Stay

Accommodations in Caracas are more expensive than elsewhere in the country and are rarely good values. On the whole, Caracas' budget hotels are poor and styleless, usually located in unprepossessing, sometimes unsafe areas. Many of the bottom-end hotels double as love hotels and some as brothels; business is particularly brisk on Fridays and Saturdays. Consequently, some hotels may turn you down on weekends.

There are two major hotel areas: the center and Sabana Grande. All hotels listed here have rooms with private baths and either fan or air-conditioning, and most have hot water.

Center This area roughly corresponds with what is covered by the left page of the Central Caracas map. The cheapest accommodations in this sector are south of Av Bolívar, but the area is unattractive and can be unsafe. One of the few acceptable places here is *Hotel Center Park* (☎ 02-541-8619), Av Lecuna, Velásquez a Miseria, which is sometimes used by travelers. It offers small singles/matrimoniales/doubles with fans for US$16/18/20.

It's more convenient for sightseeing and probably safer to stay north of Av Bolívar. One of the cheapest options here is *Hotel Caracol* (☎ 02-545-1228), Peinero a Coliseo, near La Hoyada metro station, which has

air-con matrimoniales for around US$22. Similarly priced is the basic and noisy *Hotel Hollywood* (☎ 02-561-4989), Av Fuerzas Armadas, Esquina Romualda. Both double as love hotels.

Two blocks north of the Hollywood you'll find *Hotel Metropol* (☎ 02-562-8666), Plaza López a Socorro, and *Hotel Terepaima* (☎ 02-562-0966), Socorro a San Ramón. Both have air-con rooms and are OK if noisy; both charge US$24/28/32 per matrimonial/double/triple with TV.

One block east, on Esquina Calero, is *Hotel Inter* (☎ 02-564-0251), which costs marginally more than the Metropol and Terepaima, but is quieter and better kept. It's popular with businesspeople and may often be full. If so, try *Hotel Turín* (☎ 02-561-3315), two blocks west, which offers much the same for a little less.

If you are prepared to pay more, go to *Plaza Catedral Hotel* (☎ 02-564-2111), overlooking Plaza Bolívar. It's the best-located affordable hotel in the area, and it's worth its price – US$40/54/66 per single/double/triple. There's a restaurant on its top floor.

Sabana Grande Plenty of hotels dot Sabana Grande, many of which are concentrated on Prolongación Sur Av Las Acacias and neighboring streets. Perhaps 30 hotels are packed in a small area just minutes from Plaza Venezuela metro station.

Some of the cheapest hotels are on Calles El Colegio and San Antonio, but many double as love hotels. If you don't mind this, try the basic *Hotel Capri Casanova* (☎ 02-762-7270), on Calle San Antonio at Av Casanova, which has matrimoniales/doubles with fans for about US$14/18. Another basic option is *Hotel Tanausú* (☎ 02-793-1922), charging US$20/24 per double/triple, which also rents out rooms by the hour.

Across the street is the more respectable *Hotel Odeón* (☎ 02-793-1345), which has air-con matrimoniales/doubles/triples for US$26/30/36. Next door is the better *Hotel Gabial* (☎ 02-793-1156), which charges US$36/48 per matrimonial/double. There are a dozen others (including some love hotels) within a distance of 200m south along Prolongación Sur Av Las Acacias.

Hotel Cristal (☎ 02-761-9131) is not classy but is perfectly located on Boulevard

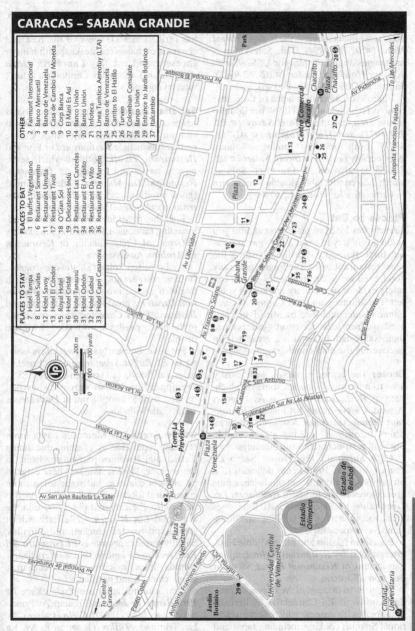

CARACAS – SABANA GRANDE

PLACES TO STAY

7 Hotel Tampa
8 Lincoln Suites
12 Hotel Savoy
13 Hotel El Cóndor
15 Royal Hotel
16 Hotel Cristal
30 Hotel Tanausú
31 Hotel Odeon
32 Hotel Gabiel
33 Hotel Capri Casanova

PLACES TO EAT

1 El Buffet Vegetariano
6 Restaurant Sorrento
17 Restaurant Urrutia
17 Restaurant Tivoli
18 O'Gran Sol
19 Delicatesses Indú
23 Restaurant Las Cancelas
34 Restaurant El Arabito
35 Restaurant Da Vito
36 Restaurant Da Marcelo

OTHER

2 Fairmont Internacional
3 Banco Mercantil
4 Banco de Venezuela
5 Casa de Cambio La Moneda
9 Corp Banca
10 El Mani Es Asi
14 Banco Unión
20 Banco Unión
21 Infoteca
22 Línea Turística Aereotuy (LTA)
24 Banco de Venezuela
25 Carritos to El Hatillo
26 Turven
27 Colombian Consulate
28 Banco Unión
29 Entrance to Jardín Botánico
37 Italcambio

de Sabana Grande and costs US$30 per double with air-con. Another convenient place near the boulevard, the tranquil *Royal Hotel* (☎ 02-762-5494), Calle San Antonio, has singles/doubles/triples for US$28/34/40. Also try *Hotel El Cóndor* (☎ 02-762-9911), 3a Av Las Delicias (US$34/40/46).

There's a reasonable choice of three-star options (costing roughly US$80 per double) in the area, including *Hotel Savoy* (☎ 02-762-1971) and *Hotel Tampa* (☎ 02-762-3771), both on Av Francisco Solano. Appreciably better is *Lincoln Suites* (☎ 02-762-8575), also on Av Francisco Solano, which has comfortable double suites with full amenities for around US$140.

Places to Eat

Caracas has loads of places to eat, and you could easily stay in town a full year and eat out three times a day without visiting the same restaurant twice. The food is generally good, even in the cheap eateries, so you can safely explore the culinary market by yourself. The annually updated *Caracas Gastronomic Guide*, published by Miro Popic and available from local bookstores, covers more than 600 restaurants and is a great help in discovering the local cooking scene.

Center The center is packed with mostly low- to mid-priced eateries, some of which, such as *Restaurant Sokol* on Av Fuerzas Armadas, serve hearty set lunches. *Restaurant Dama Antañona*, Jesuitas a Maturín, offers traditional cooking at reasonable prices in craft-decorated surroundings.

Café Sacro, in the Museo Sacro de Caracas at Plaza Bolívar, has delicious (if a bit pricey) fresh salads and sandwiches, plus great espresso. The top-floor *Restaurant Les Grisons* in the Plaza Catedral Hotel does local and international cooking, including some Swiss specialties.

For cheap felafels and other Middle Eastern fast food, try *Restaurant Kafta*, Esquina San Jacinto, or *Restaurant Beirut*, Salvador de León a Socarrás.

The area to the east of Av Fuerzas Armadas, known as La Candelaria, is literally swamped with *tascas*, which serve traditional Spanish cooking, including tapas and plenty of drinks. Some of the better tascas are marked on the Central Caracas map.

The budget *Pollo en Brasas El Coyuco*, Av Urdaneta, has good chicken and parrillas (grilled meats). Some of the best and cheapest cachapas (corncakes) with ham or cheese are at the tiny *Lunchería Doña Agapita*, off Plaza La Candelaria. Don't miss trying one.

Sabana Grande Sabana Grande boasts heaps of restaurants, cafés and snack bars to suit any budget and taste. Inexpensive restaurants include *Restaurant Da Vito* and *Restaurant Tivoli*, both of which serve mostly pasta and are on Av Casanova, *Restaurant Da Marcelo*, Calle Coromoto (good fixed menus), and *Restaurant Sorrento* (local cuisine), Av Francisco Solano.

For cheap Middle Eastern fast food, including tabbouleh, felafel and the like, try *O'Gran Sol*, Calle Villaflor, or *Restaurant El Arabito*, Av Casanova.

Av Francisco Solano shelters reasonable Italian restaurants and several Spanish tascas in addition to the upmarket *Restaurant Urrutia*, a great Basque restaurant, and *Restaurant Las Cancelas*, which has some of the better paellas in town (US$12 for two people).

For a vegetarian lunch (weekdays only) go to *El Buffet Vegetariano*, Av Los Jardines, La Florida (all you can eat for US$5). Try appetizing Indian veggie dishes (set meals are US$5) until 8 pm at *Delicatesses Indú*, Calle Villaflor.

Other Areas Las Mercedes has a long-standing reputation as a fashionable dining district that becomes particularly lively in the evening. Most restaurants here cater to an affluent clientele, but some serve more economical food, such as *Real Past*, Av Río de Janeiro, the cheapest pasta house in the area, and *Los Riviera*, Calle París, which serves spit-roasted chicken and parrillas. Slightly more expensive is *El Granjero del Este*, Av Río de Janeiro, which offers hearty comida típica, including arepas, cachapas, soups, chicken and parrillas.

Upmarket restaurants in the area are *Le Petit Bistrot de Jacques* (French), Av Principal de Las Mercedes, *Il Cielo* (Italian), Av La Trinidad, *Taiko* (Japanese), Av La Trinidad, and *Hereford Grill* (grilled beef), Calle Madrid.

Another area dotted with restaurants is Altamira and its neighboring suburbs of La Castellana and Los Palos Grandes. Commendable upscale restaurants here include **La Estancia** and **El Gran Charolais**, both on Av Principal de La Castellana and specializing in grilled meats: **Via Appia** (Italian), Av San Felipe; **El Barquero** (Spanish), Av Luis Roche; **Casa Juancho** (Spanish), Av San Juan Bosco; **El Alazán de Altamira** (steaks), Av Luis Roche, and **Hatsuhana** (Japanese), Av San Juan Bosco.

Entertainment

The Friday edition of *El Universal* carries a what's-on supplement called *La Brújula,* which covers museums, galleries, music, theater, cinemas and other cultural events. *Urbe,* a magazine published Wednesday, covers lighter entertainment, including cinema, pop music and nightspots.

For thought-provoking films, check the program of **Cinemateca Nacional,** Caracas' leading art cinema, in the Galería de Arte Nacional. **Ateneo de Caracas** and **Cine La Provisora** also feature arthouse films.

The Ateneo may also have something interesting in its theater, while the **Complejo Cultural Teresa Carreño** is the main venue for concerts and ballet. **Aula Magna,** in the Universidad Central de Venezuela, also has concerts, usually on Sunday morning.

Las Mercedes, El Rosal, Altamira and La Castellana are the scene of most nighttime entertainment. **Gran Pizzería El León,** at Plaza La Castellana, has a vast terrace that's a popular youth haunt for evening beer. **Weekends,** Av San Juan Bosco, is a North American-style short-order restaurant open until late, with pool, electronic games, darts, karaoke, music and videos.

Café L'Attico, Av Luis Roche, is an informal bar-restaurant and one of the trendiest places in town. It has good food (including North American fare), videos, music and usually great atmosphere.

Juan Sebastián Bar, Av Venezuela in El Rosal, also a bar-restaurant, is one of the few jazz spots in the city. Live jazz, performed by various groups, plays from afternoon till 2 am.

El Maní es Así, Av El Cristo, Sabana Grande, features hot live salsa for dancing, as does **O'Gran Sol,** a two-level restaurant on

Villaflor, next door to the food outlet of the same name, also in Sabana Grande. Similar is **El Solar del Vino** in La Castellana.

Boomker, Av Principal de Las Mercedes, is a large, multilevel disco, with a well-stocked bar, pool tables and all the bells and whistles. **Caramba,** Calle París, and **Ozono,** Calle Madrid, are other popular discos in Las Mercedes. **Magic Discotheque,** Calle Madrid, features lots of classics and oldies, attracting a more mature clientele than most. Also try **Khrôma,** 6a Av between 3a y 5a Transversal in Altamira or **Xanadú** at Plaza La Castellana.

Spectator Sports

Professional baseball league games are played October to February at the stadium in Universidad Central de Venezuela. The neighboring soccer stadium hosts major matches, most of which are held between December and March, with major events usually scheduled on Saturday evenings.

Caracas' horse racetrack, the Hipódromo La Rinconada, has racing on Saturday and Sunday afternoons from 1 pm on. The track is 6km southwest of the center, off the Caracas-Valencia freeway.

Getting There & Away

Air Simón Bolívar international airport is in Maiquetía on the Caribbean coast, 26km from central Caracas. It's linked to the city by a freeway with three tunnels cutting through the coastal mountain range. The airport has two separate terminals 400m apart, one for international and another for domestic flights.

The airport's international terminal has a tourist office, casas de cambio (among them Italcambio, which is open late), a Banco de Venezuela ATM, post and telephone offices and travel agencies. The domestic terminal doesn't have much apart from airline offices, car-rental companies and tour operators.

Avensa, Servivensa, Aeropostal, Air Venezuela and other domestic carriers cover major routes, including Barcelona (US$60 one way), Ciudad Bolívar (US$95), Ciudad Guayana (US$80), Coro (US$80), Maracaibo (US$75), Mérida (US$75), Porlamar (US$60), Puerto Ayacucho (US$75) and San Antonio del Táchira (US$95).

Bus The old Nuevo Circo terminal in the center has closed down; its services are now handled by two new bus terminals.

The Terminal de La Bandera, 2km south of the center near La Bandera metro station, handles all intercity runs to the west and southwest of the country, including Coro (US$14, seven hours), Maracaibo (US$21, 11 hours), Maracay (US$4, two hours), Mérida (US$23, 11 hours), San Antonio del Táchira (US$26, 14 hours) and San Cristóbal (US$24, 13 hours).

The Terminal de Oriente, on the eastern outskirts of Caracas on the highway to Barcelona, 5km beyond the suburb of Petare (accessible by local *carritos* – see Bus under Getting Around), handles all traffic to the east and southeast, including Barcelona (US$12, 4½ hours), Ciudad Bolívar (US$20, nine hours), Ciudad Guayana (US$23, 10½ hours), Cumaná (US$14, 6½ hours), Güiria (US$24, 11 hours) and Puerto La Cruz (US$12, five hours). All the fares given here are for air-con buses.

Getting Around

To/From the Airport There's half-hourly bus service between the airport in Maiquetía and Caracas. In the city, buses depart 5:30 am to 7 pm from Calle Sur 17, directly underneath Av Bolívar, next to Parque Central. There are no stairs connecting the two levels; get down to the buses by Calle Sur 17 from Av Mexico. Buses also depart from Gato Negro metro station. At the airport, buses leave from the front of the domestic and international terminals. The last bus is supposed to wait for the last incoming flight, which does not always happen.

The trip costs US$2 and normally takes about 45 minutes, but traffic jams, particularly on weekends and holidays, can double that time. If you are going from the airport to the city, it may be faster and more convenient to get off at Gato Negro metro station and continue by metro to your final destination.

A taxi from the airport to Caracas costs between US$20 and US$25. In order to avoid overcharging, check official tariffs before boarding a taxi – they are posted on the terminal's wall next to the taxi stand.

If you have just an overnight stop between flights in Maiquetía, it may be better to stay the night on the coast in Macuto (see Litoral Central in the Around Caracas section). Carritos to Macuto (US$0.75) pass by the road beyond the parking lot – get there by the passageway from the terminal's upper level. Taxis to Macuto shouldn't cost more than US$7.

After dark, don't venture outside the terminal anywhere farther than the bus stop and taxi stand (both are just at the building's doors).

Bus The bus network is extensive and covers all suburbs within the metropolitan area and some beyond. Small buses called *carritos* run frequently but may often be trapped in traffic jams. Use carritos only if going to destinations that are inaccessible by metro.

Metro The French-made metro is fast, well organized, easy to use and clean; it provides access to most major city attractions and tourist facilities. The metro system has three lines and 39 stations. The longest line, No 1, goes east-west all the way along the city axis. Line No 2 leads from the center southwest to the distant suburb of Caricuao and the zoo. The newest and shortest line, No 3, runs from Plaza Venezuela southwest to El Valle suburb, passing by the bus terminal at La Bandera. The system also includes a number of bus routes, called metrobus, that link some of the suburbs to metro stations. Metro lines and metrobus routes are marked on a Caracas map posted in every metro station.

The metro operates 5:30 am to 11 pm daily. Yellow-colored tickets cost US$0.50 for a ride up to three stations away from your starting point, US$0.55 for four to seven stations and US$0.60 for any longer route. The transfer ticket *(boleto integrado)* for the combined metro-plus-bus route costs US$0.65. Consider buying the *multiabono*, an orange ticket costing US$4.50 valid for 10 metro rides of any distance. Not only do you save money, but you also avoid lines at the ticket counters.

Bulky packages are not allowed in the metro. Small to mid-size backpacks are usually no problem, but large suitcases may be. Use common sense and don't carry bulky bags, at least during rush hours. The metro is generally safe, though be careful of pick-pockets operating in groups on the escalators of some busy stations.

AROUND CARACAS

El Hatillo

A small, old town 15km southeast of the center, El Hatillo is today an outer city suburb. Centered around Plaza Bolívar, it retains some of its colonial architecture. The plaza's **parish church** has preserved its exterior pretty well, but the interior has been radically modernized. Restored central houses have been painted in bright colors, giving the place an attractive and lively look.

El Hatillo has become a trendy getaway for *caraqueños* and is packed with cars and people on weekends. Every second house is either an eating establishment or a handicrafts shop. Frequent carritos run to El Hatillo from Av Humboldt, just off Boulevard de Sabana Grande.

Parque Nacional El Ávila

This national park is a steep, verdant mountain that looms just to the north of Caracas. The park encompasses about 90km of the range running east-west along the coast and separating the city from the sea. The highest peak is Pico Naiguatá (2765m).

The southern slope, overlooking Caracas, is uninhabited but is crisscrossed with walking trails. The northern face, running down to the sea, is dotted with hamlets and haciendas, but few tourist trails. The park is crossed north to south by a few jeepable tracks and the inoperable *teleférico* (cable car).

Built by a German company in 1956-57, the cable car was closed down in 1988, but there have been talks about privatizing the facility, which might lead to its reopening. The area around Pico El Ávila offers breathtaking views of Caracas and the Caribbean coast.

El Ávila is one of the best places in the country for walkers. There are about 200km of walking trails, most of them well signposted. Most camping grounds in the park are equipped with sanitary facilities.

A dozen entrances lead into the park from Caracas; all originate from Av Boyacá, commonly known as Cota Mil, as it runs at an altitude of 1000m. All routes have a short ascent before reaching a guard post, where you pay a nominal entrance fee. The *guardaparques* (rangers) may provide information about routes. Before you come, buy the useful *Mapa para el Excursionista – Parque Nacional El Ávila* (scale 1:40,000; look for it at Caracas or local bookstores), which has marked trails and camping facilities.

Options abound for half- and full-day hikes. A popular destination is Pico El Ávila – at least four routes lead there. Start early as it gets pretty hot by mid-morning. If you are prepared to camp, probably the most scenic route is the two-day hike to Pico Naiguatá. Take rain gear, warm clothes, water (scarce in the park) and plastic bags (for bringing your rubbish back down). The dry season is December to April, but even then there may be some rains in the upper reaches.

Litoral Central

The north face of El Ávila slopes steeply into the sea, leaving a narrow, flat strip of land between the foothills and the shore referred to as Litoral Central. The area is well urbanized and densely populated, with perhaps 400,000 people living in towns lining the waterfront. From west to east, the major urban centers are Catia La Mar, Maiquetía, La Guaira, Macuto, Caraballeda and Naiguatá. The first two towns sit at opposite ends of the airport and have little charm. La Guaira is a busy Caracas port, while the other three are popular seaside resorts for caraqueños, who come here en masse on weekends. Further east, the holiday centers thin out, though the paved road continues for another 20km to Los Caracas.

The coast is dramatic and spectacular (especially from Naiguatá to Los Caracas), but not particularly good for bathing. The shore is rocky and there are only short stretches of beach (good wild beaches begin east of Los Caracas). The straight coastline is exposed to open-sea surf, and strong currents can make swimming dangerous. Most holiday activity is confined to *balnearios*, sections of beach with facilities, and private beach clubs. Macuto, Caraballeda and Naiguatá have balnearios, and there are a few more in between. An array of hotels and restaurants has sprung up along the waterfront, providing an adequate choice of comfortable beds and good fried fish.

If you like seaside ambiance and want to escape from Caracas' rush, this might be an easy option. Also, if you fly through Maiquetía and have an overnight stop, it's probably better to stay here than in Caracas just for the night. Macuto is the most enjoyable town in the area and has the largest choice of places to stay, including a number of budget hotels. And you can visit the small **Museo Reverón**, on the grounds where a renowned painter, Armando Reverón (1889-1954), lived and worked.

Places to Stay & Eat Macuto has plenty of hotels, many of which are located on or just off Paseo La Playa, a 600m waterfront promenade. Reasonable places include *Hotel Diana* (☎ 031-461453), *Hotel Colonial* (☎ 031-461462), *Hotel Darimar* and *Hotel Plazamar*. Prices fluctuate, rising at weekends, but you shouldn't pay more than US$25 for a double in any of these. There are some cheaper but basic places around. The promenade is swamped with restaurants and snack bars.

Getting There & Away Regular carritos go from Caracas to Macuto; many go all the way up to Caraballeda. The fare is around US$1.50.

Colonia Tovar

This unusual mountain town sits at an altitude of 1800m amid lush cloud forest of the Cordillera de la Costa, about 60km west of Caracas. It was founded in 1843 by a group of 376 German settlers from the Black Forest who arrived during Venezuela's search for immigrants to cultivate the land devastated by independence wars.

Effectively isolated by a lack of roads and internal rules prohibiting marriage outside the colony, the village followed its mother culture, language and architecture for a century. Only in the 1940s was Spanish introduced as the official language and the ban on marrying outside the community abandoned. It was not until 1963 that a sealed road reached Colonia Tovar from Caracas, marking a turning point in the history of the town, which by then had a mere 1300 souls.

Today, Colonia Tovar has five times as many inhabitants and is a tourist town. Caraqueños curious to see a bit of old Germany lost in the Venezuelan mountains come on weekends to glimpse the German-style architecture; enjoy a German meal; buy bread or sausage made according to traditional recipes; and sample delicious strawberries, apples, peaches and blackberries cultivated locally.

They also call at the Museo de Historia y Artesanía (open weekends only) for a taste

of the town's history, and visit the local church, a curious L-shaped building with two perpendicular naves (one for women, the other for men) and the high altar placed in the angle where the naves join.

On weekends the town is swamped with visitors and cars; on weekdays it's almost dead, and many restaurants are closed. Whenever you come, though, take some warm clothing.

Places to Stay & Eat By and large, accommodations are good and stylish, but not cheap by Venezuelan standards, with rates starting at US$25 per double. Private bath and hot water are the norm, and some place also have heated rooms. Many hotels offer full board.

Hotel Selva Negra (☎ 033-51415) is the oldest and the best-known lodge in town. Built in the 1930s, it has about 40 cabañas of different sizes holding two to six guests and costing US$50 for two people plus US$10 for each additional person. The old-style *restaurant* is in the original house.

Cheaper options (about US$30 to US$40 per double) include *Hotel Edelweiss* (☎ 033-51260), *Hotel Drei-Tannen* (☎ 033-51246) and *Hotel Bergland* (☎ 033-51229). Still cheaper are *Cabañas Breidenbach* (☎ 033-51211), *Residencias Baden* (☎ 033-51151) and *Cabañas Silberbrunnen* (☎ 033-51490).

Getting There & Away The trip from Caracas to Colonia Tovar requires a change at El Junquito. Carritos to El Junquito (US$0.75) depart from the corner of Av Lecuna and Calle Sur 9, just south of the Nuevo Circo bullring. From El Junquito, por puestos take you the remainder of the journey (US$0.80). The whole trip takes about two hours.

Instead of returning to Caracas the same way, you can take an exciting ride south down to La Victoria. Over a distance of only 34km, the road descends about 1250m. Por puestos depart from Colonia Tovar several times a day; the ride takes one hour and costs US$1. There's regular bus transport from La Victoria to both Caracas and Maracay.

Archipiélago Los Roques

Los Roques is a beautiful archipelago of small coral islands lying about 150km north of Litoral Central. Stretching 36km east to west and 25km north to south, it consists of some 40 islands big enough to deserve a name and perhaps 250 other islets, sandbars and cays. The soft, white-sand beaches are clean and lovely, although shadeless, and the coral reefs are a paradise for snorkeling and scuba diving. The archipelago is a national park, and all visitors pay a US$12 entry fee.

Gran Roque, on the northern edge of the archipelago, is the main island and transport hub. It has a fishing village of about 1200 people, an airstrip and a wharf. From here you can visit the nearby islands, either in a local's fishing boat or on a tour. Bring enough local currency – there are no money exchange facilities.

Organized Tours The usual way of visiting the archipelago is by tour. Tours are run by several small airlines, including Rutaca, AeroEjecutivos, Chapi Air and Línea Turística Aereotuy (LTA), all of which have desks at the domestic terminal of the airport in Maiquetía. LTA is the major (and possibly the best) operator and has a main office in Caracas (☎ 02-761-9782), Edificio Gran Sabana, Boulevard de Sabana Grande.

The one-day tour includes the return flight, a boat excursion from Gran Roque to nearby islands, lunch, soft drinks, one hour of snorkeling (equipment provided) and free time on the beach and costs about US$150. The two-day tour includes accommodations in Gran Roque, meals, and it costs US$200 to US$300.

Places to Stay & Eat There are already more than 40 posadas in Gran Roque, providing about 300 beds. Most of them are small and simple, offering both lodging and dining. Food is expensive and limited, as everything, except fish, has to be shipped from the mainland. Be prepared to pay at least US$30 for a bed plus breakfast and dinner. Among the cheapest places are *Posada Doña Carmen*, *Posada Doña Magalys*, *Posada Roquelusa* and *Posada La Lagunita*.

Camping is allowed on Gran Roque and the nearby islands; get a free camping permit from the Inparques office in the village. Fishing boats can take you to the island of your choice and pick you up at a prearranged time the same day or on a later date. If you plan on camping on any island

other than Gran Roque, take food and water. Bring along snorkeling gear and good sun protection – there's almost no shade on the islands.

Getting There & Away Airlines that organize tours to Los Roques also offer flight-only service – about US$110 roundtrip from Maiquetía. LTA offers budget one-way fares of US$35 on afternoon flights to Los Roques and on morning flights to Maiquetía. In effect, you fly roundtrip for US$70, but two-night accommodations in Gran Roque can easily eat the savings on the fare unless you are camping.

There's no passenger boat service to Los Roques. Talk to the fishermen in La Guaira port, or ask around the marinas in Caraballeda and Naiguatá.

The Northwest

Venezuela's northwest shelters such diverse natural features as coral islands, beaches, rain forests, the country's only desert (near Coro) and South America's largest lake, Lago Maracaibo. The region combines the traditional with the contemporary, from living Indian cultures (such as that of the Guajiros) and colonial heritage (in Coro) to the modern city of Maracaibo. Favorite travel destinations in the region are the national parks of Henri Pittier and Morrocoy. Administratively, the northwest encompasses the states of Aragua, Carabobo, Yaracuy, Lara, Falcón and Zulia.

MARACAY

The capital of Aragua state, Maracay is a thriving city of about 500,000 people. It was founded in 1701, but its growth only really came with the rule of Juan Vicente Gómez (1908-35), an enduring and ruthless caudillo. He made Maracay his home and commissioned a number of projects, including the government house, a bullring, an aviation school, an opera house, a zoo and his own mausoleum.

Maracay is not a top not-to-be-missed destination, but has some attractions and a number of parks, including Venezuela's largest Plaza Bolívar. The city is a gateway to the Parque Nacional Henri Pittier (see that section).

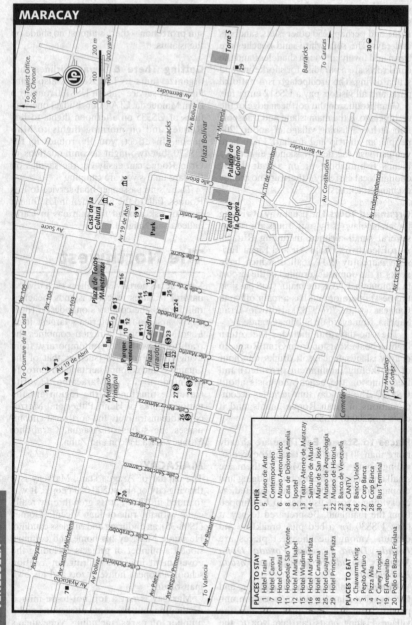

MARACAY

PLACES TO STAY
1   Hotel Traini
7   Hotel Caroní
10 Hotel Central
11 Hospedaje São Vicente
12 Hotel María Isabel
15 Hotel Wladimir
16 Hotel Mar del Plata
18 Hotel Canaima
25 Hotel Guayana
29 Hotel Princesa Plaza

PLACES TO EAT
2   Chawarma King
3   Pepito Arturo
4   Pizza Mía
17 Carey Tropical
19 El Arepanito
20 Pollo en Brasas Friulana

OTHER
5   Museo de Arte
    Contemporáneo
6   Museo Aeronáutico
8   Casa de Dolores Amelia
9   Ipostel
13 Teatro Ateneo de Maracay
14 Santuario de Madre
    María de San José
21 Museo de Arqueología
22 Museo de Historia
23 Banco de Venezuela
24 CANTV
26 Banco Unión
27 Corp Banca
28 Corp Banca
30 Bus Terminal

Information

The tourist office is in Edificio Fundaragua, in La Soledad district, north of the city center. Most of the useful banks are within a few blocks of Plaza Girardot – see the map for locations.

Things to See

The **Plaza Girardot**, the historic heart of Maracay, features the fair-size **Catedral**, completed in 1743. The south side of the plaza is occupied by an arcaded building, erected by Gómez as the seat of government. Today, it houses the **Museo de Historia** and the **Museo de Arqueología**.

One block east of the plaza is the **Santuario de Madre María de San José**, probably the most revered and visited city sight. Madre María (1875-1967), a Choroní-born nun who dedicated her life to service for the poor, was beatified in 1995 by a papal bull. Her remains were exhumed and, to everybody's surprise, the corpse was allegedly intact. You can see it in a crystal sarcophagus in the Santuario (though the face is covered with a mask). Just to the north is the large Spanish-Moorish **Plaza de Toros Maestranza**, modeled on the one in Seville and built in 1933; it's possibly the most stylish and beautiful bullring in the country.

Two blocks east, the **Museo Aeronáutico** has about 40 aircraft dating from the 1910s to the 1950s, mostly military planes that once served in the Venezuelan Air Force. There's also a replica of the famous Jimmie Angel's plane (see the Angel Falls section). The museum is only open on weekends; if you happen to come on a weekday, inquire at the side gate at the end of Av Santos Michelena and somebody may show you around. Nearby, the **Museo de Arte Contemporáneo** stages temporary exhibitions of modern art.

At the northern city limits is the **Parque Zoológico**, which features many animals typical of Venezuela. Take the Castaño-Zoológico carrito from the city center.

Places to Stay

Several budget hotels are right in the city center, of which the basic **Hospedaje São Vicente** is one of the cheapest options, costing US$10/12 for matrimoniales/doubles with fan and shared facilities. If you'd like a private bath, choose between **Hotel Guayana**, **Hotel Central** and **Hotel María**

Isabel, all of which are basic and cost about US$13/16 per matrimonial/double.

Hotel Canaima (☎ 043-338278) is one of the cheapest places with air-con rooms (US$15/18 for matrimoniales/doubles) but nothing special. Better is the quiet *Hotel Mar del Plata* (☎ 043-464313), which costs US$18/22.

More comfortable central options include *Hotel Traini* (☎ 043-455502), the *Hotel Wladimir* (☎ 043-461115), and *Hotel Caroní* (☎ 043-541817), each of which costs about US$25/30/35 for air-con singles/doubles/triples. More upmarket is *Hotel Princesa Plaza* (☎ 043-332357), near Plaza Bolívar, which charges around US$50 per double.

Places to Eat

Some of the cheapest local meals are to be found in *Mercado Principal*. *Caney Tropical* has tasty, inexpensive local cuisine, including arepas. *El Arepanito* is also good for local food and is open late.

Pizza Mía has some of the better budget pizzas in the center. *Pepito Arturo*, across the road, offers parrillas and batidos. Next door, *Chawarma King* serves felafel, kibbeh and the like. *Pollo en Brasas Friulana* is the place for chicken.

Getting There & Away

The bus terminal is on the southeastern outskirts of the city center. It's vast and handles frequent transport to most major cities. Buses to Caracas depart every 10 or 15 minutes (US$4, two hours) as do buses to Valencia (US$1, 45 minutes).

PARQUE NACIONAL HENRI PITTIER

This is Venezuela's oldest national park, created in 1937. It stretches from the Caribbean coast in the north to almost as far south as the Valencia-Caracas freeway and the city of Maracay. The park covers part of the Cordillera de la Costa, the coastal mountain range that exceeds 2000m in some areas.

Given the wide range in elevation, there's a variety of habitats in the park, including semidry deciduous woods; evergreen rain forest; lush cloud forest; arid coastal scrub and mangroves; and, accordingly, a diverse animal world. The park is particularly famous for its birds; about 600 species have been identified here – about 43% of the bird species found in Venezuela.

Orientation

Two roads, both sealed, cross the park from north to south. The western road leads from Maracay to Ocumare de la Costa and continues on to Cata; it ascends to 1128m at Paso Portachuelo. The eastern road heads from Maracay north to Choroní and reaches the coast 2km farther on at Puerto Colombia. It's narrower, poorer and more twisting, but it climbs up to 1830m and is more spectacular. Both roads are about 55km long. There's no road connection between the coastal ends of these roads; a rented boat is the only way to get from one end to the other.

The coast features rocky cliffs in some parts, interspersed with bays filled with coconut groves and bordered by beaches. The town of Puerto Colombia is the major destination, with boat-hire facilities and a choice of hotels and restaurants.

The park has something for nearly everyone, including beachgoers, bird-watchers, hikers, old-architecture buffs and fiesta lovers. Unless you are particularly interested in bird-watching, it's better to take the eastern road, which provides access to more attractions and leads along a more spectacular route.

Things to See & Do

Along the eastern road, stop in **Choroní**, a tiny colonial town with narrow streets lined with old pastel houses. The leafy Plaza Bolívar boasts a lovely parish church, Iglesia de Santa Clara, with a finely decorated interior. The feast of Santa Clara, the town's patron saint, is celebrated in August.

A 20-minute walk north will bring you to **Puerto Colombia**, the main travelers' haunt. Its major magnet is **Playa Grande**, a fine beach shaded by coconuts a five-minute walk east of town.

Boats from town take tourists to isolated beaches farther down the coast, such as **Playa Aroa** (US$30 roundtrip per boat), **Playa Chuao** (US$30) or **Playa Cepe** (US$40). From Playa Chuao, walk up a rough 4km track to the old village of **Chuao** surrounded by cocoa plantations. The town lives in almost complete isolation, with no road links to the outer world. Chuao has a very simple colonial church and is known for its Diablos Danzantes celebrations.

Drumbeats are an integral part of life in Chuzo and Puerto Colombia and can be heard year-round weekend nights and particularly during the Fiesta de San Juan on June 23 and 24. The pulsating beat immediately sparks dancing and the atmosphere is great.

The western road also leads to fine beaches, of which **Playa Cata** is the most popular and developed. Boats from Cata take tourists to the smaller but quieter **Playa Catita**, on the east side of the same bay. Farther east is the unspoiled and usually deserted **Playa Cuyagua**. It's accessible by a 2.5km sand track from the town of Cuyagua or by boat from Cata (US$30 roundtrip).

The highlight of the western road is the **Paso Portachuelo**, the lowest pass in the coastal mountain ridge. It's a natural corridor for migratory birds and insects flying inland from the sea (and vice versa) from such distant places as Argentina and Canada.

Close to the pass is the **Estación Biológica Rancho Grande**, a biological station run by the Universidad Central de Venezuela. An ecological path, traced through the forest behind the station, provides an opportunity to watch the wildlife, particularly birds (it's best to do it early in the morning and late in the afternoon). September and October are the best months for viewing migratory birds. You may also see monkeys, agoutis, peccaries, butterflies and snakes (wear proper boots).

Places to Stay & Eat

Accommodations and food are available in various areas, some of which are detailed below. You can camp free on the beaches, but never leave your tent unattended.

Puerto Colombia There are two dozen places to stay – everything from rock bottom to luxury – and locals often rent rooms if there's the demand. Prices usually rise on weekends and during major holidays (rates listed here are for off-peak times). Restaurants, too, are in good supply; fried fish is the local staple.

Budget places to stay include the simple but friendly *Posada Los Guanches* (☎ 043-911209), Calle Trino Rangel, close to the bus terminus; *Posada Playa Grande* (☎ 043-911054), above *Tasca Bahía*; the German-run *Posada Alfonso* (☎ 043-911037), Calle Morillo near the alcabala; and *Hostal Colonial* (☎ 043-911087), opposite the bus terminus. All charge around US$20 for a double with bath and fan.

Hotel Alemania (☎ 043-911157) and *Posada Don Miguel* (☎ 043-911081), near each other on Calle Morillo, are slightly better options costing around US$26 per double. Colonial-style *Hospedaje La Montañita* (☎ 043-911132), Calle Morillo just off the waterfront, has doubles for US$32. For a little more, you can stay in the small and quiet *Posada La Parchita* (☎ 043-911259), Calle Trino Rangel.

Puerto Colombia also has a choice of fine upmarket hotels, including the beautiful colonial *Hacienda El Portete* (☎ 043-911255).

Choroní The town has few tourist facilities apart from two pleasant colonial hotels on the main street: *Hostería Río Mar*, which costs US$32 per double and has a restaurant; and the four-room *Posada Colonial Choroní*, which costs US$36 per person, breakfast included.

Playa Cata & Around Many people camp on the Cata beach, either in tents or swinging in hammocks from the palms. There are toilets and changing rooms, and stalls on the beach sell cooked meals and drinks.

There are several hotels back from the beach in El Playón, including the budget *Posada Los Bertis* and the more expensive *Hotel Montemar* (☎ 043-931173). One of the best is pleasant *Posada María Luisa* (☎ 043-931184) in Ocumare de la Costa, which costs about US$36 per bed plus breakfast and dinner.

Rancho Grande The biological station has simple dormitory-style lodging facilities, essentially intended for visiting researchers. Tourists can stay if there are vacancies but are charged a hefty US$14 per head. No camping is allowed and no food is provided, but there are plans to open a café. It's cheaper and more comfortable to stay in a budget hotel in Maracay and make a day trip.

Getting There & Away
The departure point for the park is the Maracay bus terminal. Buses to Ocumare de la Costa depart every hour 7 am to 5 pm (US$3, two hours). They can let you off at Rancho Grande (28km from Maracay), but will charge the full fare to Ocumare. From Ocumare, catch a carrito to Playa Cata (US$1, 15 minutes). To Puerto Colombia, buses leave every two hours (US$3, 2¼ hours). The last bus from both Ocumare and Puerto Colombia back to Maracay departs at 5 pm (later on weekends) but is not reliable.

PARQUE NACIONAL MORROCOY
This is one of the most popular parks for beaches and snorkeling. At the eastern edge of Falcón state, the park comprises a strip of the coast and the offshore area dotted with islands, islets and cays. Many islands are skirted with white-sand beaches and surrounded by coral reefs, though some of the coral has died, believed to be the result of a chemical leak from an oil refinery in 1996.

The most popular of the islands is Cayo Sombrero, which has fine coral reefs and some of the best beaches. Other places good for snorkeling include Cayo Borracho, Cayo Peraza, Playa Mero and Playuela.

Morrocoy is also noted for its variety of wading and water birds, including ibis, herons, cormorants, ducks, pelicans and flamingos.

Orientation
The park lies between the towns of Tucacas and Chichiriviche, which are its main gateways. **Tucacas** is an ordinary, hot town on the Valencia-Coro highway, with nothing to keep you here for long. With the park just a stone's throw away, though, the town is quickly developing into a holiday center and has hotels and other facilities. The nearest island that is part of the park, Cayo Punta Brava, is over the bridge from the town's waterfront, and a 15-minute walk from the bridge will bring you to a good palm-shaded beach.

To visit other islands of the park, go to the *embarcadero* (wharf) close to the bridge, from where boats can take you for a trip along *caños* (channels) through mangroves or to one of the many islands. Boats take up to eight people and charge the same for one as for eight. Popular destinations include Cayo Sombrero (US$60 roundtrip), Playa Paiclás (US$30), Playa Mero (US$35) and Playuela (US$35). Boats will pick you up from the island in the afternoon or on a later date. Weekdays during the off-season, you can usually beat the price down.

Another popular gateway to the park is **Chichiriviche**, which provides access to neighboring cays. The town is smaller than Tucacas but equally unattractive. Boats depart from the wharf at the end of Av Zamora, the main street. As in Tucacas, the boat takes a maximum of eight passengers and the fare is per boat, regardless of the number aboard. Return fare to the closest cays, such as Cayo Muerto, Cayo Sal or Cayo Pelón, is about US$25, whereas return fare to the farthest cays, such as Cayo Borracho, Cayo Sombrero or Cayo Pescadores, is about US$45. The return time is up to you, and haggling over the price is also possible.

Information

Neither Tucacas nor Chichiriviche have tourist offices, but you can get information from staff at travelers' hotels and from Varadero Tours on Av Libertador in Tucacas (☎ 042-834745) and on Av Zamora in Chichiriviche (☎ 042-86919).

Useful banks include Banco Unión in Tucacas (which gives cash advances on Visa and MasterCard) and Banco Industrial de Venezuela in Chichiriviche (which changes cash and gives cash advances on Visa). Some travel agencies and other establishments may change your dollars and traveler's checks at poor rates.

The Inparques office (☎ 042-830069) is close to the bridge in Tucacas.

Activities

Recommended scuba-diving operators are Submatur (☎ 042-830082), on Calle Ayacucho in Tucacas, and Agua-Fun Diving (☎ 042-86265), on Calle El Sol in Chichiriviche.

Snorkeling gear can be rented from many tour and boat operators and hotel managers for about US$7 per day. Some hotels have their own boats or have arrangements with the boat owners and offer beach, snorkeling and bird-watching excursions.

Places to Stay & Eat

Islands With a tent or a hammock and a mosquito net, you can stay on the islands; without one of these, you'll be limited to one-day trips out of Tucacas or Chichiriviche. *Camping* is officially permitted on four islands – Sal, Sombrero, Muerto and Paiclás. All four have beach *restaurants* or *food kiosks*, but some may be closed week-

days in the slow season, so come prepared. Take sufficient fresh water, snorkeling gear, good sun protection and a reliable insect repellent.

Before you go camping, you have to contact the Inparques office in Tucacas and pay the camping fee of US$3 per person per night at Banco Unión in Tucacas or Banco Industrial de Venezuela in Chichiriviche.

Tucacas Most budget hotels are on Av Libertador, midway between the Morón-Coro road and the bridge. One of the cheapest is *Hotel La Esperanza* (☎ 042-830950), managed by a German, Norbert. Matrimoniales/doubles with bath and fan cost US$11/14.

Right across the road is the slightly more expensive *Posada de Carlos* (☎ 042-831493). Other budget places in the same area include *Hotel Oti Daly Mar* (☎ 042-831478), *Hotel La Suerte* (☎ 042-831332) and *Posada Johnatan* (☎ 042-830239), all costing about the same as Posada de Carlos. The Johnatan and La Suerte also have aircon matrimoniales for around US$26.

Belgian André Nahon, one of the Submatur instructors, runs the pleasant 10-room *Submar Inn* (☎ 042-831754). Good doubles/triples with bath and fan cost US$18/24, or you can sling your hammock for US$5. The place is beyond the Hospital of Tucacas on the unsafe side of the road and is unmarked. Don't look for it if you're arriving after dark; call the manager from the bus stop, and he'll probably come and accompany you to the hotel.

Budget restaurants include *Nuevo Tito*, on Calle Sucre close to the Hotel Johnatan, and *El Timón*, diagonally opposite Banco Unión.

Chichiriviche *Guest House América Mía* (☎ 042-86547), in the building of Banco Industrial de Venezuela, costs US$10 per person in doubles with bath and fan, and you can use the kitchen and fridge. The place is run by a helpful Argentine couple who also offer laundry service and organize boat trips.

The nearby *Residencia La Perrera* (☎ 042-86372), run by an Italian couple, is also good and friendly and costs the same as América Mía. Another pleasant family option is the Spanish-run *Villa Gregoria* (☎ 042-86359), Calle Mariño, one block north of Av Zamora. Singles/doubles/triples with bath and fan are US$15/22/30; rooms on the 1st floor are more attractive.

The basic *Hotel El Centro* (☎ 042-86906), near the waterfront is the cheapest place in town. The entrance is from the back of *Panadería El Centro* (which does good breakfast) on Av Zamora. Claustrophobic rooms cost US$7 per person. Next door is the unsigned *Habitaciones Rigoberto*, which offers better rooms with bath for US$7 a person.

Hotel Capri (☎ 042-86026), opposite the Panadería El Centro, is a reasonable air-con option, with matrimoniales/doubles/triples for US$22/32/40. *Hotel Caribana* (☎ 042-86837), offers similar standards and prices.

In the southern part of the town are the German-run *Posada Alemania* (☎ 042-86979), set in a pleasant coconut-palm garden (US$10 per person), and the dearer *Hotel Náutico* (☎ 042-86024) on the waterfront.

For budget food, try *El Juncal* or *Taberna de Pablo*, both on Av Zamora, or *Pizzería Casamare* on the waterfront. Among the better places are *Txalupa*, on the waterfront, and *Il Ristorante*, at the Hotel Capri.

Getting There & Away
Tucacas lies on the Valencia-Coro highway, and there are frequent buses to both Valencia (US$3, two hours) and Coro (US$6, four hours). Chichiriviche is 22km off the highway and is serviced by half-hourly *busetas* (small buses) from Valencia (US$4, 2½ hours).

There are no direct buses to Chichiriviche from Caracas or Coro. To get there from Caracas, take any of the frequent buses to Valencia (US$5, three hours) and change there. From Coro, take any bus to Valencia, get off in Sanare (the turnoff for Chichiriviche; US$5, 3¾ hours) and catch the Valencia-Chichiriviche buseta.

The last 12km stretch of the road to Chichiriviche runs along a causeway through mangrove swamps. The area is a favorite feeding ground for flamingos, which mostly gather here between August and January or February. November is usually the peak month, when up to 5000 birds can stay in the area.

CORO
Set at the base of the curiously shaped Península de Paraguaná, Coro is a pleasant, peaceful city of 140,000 people. It has some of the best colonial architecture in the country and a few good museums.

Founded in 1527, it was the first capital of the colony of Venezuela. Four years later, the Episcopal See, the first in the New World, was established in Coro. Despite its early and promising start, the town was almost deserted a century later and only revived thanks to trade with Curaçao and Bonaire during the 18th century. Most of its historic heritage dates from that time.

In 1993, Coro was made a World Heritage Site – Venezuela's only cultural site to appear on the UNESCO list (along with Canaima national park as the country's only natural site).

Information
The tourist office (☎ 068-511132) is on the pedestrian mall, Paseo La Alameda, just north of the cathedral.

Things to See
Construction on the massive, fortresslike **Catedral** began in the 1580s and was completed half a century later, making the church the oldest surviving one in Venezuela.

One block east, the **Museo de Arte de Coro**, in a beautiful colonial house, is a branch of the Caracas Museo de Arte Contemporáneo and, like its parent, focuses on modern art. Diagonally opposite, the **Museo de Arte Alberto Henríquez** also features modern art.

For insight into the colonial past, go to the **Museo de Coro Lucas Guillermo Castillo**, located in an old convent, which has an extensive collection of religious and secular art from the region and beyond. It's one of Venezuela's best museums of its kind. All visits are guided (in Spanish only) and the tour takes about an hour. Adjacent to the museum is the 18th-century **Iglesia de San Francisco**.

Across the street on a small plaza is the **Cruz de San Clemente**, said to be the cross used in the first mass celebrated after the foundation of the town. The 18th-century **Iglesia de San Clemente**, on the west side of the plaza, was laid out on the Latin-cross plan, one of the few examples of its kind in the country.

West across the street is the **Casa de los Arcaya**, noted for its long, tile-roofed balconies. The mansion houses the **Museo de**

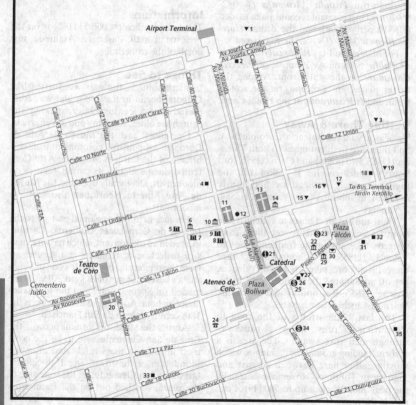

CORO

PLACES TO STAY
2   Hotel Miranda Cumberland
4   Posada Turística El Gallo
18   Hotel Intercaribe
26   Hotel Colonial
31   Hotel Martín
32   Hotel Roma
33   Posada Turística Manena
35   Apart Hotel Sahara

PLACES TO EAT
1   Il Ristorante Da Vicenzo
3   Pizzería La Barra del Jacal
15   Restaurant Casavieja
16   Pizzería Mersi
17   Comedor Popular
19   Panadería Costa Nova
27   Hostería Colonial
28   La Colmena

OTHER
5   Casa del Tesoro
6   Casa de las Ventanas de Hierro
7   Casa de los Soto
8   Casa Nazaret
9   Casa del Sol
10   Casa de los Arcaya, Museo de
     Cerámica Histórica y Loza Popular
11   Iglesia de San Clemente
12   Cruz de San Clemente
13   Iglesia de San Francisco
14   Museo de Coro Lucas
     Guillermo Castillo
20   Iglesia de San Nicolás de Bari
21   Tourist Office
22   Museo de Arte de Coro
23   Banco Federal
24   Public Telephones
25   Banco de Venezuela

29   Museo de Arte Alberto Henríquez
30   Ipostel
34   Banesco

0   100   200 m
0   100   200 yards

Cerámica Histórica y Loza Popular, which features pottery and ceramics. One block west, the Casa de las Ventanas de Hierro, noted for a splendid 8m plaster doorway, shelters a private collection of historic objects. The Casa del Tesoro houses an art gallery.

The Cementerio Judío, three blocks west along Calle Zamora, was established in the 1830s and is the oldest Jewish cemetery still in use in South America. It's normally locked and the keys are kept in the Museo de Coro Lucas Guillermo Castillo – inquire there.

Northeast of the town spreads the Médanos de Coro, a unique mini-Sahara with sandy dunes rising up to 30m, now a national park. To get there from the city center, take the city bus marked 'Carabobo' and get off past the huge Monumento a la Federación. Then, walk 10 minutes north along a wide avenue to another public sculpture, Monumento a la Madre. A few paces north, there is nothing but sand. Some cases of armed robbery have been reported here, so don't go alone and keep on guard.

About 4.5km west of the Monumento a la Federación, on the road to La Vela de Coro, is the Jardín Xerófilo, a well-kept xerophytic botanical garden. To get there, take the La Vela bus from Calle Falcón anywhere east of Av Manaure.

Places to Stay

The best budget place is the friendly *Posada Turística El Gallo* (☎ 068-529801), Calle Federación 26, which offers matrimoniales (US$12) and dorms (US$6 per bed), kitchen facilities, bike rental and tours. Alternatively, try *Posada Turística Manena* (☎ 068-516615), Calle Garcés 119, where all rooms have private baths (some with air-con), but are more expensive – a matrimonial with fan/air-con costs about US$16/24.

Three budget hotels in the center, *Hotel Colonial*, *Hotel Martín* and *Hotel Roma* are basic, filthy and run-down; they are best avoided.

Hotel Intercaribe (☎ 068-511844), Av Manaure, offers more comfort and facilities, including TV, for US$30/40/55 singles/doubles/triples. *Apart Hotel Sahara* (☎ 068-527113), on Calle Bolívar, costs about US$34/46/60.

Hotel Miranda Cumberland (☎ 068-522111), opposite the airport, is the best

place in town (US$80 per double), with a restaurant, bar, pool and sauna.

Places to Eat

Some of the cheapest meals can be had at lunchtime at the *Comedor Popular*, though don't expect much. On a similarly basic side are *Pizzería Mersi* and *Hostería Colonial*.

La Colmena, on Calle Comercio, serves better food in more pleasant surroundings, as does *Restaurant Casavieja*, Calle Zamora. Still better is the pleasant, open-air *Pizzería La Barra del Jacal*, on Calle Unión, which offers more than just pizzas. Or try the reasonable Italian *Il Ristorante Da Vicenzo*, across from Hotel Miranda Cumberland.

For breakfast, go to *Panadería Costa Nova*, opposite the Hotel Intercaribe, which is good and popular with locals.

Getting There & Away

Air The airport, a five-minute walk north of the city center, handles daily flights to Caracas (US$80); change there for other destinations. You can also use the busier Las Piedras airport, near Punto Fijo on the Paraguaná Peninsula, about 90km from Coro. From Las Piedras, Servivensa has daily flights to Aruba (US$68) and Curaçao (US$96).

From Coro airport, two small local carriers, Aerocaribe Coro (☎ 068-521837) and Aeroservicios Paraguaná (☎ 068-527626), fly light planes to Aruba and Curaçao (US$80 to either) provided they collect a minimum of three passengers.

Bus The bus terminal is on Av Los Médanos, about 2km east of the center, and is accessible by frequent city transport. Half a dozen buses run daily to Caracas (US$14, seven hours). There are a few direct buses per day to Mérida (US$21, 12 hours) via Maracaibo. Buses to Maracaibo (US$8, four hours) run every half-hour until 5 or 6 pm.

MARACAIBO

Although the region around Maracaibo was explored as early as 1499 and Maracaibo itself was founded in 1574, the town only began to grow in the 18th century as a port engaged in trade with the Netherlands Antilles. The republicans' naval victory over the Spanish fleet, fought on Lago Maracaibo in 1823, brought the town some political importance. It was not, however, until 1914 that the first oil well, Zumaque No 1, was sunk in the area and the oil boom took off. Maracaibo has developed into Venezuela's oil capital, with two-thirds of the nation's output coming from beneath the lake.

With a population of about 1.4 million, Maracaibo is today the country's largest urban center after Caracas, and it's a predominantly modern, prosperous city. Its climate is hot, humid and often windless, with an average temperature of 30°C (86°F) which is among the highest in the country.

Maracaibo doesn't rank high among tourist destinations, and there's not much to see. However, you may need to stop here on the way to the Colombian coast. If you have more time, you can explore the surrounding region, which offers some attractions, from a community living in houses on stilts on Laguna de Sinamaica to forests of oil derricks on Lago Maracaibo.

Information

Tourist Offices The Corpozulia tourist office (☎ 061-921811, 061-921840) is on Av Bella Vista between Calles 83 and 84, about 2km north of the city center; the Bella Vista por puestos from Plaza Bolívar will take you there.

Money There are several casas de cambio in the bus terminal that change Venezuelan bolívares into Colombian pesos and vice versa; some also exchange US dollars.

Things to See

If you are in Maracaibo in transit, you probably won't go far beyond downtown, the oldest part of the city. The axis here is the **Paseo de las Ciencias**, a wide greenbelt seven blocks long, made after demolishing old buildings and establishing a park.

At the western end of the paseo is the **Basílica de Chiquinquirá**, with its opulent interior decor. In the high altar is the venerated image of the Virgin of Chiquinquirá, to whom numerous miracles are attributed. Pilgrims flock here year-round, but the major celebrations are held for a full week in November, culminating in a procession on the 18th.

The eastern end of the paseo is bordered by **Plaza Bolívar**, which has the usual Bolívar statue in the middle and a 19th-century **Catedral** on the east side. To the north is the **Casa de la Capitulación**, also known as Casa Morales, where, in 1823, the act of capitulation was signed by the Spanish defeated in the naval battle of Lago Maracaibo, sealing the independence of Gran Colombia.

One block north is the **Museo Arquidiocesano** and farther north is the **Museo Antropológico**. Nearby to the west is **Museo Urdaneta**, dedicated to Maracaibo-born General Rafael Urdaneta, the city's greatest independence hero.

Calle 94 has been partly restored to its former appearance, notable for its brightly colored façades and grilled windows. The most spectacular part of the street is between Avs 6 and 8.

The sector south of the paseo is a wonder of heat, dirt and chaos. Many streets are occupied by vendors and stalls, making the area feel like a market. The most striking sight here is the imposing old market building, restored and reopened as the **Centro de Arte de Maracaibo**.

The most popular tourist sight around Maracaibo is the **Laguna de Sinamaica**, 60km north of the city, noted for lakeside hamlets whose inhabitants live in *palafitos*, houses built on piles on or off the lakeshore. Perhaps it was here that in 1499 the Spaniards first saw Indians in similar houses and gave Venezuela its name. Pleasure boats take tourists for a trip around the lagoon (US$30 per boat for up to six people). To get there from Maracaibo, take a bus heading for Guane or Los Filuos, get off in the town of Sinamaica (US$2, two hours), and take a por puesto to Puerto Cuervito (US$0.40, 10 minutes).

Places to Stay

If you're just trapped for the night in the city, there are several basic and overpriced hotels on the west side of the bus terminal, including *Hotel San Diego* and *Hotel Caroní*. The historic center has very little to offer as far as accommodations go. The cheapest hotels here, such as *Hotel Santa Ana*, *Hotel Coruña* and *Hotel Aurora No 2*, rent rooms by the hour and are really basic. Book into the *Hotel El Milagro*

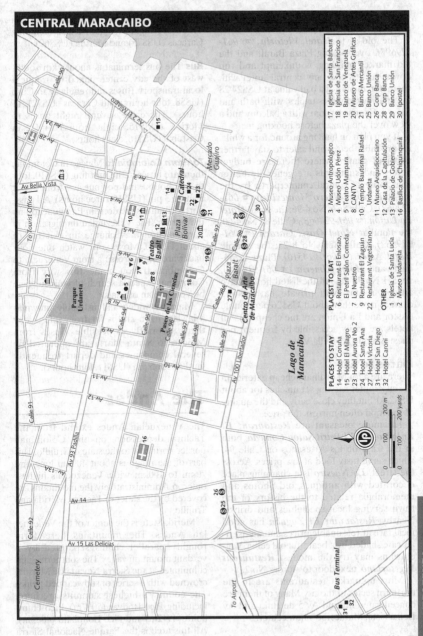

CENTRAL MARACAIBO

Av 2E J Villalobos
Av 2A
Av 2B
Av 3
Av Bella Vista
To Tourist Office
Av 3A
Mercado Guajiro
Catedral
Plaza Bolívar
Teatro Baralt
Parque Urdaneta
Paseo de las Ciencias
Plaza Baralt
Centro de Arte de Maracaibo
Lago de Maracaibo
Av 4
Av 4A
Av 5
Av 6
Av 7
Av 8
Av 9
Av 94
Av 95
Calle 94
Calle 95
Calle 96
Calle 97
Calle 98
Calle 99
Calle 98
Calle 99
Calle 91
Calle 92
Calle 93 Padilla
Av 10
Av 11
Av 12
Av 13
Av 13A
Av 14
Av 15 Las Delicias
Av 100 Libertador
Cemetery
Bus Terminal
To Airport

N

0   100   200 m
0   100   200 yards

PLACES TO STAY
14 Hotel Coruña
15 Hotel El Milagro
23 Hotel Aurora No 2
24 Hotel Santa Ana
27 Hotel Victoria
31 Hotel San Diego
32 Hotel Caroní

PLACEST TO EAT
6   Restaurant El Enlosao,
    El Petril Salón Comeda
9   Lo Nuestro
9   Restaurant El Zaguán
22 Restaurant Vegetariano

OTHER
1   Iglesia de Santa Lucía
2   Museo Urdaneta
3   Museo Antropológico
4   Museo Udón Pérez
5   Teatro Mampara
8   CANTV
10 Templo Bautismal Rafael
    Urdaneta
11 Museo Arquidiocesano
12 Casa de la Capitulación
13 Palacio de Gobierno
16 Basílica de Chiquinquirá
17 Iglesia de Santa Bárbara
18 Iglesia de San Francisco
19 Banco de Venezuela
20 Museo de Artes Gráficas
21 Banco Mercantil
25 Banco Unión
26 Corp Banca
28 Corp Banca
29 Banco Unión
30 Ipostel

VENEZUELA

(☎ 061-228934), which is more reputable and charges US$28 a double.

The old-style *Hotel Victoria (☎ 061-229697)*, overlooking Plaza Baralt and the old market building, is unkempt and run down, yet it's the only central hotel with character and is not a bad value at US$24/28 for spacious doubles/triples with bath and air-con. Choose a room with a balcony and a view over the plaza before booking in.

If you plan on hanging around for a while, it's probably better and safer to stay farther north of center, where there are budget hotels and standards are generally better than those of central counterparts. Try the old-style *Hotel Nuevo Montevideo (☎ 061-222762)*, Calle 86A No 4-96; the small *Hotel La Unión (☎ 061-924068)*, Calle 84 No 4-60; the familiar *Hotel Oasis Garden (☎ 061-979582)*, Calle 82B No 8-25; the simple *Hotel Astor (☎ 061-914510)*, Plaza República; and *Hotel Almeria (☎ 061-914424)*, Av 3H No 74-78. All the listed hotels have air-con rooms with private bath. None charges more than about US$26 per double (Astor and La Unión are the cheapest). All hotels are easily accessible by frequent por puestos along Av Bella Vista.

Places to Eat

There are a lot of ordinary cheap eateries in the city center serving set lunches for about US$2.50, but they close early and the quality of the food often mirrors the price.

Far more pleasant are *Restaurant El Enlosao* and *El Petril Salón Comeda*, both in the Casa de los Artesanos on Calle 94, which serve tasty food at low prices. Across the street, *Lo Nuestro* is a charming place decorated with antiques, old photos and memorabilia related to the history of the town serving local specialties and drinks. Nearby, *Restaurant El Zaguán* has good local fare at reasonable prices and an open-air café shaded by a beautiful old ceiba. Vegetarians may try the modest *Restaurant Vegetariano*, next door to Aurora No 2.

Most upmarket restaurants are in the northern sector of the city. Many of them are concentrated around Av 5 de Julio and Av Bella Vista, Maracaibo's new center.

Getting There & Away

Air La Chinita airport is about 12km southwest of the city center. There's no public transport; a taxi will cost about US$10. There are flights to main cities, including Caracas (US$75) and Mérida (US$60).

Bus The bus terminal is about 1km southwest of the city center, linked by frequent local transport. Buses run regularly to Coro (US$8, four hours) and Caracas (US$21, 11 hours). There are several night buses to Mérida (US$15, eight hours) and San Cristóbal (US$16, eight hours).

To/From Colombia To Maicao in Colombia, there are buses in the morning (US$10, four to five hours) and por puestos from about 5 am to 3 pm (US$15, three hours). All passport formalities are done in Paraguachón on the border. The Venezuelan immigration in Paraguachón may charge an exit tax of about US$10. Move your watch one hour backward when crossing from Venezuela to Colombia. If you come this way from Colombia, expect a search of your luggage by Venezuelan officials.

Maicao is widely and justifiably known as a lawless town and is far from safe – stay there as briefly as possible. Buses from Maicao to Santa Marta are operated by several companies and depart frequently until about 5 pm (US$11, four hours).

The Andes

The Venezuelan Andes extend from the Táchira depression on the Colombian border northeast to the state of Trujillo. This part of the range is about 400km long and 70km to 100km wide, Venezuela's highest outcrop. Administratively, the mountains are covered by the states of Táchira, Mérida and Trujillo.

Mérida state is the center of the Venezuelan Andes. The mountains here form roughly parallel chains separated by a verdant mountain valley. The southern chain culminates at the Sierra Nevada de Mérida, crowned with a series of snowcapped peaks. The country's highest summits are here, including Pico Bolívar (5007m), Pico Humboldt (4942m) and Pico Bonpland (4883m). All this area is the Parque Nacional Sierra Nevada. The northern chain, the Sierra de la Culata, reaches 4660m and is also a national park. In the deep valley sits the city of

Mérida, the region's major urban center and the country's mountain capital.

The Andes are popular hiking territory, offering a spectrum of habitats from lush rain forest to the *páramos*, open highland moors that begin at about 3300m and stretch up almost to the snow line. The most characteristic plant here is the *frailejón* (espeletia), typical only of highland areas of Venezuela, Colombia and Ecuador. Frailejones are particularly spectacular when in bloom between November and December.

The dry season in the Venezuelan Andes lasts from December to April. May through June is a period of changeable weather with a lot of sunshine but also frequent rains (or snow at high altitudes). It is usually followed by a short, relatively dry period from late June to late July, before a long, really wet season begins. August to October is the wettest, during which hiking can be miserable and without many panoramic views. The snowy period (June to October) can be dangerous for mountaineering.

MÉRIDA

Mérida is arguably Venezuela's most popular destination among backpackers. It has an unhurried and friendly atmosphere, plenty of tourist facilities, the famous teleférico and beautiful mountains, with the country's rooftop, Pico Bolívar, just 12km away.

Home to the large Universidad de los Andes (Venezuela's second-oldest university), the city has a sizable academic community that gives it a cultured and bohemian air. Mérida enjoys a mild climate, with an average temperature of 19°C (66°F). It's inexpensive and reasonably safe by Venezuelan standards.

Mérida was founded in 1558, but its transition from a town into a city really only took place over the last few decades. It sits on a flat *meseta*, a terrace stretching for a dozen kilometers between parallel rivers, its edges dropping abruptly to the riverbanks. Having filled the meseta as densely as possible, Mérida is now expanding beyond it and is approaching 250,000 inhabitants.

Information

Tourist Offices The Cormetur tourist office (☎ 074-634877) is on Av Urdaneta near the airport. Cormetur operates several tourist information outlets, including one at the airport, one at the bus terminal and another in Parque Las Heroínas.

Most major tour companies (see Organized Tours) provide information about trekking, mountaineering and other activities.

Money The Corp Banca, on Av Las Américas outside the center, changes Amex traveler's checks. Banks generally do not exchange cash; do it at Italcambio at the airport (which also changes traveler's checks). Also ask tour agents and hotel managers where to change money.

Inparques The Inparques office (☎ 074-529876), Calle 19 No 5-44, issues permits for trekking. Another Inparques outlet at the cable car station does the same. You need a permit to stay in the mountains overnight; it costs US$1 per person plus US$2 per tent per night.

E-mail & Internet Access Arassari Trek's cybercafé (☎ 074-525879), Calle 24 No 8-301, is the best facility. Also try the Internet café on Calle 18 between Avs 5 and 6, or Natoura (☎ 074-524216), Calle 24 No 8-237.

Things to See & Do

Teleférico The highlight of a visit to Mérida is the teleférico, the world's highest and longest cable car, now running after a period of being out of order. It was constructed in 1958 by a French company and runs the 12.6km from Mérida to the top of Pico Espejo, covering the 3188m climb in four stages. There are five stations: Barinitas in Mérida (1577m), Montaña (2436m), Aguada (3452m), Loma Redonda (4045m) and Pico Espejo (4765m).

The cable car normally operates Tuesday to Sunday, though in tourist season it may run every day. The first trip up goes at 7:30 am and the last at 10 am (noon on weekends). The last trip down is about 2 pm but can be later in peak season. The roundtrip ticket from Mérida to Loma Redonda costs US$15, and the last stage from Roma Redonda to Pico Espejo is another US$10; there are no student discounts. Big backpacks are charged US$4 extra. The ascent to Pico Espejo takes about an hour if you go straight through. It's best to go up as early as possible, as clouds

VENEZUELA

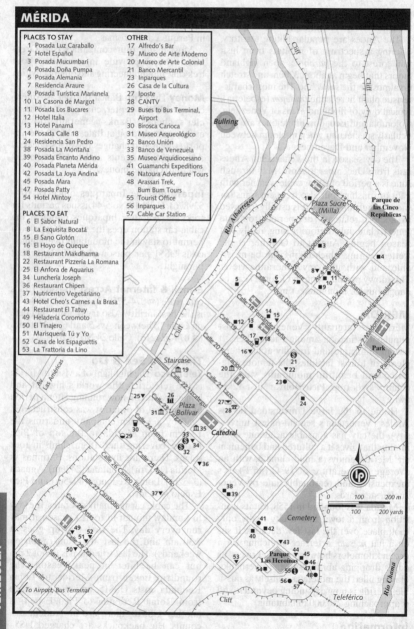

MÉRIDA

PLACES TO STAY
1 Posada Luz Caraballo
2 Hotel Español
3 Posada Mucumbarí
4 Posada Doña Pumpa
5 Posada Alemania
7 Residencia Araure
9 Posada Turística Marianela
10 La Casona de Margot
11 Posada Los Bucares
12 Hotel Italia
13 Hotel Panamá
14 Posada Calle 18
24 Residencia San Pedro
38 Posada La Montaña
39 Posada Encanto Andino
40 Posada Planeta Mérida
42 Posada La Joya Andina
45 Posada Mara
47 Posada Patty
54 Hotel Mintoy

PLACES TO EAT
6 El Sabor Natural
8 La Exquisita Bocatá
15 El Sano Glotón
16 El Hoyo de Queque
18 Restaurant Makdharma
22 Restaurant Pizzería La Romana
25 El Anfora de Aquarius
34 Lunchería Joseph
36 Restaurant Chipen
37 Nutricentro Vegetariano
43 Hotel Cheo's Carnes a la Brasa
44 Restaurant El Tatuy
49 Heladería Coromoto
50 El Tinajero
51 Marisquería Tú y Yo
52 Casa de los Espaguettis
53 La Trattoria da Lino

OTHER
17 Alfredo's Bar
19 Museo de Arte Moderno
20 Museo de Arte Colonial
21 Banco Mercantil
23 Inparques
26 Casa de la Cultura
27 Iposte
28 CANTV
29 Buses to Bus Terminal,
     Airport
30 Birosca Carioca
31 Museo Arqueológico
32 Banco Unión
33 Banco de Venezuela
35 Museo Arquidiocesano
41 Guamanchi Expeditions
46 Natoura Adventure Tours
48 Arassari Trek,
     Bum Bum Tours
55 Tourist Office
56 Inparques
57 Cable Car Station

usually obscure views later on. Don't forget to take warm clothes.

Apart from splendid views during the trip itself, the cable car provides easy access for high-mountain hiking, saving you a day or two of puffing uphill. Bear in mind, however, that acclimatization problems can easily occur by quickly reaching high altitudes.

Other Attractions The city center is quite pleasant for leisurely strolls, though there's not much in the way of colonial architecture or outstanding sights. Plaza Bolívar is the city's heart, but it's not a colonial square. Work on the **Catedral** was begun in 1800 but not completed until 1958. Next to it is the **Museo Arquidiocesano** (open Tuesday to Friday), with a collection of religious art. Note the bell cast in 909, thought to be the world's second-oldest surviving bell. Across the square, the **Casa de la Cultura** (open weekdays) hosts temporary exhibitions of local artists and craftspeople.

Universidad de los Andes, just off the square, houses the **Museo Arqueológico** (closed Monday). A small but interesting collection supported by extensive background information gives insight into pre-Hispanic times of the region.

The large and sparkling Complejo Cultural, one block north of the plaza, shelters Mérida's **Museo de Arte Moderno** (closed Monday). The **Museo de Arte Colonial** (closed Monday), two blocks northeast of the plaza, has a collection of mostly sacred art.

Organized Tours

Mérida is easily Venezuela's major center of active tourism. The region provides excellent conditions for hiking, mountaineering, rock climbing, bird-watching, paragliding and rafting, and local operators have been quick to make them accessible to visitors.

There are plenty of tour companies in Mérida and prices are reasonable. Mountain trips feature most prominently on operators' lists and include treks to Pico Bolívar and Pico Humboldt; expect to pay about US$35 to US$50 per person per day, all-inclusive.

The village of Los Nevados is probably the most popular destination among those who don't attempt to climb the peaks. Most companies offer trips there, but you can easily do it on your own. Tour companies

listed in this section will give you the details on how to do it and can arrange a jeep to Los Nevados without charging a commission. See Around Mérida for more about this trip.

The Sierra de la Culata is another attractive destination, available as a tour from most agents. It's a two- to three-day trip, costing around US$35 to US$50 per person a day, all-inclusive.

A worthwhile excursion out of Mérida is a wildlife safari in Los Llanos, Venezuela's greatest repository of wildlife, particularly birds. Several ecotourist camps in Los Llanos offer wildlife-watching tours on their ranches, but they are expensive (US$100 to US$150 per person daily). Mérida's companies organize similarly fascinating excursions for US$40 to US$60 per day. They are offered as three-to four-day all-inclusive packages.

The companies offer a lot of other destinations and activities, including mountain biking, paragliding, rock climbing, fishing and horseback riding. Some handle rental of mountaineering equipment, camping gear and bikes. Most will provide tourist information even if you don't plan on buying their services. Among the best local tour companies are:

Arassari Trek & Bum Bum Tours
    (☎ 074-525879; jvm.com/bumbum)
    Calle 24 No 8-301

Guamanchi Expeditions
    (☎ 074-522080; www.ftech.net/~geca)
    Calle 24 No 8-39

Natoura Adventure Tours
    (☎ 074-524216; www.natoura.com)
    Calle 24 No 8-237

Places to Stay

Mérida has heaps of places to stay and most are good values for the money. Most are posadas, family-run guesthouses, often with a friendly atmosphere. Many provide kitchen and laundry facilities.

One of the cheapest hotels in the city center is *Hotel Italia* (☎ 074-525737), Calle 19 No 2-55. It costs US$7/9 for a small, basic single/double without bath, US$10/12 with bath. Another ultrabudget option is *Hotel Panamá* (☎ 074-529156), Av 3 No 18-31. Matrimoniales/doubles/triples with bath are US$9/12/14.

It's more pleasant to stay in a posada. The cheapest places of that style include *Posada*

Mucumbarí (☎ *074-526015*), Av 3 No 14-73; *Posada Calle 18* (☎ *074-522986*), Calle 18 No 3-51; *Posada Patty* (☎ *074-525917*), Calle 24 No 8-265; *Posada Planeta Mérida* (☎ *074-522644*), Calle 24 No 8-14; *Posada Turística Marianela* (☎ *074-526907*), Calle 16 No 4-33; *Residencia San Pedro* (☎ *074-522735*), Calle 19 No 6-36; and *Residencia Araure* (☎ *074-525103*), Calle 16 No 3-34. All are clean and pleasant and cost US$5 to US$7 per head in doubles or triples with shared facilities.

For a little more, there's a wide choice of posada-style options, all with private bath and hot water. The cheapest (for about US$6 to US$9 per person) include *Posada La Joya Andina* (☎ *074-526055*), Calle 24 No 8-51, and *Posada Mara* (☎ *074-525507*), Calle 24 No 8-215. Better places include *Posada La Montaña* (☎ *074-525977*), Calle 24 No 6-47 (US$25 doubles); *Posada Encanto Andino* (☎ *074-526929*), Calle 24 No 6-53 (US$25/30/35 doubles/triples/quads); *Hotel Español* (☎ *074-529235*), Av 2 No 15-48 (spotlessly clean doubles for US$20); *Posada Luz Caraballo* (☎ *074-525441*), Av 2 No 13-80 (US$16/22/28 singles/doubles/triples); *Posada Los Bucares* (☎ *074-522841*), Av 4 No 15-05 (US$20/28 doubles/triples); *La Casona de Margot* (☎ *074-523312*), Av 4 No 15-17 (US$24/28/34 matrimoniales/triples/quads); *Posada Alemania* (☎ *074-524067*), Av 2 near the corner of Calle 18 (US$22/28 doubles/triples); and *Posada Doña Pumpa* (☎ *074-527286*), Calle 14 No 5-11 (US$22/28/34 doubles/triples/quads).

There are plenty of more upmarket yet affordable options, including *Hotel Mintoy* (☎ *074-523545*), Calle 25 No 8-130, just off Parque Las Heroínas, which has comfortable doubles for around US$45.

Places to Eat

If you are used to unpretentious, low-budget dining, Mérida is for you: it's one of the cheapest places to eat in Venezuela, and the food is generally good. Many restaurants serve set lunches for around US$2, such as *Lunchería Joseph*, just off Plaza Bolívar.

The inexpensive *Restaurant Pizzería La Romana*, Calle 19 No 5-13, has hearty lunches, plus pizzas and à-la-carte dishes. *Restaurant Chipen*, on Av 5, has no set meals but offers straightforward tasty food à la carte, including churrasco and lomito, at

reasonable prices. *Posada Luz Caraballo* has a good inexpensive restaurant. *Casa de los Espaguettis*, Av 4 No 28-52, is one of the cheapest pasta houses in town.

Cheap vegetarian lunches are served at *El Sano Glotón*, Av 4 No 17-76; *Restaurant Makdharma*, Av 4 No 18 58; *El Sabor Natural*, Av 3 No 16-80; *El Tinajero*, Calle 29 near Av 4; *Nutricentro Vegetariano*, Av 5 No 25-46; and *El Anfora de Aquarius*, Av 2 No 23-18.

The reasonably priced *Restaurant El Tatuy*, at Parque Las Heroínas, has a long menu including local specialties. More expensive, but worth it, is *Hotel Cheo's Carnes a la Brasa*, which serves good steaks and trout.

Marisquería Tú y Yo, Av 4 No 28-70, has excellent fish and seafood. *La Trattoria da Lino*, Pasaje Ayacucho No 25-30, serves wonderful Italian food at reasonable prices.

La Exquisita Bocatá, Av 4 No 15-24, does delicious bocatás (a sort of sandwich with a meat filling). *El Hoyo de Queque*, corner of Av 4 and Calle 19, offers budget breakfasts, crêpes and other snacks at outdoor tables.

You shouldn't miss *Heladería Coromoto*, Av 3 No 28-75, perhaps the most famous ice-cream parlor on the continent, appearing in the *Guinness Book of World Records*. The place offers nearly 700 flavors, though not all are available every day. Among the more unusual varieties are Polar beer, shrimp, trout, chicken with spaghetti or 'el vegetariano.' You can even have the Lonely Planet flavor (appearing under its Spanish name, *Planeta Solitario*). The place is open 2 to 10 pm (closed Monday).

Entertainment

For an evening beer, dance music and student atmosphere, try *Birosca Carioca*, Calle 24 No 2-04, a popular nightspot in the city center. Or try the noisy *Alfredo's Bar*, at Calle 19 and Av 4. *La Jungla*, Parque Glorias Patrias (Calle 36 at Av 4), has good music and more dance floor than Birosca.

Getting There & Away

Air The airport is right inside the city, 2km southwest of Plaza Bolívar. The runway is short, and the proximity of high mountains doesn't make landing an easy task, especially in bad weather, so flights are often diverted to El Vigía. If this is the case, the airline should provide free transport to and from Mérida – be sure to insist.

There are direct flights to Caracas (US$75) and Maracaibo (US$60) and, indirectly, to other destinations.

Bus The bus terminal is 3km southwest of the center; it's linked by frequent public transport, or you can take a taxi (US$3). A half-dozen buses a day run to Caracas (US$23, 12 hours) and to Maracaibo (US$15, eight hours). Busetas to San Cristóbal depart every two hours 8 am to 6 pm (US$11, five hours). Por puestos operate on many regional routes, including Apartaderos and Jají.

AROUND MÉRIDA

The region surrounding Mérida offers plenty of natural and cultural attractions, and you can easily spend a week or two here, walking in the mountains or exploring old villages and other sights by road. Virtually every sizable village on the Trans-Andean Highway has posadas, and there's a satisfactory number of roadside restaurants.

Things to See

The region is sprinkled with old mountain villages, the best known of which is **Jají**, 38km west of Mérida, accessible by por puesto from the bus terminal. Jají was extensively reconstructed in the late 1960s to become a manicured typical Andean town. There are two budget posadas in the village.

For something more authentic, try **Mucuchíes**, a 400-year-old town 48km east of Mérida. Several kilometers up the road is the village of **San Rafael**, noted for an amazing small stone chapel built by a local artist, Juan Félix Sánchez.

Two theme parks in the vicinity of Mérida are favorite attractions for Venezuelan tourists, though they look somewhat pretentious. **Los Aleros**, on the road to Mucuchíes, is a re-creation of a Andean village from the 1930s, with period events, crafts, food and a few surprises. Por puestos from the corner of Calle 19 and Av 4 in Mérida take you there. **Venezuela de Antier**, on the Jají road, is a sort of Venezuela in a capsule, encompassing landmarks, costumes and traditions. The Jají bus will drop you off next to the park, or take a por puesto from Calle 26.

Hiking & Mountaineering

Climbing Venezuela's highest peaks, **Pico Bolívar** (with a bust of the hero on the summit) and **Pico Humboldt**, shouldn't be attempted without a guide unless you have climbing experience and a rope with you. Trips to both are offered by a number of tour operators in Mérida (see Mérida, earlier).

On your own, you can hike along the trails leading up to both peaks. The trail to Pico Bolívar originates in Mérida and roughly follows the cable-car line, but don't go alone from Loma Redonda to Pico Espejo – the trail is not clear and it's easy to get lost. The starting point for the trek up to Pico Humboldt is La Mucuy, accessible by road from Mérida.

An easier and more popular destination is **Los Nevados**, a charming mountain village sitting at an altitude of about 2700m (budget accommodations and food are available here). The usual way of getting to the village is by jeep along a breathtaking, cliffside-hugging track (US$50 per jeep for up to five people, four to five hours). You stay the night in Los Nevados, from where you walk or ride muleback to Loma Redonda. Return by cable car to Mérida or walk downhill to the beautiful Valle Los Calderones for another night and return to Mérida on the third day.

Sierra La Culata also offers some amazing hiking territory and is particularly noted for its desertlike highland landscapes. Take a por puesto to La Culata (departing from Calle 19), a three- to four-hour hike uphill from a primitive shelter known as *El Refugio* at about 3700m. Continue the next day for about three hours to the top of Pico Pan de Azúcar (4660m). Return before 4 pm, the time the last por puesto tends to depart for Mérida.

Another interesting area for hiking is farther east, near **Pico El Águila** (4118m). Take a morning bus to Valera and get off at Venezuela's highest road pass (4007m), at the foot of the peak, about 60km from Mérida. Have a hot chocolate before you set off at the *roadside restaurant*. Locals with mules wait by the road to take tourists to **Laguna Mucubají** (3540m), 5km due south, but it's better to walk there to get a closer look at the splendid páramo. From Laguna Mucubají, it's well worth walking an hour through the reforested pine woods to **Laguna Negra**, a small but beautiful mountain lake with amazingly dark water.

Most of Mérida's tour operators, including Arassari, Guamanchi and Natoura, provide free information about these and other do-it-yourself tours. Don't ignore their comments about safety measures. Bear in mind that weather can change frequently and rapidly even in the dry season.

Mountain Biking
Several tour companies in Mérida organize bike trips and rent bikes. One of the most popular bike tours is the loop around the remote mountain villages south of Mérida known as Pueblos del Sur. Ask for recommended bike trips to do on your own. Bike rental is around US$8 to US$15 a day.

Paragliding
Paragliding is also a popular activity in the region. Most tour operators offer tandem flights with a skilled pilot, so no previous experience is necessary. The usual starting point for flights is Las González, an hour-long jeep ride from Mérida, from where you fly for 20 to 30 minutes over a 850m altitude difference. The cost of the flight is much the same with all agencies (US$60), jeep transport included.

Rafting
This is the newest craze. It was introduced in 1996 by Arassari, and other companies are now jumping on the bandwagon. Rafting is done on some of the rivers at the southern foothill of the Andes and is usually included in the tour to Los Llanos. Rafting is a wet-season activity, normally from May to November, but climate anomalies over the past few years make it difficult to determine the season.

SAN CRISTÓBAL
Set 40km from the Colombian border, San Cristóbal is the capital of Táchira state and a thriving commercial center of 340,000 people. Spread over a mountain slope at an altitude of about 800m, the city has an attractive location and an agreeable climate, with an average temperature of 21°C (70°F). However, San Cristóbal has little to offer tourists and is really just a place to pass through. It's a transit point on the Pan-American route between Venezuela and Colombia, and you'll surely pass through if you come from or go to Cúcuta in Colombia.

Information
The Cotatur tourist office (☎ 076-559578) is on the corner of Av Carabobo and Av España, northeast of the city center. Some major banks are close to Plaza Bolívar.

Places to Stay
There are plenty of budget hotels (some double as love hotels) in the city center, including *Hotel Ejecutivo* (☎ 076-446298), Calle 6 No 3-25 (US$14 for a matrimonial with bath), and *Hotel Parador del Hidalgo* (☎ 076-432839), Calle 7 No 9-35 (US$16 per double with bath). More pleasant is *Hotel Rossio* (☎ 076-432330), Carrera 9 No 10-98, which costs US$14/17 per matrimonial/double with bath and fan. The nearby *Hotel Prados del Torbes* (☎ 076-439055) costs US$18/22.

For more style and comfort, try *Hotel Bella Vista* (☎ 076-437866), on the corner of Carrera 9 and Calle 9, which has spacious singles/doubles/triples with bath going for US$28/36/44. Possibly the best place to stay in the center is *Hotel Dinastía* (☎ 076-441366), Av 7 at Calle 14, which has air-con singles/doubles/triples for US$45/55/65.

Places to Eat
There are plenty of restaurants all over the center, including numerous greasy spoons serving set lunches for US$2 (eg, the restaurant in *Hotel Parador del Hidalgo*). Just around the corner, *Restaurant El Trapiche* is slightly better and more enjoyable. More decent central eateries include *Restaurant Da Cosimo*, Av 7 No 13-51, and the restaurant of *Hotel Dinastía*.

Getting There & Away
Air San Cristóbal's airport is in Santo Domingo, about 35km southeast of the city, but there's not much air traffic going through here. The airport in San Antonio del Táchira is far busier and just about the same distance from San Cristóbal.

Bus The bus terminal is about 2km south of the city center, linked by frequent city bus services. About 10 buses daily go to Caracas (US$24, 13 hours). Most depart in the late afternoon or early evening for an overnight trip via the El Llano highway. Busetas go to Mérida every two hours until 6 pm (US$11, five hours). Por puestos to San Antonio del

Táchira, on the border, run every 15 minutes or so (US$2, 1¼ hours).

SAN ANTONIO DEL TÁCHIRA

San Antonio is a Venezuelan border town of some 50,000 people living off trade with neighboring Colombia. You'll pass through it if taking this route between the two countries; otherwise, there's no point in coming here as the town has no significant attractions. Wind your watch back one hour when crossing from Venezuela to Colombia.

Information

Tourist Offices There's a branch of the Cotatur state tourist office at the airport, but any of several travel agencies in the town's center (most of which are on Carrera 4) should solve transport problems.

Money Banks in San Antonio on the whole do not change money. Corp Banca will change American Express traveler's checks, while other banks may service Visa or MasterCard cardholders.

There are plenty of casas de cambio in the center, particularly on Carrera 4 and around the DIEX office. All change US dollars, bolívares and pesos at rates similar to those in Cúcuta across the border. The casas de cambio do not change traveler's checks.

Immigration The DIEX office is on Carrera 9, between Calles 6 and 7, and is

SAN ANTONIO DEL TÁCHIRA

COLOMBIA

Río Táchira

To Cúcuta (Colombia)

Carrera 2
To Bus Terminal,
Airport
Carrera 3
Carrera 4
Cemetery
Carrera 5
Carrera 6
Carrera 7
Av. Venezuela
Carrera 8
To San Cristóbal
Carrera 9
Carrera 10
Carrera 11
Carrera 12
Carrera 13

Plaza Bolívar
Plaza Miranda

PLACES TO STAY
9 Hotel Villa de San Antonio
11 Hotel Adriático
12 Hotel Villa Heroica
13 Hotel Terepaima
14 Hotel Frontera
17 Hotel Don Jorge
23 Hotel Colonial

OTHER
1 DAS (Colombian Immigration)
2 Avensa Office
3 Viajes Turismo Uribante (Travel Agency)
4 Expresos Mérida
5 Expresos San Cristóbal
6 Viajes Turismo Internacional (Travel Agency)
7 Expresos Los Llanos
8 Busetas to Bus Terminal, Airport
10 CANTV
15 Banco de Venezuela
16 Corp Banca
18 Por Puestos to Cúcuta (Colombia)
19 DIEX Office
20 Por Puestos to San Cristóbal
21 Ipostel
22 Banco Mercantil
24 Banco Unión

0   100   200 m
0   100   200 yards

VENEZUELA

theoretically open daily 6 am to 8 pm, though it may close earlier. You must get an exit or entry stamp in your passport here. There's a departure tax of around US$10 (it seems to change frequently), paid in bolívares, required from all tourists leaving Venezuela via this border crossing.

Nationals of most countries don't need a visa for Colombia, but all travelers must get an entry stamp from DAS (see the Cúcuta section in the Colombia chapter for further information).

Places to Stay & Eat

Hotel Frontera (☎ 076-715245), Calle 2 No 8-70, is one of the cheapest (US$10 per matrimonial) but basic. *Hotel Villa de San Antonio* (☎ 076-711023), Carrera 6 No 1-61, is also on the basic side and marginally more expensive. Another basic shelter, *Hotel Villa Heroica* (☎ 076-711910), Carrera 7 No 7-97, has matrimoniales/doubles with bath and fan for US$13/15.

A better budget bet, *Hotel Colonial* (☎ 076-712679), Carrera 11 No 2-51, has clean matrimoniales/doubles with fan and bath for US$15/18. If you need air-con, one of the cheapest options is *Hotel Terepaima* (☎ 076-711763), Carrera 8 No 1-37, which costs US$20/24. Both of the above have inexpensive restaurants.

The best accommodations in town are at *Hotel Don Jorge* (☎ 076-714089), Calle 5 No 9-20, and *Hotel Adriático* (☎ 076-715757), Calle 6 at Carrera 6. Both charge US$32/40/50 singles/doubles/triples and have restaurants.

Getting There & Away

Air The airport is a couple of kilometers northeast of town, reachable by local transport. It handles flights to Caracas (US$95), Maracaibo (US$60) and other domestic destinations. Servivensa had cheap flights to Bogotá in Colombia, but they were suspended indeterminately. It still flies to Medellín (US$63), but the future of these flights is uncertain.

Bus The bus terminal is halfway to the airport. Four bus companies – Expresos Mérida, Expresos Los Llanos, Expresos Alianza and Expresos San Cristóbal – operate buses to Caracas, with a total of seven buses daily. All depart between 4 and 7 pm and use the El Llano route (US$26,

14 hours). Bus companies also have offices in the town center, close to each other on Carrera 4, where they sell tickets.

There are no direct buses to Mérida; go to San Cristóbal and change. Por puestos to San Cristóbal leave frequently from the bus terminal and from Av Venezuela in the center (US$2, 1¼hours).

Buses and por puestos (colectivos) run frequently to Cúcuta in Colombia, 12km from San Antonio. Catch buses (US$0.40) on Calle 6 or Carrera 4 and por puestos (US$0.60) on Calle 6 near the corner of Carrera 9. Both will deposit you at the Cúcuta bus terminal, passing through the center. You can pay in bolívares or pesos.

The Northeast

Venezuela's northeast is a mosaic of diverse natural features, including white beaches, coral reefs, fresh mountains and verdant valleys. The coast has some amazing stretches here, including the marvelous Mochima national park. The region also boasts Venezuela's best cave, the Cueva del Guácharo.

Most of the cultural and historic attractions are close to the sea, for it was essentially the coast that the Spanish conquered and settled. However, even though colonists arrived here as early as 1498 and soon founded their first towns, there's not much left of the colonial legacy except for the partly preserved old quarters of Barcelona and Cumaná and some old churches and forts scattered over the region.

Administratively, the northeast covers the states of Anzoátegui, Sucre and Monagas. The Isla de Margarita, which geographically belongs to the region, is detailed separately in this chapter.

BARCELONA

Barcelona was founded in 1671 by a group of Catalan colonists and named after their home town in Spain. Today, it's a city of about 300,000 people and the capital of Anzoátegui state. It's gradually merging into a single urban sprawl with its dynamic young neighbor, Puerto La Cruz.

Central Barcelona has several leafy plazas and some colonial architecture. The historic quarter has been partly restored and whitewashed throughout, giving it a pleasant general appearance, even though the urban fabric is a mishmash of houses dating from different periods. The city doesn't seem to have rushed into modernity at the pace of Puerto La Cruz, and the yesteryear feel is still noticeable within the old town.

Information

Tourist Offices The Coranztur tourist office, (☎ 081-741142), is on the ground floor of the building of the Gobernación on Av 5 de Julio. Also try the Dirección de Cultura y Turismo (☎ 081-742978) just off Plaza Boyacá.

Money There are only a few banks in central Barcelona, and they are unlikely to

do anything more than advance cash on Visa and MasterCard. Come prepared.

Things to See

The city's historic center is **Plaza Boyacá**, with a statue of General José Antonio Anzoátegui, the Barcelona-born hero of the War of Independence, in its middle. On the west side of the square is the **Catedral**, built a century after the town's foundation.

The **Museo de Anzoátegui** (closed Monday), in the oldest surviving building in town on the south side of the plaza, features a variety of objects related to Barcelona's history. An extension of the museum is housed in the **Ateneo de Barcelona**, two blocks east. On the 1st floor is a 44-piece

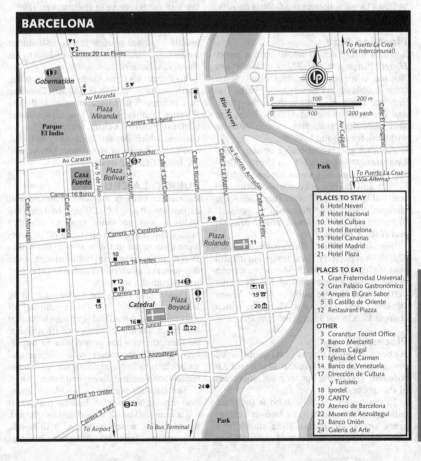

BARCELONA

0   100   200 m
0   100   200 yards

PLACES TO STAY
6   Hotel Neverí
8   Hotel Nacional
10 Hotel Cultura
13 Hotel Barcelona
15 Hotel Canarias
16 Hotel Madrid
21 Hotel Plaza

PLACES TO EAT
1   Gran Fraternidad Universal
2   Gran Palacio Gastronómico
4   Arepera El Gran Sabor
5   El Castillo de Oriente
12 Restaurant Piazza

OTHER
3   Coranztur Tourist Office
7   Banco Mercantil
9   Teatro Cajigal
11 Iglesia del Carmen
14 Banco de Venezuela
17 Dirección de Cultura y Turismo
18 Ipostel
19 CANTV
20 Ateneo de Barcelona
22 Museo de Anzoátegui
23 Banco Unión
24 Galería de Arte

VENEZUELA

collection of paintings (most date from the 1940s and 1950s) by modern Venezuelan artists. Temporary exhibitions are presented on the ground floor.

The **Plaza Rolando** is lined by more recent buildings, including the Iglesia del Carmen and the Teatro Cajigal, both dating from the 1890s. There are a few more plazas to the northwest, including Plaza Miranda and Plaza Bolívar, just one block from each other. The western side of the latter is occupied by the **Casa Fuerte**, once a Franciscan hospice, destroyed by royalists in a heavy attack in 1817. More than 1500 people died in the massacre following the takeover. Surviving parts of the walls have been left in ruins as a memorial.

The Palacio Legislativo, two blocks south of Plaza Boyacá, houses the **Galería de Arte**, which has temporary exhibitions.

Places to Stay

Set in a fine colonial house with a patio, **Hotel Plaza** (☎ 081-772843), on Plaza Boyacá, is a pleasant budget place. Some front doubles don't have private baths, but they are spacious and overlook the plaza, and are good values at US$13. There are also some less attractive air-con doubles with bath for around US$18.

Another good inexpensive option, **Hotel Canarias** (☎ 081-771034), on Carrera Bolívar, has matrimoniales with fan and bath for US$15 and matrimoniales/triples with air-con and bath for US$18/22. There are some cheaper but poorer places in the center, including **Hotel Nacional**, **Hotel Madrid** and **Hotel Cultura.**

The large **Hotel Barcelona** (☎ 081-771065) has passed its best times, but it's still reasonable at US$28/34 per air-con double/triple with bath and TV. Probably better cared for but noisy is **Hotel Neverí** (☎ 081-772373), on Av Miranda, which charges US$25 for an air-con double.

Places to Eat

A cheap and good place to eat (until about 2 pm) is the market, **Mercado Municipal La Aduana,** next to the bus terminal, southeast of the city center.

In the center, Av 5 de Julio is the main culinary artery, lined with budget restaurants, snack lyncherías, soda stands and street-food vendors. The self-service **Gran**

Palacio Gastronómico, near the Gobernación, offers inexpensive fast food and snacks. Next door, **Gran Fraternidad Universal** serves cheap vegetarian lunches. One block south, **Arepera El Gran Sabor** does good arepas and some budget local dishes at low prices. The 1st-floor **Restaurant Piazza,** next to the Hotel Barcelona, has pizzas and steaks at reasonable prices. **El Castillo de Oriente,** on Av Miranda, does parrillas.

Getting There & Away

Air The airport is 2km south of the city center and is accessible by urban transport. Flights include Caracas (US$60) and Porlamar (US$45).

Bus The bus terminal is 1km southeast of the city center, next to the market; take a buseta going south along Av 5 de Julio or walk 15 minutes. The terminal handles mostly regional routes; few long-distance buses call here. The terminal in Puerto La Cruz is far busier.

To Puerto La Cruz, catch a city bus going north on Av 5 de Julio (US$0.30). They use two routes, 'Vía Intercomunal' and 'Vía Alterna.' Either will set you down in the center of Puerto La Cruz. There are also por puestos, which depart from Av 5 de Julio, two blocks south of the Banco Unión, and are faster than the buses.

PUERTO LA CRUZ

Puerto La Cruz is a young, dynamic and expanding city of 175,000 people. Until the 1930s it was no more than an obscure village, but it boomed after rich oil deposits were discovered in the region to the south. Port facilities have been built just east of the city to serve as an oil terminal to export oil piped from the wells.

Puerto La Cruz is the major gateway to Isla de Margarita. It's also a jumping-off point to the beautiful Parque Nacional Mochima. Taking advantage of its strategic position, the city has grown into an important water-sports center, with marinas and yacht clubs, sailing and diving schools, yacht-rental facilities, and diving and fishing tours.

The city has become a popular destination among Venezuelan holiday-makers. It has a lively 10-block waterfront boulevard, Paseo Colón, which is packed with hotels, tour agencies, bars and restaurants. It comes

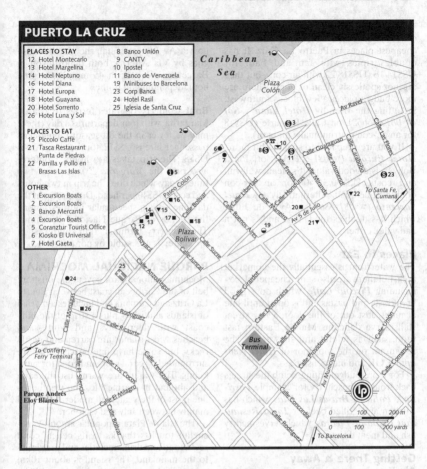

PUERTO LA CRUZ

PLACES TO STAY
12 Hotel Montecarlo
13 Hotel Margelina
14 Hotel Neptuno
16 Hotel Diana
17 Hotel Europa
18 Hotel Guayana
20 Hotel Sorrento
26 Hotel Luna y Sol

PLACES TO EAT
15 Piccolo Caffè
21 Tasca Restaurant
    Punta de Piedras
22 Parrilla y Pollo en
    Brasas Las Islas

OTHER
1   Excursion Boats
2   Excursion Boats
3   Banco Mercantil
4   Excursion Boats
5   Coranztur Tourist Office
6   Kiosko El Universal
7   Hotel Gaeta

8   Banco Unión
9   CANTV
10 Ipostel
11 Banco de Venezuela
19 Minibuses to Barcelona
23 Corp Banca
24 Hotel Rasil
25 Iglesia de Santa Cruz

Caribbean Sea

Plaza Colón

Plaza Bolívar

Bus Terminal

Parque Andrés Eloy Blanco

To Conferry Ferry Terminal

To Santa Fe, Cumaná

To Barcelona

0   100   200 m
0   100   200 yards

to life in the late afternoon and evening, when craft stalls open and a gentle breeze refreshes the heat of the day. Apart from this, the city has little to offer tourists: a block or two back from the beach and it's just an ordinary place. Some travelers may be disappointed.

Information
Tourist Offices The Coranztur tourist office (☎ 081-688170), midway along Paseo Colón, is open daily 8 am to 8 pm. City maps can bought at Kiosko El Universal.

Money Most banks are within a few blocks south of Plaza Colón. Useful banks include Banco Unión and Banco de Venezuela (Visa,

MasterCard) and Corp Banca (American Express traveler's checks). Several casas de cambio, including Oficambio in the Hotel Rasil and Asecambio in the Hotel Gaeta, exchange cash and traveler's checks.

Places to Stay
The cheapest options on Paseo Colón include *Hotel Montecarlo* (☎ 081-685678), *Hotel Neptuno* (☎ 081-653261), *Hotel Diana* (☎ 081-650017) and *Hotel Margelina* (☎ 081-687545). All have rooms with air-con and bath, but are otherwise nothing special. Check a few and inspect rooms before deciding. Expect a double to cost US$18 to US$25. The Diana has some cheaper rooms with fans.

The small *Hotel Guayana* (☎ 081-652175), on Plaza Bolívar, is one of the cheapest places in Puerto La Cruz. It has doubles/triples with fan and bath for US$14/16 (US$18/22 with air-con), but they are not spotlessly clean or good. There are more budget places a few blocks southwest, including the friendly *Hotel Luna y Sol* (☎ 081-686662), on Calle Ricaurte (US$18 for an air-con matrimonial with bath).

If you are prepared to spend a bit more, *Hotel Europa* (☎ 081-650034), off Plaza Bolívar, is a good value. It's clean, well-run and costs US$30/36/40 for an air-con double/triple/quad. Alternatively, try *Hotel Sorrento* (☎ 081-686745), Av 5 de Julio, which has doubles for US$36 and is not a bad value either.

Places to Eat

The waterfront is essentially the upmarket area, but there are also some cheaper places, including *Piccolo Caffè*, which does good breakfasts and pastas and is open until late at night. Just out of the door, a few street stalls serve delicious Middle Eastern fast food, such as felafel and shawarma. The restaurant on the top floor of *Hotel Neptuno* is OK and inexpensive.

For more budget eating, comb the streets back from the beach. Try, for example, *Parrilla y Pollo en Brasas Las Islas*, which has chicken and grilled beef, or *Tasca Restaurant Punta de Piedras*, which serves hearty fish and meat dishes.

Getting There & Away

Air The airport is in Barcelona (see that section for details).

Bus The busy bus terminal is conveniently located just three blocks from Plaza Bolívar. Frequent buses travel to Caracas (US$12, five hours) and Cumaná (US$3, 1½ hours); some of the latter continue as far as Güiria (US$10, 5½ hours). If you go eastward (to Cumaná or farther on), grab a seat on the left side of the bus – there are some spectacular views over the islands of Mochima park. There are also por puestos to Cumaná (US$5, 1½ hours) and Santa Fe (US$2, 40 minutes). Half a dozen buses run daily to Ciudad Guayana (US$12, six hours), and all go via Ciudad Bolívar (US$9, 4½ hours).

To Barcelona, take a city bus or the faster por-puesto minibus from Av 5 de Julio. Both go via Av Intercomunal; the city bus also goes by Vía Alterna; both deposit you in Barcelona's center in 45 minutes to one hour, depending on traffic.

Boat Conferry operates ferries to Isla de Margarita, with four departures a day (there may be fewer in the off-season). First-class passenger fare is US$12; tourist-class fare is US$8. The trip takes 4½ hours. Conferry also runs the *Margarita Express* boat two times a day, which does the trip in two hours and costs US$40 per head. Do this trip in the daytime – it's a spectacular journey among the islands of Parque Nacional Mochima. The Conferry terminal, 1km southwest of the center, is accessible by por puesto.

PARQUE NACIONAL MOCHIMA

Mochima national park covers the offshore belt of the Caribbean coast between Puerto La Cruz and Cumaná and includes a myriad of islands and islets, plus a strip of the hilly coast with deep bays and white-sand beaches. Most islands are barren and partly rocky, but some have fine beaches and are surrounded by coral reefs and good for snorkeling. The waters are warm, usually calm and abound in marine life. The weather is fine most of the year, with moderate rainfall mainly between July and October.

The **Isla de Plata** is popular among Venezuelan tourists thanks to its beach, coral reefs, food and drink facilities and proximity to the mainland. The island is about 10km east of Puerto La Cruz and is accessible by boat from the pier near Pamatacualito, the eastern suburb of the port of Guanta (serviced by por puestos from Puerto La Cruz). It can also be reached by excursion boats directly from Puerto La Cruz, but these are more expensive and less regular.

Other standard boat destinations offered from Puerto La Cruz include **Playa El Saco** and **Playa El Faro** (US$7 roundtrip per person to either) and a **La Piscina** tour with an hour's snorkeling (US$25 per person including lunch and equipment rental). Boats depart in the morning from the city waterfront and return in the afternoon.

Parts of the Puerto La Cruz-Cumaná road skirt the seafront, providing some spectacular glimpses of the islands. There are a dozen beaches off the road, the most popular of which are **Playa Arapito**, about 23km from Puerto La Cruz, and **Playa Colorada**, 4km farther east. There are several budget hotels near the latter, including *Quinta Jaly*, run by friendly French Canadians.

On weekends, popular beaches swarm with holiday-makers, some of whom seem to come just to drink beer and party to music at full volume. Some deserted beaches can be unsafe, particularly at night – use common sense.

About 10km east of Playa Colorada is the ordinary fishing town of **Santa Fe**, which has become popular with foreign backpackers thanks to a bit of beach. A bunch of budget restaurants and posadas have sprung up along the beach, including *Residencia La Sierra*, *Residencia Los 7 Delfines* and *Hotel Cochaima*; they offer various facilities and activities, such as Spanish lessons, boat excursions, snorkeling and horseback riding. Santa Fe has regular bus and por puesto service from Puerto La Cruz and Cumaná.

Another 10km east along the Cumaná road, a side road branches off to the north and goes 5km downhill to the village of Mochima. Mochima sits in the deep Bahía de Mochima and is a jumping-off point for nearby beaches that are inaccessible by road. The most visited of these beaches are Playa Blanca and Las Maritas, both with food facilities. The village of Mochima has some budget accommodation options, including *Posada Gaby* and *Posada Puerto Viejo*, plus several restaurants, the best of which is *El Mochimero*. Jeeps run regularly to and from Cumaná (there's no direct transport from Puerto La Cruz).

CUMANÁ

The capital of Sucre state, Cumaná is a city of 275,000 inhabitants and an important port for sardine fishing and canning. Founded by the Spaniards in 1521, it takes pride in being the oldest existing town on South America's mainland. There's not much colonial architecture, however; several earthquakes, including three serious ones in 1684, 1765 and 1929, reduced the town each time to little more than a pile of rubble, and its historic character largely disappeared in the subsequent reconstruction.

Cumaná is noted more for its environs than for the city itself. There are some beaches nearby, the closest being Playa San Luis on the southwestern outskirts of the city. Better beaches are in the Mochima national park, a little farther down the coast. To the north is the intriguing Península de Araya, while to the southeast is the Cueva del Guácharo. Cumaná is also one of the gateways to Isla de Margarita.

Information
Tourist Offices The Dirección de Turismo (☎ 093-316051) is on Calle Sucre, close to Iglesia de Santa Inés.

Money Most major banks are on Calle Mariño and Av Bermúdez. Corp Banca is farther west on Av Bermúdez, seven blocks beyond the Banco Mercantil. The only casa de cambio, Oficambio, Calle Mariño, 10 blocks west of Plaza Miranda, changes cash and traveler's checks.

Things to See
Some streets around **Iglesia de Santa Inés** retain some of their former appearance. The church itself is a 1929 construction and has few objects of an earlier date inside. The **Catedral**, on Plaza Blanco, is also relatively young and has a hodgepodge of altarpieces in its largely timbered interior.

Perhaps the best restored colonial structure in town is the **Castillo de San Antonio de la Eminencia**, on a hill just southeast of the center. Constructed in 1659 on a four-pointed star plan, it suffered pirate attacks and earthquakes, but the coral rock walls have survived in pretty good shape. The fort commands good views over the city and the bay.

The city has three modest museums. The **Casa Natal de Andrés Eloy Blanco** is the house where this poet, considered one of Venezuela's most extraordinary literary talents, was born in 1896. The **Museo Gran Mariscal de Ayacucho** is dedicated to the Cumaná-born hero of the War of Independence, General Antonio José de Sucre. The **Museo del Mar** is at the old airport, 2km southwest of the city center.

Places to Stay
One of the cheapest places to stay in the area (US$10 per matrimonial with bath) is the basic *Hospedaje La Gloria* (☎ 093-664243), Calle Sucre. More pleasant is *Hospedaje Lucila* (☎ 093-311808), Calle Bolívar. It's

VENEZUELA

VENEZUELA

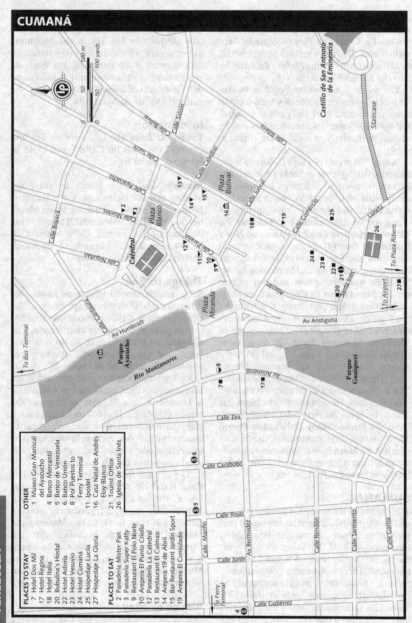

CUMANÁ

Castillo de San Antonio de la Eminencia

Staircase

Luneta

To Plaza Ribera

To Airport

Parque Guaiqueri

Av Aristiguita

Av Arismendi

Parque Ayacucho

Río Manzanares

Av Humboldt

Plaza Miranda

Plaza Bolívar

Plaza Blanco

Catedral

Calle Bolívar

Calle Salom

Calle Sucre

Calle Ribero

Calle Ayacucho

Calle Catedral

Calle Lunal

Calle Montes

Calle Boyacá

Calle Niquitao

Calle Cumaná

Calle Paraíso

Calle Comercio

Calle Mariño

Calle Bermúdez

Calle Zea

Calle Carabobo

Calle Rojas

Calle Junín

Calle Gutiérrez

Calle Rendón

Calle Sarmiento

Calle García

Santa Inés

Alacrán

To Bus Terminal

To Ferry Terminal

100 m
100 yards

PLACES TO STAY
7 Hotel Dos Mil
17 Hotel Regina
18 Hotel Italia
20 Bubulina's Hostal
22 Hotel Astoria
23 Hotel Vesuvio
24 Hotel Cumaná
25 Hospedaje Lucila
27 Hospedaje La Gloria

PLACES TO EAT
2 Panadería Míster Pan
3 Panadería Super Katty
9 Restaurant El Polo Norte
10 Arepera El Punto Criollo
12 Panadería La Catedral
13 Restaurant El Colmao
14 Arepera 19 de Abril
15 Bar Restaurant Jardín Sport
19 Arepera El Consulado

OTHER
1 Museo Gran Mariscal de Ayacucho
4 Banco Mercantil
5 Banco de Venezuela
6 Banco Unión
8 Por Puestos to Ferry Terminal
11 Ipostel
16 Casa Natal de Andrés Eloy Blanco
21 Tourist Office
26 Iglesia de Santa Inés

clean and quiet, and has matrimoniales with fan/air-con for US$12/15.

There's a choice of budget options on Calle Sucre in the city center, including *Hotel Astoria* (☎ 093-662708), *Hotel Vesuvio* (☎ 093-314077), *Hotel Cumaná* (☎ 093-310545) and *Hotel Italia* (☎ 093-663678). They all charge about US$14 to US$16 a double with bath and fan. The Astoria and Italia have rooms with air-con for a little more.

There are also some inexpensive hotels just west across the river from Plaza Miranda, the cheapest of which is the unremarkable *Hotel Dos Mil* (☎ 093-323414) at US$10/14/18 a single/double/triple with fan. Appreciably better is the nearby *Hotel Regina* (☎ 093-322581) at US$20/25/33 for an air-con single/double/triple.

Bubulina's Hostal (☎ 093-314025), around the corner from the tourist office, is more pleasant and stylish than anything listed above. Accommodated in a fine historic building, this upmarket posada offers six matrimoniales and six doubles, all with air-con, TV, bath and hot water, for about US$60 each, breakfast included.

Places to Eat
Central areperas include *Arepera 19 de Abril* (possibly the best), *Arepera El Punto Criollo* or *Arepera El Consulado*. Some of the cheapest parrillas are served at the food stalls at Plaza Ribero, one block south of Santa Inés Church. Central panaderías include *Panadería Mister Pan* (which has some tables to sit and eat at), *Panadería Super Katty* and *Panadería La Catedral*. The informal open-air *Bar Restaurant Jardín Sport*, on Plaza Bolívar, serves inexpensive snacks, though it's essentially the cheap beer that draws people in.

The restaurant in *Hotel Italia* serves unpretentious inexpensive meals, as does *Restaurant El Polo Norte*. For some better food in more pleasant surroundings check *Restaurant El Colmao*, but it's probably best to go to *Bubulina's Restaurant*, which does delicious traditional local dishes at fair prices.

Getting There & Away
Air The airport, 4km southeast of the city center, handles direct flights to Caracas (US$75) and Porlamar (US$40).

Bus The bus terminal is 1.5km northwest of the city center and linked to town by frequent urban buses. There's regular bus service to Caracas (US$14, 6½ hours); all buses go through Puerto La Cruz (US$3, 1½ hours). Half a dozen buses go daily to Ciudad Bolívar (US$11, six hours) and Güiria (US$8, 4½ hours).

For Cueva del Guácharo, take the Caripe bus (US$5, 3½ hours), which will let you off at the cave's entrance; there are two departures daily at 7:15 am and 12:30 pm.

Boat Conferry operates two ferries a day to Isla de Margarita (US$8, 3½ hours). Boats to Araya run every hour or two until about 4 pm (US$1.50, one hour). All ferries and boats depart from the ferry docks next to the mouth of Río Manzanares, 2km west of the center; por puestos go there from the door of Hotel Dos Mil.

PENINSULA DE ARAYA
This 70km-long arid peninsula stretches from east to west along the mainland's coast, with its western end lying due north of Cumaná. The population is thinly scattered in a handful of coastal villages, of which Araya, on the tip, is the largest. This is the place to go to see the peninsula's two major attractions, the *salinas* (saltpans) and the *castillo* (fort).

Salinas
The salinas were discovered by the Spaniards in 1499 and have been exploited almost uninterruptedly up to the present day. They were, and still are, Venezuela's largest salt deposits. The salt mining is operated by the ENSAL company, which has built installations on the seafront and produces half a million tons of salt per year.

Until recently, ENSAL organized tours around the salt works, but there were no tours when this book was researched. They may be reintroduced in the future – check with the Cumaná's tourist office for news. Even if there are no tours, the trip to Araya is worth considering, for the boat ride itself and the fort, and you can still see quite a bit of the salinas from outside the installations and restricted areas.

A *mirador* (lookout), built on the hill 2km north of Araya, provides a panoramic view over the salinas, which are rectangular pools filled in with salt water and left to dry out. What is particularly amazing is the unbelievable color of the water, ranging from creamy pink to deep purple.

Start early and be prepared for baking heat: a hat or other head protection is recommended, as are sunglasses and sunscreen. It's wise to carry a large bottle of water or other drink.

Castillo

The fort was built in the first half of the 17th century to protect the salinas from plunder. It was the most costly Spanish project in the New World up to that time. In 1726, a hurricane produced a tide that broke over the salt lagoon, flooding it and turning it into a gulf. Salt could no longer be exploited, and the Spanish decided to abandon the fortress. Before leaving, they tried to blow it up, but despite using huge charges of gunpowder, the structure largely resisted the efforts to destroy it. The mighty bulwarks still proudly crown the waterfront cliff. The fort is a 10-minute walk along the beach from the wharf. You can wander freely around the place, as there's no gate.

Getting There & Away

Boats go from Cumaná every two hours or so until 4 or 5 pm (US$1.50, one hour). Upon arrival at Araya, check the schedule of the boats back to Cumaná, and keep in mind that the last boat may depart earlier than scheduled or sometimes not at all. There are several simple *posadas* and *restaurants* in Araya.

CARIPE

Set in a verdant mountain valley 55km back from the coast, Caripe is a pleasant, easy-going small town renowned for its agreeable climate, attractive environs, coffee and orange plantations, and proximity to the spectacular Cueva del Guácharo. Home to about 12,000 inhabitants, the town is little more than two parallel streets, around which most activities and services are centered. The place is quite touristy, and on weekends it's full of people escaping the steamy lowlands that dominate most of the region.

Information

There's no tourist office, but two of the local tour operators, Trekking Travelers Tours

(☎ 092-51352) and Viajes y Turismo Caripe (☎ 092-51246), may provide information.

Caripe has three banks (Banco Unión, Banco de Venezuela and Banco del Orinoco), but it may be wise to bring bolívares with you.

Things to See & Do

There's nothing special to see in town, but the rugged surroundings are beautiful and pleasant for walks. The top attraction in the region is no doubt the **Cueva del Guácharo** (see the following section). Among other sights, there are two nice waterfalls: **Salto La Payla**, near the cave, and the 80m **Salto El Chorrerón**, an hour's walk from the village of Sabana de Piedra.

El Mirador (1100m), to the north of the town, commands sweeping views over the Valle del Caripe. It's an hour-long walk from town, or you can go there by road. Longer trips include the hike to the highest peak in the region, **Cerro Negro**.

Places to Stay & Eat

There are many spots for eating and sleeping in town; hotel prices tend to rise on weekends.

Parrilla Restaurant La Posada, opposite the church, is perhaps the cheapest place to stay in town (US$12 a double without bath). It's also a very cheap place to eat. Across the street, *Hotel San Francisco* (☎ 092-51018) has rooms with bath for US$14/16/20 per single/double/triple. You'll pay much the same at *Posadas Oriente* (☎ 092-51971) on Av Guzmán Blanco.

Better options include *Hotel Berlín* (☎ 092-51246), for US$26 a double; *Hotel Venezia* (☎ 092-51875), for US$22/28 per double/triple; and *Hotel Samán* (☎ 092-51183), for US$28/32. The Venezia has one of the best *restaurants* in town.

There are more places to stay and eat outside the town, particularly along the road between Caripe and the village of El Guácharo.

Getting There & Away

The bus terminal is at the northeastern end of town, behind the market. There's an evening bus that runs to Caracas via Maturín (US$20, 11 hours). Buses to Maturín depart every two hours until about 5:30 pm (US$4, three hours) and there are also por puestos (US$5, two hours). There are two buses daily to Cumaná, at 6 am and at noon (US$5, 3½ hours); they pass the Guácharo Cave on the way.

CUEVA DEL GUÁCHARO

The Guácharo Cave, 12km from Caripe on the road toward the coast, is Venezuela's longest, largest and most magnificent cave. It had been known to the local Indians long before Columbus crossed the Atlantic and was later explored by Europeans. The eminent scientist Alexander von Humboldt penetrated 472m into the cave in September 1799, and it was he who first classified its unusual inhabitant, the *guácharo*, or oilbird.

The guácharo is a nocturnal, fruit-eating bird, the only one of its kind in the world. It inhabits caves in various parts of tropical America, living in total darkness and leaving the cave only at night for food, principally the fruit of some species of palms. The guácharo has a radarlike location system similar to that used by bats, which enables it to get around. The adult bird is about 60cm long, with a wingspan of a meter.

In Venezuela, the guácharo has been seen in more than 40 caves; the biggest colony, estimated at up to 18,000 birds, is here, in the Guácharo Cave. The birds inhabit only the first chamber of the cave, the 750m-long Humboldt Hall. The cave also boasts a variety of other wildlife and amazing natural formations including a maze of stalactites and stalagmites.

A 1200m portion of the total 10.2km length of the cave plus a small museum related to the cave can be visited; both are open 8 am to 4 pm daily. All visits are guided and the tour takes about 1½ hours (US$5, no student discounts). Cameras with flashes are permitted beyond the area where the guácharos live.

You can *camp* near the entrance to the cave (but only after closing time; US$5 per tent); if you camp here, watch the hundreds of birds pouring out of the cave mouth at around 7 pm and returning about 4 am. There's a 35m waterfall, Salto La Payla, a 25-minute walk from the cave.

GÜIRIA

Güiria is the easternmost point on Venezuela's coast that you can reach by road after a 275km ride from Cumaná. Home to 25,000 people, it's the largest town of Península de Paria and an important fishing port. The town itself is rather an ordinary place with no significant tourist attractions.

Güiria is probably not worth a trip unless you plan on continuing to Trinidad or exploring the rugged Parque Nacional Península de Paria, which stretches along the northern coast. Near the eastern tip of the peninsula, about 40km east of Güiria, is the small fishing village of Macuro (accessible only by water), the place where Columbus came ashore in August 1498.

Information

The Acosta Asociados (☎ 094-81679, 81112), Calle Bolívar No 33, are representatives of Windward Lines; they provide information and sell tickets for the ferry to Trinidad (see later in this section) They may also change US dollars (at a low rate) or at least will know where to go.

The Banco del Orinoco may change traveler's checks but is likely to charge a hefty US$5 commission on each transaction. The Banco de Venezuela and Banco Unión may give advances on Visa and MasterCard.

Places to Stay & Eat

Hotel Plaza (☎ 094-820022), in the corner of Plaza Bolívar, is a popular budget place to stay, for US$12/16 per double with bath and fan/air-con; its *restaurant* serves good inexpensive food. For a similar price, you can stay in the rustic *Hotel Fortuna*, on Calle Bolívar, 50m from the plaza, or in *Hotel Miramar*, on Calle Turipiari, a little bit farther toward the port.

Posada Gran Puerto (☎ 094-81085), on Calle Vigirima, offers much the same for marginally more. *Hotel Gran Puerto* (☎ 094-81343), on Calle Pegallos, provides slightly better standards in its air-con matrimoniales/doubles/triples for US$18/24/28. Also try the marginally cheaper *Hotel El Milagro* (☎ 094-81218), Calle Valdéz, which has its own restaurant.

One of the best central places to stay is *La Posada de Chuchú* (☎ 094-81266), Calle Bideau, which has air-con doubles for US$30 and its own *restaurant*.

Getting There & Away

Bus Several bus companies have offices around the triangular Plaza Sucre, two blocks from Plaza Bolívar. There are a half-dozen buses daily to Caracas (US$24, 11 hours). They all go via Cumaná and Puerto La Cruz. Por puestos run frequently to Carúpano (US$6, two hours).

Boat Windward Lines operates a ferry on the Güiria-Trinidad-St Vincent-Barbados-St Lucia route. The ferry is supposed to arrive at Güiria from Trinidad every second Tuesday night and depart back to Trinidad on Wednesday night. On alternate weeks it goes to Pampatar on Isla de Margarita. The Güiria-Port of Spain deck fare is US$75 (US$105 roundtrip), and the trip takes seven hours. Optional air-con cabins are available for US$25 per double. Acosta Asociados (see Information) arrange all necessary formalities. They may also know about independent boats to Port of Spain, Trinidad, that depart when they have collected enough passengers.

Peñeros (open fishing boats) leave from the northern end of the Güiria port for Macuro every morning except Sunday without a fixed schedule, but normally around 11 am (US$3, 1½ to two hours). There are a few simple *posadas* in Macuro, which can also provide meals.

Isla de Margarita

With an area of 1071 sq km, Isla de Margarita is Venezuela's largest island, stretching some 60km from east to west and 32km from north to south. It lies some 40km off the mainland, due north of Cumaná, and is composed of what were once two neighboring islands, now linked by a narrow, crescent-shaped sandbank, La Restinga.

The eastern part of Margarita is the larger and more fertile and contains 95% of the island's total population of 340,000. All major towns are here, connected by a well-developed array of roads. The western part, known as the Península de Macanao, is arid and sparsely populated, with 17,000 people living in a dozen villages located mostly along the coast. Both sections of the island are mountainous, with highest peaks approaching 1000m.

Generally speaking, people are drawn to the island for two reasons. The first is the beaches which skirt its coast. Thanks to

them, Margarita has become the prime destination for Venezuelan vacationers seeking white sand and sunbathing opportunities with decent facilities. It's also popular with international visitors, most on package tours. The tourism infrastructure is well developed, and Margarita has a collection of posh hotels comparable only to those in Caracas.

The island's other magnet is shopping. Margarita is a duty-free zone, so prices of consumer goods are supposed to be lower than on the mainland, though in many cases there's no significant difference. Despite that, local shops are usually packed with bargain-seekers.

The island's climate is typical of the Caribbean, which has average temperatures ranging between 25°C (77°F) and 28°C (82°F), with the heat of the day agreeably cooled down by evening breezes. The rainy season lasts from November to January, with rain falling mostly during the night.

Administratively, Isla de Margarita and the two small islands of Cubagua and Coche make up the state of Nueva Esparta. Although Porlamar is by far the largest urban center on the island, the small, sleepy town of La Asunción is the state capital.

Getting There & Away

Air Margarita's airport is in the southern part of the island, 20km southwest of Porlamar, reached by infrequent por puestos (US$2). A taxi on this route will cost about US$10. The terminal has a tourist office, a few casas de cambio (which change both cash and traveler's checks) and a useful ATM.

Most major national airlines have flights to Caracas (US$60) and to some other domestic destinations (either directly or via Caracas). Small airlines operate flights on light planes to Los Roques, Canaima, Güiria and Tucupita.

Boat Isla de Margarita has Conferry links with Cumaná (two ferries a day, US$8, 3½ hours) and Puerto La Cruz (four ferries, US$12 first class, US$8 tourist class, 4½ hours). Conferry also operates its modern *Margarita Express* boat on Puerto La Cruz route, with two departures a day (US$40, two hours). In the off season, there may be fewer departures. Tickets for the ferry can be bought at the Conferry office in Porlamar

ISLA DE MARGARITA

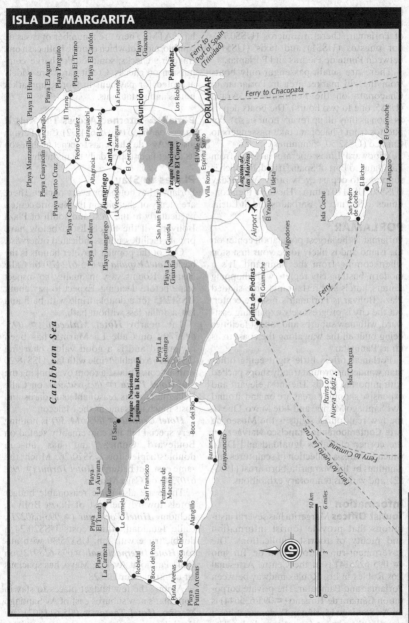

- Playa El Humo
- Playa Manzanillo
- Manzanillo
- Playa El Agua
- Playa Parguito
- Playa El Tirano
- Playa El Cardón
- Playa Guacuco
- El Tirano
- Pampatar
- La Fuente
- La Asunción
- Los Robles
- Guayacán
- El Salado
- Paraguachi
- Pedro González
- Santa Ana
- Tacarigua
- La Asunción
- Playa Guayacán
- Altagracia
- Juangriego
- El Cercado
- PORLAMAR
- Playa Puerto Cruz
- Parque Nacional Cerro El Copey
- Ferry to Port of Spain (Trinidad)
- Ferry to Chacopata
- Playa Caribe
- Playa La Galera
- Juangriego
- La Vecindad
- El Valle del Espíritu Santo
- Villa Rosa
- Playa Juangriego
- San Juan Bautista
- Laguna de las Marinas
- La Isleta
- El Guamache
- El Bichar
- El Amparo
- La Guardia
- El Yaque
- Airport
- Los Algodones
- Isla Coche
- San Pedro de Coche
- Playa La Guardia
- Caribbean Sea
- Punta de Piedras
- El Guamache
- Ferry
- Playa La Restinga
- Parque Nacional Laguna de la Restinga
- Ferry to Cumaná
- Ferry to Puerto La Cruz
- Isla Cubagua
- Ruins of Nueva Cádiz
- Boca del Río
- Barrancas
- Guayacancito
- El Saco
- Playa La Auyama
- El Tunal
- San Francisco
- La Carmela
- Península de Macanao
- Mangrillo
- Playa El Tunal
- La Carmela
- Robledal
- Boca del Pozo
- Boca Chica
- Playa La Carmela
- Punta Arenas
- Playa Punta Arenas
- 10 km
- 6 miles
- 5
- 3
- 0

(☎ 095-619235) or at the ferry terminal in Punta de Piedras (☎ 095-98148), 29km west of Porlamar. There are micros (US$0.75), por puestos (US$1) and taxis (US$10) between Punta de Piedras and Porlamar.

There are small, passenger-only boats from the old market area in Porlamar to Chacopata on the Península de Araya (US$5, one to two hours). The boats depart as soon as they fill up (every hour or so). Por puestos from Chacopata take passengers to Cariaco (US$2.50, 45 minutes).

Windward Lines operates a ferry from Pampatar to Port of Spain, Trinidad, which is supposed to depart every other Wednesday (US$80, US$110 return). The ferry then continues to St Vincent, Barbados and St Lucia.

PORLAMAR

Porlamar is the largest population center on the island and is likely to be your first stop when coming from the mainland. It's a modern, bustling city replete with shopping centers, hotels and restaurants. Tree-shaded Plaza Bolívar is Porlamar's historic center, but the city is progressively expanding eastward, with new suburbs and tourist facilities being built all the way along the coast to as far as Pampatar.

Porlamar offers little sightseeing other than wandering around trendy shops packed with imported goods. The most elegant and expensive shopping areas are on and around Avs Santiago Mariño and 4 de Mayo. One of the few real tourist sights is the **Museo de Arte Contemporáneo Francisco Narváez**, on the corner of Calles Igualdad and Díaz, which features a collection of sculptures and paintings by the Margarita-born artist (1905-82), and various temporary exhibitions.

Information
Tourist Offices Margarita has several institutions that provide tourist information and plenty of tourist publications. The government-run Corporación de Turismo (☎ 095-622514) is at the Centro Artesanal Los Robles, in Los Robles, midway between Porlamar and Pampatar. The private corporation Cámara de Turismo (☎ 095-635644) is on Av Santiago Mariño in Porlamar; it has a stand at the airport (open irregularly). The Promargarita (☎ 095-640264) is in Centro Comercial Trarimat on Av 4 de Mayo, 2km northeast of the center.

Money Many of Porlamar's banks handle foreign currency transactions, and some have ATMs. There are a number of casas de cambio, most of which change both cash and traveler's checks; some don't charge commission on checks. Credit cards are widely accepted for payment in stores, upmarket hotels and restaurants.

E-mail & Internet Access The Kids II Juegos de Video (☎ 095-634832), Calle Fermín just off Av 4 de Mayo, has Internet facilities on its upper floor (open daily till midnight).

Places to Stay
Porlamar has hotels for every pocket. There are plenty of cheapies in the historic center, particularly to the west and south of Plaza Bolívar. All the hotels listed below have private facilities, unless indicated otherwise.

One of the popular traveler haunts is the basic *Hotel España* (☎ 095-612479) on Calle Mariño. Rooms vary in quality, so inspect some before deciding. Expect to pay about US$12/15 for a double/triple with bath and fan, a dollar less without bath.

The nearby *Hotel Malecón* (☎ 095-642579), on Calle La Marina, has been revamped and is a good value, charging US$14/16 a double/triple with fan, US$18/20 with air-con. Choose a room overlooking the sea. *Hotel Plaza* (☎ 095-630395), on Calle Velázquez, offers reasonable standards and costs much the same as the Malecón.

Hotel Central (☎ 095-614757) is nothing very special but it's conveniently seated on Boulevard Gómez, and has air-con doubles/triples for US$20/26. Much the same cost, but better, is *Hotel Torino* (☎ 095-610734), on Calle Mariño.

There are also some reasonable budget hotels toward the east of Plaza Bolívar, including *Hotel Porlamar* (☎ 095-630271), Calle Igualdad, which costs US$20/24 a double/triple with fan, US$25/30 with air-con. *Hotel Internacional* (☎ 095-618912), on Calle Patiño at Av 4 de Mayo, has spacious air-con triples for US$28.

Among the few budget places to stay in Porlamar's new suburbs east of Av Santiago Mariño, *Hotel Tama* (☎ 095-611602), Av Raúl Leoni, is the most popular gringo haunt. Clean rooms cost US$14/17/20 a single/double/triple with fan, US$18/22/25 with air-con.

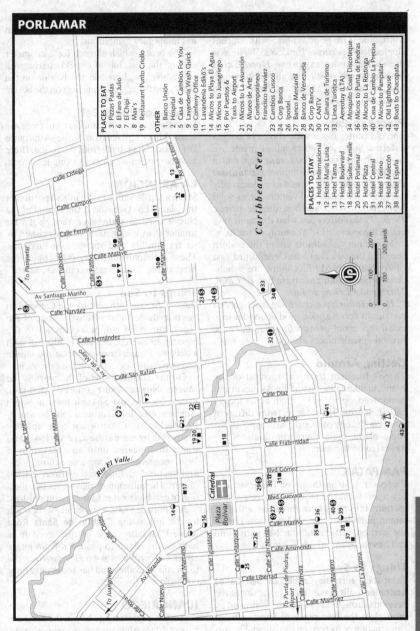

PORLAMAR

PLACES TO EAT

3 Pizzas Pastas
6 El Faro de Julio
7 El Chipi
8 Max's
19 Restaurant Punto Criollo

OTHER

1 Banco Unión
2 Hospital
5 Casa de Cambios For You
9 Lavandería Wash Quick
10 Conferry Office
11 Lavandería Edikó's
14 Micros to Playa El Agua
15 Micros to Juangriego
16 Por Puestos &
   Taxis to Airport
21 Micros to La Asunción
22 Museo de Arte
   Contemporáneo
   Francisco Narváez
23 Cambios Cusco
24 Corp Banca
26 Ipostel
27 Banco Mercantil
28 Banco de Venezuela
29 Corp Banca
30 CANTV
32 Cámara de Turismo
33 Línea Turística
   Aereotuy (LTA)
34 Mosquito Coast Discoteque
36 Micros to Punta de Piedras
39 Micros to La Restinga
40 Casa de Cambio La Precisa
41 Micros to Pampatar
42 Old Lighthouse
43 Boats to Chacopata

PLACES TO STAY

4 Hotel Internacional
12 Hotel María Luisa
13 Hotel Tama
17 Hotel Boulevard
18 Hotel Suites Yamile
20 Hotel Porlamar
25 Hotel Plaza
31 Hotel Central
35 Hotel Torino
37 Hotel Malecón
38 Hotel España

Caribbean Sea

For somewhere a bit more upmarket, *Hotel Boulevard* (☎ 095-610522), Calle Marcano, is a good value, with decent singles/doubles/triples for US$35/40/46, as is the slightly more expensive *Hotel Suites Yamile* (☎ 095-633011), Calle Fraternidad. Still better is the three-star *Hotel María Luisa* (☎ 095-610564) for US$50/60/70.

Places to Eat

The old center has a wide choice of budget eateries. Some of the cheapest meals are served in the basic *Restaurant España*, in the hotel of the same name. *Restaurant Punto Criollo*, Calle Igualdad, is deservedly popular with locals and visitors for its solid Venezuelan food and reasonable prices. *Pizzas Pastas* offers just what the name says and is a good value – take away or eat in.

Most finer restaurants are in the eastern sector of the city. On Calle Cedeño, just east of Av Santiago Mariño, there are a half-dozen good restaurants, including *El Chipi*, *Max's* and *El Faro de Julio*.

Hotel Tama has a charming front-garden restaurant serving good food at good prices, but if this is not enough for you, there are several upscale places around.

Getting Around

There's frequent transport to most of the island, including Pampatar, La Asunción and Juangriego, operated by small buses locally called micros. They leave from different points in the city center; departure points for some of the main tourist destinations are indicated on the map.

PAMPATAR

Pampatar, just northeast of Porlamar, is a town of some 12,000 people, gradually merging into a single conurbation with Porlamar. Founded in the 1530s, it was one of the earliest settlements on Margarita and still has some colonial buildings.

Things to See

Pampatar's fort, the **Castillo de San Carlos Borromeo**, built in the 1660s on the site of the previous stronghold (which was destroyed by pirates), is the best preserved and restored construction of its type on the island. The fort is on the waterfront in the center of town.

Opposite the fort is the **parish church**, dating from the mid-18th century. About 100m east of the church is the neoclassical **Casa de la Aduana**, dating from 1864, which has temporary exhibitions.

The beach, which extends for a kilometer east of the fort, has old-world charm, with rustic boats anchored in the bay or on the shore, and fishers repairing nets on the beach.

Places to Stay & Eat

Few travelers stay in Pampatar, but there are some budget places on Calle Almirante Brion, one block back from the beach. There are many open-air eateries along the beach.

LA ASUNCIÓN

Set in a fertile valley in the inland portion of the island, La Asunción is the capital of the Nueva Esparta state, even though it's far smaller than Porlamar. It's distinguished by its tranquillity and its verdant environs. There's virtually no duty-free commerce here, and hotels and restaurants are scarce.

Things to See

Built in the late 16th century, the **Catedral** on the tree-shaded Plaza Bolívar is one of the oldest surviving colonial churches in the country. Its austere exterior is adorned with a delicate Renaissance portal on the façade and two more doorways on the side walls.

On the northern side of the plaza is the **Museo Nueva Cádiz** (closed Monday), named for the first Spanish town in South America, established around 1500 on nearby Isla Cubagua. The town was completely destroyed by an earthquake in 1541, and traces disappeared until an excavation in 1950 uncovered the town foundations, some architectural details and various period objects. The museum displays a small collection of exhibits related to the region's history.

Just outside town, a 10-minute walk south up the hill, is the **Castillo de Santa Rosa** (closed Monday), one of the seven forts built on the island to protect it from pirate attacks. It provides a good view over the town and the valley and has some old armor on display.

JUANGRIEGO

Set on the edge of a fine bay in the northern part of Margarita, Juangriego is a relaxing, backwater sort of town. It has become popular with tourists, most of whom hang around the beach along the bay with rustic fishing boats and visiting yachts. Far away on the horizon, the peaks of Macanao are visible, particularly spectacular when the sun sets behind them.

The **Fortín de la Galera**, the fort crowning the hill just north of town, is today nothing more than stone walls with a terrace and a refreshment stand on the top. At sunset it is packed with tourists who come for the view, though a similarly attractive vista can be had from the beach.

Places to Stay & Eat

In the middle of the beach is the simple **Hotel Nuevo Juangriego** (☎ 095-532409). If you choose a room facing the bay (US$30 a double with bath) you'll get a postcard snap of the sunset from your window. Downstairs is an overpriced **restaurant**, with some umbrella-shaded tables outside on a terrace.

The basic **Hotel El Fortín** (☎ 095-530092), 200m north along the beach, costs US$16 per matrimonial with bath and has equally attractive sunset views if you choose the right room, although there are only three rooms facing the bay. Its restaurant and **El Búho**, next door, are pleasant places to eat, even though there appears to be a sunset-view tax on the food prices. **El Viejo Muelle**, a few paces away, is yet another romantic place for a meal or beer at sunset, though again, prices seem to be inflated.

Just back from the beach, in the Centro Comercial Juangriego on Calle La Marina, are two acceptable budget hotels: **Hotel La Coral** (☎ 095-532463), charging US$18/22 a double/triple; and **Hotel Gran Sol** (☎ 095-533216) at US$22/30. Other accommodations and food options are in the same area and farther back from the beach.

BEACHES

Isla de Margarita has some 50 beaches big enough to deserve a name, not to mention smaller bits of sandy coast. Many beaches have been developed with restaurants, bars, and deck chairs and sunshades for hire. Though the island is no longer a virgin paradise, you can still find a relatively deserted strip of sand. On the whole, Margarita's beaches have little shade, and some are virtually barren.

The postcard **Playa El Agua** is Margarita's trendiest and most developed beach. It's shaded with coconut groves and densely

dotted with palm-thatched restaurants and bars offering a good selection of food, cocktails and frequent live music. Behind the beach is a collection of hotels and holiday homes. The French-run **Hostería El Agua** (☎ 095-491297), on the Manzanillo road, half a kilometer back from the beach, is one of the cheapest places around at US$30/40 for air-con singles/doubles.

Other popular beaches include **Playa Guacuco** and **Playa Manzanillo**. Perhaps Margarita's finest beach is **Playa Puerto Cruz**, which arguably has the widest, whitest stretch of sand and still isn't overdeveloped. If you want to escape from people, head for the northern coast of **Macanao**, the wildest part of the island.

You can *camp* on the beaches, but use common sense and be cautious. Don't leave your tent unattended. Swimmers should be aware of dangerous undertows on some beaches, including Playa El Agua and Playa Puerto Cruz.

Guayana

Guayana occupies the whole of Venezuela's southeast to the south of the Orinoco River and its delta. It's an amazing and wildly diverse region, featuring mysterious tepuis, spectacular waterfalls, wild jungles and sweeping savannas. Here are the famous Angel Falls, the world's highest, and the unique Gran Sabana, a rolling savanna dotted with tepuis. One of them, Roraima, can be climbed, and this trip is an extraordinary adventure.

The only two important cities in the region are Ciudad Bolívar and Ciudad Guayana, both on the lower Orinoco; these apart, the region is very sparsely populated, without any significant urban centers. Much of the southern part of the region (30,000 sq km) has been decreed the Parque Nacional Canaima, which includes the Gran Sabana, Roraima and Angel Falls. The Ciudad Guayana-Santa Elena de Uairén highway, which cuts across the region, provides access to this fascinating land.

CIUDAD BOLÍVAR

Ciudad Bolívar is a hot city set on the southern bank of the Orinoco, about 420km upstream from the Atlantic. Founded in 1764 on a rocky elevation at the narrowest point of the river, the town was appropriately named Angostura (literally 'narrows') and grew slowly as a sleepy river port hundreds of miles away from any important centers of population. Then, suddenly and unexpectedly, Angostura became the place where much of the country's (and the continent's) history was forged.

It was here that Bolívar came in 1817, soon after the town had been liberated from Spanish control, and set up the base for the military operations against the Spaniards. The town was made the provisional capital of the country, which had yet to be liberated. It was in Angostura that the British Legionnaires joined Bolívar before all set off for a long and strenuous march across Los Llanos and up the Andes to bring independence for Colombia. And it was here that the Angostura Congress convened in 1819 and gave birth to Gran Colombia, a unified republic comprising Venezuela, Colombia and Ecuador. In honor of Bolívar, in 1846 the town was renamed Ciudad Bolívar.

Today, Ciudad Bolívar is the capital of Venezuela's largest state, Bolívar, and a city of 300,000 inhabitants. It has retained the flavor of an old river town and still conserves some of the architecture dating from its 50-year colonial era. It's a popular stop on travelers' routes, partly for the city itself and partly as a jumping-off point for Angel Falls.

Information

Tourist Offices The CIAT (Centro de Información y Atención al Turista) tourist office (☎ 085-22771) is on Av Táchira, two blocks northwest of the airport.

Money Banco Unión, Banco Mercantil and Banco de Venezuela give advances on credit cards. The Corp Banca, near the airport, changes American Express traveler's checks. The only authorized casa de cambio in town is across the road in the Hotel Laja Real; it exchanges cash and checks, but charges a 2% commission on transactions. Moneychangers hang around the entrance of the Hotel Colonial, on Paseo Orinoco, and change dollars and traveler's checks, although rates are rather poor.

Things to See

Midway along the lively waterfront, **Paseo Orinoco**, is the **Mirador Angostura**, a rocky headland that juts into the river at its narrowest point. The lookout commands good views up and down the Orinoco. About 5km upriver you'll see **Puente de Angostura**, a suspension bridge constructed in 1967; it's the only bridge across the Orinoco along its entire course.

Close to the lookout, the restored 18th-century prison building is now home to the **Instituto de Cultura del Orinoco**, which features crafts of Indian groups from Venezuela's south. Two blocks west is the **Museo de Ciudad Bolívar**, accommodated in the Casa del Correo del Orinoco. It was here that the republic's first newspaper was printed 1818-21, and you can see the original press on which it was done, along with other objects related to the town's history.

South up the hill is the historic heart of the city, **Plaza Bolívar**. Five allegorical statues on the square personify the five countries Bolívar liberated. To the east looms the massive **Catedral**, begun right after the town's foundation and completed 80 years later. Half of the west side of the plaza is taken by the **Casa del Congreso de Angostura**, built in the 1770s, which was the seat of the lengthy debates of the 1819 Angostura Congress. You can have a look around the interior.

Three blocks south of Plaza Bolívar is tree-shaded **Plaza Miranda**, bordered by the sizable **Centro de las Artes**, which features temporary exhibitions of modern art. Go upstairs to the mirador on the roof for a view of the **Fortín El Zamuro**, which crowns the top of the highest hill in the city, half a kilometer southeast. The fort is open for visitors and provides views over the old town.

Beyond the fort, on Av Táchira, is the **Museo Casa San Isidro**, in a fine colonial mansion where Bolívar stayed during the Angostura Congress. The house interior is maintained in the style of the Bolívar era.

About 1km to the southeast, on Av Briceño Irragorry, is the **Museo de Arte Moderno Jesús Soto**, which has a good collection of works by this kinetic artist (born in Ciudad Bolívar in 1923) and works by other modern artists.

In front of the airport terminal stands the legendary **airplane of Jimmie Angel** (see the Angel Falls section). This is the original plane, which was removed from the top of Auyantepui.

CIUDAD BOLÍVAR

PLACES TO STAY
5 Hotel Ritz
7 Hotel Colonial
9 Hotel Caracas
10 Hotel Italia
11 Hotel Unión

PLACES TO EAT
2 Restaurant Mirador
   Angostura
12 Tasca La Playa
18 Gran Fraternidad Universal
19 Arepera El Gran Boulevard

OTHER
1 Mirador Angostura
3 Museo de Ciudad Bolívar
4 Instituto de Cultura
   del Orinoco
6 Banco Unión
8 Banco de Venezuela
13 Casa de Tejas
14 Gobernación
15 Casa Piar
16 Casa Parroquial
17 Soana Travel
20 Iglesia de las Siervas

Organized Tours

Ciudad Bolívar is the main gateway to Angel Falls, and tours to the falls are the staple of most tour operators in the city. The most popular tour is a one-day package that includes a return flight to Canaima, a flight over Angel Falls, lunch in Canaima and a short boat excursion to Salto El Sapo. Some agents may offer Kavac as an alternative to Canaima, in which case the tour will include, apart from the Angel Falls flyover, an excursion to the Cueva de Kavac. Either tour will cost US$150 to US$180. A Canaima-Kavac two-day tour that combines all the attractions of the two one-day trips is available from some agencies for US$230 to US$270. Three-day tours are also offered, particu-

larly in the rainy season, when they include a boat trip to the foot of Angel Falls instead of a flight over it (US$240 to US$300).

Most tour operators in the city are grouped around Paseo Orinoco and the airport. In the former area, check the offers of three companies nestled in riverfront hotels – Neckar Tour (☎ 085-24402) in the Hotel Colonial; Expediciones Dearuna (☎ 085-26089) in the Hotel Caracas; and Cunaguaro Tours (☎ 085-22041) in the Hotel Italia. In the airport terminal, Turi Express (☎ 085-28910) is one of the better agencies.

Tour companies use the services of small local airlines that are based at the airport. Possibly the most reliable are Aero Servicios Caicara and Rutaca, and both have offices at the terminal. They can fly you to Canaima (US$50 to US$60 either way) and can include a flight over Angel Falls for US$40 to US$50 extra.

Other tours out of Ciudad Bolívar include trips to the Gran Sabana and Río Caura. The former is offered by most agents, usually as a four-day jeep trip (about US$200 per person, all-inclusive). The latter is probably best done with Soana Travel (☎ 085-22536), Calle Bolívar (US$350 per person for a five-day trip, all-inclusive).

Places to Stay

There's a choice of budget hotels on or just off Paseo Orinoco, arguably the most pleasant area to stay in the city. All hotels listed have rooms with private bath and fan (or air-con where indicated).

Hotel Caracas (☎ 085-26089), at Paseo Orinoco No 82, and *Hotel Italia* (☎ 085-27810), Paseo Orinoco No 131, have long been popular travelers' haunts. The Caracas is quite simple but cheap (US$12/14 a matrimonial/double) and has a lovely large terrace overlooking the Paseo, where you can sit over a bottle of beer, watch the world go by and enjoy the evening breeze. The Italia doesn't offer much luxury either, and it's been criticized by travelers for the lack of cleanliness and security. It costs US$12/14 a matrimonial/double with fan, US$16/18 with air-con. The hotel has a good budget restaurant.

Hotel Unión (☎ 085-23374), Calle Urica No 11, is clean if styleless and has rooms with fan and air-con for slightly less than those in the Italia. The Brazilian-run *Hotel Ritz* (☎ 085-23886), Calle Libertad No 3, offers air-con doubles with bath for US$18, doubles with fan but without bath for US$12.

The best place to stay on Paseo Orinoco is old-style *Hotel Colonial* (☎ 085-24402), where spacious air-con singles/doubles/triples cost US$26/32/36. Grab a room on the front side overlooking the river. You can eat in one of the two hotel restaurants.

Places to Eat

Good, inexpensive local fare is served at *Mercado La Carioca* (popularly called La Sapoara), a well-organized market at the eastern end of Paseo Orinoco, which has a row of restaurants lining the riverfront.

In the central waterfront area, the restaurant in *Hotel Italia* is the most popular budget place to eat among travelers. Alternatively, try *Restaurant Mirador Angostura*, which is even cheaper and popular with locals.

Arepera El Gran Boulevard is the best central arepera, while *Gran Fraternidad Universal*, on Calle Amor Patrio, provides cheap vegetarian lunches on weekdays. *Tasca La Playa*, on Calle Urica, has reasonable food, and the two restaurants in *Hotel Colonial* have some Italian dishes at affordable prices.

Getting There & Away

Air The airport is 2km southeast of the riverfront and is linked to the city center by local transport. There are two flights daily to Caracas (US$95). Rutaca has daily flights on light planes to Santa Elena de Uairén (US$70). For information about flights to Angel Falls, see Organized Tours, earlier, and the Angel Falls section.

Bus The bus terminal is at the junction of Avs República and Sucre, 2km south of the center. To get there, take the westbound buseta marked 'Terminal' from Paseo Orinoco.

Buses to Caracas run regularly throughout the day (US$20, nine hours). There are a dozen departures a day to Puerto Ayacucho (US$20, 10 hours). Turgar, Línea Orinoco, Travircán and Expresos Guayana service the route to Santa Elena de Uairén, with a total of nine departures daily (US$21, nine to 11 hours). To Ciudad Guayana, buses depart every 15 to 30 minutes (US$3, 1½ hours).

CIUDAD GUAYANA

Set on the southern bank of the Orinoco at its confluence with the Río Caroní, Ciudad Guayana is an unusual city. It was officially founded in 1961 to serve as an industrial center for the region and took into its metropolitan boundaries two quite different urban components: the old town of San Félix, on the eastern side of the Caroní, and the newborn Puerto Ordaz on the opposite bank. At the time of its foundation, the total population of the area was about 40,000. Forty years later, the two parts have virtually merged together into a 20km urban sprawl populated by more than 500,000 people – it's Venezuela's fastest growing city. Despite

CIUDAD GUAYANA – PUERTO ORDAZ

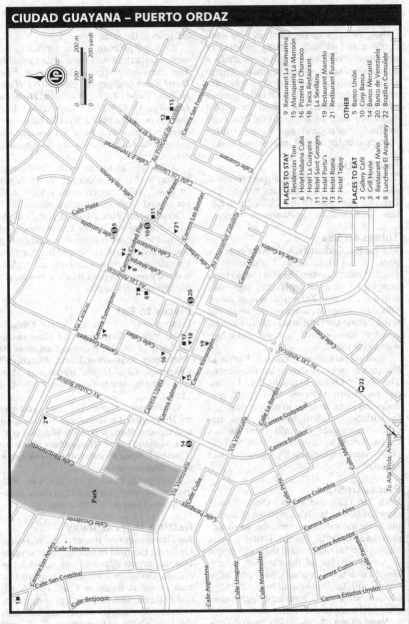

PLACES TO STAY
1 Residencias Tore
6 Hotel Habana Cuba
7 Hotel La Guayana
11 Hotel Saint Georges
12 Hotel Portu's
13 Hotel Roma
17 Hotel Tepuy

9 Restaurant La Romanina
15 Marisquería La Mansión
16 Pizzería El Churrasco
18 Tasca Restaurant
La Sevillana
19 Restaurant Marcelo
21 Restaurant Furama

OTHER
5 Banco Unión
10 Corp Banca
14 Banco Mercantil
20 Banco de Venezuela
22 Brazilian Consulate

PLACES TO EAT
2 Gallery Café
3 Grill House
4 Restaurant Mario
8 Lunchería El Araguaney

Park

To Alta Vista, Airport

its unified name, people persistently refer to San Félix and Puerto Ordaz.

San Félix was founded in the 16th century, but there's nothing historic or attractive about the town. It's essentially a workers' suburb and can be unsafe. Puerto Ordaz is quite a different story; it's modern and well planned, with a good infrastructure of roads, supermarkets and services. Yet it lacks the soul of those cities that have evolved in a natural way. Save for three scenic parks, there's not much to see or do.

Information

The tourist office is at the airport terminal, 6km west of Puerto Ordaz's center. The Brazilian consulate (☎ 086-235243) is in Edificio Amazonas, Av Las Américas.

Things to See

The **Parque Cachamay**, a pleasant riverside park, is a 15-minute walk southeast of Puerto Ordaz's center. The Río Caroní turns here into a series of rapids and eventually into a spectacular 200m-wide line of waterfalls. Adjoining the park from the southwest is the **Parque Loefling**, where there's a small zoo with some animals in cages and others wandering freely.

Another park noted for its falls, **Parque La Llovizna**, is on the islands in the Río Caroní. The highlight is the 20m Salto La Llovizna, and the drizzle (literally 'llovizna') it produces has given its name to the waterfall and the park. Several vantage points provide dramatic views over the falls from various angles. Access to the park is from Av Leopoldo Sucre Figarella. All parks are closed Monday.

Places to Stay

Both San Félix and Puerto Ordaz have a range of hotels, but it's advisable to stay in the latter for value, convenience, surroundings and security. Puerto Ordaz's main budget hotel area is around the Av Principal de Castillito. One of the cheapest here is *Hotel Portu's*, which costs US$10 per matrimonial with fan but without bath, US$12/14 a matrimonial with bath and fan/air-con. The hotel has a budget restaurant.

Hotel Roma (☎ 086-223780), next door, is basic but acceptable and costs much the same as Portu's. At first sight, you might think the hotel has been demolished, but it

hasn't. Look out for the steps and go downstairs (watch your head). There are more cheapies in the same area.

It's more pleasant to stay farther to the west and south of Av Principal de Castillito. The cheapest places in this area include *Hotel Saint Georges* (☎ 086-220079), *Hotel Habana Cuba* (☎ 086-224904) and *Hotel La Guayana* (☎ 086-227375), none of which should cost more than US$24/30 for air-con doubles/triples with bath. La Guayana is perhaps the best of the lot and has a reasonable restaurant.

A few blocks to the south, on Carrera Upata, is the more decent *Hotel Tepuy* (☎ 086-220111), which costs US$30/36/50 per air-con single/double/triple with bath.

Residencias Tore (☎ 086-231780), Calle San Cristóbal at Carrera Los Andes, is an enjoyable family-run small posada on a quiet leafy backstreet. Simple but comfortable air-con doubles with bath are US$36, and the guests can have meals in the hotel's own open-air restaurant.

Places to Eat

Inexpensive eateries in Puerto Ordaz's center include *Restaurant La Guayana* in the hotel of the same name, *Lunchería El Araguaney*, *Restaurant Mario*, *Pizzería El Churrasco*, *Grill House*, *Restaurant Marcelo* and the street stalls along Calle Los Llanos.

Of some more upmarket places, you may try *Restaurant La Romanina* (Italian food and steaks), *Marisquería La Mansión* (fish and seafood) and *Restaurant Furama* (Chinese). *Tasca Restaurant La Sevillana* is a chic place open late.

Gallery Café is a trendy, arty café with live music most days, lovely salads, sandwiches and fondue; it's open late.

Getting There & Away

Air The airport is at the west end of Puerto Ordaz on the road to Ciudad Bolívar (note that the airport appears in all schedules as Puerto Ordaz, not Ciudad Guayana). It handles direct flights to Caracas (US$80) and Porlamar (US$55) and has connections to other destinations. Servivensa has daily flights on DC-3s to Canaima (US$125) and on to Santa Elena de Uairén (another US$125, but if you don't stop in Canaima it's US$125 for the whole route).

Bus Ciudad Guayana has two bus terminals. The main one is in San Félix, on Av Gumilla, about 1.5km south of San Félix's center. The environs of the terminal can be unsafe, particularly after dark, so don't walk there; get there by carrito or taxi.

The other terminal is in Puerto Ordaz, on Av Guayana, 1km east of the airport. It's smaller, cleaner, quieter and safer and handles far fewer buses than the San Félix station.

There are regular departures from San Félix's terminal to Caracas (US$23, 10½ hours), and most buses call en route at Puerto Ordaz's terminal. Buses to Ciudad Bolívar depart from both terminals every half-hour or so (US$3, 1½ hours).

Nine buses daily come through from Ciudad Bolívar on their way to Santa Elena (US$18, eight to 10 hours); all call at San Félix, but only a few do in Puerto Ordaz.

Expresos La Guayanesa has two buses a day from San Félix to Tucupita (US$5, 3½ hours), but por puestos go there regularly (US$7, two hours). The trip involves a ferry ride across the Orinoco from San Félix to Los Barrancos.

TUCUPITA

The major urban center of the Orinoco delta, Tucupita is a hot river town of 60,000 people. It evolved in the 1920s as one of a chain of Capuchin missions that were founded in the delta to convert the Indians. For travelers, Tucupita is essentially a jumping-off point for exploring the delta rather than an attraction in itself.

Covering about 25,000 sq km, the Orinoco delta is the second-largest delta on the continent after the Amazon. The river splits into 40-odd major *caños* (channels), which carry the waters down into the Atlantic. Their *bocas* (mouths) are distributed along 360km of coast. The southernmost channel, Río Grande, is the main one and is used by ocean-going vessels sailing upriver to Ciudad Guayana.

The climate of the delta is hot and humid, with an average annual temperature around 26°C (79°F). The driest period is from January to March; the remaining part of the year is wet or very wet. The water reaches its highest level from August to September, when parts of the delta become marshy or flooded.

The delta is inhabited by the Warao Indians, the second-largest indigenous group in Venezuela (after the Guajiro), numbering about 24,000. They live along the caños, constructing palafitos on riverbanks and living mostly off fishing. Many of the Waraos still use their native language.

Information

Tourist Office The Diturda state tourist office (☎ 087-216852) is in the Edificio San Juan (2nd floor), on Calle Bolívar, just off Plaza Bolívar.

Money Banco de Venezuela and Banco Unión might give cash advances on Visa and MasterCard, but that's about it. US cash and traveler's checks may prove difficult to change in Tucupita. Most tour agencies accept US money for their services, but not credit cards or traveler's checks.

Organized Tours

A half-dozen tour operators in town focus on trips into the delta. The tourist office keeps track of the current situation and has a list of registered companies. Tours are usually all-inclusive two- to four-day trips (there are hardly any one-day tours), and the going rate is US$60 to US$100 per person a day depending on the company, the routes and conditions, and particularly on the number of people in the group. Most agencies say they can provide English or German-speaking guides, though it's better to check this by asking to meet the guide before you commit yourself.

Most agents offer tours to the northern part of the delta, toward Pedernales. Of these, Aventura Turística Delta (☎ 087-210835), Calle Centurión, receives the best comments from travelers. Other agencies operating northern routes include Trip to Nature (☎ 087-210144), Calle Bolívar; Bujana Tours (☎ 087-212776), Calle Dalla Costa; and Tucupita Expeditions (☎ 087-212986), Calle Manamo.

Delta Surs (☎ 087-212666), Calle Mariño, offers tours to the far eastern area of the delta, based at the camp in San Francisco de Guayo. Also in Guayo is the French-run Tobé Lodge. The company's office at Plaza Bolívar in Tucupita (☎ 087-210709) offers packages to the camp.

There are also independent guides who descend like vultures as soon as you arrive

VENEZUELA

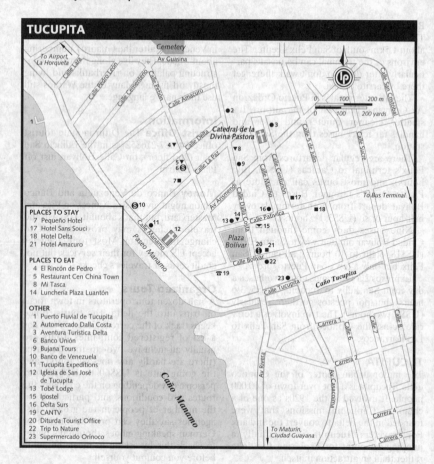

TUCUPITA

To Airport,
La Horqueta

Cemetery

Av Guasina

Calle Lara

Calle Pedro León

Calle Cementerio

Calle Petión

Calle Amacuro

Calle San Cristóbal

Catedral de la
Divina Pastora

Calle La Paz

Calle 5 de Julio

Calle Centurión

Calle Sucre

Calle Mariño

Av Arismendi

To Bus Terminal

Av Dalla Costa

Calle Pativilca

Plaza
Bolívar

Calle Bolívar

Caño Tucupita

Calle Tucupita

Carrera 1

Calle 6

Calle 7

Calle 8

Carrera 2

Av Rivera

Av Casacoima

Carrera 4

Carrera 5

Caño Manamo

Paseo Manamo

To Maturín,
Ciudad Guayana

0   100   200 m
0   100   200 yards

PLACES TO STAY
7   Pequeño Hotel
17 Hotel Sans Souci
18 Hotel Delta
21 Hotel Amacuro

PLACES TO EAT
4   El Rincón de Pedro
5   Restaurant Cen China Town
8   Mi Tasca
14 Lunchería Plaza Luantón

OTHER
1   Puerto Fluvial de Tucupita
2   Automercado Dalla Costa
3   Aventura Turística Delta
6   Banco Unión
9   Bujana Tours
10 Banco de Venezuela
11 Tucupita Expeditions
12 Iglesia de San José
    de Tucupita
13 Tobé Lodge
15 Ipostel
16 Delta Surs
19 CANTV
20 Diturda Tourist Office
22 Trip to Nature
23 Supermercado Orinoco

in town. Their tours may be cheaper, though
you never actually know what you'll get for
your money; comments are mixed (even
totally contradictory) about their services. If
you decide on these guides, clarify all the
details of the trip (the duration, the places to
be visited, food and lodging, etc), and have a
look at the boat before you commit yourself.
Make sure the boat has two engines
(required by law) and preferably a roof and
that the mosquito nets are provided for
hammocks. After you and your guide agree
on a price, pay only the money necessary for
predeparture expenses (gasoline, food).
Insist on paying the remaining part only on
your return.

Places to Stay

There are four or five hotels in the town
center, and a few more outside the central
area. All the hotels listed have rooms with
private baths.

The cheapest, *Pequeño Hotel* (☎ 087-
210523), Calle La Paz, has doubles with
fan/noisy air-con for US$12/15. *Hotel Delta*
(☎ 087-212467), Calle Pativilca, offers much
the same for US$14/17.

Hotel Amacuro (☎ 087-210404), Calle
Bolívar, is a little bit better and has quieter
air-con. Its singles/doubles/triples cost
US$15/18/22. The best of the central options
is *Hotel Sans Souci* (☎ 087-210132), Calle
Centurión, which charges US$15/20 for a

matrimonial with fan/air-con and has its own restaurant.

Places to Eat

There's a range of simple places to eat in town, of which *Mi Tasca*, Calle Dalla Costa, is popular with travelers for its hearty food at low prices. *El Rincón de Pedro*, Calle Petión, has good chicken, among other dishes, while the nearby *Restaurant Cen China Town* does some reasonable Chinese cooking. *Tasca Sans Souci* is OK and inexpensive. *Lunchería Plaza Luantón*, on Plaza Bolívar, serves good coffee and a choice of snacks. For food provisions for a trip, try *Automercado Dalla Costa* or *Supermercado Orinoco*.

Getting There & Away

The bus terminal is 1km southeast of the center; walk or take a taxi (US$2). There are two buses nightly to Caracas (US$21, 11 hours). Expresos La Guayanesa runs two buses daily to Ciudad Guayana (US$5, 3½ hours), but por puestos service this route regularly (US$7, two hours). Similarly, to Maturín, there are both buses (US$5, four hours) and the more frequent por puestos (US$8, three hours). Change in Maturín for Caripe and Cueva del Guácharo.

ANGEL FALLS

Salto Angel (known to the English-speaking world as Angel Falls) is the world's highest waterfall. Its total height is 979m, of which the uninterrupted drop is 807m, about 16 times the height of Niagara Falls. Angel Falls spill from the heart-shaped Auyantepui, one of the largest of the tepuis, with a flat top of about 700 sq km. The waterfall is in the central part of the tepui and drops into Cañón del Diablo (Devil's Canyon).

The fall is not named, as one might expect, after a divine creature, but after an American bush pilot, Jimmie Angel, who landed on the boggy top of the tepui in 1937 in his four-seater airplane in search of gold. The plane stuck in the marshy surface and Angel couldn't take off again. He, his wife and two companions trekked through rough, virgin terrain to the edge of the plateau, then descended more than a kilometer of almost vertical cliff, returning to civilization after an 11-day odyssey.

The waterfall's volume much depends on the season. In the dry months (normally January to May), it can be pretty faint – just a thin ribbon of water fading into mist halfway down its drop. In rainy months (June to December), it's often voluminous and spectacular, but frequently covered by clouds.

Orientation

The waterfall is in a distant wilderness without any road access. The village of Canaima, about 50km northwest, is the major gateway to the falls. Canaima doesn't have any overland link to the rest of the country either, but it does have an airport. The small Indian settlement of Kavac, at the southeastern foot of Auyantepui, is becoming another jumping-off point for the falls, mostly for organized tours. It's also isolated, but it has its own airstrip.

A visit to Angel Falls is normally undertaken in two stages, with Canaima (or Kavac) as the stepping stone. Most tourists fly into Canaima, where they take a light plane or boat to the falls. No walking trails go all the way from Canaima (or Kavac) to the falls.

Flights are serviced by light (usually five-seat) planes of various small airlines coming mostly from Ciudad Bolívar or via Servivensa's 22-seater DC-3s. The pilots fly two or three times back and forth over the face of the falls, circle the top of the tepui and then return. The return trip from Canaima takes about 40 minutes and costs US$40 to US$60.

Motorized canoes to the foot of Angel Falls only operate in the rainy season (usually June to December or January), when the water level is sufficiently high. The return trip can be done in one day (US$120 to US$150 per person, all-inclusive), but it's more relaxing to go for a three-day, two-night tour (US$180 to US$240).

There are a number of other attractions in the area, mostly waterfalls, of which the most popular is **Salto El Sapo**. It's a 10-minute boat trip from Canaima plus a short walk. Salto El Sapo is beautiful and unusual in that you can walk under it. You'll probably get drenched by the waterfall, so take a swimsuit. A short walk from El Sapo is **Salto El Sapito**, another attractive waterfall, normally included in the same excursion.

VENEZUELA

Salto Angel, Auyantepui, Canaima and the surrounding area lie within the boundaries of the Parque Nacional Canaima, Venezuela's second-largest national park (the country's only park appearing on the UNESCO World's Natural Heritage list), which covers 30,000 sq km. All visitors coming to Canaima pay a US$5 national park entrance fee.

Canaima

Canaima is a mixed Indian-tourist village that serves as a springboard for Angel Falls. It is spectacularly set on a peaceful, wide stretch of the Río Carrao, known as Laguna Canaima, just below the point where the river turns into a line of magnificent falls, called Saltos Hacha.

The centerpoint of the village is Campamento Canaima, a tourist camp built right on the bank of the lake. The airport is just a few minutes walk to the west.

Bring a swimsuit, plenty of film and efficient insect repellent. There are treacherous undercurrents caused by the waterfalls in Laguna de Canaima, so be careful and find out where it's safe to swim before going into deep water.

Information There's no specific tourist office here, but tour operators are knowledgeable about the region and usually helpful.

Campamento Canaima changes US dollars (but not traveler's checks). Try the Tienda Quincallería Canaima (a souvenir-grocery shop) near the airport, which is likely to change both cash and checks. The rate is lower than in the cities, so it's best to come with a sufficient amount of bolívares. Most of Canaima's tour operators will accept payment in US dollars, but not credit cards, or will charge 10% more if you pay with plastic money.

Organized Tours Hoturvensa (Hoteles y Turismo Avensa), which runs Campamento Canaima, offers packages that include accommodations and full board in its camp, a flight over Angel Falls in a DC-3 (weather permitting) and a short boat trip around the lake (but they don't include the flight in and out of Canaima). Two kinds of packages are available: a two-day and one-night stay for around US$400, and a three-day, two-night

stay for US$750 (single or double occupancy). Packages can be bought from any Avensa office in Venezuela and from most travel agencies. Hoturvensa doesn't offer any tours other than these.

There are several other operators in Canaima, including Canaima Tours, Tiuna Tours and Kamaracoto Tours; tours with these companies are generally booked upon arrival in Canaima. Canaima Tours is an agent of Hoturvensa and has its office in Campamento Canaima. The two remaining companies are cheaper and advertised prices can be negotiated to some extent – representatives wait for incoming flights at the airport. All three companies run boat trips to Angel Falls and operate other regional tours and can also arrange flights over the falls.

See Organized Tours in the Ciudad Bolívar section for tours organized from that city, which may work out to be cheaper and more convenient.

Places to Stay & Eat Canaima's main lodging and eating facility is Hoturvensa's *Campamento Canaima*. The camp consists of about 35 palm-thatched cabañas (109 rooms in all, with bath and hot water), its own *restaurant*, *bar* and *soda fountain*. Accommodations are only available as part of a package (see Organized Tours), but the camp's other facilities are open to all. The restaurant is expensive (breakfast US$12, lunch US$14, dinner US$14), but the food is good and you can eat as much as you want.

There are more than a half-dozen cheaper camps and posadas in Canaima, some of which also serve meals. At most places, expect to pay US$8 to US$12 for a hammock and US$20 to US$30 for a bed. Some camps will let you string up your own hammock under their roof (and use their facilities) for US$4 to US$8. Inquire with Tiuna and Kamaracoto agents at the airport upon arrival for information about lodging options.

Campamento Churún Vená, opposite the soccer pitch in the south part of the village, is one of the cheaper places, at US$9/20 a hammock/bed. The nearby *Restaurant Imabarí* (popularly known as Los Simons) is reasonably cheap by Canaima standards – US$10 for lunch or dinner. In the same area, *Campamento Weytüpü*, opposite the school, provides more comfortable lodgings for US$60/90 per double/triple.

In the north of the village, the cheapest hammock-type accommodations are at **Campamento Hermanos Jiménez** for US$8 per hammock. About 250m farther north are **Posada Kusarí** (US$20 a bed) and **Posada Kaikusé** (US$25).

If you have your own tent, you can camp free in Canaima, but get a permit from the Inparques officer at the airport. The usual place to camp is on the beach next to the helpful Guardia Nacional post, just off Campamento Canaima. You may be able to arrange with guards to leave your stuff at the post while you are away.

There are a few shops in Canaima that sell basic supplies, such as bread, pasta, canned fish and biscuits, but prices are high. If you plan on shopping for your own groceries, it's best to bring your own food with you to Canaima.

Getting There & Away Servivensa has one flight per day on jets between Caracas and Canaima via Ciudad Bolívar. If you buy either of Hoturvensa's packages, Servivensa will sell you a discount ticket (about US$160 roundtrip from Caracas). Otherwise, it will charge an inflated fare (US$160 one way from Caracas, US$125 from Ciudad Bolívar) and still may not want to sell tickets in advance in hopes of filling flights with package passengers. Servivensa also has (equally overpriced) daily flights on DC-3s to and from Puerto Ordaz (US$125) and Santa Elena de Uairén (US$125). Make sure to book an onward ticket; otherwise you may have to wait in Canaima for several days before an available seat appears.

Several regional carriers fly from Ciudad Bolívar to Canaima on a semiregular or charter basis for US$50 to US$60. See Organized Tours in the Ciudad Bolívar section for details.

GRAN SABANA

A rolling grassy highland in Venezuela's far southeastern corner, the Gran Sabana is vast, wild, beautiful, empty and silent. The only town in the region is Santa Elena de Uairén, near the Brazilian border. The remaining part of the sparse population are mostly Pemón Indians, the traditional inhabitants of the land, who live in scattered villages and hamlets.

Not long ago, the Gran Sabana was virtually inaccessible by land. It wasn't until 1973 that a road between El Dorado and Santa Elena was completed, and the last stretch of road was finally sealed in 1991. Today, it's one of the best highways in the country and one of the most spectacular. The road is signposted with kilometer marks from the El Dorado fork (km 0) southward to Santa Elena (km 316) – a great help in orientation.

The most striking natural features of Gran Sabana's skyline are gigantic, flat-topped tepuis. 'Tepui' (also spelled 'tepuy') is the Pemón word for mountain. More than 100 such mesas dot the vast region from the Colombian border in the west up into Guyana and Brazil in the east. The largest concentration is in the Gran Sabana. The best known of all tepuis is Roraima, one of the few that can be climbed (see Roraima, later in this chapter).

There are many other sights in the Sabana, some conveniently close to the main road. Particularly amazing are the waterfalls, and there are a maze of them. One of the best examples easily accessible from the road is lovely, 50m-high **Salto Kamá** (km 202). Go down to the foot of the waterfall for the best view.

Salto Yuruaní (km 247) is a wonderful mini-Niagara, about 7m high and 100m wide. **Quebrada de Jaspe** (km 273) is a small cascade made particularly beautiful by the red jasper rock of the creekbed.

The star attraction is probably the 105m **Salto Aponguao**, also known by its Indian name, 'Chinak Merú.' This one is harder to get to, as it's about 40km off the highway, near the small Indian hamlet of Iboribó, accessible by a rough road.

Make sure you bring plenty of good insect repellent. The Sabana is infested by a kind of small gnat known as *jején*. They are particularly voracious in the morning and late afternoon, and the bites itch for days.

Places to Stay & Eat

Simple accommodations and meals are available in a number of places throughout the Gran Sabana, including Kavanayén, Chivatón, Iboribó, Rápidos de Kamoirán (km 172), Salto Kamá (km 202), Quebrada Pacheco (km 237) and San Francisco de Yuruaní (km 250). You can *camp* virtually anywhere you wish.

VENEZUELA

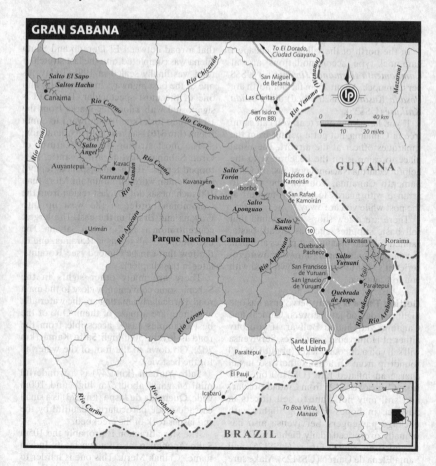

GRAN SABANA

Getting Around

Getting around the Sabana is not all that easy, as public transport only operates on the highway and is infrequent. Given time, you can visit the sights on the main road using a combination of hitchhiking and buses. Heading toward Kavanayén, however, may prove difficult, as there are no buses on this road and traffic is sporadic. A comfortable solution is a tour from Ciudad Bolívar or Santa Elena de Uairén (see those sections).

RORAIMA

Roraima, on the tripartite border of Venezuela, Guyana and Brazil, is one of the highest tepuis; its plateau is at about 2700m

and the highest peak is at 2810m. It was the first of the tepuis on which a climb was recorded (in 1884) and has been much explored by botanists. It's the easiest table mountain to ascend and is increasingly popular among travelers. The climb can be done by anyone reasonably fit and healthy, yet it's a long and strenuous hike. You need a minimum of five days to do this trip in addition to camping equipment and food.

When to Go

Dry season is from December to April, but the tops of the tepuis receive rain off the Atlantic year-round. Weather changes in a matter of minutes, with bright sunshine or heavy rain possible at any time.

What to Bring

A good tent, preferably with a fly sheet, is a must. It gets bitterly cold at night on the top, so bring a good sleeping bag and warm clothes. You also need reliable rain gear, sturdy shoes, a cooking stove and the usual hiking equipment. Bring enough food to last you one or two days more than planned – you may not be able to resist the temptation of staying longer on the top, or you may be stuck at Río Kukenán, unable to cross. A rope may be useful for crossing the river.

There are no jejenes atop Roraima, but you'll have plenty of these nasty biting gnats on the way, so take an effective insect repellent. Don't forget to bring a good supply of film. A macro lens is a great help in photographing the unique small plants. Make sure to bring along plastic bags, to take *all* your garbage back down to civilization. Don't remove anything that belongs to the mountain – no plants, rocks, crystals. Searches are sometimes conducted on returning travelers and crystals are subject to heavy fines.

San Francisco de Yuruaní

The starting point for the trip is the small village of San Francisco de Yuruaní, 66km north of Santa Elena by the highway.

Two small tour operators, Roraima Tours and Arapena Tours, offer expensive but all-inclusive tours or can arrange just guides (US$30 a day per group) and porters (US$30 a day). Both guides and porters can also be hired in the village of Paraitepui, the next stop on the way to Roraima.

Accommodation options in San Francisco include the roadside *Hospedaje Minina*, 100m north of the bus stop (US$15 per triple), and an *unmarked house* just next to Roraima Tours (US$6 per person). A few basic eateries will keep you going.

Paraitepui

Paraitepui is a nondescript Indian village of about 270 people whose identity has been largely shattered by tourists and their money. It's about 25km east of San Francisco; to get there, hire a jeep from tour operators in San Francisco (US$60, regardless of the number of passengers, up to about eight) or walk. The road to Paraitepui branches off the highway 1km south of San Francisco. It's a hot, steady, seven-hour walk, mostly uphill, to Paraitepui (back to San Francisco, it's six

hours). You may be lucky enough to hitch a jeep ride on this road, but traffic is sporadic and drivers are likely to charge you for the lift (a more reasonable fare than the jeep rental in San Francisco, though).

Upon arrival, you will invariably be greeted by one of the village headmen, who will show you the list of guides (apparently every adult male in the village is a guide) and inform you about prices (much the same as in San Francisco). Although you don't really need a guide to follow the track up to the tepui, the village headmen won't let you pass through without one.

There are no hotels in the village, but you can *camp* on the square near the school, under a thatched roof (US$4 per person). Overpriced hot meals are available in the house behind the school. A few shops in the village sell basic food (canned fish, biscuits, packet soups) at exorbitant prices.

Climbing Roraima

Once you have your guide, you can set off for Roraima. The trip to the top takes two days (total walking time is about 12 hours up and 10 hours down). There are several good places to camp (with water) on the way. The most popular campsites are on the Río Tek (four hours from Paraitepui), on the Río Kukenán (30 minutes farther on) and the so-called *campamento base* (base camp) at the foot of Roraima (three hours uphill from the Río Kukenán). The steep and tough four-hour ascent from the base camp to the top is the most spectacular (yet demanding) part of the hike.

Once you reach the top, you walk for some 15 minutes to a place called *El Hotel*, one of the few sites good for camping. It's actually a patch of sand large enough for about four small tents, partly protected by an overhanging rock. There are several other, smaller 'hotels' in the area.

The scenery all around is a moonscape, evocative of a science-fiction movie: impressive blackened rocks of every imaginable shape, gorges, creeks, pink beaches and gardens filled with unique flowering plants. Frequent and constantly changing mist and fog add to the mysterious air.

It's here that the guide finally becomes handy, as it's very easy to get lost on the vast plateau. Your guide will take you to some of the attractions, including **El Foso**, a curious

VENEZUELA

round pool in a deep rocky hole. It's about a three-hour walk from El Hotel. On the way, you'll pass by the amazingly lush **Valle Arabopo**. Beyond the pool is the **Valle de los Cristales** and the **Laberinto**, both well worth a trip. Plan on staying at least one full day on the top; it's better to allow two or three days.

Getting There & Away
San Francisco de Yuruaní is on the Ciudad Guayana-Santa Elena highway, and nine buses a day run in either direction.

SANTA ELENA DE UAIRÉN
Founded in 1924, Santa Elena de Uairén began to grow when diamonds were discovered in the 1930s in the Icabarú region, 115km to the west. Because it was isolated from the center of the country by a lack of roads, it remained a small village. The second development push came with the opening of the highway from El Dorado.

Today, Santa Elena is a pleasant, easygoing border town of 12,000 people, with an agreeable, if damp, climate and a Brazilian air, thanks to the significant number of residents from across the border.

Information
Tourist Offices Tour agencies (see Organized Tours) are likely to provide information about the region.

Brazilian Consulate The consulate is at the northeastern end of town and is open weekdays 8 am until noon. It's a good idea to play it safe and get your visa beforehand – the nearest Brazilian consulate before Santa Elena is in Ciudad Guayana.

Immigration The DEX office, behind the large building of the Prefectura, is open 7:30 to 11:30 am and 2 to 5 pm Monday to Saturday, Sunday 8 to 11:30 am. Be sure to have your passport stamped here before leaving or upon arrival in Venezuela. Brazilian passport formalities are done at the border itself. A yellow-fever vaccination certificate is required by officials if you're entering Brazil.

Money Banco Industrial de Venezuela gives cash advances on Visa credit cards. Banco del Orinoco changes American Express traveler's checks, but the transaction may take up to two hours. Money-changers hang around the corner of Calle Bolívar and Calle Urdaneta and deal with cash.

If you are heading north into Venezuela, keep in mind that the nearest place you can change money is likely to be Ciudad Guayana, 600km away. If you're heading south for Brazil, get rid of all *bolívares* in Santa Elena and buy Brazilian currency.

Organized Tours
There are a dozen tour agencies in Santa Elena. Their staple is a two or three-day jeep tour around the Gran Sabana, with visits to the most interesting sights. Count on US$30 to US$35 per day per person in a group of four and about US$5 less than that for a larger party. Prices include transport and a guide, but not accommodations or food. However, the tours normally call at budget places to stay and eat.

Another popular tour destination is the El Paují area, noted for natural attractions and gold and diamond mines. These are usually one- or two-day trips, with prices and conditions similar to those of the Gran Sabana tours.

Most operators can take you to Paraitepui (the starting point for the Roraima trek) and pick you up on a pre-arranged date, though it may work out cheaper to go by bus to San Francisco and hire a jeep there or walk.

Roberto's Mystic Tours (☎ 088-951790), run by Roberto Marrero, is one of the most respected companies. Apart from the standard Gran Sabana trips, it has tours to the El Paují area (without visiting the mines). The company also offers camping-equipment rental and Internet access. Another recommended agency is Ruta Salvaje Tours (☎ 088-951134), run by Iván Artal, which has a choice of tours, including rafting, and also rents camping gear.

Viajes Karavaré/New Frontiers (☎ 088-951443) specializes in trekking, including trips to the top of Roraima, and provides guides, porters, equipment and transport. The company also rents camping equipment. Also try Tayukasen Tours (☎ 088-951071), in the Hotel Luz, which has reasonable services and prices.

Other tour companies include Anaconda Tours (☎ 088-951016), Happy Tour (☎ 088-951339) and Rodiske Tours (☎ 088-951467).

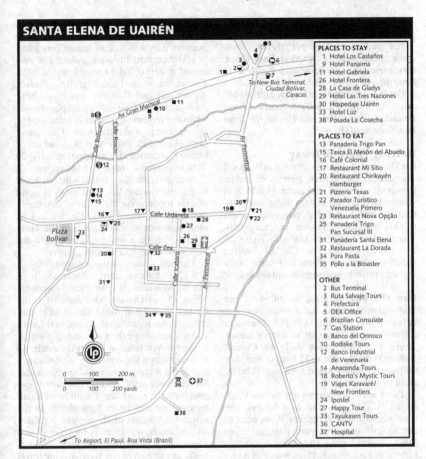

SANTA ELENA DE UAIRÉN

To New Bus Terminal,
Ciudad Bolívar,
Caracas

Av Gran Mariscal

Calle Bolívar

Calle Roscio

Av Perimetral

Plaza
Bolívar

Calle Urdaneta

Calle Icabarú

Calle Zea

Av Perimetral

0   100   200 m
0   100   200 yards

To Airport, El Paují, Boa Vista (Brazil)

PLACES TO STAY
1 Hotel Los Castaños
9 Hotel Panaima
11 Hotel Gabriela
26 Hotel Frontera
28 La Casa de Gladys
29 Hotel Las Tres Naciones
30 Hospedaje Uairén
33 Hotel Luz
38 Posada La Cosecha

PLACES TO EAT
13 Panadería Trigo Pan
15 Tasca El Mesón del Abuelo
16 Café Colonial
17 Restaurant Mi Sitio
20 Restaurant Chirikayén
    Hamburger
21 Pizzería Texas
22 Parador Turístico
    Venezuela Primero
23 Restaurant Nova Opção
25 Panadería Trigo
    Pan Sucursal III
31 Panadería Santa Elena
32 Restaurant La Dorada
34 Pura Pasta
35 Pollo a la Broaster

OTHER
2 Bus Terminal
3 Ruta Salvaje Tours
4 Prefectura
5 DEX Office
6 Brazilian Consulate
7 Gas Station
8 Banco del Orinoco
10 Rodiske Tours
12 Banco Industrial
    de Venezuela
14 Anaconda Tours
18 Roberto's Mystic Tours
19 Viajes Karavaré/
    New Frontiers
24 Ipostel
27 Happy Tour
33 Tayukasen Tours
36 CANTV
37 Hospital

Places to Stay

There's no shortage of accommodations in Santa Elena. It's easy to find a room, except in mid-August, when the town celebrates the feast of its patron saint. All hotels listed here have rooms with fans and private baths.

The friendly *La Casa de Gladys* (☎ 088-951171) has long been a popular travelers' lodge. Doubles/triples are US$12/15, and you can use the kitchen and fridge. Gladys offers laundry facilities for guests and handles camping-gear rental.

Posada La Cosecha (☎ 088-951756) is a pleasant, family-run place and a good value for US$15 a double. Other budget places (costing not more than La Cosecha) include *Hotel Las Tres Naciones* (☎ 088-951190), *Hotel Panaima* (☎ 088-951474), *Hospedaje Uairén* and the basic *Hotel Luz* (☎ 088-951050).

For a little more, you can stay in the reasonable *Hotel Gabriela* (☎ 088-951379) or *Hotel Los Castaños* (☎ 088-951450). One of the best in the town center is *Hotel Frontera* (☎ 088-951095), which has doubles with TV for US$30.

Places to Eat

There are plenty of inexpensive eateries all around central streets. *Café Colonial*, *Restaurant Nova Opçâo*, *Restaurant Mi Sitio* and *Restaurant Chirikayén Hamburger* are a few. Slightly more expensive

VENEZUELA

are *Parador Turístico Venezuela Primero* and *Tasca El Mesón del Abuelo*.

For budget pizza, try *Pizzería Texas*, while cheap pasta is served at *Pura Pasta*. *Restaurant La Dorada* and *Pollo a la Broaster* are the places for chicken.

For breakfast, there are a few central bakeries, including *Panadería Santa Elena*, *Panadería Trigo Pan* and *Panadería Trigo Pan Sucursal III*.

Getting There & Away

Air The airport is 7km southwest of town, off the road to the border. There's no public transport; a taxi will cost around US$6. Servivensa has overpriced daily flights to Puerto Ordaz (US$125), with a stopover in Canaima (US$125). These flights are serviced by 60-year-old DC-3s. Rutaca has daily flights on five-seater Cessnas to Ciudad Bolívar (US$70). Anaconda Tours and some other agencies provide information and sell tickets.

Bus The bus terminal is on Av Gran Mariscal in the town, but a new terminal is being built on the Ciudad Guayana highway, about 2km east of town's center. There are nine buses daily to Ciudad Bolívar (US$21, nine to 11 hours), and they all pass through Ciudad Guayana (US$18, eight to 10 hours).

There are three buses a day to Boa Vista, Brazil (US$12, three to four hours). The road is now sealed all the way. Remember to get an exit stamp in your passport from DEX beforehand. The border, locally known as La Línea, is 15km south of Santa Elena. The bus calls at the Brazilian border immigration post for passport formalities.

Amazonas

Venezuela's southernmost state, Amazonas, covers an area of 175,000 sq km, or approximately one-fifth of the national territory, yet it has at most 1% of the country's population. Despite its name, most of the region lies in the Orinoco drainage basin, while the Amazon basin takes up only the southwestern portion of the state. The two basins are linked by the unusual Brazo Casiquiare, a natural channel that sends a portion of the water from the Orinoco to Río Negro and down to the Amazon.

The region is predominantly a thick rain forest crisscrossed by rivers and sparsely populated by a mosaic of Indian communities. The current Indian population is estimated at 40,000, half of what it was in 1925. The three main Indian groups, Piaroa, Yanomami and Guajibo, make up about three-quarters of the indigenous population, while the remaining quarter is composed of the Yekuana (Maquiritare), Curripaco, Guarekena, Piapoco and a number of smaller communities. Approximately 20 Indian languages are used in the region.

In contrast to the central Amazon basin in Brazil, Venezuelan Amazonas is quite diverse topographically, its most noticeable feature being the tepuis. Though not as numerous nor as 'classical' as in the Gran Sabana, they do give the green carpet a distinctive and spectacular appearance.

The best known of the Amazonas tepuis is Cerro Autana, about 80km south of Puerto Ayacucho. It's the sacred mountain of the Piaroa Indians, who consider it the birthplace of the universe. The tepui is reminiscent of a gigantic tree trunk that looms about 700m above the surrounding plains.

Puerto Ayacucho, at the northwestern tip of Amazonas, is the only town of significance and is the main gateway and supply center for the entire state. It's also the chief transport hub, from where a couple of small regional airlines fly in light planes to the major settlements of the region. As there are no roads, transport is by river or air. There's no regular passenger service on virtually any stretch of any river, making travel on your own difficult, if not impossible. Tour operators in Puerto Ayacucho have swiftly filled the gap and can take you just about everywhere – at a price, of course.

The climate is not uniform throughout the region. At the northern edge, there's a distinctive dry season from December to April. April is the cruelest month, heatwise. The rest of the year is marked by frequent heavy rains. Going south, the dry season becomes shorter and not so dry, eventually disappearing. Accordingly, the southern part of Amazonas is wet year-round.

PUERTO AYACUCHO

Set on the middle reaches of the Orinoco, Puerto Ayacucho is the capital of Amazonas. It was founded in 1924, together with another port, Samariapo, 63km upriver. The two ports have been linked by road to bypass the unnavigable stretch of the Orinoco cut by a series of rapids.

For a long time, particularly during the oil boom, Amazonas was a forgotten territory, and the two ports were little more than obscure villages. The link between them was the only sealed road in the whole region; connection to the rest of the country was by a rough track. Only in the late 1980s, when this track was improved and surfaced, did Puerto Ayacucho start to grow dramatically to become now a town of some 70,000 inhabitants. Paradoxically, the port, which was responsible for the town's birth and initial growth, has lost its importance as most cargo is now trucked by road.

Puerto Ayacucho is the main gateway to Venezuelan Amazonia and is becoming a tourist center. It has a range of hotels and restaurants and a bunch of tour operators. Puerto Ayacucho is also a transit point on the way to Colombia.

Information

Tourist Offices The Cadetur tourist office (☎ 048-210033) is in the building of the Gobernación, on Plaza Bolívar.

Money Banco Unión changes American Express traveler's checks and gives cash advances on Visa and MasterCard. Banco de Venezuela and Banco Caroní don't change cash or checks, but they do service credit-card holders. Some tour agencies may change your dollars or at least accept them as payment for their services.

Immigration The DIEX office is on Av Aguerrevere and is open 8 am to noon and 2 to 6 pm weekdays, though it doesn't seem to keep to these hours very strictly. Get your passport stamped here when leaving or entering Venezuela.

Things to See

Puerto Ayacucho is hot but pleasantly shaded by luxuriant mango trees. The **Museo Etnológico de Amazonas** gives insight into the culture of regional Indian groups, including the Piaroa, Guajibo, Yekuana and Yanomami.

The **Mercado Indígena**, held every day in the morning (it's busiest from Thursday to Saturday) on the square opposite the museum, sells Indian crafts, though you may find more interesting artifacts in the handicraft shops, Artesanías Amazonas and Bazar Corotería La Colmena. Visit the **Catedral** on Plaza Bolívar to see its colorful interior.

The **Cerro Perico**, southwest of the town center, provides views over the Río Orinoco and the town. Another hill, Cerro El Zamuro, commonly known as **El Mirador**, 1.5km south of the center, overlooks the Raudales Atures, the spectacular rapids that block river navigation. They are more impressive in the wet season, when the water is high.

There are some attractions around Puerto Ayacucho. The **Parque Tobogán de la Selva** is a picnic area developed around a large, steeply inclined smooth rock with water running over it – a sort of natural slide. It's 30km south of town along the Samariapo road, then 6km off to the east. There's no transport directly to the park. You can either take a por puesto to Samariapo, get off at the turn-off and walk the remaining distance, or negotiate a taxi in Puerto Ayacucho. The rock is a favorite weekend place among townspeople, who, unfortunately, leave it littered (watch for broken glass). There's a lesser-known natural waterslide farther upriver.

The **Cerro Pintado** is a large rock with pre-Columbian petroglyphs carved high above the ground in a virtually inaccessible place. It's 17km south of town and a few kilometers off the main road to the left. The best time to see the carvings is early in the morning or late in the afternoon.

Organized Tours

Tour business has flourished, and probably as many as a dozen operators are hunting for your money. Tour agents have some standard tours, but most can arrange a tour according to your interests and time. Be sure to carry your passport and tarjeta de ingreso on all trips.

Among the popular shorter tours are a three-day trip up the Sipapo and Autana rivers to the foot of Cerro Autana and a three-day trip up the Río Cuao. Expect to pay US$40 to US$70 per person per day, all-inclusive.

The Ruta Humboldt, following the route of the great explorer, is a longer and more

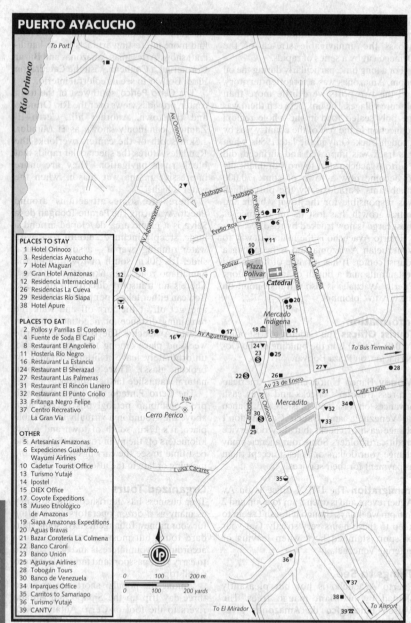

PUERTO AYACUCHO

Río Orinoco

To Port

Av Orinoco

Av Río Negro

Atabapo

Atabapo

Evelio Roa

Bolívar

Plaza Bolívar

Catedral

Av La Guardia

Av Amazonas

Mercado Indígena

Av Aguerrevere

Av Aguerrevere

To Bus Terminal

To Bus Terminal

trail

Cerro Perico

Luisa Cáceres

Calle Unión

Mercadito

Av 23 de Enero

Av Orinoco

Carabobo

To El Mirador

To Airport

0   100   200 m

0   100   200 yards

PLACES TO STAY
1   Hotel Orinoco
3   Residencias Ayacucho
7   Hotel Maguarí
9   Gran Hotel Amazonas
12   Residencia Internacional
26   Residencias La Cueva
29   Residencias Río Siapa
38   Hotel Apure

PLACES TO EAT
2   Pollos y Parrillas El Cordero
4   Fuente de Soda El Capi
8   Restaurant El Angoleño
11   Hostería Río Negro
16   Restaurant La Estancia
24   Restaurant El Sherazad
27   Restaurant Las Palmeras
31   Restaurant El Rincón Llanero
32   Restaurant El Punto Criollo
33   Fritanga Negro Felipe
37   Centro Recreativo
      La Gran Vía

OTHER
5   Artesanías Amazonas
6   Expediciones Guaharibo,
      Wayumí Airlines
10   Cadetur Tourist Office
13   Turismo Yutajé
14   Ipostel
15   DIEX Office
17   Coyote Expeditions
18   Museo Etnológico
      de Amazonas
19   Siapa Amazonas Expeditions
20   Aguas Bravas
21   Bazar Corotería La Colmena
22   Banco Caroní
23   Banco Unión
25   Aguaysa Airlines
28   Tobogán Tours
30   Banco de Venezuela
34   Inparques Office
35   Carritos to Samariapo
36   Turismo Yutajé
39   CANTV

adventurous trip. It goes along the Orinoco, Casiquiare and Guainía rivers up to Maroa. From there, the boat is transported overland to Yavita, and you then return down the Atabapo and Orinoco to Puerto Ayacucho. This trip takes eight to 10 days and will cost around US$80 to US$100 per person a day.

The far southeastern part of Amazonas, where the Yanomami live, is a restricted area requiring special permits almost impossible to get.

Probably the most reputable agency in town is Expediciones Guaharibo (☎ 048-210635), but it is also the most expensive. The company's main office is in Caracas (☎ 02-9526996), where most tours are put together and sent to Puerto Ayacucho.

Of the cheaper local companies, it's difficult to heartily recommend any particular one. Try Coyote Expeditions (☎ 048-212027) or Siapa Amazonas Expeditions (☎ 048-214958). Also check the offers of the two long-lived companies, Turismo Yutajé (☎ 048-210664) and Tobogán Tours (☎ 048-214865).

If there's a serious discrepancy between what an agency promises and what it actually provides, complain to the tourist office and insist on receiving part of your money back.

Aguas Bravas (☎ 048-210541) offers rafting over the Atures rapids. They run two trips a day (about three hours long), at US$40.

Places to Stay

The most popular choice with backpackers has long been the simple *Residencia Internacional* (☎ 048-210242), but it has almost doubled its prices over recent years – it's up to US$16/21 a double/triple with bath. *Hotel Maguarí* (☎ 048-213189) is probably less pleasant but more central and cheaper (US$13/16). Cheaper still is the basic *Residencias Ayacucho* (☎ 048-210779), which has doubles with bath for US$11.

Residencias Río Siapa (☎ 048-210138) is one of the cheapest options with air-con, costing US$20/24 per double/triple with bath. The small *Residencias La Cueva* (☎ 048-210563) has become popular with travelers. It has spotlessly clean air-con doubles/triples for US$22/28.

Gran Hotel Amazonas (☎ 048-210328) was perhaps the best hotel in town when built, but its good days have long gone. It's still probably worth US$26/30 a double/triple, and it's the only city hotel with a swimming pool. Other reasonable options include *Hotel Orinoco* (☎ 048-210285), for US$24/26 a double/triple, and *Hotel Apure* (☎ 048-210516), for US$35/44).

Places to Eat

There's quite a choice of eating outlets in town, but most are closed on Sunday. *Fuente de Soda El Capi* has savory food, including vegetable salads, at very moderate prices. For chicken and parrillas, try the cheap *Pollos y Parrillas El Cordero*, in the market on Av Orinoco. *Restaurant El Angoleño* doesn't look very elegant, but the food is good and cheap. Hearty felafel, shawarma and the like are served at *Centro Recreativo La Gran Vía*. *Restaurant Las Palmeras* is a pleasant, palm-thatched place that cooks some of the better pizzas in town.

One of the popular budget places to eat among the locals is the Mercadito (literally 'little market'), which boasts half a dozen rudimentary eateries, including *Restaurant El Rincón Llanero*, *Restaurant El Punto Criollo* and *Fritanga Negro Felipe*.

Among some more decent places, *Restaurant La Estancia* maintains good food and prices, as does *Hostería Río Negro*, Av Río Negro. *Restaurant El Sherazad* specializes in Middle Eastern cuisine.

Getting There & Away

Air The airport, 6km southeast of town, handles one flight daily to Caracas (US$75). Two small local carriers, Aguaysa and Wayumi, operate flights within Amazonas.

Bus The bus terminal is 6km east of the center on the outskirts of town. City buses go there from Av 23 de Enero, or you can take a taxi (US$3). Buses to Ciudad Bolívar depart regularly throughout the day (US$20, 10 to 11 hours). There are a half-dozen departures daily to San Fernando de Apure (US$13, eight hours), from where you can get buses to Caracas, Maracay, Valencia, Barinas and San Cristóbal. There are also direct buses from Puerto Ayacucho to Caracas, but they go via a longer route through Caicara del Orinoco.

To/From Colombia The nearest Colombian town, Puerto Carreño, at the confluence of the Meta and Orinoco rivers, is

VENEZUELA

accessible from Puerto Ayacucho in two ways. Remember to get an exit stamp in your passport at DIEX before setting off.

The first way leads via Casuarito, a Colombian hamlet right across the Orinoco from Puerto Ayacucho. A boat between Puerto Ayacucho's port (at the northeastern end of town) and Casuarito shuttles regularly throughout the day (US$1.50). From Casuarito, the *voladora* (high-speed boat) departs in the afternoon to Puerto Carreño (US$8, one hour). In the dry season (December to April), there may also be some jeeps between Casuarito and Puerto Carreño.

The other way goes via Puerto Páez, a Venezuelan village 95km north of Puerto Ayacucho. Get there by San Fernando bus (US$4, two hours); the trip includes a ferry

crossing of the Orinoco from El Burro to Puerto Páez. Take a boat from the village's wharf across the Río Meta to Puerto Carreño (US$1.50); it runs regularly between 6 am and 6 pm.

Puerto Carreño is a long, one-street town with an airport, a half-dozen budget hotels and a number of places to eat.

Don't forget to go to the DAS office, one block west of the main square, for an entry stamp in your passport. A number of shops will change bolívares to pesos.

There are two flights per week to Bogotá (US$130). Buses go only in the dry season, approximately from mid-December to mid-March. They depart once a week for the two-day journey by rough road to Villavicencio (US$75), which is four hours by bus from Bogotá.

Language

Latin American Spanish

Pronunciation

Most sounds in Spanish have English equivalents, and written Spanish is largely phonetic.

Vowels

Spanish vowels are very consistent and have easy English equivalents.

a   as in 'f**a**ther'
e   as in 'm**e**t'
i   as in 'f**ee**t'
o   as in 'f**o**r'
u   as in 'f**oo**d.' After consonants other than 'q,' the letter 'u' is more like the English 'w.' When modified by an umlaut, as in 'Güemes,' it is also pronounced 'w.'
y   is a semiconsonant, pronounced as Spanish 'i' when at the end of a word or when standing alone as a conjunction. As a consonant, it's somewhere between 'y' in 'yonder' and 'g' in 'beige,' depending on the region. In Argentina, Chile and Uruguay it sounds similar to the 's' in 'mea**s**ure.'

Diphthongs

A diphthong is a combination of two vowels forming a single syllable. In Spanish, the formation of a diphthong depends on combinations of 'weak' vowels ('i' and 'u') or strong ones ('a,' 'e' and 'o'). Two weak vowels or a strong and a weak vowel make a diphthong, but two strong ones are separate syllables.

A good example of two weak vowels forming a diphthong is the word *diurno* ('during the day'). The final syllable of *obligatorio* ('obligatory') is a combination of weak and strong vowels.

Consonants

Spanish consonants resemble their English equivalents, with some major exceptions. Pronunciation of the letters *f, k, l, m, n, p, q, s,* and *t* is virtually identical to English.

The consonants *ch, ll* and *ñ* are distinct letters, and are alphabetized accordingly. For example, *señal* follows *senyera* in the dictionary, and names beginning with 'Ch' have their own section in the telephone directory, following the Cs.

b   resembles its English equivalent; referred to as 'b larga' (see 'v')
c   like the 's' in '**s**ee' before 'e' and 'i'; otherwise like the English 'k'
d   as in '**d**og' in an initial position; otherwise like 'th' in 'fea**th**er'
g   like the 'ch' in the Scottish 'lo**ch**' before 'e' and 'i,' otherwise like 'g' in '**g**o'
h   invariably silent. If your name begins with this letter, listen carefully when immigration officials summon you to pick up your passport
j   like the 'ch' in the Scottish 'lo**ch**'
ll   as the 'y' in '**y**ellow,' except in Argentina, where it is as the 's' in 'plea**s**ure'
ñ   like 'ni' in 'o**ni**on'
r   is a short 'r,' except at the beginning of a word, and after 'l,' 'n,' or 's,' when it is often rolled
rr   very strongly rolled
v   indistinguishable from 'b,' and referred to as 'b corta'
x   as in 'ta**x**i,' except for a very few words, when it is pronounced like 'j'
z   as in '**s**un'

Stress

Stress is very important, since it can change the meaning of words. In general, words ending in vowels or the letters 'n' or 's' have stress on the next-to-last syllable, while those with other endings have stress on the last syllable. Thus *vaca* ('cow') and *caballos* ('horses') are both stressed on the next-to-last syllable, while *ciudad* ('city') and *infeliz* ('unhappy') both have stress on their last syllables.

Written accents will almost always appear in words that do not follow the rules above, such as *sótano* ('basement'), *América* and *porción* ('portion'). When counting syllables be sure to remember that diphthongs constitute only one. When a word with a written accent appears in capital letters, the accent is often not written, but is still pronounced.

Agreement

An adjective, like the definite or indefinite article, must agree in gender and number with the noun it describes.

a good boy	*un chico bueno*
the pretty house	*la casa bonita*
some pretty rooms	*unos cuartos bonitos*
the good girls	*las chicas buenas*

Greetings & Civilities

In their public behavior, South Americans are very conscious of civilities, sometimes to the point of ceremoniousness. Never, for example, approach a stranger for information without extending a greeting.

Hello.	*¡Hola!*
Good morning.	*Buenos días.*
Good afternoon.	*Buenas tardes.*
Good evening/night.	*Buenas noches.*
Goodbye.	*Adiós/Chau.*
Mr/Sir	*Señor* (formal)
Mrs/Madam	*Señora* (formal)
unmarried woman	*Señorita*
male friend	*compadre*
female friend	*comadre*
Bye, see you soon.	*Hasta luego.*

May it go well for you.
Que le vaya bien. (used when parting)

Basics

Yes.	*Sí.*
No.	*No.*
Please.	*Por favor.*
Thank you.	*Gracias.*
Many thanks.	*Muchas gracias.*
You're welcome.	*De nada.*
Excuse me.	*Permiso.*
Sorry.	*Perdón.*
Excuse me.	*Disculpe.*
Good luck!	*¡Buena suerte!*

Small Talk

How are you?
¿Cómo está? (formal)
¿Cómo estás? (familiar)
How are things going?
¿Qué tal?
Fine, thanks.
Bien, gracias.

Very well.
Muy bien.
Very badly.
Muy mal.
What is your name?
¿Cómo se llama? (formal)
¿Cómo te llamas? (familiar)
My name is…
Me llamo…
Where are you from?
¿De dónde es? (formal)
¿De dónde eres? (familiar)
I am from…
Soy de…
How old are you?
¿Cuántos años tiene?
I'm 29.
Tengo veintinueve años.
Are you married?
¿Es casado/a?
I am single.
Soy soltero/a.
I am married.
Soy casado/a.
Can I take a photo?
¿Puedo sacar una foto?
Of course. Why not. Sure.
Por supuesto. Cómo no. Claro.

Curious South Americans, from officials to casual acquaintances, will often want to know what travelers do for a living. If it's something that seems unusual (many would find it difficult to believe, for example, that a gardener could earn enough money to travel the world), it may be easiest to claim to be a student or teacher.

What do you do?
¿Qué hace?
What's your profession?
¿Cuál es su profesión?

I am a…	*Soy…*
student	*estudiante*
teacher	*profesor/a*
nurse	*enfermero/a*
lawyer	*abogado/a*
engineer	*ingeniero/a*
mechanic	*mecánico/a*

Language Difficulties

I don't speak much Spanish.
Hablo poco castellano.
I (don't) understand.
(No) entiendo.

Do you speak English?
¿Habla inglés?
Could you repeat that?
¿Puede repetirlo?
Could you speak more slowly please?
¿Puede hablar más despacio por favor?
How do you say...?
¿Cómo se dice...?
What does...mean?
¿Qué quiere decir...?

Toilets

The most common word for 'toilet' is *baño*,
but *servicios sanitarios* ('services') is a frequent alternative. Men's toilets will usually
be labeled *hombres*, *caballeros* or *varones*.
Women's will be marked *señoras* or *damas*.

Getting Around

Where is...?	*¿Dónde está...?*
the airport	*el aeropuerto*
the train station	*la estación de ferrocarril*
the bus terminal	*el terminal de buses*
the ticket office	*la boletería*
What time does...	*¿A qué hora...*
the airplane	*el avión*
the train	*el tren*
the bus	*el colectivo/micro/ camión/ómnibus/ la flota*
the ship	*el barco/buque*
leave/arrive?	*sale/llega?*

I'd like a ticket to...
Quiero un boleto/pasaje a...
What's the fare to...?
¿Cuánto cuesta hasta...?
Is there a student discount?
¿Hay descuento estudiantil?

1st class	*primera clase*
2nd class	*segunda clase*
single/one-way	*ida*
return/roundtrip	*ida y vuelta*
car	*auto/carro/coche*
taxi	*taxi*
truck	*camión*
pickup (truck)	*camioneta*
bicycle	*bicicleta*
motorcycle	*motocicleta/moto*
hitchhike	*hacer dedo*
sleeper	*camarote*
luggage checkroom	*guardería/equipaje*

Directions

How do I get to...?	*¿Cómo puedo llegar a...?*
Is it far?	*¿Está lejos?*
Go straight ahead.	*Siga/Vaya derecho.*
Turn left.	*Voltée a la izquierda.*
Turn right.	*Voltée a la derecha.*
north	*norte*
south	*sur*
east	*este/oriente*
west	*oeste/occidente*

Accommodations

Where is...?	*¿Dónde hay...?*
a hotel	*un hotel*
a boarding house	*una pensión/ residencial*
a youth hostel	*un albergue juvenil*

What does it cost per night?
¿Cuánto cuesta por noche?
Does it include breakfast?
¿Incluye el desayuno?
May I see the room?
¿Puedo ver la habitación?
I don't like it.
No me gusta.

single room	*habitación para una persona*
double room	*habitación doble*
full board	*pensión completa*
shared bath	*baño compartido*
private bath	*baño privado*
too expensive	*demasiado caro*
discount	*descuento*
cheaper	*más económico*
the bill	*la cuenta*

Around Town

I'm looking for...	*Estoy buscando...*
the bank	*el banco*
the embassy	*la embajada*
my hotel	*mi hotel*
the market	*el mercado*
the post office	*el correo*
the tourist office	*la oficina de turismo*

What time does it open/close?
¿A qué hora abre/cierra?
I want to change some money/
traveler's checks.
*Quiero cambiar dinero/
cheques de viajero.*

What is the exchange rate?
¿Cuál es el tipo de cambio?
I want to call (Canada).
Quiero llamar a (Canadá).

letter	*carta*
airmail	*correo aéreo*
registered mail	*certificado*
stamps	*estampillas*
credit card	*tarjeta de crédito*
black market	*mercado negro,*
	mercado paralelo
exchange house	*casa de cambio*

Food

breakfast	*desayuno*
lunch	*almuerzo*
dinner	*cena*
(cheap) restaurant	*restaurante (barato)*
I would like…	*Quisiera…*

Is service included in the bill?
¿El servicio está incluido en la cuenta?
I'm a vegetarian.
Soy vegetariano/a.

Shopping

Can I look at it?	*¿Puedo mirarlo/a?*
How much is it?	*¿Cuánto cuesta?*

That's too expensive for me.
Es demasiado caro para mí.
Do you accept credit cards?
¿Aceptan tarjetas de crédito?

bookstore	*la librería*
general store/shop	*la tienda*
laundry	*la lavandería*
market	*el mercado*
pharmacy, chemist	*la farmacia,*
	la droguería
supermarket	*el supermercado*

Health

I need a doctor.
Necesito un médico.
Where is the hospital?
¿Dónde está el hospital?
I'm allergic to antibiotics/penicillin.
*Soy alérgico/a a los antibióticos/
la penicilina.*
I'm pregnant.
Estoy embarazada.
I have been vaccinated.
Estoy vacunado/a.

Emergencies

Danger/Careful!	*¡Cuidado!*
Help!	*¡Socorro!*
Fire!	*¡Incendio!*
Thief!	*¡Ladrón!*
I've been robbed.	*Me robaron.*
Don't bother me!	*¡No me moleste!*
Go away!	*¡Déjeme!*
Go away! (stronger)	*¡Que se vaya!*
Get lost!	*¡Váyase!*

Time & Dates

today	*hoy*
this morning	*esta mañana*
this afternoon	*esta tarde*
tonight	*esta noche*
yesterday	*ayer*
tomorrow	*mañana*
week/month/year	*semana/mes/año*
last week	*la semana pasada*
next month	*el mes que viene*
always	*siempre*
now	*ahora*
before/after	*antes/después*

It's early/late.	*Es temprano/tarde.*
What time is it?	*¿Qué hora es?*
It's one o'clock.	*Es la una.*
It's seven o'clock.	*Son las siete.*

Days of the Week

Monday	*lunes*
Tuesday	*martes*
Wednesday	*miércoles*
Thursday	*jueves*
Friday	*viernes*
Saturday	*sábado*
Sunday	*domingo*

Numbers

1	*uno/una*
2	*dos*
3	*tres*
4	*cuatro*
5	*cinco*
6	*seis*
7	*siete*
8	*ocho*
9	*nueve*
10	*diez*
11	*once*
12	*doce*
13	*trece*
14	*catorce*
15	*quince*

16	*dieciséis*
17	*diecisiete*
18	*dieciocho*
19	*diecinueve*
20	*veinte*
21	*veintiuno*
30	*treinta*
40	*cuarenta*
50	*cincuenta*
60	*sesenta*
70	*setenta*
80	*ochenta*
90	*noventa*
100	*cien*
101	*ciento uno*
200	*doscientos*
1000	*mil*
5000	*cinco mil*
10,000	*diez mil*
50,000	*cincuenta mil*
100,000	*cien mil*
one million	*un millón*
one billion	*un billón*

Portuguese

Brazilian Portuguese is quite different from that of Portugal. The European settlers' original tongue was rapidly enriched by the local Indian dialects, as well as the languages of Africans brought over as slaves. Make sure your Portuguese dictionary or phrasebook specifies Brazilian Portuguese; Lonely Planet's *Brazilian phrasebook* is a good resource.

Pronunciation

Although written Portuguese is recognizable to Spanish speakers, the pronunciation is very different.

Vowels

Without a doubt, the most frustrating thing in learning to pronounce Portuguese is the vowels. The following lists offer only general rules, which should at least enable you to be understood.

a	as in 'up'
e	at the beginning or at the end of a word, as in 'feet,' only shorter; elsewhere, as in 'pet'
i	as in 'feet,' only shorter
o	at the end of a word or before an 'e', as in 'put,' only shorter; elsewhere as in 'or'
u	as in 'put'

Nasalization When a tilde appears over a vowel (ã), this means that the vowel should be heavily nasalized. This is done by allowing air to escape through the nose when you are pronouncing the vowel. The best way to learn is by listening to Brazilians speak, then practicing until you get it right.

Diphthongs Most diphthongs, or combinations of vowels, are pronounced by following the general rules described earlier, one after the other in the order they appear. There are, however, a few worth mentioning.

ei	as in 'day,' but slightly longer
oi	as in 'boy'
au	as in 'how'
ãe	as in 'day,' only nasalized
õe	as in 'boy,' only nasalized
ão	as in 'how,' only nasalized

Consonants

Most consonants in Portuguese are similar to their English counterparts, but there are exceptions. Only those consonants that vary considerably from English are discussed here.

c	as in 'cease' before 'e' or 'i'; elsewhere, as in 'kiss'
ç	as in 'cease'
d	as in 'jungle' before 'e' or 'i'; elsewhere, as in 'dog'
g	as in 'rouge'; before 'e' or 'i'; elsewhere as in 'game'
h	silent (see 'lh' and 'nh')
lh	as in 'million'
m & n	after a vowel, the vowel is nasalized, and neither the 'm' nor 'n' is articulated, as in 'sing'
nh	as in 'canyon'
q	as in 'keep'
r	pronounced like 'rr' at the beginning or end of a word; elsewhere as a short, rolled 'r'
rr	as in 'house'
s	as in 'star' before a vowel; as in 'ship' before 'p,' 't,' 'k' or at the end of a word; as in 'zoo,' only softer, elsewhere

ss   as in 'star'
t   as in 'chair' before 'e' or 'i'; as in 'table' elsewhere
x   as in 'ship' at the beginning of a word or after 'e,' 'ai,' 'ei,' 'ou,' or 'n'; as in 'zoo' in the initial syllable 'ex'; as in 'taxi' and sometimes 'miss' elsewhere

Stress

When a word ends in 'r' or a nasalized vowel, the stress falls on the last syllable, unless there is an accent on one of the other vowels in the word.

If a vowel has either a circumflex accent (ê) or an acute accent (é), the stress falls on that vowel no matter where it is in the word. In all other words of more than one syllable, the stress falls on the second-to-last vowel.

Basics

Hello.	*Oi.*
Goodbye.	*Tchau.*
Good morning.	*Bom dia.*
Good afternoon.	*Boa tarde.*
Good evening.	*Boa noite.*
Please.	*Por favor.*
Yes.	*Sim.*
No.	*Não.*
Maybe.	*Talvez.*
Excuse me.	*Com licença.*

Thank you (very much).
   (Muito/a) obrigado/a.
I'm sorry.
   Desculpe (meperdoe).
I (don't) understand.
   Eu (não) entendo.
Please write it down.
   Escreva por favor.
Do you speak English?
   Você fala inglês?

Small Talk

What is your name?
   Qual é seu nome?
My name is...
   Meu nome é...
How are you?
   Como vai você/Tudo bem?
I'm fine, thanks.
   Vou bem/Tudo bem, obrigado/a.
I'm a tourist/student.
   Eu sou um turista/estudante.

Where/What country are you from?
   Aonde/Da onde você é?
I am from...
   Eu sou...
How old are you?
   Quantos anos você tem?
I am...years old.
   Eu tenho...anos.

Getting Around

I want to go to...
   Eu quero ir para...
I want to book a seat for...
   Eu quero reservar um assento para...
What time does the...leave/arrive?
   A que horas...sai/chega?

bus	*onibus*
tram	*bonde*
train	*trem*
boat	*barco*

one-way/return ticket
   passagem de ida/ida e volta

station	*estação*
ticket office	*bilheteria*
timetable	*horário*

I would like to hire a...
   Eu gostaria de alugar um/uma...

bicycle	*bicicleta*
motorcycle	*moto*
car	*carro*
guide	*guia*
horse	*cavalo*
Where is...?	*Aonde é...?*
Is it near/far?	*É perto/longe?*
Go straight ahead.	*Vá em frente.*
Turn left.	*Vire a esquerda.*
Turn right.	*Vire a direita.*

Accommodations

youth hostel	*albergue da juventude*
campground	*camping*
hotel	*hotel*
guesthouse	*pousada*

Do you have a room available?
   Você tem um quarto para alugar?
How much is it per night/per person?
   Quanto é por noite/por pessoa?
Is service/breakfast included?
   O serviço/café de manha está incluído?
Can I see the room?
   Posso ver o quarto?

Where is the toilet?
Aonde é o banheiro?

Around Town

Where is the/a…?	*Aonde é o/a…?*
bank	*banco*
exchange office	*casa de câmbio*
city center	*centro da cidade*
embassy	*embaixada*
post office	*correio*
telephone center	*telefônica*
tourist office	*posto de informações turísticas*

I'd like to change some money/
traveler's checks.
Eu gostaria de trocar um pouco de dineiro/checks de viagem.

Food & Shopping

I would like the set lunch please.
Eu gostaria do prato feito por favor.
Is service included in the bill?
O serviço está incluído na conta?
I am a vegetarian.
Eu sou vegetariano/a.
How much does it cost?
Quanto custa?
It's too expensive for me.
É muito caro para mim.
Can I look at it?
Posso ver?
Do you take traveler's checks/credit cards?
Você aceita checks de viagem/cartões de crédito?

Times & Dates

What time is it?	*Que horas são?*
It's 1:15.	*São uma e quinze.*
…1:30.	*uma e meia.*
…1:45.	*uma e quarenta e cinco.*

When?	*Quando?*
o'clock	*horas*
yesterday	*ontem*
today	*hoje*
tonight	*hoje de noite*
tomorrow	*amanhã*
morning	*a manhã*
afternoon	*a tarde*
Sunday	*domingo*
Monday	*segunda-feira*
Tuesday	*terça-feira*
Wednesday	*quarta-feira*
Thursday	*quinta-feira*
Friday	*sexta-feira*
Saturday	*sábado*

Numbers

0	*zero*
1	*um/uma*
2	*dois/duas*
3	*três*
4	*quatro*
5	*cinco*
6	*seis* (when quoting telephone or house numbers, you'll hear 'meia')
7	*sete*
8	*oito*
9	*nove*
10	*dez*
11	*onze*
12	*doze*
13	*treze*
14	*catorze*
15	*quinze*
16	*dezesseis*
17	*dezessete*
18	*dezoito*
19	*dezenove*
20	*vinte*
30	*trinta*
40	*quarenta*
50	*cinqüenta*
60	*sessenta*
70	*setenta*
80	*oitenta*
90	*noventa*
100	*cem*
1000	*mil*
one million	*um milhão*

Health & Emergencies

I'm allergic to penicillin/antibiotics.
Eu sou allergico/a a penicilina/ antibióticos.

I'm…	*Eu sou…*
diabetic	*diabético/a*
epileptic	*epilético/a*
asthmatic	*asmático/a*
antiseptic	*antiséptico*
aspirin	*aspirina*
condoms	*camisinhas*
contraceptive	*contraceptivo*
sunblock cream	*creme de proteção solar*
tampons	*absorventes internos*
Help!	*Socorro!*

Go away!	*Va embora!*
Call a doctor!	*Chame o médico!*
Call the police!	*Chame a polícia!*

Slang

Brazilians pepper their language with strange oaths and odd expressions. Literal translations are in brackets:

Hello!	*Oi!*
Everything OK?	*Tudo bem?*
Everything's OK	*Tudo bom.*
That's great/Cool!	*Chocante!*
That's bad/Shit!	*Merda!*
Great/Cool/OK!	*'Ta lógico/*
	'Ta ótimo/
	'Ta legal!
My God!	*Meu deus!*
It's/You're crazy!	*'Ta louco!*
Gosh!	*Nossa!* (Our Lady!)
Whoops!	*Opa!*
Wow!	*Oba!*
You said it!	*Falou!*
I'm mad at…	*Eu estou chateado*
	com…
Is there a way?	*Tem jeito?*
There's always a way.	*Sempre tem jeito.*
shooting the breeze	*batendo um papo*
marijuana	*fumo* (smoke)
guy	*cara*
girl	*garota*
money	*grana*
bald	*careca*
mess	*bagunça*
problem	*abacaxí*
thong bikini	*fio dental*
	(dental floss)

French

The French spoken in French Guiana is not substantially different from that spoken in other parts of the world.

Basics

Hello.	*Bonjour.*
Goodbye.	*Au revoir.*
Yes/No.	*Oui/Non.*
Please.	*S'il vous plaît.*
Thank you.	*Merci.*
You're welcome	*Je vous en prie.*
Excuse me.	*Excusez-moi.*
Sorry.	*Pardon.*
Do you speak…	*Parlez-vous…*

English?	*anglais?*
Spanish?	*espagnol?*
How much is it?	*C'est combien?*
I don't understand.	*Je ne comprends pas.*

Getting Around

When does the next…leave/arrive?
À quelle heure part/arrive le prochain…?

boat	*bateau*
bus (city)	*bus*
bus (intercity)	*car*
tram	*tramway*
train	*train*
1st class	*première classe*
2nd class	*deuxième classe*
baggage checkroom	*consigne*
timetable	*horaire*
bus/tram stop	*arrêt d'autobus/*
	de tramway
train station	*gare*
ferry terminal	*gare maritime*
I'd like a…ticket.	*Je voudrais un*
	billet…
one-way	*aller simple*
return	*aller retour*
I want to go to…	*Je veux aller à…*
customs	*la douane*
border	*la frontière*
passport	*le passeport*
visa	*le visa*

I'd like to rent a car/bicycle.
Je voudrais louer une voiture/un vélo.

Where is…?	*Où est…?*
Go straight ahead.	*Continuez tout droit.*
Turn left.	*Tournez à gauche.*
Turn right.	*Tournez à droite.*
far/near	*loin/proche*

Emergencies

Help!	*Au secours!*
Call a doctor!	*Appelez un médecin!*
Call the police!	*Appelez la police!*
Leave me alone!	*Fichez-moi la paix!*
I'm lost.	*Je me suis égaré/ée.*

Around Town

a bank	*une banque*
the…embassy	*l'ambassade de…*
post office	*le bureau de poste*
market	*le marché*
chemist/pharmacy	*la pharmacie*
news agency	*l'agence de presse*

a public telephone	*une cabine téléphonique*	tomorrow	*demain*
the tourist office	*l'office de tourisme/ le syndicat d'initiative*	yesterday	*hier*
		morning/afternoon	*matin/après-midi*

What time does it open/close
Quelle est l'heure de ouverture/fermeture?

Accommodations

the hotel	*l'hôtel*
the youth hostel	*l'auberge de jeunesse*
the campground	*le camping*

Do you have any rooms available?
Est-ce que vous avez des chambres libres?

How much is it	*Quel est le prix*
per night?	*par nui?*
per person?	*par personne?*
for one person	*pour une personne*
for two people	*deux personnes*

Time, Days & Numbers

What time is it?	*Quelle heure est-il?*
today	*aujourd'hui*

Monday	*lundi*
Tuesday	*mardi*
Wednesday	*mercredi*
Thursday	*jeudi*
Friday	*vendredi*
Saturday	*samedi*
Sunday	*dimanche*

1	*un*
2	*deux*
3	*trois*
4	*quatre*
5	*cinq*
6	*six*
7	*sept*
8	*huit*
9	*neuf*
10	*dix*
100	*cent*
1000	*mille*
one million	*un million*

Quechua & Aymara

The following list of words and phrases is obviously minimal, but it should be useful in areas where these languages are spoken.

Pronounce them as you would a Spanish word. An apostrophe represents a glottal stop (the 'sound' in the middle of 'uh-oh!').

	Aymara	Quechua
Where is…?	*Kaukasa…?*	*Maypi…?*
to the left	*chchekaru*	*lokeman*
to the right	*cupiru*	*pañaman*
How do you say…?	*Cun sañasauca'ha…?*	*Imainata nincha chaita…?*
It is called…	*Ucan sutipa'h…*	*Chaipa'g sutin'ha…*
Please repeat.	*Uastata sita.*	*Ua'manta niway.*
It's a pleasure.	*Take chuima'hampi.*	*Tucuy sokoywan.*
What does that mean?	*Cuna sañasa muniucha'ha?*	*Imata'nita munanchai'ja?*
I don't know.	*Janiwa yatkti.*	*Mana yachanichu.*
I am hungry.	*Mankatawa hiu'ta.*	*Yarkaimanta wañusianiña.*
How much?	*K'gauka?*	*Maik'ata'g?*
cheap	*pisitaqui*	*pisillapa'g*
condor	*malku*	*cóndor*
distant	*haya*	*caru*
downhill	*aynacha*	*uray*
father	*auqui*	*tata*
food	*manka*	*mikíuy*
friend	*kgochu*	*kgochu*
Hello!	*Laphi!*	*Raphi!*
house	*uta*	*huasi*
I	*haya*	*ñoka*

	Aymara	Quechua
llama	yama-karhua	karhua
lodging	korpa	pascana
man	chacha	k'gari
miner	koyiri	koya'g
moon	pha'gsi	kiya
mother	taica	mama
near	maka	kailla
no	janiwa	mana
river	jawira	mayu
ruins	champir	champir
snowy peak	kollu	riti-orko
sun	yinti	inti
teacher	yatichiri	yachachi'g
thirst	phara	chchaqui
trail	tapu	chakiñan
very near	hakítaqui	kaillitalla
water	uma	yacu
when?	cunapacha?	haiká'g?
woman	warmi	warmi
yes	jisa	ari
you	huma	khan
young	wuayna	huayna
1	maya	u'
2	paya	iskai
3	quimsa	quinsa
4	pusi	tahua
5	pesca	phiska
6	zo'hta	so'gta
7	pakalko	khanchis
8	quimsakalko	pusa'g
9	yatunca	iskon
10	tunca	chunca
11	tuncamayani	chunca u'niyo'g
12	tuncapayani	chuncaiskai'niyo'g
13	tuncaquimsani	chunca quinsa'niyo'g
14	tuncapusini	chunca tahua'yo'g
15	tuncapescani	chunca phiska'nio'g
16	tunca zo'htani	chunca so'gta'nio'g
17	tuncapakalkoni	chunca khanchisniyo'g
18	tunca quimsakalkoni	chunca pusa'gniyo'g
19	tunca yatuncani	chunca iskoniyo'g
20	pa tunca	iskai chunca

Glossary

Some terms are used mainly or exclusively in specific countries or regions whereas others are more or less common in all Spanish-speaking countries. Note that regional variations in meaning are common.

abra – mountain pass
aerosilla – (Arg) chairlift (see also *telesilla*)
aguardente – (Bra) any strong drink, but usually *cachaça*
aguardiente – cane alcohol or similar drink
alameda – street lined with trees (often poplars); an avenue or boulevard
albergue – lodging house; youth hostel
alcabala – (Ven) roadside police checkpoint
alcaldía – town hall
álcool – (Bra) fuel made from sugarcane; about half of Brazil's cars, including all new ones, run on álcool
aldeia – (Bra) originally a Jesuit mission village; now any small village
alerce – large coniferous tree, once common in parts of the southern Argentine and Chilean Andes; its numbers have declined greatly due to overexploitation for timber
almuerzo – lunch; often an inexpensive fixed-price meal
altiplano – Andean high plain of Peru, Bolivia, Chile and Argentina
andar – the verb 'to walk'; (Bra) floor in a multistory building
apartado – post office box
apartamento – apartment or flat; (Bra) hotel room with private bath
api – in Central Andean countries, a syrupy *chicha* made of maize, lemon, cinnamon and sugar
apunamiento – altitude sickness, especially in the *puna* region of the high Andes; see also *soroche*
arrayán – reddish-barked tree of the myrtle family; common in forests of southern Argentina and Chile
arriero – mule driver
artesanía – handicrafts; crafts shop
asado – roasted; (Arg) barbecue; often a family outing in summer
asunceño/a – native or resident of Asunción
audiencia – colonial administrative subdivision, under a president who held civil power in areas where no viceroy was resident

autopista – freeway or motorway
Aymara – indigenous people of highland Bolivia, Peru, Chile and Argentina (also called *Kollas*); also their language
azulejos – ceramic tiles, commonly blue

balneario – bathing resort or beach
bandeirantes – (Bra) colonial slavers and gold prospectors from São Paulo who explored the interior
baño – bath, bathroom, or toilet
barraca – (Bra) any stall or hut, including food and drink stands at beaches, parks, etc
barrio – neighborhood, district or borough; (Ven) shantytown
bencina – (Chi) gasoline
bencina blanca – white gas (Shellite) used especially for camping stoves; usually available only in hardware stores or chemical supply shops
bicho de pé – (Bra) literally, foot bug; burrowing parasite found near beaches and in some rain-forest areas
bilheteria – (Bra) ticket office
blocos – (Bra) groups of musicians and dancers who perform in street parades during Brazil's Carnavals
bodega – a storage area, warehouse; wine store; (Bol) boxcar, sometimes used for train travel by 2nd-class passengers; (Ven) small shop
bofedal – in the Andean altiplano, a swampy alluvial pasture
boleadoras – heavily weighted thongs, once used for hunting guanaco and rhea; also called *bolas*
boletería – ticket office
bomba – among many meanings, a gasoline (petrol) station
burro – donkey
burundanga – (Col) drug obtained from a plant, used to intoxicate unsuspecting victims in order to rob them

cabaña – cabin
cabildo – colonial town council
cachaça – (Bra) sugarcane rum, also called *pinga* or *aguardente*, produced by hundreds of small distilleries throughout the country; the national drink
cachoeira – (Bra) waterfall

cacique – Indian chieftain; among Araucanian Indians, a *toqui*

callampas – literally, mushrooms; (Chi) shantytowns on the outskirts of Santiago

calle – street

cama matrimonial – double bed

camanchaca – (Chi) dense convective fog on the coastal hills of the Atacama desert; equivalent to Peru's *garúa*

câmara – (Bra) colonial town council

cambista – street moneychanger

camellones – (Ecu) pre-Columbian raised-field earthworks in the Guayas Basin; evidence of large early populations

camino – road, path, way

camión – truck, lorry (camiones carry both goods and passengers in Central Andean countries)

camioneta – pickup or other small truck

campesino/a – rural dweller who practices subsistence agriculture; a peasant

campo – the countryside; a field or paddock

Candomblé – (Bra) Afro-Brazilian religion of Bahia

capoeira – (Bra) martial art/dance performed to rhythms of an instrument called the *berimbau*; developed by Bahian slaves

caraqueño/a – native or resident of Caracas

carioca – native or resident of Rio de Janeiro

Carnaval – all over Latin America, pre-Lenten celebration

casa – house

casa de cambio – foreign currency exchange house

casa de familia – modest family accommodations, usually in tourist centers in Southern Cone countries

casilla de correos – post office box

casona – large house, usually a mansion; term often applied to colonial architecture in particular

catarata – waterfall

caudillo – in South American politics, a provincial or military strongman whose power rested more on personal loyalty than political ideals or party organization

ceiba – a common tropical tree; can reach a huge size

cena – dinner; often an inexpensive set menu

cerro – hill or mountain (used to refer to even very high Andean peaks)

ceviche – marinated raw seafood (be cautious about eating ceviche as it can be a source of cholera; see Health in the Facts for the Visitor chapter)

chachacoma – *Senecio graveolens*; a native Andean plant yielding a tea that helps combat mild symptoms of altitude sickness

chacra – (Arg) garden; small, independent farm

charango – Andean stringed instrument, traditionally made with an armadillo shell as a soundbox

chicha – in Andean countries, a popular beverage (often alcoholic) made from ingredients like yuca, sweet potato or maize

chifa – (mostly Per, Bol & Chi) Chinese restaurant

chilote – (Chi) a person from the island of Chiloé

chiva – goat; (Col) a basic rural bus with wooden bench seats; until the 1960s, the main means of transport throughout the country

cholo/a – Quechua- or Aymara-speaking person who has migrated to the city but continues to wear peasant dress

chullo – (Bol & Per) Andean knitted hat, often with earflaps

churrascaria – (Bra) restaurant featuring barbecued meat

coa – (Chi) working-class slang of Santiago

coima – in the Andean countries and the Southern Cone, a bribe

colectivo – depending on the country, either a bus, a minibus or a shared taxi providing public transport

comedor – basic cafeteria or dining room in a hotel

comida – food; dinner; often an inexpensive set menu

condón – condom

confitería – (Arg) café that serves coffee, tea, desserts and simple food orders

Cono Sur – Southern Cone; a collective term for Argentina, Chile, Uruguay and parts of Brazil and Paraguay

conuco – in the Andean and Caribbean countries, a small cultivated plot of land

cordillera – mountain range

corregidor – in colonial Spanish America, governor of a provincial city and its surrounding area; the corregidor was usually associated with the *cabildo*

correo – postal service, post office, mail

corrida – bullfight

cospel – (Arg) token used in public telephones; also known as a *ficha*

costanera – in the Southern Cone, a seaside, riverside or lakeside road

criollo/a – a Spaniard born in colonial South America; in modern times, a South American of European descent

curanto – Chilean seafood stew

cuy – (Col, Ecu & Per) guinea pig, a traditional food

DEA – US Drug Enforcement Agency, active in a number of South American countries

dendê – (Bra) palm-tree oil, a main ingredient in the cuisine of Bahia

denuncia – affidavit or statement, usually in connection with theft or robbery

desayuno – breakfast

dique – sea wall, jetty or dock; also a reservoir used for recreational purposes

edificio – building

empanada – baked or fried turnover filled with vegetables, egg, olive, meat, chicken, cheese, etc

encomienda – colonial labor system under which Indian communities had to provide labor and tribute to a Spanish encomendero (landholder) in exchange for religious and language instruction; usually the system benefited the Spaniards far more than the Indians

esquina – street corner (often abbreviated to 'esq')

estancia – extensive ranch, either for cattle or sheep, with dominating owner or manager and dependent resident labor force

estanciero – owner of an estancia

este – east

expreso – train making more stops than a *ferrobus*

farinha – (Bra) manioc flour, the staple food of Indians before colonization, and of many Brazilians today, especially in the northeast and the Amazon

favela – (Bra) slum or shantytown

fazenda – (Bra) large ranch or farm, roughly equivalent to Spanish American *hacienda*; also cloth or fabric

ferrobus – bus on railway wheels

ferroviária – (Bra) railway station

ficha – token used for public telephone, subway, etc, in lieu of coins

flota – fleet; often a long-distance bus line

frailejón – espeletia; plant specific to the highland areas of Venezuela, Colombia and Ecuador (spectacular in bloom in November and December)

frigorífico – (Southern Cone) meat-freezing factory

fundo – *hacienda* or farm

gamines – street children of Colombia

gamonal – local ruler or leader; (Per) rural landowner, equivalent to *hacendado*

garúa – (Per) a convective coastal fog

gaseosa – (Per) carbonated soft drink

gas-oil – in the Southern Cone, diesel fuel; generally much cheaper than gasoline

gasolina – gasoline, petrol

gaucho – Argentine cowboy; in Brazil, *gaúcho*, pronounced 'ga-oo-shoo'

golpe de estado – coup d'état

gringo/a – throughout Latin America, a foreigner or person with light hair and complexion; not necessarily a derogatory term; (Arg) a person of Italian descent

guanaco – undomesticated relative of the llama; (Chi) a water cannon

guaquero – see *huaquero*

guaraná – Amazonian shrub whose berry is believed to have magical and medicinal powers; also a popular soft drink in Brazil

guardaparque – park ranger

hacendado – owner of an hacienda

hacienda – large rural landholding, historically with a dominant owner ruling a dependent resident labor force; (Chi) the term *fundo* is more common; (Arg) a much less common form of *latifundio* than the *estancia*

hato – (Ven) large cattle ranch

hospedaje – budget lodging place, often with shared bathroom

huaquero – (also *guaquero*) robber of pre-Columbian tombs

ichu – bunch grass of the Andean *altiplano*

iglesia – church

igreja – (Bra) church

Inca – the dominant indigenous civilization of the Central Andes at the time of the Spanish conquest; refers both to the people and, individually, to their leader

indígena – native American (Indian)

indigenismo – movement in Latin American art and literature that extols aboriginal traditions, often in a romantic or patronizing manner

inquilino – tenant or tenant farmer

invierno – literally, winter; the rainy season in the South American tropics

GLOSSARY

invierno boliviano – (Chi) 'Bolivian winter'; the summer rainy season in the altiplano
IVA – impuesto de valor agregado, a value-added tax (VAT)

Kolla – another name for the *Aymara*
Kollasuyo – 'Land of the Kolla'; early indigenous name for the area now known as Bolivia

ladrão – (Bra) thief
ladrón – thief
lago – lake
laguna – lagoon; shallow lake
lanchonete – (Bra) stand-up snack bar
latifundio – large landholding, such as an *hacienda* or cattle *estancia*
leito – (Bra) luxury overnight express bus
lejía – alkaline material (often made from potato and quinoa ash) chewed with coca leaves to activate their mild stimulant properties
limeño/a – of Lima; an inhabitant of that city
llanos – plains
llareta – *Laretia compacta*, a dense, compact *altiplano* shrub, used for fuel
loma – mound or hill
lunfardo – street slang of Buenos Aires

machismo – the exaggerated masculine pride of some Latin American men
manglar – mangrove
manta – a shawl or bedspread
mate – see *yerba mate*
matrimonial – or *cama matrimonial*, a double bed
matrimonio – literally, marriage; also, a room with a double bed
menú del día – inexpensive set meal
mercado – market
mercado negro – black market
mercado paralelo – euphemism for black market
meseta – interior steppe of eastern Patagonia
mestizo/a – a person of mixed Indian and Spanish descent
micro – small bus or minibus
mineiro – (Bra) a miner; person from Minas Gerais state
minga – reciprocal labor system, common throughout the Andean region and other parts of South America
minifundio – small landholding, such as a peasant farm
minuta – (Arg) a short-order snack

mirador – viewpoint or lookout, usually on a hilltop
monte – mount or small hill; also a scrub forest or any densely vegetated area
morro – a hill or headland; (Bra) person or culture of the *favelas*
mula – mule
mulato/a – person of mixed African and European ancestry
municipalidad – city or town hall
museo – museum
museu – (Bra) museum

nafta – (Arg) gasoline (petrol)
nafta blanca – white gas (Shellite)
ñandú – the rhea: a large, flightless bird, resembling the ostrich
ñapa – a little extra over the specified amount; ask for it in markets, etc
nevado – snow-covered peak
norte – north
novela – novel
NS – (Bra) Nosso Senhor (Our Father), or Nossa Senhora (Our Lady); often used in the name of a church

oca – edible Andean tuber resembling a potato
occidente, occidental – west, western
oeste – west
oferta – promotional fare, often seasonal, for plane or bus travel
oficina – office
onces – 'elevenses'; morning or afternoon tea
oriente, oriental – east, eastern
orixás – (Bra) gods of Afro-Brazilian religions

paceño/a – of La Paz; an inhabitant of that city
palafito – a house on stilts, above water
pampero – South Atlantic cold front that brings dramatic temperature changes to Uruguay, Paraguay and the interior of northern Argentina
parada or **paradero** – bus stop
páramo – humid, high-altitude grassland of the northern Andean countries
parque – park; in a city, any small grassed area may be called a parque
parque nacional – national park
parrillada – barbecued or grilled meat served at a parilla
paseo – an outing, such as a walk in the park or downtown

pau brasil – brazil wood tree, which produces a red dye that was the colony's first commodity; the tree is now scarce

paulistano – (Bra) native of São Paulo city

peatonal – pedestrian mall

pehuén – *Araucaria auracana*, the monkey-puzzle tree of southern South America

peña – club that hosts informal folk-music gatherings; a performance at such a club

peninsulares – in colonial South America, Spaniards born in Europe (as opposed to *criollos*, who were born in the colonies)

pensión – short-term budget accommodations in a family home or small family hotel (may also have permanent lodgers)

piropo – a sexist remark, ranging from relatively innocuous to very offensive

piso – floor in a multistory building

Planalto – enormous plateau that covers much of southern Brazil

plaza – an urban open space, usually laid out with paths and gardens, often with a central fountain, statue or rotunda (the main plaza is the heart of any South American town or city, and is usually surrounded by the most important church and government buildings)

pongaje – (Bol) nonfeudal system of peonage, abolished in 1952

por puesto – (Ven) shared taxi

porteño/a – (Arg) inhabitant of Buenos Aires; (Chi) a native or resident of Valparaíso

posta – (Chi) first-aid station in a smaller town that lacks a proper hospital

pousada – (Bra) hotel

prato feito, prato do dia – (Bra) literally, made plate or plate of the day; typically an enormous and very cheap meal

precordillera – foothills of the Andes

preservativo – condom

propina – a tip, eg, in a restaurant or taxi

pucará – indigenous Andean fortification

pueblos jóvenes – literally, young towns; (Per) shantytowns surrounding Lima

puna – Andean highlands, usually higher than 3000m

quarto – (Bra) hotel room with shared bath

quebracho – 'axe-breaker' tree (*Quebrachua lorentzii*) of the Chaco, a natural source of tannin

quebrada – canyon, ravine (often dry)

Quechua – indigenous language of the Andean highlands, spread by Inca rule and widely spoken today

quena – simple reed flute

quilombo – (Bra) a community of runaway slaves; (Arg) a slang term for a brothel or a mess

quinoa – native Andean grain, the dietary equivalent of rice in the pre-Columbian era

quinto real – the 'royal fifth,' a Spanish tax on all precious metals mined in colonial America

quipu – colored, knotted cord used for record-keeping by the Incas

quiteño/a – of Quito; an inhabitant of that city

rancho – rural house; (Ven) shantytown dwelling

raudales – rapids in a river

recargo – surcharge; added by many businesses to credit-card transactions

refugio – a usually rustic shelter in a national park or remote area

residencial – cheap hotel for short-term lodging, sometimes only seasonal; also called a residencia

rio – (Bra) river; in Spanish, *río*

rodeo – annual roundup of cattle on an *estancia* or *hacienda*

rodoferroviária – (Bra) combined bus and train station

rodoviária – (Bra) bus station

ruana – (Col) traditional woolen poncho

ruta – route or highway

salar – salt lake or salt pan, usually in the high Andes or Argentine Patagonia

salteña – (Bol) meat and vegetable pastie, generally a spicier version of an *empanada*

salto – waterfall

santiaguino/a – native or resident of Santiago, Chile

selva – natural tropical rain forest

Semana Santa – all over South America, Holy Week, the week before Easter Sunday

siesta – lengthy break after lunch

s/n – sin número; indicating a street address without a number

soroche – altitude sickness

Southern Cone – see *Cono Sur*

stelling – (Guy) a ferry dock or pier

suco – (Bra) fruit juice; a fruit juice bar

sud, sur – south

taguá – Wagner's peccary; a species of wild pig thought extinct but recently rediscovered in the Paraguayan Chaco

Tahuantinsuyo – Hispanicized name of the Inca Empire; in Quechua, Tawantinsuyu

tambo – in Andean countries, a wayside market and meeting place; an inn

tapir – large hoofed mammal; a distant relative of the horse

taxista – taxi driver

teleférico – cable car

telenovela – TV soap opera

telesilla – chair lift (see also *aerosilla*)

tenedor libre – 'all-you-can-eat' restaurant

tepui – (Ven) flat-topped mountain

termales, termas – hot springs

terminal de autobuses – long-distance bus terminal

terra firme – (Bra) Amazonian uplands of limited fertility

tinto – red wine; (Col) a small cup of black coffee

todo terreno – mountain bike

toqui – Mapuche Indian chieftain (see also *cacique*)

totora – type of reed, used as a building material

tranca – (Bol) police post

tugurios – (Col) shantytowns

Tupi – (Bra) major coastal people at the time of European contact; also their language

turismo de aventura – 'adventure tourism' activities such as trekking and river rafting

tuteo – use of the pronoun tú (you, singular) and its corresponding verb forms (see also *voseo*)

vaquero – cowboy; in Brazil, vaqueiro

valle – valley

várzea – (Bra) Amazonian floodplain

verano – literally, summer; also the dry season in the South American tropics

vicuña – wild relative of the domestic llama and alpaca, found only at high altitudes in the south-central Andes

villas miserias – (Arg) shantytowns on the outskirts of Buenos Aires and other cities

vinchuca – reduviid bug; a biting insect, found in thatched dwellings with dirt floors, that transmits Chagas' disease

viviendas temporarias – literally, temporary dwellings; (Par) riverfront shantytowns of Asunción

vizcacha – also written as viscacha; wild relative of the domestic chinchilla

voladora – (Col, Ven) river speedboat

voseo – use of the pronoun vos (you, singular) and its corresponding verb forms in preference to tú; standard usage in Argentina, Uruguay and Paraguay (see also *tuteo*)

yapa – variant spelling of *ñapa*

yareta – variant spelling of *llareta*

yatire – Andean healer or witch doctor

yerba mate – 'Paraguayan tea' *(Ilex paraguariensis)*; *mate* is consumed regularly in Argentina, Paraguay, Uruguay and Brazil

yuca – manioc tuber; in Portuguese, mandioca is the most common term

zambo/a – a person of mixed African and Amerindian ancestry

zampoña – pan flute featured in traditional Andean music

zona franca – duty-free zone

zonda – (Arg) in the central Andes, a powerful, dry north wind

Climate Charts

BOGOTÁ, COLOMBIA
Elevation - 2,500m/8,200ft

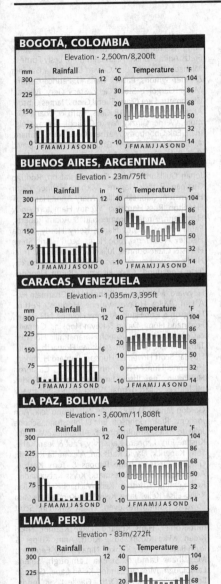

BUENOS AIRES, ARGENTINA
Elevation - 23m/75ft

CARACAS, VENEZUELA
Elevation - 1,035m/3,395ft

LA PAZ, BOLIVIA
Elevation - 3,600m/11,808ft

LIMA, PERU
Elevation - 83m/272ft

MANAUS, BRAZIL
Elevation - 50m/164ft

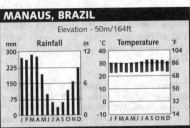

PUERTO MONTT, CHILE
Elevation - 3m/10ft

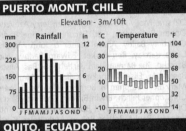

QUITO, ECUADOR
Elevation - 2,800m/9,184ft

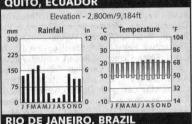

RIO DE JANEIRO, BRAZIL
Elevation - 10m/33ft

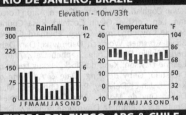

TIERRA DEL FUEGO, ARG & CHILE
Elevation - 2,467m/8,092ft

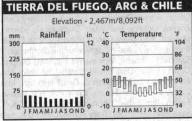

Acknowledgments

THANKS
Many thanks to the travelers who used the last edition and wrote to us with helpful hints, useful advice and interesting anecdotes:

Jadwiga Adamczuk, Esther Adams, Tamar Adelaar & Robin Bollweg, Betty Adell, Hazel Ahrens, Ximena Alfaro, Sytze Algera, Wendy Allen, Caroline Allerton, Brian Ambrosio, Ingvild W Andersen, J & C Anderson, Matt Anderson, Diu Andhlam-Gardiner, Phillip Andrus, Joeri Apontoweil & Bianca Dijkstra, Molly Arevalo, Ben Arker, Jerry Azevedo, Dorian Bachmann, Ceri Bacon, Christine Badre, Courtney Bailey, Alison Barber & John Murphy, Laura Barclay, Ben Barker, Edward Barlow, Nick Barraud, Sue Barreau, Iain Bartlett, Luc Bas, Alistair Basendale, Elise Batchelor, K Baxter, Adam Beird, Mary Bell, Stephen B Bergren, Denyse Bernard, Christopher Billich, Erwin Bittner, Charlotte Blixt & Dirk Schwensen, Daniel Boag, Ian Boag, Chantal Boisvert, Paul & Bettina Bojsen, Andy Bolas, Kristin Bolenc, J Borrel, Peter Bossew, RJ Boule, Anthony Boult, Paul Bouwman, Katja Breitenbücher, Dawson Brown, Heather Brown, Stefany & Paul Brown, Suzanne Brown, Werner Bull, Linda Broschofsky, Helen Butler, Stuart Buxton, Edward Cahill, Eileen Cameron, Robert Canter, Agustín Cardona M, Ricardo Carvalho, Salvatore Casari, Alexandra Taylor & Carmel Castellan, Marcus Castro, Mike Cavendish, Dennis Chambers, Morag Chase, Marjorie & Nilson Chaves, Philip P Chen, Kim Childs, Liam Clancy, David Clapham & Alison Hoad, Eleanor Clevenger, Steve Coats, Dale & Kevin Coghlan, Ross Spencer Cohen, Aaron Corcoran, Len Corsbie, Glenn Costello, Rosa Couras, Sophie Coyaud, James Cowie, Eberhard Cramer, Steve Creamer, Wojciech Dabrowski, Dan Dahlberg, Phillip Dale, Craig Stephen Daly, Alan & Leanne Dawson, Katia de Block, Lesus Lopez de Dicastillo, Geby de Jong, Dale & Adrienne de Kretser, James Delaney, Robyn Christie & Mark Dellar, Guy de Mondt, Amy Denman, Danielle Deutscher, Remmert DeVroome, Andrew Dick, Vanessa Dickson, Mollie Dobson, David Dolan, Eva Dolne, Annick Donkers, A Downing, Paisley Drab, Zbynek Dubsky, Jean Marc Dugauquier, Suzanne DuRard, Alex Duss, Denis Duysens, Shaun Dwyer, Brenden Dyke, Justin Edgar, Katrin Eichenberger & Claudio Hartmann, Vincent WJ Eijt, Mats Ekelund, David Eliason, Don Ellis III, Sarah-Jane Elvin, Alex Encel, John Endres, Ruth & Geoff Erickson, Josie Cali & Emmanuel Espino, Chris P Evans, William Evelyn, Igor Fabjan, Annabel Falk, Michael Falk, Salustiano Fernandes, Tracy Ferrell, Dieter & Renate Finsker, Alan Firth, Marilyn Flax, Julia Fleminger, Els Flipse, Alan D Foster, Peter Foster, Sharon Frazzini, Bente K Fremmerlid, Erith French, Paul & Sarah Fretz, Anita Frohlin, Allan L Fruman, Lesly Furness, Michael Gacquin, Juan Galvan D, Joanna Gardner & Peter Symons, Patrick Garland, Fabrice Gendre, Matija Gergolet, Stecv Gery, Stacy Gery, Michael Giacometti, Lara Giavi, Sheryl Gibbs, James Gibson, Alice Gilbey, Shaun AB Giles, Ruth & Charlie Gilmore, Werner Ginzky, Mirko Giulietti, Jeremy Goldman, Erik Goodbody, Mathew Gore, Jerry Graham, Andrea Graner, Robert Grant, DN Griffiths, David Grill, Peter Grip, Tony & Irena Grogan, Ian & Lynn Grout, Aler Grubbs, Daniel Guerro, Stephen Guest, Johan Guillaume, Anna Carin Gustafson, Rodrigo Guzman, Patrick Hagans, Michael Hahne, Viktor Håkansson, Gabriela Hallas, Mary Anne Hamer, JT Hamilton, Ross Hamilton, Wendy Hamilton, Andy Hammann, Anne Hammersbad & Adam Roberts, Paula Hanna, James Hardy, Kerry Hardy, Lynda Harpley, Fred Harris, Jude Harris, Scott Harris, Steve Harris & Claire Bonnet, Julian & Jacquie Hart, Trudi Hartley, Sue Harvey, Eric Haskell, Dave Hawkin, Birte Hegerlund, Clive Henman, Byron Heppner, Lothar Herb, Ingred Hermansen, Tom Hetley, Nicky Heyward, Matt Hickey, Richard Hill, Charmain Ho-A-Lim, Mike Hoave, Valerie Hodges, Pettina Hodgson & Rob Haub, Andrew Holmes, NH Home, Ferdinand Höng, Dawn & Kevin Hopkins, Grenville & Georgina Hopkins, Joseph Horan, Philip Horchler, Tamir Horesh, Armin Howald, Jay Howarth, Danial Hoydal, Scott Hoyer, Ed Hudson, Bernard Humpert, Hernione Hunter & Ronni Johansen, Cameron Hutchison, Tage Ibsen, Ernestein Idenburg, Rod & Jill Illidge, Ricardo Imai, Vicki Irvine, Sabriya B Ishoof, Daniel Jacks, D Jagesar, Tjasa Janovljak, Gordon Janow, D Jax, Myles Jelf, Bruno Jelk, Ann Jochems, Ripton Johnson, Eric D Johnstone, Schona Jolly, Jo Jones, Arnold Joost & Annemieke Wevers, Kristine Jürs, Leonard Kahansky, Paul & Jean Kahe, Tony Kaperick, David Karlsson, Alexandra Karpoff, Garben Karstens, Irene Pappas & Tony Karton, Arne Kasper, Tessa Katesmark, Kryss Katsiaviades, Ron Keesing, Christian Keil, Michael Keller, Allan Kelly, Elisa Kelly, Jane Kelly, Bill Kemball, Jessica Lowe & Nathan Kesteven, Hugh Kirkman, Scott Kistler, Bill Klynnk, Brigitte Knoetig, D Koch, Hartmut Köhler, Hans Kolland, Dave Kramer, Nikki Kroan, Mike Krosin, Susie Krott, Anne Kuiper & Ruth Bitterlin, Peter Kunkel, Nina Kyelby, Fernanda Magalhaes Lamego, Selena Lamlough, Selena Lamplough, Melanie Lander, Kevin Lane, Germán Bender-Pulido, Carina Ortiz, Gaëlle Léon, Andre Lannee, Nick Lansdowne, Michael Laudahn, Lewis Laura, Linda Layfield, Anneliese Lehmann, Angela Lerwill, Guy Leonard, Brian & Lorna Lewis, Colin Lewis, Laura Lewis, Peter Lewis, Peter & Dawn Lezak, Steve Lidgey, John P Linstroth, Diane Lister,

Daniel Lloyd, Stacy Long, Xavier Cordero Lopez, Agnes & Antoine Lorgnier, Dieter Lubitz, Jacqui Luff, A Lukosky, Francesco Lulli, Ian Lunt, Joana Luplin, Joanna Luplin, Jacqui Lupp, Dikrán P Lutufyan, Jo Luxmore, Jim Macgillis, Ian Mackley, Thomas Mader, Eduardo Viteri Manticha, Lynette Manuel, Nick Marbach, Rodrigo Marcus, George Markopoulos & Sarah Holman, Jane Martin, Bob Masters, Marisa Maters, Mario Mathieu, Carly Mattes, Yvonne & David McCredie, Denise & Malcolm McDonaugh, Chris Latterell & Elizabeth McInerney, Lachlan McKenzie, Rebecca Goodall & Steve McKinney, Kerstin Mechlem, Ulla Melchiorsen, Peter Mellas, Mr & Mrs Gordon R Merrick, John & Tessa Messenger, Juerg Messerli & Erika Rupp, Matthew Meyer, Lee Micholson, Sylvie Micolon, Mark Miller, Lennat Milsson, Zachary Moavani, Jamie Monk, Michael J Monsour, Darren Moody, Nicole Moore, Marina Morales, David Morris, Vennee Mortimer, Rohan Morton, Ir Moshe, Carmen Moya, Trish Quilaran & Daniel Moylan, Arun Mucherjee, Petra Mueller, Arun Mukherjee, Kerry Mullen, Alison Barber & John Murphy, Lori Murphy, R Murray, Ian Myers, Nicole Myerson, Danielle Nadeau, BJ Narkoben, Alex Nash, Gavin Nathan, Bruce & Marcia Nesbitt, Siegfried Neudorfer, Paige Newman, Liv Ng & Rag Gent, Katie Nicholls, Iris & Stefan Niederberger, Jan Nielsen, Marita Nieminen, Leo Kevin Nilon, Anders Nilsson, Jesper Nissen & Mettine Due, Maria Nordstedt & Ann Christofferson, Linda Norman, Michael Ny, Heather Nyberg, Steve Oades, Matt O'Brien, Diane O'Connor, Etain O'Carroll, Katherine Karen O'Donahoo, Elizabeth O'Donnell, J O'Donoghue, Anne Lise Opsahl, Rainer Osterreicher, Jenny Paley, Fiona Palmer, Gary Palmer, Josep Panella, Julie & Spiro Pappas, Joseph Parkhurst, Lynn H & Michele G Patterson, Theon Pearce, A Perlott, Debra Pett, Richard & Alison Pett, Laura Pezzano, Rod Phillips, Roger Phillips, Tim Phipps, Katherine Pike, Patrick Po Kin Fung, Andreas Poethen, Chris Pogson & Vivienne Avery, Thomas Polfeldt, Scott Pope, Alison & Simon Porges, Stephen Portnoy, Filip Pospisil, Michael Pößl, Tal Potishman, Julianne Power, Joel & Maria Teresa Prades, Damita & Adam Price, Malte Priesmeyer, Lori Prucha, Mike Quick, Talaat Qureshi, Will Race, Rob Rado, Hanna Ramberg, Nikolah Rasmussen, Kumi Rattenbury, Thomas Rau, Diederik Ravesloot, Christopher Rea,

Andrew Redfern, Frances Reid & Lili Pâquet, Saskia Snik & Theo Rengelink, Thomas Ribisel, Elise Richards, Eunan Robins, Margaret Roemer, Andrew Rogge, Jonathan Rosser, Miga Rossetti, Hans R Roth, Jeff Rothman, Anton Rupar, Michael Ruppert, Skarrn Rynine, Skarrn Ryvnine, Ofer Sadan, Karen Sadofschi, Rodrigo Salinas, Matt Salmon, Gil Salomon, Ian Samways, Manpal Singh Sandhu, Sarah Sarzynski, Emile Schenk, Andreas Schäfer & Iris Schick, Henrik Schinzel, Stephen Schmidt, Katrina Schneider, Mark Schottlander, Toralf Schrinner, Charlotte Blixt & Dirk Schwensen, Stephen Scott, Davide Selva, Gour Sen, Dawn Sentance & Padraig Eochaidh, Jerome Sgard, Irene & Burley Shepard, Andy Shrsozo, Ondrej Simetka, Dean Simonsen, John Simpkins, Luke Skinner, Duncan Smith, Jonathan Smith, Terry Smith, Charlotte Snowden, Frank Sorauf, Heidi Sorensen, Anita Spencer, Erika Spencer, Georg Steed, Mike Steele, Roland Steffen, Janig Stephens, Catherine Stewart & Lee Hallam, Lucy Stockbridge, Anja Stoetenborg, Ralph E Stone, John Straube, Jim & Miki Strong, Marjorie Stuehrenberg, Melanie Surry, Janice & Ed Swab, Brian Swinyard, Wilbert Sybesma, Danko Taborosi, Shona Taner, Patrick & Jayne Taylor, Paul Tetrault, Julie Tilghman, Jim Tomlinson, James Toplis, Fred Tottenham, Lina Troendle, Olivier Twiesselmann, Jacek Ture Nadzin, Jens Udsen & Signe Steninge, Jacky Upson & Martin Scott, Cheyenne Valenzuela, Tim van Bruggen, Annelies van den Berg, James van den Berg, Joseph ven den Heuvel, Koosje van der Horst, Lidy van der Ploeg, Ton van Grondelle, Gert van Lancker & Sandra van Henste, Johan van Hoof & Corneliek Bisschop, Dr A van Hoorn, Alma van Steenbergen, Margot Verhagen, Natalie Vial, Pam Wadsworth, Clive Walker, Julius Walker, Mélanie Walsh, Andy Walters, Richard Ward, Trevor Warman, Etienne Waternal, Paul Watson, Lenden Webb, Goeran Werner, Melody Hall & James West, Reto Westermann & Maria-José Blass, Stefan Westmeier, Dalma Whang, Michael Wheelahon, MC Whirter, Andy Whittaker, Cyprian Wilkowski, Jennifer Williams, Lee Williams, Lawrence Wilmshurst, Anne Wilshin, Eldon R Wilson, Mike Wilson, Bart & Patricia Wim, Michael Wingenroth, Bert Winthorst & Ineke van Hassel, Alan H Witz, Barrie Wraith, Steve Wright, Alexander Wuerfel, Masafumi Yamazaki, Yoav Yanir & Tamar Bar-El, Bill Young, S Zekkar & Johanna Zevenboom.

LONELY PLANET

Guides by Region

Lonely Planet is known worldwide for publishing practical, reliable and no-nonsense travel information in our guides and on our Web site. The Lonely Planet list covers just about every accessible part of the world. Currently there are ten series: travel guides, shoestring guides, walking guides, city guides, phrasebooks, audio packs, city maps, travel atlases, diving and snorkeling guides and travel literature.

AFRICA Africa – the South • Africa on a shoestring • Arabic (Egyptian) phrasebook • Arabic (Moroccan) phrasebook • Cairo • Cape Town • Central Africa • East Africa • Egypt • Egypt travel atlas • Ethiopian (Amharic) phrasebook • The Gambia & Senegal • Healthy Travel Africa • Kenya • Kenya travel atlas • Malawi, Mozambique & Zambia • Morocco • North Africa • South Africa, Lesotho & Swaziland • South Africa, Lesotho & Swaziland travel atlas • Swahili phrasebook • Trekking in East Africa • Tunisia • West Africa • Zimbabwe, Botswana & Namibia • Zimbabwe, Botswana & Namibia travel atlas
Travel Literature: The Rainbird: A Central African Journey • Songs to an African Sunset: A Zimbabwean Story • Mali Blues: Traveling to an African Beat

AUSTRALIA & THE PACIFIC Auckland • Australia • Australian phrasebook • Bushwalking in Australia • Bushwalking in Papua New Guinea • Fiji • Fijian phrasebook • Islands of Australia's Great Barrier Reef • Melbourne • Melbourne city map • Micronesia • New Caledonia • New South Wales & the ACT • New Zealand • Northern Territory • Outback Australia • Papua New Guinea • Papua New Guinea (Pidgin) phrasebook • Queensland • Rarotonga & the Cook Islands • Samoa • Solomon Islands • South Australia • South Pacific Languages phrasebook • Sydney • Sydney city map • Tahiti & French Polynesia • Tasmania • Tonga • Tramping in New Zealand • Vanuatu • Victoria • Western Australia
Travel Literature: Islands in the Clouds • Kiwi Tracks • Sean & David's Long Drive

CENTRAL AMERICA & THE CARIBBEAN Bahamas and Turks & Caicos • Bermuda • Central America on a shoestring • Costa Rica • Cuba • Dominican Republic & Haiti • Eastern Caribbean • Guatemala, Belize & Yucatán: La Ruta Maya • Jamaica • Mexico • Mexico City • Panama • Puerto Rico
Travel Literature: Green Dreams: Travels in Central America

EUROPE Amsterdam • Andalucía • Austria • Baltic States phrasebook • Berlin • Berlin city map• Britain • Brussels, Bruges & Antwerp • Central Europe • Central Europe phrasebook • Corsica • Czech & Slovak Republics • Denmark • Dublin • Eastern Europe • Eastern Europe phrasebook • Edinburgh • Estonia, Latvia & Lithuania • Europe • Finland • France • French phrasebook • Germany • German phrasebook • Greece • Greek phrasebook • Hungary • Iceland, Greenland & the Faroe Islands • Ireland • Italian phrasebook • Italy • Lisbon • London • London city map • Mediterranean Europe • Mediterranean Europe phrasebook • Norway • Paris • Paris city map • Poland • Portugal • Portugal travel atlas • Prague • Prague city map • Romania & Moldova • Rome • Russia, Ukraine & Belarus • Russian phrasebook • Scandinavian & Baltic Europe • Scandinavian Europe phrasebook • Scotland • Slovenia • Spain • Spanish phrasebook • St Petersburg • Switzerland • Trekking in Spain • Ukrainian phrasebook • Vienna • Walking in Britain • Walking in Italy • Walking in Switzerland • Western Europe • Western Europe phrasebook
Travel Literature: The Olive Grove: Travels in Greece

INDIAN SUBCONTINENT Bangladesh • Bengali phrasebook • Bhutan • Delhi • Goa • Hindi/Urdu phrasebook • India • India & Bangladesh travel atlas • Indian Himalaya • Karakoram Highway • Mumbai • Nepal • Nepali phrasebook • Pakistan • Rajasthan • South India • Sri Lanka • Sri Lanka phrasebook • Trekking in the Indian Himalaya • Trekking in the Karakoram & Hindukush • Trekking in the Nepal Himalaya
Travel Literature: In Rajasthan • Shopping for Buddhas

Mail Order

Lonely Planet products are distributed worldwide. They are also available by mail order from Lonely Planet, so if you have difficulty finding a title please write to us. North and South American residents should write to 150 Linden St, Oakland, CA 94607, USA; European and African residents should write to 10a Spring Place, London NW5 3BH, UK; and residents of other countries to PO Box 617, Hawthorn, Victoria 3122, Australia.

ISLANDS OF THE INDIAN OCEAN Madagascar & Comoros • Maldives • Mauritius, Réunion & Seychelles

MIDDLE EAST & CENTRAL ASIA Arab Gulf States • Central Asia • Central Asia phrasebook • Hebrew phrasebook • Iran • Israel & the Palestinian Territories • Israel & the Palestinian Territories travel atlas • Istanbul • Jerusalem • Jordan & Syria • Jordan, Syria & Lebanon travel atlas • Lebanon • Middle East on a shoestring • Syria • Turkey • Turkish phrasebook • Turkey travel atlas • Yemen

Travel Literature: The Gates of Damascus • Kingdom of the Film Stars: Journey into Jordan

NORTH AMERICA Alaska • Backpacking in Alaska • Baja California • California & Nevada • Canada • Chicago • Chicago city map • Deep South • Florida • Hawaii • Honolulu • Las Vegas • Los Angeles • Miami • New England USA • New Orleans • New York City • New York city map • New York, New Jersey & Pennsylvania • Pacific Northwest USA • Puerto Rico • Rocky Mountain States • San Francisco • San Francisco city map • Seattle • Southwest USA • Texas • USA • USA phrasebook • Vancouver • Washington, DC & the Capital Region

Travel Literature: Drive Thru America

NORTH-EAST ASIA Beijing • Cantonese phrasebook • China • Hong Kong • Hong Kong city map • Hong Kong, Macau & Guangzhou • Japan • Japanese phrasebook • Japanese audio pack • Korea • Korean phrasebook • Kyoto • Mandarin phrasebook • Mongolia • Mongolian phrasebook • North-East Asia on a shoestring • Seoul • South-West China • Taiwan • Tibet • Tibetan phrasebook • Tokyo

Travel Literature: Lost Japan

SOUTH AMERICA Argentina, Uruguay & Paraguay • Bolivia • Brazil • Brazilian phrasebook • Buenos Aires • Chile & Easter Island • Chile & Easter Island travel atlas • Colombia • Ecuador & the Galapagos Islands • Latin American Spanish phrasebook • Peru • Quechua phrasebook • Rio de Janeiro • Rio de Janeiro city map • South America on a shoestring • Trekking in the Patagonian Andes • Venezuela

Travel Literature: Full Circle: A South American Journey

SOUTH-EAST ASIA Bali & Lombok • Bangkok • Bangkok city map • Burmese phrasebook • Cambodia • Hanoi • Hill Tribes phrasebook • Ho Chi Minh City • Indonesia • Indonesian phrasebook • Indonesian audio pack • Jakarta • Java • Laos • Lao phrasebook • Laos travel atlas • Malay phrasebook • Malaysia, Singapore & Brunei • Myanmar (Burma) • Philippines • Pilipino (Tagalog) phrasebook • Singapore • South-East Asia on a shoestring • South-East Asia phrasebook • Thailand • Thailand's Islands & Beaches • Thailand travel atlas • Thai phrasebook • Thai audio pack • Vietnam • Vietnamese phrasebook • Vietnam travel atlas

ALSO AVAILABLE: Antarctica • Brief Encounters: Stories of Love, Sex & Travel • Chasing Rickshaws • Lonely Planet Unpacked • Not the Only Planet: Travel Stories from Science Fiction • Sacred India • Travel with Children • Traveller's Tales

LONELY PLANET

Phrasebooks

Lonely Planet phrasebooks are packed with essential words and phrases to help travellers communicate with the locals. With color tabs for quick reference, an extensive vocabulary and use of script, these handy pocket-sized language guides cover day-to-day travel situations.

- handy pocket-sized books
- easy to understand Pronunciation chapter
- clear & comprehensive Grammar chapter
- romanization alongside script to allow ease of pronunciation
- script throughout so users can point to phrases for every situation
- full of cultural information and tips for the traveller

'...vital for a real DIY spirit and attitude in language learning'
— *Backpacker*

'the phrasebooks have good cultural backgrounders and offer solid advice for challenging situations in remote locations'
— *San Francisco Examiner*

Arabic (Egyptian) • Arabic (Moroccan) • Australian *(Australian English, Aboriginal and Torres Strait languages)* • Baltic States *(Estonian, Latvian, Lithuanian)* • Bengali • Brazilian • Burmese • Cantonese • Central Asia • Central Europe *(Czech, French, German, Hungarian, Italian, Slovak)* • Eastern Europe *(Bulgarian, Czech, Hungarian, Polish, Romanian, Slovak)* • Ethiopian (Amharic) • Fijian • French • German • Greek • Hebrew • Hill Tribes • Hindi/Urdu • Indonesian • Italian • Japanese • Korean • Lao • Latin American Spanish • Malay • Mandarin • Mediterranean Europe *(Albanian, Croatian, Greek, Italian, Macedonian, Maltese, Serbian, Slovene)* • Mongolian • Nepali • Papua New Guinea • Pilipino (Tagalog) • Quechua • Russian • Scandinavian Europe *(Danish, Finnish, Icelandic, Norwegian, Swedish)* • South Pacific Languages • South-East Asia *(Burmese, Indonesian, Khmer, Lao, Malay, Tagalog Pilipino, Thai, Vietnamese)* • Spanish (Castilian) *(also includes Catalan, Galician and Basque)* • Sri Lanka • Swahili • Thai • Tibetan • Turkish • Ukrainian • USA *(US English, Vernacular, Native American languages, Hawaiian)* • Vietnamese • Western Europe *(Basque, Catalan, Dutch, French, German, Greek, Irish)*

Lonely Planet Journeys

JOURNEYS is a unique collection of travel writing – published by the company that understands travel better than anyone else. It is a series for anyone who has ever experienced – or dreamed of – the magical moment when they encountered a strange culture or saw a place for the first time. They are tales to read while you're planning a trip, while you're on the road or while you're in an armchair in front of a fire.

These outstanding titles explore our planet through the eyes of a diverse group of international writers. JOURNEYS books catch the spirit of a place, illuminate a culture, recount a crazy adventure or introduce a fascinating way of life. They always entertain, and always enrich the experience of travel.

FULL CIRCLE
A South American Journey
Luis Sepúlveda (translated by Chris Andrews)
'A journey without a fixed itinerary' with Chilean writer Luis Sepúlveda. Extravagant characters and extraordinary situations are memorably evoked: gauchos organising a tournament of lies, a scheming heiress on the lookout for a husband, a pilot with a corpse on board his plane…*Full Circle* brings us the distinctive voice of one of South America's most compelling writers.

WINNER 1996 Astrolabe – Etonnants Voyageurs award for the best work of travel literature published in France.

GREEN DREAMS
Travels in Central America
Stephen Benz
On the Amazon, in Costa Rica, Honduras and on the Mayan trail from Guatemala to Mexico, Stephen Benz describes his encounters with water, mud, insects and other wildlife – and not least with the ecotourists themselves. With witty insights into modern travel, *Green Dreams* discusses the paradox of cultural and 'green' tourism.

DRIVE THRU AMERICA
Sean Condon
If you've ever wanted to drive across the USA but couldn't find the time (or afford the gas), *Drive Thru America* is perfect for you. In his search for American myths and realities – along with comfort, cable TV and good, reasonably priced coffee – Sean Condon paints a hilarious road-portrait of the USA.

'entertaining and laugh-out-loud funny'– *Alex Wilber, Travel editor, Amazon.com*

SEAN & DAVID'S LONG DRIVE
Sean Condon
Sean and David are young townies who have rarely strayed beyond city limits. One day, for no good reason, they set out to discover their homeland, and what follows is a wildly entertaining adventure that covers half of Australia.

'a hilariously detailed log of two burned out friends' – *Rolling Stone*

Index

Abbreviations

Text

Bold indicates maps.

Bold indicates maps.

Bold indicates maps.

Bold indicates maps.

Bold indicates maps.

Bold indicates maps.

Bold indicates maps.

MAP LEGEND

BOUNDARIES

- International
- State, Province
- County

HYDROGRAPHY

- Water
- Reef
- Coastline
- Beach
- River, Waterfall
- Swamp, Spring

⊗ NATIONAL CAPITAL

◉ State, Provincial Capital

● LARGE CITY

● Medium City

● Small City

● Town, Village

○ Point of Interest

■ Place to Stay

▲ Campsite

⚎ RV Park

⌂ Refugio, Chalet, Hut

▼ Place to Eat

▪ Bar (Place to Drink)

▪ Café

ROUTES & TRANSPORT

- Freeway
- Toll Freeway
- Primary Road
- Secondary Road
- Tertiary Road
- Poorly Maintained Road
- Pedestrian Mall
- Trail
- Walking Tour
- Ferry Route
- Railway, Train Station
- Mass Transit Line & Station

MAP SYMBOLS

✈	Airfield	🗿	Monument
✈	Airport	☪	Mosque
∴	Archaeological Site, Ruins	▲	Mountain
$	Bank	🏛	Museum
✕	Battlefield	♨	Observatory
🏖	Beach	←	One-Way Street
✳	Border Crossing	🌲	Park
⊜	Bus Depot, Bus Stop	P	Parking
▭	Cathedral	)(	Pass
🏰	Castle, Chateau	★	Police Station
⌓	Cave	🏊	Pool
†	Church	✉	Post Office
☿	Embassy	⤢	Shipwreck
⋈	Footbridge	❖	Shopping Mall
✿	Garden	⛷	Skiing (Nordic)
🏪	Gas Station	⛷	Skiing (Alpine)
⚍	Hindu Temple	🏛	Stately Home
✛	Hospital, Clinic	🏄	Surfing
➊	Information	✡	Synagogue
⚘	Lighthouse	⬛	Tomb, Mausoleum
☼	Lookout	🐘	Zoo

ROUTE SHIELDS

ARGENTINA
- [RN 3] Ruta Nacional
- [RP 21] Ruta Provincial

BRAZIL
- [BR 262] Highway

ECUADOR
- [55] Highway

PARAGUAY
- [3] Highway

URUGUAY
- [8] Ruta Nacional
- [15] Ruta Secundaria

BOLIVIA
- [9] Red Fundamental
- [601] Red Complementaria

CHILE
- [5] Ruta Nacional

FRENCH GUIANA
- [1] Highway

PERU
- [1] Carreteras Sistema Nacional
- [113] Carreteras Sistema Departmental

VENEZUELA
- [10] Highway

Note: Not all symbols displayed above appear in this book.

LONELY PLANET OFFICES

Australia
PO Box 617, Hawthorn 3122, Victoria
☎ 03 9819 1877 fax 03 9819 6459
email talk2us@lonelyplanet.com.au

USA
150 Linden Street, Oakland, California 94607
☎ 510 893 8555, TOLL FREE 800 275 5555
fax 510 893 8572
email info@lonelyplanet.com

UK
10A Spring Place, London NW5 3BH
☎ 020 7428 4800 fax 020 7428 4828
email go@lonelyplanet.co.uk

France
1 rue du Dahomey, 75011 Paris
☎ 01 55 25 33 00 fax 01 55 25 33 01
email bip@lonelyplanet.fr
www.lonelyplanet.fr

World Wide Web: www.lonelyplanet.com or AOL keyword: lp
Lonely Planet Images: lpi@lonelyplanet.com.au